O9-ABH-142

# TIME
## ALMANAC
# 2003

with INFORMATION PLEASE®

### BORGNA BRUNNER
#### EDITOR IN CHIEF

Information
Please®
part of Family Education Network, Inc.
www.infoplease.com

**Information Please®**
part of Family Education Network, Inc.
www.infoplease.com

**Editor in Chief** Borgna Brunner

**Editor** Ann-Marie Imbornoni

**Senior Contributing Editors**
David P. Johnson, Jr., Beth Rowen

**Contributing Editors** Christine Frantz (Sports), Holly Hartman (Inventions and Discoveries)

**Production Director**
Susan Hyde

**Production Editor** Christine Frantz

**Vice President** George Kane

**Proofreading and Fact-checking**
Katie Blatt, Lauren Byrne, Susan Chicoski, Elissa Haney, Elizabeth Olson

**Editorial Assistants** Caitlin Helfrich, Kate Pritchard

**Graphics** Sean M. Dessureau, Phyllis McKee

**Technical Support** Tuna Chatterjee, Karl DeBisschop

This edition of the almanac is dedicated to our colleagues, the editors of our companion sports almanac:
Gerry Brown, John Gettings, Phyllis McKee, and Michael Morrison

**Time Inc.**
HOME ENTERTAINMENT

**Contributing Editor** Kelly Knauer

**Design** Ellen Fanning

**Pictures** Patricia Cadley

**President** Rob Gursha

**Vice President, Branded Businesses**
David Arfine

**Executive Director, Marketing Services**
Carol Pittard

**Director, Retail & Special Sales** Tom Mifsud

**Director of Finance** Tricia Griffin

**Marketing Director** Kenneth Maehlum

**Assistant Director** Ann Marie Doherty

**Prepress Manager** Emily Rabin

**Book Production Manager** Jonathan Polsky

**Associate Product Manager** Michelle Kuhr

**Special thanks to:** Suzanne DeBenedetto, Robert Dente, Gina Di Meglio, Anne-Michelle Gallero, Peter Harper, Natalie McCrea, Jessica McGrath, Mary Jane Rigoroso, Steven Sandonato, Bozena Szwagulinski, Niki Whelan

The TIME Almanac welcomes comments and suggestions from readers. Although the editors carefully consider each suggestion, because of the volume of correspondence we receive we cannot respond personally to each writer. The TIME Almanac does not rule on bets or wagers.

**Editorial Office**
**Information Please**
20 Park Plaza, Suite 1220
Boston, MA 02116
Email: ipa@infoplease.com

**Customer Service**
**Attention: TIME Almanac**
PO Box 11016
Des Moines, IA 50336-1016

ISBN: 1-929049-95-1 Paperback
ISBN: 1-929049-87-0 Hardcover
ISSN: 0073-7860

If you would like to order copies of TIME's hardcover Collector's Edition books, please call us at 1-800-327-6388 (Monday through Friday, 7:00 A.M.–8:00 P.M. or Saturday, 7:00 A.M.–6:00 P.M. Central Time).

# Keyword Index

# Section Index

Page numbers followed by "n" indicate information in footnotes.

# The News of 2002: Nation

## The War on Terrorism

Polls released shortly before the anniversary of the Sept. 11 attacks revealed how divided the public was in its assessment of the nation's vulnerability to terrorism. A Pew Research Center poll indicated that 34% of Americans felt terrorists were less able to carry out an attack on U.S. soil, 22% felt the danger of terrorism had in fact increased, and another 39% believed there was no change in our level of danger or safety. The wide divergence in public opinion seemed to reflect the difficulty of evaluating the nebulous and uncharted war on terrorism. The U.S.-led military effort in Afghanistan destroyed al-Qaeda's headquarters and training camps, yet failed in its primary goal, eliminating Osama bin Laden and al-Qaeda—two-thirds of al-Qaeda's senior leadership remain at large. More than 2,700 suspected terrorists have been questioned in 98 countries, yet U.S. intelligence estimates that terrorist training camps in Afghanistan have produced 10,000 to 15,000 terrorists over the past decade. And about $100 million in al-Qaeda assets have been frozen in more than 160 nations, yet al-Qaeda is believed to retain more than twice that amount. A synagogue bombing in Tunisia, a tanker explosion off Yemen, a nightclub bombing in Bali, and various failed or intercepted terrorist acts in recent months were ominous signs of the resurgence of al-Qaeda and its sympathizers.

## National Security

National security efforts—identified by the Bush administration as falling into the four areas of bioterrorism, emergency response, airport and border security, and intelligence—have proved somewhat less complex to judge than international efforts against terrorism, and they have come under harsher scrutiny. No one will ever know whether the country's intelligence agencies could have prevented the Sept. 11 attacks, but intelligence has clearly been the greatest failing in domestic security. On Sept. 11, the FBI had only 20 agents monitoring al-Qaeda, despite the attacks on the U.S. embassies in Africa and the bombing of the USS *Cole;* the CIA had just 40 agents assigned to counterterrorism. FBI agent Coleen Rowley's whistle-blowing memo in May, charging the agency with disregarding warning signs of the impending attacks, was just the most recent indictment of the agency's obstructionist bureaucracy and incompetence. A congressional investigation indicated that between May and July 2001, U.S. intelligence intercepted at least 33 messages about a possible terrorist attack. The ineptitude of the Immigration and Naturalization Service (INS) was shockingly underscored when it approved student visas for two of the Sept. 11 hijackers six months after they destroyed the World Trade Center. These and other failures have led to an overhaul of U.S. intelligence, but CIA director George Tenet has warned that the "threat environment we find ourselves in today is as bad as it was . . . the summer before Sept. 11," and has urged the country to accept the stark truth that safety from terrorism is fundamentally an impossibility, no matter what measures are taken: "There will be more battles won, and, sadly, more battles lost."

Reform of airport security has proceeded at a glacial pace, and it remains to be seen whether the proposed Department of Homeland Security—which would consolidate 20 federal agencies in the most massive government reorganization since 1948—proves effective, or whether, as the Brookings Institution maintains, "The new department is only a means to an end, and it is being oversold as an end in itself."

## Civil Liberties

The means used in securing the country against terrorist attacks have been questioned as well. Civil libertarians and increasingly, the courts, have condemned the compromise on civil rights and due process in the name of national security. While security measures necessarily involve restrictions, new anti-terrorism legislation has presented law enforcement officials with sweeping new powers to conduct searches without warrants, monitor financial transactions and eavesdrop, and detain and deport individuals in secret. Under the USA Patriot Act—passed in Oct. 2001 with just one vote short of unanimous bipartisan support by Congress—about 1,200 people were detained for months without access to lawyers or the release of their names. In August, a U.S. Court of Appeals ruled these secret detentions unconstitutional: "The executive branch seeks to uproot people's lives, outside the public eye, and behind a closed door. Democracies die behind closed doors."

## Targeting Iraq

President Bush's broad characterizations of the terrorist threat allowed him to expand the focus of his foreign policy from al-Qaeda and other terrorist organizations to any regimes hostile to the United States, regardless of their connection to the Sept. 11 attacks. Soon the lines began blurring between the "evil one," as he called Osama bin Laden, and the "axis of evil"—his label for Iran, North Korea, and most emphatically, Iraq. "We must take the battle to the enemy, disrupt his plans, and confront the worst threats before they emerge," was Bush's explanation of the necessity for a preemptive strike meant to bring about "regime change" by ousting Saddam Hussein. Although the Bush administration failed to link Iraq to al Qaeda, such a connection eventually became irrelevant, with Bush contending, "you can't distinguish between al-Qaeda and Saddam when you talk about the war on terror."

Bush cited the existence of weapons of mass destruction, the thwarting of UN weapons inspections, and Saddam Hussein's despotism and human rights abuses as the justification for waging war. But while few quarrelled with Bush's basic assessment of Iraq's transgressions, foreign and domestic critics remained skeptical of the allegations of the direct and imminent danger posed by Iraq, questioned the circumstantial nature of its evidence (particularly concerning Iraq's nuclear capacities), and disputed whether military means were the only answer. Critics warned that a focus on Iraq would deflect attention away from the real threat of terrorism, complicate the chance for a resolution in the Israeli-Palestinian conflict, and potentially destabilize the region. Much of the world also balked at Bush's unilateralism, contending that the U.S. would violate international law if it acted without UN approval. In September, Bush addressed the UN, challenging the organization to swiftly enforce its own resolutions against Iraq—for a decade the UN has feebly imposed weapons inspections—or else the U.S. would have no choice but to act on its own. Bush's multilateral gesture began drawing modest support from the international community, and in October he easily secured the support of Congress to pursue war, as well as that of the majority of Americans (62%; Pew Research). In the meantime the UN scrambled to secure a diplomatic alternative to the standoff between the United States and the notoriously untrustworthy Saddam Hussein.

## Sickness in the Church

In Jan. 2002, a *Boston Globe* article ignited a sexual abuse scandal in the American Catholic church that its own bishops came to describe "as a crisis without precedent in our times." It was not the conviction of pedophile priest John Geoghan itself that generated the enormous public outcry—there have been civil trials of sexual abuse by the clergy since 1985—but revelations that senior church officials had systematically covered up Geoghan's criminal behavior for decades. Boston's archbishop, Cardinal Bernard Law, as well as five other bishops, had known of Geoghan's pedophilia for more than three decades, yet had simply transferred him from position to position, during which time he sexually molested more than 130 children. A second coverup broke in Boston in April, this time involving priest Paul Shanley, an open member of the North American Man-Boy Love Association.

The publicity in Boston unleashed allegations of abuse and coverup around the country. In the first eight months of the scandal, almost 300 U.S. priests and four bishops left the church, and another 2,000 were accused of molesting children. At the U.S. Conference of Catholic Bishops in June, bishops voted to ban priests abusing children from working in parishes but did not address their own accountability: according to the *Dallas Morning News,* "two-thirds of U.S. bishops knowingly covered up

sexual abuses by priests." The Vatican, however, rejected the "zero tolerance" policy adopted by the bishops and asked for modifications to protect the rights of accused priests.

The church's culture of secrecy and denial gave rise to grass-roots reform movements, most notably Voice of the Faithful, whose motto is "keep the faith, change the church." In addition to promoting greater involvement of the laity in church affairs, the group provides support to the abused—perhaps nothing has dismayed people more than the church's minimal expression of compassion for the young victims of predatory priests.

## Capitalism Run Amok

The wave of corporate scandals in 2002 began when Enron, the country's largest energy trader, filed for bankruptcy in Dec. 2001 while under federal investigation for hiding debt and misrepresenting earnings. The company used complicated off-the-balance-sheet partnerships to inflate profits by as much as $600 million. Enron's collapse not only shook the economy, but it left most of its employees bereft of retirement funds. Arthur Andersen, Enron's accounting firm and auditor, fell next, after it was convicted of destroying Enron-related documents. In July 2002, WorldCom, the nation's second-largest telecommunications company, became the largest company to go bankrupt in U.S. history after it admitted to cooking its books. Tyco, Qwest, Global Crossing, ImClone, and Adelphia, among others, were placed under federal investigation for various misadventures in fraud and crooked accounting. And putting a face on the impersonality of Big Business were the stories of extravagantly paid CEOs who indulged in personal enrichment schemes that demonstrated astounding arrogance, greed, and a criminal disregard for their employees. The Bush administration was slow to respond to the scandals, and the measures subsequently passed by Congress were tougher than those the president had proposed.

## Mid-Term Election Issues

Corporate corruption, however, did not figure as a significant issue leading up to the mid-term elections in November—the Democrats never gained ground as the socially conscious party in comparison to the generally pro-business Republicans on the issue. Nor did terrorism or Iraq strongly engage the public. Voters were most concerned with the downturn in the economy—2 million private-sector jobs have vanished over the past two years and the stock market has continued to falter—a problem for which neither party offered compelling solutions.

# The News of 2002: World

## Afghanistan

Hamid Karzai, leader of an interim Afghan government after the fall of the Taliban, officially became head of state in June 2002. Karzai's strong international support led to the infusion of both aid ($4.5 billion has been promised) and UN peacekeeping troops to his war-ravaged nation. But Karzai's grasp on power remained tenuous, with warlords maintain-

ing tight regional control, ethnic rivalries volatile, and pockets of al-Qaeda fighters continuing to battle U.S. and allied troops—Karzai himself narrowly escaped an assassination attempt in September. While the foreign military presence has been essential to the stability of the country, it has also been responsible for hundreds of inadvertent civilian casualties. Between Oct. 2001 and March 2002, the U.S. dropped approximately 20,000 bombs on the country. In addition to political fragility, Afghanistan's troubles remain overwhelming: a devastating drought is now in the fourth year, the country's infrastructure requires massive reconstruction, and a greater-than-expected influx of 1.6 million returning refugees has desperately strained the eviscerated economy.

## Peace in Africa

Angola's seemingly unquenchable civil war, which began shortly after independence from Portugal in 1975, finally ended when the rebels' ruthless and indefatigable leader, Jonas Savimbi, was killed by government troops in February. The war was little more than a power grab between two rival parties: the MPLA, initially a Marxist group supported by Cuba and the Soviet Union, became the semidemocratic ruling party over time; and Savimbi's UNITA, which fought a proxy cold war on behalf of its supporters, South Africa and the U.S., eventually deteriorated into an international pariah interested only in diamonds and power. The exhausted UNITA rebels quickly surrendered after the death of their leader, and while peace finally seemed secure, more than a third of the population had been displaced by war and a half-million Angolans faced starvation.

Less hopeful were two other African cease-fires. The Democratic Republic of the Congo signed a series of agreements with rebel groups and the governments of Rwanda and Uganda, ending a tangled war that has raged since 1998, involved eight nations, and claimed an astounding 3 million lives. In Sudan, a cease-fire signed in July may lead to a permanent end to the brutal 19-year civil war between the Arab and strongly Islamic North, the seat of the government, and the black African animists and Christians in the South. More than 2 million have died in the conflict, primarily in the South.

## India, Pakistan, Sri Lanka

After 19 crippling years of war that left 65,000 dead, a seemingly lasting peace agreement was signed in Feb. 2002 between the Sri Lankan government and the Tamil Tiger guerrillas. The Tamil minority's (18% of the population) mounting resentment toward the Sinhalese majority's monopoly on political and economic power, exacerbated by different religions (Tamils are generally Hindu, Sinhalese Buddhist), had erupted in bloody violence in 1983. In fall peace talks, the Tamil Tigers compromised on earlier demands, asking for autonomy and self-determination rather than independence, and thus improving the chance for a permanent resolution.

India's worst Hindu-Muslim violence in a decade racked the state of Gujarat in February and March after a Muslim mob fire-bombed a train, killing Hindu activists. Hindus retaliated, and more than 1,000 died in the bloodshed. The ruling Hindu nationalist BJP was criticized for not stemming the attacks, most of which affected Muslims.

After a Dec. 2001 terrorist attack on the Indian parliament that Indian officials blamed on Pakistan-backed Islamic militants, India amassed more than half a million troops along the Pakistan border. Pakistan followed suit with its own buildup. After ten months of steadily escalating tensions that brought the two nuclear-armed countries to the brink of war, both pulled back the majority of their troops in October. But troops stationed along the Line of Control, which divides the contested state of Kashmir, remained unchanged, as did the political stalemate.

## Middle East

Palestinians carried out some of the most horrific terrorist attacks in years—Hamas and the al-Aksa Martyr Brigade claimed responsibility for most of them—killing Israeli civilians in cafes, bus stops, and supermarkets. In retaliation, Israeli troops unleashed bombing raids, razed several major Palestinian cities and refugee camps, and stepped up their occupation of Palestinian-controlled territories. Israeli troops twice surrounded Yasir Arafat at the Palestinian Authority headquarters in Ramallah, and Prime Minister Sharon called for his expulsion from the territories. Arafat, unable or unwilling to prevent the increased wave of suicide bombings, managed to hold onto power despite his growing political irrelevance. U.S. help was not forthcoming, with President Bush declaring that the U.S. will not recognize an independent Palestinian state until Arafat is replaced. By Sept. 2002, the second anniversary of the al-Aksa intifada, more than 1,500 Palestinians and 550 Israelis had been killed.

## Economic Calamity in South America

After years of recession, Argentina suffered its worst economic crisis ever, which began in Dec. 2001 when the nation defaulted on its $155 billion foreign debt payments, the largest such default in history. In response, Argentina devalued its peso, which had been pegged to the dollar for a decade. The devaluation plunged the banking industry into crisis and wiped out much of the savings of the middle class. Banking and foreign exchange were suspended. Half of Argentina's 36 million now live in poverty, unemployment has reached 22%, and protests and strikes have multiplied. The IMF has refused to bail out Argentina as it has in past years, insisting that the nation reform its ineffective economic policies first. But the IMF did not present the same tough love policy to Argentina's ailing neighbors: Uruguay received a modest $500 million and Brazil a record $30 billion.

Three nationwide strikes in Venezuela since Dec. 2001 were a massive protest against the increasing authoritarianism of populist president Hugo Chavez and the faltering economy. A strike in April led to a coup that briefly toppled Chavez; he was reinstated two days later. But while unions, business organizations, the Catholic church, and the media have called for his resignation, Chavez remained enormously popular among the working poor with his many promises to end poverty and corruption.

## A Nuclear North Korea

A reclusive and secretive North Korea stunned the world in the fall with two shocking admissions. In September, the government unexpectedly acknowledged that it had kidnapped about a dozen Japanese in the 1970s and 1980s for the purposes of training North Korean spies. In October, confronted with U.S. intelligence, North Korea admitted that it had violated a 1994 agreement freezing its nuclear-weapons program and had in fact been developing a nuclear bomb. North Korea's uncharacteristic candor and its mystifying motives left the Bush administration with the daunting task of finding a diplomatic solution to the world's newest nuclear threat.

# What Happened in 2002: Month by Month

Below are highlights of key events of the year, organized month by month, in three categories for easy reference. For the year's major Supreme Court decisions, *see* p. 94. "Countries of the World" covers specific international events, country by country. *See also* "People in the News," pp. 1030–1034, and "2002 Deaths," pp. 1035–1039, for more current-events coverage.

## January 2002

### WORLD

**Marines Secure Taliban Compounds (Jan. 1):** Two hundred soldiers leave Kandahar to wage extensive American ground operation.

**Argentina Gets Fifth President in Two Weeks (Jan. 1):** Congress appoints Sen. Eduardo Duhalde of the Peronist party to complete the term of Fernando De la Rua, who resigned in December amid protests over the failed economy.

**Euro Makes Smooth Debut (Jan. 2):** Europeans start using common currency without significant problems.

**Israel Eases West Bank Blockade (Jan. 3):** Relaxes military presence in various areas as U.S. peace envoy, Anthony Zinni, returns.

**Israel Seizes Ship Loaded with Arms (Jan. 3):** Says Palestinians are involved in the shipment of 50 tons of weapons and explosives that was intercepted in the Red Sea.

**U.S. Builds Up Bases in Afghan Region (Jan. 8):** Prepares for long-term presence in Central Asia. War in Afghanistan appears to be winding down, but U.S. continues to search for al-Qaeda and Taliban resistance fighters.

**U.S. Takes War Captives to Cuba Base (Jan. 10):** Taliban and al-Qaeda prisoners flown from Afghanistan to Guantanamo Bay in first transport of detainees.

**Russia Rejects Nuclear Storage Plan (Jan. 10):** Opposes Bush's plans to mothball rather than destroy large number of nuclear warheads.

**U.S. and Philippines Join to Fight Terrorism (Jan. 15):** Agree to have U.S. troops train Filipino soldiers to eliminate Abu Sayyaf, an Islamic terrorist organization.

**Arab Gunman Kills Six Israelis (Jan. 17–18):** Palestinian also wounds 30 in crowded reception hall in Hadera. Israeli forces retaliate by bombing governor's office in Palestinian-controlled town of Tulkarm on West Bank.

**Mass Killing in Chechnya Reported (Jan. 22):** Local officials contend Russian troops continue to execute civilians and loot property nearly two years after end of major hostilities.

**U.S. Reporter Kidnapped in Pakistan (Jan. 23):** *Wall St. Journal* South Asia bureau chief Daniel Pearl disappears while investigating alleged shoe bomber Richard Reid's ties to Muslim fundamentalists.

**Iraqi Opposition Seeks U.S. Aid (Jan. 31):** Insurgent leaders call on Bush administration to train forces seeking to overthrow Saddam Hussein.

### NATION

**FBI Extends Terrorist Alert (Jan. 3):** Tells nation's police to maintain security alert through Winter Olympic Games in Salt Lake City and March 11, six months after Sept. 11.

**Funds to Dismantle Nuclear Arms Sought (Jan. 8):** White House plans to ask Congress for 37% increase over 2001 for Energy Department programs to store and destroy weapons-grade materials.

**President Signs Education Bill (Jan. 8):** Measure, central to Bush's campaign, will broaden federal role in public education and mandate national testing.

**Judge Bars Fingerprint as Scientific Testimony (Jan. 11):** Federal judge in Philadelphia rules fingerprint evidence, used for 90 years, does not meet standards set for scientific testimony.

**President Warns World Terrorists (Jan. 29):** In first State of Union address, Bush says war against terrorists is "just beginning." Address, broadcast to nation, focuses on Iran, Iraq, and North Korea. He charges that the three constitute "an axis of evil." And Bush asserts that if he thinks necessary, he will wage war against states developing weapons of mass destruction.

### BUSINESS/SCIENCE/SOCIETY

**Ford Plans to Close Five Plants (Jan. 11):** Announces most drastic cutbacks in two decades, with 35,000 layoffs and the elimination of four models.

**Enron Collapse Takes Heavy Toll (Jan. 12):** Investors and employees hard-hit by one of the largest bankruptcies in the history of American business. They seek to learn how much executives profited by selling stock when the price was still high. **(Jan. 23):** Kenneth L. Lay resigns as Enron chairman and chief executive under pressure from outside creditors. **(Jan. 24):** Lawyers investigating the company's demise report that Enron's auditor, Arthur Andersen, shredded important documents in anticipation of a lawsuit.

**Four Former Radicals Face Trial (Jan. 16):** Sara Jane Olson and three others charged with murder in killing of woman in 1975 bank robbery in California.

**Defrocked Priest Convicted (Jan. 18):** John Geoghan, former Massachusetts priest, found guilty of indecent assault and battery for fondling a young boy in 1991. He's accused of sexually molesting about 130 children.

**Panel Opposes Cloning of Babies (Jan. 18):** Scientific experts call procedure unsafe, but support cloning techniques for treatment of disease.

**Fed Ends Series of Interest Rate Cuts (Jan. 30):** Reserve apparently finishes year-old campaign as economy shows signs of recovery.

## February 2002

### WORLD

**Taliban Official in U.S. Custody (Feb. 8):** Former foreign minister, Mullah Muttawakil, surrenders at Kandahar.

**Milosevic Trial Opens at The Hague (Feb. 12):** Former Yugoslav president faces charges of genocide and crimes against humanity. **(Feb. 12):** In opening statement, Milosevic defends himself and berates NATO for decade of violence in the Balkans.

**Afghan Government Minister Assassinated (Feb. 14):** Abdul Rahman, member of Hamid Karzai's interim government, murdered at Kabul airport.

**U.S. Air Strikes Bolster Kabul Government (Feb. 18):** New phase of Afghanistan war opens when American forces drop precision-guided missiles on "enemy troops."

**Colombia President Suspends Talks with Rebels (Feb. 20):** Andres Pastrana acts after FARC members hijack a commercial plane and kidnap a Liberal Party senator.

**Video Confirms Death of Reporter (Feb. 21):** FBI says tape delivered to Pakistani official proves *Wall Street Journal* journalist Daniel Pearl is dead.

**Angolan Rebel Leader Killed (Feb. 22):** Jonas Savimbi, leader of UNITA, which has waged a decades-long civil war, is shot in a battle with Angolan army.

**Israelis Keep Arafat Confined (Feb. 25):** Government decides to continue restricting Palestinian leader to West Bank city of Ramallah, but lifts his confinement to his compound. Arafat will need prime minister's permission to leave Ramallah.

**Bush Welcomes Saudi Peace Offer (Feb. 26):** Praises Crown Prince Abdullah's proposal for Israel to withdraw completely from West Bank and Gaza Strip in exchange for normalized relations with all Arab nations.

**Israelis Raid Refugee Camps (Feb. 28):** Troops kill at least 11 Palestinians in brutal battle. One Israeli dies in the fighting.

**Muslim Mob Attacks Trainload of Hindus (Feb. 27):** Fifty-eight people burned to death in Ahmedabad. Group returning from demonstration to support construction of a temple on a Muslim holy site in Ayodhya. **(Feb. 28):** Hindus retaliate, burning Muslims alive in their homes and setting fire to Muslim-owned restaurants, shops, cars, and apartments.

NATION

**Bush Proposes Military Budget Increase (Feb. 1):** Administration to seek additional $120 billion over next five years, bringing annual budget to $451 billion in 2007.

**American Taliban Soldier Charged (Feb. 13):** John Walker Lindh pleads not guilty to charges that he supported terrorist groups and conspired to kill U.S. citizens.

**House Votes for Campaign Reform (Feb. 14):** Approves, 240–189, broad overhaul of financing procedures, including ban on soft money.

**Bush Offers Antipollution Plan (Feb. 14):** Discloses program to slow accumulation of gases linked to climate change and cut pollution from power plants.

**Big TV Networks Win Court Victory (Feb. 19):** Federal bench in Washington rules government must reconsider number of stations a network can own and voids ban on cable operator ownership of TV stations.

**Bush Changes Toxic Waste Policy (Feb. 22):** Specifies fewer sites for restoration and transfers most costs from industry to taxpayers.

BUSINESS/SCIENCE/SOCIETY

**Queen Marks Golden Jubilee (Feb. 6):** Elizabeth II observes 50th anniversary of ascension to the throne.

**Another Company Under Inquiry (Feb. 8):** SEC investigating bankruptcy filing of optic network operator Global Crossing. Largest filing ever by a telecommunications company.

**Winter Olympics Open (Feb. 8):** 19th winter games open with festive ceremony at Salt Lake City.

**Enron Ex-Head Criticized at Hearing (Feb. 12):** Bipartisan group of 21 senators highly critical of Kenneth L. Lay, former chairman.

**Rotting Corpses Found Near Crematory (Feb. 15):** Operator of Georgia's Tri-State Crematory, Ray Marsh, allegedly dumped bodies on property when furnace failed.

**Train Fire Kills Hundreds in Egypt (Feb. 20):** More than 370 holiday travelers dead. Explosion in stove blamed.

**Operation on Fetus Called Success (Feb. 21):** Boston surgeons operate on fetus's aortic valve in utero. Baby born healthy although delivered six weeks early.

**U.S. Issues New Guidelines on Mammograms (Feb. 21):** Ending months of controversy, health officials strongly recommend breast cancer screening beginning at age 40, instead of 50.

**Former Enron Official Defiant at Hearing (Feb. 26):** Jeffrey K. Skilling, former CEO, tells Senate panel he did not lie to Congress about his role in Enron's collapse.

WORLD

**Hundreds in India Die in Rioting (March 2):** Hindu-Muslim clashes in western India claim almost 400, highest losses in nearly a decade.

**U.S. and Afghan Troops Launch Attack (March 2):** Target remaining al-Qaeda and Taliban fighters in eastern Afghanistan in mission dubbed Operation Anaconda. **(March 4):** At least seven Americans die in the mission, the first U.S.-led assault by ground troops. **(March 6):** More troops and helicopters brought in to thwart attempts by Taliban and al-Qaeda fighters to maintain their redoubts in the mountains of Shah-i-Kot.

**Afghan Allies Seize Mountain Stronghold (March 12):** U.S. troops and Afghan forces attack Shah-i-Kot Valley from three sides and gain control of the fortress.

**Lockerbie Bomber Loses Appeal (March 14):** Abdelbaset Ali Mohmed al-Megrahi, Libyan intelligence official, flown to Scotland to begin life sentence for plane crash that killed 270 in Dec. 1988.

**Mugabe Reelected President of Zimbabwe (March 13):** With 1.685 million votes, wins another six-year term, beating Morgan Tsvangirai of the Movement for Democratic Change, who tallies 1.258 million votes.

**UN Human Rights Chief to Quit Post (March 18):** In Geneva, Mary Robinson says she will not seek another term when appointment ends in September.

**Rules for War Tribunal Set (March 20):** Bush administration outlines procedures for trials of prisoners from the Afghan war. Way opened for U.S. to try, and possibly execute, foreigners.

**Pope Speaks Out on Church Scandals (March 21):** John Paul II calls wave of pedophile cases "a dark shadow of suspicion" cast over all clergy.

**U.S.-Mexico Security Pact Announced (March 21):** Border accord intended to weed out terrorists and smugglers.

**Bomb Kills at Least 19 in Israel (March 27):** More than 100 wounded as Palestinian blows himself up in a Netanya hotel during a Passover seder.

**Arab League Approves Saudi Peace Plan (March 28):** At summit, Arab nations adopt Crown Prince Abdullah's proposal to offer Israel normal relations in return for withdrawal from occupied territories, the creation of a Palestinian state, and the return of refugees.

**Israel Raids West Bank Towns (March 29):** Troops and tanks enter Jenin, Nablus, Bethlehem, and other areas in response to a string of Palestinian suicide attacks.

**Dutch Legalize Euthanasia (March 31):** Netherlands becomes first nation to legalize mercy killing for terminally ill persons wishing to die.

**Sharon Declares Israel in a War (March 31):** Israeli prime minister calls Yasir Arafat the enemy of the entire free world. Speech follows a suicide attack in a Haifa restaurant that killed 15, including bomber.

NATION

**Bush Imposes Tariffs on Steel Imports (March 5):** In a broad move to protect a major industry, president sets import tariffs as high as 30%. Higher consumer prices expected for autos, homes, and appliances.

**Case Against Clinton Dropped (March 6):** Independent Counsel Robert Ray closes the Whitewater probe, ending the threat of criminal liability for the former president.

**U.S. Aids Countries Fighting Terrorism (March 11):** Bush says nation is willing to train and provide military aid to "governments everywhere" for what he made clear would be battles beyond Afghanistan.

**Four Immigration Officials Replaced (March 15):** Top aides ousted over recent embarrassment of mailing visa extensions to two dead Sept. 11 hijackers.

**Congress Passes Campaign Reform Bill (March 20):** Bush agrees to sign measure after 60–40 Senate approval of bill allowing Senate approval of bill.

BUSINESS/SCIENCE/SOCIETY

**Fed Chief Declares Recession Over (March 7):** Alan Greenspan speaks on basis of recent economic news.

**Arthur Andersen Indicted in Enron Inquiry (March 14):** Becomes the first major firm to face criminal charge. Charged with a single count of obstruction of justice in the destruction of documents relating to case.

**Mother Escapes Death Penalty (March 15):** Texas jury recommends life sentence for Andrea Pia Yates, who was convicted of drowning her five children in a bathtub.

**Attorney Convicted in Fatal Dog Attack (March 21):** Marjorie Knoller guilty of second-degree murder in the death of Diane Whipple, 33, who was mauled to death in 2001 by a 120-pound Presa Canario dog.

**Rise in Postal Rates Approved (March 22):** Independent Postal Rate Commission approves 3-cent increase in price of mailing first-class letter to 37 cents. Part of a broad increase in most postal rates.

**Black Actors Win Top Oscars (March 24):** Denzel Washington and Halle Berry honored for *Training Day* and *Monster's Ball,* respectively.

# April 2002

## WORLD

**Fighting Escalates Between Israelis and Palestinians (April 2):** Israeli prime minister Ariel Sharon says he would allow Palestinian leader Yasir Arafat to leave his besieged Ramallah headquarters if he went into exile. Arafat refuses the proposal, saying he "would rather die." **(April 3):** More than 400 Israeli tanks enter Nablus, largest city in the West Bank, and Jenin, bulldozing buildings and questioning suspected militants. Palestinians retaliate with gunfire.

**UNITA Rebels and Angolan Government Sign a Cease-fire (April 4):** Agreement ends civil war that has ravaged the country since Angola's independence from Portugal in 1975. Accord reached six weeks after the death of UNITA leader Jonas Savimbi.

**International Criminal Court Wins UN Ratification (April 11):** Court will try criminals charged with genocide, crimes against humanity, war crimes, and crimes of aggression. The U.S. refuses to ratify the treaty, saying Americans overseas may be unfairly targeted.

**Truck Bomb Kills 19 in Tunisia (April 11):** Victims include 14 German tourists. Intelligence officials suspect al-Qaeda responsible.

**Venezuelan President Ousted (April 12):** Hugo Chávez forced by military officers to resign after massive street protests turn violent. **(April 14):** Chávez returns to power amid international criticism of the coup and overwhelming support from Venezuela's poor.

**Palestinian Suicide Bomber Strikes in Jerusalem (April 13):** Six killed at a bus stop. Secretary of State Colin Powell postpones a meeting with Yasir Arafat.

**Former Guerilla Leader Elected President of East Timor (April 14):** José Gusmão wins in a landslide. Will become the country's first president when independence is officially declared in May.

**Israel Begins West Bank Withdrawal (April 15):** Responding to plea by President Bush, Israeli prime minister Ariel Sharon begins to pull out of some towns.

**Dutch Government Resigns (April 16):** Prime Minister Wim Kok and his coalition step down after an investigation concludes that the government and military leaders should have been able to prevent the 1995 massacre of Bosnian Muslims by Bosnian Serbs at Srebrenica.

**Former Afghan King Returns to Homeland (April 18):** Mohammad Zahir Shah arrives in Kabul after 29 years in exile.

**France's Rightist Candidate to Face Chirac (April 21):** Jean-Marie Le Pen polls ahead of Prime Minister Lionel Jospin, placing second in the first round of France's presidential election.

**U.S. Cardinals Condemn Sexual Abuse by Priests (April 24):** Communique released after unprecedented two-day meeting at Vatican results in policy to oust notorious predators.

**Vote Gives Musharraf Another Five Years (April 30):** Voters approve a referendum to extend the Pakistani military leader's presidency for another five years.

## NATION

**Bush Calls for Total Ban on Human Cloning (April 10):** Urges Senate to pass legislation forbidding procedure for both reproductive and research purposes.

**Senate Passes Election Reform Bill (April 11):** Votes, 99–1, to set national election standards.

**Ohio Congressman Convicted (April 11):** James Traficant found guilty of bribery, racketeering, tax evasion, and obstruction of justice.

**U.S. and Cincinnati Agree on New Police Policy (April 12):** Pact, signed a year after protests erupted over the shooting deaths of 15 black suspects by police, calls for more patrol officers, improved inquiries into civilian complaints, and more police training.

**Senate Rejects Arctic Drilling (April 19):** Measure to permit oil exploration in the Arctic National Wildlife Refuge defeated, 46–54.

**Top Bush Aide Resigns (April 23):** Karen Hughes, president's confidant, director of communications, and spokeswoman, says her husband and son miss Texas home. She plans to advise Bush from Austin.

**Senate and House Agree on Farm Bill (April 26):** Measure, which tops $100 billion, will increase subsidies to farmers and fund conservation programs.

**House Supports Splitting INS (April 26):** Votes, 405–9, to divide agency's roles between two new bureaus, one for immigration services and one for enforcement.

### BUSINESS/SCIENCE/SOCIETY

**Plane Crashes into Milan Skyscraper (April 18):** Three die and dozens injured when a small private craft hits the city's tallest building.

**Actor Charged with Wife's Murder (April 22):** Robert Blake pleads not guilty to 2001 shooting death of wife, Bonny Lee Bakley.

**German Student Kills 18 in School Shooting (April 26):** Robert Steinhäuser, 19, recently expelled, murders students, teachers, and staff member before turning the gun on himself in Erfurt.

# May 2002

## WORLD

**Israel Releases Arafat (May 2):** Palestinian leader free to leave Ramallah compound after five-month confinement in exchange for the imprisonment in Jericho of six Palestinians. U.S. brokered deal.

**Chirac Reelected in a Landslide (May 5):** Outpolls far-right candidate, Jean-Marie Le Pen, 82% to 18% in the second round of France's presidential election.

**Burmese Pro-democracy Leader Freed (May 6):** Aung San Suu Kyi released after 19 months of house arrest.

**Dutch Politician Killed (May 6):** Pim Fortuyn, far-right, anti-immigration populist, had been a leading contender in upcoming elections.

**Madagascar's President Sworn In Again (May 6):** Marc Ravalomanana takes oath of office a week after recount of December vote favors him over rival and former president Didier Ratsiraka.

**Suicide Bomber Kills 16 in Tel Aviv (May 7):** Blast at a crowded pool hall prompts Israeli prime minister Ariel Sharon to cut short Washington visit.

**Pakistan Blast Kills 11 (May 8):** Victims in Karachi are French naval engineers. Al-Qaeda blamed.

**Siege at Bethlehem Church Ends (May 10):** Deal calls for withdrawal of Israeli troops, who had surrounded the Church of the Nativity, and the exile of 13 Palestinian militants to several European countries.

**U.S. and Russia Reach Landmark Arms Agreement (May 13):** President Bush and Russian president Vladimir Putin announce a pact to cut both countries' nuclear arsenals by up to two-thirds over the next 10 years.

**Military Camp Attacked in Kashmir (May 14):** More than 30 Indians, including 10 children, die in Jammu and Kashmir. India blames Pakistani militants.

**UN Overhauls Iraq Sanctions (May 14):** New rules, unanimously approved by the Security Council, allow import of more goods for civilians but tighten restrictions on items that could also be used by the military.

**Carter Urges U.S. to End Cuban Trade Embargo (May 14):** While visiting Cuba, former president also criticizes Fidel Castro and his communist regime for suppressing human rights and democracy.

**Arafat Vows to Reform Regime (May 15):** In a speech to parliament, Palestinian leader calls for elections and a total overhaul of the Palestinian Authority.

**Netherlands Turns to the Right (May 16):** Christian Democrats return to power after eight years of liberal leadership. Jan Peter Balkenende becomes prime minister.

**Sharon Ousts Cabinet Members (May 20):** Fires ultra-Orthodox Shas Party ministers after they vote down economic reform legislation.

**East Timor Declares Independence (May 20):** World's newest country, led by José Gusmão, debuts to grand celebration and daunting economic woes.

**Pakistan Tests Ballistic Missiles (May 25 et seq.):** Move infuriates international community, as tensions between India and Pakistan over Kashmir reach boiling point.

**Colombia Elects New President (May 26):** Alvaro Uribe, who vowed to crack down on rebel groups, wins in the first round of the election, taking 53% of the vote.

**Russia Joins NATO as Junior Partner (May 28):** Russia-NATO council to focus on terrorism, arms control, and regional crises. Russia will not have say in alliance's use of force or veto power on new members.

**Libya Reportedly Makes Offer to Lockerbie Families (May 29):** Lawyers for victims say Libya offered $2.7 billion to compensate families of the 270 victims of 1988 crash. Payment would follow the lifting of sanctions by the U.S. and the UN.

NATION

**U.S. Withdraws from International Court Treaty (May 6):** State department informs UN of its decision, saying it fears Americans overseas may be unfairly targeted and subject to arbitrary charges.

**Pentagon Looks to Scrap Artillery System (May 8):** Defense Secretary Donald Rumsfeld plans to cancel $11 billion Crusader and develop new technology.

**House Passes Defense Bill (May 10):** Votes, 359–58, in favor of $400 billion wartime legislation that funds Crusader artillery system, which the defense department wants to cancel.

**Bush Signs Farm Bill (May 13):** Ten-year, $100 billion measure will increase farm subsidies.

**White House Acknowledges Hijacking Warning (May 15):** Administration criticized for not launching an investigation last August, when the CIA told President Bush that it believed al-Qaeda was planning to attack U.S.

**House Votes to Revamp Welfare (May 17):** Votes, 229–197, to increase work requirements for welfare recipients.

**FBI Lawyer Criticizes Bureau in Letter to Director (May 21):** In a 12-page memo, Coleen Rowley accuses FBI headquarters of thwarting efforts to investigate Zacarias Moussaoui, a suspected terrorist.

**FBI Agent Testifies About Memo (May 21):** Kenneth Williams answers questions before the Senate Judiciary Committee about his July 2001 memo that posited that large numbers of al-Qaeda members enrolled in U.S. flight schools could use their training to launch a terrorist attack against the country.

**Senate Passes Trade Bill (May 30):** Votes, 68–58, to give President Bush power to negotiate trade agreements that Congress can approve or defeat but not amend.

**FBI Announces Sweeping Changes (May 30):** Following harsh criticism for handling of Sept. 11 attacks, director Robert Mueller outlines plan that will have bureau focus on counterterrorism rather than domestic crimes.

BUSINESS / SCIENCE / SOCIETY

**Arthur Andersen Trial Begins (May 7):** Accounting firm faces one charge of obstruction of justice for allegedly shredding Enron documents.

**College Student Charged in Pipe Bombings (May 7):** Lucas Helder, 21, admits that he planted 18 pipe bombs in mailboxes in five states.

**Cardinal Law Testifies in Court (May 8):** Embattled Roman Catholic archbishop of Boston says he delegated most decision making in the John Geoghan sex abuse case to subordinates and claims he has forgotten many of the details surrounding the scandal.

**Merrill Lynch Agrees to Pay Fine (May 21):** Brokerage firm to pay $100 million to settle conflict-of-interest case brought by New York attorney general.

**Former Intern's Remains Found in DC Park (May 22):** Bones of Chandra Levy discovered in a remote section of Rock Creek Park. She disappeared in April 2001.

**Former Klansman Convicted of First-Degree Murder (May 22):** Bobby Frank Cherry sentenced to life in prison for his role in the death of four young black girls in the 1963 bombing of Birmingham, Alabama's 16th Street Baptist Church.

**Hormone Linked to Obesity Identified (May 23):** Ghrelin believed to slow metabolism, cause hunger, and limit ability to burn fat.

**Plane Crashes into Taiwan Strait (May 25):** China Airlines Boeing 747–200 breaks into four pieces, killing all 225 aboard.

# June 2002

WORLD

**Arafat Outlines Plan to Reform Security Forces (June 4):** In meeting with CIA director George Tenet, Palestinian leader suggests that he will streamline police and intelligence agencies.

**Asian Leaders Meet to Talk Peace (June 4):** Kazakhstan hosts First Conference on Interaction and Confidence-Building Measures in Asia.

**Israeli Troops Attack Arafat's Compound (June 5):** Move follows Palestinian suicide attack that kills 17 Israelis, including 13 soldiers, in Galilee.

**Pakistan President Vows to Curb Kashmir Militants (June 6):** Pervez Musharraf pledges to permanently halt infiltration of militants into Indian-held Kashmir.

**American Missionary Killed in Philippines (June 7):** Martin Burnham, who had been held hostage since last May by rebel group Abu Sayyaf, shot and killed during a fire fight between the guerillas and Filipino troops.

**India Moves to Ease Tension in Kashmir (June 10):** Ends its ban on Pakistani planes flying over Indian airspace and pulls back its ships from Pakistan's coast.

**Grand Council Convenes in Afghanistan (June 11):** More than 1,500 delegates from around the country meet at loya jirga in Kabul to elect a president and government.

**U.S. Abandons Antiballistic Missile Treaty (June 13):** Thirty-year-old pact lapses six months after President Bush announced U.S. withdrawal. Decision allows U.S. to develop system to defend against missile attack.

**Hamid Karzai Elected President of Afghanistan (June 13):** Interim leader wins in a landslide. He'll serve until 2004 general election.

**Car Bomb Explodes at U.S. Consulate in Karachi (June 14):** Pakistani militants suspected in blast that kills 11 and injures more than two dozen.

**Israel Reoccupies Parts of West Bank Towns (June 20):** Troops to remain as long "as terror continues," says Prime Minister Ariel Sharon. At least ten Palestinians killed in ongoing skirmishes. Move follows three consecutive days of violence.

**Bush Announces New Mideast Policy (June 24):** Tells Palestinians that the U.S. will not recognize an independent Palestinian state until Yasir Arafat is replaced.

**Alleged Terrorist Enters Plea (June 24):** Zacarias Moussaoui, the suspected 20th hijacker in the Sept. 11 attacks, tries to plead no contest, which would have been considered an admission of guilt. Judge Leonie Brinkema enters a not guilty plea on his behalf.

**Industrialized Countries Pledge Aid to Africa (June 27):** At summit in Canada, G-8 countries, with Russia newly admitted, commit $6 billion to African nations that undergo social and government reform.

**Israeli Forces Attack Palestinian Authority Office (June 28):** Part of the four-story building in Hebron destroyed. Palestinian militants thought to be inside.

**U.S. Vetoes Peacekeeping Force in Bosnia (June 30):** Move follows Security Council's refusal to grant American peacekeepers immunity from being tried by new International Criminal Court. U.S., however, agrees to a three-day extension of the mission.

NATION

**Intelligence Committees Begin Terrorism Investigations (June 4):** House and Senate groups look into U.S. response to threats that date back to 1986.

**Anti-abortion Activist Extradited to U.S. (June 5):** James Kopp, indicted in 1999 in the 1998 shooting death of abortion doctor Barnett Slepian, returned from France.

**Bush Seeks New Cabinet Department to Fight Terrorism (June 6):** President proposes major reorganization of government that would combine 22 federal agencies into a Department of Homeland Security. **(June 13):** President sends bill to Congress.

**Dirty Bomb Plot Foiled (June 10):** Justice Dept. announces the May 8 arrest of Jose Padilla (aka Abdullah al-Muhajir), a U.S. citizen. Government, alleging he was working with al-Qaeda to launch an attack in the U.S, calls him an enemy combatant and holds him at a naval base.

**Senate Defeats Repeal of Estate Tax (June 12):** Votes to thwart president's efforts to make permanent the tax cut that expires in 2011.

**NSA Announces al-Qaeda Intercept (June 19):** Security agency collected conversations on Sept. 10 that referred to "the big match" and "zero hour" but did not translate the discussions until the day after the terrorist attacks.

**Providence Mayor Convicted (June 24):** Vincent "Buddy" Cianci, Jr., found guilty of racketeering.

**Government Loan Bails Out Amtrak (June 26):** Bush administration promises troubled railroad $100 million loan to maintain service through Sept. Congress expected to approve another $100 million. Amtrak agrees to cut next year's budget by $100 million.

**Court Declares Pledge Unconstitutional (June 26):** Federal appeals court in San Francisco rules that the words "under God" in the Pledge of Allegiance violate the separation of church and state.

**House and Senate Pass Defense Budget (June 27):** Senate votes, 97–2, in favor of $393 billion program that includes pay raises for military personnel and increased funding for hardware and research. House approves, 413–18, a similar $355 billion appropriations bill.

**House Approves Increase in Debt Limit (June 27):** Votes, 215–214, to raise ceiling on national debt $450 billion, to $6.4 trillion. Senate already passed identical bill.

**Bush Cuts Superfund Program (June 30):** Slashes funding for decontamination of 33 toxic-waste sites.

BUSINESS/SCIENCE/SOCIETY

**Business Executive Indicted (June 4):** Manhattan district attorney indicts former Tyco chief executive L. Dennis Kozlowski on charges he avoided sales taxes on art.

**Kennedy Cousin Found Guilty (June 7):** Connecticut jury finds Michael Skakel, 41, guilty of the 1975 murder of Martha Moxley.

**Biotech Executive Charged with Insider Trading (June 12):** Samuel Waksal, former CEO of ImClone Systems, accused of tipping off family members to FDA's decision not to approve company's cancer drug.

**U.S. Bishops Adopt Policy for Abusers (June 14):** At national meeting in Dallas, bishops decide to ban from all ministerial duties any priest who has ever been known to sexually abuse a minor.

**Scientists Discover New Planet (June 14):** Astronomers at the University of California-Berkeley discover a planet similar to Jupiter in planetary system similar to the Earth's own solar system.

**Arthur Andersen Guilty (June 15):** Houston jury convicts accounting firm Arthur Andersen of obstruction of justice for destroying documents relating to former client Enron Corp.

**Firefighter Accused of Starting Colorado Blaze (June 17):** Terry Barton, an employee of the U.S. Forest Service, charged with setting the largest wildfire in Colorado history.

**Murder Conviction Overturned in Dog Mauling Case (June 17):** Saying the evidence did not justify the conviction, a San Francisco judge overturns a second-degree murder conviction for Marjorie Knoller, owner of two dogs that killed a neighbor, Diane Whipple.

**Jury Favors Victim of Secondhand Smoke (June 18):** A Miami jury awards $5.5 million in damages to Lynn French, 56, a flight attendant who claimed smoky airplane cabins caused her chronic sinus problems.

**Arizona Wildfires Merge (June 22):** Two wildfires that have already burned 330,000 acres in northern Arizona join, creating a conflagration covering 250,000 acres with a front line stretching 50 mi. **(June 30):** Leonard Gregg, contract firefighter, charged with setting fire.

**Train Crash Kills Hundreds in Tanzania (June 24):** Passenger train rolls down a hill and collides with freight train. About 280 die and more than 900 are wounded.

**WorldCom Admits It Grossly Misstated Profits (June 25):** Country's second-largest long-distance carrier said it inflated cash flow over last five quarters by $3.8 billion.

**Brazil Wins World Cup (June 30):** Beats Germany, 2–0, for record-setting fifth time. Ronaldo scores both goals.

## July 2002

WORLD

**International Criminal Court Opens (July 1):** Hague-based court will try cases of genocide and war crimes. U.S. removed signature from treaty that created the court.

**U.S. Bomb Kills Dozens of Afghan Civilians (July 1):** Errant 2,000-pound bomb dropped during an Air Force attack kills about 40 members of a wedding party.

**U.S. Extends Peacekeeping Mission (July 3):** Allows force to remain in Bosnia until July 15, while U.S. and UN Security Council negotiate over U.S. demands that Americans be granted immunity from prosecution by International Criminal Court.

**Afghan Vice President Assassinated (July 6):** Abdul Qadir, a Pashtun, shot in the head by gunmen in Kabul.

**African Leaders Form New Group (July 8):** More than 30 leaders meet in Durban to dismantle Organization of African Unity, established 39 years ago to battle apartheid and colonialism, and create the African Union.

**Turkey Rocked by Cabinet Resignations (July 8):** Several legislators and ministers step down amid fears that government is crumbling. **(July 11):** Foreign minister Ismail Cem resigns, seventh cabinet-level departure.

**Security Council and U.S. Compromise on New Court (July 12):** American peacekeepers granted one-year immunity from prosecution by International Criminal Court. Move ends weeks of tense negotiations.

**Islamic Militants Attack Hindus (July 14):** Kashmir assault claims 25 and wounds more than 30.

**French President Survives Assassination Attempt (July 14):** Student, Maxime Brunerie, 25, fires at Jacques Chirac on the Champs-Élysées.

**Pearl Kidnapper Sentenced to Death (July 15):** Pakistani court convicts Ahmed Omar Sheikh of masterminding the capture and murder of *Wall Street Journal* reporter. Three others sent to prison for life.

**IRA Apologizes to Families of Victims (July 16):** In a remarkable act of contrition, the Irish Republican Army issues condolences to the relatives of 650 civilians killed during 30 years of violence in Northern Ireland.

**Spain Arrests al-Qaeda Suspects (July 16):** Police detain three men accused of belonging to terror group. Find videotapes containing surveillance of World Trade Center and other possible targets.

**Suicide Bombings Resume in Israel (July 16):** Militants ambush bus near West Bank settlement, killing 9 people. First attack in nearly a month. **(July 17):** Two Palestinian suicide bombers kill three in Tel Aviv.

**Sept. 11 Suspect Enters Guilty Plea (July 18):** Zacarias Moussaoui pleads guilty to planning terrorist attacks on U.S. and admits belonging to al-Qaeda. **(July 25):** Withdraws earlier guilty plea and denies he helped to plan the Sept. 11 attacks.

**Leader of Greek Terrorist Group Arrested (July 19):** Alexandros Yiotopoulos, a mathematician, charged with murder, bombings, and bank robberies. He headed November 17, a terrorist group that has killed 23 people since the 1980s.

**Israelis Attack Home of Hamas Leader (July 23):** Bomb strikes a house in a dense civilian area, killing militant Sheik Salah Shehada and 14 others.

**Rwanda and Congo Sign Peace Accord (July 30):** Paul Kagame and Joseph Kabila, presidents of Rwanda and Congo, respectively, agree to end 4-year-old war that has claimed 3 million people.

**Americans Die in Jerusalem Attack (July 31):** Bomb explodes at a Hebrew University cafeteria. Five of the seven casualties are U.S. citizens.

NATION

**Two Dead in Airport Shooting (July 4):** Alleged gunman, Egyptian-born Hesham Mohamed Hadayet, kills two at Los Angeles International Airport.

**Senate Approves Nuclear Waste Site (July 9):** Votes, 60–39, to store radioactive material from 39 states inside Nevada's Yucca Mountain. Site expected to open in 2010. **(July 23):** President Bush approves measure.

**Bush Speaks Out Against Corporate Malfeasance (July 10):** In first policy speech on issue, president calls for prison sentences for offenders, close scrutiny of businesses, and additional funds for enforcement.

**House Votes to Arm Pilots (July 10):** Bill passes, 310–113, to train airline pilots to become deputized flight deck officers and carry guns in cockpits.

**Bush Announces Deficit (July 12):** Shortfall, which follows four years of surpluses, expected to hit $165 billion for 2002. President blames decrease in capital gains tax revenue.

**American Taliban Member Pleads Guilty (July 15):** John Walker Lindh, 21, will serve 20 years in prison for aiding a terrorist organization.

**Bush Unveils Domestic Security Plan (July 16):** Proposal includes measures to protect the country's infrastructure, issue national drivers' licenses, review laws that ban the military from playing a role in U.S. law enforcement, and beef up border patrols. **(July 26):** House votes, 295–132, to create a Department of Homeland Security.

**EPA to Clean Up Some Toxic Sites (July 21):** In a reversal, agency decides to fund decontamination of 11 areas.

**U.S. Withholds Aid for Population Fund (July 22):** Bush administration refuses to give $34 million, which had been approved earlier to UN fund.

**House Expels Traficant (July 24):** Votes, 420–1, to oust from Congress nine-term Ohio Democrat. **(July 30):** Traficant sentenced to eight years in prison.

**Congressional Negotiators Compromise on Bankruptcy Bill (July 25):** Legislation requires individuals to repay some debt over an extended period.

**House and Senate Pass Corporate Reform Bill (July 25):** Legislation makes security fraud a criminal offense, metes stiff penalties for executives who sign off on false financial reports, and creates an accounting-industry oversight board. **(July 30):** Bush signs measure.

**House Approves Trade Authority for Bush (July 27):** Votes, 215–212, to give president the right to negotiate trade deals with other countries. Congress can only accept or reject the deals, not amend them.

**Ethics Committee Reprimands Torricelli (July 30):** Senate group "severely admonishes" New Jersey senator for accepting gifts from David Chang, a wealthy businessman and campaign contributor.

**Senate Kills Drug Plan (July 31):** Republican and Democratic proposals to help the elderly pay for prescription drugs fall short of the 60 votes necessary for passage. Manages, however, to pass bill that hastens the approval of cheaper, generic drugs.

BUSINESS/SCIENCE/SOCIETY

**Vivendi Universal Chief Steps Down (July 2):** Jean-Marie Messier forced to resign from media giant amid $32.7 billion debt.

**Dozens Die in Midair Collision (July 2):** Swiss air traffic controllers cited for lapses in crash of Russian passenger plane and German cargo plane that killed 71, including 52 Russian children headed for vacation.

**AIDS Deaths Projected to Skyrocket (July 2):** UN announces toll could reach an additional 65 million by 2020 if preventative measures are not expanded.

**Balloonist Completes Around-the-World Trip (July 2):** In sixth attempt, Steve Fossett, Chicago investment banker, circumnavigates globe in a balloon in 14 days.

**Hormone Replacement Questioned (July 9):** Study finds that drug therapy for menopausal women can cause increases in rate of breast cancer, heart attacks, blood clots, and strokes.

**Early Skull Discovered in Chad (July 11):** French scientists report in the journal *Nature* that they have unearthed a 7-million-year-old member of the human family, *Sahelanthropus tchadensis*, who has been nicknamed "Toumai." Fossil combines human and chimpanzee characteristics.

**Scientists Re-create Polio Virus (July 11):** Use virus's genome sequence and DNA purchased by mail. Move shows that terrorists may be able to make biological weapons without a live virus.

**Millions of Pounds of Beef Recalled (July 19):** Agriculture Department pulls 19 million pounds of ground beef from store shelves after 19 people fall ill. Contaminated meat traced to ConAgra plant in Greeley, Colo.

**WorldCom Files for Bankruptcy (July 21):** Largest claim in U.S. history. Lists more than $107 billion in assets.

**Adelphia Founder and Sons Arrested (July 24):** John Rigas, 78, and sons Timothy and Michael charged with bank, wire, and securities fraud. Accused of using more than $1 billion in company funds for personal use.

**Imperiled Pennsylvania Miners Rescued (July 28):** After spending 77 hours in a dark, flooded mine shaft 240 ft below ground, nine workers emerge in good health.

**Former WorldCom Executives Charged with Fraud (July 31):** Scott Sullivan, former CFO, and David Myers, former controller, accused of misstating revenue by more than $3.8 billion.

## August 2002

WORLD

**Iraq Moves to Resume Inspection Talks (Aug. 1):** Iraqi foreign minister Naji Sabri invites UN inspector Hans Blix to Baghdad to discuss weapons inspections. **(Aug. 5):** Iraq says it will give members of Congress access to areas believed to be arms-development sites.

**Judge Orders Release of Detainee Names (Aug. 2):** Rules that the Bush administration must disclose names of people arrested following Sept. 11 terrorist attacks.

**Taiwan President Says Country Separate from China (Aug. 2):** Chen Shui-bian also encourages a referendum on the issue.

**Suspected Pakistani Militants Attack Christian Sites (Aug. 5):** Six die when four men open fire at Islamabad's Murree Christian School. **(Aug. 9):** Four die in Islamabad after a grenade attack on a missionary hospital.

**UN and U.S. Refuse Inspection Talks in Iraq (Aug. 5):** Congress rejects Iraq's offer to have members personally inspect weapons sites. **(Aug. 6):** Secretary General Kofi Annan says inspectors will only go if Iraq agrees to follow rules set by UN.

**Explosions Rock Bogotá During Inauguration (Aug. 7):** FARC guerrillas suspected in attacks on presidential palace and nearby slum that claim at least 14 people as Alvaro Uribe Vélez takes oath of office nearby.

**IMF Loan Rescues Brazil (Aug. 7):** U.S. backs $30 billion loan to beleaguered nation.

**White Farmers Ordered to Leave Property (Aug. 8):** Zimbabwe redistribution policy, drafted by President Robert Mugabe, seeks to return to black farmers land that was taken during the colonial era without offering compensation to current white owners.

**Israel Indicts Palestinian Leader (Aug. 14):** Marwan Barghouit, leader in Yasir Arafat's Fatah organization, charged with murder, conspiracy to commit murder, and working with a terrorist group. He's considered a possible successor to Arafat.

**Indonesian Court Rules on Human Rights Cases (Aug. 14):** Former governor of East Timor, Abilio Soares, convicted for not stopping 1999's post-referendum killing spree by pro-Indonesian militia and government troops. **(Aug. 15):** Six military leaders and police officers acquitted of charges, outraging human rights groups.

**Bush Protests Sentencing of Activist (Aug. 15):** Refuses Egypt's request for funds, beyond $2 billion allotted annually, after Egyptian court sentences Saad Eddin Ibrahim to seven years in prison for political activism.

**Pope Returns to Homeland (Aug. 16):** Begins emotional, three-day trip to Poland, which many believe will be his last.

**Israel and Palestinians Agree on Withdrawal Plan (Aug. 18):** Agreement, "Gaza, Bethlehem first," calls for Israel to pull out of areas if Palestinians agree to rein in militants. Hamas and Islamic Jihad reject the deal.

**Videotapes Support al-Qaeda Weapons Theory (Aug. 19):** CNN broadcasts footage of al-Qaeda members giving instructions on how to build bombs and fire surface-to-air missiles and of dogs dying, allegedly from exposure to chemical agents. Network paid $30,000 for 64 tapes.

**Palestinian Terrorist Dies (Aug. 19):** Abu Nidal, blamed for deaths of 900 people in 20 countries, reportedly killed himself in Iraq.

**Protesters Seize Iraqi Embassy in Berlin (Aug. 19):** Members of Democratic Iraqi Opposition of Germany, calling for ouster of Saddam Hussein, take over building.

**Canadian Prime Minister Will Not Run for Reelection (Aug. 21):** Jean Chretien announces he will step down when his third term expires in Feb. 2004.

**Pakistan President Rewrites Constitution (Aug. 21):** Pervez Musharraf makes sweeping changes that allow him to dissolve parliament and appoint supreme court justices and military leaders.

**World Leaders Gather at Development Meeting (Aug. 26):** Thousands of officials, including about 100 heads of state, meet in Johannesburg for the United Nations' World Summit on Sustainable Development.

**Four Indicted for Terrorist Activity (Aug. 28):** Arab men in Detroit charged with running a "sleeper operational combat cell." Government alleges they provided fake licenses, bought weapons, and sheltered terrorists.

NATION

**Senate Approves Trade Authority for Bush (Aug. 1):** Votes, 64–34, to give president the right to negotiate trade deals with other countries. Congress can only accept or reject the deals, not amend them. **(Aug. 6):** Bush signs the trade bill.

**Bush Sets New Medical Privacy Rules (Aug. 9):** Rolls back protections, enacted by President Clinton, that required doctors and other health-care providers to get written permission before disclosing patient information for treatment or claim payment.

**Germ Weapon Expert Denies Role in Anthrax Attacks (Aug. 11):** Steven Hatfill also says high-profile government investigation is destroying his reputation.

**Bush Discusses Economy at Texas Forum (Aug. 13):** At Baylor University meeting, president reports that he's confident about future of U.S. economy. Also announces he will not grant Congress $5.1 billion in emergency funds.

**Amtrak Suspends High-Speed Service (Aug. 13):** Design flaws in Acela trains shelve service on Eastern seaboard route.

**Former Security Chief Advises Against Iraq Attack (Aug. 15):** In *Wall Street Journal*, Brent Scowcroft, close friend and adviser of Bush family, warns that invasion could jeopardize war on terrorism.

**Bush Scales Back Steel Tariffs (Aug. 22):** Administration revises March legislation and exempts 178 imported steel products from hefty fees.

**Budget Office Predicts Large Deficits (Aug. 27):** Forecast by Congressional Budget Office expects deficits through 2005 and expects 2002 tax revenues to come in 6.6% lower than in 2001.

BUSINESS/SCIENCE/SOCIETY

**Conjoined Twins Separated (Aug. 6):** Guatemalan girls, joined at their heads, survive 22-hour surgery at U.C.L.A. Medical Center.

**Waksal Faces More Charges (Aug. 7):** Founder and former ImClone CEO indicted on charges of insider trading, bank fraud, forgery, and obstruction of justice.

**WorldCom Discloses Inflated Revenue (Aug. 8):** Latest accounting irregularity reveals $3.3 billion in false earnings, bringing total to $7.1 billion since 1999.

**Scientists Identify Hunger Hormone (Aug. 8):** London scientists report in journal *Nature* that the hormone PYY, produced in the small intestine, triggers a feeling of fullness after eating.

**US Airways Files for Bankruptcy (Aug. 11):** Sixth-largest airline in U.S. plans to maintain service during reorganization.

**Several Die in Europe Floods (Aug. 12):** Prague and Dresden, where levels of the Elbe River rise about 30 ft above normal, suffer most, with damage estimated to top $20 billion. More than 70,000 people evacuated in worst flooding on record. Towns in Austria and Slovakia also affected by flooding of the Danube. **(Aug. 16):** Elbe reaches 29.5 ft, 9 in. higher than peak in 1845.

**Russian Helicopter Crashes in Chechnya (Aug. 19):** Transport vehicle lands in a minefield, increasing number of casualties. Toll at 117, the country's largest military air disaster.

**Conviction in California Kidnapping (Aug. 21):** David Westerfield convicted of kidnapping and murdering his neighbor, 7-year-old Danielle van Dam.

**Enron Official Pleads Guilty to Felonies (Aug. 21):** Michael J. Kopper, former division director, admits to paying kickbacks to Andrew Fastow, former CFO, conspiring to commit wire fraud, and money laundering.

**Skakel Sentenced in Moxley Murder (Aug. 29):** Michael Skakel, nephew of Ethel Kennedy, given 20 years to life in prison for 1975 killing of Martha Moxley.

**Baseball Strike Averted (Aug. 30):** Major league baseball team owners and players' union agree to revenue-sharing deal and luxury tax for big-budget teams.

# September 2002

WORLD

**Earth Summit Ends with Pact (Sept. 4):** Meeting produces plan to improve sanitation, increase accessibility of clean water, reduce the number of endangered species, and improve safety of chemical production.

**Karzai Escapes Assassination Attempt (Sept. 5):** Uniformed assailant fires at Afghan president in Kandahar. Karzai's bodyguards kill the gunman.

**Austrian Government Coalition Collapses (Sept. 9):** Chancellor Wolfgang Schüssel breaks with the right-wing Freedom Party and calls for early elections.

**Switzerland Joins UN (Sept. 10):** Abandons long-held neutrality and becomes the 190th member.

**Palestinian Cabinet Resigns (Sept. 11):** Yasir Arafat's ministers step down to avoid a no-confidence vote by Legislative Council. Arafat sets presidential and parliamentary elections for Jan. 20.

**Bush Addresses United Nations (Sept. 12):** Citing torture, oppression, and 11 years of defiance by Saddam Hussein's regime, president argues for an attack on Iraq.

**Al-Qaeda Operative Captured in Pakistan (Sept. 13):** U.S. announces that Ramzi bin al-Shibh was caught in a Karachi raid. Officials believe he has critical inside information about the Sept. 11 terrorists attacks.

**Terrorist Suspects Arrested in New York (Sept. 13 ):** Five men of Yemeni descent charged with giving "material support" to al-Qaeda terrorists. **(Sept. 15):** Sixth suspect arrested in Bahrain.

**Saudis Offer Bases for Iraq Attack (Sept. 14):** Say U.S. could launch offensive against Iraq from its military bases if a UN resolution justified the action.

**Iraq Says Weapons Inspectors May Return (Sept. 16):** Iraqi foreign minister says country will readmit inspectors unconditionally. President Bush dismisses the offer.

**State Elections Begin in Kashmir (Sept. 16):** Low turnout for State Assembly elections, with many constituencies boycotting the vote.

**Sri Lanka and Rebels Open Talks (Sept. 16):** The government and members of the separatist Tamil Tigers begin peace negotiations in Thailand.

**Japanese Leader Visits North Korea (Sept. 17):** Prime Minister Junichiro Koizumi makes unprecedented visit to Pyongyang, where North Korean president Kim Jong Il apologizes for the abduction of 11 Japanese citizens during the 1970s and 1980s.

**Suicide Bomber Strikes in Tel Aviv (Sept. 19):** Six die in second attack in less than 24 hours. Israel responds by surrounding Yasir Arafat's compound. **(Sept. 20):** Israeli troops further isolate Arafat, destroying several buildings in his compound.

**Violence Rocks Ivory Coast (Sept. 19):** Gen. Robert Guei, the country's former leader, and Interior Minister Emile Boga Doudou are killed in fighting between government troops and mutineering soldiers.

**Schröder Narrowly Reelected (Sept. 22):** German chancellor wins close battle with conservative businessman Edmund Stoiber. Victory attributed to Schröder's stance against a war in Iraq.

**North Korea Plans Free-Trade Zone (Sept. 24):** President Kim announces plans to build a special economic area near North Korea's northwest border with China.

**Gunmen Ambush Hindu Temple (Sept. 24):** Gujarat once again site of deadly violence as 33 people, including 11 Hindu militants.

**Blair Argues for Attack on Iraq (Sept. 24):** British prime minister releases 50-page dossier that outlines threat posed by Saddam Hussein and his stockpile of biological and chemical weapons.

**Iraq Refuses New Resolution (Sept. 28):** Rejects proposed Security Council resolution giving Iraq 30 days to disclose weapons inventory and calling for unfettered access to sites.

**Israeli Troops Withdraw from Arafat's Base (Sept. 29):** End 10-day siege in which forces destroyed most of Arafat's Ramallah compound and trapped him inside.

**Europeans Exempt U.S. from New War Court (Sept. 30):** European Union agrees to spare U.S. military personnel and government officials prosecution by International Criminal Court. In exchange, U.S. promises to try war crimes suspects in American courts.

NATION

**Senate Committee Rejects Bush Judicial Nominee (Sept. 5):** Votes, 10–9, on party lines against nomination of Priscilla Owen to U.S. Court of Appeals.

**Senate Agrees to Arm Pilots (Sept. 5):** Votes, 87–6, to allow pilots to voluntarily become U.S. deputies and thus carry firearms in the cockpit.

**Cianci Resigns After Sentencing (Sept. 6):** Vincent "Buddy" Cianci steps down as mayor of Providence after receiving 64-month prison sentence for a racketeering conviction.

**Bush Places Country on High Alert (Sept. 10):** Officials say they have intelligence that terrorists have planned attacks for Sept. 11. U.S. Embassies in Indonesia, Malaysia, Cambodia, and Vietnam are closed.

**U.S. Mourns on Sept. 11 Anniversary (Sept. 11):** Ceremonies held around the country to honor those who died in terrorist attacks.

**Report Reveals Early Terrorist Threats (Sept. 18):** Details of congressional investigation indicate that in 1998 the intelligence community was aware of plans by Arab terrorists to fly a plane into World Trade Center but failed to actively pursue tips.

**Number of Poor in U.S. Increased in 2001 (Sept. 24):** Newly released census figures show number of Americans living in poverty increased by 1.3 million, to 32.9 million. Median household income also dropped by 2.2%, to $42,228.

**Bush Unveils Draft Resolution on Iraq (Sept. 27):** Plan administration will present to the UN calls for immediate, unlimited access to any site in Iraq and would authorize the use of "all necessary means to restore international peace and security" if Saddam Hussein fails to comply in any way.

**Torricelli Bows Out of Senate Race (Sept. 30):** Fearing that Democrats will lose control of the Senate because of his ethical lapses in fundraising, New Jersey politician drops out 36 days before election.

**West Coast Ports Shut Down (Sept. 30):** Operators close ports, which bring in about $300 billion in cargo annually, after work slowdown by longshoremen.

BUSINESS / SCIENCE / SOCIETY

**Train Derails in India (Sept. 9):** An estimated 100 people die in accident in remote northeast India.

**Study Supports Removal of Prostate (Sept. 12):** Swedish study finds that survival rate higher for men ages 60–70 when they have the cancerous gland removed.

**Tyco Executives Indicted (Sept. 12):** L. Dennis Kozlowski, former CEO, and Mark Swartz, former CFO, charged with bilking the company out of $600 million in a stock-fraud scheme. Mark Belnick, former chief counsel, was also charged with falsifying company records.

**Church Settles with Abuse Victims (Sept. 18):** Roman Catholic Archdiocese of Boston agrees to pay $10 million to 86 victims of pedophile priest John Geoghan.

**Texas Energy Company Manipulated Gas Supply (Sept. 20):** El Paso Corp. charged with withholding supply to California and thus contributed to steep price increases during energy crisis of 2000 and 2001.

**U.S. Sets Smallpox Vaccination Plan (Sept. 23):** Centers for Disease Control and Prevention tell states to be ready to vaccinate up to 1 million people in 10 days in the wake of a bioterrorist attack.

**Federal Reserve Holds Rates Steady (Sept. 24):** But in rare dissent, 2 out of 12 members vote to lower rates.

# October 2002

WORLD

**Bosnian Serb Leader Pleads Guilty (Oct. 2):** Biljana Plavsic admits to committing crimes against humanity during the 1992–1995 Bosnian war against Croats and Muslims. In exchange, the war crimes tribunal at The Hague drops other charges, including genocide.

**Shoe Bomber Enters Guilty Plea (Oct. 2):** Richard Reid files motion indicating he plans to plead guilty to eight charges, including attempted murder.

**Suspected Terrorists Arrested (Oct. 4):** Four U.S. citizens charged in Portland, Ore., with collaborating with al-Qaeda and the Taliban in a *jihad* against the U.S.

**U.S. Marine Killed in Kuwait (Oct. 8):** Another wounded when two Kuwaitis open fire on a training exercise on Failaka Island. Officials call it a terrorist act.

**European Union Announces New Members (Oct. 9):** Ten countries—Poland, Hungary, Czech Republic, Slovakia, Slovenia, Estonia, Lithuania, Latvia, Malta, and Cyprus—expected to join in 2004. **(Oct. 20):** Irish vote to support expansion.

**Musharraf Suffers Setback in Elections (Oct. 11):** Islamic fundamentalists and other parties, led by exiled former prime ministers Benazir Bhutto and Nawaz Sharif, fare well. Vote indicates dissatisfaction with the president.

**Blast in Bali Kills Hundreds (Oct. 12):** About 200 people die when car bomb explodes in front of crowded club in a resort area. Three Americans among the victims. **(Oct. 14):** President Bush links bombing to al-Qaeda.

**Government Suspended in Northern Ireland (Oct. 14):** Move follows threat by Unionists to quit Assembly in protest of suspected military activity by Irish Republican Army.

**Dutch Prime Minister Resigns (Oct. 16):** Jan Peter Balkenende steps down amid infighting by members of the Pim Fortuyn party. New elections called.

**North Korea Admits to Developing Nuclear Arms (Oct. 16):** Bush administration announces that North Korean official recently acknowledged the country has been working on system for several years.

**Chechen Rebels Take Hostages (Oct. 23):** Seize crowded Moscow theater and detain 763 people, including 3 Americans. Guerrillas, armed and wired with explosives, demand Russian government end war in Chechnya. **(Oct. 24):** Rebels kill one hostage. **(Oct. 26):** Government forces storm the theater after rebels begin to kill other hostages. Russian troops also release a gas into the theater, which kills 116 hostages.

**Brazilian Leftist Wins Presidential Race (Oct. 27):** Luiz Inácio Lula da Silva of the Workers Party tallies 61.4%, ahead of Social Democrat José Serra, who earns 38.6%.

NATION

**Sniper Preys upon DC Suburbs (Oct. 2):** First victim dies in Wheaton, Md. **(Oct. 3):** Five people killed when a highly skilled gunman shoots randomly at civilians outside Washington, DC. **(Oct. 4):** Woman survives gunshot wound. **(Oct. 7):** Thirteen-year-old student shot and wounded outside his Bowie, Md., school. Eighth attack. **(Oct. 9):** Sniper kills seventh victim, at a gas station in Manassas, Va. **(Oct. 11):** Eighth killed while pumping gas in Fourmile Fork, Va. **(Oct. 14):** FBI analyst shot down in a parking garage after shopping at Home Depot in Falls Church, Va. **(Oct. 19):** A 37-year-old man survives attack in Ashland, Va. **(Oct. 22):** Bus driver killed in Silver Spring, Md. Tenth victim. **(Oct. 24):** Police arrest two suspects, John Allen Muhammad, 41, and John Lee Malvo, 17, in Rockville, Md. **(Oct. 25):** Muhammad and Malvo charged in Maryland with six counts of first-degree murder.

**American Taliban Member Sentenced (Oct. 4):** John Walker Lindh given 20 years to life in prison for aiding the Taliban and carrying explosives.

**Bush Intervenes in Strike (Oct. 8):** Invokes Taft-Hartley Act to halt lockout of longshoremen and open West Coast Ports.

**House and Senate Back Force in Iraq (Oct. 10):** House votes, 296–133, to give President Bush authorization to defend against the "continuing threat posed by Iraq." Senate approves resolution, 77–23.

**Congress Approves Election Bill (Oct. 16):** Senate votes, 92–2, to set federal election standards and to give

nearly $4 billion to states to update voting systems. House previously passed measure 357–48.

**U.S. Senator Killed in Plane Crash (Oct. 25):** Minnesota Democrat Paul Wellstone; his wife, Sheila; daughter, Marcia Markuson; and five others die when their turboprop goes down near Eveleth, Minn.

BUSINESS / SCIENCE / SOCIETY

**Former Enron Official Charged (Oct. 2):** Andrew Fastow, former CFO, accused of fraud, money laundering, and conspiracy in using complicated off-the-books partnerships to cover up the company's dismal finances.

**Public Health Officials Endorse Smallpox Vaccine (Oct. 4):** Recommend offering immunization to general public after 10 million health-care workers receive it. Vaccination won't be licensed for wide use until 2004.

**Former ImClone Executive Pleads Guilty (Oct. 15):** Sam Waksal faces nine years in prison for admitting to six charges, including securities fraud, perjury, obstruction of justice, conspiracy, and bank fraud.

**Vatican Rejects Abuse Policy (Oct. 18):** Demands that U.S. bishops rewrite segments of zero-tolerance policy to bring it into line with Roman Catholic Church laws.

# 2002 Nobel Prize Winners

**Peace:** Jimmy Carter, former president of the United States, was cited for "his decades of untiring effort to find peaceful solutions to international conflicts, to advance democracy and human rights, and to promote economic and social development."

**Literature:** Imre Kertész (Hungary) for "writing that upholds the fragile experience of the individual against the barbaric arbitrariness of history." Kertész often draws on his experiences as a prisoner in Auschwitz in his works, which explore "the possibility of continuing to live and think as an individual in an era in which the subjection of human beings to social forces has become increasingly complete."

**Physics:** One-half jointly to Raymond Davis, Jr. (U.S.) and Masatoshi Koshiba (Japan) for "pioneering contributions to astrophysics, in particular for the detection of cosmic neutrinos," and one-half to Riccardo Giacconi (U.S.) for "pioneering contributions to astrophysics, which have led to the discovery of cosmic X-ray sources." The laureates have used cosmic particles, the smallest components of the universe, to "increase our understanding of the very largest: the Sun, stars, galaxies, and supernovae."

**Chemistry:** One-half jointly to John B. Fenn (U.S.) and Koichi Tanaka (Japan) for "their development of soft desorption ionization methods for mass spectrometric analyses of biological macromolecules," and one-half to Kurt Wüthrich (Switzerland) for "his development of nuclear magnetic resonance spectroscopy for determining the three-dimensional structure of biological macromolecules in solution." The work of the laureates has helped researchers to quickly determine the composition of biological macromolecules, such as proteins, and understand their function in the cell. "The methods have revolutionized the development of new pharmaceuticals."

**Medicine:** Sydney Brenner (UK), H. Robert Horvitz (U.S.), and John E. Sulston (UK) for "their discoveries concerning genetic regulation of organ development and programmed cell death." The laureates have "have identified key genes regulating organ development and programmed cell death and have shown that corresponding genes exist in higher species, including man."

**Economics:** Daniel Kahneman (U.S.) for "having integrated insights from psychological research into economic science, especially concerning human judgment and decision-making under uncertainty," and Vernon L. Smith (U.S.) for "having established laboratory experiments as a tool in empirical economic analysis, especially in the study of alternative market mechanisms."

# The One Hundred Eighth Congress
## Composition of the 107th and 108th Congresses

| 108th Congress[1] | Rep. | Dem. | Ind. | Undecided | Vacant | | 107th Congress | Rep. | Dem. | Ind. | Male | Female |
|---|---|---|---|---|---|---|---|---|---|---|---|---|
| Senate | 51 | 47 | 1 | 1 | — | | Senate | 50 | 50 | — | 87 | 13 |
| House | 228 | 202 | 1 | 3 | 1 | | House | 221 | 212 | 2 | 376 | 59 |

1. Reflects immediate results of the 2002 election.

# The Senate

Dates in left column indicate term in office; birth dates are given in parentheses after party affiliation. All terms are for six years and expire in January. Senators listed in italics were elected or reelected in 2002.

**Alabama**
1987–2005 Richard Shelby (R) (1934)
*1997–2009 Jeff Sessions (R) (1946)*
**Alaska**
*1969–2009 Ted Stevens (R) (1923)*
1981–2005 Frank H. Murkowski (R) (1933)
**Arizona**
1987–2005 John McCain (R) (1936)
1995–2007 Jon Kyl (R) (1942)
**Arkansas**
*2003–2009 Mike Pryor (D) (1963)*
1999–2005 Blanche Lincoln (D) (1960)
**California**
1993–2007 Dianne Feinstein (D) (1933)
1993–2005 Barbara Boxer (D) (1940)
**Colorado**
1993–2005 Ben Nighthorse Campbell (R) (1933)
*1997–2009 Wayne Allard (R) (1943)*
**Connecticut**
1981–2005 Christopher J. Dodd (D) (1944)
1989–2007 Joseph I. Lieberman (D) (1942)
**Delaware**
*1973–2009 Joseph R. Biden, Jr. (D) (1942)*
2001–2007 Thomas R. Carper (D) (1947)
**Florida**
1987–2005 Bob Graham (D) (1936)
2001–2007 Bill Nelson (D) (1942)
**Georgia**
*2003–2009 Saxby Chambliss (R) (1943)*
2000–2005 Zell Miller (D) (1932)[1]
**Hawaii**
1963–2005 Daniel K. Inouye (D) (1924)
1990–2007 Daniel K. Akaka (D) (1924)
**Idaho**
*1991–2009 Larry E. Craig (R) (1945)*
1999–2005 Mike Crapo (R) (1951)
**Illinois**
*1997–2009 Richard J. Durbin (D) (1944)*
1999–2005 Peter G. Fitzgerald (R) (1960)
**Indiana**
1977–2007 Richard G. Lugar (R) (1932)
[illegible]
1981–2005 Chuck Grassley (R) (1933)
*1985–2009 Tom Harkin (D) (1939)*
**Kansas**
1997–2005 Sam Brownback (R) (1956)
*1997–2009 Pat Roberts (R) (1936)*
**Kentucky**
*1985–2009 Mitch McConnell (R) (1942)*
1999–2005 Jim Bunning (R) (1931)
**Louisiana**
1987–2005 John B. Breaux (D) (1944)
*1997–2003 Mary L. Landrieu (D) (1955)[2]*
**Maine**
1995–2007 Olympia J. Snowe (R) (1947)
*1997–2009 Susan M. Collins (R) (1952)*

**Maryland**
1977–2007 Paul S. Sarbanes (D) (1933)
1987–2005 Barbara A. Mikulski (D) (1936)
**Massachusetts**
1963–2007 Edward M. Kennedy (D) (1932)
*1985–2009 John F. Kerry (D) (1943)*
**Michigan**
*1979–2009 Carl Levin (D) (1934)*
2001–2007 Debbie A. Stabenow (D) (1950)
**Minnesota**
*2003–2009 Norm Coleman (R) (1949)*
2001–2007 Mark Dayton (D) (1947)
**Mississippi**
*1979–2009 Thad Cochran (R) (1937)*
1989–2007 Trent Lott (R) (1941)
**Missouri**
1987–2005 Christopher S. "Kit" Bond (R) (1939)
*2003–2009 James M. Talent (R) (1956)*
**Montana**
*1978–2009 Max Baucus (D) (1941)*
1989–2007 Conrad Burns (R) (1935)
**Nebraska**
*1997–2009 Charles Hagel (R) (1946)*
2001–2007 Ben Nelson (D) (1941)
**Nevada**
1987–2005 Harry Reid (D) (1939)
2001–2007 John Ensign (R) (1958)
**New Hampshire**
1993–2005 Judd Gregg (R) (1947)
*2003–2009 John E. Sununu (R) (1964)*
**New Jersey**
2001–2007 Jon Corzine (D) (1947)
*2003–2009 Frank R. Lautenberg (D) (1924)*
**New Mexico**
*1973–2009 Pete V. Domenici (R) (1932)*
1983–2007 Jeff Bingaman (D) (1943)
**New York**
1999–2005 Charles E. Schumer (D) (1950)
2001–2007 Hillary Rodham Clinton (D) (1947)
**North Carolina**
1999–2005 John Edwards (D) (1953)
[illegible]
**North Dakota**
1987–2007 Kent Conrad (D) (1948)
1992–2005 Byron L. Dorgan (D) (1942)
**Ohio**
1995–2007 Mike DeWine (R) (1947)
1999–2005 George Voinovich (R) (1936)
**Oklahoma**
1989–2005 Don Nickles (R) (1948)
*1994–2009 James M. Inhofe (R) (1934)*
**Oregon**
1996–2005 Ron Wyden (D) (1949)
*1997–2009 Gordon H. Smith (R) (1952)*
**Pennsylvania**
1981–2005 Arlen Specter (R) (1930)
1995–2007 Rick Santorum (R) (1958)

**Rhode Island**
*1997–2009 Jack Reed (D) (1949)*
1999–2007 Lincoln Chafee (R) (1953)
**South Carolina**
1966–2005 Ernest Hollings (D) (1922)
*2003–2009 Lindsey Graham (R) (1955)*
**South Dakota**
1987–2005 Thomas A. Daschle (D) (1947)
*1997–2009 Tim Johnson (D) (1946)*
**Tennessee**
1995–2007 William Frist (R) (1952)
*2003–2009 Lamar Alexander (R) (1940)*
**Texas**
1995–2007 Kay Bailey Hutchison (R) (1943)
*2003–2009 John Cornyn (R) (1952)*
**Utah**
1977–2007 Orrin G. Hatch (R) (1934)
1993–2005 Robert F. Bennett (R) (1933)

**Vermont**
1975–2005 Patrick Leahy (D) (1940)
1989–2007 James M. Jeffords (I) (1934)
**Virginia**
*1979–2009 John Warner (R) (1927)*
2001–2007 George Allen (R) (1952)
**Washington**
1993–2005 Patty Murray (D) (1950)
2001–2007 Maria Cantwell (D) (1958)
**West Virginia**
1959–2007 Robert C. Byrd (D) (1917)
*1985–2009 John D. "Jay" Rockefeller IV (D) (1937)*
**Wisconsin**
1989–2007 Herbert Kohl (D) (1935)
1993–2005 Russ Feingold (D) (1953)
**Wyoming**
1995–2007 Craig Thomas (R) (1933)
*1997–2009 Michael B. Enzi (R) (1944)*

1. Zell Miller was appointed and then elected to serve out the remaining term of Paul Coverdell, who died in July 2000.
2. 2002 election undecided as of Nov. 7. Senator Landrieu was the incumbent.

# The House of Representatives

In the following lists, the numeral indicates the congressional district represented; AL is for representatives at large. All terms run from Jan. 2003 to Jan. 2005.

**Alabama**
1. Jo Bonner (R)
2. Terry Everett (R)
3. Mike Rogers (R)
4. Robert B. Aderholt (R)
5. Robert E. "Bud" Cramer, Jr. (D)
6. Spencer Bachus (R)
7. Artur Davis (D)

**Alaska**
AL Don Young (R)

**Arizona**
1. Rick Renzi (R)
2. Trent Franks (R)
3. John Shadegg (R)
4. Ed Pastor (D)
5. J. D. Hayworth (R)
6. Jeff Flake (R)
7. Raul Grijalva (D)
8. Jim Kolbe (R)

**Arkansas**
1. Marion Berry (D)
2. Vic Snyder (D)
3. John Boozman (R)
4. Mike Ross (D)

**California**
1. Mike Thompson (D)
2. Wally Herger (R)
3. Doug Ose (R)
4. John T. Doolittle (R)
5. Robert T. Matsui (D)
6. Lynn C. Woolsey (D)
7. George Miller (D)
8. Nancy Pelosi (D)
9. Barbara Lee (D)
10. Ellen O. Tauscher (D)
11. Richard W. Pombo (R)
12. Tom Lantos (D)
13. Pete Stark (D)
14. Anna G. Eshoo (D)
15. Michael M. Honda (D)
16. Zoe Lofgren (D)
17. Sam Farr (D)
18. Dennis Cardoza (D)
19. George P. Radanovich (R)
20. Cal Dooley (D)
21. Devin Nunes (R)
22. Bill Thomas (R)
23. Lois Capps (D)
24. Elton Gallegly (R)
25. Howard P. "Buck" McKeon (R)
26. David Dreier (R)
27. Brad Sherman (D)
28. Howard L. Berman (D)
29. Adam B. Schiff (D)
30. Henry A. Waxman (D)
31. Xavier Becerra (D)
32. Hilda L. Solis (D)
33. Diane Watson (D)
34. Lucille Roybal-Allard (D)
35. Maxine Waters (D)
36. Jane Harman (D)
37. Juanita Millender-McDonald (D)
38. Grace F. Napolitano (D)
39. Linda T. Sanchez (D)
40. Ed Royce (R)
41. Jerry Lewis (R)
42. Gary G. Miller (R)
43. Joe Baca (D)
44. Ken Calvert (R)
45. Mary Bono (R)
46. Dana Rohrabacher (R)
47. Loretta Sanchez (D)
48. Christopher Cox (R)
49. Darrell Issa (R)
50. Randy "Duke" Cunningham (R)
51. Bob Filner (D)
52. Duncan Hunter (R)
53. Susan Davis (D)

**Colorado**
1. Diana DeGette (D)
2. Mark Udall (D)
3. Scott McInnis (R)
4. Marilyn Musgrave (R)
5. Joel Hefley (R)
6. Tom Tancredo (R)
7. (¹)

**Connecticut**
1. John B. Larson (D)
2. Rob Simmons (R)
3. Rosa L. DeLauro (D)
4. Christopher Shays (R)
5. Nancy L. Johnson (R)

**Delaware**
AL Michael N. Castle (R)

**Florida**
1. Jeff Miller (R)
2. Allen Boyd (D)
3. Corrine Brown (D)
4. Ander Crenshaw (R)
5. Virginia Brown-Waite (R)
6. Cliff Stearns (R)
7. John L. Mica (R)
8. Ric Keller (R)
9. Michael Bilirakis (R)
10. C. W. Bill Young (R)
11. Jim Davis (D)
12. Adam Putnam (R)
13. Katherine Harris (R)
14. Porter J. Goss (R)
15. Dave Weldon (R)
16. Mark Foley (R)
17. Kendrick Meek (D)
18. Ileana Ros-Lehtinen (R)
19. Robert Wexler (D)
20. Peter Deutsch (D)
21. Lincoln Diaz-Balart (R)
22. E. Clay Shaw, Jr. (R)
23. Alcee L. Hastings (D)
24. Tom Feeney (R)
25. Mario Diaz-Balart (R)

**Georgia**
1. Jack Kingston (R)
2. Sanford D. Bishop, Jr. (D)
3. Jim Marshall (D)
4. Denise Majette (D)
5. John Lewis (D)
6. Johnny Isakson (R)
7. John Linder (R)
8. Mac Collins (R)
9. Charlie Norwood (R)
10. Nathan Deal (R)
11. Phil Gingrey (R)
12. Max Burns (R)
13. David Scott (D)

**Hawaii**
1. Neil Abercrombie (D)
2. Patsy T. Mink (D)²

**Idaho**
1. C. L. "Butch" Otter (R)
2. Mike Simpson (R)

**Illinois**
1. Bobby L. Rush (D)
2. Jesse L. Jackson, Jr. (D)
3. William O. Lipinski (D)
4. Luis V. Gutierrez (D)
5. Rahm Emanuel (D)
6. Henry J. Hyde (R)

7. Danny K. Davis (D)
8. Philip M. Crane (R)
9. Janice Schakowsky (D)
10. Mark Steven Kirk (R)
11. Jerry Weller (R)
12. Jerry F. Costello (D)
13. Judy Biggert (R)
14. J. Dennis Hastert (R)
15. Timothy V. Johnson (R)
16. Donald Manzullo (R)
17. Lane Evans (D)
18. Ray LaHood (R)
19. John Shimkus (R)

**Indiana**
1. Peter J. Visclosky (D)
2. Chris Chocola (R)
3. Mark E. Souder (R)
4. Steve Buyer (R)
5. Dan Burton (R)
6. Mike Pence (R)
7. Julia Carson (D)
8. John Hostettler (R)
9. Baron P. Hill (D)

**Iowa**
1. Jim Nussle (R)
2. Jim Leach (R)
3. Leonard L. Boswell (D)
4. Tom Latham (R)
5. Steve King (R)

**Kansas**
1. Jerry Moran (R)
2. Jim Ryun (R)
3. Dennis Moore (D)
4. Todd Tiahrt (R)

**Kentucky**
1. Edward Whitfield (R)
2. Ron Lewis (R)
3. Anne M. Northup (R)
4. Ken Lucas (D)
5. Harold Rogers (R)
6. Ernie Fletcher (R)

**Louisiana**
1. David Vitter (R)
2. William J. Jefferson (D)
3. Billy Tauzin (R)
4. Jim McCrery (R)
5. (¹)
6. Richard H. Baker (R)
7. Chris John (D)

**Maine**
1. Tom Allen (D)
2. Mike Michaud (D)

**Maryland**
1. Wayne T. Gilchrest (R)
2. C. A. "Dutch" Ruppersberger (D)
3. Benjamin L. Cardin (D)
4. Albert R. Wynn (D)
5. Steny H. Hoyer (D)
6. Roscoe G. Bartlett (R)
7. Elijah E. Cummings (D)
8. Chris Van Hollen (D)

**Massachusetts**
1. John W. Olver (D)
2. Richard E. Neal (D)
3. Jim McGovern (D)
4. Barney Frank (D)
5. Martin T. Meehan (D)
6. John F. Tierney (D)
7. Edward J. Markey (D)
8. Michael E. Capuano (D)
9. Stephen F. Lynch (D)
10. Bill Delahunt (D)

**Michigan**
1. Bart Stupak (D)
2. Peter Hoekstra (R)
3. Vernon J. Ehlers (R)
4. Dave Camp (R)
5. Dale Kildee (D)
6. Fred Upton (R)
7. Nick Smith (R)
8. Mike Rogers (R)
9. Joe Knollenberg (R)
10. Candice Millor (R)
11. Thaddeus McCotter (R)
12. Sander M. Levin (D)
13. Carolyn Cheeks Kilpatrick (D)
14. John Conyers, Jr. (D)
15. John D. Dingell (D)

**Minnesota**
1. Gil Gutknecht (R)
2. John Kline (R)
3. Jim Ramstad (R)
4. Betty McCollum (D)
5. Martin Olav Sabo (D)
6. Mark Kennedy (R)
7. Collin C. Peterson (D)
8. James L. Oberstar (D)

**Mississippi**
1. Roger Wicker (R)
2. Bennie Thompson (D)
3. Charles W. "Chip" Pickering (R)
4. Gene Taylor (D)

**Missouri**
1. William Lacy Clay (D)
2. Todd Akin (R)
3. Richard A. Gephardt (D)
4. Ike Skelton (D)
5. Karen McCarthy (D)
6. Sam Graves (R)
7. Roy Blunt (R)
8. Jo Ann Emerson (R)
9. Kenny Hulshof (R)

**Montana**
AL Denny Rehberg (R)

**Nebraska**
1. Doug Bereuter (R)
2. Lee Terry (R)
3. Tom Osborne (R)

**Nevada**
1. Shelley Berkley (D)
2. Jim Gibbons (R)
3. Jon Porter (R)

**New Hampshire**
1. Jeb Bradley (R)
2. Charles Bass (R)

**New Jersey**
1. Robert E. Andrews (D)
2. Frank A. LoBiondo (R)
3. Jim Saxton (R)
4. Christopher H. Smith (R)
5. Scott Garrett (R)
6. Frank Pallone, Jr. (D)
7. Mike Ferguson (R)
8. Bill Pascrell, Jr. (D)
9. Steven R. Rothman (D)
10. Donald M. Payne (D)
11. Rodney Frelinghuysen (R)
12. Rush D. Holt (D)
13. Robert Menendez (D)

**New Mexico**
1. Heather Wilson (R)
2. Steve Pearce (R)
3. Tom Udall (D)

**New York**
1. (¹)
2. Steve Israel (D)
3. Peter T. King (R)
4. Carolyn McCarthy (D)
5. Gary L. Ackerman (D)
6. Gregory W. Meeks (D)
7. Joseph Crowley (D)
8. Jerrold Nadler (D)
9. Anthony D. Weiner (D)
10. Edolphus Towns (D)
11. Major R. Owens (D)
12. Nydia M. Velázquez (D)
13. Vito J. Fossella (R)
14. Carolyn B. Maloney (D)
15. Charles B. Rangel (D)
16. José E. Serrano (D)
17. Eliot L. Engel (D)
18. Nita M. Lowey (D)
19. Sue W. Kelly (R)
20. John E. Sweeney (R)
21. Michael R. McNulty (D)
22. Maurice D. Hinchey (D)
23. John M. McHugh (R)
24. Sherwood L. Boehlert (R)
25. James T. Walsh (R)
26. Thomas M. Reynolds (R)
27. Jack Quinn (R)
28. Louise M. Slaughter (D)
29. Amo Houghton (R)

**North Carolina**
1. Frank Ballance (D)
2. Bob Etheridge (D)
3. Walter B. Jones (R)
4. David E. Price (D)
5. Richard Burr (R)
6. Howard Coble (R)
7. Mike McIntyre (D)
8. Robin Hayes (R)
9. Sue Myrick (R)
10. Cass Ballenger (R)
11. Charles H. Taylor (R)
12. Melvin L. Watt (D)
13. Brad Miller (D)

**North Dakota**
AL Earl Pomeroy (D)

**Ohio**
1. Steve Chabot (R)
2. Rob Portman (R)
3. Mike Turner (R)
4. Michael G. Oxley (R)
5. Paul E. Gillmor (R)
6. Ted Strickland (D)
7. David L. Hobson (R)
8. John A. Boehner (R)
9. Marcy Kaptur (D)
10. Dennis J. Kucinich (D)
11. Stephanie Tubbs Jones (D)
12. Pat Tiberi (R)
13. Sherrod Brown (D)
14. Steven C. LaTourette (R)
15. Deborah Pryce (R)
16. Ralph Regula (R)
17. Timothy J. Ryan (D)
18. Robert W. Ney (R)

**Oklahoma**
1. John Sullivan (R)
2. Brad Carson (D)
3. Frank D. Lucas (R)
4. Tom Cole (R)
5. Ernest Istook (R)

**Oregon**
1. David Wu (D)
2. Greg Walden (R)
3. Earl Blumenauer (D)
4. Peter A. DeFazio (D)
5. Darlene Hooley (D)

**Pennsylvania**
1. Robert A. Brady (D)
2. Chaka Fattah (D)
3. Phil English (R)
4. Melissa Hart (R)
5. John E. Peterson (R)
6. Jim Gerlach (R)
7. Curt Weldon (R)
8. James C. Greenwood (R)
9. Bill Shuster (R)
10. Donald L. Sherwood (R)
11. Paul E. Kanjorski (D)
12. John P. Murtha (D)
13. Joseph M. Hoeffel (D)
14. Mike Doyle (D)
15. Patrick J. Toomey (R)
16. Joe Pitts (R)
17. Tim Holden (D)
18. Tim Murphy (R)
19. Todd R. Platts (R)

**Rhode Island**
1. Patrick J. Kennedy (D)
2. James R. Langevin (D)

**South Carolina**
1. Henry E. Brown, Jr. (R)
2. Joe Wilson (R)
3. J. Gresham Barrett (R)
4. Jim DeMint (R)
5. John M. Spratt, Jr. (D)
6. James E. Clyburn (D)

**South Dakota**
AL William J. Janklow (R)

**Tennessee**
1. Bill Jenkins (R)
2. John J. "Jimmy" Duncan, Jr. (R)
3. Zach Wamp (R)
4. Lincoln Davis (D)
5. Jim Cooper (D)
6. Bart Gordon (D)

7. Marsha Blackburn (R)
8. John Tanner (D)
9. Harold E. Ford, Jr. (D)

**Texas**
1. Max Sandlin (D)
2. Jim Turner (D)
3. Sam Johnson (R)
4. Ralph M. Hall (D)
5. Jeb Hensarling (R)
6. Joe L. Barton (R)
7. John Culberson (R)
8. Kevin Brady (R)
9. Nick Lampson (D)
10. Lloyd Doggett (D)
11. Chet Edwards (D)
12. Kay Granger (R)
13. William "Mac" Thornberry (R)
14. Ron Paul (R)
15. Rubén Hinojosa (D)
16. Silvestre Reyes (D)
17. Charles W. Stenholm (D)
18. Sheila Jackson-Lee (D)
19. Larry Combest (R)
20. Charlie Gonzalez (D)
21. Lamar S. Smith (R)
22. Tom DeLay (R)
23. Henry Bonilla (R)
24. Martin Frost (D)
25. Chris Bell (D)
26. Michael C. Burgess (R)
27. Solomon P. Ortiz (D)
28. Ciro D. Rodriguez (D)
29. Gene Green (D)
30. Eddie Bernice Johnson (D)
31. John R. Carter (R)
32. Pete Sessions (R)

**Utah**
1. Rob Bishop (R)
2. Jim Matheson (D)
3. Christopher B. Cannon (R)

**Vermont**
AL Bernard Sanders (I)

**Virginia**
1. Jo Ann S. Davis (R)
2. Ed Schrock (R)
3. Robert C. Scott (D)
4. Randy Forbes (R)
5. Virgil H. Goode, Jr. (R)
6. Robert W. Goodlatte (R)
7. Eric I. Cantor (R)
8. James P. Moran (D)
9. Rick Boucher (D)
10. Frank R. Wolf (R)
11. Thomas M. Davis III (R)

**Washington**
1. Jay Inslee (D)
2. Rick Larsen (D)
3. Brian Baird (D)
4. Doc Hastings (R)
5. George Nethercutt (R)
6. Norm Dicks (D)
7. Jim McDermott (D)
8. Jennifer Dunn (R)
9. Adam Smith (D)

**West Virginia**
1. Alan B. Mollohan (D)
2. Shelley Moore Capito (R)
3. Nick J. Rahall II (D)

**Wisconsin**
1. Paul D. Ryan (R)
2. Tammy Baldwin (D)
3. Ron Kind (D)
4. Gerald D. Kleczka (D)
5. F. James Sensenbrenner, Jr. (R)
6. Tom Petri (R)
7. David R. Obey (D)
8. Mark Green (R)

**Wyoming**
AL Barbara Cubin (R)

1. 2002 election undecided as of Nov. 7. 2. Died Sept. 28, 2002, but name remained on ballot. Special election will be held to fill vacancy.

# The Governors of the Fifty States

| State | Governor | Current term[1] | State | Governor | Current term[1] |
|---|---|---|---|---|---|
| *Ala.* | (2) | — | Mont. | Judy Martz (R) | 2001–2005 |
| *Alaska* | *Frank H. Murkowski (R)* | *2002–2006[3]* | Nebr. | Mike Johanns (R) | *1999–2007* |
| *Ariz.* | *Janet Napolitano (D)[4]* | *2003–2007* | Nev. | Kenny Guinn (R) | *2003–2007* |
| *Ark.* | *Mike Huckabee (R)* | *2003–2007* | N.H. | Craig Benson (R) | *2003–2005* |
| *Calif.* | *Gray Davis (D)* | *2003–2007* | N.J. | Jim McGreevey (D) | 2002–2006 |
| *Colo.* | *Bill Owens (R)* | *2003–2007* | N.M. | Bill Richardson (D) | *2003–2007* |
| *Conn.* | *John G. Rowland (R)* | *2003–2007* | N.Y. | George E. Pataki (R) | *2003–2007* |
| Del. | Ruth Ann Minner (D) | 2001–2005 | N.C. | Mike Easley (D) | 2001–2005 |
| *Fla.* | *Jeb Bush (R)* | *2003–2007* | N.D. | John Hoeven (R) | 2001–2005 |
| *Ga.* | *Sonny Perdue (R)* | *2003–2007* | Ohio | Bob Taft (R) | *2003–2007* |
| *Hawaii* | *Linda Lingle (R)* | *2002–2006[3]* | Okla. | Brad Henry (D) | *2003–2007* |
| *Idaho* | *Dirk Kempthorne (R)* | *2003–2007* | Ore. | Ted Kulongoski (D) | *2003–2007* |
| *Ill.* | *Rod R. Blagojevich (D)* | *2003–2007* | Pa. | Ed Rendell (D) | *2003–2007* |
| Ind. | Frank O'Bannon (D) | 2001–2005 | R.I. | Don Carcieri (R) | *2003–2007* |
| *Iowa* | *Tom Vilsack (D)* | *2003–2007* | S.C. | Mark Sanford (R) | *2003–2007* |
| *Kans.* | *Kathleen Sebelius (D)* | *2003–2007* | S.D. | Mike Rounds (R) | *2003–2007* |
| Ky. | Paul E. Patton (D) | 1999–2003[3] | Tenn. | Phil Bredesen (D) | *2003–2007* |
| La. | Mike Foster (R) | 2000–2004 | Tex. | Rick Perry (R) | *2003–2007* |
| *Maine* | *John Baldacci (D)* | *2003–2007* | Utah | Michael O. Leavitt (R) | 2001–2005 |
| *Md.* | *Robert L. Ehrlich, Jr. (R)* | *2003–2007* | Vt. | *Jim Douglas (R)[5]* | *2003–2007* |
| *Mass.* | *Mitt Romney (R)* | *2003–2007* | Va. | Mark Warner (D) | 2002–2006 |
| *Mich.* | *Jennifer Granholm (D)* | *2002–2007* | Wash. | Gary Locke (D) | 2001–2005 |
| *Minn.* | *Tim Pawlenty (R)* | *2003–2007* | W. Va. | Bob Wise (D) | 2001–2005 |
| Miss. | Ronnie Musgrove (D) | 2000–2004 | *Wis.* | *Jim Doyle (D)* | *2003–2007* |
| Mo. | Bob Holden (D) | 2001–2005 | *Wyo.* | *Dave Freudenthal (D)* | *2003–2007* |

NOTE: Governors listed in italics were elected or reelected in 2002. 1. Except where indicated, all terms begin and end in January. 2. 2002 election undecided as of Nov. 7. 3. Term begins and ends in December. 4. The 2002 election was undecided as of Nov. 7, but Janet Napolitano was expected to defeat her Republican rival, Matt Salmon. 5. Douglas won plurality but not majority in 2002 election; state legislature expected to elect him formally in Jan. 2003.

# Presidential Election of 2000, Electoral and Popular Vote Summary

Principal Candidates for President and Vice President:
**Republican—George W. Bush; Richard B. Cheney** (winner)
Democratic—Albert A. Gore, Jr.; Joseph I. Lieberman
Green—Ralph Nader; Winona LaDuke

| | George W. Bush | | Albert A. Gore, Jr. | | Ralph Nader | | Electoral votes | | |
|---|---|---|---|---|---|---|---|---|---|
| | Popular vote | % | Popular vote | % | Popular vote | % | R | D | G |
| Alabama | 941,173 | 56% | 692,611 | 42% | 18,323 | 1% | 9 | | |
| Alaska | 167,398 | 59 | 79,004 | 28 | 28,747 | 10 | 3 | | |
| Arizona | 781,652 | 51 | 685,341 | 45 | 45,645 | 3 | 8 | | |
| Arkansas | 472,940 | 51 | 422,768 | 46 | 13,421 | 1 | 6 | | |
| California | 4,567,429 | 42 | 5,861,203 | 53 | 418,707 | 4 | | 54 | |
| Colorado | 883,748 | 51 | 738,227 | 42 | 91,434 | 5 | 8 | | |
| Connecticut | 561,094 | 38 | 816,015 | 56 | 64,452 | 4 | | 8 | |
| Delaware | 137,288 | 42 | 180,068 | 55 | 8,307 | 3 | | 3 | |
| DC | 18,073 | 9 | 171,923 | 85 | 10,576 | 5 | | 2[1] | |
| Florida | 2,912,790 | 49 | 2,912,253 | 49 | 97,488 | 2 | 25 | | |
| Georgia | 1,419,720 | 55 | 1,116,230 | 43 | 13,432[2] | .5 | 13 | | |
| Hawaii | 137,845 | 37 | 205,286 | 56 | 21,623 | 6 | | 4 | |
| Idaho | 336,937 | 67 | 138,637 | 28 | 12,292[2] | 2 | 4 | | |
| Illinois | 2,019,421 | 43 | 2,589,026 | 55 | 103,759 | 2 | | 22 | |
| Indiana | 1,245,836 | 57 | 901,980 | 41 | 18,531[2] | .8 | 12 | | |
| Iowa | 634,373 | 48 | 638,517 | 49 | 29,374 | 2 | | 7 | |
| Kansas | 622,332 | 58 | 399,276 | 37 | 36,086 | 3 | 6 | | |
| Kentucky | 872,492 | 57 | 638,898 | 41 | 23,192 | 2 | 8 | | |
| Louisiana | 927,871 | 53 | 792,344 | 45 | 20,473 | 1 | 9 | | |
| Maine | 286,616 | 44 | 319,951 | 49 | 37,127 | 6 | | 4 | |
| Maryland | 813,797 | 40 | 1,140,782 | 56 | 53,768 | 3 | | 10 | |
| Massachusetts | 878,502 | 33 | 1,616,487 | 60 | 173,564 | 6 | | 12 | |
| Michigan | 1,953,139 | 46 | 2,170,418 | 51 | 84,165 | 2 | | 18 | |
| Minnesota | 1,109,659 | 46 | 1,168,266 | 48 | 126,696 | 5 | | 10 | |
| Mississippi | 572,844 | 58 | 404,614 | 41 | 8,122 | .8 | 7 | | |
| Missouri | 1,189,924 | 50 | 1,111,138 | 47 | 38,515 | 2 | 11 | | |
| Montana | 240,178 | 58 | 137,126 | 33 | 24,437 | 6 | 3 | | |
| Nebraska | 433,862 | 62 | 231,780 | 33 | 24,540 | 4 | 5 | | |
| Nevada | 301,575 | 50 | 279,978 | 46 | 15,008 | 2 | 4 | | |
| New Hampshire | 273,559 | 48 | 266,348 | 47 | 22,198 | 4 | 4 | | |
| New Jersey | 1,284,173 | 40 | 1,788,850 | 56 | 94,554 | 3 | | 15 | |
| New Mexico | 286,417 | 48 | 286,783 | 48 | 21,251 | 4 | | 5 | |
| New York | 2,403,374 | 35 | 4,107,697 | 60 | 244,030 | 4 | | 33 | |
| North Carolina | 1,631,163 | 56 | 1,257,692 | 43 | — | — | 14 | | |
| North Dakota | 174,852 | 61 | 95,284 | 33 | 9,486 | 3 | 3 | | |
| Ohio | 2,350,363 | 50 | 2,183,628 | 46 | 117,799 | 3 | 21 | | |
| Oklahoma | 744,337 | 60 | 474,276 | 38 | — | — | 8 | | |
| Oregon | 713,577 | 47 | 720,342 | 47 | 77,357 | 5 | | 7 | |
| Pennsylvania | 2,281,127 | 46 | 2,485,967 | 51 | 103,392 | 2 | | 23 | |
| Rhode Island | 130,555 | 32 | 249,508 | 61 | 25,052 | 6 | | 4 | |
| South Carolina | 785,937 | 57 | 565,561 | 41 | 20,200 | 1 | 8 | | |
| South Dakota | 190,700 | 60 | 118,804 | 38 | — | — | 3 | | |
| Tennessee | 1,061,040 | 51 | 981,720 | 47 | 19,781 | 1 | 11 | | |
| Texas | 3,799,639 | 59 | 2,433,746 | 38 | 137,994 | 2 | 32 | | |
| Utah | 515,096 | 67 | 203,053 | 26 | 35,850 | 5 | 5 | | |
| Vermont | 119,775 | 41 | 149,022 | 51 | 20,374 | 7 | | 3 | |
| Virginia | 1,437,490 | 52 | 1,217,290 | 44 | 59,398 | 4 | 13 | | |
| Washington | 1,108,864 | 45 | 1,247,652 | 50 | 103,002 | 4 | | 11 | |
| West Virginia | 336,475 | 52 | 295,497 | 46 | 10,680 | 2 | 5 | | |
| Wisconsin | 1,237,279 | 48 | 1,242,987 | 48 | 94,070 | 4 | | 11 | |
| Wyoming | 147,947 | 68 | 60,481 | 28 | 4,625[2] | 2 | 3 | | |
| **Total** | **50,455,156** | **47.87%** | **50,992,335** | **48.38%** | **2,882,897** | **2.74%** | **271** | **266** | |

NOTE: Total electoral votes = 538. Total electoral votes needed to win = 270. Dash (—) indicates not on ballot. 1. The District of Columbia has 3 votes. There was 1 abstention. 2. Write-in votes. *Source:* Federal Election Commission.

Voting age population (Census Bureau Population Survey for Nov. 2000): 205,815,000
Percentage of voting age population casting a vote for president: 51.3%

# How a President Is Nominated and Elected

## The Conventions

The national conventions of both major parties are held during the summer of a presidential election year. Earlier, each party selects delegates by primaries, conventions, committees, etc.

At each convention, a temporary chairman is chosen. After a credentials committee seats the delegates, a permanent chairman is elected. The convention then votes on a platform, drawn up by the platform committee.

By the third or fourth day, presidential nominations begin. The chairman calls the roll of states alphabetically. A state may place a candidate in nomination or yield to another state.

Voting, again alphabetically by roll call of states, begins after all nominations have been made and seconded. A simple majority is required in each party, although this may require many ballots.

Finally, the vice-presidential candidate is selected. Although there is no law saying that the candidates *must* come from different states, it is, practically, necessary for this to be the case. Otherwise, according to the Constitution (*see* the 12th Amendment), electors from that state could vote for only one of the candidates and would have to cast their other vote for some person of another state. This could result in a presidential candidate's receiving a majority electoral vote and his or her running mate's failing to do so.

## The Electoral College

The next step in the process is the nomination of electors in each state, according to its laws. These electors must not be federal office holders. In the November election, the voters cast their votes for electors, not for president. In some states, the ballots include only the names of the presidential and vice-presidential candidates; in others, they include only names of the electors. Nowadays, it is rare for electors to be split between parties. The last such occurrence was in North Carolina in 1968;[1] the last before that, in Tennessee in 1948. On four occasions (1824, 1876, 1888, and 2000), the presidential candidate with the largest popular vote failed to obtain an electoral vote majority.

Each state has as many electors as it has senators and representatives. For the 2000 election, the total electors were 538, based on 100 senators and 435 representatives, plus 3 electoral votes from the District of Columbia as a result of the 23rd Amendment to the Constitution.

On the first Monday after the second Wednesday in December, the electors cast their votes in their respective state capitols. Constitutionally they may vote for someone other than the party candidate but usually they do not since they are pledged to one party and its candidate on the ballot. Should the presidential or vice-presidential candidate die between the November election and the December meetings, the electors pledged to vote for him or her could vote for whomever they pleased. However, it seems certain that the national committee would attempt to get an agreement among the state party leaders for a replacement candidate.

The votes of the electors, certified by the states, are sent to Congress, where the president of the Senate opens the certificates and has them counted in the presence of both houses on Jan. 6. The new president is inaugurated at noon on Jan. 20.

Should no candidate receive a majority of the electoral vote for president, the House of Representatives chooses a president from among the three highest candidates, voting, not as individuals, but as states, with a majority (now 26) needed to elect. Should no vice-presidential candidate obtain the majority, the Senate, voting as individuals, chooses from the highest two.

1. In 1956, one of Alabama's 11 electoral votes was cast for Walter B. Jones. In 1960, six of Alabama's 11 electoral votes and one of Oklahoma's eight electoral votes were cast for Harry Flood Byrd. (Byrd also received all eight of Mississippi's electoral votes.)

## Electoral College Votes by State, 2000 Presidential Elections

### (total electoral votes: 538; majority needed to elect: 270)

| State | Votes | State | Votes | State | Votes |
|---|---|---|---|---|---|
| Alabama | 9 | Kentucky | 8 | North Dakota | 3 |
| Alaska | 3 | Louisiana | 9 | Ohio | 21 |
| Arizona | 8 | Maine | 4 | Oklahoma | 8 |
| Arkansas | 6 | Maryland | 10 | Oregon | 7 |
| California | 54 | Massachusetts | 12 | Pennsylvania | 23 |
| Colorado | 8 | Michigan | 18 | Rhode Island | 4 |
| Connecticut | 8 | Minnesota | 10 | South Carolina | 8 |
| Delaware | 3 | Mississippi | 7 | South Dakota | 3 |
| District of Columbia | 3 | Missouri | 11 | Tennessee | 11 |
| Florida | 25 | Montana | 3 | Texas | 32 |
| Georgia | 13 | Nebraska | 5 | Utah | 5 |
| Hawaii | 4 | Nevada | 4 | Vermont | 3 |
| Idaho | 4 | New Hampshire | 4 | Virginia | 13 |
| Illinois | 22 | New Jersey | 15 | Washington | 11 |
| Indiana | 12 | New Mexico | 5 | West Virginia | 5 |
| Iowa | 7 | New York | 33 | Wisconsin | 11 |
| Kansas | 6 | North Carolina | 14 | Wyoming | 3 |

# National Political Conventions Since 1856

| Opening date | Party | Where held | Opening date | Party | Where held |
|---|---|---|---|---|---|
| June 17, 1856 | Republican | Philadelphia | June 14, 1932 | Republican | Chicago |
| June 2, 1856 | Democratic | Cincinnati | June 27, 1932 | Democratic | Chicago |
| May 16, 1860 | Republican | Chicago | June 9, 1936 | Republican | Cleveland |
| April 23, 1860 | Democratic | Charleston and Baltimore | June 23, 1936 | Democratic | Philadelphia |
| June 7, 1864 | Republican[1] | Baltimore | June 24, 1940 | Republican | Philadelphia |
| Aug. 29, 1864 | Democratic | Chicago | July 15, 1940 | Democratic | Chicago |
| May 20, 1868 | Republican | Chicago | June 26, 1944 | Republican | Chicago |
| July 4, 1868 | Democratic | New York City | July 19, 1944 | Democratic | Chicago |
| June 5, 1872 | Republican | Philadelphia | June 21, 1948 | Republican | Philadelphia |
| June 9, 1872 | Democratic | Baltimore | July 12, 1948 | Democratic | Philadelphia |
| June 14, 1876 | Republican | Cincinnati | July 17, 1948 | (3) | Birmingham |
| June 28, 1876 | Democratic | St. Louis | July 22, 1948 | Progressive | Philadelphia |
| June 2, 1880 | Republican | Chicago | July 7, 1952 | Republican | Chicago |
| June 23, 1880 | Democratic | Cincinnati | July 21, 1952 | Democratic | Chicago |
| June 3, 1884 | Republican | Chicago | Aug. 20, 1956 | Republican | San Francisco |
| July 11, 1884 | Democratic | Chicago | Aug. 13, 1956 | Democratic | Chicago |
| June 19, 1888 | Republican | Chicago | July 25, 1960 | Republican | Chicago |
| June 6, 1888 | Democratic | St. Louis | July 11, 1960 | Democratic | Los Angeles |
| June 7, 1892 | Republican | Minneapolis | July 13, 1964 | Republican | San Francisco |
| June 21, 1892 | Democratic | Chicago | Aug. 24, 1964 | Democratic | Atlantic City |
| June 16, 1896 | Republican | St. Louis | Aug. 5, 1968 | Republican | Miami Beach |
| July 7, 1896 | Democratic | Chicago | Aug. 26, 1968 | Democratic | Chicago |
| June 19, 1900 | Republican | Philadelphia | July 10, 1972 | Democratic | Miami Beach |
| July 4, 1900 | Democratic | Kansas City | Aug. 21, 1972 | Republican | Miami Beach |
| June 21, 1904 | Republican | Chicago | July 12, 1976 | Democratic | New York City |
| July 6, 1904 | Democratic | St. Louis | Aug. 16, 1976 | Republican | Kansas City, Mo. |
| June 16, 1908 | Republican | Chicago | Aug. 11, 1980 | Democratic | New York City |
| July 7, 1908 | Democratic | Denver | July 14, 1980 | Republican | Detroit |
| June 18, 1912 | Republican | Chicago | Aug. 20, 1984 | Republican | Dallas |
| June 25, 1912 | Democratic | Baltimore | July 16, 1984 | Democratic | San Francisco |
| June 7, 1916 | Republican | Chicago | July 18, 1988 | Democratic | Atlanta |
| June 14, 1916 | Democratic | St. Louis | Aug. 15, 1988 | Republican | New Orleans |
| June 8, 1920 | Republican | Chicago | July 13, 1992 | Democratic | New York City |
| June 28, 1920 | Democratic | San Francisco | Aug. 17, 1992 | Republican | Houston |
| June 10, 1924 | Republican | Cleveland | Aug. 10, 1996 | Republican | San Diego |
| June 24, 1924[2] | Democratic | New York City | Aug. 26, 1996 | Democratic | Chicago |
| June 12, 1928 | Republican | Kansas City | July 29, 2000 | Republican | Philadelphia |
| June 26, 1928 | Democratic | Houston | Aug. 14, 2000 | Democratic | Los Angeles |

1. The convention adopted name Union Party to attract War Democrats and others favoring prosecution of war. 2. In session until July 10, 1924. 3. States' Rights delegates from 13 southern states.

# National Committee Chairs Since 1944

| Chairman and (state) | Term | Chairman and (state) | Term |
|---|---|---|---|
| **Republican** | | **Democratic** | |
| Herbert Brownell, Jr. (N.Y.) | 1944–1946 | Robert E. Hannegan (Mo.) | 1944–1947 |
| Carroll Reece (Tenn.) | 1946–1948 | J. Howard McGrath (R.I.) | 1947–1949 |
| Hugh D. Scott, Jr. (Pa.) | 1948–1949 | William M. Boyle, Jr. (Mo.) | 1949–1951 |
| Guy G. Gabrielson (N.J.) | 1949–1952 | Frank E. McKinney (Ind.) | 1951–1952 |
| Arthur E. Summerfield (Mich.) | 1952–1953 | Stephen A. Mitchell (Ill.) | 1952–1954 |
| Wesley Roberts (Kan.) | 1953 | Paul M. Butler (Ind.) | 1955–1960 |
| Leonard W. Hall (N.Y.) | 1953–1957 | Henry M. Jackson (Wash.) | 1960–1961 |
| Meade Alcorn (Conn.) | 1957–1959 | John M. Bailey (Conn.) | 1961–1968 |
| Thruston B. Morton (Ky.) | 1959–1961 | Lawrence F. O'Brien (Mass.) | 1968–1969 |
| William E. Miller (N.Y.) | 1961–1964 | Fred R. Harris (Okla.) | 1969–1970 |
| Dean Burch (Ariz.) | 1964–1965 | Lawrence F. O'Brien (Mass.) | 1970–1972 |
| Ray C. Bliss (Ohio) | 1966–1969 | Jean Westwood (Utah) | 1972 |
| Rogers C. B. Morton (Md.) | 1969–1971 | Robert S. Strauss (Tex.) | 1972–1977 |
| Robert Dole (Kan.) | 1971–1973 | Kenneth M. Curtis (Me.) | 1977 |
| George H. Bush (Tex.) | 1973–1974 | John C. White (Tex.) | 1977–1981 |
| Mary Louise Smith (Iowa) | 1974–1977 | Charles T. Manatt (Calif.) | 1981–1985 |
| William E. Brock III (Tenn.) | 1977–1981 | Paul G. Kirk, Jr. (Mass.) | 1985–1989 |
| Richard Richards (Utah) | 1981–1983 | Ronald H. Brown (D.C.) | 1989–1993 |
| Frank J. Fahrenkopf, Jr. (Nevada) | 1983–1989 | David Wilhelm (Ill.) | 1993–1994 |
| Lee Atwater (S.C.) | 1989–1991 | Christopher J. Dodd (Conn.) | 1995–1996 |
| Clayton K. Yeutter (Neb.) | 1991–1992 | Steven Grossman (Mass.) | 1996–1999 |
| Richard Bond (N.Y.) | 1992–1993 | Joe Andrew (Ind.) | 1999–2001 |
| Haley Barbour (Miss.) | 1993–1997 | Terry McAuliffe (Va.) | 2001– |
| Jim Nicholson (Colo.) | 1997–2001 | | |
| Jim Gilmore (Va.) | 2001–2002 | | |
| Marc Racicot (Mont.) | 2002– | | |

*Republican National Committee:* 310 First St., SE, Washington, DC 20003. *Democratic National Committee:* 430 South Capitol St., SE, Washington, DC 20003.

# Presidential Elections, 1789–2000

For the original method of electing the president and the vice president (elections of 1789, 1792, 1796, and 1800), *see* Article II, Section 1, of the Constitution. The election of 1804 was the first one in which the electors voted for president and vice president on separate ballots. (See Amendment XII to the Constitution.)

| Year | Presidential candidate | Party | Electoral votes | Year | Presidential candidate | Party | Electoral votes |
|---|---|---|---|---|---|---|---|
| 1789[1] | George Washington | (no party) | 69 | 1796 | John Adams | Federalist | 71 |
| | John Adams | (no party) | 34 | | Thomas Jefferson | Dem.-Rep. | 68 |
| | Scattering | (no party) | 35 | | Thomas Pinckney | Federalist | 59 |
| | Votes not cast | | 8 | | Aaron Burr | Dem.-Rep. | 30 |
| | | | | | Scattering | | 48 |
| 1792 | George Washington | Federalist | 132 | | | | |
| | John Adams | Federalist | 77 | 1800[2] | Thomas Jefferson | Dem.-Rep. | 73 |
| | George Clinton | Anti-Federalist | 50 | | Aaron Burr | Dem.-Rep. | 73 |
| | Thomas Jefferson | Anti-Federalist | 4 | | John Adams | Federalist | 65 |
| | Aaron Burr | Anti-Federalist | 1 | | Charles C. Pinckney | Federalist | 64 |
| | Votes not cast | | 6 | | John Jay | Federalist | 1 |

| Year | Presidential candidate | Party | Electoral votes | Vice-presidential candidate | Party | Electoral votes |
|---|---|---|---|---|---|---|
| 1804 | Thomas Jefferson | Dem.-Rep. | 162 | George Clinton | Dem.-Rep. | 162 |
| | Charles C. Pinckney | Federalist | 14 | Rufus King | Federalist | 14 |
| 1808 | James Madison | Dem.-Rep. | 122 | George Clinton | Dem.-Rep. | 113 |
| | Charles C. Pinckney | Federalist | 47 | Rufus King | Federalist | 47 |
| | George Clinton | Dem.-Rep. | 6 | John Langdon | Ind. (no party) | 9 |
| | Votes not cast | | 1 | James Madison | Dem.-Rep. | 3 |
| | | | | James Monroe | Dem.-Rep. | 3 |
| | | | | Votes not cast | | 1 |
| 1812 | James Madison | Dem.-Rep. | 128 | Elbridge Gerry | Dem.-Rep. | 131 |
| | De Witt Clinton | Federalist | 89 | Jared Ingersoll | Federalist | 86 |
| | Votes not cast | | 1 | Votes not cast | | 1 |
| 1816 | James Monroe | Dem.-Rep. | 183 | Daniel D. Tompkins | Dem.-Rep. | 183 |
| | Rufus King | Federalist | 34 | John E. Howard | Federalist | 22 |
| | Votes not cast | | 4 | James Ross | Ind (no party) | 5 |
| | | | | John Marshall | Federalist | 4 |
| | | | | Robert G. Harper | Ind. (no party) | 3 |
| | | | | Votes not cast | | 4 |
| 1820 | James Monroe | Dem-Rep | 231 | Daniel D. Tompkins | Dem.-Rep. | 218 |
| | John Quincy Adams | Ind. (no party) | 1 | Richard Stockton | Ind. (no party) | 8 |
| | Votes not cast | | 3 | Daniel Rodney | Ind. (no party) | 4 |
| | | | | Richard Rush | Ind. (no party) | 1 |
| | | | | Robert G. Harper | Ind. (no party) | 1 |
| | | | | Votes not cast | | 3 |
| 1824[3] | John Quincy Adams | (no party) | 84 | John C. Calhoun | (no party) | 182 |
| | Andrew Jackson | (no party) | 99 | Nathan Sanford | (no party) | 30 |
| | William H. Crawford | (no party) | 41 | Nathaniel Macon | (no party) | 24 |
| | Henry Clay | (no party) | 37 | Andrew Jackson | (no party) | 13 |
| | | | | Martin Van Buren | (no party) | 9 |
| | | | | Henry Clay | (no party) | 2 |
| | | | | Votes not cast | | 1 |
| 1828 | Andrew Jackson | Democratic | 178 | John C. Calhoun | Democratic | 171 |
| | John Quincy Adams | Natl. Rep. | 83 | Richard Rush | Natl. Rep. | 83 |
| | | | | William Smith | Democratic | 7 |
| 1832 | Andrew Jackson | Democratic | 219 | Martin Van Buren | Democratic | 189 |
| | Henry Clay | Natl. Rep. | 49 | John Sergeant | Natl. Rep. | 49 |
| | John Floyd | Ind. (no party) | 11 | Henry Lee | Ind. (no party) | 11 |
| | William Wirt | Antimasonic[4] | 7 | Amos Ellmaker | Antimasonic | 7 |
| | Votes not cast | | 2 | William Wilkins | Ind. (no party) | 30 |
| | | | | Votes not cast | | 2 |
| 1836 | Martin Van Buren | Democratic | 170 | Richard M. Johnson[5] | Democratic | 147 |
| | William H. Harrison | Whig | 73 | Francis Granger | Whig | 77 |
| | Hugh L. White | Whig | 26 | John Tyler | Whig | 47 |
| | Daniel Webster | Whig | 14 | William Smith | Ind. (no party) | 23 |
| | W. P. Mangum | Ind. (no party) | 11 | | | |

| Year | Presidential candidate | Party | Electoral votes | Vice-presidential candidate | Party | Electoral votes |
|------|------------------------|-------|-----------------|------------------------------|-------|-----------------|
| 1840 | William H. Harrison[6] | Whig | 234 | John Tyler | Whig | 234 |
| | Martin Van Buren | Democratic | 60 | Richard M. Johnson | Democratic | 48 |
| | | | | L. W. Tazewell | Ind. (no party) | 11 |
| | | | | James K. Polk | Democratic | 1 |
| 1844 | James K. Polk | Democratic | 170 | George M. Dallas | Democratic | 170 |
| | Henry Clay | Whig | 105 | Theo. Frelinghuysen | Whig | 105 |
| 1848 | Zachary Taylor[7] | Whig | 163 | Millard Fillmore | Whig | 163 |
| | Lewis Cass | Democratic | 127 | William O. Butler | Democratic | 127 |
| 1852 | Franklin Pierce | Democratic | 254 | William R. King | Democratic | 254 |
| | Winfield Scott | Whig | 42 | William A. Graham | Whig | 42 |
| 1856 | James Buchanan | Democratic | 174 | John C. Breckinridge | Democratic | 174 |
| | John C. Fremont | Republican | 114 | William L. Dayton | Republican | 114 |
| | Millard Fillmore | American[8] | 8 | A. J. Donelson | American[8] | 8 |
| 1860 | Abraham Lincoln | Republican | 180 | Hannibal Hamlin | Republican | 180 |
| | John C. Breckinridge | Democratic | 72 | Joseph Lane | Democratic | 72 |
| | John Bell | Const. Union | 39 | Edward Everett | Const. Union | 39 |
| | Stephen A. Douglas | Democratic | 12 | H. V. Johnson | Democratic | 12 |
| 1864 | Abraham Lincoln[9] | Union[10] | 212 | Andrew Johnson | Union[10] | 212 |
| | George B. McClellan | Democratic | 21 | G. H. Pendleton | Democratic | 21 |
| 1868 | Ulysses S. Grant | Republican | 214 | Schuyler Colfax | Republican | 214 |
| | Horatio Seymour | Democratic | 80 | Francis P. Blair, Jr. | Democratic | 80 |
| | Votes not counted[11] | | 23 | Votes not counted[11] | | 23 |

NOTE: Due to the communications constrictions of the time and the lack of formal political party organizations, the framers of the Constitution specified that the president and vice president be chosen based upon the votes cast by members of an electoral college rather than by a direct popular vote. Eventually, states began to change the method by which electors cast their votes. Today, all but two states, Maine and Nebraska, have a winner-take-all system in which a popular vote decides which candidates will be given all of a given state's electoral votes. The number of popular votes won by each presidential candidate are listed here for elections beginning in 1872.

| Year | Presidential candidate | Party | Electoral votes | Popular votes | Vice-presidential candidate and party |
|------|------------------------|-------|-----------------|---------------|----------------------------------------|
| 1872 | Ulysses S. Grant | Republican | 286 | 3,597,132 | Henry Wilson—R |
| | Horace Greeley | Dem., Liberal Rep. | (12) | 2,834,125 | B. Gratz Brown—D, LR—(47) |
| | Thomas A. Hendricks | Democratic | 42 | | Scattering—(19) |
| | B. Gratz Brown | Dem., Liberal Rep. | 18 | | Vote not counted—(14) |
| | Charles J. Jenkins | Democratic | 2 | | |
| | David Davis | Democratic | 1 | | |
| | Votes not counted | | 17 | | |
| 1876[13] | Rutherford B. Hayes | Republican | 185 | 4,033,768 | William A. Wheeler—R |
| | Samuel J. Tilden | Democratic | 184 | 4,285,992 | Thomas A. Hendricks—D |
| | Peter Cooper | Greenback | 0 | 81,737 | Samuel F. Cary—G |
| 1880 | James A. Garfield[14] | Republican | 214 | 4,449,053 | Chester A. Arthur—R |
| | Winfield S. Hancock | Democratic | 155 | 4,442,035 | William H. English—D |
| | James B. Weaver | Greenback | 0 | 308,578 | B. J. Chambers—G |
| 1884 | Grover Cleveland | Democratic | 219 | 4,911,017 | Thomas A. Hendricks—D |
| | James G. Blaine | Republican | 182 | 4,848,334 | John A. Logan—R |
| | Benjamin F. Butler | Greenback | 0 | 175,370 | A. M. West—G |
| | John P. St. John | Prohibition | 0 | 150,369 | William Daniel—P |
| 1888 | Benjamin Harrison | Republican | 233 | 5,443,610 | Levi P. Morton—R |
| | Grover Cleveland | Democratic | 168 | 5,538,233 | A. G. Thurman—D |
| | Clinton B. Fisk | Prohibition | 0 | 249,506 | John A. Brooks—P |
| | Alson J. Streeter | Union Labor | 0 | 146,935 | Charles F. Cunningham—UL |
| 1892 | Grover Cleveland | Democratic | 277 | 5,556,918 | Adlai E. Stevenson—D |
| | Benjamin Harrison | Republican | 145 | 5,176,108 | Whitelaw Reid—R |
| | James B. Weaver | People's[15] | 22 | 1,041,028 | James G. Field—Peo |
| | John Bidwell | Prohibition | 0 | 264,133 | James B. Cranfill—P |
| 1896 | William McKinley | Republican | 271 | 7,035,638 | Garret A. Hobart—R |
| | William J. Bryan | Dem., People's[15] | 176 | 6,467,946 | Arthur Sewall—D—(149) |
| | | | | | Thomas E. Watson—Peo—(27) |
| | John M. Palmer | Natl. Dem. | 0 | 133,148 | Simon B. Buckner—ND |
| | Joshua Levering | Prohibition | 0 | 132,007 | Hale Johnson—P |

| Year | Presidential candidate | Party | Electoral votes | Popular votes | Vice-presidential candidate and party |
|------|------------------------|-------|-----------------|---------------|----------------------------------------|
| 1900 | William McKinley[16] | Republican | 292 | 7,219,530 | Theodore Roosevelt—R |
|      | William J. Bryan | Dem., People's[15] | 155 | 6,358,071 | Adlai E. Stevenson—D, Peo |
|      | Eugene V. Debs | Social Democratic | 0 | 94,768 | Job Harriman—SD |
| 1904 | Theodore Roosevelt | Republican | 336 | 7,628,834 | Charles W. Fairbanks—R |
|      | Alton B. Parker | Democratic | 140 | 5,084,491 | Henry G. Davis—D |
|      | Eugene V. Debs | Socialist | 0 | 402,400 | Benjamin Hanford—S |
| 1908 | William H. Taft | Republican | 321 | 7,679,006 | James S. Sherman—R |
|      | William J. Bryan | Democratic | 162 | 6,409,106 | John W. Kern—D |
|      | Eugene V. Debs | Socialist | 0 | 402,820 | Benjamin Hanford—S |
| 1912 | Woodrow Wilson | Democratic | 435 | 6,286,214 | Thomas R. Marshall—D |
|      | Theodore Roosevelt | Progressive | 88 | 4,126,020 | Hiram Johnson—Prog |
|      | William H. Taft | Republican | 8 | 3,483,922 | Nicholas M. Butler—R[17] |
|      | Eugene V. Debs | Socialist | 0 | 897,011 | Emil Seidel—S |
| 1916 | Woodrow Wilson | Democratic | 277 | 9,129,606 | Thomas R. Marshall—D |
|      | Charles E. Hughes | Republican | 254 | 8,538,221 | Charles W. Fairbanks—R |
|      | A. L. Benson | Socialist | 0 | 585,113 | G. R. Kirkpatrick—S |
| 1920 | Warren G. Harding[18] | Republican | 404 | 16,152,200 | Calvin Coolidge—R |
|      | James M. Cox | Democratic | 127 | 9,147,353 | Franklin D. Roosevelt—D |
|      | Eugene V. Debs | Socialist | 0 | 917,799 | Seymour Stedman—S |
| 1924 | Calvin Coolidge | Republican | 382 | 15,725,016 | Charles G. Dawes—R |
|      | John W. Davis | Democratic | 136 | 8,385,586 | Charles W. Bryan—D |
|      | Robert M. LaFollette | Progressive, Socialist | 13 | 4,822,856 | Burton K. Wheeler—Prog, S |
| 1928 | Herbert Hoover | Republican | 444 | 21,392,190 | Charles Curtis—R |
|      | Alfred E. Smith | Democratic | 87 | 15,016,443 | Joseph T. Robinson—D |
|      | Norman Thomas | Socialist | 0 | 267,420 | James H. Maurer—S |
| 1932 | Franklin D. Roosevelt | Democratic | 472 | 22,821,857 | John N. Garner—D |
|      | Herbert Hoover | Republican | 59 | 15,761,841 | Charles Curtis—R |
|      | Norman Thomas | Socialist | 0 | 884,781 | James H. Maurer—S |
| 1936 | Franklin D. Roosevelt | Democratic | 523 | 27,751,597 | John N. Garner—D |
|      | Alfred M. Landon | Republican | 8 | 16,679,583 | Frank Knox—R |
|      | Norman Thomas | Socialist | 0 | 187,720 | George Nelson—S |
| 1940 | Franklin D. Roosevelt | Democratic | 449 | 27,244,160 | Henry A. Wallace—D |
|      | Wendell L. Willkie | Republican | 82 | 22,305,198 | Charles L. McNary—R |
|      | Norman Thomas | Socialist | 0 | 99,557 | Maynard C. Krueger—S |
| 1944 | Franklin D. Roosevelt[19] | Democratic | 432 | 25,602,504 | Harry S. Truman—D |
|      | Thomas E. Dewey | Republican | 99 | 22,006,285 | John W. Bricker—R |
|      | Norman Thomas | Socialist | 0 | 80,518 | Darlington Hoopes—S |
| 1948 | Harry S. Truman | Democratic | 303 | 24,179,345 | Alben W. Barkley—D |
|      | Thomas E. Dewey | Republican | 189 | 21,991,291 | Earl Warren—R |
|      | J. Strom Thurmond | States' Rights Dem. | 39 | 1,176,125 | Fielding L. Wright—SR |
|      | Henry A. Wallace | Progressive | 0 | 1,157,326 | Glen Taylor—Prog |
|      | Norman Thomas | Socialist | 0 | 139,572 | Tucker P. Smith—S |
| 1952 | Dwight D. Eisenhower | Republican | 442 | 33,936,234 | Richard M. Nixon—R |
|      | Adlai E. Stevenson | Democratic | 89 | 27,314,992 | John J. Sparkman—D |
| 1956 | Dwight D. Eisenhower | Republican | 457 | 35,590,472 | Richard M. Nixon—R |
|      | Adlai E. Stevenson | Democratic | 73[20] | 26,022,752 | Estes Kefauver—D |
| 1960 | John F. Kennedy[21] | Democratic | 303 | 34,226,731 | Lyndon B. Johnson—D |
|      | Richard M. Nixon | Republican | 219[22] | 34,108,157 | Henry Cabot Lodge—R |
| 1964 | Lyndon B. Johnson | Democratic | 486 | 43,129,484 | Hubert H. Humphrey—D |
|      | Barry M. Goldwater | Republican | 52 | 27,178,188 | William E. Miller—R |
| 1968 | Richard M. Nixon | Republican | 301 | 31,785,480 | Spiro T. Agnew—R |
|      | Hubert H. Humphrey | Democratic | 191 | 31,275,166 | Edmund S. Muskie—D |
|      | George C. Wallace | American Independent | 46 | 9,906,473 | Curtis F. LeMay—AI |
| 1972 | Richard M. Nixon[23] | Republican | 520[24] | 47,169,911 | Spiro T. Agnew—R |
|      | George McGovern | Democratic | 17 | 29,170,383 | Sargent Shriver—D |
|      | John G. Schmitz | American | 0 | 1,099,482 | Thomas J. Anderson—A |
| 1976 | Jimmy Carter | Democratic | 297 | 40,830,763 | Walter F. Mondale—D |
|      | Gerald R. Ford | Republican | 240[25] | 39,147,973 | Robert J. Dole—R |
|      | Eugene J. McCarthy | Independent | 0 | 756,631 | None |

| Year | Presidential candidate | Party | Electoral votes | Popular votes | Vice-presidential candidate and party |
|------|------------------------|-------|-----------------|---------------|----------------------------------------|
| 1980 | Ronald Reagan | Republican | 489 | 43,899,248 | George Bush—R |
|      | Jimmy Carter | Democratic | 49 | 36,481,435 | Walter F. Mondale—D |
|      | John B. Anderson | Independent | 0 | 5,719,437 | Patrick J. Lucey—I |
| 1984 | Ronald Reagan | Republican | 525 | 54,455,075 | George Bush—R |
|      | Walter F. Mondale | Democratic | 13 | 37,577,185 | Geraldine A. Ferraro—D |
| 1988 | George H. Bush | Republican | 426 | 48,886,097 | J. Danforth Quayle—R |
|      | Michael S. Dukakis | Democratic | 111[26] | 41,809,074 | Lloyd Bentsen—D |
| 1992 | William J. Clinton | Democratic | 370 | 44,909,889 | Albert A. Gore, J.—D |
|      | George H. Bush | Republican | 168 | 39,104,545 | J. Danforth Quayle—R |
|      | H. Ross Perot | Independent | 0 | 19,742,267 | James B. Stockdale—I |
| 1996 | William J. Clinton | Democratic | 379 | 47,402,357 | Albert A. Gore, Jr.—D |
|      | Robert J. Dole | Republican | 159 | 39,198,755 | Jack F. Kemp—R |
|      | H. Ross Perot | Reform Party[27] | 0 | 8,085,402 | Pat Choate—RP[27] |
| 2000 | George W. Bush | Republican | 271 | 50,455,156 | Richard B. Cheney—R |
|      | Albert A. Gore | Democratic | 266[28] | 50,992,335 | Joseph I. Lieberman—D |
|      | Ralph Nader | Green Party | 0 | 2,882,897 | Winona LaDuke—GP |

1. Only 10 states participated in the election. The New York legislature chose no electors, and North Carolina and Rhode Island had not yet ratified the Constitution. 2. As Jefferson and Burr were tied, the House of Representatives chose the president. In a vote by states, 10 votes were cast for Jefferson, 4 for Burr; 2 votes were not cast. 3. As no candidate had an electoral-vote majority, the House of Representatives chose the president from the first three. In a vote by states, 13 votes were cast for Adams, 7 for Jackson, and 4 for Crawford. 4. The Antimasonic Party on Sept. 26, 1831, was the first party to hold a nominating convention to choose candidates for president and vice president. 5. As Johnson did not have an electoral-vote majority, the Senate chose him 33–14 over Granger, the others being legally out of the race. 6. Harrison died April 4, 1841, and Tyler succeeded him April 6. 7. Taylor died July 9, 1850, and Fillmore succeeded him July 10. 8. Also known as the Know-Nothing Party. 9. Lincoln died April 15, 1865, and Johnson succeeded him the same day. 10. Name adopted by the Republican National Convention of 1864. Johnson was a War Democrat. 11. 23 Southern electoral votes were excluded. 12. Greeley died Nov. 29, 1872, before his 66 electors voted; 63 of Greeley's votes were scattered among four of the other candidates. 13. Hayes was chosen by a special electoral commission since initially neither candidate had the requisite 185 electoral votes. 14. Garfield died Sept. 19, 1881, and Arthur succeeded him Sept. 20. 15. Members of People's Party were called Populists. 16. McKinley died Sept. 14, 1901, and Roosevelt succeeded him the same day. 17. James S. Sherman, Republican candidate for vice president, died Oct. 30, 1912, and the Republican electoral votes were cast for Butler. 18. Harding died Aug. 2, 1923, and Coolidge succeeded him Aug. 3. 19. Roosevelt died April 12, 1945, and Truman succeeded him the same day. 20. One electoral vote from Alabama was cast for Walter B. Jones. 21. Kennedy died Nov. 22, 1963, and Johnson succeeded him the same day. 22. Sen. Harry F. Byrd received 15 electoral votes. 23. Nixon resigned Aug. 9, 1974, and Gerald R. Ford succeeded him the same day. 24. One electoral vote from Virginia was cast for John Hospers, Libertarian Party. 25. One electoral vote from Washington was cast for Ronald Reagan. 26. One electoral vote from West Virginia was cast for Lloyd Bentsen. 27. Perot helped establish the Reform Party following his defeat in the 1992 election. 28. One elector from the District of Columbia left her ballot blank to protest the city's lack of representation in Congress, leaving Gore with 266 electoral votes instead of 267.

## Plurality and Majority

In order to win a plurality, a candidate must receive a greater number of votes than anyone running against him. If he receives 50 votes, for example, and two other candidates receive 49 and 2, he will have a plurality of one vote over his closest opponent.

However, a candidate does not have a majority unless he receives more than 50% of the total votes cast. In the example above, the candidate does not have a majority, because his 50 votes are less than 50% of the 101 votes cast.

## Presidents Elected Without a Majority

Fifteen candidates (three of them twice) have become president of the United States with a plurality. It should be noted, however, that in elections before 1872, presidential electors were not chosen by popular vote in all states. Adams's election in 1824 was by the House of Representatives (see footnote 3 on Jackson, who had a plurality of both electoral and popular votes, but not a majority in the electoral college.

The "minority" presidents are listed below.

| Year | President | Electoral percent | Popular percent | Year | President | Electoral percent | Popular percent |
|------|-----------|-------------------|-----------------|------|-----------|-------------------|-----------------|
| 1824 | John Q. Adams | 31.8% | 29.8% | 1892 | Grover Cleveland (D) | 62.4% | 46.0% |
| 1844 | James K. Polk (D) | 61.8 | 49.3 | 1912 | Woodrow Wilson (D) | 81.9 | 41.8 |
| 1848 | Zachary Taylor (W) | 56.2 | 47.3 | 1916 | Woodrow Wilson (D) | 52.1 | 49.3 |
| 1856 | James Buchanan (D) | 58.7 | 45.3 | 1948 | Harry S. Truman (D) | 57.1 | 49.5 |
| 1860 | Abraham Lincoln (R) | 59.4 | 39.9 | 1960 | John F. Kennedy (D) | 56.4 | 49.7 |
| 1876 | Rutherford B. Hayes (R) | 50.1 | 47.9 | 1968 | Richard M. Nixon (R) | 56.1 | 43.4 |
| 1880 | James A. Garfield (R) | 57.9 | 48.3 | 1992 | William J. Clinton (D) | 68.8 | 43.0 |
| 1884 | Grover Cleveland (D) | 54.6 | 48.8 | 1996 | William J. Clinton (D) | 70.4 | 49.0 |
| 1888 | Benjamin Harrison (R) | 58.1 | 47.8 | 2000 | George W. Bush (R) | 50.3 | 47.8 |

# The Closest Presidential Races

Although the 2000 presidential race was extremely close, there have been others that were also too close to call immediately after the election. Indeed, the results of the Nov. 7 election in 1876 were not known until March 2, 1877, just three days before the inauguration. More recently, John F. Kennedy's defeat of Richard M. Nixon in 1960 wasn't official until noon the following day.

| President | Electoral votes | Popular votes | President | Electoral votes | Popular votes |
|---|---|---|---|---|---|
| **1800[1]** | | | **1916** | | |
| Thomas Jefferson (Dem.-Rep.) | 73 | — | Woodrow Wilson (D) | 277 | 9,129,606 |
| Aaron Burr (Dem.-Rep.) | 73 | — | Charles E. Hughes (R) | 254 | 8,538,221 |
| John Adams (Federalist) | 65 | — | **1960** | | |
| Charles C. Pinckney (Federalist) | 64 | — | John F. Kennedy (D) | 303 | 34,226,731 |
| John Jay (Federalist) | 1 | — | Richard M. Nixon (R) | 219 | 34,108,157 |
| **1824[2]** | | | **1968** | | |
| John Quincy Adams (no party) | 84 | — | Richard M. Nixon (R) | 301 | 31,785,480 |
| Andrew Jackson (no party) | 99 | — | Hubert H. Humphrey (R) | 191 | 31,275,166 |
| William H. Crawford (no party) | 41 | — | George C. Wallace | 46 | 9,906,473 |
| Henry Clay (no party) | 37 | — | (American Independent) | | |
| **1876** | | | **1976** | | |
| Rutherford B. Hayes (R) | 185 | 4,033,768 | Jimmy Carter (D) | 297 | 40,830,763 |
| Samuel J. Tilden (D) | 184 | 4,285,992 | Gerald R. Ford (R) | 240 | 39,147,973 |
| **1880** | | | **2000** | | |
| James A. Garfield (R) | 214 | 4,449,053 | George W. Bush (R) | 271 | 50,455,156 |
| Winfield S. Hancock (D) | 155 | 4,442,035 | Albert A. Gore (D) | 266[3] | 50,992,335 |

1. As Jefferson and Burr were tied, the House of Representatives chose the president. In a vote by states, 10 votes were cast for Jefferson, 4 for Burr; 2 votes were not cast. For the original method of electing the president and vice president (elections of 1789, 1792, 1796, and 1800), see Article II, Section 1, of the Constitution. 2. As no candidate had an electoral vote majority, the House of Representatives chose the president from the first three. In a vote by states, 13 votes were cast for Adams, 7 for Jackson, and 4 for Crawford. 3. One elector from the District of Columbia left her ballot blank to protest the city's lack of representation in Congress, leaving Gore with 266 electoral votes instead of 267.

# National Voter Turnout in Federal Elections: 1964–2000

| Year | Voting-age population | Voter registration | Voter turnout | Turnout of voting-age population (percent) |
|---|---|---|---|---|
| **2000** | **205,815,000** | **156,421,311** | **105,586,274** | **51.3%** |
| 1998 | 200,929,000 | 141,850,558 | 73,117,022 | 36.4 |
| **1996** | **196,511,000** | **146,211,960** | **96,456,345** | **49.1** |
| 1994 | 193,650,000 | 130,292,822 | 75,105,860 | 38.8 |
| **1992** | **189,529,000** | **133,821,178** | **104,405,155** | **55.1** |
| 1990 | 185,812,000 | 121,105,630 | 67,859,189 | 36.5 |
| **1988** | **182,778,000** | **126,379,628** | **91,594,693** | **50.1** |
| 1986 | 178,566,000 | 118,399,984 | 64,991,128 | 36.4 |
| **1984** | **174,466,000** | **124,150,614** | **92,652,680** | **53.1** |
| 1982 | 169,938,000 | 110,671,225 | 67,615,576 | 39.8 |
| **1980** | **164,597,000** | **113,043,734** | **86,515,221** | **52.6** |
| 1978 | 158,373,000 | 103,291,265 | 58,917,938 | 37.2 |
| **1976** | **152,309,190** | **105,037,986** | **81,555,789** | **53.6** |
| 1974 | 146,336,000 | 96,199,020[1] | 55,943,834 | 38.2 |
| **1972** | **140,776,000** | **97,328,541** | **77,718,554** | **55.2** |
| 1970 | 124,498,000 | 82,496,747[2] | 58,014,338 | 46.6 |
| **1968** | **120,328,186** | **81,658,180** | **73,211,875** | **60.8** |
| 1966 | 116,132,000 | 76,288,283[3] | 56,188,046 | 48.4 |
| **1964** | **114,090,000** | **73,715,818** | **70,644,592** | **61.9** |

n.a. = not available. NOTE: Presidential election years are in boldface. 1. Registrations from Iowa not included. 2. Registrations from Iowa and Mo. not included. 3. Registrations from Iowa, Kans., Miss., Mo., Nebr., and Wyo. not included. D.C. did not have independent status. *Source:* Federal Election Commission. Data drawn from Congressional Research Service reports, Election Data Services Inc., and State Election Offices.

# Facts About Elections

**Candidate with highest popular vote:** Reagan (1984), 54,455,075.
**Candidate with highest electoral vote:** Reagan (1984), 525.
**Candidate carrying most states:** Nixon (1972) and Reagan (1984), 49.

**Candidate running most times:** Norman Thomas (Socialist Party), six (1928, 1932, 1936, 1940, 1944, 1948).
**Candidate elected, defeated, then reelected:** Cleveland (1884, 1888, 1892).

# Presidents

| | Name and (party)[1] | Term | State of birth | Born | Died | Religion | Age at inaug. | Age at death |
|---|---|---|---|---|---|---|---|---|
| 1. | Washington (F)[2] | 1789–1797 | Va. | 2/22/1732 | 12/14/1799 | Episcopalian | 57 | 67 |
| 2. | J. Adams (F) | 1797–1801 | Mass. | 10/30/1735 | 7/4/1826 | Unitarian | 61 | 90 |
| 3. | Jefferson (DR) | 1801–1809 | Va. | 4/13/1743 | 7/4/1826 | Deist | 57 | 83 |
| 4. | Madison (DR) | 1809–1817 | Va. | 3/16/1751 | 6/28/1836 | Episcopalian | 57 | 85 |
| 5. | Monroe (DR) | 1817–1825 | Va. | 4/28/1758 | 7/4/1831 | Episcopalian | 58 | 73 |
| 6. | J. Q. Adams (DR) | 1825–1829 | Mass. | 7/11/1767 | 2/23/1848 | Unitarian | 57 | 80 |
| 7. | Jackson (D) | 1829–1837 | S.C. | 3/15/1767 | 6/8/1845 | Presbyterian | 61 | 78 |
| 8. | Van Buren (D) | 1837–1841 | N.Y. | 12/5/1782 | 7/24/1862 | Reformed Dutch | 54 | 79 |
| 9. | W. H. Harrison (W)[3] | 1841 | Va. | 2/9/1773 | 4/4/1841 | Episcopalian | 68 | 68 |
| 10. | Tyler (W) | 1841–1845 | Va. | 3/29/1790 | 1/18/1862 | Episcopalian | 51 | 71 |
| 11. | Polk (D) | 1845–1849 | N.C. | 11/2/1795 | 6/15/1849 | Methodist | 49 | 53 |
| 12. | Taylor (W)[3] | 1849–1850 | Va. | 11/24/1784 | 7/9/1850 | Episcopalian | 64 | 65 |
| 13. | Fillmore (W) | 1850–1853 | N.Y. | 1/7/1800 | 3/8/1874 | Unitarian | 50 | 74 |
| 14. | Pierce (D) | 1853–1857 | N.H. | 11/23/1804 | 10/8/1869 | Episcopalian | 48 | 64 |
| 15. | Buchanan (D) | 1857–1861 | Pa. | 4/23/1791 | 6/1/1868 | Presbyterian | 65 | 77 |
| 16. | Lincoln (R)[4] | 1861–1865 | Ky. | 2/12/1809 | 4/15/1865 | Liberal | 52 | 56 |
| 17. | A. Johnson (U)[5] | 1865–1869 | N.C. | 12/29/1808 | 7/31/1875 | (6) | 56 | 66 |
| 18. | Grant (R) | 1869–1877 | Ohio | 4/27/1822 | 7/23/1885 | Methodist | 46 | 63 |
| 19. | Hayes (R) | 1877–1881 | Ohio | 10/4/1822 | 1/17/1893 | Methodist | 54 | 70 |
| 20. | Garfield (R)[4] | 1881 | Ohio | 11/19/1831 | 9/19/1881 | Disciples of Christ | 49 | 49 |
| 21. | Arthur (R) | 1881–1885 | Vt. | 10/5/1829 | 11/18/1886 | Episcopalian | 50 | 56 |
| 22. | Cleveland (D) | 1885–1889 | N.J. | 3/18/1837 | 6/24/1908 | Presbyterian | 47 | 71 |
| 23. | B. Harrison (R) | 1889–1893 | Ohio | 8/20/1833 | 3/13/1901 | Presbyterian | 55 | 67 |
| 24. | Cleveland (D)[7] | 1893–1897 | — | — | — | — | 55 | — |
| 25. | McKinley (R)[4] | 1897–1901 | Ohio | 1/29/1843 | 9/14/1901 | Methodist | 54 | 58 |
| 26. | T. Roosevelt (R) | 1901–1909 | N.Y. | 10/27/1858 | 1/6/1919 | Reformed Dutch | 42 | 60 |
| 27. | Taft (R) | 1909–1913 | Ohio | 9/15/1857 | 3/8/1930 | Unitarian | 51 | 72 |
| 28. | Wilson (D) | 1913–1921 | Va. | 12/28/1856 | 2/3/1924 | Presbyterian | 56 | 67 |
| 29. | Harding (R)[3] | 1921–1923 | Ohio | 11/2/1865 | 8/2/1923 | Baptist | 55 | 57 |
| 30. | Coolidge (R) | 1923–1929 | Vt. | 7/4/1872 | 1/5/1933 | Congregationalist | 51 | 60 |
| 31. | Hoover (R) | 1929–1933 | Iowa | 8/10/1874 | 10/20/1964 | Quaker | 54 | 90 |
| 32. | F. D. Roosevelt (D)[3] | 1933–1945 | N.Y. | 1/30/1882 | 4/12/1945 | Episcopalian | 51 | 63 |
| 33. | Truman (D) | 1945–1953 | Mo. | 5/8/1884 | 12/26/1972 | Baptist | 60 | 88 |
| 34. | Eisenhower (R) | 1953–1961 | Tex. | 10/14/1890 | 3/28/1969 | Presbyterian | 62 | 78 |
| 35. | Kennedy (D)[4] | 1961–1963 | Mass. | 5/29/1917 | 11/22/1963 | Roman Catholic | 43 | 46 |
| 36. | L. B. Johnson (D) | 1963–1969 | Tex. | 8/27/1908 | 1/22/1973 | Disciples of Christ | 55 | 64 |
| 37. | Nixon (R)[8] | 1969–1974 | Calif. | 1/9/1913 | 4/22/1994 | Quaker | 56 | 81 |
| 38. | Ford (R) | 1974–1977 | Neb. | 7/14/1913 | — | Episcopalian | 61 | — |
| 39. | Carter (D) | 1977–1981 | Ga. | 10/1/1924 | — | Southern Baptist | 52 | — |
| 40. | Reagan (R) | 1981–1989 | Ill. | 2/6/1911 | — | Disciples of Christ | 69 | — |
| 41. | G.H.W. Bush (R) | 1989–1993 | Mass. | 6/12/1924 | — | Episcopalian | 64 | — |
| 42. | Clinton (D) | 1993–2001 | Ark. | 8/19/1946 | — | Baptist | 46 | — |
| 43. | G. W. Bush (R) | 2001– | Conn. | 7/6/46 | — | Methodist | 54 | — |

1. F—Federalist; DR—Democratic-Republican; D—Democratic; W—Whig; R—Republican; U—Union. 2. No party for first election. The party system in the U.S. made its appearance during Washington's first term. 3. Died in office. 4. Assassinated in office. 5. The Republican National Convention of 1864 adopted the name Union Party. It renominated Lincoln for president; for vice president it nominated Johnson, a War Democrat. Although frequently listed as a Republican vice president and president, Johnson undoubtedly considered himself strictly a member of the Union Party. When that party broke apart after 1868, he returned to the Democratic Party. 6. Johnson was not a professed church member; however, he admired the Baptist principles of church government. 7. Second nonconsecutive term. 8. Resigned Aug. 9, 1974.

## Vice Presidents

| | Name and (party)[1] | Term | State of birth | Birth and death dates | President served under |
|---|---|---|---|---|---|
| 1 | John Adams (F)[2] | 1789–1797 | Massachusetts | 1736–1826 | Washington |
| 2. | Thomas Jefferson (DR) | 1797–1801 | Virginia | 1743–1826 | J. Adams |
| 3. | Aaron Burr (DR) | 1801–1805 | New Jersey | 1756–1836 | Jefferson |
| 4. | George Clinton (DR)[3] | 1805–1812 | New York | 1739–1812 | Jefferson and Madison |
| 5. | Elbridge Gerry (DR)[3] | 1813–1814 | Massachusetts | 1744–1814 | Madison |
| 6. | Daniel D. Tompkins (DR) | 1817–1825 | New York | 1774–1825 | Monroe |
| 7. | John C. Calhoun[4] | 1825–1832 | South Carolina | 1782–1850 | J. Q. Adams and Jackson |
| 8. | Martin Van Buren (D) | 1833–1837 | New York | 1782–1862 | Jackson |
| 9. | Richard M. Johnson (D) | 1837–1841 | Kentucky | 1780–1850 | Van Buren |
| 10. | John Tyler (W)[5] | 1841 | Virginia | 1790–1862 | W. H. Harrison |
| 11. | George M. Dallas (D) | 1845–1849 | Pennsylvania | 1792–1864 | Polk |
| 12. | Millard Fillmore (W)[5] | 1849–1850 | New York | 1800–1874 | Taylor |
| 13. | William R. King (D)[3] | 1853 | North Carolina | 1786–1853 | Pierce |

| | Name and (party)[1] | Term | State of birth | Birth and death dates | President served under |
|---|---|---|---|---|---|
| 14. | John C. Breckinridge (D) | 1857–1861 | Kentucky | 1821–1875 | Buchanan |
| 15. | Hannibal Hamlin (R) | 1861–1865 | Maine | 1809–1891 | Lincoln |
| 16. | Andrew Johnson (U)[5] | 1865 | North Carolina | 1808–1875 | Lincoln |
| 17. | Schuyler Colfax (R) | 1869–1873 | New York | 1823–1885 | Grant |
| 18. | Henry Wilson (R)[3] | 1873–1875 | New Hampshire | 1812–1875 | Grant |
| 19. | William A. Wheeler (R) | 1877–1881 | New York | 1819–1887 | Hayes |
| 20. | Chester A. Arthur (R)[5] | 1881 | Vermont | 1829–1886 | Garfield |
| 21. | Thomas A. Hendricks (D)[3] | 1885 | Ohio | 1819–1885 | Cleveland |
| 22. | Levi P. Morton (R) | 1889–1893 | Vermont | 1824–1920 | B. Harrison |
| 23. | Adlai E. Stevenson (D) | 1893–1897 | Kentucky | 1835–1914 | Cleveland |
| 24. | Garrett A. Hobart (R)[3] | 1897–1899 | New Jersey | 1844–1899 | McKinley |
| 25. | Theodore Roosevelt (R)[5] | 1901 | New York | 1858–1919 | McKinley |
| 26. | Charles W. Fairbanks (R) | 1905–1909 | Ohio | 1852–1918 | T. Roosevelt |
| 27. | James S. Sherman (R)[3] | 1909–1912 | New York | 1855–1912 | Taft |
| 28. | Thomas R. Marshall (D) | 1913–1921 | Indiana | 1854–1925 | Wilson |
| 29. | Calvin Coolidge (R)[5] | 1921–1923 | Vermont | 1872–1933 | Harding |
| 30. | Charles G. Dawes (R) | 1925–1929 | Ohio | 1865–1951 | Coolidge |
| 31. | Charles Curtis (R) | 1929–1933 | Kansas | 1860–1936 | Hoover |
| 32. | John N. Garner (D) | 1933–1941 | Texas | 1868–1967 | F. D. Roosevelt |
| 33. | Henry A. Wallace (D) | 1941–1945 | Iowa | 1888–1965 | F. D. Roosevelt |
| 34. | Harry S. Truman (D)[5] | 1945 | Missouri | 1884–1972 | F. D. Roosevelt |
| 35. | Alben W. Barkley (D) | 1949–1953 | Kentucky | 1877–1956 | Truman |
| 36. | Richard M. Nixon (R) | 1953-1961 | California | 1913–1994 | Eisenhower |
| 37. | Lyndon B. Johnson (D)[5] | 1961–1963 | Texas | 1908–1973 | Kennedy |
| 38. | Hubert H. Humphrey (D) | 1965–1969 | South Dakota | 1911–1978 | L. B. Johnson |
| 39. | Spiro T. Agnew (R)[6] | 1969–1973 | Maryland | 1918–1996 | Nixon |
| 40. | Gerald R. Ford (R)[7] | 1973–1974 | Nebraska | 1913– | Nixon |
| 41. | Nelson A. Rockefeller (R)[8] | 1974–1977 | Maine | 1908–1979 | Ford |
| 42. | Walter F. Mondale (D) | 1977–1981 | Minnesota | 1928– | Carter |
| 43. | George Bush (R) | 1981–1989 | Massachusetts | 1924– | Reagan |
| 44. | J. Danforth Quayle (R) | 1989–1993 | Indiana | 1947– | G.H.W. Bush |
| 45. | Albert A. Gore, Jr. (D) | 1993–2001 | Washington, D.C. | 1948– | Clinton |
| 46. | Richard B. Cheney (R) | 2001– | Nebraska | 1941– | G. W. Bush |

1. F—Federalist; DR—Democratic-Republican; D—Democratic; W—Whig; R—Republican; U—Union. 2. No party for first election. The party system in the U.S. made its appearance during Washington's first term as president. 3. Died in office. 4. Democratic-Republican with J. Q. Adams; Democratic with Jackson. Calhoun resigned in 1832 to become a U.S. senator. 5. Succeeded to presidency on death of president. Prior to the passage of the 25th Amendment (ratified Feb. 10, 1967), there were no provisions for filling a vacancy in the vice presidency. In the event of a vacancy, the president pro tempore took over most of the vice president's duties. 6. Resigned Oct. 10, 1973, after pleading no contest to federal income tax evasion charges. 7. Nominated by Nixon on Oct. 12, 1973, under provisions of 25th Amendment. Confirmed by Congress on Dec. 6, 1973, and was sworn in same day. He became president Aug. 9, 1974, upon Nixon's resignation. 8. Nominated by Ford Aug. 20, 1974; confirmed by Congress on Dec. 19, 1974, and was sworn in same day.

# Presidential Libraries

These are not traditional libraries, but rather repositories for preserving and making available the papers, records, and other historical materials of the presidents since Herbert Hoover. The presidential library system formally began in 1939, when President Franklin Roosevelt donated his personal and presidential papers to the federal government.

**Hoover Library**
210 Parkside Drive
P.O. Box 488
West Branch, IA 52358-0488
http://hoover.archives.gov

**Roosevelt Library**
4079 Albany Post Road
Hyde Park, NY 12538-1999
http://www.fdrlibrary.marist.edu/

**Truman Library**
500 West U.S. Highway 24
Independence, MO 64050-1798
http://www.trumanlibrary.org

**Eisenhower Library**
200 SE 4th Street
Abilene, KS 67410-2900
http://www.eisenhower.utexas.edu

**Kennedy Library**
Columbia Point
Boston, MA 02125-3398
http://www.jfklibrary.org

**Johnson Library**
2313 Red River Street
Austin, TX 78705-5702
http://www.lbjlib.utexas.edu

**The Nixon Project[1]**
National Archives at College Park
8601 Adelphi Road
College Park, MD 20740-6001
http://www.nixon.archives.gov/

**Ford Library**
1000 Beal Avenue
Ann Arbor, MI 48109-2114
http://www.ford.utexas.edu

**Carter Library**
441 Freedom Parkway
Atlanta, GA 30307-1498
http://www.jimmycarterlibrary.org/

**Reagan Library**
40 Presidential Drive
Simi Valley, CA 93065-0666
http://www.reagan.utexas.edu

**Bush Library**
1000 George Bush Drive West
College Station, TX 77845
http://bushlibrary.tamu.edu/

1. The Nixon Project is not affiliated with the Richard Nixon Library and Birthplace in Yorba Linda, Calif., a private institution that was established by Nixon in 1990. *Source:* National Archives and Records Administration. Web: www.archives.gov/.

# Wives and Children of the Presidents

| President | Wife's name | Year and place of wife's birth | Married | Wife died | Children[1] Sons | Daughters |
|---|---|---|---|---|---|---|
| Washington | Martha Dandridge Custis | 1732, Va. | 1759 | 1802 | — | — |
| John Adams | Abigail Smith | 1744, Mass. | 1764 | 1818 | 3 | 2 |
| Jefferson [2] | Martha Wayles Skelton | 1748, Va. | 1772 | 1782 | 1 | 5 |
| Madison | Dorothy "Dolley" Payne Todd | 1768, N.C. | 1794 | 1849 | — | — |
| Monroe | Elizabeth "Eliza" Kortright | 1768, N.Y. | 1786 | 1830 | — | 2 |
| J. Q. Adams | Louisa Catherine Johnson | 1775, England | 1797 | 1852 | 3 | 1 |
| Jackson | Rachel Donelson Robards | 1767, Va. | 1791 | 1828 | — | — |
| Van Buren | Hannah Hoes | 1788, N.Y. | 1807 | 1819 | 4 | — |
| W. H. Harrison | Anna Symmes | 1775, N.J. | 1795 | 1864 | 6 | 4 |
| Tyler | Letitia Christian | 1790, Va. | 1813 | 1842 | 3 | 4 |
| | Julia Gardiner | 1820, N.Y. | 1844 | 1889 | 5 | 2 |
| Polk | Sarah Childress | 1803, Tenn. | 1824 | 1891 | — | — |
| Taylor | Margaret Smith | 1788, Md. | 1810 | 1852 | 1 | 5 |
| Fillmore | Abigail Powers | 1798, N.Y. | 1826 | 1853 | 1 | 1 |
| | Caroline Carmichael McIntosh | 1813, N.J. | 1858 | 1881 | — | — |
| Pierce | Jane Means Appleton | 1806, N.H. | 1834 | 1863 | 3 | — |
| Buchanan | (Unmarried) | — | — | — | — | — |
| Lincoln | Mary Todd | 1818, Ky. | 1842 | 1882 | 4 | — |
| A. Johnson | Eliza McCardle | 1810, Tenn. | 1827 | 1876 | 3 | 2 |
| Grant | Julia Dent | 1826, Mo. | 1848 | 1902 | 3 | 1 |
| Hayes | Lucy Ware Webb | 1831, Ohio | 1852 | 1889 | 7 | 1 |
| Garfield | Lucretia Rudolph | 1832, Ohio | 1858 | 1918 | 5 | 2 |
| Arthur | Ellen Lewis Herndon | 1837, Va. | 1859 | 1880 | 2 | 1 |
| Cleveland | Frances Folsom | 1864, N.Y. | 1886 | 1947 | 2 | 3 |
| B. Harrison | Caroline Lavinia Scott | 1832, Ohio | 1853 | 1892 | 1 | 1 |
| | Mary Scott Lord Dimmick | 1858, Pa. | 1896 | 1948 | — | 1 |
| McKinley | Ida Saxton | 1847, Ohio | 1871 | 1907 | — | 2 |
| T. Roosevelt | Alice Hathaway Lee | 1861, Mass. | 1880 | 1884 | — | 1 |
| | Edith Kermit Carow | 1861, Conn. | 1886 | 1948 | 4 | 1 |
| Taft | Helen Herron | 1861, Ohio | 1886 | 1943 | 2 | 1 |
| Wilson | Ellen Louise Axson | 1860, Ga. | 1885 | 1914 | — | 3 |
| | Edith Bolling Galt | 1872, Va. | 1915 | 1961 | — | — |
| Harding | Florence Kling DeWolfe | 1860, Ohio | 1891 | 1924 | — | — |
| Coolidge | Grace Anna Goodhue | 1879, Vt. | 1905 | 1957 | 2 | — |
| Hoover | Lou Henry | 1875, Iowa | 1899 | 1944 | 2 | — |
| F. D. Roosevelt | (Anna) Eleanor Roosevelt | 1884, N.Y. | 1905 | 1962 | 5 | 1 |
| Truman | Bess Wallace | 1885, Mo. | 1919 | 1982 | — | 1 |
| Eisenhower | Mamie Geneva Doud | 1896, Iowa | 1916 | 1979 | 2 | — |
| Kennedy | Jacqueline Lee Bouvier | 1929, N.Y. | 1953 | 1994 | 2 | 1 |
| L. B. Johnson | Claudia Alta "Lady Bird" Taylor | 1912, Tex. | 1934 | — | — | 2 |
| Nixon | Thelma Catherine "Pat" Ryan | 1912, Nev. | 1940 | 1993 | — | 2 |
| Ford | Elizabeth "Betty" Bloomer Warren | 1918, Ill. | 1948 | — | 3 | 1 |
| Carter | Rosalynn Smith | 1928, Ga. | 1946 | — | 3 | 1 |
| Reagan | Jane Wyman | 1914, Mo. | 1940[3] | — | 1[4] | 1 |
| | Nancy Davis | 1921 (?)[5], N.Y. | 1952 | — | 1 | 1 |
| G.H.W. Bush | Barbara Pierce | 1925, N.Y. | 1945 | — | 4 | 2 |
| Clinton | Hillary Rodham | 1947, Ill. | 1975 | — | — | 1 |
| G. W. Bush | Laura Welch | 1946, Tex. | 1977 | — | — | 2 |

1. Includes children who died in infancy. 2. Number of children listed [...] agree[...] accounts [...], that Jefferson may have fathered at least one child with slave Sally Hemings. 3. Divorced in 1948. 4. Adopted. 5. Birthday officially given as 1923 but her high school and college records show 1921 for year of birth.

## Biographies of the Presidents

**GEORGE WASHINGTON** was born on Feb. 22, 1732 (Feb. 11, 1731/2, old style) in Westmoreland County, Va. While in his teens, he trained as a surveyor, and at the age of 20 he was appointed adjutant in the Va. militia. For the next three years, he fought in the wars against the French and Indians, serving as Gen. Edward Braddock's aide in the disastrous campaign against Ft. Duquesne. In 1759, he resigned from the militia, married Martha Dandridge Custis, a widow with children, and settled down as a gentleman farmer at Mount Vernon, Va.

As a militiaman, Washington had been exposed to the arrogance of the British officers, and his experience as a planter with British commercial restrictions increased his anti-British sentiment. He opposed the Stamp Act of 1765 and after 1770 became increasingly prominent in organizing resistance. A delegate to the Continental Congress, Washington was selected as commander in chief of the Continental Army and took command at Cambridge, Mass., on July 3, 1775.

Inadequately supported and sometimes covertly sabotaged by the Congress, in charge of troops who were inexperienced, badly equipped, and impatient of discipline, Washington conducted the war on the policy of avoiding major engagements with the British and wearing them down by harassing tactics. His able generalship, along with the French alliance and the growing weariness within Britain, brought the war to a conclusion with the surrender of Cornwallis at Yorktown, Va., on Oct. 19, 1781.

The chaotic years under the Articles of Confederation led Washington to return to public life in the hope of promoting the formation of a strong central government. He presided over the Constitutional Convention and yielded to the universal demand that he serve as first president. He was inaugurated on April 30, 1789, in New York, the first national capital. In office, he sought to unite the nation and establish the authority of the new government at home and abroad. Greatly distressed by the emergence of the Hamilton-Jefferson rivalry, Washington worked to maintain neutrality but actually sympathized more with Hamilton. Following his unanimous re-election in 1792, his second term was dominated by the Federalists. His Farewell Address on Sept. 17, 1796 (published but never delivered) rebuked party spirit and warned against "permanent alliances" with foreign powers.

He died at Mount Vernon on Dec. 14, 1799.

**JOHN ADAMS** born on Oct. 30 (Oct. 19, old style), 1735, at Braintree (now Quincy), Mass. A Harvard graduate, he considered teaching and the ministry but finally turned to law and was admitted to the bar in 1758. Six years later, he married Abigail Smith. He opposed the Stamp Act, served as lawyer for patriots indicted by the British, and by the time of the Continental Congresses, was in the vanguard of the movement for independence. In 1778, he went to France as commissioner. Subsequently he helped negotiate the peace treaty with Britain, and in 1785 became envoy to London. Resigning in 1788, he was elected vice president under Washington and was re-elected in 1792.

Though a Federalist, Adams did not get along with Hamilton, who sought to prevent his election to the presidency in 1796 and thereafter intrigued against his administration. In 1798, Adams's independent policy averted a war with France but completed the break with Hamilton and the right-wing Federalists; at the same time, the enactment of the Alien and Sedition Acts, directed against foreigners and against critics of the government, exasperated the Jeffersonian opposition. The split between Adams and Hamilton resulted in Jefferson's becoming the next president. Adams retired to his home in Quincy. He and Jefferson died on the same day, July 4, 1826, the 50th anniversary of the adoption of the Declaration of Independence.

His *Defence of the Constitutions of Government of the United States* (1787) contains original and striking, if conservative, political ideas.

**THOMAS JEFFERSON** was born on April 13 (April 2, old style), 1743, at Shadwell in Goochland (now Albemarle) County, Va. A William and Mary graduate, he studied law, but from the start showed an interest in science and philosophy. His literary skill and political clarity brought him to the forefront of the revolutionary movement in Virginia. As delegate to the Continental Congress, he drafted the Declaration of Independence. In 1776, he entered the Virginia House of Delegates and initiated a comprehensive reform program for the abolition of feudal survivals in land tenure and the separation of church and state.

In 1779, he became governor, but constitutional limitations on his power, combined with his own lack of executive energy, caused an unsatisfactory administration, culminating in Jefferson's virtual abdication when the British invaded Virginia in 1781. He retired to his beautiful home at Monticello, Va., to his family. His wife, Martha Wayles Skelton, whom he married in 1772, died in 1782.

Jefferson's *Notes on Virginia* (1784–85) illustrate his many-faceted interests, his limitless intellectual curiosity, his deep faith in agrarian democracy. Sent to Congress in 1783, he helped lay down the decimal system and drafted basic reports on the organization of the western lands. In 1785 he was appointed minister to France, where the Anglo-Saxon liberalism he had drawn from John Locke, the British philosopher, was stimulated by contact with the thought that would soon foment in the French Revolution. In 1789, Washington appointed him secretary of state. While favoring the Constitution and a strengthened central government, Jefferson came to believe that Hamilton contemplated the establishment of a monarchy. Growing differences resulted in Jefferson's resignation on Dec. 31, 1793.

Elected vice president in 1796, Jefferson continued to serve as spiritual leader of the opposition to Federalism, particularly to the repressive Alien and Sedition Acts. He was elected president in 1801 by the House of Representatives as a result of Hamilton's decision to throw the Federalist votes to him rather than to Aaron Burr, who had tied him in electoral votes. He was the first president to be inaugurated in Washington, which he had helped to design.

The purchase of Louisiana from France in 1803, though in violation of Jefferson's earlier constitutional scruples, was the most notable act of his administration. Re-elected in 1804, with the Federalist Charles C. Pinckney opposing him, Jefferson tried desperately to keep the United States out of the Napoleonic Wars in Europe, employing to this end the unpopular embargo policy.

After his retirement to Monticello in 1809, he developed his interest in education, founding the University of Virginia and watching its development with never-flagging interest. He died at Monticello on July 4, 1826. Jefferson had an enormous variety of interests and skills, ranging from education and science to architecture and music.

**JAMES MADISON** was born in Port Conway, Va., on March 16, 1751 (March 5, 1750/1, old style). A Princeton graduate, he joined the struggle for independence on his return to Virginia in 1771. In the 1770s and 1780s he was active in state politics, where he championed the Jefferson reform program, and in the Continental Congress. Madison was influential in the Constitutional Convention as leader of the group favoring a strong central government and as recorder of the debates; and he subsequently wrote, in collaboration with Alexander Hamilton and John Jay, the *Federalist* papers to aid the campaign for the adoption of the Constitution.

Serving in the new Congress, Madison soon emerged as the leader in the House of the men who opposed Hamilton's financial program and his pro-British leanings in foreign policy. Retiring from Congress in 1797, he continued to be active in Virginia and drafted the Virginia Resolution protesting the Alien and Sedition Acts. His intimacy with Jefferson made him the natural choice for secretary of state in 1801.

In 1809, Madison succeeded Jefferson as president, defeating Charles C. Pinckney. His wife, Dolley Payne Todd, whom he married in 1794, brought a new social sparkle to the executive mansion. In the meantime, increasing tension with Britain culminated in the War of 1812—a war for which the United States was unprepared and for which Madison lacked the executive talent to clear out incompetence and mobilize the nation's energies. Madison was re-elected in 1812, running against the Federalist De Witt Clinton. In 1814, the British actually captured Washington and forced Madison to flee to Virginia.

Madison's domestic program capitulated to the Hamiltonian policies that he had resisted 20 years before and he now signed bills to establish a United States Bank and a higher tariff.

After his presidency, he remained in retirement in Virginia until his death on June 28, 1836.

**JAMES MONROE** was born on April 28, 1758, in Westmoreland County, Va. A William and Mary graduate, he served in the army during the first years of the Revolution and was wounded at Trenton. He then entered Virginia politics and later national politics under the sponsorship of Jefferson. In 1786, he married Elizabeth (Eliza) Kortright.

Fearing centralization, Monroe opposed the adoption of the Constitution and, as senator from Virginia, was highly critical of the Hamiltonian program. In 1794, he was appointed minister to France, where his ardent sympathies with the Revolution exceeded the wishes of the State Department. His troubled diplomatic career ended with his recall in 1796. From 1799 to 1802, he was governor of Virginia. In 1803, Jefferson sent him to France to help negotiate the Louisiana Purchase and for the next few years he was active in various negotiations on the Continent.

In 1808, Monroe flirted with the radical wing of the Republican Party, which opposed Madison's candidacy; but the presidential boom came to naught and, after a brief term as governor of Virginia in 1811, Monroe accepted Madison's offer of secretary of state. During the War of 1812, he vainly sought a field command and instead served as secretary of war from September 1814 to March 1815.

Elected president in 1816 over the Federalist Rufus King, and re-elected without opposition in 1820, Monroe, the last of the Virginia dynasty, pursued the course of systematic tranquilization that won for his administrations the name "the era of good feeling." He continued Madison's surrender to the Hamiltonian domestic program, signed the Missouri Compromise, acquired Florida, and with the able assistance of his secretary of state, John Quincy Adams, promulgated the Monroe Doctrine in 1823, declaring against foreign colonization or intervention in the Americas. He died in New York City on July 4, 1831, the third president to die on the anniversary of Independence.

**JOHN QUINCY ADAMS** was born on July 11, 1767, at Braintree (now Quincy), Mass., the son of John Adams, the second president. He spent his early years in Europe with his father, graduated from Harvard, and entered law practice. His anti-Paine newspaper articles won him political attention. In 1794, he became minister to the Netherlands, the first of several diplomatic posts that occupied him until his return to Boston in 1801. In 1797, he married Louisa Catherine Johnson.

In 1803, Adams was elected to the Senate, nominally as a Federalist, but his repeated displays of independence on such issues as the Louisiana Purchase and the embargo caused his party to demand his resignation and ostracize him socially. In 1809, Madison rewarded him for his support of Jefferson by appointing him minister to St. Petersburg. He helped negotiate the Treaty of Ghent in 1814, and in 1815 became minister to London. In 1817 Monroe appointed him secretary of state where he served with great distinction, gaining Florida from Spain without hostilities and playing an equal part with Monroe in formulating the Monroe Doctrine.

When no presidential candidate received a majority of electoral votes in 1824, Adams, with the support of Henry Clay, was elected by the House in 1825 over Andrew Jackson, who had the original plurality. Adams had ambitious plans of government activity to foster internal improvements and promote the arts and sciences, but congressional obstructionism, combined with his own unwillingness or inability to play the role of a politician, resulted in little being accomplished. After being defeated for re-election by Jackson in 1828, he successfully ran for the House of Representatives in 1830. There, though nominally a Whig, he pursued as ever an independent course. He led the fight to force Congress to receive antislavery petitions and fathered the Smithsonian Institution.

Adams had a stroke while on the floor of the House, and died two days later on Feb. 23, 1848. His long and detailed *Diary* gives a unique picture of the personalities and politics of the times.

**ANDREW JACKSON** was born on March 15, 1767, in what is now generally agreed to be Waxhaw, S.C. After a turbulent boyhood as an orphan and a British prisoner, he moved west to Tennessee, where he soon qualified for law practice but found income security of state practice in horse racing, cockfighting, and dueling. His marriage to Rachel Donelson Robards in 1791 was complicated by subsequent legal uncertainties about the status of her divorce. During the 1790s, Jackson served in the Tennessee Constitutional Convention, the United States House of Representatives and Senate, and on the Tennessee Supreme Court.

After some years as a country gentleman, living at the Hermitage near Nashville, Jackson in 1812 was given command of Tennessee troops sent against the Creeks. He defeated the Indians at Horseshoe Bend in 1814; subsequently he became a major general and won the Battle of New Orleans over veteran British troops, though after the treaty of peace had been signed at Ghent. In 1818, Jackson invaded Florida, captured Pensacola, and hanged two

Englishmen named Arbuthnot and Ambrister, creating an international incident. A presidential boom began for him in 1821, and to foster it, he returned to the Senate (1823–25). Though he won a plurality of electoral votes in 1824, he lost in the House when Clay threw his strength to Adams. Four years later, he easily defeated Adams.

As president, Jackson greatly expanded the power and prestige of the presidential office and carried through an unprecedented program of domestic reform, vetoing the bill to extend the United States Bank, moving toward a hard-money currency policy, and checking the program of federal internal improvements. He also vindicated federal authority against South Carolina with its doctrine of nullification and against France on the question of debts. The support given his policies by the workingmen of the East as well as by the farmers of the East, West, and South resulted in his triumphant re-election in 1832 over Clay.

After watching the inauguration of his handpicked successor, Martin Van Buren, Jackson retired to the Hermitage, where he maintained a lively interest in national affairs until his death on June 8, 1845.

**MARTIN VAN BUREN** was born on Dec. 5, 1782, at Kinderhook, N.Y. After graduating from the village school, he became a law clerk, entered practice in 1803, and soon became active in state politics as state senator and attorney general. In 1820, he was elected to the United States Senate. He threw the support of his efficient political organization, known as the Albany Regency, to William H. Crawford in 1824 and to Jackson in 1828. After leading the opposition to Adams's administration in the Senate, he served briefly as governor of New York (1828–1829) and resigned to become Jackson's secretary of state. He was soon on close personal terms with Jackson and played an important part in the Jacksonian program.

In 1832, Van Buren became vice president; in 1836, president. The Panic of 1837 overshadowed his term. He attributed it to the overexpansion of the credit and favored the establishment of an independent treasury as repository for the federal funds. In 1840, he established a 10-hour day on public works. Defeated by Harrison in 1840, he was the leading contender for the Democratic nomination in 1844 until he publicly opposed immediate annexation of Texas, and was subsequently beaten by the Southern delegations at the Baltimore convention. This incident increased his growing misgivings about the slave power.

After working behind the scenes among the antislavery Democrats, Van Buren joined in the movement that led to the Free-Soil Party and became its candidate for president in 1848. He subsequently returned to the Democratic Party while continuing to object to its pro-Southern policy. He died in Kinderhook on July 24, 1862. His *Autobiography* throws valuable sidelights on the political history of the times.

His wife, Hannah Hoes, whom he married in 1807, died in 1819.

**WILLIAM HENRY HARRISON** was born in Charles City County, Va., on Feb. 9, 1773. Joining the army in 1791, he was active in Indian fighting in the Northwest, became secretary of the Northwest

Territory in 1798 and governor of Indiana in 1800. He married Anna Symmes in 1795. Growing discontent over white encroachments on Indian lands led to the formation of an Indian alliance under Tecumseh to resist further aggressions. In 1811, Harrison won a nominal victory over the Indians at Tippecanoe and in 1813 a more decisive one at the Battle of the Thames, where Tecumseh was killed.

After resigning from the army in 1814, Harrison had an obscure career in politics and diplomacy, ending up 20 years later as a county recorder in Ohio. Nominated for president in 1835 as a military hero whom the conservative politicians hoped to be able to control, he ran surprisingly well against Van Buren in 1836. Four years later, he defeated Van Buren but caught pneumonia and died in Washington on April 4, 1841, a month after his inauguration. Harrison was the first president to die in office.

**JOHN TYLER** was born in Charles City County, Va., on March 29, 1790. A William and Mary graduate, he entered law practice and politics, serving in the House of Representatives (1817–21), as governor of Virginia (1825–27), and as senator (1827–36). A strict constructionist, he supported Crawford in 1824 and Jackson in 1828, but broke with Jackson over his United States Bank policy and became a member of the Southern state-rights group that cooperated with the Whigs. In 1836, he resigned from the Senate rather than follow instructions from the Virginia legislature to vote for a resolution expunging censure of Jackson from the Senate record.

Elected vice president on the Whig ticket in 1840, Tyler succeeded to the presidency on Harrison's death. His strict-constructionist views soon caused a split with the Henry Clay wing of the Whig party and a stalemate on domestic questions. Tyler's more considerable achievements were his support of the Webster-Ashburton Treaty with Britain and his success in bringing about the annexation of Texas.

After his presidency he lived in retirement in Virginia until the outbreak of the Civil War, when he emerged briefly as chairman of a peace convention and then as delegate to the provisional Congress of the Confederacy. He died on Jan. 18, 1862. He married Letitia Christian in 1813 and, two years after her death in 1842, Julia Gardiner.

**JAMES KNOX POLK** was born in Mecklenburg County, N.C., on Nov. 2, 1795. A graduate of the University of North Carolina, he moved west to Tennessee, was admitted to the bar, and soon became prominent in state politics. In 1825, he was elected to the House of Representatives, where he opposed Adams and, after 1829, became Jackson's floor leader in the fight against the Bank. In 1835, he became Speaker of the House. Four years later, he was elected governor of Tennessee, but was beaten in tries for re-election in 1841 and 1843.

The supporters of Van Buren for the Democratic nomination in 1844 counted on Polk as his running mate, but when Van Buren's stand on Texas alienated Southern support, the convention swung to Polk on the ninth ballot. He was elected over Henry Clay, the Whig candidate. Rapidly disillusioning those who thought that he would not run his own administration, Polk proceeded steadily and precisely to achieve four major objectives—the acquisition of California, the settlement of the Oregon question, the reduction of the tariff, and the establishment of the independent treasury. He also enlarged the Monroe Doctrine to exclude all non-American intervention in American affairs, whether forcible or not, and he forced Mexico into a war that he waged to a successful conclusion.

His wife, Sarah Childress, whom he married in 1824, was a woman of charm and ability. Polk died in Nashville, Tenn., on June 15, 1849.

**ZACHARY TAYLOR** was born at Montebello, Orange County, Va., on Nov. 24, 1784. Embarking on a military career in 1808, Taylor fought in the War of 1812, the Black Hawk War, and the Seminole War, meanwhile holding garrison jobs on the frontier or desk jobs in Washington. A brigadier general as a result of his victory over the Seminoles at Lake Okeechobee (1837), Taylor held a succession of Southwestern commands and in 1846 established a base on the Rio Grande, where his forces engaged in hostilities that precipitated the war with Mexico. He captured Monterrey in Sept. 1846 and, disregarding Polk's orders to stay on the defensive, defeated Santa Anna at Buena Vista in Feb. 1847, ending the war in the northern provinces.

Though Taylor had never cast a vote for president, his party affiliations were Whiggish and his availability was increased by his difficulties with Polk. He was elected president over the Democrat Lewis Cass. During the revival of the slavery controversy, which was to result in the Compromise of 1850, Taylor began to take an increasingly firm stand against appeasing the South; but he died in Washington on July 9, 1850, during the fight over the Compromise. He married Margaret Mackall Smith in 1810. His bluff and simple soldierly qualities won him the name Old Rough and Ready.

**MILLARD FILLMORE** was born at Locke, Cayuga County, N.Y., on Jan. 7, 1800. A lawyer, he entered politics with the Anti-Masonic Party under the sponsorship of Thurlow Weed, editor and party boss, and subsequently followed Weed into the Whig Party. He served in the House of Representatives (1833–35 and 1837–43) and played a leading role in writing the tariff of 1842. Defeated for governor of New York in 1844, he became state comptroller in 1848, was put on the Whig ticket with Taylor as a concession to the Clay wing of the party, and became president upon Taylor's death in 1850.

As president, Fillmore broke with Weed and William H. Seward and associated himself with the pro-Southern Whigs, supporting the Compromise of 1850. Defeated for the Whig nomination in 1852, he ran for president in 1856 as candidate of the American, or Know-Nothing, Party, which sought to unite the country against foreigners in the alleged hope of diverting it from the explosive slavery issue. Fillmore opposed Lincoln during the Civil War. He died in Buffalo on March 8, 1874.

He was married in 1826 to Abigail Powers, who died in 1853, and in 1858 to Caroline Carmichael McIntosh.

**FRANKLIN PIERCE** was born at Hillsboro, N.H., on Nov. 23, 1804. A Bowdoin graduate, lawyer, and Jacksonian Democrat, he won rapid political advancement in the party, in part because of the prestige of his father, Gov. Benjamin Pierce. By 1831 he was Speaker of the New Hampshire House of Representatives; from 1833 to 1837, he served in the federal House and from 1837 to 1842 in the Senate. His wife, Jane Means Appleton, whom he married in 1834, disliked Washington and the somewhat dissipated life led by Pierce; in 1842 Pierce resigned from the Senate and began a successful law practice in Concord, N.H. During the Mexican War, he was a brigadier general.

Thereafter Pierce continued to oppose antislavery tendencies within the Democratic Party. As a result, he was the Southern choice to break the deadlock at the Democratic convention of 1852 and was nominated on the 49th ballot. In the election, Pierce overwhelmed Gen. Winfield Scott, the Whig candidate.

As president, Pierce followed a course of appeasing the South at home and of playing with schemes of territorial expansion abroad. The failure of his foreign and domestic policies prevented his renomination. He died in Concord on Oct. 8, 1869, in relative obscurity.

**JAMES BUCHANAN** was born near Mercersburg, Pa., on April 23, 1791. A Dickinson graduate and a lawyer, he entered Pennsylvania politics as a Federalist. With the disappearance of the Federalist party, he became a Jacksonian Democrat. He served with ability in the House (1821–31), as minister to St. Petersburg (1832–33), and in the Senate (1834–45), and in 1845 became Polk's secretary of state. In 1853, Pierce appointed Buchanan minister to Britain, where he participated with other American diplomats in Europe in drafting the expansionist Ostend Manifesto.

He was elected president in 1856, defeating John C. Frémont, the Republican candidate, and former President Millard Fillmore of the American Party. The growing crisis over slavery presented Buchanan with problems he lacked the will to tackle. His appeasement of the South alienated the Stephen Douglas wing of the Democratic Party without reducing Southern militancy on slavery issues. While denying the right of secession, Buchanan also denied that the federal government could do anything about it. He supported the administration during the Civil War and died in Lancaster, Pa., on June 1, 1868.

The only president to remain a bachelor throughout his term, Buchanan used his charming niece, Harriet Lane, as White House hostess.

**ABRAHAM LINCOLN** was born in Hardin (now Larue) County, Ky., on Feb. 12, 1809. His family moved to Indiana and then to Illinois, and Lincoln gained what education he could along the way. While reading law, he worked in a store, managed a mill, surveyed, and split rails. In 1834, he went to the Illinois legislature as a Whig and became the party's floor leader. For the next 20 years he practiced law in Springfield, except for a single term (1847–49) in Congress, where he denounced the Mexican War. In 1855, he was a candidate for senator and the next year he joined the new Republican Party.

A leading but unsuccessful candidate for the vice-presidential nomination with Frémont, Lincoln gained national attention in 1858 when, as Republican candidate for senator from Illinois, he engaged in a series of debates with Stephen A. Douglas, the

Democratic candidate. He lost the election, but continued to prepare the way for the 1860 Republican convention and was rewarded with the presidential nomination on the third ballot. He won the election over three opponents.

From the start, Lincoln made clear that, unlike Buchanan, he believed the national government had the power to crush the rebellion. Not an abolitionist, he held the slavery issue subordinate to that of preserving the Union, but soon perceived that the war could not be brought to a successful conclusion without freeing the slaves. His administration was hampered by the incompetence of many Union generals, the inexperience of the troops, and the harassing political tactics both of the Republican Radicals, who favored a hard policy toward the South, and the Democratic Copperheads, who desired a negotiated peace. The Gettysburg Address of Nov. 19, 1863, marks the high point in the record of American eloquence. Lincoln's long search for a winning combination finally brought generals Ulysses S. Grant and William T. Sherman to the top; and their series of victories in 1864 dispelled the mutterings from both Radicals and Peace Democrats that at one time seemed to threaten Lincoln's reelection. He was reelected in 1864, defeating Gen. George B. McClellan, the Democratic candidate. His inaugural address urged leniency toward the South: "With malice toward none, with charity for all . . . let us strive on to finish the work we are in; to bind up the nation's wounds . . ." This policy aroused growing opposition on the part of the Republican Radicals, but before the matter could be put to the test, Lincoln was shot by the actor John Wilkes Booth at Ford's Theater, Washington, on April 14, 1865. He died the next morning.

Lincoln's marriage to Mary Todd in 1842 was often unhappy and turbulent, in part because of his wife's pronounced instability.

**ANDREW JOHNSON** was born at Raleigh, N.C., on Dec. 29, 1808. Self-educated, he became a tailor in Greeneville, Tenn., but soon went into politics, where he rose steadily. He served in the House of Representatives (1843–54), as governor of Tennessee (1853–57), and as a senator (1857–62). Politically he was a Jacksonian Democrat and his specialty was the fight for a more equitable land policy. Alone among the Southern Senators, he stood by the Union during the Civil War. In 1862, he became war governor of Tennessee and carried out a thankless and difficult job with great courage. Johnson became Lincoln's running mate in 1864 as a result of an attempt to give the ticket a nonpartisan and nonsectional character. Succeeding to the presidency on Lincoln's death, Johnson sought to carry out Lincoln's policy, but without his political skill. The result was a hopeless conflict with the Radical Republicans who dominated Congress, passed measures over Johnson's vetoes, and attempted to limit the power of the executive concerning appointments and removals. The conflict culminated with Johnson's impeachment for attempting to remove his disloyal secretary of war in defiance of the Tenure of Office Act which required senatorial concurrence for such dismissals. The opposition failed by one vote to get the two thirds necessary for conviction.

After his presidency, Johnson maintained an interest in politics and in 1875 was again elected to the Senate. He died near Carter Station, Tenn., on July 31, 1875. He married Eliza McCardle in 1827.

**ULYSSES SIMPSON GRANT** was born (as Hiram Ulysses Grant) at Point Pleasant, Ohio, on April 27, 1822. He graduated from West Point in 1843 and served without particular distinction in the Mexican War. In 1848 he married Julia Dent. He resigned from the army in 1854, after warnings from his commanding officer about his drinking habits, and for the next six years held a wide variety of jobs in the Middle West. With the outbreak of the Civil War, he sought a command and soon, to his surprise, was made a brigadier general. His continuing successes in the western theaters, culminating in the capture of Vicksburg, Miss., in 1863, brought him national fame and soon the command of all the Union armies. Grant's dogged, implacable policy of concentrating on dividing and destroying the Confederate armies brought the war to an end in 1865. The next year, he was made full general.

In 1868, as Republican candidate for president, Grant was elected over the Democrat, Horatio Seymour. From the start, Grant showed his unfitness for the office. His cabinet was weak, his domestic policy was confused, and many of his intimate associates were corrupt. The notable achievement in foreign affairs was the settlement of controversies with Great Britain in the Treaty of London (1871), negotiated by his able secretary of state, Hamilton Fish.

Running for reelection in 1872, he defeated Horace Greeley, the Democratic and Liberal Republican candidate. The Panic of 1873 graft scandals close to the presidency created difficulties for his second term.

After retiring from office, Grant toured Europe for two years and returned in time to accede to a third-term boom, but was beaten in the convention of 1880. Illness and bad business judgment darkened his last years, but he worked steadily at the *Personal Memoirs*, which were to be successful when published after his death at Mount McGregor, near Saratoga, N.Y., on July 23, 1885.

**RUTHERFORD BIRCHARD HAYES** was born in Delaware, Ohio, on Oct. 4, 1822. A graduate of Kenyon College and the Harvard Law School, he practiced law in Lower Sandusky (now Fremont) and then in Cincinnati. In 1852 he married Lucy Webb. A Whig, he joined the Republican party in 1855. During the Civil War he rose to major general. He served in the House of Representatives from 1865 to 1867 and then confirmed a reputation for honesty and efficiency in two terms as Governor of Ohio (1868–72). His election to a third term in 1875 made him the logical candidate for those Republicans who wished to stop James G. Blaine in 1876, and he was nominated.

The result of the election was in doubt for some time and hinged upon disputed returns from South Carolina, Louisiana, Florida, and Oregon. Samuel J. Tilden, the Democrat, had the larger popular vote but was adjudged by the strictly partisan decisions of the Electoral Commission to have one fewer electoral vote, 185 to 184. The national acceptance of this result was due in part to the general understanding that Hayes would pursue a conciliatory policy toward the South. He withdrew the troops from the South, took a conservative position on financial and labor issues, and urged civil service reform.

Hayes served only one term by his own wish and spent the rest of his life in various humanitarian endeavors. He died in Fremont on Jan. 17, 1893.

**JAMES ABRAM GARFIELD**, the last president to be born in a log cabin, was born in Cuyahoga County, Ohio, on Nov. 19, 1831. A Williams graduate, he taught school for a time and entered Republican politics in Ohio. In 1858, he married Lucretia Rudolph. During the Civil War, he had a promising career, rising to major general of volunteers; but he resigned in 1863, having been elected to the House of Representatives, where he served until 1880. His oratorical and parliamentary abilities soon made him the leading Republican in the House, though his record was marred by his unorthodox acceptance of a fee in the DeGolyer paving contract case and by suspicions of his complicity in the Crédit Mobilier scandal.

In 1880, Garfield was elected to the Senate, but instead became the presidential candidate on the 36th ballot as a result of a deadlock in the Republican convention. In the election, he defeated Gen. Winfield Scott Hancock, the Democratic candidate. Garfield's administration was barely under way when he was shot by Charles J. Guiteau, a disappointed office seeker, in Washington on July 2, 1881. He died in Elberton, N.J., on Sept. 19.

**CHESTER ALAN ARTHUR** was born at Fairfield, Vt., on Oct. 5, 1829. A graduate of Union College, he became a successful New York lawyer. In 1859, he married Ellen Herndon. During the Civil War, he held administrative jobs in the Republican state administration and in 1871 was appointed collector of the Port of New York by Grant. This post gave him control over considerable patronage. Though not personally corrupt, Arthur managed his power in the interests of the New York machine so openly that President Hayes in 1877 called for an investigation and the next year Arthur was suspended.

In 1880 Arthur was nominated for vice president in the hope of conciliating the followers of Grant and the powerful New York machine. As president upon Garfield's death, Arthur, stepping out of his familiar role as spoilsman, backed civil service reform, reorganized the cabinet, and prosecuted political associates accused of post office graft. Losing machine support and failing to gain the reformers, he was not nominated for a full term in 1884. He died in New York City on Nov. 18, 1886.

**(STEPHEN) GROVER CLEVELAND** was born at Caldwell, N.J., on March 18, 1837. He lived in various places in Buffalo, N.Y., in 1859 and lived there as a lawyer, with occasional incursions into Democratic politics, for more than 20 years. He did not participate in the Civil War. As mayor of Buffalo in 1881, he carried through a reform program so ably that the Democrats ran him successfully for governor in 1882. In 1884 he won the Democratic nomination for president. The campaign contrasted Cleveland's spotless public career with the uncertain record of James G. Blaine, the Republican candidate, and Cleveland received enough Mugwump (independent Republican) support to win.

As president, Cleveland pushed civil service reform, opposed the pension grab and attacked the high tariff rates. While in the White House, he married Frances Folsom in 1886. Renominated in 1888, Cleveland was defeated by Benjamin Harrison, polling more popular but fewer electoral votes. In 1892, he was elected over Harrison. When the Panic of 1893 burst upon the country, Cleveland's attempts to solve it by sound-money measures alienated the free-silver wing of the party, while his tariff policy alienated the protectionists. In 1894, he sent troops to break the Pullman strike. In foreign affairs, his firmness caused Great Britain to back down in the Venezuela border dispute.

In his last years Cleveland was an active and much-respected public figure. He died in Princeton, N.J., on June 24, 1908.

**BENJAMIN HARRISON** was born in North Bend, Ohio, on Aug. 20, 1833, the grandson of William Henry Harrison, the ninth president. A graduate of Miami University in Ohio, he took up the law in Indiana and became active in Republican politics. In 1853, he married Caroline Lavinia Scott. During the Civil War, he rose to brigadier general. A sound-money Republican, he was elected senator from Indiana in 1880. In 1888, he received the Republican nomination for president on the eighth ballot. Though behind on the popular vote, he won over Grover Cleveland in the electoral college by 233 to 168.

As president, Harrison failed to please either the bosses or the reform element in the party. In foreign affairs he backed Secretary of State Blaine, whose policy foreshadowed later American imperialism. Harrison was renominated in 1892 but lost to Cleveland. His wife died in the White House in 1892 and Harrison married her niece, Mary Scott (Lord) Dimmick, in 1896. After his presidency, he resumed law practice. He died in Indianapolis on March 13, 1901.

**WILLIAM McKINLEY** was born in Niles, Ohio, on Jan. 29, 1843. He taught school, then served in the Civil War, rising from the ranks to become a major. Subsequently he opened a law office in Canton, Ohio, and in 1871 married Ida Saxton. Elected to Congress in 1876, he served there until 1891, except for 1883–85. His faithful advocacy of business interests culminated in the passage of the highly protective McKinley Tariff of 1890. With the support of Mark Hanna, a shrewd Cleveland businessman interested in safeguarding tariff protection, McKinley became governor of Ohio in 1892 and Republican presidential candidate in 1896. The business community, alarmed by the progressivism of William Jennings Bryan, the Democratic candidate, spent considerable money to assure McKinley's victory.

The chief event of McKinley's administration was the war with Spain, which resulted in the United States' acquisition of the Philippines and other islands. With imperialism an issue, McKinley defeated Bryan again in 1900. On Sept. 6, 1901, he was shot at Buffalo, N.Y., by Leon F. Czolgosz, an anarchist, and he died there eight days later.

**THEODORE ROOSEVELT** was born in New York City on Oct. 27, 1858. A Harvard graduate, he was early interested in ranching, in politics, and in writing picturesque historical narratives. He was a Republican member of the New York Assembly in 1882–84, an unsuccessful candidate for mayor of

New York in 1886, a U.S. Civil Service Commissioner under Benjamin Harrison, Police Commissioner of New York City in 1895, and Assistant Secretary of the Navy under McKinley in 1897. He resigned in 1898 to help organize a volunteer regiment, the Rough Riders, and take a more direct part in the war with Spain. He was elected governor of New York in 1898 and vice president in 1900, in spite of lack of enthusiasm on the part of the bosses.

Assuming the presidency of the assassinated McKinley in 1901, Roosevelt embarked on a wide-ranging program of government reform and conservation of natural resources. He ordered antitrust suits against several large corporations, threatened to intervene in the anthracite coal strike of 1902, which prompted the operators to accept arbitration, and, in general, championed the rights of the "little man" and fought the "malefactors of great wealth." He was also responsible for such progressive legislation as the Elkins Act of 1903, which outlawed freight rebates by railroads; the bill establishing the Department of Commerce and Labor; the Hepburn Act, which gave the I.C.C. greater control over the railroads; the Meat Inspection Act; and the Pure Food and Drug Act.

In foreign affairs, Roosevelt pursued a strong policy, permitting the instigation of a revolt in Panama to dispose of Colombian objections to the Panama Canal and helping to maintain the balance of power in the East by bringing the Russo-Japanese War to an end, for which he won the Nobel Peace Prize, the first American to achieve a Nobel prize in any category. In 1904, he decisively defeated Alton B. Parker, his conservative Democratic opponent.

Roosevelt's increasing coldness toward his successor, William Howard Taft, led him to overlook his earlier disclaimer of third-term ambitions and to reenter politics. Defeated by the machine in the Republican convention of 1912, he organized the Progressive Party (Bull Moose) and polled more votes than Taft, though the split brought about the election of Woodrow Wilson. From 1915 on, Roosevelt strongly favored intervention in the European war. He became deeply embittered at Wilson's refusal to allow him to raise a volunteer division. He died in Oyster Bay, N.Y., on Jan. 6, 1919. He was married twice: in 1880 to Alice Hathaway Lee, who died in 1884, and in 1886 to Edith Kermit Carow.

**WILLIAM HOWARD TAFT** was born in Cincinnati on Sept. 15, 1857. A Yale graduate, he entered Ohio Republican politics in the 1880s. In 1886 he married Helen Herron. From 1887 to 1890, he served on the Ohio Superior Court; 1890–92, as solicitor general of the United States; 1892–1900, on the federal circuit court. In 1900 McKinley appointed him president of the Philippine Commission and in 1901 governor general. Taft had great success in pacifying the Filipinos, solving the problem of the church lands, improving economic conditions, and establishing limited self-government. His period as secretary of war (1904–08) further demonstrated his capacity as administrator and conciliator, and he was Roosevelt's hand-picked successor in 1908. In the election, he polled 321 electoral votes to 162 for William Jennings Bryan, who was running for the presidency for the third time.

Though he carried on many of Roosevelt's policies, Taft got into increasing trouble with the progressive wing of the party and displayed mounting irritability and indecision. After his defeat in 1912, he became professor of constitutional law at Yale. In 1921 he was appointed chief justice of the United States Supreme Court. He died in Washington, DC, on March 8, 1930.

**(THOMAS) WOODROW WILSON** was born in Staunton, Va., on Dec. 28, 1856. A Princeton graduate, he turned from law practice to post-graduate work in political science at Johns Hopkins University, receiving his Ph.D. in 1886. He taught at Bryn Mawr, Wesleyan, and Princeton, and in 1902 was made president of Princeton. After an unsuccessful attempt to democratize the social life of the university, he welcomed an invitation in 1910 to be the Democratic gubernatorial candidate in New Jersey, and was elected. His success in fighting the machine and putting through a reform program attracted national attention.

In 1912, at the Democratic convention in Baltimore, Wilson won the nomination on the 46th ballot and went on to defeat Roosevelt and Taft in the election. Wilson proceeded under the standard of the New Freedom to enact a program of domestic reform, including the Federal Reserve Act, the Clayton Antitrust Act, the establishment of the Federal Trade Commission, and other measures designed to restore competition in the face of the great monopolies. In foreign affairs, while privately sympathetic with the Allies, he strove to maintain neutrality in the European war and warned both sides against encroachments on American interests.

Reelected in 1916 as a peace candidate, he tried to mediate between the warring nations; but when the Germans resumed unrestricted submarine warfare in 1917, Wilson brought the United States into what he now believed was a war to make the world safe for democracy. He supplied the classic formulations of Allied war aims and the armistice of Nov. 11, 1918 was negotiated on the basis of Wilson's Fourteen Points. In 1919 he strove at Versailles to lay the foundations for enduring peace. He accepted the imperfections of the Versailles Treaty in the expectation that they could be remedied by action within the League of Nations. He probably could have secured ratification of the treaty by the Senate if he had adopted a more conciliatory attitude toward the mild reservationists; but his insistence on all or nothing eventually caused the diehard isolationists and diehard Wilsonites to unite in rejecting a compromise.

In Sept. 1919 Wilson suffered a paralytic stroke that limited his activity. After leaving the presidency he lived on in retirement in Washington, dying on Feb. 3, 1924. He was married twice—in 1885 to Ellen Louise Axson, who died in 1914, and in 1915 to Edith Bolling Galt.

**WARREN GAMALIEL HARDING** was born in Morrow County, Ohio, on Nov. 2, 1865. After attending Ohio Central College, Harding became interested in journalism and in 1884 bought the *Marion* (Ohio) *Star.* In 1891 he married a wealthy widow, Florence Kling De Wolfe. As his paper prospered, he entered Republican politics, serving as state senator (1899–1903) and as lieutenant governor (1904–06). In 1910, he was defeated for governor, but in 1914 was elected to the Senate. His reputation as an orator made him the keynoter at the 1916 Republican convention.

When the 1920 convention was deadlocked between Leonard Wood and Frank O. Lowden, Harding became the dark-horse nominee on his solemn affirmation that there was no reason in his past that he should not be. Straddling the League question, Harding was easily elected over James M. Cox, his Democratic opponent. His cabinet contained some able men, but also some manifestly unfit for public office. Harding's own intimates were mediocre when they were not corrupt. The impending disclosure of the Teapot Dome scandal in the Interior Department and illegal practices in the Justice Department and Veterans' Bureau, as well as political setbacks, profoundly worried him. On his return from Alaska in 1923, he died unexpectedly in San Francisco on Aug. 2.

**(JOHN) CALVIN COOLIDGE** was born in Plymouth, Vt., on July 4, 1872. An Amherst graduate, he went into law practice at Northampton, Mass., in 1897. He married Grace Anna Goodhue in 1905. He entered Republican state politics, becoming successively mayor of Northampton, state senator, lieutenant governor and, in 1919, governor. His use of the state militia to end the Boston police strike in 1919 won him a somewhat undeserved reputation for decisive action and brought him the Republican vice-presidential nomination in 1920. After Harding's death Coolidge handled the Washington scandals with care and finally managed to save the Republican Party from public blame for the widespread corruption.

In 1924, Coolidge was elected without difficulty, defeating the Democrat, John W. Davis, and Robert M. La Follette running on the Progressive ticket. His second term, like his first, was characterized by a general satisfaction with the existing economic order. He stated that he did not choose to run in 1928.

After his presidency, Coolidge lived quietly in Northampton, writing an unilluminating autobiography and a syndicated column. He died there on Jan. 5, 1933.

**HERBERT CLARK HOOVER** was born at West Branch, Iowa, on Aug. 10, 1874, the first president to be born west of the Mississippi. A Stanford graduate, he worked from 1896 to 1914 as a mining engineer and consultant throughout the world. In 1899, he married Lou Henry. During World War I, he served with distinction as chairman of the American Relief Committee in London, as chairman of the Commission for Relief in Belgium, and as U.S. Food Administrator. His political affiliations were still too indeterminate for him to be mentioned as a possibility for either the Republican or Democratic nomination in 1920, but after the election he served Harding and Coolidge as secretary of commerce.

In the election of 1928, Hoover overwhelmed Gov. Alfred E. Smith of New York, the Democratic candidate and the first Roman Catholic to run for the presidency. He soon faced the worst depression in the nation's history, but his attacks upon it were hampered by his devotion to the theory that the forces that brought the crisis would soon bring the revival and then by his belief that there were too many areas in which the federal government had no power to act. In a succession of vetoes, he struck down measures proposing a national employment system or national relief, he reduced income tax rates, and only at the end of his term did he yield to popular pressure and set up agencies such as the Reconstruction Finance Corporation to make emergency loans to assist business.

After his 1932 defeat, Hoover returned to private business. In 1946, President Truman charged him with various world food missions; and from 1947 to 1949 and 1953 to 1955, he was head of the Commission on Organization of the Executive Branch of the Government. He died in New York City on Oct. 20, 1964.

**FRANKLIN DELANO ROOSEVELT** was born in Hyde Park, N.Y., on Jan. 30, 1882. A Harvard graduate, he attended Columbia Law School and was admitted to the New York bar. In 1910, he was elected to the New York State Senate as a Democrat. Reelected in 1912, he was appointed assistant secretary of the navy by Woodrow Wilson the next year. In 1920, his radiant personality and his war service resulted in his nomination for vice president as James M. Cox's running mate. After his defeat, he returned to law practice in New York. In Aug. 1921, Roosevelt was stricken with infantile paralysis while on vacation at Campobello, New Brunswick. After a long and gallant fight, he recovered partial use of his legs. In 1924 and 1928, he led the fight at the Democratic national conventions for the nomination of Gov. Alfred E. Smith of New York, and in 1928 Roosevelt was himself induced to run for governor of New York. He was elected, and was reelected in 1930.

In 1932, Roosevelt received the Democratic nomination for president and immediately launched a campaign that brought new spirit to a weary and discouraged nation. He defeated Hoover by a wide margin. His first term was characterized by an unfolding of the New Deal program, with greater benefits for labor, the farmers, and the unemployed, and the progressive estrangement of most of the business community.

At an early stage, Roosevelt became aware of the menace to world peace posed by totalitarian fascism, and from 1937 on he tried to focus public attention on the trend of events in Europe and Asia. As a result, he was widely denounced as a warmonger. He was reelected in 1936 over Gov. Alfred M. Landon of Kansas by the overwhelming electoral margin of 523 to 8, and the gathering international crisis prompted him to run for an unprecedented third term in 1940. He defeated Wendell L. Willkie.

Roosevelt's program to bring maximum aid to Britain and, after June 1941, to Russia was opposed, until the Japanese attack on Pearl Harbor restored national unity. During the war, Roosevelt shelved the New Deal in the interests of conciliating the business community, both in order to get full production during the war and to prepare the way for a united acceptance of the peace settlements after the war. A series of conferences with Winston Churchill and Joseph Stalin laid down the bases for the postwar world. In 1944 he was elected to a fourth term, running against Gov. Thomas E. Dewey of New York.

On April 12, 1945, Roosevelt died of a cerebral hemorrhage at Warm Springs, Ga., shortly after his return from the Yalta Conference. His wife, (Anna) Eleanor Roosevelt, whom he married in 1905, was a woman of great ability who made significant contributions to her husband's policies.

**HARRY S. TRUMAN** was born on a farm near Lamar, Mo., on May 8, 1884. During World War I, he served in France as a captain with the 129th Field Artillery. He married Bess Wallace in 1919. After engaging briefly and unsuccessfully in the haberdashery business in Kansas City, Mo., Truman entered local politics. Under the sponsorship of Thomas Pendergast, Democratic boss of Missouri, he held a number of local offices, preserving his personal honesty in the midst of a notoriously corrupt political machine. In 1934, he was elected to the Senate and was reelected in 1940. During his first term he was a loyal but quiet supporter of the New Deal, but in his second term, an appointment as head of a Senate committee to investigate war production brought out his special qualities of honesty, common sense, and hard work, and he won widespread respect.

Elected vice president in 1944, Truman became president upon Roosevelt's sudden death in April 1945 and was immediately faced with the problems of winding down the war against the Axis and preparing the nation for postwar adjustment. Germany surrendered on May 8, and in July Truman attended the Potsdam Conference to discuss the settlement plans for postwar Europe. To end the war with Japan, he authorized the dropping of atomic bombs on Hiroshima and Nagasaki on Aug. 6 and Aug. 9, 1945. Japan surrendered on Aug. 14. Although the action undoubtedly saved many American lives by bringing the war to an end, the morality of the decision is still debated.

The years 1947–48 were distinguished by civil-rights proposals, the Truman Doctrine to contain the spread of Communism, and the Marshall Plan to aid in the economic reconstruction of war-ravaged nations. Truman's general record, highlighted by a vigorous Fair Deal campaign, brought about his unexpected election in 1948 over the heavily favored Thomas E. Dewey.

Truman's second term was primarily concerned with the cold war with the Soviet Union, the implementing of the North Atlantic Pact, the United Nations police action in Korea, and the vast rearmament program with its accompanying problems of economic stabilization.

On March 29, 1952, Truman announced that he would not run again for the presidency. After leaving the White House, he returned to his home in Independence, Mo., to write his memoirs. He further busied himself with the Harry S. Truman Library there. He died in Kansas City, Mo., on Dec. 26, 1972.

**DWIGHT DAVID EISENHOWER** was born in Denison, Tex., on Oct. 14, 1890. His ancestors lived in Germany and emigrated to America, settling in Pennsylvania, early in the 18th century. His father, David, had a general store in Hope, Kans., which failed. After a brief time in Texas, the family moved to Abilene, Kan.

After graduating from Abilene High School in 1909, Eisenhower did odd jobs for almost two years. He won an appointment to the Naval Academy at Annapolis, but was too old for admittance. Then he received an appointment in 1910 to West Point, from which he graduated as a second lieutenant in 1915.

He did not see service in World War I, having been stationed at Fort Sam Houston, Tex. There he met Mamie Geneva Doud, whom he married in Denver on July 1, 1916, and by whom he had two sons: Doud Dwight (died in infancy) and John Sheldon Doud.

Eisenhower served in the Philippines from 1935 to 1939 with Gen. Douglas MacArthur. Afterward, Gen. George C. Marshall, the army chief of staff, brought him into the War Department's General Staff and in 1942 placed him in command of the invasion of North Africa. In 1944, he was made Supreme Allied Commander for the invasion of Europe.

After the war, Eisenhower served as army chief of staff from Nov. 1945 until Feb. 1948, when he was appointed president of Columbia University.

In Dec. 1950, President Truman recalled Eisenhower to active duty to command the North Atlantic Treaty Organization forces in Europe. He held his post until the end of May 1952.

At the Republican convention of 1952 in Chicago, Eisenhower won the presidential nomination on the first ballot in a close race with Sen. Robert A. Taft of Ohio. In the election, he defeated Gov. Adlai E. Stevenson of Illinois.

Through two terms, Eisenhower hewed to moderate domestic policies. He sought peace through Free World strength in an era of new nationalisms, nuclear missiles, and space exploration. He fostered alliances pledging the United States to resist "Red" aggression in Europe, Asia, and Latin America. The Eisenhower Doctrine of 1957 extended commitments to the Middle East.

At home, the popular president lacked Republican congressional majorities after 1954, but he was reelected in 1956 by 457 electoral votes to 73 for Stevenson.

While retaining most Fair Deal programs, he stressed "fiscal responsibility" in domestic affairs. A moderate in civil rights, he sent troops to Little Rock, Ark., to enforce court-ordered school integration.

With his wartime rank restored by Congress, Eisenhower returned to private life and the role of elder statesman, with his vigor hardly impaired by a heart attack, an ileitis operation, and a mild stroke suffered while in office. He died in Washington, D.C., on March 28, 1969.

**JOHN FITZGERALD KENNEDY** was born in Brookline, Mass., on May 29, 1917. His father, Joseph P. Kennedy, was ambassador to Great Britain from 1937 to 1940.

Kennedy was graduated from Harvard University in 1940 and joined the navy the next year. He became skipper of a PT boat that was sunk in the Pacific by a Japanese destroyer. Although given up for lost, he swam to a safe island, towing an injured enlisted man.

After recovering from a war-aggravated spinal injury, Kennedy entered politics in 1946 and was elected to Congress. In 1952, he ran against Sen. Henry Cabot Lodge, Jr., of Massachusetts, and won.

Kennedy was married on Sept. 12, 1953, to Jacqueline Lee Bouvier, by whom he had three children: Caroline, John Fitzgerald, Jr. (died in a 1999 plane crash), and Patrick Bouvier (died in infancy).

In 1957 Kennedy won the Pulitzer Prize for a book he had written earlier, *Profiles in Courage*.

After strenuous primary battles, Kennedy won the Democratic presidential nomination on the first ballot at the 1960 Los Angeles convention. With a plurality of only 118,574 votes, he carried the election over Vice President Richard M. Nixon and became the first Roman Catholic president.

Kennedy brought to the White House the dynamic idea of a "New Frontier" approach in dealing with problems at home, abroad, and in the dimensions of space. Out of his leadership in his first few months in office came the 10-year Alliance for Progress to aid Latin America, the Peace Corps, and accelerated programs that brought the first Americans into orbit in the race in space.

Failure of the U.S.-supported Cuban invasion in April 1961 led to the entrenchment of the Communist-backed Castro regime, only 90 mi from United States soil. When it became known that Soviet offensive missiles were being installed in Cuba in 1962, Kennedy ordered a naval "quarantine" of the island and moved troops into position to eliminate this threat to U.S. security. The world seemed on the brink of a nuclear war until Soviet premier Khrushchev ordered the removal of the missiles.

A sudden "thaw," or the appearance of one, in the cold war came with the agreement with the Soviet Union on a limited test-ban treaty signed in Moscow on Aug. 6, 1963.

In his domestic policies, Kennedy's proposals for medical care for the aged and aid to education were defeated, but on minimum wage, trade legislation, and other measures he won important victories.

Widespread racial disorders and demonstrations led to Kennedy's proposing sweeping civil rights legislation. As his third year in office drew to a close, he also recommended an $11-billion tax cut to bolster the economy. Both measures were pending in Congress when Kennedy, looking forward to a second term, journeyed to Texas for a series of speeches.

While riding in an automobile procession in Dallas on Nov. 22, 1963, he was shot to death by an assassin firing from an upper floor of a building. The alleged assassin, Lee Harvey Oswald, was killed two days later in the Dallas city jail by Jack Ruby, owner of a strip-tease club.

At 46 years of age, Kennedy became the fourth president to be assassinated and the eighth to die in office.

**LYNDON BAINES JOHNSON** was born in Stonewall, Tex., on Aug. 27, 1908. On both sides of his family he had a political heritage mingled with a Baptist background of preachers and teachers. Both his father and his paternal grandfather served in the Texas House of Representatives.

After his graduation from Southwest Texas State Teachers College, Johnson taught school for two years. He went to Washington in 1932 as secretary to Rep. Richard M. Kleberg. During this time, he married Claudia Alta Taylor, known as "Lady Bird." They had two children: Lynda Bird and Luci Baines.

In 1935, Johnson became Texas administrator for the National Youth Administration. Two years later,

he was elected to Congress as an all-out supporter of Franklin D. Roosevelt, and served until 1949. He was the first member of Congress to enlist in the armed forces after the attack on Pearl Harbor. He served in the navy in the Pacific and won a Silver Star.

Johnson was elected to the Senate in 1948 after he had captured the Democratic nomination by only 87 votes. He was 40 years old. He became the Senate Democratic leader in 1953. A heart attack in 1955 threatened to end his political career, but he recovered fully and resumed his duties.

At the height of his power as Senate leader, Johnson sought the Democratic nomination for president in 1960. When he lost to John F. Kennedy, he surprised even some of his closest associates by accepting second place on the ticket.

Johnson was riding in another car in the motorcade when Kennedy was assassinated in Dallas on Nov. 22, 1963. He took the oath of office in the presidential jet on the Dallas airfield.

With Johnson's insistent backing, Congress finally adopted a far-reaching civil-rights bill, a voting-rights bill, a Medicare program for the aged, and measures to improve education and conservation. Congress also began what Johnson described as "an all-out war" on poverty.

Amassing a record-breaking majority of nearly 16 million votes, Johnson was elected president in his own right in 1964, defeating Sen. Barry Goldwater of Arizona.

The double tragedy of a war in Southeast Asia and urban riots at home marked Johnson's last two years in office. Faced with disunity in the nation and challenges within his own party, Johnson surprised the country on March 31, 1968, with the announcement that he would not be a candidate for reelection. He died of a heart attack suffered at his LBJ Ranch on Jan. 22, 1973.

**RICHARD MILHOUS NIXON** was born in Yorba Linda, Calif., on Jan. 9, 1913, to Midwestern-bred parents, Francis A. and Hannah Milhous Nixon, who raised their five sons as Quakers.

Nixon was a high school debater and was undergraduate president at Whittier College in California, where he was graduated in 1934. As a scholarship student at Duke University Law School in North Carolina, he graduated third in his class in 1937.

After five years as a lawyer, Nixon joined the navy in August 1942. He was an air transport officer in the South Pacific and a legal officer stateside before his discharge in 1946 as a lieutenant commander.

Running for Congress in California as a Republican in 1946, Nixon defeated Rep. Jerry Voorhis. As a member of the House Un-American Activities Committee, he made a name as an investigator of Alger Hiss, a former high State Department official, who was later jailed for perjury. In 1950, Nixon defeated Rep. Helen Gahagan Douglas, a Democrat, for the Senate. He was criticized for portraying her as a Communist dupe.

Nixon's anti-Communism ideals, his Western roots, and his youth figured into his selection in 1952 to run for vice president on the ticket headed by Dwight D. Eisenhower. Demands for Nixon's withdrawal followed disclosure that California businessmen had paid some of his Senate office expenses. His televised rebuttal, known as "the

Checkers speech" (named for a cocker spaniel given to the Nixons), brought him support from the public and from Eisenhower. The ticket won easily in 1952 and again in 1956.

Eisenhower gave Nixon substantive assignments, including missions to 56 countries. In Moscow in 1959, Nixon won acclaim for his defense of U.S. interests in an impromptu "kitchen debate" with Soviet premier Nikita S. Khrushchev.

Nixon lost the 1960 race for the presidency to John F. Kennedy.

In 1962, Nixon failed in a bid for California's governorship and seemed to be finished as a national candidate. He became a Wall Street lawyer, but kept his old party ties and developed new ones through constant travels to speak for Republicans.

Nixon won the 1968 Republican presidential nomination after a shrewd primary campaign, then made Gov. Spiro T. Agnew of Maryland his surprise choice for vice president. In the election, they edged out the Democratic ticket headed by Vice President Hubert H. Humphrey by 510,314 votes out of 73,212,065 cast.

Committed to winding down the U.S. role in the Vietnamese War, Nixon pursued "Vietnamization"—training and equipping South Vietnamese to do their own fighting. American ground combat forces in Vietnam fell steadily from 540,000 when Nixon took office to none in 1973 when the military draft was ended. But there was heavy continuing use of U.S. air power.

Nixon improved relations with Moscow and reopened the long-closed door to mainland China with a good-will trip there in Feb. 1972. In May of that same year, he visited Moscow and signed agreements on arms limitation and trade expansion and approved plans for a joint U.S.–Soviet space mission in 1975.

Inflation was a campaign issue for Nixon, but he failed to master it as president. On Aug. 15, 1971, with unemployment edging up, Nixon abruptly announced a new economic policy: a 90-day wage-price freeze, stimulative tax cuts, a temporary 10% tariff, and spending cuts. A second phase, imposing guidelines on wage, price, and rent boosts, was announced Oct. 7.

The economy responded in time for the 1972 campaign, in which Nixon played up his foreign-policy achievements. Played down was the burglary on June 17, 1972, of Democratic national headquarters in the Watergate apartment complex in Washington. The Nixon–Agnew reelection campaign cost a record $60 million and swamped the Democratic ticket headed by Sen. George McGovern of South Dakota with a plurality of 17,999,528 out of 77,718,554 votes. Only Massachusetts, with 14 electoral votes, and the District of Columbia, with 3, went for McGovern.

In Jan. 1973, hints of a cover-up emerged at the trial of six men found guilty of the Watergate burglary. With a Senate investigation under way, Nixon announced on April 30 the resignations of his top aides, H. R. Haldeman and John D. Ehrlichman, and the dismissal of White House counsel John Dean III. Dean was the star witness at televised Senate hearings that exposed both a White House cover-up of Watergate and massive illegalities in Republican fund-raising in 1972.

The hearings also disclosed that Nixon had routinely tape-recorded his office meetings and telephone conversations.

On Oct. 10, 1973, Agnew resigned as vice president, then pleaded no-contest to a negotiated federal charge of evading income taxes on alleged bribes. Two days later, Nixon nominated the House minority leader, Rep. Gerald R. Ford of Michigan, as the new vice president. Congress confirmed Ford on Dec. 6, 1973.

In June 1974, Nixon visited Israel and four Arab nations. Then he met in Moscow with Soviet leader Leonid I. Brezhnev and reached preliminary nuclear arms limitation agreements.

But, in the month after his return, Watergate ended the Nixon regime. On July 24 the Supreme Court ordered Nixon to surrender subpoenaed tapes. On July 30, the Judiciary Committee referred three impeachment articles to the full membership. On Aug. 5, Nixon bowed to the Supreme Court and released tapes showing he halted an FBI probe of the Watergate burglary six days after it occurred. It was in effect an admission of obstruction of justice, and impeachment appeared inevitable.

Nixon resigned on Aug. 9, 1974, the first president ever to do so. A month later, President Ford issued an unconditional pardon for any offenses Nixon might have committed as president, thus forestalling possible prosecution.

In 1940, Nixon married Thelma Catherine (Pat) Ryan. They had two daughters, Patricia (Tricia) and Julie, who married Dwight David Eisenhower II, grandson of the former president.

He died on April 22, 1994, in New York City of a massive stroke.

**GERALD RUDOLPH FORD** was born Leslie King Jr. in Omaha, Neb., on July 14, 1913, the only child of Leslie and Dorothy Gardner King. His parents were divorced in 1915. His mother moved to Grand Rapids, Mich., and married Gerald R. Ford. The boy was renamed for his stepfather.

Ford captained his high school football team in Grand Rapids, and a football scholarship took him to the University of Michigan, where he starred as varsity center before his graduation in 1935. A job as assistant football coach at Yale gave him an opportunity to attend Yale Law School, from which he graduated in the top third of his class in 1941.

He returned to Grand Rapids to practice law, but entered the Navy in April 1942. He saw wartime service in the Pacific on the light aircraft carrier *Monterey* and was a lieutenant commander when he returned to Grand Rapids early in 1946 to resume law practice and dabble in politics.

Ford was elected to Congress in 1948 for the first of his 13 terms in the House. He was soon assigned to the influential Appropriations Committee and rose to become the ranking Republican on the subcommittee on Defense Department appropriations.

As a legislator, Ford described himself as "a moderate on domestic issues, a conservative in fiscal affairs, and a dyed-in-the-wool internationalist." He carried the ball for Pentagon appropriations, was a hawk on the war in Vietnam, and kept a low profile on civil-rights issues.

Ford was also dependable and hard-working and popular with his colleagues. In 1963, he was elected chairman of the House Republican Conference. He served in 1963–1964 as a member of the Warren Commission, which investigated the assassination of John F. Kennedy. A revolt by dissatisfied younger Republicans in 1965 made him minority leader.

On Oct. 12, 1973, Nixon nominated Ford to fill the vice presidency left vacant by Agnew's resignation under fire. It was the first use of the procedures for filling vacancies in the vice presidency laid down in the 25th Amendment to the Constitution, which Ford had helped enact.

Congress confirmed Ford as vice president on Dec. 6, 1973. Once in office, he said he did not believe Nixon had been involved in the Watergate scandals, but he criticized Nixon's stubborn court battle against releasing tape recordings of Watergate-related conversations for use as evidence. The scandals led to Nixon's unprecedented resignation on Aug. 9, 1974, and Ford was sworn in immediately as the 38th president, the first to enter the White House without winning a national election.

Ford assured the nation when he took office that "our long national nightmare is over" and pledged "openness and candor" in all his actions. He won a warm response from the Democratic 93rd Congress when he said he wanted "a good marriage" rather than a honeymoon with his former colleagues. In Dec. 1974 congressional majorities backed his choice of former New York governor Nelson A. Rockefeller as his vice president.

The cordiality was chilled by Ford's announcement on Sept. 8, 1974, that he had granted an unconditional pardon to Nixon for any crimes he might have committed as president. Although no formal charges were pending, Ford said he feared "ugly passions" would be aroused if Nixon were brought to trial. The pardon was widely criticized.

To fight inflation, the new president first proposed fiscal restraints and spending curbs and a 5% tax surcharge that got nowhere in the Senate and House. Congress again rebuffed Ford in the spring of 1975 when he appealed for emergency military aid to help the governments of South Vietnam and Cambodia resist massive Communist offensives.

In Nov. 1974, Ford visited Japan, South Korea, and the Soviet Union, where he and Soviet leader Leonid I. Brezhnev conferred in Vladivostok and reached a tentative agreement to limit the number of strategic offensive nuclear weapons.

Politically, Ford's fortunes improved steadily in the first half of 1975. Badly divided Democrats in Congress were unable to muster votes to override his vetoes of spending bills that exceeded his budget. He faced some right-wing opposition in his own party, but moved to preempt it with an ꞏꞏꞏꞏ ꞏꞏꞏꞏꞏꞏꞏꞏꞏ ꞏꞏꞏꞏꞏ ꞏꞏ ꞏꞏ, ꞏꞏ ꞏꞏꞏ—ꞏꞏ ꞏꞏꞏ ꞏꞏꞏꞏꞏꞏꞏ ꞏꞏ be a candidate in 1976.

Early state primaries in 1976 suggested an easy victory for Ford despite Ronald Reagan's bitter attacks on administration foreign policy and defense programs. But later Reagan primary successes threatened the president's lead. At the Kansas City convention, Ford was nominated by the narrow margin of 1,187 to 1,070. But Reagan had moved the party to the right, and Ford himself was regarded as a caretaker president lacking in strength and vision. He was defeated in November by Jimmy Carter.

In 1948, Ford married Elizabeth Anne (Betty) Bloomer. They had four children, Michael Gerald, John Gardner, Steven Meigs, and Susan Elizabeth.

**JAMES EARL CARTER, JR.,** was born in the tiny village of Plains, Ga., Oct. 1, 1924, and grew up on the family farm at nearby Archery. Both parents were fifth-generation Georgians. His father, James Earl Carter, was known as a segregationist, but treated his black and white workers equally. Carter's mother, Lillian Gordy, was a matriarchal presence in home and community and opposed the then-prevailing code of racial inequality. The future president was baptized in 1935 in the conservative Southern Baptist Church and spoke often of being a "born again" Christian, although committed to the separation of church and state.

Carter married Rosalynn Smith, a neighbor, in 1946. Their first child, John William, was born a year later in Portsmouth, Va. Their other children are James Earl III, born in Honolulu in 1950; Donnel Jeffrey, born in New London, Conn., in 1952; and Amy Lynn, born in Plains in 1967.

In 1946 Carter was graduated from the U.S. Naval Academy at Annapolis and served in the nuclear-submarine program under Adm. Hyman G. Rickover. In 1954, after his father's death, he resigned from the Navy to take over the family's flourishing warehouse and cotton gin, with several thousand acres for growing seed peanuts.

Carter was elected to the Georgia Senate in 1962. In 1966 he lost the race for governor, but was elected in 1970. His term brought a state government reorganization, sharply reduced agencies, increased economy and efficiency, and new social programs, all with no general tax increase. In 1972 the peanut farmer–politician set his sights on the presidency and in 1974 built a base for himself as he criss-crossed the country as chairman of the Democratic Campaign Committee, appealing for revival and reform. In 1975 he won the support of most of the old Southern civil-rights coalition after endorsement by Rep. Andrew Young, black Democrat from Atlanta, who had been the closest aide to the Rev. Martin Luther King, Jr. Having won 19 out of 31 primaries with a broad appeal to conservatives and liberals, black and white, poor and well-to-do, he defeated Gerald R. Ford in Nov. 1976.

In his one term, Carter fought hard for his programs against resistance from an independent-minded Democratic Congress that frustrated many pet projects although it overrode only two vetoes. Public dissatisfaction with the "stagflation" economy, staff problems, friction with Congress, long gasoline lines, and the months-long Iranian crisis, including the abortive sally in April 1980 to free the hostages, came to mark public perception of the administration. Yet, assessments of his record have noted many positive elements. There was, for one thing, peace throughout his term, with no American combat deaths and with a brake on the advocates of force. Regarded as perhaps his greatest personal achievements were the Camp David accords between Israel and Egypt and the resulting treaty— the first between Israel and an Arab neighbor. The treaty with China and the Panama Canal treaties were also major achievements. Carter worked for nuclear-arms control. His concern for international human rights was credited with saving lives and reducing torture, and he supported the British policy that ended internecine warfare in Rhodesia, now Zimbabwe. Domestically, his environmental record was a major accomplishment. His judicial appointments won acclaim, with 265 choices for the federal bench that included minority members and women.

In 1980 Carter was renominated on the first ballot after vanquishing Sen. Edward M. Kennedy of Massachusetts in the primaries. In the election campaign, he attacked his rivals, Ronald Reagan and John B. Anderson, independent, with the warning that a Reagan Republican victory would heighten the risk of war and impede civil rights and economic opportunity. In November Carter lost to Reagan, who won 489 electoral college votes and 51% of the popular tally, to 49 electoral votes and 41% for Carter. He was awarded the 2002 Nobel Peace Prize.

**RONALD WILSON REAGAN** rode to the presidency in 1980 on a tide of resurgent right-wing sentiment among an electorate longing for a distant, simpler era. He left office in Jan. 1989 with two-thirds of the American people approving his performance during his two terms. It was the highest rating for any retiring president since World War II.

Reagan, an actor turned politician, a New Dealer turned conservative, came to films and politics from a thoroughly Middle-American background—middle class, Middle West, and small town. He was born in Tampico, Ill., Feb. 6, 1911, the second son of John Edward Reagan and Nelle Wilson Reagan; the family later moved to Dixon, Ill. His father was a shop clerk and merchant with Democratic sympathies. It was an impoverished family; young Ronald sold homemade popcorn at high school games and worked as a lifeguard to earn money for his college tuition. When his father got a New Deal WPA job, the future president became an ardent Roosevelt Democrat.

Reagan earned a BA degree in 1932 from Eureka (Ill.) College, where a photographic memory aided in his studies and in debating and college theatricals. During the Depression, he made $100 a week as a sports announcer for radio station WHO in Des Moines, Iowa. His career as a film and TV actor stretched from 1937 to 1966, and his salary climbed to $3,500 a week. As a World War II captain in army film studios, Reagan recoiled from what he saw as the laziness of civil service workers, and moved to the Right. As president of the Screen Actors Guild, he resisted what he considered a Communist plot to subvert the film industry. With advancing age, Reagan left leading-man roles and became a television spokesman for the General Electric Company.

With oratorical skill as his trademark, Reagan became an active Republican. In 1966, at the behest of a small group of conservative businessmen, he ran for governor of California with a pledge to cut spending; he was elected by almost a million votes over the political veteran, Democratic governor Edmund G. Brown. Reelected to a second term, he served as governor until 1975.

In the 1980 election battle against Jimmy Carter, Reagan broadened his appeal by espousing moderate policies, gaining much of his support from disaffected Democrats and blue-collar workers. The incoming administration immediately set out to "turn the government around" with a new economic program. Over strenuous congressional opposition, Reagan pushed through his "supply side" economic program to stimulate production and control inflation through tax cuts and sharp reductions in government spending. However, in 1982, as the economy declined into the worst recession in 40 years, the president's popularity slipped and support for supply-side economics faded.

Barely three months into his first term, Reagan was the target of an assassin's bullet; his courageous comeback won public admiration. The president also won high acclaim for his nomination of Sandra Day O'Connor as the first woman on the Supreme Court. His later nominations met increasing opposition and did much to tilt the Court's orientation to the Right.

Internationally, Reagan confronted numerous problems in his first term. In an effort to establish order on the Caribbean island of Grenada and eliminate the Cuban military presence there, Reagan ordered an invasion of the tiny nation on Oct. 25, 1983. The troops met strong resistance from Cuban military personnel on the island but soon occupied it. Another military effort, in Lebanon, ended in failure, however. U.S. Marines engaged as part of a multinational peacekeeping force in Beirut were forced to withdraw in 1984 after a disastrous terrorist attack left 241 marines dead.

With the economy improving and inflation under control, the popular president won reelection in a landslide in 1984. Domestically, a tax reform bill that Reagan backed became law. But the constantly growing budget deficit remained an irritant, with the president and Congress persistently at odds over priorities in spending for defense and domestic programs. Congress was also increasingly reluctant to increase spending for the Nicaraguan "Contras." But even severe critics praised Reagan's restrained but decisive handling of the crisis following the hijacking of an American plane in Beirut by Muslim extremists. The attack on Libya in April 1986 galvanized the nation, although it drew scathing disapproval from the NATO alliance.

Reagan's popularity with the public dipped sharply in 1986 when the Iran-Contra scandal broke, shortly after the Democrats gained control of the Senate. The weeks-long congressional hearings in the summer of 1987 heard an array of administration officials, present and former, reveal a web of deceit and undercover maneuvering in the White House. Yet the president's personal reputation remained untouched; on Aug. 12, 1987, he told the nation that he had not known of questionable activities but agreed that he was ultimately accountable.

Reagan's place in history will rest, perhaps, on the short- and intermediate-range missile treaty consummated on a cordial visit to the Soviet Union that he had once reviled as an "evil empire." Its provisions, including a ground-breaking agreement on verification inspection, were formulated in four days of summit talks in Moscow in May 1988 with the Soviet leader, Mikhail S. Gorbachev. Reagan could point to numerous domestic achievements as well: sharp cuts in income tax rates, creating economic growth without inflation, and reducing the unemployment rate, among others. He failed, however, to win the "Reagan Revolution" on such issues as abortion and school prayer.

Reagan married his wife, Nancy, fours years after his divorce from the screen actress Jane Wyman. The children from his first marriage are

Maureen, his daughter by Wyman, and Michael, an adopted son. He had two children by Nancy: Patricia and Ron. Reagan suffers from Alzheimer's disease, which he developed in the years following his presidency.

## GEORGE HERBERT WALKER BUSH was born
June 12, 1924, in Milton, Mass., to Prescott and Dorothy Bush. The family later moved to Connecticut. The youth studied at the elite Phillips Academy in Andover, Mass.

The future president joined the Navy after war broke out and at 18 became the Navy's youngest commissioned pilot, serving from 1942 to 1945. The man later derided by some as a "wimp" fought the Japanese on 58 missions and was shot down once. He won the Distinguished Flying Cross.

After the war, Bush earned an economics degree and a Phi Beta Kappa key in two and a half years at Yale University. While there he captained the baseball team and was initiated into "Skull and Bones," the prestigious Yale secret society.

In 1945 Bush married Barbara Pierce of Rye, N.Y., daughter of a magazine publisher. With his bride, Bush moved to Texas instead of entering his father's investment banking business. There he founded his oil company and by 1980 reported an estimated wealth of $1.4 million.

Throughout his whole career, Bush had the backing of an established family, headed by his father, Prescott Bush, who was elected to the Senate from Connecticut in 1952. The family helped the young patrician become established in his early business ventures, a rich uncle raising most of the capital required for founding the oil company.

In the 1960s, Bush won two contests for a Texas Republican seat in the House of Representatives, but lost two bids for a Senate seat. After Bush's second race for the Senate, President Nixon appointed him U.S. delegate to the United Nations with the rank of ambassador and he later became Republican National Committee chairman. He headed the U.S. liaison office in Beijing before becoming Director of Central Intelligence.

In 1980 Bush became Reagan's running mate despite earlier criticism of Reagan "voodoo economics" and by the 1984 election had won acclaim for his devotion to Reagan's conservative agenda. Die-hard right-wingers could also find satisfaction in Bush's war record and his government service, particularly with the CIA. Throughout he remained influential in White House decisions, particularly in foreign affairs.

In the 1988 presidential campaign, Bush's choice of Dan Quayle, youthful Indiana Xa vice president surprised his friends and provoked criticism and ridicule that continued even after the administration was in office. Nonetheless Bush strongly defended his choice.

George Herbert Walker Bush became president on Jan. 20, 1989, with his theme harmony and conciliation after the often-turbulent Reagan years. With his calm and unassuming manner, he emerged from his subordinate vice-presidential role with an air of quiet authority. His inaugural address emphasized "A new breeze is blowing, and the old bipartisanship must be made new again."

In his first months, the president, the nation's 41st, established himself as his own man and all but erased memories of what many had regarded as his fiercely abrasive presidential election campaign of 1988 and questionable tactics against his Democratic opponent. People liked his easy style and readiness to compromise even as he remained a staunch conservative, although that readiness had disconcerted some conservatives.

Bush's early Cabinet choices reflected a pragmatic desire for an efficient, nonideological government. And with his usual cautious instinct, in 1990 he nominated to the Supreme Court the scholarly David H. Souter, with broadly conservative views. Souter was confirmed without a bruising battle.

In his first year, Bush, a World War II hero, had won plaudits at home and abroad for his confident, competent conduct at the NATO 40th anniversary summit meeting in Brussels, the Paris economic conference, on his tour of Eastern Europe, and at the Malta conference with Gorbachev. Grave challenges in that year were the Lebanese hostage crisis and the ongoing war against drug trafficking.

Domestically, Bush had to cope with such issues as the Exxon Valdez oil spill in Alaska and the dispute over flag-burning restrictions, which was resolved, if only for a time, in mid-1990.

But in his second year, 1990, the president confronted a mounting array of problems, chief among them the staggering budget deficit and the savings and loan crisis. The president's popularity dipped sharply from its near-record public approval following the invasion of Panama in late 1989. This plunge followed Bush's recantation of his campaign "no new taxes" pledge as he sat down with congressional leaders to tame the budget deficit and deal with a faltering economy.

In 1991, the president emerged as the leader of an international coalition of Western democracies, Japan, and even some Arab states that came together to free Kuwait following an invasion of the country by Iraq in Aug. 1990. The coalition forces defeated Iraq in only a little more than a month after Operation Desert Storm was launched on Jan. 18, 1991, and a nation grateful at feeling the end of the "Vietnam syndrome" gave the president an 89% approval rating. However, the high rating fell as the year went on, as doubts persisted about the war's outcome—Iraqi president Saddam Hussein remained in power and persistently avoided complying with the terms of the peace treaty—and as concerns began to grow about the faltering U.S. economy and other domestic problems.

A major Bush accomplishment in 1991 was the Strategic Arms Reduction Treaty (START), signed in July with Soviet president Mikhail S. Gorbachev at their fourth summit conference, marking the end of the long weapons buildup.

The year also saw the president undergoing treatment for Graves' disease, a thyroid disorder, from which he suffered serious side effects.

In the 1992 presidential election, Bush was defeated by Gov. Bill Clinton of Arkansas.

The Bushes have four sons, George, Jeb, Neil, and Marvin, and a daughter, Dorothy. Another daughter, Robin, died at age three from leukemia. Son George served as governor of Texas from 1995 to 2000, when he was elected the 43rd U.S. president. Jeb Bush was elected governor of Florida in 1998.

**WILLIAM JEFFERSON CLINTON** was born William Jefferson Blythe IV in Hope, Ark., on Aug. 19, 1946. He was named for his father, who was killed in an automobile accident before Clinton's birth. Virginia Kelley, his mother, eventually married Roger Clinton, a car dealer, whose surname the future president later adopted.

In high school in Hot Springs, Ark., Clinton considered becoming a doctor, but politics beckoned after a meeting with President John F. Kennedy in Washington, DC, on a Boys' Nation trip. He earned a BS in international affairs in 1968 at Georgetown University, having spent his junior year working for Arkansas senator J. William Fulbright. He was a Rhodes scholar at Oxford between 1968 and 1970. He then attended Yale Law School, where he met his future wife, Hillary Rodham, a Wellesley graduate. The couple has one child, Chelsea.

Clinton taught at the University of Arkansas (1974–1976), was elected state attorney general (1976), and in 1979 became the nation's youngest governor. But he was defeated for reelection in 1980 by voters irate at a rise in the state's automobile license fees. In 1982 he was elected again. This time he reined in liberal tendencies to accommodate the conservative bent of the voters.

Clinton became the 42nd U.S. president following a turbulent political campaign. He overcame vigorous personal attacks on his character and on his actions during the Vietnam War, which he actively opposed. The "character issue" stemmed from allegations of infidelity, which Clinton refuted in a television interview in which he and Hillary avowed their relationship was solid. Throughout his term in office, Clinton was dogged by allegations relating to the Whitewater real estate deal in which he and Hillary were involved prior to the 1992 election. Though the Clintons were never accused of any wrongdoing, partners in the venture were convicted of fraud and conspiracy in a trial in 1996.

The problems faced by the new president were as daunting as they were varied. In Jan. 1993 he became embroiled with the military leadership over his campaign pledge to allow homosexuals to serve openly in the armed services. He ultimately agreed to a compromise, dubbed the "don't ask, don't tell" policy. Clinton's first year also saw him wrangling with Congress over the federal budget and economic policy.

In his second year, Clinton was faced with acrimonious battles over health care, welfare reform, and crime prevention. A health care reform package crafted by his wife failed to gain sufficient support. Clinton had to reduce his objective from massive overhaul to incremental reform.

Clinton won major victories with the passage of the North American Free Trade Agreement (NAFTA), which took effect Jan. 1, 1994, and the Global Agreement on Tariffs and Trade (GATT), which led to the establishment in 1995 of the World Trade Organization (WTO). Congress also approved a deficit reduction bill, rules allowing abortion counseling in federally funded clinics, a waiting period for handgun purchases (the Brady Bill), and a national service program.

Foreign affairs became a proving ground for Clinton, since he has been elected primarily on a domestic economic agenda. He improved his international image when the Israel–Jordan peace agreement was signed at the White House in the summer of 1994 by Israeli prime minister Yitzhak Rabin and Jordan's King Hussein. In the fall of that year, the administration succeeded in restoring Haiti's ousted president, Jean-Bertrand Aristide, to power. Clinton scored again by bolstering Russian president Boris Yeltsin's popularity with promises of economic aid.

The problems in Eastern Europe were Clinton's next big challenge. Though he wanted desperately to end the brutal ethnic cleansing in Bosnia, he did not want to commit American ground troops to do so. A peace accord involving American peacekeeping troops was ultimately signed in Dayton, Ohio, in Nov. 1995.

The 1994 elections resulted in a Republican-controlled Congress, and 1995 was largely a tug-of-war between the White House and Capitol Hill over budget-balancing and other key points of the GOP's "Contract with America," crafted by Speaker of the House Newt Gingrich.

In 1996, aided by a booming economy, Clinton won reelection to a second term, becoming the first Democratic president since Franklin D. Roosevelt to do so. The country's general prosperity also made it possible in 1997 for Clinton and the Republicans to reach an agreement to balance the federal budget in three decades.

However, the character issues that had followed Clinton for years soon began to emerge once again. A series of investigations was begun to determine whether Clinton and Vice President Gore had participated in questionable fund-raising practices in their 1996 campaign.

As his tenure wore on, Clinton came under increasing pressure from Kenneth Starr, the independent counsel who in 1994 took over the investigation of the Clintons' involvement in the Whitewater land deal. Over time, Starr's brief was expanded to include other matters, such as the death of White House lawyer Vincent Foster, the handling of firings in the White House travel office, and shocking allegations of sexual misconduct by Clinton.

In Jan. 1998, Clinton was called to testify in a long-pending sexual harassment suit brought against him by Paula Corbin Jones, a former Arkansas state employee. In his testimony, Clinton denied that he had had a sexual relationship with a young White House intern, Monica Lewinsky, and that he had attempted to cover it up. Although a federal judge in Arkansas threw out the Jones sexual harassment suit in April 1998, by this time the Lewinsky affair had become the focus of Kenneth Starr's investigation as well as a national obsession.

Finally, on Aug. 17, 1998, after relentless media attention, leaks, and news of Lewinsky's upcoming testimony, Clinton made history by becoming the first U.S. president to testify in front of a grand jury in an investigation of his own possibly criminal conduct. In an address to the nation that evening, he admitted to having had an "inappropriate relationship" with Lewinsky, but reaffirmed that he did not ask anyone to lie about or cover up the affair.

Paradoxically, however, in spite of the scandalous outcome of events, Clinton's overall popularity among Americans remained high. The country seemed willing to ignore his weaknesses in character, much as they did in the 1992 elections, as long as the economy was good, his policies were popular, and the United States remained strong abroad.

On Sept. 9, Starr—a conservative Republican whose investigation was seen by Clinton supporters as a politically inspired vendetta—delivered his report to the House of Representatives. While the report outlined 11 possible grounds for impeachment, none stemmed from the initial subjects of the investigation, including the Whitewater real estate deal. The real focus of the accusations seemed to be Clinton's moral conduct, and the "Starr Report" graphically detailed his sexual affair.

Despite the American population's general disapproval of a trial (which was reflected in poll after poll), Congress moved forward in its highly partisan impeachment proceedings and on Dec. 19, Clinton became the second president in American history to be impeached. Two of the four articles of impeachment passed (Article I, grand jury perjury, and Article III, obstruction of justice), the votes drawn along party lines. After a Senate trial in Jan.–Feb. 1999, Clinton was acquitted on both counts.

While the impeachment trial overshadowed all other activity in Washington for a good portion of 1998, Clinton was forced to respond to continued problems with Iraq at the end of the year. In December, Saddam Hussein blocked a weapons inspection by the United Nations. The UN responded with airstrikes that would continue on a nearly daily basis for the next three months, and then off and on through the spring and summer, as Iraq taunted the U.S. and its allies further by shooting at jets patrolling the no-fly zones set up after the Persian Gulf war.

In the spring of 1999, reports of continued ethnic cleansing in the Serbian province of Kosovo were growing. Clinton and his British counterpart, Tony Blair, led the push for NATO intervention, which resulted in a 78-day bombing campaign against Serbia that began in March. Although Clinton received some sharp criticism for holding back on the deployment of NATO ground troops, he was ultimately justified, as Serbian president Slobodan Milosevic finally agreed to a peace treaty, signed June 9.

In his final year of office, the president maintained a relatively low profile but took several major trips overseas, to South Asia, Europe, and Africa. He also prepared for the 2000 elections, lending his support not only to presidential hopeful Al Gore, but also to his wife, Hillary Clinton, who successfully ran for U.S. senator from New York.

On Jan. 19, 2001, the day before he left office, Clinton agreed to a five-year suspension of his Arkansas law license and his paying of a $25,000 fine to the Arkansas Bar Association. In exchange, Kenneth Starr's successor, Robert Ray, agreed to close the Whitewater probe, ending the threat of indictment once and for all. Clinton after he left office.

## GEORGE WALKER BUSH was born on July 6, 1946, in New Haven, Conn. the first child of President George Bush, who was then still a student at Yale. In 1948, the family moved to Odessa, Tex., where the senior Bush went to work in the oil business. George W. grew up mainly in Midland, Tex., and Houston and later attended two of his father's alma maters, Phillips Academy in Andover, Mass., and Yale.

After graduating from Yale with a history degree in 1968, Bush joined the Texas Air National Guard. He underwent two years of flight training and subsequently served as a part-time fighter pilot until 1973, when he entered Harvard Business School. After receiving an MBA in 1975, he returned to Texas, where he established his own oil and gas business in the late 1970s. In 1977 he met and married his wife, Laura Welch, a librarian. The couple has twin daughters, Jenna and Barbara, born in 1981.

Coming from a prominent political family—his grandfather Prescott Bush had been a senator from Connecticut and his father a U.S. congressman and political appointee—George W. had been immersed in politics since childhood. In 1977 Bush finally entered the fray himself, running for U.S. Congress from the West Texas district that included his hometown of Midland. Although he won the Republican primary, he ultimately lost in the general election to his Democratic opponent.

Following his defeat, Bush returned to the oil business. In 1985, however, oil prices fell sharply, and Bush's company verged on collapse until it was acquired by a Dallas firm. It was a lucky break for Bush, and also something of a turning point. Having finalized the buyout of his oil company in September, he headed to Washington to become a paid adviser to his father's 1988 presidential campaign.

After the 1988 election, Bush returned to Texas and assembled a group of investors to buy the Texas Rangers for $86 million. Although Bush invested only $606,302, he was named managing partner, a position that allowed him to build his reputation in the public eye as a Texas businessman. A baseball enthusiast from his childhood, Bush preferred to sit in the stands among the other fans rather than in the owners' box.

The younger Bush's political turn at bat finally came in 1993, when, in the wake of his father's unsuccessful bid for reelection, he announced his plans to run for the Texas governorship. Although he had a tough opponent in the immensely popular incumbent Ann Richards, he created a clear agenda focused on issues such as education and juvenile justice and won with 53% of the vote.

He was reelected in 1998, not long before he announced plans to run for president. At this point the Rangers partners decided to sell the team for $250 million. The timing was fortuitous—Bush made $14.9 million (on his $606,302 investment), which helped fund his presidential campaign as well as his new 1,500-acre ranch near Crawford, Tex.

During the campaign leading up to the 2000 election, Bush characterized himself as a "compassionate conservative," a somewhat vague description meant to evoke a kinder, gentler Republican. On the issue of foreign policy, Bush adhered closely to the traditional conservative line, favoring small government, tax cuts, a strong military, and opposing gun control and abortion. He won plaudits for his choice of running mate, Dick Cheney, who had served as secretary of defense during his father's administration and had commanded the Pentagon during the Persian Gulf War. Bush had been faulted for his lack of Washington political experience and gravitas, qualities that Cheney brought to the ticket in abundance.

With the country in a state of general prosperity and the candidates divided along only narrowly differentiated ideological lines, the 2000 election between George W. Bush and Vice President Al Gore was perceived to be one of the least dynamic on issues. As it turned out, the race was one of the closest in the country's history. By early evening on election night, it was apparent that whoever won Florida would win the election. But the vote was so close, Bush's razor thin margin of about 1,200 votes prompted an automatic recount.

On Nov. 11, after the mandatory machine recount revealed that the two candidates were only a few hundred votes apart, the election began its tortuous journey through the judicial system. The Bush camp sued in federal district court to prohibit manual recounts sought by Gore, and the case ultimately ended up in the U.S. Supreme Court.

Bush officially became the president-elect on Dec. 13, after the U.S. Supreme Court reversed a decision by the Florida Supreme Court to allow manual recounts of ballots in some Florida counties. With Florida in his column, Bush won the presidency with 271 electoral votes, just one more than he needed, although he lost the popular vote by half a million. It was the first time that the Supreme Court, and not the electorate, determined the outcome of the presidential election.

The top item on Bush's domestic agenda, a $1.6 trillion tax cut, was the subject of bitter partisan debate in Congress, with opponents (mostly Democratic) arguing that the bill primarily favored the wealthy and would not provide the desired economic stimulus. The Senate eventually trimmed the tax cut to $1.35 trillion over 11 years, and Bush signed it into law in early June 2001. Victory over the tax cut was somewhat marred, however, by the defection of Sen. James Jeffords (I-Vt.) from the Republican Party—a major blow for the president, since it resulted in the Democrats' gaining control of the Senate.

With the nation's economy in the doldrums and the federal budget surplus dwindling, the Bush team in early September was gearing up for a major battle in Congress over spending for Bush's domestic programs. The terrorist attack on the World Trade Center and the Pentagon on Sept. 11, however, instantly moved all pending issues to the back burner and irrevocably altered the direction of the Bush presidency. Rather than domestic issues, the president's primary focus would be the war on international terrorism.

On Oct. 7 the U.S. and Britain began air strikes against military installations and terrorist training camps in Afghanistan, after the Taliban government repeatedly refused to surrender Osama bin Laden—the suspected mastermind of the Sept. 11 attacks—and other al-Qaeda leaders. The Taliban collapsed on Dec. 9, but despite this outstanding military success, bin Laden remained at large.

Meanwhile, at home, an anthrax scare in October prompted the Bush administration to announce the expansion of the government's bioterrorism program and to take steps to acquire enough antibiotics for millions of people. The president had announced the creation of a White House Office of Homeland Security shortly after the Sept. 11 attacks, and his plan for a cabinet-level domestic security agency—which would consolidate 20 federal agencies in a massive government reorganization—received wide bipartisan support.

The president also formally withdrew the U.S. from the Antiballistic Missile Treaty it signed with the Soviet Union in 1972, saying "I have concluded the ABM treaty hinders our government's ways to

protect our people from future terrorist or rogue state missile attacks." However, the leaders of the two nations agreed to cut their nuclear weapons stockpiles by two-thirds over the next decade.

Into 2002 Bush continued to focus his efforts on the war against international terrorism. In his first state of the union address to Congress on Jan. 29, 2002, the president delivered strong new warnings to terrorists around the world, and in particular to Iran, Iraq, and North Korea, which he called an "axis of evil." In the months that followed, Bush designated Iraq as the primary new threat to American security, shifting the focus away from Osama bin Laden, al-Qaeda, and other terrorist groups.

In an effort to appease U.S. officials and world leaders alarmed by the prospect of a preemptive U.S. military strike against Iraq, Bush spoke before the UN General Assembly on Sept. 12. He called on the world body to force Saddam Hussein to abandon his weapons build-up program and allow UN weapons inspections. He made it clear, however, that if the UN did not act, the U.S. would not hesitate to go it alone. Although the speech was viewed favorably, critics complained that the president had not presented any evidence to show that the threat from Saddam Hussein was imminent, or that there was a direct connection between Hussein and the Sept. 11 attacks.

With his attention firmly fixed on Iraq, the president seemed to have little time or energy for international matters elsewhere. Bush had been criticized early on for the U.S.'s disengagement from the Palestinian-Israeli crisis, and in June he seemed to distance himself further, by demanding the ouster of Palestinian leader Yasir Arafat as a precondition for new negotiations.

And, nearly a year after withdrawing the U.S. from the Kyoto treaty on global warming, Bush continued to alienate friends abroad, first by imposing high tariffs on steel imports (to protect the U.S. steel industry), and then by withdrawing from a treaty to establish an international war-crimes court. European allies viewed both actions as further examples of Bush's tendency to act unilaterally and without regard for overseas partners.

On the domestic front, the Bush administration had been criticized for its slow response to the financial scandals that rocked the nation, beginning with the bankruptcy of Enron in Dec. 2001. Finally, on July 9, the president spoke on Wall Street, criticizing corporate leaders and promising reform. The measures subsequently passed by Congress were tougher than those the president had proposed; however, Bush readily signed the corporate-fraud bill into law in late July.

Also in 2002, Bush suffered a number of legislative disappointments, primarily at the hands of the narrowly divided Senate. In February and March, he reluctantly signed into law a drastically altered faith-based charity initiative; a stripped-down economic stimulus package; and a campaign-finance reform bill sponsored by his former presidential rival Sen. John McCain. The administration's energy bill, which would allow oil drilling in the Arctic National Wildlife Refuge, stalled in the Senate.

In early Oct. 2002, the president finally won authorization from Congress to use force against Iraq. The decision came following weeks of briefings and lobbying by the administration.

# Senate and House Standing Committees, 107th Congress

## Committees of the Senate

**Agriculture, Nutrition, and Forestry** (21 members)
*Chairman:* Tom Harkin (Iowa)
*Ranking Rep.:* Richard G. Lugar (Ind.)

**Appropriations** (29 members)
*Chairman:* Robert C. Byrd (W.Va.)
*Ranking Rep.:* Ted Stevens (Alaska)

**Armed Services** (25 members)
*Chairman:* Carl Levin (Mich.)
*Ranking Rep.:* John Warner (Va.)

**Banking, Housing, and Urban Affairs** (21 members)
*Chairman:* Paul S. Sarbanes (Md.)
*Ranking Rep.:* Phil Gramm (Tex.)

**Budget** (23 members)
*Chairman:* Kent Conrad (N.D.)
*Ranking Rep.:* Pete V. Domenici (N.M.)

**Commerce, Science, and Transportation** (23 members)
*Chairman:* Ernest F. Hollings (S.C.)
*Ranking Rep.:* John McCain (Ariz.)

**Energy and Natural Resources** (23 members)
*Chairman:* Jeff Bingaman (N.M.)
*Ranking Rep.:* Frank H. Murkowski (Alaska)

**Environment and Public Works** (19 members)
*Chairman:* James M. Jeffords (Vt.)
*Ranking Rep.:* Robert C. Smith (N.H.)

**Finance** (21 members)
*Chairman:* Max Baucus (Mont.)
*Ranking Rep.:* Charles E. Grassley (Iowa)

**Foreign Relations** (19 members)
*Chairman:* Joseph R. Biden, Jr. (Del.)
*Ranking Rep.:* Jesse Helms (N.C.)

**Governmental Affairs** (17 members)
*Chairman:* Joseph Lieberman (Conn.)
*Ranking Rep.:* Fred Thompson (Tenn.)

**Health, Education, Labor, and Pensions** (21 members)
*Chairman:* Edward M. Kennedy (Mass.)
*Ranking Rep.:* Judd Gregg (N.H.)

**Judiciary** (19 members)
*Chairman:* Patrick J. Leahy (Vt.)
*Ranking Rep.:* Orrin G. Hatch (Utah)

**Rules and Administration** (19 members)
*Chairman:* Christopher Dodd (Conn.)
*Ranking Rep.:* Mitch McConnell (Ky.)

**Small Business** (19 members)
*Chairman:* John Kerry (Mass.)
*Ranking Rep.:* Christopher S. Bond (Mo.)

**Veterans' Affairs** (15 members)
*Chairman:* John D. Rockefeller IV (W.Va.)
*Ranking Rep:* Arlen Specter (Pa.)

## Senate Special or Select Committees

**Aging** (21 members)
*Chairman:* John B. Breaux (La.)
*Ranking Rep.:* Larry Craig (Idaho)

**Ethics** (6 members)
*Chairman:* Harry Reid (Nev.)
*Ranking Rep.:* Pat Roberts (Kans.)

**Indian Affairs** (15 members)
*Chairman:* Daniel K. Inouye (Hawaii)
*Ranking Rep.:* Ben Nighthorse Campbell (Colo.)

**Intelligence** (17 members)
*Chairman:* Bob Graham (Fla.)
*Ranking Rep.:* Richard C. Shelby (Ala.)

## Committees of the House

**Agriculture** (51 members)
*Chairman:* Larry Combest (Tex.)
*Ranking Dem.:* Charles W. Stenholm (Tex.)

**Appropriations** (65 members)
*Chairman:* C. W. Bill Young (Fla.)
*Ranking Dem.:* David R. Obey (Wis.)

**Armed Services** (60 members)
*Chairman:* Bob Stump (Ariz.)
*Ranking Dem.:* Ike Skelton (Mo.)

**Budget** (43 members)
*Chairman:* Jim Nussle (Iowa)
*Ranking Dem.:* John M. Spratt, Jr. (S.C.)

**Education and the Workforce** (49 members)
*Chairman:* John A. Boehner (Ohio)
*Ranking Dem.:* George Miller (Calif.)

**Energy and Commerce** (57 members)
*Chairman:* W. J. Billy Tauzin (La.)
*Ranking Dem.:* John D. Dingell (Mich.)

**Financial Services** (70 members)
*Chairman:* Michael G. Oxley (Ohio)
*Ranking Dem.:* John J. LaFalce (N.Y.)

**Government Reform** (44 members)
*Chairman:* Dan Burton (Ind.)
*Ranking Dem.:* Henry A. Waxman (Calif.)

**House Administration** (9 members)
*Chairman:* Robert W. Ney (Ohio)
*Ranking Dem.:* Steny H. Hoyer (Md.)

**International Relations** (49 members)
*Chairman:* Henry J. Hyde (Ill.)
*Ranking Dem.:* Tom Lantos (Calif.)

**Judiciary** (37 members)
*Chairman:* F. James Sensenbrenner, Jr. (Wis.)
*Ranking Dem.:* John Conyers, Jr. (Mich.)

**Resources** (52 members)
*Chairman:* James V. Hansen (Utah)
*Ranking Dem.:* Nick J. Rahall II (W. Va.)

**Rules** (13 members)
*Chairman:* David Dreier (Calif.)
*Ranking Dem.:* Martin Frost (Tex.)

**Science** (47 members)
*Chairman:* Sherwood L. Boehlert (N.Y.)
*Ranking Dem.:* Ralph M. Hall (Tex.)

**Small Business** (36 members)
*Chairman:* Donald A. Manzullo (Ill.)
*Ranking Dem.:* Nydia M. Velázquez (N.Y.)

**Standards of Official Conduct** (10 members)
*Chairman:* Joel Hefley (Colo.)
*Ranking Dem.:* Howard L. Berman (Calif.)

**Transportation and Infrastructure** (75 members)
*Chairman:* Don Young (Alaska)
*Ranking Dem.:* James L. Oberstar (Minn.)

**Veterans' Affairs** (31 members)
*Chairman:* Christopher H. Smith (N.J.)
*Ranking Dem.:* Lane Evans (Ill.)

**Ways and Means** (41 members)
*Chairman:* William M. Thomas (Calif.)
*Ranking Dem.:* Charles B. Rangel (N.Y.)

# Speakers of the House of Representatives

| Dates served | Congress | Name and state | Dates served | Congress | Name and state |
|---|---|---|---|---|---|
| 1789–1791 | 1 | Frederick A. C. Muhlenberg (Pa.) | 1869–1875 | 41–43 | James G. Blaine (Maine) |
| 1791–1793 | 2 | Jonathan Trumbull (Conn.) | 1875–1876 | 44 | Michael C. Kerr (Ind.)[6] |
| 1793–1795 | 3 | Frederick A. C. Muhlenberg (Pa.) | 1876–1881 | 44–46 | Samuel J. Randall (Pa.) |
| 1795–1799 | 4–5 | Jonathan Dayton (N.J.)[1] | 1881–1883 | 47 | J. Warren Keifer (Ohio) |
| 1799–1801 | 6 | Theodore Sedgwick (Mass.) | 1883–1889 | 48–50 | John G. Carlisle (Ky.) |
| 1801–1807 | 7–9 | Nathaniel Macon (N.C.) | 1889–1891 | 51 | Thomas B. Reed (Maine) |
| 1807–1811 | 10–11 | Joseph B. Varnum (Mass.) | 1891–1895 | 52–53 | Charles F. Crisp (Ga.) |
| 1811–1814 | 12–13 | Henry Clay (Ky.)[2] | 1895–1899 | 54–55 | Thomas B. Reed (Maine) |
| 1814–1815 | 13 | Langdon Cheves (S.C.) | 1899–1903 | 56–57 | David B. Henderson (Iowa) |
| 1815–1820 | 14–16 | Henry Clay (Ky.)[3] | 1903–1911 | 58–61 | Joseph G. Cannon (Ill.) |
| 1820–1821 | 16 | John W. Taylor (N.Y.) | 1911–1919 | 62–65 | Champ Clark (Mo.) |
| 1821–1823 | 17 | Philip P. Barbour (Va.) | 1919–1925 | 66–68 | Frederick H. Gillett (Mass.) |
| 1823–1825 | 18 | Henry Clay (Ky.) | 1925–1931 | 69–71 | Nicholas Longworth (Ohio) |
| 1825–1827 | 19 | John W. Taylor (N.Y.) | 1931–1933 | 72 | John N. Garner (Tex.) |
| 1827–1834 | 20–23 | Andrew Stevenson (Va.)[4] | 1933–1934 | 73 | Henry T. Rainey (Ill.)[7] |
| 1834–1835 | 23 | John Bell (Tenn.) | 1935–1936 | 74 | Joseph W. Byrns (Tenn.)[8] |
| 1835–1839 | 24–25 | James K. Polk (Tenn.) | 1936–1940 | 74–76 | William B. Bankhead (Ala.)[9] |
| 1839–1841 | 26 | Robert M. T. Hunter (Va.) | 1940–1947 | 76–79 | Sam Rayburn (Tex.) |
| 1841–1843 | 27 | John White (Ky.) | 1947–1949 | 80 | Joseph W. Martin, Jr. (Mass.) |
| 1843–1845 | 28 | John W. Jones (Va.) | 1949–1953 | 81–82 | Sam Rayburn (Tex.) |
| 1845–1847 | 29 | John W. Davis (Ind.) | 1953–1955 | 83 | Joseph W. Martin, Jr. (Mass.) |
| 1847–1849 | 30 | Robert C. Winthrop (Mass.) | 1955–1961 | 84–87 | Sam Rayburn (Tex.)[10] |
| 1849–1851 | 31 | Howell Cobb (Ga.) | 1963–1971 | 87–91 | John W. McCormack (Mass.)[11] |
| 1851–1855 | 32–33 | Linn Boyd (Ky.) | 1971–1977 | 92–94 | Carl Albert (Okla.)[12] |
| 1855–1857 | 34 | Nathaniel P. Banks (Mass.) | 1977–1987 | 95–99 | Thomas P. O'Neill, Jr. (Mass.)[13] |
| 1857–1859 | 35 | James L. Orr (S.C.) | 1987–1989 | 100–101 | James C. Wright, Jr. (Tex.)[14] |
| 1859–1861 | 36 | Wm. Pennington (N.J.) | 1989–1995 | 101–103 | Thomas S. Foley (Wash.) |
| 1861–1863 | 37 | Galusha A. Grow (Pa.) | 1995–1999 | 104–105 | Newt Gingrich (Ga.)[15] |
| 1863–1869 | 38–40 | Schuyler Colfax (Ind.) | 1999– | 106– | Dennis Hastert (Ill.) |
| 1869–1869 | 40 | Theodore M. Pomeroy (N.Y.)[5] | | | |

1. George Dent (Md.) was elected Speaker pro tempore for April 20 and May 28, 1798. 2. Resigned during second session of 13th Congress. 3. Resigned between first and second sessions of 16th Congress. 4. Resigned during first session of 23rd Congress. 5. Elected Speaker and served the day of adjournment. 6. Died between first and second sessions of 44th Congress. During first session, there were two Speakers pro tempore: Samuel S. Cox (N.Y.), appointed for Feb. 17, May 12, and June 19, 1876, and Milton Sayler (Ohio), appointed for June 4, 1876. 7. Died in 1934 after adjournment of second session of 73rd Congress. 8. Died during second session of 74th Congress. 9. Died during third session of 76th Congress. 10. Died between first and second sessions of 87th Congress. 11. Not a candidate in 1970 election. 12. Not a candidate in 1976 election. 13. Not a candidate in 1986 election. 14. Resigned during first session of 101st Congress. 15. Resigned Jan. 3, 1999, three days before the first session of the 106th Congress. Source: Congressional Directory.

# Floor Leaders of the Senate

| Democratic | Republican |
|---|---|
| Gilbert M. Hitchcock, Neb. (Min. 1919–20) | Charles Curtis, Kan. (Maj. 1925–29) |
| Oscar W. Underwood, Ala. (Min. 1920–23) | James E. Watson, Ind. (Maj. 1929–33) |
| Joseph T. Robinson, Ark. (Min. 1923–33, Maj. 1933–37) | Charles L. McNary, Ore. (Min. 1933–44) |
| Alben W. Barkley, Ky. (Maj. 1937–46, Min. 1947–48) | Wallace H. White, Jr., Maine (Min. 1944–47, Maj. 1947–48) |
| Scott W. Lucas, Ill. (Maj. 1949–50) | Kenneth S. Wherry, Neb. (Min. 1949–51) |
| Ernest W. McFarland, Ariz. (Maj. 1951–52) | Styles Bridges, N.H. (Min. 1951–52) |
| Lyndon B. Johnson, Tex. (Min. 1953–54, Maj. 1955–60) | Robert A. Taft, Ohio (Maj. 1953) |
| Mike Mansfield, Mont. (Maj. 1961–77) | William F. Knowland, Calif. (Maj. 1953–54, Min. 1955–58) |
| Robert C. Byrd, W. Va. (Maj. 1977–81, Min. 1981–86, Maj. 1987–88) | Everett M. Dirksen, Ill. (Min. 1959–69) |
| George John Mitchell, Maine (Maj. 1989–1994) | Hugh Scott, Pa. (Min. 1969–1977) |
| Thomas A. Daschle, S.D. (Min. 1995–2001, Maj. 2001–  ) | Howard H. Baker, Jr., Tenn. (Min. 1977–81, Maj. 1981–84) |
| | Robert J. Dole, Kan. (Maj. 1985–86, Min. 1987–94, Maj. 1995–96) |
| | Trent Lott, Miss. (Maj. 1996–2001, Min. 2001–  ) |

NOTE: Min. = Minority Leader; Maj. = Majority Leader. Source: United States Senate, Secretary for the Majority.

## Composition of Congress, by Political Party, 1855–2001

| Congress | Years | Senate | | | | | House | | | | |
|---|---|---|---|---|---|---|---|---|---|---|---|
| | | Total | Dems | Reps | Others | Vacant | Total | Dems | Reps | Others | Vacant |
| 34th | 1855–1857 | 62 | 42 | 15 | 5 | — | 234 | 83 | 108 | 43 | — |
| 35th | 1857–1859 | 64 | 39 | 20 | 5 | — | 237 | 131 | 92 | 14 | — |
| 36th | 1859–1861 | 66 | 38 | 26 | 2 | — | 237 | 101 | 113 | 23 | — |
| 37th | 1861–1863 | 50 | 11 | 31 | 7 | 1 | 178 | 42 | 106 | 28 | 2 |
| 38th | 1863–1865 | 51 | 12 | 39 | — | — | 183 | 80 | 103 | — | — |
| 39th | 1865–1867 | 52 | 10 | 42 | — | — | 191 | 46 | 145 | — | — |
| 40th | 1867–1869 | 53 | 11 | 42 | — | — | 193 | 49 | 143 | — | 1 |
| 41st | 1869–1871 | 74 | 11 | 61 | — | 2 | 243 | 73 | 170 | — | — |
| 42nd | 1871–1873 | 74 | 17 | 57 | — | — | 243 | 104 | 139 | — | — |
| 43rd | 1873–1875 | 74 | 19 | 54 | — | 1 | 293 | 88 | 203 | — | 2 |
| 44th | 1875–1877 | 76 | 29 | 46 | — | 1 | 293 | 181 | 107 | 3 | 2 |
| 45th | 1877–1879 | 76 | 36 | 39 | 1 | — | 293 | 156 | 137 | — | — |
| 46th | 1879–1881 | 76 | 43 | 33 | — | — | 293 | 150 | 128 | 14 | 1 |
| 47th | 1881–1883 | 76 | 37 | 37 | 2 | — | 293 | 130 | 152 | 11 | — |
| 48th | 1883–1885 | 76 | 36 | 40 | — | — | 325 | 200 | 119 | 6 | — |
| 49th | 1885–1887 | 76 | 34 | 41 | — | 1 | 325 | 182 | 140 | 2 | 1 |
| 50th | 1887–1889 | 76 | 37 | 39 | — | — | 325 | 170 | 151 | 4 | — |
| 51st | 1889–1891 | 84 | 37 | 47 | — | — | 330 | 156 | 173 | 1 | — |
| 52nd | 1891–1893 | 88 | 39 | 47 | 2 | — | 333 | 231 | 88 | 14 | — |
| 53rd | 1893–1895 | 88 | 44 | 38 | 3 | 3 | 356 | 220 | 126 | 10 | — |
| 54th | 1895–1897 | 88 | 39 | 44 | 5 | — | 357 | 104 | 246 | 7 | — |
| 55th | 1897–1899 | 90 | 34 | 46 | 10 | — | 357 | 134 | 206 | 16 | 1 |
| 56th | 1899–1901 | 90 | 26 | 53 | 11 | — | 357 | 163 | 185 | 9 | — |
| 57th | 1901–1903 | 90 | 29 | 56 | 3 | 2 | 357 | 153 | 198 | 5 | 1 |
| 58th | 1903–1905 | 90 | 32 | 58 | — | — | 386 | 178 | 207 | — | 1 |
| 59th | 1905–1907 | 90 | 32 | 58 | — | — | 386 | 136 | 250 | — | — |
| 60th | 1907–1909 | 92 | 29 | 61 | — | 2 | 386 | 164 | 222 | — | — |
| 61st | 1909–1911 | 92 | 32 | 59 | — | 1 | 391 | 172 | 219 | — | — |
| 62nd | 1911–1913 | 92 | 42 | 49 | — | 1 | 391 | 228 | 162 | 1 | — |
| 63rd | 1913–1915 | 96 | 51 | 44 | 1 | — | 435 | 290 | 127 | 18 | — |
| 64th | 1915–1917 | 96 | 56 | 39 | 1 | — | 435 | 231 | 193 | 8 | 3 |
| 65th | 1917–1919 | 96 | 53 | 42 | 1 | — | 435 | 210[1] | 216 | 9 | — |
| 66th | 1919–1921 | 96 | 47 | 48 | 1 | — | 435 | 191 | 237 | 7 | — |
| 67th | 1921–1923 | 96 | 37 | 59 | — | — | 435 | 132 | 300 | 1 | 2 |
| 68th | 1923–1925 | 96 | 43 | 51 | 2 | — | 435 | 207 | 225 | 3 | — |
| 69th | 1925–1927 | 96 | 40 | 54 | 1 | 1 | 435 | 183 | 247 | 5 | — |
| 70th | 1927–1929 | 96 | 47 | 48 | 1 | — | 435 | 195 | 237 | 3 | — |
| 71st | 1929–1931 | 96 | 39 | 56 | 1 | — | 435 | 163 | 267 | 1 | 4 |
| 72nd | 1931–1933 | 96 | 47 | 48 | 1 | — | 435 | 216[2] | 218 | 1 | — |
| 73rd | 1933–1935 | 96 | 59 | 36 | 1 | — | 435 | 313 | 117 | 5 | — |
| 74th | 1935–1937 | 96 | 69 | 25 | 2 | — | 435 | 322 | 103 | 10 | — |
| 75th | 1937–1939 | 96 | 75 | 17 | 4 | — | 435 | 333 | 89 | 13 | — |
| 76th | 1939–1941 | 96 | 69 | 23 | 4 | — | 435 | 262 | 169 | 4 | — |
| 77th | 1941–1943 | 96 | 66 | 28 | 2 | — | 435 | 267 | 162 | 6 | — |
| 78th | 1943–1945 | 96 | 57 | 38 | 1 | — | 435 | 222 | 209 | 4 | — |
| 79th | 1945–1947 | 96 | 57 | 38 | 1 | — | 435 | 243 | 190 | 2 | — |
| 80th | 1947–1949 | 96 | 45 | 51 | — | — | 435 | 188 | 246 | 1 | — |
| 81st | 1949–1951 | 96 | 54 | 42 | — | — | 435 | 263 | 171 | 1 | — |
| 82nd | 1951–1953 | 96 | 48 | 47 | 1 | — | 435 | 234 | 199 | 2 | — |
| 83rd | 1953–1955 | 96 | 46 | 48 | 2 | — | 435 | 213 | 221 | 1 | — |
| 84th | 1955–1957 | 96 | 48 | 47 | 1 | — | 435 | 232 | 203 | — | — |
| 85th | 1957–1959 | 96 | 49 | 47 | — | — | 435 | 234 | 201 | — | — |
| 86th | 1959–1961 | 98 | 64 | 34 | — | — | 436[3] | 283 | 153 | — | — |
| 87th | 1961–1963 | 100 | 64 | 36 | — | — | 437[4] | 262 | 175 | — | — |
| 88th | 1963–1965 | 100 | 67 | 33 | — | — | 435 | 258 | 176 | — | 1 |
| 89th | 1965–1967 | 100 | 68 | 32 | — | — | 435 | 295 | 140 | — | — |
| 90th | 1967–1969 | 100 | 64 | 36 | — | — | 435 | 248 | 187 | — | — |
| 91st | 1969–1971 | 100 | 58 | 42 | — | — | 435 | 243 | 192 | — | — |
| 92nd | 1971–1973 | 100 | 54 | 44 | 2 | — | 435 | 255 | 180 | — | — |
| 93rd | 1973–1975 | 100 | 56 | 42 | 2 | — | 435 | 242 | 192 | 1 | — |
| 94th | 1975–1977 | 100 | 61 | 37 | 2 | — | 435 | 291 | 144 | — | — |
| 95th | 1977–1979 | 100 | 61 | 38 | 1 | — | 435 | 292 | 143 | — | — |
| 96th | 1979–1981 | 100 | 58 | 41 | 1 | — | 435 | 277 | 158 | — | — |
| 97th | 1981–1983 | 100 | 46 | 53 | 1 | — | 435 | 242 | 192 | 1 | — |
| 98th | 1983–1985 | 100 | 46 | 54 | — | — | 435 | 269 | 166 | — | — |
| 99th | 1985–1987 | 100 | 47 | 53 | — | — | 435 | 253 | 182 | — | — |
| 100th | 1987–1989 | 100 | 55 | 45 | — | — | 435 | 258 | 177 | — | — |
| 101st | 1989–1991 | 100 | 55 | 45 | — | — | 435 | 260 | 175 | — | — |

| Congress | Years | Senate | | | | | House | | | | |
|---|---|---|---|---|---|---|---|---|---|---|---|
| | | Total | Dems | Reps | Others | Vacant | Total | Dems | Reps | Others | Vacant |
| 102nd | 1991–1993 | 100 | 56 | 44 | — | — | 435 | 267 | 167 | 1 | — |
| 103rd | 1993–1995 | 100 | 57 | 43 | — | — | 435 | 258 | 176 | 1 | — |
| 104th | 1995–1997 | 100 | 48 | 52 | — | — | 435 | 204 | 230 | 1 | — |
| 105th | 1997–1999 | 100 | 45 | 55 | — | — | 435 | 207 | 226 | 2 | — |
| 106th | 1999–2001 | 100 | 45 | 55 | — | — | 435 | 211 | 223 | 1 | — |
| 107th | 2001–2003 | 100 | 50 | 50 | — | — | 435 | 212 | 221 | 2 | — |

NOTE: All figures reflect immediate results of elections. 1. Democrats organized House with help of other parties. 2. Democrats organized House due to Republican deaths. 3. Proclamation declaring Alaska a state issued Jan 3., 1959. 4. Proclamation declaring Hawaii a state issued Aug. 21, 1959. *Source:* Office of the Clerk of the House of Representatives. Web: http://clerkweb.house.gov/histrecs/history.htm.

# Salaries of the President, Vice President, and Other U.S. Officials, 2002

## (per year)

| Position | Salary | Position | Salary |
|---|---|---|---|
| President | | Vice President | $192,600[2] |
| 1789 | $ 25,000 | Senator | 150,000 |
| 1873 | 50,000 | Representative | 150,000 |
| 1909 | 75,000 | Majority and Minority Leaders | 166,700 |
| 1949 | 100,000[1] | Speaker of the House | 192,600 |
| 1969 | 200,000[1] | Chief Justice, U.S. Supreme Court | 192,600 |
| 2001 | 400,000[1] | Assoc. Justice, U.S. Supreme Court | 184,400 |

1. Plus $50,000 non-taxable expense allowance to assist in defraying expenses relating to or resulting from the discharge of his official duties. 2. Plus $10,000 taxable expense allowance. *Source:* Office of Personnel Management. Web: www.opm.gov/.

# Congressional Apportionment, 2000

*Source:* U.S. Census Bureau

Apportionment is the process of dividing the 435 seats in the House of Representatives among the 50 states. The number of seats, or representatives, each state is entitled to is apportioned according to the new census figures that are compiled every 10 years. States with larger populations have more representatives than states with smaller populations. Each state must have at least one representative.

Once the number of seats is assigned to each state, it is up to the individual state legislatures to redraw new congressional districts. Each representative is elected by voters from a congressional district within their state.

## Who Counts?

The population figure used to calculate the apportionment of House seats is based on the total resident population of the United States, including citizens and noncitizens, plus U.S. military personnel and federal civilian employees and their dependents living overseas. It excludes the populations of the District of Columbia, Puerto Rico, and other U.S. territories that do not have voting seats in the House of Representatives. The Census 2000 apportionment population was 281,424,177.

## Congressional District Size

The number of representatives in the U.S. House of Representatives has remained constant at 435 since 1911, except for a temporary increase to 437 at the time of admission of Alaska and Hawaii as states in 1959. However, the apportionment based on the 1960 census, which took effect for the election of 1962, reverted to 435 seats.

The average size of a congressional district based on the Census 2000 apportionment population will be 646,952, more than triple the average district size of 193,167 based on the 1900 census apportionment, and about 74,486 more than the average size of 572,466 based on the 1990 census.

## Congressional Seats Gained/Lost in the 108th Congress[1]

| Seats gained | | Seats lost | |
|---|---|---|---|
| + 2 seats | +1 seat | –1 seat | –2 seats |
| Arizona (8) | California (53) | Connecticut (5) | New York (29) |
| Florida (25) | Colorado (7) | Illinois (19) | Pennsylvania (19) |
| Georgia (13) | Nevada (3) | Indiana (9) | |
| Texas (32) | North Carolina (13) | Michigan (15) | |
| | | Mississippi (4) | |
| | | Ohio (18) | |
| | | Oklahoma (5) | |
| | | Wisconsin (8) | |

NOTE: The number of representatives based on Census 2000 is given in parentheses after each state. 1. Based on Census 2000. *Source:* U.S. Census Bureau, Census 2000. Web: www.census.gov.

# How a Bill Becomes a Law

When a senator or a representative introduces a bill, he or she sends it to the clerk of his house, who gives it a number and title. This is the *first reading,* and the bill is referred to the proper committee.

The committee may decide the bill is unwise or unnecessary and *table* it, thus killing it at once. Or it may decide the bill is worthwhile and hold hearings to listen to facts and opinions presented by experts and other interested persons. After members of the committee have debated the bill and perhaps offered amendments, a vote is taken; and if the vote is favorable, the bill is sent back to the floor of the house.

The clerk reads the bill sentence by sentence to the house, and this is known as the *second reading.* Members may then debate the bill and offer amendments. In the House of Representatives, the time for debate is limited by a *cloture rule,* but there is no such restriction in the Senate for cloture, where 60 votes are required. This makes possible a *filibuster,* in which one or more opponents hold the floor to defeat the bill.

The *third reading* is by title only, and the bill is put to a vote, which may be by voice or roll call, depending on the circumstances and parliamentary rules. Members who must be absent at the time but who wish to record their vote may be paired if each negative vote has a balancing affirmative one.

The bill then goes to the other house of Congress, where it may be defeated, or passed with or without amendments. If the bill is defeated, it dies. If it is passed with amendments, a joint congressional committee must be appointed by both houses to iron out the differences.

After its final passage by both houses, the bill is sent to the president. If he approves, he signs it, and the bill becomes a law. However, if he disapproves, he *vetoes* the bill by refusing to sign it and sending it back to the house of origin with his reasons for the veto. The objections are read and debated, and a roll-call vote is taken. If the bill receives less than a two-thirds vote, it is defeated and goes no further. But if it receives a two-thirds vote or greater, it is sent to the other house for a vote. If that house also passes it by a two-thirds vote, the president's veto is *overridden,* and the bill becomes a law.

Should the president desire neither to sign nor to veto the bill, he may retain it for ten days, Sundays excepted, after which time it automatically becomes a law without signature. However, if Congress has adjourned within those ten days, the bill is automatically killed, that process of indirect rejection being known as a *pocket veto.*

## Presidential Vetoes, 1789–1999

| President | Coincident Congresses | Regular vetoes | Pocket vetoes | Total vetoes | Vetoes overridden |
|---|---|---|---|---|---|
| Washington | 1st–4th | 2 | — | 2 | — |
| Adams | 5th–6th | — | — | — | — |
| Jefferson | 7th–10th | — | — | — | — |
| Madison | 11th–14th | 5 | 2 | 7 | — |
| Monroe | 15th–18th | 1 | — | 1 | — |
| J. Q. Adams | 19th–20th | — | — | — | — |
| Jackson | 21st–24th | 5 | 7 | 12 | — |
| Van Buren | 25th–26th | — | 1 | 1 | — |
| W. H. Harrison | 27th | — | — | — | — |
| Tyler | 27th–28th | 6 | 4 | 10 | 1 |
| Polk | 29th–30th | 2 | 1 | 3 | — |
| Taylor | 31st | — | — | — | — |
| Fillmore | 31st–32nd | — | — | — | — |
| Pierce | 33rd–34th | 9 | — | 9 | 5 |
| Buchanan | 35th–36th | 4 | 3 | 7 | — |
| Lincoln | 37th–39th | 2 | 5 | 7 | — |
| A. Johnson | 39th–40th | 21 | 8 | 29 | 15 |
| Grant | 41st–44th | 45 | 48 | 93 | 4 |
| Hayes | 45th–46th | 12 | 1 | 13 | 1 |
| Arthur | 47th–48th | 4 | 8 | 12 | 1 |
| Cleveland | 49th–50th | 304 | 110 | 414 | 2 |
| B. Harrison | 51st–52nd | 19 | 25 | 44 | 1 |
| Cleveland | 53rd–54th | 42 | 128 | 170 | 5 |
| McKinley | 55th–57th | 6 | 36 | 42 | — |
| T. Roosevelt | 57th–60th | 42 | 40 | 82 | 1 |
| Taft | 61st–62nd | 30 | 9 | 39 | 1 |
| Wilson | 63rd–66th | 33 | 11 | 44 | 6 |
| Harding | 67th | 5 | 1 | 6 | — |
| Coolidge | 68th–70th | 20 | 30 | 50 | 4 |
| Hoover | 71st–72nd | 21 | 16 | 37 | 3 |
| F. D. Roosevelt | 73rd–79th | 372 | 263 | 635 | 9 |
| Truman | 79th–82nd | 180 | 70 | 250 | 12 |
| Eisenhower | 83rd–86th | 73 | 108 | 181 | 2 |
| Kennedy | 87th–88th | 12 | 9 | 21 | — |
| L. B. Johnson | 88th–90th | 16 | 14 | 30 | — |

| President | Coincident Congresses | Regular vetoes | Pocket vetoes | Total vetoes | Vetoes overridden |
|---|---|---|---|---|---|
| Nixon | 91st–93rd | 26 | 17 | 43 | 7 |
| Ford | 93rd–94th | 48 | 18 | 66 | 12 |
| Carter | 95th–96th | 13 | 18 | 31 | 2 |
| Reagan | 97th–100th | 39 | 39 | 78 | 9 |
| G. H. W. Bush[1] | 101st–102nd | 29 | 15 | 44 | 1 |
| Clinton | 103rd–106th | 37 | 1 | 38 | 2 |
| Total | | 1,484 | 1,066 | 2,551 | 106 |

1. President Bush attempted to pocket veto two bills during intrasession recess periods. Congress considered the two bills enacted into law because of the president's failure to return the legislation. The bills are not counted as pocket vetoes in this table. *Source:* Office of the Clerk of the House. Web: http://clerk.house.gov.

## Order of Presidential Succession

According to the Presidential Succession Act of 1792, the Senate president pro tempore[1] was next in line after the vice president to succeed to the presidency, followed by the Speaker of the House.

In 1886, however, Congress changed the order of presidential succession, replacing the president pro tempore and the Speaker with the cabinet officers. Proponents of this change argued that the congressional leaders lacked executive experience, and none had served as president, while six former secretaries of state had later been elected to that office.

The Presidential Succession Act of 1947, signed by President Harry Truman, changed the order again to what it is today. The cabinet members are ordered in the line of succession according to the date their offices were established.

Prior to the ratification of the 25th Amendment in 1967, there was no provision for filling a vacancy in the vice presidency. When a president died in office, the vice president succeeded him, and the vice presidency then remained vacant. The first vice president to take office under the new procedure was Gerald Ford, who was nominated by Nixon on Oct. 12, 1973, and confirmed by Congress the following Dec. 6.

1. The Vice President
2. Speaker of the House
3. President pro tempore of the Senate[1]
4. Secretary of State
5. Secretary of the Treasury
6. Secretary of Defense
7. Attorney General
8. Secretary of the Interior
9. Secretary of Agriculture
10. Secretary of Commerce
11. Secretary of Labor
12. Secretary of Health and Human Services
13. Secretary of Housing and Urban Development
14. Secretary of Transportation
15. Secretary of Energy
16. Secretary of Education
17. Secretary of Veterans Affairs

NOTE: An official cannot succeed to the Presidency unless that person meets the Constitutional requirements.
1. The president pro tempore presides over the Senate when the vice president is absent. By tradition the position is held by the senior member of the majority party.

## Executive Departments and Agencies

*Source: United States Government Manual, 2002–2003*

Unless otherwise indicated, addresses shown are in Washington, DC. ZIP codes are in parentheses.

### White House Offices and Agencies

**Office of Administration**
*Eisenhower Executive Office Bldg., 725 17th St., N.W. (20503)*
  **Established:** Dec. 12, 1977
  **Director:** Phillip D. Larsen
**Office of National Drug Control Policy**
*Executive Office of the President (20503)*
  **Established:** Jan. 29, 1989
  **Director:** John P. Walters
**Council of Economic Advisers (CEA)**
*Old Executive Office Bldg. (20502)*
  **Members:** 3
  **Established:** Feb. 20, 1946
  **Chair:** R. Glenn Hubbard
**Council on Environmental Quality**
*722 Jackson Place, N.W. (20503)*
  **Established:** 1969
  **Chair:** James Connaughton
**Office of Management and Budget**
*Executive Office Bldg. (20503)*
  **Established:** July 1, 1939
  **Director:** Mitchell Daniels, Jr.

**Office of Science and Technology Policy**
*Eisenhower Executive Office Building (20502)*
  **Established:** May 11, 1976
  **Director:** John H. Marburger III
**National Security Council (NSC)**
*Eisenhower Executive Office Bldg. (20504)*
  **Members:** 4
  **Established:** July 26, 1947
  **Chair:** The President
  **National Security Adviser:** Condoleezza Rice
  **Other members:** Vice President; Secretary of State; Secretary of Defense
**Office of the United States Trade Representative**
*600 17th St., N.W. (20508)*
  **Established:** Jan. 15, 1963
  **Trade Representative:** Robert Zoellick

### Executive Departments

**Department of Agriculture**
*1400 Independence Ave., S.W. (20250)*
  **Established:** May 15, 1862. Administered by Commissioner of Agriculture until 1889, when it was made executive department.
  **Secretary:** Ann Veneman
**Department of Commerce**
*1401 Constitution Ave., N.W. (20230)*

**Established:** Department of Commerce and Labor was created Feb. 14, 1903. On March 4, 1913, all labor activities were transferred out of Department of Commerce and Labor and it was renamed Department of Commerce.
**Secretary:** Donald L. Evans

**Department of Defense**
*Office of the Secretary, The Pentagon (20301-1155)*
**Established:** July 26, 1947, as National Military Establishment; name changed to Department of Defense on Aug. 10, 1949. Subordinate to Secretary of Defense are Secretaries of Army, Navy, Air Force.
**Secretary:** Donald H. Rumsfeld
**Deputy Secretary:** Paul D. Wolfowitz
**Secretary of Army:** Thomas E. White
**Secretary of Navy:** Gordon R. England
**Secretary of Air Force:** James G. Roche
**Commandant of Marine Corps:** Gen. James L. Jones
**Joint Chiefs of Staff:** Gen. Richard B. Myers, Air Force, Chairman; Gen. Peter Pace, Marine Corps, Vice Chairman; Gen. Eric K. Shinseki, Army; Adm. Vernon E. Clark, Navy; Gen. John P. Jumper, Air Force; Gen. James L. Jones, Marine Corps.

**Department of Education**
*400 Maryland Ave., S.W. (20202)*
**Established:** Oct. 17, 1979
**Secretary:** Roderick R. Paige

**Department of Energy**
*1000 Independence Ave., S.W. (20585)*
**Established:** Oct. 1, 1977
**Secretary:** Spencer Abraham

**Department of Health and Human Services**
*200 Independence Ave., S.W. (20201)*
**Established:** Department of Health, Education, and Welfare was created April 11, 1953, replacing Federal Security Agency created in 1939. On Oct. 17, 1979, the Department of Education became a separate department.
**Secretary:** Tommy G. Thompson
**Surgeon General:** Dr. Richard Carmona

**Department of Housing and Urban Development**
*451 7th St., S.W. (20410)*
**Established:** Nov. 9, 1965, replacing Housing and Home Finance Agency created in 1947
**Secretary:** Melquiades R. Martinez

**Department of the Interior**
*1849 C St., N.W. (20240)*
**Established:** March 3, 1849
**Secretary:** Gale A. Norton

**Department of Justice**
*950 Pennsylvania Ave., N.W. (20530)*
**Established:** Office of Attorney General was created Sept. 24, 1789. Although one of the original cabinet members, the attorney general was not an executive department head until June 22, 1870, when the Department of Justice was established.
**Attorney General:** John Ashcroft
**Solicitor General:** Theodore B. Olson
**Director of FBI:** Robert S. Mueller, III

**Department of Labor**
*200 Constitution Ave., N.W. (20210)*
**Established:** Bureau of Labor was created in 1884 under Department of the Interior; later became independent department without executive rank. Returned to bureau status in Department of Commerce and Labor, but on March 4, 1913, became independent executive department under its present name.
**Secretary:** Elaine L. Chao

**Department of State**
*2201 C St., N.W. (20520)*
**Established:** 1781 as Department of Foreign Affairs; reconstituted, 1789, following adoption of Constitution; name changed to Department of State Sept. 15, 1789.
**Secretary:** Colin L. Powell
**UN Ambassador:** John D. Negroponte
**Deputy UN Ambassador:** James Cunningham

**Department of Transportation**
*400 7th St., S.W. (20590)*
**Established:** Oct. 15, 1966, as result of Department of Transportation Act, which became effective April 1, 1967.
**Secretary:** Norman Y. Mineta

**Department of the Treasury**
*1500 Pennsylvania Ave., N.W. (20220)*
**Established:** Sept. 2, 1789
**Secretary:** Paul H. O'Neill
**Treasurer of the U.S.:** Rosario Marin

**Department of Veterans' Affairs**
*810 Vermont Ave., N.W. (20420)*
**Established:** March 15, 1989, replacing Veterans Administration created in 1930
**Secretary:** Anthony J. Principi

## Major Independent Agencies

**Central Intelligence Agency (CIA)**
*Washington, D.C. (20505)*
**Established:** 1947
**Director of Central Intelligence:** George J. Tenet

**U.S. Commission on Civil Rights**
*624 9th St., N.W. (20425)*
**Established:** 1957
**Chair:** Mary Frances Berry

**Consumer Product Safety Commission**
*East West Towers, 4330 East West Highway, Bethesda, Md. 20814*
**Established:** Oct. 27, 1972
**Chair:** Harold D. Stratton

**Corporation for National and Community Service**
*1201 New York Ave., N.W. (20525)*
**Established:** Sept. 1993
**CEO:** Leslie Lenkowsky

**Environmental Protection Agency (EPA)**
*1200 Pennsylvania Ave., N.W. (20460)*
**Established:** Dec. 2, 1970
**Administrator:** Christine Todd Whitman

**Equal Employment Opportunity Commission (EEOC)**
*1801 L St., N.W. (20507)*
**Members:** 5
**Established:** July 2, 1965
**Chair:** Cari M. Dominguez

**Farm Credit Administration (FCA)**
*1501 Farm Credit Dr., McLean, Va. 22102-5090*
**Members:** 13
**Established:** March 27, 1933
**Chair:** Michael M. Reyna

**Federal Communications Commission (FCC)**
*445 Twelfth Street, S.W. (20554)*
**Established:** 1934
**Chair:** Michael Powell

**Federal Deposit Insurance Corporation (FDIC)**
*550 17th St., N.W. (20429)*
**Established:** June 16, 1933
**Chair:** Donald E. Powell

**Federal Election Commission (FEC)**
*999 E St., N.W. (20463)*
**Members:** 6
**Established:** 1975
**Chair:** David M. Mason

**Federal Maritime Commission**
*800 North Capitol St., N.W. (20573-0001)*
**Members:** 5
**Established:** Aug. 12, 1961
**Chair:** Steven R. Blust

**Federal Mediation and Conciliation Service (FMCS)**
*2100 K St., N.W. (20427)*
**Established:** 1947
**Director:** Peter J. Hurtgen

**Federal Reserve System (FRS), Board of Governors of**
*20th St. & Constitution Ave., N.W. (20551)*
**Members:** 7
**Established:** Dec. 23, 1913

**Chair:** Alan Greenspan
**Federal Trade Commission (FTC)**
*600 Pennsylvania Ave., N.W. (20580)*
 **Members:** 5
 **Established:** Sept. 26, 1914
 **Chair:** Timothy J. Muris
**General Services Administration (GSA)**
*1800 F St., N.W. (20405)*
 **Established:** July 1, 1949
 **Administrator:** Stephen A. Perry
**U.S. International Trade Commission**
*500 E St., S.W. (20436)*
 **Members:** 6
 **Established:** Sept. 8, 1916
 **Chair:** Deanna Tanner Okun
**National Aeronautics and Space Administration (NASA)**
*300 E St., S.W. (20546)*
 **Established:** 1958
 **Administrator:** Sean O'Keefe
**National Archives and Records Administration (NARA)**
*8601 Adelphi Road, College Park, Md. 20740-6001*
 **Established:** Oct. 19, 1984. NARA is the successor agency to the National Archives Establishment, which was created in 1934 and later incorporated into the General Services Administration as the National Archives and Records Service in 1949.
 **Archivist of the U.S.:** John W. Carlin
**National Foundation on the Arts and the Humanities**
*1100 Pennsylvania Ave., N.W. (20506-0001)*
 **Established:** 1965
 **Chairs:** National Endowment for the Arts, Chair, Eileen Mason, Acting; National Endowment for the Humanities, Chair, Bruce Cole
**National Labor Relations Board (NLRB)**
*1099 14th St., N.W. (20570)*
 **Members:** 5
 **Established:** July 5, 1935
 **Chair:** Vacant
**National Mediation Board**
*Suite 250 East, 1301 K St., N.W. (20572)*
 **Established:** June 21, 1934
 **Chair:** Francis J. Duggan
**National Science Foundation (NSF)**
*4201 Wilson Blvd., Arlington, Va. 22230*
 **Established:** 1950
 **Director:** Rita R. Colwell
**National Transportation Safety Board**
*490 L'Enfant Plaza, S.W. (20594)*
 **Members:** 5
 **Established:** April 1, 1967, as an independent agency supported by the Dept. of Transportation. Ties with Dept. of Transportation officially ended in 1975.
 **Chair:** Carol J. Carmody, Acting
**Nuclear Regulatory Commission (NRC)**
*Washington, D.C. 20555*
 **Members:** 5
 **Established:** Jan. 19, 1975
 **Chair:** Richard A. Meserve
**Office of Personnel Management (OPM)**
*1900 E St., N.W. (20415-0001)*
 **Established:** Jan. 1, 1979
 **Director:** Kay Coles James
**U.S. Postal Service**
*475 L'Enfant Plaza West, S.W. (20260-0010)*
 **Established:** In 1775 with the appointment of Benjamin Franklin as the first postmaster general under the Continental Congress. In 1970 became independent agency headed by 11-member board of governors.
 **Postmaster General:** John E. Potter
**Securities and Exchange Commission (SEC)**
*450 5th St., N.W. (20549)*
 **Members:** 5
 **Established:** July 2, 1934
 **Chair:** Harvey L. Pitt

**Selective Service System (SSS)**
*National Headquarters, Arlington, Va., 22209-2425*
 **Established:** Sept. 16, 1940
 **Director:** Alfred Rascon
**Small Business Administration (SBA)**
*409 3rd St., S.W. (20416)*
 **Established:** July 30, 1953
 **Administrator:** Hector V. Barreto
**Tennessee Valley Authority (TVA)**
*400 West Summit Hill Drive, Knoxville, Tenn. 37902. Washington office: One Massachusetts Ave., N.W. (20444-0001)*
 **Members of Board of Directors:** 3
 **Established:** May 18, 1933
 **Chairman:** Glenn L. McCullough, Jr.

## Other Independent Agencies

**American Battle Monuments Commission**—Courthouse Plaza II, Suite 500, 2300 Clarendon Blvd., Arlington, Va. (22201)
**Appalachian Regional Commission**—1666 Connecticut Ave., N.W., Suite 700 (20235)
**Commission of Fine Arts**—441 F St., N.W., Ste. 312 (20001)
**Commodity Futures Trading Commission**—1155 21st St., N.W. (20581)
**Export-Import Bank of the United States**—811 Vermont Ave., N.W. (20571)
**Federal Emergency Management Agency**—500 C St., S.W. (20472)
**Federal Housing Finance Board**—1777 F St., N.W. (20006)
**Federal Labor Relations Authority**—607 14th St., N.W. (20424-0001)
**Inter-American Foundation**—901 N. Stuart St., Arlington, Va. 22203
**National Commission on Libraries and Information Science**—1110 Vermont Ave., N.W., Ste. 820 (20005-3552)
**National Credit Union Administration**—1775 Duke St., Alexandria, Va. 22314-3428
**Occupational Safety and Health Review Commission**—1120 20th St., N.W. (20036-3419)
**U.S. Parole Commission**—Dept. of Justice, 5550 Friendship Blvd., Ste. 420, Chevy Chase, Md. 20815
**Peace Corps**—1111 20th St., N.W. (20526)
**Pension Benefit Guaranty Corporation**—1200 K St., N.W. (20005-4026)
**Postal Rate Commission**—1333 H St., N.W. (20268-0001)
**President's Council on Physical Fitness and Sports**—Dept. W, 200 Independence Ave., S.W., Room 738-H (20201-0004)
**Railroad Retirement Board (RRB)**—844 N. Rush St., Ninth Floor, Chicago, Ill. 60611-2092; Office of Legislative Affairs: 1310 G St., N.W, Ste. 500 (20005-3004).

### Legislative Department

**Architect of the Capitol**—U.S. Capitol Building (20515)
**General Accounting Office (GAO)**—441 G St., N.W. (20548)
**Government Printing Office (GPO)**—732 North Capitol St., N.W. (20401)
**Library of Congress**—101 Independence Ave., S.E. (20540)
**United States Botanic Garden**—Office of Executive Director, 245 1st St., S.W. (20024)

### Quasi-Official Agencies

**American National Red Cross**—430 17th St., N.W. (20006)
**Legal Services Corporation**—750 1st St., N.E. (20002-4250)
**National Academy of Sciences, National Academy of Engineering, National Research Council, Institute of Medicine**—2101 Constitution Ave., N.W. (20418)
**National Railroad Passenger Corporation (Amtrak)**—60 Massachusetts Ave., N.E. (20002)
**Smithsonian Institution**—1000 Jefferson Dr., S.W. (20560)

# Government Officials
## Cabinet Members with Dates of Appointment

Although the Constitution made no provision for a president's advisory group, the heads of the three executive departments (State, Treasury, and War) and the attorney general were organized by Washington into such a group; and by about 1793, the name "cabinet" was applied to it. With the exception of the attorney general up to 1870 and the postmaster general from 1829 to 1872, cabinet members have been heads of executive departments.

Cabinet members are appointed by the president, subject to the confirmation of the Senate; and as their terms are not fixed, they may be replaced at any time by the president. At a change in administration, it is customary for cabinet members to resign, but they remain in office until successors are appointed.

The table of cabinet members lists only those members who actually served after being duly commissioned. The dates shown are those of appointment. "Cont." indicates that the term continued from the previous administration for a substantial amount of time.

### Washington

| | |
|---|---|
| Secretary of State | Thomas Jefferson, 1789 |
| | Edmund Randolph, 1794 |
| | Timothy Pickering, 1795 |
| Secretary of the Treasury | Alexander Hamilton, 1789 |
| | Oliver Wolcott, Jr., 1795 |
| Secretary of War | Henry Knox, 1789 |
| | Timothy Pickering, 1795 |
| | James McHenry, 1796 |
| Attorney General | Edmund Randolph, 1789 |
| | William Bradford, 1794 |
| | Charles Lee, 1795 |

### J. Adams

| | |
|---|---|
| Secretary of State | Timothy Pickering (Cont.) |
| | John Marshall, 1800 |
| Secretary of the Treasury | Oliver Wolcott, Jr. (Cont.) |
| | Samuel Dexter, 1801 |
| Secretary of War | James McHenry (Cont.) |
| | Samuel Dexter, 1800 |
| Attorney General | Charles Lee (Cont.) |
| Secretary of the Navy | Benjamin Stoddert, 1798 |

### Jefferson

| | |
|---|---|
| Secretary of State | James Madison, 1801 |
| Secretary of the Treasury | Samuel Dexter (Cont.) |
| | Albert Gallatin, 1801 |
| Secretary of War | Henry Dearborn, 1801 |
| Attorney General | Levi Lincoln, 1801 |
| | Robert Smith, 1805 |
| | John Breckinridge, 1805 |
| | Caesar A. Rodney, 1807 |
| Secretary of the Navy | Benjamin Stoddert (Cont.) |
| | Robert Smith, 1801 |

### Madison

| | |
|---|---|
| Secretary of State | Robert Smith, 1809 |
| | James Monroe, 1811 |
| Secretary of the Treasury | Albert Gallatin (Cont.) |
| | George W. Campbell, 1814 |
| | Alexander J. Dallas, 1814 |
| | William H. Crawford, 1816 |
| Secretary of War | William Eustis, 1809 |
| | John Armstrong, 1813 |
| | James Monroe, 1814 |
| | William H. Crawford, 1815 |
| Attorney General | Caesar A. Rodney (Cont.) |
| | William Pinckney, 1811 |
| | Richard Rush, 1814 |
| Secretary of the Navy | Paul Hamilton, 1809 |
| | William Jones, 1813 |
| | B. W. Crowninshield, 1814 |

### Monroe

| | |
|---|---|
| Secretary of State | John Quincy Adams, 1817 |
| Secretary of the Treasury | William H. Crawford (Cont.) |
| Secretary of War | John C. Calhoun, 1817 |
| Attorney General | Richard Rush (Cont.) |
| | William Wirt, 1817 |

| | |
|---|---|
| Secretary of the Navy | B. W. Crowninshield (Cont.) |
| | Smith Thompson, 1818 |
| | Samuel L. Southard, 1823 |

### J. Q. Adams

| | |
|---|---|
| Secretary of State | Henry Clay, 1825 |
| Secretary of the Treasury | Richard Rush, 1825 |
| Secretary of War | James Barbour, 1825 |
| | Peter B. Porter, 1828 |
| Attorney General | William Wirt (Cont.) |
| Secretary of the Navy | Samuel L. Southard (Cont.) |

### Jackson

| | |
|---|---|
| Secretary of State | Martin Van Buren, 1829 |
| | Edward Livingston, 1831 |
| | Louis McLane, 1833 |
| | John Forsyth, 1834 |
| Secretary of the Treasury | Samuel D. Ingham, 1829 |
| | Louis McLane, 1831 |
| | William J. Duane, 1833 |
| | Roger B. Taney[1], 1833 |
| | Levi Woodbury, 1834 |
| Secretary of War | John H. Eaton, 1829 |
| | Lewis Cass, 1831 |
| Attorney General | John M. Berrien, 1829 |
| | Roger B. Taney, 1831 |
| | Benjamin F. Butler, 1833 |
| Postmaster General[2] | William T. Barry, 1829 |
| | Amos Kendall, 1835 |
| Secretary of the Navy | John Branch, 1829 |
| | Levi Woodbury, 1831 |
| | Mahlon Dickerson, 1834 |

1. Not confirmed by the Senate. 2. The postmaster general did not become a cabinet member until 1829. Earlier postmasters general were: Samuel Osgood (1789), Timothy Pickering (1791), Joseph Habersham (1795), Gideon Granger (1801), Return J. Meigs, Jr. (1814), and John McLean (1823).

### Van Buren

| | |
|---|---|
| Secretary of State | John Forsyth (Cont.) |
| Secretary of the Treasury | Levi Woodbury (Cont.) |
| Secretary of War | Joel R. Poinsett, 1837 |
| Attorney General | Benjamin F. Butler (Cont.) |
| | Felix Grundy, 1838 |
| | Henry D. Gilpin, 1840 |
| Postmaster General | Amos Kendall (Cont.) |
| | John M. Niles, 1840 |
| Secretary of the Navy | Mahlon Dickerson (Cont.) |
| | James K. Paulding, 1838 |

### W. H. Harrison

| | |
|---|---|
| Secretary of State | Daniel Webster, 1841 |
| Secretary of the Treasury | Thomas Ewing, 1841 |
| Secretary of War | John Bell, 1841 |
| Attorney General | John J. Crittenden, 1841 |
| Postmaster General | Francis Granger, 1841 |
| Secretary of the Navy | George E. Badger, 1841 |

## Tyler

| | |
|---|---|
| *Secretary of State* | Daniel Webster (Cont.) |
| | Abel P. Upshur, 1843 |
| | John C. Calhoun, 1844 |
| *Secretary of the Treasury* | Thomas Ewing (Cont.) |
| | Walter Forward, 1841 |
| | John C. Spencer[1], 1843 |
| | George M. Bibb, 1844 |
| *Secretary of War* | John Bell (Cont.) |
| | John C. Spencer, 1841 |
| | James M. Porter[1], 1843 |
| | William Wilkins, 1844 |
| *Attorney General* | John J. Crittenden (Cont.) |
| | Hugh S. Legaré, 1841 |
| | John Nelson, 1843 |
| *Postmaster General* | Francis Granger (Cont.) |
| | Charles A. Wickliffe, 1841 |
| *Secretary of the Navy* | George E. Badger (Cont.) |
| | Abel P. Upshur, 1841 |
| | David Henshaw[1], 1843 |
| | Thomas W. Gilmer, 1844 |
| | John Y. Mason, 1844 |

1. Not confirmed by the Senate.

## Polk

| | |
|---|---|
| *Secretary of State* | James Buchanan, 1845 |
| *Secretary of the Treasury* | Robert J. Walker, 1845 |
| *Secretary of War* | William L. Marcy, 1845 |
| *Attorney General* | John Y. Mason, 1845 |
| | Nathan Clifford, 1846 |
| | Isaac Toucey, 1848 |
| *Postmaster General* | Cave Johnson, 1845 |
| *Secretary of the Navy* | George Bancroft, 1845 |
| | John Y. Mason, 1846 |

## Taylor

| | |
|---|---|
| *Secretary of State* | John M. Clayton, 1849 |
| *Secretary of the Treasury* | William M. Meredith, 1849 |
| *Secretary of War* | George W. Crawford, 1849 |
| *Attorney General* | Reverdy Johnson, 1849 |
| *Postmaster General* | Jacob Collamer, 1849 |
| *Secretary of the Navy* | William B. Preston, 1849 |
| *Secretary of the Interior* | Thomas Ewing, 1849 |

## Fillmore

| | |
|---|---|
| *Secretary of State* | Daniel Webster, 1850 |
| | Edward Everett, 1852 |
| *Secretary of the Treasury* | Thomas Corwin, 1850 |
| *Secretary of War* | Charles M. Conrad, 1850 |
| *Attorney General* | John J. Crittenden, 1850 |
| *Postmaster General* | Nathan K. Hall, 1850 |
| | Samuel D. Hubbard, 1852 |
| *Secretary of the Navy* | William A. Graham, 1850 |
| | John P. Kennedy, 1852 |
| *Secretary of the Interior* | Thos. M. T. McKennan, 1850 |
| | Alex. H. H. Stuart, 1850 |

## Pierce

| | |
|---|---|
| *Secretary of State* | William L. Marcy, 1853 |
| *Secretary of the Treasury* | James Guthrie, 1853 |
| *Secretary of War* | Jefferson Davis, 1853 |
| *Attorney General* | Caleb Cushing, 1853 |
| *Postmaster General* | James Campbell, 1853 |
| *Secretary of the Navy* | James C. Dobbin, 1853 |
| *Secretary of the Interior* | Robert McClelland, 1853 |

## Buchanan

| | |
|---|---|
| *Secretary of State* | Lewis Cass, 1857 |
| | Jeremiah S. Black, 1860 |
| *Secretary of the Treasury* | Howell Cobb, 1857 |
| | Philip F. Thomas, 1860 |
| | John A. Dix, 1861 |
| *Secretary of War* | John B. Floyd, 1857 |
| | Joseph Holt, 1861 |
| *Attorney General* | Jeremiah S. Black, 1857 |
| | Edwin M. Stanton, 1860 |
| *Postmaster General* | Aaron V. Brown, 1857 |
| | Joseph Holt, 1859 |
| | Horatio King, 1861 |
| *Secretary of the Navy* | Isaac Toucey, 1857 |
| *Secretary of the Interior* | Jacob Thompson, 1857 |

## Lincoln

| | |
|---|---|
| *Secretary of State* | William H. Seward, 1861 |
| *Secretary of the Treasury* | Salmon P. Chase, 1861 |
| | William P. Fessenden, 1864 |
| | Hugh McCulloch, 1865 |
| *Secretary of War* | Simon Cameron, 1861 |
| | Edwin M. Stanton, 1862 |
| *Attorney General* | Edward Bates, 1861 |
| | James Speed, 1864 |
| *Postmaster General* | Montgomery Blair, 1861 |
| | William Dennison, 1864 |
| *Secretary of the Navy* | Gideon Welles, 1861 |
| *Secretary of the Interior* | Caleb B. Smith, 1861 |
| | John P. Usher, 1863 |

## A. Johnson

| | |
|---|---|
| *Secretary of State* | William H. Seward (Cont.) |
| *Secretary of the Treasury* | Hugh McCulloch (Cont.) |
| *Secretary of War* | Edwin M. Stanton (Cont.) |
| | John M. Schofield, 1868 |
| *Attorney General* | James Speed (Cont.) |
| | Henry Stanbery, 1866 |
| | William M. Evarts, 1868 |
| *Postmaster General* | William Dennison (Cont.) |
| | Alexander W. Randall, 1866 |
| *Secretary of the Navy* | Gideon Welles (Cont.) |
| *Secretary of the Interior* | John P. Usher (Cont.) |
| | James Harlan, 1865 |
| | Orville H. Browning, 1866 |

## Grant

| | |
|---|---|
| *Secretary of State* | Elihu B. Washburne, 1869 |
| | Hamilton Fish, 1869 |
| *Secretary of the Treasury* | George S. Boutwell, 1869 |
| | William A. Richardson, 1873 |
| | Benjamin H. Bristow, 1874 |
| | Lot M. Morrill, 1876 |
| *Secretary of War* | John A. Rawlins, 1869 |
| | William W. Belknap, 1869 |
| | Alphonso Taft, 1876 |
| | James D. Cameron, 1876 |
| *Attorney General* | Ebenezer R. Hoar, 1869 |
| | Amos T. Akerman, 1870 |
| | George H. Williams, 1871 |
| | Edwards Pierrepont, 1875 |
| | Alphonso Taft, 1876 |
| *Postmaster General* | John A. J. Creswell, 1869 |
| | Marshall Jewell, 1874 |
| | James N. Tyner, 1876 |
| *Secretary of the Navy* | Adolph E. Borie, 1869 |
| | George M. Robeson, 1869 |
| *Secretary of the Interior* | Jacob D. Cox, 1869 |
| | Columbus Delano, 1870 |
| | Zachariah Chandler, 1875 |

## Hayes

| | |
|---|---|
| *Secretary of State* | William M. Evarts, 1877 |
| *Secretary of the Treasury* | John Sherman, 1877 |
| *Secretary of War* | George W. McCrary, 1877 |
| | Alexander Ramsey, 1879 |
| *Attorney General* | Charles Devens, 1877 |
| *Postmaster General* | David M. Key, 1877 |
| | Horace Maynard, 1880 |
| | Richard W. Thompson, 1877 |
| | Nathan Goff, Jr., 1881 |
| *Secretary of the Interior* | Carl Schurz, 1877 |

## Garfield

| | |
|---|---|
| Secretary of State | James G. Blaine, 1881 |
| Secretary of the Treasury | William Windom, 1881 |
| Secretary of War | Robert T. Lincoln, 1881 |
| Attorney General | Wayne MacVeagh, 1881 |
| Postmaster General | Thomas L. James, 1881 |
| Secretary of the Navy | William H. Hunt, 1881 |
| Secretary of the Interior | Samuel J. Kirkwood, 1881 |

## Arthur

| | |
|---|---|
| Secretary of State | James G. Blaine (Cont.) |
| | F. T. Frelinghuysen, 1881 |
| Secretary of the Treasury | William Windom (Cont.) |
| | Charles J. Folger, 1881 |
| | Walter Q. Gresham, 1884 |
| | Hugh McCulloch, 1884 |
| Secretary of War | Robert T. Lincoln (Cont.) |
| Attorney General | Wayne MacVeagh (Cont.) |
| | Benjamin H. Brewster, 1881 |
| Postmaster General | Thomas L. James (Cont.) |
| | Timothy O. Howe, 1881 |
| | Walter Q. Gresham, 1883 |
| | Frank Hatton, 1884 |
| Secretary of the Navy | William H. Hunt (Cont.) |
| | William E. Chandler, 1882 |
| Secretary of the Interior | Samuel J. Kirkwood (Cont.) |
| | Henry M. Teller, 1882 |

## Cleveland

| | |
|---|---|
| Secretary of State | Thomas F. Bayard, 1885 |
| Secretary of the Treasury | Daniel Manning, 1885 |
| | Charles S. Fairchild, 1887 |
| Secretary of War | William C. Endicott, 1885 |
| Attorney General | Augustus H. Garland, 1885 |
| Postmaster General | William F. Vilas, 1885 |
| | Don M. Dickinson, 1888 |
| Secretary of the Navy | William C. Whitney, 1885 |
| Secretary of the Interior | Lucius Q. C. Lamar, 1885 |
| | William F. Vilas, 1888 |
| Secretary of Agriculture | Norman J. Colman, 1889 |

## B. Harrison

| | |
|---|---|
| Secretary of State | James G. Blaine, 1889 |
| | John W. Foster, 1892 |
| Secretary of the Treasury | William Windom, 1889 |
| | Charles Foster, 1891 |
| Secretary of War | Redfield Proctor, 1889 |
| | Stephen B. Elkins, 1891 |
| Attorney General | William H. H. Miller, 1889 |
| Postmaster General | John Wanamaker, 1889 |
| Secretary of the Navy | Benjamin F. Tracy, 1889 |
| Secretary of the Interior | John W. Noble, 1889 |
| Secretary of Agriculture | Jeremiah M. Rusk, 1889 |

## Cleveland

| | |
|---|---|
| Secretary of State | Walter Q. Gresham, 1893 |
| | Richard Olney, 1895 |
| Secretary of the Treasury | John G. Carlisle, 1893 |
| Secretary of War | Richard Olney, 1893 |
| | Judson Harmon, 1895 |
| Postmaster General | Wilson S. Bissell, 1893 |
| | William L. Wilson, 1895 |
| Secretary of the Navy | Hilary A. Herbert, 1893 |
| Secretary of the Interior | Hoke Smith, 1893 |
| | David R. Francis, 1896 |
| Secretary of Agriculture | Julius Sterling Morton, 1893 |

## McKinley

| | |
|---|---|
| Secretary of State | John Sherman, 1897 |
| | William R. Day, 1898 |
| | John Hay, 1898 |
| Secretary of the Treasury | Lyman J. Gage, 1897 |
| Secretary of War | Russell A. Alger, 1897 |
| | Elihu Root, 1899 |
| Attorney General | Joseph McKenna, 1897 |
| | John W. Griggs, 1898 |
| | Philander C. Knox, 1901 |
| Postmaster General | James A. Gary, 1897 |
| | Charles E. Smith, 1898 |
| Secretary of the Navy | John D. Long, 1897 |
| Secretary of the Interior | Cornelius N. Bliss, 1897 |
| | Ethan A. Hitchcock, 1898 |
| Secretary of Agriculture | James Wilson, 1897 |

## T. Roosevelt

| | |
|---|---|
| Secretary of State | John Hay (Cont.) |
| | Elihu Root, 1905 |
| | Robert Bacon, 1909 |
| Secretary of the Treasury | Lyman J. Gage (Cont.) |
| | Leslie M. Shaw, 1902 |
| | George B. Cortelyou, 1907 |
| Secretary of War | Elihu Root (Cont.) |
| | William H. Taft, 1904 |
| | Luke E. Wright, 1908 |
| Attorney General | Philander C. Knox (Cont.) |
| | William H. Moody, 1904 |
| | Charles J. Bonaparte, 1906 |
| Postmaster General | Charles E. Smith (Cont.) |
| | Henry C. Payne, 1902 |
| | Robert J. Wynne, 1904 |
| | George B. Cortelyou, 1905 |
| | George von L. Meyer, 1907 |
| Secretary of the Navy | John D. Long (Cont.) |
| | William H. Moody, 1902 |
| | Paul Morton, 1904 |
| | Charles J. Bonaparte, 1905 |
| | Victor H. Metcalf, 1906 |
| | Truman H. Newberry, 1908 |
| Secretary of the Interior | Ethan A. Hitchcock (Cont.) |
| | James R. Garfield, 1907 |
| Secretary of Agriculture | James Wilson (Cont.) |
| Secretary of Commerce and Labor | George B. Cortelyou, 1903 |
| | Victor H. Metcalf, 1904 |
| | Oscar S. Straus, 1906 |

## Taft

| | |
|---|---|
| Secretary of State | Philander C. Knox, 1909 |
| Secretary of the Treasury | Franklin MacVeagh, 1909 |
| Secretary of War | Jacob M. Dickinson, 1909 |
| | Henry L. Stimson, 1911 |
| Attorney General | George W. Wickersham, 1909 |
| Postmaster General | Frank H. Hitchcock, 1909 |
| Secretary of the Navy | George von L. Meyer, 1909 |
| Secretary of the Interior | Richard A. Ballinger, 1909 |
| | Walter L. Fisher, 1911 |
| Secretary of Agriculture | James Wilson (Cont.) |
| Secretary of Commerce and Labor | Charles Nagel, 1909 |

## Wilson

| | |
|---|---|
| Secretary of State | William J. Bryan, 1913 |
| | Robert Lansing, 1915 |
| Secretary of the Treasury | William G. McAdoo, 1913 |
| | Carter Glass, 1918 |
| | David F. Houston, 1920 |
| Secretary of War | Lindley M. Garrison, 1913 |
| | Newton D. Baker, 1916 |
| Attorney General | James C. McReynolds, 1913 |
| | Thomas W. Gregory, 1914 |
| | A. Mitchell Palmer, 1919 |
| Postmaster General | Albert S. Burleson, 1913 |
| Secretary of the Navy | Josephus Daniels, 1913 |
| Secretary of the Interior | Franklin K. Lane, 1913 |
| | John B. Payne, 1920 |
| Secretary of Agriculture | David F. Houston, 1913 |
| | Edwin T. Meredith, 1920 |
| Secretary of Commerce | William C. Redfield, 1913 |
| | Joshua W. Alexander, 1919 |
| Secretary of Labor | William B. Wilson, 1913 |

## Harding

| | |
|---|---|
| Secretary of State | Charles E. Hughes, 1921 |
| Secretary of the Treasury | Andrew W. Mellon, 1921 |
| Secretary of War | John W. Weeks, 1921 |
| Attorney General | Harry M. Daugherty, 1921 |
| Postmaster General | Will H. Hays, 1921 |
| | Hubert Work, 1922 |
| | Harry S. New, 1923 |
| Secretary of the Navy | Edwin Denby, 1921 |
| Secretary of the Interior | Albert B. Fall, 1921 |
| | Hubert Work, 1923 |
| Secretary of Agriculture | Henry C. Wallace, 1921 |
| Secretary of Commerce | Herbert Hoover, 1921 |
| Secretary of Labor | James J. Davis, 1921 |

## Coolidge

| | |
|---|---|
| Secretary of State | Charles E. Hughes (Cont.) |
| | Frank B. Kellogg, 1925 |
| Secretary of the Treasury | Andrew W. Mellon (Cont.) |
| Secretary of War | John W. Weeks (Cont.) |
| | Dwight F. Davis, 1925 |
| Attorney General | Harry M. Daughtery (Cont.) |
| | Harlan F. Stone, 1924 |
| | John G. Sargent, 1925 |
| Postmaster General | Harry S. New (Cont.) |
| Secretary of the Navy | Edwin Denby (Cont.) |
| | Curtis D. Wilbur, 1924 |
| Secretary of the Interior | Hubert Work (Cont.) |
| | Roy O. West, 1928 |
| Secretary of Agriculture | Henry C. Wallace (Cont.) |
| | Howard M. Gore, 1924 |
| | William M. Jardine, 1925 |
| Secretary of Commerce | Herbert Hoover (Cont.) |
| | William F. Whiting, 1928 |
| Secretary of Labor | James J. Davis (Cont.) |

## Hoover

| | |
|---|---|
| Secretary of State | Frank B. Kellogg (Cont.) |
| | Henry L. Stimson, 1929 |
| Secretary of the Treasury | Andrew W. Mellon (Cont.) |
| | Ogden L. Mills, 1932 |
| Secretary of War | James W. Good, 1929 |
| | Patrick J. Hurley, 1929 |
| Attorney General | William D. Mitchell, 1929 |
| Postmaster General | Walter F. Brown, 1929 |
| Secretary of the Navy | Charles F. Adams, 1929 |
| Secretary of the Interior | Ray Lyman Wilbur, 1929 |
| Secretary of Agriculture | Arthur M. Hyde, 1929 |
| Secretary of Commerce | Robert P. Lamont, 1929 |
| | Roy D. Chapin, 1932 |
| Secretary of Labor | James J. Davis (Cont.) |
| | William N. Doak, 1930 |

## F. D. Roosevelt

| | |
|---|---|
| Secretary of State | Cordell Hull, 1933 |
| | E. R. Stettinius, Jr., 1944 |
| Secretary of the Treasury | William H. Woodin, 1933 |
| | Henry Morgenthau, Jr., 1934 |
| Secretary of War | George H. Dern, 1933 |
| | Harry H. Woodring, 1936 |
| | Henry L. Stimson, 1940 |
| Attorney General | Homer S. Cummings, 1933 |
| | Frank Murphy, 1939 |
| | Robert H. Jackson, 1940 |
| | Francis Biddle, 1941 |
| Postmaster General | James A. Farley, 1933 |
| | Frank C. Walker, 1940 |
| Secretary of the Navy | Claude A. Swanson, 1933 |
| | Charles Edison, 1940 |
| | Frank Knox, 1940 |
| | James Forrestal, 1944 |
| Secretary of the Interior | Harold L. Ickes, 1933 |
| Secretary of Agriculture | Henry A. Wallace, 1933 |
| | Claude R. Wickard, 1940 |

| | |
|---|---|
| Secretary of Commerce | Daniel C. Roper, 1933 |
| | Harry L. Hopkins, 1938 |
| | Jesse H. Jones, 1940 |
| | Henry A. Wallace, 1945 |
| Secretary of Labor | Frances Perkins, 1933 |

## Truman

| | |
|---|---|
| Secretary of State | E. R. Stettinius, Jr. (Cont.) |
| | James F. Byrnes, 1945 |
| | George C. Marshall, 1947 |
| | Dean Acheson, 1949 |
| Secretary of the Treasury | Henry Morgenthau, Jr. (Cont.) |
| | Frederick M. Vinson, 1945 |
| | John W. Snyder, 1946 |
| Secretary of Defense | James Forrestal, 1947 |
| | Louis A. Johnson, 1949 |
| | George C. Marshall, 1950 |
| | Robert A. Lovett, 1951 |
| Attorney General | Francis Biddle (Cont.) |
| | Tom C. Clark, 1945 |
| | J. Howard McGrath, 1949 |
| | James P. McGranery, 1952 |
| Postmaster General | Frank C. Walker (Cont.) |
| | Robert E. Hannegan, 1945 |
| | Jesse M. Donaldson, 1947 |
| Secretary of the Interior | Harold L. Ickes (Cont.) |
| | Julius A. Krug, 1946 |
| | Oscar L. Chapman, 1949 |
| Secretary of Agriculture | Claude R. Wickard (Cont.) |
| | Clinton P. Anderson, 1945 |
| | Charles F. Brannan, 1948 |
| Secretary of Commerce | Henry A. Wallace (Cont.) |
| | W. Averell Harriman, 1946 |
| | Charles Sawyer, 1948 |
| Secretary of Labor | Frances Perkins (Cont.) |
| | Lewis B. Schwellenbach, 1945 |
| | Maurice J. Tobin, 1948 |
| Secretary of War[1] | Henry L. Stimson, 1945 |
| | Robert P. Patterson, 1945 |
| | Kenneth C. Royall, 1947 |
| Secretary of the Navy[1] | James Forrestal (Cont.) |

1. On July 26, 1947, the Departments of War and of the Navy were incorporated into the Department of Defense.

## Eisenhower

| | |
|---|---|
| Secretary of State | John Foster Dulles, 1953 |
| | Christian A. Herter, 1959 |
| Secretary of the Treasury | George M. Humphrey, 1953 |
| | Robert B. Anderson, 1957 |
| Secretary of Defense | Charles E. Wilson, 1953 |
| | Neil H. McElroy, 1957 |
| | Thomas S. Gates, Jr., 1959 |
| Attorney General | Herbert Brownell, Jr., 1953 |
| | William P. Rogers, 1958 |
| Postmaster General | Arthur E. Summerfield, 1953 |
| Secretary of the Interior | Douglas McKay, 1953 |
| | Frederick A. Seaton, 1956 |
| Secretary of Agriculture | Ezra Taft Benson, 1953 |
| Secretary of Commerce | Sinclair Weeks, 1953 |
| | Lewis L. Strauss[1], 1958 |
| | Frederick H. Mueller, 1959 |
| Secretary of Health, Education, and Welfare | Oveta Culp Hobby, 1953 |
| | Marion B. Folsom, 1955 |
| | Arthur S. Flemming, 1958 |
| Secretary of Labor | Martin P. Durkin, 1953 |
| | James P. Mitchell, 1953 |

1. Not confirmed by the Senate.

## Kennedy

| | |
|---|---|
| Secretary of State | Dean Rusk, 1961 |
| Secretary of the Treasury | C. Douglas Dillon, 1961 |
| Secretary of Defense | Robert S. McNamara, 1961 |
| Attorney General | Robert F. Kennedy, 1961 |
| Postmaster General | J. Edward Day, 1961 |
| | John A. Gronouski, 1963 |

| | |
|---|---|
| Secretary of the Interior | Stewart L. Udall, 1961 |
| Secretary of Agriculture | Orville L. Freeman, 1961 |
| Secretary of Commerce | Luther H. Hodges, 1961 |
| Secretary of Labor | Arthur J. Goldberg, 1961 |
| | W. Willard Wirtz, 1962 |
| Secretary of Health, Education, and Welfare | Abraham A. Ribicoff, 1961 |
| | Anthony J. Celebrezze, 1962 |

## L. B. Johnson

| | |
|---|---|
| Secretary of State | Dean Rusk (Cont.) |
| Secretary of the Treasury | C. Douglas Dillon (Cont.) |
| | Henry H. Fowler, 1965 |
| | Joseph W. Barr[1], 1968 |
| Secretary of Defense | Robert S. McNamara (Cont.) |
| | Clark M. Clifford, 1968 |
| Attorney General | Robert F. Kennedy (Cont.) |
| | N. de B. Katzenbach, 1965 |
| | Ramsey Clark, 1967 |
| Postmaster General | John A. Gronouski (Cont.) |
| | Lawrence F. O'Brien, 1965 |
| | W. Marvin Watson, 1968 |
| Secretary of the Interior | Stewart L. Udall (Cont.) |
| Secretary of Agriculture | Orville L. Freeman (Cont.) |
| Secretary of Commerce | Luther H. Hodges (Cont.) |
| | John T. Connor, 1964 |
| | A. B. Trowbridge, 1967 |
| | C. R. Smith, 1968 |
| Secretary of Labor | W. Willard Wirtz (Cont.) |
| Secretary of Health, Education, and Welfare | Anthony J. Celebrezze (Cont.) |
| | John W. Gardner, 1965 |
| | Wilbur J. Cohen, 1968 |
| Secretary of Housing and Urban Development | Robert C. Weaver, 1966 |
| | Robert C. Wood[1], 1969 |
| Secretary of Transportation | Alan S. Boyd, 1966 |

1. Recess appointment.

## Nixon

| | |
|---|---|
| Secretary of State | William P. Rogers, 1969 |
| | Henry A. Kissinger, 1973 |
| Secretary of the Treasury | David M. Kennedy, 1969 |
| | John B. Connally, 1971 |
| | George P. Shultz, 1972 |
| | William E. Simon, 1974 |
| Secretary of Defense | Melvin R. Laird, 1969 |
| | Elliot L. Richardson, 1973 |
| | James R. Schlesinger, 1973 |
| Attorney General | John N. Mitchell, 1969 |
| | Richard G. Kleindienst, 1972 |
| | Elliot L. Richardson, 1973 |
| | William B. Saxbe, 1974 |
| Postmaster General[1] | William M. Blount, 1969 |
| Secretary of the Interior | Walter J. Hickel, 1969 |
| | Rogers C. B. Morton, 1971 |
| Secretary of Agriculture | Clifford M. Hardin, 1969 |
| | Earl L. Butz, 1971 |
| Secretary of Commerce | Maurice H. Stans, 1969 |
| | Peter G. Peterson, 1972 |
| | Frederick B. Dent, 1973 |
| Secretary of Labor | George P. Shultz, 1969 |
| | James D. Hodgson, 1970 |
| | Peter J. Brennan, 1973 |
| Secretary of Health, Education, and Welfare | Robert H. Finch, 1969 |
| | Elliot L. Richardson, 1970 |
| | Caspar W. Weinberger, 1973 |
| Secretary of Housing and Urban Development | George Romney, 1969 |
| | James T. Lynn, 1973 |
| Secretary of Transportation | John A. Volpe, 1969 |
| | Claude S. Brinegar, 1973 |

1. The postmaster general is no longer a cabinet member.

## Ford

| | |
|---|---|
| Secretary of State | Henry A. Kissinger (Cont.) |
| Secretary of the Treasury | William E. Simon (Cont.) |
| Secretary of Defense | James R. Schlesinger (Cont.) |
| | Donald H. Rumsfeld, 1975 |

| | |
|---|---|
| Attorney General | William B. Saxbe (Cont.) |
| | Edward H. Levi, 1975 |
| Secretary of the Interior | Rogers C. B. Morton (Cont.) |
| | Stanley K. Hathaway, 1975 |
| | Thomas S. Kleppe, 1975 |
| Secretary of Agriculture | Earl L. Butz (Cont.) |
| | John Knebel, 1976 |
| Secretary of Commerce | Frederick B. Dent (Cont.) |
| | Rogers C. B. Morton, 1975 |
| | Elliot L. Richardson, 1976 |
| Secretary of Labor | Peter J. Brennan (Cont.) |
| | John T. Dunlop, 1975 |
| | William J. Usery, Jr., 1976 |
| Secretary of Health, Education, and Welfare | Caspar W. Weinberger (Cont.) |
| | F. David Mathews, 1975 |
| Secretary of Housing and Urban Development | James T. Lynn (Cont.) |
| | Carla A. Hills, 1975 |
| Secretary of Transportation | Claude S. Brinegar (Cont.) |
| | William T. Coleman, Jr., 1975 |

## Carter

| | |
|---|---|
| Secretary of State | Cyrus R. Vance, 1977 |
| | Edmund S. Muskie, 1980 |
| Secretary of the Treasury | W. Michael Blumenthal, 1977 |
| | G. William Miller, 1979 |
| Secretary of Defense | Harold Brown, 1977 |
| Attorney General | Griffin B. Bell, 1977 |
| | Benjamin R. Civiletti, 1979 |
| Secretary of the Interior | Cecil D. Andrus, 1977 |
| Secretary of Agriculture | Bob S. Bergland, 1977 |
| Secretary of Commerce | Juanita M. Kreps, 1977 |
| | Philip M. Klutznick, 1979 |
| Secretary of Labor | F. Ray Marshall, 1977 |
| Secretary of Health and Human Services[1] | Joseph A. Califano, Jr., 1977 |
| | Patricia Roberts Harris, 1979 |
| Secretary of Housing and Urban Development | Patricia Roberts Harris, 1977 |
| | Moon Landrieu, 1979 |
| Secretary of Transportation | Brock Adams, 1977 |
| | Neil E. Goldschmidt, 1979 |
| Secretary of Energy | James R. Schlesinger, 1977 |
| | Charles W. Duncan, Jr., 1979 |
| Secretary of Education | Shirley Mount Hufstedler, 1979 |

1. Known as Department of Health, Education, and Welfare until May 1980.

## Reagan

| | |
|---|---|
| Secretary of State | Alexander M. Haig, Jr., 1981 |
| | George P. Shultz, 1982 |
| Secretary of the Treasury | Donald T. Regan, 1981 |
| | James A. Baker 3rd, 1985 |
| | Nicholas F. Brady, 1988 |
| Secretary of Defense | Caspar W. Weinberger, 1981 |
| | Frank C. Carlucci, 1987 |
| Attorney General | William French Smith, 1981 |
| | Edwin Meese 3rd, 1985 |
| | Richard L. Thornburgh, 1988 |
| Secretary of the Interior | James G. Watt, 1981 |
| | William P. Clark, 1983 |
| | Donald P. Hodel, 1985 |
| Secretary of Agriculture | John R. Block, 1981 |
| | Richard E. Lyng, 1986 |
| Secretary of Commerce | Malcolm Baldrige, 1981 |
| | C. William Verity, Jr., 1987 |
| Secretary of Labor | Raymond J. Donovan, 1981 |
| | William E. Brock, 1985 |
| | Ann Dore McLaughlin, 1987 |
| Secretary of Health and Human Services | Richard S. Schweiker, 1981 |
| | Margaret M. Heckler, 1983 |
| | Otis R. Bowen, 1985 |
| Secretary of Housing and Urban Development | Samuel R. Pierce, Jr., 1981 |
| Secretary of Transportation | Andrew L. Lewis, Jr., 1981 |
| | Elizabeth H. Dole, 1983 |
| | James H. Burnley 4th, 1987 |

| | |
|---|---|
| Secretary of Energy | James B. Edwards, 1981 |
| | Donald P. Hodel, 1983 |
| | John S. Herrington, 1985 |
| Secretary of Education | T. H. Bell, 1981 |
| | William J. Bennett, 1985 |
| | Lauro F. Cavazos, 1988 |

## G. H. W. Bush

| | |
|---|---|
| Secretary of State | James A. Baker 3d, 1989 |
| | Lawrence S. Eagleburger, 1992 |
| Secretary of the Treasury | Nicholas F. Brady (Cont.) |
| Secretary of Defense | Richard Cheney, 1989 |
| Attorney General | Richard L. Thornburgh (Cont.) |
| | William P. Barr, 1992 |
| Secretary of the Interior | Manuel Lujan Jr., 1989 |
| Secretary of Agriculture | Clayton K. Yeutter, 1989 |
| | Edward Madigan, 1991 |
| Secretary of Commerce | Robert A. Mosbacher Sr., 1989 |
| | Barbara H. Franklin, 1992 |
| Secretary of Labor | Elizabeth H. Dole, 1989 |
| | Lynn Martin, 1991 |
| Secretary of Health and Human Services | Louis W. Sullivan, 1989 |
| Secretary of Housing and Urban Development | Jack F. Kemp, 1989 |
| Secretary of Transportation | Samuel K. Skinner, 1989 |
| | Andrew Card, 1992 |
| Secretary of Energy | James D. Watkins, 1989 |
| Secretary of Education | Lauro F. Cavazos (Cont.) |
| | Lamar Alexander, 1991 |
| Secretary of Veterans' Affairs | Edward J. Derwinski, 1989 |

## Clinton

| | |
|---|---|
| Secretary of State | Warren M. Christopher, 1993 |
| | Madeleine Albright, 1996 |
| Secretary of the Treasury | Lloyd Bentsen, 1993 |
| | Robert E. Rubin, 1995–1999 |
| | Lawrence H. Summers, 1999 |
| Secretary of Defense | Les Aspin, 1993 |
| | William J. Perry, 1994 |
| | William S. Cohen, 1997 |
| Attorney General | Janet Reno, 1993 |

| | |
|---|---|
| Secretary of the Interior | Bruce Babbitt, 1993 |
| Secretary of Agriculture | Mike Espy, 1993 |
| | Dan Glickman, 1995 |
| Secretary of Commerce | Ronald H. Brown, 1993 |
| | Mickey Kantor, 1996 |
| | William M. Daley, 1997 |
| | Norman Y. Mineta, 2000 |
| Secretary of Labor | Robert B. Reich, 1993 |
| | Alexis Herman, 1997 |
| Secretary of Health and Human Services | Donna E. Shalala, 1993 |
| Secretary of Housing and Urban Development | Henry G. Cisneros, 1993 |
| | Andrew M. Cuomo, 1997 |
| Secretary of Transportation | Federico F. Pena, 1993 |
| | Rodney Slater, 1997 |
| Secretary of Energy | Hazel R. O'Leary, 1993 |
| | Frederico F. Pena, 1997 |
| | Bill Richardson, 1998 |
| Secretary of Education | Richard W. Riley, 1993 |
| Secretary of Veterans' Affairs | Jesse Brown, 1993 |
| | Togo D. West, Jr., 1998 |

## G. W. Bush

| | |
|---|---|
| Secretary of State | Gen. Colin L. Powell, 2001 |
| Secretary of the Treasury | Paul H. O'Neill, 2001 |
| Secretary of Defense | Donald H. Rumsfeld, 2001 |
| Attorney General | John Ashcroft, 2001 |
| Secretary of the Interior | Gale A. Norton, 2001 |
| Secretary of Agriculture | Ann M. Veneman, 2001 |
| Secretary of Commerce | Donald L. Evans, 2001 |
| Secretary of Labor | Elaine L. Chao, 2001 |
| Secretary of Health and Human Services | Tommy G. Thompson, 2001 |
| Secretary of Housing and Urban Development | Melquiades R. Martinez, 2001 |
| Secretary of Transportation | Norman Y. Mineta, 2001 |
| Secretary of Energy | Spencer Abraham, 2001 |
| Secretary of Education | Roderick R. Paige, 2001 |
| Secretary of Veterans' Affairs | Anthony Principi, 2001 |

# Impeachments of Federal Officials

*Source:* Congressional Directory

The procedure for the impeachment of federal officials is detailed in Article I, Section 3, of the Constitution. The Senate has sat as a court of impeachment in the following cases:

**William Blount,** senator from Tennessee; charges dismissed for want of jurisdiction, Jan. 14, 1799.

**John Pickering,** judge of the U.S. District Court for New Hampshire; removed from office March 12, 1804.

**Samuel Chase,** associate justice of the Supreme Court; acquitted March 1, 1805.

**James H. Peck,** judge of the U.S. District Court for Missouri; acquitted Jan. 31, 1831.

**West H. Humphreys,** judge of the U.S. District Court for the middle, eastern, and western districts of Tennessee; removed from office June 26, 1862.

**Andrew Johnson,** president of the United States; acquitted May 26, 1868.

**William W. Belknap,** secretary of war; acquitted Aug. 1, 1876.

**Charles Swayne,** judge of the U.S. District Court for the northern district of Florida; acquitted Feb. 27, 1905.

**Robert W. Archbald,** associate judge, U.S. Commerce Court; removed Jan. 13, 1913.

**George W. English,** judge of the U.S. District Court for eastern district of Illinois; resigned Nov. 4, 1926; proceedings dismissed.

**Harold Louderback,** judge of the U.S. District Court for the northern district of California; acquitted May 24, 1933.

**Halsted L. Ritter,** judge of the U.S. District Court for the southern district of Florida; removed from office April 17, 1936.

**Harry E. Claiborne,** judge of the U.S. District Court for the district of Nevada; removed from office Oct. 9, 1986.

**Alcee L. Hastings,** judge of the U.S. District Court for the southern district of Florida; removed from office Oct. 20, 1988.

**Walter L. Nixon,** judge of the U.S. District Court for Mississippi; removed from office Nov. 3, 1989.

**William J. Clinton,** president of the United States; acquitted Feb. 12, 1999.

# Members of the Supreme Court of the United States

**Mailing address for the Supreme Court: U.S. Supreme Court Building, 1 First Street NE Washington, DC 20543**

| Name, state | Service Term | Service Yrs | Birth Place | Birth Date | Died | Religion |
|---|---|---|---|---|---|---|
| **Chief Justices** | | | | | | |
| John Jay, N.Y. | 1789–1795 | 5 | N.Y. | 1745 | 1829 | Episcopal |
| John Rutledge, S.C. | 1795 | 0 | S.C. | 1739 | 1800 | Church of England |
| Oliver Ellsworth, Conn. | 1796–1800 | 4 | Conn. | 1745 | 1807 | Congregational |
| John Marshall, Va. | 1801–1835 | 34 | Va. | 1755 | 1835 | Episcopal |
| Roger B. Taney, Md. | 1836–1864 | 28 | Md. | 1777 | 1864 | Roman Catholic |
| Salmon P. Chase, Ohio | 1864–1873 | 8 | N.H. | 1808 | 1873 | Episcopal |
| Morrison R. Waite, Ohio | 1874–1888 | 14 | Conn. | 1816 | 1888 | Episcopal |
| Melville W. Fuller, Ill. | 1888–1910 | 21 | Maine | 1833 | 1910 | Episcopal |
| Edward D. White, La. | 1910–1921 | 10 | La. | 1845 | 1921 | Roman Catholic |
| William H. Taft, Conn. | 1921–1930 | 8 | Ohio | 1857 | 1930 | Unitarian |
| Charles E. Hughes, N.Y. | 1930–1941 | 11 | N.Y. | 1862 | 1948 | Baptist |
| Harlan F. Stone, N.Y. | 1941–1946 | 4 | N.H. | 1872 | 1946 | Episcopal |
| Frederick M. Vinson, Ky. | 1946–1953 | 7 | Ky. | 1890 | 1953 | Methodist |
| Earl Warren, Calif. | 1953–1969 | 15 | Calif. | 1891 | 1974 | Protestant |
| Warren E. Burger, Va. | 1969–1986 | 17 | Minn. | 1907 | 1995 | Presbyterian |
| William H. Rehnquist, Ariz. | 1986– | — | Wis. | 1924 | — | Lutheran |
| **Associate Justices** | | | | | | |
| James Wilson, Pa. | 1789–1798 | 8 | Scotland | 1742 | 1798 | Episcopal |
| John Rutledge, S.C. | 1790–1791 | 1 | S.C. | 1739 | 1800 | Church of England |
| William Cushing, Mass. | 1790–1810 | 20 | Mass. | 1732 | 1810 | Unitarian |
| John Blair, Va. | 1790–1796 | 5 | Va. | 1732 | 1800 | Presbyterian |
| James Iredell, N.C. | 1790–1799 | 9 | England | 1751 | 1799 | Episcopal |
| Thomas Johnson, Md. | 1792–1793 | 0 | Md. | 1732 | 1819 | Episcopal |
| William Paterson, N.J. | 1793–1806 | 13 | Ireland | 1745 | 1806 | Protestant |
| Samuel Chase, Md. | 1796–1811 | 15 | Md. | 1741 | 1811 | Episcopal |
| Bushrod Washington, Va. | 1799–1829 | 30 | Va. | 1762 | 1829 | Episcopal |
| Alfred Moore, N.C. | 1800–1804 | 3 | N.C. | 1755 | 1810 | Episcopal |
| William Johnson, S.C. | 1804–1834 | 30 | S.C. | 1771 | 1834 | Presbyterian |
| Brockholst Livingston, N.Y. | 1807–1823 | 16 | N.Y. | 1757 | 1823 | Presbyterian |
| Thomas Todd, Ky. | 1807–1826 | 18 | Va. | 1765 | 1826 | Presbyterian |
| Gabriel Duval, Md. | 1811–1835 | 23 | Md. | 1752 | 1844 | French Protestant |
| Joseph Story, Mass. | 1812–1845 | 33 | Mass. | 1779 | 1845 | Unitarian |
| Smith Thompson, N.Y. | 1823–1843 | 20 | N.Y. | 1768 | 1843 | Presbyterian |
| Robert Trimble, Ky. | 1826–1828 | 2 | Va. | 1777 | 1828 | Protestant |
| John McLean, Ohio | 1830–1861 | 31 | N.J. | 1785 | 1861 | Methodist-Epis. |
| Henry Baldwin, Pa. | 1830–1844 | 14 | Conn. | 1780 | 1844 | Trinity Church |
| James M. Wayne, Ga. | 1835–1867 | 32 | Ga. | 1790 | 1867 | Protestant |
| Philip P. Barbour, Va. | 1836–1841 | 4 | Va. | 1783 | 1841 | Episcopal |
| John Catron, Tenn. | 1837–1865 | 28 | Pa. | 1786 | 1865 | Presbyterian |
| John McKinley, Ala. | 1837–1852 | 14 | Va. | 1780 | 1852 | Protestant |
| Peter V. Daniel, Va. | 1841–1860 | 18 | Va. | 1784 | 1860 | Episcopal |
| Samuel Nelson, N.Y. | 1845–1872 | 27 | N.Y. | 1792 | 1873 | Protestant |
| Levi Woodbury, N.H. | 1845–1851 | 5 | N.H. | 1789 | 1851 | Protestant |
| Robert C. Grier, Pa. | 1846–1870 | 23 | Pa. | 1794 | 1870 | Presbyterian |
| Benjamin R. Curtis, Mass. | 1851–1857 | 5 | Mass. | 1809 | 1874 | (²) |
| John A. Campbell, Ala. | 1853–1861 | 8 | Ga. | 1811 | 1889 | Episcopal |
| Nathan Clifford, Maine | 1858–1881 | 00 | Maine | 1804 | 1884 | Quaker |
| Samuel F. Miller, Iowa | 1862–1890 | 28 | Ky. | 1816 | 1890 | Unitarian |
| David Davis, Ill. | 1862–1877 | 14 | Md. | 1815 | 1886 | (¹) |
| Stephen J. Field, Calif. | 1863–1897 | 34 | Conn. | 1816 | 1899 | Episcopal |
| William Strong, Pa. | 1870–1880 | 10 | Conn. | 1808 | 1895 | Presbyterian |
| Joseph P. Bradley, N.J. | 1870–1892 | 21 | N.Y. | 1813 | 1892 | Presbyterian |
| Ward Hunt, N.Y. | 1872–1882 | 9 | N.Y. | 1810 | 1886 | Episcopal |
| John M. Harlan, Ky. | 1877–1911 | 33 | Ky. | 1833 | 1911 | Presbyterian |
| William B. Woods, Ga. | 1880–1887 | 6 | Ohio | 1824 | 1887 | Protestant |
| Stanley Matthews, Ohio | 1881–1889 | 7 | Ohio | 1824 | 1889 | Presbyterian |
| Horace Gray, Mass. | 1882–1902 | 20 | Mass. | 1828 | 1902 | (³) |
| Samuel Blatchford, N.Y. | 1882–1893 | 11 | N.Y. | 1820 | 1893 | Presbyterian |
| Lucius Q. C. Lamar, Miss. | 1888–1893 | 5 | Ga. | 1825 | 1893 | Methodist |
| David J. Brewer, Kan. | 1889–1910 | 20 | Asia Minor | 1837 | 1910 | Protestant |
| Henry B. Brown, Mich. | 1890–1906 | 15 | Mass. | 1836 | 1913 | Protestant |

| Name, state | Service Term | Yrs | Birth Place | Date | Died | Religion |
|---|---|---|---|---|---|---|
| George Shiras, Jr., Pa. | 1892–1903 | 10 | Pa. | 1832 | 1924 | Presbyterian |
| Howell E. Jackson, Tenn. | 1893–1895 | 2 | Tenn. | 1832 | 1895 | Baptist |
| Edward D. White, La.* | 1894–1910 | 16 | La. | 1845 | 1921 | Roman Catholic |
| Rufus W. Peckham, N.Y. | 1895–1909 | 13 | N.Y. | 1838 | 1909 | Episcopal |
| Joseph McKenna, Calif. | 1898–1925 | 26 | Pa. | 1843 | 1926 | Roman Catholic |
| Oliver W. Holmes, Mass. | 1902–1932 | 29 | Mass. | 1841 | 1935 | Unitarian |
| William R. Day, Ohio | 1903–1922 | 19 | Ohio | 1849 | 1923 | Protestant |
| William H. Moody, Mass. | 1906–1910 | 3 | Mass. | 1853 | 1917 | Episcopal |
| Horace H. Lurton, Tenn. | 1909–1914 | 4 | Ky. | 1844 | 1914 | Episcopal |
| Charles E. Hughes, N.Y.* | 1910–1916 | 5 | N.Y. | 1862 | 1948 | Baptist |
| Willis Van Devanter, Wyo. | 1910–1937 | 26 | Ind. | 1859 | 1941 | Episcopal |
| Joseph R. Lamar, Ga. | 1910–1916 | 4 | Ga. | 1857 | 1916 | Ch. of Disciples |
| Mahlon Pitney, N.J. | 1912–1922 | 10 | N.J. | 1858 | 1924 | Presbyterian |
| James C. McReynolds, Tenn. | 1914–1941 | 26 | Ky. | 1862 | 1946 | Disciples of Christ |
| Louis D. Brandeis, Mass. | 1916–1939 | 22 | Ky. | 1856 | 1941 | Jewish |
| John H. Clarke, Ohio | 1916–1922 | 5 | Ohio | 1857 | 1945 | Protestant |
| George Sutherland, Utah | 1922–1938 | 15 | England | 1862 | 1942 | Episcopal |
| Pierce Butler, Minn. | 1923–1939 | 16 | Minn. | 1866 | 1939 | Roman Catholic |
| Edward T. Sanford, Tenn. | 1923–1930 | 7 | Tenn. | 1865 | 1930 | Episcopal |
| Harlan F. Stone, N.Y.* | 1925–1941 | 16 | N.H. | 1872 | 1946 | Episcopal |
| Owen J. Roberts, Pa. | 1930–1945 | 15 | Pa. | 1875 | 1955 | Episcopal |
| Benjamin N. Cardozo, N.Y. | 1932–1938 | 6 | N.Y. | 1870 | 1938 | Jewish |
| Hugo L. Black, Ala. | 1937–1971 | 34 | Ala. | 1886 | 1971 | Baptist |
| Stanley F. Reed, Ky. | 1938–1957 | 19 | Ky. | 1884 | 1980 | Protestant |
| Felix Frankfurter, Mass. | 1939–1962 | 23 | Austria | 1882 | 1965 | Jewish |
| William O. Douglas, Conn. | 1939–1975 | 36 | Minn. | 1898 | 1980 | Presbyterian |
| Frank Murphy, Mich. | 1940–1949 | 9 | Mich. | 1890 | 1949 | Roman Catholic |
| James F. Byrnes, S.C. | 1941–1942 | 1 | S.C. | 1879 | 1972 | Episcopal |
| Robert H. Jackson, Pa. | 1941–1954 | 13 | N.Y. | 1892 | 1954 | Episcopal |
| Wiley B. Rutledge, Iowa | 1943–1949 | 6 | Ky. | 1894 | 1949 | Unitarian |
| Harold H. Burton, Ohio | 1945–1958 | 13 | Mass. | 1888 | 1964 | Unitarian |
| Tom C. Clark, Tex. | 1949–1967 | 17 | Tex. | 1899 | 1977 | Presbyterian |
| Sherman Minton, Ind. | 1949–1956 | 7 | Ind. | 1890 | 1965 | Roman Catholic |
| John M. Harlan, N.Y. | 1955–1971 | 16 | Ill. | 1899 | 1971 | Presbyterian |
| William J. Brennan, Jr., N.J. | 1956–1990 | 33 | N.J. | 1906 | 1997 | Roman Catholic |
| Charles E. Whittaker, Mo. | 1957–1962 | 5 | Kan. | 1901 | 1973 | Methodist |
| Potter Stewart, Ohio | 1958–1981 | 23 | Mich. | 1915 | 1985 | Episcopal |
| Byron R. White, Colo. | 1962–1993 | 31 | Colo. | 1917 | 2002 | Episcopal |
| Arthur J. Goldberg, Ill. | 1962–1965 | 2 | Ill. | 1908 | 1990 | Jewish |
| Abe Fortas, Tenn. | 1965–1969 | 3 | Tenn. | 1910 | 1982 | Jewish |
| Thurgood Marshall, N.Y. | 1967–1991 | 24 | Md. | 1908 | 1993 | Episcopal |
| Harry A. Blackmun, Minn. | 1970–1994 | 24 | Ill. | 1908 | 1999 | Methodist |
| Lewis F. Powell, Jr., Va. | 1972–1987 | 15 | Va. | 1907 | 1998 | Presbyterian |
| William H. Rehnquist, Ariz.* | 1972–1986 | 14 | Wis. | 1924 | — | Lutheran |
| John Paul Stevens, Ill. | 1975– | — | Ill. | 1920 | — | Protestant |
| Sandra Day O'Connor, Ariz. | 1981– | — | Tex. | 1930 | — | Episcopal |
| Antonin Scalia, D.C. | 1986– | — | N.J. | 1936 | — | Roman Catholic |
| Anthony M. Kennedy, Calif. | 1988– | — | Calif. | 1936 | — | Roman Catholic |
| David H. Souter, N.H. | 1990– | — | Mass. | 1939 | — | Episcopal |
| Clarence Thomas, D.C. | 1991– | — | Ga. | 1948 | — | Roman Catholic |
| Ruth Bader Ginsburg, D.C. | 1993– | — | N.Y. | 1933 | — | Jewish |
| Stephen G. Breyer, Mass. | 1994– | — | Calif. | 1938 | — | n.a. |

NOTE: n.a. = not available. *Served as both chief justice and associate justice. 1. Congregational; later Unitarian. 2. Unitarian; then Episcopal. 3. Unitarian or Congregational. 4. Not a member of any church.

## Supreme Court Facts

**Youngest justice appointed:** Joseph Story (age 32)

**Oldest justice appointed:** Horace Lurton (age 65)

**Oldest justice to serve:** Oliver Wendell Holmes (retired at age 90)

**Shortest term:** John Rutledge (1 year associate justice; 4 months chief justice)

**Longest term:** William O. Douglas (36 years, 209 days)

**First African-American justice:** Thurgood Marshall

**First woman justice:** Sandra Day O'Connor

**President to appoint the most justices:** George Washington (11)

**President to appoint the most justices in the 20th century:** Franklin Roosevelt (9)

**Presidents to appoint current justices:** Nixon (Rehnquist); Ford (Stevens); Reagan (O'Connor, Scalia, Kennedy); G.H.W. Bush (Souter, Thomas); Clinton (Ginsburg, Breyer)

# Milestone Cases in Supreme Court History

**1803** *Marbury* v. *Madison* was the first instance in which a law passed by Congress was declared unconstitutional. The decision greatly expanded the power of the Court by establishing its right to overturn acts of Congress, a power not explicitly granted by the Constitution. Initially the case involved Secretary of State James Madison, who refused to seat four judicial appointees although they had been confirmed by the Senate.

**1824** *Gibbons* v. *Ogden* defined broadly Congress's right to regulate commerce. Aaron Ogden had filed suit in New York against Thomas Gibbons for operating a rival steamboat service between New York and New Jersey ports. Ogden had exclusive rights to operate steamboats in New York under a state law, while Gibbons held a federal license. Gibbons lost the case and appealed to the U.S. Supreme Court, which reversed the decision. The Court held that the New York law was unconstitutional, since the power to regulate interstate commerce, which extended to the regulation of navigation, belonged exclusively to Congress. In the 20th century, Chief Justice John Marshall's broad definition of commerce was used to uphold civil rights.

**1857** *Dred Scott* v. *Sanford* was a highly controversial case that intensified the national debate over slavery. The case involved Dred Scott, a slave, who was taken from a slave state to a free territory. Scott filed a lawsuit claiming that because he had lived on free soil he was entitled to his freedom. Chief Justice Roger B. Taney disagreed, ruling that blacks were not citizens and therefore could not sue in federal court. Taney further inflamed antislavery forces by declaring that Congress had no right to ban slavery from U.S. territories.

**1896** *Plessy* v. *Ferguson* was the infamous case that asserted that "equal but separate accommodations" for blacks on railroad cars did not violate the "equal protection under the laws" clause of the 14th Amendment. By defending the constitutionality of racial segregation, the Court paved the way for the repressive Jim Crow laws of the South. The lone dissenter on the Court, Justice John Marshall Harlan, pro tested, "The thin disguise of 'equal' accommodations . . . will not mislead anyone."

**1954** *Brown* v. *Board of Education of Topeka* invalidated racial segregation in schools and led to the unraveling of de jure segregation in all areas of public life. In the unanimous decision spearheaded by Chief Justice Earl Warren, the Court invalidated the Plessy ruling, declaring "in the field of public education, the doctrine of 'separate but equal' has no place" and contending that "separate educational facilities are inherently unequal." Future Supreme Court justice Thurgood Marshall was one of the NAACP lawyers who successfully argued the case.

**1963** *Gideon* v. *Wainwright* guaranteed a defendant's right to legal counsel. The Supreme Court overturned the Florida felony conviction of Clarence Earl Gideon, who had defended himself after having been denied a request for free counsel. The Court held that the state's failure to provide counsel for a defendant charged with a felony violated the Fourteenth Amendment's due process clause. Gideon was given another trial, and with a court-appointed lawyer defending him, he was acquitted.

**1964** *New York Times* v. *Sullivan* extended the protection offered the press by the First Amendment. L.B. Sullivan, a police commissioner in Montgomery, Ala., had filed a libel suit against the *New York Times* for publishing inaccurate information about certain actions taken by the Montgomery police department. In overturning a lower court's decision, the Supreme Court held that debate on public issues would be inhibited if public officials could sue for inaccuracies that were made by mistake. The ruling made it more difficult for public officials to bring libel charges against the press, since the official had to prove that a harmful untruth was told maliciously and with reckless disregard for truth.

**1966** *Miranda* v. *Arizona* was another case that helped define the due process clause of the 14th Amendment. At the center of the case was Ernesto Miranda, who had confessed to a crime during police questioning without knowing he had a right to have an attorney present. Based on his confession, Miranda was convicted. The Supreme Court overturned the conviction, ruling that criminal suspects must be warned of their rights before they are questioned by police. These rights are: the right to remain silent, to have an attorney present, and, if the suspect cannot afford an attorney, to have one appointed by the state. The police must also warn suspects that any statements they make can be used against them in court. Miranda was retried without the confession and convicted.

**1973** *Roe* v. *Wade* legalized abortion and is at the center of the current controversy between "pro-life" and "pro-choice" advocates. The Court ruled that a woman has the right to an abortion without interference from the government in the first trimester of pregnancy, contending that it is part of her "right to privacy." The Court maintained that right to privacy is not absolute, however, and granted states the right to intervene in the second and third trimesters of pregnancy.

**1978** *Regents of the University of California* v. *Bakke* imposed limitations on affirmative action to ensure that providing greater opportunities for minorities did not come at the expense of the rights of the majority. In other words, affirmative action was unfair if it lead to reverse discrimination. The case involved the University of Calif., Davis, Medical School and Allan Bakke, a white applicant who was rejected twice even though there were minority applicants admitted with significantly lower scores than his. A closely divided Court ruled that while race was a legitimate factor in school admissions, the use of rigid quotas was not permissible.

# Notable Decisions of the U.S. Supreme Court, 2001–2002 Term

**Law on Disabilities Narrowed (Jan. 8, 2002):** Justices rule unanimously that persons seeking to qualify for protection under the Americans with Disabilities Act must have impairment that limits activities that are central to daily life and not just to their job.

**Due Process Guarantees Upheld (Jan. 9, 2002):** In narrow 5–4 split, justices rule that jury must be informed of life without parole option when defendant's future dangerousness is an issue and death sentence is only alternative to life imprisonment.

**Due Process for Sex Offenders (Jan. 22, 2002):** Justices, 7–2, hold that state does not have to show that sex offender is completely unable to control dangerous behavior to justify confinement in a civil commitment center following prison; however, state must show defendant has some difficulty controlling behavior.

**Student Grading Does Not Violate Student Privacy (Feb. 19, 2002):** Court holds unanimously that student grading of classroom assignments does not violate students' privacy rights.

**Tenants Evicted Under Drug Law (March 26, 2002):** In 8–0[1] decision, Court upholds fairness of federal drug law that permits the eviction of public housing tenants because of drug use by any household member or guest, even if the drug use takes place off site without the tenant's knowledge.

**Illegal Immigrants Denied Back Pay (March 27, 2002):** Court, in 5–4 split, rules that companies cannot be forced to give back pay to undocumented workers who have been wrongly fired or demoted.

**Virtual Child Pornography Protected (April 16, 2002):** Court, 6–3, holds that 1996 child pornography prevention law went too far in banning computer-generated child pornography.

**Court Deals Setback to Property Rights Movement (April 23, 2002):** Court, 6–3, rules that a government-imposed moratorium on property development does not automatically amount to a "taking" of private property, for which property owners must be compensated by the government.

**Seniority Prevails over Disability (April 29, 2002):** In 5–4 decision, Court rules that in accommodating a disabled employee, an employer is not required to make a placement that overrides a valid seniority system.

**Ban Lifted on Advertising of Drugs (April 29, 2002):** In 5–4 decision, Court invalidates a 1997 federal law that banned pharmacies from advertising special compound drugs made to order by pharmacists. Ruling marks shift in favor of free speech in commercial advertising.

**Internet Pornography Law Gets Temporary Reprieve (May 13, 2002):** Court, 8–1, rules that case involving Child Online Protection Act (COPA) be sent back to lower court for further analysis. According to a majority of the justices, COPA's use of "community standards" to define what is harmful to children does not make the law unconstitutional; however, most feel there are other potential constitutional problems with the law. Meanwhile, as a result of the decision, enforcement of the 1998 law remains blocked.

**Right to Counsel Expanded (May 20, 2002):** Court, 5–4, rules that a state may not impose even a suspended sentence—in which the possibility of incarceration is remote—on a defendant who has not had a lawyer.

**States' Rights Upheld (May 28, 2002):** Court, 5–4, holds that the Federal Maritime Commission does not have the authority to decide a dispute between a private casino-boat company and South Carolina port officials.

**Patent Protection Upheld (May 28, 2002):** In unanimous decision, Court upholds "doctrine of equivalents," which states that patent protection extends to very similar devices even if they do not fall literally within the scope of a particular patent.

**Court Backs SEC (June 3, 2002):** In unanimous decision, Court overturns an appeals court ruling that said the Securities and Exchange Commission (SEC) could not sue to recover money from a broker convicted of fraud since the crime did not involve the sale or purchase of securities. Ruling ensures SEC has authority to protect consumers from unscrupulous brokers.

**Court Backs Employers in Americans with Disabilities Act Case (June 10, 2002):** Court rules, 9–0, that an employer can refuse to hire someone whose disability makes a job physically dangerous for him. The justices agree that such a refusal does not constitute discrimination.

**Jehovah's Witnesses Win Free Speech Dispute (June 17, 2002):** In 8–1 ruling, Court decides that a Stratton, Ohio, ordinance requiring permits for door-to-door solicitation is too broad and violates First Amendment's guarantee of free speech.

**Utah Loses Census Battle (June 20, 2002):** Justices, in 5–4 decision, reject Utah's claim that Census Bureau used a banned counting method for 2000 Census, which resulted in Utah's losing one congressional seat.

**States Have Authority to Protect Medical Patients (June 20, 2002):** In 5–4 decision, justices uphold Illinois state law that requires health maintenance organizations to provide for independent review in disputed cases where physician-prescribed treatment is being denied by HMO. Although Congress has yet to enact a patients' bill of rights that would include the right to independent review, 42 states and the District of Columbia currently have medical review laws.

**Court Bars Execution of Mentally Retarded (June 20, 2002):** Court rules, 6–3, that executing murderers who are mentally retarded is unconstitutional.

**Death Penalty Law Invalidated (June 25, 2002):** In 7–2 decision, justices rule that juries rather than judges must decide who gets death penalty. In five states, including Ariz., Colo., Idaho, Mont., and Nebr., judges have had sole authority to sentence prisoners to death. In four other states, Ala., Del., Fla., and Ind., juries may give sentencing recommendation, but final decision rests with judge.

**Federal Sentencing Guidelines Upheld (June 25, 2002):** In 5–4 decision, Court holds that it is permissible for a judge to impose a tougher sentence based on aggravating factors with which the defendent was not formally charged as long as the sentence remains within the statutory range for the crime. The decision clarifies a Supreme Court ruling from two years ago (Apprendi decision) that held that any factor that led to a sentence beyond the statutory maximum must be included in the indictment and found by a jury.

**Random Drug Tests for Students (June 27, 2002):** Justices, 5–4, approve drug testing as a condition for participation in any extracurricular activities involving interscholastic competition.

**School Voucher Victory (June 27, 2002):** Court, 5–4, upholds use of public funds for tuition at private religious schools under Cleveland voucher program.

1. Justice Breyer took no part in the consideration or decision of the case.

# U.S. History Timeline

NOTES: o.s. = old style (according to the Julian calendar). *See also,* States by Order of Entry into the Union; Presidential Elections 1789–2000; the Confederate States of America; National Censuses; Milestone Cases in Supreme Court History; World History; and Current Events.

**1607** Jamestown, the first permanent English settlement in America, is established by the London Company in southeast Virginia (**May 14 o.s.**).

**1619** The House of Burgesses, the first representative assembly in America, meets for the first time in Virginia (**July 30 o.s.**). The first African slaves are brought to Jamestown (**summer**).

**1620** The Plymouth Colony in Massachusetts is established by Pilgrims from England (**Dec. 11 o.s.**). Before disembarking from their ship, the *Mayflower,* 41 male passengers sign the Mayflower Compact, an agreement that forms the basis of the colony's government.

**1650** Colonial population is estimated at 50,400.

**1752** Britain and the British colonies switch from the Julian to the Gregorian calendar (**Sept. 2**).

**1754–1763** French and Indian War: Final conflict in the ongoing struggle between the British and French for control of eastern North America. The British win a decisive victory over the French on the Plains of Abraham outside Quebec (**Sept. 13, 1759**) and, by the Treaty of Paris (signed **Feb. 10, 1763**), formally gain control of Canada and all the French possessions east of the Mississippi.

**1770** Boston Massacre: British troops fire into a mob, killing five men and leading to intense public protests (**March 5**).

**1773** Boston Tea Party: Group of colonial patriots disguised as Mohawk Indians board three ships in Boston harbor and dump more than 300 crates of tea overboard as a protest against the British tea tax (**Dec. 16**).

**1774** First Continental Congress meets in Philadelphia, with 56 delegates representing every colony except Georgia. Delegates include Patrick Henry, George Washington, and Samuel Adams (**Sept. 5–Oct. 26**).

**1775–1783** American Revolution: War of independence fought between Great Britain and the 13 British colonies on the eastern seaboard of North America. Battles of Lexington and Concord, Mass., between the British Army and colonial minutemen, mark the beginning of the war (**April 19, 1775**). Battle-weary and destitute Continental army spends brutally cold winter and following spring at Valley Forge, Pa. (1777–1778). British general Charles Cornwallis surrenders to Gen. George Washington at Yorktown, Va. (**Oct. 19, 1781**). Great Britain formally acknowledges American Independence in the Treaty of Paris, which officially brings the war to a close (**Sept. 3, 1783**).

**1776** Continental Congress adopts the Declaration of Independence in Philadelphia (**July 4**).

**1777** Continental Congress approves the first official flag of the United States (**June 14**). Continental Congress adopts the Articles of Confederation, the first U.S. constitution (**Nov. 15**).

**1786** Shays's Rebellion erupts (**Aug.**); farmers from New Hampshire to South Carolina take up arms to protest high state taxes and stiff penalties for failure to pay.

**1787** Constitutional Convention, made up of delegates from 12 of the original 13 colonies, meets in Philadelphia to draft the U.S. Constitution (**May–Sept.**).

**1789** George Washington is unanimously elected president of the United States in a vote by state electors (**Feb. 4**). U.S. Constitution goes into effect, having been ratified by nine states (**March 4**). U.S. Congress meets for the first time at Federal Hall in New York City (**March 4**). Washington is inaugurated as president at Federal Hall in New York City (**April 30**).

**1790** U.S. Supreme Court meets for the first time at the Merchants Exchange Building in New York City (**Feb. 2**). The court, made up of one chief justice and five associate justices, hears its first case in 1792. The nation's first census shows that the population has climbed to nearly 4 million.

**1791** First ten amendments to the Constitution, known as the Bill of Rights, are ratified (**Dec. 15**).

**1793** Washington's second inauguration is held in Philadelphia (**March 4**).

**1797** John Adams is inaugurated as the second president in Philadelphia (**March 4**).

**1800** The U.S. capital is moved from Philadelphia to Washington, DC (**June 15**). U.S. Congress meets in Washington, DC, for the first time (**Nov. 17**).

**1801** Thomas Jefferson is inaugurated as the third president in Washington, DC (**March 4**).

**1803** Louisiana Purchase: United States agrees to pay France $15 million for the Louisiana Territory, which extends west from the Mississippi River to the Rocky Mountains and comprises about 830,000 sq mi (treaty signed **May 2**). As a result, the U.S. nearly doubles in size.

**1804** Lewis and Clark set out from St. Louis, Mo., on expedition to explore the West and find a route to the Pacific Ocean. (**May 14**).

**1805** Jefferson's second inauguration (**March 4**). Lewis and Clark reach the Pacific Ocean (**Nov. 15**).

**1809** James Madison is inaugurated as the fourth president in Washington, DC (**March 4**).

**1812–1814** War of 1812: U.S. declares war on Britain over British interference with American maritime shipping and westward expansion (**June 18, 1812**). Madison's second inauguration (**March 4, 1813**). British capture Washington, DC, and set fire to White House and Capitol (**Aug. 1814**). Francis Scott Key writes *Star-Spangled Banner* as he watches British attack on Fort McHenry at Baltimore (**Sept. 13–14, 1814**). Treaty of Ghent is signed, officially ending the war (**Dec. 24, 1814**).

**1817** James Monroe is inaugurated as the fifth president (**March 4**).

**1819** Spain agrees to cede Florida to the United States (**Feb. 22**).

**1820** Missouri Compromise: In an effort to maintain the balance between free and slave states, Maine (formerly part of Massachusetts) is admitted as a free state so that Missouri can be admitted as a slave state; except for Missouri, slavery is prohibited in the Louisiana Purchase lands north of latitude 36°30′ **(March 3).**

**1821** Monroe's second inauguration **(March 5).**

**1823** Monroe Doctrine: In his annual address to Congress, President Monroe declares that the American continents are henceforth off-limits for further colonization by European powers **(Dec. 2).**

**1825** John Quincy Adams is inaugurated as the sixth president **(March 4).** Erie Canal, linking the Hudson River to Lake Erie, is opened for traffic **(Oct. 26).**

**1828** Construction is begun on the Baltimore and Ohio Railroad, the first public railroad in the U.S. **(July 4).**

**1829** Andrew Jackson is inaugurated as seventh president **(March 4).**

**1830** President Jackson signs the Indian Removal Act, which authorizes the forced removal of Native Americans living in the eastern part of the country to lands west of the Mississippi River **(May 28).** By the late 1830s the Jackson administration has relocated nearly 50,000 Native Americans.

**1833** Jackson's second inauguration **(March 4).**

**1836** Texas declares its independence from Mexico **(March 1).** Texan defenders of the Alamo are all killed during siege by the Mexican Army **(Feb. 24–March 6).** Texans defeat Mexicans at San Jacinto **(April 21).**

**1837** Martin Van Buren is inaugurated as the eighth president **(March 4).**

**1838** More than 15,000 Cherokee Indians are forced to march from Georgia to Indian Territory in present-day Oklahoma. Approximately 4,000 die from starvation and disease along the "Trail of Tears."

**1841** William Henry Harrison is inaugurated as the ninth president **(March 4).** He dies one month later **(April 4)** and is succeeded in office by his vice president, John Tyler.

**1845** U.S. annexes Texas by joint resolution of Congress **(March 1).** James Polk is inaugurated as the 11th president **(March 4).** The term "manifest destiny" appears for the first time in a magazine article by John L. O'Sullivan **(July–August).** It expresses the belief held by many white Americans that the United States is destined to expand across the continent.

**1846** Oregon Treaty fixes U.S.-Canadian border at 49th parallel; U.S. acquires Oregon territory **(June 15).**

**1846–1848** Mexican War: U.S. declares war on Mexico in effort to gain California and other territory in Southwest **(May 13, 1846).** War concludes with signing of Treaty of Guadalupe Hidalgo **(Feb. 2, 1848).** Mexico recognizes Rio Grande as new boundary with Texas and, for $15 million, agrees to cede territory comprising present-day California, Nevada, Utah, most of New Mexico and Arizona, and parts of Colorado and Wyoming.

**1848** Gold is discovered at Sutter's Mill in California **(Jan. 24)**; gold rush reaches its height the following year. Women's rights convention is held at Seneca Falls, N.Y. **(July 19–20).**

**1849** Zachary Taylor is inaugurated as the 12th president **(March 5).**

**1850** President Taylor dies **(July 9)** and is succeeded by his vice president, Millard Fillmore.

**1853** Franklin Pierce is inaugurated as the 14th president **(March 4).** Gadsden Purchase treaty is signed; U.S. acquires border territory from Mexico for $10 million **(Dec. 30).**

**1854** Congress passes the Kansas-Nebraska Act, establishing the territories of Kansas and Nebraska **(May 30).** The legislation repeals the Missouri Compromise of 1820 and renews tensions between anti- and proslavery factions.

**1857** James Buchanan is inaugurated as the 15th president **(March 4).**

**1858** Abraham Lincoln comes to national attention in a series of seven debates with Sen. Stephen A. Douglas during Illinois state election campaign **(Aug.–Oct.).**

**1859** Abolitionist John Brown and 21 followers capture federal arsenal at Harper's Ferry, Va. (now W. Va.), in an attempt to spark a slave revolt **(Oct. 16).**

**1860** Abraham Lincoln is elected president **(Nov. 6).** South Carolina secedes from the Union **(Dec. 20).**

**1861** Mississippi, Florida, Alabama, Georgia, and Louisiana secede **(Jan.).** Confederate States of America is established **(Feb. 8).** Jefferson Davis is elected president of the Confederacy **(Feb. 9).** Texas secedes **(March 2).** Abraham Lincoln is inaugurated as the 16th president **(March 4).**

**1861–1865** Civil War: Conflict between the North (the Union) and the South (the Confederacy) over the expansion of slavery into western states. Confederates attack Ft. Sumter in Charleston, S.C., marking the start of the war **(April 12, 1861).** Virginia, Arkansas, North Carolina, and Tennessee secede **(April–June).** Emancipation Proclamation is issued, freeing slaves in the Confederate states **(Jan. 1, 1863).** Gen. William T. Sherman captures Atlanta **(Sept. 2, 1864).** Lincoln's second inauguration **(March 4, 1865).** Gen. Ulysses S. Grant captures Richmond, Va., the capital of the Confederacy **(April 3).** Confederate general Robert E. Lee surrenders to Ulysses S. Grant at Appomattox Courthouse, Va., **(April 9).**

**1863** Homestead Act becomes law, allowing settlers to claim land (160 acres) after they have lived on it for five years **(Jan. 1).**

**1865** Lincoln is assassinated **(April 14)** by John Wilkes Booth in Washington, DC, and is succeeded by his vice president, Andrew Johnson. Thirteenth Amendment to the Constitution is ratified, prohibiting slavery **(Dec. 6).**

**1867** U.S. acquires Alaska from Russia for the sum of $7.2 million (treaty concluded **March 30).**

**1868** President Johnson is impeached by the House of Representatives **(Feb. 24),** but he is acquitted at his trial in the Senate **(May 26).** Fourteenth Amendment to the Constitution is ratified, defining citizenship **(July 9).**

**1869** Ulysses S. Grant is inaugurated as the 18th president **(March 4).** Central Pacific and Union Pacific railroads are joined at Promontory, Utah, creating first transcontinental railroad **(May 10).**

**1870** Fifteenth Amendment to the Constitution is ratified, giving blacks the right to vote **(Feb. 3)**.

**1871** Chicago fire kills 300 and leaves 90,000 people homeless **(Oct. 8–9)**.

**1872** Crédit Mobilier scandal breaks, involving several members of Congress **(Sept.)**.

**1873** Grant's second inauguration **(March 4)**.

**1876** Lt. Col. George A. Custer's regiment is wiped out by Sioux Indians under Sitting Bull at the Little Bighorn River, Mont. **(June 25)**.

**1877** Rutherford B. Hayes is inaugurated as the 19th president **(March 5)**. The first telephone line is built from Boston to Somerville, Mass.; the following year, President Hayes has the first telephone installed in the White House.

**1881** James A. Garfield is inaugurated as the 20th president **(March 4)**. He is shot **(July 2)** by Charles Guiteau in Washington, DC, and later dies from complications of his wounds in Elberon, N.J. **(Sept. 19)**. Garfield's vice president, Chester Alan Arthur, succeeds him in office.

**1882** U.S. adopts standard time **(Nov. 18)**.

**1885** Grover Cleveland is inaugurated as the 22nd president **(March 4)**.

**1886** Statue of Liberty is dedicated **(Oct. 28)**. American Federation of Labor is organized **(Dec.)**.

**1889** Benjamin Harrison is inaugurated as the 23rd president **(March 4)**. Oklahoma is opened to settlers **(April 22)**.

**1890** National American Woman Suffrage Association (NAWSA) is founded, with Elizabeth Cady Stanton as president. Sherman Antitrust Act is signed into law, prohibiting commercial monopolies **(July 2)**. Last major battle of the Indian Wars occurs at Wounded Knee in South Dakota **(Dec. 29)**. In reporting the results of the 1890 census, the Census Bureau announces that the West has been settled and the frontier is closed.

**1892** Ellis Island becomes chief immigration station of the U.S. **(Jan. 1)**.

**1893** Grover Cleveland is inaugurated a second time, as the 24th president **(March 4)**. He is the only president to serve two nonconsecutive terms.

**1897** William McKinley is inaugurated as the 25th president **(March 4)**.

**1898** Spanish-American War: USS *Maine* is blown up in Havana harbor **(Feb. 15)**, prompting U.S. to declare war on Spain **(April 25)**. Treaty of Paris is signed, ending the Spanish-American War **(Dec. 10)**; Spain gives up control of Cuba, which becomes an independent republic, and cedes Puerto Rico, Guam, and (for $20 million) the Philippines to the U.S.

**1898** U.S. annexes Hawaii by an act of Congress **(July 7)**.

**1899** U.S. acquires American Samoa by treaty with Great Britain and Germany **(Dec. 2)**.

**1900** Galveston hurricane leaves an estimated 6,000 to 8,000 dead **(Sept. 8)**. According to the census, the nation's population numbers nearly 76 million.

**1901** McKinley's second inauguration **(March 4)**. He is shot **(Sept. 6)** by anarchist Leon Czolgosz in Buffalo, N.Y., and later dies from his wounds **(Sept. 14)**. He is succeeded by his vice president, Theodore Roosevelt.

**1903** U.S. acquires Panama Canal Zone (treaty signed **Nov. 17**). Wright brothers make the first controlled, sustained flight in heavier-than-air aircraft at Kitty Hawk, N.C. **(Dec. 17)**.

**1905** Theodore Roosevelt's second inauguration **(March 4)**.

**1906** San Francisco earthquake leaves 500 dead or missing and destroys about 4 sq mi of the city **(April 18)**.

**1908** Bureau of Investigation, forerunner of the FBI, is established **(July 26)**.

**1909** William Howard Taft is inaugurated as the 27th president **(March 4)**. Mrs. Taft has 80 Japanese cherry trees planted along the banks of the Potomac River.

**1913** Woodrow Wilson is inaugurated as the 28th president **(March 4)**. Seventeenth Amendment to the Constitution is ratified, providing for the direct election of U.S. senators by popular vote rather than by the state legislatures **(April 8)**.

**1914–1918** World War I: U.S. enters World War I, declaring war on Germany **(April 6, 1917)** and Austria-Hungary **(Dec. 7, 1917)** three years after conflict began in 1914. Armistice ending World War I is signed **(Nov. 11, 1918)**.

**1914** Panama Canal opens to traffic **(Aug. 15)**.

**1915** First long distance telephone service, between New York and San Francisco, is demonstrated **(Jan. 25)**.

**1916** U.S. agrees to purchase Danish West Indies (Virgin Islands) for $25 million (treaty signed **Aug. 14**). Jeannette Rankin of Montana is the first woman elected to the U.S. House of Representatives **(Nov. 7)**.

**1917** Wilson's second inauguration **(March 5)**. First regular airmail service begins, with one round trip a day between Washington, DC, and New York **(May 15)**.

**1918** Eighteenth Amendment to the Constitution is ratified, prohibiting the manufacture, sale, and transportation of liquor **(Jan. 16)**. It is later repealed by the Twenty-First Amendment in 1933.

**1919** League of Nations meets for the first time; U.S. is not represented **(Jan. 13)**. Nineteenth Amendment to the Constitution is ratified, granting women the right to vote **(Aug. 18)**. President Wilson suffers a stroke **(Sept. 26)**. Treaty of Versailles, outlining terms for peace at the end of World War I, is rejected by the Senate **(Nov. 19)**.

**1921** Warren G. Harding is inaugurated as the 29th president **(March 4)**. He signs a resolution declaring peace with Austria and Germany **(July 2)**.

**1923** President Harding dies suddenly **(Aug. 2)**. He is succeeded by his vice president, Calvin Coolidge. Teapot Dome scandal breaks, as Senate launches an investigation into improper leasing of naval oil reserves during Harding administration **(Oct.)**.

**1925** Coolidge's second inauguration **(March 4)**. Tennessee passes a law against the teaching of evolution in public schools **(March 23)**, setting the stage for the Scopes Monkey Trial **(July 10–25)**.

**1927** Charles Lindbergh makes the first solo nonstop transatlantic flight in his plane *The Spirit of St. Louis* **(May 20–21)**.

**1929** Herbert Hoover is inaugurated as the 31st president (**March 4**). Stock market crash precipitates the Great Depression (**Oct. 29**).

**1931** *The Star-Spangled Banner* is adopted as the national anthem (**March 3**).

**1932** Hattie Wyatt Caraway of Arkansas is the first woman elected to the U.S. Senate, to fill a vacancy caused by the death of her husband (**Jan. 12**). She is reelected in 1932 and 1938. Amelia Earhart completes first solo nonstop transatlantic flight by a woman (**May 21**).

**1933** Twentieth Amendment to the Constitution, sometimes called the "Lame Duck Amendment," is ratified, moving the president's inauguration date from March 4 to Jan. 20 (**Jan. 23**). Franklin Roosevelt is inaugurated as the 32nd president (**March 4**). New Deal recovery measures are enacted by Congress (**March 9–June 16**). Twenty-First Amendment to the Constitution is ratified, repealing Prohibition (**Dec. 5**).

**1935** Works Progress Administration is established (**April 8**). Social Security Act is passed (**Aug. 14**). Bureau of Investigation (established 1908) becomes the Federal Bureau of Investigation under J. Edgar Hoover.

**1937** F. Roosevelt's second inauguration (**Jan. 20**).

**1938** Fair Labor Standards Act is passed, setting the first minimum wage in the U.S. at 25 cents per hour (**June 25**).

**1939–1945** World War II: U.S. declares its neutrality in European conflict (**Sept. 5, 1939**). F. Roosevelt's third inauguration (**Jan. 20, 1941**). He is the first and only president elected to a third term. Japan attacks Hawaii, Guam, and the Philippines (**Dec. 7, 1941**). U.S. declares war on Japan (**Dec. 8**). Germany and Italy declare war on the United States; U.S. reciprocates by declaring war on both countries (**Dec. 11**). Allies invade North Africa (**Oct.–Dec. 1942**) and Italy (**Sept.–Dec. 1943**). Allies invade France on D-Day (**June 6, 1944**). F. Roosevelt's fourth inauguration (**Jan. 20, 1945**). President Roosevelt, Churchill, and Stalin meet at Yalta in the USSR to discuss postwar occupation of Germany (**Feb. 4–11**). President Roosevelt dies of a stroke (**April 12**) and is succeeded by his vice president, Harry Truman. Germany surrenders unconditionally (**May 7**). First atomic bomb is detonated at Alamogordo, N.M. (**July 16**). President Truman, Churchill, and Stalin meet at Potsdam, near Berlin, Germany, to demand Japan's unconditional surrender and to discuss plans for postwar Europe (**July 17–Aug. 2**). U.S. drops atomic bomb on Hiroshima, Japan (**Aug. 6**). U.S. drops atomic bomb on Nagasaki, Japan (**Aug. 9**). Japan agrees to unconditional surrender (**Aug. 14**). Japanese envoys sign surrender terms aboard the USS *Missouri* in Tokyo harbor (**Sept. 2**).

**1945** United Nations is established (**Oct. 24**).

**1946** The Philippines, which had been ceded to the U.S. by Spain at the end of the Spanish-American War, becomes an independent republic (**July 4**).

**1947** Central Intelligence Agency is established.

**1948** Congress passes foreign aid bill including the Marshall Plan, which provides for European postwar recovery (**April 2**). Soviets begin blockade of Berlin in the first major crisis of the cold war (**June 24**). In response, U.S. and Great Britain begin airlift of food and fuel to West Berlin (**June 26**).

**1949** Truman's second inauguration (**Jan. 20**). North Atlantic Treaty Organization (NATO) is established (**April 4**). Soviets end blockade of Berlin (**May 12**), but airlift continues until Sept. 30.

**1950–1953** Korean War: Cold war conflict between Communist and non-Communist forces on Korean Peninsula. North Korean communists invade South Korea (**June 25, 1950**). President Truman, without the approval of Congress, commits American troops to battle (**June 27**). Armistice agreement is signed (**July 27, 1953**).

**1950–1975** Vietnam War: Prolonged conflict between Communist forces of North Vietnam, backed by China and the USSR, and non-Communist forces of South Vietnam, backed by the United States. President Truman authorizes $15 million in economic and military aid to the French, who are fighting to retain control of French Indochina, including Vietnam. As part of the aid package, Truman also sends 35 military advisers (**May 1950**). North Vietnamese torpedo boats allegedly attack U.S. destroyer in Gulf of Tonkin off the coast of North Vietnam (**Aug. 2, 1964**). Congress approves Gulf of Tonkin resolution, authorizing President Johnson to take any measures necessary to defend U.S. forces and prevent further aggression (**Aug. 7**). U.S. planes begin bombing raids of North Vietnam (**Feb. 1965**). First U.S. combat troops arrive in South Vietnam (**March 8–9**). North Vietnamese army and Viet Cong launch Tet Offensive, attacking Saigon and other key cities in South Vietnam (**Jan.–Feb. 1968**). American soldiers kill 300 Vietnamese villagers in My Lai massacre (**March 16**). U.S. troops invade Cambodia (**May 1, 1970**). Representatives of North and South Vietnam, the Viet Cong, and the U.S. sign a cease-fire agreement in Paris (**Jan. 27, 1973**). Last U.S. troops leave Vietnam (**March 29**). South Vietnamese government surrenders to North Vietnam; U.S. embassy Marine guards and last U.S. civilians are evacuated (**April 30, 1975**).

**1951** Twenty-Second Amendment to the Constitution is ratified, limiting the president to two terms (**Feb. 27**). President Truman speaks in first coast-to-coast live television broadcast (**Sept. 4**).

**1952** Puerto Rico becomes a U.S. commonwealth (**July 25**). First hydrogen bomb is detonated by the U.S. on Eniwetok, an atoll in the Marshall Islands (**Nov. 1**).

**1953** Dwight Eisenhower is inaugurated as the 34th president (**Jan. 20**). Julius and Ethel Rosenberg are executed for passing secret information about U.S. atomic weaponry to the Soviets (**June 19**).

**1954** Sen. Joseph R. McCarthy accuses army officials, members of the media, and other public figures of being Communists during highly publicized hearings (**April 22–June 17**).

**1957** Eisenhower's second inauguration (**Jan. 21**). President sends federal troops to Central High School in Little Rock, Ark., to enforce integration of black students (**Sept. 24**).

**1958** *Explorer I,* first American satellite, is launched (**Jan. 31**).

**1959** Alaska becomes the 49th state (**Jan. 3**) and Hawaii becomes the 50th state (**Aug. 21**).

**1961** U.S. severs diplomatic relations with Cuba (**Jan. 3**). John F. Kennedy is inaugurated as the 35th president (**Jan. 20**). Bay of Pigs invasion of Cuba fails (**April 17–20**). A mixed-race group of volunteers sponsored by the Committee on Racial Equality—the so-called Freedom Riders—travel on buses through the South in order to protest racially segregated interstate bus facilities (**May**).

**1962** Lt. Col. John Glenn becomes first U.S. astronaut to orbit Earth (**Feb. 20**). Cuban Missile Crisis: President Kennedy denounces Soviet Union for secretly installing missile bases on Cuba and initiates a naval blockade of the island (**Oct. 22–Nov. 20**).

**1963** Rev. Martin Luther King, Jr., delivers his "I Have a Dream" speech before a crowd of 200,000 during the civil rights march on Washington, DC (**Aug. 28**). President Kennedy is assassinated in Dallas, Tex. (**Nov. 22**). He is succeeded in office by his vice president, Lyndon B. Johnson.

**1964** President Johnson signs the Civil Rights Act (**July 2**).

**1965** In his annual state of the Union address, President Johnson proposes his Great Society program (**Jan. 4**). L. Johnson's second inauguration (**Jan. 20**). State troopers attack peaceful demonstrators led by Rev. Martin Luther King, Jr., as they try to cross bridge in Selma, Ala. (**March 7**). President Johnson signs the Voting Rights Act, which prohibits discriminatory voting practices (**Aug. 6**). In six days of rioting in Watts, a black section of Los Angeles, 35 people are killed and 883 injured (**Aug. 11–16**).

**1967** Twenty-Fifth Amendment to the Constitution is ratified, outlining the procedures for filling vacancies in the presidency and vice presidency (**Feb. 10**).

**1968** Rev. Martin Luther King, Jr., is assassinated in Memphis, Tenn. (**April 4**). Sen. Robert F. Kennedy is assassinated in Los Angeles, Calif. (**June 5–6**).

**1969** Richard Nixon is inaugurated as the 37th president (**Jan. 20**). Astronauts Neil Armstrong and Edwin Aldrin, Jr., become the first men to land on the Moon (**July 20**).

**1970** Four students are shot to death by National Guardsmen during an antiwar protest at Kent State University (**May 1**).

**1971** The Twenty-Sixth Amendment to the Constitution is ratified, lowering the voting age from 21 to 18 (**July 1**).

**1972** Nixon makes historic visit to Communist China (**Feb. 21–27**). U.S. and Soviet Union sign strategic arms control agreement known as SALT I (**May 26**). Five men, all employees of Nixon's reelection campaign, are caught breaking into rival Democratic headquarters at the Watergate complex in Washington, DC (**June 17**).

**1973** Nixon's second inauguration (**Jan. 20**). Senate Select Committee begins televised hearings to investigate Watergate cover-up (**May 17–Aug. 7**). Vice President Spiro T. Agnew resigns over charges of corruption and income tax evasion

(**Oct. 10**). President Nixon nominates Gerald R. Ford as vice president (**Oct. 12**). Ford is confirmed by Congress and sworn in (**Dec. 6**).

**1974** House Judiciary Committee recommends to full House that Nixon be impeached on grounds of obstruction of justice, abuse of power, and contempt of Congress (**July 27–30**). Nixon resigns; he is succeeded in office by his vice president, Gerald Ford (**Aug. 9**). Nixon is granted an unconditional pardon by President Ford (**Sept. 8**). Five former Nixon aides go on trial for their involvement in the Watergate cover-up (**Oct. 15**); H. R. Haldeman, John D. Ehrlichman, and John Mitchell eventually serve time in prison. Nelson Rockefeller is confirmed and sworn in as vice president (**Dec. 19**).

**1977** Jimmy Carter is inaugurated as the 39th president (**Jan. 20**). President Carter signs treaty (**Sept. 7**) agreeing to turn control of Panama Canal over to Panama on Dec. 31, 1999.

**1978** President Carter meets with Egyptian president Anwar Sadat and Israeli prime minister Menachem Begin at Camp David (**Sept. 6**); Sadat and Begin sign Camp David Accord, ending 30-year conflict between Egypt and Israel (**Sept. 17**).

**1979** U.S. establishes diplomatic ties with mainland China for the first time since Communist takeover in 1949 (**Jan. 1**). Malfunction at Three Mile Island nuclear reactor in Pennsylvania causes near meltdown (**March 28**). Panama takes control of the Canal Zone, formerly administered by U.S. (**Oct. 1**). Iranian students storm U.S. embassy in Teheran and hold 66 people hostage (**Nov. 4**); 13 of the hostages are released (**Nov. 19–20**).

**1980** President Carter announces that U.S. athletes will not attend Summer Olympics in Moscow unless Soviet Union withdraws from Afghanistan (**Jan. 20**). FBI's undercover bribery investigation, code named Abscam, implicates a U.S. senator, seven members of the House, and 31 other public officials (**Feb. 2**). U.S. mission to rescue hostages in Iran is aborted after a helicopter and cargo plane collide at the staging site in a remote part of Iran and 8 servicemen are killed (**April 25**).

**1981** Ronald Reagan is inaugurated as the 40th president (**Jan. 20**). U.S. hostages held in Iran are released after 444 days in captivity (**Jan. 20**). President Reagan is shot in the chest by John Hinckley, Jr. (**March 30**). Sandra Day O'Connor is sworn in as the first woman Supreme Court justice (**Sept. 25**).

**1982** Deadline for ratification of the Equal Rights Amendment to the Constitution passes without the necessary votes (**June 30**).

**1983** U.S. invades Caribbean island of Grenada after a coup by Marxist faction in the government (**Oct. 25**).

**1985** Reagan's second inauguration (**Jan. 21**).

**1986** Space shuttle *Challenger* explodes 73 seconds after liftoff, killing all seven crew members (**Jan. 28**). It is the worst accident in the history of the U.S. space program. U.S. bombs military bases in Libya in effort to deter terrorist strikes on American targets (**April 14**). Iran-Contra scandal breaks when White House is forced to reveal secret arms-for-hostages deals (**Nov.**).

**1987** Congress holds public hearings in Iran-Contra investigation (**May 5–Aug. 3**). In a speech in Berlin, President Reagan challenges Soviet leader Mikhail Gorbachev to "tear down this wall" and open Eastern Europe to political and economic reform (**June 12**). Reagan and Gorbachev sign INF treaty, the first arms-control agreement to reduce the superpowers' nuclear weapons (**Dec. 8**).

**1989** George H. W. Bush is inaugurated as the 41st president (**Jan. 20**). Oil tanker *Exxon Valdez* runs aground in Prince William Sound, spilling more than 10 million gallons of oil (**March 24**). It is the largest oil spill in U.S. history. President Bush signs legislation to provide for federal bailout of nearly 800 insolvent savings and loan institutions (**Aug. 9**). U.S. forces invade Panama in an attempt to capture Gen. Manuel Noriega, who previously had been indicted in the U.S. on drug trafficking charges (**Dec. 20**).

**1991** Persian Gulf War: U.S. leads international coalition in military operation (code named "Desert Storm") to drive Iraqis out of Kuwait (**Jan. 16–Feb. 28**). Iraq accepts terms of UN ceasefire, marking an end of the war (**April 6**).

**1991** U.S. and Soviet Union sign START I treaty, agreeing to further reduce strategic nuclear arms (**July 31**). Senate Judiciary Committee conducts televised hearings to investigate allegations of past sexual harassment brought against Supreme Court nominee Clarence Thomas by Anita Hill, a law professor at the University of Oklahoma (**Oct. 11–13**).

**1992** Following the breakup of the Soviet Union in Dec. 1991, President Bush and Russian president Boris Yeltsin meet at Camp David and formally declare an end to the cold war (**Feb. 1**). The acquittal of four white police officers charged in the 1991 beating of black motorist Rodney King in Los Angeles sets off several days of rioting, leading to more than 50 deaths, thousands of injuries and arrests, and $1 billion in property damage (**April 29**). President Bush authorizes sending U.S. troops to Somalia as part of UN relief effort (**Dec. 4**). President Bush grants pardons to six officials convicted or indicted in the Iran-Contra scandal, leading some to suspect a cover-up (**Dec. 24**).

**1993** Bill Clinton is inaugurated as the 42nd president (**Jan. 20**). Bomb explodes in basement garage of World Trade Center, killing 6, injuring 1,000, and causing more than $500 million in damage (**Feb. 26**). After 51-day standoff with federal agents, Branch Davidian compound in Waco, Tex., burns to the ground, killing 80 cult members (**April 19**). President Clinton orders missile attack against Iraq in retaliation for alleged plot to assassinate former President Bush (**June 26**). Eighteen U.S. soldiers are killed in ambush by Somali militiamen in Mogadishu (**Oct. 3–4**). President Clinton signs North American Free Trade Agreement into law (**Dec. 8**).

**1994** Paula Jones, a former Arkansas state employee, files a federal lawsuit against President Clinton for sexual harassment (**May 6**).

**1995** Bombing of federal office building in Oklahoma City kills 168 people (**April 19**). U.S.

establishes full diplomatic relations with Vietnam (**July 11**). President Clinton sends first 8,000 of 20,000 U.S. troops to Bosnia for 12-month peacekeeping mission (**Dec.**). Budget standoff between President Clinton and Congress results in partial shutdown of U.S. government (**Dec. 16–Jan. 6**).

**1997** Clinton's second inauguration (**Jan. 20**).

**1998** President Clinton denies having had a sexual relationship with a White House intern named Monica Lewinsky (**Jan. 17**). President Clinton releases 1999 federal budget plan; it is the first balanced budget since 1969 (**Feb. 2**). In televised address, President Clinton admits having had a sexual relationship with Monica Lewinsky (**Aug. 17**). U.S. launches missile attacks on targets in Sudan and Afghanistan following terrorist attacks on U.S. embassies in Kenya and Tanzania (**Aug. 20**). U.S. and Britain launch air strikes against weapons sites in Iraq (**Dec. 16**). House of Representatives votes to impeach President Clinton on charges of perjury and obstruction of justice (**Dec. 19**).

**1999** Senate acquits Clinton of impeachment charges (**Feb. 12**). NATO wages air campaign against Yugoslavia over killing and deportation of ethnic Albanians in Kosovo (**March 24–June 10**). School shooting at Columbine High School in Littleton, Colo., leaves 14 students (including the 2 shooters) and 1 teacher dead and 23 others wounded (**April 20**).

**2000** According to the census, the nation's population numbers more than 280 million (**April 1**). No clear winner is declared in close presidential election contest between Vice President Al Gore and Texas governor George W. Bush (**Nov. 7**). Bush's tiny lead prompts automatic recount of votes in Florida (**Nov. 8**). More than a month after presidential election, U.S. Supreme Court determines the outcome by ruling against a manual recount of ballots in certain Florida counties (**Dec. 12**). Bush formally accepts the presidency, having won a slim majority in the electoral college but not a majority of the popular vote (**Dec. 13**).

**2001** George W. Bush is inaugurated as the 43rd president (**Jan. 20**). Two hijacked jetliners ram twin towers of World Trade Center in worst terrorist attack against U.S.; a third hijacked plane flies into the Pentagon, and a fourth crashes in rural Pennsylvania. More than 3,000 people die in the attacks (**Sept. 11**). U.S. and Britain launch air attacks against targets in Afghanistan after Taliban government fails to hand over Saudi terrorist Osama bin Laden, the suspected mastermind behind the Sept. 11 attacks (**Oct. 7**). Following air campaign and ground assault by Afghani opposition troops, the Taliban regime topples (**Dec. 9**); however, the hunt for bin Laden and other members of al-Qaeda terrorist organization continues.

**2002** In his first State of the Union address, President Bush labels Iran, Iraq, and North Korea an "axis of evil" and declares that U.S. will wage war against states that develop weapons of mass destruction (**Jan. 29**).

*See* What Happened in 2002: Month-by-Month, National News, pp. 36–44.

# The Early Congresses

At the urging of Massachusetts and Virginia, the First Continental Congress met in Philadelphia on Sept. 5, 1774, and was attended by representatives of all the colonies except Georgia. Patrick Henry of Virginia declared: "The distinctions between Pennsylvanians, New Yorkers, and New Englanders are no more. I am not a Virginian but an American." This Congress, which adjourned Oct. 26, 1774, passed intercolonial resolutions calling for extensive boycott by the colonies against British trade.

The following year, most of the delegates from the colonies were chosen by popular election to attend the Second Continental Congress, which assembled in Philadelphia on May 10. As war had already begun between the colonies and England, the chief problems before the Congress were the procuring of military supplies, the establishment of an army and proper defenses, the issuing of continental bills of credit, etc. On June 15, 1775, George Washington was elected to command the Continental army. Congress adjourned Dec. 12, 1776.

Other Continental Congresses were held in Baltimore (1776–1777), Philadelphia (1777), Lancaster, Pa. (1777), York, Pa. (1777–1778), and Philadelphia (1778–1781).

In 1781, the Articles of Confederation, although establishing a league of the thirteen states rather than a strong central government, provided for the continuance of Congress. Known thereafter as the Congress of the Confederation, it held sessions in Philadelphia (1781–1783), Princeton, N.J. (1783), Annapolis, Md. (1783–1784), and Trenton, N.J. (1784). Five sessions were held in New York City between the years 1785 and 1789.

The Congress of the United States, established by the ratification of the Constitution, held its first meeting on March 4, 1789, in New York City. Several sessions of Congress were held in Philadelphia, and the first meeting in Washington, DC, was on Nov. 17, 1800.

## Presidents of the Continental Congresses

| Name | Elected | Birth and death dates | Name | Elected | Birth and death dates |
|---|---|---|---|---|---|
| Peyton Randolph, Va. | 9/5/1774 | c.1721–1775 | John Hanson, Md. | 11/5/1781 | 1715–1783 |
| Henry Middleton, S.C. | 10/22/1774 | 1717–1784 | Elias Boudinot, N.J. | 11/4/1782 | 1740–1821 |
| Peyton Randolph, Va. | 5/10/1775 | c.1721–1775 | Thomas Mifflin, Pa. | 11/3/1783 | 1744–1800 |
| John Hancock, Mass. | 5/24/1775 | 1737–1793 | Richard Henry Lee, Va. | 11/30/1784 | 1732–1794 |
| Henry Laurens, S.C. | 11/1/1777 | 1724–1792 | John Hancock, Mass.[1] | 11/23/1785 | 1737–1793 |
| John Jay, N.Y. | 12/10/1778 | 1745–1829 | Nathaniel Gorham, Mass. | 6/6/1786 | 1738–1796 |
| Samuel Huntington, Conn. | 9/28/1779 | 1731–1796 | Arthur St. Clair, Pa. | 2/2/1787 | 1734–1818 |
| Thomas McKean, Del. | 7/10/1781 | 1734–1817 | Cyrus Griffin, Va. | 1/22/1788 | 1748–1810 |

1. Resigned May 29, 1786, never having served, because of continued illness.

## States by Order of Entry into Union

| State | Entered Union | Year settled | State | Entered Union | Year settled |
|---|---|---|---|---|---|
| 1. Delaware | Dec. 7, 1787 | 1638 | 26. Michigan | Jan. 26, 1837 | 1668 |
| 2. Pennsylvania | Dec. 12, 1787 | 1682 | 27. Florida | Mar. 3, 1845 | 1565 |
| 3. New Jersey | Dec. 18, 1787 | 1660 | 28. Texas | Dec. 29, 1845 | 1682 |
| 4. Georgia | Jan. 2, 1788 | 1733 | 29. Iowa | Dec. 28, 1846 | 1788 |
| 5. Connecticut | Jan. 9, 1788 | 1634 | 30. Wisconsin | May 29, 1848 | 1766 |
| 6. Massachusetts | Feb. 6, 1788 | 1620 | 31. California | Sept. 9, 1850 | 1769 |
| 7. Maryland | Apr. 28, 1788 | 1634 | 32. Minnesota | May 11, 1858 | 1805 |
| 8. South Carolina | May 23, 1788 | 1670 | 33. Oregon | Feb. 14, 1859 | 1811 |
| 9. New Hampshire | June 21, 1788 | 1623 | 34. Kansas | Jan. 29, 1861 | 1727 |
| 10. Virginia | June 25, 1788 | 1607 | 35. West Virginia | June 20, 1863 | 1727 |
| 11. New York | July 26, 1788 | 1614 | 36. Nevada | Oct. 31, 1864 | 1849 |
| 12. North Carolina | Nov. 21, 1789 | 1660 | 37. Nebraska | Mar. 1, 1867 | 1823 |
| 13. Rhode Island | May 29, 1790 | 1636 | 38. Colorado | Aug. 1, 1876 | 1858 |
| 14. Vermont | Mar. 4, 1791 | 1724 | 39. North Dakota | Nov. 2, 1889 | 1812 |
| 15. Kentucky | June 1, 1792 | 1774 | 40. South Dakota | Nov. 2, 1889 | 1859 |
| 16. Tennessee | June 1, 1796 | 1709 | 41. Montana | Nov. 8, 1889 | 1809 |
| 17. Ohio | Mar. 1, 1803 | 1788 | 42. Washington | Nov. 11, 1889 | 1811 |
| 18. Louisiana | Apr. 30, 1812 | 1699 | 43. Idaho | July 3, 1890 | 1842 |
| 19. Indiana | Dec. 11, 1816 | 1733 | 44. Wyoming | July 10, 1890 | 1834 |
| 20. Mississippi | Dec. 10, 1817 | 1699 | 45. Utah | Jan. 4, 1896 | 1847 |
| 21. Illinois | Dec. 3, 1818 | 1720 | 46. Oklahoma | Nov. 16, 1907 | 1889 |
| 22. Alabama | Dec. 14, 1819 | 1702 | 47. New Mexico | Jan. 6, 1912 | 1610 |
| 23. Maine | Mar. 15, 1820 | 1624 | 48. Arizona | Feb. 14, 1912 | 1776 |
| 24. Missouri | Aug. 10, 1821 | 1735 | 49. Alaska | Jan. 3, 1959 | 1784 |
| 25. Arkansas | June 15, 1836 | 1686 | 50. Hawaii | Aug. 21, 1959 | 1820 |

Source: Compiled from various sources by the editors.

## The Confederate States of America

| State | Seceded from Union | Readmitted to Union[1] | State | Seceded from Union | Readmitted to Union[1] |
|---|---|---|---|---|---|
| 1. South Carolina | Dec. 20, 1860 | July 9, 1868 | 7. Texas | March 2, 1861 | March 30, 1870 |
| 2. Mississippi | Jan. 9, 1861 | Feb. 23, 1870 | 8. Virginia | April 17, 1861 | Jan. 26, 1870 |
| 3. Florida | Jan. 10, 1861 | June 25, 1868 | 9. Arkansas | May 6, 1861 | June 22, 1868 |
| 4. Alabama | Jan. 11, 1861 | July 13, 1868 | 10. North Carolina | May 20, 1861 | July 4, 1868 |
| 5. Georgia | Jan. 19, 1861 | July 15, 1870[2] | 11. Tennessee | June 8, 1861 | July 24, 1866 |
| 6. Louisiana | Jan. 26, 1861 | July 9, 1868 | | | |

NOTE: Four other slave states—Delaware, Maryland, Kentucky, and Missouri—remained in the Union. The latter two were actually represented on the Confederate flag, which, like the Stars and Stripes, featured a star for every state. 1. Date of readmission to representation in U.S. House of Representatives. 2. Second readmission date. First date was July 21, 1868, but the representatives were unseated March 5, 1869.

## Territorial Expansion

| Accession | Date | Area[1] | Accession | Date | Area[1] |
|---|---|---|---|---|---|
| United States | — | 3,717,796 | Other territory | | |
|   Territory in 1790 | — | 891,364 |   Philippines[2] | 1898 | 115,600 |
|   Louisiana Purchase | 1803 | 831,321 |   Puerto Rico | 1899 | 3,508 |
|   Florida | 1819 | 69,866 |   Guam | 1899 | 217 |
|   Texas | 1845 | 384,958 |   American Samoa | 1900 | 90 |
|   Oregon | 1846 | 283,439 |   Canal Zone[3] | 1904 | 553 |
|   Mexican Cession | 1848 | 530,706 |   Virgin Islands of U.S. | 1917 | 171 |
|   Gadsden Purchase | 1853 | 29,640 |   Trust Territory of Pacific Islands[4] | 1947 | 241 |
|   Alaska | 1867 | 591,004 |   Northern Mariana Islands | 1986 | 189 |
|   Hawaii | 1898 | 6,471 |   All other | — | 16 |
| | | | Total, 1990 | — | 3,722,228 |

1. Total area (land and water), in square miles. 2. Became independent in 1946. 3. Reverted to Panama in 1979. 4. Palau, the last remaining trust territory, became a sovereign state in 1994. *Source:* U.S. Bureau of the Census, Web: www.census.gov.

## History of the American Flag

According to popular legend, the first American flag was made by Betsy Ross, a Philadelphia seamstress who was acquainted with George Washington, leader of the Continental Army, and other influential Philadelphians. In May 1776, so the story goes, General Washington and two representatives from the Continental Congress visited Ross at her upholstery shop and showed her a rough design of the flag. Although Washington initially favored using a star with six points, Ross advocated for a five-pointed star, which could be cut with just one quick snip of the scissors, and the gentlemen were won over.

Unfortunately, historians have never been able to verify this charming version of events, although it is known that Ross made flags for the navy of Pennsylvania. The story of Washington's visit to the flagmaker became popular about the time of the country's first centennial, after William Canby, a grandson of Ross, told about her role in shaping U.S. history in a speech given at the Philadelphia Historical Society in March 1870.

What is known is that the first unofficial national flag, called the Grand Union Flag or the Continental Colours, was raised at the behest of General Washington near his headquarters outside Boston, Mass.,

on Jan. 1, 1776. The flag had 13 alternating red and white horizontal stripes and the British Union Flag (a predecessor of the Union Jack) in the canton. Another early flag had a rattlesnake and the motto "Don't Tread on Me."

The first official national flag, also known as the Stars and Stripes, was approved by the Continental Congress on June 14, 1777. The blue canton contained 13 stars, representing the original 13 colonies, but the layout varied. Although nobody knows for sure who designed the flag, it may have been Continental Congress member Francis Hopkinson.

After Vermont and Kentucky were admitted to the Union in 1791 and 1792, respectively, two more stars and two more stripes were added in 1795. This 15-star, 15-stripe flag was the "star-spangled banner" that inspired lawyer Francis Scott Key to write the poem that later became the U.S. national anthem.

In 1818, after five more states had gained admittance, Congress passed legislation fixing the number of stripes at 13 and requiring that the number of stars equal the number of states. The last new star, bringing the total to 50, was added on July 4, 1960, after Hawaii became a state.

## The Pledge of Allegiance to the Flag[1]

I pledge allegiance to the Flag of the United States of America, and to the Republic for which it stands, one Nation under God,[2] indivisible, with liberty and justice for all.

1. The original pledge was published in the Sept. 8, 1892, issue of *The Youth's Companion* in Boston. For years, the authorship was in dispute between James B. Upham and Francis Bellamy of the magazine's staff. In 1939, after a study of the controversy, the United States Flag Association decided that authorship be credited to Bellamy. 2. The phrase "under God" was added to the pledge on June 14, 1954.

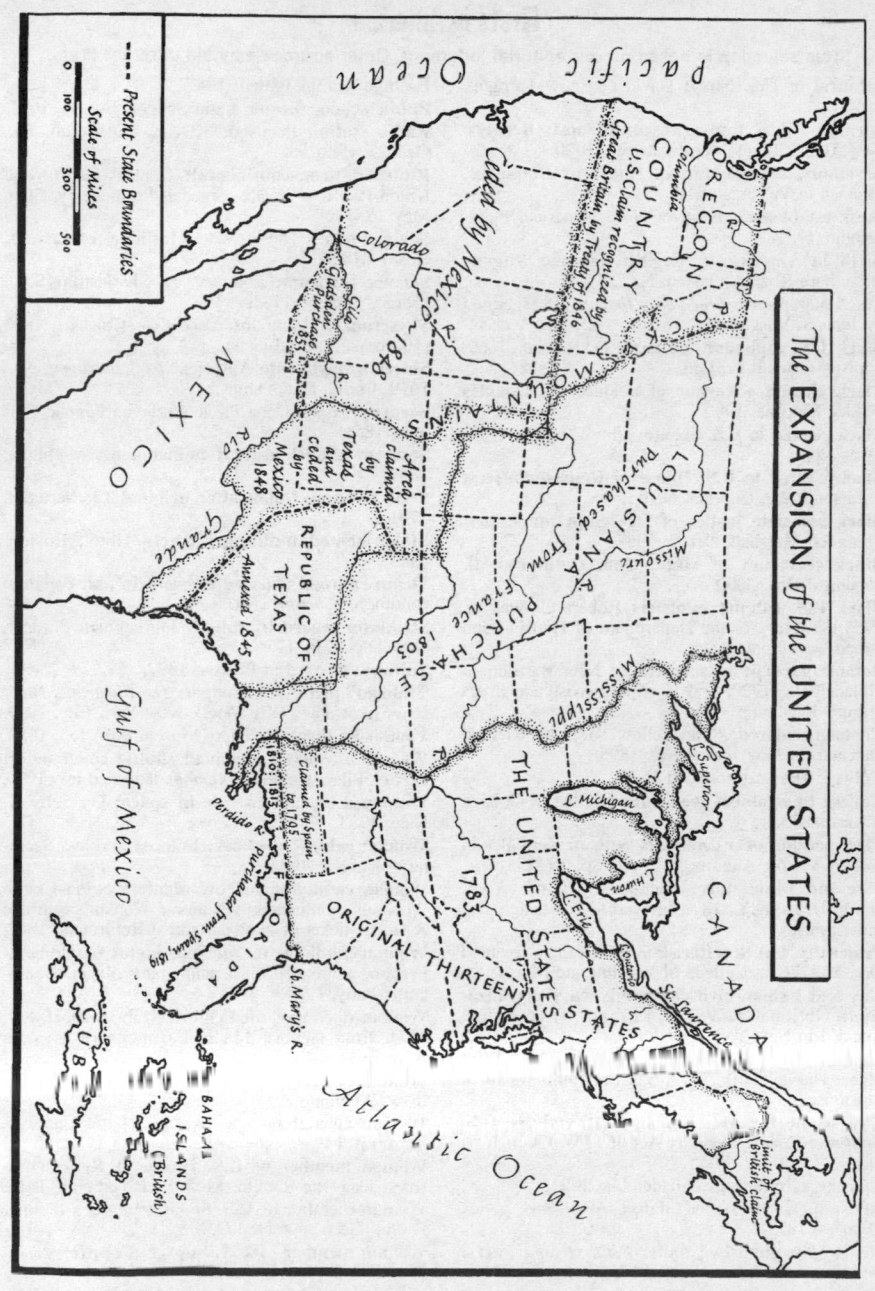

The EXPANSION of the UNITED STATES

Present State Boundaries

Scale of Miles
0  100  300  500

# Firsts in America

This selection is based on our editorial judgment. Other sources may list different firsts.

**Admiral in U.S. Navy:** David Glasgow Farragut, 1866.

**Airmail route, first transcontinental:** Between New York City and San Francisco, 1920.

**Assembly, representative:** House of Burgesses, founded in Virginia, 1619.

**Bank established:** Bank of North America, Philadelphia, 1781.

**Birth in America to English parents:** Virginia Dare, born Roanoke Island, N.C., 1587.

**Black newspaper:** *Freedom's Journal*, 1827, edited by John B. Russworm.

**Black U.S. diplomat:** Ebenezer D. Bassett, 1869, minister-resident to Haiti.

**Black elected governor of a state:** L. Douglas Wilder, Virginia, 1990.

**Black elected to U.S. Senate:** Hiram Revels, 1870, Mississippi.

**Black elected to U.S. House of Representatives:** Jefferson Long, Georgia, 1870.

**Black associate justice of U.S. Supreme Court:** Thurgood Marshall, Oct. 2, 1967.

**Black secretary of state:** Gen. Colin Powell, appointed Dec. 2000.

**Black U.S. cabinet minister:** Robert C. Weaver, 1966, Secretary of the Department of Housing and Urban Development.

**Botanic garden:** Established by John Bartram in Philadelphia, 1728, and is still in existence in its original location.

**Cartoon, colored:** "The Yellow Kid," by Richard Outcault, in *New York World*, 1895.

**College:** Harvard, founded 1636.

**College to establish coeducation:** Oberlin College (Ohio), 1833.

**Electrocution of a criminal:** William Kemmler in Auburn Prison, Auburn, N.Y., Aug. 6, 1890.

**Five and Dime store:** Founded by Frank Woolworth, Utica, N.Y., 1879 (moved to Lancaster, Pa., same year).

**Fraternity, Greek-letter:** Phi Beta Kappa; founded Dec. 5, 1776, at College of William and Mary.

**Gay and lesbian civil rights advocacy organization:** National Gay and Lesbian Task Force, founded in New York City, 1973.

**Homosexual, acknowledged, elected to high local office:** Harvey Milk, 1977, San Francisco Board of Supervisors.

**Law to be declared unconstitutional by U.S. Supreme Court:** Judiciary Act of 1789. Case: *Marbury v. Madison*, 1803.

**Library, circulating:** Philadelphia, 1731.

**Newspaper, illustrated daily:** *New York Daily Graphic*, 1873.

**Newspaper published daily:** *Pennsylvania Packet and General Advertiser*, Philadelphia, Sept. 1784.

**Newspaper published over a continuous period:** *The Boston News-Letter*, April 1704.

**Oil well, commercial:** Titusville, Pa., 1859.

**Panel quiz show on radio:** *Information Please*, May 17, 1938.

**Postage stamps issued:** 1847.

**Public school:** Boston Latin School, Boston, 1635.

**Radio station licensed:** KDKA, Pittsburgh, Pa., Oct. 27, 1920.

**Railroad, transcontinental:** Central Pacific and Union Pacific railroads, joined at Promontory, Utah, May 10, 1869.

**Savings bank:** The Provident Institute for Savings, Boston, 1816.

**Science museum:** Founded by Charleston (S.C.) Library Society, 1773.

**Skyscraper:** Home Insurance Co., Chicago, 1885 (10 floors, 2 added later).

**Slaves brought into America:** At Jamestown, Va., 1619, from a Dutch ship.

**Sorority:** Alpha Delta Pi, at Wesleyan Female College, 1851.

**State to abolish capital punishment:** Michigan, 1847.

**State to enter Union after original 13:** Vermont, 1791.

**Steam-heated building:** Eastern Hotel, Boston, 1845.

**Steam railroad (carried passengers and freight):** Baltimore & Ohio, 1830.

**Strike on record by union:** Journeymen Printers, New York City, 1776.

**Subway:** Opened in Boston, 1897.

**"Tabloid" picture newspaper:** *The Illustrated Daily News* (now *The Daily News*), New York City, 1919.

**Vaudeville theater:** Gaiety Museum, Boston, 1883.

**Woman astronaut appointed shuttle commander:** Lt. Col. Eileen Collins, *Columbia*, launched July 1999.

**Woman astronaut to ride in space:** Dr. Sally K. Ride, 1983.

**Woman cabinet member:** Frances Perkins, Secretary of Labor, 1933.

**Woman candidate for president:** Victoria Claflin Woodhull, nominated by National Woman's Suffrage Assn. on ticket of Nation Radical Reformers, 1872.

**Woman candidate for vice president:** Geraldine A. Ferraro, nominated on a major party ticket, Democratic Party, 1984.

**Woman doctor of medicine:** Elizabeth Blackwell; M.D. from Geneva Medical College of Western New York, 1849.

**Woman elected governor of a state:** Nellie Tayloe Ross, Wyoming, 1925.

**Woman elected to U.S. Senate:** Hattie Caraway, Arkansas; elected Nov. 1932.

**Woman member of U.S. House of Representatives:** Jeannette Rankin (Mont.); elected Nov. 1916.

**Woman member of U.S. Senate:** Rebecca Latimer Felton (Ga.); appointed Oct. 3, 1922.

**Woman member of U.S. Supreme Court:** Sandra Day O'Connor; appointed July 1981.

**Woman secretary of state:** Madeleine Albright, appointed Dec. 1996.

**Woman suffrage granted:** Wyoming Territory, 1869.

**Written constitution:** *Fundamental Orders of Connecticut*, 1639.

## The Great Seal of the U.S.

On July 4, 1776, the Continental Congress appointed a committee consisting of Benjamin Franklin, John Adams, and Thomas Jefferson "to bring in a device for a seal of the United States of America." After many delays, a verbal description of a design by William Barton was finally approved by Congress on June 20, 1782. The seal shows an American bald eagle with a ribbon in its mouth bearing the device *E pluribus unum* (One out of many). In its talons are the arrows of war and an olive branch of peace. On the reverse side it shows an unfinished pyramid with an eye (the eye of Providence) above it. Although this description was adopted in 1782, the first drawing was not made until four years later, and no die has ever been cut.

## The Star-Spangled Banner

### Francis Scott Key, 1814

*O say, can you see, by the dawn's early light,*
*What so proudly we hail'd at the twilight's last gleaming?*
*Whose broad stripes and bright stars, thro' the perilous fight,*
*O'er the ramparts we watch'd, were so gallantly streaming?*
*And the rockets' red glare, the bombs bursting in air,*
*Gave proof thro' the night that our flag was still there.*
*O say, does that star-spangled banner yet wave*
*O'er the land of the free and the home of the brave?*

*On the shore dimly seen thro' the mists of the deep,*
*Where the foe's haughty host in dread silence reposes,*
*What is that which the breeze, o'er the towering steep,*
*As it fitfully blows, half conceals, half discloses?*
*Now it catches the gleam of the morning's first beam,*
*In full glory reflected, now shines on the stream:*
*'Tis the star-spangled banner: O, long may it wave*
*O'er the land of the free and the home of the brave!*

*And where is that band who so vauntingly swore*
*That the havoc of war and the battle's confusion,*
*A home and a country should leave us no more?*
*Their blood has wash'd out their foul footsteps' pollution.*
*No refuge could save the hireling and slave*
*From the terror of flight or the gloom of the grave:*
*And the star-spangled banner in triumph doth wave*
*O'er the land of the free and the home of the brave.*

*O thus be it ever when free-men shall stand*
*Between their lov'd home and the war's desolation;*
*Blest with vict'ry and peace, may the heav'n-rescued land*
*Praise the power that hath made and preserv'd us a nation!*
*Then conquer we must, when our cause it is just,*
*And this be our motto: "In God is our trust!"*
*And the star-spangled banner in triumph shall wave*
*O'er the land of the free and the home of the brave!*

On Sept. 13, 1814, Francis Scott Key visited the British fleet in Chesapeake Bay to secure the release of Dr. William Beanes, who had been captured after the burning of Washington, DC. The release was secured, but Key was detained on ship overnight during the shelling of Fort McHenry, one of the forts defending Baltimore. In the morning, he was so delighted to see the American flag still flying over the fort that he began a poem to commemorate the occasion. First published under the title "Defense of Fort M'Henry," the poem soon attained wide popularity as sung to the tune "To Anacreon in Heaven." The origin of this tune is obscure, but it may have been written by John Stafford Smith, a British composer born in 1750. "The Star-Spangled Banner" was officially made the national anthem by Congress in 1931, although it already had been adopted as such by the army and the navy.

# The Liberty Bell

The Liberty Bell was cast in England in 1752 for the Pennsylvania Statehouse (now named Independence Hall) in Philadelphia. It was recast in Philadelphia in 1753. It is inscribed with the words, "Proclaim liberty throughout all the land unto all the inhabitants thereof" (Lev. 25:10). The bell was rung on July 8, 1776, for the first public reading of the Declaration of Independence. Hidden in Allentown during the British occupation of Philadelphia, it was re-placed in Independence Hall in 1778. The bell cracked on July 8, 1835, while tolling the death of Chief Justice John Marshall. In 1976 the Liberty Bell was moved to a special exhibition building near Independence Hall.

# The Declaration of Independence

On April 12, 1776, the legislature of North Carolina authorized its delegates to the Continental Congress to join with others in a declaration of separation from Great Britain; the first colony to instruct its delegates to take the actual initiative was Virginia on May 15. On June 7, 1776, Richard Henry Lee of Virginia offered a resolution to the Congress to the effect "that these United Colonies are, and of right ought to be, free and independent States. . . ." A committee consisting of Thomas Jefferson, John Adams, Benjamin Franklin, Robert R. Livingston, and Roger Sherman was organized to "prepare a declaration to the effect of the said first resolution." The Declaration of Independence was adopted on July 4, 1776. Most delegates signed the Declaration August 2, but George Wythe (Va.) signed August 27; Richard Henry Lee (Va.), Elbridge Gerry (Mass.), and Oliver Wolcott (Conn.) in September; Matthew Thornton (N.H.), not a delegate until September, in November; and Thomas McKean (Del.), although present on July 4, not until 1781 by special permission, having served in the army in the interim.

**In Congress, July 4, 1776**

**The unanimous Declaration of the thirteen United States of America**

When in the Course of human events it becomes necessary for one people to dissolve the political bands which have connected them with another, and to assume among the powers of the earth, the separate and equal station to which the Laws of Nature and of Nature's God entitle them, a decent respect to the opinions of mankind requires that they should declare the causes which impel them to the separation.

We hold these truths to be self-evident, that all men are created equal, that they are endowed by their Creator with certain unalienable Rights, that among these are Life, Liberty and the pursuit of Happiness.—That to secure these rights, Governments are instituted among Men, deriving their just powers from the consent of the governed.—That whenever any Form of Government becomes destructive of these ends, it is the Right of the People to alter or to abolish it, and to institute new Government, laying its foundation on such principles and organizing its powers in such form, as to them shall seem most likely to effect their Safety and Happiness. Prudence, indeed, will dictate that Governments long established should not be changed for light and transient causes; and accordingly all experience hath shewn that mankind are more disposed to suffer, while evils are sufferable, than to right themselves by abolishing the forms to which they are accustomed. But when a long train of abuses and usurpations, pursuing invariably the same Object evinces a design to reduce them under absolute Despotism, it is their right, it is their duty, to throw off such Government, and to provide new Guards for their future security.—Such has been the patient sufferance of these Colonies; and such is now the necessity which constrains them to alter their former Systems of Government. The history of the present King of Great Britain is a history of repeated injuries and usurpations, all having in direct object the establishment of an absolute Tyranny over these States. To prove this, let Facts be submitted to a candid world.

He has refused his Assent to Laws, the most wholesome and necessary for the public good.

He has forbidden his Governors to pass Laws of immediate and pressing importance, unless suspended in their operation till his Assent should be obtained; and when so suspended, he has utterly neglected to attend to them.

He has refused to pass other Laws for the accommodation of large districts of people, unless those people would relinquish the right of Representation in the Legislature, a right inestimable to them and formidable to tyrants only.

He has called together legislative bodies at places unusual, uncomfortable, and distant from the depository of their Public Records, for the sole purpose of fatiguing them into compliance with his measures.

He has dissolved Representative Houses repeatedly, for opposing with manly firmness his invasions on the rights of the people.

He has refused for a long time, after such dissolutions, to cause others to be elected; whereby the Legislative Powers, incapable of Annihilation, have returned to the People at large for their exercise; the State remaining in the mean time exposed to all the dangers of invasion from without, and convulsions within.

He has endeavoured to prevent the population of these States; for that purpose obstructing the Laws for Naturalization of Foreigners; refusing to pass others to encourage their migrations hither, and raising the conditions of new Appropriations of Lands.

He has obstructed the Administration of Justice, by refusing his Assent to Laws for establishing Judiciary Powers.

He has made Judges dependent on his Will alone, for the tenure of their offices, and the amount and payment of their salaries.

He has erected a multitude of New Offices, and sent hither swarms of Officers to harass our people, and eat out their substance.

He has kept among us, in times of peace, Standing Armies without the Consent of our legislatures.

He has affected to render the Military independent of and superior to the Civil Power.

He has combined with others to subject us to a jurisdiction foreign to our constitution, and unacknowledged by our laws; giving his Assent to their Acts of pretended Legislation:

For quartering large bodies of armed troops among us:

For protecting them, by a mock Trial, from punishment for any Murders which they should commit on the Inhabitants of these States:

For cutting off our Trade with all parts of the world:

For imposing Taxes on us without our Consent:

For depriving us in many cases, of the benefits of Trial by Jury:

For transporting us beyond Seas to be tried for pretended offences:

For abolishing the free System of English Laws in a neighbouring Province, establishing therein an Arbitrary government, and enlarging its Boundaries so as to render it at once an example and fit instrument for introducing the same absolute rule into these Colonies:

For taking away our Charters, abolishing our most valuable Laws and altering fundamentally the Forms of our Governments:

For suspending our own Legislatures, and declaring themselves invested with power to legislate for us in all cases whatsoever.

He has abdicated Government here, by declaring us out of his Protection and waging War against us.

He has plundered our seas, ravaged our Coasts, burnt our towns, and destroyed the lives of our people.

He is at this time transporting large Armies of foreign Mercenaries to compleat the works of death, desolation, and tyranny, already begun with circumstances of Cruelty & Perfidy scarcely paralleled in the most barbarous ages, and totally unworthy the Head of a civilized nation.

He has constrained our fellow Citizens taken Captive on the high Seas to bear Arms against their Country, to become the executioners of their friends and Brethren, or to fall themselves by their Hands.

He has excited domestic insurrections amongst us, and has endeavoured to bring on the inhabitants of our frontiers, the merciless Indian Savages, whose known rule of warfare, is an undistinguished destruction of all ages, sexes and conditions.

In every stage of these Oppressions We have Petitioned for Redress in the most humble terms: Our repeated Petitions have been answered only by repeated injury. A Prince, whose character is thus marked by every act which may define a Tyrant, is unfit to be the ruler of a free people.

Nor have We been wanting in attentions to our British brethren. We have warned them from time to time of attempts by their legislature to extend an unwarrantable jurisdiction over us. We have reminded them of the circumstances of our emigration and settlement here. We have appealed to their native justice and magnanimity, and we have conjured them by the ties of our common kindred to disavow these usurpations, which would inevitably interrupt our connections and correspondence. They too have been deaf to the voice of justice and of consanguinity. We must, therefore, acquiesce in the necessity, which denounces our Separation, and hold them, as we hold the rest of mankind, Enemies in War, in Peace Friends.

We, therefore, the Representatives of the United States of America, in General Congress, Assembled, appealing to the Supreme Judge of the world for the rectitude of our intentions, do, in the Name, and by Authority of the good People of these Colonies, solemnly publish and declare, That these United Colonies are, and of Right ought to be Free and Independent States; that they are Absolved from all Allegiance to the British Crown, and that all political connection between them and the State of Great Britain, is and ought to be totally dissolved; and that as Free and Independent States, they have full Power to levy War, conclude Peace, contract Alliances, establish Commerce, and to do all other Acts and Things which Independent States may of right do.—And for the support of this Declaration, with a firm reliance on the protection of Divine Providence, we mutually pledge to each other our Lives, our Fortunes and our sacred Honor.

—John Hancock

| | | | |
|---|---|---|---|
| **New Hampshire** | **New Jersey** | John Adams | Benj. Harrison |
| Josiah Bartlett | Richd. Stockton | Robt. Treat Paine | Ths. Nelson, Jr. |
| Wm. Whipple | Jno. Witherspoon | Elbridge Gerry | Francis Lightfoot Lee |
| Matthew Thornton | Fras. Hopkinson | | Carter Braxton |
| | John Hart | **Delaware** | |
| **Rhode Island** | Abra. Clark | Caesar Rodney | **North Carolina** |
| Step. Hopkins | | [illegible] | [illegible] |
| William Ellery | **Pennsylvania** | Tho. M'Kean | Joseph Hewes |
| | Robt. Morris | | John Penn |
| **Connecticut** | Benjamin Rush | **Maryland** | |
| Roger Sherman | Benj. Franklin | Samuel Chase | **South Carolina** |
| Sam el Huntington | John Morton | Wm. Paca | Edward Rutledge |
| Wm. Williams | Geo. Clymer | Thos. Stone | Thos. Heyward, Junr. |
| Oliver Wolcott | Jas. Smith | Charles Carroll of | Thomas Lynch, Junr. |
| | Geo. Taylor | Carrollton | Arthur Middleton |
| **New York** | James Wilson | | |
| Wm. Floyd | Geo. Ross | **Virginia** | **Georgia** |
| Phil. Livingston | | George Wythe | Button Gwinnett |
| Frans. Lewis | **Massachusetts-Bay** | Richard Henry Lee | Lyman Hall |
| Lewis Morris | Saml. Adams | Th. Jefferson | Geo. Walton |

# Constitution of the United States of America

(Historical text has been edited to conform to contemporary American usage. The bracketed words are designations for your convenience; they are not part of the Constitution.)

*The oldest federal constitution in existence was framed by a convention of delegates from twelve of the thirteen original states in Philadelphia in May 1787, Rhode Island failing to send a delegate. George Washington presided over the session, which lasted until September 17, 1787. The draft (originally a preamble and seven Articles) was submitted to all thirteen states and was to become effective when ratified by nine states. It went into effect on the first Wednesday in March 1789, having been ratified by New Hampshire, the ninth state to approve, on June 21, 1788. The states ratified the Constitution in the following order:*

| | | | |
|---|---|---|---|
| Delaware | December 7, 1787 | South Carolina | May 23, 1788 |
| Pennsylvania | December 12, 1787 | New Hampshire | June 21, 1788 |
| New Jersey | December 18, 1787 | Virginia | June 25, 1788 |
| Georgia | January 2, 1788 | New York | July 26, 1788 |
| Connecticut | January 9, 1788 | North Carolina | November 21, 1789 |
| Massachusetts | February 6, 1788 | Rhode Island | May 29, 1790 |
| Maryland | April 28, 1788 | | |

## [Preamble]

We the people of the United States, in order to form a more perfect Union, establish justice, insure domestic tranquility, provide for the common defence, promote the general welfare, and secure the blessings of liberty to ourselves and our posterity, do ordain and establish this Constitution for the United States of America.

## Article I

### Section 1

[Legislative powers vested in Congress.] All legislative powers herein granted shall be vested in a Congress of the United States, which shall consist of a Senate and House of Representatives.

### Section 2

[Composition of the House of Representatives.—1.] The House of Representatives shall be composed of members chosen every second year by the people of the several States, and the electors in each State shall have the qualifications requisite for electors of the most numerous branch of the State Legislature.

[Qualifications of Representatives.—2.] No Person shall be a Representative who shall not have attained to the age of twenty-five years, and been seven years a citizen of the United States, and who shall not, when elected, be an inhabitant of that State in which he shall be chosen.

[Apportionment of Representatives and direct taxes—census.[1]—3.] (Representatives and direct taxes shall be apportioned among the several States which may be included within this Union, according to their respective numbers, which shall be determined by adding to the whole number of free persons, including those bound to service for a term of years, and excluding Indians not taxed, three fifths of all other persons.) The actual enumeration shall be made within three years after the first meeting of the Congress of the United States, and within every subsequent term of ten years, in such manner as they shall by law direct. The number of Representatives shall not exceed one for every thirty thousand, but each State shall have at least one Representa-

tive; and until such enumeration shall be made, the State of New Hampshire shall be entitled to choose three, Massachusetts eight, Rhode-Island and Providence Plantations one, Connecticut five, New York six, New Jersey four, Pennsylvania eight, Delaware one, Maryland six, Virginia ten, North Carolina five, South Carolina five, and Georgia three.

[Filling of vacancies in representation.—4.] When vacancies happen in the representation from any State, the Executive Authority thereof shall issue writs of election to fill such vacancies.

[Selection of officers; power of impeachment.—5.] The House of Representatives shall choose their Speaker and other officers; and shall have the sole power of impeachment.

### Section 3[2]

[The Senate.—1.] The Senate of the United States shall be composed of two Senators from each State, chosen by the Legislature thereof, for six years; and each Senator shall have one vote.

[Classification of Senators; filling of vacancies.—2.] Immediately after they shall be assembled in consequence of the first election, they shall be divided as equally as may be into three classes. The seats of the Senators of the first class shall be vacated at the expiration of the second year, of the second class at the expiration of the fourth year, and of the third class at the expiration of the sixth year, so that one-third may be chosen every second year; and if vacancies happen by resignation, or otherwise, during the recess of the Legislature of any State, the Executive thereof may make temporary appointments (until the next meeting of the Legislature, which shall then fill such vacancies).

[Qualification of Senators.—3.] No person shall be a Senator who shall not have attained to the age of thirty years, and been nine years a citizen of the United States, and who shall not, when elected, be an inhabitant of that State for which he shall be chosen.

[Vice President to be President of Senate.—4.] The Vice President of the United States shall be President of the Senate, but shall have no vote, unless they be equally divided.

[Selection of Senate officers; President pro tempore.—5.] The Senate shall choose their other

1. The clause included in parentheses is amended by the 14th Amendment, Section 2. 2. The first paragraph of this section and the part of the second paragraph included in parentheses are amended by the 17th Amendment.

officers, and also a President pro tempore, in the absence of the Vice President, or when he shall exercise the office of President of the United States.

**[Senate to try impeachments.—6.]** The Senate shall have the sole power to try all impeachments. When sitting for that purpose, they shall be on oath or affirmation. When the President of the United States is tried, the Chief Justice shall preside: and no person shall be convicted without the concurrence of two thirds of the members present.

**[Judgment in cases of Impeachment.—7.]** Judgment in cases of impeachment shall not extend further than to removal from office, and disqualification to hold and enjoy any office of honor, trust, or profit under the United States: but the party convicted shall nevertheless be liable and subject to indictment, trial, judgment and punishment, according to Law.

### Section 4

**[Control of congressional elections.—1.]** The times, places, and manner of holding elections for Senators and Representatives, shall be prescribed in each State by the Legislature thereof; but the Congress may at any time by law make or alter such regulations, except as to the places of choosing Senators.

**[Time for assembling of Congress[3]—2.]** The Congress shall assemble at least once in every year, and such meeting shall be on the first Monday in December, unless they shall by law appoint a different day.

### Section 5

**[Each house to be the judge of the election and qualifications of its members; regulations as to quorum.—1.]** Each House shall be the judge of the elections, returns, and qualifications of its own members, and a majority of each shall constitute a quorum to do business; but a smaller number may adjourn from day to day, and may be authorized to compel the attendance of absent members, in such manner, and under such penalties as each House may provide.

**[Each house to determine its own rules.—2.]** Each House may determine the rules of its proceedings, punish its members for disorderly behavior, and, with the concurrence of two thirds, expel a member.

**[Journals and yeas and nays.—3.]** Each House shall keep a journal of its proceedings, and from time to time publish the same, excepting such parts as may in their judgment require secrecy; and the yeas and nays of the members of either House on ⸺⸺⸺⸺⸺⸺⸺⸺⸺⸺⸺ present, be entered on the journal.

**[Adjournment.—4.]** Neither House, during the session of Congress, shall, without the consent of the other, adjourn for more than three days, nor to any other place than that in which the two Houses shall be sitting.

### Section 6

**[Compensation and privileges of members of Congress.—1.]** The Senators and Representatives shall receive a compensation for their services, to be ascertained by law, and paid out of the Treasury of the United States. They shall in all cases, except

treason, felony, and breach of the peace, be privileged from arrest during their attendance at the session of their respective Houses, and in going to and returning from the same; and for any speech or debate in either House, they shall not be questioned in any other place.

**[Incompatible offices; exclusions.—2.]** No Senator or Representative shall, during the time for which he was elected, be appointed to any civil office under the authority of the United States, which shall have been created, or the emoluments whereof shall have been increased during such time; and no person holding any office under the United States shall be a member of either House during his continuance in office.

### Section 7

**[Revenue bills to originate in House.—1.]** All bills for raising revenue shall originate in the House of Representatives; but the Senate may propose or concur with amendments as on other bills.

**[Manner of passing bills; veto power of President.—2.]** Every bill which shall have passed the House of Representatives and the Senate, shall, before it becomes a law, be presented to the President of the United States; if he approve he shall sign it, but if not he shall return it, with his objections to that House in which it shall have originated, who shall enter the objections at large on their journal, and proceed to reconsider it. If after such reconsideration two thirds of that House shall agree to pass the bill, it shall be sent, together with the objections, to the other House, by which it shall likewise be reconsidered, and if approved by two thirds of that House, it shall become a law. But in all such cases the votes of both Houses shall be determined by yeas and nays, and the names of the persons voting for and against the bill shall be entered on the journal of each house, respectively. If any bill shall not be returned by the President within ten days (Sundays excepted) after it shall have been presented to him, the same shall be a law, in like manner as if he had signed it, unless the Congress by their adjournment prevent its return, in which case it shall not be a law.

**[Concurrent orders or resolutions, to be passed by President.—3.]** Every order, resolution, or vote to which the concurrence of the Senate and House of Representatives may be necessary (except on a question of adjournment) shall be presented to the President of the United States; and before the same shall take effect, shall be approved by him, or being ⸺⸺⸺⸺⸺⸺⸺⸺⸺⸺⸺⸺⸺⸺⸺ of the Senate and House of Representatives, according to the rules and limitations prescribed in the case of a bill.

### Section 8

**[General powers of Congress.[4]]**

**[Taxes, duties, imposts, and excises.—1.]** The Congress shall have power to lay and collect taxes, duties, imposts and excises, to pay the debts and provide for the common defense and general welfare of the United States; but all duties, imposts and excises shall be uniform throughout the United States;

---

3. Amended by the 20th Amendment, Section 2. 4. By the 16th Amendment, Congress is given the power to lay and collect taxes on income.

[Borrowing of money.—2.] To borrow money on the credit of the United States;

[Regulation of commerce.—3.] To regulate commerce with foreign nations, and among the several States, and with the Indian tribes;

[Naturalization and bankruptcy.—4.] To establish a uniform rule of naturalization, and uniform laws on the subject of bankruptcies throughout the United States;

[Money, weights and measures.—5.] To coin money, regulate the value thereof, and of foreign coin, and fix the standard of weights and measures;

[Counterfeiting.—6.] To provide for the punishment of counterfeiting the securities and current coin of the United States;

[Post offices.—7.] To establish post offices and post roads;

[Patents and copyrights.—8.] To promote the progress of science and useful arts, by securing for limited times to authors and inventors the exclusive right to their respective writings and discoveries;

[Inferior courts.—9.] To constitute tribunals inferior to the Supreme Court;

[Piracies and felonies.—10.] To define and punish piracies and felonies committed on the high seas, and offences against the law of nations;

[War; marque and reprisal.—11.] To declare war, grant letters of marque and reprisal, and make rules concerning captures on land and water;

[Armies.—12.] To raise and support armies, but no appropriation of money to that use shall be for a longer term than two years;

[Navy.—13.] To provide and maintain a navy;

[Land and naval forces.—14.] To make rules for the government and regulation of the land and naval forces;

[Calling out militia.—15.] To provide for calling forth the militia to execute the laws of the Union, suppress insurrections, and repel invasions;

[Organizing, arming, and disciplining militia. —16.] To provide for organizing, arming, and disciplining, the militia, and for governing such part of them as may be employed in the service of the United States, reserving to the States, respectively, the appointment of the officers, and the authority of training the militia according to the discipline prescribed by Congress;

[Exclusive legislation over District of Columbia.—17.] To exercise exclusive legislation in all cases whatsoever, over such district (not exceeding ten miles square) as may, by cession of particular States, and the acceptance of Congress, become the seat of the Government of the United States, and to exercise like authority over all places purchased by the consent of the Legislature of the State in which the same shall be, for the erection of forts, magazines, arsenals, dock-yards, and other needful buildings;—And

[To enact laws necessary to enforce Constitution.—18.] To make all laws which shall be necessary and proper for carrying into execution the foregoing powers, and all other powers vested by this Constitution in the Government of the United States, or in any department or officer thereof.

## Section 9

[Migration or importation of certain persons not to be prohibited before 1808.—1.] The migration or importation of such persons as any of the States now existing shall think proper to admit, shall not be prohibited by the Congress prior to the year one thousand eight hundred and eight, but a tax or duty may be imposed on such importation, not exceeding ten dollars for each person.

[Writ of habeas corpus not to be suspended; exception.—2.] The privilege of the writ of habeas corpus shall not be suspended, unless when in cases of rebellion or invasion the public safety may require it.

[Bills of attainder and ex post facto laws prohibited.—3.] No bill of attainder or ex post facto law shall be passed.

[Capitation and other direct taxes.—4.] No capitation, or other direct, tax shall be laid, unless in proportion to the census or enumeration herein before directed to be taken.[5]

[Exports not to be taxed.—5.] No tax or duty shall be laid on articles exported from any State.

[No preference to be given to ports of any States; interstate shipping.—6.] No preference shall be given by any regulation of commerce or revenue to the ports of one State over those of another: nor shall vessels bound to, or from, one State, be obliged to enter, clear, or pay duties in another.

[Money, how drawn from treasury; financial statements to be published.—7.] No money shall be drawn from the Treasury, but in consequence of appropriations made by law; and a regular statement and account of the receipts and expenditures of all public money shall be published from time to time.

[Titles of nobility not to be granted; acceptance by government officers of favors from foreign powers.—8.] No title of nobility shall be granted by the United States: and no person holding any office of profit or trust under them, shall, without the consent of the Congress, accept of any present, emolument, office, or title, of any kind whatever, from any king, prince, or foreign state.

## Section 10

[Limitations of the powers of the several States.—1.] No State shall enter into any treaty, alliance, or confederation; grant letters of marque and reprisal; coin money; emit bills of credit; make any thing but gold and silver coin a tender in payment of debts; pass any bill of attainder, ex post facto law, or law impairing the obligation of contracts, or grant any title of nobility.

[State imposts and duties.—2.] No State shall, without the consent of the Congress, lay any imposts or duties on imports or exports, except what may be absolutely necessary for executing its inspection laws; and the net produce of all duties and imposts, laid by any State on imports or exports, shall be for the use of the Treasury of the United States; and all such laws shall be subject to the revision and control of the Congress.

[Further restrictions on powers of States.—3.] No State shall, without the consent of Congress, lay any duty of tonnage, keep troops, or ships of war in time of peace, enter into any agreement or compact

5. *See* the 16th Amendment.

with another state, or with a foreign power, or engage in war, unless actually invaded, or in such imminent danger as will not admit of delay.

# Article II

## Section 1

[The president; the executive power.—1.] The executive power shall be vested in a President of the United States of America. He shall hold his office during the term of four years, and, together with the Vice President, chosen for the same term, be elected, as follows

[Appointment and qualifications of presidential electors.—2.] Each State shall appoint, in such manner as the Legislature thereof may direct, a number of electors, equal to the whole number of Senators and Representatives to which the State may be entitled in the Congress: but no Senator or Representative, or person holding an office of trust or profit under the United States, shall be appointed an elector.

[Original method of electing the president and vice president.6] (The electors shall meet in their respective States, and vote by ballot for two persons, of whom one at least shall not be an inhabitant of the same State with themselves. And they shall make a list of all the persons voted for, and of the number of votes for each; which list they shall sign and certify, and transmit sealed to the seat of the Government of the United States, directed to the President of the Senate. The President of the Senate shall, in the presence of the Senate and House of Representatives, open all the certificates, and the votes shall then be counted. The person having the greatest number of votes shall be the President, if such number be a majority of the whole number of electors appointed; and if there be more than one who have such majority, and have an equal number of votes, then the House of Representatives shall immediately choose by ballot one of them for President; and if no person have a majority, then from the five highest on the list the said House shall in like manner choose the President. But in choosing the President, the votes shall be taken by States, the representation from each State having one vote; A quorum for this purpose shall consist of a member or members from two thirds of the States, and a majority of all the states shall be necessary to a choice. In every case, after the choice of the President, the person having the greatest number of votes of the electors shall be the Vice President. But if there should remain two or more who have equal votes, the Senate should choose from them by ballot the Vice President.)

[Congress may determine time of choosing electors and day for casting their votes. 3.] The Congress may determine the time of choosing the electors, and the day on which they shall give their votes; which day shall be the same throughout the United States.

[Qualifications for the office of president.7—4.] No person except a natural born citizen, or a citizen of the United States, at the time of the adoption of this Constitution, shall be eligible to the office of President; neither shall any person be eligible to that office who shall not have attained to the age of thirty-five years, and been fourteen years a resident within the United States.

[Filling vacancy in the office of president.8—5.] In case of the removal of the President from office, or of his death, resignation, or inability to discharge the powers and duties of the said office, the same shall devolve on the Vice President, and the Congress may by law provide for the case of removal, death, resignation or inability, both of the President and Vice President, declaring what officer shall then act as President, and such officer shall act accordingly, until the disability be removed, or a President shall be elected.

[Compensation of the president.—6.] The President shall, at stated times, receive for his services, a compensation, which shall neither be increased nor diminished during the period for which he shall have been elected, and he shall not receive within that period any other emolument from the United States, or any of them.

[Oath to be taken by the president.—7.] Before he enter on the execution of his office, he shall take the following oath or affirmation:—"I do solemnly swear (or affirm) that I will faithfully execute the office of President of the United States, and will to the best of my ability, preserve, protect, and defend the Constitution of the United States."

## Section 2

[The president to be commander in chief of army and navy and head of executive departments; may grant reprieves and pardons.—1.] The President shall be Commander in Chief of the Army and Navy of the United States, and of the militia of the several States, when called into the actual service of the United States; he may require the opinion, in writing, of the principal officer in each of the executive departments, upon any subject relating to the duties of their respective offices, and he shall have power to grant reprieves and pardons for offences against the United States, except in cases of impeachment.

[President may, with concurrence of Senate, make treaties, appoint ambassadors, etc.; appointment of inferior officers, authority of Congress over.—2.] He shall have power, by and with the advice and consent of the Senate, to make treaties, provided two thirds of the Senators present concur; and he shall nominate, and by and with the advice and consent of the Senate, shall appoint ambassadors, other public ministers and consuls, judges of the Supreme Court, and all other officers of the United States, whose appointments are not herein otherwise provided for, and which shall be established by law: but the Congress may by law vest the appointment of such inferior officers, as they think proper, in the President alone, in the courts of law, or in the heads of departments.

[President may fill vacancies in office during recess of Senate.—3.] The President shall have power to fill up all vacancies that may happen during the recess of the Senate, by granting commissions which shall expire at the end of their session.

6. This clause has been superseded by the 12th Amendment. 7. For qualifications of the vice president, *see* the 12th Amendment. 8. Amended by the 20th Amendment, Sections 3 and 4.

### Section 3
[**President to give advice to Congress; may convene or adjourn it on certain occasions; to receive ambassadors, etc.; have laws executed and commission all officers.**] He shall from time to time give to the Congress information of the state of the Union, and recommend to their consideration such measures as he shall judge necessary and expedient; he may, on extraordinary occasions, convene both Houses, or either of them, and in case of disagreement between them, with respect to the time of adjournment, he may adjourn them to such time as he shall think proper; he shall receive ambassadors and other public ministers: he shall take care that the laws be faithfully executed, and shall commission all the officers of the United States.

### Section 4
[**All civil officers removable by impeachment.**] The President, Vice President, and all civil officers of the United States shall be removed from office on impeachment for, and conviction of, treason, bribery, or other high crimes and misdemeanors.

## Article III
### Section 1
[**Judicial powers; how vested; term of office and compensation of judges.**] The judicial Power of the United States, shall be vested in one Supreme Court, and in such inferior courts as the Congress may from time to time ordain and establish. The judges, both of the supreme and inferior courts, shall hold their offices during good behavior, and shall, at stated times, receive for their services, a compensation, which shall not be diminished during their continuance in office.

### Section 2
[**Jurisdiction of federal courts[9]—1.**] The judicial power shall extend to all cases, in law and equity, arising under this Constitution, the laws of the United States, and treaties made, or which shall be made, under their authority; to all cases affecting ambassadors, other public ministers and consuls; to all cases of admiralty and maritime jurisdiction; to controversies to which the United States, shall be a party; to controversies between two or more States; between a State and citizens of another State; between citizens of different States; between citizens of the same State claiming lands under grants of different states, and between a State, or the citizens thereof, and foreign states, citizens, or subjects.

[**Original and appellate jurisdiction of Supreme Court.—2.**] In all cases affecting ambassadors, other public ministers and consuls, and those in which a State shall be party, the Supreme Court shall have original jurisdiction. In all the other cases before mentioned, the Supreme Court shall have appellate jurisdiction, both as to law and fact, with such exceptions, and under such regulations, as the Congress shall make.

[**Trial of all crimes, except impeachment, to be by jury.—3.**] The trial of all crimes, except in cases of impeachment, shall be by jury; and such trial shall be held in the State where the said crimes shall have been committed; but when not committed within any State, the trial shall be at such place or places as the Congress may by law have directed.

### Section 3
[**Treason defined; conviction of.—1.**] Treason against the United States, shall consist only in levying war against them, or, in adhering to their enemies, giving them aid and comfort. No person shall be convicted of treason unless on the testimony of two witnesses to the same overt act, or on confession in open court.

[**Congress to declare punishment for treason; proviso.—2.**] The Congress shall have power to declare the punishment of treason, but no attainder of treason shall work corruption of blood, or forfeiture except during the life of the person attained.

## Article IV
### Section 1
[**Each state to give full faith and credit to the public acts and records of other states.**] Full faith and credit shall be given in each State to the public acts, records, and judicial proceedings of every other State. And the Congress may by general laws prescribe the manner in which such acts, records, and proceedings shall be proved, and the effect thereof.

### Section 2
[**Privileges of citizens.—1.**] The citizens of each State shall be entitled to all privileges and immunities of citizens in the several States.

[**Extradition between the several states.—2.**] A person charged in any State with treason, felony, or other crime, who shall flee from justice, and be found in another State, shall on demand of the Executive authority of the State from which he fled, be delivered up, to be removed to the State having jurisdiction of the crime.

[**Persons held to labor or service in one state, fleeing to another, to be returned.—3.**] No person held to service or labor in one State, under the laws thereof, escaping into another, shall, in consequence of any law or regulation therein, be discharged from such service or labor, but shall be delivered up on claim of the party to whom such service or labor may be due.

### Section 3
[**New states.—1.**] New States may be admitted by the Congress into this Union; but no new State shall be formed or erected within the jurisdiction of any other State; nor any State be formed by the junction of two or more States, or parts of States, without the consent of the Legislatures of the States concerned as well as of the Congress.

[**Regulations concerning territory.—2.**] The Congress shall have power to dispose of and make all needful rules and regulations respecting the territory or other property belonging to the United States; and nothing in this Constitution shall be so construed as to prejudice any claims of the United States, or of any particular State.

### Section 4
[**Republican form of government and protection guaranteed the several states.**] The United States shall guarantee to every State in this Union a Republican form of government, and shall protect each of them against invasion; and on application of the Legislature, or of the Executive (when the Legislature cannot be convened) against domestic violence.

9. This section is abridged by the 11th Amendment.

## Article V

[**Ways in which the Constitution can be amended.**] The Congress, whenever two thirds of both Houses shall deem it necessary, shall propose amendments to this Constitution, or, on the application of the Legislatures of two thirds of the several States shall call a convention for proposing amendments, which, in either case, shall be valid to all intents and purposes, as part of this Constitution, when ratified by the Legislatures of three fourths of the several States, or by conventions in three fourths thereof, as the one or the other mode of ratification may be proposed by the Congress; provided that no amendment which may be made prior to the year one thousand eight hundred and eight shall in any manner affect the first and fourth clauses in the ninth Section of the first Article; and that no State, without its consent, shall be deprived of its equal suffrage in the Senate.

## Article VI

[**Debts contracted under the confederation secured.—1.**] All debts contracted and engagements entered into, before the adoption of this Constitution, shall be as valid against the United States under this Constitution, as under the Confederation.
[**Constitution, laws, and treaties of the United States to be supreme.—2.**] This Constitution, and the laws of the United States which shall be made in pursuance thereof; and all treaties made, or which shall be made, under the authority of the United States, shall be the supreme law of the land; and the judges in every State shall be bound thereby, any thing in the Constitution or laws of any State to the contrary notwithstanding.
[**Who shall take constitutional oath; no religious test as to official qualification.—3.**] The Senators and Representatives before mentioned, and the members of the several State Legislatures, and all executive and judicial officers, both of the United States and of the several States, shall be bound by oath or affirmation, to support this Constitution; but no religious test shall ever be required as a qualification to any office or public trust under the United States.

## Article VII

[**Constitution to be considered adopted when ratified by nine states.**] The ratification of the conventions of nine States shall be sufficient for the establishment of this Constitution between the States so ratifying the same.
Done in convention by the unanimous consent of the States present the seventeenth day of September in the year of our Lord one thousand seven hundred and eighty seven and of the independence of the United States of America the Twelfth. In witness whereof we have hereunto subscribed our names.

George Washington
*President and Deputy from Virginia*

| | | | |
|---|---|---|---|
| **New Hampshire** | David Brearley | John Dickinson | **South Carolina** |
| John Langdon | Jona. Dayton | Richard Bassett | J. Rutledge |
| Nicholas Gilman | | Jaco. Broom | Charles Cotesworth |
| **Massachusetts** | **Pennsylvania** | **Maryland** | Pinckney |
| Nathaniel Gorham | B. Franklin | James McHenry | Charles Pinckney |
| Rufus King | Thomas Mifflin | Dan. of St. Thos. Jenifer | Pierce Butler |
| **Connecticut** | Robt. Morris | Danl. Carroll | **Georgia** |
| Wm. Saml. Johnson | Geo. Clymer | **Virginia** | William Few |
| Roger Sherman | Thos. FitzSimons | John Blair | Abr. Baldwin |
| **New York** | Jared Ingersoll | James Madison, Jr. | Attest: William Jackson, |
| Alexander Hamilton | James Wilson | **North Carolina** | Secretary |
| **New Jersey** | Gouv. Morris | Wm. Blount | |
| Wil. Livingston | **Delaware** | Richd Dobbs Spaight | |
| Wm. Paterson | Geo. Read | Hu. Williamson | |
| | Gunning Bedford Jun. | | |

## Amendments to the Constitution of the United States

(Amendments I to X inclusive, popularly known as the Bill of Rights, were proposed and sent to the states by the first session of the First Congress. They were ratified Dec. 15, 1791.)

## Amendment I

[**Freedom of religion, speech, of the press, and right of petition.**] Congress shall make no law respecting an establishment of religion, or prohibiting the free exercise thereof; or abridging the freedom of speech, or of the press; or the right of the people peaceably to assemble, and to petition the Government for a redress of grievances.

## Amendment II

[**Right of people to bear arms not to be infringed.**] A well regulated militia, being necessary to the security of a free State, the right of the people to keep and bear arms, shall not be infringed.

## Amendment III

[**Quartering of troops.**] No soldier shall, in time of peace be quartered in any house, without the consent of the owner, nor in time of war, but in a manner to be prescribed by law.

## Amendment IV

[**Persons and houses to be secure from unreasonable searches and seizures.**] The right of the people to be secure in their persons, houses, papers, and effects, against unreasonable searches and seizures, shall not be violated, and no warrants shall issue, but upon probable cause, supported by oath or affirmation, and particularly describing the place to be searched, and the persons or things to be seized.

## Amendment V

[**Trials for crimes; just compensation for private property taken for public use.**] No person shall be held to answer for a capital, or otherwise infamous crime, unless on a presentment or indictment of a Grand Jury, except in cases arising in the land or naval forces, or in the militia, when in actual service in time of war or public danger; nor shall any person be subject for the same offence to be twice put in jeopardy of life or limb; nor shall be compelled in any criminal case to be a witness, against himself, nor be deprived of life, liberty, or property, without due process of law; nor shall private property be taken for public use, without just compensation.

## Amendment VI

[**Civil rights in trials for crimes enumerated.**] In all criminal prosecutions, the accused shall enjoy the right to a speedy and public trial, by an impartial jury of the State and district wherein the crime shall have been committed, which district shall have been previously ascertained by law, and to be informed of the nature and cause of the accusation; to be confronted with the witnesses against him; to have compulsory process for obtaining witnesses in his favor, and to have the assistance of counsel for his defense.

## Amendment VII

[**Civil rights in civil suits.**] In suits at common law, where the value in controversy shall exceed twenty dollars, the right of trial by jury shall be preserved, and no fact tried by a jury, shall be otherwise re-examined in any court of the United States, than according to the rules of the common law.

## Amendment VIII

[**Excessive bail, fines, and punishments prohibited.**] Excessive bail shall not be required, nor excessive fines imposed, nor cruel and unusual punishments inflicted.

## Amendment IX

[**Reserved rights of people.**] The enumeration in the Constitution, of certain rights, shall not be construed to deny or disparage others retained by the people.

## Amendment X

[**Powers not delegated, reserved to states and people respectively.**] The powers not delegated to the United States by the Constitution, nor prohibited by it to the States, are reserved to the States, respectively, or to the people.

## Amendment XI

(**The proposed amendment was sent to the states Mar. 5, 1794, by the Third Congress. It was ratified Feb. 7, 1795.**)

[**Judicial power of United States not to extend to suits against a state.**] The judicial power of the United States shall not be construed to extend to any suit in law or equity, commenced or prosecuted against one of the United States by citizens of another State, or by citizens or subjects of any foreign state.

## Amendment XII

(**The proposed amendment was sent to the states Dec. 12, 1803, by the Eighth Congress. It was ratified July 27, 1804.**)

[**Present mode of electing president and vice president by electors.**[1]]

The electors shall meet in their respective states, and vote by ballot for President and Vice President, one of whom, at least, shall not be an inhabitant of the same state with themselves; they shall name in their ballots the person voted for as President, and in distinct ballots the person voted for as Vice President, and they shall make distinct lists of all persons voted for as President, and of all persons voted for as Vice President, and of the number of votes for each, which lists they shall sign and certify, and transmit sealed to the seat of the government of the United States, directed to the President of the Senate; the President of the Senate shall, in the presence of the Senate and House of Representatives, open all the certificates and the votes shall then be counted; the person having the greatest number of votes for President, shall be the President, if such number be a majority of the whole number of electors appointed; and if no person have such majority, then from the persons having the highest numbers not exceeding three on the list of those voted for as President, the House of Representatives shall choose immediately, by ballot, the President. But in choosing the President, the votes shall be taken by states, the representation from each State having one vote; a quorum for this purpose shall consist of a member or members from two thirds of the states, and a majority of all the states shall be necessary to a choice. And if the House of Representatives shall not choose a President whenever the right of choice shall devolve upon them, before the fourth day of March next following, then the Vice President shall act as President, as in the case of the death or other constitutional disability of the President. The person having the greatest number of votes as Vice President, shall be the Vice President, if such number be a majority of the whole number of electors appointed, and if no person have a majority, then from the two highest numbers on the list, the Senate shall choose the Vice President; a quorum for the purpose shall consist of two thirds of the whole

1. Amended by the 20th Amendment, Sections 3 and 4.

number of Senators, and a majority of the whole number shall be necessary to a choice. But no person constitutionally ineligible to the office of President shall be eligible to that of Vice President of the United States.

## Amendment XIII

(The proposed amendment was sent to the states Feb. 1, 1865, by the Thirty-eighth Congress. It was ratified Dec. 6, 1865.)

### Section 1

[Slavery prohibited.] Neither slavery nor involuntary servitude, except as a punishment for crime whereof the party shall have been duly convicted, shall exist within the United States, or any place subject to their jurisdiction.

### Section 2

[Congress given power to enforce this article.] Congress shall have power to enforce this article by appropriate legislation.

## Amendment XIV

(The proposed amendment was sent to the states June 16, 1866, by the Thirty-ninth Congress. It was ratified July 9, 1868.)

### Section 1

[Citizenship defined; privileges of citizens.] All persons born or naturalized in the United States, and subject to the jurisdiction thereof, are citizens of the United States and of the State wherein they reside. No State shall make or enforce any law which shall abridge the privileges or immunities of citizens of the United States; nor shall any State deprive any person of life, liberty, or property, without due process of law; nor deny to any person within its jurisdiction the equal protection of the laws.

### Section 2

[Apportionment of Representatives.] Representatives shall be apportioned among the several States according to their respective numbers, counting the whole number of persons in each State, excluding Indians not taxed. But when the right to vote at any election for the choice of electors for President and Vice President of the United States, Representatives in Congress, the executive and judicial officers of a State, or the members of the Legislature thereof, is denied to any of the male inhabitants of such State, being twenty-one years of age, and citizens of the United States, or in any way abridged, except for participation in rebellion, or other crime, the basis of representation therein shall be reduced in the proportion which the number of such male citizens shall bear to the whole number of male citizens twenty-one years of age in such State.

### Section 3

[Disqualification for office; removal of disability.] No person shall be a Senator or Representative in Congress, or elector of President and Vice President, or hold any office, civil or military, under the United States, or under any State, who, having previously taken an oath, as a member of Congress, or as an officer of the United States, or as a member of any State Legislature, or as an executive or judicial officer of any State, to support the Constitution of the United States, shall have engaged in insurrection or rebellion against the same, or given aid or comfort to the enemies thereof. But Congress may, by a vote of two thirds of each House, remove such disability.

### Section 4

[Public debt not to be questioned; payment of debts and claims incurred in aid of rebellion forbidden.] The validity of the public debt of the United States, authorized by law, including debts incurred for payment of pensions and bounties for services in suppressing insurrection or rebellion, shall not be questioned. But neither the United States nor any State shall assume or pay any debt or obligation incurred in aid of insurrection or rebellion against the United States, or any claim for the loss or emancipation of any slave; but all such debts, obligations, and claims shall be held illegal and void.

### Section 5

[Congress given power to enforce this article.] The Congress shall have power to enforce, by appropriate legislation, the provisions of this article.

## Amendment XV

(The proposed amendment was sent to the states Feb. 27, 1869, by the Fortieth Congress. It was ratified Feb. 3, 1870.)

### Section 1

[Right of certain citizens to vote established.] The right of citizens of the United States to vote shall not be denied or abridged by the United States or by any State on account of race, color, or previous condition of servitude.

### Section 2

[Congress given power to enforce this article.] The Congress shall have power to enforce this article by appropriate legislation.

## Amendment XVI

(The proposed amendment was sent to the states July 12, 1909, by the Sixty-first Congress. It was ratified Feb. 3, 1913.)

[Taxes on income; Congress given power to lay and collect.] The Congress shall have power to lay and collect taxes on incomes, from whatever source derived, without apportionment among the several States, and without regard to any census or enumeration.

## Amendment XVII

(The proposed amendment was sent to the states May 16, 1912, by the Sixty-second Congress. It was ratified April 8, 1913.)

[Election of U.S. senators; filling of vacancies; qualifications of electors.] The Senate of the United States shall be composed of two Senators from each State, elected by the people thereof, for six years; and each Senator shall have one vote. The electors in each State shall have the qualifications requisite for electors of the most numerous branch of the State Legislatures.

When vacancies happen in the representation of any State in the Senate, the executive authority of such State shall issue writs of election to fill such vacancies: Provided, that the legislature of any State may empower the executive thereof to make temporary appointment until the people fill the vacancies by election as the legislature may direct.

This amendment shall not be so construed as to affect the election or term of any Senator chosen before it becomes valid as part of the Constitution.

## Amendment XVIII[2]

**(The proposed amendment was sent to the states Dec. 18, 1917, by the Sixty-fifth Congress. It was ratified by three quarters of the states by Jan. 16, 1919, and became effective Jan. 16, 1920.)**

### Section 1

**[Manufacture, sale, or transportation of intoxicating liquors, for beverage purposes, prohibited.]** After one year from the ratification of this article the manufacture, sale, or transportation of intoxicating liquors within, the importation thereof into, or the exportation thereof from the United States and all territory subject to the jurisdiction thereof for beverage purposes is hereby prohibited.

### Section 2

**[Congress and the several states given concurrent power to pass appropriate legislation to enforce this article.]** The Congress and the several States shall have concurrent power to enforce this article by appropriate legislation.

### Section 3

**[Provisions of article to become operative, when adopted by three fourths of the states.]** This article shall be inoperative unless it shall have been ratified as an amendment to the Constitution by the legislatures of the several States, as provided in the Constitution, within seven years from the date of the submission hereof to the States by Congress.

## Amendment XIX

**(The proposed amendment was sent to the states June 4, 1919, by the Sixty-sixth Congress. It was ratified Aug. 18, 1920.)**

**[The right of citizens to vote shall not be denied because of sex.]** The right of citizens of the United States to vote shall not be denied or abridged by the United States or by any State on account of sex.

**[Congress given power to enforce this article.]** Congress shall have power to enforce this article by appropriate legislation.

## Amendment XX

**(The proposed amendment, sometimes called the "Lame Duck Amendment," was sent to the states Mar. 3, 1932, by the Seventy-second Congress. It was ratified Jan. 23, 1933; but, in accordance with Section 5, Sections 1 and 2, did not go into effect until Oct. 15, 1933.)**

### Section 1

**[Terms of president, vice president, senators, and representatives.]** The terms of the President and Vice President shall end at noon on the twentieth day of January, and the terms of Senators and Representatives at noon on the third day of January, of the years in which such terms would have ended if this article had not been ratified; and the terms of their successors shall then begin.

### Section 2

**[Time of assembling Congress.]** The Congress shall assemble at least once in every year, and such meeting shall begin at noon on the third day of January, unless they shall by law appoint a different day.

### Section 3

**[Filling vacancy in office of president.]** If, at the time fixed for the beginning of the term of the President, the President-elect shall have died, the Vice President-elect shall become President. If a President shall not have been chosen before the time fixed for the beginning of his term, or if the President-elect shall have failed to qualify, then the Vice President shall have qualified; and the Congress may by law provide for the case wherein neither a President-elect nor a Vice President-elect shall have qualified, declaring who shall then act as President, or the manner in which one who is to act shall be selected, and such person shall act accordingly until a President or Vice President shall have qualified.

### Section 4

**[Power of Congress in presidential succession.]** The Congress may by law provide for the case of the death of any of the persons from whom the House of Representatives may choose a President whenever the right of choice shall have devolved upon them, and for the case of the death of any of the persons from whom the Senate may choose a Vice President whenever the right of choice shall have devolved upon them.

### Section 5

**[Time of taking effect.]** Sections 1 and 2 shall take effect on the 15th day of October following the ratification of this article.

### Section 6

**[Ratification.]** This article shall be inoperative unless it shall have been ratified as an amendment to the Constitution by the legislatures of three fourths of the several States within seven years from the date of its submission.

## Amendment XXI

**(The proposed amendment was sent to the states Feb. 20, 1933, by the Seventy-second Congress. It was ratified Dec. 5, 1933.)**

### Section 1

**[Repeal of Prohibition Amendment.]** The eighteenth article of amendment to the Constitution of the United States is hereby repealed.

### Section 2

**[Transportation of intoxicating liquors.]** The transportation or importation into any State, territory, or possession of the United States for delivery or use therein of intoxicating liquors, in violation of the laws thereof, is hereby prohibited.

### Section 3

**[Ratification.]** This article shall be inoperative unless it shall have been ratified as an amendment to the Constitution by convention in the several States, as provided in the Constitution, within seven years from the date of the submission thereof to the States by the Congress.

## Amendment XXII

**(The proposed amendment was sent to the states Mar. 21, 1947, by the Eightieth Congress. It was ratified Feb. 27, 1951.)**

2. Repealed by the 21st Amendment.

## Section 1

[Limit to number of terms a president may serve.] No person shall be elected to the office of the President more than twice, and no person who has held the office of President, or acted as President, for more than two years of a term to which some other person was elected President shall be elected to the office of the President more than once. But this article shall not apply to any person holding the office of President when this article was proposed by the Congress, and shall not prevent any person who may be holding the office of President, or acting as President, during the term within which this article becomes operative from holding the office of President or acting as President during the remainder of such term.

## Section 2

[Ratification.] This article shall be inoperative unless it shall have been ratified as an amendment to the Constitution by the legislatures of three fourths of the several States within seven years from the date of its submission to the States by the Congress.

# Amendment XXIII

(The proposed amendment was sent to the states June 16, 1960, by the Eighty-sixth Congress. It was ratified March 29, 1961.)

## Section 1

[Electors for the District of Columbia.] The District constituting the seat of Government of the United States shall appoint in such manner as the Congress may direct: A number of electors of President and Vice President equal to the whole number of Senators and Representatives in Congress to which the District would be entitled if it were a State, but in no event more than the least populous State; they shall be in addition to those appointed by the States, but they shall be considered, for the purposes of the election of President and Vice President, to be electors appointed by a State; and they shall meet in the District and perform such duties as provided by the twelfth article of amendment.

## Section 2

[Congress given power to enforce this article.] The Congress shall have the power to enforce this article by appropriate legislation.

# Amendment XXIV

(The proposed amendment was sent to the states Aug. 27, 1962, by the Eighty-seventh Congress.)

## Section 1

[Payment of poll tax or other taxes not to be prerequisite for voting in federal elections.] The right of citizens of the United States to vote in any primary or other election for President or Vice President, for electors for President or Vice President, or for Senator or Representative in Congress, shall not be denied or abridged by the United States or any State by reasons of failure to pay any poll tax or other tax.

## Section 2

[Congress given power to enforce this article.] The Congress shall have the power to enforce this article by appropriate legislation.

# Amendment XXV

(The proposed amendment was sent to the states July 6, 1965, by the Eighty-ninth Congress. It was ratified Feb. 10, 1967.)

## Section 1

[Succession of vice president to presidency.] In case of the removal of the President from office or of his death or resignation, the Vice President shall become President.

## Section 2

[Vacancy in office of vice president.] Whenever there is a vacancy in the office of the Vice President, the President shall nominate a Vice President who shall take office upon confirmation by a majority vote of both Houses of Congress.

## Section 3

[Vice president as acting president.] Whenever the President transmits to the President pro tempore of the Senate and the Speaker of the House of Representatives his written declaration that he is unable to discharge the powers and duties of his office, and until he transmits to them a written declaration to the contrary, such powers and duties shall be discharged by the Vice President as Acting President.

## Section 4

[Vice president as acting president.] Whenever the Vice President and a majority of either the principal officers of the executive departments or of such other body as Congress may by law provide, transmit to the President pro tempore of the Senate and the Speaker of the House of Representatives their written declaration that the President is unable to discharge the powers and duties of his office, the Vice President shall immediately assume the powers and duties of the office as Acting President.

Thereafter, when the President transmits to the President pro tempore of the Senate and the Speaker of the House of Representatives his written declaration that no inability exists, he shall resume the powers and duties of his office unless the Vice President and a majority of either the principal officers of the executive department or of such other body as Congress may by law provide, transmit within four days to the President pro tempore of the Senate and the Speaker of the House of Representatives their written declaration that the President is unable to discharge the powers and duties of his office. Thereupon Congress shall decide the issue, assembling within forty-eight hours for that purpose if not in session. If the Congress, within twenty-one days after receipt of the written declaration, or, if Congress is not in session, within twenty-one days after Congress is required to assemble, determines by two thirds vote of both Houses that the President is unable to discharge the powers and duties of his office, the Vice President shall continue to discharge the same as Acting President; otherwise, the President shall resume the powers and duties of his office.

# Amendment XXVI

(The proposed amendment was sent to the states Mar. 23, 1971, by the Ninety-second Congress. It was ratified July 1, 1971.)

## Section 1

[Voting for 18-year-olds.] The right of citizens of the United States, who are 18 years of age or older, to vote shall not be denied or abridged by the United States or by any state on account of age.

### Section 2
**[Congress given power to enforce this article.]** The Congress shall have power to enforce this article by appropriate legislation.

## Amendment XXVII
**(Ratified May 7, 1992.)**
**[Congressional raises.]** No law, varying the compensation for the services of the Senators and Representatives, shall take effect, until an election of Representatives shall have intervened.

## Lincoln's Gettysburg Address

The Battle of Gettysburg, one of the most noted battles of the Civil War, was fought on July 1–3, 1863. On Nov. 19, 1863, the field was dedicated as a national cemetery by President Lincoln in a two-minute speech that was to become immortal. At the time of its delivery the speech was relegated to the inside pages of the papers, while a two-hour address by Edward Everett, the leading orator of the time, caught the headlines.

Fourscore and seven years ago our fathers brought forth on this continent a new nation conceived in liberty and dedicated to the proposition that all men are created equal. Now we are engaged in a great civil war testing whether that nation, or any nation so conceived and so dedicated, can long endure. We are met on a great battlefield of that war. We have come to dedicate a portion of that field as a final resting-place for those who here gave their lives that that nation might live. It is altogether fitting and proper that we should do this. But, in a larger sense, we cannot dedicate, we cannot consecrate, we cannot hallow this ground. The brave men, living and dead, who struggled here have consecrated it far above our poor power to add or detract. The world will little note nor long remember what we say here, but it can never forget what they did here. It is for us the living rather to be dedicated here to the unfinished work which they who fought here have thus far so nobly advanced. It is rather for us to be here dedicated to the great task remaining before us—that from these honored dead we take increased devotion to that cause for which they gave the last full measure of devotion—that we here highly resolve that these dead shall not have died in vain, that this nation under God shall have a new birth of freedom, and that government of the people, by the people, for the people shall not perish from the earth.

## Assassinations and Attempts in U.S. Since 1865

**Lincoln, Abraham (president of U.S.):** Shot April 14, 1865, in Washington, DC, by John Wilkes Booth; died April 15.

**Seward, William H. (secretary of state):** Escaped assassination (though injured) April 14, 1865, in Washington, DC, by Lewis Powell (or Paine), accomplice of John Wilkes Booth.

**Garfield, James A. (president of U.S.):** Shot July 2, 1881, in Washington, DC, by Charles J. Guiteau; died Sept. 19.

**McKinley, William (president of U.S.):** Shot Sept. 6, 1901, in Buffalo by Leon Czolgosz; died Sept. 14.

**Roosevelt, Theodore (ex-president of U.S.):** Escaped assassination (though shot) Oct. 14, 1912, in Milwaukee while campaigning for president.

**Cermak, Anton J. (mayor of Chicago):** Shot Feb. 15, 1933, in Miami by Giuseppe Zangara, who attempted to assassinate Franklin D. Roosevelt; Cermak died March 6.

**Roosevelt, Franklin D. (president-elect of U.S.):** Escaped assassination Feb. 15, 1933, in Miami.

**Long, Huey P. (U.S. senator from Louisiana):** Shot Sept. 8, 1935, in Baton Rouge by Dr. Carl A. Weiss; died Sept. 10.

**Truman, Harry S. (president of U.S.):** Escaped assassination unhurt Nov. 1, 1950, in Washington, DC, as 2 Puerto Rican nationalists attempted to shoot their way into Blair House.

**Kennedy, John F. (president of U.S.):** Shot Nov. 22, 1963, in Dallas, Tex., allegedly by Lee Harvey Oswald; died same day. Injured was Gov. John B. Connally of Texas. Oswald was shot and killed two days later by Jack Ruby.

**Malcolm X, also known as El-Hajj Malik El-Shabazz (black activist):** Shot and killed in a New York City auditorium, Feb. 21, 1965; his killer(s) were never positively identified.

**King, Martin Luther, Jr. (civil rights leader):** Shot April 4, 1968, in Memphis by James Earl Ray; died same day.

**Kennedy, Robert F. (U.S. senator from New York):** Shot June 5, 1968, in Los Angeles by Sirhan Bishara Sirhan; died June 6.

**Wallace, George C. (governor of Alabama):** Shot and critically wounded in assassination attempt May 15, 1972, at Laurel, Md., by Arthur Herman Bremer. Wallace paralyzed from waist down.

**Ford, Gerald R. (president of U.S.):** Escaped assassination attempt Sept. 5, 1975, in Sacramento, Calif., by Lynette Alice (Squeaky) Fromme, who pointed but did not fire .45-caliber pistol. Escaped assassination attempt in San Francisco, Calif., Sept. 22, 1975, by Sara Jane Moore, who fired one shot from a .38-caliber pistol that was deflected.

**Jordan, Vernon E., Jr. (civil rights leader):** Shot and critically wounded in assassination attempt May 29, 1980, in Fort Wayne, Ind.

**Reagan, Ronald (president of U.S.):** Shot in left lung in Washington by John W. Hinckley, Jr., on March 30, 1981; three others also wounded.

# Profile of the United States

This profile was created by the editors of the almanac from many data sources. Most figures are approximate. For additional details about the U.S., please refer to the appropriate sections of the almanac.

## Geography

Number of states: 50
Territories: 14
Area (2000): total: 3,794,083 sq mi (9,826,675 sq km), land only: 3,537,438 sq mi (9,161,964 sq km), water: 256,645 sq mi (664,711 sq km). Share of world land area (1990): 6.2%
Northernmost point: Point Barrow, Alaska
Easternmost point: West Quoddy Head, Maine
Southernmost point: Ka Lae (South Cape), Hawaii
Westernmost point: Cape Wrangell, Alaska[1]
Geographic center (50 states): in Butte County, S.D. (44′ 58′ N. lat., 103′ 46′ W. long.)
Highest point: Mt. McKinley, Alaska (20,320 ft)
Lowest point: Death Valley, Calif. (282 ft below sea level)

1. The extreme points are measured from the geographic center of the United States (incl. Alaska and Hawaii), west of Castle Rock, S.D., 44° 58′ N. lat., 103° 46′ W. long. If measured from the prime meridian in Greenwich, England, Cape Wrangell, Alaska, would be the easternmost point.

## Population

**(Based on Census 2000 data unless otherwise noted.)**

Total Resident Pop. (July 2001 est.)[1]: 284,796,887
Population density: 79.6 people per sq mi
Mean center of population: 3 mi east of Edgar Springs in Phelps County, Mo.
Males: 138,053,563 (49.1% of pop.)
Females: 143,368,343 (50.9% of pop.)
White: 211,460,626 (75.1% of pop.)
Black: 34,658,190 (12.3% of pop.)
Asian: 10,242,998 (3.6% of pop.)
American Indian and Alaska Native: 2,475,956 (0.9% of pop.)
Hispanic/Latino[2]: 35,305,818 (12.5% of pop.)
Native Hawaiian and Other Pacific Islander: 398,835 (0.1% of pop.)
Median age: 35.3
Metropolitan population: 225,981,679
Nonmetropolitan population: 55,440,227
Families: 71,787,347
Average family size: 3.14
Homeownership (2000): 67.4% of pop.
Married couples (2000): 56,497,000
Unmarried couples (1999): 4,486,000
Never married (2000): 48,200,000
Divorced (2000): 19,800,000

1. Excludes the U.S. Armed Forces overseas. 2. People of Hispanic or Latino origin may be of any race.

## Vital Statistics

Births (2000): 4,058,814 (14.7 per 1,000 pop.)
Deaths (2000): 2,404,624 (8.7 per 1,000 pop.)
Marriages (2000): 2,329,000 (8.5 per 1,000 pop.)
Divorces (1998): 1,135,000 (4.2 per 1,000 pop.)
Infant mortality rate (1999): (7.1 per 1,000 live births)
Legal abortions (1997): 1,186,039
Life expectancy (2000)[1]: Total U.S., both sexes, 76.9; total men, 74.1; total women, 79.5; white men, 74.8; white women, 80.0; black men, 68.3; black women, 75.0

1. Preliminary.

## Civilian Labor Force

All (2001): 141,815,000 (4.8% unemployed)
Men (2001): 75,743,000 (4.7% unemployed)
Women (2001): 62,992,000 (4.7% unemployed)
Work at home (2001 est.): 19.8 million
Farms (2001): 2,157,780; total acres (2001): 941,210,000
Avg. weekly earnings of workers (2001): $597
Avg. weekly hours of workers (2000): 34.5

## Income and Credit

GDP (2001): $10,208.1 billion
Fed. Budget (2001 est.): total receipts, $2,136,900 million; total outlays, $1,856,000 million; (2002 est.): total receipts, $2,191,700 million; total outlays, $1,960,600 million
Personal income per capita (2001): $30,511
Median four-person family income (2000): $65,381
Consumer credit outstanding (2001): $1,702.8 billion
Number below poverty level (2000): total, 31,139,000; white, 21,291,000; black, 7,901,000; Hispanic, 7,155,000; Asian and Pacific Islander, 1,226,000

## Education

Public elementary school pupils, pre-K–grade 8 (2000)[1]: 33,622,000
Public secondary school pupils, grades 9–12 (2000)[1]: 13,537,000
Private elementary school pupils, K–grade 8 (2000)[1]: 4,678,000
Private secondary school pupils, grades 9–12 (2000)[1]: 1,266,000
High school dropout rate, ages 16–24 (2000): 10.9%
College and university enrollment (2000)[1]: 14,979,000
Total funding for public elementary and secondary education (1998–1999): $347,329,664,000
Public school teachers (2001)[1]: 3,100,000
Private school teachers (2001)[1]: 400,000
Average salary for public school teachers (2000–2001)[1]: $42,898

1. Estimated

## Conveniences

Radio stations (Sept. 1999): AM, 4,783; FM, 5,766
Television stations (Sept. 1999): 1,585
Registered automobiles (1999): 132,432,000
Daily newspaper circulation (2000): 55,800,000
Total TV households (2002): 105,500,000
Avg. number TV sets per household (1999): 2.1
Cable TV households (2001): 80%
Avg. number TV households with VCRs (2001): 91%
Percent households with a computer (2001): 56.5%
Percent households with Internet access (2001): 50.5%

## Crime

Total arrests (2000): 9,116,967
State, federal, and local prison inmates (2001): 1,965,495
Prisoners under sentence of death (1999): 3,527
Persons executed under civil authority (2000): 85
Law enforcement officers killed (1999): 107
Total murder victims (2000): 12,943
Violent crimes per 100,000 people (2000): 506.1
Property crimes per 100,000 people (2000): 3,617.9
Homicides per 100,000 people (2000): 5.5
Hate crime victims (2000): 7,530

# U.S. Census Timeline

**1787** Article 1, Section 2 of the U.S. Constitution requires that a census of the population be conducted every ten years so that the representatives in Congress and direct taxes might be apportioned.

**1790** Federal marshals conduct the first census by going door-to-door through the 13 states plus the districts of Maine, Vermont, Kentucky, and the Southwest Territory (Tennessee). The marshals record the name of every householder and count the occupants in each house. African-American slaves are counted as three-fifths of a person, and American Indians who do not pay taxes are excluded. The census is completed in 18 months at a cost of $45,000. The census counts 3.9 million people.

**1830** The first printed forms are used for collecting census data. Prior to this, marshals used sheets of paper or notebooks.

**1850** All free persons, rather than just the head of house, are recorded by name, along with their occupation and place of birth.

**1868** The Fourteenth Amendment to the Constitution is ratified, ending the three-fifths counting rule for African Americans.

**1870** Although individuals have been identified as white or black since the 1790 census, American Indians are first enumerated in the 1870 census. (However, those in the Indian Territory or on reservations are not included in the official U.S. population count used for congressional apportionment until 1890.) The Chinese population is also counted for the first time in the 1870 census.

**1880** Congress establishes a census office in the Department of the Interior, and the U.S. marshals who have previously collected census data are replaced by professional enumerators.

**1890** For the first time simple machines are used to tabulate census data.

**1902** Congress authorizes a permanent census office, which is transferred the following year to the Department of Commerce and Labor. (In 1913, when Commerce and Labor become separate departments, the U.S. Census Bureau is placed in the Department of Commerce.)

**1940** Statistical sampling techniques are introduced, which allow the Census Bureau to create a "long form" answered by only a subset of the population.

**1950** For the first time an electronic computer, UNIVAC I, is used to help tabulate results.

**1960** In an effort to move toward self-enumeration, census forms are mailed to urban households to be completed and mailed back to the Census Bureau.

**1970** Mail-in forms take precedence over door-to-door enumerators. For the first time, respondents are asked to check off whether they are of Spanish or Hispanic origin or descent.

**1980** Although 1980 census was considered one of the most accurate in recent decades, New York City and civil rights groups file numerous lawsuits challenging the final results.

**1990** The 1990 census is the first to be less accurate than the one preceding it (an estimated 8.4 million people were missed while another 4.4 million were counted twice). The problem is partly blamed on declining census participation: the response rate for Census 1990 was only 65%.

**1999** The Supreme Court rules that statistical sampling—which allows for the estimation of certain populations, such as the homeless or minorities—could not be used to apportion congressional seats, although it could be used for other purposes.

**2000** Employing some 860,000 temporary workers and costing $6 billion, Census 2000 is the largest peacetime mobilization of resources and personnel. For the first time, the Census Bureau runs a nationwide advertising campaign to encourage people to fill out their forms.

## Colonial Population Estimates

### (in round numbers)

| Year | Population | Year | Population |
|------|-----------:|------|-----------:|
| 1610 | 350 | 1700 | 250,900 |
| 1620 | 2,300 | 1710 | 331,700 |
| 1630 | 4,600 | 1720 | 466,200 |
| 1640 | 26,600 | 1730 | 629,400 |
| 1650 | 50,400 | 1740 | 905,600 |
| 1660 | 75,100 | 1750 | 1,170,800 |
| 1670 | 111,900 | 1760 | 1,593,600 |
| 1680 | 151,500 | 1770 | 2,148,100 |
| 1690 | 210,400 | 1780 | 2,780,400 |

Covers years before the establishment of the U.S. Census in 1790.

## National Censuses[1]

| Year | Resident population[2] | Land area, sq mi | Pop. per sq mi | Year | Resident population[2] | Land area, sq mi | Pop. per sq mi |
|------|-----------:|---------:|-----:|------|-----------:|---------:|-----:|
| 1790 | 3,929,214 | 864,746 | 4.5 | 1900 | 75,994,575 | 2,969,834 | 25.6 |
| 1800 | 5,308,483 | 864,746 | 6.1 | 1910 | 91,972,266 | 2,969,565 | 31.0 |
| 1810 | 7,239,881 | 1,681,828 | 4.3 | 1920 | 105,710,620 | 2,969,451 | 35.6 |
| 1820 | 9,638,453 | 1,749,462 | 5.5 | 1930 | 122,775,046 | 2,977,128 | 41.2 |
| 1830 | 12,866,020 | 1,749,462 | 7.4 | 1940 | 131,669,275 | 2,977,128 | 44.2 |
| 1840 | 17,069,453 | 1,749,462 | 9.8 | 1950 | 150,697,361 | 2,974,726 | 50.7 |
| 1850 | 23,191,876 | 2,940,042 | 7.9 | 1960 | 179,323,175 | 3,540,911 | 50.6 |
| 1860 | 31,443,321 | 2,969,640 | 10.6 | 1970 | 203,302,031 | 3,540,023 | 57.4 |
| 1870 | 39,818,449 | 2,969,640 | 13.4 | 1980 | 226,545,805 | 3,539,289 | 64.0 |
| 1880 | 50,155,783 | 2,969,640 | 16.9 | 1990 | 248,709,873 | 3,536,278 | 70.3 |
| 1890 | 62,947,714 | 2,969,640 | 21.2 | 2000 | 281,421,906 | 3,537,441 | 79.6 |

1. Beginning with 1960, figures include Alaska and Hawaii. 2. Excludes armed forces overseas. *Source:* U.S. Bureau of the Census; Web: www.census.gov.

## Profile of General Demographic Characteristics, 2000

| Subject | Number | Percent | Subject | Number | Percent |
|---|---|---|---|---|---|
| **Total population** | **281,421,906** | **100.0%** | **Hispanic or Latino and race** | | |
| **Sex and age** | | | Total population | 281,421,906 | 100.0% |
| Male | 138,053,563 | 49.1 | Hispanic or Latino (of any | | |
| Female | 143,368,343 | 50.9 | race) | 35,305,818 | 12.5 |
| | | | Mexican | 20,640,711 | 7.3 |
| Under 5 years | 19,175,798 | 6.8 | Puerto Rican | 3,406,178 | 1.2 |
| 5 to 9 years | 20,549,505 | 7.3 | Cuban | 1,241,685 | 0.4 |
| 10 to 14 years | 20,528,072 | 7.3 | Other Hispanic or Latino | 10,017,244 | 3.6 |
| 15 to 19 years | 20,219,890 | 7.2 | Not Hispanic or Latino | 246,116,088 | 87.5 |
| 20 to 24 years | 18,964,001 | 6.7 | White alone | 194,552,774 | 69.1 |
| 25 to 34 years | 39,891,724 | 14.2 | | | |
| 35 to 44 years | 45,148,527 | 16.0 | **Relationship** | | |
| 45 to 54 years | 37,677,952 | 13.4 | Total population | 281,421,906 | 100.0% |
| 55 to 59 years | 13,469,237 | 4.8 | In households | 273,643,273 | 97.2 |
| 60 to 64 years | 10,805,447 | 3.8 | Householder | 105,480,101 | 37.5 |
| 65 to 74 years | 18,390,986 | 6.5 | Spouse | 54,493,232 | 19.4 |
| 75 to 84 years | 12,361,180 | 4.4 | Child | 83,393,392 | 29.6 |
| 85 years and over | 4,239,587 | 1.5 | Own child under 18 | 64,494,637 | 22.9 |
| | | | Other relatives | 15,684,318 | 5.6 |
| Median age (years) | 35.3 | n.a. | Under 18 | 6,042,435 | 2.1 |
| | | | Nonrelatives | 14,592,230 | 5.2 |
| 18 years and over | 209,128,094 | 74.3 | Unmarried partner | 5,475,768 | 1.9 |
| Male | 100,994,367 | 35.9 | In group quarters | 7,778,633 | 2.8 |
| Female | 108,133,727 | 38.4 | Institutionalized pop. | 4,059,039 | 1.4 |
| 21 years and over | 196,899,193 | 70.0 | Noninstitutionalized pop. | 3,719,594 | 1.3 |
| 62 years and over | 41,256,029 | 14.7 | | | |
| 65 years and over | 34,991,753 | 12.4 | **Household by type** | | |
| Male | 14,409,625 | 5.1 | Total households | 105,480,101 | 100.0 |
| Female | 20,582,128 | 7.3 | Family households (families) | 71,787,347 | 68.1 |
| | | | With own children under 18 | 34,588,368 | 32.8 |
| **Race** | | | Married-couple family | 54,493,232 | 51.7 |
| One race | 274,595,678 | 97.6 | With own children under 18 | 24,835,505 | 23.5 |
| White | 211,460,626 | 75.1 | Female householder, | | |
| Black or African American | 34,658,190 | 12.3 | no husband present | 12,900,103 | 12.2 |
| American Indian and Alaska | | | With own children under 18 | 7,561,874 | 7.2 |
| Native | 2,475,956 | 0.9 | Nonfamily households | 33,692,754 | 31.9 |
| Asian | 10,242,998 | 3.6 | Householder living alone | 27,230,075 | 25.8 |
| Asian Indian | 1,678,765 | 0.6 | Householder 65 and over | 9,722,857 | 9.2 |
| Chinese | 2,432,585 | 0.9 | Households with individuals | | |
| Filipino | 1,850,314 | 0.7 | under 18 | 38,022,115 | 36.0 |
| Japanese | 796,700 | 0.3 | Households with individuals 65 | | |
| Korean | 1,076,872 | 0.4 | and over | 24,672,708 | 23.4 |
| Vietnamese | 1,122,528 | 0.4 | | | |
| Other Asian[1] | 1,285,234 | 0.5 | Average household size | 2.59 | n.a. |
| Native Hawaiian and Other | | | Average family size | 3.14 | n.a. |
| Pacific Islander | 398,835 | 0.1 | | | |
| Native Hawaiian | 140,652 | — | **Housing occupancy** | | |
| Guamanian or Chamorro | 58,240 | — | Total housing units | 115,904,641 | 100.0 |
| Samoan | 91,029 | — | Occupied housing units | 105,480,101 | 91.0 |
| Other Pacific Islander[2] | 108,914 | — | Vacant housing units | 10,424,540 | 9.0 |
| Some other race | 15,359,073 | 5.5 | For seasonal, recreational, | | |
| Two or more races | 6,826,228 | 2.4 | or occasional use | 3,578,718 | 3.1 |
| | | | Homeowner vacancy rate (%) | 1.7 | n.a. |
| **with one or more other races:[3]** | | | | | |
| White | 216,930,975 | 77.1 | **Housing tenure** | | |
| Black or African American | 36,419,434 | 12.9 | Occupied housing units | 105,480,101 | 100.0 |
| American Indian and Alaska | | | Owner-occupied housing units | 69,815,753 | 66.2 |
| Native | 4,119,301 | 1.5 | Renter-occupied housing units | 35,664,348 | 33.8 |
| Asian | 11,898,828 | 4.2 | Average household size of | | |
| Native Hawaiian and Other | | | owner-occupied units | 2.69 | n.a. |
| Pacific Islander | 874,414 | 0.3 | Average household size of | | |
| Some other race | 18,521,486 | 6.6 | renter-occupied units | 2.40 | n.a. |

NOTES: (—) represents zero or rounds to zero; n.a. = not applicable. 1. Other Asian alone, or two or more Asian categories. 2. Other Pacific Islander alone, or two or more Native Hawaiian and Other Pacific Islander categories. 3. In combination with one or more of the other races listed. The six numbers may add to more than the total population and the six percentages may add to more than 100% because individuals may report more than one race. *Source:* U.S. Census Bureau, Census 2000. Web: www.census.gov.

# U.S. STATISTICS

## Population by State

| State | 2000 | Percent change, 1990–2000 | Pop. per sq mi, 2000 | Pop. rank, 2000 | 1990 | 1950 | 1900 | 1790 |
|---|---|---|---|---|---|---|---|---|
| Alabama | 4,447,100 | 10.1% | 87.6 | 23 | 4,040,587 | 3,061,743 | 1,828,697 | — |
| Alaska | 626,932 | 14.0 | 1.1 | 48 | 550,043 | 128,643 | 63,592 | — |
| Arizona | 5,130,632 | 40.0 | 45.2 | 20 | 3,665,228 | 749,587 | 122,931 | — |
| Arkansas | 2,673,400 | 13.7 | 51.3 | 33 | 2,350,725 | 1,909,511 | 1,311,564 | — |
| California | 33,871,648 | 13.8 | 217.2 | 1 | 29,760,021 | 10,586,223 | 1,485,053 | — |
| Colorado | 4,301,261 | 30.6 | 41.5 | 24 | 3,294,394 | 1,325,089 | 539,700 | — |
| Connecticut | 3,405,565 | 3.6 | 702.9 | 29 | 3,287,116 | 2,007,280 | 908,420 | 237,946 |
| Delaware | 783,600 | 17.6 | 401.0 | 45 | 666,168 | 318,085 | 184,735 | 59,096 |
| DC | 572,059 | −5.7 | 9,378.0 | — | 606,900 | 802,178 | 278,718 | — |
| Florida | 15,982,378 | 23.5 | 296.4 | 4 | 12,937,926 | 2,771,305 | 528,542 | — |
| Georgia | 8,186,453 | 26.4 | 141.4 | 10 | 6,478,216 | 3,444,578 | 2,216,331 | 82,548 |
| Hawaii | 1,211,537 | 9.3 | 188.6 | 42 | 1,108,229 | 499,794 | 154,001 | — |
| Idaho | 1,293,953 | 28.5 | 15.6 | 39 | 1,006,749 | 588,637 | 161,772 | — |
| Illinois | 12,419,293 | 8.6 | 223.4 | 5 | 11,430,602 | 8,712,176 | 4,821,550 | — |
| Indiana | 6,080,485 | 9.7 | 169.5 | 14 | 5,544,159 | 3,934,224 | 2,516,462 | — |
| Iowa | 2,926,324 | 5.4 | 52.4 | 30 | 2,776,755 | 2,621,073 | 2,231,853 | — |
| Kansas | 2,688,418 | 8.5 | 32.9 | 32 | 2,477,574 | 1,905,299 | 1,470,495 | — |
| Kentucky | 4,041,769 | 9.7 | 101.7 | 25 | 3,685,296 | 2,944,806 | 2,147,174 | 73,677 |
| Louisiana | 4,468,976 | 5.9 | 102.6 | 22 | 4,219,973 | 2,683,516 | 1,381,625 | — |
| Maine | 1,274,923 | 3.8 | 41.3 | 40 | 1,227,928 | 913,774 | 694,466 | 96,540 |
| Maryland | 5,296,486 | 10.8 | 541.9 | 19 | 4,781,468 | 2,343,001 | 1,188,044 | 319,728 |
| Massachusetts | 6,349,097 | 5.5 | 809.8 | 13 | 6,016,425 | 4,690,514 | 2,805,346 | 378,787 |
| Michigan | 9,938,444 | 6.9 | 175.0 | 8 | 9,295,297 | 6,371,766 | 2,420,982 | — |
| Minnesota | 4,919,479 | 12.4 | 61.8 | 21 | 4,375,099 | 2,982,483 | 1,751,394 | — |
| Mississippi | 2,844,658 | 10.5 | 60.6 | 31 | 2,573,216 | 2,178,914 | 1,551,270 | — |
| Missouri | 5,595,211 | 9.3 | 81.2 | 17 | 5,117,073 | 3,954,653 | 3,106,665 | — |
| Montana | 902,195 | 12.9 | 6.2 | 44 | 799,065 | 591,024 | 243,329 | — |
| Nebraska | 1,711,263 | 8.4 | 22.3 | 38 | 1,578,385 | 1,325,510 | 1,066,300 | — |
| Nevada | 1,998,257 | 66.3 | 18.2 | 35 | 1,201,833 | 160,083 | 42,335 | — |
| New Hampshire | 1,235,786 | 11.4 | 137.8 | 41 | 1,109,252 | 533,242 | 411,588 | 141,885 |
| New Jersey | 8,414,350 | 8.9 | 1,134.5 | 9 | 7,730,188 | 4,835,329 | 1,883,669 | 184,139 |
| New Mexico | 1,819,046 | 20.1 | 15.0 | 36 | 1,515,069 | 681,187 | 195,310 | — |
| New York | 18,976,457 | 5.5 | 401.9 | 3 | 17,990,455 | 14,830,192 | 7,268,894 | 340,120 |
| North Carolina | 8,049,313 | 21.4 | 165.2 | 11 | 6,628,637 | 4,061,929 | 1,893,810 | 393,751 |
| North Dakota | 642,200 | 0.5 | 9.3 | 47 | 638,800 | 619,636 | 319,146 | — |
| Ohio | 11,353,140 | 4.7 | 277.3 | 7 | 10,847,115 | 7,946,627 | 4,157,545 | — |
| Oklahoma | 3,450,654 | 9.7 | 50.3 | 27 | 3,145,585 | 2,233,351 | 790,391[1] | — |
| Oregon | 3,421,399 | 20.4 | 35.6 | 28 | 2,842,321 | 1,521,341 | 413,536 | — |
| Pennsylvania | 12,281,054 | 3.4 | 274.0 | 6 | 11,881,643 | 10,498,012 | 6,302,115 | 434,373 |
| Rhode Island | 1,048,319 | 4.5 | 1,003.2 | 43 | 1,003,464 | 791,896 | 428,556 | 68,825 |
| South Carolina | 4,012,012 | 15.1 | 133.2 | 26 | 3,486,703 | 2,117,027 | 1,340,316 | 249,073 |
| South Dakota | 754,844 | 8.5 | 9.9 | 46 | 696,004 | 652,740 | 401,570 | — |
| Tennessee | 5,689,283 | 16.7 | 138.0 | 16 | 4,877,185 | 3,291,718 | 2,020,616 | 35,691 |
| Texas | 20,851,820 | 22.8 | 79.6 | 2 | 16,986,510 | 7,711,194 | 3,048,710 | — |
| Utah | 2,233,169 | 29.6 | 27.2 | 34 | 1,722,850 | 688,862 | 276,749 | — |
| Vermont | 608,827 | 8.2 | 65.8 | 49 | 562,758 | 377,747 | 343,641 | 85,425 |
| Virginia | 7,078,515 | 14.4 | 178.8 | 12 | 6,187,358 | 3,318,680 | 1,854,184 | 747,610[2] |
| Washington | 5,894,121 | 21.1 | 88.6 | 15 | 4,866,692 | 2,378,963 | 518,103 | — |
| West Virginia | 1,808,344 | 0.8 | 75.1 | 37 | 1,793,477 | 2,005,552 | 958,800 | — |
| Wisconsin | 5,363,675 | 9.6 | 98.8 | 18 | 4,891,769 | 3,434,575 | 2,069,042 | — |
| Wyoming | 493,782 | 8.9 | 5.1 | 50 | 453,588 | 290,529 | 92,531 | — |
| **Total U.S.** | **281,421,906** | **13.2** | **—** | **—** | **248,709,873** | **151,325,798** | **76,212,168** | **3,929,214** |

1. Includes population of Indian Territory, 1900: 392,960. 2. Until 1863, Virginia included what is now West Virginia. *Source:* U.S. Bureau of the Census. Web: www.census.gov.

## Total U.S. Population

| Area | 2000 | 1990 | 1980 | Area | 2000 | 1990 | 1980 |
|---|---|---|---|---|---|---|---|
| 50 states[1] | 281,421,906 | 248,709,873 | 226,545,805 | N. Mariana Is.[3] | 69,221 | 43,345 | [4] |
| 48 coterminous[1] | 279,583,437 | 247,051,601 | 225,179,263 | Puerto Rico | 3,808,610 | 3,522,037 | 3,196,520 |
| Alaska | 626,932 | 550,043 | 401,851 | Trust Ter. of Pac. Is. | [7] | 15,122[6] | 132,929[5] |
| Hawaii | 1,211,537 | 1,108,229 | 964,691 | Virgin Is. of U.S. | 108,612 | 101,809 | 96,569 |
| American Samoa | 57,291 | 46,773 | 32,297 | Wake Island | [2] | [2] | 302 |
| Guam | 154,805 | 133,152 | 105,979 | Population abroad | 576,367[8] | 922,819 | 995,546 |
| Johnston Atoll | [2] | [2] | 327 | Armed forces | n.a. | 910,611 | 515,408 |
| Midway | [2] | [2] | 453 | **Total** | **286,196,812** | **253,451,585** | **231,106,727** |

NOTE: n.a. = not available. 1. Includes the District of Columbia. 2. No indigenous population. 3. The Commonwealth of the Northern Mariana Islands (CNMI) became part of the United States in 1986. 4. Included under trust territory of the Pacific Islands. 5. Includes Northern Mariana Islands. 6. Palau only trust territory remaining. 7. Palau, the last remaining trust territory, became an independent country in 1994. 8. Includes overseas U.S. military and federal civilian employees and their dependents living with them. *Source:* U.S. Bureau of the Census. Web: www.census.gov.

## U.S. Population by Region, 1990–2000

| Area | Population | | Change, 1990–2000 | |
|---|---|---|---|---|
| | April 1, 1990 | April 1, 2000 | Number | Percent |
| United States | 248,709,873 | 281,421,906 | 32,712,033 | 13.2% |
| Region[1] | | | | |
| Northeast | 50,809,229 | 53,594,378 | 2,785,149 | 5.5 |
| Midwest | 59,668,632 | 64,392,776 | 4,724,144 | 7.9 |
| South | 85,445,930 | 100,236,820 | 14,790,890 | 17.3 |
| West | 52,786,082 | 63,197,932 | 10,411,850 | 19.7 |

1. The Northeast region includes Connecticut, Maine, Massachusetts, New Hampshire, New Jersey, New York, Pennsylvania, Rhode Island, and Vermont. The Midwest includes Illinois, Indiana, Iowa, Kansas, Michigan, Minnesota, Missouri, Nebraska, North Dakota, Ohio, South Dakota, and Wisconsin. The South includes Alabama, Arkansas, Delaware, the District of Columbia, Florida, Georgia, Kentucky, Louisiana, Maryland, Mississippi, North Carolina, Oklahoma, South Carolina, Tennessee, Texas, Virginia, and West Virginia. The West includes Alaska, Arizona, California, Colorado, Hawaii, Idaho, Montana, Nevada, New Mexico, Oregon, Utah, Washington, and Wyoming. Source: U.S. Census Bureau, Census 2000; 1990 Census. Web: www.census.gov.

## Resident Population—Selected Characteristics, 1790–2000

### (in thousands)

| Date | Male | Female | White | Black | Total other | Other American Indian, Eskimo, Aleut | Asian and Pacific Islanders | Hispanic origin[1] |
|---|---|---|---|---|---|---|---|---|
| 1790 (Aug. 2)[2] | n.a. | n.a. | 3,172 | 757 | n.a. | n.a. | n.a. | n.a. |
| 1800 (Aug. 4)[2] | n.a. | n.a. | 4,306 | 1,002 | n.a. | n.a. | n.a. | n.a. |
| 1850 (June 1)[2] | 11,838 | 11,354 | 19,553 | 3,639 | n.a. | n.a. | n.a. | n.a. |
| 1900 (June 1)[2] | 38,816 | 37,178 | 66,809 | 8,834 | 351 | n.a. | n.a. | n.a. |
| 1910 (Apr. 15)[2] | 47,332 | 44,640 | 81,732 | 9,828 | 413 | n.a. | n.a. | n.a. |
| 1920 (Jan. 1)[2] | 53,900 | 51,810 | 94,821 | 10,463 | 427 | n.a. | n.a. | n.a. |
| 1930 (Apr. 1)[2] | 62,137 | 60,638 | 110,287 | 11,891 | 597 | n.a. | n.a. | n.a. |
| 1940 (Apr. 1)[2] | 66,062 | 65,608 | 118,215 | 12,866 | 589 | n.a. | n.a. | n.a. |
| 1950 (Apr. 1)[2] | 74,833 | 75,864 | 134,942 | 15,042 | 713 | n.a. | n.a. | n.a. |
| 1950 (Apr. 1) | 75,187 | 76,139 | 135,150 | 15,045 | 1,131 | n.a. | n.a. | n.a. |
| 1960 (Apr. 1) | 88,331 | 90,992 | 158,832 | 18,872 | 1,620 | n.a. | n.a. | n.a. |
| 1970 (Apr. 1)[3] | 98,926 | 104,309 | 178,098 | 22,581 | 2,557 | n.a. | n.a. | n.a. |
| 1980 (Apr. 1)[4, 5] | 110,053 | 116,493 | 194,713 | 26,683 | 5,150 | 1,420 | 3,729 | 14,609 |
| 1990 (Apr. 1)[4, 6] | 121,271 | 127,494 | 208,727 | 30,511 | 9,527 | 2,065 | 7,462 | 22,372 |
| 2000 (Apr. 1)[4] | 138,054 | 143,368 | 211,461 | 34,658 | 13,118 | 2,476 | 10,642 | 35,306 |

NOTES: n.a. = not available. 1. Persons of Hispanic origin may be of any race. 2. Excludes Alaska and Hawaii. 3. The revised 1970 resident population count is 203,302,031, which incorporates changes due to errors found after tabulations were completed. The race and sex data shown here reflect the official 1970 census count. 4. The race data shown have been modified to be consistent with the guidelines in Federal Statistical Directive No. 15 issued by the Office of Management and Budget and are not comparable to data for earlier years. 5. Total population count has been revised since the 1980 census publications. Numbers by age, race, Hispanic origin, and sex have not been corrected. 6. The April 1, 1990, census count (248,765,170) includes count resolution corrections processed through Aug. 1997, and does not include adjustments for census coverage errors except for adjustments estimated for the 1995 Census Test in Oakland, Calif.; Paterson, N.J., and six Louisiana parishes. These adjustments amounted to a total of 55,297 persons. Source: Statistical Abstract of the United States and Census 2000. Web (Census 2000): www.census.gov.

## Ratio of Males to Females, by Age Group, 1950–2000

### (number of males per 100 females, total resident population)

| Age | 1950 | 1960 | 1970 | 1980 | 1990[1] | 2000 |
|---|---|---|---|---|---|---|
| All ages | 98.6 | 97.1 | 94.8 | 94.5 | 95.1 | 96.3 |
| Under 14 years | 103.7 | 103.4 | 103.9 | 104.6 | 104.9 | 104.9 |
| 14 to 24 years | 98.2 | 98.7 | 98.7 | 101.9 | 104.6 | 105.1 |
| 25 to 44 years | 96.4 | 95.7 | 95.5 | 97.4 | 98.9 | 100.2 |
| 45 to 64 years | 100.1 | 95.7 | 91.6 | 90.7 | 92.5 | 94.8 |
| 65 years and over | 89.6 | 82.8 | 72.1 | 67.6 | 67.2 | 70.8 |

NOTES: As of April 1 for all years. 1. The April 1, 1990, census count (248,765,170) includes count resolution corrections processed through August 1997, and does not include adjustments for census coverage errors except for adjustments estimated for the 1995 Census Test in Oakland, Calif.; Paterson, N.J.; and six Louisiana parishes. These adjustments amounted to a total of 55,297 persons. Source: U.S. Census Bureau, Current Population Reports, P25-1095 and P25-1130; and unpublished data. From Statistical Abstract of the United States 1999. 2000 data are from Census 2000.

## Population Distribution by Age, Race, Nativity, and Sex Ratio

| Year | Total | Age Under 5 | 5–19 | 20–44 | 45–64 | 65 and over | White[1] Total | Native born | Foreign born | Black | Other races[1] |
|------|-------|---------|------|-------|-------|-------------|-------|-------------|--------------|-------|-------|
| **Percent Distribution** | | | | | | | | | | | |
| 1860[2] | 100.0% | 15.4% | 35.8% | 35.7% | 10.4% | 2.7% | 85.6% | 72.6% | 13.0% | 14.1% | 0.3% |
| 1870[2] | 100.0 | 14.3 | 35.4 | 35.4 | 11.9 | 3.0 | 87.1 | 72.9 | 14.2 | 12.7 | 0.2 |
| 1880[2] | 100.0 | 13.8 | 34.3 | 35.9 | 12.6 | 3.4 | 86.5 | 73.4 | 13.1 | 13.1 | 0.3 |
| 1890[3] | 100.0 | 12.2 | 33.9 | 36.9 | 13.1 | 3.9 | 87.5 | 73.0 | 14.5 | 11.9 | 0.3 |
| 1900 | 100.0 | 12.1 | 32.3 | 37.7 | 13.7 | 4.1 | 87.9 | 74.5 | 13.4 | 11.6 | 0.5 |
| 1910 | 100.0 | 11.6 | 30.4 | 39.0 | 14.6 | 4.3 | 88.9 | 74.4 | 14.5 | 10.7 | 0.4 |
| 1920 | 100.0 | 10.9 | 29.8 | 38.4 | 16.1 | 4.7 | 89.7 | 76.7 | 13.0 | 9.9 | 0.4 |
| 1930 | 100.0 | 9.3 | 29.5 | 38.3 | 17.4 | 5.4 | 89.8 | 78.4 | 11.4 | 9.7 | 0.5 |
| 1940 | 100.0 | 8.0 | 26.4 | 38.9 | 19.8 | 6.8 | 89.8 | 81.1 | 8.7 | 9.8 | 0.4 |
| 1950 | 100.0 | 10.7 | 23.2 | 37.6 | 20.3 | 8.1 | 89.5 | 82.8 | 6.7 | 10.0 | 0.5 |
| 1960 | 100.0 | 11.3 | 27.1 | 32.2 | 20.1 | 9.2 | 88.6 | 83.4 | 5.2 | 10.5 | 0.9 |
| 1970[2] | 100.0 | 8.4 | 29.5 | 31.7 | 20.6 | 9.8 | 87.6 | 83.4 | 4.3 | 11.1 | 1.4 |
| 1980 | 100.0 | 7.2 | 24.8 | 37.1 | 19.6 | 11.3 | 83.1 | — | — | 11.7 | 5.2 |
| 1990 | 100.0 | 7.6 | 21.3 | 40.1 | 18.6 | 12.5 | 83.9 | — | — | 12.3 | 3.8 |
| 2000 | 100.0 | 6.8 | 21.8 | 37.0 | 22.0 | 12.4 | 75.1[4] | — | — | 12.3[4] | 10.1[5] |
| **Males per 100 Females** | | | | | | | | | | | |
| 1860[2] | 104.7 | 102.4 | 101.2 | 107.9 | 111.5 | 98.3 | 105.3 | 103.7 | 115.1 | 99.6 | 260.8 |
| 1870[2] | 102.2 | 102.9 | 101.2 | 99.2 | 114.5 | 100.5 | 102.8 | 100.6 | 115.3 | 96.2 | 400.7 |
| 1880[2] | 103.6 | 103.0 | 101.3 | 104.0 | 110.2 | 101.4 | 104.0 | 102.1 | 115.9 | 97.8 | 362.2 |
| 1890[3] | 105.0 | 103.6 | 101.4 | 107.3 | 108.3 | 104.2 | 105.4 | 102.9 | 118.7 | 99.5 | 165.2 |
| 1900 | 104.4 | 102.1 | 100.9 | 105.8 | 110.7 | 102.0 | 104.9 | 102.8 | 117.4 | 98.6 | 185.2 |
| 1910 | 106.0 | 102.5 | 101.3 | 108.1 | 114.4 | 101.1 | 106.6 | 102.7 | 129.2 | 98.9 | 185.6 |
| 1920 | 104.0 | 102.5 | 100.8 | 102.8 | 115.2 | 101.3 | 104.4 | 101.7 | 121.7 | 99.2 | 156.6 |
| 1930 | 102.5 | 103.0 | 101.4 | 100.5 | 109.1 | 100.5 | 102.9 | 101.1 | 115.8 | 97.0 | 150.6 |
| 1940 | 100.7 | 103.2 | 102.0 | 98.1 | 105.2 | 95.5 | 101.2 | 100.1 | 111.1 | 95.0 | 140.5 |
| 1950 | 98.6 | 103.9 | 102.5 | 96.2 | 100.1 | 89.6 | 99.0 | 98.8 | 102.0 | 93.7 | 129.7 |
| 1960 | 97.1 | 103.4 | 102.7 | 95.6 | 95.7 | 82.8 | 97.4 | 97.6 | 94.2 | 93.3 | 109.7 |
| 1970[2] | 94.8 | 104.0 | 103.3 | 95.1 | 91.6 | 72.1 | 95.3 | 95.9 | 83.8 | 90.8 | 100.2 |
| 1980 | 94.5 | 104.7 | 104.0 | 98.1 | 90.7 | 67.6 | 94.8 | — | — | 89.6 | 100.3 |
| 1990 | 95.1 | 104.8 | 105.0 | 99.8 | 92.5 | 67.2 | 95.9 | — | — | 89.8 | 96.5 |
| 2000 | 96.3 | 104.8 | 105.3 | 101.0 | 94.8 | 70.0 | 96.4[4] | — | — | 90.5[4] | 102.2[5] |

NOTES: Data exclude armed forces overseas. Beginning in 1960, includes Alaska and Hawaii. (—) Data not available. 1. The 1980 and 1990 census data for white and other race categories are not directly comparable to those shown for the preceding years because of changes in the way some persons reported their race, as well as changes in procedures relating to racial classification. 2. Excludes persons for whom age is not available. 3. Excludes persons enumerated in the Indian Territory and on Indian reservations. 4. Includes only those claiming one race only. 5. Includes American Indian and Alaska Native, Asian, Native Hawaiian and other Pacific Islander, and some other race. *Source:* U.S. Bureau of the Census. Web: www.census.gov.

## Households by Size, 1790–2000

| Year | Number of households (in thousands) | Percent distribution of number of households 1 person | 2 persons | 3 persons | 4 persons | 5 persons | 6 persons | 7 or more persons |
|------|------|------|------|------|------|------|------|------|
| 1790 (Mar.) | 558 | 3.7% | 7.8% | 11.7% | 13.8% | 13.9% | 13.2% | 35.8% |
| 1890 (June) | 12,690 | 3.6 | 13.2 | 16.7 | 16.8 | 15.1 | 11.6 | 23.0 |
| 1900 (Mar.) | 15,964 | 5.1 | 15.0 | 17.6 | 16.9 | 14.2 | 10.9 | 20.4 |
| 1930 (Apr.) | 29,905 | 7.9 | 23.4 | 20.8 | 17.5 | 12.0 | 7.6 | 10.9 |
| 1940 (Apr.) | 34,949 | 7.1 | 24.8 | 22.4 | 18.1 | 11.5 | 6.8 | 9.3 |
| 1950 (Apr.)[1] | 43,468 | 10.9 | 28.8 | 22.6 | 17.8 | 10.0 | 5.1 | 4.9 |
| 1955 (Mar.) | 47,788 | 10.9 | 28.5 | 20.4 | 18.9 | 11.1 | 5.4 | 4.9 |
| 1960 (Mar.)[2] | 52,610 | 13.1 | 27.8 | 18.9 | 17.6 | 11.5 | 5.7 | 5.4 |
| 1965 (Mar.) | 57,251 | 15.0 | 28.1 | 17.9 | 16.1 | 11.0 | 5.8 | 6.1 |
| 1970 (Mar.) | 62,874 | 17.0 | 28.8 | 17.3 | 15.8 | 10.4 | 5.6 | 5.1 |
| 1975 (Mar.) | 71,120 | 19.6 | 30.6 | 17.4 | 15.6 | 9.0 | 4.3 | 3.5 |
| 1980 (Mar.) | 80,776 | 22.7 | 31.3 | 17.5 | 15.7 | 7.5 | 3.1 | 2.2 |
| 1985 (Mar.) | 86,789 | 23.7 | 31.6 | 17.8 | 15.7 | 7.0 | 2.6 | 1.5 |
| 1990 (Mar.) | 93,347 | 24.6 | 32.2 | 17.2 | 15.5 | 6.7 | 2.3 | 1.4 |
| 1995 (Mar.) | 98,990 | 25.0 | 32.1 | 17.0 | 15.5 | 6.7 | 2.3 | 1.4 |
| 2000 (Mar.) | 104,705 | 25.5 | 33.1 | 16.4 | 14.6 | 6.7 | 2.3 | 1.4 |

1. Covers related persons only; therefore, not strictly comparable with other years. 2. Denotes first year for which figures include Alaska and Hawaii. *Source:* U.S. Census Bureau. Web: www.census.gov.

# Population Explosion Among Older Americans

The United States saw a rapid growth in its elderly population during the 20th century. The number of Americans aged 65 and older climbed above 34.9 million in 2000, compared with 3.1 million in 1900. For the same years, the ratio of elderly Americans to the total population jumped from one in 25 to one in eight. The trend is guaranteed to continue in the coming century as the baby-boom generation grows older. Between 1990 and 2020, the population aged 65 to 74 is projected to grow 74%.

The elderly population explosion is a result of impressive increases in life expectancy. When the nation was founded, the average American could expect to live to the age of 35. Life expectancy at birth had increased to 47.3 by 1900 and in 1997 stood at 76.5.

Along with the growth of the general elderly population has come a remarkable increase in the number of Americans reaching age 100. In 2000 there were 50,454 centenarians (people aged 100 or over), representing 1 out of every 5,578 people. In 1990 centenarians numbered 37,306 people, or 1 out of every 6,667 people.

*Source:* Based on U.S. Census Bureau data.

## Population 65 Years and Over by Age, 1990 and 2000

| Age | 1990 Number | 1990 Percent | 2000 Number | 2000 Percent | Percent of U.S. total 1990 | Percent of U.S. total 2000 | Percent change, 1990 to 2000 |
|---|---|---|---|---|---|---|---|
| **65 years and over** | 31,241,831 | 100.0% | 34,991,753 | 100.0% | 12.6% | 12.4% | 12.0% |
| 65 to 74 years | 18,106,558 | 58.0 | 18,390,986 | 52.6 | 7.3 | 6.5 | 1.6 |
| 65 to 69 years | 10,111,735 | 32.4 | 9,533,545 | 27.2 | 4.1 | 3.4 | −5.7 |
| 70 to 74 years | 7,994,823 | 25.6 | 8,857,441 | 25.3 | 3.2 | 3.1 | 10.8 |
| 75 to 84 years | 10,055,108 | 32.2 | 12,361,180 | 35.3 | 4.0 | 4.4 | 22.9 |
| 75 to 79 years | 6,121,369 | 19.6 | 7,415,813 | 21.2 | 2.5 | 2.6 | 21.1 |
| 80 to 84 years | 3,933,739 | 12.6 | 4,945,367 | 14.1 | 1.6 | 1.8 | 25.7 |
| 85 to 94 years | 2,829,728 | 9.1 | 3,902,349 | 11.2 | 1.1 | 1.4 | 37.9 |
| 85 to 89 years | 2,060,247 | 6.6 | 2,789,818 | 8.0 | 0.8 | 1.0 | 35.4 |
| 90 to 94 years | 769,481 | 2.5 | 1,112,531 | 3.2 | 0.3 | 0.4 | 44.6 |
| 95 years and over | 250,437 | 0.8 | 337,238 | 1.0 | 0.1 | 0.1 | 34.7 |

*Source:* U.S. Census Bureau, Census 2000; 1990 Census of Population, *General Population Characteristics, United States* (1990 CP-1-1). Web: www.census.gov.

## Persons 65 Years Old and Over—Characteristics by Sex, 1980–2000

| Characteristic | Total 1980 | Total 1990 | Total 2000 | Male 1980 | Male 1990 | Male 2000 | Female 1980 | Female 1990 | Female 2000 |
|---|---|---|---|---|---|---|---|---|---|
| **Total[1] (million)** | 24.2 | 29.6 | 32.6 | 9.9 | 12.3 | 13.9 | 14.2 | 17.2 | 18.7 |
| White (million) | 21.9 | 26.5 | n.a. | 9.0 | 11.0 | n.a. | 12.9 | 15.4 | n.a. |
| Black (million) | 2.0 | 2.5 | n.a. | 0.8 | 1.0 | n.a. | 1.2 | 1.5 | n.a. |
| Percent below poverty level[2] | 15.2% | 11.4% | 9.7% | 11.1% | 7.8% | 6.9% | 17.9% | 13.9% | 11.8% |
| **Percent distribution** | | | | | | | | | |
| **Marital status:** | | | | | | | | | |
| Single | 5.5% | 4.6% | 3.9% | 4.9% | 4.2% | 4.2% | 5.9% | 4.9% | 3.6% |
| Married | 55.4 | 56.1 | 57.2 | 78.0 | 76.5 | 75.2 | 39.5 | 41.4 | 43.8 |
| Spouse present | 53.6 | 54.1 | 54.6 | 76.1 | 74.2 | 72.6 | 37.9 | 39.7 | 41.3 |
| Spouse absent | 1.8 | 2.0 | 2.6 | 1.9 | 2.3 | 2.6 | 1.7 | 1.7 | 2.5 |
| Widowed | 35.7 | 34.2 | 32.1 | 13.5 | 14.2 | 14.4 | 51.2 | 48.6 | 45.3 |
| Divorced | 3.5 | 5.0 | 6.7 | 3.6 | 5.0 | 6.1 | 3.4 | 5.1 | 7.2 |
| **Years of school completed:** | | | | | | | | | |
| 8 years or fewer | 43.1% | 28.5% | 16.7% | 45.3% | 29.9% | 12.7%[3] | 41.1% | 11.11 | 18.11% |
| 1 to 3 years of high school | 11.11 | 11.11 | 13.0% | 18.5 | 15.7 | 12.7[3] | 16.7 | 16.4 | 14.7[3] |
| 4 years of high school | 24.0 | 32.9 | 35.9[4] | 21.4 | 29.0 | 30.4[4] | 25.8 | 35.6 | 39.9[4] |
| 1 to 3 years of college | 8.2 | 10.9 | 18.0[5] | 7.5 | 10.8 | 17.9[5] | 0.0 | 11.0 | 18.0[5] |
| 4 years or more of college | 8.0 | 11.6 | 15.6[6] | 10.2 | 14.5 | 21.4[6] | 7.4 | 9.5 | 11.4[6] |
| **Labor force participation[7]:** | | | | | | | | | |
| Employed | 12.2% | 11.5% | 12.4% | 18.4% | 15.9% | 16.9% | 7.8% | 8.4% | 9.1% |
| Unemployed | 0.4 | 0.4 | 0.4 | 0.6 | 0.5 | 0.6 | 0.3 | 0.3 | 0.3 |
| Not in labor force | 87.5 | 88.1 | 87.2 | 81.0 | 83.6 | 82.5 | 91.9 | 91.3 | 90.6 |

NOTES: n.a. = not available. (—) Represents zero. 1. Includes other races, not shown separately. 2. Poverty status based on income in preceding year. 3. Represents those who completed 9th to 12th grade, but have no high school diploma. 4. High school graduate. 5. Some college or associate degree. 6. Bachelor's or advanced degree. 7. Annual averages of monthly figures (from U.S. Bureau of Labor Statistics, *Employment and Earnings,* January issues. Data beginning 1994 not directly comparable with earlier years). *Source:* Except as noted, U.S. Bureau of the Census, *Current Population Reports.* From *Statistical Abstract of the United States 2001.*

# Marital Status and Household Characteristics

## Marriages and Divorces, 1900–2000

| Year | Marriage Number | Marriage Rate[2] | Divorce[1] Number | Divorce[1] Rate[2] | Year | Marriage Number | Marriage Rate[2] | Divorce[1] Number | Divorce[1] Rate[2] |
|---|---|---|---|---|---|---|---|---|---|
| 1900 | 709,000 | 9.3 | 55,751 | 0.7 | 1986 | 2,400,000 | 10.0 | 1,159,000 | 4.8 |
| 1910 | 948,166 | 10.3 | 83,045 | 0.9 | 1987 | 2,421,000 | 9.9 | 1,157,000 | 4.8 |
| 1920 | 1,274,476 | 12.0 | 170,505 | 1.6 | 1988 | 2,389,000 | 9.7 | 1,183,000 | 4.8 |
| 1930 | 1,126,856 | 9.2 | 195,961 | 1.6 | 1989 | 2,404,000 | 9.7 | 1,163,000 | 4.7 |
| 1940 | 1,595,879 | 12.1 | 264,000 | 2.0 | 1990 | 2,448,000 | 9.8 | 1,175,000 | 4.7 |
| 1950 | 1,667,231 | 11.1 | 385,144 | 2.6 | 1991 | 2,371,000 | 9.4 | 1,187,000 | 4.7 |
| 1960 | 1,523,000 | 8.5 | 393,000 | 2.2 | 1992 | 2,362,000 | 9.2 | 1,215,000 | 4.8 |
| 1965 | 1,800,000 | 9.3 | 479,000 | 2.5 | 1993 | 2,334,000 | 9.0 | 1,187,000 | 4.6 |
| 1970 | 2,158,802 | 10.6 | 708,000 | 3.5 | 1994 | 2,362,000 | 9.1 | 1,191,000 | 4.6 |
| 1975 | 2,152,662 | 10.1 | 1,036,000 | 4.9 | 1995 | 2,336,000 | 8.9 | 1,169,000 | 4.4 |
| 1980 | 2,406,708 | 10.6 | 1,182,000 | 5.2 | 1996 | 2,344,000 | 8.8 | 1,150,000 | 4.3 |
| 1982 | 2,495,000 | 10.8 | 1,180,000 | 5.1 | 1997 | 2,384,000 | 8.9 | 1,163,000 | 4.3 |
| 1983 | 2,444,000 | 10.5 | 1,179,000 | 5.0 | 1998 | 2,256,000 | 8.4 | 1,135,000 | 4.2 |
| 1984 | 2,487,000 | 10.5 | 1,155,000 | 4.9 | 1999 | 2,358,000 | 8.6 | — | 4.1 |
| 1985 | 2,425,000 | 10.2 | 1,187,000 | 5.0 | 2000 | 2,329,000 | 8.5 | — | 4.1 |

NOTE: (—) Data not available. Marriage and divorce figures for most years include some estimated data. Alaska is included beginning 1959, Hawaii beginning 1960. 1. Includes annulments. 2. Per 1,000 population. *Source:* U.S. Dept. of Health and Human Services, National Center for Health Statistics; Web: www.cdc.gov/nchs/.

## Median Age at First Marriage

| Year | Males | Females | Year | Males | Females | Year | Males | Females |
|---|---|---|---|---|---|---|---|---|
| 1890 | 26.1 | 22.0 | 1950 | 22.8 | 20.3 | 1996 | 27.1 | 24.8 |
| 1900 | 25.9 | 21.9 | 1960 | 22.8 | 20.3 | 1997 | 26.8 | 25.0 |
| 1910 | 25.1 | 21.6 | 1970 | 23.2 | 20.8 | 1998 | 26.7 | 25.0 |
| 1920 | 24.6 | 21.2 | 1980 | 24.7 | 22.0 | 1999 | 26.9 | 25.1 |
| 1930 | 24.3 | 21.3 | 1990 | 26.1 | 23.9 | 2000 | 26.8 | 25.1 |
| 1940 | 24.3 | 21.5 | 1995 | 26.9 | 24.5 | | | |

*Source:* U.S. Bureau of the Census; Web: www.census.gov.

## Marital Status of the Population, 1980–2000

### (numbers are in millions)

| Marital status | Total 2000 | Total 1995 | Total 1990 | Total 1980 | Male 2000 | Male 1995 | Male 1990 | Male 1980 | Female 2000 | Female 1995 | Female 1990 | Female 1980 |
|---|---|---|---|---|---|---|---|---|---|---|---|---|
| **Total** | 201.8 | 191.6 | 181.8 | 159.5 | 96.9 | 92.0 | 86.9 | 75.7 | 104.9 | 99.6 | 95.0 | 83.8 |
| Never married | 48.2 | 43.9 | 40.4 | 32.3 | 26.1 | 24.6 | 22.4 | 18.0 | 22.1 | 19.3 | 17.9 | 14.3 |
| Married | 120.1 | 116.7 | 112.6 | 104.6 | 59.6 | 57.7 | 55.8 | 51.8 | 60.4 | 58.9 | 56.7 | 52.8 |
| Widowed | 13.7 | 13.4 | 13.8 | 12.7 | 2.6 | 2.3 | 2.3 | 2.0 | 11.1 | 11.1 | 11.5 | 10.8 |
| Divorced | 19.8 | 17.6 | 15.1 | 9.9 | 8.5 | 7.4 | 6.3 | 3.9 | 11.3 | 10.3 | 8.8 | 6.0 |
| **Percent of total** | 100.0% | 100.0% | 100.0% | 100.0% | 100.0% | 100.0% | 100.0% | 100.0% | 100.0% | 100.0% | 100.0% | 100.0% |
| Never married | 23.9 | 22.9 | 22.2 | 20.3 | 27.0 | 26.8 | 25.8 | 23.8 | 21.1 | 19.4 | 18.9 | 17.1 |
| Married | 59.5 | 60.9 | 61.9 | 65.5 | 61.5 | 62.7 | 64.3 | 68.4 | 57.6 | 59.2 | 59.7 | 63.0 |
| Widowed | 6.8 | 7.0 | 7.6 | 8.0 | 2.7 | 2.5 | 2.7 | 2.6 | 10.5 | 11.1 | 12.1 | 12.8 |
| Divorced | 9.8 | 9.2 | 8.3 | 6.2 | 8.8 | 8.0 | 7.2 | 5.2 | 10.8 | 10.3 | 9.3 | 7.1 |

*Source:* U.S. Bureau of the Census, *Current Population Reports,* P20-491, and earlier reports; and unpublished data. From *Statistical Abstract of the United States 2001.*

## Percent Never Married, 1970, 1999, and 2000

| Age | 1970 | 1999 | 2000 | Age | 1970 | 1999 | 2000 |
|---|---|---|---|---|---|---|---|
| **Male:** | | | | **Female:** | | | |
| 20 to 24 years | 35.8% | 83.2% | 83.7% | 20 to 24 years | 54.7% | 72.3% | 72.8% |
| 25 to 29 years | 10.5 | 52.1 | 51.7 | 25 to 29 years | 19.1 | 38.9 | 38.9 |
| 30 to 34 years | 6.2 | 30.7 | 30.0 | 30 to 34 years | 9.4 | 22.1 | 21.9 |
| 35 to 39 years | 5.4 | 21.1 | 20.3 | 35 to 39 years | 7.2 | 15.2 | 14.3 |
| 40 to 44 years | 4.9 | 15.8 | 15.7 | 40 to 44 years | 6.3 | 10.9 | 11.8 |

NOTE: Data apply to the U.S. *Source:* U.S. Bureau of the Census. From *Statistical Abstract of the United States 2001.*

## Persons Living Alone, by Sex and Age

### (in thousands)

| Sex and Age | 2000 Number | 2000 Percent | 1995 Number | 1995 Percent | 1990 Number | 1990 Percent | 1980 Number | 1980 Percent |
|---|---|---|---|---|---|---|---|---|
| **Both sexes** | | | | | | | | |
| 15 to 24 years | 1,144 | 4% | 1,196 | 5% | 1,210 | 5% | 1,726 | 9% |
| 25 to 34 years | 3,848 | 14 | 3,653 | 15 | 3,972 | 17 | 4,729[1] | 26[1] |
| 35 to 44 years | 4,109 | 15 | 3,663 | 15 | 3,138 | 14 | (1) | (1) |
| 45 to 64 years | 7,842 | 29 | 6,377 | 26 | 5,502 | 24 | 4,514 | 25 |
| 65 to 74 years | 4,091 | 15 | 4,374 | 18 | 4,350 | 19 | 3,851 | 21 |
| 75 years and over | 5,692 | 21 | 5,470 | 22 | 4,825 | 21 | 3,477 | 19 |
| **Total, 15 years and over** | 26,724 | 100 | 24,732 | 100 | 22,999 | 100 | 18,296 | 100 |
| **Male** | | | | | | | | |
| 15 to 24 years | 556 | 2 | 623 | 3 | 674 | 3 | 947 | 5 |
| 25 to 34 years | 2,279 | 9 | 2,213 | 9 | 2,395 | 10 | 2,920[1] | 16[1] |
| 35 to 44 years | 2,569 | 10 | 2,263 | 9 | 1,836 | 8 | (1) | (1) |
| 45 to 64 years | 3,422 | 13 | 2,787 | 11 | 2,203 | 10 | 1,613 | 9 |
| 65 to 74 years | 1,108 | 4 | 1,134 | 5 | 1,042 | 5 | 775 | 4 |
| 75 years and over | 1,247 | 5 | 1,120 | 5 | 901 | 4 | 711 | 4 |
| **Total, 15 years and over** | 11,181 | 42 | 10,140 | 41 | 9,049 | 39 | 6,966 | 38 |
| **Female** | | | | | | | | |
| 15 to 24 years | 588 | 2 | 572 | 2 | 536 | 2 | 779 | 4 |
| 25 to 34 years | 1,568 | 6 | 1,440 | 6 | 1,578 | 7 | 1,809[1] | 10[1] |
| 35 to 44 years | 1,540 | 6 | 1,399 | 6 | 1,303 | 6 | (1) | (1) |
| 45 to 64 years | 4,420 | 17 | 3,589 | 15 | 3,300 | 14 | 2,901 | 16 |
| 65 to 74 years | 2,983 | 11 | 3,240 | 13 | 3,309 | 14 | 3,076 | 17 |
| 75 years and over | 4,444 | 17 | 4,351 | 18 | 3,924 | 17 | 2,766 | 15 |
| **Total, 15 years and over** | 15,543 | 58 | 14,592 | 59 | 13,950 | 61 | 11,330 | 62 |

NOTE: As of March. 1. Data for persons 35 to 44 years old included with persons 25 to 34 years old. *Source:* U.S. Bureau of the Census, *Current Population Reports*, P20-491, and earlier reports; and unpublished data. From *Statistical Abstract of the United States 2001.*

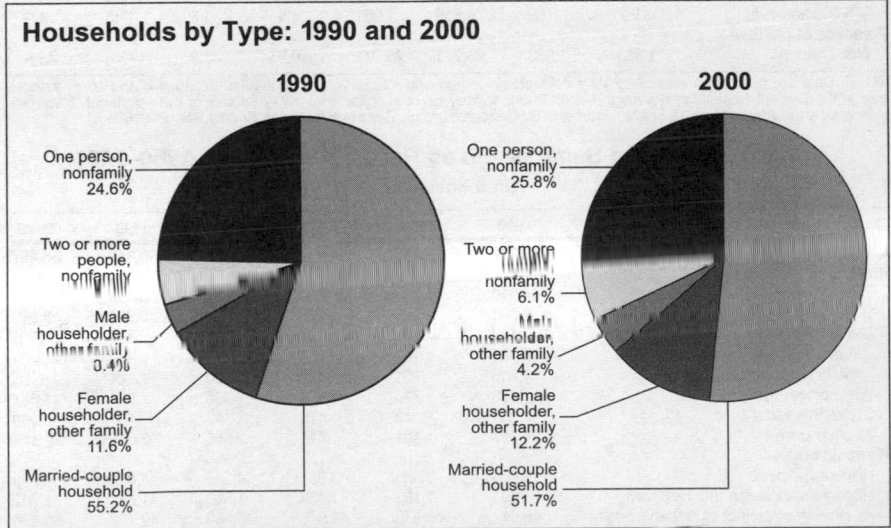

# Households by Type: 1990 and 2000

## 1990

One person, nonfamily 24.6%

Two or more people, nonfamily

Male householder, other family 0.4%

Female householder, other family 11.6%

Married-couple household 55.2%

## 2000

One person, nonfamily 25.8%

Two or more nonfamily 6.1%

Male householder, other family 4.2%

Female householder, other family 12.2%

Married-couple household 51.7%

Source: U.S. Census Bureau, Census 2000; 1990 Census of Population, *Summary Population and Housing Characteristics, United States* (1990 CPH-1-1).

## Characteristics of Unmarried Partners and Married Spouses, 2000

### (in thousands)

| | Number | | | | Percent | | | |
|---|---|---|---|---|---|---|---|---|
| | Unmarried partners | | Married spouses | | Unmarried partners | | Married spouses | |
| Characteristic | Men | Women | Men | Women | Men | Women | Men | Women |
| **Total** | **3,822** | **3,822** | **56,497** | **56,497** | **100.0%** | **100.0%** | **100.0%** | **100.0%** |
| **Age:** | | | | | | | | |
| 15 to 24 years old | 597 | 937 | 1,321 | 2,386 | 15.6 | 24.5 | 2.3 | 4.2 |
| 25 to 34 years old | 1,413 | 1,269 | 9,296 | 10,964 | 37.0 | 33.2 | 16.5 | 19.4 |
| 35 years old and over | 1,811 | 1,616 | 45,881 | 43,146 | 47.4 | 42.3 | 81.2 | 76.4 |
| **Race and Hispanic origin** | | | | | | | | |
| White | 3,127 | 3,147 | 49,668 | 49,581 | 81.8 | 82.3 | 87.9 | 87.8 |
| Non-Hispanic | 2,710 | 2,742 | 44,350 | 44,142 | 70.9 | 71.7 | 78.5 | 78.1 |
| Black | 562 | 498 | 4,294 | 4,097 | 14.7 | 13.0 | 7.6 | 7.3 |
| Asian and Pacific Islander | 63 | 105 | 2,118 | 2,393 | 1.6 | 2.7 | 3.7 | 4.2 |
| Hispanic (of any race) | 453 | 433 | 5,550 | 5,671 | 11.9 | 11.3 | 9.8 | 10.0 |
| **Education** | | | | | | | | |
| Less than high school | 683 | 599 | 8,314 | 7,160 | 17.9 | 15.7 | 14.7 | 12.7 |
| High school graduate | 1,441 | 1,357 | 17,506 | 19,950 | 37.7 | 35.5 | 31.0 | 35.3 |
| Some college | 996 | 1,223 | 14,002 | 14,968 | 26.1 | 32.0 | 24.8 | 26.5 |
| College graduate | 702 | 643 | 16,674 | 14,419 | 18.4 | 16.8 | 29.5 | 25.5 |
| **Labor force status** | | | | | | | | |
| Employed | 3,179 | 2,894 | 42,854 | 34,067 | 83.2 | 75.7 | 75.9 | 60.3 |
| Unemployed | 187 | 178 | 992 | 961 | 4.9 | 4.7 | 1.8 | 1.7 |
| Not in labor force | 453 | 747 | 12,650 | 21,468 | 11.9 | 19.5 | 22.4 | 38.0 |
| **Personal earnings** | | | | | | | | |
| Without earnings | 402 | 642 | 11,353 | 19,368 | 10.5 | 16.8 | 20.1 | 34.3 |
| With earnings | 3,419 | 3,178 | 45,144 | 37,132 | 89.5 | 83.2 | 79.9 | 65.7 |
| Under $5,000 | 184 | 373 | 1,874 | 4,683 | 4.8 | 9.8 | 3.3 | 8.3 |
| $5,000 to $9,999 | 286 | 395 | 1,665 | 4,183 | 7.5 | 10.3 | 2.9 | 7.4 |
| $10,000 to $14,999 | 360 | 445 | 2,401 | 4,497 | 9.4 | 11.6 | 4.2 | 8.0 |
| $15,000 to $19,999 | 410 | 441 | 3,101 | 4,427 | 10.7 | 11.5 | 5.5 | 7.8 |
| $20,000 to $24,999 | 401 | 397 | 3,561 | 4,249 | 10.5 | 10.4 | 6.3 | 7.5 |
| $25,000 to $29,999 | 336 | 315 | 3,595 | 3,429 | 8.8 | 8.2 | 6.4 | 6.1 |
| $30,000 to $39,999 | 548 | 405 | 7,492 | 4,954 | 14.3 | 10.6 | 13.3 | 8.8 |
| $40,000 to $49,999 | 337 | 201 | 6,096 | 2,976 | 8.8 | 5.3 | 10.8 | 5.3 |
| $50,000 to $74,999 | 370 | 137 | 8,703 | 2,683 | 9.7 | 3.6 | 15.4 | 4.7 |
| $75,000 and over | 187 | 69 | 6,656 | 1,051 | 4.9 | 1.8 | 11.8 | 1.9 |
| **Presence of children** | | | | | | | | |
| With children[1] | 1,563 | 1,563 | 25,771 | 25,771 | 40.9 | 40.9 | 45.6 | 45.6 |

NOTE: Data are not shown separately for the American Indian and Alaska Native population because of the small sample size in the Current Population Survey in March 2000. 1. May be own children of either partner or both partners. Excludes ever married children under 18 years. Source: U.S. Census Bureau, Current Population Survey, March 2000.

## Married Couples of Same or Mixed Races and Origins, 1980–2000

### (in thousands)

| Race and origin of spouse | 1980 | 1990 | 1995 | 1998 | 1999 | 2000 |
|---|---|---|---|---|---|---|
| **Married couples, total** | **49,714** | **53,256** | **54,937** | **55,305** | **55,849** | **56,497** |
| **Race** | | | | | | |
| White/white | 44,910 | 47,202 | 48,030 | 48,050 | 48,455 | 48,917 |
| Black/black | 3,354 | 3,687 | 3,703 | 3,839 | 3,868 | 3,989 |
| Black/white | 167 | 211 | 328 | 330 | 364 | 363 |
| Black husband/white wife | 122 | 150 | 206 | 210 | 240 | 268 |
| White husband/black wife | 45 | 61 | 122 | 120 | 124 | 95 |
| White/other race[1] | 450 | 720 | 988 | 975 | 1,086 | 1,051 |
| Black/other race[1] | 34 | 33 | 76 | 43 | 31 | 50 |
| All other couples[1] | 799 | 1,401 | 1,811 | 2,068 | 2,045 | 2,127 |
| **Hispanic origin** | | | | | | |
| Hispanic/Hispanic | 1,906 | 3,085 | 3,857 | 4,279 | 4,480 | 4,739 |
| Hispanic/other origin (not Hispanic) | 891 | 1,193 | 1,434 | 1,662 | 1,647 | 1,742 |
| All other couples (not of Hispanic origin) | 46,917 | 48,979 | 49,646 | 49,363 | 49,722 | 50,016 |

NOTE: Persons 15 years old and over. Persons of Hispanic origin may be of any race. 1. Excluding white and black. Source: U.S. Census Bureau, Current Population Reports. From Statistical Abstract of the United States 2001.

# Births

## Births, Birth Rates, and Fertility Rates by State, 2000

| State | Number of births | Birth rate[1] | Fertility rate[2] | State | Number of births | Birth rate[1] | Fertility rate[2] |
|---|---|---|---|---|---|---|---|
| United States[3] | 4,058,814 | 14.7 | 67.5 | Nevada | 30,829 | 16.4 | 79.8 |
| Alabama | 63,299 | 14.4 | 65.0 | New Hampshire | 14,609 | 12.0 | 52.2 |
| Alaska | 9,974 | 16.0 | 74.6 | New Jersey | 115,632 | 14.1 | 65.8 |
| Arizona | 85,273 | 17.5 | 84.4 | New Mexico | 27,223 | 15.6 | 72.7 |
| Arkansas | 37,783 | 14.7 | 69.1 | New York | 258,737 | 14.2 | 65.0 |
| California | 531,959 | 15.8 | 70.7 | North Carolina | 120,311 | 15.5 | 71.6 |
| Colorado | 65,438 | 15.8 | 73.1 | North Dakota | 7,676 | 12.2 | 58.7 |
| Connecticut | 43,026 | 13.0 | 61.2 | Ohio | 155,472 | 13.8 | 63.0 |
| Delaware | 11,051 | 14.5 | 63.5 | Oklahoma | 49,782 | 14.7 | 69.9 |
| District of Columbia | 7,666 | 14.8 | 63.0 | Oregon | 45,804 | 13.7 | 65.8 |
| Florida | 204,125 | 13.3 | 66.9 | Pennsylvania | 146,281 | 12.2 | 58.2 |
| Georgia | 132,644 | 16.7 | 71.4 | Rhode Island | 12,505 | 12.6 | 58.1 |
| Hawaii | 17,551 | 14.9 | 72.3 | South Carolina | 56,114 | 14.3 | 63.3 |
| Idaho | 20,366 | 16.0 | 74.8 | South Dakota | 10,345 | 14.0 | 66.7 |
| Illinois | 185,036 | 15.2 | 69.5 | Tennessee | 79,611 | 14.4 | 65.2 |
| Indiana | 87,699 | 14.7 | 66.8 | Texas | 363,414 | 17.8 | 80.0 |
| Iowa | 38,266 | 13.3 | 64.0 | Utah | 47,353 | 21.9 | 94.5 |
| Kansas | 39,666 | 14.9 | 69.2 | Vermont | 6,500 | 10.9 | 48.8 |
| Kentucky | 56,029 | 14.1 | 63.6 | Virginia | 98,938 | 14.2 | 61.2 |
| Louisiana | 67,898 | 15.5 | 69.1 | Washington | 81,036 | 13.9 | 63.2 |
| Maine | 13,603 | 10.8 | 49.5 | West Virginia | 20,865 | 11.6 | 55.9 |
| Maryland | 74,316 | 14.2 | 61.9 | Wisconsin | 69,326 | 13.1 | 60.4 |
| Massachusetts | 81,614 | 13.2 | 59.2 | Wyoming | 6,253 | 13.0 | 62.7 |
| Michigan | 136,171 | 13.7 | 62.0 | Puerto Rico | 59,333 | 15.2 | 64.9 |
| Minnesota | 67,604 | 14.0 | 63.8 | Virgin Islands | 1,564 | 12.9 | 57.6 |
| Mississippi | 44,075 | 15.8 | 70.3 | Guam | 3,766 | 24.4 | 113.8 |
| Missouri | 76,463 | 13.9 | 64.0 | American Samoa | 1,731 | 26.4 | 108.2 |
| Montana | 10,957 | 12.3 | 61.3 | Northern Marianas | 1,431 | 19.9 | 60.5 |
| Nebraska | 24,646 | 14.8 | 68.9 | | | | |

NOTE: Data by place of residence. 1. Birth rates are live births per 1,000 estimated population in each area. 2. Fertility rates are live births per 1,000 women aged 15–44 years estimated in each area. 3. Excludes data for Puerto Rico, Virgin Islands, Guam, American Samoa, and Northern Marianas. *Source:* National Center for Health Statistics, *National Vital Statistics Reports*, vol. 50, no. 5, Feb. 12, 2002. Web: www.cdc.gov/nchs.

## Live Births by Age and Race of Mother, 1940–2000

| Year[1]/race | Total | Under 15 | 15–19 | 20–24 | 25–29 | 30–34 | 35–39 | 40–44 | 45–49[2] |
|---|---|---|---|---|---|---|---|---|---|
| 1940 | 2,558,647 | 3,865 | 332,667 | 799,537 | 693,268 | 431,468 | 222,015 | 68,269 | 7,558 |
| 1945 | 2,858,449 | 4,028 | 298,868 | 832,746 | 785,299 | 554,906 | 296,852 | 78,853 | 6,897 |
| 1950 | 3,631,512 | 5,413 | 432,911 | 1,155,167 | 1,041,360 | 610,816 | 302,780 | 77,743 | 5,322 |
| 1955 | 4,014,112 | 6,181 | 493,770 | 1,290,939 | 1,133,155 | 732,540 | 352,320 | 89,777 | 5,430 |
| 1960 | 4,257,850 | 6,780 | 586,966 | 1,426,912 | 1,092,816 | 687,722 | 359,908 | 91,564 | 5,182 |
| 1965 | 3,760,358 | 7,768 | 590,894 | 1,337,350 | 925,732 | 529,376 | 282,908 | 81,716 | 4,614 |
| 1970 | 3,731,386 | 11,752 | 644,708 | 1,418,874 | 994,904 | 427,806 | 180,244 | 49,952 | 3,146 |
| 1975 | 3,144,198 | 12,642 | 582,238 | 1,093,676 | 936,786 | 375,500 | 115,409 | 26,319 | 1,628 |
| 1980 | 3,612,258 | 10,169 | 552,161 | 1,226,200 | 1,108,291 | 550,354 | 140,793 | 23,090 | 1,200 |
| 1985 | 3,760,561 | 10,220 | 467,485 | 1,141,320 | 1,201,350 | 696,354 | 214,336 | 22,981 | 1,300 |
| 1990 | 4,158,212 | 11,657 | 521,000 | 1,096,529 | 965,547 | 904,666 | 211,303 | 48,607 | 1,638 |
| 1995 | 3,899,589 | 12,242 | 499,873 | 965,547 | 1,063,539 | 904,666 | 383,745 | 67,250 | 2,727 |
| 1998 | 3,941,553 | 9,462 | 484,895 | 965,122 | 1,083,010 | 889,365 | 424,890 | 81,027 | 3,782[2] |
| 1999 | 3,959,417 | 9,054 | 476,050 | 981,929 | 1,078,252 | 902,100 | 434,234 | 83,090 | 4,349[2] |
| 2000 | 4,058,814 | 8,519 | 468,990 | 1,017,806 | 1,087,547 | 929,278 | 452,057 | 90,013 | 4,604[2] |
| White | 3,104,003 | 4,439 | 333,013 | 772,811 | 874,180 | 764,708 | 368,711 | 72,414 | 3,729[2] |
| Black | 622,598 | 3,808 | 118,954 | 202,596 | 141,968 | 94,808 | 49,295 | 10,699 | 470[2] |
| American Indian[3] | 41,668 | 160 | 8,055 | 13,633 | 10,053 | 6,097 | 2,983 | 658 | 29[2] |
| Asian or Pacific Islander | 200,543 | 112 | 8,968 | 28,766 | 61,346 | 63,665 | 31,068 | 6,242 | 376[2] |
| Hispanic origin[4] | 815,868 | 2,638 | 129,469 | 247,552 | 218,167 | 141,493 | 62,993 | 12,987 | 569[2] |

NOTE: Data refer only to births occurring within the U.S. 1. Data for 1940–1955 are adjusted for under-registration. Beginning 1960, only registered births are shown. Data for 1960–1970 based on a 50% sample of births. For 1972–1984, based on 100% of births in selected states and on 50% sample in all other states. Beginning 1989, births are tabulated by race of mother; previously based on race of child. 2. Beginning 1998, ages 45–54. 3. Includes births to Aleuts and Eskimos. 4. Persons of Hispanic origin may be any race. *Source:* National Center for Health Statistics, *National Vital Statistics Reports,* vol. 50, no. 5, Feb. 12, 2002. Web: www.cdc.gov/nchs.

## Live Births by Sex and Sex Ratio

| | Total[1, 2] | | | White | | | Black | | |
|---|---|---|---|---|---|---|---|---|---|
| Year | Male | Female | Males per 1,000 females | Male | Female | Males per 1,000 females | Male | Female | Males per 1,000 females |
| 1985 | 1,927,983 | 1,832,578 | 1,052 | 1,536,646 | 1,454,727 | 1,056 | 308,575 | 299,618 | 1,030 |
| 1986 | 1,924,868 | 1,831,679 | 1,051 | 1,523,914 | 1,446,525 | 1,053 | 315,788 | 305,433 | 1,034 |
| 1987 | 1,951,153 | 1,858,241 | 1,050 | 1,535,517 | 1,456,971 | 1,054 | 325,259 | 316,308 | 1,028 |
| 1988 | 2,002,424 | 1,907,086 | 1,050 | 1,562,675 | 1,483,487 | 1,053 | 341,441 | 330,535 | 1,033 |
| 1989 | 2,069,490 | 1,971,468 | 1,050 | 1,606,757 | 1,525,234 | 1,053 | 360,131 | 349,264 | 1,031 |
| 1990 | 2,129,495 | 2,028,717 | 1,050 | 1,654,928 | 1,570,415 | 1,054 | 367,455 | 357,121 | 1,029 |
| 1991 | 2,101,518 | 2,009,389 | 1,046 | 1,659,077 | 1,582,196 | 1,049 | 346,455 | 336,147 | 1,031 |
| 1992 | 2,082,097 | 1,982,917 | 1,050 | 1,641,811 | 1,559,867 | 1,053 | 342,726 | 330,907 | 1,036 |
| 1993 | 2,048,861 | 1,951,379 | 1,050 | 1,616,332 | 1,533,501 | 1,054 | 333,984 | 324,891 | 1,028 |
| 1994 | 2,022,589 | 1,930,178 | 1,048 | 1,599,803 | 1,521,401 | 1,051 | 322,554 | 313,837 | 1,028 |
| 1995 | 1,996,355 | 1,930,234 | 1,049 | 1,588,427 | 1,510,458 | 1,052 | 308,115 | 297,024 | 1,031 |
| 1996 | 1,990,480 | 1,901,014 | 1,047 | — | — | 1,050 | — | — | 1,028 |
| 1997 | 1,985,596 | 1,895,298 | 1,048 | — | — | 1,052 | — | — | 1,031 |
| 1998 | 2,016,205 | 1,925,348 | 1,047 | — | — | 1,052 | — | — | 1,034 |
| 1999 | 2,026,854 | 1,932,563 | 1,049 | — | — | 1,052 | — | — | 1,031 |
| 2000 | 2,076,969 | 1,981,845 | 1,048 | — | — | 1,050 | — | — | 1,031 |

NOTE: (—) Data not available. 1. Excludes births to nonresidents of U.S. 2. Includes races other than white and black. *Source:* National Center for Health Statistics, *National Vital Statistics Reports*, vol. 50, no. 5, Feb. 12, 2002. Web: www.cdc.gov/nchs.

## Selected Characteristics of Births by Race of Mother, 2000

| Characteristic | All races | White | Black | American Indian[1] | Asian or Pacific Islander | Hispanic origin[2] |
|---|---|---|---|---|---|---|
| **Percentage of mothers who:** | | | | | | |
| Had prenatal care beginning in the first trimester | 83.2% | 85.0% | 74.3% | 69.3% | 84.0% | 74.4% |
| Had late or no prenatal care | 3.9 | 3.3 | 6.7 | 8.6 | 3.3 | 6.3 |
| Were tobacco users[3] | 12.2 | 13.2 | 9.1 | 20.0 | 2.8 | 3.5 |
| Were alcohol users[4] | 0.9 | 0.9 | 1.0 | 2.9 | 0.4 | 0.5 |
| Gained less than 16 lbs[5] | 11.6 | 10.5 | 16.7 | 16.5 | 9.3 | 13.9 |
| Median weight gain[5] | 30.5 | 30.1 | 30.0 | 30.2 | 30.4 | 29.6 |
| Had cesarean births | 22.9 | 22.8 | 24.3 | 20.2 | 21.1 | 22.1 |
| **Percentage of infants who:** | | | | | | |
| Were born prior to 37 full weeks | 11.6 | 10.6 | 17.3 | 12.7 | 9.9 | 11.2 |
| Weighed less than 1,500 grams (3 lb 4 oz.) | 1.4 | 1.1 | 3.1 | 1.2 | 1.0 | 1.1 |
| Weighed less than 2,500 grams (5 lb 8 oz.) | 7.6 | 6.5 | 13.0 | 6.8 | 7.3 | 6.4 |
| Weighed 4,000 grams (8 lb 14 oz.) or more | 9.9 | 11.0 | 5.4 | 11.8 | 5.8 | 9.0 |
| Had five-minute Apgar scores of less than 7[6] | 1.4 | 1.2 | 2.4 | 1.4 | 1.0 | 1.1 |

1. Includes births to Aleuts and Eskimos. 2. Hispanic origin may be of any race. 3. Excludes data for Calif., which did not report tobacco use on birth certificate. 4. Excludes data for Calif., which did not report alcohol use on birth certificate. 5. Excludes data for Calif., which did not report weight gain on birth certificate. Median weight gain shown in pounds. 6. Excludes data for Calif. and Tex., which did not report Apgar scores on birth certificate. Apgar scores are derived from evaluations of five major signs at one minute and five minutes after birth. Each sign is given a score of 0–2 for a total of ten possible points; scores of 7–10 are considered normal, 4–7 may require resuscitative measures, and 0–3 require immediate resuscitation. The signs and scores (0-1-2) are as follows: Activity or muscle tone (absent—arms and legs flexed—active movement); Pulse (absent—below 100 bpm—above 100 bpm); Grimace or reflex irritability (no response—grimace—sneeze, cough, pulls away); Appearance or skin color (blue-gray, pale all over—normal, except for extremities—normal over entire body); Respiration (absent—slow, irregular—good, crying). *Source:* National Center for Health Statistics, *National Vital Statistics Reports,* vol. 50, no. 5, Feb. 12, 2002. Web: www.cdc.gov/nchs.

## Births: Other Data for 2000

The source for the data on U.S. births, birth rates, and fertility rates in this section is the *National Vital Statistics Reports* series published by the National Center for Health Statistics, a part of the Centers for Disease Control and Prevention. The report issued on Feb. 12, 2002, showing final birth data for 2000 also highlighted these findings:

**Births** in the United States increased 3% for 2000, to 4,058,814, the third consecutive increase following a 7% decline from 1990 to 1997. The **birth rate** also rose, but slightly, to 14.7 births per 1,000 total population for 2000. The **fertility rate,** which relates births to the number of women of childbearing age, was up 2% for 2000, to 67.5 births per 1,000 women aged 15–44 years.

The **birth rate for teenagers** declined again in 2000, falling 2% to 48.5 births per 1,000 women aged 15–19 years, a record low for the nation. The rate has declined 22% since 1991.

The **birth rates for women in their twenties** have been relatively stable over the past 20 years. In 2000, the rate for women in their early twenties increased slightly to 112.3 per 1,000 women aged 20–24 years. The rate for women aged 25–29 years rose 3% to 121.4 per 1,000, its highest level since 1971. **Birth rates for women in their thirties** increased 5%, to 94.1 per 1,000 women aged 30–34 years, and to 40.4 per 1,000 women aged 35–39 years. The birth rate for women 40–44 years increased again in 2000 to 7.9 per 1,000. Rates for women aged 45–49 years also rose in 2000.

In 2000, the **median age at first birth** increased to 24.6 years. The median age of first-time mothers has risen fairly consistently over the last three decades.

**Cigarette smoking during pregnancy** declined again in 2000, to 12.2%. The overall rate has fallen steadily since 1989, by 37%. However, whereas tobacco use declined for teenagers and women aged 25–39 years, it increased slightly for women aged 20–24 years. Infant birth weight is seriously compromised by maternal smoking: In 2000, 11.9% of infants born to smokers weighed less than 2,500 grams (5 lb 8 oz), compared with 7.2% of infants born to nonsmokers.

The **cesarean delivery rate** increased for the fourth consecutive year, to 22.9% of all births, a 4%

increase from 1999 (22%). Following declines between 1989 and 1996, the rate has increased steadily; the 2000 rate is the highest reported since 1989, when these data first became available from birth certificates. (A total of 923,991 infants were born by cesarean delivery in 2000, compared to 3,108,188 vaginal births.)

The **preterm birth rate,** or percentage of infants born after less than 37 completed weeks of gestation, was down for the first year in almost a decade, from 11.8% in 1999 to 11.6% in 2000. The preterm birth rate rose fairly steadily, by 25% between 1981 and 1999.

The number and rate of **twin births** continued to climb for 2000, rising to 118,916 or 29.3 per 1,000 total births. The twinning rate has risen 55%, from 18.9 per 1,000 since 1980. The dramatic upsurge in **triplet-plus births** over the last two decades, however, may be at an end—the triplet-plus birth rate declined for the second consecutive year to 180.5 triplet-plus births per 100,000 live births. (The rate had surged from 37.0 to 193.5 between 1980 and 1998.) There were 7,325 births in triplet-plus deliveries in 2000, about the same as that for 1999.

## Contraceptive Use by Women, 15 to 44 Years Old, 1995

| Contraceptive status and method | All women | Age | | | Marital status | | |
|---|---|---|---|---|---|---|---|
| | | 15–24 years | 25–34 years | 35–44 years | Never married | Currently married | Formerly married |
| All women (in thousands) | 60,201 | 18,002 | 20,758 | 21,440 | 22,679 | 29,673 | 7,849 |
| **Percent distribution** | | | | | | | |
| Sterile[1] | 29.7% | 2.6% | 25.0% | 57.0% | 6.9% | 43.2% | 45.1% |
| Surgically sterile | 27.9 | 1.8 | 23.6 | 54.0 | 5.7 | 41.1 | 42.5 |
| Nonsurgically sterile[2] | 1.7 | 0.7 | 1.3 | 2.8 | 1.1 | 2.0 | 2.2 |
| Pill | 17.3 | 23.1 | 23.7 | 6.3 | 20.4 | 15.6 | 14.6 |
| IUD | 0.5 | 0.1 | 0.6 | 0.8 | 0.3 | 0.7 | 0.4 |
| Diaphragm | 1.2 | 0.2 | 1.2 | 2.0 | 0.5 | 1.8 | 0.9 |
| Condom | 13.1 | 13.9 | 15.0 | 10.7 | 13.9 | 13.3 | 10.1 |
| Periodic abstinence | 1.5 | 0.5 | 1.8 | 2.0 | 0.6 | 2.3 | 0.7 |
| Withdrawal | 2.0 | 1.6 | 2.3 | 1.9 | 1.5 | 2.3 | 1.8 |
| Other methods[3] | 3.9 | 5.6 | 4.2 | 2.1 | 4.6 | 3.3 | 3.9 |

1. Total sterile includes male sterile for unknown reasons. 2. Persons sterile from illness, accident, or congenital conditions. 3. Includes implants, injectables, morning-after-pill, suppository, Today™ sponge, and less frequently used methods. *Source:* U.S. National Center for Health Statistics. From *Statistical Abstract of the United States 2001.*

## Abortion Statistics, 1972–1997

| | 1972 | 1980 | 1985 | 1990 | 1995 | 1997 |
|---|---|---|---|---|---|---|
| Reported no. legal abortions | 000 100 | 1 001 010 | 1,028,013 | 1,429,577 | 1,210,883 | 1,186,039 |
| Abortion ratio[1] | 180 | 359 | 354 | 345 | 311 | 306 |
| Abortion rate[2] | 13 | 25 | 24 | 24 | 20 | 20 |
| | Percentage distribution | | | | | |
| **Age group (yrs)** | | | | | | |
| ≤19 | 32.6% | 29.2% | 26.3% | 22.4% | 20.1% | 20.1% |
| 20–24 | 32.5 | 35.5 | 34.7 | 33.2 | 32.5 | 31.7 |
| ≥25 | 34.9 | 35.3 | 39.0 | 44.4 | 47.4 | 48.2 |
| **Marital status** | | | | | | |
| Married | 29.7 | 23.1 | 19.3 | 21.7 | 19.7 | 19.0 |
| Unmarried | 70.3 | 76.9 | 80.7 | 78.3 | 80.3 | 81.0 |

NOTE: The number of areas reporting a given characteristic varied. 1. Number of legal induced abortions per 1,000 live births. 2. Number of legal induced abortions per 1,000 women aged 15–44 years. *Source:* U.S. Centers for Disease Control and Prevention. *Abortion Surveillance: Preliminary Analysis—United States, 1997.* Jan. 7, 2000.

# Mortality

## 15 Leading Causes of Death in the U.S., 2000[1]

| Rank[2] | Causes of death | Number | Deaths per 100,000 population |
|---|---|---|---|
| | All causes | 2,404,624 | 873.6 |
| 1 | Diseases of heart | 709,894 | 257.9 |
| 2 | Malignant neoplasms (cancer) | 551,833 | 200.5 |
| 3 | Cerebrovascular diseases (stroke) | 166,028 | 60.3 |
| 4 | Chronic lower respiratory diseases | 123,550 | 44.9 |
| 5 | Accidents (unintentional injuries) | 93,592 | 34.0 |
| |    Motor vehicle accidents | 41,804 | 15.2 |
| |    All other accidents | 51,788 | 18.8 |
| 6 | Diabetes mellitus | 68,662 | 24.9 |
| 7 | Pneumonia and influenza | 67,024 | 24.3 |
| 8 | Alzheimer's disease | 49,044 | 17.8 |
| 9 | Nephritis, nephrotic syndrome, and nephrosis | 37,672 | 13.7 |
| 10 | Septicemia | 31,613 | 11.5 |
| 11 | Suicide | 28,332 | 10.3 |
| 12 | Chronic liver disease and cirrhosis | 26,219 | 9.5 |
| 13 | Hypertension and hypertensive renal disease | 17,964 | 6.5 |
| 14 | Pneumonitis due to solids and liquids | 16,659 | 6.1 |
| 15 | Homicide | 16,137 | 5.9 |
| | All other causes | 400,401 | 145.5 |

1. Preliminary. 2. Rank based on number of deaths. *Source:* U.S. National Center for Health Statistics, *National Vital Statistics Reports,* vol. 49, no. 12, Oct. 9, 2001. Web: www.cdc.gov/nchs.

## Life Expectancy at Birth by Race and Sex, 1940–2000

| | All races | | | White | | | Black | | |
|---|---|---|---|---|---|---|---|---|---|
| Year | Both sexes | Male | Female | Both sexes | Male | Female | Both sexes | Male | Female |
| 2000[1] | 76.9 | 74.1 | 79.5 | 77.4 | 74.8 | 80.0 | 71.8 | 68.3 | 75.0 |
| 1999 | 76.7 | 73.9 | 79.4 | 77.3 | 74.6 | 79.9 | 71.4 | 67.8 | 74.7 |
| 1998 | 76.7 | 73.8 | 79.5 | 77.3 | 74.5 | 80.0 | 71.3 | 67.6 | 74.8 |
| 1997 | 76.5 | 73.6 | 79.4 | 77.1 | 74.3 | 79.9 | 71.1 | 67.2 | 74.7 |
| 1996 | 76.1 | 73.1 | 79.1 | 76.8 | 73.9 | 79.7 | 70.2 | 66.1 | 74.2 |
| 1995 | 75.8 | 72.5 | 78.9 | 76.5 | 73.4 | 79.6 | 69.6 | 65.2 | 73.9 |
| 1994 | 75.7 | 72.4 | 79.0 | 76.5 | 73.3 | 79.6 | 69.5 | 64.9 | 73.9 |
| 1993 | 75.5 | 72.2 | 78.8 | 76.3 | 73.1 | 79.5 | 69.2 | 64.6 | 73.7 |
| 1992 | 75.8 | 72.3 | 79.1 | 76.5 | 73.2 | 79.8 | 69.6 | 65.0 | 73.9 |
| 1991 | 75.5 | 72.0 | 78.9 | 76.3 | 72.9 | 79.6 | 69.3 | 64.6 | 73.8 |
| 1990 | 75.4 | 71.8 | 78.8 | 76.1 | 72.7 | 79.4 | 69.1 | 64.5 | 73.6 |
| 1989 | 75.1 | 71.7 | 78.5 | 75.9 | 72.5 | 79.2 | 68.8 | 64.3 | 73.3 |
| 1988 | 74.9 | 71.4 | 78.3 | 75.6 | 72.2 | 78.9 | 68.9 | 64.4 | 73.2 |
| 1987 | 74.9 | 71.4 | 78.3 | 75.6 | 72.1 | 78.9 | 69.1 | 64.7 | 73.4 |
| 1986 | 74.7 | 71.2 | 78.2 | 75.4 | 71.9 | 78.8 | 69.1 | 64.8 | 73.4 |
| 1985 | 74.7 | 71.1 | 78.2 | 75.3 | 71.8 | 78.7 | 69.3 | 65.0 | 73.4 |
| 1984 | 74.7 | 71.1 | 78.2 | 75.3 | 71.8 | 78.7 | 69.5 | 65.3 | 73.6 |
| 1983 | 74.6 | 71.0 | 78.1 | 75.2 | 71.6 | 78.7 | 69.4 | 65.2 | 73.5 |
| 1982 | 74.5 | 70.8 | 78.1 | 75.1 | 71.5 | 78.7 | 69.4 | 65.1 | 73.6 |
| 1981 | 74.1 | 70.4 | 77.8 | 74.8 | 71.1 | 78.4 | 68.9 | 64.5 | 73.2 |
| 1980 | 73.7 | 70.0 | 77.4 | 74.4 | 70.7 | 78.1 | 68.1 | 63.8 | 72.5 |
| 1979 | 73.9 | 70.0 | 77.8 | 74.6 | 70.8 | 78.4 | 68.5 | 64.0 | 72.9 |
| 1978 | 73.5 | 69.6 | 77.3 | 74.1 | 70.4 | 78.0 | 68.1 | 63.7 | 72.4 |
| 1977 | 73.3 | 69.5 | 77.2 | 74.0 | 70.2 | 77.9 | 67.7 | 63.4 | 72.0 |
| 1976 | 72.9 | 69.1 | 76.8 | 73.6 | 69.9 | 77.5 | 67.2 | 62.9 | 71.6 |
| 1975 | 72.6 | 68.8 | 76.6 | 73.4 | 69.5 | 77.3 | 66.8 | 62.4 | 71.3 |
| 1974 | 72.0 | 68.2 | 75.9 | 72.8 | 69.0 | 76.7 | 66.0 | 61.7 | 70.3 |
| 1973 | 71.4 | 67.6 | 75.3 | 72.2 | 68.5 | 76.1 | 65.0 | 60.9 | 69.3 |
| 1972[2] | 71.2 | 67.4 | 75.1 | 72.0 | 68.3 | 75.9 | 64.7 | 60.4 | 69.1 |
| 1971 | 71.1 | 67.4 | 75.0 | 72.0 | 68.3 | 75.8 | 64.6 | 60.5 | 68.9 |
| 1970 | 70.8 | 67.1 | 74.7 | 71.7 | 68.0 | 75.6 | 64.1 | 60.0 | 68.3 |
| 1960 | 69.7 | 66.6 | 73.1 | 70.6 | 67.4 | 74.1 | — | — | — |
| 1950 | 68.2 | 65.6 | 71.1 | 69.1 | 66.5 | 72.2 | — | — | — |
| 1940 | 62.9 | 60.8 | 65.2 | 64.2 | 62.1 | 66.6 | — | — | — |

(—) Data not available. 1. Preliminary. 2. Deaths based on a 50% sample. *Source:* National Center for Health Statistics, *National Vital Statistics Reports,* vol. 49, no. 12, Oct. 9, 2001. Web: www.cdc.gov/nchs.

# Life Expectancy by Age, 1850–2000

The expectation of life at a specified age is the average number of years that members of a hypothetical group of people of the same age would continue to live if they were subject throughout the remainder of their lives to the same mortality rate.

| Calendar period | \ 0 | 10 | 20 | 30 | Age \ 40 | 50 | 60 | 70 | 80 |
|---|---|---|---|---|---|---|---|---|---|
| **White males** | | | | | | | | | |
| 1850[1] | 38.3 | 48.0 | 40.1 | 34.0 | 27.9 | 21.6 | 15.6 | 10.2 | 5.9 |
| 1890[1] | 42.50 | 48.45 | 40.66 | 34.05 | 27.37 | 20.72 | 14.73 | 9.35 | 5.40 |
| 1900–1902[2] | 48.23 | 50.59 | 42.19 | 34.88 | 27.74 | 20.76 | 14.35 | 9.03 | 5.10 |
| 1909–1911[2] | 50.23 | 51.32 | 42.71 | 34.87 | 27.43 | 20.39 | 13.98 | 8.83 | 5.09 |
| 1919–1921[3] | 56.34 | 54.15 | 45.60 | 37.65 | 29.86 | 22.22 | 15.25 | 9.51 | 5.47 |
| 1929–1931 | 59.12 | 54.96 | 46.02 | 37.54 | 29.22 | 21.51 | 14.72 | 9.20 | 5.26 |
| 1939–1941 | 62.81 | 57.03 | 47.76 | 38.80 | 30.03 | 21.96 | 15.05 | 9.42 | 5.38 |
| 1949–1951 | 66.31 | 58.98 | 49.52 | 40.29 | 31.17 | 22.83 | 15.76 | 10.07 | 5.88 |
| 1959–1961[5] | 67.55 | 59.78 | 50.25 | 40.98 | 31.73 | 23.22 | 16.01 | 10.29 | 5.09 |
| 1969–1971[6] | 67.94 | 59.69 | 50.22 | 41.07 | 31.87 | 23.34 | 16.07 | 10.38 | 6.18 |
| 1979–1981 | 70.82 | 61.98 | 52.45 | 43.31 | 34.04 | 25.26 | 17.56 | 11.35 | 6.76 |
| 1990 | 72.7 | 63.5 | 54.0 | 44.7 | 35.6 | 26.7 | 18.7 | 12.1 | 7.1 |
| 2000[7] | 74.8 | 65.4 | 55.7 | 46.4 | 37.1 | 28.2 | 20.0 | 13.0 | 7.6 |
| **White females** | | | | | | | | | |
| 1850[1] | 40.5 | 47.2 | 40.2 | 35.4 | 29.8 | 23.5 | 17.0 | 11.3 | 6.4 |
| 1890[1] | 44.46 | 49.62 | 42.03 | 35.36 | 28.76 | 22.09 | 15.70 | 10.15 | 5.75 |
| 1900–1902[2] | 51.08 | 52.15 | 43.77 | 36.42 | 29.17 | 21.89 | 15.23 | 9.59 | 5.50 |
| 1909–1911[2] | 53.62 | 53.57 | 44.88 | 36.96 | 29.26 | 21.74 | 14.92 | 9.38 | 5.35 |
| 1919–1921[3] | 58.53 | 55.17 | 46.46 | 38.72 | 30.94 | 23.12 | 15.93 | 9.94 | 5.70 |
| 1929–1931 | 62.67 | 57.65 | 48.52 | 39.99 | 31.52 | 23.41 | 16.05 | 9.98 | 5.63 |
| 1939–1941 | 67.29 | 60.85 | 51.38 | 42.21 | 33.25 | 24.72 | 17.00 | 10.50 | 5.88 |
| 1949–1951 | 72.03 | 64.26 | 54.56 | 45.00 | 35.64 | 26.76 | 18.64 | 11.68 | 6.59 |
| 1959–1961[5] | 74.19 | 66.05 | 56.29 | 46.63 | 37.13 | 28.08 | 19.69 | 12.38 | 6.67 |
| 1969–1971[6] | 75.49 | 66.97 | 57.24 | 47.60 | 38.12 | 29.11 | 20.79 | 13.37 | 7.59 |
| 1979–1981 | 78.22 | 69.21 | 59.44 | 49.76 | 40.16 | 30.96 | 22.45 | 14.89 | 8.65 |
| 1990 | 79.4 | 70.1 | 60.3 | 50.6 | 41.0 | 31.6 | 23.0 | 15.4 | 9.0 |
| 2000[7] | 80.0 | 70.5 | 60.7 | 50.9 | 41.3 | 32.0 | 23.2 | 15.5 | 9.1 |
| **All other males[4]** | | | | | | | | | |
| 1900–1902[2] | 32.54 | 41.90 | 35.11 | 29.25 | 23.12 | 17.34 | 12.62 | 8.33 | 5.12 |
| 1909–1911[2] | 34.05 | 40.65 | 33.46 | 27.33 | 21.57 | 16.21 | 11.67 | 8.00 | 5.53 |
| 1919–1921[3] | 47.14 | 45.99 | 38.36 | 32.51 | 26.53 | 20.47 | 14.74 | 9.58 | 5.83 |
| 1929–1931 | 47.55 | 44.27 | 35.95 | 29.45 | 23.36 | 17.92 | 13.15 | 8.78 | 5.42 |
| 1939–1941 | 52.33 | 48.54 | 39.74 | 32.25 | 25.23 | 19.18 | 14.38 | 10.06 | 6.46 |
| 1949–1951 | 58.91 | 52.96 | 43.73 | 35.31 | 27.29 | 20.25 | 14.91 | 10.74 | 7.07 |
| 1959–1961[5] | 61.48 | 55.19 | 45.78 | 37.05 | 28.72 | 21.28 | 15.29 | 10.81 | 6.87 |
| 1969–1971[6] | 60.98 | 53.67 | 44.37 | 36.20 | 28.29 | 21.24 | 15.35 | 10.68 | 7.57 |
| 1979–1981 | 65.63 | 57.40 | 47.87 | 39.13 | 30.64 | 22.92 | 16.54 | 11.36 | 7.22 |
| 1990 | 67.0 | 58.5 | 49.0 | 40.3 | 31.9 | 23.9 | 17.0 | 11.4 | 7.0 |
| 2000[7] | 68.3 | 59.6 | 50.0 | 41.1 | 32.3 | 24.3 | 17.5 | 11.8 | 7.4 |
| **All other females[4]** | | | | | | | | | |
| 1900–1902[2] | 35.04 | 43.02 | 36.89 | 30.70 | 24.85 | 17.65 | 12.78 | 9.22 | 6.05 |
| 1919–1921[3] | 46.92 | 44.54 | 37.15 | 31.48 | 25.60 | 19.76 | 14.69 | 10.25 | 6.58 |
| 1929–1931 | 49.51 | 45.33 | 37.22 | 30.67 | 24.30 | 18.60 | 14.00 | 10.30 | 6.90 |
| 1939–1941 | 55.51 | 50.83 | 42.14 | 34.52 | 27.01 | 21.04 | 16.14 | 11.81 | 8.00 |
| 1949–1951 | 62.70 | 56.17 | 46.77 | 38.02 | 29.82 | 22.67 | 16.95 | 12.29 | 8.15 |
| 1959–1961[5] | 66.47 | 59.72 | 50.07 | 40.83 | 32.16 | 24.31 | 17.83 | 12.46 | 7.66 |
| 1969–1971[6] | 69.05 | 61.49 | 51.85 | 42.61 | 33.87 | 25.97 | 19.02 | 13.30 | 9.01 |
| 1979–1981 | 74.00 | 65.64 | 55.88 | 46.39 | 37.16 | 28.59 | 20.49 | 14.44 | 9.17 |
| 1990 | 75.2 | 66.6 | 56.8 | 47.3 | 38.1 | 29.2 | 21.3 | 14.5 | 8.8 |
| 2000[7] | 75.0 | 66.2 | 56.4 | 46.8 | 37.6 | 29.0 | 21.0 | 14.1 | 8.7 |

1. Massachusetts only; white and nonwhite combined, the latter being about 1% of the total. *Source:* U.S. Dept. of Commerce, Bureau of the Census, *Historical Statistics of the United States.* 2. Original Death Registration States. 3. Death Registration States of 1920. 4. Data for periods 1900–1902, 1929–1931, and 2000 relate to blacks only. 5. Alaska and Hawaii included beginning in 1959. 6. Deaths of nonresidents of the United States excluded starting in 1970. 7. Preliminary. *Sources:* Department of Health and Human Services, National Center for Health Statistics; Web: www.dhhs.gov.

## U.S. Annual Death Rates per 1,000 Population

| Year | Rate | Year | Rate | Year | Rate | Year | Rate | Year | Rate | Year | Rate | Year | Rate |
|------|------|------|------|------|------|------|------|------|------|------|------|------|------|
| 1900 | 17.2 | 1935 | 10.9 | 1946 | 10.0 | 1957 | 9.6 | 1969 | 9.5 | 1980 | 8.7 | 1991 | 8.5 |
| 1905 | 15.9 | 1936 | 11.6 | 1947 | 10.1 | 1958 | 9.5 | 1970[1] | 9.5 | 1981 | 8.6 | 1992 | 8.5 |
| 1910 | 14.7 | 1937 | 11.3 | 1948 | 9.9 | 1959 | 9.4 | 1971 | 9.3 | 1982 | 8.5 | 1993 | 8.8 |
| 1915 | 13.2 | 1938 | 10.6 | 1949 | 9.7 | 1960 | 9.5 | 1972 | 9.4 | 1983 | 8.6 | 1994 | 8.8 |
| 1920 | 13.0 | 1939 | 10.6 | 1950 | 9.6 | 1962 | 9.5 | 1973 | 9.3 | 1984 | 8.6 | 1995 | 8.8 |
| 1925 | 11.7 | 1940 | 10.8 | 1951 | 9.7 | 1963 | 9.6 | 1974 | 9.1 | 1985 | 8.7 | 1996 | 8.8 |
| 1930 | 11.3 | 1941 | 10.5 | 1952 | 9.6 | 1964 | 9.4 | 1975 | 8.8 | 1986 | 8.7 | 1997 | 8.6 |
| 1931 | 11.1 | 1942 | 10.3 | 1953 | 9.6 | 1965 | 9.4 | 1976 | 8.8 | 1987 | 8.7 | 1998 | 8.6 |
| 1932 | 10.9 | 1943 | 10.9 | 1954 | 9.2 | 1966 | 9.5 | 1977 | 8.6 | 1988 | 8.8 | 1999 | 8.8 |
| 1933 | 10.7 | 1944 | 10.6 | 1955 | 9.3 | 1967 | 9.4 | 1978 | 8.7 | 1989 | 8.7 | 2000[2] | 8.7 |
| 1934 | 11.1 | 1945 | 10.6 | 1956 | 9.4 | 1968 | 9.7 | 1979 | 8.5 | 1990 | 8.6 | | |

NOTES: Includes only deaths occurring within the registration states. Beginning with 1933, area includes entire U.S.; with 1959 includes Alaska, and with 1960 includes Hawaii. Excludes fetal deaths. Rates as of April 1 for 1940, 1950, 1960, 1970, and 1980, and estimated as of July 1 for all other years. 1. First year for which deaths of nonresidents are excluded. 2. Preliminary. *Sources:* Department of Health and Human Services, National Center for Health Statistics. Web: www.dhhs.gov.

## Infant Mortality Rates, 1950–1999

| | | Deaths per 1,000 live births | | | | |
|---|---|---|---|---|---|---|
| | | **Neonatal** | | | **Fetal mortality rate[1]** | **Late fetal mortality rate[2]** |
| Year | Infant | Under 28 days | Under 7 days | Postneonatal | | |
| 1950[3] | 29.2 | 20.5 | 17.8 | 8.7 | 18.4 | 14.9 |
| 1960[3] | 26.0 | 18.7 | 16.7 | 7.3 | 15.8 | 12.1 |
| 1970 | 20.0 | 15.1 | 13.6 | 4.9 | 14.0 | 9.5 |
| 1980 | 12.6 | 8.5 | 7.1 | 4.1 | 9.1 | 6.2 |
| 1985 | 10.6 | 7.0 | 5.8 | 3.7 | 7.8 | 4.9 |
| 1990 | 9.2 | 5.8 | 4.8 | 3.4 | 7.5 | 4.3 |
| 1991 | 8.9 | 5.6 | 4.6 | 3.4 | 7.3 | 4.1 |
| 1992 | 8.5 | 5.4 | 4.4 | 3.1 | 7.4 | 4.1 |
| 1993 | 8.4 | 5.3 | 4.3 | 3.1 | 7.1 | 3.8 |
| 1994 | 8.0 | 5.1 | 4.2 | 2.9 | 7.0 | 3.7 |
| 1995 | 7.6 | 4.9 | 4.0 | 2.7 | 7.0 | 3.6 |
| 1996 | 7.3 | 4.8 | 3.8 | 2.5 | 6.9 | 3.6 |
| 1997 | 7.2 | 4.8 | 3.8 | 2.5 | 6.8 | 3.5 |
| 1998 | 7.2 | 4.8 | 3.8 | 2.4 | 6.7 | 3.4 |
| 1999 | 7.1 | 4.7 | 3.8 | 2.3 | — | — |

NOTES: "Infant" is defined as under 1 year of age; "neonatal" is under 28 days; "postneonatal" is 28–365 days. (—) Data not available. 1. Number of fetal deaths of 20 weeks or more gestation per 1,000 live births plus fetal deaths. 2. Number of fetal deaths of 28 weeks or more gestation per 1,000 live births plus late fetal deaths. 3. Includes birth and deaths of persons who were not residents of the 50 states and the District of Columbia. *Sources:* Centers for Disease Control and Prevention, National Center for Health Statistics. From *Health, United States, 2001.*

## Deaths and Death Rates from Accidents, by Type: 1980–1998

| | Deaths (number) | | | | | Rate per 100,000 population | | | | |
|---|---|---|---|---|---|---|---|---|---|---|
| Type of accident | 1980 | 1990 | 1996 | 1997 | 1998 | 1980 | 1990 | 1996 | 1997 | 1998 |
| Motor vehicle accidents | 53,172 | 46,814 | 43,649 | 43,458 | 43,501 | 23.5 | 18.8 | 16.5 | 16.2 | 16.1 |
| Traffic | 51,930 | 45,827 | 42,522 | 42,340 | 42,191 | 22.9 | 18.4 | 16.0 | 15.8 | 15.6 |
| Nontraffic | 1,242 | 987 | 1,127 | 1,118 | 1,310 | 0.5 | 0.4 | 0.4 | 0.4 | 0.5 |
| Water-transport accidents | 1,429 | 923 | 675 | 758 | 692 | 0.6 | 0.4 | 0.3 | 0.3 | 0.3 |
| Air and space transport accidents | 1,494 | 941 | 1,061 | 734 | 692 | 0.7 | 0.4 | 0.4 | 0.3 | 0.3 |
| Railway accidents | 632 | 663 | 565 | 527 | 515 | 0.3 | 0.3 | 0.2 | 0.2 | 0.2 |
| Accidental falls | 13,294 | 12,313 | 14,986 | 15,447 | 16,274 | 5.9 | 5.0 | 5.6 | 5.8 | 6.0 |
| Accidental drowning | 6,043 | 3,979 | 3,488 | 3,561 | 3,964 | 2.7 | 1.6 | 1.3 | 1.3 | 1.5 |
| Accidents caused by— | | | | | | | | | | |
| Fires and flames | 5,822 | 4,175 | 3,741 | 3,490 | 3,255 | 2.6 | 1.7 | 1.4 | 1.0 | 1.0 |
| Firearms, unspecified and other | 1,667 | 1,175 | 947 | 820 | 726 | 0.7 | 0.5 | 0.4 | 0.3 | 0.3 |
| Handguns | 288 | 241 | 187 | 161 | 140 | 0.1 | 0.1 | 0.1 | 0.1 | 0.1 |
| Electric current | 1,095 | 670 | 482 | 488 | 548 | 0.5 | 0.3 | 0.2 | 0.2 | 0.2 |
| Accidental poisoning by— | | | | | | | | | | |
| Drugs and medicines | 2,492 | 4,506 | 8,431 | 9,099 | 9,838 | 1.1 | 1.8 | 3.2 | 3.4 | 3.6 |
| Other solid and liquid substances | 597 | 549 | 441 | 488 | 417 | 0.3 | 0.2 | 0.2 | 0.2 | 0.2 |
| Gases and vapors | 1,242 | 748 | 638 | 576 | 546 | 0.5 | 0.3 | 0.2 | 0.2 | 0.2 |
| Complications due to medical procedures | 2,282 | 2,669 | 2,919 | 3,043 | 3,228 | 1.0 | 1.1 | 1.1 | 1.1 | 1.2 |
| Inhalation and ingestion of objects | 3,249 | 3,303 | 3,206 | 3,275 | 3,515 | 1.4 | 1.3 | 1.2 | 1.2 | 1.3 |

NOTE: Excludes deaths of nonresidents of the United States. *Source: Statistical Abstract of the United States 2001.*

## Deaths by Firearms, 1979–1999

### (per 100,000 population in specified group)

| Year | All races Number of deaths | All races Death rate[1] | White Number of deaths | White Death rate[1] | Black Number of deaths | Black Death rate[1] |
|------|---------|---------|---------|---------|---------|---------|
| 1979 | 33,019 | 14.7 | 24,234 | 12.5 | 8,304 | 31.6 |
| 1980 | 33,780 | 14.9 | 24,849 | 12.8 | 8,505 | 31.9 |
| 1981 | 34,050 | 14.8 | 25,237 | 12.8 | 8,324 | 30.7 |
| 1982 | 32,957 | 14.2 | 25,071 | 12.7 | 7,415 | 27.0 |
| 1983 | 31,099 | 13.3 | 24,038 | 12.1 | 6,589 | 23.6 |
| 1984 | 31,331 | 13.3 | 24,419 | 12.2 | 6,449 | 22.9 |
| 1985 | 31,566 | 13.3 | 24,507 | 12.1 | 6,565 | 23.0 |
| 1986 | 33,373 | 13.9 | 25,339 | 12.5 | 7,494 | 25.9 |
| 1987 | 32,895 | 13.6 | 24,789 | 12.1 | 7,586 | 25.9 |
| 1988 | 33,989 | 13.9 | 24,892 | 12.1 | 8,475 | 28.5 |
| 1989 | 34,776 | 14.1 | 25,023 | 12.1 | 9,077 | 30.1 |
| 1990 | 37,155 | 14.9 | 26,299 | 12.6 | 10,175 | 33.4 |
| 1991 | 38,317 | 15.2 | 26,455 | 12.5 | 11,025 | 35.4 |
| 1992 | 37,776 | 14.8 | 26,120 | 12.3 | 10,906 | 34.5 |
| 1993 | 39,595 | 15.4 | 26,948 | 12.5 | 11,763 | 36.6 |
| 1994 | 38,505 | 14.8 | 26,403 | 12.2 | 11,223 | 34.4 |
| 1995 | 35,957 | 13.7 | 25,438 | 11.7 | 9,643 | 29.1 |
| 1996 | 34,040 | 12.8 | 24,114 | 11.0 | 9,175 | 27.4 |
| 1997 | 32,436 | 12.1 | 23,270 | 10.5 | 8,389 | 24.7 |
| 1998 | 30,708 | 11.4 | 22,480 | 10.1 | 7,503 | 21.8 |
| 1999 | 28,874 | 10.6 | 21,143 | 9.4 | 7,017 | 20.1 |

1. On an annual basis, per 100,000 population in specified group. *Source:* Centers for Disease Control and Prevention, *National Vital Statistics Reports,* vol. 49, no. 8, Sept. 21, 2001.

## Death Rates for Suicide, 1950–1999

### (deaths per 100,000 resident population)

| Characteristic | 1950[1] | 1960[1] | 1970 | 1980 | 1990 | 1996 | 1997 | 1998 | 1999 |
|------|------|------|------|------|------|------|------|------|------|
| All ages[2] | 13.6 | 12.5 | 13.1 | 12.2 | 12.0 | 11.7 | 11.4 | 11.3 | 10.7 |
| 5 to 14 years | 0.2 | 0.3 | 0.3 | 0.4 | 0.8 | 0.8 | 0.8 | 0.8 | 0.6 |
| 15 to 24 years | 4.5 | 5.2 | 8.8 | 12.3 | 13.2 | 12.0 | 11.4 | 11.1 | 10.3 |
| 25 to 34 years | 9.1 | 10.0 | 14.1 | 16.0 | 15.4 | 14.5 | 14.3 | 13.8 | 13.5 |
| 35 to 44 years | 14.3 | 14.2 | 16.9 | 15.4 | 15.2 | 15.5 | 15.3 | 15.4 | 14.4 |
| 45 to 54 years | 20.9 | 20.7 | 20.0 | 15.9 | 14.6 | 14.9 | 14.7 | 14.8 | 14.2 |
| 55 to 64 years | 26.8 | 23.7 | 21.4 | 15.9 | 13.3 | 13.7 | 13.5 | 13.1 | 12.4 |
| 65 to 74 years | 29.6 | 23.0 | 20.8 | 16.9 | 15.8 | 15.0 | 14.4 | 14.1 | 13.6 |
| 75 to 84 years | 31.1 | 27.9 | 21.2 | 19.1 | 20.7 | 20.0 | 19.3 | 19.7 | 16.3 |
| 85 years and over | 28.8 | 26.0 | 19.0 | 19.2 | 21.6 | 20.2 | 20.8 | 21.0 | 19.2 |
| Male, all ages[2] | 21.2 | 20.0 | 19.8 | 19.9 | 20.6 | 20.0 | 19.4 | 19.2 | 18.2 |
| Female, all ages[2] | 5.6 | 5.6 | 7.4 | 5.7 | 4.4 | 4.3 | 4.4 | 4.3 | 4.1 |

1. Includes deaths of persons who were not residents of the 50 states and the District of Columbia. 2. Data are age-adjusted. *Sources:* Centers for Disease Control and Prevention, National Center for Health Statistics. From *Health, United States, 2001.*

# Miscellaneous

## Most Common Last Names in the U.S.

| Rank | Name | Frequency[1] | Rank | Name | Frequency[1] | Rank | Name | Frequency[1] |
|------|------|------|------|------|------|------|------|------|
| 1. | Smith | 1.01% | 11. | Anderson | 0.31 | 21. | Clark | 0.23 |
| 2. | Johnson | 0.81 | 12. | Thomas | 0.31 | 22. | Rodriguez | 0.23 |
| 3. | Williams | 0.70 | 13. | Jackson | 0.31 | 23. | Lewis | 0.23 |
| 4. | Jones | 0.62 | 14. | White | 0.28 | 24. | Lee | 0.22 |
| 5. | Brown | 0.62 | 15. | Harris | 0.28 | 25. | Walker | 0.22 |
| 6. | Davis | 0.48 | 16. | Martin | 0.27 | 26. | Hall | 0.20 |
| 7. | Miller | 0.42 | 17. | Thompson | 0.27 | 27. | Allen | 0.20 |
| 8. | Wilson | 0.34 | 18. | Garcia | 0.25 | 28. | Young | 0.19 |
| 9. | Moore | 0.31 | 19. | Martinez | 0.23 | 29. | Hernandez | 0.19 |
| 10. | Taylor | 0.31 | 20. | Robinson | 0.23 | 30. | King | 0.19 |

NOTE: Based on 1990 Census data. Numbers are rounded. 1. Percent of U.S. population sample. *Source:* U.S. Census Bureau. Web: www.census.gov/genealogy/names/dist.all.last.

## Most Popular Given Names, 1880–2000

**Boys**

**1880:** John, William, Charles, George, James, Joseph, Frank, Henry, Thomas, Harry
**1890:** John, William, James, George, Charles, Joseph, Frank, Harry, Henry, Edward
**1900:** John, William, James, George, Charles, Joseph, Frank, Henry, Robert, Harry
**1910:** John, William, James, Robert, Joseph, Charles/George (tie), Edward, Frank, Henry
**1920:** John, William, James, Robert, Joseph, Charles, George, Edward, Thomas, Frank
**1930:** Robert, James, John, William, Richard, Charles, Donald, George, Joseph, Edward
**1940:** James, Robert, John, William, Richard, Charles, David, Thomas, Donald, Ronald
**1950:** John, James, Robert, William, Michael, David, Richard, Thomas, Charles, Gary
**1960:** David, Michael, John, James, Robert, Mark, William, Richard, Thomas, Steven
**1970:** Michael, David, John, James, Robert, Christopher, William, Mark, Richard, Brian
**1980:** Michael, Jason, Christopher, David, James, Matthew, John, Joshua, Robert, Daniel
**1990:** Michael, Christopher, Joshua, Matthew, David, Daniel, Andrew, Joseph, Justin, James
**2000:** Jacob, Michael, Matthew, Joshua, Christopher, Nicholas, Andrew, Joseph, Daniel, Tyler

**Girls**

**1880:** Mary, Anna, Elizabeth, Margaret, Minnie, Emma, Martha, Alice, Marie, Annie/Sarah (tie)
**1890:** Mary, Anna, Elizabeth, Emma, Margaret, Rose, Ethel, Florence, Ida, Bertha/Helen (tie)
**1900:** Mary, Helen, Anna, Margaret, Ruth, Elizabeth, Marie, Rose, Florence, Bertha
**1910:** Mary, Helen, Margaret, Dorothy, Ruth, Anna, Mildred, Elizabeth, Alice, Ethel
**1920:** Mary, Dorothy, Helen, Margaret, Ruth, Virginia, Elizabeth, Anna, Mildred, Betty
**1930:** Mary, Betty, Dorothy, Helen, Barbara, Margaret, Maria, Patricia, Doris, Joan/Ruth (tie)
**1940:** Mary, Barbara, Patricia, Carol, Judith, Betty, Nancy, Maria, Margaret, Linda
**1950:** Linda, Mary, Patricia, Barbara, Susan, Maria, Sandra, Nancy, Deborah, Kathleen
**1960:** Mary, Susan, Maria, Karen, Lisa, Linda, Donna, Patricia, Debra, Deborah
**1970:** Jennifer, Lisa, Kimberly, Michelle, Angela, Maria, Amy, Melissa, Mary, Tracy
**1980:** Jennifer, Jessica, Amanda, Melissa, Sarah, Nicole, Heather, Amy, Michelle, Elizabeth
**1990:** Jessica, Ashley, Brittany, Amanda, Stephanie, Jennifer, Samantha, Sarah, Megan, Lauren
**2000:** Emily, Hannah, Madison, Ashley, Sarah, Alexis, Samantha, Jessica, Taylor, Elizabeth

NOTE: Represents the most frequently used given names for births, based on a sampling of Social Security Number card applications. *Source:* Social Security Administration. Web: www.ssa.gov/OACT/NOTES/note139/note139.html.

## Most Popular Pet Names

The American Society for the Prevention of Cruelty to Animals (ASPCA) has conducted a veterinarian survey to find out which pet names are most popular in the United States today. Here are the top 30:

| | | | | |
|---|---|---|---|---|
| 1. Max | 7. Kitty | 13. Misty | 19. Samantha | 25. Sheba |
| 2. Sam | 8. Molly | 14. Missy | 20. Lucky | 26. Rocky |
| 3. Lady | 9. Buddy | 15. Pepper | 21. Muffin | 27. Patches |
| 4. Bear | 10. Brandy | 16. Jake | 22. Princess | 28. Tigger |
| 5. Smokey | 11. Ginger | 17. Bandit | 23. Maggie | 29. Rusty |
| 6. Shadow | 12. Baby | 18. Tiger | 24. Charlie | 30. Buster |

## Household Pet Ownership, 1996

| Item | Dog | Cat | Pet bird | Horse |
|---|---|---|---|---|
| Households owning companion pets[1] (millions) | 31.20 | 27.00 | 4.60 | 1.50 |
| Percent of all households | 31.60% | 27.30% | 4.60% | 1.50% |
| Average number owned | 1.70 | 2.20 | 2.70 | 2.70 |
| Total companion pet population[1] (millions) | 52.90 | 59.10 | 12.60 | 4.00 |
| Households obtaining veterinary care[2] | 88.70% | 72.90% | 15.80% | 66.30% |
| Average visits per household per year | 2.60 | 1.90 | 0.20 | 2.30 |
| Average annual costs per household | $ 186.80 | $ 112.24 | $10.95 | $226.26 |
| Total expenditures (millions) | $5,828.00 | $3,030.00 | $50.00 | $339.00 |
| **Percent distribution of households owning pets** | | | | |
| Annual household income: | | | | |
| Under $12,500 | 12.70% | 13.90% | 17.30% | 9.50% |
| $12,500 to $24,999 | 19.10 | 19.70 | 20.90 | 20.30 |
| $25,000 to $39,999 | 21.60 | 21.50 | 22.00 | 21.80 |
| $40,000 to $59,999 | 21.50 | 21.20 | 17.50 | 23.10 |
| $60,000 and over | 25.20 | 23.70 | 22.30 | 25.40 |
| Family size:[1] | | | | |
| One person | 13.20% | 16.80% | 12.70% | 12.10% |
| Two persons | 31.00 | 32.60 | 27.90 | 29.10 |
| Three persons | 21.40 | 20.60 | 20.40 | 22.00 |
| Four or more persons | 34.50 | 29.90 | 38.90 | 36.70 |

NOTE: Based on a sample survey of 80,000 households in 1996. 1. As of December. 2. During 1996. *Source:* American Veterinary Medical Association, Schaumburg, Ill., *U.S. Pet Ownership and Demographics Sourcebook, 1997.* Reprinted with permission.

## Hunger Still a Problem in U.S.

Source: Economic Research Service, U.S. Dept. of Agriculture, Household Food Security in the United States, 2000

Nearly 90% of U.S. households were food secure throughout the entire year ending in Sept. 2000. "Food secure" means that all household members had access at all times to enough food for an active, healthy life. The remaining 11 million U.S. households (10.5% of all households) were food insecure at some time during the year. That is, they were uncertain of having, or unable to acquire, enough food to meet basic needs for all household members because they had insufficient money and other resources. About two-thirds of food-insecure households avoided hunger, in many cases by relying on a few basic foods and reducing variety in their diets. But 3.3 million households (3.1% of all U.S. house-

holds) were food insecure to the extent one or more household members were hungry due to inadequate resources at least some time during the year.

The prevalence of food insecurity and hunger varied considerably among household types, and some groups, including 31% of households with children headed by a single woman, 20.5% of black households, and 21.4% of Hispanic households, experienced rates of food insecurity greater than the national average. Overall, households with children experienced food insecurity at more than double the rate for households without children (16.2% versus 7.3%).

### Food Insecurity and Hunger, 2000

(numbers in thousands)

| Category | Total number[1] | Food secure | | Food insecure | | | | | |
|---|---|---|---|---|---|---|---|---|---|
| | | | | Total | | Without hunger | | With hunger | |
| | | Number | Percent | Number | Percent | Number | Percent | Number | Percent |
| All households | 106,043 | 94,942 | 89.5% | 11,101 | 10.5% | 7,786 | 7.3 | 3,315 | 3.1 |
| Household composition: | | | | | | | | | |
| With children < 18 | 38,113 | 31,942 | 83.8 | 6,171 | 16.2 | 4,748 | 12.5 | 1,423 | 3.7 |
| Married couple families | 26,366 | 23,500 | 89.1 | 2,866 | 10.9 | 2,355 | 8.9 | 511 | 1.9 |
| Female head, no spouse | 9,070 | 6,255 | 69.0 | 2,815 | 31.0 | 2,002 | 22.1 | 813 | 9.0 |
| Male head, no spouse | 2,099 | 1,728 | 82.3 | 371 | 17.7 | 290 | 13.8 | 81 | 3.9 |
| Other household with child[2] | 578 | 457 | 79.1 | 121 | 20.9 | 102 | 17.6 | 19 | 3.3 |
| With no children < 18 | 67,930 | 63,000 | 92.7 | 4,930 | 7.3 | 3,038 | 4.5 | 1,892 | 2.8 |
| More than one adult | 40,436 | 38,160 | 94.4 | 2,276 | 5.6 | 1,512 | 3.7 | 764 | 1.9 |
| Women living alone | 16,157 | 14,527 | 89.9 | 1,630 | 10.1 | 976 | 6.0 | 654 | 4.0 |
| Men living alone | 11,336 | 10,313 | 91.0 | 1,023 | 9.0 | 549 | 4.8 | 474 | 4.2 |
| Households with elderly | 24,926 | 23,447 | 94.1 | 1,479 | 5.9 | 1,097 | 4.4 | 382 | 1.5 |
| Elderly living alone | 10,125 | 9,409 | 92.9 | 716 | 7.1 | 523 | 5.2 | 193 | 1.9 |
| Race/ethnicity of households: | | | | | | | | | |
| White non-Hispanic | 79,697 | 73,633 | 92.4 | 6,064 | 7.6 | 4,147 | 5.2 | 1,917 | 2.4 |
| Black non-Hispanic | 12,813 | 10,182 | 79.5 | 2,631 | 20.5 | 1,802 | 14.1 | 829 | 6.5 |
| Hispanic[3] | 9,445 | 7,428 | 78.6 | 2,017 | 21.4 | 1,562 | 16.5 | 455 | 4.8 |
| Other non-Hispanic | 4,088 | 3,699 | 90.5 | 389 | 9.5 | 275 | 6.7 | 114 | 2.8 |

1. Total households in each category exclude households whose food security status is unknown. 2. Households with children in complex living arrangements, e.g., children of other relatives or unrelated roommate or boarder. 3. Hispanics may be of any race. Source: Economic Research Service, U.S. Dept. of Agriculture, Household Food Security in the United States, 2000. Web: www.ers.usda.gov/briefing/foodsecurity/.

### Food Stamp Households, 1999

(for year ending Sept. 30)

| | Households | | | Participants | |
|---|---|---|---|---|---|
| | Num. (1,000) | Percent | and Hispanic origin | (1,000) | Percent |
| Total | 7,670 | 100.0% | Total[1] | 18,149 | 100.0% |
| With children | 4,275 | 55.7 | Male | 7,226 | 39.8 |
| Single-parent households | 2,928 | 38.2 | Female | 10,878 | 59.9 |
| Married-couple households | 964 | 12.6 | White, non-Hispanic | 7,363 | 40.6 |
| Other | 702 | 9.1 | Black, non-Hispanic | 6,543 | 36.1 |
| With elderly | 1,543 | 20.1 | Hispanic | 3,279 | 18.1 |
| Living alone | 1,212 | 15.8 | Asian | 564 | 3.1 |
| Not living alone | 330 | 4.3 | Native American | 281 | 1.5 |
| Disabled | 2,031 | 26.5 | Other | 119 | 0.7 |
| Living alone | 1,162 | 15.1 | | | |
| Not living alone | 869 | 11.3 | | | |

1. Includes persons of unknown age not shown separately. Source: U.S. Dept. of Agriculture, Food and Nutrition Service, Characteristics of Food Stamp Households: Fiscal Year 1999, Dec. 2000. From Statistical Abstract of the United States, 2001.

## U.S. Charities Receiving Highest Donations in 2000

| 2000 Rank | Charity | Private support | Year Ending | 1999 rank |
|---|---|---|---|---|
| 1. | Salvation Army[1] | $1,440,442,000 | 9/30/2000 | 1. |
| 2. | Fidelity Investments Charitable Gift Fund | 1,087,748,356 | 6/30/2000 | 5. |
| 3. | YMCA of the USA[1, 2] | 812,098,000 | 12/31/2000 | 2. |
| 4. | American Cancer Society[1] | 746,391,000 | 8/31/2000 | 4. |
| 5. | Lutheran Services in America[1, 2] | 710,263,416 | 6/30/1999 | 6. |
| 6. | American Red Cross[1] | 637,664,249 | 6/30/2000 | 3. |
| 7. | Gifts in Kind International[1] | 601,926,952 | 12/31/2000 | 15. |
| 8. | Stanford University | 580,473,838 | 8/31/2000 | 19. |
| 9. | Harvard University | 485,238,498 | 6/30/2000 | 10. |
| 10. | Nature Conservancy[1, 3] | 445,326,081 | 6/30/2000 | 12. |
| 11. | Boys and Girls Clubs of America[1] | 425,125,115 | 12/31/2000 | 13. |
| 12. | America's Second Harvest[4] | 421,665,967 | 6/30/2000 | 8. |
| 13. | Catholic Charities USA[1] | 414,440,601 | 12/31/1999 | 11. |
| 14. | Duke University[1] | 407,952,525 | 6/30/2000 | 18. |
| 15. | American Heart Association[1] | 396,388,909 | 6/30/2000 | 14. |
| 16. | Feed the Children | 395,581,981 | 9/30/2000 | 19. |
| 17. | World Vision | 372,045,000 | 9/30/2000 | 17. |
| 18. | Habitat for Humanity International[1] | 371,086,000 | 6/30/2000 | 9. |
| 19. | Yale University | 358,102,600 | 6/30/2000 | 30. |
| 20. | AmeriCares Foundation | 326,373,880 | 6/30/2000 | 25. |
| 21. | Campus Crusade for Christ International[1] | 325,792,000 | 8/31/2000 | 20. |
| 22. | Cornell University | 308,676,394 | 6/30/2000 | 16. |
| 23. | Johns Hopkins University[1] | 304,043,508 | 6/30/2000 | 36. |
| 24. | Columbia University | 292,267,910 | 6/30/2000 | 22. |
| 25. | University of Pennsylvania | 288,152,160 | 6/30/2000 | 24. |

1. Includes affiliates. 2. Affiliates have different fiscal years. Fiscal year is for the national office. 3. Another $191,938,179 was spent to purchase land, which is not included in program services. An additional $137,396,666 was put into an endowment to be used for future land acquisitions and land management. 4. Figure includes food donated and passed to affiliated food banks. Value of food donated is estimated by the organization. *Source: The Chronicle of Philanthropy,* Nov. 1, 2001. Reprinted with permission.

## Percent of Adult Population Doing Volunteer Work, 1998

| Age, sex, race, and Hispanic origin | Percent of population volunteering | Average hours volunteered per week | Educational attainment and household income | Percent of population volunteering | Average hours volunteered per week |
|---|---|---|---|---|---|
| **Total** | **55.5%** | **3.5** | Elementary school | 29.4% | (B) |
| | | | Some high school | 43.0 | 3.9 |
| 18–24 years | 48.5 | 3.0 | High-school graduate | 43.2 | 2.8 |
| 25–34 years | 54.9 | 3.5 | Technical, trade, or | | |
| 35–44 years | 67.3 | 3.7 | business school | 53.5 | 3.5 |
| 45–54 years | 62.7 | 3.8 | Some college | 67.2 | 4.8 |
| 55–64 years | 50.3 | 3.3 | College graduate | 67.7 | 3.1 |
| 65–74 years | 46.6 | 3.6 | | | |
| 75 years and over | 43.0 | 3.1 | Under $10,000 | 42.1 | 3.4 |
| | | | $10,000–19,999 | 42.2 | 2.9 |
| Male | 49.4 | 3.6 | $20,000–29,999 | 43.7 | 4.0 |
| Female | 61.7 | 3.4 | $30,000–39,999 | 54.4 | 3.4 |
| | | | $40,000–49,999 | 67.5 | 3.6 |
| White | 58.6 | 3.5 | $50,000–59,999 | 62.8 | 4.3 |
| Black | 46.6 | 4.7 | $60,000–74,999 | 71.2 | 2.9 |
| Hispanic[1] | 46.4 | 2.1 | $75,000–99,999 | 64.2 | 3.5 |
| | | | $100,000 or more | 70.5 | 3.5 |

| Type of activity | Percent of population involved in activity | Type of activity | Percent of population involved in activity |
|---|---|---|---|
| Arts, culture, humanities | 8.6% | Political organizations | 4.6% |
| Education | 17.3 | Private, community foundations | 3.4 |
| Environment | 9.2 | Public and societal benefit | 7.9 |
| Health | 11.4 | Recreation—adults | 8.6 |
| Human services | 15.9 | Religion | 22.8 |
| Informal | 24.4 | Work-related organizations | 10.3 |
| International, foreign | 2.5 | Youth development | 17.5 |

(B) = Base figure too small to meet statistical standards for reliability. 1. Hispanic persons may be of any race. NOTE: Covers persons 18 years and over. Volunteers are persons who worked in some way to help others for no monetary pay during the previous year. Based on a sample survey conducted during the spring of the following year and subject to sampling variability. *Source: Statistical Abstract of the United States 2001.*

## Homeownership Rates by Race and Ethnicity of Householder

| | 1994 | 1995 | 1996 | 1997 | 1998 | 1999 | 2000 |
|---|---|---|---|---|---|---|---|
| **U.S. total** | **64.0** | **64.7** | **65.4** | **65.7** | **66.3** | **66.8** | **67.4** |
| White, total | 67.7 | 68.7 | 69.1 | 69.3 | 70.0 | 70.5 | 71.1 |
| White, non-Hispanic | 70.0 | 70.9 | 71.7 | 72.0 | 72.6 | 73.2 | 73.8 |
| Black, total | 42.3 | 42.7 | 44.1 | 44.8 | 45.6 | 46.3 | 47.2 |
| Other race[1] | 47.7 | 47.2 | 51.0 | 52.5 | 53.0 | 53.7 | 53.5 |
| American Indian, Aleut, Eskimo | 51.7 | 55.8 | 51.6 | 51.7 | 54.3 | 56.1 | 56.2 |
| Asian or Pacific Islander | 51.3 | 50.8 | 50.8 | 52.8 | 52.6 | 53.1 | 52.8 |
| Other | 36.1 | 37.4 | n.a. | n.a. | n.a. | n.a. | n.a. |
| Hispanic | 41.2 | 42.1 | 42.8 | 43.3 | 44.7 | 45.5 | 46.3 |
| Non-Hispanic | 65.9 | 66.7 | 67.4 | 67.8 | 68.3 | 68.9 | 69.5 |

NOTE: n.a. = not applicable. 1. Beginning in 1996, those answering "other" for race were allocated to one of the 4 race categories—white, black, American Indian, Aleut, or Eskimo (one category), or Asian or Pacific Islander. Source: U.S. Census Bureau. Web: www.census.gov.

## Homeownership by State, 1990 and 2000

| State | Homeownership rate (%) 1990 | 2000 | State | Homeownership rate (%) 1990 | 2000 | State | Homeownership rate (%) 1990 | 2000 |
|---|---|---|---|---|---|---|---|---|
| **U.S. total** | **63.9%** | **67.4%** | Kentucky | 65.8% | 73.4% | Ohio | 68.7% | 71.3% |
| Alabama | 68.4 | 73.2 | Louisiana | 67.8 | 68.1 | Oklahoma | 70.3 | 72.7 |
| Alaska | 58.4 | 66.4 | Maine | 74.2 | 76.5 | Oregon | 64.4 | 65.3 |
| Arizona | 64.5 | 68.0 | Maryland | 64.9 | 69.9 | Pennsylvania | 73.8 | 74.7 |
| Arkansas | 67.8 | 68.9 | Massachusetts | 58.6 | 59.9 | Rhode Island | 58.5 | 61.5 |
| California | 53.8 | 57.1 | Michigan | 72.3 | 77.2 | South Carolina | 71.4 | 76.5 |
| Colorado | 59.0 | 68.3 | Minnesota | 68.0 | 76.1 | South Dakota | 66.2 | 71.2 |
| Connecticut | 67.9 | 70.0 | Mississippi | 69.4 | 75.2 | Tennessee | 68.3 | 70.9 |
| Delaware | 67.7 | 72.0 | Missouri | 64.0 | 74.2 | Texas | 59.7 | 63.8 |
| DC | 36.4 | 41.9 | Montana | 69.1 | 70.2 | Utah | 70.1 | 72.7 |
| Florida | 65.1 | 68.4 | Nebraska | 67.3 | 70.2 | Vermont | 72.6 | 68.7 |
| Georgia | 64.3 | 69.8 | Nevada | 55.8 | 64.0 | Virginia | 69.8 | 73.9 |
| Hawaii | 55.5 | 55.2 | New Hampshire | 65.0 | 69.2 | Washington | 61.8 | 63.6 |
| Idaho | 69.4 | 70.5 | New Jersey | 65.0 | 66.2 | West Virginia | 72.0 | 75.9 |
| Illinois | 63.0 | 67.9 | New Mexico | 68.6 | 73.7 | Wisconsin | 68.3 | 71.8 |
| Indiana | 67.0 | 74.9 | New York | 53.3 | 53.4 | Wyoming | 68.9 | 71.0 |
| Iowa | 70.7 | 75.2 | North Carolina | 69.0 | 71.1 | | | |
| Kansas | 69.0 | 69.3 | North Dakota | 67.2 | 70.7 | | | |

Source: U.S. Census Bureau. Web: www.census.gov.

## Characteristics of the Homeless, 1996

| Characteristic | U.S. adult population (1996) | All homeless persons | Persons in homeless families | Single homeless persons |
|---|---|---|---|---|
| **Sex:** | | | | |
| Male | 48% | 68% | 16% | 77% |
| Female | 52 | 32 | 84 | 23 |
| **Race/ethnicity:** | | | | |
| White non-Hispanic | 75 | 41 | 38 | 41 |
| Black non-Hispanic | 11 | 40 | 43 | 40 |
| Hispanic | 10 | 11 | 11 | 11 |
| Native American | 1 | 8 | 3 | 8 |
| **Marital status:** | | | | |
| Never married | 23 | 48 | 41 | 50 |
| Married | 60 | 9 | 20 | 7 |
| Separated | (2) | 15 | 23 | 14 |
| Divorced | 10 | 24 | 13 | 26 |
| Widowed | 7 | 3 | 0 | 4 |
| **Educational attainment:** | | | | |
| Less than high school | 25 | 38 | 53 | 37 |
| High school graduate/G.E.D. | 30 | 34 | 21 | 36 |
| More than high school | 45 | 28 | 27 | 28 |
| **Veteran** | 13 | 23 | 5 | 26 |

NOTE: Numbers do not add up to 100% due to rounding. 1. Denotes percentage less than 0.5 percent but greater than 0. 2. Included in "married." Source: U.S. Bureau of the Census. From Interagency Council on the Homeless, Homelessness: Programs and the People They Serve, 1999.

# States

Data for state populations are the latest available from the U.S. Census Bureau. NOTE: Persons of Hispanic origin can be of any race. "American Indian" includes American Indians, Eskimos, and Aleuts. "Asian" includes Asian Indians, Chinese, Filipino, Japanese, Korean, and Vietnamese. Largest cities include incorporated places only, as defined by the U.S. Census Bureau. They do not include adjacent or suburban areas. Population data for U.S. cities are also the latest available from the U.S. Census Bureau.

For secession and readmission dates of the former Confederate states, *see* U.S. Government & History: The Confederate States of America. For a separate list of governors, and lists of senators and representatives elected to terms beginning in 2003, *see* U.S. Government & History: The Governors of the Fifty States, The Senate, and The House of Representatives. For U.S. Territories, *see* Countries of the World: United States.

## Alabama

**Capital:** Montgomery
**Governor:** Don Siegelman, D (to Jan. 2003)
**Lieut. Governor:** Steve Windom, R (to Jan. 2003)
**Senators:** Jeff Sessions, R (to Jan. 2003); Richard C. Shelby, R (to Jan. 2005)
**Secy. of State:** Jim Bennett, R (to Jan. 2003)
**Treasurer:** Lucy Baxley, D (to Jan. 2003)
**Atty. General:** William Pryor, R (to Jan. 2003)
**Organized as territory:** March 3, 1817
**Entered Union (rank):** Dec. 14, 1819 (22)
**Present constitution adopted:** 1901
**Motto:** *Audemus jura nostra defendere* (We dare defend our rights)
**State Symbols: flower,** camellia (1959); **bird,** yellowhammer (1927); **song,** "Alabama" (1931); **tree,** Southern longleaf pine (1949, 1997); **salt water fish,** fighting tarpon (1955); **fresh water fish,** largemouth bass (1975); **horse,** racking horse (1975); **mineral,** hematite (1967); **rock,** marble (1969); **game bird,** wild turkey (1980); **dance,** square dance (1981); **nut,** pecan (1982); **fossil,** species *Basilosaurus Cetoides* (1984); **official mascot and butterfly,** eastern tiger swallowtail (1989); **insect,** monarch butterfly (1989); **reptile,** Alabama red-bellied turtle (1990); **gemstone,** star blue quartz (1990); **shell,** *scaphella junonia johnstoneae* (1990);
**Nickname:** Yellowhammer State
**Origin of name:** May come from Choctaw meaning "thicket-clearers" or "vegetation-gatherers"
**10 largest cities (2000):** Birmingham, 242,820; Montgomery, 201,568; Mobile, 198,915; Huntsville, 158,216; Tuscaloosa, 77,906; Hoover, 62,742; Dothan, 57,737; Decatur, 53,929; Auburn, 42,987; Gadsden, 38,978
**Land area:** 50,744 sq mi. (131,427 sq km)
**Geographic center:** In Chilton Co., 12 mi. SW of Clanton
**Number of counties:** 67
**Largest county by population and area:** Jefferson, 659,743 (2001); Baldwin, 1,596 sq mi.
**State forests:** 21 (48,000 ac.)
**State parks:** 22 (45,614 ac.)
**Residents:** Alabamian, Alabaman
**2001 resident population est.:** 4,464,356
**2000 resident census population (rank):** 4,447,100 (23). **Male:** 2,146,504 (48.3%); **Female:** 2,300,596 (51.7%). **White:** 3,162,808 (71.1%); **Black:** 1,155,930 (26.0%); **American Indian:** 22,430 (0.5%); **Asian:** 31,346 (0.7%); **Other race:** 28,998 (0.7%); **Two or more races:** 44,179 (1.0%); **Hispanic/Latino:** 75,830 (1.7%). **2000 percent population 18 and over:** 74.7; **65 and over:** 13.0; **median age:** 35.8.

Spanish explorers are believed to have arrived at Mobile Bay in 1519, and the territory was visited in 1540 by the explorer Hernando de Soto. The first permanent European settlement in Alabama was founded by the French at Fort Louis de la Mobile in 1702. The British gained control of the area in 1763 by the Treaty of Paris but had to cede almost all the Alabama region to the U.S. and Spain after the American Revolution. The Confederacy was founded at Montgomery in Feb. 1861, and, for a time, the city was the Confederate capital.

During the later 19th century, the economy of the state slowly improved with industrialization. At Tuskegee Institute, founded in 1881 by Booker T. Washington, Dr. George Washington Carver carried out his famous agricultural research.

In the 1950s and '60s, Alabama was the site of such landmark civil-rights actions as the bus boycott in Montgomery (1955–56) and the "Freedom March" from Selma to Montgomery (1965).

Today paper, chemicals, rubber and plastics, apparel and textiles, primary metals, and automobile manufacturing constitute the leading industries of Alabama. Continuing as a major manufacturer of coal, iron, and steel, Birmingham is also noted for its world-renowned medical center. The state ranks high in the production of poultry, soybeans, milk, vegetables, livestock, wheat, cattle, cotton, peanuts, fruits, hogs, and corn.

Points of interest include the Helen Keller birthplace at Tuscumbia, the Space and Rocket Center at Huntsville, the White House of the Confederacy, the restored state Capitol, the Civil Rights Memorial, the Rosa Parks Museum & Library, and the Shakespeare Festival Theater Complex in Montgomery; the Civil Rights Institute and the McWane Center in Birmingham; the Russell Cave near Bridgeport; the Bellingrath Gardens at Theodore; the USS *Alabama* at Mobile; Mound State Monument near Tuscaloosa; and the Gulf Coast area.

Famous natives and residents: Hank Aaron, baseball player; Ralph Abernathy, civil rights activist; Tallulah Bankhead, actress; Hugo L. Black, jurist; George Washington Carver, educator, agricultural chemist; Nat "King" Cole, entertainer; Lionel Hampton, jazz musician; W. C. Handy, composer; Courtney Cox-Arquette, actress; Helen Keller, author and educator; Coretta Scott King, civil rights leader; Harper Lee, writer; Joe Louis, boxer; Willie Mays, baseball player; Jim Nabors, actor; Jesse Owens, athlete; Rosa Parks, civil rights activist; Wayne Rogers, actor; Tascaluza, Choctaw chief; George Wallace, governor; William Weatherford (Red Eagle), Creek leader; Heather Whitestone, Miss America (1995).

# Alaska

**Capital:** Juneau
**Governor:** Tony Knowles, D (to Dec. 2002)
**Lieut. Governor:** Fran Ulmer, D (to Dec. 2002)
**Senators:** Frank H. Murkowski, R (to Jan. 2005); Ted Stevens, R (to Jan. 2003)
**Atty. General:** Bruce M. Bothelho, D
**Organized as territory:** 1912
**Entered Union (rank):** Jan. 3, 1959 (49)
**Constitution ratified:** April 24, 1956
**Motto:** North to the Future
**State Symbols: flower,** forget-me-not (1949); **tree,** sitka spruce (1962); **bird,** willow ptarmigan (1955); **fish,** king salmon (1962); **song,** "Alaska's Flag" (1955); **gem,** jade (1968); **marine mammal,** bowhead whale (1983); **fossil,** woolly mammoth (1986); **mineral,** gold (1968); **sport,** dog mushing (1972);
**Nickname:** The state is commonly called "The Last Frontier" or "Land of the Midnight Sun"
**Origin of name:** Corruption of Aleut word meaning "great land" or "that which the sea breaks against"
**10 largest cities (2000):** Anchorage, 260,283; Juneau, 30,711; Fairbanks, 30,224; Sitka, 8,835; Ketchikan, 7,922; Kenai, 6,942; Kodiak, 6,334; Bethel, 5,471; Wasilla, 5,469; Barrow, 4,581
**Land area:** 571,951 sq mi. (1,4 81,353 sq km)
**Geographic center:** 60 mi. NW of Mt. McKinley
**Number of boroughs (counties):** 27
**Largest borough by population and area:** Anchorage, 264,937 (2001); Yukon-Koyukuk, 157,121 sq mi.
**State parks:** more than 100 (3.5 million acres)
**Residents:** Alaskan
**2001 resident population est.:** 634,892
**2000 resident census population (rank):** 626,932 (48).
  **Male:** 324,112 (51.7%); **Female:** 302,820 (48.3%).
  **White:** 434,534 (69.3%); **Black:** 21,787 (3.5%);
  **American Indian and Alaska Native:** 98,043 (15.6%);
  **Asian:** 25,116 (4.0%); **Other race:** 9,997 (1.6%);
  **Two or more races:** 34,146 (5.4%); **Hispanic/Latino:** 25,852 (4.1%). **2000 percent population 18 and over:** 69.6; **65 and over:** 5.7; **median age:** 32.4.

Vitus Bering, a Dane working for the Russians, and Alexei Chirikov discovered the Alaskan mainland and the Aleutian Islands in 1741. The tremendous land mass of Alaska—equal to one-fifth of the continental U.S.—was unexplored in 1867 when Secretary of State William Seward arranged for its purchase from the Russians for $7,200,000. The transfer of the territory took place on Oct. 18, 1867. Despite a price of about two cents an acre, the purchase was widely ridiculed as "Seward's Folly." The first official census (1880) reported a total of 33,426 Alaskans, all but 430 being of aboriginal stock. The Gold Rush of 1898 resulted in a mass influx of more than 30,000 people. Since then, Alaska has contributed billions of dollars' worth of products to the U.S. economy.

In 1968, a large oil and gas reservoir near Prudhoe Bay on the Arctic Coast was found. The Prudhoe Bay reservoir, with an estimated recoverable 10 billion barrels of oil and 27 trillion cubic feet of gas, is twice as large as any other oil field in North America. The Trans-Alaska pipeline was completed in 1977 at a cost of $7.7 billion. Oil flows through the 800-mile-long pipeline from Prudhoe Bay to the port of Valdez.

Other important industries are fisheries, wood and wood products, furs, and tourism.

Denali National Park and Mendenhall Glacier in North Tongass National Forest are of interest, as is the large totem pole collection at Sitka National His-

torical Park. The Katmai National Park includes the "Valley of Ten Thousand Smokes," an area of active volcanoes.

The Alaska Native population includes Eskimos, Indians, and Aleuts. About half of all Alaska Natives are Eskimos. (*Eskimo* is used for Alaska Natives; *Inuit* is used for Eskimos living in Canada.) The two main Eskimo groups, Inupiat and Yupik, are distinguished by their language and geography. The former live in the north and northwest parts of Alaska and speak Inupiaq, while the latter live in the south and southwest and speak Yupik.

About a third of Alaska Natives are American Indians. The major tribes are the Alaskan Athabaskan in the central part of the state, and the Tlingit, Tsimshian, and Haida in the southeast.

The Aleuts, native to the Aleutian Islands, Kodiak Island, the lower Alaska and Kenai Peninsulas, and Prince William Sound, are physically and culturally related to the Eskimos. About 15% of Alaska Natives are Aleuts.

Famous natives and residents: Clarence L. Andrews, author; Aleksandr Baranov, first governor of Russian America; Margaret Elizabeth Bell, author; Benny Benson, designed state flag at age 13; Vitus Bering, explorer; Charles E. Bunnell, educator; Susan Butcher, sled-dog racer; William A. Egan, first state governor; Carl Ben Eielson, pioneer pilot; Henry E. Gruennig, political leader; B. Frank Heintzleman, territorial governor; Walter J. Hickel, governor; Sheldon Jackson, educator and missionary; Joe Juneau, prospector; Austin Lathrop, industrialist; Sydney Lawrence, painter; Ray Mala, actor; Virgil F. Partch, cartoonist; Joe Redington, Sr., sled-dog musher and promoter; Peter Trinble Rowe, first Episcopal bishop; Ivan Popov-Veniaminov (St. Innocent), Russian Orthodox missionary; Ferdinand Wrangel, educator; Samuel Hall Young, founder of first American church.

# Arizona

**Capital:** Phoenix
**Governor:** Jane Dee Hull, R (to Jan. 2003)
**Senators:** Jon Kyl, R (to Jan. 2007); John McCain, R (to Jan. 2005)
**Secy. of State:** Betsey Bayless, R (to Jan. 2003)
**Atty. General:** Janet Napolitano, D (to Jan. 2003)
**Treasurer:** Carol Springer, R (to Jan. 2003)
**Organized as territory:** Feb. 24, 1863
**Entered Union (rank):** Feb. 14, 1912 (48)
**Present constitution adopted:** 1911
**Motto:** *Ditat Deus* (God enriches)
**State Symbols: flower,** flower of saguaro cactus (1931); **bird,** cactus wren (1931); **colors,** blue and old gold (1915); **song,** "Arizona" (1919); **tree,** palo verde (1954); **neckwear,** bola tie (1971); **fossil,** petrified wood (1988); **gemstone,** turquoise (1974); **mammal,** ringtail (1986); **reptile,** Arizona ridgenose rattlesnake (1986); **fish,** Arizona trout (1986); **amphibian,** Arizona tree frog (1986); **butterfly,** two-tailed swallowtail (2001);
**Nickname:** Grand Canyon State
**Origin of name:** From the Indian "Arizonac," meaning "little spring" or "young spring"
**10 largest cities (2000):** Phoenix, 1,321,045; Tucson, 486,699; Mesa, 396,375; Glendale, 218,812; Scottsdale, 202,705; Chandler, 176,581; Tempe, 158,625; Gilbert, 109,697; Peoria, 108,364; Yuma, 77,515
**Land area:** 113,635 sq mi. (294,315 sq km)
**Geographic center:** In Yavapai Co., 55 mi. ESE of Prescott
**Number of counties:** 15
**Largest county by population and area:** Maricopa, 3,194,798 (2001); Coconino, 18,562 sq mi.
**State parks:** 28

**Residents:** Arizonan, Arizonian
**2001 resident population est.:** 5,307,331
**2000 resident census population (rank):** 5,130,632 (20). **Male:** 2,561,057 (49.9%); **Female:** 2,569,575 (50.1%). **White:** 3,873,611 (75.5%); **Black:** 158,873 (3.1%); **American Indian:** 255,879 (5.0%); **Asian:** 92,236 (1.8%); **Other race:** 596,774 (11.6%); **Two or more races:** 146,526 (2.9%); **Hispanic/Latino:** 1,295,617 (25.3%). **2000 percent population 18 and over:** 73.4; **65 and over:** 13.0; **median age:** 34.2.

Marcos de Niza, a Spanish Franciscan friar, was the first European to explore Arizona. He entered the area in 1539 in search of the mythical Seven Cities of Gold. Although he was followed a year later by another gold seeker, Francisco Vásquez de Coronado, most of the early settlement was for missionary purposes. In 1775 the Spanish established Fort Tucson. In 1848, after the Mexican War, most of the Arizona territory became part of the U.S., and the southern portion of the territory was added by the Gadsden Purchase in 1853.

Arizona history is rich in legends of America's Old West. It was here that the great Indian chiefs Geronimo and Cochise led their people against the frontiersmen. Tombstone, Ariz., was the site of the West's most famous shoot-out—the gunfight at the O.K. Corral. Today, Arizona has one of the largest U.S. Indian populations; more than 14 tribes are represented on 20 reservations.

Manufacturing has become Arizona's most important industry. Principal products include electrical, communications, and aeronautical items. The state produces over half of the country's copper. Agriculture is also important to the state's economy. Top commodities are cattle and calves, dairy products, and cotton. In 1973 one of the world's most massive dams, the New Cornelia Tailings, was completed near Ajo.

State attractions include the Grand Canyon, the Petrified Forest, the Painted Desert, Hoover Dam, Lake Mead, Fort Apache, and the reconstructed London Bridge at Lake Havasu City.

Famous natives and residents: Apache Kid, Indian outlaw; Erma Bombeck, humorist and writer; Glen Campbell, singer; Lynda Carter, actress; Cesar Chavez, labor leader; Cochise, Apache chief; Alice Cooper, singer and songwriter; Wyatt Earp, marshall; Max Ernst, painter; Geronimo (Goyathlay), Apache chief; Barry Goldwater, politician; Zane Grey, novelist; Carl Trumbull Hayden, politician; George W. P. Hunt, first state governor; Bill Keane, cartoonist; Eusebio Kino, missionary; Percival Lowell, astronomer; Frank Luke, Jr., WWI fighter ace; Charles Mingus, jazz musician and composer; Carlos Montezuma, doctor and Indian spokesman; Stevie Nicks, singer; Sandra Day O'Connor, jurist; William O'Neill, frontier sheriff; Alexander M. Patch, general; William H. Pickering, astronomer; Linda Ronstadt, singer; Paolo Soleri, architect; Clyde W. Tombaugh, astronomer; Tanya Tucker, singer; Stewart Udall, secretary of the Interior; Frank Lloyd Wright, architect.

# Arkansas

**Capital:** Little Rock
**Governor:** Mike Huckabee, R (to Jan. 2003)
**Lieut. Governor:** Winthrop Rockefeller, R (to Jan. 2003)
**Senators:** Tim Hutchinson, R (to Jan. 2003);
Blanche Lambert Lincoln, D (to Jan. 2005)
**Secy. of State:** Sharon Priest, D (to Jan. 2003)
**Atty. General:** Mark Pryor (to Jan. 2003)
**Treasurer:** Jimmie Lou Fisher, D
(to Jan. 2003)
**Organized as territory:** March 2, 1819
**Entered Union (rank):** June 15, 1836 (25)

**Present constitution adopted:** 1874
**Motto:** *Regnat populus* (The people rule)
**State Symbols: flower,** apple blossom (1901); **tree,** pine (1939); **bird,** mockingbird (1929); **insect,** honeybee (1973); **song,** "Arkansas" (1963);
**Nickname:** The Natural State
**Origin of name:** From the Quapaw Indians
**10 largest cities (2000):** Little Rock, 183,133; Fort Smith, 80,268; North Little Rock, 60,433; Fayetteville, 58,047; Jonesboro, 55,515; Pine Bluff, 55,085; Springdale, 45,798; Conway, 43,167; Rogers, 38,829; Hot Springs, 35,750
**Land area:** 52,068 sq mi. (134,856 sq km)
**Geographic center:** In Pulaski Co., 12 mi. SW of Little Rock
**Number of counties:** 75
**Largest county by population and area:** Pulaski, 361,967 (2001); Union, 1,039 sq mi.
**State parks:** 50
**Residents:** Arkansan
**2001 resident population est.:** 2,692,090
**2000 resident census population (rank):** 2,673,400 (33). **Male:** 1,304,693 (48.8%); **Female:** 1,368,707 (51.2%). **White:** 2,138,598 (80.0%); **Black:** 418,950 (15.7%); **American Indian:** 17,808 (0.7%); **Asian:** 20,220 (0.8%); **Other race:** 40,412 (1.5%); **Two or more races:** 35,744 (1.3%); **Hispanic/Latino:** 86,866 (3.2%). **2000 percent population 18 and over:** 74.6; **65 and over:** 14.0; **median age:** 36.0.

Spaniard Hernando de Soto was among the early European explorers to visit the territory in the mid-16th century, but it was a Frenchman, Henri de Tonti, who in 1686 founded the first permanent white settlement—the Arkansas Post. In 1803 the area was acquired by the U.S. as part of the Louisiana Purchase.

Part of the Territory of Missouri from 1812, the area became a separate entity in 1819 after the first large wave of settlers arrived. The next several decades were marked by the development of the cotton industry and the spread of the Southern plantation system west into Arkansas. Arkansas joined the Confederacy in 1861, but from 1863 the northern part of the state was occupied by Union troops.

Food products are the state's largest employing sector, with lumber and wood products a close second. Arkansas is also a leader in the production of cotton, rice, and soybeans. It also has the country's only active diamond mine; located near Murfreesboro, it is operated as a tourist attraction.

Hot Springs National Park and Buffalo National River in the Ozarks are major state attractions. Blanchard Springs Caverns, the Historic Arkansas Museum at Little Rock, the William J. Clinton Birthplace in Hope, and the Arkansas Folk Center in Mountain View are also of interest.

Famous natives and residents: Maya Angelou, author and poet; Daisy Bates, social reformer; Dee Brown, author; Helen Gurley Brown, editor; Dale Bumpers, governor and senator; Glen Campbell, singer; Hattie Caraway, first elected woman senator; Johnny Cash, singer; Eldridge Cleaver, social activist; William Jefferson Clinton, former president; William Darby, founder of the Darby Rangers; Dizzy Dean, baseball player; Orval Faubus, governor; John Gould Fletcher, poet; J. William Fulbright, former senator; John Grisham, author; Tess Harper, actress; John H. Johnson, publisher; E. Fay Jones, architect; Scott Joplin, composer; Douglas MacArthur, general; Patsy Montana, singer; Isaac C. Parker, judge; Albert Pike, pioneer teacher and lawyer; Mary Steenburgen, actress; Billy Bob Thornton, actor; Sam Walton, founder of Wal-Mart; William C. Warfield, concert singer and actor.

# California

**Capital:** Sacramento
**Governor:** Gray Davis, D (to Jan. 2003)
**Lieut. Governor:** Cruz M. Bustamante, D (to Jan. 2003)
**Senators:** Barbara Boxer, D (to Jan. 2005);
Dianne Feinstein, D (to Jan. 2007)
**Secy. of State:** Bill Jones, R (to Jan. 2003)
**Atty. General:** Bill Lockyer, D (to Jan. 2003)
**Treasurer:**Phil Angelides, D (to Jan. 2003)
**Entered Union (rank):** Sept. 9, 1850 (31)
**Present constitution adopted:** 1879
**Motto:** *Eureka* (I have found it)
**State Symbols: flower,** golden poppy (1903); **tree,**
California redwoods (*Sequoia sempervirens &
Sequoiadendron giganteum*) (1937, 1953); **bird,**
California valley quail (1931); **animal,** California grizzly
bear (1953); **fish,** California golden trout (1947);
**colors,** blue and gold (1951); **song,** "I Love You,
California" (1951);
**Nickname:** Golden State
**Origin of name:** From a book, *Las Sergas de Espland-
ián,* by Garcia Ordóñez de Montalvo, c. 1500
**10 largest cities (2000):** Los Angeles, 3,694,820; San
Diego, 1,223,400; San Jose, 894,943; San Francisco,
776,733; Long Beach, 461,522; Fresno, 427,652;
Sacramento, 407,018; Oakland, 399,484; Santa Ana,
337,977; Anaheim, 328,014
**Land area:** 155,959 sq mi. (403,934 sq km)
**Geographic center:** In Madera Co., 38 mi. E of
Madera
**Number of counties:** 58
**Largest county by population and area:** Los Angeles,
9,637,494 (2001); San Bernardino, 20,062 sq mi.
**National forests:** 18
**State parks and beaches:** 264
**Residents:** Californian
**2001 resident population est.:** 34,501,130
**2000 resident census population (rank):** 33,871,648
(1). **Male:** 16,874,892 (49.8%); **Female:** 16,996,756
(50.2%). **White:** 20,170,059 (59.5%); **Black:**
2,263,882 (6.7%); **American Indian:** 333,346 (1.0%);
**Asian:** 3,697,513 (10.9%); **Other race:** 5,682,241
(16.8%); **Two or more races:** 1,607,646 (4.7%);
**Hispanic/Latino:** 10,966,556 (32.4%). **2000 percent
population 18 and over:** 72.7; **65 and over:** 10.6;
**median age:** 33.3.

Although California was sighted by Spanish navigator Juan Rodríguez Cabrillo in 1542, its first
Spanish mission (at San Diego) was not established
until 1769. California became a U.S. territory in
1847 when Mexico surrendered it to John C. Frémont. On Jan. 24, 1848, James W. Marshall discovered gold at Sutter's Mill, starting the California
Gold Rush and bringing settlers to the state in large
numbers. By1964, California had surpassed New
York to become the most populous state.
Air this may be that more immigrants settle in California than any other state—more than one-third of
the nation's total in 1994. Asians and Pacific Islanders led the influx.

Leading industries include agriculture, manufacturing (transportation equipment, machinery, and
electronic equipment), biotechnology, aerospace-
defense, and tourism. Principal natural resources
include timber, petroleum, cement, and natural gas.

Death Valley, in the southeast, is 282 ft below sea
level, the lowest point in the nation. Mt. Whitney
(14,491 ft) is the highest point in the contiguous 48
states. Lassen Peak is one of two active U.S. volcanoes outside of Alaska and Hawaii; its last eruptions
were recorded in 1917.

Other points of interest include Yosemite National
Park, Disneyland, Hollywood, the Golden Gate
Bridge, Sequoia National Park, San Simeon State
Park, and Point Reyes National Seashore.

**Famous natives and residents:** Gertrude Atherton, author;
David Belasco, playwright and producer; Shirley Temple
Black, actress, ambassador; Dave Brubeck, musician;
Luther Burbank, horticulturalist; Julia Child, chef; Joe
DiMaggio, baseball player; James H. Doolittle, air force
general; Isadora Duncan, dancer; John Frémont, explorer;
Robert Frost, poet; Henry George, economist; Richard
"Pancho" Gonzales, tennis player; George E. Hale,
astronomer; Bret Harte, writer; William Randolph Hearst,
publisher; Sidney Howard, playwright; Collis Potter
Huntington, financier; Helen Hunt Jackson, writer;
Robinson Jeffers, poet; Anthony M. Kennedy, jurist; Jack
London, author; James W. Marshall, first discovered gold;
Aimee Semple McPherson, evangelist; Marilyn Monroe,
actress; John Muir, naturalist; Richard M. Nixon, president;
Isamu Noguchi, sculptor; Frank Norris, novelist; Kathleen
Norris, novelist; George S. Patton, Jr., general; Robert
Redford, actor; Sally K. Ride, astronaut; William Saroyan,
author; Junípero Serra, missionary; Upton Sinclair,
novelist; Leland Stanford, railroad magnate; Lincoln
Steffens, journalist, author; John Steinbeck, author; Adlai
Stevenson, statesman; Johann Sutter, pioneer; Michael
Tilson Thomas, conductor; Earl Warren, jurist.

# Colorado

**Capital:** Denver
**Governor:** Bill Owens, R (to Jan. 2003)
**Lieut. Governor:** Joe Rogers, D (to Jan. 2003)
**Senators:** Wayne A. Allard, R (to Jan. 2003);
Ben Nighthorse Campbell, R (to Jan. 2005)
**Secy. of State:** Donetta Davidson, R (to Jan. 2003)
**Treasurer:** Mike Coffman, R (to Jan. 2003)
**Atty. General:** Ken Salazar, D (to Jan. 2003)
**Organized as territory:** Feb. 28, 1861
**Entered Union (rank):** Aug. 1, 1876 (38)
**Present constitution adopted:** 1876
**Motto:** *Nil sine Numine* (Nothing without Providence)
**State Symbols: flower,** Rocky Mountain columbine
(1899); **tree,** Colorado blue spruce (1939); **bird,** lark
bunting (1931); **animal,** Rocky Mountain bighorn
sheep (1961); **gemstone,** aquamarine (1971); **colors,**
blue and white (1911); **song,** "Where the Columbines
Grow" (1915); **fossil,** stegosaurus (1991);
**Nickname:** Centennial State
**Origin of name:** From the Spanish, "ruddy" or "red"
**10 largest cities (2000):** Denver, 554,636; Colorado
Springs, 360,890; Aurora, 276,393; Lakewood,
144,126; Fort Collins, 118,652; Arvada, 102,153;
Pueblo, 102,121; Westminster, 100,940; Boulder,
94,673; Thornton, 82,384
**Land area:** 103,717 sq mi. (268,627 sq km)
**Geographic center:** In Park Co., 30 mi. NW of
Pikes Peak
**Number of counties:** 63
**Largest county by population and area:** Denver,
554,446 (2001); Las Animas, 4,773 sq mi.
**State forests:** 1 (71,000 ao.)
**State parks:** 44 (160,000 ac.)
**Residents:** Coloradan, Coloradoan
**2001 resident population est.:** 4,417,714
**2000 resident census population (rank):** 4,301,261
(24). **Male:** 2,165,983 (50.4%); **Female:** 2,135,278
(49.6%). **White:** 3,560,005 (82.8%); **Black:** 165,063
(3.8%); **American Indian:** 44,241 (1.0%); **Asian:**
95,213 (2.2%); **Other race:** 309,931 (7.2%); **Two or
more races:** 122,187 (2.8%); **Hispanic/Latino:**
735,601 (17.1%). **2000 percent population 18 and
over:** 74.4; **65 and over:** 9.7; **median age:** 34.3.

First visited by Spanish explorers in the 1500s,
the territory was claimed for Spain by Juan de Uli-
barri in 1706. The U.S. obtained eastern Colorado as

part of the Louisiana Purchase in 1803, the central portion in 1845 with the admission of Texas as a state, and the western part in 1848 as a result of the Mexican War.

Colorado has the highest mean elevation of any state, with more than 1,000 Rocky Mountain peaks over 10,000 ft high and 54 towering above 14,000 ft. Pikes Peak, the most famous of these mountains, was discovered by U.S. Army lieutenant Zebulon M. Pike in 1806.

Once primarily a mining and agricultural state, Colorado's economy is now driven by the service industries, including medical providers and other business and professional services. Colorado's economy also has a strong manufacturing base. The primary manufactures are food products, printing and publishing, machinery, and electrical instruments. The state is also a communications and transportation hub for the Rocky Mountain region.

The farm industry, which is primarily concentrated in livestock, is also an important element of the state's economy. The primary crops in Colorado are corn, hay, and wheat.

Breathtaking scenery and world-class skiing make Colorado a prime tourist destination. The main tourist attractions in the state include Rocky Mountain National Park, Mesa Verde National Park, the Great Sand Dunes and Dinosaur National Monuments, Colorado National Monument, and the Black Canyon of the Gunnison National Monument.

Famous natives and residents: Tim Allen, actor and comedian; William E. Barrett, writer; William Bent, fur trader and pioneer; Charles F. Brannan, lawyer and public official; M. Scott Carpenter, astronaut; Lon Chaney, actor; Mary Coyle Chase, playwright; Jack Dempsey, boxer; John Evans, physician, educator; Douglas Fairbanks, actor; Eugene Fodor, violinist; Gene Fowler, writer; Erick Hawkins, choreographer; Helen Hunt Jackson, novelist and Indian rights activist; Homer Lea, soldier, writer; Ted Mack, TV host; Jaye P. Morgan, singer; Peg Murray, actress; Ouray, Ute Indian chief; Anne Parrish, writer; Barbara Rush, actress; Horace A. Tabor, silver king and lieut. governor; Lowell Thomas, commentator and author; Dalton Trumbo, screenwriter, novelist; Amy Van Dyken, athlete; Byron R. White, jurist; Paul Whiteman, conductor; Don Wilson, announcer.

# Connecticut

**Capital:** Hartford
**Governor:** John G. Rowland, R (to Jan. 2003)
**Lieut. Governor:** M. Jodi Rell, R (to Jan. 2003)
**Senators:** Christopher J. Dodd, D (to Jan. 2005); Joseph I. Lieberman, D (to Jan. 2007)
**Secy. of the State:** Susan Bysiewicz, D (to Jan. 2003)
**Treasurer:** Denise Nappier, D (to Jan. 2003)
**Atty. General:** Richard Blumenthal, D (to Jan. 2003)
**Entered Union (rank):** Jan. 9, 1788 (5)
**Present constitution adopted:** Dec. 30, 1965
**Motto:** *Qui transtulit sustinet* (He who transplanted still sustains)
**State Symbols: flower,** mountain laurel (1907); **tree,** white oak (1947); **animal,** sperm whale (1975); **bird,** American robin (1943); **hero,** Nathan Hale (1985); **heroine,** Prudence Crandall (1995); **insect,** praying mantis (1977); **mineral,** garnet (1977); **song,** "Yankee Doodle" (1978); **ship,** USS *Nautilus* (1983); **shellfish,** eastern oyster (1989); **fossil,** *Eubrontes Giganteus* (1991); **composer,** Charles Edward Ives (1991);
**Nickname:** Constitution State (official, 1959); Nutmeg State
**Origin of name:** From an Indian word (Quinnehtukqut) meaning "beside the long tidal river"
**10 largest cities (2000):** Bridgeport, 139,529; New Haven, 123,626; Hartford, 121,578; Stamford, 117,083; Waterbury, 107,271; Norwalk, 82,951; Danbury, 74,848; New Britain, 71,538; West Hartford, 63,589; Greenwich, 61,101
**Land area:** 4,844 sq mi. (12,545 sq km)
**Geographic center:** In Hartford Co., at East Berlin
**Number of counties:** 8
**Largest county by population and area:** Fairfield, 885,368 (2001); Litchfield, 920 sq mi.
**State forests:** 30 (149,352 ac.)
**State parks:** 93 (32,960 ac.)
**Residents:** Connecticuter; Nutmegger
**2001 resident population est.:** 3,425,074
**2000 resident census population (rank):** 3,405,565 (29). **Male:** 1,649,319 (48.4%); **Female:** 1,756,246 (51.6%). **White:** 2,780,355 (81.6%); **Black:** 309,843 (9.1%); **American Indian:** 9,639 (0.3%); **Asian:** 82,313 (2.4%); **Other race:** 147,201 (4.3%); **Two or more races:** 74,848 (2.2%); **Hispanic/Latino:** 320,323 (9.4%). **2000 percent population 18 and over:** 75.3; **65 and over:** 13.8; **median age:** 37.4.

The Dutch navigator, Adriaen Block, was the first European of record to explore the area, sailing up the Connecticut River in 1614. In 1633, Dutch colonists built a fort and trading post near present-day Hartford but soon lost control to English Puritans from the Massachusetts Bay Colony. English settlements established in the 1630s at Windsor, Wethersfield, and Hartford united in 1639 to form the Connecticut Colony under the *Fundamental Orders*, the first modern constitution.

Connecticut played a prominent role in the Revolutionary War, serving as the Continental Army's major supplier. Sometimes called the "Arsenal of the Nation," the state became one of the most industrialized in the nation.

Today, Connecticut factories produce weapons, sewing machines, jet engines, helicopters, motors, hardware and tools, cutlery, clocks, locks, silverware, and submarines. Hartford has the oldest U.S. newspaper still being published—the *Hartford Courant*, established 1764—and is the insurance capital of the nation.

Connecticut leads New England in the production of eggs, pears, peaches, and mushrooms, and its oyster crop is the nation's second largest. Poultry and dairy products also account for a large portion of farm income.

Connecticut is a popular resort area with its 250-mile Long Island Sound shoreline and many inland lakes. Among the major points of interest are Yale University's Gallery of Fine Arts and Peabody Museum. Other famous museums include the P. T. Barnum, Winchester Gun, and American Clock and Watch. The town of Mystic features a recreated 19th-century New England seaport and the Mystic Marinelife Aquarium.

Famous natives and residents: Dean Acheson, statesman; Ethan Allan, American Revolutionary soldier; Benedict Arnold, American Revolutionary general; P. T. Barnum, showman; Henry Ward Beecher, clergyman; John Brown, abolitionist; Prudence Crandall, educator and reformer; Oliver Ellsworth, jurist; Eileen Farrell, soprano; Charles Goodyear, inventor; Nathan Hale, American Revolutionary officer; Dorothy Hamill, ice skater; Katharine Hepburn, actress; Charles Ives, composer; Edwin H. Land, inventor; John Pierpont Morgan, financier; Frederick Law Olmsted, landscape designer; Rosa Ponselle, soprano; Adam Clayton Powell, Jr., congressman; Benjamin Spock, pediatrician; Harriet Beecher Stowe, author; Mark Twain, author; Morris R. Waite, jurist; Noah Webster, lexicographer.

# Delaware

**Capital:** Dover
**Governor:** Ruth Ann Minner, D (to Jan. 2005)
**Lieut. Governor:** John C. Carney, Jr., D (to Jan. 2005)
**Senators:** Joseph R. Biden, Jr., D (to Jan. 2003);
   Thomas R. Carper, D (to Jan. 2007)
**Secy. of State:** Harriet Smith Windsor
**Treasurer:** Jack Markell, D (to Jan. 2003)
**Atty. General:** M. Jane Brady, R (to Jan. 2003)
**Entered Union (rank):** Dec. 7, 1787 (1)
**Present constitution adopted:** 1897
**Motto:** Liberty and independence
**State Symbols: colors,** colonial blue and buff; **flower,**
   peach blossom (1895); **tree,** American holly (1939);
   **bird,** blue hen chicken (1939); **insect,** ladybug (1974);
   **butterfly,** tiger swallowtail (1999); **fish,** weakfish,
   *cynoscion regalis* (1981); **song,** "Our Delaware";
   **beverage,** milk; **fossil,** belemnite;
**Nicknames:** Diamond State; First State; Small Wonder
**Origin of name:** From Delaware River and Bay; named
   in turn for Sir Thomas West, Baron De La Warr
**10 largest cities (2000):** Wilmington, 72,664; Dover,
   32,135; Newark, 28,547; Milford, 6,732; Seaford,
   6,699; Middletown, 6,161; Elsmere, 5,800; Smyrna,
   5,679; New Castle, 4,862; Georgetown, 4,643
**Land area:** 1,954 sq mi. (5,161 sq km)
**Geographic center:** In Kent Co., 11 mi. S of Dover
**Number of counties:** 3
**Largest county by population and area:** New Castle,
   505,829 (2001); Sussex, 938 sq mi.
**State forests:** 3 (over 15,000 ac.)
**State parks:** 14
**Residents:** Delawarean
**2001 resident population est.:** 796,165
**2000 resident census population (rank):** 783,600 (45).
   **Male:** 380,541 (48.6%); **Female:** 403,059 (51.4%).
   **White:** 584,773 (74.6%); **Black:** 150,666 (19.2%);
   **American Indian:** 2,731 (0.3%); **Asian:** 16,259 (2.1%);
   **Other race:** 15,855 (2.0%); **Two or more races:**
   13,033 (1.7%); **Hispanic/Latino:** 37,277 (4.8%). **2000
   percent population 18 and over:** 75.2; **65 and over:**
   13.0; **median age:** 36.0.

Henry Hudson, sailing under the Dutch flag, is credited with Delaware's discovery in 1609. The following year, Capt. Samuel Argall of Virginia named Delaware for his colony's governor, Thomas West, Baron De La Warr. An attempted Dutch settlement failed in 1631. Swedish colonization began at Fort Christina (now Wilmington) in 1638, but New Sweden fell to Dutch forces led by New Netherlands' governor Peter Stuyvesant in 1655.

England took over the area in 1664, and it was transferred to William Penn as the lower Three Counties in 1682. Semiautonomous after 1704, Delaware fought as a separate state in the American Revolution and became the first state to ratify the Constitution in 1787.

During the Civil War, although a slave state, Delaware did not secede from the Union.

In 1802, Eleuthère Irénée du Pont established a gunpowder mill near Wilmington that laid the foundation for Delaware's huge chemical industry. Delaware's manufactured products now also include vulcanized fiber, textiles, paper, medical supplies, metal products, machinery, machine tools, and automobiles.

Delaware also grows a great variety of fruits and vegetables and is a U.S. pioneer in the food-canning industry. Corn, soybeans, potatoes, and hay are important crops. Delaware's broiler-chicken farms supply the big Eastern markets, and fishing and dairy products are other important industries.

Points of interest include the Fort Christina Monument, Hagley Museum, Holy Trinity Church (erected in 1698, the oldest Protestant church in the United States still in use), and Winterthur Museum, in and near Wilmington; central New Castle, an almost unchanged late 18th-century capital; and the Delaware Museum of Natural History.

Popular recreation areas include Cape Henlopen, Delaware Seashore, Trap Pond State Park, and Rehoboth Beach.

**Famous natives and residents:** Richard Allen, founder of the African Methodist Episcopal Church; Valerie Bertinelli, actress; Robert Montgomery Bird, writer and artist; Henry S. Canby, editor and author; Annie Jump Cannon, astronomer; Elizabeth Margaret Chandler, author; Felix Darley, artist; John Dickinson, statesman; E. I. du Pont, industrialist; Oliver Evans, inventor; Thomas Garrett, abolitionist; Henry Heimlich, surgeon, inventor; William Julius "Judy" Johnson, baseball player; J. P. Marquand, novelist; Howard Pyle, artist and author; George Read, jurist, signer of Declaration of Independence; Jay Saunders Redding, educator and author; Caesar Rodney, patriot, signer of Declaration of Independence; Frank Stephens, sculptor; Estelle Taylor, actress; George Alfred Townsend, journalist and author.

# District of Columbia

*See* Washington, D.C., listing in U.S. Cities.

# Florida

**Capital:** Tallahassee
**Governor:** Jeb Bush, R (to Jan. 2003)
**Lieut. Governor:** Frank Brogan, R (to Jan. 2003)
**Senators:** Bob Graham, D (to Jan. 2005); Bill Nelson, D
   (to Jan. 2007)
**Secy. of State:** Katherine Harris, R (to Jan. 2003)
**Atty. General:** Bob Butterworth, D (to Jan. 2003)
**Organized as territory:** March 30, 1821
**Entered Union (rank):** March 3, 1845 (27)
**Present constitution adopted:** 1969
**Motto:** In God we trust (1868)
**State Symbols: flower,** orange blossom (1909); **bird,**
   mockingbird (1927); **song,** "Suwannee River" (1935);
**Nickname:** Sunshine State (1970)
**Origin of name:** From the Spanish, meaning "feast of
   flowers" (Easter)
**10 largest cities (2000):** Jacksonville, 735,617; Miami,
   362,470; Tampa, 303,447; St. Petersburg, 248,232;
   Hialeah, 226,419; Orlando, 185,951; Fort Lauderdale,
   152,397; Tallahassee, 150,624; Hollywood, 139,357;
   Pembroke Pines, 137,427
**Land area:** 53,927 sq mi. (139,671 sq km)
**Geographic center:** In Hernando Co., 12 mi. NNW of
   Brooksville
**Number of counties:** 67
**Largest county by population** and area: Palm Beach, 1,131,184 (2001); Palm Beach, 2,034 sq mi.
**State forests:** 31 (more than 890,000 ac.)
**State parks:** 151 (523,920 ac.)
**Residents:** Floridian, Floridan
**2001 resident population est.:** 16,396,515
**2000 resident census population (rank):** 15,982,378
   (4). **Male:** 7,797,715 (48.8%); **Female:** 8,184,663
   (51.2%). **White:** 12,465,029 (78.0%); **Black:**
   2,335,505 (14.6%); **American Indian:** 53,541 (0.3%);
   **Asian:** 266,256 (1.7%); **Other race:** 477,107 (3.0%);
   **Two or more races:** 376,315 (2.4%); **Hispanic/
   Latino:** 2,682,715 (16.8%). **2000 percent population
   18 and over:** 77.2; **65 and over:** 17.6; **median age:**
   38.7.

In 1513, Ponce de León, seeking the mythical "Fountain of Youth," discovered and named Florida, claiming it for Spain. Later, Florida would be held at different times by Spain and England until Spain finally sold it to the United States in 1819. (Incidentally, France established a colony named Fort Caroline in 1564 in the state that was to become Florida.)

Florida's history in the early 19th century was marked by wars with the Seminole Indians, which did not end until 1842.

Florida's economy rests on a solid base of tourism, manufacturing, and agriculture. Leading the manufacturing sector are electrical equipment and electronics, printing and publishing, transportation equipment, food processing, and machinery. Oranges, grapefruit, and other citrus fruits lead Florida's agricultural products list, followed by potatoes, melons, strawberries, sugar cane, peanuts, dairy products, and cattle.

Major tourist attractions are Miami Beach, Palm Beach, St. Augustine (founded in 1565, thus the oldest permanent city in the U.S.), Daytona Beach, and Fort Lauderdale on the East Coast; Sarasota, Tampa, and St. Petersburg on the West Coast; and Key West off the southern tip of Florida. The Orlando area, where Disney World is located on a 27,000-acre site, is Florida's most popular tourist destination. Also drawing many visitors are the NASA Kennedy Space Center's Spaceport USA, Everglades National Park, and the Epcot Center.

Famous natives and residents: Julian "Cannonball" Adderley, jazz saxophonist; Pat Boone, singer; Fernando Bujones, ballet dancer; Steve Carlton, baseball player; Faye Dunaway, actress; Stepin Fetchit (Lincoln Theodore Perry), comedian; Lue Gim Gong, horticulturist; Dwight Gooden, baseball player; Zora Neale Hurston, writer; Daniel James, air force general; James Weldon Johnson, author and educator; Frances Langford, singer; Butterfly McQueen, actress; Jim Morrison, singer; Osceola, Seminole Indian leader; Sidney Poitier, actor; A. Philip Randolph, labor leader; Marjorie Kinnan Rawlings, author; Burt Reynolds, actor; Charles and John Ringling, circus entrepreneurs; Joseph W. Stilwell, army general; Norman E. Thargard, astronaut; Clarence Thomas, jurist; Ben Vereen, actor.

# Georgia

**Capital:** Atlanta
**Governor:** Roy E. Barnes, D (to Jan. 2003)
**Lieut. Governor:** Mark Taylor, D (to Jan. 2003)
**Senators:** Max Cleland, D (to Jan. 2003); Zell Miller, D (to Jan. 2005)
**Secy. of State:** Cathy Cox, D (to Jan. 2003)
**Insurance Commissioner:** John Oxendine, R (to Jan. 2003)
**Atty. General:** Thurbert Baker, D (to Jan. 2003)
**Entered Union (rank):** Jan. 2, 1788 (4)
**Present constitution adopted:** 1977
**Motto:** Wisdom, justice, and moderation
**State Symbols: flower,** Cherokee rose (1916); **tree,** live oak (1937); **bird,** brown thrasher (1935); **song,** "Georgia on My Mind" (1922);
**Nicknames:** Peach State, Empire State of the South
**Origin of name:** In honor of George II of England
**10 largest cities (2000):** Atlanta, 416,474; Augusta-Richmond County[1], 199,775; Columbus[1], 186,291; Savannah, 131,510; Athens-Clarke County[1], 101,489; Macon, 97,255; Roswell, 79,334; Albany, 76,939; Marietta, 58,748; Warner Robins, 48,804
**Land area:** 57,906 sq mi. (149,977 sq km)
**Geographic center:** In Twiggs Co., 18 mi. SE of Macon
**Number of counties:** 159
**Largest county by population and area:** Fulton, 816,638 (2001); Ware, 903 sq mi.
**State forests:** 25,258,000 ac. (67% of total state area)
**State parks:** 53 (42,600 ac.)

**Residents:** Georgian
**2001 resident population est.:** 8,383,915
**2000 resident census population (rank):** 8,186,453 (10). **Male:** 4,027,113 (49.2%); **Female:** 4,159,340 (50.8%). **White:** 5,327,281 (65.1%); **Black:** 2,349,542 (28.7%); **American Indian:** 21,737 (0.3%); **Asian:** 173,170 (2.1%); **Other race:** 196,289 (2.4%); **Two or more races:** 114,188 (1.4%); **Hispanic/Latino:** 435,227 (5.3%). **2000 percent population 18 and over:** 73.5; **65 and over:** 9.6; **median age:** 33.4.

1. The city is part of a consolidated city-county government; the city and county are coextensive.

Hernando de Soto, the Spanish explorer, first traveled parts of Georgia in 1540. British claims later conflicted with those of Spain. After obtaining a royal charter, Gen. James Oglethorpe established the first permanent settlement in Georgia in 1733 as a refuge for English debtors. In 1742, Oglethorpe defeated Spanish invaders in the Battle of Bloody Marsh.

A Confederate stronghold, Georgia was the scene of extensive military action during the Civil War. Union general William T. Sherman burned Atlanta and destroyed a 60-mile-wide path to the coast, where he captured Savannah in 1864.

The largest state east of the Mississippi, Georgia is typical of the changing South with an ever-increasing industrial development. Atlanta, largest city in the state, is the communications and transportation center for the Southeast and the area's chief distributor of goods.

Georgia leads the nation in the production of paper and board, tufted textile products, and processed chicken. Other major manufactured products are transportation equipment, food products, apparel, and chemicals.

Important agricultural products are corn, cotton, tobacco, soybeans, eggs, and peaches. Georgia produces twice as many peanuts as the next leading state. From its vast stands of pine come more than half of the world's resins and turpentine and 74.4 percent of the U.S. supply. Georgia is a leader in the production of marble, kaolin, barite, and bauxite.

Principal tourist attractions in Georgia include the Okefenokee National Wildlife Refuge, Andersonville Prison Park and National Cemetery, Chickamauga and Chattanooga National Military Park, the Little White House at Warm Springs where Pres. Franklin D. Roosevelt died in 1945, Sea Island, the enormous Confederate Memorial at Stone Mountain, Kennesaw Mountain National Battlefield Park, and Cumberland Island National Seashore.

Famous natives and residents: Conrad Aiken, poet; James Bowie, soldier; James Brown, singer; Jim Brown, actor and athlete; Erskine Caldwell, writer; James E. Carter, former president; Ray Charles, singer; Lucius D. Clay, banker and general; Ty Cobb, baseball player; Ossie Davis, actor and writer; James Dickey, poet; Melvyn Douglas, actor; Rebecca Latimer Felton, first appointed woman U.S. senator; Roosevelt Grier, entertainer and former athlete; Oliver Hardy, comedian; Joel Chandler Harris, journalist and author; Larry Holmes, boxer; Miriam Hopkins, actress; Alan Jackson, singer; Harry James, trumpeter; Jasper Johns, painter and sculptor; Bobby Jones, golfer; Stacy Keach, actor; DeForest Kelley, actor; Martin Luther King, Jr., civil rights leader; Gladys Knight, singer; Joseph R. Lamar, jurist; Little Richard, singer; Juliette Gordon Low, U.S. Girl Scouts founder; Carson McCullers, novelist; Johnny Mercer, songwriter; Margaret Mitchell, novelist; Elijah Muhammad, religious leader; Jessye Norman, soprano; Otis Redding, singer; Burt Reynolds, actor; Jackie Robinson, baseball player; Dean Rusk, former secretary of state; Nipsey Russell, comedian; Travis Tritt, singer; Alice Walker, author; Joanne Woodward, actress. Trisha Yearwood, singer;

# Hawaii

**Capital:** Honolulu (on Oahu)
**Governor:** Benjamin Cayetano, D (to Dec. 2002)
**Lieut. Governor:** Mazie Hirono, D
**Senators:** Daniel K. Akaka, D (to Jan. 2007); Daniel K. Inouye, D (to Jan. 2005)
**Comptroller:** Wayne Kimura (to Dec. 2002)
**Atty. General:** Earl Anzai (to Dec. 2002)
**Organized as territory:** 1900
**Entered Union (rank):** Aug. 21, 1959 (50)
**Motto:** *Ua Mau Ke Ea O Ka Aina I Ka Pono* (The life of the land is perpetuated in righteousness)
**State Symbols: flower,** hibiscus (yellow) (1988); **song,** "Hawaii Ponoi" (1967); **bird,** nene (Hawaiian goose) (1957); **tree,** kukui (candlenut) (1959);
**Nickname:** Aloha State (1959)
**Origin of name:** Uncertain. The islands may have been named by Hawaii Loa, their traditional discoverer. Or they may have been named after Hawaii or Hawaiki, the traditional home of the Polynesians.
**10 largest cities[1] (2000):** Honolulu, 371,657; Hilo, 40,759; Kailua, 36,513; Kaneohe, 34,970; Waipahu, 33,108; Pearl City, 30,976; Waimalu, 29,371; Mililani Town, 28,608; Kahului, 20,146; Kihei, 16,749
**Land area:** 6,423 sq mi. (16,637 sq km)
**Geographic center:** Between islands of Hawaii and Maui
**Number of counties:** 5 (Kalawao non-functioning)
**Largest county by population and area:** Honolulu, 881,295 (2001); Hawaii, 4,028 sq mi.
**State parks and historic sites:** 69
**Residents:** Hawaiian, also kamaaina (native-born nonethnic Hawaiian), malihini (newcomer)
**2001 resident population est.:** 1,224,398
**2000 resident census population (rank):** 1,211,537 (42). **Male:** 608,671 (50.2%); **Female:** 602,866 (49.8%). **White:** 294,102 (24.3%); **Black:** 22,003 (1.8%); **American Indian:** 3,535 (0.3%); **Asian:** 503,868 (41.6%); **Native Hawaiian and Other Pacific Islander:** 113,539 (9.4%); **Other race:** 15,147 (1.3%); **Two or more races:** 259,343 (21.4%); **Hispanic/ Latino:** 87,699 (7.2%). **2000 percent population 18 and over:** 75.6; **65 and over:** 13.3; **median age:** 36.2.

1. Census Designated Places.

First settled by Polynesians sailing from other Pacific islands between A.D. 300 and 600, Hawaii was visited in 1778 by British captain James Cook, who called the group the Sandwich Islands.

Hawaii was a native kingdom throughout most of the 19th century, when the expansion of the sugar industry (pineapple came after 1898) meant increasing U.S. business and political involvement. In 1893, Queen Liliuokalani was deposed, and a year later the Republic of Hawaii was established with Sanford B. Dole as president. Following annexation (1898), Hawaii became a U.S. territory in 1900.

The Japanese attack on the naval base at Pearl Harbor on Dec. 7, 1941, was directly responsible for U.S. entry into World War II.

Hawaii, 2,397 mi west-southwest of San Francisco, is a 1,523-mile chain of islets and eight main islands—Hawaii, Kahoolawe, Maui, Lanai, Molokai, Oahu, Kauai, and Niihau. The Northwestern Hawaiian Islands, other than Midway, are administratively part of Hawaii.

The temperature is mild, and cane sugar, pineapple, and flowers and nursery products are the chief products. Hawaii also grows coffee beans, bananas, and macadamia nuts. The tourist business is Hawaii's largest source of outside income.

Hawaii's highest peak is Mauna Kea (13,796 ft). Mauna Loa (13,679 ft) is the largest volcanic mountain in the world by volume.

Among the major points of interest are Hawaii Volcanoes National Park (Hawaii), Haleakala National Park (Maui), Puuhonua o Honaunau National Historical Park (Hawaii), Polynesian Cultural Center (Oahu), the USS *Arizona* and USS *Missouri* Memorial at Pearl Harbor, The National Memorial Cemetery of the Pacific (Oahu), and Iolani Palace (the only royal palace in the U.S.), Bishop Museum, and Waikiki Beach (all in Honolulu).

Famous natives and residents: Salevaa Atisanoe (Konishiki), sumo wrestler; George Ariyoshi, first Japanese-American elected governor; Angela Perez Baraquio, Miss America (2001); Tia Carrere, singer, actress; Steve Case, business executive; Father Damien, priest; Hiram L. Fong, first Chinese-American senator; Don Ho, entertainer; Kaahumanu, Hawaiian queen; Duke Paoa Kahanamoku, Olympic swimming champion; Kamehameha I, first Hawaiian king; Kamehameha V, last of the dynasty; Liliuokalani, queen, last Hawaiian monarch; Bette Midler, singer; Ellison Onizuka, astronaut; Chad Rowan (Akebono), sumo wrestler; Carolyn Suzanne Sapp, Miss America (1991); John Waihee, first Hawaiian elected governor.

# Idaho

**Capital:** Boise
**Governor:** Dirk Kempthorne, R (to Jan. 2003)
**Lieut. Governor:** Jack T. Riggs, MD, R (to Jan. 2003)
**Senators:** Larry E. Craig, R (to Jan. 2003); Mike Crapo, R (to Jan. 2005)
**Secy. of State:** Pete T. Cenarrusa, R (to Jan. 2003)
**Atty. General:** Alan G. Lance, R (to Jan. 2003)
**Treasurer:** Ron G. Crane, R (to Jan. 2003)
**Organized as territory:** March 3, 1863
**Entered Union (rank):** July 3, 1890 (43)
**Present constitution adopted:** 1890
**Motto:** *Esto perpetua* (It is forever)
**State Symbols: flower,** syringa (1931); **tree,** white pine (1935); **bird,** mountain bluebird (1931); **horse,** Appaloosa (1975); **gem,** star garnet (1967); **song,** "Here We Have Idaho"; **folk dance,** square dance; **fish,** cutthroat trout (1990); **fossil,** Hagerman horse fossil (1988);
**Nickname:** Gem State
**Origin of name:** Though popularly believed to be an Indian word, it is an invented name whose meaning is unknown.
**10 largest cities (2000):** Boise, 185,787; Nampa, 51,867; Pocatello, 51,466; Idaho Falls, 50,730; Meridian, 34,919; Coeur d'Alene, 34,514; Twin Falls, 34,469; Lewiston, 30,904; Caldwell, 25,967; Moscow, 21,291
**Land area:** 82,747 sq mi. (214,315 sq km)
**Geographic center:** In Custer Co. at Custer, SW of Challis
**Number of counties:** 44, plus small part of Yellowstone National Park
**Largest county by population and area:** Ada, 012,037 (2001); Idaho, 8,485 sq mi.
**State forests:** 881,000 ac.
**State parks:** 27 (43,000+ ac.)
**Residents:** Idahoan
**2001 resident population est.:** 1,321,006
**2000 resident census population (rank):** 1,293,953 (39). **Male:** 648,660 (50.1%); **Female:** 645,293 (49.9%). **White:** 1,177,304 (91.0%); **Black:** 5,456 (0.4%); **American Indian:** 17,645 (1.4%); **Asian:** 11,889 (0.9%); **Other race:** 54,742 (4.2%); **Two or more races:** 25,609 (2.0%); **Hispanic/Latino:** 101,690 (7.9%). **2000 percent population 18 and over:** 71.5; **65 and over:** 11.3; **median age:** 33.2.

After its acquisition by the U.S. as part of the Louisiana Purchase in 1803, the region was explored by Meriwether Lewis and William Clark in 1805–1806. Northwest boundary disputes with Great Britain were settled by the Oregon Treaty in 1846, and the first permanent U.S. settlement in Idaho was established by the Mormons at Franklin in 1860.

After gold was discovered at Orofino Creek in 1860, prospectors swarmed into the territory, but they left little more than a number of ghost towns.

In the 1870s, growing white occupation of Indian lands led to a series of battles between U.S. forces and the Nez Percé, Bannock, and Sheepeater tribes.

Mining and lumbering have been important for years. Idaho ranks high among the states in silver, antimony, lead, cobalt, garnet, phosphate rock, vanadium, zinc, and mercury.

Agriculture is a major industry: The state produces about one fourth of the nation's potato crop, as well as wheat, apples, corn, barley, sugar beets, and hops.

The 1990s saw a remarkable growth in the high technology industries, concentrated in the metropolitan Boise area.

With the growth of winter sports, tourism now outranks other industries in revenue. Idaho's many streams and lakes provide fishing, camping, and boating sites. The nation's largest elk herds draw hunters from all over the world, and the famed Sun Valley resort attracts thousands of visitors to its swimming, golfing, and skiing facilities.

Points of interest are the Craters of the Moon National Monument; Nez Percé National Historic Park, which includes many sites visited by Lewis and Clark; and the State Historical Museum in Boise. Other attractions are the Snake River Birds of Prey National Conservation Area south of Boise, Hells Canyon on the Idaho-Oregon border, and the Sawtooth National Recreation Area in south-central Idaho.

Famous natives and residents: Joe Albertson, grocery chain founder; Cecil Andrus, governor; T. H. Bell, educator; Ezra Taft Benson, secretary of Agriculture, pres. LDS church, marketing specialist; William E. Borah, senator; Gutzon Borglum, Mt. Rushmore sculptor; Carol R. Brink, author; Frank F. Church, senator; Fred Dubois, senator; Vardis Fisher, novelist; Lawrence H. Gipson, historian; Ernest Hemingway, author; Mariel Hemingway, actress; Chief Joseph, Nez Percé chief; Harmon Killebrew, baseball player; Jerry Kramer, football player, author; Ezra Pound, poet; Sacagawea, Shoshonean guide; J. R. Simplot, industrialist; Robert E. Smylie, political leader; Henry Spalding, missionary; Frank Steunenberg, governor; Picabo Street, skier; David Tompson, founded first trading post; Lana Turner, actress.

## Illinois

**Capital:** Springfield
**Governor:** George H. Ryan, R (to Jan. 2003)
**Lieut. Governor:** Corinne G. Wood, R (to Jan. 2003)
**Senators:** Richard J. Durbin, D (to Jan. 2003); Peter G. Fitzgerald, R (to Jan. 2005)
**Atty. General:** Jim Ryan, R (to Jan. 2003)
**Secy. of State:** Jesse White, D (to Jan. 2003)
**Treasurer:** Judith Barr Topinka, R (to Jan. 2003)
**Organized as territory:** Feb. 3, 1809
**Entered Union (rank):** Dec. 3, 1818 (21)
**Present constitution adopted:** 1970
**Motto:** State sovereignty, national union
**State Symbols: flower,** violet (1908); **tree,** white oak (1973); **bird,** cardinal (1929); **animal,** white-tailed deer

(1982); **fish,** bluegill (1987); **insect,** monarch butterfly (1975); **song,** "Illinois" (1925); **mineral,** fluorite (1965);
**Nickname:** Prairie State
**Origin of name:** Algonquin for "tribe of superior men"
**10 largest cities (2000):** Chicago, 2,896,016; Rockford, 150,115; Aurora, 142,990; Naperville, 128,358; Peoria, 112,936; Springfield, 111,454; Joliet, 106,221; Elgin, 94,487; Waukegan, 87,901; Cicero, 85,616
**Land area:** 55,584 sq mi. (143,963 sq km)
**Geographic center:** In Logan Co., 28 mi. NE of Springfield
**Number of counties:** 102
**Largest county by population and area:** Cook, 5,350,269 (2001); McLean, 1,184 sq mi.
**Public use areas:** 186 (275,000 ac.), incl. state parks, memorials, forests and conservation areas
**Residents:** Illinoisan
**2001 resident population est.:** 12,482,301
**2000 resident census population (rank):** 12,419,293 (5). **Male:** 6,080,336 (49.0%); **Female:** 6,338,957 (51.0%). **White:** 9,125,471 (73.5%); **Black:** 1,876,875 (15.1%); **American Indian:** 31,006 (0.2%); **Asian:** 423,603 (3.4%); **Other race:** 722,712 (5.8%); **Two or more races:** 235,016 (1.9%); **Hispanic/Latino:** 1,530,262 (12.3%). **2000 percent population 18 and over:** 73.9; **65 and over:** 12.1; **median age:** 34.7.

French explorers Jacques Marquette and Louis Joliet, in 1673, were the first Europeans of record to visit the region. In 1699 French settlers established the first permanent settlement at Cahokia, near present-day East St. Louis. Great Britain obtained the region at the end of the French and Indian Wars in 1763. The area figured prominently in frontier struggles during the Revolutionary War and in Indian wars during the early 19th century.

Significant episodes in the state's early history include the influx of settlers following the opening of the Erie Canal in 1825; the Black Hawk War, which virtually ended the Indian troubles in the area; and the rise of Abraham Lincoln from farm laborer to president.

Today, Illinois stands high in manufacturing, coal mining, agriculture, and oil production. The state's manufactures include food and agricultural products, transportation equipment, chemicals, industrial machinery, and computer equipment. The sprawling Chicago district (including a slice of Indiana) is a great iron and steel producer, meat packer, grain exchange, and railroad center. Chicago is also famous as a Great Lakes port.

Illinois is a leading producer of soybeans, corn, and hogs. Other agricultural commodities include cattle, wheat, oats, sorghum, and hay.

Central Illinois is noted for shrines and memorials associated with the life of Abraham Lincoln. In Springfield are the Lincoln Home, the Lincoln Tomb, and the restored Old State Capitol. Other points of interest are the home of Mormon leader Joseph Smith in Nauvoo and, in Chicago: the Art Institute, Field Museum, Museum of Science and Industry, Shedd Aquarium, Adler Planetarium, Merchandise Mart, and Chicago Portage National Historic Site.

Famous natives and residents: Franklin Pierce Adams, author; Jane Addams, social worker; Mary Astor, actress; Jack Benny, comedian; Black Hawk, Sauk Indian chief; Harry A. Blackmun, jurist; Ray Bradbury, author; William Jennings Bryan, orator and politician; Edgar Rice Burroughs, novelist; Gower Champion, choreographer; John Chancellor, TV commentator; Raymond Chandler, author; Jimmy Connors, tennis champion; James Gould Cozzens, novelist; Richard J. Daley, mayor of Chicago; Miles Davis, musician; Peter DeVries, novelist; Everett Dirksen, senator; Walt Disney, film animator and producer; John Dos Passos, author; James T. Farrell, novelist; Dan Fogelberg, singer and songwriter; Betty Friedan, feminist; Benny Goodman, musician; John Gunther, author; Ernest Hemingway, author; Charlton Heston, actor; Wild Bill Hickok, scout; William Holden, actor; Rock Hudson, actor; Burl Ives, singer; James Jones, novelist; John Jones, civil rights leader; Quincy Jones, composer; Keokuk (Watchful Fox), chief of the Sac and Fox Indians; Walter Kerr, drama critic; Archibald MacLeish, poet; David Mamet, playwright; Robert A. Millikan, physicist; Sherrill Milnes, baritone; Bill Murray, actor; Bob Newhart, actor and comedian; William S. Paley, broadcasting executive; Drew Pearson, columnist; Richard Pryor, comedian and actor; Ronald Reagan, former president and actor; Carl Sandburg, poet; Sam Shepard, playwright; William L. Shirer, author and historian; John Paul Stevens, jurist; McLean Stevenson, actor; Preston Sturges, director; Gloria Swanson, actress; Carl Van Doren, writer and educator; Melvin Van Peebles, playwright; Irving Wallace, novelist; Alfred Wallenstein, conductor; Raquel Welch, actress; Oprah Winfrey, television talk show host and actress; Florenz Ziegfield, theatrical producer.

# Indiana

**Capital:** Indianapolis
**Governor:** Frank O'Bannon, D (to Jan. 2005)
**Lieut. Governor:** Joseph E. Kernan, D (to Jan. 2005)
**Senators:** Evan Bayh, D (to Jan. 2005); Richard G. Lugar, R (to Jan. 2007)
**Secy. of State:** Sue Anne Gilroy, R (to Dec. 2002)
**Treasurer:** Tim Berry, R (to Feb. 2003)
**Atty. General:** Stephen Carter, R (to Jan. 2005)
**Organized as territory:** May 7, 1800
**Entered Union (rank):** Dec. 11, 1816 (19)
**Present constitution adopted:** 1851
**Motto:** The Crossroads of America
**State Symbols: flower,** peony (1957); **tree,** tulip tree (1931); **bird,** cardinal (1933); **song,** "On the Banks of the Wabash, Far Away" (1913); **river,** Wabash; **stone,** limestone;
**Official language:** English
**Nickname:** Hoosier State
**Origin of name:** Meaning "land of Indians"
**10 largest cities (2000):** Indianapolis, 791,926; Fort Wayne, 205,727; Evansville, 121,582; South Bend, 107,789; Gary, 102,746; Hammond, 83,048; Bloomington, 69,291; Muncie, 67,430; Anderson, 59,734; Terre Haute, 59,614
**Land area:** 35,867 sq mi. (92,896 sq km)
**Geographic center:** In Boone Co., 14 mi. NNW of Indianapolis
**Number of counties:** 92
**Largest county by population and area:** Marion, 856,938 (2001); Allen, 657 sq mi.
**State parks:** 23 (56,409 ac.)
**State historic sites:** 17 (2,007 ac.)
**Residents:** Indianan, Indianian, Hoosier
**2001 resident population est.:** 6,114,745
**2000 resident census population (rank):** 6,080,485 (14). **Male:** 3,000,471 (49.4%); **Female:** 3,020,022 (87.5%); **Black:** 510,034 (8.4%); **American Indian:** 15,815 (0.3%); **Asian:** 59,126 (1.0%); **Other race:** 97,811 (1.6%); **Two or more races:** 75,672 (1.2%); **Hispanic/Latino:** 214,536 (3.5%). **2000 percent population 18 and over:** 74.1; **65 and over:** 12.4; **median age:** 35.2.

First explored for France by Robert Cavelier, Sieur de la Salle, in 1679–1680, the region figured importantly in the Franco-British struggle for North America that culminated with British victory in 1763. George Rogers Clark led American forces against the British in the area during the Revolutionary War and, prior to becoming a state, Indiana was the scene of frequent Indian uprisings until the victories of Gen. Anthony Wayne at Fallen Timbers in 1794 and Gen. William Henry Harrison at Tippecanoe in 1811.

During the 19th century, Indiana was the site of several experimental communities, including those established by George Rapp and Robert Owen at New Harmony.

Indiana's 41-mile Lake Michigan waterfront—one of the world's great industrial centers—turns out iron, steel, and oil products. Products include automobile parts and accessories, mobile homes and recreational vehicles, truck and bus bodies, aircraft engines, farm machinery, and fabricated structural steel. Wood office furniture and pharmaceuticals are also manufactured.

The state is a leader in agriculture with corn the principal crop. Hogs, soybeans, wheat, oats, rye, tomatoes, onions, and poultry also contribute heavily to Indiana's agricultural output.

Much of the building limestone used in the U.S. is quarried in Indiana, which is also a large producer of coal. Other mineral commodities include crushed stone, cement, and sand and gravel.

Wyandotte Cave, one of the largest in the U.S., is located in Crawford County in southern Indiana, and West Baden and French Lick are well known for their mineral springs. Other attractions include Indiana Dunes National Lakeshore, Indianapolis Motor Speedway, Lincoln Boyhood National Memorial, and the George Rogers Clark National Historical Park.

Famous natives and residents: George Ade, humorist; Leon Ames, actor; Anne Baxter, actress; Albert J. Beveridge, political leader; Larry Bird, basketball player; Bill Blass, fashion designer; Frank Borman, astronaut; Hoagy Carmichael, songwriter; James Dean, actor; Eugene V. Debs, Socialist leader; Lloyd C. Douglas, author; Theodore Dreiser, writer; Bernard F. Gimbel, merchant; Virgil Grissom, astronaut; Phil Harris, actor and band leader; John Milton Hay, statesman; James R. Hoffa, labor leader; Michael Jackson, singer; Buck Jones, actor; Alfred C. Kinsey, zoologist; David Letterman, TV host and comedian; Eli Lilly, pharmaceuticals manufacturer; Carole Lombard, actress; Shelley Long, actress; Marjorie Main, actress; James McCracken, tenor; Joaquin Miller, poet; Paul Osborn, playwright; Cole Porter, songwriter; Gene Stratton Porter, naturalist and author; Ernest Taylor Pyle, journalist; J. Danforth Quayle, former vice president; James Whitcomb Riley, poet; Knute Rockne, football coach; Ned Rorem, composer; Red Skelton, comedian; Rex Stout, mystery writer; Booth Tarkington, author; Twyla Tharp, dancer and choreographer; Forrest Tucker, actor; Harold C. Urey, physicist; Kurt Vonnegut, Jr., author; Dan Wakefield, author; Robert Wise, director; Jessamyn West, novelist; Wendell Willkie, lawyer; Wilbur Wright, inventor.

# Iowa

**Capital:** Des Moines
**Governor:** Thomas J. Vilsack, D (to Jan. 2003)
**Lieut. Governor:** Sally Pederson, D (to Jan. 2003)
**Senators:** Chuck Grassley, R (to Jan. 2005); Tom Harkin, D (to Jan. 2003)
**Secy. of State:** Chet Culver, D (to Jan. 2003)
**Treasurer:** Michael L. Fitzgerald, D (to Jan. 2003)
**Atty. General:** Tom Miller, D (to Jan. 2003)
**Organized as territory:** June 12, 1838
**Entered Union (rank):** Dec. 28, 1846 (29)
**Present constitution adopted:** 1857
**Motto:** Our liberties we prize and our rights we will maintain
**State Symbols: flower,** wild rose (1897); **bird,** eastern goldfinch (1933); **colors,** red, white, and blue (in state flag); **song,** "Song of Iowa";
**Nickname:** Hawkeye State
**Origin of name:** Probably from an Indian word meaning "this is the place" or "the Beautiful Land"

**10 largest cities (2000):** Des Moines, 198,682; Cedar Rapids, 120,758; Davenport, 98,359; Sioux City, 85,013; Waterloo, 68,747; Iowa City, 62,220; Council Bluffs, 58,268; Dubuque, 57,686; Ames, 50,731; West Des Moines, 46,403
**Land area:** 55,869 sq mi. (144,701 sq km)
**Geographic center:** In Story Co., 5 mi. NE of Ames
**Number of counties:** 99
**Largest county by population and area:** Polk, 379,029 (2001); Kossuth, 973 sq mi.
**State forests:** 8 (40,706 ac.)
**State parks:** 83 (53,000 ac.)
**Residents:** Iowan
**2001 resident population est.:** 2,923,179
**2000 resident census population (rank):** 2,926,324 (30). **Male:** 1,435,515 (49.1%); **Female:** 1,490,809 (50.9%). **White:** 2,748,640 (93.9%); **Black:** 61,853 (2.1%); **American Indian:** 8,989 (0.3%); **Asian:** 36,635 (1.3%); **Other race:** 37,420 (1.3%); **Two or more races:** 31,778 (1.1%); **Hispanic/Latino:** 82,473 (2.8%). **2000 percent population 18 and over:** 74.9; **65 and over:** 14.9; **median age:** 36.6.

The first Europeans to visit the area were the French explorers Jacques Marquette and Louis Joliet in 1673. The U.S. obtained control of the area in 1803 as part of the Louisiana Purchase, and during the first half of the 19th century, there was heavy fighting between white settlers and Indians. Lands were taken from the Indians after the Black Hawk War in 1832 and again in 1836 and 1837.

When Iowa became a state in 1846, its capital was Iowa City; the more centrally located Des Moines became the new capital in 1857. At that time, the state's present boundaries were also drawn.

Although Iowa produces a tenth of the nation's food supply, the value of Iowa's manufactured products is twice that of its agriculture. Major industries are food and associated products, non-electrical machinery, electrical equipment, printing and publishing, and fabricated products.

Iowa stands in a class by itself as an agricultural state. Its farms sell over $10 billion worth of crops and livestock annually. Iowa leads the nation in all corn, soybean, and hog marketings, and comes in third in total livestock sales. Iowa's forests produce hardwood lumber, particularly walnut, and its mineral products include cement, limestone, sand, gravel, gypsum, and coal.

Tourist attractions include the Herbert Hoover birthplace and library near West Branch; the Amana Colonies; Fort Dodge Historical Museum, Fort, and Stockade; the Iowa State Fair at Des Moines in August; and the Effigy Mounds National Monument, a prehistoric Indian burial site at Marquette.

Famous natives and residents: Bix Beiderbecke, jazz musician; Norman Borlaug, plant pathologist, geneticist, and Nobel Peace Prize winner; William "Buffalo Bill" F. Cody, scout; Johnny Carson, TV entertainer; Gardner Cowles, Jr., publisher; Simon Estes, bass-baritone; William Frawley, actor; George H. Gallup, poll taker; Susan Glaspell, writer; Herbert Hoover, president; MacKinlay Kantor, novelist; Charles A. Kettering, inventor; Ann Landers, columnist; Cloris Leachman, actress; John L. Lewis, labor leader; Glenn L. Martin, aviator and manufacturer; Elsa Maxwell, writer; Frederick L. Maytag, inventor and manufacturer; Glenn Miller, bandleader; Kate Mulgrew, actress; Harriet Nelson, actress; Nathan M. Pusey, educator; David Rabe, playwright; Harry Reasoner, TV commentator; Donna Reed, actress; Lillian Russell, soprano; Robert Schuller, evangelist; Wallace Stegner, novelist and critic; Billy Sunday, evangelist; James A. Van Allen, space physicist; Abigail Van Buren, columnist; Henry A. Wallace, statesman and vice president; John Wayne, actor; Andy Williams, singer; Meredith Willson, composer; Grant Wood, painter.

# Kansas

**Capital:** Topeka
**Governor:** Bill Graves, R (to Jan. 2003)
**Lieut. Governor:** Gary Sherrer, R (to Jan. 2003)
**Senators:** Sam Brownback, R (to Jan. 2005); Pat Roberts, R (to Jan. 2003)
**Secy. of State:** Ron Thornburgh, R (to Jan. 2003)
**Treasurer:** Tim Shallenburger, R (to Jan. 2003)
**Atty. General:** Carla Stovall, R (to Jan. 2003)
**Organized as territory:** May 30, 1854
**Entered Union (rank):** Jan. 29, 1861 (34)
**Present constitution adopted:** 1859
**Motto:** *Ad astra per aspera* (To the stars through difficulties)
**State Symbols: flower,** sunflower (1903); **tree,** cottonwood (1937); **bird,** western meadowlark (1937); **animal,** buffalo (1955); **song,** "Home on the Range" (1947);
**Nicknames:** Sunflower State; Jayhawk State
**Origin of name:** From a Sioux word meaning "people of the south wind"
**10 largest cities (2000):** Wichita, 344,284; Overland Park, 149,080; Kansas City, 146,866; Topeka, 122,377; Olathe, 92,962; Lawrence, 80,098; Shawnee, 47,996; Salina, 45,679; Manhattan, 44,831; Hutchinson, 40,787
**Land area:** 81,815 sq mi. (211,901 sq km)
**Geographic center:** In Barton Co., 15 mi. NE of Great Bend
**Number of counties:** 105
**Largest county by population and area:** Johnson, 465,058 (2001); Butler, 1,428 sq mi.
**State parks:** 22 (14,394 ac.)
**Residents:** Kansan
**2001 resident population est.:** 2,694,641
**2000 resident census population (rank):** 2,688,418 (32). **Male:** 1,328,474 (49.4%); **Female:** 1,359,944 (50.6%). **White:** 2,313,944 (86.1%); **Black:** 154,198 (5.7%); **American Indian:** 24,936 (0.9%); **Asian:** 46,806 (1.7%); **Other race:** 90,725 (3.4%); **Two or more races:** 56,496 (2.1%); **Hispanic/Latino:** 188,252 (7.0%). **2000 percent population 18 and over:** 73.5; **65 and over:** 13.3; **median age:** 35.2.

Spanish explorer Francisco de Coronado, in 1541, is considered the first European to have traveled this region. Sieur de la Salle's extensive land claims for France (1682) included present-day Kansas. Ceded to Spain by France in 1763, the territory reverted to France in 1800 and was sold to the U.S. as part of the Louisiana Purchase in 1803.

Lewis and Clark, Zebulon Pike, and Stephen H. Long explored the region between 1803 and 1819. The first permanent white settlements in Kansas were outposts—Fort Leavenworth (1827), Fort Scott (1842), and Fort Riley (1853)—established to protect travelers along the Santa Fe and Oregon Trails.

Just before the Civil War, the conflict between the pro- and anti-slavery forces earned the region the grim title of Bleeding Kansas.

Today, wheat fields, oil-well derricks, herds of cattle, and grain-storage elevators are chief features of the Kansas landscape. A leading wheat-growing state, Kansas also raises corn, sorghum, oats, barley, soybeans, and potatoes. Kansas stands high in petroleum production and mines zinc, coal, salt, and lead. It is also the nation's leading producer of helium.

Wichita is one of the nation's leading aircraft-manufacturing centers, ranking first in production of private aircraft. Kansas City is an important transportation, milling, and meat-packing center.

Points of interest include the Kansas History Center at Topeka, the Eisenhower boyhood home and the Eisenhower Memorial Museum and Presidential Library at Abilene, John Brown's cabin at Osawatomie, re-created Front Street in Dodge City, Fort Larned (an important military post on the Santa Fe Trail), Fort Leavenworth, and Fort Riley.

Famous natives and residents: Roscoe "Fatty" Arbuckle, actor; Clarence D. Batchelor, political cartoonist; Gwendolyn Brooks, poet; Walter P. Chrysler, auto manufacturer; Clark M. Clifford, secretary of defense; John Steuart Curry, painter; Charles Curtis, vice president; Robert Dole, senator; Amelia Earhart, aviator; Dwight D. Eisenhower, general and president; Milton S. Eisenhower, educator; Gary Hart, politician; William Inge, playwright; Walter Johnson, baseball pitcher; Osa L. Johnson, documentary film producer; Buster Keaton, comedian; Emmett Kelly, clown; Stan Kenton, jazz musician; James Lehrer, broadcast journalist; Edgar Lee Masters, poet; Mary McCarthy, actress; Hattie McDaniel, actress; Karl Menninger, psychiatrist; Carry A. Nation, temperance leader; Gordon Parks, film director; ZaSu Pitts, actress; Samuel Ramey, opera singer; Charles Robinson, statesman and first governor; Charles (Buddy) Rogers, actor; Damon Runyon, journalist; Gale Sayers, football player; Eugene W. Smith, photojournalist; Milburn Stone, actor; John Cameron Swayze, news commentator; William Allen White, journalist; Charles E. Whittaker, jurist; Jess Willard, boxer.

# Kentucky

**Capital:** Frankfort
**Governor:** Paul E. Patton, D (to Dec. 2003)
**Lieut. Governor:** Stephen L. Henry, D (to Dec. 2003)
**Senators:** Jim Bunning, R (to Jan. 2005); Mitch McConnell, R (to Jan. 2003)
**Secy. of State:** John Y. Brown III, D (to Dec. 2003)
**Treasurer:** Jonathan Miller, D (to Dec. 2003)
**Atty. General:** A. B. "Ben" Chandler III, D (to Dec. 2003)
**Entered Union (rank):** June 1, 1792 (15)
**Present constitution adopted:** 1891
**Motto:** United we stand, divided we fall
**State Symbols: tree,** tulip poplar (1994); **flower,** goldenrod; **bird,** Kentucky cardinal; **song,** "My Old Kentucky Home";
**Nickname:** Bluegrass State
**Origin of name:** From an Iroquoian word "Ken-tah-ten" meaning "land of tomorrow"
**10 largest cities (2000):** Lexington-Fayette[1], 260,512; Louisville, 256,231; Owensboro, 54,067; Bowling Green, 49,296; Covington, 43,370; Hopkinsville, 30,089; Frankfort, 27,741; Henderson, 27,373; Richmond, 27,152; Jeffersontown, 26,633
**Land area:** 39,728 sq mi. (102,896 sq km)
**Geographic center:** In Marion Co., 3 mi. NNW of Lebanon
**Number of counties:** 120
**Largest county by population and area:** Jefferson, 692,910 (2001); Pike, 787 sq mi.
**State forests:** 4 (30,200 ac.)
**Residents:** Kentuckian
**2001 resident population est.:** 4,065,556
**2000 resident census population (rank):** 4,041,760 (25). **Male.** 1,975,368 (48.9%); **Female:** 2,066,401 (51.1%). **White:** 3,640,889 (90.1%); **Black:** 295,994 (7.3%); **American Indian:** 8,616 (0.2%); **Asian:** 29,744 (0.7%); **Other race:** 22,623 (0.6%); **Two or more races:** 42,443 (1.1%); **Hispanic/Latino:** 59,939 (1.5%). **2000 percent population 18 and over:** 75.4; **65 and over:** 12.5; **median age:** 35.9.

1. Coextensive with Fayette County.

Kentucky was the first region west of the Allegheny Mountains to be settled by American pioneers. James Harrod established the first permanent settlement at Harrodsburg in 1774; the following year Daniel Boone, who had explored the area in 1767, blazed the Wilderness Trail through the Cumberland Gap and founded Boonesboro.

Politically, the Kentucky region was originally part of Virginia, but statehood was gained in 1792. Gen. Anthony Wayne's victory in 1794 at Fallen Timbers in Ohio marked the end of Native American resistance in the area and secured the Kentucky frontier.

As a slaveholding state with a considerable abolitionist population, Kentucky was caught in the middle during the Civil War, supplying both Union and Confederate forces with thousands of troops.

Kentucky prides itself on producing some of the nation's best tobacco, horses, and whiskey. Corn, soybeans, wheat, fruit, hogs, cattle, and dairy products are among the agricultural items produced.

Among the manufactured items produced in the state are motor vehicles, furniture, aluminum ware, brooms, apparel, lumber products, machinery, textiles, and iron and steel products. Kentucky also produces significant amounts of petroleum, natural gas, fluorspar, clay, and stone. However, coal accounts for 85% of the total mineral income.

Louisville is famous for the Kentucky Derby at Churchill Downs, and the Bluegrass country around Lexington is the home of some of the world's finest race horses. Other attractions are Mammoth Cave, the George S. Patton, Jr., Military Museum at Fort Knox, and Old Fort Harrod State Park.

Famous natives and residents: John Adair, pioneer and political leader; Muhammad Ali, boxer; Alben W. Barkley, vice president; Louis D. Brandeis, jurist; John Mason Brown, critic; Kit Carson, scout; Champ Clark, politician; George Clooney, actor; Rosemary Clooney, singer; Irvin S. Cobb, humorist; Jefferson Davis, president of the Confederacy; Johnny Depp, actor; Irene Dunne, actress; Crystal Gayle, singer; David W. Griffith, film producer; John M. Harlan, jurist; Elizabeth Hardwick, writer; Casey Jones, locomotive engineer; Ashley Judd, actress; Naomi Judd, singer; Wynona Judd, singer; Barbara Kingsolver, writer; Abraham Lincoln, president; Loretta Lynn, singer; Bill Monroe, bluegrass musician; Carry A. Nation, temperance leader; Patricia Neal, actress; George Reeves, actor; Wiley B. Rutledge, jurist; Diane Sawyer, broadcast journalist; Phil Simms, football player; Adlai Stevenson, vice president; Allen Tate, poet and critic; Hunter Thompson, writer; Frederick M. Vinson, jurist; Robert Penn Warren, novelist.

# Louisiana

**Capital:** Baton Rouge
**Governor:** Murphy J. "Mike" Foster, R (to Jan. 2004)
**Lieut. Governor:** Kathleen Blanco, D (to Jan. 2004)
**Senators:** John B. Breaux, D (to Jan. 2005); Mary Landrieu, D (to Jan. 2003)
**Secy. of State:** Fox McKeithen, R (to Jan. 2004)
**Treasurer:** John Neely Kennedy, D (to Jan. 2004)
**Atty. General:** Richard P. Ieyoub, D (to Jan. 2004)
**Organized as territory:** March 26, 1804
**Entered Union (rank):** April 30, 1812 (18)
**Present constitution adopted:** 1974
**Motto:** Union, justice, and confidence
**State Symbols: flower,** magnolia (1900); **tree,** bald cypress (1963); **bird,** eastern brown pelican (1958); **songs,** "Give Me Louisiana" and "You Are My Sunshine";
**Nickname:** Pelican State
**Origin of name:** In honor of Louis XIV of France
**10 largest cities (2000):** New Orleans, 484,674; Baton Rouge, 227,818; Shreveport, 200,145; Lafayette, 110,257; Lake Charles, 71,757; Kenner, 70,517; Bossier City, 56,461; Monroe, 53,107; Alexandria, 46,342; New Iberia, 32,623

**Land area:** 43,562 sq mi. (112,826 sq km)
**Geographic center:** In Avoyelles Parish, 3 mi.
SE of Marksville
**Number of parishes (counties):** 64
**Largest parish by population and area:** Orleans,
476,492 (2001); Vernon, 1,328 sq mi.
**State forests:** 1 (8,000 ac.)
**State parks:** 30 (13,932 ac.)
**Residents:** Louisianan, Louisianian
**2001 resident population est.:** 4,465,430
**2000 resident census population (rank):** 4,468,976
(22). **Male:** 2,162,903 (48.4%); **Female:** 2,306,073
(51.6%). **White:** 2,856,161 (63.9%); **Black:** 1,451,944
(32.5%); **American Indian:** 25,477 (0.6%); **Asian:**
54,758 (1.2%); **Other race:** 31,131 (0.7%); **Two or
more races:** 48,265 (1.1%); **Hispanic/Latino:**
107,738 (2.4%). **2000 percent population 18 and
over:** 72.7; **65 and over:** 11.6; **median age:** 34.0.

Louisiana has a rich, colorful historical background. Early Spanish explorers were Alvárez
Piñeda, 1519; Álvar Núñez Cabeza de Vaca, 1528;
and Hernando De Soto in 1541. Sieur de la Salle
reached the mouth of the Mississippi and claimed
all the land drained by it and its tributaries for Louis
XIV of France in 1682.

Louisiana became a French crown colony in 1731
but was ceded to Spain in 1763 after the French and
Indian Wars. (The portion east of the Mississippi
came under British control in 1764.) Louisiana
reverted to France in 1800 and was sold by Napoleon to the U.S. in 1803. The southern part, known
as the territory of Orleans, became the state of Louisiana in 1812.

During the Civil War, Louisiana joined the Confederacy, but New Orleans was captured by Union
Adm. David Farragut in April 1862. The state's
economy suffered during Reconstruction; however,
the situation improved at the turn of the 20th century, with the discovery of oil and natural gas and
the growth of industry.

Louisiana is a leader in natural gas, salt, petroleum, and sulfur production. Much of the oil and
sulfur comes from offshore deposits. The state also
produces large crops of sweet potatoes, rice, sugar
cane, pecans, soybeans, corn, and cotton. Leading
manufactured items include chemicals, processed
food, petroleum and coal products, paper, lumber
and wood products, transportation equipment, and
apparel.

The state has become a popular tourist destination. New Orleans is the major draw, known particularly for its picturesque French Quarter and the
annual Mardi Gras celebration, held since 1838.

Other major points of interest include the Superdome in New Orleans, historic plantation homes
near Natchitoches and New Iberia, Cajun country in
the Mississippi Delta Region, Chalmette National
Historic Park, and the state capital at Baton Rouge.

Famous natives and residents: Louis Armstrong, musician;
Geoffrey Beene, fashion designer; Truman Capote, writer;
Kitty Carlisle, singer and actress; Van Cliburn, concert
pianist; Michael De Bakey, heart surgeon; Fats Domino,
musician; Louis Moreau Gottschalk, pianist and composer;
Bryant Gumbel, TV newscaster; Lillian Hellman, playwright;
Al Hirt, trumpeter; Mahalia Jackson, gospel singer; Jean
Laffite, privateer; Dorothy Lamour, actress; John A. Lejeune,
Marine Corps general; Elmore Leonard, author; Jerry Lee
Lewis, singer; Huey P. Long, politician; Wynton Marsalis,
musician; Jelly Roll Morton, jazz musician and composer;
Huey Newton, black activist; Paul Prudhomme, chef; Howard
K. Smith, TV commentator; Ben Turpin, comedian; Ray
Walston, actor; Edward Douglas White, jurist.

# Maine

**Capital:** Augusta
**Governor:** Angus S. King, Jr., I (to Jan. 2003)
**Senators:** Susan Collins, R (to Jan. 2003);
Olympia J. Snowe, R (to Jan. 2007)
**Secy. of State:** Dan A. Gwadosky, D (to Jan. 2003)
**Treasurer:** Dale McCormick (to Jan. 2003)
**Atty. General:** G. Steven Rowe (to Jan. 2003)
**Entered Union (rank):** March 15, 1820 (23)
**Present constitution adopted:** 1820
**Motto:** *Dirigo* (I lead)
**State Symbols: flower,** white pine cone and tassel
(1895); **tree,** white pine tree (1945); **bird,** chickadee
(1927); **fish,** landlocked salmon (1969); **mineral,**
tourmaline (1971); **song,** "State of Maine Song"
(1937); **animal,** moose (1979); **cat,** Maine coon cat
(1985); **fossil,** *pertica quadrifaria* (1985); **insect,**
honeybee (1975);
**Nickname:** Pine Tree State
**Origin of name:** First used to distinguish the mainland
from the offshore islands. It has been considered a
compliment to Henrietta Maria, queen of Charles I of
England. She was said to have owned the province of
Mayne in France.
**10 largest cities (2000):** Portland, 64,249; Lewiston,
35,690; Bangor, 31,473; South Portland, 23,324;
Auburn, 23,203; Brunswick, 21,172; Biddeford, 20,942;
Sanford, 20,806; Augusta, 18,560; Scarborough,
16,970
**Largest town (1990 census):** Brunswick, 20,906
**Land area:** 30,862 sq mi. (79,933 sq km)
**Geographic center:** In Piscataquis Co., 18 mi. N of
Dover-Foxcroft
**Number of counties:** 16
**Largest county by population and area:** Cumberland,
266,988 (2001); Aroostook, 6,672 sq mi.
**State forests:** 1 (21,000 ac.)
**State parks:** 26 (247,627 ac.)
**State historic sites:** 18 (403 ac.)
**Residents:** Mainer
**2001 resident population est.:** 1,286,670
**2000 resident census population (rank):** 1,274,923
(40). **Male:** 620,309 (48.7%); **Female:** 654,614
(51.3%). **White:** 1,236,014 (96.9%); **Black:** 6,760
(0.5%); **American Indian:** 7,098 (0.6%); **Asian:** 9,111
(0.7%); **Other race:** 2,911 (0.2%); **Two or more
races:** 12,647 (1.0%); **Hispanic/Latino:** 9,360 (0.7%);
**2000 percent population 18 and over:** 76.4; **65
and over:** 14.4; **median age:** 38.6.

John Cabot and his son, Sebastian, are believed to
have visited the Maine coast in 1498. However, the
first permanent English settlements were not established until more than a century later, in 1623.

The first naval action of the Revolutionary War
occurred in 1775 when colonials captured the British sloop *Margaretta* off Machias on the Maine
coast. In that same year, the British burned Falmouth (now Portland).

Long governed by Massachusetts, Maine
became the 23rd state as part of the Missouri Compromise in 1820.

Maine produces 98% of the nation's low-bush
blueberries. Farm income is also derived from
apples, potatoes, dairy products, and vegetables,
with poultry and eggs the largest selling items.

The state is one of the world's largest pulp-paper
producers. With almost 89% of its area forested,
Maine turns out wood products from boats to toothpicks. Maine also leads the world in the production
of the familiar flat tins of sardines, producing more
than 75 million of them annually. In 2001, Maine

lobstermen landed nearly 48 million pounds of lobster, compared with an estimated 53 million pounds in 2000.

A scenic seacoast, beaches, lakes, mountains, and resorts make Maine a popular vacationland. There are more than 2,500 lakes and 5,000 streams, plus 26 state parks to attract hunters, fishermen, skiers, and campers.

Major points of interest are Bar Harbor, Acadia National Park, Allagash National Wilderness Waterway, the Wadsworth Longfellow House in Portland, Roosevelt Campobello International Park, and the St. Croix Island National Monument.

Famous natives and residents: F. Lee Bailey, defense attorney; Charles F. Browne (Artemus Ward), humorist; Cyrus Curtis, publisher; Dorothea Dix, civil rights reformer; John Ford, film director; Melville Fuller, jurist; Marsden Hartley, painter; Henry Wadsworth Longfellow, poet; Sarah Orne Jewett, author; Stephen King, writer; Linda Lavin, actress; Edna St. Vincent Millay, poet; Marston Morse, mathematician; Frank Munsey, publisher; Walter Piston, composer; George Putnam, publisher; Kenneth Roberts, historical novelist; Edwin Arlington Robinson, poet; Margaret Chase Smith, politician; Samantha Smith, peacemaker and actress; John Hay Whitney, publisher.

# Maryland

**Capital:** Annapolis
**Governor:** Parris N. Glendening, D (to Jan. 2003)
**Lieut. Gov.:** Kathleen Kennedy Townsend, D (to Jan. 2003)
**Senators:** Barbara A. Mikulski, D (to Jan. 2005); Paul S. Sarbanes, D (to Jan. 2007)
**Secy. of State:** John T. Willis, D (to Jan. 2003)
**Treasurer:** Richard N. Dixon, D (to Jan. 2003)
**Atty. General:** J. Joseph Curran, Jr., D (to Jan. 2003)
**Entered Union (rank):** April 28, 1788 (7)
**Present constitution adopted:** 1867
**Motto:** *Fatti maschii, parole femine* (Manly deeds, womanly words)
**State Symbols: bird,** Baltimore oriole (1947); **boat,** skipjack (1985); **crustacean,** Maryland blue crab (1989); **dinosaur,** Astrodon johnstoni (1998); **dog,** Chesapeake Bay retriever (1964); **beverage,** milk (1998); **flower,** black-eyed susan (1918); **fish,** rockfish (1965); **folk dance,** square dance (1994); **fossil shell,** *ecphora gardnerae gardnerae* (Wilson) (1994); **insect,** Baltimore checkerspot butterfly (1973); **reptile,** Diamondback terrapin (1994); **song,** "Maryland! My Maryland!" (1939); **sport,** jousting (1962); **tree,** white oak (1941);
**Nicknames:** Free State; Old Line State
**Origin of name:** In honor of Henrietta Maria (queen of Charles I of England)
**10 largest cities (2000):** Baltimore, 651,154; Frederick, 52,767; Gaithersburg, 52,613; Bowie, 50,269; Rockville, 47,388; Hagerstown, 36,687; Annapolis, 35,838; College Park, 24,657; Salisbury, 23,743; Cumberland, 21,518
**Land area:** 9,774 sq mi. (25,315 sq km)
**Geographic center:** In Prince Georges Co., 4½ mi. NW of Davidsonville
**Number of counties:** 23, and 1 independent city
**Largest county by population and area:** Montgomery, 891,347 (2001); Frederick, 663 sq mi.
**State forests:** 13 (132,944 ac.)
**State parks:** 47 (87,670 ac.)
**Residents:** Marylander
**2001 resident population est.:** 5,375,156
**2000 resident census population (rank):** 5,296,486 (19). **Male:** 2,557,794 (48.3%); **Female:** 2,738,692 (51.7%). **White:** 3,391,308 (64.0%); **Black:** 1,477,411 (27.9%); **American Indian:** 15,423 (0.3%); **Asian:**

210,929 (4.0%); **Other race:** 95,525 (1.8%); **Two or more races:** 103,587 (2.0%); **Hispanic/Latino:** 227,916 (4.3%). **2000 percent population 18 and over:** 74.4; **65 and over:** 11.3; **median age:** 36.0.

In 1608, Capt. John Smith explored Chesapeake Bay. Charles I granted a royal charter for Maryland to Cecil Calvert, Lord Baltimore, in 1632, and English settlers, many of whom were Roman Catholic, landed on St. Clement's (now Blakistone) Island in 1634. Religious freedom, granted all Christians in the Toleration Act passed by the Maryland assembly in 1649, was ended by a Puritan revolt, 1654–1658.

From 1763 to 1767, Charles Mason and Jeremiah Dixon surveyed Maryland's northern boundary line with Pennsylvania. In 1791, Maryland ceded land to form the District of Columbia.

In 1814, during the British attempt to capture Baltimore, the bombardment of Fort McHenry inspired Francis Scott Key to write the words to "The Star-Spangled Banner." During the Civil War, Maryland was a slave state but remained in the Union. Consequently, Marylanders fought on both sides and many families were divided.

Maryland's Eastern Shore and Western Shore embrace the Chesapeake Bay, and the many estuaries and rivers create one of the longest waterfronts of any state. The Bay produces more seafood—oysters, crabs, clams, fin fish—than any comparable body of water. Important agricultural products are greenhouse and nursery products, chickens, dairy products, eggs, and soybeans. Stone, coal, sand, gravel, cement, and clay are the chief mineral products.

Manufacturing industries include food products, chemicals, computer and electronic products, transportation equipment, and primary metals. Baltimore, home of the Johns Hopkins University and Hospital, ranks as the nation's second port in foreign tonnage. The capital, Annapolis, is the site of the U.S. Naval Academy.

Among the popular attractions in Maryland are the Fort McHenry National Monument; Harpers Ferry and Chesapeake and Ohio Canal National Historic Parks; Antietam National Battlefield; National Aquarium, USS *Constellation,* and Maryland Science Center at Baltimore's Inner Harbor; Historic St. Mary's City; Jefferson Patterson Historical Park and Museum at St. Leonard; U.S. Naval Academy in Annapolis; Goddard Space Flight Center at Greenbelt; Assateague Island National Park Seashore; Ocean City beach resort; and Catoctin Mountain, Fort Frederick, and Piscataway parks.

Famous natives and residents: Benjamin Banneker, mathematician and astronomer; John Barth, writer; Eubie Blake, musician; John Wilkes Booth, actor and Lincoln assassin; Francis X. Bushman, actor; James M. Cain, writer; Samuel Chase, jurist; Frederick Douglass, abolitionist; John Fletcher Hurst, Methodist bishop and educator; Christopher Gist, frontiersman; Philip Glass, composer; John Hanson, president of Continental Congress; Matthew Henson, polar explorer; Billie Holiday, jazz-blues singer; Johns Hopkins, financier; Reverdy Johnson, lawyer and statesman; Thomas Johnson, political leader; Francis Scott Key, lawyer and poet; Thurgood Marshall, jurist; H. L. Mencken, writer; Hezekiah Niles, journalist; Charles Willson Peale, painter; Frank Perdue, farmer, businessman; James R. Randall, journalist and writer of the state song; Babe Ruth, baseball player; Upton Sinclair, novelist; Roger B. Taney, jurist; George Alfred Townsend (Gath), journalist; Harriet Tubman, abolitionist; Leon Uris, novelist; Frank Zappa, singer.

# Massachusetts

**Capital:** Boston
**Acting Governor:** Jane Swift, R (to Jan. 2003)
**Lieut. Governor:** vacant
**Senators:** Edward M. Kennedy, D (to Jan. 2007);
John F. Kerry, D (to Jan. 2003)
**Secy. of the Commonwealth:** William F. Galvin, D
(to Jan. 2003)
**Treasurer:** Shannon P. O'Brien, D (to Jan. 2003)
**Atty. General:** Thomas F. Reilly, D (to Jan. 2003)
**Present constitution drafted:** 1780 (oldest U.S. state
constitution in effect today)
**Entered Union (rank):** Feb. 6, 1788 (6)
**Motto:** *Ense petit placidam sub libertate quietem*
(By the sword we seek peace, but peace only
under liberty)
**State Symbols: flower,** mayflower (1918); **tree,**
American elm (1941); **bird,** chickadee (1941); **song,**
"All Hail to Massachusetts" (1966); **beverage,**
cranberry juice (1970); **insect,** ladybug (1974);
**cookie,** chocolate chip (1997); **muffin,** corn muffin
(1986); **dessert,** Boston cream pie (1996);
**Nicknames:** Bay State; Old Colony State
**Origin of name:** From Massachusett tribe of Native
Americans, meaning "at or about the great hill"
**10 largest cities (2000):** Boston, 589,141; Worcester,
172,648; Springfield, 152,082; Lowell, 105,167;
Cambridge, 101,355; Brockton, 94,304; New Bedford,
93,768; Fall River, 91,938; Lynn, 89,050; Quincy,
88,025
**Land area:** 7,840 sq mi. (20,306 sq km)
**Geographic center:** In Worcester Co., in N part of city
of Worcester
**Number of counties:** 14
**Largest county by population and area:** Middlesex,
1,463,454 (2001); Worcester, 1,513 sq mi.
**State forests and parks:** 144 (300,000 ac.)[1]
**Residents:** Bay Stater
**2001 resident population est.:** 6,379,304
**2000 resident census population (rank):** 6,349,097
(13). **Male:** 3,058,816 (48.2%); **Female:** 3,290,281
(51.8%). **White:** 5,367,286 (84.5%); **Black:** 343,454
(5.4%). **American Indian:** 15,015 (0.2%); **Asian:**
238,124 (3.8%); **Other race:** 236,724 (3.7%); **Two or
more races:** 146,005 (2.3%); **Hispanic/Latino:**
428,729 (6.8%). **2000 percent population 18 and
over:** 76.4; **65 and over:** 13.5; **median age:** 36.5.

1. The Metropolitan District Commission, an agency of
the Commonwealth serving municipalities in the Boston
area, has about 20,000 acres of woodlands, wetlands,
and urban parks under its jurisdiction.

Massachusetts has played a significant role in
American history since the Pilgrims, seeking religious freedom, founded Plymouth Colony in 1620.
As one of the most important of the 13 colonies,
Massachusetts became a leader in resisting British
oppression. In 1773, the Boston Tea Party protested
unjust taxation. The Minute Men started the American Revolution by battling British troops at Lexington and Concord on April 19, 1775.

During the 19th century, Massachusetts was
famous for the intellectual activity of its writers and
educators and for its expanding commercial fishing,
shipping, and manufacturing interests. Massachusetts pioneered the manufacture of textiles and
shoes. Today, these industries have been replaced in
importance by the electronics and communications
equipment fields.

The state's cranberry crop is the nation's second-
largest (after Wisconsin). Also important are dairy
and poultry products, nursery and greenhouse produce, vegetables, and fruit.

Tourism has become an important factor in the
economy of the state because of its numerous recreational areas and historical landmarks. Cape Cod
has beaches, summer theaters, and an artists' colony
at Provincetown. The Berkshires, in the western part
of the state, is the site of Tanglewood, the summer
home of the Boston Symphony; art museums,
including Mass MoCA and the Clark Institute; and
Jacob's Pillow, a world renowned dance center.

Among the many other points of interest are Old
Sturbridge Village in Sturbridge, Minute Man
National Historical Park between Lexington and
Concord, and Plimoth Plantation in Plymouth. In
Boston there are many places of historical interest,
including Old North Church, Old State House,
Faneuil Hall, the USS *Constitution*, and the John F.
Kennedy Library and Museum.

Famous natives and residents: John Adams, president;
John Quincy Adams, president; Samuel Adams, patriot;
Bronson Alcott, educator and social reformer; Louisa May
Alcott, writer; Horatio Alger, novelist; Susan B. Anthony,
woman suffragist; Clara Barton, American Red Cross
founder; Leonard Bernstein, conductor; George Bush,
former president; William Cullen Bryant, poet and editor;
Luther Burbank, horticulturalist; John Cheever, novelist;
John Singleton Copley, painter; e.e. cummings, poet;
Jacques d'Amboise, ballet dancer; Bette Davis, actress;
Cecil B. DeMille, film director; Emily Dickinson, poet; Ralph
Waldo Emerson, philosopher and poet; Geraldine Farrar,
soprano, actress; Benjamin Franklin, statesman and
scientist; Buckminster Fuller, architect and educator;
Robert Goddard, father of modern rocketry; John Hancock,
statesman; Nathaniel Hawthorne, novelist; Oliver Wendell
Holmes, jurist; Winslow Homer, painter; Elias Howe,
inventor; John F. Kennedy, president; Amy Lowell, poet;
James Russell Lowell, poet; Robert Lowell, poet; Horace
Mann, educator; Cotton Mather, clergyman; Herman
Melville, writer; Samuel F. B. Morse, painter and inventor;
Edgar Allan Poe, writer; Paul Revere, silversmith and
Revolutionary War figure; Norman Rockwell, artist; Dr.
Seuss (Theodore Geisel), author and illustrator; David
Souter, jurist; Lucy Stone, woman suffragist; Louis Henry
Sullivan, architect; Henry David Thoreau, author; Barbara
Walters, TV commentator; James McNeill Whistler, painter;
Eli Whitney, inventor; John Greenleaf Whittier, poet.

# Michigan

**Capital:** Lansing
**Governor:** John Engler, R (to Jan. 2003)
**Lieut. Governor:** Dick Posthumus, R (to Jan. 2003)
**Senators:** Carl Levin, D (to Jan. 2003);
Debbie A. Stabenow, D (to Jan. 2007)
**Secy. of State:** Candace S. Miller, R (to Jan. 2003)
**Atty. General:** Jennifer Granholm, D (to Jan. 2003)
**Organized as territory:** Jan. 11, 1805
**Entered Union (rank):** Jan. 26, 1837 (26)
**Present constitution adopted:** April 1, 1963, (effective
Jan. 1, 1964)
**Motto:** *Si quaeris peninsulam amoenam circumspice*
(If you seek a pleasant peninsula, look around you)
**State Symbols: flower,** apple blossom (1897); **bird,**
robin (1931); **mammal,** white-tailed deer (1997);
**fishes,** trout (1965), brook trout (1988); **gem,** isle
royal greenstone (chlorastrolite) (1972); **stone,**
petoskey stone (1965); **tree,** white pine (1955); **soil,**
kalkaska soil series (1990); **reptile,** painted turtle
(1995); **flag,** "Blue charged with the arms of the state"
(1911); **wildflower,** Dwarf Lake iris (1998);
**Nickname:** Wolverine State
**Origin of name:** From Indian word "Michigana" meaning
"great or large lake"
**10 largest cities (2000):** Detroit, 951,270; Grand
Rapids, 197,800; Warren, 138,247; Flint, 124,943;
Sterling Heights, 124,471; Lansing, 119,128; Ann

Arbor, 114,024; Livonia, 100,545; Dearborn, 97,775; Westland, 86,602
**Land area:** 56,804 sq mi. (147,122 sq km)
**Geographic center:** In Wexford Co., 5 mi. NNW of Cadillac
**Number of counties:** 83
**Largest county by population and area:** Wayne, 2,045,473 (2001); Marquette, 1,821 sq mi.
**State parks and recreation areas:** 96 (265,000 ac.)
**Residents:** Michigander, Michiganite
**2001 resident population est.:** 9,990,817
**2000 resident census population (rank):** 9,938,444 (8). **Male:** 4,873,095 (49.0%); **Female:** 5,065,349 (51.0%). **White:** 7,966,053 (80.2%); **Black:** 1,412,742 (14.2%); **American Indian:** 58,479 (0.6%); **Asian:** 176,510 (1.8%); **Other race:** 129,552 (1.3%); **Two or more races:** 192,416 (1.9%); **Hispanic/Latino:** 323,877 (3.3%). **2000 percent population 18 and over:** 73.9; **65 and over:** 12.3; **median age:** 35.5.

Indian tribes were living in the Michigan region when the first European, Étienne Brulé of France, arrived in 1618. Other French explorers, including Jacques Marquette, Louis Joliet, and Sieur de la Salle, followed, and the first permanent settlement was established in 1668 at Sault Ste. Marie. France was ousted from the territory by Great Britain in 1763, following the French and Indian Wars.

After the Revolutionary War, the U.S. acquired most of the region, which remained the scene of constant conflict between the British and U.S. forces and their respective Indian allies through the War of 1812.

Bordering on four of the five Great Lakes, Michigan is divided into Upper and Lower peninsulas by the Straits of Mackinac, which link lakes Michigan and Huron. The two parts of the state are connected by the Mackinac Bridge, one of the world's longest suspension bridges. To the north, connecting lakes Superior and Huron, are the busy Sault Ste. Marie Canals.

While Michigan ranks first among the states in production of motor vehicles and parts, it is also a leader in many other manufacturing and processing lines, including prepared cereals, machine tools, airplane parts, refrigerators, hardware, and furniture.

The state produces important amounts of iron, copper, iodine, gypsum, bromine, salt, lime, gravel, and cement. Michigan's farms grow apples, cherries, beans, pears, grapes, potatoes, and sugar beets. Michigan's forests contribute significantly to the state's economy, supporting thousands of jobs in the wood-product, tourism, and recreation industries. With 10,083 inland lakes and 3,288 mi of Great Lakes shoreline, Michigan is a prime area for both commercial and sport fishing.

Points of interest are the automobile plants in Dearborn, Detroit, Flint, Lansing, and Pontiac; Mackinac Island; Pictured Rocks and Sleeping Bear Dunes National Lakeshores; Greenfield Village in Dearborn; and the many summer resorts along both the inland lakes and Great Lakes.

**Famous natives and residents:** Nelson Algren, novelist; Tim Allen, actor and comedian; Anita Baker, singer; William Boeing, Sr., airplane manufacturer; Ralph J. Bunche, statesman; Ellen Burstyn, actress; Bruce Catton, historian; Roger Chaffee, astronaut; Francis Ford Coppola, film director; Thomas E. Dewey, politician; Edna Ferber, novelist; Gerald Ford, former president; Henry Ford, industrialist; Ali Haji-Sheikh, football player; Julie Harris, actress; Earvin "Magic" Johnson, basketball player; Casey Kasem, radio personality; John Harvey Kellogg, surgeon and health reformer; Ring Lardner, writer; Charles A. Lindbergh, aviator; Madonna, singer; Dick Martin, comedian; Terry McMillan, author; John N. Mitchell, attorney general; Ted Nugent, singer; Chief Pontiac, Ottawa chief; Iggy Pop, musician; Gilda Radner, comedienne; Della Reese, singer; Jason Robards, Sr., actor; Diana Ross, singer; Steven Seagal, actor; Bob Seger, singer; Tom Selleck, actor; Thomas Schippers, conductor; Potter Stewart, jurist; Lily Tomlin, actress; Danny Thomas, entertainer; William E. Upjohn, pharmaceuticals manufacturer; Margaret Whiting, singer; Robin Williams, comedian and actor; Stevie Wonder, singer.

# Minnesota

**Capital:** St. Paul
**Governor:** Jesse Ventura, IP[1] (to Jan. 2003)
**Lieut. Governor:** Mae Schunk, IP[1] (to Jan. 2003)
**Senators:** Paul Wellstone, D (to Jan. 2003)
Mark Dayton, D (to Jan. 2007)
**Secy. of State:** Mary Kiffmeyer, R (to Jan. 2003)
**Atty. General:** Mike Hatch, D (to Jan. 2003)
**State Treasurer:** Carol Johnson, D (to Jan. 2003)
**Organized as territory:** March 3, 1849
**Entered Union (rank):** May 11, 1858 (32)
**Present constitution adopted:** 1858
**Motto:** L'Étoile du Nord (The North Star)
**State Symbols: flower,** lady slipper (1902); **tree,** red (or Norway) pine (1953); **bird,** common loon (also called great northern diver) (1961); **song,** "Hail Minnesota" (1945); **fish,** walleye (1965); **mushroom,** morel (1984);
**Nicknames:** North Star State; Gopher State; Land of 10,000 Lakes
**Origin of name:** From a Dakota Indian word meaning "sky-tinted water"
**10 largest cities (2000):** Minneapolis, 382,618; St. Paul, 287,151; Duluth, 86,918; Rochester, 85,806; Bloomington, 85,172; Brooklyn Park, 67,338; Plymouth, 65,894; Eagan, 63,557; Coon Rapids, 61,607; Burnsville, 60,220
**Land area:** 79,610 sq mi. (206,190 sq km)
**Geographic center:** In Crow Wing Co., 10 mi. SW of Brainerd
**Number of counties:** 87
**Largest county by population and area:** Hennepin, 1,114,977 (2001); St. Louis, 6,226 sq mi.
**State forests:** 55
**State parks:** 66 (226,000 ac.)
**Residents:** Minnesotan
**2001 resident population est.:** 4,972,294
**2000 resident census population (rank):** 4,919,479 (21). **Male:** 2,435,631 (49.5%); **Female:** 2,483,848 (50.5%). **White:** 4,400,282 (89.4%); **Black:** 171,731 (3.5%); **American Indian:** 54,967 (1.1%); **Asian:** 141,968 (2.9%); **Other race:** 65,810 (1.3%); **Two or more races:** 82,742 (1.7%); **Hispanic/Latino:** 143,382 (2.9%). **2000 percent population 18 and over:** 73.9; **65 and** over, 12.3; **median age:** 35.4.

Independence Party.

Following the visits of several French explorers, fur traders, and missionaries, including Jacques Marquette, Louis Joliet, and Robert Cavelier, Sieur de la Salle, the region was claimed for Louis XIV by Daniel Greysolon, Sieur Duluth, in 1679.

The U.S. acquired eastern Minnesota from Great Britain after the Revolutionary War and 20 years later bought the western part from France in the Louisiana Purchase of 1803. Much of the region was explored by U.S. Army lieutenant Zebulon M. Pike before the northern strip of Minnesota bordering Canada was ceded by Britain in 1818.

The state is rich in natural resources. A few square miles of land in the north in the Mesabi, Cuyuna, and Vermilion ranges produce more than

75% of the nation's iron ore. The state's farms rank high in yields of corn, wheat, rye, alfalfa, and sugar beets. Other leading farm products include butter, eggs, milk, potatoes, green peas, barley, soybeans, oats, and livestock.

Minnesota's factories produce nonelectrical machinery, fabricated metals, flour-mill products, plastics, electronic computers, scientific instruments, and processed foods. The state is also a leader in the printing and paper-products industries.

Minneapolis is the trade center of the Midwest, and the headquarters of the world's largest super-computer and grain distributor. St. Paul is the nation's biggest publisher of calendars and law books. These "twin cities" are the nation's third-largest trucking center. Duluth has the nation's largest inland harbor and now handles a significant amount of foreign trade. Rochester is home to the Mayo Clinic, a world-famous medical center.

Tourism is a major revenue producer in Minnesota, with arts, fishing, hunting, water sports, and winter sports bringing in millions of visitors each year.

Among the most popular attractions are the St. Paul Winter Carnival; the Tyrone Guthrie Theatre, the Institute of Arts, Walker Art Center, and Minnehaha Park, in Minneapolis; Boundary Waters Canoe Area; Voyageurs National Park; North Shore Drive; the Minnesota Zoological Gardens; and the state's more than 10,000 lakes.

Famous natives and residents: LaVerne, Maxene, and Patti Andrews, singers; Warren E. Burger, jurist; William E. Colby, CIA director; William Demarest, actor; William O. Douglas, jurist; Bob Dylan, singer and composer; F. Scott Fitzgerald, novelist; Judy Garland, singer and actress; J. Paul Getty, oil executive; Cass Gilbert, architect; Duane Hanson, sculptor; Hubert H. Humphrey, senator and vice president; Jessica Lange, actress; Sinclair Lewis, novelist; Cornell MacNeil, baritone; Roger Maris, baseball player; E. G. Marshall, actor; Charles H. Mayo, surgeon; William J. Mayo, surgeon; Eugene J. McCarthy, former senator; Kate Millett, feminist; Walter F. Mondale, former vice president; Gen. Lauris Norstad, NATO commander; Westbrook Pegler, columnist; John Sargent Pillsbury, businessman; Marion Ross, actress; Jane Russell, actress; Harrison E. Salisbury, journalist; Charles M. Schulz, cartoonist; Max Shulman, novelist; Maurice H. Stans, secretary of commerce; Harold E. Stassen, government official; Michael Todd, producer; Frederick Weyerhaeuser, businessman; Gig Young, actor.

# Mississippi

**Capital:** Jackson
**Governor:** Ronnie Musgrove, D (to Jan. 2004)
**Lieut. Governor:** Amy Tuck, D (to Jan. 2004)
**Senators:** Thad Cochran, R (to Jan. 2003);
Trent Lott, R (to Jan. 2007)
**Secy. of State:** Eric Clark, D (to Jan. 2004)
**Treasurer:** Marshall Bennett, D (to Jan. 2004)
**Atty. General:** Mike Moore, D (to Jan. 2004)
**Organized as territory:** April 7, 1798
**Entered Union (rank):** Dec. 10, 1817 (20)
**Present constitution adopted:** 1890
**Motto:** *Virtute et armis* (By valor and arms)
**State Symbols: flower,** flower or bloom of the magnolia or evergreen magnolia (1952); **wildflower,** coreopsis (1991); **tree,** magnolia (1938); **bird,** mockingbird (1944); **song,** "Go, Mississippi" (1962); **stone,** petrified wood (1976); **fish,** largemouth or black bass (1974); **insect,** honeybee (1980); **shell,** oyster shell (1974); **water mammal,** bottlenosed dolphin or porpoise (1974); **fossil,** prehistoric whale (1981); **land mammal,** white-tailed deer (1974), red fox (1997);

**waterfowl,** wood duck (1974); **beverage,** milk (1984); **butterfly,** spicebush swallowtail (1991); **dance,** square dance (1995);
**Nickname:** Magnolia State
**Origin of name:** From an Indian word meaning "Father of Waters"
**10 largest cities (2000):** Jackson, 184,256; Gulfport, 71,127; Biloxi, 50,644; Hattiesburg, 44,779; Greenville, 41,663; Meridian, 39,968; Tupelo, 34,211; Southhaven, 28,977; Vicksburg, 26,407; Pascagoula, 26,200
**Land area:** 46,907 sq mi. (121,489 sq km)
**Geographic center:** In Leake Co., 9 mi. WNW of Carthage
**Number of counties:** 82
**Largest county by population and area:** Hinds, 249,495 (2001); Yazoo, 920 sq mi.
**State forests:** 1 (1,760 ac.)
**State parks:** 29 (24,521 ac.)
**Residents:** Mississippian
**2001 resident population est.:** 2,858,029
**2000 resident census population (rank):** 2,844,658 (31). **Male:** 1,373,554 (48.3%); **Female:** 1,471,104 (51.7%). **White:** 1,746,099 (61.4%); **Black:** 1,033,809 (36.3%); **American Indian:** 11,652 (0.4%); **Asian:** 18,626 (0.7%); **Other race:** 13,784 (0.5%); **Two or more races:** 20,021 (0.7%); **Hispanic/Latino:** 39,569 (1.4%). **2000 percent population 18 and over:** 72.7; **65 and over:** 12.1; **median age:** 33.8.

First explored for Spain by Hernando De Soto, who discovered the Mississippi River in 1540, the region was later claimed by France. In 1699, a French group under Sieur d'Iberville established the first permanent settlement near present-day Ocean Springs.

Great Britain took over the area in 1763 after the French and Indian Wars, ceding it to the U.S. in 1783 after the Revolution. Spain did not relinquish its claims until 1798, and in 1810 the U.S. annexed West Florida from Spain, including what is now southern Mississippi.

For a little more than one hundred years, from shortly after the state's founding through the Great Depression, cotton was the undisputed king of Mississippi's largely agrarian economy. Over the last half-century, however, Mississippi has diversified its economy by balancing agricultural output with increased industrial activity.

Today, agriculture continues as a major segment of the state's economy. For almost four decades soybeans occupied the most acreage, while cotton remained the largest cash crop. In 2001, however, more acres of cotton were planted than soybeans, and Mississippi jumped to second in the nation in cotton production (exceeded only by Texas). The state's farmlands also yield important harvests of corn, peanuts, pecans, rice, sugar cane, and sweet potatoes as well as poultry, eggs, meat animals, dairy products, feed crops, and horticultural crops. Mississippi remains the world's leading producer of pond-raised catfish.

The state abounds in historical landmarks and is the home of the Vicksburg National Military Park. Other National Park Service areas are Brices Cross Roads National Battlefield Site, Tupelo National Battlefield, and part of Natchez Trace National Parkway. Pre–Civil War mansions are the special pride of Natchez, Oxford, Columbus, Vicksburg, and Jackson.

Famous natives and residents: Red Barber, sportscaster; Jimmy Buffett, singer and songwriter; Craig Claiborne, columnist and restaurant critic; Bo Diddley, guitarist;

Charles Evers, civil rights leader; Medgar Evers, civil rights leader; William Faulkner, novelist; Brett Favre, football player; Shelby Foote, historian; Richard Ford, novelist; John Grisham, novelist; Barry Hannah, novelist; Beth Henley, playwright and actress; Jim Henson, puppeteer; James Earl Jones, actor; B. B. King, guitarist; Steve McNair, football player; Mary Ann Mobley, actress; Willie Morris, writer; Elvis Presley, singer and actor; Leontyne Price, soprano; William Raspberry, columnist; Jerry Rice, football player; Jimmie Rodgers, singer; Sela Ward, actress; Muddy Waters, singer and guitarist; Eudora Welty, novelist; Tennessee Williams, playwright; Oprah Winfrey, talk-show host and actress; Richard Wright, novelist; Tammy Wynette, singer.

# Missouri

**Capital:** Jefferson City
**Governor:** Bob Holden, D (to Jan. 2005)
**Lieut. Governor:** Joe Maxwell, D (to Jan. 2005)
**Senators:** Christopher S. Bond, R (to Jan. 2005); Jean Carnahan, D (to Jan. 2003)
**Secy. of State:** Matt Blunt, R (to Jan. 2005)
**Auditor:** Claire C. McCaskill, D (to Jan. 2003)
**Treasurer:** Nancy Farmer, D (to Jan. 2005)
**Atty. General:** Jeremiah "Jay" W. Nixon, D (to Jan. 2005)
**Organized as territory:** June 4, 1812
**Entered Union (rank):** Aug. 10, 1821 (24)
**Present constitution adopted:** 1945
**Motto:** *Salus populi suprema lex esto* (The welfare of the people shall be the supreme law)
**State Symbols: flower,** hawthorn (1923); **bird,** bluebird (1927); **aquatic animal,** paddlefish (1997); **fish,** channel catfish (1997); **song,** "Missouri Waltz" (1949); **fossil,** crinoid (1989); **musical instrument,** fiddle (1987); **rock,** mozarkite (1967); **mineral,** galena (1967); **insect,** honeybee (1985); **tree,** flowering dogwood (1955); **tree nut,** eastern black walnut (1990); **animal,** mule (1995); **dance,** square dance (1995); **Missouri Day,** third Wednesday in October (1969);
**Nickname:** Show-me State
**Origin of name:** Named after the Missouri Indian tribe. "Missouri" means "town of the large canoes."
**10 largest cities (2000):** Kansas City, 441,545; St. Louis, 348,189; Springfield, 151,580; Independence, 113,288; Columbia, 84,531; St. Joseph, 73,990; Lee's Summit, 70,700; St. Charles, 60,321; St. Peter's, 51,381; Florissant, 50,497
**Land area:** 68,886 sq mi. (178,415 sq km)
**Geographic center:** In Miller Co., 20 mi. SW of Jefferson City
**Number of counties:** 114, plus 1 independent city
**Largest county by population and area:** St. Louis, 1,015,417 (2001); Texas, 1,179 sq mi.
**Conservation areas[1]:** leased, 315 (197, 661 ac.); owned, 775 (770,574 ac.)
**Conservation accesses:** leased, 77; owned, 237
**State parks and historic sites:** 81
**Residents:** Missourian
**2001 resident population est.:** 5,629,707
**2000 resident census population (rank):** 5,595,211 (17). **Male:** 2,720,177 (48.6%); **Female:** 2,875,034 (51.4%). **White:** 4,748,083 (84.9%); **Black:** 629,391 (11.2%); **American Indian:** 25,076 (0.4%); **Asian:** 61,595 (1.1%); **Other race:** 45,827 (0.8%); **Two or more races:** 82,061 (1.5%); **Hispanic/Latino:** 118,592 (2.1%). **2000 percent population 18 and over:** 74.5; **65 and over:** 13.5; **median age:** 36.1.

1. Includes wildlife areas, natural history areas, state forests, and tower sites.

Hernando De Soto visited the Missouri area in 1541. France's claim to the entire region was based on Sieur de la Salle's travels in 1682. French fur traders established Ste. Genevieve in 1735, and St. Louis was first settled in 1764.

The U.S. gained Missouri from France as part of the Louisiana Purchase in 1803, and the territory was admitted as a state following the Missouri Compromise of 1820. Throughout the pre–Civil War period and during the war, Missourians were sharply divided in their opinions about slavery and in their allegiances, supplying both Union and Confederate forces with troops. However, the state itself remained in the Union.

Historically, Missouri played a leading role as a gateway to the West, St. Joseph being the eastern starting point of the Pony Express, while the much-traveled Santa Fe and Oregon trails began in Independence.

Missouri's economy is highly diversified. Service industries provide more income and jobs than any other segment, and include a growing tourism and travel sector. Wholesale and retail trade, manufacturing, and agriculture also play significant roles in the state's economy.

Missouri is a leading producer of transportation equipment (including automobile manufacturing and auto parts), beer and beverages, and defense and aerospace technology. Food processing is the state's fastest-growing industry.

Missouri mines produce 90% of the nation's principal (non-recycled) lead supply. Other natural resources include iron ore, zinc, barite, limestone, and timber.

The state's top agricultural products include grain, sorghum, hay, corn, soybeans, and rice. Missouri also ranks high among the states in cattle and calves, hogs, and turkeys and broilers. A vibrant wine industry also contributes to the economy.

Tourism draws hundreds of thousands of visitors to a number of Missouri points of interest: the country-music shows of Branson; Bass Pro Shops national headquarters (Springfield); the Gateway Arch at the Jefferson National Expansion (St. Louis); Mark Twain's boyhood home (Hannibal); the Harry S Truman home and library (Independence); the scenic beauty of the Ozark National Scenic Riverways; and the Pony Express and Jesse James museums (St. Joseph). The state's different lake regions also attract fishermen and sun-seekers from throughout the Midwest.

Famous natives and residents: Robert Altman, film director; Burt Bacharach, songwriter; Josephine Baker, singer and dancer; Wallace Beery, actor; Robert Russell Bennett, composer; Yogi Berra, baseball player; Thomas Hart Benton, painter; Bill Bradley, basketball player and N.J. senator; Omar N. Bradley, general; Tom Bass, equestrian; William Burroughs, writer; Sarah Caldwell, opera director and conductor; Martha Jane Canary (Calamity Jane), frontierswoman; George Washington Carver, scientist; Don Cheadle, actor; Walter Cronkite, TV newscaster; Robert Cummings, actor; Jane Darwell, actress; Walt Disney, artist; T. S. Eliot, poet; Redd Foxx, actor and comedian; Betty Grable, actress; Dick Gregory, comic and activist; Jean Harlow, actress; Coleman Hawkins, jazz musician; George Hearn, actor; Edwin Hubble, astronomer; Langston Hughes, poet; John Huston, film director; Jesse James, outlaw; Scott Joplin, composer; Marianne Moore, poet; Geraldine Page, actress; James C. Penney, merchant; John Joseph Pershing, general; Vincent Price, actor; Joseph Pulitzer, journalist; Ginger Rogers, dancer and actress; Casey Stengel, baseball player; Gladys Swarthout, soprano; Sara Teasdale, poet; Virgil Thomson, composer; Harry S. Truman, president; Mark Twain, author; Dick Van Dyke, actor; Ruth Warrick, actress; Dennis Weaver, actor; Mary Wickes, actress; Laura Ingalls Wilder, author; Roy Wilkins, civil rights leader.

# Montana

**Capital:** Helena
**Governor:** Judy Martz, R (to Jan. 2005)
**Lieut. Governor:** Karl Ohs, R (to Jan. 2005)
**Senators:** Max Baucus, D (to Jan. 2003);
  Conrad R. Burns, R (to Jan. 2007)
**Secy. of State:** Bob Brown, R (to Jan. 2005)
**Auditor:** John Morrison, D (to Jan. 2005)
**Atty. General:** Mike McGrath, D (to Jan. 2005)
**Organized as territory:** May 26, 1864
**Entered Union (rank):** Nov. 8, 1889 (41)
**Present constitution adopted:** 1972
**Motto:** *Oro y plata* (Gold and silver)
**State Symbols: flower,** bitterroot (1895); **tree,**
ponderosa pine (1949); **stones,** sapphire and agate
(1969); **bird,** Western meadowlark (1981); **song,**
"Montana" (1945);
**Nickname:** Treasure State
**Origin of name:** Chosen from Latin dictionary by J. M.
Ashley. It is a Latinized Spanish word meaning
"mountainous."
**10 largest cities (2000):** Billings, 89,847; Missoula,
57,053; Great Falls, 56,690; Butte-Silver Bow[1],
34,606; Bozeman, 27,509; Helena, 25,780; Kalispell,
14,223; Havre, 9,621; Anaconda–Deer Lodge County,
9,417; Miles City, 8,487
**Land area:** 145,552 sq mi. (376,980 sq km)
**Geographic center:** In Fergus Co., 11 mi. W
of Lewistown
**Number of counties:** 56
**Largest county by population and area:** Yellowstone,
130,398 (2001); Beaverhead, 5,543 sq mi.
**State forests:** 7 (214,000 ac.)
**State parks and recreation areas:** 110 (18,273 ac.)
**Residents:** Montanan
**2001 resident population est.:** 904,433
**2000 resident census population (rank):** 902,195 (44).
**Male:** 449,480 (49.8%); **Female:** 452,715 (50.2%).
**White:** 817,229 (90.6%); **Black:** 2,692 (0.3%); **American Indian:** 56,068 (6.2%); **Asian:** 4,691 (0.5%);
**Other race:** 5,315 (0.6%); **Two or more races:**
15,730 (1.7%); **Hispanic/Latino:** 18,081 (2.0%). **2000
percent population 18 and over:** 74.5; **65 and over:**
13.4; **median age:** 37.5.

1. The city is part of a consolidated city-county government and is coextensive with Silver Bow County.

First explored for France by François and Louis-
Joseph Verendrye in the early 1740s, much of the
region was acquired by the U.S. from France as part
of the Louisiana Purchase in 1803. Before western
Montana was obtained from Great Britain in the
Oregon Treaty of 1846, American trading posts and
forts had been established in the territory.

The major Indian Wars (1867–1877) included the
famous 1876 Battle of the Little Big Horn, better
known as "Custer's Last Stand," in which Cheyenne
and Sioux defeated George A. Custer and more than
200 of his men in southeast Montana.

Much of Montana's early history was concerned
with mining, with copper, lead, zinc, silver, coal,
and oil as principal products. Butte is the center of
the area that once supplied half of the U.S. copper.

Fields of grain cover much of Montana's plains. It
ranks high among the states in wheat and barley,
with rye, oats, flaxseed, sugar beets, and potatoes as
other important crops. Sheep and cattle raising make
significant contributions to the economy.

Tourist attractions include hunting, fishing, skiing,
and dude ranching. Glacier National Park, on the
Continental Divide, has 60 glaciers, 200 lakes, and
many streams with good trout fishing. Other major

points of interest include the Little Bighorn Battlefield National Monument, Virginia City, Yellowstone National Park, Fort Union Trading Post and
Grant-Kohr's Ranch National Historic Sites, and the
Museum of the Plains Indians at Browning.

Famous natives and residents: Dorothy Baker, author; Dirk
Benedict, actor; W. A. (Tony) Boyle, labor union official;
Gary Cooper, actor; John Cowan, prospector and founder
of Last Chance Gulch (now Helena); Alfred Bertram
Guthrie, Pulitzer Prize–winning author; Chet Huntley, TV
newscaster; Will James, writer and artist; Dorothy
Johnson, author; Evel Knievel, daredevil motorcyclist;
Myrna Loy, actress; David Lynch, filmmaker; Mike
Mansfield, senator; George Montgomery, actor; Jeannette
Rankin, first woman elected to Congress; Martha Raye,
actress; Charles M. Russell, painter; Michael Smuin,
choreographer; Lester C. Thurow, economist and educator.

# Nebraska

**Capital:** Lincoln
**Governor:** Mike Johanns, R (to Jan. 2003)
**Lieut. Governor:** Dave Maurstad, R (to Jan. 2003)
**Senators:** Chuck Hagel, R (to Jan. 2003);
  Ben Nelson, D (to Jan. 2007)
**Secy. of State:** Scott Moore, R (to Jan. 2003)
**Atty. General:** Don Stenberg, R (to Jan. 2003)
**Treasurer:** David Heineman, R (to Jan. 2003)
**Organized as territory:** May 30, 1854
**Entered Union (rank):** March 1, 1867 (37)
**Present constitution adopted:** Oct. 12, 1875 (exten-
sively amended 1919–20)
**Motto:** Equality before the law
**State Symbols: flower,** goldenrod (1895); **fish,** channel
catfish (1997); **American folk dance,** square dance
(1997); **ballad,** "A Place Like Nebraska" (1997); **tree,**
cottonwood (1972); **bird,** Western meadowlark (1929);
**insect,** honeybee (1975); **gemstone,** blue agate
(1967); **rock,** prairie agate (1967); **fossil,** mammoth
(1967); **song,** "Beautiful Nebraska" (1967); **soil,** typic
argiustolls, holdreges series (1979); **mammal,** whitetail
deer (1981); **grass,** little bluestem (1969); **beverage,**
milk (1998);
**Nicknames:** Cornhusker State (1945); Beef State
**Origin of name:** From an Oto Indian word meaning
"flat water"
**10 largest cities (2000):** Omaha, 390,007; Lincoln,
225,581; Bellevue, 44,382; Grand Island, 42,940;
Kearney, 27,431; Fremont, 25,174; Hastings, 24,064;
North Platte, 23,878; Norfolk, 23,516; Columbus,
20,971
**Land area:** 76,872 sq mi. (199,098 sq km)
**Geographic center:** In Custer Co., 10 mi. NW of
Broken Bow
**Number of counties:** 93
**Largest county by population and area:** Douglas,
465,683 (2001); Cherry, 5,961 sq mi.
**State parks:** 85 areas, historical and recreational;
8 major areas
**Residents:** Nebraskan
**2001 resident population est.:** 1,713,235
**2000 resident census population (rank):** 1,711,263
(38). **Male:** 843,351 (49.3%); **Female:** 867,912
(50.7%). **White:** 1,533,261 (89.6%); **Black:** 68,541
(4.0%); **American Indian:** 14,896 (0.9%); **Asian:**
21,931 (1.3%); **Other race:** 47,845 (2.8%); **Two or
more races:** 23,953 (1.4%); **Hispanic/Latino:** 94,425
(5.5%). **2000 percent population 18 and over:** 73.7;
**65 and over:** 13.6; **median age:** 35.3.

French fur traders first visited Nebraska in the late
1600s. Part of the Louisiana Purchase in 1803, eastern Nebraska was explored by Lewis and Clark in
1804–1806. A few years later, Robert Stuart pioneered the Oregon Trail across Nebraska in 1812–

1813, and the first permanent white settlement was established at Bellevue in 1823.

Western Nebraska was acquired by treaty following the Mexican War in 1848. The Union Pacific began its transcontinental railroad at Omaha in 1865. In 1937, Nebraska became the only state in the Union to have a unicameral (one-house) legislature. Members are elected to it without party designation.

Nebraska is a leading grain-producer with bumper crops of sorghum, corn, and wheat. More varieties of grass, valuable for forage, grow in this state than in any other in the nation. The state's sizable cattle and hog industries make Dakota City and Lexington among the nation's largest meat-packing centers.

Manufacturing has become diversified: Firms making electronic components, auto accessories, pharmaceuticals, and mobile homes have joined such older industries as clothing, farm machinery, chemicals, and transportation equipment. Oil was discovered in 1939 and natural gas in 1949.

Among the principal attractions are Agate Fossil Beds, Homestead, and Scotts Bluff National Monuments; Chimney Rock National Historic Site; a recreated pioneer village at Minden; SAC Museum near Ashland; the Stuhr Museum of the Prairie Pioneer Grand Island; Boys Town; the Sheldon Memorial Art Gallery and the Lied Center for the Performing Arts at the University of Nebraska in Lincoln; the State Capitol in Lincoln; the Joslyn Art Museum in Omaha; the Henry Doorly Zoo in Omaha; Museum of Nebraska Art in Kearney; Museum of Nebraska History in Lincoln; and the University of Nebraska State Museum in Lincoln.

Famous natives and residents: Grace Abbott, social worker; Bess Streeter Aldrich, author; Grover Cleveland Alexander, baseball pitcher; Fred Astaire, dancer and actor; Max Baer, boxer; Bil Baird, puppeteer; George Beadle, geneticist; Marlon Brando, actor; William Jennings Bryan, political leader; Warren Buffett, investor; Johnny Carson, TV host; Willa Cather, author; Dick Cavett, TV entertainer; Richard B. Cheney, vice president; Montgomery Clift, actor; James Coburn, actor; William "Buffalo Bill" Cody, showman; Sandy Dennis, actress; Mignon Eberhart, author; Harold "Doc" Edgerton, inventor; Ruth Etting, singer and actress; Fr. Edward J. Flanagan, founder of Boys Town; Henry Fonda, actor; Gerald Ford, former president; Bob Gibson, baseball player; Howard Hanson, conductor; Leland Hayward, producer; Robert Henri, painter; David Janssen, actor; Francis La Flesche, ethnologist; Melvin Laird, politician; Frank W. Leahy, football coach; Harold Lloyd, actor; Malcolm X, civil rights advocate; Dorothy McGuire, actress; Julius Sterling Morton, politician and journalist; John G. Neihardt, epic poet; Nick Nolte, actor; George W. Norris, senator; John J. Pershing, army general; Nathan Roscoe Pound, educator and botanist; Red Cloud, Indian rights advocate; Mari Sandoz, author; Standing Bear, Indian rights advocate; Robert Taylor, actor; Fred the Alvino Williams, singer, composer, and actor; Julie Wilson, singer and actress; Darryl F. Zanuck, film producer.

## Nevada

**Capital:** Carson City
**Governor:** Kenny Guinn, R (to Jan. 2003)
**Lieut. Governor:** Lorraine Hunt, R (to Jan. 2003)
**Senators:** Harry Reid, D (to Jan. 2005);
  John Ensign, R (to Jan. 2007)
**Secy. of State:** Dean Heller, R (to Jan. 2003)
**Treasurer:** Brian Krolicki, R (to Jan. 2003)
**Atty. General:** Frankie Sue Del Papa, D (to Jan. 2003)
**Organized as territory:** March 2, 1861
**Entered Union (rank):** Oct. 31, 1864 (36)
**Present constitution adopted:** 1864

**Motto:** All for Our Country
**State Symbols: flower,** sagebrush (1959); **trees,** single-leaf pinon (1953) and bristlecone pine (1987); **bird,** mountain bluebird (1967); **animal,** desert bighorn sheep (1973); **colors,** silver and blue (1983); **song,** "Home Means Nevada" (1933); **rock,** sandstone (1987); **precious gemstone,** virgin valley black fire opal (1987); **semiprecious gemstone,** Nevada turquoise (1987); **grass,** Indian ricegrass (1977); **metal,** silver (1977); **fossil,** ichthyosaur (1977); **fish,** lahontan cutthroat trout (1981); **reptile,** desert tortoise (1989); **state artifact,** tule duck decoy (1995);
**Nicknames:** Sagebrush State; Silver State; Battle Born State
**Origin of name:** Spanish: "snowcapped"
**10 largest cities (2000):** Las Vegas, 478,434; Reno, 180,480; Henderson, 175,381; North Las Vegas, 115,488; Sparks, 66,346; Carson City, 52,457; Elko, 16,708; Boulder City, 14,966; Mesquite, 9,389; Fallon, 7,536
**Land area:** 109,826 sq mi. (284,449 sq km)
**Geographic center:** In Lander Co., 26 mi. SE of Austin
**Number of counties:** 16, plus 1 independent city
**Largest county by population and area:** Clark, 1,464,653 (2001); Nye, 18,147 sq mi.
**State parks:** 20 (150,000 ac., including leased lands)
**Residents:** Nevadan, Nevadian
**2001 resident population est.:** 2,106,074
**2000 resident census population (rank):** 1,998,257 (35). **Male:** 1,018,051 (50.9%); **Female:** 980,206 (49.1%). **White:** 1,501,886 (75.2%); **Black:** 135,477 (6.8%); **American Indian:** 26,420 (1.3%); **Asian:** 90,266 (4.5%); **Other race:** 159,354 (8.0%); **Two or more races:** 76,428 (3.8%); **Hispanic/Latino:** 393,970 (19.7%). **2000 percent population 18 and over:** 74.4; **65 and over:** 11.0; **median age:** 35.0.

Trappers and traders, including Jedediah Smith and Peter Skene Ogden, entered the Nevada area in the 1820s. In 1843–1845, John C. Frémont and Kit Carson explored the Great Basin and Sierra Nevada. The U.S. obtained the region in 1848 following the Mexican War, and the first permanent settlement was a Mormon trading post near present-day Genoa.

The driest state in the nation, with an average annual rainfall of only about 7 in., much of Nevada is uninhabited, sagebrush-covered desert. The wettest part of the state receives about 40 in. of precipitation per year, while the driest spot has less than 4 in. per year.

Nevada was made famous by the discovery of the Comstock Lode, the richest known U.S. silver deposit, in 1859, and its mines have produced large quantities of gold, silver, copper, lead, zinc, mercury, barite, and tungsten. Oil was discovered in 1954. Gold now far outstrips all other minerals in value of production.

In 1931, the state created two industries, divorce and gambling. For many years, Reno and Las Vegas were the "divorce capitals of the nation." More liberal divorce laws in many states have ended this distinction, but Nevada is still the gambling capital of the U.S. and a leading entertainment center. State gambling taxes account for 34.1% of general fund tax revenues.

The state's leading agricultural industry is cattle and calves. Agricultural crops consist mainly of hay, alfalfa seed, barley, wheat, and potatoes.

Nevada manufactures gaming equipment; lawn and garden irrigation devices; titanium products; seismic and machinery monitoring devices; and specialty printing.

Lake Tahoe, Reno, and Las Vegas are major resorts. Recreation areas include Pyramid Lake, Lake Tahoe, and Lake Mead and Lake Mohave, both in Lake Mead National Recreation Area. Other attractions are Hoover Dam, Virginia City, and Great Basin National Park (includes Lehman Caves).

Famous natives and residents: Eva Adams, director of U.S. Mint; Andre Agassi, tennis player; Raymond T. Baker, director of U.S. Mint; Helen Delich Bentley, government official and newspaperwoman; Robert Caples, painter; Walter Van Tilburg Clark, writer; Henry Comstock, prospector; Abby Dalton, actress; Michele Greene, actress; Sarah Winnemucca Hopkins, author and Paiute interpreter and peacemaker; Jack Kramer, tennis player; Paul Laxalt, politician; Robert Laxalt, writer; William Lear, aviation inventor; Robert C. Lynch, surgeon; John W. Mackay, benefactor, one of Big Four of Comstock Lode; Emma Nevada, opera singer; Thelma "Pat" Nixon, first lady; James W. Nye, territory governor and senator; Lute Pease, cartoonist and Pulitzer Prize winner; Edna Purviance, actress; Patty Sheehan, golfer; Jack Wilson, Paiute Indian prophet; George Wingfield, mining millionaire.

# New Hampshire

**Capital:** Concord
**Governor:** Jeanne Shaheen, D (to Jan. 2005)
**Senators:** Judd Gregg, R (to Jan. 2005); Bob Smith, R (to Jan. 2003)
**Treasurer:** Michael Ablowich, R (to Dec. 2002)
**Secy. of State:** William M. Gardner, D (to Dec. 2002)
**Atty. General:** Philip T. McLaughlin (to March 2001)
**Entered Union (rank):** June 21, 1788 (9)
**Present constitution adopted:** 1784
**Motto:** Live free or die
**State Symbols: flower,** purple lilac (1919); **tree,** white birch (1947); **animal,** white-tailed deer (1983); **insect,** ladybug (1977); **saltwater fish,** striped bass (1994); **freshwater fish,** brook trout (1995); **amphibian,** spotted newt (1985); **butterfly,** karner blue (1992); **bird,** purple finch (1957); **songs,** "Old New Hampshire" (1949) and "New Hampshire, My New Hampshire" (1963);
**Nickname:** Granite State
**Origin of name:** From the English county of Hampshire
**10 largest cities (2000):** Manchester, 107,006; Nashua, 86,605; Concord, 40,687; Derry, 34,021; Rochester, 28,461; Salem, 28,112; Dover, 26,884; Merrimack, 25,119; Londonderry, 23,236; Hudson, 22,928
**Land area:** 8,968 sq mi. (23,227 sq km)
**Geographic center:** In Belknap Co., 3 mi. E of Ashland
**Number of counties:** 10
**Largest county by population and area:** Hillsborough, 387,674 (2001); Coos, 1,801 sq mi.
**State parks:** 65 (50,000+ ac.)
**Residents:** New Hampshirite
**2001 resident population est.:** 1,259,181
**2000 resident census population (rank):** 1,235,786 (41). **Male:** 607,687 (49.2%); **Female:** 628,099 (50.8%). **White:** 1,186,851 (96.0%); **Black:** 9,035 (0.7%); **American Indian:** 2,964 (0.2%); **Asian:** 15,931 (1.3%); **Other race:** 7,420 (0.6%); **Two or more races:** 13,214 (1.1%); **Hispanic/Latino:** 20,489 (1.7%). **2000 percent population 18 and over:** 75.0; **65 and over:** 12.0; **median age:** 37.1.

Under an English land grant, Capt. John Smith sent settlers to establish a fishing colony at the mouth of the Piscataqua River, near present-day Rye and Dover, in 1623. Capt. John Mason, who participated in the founding of Portsmouth in 1630, gave New Hampshire its name.

After a 38-year period of union with Massachusetts, New Hampshire was made a separate royal colony in 1679. As leaders in the revolutionary cause, New Hampshire delegates received the honor of being the first to vote for the Declaration of Independence on July 4, 1776. New Hampshire gained a measure of international attention in 1905 when Portsmouth Naval Base played host to the signing of the treaty ending the Russo-Japanese War, known as the Treaty of Portsmouth.

Abundant water power turned New Hampshire into an industrial state early on, and manufacturing is the principal source of income. The most important industrial products are electrical and other machinery, textiles, pulp and paper products, and stone and clay products. Dairy and poultry, and growing fruit, truck vegetables, corn, potatoes, and hay are the major agricultural pursuits.

Because of New Hampshire's scenic and recreational resources, tourism now brings over $3.5 billion into the state annually.

Vacation attractions include Lake Winnipesaukee, largest of 1,300 lakes and ponds; the 724,000-acre White Mountain National Forest; Daniel Webster's birthplace near Franklin; Strawbery Banke, restored buildings of the original settlement at Portsmouth; and the famous "Old Man of the Mountain" granite head profile, the state's official emblem, at Franconia.

Famous natives and residents: Sherman Adams, former governor and presidential advisor; Salmon P. Chase, jurist; Charles Anderson Dana, editor; Mary Baker Eddy, founder of the Christian Science Church; Dustin Farnum, actor; Thomas Green Fessenden, journalist and satirical poet; Daniel Chester French, sculptor; Robert Frost, poet; Horace Greeley, journalist and politician; Sarah J. Hale, editor; John Irving, writer; Benjamin F. Keith, theater entrepreneur; Jackson Hall Kelly, promoter of Oregon settlement; John Langdon, political leader; Sharon Christa McAuliffe, teacher and astronaut; Franklin Pierce, former president; Augustus Saint-Gaudens, sculptor; Alan Shepard, astronaut; Harlan F. Stone, jurist; Daniel Webster, statesman; Henry Wilson, politician and former vice president; Noah Worcester, clergyman and pacifist.

# New Jersey

**Capital:** Trenton
**Governor:** Jim McGreevey, D (to Jan. 2006)
**Senators:** Robert Torricelli, D (to Jan. 2003); Jon Corzine, D (to Jan. 2007)
**Secy. of State:** Regena L. Thomas (to Jan. 2006)
**Treasurer:** John E. McCormac
**Atty. General:** David Samson (to Jan. 2006)
**Entered Union (rank):** Dec. 18, 1787 (3)
**Present constitution adopted:** 1947
**Motto:** Liberty and prosperity
**State Symbols: flower,** purple violet (1913); **bird,** eastern goldfinch (1935); **insect,** honeybee (1974); **tree,** red oak (1950); **animal,** horse (1977); **colors,** buff and blue (1965); **folk dance,** square dance; **dinosaur,** hadrosaurus foulkii; **fish,** brook trout; **shell,** knobbed whelk;
**Nickname:** Garden State
**Origin of name:** From the Channel Isle of Jersey
**10 largest cities (2000):** Newark, 273,546; Jersey City, 240,055; Paterson, 149,222; Elizabeth, 120,568; Edison, 97,687; Woodbridge, 97,203; Dover, 89,706; Hamilton, 87,109; Trenton, 85,403; Camden, 79,904
**Land area:** 7,417 sq mi. (19,210 sq km)
**Geographic center:** In Mercer Co., 5 mi. SE of Trenton
**Number of counties:** 21
**Largest county by population and area:** Bergen, 886,680 (2001); Burlington, 805 sq mi.
**State forests:** 11
**State parks:** 35 (67,111 ac.)

**Residents:** New Jerseyite, New Jerseyan
**2001 resident population est.:** 8,484,431
**2000 resident census population (rank):** 8,414,350 (9). **Male:** 4,082,813 (48.5%); **Female:** 4,331,537 (51.5%). **White:** 6,104,705 (72.6%); **Black:** 1,141,821 (13.6%); **American Indian:** 19,492 (0.2%); **Asian:** 480,276 (5.7%); **Other race:** 450,972 (5.4%); **Two or more races:** 213,755 (2.5%); **Hispanic/Latino:** 1,117,191 (13.3%). **2000 percent population 18 and over:** 75.2; **65 and over:** 13.2; **median age:** 36.7.

New Jersey's early colonial history was involved with that of New York (New Netherlands), of which it was a part. One year after the Dutch surrender to England in 1664, New Jersey was organized as an English colony under Gov. Philip Carteret.

In 1676 the colony was divided between Carteret and a company of English Quakers who had obtained the rights belonging to John, Lord Berkeley. New Jersey became a united crown colony in 1702, administered by the royal governor of New York. Finally, in 1738, New Jersey was separated from New York under its own royal governor, Lewis Morris. Because of its key location between New York City and Philadelphia, New Jersey saw much fighting during the American Revolution.

Today, New Jersey, an area of wide industrial diversification, is known as the Crossroads of the East. Products from over 15,000 factories can be delivered overnight to almost 60 million people, representing 12 states and the District of Columbia. The greatest single industry is chemicals; New Jersey is one of the foremost research centers in the world. Many large oil refineries are located in northern New Jersey. Other important manufactured items are pharmaceuticals, instruments, machinery, electrical goods, and apparel.

Productive farmland covers nearly one million acres, about 20% of New Jersey's land area. The state ranks high in the production of almost all garden vegetables, as well as cranberries, blueberries, and peaches. Poultry, dairy products, and seafood are also top commodities.

Tourism is the second-largest industry in New Jersey. The state has numerous resort areas on 127 mi of Atlantic coastline. In 1977, New Jersey voters approved legislation allowing legalized casino gambling in Atlantic City. Points of interest include the Delaware Water Gap, the Edison National Historic Site in West Orange, Princeton University, Liberty State Park, Jersey City, and the N.J. State Aquarium in Camden.

Famous natives: J. Valentine Lou Abbott, comedian, Charles Addams, cartoonist; Edwin Aldrin, astronaut; Count Basie, band leader; Joan Bennett, actress; Jon Bon Jovi, musician; William J. Brennan, jurist; Aaron Burr, political leader; James Fenimore Cooper, novelist; Lou Costello, comedian; Stephen Crane, writer; Helen Gahagan Douglas, representative; Allen Ginsberg, poet; William Frederick Halsey, Jr., admiral; Alfred Joyce Kilmer, poet; Ernie Kovacs, comedian; Jerry Lewis, comedian and film director; Anne Morrow Lindbergh, author; Norman Mailer, novelist; Patricia McBride, ballerina; Richard Nixon, president; Dorothy Parker, author; Joe Piscopo, comedian and actor; Paul Hobeson, singer and actor; Philip Roth, novelist; Ruth St. Denis, dancer and choreographer; Antonin Scalia, jurist; H. Norman Schwarzkopf, general; Frank Sinatra, singer and actor; Bruce Springsteen, musician; Alfred Stieglitz, photographer; Albert Payson Terhune, journalist and novelist; Sarah Vaughan, singer; William Carlos Williams, physician and poet; Edmund Wilson, literary critic and author.

# New Mexico

**Capital:** Santa Fe
**Governor:** Gary E. Johnson, R (to Jan. 2003)
**Lieut. Governor:** Walter Bradley, R (to Jan. 2003)
**Senators:** Jeff Bingaman, D (to Jan. 2007); Pete V. Domenici, R (to Jan. 2003)
**Secy. of State:** Rebecca Vigil-Giron, D (to Jan. 2003)
**Atty. General:** Patricia A. Madrid, D (to Jan. 2003)
**State Treasurer:** Michael A. Montoya, D (to Jan. 2003)
**Organized as territory:** Sept. 9, 1850
**Entered Union (rank):** Jan. 6, 1912 (47)
**Present constitution adopted:** 1911
**Motto:** *Crescit eundo* (It grows as it goes)
**State Symbols: flower,** yucca (1927); **tree,** pinon (1949); **animal,** black bear (1963); **bird,** roadrunner (1949); **fish,** cutthroat trout (1955); **vegetables,** chili and frijol (1965); **gem,** turquoise (1967); **song,** "O Fair New Mexico" (1917); **Spanish-language song,** "Asi Es Nuevo Méjico" (1971); **poem,** A Nuevo México (1991); **grass,** blue gramma (1973); **fossil,** coelophysis (1981); **cookie,** bizcochito (1989); **insect,** tarantula hawk wasp (1989); **ballad,** "Land of Enchantment" (1989); **bilingual song,** "New Mexico—Mi Lindo Nuevo Mexico", (1995); **question,** "Red or Green?" (1999);
**Nickname:** Land of Enchantment (1999)
**Origin of name:** From the country of Mexico
**10 largest cities (2000):** Albuquerque, 448,607; Las Cruces, 74,267; Santa Fe, 62,203; Rio Rancho, 51,765; Roswell, 45,293; Farmington, 37,844; Alamogordo, 35,582; Clovis, 32,667; Hobbs, 28,657; Carlsbad, 25,625
**Land area:** 121,356 sq mi. (314,312 sq km)
**Geographic center:** In Torrance Co., 12 mi. SSW of Willard
**Number of counties:** 33
**Largest county by population and area:** Bernalillo, 562,458 (2001); Catron, 6,928 sq mi.
**State-owned forested land:** 933,000 ac.
**State parks:** 31 (267,302 ac.)
**Residents:** New Mexican
**2001 resident population est.:** 1,829,146
**2000 resident census population (rank):** 1,819,046 (36). **Male:** 894,317 (49.2%); **Female:** 924,729 (50.8%). **White:** 1,214,253 (66.8%); **Black:** 34,343 (1.9%); **American Indian:** 173,483 (9.5%); **Asian:** 19,255 (1.1%); **Other race:** 309,882 (17.0%); **Two or more races:** 66,327 (3.6%); **Hispanic/Latino:** 765,386 (42.1%). **2000 percent population 18 and over:** 72.0; **65 and over:** 11.7; **median age:** 34.6.

Francisco Vásquez de Coronado, a Spanish explorer searching for gold, traveled the region that became New Mexico in 1540–1542. In 1598 the first Spanish settlement was established on the Rio Grande. Don Juan de Oñate in 1610 Santa Fe was founded and made the capital of New Mexico.

The U.S. acquired most of New Mexico in 1848, as a result of the Mexican War, and the remainder in the 1853 Gadsden Purchase. Union troops captured the territory from the Confederates during the Civil War. With the surrender of Geronimo in 1886, the Apache Wars and most of the Indian conflicts in the area were ended.

Since 1945, New Mexico has been a leader in energy research and development with extensive experiments conducted at Los Alamos Scientific Laboratory and Sandia Laboratories in the nuclear, solar, and geothermal areas.

Minerals are the state's richest natural resource, and New Mexico is one of the U.S. leaders in output of uranium and potassium salts. Petroleum, natural gas, copper, gold, silver, zinc, lead, and molybdenum also contribute heavily to the state's income.

The principal manufacturing industries include food products, chemicals, transportation equipment, lumber, electrical machinery, and stone-clay-glass products. More than two-thirds of New Mexico's farm income comes from livestock products, especially sheep. Cotton, pecans, and sorghum are the most important field crops. Corn, peanuts, beans, onions, chilies, and lettuce are also grown.

Tourist attractions include the Carlsbad Caverns National Park, Inscription Rock at El Morro National Monument, the ruins at Fort Union, Billy the Kid mementos at Lincoln, the White Sands and Gila Cliff Dwellings National Monuments, Bandelier National Monument, and the Chaco Culture National Historical Park.

Famous natives and residents: Kathy Baker, actress; Notah Begay III, golfer; Judy Blume, author; Ernest L. Blumenshein, artist; William "Billy the Kid" Bonney, outlaw; Richard Bradford, author; Ralph Bunche, Nobel Peace Prize winner; Bruce Cabot, actor; Glen Campbell, singer; Kit Carson, army scout and trapper; Dennis Chavez, former senator; John Chisum, cattle king; Mangus Coloradas, Apache leader; Edward Condon, physicist; Bill Daily, actor; John Denver, singer; Bo Diddley, blues guitarist; Patrick Garrett, lawman; Greer Garson, actress; Sid Gutierrez, astronaut; William Hanna, animator; Neil Patrick Harris, actor; Carl Hatch, senator; Tony Hillerman, author; Conrad Hilton, hotel executive; Dennis Hopper, actor; Peter Hurd, artist; Preston Jones, playwright and actor; Ralph Kiner, baseball player and sportscaster; Nancy Lopez, golfer; Maria Martínez, San Ildefonso Pueblo potter; Demi Moore, actress; Jim Morrison, singer and songwriter; Bill Mauldin, political cartoonist; Popé, San Juan Pueblo medicine man and leader; Georgia O'Keeffe, painter; Harrison Schmitt, astronaut and representative; Kim Stanley, actress; Slim Summerville, actor; Clyde Tombaugh, astronomer; Al Unser, Bobby Unser, auto racers; Victorio, Apache chief; Linda Wertheimer, NPR correspondent; Kathy Whitworth, golfer.

# New York

**Capital:** Albany
**Governor:** George E. Pataki, R (to Jan. 2003)
**Lieut. Governor:** Mary Donohue, R (to Jan. 2003)
**Senators:** Charles E. Schumer, D (to Jan. 2005); Hillary Rodham Clinton, D (to Jan. 2007)
**Secy. of State:** Randy A. Daniels, R (apptd. by governor)
**Comptroller:** Carl McCall, D (to Jan. 2003)
**Atty. General:** Eliot Spitzer, D (to Jan. 2003)
**Entered Union (rank):** July 26, 1788 (11)
**Present constitution adopted:** 1777 (last revised 1938)
**Motto:** *Excelsior* (Ever upward)
**State Symbols: animal,** beaver (1975); **fish,** brook trout (1975); **gem,** garnet (1969); **flower,** rose (1955); **tree,** sugar maple (1956); **bird,** bluebird (1970); **insect,** ladybug (1989); **song,** "I Love New York" (1980);
**Nickname:** Empire State
**Origin of name:** In honor of the Duke of York
**10 largest cities (2000):** New York, 8,008,278; Buffalo, 292,648; Rochester, 219,773; Yonkers, 196,086; Syracuse, 147,306; Albany, 95,658; New Rochelle, 72,182; Mount Vernon, 68,381; Schenectady, 61,821; Utica, 60,651
**Land area:** 47,214 sq mi. (122,284 sq km)
**Geographic center:** In Madison Co., 12 mi. S of Oneida and 26 mi. SW of Utica
**Number of counties:** 62
**Largest county by population and area:** Kings, 2,465,286 (2001); St. Lawrence, 2,686 sq mi.
**State forest preserves:** Adirondacks, 2,500,000 ac.; Catskills, 250,000 ac.
**State parks:** 152
**Residents:** New Yorker
**2001 resident population est.:** 19,011,378

**2000 resident census population (rank):** 18,976,457 (3). **Male:** 9,146,748 (48.2%); **Female:** 9,829,709 (51.8%). **White:** 12,893,689 (67.9%); **Black:** 3,014,385 (15.9%); **American Indian:** 82,461 (0.4%); **Asian:** 1,044,976 (5.5%); **Other race:** 1,341,946 (7.1%); **Two or more races:** 590,182 (3.1%); **Hispanic/Latino:** 2,867,583 (15.1%). **2000 percent population 18 and over:** 75.3; **65 and over:** 12.9; **median age:** 35.9.

Giovanni da Verrazano, an Italian-born navigator sailing for France, discovered New York Bay in 1524. Henry Hudson, an Englishman employed by the Dutch, reached the bay and sailed up the river now bearing his name in 1609, the same year that northern New York was explored and claimed for France by Samuel de Champlain.

In 1624 the first permanent Dutch settlement was established at Fort Orange (now Albany). One year later Peter Minuit purchased Manhattan Island from the Indians for trinkets worth about 60 Dutch guilders and founded the Dutch colony of New Amsterdam (now New York City), which was surrendered to the English in 1664.

New York's extremely rapid commercial growth may be partly attributed to Gov. De Witt Clinton, who pushed through the construction of the Erie Canal (Buffalo to Albany), which was opened in 1825. Today, the 641-mile Gov. Thomas E. Dewey Thruway connects New York City with Buffalo and with Connecticut, Massachusetts, and Pennsylvania express highways. Two toll-free superhighways, the Adirondack Northway (linking Albany with the Canadian border) and the North-South Expressway (crossing central New York from the Pennsylvania border to the Thousand Islands), have been opened.

The great metropolis of New York City is the nerve center of the nation. It is a leader in manufacturing, foreign trade, commerce and banking, book and magazine publishing, and theatrical production. A leading seaport, its John F. Kennedy International Airport is one of the busiest airports in the world. New York is also home to the New York Stock Exchange, the largest in the world. The printing and publishing industry is the city's largest manufacturing employer, with the apparel industry second.

Nearly all the rest of the state's manufacturing is done on Long Island, along the Hudson River north to Albany, and through the Mohawk Valley, Central New York, and Southern Tier regions to Buffalo. The St. Lawrence seaway and power projects have opened the North Country to industrial expansion and have given the state a second seacoast.

The state ranks seventh in the nation in manufacturing, with 805,200 employees in 2002. The principal industries are printing and publishing, industrial machinery and equipment, electronic equipment, and instruments. The convention and tourist business is also an important source of income.

New York farms produce cattle and calves, corn and poultry, and vegetables and fruits. The state is a leading wine producer.

Major points of interest are Castle Clinton, Fort Stanwix, and Statue of Liberty National Monuments; Niagara Falls; U.S. Military Academy at West Point; National Historic Sites that include homes of Franklin D. Roosevelt at Hyde Park and Theodore Roosevelt in Oyster Bay and New York City; the Women's Rights National Historical Park in Seneca Falls; National Memorials, including

Grant's Tomb and Federal Hall in New York City; Fort Ticonderoga; the Baseball Hall of Fame in Cooperstown; and the United Nations, skyscrapers, museums, theaters, and parks in New York City.

Famous natives and residents: Kareem Abdul-Jabbar, basketball player; Lucille Ball, actress; Humphrey Bogart, actor; James Cagney, actor; Maria Callas, opera singer; Benjamin N. Cardozo, jurist; Paddy Chayefsky, playwright; Peter Cooper, industrialist and philanthropist; Aaron Copland, composer; Tom Cruise, actor; Sammy Davis, Jr., actor and singer; Agnes de Mille, choreographer; Eamon De Valera, president of Ireland; George Eastman, inventor; Millard Fillmore, president; Lou Gehrig, baseball player; George Gershwin, composer; Learned Hand, jurist; Edward Hopper, painter; Julia Ward Howe, poet and reformer; Charles Evans Hughes, jurist; Washington Irving, author; Henry James, novelist; John Jay, jurist; Michael Jordan, basketball player; Jerome Kern, composer; Rockwell Kent, painter; Vince Lombardi, football coach; Chico, Groucho, Harpo, and Zeppo Marx, comedians; Herman Melville, author; Ethel Merman, singer and actress; Ogden Nash, poet; Rosie O'Donnell, comedian; Eugene O'Neill, playwright; Red Jacket, Seneca chief; John D. Rockefeller, industrialist; Norman Rockwell, painter and illustrator; Mickey Rooney, actor; Anna Eleanor Roosevelt, reformer and humanitarian; Franklin D. Roosevelt, president; Theodore Roosevelt, president; Jonas Salk, polio researcher; Margaret Sanger, birth control advocate; Beverly Sills, opera singer; Barbara Stanwyck, actress; Risë Stevens, opera singer; Joe Torre, baseball player and manager; Richard Tucker, tenor; Martin Van Buren, president; Mae West, actress; Walt Whitman, poet; Edith Wharton, novelist.

# North Carolina

**Capital:** Raleigh
**Governor:** Mike Easley, D (to Jan. 2005)
**Lieut. Governor:** Beverly Perdue, D (to Jan. 2005)
**Senators:** John Edwards, D (to Jan. 2005);
  Jesse Helms, R (to Jan. 2003)
**Secy. of State:** Elaine F. Marshall, D (to Jan. 2005)
**Treasurer:** Richard H. Moore, D (to Jan. 2005)
**Atty. General:** Roy Cooper, D (to Jan. 2005)
**Entered Union (rank):** Nov. 21, 1789 (12)
**Present constitution adopted:** 1971
**Motto:** *Esse quam videri* (To be rather than to seem)
**State Symbols: flower,** dogwood (1941); **tree,** pine (1963); **bird,** cardinal (1943); **mammal,** gray squirrel (1969); **insect,** honeybee (1973); **reptile,** eastern box turtle (1979); **gemstone,** emerald (1973); **shell,** scotch bonnet (1965); **historic boat,** shad boat (1987); **beverage,** milk (1987); **rock,** granite (1979); **dog,** plott hound (1989); **song,** "The Old North State" (1927); **colors,** red and blue (1945); **fruit,** scuppernong grape (2001);
**Nickname:** Tar Heel State
**Origin of name:** In honor of Charles I of England
**10 largest cities (2000):** Charlotte, 540,828; Raleigh, 276,093; Greensboro, 223,891; Durham, 187,095; Winston-Salem, 185,776; Fayetteville, 121,015; Cary, 94,536; High Point, 85,839; Wilmington, 75,838; Asheville, 68,889
**Land area:** 48,711 sq mi. (126,101 sq km)
**Geographic center:** In Chatham Co., 10 mi. NW of Sanford
**Number of counties:** 100
**Largest county by population and area:** Mecklenburg, 716,407 (2001); Robeson, 949 sq mi.
**State forests:** 6
**State parks:** 33 (125,000 ac.)
**Residents:** North Carolinian
**2001 resident population est.:** 8,186,268
**2000 resident census population (rank):** 8,049,313 (11). **Male:** 3,942,695 (49.0%); **Female:** 4,106,618 (51.0%). **White:** 5,804,656 (72.1%); **Black:** 1,737,545 (21.6%); **American Indian:** 99,551 (1.2%); **Asian:** 113,689 (1.4%); **Other race:** 186,629 (2.3%); **Two or more races:** 103,260 (1.3%); **Hispanic/Latino:** 378,963 (4.7%). **2000 percent population 18 and over:** 75.6; **65 and over:** 12.0; **median age:** 35.3.

English colonists, sent by Sir Walter Raleigh, unsuccessfully attempted to settle Roanoke Island in 1585 and 1587. Virginia Dare, born there in 1587, was the first child of English parentage born in America.

In 1653 the first permanent settlements were established by English colonists from Virginia near the Roanoke and Chowan rivers. The region was established as an English proprietary colony in 1663–1665 and in its early history was the scene of Culpepper's Rebellion (1677), the Quaker-led Cary Rebellion (1708), the Tuscarora Indian War (1711–1713), and many pirate raids.

During the American Revolution, there was relatively little fighting within the state, but many North Carolinians saw action elsewhere. Despite considerable pro-Union, antislavery sentiment, North Carolina joined the Confederacy during the Civil War.

North Carolina is the nation's largest furniture, tobacco, brick, and textile producer. Metalworking, chemicals, and paper are also important industries. The major agricultural products are tobacco, corn, cotton, hay, peanuts, and vegetable crops. The state is the country's leading producer of mica and lithium.

Tourism is also important, with visitors spending more than $1 billion annually. Sports include year-round golfing, skiing at mountain resorts, both fresh- and salt-water fishing, and hunting.

Among the major attractions are the Great Smoky Mountains, the Blue Ridge National Parkway, the Cape Hatteras and Cape Lookout National Seashores, the Wright Brothers National Memorial at Kitty Hawk, Guilford Courthouse and Moores Creek National Military Parks, Carl Sandburg's home near Hendersonville, and the Old Salem Restoration in Winston-Salem.

Famous natives and residents: David Brinkley, TV newscaster; Howard Cosell, sportscaster; Virginia Dare, first person born in America to English parents; Elizabeth Dole, government official; James B. Duke, industrialist; Donna Fargo, singer; Roberta Flack, singer; Ava Gardner, actress; Richard Gatling, inventor; Billy Graham, evangelist; Kathryn Grayson, singer and actress; Andy Griffith, actor; Jesse Helms, politician; O. Henry, writer; Barbara Howar, broadcaster and writer; Andrew Johnson, president; Charles Kuralt, TV journalist; Sugar Ray Leonard, boxer; Dolley Madison, first lady; Ronnie Milsap, singer; Thelonious Monk, pianist; Alfred Moore, jurist; Edward R. Murrow, commentator and government official; Walter Hines Page, journalist and ambassador; Floyd Patterson, boxer; James K. Polk, president; Soupy Sales, comedian; Earl Scruggs, bluegrass musician; Randy Travis, musician; John Scott Trotter, orchestra leader; Thomas Wolfe, novelist.

# North Dakota

**Capital:** Bismarck
**Governor:** John Hoeven, R (to Dec. 15, 2004)
**Lieut. Governor:** Jack Dalrymple, R (to Dec. 15, 2004)
**Senators:** Kent Conrad, D (to Jan. 2007);
  Byron L. Dorgan, D (to Jan. 2005)
**Secy. of State:** Alvin A. Jaeger, R (to Dec. 31, 2004)
**Treasurer:** Kathi Gilmore, D (to Dec. 31, 2004)
**Atty. General:** Wayne Stenehjem, R (to Dec. 31, 2004)
**Organized as territory:** March 2, 1861
**Entered Union (rank):** Nov. 2, 1889 (39)
**Present constitution adopted:** 1889

**Motto:** Liberty and union, now and forever: one and inseparable
**State Symbols: tree,** American elm (1947); **bird,** western meadowlark (1947); **song,** "North Dakota Hymn" (1947); **fish,** northern pike (1969); **grass,** western wheatgrass (1977); **fossil,** teredo petrified wood (1967); **beverage,** milk (1983); **state march,** Spirit of the Land (1975); **flower,** wild prairie rose (1907); **equine,** Nokota horse (1993); **dance,** square dance (1995);
**Nickname:** Sioux State; Flickertail State; Peace Garden State; Rough Rider State
**Origin of name:** From the Sioux tribe, meaning "allies"
**10 largest cities (2000):** Fargo, 90,599; Bismarck, 55,532; Grand Forks, 49,321; Minot, 36,567; Mandan, 16,718; Dickinson, 16,010; Jamestown, 15,527; West Fargo, 14,940; Williston, 12,512; Wahpeton, 8,586
**Land area:** 68,976 sq mi. (178,648 sq km)
**Geographic center:** In Sheridan Co., 5 mi. SW of McClusky
**Number of counties:** 53
**Largest county by population and area:** Cass, 124,021 (2001); McKenzie, 2,742 sq mi.
**State parks:** 20 (14,822 ac.)
**Residents:** North Dakotan
**2001 resident population est.:** 634,448
**2000 resident census population (rank):** 642,200 (47). **Male:** 320,524 (49.9%); **Female:** 321,676 (50.1%). **White:** 593,181 (92.4%); **Black:** 3,916 (0.6%); **American Indian:** 31,329 (4.9%); **Asian:** 3,606 (0.6%); **Other race:** 2,540 (0.4%); **Two or more races:** 7,398 (1.2%); **Hispanic/Latino:** 7,786 (1.2%). **2000 percent population 18 and over:** 75.0; **65 and over:** 14.7; **median age:** 36.2.

North Dakota was explored in 1738–1740 by French Canadians led by Sieur de la Verendrye. In 1803, the U.S. acquired most of North Dakota from France in the Louisiana Purchase. Lewis and Clark explored the region in 1804–1806, and the first settlements were made at Pembina in 1812 by Scottish and Irish families while this area was still in dispute between the U.S. and Great Britain. In 1818, the U.S. obtained the northeast part of North Dakota by treaty with Great Britain and took possession of Pembina in 1823. However, the region remained largely unsettled until the construction of the railroad in the 1870s and 1880s.

North Dakota is the most rural of all the states, with farms covering more than 90% of the land. North Dakota ranks first in the nation's production of spring and durum wheat; other agricultural products include barley, rye, sunflowers, dry edible beans, honey, oats, flaxseed, sugar beets, hay, beef cattle, sheep, and hogs.

Recently, manufacturing industries have grown, especially food processing and farm equipment. The state's coal and oil reserves are plentiful, and it also produces natural gas, lignite, clay, sand, and gravel.

The Garrison Dam on the Missouri River provides extensive irrigation and produces 400,000 kilowatts of electricity for the Missouri Basin areas.

Known for its waterfowl, grouse, pheasant, and deer hunting and bass, trout, and pike fishing, North Dakota has 20 state parks and recreation areas. Points of interest include the International Peace Garden near Dunseith, Fort Union Trading Post National Historic Site near Williston, Knife River Indian Villages National Historic Site in Stanton, the State Capitol at Bismarck, the Badlands, Theodore Roosevelt National Park, and Fort Abraham Lincoln State Park.

**Famous natives and residents:** Lynn Anderson, singer; Maxwell Anderson, playwright; Elizabeth Bodine, humanitarian; Dr. Anne Carlsen, educator; Warren Christopher, statesman; Ronald N. Davies, jurist; Angie Dickinson, actress; Ivan Dmitre, artist; Carl Ben Eielson, aviator; Phyllis Frelich, actress; Bertin C. Gamble, founder of Gamble-Skogmo; William H. Gass, writer and philosopher; Brynhild Haugland, state legislator; Phil D. Jackson, basketball player and coach; Dr. Leon O. Jacobson, researcher and educator; Harold K. Johnson, general; David C. Jones, general; Louis L'Amour, author; Peggy Lee, singer; William Lemke, representative; Roger Maris, baseball player; Marquis de Mores, cattleman who established Medora; Gerald P. Nye, senator; Casper Oimoen, skier; William A. Owens, admiral; Arthur Peterson, radio and TV actor; Cliff (Fido) Purpur, hockey player and coach; James Rosenquist, painter; Harold Schafer, founder of Gold Seal Co.; Eric Sevareid, TV commentator; Ann Sothern, actress; Dorothy Stickney, actress; Edward K. Thompson, editor; Era Bell Thompson, editor; Tommy Tucker, band leader; Lawrence Welk, band leader; Larry Woiwode, writer.

# Ohio

**Capital:** Columbus
**Governor:** Bob Taft, R (to Jan. 2003)
**Lieut. Governor:** Maureen O'Connor, R (to Jan. 2003)
**Senators:** Mike DeWine, R (to Jan. 2007); George V. Voinovich, R (to Jan. 2005)
**Secy. of State:** J. Kenneth Blackwell, R (to Jan. 2003)
**Treasurer:** Joseph T. Deters, R (to Jan. 2003)
**Atty. General:** Betty D. Montgomery, R (to Jan. 2003)
**Entered Union (rank):** March 1, 1803 (17)
**Present constitution adopted:** 1851
**Motto:** With God all things are possible
**State Symbols: flower,** scarlet carnation (1904); **tree,** buckeye (1953); **bird,** cardinal (1933); **insect,** ladybug (1975); **gemstone,** flint (1965); **song,** "Beautiful Ohio" (1969); **beverage,** tomato juice (1965); **fossil,** trilobite (1985); **animal,** white-tailed deer (1988); **wildflower,** large white trillium (1987);
**Nickname:** Buckeye State
**Origin of name:** From an Iroquoian word meaning "great river"
**10 largest cities (2000):** Columbus, 711,470; Cleveland, 478,403; Cincinnati, 331,285; Toledo, 313,619; Akron, 217,074; Dayton, 166,179; Parma, 85,655; Youngstown, 82,026; Canton, 80,806; Lorain, 68,652
**Land area:** 40,948 sq mi. (106,055 sq km)
**Geographic center:** In Delaware Co., 25 mi. NNE of Columbus
**Number of counties:** 88
**Largest county by population and area:** Cuyahoga, 1,380,421 (2001); Ashtabula, 703 sq mi.
**State forests:** 20 (more than 183,000 ac.)
**State parks:** 73 (more than 204,000 ac.)
**Residents:** Ohioan
**2001 resident population est.:** 11,373,541
**2000 resident census population (rank):** 11,353,140 (7). **Male:** 5,512,262 (48.6%); **Female:** 5,840,878 (51.4%). **White:** 9,645,453 (85.0%); **Black:** 1,301,307 (11.5%); **American Indian:** 24,486 (0.2%); **Asian:** 132,633 (1.2%); **Other race:** 88,627 (0.8%); **Two or more races:** 157,885 (1.4%); **Hispanic/Latino:** 217,123 (1.9%). **2000 percent population 18 and over:** 74.6; **65 and over:** 13.3; **median age:** 36.2.

First explored for France by Robert Cavelier, Sieur de la Salle, in 1669, the Ohio region became British property after the French and Indian Wars. Ohio was acquired by the U.S. after the Revolutionary War in 1783. In 1788, the first permanent settlement was established at Marietta, capital of the Northwest Territory.

The 1790s saw severe fighting with the Indians in Ohio; a major battle was won by Maj. Gen. Anthony

Wayne at Fallen Timbers in 1794. In the War of 1812, Commodore Oliver H. Perry defeated the British in the Battle of Lake Erie on Sept. 10, 1813.

Ohio is one of the nation's industrial leaders, ranking third in manufacturing employment nationwide. Important manufacturing centers are located in or near Ohio's major cities. Akron is known for rubber; Canton for roller bearings; Cincinnati for jet engines and machine tools; Cleveland for auto assembly, auto parts, and steel; Dayton for office machines, refrigeration, and heating and auto equipment; Youngstown and Steubenville for steel; and Toledo for glass and auto parts.

The state's fertile soil produces soybeans, corn, oats, greenhouse and nursery products, wheat, hay, and fruit, including apples, peaches, strawberries, and grapes. More than half of Ohio's farm receipts come from dairy farming and sheep and hog raising. Ohio ranks fourth among the states in lime production and also ranks high in sand and gravel and crushed stone production.

Tourism is a valuable revenue producer, bringing in $25.7 billion in 2000. Attractions include the Rock and Roll Hall of Fame, Indian burial grounds at Mound City Group National Monument, Perry's Victory International Peace Memorial, the Pro Football Hall of Fame at Canton, and the homes of presidents Grant, Taft, Hayes, Harding, and Garfield.

Famous natives and residents: Neil Armstrong, astronaut; Kathleen Battle, soprano; George Bellows, painter and lithographer; Ambrose Bierce, journalist; Erma Bombeck, columnist; Bill Boyd (Hopalong Cassidy), actor; Milton Caniff, cartoonist; Hart Crane, poet; George Armstrong Custer, army officer; Dorothy Dandridge, actress; Doris Day, singer and actress; Clarence Darrow, lawyer; Ruby Dee, actress; Rita Dove, poet; Hugh Downs, TV broadcaster; Thomas A. Edison, inventor; Clark Gable, actor; James A. Garfield, president; Lillian Gish, actress; John Glenn, astronaut and senator; Ulysses S. Grant, president; Warren G. Harding, president; Rutherford Hayes, president; Benjamin Harrison, president; William Dean Howells, novelist and critic; Zane Grey, author; Robert Henri, painter; Kenisaw Mountain Landis, first baseball commissioner; Dean Martin, singer and actor; William McKinley, president; Paul Newman, actor; Jack Nicklaus, golfer; Annie Oakley, markswoman; Norman Vincent Peale, clergyman; Tyrone Power, actor; Judith Resnik, astronaut; Eddie Rickenbacker, aviator; Roy Rogers, actor and singer; Arthur M. Schlesinger, Jr., historian; William Tecumseh Sherman, army general; Gloria Steinem, feminist; William H. Taft, president; Tecumseh, Shawnee Indian chief; Lowell Thomas, explorer and commentator; James Thurber, author and cartoonist; Orville Wright, inventor; Cy Young, baseball player.

# Oklahoma

**Capital:** Oklahoma City
**Governor:** Frank Keating, R (to Jan. 2003)
**Lieut. Governor:** Mary Fallin, R (to Jan. 2003)
**Senators:** James M. Inhofe, R (to Jan. 2003); Don Nickles, R (to Jan. 2005)
**Secy. of State:** Mike Hunter, R (to Jan. 2003)
**Treasurer:** Robert Butkin, D (to Jan. 2003)
**Atty. General:** Drew Edmondson, D (to Jan. 2003)
**Organized as territory:** May 2, 1890
**Entered Union (rank):** Nov. 16, 1907 (46)
**Present constitution adopted:** 1907
**Motto:** *Labor omnia vincit* (Labor conquers all things)
**State Symbols: flower,** mistletoe (1893); **tree,** redbud (1937); **bird,** scissor-tailed flycatcher (1951); **animal,** bison (1972); **reptile,** mountain boomer lizard (1969); **stone,** rose rock (barite rose) (1968); **colors,** green and white (1915); **song,** "Oklahoma" (1953); **beverage,** milk; **butterfly,** black swallowtail; **fish,**

white or sand bass; **folk dance,** square dance; **furbearer,** raccoon; **game animal,** white-tailed deer; **grass,** Indiangrass; **insect,** honeybee; **musical instrument,** fiddle; **poem,** "Howdy Folks," David Randolph Milsten; **waltz,** "Oklahoma Wind"; **wildflower,** Indian blanket;
**Nickname:** Sooner State
**Origin of name:** From two Choctaw Indian words meaning "red people"
**10 largest cities (2000):** Oklahoma City, 506,132; Tulsa, 393,049; Norman, 95,694; Lawton, 92,757; Broken Arrow, 74,859; Edmond, 68,315; Midwest City, 54,088; Enid, 47,045; Moore, 41,138; Stillwater, 39,065
**Land area:** 68,667 sq mi. (177,848 sq km)
**Geographic center:** In Oklahoma Co., 8 mi. N of Oklahoma City
**Number of counties:** 77
**Largest county by population and area:** Oklahoma, 662,153 (2001); Osage, 2,251 sq mi.
**State parks:** 51 (72,000 ac.)
**Residents:** Oklahoman
**2001 resident population est.:** 3,460,097
**2000 resident census population (rank):** 3,450,654 (27). **Male:** 1,696,895 (49.1%); **Female:** 1,754,759 (50.9%). **White:** 2,628,434 (76.2%); **Black:** 260,968 (7.6%); **American Indian:** 273,230 (7.9%); **Asian:** 46,767 (1.4%); **Other race:** 82,898 (2.4%); **Two or more races:** 155,985 (4.5%); **Hispanic/Latino:** 179,304 (5.2%). **2000 percent population 18 and over:** 74.1; **65 and over:** 13.2; **median age:** 35.5.

Francisco Vásquez de Coronado first explored the region for Spain in 1541. The U.S. acquired most of Oklahoma in 1803 in the Louisiana Purchase from France; the Western Panhandle region became U.S. territory with the annexation of Texas in 1845.

Set aside as Indian Territory in 1834, the region was divided into Indian Territory and Oklahoma Territory on May 2, 1890. The two were combined to make a new state, Oklahoma, on Nov. 16, 1907.

On April 22, 1889, the first day homesteading was permitted, 50,000 people swarmed into the area. Those who tried to beat the noon starting gun were called "Sooners," hence the state's nickname.

Oil made Oklahoma a rich state, but natural-gas production has now surpassed it. Oil refining, meat packing, food processing, and machinery manufacturing (especially construction and oil equipment) are important industries. Minerals produced in Oklahoma include helium, gypsum, zinc, cement, coal, copper, and silver.

Oklahoma's rich plains produce bumper yields of wheat, as well as large crops of sorghum, hay, cotton, and peanuts. More than half of Oklahoma's annual farm receipts are contributed by livestock and their products, dairy products, swine, and broilers.

Tourist attractions include the National Cowboy Hall of Fame in Oklahoma City, the Will Rogers Memorial in Claremore, the Cherokee Cultural Center with a restored Cherokee village, the restored Fort Gibson Stockade near Muskogee, the Lake Texoma recreation area, pari-mutuel horse racing at Remington Park in Oklahoma City, and Blue Ribbon Downs in Sallisaw.

Famous natives and residents: Johnny Bench, baseball player; John Berryman, poet; Garth Brooks, singer; Iron Eyes Cody, Cherokee actor; L. Gordon Cooper, astronaut; Ralph Ellison, writer; James Garner, actor; Owen K. Garriott, astronaut; Vince Gill, singer; Chester Gould, cartoonist; Woody Guthrie, singer and composer; Roy Harris, composer; Paul Harvey, broadcaster; Van Heflin, actor; Ron Howard, actor and director; Ben Johnson, actor; Jennifer Jones, actress; Jeane Kirkpatrick, educator and public-affairs spokesperson; Shannon Lucid, astronaut; Wilma P. Mankiller, principal chief of the Cherokee Nation of Oklahoma; Mickey Mantle, baseball player; Reba McEntire, singer; Shannon Miller, Olympic gymnast; Bill Moyers, journalist; Daniel Patrick Moynihan, N.Y. senator; Patti Page, singer; Mary Kay Place, actress and writer; Tony Randall, actor; Oral Roberts, evangelist; Dale Robertson, actor; Will Rogers, humorist; Dan Rowan, comedian; Thomas P. Stafford, astronaut; Maria Tallchief, ballerina; Jim Thorpe, athlete; Alfre Woodard, actress.

# Oregon

**Capital:** Salem
**Governor:** John A. Kitzhaber, D (to Jan. 2003)
**Senators:** Gordon Smith, R (to Jan. 2003);
   Ron Wyden, D (to Jan. 2005)
**Secy. of State:** Bill Bradbury, D (to Jan. 2005)
**Treasurer:** Randall Edwards, D (to Jan. 2005)
**Atty. General:** Hardy Myers, D (to Jan. 2005)
**Organized as territory:** Aug. 14, 1848
**Entered Union (rank):** Feb. 14, 1859 (33)
**Present constitution adopted:** 1859
**Motto:** *Alis volat Propriis* (She flies with her own wings) (1987)
**State Symbols: flower,** Oregon grape (1899); **tree,** douglas fir (1939); **animal,** beaver (1969); **bird,** western meadowlark (1927); **fish,** chinook salmon (1961); **rock,** thunderegg (1965); **colors,** navy blue and gold (1959); **song,** "Oregon, My Oregon" (1927); **insect,** swallowtail butterfly (1979); **dance,** square dance (1977); **nut,** hazelnut (1989); **gemstone,** sunstone (1987); **seashell,** Oregon hairy triton (1991); **beverage,** milk (1997); **mushroom,** Pacific golden chanterelle (1999);
**Nickname:** Beaver State
**Origin of name:** Unknown. However, it is generally accepted that the name, first used by Jonathan Carver in 1778, was taken from the writings of Maj. Robert Rogers, an English army officer.
**10 largest cities (2000):** Portland, 529,121; Eugene, 137,893; Salem, 136,924; Gresham, 90,205; Beaverton, 76,129; Hillsboro, 70,186; Medford, 63,154; Springfield, 52,864; Bend, 52,029; Corvallis, 49,322
**Land area:** 95,997 sq mi. (248,632 sq km)
**Geographic center:** In Crook Co., 25 mi. SSE of Prineville
**Number of counties:** 36
**Largest county by population and area:** Multnomah, 665,810 (2001); Harney, 10,135 sq mi.
**State forests:** 820,000 ac.
**State parks:** 240 (93,330 ac.)
**Residents:** Oregonian
**2001 resident population est.:** 3,472,867
**2000 resident census population (rank):** 3,421,399 (28). **Male:** 1,696,550 (49.6%); **Female:** 1,724,849 (50.4%). **White:** 2,961,623 (86.6%); **Black:** 55,662 (1.6%); **American Indian:** 45,211 (1.3%); **Asian:** 101,350 (3.0%); **Other race:** 144,832 (4.2%); **Two or more races:** 104,745 (3.1%); **Hispanic/Latino:** 275,314 (8.0%). **2000 percent population 18 and over:** 75.3; **65 and over:** 12.8; **median age:** 36.3.

Spanish and English sailors are believed to have sighted the Oregon coast in the 1500s and 1600s. Capt. James Cook, seeking the Northwest Passage, charted some of the coastline in 1778. In 1792, Capt. Robert Gray, in the *Columbia,* discovered the river named after his ship and claimed the area for the U.S.

In 1805 the Lewis and Clark expedition explored the area. John Jacob Astor's fur depot, Astoria, was founded in 1811. Disputes for control of Oregon between American settlers and the Hudson Bay

Company were finally resolved in the 1846 Oregon Treaty, in which Great Britain gave up claims to the region.

Oregon has a $3.3 billion lumber and wood products industry, and an $859 million paper and allied manufacturing industry. Oregon has the only nickel smelter in the United States. Its salmon-fishing industry is one of the world's largest.

In agriculture, the state leads in growing peppermint, cover seed crops, blackberries, boysenberries, loganberries, black raspberries, and hazelnuts. It is second in raising hops, red raspberries, prunes, snap beans, and onions.

With the low-cost electric power provided by dams, Oregon has developed steadily as a manufacturing state. Leading manufactured items are lumber and plywood, metalwork, machinery, aluminum, chemicals, paper, food packing, and electronic equipment.

Crater Lake National Park, Mount Hood, and Bonneville Dam on the Columbia are major tourist attractions. Other points of interest include the Oregon Dunes National Recreation Area, Oregon Caves National Monument, Cape Perpetua in Siuslaw National Forest, Columbia River Gorge between The Dalles and Troutdale, Hells Canyon, Newberry Volcanic National Monument, and John Day Fossil Beds National Monument.

Famous natives and residents: James Beard, food expert; Raymond Carver, writer and poet; Homer C. Davenport, political cartoonist; David Douglas, botanist; Abigail Scott Duniway, women's suffrage advocate; Robert Gray, sea captain and discoverer of Columbia River; Matt Groening, cartoonist; Mark Hatfield, senator; Donald P. Hodel, secretary of the Interior; Chief Joseph, Nez Percé chief; Dave Kingman, baseball player; Ursula LeGuin, writer; Edwin Markham, poet; Phyllis McGinley, author; Linus Pauling, chemist; Jane Powell, actress and singer; John Reed, poet and author; Harvey W. Scott, editor; Doc Severinsen, band leader; Norton Simon, business executive; Paul M. Simon, Illinois senator; William E. Stafford, poet; Sally Struthers, actress.

# Pennsylvania

**Capital:** Harrisburg
**Governor:** Mark Schweiker, R (to Jan. 2003)
**Lieut. Governor:** Robert Jubelirer, R (to Jan. 2003)
**Senators:** Rick Santorum, R (to Jan. 2007);
   Arlen Specter, R (to Jan. 2005)
**Acting Secy. of the Commonwealth:** C. Michael Weaver, R (at the pleasure of the governor)
**Auditor General:** Robert P. Casey, Jr., D (to Jan. 2005)
**Atty. General:** Mike Fisher, R (to Jan. 2005)
**Entered Union (rank):** Dec. 12, 1787 (2)
**Present constitution adopted:** 1968
**Motto:** Virtue, liberty, and independence
**State Symbols: flower,** mountain laurel (1933); **tree,** hemlock (1931); **bird,** ruffed grouse (1931); **dog,** Great Dane (1965); **colors,** blue and gold (1907); **song,** "Pennsylvania" (1990);
**Nickname:** Keystone State
**Origin of name:** In honor of Adm. Sir William Penn, father of William Penn. It means "Penn's Woodland."
**10 largest cities (2000):** Philadelphia, 1,517,550; Pittsburgh, 334,563; Allentown, 106,632; Erie, 103,717; Upper Darby, 81,821; Reading, 81,207; Scranton, 76,415; Bethlehem, 71,329; Lower Merion, 59,850; Bensalem, 58,434
**Land area:** 44,817 sq mi. (116,076 sq km)
**Geographic center:** In Centre Co., 2½ mi. SW of Bellefonte
**Number of counties:** 67

**Largest county by population and area:** Philadelphia, 1,491,812 (2001); Lycoming, 1,235 sq mi.
**State forests:** over 2 mil. ac.
**State parks:** 116
**Residents:** Pennsylvanian
**2001 resident population est.:** 12,287,150
**2000 resident census population (rank):** 12,281,054 (6). **Male:** 5,929,663 (48.3%); **Female:** 6,351,391 (51.7%). **White:** 10,484,203 (85.4%); **Black:** 1,224,612 (10.0%); **American Indian:** 18,348 (0.1%); **Asian:** 219,813 (1.8%); **Other race:** 188,437 (1.5%); **Two or more races:** 142,224 (1.2%); **Hispanic/ Latino:** 394,088 (3.2%). **2000 percent population 18 and over:** 76.2; **65 and over:** 15.6; **median age:** 38.0.

Rich in historic lore, Pennsylvania territory was disputed in the early 1600s among the Dutch, the Swedes, and the English. England acquired the region in 1664 with the capture of New York, and in 1681 Pennsylvania was granted to William Penn, a Quaker, by King Charles II.

Philadelphia was the seat of the federal government almost continuously from 1776 to 1800; there the Declaration of Independence was signed in 1776 and the U.S. Constitution drawn up in 1787. Valley Forge, of Revolutionary War fame, and Gettysburg, site of the pivotal battle of the Civil War, are both in Pennsylvania. The Liberty Bell is located in a glass pavilion across from Independence Hall in Philadelphia.

The nation's first oil well was dug at Titusville in 1859, and the mining of iron ore and coal led to the development of the state's steel industry. More recently Pennsylvania's industry has diversified, although the state still leads the country in the production of specialty steel. The service, retail trade, and manufacturing sectors provide the most jobs; Pennsylvania is a leader in the production of chemicals and pharmaceuticals, food products, and electronic equipment.

Pennsylvania's 59,000 farms (occupying nearly 8 million acres) are the backbone of the state's economy, producing a wide variety of crops. Leading commodities are dairy products, cattle and calves, mushrooms, greenhouse and nursery products, poultry and eggs, a variety of fruits, sweet corn, potatoes, maple syrup, and Christmas trees.

Pennsylvania's rich heritage draws billions of tourist dollars annually. Among the chief attractions are the Gettysburg National Military Park, Valley Forge National Historical Park, Independence National Historical Park in Philadelphia, the Pennsylvania Dutch region, the Eisenhower farm near [illegible], and the [illegible] Recreation Area.

Famous natives and residents: Louisa May Alcott, novelist; Marian Anderson, contralto; Maxwell Anderson, dramatist; Samuel Barber, composer; John Barrymore, actor; Donald Barthelme, author; Stephen Vincent Benét, poet and story writer; Daniel Boone, frontiersman; Ed Bradley, TV anchorman; James Buchanan, former president; Alexander Calder, sculptor; Rachel Carson, biologist and author; Mary Cassatt, painter; Henry Steele Commager, historian; Bill Cosby, actor; Stuart Davis, painter; Jimmy and Tommy Dorsey, band leaders; W. C. Fields, comedian; Stephen Foster, composer; Robert Fulton, inventor; Grace, Princess of Monaco; Martha Graham, choreographer; Alexander Haig, secretary of state; Marilyn Horne, mezzo-soprano; Lee Iacocca, auto executive; Reggie Jackson, baseball player; Gene Kelly, dancer and actor; Gelsey Kirkland, ballerina; S. S. Kresge, merchant; Mario Lanza, actor and singer; George C. Marshall, general; George McClellan, general; Margaret Mead, anthropologist; Andrew Mellon,

financier; Tom Mix, actor; Arnold Palmer, golfer; Robert E. Peary, explorer; Man Ray, painter; Mary Roberts Rinehart, novelist; Betsy Ross, flagmaker; B. F. Skinner, psychologist; John Sloan, painter; Gertrude Stein, author; James Stewart, actor; John Updike, novelist; Honus Wagner, baseball player; Fred Waring, band leader; Ethel Waters, singer and actress; Anthony Wayne, military officer; August Wilson, poet, writer, and playwright; Wallis Warfield, Duchess of Windsor; Andrew Wyeth, painter.

# Rhode Island

**Capital:** Providence
**Governor:** Lincoln C. Almond, R (to Jan. 2003)
**Lieut. Governor:** Charles J. Fogarty, D (to Jan. 2003)
**Senators:** Jack Reed, D (to Jan. 2003); Lincoln Chafee, R (to Jan. 2007)
**Secy. of State:** Edward S. Inman, D (to Jan. 2003)
**Atty. General:** Sheldon Whitehouse, D (to Jan. 2003)
**General Treasurer:** Paul J. Tavares, D (to Jan. 2003)
**Entered Union (rank):** May 29, 1790 (13)
**Present constitution adopted:** 1843
**Motto:** Hope
**State Symbols: flower,** violet (unofficial) (1968); **tree,** red maple (official) (1964); **bird,** Rhode Island red hen (official) (1954); **shell,** quahog (official) (1954); **mineral,** bowenite (1966); **stone,** cumberlandite (1966); **colors,** blue, white, and gold (in state flag); **song,** "Rhode Island" (1946);
**Nickname:** The Ocean State
**Origin of name:** From the Greek Island of Rhodes
**10 largest cities (2000):** Providence, 173,618; Warwick, 85,808; Cranston, 79,269; Pawtucket, 72,958; East Providence, 48,688; Woonsocket, 43,224; Coventry, 33,668; North Providence, 32,411; Cumberland, 31,840; West Warwick, 29,581
**Land area:** 1,045 sq mi. (2,706 sq km)
**Geographic center:** In Kent Co., 1 mi. SSW of Crompton
**Number of counties:** 5
**Largest county by population and area:** Providence, 627,314 (2001); Providence, 413 sq mi.
**State forests:** 11 (20,900 ac.)
**State parks:** 14
**Residents:** Rhode Islander
**2001 resident population est.:** 1,058,920
**2000 resident census population (rank):** 1,048,319 (43). **Male:** 503,635 (48.0%); **Female:** 544,684 (52.0%). **White:** 891,191 (85.0%); **Black:** 46,908 (4.5%); **American Indian:** 5,121 (0.5%); **Asian:** 23,665 (2.3%); **Other race:** 52,616 (5.0%); **Two or more races:** 28,251 (2.7%); **Hispanic/Latino:** 90,820 (8.7%). **2000 percent population 18 and over:** 76.4; **65 and over:** 14.5; **median age:** 36.7.

From its beginnings, Rhode Island has been distinguished by its support for freedom of conscience and national independence. Roger Williams founded the present state capital, Providence, after being exiled by the Massachusetts Bay Colony Puritans in 1636. Williams was followed by other religious exiles who founded Pocasset, now Portsmouth, in 1638 and Newport in 1639.

Rhode Island's rebellious, authority-defying nature was further demonstrated by the burnings of the British revenue cutters *Liberty* and *Gaspee* prior to the Revolution; by its early declaration of independence from Great Britain in May 1776; by its refusal to participate actively in the War of 1812; and by Dorr's Rebellion of 1842, which protested property requirements for voting.

Rhode Island, smallest of the fifty states, is densely populated and highly industrialized. It is a major center for jewelry manufacturing. Electronics, metal, plastic products, and boat and ship construction are other important industries. Non-manufacturing employment includes research in health, medicine, and the ocean environment. Providence is a wholesale distribution center for New England.

Fishing ports are at Galilee and Newport. Rural areas of the state support small-scale farming, including grapes for local wineries, turf grass, and nursery stock. Tourism generates over a billion dollars a year in revenue.

Newport became famous as the summer capital of high society in the mid-19th century. Touro Synagogue (1763) is the oldest in the U.S. Other points of interest include the Roger Williams National Memorial in Providence, Samuel Slater's Mill in Pawtucket, the General Nathanael Greene Homestead in Coventry, and Block Island.

Famous natives and residents: Harry Anderson, actor; George M. Cohan, actor and dramatist; Eddie Dowling, actor and stage producer; Nelson Eddy, baritone and actor; Ann Smith Franklin, printer and almanac publisher; Charles Gorham, silversmith; Spalding Gray, writer, performance artist; Bobby Hackett, trumpeter; David Hartman, TV newscaster; Ruth Hussey, actress; Anne Hutchinson, religious leader; Thomas H. Ince, film producer; Wilbur John, Quaker leader; Van Johnson, actor; Clarence King, first director of the U.S. Geological Survey; Galway Kinnell, poet; Oliver La Farge, writer; Irving R. Levine, news correspondent; H. P. Lovecraft, author; Ida Lewis, lighthouse keeper; John McLaughlin, political commentator, broadcaster; Dana C. Munro, educator and historian; Matthew C. Perry, naval officer; Oliver Hazard Perry, naval officer; King Philip (Metacomet), Indian leader; Anthony Quinn, actor; Gilbert Stuart, painter; Sarah Helen (Power) Whitman, poet; Jemima Wilkinson, religious leader; Roger Williams, clergyman and founder of Rhode Island; Leonard Woodcock, labor union official; James Woods, actor.

# South Carolina

**Capital:** Columbia
**Governor:** Jim Hodges, D (to Jan. 2003)
**Lieut. Governor:** Robert L. Peeler, R (to Jan. 2003)
**Senators:** Ernest Hollings, D (to Jan. 2005);
  Strom Thurmond, R (to Jan. 2003)
**Secy. of State:** Jim Miles, R (to Jan. 2003)
**Comptroller General:** Jim Lander, D
  (to Jan. 2003)
**Atty. General:** Charles M. Condon, R (to Jan. 2003)
**Entered Union (rank):** May 23, 1788 (8)
**Present constitution adopted:** 1895
**Mottoes:** *Animis opibusque parati* (Prepared in mind
  and resources) and *Dum spiro spero* (While I breathe,
  I hope)
**State Symbols: flower,** Carolina yellow jessamine
  (1924); **tree,** palmetto tree (1939); **bird,** Carolina wren
  (1948); **song,** "Carolina" (1911);
**Nickname:** Palmetto State
**Origin of name:** In honor of Charles I of England
**10 largest cities (2000):** Columbia, 116,278;
  Charleston, 96,650; North Charleston, 79,641;
  Greenville, 56,002; Rock Hill, 49,765; Mount Pleasant,
  47,609; Spartanburg, 39,673; Sumter, 39,643; Hilton
  Head Island, 33,862; Florence, 30,248
**Land area:** 30,109 sq mi. (77,982 sq km)
**Geographic center:** In Richland Co., 13 mi. SE of
  Columbia
**Number of counties:** 46
**Largest county by population and area:** Greenville,
  386,693 (2001); Horry, 1,134 sq mi.
**State forests:** 4 (124,052 ac.)
**State parks:** 50 (61,726 ac.)
**Residents:** South Carolinian
**2001 resident population est.:** 4,063,011

**2000 resident census population (rank):** 4,012,012
(26). **Male:** 1,948,929 (48.6%); **Female:** 2,063,083
(51.4%). **White:** 2,695,560 (67.2%); **Black:** 1,185,216
(29.5%); **American Indian:** 13,718 (0.3%); **Asian:**
36,014 (0.9%); **Other race:** 39,926 (1.0%); **Two or
more races:** 39,950 (1.0%); **Hispanic/Latino:** 95,076
(2.4%). **2000 percent population 18 and over:** 74.8;
**65 and over:** 12.1; **median age:** 35.4.

Following exploration of the coast in 1521 by Francisco de Gordillo, the Spanish tried unsuccessfully to establish a colony near present-day Georgetown in 1526, and the French also failed to colonize Parris Island near Fort Royal in 1562. The first English settlement was made in 1670 at Albemarle Point on the Ashley River, but poor conditions drove the settlers to the site of Charleston (originally called Charles Town).

South Carolina, officially separated from North Carolina in 1729, was the scene of extensive military action during the Revolution and again during the Civil War. The Civil War began in 1861 as South Carolina troops fired on federal Fort Sumter in Charleston Harbor, and the state was the first to secede from the Union.

Once primarily agricultural, South Carolina today has many large textile and other mills that produce several times the output of its farms in cash value. Charleston makes asbestos, wood, pulp, steel products, chemicals, machinery, and apparel.

Farms have become fewer but larger in recent years. South Carolina ranks third in peach production; it ranks fourth in overall tobacco production. Other top agricultural commodities include nursery and greenhouse products, watermelons, peanuts, broilers and turkeys, and cattle and calves. The only commercial tea plantation in America is 20 mi south of Charleston on Wadmalaw Island.

Points of interest include Fort Sumter National Monument, Fort Moultrie, Fort Johnson, and aircraft carrier USS *Yorktown* in Charleston Harbor; the Middleton, Magnolia, and Cypress Gardens in Charleston; Cowpens National Battlefield; the Hilton Head resorts; and the Riverbanks 200 and Botanical Garden in Columbia.

Famous natives and residents: Bernard Baruch, statesman; Mary McLeod Bethune, educator; James F. Byrnes, senator, jurist and secretary of state; John C. Calhoun, statesman; Mark Clark, general; Joe Frazier, prize fighter; Althea Gibson, tennis champion; Dizzy Gillespie, jazz trumpeter; DuBose Heyward, poet, playwright, and novelist; Andrew Jackson, president; Jesse Jackson, civil rights leader; Eartha Kitt, singer; Francis Marion ("Swamp Fox"), Revolutionary general; Ronald McNair, astronaut; John Rutledge, jurist; Strom Thurmond, politician; Charles Townes, physicist; William Westmoreland, general; Vanna White, TV personality.

# South Dakota

**Capital:** Pierre
**Governor:** William J. Janklow, R (to Jan. 2003)
**Lieut. Governor:** Carole Hillard, R (to Jan. 2003)
**Senators:** Thomas A. Daschle, D (to Jan. 2005);
  Tim Johnson, D (to Jan. 2003)
**Atty. General:** Mark Barnett, R (to Jan. 2003)
**Secy. of State:** Joyce Hazeltine, R (to Jan. 2003)
**Treasurer:** Richard Butler, D (to Jan. 2003)
**Organized as territory:** March 2, 1861
**Entered Union (rank):** Nov. 2, 1889 (40)
**Present constitution adopted:** 1889
**Motto:** Under God the people rule
**State Symbols: flower,** American pasqueflower (1903);
  **grass,** Western wheat grass (1970); **soil,** houdek

(1990); **tree,** black hills spruce (1947); **bird,**
ring-necked pheasant (1943); **insect,** honeybee
(1978); **animal,** coyote (1949); **mineral stone,** rose
quartz (1966); **gemstone,** fairburn agate (1966);
**colors,** blue and gold (in state flag); **song,** "Hail!
South Dakota" (1943); **fish,** walleye (1982); **musical
instrument,** fiddle (1989); **dessert,** kuchen (2000);
**Nicknames:** Mount Rushmore State; Coyote State
**Origin of name:** From the Sioux tribe, meaning "allies"
**10 largest cities (2000):** Sioux Falls, 123,975; Rapid
City, 59,607; Aberdeen, 24,658; Watertown, 20,237;
Brookings, 18,504; Mitchell, 14,558; Pierre, 13,876;
Yankton, 13,528; Huron, 11,893; Vermillion, 9,765
**Land area:** 75,885 sq mi. (196,542 sq km)
**Geographic center:** In Hughes Co., 8 mi. NE of Pierre
**Number of counties:** 66 (64 county governments)
**Largest county by population and area:** Minnehaha,
150,327 (2001); Meade, 3,471 sq mi.
**State forests:** None[1]
**State parks:** 12 plus 39 recreational areas (87,269 ac.)[2]
**Residents:** South Dakotan
**2001 resident population est.:** 756,600
**2000 resident census population (rank):** 754,844 (46).
**Male:** 374,558 (49.6%); **Female:** 380,286 (50.4%).
**White:** 669,404 (88.7%); **Black:** 4,685 (0.6%); **Ameri-
can Indian:** 62,283 (8.3%); **Asian:** 4,378 (0.6%);
**Other race:** 3,677 (0.5%); **Two or more races:**
10,156 (1.3%); **Hispanic/Latino:** 10,903 (1.4%). **2000
percent population 18 and over:** 73.2; **65 and over:**
14.3; **median age:** 35.6.

1. No designated state forests; about 13,000 ac. of
state land is forestland. 2. Acreage includes 39 recreation areas and 80 roadside parks, in addition to 12
state parks.

Exploration of this area began in 1743 when
Louis-Joseph and François Verendrye came from
France in search of a route to the Pacific.

The U.S. acquired the region as part of the Louisiana Purchase in 1803, and it was explored by
Lewis and Clark in 1804–1806. Fort Pierre, the first
permanent settlement, was established in 1817.

Settlement of South Dakota did not begin in earnest until the arrival of the railroad in 1873 and the
discovery of gold in the Black Hills in 1874.

Agriculture is a cultural and economic mainstay,
but it no longer leads the state in employment or
share of gross state product. Durable-goods manufacturing and private services have evolved as the
drivers of the economy. Tourism is also a booming
industry in the state, generating over a billion dollars' worth of economic activity each year.

South Dakota is the second-largest producer of
flaxseed and sunflower seed in the nation. It is the
third-largest producer of hay and rye.

The Black Hills are the highest mountains east of
the Rockies. Mt. Rushmore is world-famous for the
101 ft. likenesses of Washington, Jefferson, Lincoln,
and Theodore Roosevelt, which were carved in
granite by Gutzon Borglum. A memorial to Crazy
Horse is also being carved in granite near Custer.

Other tourist attractions include the Badlands; the
World's Only Corn Palace, in Mitchell; and the city
of Deadwood, where Wild Bill Hickok was killed in
1876 and where gambling was recently legalized.

Famous natives and residents: Sparky Anderson, baseball
manager; Gertrude Bonnin (Zitkala-Sa), Sioux writer and
pan-Indian activist; Tom Brokaw, TV newscaster; Robert
Casey, writer; Myron Floren, accordionist; Joseph J. Foss,
WW II Marine fighter ace; Mary Hart, TV host; Crazy
Horse, Oglala chief; Oscar Howe, Sioux artist; Hubert H.
Humphrey, vice president; Cheryl Ladd, actress; Ernest
Orlando Lawrence, physicist; Russell Means, American

Indian activist; George McGovern, politician; Arthur C.
Mellette, first governor; Dorothy Provine, actress;
Rain-in-the-Face, Hunkpapa Sioux chief; Red Cloud, chief
of the Oglala Sioux; Ben Reifel, Brulé Sioux congressman;
Ole Edvart Rølvaag, writer; Sitting Bull, chief of
Hunkpappa Sioux; Norm Van Brocklin, football player;
Mamie Van Doren, actress.

# Tennessee

**Capital:** Nashville
**Governor:** Don Sundquist, R (to Jan. 2003)
**Lieut. Governor:** John S. Wilder, D (to Jan. 2005)
**Senators:** Fred Thompson, R (to Jan. 2003);
William Frist, R (to Jan. 2007)
**Secy. of State:** Riley C. Darnell, D (to Jan. 2005)
**Atty. General:** Paul G. Summers, D (to Aug. 2005)
**Treasurer:** Steve Adams, D (to Jan. 2003)
**Comptroller:** John G. Morgan (to Jan. 2003)
**Entered Union (rank):** June 1, 1796 (16)
**Present constitution adopted:** 1870; amended 1953,
1960, 1966, 1972, 1978
**Motto:** Agriculture and Commerce (1987)
**Slogan:** Tennessee—America at its best! (1965)
**State Symbols: flower,** iris (1933); **tree,** tulip poplar
(1947); **bird,** mockingbird (1933); **horse,** Tennessee
walking horse; **animal,** raccoon (1971); **wild flower,**
passion flower (1973); **songs,** "Tennessee Waltz"
(1965); "My Homeland, Tennessee" (1925); "When It's
Iris Time in Tennessee" (1935); "My Tennessee"
(1955); "Rocky Top" (1982); "Tennessee" (1992);
**Nickname:** Volunteer State
**Origin of name:** Of Cherokee origin; the exact meaning
is unknown
**10 largest cities (2000):** Memphis, 650,100;
Nashville-Davidson [1], 569,891; Knoxville, 173,890;
Chattanooga, 155,554; Clarksville, 103,455;
Murfreesboro, 68,816; Jackson, 59,643; Johnson City,
55,469; Kingsport, 44,905; Franklin, 41,842
**Land area:** 41,217 sq mi. (106,752 sq km)
**Geographic center:** In Rutherford Co., 5 mi. NE
of Murfreesboro
**Number of counties:** 95
**Largest county by population and area:** Shelby,
896,013 (2001); Shelby, 755 sq mi.
**State forests:** 5
**State parks:** 80
**Residents:** Tennessean, Tennesseean
**2001 resident population est.:** 5,740,021
**2000 resident census population (rank):** 5,689,283
(16). **Male:** 2,770,275 (48.7%); **Female:** 2,919,008
(51.3%). **White:** 4,563,310 (80.2%); **Black:** 932,809
(16.4%); **American Indian:** 15,152 (0.3%); **Asian:**
56,662 (1.0%); **Other race:** 56,036 (1.0%); **Two or
more races:** 63,109 (1.1%); **Hispanic/Latino:**
123,838 (2.2%). **2000 percent population 18 and
over:** 75.0; **65 and over:** 12.4; **median age:** 35.9.

1. The city is part of a consolidated city-county government and is coextensive with Davidson County.

First visited by the Spanish explorer Hernando de
Soto in 1540, the Tennessee area would later be
claimed by both France and England as a result of
the 1670s and 1680s explorations of Jacques Marquette and Louis Joliet, Sieur de la Salle, and James
Needham and Gabriel Arthur. Great Britain obtained
the area after the French and Indian Wars in 1763.

During 1784–1787, the settlers formed the "state"
of Franklin, which was disbanded when the region
was allowed to send representatives to the North
Carolina legislature. In 1790 Congress organized the
territory south of the Ohio River, and Tennessee
joined the Union in 1796.

Although Tennessee joined the Confederacy during the Civil War, there was much pro-Union sentiment in the state, which was the scene of extensive military action.

The state is now predominantly industrial; the majority of its population lives in urban areas. Among the most important products are chemicals, textiles, apparel, electrical machinery, furniture, and leather goods. Other lines include food processing, lumber, primary metals, and metal products. The state ranks high in the production of marble, zinc, pyrite, and ball clay.

Tennessee is a leading tobacco-producing state. Other farming income is derived from livestock and dairy products, as well as greenhouse and nursery products and cotton.

With six other states, Tennessee shares the extensive federal reservoir developments on the Tennessee and Cumberland River systems. The Tennessee Valley Authority operates a number of dams and reservoirs in the state.

Among the major points of interest are the Andrew Johnson National Historic Site at Greeneville, the American Museum of Atomic Energy at Oak Ridge, Great Smoky Mountains National Park, the Hermitage (home of Andrew Jackson near Nashville), Rock City Gardens near Chattanooga, and three National Military Parks.

Famous natives and residents: James Agee, writer; Eddy Arnold, singer; Chet Atkins, guitarist; Julian Bond, Georgia legislator; Davy Crockett, frontiersman; David G. Farragut, first American admiral; Lester Flatt, bluegrass musician; Tennessee Ernie Ford, singer; Abe Fortas, jurist; Aretha Franklin, singer; Nikki Giovanni, poet; Al Gore, Jr., former vice president; Red Grooms, artist; Isaac Hayes, composer; Benjamin L. Hooks, civil rights activist; Cordell Hull, secretary of state; Andrew Jackson, president; Andrew Johnson, president; Estes Kefauver, legislator; Anita Kerr, singer; Grace Moore, soprano; Dolly Parton, singer; Minnie Pearl, singer and comedienne; James K. Polk, president; Grantland Rice, sportswriter; Carl Rowan, journalist; Wilma Rudolph, sprinter; Sequoyah, Cherokee scholar and educator; Cybil Shepherd, actress; Dinah Shore, actress and singer; Tina Turner, singer; Alvin York, World War I hero.

# Texas

**Capital:** Austin
**Governor:** Rick Perry, R (to Jan. 2003)
**Lieut. Governor:** Bill Ratliff, R (to Jan. 2003)
**Senators:** Phil Gramm, R (to Jan. 2003);
  Kay Bailey Hutchison, R (to Jan. 2007)
**Secy. of State:** Guyn Shea (apptd. by gov.)
**Comptroller:** Carole Keeton Rylander, R (to Jan. 2003)
**Atty. General:** John Cornyn, R (to Jan. 2003)
**Entered Union (rank):** Dec. 29, 1845 (28)
**Present constitution adopted:** 1876
**Motto:** Friendship
**State Symbols: flower,** bluebonnet (1901); **tree,** pecan (1919); **bird,** mockingbird (1927); **song,** "Texas, Our Texas" (1929); **fish,** guadalupe bass (1989); **seashell,** lightning whelk (1987); **dish,** chili (1977); **folk dance,** square dance (1991); **fruit,** Texas red grapefruit (1993); **gem,** Texas blue topaz (1969); **gemstone cut,** Lone Star cut (1977); **grass,** sideoats grass (1971); **reptile,** horned lizard (1993); **stone,** petrified palmwood (1969); **plant,** prickly pear cactus; **insect,** monarch butterfly; **pepper,** jalapeño pepper; **mammal,** longhorn; **small mammal,** armadillo; **flying mammal,** Mexican free-tailed bat;
**Nickname:** Lone Star State
**Origin of name:** From an Indian word meaning "friends"
**10 largest cities (2000):** Houston, 1,953,631; Dallas,

1,188,580; San Antonio, 1,144,646; Austin, 656,562; El Paso, 563,662; Fort Worth, 534,694; Arlington, 332,969; Corpus Christi, 277,454; Plano, 222,030; Garland, 215,768
**Land area:** 261,797 sq mi. (678,054 sq km)
**Geographic center:** In McCulloch Co., 15 mi. NE of Brady
**Number of counties:** 254
**Largest county by population and area:** Harris, 3,460,589 (2001); Brewster, 6,193 sq mi.
**State forests:** 5 (7,314 ac.)
**State parks[1]:** 125 (587,216 ac.)
**Residents:** Texan
**2001 resident population est.:** 21,325,018
**2000 resident census population (rank):** 20,851,820 (2). **Male:** 10,352,910 (49.6%); **Female:** 10,498,910 (50.4%). **White:** 14,799,505 (71.0%); **Black:** 2,404,566 (11.5%); **American Indian:** 118,362 (0.6%); **Asian:** 562,319 (2.7%); **Other race:** 2,438,001 (11.7%); **Two or more races:** 514,633 (2.5%); **Hispanic/Latino:** 6,669,666 (32.0%). **2000 percent population 18 and over:** 71.8; **65 and over:** 9.9; **median age:** 32.3.

1. Includes state parks and natural areas, two state fishing piers, and one county park.

Spanish explorers, including Álvar Núñez Cabeza de Vaca and Francisco Vásquez de Coronado, were the first to visit the region in the 16th and 17th centuries, settling at Ysleta near El Paso in 1682. In 1685, Robert Cavelier, Sieur de la Salle, established a short-lived French colony at Matagorda Bay.

Americans, led by Stephen F. Austin, began to settle along the Brazos River in 1821 when Texas was controlled by Mexico, recently independent from Spain. In 1836, following a brief war between the American settlers in Texas and the Mexican government, the Independent Republic of Texas was proclaimed with Sam Houston as president. This war was famous for the battles of the Alamo and San Jacinto. After Texas became the state in 1845, border disputes led to the Mexican War of 1846–1848.

Possessing enormous natural resources, Texas is a major agricultural state and an industrial giant. Second only to Alaska in land area, it leads all other states in such categories as oil, cattle, sheep, and cotton. Texas ranches and farms also produce poultry and eggs, dairy products, greenhouse and nursery products, wheat, hay, rice, sugar cane, and peanuts, and a variety of fruits and vegetables.

Sulfur, salt, helium, asphalt, graphite, bromine, natural gas, cement, and clays are among the state's valuable resources. Chemicals, oil refining, food processing, machinery, and transportation equipment are among the major Texas manufacturing industries.

Millions of tourists spend well over $20.6 billion annually visiting more than 100 state parks, recreation areas, and points of interest such as the Gulf Coast resort area, the Lyndon B. Johnson Space Center in Houston, the Alamo in San Antonio, the state capital in Austin, and the Big Bend and Guadalupe Mountains National Park.

Famous natives and residents: Alvin Ailey, choreographer; Mary Kay Ash, cosmetics entrepreneur; Steven Fuller Austin, founding father of Texas; Gene Autry, singer and actor; Carol Burnett, comedienne; George W. Bush, president and governor; Cyd Charisse, actress and dancer; Denton A. Cooley, heart surgeon; Joan Crawford, actress; Dwight David Eisenhower, president and general; A. J. Foyt, auto racer; Ben Hogan, golfer; Sam Houston, general and statesman; Howard Hughes, industrialist and film producer; Jack Johnson, boxer; Lyndon B. Johnson, president; George Jones, singer; Tommy Lee Jones, actor; Janis Joplin, singer; Scott Joplin, composer; Trini Lopez, singer; Mary Martin, singer and actress; Spanky McFarland, actor; Audie Murphy, actor and war hero; Chester Nimitz, admiral; Sandra Day O'Connor, jurist; Buck Owens, singer; Selena Pérez, singer; Lou Diamond Phillips, actor; Katherine Anne Porter, novelist; Wiley Post, aviator; Dan Rather, TV newscaster; Robert Rauschenberg, painter; Tex Ritter, singer; Rip Torn, actor and director; Tommy Tune, dancer and choreographer; Stevie Ray Vaughan, guitarist and singer; Lupe Velez, actress; Dooley Wilson, actor and musician; Babe Didrikson Zaharias, athlete and golfer.

# Utah

**Capital:** Salt Lake City
**Governor:** Michael O. Leavitt, R (to Jan. 2005)
**Lieut. Governor:** Olene Walker, R (to Jan. 2005)
**Senators:** Robert F. Bennett, R (to Jan. 2005);
 Orrin G. Hatch, R (to Jan. 2007)
**Treasurer:** Edward T. Alter, R. (Jan. 2005)
**Auditor:** Auston G. Johnson, R (Jan. 2005)
**Atty. General:** Mark Shurtleff, R (to Jan. 2005)
**Organized as territory:** Sept. 9, 1850
**Entered Union (rank):** Jan. 4, 1896 (45)
**Present constitution adopted:** 1896
**Motto:** Industry
**State Symbols: flower,** sego lily (1911); **tree,** blue spruce (1933); **bird,** California gull (1955); **emblem,** beehive (1959); **song,** "Utah, We Love Thee" (1953); **gem,** topaz; **animal,** Rocky Mountain elk (1971); **insect,** honeybee (1983); **grass,** Indian rice grass (1990); **fossil,** allosaurus (1988); **cooking pot,** dutch oven (1997); **fish,** Bonneville cutthroat trout (1997); **fruit,** cherry (1997); **mineral,** copper; **rock,** coal (1991);
**Nickname:** Beehive State
**Origin of name:** From the Ute tribe, meaning "people of the mountains"
**10 largest cities (2000):** Salt Lake City, 181,743; West Valley City, 108,896; Provo, 105,166; Sandy, 88,418; Orem, 84,324; Ogden, 77,226; West Jordan, 68,336; Layton, 58,474; Taylorsville, 57,439; St. George, 49,663
**Land area:** 82,144 sq mi. (212,753 sq km)
**Geographic center:** In Sanpete Co., 3 mi. N. of Manti
**Number of counties:** 29
**Largest county by population and area:** Salt Lake, 904,331 (2001); San Juan, 7,821 sq mi.
**National parks:** 5
**National monuments:** 7
**State parks/forests:** 45 (64,097 ac.)
**Residents:** Utahan, Utahn
**2001 resident population est.:** 2,269,789
**2000 resident census population (rank):** 2,233,169 (34). **Male:** 1,119,031 (50.1%); **Female:** 1,114,138 (49.9%). **White:** 1,992,975 (89.2%); **Black:** 17,657 (0.8%); **American Indian:** 29,684 (1.3%); **Asian:** 37,108 (1.7%); **Other race:** 93,405 (4.2%); **Two or more races:** 31,309 (1.4%)]. **2000 percent population 18 and over:** 67.8; **65 and over:** 8.5; **median age:** 27.1.

The region was first explored for Spain by Franciscan friars Escalante and Domínguez in 1776. In 1824 the famous American frontiersman Jim Bridger discovered the Great Salt Lake.

Fleeing religious persecution in the East and Midwest, the Mormons arrived in 1847 and began to build Salt Lake City. The U.S. acquired the Utah region in the treaty ending the Mexican War in 1848, and the first transcontinental railroad was completed with the driving of a golden spike at Promontory Summit in 1869.

Mormon difficulties with the federal government about polygamy did not end until the Mormon Church renounced the practice in 1890, six years before Utah became a state.

Rich in natural resources, Utah has long been a leading producer of copper, gold, silver, lead, zinc, and molybdenum. Oil has also become a major product. Utah shares rich oil shale deposits with Colorado and Wyoming. Utah also has large deposits of low sulphur coal.

The state's top agricultural commodities include cattle and calves, dairy products, hay, greenhouse and nursery products, and hogs.

Utah's traditional industries of agriculture and mining are complemented by increased tourism and growing aerospace, biomedical, and computer-related businesses.

Utah is a great vacationland with 11,000 mi of fishing streams and 147,000 acres of lakes and reservoirs. Among the many tourist attractions are Arches, Bryce Canyon, Canyonlands, Capitol Reef, and Zion National Parks; Cedar Breaks, Dinosaur, Hovenweep, Natural Bridges, Rainbow Bridge, Timpanogos Cave, and Grand Staircase (Escalante) National Monuments; the Mormon Tabernacle in Salt Lake City; and Monument Valley. Salt Lake City hosted the 2002 Winter Olympics.

Famous natives and residents: Maude Adams, actress; Roseanne, actress; Frank Borzage, film director and producer; John M. Browning, inventor; Butch Cassidy, outlaw; Laraine Day, actress; Bernard De Voto, writer; Avard Fairbanks, sculptor; Philo Farnsworth, television pioneer; Jake Garn, senator; John Gilbert, actor; J. Willard Marriott, restaurant and hotel chain founder; Peter Skene Ogden, fur trader and trapper; Merlin Olsen, football player; Donny Osmond, Marie Osmond, singers; Ivy Baker Priest, U.S. treasurer; Lee Greene Richards, painter; Leroy Robertson, composer; Brent Scowcroft, business executive and consultant; Reed Smoot, first Mormon elected to U.S. Senate; Mack Swain, actor; Everett Thorpe, painter; Robert Walker, actor; James Woods, actor; Brigham Young, territory governor and religious leader; Loretta Young, actress.

# Vermont

**Capital:** Montpelier
**Governor:** Howard Dean, D (to Jan. 2003)
**Lieut. Governor:** Douglas A. Racine, D (to Jan. 2003)
**Senators:** James M. Jeffords, I (to Jan. 2007);
 Patrick Leahy, D (to Jan. 2005)
**Secy. of State:** Deborah L. Markowitz, D (to Jan. 2003)
**Treasurer:** James H. Douglas, R (to Jan. 2003)
**Atty. General:** William Sorrell, D (to Jan. 2003)
**Entered Union (rank):** March 4, 1791 (14)
**Present constitution adopted:** 1793
**Motto:** Vermont, Freedom and Unity
**State Symbols: flower,** red clover (1894); **tree,** sugar maple (1949); **bird,** hermit thrush (1941); **animal,** Morgan horse (1961); **insect,** honeybee (1978); **song,** "These Green Mountains" (2000);
**Nickname:** Green Mountain State
**Origin of name:** From the French "vert mont," meaning "green mountain"
**10 largest cities (2000):** Burlington, 38,889; Essex, 18,626; Rutland, 17,292; Colchester, 16,986; South Burlington, 15,814; Bennington, 15,737; Brattleboro, 12,005; Hartford, 10,367; Milton, 9,479; Barre, 9,291
**Land area:** 9,250 sq mi. (23,958 sq km)
**Geographic center:** In Washington Co., 3 mi. E of Roxbury
**Number of counties:** 14
**Largest county by population and area:** Chittenden, 147,591 (2001); Windsor, 971 sq mi.
**State forests:** 38 (167,769.5 ac.)
**State parks:** 59 (47,756.5 ac.)

**Residents:** Vermonter
**2001 resident population est.:** 613,090
**2000 resident census population (rank):** 608,827 (49).
**Male:** 298,337 (49.0%); **Female:** 310,490 (51.0%).
**White:** 589,208 (96.8%); **Black:** 3,063 (0.5%); **American Indian:** 2,420 (0.4%); **Asian:** 5,217 (0.9%); **Other race:** 1,443 (0.2%); **Two or more races:** 7,335 (1.2%); **Hispanic/Latino:** 5,504 (0.9%). **2000 percent population 18 and over:** 75.8; **65 and over:** 12.7; **median age:** 37.7.

The Vermont region was explored and claimed for France by Samuel de Champlain in 1609, and the first French settlement was established at Fort Ste. Anne in 1666. The first English settlers moved into the area in 1724 and built Fort Dummer on the site of present-day Brattleboro. England gained control of the area in 1763 after the French and Indian Wars.

First organized to drive settlers from New York out of Vermont, the Green Mountain Boys, led by Ethan Allen, won fame by capturing Fort Ticonderoga from the British on May 10, 1775, in the early days of the Revolutionary War. In 1777 Vermont adopted its first constitution, abolishing slavery and providing for universal male suffrage without property qualifications.

Vermont leads the nation in the production of monument granite, marble, and maple syrup. It is also a leader in the production of talc. Vermont's rugged, rocky terrain discourages extensive agricultural farming, but is well suited to raising fruit trees and to dairy farming.

Principal industrial products include electrical equipment, fabricated metal products, printing and publishing, and paper and allied products.

Tourism is a major industry in Vermont. Vermont's many famous ski areas include Stowe, Killington, Mt. Snow, Bromley, Jay Peak, and Sugarbush. Hunting and fishing also attract many visitors to Vermont each year. Among the many points of interest are the Green Mountain National Forest, Bennington Battle Monument, the Calvin Coolidge Homestead at Plymouth, and the Marble Exhibit in Proctor.

Famous natives and residents: Chester A. Arthur, president; Orson Bean, actor; Calvin Coolidge, president; George Dewey, admiral; John Dewey, philosopher and educator; Stephen A. Douglas, politician; James Fisk, financial speculator; Willbur Fisk, clergyman and educator; Richard Morris Hunt, architect; William Morris Hunt, painter; Elisha Otis, inventor; Moses Pendleton, choreographer; Joseph Smith, religious leader; Ernest Thompson, actor and writer; Rudy Vallee, singer and band leader; Henry Wells, pioneer entrepreneur (Wells Fargo & Co.); Brigham Young, religious leader.

# Virginia

**Capital:** Richmond
**Governor:** Mark Warner, D (to Jan. 2006)
**Senators:** John Warner, R (to Jan. 2003); George Allen, R (to Jan. 2007)
**Secy. of the Commonwealth:** Anita Rimler
**Comptroller:** David A. Von Moll
**Atty. General:** Jerry W. Kilgore
**Entered Union (rank):** June 25, 1788 (10)
**Present constitution adopted:** 1970
**Motto:** *Sic semper tyrannis* (Thus always to tyrants)
**State Symbols: flower,** American dogwood (1918); **bird,** cardinal (1950); **dog,** American foxhound (1966); **shell,** oyster shell (1974); **tree,** dogwood (1956);
**Nicknames:** The Old Dominion; Mother of Presidents
**Origin of name:** In honor of Elizabeth "Virgin Queen" of England

**10 largest cities (2000):** Virginia Beach, 425,257; Norfolk, 234,403; Chesapeake, 199,184; Richmond, 197,790; Newport News, 180,150; Hampton, 146,437; Alexandria, 128,283; Portsmouth, 100,565; Roanoke, 94,911; Lynchburg, 65,269
**Land area:** 39,594 sq mi. (102,558 sq km)
**Geographic center:** In Buckingham Co., 5 mi. SW of Buckingham
**Number of counties:** 95, plus 40 independent cities
**Largest county by population and area:** Fairfax, 985,161 (2001); Augusta, 972 sq mi.
**State forests:** 15 (50,869 ac.)
**State parks:** 34 (plus 33 natural areas)
**Residents:** Virginian
**2001 resident population est.:** 7,187,734
**2000 resident census population (rank):** 7,078,515 (12). **Male:** 3,471,895 (49.0%); **Female:** 3,606,620 (51.0%). **White:** 5,120,110 (72.3%); **Black:** 1,390,293 (19.6%); **American Indian:** 21,172 (0.3%); **Asian:** 261,025 (3.7%); **Other race:** 138,900 (2.0%); **Two or more races:** 143,069 (2.0%); **Hispanic/Latino:** 329,540 (4.7%). **2000 percent population 18 and over:** 75.4; **65 and over:** 11.2; **median age:** 35.7.

The history of America is closely tied to that of Virginia, particularly during the Colonial period. Jamestown, founded in 1607, was the first permanent English settlement in North America and slavery was introduced there in 1619. The surrenders ending both the American Revolution (Yorktown) and the Civil War (Appomattox) occurred in Virginia. The state is called the "Mother of Presidents" because eight U.S. presidents were born there.

Today, the service sector provides one-third of all jobs in Virginia, generating as much income as the manufacturing and retail industries combined in 1999 and accounting for 23% of gross state product. (The largest component of the service sector is business services, which includes computer and data processing services.)

Virginia has a large number of manufacturing industries, including transportation equipment, food processing, electronic and other electrical equipment, chemicals, textiles and apparel, lumber and wood products, and furniture.

Agriculture remains an important sector, and the state ranks among the top ten in a variety of agricultural products, including tomatoes, tobacco, peanuts, apples, summer potatoes, sweet potatoes, snap beans, and turkeys and broilers. Virginia also has a large dairy industry.

Virginia is one of the top ten coal producers in the U.S. Coal accounts for roughly 70% of Virginia's mineral value; crushed stone, sand and gravel, lime, and kyanite are also mined.

Points of interest include Mt. Vernon, home of George Washington; Monticello, home of Thomas Jefferson; Stratford, home of the Lees; Richmond, capital of the Confederacy and of Virginia; and Williamsburg, the restored Colonial capital.

Other attractions are the Shenandoah National Park, Colonial National Historical Park, Fredericksburg and Spotsylvania National Military Park, the Booker T. Washington birthplace near Roanoke, Arlington House (the Robert E. Lee Memorial), Luray Caverns, the Skyline Drive, and the Blue Ridge National Parkway.

Famous natives and residents: Richard Arlen, actor; Arthur Ashe, tennis player; Pearl Bailey, singer; Russell Baker, columnist; Warren Beatty, actor; George Bingham, painter; Richard E. Byrd, polar explorer; Willa Cather, novelist; Roy Clark, country music artist; William Clark, explorer; Henry

Clay, statesman; Joseph Cotten, actor; Ella Fitzgerald, singer; William H. Harrison, president; Patrick Henry, statesman; Sam Houston, political leader; Thomas Jefferson, president; Robert E. Lee, Confederate general; Meriwether Lewis, explorer; Shirley MacLaine, actress; James Madison, president; Moses Malone, basketball player; John Marshall, jurist; Cyrus McCormick, inventor; James Monroe, president; Opechancanough, Powhatan leader; John Payne, actor; Walter Reed, army surgeon; Matthew Ridgway, general; Bill "Bojangles" Robinson, dancer; George C. Scott, actor; Sam Snead, golfer; James "Jeb" Stuart, Confederate army officer; Thomas Sumter, general; Zachary Taylor, president; Nat Turner, leader of slave uprising; John Tyler, president; Booker T. Washington, educator; George Washington, first president; James E. West,, inventor; Woodrow Wilson, president; Tom Wolfe, journalist.

# Washington

**Capital:** Olympia
**Governor:** Gary Locke, D (to Jan. 2005)
**Lieut. Governor:** Brad Owen, D (to Jan. 2005)
**Senators:** Patty Murray, D (to Jan. 2005);
Maria Cantwell, D (to Jan. 2007)
**Secy. of State:** Sam Reed, R (to Jan. 2005)
**Treasurer:** Michael J. Murphy (to Jan. 2005)
**Atty. General:** Christine Gregoire, D (to Jan. 2005)
**Auditor:** Brian Sonntag, D (to Jan. 2005)
**Organized as territory:** March 2, 1853
**Entered Union (rank):** Nov. 11, 1889 (42)
**Present constitution adopted:** 1889
**Motto:** Al-Ki (Indian word meaning "by and by")
**State Symbols: flower,** coast rhododendron (1892); **tree,** western hemlock (1947); **bird,** willow goldfinch (1951); **fish,** steelhead trout (1969); **gem,** petrified wood (1975); **colors,** green and gold (1925); **song,** "Washington, My Home" (1959); **folk song,** "Roll On Columbia, Roll On" (1987); **dance,** square dance (1979); **grass,** bluebunch wheatgrass (1989); **insect,** blue darner dragonfly (1997); **fossil,** Columbian mammoth (1998); **fruit,** apple (1989);
**Nicknames:** Evergreen State
**Origin of name:** In honor of George Washington
**10 largest cities (2000):** Seattle, 563,374; Spokane, 195,629; Tacoma, 193,556; Vancouver, 143,560; Bellevue, 109,569; Everett, 91,488; Federal Way, 83,259; Kent, 79,524; Yakima, 71,845; Bellingham, 67,171
**Land area:** 66,544 sq mi. (172,349 sq km)
**Geographic center:** In Chelan Co., 10 mi. WSW of Wenatchee
**Number of counties:** 39
**Largest county by population and area:** King, 1,741,785 (2001); Okanogan, 5,268 sq mi.
**State forest lands:** 2.1 million ac.
**State parks:** 215 (260,000 ac.)[1]
**Residents:** Washingtonian
**2001 resident population est.:** 5,987,973
**2000 resident census population (rank) 5,894,121** (50.2%). **White:** 4,821,823 (81.8%); **Black:** 190,267 (3.2%); **American Indian:** 93,301 (1.6%); **Asian:** 322,335 (5.5%); **Other race:** 228,923 (3.9%); Two or more races: 213,519 (3.6%); **Hispanic/Latino:** 441,509 (7.5%). **2000 percent population 18 and over:** 74.3; **65 and over:** 11.2; **median age:** 35.3.

1. Parks and undeveloped areas administered by State Parks and Recreation Commission. Dept. of Wildlife administers wildlife and recreation areas totaling 428,989.5 acres.

As part of the vast Oregon Country, Washington territory was visited by Spanish, American, and British explorers—Bruno Heceta for Spain in 1775, the American Capt. Robert Gray in 1792, and Capt. George Vancouver for Britain in 1792–1794. Lewis and Clark explored the Columbia River region and coastal areas for the U.S. in 1805–1806.

Rival American and British settlers and conflicting territorial claims threatened war in the early 1840s. However, in 1846 the Oregon Treaty set the boundary at the 49th parallel and war was averted.

Washington is a leading lumber producer. Its rugged surface is rich in stands of Douglas fir, hemlock, ponderosa and white pine, spruce, larch, and cedar. The state holds first place in apples, lentils, dry edible peas, hops, pears, red raspberries, spearmint oil, and sweet cherries, and ranks high in apricots, asparagus, grapes, peppermint oil, and potatoes. Livestock and livestock products make important contributions to total farm revenue and the commercial fishing catch of salmon, halibut, and bottomfish makes a significant contribution to the state's economy.

Manufacturing industries in Washington include aircraft and missiles, shipbuilding and other transportation equipment, lumber, food processing, metals and metal products, chemicals, and machinery.

Washington has over 1,000 dams, including the Grand Coulee, built for a variety of purposes including irrigation, power, flood control, and water storage. Its abundance of electrical power makes Washington one of the nation's major producers of refined aluminum.

Among the major points of interest: Mt. Rainier, Olympic, and North Cascades National Parks. Mount St. Helens, a peak in the Cascade Range, erupted in May 1980. Also of interest are Whitman Mission and Fort Vancouver National Historic Sites; and the Pacific Science Center and the Space Needle, in Seattle.

Famous natives and residents: Earl Anthony, professional bowler; Mildred Bailey, singer; Bob Barker, TV host; Dyan Cannon, actress; Raymond Carver, writer; Carol Channing, actress; Ray Charles, singer and musician; Kurt Cobain, rock musician; Judy Collins, singer; Chris Cornell, rock musician; Fred Couples, professional golfer; Bing Crosby, singer and actor; Bob Crosby, musician; Merce Cunningham, choreographer; Howard Duff, actor; Frances Farmer, actress; Kenny G., saxophonist; Bill Gates, software executive; Jimi Hendrix, guitarist; Frank Herbert, writer; Robert Joffrey, choreographer; Chuck Jones, animator; Quincy Jones, music producer; Hank Ketcham, cartoonist; Gary Larson, cartoonist; Gypsy Rose Lee, entertainer; Kenny Loggins, rock musician; Mary McCarthy, novelist; Guthrie McClintic, theatrical producer and director; John McIntire, actor; Steve Miller, rock musician; Robert Motherwell, artist; Patrice Munsel, soprano; Craig T. Nelson, actor; Ella Raines, actress; Ahmad Rashad, football player; Ann Reinking, dancer and actress; Tom Robbins, novelist; Ann Rule, writer; Francis Scobee, astronaut; Seattle, Suquamish chief; Smohalla, Indian prophet and chief; Hillary Swank, actress; Julia Sweeney, actress; Adam West, actor; Audrey Wurdemann, poet.

# West Virginia

**Capital:** Charleston
**Governor:** Bob Wise, D (to Jan. 2005)
**Senators:** Robert C. Byrd, D (to Jan. 2007);
John D. "Jay" Rockefeller IV, D (to Jan. 2003)
**Secy. of State:** Joe Manchin, D (to Jan. 2005)
**Treasurer:** John D. Perdue, D (to Jan. 2005)
**Atty. General:** Darrell McGraw, D (to Jan. 2005)
**Entered Union (rank):** June 20, 1863 (35)
**Present constitution adopted:** 1872
**Motto:** Montani semper liberi (Mountaineers are always free)
**State Symbols: flower,** rhododendron (1903); **tree,** sugar maple (1949); **bird,** cardinal (1949); **animal,** black bear (1973); **colors,** blue and gold (official)

(1863); **songs,** "West Virginia, My Home Sweet Home," "The West Virginia Hills," and "This Is My West Virginia" (adopted by Legislature in 1947, 1961, and 1963 as official state songs);
**Nickname:** Mountain State
**Origin of name:** In honor of Elizabeth, "Virgin Queen" of England
**10 largest cities (2000):** Charleston, 53,421; Huntington, 51,475; Parkersburg, 33,099; Wheeling, 31,419; Morgantown, 26,809; Weirton, 20,411; Fairmont, 19,097; Beckley, 17,254; Clarksburg, 16,743; Martinsburg, 14,972
**Land area:** 24,077 sq mi. (62,359 sq km)
**Geographic center:** In Braxton Co., 4 mi. E of Sutton
**Number of counties:** 55
**Largest county by population and area:** Kanawha, 197,338 (2001); Randolph, 1,040 sq mi.
**State forests:** 9 (79,502 ac.)
**State parks:** 37 (74,508 ac.)
**Residents:** West Virginian
**2001 resident population est.:** 1,801,916
**2000 resident census population (rank):** 1,808,344 (37). **Male:** 879,170 (48.6%); **Female:** 929,174 (51.4%). **White:** 1,718,777 (95.0%); **Black:** 57,232 (3.2%); **American Indian:** 3,606 (0.2%); **Asian:** 9,434 (0.5%); **Other race:** 3,107 (0.2%); **Two or more races:** 15,788 (0.9%); **Hispanic/Latino:** 12,279 (0.7%). **2000 percent population 18 and over:** 77.7; **65 and over:** 15.3; **median age:** 38.9.

West Virginia's early history from 1609 until 1863 is largely shared with Virginia, of which it was a part until Virginia seceded from the Union in 1861. The delegates of the 40 western counties who opposed secession formed their own government, which was granted statehood in 1863.

In 1731 Morgan Morgan established the first permanent white settlement on Mill Creek in present-day Berkeley County. Coal, a mineral asset that would figure significantly in West Virginia's history, was discovered in 1742. Other important natural resources are oil, natural gas, and hardwood forests, which cover about 75% of the state's area.

The state's rapid industrial expansion began in the 1870s, drawing thousands of European immigrants and African Americans into the region. Miners' strikes between 1912 and 1921 required the intervention of state and federal troops to quell the violence.

Today, the state ranks second in total coal production, with about 15% of the U.S. total. It is also a leader in steel, glass, aluminum, and chemical manufactures. Major agricultural commodities are poultry and eggs, dairy products, and apples.

Tourism is increasingly popular in mountainous West Virginia. More than a million acres have been set aside in 37 state parks and recreation areas and in 9 state forests and 2 national forests. Major points of interest include Harpers Ferry and New River Gorge National River, The Greenbrier and Berkeley Springs resorts, the scenic railroad at Cass, and the historic homes in the Eastern Panhandle.

Famous natives and residents: George Brett, baseball player; Pearl S. Buck, author; Phyllis Curtin, soprano; Martin R. Delany, first black army major; Billy Dixon, frontiersman and scout; Joanne Dru, actress; Thomas "Stonewall" Jackson, Confederate general; John S. Knight, publisher; Don Knotts, actor; Peter Marshall, TV host; Kathy Mattea, singer; Whitney D. Morrow, banker and diplomat; Mary Lou Retton, gymnast; Walter Reuther, labor leader; Eleanor Steber, soprano; Lewis L. Strauss, naval officer and scientist; Cyrus Vance, government official; Jerry West, basketball player; William Lyne Wilson, legislator and university president; Chuck Yeager, test pilot and Air Force general.

# Wisconsin

**Capital:** Madison
**Governor:** Scott McCallum, R (to Jan. 2003)
**Lieut. Governor:** Margaret Farrow, R (to Jan. 2003)
**Senators:** Russell D. Feingold, D (to Jan. 2005); Herbert Kohl, D (to Jan. 2007)
**Secy. of State:** Douglas J. La Follette, D (to Jan. 2003)
**State Treasurer:** Jack C. Voight, R (to Jan. 2003)
**Atty. General:** James E. Doyle, D (to Jan. 2003)
**Superintendent of Public Instruction:** Elizabeth Burmaster, Nonpartisan (to July 2005)
**Organized as territory:** July 4, 1836
**Entered Union (rank):** May 29, 1848 (30)
**Present constitution adopted:** 1848
**Motto:** Forward
**State Symbols: flower,** wood violet (1949); **tree,** sugar maple (1949); **grain,** corn (1990); **bird,** robin (1949); **animal,** badger; **wild life animal,** white-tailed deer (1957); **domestic animal,** dairy cow (1971); **insect,** honeybee (1977); **fish,** musky (muskellunge) (1955); **song,** "On Wisconsin"; **mineral,** galena (1971); **rock,** red granite (1971); **symbol of peace,** mourning dove (1971); **soil,** antigo silt loam (1983); **fossil,** trilobite (1985); **dog,** American Water Spaniel (1986); **beverage,** milk (1988); **dance,** polka (1994); **walts,** "The Wisconsin Waltz" (2001); **ballad,** "Oh Wisconsin, Land of My Dreams" (2001);
**Nickname:** Badger State
**Origin of name:** French corruption of an Indian word whose meaning is disputed
**10 largest cities (2000):** Milwaukee, 596,974; Madison, 208,054; Green Bay, 102,313; Kenosha, 90,352; Racine, 81,855; Appleton, 70,087; Waukesha, 64,825; Oshkosh, 62,916; Eau Claire, 61,704; West Allis, 61,254
**Land area:** 54,310 sq mi. (140,673 sq km)
**Geographic center:** In Wood Co., 9 mi. SE of Marshfield
**Number of counties:** 72
**Largest county by population and area:** Milwaukee, 932,012 (2001); Marathon, 1,545 sq mi.
**State forests:** 12 (493,975 ac.)
**State parks & scenic trails:** 43 parks, 14 trails (68,355 ac.)
**Residents:** Wisconsinite
**2001 resident population est.:** 5,401,906
**2000 resident census population (rank):** 5,363,675 (18). **Male:** 2,649,041 (49.4%); **Female:** 2,714,634 (50.6%). **White:** 4,769,857 (88.9%); **Black:** 304,460 (5.7%); **American Indian:** 47,228 (0.9%); **Asian:** 88,763 (1.7%); **Other race:** 84,842 (1.6%); **Two or more races:** 66,895 (1.2%); **Hispanic/Latino:** 192,921 (3.6%). **2000 percent population 18 and over:** 74.5; **65 and over:** 13.1; **median age:** 36.0.

The Wisconsin region was first explored for France by Jean Nicolet, who landed at Green Bay in 1634. In 1660 a French trading post and Roman Catholic mission were established near present-day Ashland.

Great Britain obtained the region in settlement of the French and Indian Wars in 1763; the U.S. acquired it in 1783 after the Revolutionary War. However, Great Britain retained actual control until after the War of 1812. The region was successively governed as part of the territories of Indiana, Illinois, and Michigan between 1800 and 1836, when it became a separate territory.

Wisconsin is a leading state in milk and cheese production. Other important farm products are peas, beans, beets, corn, potatoes, oats, hay, and cranberries.

The chief industrial products of the state are automobiles, machinery, furniture, paper, beer, and processed foods. Wisconsin ranks second among the 47 paper-producing states. The state's mines produce copper, iron ore, lead, and zinc.

Wisconsin is a pioneer in social legislation, providing pensions for the blind (1907), aid to dependent children (1913), and old-age assistance (1925). In labor legislation, the state was the first to enact an unemployment compensation law (1932) and the first in which a workman's compensation law actually took effect. In 1984, Wisconsin became the first state to adopt the Uniform Marital Property Act.

The state has over 14,000 lakes, of which Winnebago is the largest. Water sports, ice-boating, and fishing are popular, as are skiing and hunting. Public parks and forests take up one-seventh of the land, with 43 state parks, 12 state forests, 14 state trails, 3 recreational areas, and 2 national forests.

Among the many points of interest are the Apostle Islands National Lakeshore; Ice Age National Scientific Reserve; the Circus World Museum at Baraboo; the Wolf, St. Croix, and Lower St. Croix national scenic riverways; and the Wisconsin Dells.

Famous natives and residents: Don Ameche, actor; Roy Chapman Andrews, naturalist and explorer; Walter Annenberg, media tycoon and philanthropist; Carrie Catt, woman suffragist; John R. Commons, economist; Tyne Daly, actress; August Derleth, author; Jeanne Dixon, seer; Zona Gale, novelist; Eric Heiden, skater; Woody Herman, band leader; Hildegarde, singer; Harry Houdini, magician; Hans V. Kaltenborne, journalist; Pee Wee King, singer; George F. Kennan, diplomat; Robert La Follette, politician; William D. Leahy, admiral; Liberace, pianist; Charles Litel, actor; Allen Ludden, TV host; Alfred Lunt, actor; Frederic March, actor; Jackie Mason, comedian; John Ringling North, circus director; Pat O'Brien, actor; Georgia O'Keeffe, painter; Charlotte Rae, actress; William H. Rehnquist, jurist; Gena Rowlands, actress; Tom Snyder, newscaster; Spencer Tracy, actor; Thorstein Veblen, economist; Orson Welles, actor and producer; Thornton Wilder, author; Charles Winninger, actor; Frank Lloyd Wright, architect.

# Wyoming

**Capital:** Cheyenne
**Governor:** Jim Geringer, R (to Jan. 2003)
**Senators:** Michael B. Enzi, R (to Jan. 2003); Craig Thomas, R (to Jan. 2007)
**Secy. of State:** Joe Meyer, R (to Jan. 2003)
**Treasurer:** Cynthia M. Lummis, R (to Jan. 2003)
**Atty. General:** Hoke MacMillan, R
**Organized as territory:** May 19, 1869
**Entered Union (rank):** July 10, 1890 (44)
**Present constitution adopted:** 1890
**Motto:** Equal rights (1893)
**State Symbols: flower,** Indian paintbrush (1917); **tree,** cottonwood (1947); **bird,** western meadowlark (1927); **dinosaur,** Triceratops (1994); **fish,** cutthroat trout (1987); **fossil,** Knightia (1987); **gemstone,** jade (1967); **insignia,** bucking horse (unofficial); **mammal,** bison (1985); **reptile,** horned toad (1993); **soil,** Forkwood series (unofficial); **song,** "Wyoming" (1955);
**Nickname:** Equality State
**Origin of name:** From the Delaware Indian word, meaning "mountains and valleys alternating"; the same as the Wyoming Valley in Pennsylvania
**10 largest cities (2000):** Cheyenne, 53,011; Casper, 49,644; Laramie, 27,204; Gillette, 19,646; Rock Springs, 18,708; Sheridan, 15,804; Green River, 11,808; Evanston, 11,507; Riverton, 9,310; Cody, 8,835

**Land area:** 97,100 sq mi. (251,501 sq km)
**Geographic center:** In Fremont Co., 58 mi. ENE of Lander
**Number of counties:** 23, plus Yellowstone National Park
**Largest county by population and area:** Laramie, 81,958 (2001); Sweetwater, 10,426 sq mi.
**State parks and historic sites:** 23 (58,498 ac.)
**Residents:** Wyomingite
**2001 resident population est.:** 494,423
**2000 resident census population (rank):** 493,782 (50). **Male:** 248,374 (50.3%); **Female:** 245,408 (49.7%). **White:** 454,670 (92.1%); **Black:** 3,722 (0.8%); **American Indian:** 11,133 (2.3%); **Asian:** 2,771 (0.6%); **Other race:** 12,301 (2.5%); **Two or more races:** 8,883 (1.8%); **Hispanic/Latino:** 31,669 (6.4%). **2000 percent population 18 and over:** 73.9; **65 and over:** 11.7; **median age:** 36.2.

The U.S. acquired the land comprising Wyoming from France as part of the Louisiana Purchase in 1803. John Colter, a fur-trapper, is the first white man known to have entered the region. In 1807 he explored the Yellowstone area and brought back news of its geysers and hot springs.

Robert Stuart pioneered the Oregon Trail across Wyoming in 1812–1813 and, in 1834, Fort Laramie, the first permanent trading post in Wyoming, was built. Western Wyoming was obtained by the U.S. in the 1846 Oregon Treaty with Great Britain and as a result of the treaty ending the Mexican War in 1848.

When the Wyoming Territory was organized in 1869, Wyoming women became the first in the nation to obtain the right to vote. In 1925 Mrs. Nellie Tayloe Ross became the first woman governor in the United States.

Wyoming's towering mountains and vast plains provide spectacular scenery, grazing lands for sheep and cattle, and rich mineral deposits.

Mining, particularly oil and natural gas, is the most important industry. Wyoming has the world's largest sodium carbonate (natrona) deposits and has the nation's second largest uranium deposits.

In 2000 Wyoming ranked second among the states in wool production (exceeded only by Texas) and third in sheep and lambs (exceeded only by Texas and California); it also had 1,580,000 cattle. Principal crops include wheat, oats, sugar beets, corn, barley, and alfalfa.

Second in mean elevation to Colorado, Wyoming has many attractions for the tourist trade, notably Yellowstone National Park. Hikers, campers and skiers are attracted to Grand Teton National Park and Jackson Hole National Monument in the Teton Range of the Rockies. Cheyenne is famous for its annual "Frontier Days" celebration. Flaming Gorge, the Fort Laramie National Historic Site, and Devils Tower and Fossil Butte National Monuments are other points of interest.

Famous natives and residents: James Bridger, trapper, guide, and storyteller; Dick Cheney, vice president; Buffalo Bill Cody, scout; John Colter, trader and first white man to enter Wyoming; June E. Downey, educator; Thomas Fitzpatrick, mountain man and guide; Curt Gowdy, sportscaster; Tom Horn, detective; Isabel Jewell, actress; Velma Linford, writer; Esther Morris, first woman judge; Ted Olson, writer; John "Portugee" Phillips, frontiersman; Jackson Pollock, painter; Nellie Tayloe Ross, first woman elected governor of a state; Alan K. Simpson, senator; Jedediah S. Smith, mountain man and first American to reach California from the East; Alan Swallow, publisher and author; Willis Van Devanter, jurist; Francis E. Warren, first state governor; Chief Washakie, chief of the Shoshone; James G. Watt, secretary of the Interior.

## Tabulated Data on State Governments

| State | Governor Term, years | Governor Annual salary | Legislature[1] Membership U[3] | Legislature[1] Membership L[4] | Legislature[1] Term, years U[3] | Legislature[1] Term, years L[4] | Legislature[1] Salaries of members[5] | Highest Court[2] Members | Highest Court[2] Term, years | Highest Court[2] Annual salary |
|---|---|---|---|---|---|---|---|---|---|---|
| Alabama | 4[6] | $ 94,655 | 35 | 105 | 4 | 4 | $ 10 per diem | 9 | 6 | $185,376[7] |
| Alaska | 4 | 83,281 | 20 | 40 | 4 | 2 | 24,012[8] per annum | 5 | 3[9] | 109,908[7] |
| Arizona | 4 | 95,000 | 30 | 60 | 2 | 2 | 25,000 per annum | 5 | 6[14] | 126,525[7] |
| Arkansas | 4 | 73,603 | 35 | 100 | 4 | 2 | 13,442[8] per annum | 7 | 8 | 123,475[7] |
| California | 4 | 165,000 | 40 | 80 | 4 | 2 | 99,000 per annum | 7 | 12 | 162,409[7] |
| Colorado | 4 | 90,000 | 35 | 65 | 4 | 2 | 30,000 per annum | 7 | 10 | 79,500[7] |
| Connecticut | 4 | 78,000 | 36 | 151 | 2 | 2 | 28,000[8] per annum | 7 | 8 | 129,404[7] |
| Delaware | 4[10] | 114,000 | 21 | 41 | 4 | 2 | 34,100 per annum | 5 | 12 | 144,100[7] |
| Florida | 4[6] | 120,171 | 40 | 120 | 4[6] | 2[11] | 29,328[8] per annum | 7 | 6[14] | 153,750 |
| Georgia | 4[6] | 127,303 | 56 | 180 | 2 | 2 | 16,200 per session | 7 | 6 | 153,086 |
| Hawaii | 4 | 94,780 | 25 | 51 | 4 | 2 | 32,000[8] per annum | 5 | 10 | 115,547[7] |
| Idaho | 4 | 95,500 | 35 | 70 | 2 | 2 | 15,646[8] per annum | 5 | 6 | 102,125[7] |
| Illinois | 4 | 151,771 | 59 | 118 | 4-2 | 2 | 57,619 per annum | 7 | 10 | 159,235 |
| Indiana | 4[6] | 95,000 | 50 | 100 | 4 | 2 | 11,600 per annum | 5 | 2[9] | 115,000 |
| Iowa | 4 | 107,482 | 50 | 100 | 4 | 2 | 21,381 per annum | 9 | 8 | 116,600[7] |
| Kansas | 4 | 94,036 | 40 | 125 | 4 | 2 | 76 per diem[12] | 7 | 6 | 109,756[7] |
| Kentucky | 4 | 104,619 | 38 | 100 | 4 | 2 | 164 per diem[13] | 7 | 8 | 123,335[7] |
| Louisiana | 4 | 95,000 | 39 | 105 | 4 | 4 | 16,800 per annum | 7 | 10 | 85,000 |
| Maine | 4 | 70,000 | 35 | 151 | 2 | 2 | 18,803 per biennium | 7 | 7 | 96,000 |
| Maryland | 4[6] | 120,000 | 47 | 141 | 4 | 4 | 31,509[8] per annum | 7 | 10 | 131,600[7] |
| Massachusetts | 4 | 135,000 | 40 | 160 | 2 | 2 | 46,410[8] per annum | 7 | (14) | 95,880[7] |
| Michigan | 4 | 177,000 | 38 | 110 | 4 | 2 | 79,650 per annum | 7 | 8 | 164,610 |
| Minnesota | 4 | 120,303 | 67 | 134 | 4[15] | 2 | 31,140 per annum | 7 | 6 | 125,897[7] |
| Mississippi | 4 | 101,800 | 52 | 122 | 4 | 4 | 10,000 per session | 9 | 8 | 102,300[7] |
| Missouri | 4[10] | 120,086 | 34 | 163 | 4[16] | 2 | 31,351 per annum | 7 | 12 | 123,000[7] |
| Montana | 4 | 88,190 | 50 | 100 | 4 | 2 | 55 per diem | 7 | 8 | 83,550 |
| Nebraska | 4[6] | 85,000 | 49[17] | — | 4[17] | — | 12,000 per annum | 7 | 6 | 119,276 |
| Nevada | 4[6] | 117,000 | 21 | 42 | 4 | 2 | 7,800 per biennium | 7 | 6 | 140,000 |
| New Hampshire | 2 | 100,690 | 24 | (18) | 2 | 2 | 200 per biennium | 5 | (14) | 111,045[7] |
| New Jersey | 4[6] | 130,000 | 40 | 80 | 4[15] | 2 | 49,000 per annum | 7 | 7[19] | 158,500[7] |
| New Mexico | 4[6] | 90,000 | 42 | 70 | 4 | 2 | 136 per diem | 5 | 8 | 96,283[7] |
| New York | 4 | 179,000 | 61 | 150 | 2 | 2 | 79,500 per annum | 7 | 14 | 151,200[7] |
| North Carolina | 4[6] | 118,430 | 50 | 120 | 2 | 2 | 13,951[8] per annum | 7 | 8 | 115,336[7] |
| North Dakota | 4 | 87,216 | 47 | 94 | 4 | 4 | 125 per diem[20] | 5 | 10 | 99,122[7] |
| Ohio | 4 | 130,292 | 33 | 99 | 4 | 2 | 53,018[8] per annum | 7 | 6 | 127,600[7] |
| Oklahoma | 4 | 101,140 | 48 | 101 | 4 | 2 | 38,400 per annum | (21) | 6 | 106,706[7] |
| Oregon | 4[6] | 99,200 | 30 | 60 | 4 | 2 | 1,092 per month | 7 | 6[22] | 105,200[7] |
| Pennsylvania | 4[6] | 138,270 | 50 | 203 | 4 | 2 | 63,629 per annum | 7 | 10 | 137,386[7] |
| Rhode Island | 4 | 95,000 | 38 | 75 | 2 | 2 | 12,407[23] per annum | 5 | (24) | 152,000[7] |
| South Carolina | 4 | 106,078 | 46 | 124 | 4 | 2 | 10,400 per annum | 5 | 10 | 106,061[7] |
| South Dakota | 4[6] | 95,389 | 35 | 70 | 2 | 2 | 6,000 per annum | 5 | 3[25] | 100,671[7] |
| Tennessee | 4 | 85,000 | 33 | 99 | 4 | 2 | 16,500 per annum | 5 | 8 | 101,820 |
| Texas | 4 | 99,122 | 31 | 150 | 4 | 2 | 7,200 per annum | 9 | 6 | 94,686[7] |
| Utah | 4 | 100,600 | 29 | 75 | 4 | 2 | 120[8] per diem | 5 | 3[22] | 114,050[7] |
| Vermont | 2 | 119,615 | 30 | 150 | 2 | 2 | 536[26] per week | 5 | 6 | 103,019[7] |
| Virginia | 4 | 124,855 | 40 | 100 | 4 | 2 | 17,640[27] per annum | 7 | 12 | 132,523[7] |
| Washington | 4[28] | 139,087 | 49 | 98 | 4[11] | 2 | 32,801[8] per annum | 9 | 6 | 134,584 |
| West Virginia | 4[6] | 90,000 | 34 | 100 | 4 | 2 | 15,000 per annum | 5 | 12 | 95,000 |
| Wisconsin | 4 | 122,406 | 33 | 99 | 4 | 2 | 44,233 per annum | 7 | 10 | 122,418[7] |
| Wyoming | 4 | 150,000 | 30 | 60 | 4 | 2 | 125 per diem | 5 | 8 | 105,000 |

NOTE: Salaries are rounded to nearest dollar. 1. Known as *General Assembly* in Ark., Colo., Conn., Del., Ga., Ill., Iowa, Ind., Ky., Md., Mo., N.C., Ohio, Pa., R.I., S.C., Tenn., Vt., Va.; *Legislative Assembly* in N.D., Ore.; *General Court* in Mass., N.H.; *Legislature* in other states. Meets biennially in Ark., Ky., Mont., Nev., N.D., Ore., Texas. Wyoming Legislature has regular general session on odd-numbered years and a budget session on even-numbered years. Arkansas General Assembly meets every other year for 60 days in odd numbered years. Ohio General Assembly meets when deemed necessary. Legislative bodies meet annually in other states. 2. Known as *Court of Appeals* in Md., N.Y.; *Supreme Court of Virginia* in Va.; *Supreme Judicial Court* in Maine, Mass.; *Supreme Court* in other states. 3. Upper house: *Senate* in all states except Neb., which has a single-house legislative body, "the Legislature." 4. Lower house: *Assembly* in Calif., Nev., N.Y., Wis.; *House of Delegates* in Md., Va., W.Va.; *General Assembly* in N.J.; *House of Representatives* in other states. 5. Base salary. Does not include additional payments for expenses, mileage, special sessions, etc., or additional per diem payments. 6. May not serve third consecutive term. 7. Chief justice receives a higher salary. 8. Leaders receive a higher salary. 9. Initial term; thereafter elected popularly for 10-year term. 10. May serve only two terms, consecutive or otherwise. 11. Have term limitations. 12. When in session, plus $85 per day for expenses. There is also an out-of-session expense allowance of $5,400. Leaders receive an additional sum. 13. For days worked whether or not legislature is in session. 14. Until 70 years old. 15. Every 10 years (the year after census) term is only for 2 years. 16. Legislators may serve only 8 years in each house, 16 combined. 17. Unicameral legislature. 18. Constitutional number: 375-400. 19. Second term receive tenure, mandatory retirement at 70. 20. When in session, plus $250 per month when not in session. 21. Nine members in Supreme Court, highest in civil cases; five in Court of Criminal Appeals. 22. Until 75 years old. 23. Upper house receives slightly lower salary. 24. Term of good behavior. 25. Subsequent terms, eight years. 26. To limit of $13,000 per biennium; $105 per diem for Special Session. 27. Upper house receives higher salary. 28. No person is eligible who would have served during 8 of the previous 14 years. *Source:* questionnaires to the states.

## Land and Water Area of States, 2000

### (in square miles)

| State | Rank (total area) | Land[1] area | Water[2] area | Total area | State | Rank (total area) | Land[1] area | Water[2] area | Total area |
|---|---|---|---|---|---|---|---|---|---|
| Alabama | 30 | 50,744.00 | 1,675.01 | 52,419.02 | Montana | 4 | 145,552.43 | 1,489.96 | 147,042.40 |
| Alaska | 1 | 571,951.26 | 91,316.00 | 663,267.26 | Nebraska | 16 | 76,872.41 | 481.31 | 77,353.73 |
| Arizona | 6 | 113,634.57 | 363.73 | 113,998.30 | Nevada | 7 | 109,825.99 | 734.71 | 110,560.71 |
| Arkansas | 29 | 52,068.17 | 1,110.45 | 53,178.62 | New | | | | |
| California | 3 | 155,959.34 | 7,736.23 | 163,695.57 | Hampshire | 46 | 8,968.10 | 381.84 | 9,349.94 |
| Colorado | 8 | 103,717.53 | 376.04 | 104,093.57 | New Jersey | 47 | 7,417.34 | 1,303.96 | 8,721.30 |
| Connecticut | 48 | 4,844.80 | 698.53 | 5,543.33 | New Mexico | 5 | 121,355.53 | 233.96 | 121,589.48 |
| Delaware | 49 | 1,953.56 | 535.71 | 2,489.27 | New York | 27 | 47,213.79 | 7,342.22 | 54,556.00 |
| Dist. of | | | | | North Carolina | 28 | 48,710.88 | 5,107.63 | 53,818.51 |
| Columbia | — | 61.4 | 6.94 | 68.34 | North Dakota | 19 | 68,975.93 | 1,723.86 | 70,699.79 |
| Florida | 22 | 53,926.82 | 11,827.77 | 65,754.59 | Ohio | 34 | 40,948.38 | 3,876.53 | 44,824.90 |
| Georgia | 24 | 57,906.14 | 1,518.63 | 59,424.77 | Oklahoma | 20 | 68,667.06 | 1,231.13 | 69,898.19 |
| Hawaii | 43 | 6,422.62 | 4,508.36 | 10,930.98 | Oregon | 9 | 95,996.79 | 2,383.85 | 98,380.64 |
| Idaho | 14 | 82,747.21 | 822.87 | 83,570.08 | Pennsylvania | 33 | 44,816.61 | 1,238.63 | 46,055.24 |
| Illinois | 25 | 55,583.58 | 2,330.79 | 57,914.38 | Rhode Island | 50 | 1,044.93 | 500.12 | 1,545.05 |
| Indiana | 38 | 35,866.90 | 550.83 | 36,417.73 | South Carolina | 40 | 30,109.47 | 1,910.73 | 32,020.20 |
| Iowa | 26 | 55,869.36 | 402.2 | 56,271.55 | South Dakota | 17 | 75,884.64 | 1,231.85 | 77,116.49 |
| Kansas | 15 | 81,814.88 | 461.96 | 82,276.84 | Tennessee | 36 | 41,217.12 | 926.15 | 42,143.27 |
| Kentucky | 37 | 39,728.18 | 680.85 | 40,409.02 | Texas | 2 | 261,797.12 | 6,783.70 | 268,580.82 |
| Louisiana | 31 | 43,561.85 | 8,277.85 | 51,839.70 | Utah | 13 | 82,143.65 | 2,755.18 | 84,898.83 |
| Maine | 39 | 30,861.55 | 4,523.10 | 35,384.65 | Vermont | 45 | 9,249.56 | 364.7 | 9,614.26 |
| Maryland | 42 | 9,773.82 | 2,632.86 | 12,406.68 | Virginia | 35 | 39,594.07 | 3,180.13 | 42,774.20 |
| Massachusetts | 44 | 7,840.02 | 2,714.55 | 10,554.57 | Washington | 18 | 66,544.06 | 4,755.58 | 71,299.64 |
| Michigan | 11 | 56,803.82 | 39,912.28 | 96,716.11 | West Virginia | 41 | 24,077.73 | 152.03 | 24,229.76 |
| Minnesota | 12 | 79,610.08 | 7,328.79 | 86,938.87 | Wisconsin | 23 | 54,310.10 | 11,187.72 | 65,497.82 |
| Mississippi | 32 | 46,906.96 | 1,523.24 | 48,430.19 | Wyoming | 10 | 97,100.40 | 713.16 | 97,813.56 |
| Missouri | 21 | 68,885.93 | 818.39 | 69,704.31 | U.S. total | | 3,537,438.44 | 256,644.62 | 3,794,083.06 |

1. Dry land and land temporarily or partially covered by water, such as marshland, swamps, etc.; streams and canals under one-eighth statute mile wide; and lakes, reservoirs, and ponds under 40 acres. 2. Permanent inland water surface, such as lakes, reservoirs, and ponds having an area of 40 acres or more; streams, sloughs, estuaries, and canals one-eighth statute mile or more in width; deeply indented embayments and sounds, and other coastal waters behind or sheltered by headlands or islands separated by less than 1 nautical mile of water, and islands under 40 acres in area. Excludes areas of oceans, bays, sounds, etc. lying within U.S. jurisdiction but not defined as inland water. *Source:* Department of Commerce, Bureau of the Census.

## State Capitals and Largest Cities

| State | Capital | Largest city | State | Capital | Largest city |
|---|---|---|---|---|---|
| Alabama | Montgomery | Birmingham | Montana | Helena | Billings |
| Alaska | Juneau | Anchorage | Nebraska | Lincoln | Omaha |
| Arizona | Phoenix | Phoenix | Nevada | Carson City | Las Vegas |
| Arkansas | Little Rock | Little Rock | New Hampshire | Concord | Manchester |
| California | Sacramento | Los Angeles | New Jersey | Trenton | Newark |
| Colorado | Denver | Denver | New Mexico | Santa Fe | Albuquerque |
| Connecticut | Hartford | Bridgeport | New York | Albany | New York City |
| Delaware | Dover | Wilmington | North Carolina | Raleigh | Charlotte |
| Florida | Tallahassee | Jacksonville | North Dakota | Bismarck | Fargo |
| Georgia | Atlanta | Atlanta | Ohio | Columbus | Columbus |
| Hawaii | Honolulu | Honolulu | Oklahoma | Oklahoma City | Oklahoma City |
| Idaho | Boise | Boise | Oregon | Salem | Portland |
| Illinois | Springfield | Chicago | Pennsylvania | Harrisburg | Philadelphia |
| Indiana | Indianapolis | Indianapolis | Rhode Island | Providence | Providence |
| Iowa | Des Moines | Des Moines | South Carolina | Columbia | Columbia |
| Kansas | Topeka | Wichita | South Dakota | Pierre | Sioux Falls |
| Kentucky | Frankfort | Lexington | Tennessee | Nashville | Memphis |
| Louisiana | Baton Rouge | New Orleans | Texas | Austin | Houston |
| Maine | Augusta | Portland | Utah | Salt Lake City | Salt Lake City |
| Maryland | Annapolis | Baltimore | Vermont | Montpelier | Burlington |
| Massachusetts | Boston | Boston | Virginia | Richmond | Virginia Beach |
| Michigan | Lansing | Detroit | Washington | Olympia | Seattle |
| Minnesota | St. Paul | Minneapolis | West Virginia | Charleston | Charleston |
| Mississippi | Jackson | Jackson | Wisconsin | Madison | Milwaukee |
| Missouri | Jefferson City | Kansas City | Wyoming | Cheyenne | Cheyenne |

*Source:* U.S. Bureau of the Census, 2000 figures.

# 50 Largest Cities of the United States

Data supplied by U.S. Census Bureau and by the cities in response to questionnaires. Per capita personal income data are given for the Metropolitan Statistical Area (MSA), the Primary Metropolitan Statistical Area (PMSA), the New England County Metropolitan Area (NECMA), or the Consolidated Metropolitan Statistical Area (CMSA), as noted. NOTE: Persons of Hispanic origin may be of any race.

## Albuquerque, N.M.

**Mayor:** Martin Chavez (to Nov. 2005)
**2000 census population (rank):** 448,607 (35); **% change:** 16.6; **Male:** 217,887 (48.6%); **Female:** 230,720 (51.4%); **White:** 321,179 (71.6%); **Black:** 13,854 (3.1%); **American Indian and Alaska Native:** 17,444 (3.9%); **Asian:** 10,068 (2.2%); **Other race:** 66,292 (14.8%); **Two or more races:** 19,318 (4.3%); **Hispanic/Latino:** 179,075 (39.9%). **2000 percent population 18 and over:** 75.5%; **65 and over:** 12.0%; **median age:** 34.9.
**Land area:** 181 sq mi. (469 sq km); **Alt.:** 4,958 ft.
**Avg. daily temp.:** Jan., 34.2° F; July, 78.5° F
**Churches:** 211; **City-owned parks:** 189; **Radio stations:** 43 (AM, 17; FM, 26); **Television stations:** 11
**Civilian Labor Force (MSA) 2001:** 370,845; **Unemployed:** 13,468, **Percent:** 3.6; **Per capita personal income (MSA) 2000:** $25,894
**Chamber of Commerce:** Greater Albuquerque Chamber of Commerce, 401 2nd St. N.W., Albuquerque, N.M. 87125. Albuquerque Hispanic Chamber of Commerce, 202 Central Ave. S.E., Albuquerque, N.M. 87102

Albuquerque is the largest city in New Mexico and the seat of Bernalillo County. It is situated in west-central New Mexico on the upper Rio Grande.

Spanish settlers arrived in the mid-1600s, but they retreated from the area in 1680 after the Pueblo revolt. The old town was founded in 1706 by Don Francisco Cuervo y Valdés, the governor of New Mexico, and named after the Duke of Alburquerque, the viceroy of New Spain.

The opening of the Santa Fe Trail in the early 19th century brought an influx of settlers, and an army post was established following U.S. occupation in 1846. Albuquerque remained loyal to the Union during the Civil War, although it was briefly occupied by Confederate forces in 1862. The new town was laid out in 1880 after the Santa Fe Railroad was built one mile east of the original plaza. The Spanish old town and the mission church of San Felipe de Neri (1706) were soon enveloped by the new construction but survive today.

The city is noted as a center for health and medical services in the region, and government agencies, nuclear research, banking, and tourism are important to the economy. There is a growing high-tech center in Albuquerque, and Intel Corp.'s largest manufacturing facility is located there.

Albuquerque is the seat of the University of New Mexico (1889). Its numerous attractions include the Albuquerque Biological Park, the Indian Pueblo Cultural Center, the National Atomic Museum, Petroglyph National Monument, and the Sandia Mountain Wilderness.

Famous natives: Annabeth Gish, actress; Fred Haney, baseball player; Ernie Pyle, war correspondent; Al and Bobby Unser, auto racers.

## Atlanta, Ga.

**Mayor:** Shirley Franklin (to Jan. 2006)
**2000 census population (rank):** 416,474 (39); **% change:** 5.7; **Male:** 206,725 (49.6%); **Female:** 209,749 (50.4%); **White:** 138,352 (33.2%); **Black:** 255,689 (61.4%); **American Indian and Alaska Native:** 765 (0.2%); **Asian:** 8,046 (1.9%); **Other race:** 8,272 (2.0%); **Two or more races:** 5,177 (1.2%); **Hispanic/Latino:** 18,720 (4.5%). **2000 percent population 18 and over:** 77.7%; **65 and over:** 9.7%; **median age:** 31.9.
**City land area:** 132 sq mi. (341 sq km); **Alt.:** Highest, 1,050 ft.; lowest, 940 ft.
**Avg. daily temp.:** Jan., 41.0° F; July, 78.8° F
**Churches:** 1,500; **City-owned parks:** 277 (3,178 ac.); **Radio stations:** AM, 7; FM, 20; **Television stations:** 8 commercial; 2 PBS
**Civilian Labor Force (MSA) 2001:** 2,280,402; **Unemployed:** 79,641, **Percent:** 3.5; **Per capita personal income (MSA) 2000:** $33,013
**Chamber of Commerce:** Metro Atlanta Chamber of Commerce, 235 International Blvd., Atlanta, Ga. 30303

Atlanta, the largest city and capital of Georgia, is the seat of Fulton County. It is situated in the northwest part of the state at the base of the Blue Ridge Mountains near the Chattahoochee River. The first European settler was Hardy Ivy, who built a cabin there in 1833.

Founded as Terminus in 1837, the town served as the end of the Georgia railroad line (Western and Atlantic Railroad) and later became incorporated as Marthasville in 1843 in honor of ex-governor Lumpkin's daughter Martha. It was renamed Atlanta in 1845 and incorporated as a city in 1847. The name was suggested by the railroad's chief engineer, J. Edgar Thomson, and was derived from its location at the end of the Georgia and Atlantic railroad line. The city became the capital of Georgia in 1868.

During the Civil War, the city was burned and almost completely destroyed while occupied by Gen. William T. Sherman's troops in Nov. 1864. It was rebuilt after the war and grew rapidly due to the expansion of the railroads in the southwest.

Today, Atlanta is the major commercial and transportation hub of the southeast United States, and its international airport is one of the busiest in the world. The city's economy is led by the service, communications, retail trade, manufacturing, finance, and insurance industries. The convention business is also important, and Atlanta is home to many major corporations, including Coca-Cola, which was founded there in 1892.

Atlanta is also a major educational center, with many prestigious universities and colleges, including Emory University (1836), Georgia Institute of Technology (1885), and Georgia State University

(1913). Morehouse College (1867), Spelman College (1881), and Clark Atlanta University (1865; 1869) are important historically black colleges.

Major attractions include Martin Luther King, Jr., National Historic Site, Grant Park, and the Carter Presidential Center. The 1996 Summer Olympics were held in Atlanta.

Famous natives: Hank Aaron, baseball player; Arrested Development, recording artists; Jimmy Carter, former president; Ray Charles, singer; James Dickey, poet; Mattivilda Dobbs, soprano; Walt Frazier, basketball player; Oliver Hardy, comedian; Evander Holyfield, boxer; Allan Jackson, singer; Bobby Jones, golfer; DeForest Kelley, actor; Martin Luther King, Jr., civil rights leader and Nobel Peace Prize winner; Gladys Knight, singer; Kriss Kross, recording artists; Margaret Mitchell, novelist; Bert Parks, entertainer; Eric Roberts, actor; Julia Roberts, actress; Doug Stone, singer; Gwen Torrence, Olympic athlete; Lee Tracy, actor; Travis Tritt, singer; Ted Turner, TBS and CNN founder; Jane Withers, actress; Joanne Woodward, actress; Andrew Young, civil rights activist.

## Austin, Tex.

**Mayor:** Gus Garcia (to June 15, 2003)
**2000 census population (rank):** 656,562 (16); **% change:** 41.0; **Male:** 337,569 (51.4%); **Female:** 318,993 (48.6%); **White:** 429,100 (65.4%); **Black:** 65,956 (10.0%); **American Indian and Alaska Native:** 3,889 (0.6%); **Asian:** 30,960 (4.7%); **Other race:** 106,538 (16.2%); **Two or more races:** 19,650 (3.0%); **Hispanic/Latino:** 200,579 (30.5%). **2000 percent population 18 and over:** 77.5%; **65 and over:** 6.7%; **median age:** 29.6
**Land area:** 252 sq mi. (653 sq km), **Alt.:** From 425 ft. to over 1000 ft.
**Avg. daily temp.:** Jan., 48.8° F; July, 84.5° F
**Churches:** 353 churches, representing 45 denominations; **City-owned parks and playgrounds:** 169 (11,800 ac.); **Radio stations:** AM, 12; FM, 27; **Television stations:** 7 commercial; 1 PBS; 1 independent
**Civilian Labor Force (MSA) 2001:** 754,269[1]; **Unemployed:** 29,020, **Percent:** 3.8; **Per capita personal income (MSA) 2000:** $32,039[1]
**Chamber of Commerce:** Greater Austin Chamber of Commerce, P.O. Box 1967, Austin, Tex. 78767

1. Austin–San Marcos, Tex.

Austin, the state capital of Texas and seat of Travis County, is the fourth-largest city in Texas. It is situated in the south-central part of the state on the Colorado River.

The site was called Waterloo in 1838, and in 1839 it was incorporated as a city and chosen as the capital of the independent Republic of Texas. Waterloo was renamed Austin in honor of Stephen F. Austin, the founder of the Texas Republic. It became the permanent capital of the state of Texas in 1870. Austin's population and commercial developments after the Civil War—the railroads reached the city in the 1870s; it was crossed by the important Chisholm cattle trail; and it became the seat of the state university in 1883.

Austin has a growing commercial and diversified manufacturing sector. Civilian government employment is 20% of the labor force and is important to the economy. As home to the University of Texas, Austin is a major center for research and development and is nationally recognized as a high-technology center.

Austin's visitor attractions include the Austin Museum of Art, the Lyndon B. Johnson Library and Museum, the Lady Bird Johnson Wildflower Center, and the Austin Zoo.

Famous natives: Don Baylor, baseball player and manager; Earl Campbell, football player; Liz Carpenter, author; Dabney Coleman, actor; Ben Crenshaw, golfer; Michael Dell, founder Dell Computer Corp.; Tobe Hooper, film director; Lady Bird Johnson, former first lady; Tom Kite, golfer; James Michener, author; Willie Nelson, musician; Amado Pena, artist; Darrell Royal, football coach; Zachary Scott, actor; Jerry Jeff Walker, musician; Dalhart Windberg, artist.

## Baltimore, Md.

**Mayor:** Martin O'Malley (to Dec. 2004)
**2000 census population (rank):** 651,154 (17); **% change:** –11.5; **Male:** 303,687 (46.6%); **Female:** 347,467 (53.4%); **White:** 205,982 (31.6%); **Black:** 418,951 (64.3%); **American Indian and Alaska Native:** 2,097 (0.3%); **Asian:** 9,985 (1.5%); **Other race:** 4,363 (0.7%); **Two or more races:** 9,554 (1.5%); **Hispanic/Latino:** 11,061 (1.7%). **2000 percent population 18 and over:** 75.2%; **65 and over:** 13.2%; **Median age:** 35.0.
**Land area:** 81 sq mi. (210 sq km), **Alt.:** Highest, 490 ft.; lowest, sea level
**Avg. daily temp.:** Jan., 31.8° F; July, 77.0° F
**Churches:** Roman Catholic, 72; Jewish, 50; Protestant and others, 344; **City-owned parks:** 347 park areas and tracts (6,314 ac.); **Radio stations:** AM, 10; FM, 11; **Television stations:** 7
**Civilian Labor Force (PMSA) 2001:** 1,324,690; **Unemployed:** 51,274, **Percent:** 3.9; **Per capita personal income (PMSA) 2000:** $32,265
**Chamber of Commerce:** Greater Baltimore Committee, 111 S. Calvert St., Ste. 1700, Baltimore, Md. 21202

Baltimore, the largest city in Maryland, is situated in the northern part of the state on the Patapsco River estuary, an arm of Chesapeake Bay. The city is independent and does not fall within any county.

The site was settled in the early 17th century and founded as a town in 1729. The town was named after Lord Baltimore, the founder of Maryland, and was incorporated as a city in 1797. It has an excellent harbor and has been a principal port since the 18th century. Baltimore was a pioneer shipbuilding center, and the Baltimore clipper was used extensively in world trade.

The city has been greatly affected by the nation's wars. During the War of 1812, the British bombarded nearby Fort McHenry, inspiring Francis Scott Key to write the *Star-Spangled Banner.* And although Maryland never seceded from the Union, Baltimore was occupied by Union troops throughout the Civil War. The city was also an important shipbuilding and supply center during the World Wars.

Baltimore's economy is very diverse, with strong financial, legal, and nonprofit service industries. The city also leads in research and development through two highly acclaimed medical institutions, Johns Hopkins Hospital and University of Maryland Hospital. There is also a significant tourist sector. Major attractions include the the National Aquarium, Harborplace, the Maryland Science Center, the Babe Ruth Museum, Fort McHenry National Monument, and Pimlico Race Course, site of the Preakness.

Famous natives: Larry Adler, musician; John Astin, actor; Eubie Blake, pianist; Francis X. Bushman, actor; Charlie Chase, actor; Hans Conried, actor; Mildred Dunnock, actress; "Mama" Cass Elliot, singer; Barry Farber, broadcaster; Paul Ford, actor; Philip Glass, composer; Billie Holiday, singer; Barry Levinson, director; H. L. Mencken, writer; Babe Ruth, baseball player; Upton Sinclair, novelist; Leon Uris, novelist; John Waters, film director, writer, and actor; Frank Zappa, musician.

## Boston, Mass.

**Mayor:** Thomas Menino (to Jan. 2006)
**2000 census population (rank):** 589,141
(20); **% change:** 2.6; **Male:** 283,588 (48.1%); **Female,**
305,553 (51.9%); **White:** 320,944 (54.5%); **Black:**
149,202 (25.3%); **American Indian and Alaska
Native:** 2,365 (0.4%); **Asian:** 44,284 (7.5%); **Other
race:** 46,102 (7.8%); **Two or more races:** 25,878
(4.4%); **Hispanic/Latino:** 85,089 (14.4%). **2000 percent population 18 and over:** 80.2%; **65 and over:**
10.4%; **median age:** 31.1.
**Land area:** 48 sq mi. (124 sq km); **Alt.:** Highest, 330 ft.;
lowest, sea level
**Avg. daily temp.:** Jan., 28.6° F; July, 73.5° F
**Churches:** Protestant, 187; Roman Catholic, 70; Jewish,
13; others, 100; **City-owned parks, playgrounds,
etc.:** 2,260 ac.; **Radio stations[1]:** AM, 24; FM, 22;
**Television stations[1]:** 27
**Civilian Labor Force (PMSA) 2001:** 1,850,736;
**Unemployed:** 59,161, **Percent:** 3.2; **Per capita personal income (NECMA) 1999:** $38,758[2]
**Chamber of Commerce:** Greater Boston Chamber of
Commerce, One Beacon St., 4th fl., Boston, Mass.
02108

1. Metropolitan area. 2. Boston–Worcester–Lawrence–
Lowell–Brockton, Mass.–N.H.

Boston is the state capital, the seat of Suffolk
County, and the largest city in Massachusetts. It is
located in the eastern part of the state on Massachusetts Bay. It was incorporated as a city in 1822. No
city in the U.S. is richer in historical associations
than Boston, and no city has retained more of its
original buildings as memorials to America's past.

The first European settler was Rev. William
Blackstone, who arrived in 1623, just three years
after the Pilgrims had landed at Plymouth in 1620.
He was joined by Puritans from England in 1630.
They named their new town Boston, after the former
home of many of them in Lincolnshire, England.
Fourteen years later, the pioneer Bostonians set
aside the first public park in the U.S.—the Boston
Common. The following year, 1635, they opened
the first free public school in America. Today, the
Boston area is home to 68 colleges and universities.

Boston is a major industrial, financial, and educational hub and has one of the finest ports in the
world. The city's banking and financial services,
insurance, and real estate sectors continue to drive
Boston's economy. Boston is also a leading city in
health care, with 25 inpatient hospitals and numerous community health centers. The city's unique
cultural and historic heritage makes it a center of
tourism, and its hotel industry ranks among the
highest in the nation in occupancy. Boston's other
businesses are in high technology, biotechnology,
software, and electronics.

The city's tourist attractions include Faneuil Hall
Marketplace, the JFK Library and Museum, the
Museum of Fine Arts, the New England Aquarium,
the USS *Constitution*, and many historic buildings
and neighborhoods.

Famous natives: Samuel Adams, patriot; Louisa May
Alcott, author; John Singleton Copley, painter; Ralph
Waldo Emerson, philosopher and poet; Arthur Fiedler,
conductor; Benjamin Franklin, statesman and scientist;
Edward Everett Hale, clergyman and author; Oliver
Wendell Holmes, Supreme Court justice; Winslow Homer,
painter; Joseph P. Kennedy, financier; Jack Lemmon,
actor; Robert Lowell, poet; Edgar Allan Poe, writer; Paul
Revere, patriot and silversmith; John L. Sullivan, boxer;
Barbara Walters, TV journalist.

## Charlotte, N.C.

**Mayor:** Pat McCrory (to Nov. 2003)
**2000 census population (rank):** 540,828 (26);
**% change:** 36.6; **Male:** 264,978 (49.0%); **Female:**
275,850 (51.0%); **White:** 315,061 (58.3%); **Black:**
176,964 (32.7%); **American Indian and Alaska
Native:** 1,863 (0.3%); **Asian:** 18,418 (3.4%); **Other
race:** 19,242 (3.6%); **Two or more races:** 8,997
(1.7%); **Hispanic/Latino:** 39,800 (7.4%). **2000 percent population 18 and over:** 75.3%; **65 and over:**
8.8%; **median age:** 32.7.
**Land area:** 242 sq mi. (627 sq km); **Alt.:** 765 ft.
**Avg. daily temp.:** Jan., 39.3° F; July, 79.3° F
**Churches:** Protestant, over 500; Roman Catholic, 13;
Jewish, 3; Greek Orthodox, 1; **City-owned parks
and parkways:** 130; **Radio stations:** AM, 10; FM, 19;
**Television stations:** 6 commercial; 1 PBS
**Civilian Labor Force (MSA) 2001:** 811,045[1];
**Unemployed:** 41,650, **Percent:** 5.1; **Per capita personal income (MSA) 2000:** $30,901[1]
**Chamber of Commerce:** Charlotte Chamber, P.O. Box
32785, Charlotte, N.C., 28232

1. Charlotte–Gastonia–Rock Hill, N.C.–S.C.

Charlotte, North Carolina's largest city and the
seat of Mecklenburg County, is located in the southern part of the state near the South Carolina border.
It was named for King George III of England's wife,
Charlotte Sophia of Mecklenburg-Strelitz.

Settled about 1750, Charlotte was incorporated as
a city in 1768 and made the county seat in 1774.
From 1800 to 1848, Charlotte was the center of U.S.
gold production. A branch of the U.S. mint operated
there from 1837 to 1913. Charlotte was a leading
Confederate city during the Civil War and was the
last meeting place of the full Confederate cabinet.

Charlotte is the second-largest banking center in
the United States, and two of the nation's top banks,
Wachovia and Bank of America, are headquartered
there. Other major employers are the education,
health care, government, technology, and communications sectors. The city is a hub for US Airways.

Charlotte is the home of the University of North
Carolina (1946) as well as the Carolina Panthers
(football) and Lowe's Motor Speedway.

Famous natives: Romare Bearden, artist; Billy Graham,
evangelist; Charles Gwathmey, architect; Hamilton Jordan,
government official; Randolph Scott, actor.

## Chicago, Ill.

**Mayor:** Richard M. Daley (to April 2003)
**2000 census population (rank):** 2,896,016 (3);
**% change:** 4.0; **Male:** 1,405,107 (48.5%); **Female:**
1,490,909 (51.5%); **White:** 1,215,315 (42.0%); **Black:**
1,065,009 (36.8%); **American Indian and Alaska
Native:** 10,290 (0.4%); **Asian:** 125,974 (4.3%); **Other
race:** 393,203 (13.6%); **Two or more races:** 84,437
(2.9%); **Hispanic/Latino:** 753,644 (26.0%). **2000 percent population 18 and over:** 73.8%; **65 and over:**
10.3%; **median age:** 31.5.
**Land area:** 227 sq mi. (588 sq km); **Alt.:** Highest, 672
ft.; lowest, 578.5 ft.
**Avg. daily temp.:** Jan., 22.4° F; July, 75.1° F
**Churches:** Protestant, 850; Roman Catholic, 252; Jewish, 51; **City-owned parks:** 551; **Radio stations:** AM,
21; FM, 37; **Television stations:** 31
**Civilian Labor Force (PMSA) June 2002:** 4,282,649;
**Unemployed:** 293,545, **Percent:** 6.9; **Per capita
personal income (PMSA) 2000:** $35,336
**Chamber of Commerce:** Chicagoland Chamber of
Commerce, One IBM Plaza, 330 N. Wabash, Suite
2800, Chicago, Ill. 60611

Chicago is the largest city in Illinois and the seat of Cook County. It stretches for 22 mi along the southwest shore of Lake Michigan in the northeast part of the state.

The first white men known to have visited the region were Louis Joliet and Jacques Marquette in 1673. The first permanent white settler was John Kinzie, who is sometimes called the Father of Chicago. He took over a trading post in 1796 that had been established in 1791 by Jean-Baptiste Point du Sable, a black fur trapper. Fort Dearborn, a blockhouse and stockade, was built in 1804 but was evacuated in 1812, at which time more than half of its garrison was massacred by Potawatomi and Ottawa Indians loyal to the British.

The name Chicago is thought to come from an Algonquian word meaning "onion" or "skunk."

Laid out in 1830, Chicago was incorporated as a village in 1833 and as a city in 1837. In the Great Chicago Fire of 1871, an area of the city about 4 mi long and nearly a mile wide—more than two thousand acres—was totally destroyed. However, much of the city, including the railroads and stockyards, survived intact, and from the ashes of the old wooden structures there arose more modern constructions in steel and stone.

Today, Chicago is a major Great Lakes port and the commercial, financial, industrial, and cultural center of the Midwest. The manufacturing industries dominate the wholesale and retail trade, and trade in agricultural commodities is important to the economy. The Chicago Board of Trade is the largest agricultural futures market in the world.

Among Chicago's many attractions are the Art Institute of Chicago, the Field Museum of Natural History, the Jane Addams–Hull House Museum, Navy Pier, and numerous architectural landmarks such as the Sears Tower and Frank Lloyd Wright's Robie House.

Famous natives: Jack Benny, comedian; Edgar Rice Burroughs, author; Raymond Chandler, author; Hillary Rodham Clinton, U.S. senator, lawyer, and former first lady; Michael Crichton, author; Walt Disney, filmmaker; John Dos Passos, author; Bobby Fischer, chess player; Bob Fosse, choreographer and director; Benny Goodman, clarinetist; Dorothy Hamill, figure skater; Quincy Jones, composer; Gene Krupa, drummer; David Mamet, playwright; Bob Newhart, comedian; Kim Novak, actress; Donald O'Connor, actor; William L. Shirer, journalist and historian; Gloria Swanson, actress; Melvin Van Peebles, playwright; Alfred Wallenstein, conductor; Robin Williams, comedian and actor; Robert Young, actor.

# Cleveland, Ohio

2000 census population (rank): 478,403 (33); % change: -5.4; Male: 226,550 (47.4%); Female: 251,853 (52.6%); White: 108,610 (41.5%); Black: 243,020 (51.0%); American Indian and Alaska Native: 1,458 (0.3%); Asian: 6,444 (1.3%); Other race: 17,173 (3.6%); Two or more races: 10,701 (2.2%); Hispanic/Latino: 34,728 (7.3%). 2000 percent population 18 and over: 71.5%; 65 and over: 12.5%; median age: 33.0.
Land area: 78 sq mi. (202 sq km), Alt.: Highest, 1048 ft.; lowest, 573 ft.
Avg. daily temp.: Jan., 24.8° F; July, 71.9° F
Churches [1]: Protestant, 980; Roman Catholic, 187; Jewish, 31; Eastern Orthodox, 22; City-owned parks: 41 (1,930 ac.); Radio stations: AM, 9; FM, 19; Television stations: 22

Civilian Labor Force (PMSA) 2001: 1,139,000[1]; Unemployed: 43,000, Percent: 3.8; Per capita personal income (PMSA) 2000: $30,909[1]
Chamber of Commerce: Greater Cleveland Growth Association, 200 Tower City Center, Cleveland, Ohio 44113
1. Cleveland–Lorain–Elyria, Ohio.

Cleveland is the second-largest city in Ohio and the seat of Cuyahoga County. It is located in the northeast part of the state on Lake Erie.

In the colonial era, the Cleveland area was known as the Connecticut Western Reserve, part of a land grant made to Connecticut by King Charles II in 1662. The city was founded in 1796 by Gen. Moses Cleaveland, who was the head surveyor of the Connecticut Land Company. This company had bought 3 million acres in what is now northern Ohio. A permanent settlement was founded in 1799, named after the general, and the spelling was shortened to Cleveland. The city was incorporated in 1836.

Cleveland's industrial growth was stimulated by the opening of the Ohio and Erie canals in 1832 and, later, by the advent of the Civil War, with the increasing demand for machinery, railroad equipment, ships, and other items. Today, the port of Cleveland is the largest overseas general cargo port on Lake Erie.

Greater Cleveland has long been famous as a durable goods manufacturing area. Following the national trend, however, Cleveland has been shifting to a more services-based economy. Greater Cleveland is a world corporate center for leading national and multinational companies in industries ranging from transportation, insurance, retailing, and utilities, to commercial banking and finance.

The city's cultural attractions include the Cleveland Museum of Art and the Cleveland Orchestra, one of the country's most highly acclaimed symphony orchestras. Jacobs Field, a new major league ballpark, and the Rock & Roll Hall of Fame also draw thousands of visitors to the city.

Famous natives: Jim Backus, actor; Drew Carey, actor and comedian; Dorothy Dandridge, actress; Ruby Dee, actress; Phil Donahue, talk-show host; Joel Grey, actor; Arsenio Hall, talk-show host; Margaret Hamilton, actress; Philip Johnson, architect; Henry Mancini, composer; Burgess Meredith, actor; Paul Newman, actor; Carl Stokes, jurist.

# Colorado Springs, Colo.

Mayor: Mary Lou Makepeace (to April 2005)
2000 census population (rank): 360,890 (48); % change: 28.4; Male: 178,469 (49.5%); Female: 182,421 (50.5%); White: 291,095 (80.7%); Black: 00,977 (0.9%); Asian: 10,179 (2.8%); Other race: 18,091 (5.0%); Two or more races: 13,909 (3.9%); Hispanic/Latino: 43,330 (12.0%). 2000 percent population 18 and over: 73.6%; 65 and over: 9.6%; median age: 33.6.
Land area: 186 sq mi. (482 sq km); Alt.: 6,035 ft.
Avg. daily temp.: Jan., 28.8° F; July, 70.8° F
Churches: Protestant, 400+; Roman Catholic, 20; Jewish, 3; others, City parks and playgrounds: 156 (10,762 ac.); Radio stations: AM, 7; FM, 17; Television stations: 7
Civilian Labor Force (MSA) 2001: 262,300; Unemployed: 8,000, Percent: 3.0; Per capita personal income (MSA) 2000: $28,804
Chamber of Commerce: Colorado Springs Chamber of Commerce, 2 N. Cascade Ave., Suite 110, Colorado Springs, Colo. 80903

Colorado Springs is the second-largest city in Colorado, after Denver. It is the seat of El Paso County, making up about three-quarters of the county's population. It is located on the edge of the Rocky Mountains, with Pikes Peak (14,110 ft) towering beside it to the west. To the east begin the Great Plains.

The city was founded in 1871. Gen. William Jackson Palmer, a Pennsylvania-born Civil War veteran, came across the scenic spot in his railroad travels and was inspired to begin a new resort community there. The subsequent development of Colorado Springs was influenced in part by an influx of English tourists later in the 1870s and by the discovery of gold in nearby Cripple Creek in the 1890s. Millionaire businessmen and philanthropists, such as Spencer Penrose, Charles Tutt, and Winfield Scott Stratton, helped to establish the city's infrastructure and shape its popularity as a tourist destination.

During World War II, Colorado Springs sold a large amount of land just south of the city to the military. The U.S. Army established Fort Carson as a training facility. The military presence in Colorado Springs continued to grow with the establishment of the U.S. Air Force Academy there in the 1950s, and later, the construction of Peterson Air Force Base, Falcon Air Force Base, and Cheyenne Mountain Air Force Base. The bases are all home to space command centers (with Cheyenne Mountain housing the headquarters for the North American Aerospace Defense Command [NORAD]) and have collectively earned Colorado Springs its national reputation as the leading center for military space operations.

The city's economy is still based heavily on tourism, although in more recent years, Colorado Springs has gained a strong foothold in the electronics, high-technology, and manufacturing industries. The city is the headquarters of the U.S. Olympic Committee and Olympic Training Center facility.

Famous natives: Bert Andrews, journalist; Kelly Bishop, actress; Spring Byington, actress; Lon Chaney, actor; Marjorie Daw, actress; Marceline Day, actress; Rich "Goose" Gossage, baseball player; Helen Hunt Jackson, writer and poet; Chase Masterson, actress; Sherry Stringfield, actress.

## Columbus, Ohio

**Mayor:** Michael B. Coleman (to Nov. 2003)
**2000 census population (rank):** 711,470 (15);
  **% change:** 12.4; **Male:** 345,878 (48.6%); **Female:** 365,592 (51.4%); **White:** 483,332 (67.9%); **Black:** 174,065 (24.5%); **American Indian and Alaska Native:** 2,090 (0.3%); **Asian:** 24,495 (3.4%); **Other race:** 8,292 (1.2%); **Two or more races:** 18,829 (2.6%); **Hispanic/Latino:** 17,471 (2.5%). **2000 percent population 18 and over:** 75.8%; **65 and over:** 8.9%; **median age:** 30.6.
**Land area:** 210 sq mi. (544 sq km); **Alt.:** Highest, 902 ft.; lowest, 702 ft.
**Avg. daily temp.:** Jan., 26.4° F; July, 73.2° F
**Churches:** Protestant, 436; Roman Catholic, 62; Jewish, 5; Other, 8; **City-owned parks:** 203 (12,891 ac.); **Radio stations:** AM, 10; FM, 16; **Television stations:** 9 commercial, 3 PBS
**Civilian Labor Force (MSA) 2001:** 874,100;
  **Unemployed:** 20,400, **Percent:** 2.3; **Per capita personal income (MSA) 2000:** $30,619
**Chamber of Commerce:** Columbus Area Chamber of Commerce, P.O. Box 1527, Columbus, Ohio 43216

Columbus, the largest city in Ohio, is the state capital and the seat of Franklin County. It is located in central Ohio on the Scioto River.

The first structures near the site of downtown Columbus were earthen mounds constructed by Indian tribes known as Mound Builders. Native Americans lived undisturbed in Central Ohio until the 1700s, when the first white explorers entered the Midwest. The first permanent white settlement in the area was founded by a surveyor from Kentucky, Lucas Sullivant, in 1797 and was named Franklinton. The state capital was laid out nearby in 1812 and named after Christopher Columbus. It became the capital in 1816. Columbus was chartered as a city in 1834 and annexed Franklinton in 1870. The city's growth was stimulated by the development of transportation facilities—a feeder to the Ohio Canal completed in 1832, the National Road in 1833, and the arrival of the railroad in 1850.

Columbus is a port of entry and a major commercial, distribution, and cultural center. It is the seat of Ohio State University (1870). The city has enjoyed steady growth over the years due to its economic diversity, and no single activity dominates the economy.

Famous natives: Warner Baxter, actor; George Bellows, painter; Michael Feinstein, singer and pianist; Eileen Heckart, actress; Jack Nicklaus, golfer; Tom Poston, actor; Eddie Rickenbacker, aviator; Arthur M. Schlesinger, historian; James Thurber, writer and cartoonist; Nancy Wilson, singer.

## Dallas, Tex.

**Mayor:** Laura Miller (to May 2003)
**City Manager:** Teodoro J. Benavides
**2000 census population (rank):** 1,188,580 (8);
  **% change:** 18.0; **Male:** 598,991 (50.4%); **Female:** 589,589 (49.6%); **White:** 604,209 (50.8%); **Black:** 307,957 (25.9%); **American Indian and Alaska Native:** 6,472 (0.5%); **Asian:** 32,118 (2.7%); **Other race:** 204,883 (17.2%); **Two or more races:** 32,351 (2.7%); **Hispanic/Latino:** 422,587 (35.6%). **2000 percent population 18 and over:** 73.4%; **65 and over:** 8.6%; **median age:** 30.5.
**Land area:** 343 sq mi. (888 sq km); **Alt.:** Highest, 750 ft.; lowest, 375 ft.
**Avg. daily temp.:** Jan., 44.6° F; July, 85.9° F
**Churches:** 1,974 (in Dallas Co.); **City-owned parks:** 406 (22,743 ac.); **Radio stations:** AM, 19; FM, 30; **Television stations:** 10 commercial, 1 PBS
**Civilian Labor Force (PMSA) 2001:** 2,032,500;
  **Unemployed:** 79,300, **Percent:** 3.9; **Per capita personal income (PMSA) 2000:** $35,216
**Chamber of Commerce:** Dallas Chamber of Commerce, 1201 Elm, Dallas, Tex. 75270

Dallas is the second-largest city in Texas and the seat of Dallas County. It is situated 185 mi northeast of Austin on the Trinity River near the junction of its three forks.

Dallas was first settled by Tennessee lawyer John Neely Bryan as a trading post on the Trinity River in 1841. Many historians believe that Bryan named the city after George Mifflin Dallas, vice president under James K. Polk, but there is no official agreement on this. It was incorporated as a town in 1856 and as a city in 1871. Located in the chief cotton-producing region of Texas, the city developed as a cotton market in the 1870s.

The economy is highly diversified, and the city is the leading commercial, marketing, and industrial center of the southwest. The insurance business is important, and the service sector has experienced rapid growth. Dallas is also a popular tourist and convention city.

Famous natives: Tex Avery, animator and director; Robby Benson, actor; Ernie Banks, baseball player; Bebe Daniels, actress; Linda Darnell, actress; Lee Elder, golfer; Morgan Fairchild, actress; Trini Lopez, singer; Aaron Spelling, producer; Stephen Stills, singer; Sharon Tate, actress; Lee Trevino, golfer.

## Denver, Colo.

**Mayor:** Wellington Webb (to June 30, 2003)
**2000 census population (rank):** 554,636 (25); **% change:** 18.6; **Male:** 280,207 (50.5%); **Female:** 274,429 (49.5%); **White:** 362,180 (65.3%); **Black:** 61,649 (11.1%); **American Indian and Alaska Native:** 7,290 (1.3%); **Asian:** 15,611 (2.8%); **Other race:** 86,464 (15.6%); **Two or more races:** 20,794 (3.7%); **Hispanic/Latino:** 175,704 (31.7%); **2000 percent population 18 and over:** 78.0%; **65 and over:** 11.3%; **median age:** 33.1.
**Land area:** 153 sq mi. (396 sq km); **Alt.:** Highest, 5,494 ft.; lowest, 5,140 ft.
**Avg. daily temp.:** Jan., 29.7° F; July, 73.5° F
**Churches[1]:** Protestant, 859; Roman Catholic, 60; Jewish, 13; **City-owned parks:** 205 (4,166 ac.); **City-owned mountain parks:** 40 (13,600 ac.); **Radio stations[1]:** AM, 23; FM, 20; **Television stations[1]:** 10
**Civilian Labor Force (PMSA) 2001:** 1,176,200; **Unemployed:** 26,300; **Percent:** 2.2; **Per capita personal income (PMSA) 2000:** $37,153
**Chamber of Commerce:** Denver Metro Chamber of Commerce, 1445 Market Street, Denver, Colo. 80202

1. Metropolitan area.

Denver is the largest city in Colorado, the state capital, and the seat of Denver County. It lies at the foot of the Rocky Mountains at the junction of the South Platte River and Cherry Creek.

The city was born in 1858, when gold was discovered in the sands of Cherry Creek, at first just a tough village of cabins, shacks, and tents. It was incorporated as a city in 1861 and became the territorial capital in 1867. The city is named for James W. Denver, governor of the Kansas Territory, which included part of Colorado. The city prospered following the opening of the famous gold and silver mines of the 1870s and 1880s.

Today, Denver is an important communications, transportation, manufacturing, and agribusiness hub. Telecommunications and biomedical technology are two of the largest industries; construction, real estate, and retail trade are among the fastest-growing industries. The city is also home to many environmental organizations, including federal government agencies such as the Environmental Protection Agency and the National Oceanic and Atmospheric Administration.

Denver International Airport, the first major new airport constructed in the U.S. in 21 years, opened to passenger traffic in 1995. At 53 sq mi, it is the largest airport in North America.

The city's tourist attractions include the Denver Zoo, the Six Flags Elitch Gardens amusement park, the Red Rocks Amphitheatre, the Coors Brewery, and nearby Rocky Mountain National Park.

Famous natives: Tim Allen, comedian and actor; Ward Bond, actor; Douglas Fairbanks, Sr., actor; John Hart, newsman; Pat Hingle, actor; Ted Mack, TV host; Barbara Rush, actress; Alan K. Simpson, U.S. senator; Paul Whiteman, bandleader; Don Wilson, announcer.

## Detroit, Mich.

**Mayor:** Kwame Kilpatrick (to Jan. 2006)
**2000 census population (rank):** 951,270 (10); **% change:** –7.5; **Male:** 448,319 (47.1%); **Female:** 502,951 (52.9%); **White:** 116,599 (12.3%); **Black:** 775,772 (81.6%); **American Indian and Alaska Native:** 3,140 (0.3%); **Asian:** 9,268 (1.0%); **Other race:** 24,199 (2.5%); **Two or more races:** 22,041 (2.3%); **Hispanic/Latino:** 47,167 (5.0%). **2000 percent population 18 and over:** 68.9%; **65 and over:** 10.4%; **median age:** 30.9.
**Land area:** 139 sq mi. (360 sq km); **Alt.:** Highest, 685 ft.; lowest, 574 ft.
**Avg. daily temp.:** Jan., 24.7° F; July, 74.2° F
**Churches[1]:** Protestant, 1,165; Roman Catholic, 89; Jewish, 2; **City-owned parks:** 56 parks (3,843 ac.); 393 sites (5,838 ac.); **Radio stations:** AM, 27; FM, 30 (includes 3 in Windsor, Ont.); **Television stations:** 8[2] (includes 1 in Windsor, Ont.)
**Civilian Labor Force (PMSA) 2001:** 2,337,900; **Unemployed:** 104,700; **Percent:** 4.5; **Per capita personal income (PMSA) 2000:** $33,259
**Chamber of Commerce:** Detroit Regional Chamber of Commerce, One Woodward Avenue, P.O. Box 33840, Detroit MI 48232-0840

1. Six-county metropolitan area. 2. Within four counties of Metro Detroit.

Detroit, the largest city in Michigan, is situated in the southeast part of the state on the Detroit River. The seat of Wayne County, Detroit was incorporated as a city in 1815 and reincorporated in 1824.

Detroit is the oldest city of any size west of the seaboard colonies, having been founded by Antoine de la Mothe Cadillac on July 24, 1701, more than a century before Chicago was founded. The French were the first settlers, and they gave the city its name from their word meaning "strait," referring to the 27-mile-long Detroit River, which connects Lake Erie and Lake St. Clair. The river forms part of the international boundary, and marks the only point where Canada lies directly south of U.S. territory.

Because of its strategic location, Detroit was fought over by the French, the British, and the Indians during the French and Indian Wars. It was the headquarters for the British forces in the Northwest Territory during the American Revolutionary War.

The first steam vessel, the *Walk-in-the-Water*, made its appearance on the Great Lakes in 1818, and Detroit was the western terminus for most of its voyages from Buffalo. Its link to all the important cities on the Great Lakes made it a major exporting center.

Detroit is one of the largest manufacturing cities in the U.S. and is the center of the automobile manufacturing industry, which has experienced a decline due to foreign competition in the past decade. The health and medical care sector is important to the economy, and employment in the finance, insurance, and real-estate industries has inched up in the Detroit metropolitan area since the early 1990s.

Famous natives: Anita Baker, singer; Sonny Bono, congressman and singer; Ralph Bunche, statesman; Ellen Burstyn, actress; Francis Ford Coppola, director; Aretha Franklin, singer; Casey Kasem, radio personality; Charles Lindbergh, aviator; Madonna, singer and actress; John Mitchell, former U.S. attorney general; Harry Morgan, actor; Rosa Parks, activist; George Peppard, actor; Gilda Radner, comedian; Della Reese, singer; Smokey Robinson, singer; Sugar Ray Robinson, boxer; Diana Ross, singer; George C. Scott, actor; Tom Selleck, actor; Lily Tomlin, comedian and actress; Margaret Whiting, singer.

# El Paso, Tex.

**Mayor:** Raymond C. Caballero (to May 2003)
**2000 census population (rank):** 563,662 (23);
  **% change:** 9.4; **Male:** 267,651 (47.5%); **Female:**
  296,011 (52.5%); **White:** 413,061 (73.3%); **Black:**
  17,586 (3.1%); **American Indian and Alaska Native:**
  4,601 (0.8%); **Asian:** 6,321 (1.1%); **Other race:**
  102,320 (18.2%); **Two or more races:** 19,190 (3.4%);
  **Hispanic/Latino:** 431,875 (76.6%). **2000 percent**
  **population 18 and over:** 69.0%; **65 and over:**
  10.7%; **median age:** 31.1
**Land area:** 249 sq mi. (645 sq km); **Alt.:** 4,000 ft.
**Avg. daily temp.:** Jan., 42.8° F; July, 82.3° F
**Churches:** Protestant, 320; Roman Catholic, 39; Jewish,
  3; others, 20; **City-owned parks:** 145 (2,150 ac.)[1];
  **Radio Stations:** AM, 18; FM, 17; **Television**
  **stations:** 6
**Civilian Labor Force (MSA) 2001:** 285,200;
  **Unemployed:** 21,800, **Percent:** 7.7; **Per capita per-**
  **sonal income (MSA) 2000:** $18,535
**Chamber of Commerce:** El Paso Chamber of Com-
  merce, Hispanic Chamber of Commerce, Black Chamber of Commerce, and Korean Chamber of Commerce, 10 Civic Center Plaza, El Paso, Tex. 79944

1. Includes 129 developed and 16 undeveloped parks.

El Paso, the fifth-largest city in Texas and the seat of El Paso County, is located in the far western part of the state on the north bank of the Rio Grande, opposite the Mexican city of Ciudad Juárez on the south bank.

On April 30, 1598, Juan de Oñate took formal possession of the area for King Philip II of Spain. Subsequently he crossed the Rio Grande near a site west of present downtown El Paso, which he called "El Paso del Rio del Norte," meaning the crossing of the river—the first use of the name "El Paso." In 1659, the mission of Nuestra Señora de Guadalupe was founded on a site that is present-day downtown Ciudad Juárez; the mission is still in use today. In 1682, Spanish colonists from Mexico founded the settlement of Ysleta on the site of the present-day city. However, it wasn't until 1827 that the first per-manent settlement at El Paso was established by Juan María Ponce de León. The city's real growth started with the arrival of the Southern Pacific Rail-road in 1881. El Paso was incorporated as a city in 1873.

In 1888, Mexico changed the name of Paso del Norte to Ciudad Juárez in honor of Benito Juárez. Later, in 1967, the U.S. agreed to cede a long-disputed part of El Paso to Mexico due to changes in the course of the Rio Grande, which forms the international boundary between the two countries. El Paso and its sister city of Ciudad Juárez across the U.S./Mexico border are inexorably joined by culture and economy. El Paso and Juárez make up the largest international metroplex in the world.

El Paso is an important port of entry to the U.S. from Mexico. The high technology, medical device manufacturing, plastics, refining, automotive, food processing, and defense-related industries are important to the economy. El Paso's service sector has experienced healthy growth since the 1980s. El Paso is also a major tourist resort.

Famous natives: Manuel Acosta, artist; Don Bluth, animation director; Vicki Carr, singer; Jose Cisneros, artist; Sam Donaldson, newsman; Albert Fall, government official; Judith Ivey, actress; Guy Kibbee, actor; Sandra Day O'Connor, Supreme Court justice; Debbie Reynolds, actress; Irene Ryan, actress.

# Fort Worth, Tex.

**Mayor:** Kenneth Barr (to May 2003)
**City Manager:** Gary W. Jackson
**2000 census population (rank):** 534,694 (27);
  **% change:** 19.5; **Male:** 263,720 (49.3%); **Female:**
  270,974 (50.7%); **White:** 319,159 (59.7%); **Black:**
  108,310 (20.3%); **American Indian and Alaska**
  **Native:** 3,144 (0.6%); **Asian:** 14,105 (2.6%); **Other**
  **race:** 75,100 (14.0%); **Two or more races:** 14,535
  (2.7%); **Hispanic/Latino:** 159,368 (29.8%). **2000 per-**
  **cent population 18 and over:** 71.7%; **65 and over:**
  9.6%; **median age:** 30.9
**Land area:** 293 sq mi. (759 sq km); **Alt.:** Highest, 780
  ft.; lowest, 520 ft.
**Avg. daily temp.:** Jan., 43.4° F; July, 85.3° F
**Churches:** 1,032, representing 72 denominations; **City-**
  **owned parks:** 222 (10,380 ac.); **Radio stations**[1]:
  AM, 29; FM, 48; **Television stations:** 13
**Civilian Labor Force (PMSA) June 2002:** 967,500[2];
  **Unemployed:** 62,355, **Percent:** 6.4; **Per capita**
  **personal income (PMSA) 2000:** $29,305[2]
**Chamber of Commerce:** Fort Worth Chamber of Com-
  merce, 777 Taylor Street, Suite 900, Fort Worth,
  Tex. 76102

1. Dallas–Fort Worth area. 2. Fort Worth–Arlington, Tex.

Fort Worth, seat of Tarrant County, is situated in the north-central part of Texas on the Trinity River.

The city was founded by Maj. Ripley Arnold in 1849 as a military outpost on the Trinity River to protect settlers moving westward from frequent Indian attacks. It was named after Gen. William J. Worth, the commander of the Texas army. Fort Worth was incorporated in 1873. Its growth was stimulated in the 1870s by its proximity to the Chisholm cattle trail. It prospered as a meat-packing and shipping center when the Texas and Pacific Railway arrived in 1876 and later experienced a new boom when oil was discovered nearby in 1917. The establishment of military installations in the area during both world wars also spurred the economy.

Fort Worth has traditionally been a diverse center of manufacturing and is not dependent on the oil or financial sectors. The city's industries range from clothing and food products to jet fighters, helicop-ters, computers, pharmaceuticals, and plastics. Fort Worth is a national leader in aviation products, elec-tronic equipment, and refrigeration equipment. It is home to a multitude of major corporate headquar-ters, offices, and distribution centers.

Famous natives: Robert Bass, financier; Mark Brooks, golfer; Betty Buckley, singer and actress; Kate Capshaw, actress; Ornette Coleman, composer; Sandra Haynie, golfer; Patricia Highsmith, writer; Spanky McFarland, actor; R. Bruce Merrifield, Nobelist in chemistry; Roger Miller, singer; Fess Parker, actor; Bill Paxton, actor; Rex Reed, critic; Johnny Rutherford, auto racer; Liz Smith, columnist.

# Fresno, Calif.

**Mayor:** Alan Autry (to Jan. 2005)
**City Manager:** Daniel G. Hobbs
**2000 census population (rank):** 427,652 (37);
  **% change:** 20.7; **Male:** 210,107 (49.1%); **Female:**
  217,545 (50.9%); **White:** 214,556 (50.2%); **Black:**
  35,763 (8.4%); **American Indian and Alaska Native:**
  6,763 (1.6%); **Asian:** 48,028 (11.2%); **Other race:**
  99,898 (23.4%); **Two or more races:** 22,061 (5.2%);
  **Hispanic/Latino:** 170,520 (39.9%). **2000 percent**
  **population 18 and over:** 67.1%; **65 and over:** 9.3%;
  **median age:** 28.5.
**Land area:** 104 sq mi. (269 sq km); **Alt.:** 328 ft.
**Avg. daily temp.:** Jan., 45.7° F; July, 81.9° F

**Churches:** 450 (approximate); **City-owned parks:** 38 (690 ac.); **Radio stations:** AM, 11[1]; FM, 13[1]; Bilingual 1; **Television stations:** 8[1]
**Civilian Labor Force (CMSA) 2001:** 447,800;
  **Unemployed:** 56,200, **Percent:** 12.6; **Per capita personal income (MSA) 2000:** $21,121
**Chamber of Commerce:** Fresno Chamber of Commerce, 2331 Fresno St., Fresno, Calif. 93721

1. Metropolitan area.

Fresno is located in central California, 184 mi southeast of San Francisco and 222 mi northwest of Los Angeles. It is the seat of Fresno County. Fresno was incorporated as a city in 1885.

Fresno began as a station for the Central Pacific Railroad in 1872 and was made the seat of Fresno County in 1874. The city's name is Spanish for the ash trees that the early explorers found in the area.

Fresno is a leading agribusiness hub, with 250 different crops produced by 7,500 farmers on 1.9 million irrigated acres, worth $3 billion a year. Fresno County's top agricultural products are grapes, cotton, tomatoes, cattle and calves, and turkeys.

The city is also a distribution and manufacturing center. Its diverse industries include agricultural chemicals, farm equipment, canned fruit and vegetables, clothing, computer software, electric wire, pumps, glass, and plastic products.

Famous natives: Mike Connors, actor; Maynard Dixon, painter; Bruce Furniss, swimmer; Jon Hall, actor; Daryle Lamonica, football player; Sam Peckinpah, director; William Saroyan, novelist; Tom Seaver, baseball player.

# Honolulu, Hawaii

**Mayor:** Jeremy Harris (to Jan. 2005)
**2000 census population (rank)[1]:** 371,657 (46);
  **% change:** 1.7; **Male:** 182,628 (49.1%); **Female:** 189,029 (50.9%); **White:** 73,093 (19.7%); **Black:** 6,038 (1.6%); **American Indian and Alaska Native:** 689 (0.2%); **Asian:** 207,588 (55.9%); **Native Hawaiian and Other Pacific Islander:** 25,457 (6.8%); **Other race:** 3,318 (0.9%); **Two or more races:** 55,474 (14.9%); **Hispanic/Latino:** 16,229 (4.4%). **2000 percent population 18 and over:** 80.8%; **65 and over:** 17.8%; **median age:** 39.7
**Land area:** 85.7 sq mi. (221.9 sq km)[1]; **Alt.:** Highest, 2,013 ft.[1]; lowest, sea level
**Avg. daily temp.:** Jan., 71.4° F; July, 78.9° F
**Churches:** Roman Catholic, 39; Buddhist, 51; Jewish, 2; Protestant and others, 402; **City-owned parks[1]:** 2,056 ac.; **Radio stations[1]:** AM, 17; FM, 11; **Television stations[1]:** 12
**Civilian Labor Force (MSA) 2001:** 425,700[2];
  **Unemployed:** 15,500[2], **Percent:** 3.6[2]; **Per capita personal income** [illegible]
**Chamber of Commerce:** Chamber of Commerce of Hawaii, 1132 Bishop St., Suite 402, Honolulu, Hawaii 96813

1. Census Designated Place, approximately Salt Lake to Hawaii Kai. 2. City and county.

Honolulu is the capital and largest city of Hawaii, on the southeast coast of the island of Oahu. The city is legally coextensive with the county of Honolulu, which includes the entire island of Oahu and most of the Northwest Hawaiian Islands, from Nihoa to Kure Atoll, except Midway. The population of Oahu makes up 73% of the state's total population. It is situated in the central Pacific Ocean 2,397 mi west-southwest of San Francisco. Honolulu's name derives from the native words *hono*, meaning "a bay," and *lulu*, meaning "sheltered."

Honolulu's early history was one of turbulence and conflict. One of the last areas on the globe to be explored and exploited by Europeans (it was first visited by British captain James Cook in 1778), Hawaii was subject to strong pressures from many forces, including American missionaries, who arrived in 1820, and opportunistic whalers. These whalers were among those who built Honolulu originally, bringing trade, commerce, and prosperity that led to expansion into the sugar and pineapple industries.

As early as 1814, Russia tried to move in, and Russian soldiers built a bastion at the harbor's edge. The British flag was raised in 1843 and French forces occupied Honolulu in 1849. Each time control was returned to the independent native kingdom without bloodshed. In 1898, a group of Americans completed a project attempted at intervals during the previous 65 years—annexation to the United States. Honolulu was incorporated as a city in 1907.

The Honolulu area was bombed by Japan in a surprise attack on the unprepared U.S. naval base at Pearl Harbor on Dec. 7, 1941. This action forced the United States to enter World War II. "Remember Pearl Harbor" became a famous American wartime slogan.

Hawaiian statehood in 1959 and the viability of commercial air travel to the island brought boom times to Honolulu. Tourism is the city's principal industry, followed by federal defense expenditures and agricultural exports (chiefly pineapples).

Famous natives: Hiram Bingham, explorer; Jean Erdman, dancer and choreographer; Hiram Fong, senator; Daniel Inouye, senator; Duke Kahanamoku, surfer and Olympian swimmer; Bette Midler, actress and singer; Kelly Preston, actress; Louise Morgan Sill, author; Don Stroud, actor; Merlin D. Tuttle, biologist and wildlife photographer.

# Houston, Tex.

**Mayor:** Lee P. Brown (to Dec. 31, 2003)
**2000 census population (rank):** 1,953,631 (4);
  **% change:** 19.8; **Male:** 975,551 (49.9%); **Female:** 978,080 (50.1%); **White:** 962,610 (49.3%); **Black:** 494,496 (25.3%); **American Indian and Alaska Native:** 8,568 (0.4%); **Asian:** 103,694 (5.3%); **Other race:** 321,603 (16.5%); **Two or more races:** 61,478 (3.1%); **Hispanic/Latino:** 730,865 (37.4%). **2000 percent population 18 and over:** 72.5%; **65 and over:** 8.4%; **median age:** 30.9
**Land area:** 579 sq mi. (1,500 sq km); **Alt.:** Highest, 120 ft.; lowest, sea level
**Avg. daily temp.:** Jan., 52.2° F; July, 83.5° F
**Churches[1]:** 1,750; **City-owned parks:** 293 (32,733 ac.); **Radio stations[1]:** AM, 23; FM, 32; **Television stations:** 15 commercial, 1 PBS [illegible]
**Unemployed:** 84,700, **Percent:** 3.9; **Per capita personal income (PMSA) 2000:** $33,891
**Chamber of Commerce:** Greater Houston Partnership, 1200 Smith, Suite 700, Houston, Tex. 77002-4400

1. Harris County.

Houston, the largest city in Texas and seat of Harris County, is located in the southeast part of the state near the Gulf of Mexico.

Sam Houston was the commander-in-chief of the Texas troops who fought a successful war of rebellion against Mexico, which had been in possession of Texas. On April 21, 1836, Houston's men won a decisive victory in which the Mexican dictator, Gen. Santa Anna, was taken prisoner and forced to sign the treaty that launched the Republic of Texas. In September, a constitution was ratified, and Houston was elected president. The Texas Republic was recognized by the U.S. and by the major European powers. The present city of Houston was incorporated in 1837 and named after Sam Houston; it was the Republic's first capital.

The port of Houston ranks high among U.S. ports in foreign tonnage handled. The city is a major business, financial, science, and technology center. Houston is outstanding in oil and natural-gas production and is the energy capital of the world. It is the home of one of the largest medical facilities in the world—the Texas Medical Center—and the focus of the aerospace industry. The Lyndon B. Johnson Space Center is the nation's headquarters for staffed spaceflight.

Among the city's many visitor attractions are Space Center Houston, the Houston Arboretum and Nature Center, Six Flags AstroWorld, George Ranch Historical Park, the Astrodome baseball stadium, and nearby San Jacinto Battlefield.

Famous natives: Debbie Allen, choreographer; Lance Alworth, football player; Denton Cooley, heart surgeon; Jim Demaret, golfer; Allen Drury, novelist; Shelly Duvall, actress; A. J. Foyt, auto racer; Howard Hughes, industrialist and film producer; Barbara C. Jordan, educator, lawyer, and politician; Barbara Mandrell, singer; Annette O'Toole, actress; Dennis and Randy Quaid, actors; Kenny Rogers, singer; Patrick Swayze, actor and dancer.

# Indianapolis, Ind.

**Mayor:** Bart Peterson (to Dec. 31, 2003)
**2000 census population (rank):** 781,870 (12);
   **% change:** 6.7; **Male:** 378,310 (48.4%); **Female:** 403,560 (51.6%); **White:** 540,212 (69.1%); **Black:** 199,412 (25.5%); **American Indian and Alaska Native:** 1,985 (0.3%); **Asian:** 11,161 (1.4%); **Other race:** 15,921 (2.0%); **Two or more races:** 12,857 (1.6%); **Hispanic/Latino:** 30,636 (3.9%). **2000 percent population 18 and over:** 74.3%; **65 and over:** 11.0%; **median age:** 33.5.
**Land area:** 366 sq mi. (948 sq km); **Alt.:** Highest, 840 ft.; lowest, 700 ft.
**Avg. daily temp.:** Jan., 25.5 F; July, 75.4° F
**Churches[1]:** 1,191; **City-owned parks:** 172 (10,174 ac.); **Radio stations[2]:** AM, 8; FM, 17; **Television stations[1]:** 7
**Civilian Labor Force (MSA) 2001:** 869,800;
   **Unemployed:** 19,600, **Percent:** 2.2; **Per capita personal income (MSA) 2000:** $30,906
**Chamber of Commerce:** Indianapolis Chamber of Commerce, 320 N. Meridian St., Indianapolis, Ind. 46204

1. Marion County. 2. Metropolitan area.

Indianapolis, the largest city in Indiana and seat of Marion County, is located in the central part of the state on the West Fork of the White River. Its name derives from combining "Indiana" with "polis," the Greek word for city.

Indianapolis was settled in 1820, and five years later it was chosen as the state capital. It was incorporated as a city in 1832 and reincorporated in 1838. The city's growth began when the railroad reached it in 1847. Toward the end of the 19th century, the discovery of nearby natural gas and the start of the automobile industry hastened its industrial expansion. In 1970, Indianapolis merged with surrounding Marion County.

Indianapolis is at the center of a rich agricultural region and is a major grain and livestock market. It is also a focal point of commerce, transportation, and manufacturing for the region. Some leading industries are electronics, pharmaceuticals, and food

processing. The financial sector and service and insurance industries are growing rapidly.

Indianapolis is the site of the world-famous 500-mile automobile race and the Indiana State Fair.

Famous natives: Monte Blue, actor; David Letterman, TV host; Steve McQueen, actor; Jane Pauley, TV newscaster; Booth Tarkington, author; Kurt Vonnegut, Jr., author; Harry Von Zell, announcer; Clifton Webb, actor.

# Jacksonville, Fla.

**Mayor:** John Delaney (to June 30, 2003)
**2000 census population (rank):** 735,617 (14);
   **% change:** 15.8; **Male:** 356,284 (48.4%); **Female:** 379,333 (51.6%); **White:** 474,307 (64.5%); **Black:** 213,514 (29.0%); **American Indian and Alaska Native:** 2,474 (0.3%); **Asian:** 20,427 (2.8%); **Other race:** 9,816 (1.3%); **Two or more races:** 14,631 (2.0%); **Hispanic/Latino:** 30,594 (4.2%). **2000 percent population 18 and over:** 73.3%; **65 and over:** 10.3%; **median age:** 33.8.
**Land area:** 758 sq mi. (1,963 sq km); **Alt.:** Highest, 71 ft.; lowest, sea level
**Avg. daily temp.:** Jan., 52.4° F; July, 81.6° F
**Churches:** Protestant, 794; Roman Catholic, 21; Jewish, 5; others, 22; **City-owned parks and playgrounds:** 19 (7,404 ac.); **Radio stations:** AM, 14; FM, 16; **Television stations:** 6 commercial, 1 PBS, 1 religious
**Civilian Labor Force (MSA) 2001:** 580,100;
   **Unemployed:** 20,100, **Percent:** 3.5; **Per capita personal income (MSA) 2000:** $28,456
**Chamber of Commerce:** Jacksonville Area Chamber of Commerce, 3 Independent Dr., Jacksonville, Fla. 32202

Jacksonville, Florida's largest city, is located in Duval County in the northeast corner of Florida, on the banks of the St. Johns River and adjacent to the Atlantic Ocean. It is the largest metropolitan area in northeast Florida and southeast Georgia.

Starting in the 16th century, French, Spanish, and English explorers and colonists were attracted to the region by the St. Johns River. The site was settled by Lewis Hogans in 1816. Jacksonville was laid out in 1822 and was named after Gen. Andrew Jackson, the first military governor of Florida. It was incorporated as a city in 1832.

During the Civil War, much of the city was destroyed by Union forces, who occupied Jacksonville four times. The city was rebuilt and, following the development of its harbor and the railroads, quickly became the transportation hub and leading industrial city in Florida by the 1880s. In 1968, the city and county governments consolidated.

Jacksonville is the leading transportation and distribution hub in the state. However, the strength of the city's economy lies in its broad diversification. The area's economy is balanced among distribution, financial services, biomedical technology, consumer goods, information services, manufacturing, and other industries. Jacksonville has the largest deepwater port in the South Atlantic and is a leading port in the U.S. for automobile imports.

Famous natives: Pat Boone, singer; Judy Canova, comedian; Harold Carmichael, football player; Billy Daniels, vocalist; Storm Davis, athlete; Bob Hayes, athlete; Wanda Hendrix, actress; James Weldon Johnson, author and educator; John Rosamond Johnson, musician and composer; Mark McCumber, pro golfer; Ray Mercer, boxer; Charles "Hoss" Singleton, songwriter; Bill Terry, baseball player and manager; Donnie Van Zant, rock musician; Ronnie Van Zant, rock musician; Leeroy Yarbrough, auto racer.

# Kansas City, Mo.

**Mayor:** Kay Barnes (to April 2003)
**City Manager:** Robert L. Collins (apptd. July 1997)
**2000 census population (rank):** 441,545 (36);
**% change:** 1.5; **Male:** 213,141 (48.3%); **Female:**
228,404 (51.7%); **White:** 267,931 (60.7%); **Black:**
137,879 (31.2%); **American Indian and Alaska
Native:** 2,122 (0.5%); **Asian:** 8,182 (1.9%); **Other
race:** 14,158 (3.2%); **Two or more races:** 10,780
(2.4%); **Hispanic/Latino:** 30,604 (6.9%). **2000 percent population 18 and over:** 74.6%; **65 and over:**
11.7%; **median age:** 34.0.
**Land area:** 314 sq mi. (813 sq km), **Alt.:** Highest, 1,014
ft.; lowest, 722 ft.
**Avg. daily temp.:** Jan., 25.7° F; July, 78.5° F
**Churches:** 1,100 churches of all denominations[1]; **City-
owned parks and playgrounds:** 189 (10,647 ac.);
**Radio stations**[1]: AM, 14; FM, 19; **Television
stations**[1]: 7
**Civilian Labor Force (MSA) 2001:** 1,009,012[2];
**Unemployed:** 44,160, **Percent:** 4.4; **Per capita per-
sonal income (MSA) 2000:** $31,765[2]
**Chamber of Commerce:** Greater Kansas City Chamber
of Commerce, 911 Main St., Kansas City, Mo. 64105

1. Metropolitan area. 2. Kansas City, Mo.–Kan.

Kansas City is the largest city in Missouri. It is
located in the western part of the state, at the junction of the Missouri and Kansas rivers. Kansas City
is located in Jackson, Clay, Platte, and Cass counties.

In 1821, the year Missouri entered the Union,
French trader François Chouteau came from St.
Louis to establish a trading post on the site of the
present city to take advantage of the growing fur
trade with the Kansa, Osage, Wyandotte, and other
tribes. In 1833, a settlement called Westport Landing
was laid out by John Calvin McCoy and developed.
The community became the Town of Kansas and was
incorporated as a city in 1850 and renamed Kansas
City in 1889. The city's name reflects its Native
American heritage—its site was within the territory
of the Kansa, or Kaw, Indians.

The city grew rapidly in the mid-1880s as the
starting point for gold prospectors and settlers heading westward. The coming of the Missouri-Pacific
Railroad in 1865 and the spanning of the Missouri
River by the Hannibal Bridge in 1869 also contributed to the city's growth. It also prospered as a center for the nation's cattle business.

The Kansas City metropolitan area, once known
primarily for agriculture and manufacturing, has
expanded its economic base to include strong
growth in areas of telecommunications, banking and
finance, and the service industry. A transportation
hub since the 1800s, the area enjoys a national and
regional production as a distribution and trans-
muting center. Kansas City ranks nationally as first in
greeting-card publishing (Hallmark Cards is located
there), frozen food storage and distribution, and
hard winter wheat marketing; second in wheat flour
production; and third in auto and truck assembly.
The area is one of ten federal regional centers, and
the federal, state, and local governments are among
the top employers. The city is also a regional center
for health care.

Famous natives: Robert Altman, director; Edward Asner,
actor; Burt Bacharach, composer; Noah and Wallace
Beery, actors; Robert Russell Bennett, composer; Jeanne
Eagels, actress; Jean Harlow, actress; Ted Shawn, dancer
and choreographer; Casey Stengel, baseball player; Virgil
Thompson, composer; Tom Watson, golfer.

# Las Vegas, Nev.

**Mayor:** Oscar Goodman (to May 2003)
**2000 census population (rank):** 478,434 (32);
**% change:** 85.2; **Male:** 243,077 (50.8%); **Female:**
235,357 (49.2%); **White:** 334,230 (69.9%); **Black:**
49,570 (10.4%); **American Indian and Alaska Native:**
3,570 (0.7%); **Asian:** 22,879 (4.8%); **Other race:**
46,643 (9.7%); **Two or more races:** 19,397 (4.1%);
**Hispanic/Latino:** 112,962 (23.6%); **2000 percent
population 18 and over:** 74.1%; **65 and over:**
11.6%; **median age:** 34.5.
**Land area:** 113 sq mi. (293 sq km), **Alt.:** 2,174 ft.
**Avg. daily temp.:** Jan., 45.5° F; July, 91.1° F
**Churches:** over 500 churches and synagogues; **Radio
stations:** AM, 4; FM, 8; **Television stations:** 7
**Civilian Labor Force (MSA) 2001:** 803,157[1];
**Unemployed:** 43,840, **Percent:** 5.5; **Per capita per-
sonal income (MSA) 2000:** $27,558[1]
**Chamber of Commerce:** 3720 Howard Hughes Park-
way, Las Vegas, NV 89109

1. Las Vegas, Nev.–Ariz.

Las Vegas, seat of Clark County in southeast
Nevada, is the largest city in the state and one of the
fastest-growing cities in the United States. Between
April 1990 and April 2000, the Las Vegas metropolitan area population increased by 83%, growing
from 852,737 to 1,563,282.

The area was discovered by Spanish explorers in
1829. The site of Las Vegas ("The Meadows" in
Spanish) was originally a watering place for travelers on their way to southern California. It was
first settled by Mormons in 1855, who were
attracted by its artesian springs. They abandoned
their settlement two years later in 1857, and the
U.S. Army established Fort Baker there in 1864. In
1867, Las Vegas was detached from the Arizona
Territory and joined with Nevada.

The town was established and started to grow
with the arrival of the railroad in 1905. However, its
growth did not really take off until shortly after
1931, when the Nevada legislature legalized gambling in an effort to lift the state from the Great
Depression. The construction of nearby Hoover
Dam aided the area economically as well.

The Las Vegas that we know today basically
began after World War II, when the idea of large
hotels along the brand new "strip" was developed.
Las Vegas is the "marriage capital" of America;
there are 50 wedding chapels in the city. Tourism
and the convention industry are the city's major
sources of income. In addition, manufacturing, government, warehousing, and trucking are major
sources of employment. Many high-technology
companies are also located in Las Vegas.

Las Vegas has a favorable business climate: taxes
are relatively low, and there are neither city nor state
income taxes. This is because gambling and sales
taxes, paid by tourists, have allowed the city and
state governments to avoid personal and corporate
income taxes.

Popular nearby tourist attractions are Hoover
Dam and Lake Mead (the largest man-made lake in
the U.S.), Lake Mojave, the Mt. Charleston Recreation Area, Red Rock Canyon, and the Death Valley
National Monument.

Famous natives: Andre Agassi, tennis player; Clara Bow,
actress; Jack Kramer, tennis player; Phyllis McGuire,
singer; Benjamin Siegel, hotel-casino promoter; Orson
Welles, actor and producer; Joe Williams, jazz singer.

# Long Beach, Calif.

**Mayor:** Beverly O'Neill (to April 2002)
**City Manager:** Henry Taboada
**2000 census population (rank):** 461,522 (34);
**% change:** 7.5; **Male:** 226,718 (49.1%); **Female:**
234,804 (50.9%); 1996 est. population breakdown:
**White:** 208,410 (45.2%); **Black:** 68,618 (14.9%);
**American Indian and Alaska Native:** 3,881 (0.8%);
**Asian:** 55,591 (12.0%); **Other race:** 95,107 (20.6%);
**Two or more races:** 24,310 (5.3%); **Hispanic/Latino:**
165,092 (35.8%). **2000 percent population 18 and
over:** 70.8%; **65 and over:** 9.1%; **median age:** 30.8.
**Land area:** 50 sq mi. (130 sq km); **Alt.:** Highest,
170 ft.; lowest, sea level
**Avg. daily temp.:** Jan., 55.9° F; July, 73.1° F
**Churches:** 236; **City-owned parks:** 58 (plus 5 golf
courses); **Radio stations:** AM, 2; FM, 2; **Television
stations:** 8 (metro area)
**Civilian Labor Force (PMSA) 2001:** 4,818,100[1];
**Unemployed:** 234,300, **Percent:** 4.9; **Per capita per-
sonal income (PMSA) 2000:** $29,522[1]
**Chamber of Commerce:** Long Beach Area Chamber of
Commerce, One World Trade Center, Suite 206, Long
Beach, Calif. 90831-0350
1. Los Angeles–Long Beach, Calif.

Long Beach is the fifth-largest city in California
and is situated on San Pedro Bay, south of Los
Angeles, in Los Angeles County.

The town was laid out and settled in 1881 by
developer W. E. Willmore, who sold lots on the site
as a seaside resort community called Willmore City.
It was renamed Long Beach for its 8½-mile beach
in 1884. The city was incorporated in 1888 and reincorporated in 1897.

Long Beach is a major industrial port, ranked
second-busiest in the U.S. and tenth-busiest in the
world. In addition to international trade through the
port, high technology has also been an important
economic engine for the Long Beach area. Major
technology and aerospace corporations such Gulf-
stream and Raytheon have large facilities in Long
Beach, and Boeing continues to be the top
employer, with over 17,000 employees.

Tourism is also important to the economy. Major
attractions are the RMS *Queen Mary,* the Aquarium
of the Pacific, whale watching tours, and water
sports.

Famous natives: Jack Anderson, journalist; Jennifer
Bartlett, artist; Barbara Britton, actress; Nicholas Cage,
actor; Spike Jones, orchestra leader; Sally Kellerman,
actress; Billie Jean King, tennis player; Martha Rae
Watson, track star; Heather Watts, dancer.

# Los Angeles, Calif.

**Mayor:** James K. Hahn (to June 2005)
**2000 census population (rank):** 3,694,820 (2);
**% change:** 6.0; **Male:** 1,841,805 (49.8%); **Female:**
1,853,015 (50.2%); **White:** 1,734,036 (46.9%); **Black:**
415,195 (11.2%); **American Indian and Alaska
Native:** 29,412 (0.8%); **Asian:** 369,254 (10.0%);
**Other race:** 949,720 (25.7%); **Two or more races:**
191,288 (5.2%); **Hispanic/Latino:** 1,719,073 (46.5%).
**2000 percent population 18 and over:** 73.4%; **65
and over:** 9.7%; **median age:** 31.6.
**Land area:** 469 sq mi. (1,215 sq km); **Alt.:** Highest,
5,081 ft.; lowest, sea level
**Avg. daily temp.:** Jan., 58.3° F; July, 74.3° F
**Churches:** 2,000 of all denominations; **City-owned
parks:** 355 (15,357 ac.); **Radio stations:** AM, 35; FM,
53; **Television stations:** 19

**Civilian Labor Force (PMSA) 2001:** 4,818,100[1];
**Unemployed:** 234,300, **Percent:** 4.9; **Per capita per-
sonal income (PMSA) 2000:** $29,522[1]
**Chamber of Commerce:** Los Angeles Chamber of
Commerce, 404 S. Bixel St., Los Angeles, Calif. 90017
1. Los Angeles–Long Beach, Calif.

Los Angeles is the largest city in California and
the second-largest urban area in the nation. It is
located in the southern part of the state on the
Pacific Ocean. It is the seat of Los Angeles County.
Geographically, it extends more than 40 mi from the
mountains to the sea.

The Spanish explorer Gaspar de Portolá visited
the site in 1769. On Sept. 4, 1781, the Mexican provincial governor, Filipe de Neve, founded "El
Pueblo de Nuestra Señora la Reina de Los Angeles,"
meaning "The Village of Our Lady, the Queen of the
Angels." The pueblo became the capital of the
Mexican province, Alta California, and it was the
last place to surrender to the United States at the
time of the American occupation in 1847. By the
Treaty of Guadalupe Hidalgo in 1848, Mexico
ceded California to the United States, and Los
Angeles was incorporated as a city in 1850.

The city's phenomenal growth was brought about
by its equable climate, which attracted people and
industry from all parts of the nation; the development of its citrus-fruit industry; the discovery of oil
in the area during the early 1890s; the development
of its man-made harbor—its port is one of the busiest in the United States; and the growth of the
motion picture industry in the early 20th century.
Today, Hollywood is a suburb of Los Angeles.

Los Angeles is a major hub of shipping, manufacturing, industry, and finance, and is world-renowned
in the entertainment and communications fields. It is
a favorite vacation destination and attracts millions
of tourists to the area each year from all over the
world. Apart from the movie studios and other landmarks associated with the movie industry, points of
interest include the J. Paul Getty Museum, the Los
Angeles County Museum of Art, the La Brea Tar
Pits (famous for Ice Age fossils), Disneyland (Anaheim), and the Santa Anita and Hollywood race-
tracks.

Los Angeles County is the nation's largest manufacturing center, and the ports of Los Angeles and
Long Beach are second only to New York as the
largest customs district in the United States. Major
employers in the Los Angeles Five-County area are
in the business and management sector. Growth in
the key wholesale industries—apparel and textiles,
furniture, jewelry, and toys—and the boom in industrial trade were the trend for the region in the 1990s.
Other important sectors are health services and international trade and investment. After some lean years,
the aerospace industry is making a modest comeback
as a result of increased federal defense spending.

Famous natives: Busby Berkeley, choreographer and
director; Marge Champion, dancer and choreographer;
Jackie Coogan, actor; Jackie Cooper, actor; Linda
Fratianne, figure skater; Jodie Foster, actress and director;
John Gavin, actor and diplomat; Pancho Gonzalez, tennis
player; Cynthia Gregory, ballerina; Jerome Hines, basso;
Dustin Hoffman, actor; Theodore Harold Maiman, laser
inventor; Marilyn Monroe, actress; Isamu Noguchi,
sculptor; Leonard Slotkin, conductor; Duke Snider,
baseball player; Adlai E. Stevenson, statesman; Madeleine
Stowe, actress; Darryl Strawberry, baseball player.

# Memphis, Tenn.

**Mayor:** W. W. Herenton (to Dec. 2003)
**2000 census population (rank):** 650,100 (18);
**% change:** 6.5; **Male:** 307,643 (47.3%); **Female:** 342,457 (52.7%); **White:** 223,728 (34.4%); **Black:** 399,208 (61.4%); **American Indian and Alaska Native:** 1,217 (0.2%); **Asian:** 9,482 (1.5%); **Other race:** 9,438 (1.5%); **Two or more races:** 6,788 (1.0%); **Hispanic/Latino:** 19,317 (3.0%). **2000 percent population 18 and over:** 72.1%; **65 and over:** 10.9%; **median age:** 31.9.
**Land area:** 279 sq mi. (723 sq km); **Alt.:** Highest, 417 ft.
**Avg. daily temp.:** Jan., 39.7° F; July, 82.6° F
**Churches:** 2000+; **Parks and playgrounds:** 230 (13,291 ac.); **Radio stations:** AM, 17; FM, 25; **Television stations:** 6
**Civilian Labor Force (MSA) 2001:** 564,488[1];
**Unemployed:** 23,629; **Percent:** 4.2; **Per capita personal income (MSA) 2000:** $29,275[1]
**Chamber of Commerce:** Memphis Area Chamber of Commerce, P.O. Box 224, Memphis, Tenn. 38103

1. Memphis, Tenn.–Ark.–Miss.

Memphis, the largest city in Tennessee and the seat of Shelby County, is located in the southwest corner of the state, on the Mississippi River near the borders of Arkansas and Mississippi.

The first settlers of Memphis were the Chickasaw Indians, who had a village named Chisca there on the bluffs overlooking the Mississippi River. Hernando de Soto, in 1541, is said to have had his first glimpse of the Mississippi from the site of Memphis; in the next century, Louis Joliet and Jacques Marquette stopped there to trade with the Indians. The French explorer Robert Cavelier, Sieur de La Salle, tried to claim the region for France in 1682 and built Fort Prudhomme on the site.

The area was ceded to the United States by the Chickasaw Indians in 1818. Memphis was officially established in 1819 by three enterprising businessmen from Nashville, James Winchester, John Overton, and future president Andrew Jackson. Jackson named it after the ancient Egyptian city because of its site on the Nile-like Mississippi River. Memphis was incorporated as a city in 1826 and became an important Mississippi River port.

During the Civil War, Memphis was a Confederate military center. In 1862, federal forces won a gunboat battle on the river at Memphis, and General Sherman was able to take the city. After the war, Memphis's population was devastated by several yellow-fever epidemics during the 1870s. As a result, the city fell into decline and went bankrupt, losing its charter in 1879. However, owing to its superior location, the city was able to recover and nominally, and it in the city charter was granted in 1893.

Memphis is known as "America's Distribution Center," serving the northeast, southeast, and south west regions of the country. The city has one of the country's largest inland ports and is the national headquarters for the Fed Ex air-courier company. Health care and related activities such as medical education and biomedical research are Memphis's largest industries, bringing over $5 billion a year to the local economy. Also important are high-technology communications.

Many of the city's tourist attractions are landmarks associated with the great Memphis music legends, such as Graceland, Elvis Presley's home.

Famous natives: Kathy Bates, actress; Dixie Carter, actress; Rosalind Cash, singer; Abe Fortas, jurist; Aretha Franklin, singer; Morgan Freeman, actor; Al Green, singer; George Hamilton, actor; Anfernee "Penny" Hardaway, basketball player; Isaac Hayes, singer; Hal Holbrook, actor; Benjamin Hooks, organization official; Elvis Presley, singer and actor; Charlie Rich, singer; Cybill Shepherd, actress; Robert Siodmak, director; Fred Smith, business executive; Rufus Thomas, singer; Kemmons Wilson, business executive.

# Mesa, Ariz.

**Mayor:** Keno Hawker (to June 2004)
**City Manager:** Mike Hutchinson
**2000 census population (rank):** 396,375 (42);
**% change:** 37.6; **Male:** 196,378 (49.5%); **Female:** 199,997 (50.5%); **White:** 323,655 (81.7%); **Black:** 9,977 (2.5%); **American Indian and Alaska Native:** 6,572 (1.7%); **Asian:** 5,917 (1.5%); **Other race:** 38,271 (9.7%); **Two or more races:** 11,051 (2.8%); **Hispanic/Latino:** 78,281 (19.7%). **2000 percent population 18 and over:** 72.7%; **65 and over:** 13.3%; **median age:** 32.0
**Land area:** 125 sq mi. (324 sq km); **Alt.:** 1,241 ft.
**Avg. daily temp.:** Jan., 52.9° F; July, 91.2° F
**City-owned parks:** 55; **Radio stations:** AM, 23; FM, 12; **Television stations:** 7
**Civilian Labor Force (MSA) 2001:** 1,620,060[1];
**Unemployed:** 63,610, **Percent:** 3.9; **Per capita personal income (MSA) 2000:** $27,564[1]
**Chamber of Commerce:** 120 N. Center St., P.O. Box 5820, Mesa, Ariz. 85201

1. Phoenix–Mesa, Ariz.

Mesa is the third-largest city in Arizona and is located in the south-central portion of the state in Maricopa County. Sitting atop a plateau overlooking the Valley of the Sun, the city gets its name from the Spanish word for "tabletop."

Prior to the arrival of Europeans, the area had been inhabited for centuries by native peoples, including the Hohokam and later the Pima. The Hohokam culture developed an extensive system of irrigation canals, some of which are still used today.

Controlled by Spain and then by Mexico, the area was ceded to the U.S. following the Mexican War (1846–1848). Mormon settlers arrived on the site in 1878 and used the old irrigation canals for farming in the Salt River valley. Mesa was incorporated as a town in 1883 and as a city in 1930.

Falcon Field Airport and Williams Air Force Base were built in 1941 to train fighter pilots during World War II. After the war, the city grew rapidly, as many military families decided to settle in Mesa permanently, and tourism also became a major factor. Williams was closed in the early 1990s, but Falcon Field has become one of the ten largest U.S. airports in terms of based aircraft and supports more than 30 aviation related businesses.

Currently Mesa is one of the fastest-growing cities in the United States, due to its excellent climate and strong local economy, which boasts some of the country's top manufacturers. Electronics, automotive testing, propulsion equipment, aerospace, and heavy machinery firms are among the most significant in the region.

With 313 days of sunshine a year, Mesa has been an ideal choice for several major-league baseball spring training camps.

Famous natives: Danielle Fishel, actress; Liz Reney, actress; John J. Rhodes, politician; Keri Russell, actress.

# Miami, Fla.

**Mayor:** Manuel A. Diaz (to Nov. 2005)
**City Manager:** Carlos Gimenez (apptd. May 2000)
**2000 census population (rank):** 362,470 (47);
**% change:** 1.1; **Male:** 180,194 (49.7%); **Female:**
182,276 (50.3%); **White:** 241,470 (66.6%); **Black:**
80,858 (22.3%); **American Indian and Alaska
Native:,** 810 (0.2%); **Asian:** 2,376 (0.7%); **Other
race:** 19,644 (5.4%); **Two or more races:** 17,182
(4.7%); **Hispanic/Latino:** 238,351 (65.8%). **2000 percent population 18 and over:** 78.3%; **65 and over:**
17.0%; **median age:** 37.7.
**Land area:** 36 sq mi. (93 sq km); **Water area:** 19.5 sq
mi.; **Alt.:** Average, 12 ft.
**Avg. daily temp.:** Jan., 67.2° F; July, 82.6° F
**Churches**[1]**:** Protestant, 850; Roman Catholic, 61; Jewish, 64; **City-owned parks:** 109; **Radio stations**[1]**:**
29; **Television stations**[1]**:** 9 TV, 1 Cable
**Civilian Labor Force (PMSA) 2001:** 1,080,432;
**Unemployed:** 74,622, **Percent:** 6.9; **Per capita per-
sonal income (PMSA) 2000:** $25,320
**Chamber of Commerce:** Greater Miami Chamber of
Commerce, 1601 Biscayne Blvd., Miami, Fla. 33132

1. Dade County.

Miami, the second-largest city in Florida and seat
of Miami-Dade County, is located in the southeast
part of the state, on Biscayne Bay.

The area was once the home of the Tequesta Indians until they were nearly wiped out by European
diseases and warfare brought on by two centuries of
Spanish control of Florida. Miami was founded in
1870 near the site of Ft. Dallas, built in 1835 during
the Seminole Indian wars. The city's name is probably derived from "Mayaimi," an Indian word for
"big water."

Miami is the only U.S. city to have been planned
by a woman. Julia Tuttle, a Clevelander, arrived
there in 1891 and bought several hundred acres on
the bank of the Miami River. She convinced New
York financier Henry M. Flagler of the area's vast
potential and persuaded him to extend his Florida
East Coast Railroad to Miami in 1896, the year the
city was incorporated. Flagler dredged Miami Harbor, built the renowned Royal Palm Hotel, and promoted the area as a winter playground. Tourists
flocked there, and by 1910 the city was a thriving
recreational area. Miami survived the collapse of a
land speculation boom in the 1920s and severe hurricanes in 1926 and 1935 and continued to grow. It
experienced a monumental population boost during
the 1960s, when about 260,000 Cuban refugees
arrived on its shore. They made a great impact on
Miami, which is now a bilingual metropolis.

Miami is an international banking and finance
center and has the greatest concentration of international and Edge Act banks (banks making only foreign loans and deposits) in North America; these
constitute a major employment base. Greater Miami
has a highly diversified economy with numerous
multinational and Fortune 500 companies. It is a
national leader in biomedical technology, and the
health care sector is a major industry. Greater Miami
is also part of an area known as the Computer Coast
of Florida, and its growing technologies include
computers, electrical engineering, and plastics
manufacturing.

Miami is one of the world's leading year-round
resort centers. The city is a major transportation
hub, and the port of Miami is the world's largest
cruise port and a major seaport for cargo. The
famous island resort of Miami Beach, incorporated
in 1915, is connected to Miami by four causeways.

Famous natives: Fernando Bujones, dancer; Steve
Carlton, baseball player; Debbie Harry, singer; Dick
Howser, baseball player and manager; Sidney Poitier,
actor; Janet Reno, former attorney general of the U.S.;
Ben Vereen, actor; Ellen Zwilich, composer.

# Milwaukee, Wis.

**Mayor:** John O. Norquist (to April 2004)
**2000 census population (rank):** 596,974 (19);
**% change:** -5.0; **Male:** 285,363 (47.8%); **Female:**
311,611 (52.2%); **White:** 298,379 (50.0%); **Black:**
222,933 (37.3%); **American Indian and Alaska
Native:** 5,212 (0.9%); **Asian:** 17,571 (2.9%); **Other
race:** 36,428 (6.1%); **Two or more races:** 16,150
(2.7%); **Hispanic/Latino:** 71,646 (12.0%). **2000 percent population 18 and over:** 71.4%; **65 and over:**
10.9%; **median age:** 30.6.
**Land area:** 96 sq mi. (249 sq km); **Alt.:** 580.60 ft.
**Avg. daily temp.:** Jan., 19.9° F; July, 73.6° F
**Churches:** 411; **County-owned parks:** 14,785 ac.;
**Radio stations:** AM, 6; FM, 13; **Television
stations:** 11
**Civilian Labor Force (PMSA) 2001:** 817,900[1];
**Unemployed:** 34,600; **Percent:** 4.2; **Per capita per-
sonal income (PMSA) 2000:** $32,538[1]
**Chamber of Commerce:** Metropolitan Milwaukee Asso-
ciation of Commerce, 756 N. Milwaukee St., Milwau-
kee, Wis. 53202; Milwaukee Minority Chamber of
Commerce, 509 W. Wisconsin Ave. #606, Milwaukee,
Wis. 53203; Hispanic Chamber of Commerce, 816
W. National Ave., Milwaukee, Wis. 53204

1. Milwaukee–Waukesha, Wis.

Milwaukee, the largest city in Wisconsin and seat
of Milwaukee County, is located in the southeast
part of the state on Lake Michigan.

French missionaries visited the site of Milwaukee
in the 17th century, but it was not until 1795 that
Jacques Vieau established a fur-trading post there.
The first permanent white settler, Vieau's son-in-
law, Solomon Juneau, an agent of the American Fur
Company, made his home there in 1818. The settlement merged with several neighboring villages in
1838 to form Milwaukee, and the city was incorporated in 1846. A large wave of German immigrants
arrived after 1848 and contributed greatly to the
city's political, economic, and cultural development.

The origins of the word "Milwaukee" are disputed; it may come from the Potawatomi "Mahn-ah-
wauk," meaning council grounds of the Potawatomi;
"Mah-an-wauk-seepe," meaning gathering place of
rivers; or the Algonquian "Milo-aki," meaning beautiful land.

Milwaukee is one of the great industrial centers in
the country and one of the largest Great Lakes ports.
Manufacturing remains strong, and Milwaukee
manufacturers are national leaders in lithographic
commercial printing and the production of medical
diagnostic instruments, small gasoline engines, malt
beverages, iron and steel forgings, mining machinery, and robotics. Milwaukee's high-tech manufacturing community is one of the largest among the
nation's major metropolitan areas.

Though Milwaukee was once known as a "beer
town," only a small percentage of its workforce is
now involved in beer production. However, beer
still plays an important role, and almost 11% of the
nation's malt beverage is produced there.

Famous natives: Donald Gramm, bass-baritone; Woody Herman, band leader; Al Jarreau, singer; Kristen Johnston, actress; George F. Kennan, diplomat; Alfred Lunt, actor; Douglas MacArthur, army general; Pat O'Brien, actor; Tom Snyder, TV personality; Speech, member of the rap group "Arrested Development"; Spencer Tracy, actor; Gene Wilder, actor; Jerry and David Zucker, film producers.

# Minneapolis, Minn.

**Mayor:** R. T. Rybak (to Jan. 2006)
**2000 census population (rank):** 382,618 (45); **% change:** 3.9; **Male:** 192,232 (50.2%); **Female:** 190,386 (49.8%); **White:** 249,186 (65.1%); **Black:** 68,818 (18.0%); **American Indian and Alaska Native:** 8,378 (2.2%); **Asian:** 23,455 (6.1%); **Other race:** 15,798 (4.1%); **Two or more races:** 16,694 (4.4%); **Hispanic/Latino:** 29,175 (7.6%). **2000 percent population 18 and over:** 78.0%; **65 and over:** 9.1%; **median age:** 31.2
**Land area:** 55 sq mi. (142 sq km); **Alt.:** Highest, 945 ft.; lowest, 695 ft.
**Avg. daily temp.:** Jan., 11.8° F; July, 73.6° F
**Churches:** 419; **City-owned parks:** 153; **Radio stations[1]:** AM, 17; FM, 15; **Television stations[1]:** 6
**Civilian Labor Force (MSA) 2001:** 1,765,600[2]; **Unemployed:** 52,100, **Percent:** 3.0; **Per capita personal income (MSA) 2000:** $36,666[2]
**Chamber of Commerce:** Minneapolis Regional Chamber of Commerce, Young Quinlan Building, 81 S. Ninth St., Suite 200, Minneapolis, Minn. 55402-3223

1. Metropolitan area. 2. Minneapolis–St. Paul, Minn.–Wis.

Minneapolis, the largest city in Minnesota and the seat of Hennepin County, is located in the southeast central part of the state on the Mississippi River. It is adjacent to its "twin city" of St. Paul.

In 1680, Father Louis Hennepin visited the future site of Minneapolis and gave the Falls of St. Anthony their name. Lt. Zebulon Pike made a treaty with the Sioux Indians in 1805–1806, by which they ceded to the whites much land, including the Falls of St. Anthony and the site of Minneapolis. Fort Snelling was built in 1819–1820, and in 1823 the government built a lumber and flour mill. Flour milling became the major industry of early Minneapolis and made the city the milling capital of the world. The town of St. Anthony was established on the east bank of the Mississippi in 1848, and the town of Minneapolis grew up on the opposite bank of the river. The name Minneapolis is a combination of the Dakota Sioux word "minna," for water, and the Greek word "polis," for city. Minneapolis was incorporated as a city in 1867, and in 1872 the city of St. Anthony (chartered in 1860) was annexed to it. After the spread of the railroads in the 1870s, Minneapolis became the gateway to the Northwest grain trade.

Minneapolis is a center of industry and commerce serving a large agricultural region. During the 20th century, manufacturing, food processing, milling, computers, health services, and graphic arts developed as Minneapolis's major industries. Fifteen Fortune 500 companies are headquartered in the Minneapolis–St. Paul metropolitan area. The city is the headquarters of the Ninth Federal Reserve Bank.

The Twin Cities are known for their wide array of cultural attractions, and Minneapolis is home to many fine museums, including the Minneapolis Institute of Arts, the Walker Center, and the Frederick R. Weisman Art Museum at the University of Minnesota's Minneapolis campus.

Famous natives: La Verne, Maxene, and Patti Andrews, singers; James Arness, actor; Lew Ayres, actor; Patty Berg, golfer; Virginia Bruce, actress; J. Paul Getty, oil executive; Peter Graves, actor; George Roy Hill, director; Cornell MacNeil, baritone; Ralph Meeker, actor; Westbrook Pegler, columnist; The Artist (formerly known as Prince), singer; Harrison Salisbury, journalist; Charles Schulz, cartoonist; Anne Tyler, writer; Bud Wilkinson, football coach; David Winfield, baseball player.

# Nashville-Davidson, Tenn.

**Mayor:** Bill Purcell (to Oct. 2003)
**2000 census population (rank)[1]:** 545,524 (22); **% change:** 11.6; **Male:** 264,095 (48.4%); **Female:** 281,429 (51.6%); **White:** 359,581 (65.9%); **Black:** 146,235 (26.8%); **American Indian and Alaska Native:** 1,639 (0.3%); **Asian:** 12,992 (2.4%); **Other race:** 13,677 (2.5%); **Two or more races:** 11,000 (2.0%); **Hispanic/Latino:** 25,774 (4.7%). **2000 percent population 18 and over:** 77.9%; **65 and over:** 11.0%; **median age:** 33.9.
**Land area:** 502 sq mi. (1,300 sq km); **Altitude:** Highest, 1,100 ft.; lowest, approx. 400 ft.
**Avg. daily temp.:** Jan., 36.2° F; July, 79.3° F
**Churches:** Protestant, 781; Roman Catholic, 18; Jewish, 3; **City-owned parks:** 76 (6,650 ac.); **Radio stations:** AM, 15; FM, 19; **Television stations:** 11
**Civilian Labor Force (MSA) 2001:** 670,434; **Unemployed:** 22,257, **Percent:** 3.3; **Per capita personal income (MSA) 2000:** $30,962
**Chamber of Commerce:** Nashville Area Chamber of Commerce, 211 Commerce Street, Suite 100, Nashville, Tenn. 37201

1. Nashville-Davidson city is consolidated with Davidson County.

Nashville-Davidson is the state capital and second-largest city in Tennessee and is located in the north-central part of the state on the Cumberland River. It is coextensive with Davidson County.

During the winter of 1779–1780, James Robertson and John Donelson founded a settlement at Big Salt Lick by the Cumberland River at the present site of the city. They built forts on both sides of the river, naming one of them Fort Nashborough in honor of Francis Nash, a Revolutionary War general. In 1784, the town was named Nashville, and it was incorporated as a city in 1806.

Nashville became the capital of Tennessee in 1843 and was the seat of Davidson County until 1963, when it merged with the county to become Nashville-Davidson.

The city is a port of entry and an important industrial and commercial center serving the Upper South. Its economy is based on a number of industries, including automobile, apparel, publishing, insurance, and banking. Health care services are the largest sector, but Nashville is best known for its music industry. It is a major recording center, especially for country music.

Nashville is home to several religious organizations and is a major tourist attraction and convention center. Its many institutions of higher education include Vanderbilt University, Fisk University, and the University of Tennessee.

Famous natives: Roy Acuff, singer; Gregg Allman, singer; Pat Boone, singer; Rita Coolidge, singer; Jeff Gordon, race car driver; Al Gore, former vice president; Red Grooms, artist; Alex Haley, author; Barbara Howar, hostess and writer; Brenda Lee, singer; Minnie Pearl, comedienne; Annie Potts, actress; Paula Robeson, flutist; Wilma Rudolph, athlete; Dinah Shore, actress and singer; Tina Turner, singer; Oprah Winfrey, entertainer.

# New Orleans, La.

**Mayor:** Marc H. Morial (to Feb. 2002)
**2000 census population (rank):** 484,674 (31);
**% change:** −2.5; **Male:** 227,094 (46.9%); **Female:**
257,580 (53.1%); **White:** 135,956 (28.1%); **Black:**
325,947 (67.3%); **American Indian and Alaska
Native:** 991 (0.2%); **Asian:** 10,972 (2.3%); **Other
race:** 4,498 (0.9%); **Two or more races:** 6,201
(1.3%); **Hispanic/Latino:** 14,826 (3.1%). **2000 percent population 18 and over:** 73.3%; **65 and over:**
11.7%; **median age:** 33.1.
**Land area:** 181 sq mi. (469 sq km); **Alt.:** Highest, 15 ft.;
lowest, −4 ft.
**Avg. daily temp.:** Jan., 51.3° F; July, 81.9° F
**Churches:** 712; **City-owned parks:** 165 (299 ac.);
**Radio stations:** AM, 12; FM, 14; **Television
stations:** 7
**Civilian Labor Force (MSA) 2001:** 612,449;
**Unemployed:** 31,759, **Percent:** 5.2; **Per capita per-
sonal income (MSA) 2000:** $26,056
**Chamber of Commerce:** New Orleans Regional Cham-
ber of Commerce, 601 Poydras St., Suite 1700, New
Orleans, La. 70130

New Orleans, the largest city in Louisiana, is
located in the southeast part of the state, between
the Mississippi River and Lake Ponchartrain. It is
coextensive with Orleans Parish.

One of the few cities of the nation that has been
under three flags, New Orleans has belonged to
Spain, France, and the United States. The French
founded it in 1718 and named it in honor of the
Duke of Orleans. In 1762, France ceded the city and
the territory to Spain. In 1800, the territory was
returned to France, but government authorities did
not take over until 1803, just 20 days before the
region became part of the United States in the Louisiana Purchase.

New Orleans is famous for its French Quarter,
with its mixture of French, Spanish, and native
architectural styles. The Mardi Gras—a week of carnival held in New Orleans before the beginning of
Lent—is the most spectacular festival in the U.S.
and is a popular tourist attraction. Tourism has
grown rapidly in recent years, and New Orleans
hosts more than seven million visitors annually.

New Orleans has one of the world's greatest international ports, one of the largest in the nation, and it
is a major focus of the city's economy. New Orleans
is home to the corporate offices of oil companies
with major offshore operations in the Gulf of
Mexico, as well as the distribution and service centers of offshore equipment suppliers and fabricators.

The manufacturing industry is a significant part of
the economy, with petroleum, petrochemical, shipbuilding, and aerospace industries all playing a role.
The New Orleans region also functions as a mining,
processing, and transportation center for other minerals, principally sulfur. Service industries are playing a larger role, with health care and telecommunications leading the way. The New Orleans region is
widely regarded as a leading center of medicine and
health care in the South.

Famous natives: Louis Armstrong, musician; Truman
Capote, author; Fats Domino, musician; Louis Gottschalk,
pianist and composer; Bryant Gumbel, TV personality;
Lillian Hellman, playwright and author; Al Hirt, musician;
Mahalia Jackson, singer; Dorothy Lamour, actress; Wynton
Marsalis, musician; Huey Newton, activist; Marguerite
Piazza, soprano; Rusty Staub, baseball player; Ben
Turpin, comedian; Shirley Verrett, mezzo-soprano; Carl
Weathers, actor; Del Williams, football player.

# New York, N.Y.

**Mayor:** Michael R. Bloomberg (to Dec. 2005)
**Borough Presidents:** Bronx, Adolfo Carrion; Brooklyn,
Marty Markowitz; Manhattan, C. Virginia Fields;
Queens, Helen M. Marshall; Staten Island,
James P. Molinaro
**2000 census population (rank):** 8,008,278 (1);
**% change:** 9.4; **Male:** 3,794,204 (47.4%); **Female:**
4,214,074 (52.6%); **White:** 3,576,385 (44.7%); **Black:**
2,129,762 (26.6%); **American Indian and Alaska
Native:** 41,289 (0.5%); **Asian:** 787,047 (9.8%); **Other
race:** 1,074,406 (13.4%); **Two or more races:**
393,959 (4.9%); **Hispanic/Latino:** 2,160,554 (27.0%).
**2000 percent population 18 and over:** 75.8%; **65
and over:** 11.7%; **median age:** 34.2.
**Land area:** 303 sq mi. (785 sq km) (Queens, 109;
Brooklyn, 71; Staten Island, 58; Bronx, 42; Manhattan,
23); **Alt.:** Highest, 426 ft.; lowest, sea level
**Avg. daily temp.:** Jan., 31.5° F; July, 76.8° F
**Churches:** Protestant, 1,766; Jewish, 1,256; Roman
Catholic, 437; Orthodox, 66; **City-owned parks:** 1,701
(28,312 ac.); **Radio stations:** AM, 13; FM, 18;
**Television stations:** 6 commercial, 1 public
**Civilian Labor Force (PMSA) 2001:** 4,137,900;
**Unemployed:** 188,000, **Percent:** 4.5; **Per capita per-
sonal income (PMSA) 2000:** $39,259
**Chamber of Commerce:** New York Chamber of Com-
merce and Industry, 172 Madison Ave., New York,
N.Y. 10016

New York City is the largest city in the United
States. It is located in the southern part of New York
State, at the mouth of the Hudson River (also known
as North River as it passes Manhattan Island).

In 1609, Henry Hudson, who worked for the
Dutch East India Company, sailed up the river that
now bears his name and went as far as Albany. Five
years later, a permanent settlement was established
at what is now New York, but it was originally
called New Amsterdam by the Dutch governors.
One of them, Peter Minuit, was said to have bought
Manhattan Island from the Indians in exchange for
beads, buttons, and trinkets. In 1664, Great Britain's
Duke of York sent a fleet that quietly seized the
settlement from the Dutch without bloodshed and
rechristened the colony in honor of the duke.

Control of New York passed to the young U.S. at
the end of the Revolutionary War, and George
Washington was inaugurated president in New
York's old City Hall. Congress met in New York
from 1785 to 1790.

In 1898, when Greater New York was chartered,
the city expanded to include the following five bor-
oughs, which are also counties in New York State:
Manhattan (New York County); Brooklyn (Kings
County); Bronx (Bronx County); Queens (Queens
County); and Staten Island (Richmond County).

"The Big Apple" is a major world capital and a
world leader in finance, the arts, and communications. The port of New York is one of the finest in
the world and ranks as the largest port complex on
the East Coast. The city is the home of the United
Nations and is headquarters for some of the world's
largest corporations. The city is also the center of
advertising, fashion, publishing, and radio broadcasting in the United States.

The city suffered incredible devastation in Sept.
2001, when terrorist hijackers crashed two commercial jets into the World Trade Center in lower Manhattan, causing the complete destruction of the twin
towers and major loss of life.

Famous natives: Kareem Abdul-Jabbar, basketball player; Woody Allen, actor and director; Lauren Bacall, actress; James Baldwin, novelist; Harry Belafonte, singer and actor; Humphrey Bogart, actor; James Cagney, actor; Maria Callas, soprano; Aaron Copland, composer; Sammy Davis, Jr., singer and actor; Agnes de Mille, choreographer; Robert De Niro, actor; Eamon De Valera, former president of Ireland; Gertrude Elion, Nobel Prize winner in medicine; Lou Gehrig, baseball player; George Gershwin, composer; Ira Gershwin, lyricist; Jackie Gleason, actor; Rita Hayworth, actress; Lena Horne, singer; Julia Ward Howe, poet and reformer; Washington Irving, author; Henry James, novelist; Michael Jordan, basketball player; Sandy Koufax, baseball player; Roy Lichtenstein, painter; Vince Lombardi, football player and coach; Chico, Groucho, Harpo, and Zeppo Marx, comedians; Herman Melville, novelist; Yehudi Menuhin, violinist; James Michener, novelist; Arthur Miller, playwright; Eugene O'Neill, playwright; J. Robert Oppenheimer, nuclear physicist; Al Pacino, actor; Jerome Robbins, choreographer; Eleanor Roosevelt, reformer and humanitarian; Theodore Roosevelt, former president; Jonas Salk, polio researcher; Beverly Sills, soprano; Neil Simon, playwright; Barbra Streisand, singer and actress; Ed Sullivan, TV personality; Mae West, actress; Edith Wharton, novelist.

## Oakland, Calif.

**Mayor:** Jerry Brown (to 2003)
**City Manager:** Robert C. Bobb
**2000 census population (rank):** 399,484 (41);
  **% change:** 7.3; **Male:** 192,757 (48.3%); **Female:** 206,727 (51.7%); **White:** 125,013 (31.3%); **Black:** 142,460 (35.7%); **American Indian and Alaska Native:** 2,655 (0.7%); **Asian:** 60,851 (15.2%); **Other race:** 46,592 (11.7%); **Two or more races:** 19,911 (5.0%); **Hispanic/Latino:** 87,467 (21.9%). **2000 percent population 18 and over:** 75.0%; **65 and over:** 10.5%; **median age:** 33.3.
**Land area:** 56 sq mi. (145 sq km); **Alt.:** Highest, 1,700 ft.; lowest, sea level
**Avg. daily temp.:** Jan., 49.9° F; July, 62.1° F
**Churches:** 374, representing over 78 denominations in the city; over 500 churches in Alameda County; **City-owned parks:** 2,196 ac.; **Radio stations:** AM, 1; **Television stations:** 1 commercial, 1 government access, 2 education access, 1 local
**Civilian Labor Force (PMSA) 2001:** 1,264,667;
  **Unemployed:** 50,578, **Percent:** 4.0; **Per capita personal income (PMSA) 2000:** $39,611
**Chamber of Commerce:** Oakland Chamber of Commerce, 475 Fourteenth St., Oakland, Calif. 94612

Oakland is located in the west-central part of California on the east side of San Francisco Bay. It is the seat of Alameda County.

Don Luis Peralta first settled the site of Oakland in 1820 when he established the Rancho San Antonio. The gold rush of 1849 attracted more people to the area, and the city's population continued to grow until a ferry service to San Francisco was started in 1851. Oakland was incorporated as a town in 1852 and as a city in 1854. It was named after the numerous oak trees found in the area. Oakland became the western terminus of the Central Pacific Railroad in 1869 and the seat of Alameda County in 1873.

In the latter part of the 19th century and also in 1910, additional territory was annexed to Oakland and the city assumed its present size. In 1906, thousands of people fled to Oakland in the aftermath of the San Francisco earthquake and settled there permanently, furthering the city's growth. Oakland's economic development continued to rise with the opening of the San Francisco–Oakland Bay Bridge in 1936.

Oakland is a major center of culture and commerce. It is an important container shipping port and the terminus of three transcontinental railroads. Oakland's industries include food processing, transportation, software, telecommunications, pharmaceuticals, and electrical and high technology manufacturing. The city is the headquarters of many national and international corporations.

Famous natives: Buster Crabbe, actor; Frederick Cottrell, inventor; Clint Eastwood, actor and director; Dennis Eckersley, athlete; Mark Hamill, singer, dancer, and songwriter; Hammer, actor; Tom Hanks, actor; Rod McKuen, singer and composer; Russ Meyer, producer and director; Eddie (Anderson) Rochester, actor; George Stevens, director; Amy Tan, writer; Jo Van Fleet, actress.

## Oklahoma City, Okla.

**Mayor:** Kirk Humphreys (to April 2006)
**City Manager:** Glen E. Deck
**2000 census population (rank):** 506,132 (29);
  **% change:** 13.8; **Male:** 247,313 (48.9%); **Female:** 258,819 (51.1%); **White:** 346,226 (68.4%); **Black:** 77,810 (15.4%); **American Indian and Alaska Native:** 17,743 (3.5%); **Asian:** 17,595 (3.5%); **Other race:** 26,705 (5.3%); **Two or more races:** 19,693 (3.9%); **Hispanic/Latino:** 51,368 (10.1%). **2000 percent population 18 and over:** 74.5%; **65 and over:** 11.5%; **median age:** 34.0.
**Land area:** 607 sq mi. (1,572 sq km); **Alt.:** Highest, 1,320 ft.; lowest, 1,140 ft.
**Avg. daily temp.:** Jan., 35.9° F; July, 82.0° F
**Churches:** Roman Catholic, 25; Jewish, 4; Protestant and others, 741; **City-owned parks:** 144 (5,225 ac.); **Radio stations:** AM, 10; FM, 14; **Television stations:** 8
**Civilian Labor Force (MSA) 2001:** 554,929;
  **Unemployed:** 21,511; **Percent:** 3.9; **Per capita personal income (MSA) 2000:** $25,436
**Chamber of Commerce:** Greater Oklahoma City Chamber of Commerce, 123 Park Ave., Oklahoma City, Okla. 73102

Oklahoma City, the state capital and seat of Oklahoma County, is the largest city in Oklahoma. It is located in the central part of the state on the North Canadian River.

Oklahoma City sprang into being almost overnight. On April 22, 1889, the U.S. government opened the territory for settlement, and there was a rush across the border line to stake claims. A sprawling tent city sprang up near the Santa Fe railroad tracks, and within a short time Oklahoma City was a bustling town of 10,000. The city was incorporated in 1890 and replaced Guthrie as the state capital in 1910. Oil was discovered in the city in 1928, and petroleum production became a mainstay of the city's economy.

Oklahoma City is the wholesale and distributing center for the state, and the city's stockyards are the largest stocker and feeder cattle market in the world. Following the decline of the energy sector, Oklahoma City is fostering a private entrepreneurial environment and a more diversified economy. Within the service sector, health services are projected to grow, followed by retail trade and business services. Nearby Tinker Air Force Base, one of the world's largest air depots, is a major city employer.

In 1995 the city was the scene of a devastating terrorist attack, when a bomb destroyed a federal office building, killing 168 people.

Famous natives: Johnny Bench, baseball player; Lon Chaney, Jr., actor; Ralph Ellison, writer; Kay Francis, actress; Vince Gill, country singer; Dale Robertson, actor; Ted Shackleford, actor; Pamela Tiffin, actress.

# Omaha, Neb.

**Mayor:** Michael Fahey (to June 2005)
**2000 census population (rank):** 390,007 (44);
  **% change:** 16.1; **Male:** 190,032 (48.7%); **Female:**
  199,975 (51.3%); **White:** 305,745 (78.4%); **Black:**
  51,917 (13.3%); **American Indian and Alaska Native:**
  2,616 (0.7%); **Asian:** 6,773 (1.7%); **Other race:**
  15,250 (3.9%); **Two or more races:** 7,478 (1.9%);
  **Hispanic/Latino:** 29,397 (7.5%). **2000 percent population 18 and over:** 74.4%; **65 and over:** 11.8%;
  **median age:** 33.5.
**Land area:** 116 sq mi. (300 sq km); **Alt.:** Highest,
  1,270 ft.
**Avg. daily temp.:** Jan., 21.1° F; July, 76.9° F
**Churches:** Protestant, 192; Roman Catholic, 44; Jewish,
  4; **City-owned parks:** 192 (over 8,000 ac.); **Radio
  stations:** AM, 7; FM, 13; **Television stations:** 4
**Civilian Labor Force (MSA) 2001:** 395,632[1];
  **Unemployed:** 12,673, **Percent:** 3.2; **Per capita personal income (MSA) 2000:** $31,866[1]
**Chamber of Commerce:** Omaha Chamber of Commerce, 1301 Harney St., Omaha, Neb. 68102

1. Omaha, Neb.–Iowa.

Omaha, the largest city in Nebraska and the seat
of Douglas County, is located in the eastern part of
the state on the west bank of the Missouri River,
opposite Council Bluffs, Iowa.

The Lewis and Clark expedition visited the area
in 1804, and the U.S. Army built Ft. Atkinson
nearby in 1819. Pierre Cabanne established a furtrading post at the site in 1825. The first Mormon
migrants wintered there in 1846–1847 on their way
to Utah. The city grew rapidly as the most northerly
supply point for overland wagons to the Far West.

The city was officially founded in 1854 after the
Nebraska Territory was opened for settlement. It
was named for the Omaha Indians living nearby,
whose tribal name means "those who go upstream
or against the current." Omaha was incorporated as
a city in 1857 and was the capital of the Nebraska
Territory from 1855 to 1867. The city continued to
thrive as a point of entry and a major transportation
center when the Union Pacific transcontinental railroad arrived in 1869.

Omaha is a major market for grain and livestock,
food processing, telecommunications, and insurance. Other important industries include electrical
equipment and finance as well as printing and publishing. It continues to be a major railroad hub.

Famous natives: Fred Astaire, dancer and actor; Max
Baer, boxer; Robert Boozer, basketball player; Marlon
Brando, actor; Montgomery Clift, actor; Gerald Ford,
former president; Bob Gibson, baseball player; Swoosie
Kurtz, actress; Melvin Laird, former secretary of defense;
Dorothy McGuire, actress; Nick Nolte, actor; Gale Sayers,
football player; Malcolm X, political activist; Paul Williams,
singer and composer.

# Philadelphia, Pa.

**Mayor:** John F. Street (to Jan. 2004)
**2000 census population (rank):** 1,517,550 (5);
  **% change:** –4.3; **Male:** 705,107 (46.5%); **Female:**
  812,443 (53.5%); **White:** 683,267 (45.0%); **Black:**
  655,824 (43.2%); **American Indian and Alaska
  Native:** 4,073 (0.3%); **Asian:** 67,654 (4.5%); **Other
  race:** 72,429 (4.8%); **Two or more races:** 33,574
  (2.2%); **Hispanic/Latino:** 128,928 (8.5%). **2000 percent population 18 and over:** 74.7%; **65 and over:**
  14.1%; **median age:** 34.2.
**Land area:** 135 sq mi. (350 sq km); **Alt.:** Highest, 440
  ft.; lowest, sea level
**Avg. daily temp.:** Jan., 30.4° F; July, 76.7° F
**Churches:** Roman Catholic, 133; Jewish, 55; Protestant
  and others, 830; **City-owned parks:** 630 (10,252 ac.);
  **Radio stations[1]:** AM, 40; FM, 43; **Television
  stations:** 14
**Civilian Labor Force (PMSA) 2001:** 2,534,787[2];
  **Unemployed:** 109,698, **Percent:** 4.3; **Per capita personal income (PMSA) 2000:** $33,742[2]
**Chamber of Commerce:** Philadelphia Chamber of Commerce, 200 South Broad St., Suite 700, Philadelphia,
  Pa. 19102

1. Metropolitan area. 2. Philadelphia, Pa.–N.J.

Philadelphia, the largest city in Pennsylvania, is
located in the southeast part of the state at the junction of the Schuylkill and Delaware Rivers. It is
coextensive with Philadelphia County.

Philadelphia, the City of Brotherly Love, was
settled in 1681 by Capt. William Markham, who,
with a small band of colonists, had been sent out by
his cousin, William Penn. Penn arrived the following year with the intention of creating a refuge for
the Quakers.

In the period before the American Revolution, the
city outstripped all others in the colonies in education, arts, science, industry, and commerce. In 1774–
1776, the First and Second Continental Congresses
met in Philadelphia, and, from 1781–1783, the city
was the capital of the United States under the
Articles of Confederation. In 1790, it became the
nation's capital under the Constitution and remained
so until the seat of the federal government moved to
Washington in 1800.

Within a half-century of the founding of the
nation at Independence Hall, Philadelphia had
emerged as a leader in America's Industrial Revolution. Today the steam locomotives and hat factories
of the 19th century have been replaced by diverse
manufacturing specialties such as chemicals (including pharmaceuticals), medical devices, transportation equipment, and printing and publishing. In the
services sector, Philadelphia leads in subsectors
such as health services, insurance carriers, legal services, and architecture and engineering services.
Philadelphia is also home to branches of the U.S.
Mint, the Federal Reserve System, and the Internal
Revenue Service.

The city's harbor, one of the largest freshwater
ports in the world, is the centerpiece of the AmeriPort facility in south Philadelphia, a major shipping
center with rail links to the Midwest and Canada.

The city abounds in landmarks of early American
history, including Independence Hall, where the
Declaration of Independence was signed, and the
Liberty Bell. Other significant tourist attractions are
the Philadelphia Museum of Art, the Franklin Institute Science Museum, and the Philadelphia Zoological Gardens.

Famous natives: Marian Anderson, contralto; Frankie
Avalon, singer and actor; John, Lionel, and Ethel
Barrymore, actors; Kevin Bacon, actor; Boyz II Men, R&B
group; Mary Cassatt, artist; Wilt Chamberlain, basketball
player; Chubby Checker, singer; Bill Cosby, actor; Stuart
Davis, painter; Thomas Eakins, painter and sculptor; W. C.
Fields, comedian; Benjamin Franklin, inventor and
statesman; Grace (Kelly), actress and princess of Monaco;
Walt Kelly, cartoonist; Patti LaBelle, singer; Mario Lanza,
singer and actor; George McClellan, general; Margaret
Mead, anthropologist; Edgar Allen Poe, author; Anna
Quindlen, writer and Pulitzer Prize winner; Man Ray,
painter; Betsy Ross, flagmaker; Will Smith, actor;
Jacqueline Susann, novelist; Robert Venturi, architect.

# Phoenix, Ariz.

**Mayor:** Skip Rimsza (to Oct. 2003)
**2000 census population (rank):** 1,321,045 (6);
% change: 34.3; **Male:** 671,760 (50.9%); **Female:**
649,285 (49.1%); **White:** 938,853 (71.1%); **Black:**
67,416 (5.1%); **American Indian and Alaska Native:**
26,696 (2.0%); **Asian:** 26,449 (2.0%); **Other race:**
216,589 (16.4%); **Two or more races:** 43,276 (3.3%);
**Hispanic/Latino:** 449,972 (34.1%). **2000 percent
population 18 and over:** 71.1%; **65 and over:** 8.1%;
**median age:** 30.7.
**Land area:** 475 sq mi. (1,230 sq km); **Alt.:** Highest,
2,740 ft.; lowest, 1,017 ft.
**Avg. daily temp.:** Jan., 53.6° F; July, 93.5° F
**City-owned parks:** 170 (25,235 ac.); **Radio stations:**
AM, 20; FM, 20; **Television stations:** 9 commercial;
1 PBS
**Civilian Labor Force (MSA) 2001:** 1,620,060[1];
**Unemployed:** 63,610, **Percent:** 3.9; **Per capita per-
sonal income (MSA) 2000:** $27,564[1]
**Chamber of Commerce:** Phoenix Chamber of Com-
merce, 201 N. Central, Phoenix, Ariz. 85073

1. Phoenix–Mesa, Ariz.

Phoenix, the capital of Arizona and seat of Maricopa County, is the largest city in the state. It is
located in the center of Arizona, on the Salt River.

The prehistoric Hohokam Indians first settled the
area about 300 B.C. and dug a system of extensive
irrigation canals for farming. The Indian culture
mysteriously broke up in the 1400s.

The site was permanently resettled by Jack Swill-
ing and "Lord Darrell" Duppa about 1867. Because
the city was founded on the ruins of the ancient civilization, it was named Phoenix after the legendary
bird that could regenerate itself. The irrigation canals
were restored for farming, and ranching and pros-
pecting began in the surrounding area. The city
quickly grew as an important trading center. Phoenix
was incorporated as a city in 1881 and was made the
territorial capital in 1889. It became the state capital
when Arizona was admitted to the Union in 1912.

Partly owing to its warm, dry climate, the city
developed rapidly in the decades after World War II.
Between 1950 and 1990 the population increased
from 100,000 to 980,000. And Phoenix continues to
be one of the fastest growing cities in the U.S.;
between 1990 and 2000, its population increased
another 34%, to 1.3 million.

Phoenix is a commercial and manufacturing center in an agricultural region. Major industries
include government, agricultural products, aerospace technology, electronics, air-conditioning,
leather goods, and Indian arts and crafts. Mining,
timbering, and tourism also contribute to the
economy.

Famous natives: Lynda Carter, actress; Alice Cooper,
musician; Arthur A. Fletcher, government official; Barry
Goldwater, politician; Stevie Nicks, musician; Charles O.
Robb, politician; Mare Winningham, actress.

# Portland, Ore.

**Mayor:** Vera Katz (to Dec. 2004)
**2000 census population (rank):** 529,121 (28);
% change: 21.0; **Male:** 261,565 (49.4%); **Female:**
267,556 (50.6%); **White:** 412,241 (77.9%); **Black:** 35,115
(6.6%); **American Indian and Alaska Native:** 5,587
(1.1%); **Asian:** 33,470 (6.3%); **Other race:** 18,760
(3.5%); **Two or more races:** 21,955 (4.1%); **Hispanic/
Latino:** 36,058 (6.8%). **2000 percent population 18 and
over:** 78.9%; **65 and over:** 11.6%; **median age:** 35.2.

**Land area:** 134 sq mi. (347 sq km); **Alt.:** Highest, 1073
ft.; lowest, sea level
**Avg. daily temp.:** Jan., 39.6° F; July, 68.2° F
**Churches:** Protestant, 450; Roman Catholic, 48; Jewish,
9; Buddhist, 6; other, 190; **City-owned parks:** 200
(over 9,400 ac.); **Radio stations:** AM: 14, FM: 14;
**Television stations:** 5 commercial, 1 public
**Civilian Labor Force (PMSA) 2001:** 1,068,400[1];
**Unemployed:** 48,900, **Percent:** 4.6; **Per capita per-
sonal income (PMSA) 2000:** $31,620[1]
**Chamber of Commerce:** Portland Chamber of Com-
merce, 221 NW 2nd Ave., Portland, Ore. 97209

1. Portland–Vancouver, Ore.–Wash.

Portland, the largest city in Oregon and seat of
Multnomah County, is located in the northwest part
of the state on the Willamette River.

Lewis and Clark camped at the site of Portland in
1805 on their expedition across the continent. Portland was founded in 1845 and was almost called
Boston after the city in Massachusetts. Founders
Amos Lovejoy from Massachusetts and Francis Pettygrove from Maine flipped a coin to decide the
name of the new town. Pettygrove won the toss and
named the place Portland after his hometown. Portland was incorporated as a city in 1851.

In the 1850s Portland served as a supply base for
the California gold rush, and it grew with the development of its salmon and lumber industries and the
arrival of the railroad in 1883. The city continued to
grow from 1879 to 1900 as a supply point for the
Alaska gold rush and as the site of the Lewis and
Clark Centennial Exposition in 1905.

The port of Portland leads the West in grain
exports and is among the top five auto-import centers in the United States.

Portland has a diverse economy with a broad base
of manufacturing, distribution, wholesale and retail
trade, regional government, and business services.
Major manufacturing industries include machinery,
electronics, metals, transportation equipment, and
lumber and wood products. Technology is a thriving
part of Portland's economy, with over 1,700 high-
tech companies located in the metropolitan area.
Tourism is also important to Portland's economy,
drawing more than 7 million visitors annually.

Famous natives: James Beard, food expert; Pietro Belluschi,
architect; Richard Fosbury, high jumper; Matt Groening,
cartoonist; Margaux Hemingway, actress; Phil Knight,
founder of Nike; Terrance Knox, actor; Jeff Lorber, jazz
musician; Linus Pauling, chemist; Jane Powell, singer and
actress; Ahmad Rashad, football player and sportscaster;
Susan Ruttan, actress; Doc Severinson, band leader; Norton
Simon, business executive; Sally Ann Struthers, actress;
Gus Van Sant, film director; Lindsay Wagner, actress; Mitch
Williams, baseball pitcher.

# Sacramento, Calif.

**Mayor:** Heather Fargo (to Nov. 2004)
**City Manager:** Robert P. Thomas
**2000 census population (rank):** 407,018 (40);
% change: 10.2; **Male:** 197,784 (48.6%); **Female:**
209,234 (51.4%); **White:** 196,549 (48.3%); **Black:**
62,968 (15.5%); **American Indian and Alaska Native:**
5,300 (1.3%); **Asian:** 67,635 (16.6%); **Other race:**
44,627 (11.0%); **Two or more races:** 26,078 (6.4%);
**Hispanic/Latino:** 87,974 (21.6%). **2000 percent
population 18 and over:** 72.7%; **65 and over:**
11.4%; **median age:** 32.8.
**Land area:** 97 sq mi. (251 sq km)
**Avg. daily temp.:** Jan., 45.2° F; July, 75.7° F
**City park & recreational facilities:** 134+ (1,427+ ac.);
**Television stations:** 7

**Civilian Labor Force (PMSA) 2001:** 829,833; **Unemployed:** 33,584, **Percent:** 4.0; **Per capita personal income (PMSA) 2000:** $30,252
**Chamber of Commerce:** Sacramento Chamber of Commerce, 917 7th St., Sacramento, Calif. 95814; West Sacramento Chamber of Commerce, 834-C Jefferson Blvd., Sacramento, Calif. 95691

Sacramento is the capital of California and the seat of Sacramento County. It is located in the north-central part of the state at the confluence of the Sacramento and American rivers.

In 1839, German-born Swiss citizen John Augustus Sutter obtained a grant from the Mexican governor to establish a colony for fellow Swiss emigrants on a large tract of land that he named New Helvetia (New Switzerland). He established Fort Sutter there as a trading post.

After gold was discovered on Sutter's property in 1848, the settlement rapidly expanded as the prominent supply point for gold prospectors coming from the East. Sacramento was laid out in 1848 and named after California's principal river, which ran beside it. The river's name in Spanish honors the Holy Sacrament. It became incorporated as a city in 1849 and was made the state capital in 1854. Sacramento was the terminus of the first railroad in 1856 and the western terminus of the Pony Express in 1860.

The city has always been a hub of river transportation and is a major deep-water port connected to the Pacific Ocean. Sacramento's economy is highly diversified and, along with state government and military installations, its industries include aerospace, high technology, furniture, chemicals, pharmaceuticals, meat packing, and food processing of crops from the Central Valley.

Famous natives: Joan Didion, author; Mark Goodson, TV producer; Tom Hanks, actor; Henry Hathaway, director; Anthony M. Kennedy, Supreme Court justice; Molly Ringwald, actress.

## St. Louis, Mo.

**Mayor:** Francis G. Slay (to April 2005)
**2000 census population (rank):** 348,189 (49); **% change:** –12.2; **Male:** 163,567 (47.0%); **Female:** 184,622 (53.0%); **White:** 152,666 (43.8%); **Black:** 178,266 (51.2%); **American Indian and Alaska Native:** 950 (0.3%); **Asian:** 6,891 (2.0%); **Other race:** 2,783 (0.8%); **Two or more races:** 6,539 (1.9%); **Hispanic/Latino:** 7,022 (2.0%). **2000 percent population 18 and over:** 74.3%; **65 and over:** 13.7%; **median age:** 33.7.
**Land area:** 62 sq mi. (161 sq km), **Alt.:** Highest, 616 ft.; lowest, 413 ft.
**Avg. daily temp.:** Jan., 28.4° F; July, 78.4° F
**Churches:** 900[1]; **City-owned parks:** 106 (3,136 ac.); **Radio stations:** AM, 21; FM 27[1]; **Television stations:** 6 commercial; 1 PBS
**Civilian Labor Force (MSA) 2001:** 1,359,505[2]; **Unemployed:** 66,060, **Percent:** 4.9; **Per capita personal income (MSA) 2000:** $31,354[2]
**Chamber of Commerce:** St. Louis Regional Chamber and Growth Association, One Metropolian Square, Suite 1300, St. Louis, Mo. 63102

1. Metropolitan area. 2. St. Louis, Mo.–Ill.

St. Louis, the second-largest city in Missouri, is located in the east central part of the state on the Mississippi River. The city is independent and is not part of any county.

St. Louis was founded by the French in 1764 when Auguste Chouteau established a fur-trading post and Pierre Laclède Liguest, a New Orleans merchant, founded a town at the present site. They named it after King Louis XV of France and his patron saint, Louis IX. From 1770 to 1803, St. Louis was a Spanish possession, but it was ceded back to France in 1803 in accordance with the Treaty of San Ildefonso (1800), only to be acquired by the U.S. as part of the Louisiana purchase later that year.

The town was incorporated in 1809. From 1812 to 1821, St. Louis was the capital of the Missouri Territory, and it was incorporated as a city in 1822.

John Jacob Astor opened the Western branch of the American Fur Company in 1819, and the city prospered during the early part of the 19th century as a commercial center for the fur trade. St. Louis continued to grow as a major transportation hub with the development of steamboat traffic and the later expansion of the railroads in the 1850s. The world-famous Louisiana Purchase Exposition was held here in 1904.

Manufacturing is important to the city's economy, and its highly developed industries include automobiles, aircraft and space technology, metal fabrication, beer, steelmaking, chemicals, food processing, and storage and distribution.

The giant stainless steel Gateway Arch, 630 ft high, standing on the banks of the Mississippi, symbolizes St. Louis as the Gateway to the West.

Famous natives: Josephine Baker, singer; Yogi Berra, baseball player; Chuck Berry, singer and guitarist; Grace Bumbry, mezzo-soprano; T. S. Eliot, poet; Eugene Field, poet; Redd Foxx, comedian; Joe Garagiola, baseball player; John Goodman, actor; Betty Grable, actress; Dick Gregory, comedian; Al Hirschfeld, cartoonist; Kevin Kline, actor; David Merrick, producer; Vincent Price, actor; Judy Rankin, golfer; Leon Spinks, boxer; Herbert Bayard Swope, journalist; Sara Teasdale, poet; Helen Traubel, soprano; Roy Wilkins, civil rights leader.

## San Antonio, Tex.

**Mayor:** Ed Garza (to May 2003)
**City Manager:** Terry M. Brechtel
**2000 census population (rank):** 1,144,646 (9); **% change:** 22.3; **Male:** 553,245 (48.3%); **Female:** 591,401 (51.7%); **White:** 774,708 (67.7%); **Black:** 78,120 (6.8%); **American Indian and Alaska Native:** 9,584 (0.8%); **Asian:** 17,934 (1.6%); **Other race:** 221,362 (19.3%); **Two or more races:** 41,871 (3.7%); **Hispanic/Latino:** 671,394 (58.7%). **2000 percent population 18 and over:** 71.5%; **65 and over:** 10.4%; **median age:** 31.7.
**Land area:** 408 sq mi. (1,057 sq km), **Alt.:** 700 ft.
**Avg. daily temp.:** Jan., 49.3° F; July, 85.0° F
**City-owned parks:** 6,717 ac.; **Radio stations:** AM, 20; FM, 22; **Television stations:** 9
**Civilian Labor Force (MSA) 2001:** 788,521; **Unemployed:** 31,223, **Percent:** 4.0; **Per capita personal income (MSA) 2000:** $25,741
**Chamber of Commerce:** Greater San Antonio Chamber of Commerce, 602 E. Commerce, San Antonio, Tex. 78296

San Antonio, the third-largest city in Texas and the seat of Bexar County, is located in the south-central part of the state, on the San Antonio River.

The site of San Antonio was first visited in 1691 by a Franciscan friar on the feast day of St. Anthony and was named San Antonio de Padua in his honor. San Antonio was permanently settled on May 1, 1718, when the Spanish governor of Coahuila and Texas, Martín de Alarcón, founded the presidio (a fort) of San Antonio de Bejar (Bexar) and the mission of San Antonio de Valero (later called the

Alamo) on the site of a Coahuiltecan Indian village. San Antonio remained almost continuously under Spanish rule until 1812, when Mexico won its independence from Spain.

During the outbreak of the Texas revolution (1835) against the tyranny of Mexican dictator General Santa Anna, San Antonio was captured by a small band of rebels who occupied the fortified mission of the Alamo in Dec. 1835. The historic battle of the Alamo was fought there (Feb. 24 to March 6, 1836), and its 183 besieged defenders were massacred by Santa Anna's troops. Their heroism aroused the anger and fighting spirit of Texans and led them to shout their famous battle cry "Remember the Alamo!" and defeat the Mexicans six weeks later (April 21, 1836) at the battle of San Jacinto. Texas became an independent republic in 1836, and San Antonio was incorporated as a city on Jan. 5, 1837.

After the Civil War, with the arrival of the railroad in 1877, San Antonio prospered as a major shipping point for cattle. The city has been an important military center since World War II and is the home to five of the largest military installations in the nation, including Fort Sam Houston, constructed in 1876. San Antonio is a leading livestock center and one of the largest produce exchange markets. The city's industries are highly diversified, and tourism is also important to the economy.

Famous natives: Carol Burnett, comedienne; Cody Carlson, football player; Henry G. Cisneros, secretary of HUD; Joan Crawford, actress; Cito Gaston, baseball manager; Ann Harding, actress; Jesse James Leija, boxer; Emilio Navaira, Tejano music singer; Oliver North, military officer and government official; Suzy Parker, model and actress; Paula Prentiss, actress; Kyle Rote, football player; David R. Scott, astronaut; John Silber, university president; Patsy Torres, Tejano music singer; Edward H. White, astronaut.

# San Diego, Calif.

**Mayor:** Dick Murphy (to Dec. 2004)
**City Manager:** Michael Uberuaga (apptd. Nov. 1997)
**2000 census population (rank):** 1,223,400 (7);
    **% change:** 10.2; **Male:** 616,884 (50.4%); **Female:** 606,516 (49.6%); **White:** 736,207 (60.2%); **Black:** 96,216 (7.9%); **American Indian and Alaska Native:** 7,543 (0.6%); **Asian:** 166,968 (13.6%); **Other race:** 151,532 (12.4%); **Two or more races:** 59,081 (4.8%); **Hispanic/Latino:** 310,752 (25.4%). **2000 percent population 18 and over:** 76.0%; **65 and over:** 10.5%; **median age:** 32.5.
**Land area:** 324 sq miles (839 sq km); **Alt.:** Highest, 1,591 ft.; lowest, sea level
**Avg. daily temp.:** Jan., 57.4° F; July, 71.0° F
**Churches:** Roman Catholic, 39; Jewish, 9; Protestant, 334; Eastern Orthodox, 8; other, 18; **City park and recreation facilities:** 18; **AM, 20; FM, 25; Television stations:** 9
**Civilian Labor Force (MSA) 2001:** 1,424,852;
    **Unemployed:** 45,698, **Percent:** 3.2; **Per capita personal income (MSA) 2000:** $32,515
**Chamber of Commerce:** San Diego Chamber of Commerce, 402 West Broadway, Suite 1000, San Diego, Calif. 92101

San Diego is the second-largest city in California. It is located in the southwest part of the state, on San Diego Bay.

Portuguese navigator Juan Rodríguez Cabrillo claimed the bay for Spain in 1542. The site was named San Miguel by Cabrillo. On Nov. 12, 1602, Don Sebastian de Viscaíno came ashore with his party on the day of St. Didacus (San Diego in Span-

ish) and celebrated a mass in the saint's honor. By coincidence, Viscaíno's flagship was named San Diego. He renamed the place San Diego after the 15th-century saint.

In 1769, Franciscan father Junípero Serra established the first California mission there—San Diego del Alcala. In 1822, Mexico won control of the town after declaring its independence from Spain. In 1846, during the Mexican War, San Diego was seized by the U.S., and it was incorporated as a city in 1850, just after California joined the Union.

Today, San Diego's excellent natural harbor is a busy commercial port and a hub of U.S. naval operations (although the naval training center at San Diego has closed due to defense cutbacks). Other leading industries are electronics, aerospace and missiles, medical and scientific research, oceanography, and agriculture. Its magnificent climate and proximity to Mexico have made tourism a significant part of the city's economy.

Famous natives: Billy Casper, golfer; Florence Chadwick, swimmer; Dennis Conner, yacht racer; Ted Danson, actor; Robert Duvall, actor; Nanette Fabray, actress; Margaret O'Brien, actress; Carol Vaness, soprano; Ted Williams, baseball player; Mickey Wright, golfer.

# San Francisco, Calif.

**Mayor:** Willie L. Brown, Jr. (to Jan. 2004)
**2000 census population (rank):** 776,733 (13);
    **% change:** 7.3; **Male:** 394,828 (50.8%); **Female:** 381,905 (49.2%); **White:** 385,728 (49.7%); **Black:** 60,515 (7.8%); **American Indian and Alaska Native:** 3,458 (0.4%); **Asian:** 239,565 (30.8%); **Other race:** 50,368 (6.5%); **Two or more races:** 33,255 (4.3%); **Hispanic/Latino:** 109,504 (14.1%). **2000 percent population 18 and over:** 85.5%; **65 and over:** 13.7%; **median age:** 36.5.
**Land area:** 47 sq mi. (122 sq km); **Alt.:** Highest, 925 ft.; lowest, sea level
**Avg. daily temp.:** Jan., 51.1° F; July, 59.1° F
**Churches:** 540 of all denominations; **City-owned parks and squares:** 225; **Radio stations:** 29; **Television stations:** 10
**Civilian Labor Force (PMSA) 2001:** 982,908;
    **Unemployed:** 37,403, **Percent:** 3.8; **Per capita personal income (PMSA) 2000:** $57,414
**Chamber of Commerce:** San Francisco Chamber of Commerce, 235 Montgomery St., San Francisco, Calif. 94104

San Francisco, the fourth-largest city in California, is coextensive with San Francisco County. It is located in the northern part of the state between the Pacific Ocean and San Francisco Bay on a narrow arm of land that embraces San Francisco Bay, one of the finest landlocked harbors in the world.

A Franciscan father who was sailing with Sebastián Rodríguez Cermeño named the bay San Francisco on Nov. 7, 1595. In 1776, the Spaniards established a presidio, or military post, and a Franciscan mission on the end of the beautiful peninsula. In the following year, a little town was founded around the mission. It was called Yerba Buena, Spanish for "Good Herb," because mint grew in abundance there. In 1846, during the Mexican War, Yerba Buena was taken over by the United States. It was renamed San Francisco in 1847 and became incorporated as a city in 1850.

When gold was discovered in California in 1848, the city's population jumped to 10,000, and it experienced turbulent years until order was established by Vigilance Committees, first in 1851, and again in 1856. Then followed a period of more orderly growth, and the foundations of the great commerce and industry of today were laid.

In 1906, San Francisco experienced the nation's most destructive earthquake, which, together with the fire that followed, practically destroyed the city. The city was quickly rebuilt and grew rapidly as a leading transportation, industrial, and cultural center. In the 19th century, the American explorer and soldier John C. Frémont, known as The Pathfinder, named the entrance to the bay the Golden Gate, and the famous bright orange Golden Gate Bridge was dedicated in May 1937.

A vital part of the economic and cultural fabric of northern California, the port of San Francisco covers 7½ mi of waterfront. The port is home to a broad range of commercial, maritime, and public activities. Its major shipping terminals serve shipping lines from around the world. Fisherman's Wharf, Alcatraz, Hyde St. Pier, and Pier 39 all make the port of San Francisco one of the world's leading visitor destinations.

The electronics and biotechnology industries are well represented throughout the Bay Area. With nearly 30% of the worldwide biotechnology labor force and 360 biotech firms, the Bay Area has been appropriately called "Bionic Bay."

Tourism is one of San Francisco's largest industries and the largest employer of city residents. In 2000, more than 17 million people visited San Francisco, and visitor spending was $7.6 billion, providing 82,000 jobs.

San Francisco is also the banking and financial center of the West and is home to a Federal Reserve Bank and a United States Mint. More than 60 foreign banks maintain offices there.

Famous natives: Gracie Allen, comedienne; Luis Walter Alvarez, Nobel Prize winner in physics; David Belasco, dramatist and producer; Mel Blanc, actor and voice specialist; Rosemary Casals, tennis player; Isadora Duncan, dancer; Clint Eastwood, actor; Robert Frost, poet; Rube Goldberg, cartoonist; William Randolph Hearst, publisher; Bruce Lee, actor; Mervyn LeRoy, director; Jack London, novelist; Johnny Mathis, singer; Lloyd Nolan, actor; O. J. Simpson, football player; Robert G. Sproul, educator; Irving Stone, novelist; Natalie Wood, actress.

# San Jose, Calif.

**Mayor:** Ron Gonzales (to Dec. 31, 2002)
**Acting City Manager:** Debra Figone
**2000 census population (rank):** 894,943 (11); **% change:** 14.4; **Male:** 454,798 (50.8%); **Female:** 440,145 (49.2%); **White:** 425,017 (47.5%); **Black:** 31,349 (3.5%); **American Indian and Alaska Native:** 6,865 (0.8%); **Asian:** 240,375 (26.9%); **Other race:** 142,691 (15.9%); **Two or more races:** 45,062 (5.0%); **Hispanic/Latino:** 269,989 (30.2%). **2000 percent population 18 and over:** 73.6%; **65 and over:** 8.3%; **median age:** 32.6.
**Land area:** 175 sq mi. (453 sq km); **Alt.:** Highest, 4,372 ft.; lowest, sea level
**Avg. daily temp.:** Jan., 49.4° F; July, 69.5° F
**Churches:** 403; **City-owned parks and playgrounds:** 152 (3,136 ac.); **Radio stations:** 14; **Television stations:** 4
**Civilian Labor Force (PMSA) 2001:** 1,012,671; **Unemployed:** 45,190, **Percent:** 4.5; **Per capita personal income (PMSA) 2000:** $55,157
**Chamber of Commerce:** San Jose Chamber of Commerce, 310 S. First St., San Jose, Calif. 95113

San Jose, the third-largest city in California and seat of Santa Clara County, is located in the northern part of the state in the Santa Clara Valley, 50 mi south of downtown San Francisco.

San Jose was founded on Nov. 29, 1777, by Spanish colonizers who named the settlement Pueblo de San José de Guadalupe in honor of Saint Joseph and after the Guadalupe River on which the pueblo (town) was situated. San Jose was the first city to be established in California.

After California became a U.S. territory in 1847, San Jose was the state capital from 1849 to 1852 and was incorporated as a city in 1850. It developed commercially as a supply base for gold prospectors and, when the railroad connected it with San Francisco in 1864, it became the distribution point for agricultural products from the Santa Clara Valley.

Today, the city continues to be the distribution and food-processing center for the surrounding rich agricultural region, which produces seasonal fruits and grapes. More than 50 wineries grace the valley.

San Jose is the capital of Silicon (Santa Clara) Valley, where more than 6,500 (as of 1999) high-tech companies are located. The area is also one of the world's leading centers for medical treatment and research. Heart transplants, gene splicing, and transportable baby incubators were developed there.

San Jose has healthy retail, transportation, and tourism industries and is the primary center for real estate and industrial development in the area. In 2001, it ranked second in the U.S. based on the median household income of $71,000.

Famous natives: "Fatty" Arbuckle, actor; Cesar Chavez, labor leader; Peggy Fleming, figure skater; Farley Granger, actor; Edmund Lowe, actor; Jim Plunkett, football player.

# Seattle, Wash.

**Mayor:** Greg Nickels (to Dec. 31, 2005)
**2000 census population (rank):** 563,374 (24); **% change:** 9.1; **Male:** 280,973 (49.9%); **Female:** 282,401 (50.1%); **White:** 394,889 (70.1%); **Black:** 47,541 (8.4%); **American Indian and Alaska Native:** 5,659 (1.0%); **Asian:** 73,910 (13.1%); **Other race:** 13,423 (2.4%); **Two or more races:** 25,148 (4.5%); **Hispanic/Latino:** 29,719 (5.3%). **2000 percent population 18 and over:** 84.4%; **65 and over:** 12.0%; **median age:** 35.4.
**Land area:** 84 sq mi. (218 sq km); **Alt.:** Highest, 521 ft.; lowest, sea level
**Avg. daily temp.:** Jan., 40.1° F; July, 65.2° F
**Churches:** Roman Catholic, 35; Jewish, 12; Protestant, 447; others, 42; **City-owned parks, playgrounds, etc.:** 397 (6,000+ ac.); **Radio stations:** AM, 15; FM, 22; **Television stations:** 6
**Civilian Labor Force (PMSA) 2001:** 1,363,035[1]; **Unemployed:** 70,407, **Percent:** 5.2; **Per capita personal income (PMSA) 2000:** $40,686[1]
**Chamber of Commerce:** Greater Seattle Chamber of Commerce, 1301 5th Ave., Suite 2400, Seattle, Wash. 98101-2603

1. Seattle–Bellevue–Everett, Wash.

Seattle is the largest city in Washington and the seat of King County. A city of steep hills, Seattle lies in western Washington between two bodies of water—Puget Sound on the west and Lake Washington on the east. Its fine landlocked harbor has made Seattle one of the major ports in the United States.

Seattle was first settled by five pioneer families from Illinois at Alki Point at the south end of Elliott Bay in 1851. They moved in 1852 to the eastern shore of the bay and laid out a town in 1853. It was named Seattle after a friendly Suquamish Indian chief (Seattle is only an approximation of his name).

Seattle successfully withstood an Indian attack in 1856 and was incorporated as a city in 1869. A disastrous fire almost destroyed the entire business district in 1889. When the Great Northern Railway arrived in 1893, the city became a major rail terminus and it grew rapidly. It was a boom town during the Alaska gold rush of 1897 and continued to prosper as a major Pacific port of entry with the opening of the Panama Canal in 1914.

Seattle is the region's commercial and transportation hub and the center of manufacturing, trade, and finance. Its important diversified industries include aircraft, lumber and forest products, fishing, high technology, food processing, boat building, machinery, fabricated metals, chemicals, pharmaceuticals, and apparel.

Famous natives: Chester Carlson, Xerox inventor; Carol Channing, actress; Judy Collins, singer; Fred Couples, golfer; Gail Devers, athlete; Frances Farmer, actress; William Gates, Microsoft founder; June Havoc, actress; Jimi Hendrix, guitarist; Robert Joffrey, choreographer; Gypsy Rose Lee, entertainer; Mary Livingstone, comedienne; Kevin McCarthy, actor; Mary McCarthy, novelist; Jeff Smith, food expert; Martha Wright, singer.

## Tucson, Ariz.

**Mayor:** Bob Walkup (to Dec. 2003)
**2000 census population (rank):** 486,699 (30);
  **% change:** 20.1; **Male:** 238,408 (49.0%); **Female:**
  248,291 (51.0%); **White:** 341,424 (70.2%); **Black:**
  21,057 (4.3%); **American Indian and Alaska Native:**
  11,038 (2.3%); **Asian:** 11,959 (2.5%); **Other race:**
  81,938 (16.8%); **Two or more races:** 18,437 (3.8%);
  **Hispanic/Latino:** 173,868 (35.7%). **2000 percent**
  **population 18 and over:** 75.4%; **65 and over:**
  11.9%; **median age:** 32.1.
**Land area:** 195 sq mi. (505 sq km); **Alt.:** 2,400 ft.
**Avg. daily temp.:** Jan., 51.3° F; July, 86.6° F
**Churches:** Protestant, 340; Roman Catholic, 42; other,
  150; **City-owned parks and parkways:** (25,349 ac.);
  **Radio stations:** AM, 15; FM, 17; **Television stations:**
  3 commercial; 1 educational; 3 other
**Civilian Labor Force (MSA) 2001:** 392,593;
  **Unemployed:** 13,561, **Percent:** 3.5; **Per capita per-**
  **sonal income (MSA) 2000:** $23,705
**Chamber of Commerce:** Tucson Metropolitan Chamber
  of Commerce, P.O. Box 991, Tucson, Ariz. 85702

Tucson is the second-largest city in Arizona and the seat of Pima County. It is located in the southeast part of the state on the Santa Cruz River.

The site was originally settled by the prehistoric Hohokam Indians (300 B.C.–A.D. 1400s). The first Europeans to visit the area were Spanish explorers in the 17th century. In 1700, the Jesuit missionary explorer Father Eusebio Francisco Kino founded the mission of San Xavier del Bac close by the Papago Indian village of Stjukshon (later called Tucson). Stjukshon is an Indian word meaning "village of the dark spring at the foot of the mountain." The Papago Indians are descendants of the ancient Hohokam peoples.

In 1776, Spanish colonists from Mexico constructed a presidio (fort) at Tucson as protection against the hostile Apache Indians and also established the mission of San Jose de Tucson nearby. Tucson remained a military outpost under Spanish and later Mexican control until the area was sold to the United States as part of the Gadsden Purchase in

1853. Tucson was the capital of the Arizona Territory from 1867 to 1877. It was incorporated as a city in 1877. The town grew rapidly when the Southern Pacific Railroad arrived in 1880 and silver and copper deposits were discovered nearby.

Tucson is a popular vacation and health resort due to its sunny, mild, dry climate and unique desert location. Tourism is important to the city's economy. Major industries include aerospace and missile production, high technology, optics, biotechnology, environmental technology, software, and electronics. Tucson is also the commercial center for the surrounding area's agricultural and mining industries. The city is the home of the University of Arizona.

Famous natives: Rose E. Bird, jurist; Dennis De Concini, senator; Barbara Eden, actress; Linda Ronstadt, singer.

## Tulsa, Okla.

**Mayor:** Bill LaFortune (to April 2006)
**2000 census population (rank):** 393,049 (43);
  **% change:** 7.0; **Male:** 189,937 (48.3%); **Female:**
  203,112 (51.7%); **White:** 275,488 (70.1%); **Black:**
  60,794 (15.5%); **American Indian and Alaska Native:**
  18,551 (4.7%); **Asian:** 7,150 (1.8%); **Other race:**
  13,564 (3.5%); **Two or more races:** 17,300 (4.4%);
  **Hispanic/Latino:** 28,111 (7.2%). **2000 percent popu-**
  **lation 18 and over:** 75.2%; **65 and over:** 12.9%;
  **median age:** 34.5.
**Land area:** 183 sq mi. (474 sq km); **Alt.:** 674 ft.
**Avg. daily temp.:** Jan., 35.2° F; July, 83.3° F
**Churches:** Protestant, 290; Roman Catholic, 40; Jewish,
  3; others, 4; **City parks and playgrounds:** 140 (6,000
  ac.); **Radio stations:** AM, 10; FM, 16; **Television**
  **stations:** 7 commercial; 1 PBS; 123 cable
**Civilian Labor Force (MSA) 2001:** 421,170;
  **Unemployed:** 14,227, **Percent:** 3.4; **Per capita per-**
  **sonal income (MSA) 2000:** $28,775
**Chamber of Commerce:** Metropolitan Tulsa Chamber of
  Commerce, 616 S. Boston, Tulsa, Okla. 74119

Tulsa, the second-largest city in Oklahoma and seat of Tulsa County, is located in the northeast part of the state on the Arkansas River.

Tulsa was settled in the 1830s by Creek Indians from Alabama who were forcibly sent to the area (then part of Indian Territory) under the Indian Removal Act of 1830. Creek medicine men planted ashes from their old home at the new site, and the Creeks named their new village "Tulsy," meaning old town, in memory of their former home in Tallassee, Ala. In time, the village became the town of Tulsa.

The coming of the first railroad in 1882 attracted white settlers to Tulsa, and the town developed into a cattle-shipping center. When enormous oil depos its were discovered in nearby Red Fork in 1901 and at Glenn Pool in 1905, the city experienced rapid growth as a center of a booming petroleum industry. Tulsa was incorporated as a city in 1898 and chartered in 1908.

Tulsa is the center of the state's petroleum and telecommunications industries and has a diversified economy. Other important industries include aerospace, chemicals, computer parts, automobile glass, fabricated metals, and industrial machinery. The city became a major inland port when the Tulsa port of Catoosa opened in 1971.

Famous natives: Garth Brooks, singer; Blake Edwards, director; Paul Harvey, commentator; Jennifer Jones, actress; Henry R. Kravis, investment banker; Daniel Patrick Moynihan, senator; Tony Randall, actor; Alfre Woodard, actress; Judy Woodruff, journalist.

# Virginia Beach, Va.

**Mayor:** Meyera E. Oberndorf (to June 2004)
**2000 census population (rank):** 425,257 (38);
**% change:** 8.2; **Male:** 210,524 (49.5%); **Female:**
214,733 (50.5%); **White:** 303,681 (71.4%); **Black:**
80,593 (19.0%); **American Indian and Alaska Native:**
1,619 (0.4%); **Asian:** 20,869 (4.9%); **Other race:**
6,402 (1.5%); **Two or more races:** 11,677 (2.7%);
**Hispanic/Latino:** 17,770 (4.2%); **2000 percent population 18 and over:** 72.5%; **65 and over:** 8.4%;
**median age:** 32.7.
**Land area:** 248 sq mi. (642 sq km); **Alt.:** 12 ft.
**Avg. daily temp.:** Jan., 39.1° F; July, 78.2° F
**Churches:** Protestant, 235; Catholic, 13; Jewish, 5;
**City-owned parks:** 182 (1,748 ac.); **Radio stations:**
AM 13, FM 31; **Television stations:** 8 commercial,
1 PBS, 1 cable
**Civilian Labor Force (MSA) 2001:** 754,088[1];
**Unemployed:** 27,091, **Percent:** 3.6; **Per capita per-
sonal income (MSA) 2000:** $26,159[1]
**Chamber of Commerce:** Hampton Roads Chamber of
Commerce, 420 Bank St., Norfolk, Va. 23510

1. Norfolk–Virginia Beach–Newport News, Va.–N.C.

Virginia Beach, the most populous city in Virginia, is located in the southeast part of the state on
the Atlantic coastline. It is independent and is not
part of any county.

The first English settlers to set foot in America
landed at Cape Henry at the tip of Virginia Beach on
April 29, 1607. They were led by John Smith on his
way to establishing Jamestown. The first permanent
settlement within the city limits was made at
Lynnhaven Bay in 1621. Cape Henry became an
important port for British merchant ships calling on
America, and it was here that the French fleet led by
Admiral Comte de Grasse blockaded the British
fleet during the American Revolution.

Virginia Beach gained its reputation as a famous
vacation resort in the 19th century, following the
building of a railroad connecting its oceanfront with
Norfolk and the construction of its first hotel in
1883. Virginia Beach was incorporated as a town in
1906 and as a city in 1952.

Tourism is a mainstay of the economy; more than
3 million people visit Virginia Beach each year. Virginia Beach's economy is also supported by four
military bases and diverse industries, including agriculture, computer software, engineering, and technical services.

Famous natives and residents: V. C. Andrews, novelist;
D. J. Dozier, football and baseball player; George
Eastman, inventor; Juice Newton, singer; Kenneth S.
Reightler, Jr., astronaut; Pat Robertson, evangelist; Henry
Walke, naval officer; Pernell "Sweet Pea" Whitaker, boxer;
Skip Wilkins, wheelchair athlete.

# Washington, DC

**Created municipal corporation:** Feb. 21, 1871
**Mayor:** Anthony Williams (to Jan. 2003)
**Motto:** Justitia omnibus (Justice to all)
**Flower:** American beauty rose; **Tree:** Scarlet oak
**2000 census population (rank):** 572,059 (21);
**% change:** −5.7; **Male:** 269,366 (47.1%); **Female:**
302,693 (52.9%); **White:** 176,101 (30.8%); **Black:**
343,312 (60.0%); **American Indian and Alaska
Native:** 1,713 (0.3%); **Asian:** 15,189 (2.7%); **Other
race:** 21,950 (3.8%); **Two or more races:** 13,446
(2.4%); **Hispanic/Latino:** 44,953 (7.9%); **2000 percent population 18 and over:** 79.9%; **65 and over:**
12.2%; **median age:** 34.6.
**Land area:** 61 sq mi. (158 sq km); **Alt.:** Highest, 420 ft.;
lowest, sea level
**Avg. daily temp.:** Jan., 34.6° F; July, 80.0° F
**Churches:** Protestant, 610; Roman Catholic, 132; Jewish, 9; **City parks:** 753 (7,725 ac.); **Radio stations:**
AM, 9; FM, 38; **Television stations:** 19
**Civilian Labor Force (PMSA) 2001:** 2,784,700[1];
**Unemployed:** 67,800, **Percent:** 2.4; **Per capita per-
sonal income (PMSA) 2000:** $40,046[1]
**Board of Trade:** Greater Washington Board of Trade,
1129 20th Street, N.W., Washington, D.C. 20036
**Chamber of Commerce:** D.C. Chamber of Commerce,
1213 K St., NW, Washington, D.C. 20005

1. Washington, D.C.–Md.–Va.–W.Va.

The District of Columbia—identical with the city
of Washington—is the capital of the United States. It
is located between Virginia and Maryland on the
Potomac River. The district is named after Columbus.

DC history began in 1790 when Congress
directed selection of a new capital site, 100 sq mi,
along the Potomac. When the site was determined,
it included 30.75 sq mi on the Virginia side of the
river. In 1846, however, Congress returned that area
to Virginia, leaving the 68.25 sq mi ceded by Maryland in 1788. The seat of government was transferred from Philadelphia to Washington on Dec. 1,
1800, and President John Adams became the first
resident in the White House.

The city was planned and partly laid out by Maj.
Pierre Charles L'Enfant, a French engineer. This
work was perfected and completed by Maj. Andrew
Ellicott and Benjamin Banneker, a freeborn black
man who was an astronomer and mathematician. In
1814, during the War of 1812, a British force burned
the capital including the White House.

Until Nov. 3, 1967, the District of Columbia was
administered by three commissioners appointed by
the president. On that day, a government consisting
of a mayor-commissioner and a 9-member council,
all appointed by the president with the approval of
the Senate, took office. On May 7, 1974, the citizens
of the District of Columbia approved a Home Rule
Charter, giving them an elected mayor and
13-member council—their first elected municipal
government in more than a century. The district also
has one nonvoting member in the House of Representatives and an elected Board of Education.

On Aug. 22, 1978, Congress passed a proposed
constitutional amendment to give Washington, DC,
voting representation in the Congress. The amendment had to be ratified by at least 38 state legislatures within seven years to become effective. It died
in 1985. A petition asking for the district's admission to the Union as the 51st state was filed in Congress on Sept. 9, 1983, and new statehood bills were
introduced in 1993. The district is continuing this
drive for statehood.

The federal government and tourism are the main-
stays of the city's economy, and many unions, business, professional, and nonprofit organizations are
headquartered there. Among the city's many educational institutions are the Catholic University of
America, Georgetown University, Howard University, and Gallaudet University. Cultural attractions
include the National Gallery of Art, the Smithsonian
Institution, the John F. Kennedy Center for the Performing Arts, and the Folger Shakespeare Library.

Famous natives: Edward Albee, playwright; Billie Burke,
comedienne; Ina Claire, actress; John Foster Dulles,
statesman; Duke Ellington, musician; Jane Greer, actress;
Goldie Hawn, actress; Helen Hayes, actress; J. Edgar

Hoover, former director of the F.B.I.; William Hurt, actor; Noor al-Hussein, queen of Jordan; Michael Learned, actress; Roger Mudd, newscaster; Eleanor Holmes Norton, government official; Chita Rivera, dancer and actress; Leonard Rose, cellist; John Philip Sousa, composer; Frances Sternhagen, actress.

## Wichita, Kans.

**Mayor:** Bob Knight (to April 2003)
**City Manager:** Chris Cherches
**2000 census population (rank):** 344,284 (50); **% change:** 13.2; **Male:** 169,604 (49.3%); **Female:** 174,680 (50.7%); **White:** 258,900 (75.2%); **Black:** 39,325 (11.4%); **American Indian and Alaska Native:** 3,986 (1.2%); **Asian:** 13,647 (4.0%); **Other race:** 17,566 (5.1%); **Two or more races:** 10,662 (3.1%); **Hispanic/Latino:** 33,112 (9.6%); **2000 percent population 18 and over:** 72.9%; **65 and over:** 11.9%; **median age:** 33.4.
**Land area:** 136 sq mi. (352 sq km); **Alt.:** 1,333 ft.
**Avg. daily temp.:** Jan., 29.5° F; July, 81.4° F
**Churches:** Protestant, 512; Roman Catholic, 20; Jewish, 2; other, 66; **City parks:** 110 (4,388 ac.); **Radio stations:** 22; **Television stations:** 7
**Civilian Labor Force (MSA)** 2001: 289,300; **Unemployed:** 9,400, **Percent:** 3.2; **Per capita personal income (MSA) 2000:** $27,904
**Chamber of Commerce:** Wichita Chamber of Commerce, 350 W. Douglas, Wichita, Kans. 67202

Wichita is the largest city in Kansas and the seat of Sedgwick County. It is located in the south-central part of the state, at the confluence of the Arkansas and Little Arkansas rivers. Incorporated as a city in 1870, Wichita is the chief commercial and industrial center of southern Kansas.

More or less uninhabited at the time of Kansas's entry into the Union in 1861, the area was first settled by Wichita Indians, who came north from Texas and Oklahoma during the Civil War. At about the same time (during the mid-1860s) a number of trading posts were established at or near the river junction. One of the traders, Jesse Chisholm, pioneered the Chisholm Trail, which passed through Wichita and was the main cattle-drive route from Texas to the railroad in Abilene. After the railroad was extended to Wichita in 1872, the city boomed first as a cow town and then later as the trading center in an agricultural and livestock region. Although the city experienced an economic slump at the end of the 19th century, oil was discovered nearby in 1915, and subsequently the population almost doubled.

Aircraft manufacturing began in the 1920s, and Wichita remains a center of the aircraft industry today. In addition, the city also has flour mills, meatpacking plants, and oil refineries. Major manufactures include camping equipment, heaters and air conditioners, and electronics. Wichita has a number of art and historical museums, a zoo, and a planetarium. It is the site of several universities, including Wichita State University (1895). McConnell Air Force Base is nearby.

Famous natives: Kirstie Alley, actress; Alan Fudge, actor; Dan Glickman, former congressman and U.S. secretary of agriculture; Laurel Goodwin, actress; Stan Kenton, musician; Jim Lehrer, news anchor; Fred, Thomas, and Edwin McConnell, WWII pilots; Hattie McDaniel, actress; Barry Sanders, football player; Gale Sayers, football player; Arlen Specter, U.S. senator from Pennsylvania; Ron Wyden, U.S. senator from Oregon.

## U.S. Cities and Metro Areas: Census 2000

Source: U.S. Census Bureau

Overall, cities expanded rapidly during the 1990s, growing nearly twice as fast as in the 1980s. Western and southern cities grew the fastest, while urban industrial centers in the Midwest and Northeast declined in population. New York remained the country's largest city, however, passing the 8 million mark.

In 2000, 80.3% of Americans (226 million people) lived in metropolitan areas, up slightly from 79.8% (198.4 million people) in 1990. (A metropolitan area is a city plus the adjacent communities to which it is linked economically.) All of the metropolitan areas with populations of at least 5 million grew over the period, ranging from 29% for the Dallas metropolitan area to 5% for Philadelphia. The total population within metropolitan areas increased by 14%, while the nonmetropolitan population grew by 10%.

## Top Ten U.S. Cities by Percent Population Change, 1990–2000

| Rank | Place name | Population | | Change, 1990 to 2000 | |
|---|---|---|---|---|---|
| | | April 1, 2000 | April 1, 1990 | Number | Percent |
| 1. | Augusta-Richmond County[1], Ga. | 199,775 | 44,639 | 155,136 | 347.5% |
| 2. | Gilbert, Ariz. | 109,697 | 29,188 | 80,509 | 275.8 |
| 3. | Vancouver, Wash. | 110,500 | 46,380 | 97,180 | 209.5 |
| 4. | Henderson, Nev. | 175,381 | 64,942 | 110,439 | 170.1 |
| 5. | North Las Vegas, Nev. | 115,488 | 47,707 | 67,781 | 142.1 |
| 6. | Athens-Clark County[2], Ga. | 101,489 | 45,734 | 55,755 | 121.9 |
| 7. | Peoria, Ariz. | 108,364 | 50,618 | 57,746 | 114.1 |
| 8. | Pembroke Pines, Fla. | 137,427 | 65,452 | 71,975 | 110.0 |
| 9. | Chandler, Ariz. | 176,581 | 90,533 | 86,048 | 95.0 |
| 10. | Las Vegas, Nev. | 478,434 | 258,295 | 220,139 | 85.2 |

1. In 2000, Richmond County and the incorporated place of Augusta-Richmond County are coextensive. The 1990 population is for the incorporated place of Augusta city before consolidation of the city and county governments. 2. In 2000, Clarke County and the incorporated place of Athens-Clarke County are coextensive. The 1990 population is for the incorporated place of Athens city before consolidation of the city and county governments. Source: U.S. Census Bureau, Census 2000; 1990 Census. Web: www.census.gov.

## The Five Fastest-Growing Metropolitan Areas, 1990–2000

| Metropolitan area | Population | | Change, 1990–2000 | |
|---|---|---|---|---|
| | April 1, 1990 | April 1, 2000 | Number | Percent |
| Las Vegas, Nev., Ariz. | 852,737 | 1,563,282 | 710,545 | 83.3% |
| Naples, Fla. | 152,099 | 251,377 | 99,278 | 65.3 |
| Yuma, Ariz. | 106,895 | 160,026 | 53,131 | 49.7 |
| McAllen-Edinburg-Mission, Tex. | 383,545 | 569,463 | 185,918 | 48.5 |
| Austin-San Marcos, Tex. | 846,227 | 1,249,763 | 403,536 | 47.7 |

*Source:* U.S. Census Bureau, Census 2000; 1990 Census. Web: www.census.gov.

## Top 50 Cities in the U.S. by Population and Rank, 1990 and 2000

| | 4/1/2000 census population | 4/1/1990 census population | Numeric population change 1990–2000 | Percent population change 1990–2000 | Size rank 1990 | Size rank 2000 |
|---|---|---|---|---|---|---|
| New York, N.Y. | 8,008,278 | 7,322,564 | 685,714 | 9.4 | 1 | 1 |
| Los Angeles, Calif. | 3,694,820 | 3,485,398 | 209,422 | 6.0 | 2 | 2 |
| Chicago, Ill. | 2,896,016 | 2,783,726 | 112,290 | 4.0 | 3 | 3 |
| Houston, Tex. | 1,953,631 | 1,630,553 | 323,078 | 19.8 | 4 | 4 |
| Philadelphia, Pa. | 1,517,550 | 1,585,577 | −68,027 | −4.3 | 5 | 5 |
| Phoenix, Ariz. | 1,321,045 | 983,403 | 337,642 | 34.3 | 10 | 6 |
| San Diego, Calif. | 1,223,400 | 1,110,549 | 112,851 | 10.2 | 6 | 7 |
| Dallas, Tex. | 1,188,580 | 1,006,877 | 181,703 | 18.0 | 8 | 8 |
| San Antonio, Tex. | 1,144,646 | 935,933 | 208,713 | 22.3 | 9 | 9 |
| Detroit, Mich. | 951,270 | 1,027,974 | −76,704 | −7.5 | 7 | 10 |
| San Jose, Calif. | 894,943 | 782,248 | 112,695 | 14.4 | 11 | 11 |
| Indianapolis, Ind. | 791,926 | 741,952 | 49,974 | 6.7 | 13 | 12 |
| San Francisco, Calif. | 776,733 | 723,959 | 52,774 | 7.3 | 14 | 13 |
| Jacksonville, Fla. | 735,617 | 635,230 | 100,387 | 15.8 | 16 | 14 |
| Columbus, Ohio | 711,470 | 632,910 | 78,560 | 12.4 | 15 | 15 |
| Austin, Tex. | 656,562 | 465,622 | 190,940 | 41.0 | 25 | 16 |
| Baltimore, Md. | 651,154 | 736,014 | −84,860 | −11.5 | 12 | 17 |
| Memphis, Tenn. | 650,100 | 610,337 | 39,763 | 6.5 | 18 | 18 |
| Milwaukee, Wis. | 596,974 | 628,088 | −31,114 | −5.0 | 17 | 19 |
| Boston, Mass. | 589,141 | 574,283 | 14,858 | 2.6 | 20 | 20 |
| Washington, DC | 572,059 | 606,900 | −34,841 | −5.7 | 19 | 21 |
| Nashville-Davidson, Tenn.[1] | 569,891 | 510,784 | 59,107 | 11.6 | 26 | 22 |
| El Paso, Tex. | 563,662 | 515,342 | 48,320 | 9.4 | 22 | 23 |
| Seattle, Wash. | 563,374 | 516,259 | 47,115 | 9.1 | 21 | 24 |
| Denver, Colo. | 554,636 | 467,610 | 87,026 | 18.6 | 28 | 25 |
| Charlotte, N.C. | 540,828 | 395,934 | 144,894 | 36.6 | 33 | 26 |
| Fort Worth, Tex. | 534,694 | 447,619 | 87,075 | 19.5 | 29 | 27 |
| Portland, Ore. | 529,121 | 437,319 | 91,802 | 21.0 | 27 | 28 |
| Oklahoma City, Okla. | 506,132 | 444,719 | 61,413 | 13.8 | 30 | 29 |
| Tucson, Ariz. | 486,699 | 405,390 | 81,309 | 20.1 | 34 | 30 |
| New Orleans, La. | 484,674 | 496,938 | −12,264 | −2.5 | 24 | 31 |
| Las Vegas, Nev. | 478,434 | 258,295 | 220,139 | 85.2 | 63 | 32 |
| Cleveland, Ohio | 478,403 | 505,616 | −27,213 | −5.4 | 23 | 33 |
| Long Beach, Calif. | 461,522 | 429,433 | 32,089 | 7.5 | 32 | 34 |
| Albuquerque, N.M. | 448,607 | 384,736 | 63,871 | 16.6 | 40 | 35 |
| Kansas City, Mo. | 441,545 | 435,146 | 6,399 | 1.5 | 31 | 36 |
| Fresno, Calif. | 427,652 | 354,202 | 73,450 | 20.7 | 48 | 37 |
| Virginia Beach, Va. | 425,257 | 393,069 | 32,188 | 8.2 | 39 | 38 |
| Atlanta, Ga. | 416,474 | 394,017 | 22,457 | 5.7 | 38 | 39 |
| Sacramento, Calif. | 407,018 | 369,365 | 37,653 | 10.2 | 37 | 40 |
| Oakland, Calif. | 399,484 | 372,242 | 27,242 | 7.3 | 35 | 41 |
| Mesa, Ariz. | 396,375 | 288,091 | 108,284 | 37.6 | 53 | 42 |
| Tulsa, Okla. | 393,049 | 367,302 | 25,747 | 7.0 | 44 | 43 |
| Omaha, Neb. | 390,007 | 335,795 | 54,212 | 16.1 | 47 | 44 |
| Minneapolis, Minn. | 382,618 | 368,383 | 14,235 | 3.9 | 43 | 45 |
| Honolulu CDP,[2] Hawaii | 371,657 | 365,272 | 6,385 | 1.7 | 41 | 46 |
| Miami, Fla. | 362,470 | 358,548 | 3,922 | 1.1 | 46 | 47 |
| Colorado Springs, Colo. | 360,890 | 281,140 | 79,750 | 28.4 | 54 | 48 |
| St. Louis, Mo. | 348,189 | 396,685 | −48,496 | −12.2 | 42 | 49 |
| Wichita, Kans. | 344,284 | 304,011 | 40,273 | 13.2 | 51 | 50 |

1. Nashville-Davidson city is consolidated with Davidson County. 2. Honolulu Census Designated Place; by agreement with the State of Hawaii, the Census Bureau does not show data separately for the city of Honolulu, which is coextensive with Honolulu County. *Source:* U.S. Census Bureau. Web: www.census.gov.

## Tabulated Data on City Governments

| City | Mayor | | City manager's salary[1,2] | Council or Commission | | | |
|------|-------|-----|------|------|------|------|------|
| | Term, years | Salary[1] | | Name | Members | Term, years | Salary[1,3] |
| Albuquerque, N.M. | 4 | $ 90,314 | $115,003 | Council | 9 | 4 | $ 9,027 |
| Atlanta, Ga. | 4 | 141,490 | — | Council | 18 | 4 | 32,473 |
| Austin, Tex. | 3 | 35,006 | 188,115 | Council | 7 | 3 | 45,011 |
| Baltimore, Md. | 4 | 125,000 | — | Council | 19 | 4 | 48,000 |
| Boston, Mass. | 4 | 125,000 | — | Council | 13 | 2 | 62,500 |
| Charlotte, N.C. | 2 | 18,262 | 153,773 | Council | 11 | 2 | 13,044 |
| Chicago, Ill. | 4 | 192,100 | — | Council | 50 | 4 | 85,000 |
| Cleveland, Ohio | 4 | 101,286 | — | Council | 21 | 4 | 47,751 |
| Colorado Springs, Colo. | 4 | 6,250 | 137,000 | Council | 9 | 4 | 6,200 |
| Columbus, Ohio | 4 | 120,000 | — | Council | 7 | 4 | 35,000 |
| Dallas, Tex. | 4 | 60,000 | 263,000 | Council | 15[5] | 2 | 37,500 |
| Denver, Colo. | 4 | 113,184 | — | Council | 13 | 4 | 57,432 |
| Detroit, Mich. | 4 | 176,176 | — | Council | 9 | 4 | 81,312 |
| El Paso, Tex. | 2 | 25,000 | — | Council | 9[5] | 2 | 15,000 |
| Fort Worth, Tex. | 2 | 75[4] | 189,010 | Council | 9[5] | 2 | 75[4] |
| Fresno, Calif. | 4 | 99,360 | 149,004 | Council | 7 | 4 | 44,511 |
| Honolulu, Hawaii | 4 | 112,200 | 107,100[6] | Council | 9 | 4 | 43,350 |
| Houston, Tex. | 2 | 165,816 | — | Council | 14 | 2 | 44,218 |
| Indianapolis, Ind. | 4 | 95,000 | — | Council | 29 | 4 | 11,400 |
| Jacksonville, Fla. | 2 | 110,000 | 105,000[7] | Council | 19 | 4 | 24,000 |
| Kansas City, Mo. | 4 | 89,988 | 151,740 | Council | 13[5] | 4 | 44,988 |
| Las Vegas, Nev. | 4 | 52,633 | 167,747 | Council | 6 | 4 | 40,063 |
| Long Beach, Calif. | 4 | 98,935 | 199,500 | Council | 9 | 4 | 24,734 |
| Los Angeles, Calif. | 4[8] | 177,091 | 210,178[6] | Council | 15 | 4[8] | 136,224 |
| Memphis, Tenn. | 4 | 140,000 | 107,000[6] | Council | 13 | 4 | 20,100 |
| Mesa, Ariz. | 4 | 34,450 | 152,880 | Council | 6 | 4 | 17,238 |
| Miami, Fla. | 4 | 97,000 | 157,538 | Commission | 5 | 4 | 5,000 |
| Milwaukee, Wis. | 4 | 124,625 | — | Council | 17 | 4 | 61,934 |
| Minneapolis, Minn. | 4 | 86,288 | 119,606 | Council | 13 | 4 | 65,679 |
| Nashville, Tenn. | 4 | 75,000 | 8,900[9] | Council | 40 | 4 | 6,900 |
| New Orleans, La. | 4 | 90,000 | 57,900 | Council | 7 | 4 | 42,500 |
| New York, N.Y. | 4 | 195,000 | 156,000[9] | Council | 51 | 4 | 90,000 |
| Oakland, Calif. | 4 | 115,371 | 224,416[10] | Council | 9[5] | 4 | 60,000[11] |
| Oklahoma City, Okla. | 4 | 24,000 | 133,500 | Council | 8 | 4 | 12,000 |
| Omaha, Neb. | 4 | 95,205 | — | Council | 7 | 4 | 27,813 |
| Philadelphia, Pa. | 4 | 130,000 | 140,000[7] | Council | 17 | 4 | 80,000 |
| Phoenix, Ariz. | 4 | 56,000 | 190,672 | Council | 9[5] | 4 | 35,999 |
| Portland, Ore. | 4 | 100,901 | — | Council | 4 | 4 | 84,989 |
| Sacramento, Calif. | 4 | 3,325[12] | 151,715 | Council | 9 | 4 | 2,300[12] |
| St. Louis, Mo. | 4 | 116,142 | — | Board of Alderman | 29 | 4 | 28,745 |
| San Antonio, Tex. | 2 | 3,000[13] | 200,000 | Council | 11[5] | 2 | 20[4] |
| San Diego, Calif. | 4 | 95,000 | 000,000 | Council | 11 | 1 | 11,190 |
| San Francisco, Calif. | 4 | 161,538 | 163,725 | Bd. of Supvrs. | 11 | 4 | 37,584 |
| San Jose, Calif. | 4 | 105,000 | 000,101 | Council | 11 | 4 | 75,000 |
| Seattle, Wash. | 4 | 136,156 | — | Council | 9 | 4 | 84,800 |
| Tucson, Ariz. | 4 | 42,000 | 163,200 | Council | 7[5] | 4 | 24,000 |
| Tulsa, Okla. | 4 | 105,000 | — | Council | 9 | 2 | 18,000 |
| Virginia Beach, Va. | 4 | 20,000 | 167,200 | Council | 11[5] | 4 | 18,000 |
| Washington, DC | 4 | 138,200 | 135,000 | Council | 13 | 4 | 92,520 |
| Wichita, Kans. | 4 | 65,240 | 141,260 | Council | 7[5] | 4 | 24,850 |

1. Annual salary unless otherwise indicated; does not include additional payments for expenses, special sessions, etc. 2. City manager's term is indefinite and at will of council (or mayor). 3. In some cities, leaders receive a higher salary. 4. Per council meeting; with an annual cap. 5. Including mayor. 6. Appointed by mayor, approved by council. 7. Appointed by mayor; not subject to council confirmation. 8. Limited to 2 terms per city charter. 9. No city manager; salary is for deputy or vice mayor. 10. Denotes average based on range. 11. Council also serves as the Redevelopment Agency for which there is additional compensation. 12. Per month. 13. Plus council pay. *Source:* Questionnaires to the cities.

## U.S. Cities with Population over 100,000

ZIP codes provided below indicate the primary ZIP code for each city. Consult a ZIP code directory to find the appropriate ZIP code for a particular address, or try the U.S. Postal Service's online "ZIP Code Lookup," www.usps.gov/zip4/.

| City | 2000 Pop. | 2000 Rank | ZIP Code | City | 2000 Pop. | 2000 Rank | ZIP Code |
|---|---|---|---|---|---|---|---|
| **Alabama** | | | | Santa Ana | 337,977 | 52 | 92711 |
| Birmingham | 242,820 | 72 | 35203 | Santa Clara | 102,361 | 232 | 95050 |
| Huntsville | 158,216 | 130 | 35813 | Santa Clarita | 151,088 | 137 | 91355 |
| Mobile | 198,915 | 94 | 36601 | Santa Rosa | 147,595 | 144 | 95402 |
| Montgomery | 201,568 | 89 | 36119 | Simi Valley | 111,351 | 206 | 93065 |
| **Alaska** | | | | Stockton | 243,771 | 71 | 95208 |
| Anchorage | 260,283 | 66 | 99599 | Sunnyvale | 131,760 | 165 | 94086 |
| **Arizona** | | | | Thousand Oaks | 117,005 | 192 | 91362 |
| Chandler | 176,581 | 116 | 85225 | Torrance | 137,946 | 159 | 90503 |
| Gilbert | 109,697 | 208 | 85296 | Vallejo | 116,760 | 193 | 94590 |
| Glendale | 218,812 | 81 | 85302 | West Covina | 105,080 | 224 | 91793 |
| Mesa | 396,375 | 43 | 85201 | **Colorado** | | | |
| Peoria | 108,364 | 214 | 85381 | Arvada | 102,153 | 235 | 80004 |
| Phoenix | 1,321,045 | 6 | 85026 | Aurora | 276,393 | 62 | 80017 |
| Scottsdale | 202,705 | 88 | 85251 | Colorado Springs | 360,890 | 49 | 80903 |
| Tempe | 158,625 | 129 | 85282 | Denver | 554,636 | 25 | 80202 |
| Tucson | 486,699 | 30 | 85726 | Fort Collins | 118,652 | 189 | 80525 |
| **Arkansas** | | | | Lakewood | 144,126 | 148 | 80202 |
| Little Rock | 183,133 | 112 | 72202 | Pueblo | 102,121 | 236 | 81003 |
| **California** | | | | Westminster | 100,940 | 239 | 80030 |
| Anaheim | 328,014 | 56 | 92803 | **Connecticut** | | | |
| Bakersfield | 247,057 | 70 | 93380 | Bridgeport | 139,529 | 156 | 06602 |
| Berkeley | 102,743 | 231 | 94704 | Hartford | 121,578 | 183 | 06101 |
| Burbank | 100,316 | 243 | 91505 | New Haven | 123,626 | 179 | 06511 |
| Chula Vista | 173,556 | 122 | 91910 | Stamford | 117,083 | 191 | 06904 |
| Concord | 121,780 | 181 | 94520 | Waterbury | 107,271 | 217 | 06702 |
| Corona | 124,966 | 174 | 91718 | **District of Columbia** | | | |
| Costa Mesa | 108,724 | 213 | 92628 | Washington[1] | 572,059 | 21 | 20090 |
| Daly City | 103,621 | 227 | 94015 | **Florida** | | | |
| Downey | 107,323 | 216 | 90241 | Cape Coral | 102,286 | 234 | 33909 |
| El Monte | 115,965 | 196 | 91734 | Clearwater | 108,787 | 212 | 33990 |
| Escondido | 133,559 | 164 | 92025 | Coral Springs | 117,549 | 190 | 33075 |
| Fontana | 128,929 | 167 | 92335 | Fort Lauderdale | 152,397 | 134 | 33310 |
| Fremont | 203,413 | 87 | 94537 | Hialeah | 226,419 | 76 | 33010 |
| Fresno | 427,652 | 37 | 93706 | Hollywood | 139,357 | 157 | 33022 |
| Fullerton | 126,003 | 173 | 92834 | Jacksonville | 735,617 | 14 | 32203 |
| Garden Grove | 165,196 | 127 | 92842 | Miami | 362,470 | 48 | 33152 |
| Glendale | 194,973 | 100 | 91205 | Orlando | 185,951 | 107 | 32802 |
| Hayward | 140,030 | 154 | 94544 | Pembroke Pines | 137,427 | 161 | 33024 |
| Huntington Beach | 189,594 | 103 | 92647 | St. Petersburg | 248,232 | 69 | 33730 |
| Inglewood | 112,580 | 204 | 90301 | Tallahassee | 150,624 | 139 | 32301 |
| Irvine | 143,072 | 150 | 92619 | Tampa | 303,447 | 58 | 33630 |
| Lancaster | 118,718 | 188 | 93534 | **Georgia** | | | |
| Long Beach | 461,522 | 34 | 90802 | Athens-Clarke County[2] | 101,489 | 237 | 30608 |
| Los Angeles | 3,694,820 | 2 | 90052 | Atlanta | 416,474 | 40 | 30304 |
| Modesto | 188,856 | 104 | 95350 | Augusta-Richmond County[3] | 199,775 | 91 | 30901 |
| Moreno Valley | 142,381 | 152 | 92553 | Columbus | 186,291 | 106 | 31908 |
| Norwalk | 103,298 | 229 | 90650 | Savannah | 131,510 | 166 | 31402 |
| Oakland | 399,484 | 42 | 94612 | **Hawaii** | | | |
| Oceanside | 161,029 | 128 | 92054 | Honolulu CDP[4] | 371,657 | 47 | 96820 |
| Ontario | 158,007 | 131 | 91761 | **Idaho** | | | |
| Orange | 128,821 | 168 | 92863 | Boise | 185,787 | 108 | 83708 |
| Oxnard | 170,358 | 124 | 93030 | **Illinois** | | | |
| Palmdale | 116,670 | 194 | 93550 | Aurora | 142,990 | 151 | 60505 |
| Pasadena | 133,936 | 163 | 91103 | Chicago | 2,896,016 | 3 | 60607 |
| Pomona | 149,473 | 141 | 91769 | Joliet | 106,221 | 221 | 60436 |
| Rancho Cucamonga | 127,743 | 171 | 91729 | Naperville | 128,358 | 169 | 60540 |
| Riverside | 255,166 | 68 | 92507 | Peoria | 112,936 | 203 | 61601 |
| Sacramento | 407,018 | 41 | 95813 | Rockford | 150,115 | 140 | 61125 |
| Salinas | 151,060 | 138 | 93907 | Springfield | 111,454 | 205 | 62703 |
| San Bernardino | 185,401 | 110 | 92401 | **Indiana** | | | |
| San Buenaventura (Ventura) | 100,916 | 240 | 93001 | Evansville | 121,582 | 182 | 47708 |
| San Diego | 1,223,400 | 7 | 92199 | Fort Wayne | 205,727 | 85 | 46802 |
| San Francisco | 776,733 | 13 | 94188 | Gary | 102,746 | 230 | 46401 |
| San Jose | 894,943 | 11 | 95101 | Indianapolis | 791,926 | 12 | 46206 |

| City | 2000 Pop. | 2000 Rank | ZIP Code |
|---|---|---|---|
| South Bend | 107,789 | 215 | 46624 |
| **Iowa** | | | |
| Cedar Rapids | 120,758 | 185 | 52401 |
| Des Moines | 198,682 | 95 | 50318 |
| **Kansas** | | | |
| Kansas City | 146,866 | 146 | 66106 |
| Overland Park | 149,080 | 143 | 66204 |
| Topeka | 122,377 | 180 | 66603 |
| Wichita | 344,284 | 51 | 67276 |
| **Kentucky** | | | |
| Lexington-Fayette | 260,512 | 65 | 40511 |
| Louisville | 256,231 | 67 | 40231 |
| **Louisiana** | | | |
| Baton Rouge | 227,818 | 75 | 70826 |
| Lafayette | 110,257 | 207 | 70509 |
| New Orleans | 484,674 | 31 | 70113 |
| Shreveport | 200,145 | 90 | 71102 |
| **Maryland** | | | |
| Baltimore | 651,154 | 17 | 21202 |
| **Massachusetts** | | | |
| Boston | 589,141 | 20 | 02205 |
| Cambridge | 101,355 | 238 | 02139 |
| Lowell | 105,167 | 222 | 01853 |
| Springfield | 152,082 | 135 | 01101 |
| Worcester | 172,648 | 123 | 01613 |
| **Michigan** | | | |
| Ann Arbor | 114,024 | 199 | 48104 |
| Detroit | 951,270 | 10 | 48233 |
| Flint | 124,943 | 175 | 48502 |
| Grand Rapids | 197,800 | 96 | 49501 |
| Lansing | 119,128 | 187 | 48924 |
| Livonia | 100,545 | 242 | 48150 |
| Sterling Heights | 124,471 | 177 | 48311 |
| Warren | 138,247 | 158 | 48090 |
| **Minnesota** | | | |
| Minneapolis | 382,618 | 46 | 55401 |
| St. Paul | 287,151 | 60 | 55109 |
| **Mississippi** | | | |
| Jackson | 184,256 | 111 | 39205 |
| **Missouri** | | | |
| Independence | 113,288 | 202 | 64052 |
| Kansas City | 441,545 | 36 | 64108 |
| St. Louis | 348,189 | 50 | 63155 |
| Springfield | 151,580 | 136 | 65801 |
| **Nebraska** | | | |
| Lincoln | 225,581 | 77 | 68501 |
| Omaha | 390,007 | 45 | 68108 |
| **Nevada** | | | |
| Henderson | 175,381 | 118 | 89015 |
| Las Vegas | 478,434 | 32 | 89199 |
| North Las Vegas | 115,488 | 198 | 89030 |
| Reno | 180,480 | 114 | 89510 |
| **New Hampshire** | | | |
| Manchester | 107,006 | 218 | 03103 |
| **New Jersey** | | | |
| Elizabeth | 120,568 | 186 | 07208 |
| Jersey City | 240,055 | 70 | 07302 |
| Newark | 273,546 | 64 | 07102 |
| Paterson | 149,222 | 142 | 07510 |
| **New Mexico** | | | |
| Albuquerque | 448,607 | 35 | 87101 |
| **New York** | | | |
| Buffalo | 292,648 | 59 | 14240 |
| New York | 8,008,278 | 1 | 10199 |
| Rochester | 219,773 | 80 | 14692 |
| Syracuse | 147,306 | 145 | 13220 |
| Yonkers | 196,086 | 98 | 10701 |
| **North Carolina** | | | |
| Charlotte | 540,828 | 26 | 28228 |
| Durham | 187,035 | 105 | 27701 |
| Fayetteville | 121,015 | 184 | 28302 |
| Greensboro | 223,891 | 78 | 27420 |
| Raleigh | 276,093 | 63 | 27613 |
| Winston-Salem | 185,776 | 109 | 27102 |
| **Ohio** | | | |
| Akron | 217,074 | 82 | 44309 |
| Cincinnati | 331,285 | 55 | 45225 |
| Cleveland | 478,403 | 33 | 44101 |
| Columbus | 711,470 | 15 | 43216 |
| Dayton | 166,179 | 126 | 45401 |
| Toledo | 313,619 | 57 | 43601 |
| **Oklahoma** | | | |
| Oklahoma City | 506,132 | 29 | 73125 |
| Tulsa | 393,049 | 44 | 74107 |
| **Oregon** | | | |
| Eugene | 137,893 | 160 | 97401 |
| Portland | 529,121 | 28 | 97208 |
| Salem | 136,924 | 162 | 97309 |
| **Pennsylvania** | | | |
| Allentown | 106,632 | 219 | 18101 |
| Erie | 103,717 | 226 | 16515 |
| Philadelphia | 1,517,550 | 5 | 19104 |
| Pittsburgh | 334,563 | 53 | 15290 |
| **Rhode Island** | | | |
| Providence | 173,618 | 121 | 02904 |
| **South Carolina** | | | |
| Columbia | 116,278 | 195 | 29201 |
| **South Dakota** | | | |
| Sioux Falls | 123,975 | 178 | 57104 |
| **Tennessee** | | | |
| Chattanooga | 155,554 | 132 | 37421 |
| Clarksville | 103,455 | 228 | 37043 |
| Knoxville | 173,890 | 119 | 37950 |
| Memphis | 650,100 | 18 | 38101 |
| Nashville-Davidson[5] | 569,891 | 22 | 37230 |
| **Texas** | | | |
| Abilene | 115,930 | 197 | 79604 |
| Amarillo | 173,627 | 120 | 79120 |
| Arlington | 332,969 | 54 | 76004 |
| Austin | 656,562 | 16 | 78710 |
| Beaumont | 113,866 | 200 | 77707 |
| Brownsville | 139,722 | 155 | 78520 |
| Carrollton | 109,576 | 209 | 75006 |
| Corpus Christi | 277,454 | 61 | 78469 |
| Dallas | 1,188,580 | 8 | 75260 |
| El Paso | 563,662 | 23 | 79910 |
| Fort Worth | 534,694 | 27 | 76161 |
| Garland | 215,768 | 83 | 75040 |
| Grand Prairie | 127,427 | 172 | 75051 |
| Houston | 1,953,631 | 4 | 77201 |
| Irving | 191,615 | 102 | 75061 |
| Laredo | 176,576 | 117 | 78041 |
| Lubbock | 199,564 | 92 | 79402 |
| McAllen | 106,414 | 220 | 78501 |
| Mesquite | 124,523 | 176 | 75149 |
| Pasadena | 141,674 | 153 | 77501 |
| Plano | 222,030 | 79 | 75074 |
| San Antonio | 1,144,646 | 9 | 78284 |
| Waco | 113,726 | 201 | 76702 |
| Wichita Falls | 104,197 | 225 | 76307 |
| **Utah** | | | |
| Provo | 105,166 | 223 | 84601 |
| Salt Lake City | 181,743 | 113 | 84199 |
| West Valley City | 108,896 | 211 | 84199 |
| **Virginia** | | | |
| Alexandria | 128,283 | 170 | 22314 |
| Chesapeake | 199,184 | 93 | 23320 |
| Hampton | 146,437 | 147 | 23670 |

| City | 2000 Pop. | 2000 Rank | ZIP Code | City | 2000 Pop. | 2000 Rank | ZIP Code |
|------|-----------|-----------|----------|------|-----------|-----------|----------|
| Newport News | 180,150 | 115 | 23607 | Spokane | 195,629 | 99 | 99201 |
| Norfolk | 234,403 | 74 | 23501 | Tacoma | 193,556 | 101 | 98413 |
| Portsmouth | 100,565 | 241 | 23707 | Vancouver | 143,560 | 149 | 98668 |
| Richmond | 197,790 | 97 | 23232 | **Wisconsin** | | | |
| Virginia Beach | 425,257 | 38 | 23450 | Green Bay | 102,313 | 233 | 54303 |
| **Washington** | | | | Madison | 208,054 | 84 | 53714 |
| Bellevue | 109,569 | 210 | 98009 | Milwaukee | 596,974 | 19 | 53203 |
| Seattle | 563,374 | 24 | 98108 | | | | |

1. Washington city is coextensive with the District of Columbia. 2. In 2000, Clarke County and the incorporated place of Athens-Clarke County are coextensive. 3. In 2000, Richmond County and the incorporated place of Augusta-Richmond County are coextensive. 4. Honolulu Census Designated Place; data are not given separately for the city of Honolulu, which is coextensive with Honolulu County. 5. Nashville-Davidson city is consolidated with Davidson County. *Source:* U.S. Census Bureau. Web: www.census.gov.

## Area Codes: United States, Canada, Caribbean

| Area codes | Selected cities | Area codes | Selected cities | Area codes | Selected cities |
|------------|-----------------|------------|-----------------|------------|-----------------|
| **UNITED STATES** | | **District of Columbia** | | **Kansas** | |
| **Alabama** | | 202 | | 316 | Wichita |
| 205 | Birmingham, Tuscaloosa | **Florida** | | 620 | Fort Scott |
| 251 | Jackson, Mobile | 239 | Fort Myers | 785 | Topeka |
| 256 | Huntsville, Florence | 305 | Miami, Key West | 913 | Kansas City |
| 334 | Montgomery, Dothan | 321 | Orlando, Cape Canaveral | **Kentucky** | |
| **Alaska** | | 352 | Gainesville, Ocala | 270 | Owensboro |
| 907 | Entire state | 386 | Daytona Beach | 502 | Frankfort, Louisville |
| **Arizona** | | 407 | Kissimmee, Orlando | 606 | Morehead |
| 480 | Chandler | 561, 772 | West Palm Beach | 859 | Lexington |
| 520 | Tucson, Flagstaff | 727 | Clearwater | **Louisiana** | |
| 602 | Phoenix | 786 | Miami | 225 | Baton Rouge |
| 623 | Buckeye, Peoria | 813 | Tampa | 318 | Shreveport |
| 928 | Flagstaff, Yuma | 850 | Tallahassee, Pensacola | 337 | Lafayette |
| **Arkansas** | | 863 | Avon Park, Clewiston | 504 | New Orleans |
| 479 | Fayetteville, Fort Smith | 904 | Jacksonville | 985 | Hammond |
| 501 | Hot Springs, Little Rock | 941 | Port Charlotte | **Maine** | |
| 870 | Jonesboro, Texarkana | 954, 754 | Ft. Lauderdale | 207 | Entire state |
| **California** | | **Georgia** | | **Maryland** | |
| 209 | Stockton | 229 | Albany | 240, 301 | Frederick, Hagerstown |
| 213, 323 | Los Angeles | 404 | Atlanta, Decatur | 410, 443 | Baltimore, Salisbury |
| 310 | Malibu, Torrance | 478 | Macon | **Massachusetts** | |
| 408 | San Jose | 678 | Atlanta, Roswell | 413 | Springfield |
| 415 | San Francisco, San Rafael | 706 | Athens, Augusta | 508, 774 | Worcester |
| 510 | Oakland | 770 | Marietta | 617, 857 | Boston |
| 530 | Redding | 912 | Savannah | 781, 339 | Waltham |
| 559 | Fresno | **Hawaii** | | 978, 351 | Lowell |
| 562 | Long Beach | 808 | Entire state | **Michigan** | |
| 619 | San Diego | **Idaho** | | 231 | Traverse City, Muskegon |
| 626 | Pasadena | 208 | Entire state | 248, 947 | Troy |
| 650 | Palo Alto | **Illinois** | | 269 | Kalamazoo |
| 661 | Bakersfield | 217 | Springfield, Champaign | 313 | Detroit |
| 707 | Vallejo, Eureka | 224, 847 | Waukegan | 517 | Lansing, Jackson |
| 714 | Orange | 309 | Peoria | 586 | Romeo, Warren |
| 760 | Bishop | 312, 773 | Chicago | 616 | Grand Rapids, Kalamazoo |
| 805 | San Luis Obispo | 618 | Carbondale | 734 | Ann Arbor, Monroe |
| 818 | San Fernando | 630 | Aurora, Naperville | 810 | Flint, Port Huron |
| 831 | Santa Cruz, Salinas | 708 | Chicago Heights, Cicero | 906 | Sault Ste. Marie |
| 858 | Solana Beach | 815 | Rockford | 989 | Saginaw |
| 909 | Pomona | **Indiana** | | **Minnesota** | |
| 916 | Sacramento | 219 | Gary | 218 | Duluth |
| 925 | Concord | 260 | Fort Wayne | 320 | St.Cloud |
| 949 | Irvine | 317 | Indianapolis | 507 | Rochester |
| **Colorado** | | 574 | South Bend | 612 | Minneapolis |
| 303, 720 | Denver, Boulder | 765 | Muncie | 651 | St. Paul |
| 719 | Colorado Springs, Pueblo | 812 | Bloomington, Terre Haute | 763 | Maple Grove |
| 970 | Aspen, Fort Collins | **Iowa** | | 952 | Bloomington |
| **Connecticut** | | 319 | Cedar Rapids | **Mississippi** | |
| 203 | Bridgeport, New Haven | 515 | Des Moines | 228 | Gulfport |
| 860 | Hartford, Norwich | 563 | Dubuque, Davenport | 601 | Jackson |
| **Delaware** | | 641 | Mason City | 662 | Tupelo |
| 302 | Entire state | 712 | Sioux City | | |

| Area codes | Selected cities | Area codes | Selected cities | Area codes | Selected cities |
|---|---|---|---|---|---|
| **Missouri** | | **Pennsylvania** | | 414 | Milwaukee |
| 314 | St. Louis | 215, | Philadelphia | 608 | Madison |
| 417 | Springfield | 267, 445 | | 715 | Eau Claire |
| 573 | Jefferson City | 412 | Pittsburgh | 920 | Green Bay |
| 636 | Chesterfield | 484, | Allentown | **Wyoming** | |
| 660 | Sedalia, Maryville | 610, 835 | | 307 | Entire state |
| 816 | Kansas City, Independence | 570 | Scranton | **U.S. TERRITORIES** | |
| **Montana** | | 717 | Harrisburg | 684 | American Samoa |
| 406 | Entire state | 724 | Uniontown, New Castle | 671 | Guam |
| **Nebraska** | | 814 | Erie | 670 | Marianas Islands |
| 308 | Grand Island, Scottsbluff | 878 | Pittsburgh, Uniontown | 787, 939 | Puerto Rico |
| 402 | Lincoln, Omaha | **Rhode Island** | | 340 | U.S. Virgin Islands |
| **Nevada** | | 401 | Entire state | **CANADA** | |
| 702 | Las Vegas | **South Carolina** | | **Alberta** | |
| 775 | Carson City, Reno | 803 | Columbia | 403 | Calgary |
| **New Hampshire** | | 843 | Charleston | 780 | Edmonton |
| 603 | Entire state | 864 | Greenville | **British Columbia** | |
| **New Jersey** | | **South Dakota** | | 250 | Victoria |
| 201, 551 | Jersey City | 605 | Entire state | 604 | Vancouver, Abbotsford |
| 609 | Trenton, Atlantic City | **Tennessee** | | 778 | Vancouver |
| 732, 848 | New Brunswick | 423 | Chattanooga | **Manitoba** | |
| 856 | Cherry Hill, Vineland | 615 | Nashville | 204 | Entire province |
| 862, 973 | Newark, Paterson | 731 | Jackson | **New Brunswick** | |
| 908 | Elizabeth | 865 | Knoxville | 506 | Entire province |
| **New Mexico** | | 901 | Memphis | **Newfoundland** | |
| 505 | Entire state | 931 | Columbia | 709 | Entire province |
| **New York** | | **Texas** | | **Nova Scotia** | |
| 212, 646 | Manhattan | 210 | San Antonio | 902 | Nova Scotia, Prince |
| 315 | Syracuse | 214, | Dallas | | Edward Island |
| 347, 718 | Bronx, Brooklyn, Queens, | 469, 972 | | **Ontario** | |
| | Staten Island | 254 | Waco | 289, 905 | Hamilton |
| 516 | Mineola | 281, | Houston | 416, 647 | Toronto |
| 518 | Albany | 713, 832 | | 519 | Windsor |
| 585 | Rochester | 361 | Corpus Christi | 613 | Ottawa |
| 607 | Binghamton | 409 | Galveston | 705 | Sudbury |
| 631 | Riverhead | 512 | Austin | 807 | Thunder Bay |
| 716 | Buffalo | 682, 817 | Fort Worth | **Quebec** | |
| 845 | Poughkeepsie | 806 | Lubbock | 418 | Quebec |
| 914 | White Plains | 830 | Uvalde | 450 | Laval |
| 917 | Manhattan, Bronx, Queens, | 903 | Tyler, Texarkana | 514 | Montreal |
| | Staten Island, Brooklyn | 915 | El Paso | 819 | Trois-Rivieres |
| **North Carolina** | | 936 | Huntsville | **Saskatchewan** | |
| 252 | Greenville | 940 | Wichita Falls | 306 | Entire province |
| 336 | Winston-Salem | 956 | Laredo | **Yukon, Northwest Territories, &** | |
| 704, 980 | Charlotte | 979 | Bryan | **Nunavut** | |
| 828 | Asheville | **Utah** | | 867 | All provinces |
| 910 | Fayetteville | 435 | Moab | **CARIBBEAN AND ATLANTIC** | |
| 919 | Raleigh | 801 | Salt Lake City, Provo | **ISLANDS** | |
| **North Dakota** | | **Vermont** | | 264 | Anguilla |
| 701 | Entire state | 802 | Entire state | 268 | Antigua and Barbuda |
| **Ohio** | | **Virginia** | | 242 | Bahamas |
| 216 | Cleveland | 276 | Abingdon, Wytheville | 519 | Barbados |
| 937, 666 | North Youngstown | 434 | Danville, Lynchburg | 441 | Bermuda |
| 419, 567 | Toledo | 540 | Roanoke | 284 | British Virgin Islands |
| 440 | Ashtabula | 571, 703 | Alexandria | 345 | Cayman Islands |
| 513 | Cincinnati | 757 | Norfolk, Virginia Beach | 809 | Dominican Republic |
| 614 | Columbus | 804 | Richmond, Charlottesville | 767 | Dominica |
| 740 | Marion, Jackson | **Washington** | | 473 | Grenada |
| 937 | Dayton | 206 | Seattle | 876 | Jamaica |
| **Oklahoma** | | 253 | Tacoma | 664 | Montserrat |
| 405 | Oklahoma City | 360 | Olympia | 869 | St. Kitts & Nevis |
| 580 | Enid, Lawton | 425 | Bellevue | 758 | St. Lucia |
| 918 | Tulsa | 509 | Spokane | 784 | St. Vincent & the |
| **Oregon** | | **West Virginia** | | | Grenadines |
| 503 | Salem, Portland, Astoria | 304 | Entire state | 868 | Trinidad & Tobago |
| 541 | Eugene | **Wisconsin** | | 649 | Turks & Caicos |
| 971 | Salem, Portland | 262 | Racine | | |

*Source:* North American Numbering Plan Administration. Web: www.nanpa.com.

# U.S. Postal Rates and Fees

**Domestic Rates, last revised by the U.S. Postal Service on June 30, 2002**

## First-Class Mail

First-Class Mail includes all personal correspondence, all bills and statements of accounts, all matter sealed or otherwise closed against inspection, and matter wholly or partly in writing or typewriting. Any mailable items may be sent as First-Class Mail. Each piece must weigh 13 oz or less. Pieces over 13 oz can be sent as Priority Mail.

### Single-Piece Letter/Flat Rates

| | |
|---|---|
| 1st oz | $0.37 |
| Each additional oz | 0.23 |

| Weight not over (oz) | Rate | Weight not over (oz) | Rate |
|---|---|---|---|
| 1* | $0.37 | 9 | $2.21 |
| 2 | 0.60 | 10 | 2.44 |
| 3 | 0.83 | 11 | 2.67 |
| 4 | 1.06 | 12 | 2.90 |
| 5 | 1.29 | 13 | 3.13 |
| 6 | 1.52 | Over 13 oz, see | |
| 7 | 1.75 | Priority Mail. | |
| 8 | 1.98 | | |

*Nonstandard surcharge may apply to pieces weighing 1 oz or less based on size.

### Card Rates

| | |
|---|---|
| Single postcard (commercial) | $0.23 |
| Single postal card sold by United States Postal Service | 0.25 |

Postcard Dimensions: Not larger than 4¼ by 6 in. by 0.016 in. thick. Not smaller than 3½ by 5 in. by 0.007 in. thick.

## Express Mail

Express Mail is the fastest service, with next day delivery by 12 noon to most destinations. Express Mail is delivered 365 days a year—with no extra charge for Saturday, Sunday, or holiday delivery. Items must weigh 70 lbs or less and measure 108 in. or less in combined length and girth.

**Customer Service**—1-800-222-1811. Order Express Mail supplies and labels, arrange pickup service, obtain delivery information between ZIP Codes, and determine delivery status.

### Post Office to Addressee Service

| | |
|---|---|
| Up to 8 oz | $13.65 |
| Up to 2 lbs | 17.85 |
| Up to 3 lbs | 21.05 |
| Up to 4 lbs | 24.20 |
| Up to 5 lbs | 27.30 |
| Up to 6 lbs | 30.40 |
| Up to 7 lbs | 33.45 |
| Over 7 lbs, see postmaster. | |

### Express Mail Flat-Rate Envelope

$13.65, regardless of weight or destination, for matter sent in a flat-rate envelope provided by the Postal Service.

## Priority Mail

Priority Mail offers 2-day service to most domestic destinations. Items must weigh 70 lbs or less and measure 108 in. or less in combined length and girth. Items that weigh less than 15 lbs but measure more than 84 in. (combined length and girth) are charged the 15 lb rate ($11.05)*.

### Single-Piece Rates*

| | |
|---|---|
| Up to 1 lb | $3.85 |
| Up to 2 lbs | 3.95 |
| Up to 3 lbs | 4.75 |
| Up to 4 lbs | 5.30 |
| Up to 5 lbs | 5.85 |
| Over 5 pounds, see postmaster. | |

*Rates are given for zones local through 3.

### Priority Mail Flat-Rate Envelope

$3.85, regardless of weight or destination, for matter sent in a flat-rate envelope provided by the Postal Service.

## Media Mail (Book Rate)

Generally used for books (at least eight pages), film (16 mm or narrower), printed music, printed test materials, sound recordings, play scripts, printed educational charts, loose-leaf pages and binders consisting of medical information, and computer-readable media. Advertising restrictions apply. Packages must measure 108 in. or less in combined length and girth.

| Weight not over (lbs) | Rate | Weight not over (lbs) | Rate |
|---|---|---|---|
| 1 | $1.42 | 9 | $4.54 |
| 2 | 1.84 | 10 | 4.84 |
| 3 | 2.26 | 11 | 5.14 |
| 4 | 2.68 | 12 | 5.44 |
| 5 | 3.10 | 13 | 5.74 |
| 6 | 3.52 | 14 | 6.04 |
| 7 | 3.94 | 15 | 6.34 |
| 8 | 4.24 | 16 | 6.64 |

## Special Services (Domestic Mail)

### Certificate of Mailing

Provides evidence of mailing only. Certificate of mailing does not provide a record of delivery. Must be purchased at time of mailing. Available for First-Class Mail, Priority Mail, Parcel Post, Bound Printed Matter, and Media Mail.

Fee, in addition to postage—$0.90

### Certified Mail

Provides the sender with a mailing receipt. A delivery record is maintained by the USPS. No insurance provided. Available with First-Class Mail and Priority Mail. For an additional fee, certified mail may be combined with restricted delivery or return receipt.

Fee, in addition to postage—$2.30

## Insurance

Provides coverage against loss or damage. Coverage up to $5,000 for Parcel Post, Bound Printed Matter, and Media Mail matter as well as merchandise mailed at Priority Mail or First-Class Mail rates. Items must not be insured for more than their value. Insured mail must be presented to a retail employee at a post office or a rural carrier.

| Liability | Fee, in addition to postage |
|---|---|
| $.01 to $50.00 | $1.30 |
| $50.01 to $100.00 | 2.20 |
| $100.01 to $200.00 | 3.20 |
| $200.01 to $300.00 | 4.20 |
| $300.01 to $400.00 | 5.20 |
| $400.01 to $500.00 | 6.20 |
| $500.01 to $600.00 | 7.20 |
| $600.01 to $5,000 | * |

*$7.00 plus $1.00 for each $100 or fraction over $600 in declared value.

## Money Orders

Provides safe transmission of money. Available in amounts up to $1,000.
Fee up to $500, in addition to postage—$0.90
Fee up to $1,000, in addition to postage—$1.25

## Registered Mail

Provides maximum protection and security for valuables. Provides sender with mailing receipt and a delivery record is maintained by the USPS. A record of mailing is maintained at the mailing post office. Available only for items paid at Priority Mail and First-Class Mail rates.

| Declared Value | Fee, in addition to postage |
|---|---|
| Without Insurance $0.00 | $ 7.50 |
| With Insurance $0.01 to $100 | 8.00 |
| $100.01 to $500.00 | 8.85 |
| $500.01 to $1,000.00 | 9.70 |
| $1,000.01 to $2,000.00 | 10.55 |

For higher values, consult your postmaster.

## Restricted Delivery

Permits a mailer to direct delivery only to the addressee or addressee's authorized agent. The addressee must be an individual specified by name. Available for First-Class Mail, Priority Mail, Parcel Post, Bound Printed Matter, and Media Mail that is sent certified, COD, mail insured for more than $50, or registered mail.
Fee in addition to postage: $2.60

## Return Receipt

Available only for Express Mail, Certified Mail, COD, Insured Mail for more than $50.00, or Registered Mail.

**Requested at time of mailing:**
Showing to whom (signature), date, and addressee's address (in conjunction with another service) $1.75
**Requested after mailing:**
Showing to whom (signature) and date delivered $3.25

## Special Handling

Provides preferential handling, but not preferential delivery, to extent practicable in dispatch and transportation. Available for First-Class Mail, Priority Mail, Parcel Post, Bound Printed Matter, and Media Mail.

Fee, in addition to postage:
Pieces weighing not more than 10 pounds—$5.95
Pieces weighing more than 10 pounds—$8.25

## Collect on Delivery (COD)

Allows mailers to collect the price of goods and/or postage on merchandise ordered by addressee when it is delivered. Fees include insurance. Maximum amount $1,000; see postmaster for details.

# Sizes for Domestic Mail

Mail must meet these standards:
• Thickness—No less than 0.007 in. thick. Pieces that are ¼ in. thick or less must be at least 3½ in. high, 5 in. long, and rectangular in shape.
• Combined length and girth—No more than 108 in.
• Weight—No more than 70 lbs.
Postcards must be:
• Minimum 3½ in. high, 5 in. long by .007 in. thick.
• Maximum 4¼ in. high, 6 in. long by .016 in. thick.

# The Mail-Order Merchandise Rule

The mail-order rule adopted by the Federal Trade Commission in October 1975 provides that when you order by mail:
• You must receive the merchandise when the seller says you will.
• If you are not promised delivery within a certain time period, the seller must ship the merchandise to you no later than 30 days after your order comes in.
• If you don't receive it shortly after that 30-day period, you can cancel your order and get your money back.

# ZIP Codes

The ZIP Code was instituted in 1963 and allows for electronic processing and delivery of mail. An envelope that does not include a ZIP Code in the delivery address must be manually sorted, which increases the cost of sorting the mail and causes mail to be delayed en route to the delivery address. ZIP Code directories are available for use or sale at your local post office, or you can look up ZIP Codes on-line: www.usps.gov/ncsc/.
In 1990, the Postal Service instituted an expanded ZIP Code called ZIP+4. It is composed of the original five-digit code plus a four-digit add-on. The four-digit add-on number identifies a geographic segment within the five-digit delivery area such as a city block, an office building, an individual high-volume receiver of mail, or any other unit that would aid efficient mail sorting and delivery.

---

## Postal Information Websites

**United States Postal Service:** http://www.usps.gov/
**ZIP Code Lookup:** http://www.usps.gov/zip4/
**U.S. Postal Service Rate Calculators:**
  domestic: http://postcalc.usps.gov/
  international: http://ircalc.usps.gov/
  business: http://dbcalc.usps.gov/

# International Postal Rates

Last revised by the U.S. Postal Service on June 30, 2002

## Single Piece Letter-Post

| Weight not over (oz) | Canada | Mexico | Western Europe and Israel | Australia, Japan, New Zealand | Other countries |
|---|---|---|---|---|---|
| 1 | $ 0.60 | $ 0.60 | $ 0.80 | $ 0.80 | $ 0.80 |
| 2 | 0.85 | 0.85 | 1.60 | 1.70 | 1.55 |
| 3 | 1.10 | 1.25 | 2.40 | 2.60 | 2.30 |
| 4 | 1.35 | 1.65 | 3.20 | 3.50 | 3.05 |
| 5 | 1.60 | 2.05 | 4.00 | 4.40 | 3.80 |
| 6 | 1.85 | 2.45 | 4.80 | 5.30 | 4.55 |
| 7 | 2.10 | 2.85 | 5.60 | 6.20 | 5.30 |
| 8 | 2.35 | 3.25 | 6.40 | 7.10 | 6.05 |
| 12 | 3.10 | 4.00 | 7.55 | 8.40 | 7.65 |
| 16 | 3.75 | 5.15 | 8.70 | 9.70 | 9.25 |
| 20 | 4.40 | 6.30 | 9.85 | 11.00 | 10.85 |
| 24 | 5.05 | 7.45 | 11.00 | 12.30 | 12.45 |
| 28 | 5.70 | 8.60 | 12.15 | 13.60 | 14.05 |
| 32 | 6.35 | 9.75 | 13.30 | 14.90 | 15.65 |
| 36 | 7.00 | 10.95 | 14.50 | 16.25 | 17.35 |
| 40 | 7.65 | 12.15 | 15.70 | 17.60 | 19.05 |
| 44 | 8.30 | 13.35 | 16.90 | 18.95 | 20.75 |
| 48 | 8.95 | 14.55 | 18.10 | 20.30 | 22.45 |
| 52 | 9.65 | 15.80 | 19.35 | 21.70 | 24.20 |
| 56 | 10.35 | 17.05 | 20.60 | 23.10 | 25.95 |
| 60 | 11.05 | 18.30 | 21.85 | 24.50 | 27.70 |
| 64 | 11.75 | 19.55 | 23.10 | 25.90 | 29.45 |

Maximum weight: 64 oz. **Postcards and Postal Rates:** Canada and Mexico—$0.50; all others—$0.70.

## All-Time Top 10 Most Popular Commemorative Stamps

| Issue | No. saved (millions) |
|---|---|
| Elvis '93 | 124.0 |
| Wildflowers '92 | 76.2 |
| Rock and Roll '93 | 75.8 |
| Civil War '95 | 46.6 |
| Legends of the West '94 | 46.5 |
| Marilyn Monroe '95 | 46.3 |
| Bugs Bunny '97 | 45.3 |
| Summer Olympics '92 | 39.6 |
| The World of Dinosaurs | 38.5 |
| Centennial Olympic Games '96 | 38.1 |

*Source:* U.S.P.S., 1998; latest data available. Popularity of stamps is measured by number saved, not used.

## Postal Workers Bitten by Dogs, by City

| City | Dog bites |
|---|---|
| 1. Houston | 58 |
| 2. Los Angeles | 38 |
| 3. Chicago | 31 |
| 4. Cleveland, Miami[1] | 27 |
| 5. Dallas | 26 |
| 6. Boston, Detroit[1] | 21 |
| 7. Denver | 20 |
| 8. San Diego | 19 |
| 9. Fort Lauderdale, San Antonio[1] | 18 |
| 10. Indianapolis | 17 |

1. ties. *Source:* U.S.P.S., 2000. A total of 2,725 postal workers were bitten by dogs in FY1999.

## State Abbreviations and State Postal Codes

| State | Abbreviation | Postal code | State | Abbreviation | Postal code | State | Abbreviation | Postal code |
|---|---|---|---|---|---|---|---|---|
| Alabama | Ala. | AL | Kentucky | Ky. | KY | Ohio | Ohio | OH |
| Alaska | Alaska | AK | Louisiana | La. | LA | Oklahoma | Okla. | OK |
| Arizona | Ariz. | AZ | Maine | Maine | ME | Oregon | Ore. | OR |
| Arkansas | Ark. | AR | Maryland | Md. | MD | Pennsylvania | Pa. | PA |
| California | Calif. | CA | Massachusetts | Mass. | MA | Puerto Rico | P.R. | PR |
| Colorado | Colo. | CO | Michigan | Mich. | MI | Rhode Island | R.I. | RI |
| Connecticut | Conn. | CT | Minnesota | Minn. | MN | South Carolina | S.C. | SC |
| Delaware | Del. | DE | Mississippi | Miss. | MS | South Dakota | S.D. | SD |
| Dist. of Columbia | D.C. | DC | Missouri | Mo. | MO | Tennessee | Tenn. | TN |
| Florida | Fla. | FL | Montana | Mont. | MT | Texas | Tex. | TX |
| Georgia | Ga. | GA | Nebraska | Nebr. | NE | Utah | Utah | UT |
| Guam | Guam | GU | Nevada | Nev. | NV | Vermont | Vt. | VT |
| Hawaii | Hawaii | HI | New Hampshire | N.H. | NH | Virginia | Va. | VA |
| Idaho | Idaho | ID | New Jersey | N.J. | NJ | Virgin Islands | V.I. | VI |
| Illinois | Ill. | IL | New Mexico | N.M. | NM | Washington | Wash. | WA |
| Indiana | Ind. | IN | New York | N.Y. | NY | West Virginia | W.Va. | WV |
| Iowa | Iowa | IA | North Carolina | N.C. | NC | Wisconsin | Wis. | WI |
| Kansas | Kans. | KS | North Dakota | N.D. | ND | Wyoming | Wyo. | WY |

# Where the Wild Things Are

Looking for the perfect outdoor family vacation? Log on to find the best parks, hikes, and campsites

**By ANITA HAMILTON** TIME

I could wax poetic about the joys of vacationing in the great outdoors, like roasting marshmallows, collecting pine cones, and wandering aimlessly through the woods. But let's face it—communing with nature doesn't always mean one breathtaking vista after another. It rains. There are too many bugs. There's no hot water. And those darned chirping crickets keep you up all night.

Still, it's worth it—especially if you plan ahead and figure out how to avoid the insects and discover the waterfalls. Not only will this give the biggest gripers in your family less to complain about but you'll also be able to take a weeklong vacation for less than the price of a weekend at Disney World.

## Click and Go

The best place to do your research is on the Web, where you can find everything from the best swimming holes to tips on keeping the bears from sniffing around your tent. I always head first to the National Park Service website at **www.nps.gov**. Just select a state, and the site lists all the national parks and recreation areas in the region. Printable travel guides tell you the peak season, what each park is like, how much campsites cost, and where the nearest hotels are. Cool extras include live webcam views and a weather map of each park as well as a "for kids" section that details special activities for them. You can even book a campsite directly on the NPS site.

My favorite unofficial site for outdoor adventures is **gorp.com**, which features magazine-style articles on topics like "10 Best Adventure Lodges" and "Death Valley's Vital Signs," along with thorough listings for national, state, and local parks. I especially like Gorp's Zagat-style ratings of parks and trails (best national park: Glacier in Montana) as well as helpful tips on when to avoid the crowds and the mosquitoes. When the time comes to book a campsite at a state or local park, I head to **reserveamerica.com**. It shows the exact layout of thousands of campgrounds, so that you can see how close each site is to the main road, other campers, and even the rest rooms.

If your family is the adventurous type, there are a couple of specialty websites that are worth exploring. **Swimmingholes.org** features more than 500 unofficial swimming spots in the 22 Eastern states, plus links to more in the West. Many are near waterfalls or at scenic lakes. For those who want to rough it, **thebackpacker.com** has everything from tips for beginners (like how to keep your tent dry) to trail reviews and extensive message boards on topics ranging from "best frying pan" to "Kentucky hiking."

And if you really want to dream, check out **onedayhikes.com**, which features hundreds of exquisite hikes around the world, from a four-day expedition along the Inca Trail to the "lost city" of Machu Picchu, Peru, to an hour-and-a-half-long amble through the coastal redwoods in Northern California's Muir Woods. The awe-inspiring photos alone will make you and your family want to pack your bags—don't forget the bug spray!—and head for the hills. □

## Travel Websites

**Adventure Travel & Ecotourism**
Adventure Travel Tips: www.adventuretraveltips.com
iExplore (National Geographic): www.iexplore.com
International Ecotourism Society: www.ecotourism.org
IE Adventure Travel: www.xpandventure.com

**Backpacking and Hiking**
American Hiking Society: www.americanhiking.org
Appalachian Mountain Club: www.outdoors.org
Rocky Mountain National Park: www.explore-rocky.com

**Fares & Reservations**
Expedia (Microsoft): www.expedia.com
Orbitz: www.orbitz.com
Priceline: www.priceline.com
Travelocity: www.travelocity.com

**Student Travel**
Council Travel: www.counciltravel.com
Hostelling International: www.iyhf.org
STA Travel: www.sta-travel.com
Student Universe: www.studentuniverse.com

**Travel Abroad**
Exchange Rates: www.x-rates.com
Intellicast (weather): www.intellicast.com
Rail Connection (Europe): www.railconnection.com

**Travel Guides**
Adventurous Traveler Bookstore:
    www.adventuroustraveler.com
Fodor's Travel Online: www.fodors.com
Frommer's: www.frommers.com
Lonely Planet: www.lonelyplanet.com
Rough Guides: www.roughguides.com
Travel Notes: www.travelnotes.org
Zagat (restaurants): www.zagat.com

**Volunteer Vacations**
Charity Guide: charityguide.org/charity/vacation.htm
Earthwatch Institute: www.earthwatch.org
Global Volunteers: www.globalvolunteers.org
GoNOMAD: www.gonomad.com
Volunteer America: www.volunteeramerica.net

## The World's Top Tourism Destinations[1]

### (international tourist arrivals)

| 2000 rank | Country | Arrivals (million) 1999 | Arrivals (million) 2000 | Percent change 1999/2000 | 2000 market share | 2000 rank | Country | Arrivals (million) 1999 | Arrivals (million) 2000 | Percent change 1999/2000 | 2000 market share |
|---|---|---|---|---|---|---|---|---|---|---|---|
| 1. | France | 73.0 | 75.5 | 3.4% | 10.8% | 9. | Canada | 19.5 | 20.4 | 4.9% | 2.9% |
| 2. | United States | 48.5 | 50.9 | 4.9 | 7.3 | 10. | Germany | 17.1 | 19.0 | 10.9 | 2.7 |
| 3. | Spain | 46.8 | 48.2 | 3.0 | 6.9 | 11. | Austria | 17.5 | 18.0 | 2.9 | 2.6 |
| 4. | Italy | 36.5 | 41.2 | 12.8 | 5.9 | 12. | Poland | 18.0 | 17.4 | -3.1 | 2.5 |
| 5. | China | 27.0 | 31.2 | 15.5 | 4.5 | 13. | Hungary | 14.4 | 15.6 | 8.1 | 2.2 |
| 6. | United Kingdom | 25.4 | 25.2 | -0.8 | 3.6 | 14. | Hong Kong (China) | 11.3 | 13.1 | 15.3 | 1.9 |
| 7. | Russian Fed. | 18.5 | 21.2 | 14.5 | 3.0 | | | | | | |
| 8. | Mexico | 19.0 | 20.6 | 8.4 | 3.0 | 15. | Greece | 12.2 | 12.5 | 2.8 | 1.8 |

1. Data collected through Aug. 2001. *Source:* World Tourism Organization (WTO). Web: www.world-tourism.org.

## Top Nationalities of Travelers to the U.S.

| 2000 rank | Country of residence | 2000 total | Percent of total travelers to U.S. | 2000 rank | Country of residence | 2000 total | Percent of total travelers to U.S. |
|---|---|---|---|---|---|---|---|
| 1. | Canada | 14,594,000 | 29% | 9. | Italy | 612,357 | 1% |
| 2. | Mexico | 10,322,000 | 20 | 10. | Venezuela | 576,663 | 1 |
| 3. | Japan | 5,061,377 | 10 | 11. | Netherlands | 553,297 | 1 |
| 4. | United Kingdom | 4,703,008 | 9 | 12. | Australia | 539,559 | 1 |
| 5. | Germany | 1,786,045 | 4 | 13. | Argentina | 533,936 | 1 |
| 6. | France | 1,087,087 | 2 | 14. | Taiwan | 457,302 | — |
| 7. | Brazil | 737,245 | 1 | 15. | Colombia | 417,065 | — |
| 8. | South Korea | 661,844 | 1 | | | | |

NOTE: (—) = less than 1%. *Source:* U.S. Dept. of Commerce, International Trade Administration. Web: www.tinet.ita.doc.gov/research/reports.

## Top States and Cities Visited by Overseas Travelers, 2000

| State | Overseas visitors (thousands) | Market share (percent) | City | Overseas visitors (thousands) | Market share (percent) |
|---|---|---|---|---|---|
| Total overseas travelers[1] | 25,975 | 100.0% | Total overseas travelers[1] | 25,975 | 100.0% |
| California | 6,364 | 24.5 | New York, N.Y. | 5,714 | 22.0 |
| Florida | 6,026 | 23.2 | Los Angeles, Calif. | 3,533 | 13.6 |
| New York | 5,922 | 22.8 | Orlando, Fla. | 3,013 | 11.6 |
| Hawaiian Islands | 2,727 | 10.5 | Miami, Fla. | 2,935 | 11.3 |
| Nevada | 2,364 | 9.1 | San Francisco, Calif. | 2,831 | 10.9 |
| Massachusetts | 1,429 | 5.5 | Las Vegas, Nev. | 2,260 | 8.7 |
| Illinois | 1,377 | 5.3 | Oahu/Honolulu, Hawaii | 2,234 | 8.6 |
| Guam | 1,325 | 5.1 | Washington, DC | 1,481 | 5.7 |
| Texas | 1,169 | 4.5 | Chicago, Ill. | 1,351 | 5.2 |
| New Jersey | 909 | 3.5 | Boston, Mass. | 1,325 | 5.1 |
| Arizona | 883 | 3.4 | San Diego, Calif. | 701 | 2.7 |
| Georgia | 805 | 3.1 | Atlanta, Ga. | 701 | 2.7 |
| Pennsylvania | 649 | 2.5 | Tampa/St. Petersburg, Fla. | 519 | 2.0 |
| Colorado | 519 | 2.0 | San Jose, Calif. | 494 | 1.9 |

NOTE: Includes travelers for business and pleasure, international travelers in transit through the United States, and students; excludes travel by international personnel and international businessmen employed in the United States. 1. Includes other states and cities, not shown separately. *Source:* U.S. Dept. of Commerce, International Trade Administration. Web: www.tinet.ita.doc.gov. From *Statistical Abstract of the United States, 2001.*

## Top International Destinations of American Tourists

### (numbers in thousands)

| 2000 rank | Country[1] | 2000 travelers | 2000 rank | Country[1] | 2000 travelers | 2000 rank | Country[1] | 2000 travelers |
|---|---|---|---|---|---|---|---|---|
| 1. | Mexico | 18,849 | 9. | Switzerland | 994 | 17. | China | 644 |
| 2. | Canada | 15,114 | 10. | Bahamas | 913 | 18. | Israel | 618 |
| 3. | United Kingdom | 4,189 | 11. | Jamaica | 886 | 19. | Austria | 564 |
| 4. | France | 2,927 | 12. | Hong Kong | 832 | 20. | Philippines | 457 |
| 5. | Germany | 2,309 | 13. | Republic of Korea | 779 | 20. | Belgium | 457 |
| 6. | Italy | 2,148 | 14. | Ireland | 725 | 20. | Greece | 457 |
| 7. | Japan | 1,262 | 15. | Australia | 698 | 20. | India | 457 |
| 7. | Spain | 1,262 | 16. | Brazil | 671 | 20. | New Zealand | 457 |
| 8. | Netherlands | 1,101 | 16. | Taiwan | 671 | 20. | Singapore | 457 |

1. Ranked by 2000 visitation volume. *Source:* U.S. Dept. of Commerce, International Trade Administration. Web: www.tinet.ita.doc.gov/research/reports.

# Current Travel Warnings

## (for U.S. citizens; as of Sept. 2002)

Travel Warnings are issued when the State Department recommends that Americans avoid a certain country. The countries listed below are currently on that list. In addition to this list, the State Department issues Consular Information Sheets for every country of the world with information on such matters as the health conditions, crime, unusual currency or entry requirements, any areas of instability, and the location of the nearest U.S. embassy or consulate in the subject country.

| Country | Most recent warning issued | Country | Most recent warning issued |
|---|---|---|---|
| Afghanistan | 7/3/02 | Israel | 8/2/02 |
| Algeria | 12/11/01 | Lebanon | 4/29/02 |
| Angola | 8/23/02 | Liberia | 5/21/02 |
| Bosnia and Herzegovina | 6/4/02 | Libya | 6/6/01 |
| Burundi | 8/9/02 | Macedonia | 5/21/02 |
| Central African Republic | 11/8/01 | Nigeria | 8/8/02 |
| Colombia | 7/3/02 | Pakistan | 8/12/02 |
| Côte d'Ivoire | 9/26/02 | Somalia | 8/23/02 |
| Dem. Rep. of the Congo (formerly Zaire) | 7/1/02 | Sudan | 7/9/02 |
| Guinea-Bissau | 4/30/01 | Tajikistan | 9/26/01 |
| Indonesia | 11/23/01 | Yemen | 3/18/02 |
| Iran | 1/30/02 | Yugoslavia | 2/13/01 |
| Iraq | 7/20/01 | | |

NOTE: In the wake of the terrorist attacks on the World Trade Center and the Pentagon on Sept. 11, 2001, the State Department issued a worldwide caution for U.S. citizens traveling abroad. *Source:* U.S. Department of State. Web: http://travel.state.gov.

## U.S. Passport Information

With a few exceptions, a passport is required for all U.S. citizens to depart and enter the United States and to enter most foreign countries. Persons who travel to a country where a U.S. passport is not required should be in possession of documentary evidence of their U.S. citizenship and identity to facilitate reentry into the United States. Travelers should check passport and visa requirements with consular officials of the countries to be visited well in advance of their departure date.

Application for a passport may be made at a passport agency, many federal and state courts, probate courts, some county and municipal offices, and some post offices. The thirteen major cities with U.S. passport agencies are Boston, Chicago, Honolulu, Houston, Los Angeles, Miami, New Orleans, New York, Norwalk, Conn., Philadelphia, San Francisco, Seattle, and Washington, DC.

All persons are required to obtain individual passports in their own names. Neither spouses nor children may be included in each other's passports.

Applicants age 14 years and older must appear in person before the clerk or agent executing the application if it is their first time applying. For children age 13 and under, a parent or legal guardian may execute an application for them.

The State Dept. suggests you make two copies of the identification page—one to leave with a friend or relative at home in case of an emergency, and one to keep with you in the event that your passport is lost or stolen while abroad. This will make it easier to get a new passport, should it be necessary. It is also a good idea to carry two extra passport-size photos with you.

If you would like more information about obtaining or renewing a passport, visit the State Dept. website (http://travel.state.gov) or call the National Passport Information Center, 1-888-362-8668.

*Source:* Department of State, Bureau of Consular Affairs. Web: http://travel.state.gov.

## A Safe Trip Abroad

The U.S. Department of State offers the following tips for safe travel abroad:
- Dress conservatively. Thieves often target tourists, so avoid wearing anything that will make you stand out, and leave your expensive jewelry at home.
- Travel light. You will be able to move more quickly and will be more likely to have a free hand. Also, you will be less tired and less likely to set your luggage down and leave it unattended.
- Conceal your valuables. Leave your passport, cash, and credit cards locked in a hotel safe if possible. When you carry them on you, conceal them in several different places rather than all in one wallet, pocket, or bag. Avoid using handbags,

fanny packs, and outside pockets that are easy targets for thieves.

- If you wear glasses, pack an extra pair. Pack your glasses and any medicines you need in your carry-on luggage.

- Keep medicines in their original labeled containers. This will help you to avoid problems when passing through customs. Bring copies of your prescriptions and the generic names for the drugs. If a medication contains narcotics, carry a letter from your doctor attesting to your need to take the drug. If you have any doubt about the legality of carrying a certain drug into a foreign country, consult the embassy or consulate of that country first.

- Bring travelers' checks and a major credit card instead of cash.
- Leave a copy of the serial numbers of your travelers' checks with a friend or relative at home. Carry your copy with you in a separate place, and as you cash the checks, cross them off the list.
- Bring an extra set of passport photos and a photocopy of your passport information page. This will make it easier to get a replacement if your passport is lost or stolen.
- Put your name, address, and telephone number inside each piece of luggage. Use covered luggage tags to avoid casual observation of your name, address, and nationality. Always lock your luggage.

- Consider getting a telephone calling card that can be used from overseas locations. Access numbers to U.S. operators are published in many international papers, but find out your access number before you go.

*Source:* U.S. Dept. of State, Bureau of Consular Affairs. Web: http://travel.state.gov.

## Average Daily Temperatures (°F) in Tourist Cities

(For U.S. cities, *see* Climate of Selected U.S. Cities, pp. 610–611)

| Location | January High | January Low | April High | April Low | July High | July Low | October High | October Low |
|---|---|---|---|---|---|---|---|---|
| Acapulco (Mexico) | 87 | 72 | 87 | 73 | 89 | 77 | 89 | 77 |
| Amsterdam (Netherlands) | 41 | 34 | 53 | 40 | 69 | 55 | 57 | 46 |
| Athens (Greece) | 54 | 42 | 67 | 52 | 90 | 72 | 74 | 60 |
| Auckland (New Zealand) | 73 | 60 | 67 | 56 | 56 | 46 | 63 | 52 |
| Bangkok (Thailand) | 89 | 69 | 94 | 78 | 91 | 77 | 89 | 76 |
| Beijing (China) | 35 | 15 | 68 | 44 | 87 | 71 | 67 | 44 |
| Belgrade (Yugoslavia) | 38 | 28 | 62 | 43 | 81 | 60 | 64 | 46 |
| Berlin (Germany) | 35 | 26 | 55 | 38 | 74 | 55 | 55 | 41 |
| Bombay (India) | 83 | 67 | 89 | 76 | 85 | 77 | 89 | 76 |
| Cairo (Egypt) | 65 | 47 | 83 | 57 | 96 | 70 | 86 | 65 |
| Calcutta (India) | 80 | 55 | 97 | 75 | 89 | 79 | 89 | 74 |
| Cape Town (South Africa) | 69 | 56 | 66 | 54 | 60 | 50 | 65 | 53 |
| Caracas (Venezuela) | 75 | 56 | 81 | 60 | 78 | 61 | 79 | 61 |
| Copenhagen (Denmark) | 36 | 29 | 50 | 37 | 72 | 55 | 53 | 42 |
| Dublin (Ireland) | 47 | 35 | 54 | 38 | 67 | 51 | 57 | 43 |
| Glasgow (Scotland) | 43 | 34 | 53 | 38 | 66 | 52 | 54 | 43 |
| Hamilton (Bermuda) | 68 | 58 | 71 | 59 | 85 | 73 | 79 | 69 |
| Helsinki (Finland) | 27 | 17 | 43 | 31 | 71 | 57 | 45 | 37 |
| Hong Kong (China) | 67 | 51 | 79 | 67 | 90 | 78 | 84 | 70 |
| Istanbul (Turkey) | 48 | 36 | 59 | 45 | 78 | 64 | 66 | 53 |
| Jerusalem (Israel) | 55 | 41 | 73 | 50 | 87 | 63 | 81 | 59 |
| Kingston (Jamaica) | 86 | 67 | 87 | 70 | 90 | 73 | 88 | 73 |
| Lagos (Nigeria) | 88 | 74 | 89 | 77 | 82 | 74 | 85 | 74 |
| Lisbon (Portugal) | 56 | 46 | 64 | 52 | 79 | 63 | 69 | 57 |
| London (United Kingdom) | 44 | 35 | 56 | 40 | 73 | 55 | 58 | 44 |
| Madrid (Spain) | 50 | 34 | 63 | 43 | 89 | 61 | 67 | 48 |
| Mexico City (Mexico) | 66 | 42 | 77 | 51 | 73 | 53 | 70 | 50 |
| Montreal (Canada) | 22 | 6 | 51 | 33 | 79 | 60 | 56 | 39 |
| Moscow (Russia) | 21 | 9 | 47 | 31 | 76 | 55 | 46 | 34 |
| Nairobi (Kenya) | 77 | 53 | 75 | 57 | 69 | 51 | 77 | 54 |
| Nassau (Bahamas) | 77 | 65 | 81 | 69 | 88 | 75 | 85 | 73 |
| Oslo (Norway) | 30 | 20 | 50 | 34 | 73 | 56 | 49 | 37 |
| Paris (France) | 42 | 32 | 60 | 41 | 76 | 55 | 59 | 44 |
| Prague (Czech Republic) | 34 | 25 | 55 | 40 | 74 | 58 | 54 | 44 |
| Quebec (Canada) | 19 | 3 | 45 | 30 | 77 | 58 | 51 | 37 |
| Rio de Janeiro (Brazil) | 84 | 73 | 80 | 69 | 75 | 63 | 77 | 66 |
| Rome (Italy) | 54 | 39 | 68 | 46 | 88 | 64 | 73 | 53 |
| San José (Costa Rica) | 75 | 58 | 79 | 62 | 77 | 62 | 77 | 60 |
| San Juan (Puerto Rico) | 81 | 70 | 83 | 72 | 86 | 76 | 86 | 75 |
| Seoul (Korea) | 33 | 17 | 62 | 42 | 84 | 70 | 67 | 47 |
| Singapore | 86 | 73 | 89 | 75 | 87 | 75 | 88 | 74 |
| Stockholm (Sweden) | 31 | 23 | 45 | 32 | 70 | 55 | 48 | 39 |
| Sydney (Australia) | 79 | 65 | 73 | 57 | 62 | 44 | 72 | 55 |
| Taipei (Taiwan) | 66 | 54 | 77 | 63 | 92 | 76 | 81 | 67 |
| Tokyo (Japan) | 48 | 31 | 64 | 48 | 84 | 71 | 70 | 56 |
| Toronto (Canada) | 30 | 17 | 51 | 35 | 79 | 60 | 57 | 42 |
| Vancouver (Canada) | 42 | 32 | 55 | 41 | 71 | 55 | 57 | 44 |
| Vienna (Austria) | 34 | 26 | 57 | 41 | 75 | 59 | 55 | 44 |
| Zurich (Switzerland) | 36 | 26 | 60 | 41 | 77 | 56 | 57 | 43 |

# State and Territory Tourism Offices

The following is a selected list of state tourism office Web addresses and phone numbers. Where a toll-free 800 or 888 number is available, it is given. However, the numbers are subject to change.

**Alabama**
1-800-ALABAMA
www.touralabama.org

**Alaska**
907-929-2200
www.travelalaska.com

**Arizona**
1-888-520-3434
www.arizonaguide.com

**Arkansas**
1-800-NATURAL
www.arkansas.com

**California**
1-800-GOCALIF
www.gocalif.ca.gov

**Colorado**
1-800-COLORADO
www.colorado.com

**Connecticut**
1-800-CT-BOUND
www.ctbound.org

**Delaware**
1-866-2-VISIT-DE
www.state.de.us/tourism

**District of Columbia
(Washington, DC)**
202-789-7000
www.washington.org

**Florida**
888-7FLA-USA
www.flausa.com

**Georgia**
1-800-VISIT-GA
www.georgiaonmymind.org

**Guam**
671-646-5278/9
www.visitguam.org

**Hawaii**
1-800-GO-HAWAII
www.gohawaii.com

**Idaho**
1-800-635-7820
www.visitid.org

**Illinois**
1-800-2-CONNECT
www.enjoyillinois.com

**Indiana**
1-888-ENJOY-IN
www.enjoyindiana.com

**Iowa**
1-888-472-6035
www.traveliowa.com/

**Kansas**
1-800-2-KANSAS
www.travelks.com

**Kentucky**
1-502-223-8687
www.tourky.com

**Louisiana**
1-800-677-4082
www.louisianatravel.com

**Maine**
1-888-MAINE-45
www.visitmaine.com

**Maryland**
1-800-MDISFUN
www.mdisfun.org

**Massachusetts**
1-800-227-MASS
www.massvacation.com

**Michigan**
1-888-78-GREAT
www.michigan.org

**Minnesota**
1-800-657-3700
www.exploreminnesota.com

**Mississippi**
1-800-WARMEST
www.visitmississippi.org

**Missouri**
1-800-810-5500
www.missouritourism.org

**Montana**
1-800-VISIT-MT
www.visitmt.com

**Nebraska**
1-877-NEBRASKA
www.visitnebraska.org

**Nevada**
1-800-NEVADA-8
www.travelnevada.com

**New Hampshire**
1-800-FUN-IN-NH
www.visitnh.gov

**New Jersey**
1-800-VISIT-NJ
www.state.nj.us/travel

**New Mexico**
1-800-733-6396
www.newmexico.org

**New York**
1-800-CALL-NYS
www.iloveny.com

**North Carolina**
1-800-VISIT-NC
www.visitnc.com

**North Dakota**
1-800-HELLO-ND
www.ndtourism.com

**Ohio**
1-800-BUCKEYE
www.ohiotourism.com

**Oklahoma**
1-800-654-8240
www.touroklahoma.com

**Oregon**
1-800-547-7842
www.traveloregon.com

**Pennsylvania**
1-800-VISIT-PA
www.experiencepa.com

**Puerto Rico**
1-800-866-7827
www.gotopuertorico.com

**Rhode Island**
1-800-556-2484
www.visitrhodeisland.com

**South Carolina**
1-800-SCSMILE
www.travelsc.com

**South Dakota**
1-800-S-DAKOTA
www.travelsd.com

**Tennessee**
1-800-610-2-TENN
www.tourism.state.tn.us/

**Texas**
1-800-452-9292
www.state.tx.us/Travel

**U.S. Virgin Islands**
1-800-372-USVI
www.usvi.org/tourism/

**Utah**
1-800-UTAH-FUN
www.state.ut.us/visiting/
travel.html

**Vermont**
1-800-VERMONT
www.1-800-vermont.com

**Virginia**
1-800-321-3244
www.virginia.org

**Washington**
800-544-1800
www.tourism.wa.gov

**Washington, DC**
See District of Columbia

**West Virginia**
1-800-CALL-WVA
www.callwva.com

**Wisconsin**
1-800-432-TRIP
www.travelwisconsin.com

**Wyoming**
1-800-225-5996
www.wyomingtourism.org

# Transportation

## Consumer Complaints Against Top U.S. Airlines by Airline[1]

| Rank | Airline | Complaints | System-wide passenger boardings[2] | Complaints per 100,000 passenger boardings[2] |
|---|---|---|---|---|
| 1. | America West | 729 | 19,576,031 | 3.72 |
| 2. | United | 2,448 | 75,453,979 | 3.24 |
| 3. | TWA | 528 | 20,791,995 | 2.54 |
| 4. | American | 1,964 | 78,115,155 | 2.51 |
| 5. | Continental | 952 | 42,779,867 | 2.23 |
| 6. | Delta | 2,021 | 93,386,645 | 2.16 |
| 7. | Northwest | 1,065 | 54,171,658 | 1.97 |
| 8. | U.S. Airways | 1,049 | 56,146,174 | 1.87 |
| 9. | American Eagle | 204 | 11,973,856 | 1.70 |
| 10. | Alaska | 174 | 13,667,526 | 1.27 |
| 11. | Southwest | 281 | 73,742,867 | 0.38 |
|  | **Total** | **11,415** | **539,805,753** | **2.11** |

NOTE: Data for Jan. 2001–Dec. 2001. 1. Includes U.S. airlines with at least 1% of total domestic scheduled-service passenger revenues. 2. Refers to individual passenger boardings. *Source:* Office of Aviation Enforcement and Proceedings, U.S. Dept. of Transportation, *Air Travel Consumer Report.* Web: www.dot.gov/airconsumer/index1.htm.

## Consumer Complaints Against Top U.S. Airlines by Category

| Complaint category | 1991 | 1992 | 1993 | 1994 | 1995 | 1996 | 1997 | 1998 | 1999 | 2000 | 2001 |
|---|---|---|---|---|---|---|---|---|---|---|---|
| **TOTAL** | **6,106** | **5,639** | **4,438** | **5,179** | **4,629** | **5,782** | **6,394** | **7,994** | **17,381** | **20,564** | **14,076** |
| Flight problems[1] | 1,877 | 1,624 | 1,211 | 1,586 | 1,133 | 1,628 | 1,699 | 2,277 | 6,469 | 8,698 | 5,046 |
| Customer service[2] | 714 | 695 | 599 | 805 | 667 | 999 | 1,418 | 1,715 | 3,664 | 4,074 | 2,700 |
| Baggage | 883 | 752 | 627 | 761 | 628 | 882 | 826 | 1,108 | 2,353 | 2,753 | 1,965 |
| Reservations/ticketing/boarding[3] | 659 | 680 | 577 | 598 | 666 | 857 | 904 | 1,137 | 1,328 | 1,405 | 1,310 |
| Refunds | 783 | 721 | 482 | 393 | 576 | 521 | 531 | 602 | 940 | 803 | 942 |
| Oversales[4] | 301 | 265 | 257 | 301 | 263 | 353 | 414 | 388 | 673 | 759 | 539 |
| Fares[5] | 388 | 573 | 398 | 267 | 185 | 180 | 195 | 277 | 584 | 708 | 568 |
| Disability[3] | n.a. | n.a. | n.a. | n.a. | n.a. | n.a. | n.a. | n.a. | 526 | 612 | 454 |
| Advertising | 96 | 54 | 51 | 94 | 66 | 61 | 57 | 40 | 57 | 42 | 42 |
| Tours | 23 | 12 | 16 | 127 | 18 | 16 | 13 | 23 | 28 | 25 | 11 |
| Smoking[6] | 30 | 25 | 30 | 20 | 15 | 13 | 5 | 4 | n.a. | n.a. | n.a. |
| Credit[6] | 10 | 10 | 4 | 2 | 4 | 3 | 1 | 1 | n.a. | n.a. | n.a. |
| Other[6] | 342 | 228 | 186 | 225 | 408 | 269 | 331 | 422 | 759 | 675 | 493 |
| Animals[7] | n.a. | n.a. | n.a. | n.a. | n.a. | n.a. | n.a. | n.a. | 0 | 1 | 6 |

1. Cancellations, delays, and other deviations from schedule. 2. Rude or unhelpful employees, inadequate meals or cabin service, treatment of delayed passengers. 3. Effective with the Sept. 1999 report, "disability" complaints are listed as a separate category. Previously, disability complaints were included in the "Reservations/ticketing/boarding" category. 4. All bumping problems, whether or not airline complied with DOT regulations. 5. Incorrect or incomplete information about fares, discount fare conditions and availability, overcharges, fare increases, and level of fares in general. 6. Complaints about "smoking" and "credit," which were formerly separate categories, are now included in the "other" category. 7. Effective with the Oct. 2000 report, "Animals" was added as a new category. *Source:* Office of Aviation Enforcement and Proceedings, U.S. Dept. of Transportation, *Air Travel Consumer Report.* Web: www.dot.gov/airconsumer/index1.htm.

## Passengers Denied Boarding by Top U.S. Airlines,[1] 2001

| Rank Airline | Denied boardings (DBs) | | Enplaned passengers | Involuntary DBs per 10,000 passengers |
|---|---|---|---|---|
|  | Voluntary | Involuntary |  |  |
| 1. TWA | 30,440 | 3,303 | 16,413,933 | 2.01 |
| 2. American Eagle | 1,463 | 270 | 1,433,495 | 1.88 |
| 3. Southwest | 63,289 | 9,215 | 56,439,110 | 1.63 |
| 4. Alaska | 25,922 | 1,567 | 10,624,014 | 1.47 |
| 5. United | 120,191 | 5,499 | 54,721,034 | 1.00 |
| 6. Continental | 54,383 | 2,599 | 29,749,486 | 0.87 |
| 7. Delta | 135,690 | 4,544 | 69,750,219 | 0.65 |
| 8. Northwest | 58,054 | 1,557 | 38,495,416 | 0.40 |
| 9. America West | 40,010 | 604 | 15,622,332 | 0.39 |
| 10. American | 103,966 | 1,937 | 55,466,583 | 0.35 |
| 11. U.S. Airways | 65,589 | 1,357 | 43,258,363 | 0.31 |
| **Total** | **698,997** | **32,452** | **391,973,985** | **0.83** |

NOTE: Data for Jan. 2001–Sept. 2001. 1. Includes U.S. airlines with at least 1% of total domestic scheduled-service passenger revenues. *Source:* Office of Aviation Enforcement and Proceedings, U.S. Dept. of Transportation, *Air Travel Consumer Report.* Web: www.dot.gov/airconsumer/index1.htm.

## World's 25 Busiest Airports by Passengers and Cargo, 2001

| Airport | Total passengers[1] | 2000–2001 percent change | Airport | Total cargo[1] | 2000–2001 percent change |
|---|---|---|---|---|---|
| 1. Atlanta, Hartsfield (ATL) | 75,849,375 | −5.4% | Memphis (MEM) | 2,631,239 | 5.7% |
| 2. Chicago, O'Hare (ORD) | 66,805,339 | −6.9 | Los Angeles (LAX) | 2,122,874 | −14.1 |
| 3. Los Angeles (LAX) | 61,024,541 | −8.3 | Hong Kong (HKG) | 2,099,605 | −7.4 |
| 4. London, Heathrow (LHR) | 60,743,154 | −6.0 | Anchorage (ANC)[2] | 1,691,027 | −10.0 |
| 5. Tokyo, Haneda (HND) | 58,692,688 | 4.1 | Tokyo, Narita (NRT) | 1,680,938 | −13.0 |
| 6. Dallas/Ft. Worth (DFW) | 55,150,689 | −9.2 | Miami (MIA) | 1,639,762 | −0.2 |
| 7. Frankfurt-Main (FRA) | 48,559,980 | −1.6 | Frankfurt-Main (FRA) | 1,613,292 | −5.7 |
| 8. Paris, Charles de Gaulle (CDG) | 47,996,223 | −0.5 | Singapore (SIN) | 1,529,930 | −10.3 |
| 9. Amsterdam, Schiphol (AMS) | 39,538,483 | −0.2 | New York (JFK) | 1,500,000[3] | −16.9 |
| 10. Denver (DEN) | 36,086,751 | −6.9 | Paris, Charles de Gaulle (CDG) | 1,479,304 | −3.5 |
| 11. Phoenix, Sky Harbor (PHX) | 35,481,950 | −1.6 | Louisville (SDF) | 1,469,013 | −3.3 |
| 12. Las Vegas (LAS) | 35,195,675 | −4.2 | Chicago, O'Hare (ORD) | 1,284,822 | −16.1 |
| 13. Minneapolis/St. Paul (MSP) | 35,170,528 | −4.4 | London, Heathrow (LHR) | 1,263,542 | −9.8 |
| 14. Houston (IAH) | 34,794,868 | −1.3 | Amsterdam, Schiphol (AMS) | 1,232,031 | −2.6 |
| 15. San Francisco (SFO) | 34,626,668 | −15.7 | Inchon (ICN) | 1,196,845 | — |
| 16. Madrid (MAD) | 33,984,413 | 3.3 | Taipei (TPE) | 1,189,874 | −1.6 |
| 17. Hong Kong (HKG) | 32,553,000 | −0.6 | Indianapolis (IND) | 1,151,105 | −2.9 |
| 18. Detroit (DTW) | 32,294,121 | −9.1 | Osaka (KIX) | 871,161 | −12.9 |
| 19. Miami (MIA) | 31,668,450 | −5.7 | Bangkok (BKK) | 842,588 | −3.3 |
| 20. London, Gatwick (LGW) | 31,182,361 | −2.8 | Newark (EWR) | 800,000[3] | −26.0 |
| 21. Bangkok (BKK) | 30,623,764 | 3.4 | Dallas/Ft. Worth (DFW) | 793,974 | −12.1 |
| 22. Newark (EWR) | 30,500,000[3] | −10.7 | Atlanta, Hartsfield (ATL) | 743,717 | −14.0 |
| 23. New York (JFK) | 29,400,000[3] | −10.5 | Tokyo, Haneda (HND) | 725,124 | −5.8 |
| 24. Orlando (MCO) | 28,166,612 | −8.4 | San Francisco (SFO) | 635,060 | −27.2 |
| 25. Singapore (SIN) | 28,093,759 | −1.8 | Dubai (DXB) | 632,224 | 8.6 |

NOTES: Total passengers enplaned and deplaned, passengers in transit counted once. Total cargo loaded and unloaded, freight and mail (in metric tons). 1. Results are preliminary. 2. Includes transit freight. 3. Estimated. *Source:* Airports Council International World Headquarters, Geneva, Switzerland. Web: www.airports.org.

## Getting to Work in the City
**Commuting characteristics for the 15 largest U.S. cities by population, 2000**

| 2000 rank | City of residence | Total workers 16 years and over | Means of transportation (%) | | | | | Worked at home | Average travel time to work (min.) |
|---|---|---|---|---|---|---|---|---|---|
| | | | Drove alone | Carpool | Public transit | Walked | Other means | | |
| 1. | New York, N.Y. | 3,332,698 | 24.1% | 6.4% | 56.3% | 9.3% | 1.4% | 2.5% | 39.0 |
| 2. | Los Angeles, Calif. | 1,592,463 | 67.1 | 14.9 | 9.5 | 2.9 | 1.6 | 4.0 | 28.1 |
| 3. | Chicago, Ill. | 1,252,949 | 50.5 | 12.8 | 27.6 | 5.6 | 0.9 | 2.5 | 33.1 |
| 4. | Houston, Tex. | 919,762 | 72.9 | 14.7 | 6.0 | 2.6 | 1.2 | 2.6 | 25.9 |
| 5. | Philadelphia, Pa. | 587,156 | 47.6 | 10.4 | 28.0 | 10.4 | 1.7 | 1.9 | 29.2 |
| 6. | Phoenix, Ariz. | 589,860 | 71.9 | 17.0 | 3.6 | 1.9 | 2.5 | 3.2 | 24.7 |
| 7. | San Diego, Calif. | 579,615 | 78.5 | 10.4 | 4.6 | 2.3 | 1.2 | 2.9 | 22.6 |
| 8. | Dallas, Tex. | 560,913 | 73.4 | 14.5 | 5.1 | 2.2 | 2.3 | 2.5 | 25.2 |
| 9. | San Antonio, Tex. | 490,076 | 78.7 | 13.9 | 3.6 | 1.6 | 0.9 | 1.4 | 21.5 |
| 10. | Detroit, Mich. | 317,179 | 76.4 | 12.8 | 6.2 | 2.3 | 1.2 | 1.0 | 24.2 |
| 11. | San Jose, Calif. | 450,093 | 73.0 | 16.9 | 4.9 | 1.7 | 0.8 | 2.7 | 26.4 |
| 12. | Indianapolis, Ind. | 407,377 | 81.9 | 10.2 | 2.2 | 2.5 | 1.5 | 1.7 | 21.6 |
| 13. | San Francisco, Calif. | 419,601 | 41.1 | 9.3 | 32.1 | 8.8 | 3.9 | 4.8 | 29.6 |
| 14. | Jacksonville, Fla. | 350,797 | 81.9 | 11.4 | 1.9 | 1.5 | 1.5 | 1.8 | 22.6 |
| 15. | Columbus, Ohio | 353,192 | 82.5 | 9.3 | 3.0 | 2.0 | 0.7 | 2.5 | 20.7 |
| | Total for U.S. | 127,448,586 | 76.3 | 11.2 | 5.2 | 2.7 | 1.4 | 3.2 | 24.3 |

NOTES: ... available. Percentages may not add up to 100%, due to rounding. Source: U.S. Bureau of the Census. Web: www.census.gov.

## World's Largest Subway Systems
**(by ridership)**

| City | Date system completed | Number of riders (year) | Length (km) | City | Date system completed | Number of riders (year) | Length (km) |
|---|---|---|---|---|---|---|---|
| Moscow | 1935 | 3.2 bil (1997) | 340 | Paris | 1900 | 1.2 bil (1998) | 211 |
| Tokyo | 1927 | 2.6 bil (1997/98) | 281+ | Osaka | 1933 | 957 mil (1997) | 114 |
| Seoul | 1974 | 1.4 bil (1993) | 278+ | London | 1863 | 866 mil (1999) | 415 |
| Mexico City | 1969 | 1.4 bil (1996) | 202 | Hong Kong | 1979 | 790 mil (1999) | 82 |
| New York City | 1904 | 1.3 bil (2001) | 371 | St. Petersburg | 1955 | 721 mil (1996) | 110 |

*Sources: Jane's Urban Transport Systems,* 2002–2003 edition, and individual subway websites.

# The U.S. Interstate System

At the beginning of the 20th century, an uninterrupted system of nationwide highways did not exist. Beginning in 1811, a National Road had been constructed between Cumberland in western Maryland and Vandalia, the then capital of Illinois, to facilitate immigration to the frontier; however, this road fell into disrepair. It wasn't until the late 1930s that interest in a transcontinental system of highways began to grow. President Franklin Roosevelt urged the construction of a network of highways as a way to provide jobs for people out of work.

## Congress Acts

The Federal-Aid Highway Act of 1938 was the first serious attempt to develop a national roadway system. The legislation directed the Bureau of Public Roads to study the feasibility of a toll-financed system of three east-west and three north-south superhighways. From this study officials determined that the amount of transcontinental traffic was insufficient to support a network of toll highways. Instead they recommended a 43,000-kilometer (26,700-mile) network of nontoll highways.

Congress passed further legislation in the form of the Federal-Aid Highway Act of 1944. This act expanded the network to 65,000 km (40,391 mi) and charged state highway agencies and the Department of Defense with planning nationwide routes that would directly connect the country's major cities and industrial centers. However, no specific funds were authorized for construction, and progress was slow.

## Eisenhower Makes It a Reality

Dwight Eisenhower had long realized the importance of highways, even before he became president in 1953. In 1919 as a young lieutenant colonel in the army he had accompanied the first transcontinental military motor convoy from Washington, DC, to San Francisco. Like most American motorists, the soldiers traveled on dirt roads and crumbling bridges; it took about two months for them to cross the country. And years later, during World War II, he

observed the advantages of the German autobahn network, which made for safe and efficient mobility.

The Federal-Aid Highway Act of 1954 set aside $175 million for the construction of an interstate highway system. However, even more money was needed for the system that Eisenhower envisioned, and he continued to press for funds. Two years later, the expanded Federal-Aid Highway Act of 1956 authorized a budget of $25 billion, of which the federal share was to be 90%.

## A Standard Design

The legislation of 1956 also provided for an extended network of 66,000 km (41,012 mi) and nationwide design standards, including:
- a minimum of two lanes in each direction
- lanes that were 12 ft in width
- a 10-foot right paved shoulder
- design speeds of 50–70 mph

Further legislation over the years continued to expand the total length of the system, which now stretches for more than 74,600 km (46,380 mi). In 1990, in recognition of President Eisenhower's pivotal role in building the national system of interstate highways, President George Bush signed legislation officially renaming it the Dwight D. Eisenhower System of Interstate and Defense Highways.

## Naming the Interstates

The procedure for naming the highways is systematic. Major routes are designated by single- or two-digit numbers. If a route runs north-south, it is given an odd number, and if a route runs east-west, an even number. For north-south routes, numbering conventions begin in the west. Thus I-5 runs north and south along the West Coast, while I-95 runs north and south along the East Coast. For east-west routes, numbers begin in the south.

Major routes usually traverse cities and are the shortest and most direct line of travel. Connecting interstate routes that travel around a city carry three-digit numbers.

## Automobile Registrations for Selected Countries

### Number of Automobiles

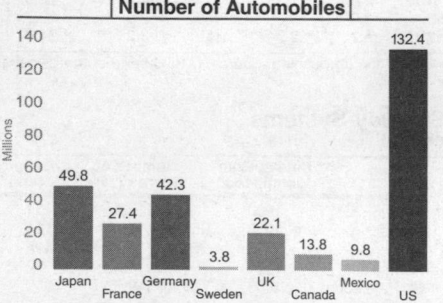

| Japan | France | Germany | Sweden | UK | Canada | Mexico | US |
|---|---|---|---|---|---|---|---|
| 49.8 | 27.4 | 42.3 | 3.8 | 22.1 | 13.8 | 9.8 | 132.4 |

### Automobiles per 1,000 Persons

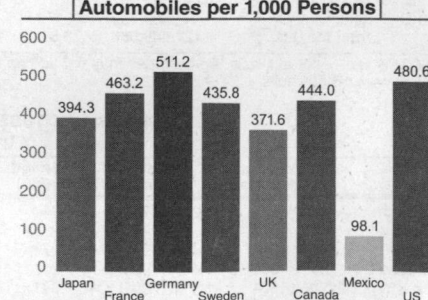

| Japan | France | Germany | Sweden | UK | Canada | Mexico | US |
|---|---|---|---|---|---|---|---|
| 394.3 | 463.2 | 511.2 | 435.8 | 371.6 | 444.0 | 98.1 | 480.6 |

NOTE: Figures for Japan, the United Kingdom, and Canada are for 1998; the rest are for 1999. *Source:* Office of Highway Policy Information, Federal Highway Administration, *Highway Statistics 2000.* Web: www.fhwa.dot.gov.

# Driving Laws, 2002

Currently all states plus DC have child safety seat laws and enforce a drinking age of 21. A national speed limit of 55 mph was imposed in 1974, and in 1987 it was modified to allow 65-mile-per-hour speeds on some rural freeways. The federal law was entirely repealed in 1995, giving states the right to set their own limits. Montana, which had been the only state with no speed limit, imposed a 75-mile-an-hour limit in 1999. As of Jan. 2000, graduated licensing laws were in effect in 40 states, 30 of which prohibit young drivers from driving during high-risk nighttime and early morning hours.

| State | Age for driver's license[1] | License revocation for alcohol offenses since | Blood alcohol concentration limit[2] | Alcohol ignition interlock device[3] | Mandatory belt-use law seating positions | Motorcycle helmet law[4] | Maximum allowable speed limit 1995[5] | 1999 |
|---|---|---|---|---|---|---|---|---|
| Alabama | 17 | 1996 | 0.08 | no | front | yes | 65 | 70 |
| Alaska | 16 | 1983 | 0.10 | yes | all | 18[6] | — | 65 |
| Arizona | 18 | 1992 | 0.10 | yes | front | 18 | 55 | 75 |
| Arkansas | 16 | 1995 | 0.10 | yes | front | 21 | 65 | 70 |
| California | 17 | 1989 | 0.08 | yes | all | yes | 55 | 70 |
| Colorado | 17 | 1983 | 0.10 | yes | front | no | 65 | 75 |
| Connecticut | 16 + 6 mo. | 1990 | 0.10 | no | front[7] | 18 | 55 | 65 |
| Delaware | 16 + 10 mo. | yes | 0.10 | yes | front | 19[8] | — | 65 |
| DC | 18 | yes | 0.08 | no | all | yes | — | — |
| Florida | 18 | 1990 | 0.08 | yes | front | yes | 65 | 70 |
| Georgia | 18 | 1995 | 0.10 | yes | front[7] | yes | 55 | 70 |
| Hawaii | 15 + 3 mo. | 1990 | 0.08 | no | front | 18 | — | 55 |
| Idaho | 16 | 1994 | 0.08 | yes | front | 18 | 65 | 75 |
| Illinois | 17 | 1986 | 0.08 | yes | front | no | 65 | 65 |
| Indiana | 18 | yes | 0.10 | yes | front | 18 | 65 | 65 |
| Iowa | 17 | 1982 | 0.10 | yes | front | no | 55 | 65 |
| Kansas | 16 | 1988 | 0.08 | yes | front | 18 | 65 | 70 |
| Kentucky | 18 | no | 0.10 | no | all | 21[9, 10, 11] | 65 | 65 |
| Louisiana | 17 | 1984 | 0.10 | yes | front[7] | 18[9] | 65 | 70 |
| Maine | 16 | 1984 | 0.08 | yes | all | 15 | 65 | 65 |
| Maryland | 18 | 1989 | 0.10 | yes | front[7] | yes | 55 | 65 |
| Massachusetts | 18 | 1994 | 0.08 | no | all | yes | 55 | 65 |
| Michigan | 17 | no | 0.10 | yes | front[7] | yes | 55 | 70 |
| Minnesota | 16 | 1976 | 0.10 | no | front[7] | 18 | 65 | 70 |
| Mississippi | 16 | 1983 | 0.10 | no | front | yes | 65 | 70 |
| Missouri | 16 | 1987 | 0.10 | yes | front[7] | yes | 70 | 70 |
| Montana | 15 | no | 0.10 | yes | all | 18 | 65 | 75 |
| Nebraska | 18 | 1993 | 0.10 | yes | front[7] | yes | 65 | 75 |
| Nevada | 16 | 1983 | 0.10 | yes | all | yes | 55 | 75 |
| New Hampshire | 18 | 1994 | 0.08 | no | — | 18 | 65 | 65 |
| New Jersey | 18 | no | 0.10 | yes | front | yes | — | 65 |
| New Mexico | 16 + 6 mo. | 1984 | 0.08 | yes | front | 18 | 65 | 75 |
| New York | 17 | 1994 | 0.10 | yes | front[7] | yes | 55 | 65 |
| North Carolina | 16 + 6 mo. | 1983 | 0.08 | yes | front[7] | yes | 55 | 70 |
| North Dakota | 18 | 1983 | 0.10 | yes | front | 18 | 65 | 70 |
| Ohio | 17 | 1993 | 0.10 | yes | front | 18[11] | 65 | 65 |
| Oklahoma | 16 | 1983 | 0.10 | yes | front | 18 | 65 | 75 |
| Oregon | 18 | 1983 | 0.08 | yes | all | yes | 65 | 65 |
| Pennsylvania | 18 | no | 0.10 | no | front | yes | 55 | 65 |
| Rhode Island | 17 + 6 mo. | no | 0.10 | yes | all | 21[6, 11] | 55 | 65 |
| South Carolina | 16 + 3 mo. | 1998 | 0.10 | no | front[7] | 21 | 65 | 70 |
| South Dakota | 16 | no | 0.10 | no | front | 18 | 65 | 75 |
| Tennessee | 16 | no | 0.10 | yes | front[7] | yes | 65 | 70 |
| Texas | 16 | 1995 | 0.08 | yes | front[7] | 21[8] | 65 | 70 |
| Utah | 16 | 1983 | 0.08 | yes | all | 18 | 55 | 75 |
| Vermont | 18 | 1969 | 0.08 | no | all | yes | 65 | 65 |
| Virginia | 17 | 1995 | 0.08 | yes | front | yes | 65 | 65 |
| Washington | 18 | 1998 | 0.08 | yes | all | yes | 55 | 70 |
| West Virginia | 17 | 1981 | 0.10 | yes | front[7] | yes | 65 | 70 |
| Wisconsin | 19 | 1988 | 0.10[12] | yes | front | 18[10] | 65 | 65 |
| Wyoming | 16 | 1973 | 0.10 | yes | front | 18 | 65 | 75 |

NOTES: A driver's license is required in every state. 1. Refers to minimum age for unrestricted driver's license. 2. Blood alcohol concentration that constitutes the threshold of legal intoxication. 3. Legislation for instruments designed to prevent drivers from starting their cars when breath alcohol content is at or above a set point. 4. Presence of law, or age below which riders are required to wear helmet. 5. In 1995, Congress repealed the national 55-miles-per-hour speed limit. 6. All passengers required to wear helmet. 7. Required for certain ages at all seating positions. 8. Helmet must also be carried on the motorcycle, whether or not it is worn, for persons 19 and older. 9. Helmet optional for those over listed age if they have proper insurance. 10. Helmets must be worn by cyclists holding learners' permits. 11. First-year novices required to wear helmet. 12. 0.08 after second DUI conviction. Sources: National Safety Council, Injury Facts, 2000 Edition; Web: www.nsc.org. U.S. Dept. of Transportation, National Highway Traffic Safety Administration, Traffic Safety Facts, 1999; Web: www.nhtsa.dot.gov. Insurance Institute for Highway Safety. Web: www.hwysafety.org.

## Traffic Congestion in U.S. Cities, 2000

| Urban area | Travel Rate Index[1] | | Annual delay per person | | Annual congestion cost | | | |
| | TRI | Rank | Hours | Rank | Total (millions) | Rank | Per person | Rank |
|---|---|---|---|---|---|---|---|---|
| Los Angeles, Calif. | 1.90 | 1 | 62 | 1 | $14,635 | 1 | $1,155 | 1 |
| San Francisco-Oakland, Calif. | 1.59 | 2 | 41 | 2 | 3,210 | 4 | 795 | 2 |
| Chicago, Ill.-Northwestern Ind. | 1.47 | 3 | 27 | 17 | 4,095 | 3 | 505 | 17 |
| Washington, D.C.-Md.-Va. | 1.46 | 4 | 35 | 5 | 2,325 | 6 | 655 | 6 |
| Seattle-Everett, Wash. | 1.45 | 5 | 34 | 7 | 1,315 | 14 | 660 | 5 |
| Miami-Hialeah, Fla. | 1.45 | 5 | 33 | 8 | 1,365 | 11 | 600 | 10 |
| Boston, Mass. | 1.45 | 5 | 28 | 13 | 1,595 | 10 | 525 | 14 |
| San Jose, Calif. | 1.42 | 8 | 33 | 8 | 1,065 | 18 | 635 | 8 |
| Denver, Colo. | 1.42 | 8 | 35 | 5 | 1,225 | 16 | 640 | 7 |
| New York, N.Y.-Northeastern N.J. | 1.41 | 10 | 23 | 21 | 7,660 | 2 | 450 | 21 |
| Phoenix, Ariz. | 1.40 | 11 | 28 | 13 | 1,360 | 12 | 525 | 14 |
| Portland-Vancouver, Ore.-Wash. | 1.40 | 11 | 23 | 21 | 670 | 25 | 445 | 22 |
| Houston, Tex. | 1.38 | 13 | 36 | 4 | 2,285 | 7 | 675 | 4 |
| Minneapolis-St. Paul, Minn. | 1.38 | 13 | 26 | 18 | 1,220 | 17 | 495 | 18 |
| Ft. Lauderdale-Hollywood-Pompano Bch., Fla. | 1.37 | 15 | 28 | 13 | 810 | 20 | 520 | 16 |
| San Diego, Calif. | 1.37 | 15 | 24 | 20 | 1,295 | 15 | 480 | 19 |
| Atlanta, Ga. | 1.36 | 17 | 33 | 8 | 1,885 | 9 | 635 | 8 |
| Las Vegas, Nev. | 1.35 | 18 | 18 | 36 | 415 | 29 | 345 | 36 |
| San Bernardino-Riverside, Calif. | 1.34 | 19 | 30 | 12 | 810 | 20 | 575 | 11 |
| Detroit, Mich. | 1.34 | 19 | 25 | 19 | 1,905 | 8 | 475 | 20 |

NOTE: Study conducted in 75 urbanized areas. 1. The Travel Rate Index is defined as the travel rate (in minutes per mile) during the peak period divided by the rate in the off-peak. A TRI of 1.30 indicates the average peak trip takes 30% longer than in uncongested conditions—a 20-minute trip becomes a 26-minute trip. *Source:* Texas Transportation Institute, the Texas A&M University System. *The 2002 Urban Mobility Report,* David Schrank and Tim Lomax. Web: http://mobility.tamu.edu.

## Improper Driving as a Factor in Accidents

| Kind of improper driving | Fatal accidents | | | Injury accidents | | | All accidents | | |
| | 2000 | 1999 | 1995 | 2000 | 1999 | 1995 | 2000 | 1999 | 1995 |
|---|---|---|---|---|---|---|---|---|---|
| **Improper driving** | **61.6%** | **72.6%** | **68.1%** | **60.3%** | **67.2%** | **73.5%** | **57.8%** | **62.2%** | **75.5%** |
| Speed too fast or unsafe | 23.7 | 23.0 | 19.8 | 16.3 | 13.0 | 13.9 | 13.6 | 10.6 | 14.0 |
| Right of way | 18.6 | 20.1 | 15.2 | 19.9 | 25.8 | 25.5 | 20.1 | 22.9 | 22.9 |
| Failed to yield | 10.1 | 10.8 | 10.2 | 15.0 | 19.2 | 18.1 | 12.7 | 13.8 | 17.0 |
| Disregarded signal | 4.6 | 4.7 | 3.0 | 3.6 | 4.9 | 5.0 | 5.3 | 5.9 | 4.0 |
| Passed stop sign | 3.8 | 4.6 | 2.2 | 1.3 | 1.7 | 2.4 | 2.2 | 3.2 | 1.9 |
| Drove left of center | 8.2 | 9.6 | 9.1 | 1.1 | 1.7 | 2.4 | 1.0 | 1.3 | 2.2 |
| Made improper turn | 0.7 | 1.2 | 2.3 | 2.0 | 2.4 | 2.8 | 2.4 | 3.0 | 4.2 |
| Improper overtaking | 0.9 | 1.1 | 1.5 | 0.6 | 0.9 | 1.3 | 0.9 | 1.2 | 1.5 |
| Followed too closely | 0.5 | 0.5 | 0.5 | 4.3 | 3.4 | 7.0 | 5.7 | 6.3 | 7.2 |
| Other improper driving | 9.0 | 17.1 | 19.7 | 16.1 | 20.3 | 20.7 | 14.1 | 16.9 | 23.6 |
| **No improper driving stated** | **38.4** | **27.4** | **31.9** | **39.7** | **32.8** | **26.5** | **42.2** | **37.8** | **24.5** |
| **Total** | **100.0%** | **100.0%** | **100.0%** | **100.0%** | **100.0%** | **100.0%** | **100.0%** | **100.0%** | **100.0%** |

NOTE: Based on reports from 7 state traffic authorities. *Source:* National Safety Council, *Injury Facts, 2001 Edition.* Web: www.nsc.org.

## Alcohol-Related Traffic Fatalities on Holidays, 2000

| Holiday 2000 | Total traffic fatalities | Total fatalities alcohol-related | Percent fatalities alcohol-related | Time period monitored |
|---|---|---|---|---|
| New Year's Eve (1999) | 149 | 75 | 50.3% | 12/31/99 |
| New Year's Day | 163 | 114 | 69.6 | 1/1/00 |
| New Year's Holiday | 354 | 216 | 61.1 | 6:00 p.m. 12/31/99–5:59 a.m. 1/3/00 |
| Super Bowl Sunday | 105 | 62 | 59.1 | 6:00 p.m. 1/30/00–5:59 a.m. 1/31/00 |
| St. Patrick's Day | 151 | 70 | 46.4 | 6 p.m. 3/17/00–5:59 a.m. 3/18/00 |
| Memorial Day | 348 | 127 | 36.5 | 6 p.m. 5/29/00–5:59 a.m. 6/2/00 |
| Fourth of July | 212 | 98 | 46.2 | 6 p.m. 7/3/00–5:59 a.m. 7/5/00 |
| Labor Day weekend | 529 | 275 | 52.0 | 6 p.m. 9/1/00–5:59 a.m. 9/5/00 |
| Halloween | 201 | 66 | 32.8 | 10/31/00–11/1/00 |
| Thanksgiving | 503 | 257 | 51.2 | 6 p.m. 11/22/00–5:59 a.m. 11/27/00 |
| Thanksgiving–New Year's | 4,398 | 1,708 | 38.8 | 11/22/00–12/31/00 |
| Christmas | 439 | 221 | 50.4 | 6 p.m. 12/22/00–5:59 a.m. 12/26/00 |
| New Year's Eve (2000) | 81 | 32 | 40.0 | 12/31/00 |

*Source:* Mothers Against Drunk Driving (MADD).

## Fatalities by Transportation Mode, 1970–1999

| Mode | 1970 | 1980 | 1990 | 1998 | 1999[1] | Mode | 1970 | 1980 | 1990 | 1998 | 1999[1] |
|---|---|---|---|---|---|---|---|---|---|---|---|
| Passenger car | n.a. | 27,449 | 24,092 | 21,194 | 20,818 | Railroad[2] | 785 | 584 | 599 | 577 | 530 |
| Light truck | n.a. | n.a. | n.a. | 10,705 | 11,243 | Heavy rail transit[3] | n.a. | n.a. | 339 | 286 | 299 |
| Motorcycle | 2,280 | 5,144 | 3,244 | 2,294 | 2,472 | Bus[4] | n.a. | 46 | 32 | 38 | 58 |
| Large truck | n.a. | n.a. | n.a. | 742 | 758 | Waterborne | | | | | |
| Large air carrier | 146 | 1 | 39 | 1 | 12 |   Vessel casualties | 178 | 206 | 85 | 59 | 44 |
| Commuter air | n.a. | 37 | 7 | 0 | 12 |   Nonvessel | 420 | 281 | 101 | 76 | 67 |
| On-demand air taxi | n.a. | 105 | 51 | 45 | 38 |   casualties | | | | | |
| General aviation | 1,310 | 1,239 | 767 | 624 | 631 | Recreational boating | 1,418 | 1,360 | 865 | 815 | 734 |

NOTES: n.a. = not available. 1. Preliminary data. 2 Includes fatalities from nontrain incidents, as well as train incidents and accidents. Also includes train occupants and nonoccupants, except motor vehicle occupants at grade crossings. 3. Subway. 4. School, intercity, and transit. *Source:* U.S. Dept. of Transportation, Bureau of Transportation Statistics, *National Transportation Statistics, 2000.*

## Most Popular Car Colors, 1999–2001

### (percentage of vehicles manufactured during 2001 model year in North America)

| Luxury (2000 rank) | 2001 | 2000 | 1999 | Sport compact (2000 rank) | 2001 | 2000 | 1999 |
|---|---|---|---|---|---|---|---|
| 1. Silver (2) | 18.4% | 17.2% | 15.8% | 1. Silver (1) | 25.4% | 22.3% | 16.2% |
| 2. Med. Gray (7) | 17.3 | 6.6 | 8.3 | 2. Black (2) | 14.5 | 14.4 | 14.7 |
| 3. White Pearl (n.a.) | 14.8 | n.a. | n.a. | 3. Med./Dk. Blue (8) | 11.3 | 5.0 | 8.5 |
| 4. Black (3) | 11.1 | 10.8 | 9.4 | 4. White (3) | 9.8 | 11.4 | 14.0 |
| 5. Med./Dk. Blue (6) | 9.4 | 7.1 | 4.9 | 5. Med. Red (6) | 7.4 | 8.3 | 7.0 |
| 6. White (5) | 9.0 | 7.1 | 10.3 | 6. Med./Dk. Green (5) | 6.7 | 9.7 | 12.4 |
| 7. Med. Red (8) | 6.0 | 6.1 | 6.0 | 7. Lt. Brown (4) | 6.2 | 9.9 | 8.5 |
| 8. Gold (9) | 5.4 | 5.3 | 7.0 | 8. Bright Red (7) | 5.3 | 7.5 | 7.5 |
| 9. Med./Dk. Green (10) | 3.1 | 4.3 | 6.1 | 9. Dk. Red (n.a.) | 2.6 | n.a. | n.a. |
| 10. Med./Dk. Red (n.a.) | 2.2 | n.a. | n.a. | 10. Med./Dk. Gray (n.a.) | 2.0 | n.a. | n.a. |

| Full/Intermediate (2000 rank) | 2001 | 2000 | 1999 | SUV/Truck/Van (2000 rank) | 2001 | 2000 | 1999 |
|---|---|---|---|---|---|---|---|
| 1. Silver (1) | 24.9% | 21.5% | 14.1% | 1. White (1) | 19.6% | 23.1% | 26.2% |
| 2. White (2) | 14.1 | 13.0 | 15.4 | 2. Silver (2) | 17.8 | 14.1 | 7.7 |
| 3. Med./Dk. Green (4) | 10.0 | 10.7 | 13.9 | 3. Black (4) | 11.2 | 10.6 | 11.2 |
| 4. Black (3) | 9.8 | 11.5 | 11.7 | 4. Med./Dk. Blue (3) | 10.4 | 11.1 | 8.4 |
| 5. Med./Dk. Blue (6) | 8.9 | 7.0 | 6.4 | 5. Med. Red (6) | 8.4 | 6.2 | 7.4 |
| 6. Lt. Brown (5) | 8.1 | 8.5 | 14.0 | 6. Med./Dk. Green (5) | 7.4 | 8.3 | 11.0 |
| 7. Gold (10) | 7.2 | 3.5 | 1.8 | 7. Bright Red (7) | 5.3 | 5.4 | 6.1 |
| 8. Dk. Red (n.a.) | 4.9 | n.a. | n.a. | 8. Lt. Brown (n.a.) | 4.6 | n.a. | n.a. |
| 9. Med. Red (7) | 4.8 | 6.9 | 5.7 | 9. Gold (8) | 3.8 | 4.1 | n.a. |
| 10. Bright Red (9) | 3.1 | 3.8 | 4.9 | 10. Med/Dk. Gray (n.a.) | 2.5 | n.a. | n.a. |

*See also* tables on top-selling cars and trucks, p. 656. *Source:* DuPont Herberts Automotive Systems, Troy, Mich. 2001 DuPont Automotive Color Popularity Survey Results. Web: www.dupont.com.

## Two Centuries of Railroading

*Source:* Association of American Railroads. Web: www.aar.org.

**1797** The steam locomotive is invented in England.

**1823** The first public railway in the world opens in England.

**1827** The first railroad in North America—the Baltimore & Ohio—is chartered by Baltimore merchants.

**1830** The first regularly scheduled steam-powered rail passenger service in the U.S. begins operation in South Carolina, utilizing the U.S. built locomotive *The Best Friend of Charleston.*

**1833** Andrew Jackson travels from Baltimore to Ellicott's Mills, becoming the first sitting U.S. president to ride the rails.

**1838** Five of the six New England states have rail service, as do such frontier states as Kentucky and Indiana.

**1840** More than 2,800 miles of track are in operation.

**1850** More than 9,000 miles of track are in operation in the U.S., as much as in the rest of the world combined.

**1860** More than 30,000 miles of track are in operation in the U.S.

**1862** President Abraham Lincoln signs the Pacific Railroad Act for the construction of the transcontinental railroad that will ultimately link California with the rest of the nation.

**1865** The "golden age" of railroads begins. For nearly half a century, no other mode of transportation challenges railroads. During these years, the rail network grows from 35,000 to a peak of 254,000 miles in 1916.

**1869** On May 10, at Promontory, in the Utah Territory, the "Golden Spike" joins the Union Pacific and Central Pacific railroads, marking completion of the first transcontinental railroad.

**1917** The federal government seizes control of the railroads for the duration of World War I.

**1900–1940** By the eve of World War II, automobiles, large buses, trucks, planes, and pipelines—supported by government subsidies and less burdened by regulation than railroads—have become full-fledged competitors to railroads.

**1945–1970** Railroads enter the postwar era with a new sense of optimism that leads them to invest billions of dollars in new locomotives, freight equipment, and passenger trains. That investment would see retirement of the last steam locomotive by the late 1950s in favor of diesel engines. In spite of this modernization, the decline in rail market share that began before the war resumes.

**1970–1975**   Burdened by regulation and faced with subsidized competition, nine Class I railroads, representing almost one-quarter of the industry's trackage, file for bankruptcy protection.

**1970**   The Rail Passenger Service Act creates Amtrak to take over intercity rail passenger service.

**1971**   Amtrak officially begins service on May 1.

**1980**   The Staggers Rail Act reduces the Interstate Commerce Commission's regulatory jurisdiction over railroads and sparks competition that stimulates advances in technology and a restructuring of the industry.

**1987**   Conrail is privatized in what—at that time—was the largest share offering in U.S. history as investors pay $1.9 billion to buy shares in the railroad.

**1996**   After 108 years, the Interstate Commerce Commission is disbanded and replaced by the Surface Transportation Board, which assumes oversight responsibility for the railroads.

**2000**   U.S. freight railroads move 1.47 trillion ton-miles of freight, more than ever before, setting new safety records in the process.

## Railroad Ridership, 1989–2001

### (millions)

| | 1989 | 1990 | 1991 | 1992 | 1993 | 1994 | 1995 | 1996 | 1997 | 1998 | 1999 | 2000 | 2001 |
|---|---|---|---|---|---|---|---|---|---|---|---|---|---|
| Amtrak system | 21.4 | 22.2 | 22.0 | 21.3 | 22.1 | 21.2 | 20.7 | 19.7 | 20.2 | 21.1 | 21.5 | 22.5 | 23.5 |
| Northeast Corridor | 11.1 | 11.2 | 10.9 | 10.1 | 10.3 | 11.7 | 11.6 | 11.0 | 11.1 | 11.9 | 12.3 | 12.9 | 13.5 |
| Intercity + West | 10.3 | 11.0 | 11.1 | 11.2 | 11.8 | 9.4 | 9.1 | 8.7 | 9.1 | 9.2 | 9.2 | 9.6 | 10.0 |
| Commuter trains[1] | 17.4 | 18.0 | 18.1 | 20.3 | 32.9 | 39.5 | 42.2 | 45.9 | 48.5 | 54.0 | 58.3 | 61.6 | n.a. |
| Total | 38.8 | 40.2 | 40.1 | 41.6 | 55.0 | 60.7 | 62.9 | 65.6 | 68.7 | 75.1 | 79.8 | 84.1 | n.a. |

NOTE: n.a. = not available. 1. Includes only commuter trains run by Amtrak under contract. *Source:* National Assoc. of Railroad Passengers. Based on Amtrak annual reports. Web: www.narprail.org.

## Ten Famous Trains

### Trans-Siberian Express

Traveling between Moscow and Vladivostok, the *Trans-Siberian Express* makes the longest regular train trip in the world, covering 5,778 mi and making 91 stops over the course of nine days. During the Cold War, Westerners could travel only in compartments, where they were subject to Stalinist propaganda played on loudspeakers.

### Blue Train

The *Blue Train* has run between Cape Town and Pretoria, South Africa, since 1939 and derives its name from its blue locomotives, railroad cars, and leather seats. It is still considered one of the most luxurious trains running, having been upgraded in 1997 to include televisions and phones in all of its suites.

### Indian Pacific

Connecting the east and west coasts of Australia, the *Indian Pacific* runs from Sydney to Perth in three days, over a distance of 2,461 mi. This route has the world's longest stretch of straight track, which lasts for 297 mi.

### Super Chief

Originally operated by the Santa Fe Railroad beginning in 1936, the *Super Chief* ran from Chicago to Los Angeles. It was considered one of the best long-distance trains in the U.S. and was renowned for its gourmet food and Hollywood clientele. Amtrak currently operates a version of this train.

### TGV

The French *TGV* (train à grande vitesse, or high speed train) is an electric train that runs between Paris and Lyon, regularly traveling at an average speed of 132 mph, with top speeds as high as 186 mph. A modified *TGV* set a world speed record in 1990 when it hit 320 mph in trial runs.

### Orient Express

In 1883 the *Orient Express* began service from Paris to Istanbul, crossing six countries. The train was famous for its five-course French meals and for its passengers, who were often diplomats, royalty, or government couriers.

### 20th Century Limited

The *20th Century Limited* debuted in 1902 as the New York Central's luxury train, operating between New York and Chicago. It traveled the smooth "water level route" alongside the Hudson River and the shores of Lake Erie. The railroad would roll out a crimson carpet to welcome passengers to the train, giving rise to the phrase the "red carpet treatment."

### The Flying Scotsman

Running between King's Cross station in London and Edinburgh, Scotland, the *Flying Scotsman* was a luxury express train full of amenities. It featured a hairdressing salon, a Louis the XVI–style restaurant and bar, and, for a short time, a cinema coach.

### Peruvian Central Railway

The highest railway in the world, the Peruvian Central Railway is an engineering marvel, climbing 13,000 ft on its trip from La Oroya to Lima, Peru. The railroad, which features 66 tunnels and 59 bridges, zigzags across valleys in order to minimize the steepness of its climb. There is an onboard doctor who administers oxygen to passengers who get altitude sickness.

### Bullet Train

The Japanese *Shinkansen,* or *Bullet Train,* runs at speeds of more than 100 mph over special tracks with minimal curves. In 1997, a newer version of the *Bullet Train* became the fastest scheduled train in the world, regularly reaching speeds of up to 186 mph.

# PEOPLE

Many public figures not listed here may be found elsewhere in the almanac.

| | |
|---|---|
| U.S. Presidents | British Prime Ministers |
| U.S. Vice Presidents | Rulers of England |
| Families of U.S. Presidents | Rulers of France |
| U.S. Governors | Rulers of Judah and Israel |
| U.S. Congress | Rulers of Prussia |
| U.S. Supreme Court Justices | Rulers of Russia |
| U.S. Government Officials | Sports Personalities |

Names in parentheses indicate a person's original name or nickname. Locations in parentheses are the present-day name of the birthplace. Dates of birth appear as month/day/year. **Boldface** years in parentheses are dates of **(birth–death).**

Information has been gathered from many sources, including the individuals themselves. However, the almanac cannot guarantee the accuracy of every item.

# A

Aalto, Alvar (architect); Kuortane, Finland **(1898–1976)**
Abbado, Claudio (orchestra conductor); Milan, Italy, 6/26/33
Abbott, Bud (William Abbott) (comedian); Asbury Park, N.J. **(1898–1974)**
Abbott, George (stage producer); Forestville, N.Y. **(1887–1995)**
Abelard, Peter (theologian); nr. Nantes, France **(1079–1142)**
Abernathy, Ralph (civil rights leader); Linden, Ala. **(1926–1990)**
Abraham, F(ahrid) Murray (actor); Pittsburgh, 10/24/39
Achebe, Chinua (writer); Ogidi, Nigeria, 11/16/30
Acheson, Dean (statesman); Middletown, Conn. **(1893–1971)**
Acuff, Roy Claxton (musician); nr. Maynardsville, Tenn. **(1903–1992)**
Adams, Abigail (First Lady, writer); Weymouth, Mass. **(1744–1818)**
Adams, Bryan (singer, songwriter); Kingston, Ont., Canada, 11/5/59
Adams, Charles Francis (diplomat); Boston **(1807–1886)**
Adams, Don (actor); New York City, 4/19/26
Adams, Edie (Edie Enke) (actress); Kingston, Pa., 4/16/29
Adams, Franklin Pierce (columnist, author); Chicago **(1881–1960)**
Adams, Gerry (political leader); West Belfast, Northern Ireland, 10/6/48
Adams, Henry Brooks (historian); Boston **(1838–1918)**
Adams, Joey (comedian); New York City **(1911–1999)**
Adams, John (2nd U.S. president); Braintree (Quincy), Mass. **(1735–1826)**
Adams, John Quincy (6th U.S. president); Braintree (Quincy), Mass. **(1767–1848)**
Adams, Maude (Maude Kiskadden) (actress); Salt Lake City **(1872–1953)**
Adams, Samuel (American Revolutionary patriot); Boston **(1722–1803)**
Adams, Scott (cartoonist); Catskill, N.Y., 6/8/57
Adamson, Joy (naturalist, writer); Troppau, Silesia **(1910–1980)**
Addams, Charles (cartoonist); Westfield, N.J. **(1912–1988)**
Addams, Jane (social worker, Nobel laureate); Cedarville, Ill. **(1860–1935)**
Adderley, Julian "Cannonball" (jazz saxophonist); Tampa, Fla. **(1928–1975)**
Ade, George (humorist); Kentland, Ind. **(1866–1944)**
Adenauer, Konrad (statesman); Cologne, Germany **(1876–1967)**
Adler, Alfred (psychoanalyst); Vienna **(1870–1937)**
Adler, Larry (musician); Baltimore **(1914–2001)**
Aeschylus (dramatist); Eleusis, Greece **(525–456 B.C.)**
Aesop (fabulist); Samos?, Greece, fl. c. 500 B.C.
Agnew, Spiro (political figure); Baltimore **(1908–1996)**
Aiello, Danny (actor); New York City, 6/20/33
Aiken, Conrad (poet); Savannah, Ga. **(1889–1973)**
Ailey, Alvin (choreographer); Rogers, Tex. **(1931–1989)**
Akhmatova, Anna (poet); Odessa, Ukraine **(1889–1966)**
Akihito, Tsugunomiya (Emperor of Japan); Tokyo, 12/23/33
Albanese, Licia (operatic soprano); Bari, Italy, 7/22/13
Albee, Edward (playwright); Washington, D.C., 3/12/28
Albers, Josef (painter); Bottrop, Germany **(1888–1976)**
Albert (Edward Albert Heimberger) (actor); Rock Island, Ill., 4/22/08
Albert, Edward (actor); Los Angeles, 2/20/51
Albertson, Jack (actor); Malden, Mass. **(1907–1981)**
Albright, Madeleine (diplomat, U.S. secretary of state); Prague, Czechoslovakia, 5/15/37

Alcott, Louisa May (novelist); Germantown, Pa. **(1832–1888)**
Alda, Alan (actor); New York City, 1/28/36
Alden, John (American Pilgrim); England **(c. 1599–1687)**
Alexander, Jane (Quigley) (actress); Boston, 10/28/39
Alexander, Jason (Jay Scott Greenspan) (actor); Newark, N.J., 9/23/59
Alexander the Great (monarch, conqueror); Pella, Macedonia, Greece **(356–323 B.C.)**
Alger, Horatio (author); Revere, Mass. **(1834–1899)**
Algren, Nelson (novelist); Detroit **(1909–1981)**
Allen, Debbie (dancer-choreographer, actress); Houston, 1/16/50
Allen, Ethan (American Revolutionary soldier); Litchfield, Conn. **(1738–1789)**
Allen, Fred (John Florence Sullivan) (comedian); Cambridge, Mass. **(1894–1956)**
Allen, Gracie (Grace Ethel Cecile Rosalie Allen) (comedienne); San Francisco **(1906–1964)**
Allen, Joan (actress); Rochelle, Ill., 8/20/56
Allen, Mel (Melvin Israel) (sportscaster); Birmingham, Ala. **(1913–1996)**
Allen, Peter (actor, songwriter); Tenterfield, Australia **(1944–1992)**
Allen, Steve (TV entertainer); New York City **(1921–2000)**
Allen, Woody (Allen Stewart Konigsberg) (actor, writer, director); Brooklyn, N.Y., 12/1/35
Allende, Isabel (novelist); Lima, Peru, 8/2/42
Alley, Kirstie (actress); Wichita, Kans., 1/12/55
Allison, Fran (actress); LaPorte City, Iowa **(1908?–1989)**
Allman, Gregg (singer); Nashville, Tenn., 12/8/47
Allyson, June (Ella Geisman) (actress); New York City, 10/7/17
Alonso, Alicia (ballet dancer); Havana, 12/21/21?
Alpert, Herb (band leader); Los Angeles, 3/31/35?
Alsop, Joseph W., Jr. (journalist); Avon, Conn. **(1910–1989)**
Alsop, Stewart (journalist); Avon, Conn. **(1914–1974)**
Alt, Carol (model); Flushing, New York, 12/1/60
Altman, Robert (director); Kansas City, Mo., 2/20/25
Amanpour, Christiane (broadcast journalist); London, 1958
Amati, Nicola (violin maker); Cremona, Italy **(1596–1684)**
Ambler, Eric (suspense writer); London **(1909–1998)**
Ambrose, Stephen (author, historian); Whitewater, Wis., 1936
Ameche, Don (Dominic Amici) (actor); Kenosha, Wis. **(1908–1993)**
Amis, Kingsley (novelist); London **(1922–1995)**
Amis, Martin (novelist); Oxford, England, 8/25/49
Amos, 'n' Andy (radio characters) (Freeman F. Gosden) (radio comedian); Richmond, Va. **(1899–1982)**
Amos, John (actor); Newark, N.J., 12/27/41
Amos, Tori (singer); Newton, N.C., 8/22/63
Amsterdam, Morey (actor); Chicago **(1914–1996)**
Andersen, Hans Christian (author of fairy tales); Odense, Denmark **(1805–1875)**
Anderson, Eddie (Rochester) (actor); Oakland, Calif. **(1905–1977)**
Anderson, Gillian (actress); Chicago, 8/9/68
Anderson, Harry (actor); Newport, R.I., 10/14/52
Anderson, Ib (ballet dancer); Copenhagen, 12/14/54
Anderson, Jack (journalist); Long Beach, Calif., 10/19/22
Anderson, Dame Judith (actress); Adelaide, Australia **(1898–1992)**
Anderson, Lindsay (Gordon) (director); Bangalore, India **(1923–1994)**
Anderson, Loni (actress); St. Paul, Minn., 8/5/45
Anderson, Lynn (singer); Grand Forks, N.D., 9/26/47
Anderson, Marian (contralto); Philadelphia **(1897–1993)**

Anderson, Maxwell (dramatist); Atlantic, Pa. **(1888–1959)**
Anderson Lee, Pamela (Pamela Anderson) (model, actress); Ladysmith, B.C., Canada, 7/1/67
Anderson, Richard Dean (actor); Minneapolis, Minn., 1/23/50
Anderson, Robert (playwright); New York City, 4/28/17
Anderson, Sherwood (novelist); Camden, Ohio **(1876–1941)**
Andress, Ursula (actress); Bern, Switzerland, 3/19/38
Andrews, Julie (Julia Wells) (actress, singer); Walton-on-Thames, England, 10/1/35
Andrews, La Verne (singer); Minneapolis **(1916–1967)**
Andrews, Maxene (singer); Minneapolis **(1918–1995)**
Andrews, Patti (singer); Minneapolis, 2/16/20
Andy (Charles J. Correll) (radio comedian); Peoria, Ill. **(1890–1972)**
Angelico, Fra (Guido di Pietro; Giovanni de Fiesole) (painter); nr. Florence **(c. 1400–1455)**
Angelou, Maya (Marguerite Johnson) (poet, novelist); St. Louis, 4/4/28
Aniston, Jennifer (Jennifer Anistonapoulos) (actress); Sherman Oaks, Calif., 2/11/69
Anka, Paul (singer, composer); Ottawa, Ont., Canada, 7/30/41
Annan, Kofi (diplomat, UN secretary general); Kumasi, Ghana, 4/8/38
Ann-Margret (Ann-Margaret Olsson) (actress); Valsjobyn, Sweden, 4/28/41
Anouilh, Jean (playwright); Bordeaux, France **(1910–1987)**
Anthony, Susan Brownell (woman suffragist); Adams, Mass. **(1820–1906)**
Antonioni, Michelangelo (director); Ferrara, Italy, 9/29/12
Antony, Mark (Marcus Antonius) (statesman); Rome **(c. 83–30 B.C.)**
Anuszkiewicz, Richard (painter); Erie, Pa., 5/23/30
Apple, Fiona (singer); New York City, 4/8/68
Applegate, Christina (actress); Los Angeles, Calif., 11/25/71
Aquinas, St. Thomas (philosopher); nr. Aquino, Italy **(1225–1274)**
Arafat, Yasir (Mohammed Abdel-Raouf Arafat al Qudwa al Husseini) (chairman of the Palestine Liberation Organization); Cairo, Egypt, 8/24/29
Arbuckle, Roscoe "Fatty" (actor, director); Smith Center, Kans. **(1887–1933)**
Archimedes (physicist, mathematician); Syracuse, Sicily **(287–212 B.C.)**
Archipenko, Alexandre (sculptor); Kiev, Ukraine **(1887–1964)**
Arden, Elizabeth (Florence Nightingale Graham) (cosmetics executive); Woodbridge, Canada **(1878–1966)**
Arden, Eve (Eunice Quedens) (actress); Mill Valley, Calif. **(1912–1990)**
Arendt, Hannah (historian); Hanover, Germany **(1906–1975)**
Aristophanes (dramatist); Athens **(c. 448–c. 385 B.C.)**
Aristotle (philosopher); Stagirus, Macedonia **(384–322 B.C.)**
Arkin, Adam (actor); New York City, 8/19/57
Arkin, Alan (actor, director); New York City, 3/26/34
Arledge, Roone (TV executive); Forest Hills, N.Y., 7/8/31
Arlen, Harold (Hyman Arluck) (composer); Buffalo, N.Y. **(1905–1986)**
Armani, Georgio (fashion designer); Piacenza, Italy, 7/11/34
Armstrong, Louis ("Satchmo") (musician); New Orleans **(1900–1971)**
Arnaz, Desi (Desiderio Alberto Araz y de Acha III) (actor, producer); Santiago, Cuba **(1917–1986)**
Arness, James (James Aurness) (actor); Minneapolis, 5/26/23
Arno, Peter (cartoonist); New York City **(1904–1968)**
Arnold, Benedict (American Revolutionary War general, charged with treason); Norwich, Conn. **(1741–1801)**
Arnold, Matthew (poet, critic); Laleham, England **(1822–1888)**
Arp, Jean (sculptor, painter); Strasbourg, France **(1887–1966)**
Arquette, Cliff (actor); Toledo, Ohio **(1905–1974)**
Arquette, Patricia (actress); Chicago, 4/8/68
Arquette, Rosanna (actress); New York City, 8/10/59
Arrau, Claudio (pianist); Chillán, Chile **(1903–1991)**
Arroyo, Martina (soprano); New York City, 2/2/40
Arthur, Bea (Bernice Frankel) (actress); New York City, 5/13/23
Arthur, Chester Alan (21st U.S. president); Fairfield, Vt. **(1829–1886)**
Ashcroft, John (U.S. attorney general); Chicago, Ill., 5/9/42
Ashcroft, Dame Peggy (actress); Croydon, England **(1907–1991)**
Ashkenazy, Vladimir (concert pianist); Nizhni Novgorod, U.S.S.R., 7/6/37
Ashley, Elizabeth (actress); Ocala, Fla., 8/30/39
Ashton, Sir Frederick William Mallandaine (choreographer); Guayaquil, Ecuador **(1904–1988)**
Asimov, Isaac (author); Petrovichi, Russia **(1920–1992)**
Asner, Edward (actor); Kansas City, Mo., 11/15/29
Assante, Armand (actor); New York City, 10/4/49

Astaire, Fred (Frederick Austerlitz) (dancer, actor); Omaha, Neb. **(1899–1987)**
Astin, John (actor, director); Baltimore, 3/30/30
Astor, Brooke (socialite, philanthropist); Portsmouth, N.H., 3/30/1902
Astor, John Jacob (financier); Waldorf, Germany **(1763–1848)**
Astor, Mary (Lucile Langhanke) (actress); Quincy, Ill. **(1906–1987)**
Ataturk, Kemal (Mustafa Kemal) (Turkish soldier, statesman); Salonika, Greece **(1881–1938)**
Atkins, Chet (guitarist); nr. Luttrell, Tenn. **(1924–2001)**
Atkinson, Rowan (actor); Newcastle-Upon-Tyne, England, 1/6/55
Attenborough, Richard (actor, director); Cambridge, England, 8/29/23
Attila (King of Huns); **(406?–453)**
Attucks, Crispus (American Revolutionary patriot); Boston **(c. 1723–1770)**
Auberjonois, Rene (actor); New York City, 6/1/40
Auchincloss, Louis (author); Lawrence, N.Y., 9/27/17
Auden, W(ystan) H(ugh) (poet); York, England **(1907–1973)**
Audubon, John James (naturalist, painter); Haiti **(1785–1851)**
Auer, Leopold (violinist, teacher); Veszprém, Hungary **(1845–1930)**
Augustine, Saint (Aurelius Augustinus) (theologian); Tagaste, Numidia, Algeria **(354–430)**
Augustus (Gaius Octavius) (Roman emperor); Rome **(63 B.C.– A.D. 14)**
Aung San Suu Kyi (human rights activist); Rangoon, Burma, 6/19/45
Austen, Jane (novelist); Steventon, England **(1775–1817)**
Autry, Gene (singer, actor); Tioga, Tex. **(1907–1998)**
Avalon, Frankie (singer); Philadelphia, 9/18/39
Avedon, Richard (photographer); New York City, 5/15/23
Avery, Milton (painter); Altmar, N.Y. **(1893–1965)**
Ax, Emanuel (pianist); Lvov, Ukraine, 6/8/49
Axelrod, George (playwright); New York City, 6/9/22
Ayckbourn, Alan (playwright); London, 4/12/39
Aykroyd, Dan (actor); Ottawa, Ont., Canada, 7/1/52
Ayres, Lew (actor); Minneapolis **(1908–1996)**

#

Bacall, Lauren (Betty Joan Perske) (actress); New York City, 9/16/24
Bach, Carl Phillipp Emanuel (composer); Weimar, Germany **(1714–1788)**
Bach, Johann Sebastian (composer); Eisenach, Germany **(1685–1750)**
Bacharach, Burt (songwriter); Kansas City, Mo., 5/12/29
Backus, Jim (actor); Cleveland **(1913–1989)**
Bacon, Francis (philosopher, essayist); London **(1561–1626)**
Bacon, Francis (painter); Dublin **(1910–1992)**
Bacon, Kevin (actor); Philadelphia, 7/8/58
Bacon, Roger (philosopher, scientist); Ilchester, England **(c. 1214–1294?)**
Badu, Erykah (Erykah Wright) (singer); Dallas, 1971
Baez, Joan (folk singer); Staten Island, N.Y., 1/9/41
Bailey, F. Lee (lawyer); Waltham, Mass., 6/10/33
Bailey, Pearl (singer); Newport News, Va. **(1918–1990)**
Bain, Conrad (actor); Lethbridge, Alba., Canada, 2/4/23
Baio, Scott (actor); Brooklyn, N.Y., 9/22/61
Baird, Bil (William B. Baird) (puppeteer); Grand Island, Neb. **(1904–1987)**
Baker, Anita (singer); Toledo, Ohio, 1958?
Baker, Carroll (actress); Johnstown, Pa., 5/28/31
Baker, Josephine (singer, dancer); St. Louis **(1906–1975)**
Baker, Russell (columnist); Loudoun County, Va., 8/14/25
Balanchine, George (choreographer); St. Petersburg, Russia **(1904–1983)**
Balboa, Vasco Nuñez de (explorer); Jerez de los Caballeros, Spain **(1475–1517)**
Baldwin, Alec (actor); Massapequa, N.Y., 4/3/58
Baldwin, James (novelist); New York City **(1924–1987)**
Bale, Christian (actor); Pembrokeshire, Wales, 1/30/74
Balenciaga, Cristóbal (fashion designer); Guetaria, Spain **(1895–1972)**
Ball, Lucille (Lucille Désirée Ball) (actress, producer); Celoron (nr. Jamestown), N.Y. **(1911–1989)**
Balsam, Martin (actor); Bronx, New York **(1919–1996)**
Balzac, Honoré de (novelist); Tours, France **(1799–1850)**
Bancroft, Anne (Annemarie Italiano) (actress); New York City, 9/17/31
Banderas, Antonio (José Antonio Dominguez Banderas) (actor, model); Málaga, Spain, 8/10/60
Bankhead, Tallulah (actress); Huntsville, Ala. **(1903–1968)**

Banks, Tyra (model); Los Angeles, 12/4/73
Banting, Fredrick Grant (physiologist); Alliston, Ont., Canada (1891–1941)
Bara, Theda (Theodosia Goodman) (actress); Cincinnati (1890–1955)
Barak, Ehud (former Israeli prime minister); Kibbutz Mishmar Hasharon, Israel, 2/12/42
Barbera, Joseph (animator, producer); New York City, 1911
Baraka, Imamu Amiri (LeRoi Jones) (playwright); Newark, N.J., 10/7/34
Baranski, Christine (actress); Buffalo, N.Y., 5/2/52
Barber, Red (Walter Lanier) (sportscaster); Columbus, Miss. (1908–1992)
Barber, Samuel (composer); West Chester, Pa. (1910–1981)
Barbie, Klaus (Nazi, "The Butcher of Lyon"); Bad Godesberg, Germany (1913–1991)
Bardem, Javier (actor); Gran Canaria, Spain, 5/1/69
Bardot, Brigitte (Camille Javal) (actress); Paris, 9/28/34
Barenboim, Daniel (concert pianist, conductor); Buenos Aires, 11/15/42
Barker, Bob (game-show host); Darrington, Wash., 12/12/23
Barkin, Ellen (actress); Bronx, N.Y., 4/16/54
Barnard, Christiaan N. (heart surgeon); Beauford West, South Africa (1922–2001)
Barnum, Phineas Taylor (showman); Bethel, Conn. (1810–1891)
Barrie, Sir James Matthew (author); Kirriemuir, Scotland (1860–1937)
Barry, John (naval officer); County Wexford, Ireland (1745–1803)
Barrymore, Diana (actress); New York City (1921–1960)
Barrymore, Drew (actress); Los Angeles, 2/22/75
Barrymore, Ethel (Ethel Blythe) (actress); Philadelphia (1879–1959)
Barrymore, Georgiana Drew (actress); Philadelphia (1856–1893)
Barrymore, John (John Blythe) (actor); Philadelphia (1882–1942)
Barrymore, Lionel (Lionel Blythe) (actor); Philadelphia (1878–1954)
Barrymore, Maurice (Herbert Blythe) (actor, playwright); Agra, India (1847–1905)
Barth, John (novelist); Cambridge, Md., 5/27/30
Barthelme, Donald (novelist); Philadelphia (1931–1989)
Bartók, Béla (composer); Nagyszentmiklo, Hungary (1881–1945)
Barton, Clara (founder of American Red Cross); Oxford, Mass. (1821–1912)
Baruch, Bernard Mannes (statesman); Camden, S.C. (1870–1965)
Baryshnikov, Mikhail Nikolayevich (ballet dancer, artistic director); Riga, Latvia, 1/27/48
Basie, Count (William Basie) (band leader); Red Bank, N.J. (1904–1984)
Basinger, Kim (actress); Athens, Ga., 12/8/53
Bassett, Angela (actress); New York City, 8/16/58
Bassey, Shirley (singer); Cardiff, Wales, 1/8/37
Batchelor, Clarence Daniel (political cartoonist); Osage City, Kans. (1888–1977)
Bateman, Jason (actor); Rye, N.Y., 1/14/69
Bateman, Justine (actress); Rye, N.Y., 2/19/66
Bates, Alan (actor); Allestree, England, 2/17/34
Bates, Kathy (Kathleen Doyle Bates) (actress); Memphis, Tenn., 6/28/48
Battle, Kathleen (soprano); Portsmouth, Ohio, 8/13/48
Baudelaire, Charles Pierre (poet); Paris (1821–1867)
Baxter, Anne (actress); Michigan City, Ind. (1923–1985)
Baxter, Meredith (actress); Los Angeles, 6/21/47
Beardsley, Aubrey Vincent (illustrator); Brighton, England (1872–1898)
Deaton, Cecil (photographer, designer); London (1904–1980)
Beatty, Clyde (animal trainer); Bainbridge, Ohio (1903–1965)
Beatty, Warren (Henry Warren Beaty) (actor, producer); Richmond Va., 3/30/37
Beaumont, Francis (dramatist); Grace-Dieu, England (1584–1616)
Becket, Thomas à (archbishop of Canterbury); London (1118?–1170)
Beckett, Samuel (playwright); Dublin (1906–1989)
Beckmann, Max (painter); Leipzig, Germany (1884–1950)
Bede, Saint ("The Venerable Bede") (scholar); Monkwearmouth, England (673–735)
Beecham, Sir Thomas (conductor); St. Helens, England (1879–1961)
Beecher, Henry Ward (clergyman); Litchfield, Conn. (1813–1887)
Beerbohm, Sir Max (author); London (1872–1956)
Beery, Noah (actor); Kansas City, Mo. (1884–1946)
Beery, Noah, Jr. (actor); New York City (1913–1994)
Beery, Wallace (actor); Kansas City, Mo. (1886–1949)
Beethoven, Ludwig van (composer); Bonn, Germany (1770–1827)

Begin, Menachem (Israeli prime minister); Brest-Litovsk, Belarus (1913–1992)
Begley, Ed (actor); Hartford, Conn. (1901–1970)
Beiderbecke, Bix (jazz musician); Davenport, Iowa (1903–1931)
Beineix, Jean-Jacques (director, producer, screenwriter) 1946
Belafonte, Harry (singer, actor); New York City, 3/1/27
Belafonte-Harper, Shari (actress); New York City, 9/22/54
Belasco, David (dramatist, producer); San Francisco (1854–1931)
Bel Geddes, Barbara (actress); New York City, 10/31/22
Bell, Alexander Graham (inventor); Edinburgh, Scotland (1847–1922)
Bell, Quentin (author, artist); England (1910–1996)
Bellamy, Edward (author); Chicopee Falls, Mass. (1850–1898)
Bellamy, Ralph (actor); Chicago (1904–1991)
Bellini, Giovanni (painter); Venice (c. 1430–1516)
Bellow, Saul (novelist); Lachine, Que., Canada, 6/10/15
Bellows, George Wesley (painter, lithographer); Columbus, Ohio (1882–1925)
Belushi, Jim (actor); Chicago, 6/15/54
Belushi, John (comedian, actor); Chicago (1949–1982)
Benchley, Peter Bradford (novelist); New York City, 5/8/40
Benchley, Robert Charles (humorist); Worcester, Mass. (1889–1945)
Bendix, William (actor); New York City (1906–1964)
Benedict, Ruth Fulton (anthropologist); New York City (1887–1948)
Benes, Eduard (statesman); Kozlany, former Czechoslovakia (1884–1948)
Benét, Stephen Vincent (poet, story writer); Bethlehem, Pa. (1898–1943)
Benét, William Rose (poet, novelist); Ft. Hamilton, Brooklyn, N.Y. (1886–1950)
Ben-Gurion, David (David Green) (statesman); Plónsk, Poland (1886–1973)
Benigni, Roberto (actor, director, screenwriter); Misericordia, Arezzo, Italy, 10/27/52
Bening, Annette (actress); Topeka, Kans., 5/29/58
Bennett, Enoch Arnold (novelist, dramatist); Hanley, England (1867–1931)
Bennett, James Gordon (editor); Keith, Scotland (1795–1872)
Bennett, Joan (actress); Palisades, N.J. (1910–1990)
Bennett, Robert Russell (composer); Kansas City, Mo. (1894–1981)
Bennett, Tony (Anthony Benedetto) (singer); Astoria, Queens, N.Y., 8/3/26
Benny, Jack (Benjamin Kubelsky) (comedian); Chicago (1894–1974)
Benson, Robby (Robert Segal) (actor); Dallas, 1/21/56
Bentham, Jeremy Heinrich (economist); London (1748–1832)
Benton, Thomas Hart (painter); Neosho, Mo. (1889–1975)
Berendt, John (writer); Syracuse, N.Y., 12/5/39
Berenger, Tom (actor); Chicago, 5/31/50
Berg, Alban (composer); Vienna (1885–1935)
Berg, Gertrude (writer, actress); New York City (1899–1966)
Bergen, Candice (actress); Beverly Hills, Calif., 5/9/46
Bergen, Edgar (ventriloquist); Chicago (1903–1978)
Bergen, Polly (Nellie Paulina Burgin) (actress, singer); Knoxville, Tenn., 7/14/30
Bergerac, Cyrano de (poet); Paris (1619–1655)
Bergman, Ingmar (film director); Uppsala, Sweden, 7/14/18
Bergman, Ingrid (actress); Stockholm (1918–1982)
Bergson, Henri (philosopher); Paris (1859–1941)
Berkeley, Busby (William Berkeley Enos) (choreographer, director); Los Angeles (1895–1976)
Berle, Milton (Milton Borlinger) (comedian); New York City (1908–2002)
Berlin, Irving (Israel Baline) (songwriter); Temum, Russia (1888–1989)
Berlioz, Louis Hector (composer); La Côte-Saint-André, France (1803–1869)
Berman, Lazar (concert pianist); Leningrad (St. Petersburg), Russia, 2/26/30
Bernardin, Joseph Cardinal (prelate); Columbia, S.C. (1928–1996)
Bernhard, Sandra (actress, comedian); Flint, Mich., 6/6/55
Bernhardt, Sarah (Rosine Bernard) (actress); Paris (1844–1923)
Bernini, Gian Lorenzo (sculptor, painter); Naples, Italy (1598–1680)
Bernoulli, Jacques (scientist); Basel, Switzerland (1654–1705)
Bernsen, Corbin (actor); North Hollywood, Calif., 7/7/54
Bernstein, Leonard (conductor); Lawrence, Mass. (1918–1990)
Berry, Chuck (Charles Edward Berry) (singer, guitarist); St. Louis, Mo., 10/19/26
Berry, Halle (actress, model); Cleveland, Ohio, 8/14/68
Berry, Ken (actor); Moline, Ill., 11/3/30
Berry, Richard (songwriter); Extension, S.C. (1935–1997)

Berryman, John (poet); McAlester, Okla. **(1914–1972)**
Bertinelli, Valerie (actress); Wilmington, Del., 4/23/60
Bertolucci, Bernardo (actor); Parma, Italy, 3/16/40
Bethune, Mary McLeod (educator); Mayesville, S.C. **(1875–1955)**
Betjeman, Sir John (poet laureate); London **(1906–1984)**
Bettelheim, Bruno (psychoanalyst); Vienna **(1903–1990)**
Bierce, Ambrose Gwinnett (journalist); Meigs County, Ohio **(1842–1914?)**
Bikel, Theodore (actor, folk singer); Vienna, 5/2/24
Bing, Sir Rudolf (opera manager); Vienna **(1902–1997)**
Bingham, George Caleb (painter); Augusta Co., Va. **(1811–1879)**
Binoche, Juliette (actress); Paris, 3/9/64
Bishop, Joey (Joseph Gottlieb) (comedian); New York City, 2/3/19
Bismarck-Schönhausen, Prince Otto Eduard Leopold von (statesman); Schönhausen, Germany **(1815–1898)**
Bisset, Jacqueline (actress); Weybridge, England, 9/13/44
Bixby, Bill (actor); San Francisco **(1934–1993)**
Bizet, Georges (Alexandre César Léopold Bizet) (composer); Paris **(1838–1875)**
Bjoerling, Jussi (tenor); Stora Tuna, Sweden **(1911–1960)**
Björk (Björk Gudmundsdottir) (pop musician, singer); Reykjavik, Iceland, 11/21/65
Black, Clint (singer, songwriter); Long Branch, N.J., 2/4/62
Black, Karen (Karen Ziegler) (actress); Park Ridge, Ill., 7/1/42
Black, Shirley Temple (child actress, former ambassador); Santa Monica, Calif., 4/23/28
Blackstone, Sir William (jurist); London **(1723–1780)**
Blackwell, Elizabeth (physician, educator); England **(1821–1910)**
Blades, Ruben (actor, musician, composer); Panama City, Panama, 7/16/48
Blair, Tony (British prime minister); Edinburgh, Scotland, 5/6/53
Blake, Amanda (Beverly Louise Neill) (actress); Buffalo, N.Y. **(1929–1989)**
Blake, Eubie (James Hubert) (pianist); Baltimore **(1883–1983)**
Blake, Robert (Michael Gubitosi) (actor); Nutley, N.J., 9/18/33
Blake, William (poet, artist); London **(1757–1827)**
Blanc, Mel (Melvin Jerome) (actor, voice specialist); San Francisco **(1908–1989)**
Blass, Bill (fashion designer); Fort Wayne, Ind. **(1922–2002)**
Bleeth, Yasmine (model, actress); New York City, 6/14/68
Blige, Mary J. (hip-hop singer); Bronx, N.Y., 1/11/71
Bloch, Ernest (composer); Geneva **(1880–1959)**
Bloom, Claire (actress); London, 2/15/31
Bloomberg, Michael (mayor of New York); Melrose, Mass., 2/14/42
Bloomgarden, Kermit (producer); Brooklyn, N.Y. **(1904–1976)**
Blume, Judy (Judy Sussman) (young adult novelist); Elizabeth, N.J., 2/12/38
Bly, Nellie (pseud. for Elizabeth Seaman) (journalist); Cochrane Mills, Pa. **(1867–1922)**
Bly, Robert (poet, critic); Madison, Minn., 12/23/26
Boccaccio, Giovanni (author); Paris **(1313–1375)**
Boccherini, Luigi (Rodolfo) (composer); Lucca, Italy **(1743–1805)**
Boccioni, Umberto (painter, sculptor); Reggio di Calabria, Italy **(1882–1916)**
Bochco, Steven (TV producer, writer); New York City, 12/16/43
Bock, Jerry (composer); New Haven, Conn., 11/23/28
Bogarde, Dirk (Derek Van den Bogaerde) (film actor, director); London **(1921–1999)**
Bogart, Humphrey DeForest (actor); New York City **(1899–1957)**
Bogdanovich, Peter (producer, director); Kingston, N.Y., 7/30/39
Bogosian, Eric (playwright, screenwriter, actor, monologuist); Woburn, Mass., 4/24/53
Bohr, Niels (atomic physicist); Copenhagen **(1885–1962)**
Bok, Sissela (Sissela Ann Myrdal) (scholar); Stockholm, 12/2/34
Bolger, Ray (dancer, actor); Dorchester, Mass **(1904–1987)**
Bolívar, Simón (South American liberator); Caracas, Venezuela **(1783–1830)**
Bologna, Giovanni da (sculptor); Douai, France **(1529–1608)**
Bombeck, Erma (author, columnist); Dayton, Ohio **(1927–1996)**
Bonaparte, Napoléon (Emperor of the French); Ajaccio, Corsica, France **(1769–1821)**
Bond, Julian (Georgia legislator); Nashville, Tenn., 1/14/40
Bonet, Lisa (actress); San Francisco, 11/16/67
Bonham Carter, Helena (actress); London, 5/23/66
Bon Jovi, Jon (musician, songwriter); Sayreville, N.J., 3/2/62
Bonnard, Pierre (painter); Fontenayaux-Roses, France **(1867–1947)**
Bono (Paul Hewson) (singer, songwriter); Dublin, Ireland, 5/10/60
Bono, Sonny (Salvatore Bono) (singer, politician); Detroit **(1935–1998)**
Boone, Daniel (frontiersman); nr. Reading, Pa. **(1734–1820)**
Boone, Pat (Charles Boone) (singer); Jacksonville, Fla., 6/1/34
Boone, Richard (actor); Los Angeles **(1917–1981)**

Boorstin, Daniel (historian); Atlanta, 10/1/14
Booth, Edwin Thomas (actor); Bel Air, Md. **(1833–1893)**
Booth, Evangeline Cory (religious leader); London **(1865–1950)**
Booth, John Wilkes (actor; assassin of Lincoln); Harford County, Md. **(1838–1865)**
Booth, Shirley (Thelma Booth Ford) (actress); New York City **(1907–1992)**
Borden, Lizzie (Elizabeth Andrew Borden) (accused murderer); Fall River, Mass. **(1860–1927)**
Borge, Victor (pianist, comedian); Copenhagen **(1909–2000)**
Borgia, Cesare (nobleman, soldier); Rome **(1476–1507)**
Borgia, Lucrezia (Duchess of Ferrara); Rome **(1480–1519)**
Borgnine, Ernest (actor); Hamden, Conn., 1/24/17
Borromini, Francesco (architect); Bissone, Italy **(1599–1667)**
Bosch, Hieronymus (Hieronymus van Aeken) (painter); Hertogenbosch, Netherlands **(c. 1450–1516)**
Bosley, Tom (actor); Chicago, 10/1/27
Bostwick, Barry (actor); San Mateo, Calif., 2/24/45
Boswell, James (diarist, biographer); Edinburgh, Scotland **(1740–1795)**
Botticelli, Sandro (Alessandro di Mariano dei Filipepi) (painter); Florence, Italy **(1444–1510)**
Bottoms, Timothy (actor); Santa Barbara, Calif., 8/30/50
Boulez, Pierre (conductor); Montbrison, France, 3/26/25
Bourke-White, Margaret (photographer); New York City **(1906–1971)**
Boutros-Ghali, Boutros (ex-secretary general of the UN); Cairo, Egypt, 11/14/22
Bow, Clara (actress); Brooklyn, N.Y. **(1905–1965)**
Bowen, Catherine Drinker (biographer); Haverford, Pa. **(1897–1973)**
Bowie, David (David Robert Jones) (actor, musician); London, 1/8/47
Bowie, James (soldier); Burke County, Ga. **(1799–1836)**
Bowles, Chester (diplomat); Springfield, Mass. **(1901–1986)**
Boxleitner, Bruce (actor); Elgin, Ill., 5/12/50
Boyce, William (composer); London? **(1710–1779)**
Boyd, Bill ("Hopalong Cassidy") (actor); Cambridge, Ohio **(1895–1972)**
Boyd, Stephen (Stephen Millar) (actor); Belfast, Northern Ireland **(1928–1977)**
Boyer, Charles (actor); Figeac, France **(1897–1978)**
Boy George (George Alan O'Dowd) (singer); London, 6/14/61
Boyle, Peter (actor); Philadelphia, 10/18/33
Boyle, Robert (scientist); Lismore Castle, Munster, Ireland **(1627–1691)**
Bradbury, Ray Douglas (science-fiction writer); Waukegan, Ill., 8/22/20
Bradlee, Benjamin C. (editor); Boston, 8/26/21
Bradley, Ed (broadcast journalist); Philadelphia, 6/22/41
Bradley, Omar N. (5-star general); Clark, Mo. **(1893–1981)**
Bradley, Thomas (mayor of Los Angeles); Calvert, Tex. **(1917–1998)**
Brady, Mathew (early photographer); Warren Co., N.Y. **(c. 1823–1896)**
Brahe, Tycho (astronomer); Knudstrup, Denmark **(1546–1601)**
Bragg, Billy (singer, songwriter); Barking, England, 12/20/57
Brahms, Johannes (composer); Hamburg, Germany **(1833–1897)**
Braille, Louis (teacher of blind); Coupvray, France **(1809–1862)**
Brailowsky, Alexander (pianist); Kiev, Ukraine **(1896–1976)**
Bramante, Donato D'Agnolo (architect); Monte Asdrualdo (now Fermignano), Italy **(1444–1514)**
Branagh, Kenneth (actor, director, writer, producer); Belfast, Northern Ireland, 12/10/60
Brancusi, Constantin (sculptor); Pestisansi, Romania **(1876–1957)**
Brandauer, Klaus Maria (Klaus Maria Steng) (actor); Bad Aussee, Steiermark, Austria , 6/22/44
Brando, Marlon (actor); Omaha, Neb., 4/3/24
Brandt, Willy (Herbert Frahm) (ex-chancellor); Lübeck, Germany **(1913– 1992)**
Brandy (Brandy Norwood) (actress, singer); McComb, Miss., 2/11/79
Braque, Georges (painter); Argenteuil, France **(1882–1963)**
Bratt, Benjamin (actor); San Francisco, 12/16/63
Braugher, André (actor); Chicago, 7/1/62
Braxton, Toni (R&B singer); Severn, Maryland, 10/7/67
Brazelton, T(homas) Berry II (pediatrician, writer); Waco, Tex., 5/10/18
Brecht, Bertolt (dramatist, poet); Augsburg, Bavaria **(1898–1956)**
Brel, Jacques (singer, composer); Brussels **(1929–1978)**
Brennan, Walter (actor); Lynn, Mass. **(1894–1974)**
Brennan, William J., Jr. (Supreme Court justice); Newark, N.J. **(1906–1997)**

## C

**Callas,** Maria (Maria Calogeropoulos) (operatic soprano); New York City **(1923–1977)**

**Calloway,** Cab (Cabell Calloway) (band leader); Rochester, N.Y. **(1907–1994)**

**Calvin,** John (Jean Chauvin) (religious reformer); Noyon, Picardy **(1509–1564)**

**Calvin,** Melvin (chemist, Nobel laureate); St. Paul, Minn. **(1911–1997)**

**Cambridge,** Godfrey (comedian); New York City **(1933–1976)**

**Cameron,** James (director); Kapuskasing, Ont., Canada, 8/16/54

**Cameron,** Rod (Rod Cox) (actor); Calgary, Alba., Canada **(1912–1983)**

**Campbell,** Glen (singer); nr. Delight, Ark., 4/22/38

**Campbell,** Naomi (model); London, England, 5/22/70

**Campbell,** Neve (actress); Guelph, Ont., Canada, 10/3/73

**Campion,** Jane (director, screenwriter); Waikanae, New Zealand, 1954

**Camus,** Albert (author); Mondovi, Algeria **(1913–1960)**

**Canaletto** (Giovanni Antonio Canale) (painter); Venice **(1697–1768)**

**Candy,** John (actor, comedian); Toronto **(1950–1994)**

**Caniff,** Milton (cartoonist); Hillsboro, Ohio **(1907–1988)**

**Cannon,** Dyan (Samille Diane Friesen) (actress); Tacoma, Wash., 1/4/37

**Cantinflas** (Mario Moreno-Reyes) (comedian); Mexico City **(1911–1993)**

**Cantor,** Eddie (Edward Iskowitz) (actor); New York City **(1892–1964)**

**Capone,** Al(fonse) (gangster); Brooklyn, N.Y. **(1899–1947)**

**Capote,** Truman (Truman Streckfus Persons) (novelist); New Orleans **(1924–1984)**

**Capp,** Al (Alfred Gerald Caplin) (cartoonist); New Haven, Conn. **(1909–1979)**

**Capra,** Frank (film producer, director); Palermo, Italy **(1897–1991)**

**Caputo,** Phil (Philip Joseph Caputo) (author, journalist); Chicago, 6/10/41

**Caravaggio,** Michelangelo Merisi da (painter); Caravaggio, Italy **(1573–1610)**

**Cardin,** Pierre (fashion designer); nr. Venice, 7/7/22

**Cardinale,** Claudia (actress); Tunis, Tunisia, 4/15/39

**Carey,** Drew (actor, producer); Cleveland, 5/23/58

**Carey,** Harry (actor); New York City **(1878–1947)**

**Carey,** Macdonald (actor); Sioux City, Iowa **(1913–1994)**

**Carlin,** George (comedian); Bronx, N.Y., 5/12/37

**Carlisle,** Kitty (singer, actress); New Orleans, 9/3/15

**Carlyle,** Robert (actor); Glasgow, Scotland, 4/14/61

**Carlyle,** Thomas (essayist, historian); Ecclefechan, Scotland **(1795–1881)**

**Carmichael,** Hoagy (Hoagland Howard) (songwriter); Bloomington, Ind. **(1899–1981)**

**Carne,** Judy (Joyce Botterill) (singer, actress); Northampton, England, 4/27/39

**Carnegie,** Andrew (industrialist); Dunfermline, Scotland **(1835–1919)**

**Carney,** Art (actor); Mt. Vernon, N.Y., 11/4/18

**Caron,** Leslie (actress); Paris, 7/1/31

**Carpenter,** Mary Chapin (singer, songwriter); Princeton, N.J., 2/21/58

**Carr,** Vikki (Florencia Bisenta de Casillas Martinez Cardona) (singer); El Paso, Tex., 7/19/42

**Carracci,** Annibale (painter); Bologna, Italy **(1560–1609)**

**Carracci,** Lodovico (painter); Bologna, Italy **(1555–1619)**

**Carradine,** David (actor); Hollywood, Calif., 12/8/36

**Carradine,** John (actor); New York City **(1906–1988)**

**Carradine,** Keith (actor); San Mateo, Calif., 8/8/49

**Carreras,** José (tenor); Barcelona, Spain, 12/5/46

**Carroll,** Diahann (Carol Diahann Johnson) (singer, actress); Bronx, N.Y., 7/17/35

**Carroll,** Leo G. (actor); Weedon, England **(1892–1972)**

**Carroll,** Lewis (Charles Lutwidge Dodgson) (author, mathematician); Daresbury, England **(1832–1898)**

**Carson,** Johnny (TV entertainer); Corning, Iowa, 10/23/25

**Carson,** Kit (Christopher Carson) (scout); Madison County, Ky. **(1809–1868)**

**Carson,** Rachel (biologist, author); Springdale, Pa. **(1907–1964)**

**Carter,** Betty (jazz singer, composer); Flint, Mich. **(1930–1998)**

**Carter,** Chris (television and film writer, director, producer); Bellflower, Calif., 10/13/57

**Carter,** Dixie (actress); McLemoresville, Tenn., 5/25/39

**Carter,** Jack (comedian); New York City, 6/24/23

**Carter,** James Earl, Jr. (39th U.S. president); Plains, Ga., 10/1/24

**Carter,** Lynda (actress); Phoenix, Ariz., 7/24/51

**Cartier,** Jacques (explorer); Saint-Malo, Brittany, France **(1491–1557)**

**Cartier-Bresson,** Henri (photographer); Chanteloup, France, 8/22/08

**Cartland,** Barbara (author); England **(1901–2000)**

**Caruso,** Enrico (Errico Caruso) (tenor); Naples, Italy **(1873–1921)**

**Carver,** George Washington (botanist); Diamond Grove, Mo. **(1864–1943)**

**Cary,** Arthur Joyce Lunel (novelist); Londonderry, Ireland **(1888–1957)**

**Casals,** Pablo (cellist); Vendrell, Spain **(1876–1973)**

**Casanova de Seingalt,** Giovanni Jacopo (adventurer); Venice **(1725–1798)**

**Case,** Steve (business executive); Honolulu, 8/21/58

**Cash,** Johnny (singer); nr. Kingsland, Ark., 2/26/32

**Cass,** Peggy (Mary Margaret Cass) (comedienne); Boston **(1924–1999)**

**Cassatt,** Mary (painter); Allegheny, Pa. **(1844–1926)**

**Cassavetes,** John (director); New York City **(1929–1989)**

**Cassidy,** David (singer); New York City, 4/12/50

**Cassidy,** Jack (actor); Richmond Hill, Queens, N.Y. **(1927–1976)**

**Cassidy,** Shaun (actor, television producer, singer); Los Angeles, 9/27/58

**Cassini,** Oleg (Oleg Lolewski-Cassini) (fashion designer); Paris, 4/11/13

**Castagno,** Andrea del (painter); San Martino a Corella, Italy **(c. 1421–1457)**

**Castaneda,** Carlos (cultural anthropologist, author); São Paulo, Brazil **(1931–1998)**

**Castle,** Irene (Irene Foote) (actress, dancer); New Rochelle, N.Y. **(1893–1969)**

**Castle,** Vernon Blythe (dancer, aviator); Norwich, England **(1887–1918)**

**Castro Ruz,** Fidel (premier); Mayari, Oriente, Cuba, 8/13/26

**Cather,** Willa Sibert (novelist); Winchester, Va. **(1876–1947)**

**Cato,** Marcus Porcius (called Cato the Elder) (statesman); Tusculum, Italy **(234–149 b.c.)**

**Catt,** Carrie Lane Chapman (woman suffragist); Ripon, Wis. **(1859–1947)**

**Catton,** Bruce (historian); Petoskey, Mich. **(1899–1978)**

**Catullus,** Gaius Valerius (poet); Verona **(c. 84–c. 54 b.c.)**

**Cavallaro,** Carmen (band leader); New York City **(1913–1989)**

**Cavett,** Dick (Richard Cavett) (TV entertainer); Gibbon, Neb., 11/19/36

**Ceausescu,** Nicolae (head of state); Scorniscesti, Romania **(1918–1989)**

**Céline,** Louis Ferdinand (pseud. of Louis Fuch Destouches) (novelist); Paris **(1894–1961)**

**Cellini,** Benvenuto (goldsmith, sculptor); Florence, Italy **(1500–1571)**

**Cervantes Saavedra,** Miguel de (novelist); Alcalá de Henares, Spain **(1547–1616)**

**Cézanne,** Paul (painter); Aix-en-Provence, France **(1839–1906)**

**Chagall,** Marc (painter); Vitebsk, Russia **(1887–1985)**

**Chaliapin,** Feodor Ivanovitch (operatic basso); Kazan, Russia **(1873–1938)**

**Chamberlain,** Arthur Neville (statesman); Edgbaston, England **(1869–1940)**

**Chamberlain,** Richard (actor, producer); Los Angeles, 3/31/35

**Champion,** Gower (choreographer); Geneva, Ill. **(1921–1980)**

**Champion,** Marge (Marjorie Celeste Belcher) (actress, dancer); Los Angeles, 9/2/23

**Champlain,** Samuel de (explorer); nr. Rochefort, France **(1567–1635)**

**Chan,** Jackie (Chan Kwong Sang) (actor); Hong Kong, 4/7/54

**Chancellor,** John (TV commentator); Chicago **(1927–1996)**

**Chandler,** Jeff (Ira Grossel) (actor); Brooklyn, N.Y. **(1918–1961)**

**Chandler,** Raymond (writer); Chicago **(1883–1959)**

**Chanel,** "Coco" (Gabriel Bonheur) (fashion designer); Issoire, France **(1883–1971)**

**Chaney,** Lon (actor); Colorado Springs, Colo. **(1883–1930)**

**Channing,** Carol (actress); Seattle, 1/31/23

**Channing,** Stockard (Susan Stockard) (actress); New York City, 2/13/44

**Chaplin,** Geraldine (actress); Santa Monica, Calif., 7/31/44

**Chaplin,** Sir Charles (actor); London **(1889–1977)**

**Charisse,** Cyd (Tula Finklea) (dancer, actress); Amarillo, Tex., 3/8/21

**Charlemagne** (Holy Roman Emperor); birthplace unknown **(742–814)**

**Charles,** Ray (Ray Charles Robinson) (pianist, singer, songwriter); Albany, Ga., 9/23/30

**Charo** (Maria Rosario Pilar Martinez) (actress); Murcia, Spain, 1/15/51

Chase, Chevy (Cornelius Crane Chase) (comedian); New York City, 10/8/43

Chase, Lucia (founder Ballet Theatre [now American Ballet Theatre]); Waterbury, Conn. **(1907–1986)**

Chateaubriand, François René de (writer, statesman); St. Malo, France **(1768–1848)**

Chaucer, Geoffrey (poet); London **(c. 1340–1400)**

Chuan, Leekpai (prime minister of Thailand); Muang District, Thailand, 7/28/38

Chávez, Carlos (composer); nr. Mexico City **(1899–1978)**

Chavez, Cesar (labor leader); nr. Yuma, Ariz. **(1927–1993)**

Chayefsky, Paddy (Sidney Chayefsky) (playwright); New York City **(1923–1981)**

Checker, Chubby (Ernest Evans) (performer); Philadelphia, 10/3/41

Cheever, John (novelist); Quincy, Mass. **(1912–1982)**

Chekhov, Anton Pavlovich (dramatist, short-story writer); Taganrog, Russia **(1860–1904)**

Chen Shui-bian (president of Taiwan); Taiwan, 2/18/51

Cher (Cherilyn Sarkisian La Piere) (actress, singer); El Centro, Calif., 5/20/46

Cherubini, Luigi (composer); Florence **(1760–1842)**

Chesterton, Gilbert Keith (author); Kensington, England **(1874–1936)**

Chesnutt, Charles Waddell (author); Cleveland **(1858–1932)**

Chevalier, Maurice (entertainer); Paris **(1888–1972)**

Chiang Kai-shek (chief of state); Feng-hwa, China **(1887–1975)**

Child, Julia (food expert); Pasadena, Calif., 8/15/12

Chippendale, Thomas (cabinet-maker); Otley, England **(1718–1779)**

Chirac, Jacques (president of France); Paris, 11/29/32

Chirico, Giorgio de (painter); Vólos, Greece **(1888–1978)**

Chisholm, Shirley Anita St. Hill (U.S. representative); Brooklyn, N.Y., 11/30/24

Chlumsky, Anna (actress); Chicago, 12/3/80

Chomsky, (Avram) Noam (linguist, educator, activist); Philadelphia, 12/7/28

Chopin, Frédéric François (composer); nr. Warsaw **(1810–1849)**

Chopin, Kate O'Flaherty (author); St. Louis **(1851–1904)**

Chow, Yun-Fat (actor); Hong Kong, 5/18/55

Chrétien, Jean Joseph-Jacques (prime minister of Canada); Shawinigan, Que., Canada, 1/11/34

Christie, Agatha (mystery writer); Torquay, England **(1890–1976)**

Christie, Julie (actress); Chukua, India, 4/14/41

Chung, Connie (broadcast journalist); Washington, D.C., 8/20/46

Churchill, Sir Winston Leonard Spencer (statesman); Blenheim Palace, Oxfordshire, England **(1874–1965)**

Cicero, Marcus Tullius (orator, statesman); Arpinum, Italy **(106–43 B.C.)**

Cid, El (Rodrigo [or Ruy] Diez de Bivar) (Spanish national hero); nr. Burgos, Spain **(c. 1043–1099)**

Cilento, Diane (actress); Queensland, Australia, 10/5/33

Cimabue, Giovanni (painter); Florence, Italy **(c. 1240–c. 1302)**

Cimino, Michael (director, writer, producer); New York City, 11/16/43

Claire, Ina (Ina Fagan) (actress); Washington, D.C. **(1895–1985)**

Clancy, Tom (novelist); Baltimore, 4/12/47

Clapton, Eric (singer, guitarist); Ripley, England, 3/30/45

Clark, Dick (TV personality); Mt. Vernon, N.Y., 11/30/29

Clark, Mary Higgins (writer); New York City, 12/24/31

Clark, Petula (singer); Epsom, England, 11/15/34

Clark, Roy (country music artist); Meherrin, Va., 4/15/33

Clark, William (explorer); Caroline County, Va. **(1770–1838)**

Clarke, Arthur C. (science fiction writer); Minehead, England, 10/16/17

Claude Lorrain (Claude Gellée) (painter); Champagne, France **(1600–1682)**

Clausewitz, Karl von (military strategist); Burg, Germany **(1780–1831)**

Olay, Henry (statesman); Hanover County, Va. **(1777–1852)**

Clay, Lucius D. (banker, ex-general); Marietta, Ga. **(1897–1978)**

Clayburgh, Jill (actress); New York City, 4/30/44

Cleary, Beverly (Beverly Atlee Bunn) (children's author); McMinnville, Ore., 1916

Cleaver, Eldridge (Leroy) (author, activist); Wabbaseka, Ark. **(1935–1998)**

Cleese, John (writer, actor); Weston-super-Mare, England, 10/27/39

Clemenceau, Georges (statesman); Mouilleron-en-Pareds, Vondée, France **(1841–1929)**

Cleopatra (queen of Egypt); Alexandria, Egypt **(69–30 B.C.)**

Cleveland, Stephen Grover (22nd & 24th U.S. president); Caldwell, N.J. **(1837–1908)**

Cliburn, Van (Harvey Lavan Cliburn, Jr.) (concert pianist); Shreveport, La., 7/12/34

Clift, Montgomery (actor); Omaha, Neb. **(1920–1966)**

Cline, Patsy (singer); Winchester, Va. **(1932–1963)**

Clinton, Hillary Rodham (ex-first lady, U.S. senator); Park Ridge, Ill., 10/26/47

Clinton, William Jefferson (42nd U.S. president); Hope, Ark., 8/19/46

Clooney, George (actor); Lexington, Ky., 5/6/61

Clooney, Rosemary (singer); Maysville, Ky. **(1928–2002)**

Close, Glenn (actress); Greenwich, Conn., 3/19/47

Cobain, Kurt (musician); Hoquiam, Wash. **(1967–1994)**

Cobb, Irvin Shrewsbury (humorist); Paducah, Ky. **(1876–1944)**

Cobb, Lee J. (Leo Jacob Cobb) (actor); New York City **(1911–1976)**

Coburn, Charles Douville (actor); Savannah, Ga. **(1877–1961)**

Coburn, James (actor); Laurel, Neb., 8/31/28

Coca, Imogene (comedienne); Philadelphia **(1908–2001)**

Cocker, Jarvis (singer, songwriter); Sheffield, England, 9/19/63

Cocker, Joe (John Robert Cocker) (singer); Sheffield, England, 5/20/44

Coco, James (actor); New York City **(1929–1987)**

Cocteau, Jean (author); Maison-Lafitte, France **(1889–1963)**

Cohan, George Michael (actor, dramatist); Providence, R.I. **(1878–1942)**

Cohen, Leonard (composer); Montreal, Que., Canada, 9/21/34

Colbert, Claudette (Lily Chauchoin) (actress); Paris **(1903–1996)**

Cole, Nat "King" (singer); Montgomery, Ala. **(1919–1965)**

Cole, Natalie (singer); Los Angeles, 2/6/50

Cole, Thomas (painter); Lancashire, England **(1801–1848)**

Coleman, Dabney (actor); Austin, Tex., 1/3/32

Coleridge, Samuel Taylor (poet); Ottery St. Mary, England **(1772–1834)**

Colette (Sidonie-Gabrielle Colette) (novelist); St.-Sauveur, France **(1873–1954)**

Collingwood, Charles (TV commentator); Three Rivers, Mich. **(1917–1985)**

Collins, Joan (actress); London, 5/23/33

Collins, Judy (singer); Seattle, 5/1/39

Colman, Ronald (actor); Richmond, England **(1891–1958)**

Colonna, Jerry (comedian); Boston **(1905–1986)**

Coltrane, John (jazz musician); Hamlet, N.C. **(1926–1967)**

Columbus, Chris (director, screenwriter); Spangler, Pa., 9/10/58

Columbus, Christopher (Cristoforo Colombo) (explorer); Genoa, Italy **(1451–1506)**

Colvin, Shawn (folk singer); Vermillion, S.D., 1/10/58

Combs, Sean "Puffy" (singer, record producer); New York City, 11/9/69

Comden, Betty (writer); New York City, 5/3/19

Comenius, Johann Amos (educational reformer); Nivnice, Moravia, Czech Republic **(1592–1670)**

Commager, Henry Steele (historian); Pittsburgh **(1902–1998)**

Como, Perry (Pierino Como) (singer); Canonsburg, Pa. **(1912–2001)**

Compton, Karl Taylor (physicist); Wooster, Ohio **(1887–1954)**

Comte, Auguste (philosopher); Montpellier, France **(1798–1857)**

Conant, James B. (educator, statesman); Dorchester, Mass. **(1893–1978)**

Condon, Eddie (jazz musician); Goodland, Ind. **(1905–1973)**

Confucius (K'ung Fu-tzu) (philosopher); Shantung province, China **(c. 551– 479 B.C.)**

Congreve, William (dramatist); nr. Leeds, England **(1670–1729)**

Connelly, Marc (playwright); McKeesport, Pa. **(1890–1980)**

Connery, Sean (actor); Edinburgh, Scotland, 8/25/30

Connick, Jr., Harry (musician, actor); New Orleans, La., 9/11/67

Conniff, Ray (band leader); Attleboro, Mass. 11/6/16

Connors, Mike (Krekor Ohanian) (actor); Fresno, Calif., 8/15/25

Conrad, Joseph (Teodor Jozef Konrad Korzeniowski) (novelist); Berdichev, Ukraine **(1857–1924)**

Conrad, Robert (Conrad Robert Falk) (actor); Chicago, 3/1/35

Conrad, William (actor); Louisville, Ky. **(1920–1994)**

Conried, Hans (Frank Foster) (actor); Baltimore **(1915–1982)**

Conroy, Pat (author); Atlanta, 10/26/45

Constable, John (painter); East Bergholt, Suffolk, England **(1776–1837)**

Constantine II (ex-king of Greece); Athens, 6/2/40

Constantine, Michael (actor); Reading, Pa., 5/22/27

Conte, Richard (actor); New York City **(1916–1975)**

Conti, Tom (actor); Paisley, Scotland, 11/22/41

Convy, Bert (actor, host); St. Louis **(1933–1991)**

Conway, Tim (comedian); Chagrin Falls, Ohio, 12/15/33

Coogan, Jackie (actor); Los Angeles **(1914–1984)**

Cook, Peter (actor, writer); Torquay, England **(1937–1995)**

Cooke, Alistair (Alfred Alistair) (TV narrator, journalist); Manchester, England, 11/20/08

Cooke, Jack Kent (business executive); Hamilton, Ont., Canada (1912–1997)
Cooley, Denton A(rthur) (heart surgeon); Houston, 8/22/20
Coolidge, (John) Calvin (30th U.S. president); Plymouth, Vt. (1872–1933)
Coolidge, Rita (singer); Nashville, Tenn., 5/1/45
Coolio (Artis Ivey, Jr.) (rap artist ); Los Angeles, Calif., 8/1/63
Cooper, Alice (Vincent Furnier) (rock musician); Detroit, 2/4/48
Cooper, Gary (Frank James Cooper) (actor); Helena, Mont. (1901–1961)
Cooper, Dame Gladys (actress); Lewisham, England (1898–1971)
Cooper, Jackie (actor, director); Los Angeles, 9/15/22
Cooper, James Fenimore (novelist); Burlington, N.J. (1789–1851)
Cooper, Peter (industrialist, philanthropist); New York City (1791–1883)
Copernicus, Nicolaus (Mikolaj Kopernik) (astronomer); Thorn, Poland (1473–1543)
Copland, Aaron (composer); Brooklyn, N.Y. (1900–1990)
Copley, John Singleton (painter); Boston (1738–1815)
Copperfield, David (David Kotkin) (illusionist); Metuchen, N.J., 9/16/56
Coppola, Francis Ford (film director); Detroit, 4/7/39
Corelli, Arcangelo (composer); Fusignano, Italy (1653–1713)
Corelli, Franco (operatic tenor); Ancona, Italy, 4/8/23
Corgan, Billy (musician); Elk Grove, Ill., 3/17/67
Corneille, Pierre (dramatist); Rouen, France (1606–1684)
Cornell, Katharine (actress); Berlin (1893–1974)
Corot, Jean Baptiste Camille (painter); Paris (1796–1875)
Corella, Angel (ballet dancer); Madrid, Spain, 11/8/75
Correggio, Antonio Allegri da (painter); Correggio, Italy (1494–1534)
Corsaro, Frank (opera director); New York harbor, 12/22/24
Cortés (or Cortez), Hernando (explorer); Medellin, Spain (1485–1547)
Cosby, Bill (actor); Philadelphia, 7/12/37
Cosell, Howard (Howard Cohen) (sportscaster); Winston-Salem, N.C. (1918–1995)
Costello, Elvis (Declan Patrick McManus) (singer, musician, songwriter); London, 1954
Costello, Lou (Louis Cristillo) (comedian); Paterson, N.J. (1908–1959)
Costner, Kevin (actor); Los Angeles, 1/18/55
Cotten, Joseph (actor); Petersburg, Va. (1905–1994)
Couperin, François (composer); Paris (1668–1733)
Courbet, Gustave (painter); Ornans, France (1819–1877)
Couric, Katie (TV host); Arlington, Va., 1/7/57
Courtenay, Tom (actor); Hull, England, 2/25/37
Cousins, Norman (publisher); Union Hill, N.J. (1915–1990)
Cousteau, Jacques-Yves (marine explorer); St. André-de-Cubzac, France (1910–1997)
Covey, Stephen R. (author); Salt Lake City, 10/24/32
Coward, Sir Noel (playwright, actor); Teddington, England (1899–1973)
Cowles, Gardner, Jr. (newspaper publisher); Algona, Iowa (1903–1985)
Cowper, William (poet); Great Berkhamstead, England (1731–1800)
Cox, Archibald (Watergate prosecutor); Plainfield, N.J., 5/17/12
Cox, Courteney (actress); Birmingham, Ala., 6/15/64
Coyote, Peter (actor); New York City, 10/10/41
Cozzens, James Gould (novelist); Chicago (1903–1978)
Crabbe, Buster (Clarence Crabbe) (actor); Oakland, Calif. (1908–1983)
Cranach, Lucas, the elder (painter); Kronach, Germany (1472–1553)
Crane, Hart (poet); Garrettsville, Ohio (1899–1932)
Crane, Stephen (novelist, poet); Newark, N.J. (1871–1900)
Cranmer, Thomas (churchman); Aslacton, England (1489–1556)
Craven, Wes (director, producer, screenwriter); Cleveland, 8/2/39
Crawford, Broderick (actor); Philadelphia (1911–1986)
Crawford, Cheryl (stage producer); Akron, Ohio (1902–1986)
Crawford, Cindy (model, actress); De Kalb, Illinois, 2/20/66
Crawford, Joan (Lucille LeSueur) (actress, business executive); San Antonio (1908–1977)
Crazy Horse (Lakota Indian leader); nr. Bear Butte, S.D. (1840?–1877)
Crenna, Richard (actor); Los Angeles, 11/30/27
Crespin, Régine (operatic soprano); Marseilles, France, 2/23/29
Crichton, (John) Michael (novelist, film producer); Chicago, 10/23/42
Crick, Francis Harry Compton (scientist, Nobel laureate); Northampton, England, 6/8/16
Crisp, Donald (actor); London (1880–1974)

Croce, Benedetto (philosopher); Peseasseroli, Aquila, Italy (1866–1952)
Croce, Jim (singer); Philadelphia (1942–1973)
Crockett, Davy (David) (frontiersman); Greene County, Tenn. (1786–1836 )
Cromwell, Oliver (statesman); Huntingdon, England (1599–1658)
Cronenberg, David (film director); Toronto, Canada, 3/15/43
Cronin, A. J. (Archibald J. Cronin) (novelist); Cardross, Scotland (1896–1981)
Cronkite, Walter (TV newscaster); St. Joseph, Mo., 11/4/16
Cronyn, Hume (actor); London, Ont., Canada, 7/18/11
Crosby, Bing (Harry Lillis) (singer, actor); Tacoma, Wash. (1904–1977)
Crosby, Bob (musician); Spokane, Wash. (1913–1993)
Crosby, Cathy Lee (actress); Los Angeles, 12/2/48
Crosby, Norm (comedian); Boston, 9/15/27
Cross, Ben (Bernard) (actor); Paddington, England, 12/16/47
Cross, Milton (opera commentator); New York City (1897–1975)
Crouse, Russell (playwright); Findlay, Ohio (1893–1966)
Crow, Sheryl (musician, record producer); Kennett, Mo., 2/11/62
Crowe, Russell (actor, musician); Auckland, New Zealand, 4/7/64
Crudup, Billy (actor); Manhasset, N.Y., 7/8/68
Cruise, Tom (Thomas Mapother IV) (actor, producer); Syracuse, N.Y., 7/3/62
Crystal, Billy (comedian, actor); Long Beach, N.Y., 3/14/47
Cugat, Xavier (band leader); Barcelona, Spain (1900–1990)
Cukor, George (film director); New York City (1899–1983)
Culkin, Macaulay (actor); New York City, 8/26/80
Cullen, Bill (William Lawrence Cullen) (radio and TV entertainer); Pittsburgh (1920–1990)
Cullen, Countee (poet); New York City (1903–1946)
Culp, Robert (actor); Berkeley, Calif., 8/16/30
cummings, e. e. (Edward Estlin Cummings) (poet); Cambridge, Mass. (1894–1962)
Cummings, Robert (actor); Joplin, Mo. (1908–1990)
Cunningham, Merce (choreographer); Centralia, Wash., 4/16/19
Curie, Marie (Marja Skłodowska) (physical chemist, Nobel laureate); Warsaw (1867–1934)
Curie, Pierre (physicist); Paris (1859–1906)
Curtin, Jane (actress); Cambridge, Mass., 9/6/47
Curtin, Phyllis (soprano); Clarksburg, W. Va., 12/3/27
Curtis, Jamie Lee (actress); Los Angeles, 11/22/58
Curtis, Tony (Bernard Schwartz) (actor); Bronx, N.Y., 6/3/25
Curzon, Clifford (concert pianist); London (1907–1982)
Cusack, Joan (actress); New York City, 10/11/62
Cusack, John (actor); Chicago, 6/28/66
Custer, George Armstrong (army officer); New Rumley, Ohio (1839–1876)

# D

Dafoe, Willem (William Dafoe, Jr.) (actor); Appleton, Wis., 7/22/55
da Gama, Vasco (explorer); Sines, Portugal (1460–1524)
Daguerre, Louis (photographic pioneer); nr. Paris (1787–1851)
Dahl, Arlene (actress); Minneapolis, 8/11/28
Dahl, Roald (writer); Llandaff, Wales (1916–1990)
Dalai Lama (Tenzin Gyatso) (spiritual and temporal head of Tibet); Taktser, China, 1935
Daley, Richard J. (mayor of Chicago); Chicago (1902–1976)
Dali, Salvador (painter); Figueras, Spain (1904–1989)
Dalton, John (chemist); nr. Cockermouth, England (1766–1844)
Dalton, Timothy (actor); Colwyn Bay, Wales, U.K., 3/21/46
Daly, Tyne (actress); Madison, Wis., 2/21/46
d'Amboise, Jacques (ballet dancer); Dedham, Mass., 7/28/34
Damone, Vic (Vito Farinola) (singer); Brooklyn, N.Y., 6/12/28
Damrosch, Walter Johannes (orchestra conductor); Breslau, Poland (1862–1950)
Dana, Charles Anderson (editor); Hinsdale, N.H. (1819–1897)
Dandridge, Dorothy (actress); Cleveland (1923–1965)
Danes, Claire (actress); New York City, 4/12/79
Dangerfield, Rodney (Jacob Cohen) (actor, comedian); Babylon, N.Y., 11/22/22
Daniels, Jeff (actor); Chelsea, Mich., 2/19/55
Daniels, William (actor); Brooklyn, N.Y., 3/31/27
Danilova, Alexandra (ballet dancer); Peterhof, Russia (1904–1997)
Dannay, Frederic (novelist, pseudonym Ellery Queen); Brooklyn, N.Y. (1905–1982)
Danner, Blythe (actress); Philadelphia, 2/3/43
D'Annunzio, Gabriele (soldier, author); Francaville at Mare, Pescara, Italy (1863–1938)
Danson, Ted (actor); San Diego, Calif., 12/29/47
Dante (or Durante) Alighieri (poet); Florence, Italy (1265–1321)

Danton, Georges Jacques (French Revolutionary leader); Arcis-sur-Aube, France (1759–1794)

Danza, Tony (actor); Brooklyn, N.Y., 4/21/51

Darren, James (actor); Philadelphia, 6/8/36

Darrow, Clarence Seward (lawyer); Kinsman, Ohio (1857–1938)

Darwin, Charles Robert (naturalist); Shrewsbury, England (1809–1882)

Dassin, Jules (film director); Middletown, Conn., 12/18/11

Daumier, Honoré (caricaturist); Marseilles, France (1808–1879)

David, Jacques-Louis (painter); Paris (1748–1825)

David (king of Israel and Judah); died c. 973 B.C.

Davidson, John (singer, actor); Pittsburgh, 12/13/41

Davies, Marion (Marion Douras) (actress); New York City (1897–1961)

Davies, (William) Robertson (writer); Thamesville, Ont., Canada (1913–1996)

Davis, Angela (social activist); Birmingham, Ala., 1/26/44

Davis, Ann B. (actress); Schenectady, N.Y., 5/5/26

Davis, Lt. Gen. Benjamin O., Jr. (Air Force general); Washington, D.C. (1912–2002)

Davis, Brig. Gen. Benjamin O., Sr. (U.S. Army general); Washington, D.C. (1877–1970)

Davis, Bette (actress); Lowell, Mass. (1908–1989)

Davis, Geena (Virginia Davis) (actress); Wareham, Mass., 1/21/57

Davis, Jefferson (president of the Confederacy); Christian (now Todd) County, Ky. (1808–1889 )

Davis, Judy (actress); Perth, Australia, 1955

Davis, Mac (singer); Lubbock, Tex., 1/21/42

Davis, Miles (jazz trumpeter); Alton, Ill. (1926–1991)

Davis, Ossie (actor, writer); Cogdell, Ga., 12/18/17

Davis, Sammy, Jr. (actor, singer); New York City (1925–1990)

Davis, Stuart (painter); Philadelphia (1894–1964)

Dawson, Richard (actor, host); Gosport, Hampshire, England, 11/20/32

Day, Doris (Doris von Kappelhoff) (singer, actress); Cincinnati, 4/3/24

Dayan, Moshe (ex-defense minister of Israel); Dagania, Palestine (1915–1981)

Day-Lewis, Daniel (actor); London, 4/29/58

Dean, James (actor); Marion, Ind. (1931–1955)

Dean, Jimmy (singer); Seth Ward, nr. Plainview, Tex., 8/10/28

De Bakey, Michael E. (heart surgeon); Lake Charles, La., 9/7/08

de Beauvoir, Simone (novelist, philosopher); Paris (1908–1986)

Debs, Eugene Victor (Socialist leader); Terre Haute, Ind. (1855–1926)

Debussy, Claude Achille (composer); St. Germain-en-Laye, France (1862–1918)

De Carlo, Yvonne (Peggy Yvonne Middleton) (actress); Vancouver, B.C., Canada, 9/1/24

Dee, Ruby (Ruby Ann Wallace) (actress); Cleveland, 10/27/24

Dee, Sandra (Alexandra Zuck) (actress); Bayonne, N.J., 4/23/42

Degas, Hilaire Germain Edgar (painter); Paris (1834–1917)

de Gaulle, Charles André Joseph Marie (soldier, statesman); Lille, France (1890–1970 )

de Havilland, Olivia (actress); Tokyo, 7/1/16

de Kooning, Willem (artist); Rotterdam (1904–1997)

Delacroix, Eugène (painter); Charenton-St. Maurice, France (1798–1863)

Delany, Dana (actress); New York City, 3/15/56

de la Renta, Oscar (fashion designer); Santo Domingo, Dominican Republic, 7/22/32

Delaunay, Robert (painter); Paris (1885–1941)

De Laurentiis, Dino (film producer); Torre Annunziata, Bay of

della Robbia, Andrea (sculptor); Florence (1435–1525)

della Robbia, Luca (sculptor); Florence (1400–1482)

Delon, Alain (actor); Sceaux, France, 11/8/35

del Toro, Benicio (actor); Santurce, Puerto Rico, 2/10/67

DeLuise, Dom (actor, comedian); Brooklyn, N.Y., 8/1/33

Demarest, William (actor); St. Paul, Minn. (1892–1983)

de Mille, Agnes (choreographer); New York City (1905–1993)

De Mille, Cecil Blount (film director); Ashfield, Mass. (1881–1959)

Demme, Jonathan (director, producer, screenwriter); Baldwin, N.Y., 2/22/44

Demosthenes (orator); Athens (384?–322 B.C.)

Dench, Dame Judi (film and stage actress); York, England, 12/9/34

Deneuve, Catherine (actress); Paris, 10/22/43

Deng Xiaoping (Chinese leader); Sichuan province, China (1904–1997)

De Niro, Robert (actor, director); New York City, 8/17/43

Dennehy, Brian (actor); Bridgeport, Conn., 7/9/39

Dennis, Sandy (actress); Hastings, Neb. (1937–1992)

Denny, Reginald (actor); Richmond, England (1891–1967)

Denver, John (Henry John Deutschendorf, Jr.) (singer, actor); Roswell, N.M. (1943–1997)

De Palma, Brian (film director); Newark, N.J., 9/11/40

Depp, Johnny (actor); Owensboro, Ky., 6/9/63

Derain, André (painter); Chatou, Seine-et-Oise, France (1880–1954)

Derek, John (Derek Harris) (actor, director); Los Angeles (1926–1998)

Dern, Bruce (actor); Winnetka, Ill., 6/4/36

Dern, Laura (actress); Los Angeles, 2/10/67

Dershowitz, Alan (lawyer); Brooklyn, N.Y., 9/1/38

Derrida, Jacques (philosopher); El-Biar, Algeria, 7/15/30

Descartes, René (philosopher, mathematician); La Haye, France (1596–1650)

De Seversky, Alexander P. (aviator); Tiflis (Tbilisi), Georgia (1894–1974)

De Sica, Vittorio (film director); Sora, Italy (1901–1974)

Desmond, Johnny (singer, composer); Detroit (1921–1985)

De Soto, Hernando (explorer); Barcarrota, Spain (c. 1500–1542)

De Valera, Eamon (ex-president of Ireland); New York City (1882–1975)

Devane, William (actor); Albany, N.Y., 9/5/39

Devine, Andy (actor); Flagstaff, Ariz. (1905–1977)

DeVito, Danny (Daniel Michael DeVito) (actor, director, producer); Neptune, N.J., 11/17/44

De Vries, Peter (novelist); Chicago (1910–1993)

de Waart, Edo (conductor); Amsterdam, the Netherlands, 6/1/41

Dewey, George (admiral); Montpelier, Vt. (1837–1917)

Dewey, John (philosopher, educator); Burlington, Vt. (1859–1952)

Dewey, Thomas E. (political figure); Owosso, Mich. (1902–1971)

Dewhurst, Colleen (actress); Montreal (1926–1991)

Dey, Susan (actress); Pekin, Ill., 12/10/52

Diaghilev, Sergei (ballet impressario); Novgorod, Russia (1872–1929)

Diamond, Neil (singer); Brooklyn, N.Y., 1/24/41

Diaz, Cameron (actress, model); San Diego, Calif., 8/30/72

DiCaprio, Leonardo (actor); Los Angeles, 11/11/74

Dichter, Misha (pianist); Shanghai, 9/27/45

Dickens, Charles John Huffam (novelist); Portsea, England (1812–1870)

Dickey, James (writer); Atlanta (1923–1997)

Dickinson, Angie (Angeline Brown) (actress); Kulm, N.D., 9/30/31

Dickinson, Emily Elizabeth (poet); Amherst, Mass. (1830–1886)

Diddley, Bo (Elias McDaniel) (guitarist); McComb, Miss., 12/30/28

Diderot, Denis (encyclopedist); Langres, France (1713–1784)

Dietrich, Marlene (Maria Magdalena von Losch) (actress); Berlin (1901–1992)

DiFranco, Ani (singer, songwriter); Buffalo, N.Y., 9/23/70

Diller, Phyllis (Phyllis Driver) (comedienne); Lima, Ohio, 7/17/17

Dillon, Matt (actor); New Rochelle, N.Y., 2/18/64

Dine, Jim (painter); Cincinnati, 6/16/35

Dinesen, Isak (Karen Blixen) (author); Rungsted, Denmark (1885–1962)

Dinkins, David (ex-mayor of New York City); Trenton, N.J., 7/10/27

Diogenes (philosopher); Sinope, Turkey (c. 412–323 B.C.)

Dion (Dion DiMucci) (singer); Bronx, N.Y., 7/18/39

Dion, Celine (musician); Charlemagne, Que., Canada, 3/30/68

Dior, Christian (fashion designer); Granville, France (1905–1957)

Disney, Walt(er) Elias (film animator, producer); Chicago (1901–1966)

Disraeli, Benjamin (Earl of Beaconsfield) (statesman); London (1804–1881)

Dix, Dorothea (social reformer); (1802), Hampden, Maine (1818–1887)

Dobbs, Mattiwilda (soprano); Atlanta, 7/11/25

Doctorow, E(dgar) L(aurence) (novelist); New York City, 1/6/31

Dogg, Snoop Diggy (Calvin Broadus) (musician); Long Beach, Calif., 10/20/72

Doherty, Shannen (actress); Memphis, Tenn., 4/21/71

Dole, Elizabeth Hanford (public official); Salisbury, N.C., 7/29/36

Dole, Robert (political figure); Russell, Kans., 7/22/23

Dolin, Anton (dancer); Slinfold, England (1904–1983)

Domingo, Placido (tenor); Madrid, 1/21/41

Domino, Fats (Antoine) (musician); New Orleans, 2/26/28

Donahue, Phil (TV host); Cleveland, 12/21/35

Donahue, Troy (Merle Johnson) (actor); New York City (1936–2001)

Donaldson, Sam (broadcast journalist); El Paso, Tex., 3/11/34

Donat, Robert (actor); Withington, England (1905–1958)

Donatello (Donato Niccolò di Betto Bardi) (sculptor); Florence (c. 1386–1466)

Donlevy, Brian (actor); Portadown, Ireland (1899–1972)

Donne, John (poet); London (1573–1631)

**Donner,** Richard (director, producer); New York City, 1939

**D'Onofrio,** Vincent (actor); Brooklyn, N.Y., 6/30/59

**Donovan** (Donovan Leitch) (singer, songwriter); Glasgow, Scotland, 2/10/46

**Doolittle,** James H. (ex-Air Force general); Alameda, Calif. **(1896–1993)**

**Doohan,** James (actor); Vancouver, B.C., 3/20/20

**Dorati,** Antal (orchestra conductor); Budapest **(1906–1988)**

**Dorn,** Michael (actor); Luling, Tex., 12/9/52

**Dorris,** Michael (anthropologist, writer); Louisville, Ky. **(1945–1997)**

**Dorsey,** Jimmy (band leader); Shenandoah, Pa. **(1904–1957)**

**Dorsey,** Thomas Andrew (father of gospel music); Villa Rice, Ga. **(1899–1993)**

**Dorsey,** Tommy (band leader); Mahanoy Plane, Pa. **(1905–1956)**

**Dos Passos,** John (author); Chicago **(1896–1970)**

**Dostoevski,** Fyodor Mikhailovich (novelist); Moscow **(1821–1881)**

**Dotrice,** Roy (actor); Guernsey, Channel Islands, England, 5/26/23

**Douglas,** Aaron (painter); Topeka, Kans. **(1900–1979)**

**Douglas,** Helen Gahagan (ex-representative); Boonton, N.J. **(1900–1980)**

**Douglas,** Kirk (Issur Danielovitch) (actor); Amsterdam, N.Y., 12/9/16

**Douglas,** Melvyn (Melvyn Hesselberg) (actor); Macon, Ga. **(1901–1981)**

**Douglas,** Michael (actor, producer); New Brunswick, N.J., 9/25/44

**Douglas,** Mike (Michael D. Dowd, Jr.) (TV host); Chicago, 8/11/25

**Douglas,** Stephen Arnold (politician); Brandon, Vt. **(1813–1861)**

**Douglass,** Frederick (abolitionist, author, orator); Tuckahoe, Md. **(1817–1895)**

**Dow,** Charles (financier); Sterling, Conn. **(1851–1902)**

**Down,** Lesley-Ann (actress); London, 3/17/54

**Downey,** Robert, Jr. (actor, director); New York City, 4/4/65

**Downs,** Hugh (broadcast journalist); Akron, Ohio, 2/14/21

**Doyle,** Sir Arthur Conan (novelist, spiritualist); Edinburgh, Scotland **(1859–1930)**

**Doyle,** David (actor); Lincoln, Neb. **(1929–1997)**

**Drake,** Sir Francis (navigator); Tavistock, England **(1545–1596)**

**Dr. Dre** (Andre Young) (rap singer); Los Angeles, 2/18/66

**Dreiser,** Theodore (writer); Terre Haute, Ind. **(1871–1945)**

**Drescher,** Fran (television and film actress); New York City, 9/30/57

**Dreyfus,** Alfred (French army officer); Mulhouse, France **(1859–1935)**

**Dreyfuss,** Richard (actor); Brooklyn, N.Y., 10/29/47

**Drury,** Allen (novelist); Houston **(1918–1998)**

**Dryden,** John (poet); Northamptonshire, England **(1631–1700)**

**Dryer,** Fred (ex-NFL player, actor); Hawthorne, Calif., 7/6/46

**Dubček,** Alexander (ex-president of Czechoslovakia); Uhrovek, Slovakia **(1921–1992)**

**Dubinsky,** David (David Dobnievski) (labor leader); Brest-Litovsk, Belarus **(1892–1982)**

**Du Bois,** W(illiam) E(dward) B(urghardt) (scholar, civil rights activist); Great Barrington, Mass. **(1868–1963)**

**Duchamp,** Marcel (painter); Blainville, France **(1887–1968)**

**Duchin,** Eddy (pianist, bandleader); Cambridge, Mass. **(1909–1951)**

**Duchin,** Peter (pianist, band leader); New York City, 7/28/37

**Duchovny,** David (actor); New York City, 8/7/60

**Dufay,** Guillaume (composer); Cambrai, France **(c. 1400–1474)**

**Duffy,** Julia (actress); Minneapolis, Minn., 6/27/50

**Dufy,** Raoul (painter); Le Havre, France **(1877–1953)**

**Dukakis,** Olympia (actress); Lowell, Mass., 6/20/31

**Duke,** James B. (industrialist); nr. Durham, N.C. **(1856–1925)**

**Duke,** Patty (Anna Marie Duke) (actress); New York City, 12/14/46

**Dulles,** Allen Welsh (ex-director of CIA); Watertown, N.Y. **(1893–1969)**

**Dulles,** John Foster (political figure); Washington, D.C. **(1888–1959)**

**Dumas,** Alexandre (called Dumas fils) (novelist); Paris **(1824–1895)**

**Dumas,** Alexandre (called Dumas père) (novelist); Villers-Cotterets, France **(1802–1870)**

**du Maurier,** Daphne (novelist); London **(1907–1989)**

**du Maurier,** George Louis Palmella Busson (novelist); Paris **(1834–1896)**

**Dumont,** Margaret (actress); Brooklyn, N.Y. **(1889–1965)**

**Dunaway,** Faye (actress); Bascom, Fla., 1/14/41

**Dunbar,** Paul Laurence (poet, novelist); Dayton, Ohio **(1872–1906)**

**Duncan,** Isadora (dancer); San Francisco **(1878–1927)**

**Duncan,** Michael Clarke (actor); Chicago, 12/10/57

**Duncan,** Sandy (actress); Henderson, Tex., 2/20/46

**Dunham,** Katherine (dancer, choreographer); Chicago, 6/22/09

**Dunne,** Irene (actress); Louisville, Ky. **(1898–1990)**

**Duns Scotus,** John (theologian); Duns, Scotland **(1265–1303)**

**Dunst,** Kirsten (actress); Point Pleasant, N.J., 4/30/82

**Du Pont,** Pierre S. (economist); Paris **(1739–1817)**

**Durante,** Jimmy (comedian); New York City **(1893–1980)**

**Duras,** Marguerite (Donnadieu) (novelist, dramatist); Gia Dinh, Vietnam **(1914–1996)**

**Durbin,** Deanna (Edna Mae) (actress); Winnipeg, Canada, 12/4/21

**Dürer,** Albrecht (painter, engraver); Nürnberg, Germany **(1471–1528)**

**Durning,** Charles (actor); Highland Falls, N.Y., 2/28/23

**Durrell,** Lawrence George (novelist); Julundur, India **(1912–1990)**

**Duse,** Eleonora (actress); Chioggia, Italy **(1859–1924)**

**Dussault,** Nancy (actress); Pensacola, Fla., 6/30/36

**Duvall,** Robert (actor, director, producer); San Diego, Calif., 1/5/31

**Duvall,** Shelley (actress); Houston, 7/7/49

**Dvořák,** Antonin (composer); Nelahozeves, Czechoslovakia **(1841–1904)**

**Dylan,** Bob (Robert Zimmerman) (singer, songwriter, guitarist); Duluth, Minn., 5/24/41

**Dysart,** Richard (actor); Brighton, Mass., 3/30/29

# E

**Eakins,** Thomas (painter, sculptor); Philadelphia **(1844–1916)**

**Earhart,** Amelia (aviator); Atchison, Kans. **(1897–1937)**

**Earp,** Wyatt (Berry Stapp) (sheriff, gunfighter); Monmouth, Ill. **(1848–1929)**

**Eastman,** George (camera inventor); Waterville, N.Y. **(1854–1932)**

**Eastwood,** Clint (actor, director, producer); San Francisco, 5/31/30

**Ebert,** Roger (film critic); Urbana, Ill., 6/18/42

**Ebsen,** Buddy (Christian Ebsen, Jr.) (actor); Belleville, Ill., 4/2/08

**Eckstine,** Billy (singer); Pittsburgh **(1914–1993)**

**Eddy,** Mary Baker (founder of Christian Science Church); Bow, N.H. **(1821–1910)**

**Eddy,** Nelson (baritone, actor); Providence, R.I. **(1901–1967)**

**Edel,** Leon (author); Pittsburgh **(1907–1997)**

**Edelman,** Marian Wright (social activist); Bennettsville, S.C., 6/6/39

**Eden,** Sir Anthony (Earl of Avon) (ex-prime minister); Durham, England **(1897–1977)**

**Eden,** Barbara (Barbara Huffman) (actress); Tucson, Ariz., 8/23/34

**Edison,** Thomas Alva (inventor); Milan, Ohio **(1847–1931)**

**Edwards,** Anthony (actor); Santa Barbara, Calif., 7/19/62

**Edwards,** Blake (film writer, producer); Tulsa, Okla., 7/26/22

**Edwards,** Jonathan (theologian); East Windsor, Conn. **(1703–1758)**

**Edwards,** Ralph (TV and radio producer); Merino, Colo., 6/13/13

**Edwards,** Vincent (Vincent Edward Zoino) (actor); Brooklyn, N.Y. **(1928–1996)**

**Eglevsky,** André (ballet dancer); Moscow **(1917–1977)**

**Egoyan,** Atom (film director, writer, editor); Cairo, 7/19/60

**Ehrlich,** Paul (bacteriologist); Strzelin, Poland **(1854–1915)**

**Eichmann,** (Karl) Adolf (Nazi, mass murderer); Solingen, Germany **(1906–1962)**

**Eikenberry,** Jill (actress); New Haven, Conn., 1/21/47

**Einstein,** Albert (physicist); Ulm, Germany **(1879–1955)**

**Eisner,** Michael (entertainment executive); Mt. Kisco, N.Y., 3/7/42

**Eisenhower,** Dwight David (34th U.S. president); Denison, Tex. **(1890–1969)**

**Eisenhower,** Milton S. (educator); Abilene, Kans. **(1899–1985)**

**Eisenstaedt,** Alfred (photographer, photojournalist); Dirschau (Prussia, now Tczew), Poland **(1898–1995)**

**Ekland,** Britt (Britt-Marie) (actress); Stockholm, 10/6/42

**Electra,** Carmen (Tara Patrick) (model, actress); Cincinnati, Ohio, 4/20/73

**Elfman,** Jenna (Jennifer Mary Butala) (actress); Los Angeles, 9/30/71

**Elgar,** Sir Edward (composer); Worcester, England **(1857–1934)**

**Elgart,** Larry (band leader); New London, Conn., 3/20/22

**El Greco** (Domenicos Theotocopoulos) (painter); Candia, Crete, Greece **(c. 1541–1614)**

**Elion,** Gertrude B. (chemist, Nobel laureate); New York City **(1918–1999)**

**Eliot,** George (Mary Ann Evans) (novelist); Chilvers Coton, England **(1819–1880)**

**Eliot,** Thomas Stearns (poet); St. Louis **(1888–1965)**

**Elizabeth I** (queen of England); Greenwich, England **(1533–1603)**

**Elizabeth II** (queen of England); London, 4/21/26

**Elizondo,** Hector (actor); New York City, 12/22/36

**Ellington,** Duke (Edward Kennedy) (jazz musician); Washington, D.C. **(1899–1974)**

**Elliot,** "Mama" Cass (Ellen Naomi Cohen) (singer); Baltimore **(1941–1974)**

**Elliott,** Sam (actor); Sacramento, Calif., 8/9/44

**Ellison,** Lawrence J. (computer industry executive); New York City, 1944

**Ellison,** Ralph (novelist); Oklahoma City, Okla. **(1914–1994)**

**Ellsberg,** Daniel (activist); Chicago, 4/7/31

Elman, Mischa (violinist); Stalnoye, Ukraine (1891–1967)
Emerson, Ralph Waldo (philosopher, poet); Boston (1803–1882)
Enesco, Georges (composer); Dorohoi, Romania (1881–1955)
Engels, Friedrich (Socialist writer); Barmen, Germany (1820–1895)
Englund, Robert (actor); Glendale, Calif., 6/6/49
Entremont, Philippe (concert pianist); Rheims, France, 6/7/34
Ephron, Nora (writer, director); New York City, 5/19/41
Epicurus (philosopher); Samos, Greece (341–270 B.C.)
Epstein, Sir Jacob (sculptor); New York City (1880–1959)
Erasmus, Desiderius (Gerhard Gerhards) (scholar); Rotterdam (1469–1536)
Erdrich, (Karen) Louise (writer); Little Falls, Minn., 7/6/54
Erickson, Leif (actor); Alameda, Calif. (1911–1986)
Ericsson, Leif (navigator) c. 10th century A.D.
Erikson, Erik H. (psychoanalyst); Frankfurt, Germany (1902–1994)
Ernst, Max (painter); Bruhl, Germany (1891–1976)
Erté (Romain de Tirtoff) (artist, designer); St. Petersburg, Russia (1892–1990)
Estevez, Emilio (actor, director, screenwriter); New York City, 5/12/62
Eszterhas, Joe (screenwriter); Csakanydoroslo, Hungary, 11/23/44
Euclid (mathematician); Megara, Greece, fl. 300 B.C.
Euler, Leonhard (mathematician); Basel, Switzerland (1707–1783)
Euripides (dramatist); Salamis, Greece (c. 484–407 B.C.)
Evangelista, Linda (model); St. Catharines, Ont., Canada, 5/10/65
Evans, Dale (born Lucille Wood Smith but raised as Frances Octavia Smith) (actress, singer); Uvalde, Tex. (1912–2001)
Evans, Dame Edith (actress); London (1888–1976)
Evans, Linda (actress); Hartford, Conn., 11/18/42
Evans, Maurice (actor); Dorchester, England (1901–1989)
Everett, Chad (Raymond Lee Cramton) (actor); South Bend, Ind., 6/11/36
Everett, Rupert (actor, model, musician); Norfolk, England, 5/29/59
Everhart, Angie (model, actress); Akron, Ohio, 9/6/69
Evers, Charles (civil rights leader); Decatur, Miss., 9/14/22
Evers, Medgar (civil rights leader); Decatur, Miss. (1925–1963)
Evers-Williams, Myrlie (civil rights leader); Vicksburg, Miss., 3/17/33

# F

Fabares, Shelley (actress); Santa Monica, Calif., 1/19/44
Fabian (Fabian Anthony Forte) (singer); Philadelphia, 2/6/43
Fabray, Nanette (Nanette Fabarés) (actress); San Diego, Calif., 10/27/22
Fahrenheit, Gabriel (German physicist); Danzig, Poland (1686–1736)
Fairbanks, Douglas (Douglas Ulman) (actor); Denver (1883–1939)
Fairbanks, Douglas, Jr. (actor); New York City (1909–2000)
Fairchild, Morgan (Patsy Ann McClenny) (actress); Dallas, 2/3/50
Faith, Percy (conductor); Toronto (1908–1976)
Falk, Peter (actor); New York City, 9/16/27
Falla, Manuel de (composer); Cadiz, Spain (1876–1946)
Faludi, Susan (journalist, writer); New York City, 4/18/59
Falwell, Jerry (fundamentalist preacher); Lynchburg, Va., 8/11/33
Faraday, Michael (physicist); Newington, England (1791–1867)
Farentino, James (actor); Brooklyn, N.Y., 2/24/38
Farley, Chris (actor, comedian); Madison, Wis. (1964–1997)
Farmer, James (civil rights leader); Marshall, Tex. (1920–1999)
Farnsworth, Richard (actor); Los Angeles (1920–2000)
Farr, Jamie (Jameel Joseph Farah) (actor); Toledo, Ohio, 7/1/34
Farrar, Geraldine (soprano, actress); Melrose, Mass. (1882–1967)
Farrell, Eileen (operatic soprano); Willimantic, Conn. (1920–2002)
Farrell, James T. (novelist); Chicago (1904–1979)
Farrell, Perry (Perry Bernstein) (lead singer); Queens, N.Y., 3/29/59
Farrell, Suzanne (Roberta Sue Ficker) (ballet dancer); Cincinnati, 8/16/45
Farrow, Mia (actress); Los Angeles, 2/9/46
Fasanella, Ralph (painter); New York City (1914–1997)
Fassbinder, Rainer Werner (film, stage director); Bad Wörishofen, Germany (1946–1982)
Fast, Howard (novelist); New York City, 11/11/14
Faubus, Orval E(ugene) (governor of Arkansas); Combs, Ark. (1910–1994)
Faulkner, William (novelist); New Albany, Miss. (1897–1962)
Fauré, Gabriel Urbain (composer); Pamiers, France (1845–1924)
Fawcett, Farrah (Mary Farrah Leni Fawcett) (actress); Corpus Christi, Tex., 2/2/47
Faye, Alice (Ann Leppert) (actress); New York City (1912–1998)
Feiffer, Jules (cartoonist); New York City, 1/26/29
Feininger, Lyonel (painter); New York City (1871–1956)
Feldman, Marty (actor, screenwriter, director); London (1938–1982)

Feldon, Barbara (actress); Pittsburgh, 3/12/41
Feliciano, José (singer); Larez, Puerto Rico, 9/10/45
Felker, Clay S. (editor, publisher); St. Louis, 10/2/25
Fell, Norman (actor); Philadelphia (1923–1998)
Fellini, Federico (film director); Rimini, Italy (1920–1993)
Fender, Freddie (Baldemar Huerta) (singer); San Benito, Tex., 6/4/37
Ferber, Edna (novelist); Kalamazoo, Mich. (1885–1968)
Ferguson, Maynard (jazz trumpeter); Verdun, Que., Canada, 5/4/28
Ferlinghetti, Lawrence (poet, writer, translator); Yonkers, N.Y., 3/24/19
Fermi, Enrico (atomic physicist); Rome (1901–1954)
Fernandel (Fernand Joseph Desire Contandin) (actor); Marseilles, France (1903–1971)
Ferraro, Geraldine Anne (political figure); New York City, 8/26/35
Ferrer, José (actor, director); Santurce, Puerto Rico (1912–1992)
Ferrer, Mel (actor); Elberon, N.J., 8/25/17
Fiedler, Arthur (conductor); Boston (1894–1979)
Field, Eugene (poet); St. Louis (1850–1895)
Field, Marshall (merchant); nr. Conway, Mass. (1834–1906)
Field, Sally (actress); Pasadena, Calif., 11/6/46
Fielding, Henry (novelist); nr. Glastonbury, England (1707–1754)
Fields, W. C. (William Claude Dukenfield) (comedian); Philadelphia (1880–1946)
Fiennes, Joseph (actor); Salisbury, England, 5/27/70
Fiennes, Ralph (actor); Suffolk, England, 12/22/62
Fierstein, Harvey (Forbes) (playwright, actor); Brooklyn, 6/6/54
Figgis, Mike (director, screenwriter, composer, actor); Carlisle, England, 2/28/48
Filene, Edward A. (merchant) (1860–1937)
Fillmore, Millard (13th U.S. president); Locke, Cayuga County, N.Y. (1800–1874)
Finch, Peter (actor); Kensington, England (1916–1977)
Finney, Albert (actor); Salford, England, 5/9/36
Fiorentino, Linda (Clorinda Fiorentino) (actress); Philadelphia, 3/9/60
Firkusny, Rudolf (pianist); Napajedia, former Czechoslovakia (1912–1994)
Firth, Colin (actor); Grayshot, England, 9/10/60
Fischer-Dieskau, Dietrich (baritone); Berlin, 5/28/25
Fishburne, Laurence (actor); Augusta, Ga., 7/30/61
Fisher, Carrie (actress); Los Angeles, 10/21/56
Fisher, Eddie (Edwin) (singer); Philadelphia, 8/10/28
Fitzgerald, Barry (William Joseph Shields) (actor); Dublin (1888–1961)
Fitzgerald, Ella (singer); Newport News, Va. (1918–1996)
Fitzgerald, F. Scott (Francis Scott Key Fitzgerald) (novelist); St. Paul, Minn. (1896–1940)
Fitzgerald, Geraldine (actress); Dublin, 11/24/14
Fitzgerald, Pegeen (radio broadcaster); Norcatur, Kans. (1910–1989)
Flack, Roberta (singer); Black Mountain, N.C., 2/10/40
Flagstad, Kirsten (Wagnerian soprano); Hamar, Norway (1895–1962)
Flatt, Lester Raymond (bluegrass musician); Overton County, Tenn. (1914–1979)
Flaubert, Gustave (novelist); Rouen, France (1821–1880)
Fleming, Sir Alexander (bacteriologist); Lochfield, Scotland (1881–1955)
Fletcher, John (dramatist); Rye, Sussex, England (1579–1625)
Flockhart, Calista (actress); Freeport, Ill., 11/11/64
Flynn, Errol (actor); Hobart, Tasmania (1909–1959)
Fodor, Eugene (violinist); Turkey Creek, Colo., 3/5/50
Fokine, Michel (dancer, choreographer); St. Petersburg, Russia (1880–1942)
Fonda, Bridget (actress); Los Angeles, 1/27/64
Fonda, Henry (actor); Grand Island, Neb. (1905–1982)
Fonda, Jane (actress); New York City, 12/21/37
Fonda, Peter (actor); New York City, 2/20/39
Fontaine, Frank (singer, comedian); Cambridge, Mass. (1920–1979)
Fontaine, Joan (Joan de Havilland) (actress); Tokyo, 10/22/17
Fontanne, Lynn (actress); London (1887–1983)
Fonteyn, Dame Margot (Margaret Hookham) (ballet dancer); Reigate, England (1919–1991)
Foote, Shelby (historian); Greenville, Miss., 11/17/16
Forbes, Malcolm S(tevenson) (publisher, sportsman); Brooklyn, N.Y. (1919–1990)
Ford, Gerald Rudolph (38th U.S. president); Omaha, Neb., 7/14/13
Ford, Glenn (Gwyllyn Ford) (actor); Ste.-Christine, Que., Canada, 5/1/16
Ford, Harrison (actor); Chicago, 7/13/42
Ford, Henry (industrialist); Greenfield, Mich. (1863–1947)
Ford, John (film director); Cape Elizabeth, Maine (1895–1973)

**Ford,** Tennessee Ernie (Ernie Jennings Ford) (singer); Bristol, Tenn. **(1919–1991)**
**Foreman,** George (boxer, actor); Marshall, Tex., 1/10/49
**Forrester,** Maureen (contralto); Montreal, 7/25/30
**Forsythe,** John (John Lincoln Freund) (actor); Penn's Grove, N.J., 1/29/18
**Fosdick,** Harry Emerson (clergyman); Buffalo, N.Y. **(1878–1968)**
**Fosse,** Bob (Robert Louis Fosse) (choreographer, director); Chicago **(1927–1987)**
**Foster,** Jodie (Alicia Christian Foster) (actress, director, producer); Los Angeles, 11/19/62
**Foster,** Stephen Collins (composer); nr. Pittsburgh **(1826–1864)**
**Fountain,** Pete (jazz musician); New Orleans, 7/3/30
**Fox,** Matthew (actor); Crowheart, Wyo., 7/14/66
**Fox,** Michael J. (actor, producer); Edmonton, Alta., Canada, 6/9/61
**Foxx,** Redd (John Elroy Sanford) (actor, comedian); St. Louis **(1922–1991)**
**Foy,** Eddie, Jr. (dancer, actor); New Rochelle, N.Y. **(1905–1983)**
**Fracci,** Carla (ballet dancer); Milan, Italy, 8/20/36
**Fragonard,** Jean Honoré (painter); Grasse, France **(1732–1806)**
**Frakes,** Jonathan (actor); Bethlehem, Pa., 8/19/52
**Frampton,** Peter (rock musician); Beckenham, England, 4/20/50
**France,** Anatole (Jacques Anatole François Thibault) (author); Paris **(1844–1924)**
**Francescatti,** Zino (violinist); Marseilles, France **(1902–1991)**
**Franciosa,** Anthony (Anthony Papaleo) (actor); New York City, 10/25/28
**Francis,** Anne (actress); Ossining, N.Y., 7/16/30
**Francis,** Connie (Concetta Franconero) (singer); Newark, N.J., 12/12/38
**Francis,** Genie (actress); Englewood, N.J., 5/26/62
**Francis of Assisi,** Saint (Giovanni Francesco Barnardone) (founder of Franciscans); Assisi, Italy **(1182–1226)**
**Franck,** César Auguste (composer); Liège, Belgium **(1822–1890)**
**Franco Bahamonde,** Francisco (chief of state); El Ferrol, Spain **(1892–1975)**
**Frankenheimer,** John (movie director, producer); New York City, 1930
**Frankenthaler,** Helen (artist); New York City, 12/12/28
**Frankl,** Victor E. (psychiatrist); Vienna **(1905–1997)**
**Franklin,** Aretha (singer); Memphis, Tenn., 3/25/42
**Franklin,** Benjamin (statesman, scientist); Boston **(1706–1790)**
**Franklin,** Bonnie (actress); Santa Monica, Calif., 1/6/44
**Franklin,** John Hope (historian); Rentiesville, Okla., 1/2/15
**Frann,** Mary (actress); St. Louis **(1943–1998)**
**Franz,** Dennis (Dennis Schlachta) (actor); Chicago, 10/28/44
**Fraser,** Brendan (actor); Indianapolis, Indiana, 12/3/67
**Frazer,** Sir James George (anthropologist); Glasgow, Scotland **(1854–1941)**
**Freeman,** Morgan (actor); Memphis, Tenn., 6/1/37
**Freud,** Sigmund (psychoanalyst); Moravia, Czech Repubic **(1856–1939)**
**Frey,** Glenn (musician); Detroit, 11/6/48
**Frick,** Henry Clay (industrialist); Westmoreland Co., Pa. **(1849–1919)**
**Friedan,** Betty (Betty Naomi Goldstein) (feminist, writer); Peoria, Ill., 2/4/21
**Fromm,** Erich (psychoanalyst); Frankfurt-am-Main, Germany **(1900–1980)**
**Frost,** David (TV entertainer); Tenterden, England, 4/7/39
**Frost,** Robert Lee (poet); San Francisco **(1874–1963)**
**Fry,** Christopher (playwright); Bristol, England, 12/18/07
**Fugard,** Athol (playwright); Middleburg, South Africa, 6/11/32
**Fulbright,** J. William (politician); Sumner, Mo. **(1905–1995)**
**Fuller,** Charles (playwright); Philadelphia, 3/5/39
**Fuller,** R(ichard) Buckminster (Jr.) (architect, educator); Milton, Mass. **(1895–1983)**
**Fulton,** Robert (inventor); Lancaster County, Pa. **(1765–1815)**
**Funicello,** Annette (actress); Utica, N.Y., 10/22/42
**Funt,** Allen (TV producer); Brooklyn, N.Y. **(1914–1999)**

## G

**Gabin,** Jean (actor); Paris **(1904–1976)**
**Gable,** (William) Clark (actor); Cadiz, Ohio **(1901–1960)**
**Gabo,** Naum (sculptor); Briansk, Russia **(1890–1977)**
**Gabor,** Eva (actress); Budapest **(1920–1995)**
**Gabor,** Zsa Zsa (Sari) (actress); Budapest, 2/6/17
**Gabriel,** Peter (musician); Cobham, England, 2/13/50
**Gabrieli,** Giovanni (composer); Venice (c. 1557–1612)
**Gaddis,** William (novelist); New York City **(1922–1998)**
**Gainsborough,** Thomas (painter); Sudbury, Suffolk, England **(1727–1788)**

**Galbraith,** John Kenneth (economist); Iona Station, Ont., Canada, 10/15/08
**Galilei,** Galileo (astronomer, physicist); Pisa, Italy **(1564–1642)**
**Gallico,** Paul (novelist); New York City **(1897–1976)**
**Gallup,** George H. (poll taker); Jefferson, Iowa **(1901–1984)**
**Galsworthy,** John (novelist, dramatist); Coombe, England **(1867–1933)**
**Galway,** James (flutist); Belfast, Northern Ireland, 12/8/39
**Gambling,** John A. (radio broadcaster); New York City, 1930
**Gandhi,** Indira (Indira Nehru) (former prime minister); Allahabad, India **(1917– 1984)**
**Gandhi,** Mohandas Karamchand (called Mahatma Gandhi) (Hindu leader); Porbandar, India **(1869–1948)**
**Gannett,** Frank E. (editor, publisher) **(1876–1957)**
**Garagiola,** Joe (Joseph Henry Garagiola) (sportscaster); St. Louis, 2/12/26
**Garbo,** Greta (Greta Gustafsson) (actress); Stockholm **(1905–1990)**
**Garcia,** Andy (Andres Arturo Garcia-Menendez) (actor); Havana, Cuba, 4/12/56
**Garcia,** Jerry (rock musician); San Francisco **(1942–1995)**
**Garcia Lorca,** Frederico (poet, dramatist); Fuente Vaqueros, Spain **(1898–1936)**
**Garden,** Mary (soprano); Aberdeen, Scotland **(1874–1967)**
**Gardenia,** Vincent (Vincente Scognamiglio) (actor); Naples, Italy **(1922–1992)**
**Gardner,** Ava (actress); Smithfield, N.C. **(1922–1990)**
**Gardner,** Erle Stanley (novelist); Malden, Mass. **(1889–1970)**
**Garfield,** James Abram (20th U.S. president); Cuyahoga County, Ohio **(1831–1881)**
**Garfunkel,** Art (Arthur) (singer); Newark, N.J., 11/5/41
**Garibaldi,** Giuseppe (Italian nationalist leader); Nice, France **(1807–1882)**
**Garland,** Judy (Frances Gumm) (actress, singer); Grand Rapids, Minn. **(1922–1969)**
**Garner,** Erroll (jazz pianist); Pittsburgh **(1921–1977)**
**Garner,** James (James Bumgarner) (actor); Norman, Okla., 4/7/28
**Garofalo,** Janeane (actress, comedienne); Newton, N.J., 9/28/64
**Garr,** Teri (actress); Lakewood, Ohio, 12/11/49
**Garrison,** William Lloyd (abolitionist); Newburyport, Mass. **(1805–1879)**
**Garroway,** Dave (TV host); Schenectady, N.Y. **(1913–1982)**
**Garson,** Greer (actress); County Down, Northern Ireland **(1903–1996)**
**Garth,** Jennie (actress); Urbana, Ill., 4/3/72
**Garvey,** Marcus Moziah (black nationalist leader); Jamaica **(1887–1940)**
**Gassman,** Vittorio (film actor, director); Genoa, Italy **(1922–2000)**
**Gates,** Bill (William Henry Gates III) (software pioneer); Seattle, 10/28/55
**Gates,** Henry Louis, Jr. (scholar); Keyser, W. Va., 9/16/50
**Gaudí,** Antonio (architect); Reus, Spain **(1852–1926)**
**Gauguin,** (Eugène Henri) Paul (painter); Paris **(1848–1903)**
**Gautama Buddha** (Prince Siddhartha) (philosopher); Kapilavastu, India **(c. 563–c. 483 B.C.)**
**Gavin,** John (actor, diplomat); Los Angeles, 4/8/35
**Gavras,** Konstantinos (Costa-Gavras) (film director); Loutra-Iraias, Greece, 2/13/33
**Gaye,** Marvin (singer); Washington, D.C. **(1939–1984)**
**Gayle,** Crystal (Brenda Gayle Webb) (singer); Paintsville, Ky., 1/9/51
**Gaynor,** Janet (actress); Philadelphia **(1906–1984)**
**Gaynor,** Mitzi (Francesca Mitzi Marlene de Czanyi von Gerber) (actress); Chicago, 9/4/31
**Gazzara,** Ben (Biagio Anthony Gazzara) (actor); New York City, 8/28/30
**Gedda,** Nicolai (tenor); Stockholm, 7/11/25
**Gellar,** Sarah Michelle (actress); New York City, 4/14/77
**Genet,** Jean (playwright); Paris **(1910–1986)**
**Genghis Khan** (Temujin) (conqueror); nr. Lake Baikal, Russia **(1162–1227 )**
**Gentry,** Bobbie (Roberta Streeter) (singer); Chickasaw Co., Miss., 7/27/44
**George,** David Lloyd (statesman); Manchester, England **(1863–1945)**
**George,** Henry (economist, reformer); Philadelphia **(1839–1897)**
**Gere,** Richard (actor); Philadelphia, 8/29/49
**Géricault,** Jean Louis (painter); Rouen, France **(1791–1824)**
**Geronimo** (Goyathlay) (Apache chieftain); Arizona **(1829–1909)**
**Gershwin,** George (composer); Brooklyn, N.Y. **(1898–1937)**
**Gershwin,** Ira (lyricist); New York City **(1896–1983)**
**Getty,** J. Paul (oil executive); Minneapolis **(1892–1976)**
**Getz,** Stan (saxophonist); Philadelphia **(1927–1991)**

**Ghiberti,** Lorenzo (goldsmith, sculptor); Florence **(1378–1455)**
**Ghostley,** Alice (actress); Eve, Mo., 8/14/26
**Giacometti,** Alberto (sculptor); Switzerland **(1901–1966)**
**Giannini,** Giancarlo (actor); La Spezia, Italy, 8/1/42
**Gibbon,** Edward (historian); Putney, England **(1737–1794)**
**Gibson,** Charles Dana (illustrator); Roxbury, Mass. **(1867–1944)**
**Gibson,** Henry (actor, comedian); Germantown, Pa., 9/21/35
**Gibson,** Mel (actor, director, producer); Peekskill, N.Y., 1/3/56
**Gide,** André (author); Paris **(1869–1951)**
**Gielgud,** Sir John (actor); London **(1904–2000)**
**Gifford,** Kathie Lee (Kathie Lee Epstein) (talk show host); Paris, 8/16/53
**Gilbert,** Melissa (actress); Los Angeles, 5/8/64
**Gilbert,** Walter (chemist, Nobel laureate); Boston, 3/21/32
**Gilbert,** Sir William Schwenck (librettist); London **(1836–1911)**
**Gilels,** Emil (concert pianist); Odessa, Ukraine **(1916–1985)**
**Gillespie,** Dizzy (John Birks Gillespie) (jazz trumpeter); Cheraw, S.C. **(1917–1993)**
**Gilligan,** Carol (Friedman) (psychologist); New York City, 11/28/36
**Gilpin,** Peri (actress); Waco, Tex., 5/27/61
**Gimbel,** Bernard F. (merchant); Vincennes, Ind. **(1885–1966)**
**Gingrich,** Newt (politician); Harrisburg, Pa., 6/17/43
**Ginsberg,** Allen (poet); Newark, N.J. **(1926–1997)**
**Giordano,** Luca (painter); Naples, Italy **(1632–1705)**
**Giorgione** (painter); Castelfranco, Italy **(c. 1477–1510)**
**Giotto di Bondone** (painter); Vespignamo, Italy **(c. 1266–1337)**
**Giovanni,** Nikki (poet); Knoxville, Tenn., 6/7/43
**Giroud,** Françoise (French government official); Geneva, 9/21/16
**Gish,** Dorothy (actress); Massillon, Ohio **(1898–1968)**
**Gish,** Lillian (Lillian de Guiche) (actress); Springfield, Ohio **(1893–1993)**
**Giuliani, Rudolph** (public official); Brooklyn, N.Y., 5/24/44
**Givenchy,** Hubert (fashion designer); Beauvais, France, 2/21/27
**Gladstone,** William Ewart (statesman); Liverpool, England **(1809–1898)**
**Glaser,** Paul Michael (actor, director); Cambridge, Mass., 3/25/43
**Glass,** Philip (composer); Baltimore, 1/31/37
**Gleason,** Jackie (comedian); Brooklyn, N.Y. **(1916–1987)**
**Glenn,** John (legislator, astronaut); Cambridge, Ohio, 7/18/21
**Gless,** Sharon (actress); Los Angeles, 5/31/43
**Glover,** Danny (actor); San Francisco, 7/22/47
**Gluck,** Christoph Willibald (composer); Erasbach, Germany **(1714–1787)**
**Gobel,** George (comedian); Chicago **(1920–1991)**
**Godard,** Jean Luc (film director); Paris, 12/3/30
**Goddard,** Paulette (Marion Levy) **(actress);** Great Neck, N.Y. **(1911–1990)**
**Goddard,** Robert Hutchings (father of modern rocketry); Worcester, Mass. **(1882–1945)**
**Godfrey,** Arthur (entertainer); New York City **(1903–1983)**
**Goebbels,** Joseph Paul (Nazi leader); Rheydt, Germany **(1897–1945)**
**Goering,** Hermann (Nazi leader); Rosenheim, Germany **(1893–1946)**
**Goethals,** George Washington (engineer); Brooklyn, N.Y. **(1858–1928)**
**Goethe,** Johann Wolfgang von (poet, playwright, novelist); Frankfurt-am-Main, Germany **(1749–1832)**
**Gogol,** Nikolai Vasilievich (novelist); nr. Mirgorod, Ukraine **(1809–1852)**
**Goldberg,** Rube (cartoonist); San Francisco **(1883–1970)**
**Goldberg,** Whoopi (Caryn Johnson) (actress); New York City, 11/13/49
**Goldblum,** Jeff (actor); Pittsburgh, 10/22/52
**Golding,** Henry (Henry Goulding) (author); New York City (1.... 1981)
**Goldman,** Emma (anarchist); Kovno, Lithuania **(1869–1940)**
**Goldsmith,** Oliver (dramatist, poet); County Longford, Ireland **(1728–1774)**
**Goldwyn,** Samuel (Schmuel Gelbfisz) (film producer); Warsaw **(1879–1974)**
**Gompers,** Samuel (labor leader); London **(1850–1924)**
**Goodall,** Jane (Baroness van Lawick-Goodall) (ethologist); London, 4/3/34
**Gooding, Jr.,** Cuba (actor); Bronx, New York, 1/2/68
**Goodman,** Benny (clarinetist); Chicago **(1909–1986)**
**Goodman,** John (actor); St. Louis, 6/20/52
**Goodwin,** Doris (Helen) Kearns (historian); Rockville Center, N.Y., 1/4/43
**Goodyear,** Charles (inventor); New Haven, Conn. **(1800–1860)**
**Gorbachev,** Mikhail Sergeyevich (former Soviet leader); Privolnoye, Russia, 3/2/31

**Gordimer,** Nadine (novelist, short-story writer); Springs, South Africa, 12/20/23
**Gordon,** Dexter (jazz musician); Los Angeles **(1923–1990)**
**Gordon,** Ruth (actress); Wollaston, Mass. **(1896–1985)**
**Gore,** Albert, Jr. (ex-vice president of the U.S.); Washington, D.C., 3/31/48
**Gordy,** Berry, Jr. (record company executive); Detroit, 11/28/29
**Gorey,** Edward (St. John) (illustrator, author); Chicago **(1925–2000)**
**Gorki,** Maxim (Alexei Maximovich Peshkov) (author); Nizhni Novgorod, Russia **(1868–1936)**
**Gorky,** Arshile (painter); Armenia **(1904–1948)**
**Gormé,** Eydie (singer); Bronx, N.Y., 8/16/32
**Gorshin,** Frank (actor); Pittsburgh, 4/5/34
**Gossett,** Louis, Jr. (actor); Brooklyn, N.Y., 5/27/36
**Gottschalk,** Louis Moreau (pianist, composer); New Orleans **(1829–1869)**
**Gould,** Chester (cartoonist); Pawnee, Okla. **(1900–1985)**
**Gould,** Elliott (Elliott Goldstein) (actor); Brooklyn, N.Y., 8/29/38
**Gould,** Glenn (concert pianist); Toronto **(1932–1982)**
**Gould,** Morton (composer); Richmond Hill, Queens, N.Y. **(1913–1996)**
**Gould,** Stephen Jay (paleontologist, science writer); New York City **(1941–2002)**
**Goulet,** Robert (singer); Lawrence, Mass., 11/26/33
**Gounod,** Charles François (composer); Paris **(1818–1893)**
**Goya y Lucientes,** Francisco José de (painter); Fuendetodos, Spain **(1746–1828)**
**Grable,** Betty (actress); St. Louis **(1916–1973)**
**Grace,** Princess of Monaco (Grace Kelly) (ex-actress); Philadelphia **(1929–1982)**
**Graham,** Bill (Wolfgang Grajonca) (rock impresario); Berlin **(1930–1991)**
**Graham,** Billy (William F. Graham) (evangelist); Charlotte, N.C., 11/7/18
**Graham,** Katharine Meyer (newspaper publisher); New York City **(1917–2001)**
**Graham,** Martha (choreographer); Pittsburgh **(1894–1991)**
**Grainger,** Percy Aldridge (pianist, composer); Melbourne, Australia **(1882–1961)**
**Gramm,** Donald (Grambach) (bass-baritone); Milwaukee **(1927–1983)**
**Grammer,** Kelsey (actor); St. Thomas, V.I., 2/21/55
**Granger,** Stewart (James Stewart) (actor); London **(1913–1993)**
**Grant,** Cary (Alexander Archibald Leach) (actor); Bristol, England **(1904–1986)**
**Grant,** Hugh (actor); London, England, 9/9/60
**Grant,** Lee (Lyova Haskell Rosenthal) (actress); New York City, 10/31/30
**Grant,** Ulysses Simpson (18th U.S. president); Point Pleasant, Ohio **(1822–1885)**
**Grass,** Günter (novelist); Danzig, Poland, 10/16/27
**Graves,** Nancy (Stevenson) (artist); Pittsfield, Mass. **(1940–1996)**
**Graves,** Peter (Peter Aurness) (actor); Minneapolis, 3/18/26
**Graves,** Robert (writer); London **(1895–1985)**
**Gray,** Linda (actress); Santa Monica, Calif., 9/12/40
**Gray,** Thomas (poet); London **(1716–1771)**
**Greco,** José (dancer); Montorio nei Frentani, Italy **(1918–2000)**
**Greeley,** Horace (journalist, politician); Amherst, N.H. **(1811–1872)**
**Green,** Adolph (actor, lyricist); New York City, 12/2/15
**Green,** Al (singer); Forrest City, Ark., 4/13/46
**Greene,** Graham (novelist); Berkhamsted, England **(1904–1991)**
**Greene,** Lorne (actor); Ottawa, Ont., Canada **(1915–1987)**
**Greene,** Shecky (comedian, actor); Chicago, 4/8/26
**Greenstreet,** Sydney (actor); Sandwich, England (1879–1.....)
**Greenspan,** Alan (chairman of the Federal Reserve); New York City, 3/6/26
**Greer,** Germaine (feminist, writer); Melbourne, Australia, 1/29/39
**Gregory,** Cynthia (ballet dancer); Los Angeles, 7/8/46
**Gregory,** Dick (comedian); St. Louis, 10/12/32
**Gregory,** Lady (Isabella) Augusta (playwright); Roxborough, Ireland **(1852–1932)**
**Greuze,** Jean-Baptiste (painter); Tournus, France **(1725–1805)**
**Grey,** Joel (Joel Katz) (actor, dancer); Cleveland, 4/11/32
**Grey,** Zane (author); Zanesville, Ohio **(1875–1939)**
**Grieg,** Edvard Hagerup (composer); Bergen, Norway **(1843–1907)**
**Grier,** Pam (actress); Winston-Salem, N.C., 5/26/49
**Griffin,** Merv (TV host, producer); San Mateo, Calif., 7/6/25
**Griffith,** Andy (actor); Mount Airy, N.C., 6/1/26
**Griffith,** David Lewelyn Wark (film producer); La Grange, Ky. **(1875–1948)**
**Griffith,** Melanie (actress); New York City, 8/9/57

**Grigorovich,** Yuri (choreographer); Leningrad (St. Petersburg), Russia, 1/1/27

**Grimes,** Tammy (actress); Lynn, Mass., 1/30/34

**Grimm,** Jacob (author of fairy tales); Hanau, Germany **(1785–1863)**

**Grimm,** Wilhelm (author of fairy tales); Hanau, Germany **(1786–1859)**

**Gris,** Juan (José Victoriano González) (painter); Madrid **(1887–1927)**

**Grisham,** John (attorney, author); Jonesboro, Ark., 2/8/55

**Grodin,** Charles (actor); Pittsburgh, 4/21/35

**Groening,** Matt (animator, producer); Portland, Ore., 2/14/54

**Gromyko,** Andrei A. (diplomat); Starye Gromyki, Russia **(1909–1989)**

**Gropius,** Walter (architect); Berlin **(1883–1969)**

**Gropper,** William (painter, illustrator); New York City **(1897–1977)**

**Gross,** Michael (actor); Chicago, 6/21/47

**Grosz,** George (painter); Germany **(1893–1959)**

**Grove,** Andrew (Andras Grof) (computer industry executive); Budapest, Hungary, 9/2/36

**Grünewald,** Matthias (Mathis Gothart Neithart) (painter); Würzburg, Germany **(c. 1470–1528)**

**Guest,** Christopher (Christopher Haden-Guest) (actor, writer, director); New York City, 2/5/48

**Guggenheim,** Meyer (capitalist); Langnau, Switzerland **(1828–1905)**

**Guillaume,** Robert (Robert Williams) (actor); St. Louis, 11/30/27

**Guinness,** Sir Alec (actor); London **(1914–2000)**

**Guitry,** Sacha (Alexandre Guitry) (actor, film director); St. Petersburg, Russia **(1885–1957)**

**Gumbel,** Bryant Charles (TV newscaster); New Orleans, 9/29/48

**Gunther,** John (author); Chicago **(1901–1970)**

**Gutenberg,** Johann (printer); Mainz, Germany **(c. 1397–1468)**

**Guthrie,** Arlo (singer); New York City, 7/10/47

**Guthrie,** Woody (folk singer, composer); Okemah, Okla. **(1912–1967)**

**Gwenn,** Edmund (actor); London **(1875–1959)**

**Gwynne,** Fred (actor); New York City **(1926–1993)**

# H

**Habibie,** Bacharuddin, Jusuf (president of Indonesia); Pare-Pare, Indonesia, 6/25/36

**Hackett,** Bobby (trumpeter); Providence, R.I. **(1915–1976)**

**Hackett,** Buddy (Leonard Hacker) (comedian, actor); Brooklyn, N.Y., 8/31/24

**Hackman,** Gene (actor); San Bernardino, Calif., 1/30/31

**Hagen,** Uta (actress); Göttingen, Germany, 6/12/19

**Haggard,** Merle (songwriter, singer); Bakersfield, Calif., 4/6/37

**Hagman,** Larry (Larry Hageman) (actor); Weatherford, Tex., 9/21/31

**Haig,** Alexander Meigs, Jr. (ex-secretary of state, ex-general); Bala-Cynwyd, Pa., 12/2/24

**Haile** Selassie (Ras Tafari Makonnen) (ex-emperor); Ethiopia **(1892–1975)**

**Hailey,** Arthur (novelist); Luton, England, 4/5/20

**Halberstam,** David (journalist); New York City, 4/10/34

**Hale,** Alan (actor, director); Washington, D.C. **(1892–1950)**

**Hale,** Barbara (actress); DeKalb, Ill., 4/18/21

**Hale,** Edward Everett (clergyman, author); Boston **(1822–1909)**

**Hale,** Nathan (American Revolutionary officer); Coventry, Conn. **(1755–1776)**

**Halevi,** Judah (Jewish poet); Toledo, Spain **(1085–1140)**

**Haley,** Alex (writer); Ithaca, N.Y. **(1921–1992)**

**Haley,** Jack (actor); Boston **(1899–1979)**

**Hall,** Anthony Michael (Michael Anthony Thomas Charles Hall) (actor, singer); Boston, 4/14/68

**Hall,** Arsenio (comedian, talk-show host); Cleveland, 2/12/58

**Hall,** Donald (Andrew, Jr.) (poet); New Haven, Conn., 9/20/28

**Hall,** Huntz (actor); New York City **(1919–1999)**

**Hall,** Jerry (model, actress); Mesquite, Texas, 7/2/56

**Hall,** Monty (TV personality); Winnipeg, Canada, 8/25/23

**Halley,** Edmund (astronomer); London **(1656–1742)**

**Hals,** Frans (painter); Antwerp, Netherlands **(c. 1580–1666)**

**Halsey,** William Frederick, Jr. (naval officer); Elizabeth, N.J. **(1882–1959)**

**Hamel,** Veronica (actress); Philadelphia, 11/20/43

**Hamill,** Mark (actor); Oakland, 9/25/52

**Hamilton,** Alexander (statesman); Nevis, British West Indies **(1755–1804)**

**Hamilton,** Alice (physician, reformer); New York City **(1869–1970)**

**Hamilton,** Edith (scholar); Dresden, Germany **(1867–1963)**

**Hamilton,** George (actor); Memphis, Tenn., 8/12/39

**Hamlin,** Harry (actor); Pasadena, Calif., 10/30/51

**Hamlisch,** Marvin (composer, pianist); New York City, 6/2/44

**Hammarskjöld,** Dag (UN secretary-general); Jönköping, Sweden **(1905–1961 )**

**Hammerstein,** Oscar, II (librettist, stage producer); New York City **(1895–1960)**

**Hampton,** Lionel (vibraharpist, band leader); Birmingham, Ala. **(1913–2002)**

**Hamsun,** Knut (Knut Pedersen) (novelist); Lom, Norway **(1859–1952)**

**Hancock,** Herbie (jazz musician); Chicago, 4/12/40

**Hancock,** John (statesman); Braintree, Mass. **(1737–1793)**

**Hand,** Learned (jurist); Albany, N.Y. **(1872–1961)**

**Handel,** George Frideric (Georg Friedrich Händel) (composer); Halle, Germany **(1685–1759)**

**Handy,** William Christopher (blues composer); Florence, Ala. **(1873–1958)**

**Hanks,** Tom (actor, director, writer); Concord, Calif., 7/9/56

**Hannah,** Daryl (actress); Chicago, 12/19/60

**Hannibal** (Carthaginian general); North Africa **(247–182 B.C.)**

**Hansberry,** Lorraine (playwright); Chicago **(1930–1965)**

**Hanson,** Howard (conductor); Wahoo, Neb. **(1896–1981)**

**Harburg,** E. Y. "Yip" (songwriter); New York City **(1896–1981)**

**Harden,** Marcia Gay (actress); La Jolla, Calif., 8/14/59

**Harding,** Warren Gamaliel (29th U.S. president); Morrow County, Ohio **(1865–1923)**

**Hardwicke,** Sir Cedric (actor); Stourbridge, England **(1893–1964)**

**Hardy,** Oliver (comedian); Atlanta **(1892–1957)**

**Hardy,** Thomas (novelist); Dorsetshire, England **(1840–1928)**

**Harkness,** Edward S. (business executive); Cleveland **(1874–1940)**

**Harlow,** Jean (Harlean Carpentier) (actress); Kansas City, Mo. **(1911–1937)**

**Harlow,** Shalom (model, TV personality); Oshawa, Ontario, Canada, 12/5/73

**Harmon,** Mark (actor); Burbank, Calif., 9/2/51

**Harnick,** Sheldon (lyricist); Chicago, 4/30/24

**Harper,** Valerie (actress); Suffern, N.Y., 8/22/40

**Harrell,** Lynn (cellist); New York City, 1/30/44

**Harrelson,** Woody (actor); Midland, Tex., 7/23/61

**Harriman,** Pamela (ambassador); Farnborough, England **(1920–1997)**

**Harriman,** W. (William) Averell (ex-governor of New York); New York City **(1891–1986)**

**Harrington,** Pat, Jr. (actor, comedian); New York City, 8/13/29

**Harris,** Barbara (Sandra Markowitz) (actress); Evanston, Ill., 7/25/35

**Harris,** Ed (actor); Englewood, N.J., 11/28/50

**Harris,** Emmylou (singer); Birmingham, Ala., 4/2/47

**Harris,** Julie (actress); Grosse Pointe Park, Mich., 12/2/25

**Harris,** Phil (actor, band leader); Linton, Ind. **(1906–1995)**

**Harris,** Richard (actor); Limerick, Ireland, 10/1/33

**Harris,** Rosemary (actress); Ashby, England, 9/19/30

**Harris,** Roy (composer); Lincoln County, Okla. **(1898–1979)**

**Harrison,** Benjamin (23rd U.S. president); North Bend, Ohio **(1833–1901)**

**Harrison,** George (singer, songwriter); Liverpool, England **(1943–2001)**

**Harrison,** Gregory (actor); Avalon, Catalina Island, Calif., 5/31/50

**Harrison,** Sir Rex (Reginald Carey) (actor); Huyton, England **(1908–1990)**

**Harrison,** William Henry (9th U.S. president); Charles City County, Va. **(1773–1841)**

**Harry,** Deborah (Blondie) (musician); Miami, Fla., 7/1/45

**Hart,** Lorenz (lyricist); New York City **(1895–1943)**

**Hart,** Mary (Mary Johanna Harum) (host); Sioux Falls, S.D., 11/8/50

**Hart,** Melissa Joan (actress); Sayville, N.Y., 4/18/76

**Hart,** Moss (playwright); New York City **(1904–1961)**

**Harte,** Bret (Francis Brett Harte) (author); Albany, N.Y. **(1836–1902)**

**Hartford,** Huntington (George Huntington Hartford II) (A.&P. heir); New York City, 4/18/11

**Hartford,** John (singer, banjoist); New York City **(1937–2001)**

**Hartley,** Mariette (actress); New York City, 6/21/40

**Hartman,** David Downs (TV newscaster); Pawtucket, R.I., 5/19/35

**Hartman,** Phil (actor, comedian); Brantford, Ont., Canada **(1948–1998)**

**Hartman Black,** Lisa (actress); Houston, 6/1/56

**Harvey,** Laurence (Larushka Skikne) (actor); Joniskis, Lithuania **(1928–1973)**

**Harvey,** Polly Jean (PJ Harvey) (singer, songwriter); Yeovil, England, 10/9/69

**Harvey,** William (physician); Folkestone, England **(1578–1657)**

**Hasselhoff,** David (actor, producer); Baltimore, 7/17/52

**Hatcher,** Teri (actress); Sunnyvale, Calif., 12/8/64

**Havel,** Vaclav (political leader, dramatist, poet); Prague, 10/5/36

**Havens,** Richie (musician); Brooklyn, N.Y., 1/21/41

Hawke, Ethan (actor); Austin, Tex., 11/6/70
Hawking, Stephen (physicist, astronomer); Oxford, England, 1/8/42
Hawkins, Coleman (jazz musician); St. Joseph, Mo. **(1904–1969)**
Hawkins, Jack (actor); London **(1910–1973)**
Hawn, Goldie (actress, producer); Washington, D.C., 11/21/45
Haworth, Jill (actress); Sussex, England, 8/15/45
Hawthorne, Nathaniel (novelist); Salem, Mass. **(1804–1864)**
Hay, John Milton (statesman); Salem, Ind. **(1838–1905)**
Hayakawa, Sessue (actor); Honshu, Japan **(1890–1973)**
Hayden, Melissa (ballet dancer); Toronto, 4/25/23
Hayden, Sterling (Sterling Relyea Walter) (actor, writer); Montclair, N.J. **(1916–1986)**
Haydn, Franz Joseph (composer); Rohrau, Austria **(1732–1809)**
Hayek, Salma (actress); Coatzacoalcos, Mexico, 9/2/68
Hayes, Helen (Helen Hayes Brown) (actress); Washington, D.C. **(1900–1993)**
Hayes, Isaac (composer); Covington, Tenn., 8/20/42
Hayes, Peter Lind (comedian, singer); San Francisco **(1915–1998)**
Hayes, Rutherford Birchard (19th U.S. president); Delaware, Ohio **(1822–1893)**
Hayward, Leland (producer); Nebraska City, Neb. **(1902–1971)**
Hayward, Susan (Edythe Marrener) (actress); Brooklyn, N.Y. **(1918–1975)**
Hayworth, Rita (Margarita Cansino) (actress); New York City **(1918–1987)**
Head, Edith (costume designer); Los Angeles **(1907–1981)**
Heaney, Seamus (poet); Londonderry, Northern Ireland, 4/13/39
Hearst, Patricia (Campbell) (heiress); San Francisco, 2/20/54
Hearst, William Randolph (publisher); San Francisco **(1863–1951)**
Hearst, William Randolph, Jr. (publisher); New York City **(1908–1993)**
Heatherton, Joey (actress); Rockville Centre, N.Y., 9/14/44
Heche, Anne (actress); Aurora, Ohio, 5/25/69
Hecht, Ben (author); New York City **(1894–1964)**
Heckart, Eileen (actress); Columbus, Ohio **(1919–2001)**
Heflin, Van (Emmet Evan Heflin) (actor); Walters, Okla. **(1910–1971)**
Hefner, Hugh (publisher); Chicago, 4/9/26
Hegel, Georg Wilhelm Friedrich (philosopher); Stuttgart, Germany **(1770–1831)**
Heidegger, Martin (existentialist philosopher); Messkirch, Germany **(1889–1976)**
Heifetz, Jascha (concert violinist); Vilna, Russia **(1901–1987)**
Heine, Heinrich (Harry) (poet); Düsseldorf, Germany **(1797–1856)**
Heinemann, Gustav (ex-president of Germany); Schweim, Germany **(1899–1976)**
Heisenberg, Werner Karl (physicist); Würzburg, Germany **(1901–1976)**
Heller, Joseph (novelist); Brooklyn, N.Y. **(1923–1999)**
Hellman, Lillian (playwright); New Orleans **(1905–1984)**
Helmond, Katherine (actress); Galveston, Tex., 7/5/34
Helms, Jesse (politician); Monroe, N.C., 10/18/21
Helmsley, Harry Brakmann (business executive); New York City **(1909–1997)**
Hemingway, Ernest Miller (novelist); Oak Park, Ill. **(1899–1961)**
Hemingway, Margaux (actress); Portland, Ore. **(1955–1996)**
Hemmings, David (actor); Guilford, England, 11/2/41
Henderson, Florence (actress); Dale, Ind., 2/14/34
Henderson, Skitch (Lyle Russell Cedric) (conductor, pianist); Birmingham, England?, 1/27/18
Hendrix, Jimi (James Marshall Hendrix) (guitarist); Seattle **(1942–1970)**
Henley, Beth (playwright-actress); Jackson, Miss., 5/8/52
Henley, Don (musician); Linden, Tex., 7/22/47
Hannan, Mc_i (ast_oud), Chicago, 10/6/62
Henning, Doug (magician, actor); Winnipeg, Canada **(1947–2000)**
Henri, Robert (painter); Cincinnati **(1865–1929)**
Henriksen, Lance (actor, screenwriter); New York City, 5/4/40
Henry VIII (king of England); Greenwich, England **(1491–1547)**
Henry, O. (William Sydney Porter) (story writer); Greensboro, N.C. **(1862–1910)**
Henry, Patrick (statesman); Hanover County, Va. **(1736–1799)**
Henson, Jim (puppeteer); Greenville, Miss. **(1936–1990)**
Hepburn, Audrey (actress); Brussels **(1929–1993)**
Hepburn, Katharine (actress); Hartford, Conn., 5/12/07
Hepplewhite, George (furniture designer); England **(?–1786)**
Hepworth, Barbara (sculptor); Wakefield, England **(1903–1975)**
Herbert, George (poet); Montgomery Castle, Wales **(1593–1633)**
Herbert, Victor (composer); Dublin **(1859–1924)**
Herblock (Herbert L. Block) (political cartoonist); Chicago **(1909–2001)**
Herman, Pee-wee (Paul Rubenfeld) (comedian); Peekskill, N.Y., 8/27/52

Herman, Woody (Woodrow Charles Herman) (band leader); Milwaukee **(1913–1987)**
Herod (called Herod the Great) (king of Judea) **(73–4 B.C.)**
Herodotus (historian); Halicarnassus, Asia Minor (Turkey) **(c. 484–425 B.C.)**
Herrick, Robert (poet); London **(1591–1674)**
Herschbach, Dudley Robert (chemist, Nobel laureate); San Jose, Calif., 6/18/32
Herschel, William (Frederich Wilhelm Herschel) (astronomer); Hannover, Germany **(1738–1822)**
Hershey, Barbara (Barbara Herzstein) (actress); Hollywood, Calif., 2/5/48
Herzog, Chaim (Israeli statesman); Belfast, Northern Ireland **(1918–1997)**
Hesburgh, Theodore M. (educator); Syracuse, N.Y., 5/2/17
Hesseman, Howard (actor); Salem, Ore., 2/27/40
Heston, Charlton (actor); Evanston, Ill., 10/4/24
Heyerdahl, Thor (ethnologist, explorer); Larvik, Norway **(1914–2002)**
Hill, Anita (lawyer, professor); Lone Tree, Okla., 7/30/56
Hill, Benny (comedian); Southampton, England **(1925–1992)**
Hill, Lauryn (actress, musician); South Orange, N.J., 5/25/75
Hillary, Sir Edmund (mountain climber); New Zealand, 7/20/19
Hillerman, John (actor); Denison, Tex., 12/20/32
Hilton, Conrad (hotelier); San Antonio, N.M. **(1887–1979)**
Hindemith, Paul (composer); Hanau, Germany **(1895–1963)**
Hindenburg, Paul von (Paul Ludwig Hans Anton von Hindenburg und Beneckendorff) (German field marshal, president); Poznan, Poland **(1847– 1934)**
Hines, Earl "Fatha" (jazz pianist); Duquesne, Pa. **(1905–1983)**
Hines, Gregory (dancer, actor); New York City, 2/14/46
Hines, Jerome (Jerome Heinz) (basso); Los Angeles, 11/8/21
Hippocrates (physician); Cos, Greece **(c. 460–c. 377 B.C.)**
Hirohito (Emperor of Japan); Tokyo **(1901–1989)**
Hiroshige, Ando (painter); Edo, Tokyo **(1797–1858)**
Hirsch, Judd (actor); New York City, 3/15/35
Hirschfeld, Al (Albert) (cartoonist); St. Louis, 6/21/03
Hirschhorn, Joseph Herman (financier, speculator, art collector); Mitau, Latvia **(1899–1981)**
Hirt, Al (trumpeter); New Orleans **(1922–1999)**
Hiss, Alger (public official); Baltimore **(1904–1996)**
Hitchcock, Alfred J. (film director); London **(1899–1980)**
Hitler, Adolf (German dictator); Braunau, Austria **(1889–1945)**
Hobbes, Thomas (philosopher); Westport, England **(1588–1679)**
Hobson, Laura Z. (Laura K. Zametkin) (novelist); New York City **(1900–1986)**
Ho Chi Minh (Nguyen That Tranh) (Vietnamese nationalist leader); Kim Lien, Vietnam **(1890–1969)**
Hockney, David (artist); Bradford, England, 7/9/37
Hodgkin, Dorothy Mary Crowfoot (chemist, Nobel laureate); Cairo, Egypt **(1910–1994)**
Hoffa, "Jimmy" James R(iddle) (labor leader); Brazil, Ind. **(1913–1975?; presumed murdered.)**
Hoffman, Dustin (actor, director); Los Angeles, 8/8/37
Hoffman, Phillip Seymour (actor); Fairport, N.Y., 1968
Hofmann, Hans (painter); Germany **(1880–1966)**
Hoffmann, Roald (chemist, Nobel laureate); Zloczow, Poland, 7/18/37
Hofstadter, Richard (historian); Buffalo, N.Y. **(1916–1970)**
Hogan, Paul (actor); Lightning Ridge, N.S.W., Australia, 10/8/39
Hogarth, William (painter, engraver); London **(1697–1764)**
Hokusai, Katsushika (artist); Yedo, Japan **(1760–1849)**
Holbein, Hans (the Elder) (painter); Augsburg, Germany **(c. 1465–1524)**
Holbein, Hans (the Younger) (painter); Augsburg, Germany **(c. 1497–1543)**
Holbrook, Hal (actor); Cleveland, 2/17/25
Holden, William (William Franklin Beedle, Jr.) (actor); O'Fallon, Ill. **(1918–1981)**
Holder, Geoffrey (dancer); Port-of-Spain, Trinidad, 8/1/30
Holiday, Billie (Eleanora Fagan) (jazz-blues singer); Baltimore **(1915–1959)**
Holliman, Earl (Henry Earl Holliman) (actor); Delhi, La., 9/11/28
Holly, Buddy (singer); Lubbock, Tex. **(1936–1959)**
Holly, Lauren (actress); Geneva, N.Y., 10/28/63
Holm, Celeste (actress); New York City, 4/29/19
Holmes, Katie (actress); Toledo, Ohio, 12/18/78
Holmes, Oliver Wendell (jurist); Boston **(1841–1935)**
Home, Lord (Alexander Frederick Douglas-Home) (diplomat); London **(7/2/1903–10/9/1995)**
Homer, Winslow (painter); Boston **(1836–1910)**
Homer (Greek poet) fl. 850 B.C.
Honegger, Arthur (composer); Le Havre, France **(1892–1955)**

**Hook,** Sidney (philosopher); New York City **(1902–1989)**
**Hooker,** John Lee (blues guitarist, singer, songwriter); Clarksdale, Miss. **(1920–2001)**
**Hoover,** Herbert Clark (31st U.S. president); West Branch, Iowa **(1874–1964)**
**Hoover,** J. Edgar (FBI director); Washington, D.C. **(1895–1972)**
**Hope,** Bob (Leslie Townes Hope) (comedian); London, 5/29/03
**Hopkins,** Sir Anthony (actor); Port Talbot, Wales, 12/31/37
**Hopkins,** Gerald Manley (poet); Stratford, England **(1844–1899)**
**Hopkins,** Johns (financier); Anne Arundel County, Md. **(1795–1873)**
**Hopper,** Dennis (actor); Dodge City, Kans., 5/17/36
**Hopper,** Edward (painter); Nyack, N.Y. **(1882–1967)**
**Horace** (Quintus Horatius Flaccus) (poet); Venosa, Italy **(65–8 B.C.)**
**Horne,** Lena (singer); Brooklyn, N.Y., 6/30/17
**Horne,** Marilyn (mezzo-soprano); Bradford, Pa., 1/16/34
**Horowitz,** Vladimir (pianist); Kiev, Ukraine **(1903–1989)**
**Horsley,** Lee (actor); Muleshoe, Tex., 5/15/55
**Horton,** Edward Everett (comedian); Brooklyn, N.Y. **(1887–1970)**
**Hoskins,** Bob (actor); Bury St. Edmunds, England, 10/26/42
**Houdini,** Harry (Ehrich Weiss) (magician); Budapest, Hungary **(1874–1926)**
**Houseman,** John (Jacques Haussmann) (producer, director, actor); Bucharest **(1902–1988)**
**Housman,** A(lfred) E(dward) (poet); Fockburg, England **(1859–1936)**
**Houston,** Charles Hamilton (civil rights lawyer); Washington, D.C. **(1895–1950)**
**Houston,** Samuel (political leader); Rockbridge County, Va. **(1793–1863)**
**Houston,** Whitney (singer); Newark, N.J., 8/9/63
**Howard,** Ken (actor); El Centro, Calif., 3/28/44
**Howard,** Leslie (Leslie Stainer) (actor); London **(1893–1943)**
**Howard,** Ron (actor, producer, director); Duncan, Okla., 3/1/54
**Howard,** Trevor (actor); Kent, England **(1916–1988)**
**Howe,** Elias (inventor); Spencer, Mass. **(1819–1867)**
**Howe,** Irving (literary critic); New York City **(1920–1993)**
**Howe,** Julia Ward (poet, reformer); New York City **(1819–1910)**
**Hudson,** Henry (English navigator) **(fl. 1607–1611)**
**Hudson,** Rock (born Roy Scherer, Jr.; took Roy Fitzgerald as legal name) (actor); Winnetka, Ill. **(1925–1985)**
**Huggins,** Nathan Irvin (historian); Chicago **(1927–1989)**
**Hughes,** Charles Evans (jurist); Glens Falls, N.Y. **(1862–1948)**
**Hughes,** Howard (industrialist, film producer); Houston **(1905–1976)**
**Hughes,** Langston (poet); Joplin, Mo. **(1902–1967)**
**Hughes,** Ted (poet); Mytholmroyd, England **(1930–1998)**
**Hugo,** Victor Marie (author); Besançon, France **(1802–1885)**
**Hulce,** Tom (actor); Detroit, 12/6/53
**Hume,** David (philosopher); Edinburgh, Scotland **(1711–1776)**
**Hume,** Kirsty (model); Glasgow, Scotland, 9/4/76
**Humperdinck,** Engelbert (composer); Siegburg, Germany **(1854–1921)**
**Humperdinck,** Engelbert (Arnold Dorsey) (singer); Madras, India, 5/2/36
**Hunt,** Helen (actress); Los Angeles, 6/15/63
**Hunt,** Linda (actress); Morristown, N.J., 4/2/45
**Hunter,** Holly (actress); Atlanta, 3/20/58
**Hunter,** Kim (Janet Cole) (actress); Detroit **(1922–2002)**
**Hunter,** Tab (Arthur Andrew Gelien) (actor); New York City, 7/11/31
**Hunter-Gault,** Charlayne (activist, broadcast journalist); Due West, S.C., 2/27/42
**Huntley,** Chet (TV newscaster); Cardwell, Mont. **(1911–1974)**
**Hurley,** Elizabeth (actress, model); Backingstoke, England, 6/10/65
**Hurok,** Sol (Solomon Hurok) (impresario); Pogar, Russia **(1884–1974)**
**Hurst,** Fannie (novelist); Hamilton, Ohio **(1889–1968)**
**Hurston,** Zora Neale (author); Eatonville, Fla. **(1901–1960)**
**Hurt,** John (actor); Shirebrook, England, 1/22/40
**Hurt,** William (actor); Washington, D.C., 3/20/50
**Hus,** Jan (Bohemian religious reformer); Husinetz, nr. Budweis, Czech Republic **(c. 1369–1415)**
**Husing,** Ted (sportscaster); New York City **(1901–1962)**
**Hussein I** (king); Jordan **(1935–1999)**
**Hussein,** Saddam (al-Tikriti) (Iraqi president); Tikrit, Iraq, 4/28/37
**Huston,** Anjelica (actress); Los Angeles, 7/8/51
**Huston,** John (actor, director, writer); Nevada, Mo. **(1906–1987)**
**Huston,** Walter (Walter Houghston) (actor); Toronto **(1884–1950)**
**Hutchins,** Robert M. (educator); Brooklyn, N.Y. **(1899–1977)**
**Hutton,** Betty (Betty Thornburg) (actress); Battle Creek, Mich., 2/26/21
**Hutton,** Lauren (actress, model); Charleston, S.C., 11/17/43
**Hutton,** Timothy (actor); Los Angeles, 8/16/60
**Huxley,** Aldous (author); Godalming, England **(1894–1963)**

**Huxley,** Sir Julian S. (biologist, author); London **(1887–1975)**
**Huxley,** Thomas Henry (biologist); Ealing, England **(1825–1895)**
**Hynde,** Chrissie (singer); Akron, Ohio, 9/7/51

# I

**Iacocca,** Lee (Lido Anthony) (business executive); Allentown, Pa., 10/15/24
**Ian,** Janis (singer); New York City, 5/7/51
**Ibsen,** Henrik (dramatist); Skien, Norway **(1828–1906)**
**Ice Cube** (O'Shea Jackson) (musician, actor); Los Angeles, 6/15/69
**Ice-T** (Tracy Morrow) (rap musician, actor); Newark, N.J., 2/16/68
**Inge,** William (playwright); Independence, Kans. **(1913–1973)**
**Ingres,** Jean Auguste Dominique (painter); Montauban, France **(1780–1867)**
**Inness,** George (painter); nr. Newburgh, N.Y. **(1825–1894)**
**Ionesco,** Eugene (playwright); Slatina, Romania **(1912–1994)**
**Ireland,** Jill (actress); London **(1936–1990)**
**Ireland,** Kathy (model, actress); Glendale, Calif., 3/8/63
**Ireland,** Patricia (feminist, social activist); Oak Park, Ill., 10/19/45
**Irons,** Jeremy (actor); Cowes, Isle of Wight, England, 9/19/48
**Irving,** Amy (actress); Palo Alto, Calif., 9/10/53
**Irving,** John (Winslow) (writer); Exeter, N.H., 3/2/42
**Irving,** Washington (author); New York City **(1783–1859)**
**Isaak,** Chris (musician, actor); Stockton, Calif., 6/26/56
**Isherwood,** Christopher (novelist, playwright); nr. Dilsey and High Lane, England **(1904–1986)**
**Iturbi,** José (concert pianist); Valencia, Spain **(1895–1980)**
**Ives,** Burl (Icle Ivanhoe) (singer); Hunt, Ill. **(1909–1995)**
**Ives,** Charles E(dward) (composer); Danbury, Conn. **(1874–1954)**
**Ivins,** Molly (journalist); Monterey, Calif., 8/30/44
**Ivory,** James (director, producer); Berkeley, Calif., 6/7/28

# J

**Jackson,** Andrew (7th U.S. president); Waxhaw, S.C. **(1767–1845)**
**Jackson,** Anne (actress); Millvale, Pa., 9/3/26
**Jackson,** Glenda (actress); Cheshire, England, 5/9/36
**Jackson,** Janet (singer); Gary, Ind., 5/16/66
**Jackson,** Rev. Jesse (civil rights leader); Greenville, S.C., 10/8/41
**Jackson,** Kate (actress); Birmingham, Ala., 10/29/49
**Jackson,** Mahalia (gospel singer); New Orleans **(1911–1972)**
**Jackson,** Maynard (mayor of Atlanta); Dallas, 3/23/38
**Jackson,** Michael (singer); Gary, Ind., 8/29/58
**Jackson,** Peter (director); Wellington, New Zealand, Oct. 31, 1961
**Jackson,** Samuel L. (actor); Washington, D.C., 12/21/48
**Jackson,** Thomas Jonathan ("Stonewall") (general); Clarksburg, Va. (now W. Va.) **(1824–1863)**
**Jacobi,** Derek (actor); Leytonstone, England, 10/22/38
**Jacobs,** Jane (urbanologist); Scranton, Pa., 5/1/16
**Jagger,** Mick (Michael Phillip Jagger) (singer); Dartford, England, 7/26/43
**James,** Harry (trumpeter); Albany, Ga. **(1916–1983)**
**James,** Henry (novelist); New York City **(1843–1916)**
**James,** Jesse Woodson (outlaw); Clay County, Mo. **(1847–1882)**
**James,** William (psychologist); New York City **(1842–1910)**
**Jameson,** (Margaret) Storm (novelist); Whitby, England **(1897–1986)**
**Janis,** Byron (pianist); McKeesport, Pa., 3/24/28
**Janis,** Conrad (actor, musician); New York City, 2/11/28
**Janssen,** David (David Meyer) (actor); Naponee, Neb. **(1930–1980)**
**Jaworkski,** Leon (Watergate special prosecutor); Waco, Tex. **(1905–1982)**
**Jay,** John (statesman, jurist); New York City **(1745–1829)**
**Jeanmaire,** Renée (dancer); Paris, 4/29/24
**Jefferson,** Thomas (3rd U.S. president); Shadwell, Va. **(1743–1826)**
**Jemison,** Mae C. (astronaut, physician); Decatur, Ala., 10/17/56
**Jenner,** Edward (physician); Berkeley, England **(1749–1823)**
**Jennings,** Peter (news anchor); Toronto, 7/29/38
**Jennings,** Waylon (singer); Littlefield, Tex. **(1937–2002)**
**Jessel,** George (entertainer); New York City **(1898–1981)**
**Jessup,** Philip C. (diplomat); New York City **(1897–1986)**
**Jillian,** Ann (Ann Jura Nauseda) (actress); Cambridge, Mass., 1/29/51
**Joan of Arc** (Jeanne d'Arc) (saint, patriot); Domremy-la-Pucelle, France **(1412–1431)**
**Jobs,** Steven Paul (computer industry pioneer); San Francisco, 1955
**Joel,** Billy (singer); New York City, 5/9/49
**Joffrey,** Robert (Abdullah Jaffa Bey Khan) (choreographer); Seattle **(1930–1988)**

John, Elton (Reginald Kenneth Dwight) (singer, pianist); Pinner, England, 3/25/47
Johns, Jasper (painter, sculptor); Augusta, Ga., 5/15/30
Johnson, Andrew (17th U.S. president); Raleigh, N.C. (1808–1875)
Johnson, Don (actor); Flatt Creek, Mo., 12/15/49
Johnson, James Weldon (author, educator); Jacksonville, Fla. (1871–1938)
Johnson, Lyndon Baines (36th U.S. president); Stonewall, Tex. (1908–1973)
Johnson, Philip Cortelyou (architect); Cleveland, 7/8/06
Johnson, Samuel (lexicographer, author); Lichfield, England (1709–1784)
Johnson, Van (actor); Newport, R.I., 8/20/16
Johnson, Virginia (human sexuality expert); Springfield, Mo., 2/11/25
Jolie, Angelina (actress); Los Angeles, 6/5/75
Joliot-Curie, Frédéric (chemist, Nobel laureate); Paris (1900–1958)
Joliot-Curie, Irène (Irène Curie) (chemist, Nobel laureate); France (1897–1956)
Jolliet, Louis (Louis Joliet) (explorer); Beaupré, Canada (1645–1700)
Jolson, Al (Asa Yoelson) (actor, singer); St. Petersburg, Russia (1886–1950)
Jones, Dean (actor); Morgan County, Ala., 1/25/35
Jones, George (singer); Saratoga, Tex., 9/12/31
Jones, Inigo (architect); London (1573–1652)
Jones, James (novelist); Robinson, Ill. (1921–1977)
Jones, James Earl (actor); Arkabutla, Miss., 1/17/31
Jones, Jennifer (Phylis Isley) (actress); Tulsa, Okla., 3/2/19
Jones, John Paul (John Paul) (naval officer); Scotland (1747–1792)
Jones, Quincy (composer); Chicago, 3/14/33
Jones, Shirley (singer, actress); Smithtown, Pa., 3/31/34
Jones, Spike (host, orchestra leader); Long Beach, Calif. (1911–1965)
Jones, Tom (Thomas Jones Woodward) (singer); Pontypridd, Wales, 6/7/40
Jones, Tommy Lee (actor); San Saba, Tex., 9/15/46
Jong, Erica (writer); New York City, 3/26/42
Jonson, Ben (Benjamin Jonson) (poet, dramatist); Westminster, England (1572–1637)
Joplin, Janis (singer); Port Arthur, Tex. (1943–1970)
Joplin, Scott (ragtime pianist, composer); Texarkansas, Tex. (1868–1917)
Jordan, Barbara (U.S. representative); Houston (1936–1996)
Jordan, Neil (film director, screenwriter); Sligo, Ireland, 2/25/50
Joseph (Chief Joseph) (Nez Perce Indian leader); eastern Ore. (1841–1904)
Josquin des Prés (usually known as Josquin) (composer); Conde-sur-L'Escaut?, Hainaut, Belgium (c. 1445–1521)
Jovovich, Milla (actress, model, singer); Kiev, Ukraine, 12/19/75
Joyce, James (novelist); Dublin (1882–1941)
Juárez, Benito (statesman); Guelatao, Mexico (1806–1872)
Judd, Ashley (actress); Los Angeles, 4/19/68
Julia, Raul (Raúl Rafael Carlos Julia y Arcelay) (actor); San Juan, P.R. (1940–1994)
Jung, Carl Gustav (psychoanalyst); Basel, Switzerland (1875–1961)
Jurado, Katy (Maria Christina Jurado Garcia) (actress); Guadalajara, Mexico (1924–2002)


# K

Kabalevsky, Dmitri (composer); St. Petersburg, Russia (1904–1987)
Kafka, Franz (author); Prague (1883–1924)
Kádár, János (Communist Party leader); Hungary (1912–1989)
Kahn, Gus (songwriter); Coblenz, Germany (1886–1941)
Kahn, Louis I. (architect); Oesel Island, Estonia (1901–1974)
Kahn, Madeline (actress); Boston (1942–1999)
Kandinsky, Wassily (painter); Moscow (1866–1944)
Kanin, Garson (playwright); Rochester, N.Y. (1912–1999)
Kant, Immanuel (philosopher); Königsberg (Kaliningrad), Russia (1724–1804)
Kantor, MacKinlay (novelist); Webster City, Iowa (1904–1977)
Kaplan, Justin (writer, editor); New York City, 9/5/25
Karan, Donna (fashion designer); Forest Hills, N.Y., 10/2/48
Karloff, Boris (William Henry Pratt) (actor); London (1887–1969)
Kasdan, Lawrence (film director, writer, actor, producer); Miami, 1/14/49
Kasem, Casey (disc jockey); Detroit, 4/27/32
Kaufman, Andy (actor, comedian); New York City (1949–1984)
Kaufman, George S. (playwright); Pittsburgh (1889–1961)
Kavner, Julie (actress); Los Angeles, 9/7/51

Kaye, Danny (David Daniel Kominski) (comedian); Brooklyn, N.Y. (1913–1987)
Kaye, Sammy (band leader); Cleveland (1910–1987)
Kazan, Elia (director); Constantinople, Turkey, 9/7/09
Kazan, Lainie (Levine) (singer); New York City, 5/15/40
Kazantzakis, Nikos (writer); Herakleion, Crete (1883–1957)
Keach, Stacy (actor); Savannah, Ga., 6/2/41
Keaton, Buster (Joseph Frank Keaton) (comedian); Piqua, Kans. (1896–1966)
Keaton, Diane (actress); Los Angeles, 1/5/46
Keaton, Michael (Michael Douglas) (actor); Robinson Township, Pa., 9/9/51
Keats, John (poet); London (1795–1821)
Keel, Howard (Harold Clifford Leek) (singer, actor); Gillespie, Ill., 4/13/19
Keeler, Ruby (Ethel Hilde Keeler) (actress, dancer); Halifax, N.S., Canada (1910–1993)
Keener, Catherine (actress); Miami, Fla., 1959(?)
Kefauver, Estes (legislator); Madisonville, Tenn (1903–1963)
Keitel, Harvey (actor); Brooklyn, N.Y., 5/13/39
Keith, Brian (Robert Brian Keith, Jr.) (actor); Bayonne, N.J. (1921–1997)
Keller, Helen Adams (author, educator); Tuscumbia, Ala. (1880–1968)
Kelley, DeForest (actor); Atlanta (1920–1999)
Kelly, Emmett (clown); Sedan, Kans. (1898–1979)
Kelly, Gene (dancer, actor); Pittsburgh (1912–1996)
Kelly, Grace (actress, Princess of Monaco); Philadelphia (1929–1982)
Kelly, R. (Robert Kelly) (singer, record producer, actor); Chicago, 1969
Kempis, Thomas à (mystic); Kempis, Prussia (Germany) (1380–1471)
Kendall, Henry W. (physicist, Nobel laureate); Boston (1926–1999)
Kennan, George F. (diplomat); Milwaukee, 2/16/04
Kennedy, Anthony (jurist); Sacramento, Calif., 7/23/36
Kennedy, Caroline Bessette (socialite); White Plains, N.Y. (1966–1999)
Kennedy, George (actor); New York City, 2/18/25
Kennedy, John Fitzgerald (35th U.S. president); Brookline, Mass. (1917–1963)
Kennedy, John F., Jr. (publisher); Washington, D.C. (1960–1999)
Kennedy, Joseph P. (financier); Boston (1888–1969)
Kennedy, Robert Francis (legislator); Brookline, Mass. (1925–1968)
Kennedy, Rose Fitzgerald (president's mother); Boston (1890–1995)
Kent, Allegra (ballet dancer); Santa Monica, Calif., 8/11/38
Kent, Rockwell (painter); Tarrytown Heights, N.Y. (1882–1971)
Kenton, Stan (Stanley Newcomb) (jazz musician); Wichita, Kans. (1912–1979)
Kepler, Johannes (astronomer); Weil, Germany (1571–1630)
Kercheval, Ken (actor); Wolcottville, Ind., 7/15/35
Kerensky, Alexander Fedorovich (statesman); Simbirsk, Russia (1881–1970)
Kern, Jerome David (composer); New York City (1885–1945)
Kerns, Joanna (actress); San Francisco, 2/12/53
Kerouac, Jack (Jean-Louis Kerouac) (writer); Lowell, Mass. (1922–1969)
Kerr, Deborah (actress); Helensburgh, Scotland, 9/30/21
Kettering, Charles F. (engineer, inventor); nr. Loudonville, Ohio (1876–1958)
Kevorkian, Jack (medical pathologist); Pontiac, Mich., 3/26/28
Key, Francis Scott (lawyer, author of national anthem); Frederick (Carroll) County, Md. (1779–1843)
Keynes, John Maynard (1st Baron of Tilton) (economist); Cambridge, England (1883–1946)
Khachaturian, Aram (composer); Tiflis, Russia (1903–1978)
Khomeini, Ayatollah Ruhollah (Islamic religious leader); Iran (1900–1989)
Khrushchev, Nikita S. (Soviet leader); Kalinovka, nr. Kursk, Ukraine (1894–1971)
Kidd, Michael (Milton Greenwald) (choreographer); Brooklyn, N.Y., 8/12/19
Kidd, William (called Captain Kidd) (pirate); Greenock, Scotland (c. 1645–1701)
Kidder, Margot (actress); Yellowknife, N.W.T., Canada, 10/17/48
Kidman, Nicole (actress); Honolulu, 6/20/67
Kiepura, Jan (tenor); Sosnowiec, Poland (1902–1966)
Kieran, John (writer); New York City (1892–1981)
Kierkegaard, Sören Aalys (philosopher); Copenhagen (1813–1855)
Kiesinger, Kurt Georg (diplomat); Ebingen, Germany (1904–1988)
Kiley, Richard (actor, singer); Chicago (1922–1999)

Kilmer, Alfred Joyce (poet); New Brunswick, N.J. (1886–1918)
Kilmer, Val (actor); Los Angeles,, 12/31/59
King, Alan (Irwin Alan Kniberg) (entertainer); Brooklyn, N.Y., 12/26/27
King, B.B. (Riley King) (guitarist); Itta Bena, Miss., 9/16/25
King, Carole (singer, songwriter); Brooklyn, N.Y., 2/9/41
King, Coretta Scott (civil rights leader); Marion, Ala., 4/27/27
King, Larry (Lawrence Harvey Zeigler) (TV host); New York City, 11/19/33
King, Martin Luther, Jr. (civil rights leader); Atlanta (1929–1968)
King, Stephen (writer); Portland, Maine, 9/21/47
Kingsley, Ben (Krishna Bhanji) (actor); Snainton, England, 12/31/43
Kingsley, Sidney (Sidney Kirschner) (playwright); New York City (1906–1995)
Kingsolver, Barbara (writer); Annapolis, Md., 4/8/55
Kingston, Maxine Hong (novelist); Stockton, Calif., 10/27/40
Kinsey, Alfred Charles (human sexuality expert); Hoboken, N.J. (1894–1956)
Kinski, Nastassja (Nastassja Nakszynski) (actress); West Berlin, 1/24/61
Kipling, Rudyard (author); Bombay (Mumbai) (1865–1936)
Kipnis, Alexander (basso); Ukraine (1891–1978)
Kirby, George (comedian); Chicago (1923–1995)
Kirchner, Ernst Ludwig (painter); Aschaffenburg, Germany (1880–1938)
Kirk, Grayson (educator); Jeffersonville, Ohio (1903–1997)
Kirkland, Gelsey (ballet dancer); Bethlehem, Pa., 12/29/52
Kirkpatrick, Jeane Jordan (educator-public affairs); Duncan, Okla., 11/19/26
Kirkpatrick, Ralph (harpsichordist); Leominster, Mass. (1911–1984)
Kirstein, Lincoln (dance, theater executive); Rochester, N.Y. (1907–1996)
Kirsten, Dorothy (soprano); Montclair, N.J. (1910–1992)
Kissinger, Henry (Heinz Alfred Kissinger) (ex-U.S. secretary of state); Furth, Germany, 5/27/23
Kitt, Eartha (singer); North, S.C., 1/26/28
Klee, Paul (painter); Münchenbuchsee, nr. Bern, Switzerland (1879–1940)
Klein, Calvin (fashion designer); Bronx, N.Y., 11/19/42
Klein, Robert (comedian); New York City, 2/8/42
Kleist, Henrich von (poet); Frankfurt an der Oder, Germany (1777–1811)
Klemperer, Otto (conductor); Breslau, Poland (1885–1973)
Klemperer, Werner (actor); Cologne, Germany (1920–2000)
Klimt, Gustav (painter); Vienna (1862–1918)
Kline, Kevin (actor); St. Louis, 10/24/47
Klugman, Jack (actor); Philadelphia, 4/27/22
Knight, Gladys (singer); Atlanta, 5/28/44
Knight, John S. (publisher); Bluefield, W. Va. (1894–1981)
Knight, Ted (Tadeus Wladyslaw Konopka) (actor); Terryville, Conn. (1923–1986)
Knight, Wayne (actor); Cartersville, Ga., 8/7/55
Knopf, Alfred A. (publisher); New York City (1892–1984)
Knopfler, Mark (musician); Glasgow, Scotland, 8/12/49
Knotts, Don (actor); Morgantown, W. Va., 7/21/24
Knox, John (religious reformer); Haddington, East Lothian, Scotland (1505–1572)
Koch, Robert (physician); Klausthal, Germany (1843–1910)
Koenig, Walter (actor); Chicago, 9/14/36
Koestler, Arthur (novelist); Budapest (1905–1983)
Kokoschka, Oskar (painter); Pöchlarn, Austria (1886–1980)
Kollwitz, Käthe (graphic artist, sculptor); Königsberg, Russia (1867–1945)
Koop, C. Everett (ex-surgeon general); Brooklyn, N.Y., 10/14/16
Kooper, Al (singer, pianist); Brooklyn, N.Y., 2/5/44
Kopell, Bernie (actor); New York City, 6/21/33
Koppel, Ted (broadcast journalist); Lancashire, England, 2/8/40
Korman, Harvey (actor); Chicago, 2/15/27
Kosciusko, Thaddeus (Tadeusz Andrzej Bonawentura Kosciuszko) (military officer and statesman) (1746–1817)
Kossuth, Lajos (patriot); Monok, Hungary (1802–1894)
Kostelanetz, André (orchestra conductor); St. Petersburg, Russia (1901–1980)
Kostunica, Vojislav (president of Yugoslavia); Belgrade, 3/24/44
Kosygin, Aleksei N. (premier); St. Petersburg, Russia (1904–1980)
Kotto, Yaphet (actor); New York City, 11/15/37
Koussevitzky, Serge (Sergei) Alexandrovitch (orchestra conductor); Vishni Volochek, Tver, Russia (1874–1951)
Kramer, Stanley E. (film producer, director); New York City (1913–2001)
Kraus, Lili (pianist); Budapest (1905–1986)

Kravitz, Lenny (musician); New York City, 5/26/64
Kreisler, Fritz (violinist, composer); Vienna (1875–1962)
Kresge, S. S. (merchant); Bald Mount, Pa. (1867–1966)
Krips, Josef (orchestra conductor); Vienna (1902–1974)
Kristofferson, Kris (singer); Brownsville, Tex., 6/22/36
Krupa, Gene (drummer); Chicago (1909–1973)
Krupp, Alfred (munitions magnate); Essen, Germany (1812–1887)
Kubelik, Rafael (conductor); Bychory, former Czechoslovakia (1914–1996)
Kublai Khan (Mongol conqueror) (1216–1294)
Kubrick, Stanley (film director, producer); New York City (1928–1999)
Kudrow, Lisa (actress); Encino, Calif., 7/30/63
Kuralt, Charles (TV journalist); Wilmington, N.C. (1934–1997)
Kurosawa, Akira (film director); Tokyo (1910–1998)
Kurtz, Efrem (conductor); St. Petersburg, Russia (1900–1995)
Kurtz, Swoosie (actress); Omaha, Neb., 9/6/44

# L

LaBelle, Patti (singer, actress); Philadelphia, 5/24/44
Ladd, Cheryl (Cheryl Stoppelmoor) (actress); Huron, S.D., 7/12/51
Ladd, Diane (actress); Meridian, Miss., 11/29/32
Laden, Osama bin (terrorist); Riyadh, Saudi Arabia, c. 1957
Lafayette, Marquis de (Marie Joseph Paul Yves Roch Gilbert du Motier) (military officer); Auvergne, France (1757–1834)
Lafitte, Jean (pirate); Bayonne?, France (1780–1826)
La Follette, Robert Marin (politician); Primrose, Wis. (1855–1925)
La Fontaine, Jean de (poet); Château-Thierry, France (1621–1695)
La Guardia, Fiorello Henry (mayor of New York); New York City (1882–1947)
Lahti, Christine (actress, director); Birmingham, Mich., 4/4/50
Laine, Frankie (Frank Paul LoVecchio) (singer); Chicago, 3/30/13
Laird, Melvin (ex-secretary of defense); Omaha, Neb., 9/1/22
Lamarck, Chevalier de (Jean Baptiste Pierre Antoine de Monet) (naturalist); Bazantin, France (1744–1829)
Lamas, Lorenzo (actor); Los Angeles, 1/20/58
Lamb, Charles (Elia) (essayist); London (1775–1834)
L'Amour, Louis (author); Jamestown, N.D. (1908–1988)
Lancaster, Burt (actor); New York City (1913–1994)
Landau, Martin (actor); Brooklyn, N.Y., 6/20/31
Landers, Ann (Esther Pauline Friedman) (columnist); Sioux City, Iowa (1918–2002)
Landon, Michael (Eugene Maurice Orowitz) (actor, director, producer); Forest Hills, Queens, N.Y. (1936–1991)
Lane, Abbe (Abigail Francine Lassman) (singer); New York City, 1933
Lane, Burton (songwriter); New York City (1912–1997)
Lane, Nathan (Joseph Lane) (actor, singer); Jersey City, N.J., 2/3/56
Lang, Fritz (film director); Vienna (1890–1976)
Lange, Hope (actress); Redding Ridge, Conn., 11/28/33
Lange, Jessica (actress); Cloquet, Minn., 4/20/49
Langella, Frank (actor); Bayonne, N.J., 1/1/40
Langmuir, Irving (chemist); Brooklyn, N.Y. (1881–1957)
Langtry, Lillie (Emily Le Breton) (actress); Island of Jersey (1852–1929)
Lansbury, Angela (actress, producer); London, 10/16/25
Lansing, Robert (Robert Howell Brown) (actor); San Diego, Calif. (1928–1994)
Lanza, Mario (Alfred Arnold Cocozza) (singer, actor); Philadelphia (1921–1959)
Lao-tse (Li Erh) (philosopher); Honan Province, China (c. 604–531 B.C.)
Lardner, Ring (Ringgold Wilmar Lardner) (story writer); Niles, Mich. (1885–1933)
La Rouchefoucauld, Francois duc de (author); Paris (1613–1680)
Larroquette, John (actor); New Orleans, 11/25/47
Larson, Gary (cartoonist); Tacoma, Wash., 8/14/50
La Salle, Eriq (actor); Hartford, Conn., 7/23/62
La Salle, Sieur de (Robert Cavelier) (explorer); Rouen, France (1643–1687)
Lasch, Christopher (historian, social critic); Omaha, Neb. (1932–1994)
La Tour, Georges de (painter); Vic-sur-Seille, France (1593–1652)
Lauer, Matt (TV host); New York City, 12/20/57
Laughton, Charles (actor); Scarborough, England (1899–1962)
Lauper, Cyndi (singer); New York City, 6/20/53
Laurel, Stan (Arthur Jefferson) (comedian); Ulverston, England (1890–1965)
Laurents, Arthur (playwright); New York City, 7/14/18
Laurie, Piper (Rosetta Jacobs) (actress); Detroit, 1/22/32
Lavin, Linda (actress); Portland, Maine, 10/15/37
Lavoisier, Antoine-Laurent (chemist); Paris (1743–1794)

Lawford, Peter (actor); London (1923–1984)

Lawless, Lucy (Lucy Ryan) (actress); Auckland, New Zealand, 3/29/68

Lawrence, David Herbert (novelist); Nottingham, England (1885–1930)

Lawrence, Jacob (painter); Atantic City, N.J. (1917–2000)

Lawrence, Martin (actor); Frankfurt, Germany, 4/16/65

Lawrence, Sharon (actress); Charlotte, N.C., 6/29/62

Lawrence, Steve (Sidney Leibowitz) (singer); Brooklyn, N.Y., 7/8/35

Lawrence of Arabia (Thomas Edward Lawrence, later changed to Shaw) (author, soldier); Tremadoc, Wales (1888–1935)

Lawrence, Vicki (actress); Inglewood, Calif., 3/26/49

Leach, Penelope (Balchin) (child psychologist, writer); London, 11/19/37

Leach, Robin (host, producer); London, 8/29/41

Leachman, Cloris (actress); Des Moines, Iowa, 4/30/26

Leadbelly, (Huddie Ledbetter) (blues singer, guitarist); Mooringsport, La. (1885–1949)

Leakey, Louis Seymour Bazett (anthropologist); Kabete, Kenya (1903–1972)

Leakey, Mary (anthropologist); London (1913–1996)

Leakey, Richard (paleoanthropologist, wildlife conservationist); Kenya, 12/19/44

Lean, David (film director); Croydon, England (1908–1991)

Lear, Edward (nonsense poet); London (1812–1888)

Lear, Evelyn (Shulman) (soprano); Brooklyn, N.Y., 1/8/26

Lear, Norman (TV producer); New Haven, Conn., 7/27/22

Learned, Michael (actress); Washington, D.C., 4/9/39

Leary, Denis (actor, screenwriter, film director); Worcester, Mass., 8/18/57

Leary, Timothy (psychologist, LSD advocate); Springfield, Mass. (1920–1996)

Le Blanc, Matt (actor); Newton, Mass., 7/25/67

le Carré, John (David John Moore Cornwell) (novelist); Poole, England, 10/19/31

Le Corbusier (Charles Edouard Jeanneret) (architect); La Chaux-de-Fonds, Switzerland (1887–1965)

Lee, Ang (film director); Pingtung, Taiwan, 10/23/54

Lee, Christopher (actor); London, 5/27/22

Lee, Manfred B. (pseudonym Ellery Queen) (novelist); Brooklyn, N.Y. (1905–1971)

Lee, Peggy (Norma Engstrom) (singer); Jamestown, N.D. (1920–2002)

Lee, Robert E(dward) (Confederate general); Stratford Estate, Va. (1807–1870)

Lee, Spike (Shelton Jackson Lee) (actor, director, writer, producer); Atlanta, 3/20/57

Leeuwenhoek, Anton van (zoologist); Delft, Netherlands (1632–1723)

Lehár, Franz (composer); Komárom, Hungary (1870–1948)

Lehman, Herbert H. (governor, senator); New York City (1878–1963)

Lehmann, Lotte (soprano); Perleberg, Germany (1888–1976)

Lehrer, Jim (TV newscaster); Wichita, Kans., 5/19/34

Leibniz, Gottfried W. von (scientist); Leipzig, Germany (1646–1716)

Leibovitz, Annie (photographer); Westbury, Conn., 10/2/49

Leigh, Janet (Jeanette Helen Morrison) (actress); Merced, Calif., 7/6/27

Leigh, Jennifer Jason (Jennifer Morrow) (actress); Los Angeles, 2/5/62

Leigh, Mike (film director, screenwriter); Manchester, England, 2/20/43

Leigh, Vivien (Vivian Mary Hartley) (actress); Darjeeling, India (1913–1967)

Leinsdorf, Erich (symphony conductor); Vienna (1912–1993)

Lemmon, Jack (actor); Boston (1925–2001)

Lenin, Vladimir (Vladimir Ilich Ulyanov) (Soviet leader); Simbirsk, Russia (1870–1924)

Lennon, John (singer, songwriter); Liverpool, England (1940–1980)

Leno, Jay (comedian, TV host); New Rochelle, N.Y., 4/28/50

Leonard, Sheldon (Sheldon Leonard Bershad) (actor, producer); New York City (1907–1997)

Leonardo da Vinci, (painter, scientist); Vinci, Tuscany, Italy (1452–1519)

Leoni, Téa (actress); New York City, 2/25/66

Lerner, Alan Jay (lyricist); New York City (1918–1986)

Lerner, Max (columnist); Minsk, Russia (1902–1992)

Lessing, Doris (novelist); Kermanshah, Iran, 10/22/19

Leto, Jared (actor); Bossier City, La., 12/26/71

Letterman, David (TV host, producer); Indianapolis, 4/12/47

Levant, Oscar (pianist); Pittsburgh (1906–1972)

Levenson, Sam (humorist); New York City (1911–1980)

Levi, Carlo (novelist); Turin, Italy (1902–1975)

Levine, James (artistic director, Metropolitan Opera); Cincinnati, 6/23/43

Levine, Joseph E. (film producer); Boston (1905–1987)

Levinson, Barry (screenwriter, director, producer, actor); Baltimore, 4/6/42

Lewis, C(live) S(taples) (author); Belfast, Northern Ireland (1898–1963)

Lewis, Gilbert Newton (chemist, Nobel laureate); Weymouth, Mass. (1875–1946)

Lewis, Jerry (Joseph Levitch) (comedian, film director); Newark, N.J., 3/16/26

Lewis, Jerry Lee (singer); Ferriday, La., 9/29/35

Lewis, John Llewellyn (labor leader); Lucas, Iowa (1880–1969)

Lewis, Juliette (actress); Los Angeles, 12/21/73

Lewis, Meriwether (explorer); Albemarle Co., Va. (1774–1809)

Lewis, (Percy) Wyndham (artist, writer); Bay of Fundy, Maine (at sea) (1884–1957)

Lewis, Shari (Shari Hurwitz) (puppeteer); New York City (1934–1998)

Lewis, Sinclair (novelist); Sauk Centre, Minn. (1885–1951)

Ley, Willy (science writer); Berlin (1906–1969)

Liberace (Wladziu Liberace) (pianist); West Allis, Wis. (1919–1987)

Lichtenstein, Roy (painter); New York City (1923–1997)

Lie, Trygve Halvdan (first U.N. secretary-general); Oslo (1896–1968)

Light, Judith (actress); Trenton, N.J., 2/9/49

Lightfoot, Gordon (singer, songwriter); Orillia, Ont., Canada, 11/17/38

Limbaugh, Rush (political commentator); Cape Girardeau, Mo., 1/12/51

Lin, Maya (architect, sculptor); Athens, Ohio, 10/5/59

Lin Yutang (author); Changchow, China (1895–1976)

Lincoln, Abraham (16th U.S. president); Hardin (Larue) County, Ky. (1809–1865)

Lind, Jenny (Johanna Maria Lind) (soprano); Stockholm (1820–1887)

Lindbergh, Anne Morrow (author); Englewood, N.J. (1906–2001)

Lindbergh, Charles A. (aviator); Detroit (1902–1974)

Linden, Hal (Harold Lipshitz) (actor); New York City, 3/20/31

Lindsay, Howard (playwright); Waterford, N.Y. (1889–1968)

Linkletter, Art (radio-TV personality); Moose Jaw, Sask., Canada, 7/17/12

Linnaeus, Carolus (Carl von Linné) (botanist); Råshult, Sweden (1707–1778)

Linney, Laura (actress); New York City, 2/5/64

Liotta, Ray (actor); Union, N.J., 12/18/55

Lipchitz, Jacques (sculptor); Druskieniki, Latvia (1891–1973)

Lippi, Fra Filippo (painter); Florence (1406–1469)

Lippmann, Walter (columnist, author, political analyst); New York City (1889–1974)

Lister, Joseph (1st Baron of Lyme Regis) (surgeon); Upton, England (1827–1912)

Liszt, Franz (composer, pianist); Raiding, Hungary (1811–1886)

Lithgow, John (actor); Rochester, N.Y., 6/6/45

Little, Rich (impressionist); Ottawa, Ont., Canada, 11/26/38

Livingstone, David (missionary, explorer); Lanarkshire, Scotland (1813–1873)

L. L. Cool J (James Todd Smith) (rap artist); New York City, 1/14/68

Llewellyn, Richard (novelist); St. David's, Wales (1906–1983)

Lloyd Webber, Andrew (composer); London, 3/22/48

Lloyd George, David (Earl of Dwyfor) (statesman); Manchester, England (1863–1945)

Lloyd, Jake (actor); Fort Collins, Colo. 3/5/90

Lloyd, Harold (comedian); Burchard, Neb. (1893–1971)

Locke, John (philosopher); Somersetshire, England (1632–1704)

Lockhart, June (actress); New York City, 6/25/25

Locklear, Heather (actress); Los Angeles, 9/25/61

Lodge, Henry Cabot (legislator); Boston (1850–1924)

Lodge, Henry Cabot, Jr. (diplomat); Nahant, Mass. (1902–1985)

Loesser, Frank (composer); New York City (1910–1969)

Loewe, Frederick (composer); Vienna (1901–1988)

Logan, Joshua (director, producer); Texarkana, Tex. (1908–1988)

Lollobrigida, Gina (Luigina Lollobrigida) (actress); Subiaco, Italy, 7/4/27

Lombard, Carole (Jane Alice Peters) (actress); Ft. Wayne, Ind. (1908–1942)

Lombardo, Guy (band leader); London, Ont., Canada (1902–1977)

London, George (baritone); Montreal (1920–1985)

London, Jack (John Griffith London) (novelist); San Francisco (1876–1916)

Long, Huey Pierce (politician); Winnfield, La. (1893–1935)

Long, Shelley (actress); Fort Wayne, Ind., 8/23/49

Longfellow, Henry Wadsworth (poet); Portland, Maine (1807–1882)

**Longworth,** Alice Roosevelt (social figure); New York City **(1884–1980)**
**Loos,** Ánita (novelist); Sissons, Calif. **(1888–1981)**
**Lopez,** Jennifer (actress, singer); Bronx, N.Y., 12/24/70
**Lopez,** Trini (singer); Dallas, 5/15/37
**Lopez,** Vincent (band leader); Brooklyn, N.Y. **(1895–1975)**
**Lord,** Jack (John Joseph Ryan) (actor); New York City **(1920–1998)**
**Loren,** Sophia (Sofia Scicolone) (actress); Rome, 9/20/34
**Lorenz,** Konrad (ethologist); Vienna **(1903–1989)**
**Lorre,** Peter (Laszlo Löewenstein) (actor); Rosenberg, former Czechoslovakia **(1904–1964)**
**Loudon,** Dorothy (actress, singer); Boston, 9/17/33
**Louis-Dreyfus,** Julia (actress); New York City, 1/13/61
**Louis XIV** (King of France); St.-Germain-en-Laye, France **(1638–1715)**
**Louise,** Tina (actress); New York City, 2/11/37
**Love,** Susan (surgeon, oncologist, activist); Long Branch, N.J., 2/9/48
**Lovecraft,** Howard Phillips (author); Providence, R.I. **(1890–1937)**
**Lovett,** Lyle (country singer, songwriter); Klein, Tex., 11/1/56
**Lowe,** Rob (actor); Charlottesville, Va., 3/17/64
**Lowell,** Amy (poet); Brookline, Mass. **(1874–1925)**
**Lowell,** James Russell (poet); Cambridge, Mass. **(1819–1891)**
**Lowell,** Robert (poet); Boston **(1917–1977)**
**Loy,** Myrna (Myrna Williams) (actress); nr. Helena, Mont. **(1905–1993)**
**Loyola,** St. Ignatius (of Iñigo de Oñez y Loyola) (founder of Jesuits); Guipuzcoa Province, Spain **(1491– 1556)**
**Lubitsch,** Ernst (film director); Berlin **(1892–1947)**
**Lucas,** George (film director); Modesto, Calif., 5/14/44
**Lucci,** Susan (actress); Scarsdale, N.Y., 12/23/46
**Luce,** Clare Boothe (playwright, former ambassador); New York City **(1903–1987)**
**Luce,** Henry Robinson (editor, publisher); Tengchow, China **(1898–1967)**
**Ludlum,** Robert (author); New York City **(1927–2001)**
**Lugosi,** Béla (Béla Blasko) (actor); Lugos, Hungary **(1888–1956)**
**Lukas,** J. Anthony (author); New York City **(1933–1997)**
**Lukas,** Paul (actor); Budapest **(1895–1971)**
**Lully,** Jean Baptiste (French composer); Florence **(1639–1687)**
**Lumet,** Sidney (director); Philadelphia, 6/25/24
**Lunden,** Joan (TV host); Fair Oaks, Calif., 9/19/50
**Lunt,** Alfred (actor); Milwaukee **(1892–1977)**
**Lupino,** Ida (actress, director); London **(1918–1995)**
**LuPone,** Patti (actress, singer); Northport, N.Y., 4/21/49
**Luther,** Martin (religious reformer); Eisleben, East Germany **(1483–1546)**
**Lynch,** David (film director); Missoula, Mont., 1/20/46
**Lynn,** Loretta (singer); Butcher's Hollow, Ky., 4/14/35

# M

**Ma,** Yo-Yo (cellist); Paris, 10/7/55
**Maazel,** Lorin (conductor); Neuilly, France, 3/5/30
**MacArthur,** Charles (playwright); Scranton, Pa. **(1895–1956)**
**MacArthur,** Douglas (five-star general); Little Rock Barracks, Ark. **(1880–1964)**
**MacArthur,** James (actor); Los Angeles, 12/8/37
**Macaulay,** Thomas Babington (author); Rothley Temple, England **(1800–1859)**
**MacDermot,** Galt (composer); Montreal, 12/19/28
**MacDonald,** James Ramsay (statesman); Lossiemouth, Scotland **(1866–1937)**
**MacDonald,** Jeanette (actress, soprano); Philadelphia **(1907–1965)**
**Macdonald,** Ross (Kenneth Millar) (mystery writer); Los Gatos, Calif. **(1915–1983)**
**MacDowell,** Edward Alexander (composer); New York City **(1861–1908)**
**MacDowell,** Andie (Rosalie Anderson MacDowell) (actress); Gaffney, S.C., 4/21/58
**MacFadden,** Bernarr (physical culturist); nr. Mill Spring, Mo. **(1868–1955)**
**Machaut,** Guillaume de (composer); Marchault, France **(1300–1377)**
**Machiavelli,** Niccolò (political philosopher); Florence, Italy **(1469–1527)**
**Mackie,** Bob (designer); Monterey Park, Calif., 3/24/40
**MacLaine,** Shirley (Shirley MacLean Beaty) (actress); Richmond, Va., 4/24/34
**MacLeish,** Archibald (poet); Glencoe, Ill. **(1892–1982)**
**Macmillan,** Harold (ex-prime minister); London **(1894–1986)**
**MacMurray,** Fred (actor); Kankakee, Ill. **(1908–1991)**
**MacNeil,** Cornell (baritone); Minneapolis, 9/24/22

**MacNeil,** Robert (TV newscaster); Montreal, 1/19/31
**MacNicol,** Peter (actor); Dallas, 4/10/54
**Macpherson,** Elle (Eleanor Gow) (model, actress); Sydney, Australia, 3/29/64
**MacRae,** Gordon (singer, actor); East Orange, N.J. **(1921–1986)**
**MacRae,** Sheila (comedienne); London, 9/24/24
**Madison,** James (4th U.S. president); Port Conway, Va. **(1751–1836)**
**Madonna** (Madonna Louise Ciccone) (singer, actress); Bay City, Mich., 8/16/58
**Maeterlinck,** Count Maurice (author); Ghent, Belgium **(1862–1949)**
**Magellan,** Ferdinand (Fernando de Magalhaes) (navigator); Sabrosa, Portugal **( c. 1480–1521)**
**Magliozzi,** Ray ("Car Talk" host); Cambridge, Mass., 3/30/49
**Magliozzi,** Tom ("Car Talk" host); Cambridge, Mass., 6/28/37
**Magritte,** René (painter); Belgium **(1898–1967)**
**Magsaysay,** Ramón (statesman); Iba, Luzon, Philippines **(1907–1957)**
**Maguire,** Tobey (actor); Santa Monica, Calif., 6/27/75
**Mahan,** Alfred Thayer (naval historian); West Point, N.Y. **(1840–1914)**
**Mahler,** Gustav (composer, conductor); Kalischt, Czechoslovakia **(1860–1911)**
**Mahoney,** John (actor); Manchester, England, 6/20/40
**Mailer,** Norman (novelist); Long Branch, N.J., 1/31/23
**Maillol,** Aristide (sculptor); Banyuls-sur-Mer, Rousillion, France **(1861–1944)**
**Maimonides,** Moses (Jewish philosopher); Cordoba, Spain **(1135–1204)**
**Mainbocher** (Main Rousseau Bocher) (fashion designer); Chicago **(1891–1976)**
**Majors,** Lee (Harvey Lee Yeary) (actor); Wyandotte, Mich., 4/23/40
**Makarova,** Natalia (ballet dancer); Leningrad (St. Petersburg), Russia, 11/21/40
**Makeba,** Miriam (singer); Johannesburg, South Africa, 3/4/32
**Malamud,** Bernard (novelist); Brooklyn, N.Y. **(1914–1986)**
**Malcolm X** (Malcolm Little; el Hajj Malik el-Shabazz) (Black nationalist, religious leader); Omaha, Neb. **(1925–1965)**
**Malden,** Karl (Karl Mladen Sekulovich) (actor); Chicago, 3/22/13
**Malkovich,** John (actor); Christopher, Ill., 12/9/53
**Mallarmé,** Stephane (poet, essayist); Paris **(1842–1898)**
**Malle,** Louis (director); Thumeries, France **(1932–1995)**
**Malraux,** André (author); Paris **(1901–1976)**
**Malthus,** Thomas Robert (economist); nr. Dorking, England **(1766–1834)**
**Maltin,** Leonard (film critic and historian); New York City, 12/18/50
**Mamet,** David (playwright); Chicago, 11/30/47
**Manchester,** Melissa (singer); Bronx, N.Y., 2/15/51
**Manchester,** William (writer); Attleboro, Mass., 4/1/22
**Mancini,** Henry (composer, conductor); Cleveland **(1924–1994)**
**Mandela,** Nelson (Rolihlahla) (former president of South Africa); Umtata, Transkei, 7/18/18
**Mandela,** Winnie (Nomzamo) (South African political activist); Pondoland district of the Transkei, 1936?
**Mandrell,** Barbara (singer); Houston, 12/25/48
**Manet,** Edouard (painter); Paris **(1832–1883)**
**Mangione,** Chuck (hornist, pianist, composer); Rochester, N.Y., 11/29/40
**Manheim,** Camryn (actress); New York City, 3/8/61
**Manilow,** Barry (singer); Brooklyn, N.Y., 6/17/46
**Mankiewicz,** Frank F. (columnist); New York City, 5/16/24
**Mankiewicz,** Joseph L. (film writer, director); Wilkes-Barre, Pa. **(1909–1993)**
**Mann,** Horace (educator); Franklin, Mass. **(1796–1859)**
**Mann,** Thomas (novelist); Lübeck, Germany **(1875–1955)**
**Mannes,** Marya (writer); New York City **(1904–1990)**
**Mansfield,** Jayne (Jayne Palmer) (actress); Bryn Mawr, Pa. **(1932–1967)**
**Mansfield,** Katherine (story writer); Wellington, New Zealand **(1888–1923)**
**Manson,** Marilyn (Brian Warner) (rock musician); Canton, Ohio, 1/5/69
**Mantegna,** Andrea (painter); Isola di Carturo, Italy **(1431–1506)**
**Mantegna,** Joe (actor); Chicago, 11/13/47
**Mantovani,** Annunzio (conductor); Venice **(1905–1980)**
**Mao Zedong** (Tse-tung) (Chinese leader); Shao Shan, China **(1893– 1976)**
**Mapplethorpe,** Robert (photographer); Floral Park, Queens, N.Y. **(1946–1989)**
**Marat,** Jean Paul (French revolutionist); Boudry, Neuchâtel, Switzerland **(1743–1793)**
**Marceau,** Marcel (mime); Strasbourg, France, 3/22/23
**Marceau,** Sophie (actress); Paris, 11/17/66

**March,** Fredric (Frederick Bickel) (actor); Racine, Wis. **(1897–1975)**
**Marchand,** Nancy (actress); Buffalo, N.Y. **(1928–2000)**
**Marconi,** Guglielmo (inventor); Bologna, Italy **(1874–1937)**
**Marcus Aurelius** (Marcus Annius Vorus) (Roman emperor); Rome **(121–180)**
**Marcus,** Rudolph Arthur (chemist, Nobel laureate); Montreal, 7/21/23
**Marcuse,** Herbert (philosopher); Berlin **(1898–1979)**
**Margaret Rose** (princess of England); Glamis Castle, Angus, Scotland, 8/21/30
**Margrethe II** (queen of Denmark); Copenhagen, 4/16/40
**Margulies,** Julianna (actress); Spring Valley, N.Y., 6/8/65
**Marie Antoinette** (Josephe Jeanne Marie Antoinette) (queen of France); Vienna **(1755 –1793)**
**Marisol** (Escobar) (Venezuelan-American sculptor); Paris, 1930
**Markham,** Edwin (poet); Oregon City, Ore. **(1852–1940)**
**Markova,** Dame Alicia (Lilian Alice Marks) (ballet dancer); London, 12/1/10
**Marley,** Bob (singer, songwriter); Kingston, Jamaica **(1945–1981)**
**Marlowe,** Christopher (dramatist); Canterbury, England **(1564–1593)**
**Marquand,** J(ohn) P(hillips) (novelist); Wilmington, Del. **(1893–1960)**
**Marquette,** Jacques (missionary, explorer); Laon, France **(1637–1675)**
**Marriner,** Neville (conductor); Lincoln, England, 4/15/24
**Marsalis,** Wynton (musician); New Orleans, 10/18/61
**Marshall,** E.G. (actor); Owatonna, Minn. **(1910–1998)**
**Marshall,** Garry (director, producer, screenwriter, actor); New York City, 11/13/34
**Marshall,** George Catlett (general); Uniontown, Pa. **(1880–1959)**
**Marshall,** Herbert (actor); London **(1890–1968)**
**Marshall,** John (jurist); nr. Germantown, Va. **(1755–1835)**
**Marshall,** Penny (Penny Marscharelli) (actress, director, producer); Bronx, N.Y., 10/15/42
**Marshall,** Thurgood (U.S. Supreme Court justice); Baltimore **(1908–1993)**
**Martin,** Dean (Dino Crocetti) (singer, actor); Steubenville, Ohio **(1917–1995)**
**Martin,** Mary (singer, actress); Weatherford, Tex. **(1913–1990)**
**Martin,** Steve (actor, writer, producer); Waco, Tex., 8/14/45
**Martin,** Tony (Alvin Morris) (singer); San Francisco, 12/25/12
**Martinelli,** Giovanni (tenor); Montagnana, Italy **(1885–1969)**
**Martins,** Peter (dancer, choreographer); Copenhagen, 10/27/45
**Marvell,** Andrew (poet); Winestead, England **(1621–1678)**
**Marvin,** Lee (actor); New York City **(1924–1987)**
**Marx,** Chico (Leonard) (comedian); New York City **(1887–1961)**
**Marx,** Groucho (Julius) (comedian); New York City **(1890–1977)**
**Marx,** Harpo (Arthur) (comedian); New York City **(1893–1964)**
**Marx,** Karl (Socialist writer); Treves, Germany **(1818–1883)**
**Marx,** Zeppo (Herbert) (comedian); New York City **(1901–1979)**
**Mary Stuart** (Mary, Queen of Scots) (queen of Scotland); Linlithgow, Scotland **(1542–1587)**
**Masaccio,** (Tommaso di Giovanni di Simone Cassai) (painter); San Giovanni Valdarno, Tuscany **(1401–c. 1428)**
**Masaryk,** Jan Garrigue (statesman); Prague **(1886–1948)**
**Masaryk,** Thomas Garrigue (statesman); Hodonin, Czech Republic **(1850–1937)**
**Masefield,** John (poet); Ledbury, England **(1878–1967)**
**Masekela,** Hugh (trumpeter); Wilbank, South Africa, 4/4/39
**Mason,** Jackie (Jacob Moshe Maza) (comedian); Sheboygan, Wis., 6/9/31
**Mason,** James (actor); Huddersfield, England **(1909–1984)**
**Mason,** Marsha (actress); St. Louis, 4/3/42
**Massenet,** Jules Emile Frédéric (composer); Montaud, France **(1842–1912)**
**Massine,** Léonide (choreographer); Moscow **(1895–1979)**
**Masters,** Edgar Lee (poet); Garnett, Kans. **(1869–1950)**
**Masters,** William (human sexuality expert); Cleveland **(1915–2001)**
**Masterson,** Mary Stuart (actress, writer, director); New York City, 6/28/66
**Mastroianni,** Marcello (actor); Fontana Liri, Italy **(1924–1996)**
**Mather,** Cotton (clergyman); Boston **(1663–1728)**
**Mathis,** Johnny (singer); Gilmer, Texas, 9/30/35
**Matisse,** Henri (painter); Le Cateau, France **(1869–1954)**
**Matthau,** Walter (Walter Matuschanskayasky) (actor); New York City **(1920–2000)**
**Mature,** Victor (actor); Louisville, Ky. **(1915–1999)**
**Maugham,** W(illiam) Somerset (author); Paris **(1874–1965)**
**Mauldin,** Bill (political cartoonist); Mountain Park, N.M., 10/29/21
**Maupassant,** Henri René Albert Guy de (story writer); Normandy, France **(1850–1893)**

**Maurois,** André (Emile Herzog) (author); Elbauf, France **(1885–1967)**
**Maximillan** (Ferdinand Maximilian Joseph) (emperor of Mexico); Vienna **( 1832–1867)**
**Maxwell,** James Clerk (physicist); Edinburgh, Scotland **(1831–1879)**
**Maxwell,** (Ian) Robert (publisher); Selo Slatina, Czechoslavakia **(1923–1991)**
**May,** Elaine (Elaine Berlin) (entertainer, writer); Philadelphia, 4/21/32
**May,** Rollo (psychologist); Ada, Ohio **(1909–1994)**
**Mayer,** Louis B. (movie executive); Minsk, Russia **(1885–1957)**
**Mayo,** Charles H. (surgeon); Rochester, Minn. **(1865–1939)**
**Mayo,** Charles W. (surgeon); Rochester, Minn. **(1898–1968)**
**Mayo,** Virginia (Jones) (actress); St. Louis, 11/30/20
**Mayo,** William J. (surgeon); Le Sueur, Minn. **(1861–1939)**
**Mayron,** Melanie (actress); Philadelphia, 10/20/52
**Mazzini,** Giuseppe (patriot); Genoa **(1805–1872)**
**McBride,** Patricia (ballet dancer); Teaneck, N.J., 8/23/42
**McCallum,** David (actor); Glasgow, Scotland, 9/19/33
**McCambridge,** Mercedes (actress); Joliet, Ill., 3/17/18
**McCarthy,** Eugene J. (ex-senator); Watkins, Minn., 3/29/16
**McCarthy,** Joseph Raymond (senator); Grand Chute, Wis. **(1908–1957)**
**McCarthy,** Mary (novelist); Seattle **(1912–1989)**
**McCartney,** Linda (photographer, singer); New York City **(1941–1998)**
**McCartney,** Paul (singer, songwriter); Liverpool, England, 6/18/42
**McClanahan,** Rue (actress); Healdton, Okla., 2/21/35
**McClellan,** George Brinton (general); Philadelphia **(1826–1885)**
**McClintock,** Barbara (geneticist, Nobel laureate) **(1902–1992)**
**McCloy,** John J. (lawyer, banker); Philadelphia **(1895–1989)**
**McCormack,** John (tenor); Athlone, Ireland **(1884–1945)**
**McCormack,** John W. (ex-Speaker of House); Boston **(1891–1980)**
**McCormick,** Cyrus Hall (inventor); Rockbridge County, Va. **(1809–1884)**
**McCourt,** Frank (writer); Brooklyn, N.Y., 8/19/30
**McCracken,** James (dramatic tenor); Gary, Ind. **(1926–1988)**
**McCrea,** Joel (actor); Los Angeles **(1905–1990)**
**McCullers,** Carson (novelist); Columbus, Ga. **(1917–1967)**
**McCullough,** David (author, historian); Pittsburgh, 7/7/33
**McDermott,** Dylan (actor); Waterbury, Conn., 10/26/62
**McDormand,** Frances (actress); Illinois, 6/23/57
**McDowall,** Roddy (actor); London **(1928–1998)**
**McDowell,** Malcolm (actor); Leeds, England, 6/15/43
**McFadden,** Gates (actress); Cuyahoga Falls, Ohio, 3/2/49
**McGavin,** Darren (actor); San Joaquin, Calif., 5/7/22
**McGillis,** Kelly (actress); Newport Beach, Calif., 7/9/57
**McGinley,** Phyllis (poet, writer); Ontario, Ore. **(1905–1978)**
**McGoohan,** Patrick (actor); Astoria, Queens, N.Y., 3/19/28
**McGovern,** Elizabeth (actress); Evanston, Ill., 7/18/61
**McGovern,** Maureen (singer); Youngstown, Ohio, 7/27/49
**McGregor,** Ewan (actor); Crieff, Scotland, 3/31/71
**McKellen,** Ian (actor); Burnley, England, 5/25/39
**McKinley,** William (25th U.S. president); Niles, Ohio **(1843–1901)**
**McKuen,** Rod (singer, composer); Oakland, Calif., 4/29/33
**McLachlan,** Sarah (singer, songwriter); Halifax, N.S., 1/28/68
**McLaughlin,** John (guitarist); Yorkshire, England, 1/4/42
**McLean,** Don (singer, songwriter); New Rochelle, N.Y., 10/2/45
**McLuhan,** Marshall (Herbert Marshall) (communications writer); Edmonton, Alta., Canada **(1911–1980)**
**McMahon,** Ed (TV personality); Detroit, 3/6/23
**McMurtry,** Larry (novelist); Wichita Falls, Tex., 6/3/36
**McQueen,** Butterfly (Thelma McQueen); Tampa, Fla. **(1911–1995)**
**McQueen,** Steve (Terence Stephen McQueen) (actor); Beech Grove, Indiana **(1930–1980)**
**McRaney,** Gerald (actor); Collins, Miss., 8/19/47
**McTeer,** Janet (actress); York, England, 1962
**Mead,** Margaret (anthropologist); Philadelphia **(1901–1978)**
**Meadows,** Audrey (actress); Wu Chang, China **(1924–1996)**
**Meadows,** Jayne (actress); Wu Chang, China, 9/27/26
**Meaney,** Colm (actor); Dublin, 5/30/53
**Meany,** George (labor leader); New York City **(1894–1980)**
**Meara,** Anne (actress); New York City, 9/20/29
**Medici,** Lorenzo de' (called Lorenzo the Magnificent) (Florentine ruler); Florence, Italy **(1449–1492)**
**Mehta,** Zubin (conductor); Bombay (Mumbai), 4/29/36
**Meir,** Golda (Golda Myerson, nee Mabovitz) (ex-premier of Israel); Kiev, Ukraine **(1898–1978)**
**Melba,** Dame Nellie (Helen Porter Mitchell) (soprano); nr. Melbourne, Australia **(1861–1931)**
**Melchior,** Lauritz (Lebrecht Hommel) (heroic tenor); Copenhagen **(1890–1973)**

**Mellon,** Andrew William (financier); Pittsburgh **(1855–1937)**
**Melville,** Herman (novelist); New York City **(1819–1891)**
**Mencken,** Henry Louis (writer); Baltimore **(1880–1956)**
**Mendel,** Gregor Johann (geneticist); Heinzendorf, Austrian Silesia **(1822–1884)**
**Mendeleyev,** Dmitri Ivanovich (chemist); Tobolsk, Russia **(1834–1907)**
**Mendelssohn-Bartholdy,** Jakob Ludwig Felix (composer); Hamburg **(1809–1847)**
**Mendès-France,** Pierre (ex-Premier); Paris **(1905–1982)**
**Mengele,** Josef (Nazi, "Angel of Death"); Günzberg, Germany **(1911–1979)**
**Mennin,** Peter (Peter Mennini) (composer); Erie, Pa. **(1923–1983)**
**Menninger,** William C. (psychiatrist); Topeka, Kans. **(1899–1966)**
**Menotti,** Gian Carlo (composer); Cadegliano, Italy, 7/7/11
**Menuhin,** Yehudi (violinist, conductor); New York City **(1916–1999)**
**Menzies,** Robert Gordon (ex-prime minister); Jeparit, Australia **(1894–1978)**
**Mercer,** Johnny (songwriter); Savannah, Ga. **(1909–1976)**
**Mercer,** Mabel (singer); Burton-on-Trent, England **(1900–1984)**
**Merchant,** Ismall (Ismail Noormohamed Abdul Rehman) (film producer); Bombay (Mumbai), 12/25/36
**Merchant,** Natalie (singer, songwriter); Jamestown, N.Y., 10/26/63
**Mercury,** Freddie (Farookh Bulsara) (musician, singer); Zanzibar **(1946–1991)**
**Meredith,** Burgess (actor); Cleveland **(1908–1997)**
**Meredith,** James (author, civil-rights leader); Kosciusko, Miss., 6/26/23
**Merman,** Ethel (Ethel Zimmerman) (singer, actress); Astoria, Queens, N.Y. **(1909–1984)**
**Merrick,** David (David Margulois) (stage producer); St. Louis **(1912–2000)**
**Merton,** Thomas (clergyman, writer); France **(1915–1968)**
**Mesmer,** Franz Anton (physician); Itzmang, nr. Constance, Germany **(1733–1815)**
**Mesta,** Perle (social figure); Sturgis, Mich. **(1889–1975)**
**Metacom,** (King Philip) (Wampanoag Indian sachem); southeastern Mass. **(1640–1676)**
**Metternich,** Prince Klemens Wenzel Nepomuk Lothar von (statesman); Coblenz, Germany **(1773–1859)**
**Mfume,** Kweisi (Frizzell Gray) (politician, NAACP leader); Baltimore, 10/24/48
**Michaels,** Lorne (producer); Toronto, 11/17/44
**Michelangelo Buonarroti** (painter, sculptor, architect); Caprese, Italy **(1475–1564)**
**Michener,** James A. (novelist); New York City **(1907–1997)**
**Mickiewicz,** Adam (Polish poet); Zozie, Belorussia (Belarus) **(1798–1855)**
**Midler,** Bette (singer, actress, producer); Honolulu, 12/1/45
**Mielziner,** Jo (stage designer); Paris **(1901–1976)**
**Mifune,** Toshiro (actor, film producer); Tsingtao, China **(1920–1997)**
**Mies van der Rohe,** Ludwig (architect, designer); Aachen, Germany **(1886–1969)**
**Mikoyan,** Anastas I. (diplomat); Sanain, Armenia **(1895–1978)**
**Milano,** Alyssa (actress); Brooklyn, New York, 12/19/72
**Milhaud,** Darius (composer); Aix-en-Provence, France **(1892–1974)**
**Mill,** John Stuart (philosopher); London **(1806–1873)**
**Milland,** Ray (Reginald Truscott-Jones) (actor); Neath, Wales **(1907–1986)**
**Millay,** Edna St. Vincent (poet); Rockland, Maine **(1892–1950)**
**Miller,** Ann (Lucille Ann Collier) (dancer, actress); Cherino, Tex., 4/12/23
**Miller,** Arthur (playwright); New York City, 10/17/15
**Miller,** Glenn (band leader); Clarinda, Iowa **(1904–1944)**
**Miller,** Henry (novelist); New York City **(1891–1980)**
**Miller,** Jason (John Miller) (playwright, actor); New York City **(1939–2001)**
**Miller,** Mitch (Mitchell) (musician); Rochester, N.Y., 7/4/11
**Miller,** Roger (singer); Fort Worth **(1936–1992)**
**Millet,** Jean François (painter); Gruchy, France **(1814–1875)**
**Millett,** Kate (feminist, writer); St. Paul, Minn., 9/14/34
**Millikan,** Robert A. (physicist); Morrison, Ill. **(1869–1953)**
**Mills,** Donna (actress); Chicago, 12/11/41
**Mills,** Hayley (actress); London, 4/18/46
**Mills,** Juliet (actress); London, 11/21/41
**Milne,** A(lan) A(lexander) (author); London **(1882–1956)**
**Milner,** Martin (actor); Detroit, 12/28/31
**Milnes,** Sherrill (baritone); Downers Grove, Ill., 1/10/35
**Milosevic,** Slobodan (Yugoslav President); Pozarevac, Serbia, 8/29/41
**Milstein,** Nathan (concert violinist); Odessa, Ukraine **(1904–1992)**
**Milton,** John (poet); London **(1608–1674)**
**Mingus,** Charles (jazz composer); Nogales, Ariz. **(1922–1979)**

**Minnelli,** Liza (singer, actress); Hollywood, Calif., 3/12/46
**Minnelli,** Vincente (film director); Chicago **(1913–1986)**
**Minuit,** Peter (Governor of New Amsterdam); Wesel, Germany **(1580–1638)**
**Miranda,** Carmen (Maria do Carmo da Cunha) (singer, dancer); Lisbon **(1909–1955)**
**Miró,** Joan (painter); Barcelona **(1893–1983)**
**Mirren,** Helen (Ilynea Lydia Mironoff) (actress); London, 7/26/45
**Mitchell,** John N. (former Attorney General); Detroit **(1913–1988)**
**Mitchell,** Joni (Roberta Joan Anderson) (singer, songwriter); Ft. Macleod, Alb., Canada, 11/7/43
**Mitchell,** Margaret (novelist); Atlanta **(1900–1949)**
**Mitchell,** Maria (astronomer); Nantucket, Mass. **(1818–1889)**
**Mitchum,** Robert (actor); Bridgeport, Conn. **(1917–1997)**
**Mitropoulos,** Dimitri (orchestra conductor); Athens **(1896–1960)**
**Mitterand,** François (Maurice) (ex-prime minister of France); Jarnac, France **(1916–1996)**
**Mix,** Tom (actor); Mix Run, Pa. **(1880–1940)**
**Mobutu Sese Seko** (Zairean dictator); Lisala, Congo **(1930–1997)**
**Modigliani,** Amedeo (painter); Leghorn, Italy **(1884–1920)**
**Moffo,** Anna (soprano); Wayne, Pa., 6/27/34
**Mohammed** (prophet); Mecca, Saudi Arabia **(570–632)**
**Molière** (Jean Baptiste Poquelin) (dramatist); Paris **(1622–1673)**
**Molina,** Mario (chemist, Nobel laureate); Mexico City, 3/19/43
**Moll,** Richard (actor); Pasadena, Calif., 1/13/43?
**Molnar,** Ferenc (dramatist); Budapest **(1878–1952)**
**Molotov,** Vyacheslav M. (V. M. Skryabin) (diplomat); Kukarka, Russia **(1890–1986)**
**Mondrian,** Piet (painter); Amersfoort, Netherlands **(1872–1944)**
**Monet,** Claude (painter); Paris **(1840–1926)**
**Monica** Monica Arnold (singer); Atlanta, Ga., 10/24/80
**Monk,** Meredith (choreographer, composer, performing artist); Lima, Peru, 11/20/42
**Monk,** Thelonious (pianist); Rocky Mount, N.C. **(1918–1982)**
**Monroe,** James (5th U.S. president); Westmoreland County, Va. **(1758–1831)**
**Monroe,** Marilyn (Norma Jean Mortenson or Baker) (actress); Los Angeles **(1926–1962)**
**Monsarrat,** Nicholas (novelist); Liverpool, England **(1910–1979)**
**Montaigne,** Michel Eyquem de (essayist); nr. Bordeaux, France **(1533–1592)**
**Montalban,** Ricardo (actor); Mexico City, 11/25/20
**Montand,** Yves (Ivo Livi) (actor, singer); Florence, Italy **(1921–1991)**
**Montesquieu,** Charles-Louis de Secondat, baron de La Brède and de (philosopher); nr. Bordeaux, France **(1689–1755)**
**Montessori,** Maria (physician, educator); Chiaravalle, Italy **(1870–1952)**
**Monteux,** Pierre (conductor); Paris **(1875–1964)**
**Monteverdi,** Claudio (composer); Cremona Italy **(1567–1643)**
**Montezuma II** (Aztec emperor); Mexico **(1466–1520)**
**Montgomery,** Elizabeth (actress); Hollywood, Calif. **(1933–1995)**
**Montgomery,** Robert (Henry, Jr.) (actor); Beacon, N.Y. **(1904–1981)**
**Montgomery of Alamein,** 1st Viscount of Hindhead (Sir Bernard Law Montgomery) (military leader); London **(1887–1976)**
**Montoya,** Carlos (guitarist); Madrid **(1903–1993)**
**Moore,** Clayton (Jack Moore) (actor); Chicago **(1914–1999)**
**Moore,** Clement Clarke (author); New York City **(1779–1863)**
**Moore,** Demi (Demi Guynes) (actress); Roswell, N.M., 11/11/62
**Moore,** Dudley (actor, writer, musician); Dagenham, England **(1935–2002)**
**Moore,** Grace (soprano); Jellico, Tenn. **(1901–1947)**
**Moore,** Henry (sculptor); Castleford, England **(1898–1986)**
**Moore,** Julianne (actress); Fayetteville, N.C., 12/3/60
**Moore,** Marianne (poet); Kirkwood, Mo. **(1887–1972)**
**Moore,** Mary Tyler (actress); Brooklyn, N.Y., 12/29/36
**Moore,** Melba (Beatrice) (singer, actress); New York City, 10/27/45
**Moore,** Roger (actor); London, 10/14/27
**Moore,** Thomas (poet); Dublin **(1779–1852)**
**Moorehead,** Agnes (actress); Clinton, Mass. **(1906–1974)**
**Moranis,** Rick (actor); Toronto, 4/18/53
**More,** Henry (philosopher); Grantham, England **(1614–1687)**
**More,** Sir Thomas (statesman, author); London **(1478–1535)**
**Moreno,** Rita (Rosita Dolores Alverio) (actress); Humacao, P.R., 12/11/31
**Morgan,** Harry (Harry Bratsburg) (actor); Detroit, 4/10/15
**Morgan,** John Pierpont (financier); Hartford, Conn. **(1837–1913)**
**Moriarty,** Michael (actor); Detroit, 4/5/41
**Morini,** Erica (concert violinist); Vienna **(1904–1995)**
**Morison,** Samuel Eliot (historian); Boston **(1887–1976)**
**Morita,** Pat (Noriyuki Morita) (actor); Berkeley, Calif., 8/28/32
**Morley,** Christopher Darlington (novelist); Haverford, Pa. **(1890–1957)**
**Morley,** Robert (actor); Semley, England **(1908–1992)**

Morris, Mark (choreographer); Seattle, 8/29/56

Morris, William (poet, craftsman); Walthamstow, England (1834–1896)

Morrison, Jim (James Douglas Morrison) (singer, songwriter); Melbourne, Fla. (1943–1971)

Morrison, Toni (Chloe Anthony Wofford) (novelist); Lorain, Ohio, 2/18/31

Morrison, Van (singer); Belfast, Northern Ireland, 8/31/45

Morse, Marston (mathematician); Waterville, Maine (1892–1977)

Morse, Samuel Finley Breese (painter, inventor); Charlestown, Mass. (1791–1872 )

Morton, Jelly Roll (Ferdinand Joseph La Menthe) (jazz composer); New Orleans (1890–1941)

Moseley-Braun, Carol (U.S. Senator); Chicago, 8/16/47

Moses, Grandma (Mrs. Anna Mary Robertson Moses) (painter); Greenwich, N.Y. (1860–1961)

Moses, Robert (urban planner); New Haven, Conn. (1888–1981)

Moss, Kate (model); London, England, 1/16/74

Mostel, Zero (Samuel Joel Mostel) (actor); Brooklyn, N.Y. (1915–1977)

Mother Teresa (Agnes Gonxha Bojaxhiu) (nun); Skopje, Macedonia (1910–1997)

Motherwell, Robert (artist, "action" painter); Aberdeen, Wash. (1915–1991)

Mott, Lucretia (Coffin) (feminist, reformer, abolitionist); Nantucket, Mass. (1793–1880)

Moussorgsky, Modest Petrovich (composer); Karev, Russia (1839–1881)

Moyers, Bill D. (Billy Don) (journalist); Hugo, Okla., 6/5/34

Moynihan, Daniel Patrick (New York senator); Tulsa, Okla., 3/16/27

Mozart, Wolfgang Amadeus (Johannes Chrysostomus Wolfgangus Theophilus Mozart) (composer); Salzburg, Austria (1756–1791)

Mudd, Roger (TV newscaster); Washington, D.C., 2/9/28

Muggeridge, Malcolm (Thomas) (writer); Croydon, England (1903–1990)

Muhammad (founder of Islam); Mecca, Saudi Arabia (c. 570–632)

Muhammad, Elijah (Elijah Poole) (religious leader); Sandersville, Ga. (1897–1975)

Mulgrew, Kate (actress); Dubuque, Iowa, 4/29/55

Mulhare, Edward (actor); Ireland (1923–1997)

Mulliken, Robert Sanderson (chemist, Nobel laureate); Newburyport, Mass. (1896–1986)

Mulroney, Dermot (actor, musician, producer); Alexandria, Va., 10/31/63

Mumford, Lewis (cultural historian, city planner); Flushing, Queens, N.Y. (1895–1990)

Munch, Edvard (painter); Löten, Norway (1863–1944)

Munchhausen, Karl Friedrick Hieronymus, baron von (anecdotist); Hannover, Germany (1720–1797)

Muni, Paul (Muni Weisenfreund) (actor); Lemburg, Austria (1895–1967)

Muñoz Marín, Luis (ex-governor of Puerto Rico); San Juan, P.R. (1898–1980)

Munsel, Patrice (soprano); Spokane, Wash., 5/14/25

Murdoch, Iris (novelist); Dublin (1919–1999)

Murdoch, Rupert (publisher); Melbourne, Australia, 3/11/31

Murillo, Bartolomé Esteban (painter); Seville, Spain (1617–1682)

Murphy, Audie (actor, war hero); Kingston, Tex. (1924–1971)

Murphy, Eddie (actor, comedian); Brooklyn, N.Y., 4/3/61

Murphy, George (actor, dancer, ex-senator); New Haven, Conn. (1902–1992)

Murray, Arthur (dance teacher); New York City (1895–1991)

Murray, Bill (actor, comedian); Wilmette, Ill., 9/21/50

Murray, Kathryn (dance teacher); Jersey City, N.J. (1906–1999)

Murrow, Edward R. (commentator, ...)

Musil, Robert (novelist); Klagenfurt, Austria (1880–1942)

Muskie, Edmund (political figure); Rumford, Maine (1914–1996)

Mussolini, Benito (Italian dictator); Dovia, Forli, Italy (1883–1945)

Muti, Riccardo (orchestra conductor); Naples, Italy, 7/28/41

Mutter, Anne-Sophie (violinist); Rheinfelden, Germany, 6/29/63

Myers, Mike (actor, writer, comedian); Scarborough, Ont., Canada, 5/25/63

Myerson, Bess (consumer advocate); Bronx, N.Y., 7/16/24

Myrdal, Gunnar (sociologist, economist); Gustaf Parish, Sweden (1898–1987)

# N

Nabokov, Vladimir (novelist); St. Petersburg, Russia (1899–1977)

Nabors, Jim (actor, singer); Sylacauga, Ala., 6/12/32

Nader, Ralph (consumer advocate); Winsted, Conn., 2/27/34

Nair, Mira (director, screenwriter); Bhubaneswar, India, 10/15/57

Nash, Graham (singer); Blackpool, England, 1942

Nash, Ogden (poet); Rye, N.Y. (1902–1971)

Nasser, Gamal Abdel (statesman); Beni Mor, Egypt (1918–1970)

Nast, Thomas (cartoonist); Landau, Germany (1840–1902)

Nation, Carry Amelia (temperance leader); Garrard County, Ky. (1846–1911)

Natta, Giulio (chemist, Nobel laureate); Imperia, Italy (1903–1979)

Natwick, Mildred (actress); Baltimore (1905–1994)

Neagle, Anna (Marjorie Robertson) (actress); London (1908–1986)

Neal, Patricia (actress); Packard, Ky., 1/20/26

Neeson, Liam (William John) (actor); Ballymena, Northern Ireland, 6/7/52

Negri, Pola (Apolina Mathias-Chalupec) (actress); Bromberg, Poland (1899–1987)

Nehru, Jawaharlal (first prime minister of India); Allahabad, India (1889–1964)

Neill, Sam (Nigel Neill) (actor); Omagh, Northern Ireland, 9/14/47

Nelligan, Kate (actress); London, Ont., Canada, 3/16/51

Nelson, Barry (Robert Haakon Nielsen) (actor); San Francisco, 4/16/20

Nelson, David (actor); New York City, 10/24/36

Nelson, Harriet Hilliard (Peggy Lou Snyder) (actress); Des Moines, Iowa (1909–1994)

Nelson, Ozzie (Oswald) (actor); Jersey City, N.J. (1907–1975)

Nelson, Ricky (Eric) (singer, actor); Teaneck, N.J. (1940–1985)

Nelson, Viscount Horatio (naval officer); Burnham Thorpe, England (1758–1805)

Nelson, Willie (singer); Waco, Tex., 4/30/33

Nenni, Pietro (Socialist leader); Faenza, Italy (1891–1980)

Nero (Nero Claudius Caesar Drusus Germanicus) (Roman emperor); Antium, Italy (37–68)

Nero, Peter (pianist); New York City, 5/22/34

Netanyahu, Benjamin (Binyamin) (former Israeli prime minister); Tel Aviv, Israel, 10/21/49

Neuwirth, Bebe (Beatrice Neuwirth) (actress); Newark, N.J., 12/31/58

Nevelson, Louise (sculptor); Kiev, Russia (1899–1988)

Neville, Aaron (singer); New Orleans, 1/24/41

Newhart, Bob (actor); Chicago, 9/5/29

Newhouse, Samuel I. (publisher); New York City (1895–1979)

Newley, Anthony (actor, songwriter); London (1931–1999)

Newman, Edwin (news commentator); New York City, 1/25/19

Newman, John Henry (prelate); London (1801–1890)

Newman, Paul (actor, director); Cleveland, 1/26/25

Newman, Randy (singer); Los Angeles, 11/28/43

Newton, Huey (black activist); New Orleans (1942–1989)

Newton, Sir Isaac (mathematician, scientist); nr. Grantham, England (1642–1727)

Newton, Wayne (singer); Norfolk, Va., 4/3/42

Newton-John, Olivia (singer); Cambridge, England, 9/26/48

Nichols, Nichelle (actress); Robbins, Ill., 12/28/33

Nichols, Mike (Michael Peschkowsky) (stage and film director); Berlin, 11/6/31

Nicholson, Jack (actor, director, writer); Neptune, N.J., 4/22/37

Nicks, Stevie (Stephanie Lynn Nicks) (singer, songwriter); Phoenix, Ariz., 5/26/48

Nielsen, Leslie (actor); Regina, Sask., Canada, 2/11/26

Nietzsche, Friedrich Wilhelm (philosopher); nr. Lützen, Saxony, Germany (1844–1900)

Nightingale, Florence (nurse); Florence, Italy (1820–1910)

Nijinsky, Vaslav (ballet dancer); Warsaw (1890–1950)

Nilsson, Birgit (soprano); West Karup, Sweden, 5/17/23

Nilsson, Harry (singer, songwriter); Brooklyn, N.Y. (1941–1994)

Nimoy, Leonard (actor, director, writer, producer); Boston, 3/26/31

Nin, Anaïs (author, diarist); Neuilly, France (1903–1977)

Niven, David (actor); Kirriemuir, Scotland (1910–1983)

Nixon, Richard Milhous (37th U.S. president); Yorba Linda, Calif. (1913–1994)

Nizer, Louis (lawyer, author); London (1902–1994)

Nobel, Alfred Bernhard (industrialist); Stockholm (1833–1896)

Noguchi, Isamu (sculptor); Los Angeles (1904–1988)

Nolan, Lloyd (actor); San Francisco (1902–1985)

Nolte, Nick (actor); Omaha, Neb., 2/8/40

Norell, Norman (Norman Levinson) (fashion designer); Noblesville, Ind. (1900–1972)

Norman, Jessye (soprano); Augusta, Ga., 9/15/45

Norman, Marsha (Marsha Williams) (playwright); Louisville, Ky., 9/21/47

Normand, Mabel (actress); Boston (1894–1930)

Norris, Chuck (Carlos Ray Norris) (actor, athlete); Ryan, Oklahoma, 3/10/40

Norstad, Gen. Lauris (ex-commander of NATO forces);
   Minneapolis (1907–1988)
North, John Ringling (circus director); Baraboo, Wis. (1903–1985)
North, Oliver (ex-military officer); San Antonio, 10/7/43
North, Sheree (actress); Los Angeles, 1/17/33
Norton, Edward (actor); Columbia, Md., 8/18/69
Norton, Eleanor Holmes (New York City government official,
   lawyer); Washington, D.C., 6/13/37
Nostradamus (Michel de Notredame) (astrologer); St. Rémy,
   France (1503–1566)
Novaes, Guiomar (pianist); São João de Boa Vista, Brazil (1895–
   1979)
Novak, Kim (Marilyn Novak) (actress); Chicago, 2/13/33
Novarro, Ramon (Ramon Samaniegoes) (actor); Durango, Mexico
   (1899–1968)
Novello, Ivor (actor, playwright, composer); Cardiff, Wales (1893–
   1951)
Nugent, Elliott (actor, director); Dover, Ohio (1899–1980)
Nureyev, Rudolf (ballet dancer); Siberia (1938–1993)
Nyro, Laura (singer, songwriter); Bronx, N.Y. (1947–1997)

# O

Oakie, Jack (actor); Sedalia, Mo. (1903–1978)
Oakley, Annie (Phoebe Anne Oakley Mozee) (markswoman); Darke
   County, Ohio (1860–1926)
Oates, Joyce Carol (novelist); Lockport, N.Y., 6/16/38
Oberon, Merle (Estelle Merle O'Brien Thompson) (actress);
   Bombay, India (1911–1979)
Oberth, Hermann (rocketry and space flight pioneer); Nagyszeben,
   Austria-Hungary (Sibiu, Romania) (1894–1989)
O'Brian, Hugh (Hugh J. Krampe) (actor); Rochester, N.Y., 4/19/25
O'Brien, Conan (TV personality); Brookline, Mass., 4/18/63
O'Brien, Edmond (actor); New York City (1915–1985)
O'Brien, Margaret (Angela Maxine O'Brien) (actress); San Diego,
   Calif., 1/15/37
O'Brien, Pat (William Joseph O'Brien, Jr.) (actor); Milwaukee
   (1899–1983)
O'Brien, Tim (novelist); Austin, Minn., 10/1/46
Obuchi, Keizo (former prime minister of Japan); Nakanojo, Japan
   (1937–2000)
O'Casey, Sean (playwright); Dublin (1881–1964)
Ochs, Adolph Simon (publisher); Cincinnati (1858–1935)
O'Connor, Carroll (actor); New York City (1924–2001)
Odets, Clifford (playwright); Philadelphia (1906–1963)
Odetta (Odetta Holmes) (folk singer, actress); Birmingham, Ala.,
   12/31/30
O'Donnell, Chris (actor); Winnetka, Ill., 6/26/70
O'Donnell, Rosie (actress, talk show host); Commack, N.Y.,
   3/21/62
Offenbach, Jacques (composer); Cologne, Germany (1819–1880)
O'Hara, John (novelist); Pottsville, Pa. (1905–1970)
O'Hara, Maureen (Maureen FitzSimons) (actress); Dublin, 8/17/20
Ohlsson, Garrick (pianist); Bronxville, N.Y., 4/3/48
Oistrakh, David (concert violinist); Odessa, Russia (1908–1974)
O'Keeffe, Georgia (painter); Sun Prairie, Wis. (1887–1986)
Oland, Warner (actor); Umea, Sweden (1880–1938)
Oldenburg, Claes (painter); Stockholm, 1/28/29
Oldman, Gary (actor, director); London, 3/21/58
Olin, Lena (actress); Stockholm, 3/22/55
Oliphant, Patrick B. (editorial cartoonist); Adelaide, Australia,
   7/24/35
Olivier, Sir Laurence (actor); Dorking, England (1907–1989)
Olmos, Edward James (actor); East Los Angeles, 2/24/47
Olmsted, Frederick Law (landscape architect); Hartford, Conn.
   (1822–1903)
Olsen, Ole (John Sigvard Olsen) (comedian); Peru, Ind. (1892–1963)
Omar Khayyam (poet, astronomer); Nishapur, Iran (died c. 1123)
Onassis, Aristotle (shipping executive); Smyrna, Turkey (1906–
   1975)
Onassis, Christina (shipping executive); New York City (1950–1988)
Onassis, Jacqueline Kennedy (Jacqueline Bouvier) (first lady);
   Southampton, N.Y. (1929–1994)
O'Neal, Ryan (Patrick) (actor); Los Angeles, 4/20/41
O'Neal, Tatum (actress); Los Angeles, 11/5/63
O'Neill, Eugene Gladstone (playwright); New York City (1888–1953)
O'Neill, Jennifer (actress); Rio de Janeiro, 2/20/49
Oppenheimer, J. Robert (nuclear physicist); New York City (1904–
   1967)
Orbach, Jerry (actor); New York City, 10/20/35
Orff, Carl (composer); Munich, Germany (1895–1982)
Orlando, Tony (Michael Anthony Orlando Cassavitis) (singer); New
   York City, 4/3/44

Ormandy, Eugene (conductor); Budapest (1899–1985)
Ormond, Julia (actress); Epsom, Surrey, England, 1/4/65
Orozco, José Clemente (painter); Zapotlán, Jalisco, Mexico (1883–
   1949)
Orwell, George (Eric Arthur Blair) (British author); Motihari, India
   (1903–1950)
Osborn, Paul (playwright); Evansville, Ind. (1901–1988)
Osborne, John (playwright); London (1929–1994)
Osbourne, Ozzy (John Osbourne) (singer); Birmingham, England,
   12/3/48
Osler, Sir William (physician); Bondhead, Ont., Canada (1849–1919)
Osmond, Donny (singer, actor); Ogden, Utah, 12/9/57
Osmond, Marie (Olive Marie) (singer, actress); Ogden, Utah,
   10/13/59
O'Sullivan, Maureen (actress); County Roscommon, Ireland
   (1911–1998)
Oswald, Lee Harvey (presumed assassin); New Orleans (1939–
   1963)
Otis, Elisha (inventor); Halifax, Vt. (1811–1861)
O'Toole, Peter (actor); Connemara, Ireland, 8/2/32
Ovid (Publius Ovidius Naso) (poet); Sulmona, Italy (43 B.C.–A.D. 17)
Ovitz, Michael (entertainment executive); Chicago, 12/14/46
Owens, Buck (Alvis Edgar Owens) (singer); Sherman, Tex., 8/12/29
Ozawa, Seiji (orchestra conductor); Fentian (Shenyan), Manchuria,
   7/1/35

# P

Paar, Jack (TV personality); Canton, Ohio, 5/1/18
Pacino, Al (Alfred) (actor); New York City, 4/25/40
Packard, Vance (author); Granville Summit, Pa. (1914–1996)
Paderewski, Ignace Jan (pianist, statesman); Kurylowka, Russian
   Podolia (1860–1941)
Paganini, Nicolò (violinist); Genoa, Italy (1782–1840)
Page, Geraldine (actress); Kirksville, Mo. (1924–1987)
Page, Jimmy (musician); Heston, Ireland, 1/9/44
Page, Patti (Clara Ann Fowler) (singer, entertainer); Claremore,
   Okla., 11/8/27
Pagels, Elaine Hiesey (religious scholar); Palo Alto, Calif., 2/13/43
Paglia, Camille (writer, social critic); Endicott, N.Y., 4/2/47
Paine, Thomas (political philosopher); Thetford, England (1737–
   1809)
Pakula, Alan J. (film director); New York City (1928–1998)
Palance, Jack (Walter Palanuik) (actor); Lattimer, Pa., 2/18/19
Palestrina, Giovanni Pierluigi da (composer); Palestrina, Italy
   (1526–1594)
Paley, William S. (broadcasting executive); Chicago (1901–1990)
Palladio, Andrea (architect); Padua or Vicenza, Italy (1508–1580)
Palmer, Robert (rock musician); Batley, England, 1/19/49
Palmerston, Henry John Templeton (3rd Viscount) (statesman);
   Broadlands, England (1784–1865)
Palminteri, Chazz (Calogero Lorenzo Palminteri) (actor, writer);
   Bronx, New York, 5/15/51
Paltrow, Gwyneth (actress); Los Angeles, 9/27/72
Papanicolaou, George N. (physician); Coumi, Greece (1883–1962)
Papas, Irene (Lelekou) (actress); Chiliomodian, Greece, 3/9/26
Papp, Joseph (Joseph Papirofsky) (stage producer, director);
   Brooklyn, N.Y. (1921–1991)
Paracelsus, Philippus (Aureolus Theophrastus Bombastus von
   Hohenheim) (physican); Einsiedeln, Switzerland (1493–1541)
Park, Chung Hee (ex-president of South Korea); Sangmo-ri, Korea
   (1917–1979)
Parker, Alan (director); London, 2/14/44
Parker, Charlie "Bird" (jazz musician); Kansas City, Kans. (1920–
   1955)
Parker, Dorothy (Dorothy Rothschild) (author); West End, N.J.
   (1893–1967)
Parker, Fess (actor); Fort Worth, Tex., 8/16/25
Parker, Sarah Jessica (actress); Nelsonville, Ohio, 3/25/65
Parker, Suzy (model, actress); San Antonio, 10/28/33
Parkinson, C(yril) Northcote (historian); Durham, England (1909–
   1993)
Parkman, Francis (historian); Boston (1823–1893)
Parks, Bert (Bert Jacobson) (entertainer); Atlanta (1914–1992)
Parks, Gordon (film director); Ft. Scott, Kans., 11/30/12
Parks, Rosa (civil rights activist); Tuskegee, Ala., 2/4/13
Parnell, Charles Stewart (statesman); Avondale, Ireland (1846–
   1891)
Parnis, Mollie (Mollie Parnis Livingston) (fashion designer); New
   York City (1905?–1992)
Parsons, Estelle (actress); Marblehead, Mass., 11/20/27
Parton, Dolly (singer); Locust Ridge, Tenn., 1/19/46
Pascal, Blaise (philosopher); Clermont, France (1623–1662)

**Pasternak,** Boris Leonidovich (author); Moscow **(1890–1960)**
**Pasternak,** Joseph (film producer); Szilagy-Somlyo, Hungary **(1901–1991)**
**Pasteur,** Louis (chemist); Dôle, France **(1822–1895)**
**Pastor,** Tony (Antonio) (actor, theater manager); New York City **(1837–1908)**
**Pater,** Walter (Horatio) (writer); London **(1839–1894)**
**Patinkin,** Mandy (Mandel) (actor, singer); Chicago, 11/30/52
**Paton,** Alan (author); Pietermaritzburg, South Africa **(1903–1988)**
**Patric,** Jason (actor); Queens, N.Y., 6/17/66
**Patti,** Adelina (soprano); Madrid **(1843–1919)**
**Patton,** George Smith, Jr. (general); San Gabriel, Calif. **(1885–1945)**
**Paul,** Alice (feminist, woman suffragist); Moorestown, N.J. **(1885–1977)**
**Paul,** Les (Lester William Polfus) (guitarist); Waukesha, Wis., 6/9/15
**Paul VI** (Giovanni Battista Montini) (Pope); Concesio, nr. Brescia, Italy **(1897–1978)**
**Pauley,** Jane (Margaret Jane Pauley) (TV newscaster); Indianapolis, 10/31/50
**Pauling,** Linus Carl (chemist, Nobel laureate); Portland, Ore. **(1901–1994)**
**Pavarotti,** Luciano (tenor); Modena, Italy, 10/12/35
**Pavlov,** Ivan Petrovich (physiologist); Ryazan district, Russia **(1849–1936)**
**Pavlova,** Anna (ballet dancer); St. Petersburg, Russia **(1885–1931)**
**Paxton,** Bill (actor); Fort Worth, Texas, 5/17/55
**Peale,** Norman Vincent (clergyman); Bowersville, Ohio **(1898–1993)**
**Pearl,** Minnie (Sarah Ophelia Colley Cannon) (comedienne, singer); Centerville, Tenn. **(1912–1996)**
**Pears,** Peter (tenor); Farnham, England **(1910–1986)**
**Pearson,** Drew (Andrew Russel Pearson) (columnist); Evanston, Ill. **(1897–1969)**
**Pearson,** Lester B. (statesman); Toronto **(1897–1972)**
**Peary,** Robert Edwin (explorer); Cresson, Pa. **(1856–1920)**
**Peck,** Gregory (Eldred Gregory Peck) (actor); La Jolla, Calif., 4/5/16
**Peckinpah,** Sam (film director); Fresno, Calif. **(1925–1984)**
**Peerce,** Jan (tenor); New York City **(1904–1984)**
**Pegler,** (James) Westbrook (columnist); Minneapolis **(1894–1969)**
**Pei,** I(eoh) M(ing) (architect); Canton, China, 4/26/17
**Penn,** Arthur (director); Philadelphia, 9/27/22
**Penn,** Sean (actor, filmmaker); Los Angeles, 8/17/60
**Penn,** William (American colonist); London **(1644–1718)**
**Penney,** James C. (merchant); Hamilton, Mo. **(1875–1971)**
**Peppard,** George (actor); Detroit **(1928–1994)**
**Pepys,** Samuel (diarist); Bampton, England **(1633–1703)**
**Perelman,** S(idney) J(oseph) (writer); Brooklyn, N.Y. **(1904–1979)**
**Perez,** Rosie (actress, dancer, choreographer); Brooklyn, New York, 5/16/63
**Pergolesi,** Giovanni Battista (composer); Jesi, Italy **(1710–1736)**
**Pericles** (statesman); Athens died 429 B.C.
**Perkins,** Anthony (actor); New York City **(1932–1992)**
**Perkins,** Frances (social reformer); Boston **(1882–1965)**
**Perlman,** Itzhak (violinist); Tel Aviv, Israel, 8/31/45
**Perlman,** Rhea (actress); Brooklyn, N.Y., 3/31/48
**Perón,** Isabel (María Estela Martínez Cartas) (former chief of state); La Rioja, Argentina, 2/4/31
**Perón,** Juan D. (statesman); nr. Lobos, Argentina **(1895–1974)**
**Perón,** Maria Eva Duarte de (political leader); Los Toldos, Argentina **(1919–1952)**
**Perot,** H. Ross (business executive); Texarkana, Tex., 6/27/30
**Perrine,** Valerie (actress, dancer); Galveston, Tex., 9/3/43
**Perry, Luke (Coy Luther Perry III)** (actor); Fredericktown, Ohio, 10/11/66
**Perry,** Matthew (actor); Williamstown, Mass., 8/19/69
**Pershing,** John Joseph (general); Laclede, Mo. (1860–1948)
**Pestalozzi,** Johann (educator); Zürich, Switzerland **(1746–1827)**
**Peters,** Bernadette (Bernadette Lazzara) (actress); New York City, 2/28/48
**Peters,** Brock (actor, singer); New York City, 7/2/27
**Peters,** Jean (actress); Canton, Ohio **(1926–2000)**
**Peters,** Roberta (Roberta Peterman) (soprano); New York City, 5/4/30
**Petit,** Roland (choreographer, dancer); Villemombe, France, 1924
**Petrarch** (Francesco Petrarca) (poet); Arezzo, Italy **(1304–1374)**
**Petty,** Tom (folk/rock musician); Gainesville, Fla., 10/20/50
**Pfeiffer,** Michelle (actress); Santa Ana, Calif., 4/29/58
**Philbin,** Regis (talk show host); New York City, 8/25/33
**Philip** (Philip Mountbatten) (Duke of Edinburgh); Corfu, Greece, 6/10/21
**Phillippe,** Ryan (actor); New Castle, Del., 9/10/75
**Phoenix,** Joaquin (actor); San Juan, Puerto Rico, 10/28/74
**Phoenix,** River (actor); Madras, Ore. **(1970–1993)**
**Piaf,** Edith (Edith Gassion) (singer); Paris **(1916–1963)**

**Piatigorsky,** Gregor (cellist); Ekaterinoslav, Russia **(1903–1976)**
**Piazza,** Marguerite (soprano); New Orleans, 5/6/26
**Picasso,** Pablo (painter, sculptor); Málaga, Spain **(1881–1973)**
**Pickett,** Wilson (singer); Prattville, Ala., 3/18/41
**Pickford,** Mary (Gladys Mary Smith) (actress); Toronto **(1893–1979)**
**Picon,** Molly (actress); New York City **(1898–1992)**
**Pidgeon,** Walter (actor); East St. John, N.B., Canada **(1898–1984)**
**Pierce,** David Hyde (actor); Saratoga Springs, N.Y., 4/3/59
**Pierce,** Franklin (14th U.S. president); Hillsboro, N.H. **(1804–1869)**
**Pileggi,** Mitch (actor); Portland, Ore., 4/5/52
**Pinkett-Smith,** Jada (actress); Baltimore, 9/18/71
**Pinsky,** Robert (ex-poet laureate of the U.S.); Long Branch, N.J., 10/20/40
**Pinochet (Ugarte),** Augusto (former leader of Chile's military government); Valparaiso, Chile, 11/25/15
**Pinter,** Harold (playwright); London, 10/10/30
**Pinza,** Ezio (basso); Rome **(1892–1957)**
**Pirandello,** Luigi (dramatist, novelist); nr. Girgenti, Italy **(1867–1936)**
**Piranesi,** Giambattista (artist); Mestre, Italy **(1720–1778)**
**Pissaro,** Camille Jacob (painter); St. Thomas, U.S. Virgin Islands **(1830–1903)**
**Piston,** Walter (composer); Rockland, Maine **(1894–1976)**
**Pitman,** Sir [Isaac] James (educator, publisher); Bath, England **(1901–1985)**
**Pitt,** Brad (actor); Shawnee, Okla., 12/18/63
**Pitt,** William ("Younger Pitt") (statesman); nr. Bromley, England **(1759–1806)**
**Pitts,** ZaSu (actress); Parsons, Kans. **(1898–1963)**
**Pius XII** (Eugenio Pacelli) (Pope); Rome **(1876–1958)**
**Pizarro,** Francisco (explorer); Trujillo, Spain (c. 1476–1541)
**Planck,** Max (physicist); Kiel, Germany **(1858–1947)**
**Plant,** Robert (musician, singer, song writer); West Bromwich, Staffordshire, England , 8/20/48
**Plath,** Sylvia (poet); Boston **(1932–1963)**
**Plato** (Aristocles) (philosopher); Athens (c. 427–347 B.C.)
**Pleasence,** Donald (actor); Worksop, England **(1919–1995)**
**Pleshette,** Suzanne (actress); New York City, 1/31/37
**Plimpton,** George (author); New York City, 3/18/27
**Plimpton,** Martha (actress); New York City, 11/16/70
**Plisetskaya,** Maya (ballet dancer); Moscow, 11/20/25
**Plowright,** Joan (actress); Brigg, England, 10/28/29
**Plummer,** Christopher (actor); Toronto, 12/13/29
**Plutarch** (biographer); Chaeronea, Greece (c. 46–c. 120)
**Pocahontas** (Matoaka) (American Indian princess); Virginia (c. 1595–1617)
**Podhoretz,** Norman (author); Brooklyn, N.Y., 1/16/30
**Poe,** Edgar Allan (poet, story writer); Boston **(1809–1849)**
**Poitier,** Sidney (actor, director); Miami, Fla., 2/20/24
**Polanski,** Roman (director); Paris, 8/18/33
**Polk,** James Knox (11th U.S. president); Mecklenburg County, N.C. **(1795–1849)**
**Pollack,** Sydney (film director, producer, actor); Lafayette, Ind., 7/1/34
**Pollard,** Michael J. (actor); Passaic, N.J., 5/30/39
**Pollock,** Jackson (painter); Cody, Wyo. **(1912–1956)**
**Polo,** Marco (traveler); Venice (c. 1254–1324)
**Pol Pot** (Cambodian dictator); Kompong Thom, Cambodia **(1925–1998)**
**Pompadour,** Mme. de (Jeanne Antoinette Poisson) (courtesan); Versailles **(1721–1764)**
**Pompey** (Gnaeus Pompeius Magnus) (general); Rome (106–48 B.C.)
**Ponce de León,** Juan (explorer); San Tervás de Campos, Spain (c. 1460–1521)
**Pons,** Lily (coloratura soprano); Cannes, France **(1904–1976)**
**Ponselle,** Rosa (soprano); Meriden, Conn. **(1897–1981)**
**Ponti,** Carlo (director); Milan, Italy, 12/11/13
**Pontormo,** Jacopo da (painter); Pontormo, Italy **(1493–1557)**
**Pope,** Alexander (poet); London **(1688–1744)**
**Porter,** Cole (songwriter); Peru, Ind. **(1891–1964)**
**Porter,** Katherine Anne (novelist); Indian Creek, Tex. **(1891–1980)**
**Portman,** Natalie (actress); Jerusalem, 6/9/81
**Posey,** Parker (actress); Baltimore, 11/8/68
**Post,** Wiley (aviator); Grand Plain, Tex. **(1900–1935)**
**Poston,** Tom (actor); Columbus, Ohio, 10/17/27
**Potëmkin,** Grigori Aleksandrovich, Prince (statesman); Khizovo (Khizov), Belarus **(1739–1791)**
**Potok,** Chaim (author); New York City **(1929–2002)**
**Potter,** (Helen) Beatrix (author, illustrator); South Kensington, Middlesex, England **(1866–1943)**
**Potts,** Annie (actress); Nashville, Tenn., 10/28/52
**Poulenc,** Francis (composer); Paris **(1899–1963)**
**Pound,** Ezra (poet); Hailey, Idaho **(1885–1972)**

**Poussin,** Nicolas (painter); Villers, France **(1594–1665)**
**Powell,** Adam Clayton, Jr. (congressman); New Haven, Conn. **(1908–1972)**
**Powell,** Colin L. (secretary of state); New York City, 4/5/37
**Powell,** Dick (actor); Mt. View, Ark. **(1904–1963)**
**Powell,** Eleanor (actress, tap dancer); Springfield, Mass. **(1912–1982)**
**Powell,** Jane (Suzanne Burce) (actress, singer); Portland, Ore., 4/1/29
**Powell,** William (actor); Pittsburgh **(1892–1984)**
**Power,** Tyrone (actor); Cincinnati, Ohio **(1914–1958)**
**Powers,** Stefanie (Stefania Zofia Federkiewicz) (actress); Hollywood, Calif., 11/12/42
**Praxiteles** (sculptor); Athens **(c. 370–c. 330** B.C.**)**
**Preminger,** Otto (director, producer); Vienna **(1906–1986)**
**Prentiss,** Paula (Paula Ragusa) (actress); San Antonio, 3/4/39
**Presley,** Elvis (singer, actor); Tupelo, Miss. **(1935–1977)**
**Presley,** Priscilla (actress); Brooklyn, N.Y., 5/24/45
**Preston,** Robert (Robert Preston Meservey) (actor); Newton Highlands, Mass. **(1918–1987)**
**Previn,** André (conductor); Berlin, 4/6/29
**Price,** Leontyne (Mary) (soprano); Laurel, Miss., 2/10/27
**Price,** Ray (country music artist); Perryville, Tex., 1/12/26
**Price,** Vincent (actor); St. Louis **(1911–1993)**
**Pride,** Charley (singer); Sledge, Miss., 3/18/38?
**Priestley,** Jason (actor, producer); Vancouver, B.C., Canada, 8/28/69
**Priestley,** J. B. (John B.) (author); Bradford, England **(1894–1984)**
**Priestley,** Joseph (chemist); nr. Leeds, England **(1733–1804)**
**Primakov,** Yevgeny (Russian political leader); Kiev, Ukraine, 10/29/29
**Primrose,** William (violist); Glasgow, Scotland **(1904–1982)**
**Prince** (Prince Rogers Nelson) (singer); Minneapolis, 6/7/58
**Prince,** Harold (stage producer); New York City, 1/30/28
**Principal,** Victoria (actress); Fukuoka, Japan, 1/3/45
**Prinze,** Freddie (actor); New York City **(1954–1977)**
**Pritchett,** V(ictor) S(awdon) (literary critic); Ipswich, England **(1900–1997)**
**Procter,** William (scientist); Cincinnati **(1872–1951)**
**Prokofiev,** Sergei Sergeevich (composer); St. Petersburg, Russia **(1891–1953)**
**Proulx,** E. Annie (novelist); Norwich, Conn., 8/22/35
**Proust,** Marcel (novelist); Paris **(1871–1922)**
**Provine,** Dorothy (actress); Deadwood, S.D., 1/20/37
**Prowse,** Juliet (actress, dancer); Bombay (Mumbai) **(1936–1996)**
**Pryce,** Jonathan (actor); Holywell, Wales, 6/1/47
**Pryor,** Richard (comedian); Peoria, Ill., 12/1/40
**Ptolemy** (Claudius Ptolemaeus) (astronomer, geographer); Ptolemais Hermii, Egypt, fl. 2nd cent.
**Pucci,** Emilio (Marchese di Barsento) (fashion designer); Naples, Italy **(1914–1992)**
**Puccini,** Giacomo (composer); Lucca, Italy **(1858–1924)**
**Puente,** Tito (band leader); New York City **(1923–2000)**
**Pulaski,** Casimir (military officer); Podolia, Poland **(1748–1779)**
**Pulitzer,** Joseph (publisher); Makó, Hungary **(1847–1911)**
**Pullman,** Bill (actor); Delphi, N.Y., 12/17/53
**Pullman,** George (inventor); Brockton, N.Y. **(1831–1897)**
**Purcell,** Henry (composer); London **(1658–1695)**
**Pusey,** Nathan M. (educator); Council Bluffs, Iowa **(1907–2001)**
**Pushkin,** Alexander Sergeevich (poet, dramatist); Moscow **(1799–1837)**
**Putin, Vladimir** (president of Russia); Leningrad, 1952
**Puzo,** Mario (novelist); New York City **(1920–1999)**
**Pyle,** Ernest Taylor (journalist); Dana, Ind. **(1900–1945)**
**Pythagoras** (mathematician, philosopher); Samos, Greece **(c. 582–c. 507**A.D.**)**

# Q

**Qaddafi,** Muammar al- (Libyan leader); Libya, 1942
**Quaid,** Dennis (actor); Houston, 4/9/54
**Quaid,** Randy, (actor); Houston, 10/1/50
**Quayle,** Anthony (actor); Ainsdale, England **(1913–1989)**
**Queen, Ellery:** pen name of Frederic Dannay and Manfred B. Lee
**Queen Latifah** (Dana Owens) (rap musician, actress); Newark, New Jersey, 3/18/70
**Queler,** Eve (conductor); New York City, 1/1/36
**Quennell,** Sir Peter Courtney (biographer); Bromley, England **(1905–1993)**
**Quindlen,** Anna (writer); Philadelphia, 7/8/53
**Quinn,** Aidan (actor); Chicago, 3/8/59
**Quinn,** Anthony (Antonio Quiñones) (actor); Chihuahua, Mexico **(1916–2001)**

# R

**Rabe,** David (playwright); Dubuque, Iowa, 3/10/40
**Rabelais,** François (satirist); nr. Chinon, France **(c. 1490–1553)**
**Rabi,** I(sidor) I(saac) (physicist); Rymanow, Poland **(1898–1988)**
**Rabin,** Yitzhak (former Israeli prime minister); Jerusalem **(1922–1995)**
**Rachmaninoff,** Sergei Wassilievitch (pianist, composer); Oneg Estate, Novgorod, Russia **(1873–1943)**
**Racine,** Jean Baptiste (dramatist); La Ferté-Milon, France **(1639–1699)**
**Radner,** Gilda (comedienne); Detroit **(1946–1989)**
**Raft,** George (actor); New York City **(1895–1980)**
**Rainier III** (Prince); Monaco, 5/31/23
**Rains,** Claude (actor); London **(1889–1967)**
**Raitt,** Bonnie (singer); Burbank, Calif., 11/8/49
**Raitt,** John (actor, singer); Santa Ana, Calif., 1/19/17
**Raleigh,** Sir Walter (courtier, navigator); London **(1552?–1618)**
**Rambeau,** Marjorie (actress); San Francisco **(1889–1970)**
**Rameau,** Jean-Philippe (composer); Dijon, France **(1683–1764)**
**Rampal,** Jean-Pierre (Louis) (flutist); Marseilles, France **(1922–2000)**
**Rand,** Ayn (novelist, philosopher); St. Petersburg, Russia **(1905–1982)**
**Randall,** Tony (Leonard Rosenberg) (actor); Tulsa, Okla., 2/26/20
**Randolph,** A(sa) Philip (labor leader); Crescent City, Fla. **(1889–1979)**
**Rankin,** Jeannette (politician, pacifist); Missoula, Mont. **(1880–1973)**
**Raphael** (Raffaello Santi) (painter, architect); Urbino, Italy **(1483–1520)**
**Rasputin,** Grigori Efimovich (monk); Tobolsk Province, Russia **(1872–1916)**
**Rathbone,** Basil (Philip St. John Basil Rathbone) (actor); Johannesburg, South Africa **(1892–1967)**
**Rather,** Dan (TV newscaster); Wharton, Tex., 10/31/31
**Rattigan,** Terence (playwright); London **(1911–1977)**
**Ratzenberger,** John (actor); Bridgeport, Conn., 4/6/47
**Rauschenberg,** Robert (painter); Port Arthur, Tex., 10/22/25
**Ravel,** Maurice Joseph (composer); Ciboure, France **(1875–1937)**
**Ray,** Aldo (DaRe) (actor); Pen Argyl, Pa. **(1926–1991)**
**Ray,** Gene Anthony (actor, dancer); Harlem, N.Y., 5/24/63
**Ray,** Man (painter); Philadelphia **(1890–1976)**
**Ray,** Satyajit (film director); Calcutta **(1921–1992)**
**Raye,** Martha (Margie Yvonne Reed) (comedienne, actress); Butte, Mont. **(1916–1994)**
**Rea,** Stephen (actor); Belfast, Ireland, 10/31/43
**Reagan,** Ronald Wilson (40th U.S. president, actor); Tampico, Ill., 2/6/11
**Reasoner,** Harry (TV commentator); Dakota City, Iowa **(1923–1991)**
**Redding,** Otis (singer); Dawson, Ga. **(1941–1967)**
**Reddy,** Helen (singer); Melbourne, Australia, 10/25/41
**Redford,** Robert (Charles Robert Redford, Jr.) (actor); Santa Monica, Calif., 8/18/37
**Redgrave,** Lynn (actress); London, 3/8/43
**Redgrave,** Sir Michael (actor); Bristol, England **(1908–1985)**
**Redgrave,** Vanessa (actress); London, 1/30/37
**Redon,** Odilon (artist); Bordeaux, France **(1840–1916)**
**Reed,** Donna (Donna Belle Mullenger) (actress); Denison, Iowa **(1921–1986)**
**Reed,** Lou (Lewis Allen Reed) (musician, guitarist, singer, song writer); Freeport, N.Y., 3/ 2/42
**Reed,** Rex (critic); Ft. Worth, 10/2/40
**Reed,** Walter (army surgeon); Belroi, Va. **(1851–1902)**
**Reese,** Della (Deloreese Patricia Early) (singer, actress); Detroit, 7/6/32
**Reeve,** Christopher (actor, activist); New York City, 9/25/52
**Reeves,** Jim (singer); Panola County, Tex. **(1923–1964)**
**Reeves,** Keanu (actor, musician); Beirut, Lebanon, 9/2/64
**Reich,** Robert (Clinton cabinet member); Scranton, Pa., 6/24/46
**Reich,** Steve (composer); New York City, 10/3/36
**Reid,** Wallace (actor); St. Louis **(1891–1923)**
**Reiner,** Carl (actor); New York City, 3/20/22
**Reiner,** Fritz (conductor); Budapest **(1888–1963)**
**Reiner,** Robert (actor, director, writer, producer); Bronx, N.Y., 3/6/45
**Reinhardt,** Max (Max Goldmann) (theater producer); nr. Vienna **(1873–1943)**
**Reiser,** Paul (actor, producer); New York City, 3/30/57
**Remarque,** Erich Maria (novelist); Osnabrük, Germany **(1898–1970)**
**Rembrandt** (Rembrandt Harmensz van Rijn) (painter); Leyden, Netherlands **(1605–1669)**
**Remick,** Lee (Ann) (actress); Boston **(1935–1991)**
**Remnick,** David (writer, editor); Hackensack, N.J., 10/29/58

Renfro, Brad (actor); Knoxville, Tenn., 7/25/82
Rennert, Günther (opera director, producer); Essen, Germany, 4/1/11
Rennie, Michael (actor); Bradford, England (1909–1971)
Reno, Janet (ex-U.S. attorney general); Miami, Fla., 7/21/38
Renoir, Jean (film director, writer); Paris (1894–1979)
Renoir, Pierre Auguste (painter); Limoges, France (1841–1919)
Resnais, Alain (film director); Vannes, France, 6/3/22
Resnik, Regina (mezzo-soprano); New York City, 8/30/22
Respighi, Ottorino (composer); Bologna, Italy (1879–1936)
Reston, James (journalist); Clydebank, Scotland (1909–1995)
Reuther, Walter (labor leader); Wheeling, W. Va. (1907–1970)
Revere, Paul (silversmith, hero of famous ride); Boston (1735–1818)
Revson, Charles (business executive); Boston (1906–1975)
Reynolds, Burt (actor, director, producer); Waycross, Ga., 2/11/36
Reynolds, Debbie (Marie Frances Reynolds) (actress); El Paso, Tex., 4/1/32
Reynolds, Sir Joshua (painter); nr. Plymouth, England (1723–1792)
Reynolds, Marjorie (Marjorie Goodspeed) (actress); Buhl, Idaho (1921–1997)
Reznor, Trent (musician); Mercer, Pa., 5/17/65
Rhodes, Cecil John (South African statesman); Bishop Stortford, England (1853–1902)
Ricci, Christina (actress); Santa Monica, Calif., 2/12/80
Rice, Anne (novelist); New Orleans, 10/14/41
Rice, Elmer (Elmer Leopold Reizenstein) (playwright); New York City (1892–1967)
Rice, Grantland (sports writer); Murfreesboro, Tenn. (1880–1954)
Rich, Buddy (Bernard) (drummer); Brooklyn, N.Y. (1917–1987)
Rich, Charlie (singer); Colt, Ark. (1932–1995)
Richard I the Lion-hearted (king of England); Oxford, England (1157–1199)
Richards, Ann (Dorothy Ann Willis) (ex-governor of Texas); Lakeview, Tex., 9/1/33
Richards, Keith (rock singer); Dartford, England, 12/18/43
Richards, Michael (actor); California, 7/21/48
Richardson, Elliot L. (ex-cabinet member); Boston (1920–1999)
Richardson, Sir Ralph (actor); Cheltenham, England (1902–1983)
Richardson, Tony (director); Shipley, England (1928–1991)
Richelieu, Duc de (Armand Jean du Plessis) (cardinal); Paris (1585–1642)
Richie, Lionel (singer, songwriter); Tuskegee, Ala., 6/20/49
Richter, Charles Francis (seismologist); Hamilton, Ohio (1900–1985)
Richter, Sviatoslav (pianist); Zhitomir, Ukraine (1914–1997)
Rickenbacker, Eddie (Edward V.) (aviator); Columbus, Ohio (1890–1973)
Rickles, Don (comedian); New York City, 5/8/26
Rickover, Vice Admiral Hyman G. (atomic energy expert); Russia (1900–1986)
Riddle, Nelson (composer); Hackensack, N.J. (1921–1985)
Ride, Sally K(risten) (astronaut, astrophysicist); Encino, Calif., 5/26/51
Ridgway, General Matthew B. (ex-Army chief of staff); Ft. Monroe, Va. (1895–1993)
Riemenschneider, Tilman (sculptor); Osterode, Germany (c. 1460–1531)
Rigg, Diana (actress); Doncaster, England, 7/20/38
Riley, James Whitcomb (poet); Greenfield, Ind. (1849–1916)
Rilke, Rainer Maria (poet); Prague (1875–1926)
Rimbaud, (Jean Nicolas) Arthur (poet); Charleville, France (1854–1891)
Rimes, LeAnn (singer); Jackson, Miss., 8/28/82
Rimsky-Korsakov, Nikolai Andreevich (composer); Tikhvin, Russia (1844–1908)
Rinehart, Mary (née Roberts) (author); Pittsburgh, Calif., 2/18/68
Rittenhouse, David (astronomer); nr. Philadelphia, Pa. (1732–1796)
Ritchard, Cyril (actor; director); Sydney, Australia (1898–1977)
Ritter, John (Jonathan) (actor); Burbank, Calif., 9/17/48
Ritter, Tex (Woodward Maurice Ritter) (singer); Panola County, Tex. (1905–1973)
Ritter, Thelma (actress); Brooklyn, N.Y. (1905–1969)
Rivera, Chita (Dolores Conchita Figuero del Rivero) (dancer, actress, singer); Washington, D.C., 1/23/33
Rivera, Diego (painter); Guanajuato, Mexico (1886–1957)
Rivera, Geraldo (Miguel Rivera) (TV host); New York City, 7/4/43
Rivers, Joan (comedienne); Brooklyn, N.Y., 6/8/33
Rivers, Larry (Yitzroch Loiza Grossberg) (painter); New York City (1923–2002)
Roach, Hal (film producer); Elmira, N.Y. (1892–1992)
Robards, Jason, Jr. (actor); Chicago (1922–2000)
Robards, Jason, Sr. (actor); Hillsdale, Mich. (1892–1963)
Robbins, Harold (Harold Rubin) (novelist); New York City (1916–1997)

Robbins, Jerome (Jerome Rabinowitz) (choreographer); New York City (1918–1998)
Robbins, Marty (singer); Glendale, Ariz. (1925–1982)
Robbins, Tim (Timothy Francis) (actor, director); West Covina, Calif., 10/16/58
Roberts, Cokie (Mary Martha Corinne Morrison Claiborne Boggs) (broadcast journalist); New Orleans, 12/27/43
Roberts, Eric (actor); Biloxi, Miss., 4/18/56
Roberts, Julia (actress); Smyrna, Ga., 10/28/67
Roberts, Oral (Granville) (evangelist, publisher); nr. Ada, Okla., 1/24/18
Robertson, Cliff (Clifford Parker Robertson III) (actor); La Jolla, Calif., 9/9/25
Robertson, Dale (Dayle) (actor); Oklahoma City, 7/14/23
Robeson, Paul (singer, actor); Princeton, N.J. (1898–1976)
Robespierre, Maximilien François Marie Isidore de (French Revolutionist); Arras, France (1758–1794)
Robinson, Bill "Bojangles" (Luther) (dancer); Richmond, Va. (1878–1949)
Robinson, Edward G. (Emanuel Goldenberg) (actor); Bucharest (1893–1973)
Robinson, Edwin Arlington (poet); Head Tide, Maine (1869–1935)
Robinson Peete, Holly (Holly Robinson) (actress); Philadelphia, 9/18/64
Robinson, Robert (chemist, Nobel laureate); Chesterfield, Derbyshire, England (1885–1975)
Robinson, Smokey (singer, songwriter); Detroit, 2/19/40
Rock, Chris (comedian, actor); Brooklyn, New York, 2/7/66
Rockefeller, David (banker); New York City, 6/12/15
Rockefeller, John Davison (business executive); Richford, N.Y. (1839–1937)
Rockefeller, John Davison, Jr. (industrialist); Cleveland (1874–1960)
Rockefeller, John D., 3rd (philanthropist); New York City (1906–1978)
Rockefeller, Laurance S. (conservationist); New York City, 5/26/10
Rockwell, Norman (painter, illustrator); New York City (1894–1978)
Roddenberry, Gene (creator of Star Trek); El Paso, Tex. (1921–1991)
Rodgers, Jimmie (singer); Meridian, Miss. (1897–1933)
Rodgers, Richard (composer); New York City (1902–1979)
Rodin, François Auguste René (sculptor); Paris (1840–1917)
Rodzinski, Artur (conductor); Spalato, Dalmatia (1894–1958)
Roeg, Nicolas (film director); London, 8/15/28
Roentgen, Wilhelm Konrad (physicist); Lennep, Prussia (1845–1923)
Roethke, Theodore (poet); Saginaw, Mich. (1908–1963)
Rogers, Buddy (Charles Rogers) (actor); Olathe, Kans. (1904–1999)
Rogers, Carl (psychologist); Oak Park, Ill. (1902–1987)
Rogers, Fred (TV producer, host); Latrobe, Pa., 3/20/28
Rogers, Ginger (Virginia McMath) (dancer, actress); Independence, Mo. (1911–1995)
Rogers, Kenny (singer); Houston, 8/21/38
Rogers, Mimi (actress); Coral Gables, Fla., 1/27/56
Rogers, Roy (Leonard Frank Slye) (actor, singer); Cincinnati (1911–1998)
Rogers, Wayne (actor); Birmingham, Ala., 4/7/33
Rogers, Will (William Penn Adair Rogers) (humorist); Oologah, Okla. (1879–1935)
Rogers, William P. (ex-secretary of state); Norfolk, N.Y. (1913–2001)
Roland, Gilbert (Luis Antonio Damaso de Alonso) (actor); Juarez, Mexico (1905–1994)
Rolland, Romain (author); Clamecy, France (1866–1944)
Rollins, Sonny (saxophonist); New York City, 9/7/30
Romberg, Sigmund (composer); Szeged, Hungary (1887–1951)
Romero, Mario (composer); Hartford, Conn. (1908–1993)
Romero, Cesar (actor); New York City (1907–1994)
Romney, George W (automobile executive, governor); Chihuahua, Mexico (1907–1995)
Romulo, Carlos P. (diplomat, educator); Manila (1899–1985)
Ronsard, Pierre de (poet); La Possonnière nr. Couture, France (1524–1585)
Ronstadt, Linda (singer); Tucson, Ariz., 7/30/46
Rooney, Andy (TV personality); Albany, N.Y., 1/14/19
Rooney, Mickey (Joe Yule, Jr.) (actor); Brooklyn, N.Y., 9/23/20
Roosevelt, (Anna) Eleanor (reformer, humanitarian); New York City (1884–1962)
Roosevelt, Franklin Delano (32nd U.S. president); Hyde Park, N.Y. (1882–1945)
Roosevelt, Theodore (26th U.S. president); New York City (1858–1919)
Rorem, Ned (composer); Richmond, Ind., 10/23/23
Rose, Billy (showman); New York City (1899–1966)
Rose, Leonard (concert cellist); Washington, D.C. (1918–1984)

Roseanne (Roseanne Barr) (actress); Salt Lake City, 11/3/52
Rosenberg, Ethel (spy); New York City (1915–1953)
Rosenberg, Julius (spy); New York City (1918–1953)
Ross, Betsy (Betsey Griscom) (flagmaker); Philadelphia (1752–1836)
Ross, Diana (singer); Detroit, 3/26/44
Ross, Katharine (actress); Hollywood, Calif., 1/29/42
Rossellini, Isabella (model, actress); Rome, Italy, 6/18/52
Rossellini, Roberto (film director); Rome (1906–1977)
Rossetti, Christina Georgina (poet); London (1830–1894)
Rossetti, Dante Gabriel (painter, poet); London (1828–1882)
Rossini, Gioacchino Antonio (composer); Pesaro, Italy (1792–1868)
Rosten, Leo (writer); Lódz, Poland (1908–1997)
Rostand, Edmond (dramatist); Marseilles, France (1868–1918)
Rostow, Walt Whitman (economist); New York City, 10/7/16
Rostropovich, Mstislav (cellist, conductor); Baku, Azerbaijan, 3/27/27
Roth, Henry (writer); Tysmenica, Ukraine (1906–1995)
Roth, Philip (novelist); Newark, N.J., 3/19/33
Roth, Tim (actor); London, 5/14/64
Rothko, Mark (Marcus Rothkovich) (painter); Russia (1903–1970)
Rouault, Georges (painter); Paris (1871–1958)
Roundtree, Richard (actor); New Rochelle, N.Y., 9/7/42
Rousseau, Henri (painter); Laval, France (1844–1910)
Rousseau, Jean Jacques (philosopher); Geneva (1712–1778)
Rovere, Richard H. (journalist); Jersey City, N.J., 5/5/15
Rowan, Carl Thomas (journalist); Ravenscroft, Tenn. (1925–2000)
Rowan, Dan (comedian); Beggs, Okla. (1922–1987)
Rowlands, Gena (actress); Cambria, Wis., 6/19/30
Rowling, J(oanne) K(athleen) (novelist); Chipping Sodbury, England, 7/31/65
Royko, Mike (columnist); Chicago (1932–1997)
Rubens, Sir Peter Paul (painter); Siegen, Germany (1577–1640)
Rubinstein, Arthur (concert pianist); Lódz, Poland (1887–1982)
Rubinstein, Helena (cosmetics executive); Kraków, Poland (1870–1965)
Rubinstein, John (actor, composer); Los Angeles, 12/8/46
Rucker, Darius (musician, singer, songwriter); Charleston, S.C., 5/13/66
Rudel, Julius (conductor); Vienna, 3/6/21
Ruffo, Titta (baritone); Italy (1878–1953)
Rumsfeld, Donald (sec. of defense); Chicago, 7/9/32
Runyon, (Alfred) Damon (journalist); Manhattan, Kans. (1884–1945)
Rush, Geoffrey (actor); Toowoomba, Australia, 7/6/51
Rushdie, (Ahmed) Salman (novelist); Bombay (Mumbai), 6/19/47
Rusk, Dean (ex-sec. of state); Cherokee County, Ga. (1909–1994)
Ruskin, John (art critic); London (1819–1900)
Russell, Keri (actress); Fountain Valley, Calif., 3/23/76
Russell, Lord Bertrand (Arthur William) (mathematician, philosopher); Trelleck, Wales (1872–1970)
Russell, Jane (actress); Bemidji, Minn., 6/21/21
Russell, Ken (film director); Southhampton, England, 4/3/27
Russell, Kurt (actor); Springfield, Mass., 3/17/51
Russell, Leon (pianist, singer); Lawton, Okla., 4/2/41
Russell, Lillian (Helen Louise Leonard) (soprano); Clinton, Iowa (1861–1922)
Russell, Mark (satirist); Buffalo, N.Y., 8/23/32
Russell, Nipsy (comedian); Atlanta, 10/13/24
Russell, Rosalind (actress); Waterbury, Conn. (1912–1976)
Russo, Rene (actress); Burbank, Calif., 2/17/54
Rustin, Bayard (civil rights leader); West Chester, Pa. (1910–1987)
Rutherford, Dame Margaret (actress); London (1892–1972)
Ryan, Meg (Margaret Mary Emily Anne Hyra) (actress); Fairfield, Conn., 11/19/61
Ryan, Robert (actor); Chicago (1909–1973)
Rydell, Bobby (Robert Ridarelli) (singer); Philadelphia, 4/26/42
Ryder, Winona (Winona Laura Horowitz) (actress); Winona, Minn., 10/29/71
Rysanek, Leonie (dramatic soprano); Vienna (1928–1998)

# S

Saarinen, Eero (architect); Finland (1910–1961)
Sabin, Albert B. (polio researcher); Bialystok, Poland (1906–1993)
Sabu (Dastagir) (actor); Karapur, India (1924–1963)
Sacagawea (Shoshone Indian guide); Lemhi River valley (Idaho) (c. 1786–1812)
Sachs, Jeffrey D. (economist, educator); Michigan, 1954
Sadat, Anwar (former president); Egypt (1918–1981)
Sade, Marquis de (Donatien Alphonse François, Comte de Sade) (libertine, writer); Paris (1740–1814)
Safer, Morley (TV newscaster); Toronto, 11/8/31

Sagan, Carl (Edward) (astronomer, science writer); New York City (1934–1996)
Sagan, Françoise (novelist); Cajarc, France, 6/21/35
Sahl, Mort (Morton Lyon Sahl) (comedian); Montreal, 5/11/27
Saint, Eva Marie (actress); Newark, N.J., 7/4/24
St. Denis, Ruth (dancer, choreographer); Newark, N.J. (1878–1968)
St. James, Susan (Susan Miller) (actress); Los Angeles, 8/14/46
St. John, Jill (actress); Los Angeles, 8/19/40
St. Johns, Adela Rogers (journalist, author); Los Angeles (1894–1988)
Sainte-Marie, Buffy (Beverly) (folk singer); Craven, Sask., Canada, 2/20/41
Saint-Gaudens, Augustus (sculptor); Dublin (1848–1907)
Saint-Laurent, Yves (Henri Donat Mathieu) (fashion designer); Oran, Algeria, 8/1/36
Saint-Saens, Charles Camille (composer); Paris (1835–1921)
Sakharov, Andrei Dmitriyevich (nuclear physicist, peace activist); Russia (1921–1989)
Sales, Soupy (Milton Hines) (television entertainer); Franklinton, N.C., 1/6/26
Salinger, J(erome) D(avid) (novelist); New York City, 1/1/19
Salisbury, Harrison E. (journalist); Minneapolis (1908–1993)
Salk, Jonas (polio researcher); New York City (1914–1995)
Salk, Lee (psychologist); New York City (1926–1992)
Salomon, Haym (American Revolution financier); Leszno, Poland (1740–1785)
Sand, George (Amandine Lucille Aurore Dudevant, née Dupin) (novelist); Paris (1804–1876)
Sandburg, Carl (poet, biographer); Galesburg, Ill. (1878–1967)
Sanders, George (actor); St. Petersburg, Russia (1906–1972)
Sandler, Adam (comedian, musician, actor, screenwriter, singer); Brooklyn, N.Y., 9/9/66
Sands, Tommy (singer); Chicago, 8/27/37
Sanger, Margaret (birth-control advocate); Corning, N.Y. (1879–1966)
San Giacomo, Laura (actress); Hoboken, N.J., 11/14/62
Santayana, George (philosopher); Madrid (1863–1952)
Sappho (poet); Lesbos, Greece (610 b.c.–580 b.c.)
Sarandon, Susan (Susan Tomalin) (actress); New York City, 10/4/46
Sargent, John Singer (painter); Florence, Italy (1856–1925)
Sarnoff, David (radio executive); Minsk, Belarus (1891–1971)
Saroyan, William (novelist); Fresno, Calif. (1908–1981)
Sarto, Andrea del (Andrea Domenico d'Agnolo di Francesco) (painter); Florence, Italy (1486–1531)
Sartre, Jean-Paul (existentialist writer); Paris (1905–1980)
Sassoon, Vidal (hair stylist); London, 1/17/28
Satie, Erik (Alfred Leslie) (composer); Paris (1866–1925)
Saul (king of Israel) fl. 11th cent. b.c.
Savage, Fred (actor); Highland Park, Ill., 7/9/76
Savalas, Telly (Aristoteles) (actor); Garden City, N.Y. (1924–1994)
Savonarola, Girolamo (religious reformer); Ferrara, Italy (1452–1498)
Sawyer, Diane (broadcast journalist); Glasgow, Ky., 12/22/45
Sayão, Bidú (soprano); Rio de Janeiro (1904–1999)
Sayles, John (director, screenwriter, actor); Schenectady, N.Y., 9/28/50
Scarlatti, Alessandro (composer); Palermo, Italy (1659–1725)
Scarlatti, Domenico (composer); Naples, Italy (1685–1757)
Scavullo, Francesco (photographer); Staten Island, N.Y., 1/16/29
Schama, Simon (historian); London, 2/13/45
Schapiro, Meyer (Meir) (art historian); Siauliai, Lithuania (1904–1996)
Schary, Dore (producer, writer); Newark, N.J. (1905–1980)
Schell, Maximilian (actor); Vienna, 12/8/30
Schiaparelli, Elsa (fashion designer); Rome (1890–1973)
Schiff, Dorothy (newspaper publisher); New York City (1903–1989)
Schiffer, Claudia (model, actress); Rheinberg/Dusseldorf, Germany, 8/25/70
Schiller, Johann Christoph Friedrich von (dramatist, poet); Marbach, Germany (1759–1805)
Schipa, Tito (tenor); Lecce, Italy (1890–1965)
Schippers, Thomas (conductor); Kalamazoo, Mich. (1930–1977)
Schlegel, Friedrich von (philosopher); Hanover, Germany (1772–1829)
Schlesinger, Arthur M., Jr. (historian); Columbus, Ohio, 10/15/17
Schnabel, Artur (pianist, composer); Lipnik, Austria (1882–1951)
Schneider, Romy (Rose-Marie Albach-Retty) (actress); Vienna (1938–1982)
Schoenberg, Arnold (composer); Vienna (1874–1951)
Schomberg, Arthur (bibliophile, antiquarian); San Juan, P.R. (1874–1938)

Schopenhauer, Arthur (philosopher); Danzig, Poland (1788–1860)

Schröder, Gerhard (chancellor of Germany); Mossenberg, Germany, 4/7/44

Schubert, Franz Peter (composer); Vienna (1797–1828)

Schulberg, Budd (novelist); New York City, 3/27/14

Schulz, Charles M. (cartoonist); Minneapolis (1922–2000)

Schumacher, Joel (film director, producer, screenwriter); New York City, 8/29/39

Schuman, Robert (statesman); Luxembourg (1886–1963)

Schuman, William (composer); New York City (1910–1992)

Schumann, Robert Alexander (composer); Zwickau, Germany (1810–1856)

Schwartz, Arthur (songwriter); Brooklyn, N.Y. (1900–1984)

Schwarzenegger, Arnold (bodybuilder, actor); Graz, Austria, 7/30/47

Schwarzkopf, Elisabeth (soprano); Poznán, Poland, 12/9/15

Schwarzkopf, H. Norman (retired general); Trenton, N.J., 8/22/34

Schweitzer, Albert (humanitarian, Nobel laureate); Kaysersburg, Upper Alsace (1875–1965)

Schwimmer, David (actor); New York City, 11/12/66

Scofield, Paul (actor); Hurstpierpoint, England, 1/21/22

Scorsese, Martin (actor, writer, director, producer); Flushing, N.Y., 11/17/42

Scott, George C. (actor); Wise, Va. (1927–1999)

Scott, Hazel (singer, pianist); Port of Spain, Trinidad (1920–1981)

Scott, Lizabeth (Emma Matzo) (actress); Scranton, Pa., 9/29/23

Scott, Randolph (Randolph Crane) (actor); Orange County, Va. (1898–1987)

Scott, Robert Falcon (explorer); Devonport, England (1868–1912)

Scott, Sir Walter (novelist); Edinburgh, Scotland (1771–1832)

Scott, Zachary (actor); Austin, Tex. (1914–1965)

Scotto, Renata (operatic soprano); Savona, Italy, 2/24/36

Scruggs, Earl Eugene (bluegrass musician); Cleveland County, N.C., 1/6/24

Seaborg, Glenn Theodore (chemist, Nobel laureate); Ishpeming, Mich. (1912–1999)

Seagal, Steven (actor); Lansing, Mich., 4/10/52

Seal (Sealhenry Olumide Samuel) (singer, songwriter); London, England, 2/19/63

Seattle (Chief Seattle) (Suquamish Indian leader); Blake Island (Wash.) (c. 1786–1866)

Sebastian, John (composer, singer); New York City, 3/17/44

Seberg, Jean (actress); Marshalltown, Iowa (1938–1979)

Sedaka, Neil (singer); Brooklyn, N.Y., 3/13/39

Sedgwick, Kyra (actress); New York City, 8/19/65

Seeger, Pete (folk singer); New York City, 5/3/19

Segal, Erich (novelist); Brooklyn, N.Y., 6/16/37

Segal, George (actor); New York City, 2/13/36

Segovia, Andrés (guitarist); Linares, Spain (1893–1987)

Seinfeld, Jerry (comedian); Brooklyn, N.Y., 4/29/54

Selena (Selena Quintanilla Perez) (singer); Lake Jackson, Tex. (1971–1995)

Selleck, Tom (actor); Detroit, 1/29/45

Sellars, Peter (theater director); Pittsburgh, 1958?

Sellers, Peter (actor); Southsea, England (1925–1980)

Selznick, David O. (producer); Pittsburgh (1902–1965)

Sendak, Maurice (Bernard) (children's book author, illustrator); Brooklyn, N.Y., 6/10/28

Sennett, Mack (Michael Sinnott) (film producer); Richmond, Que., Canada (1880–1960)

Sequoyah (Cherokee linguist); Taskigi, Tenn. (c. 1770–1843)

Serkin, Peter (pianist); New York City, 7/24/47

Serkin, Rudolf (pianist); Eger, Czech Republic (1903–1991)

Serling, Rod (writer, TV host); Syracuse, N.Y. (1924–1975)

Serra, Georges (painter); Paris (1859–1891)

Seuss, Dr. (Theodor Seuss Geisel) (author, illustrator); Springfield, Mass. (1904–1991)

Sevareid, Eric (TV commentator); Velva, N.D. (1912–1991)

Severinsen, Doc (Carl) (band leader); Arlington, Ore., 7/7/27

Sevigny, Chlöe (actress); Darien, Conn., 1975

Sewell, Rufus (actor, musician); London, 10/29/67

Sexton, Anne (poet); Newton, Mass. (1928–1974)

Seymour, Jane (Joyce Penelope Wilhelmina Frankenburg) (actress); Wimbledon, England, 2/15/51

Shabazz, Betty (Betty Sanders) (civil rights activist); Detroit (1936–1997)

Shaffer, Peter (playwright); Liverpool, England, 5/15/26

Shaham, Gil (violinist); Urbana, Ill., 1971

Shahn, Ben(jamin) (painter); Kaunas, Lithuania (1898–1969)

Shakespeare, William (dramatist); Stratford on Avon, England (1564–1616)

Shakur, Tupac (Amaru Shakur) (singer, actor); Brooklyn, N.Y. (1971–1996)

Shandling, Garry (comedian, actor, producer); Chicago, 11/29/49

Shange, Ntozake (Paulette Williams) (poet, playwright); Trenton, N.J., 10/18/48

Shankar, Ravi (sitar player); Benares, India, 4/7/20

Sharif, Omar (Michael Shalhoub) (actor); Alexandria, Egypt, 4/10/32

Shatner, William (actor); Montreal, 3/22/31

Shaw, Artie (Arthur Arshawsky) (band leader); New York City, 5/23/10

Shaw, George Bernard (dramatist); Dublin (1856–1950)

Shaw, Irwin (novelist); Brooklyn, N.Y. (1913–1984)

Shaw, Robert (actor); Lancashire, England (1927–1978)

Shaw, Robert (chorale conductor); Red Bluff, Calif. (1916–1999)

Shawn, Ted (Edwin Myers Shawn) (dancer, choreographer); Kansas City, Mo. (1891–1972)

Shawn, Wallace (actor); New York City, 11/12/43

Shearer, Moira (ballet dancer); Dunfermline, Scotland, 1/17/26

Shearer, Norma (actress); Montreal (1900–1983)

Shearing, George (pianist); London, 8/13/20

Sheedy, Ally (Alexandra Sheedy) (actress, writer); New York City, 6/12/62

Sheen, Charlie (actor); Los Angeles, 9/3/65

Sheen, Fulton J. (Peter Sheen) (Roman Catholic bishop); El Paso, Ill. (1895–1979)

Sheen, Martin (Ramon Estevez) (actor); Dayton, Ohio, 8/3/40

Shelley, Mary Wollstonecraft Godwin (writer); London (1797–1851)

Shelley, Percy Bysshe (poet); nr. Horsham, England (1792–1822)

Shelton, Henry (chairman of the Joint Chiefs of Staff); Tarboro, N.C., 1/2/42

Shepard, Sam (Samuel Shepard Rogers) (playwright); Ft. Sheridan, Ill., 11/5/43

Shepherd, Cybill (actress); Memphis, Tenn., 2/18/50

Sheraton, Thomas (furniture designer); Stockton-on-Tees, England (1751–1806)

Sheridan, Ann (Clara Lou Sheridan) (actress); Denton, Tex. (1915–1967)

Sheridan, Philip (army officer); Albany, N.Y. (1831–1888)

Sheridan, Richard Brinsley (dramatist); Dublin (1751–1816)

Sherman, William Tecumseh (army officer); Lancaster, Ohio (1820–1891)

Sherwood, Robert Emmet (playwright); New Rochelle, N.Y. (1896–1955)

Shevardnadze, Eduard Amvrosiyevich (State Council chairman, Georgia); Mamati, Georgia, 1/25/28

Shields, Brooke (actress); New York City, 5/31/65

Shire, Talia (Coppola) (actress); Lake Success, N.Y., 4/25/46

Shirer, William L. (journalist, historian); Chicago (1904–1993)

Sholokhov, Mikhail (novelist); Veshenskaya, Russia (1905–1984)

Shore, Dinah (Frances Rose Shore) (singer); Winchester,Tenn. (1917–1994)

Short, Bobby (Robert Waltrip Short) (singer, pianist); Danville, Ill., 9/15/24

Short, Martin (actor); Hamilton, Ont., Canada, 3/26/50

Shostakovich, Dmitri (composer); St. Petersburg, Russia (1906–1975)

Shriner, Herb (humorist, host); Toledo, Ohio (1918–1970)

Shriver, Maria (TV co-host); Chicago, 11/6/55

Shriver, Sargent (Robert Sargent Shriver, Jr.) (business executive); Westminster, Md., 11/9/15

Shue, Andrew (actor, soccer player); South Orange, N.J., 2/20/67

Shue, Elisabeth (actress); Wilmington, Del. (1961)

Shula, Don (football coach); Grand River, Ohio (1930–1938)

Sibelius, Jean (Johann Julius Christian Sibelius) (composer); Tavastehus, Finland (1865–1957)

Sidney, Sir Philip (poet); Penshurst, England (1554–1586)

Sidney, Sylvia (Sophia Kosow) (actress); New York City (1910–1999)

Siegfried and Roy (illusionists) Siegfried Fischbacher; Rosenheim, Bavaria, Germany, 1939 Roy Uwe Ludwig Horn; Nordenham, nr. Bremen, Germany, 1944

Siepi, Cesare (basso); Milan, Italy, 2/10/23

Signoret, Simone (Simone Kaminker) (actress); Wiesbaden, Germany (1921–1985)

Sihanouk, Norodom (king of Cambodia); Cambodia, 10/31/22

Sikorsky, Igor I. (inventor); Kiev, Ukraine (1889–1972)

Sills, Beverly (Belle Silverman) (soprano, opera director); Brooklyn, N.Y., 5/25/29

Sills, Milton (actor); Chicago (1882–1930)

Silone, Ignazio (Secondo Tranquilli) (novelist); Pescina del Marsi, Italy (1900–1978)

Silver, Ron (Ron Zimelman) (actor); New York City, 7/2/46

Stefani, Gwen (singer); Orange County, Calif., 10/3/69
Stegner, Wallace (Earle) (novelist, critic); Lake Mills, Iowa (1909–1993)
Steichen, Edward Jean (photographer, artist); Luxembourg (1879–1973)
Steiger, Rod (Rodney) (actor); Westhampton, N.Y. (1925–2002)
Stein, Gertrude (author); Allegheny, Pa. (1874–1946)
Steinbeck, John Ernst (novelist); Salinas, Calif. (1902–1968)
Steinberg, David (comedian); Winnipeg, Man., Canada, 8/19/42
Steinberg, William (conductor); Cologne, Germany (1899–1978)
Steinem, Gloria (feminist, publisher); Toledo, Ohio, 3/25/34
Steinmetz, Charles (electrical engineer); Breslau, Poland (1865–1923)
Steenburgen, Mary (actress); Newport, Ark., 2/8/53
Stendhal (Marie Henri Beyle) (novelist); Grenoble, France (1783–1842)
Stern, Howard (radio personality); New York City, 1/2/54
Stern, Isaac (concert violinist); Kreminlecz, Russia (1920–2001)
Sterne, Laurence (novelist); Clonmel, Ireland (1713–1768)
Stevens, Cat (Steven Georgiou) (singer, songwriter); London, 7/21/47
Stevens, Connie (Concetta Ingolia) (singer); Brooklyn, N.Y., 8/8/38
Stevens, George (film director); Oakland, Calif. (1905–1975)
Stevens, Risë (mezzo-soprano); New York City, 6/11/13
Stevens, Wallace (poet); Reading, Pa. (1879–1955)
Stevenson, Adlai Ewing (statesman); Los Angeles (1900–1965)
Stevenson, McLean (actor); Bloomington, Ill. (1929–1996)
Stevenson, Parker (actor); Philadelphia, 6/4/52
Stevenson, Robert Louis Balfour (novelist, poet); Edinburgh, Scotland (1850–1894)
Stewart, James (actor); Indiana, Pa. (1908–1997)
Stewart, Jon (Jonathan Stewart Leibowitz) (comedian, actor); Trenton, N.J., 11/28/62
Stewart, Martha (entrepreneurial home stylist); Nutley, N.J., 8/3/41
Stewart, Patrick (actor); Mirfield, England, 7/13/40
Stewart, Rod (Roderick David) (singer); London, 1/10/45
Stieglitz, Alfred (photographer); Hoboken, N.J. (1864–1946)
Stiers, David Ogden (actor); Peoria, Ill., 10/31/42
Stiller, Ben (actor, director, comic); New York City, 11/30/65
Stiller, Jerry (actor); Brooklyn, N.Y., 6/8/29
Stills, Stephen (singer, songwriter); Dallas, 1/3/45
Stine, R. L. (Robert Lawrence Stine) (writer); Columbus, Ohio, 10/8/43
Sting (Gordon Matthew Sumner) (singer, composer); Wallsend, England, 10/2/51
Stipe, Michael (singer); Decatur, Ga., 1/4/60
Stockwell, Dean (actor); North Hollywood, Calif., 3/5/36
Stoker, Bram (novelist); Dublin (1847–1912)
Stokes, Carl (TV newscaster); Cleveland (1927–1996)
Stokowski, Leopold (conductor); London (1882–1977)
Stoltz, Eric (actor); Whittier, Calif., 9/30/61
Stone, Edward Durell (architect); Fayetteville, Ark. (1902–1978)
Stone, I(sidor) F(einstein) (journalist); Philadelphia (1907–1989)
Stone, Irving (Irving Tennenbaum) (novelist); San Francisco (1903–1989)
Stone, Lucy (woman suffragist); nr. West Brookfield, Mass. (1818–1893)
Stone, Oliver (director, writer, producer); New York City, 9/15/46
Stone, Robert (novelist); Brooklyn, N.Y., 8/21/37
Stone, Sharon (actress); Meadville, Pa., 3/10/58
Stone, Sly (Sylvester Stone) (rock musician) 1944
Stooges, The Three (comedy team) Moe Howard (Moses Horwitz); Brooklyn, N.Y. (1897–1975;) Shemp Howard (Samuel Horwitz); Brooklyn, N.Y. (1900–1955;) Larry Fine (Laurence Feinburn); Philadelphia (1911–1975;) Curly Howard (Jerome Horwitz); Brooklyn, N.Y. (1906–1952)
Stoppard, Tom (Thomas Straussler) (playwright); Zlin, Slovakia, 7/3/37
Stout, Rex (mystery writer); Noblesville, Ind. (1886–1975)
Stowe, Harriet Elizabeth Beecher (novelist); Litchfield, Conn. (1811–1896)
Stowe, Madeleine (actress); Eagle Rock, Calif., 8/18/58
Strachey, (Giles) Lytton (biographer); London (1880–1932)
Stradivari, Antonio (violinmaker); Cremona, Italy (1644–1737)
Straight, Beatrice (actress); Old Westbury, N.Y. (1918–2001)
Strasberg, Lee (stage director); Budanov, Austria (1901–1982)
Strasberg, Susan (actress); New York City (1938–1999)
Stratas, Teresa (soprano); Toronto, 5/26/38
Straus, Oskar (composer); Vienna (1870–1954)
Strauss, Johann (composer); Vienna (1825–1899)
Strauss, Lewis L. (naval officer, scientist); Charleston, W. Va. (1896–1974)
Strauss, Peter (actor); New York City, 2/20/47

Strauss, Richard (composer); Munich, Germany (1864–1949)
Stravinsky, Igor (composer); Orlenbaum, Russia (1882–1971)
Streep, Meryl (Mary Louise) (actress); Summit, N.J., 6/22/49
Streisand, Barbra (singer, actress, director, producer, writer); Brooklyn, N.Y., 4/24/42
Strindberg, (Johan) August (dramatist); Stockholm (1849–1912)
Stritch, Elaine (actress); Detroit, 2/2/25
Struthers, Sally Ann (actress); Portland, Ore., 7/28/48
Stuart, Gilbert Charles (painter); Rhode Island (1755–1828)
Stuart, Gloria (film actress); Santa Monica, Calif., 7/4/10
Stuart, James Ewell Brown (known as Jeb) (Confederate army officer); Patrick County, Va. (1833–1864)
Sturges, Preston (Edmond P. Biden) (director, screenwriter, playwright); Chicago (1898–1959)
Stuyvesant, Peter (Governor of New Amsterdam); West Friesland, Netherlands (1592–1672)
Styne, Jule (Julius Kerwin Stein) (songwriter); London (1905–1994)
Styron, William (William Clark Styron, Jr.) (novelist); Newport News, Va., 6/11/25
Suharto (president of Indonesia); Sedaju-Godean, Java, 2/20/21
Sukarno (Indonesian leader); Surabaja, Java (1901–1970)
Sullavan, Margaret Brooke (actress); Norfolk, Va. (1911–1960)
Sullivan, Sir Arthur Seymour (composer); London (1842–1900)
Sullivan, Barry (Patrick Barry) (actor); New York City (1912–1994)
Sullivan, Ed (columnist, TV personality); New York City (1901–1974)
Sullivan, Frank (Francis John) (humorist); Saratoga Springs, N.Y. (1892–1976)
Sullivan, Louis Henry (architect); Boston (1856–1924)
Sulzberger, Arthur Ochs (newspaper publisher); New York City, 2/5/26
Sumac, Yma (singer); Ichocan, Peru, 9/10/27
Summer, Donna (La Donna Andrea Gaines) (singer); Boston, 12/31/48
Sun Ra (Herman "Sunny" Blount) (jazz composer); Birmingham, Ala. (1914?–1993)
Sun Tzu (writer, military strategist); China (fl. c. 500–320 B.C.)
Sun Yat-sen (statesman); nr. Macao (1866–1925)
Susann, Jacqueline (novelist); Philadelphia (1918–1974)
Susskind, David (TV producer); New York City (1920–1987)
Sutherland, Donald (actor); St. John, N.B., Canada, 7/17/34
Sutherland, Joan (soprano); Sydney, Australia, 11/7/26
Sutherland, Kiefer (actor); London, 12/18/66
Suzuki, Pat (actress); Cressey, Calif., 1931
Swados, Elizabeth (composer, playwright); Buffalo, N.Y., 2/5/51
Swank, Hilary (actress); Bellingham, Wash., 7/30/74
Swanson, Gloria (Gloria May Josephine Svensson) (actress); Chicago (1899–1983)
Swarthout, Gladys (soprano); Deepwater, Mo. (1904–1969)
Swayze, John Cameron (news commentator); Wichita, Kans. (1906–1995)
Swayze, Patrick (actor, dancer); Houston, 8/18/54
Swedenborg, Emanuel (scientist, philosopher, mystic); Stockholm (1688–1772)
Swift, Jonathan (satirist); Dublin (1667–1745)
Swinburne, Algernon Charles (poet); London (1837–1909)
Swit, Loretta (actress); Passaic, N.J., 11/4/37
Swope, Herbert Bayard (journalist); St. Louis (1882–1958)
Sydow, Max von (Carl Adolf von Sydow) (actor); Lund, Sweden, 4/10/29
Symons, Arthur (poet, critic); Milford Haven, Wales (1865–1945)
Synge, John Millington (dramatist); nr. Dublin (1871–1909)
Szilard, Leo (physicist); Budapest (1898–1964)

# T

Taft, Robert Alphonso (legislator); Cincinnati (1889–1953)
Taft, William Howard (27th U.S. president); Cincinnati (1857–1930)
Tagore, Sir Rabindranath (poet); Calcutta (1861–1941)
Tallchief, Maria (ballet dancer); Fairfax, Okla., 1/24/25
Talleyrand-Périgord, Charles Maurice de (statesman); Paris (1754–1838)
Talmadge, Norma (actress); Niagara Falls, N.Y. (1897–1957)
Talvela, Martti (basso); Hiitola, Finalnd (1935–1989)
Tamerlane (Timur) (Mongol conqueror); nr. Samarkand, Turkestan (c. 1336–1405)
Tamiroff, Akim (actor); Baku, Azerbaijan (1899–1972)
Tan, Amy (novelist); Oakland, Calif., 2/19/52
Tanaka, Tomoyuki (film producer); Osaka, Japan (1910–1997)
Tandy, Jessica (actress); London (1909–1994)
Tarbell, Ida Minerva (author, muckraker); Erie Co., Pa. (1857–1944)
Tarkington, (Newton) Booth (novelist); Indianapolis (1869–1946)

**Tartikoff,** Brandon (television executive); Freeport, N.Y. **(1949–1997)**
**Tate,** Allen (John Orley) (poet, critic); Winchester, Ky. **(1899–1979)**
**Tate,** Sharon (actress); Dallas **(1943–1969)**
**Taylor,** Deems (composer); New York City **(1885–1966)**
**Taylor,** Elizabeth (actress); London, 2/27/32
**Taylor,** Harold (educator); Toronto, 9/28/14
**Taylor,** James (singer, songwriter); Boston, 3/12/48
**Taylor,** Laurette (Laurette Cooney) (actress); New York City **(1884–1946)**
**Taylor,** Lili (actress); Glenco, Ill., 2/20/67
**Taylor,** Gen. Maxwell D. (former Army chief of staff); Keytesville, Mo. **(1901–1987)**
**Taylor,** Niki (model); Pembroke Pines, Fla., 3/5/75
**Taylor,** Paul (choreographer); Wilkinsburg, Pa., 7/29/30
**Taylor,** Rod (actor); Sydney, Australia, 1/11/30
**Taylor,** Zachary (12th U.S. president); Montebello, Orange County, Va. **(1784–1850)**
**Tchaikovsky,** Peter (Pëtr) Ilich (composer); Votkinsk, Russia **(1840–1893)**
**Teasdale,** Sara (poet); St. Louis **(1884–1933)**
**Tebaldi,** Renata (lyric soprano); Pesaro, Italy, 1/2/22
**Tecumseh** (Shawnee Indian chief); nr. Springfield, Ohio **(1768–1813)**
**Te Kanawa,** Kiri (soprano); Gisborne, New Zealand, 3/6/44
**Telemann,** Georg Philipp (composer); Magdeburg, Germany **(1681–1767)**
**Teller,** Edward (atomic physicist); Budapest, 1/15/08
**Templeton,** Alec Andrew (pianist, composer); Cardiff, Wales **(1910–1963)**
**Tennille,** Toni (singer); Montgomery, Ala., 5/8/43
**Tennyson,** Alfred (1st Baron Tennyson) (poet); Somersby, England **(1809–1892)**
**Tenskwatawa** (Shawnee prophet); Old Piqua, Ohio **(c. 1770–c. 1835)**
**Terhune,** Albert Payson (novelist, journalist); Newark, N.J. **(1872–1942)**
**Terkel,** Studs (writer, interviewer); New York City, 5/16/12
**Terry,** Ellen Alicia (actress); Coventry, England **(1848–1928)**
**Terry-Thomas** (Thomas Terry Hoar Stevens) (actor); London **(1911–1990)**
**Tesla,** Nikola (electrical engineer, inventor); Smiljan, Lika, Croatia **(1856–1943)**
**Thackeray,** William Makepeace (novelist); Calcutta **(1811–1863)**
**Thalberg,** Irving G. (producer); Brooklyn, N.Y. **(1899–1936)**
**Thant,** U (U.N. statesman); Pantanaw, Burma **(1909–1974)**
**Tharp,** Twyla (dancer, choreographer); Portland, Ind., 7/1/42
**Thatcher,** Margaret (former prime minister); Grantham, England, 10/13/25
**Thebom,** Blanche (mezzo-soprano); Monessen, Pa., 9/19/19
**Theodorakis,** Mikis (composer); Chios, Greece, 7/29/25
**Thicke,** Alan (actor, composer); Kirland Lake, Ont., Canada, 3/1/47
**Thieu,** Nguyen Van (ex-president of South Vietnam); Trithuy, Vietnam, 4/5/23
**Thomas,** Danny (Amos Jacobs) (entertainer, TV producer); Deerfield, Mich. **(1912–1991)**
**Thomas,** Dylan Marials (poet); Carmarthenshire, Wales **(1914–1953)**
**Thomas,** JonathanTaylor (actor); Bethlehem, Pa., 9/8/81
**Thomas,** Kristen Scott (actress); Redruth, Cornwall, England, 1960
**Thomas,** Lowell (explorer, commentator); Woodington, Ohio **(1892–1981)**
**Thomas,** Marlo (actress); Detroit, 11/21/43
**Thomas,** Michael Tilson (conductor); Hollywood, Calif., 12/21/44
**Thomas,** Norman Mattoon (Socialist leader); Marion, Ohio **(1884–1968)**
**Thomas,** Philip Michael (actor); Columbus, Ohio, 5/26/49
**Thomas,** Richard (actor); New York City, 6/13/51
**Thompson,** Dorothy (writer); Lancaster, N.Y. **(1894–1961)**
**Thompson,** Emma (actress); London, 4/15/59
**Thompson,** Hunter (Stockton) (writer); Louisville, Ky., 7/18/39
**Thompson,** Lea (actress); Rochester, Minn., 5/31/61
**Thompson,** Sada (actress); Des Moines, Iowa, 9/27/29
**Thomson,** Virgil (Garnett) (composer); Kansas City, Mo. **(1896–1989)**
**Thoreau,** Henry David (naturalist, author); Concord, Mass. **(1817–1862)**
**Thorndike,** Dame Sybil (actress); Gainsborough, England **(1882–1976)**
**Thorne-Smith,** Courteney (actress); San Francisco, 11/8/67
**Thornton,** Billy Bob (actor, screenwriter); Hot Springs, Ark., 8/4/55
**Thurber,** James Grover (author, cartoonist); Columbus, Ohio **(1894–1961)**
**Thurman,** Robert A. F. (scholar, Indo-Tibetan Buddhist studies); New York City, 8/6/40

**Thurman,** Uma (actress); Boston, 4/29/70
**Thurmond,** (James) Strom (U.S. senator); Edgefield, S.C., 12/5/02
**Tibbett,** Lawrence (baritone); Bakersfield, Calif. **(1896–1960)**
**Tiberius** Caesar Augustus (Roman emperor); Capri **(42 B.C.–A.D. 37)**
**Tiegs,** Cheryl (model, actress); Minnesota, 9/25/47
**Tierney,** Gene (actress); Brooklyn, N.Y. **(1920–1991)**
**Tillich,** Paul (philosopher, theologian); Starzeddel, Germany **(1886–1965)**
**Tilly,** Meg (Margaret Tilly) (actress); Texada Island, B.C., Canada, 2/14/60
**Tintoretto,** Il (Jacopo Robusti) (painter); Venice **(1518–1594)**
**Tiny Tim** (Herbert Khaury) (entertainer); New York City **(1932–1996)**
**Tiomkin,** Dmitri (composer); St. Petersburg, Russia **(1894–1979)**
**Titian** (Tiziano Vecelli) (painter); Pieve di Cadore, Italy **(1477–1576)**
**Tito** (Josip Broz or Brozovich) (president of Yugoslavia); Croatia (former Yugoslavia) **(1892–1980)**
**Tocqueville,** Alexis de (writer); Verneuil, France **(1805–1859)**
**Todd,** Michael (producer); Minneapolis **(1907–1958)**
**Todd,** Thelma (actress); Lawrence, Mass. **(1905–1935)**
**Tolkien,** J(ohn) R(onald) R(euel) (fantasy writer); Bloemfontein, South Africa **(1892–1973)**
**Tolstoy,** Count Leo (Lev) Nikolaevich (novelist); Tula Province, Russia **(1828–1910)**
**Tomei,** Marisa (actress); Brooklyn, N.Y., 12/4/64
**Tomlin,** Lily (actress, comedienne); Detroit, 9/1/36
**Tone,** Franchot (actor); Niagara Falls, N.Y. **(1905–1968)**
**Tormé,** Mel (Melvin) (singer); Chicago **(1925–1999)**
**Torn,** Rip (Elmore Torn, Jr.) (actor, director); Temple, Tex., 2/6/31
**Torquamada,** Tomásde (Spanish Inquisitor); Valladolid, Spain **(1420–1498)**
**Toscanini,** Arturo (orchestra conductor); Parma, Italy **(1867–1957)**
**Totenberg,** Nina (broadcast journalist); New York City, 1/14/44
**Toulouse-Lautrec** (Henri Marie Raymond de Toulouse-Lautrec Monfa) (painter); Albi, France **(1864–1901)**
**Toynbee,** Arnold J. (historian); London **(1889–1975)**
**Tracy,** Spencer (actor); Milwaukee **(1900–1967)**
**Traubel,** Helen (Wagnerian soprano); St. Louis **(1903–1972)**
**Travanti,** Daniel J. (actor); Kenosha, Wis., 3/7/40
**Travolta,** John (actor); Englewood, N.J., 2/18/54
**Treacher,** Arthur (actor); Brighton, England **(1894–1975)**
**Tree,** Sir Herbert Beerbohm (actor, manager); London **(1853–1917)**
**Trevor,** Claire (Wemlinger) (actress); New York City **(1909–2000)**
**Trigère,** Pauline (fashion designer); Paris, 11/4/12
**Trilling,** Diana (writer); New York City **(1905–1996)**
**Trilling,** Lionel (author, educator); New York City **(1905–1975)**
**Trollope,** Anthony (novelist); London **(1815–1882)**
**Trotsky,** Leon (Lev Davidovich Bronstein) (statesman); Elisavetgrad, Russia **(1879–1940)**
**Troyanos,** Tatiana (mezzo-soprano); New York City **(1938–1993)**
**Trudeau,** Garry (cartoonist); New York City, 1948
**Trudeau,** Pierre Elliott (former prime minister); Montreal **(1919–2000)**
**Truffaut,** François (film director); Paris **(1932–1984)**
**Trujillo y Molina,** Rafael Leonidas (dictator); San Cristóbal, Dominican Republic **(1891–1961)**
**Truman,** Harry S. (33rd U.S. president); near Lamar, Mo. **(1884–1972)**
**Truman,** Margaret (author); Independence, Mo., 2/17/24
**Trump,** Donald (business executive); New York City, 6/14/46
**Truth,** Sojourner (Isabella) (preacher, abolitionist); Ulster Co., N.Y. **(c. 1797–1883)**
**Tryon,** Thomas (actor, novelist); Hartford, Conn. **(1926–1991)**
**Tsiolkovsky,** Konstantin E. (father of cosmonautics); Izhevskoye, Russia **(1857–1935)**
**Tsongas,** Paul E. (politician); Lowell, Mass. **(1941–1997)**
**Tubman,** Harriet (Araminta) (abolitionist); Dorchester Co., Md. **(c. 1820–1913)**
**Tuchman,** Barbara (Wertheim) (historian, author); New York City **(1912–1989)**
**Tucker,** Forrest (actor); Plainfield, Ind. **(1919–1986)**
**Tucker,** Richard (tenor); New York City **(1914–1975)**
**Tucker,** Sophie (Sophia Kalish) (singer); Russia **(1884–1966)**
**Tudor,** Antony (choreographer); London **(1909–1987)**
**Tune,** Tommy (dancer, choreographer); Wichita Falls, Tex., 2/28/39
**Turgenev,** Ivan Sergeevich (novelist); Orel, Russia **(1818–1883)**
**Turlington,** Christy (model); San Francisco, 1/2/69
**Turner,** Frederick J. (historian); Portage, Wis. **(1861–1932)**
**Turner,** Ike (singer); Clarksdale, Miss., 11/5/31
**Turner,** Janine (actress); Lincoln, Neb., 12/6/62
**Turner,** Joseph M.W. (painter); London **(1775–1851)**
**Turner,** Kathleen (actress); Springfield, Mo., 6/19/54

Turner, Lana (Julia Jean Mildred Frances Turner) (actress); Wallace, Idaho (1920–1995)

Turner, Nat (civil rights leader); Southampton County, Va. (1800–1831)

Turner, Ted (business executive); Cincinnati, 11/19/38

Turner, Tina (Annie Mae Bullock) (singer); Nut Bush, Tenn., 11/26/39

Turpin, Ben (comedian); New Orleans (1874–1940)

Turturro, John (actor); Brooklyn, N.Y., 2/28/57

Twain, Mark (Samuel Langhorne Clemens) (author); Florida, Mo. (1835–1910)

Twain, Shania (Eileen Regina Twain) (country singer); Windsor, Ont., Canada, 8/28/65

Tweed, William Marcy (politician); New York City (1823–1878)

Twiggy (Leslie Hornby) (model); London, 9/19/49

Twining, Gen. Nathan F. (former Air Force chief of staff); Monroe, Wis. (1897–1982)

Twitty, Conway (Harold Lloyd Jenkins) (singer, guitarist); Friars Point, Miss. (1933–1993)

Tyler, John (10th U.S. president); Charles City County, Va. (1790–1862)

Tyler, Liv (actress, model); Portland, Maine, 7/1/77

Tyler, Steven (singer); New York City, 3/26/48

Tyson, Cicely (actress); New York City, 12/19/33

# U

Uccello, Paolo (painter); Florence (1397–1475)

Udall, Stewart L. (ex-secretary of the interior); St. Johns, Ariz., 1/31/20

Uggams, Leslie (singer, actress); New York City, 5/25/43

Ulanova, Galina (ballet dancer); St. Petersburg, Russia (1910–1998)

Ullman, Tracey (actress, singer); Slough, England, 12/30/59

Ullmann, Liv (actress); Tokyo, 12/16/39

Ulrich, Skeet (actor, model); North Carolina, 1/20/70

Untermeyer, Louis (anthologist, poet); New York City (1885–1977)

Updike, John (novelist); Shillington, Pa., 3/18/32

Urey, Harold C. (chemist, Nobel laureate); Walkerton, Ind. (1893–1981)

Uris, Leon (novelist); Baltimore, 8/3/24

Ustinov, Peter (actor, producer); London, 4/16/21

Utrillo, Maurice (painter); Paris (1883–1955)

# V

Vaccaro, Brenda (actress); Brooklyn, N.Y., 11/18/39

Vadim, Roger (Roger Vadim Plemiannikov) (film director); Paris (1928–2000)

Valentine, Karen (actress); Sabastopol, Calif., 5/25/47

Valentino, Rudolph (Rodolpho d'Antonguolla) (actor); Castellaneta, Italy (1895–1926)

Valentino (Valentino Garavani) (fashion designer); nr. Milan, Italy, 5/11/32

Valéry, Paul (Ambroise Toussaint Jules) (poet, critic); Sète, France (1871–1945)

Vallee, Rudy (Hubert Prior Rudy Vallée) (band leader, singer); Island Pond, Vt. (1901–1986)

Valli, Frankie (Frank Castellaccio) (singer); Newark, N.J., 5/3/37

Van Allen, James Alfred (space physicist); Mt. Pleasant, Iowa, 9/7/14

Van Buren, Abigail (Pauline Esther Friedman) (columnist); Sioux City, Iowa, 7/4/18

Van Damme, Jean-Claude (actor); Brussels, Belgium, 10/18/60

Vance, Vivian (Vivian Jones) (actress); Cherryvale, Kans. (1909–1979)

Van Der Beek, James (actor); Cheshire, Conn., 3/8/77

Vanderbilt, Alfred G. (sportsman); London (1912–1999)

Vanderbilt, Cornelius (financier); Port Richmond, N.Y. (1794–1877)

Vanderbilt, Gloria (fashion designer); New York City, 2/20/24

Van Doren, Carl (writer, educator); Hope, Ill. (1885–1950)

Van Doren, Mamie (actress); Rowena, S.D., 2/6/33

Vandross, Luther (R&B singer); New York City, 4/20/51

Van Dyke, Dick (actor); West Plains, Mo., 12/13/25

Vandyke (or Van Dyck), Sir Anthony (painter); Antwerp, Belgium (1599–1641)

Van Eyck, Jan (painter); Maeseyck, Belgium (c. 1390–1441)

Van Fleet, Jo (actress); Oakland, Calif. (1915–1996)

van Gogh, Vincent (painter); Groot Zundert, Brabant, The Netherlands (1853–1890)

van Hamel, Martine (ballet dancer); Brussels, 11/16/45

Van Heusen, Jimmy (Edward Chester Babcock) (songwriter); Syracuse, N.Y. (1913–1990)

Van Patten, Dick (actor); Richmond Hill, N.Y., 12/9/28

Van Peebles, Melvin (playwright); Chicago, 9/21/32

Vasari, Giorgio (art historian); Arezzo, Italy (1511–1574)

Vaughan, Sarah (singer); Newark, N.J. (1924–1990)

Vaughan Williams, Ralph (composer); Down Ampney, England (1872–1958)

Vaughn, Robert (actor); New York City, 11/22/32

Vaughn, Vince (actor); Minneapolis, 3/28/70

Veblen, Thorstein (economist, social critic); Cato Township, Wis. (1857–1929)

Veidt, Conrad (actor); Potsdam, Germany (1893–1943)

Velázquez, Diego Rodriguez de Silva y (painter); Seville, Spain (1599–1660)

Venturi, Robert (Charles) (architect); Philadelphia, 6/25/25

Verdi, Giuseppe (composer); Roncole, Italy (1813–1901)

Verdon, Gwen (actress); Culver City, Calif. (1925–2000)

Vereen, Ben (actor, singer); Miami, Fla., 10/10/46

Verlaine, Paul (poet); Metz, France (1844–1896)

Vermeer, Jan (or Jan van der Meer van Delft) (painter); Delft, Netherlands (1632–1675)

Verne, Jules (author); Nantes, France (1828–1905)

Veronese, Paolo (Paolo Cagliari) (painter); Verona, Italy (1528–1588)

Verrazano, Giovanni da (navigator); Florence, Italy (c. 1485–1528)

Verrett, Shirley (mezzo-soprano); New Orleans, 5/31/33

Versace, Gianni (fashion designer); Reggio di Calabria, Italy (1946–1997)

Vesalius, Andreas (anatomist); Brussels (1515–1564)

Vespucci, Amerigo (navigator); Florence, Italy (1454–1512)

Vico, Giovanni Battista (philosopher); Naples, Italy (1668–1744)

Victoria (queen of England); London (1819–1901)

Vidal, Gore (novelist); West Point, N.Y., 10/3/25

Vidor, King (film director, producer); Galveston, Tex. (1895–1982)

Vigoda, Abe (actor); New York City, 2/24/21

Villa, Pancho (Doroteo Arango) (revolutionary); Hacienda de Rio Grande, San Juan del Rio, Mexico (1877–1923)

Villella, Edward (ballet dancer); Bayside, Queens, N.Y., 10/1/36

Villon, François (François de Montcorbier) (poet); Paris (1431–1463)

Vinton, Bobby (singer); Canonsburg, Pa., 4/16/35

Virgil (or Vergil) (Publius Vergilius Maro) (poet); nr. Mantua, Italy (70–19 B.C.)

Vishnevskaya, Galina (soprano); St. Petersburg, Russia, 10/25/26

Vivaldi, Antonio (composer); Venice (1678–1741)

Vlaminck, Maurice de (painter); Paris (1876–1958)

Voight, Jon (actor); Yonkers, N.Y., 12/29/38

Volta, Alessandro (scientist); Como, Italy (1745–1827)

Voltaire (François Marie Arouet) (author); Paris (1694–1778)

von Braun, Wernher (rocket scientist); Wirsitz, Germany (1912–1977)

von Furstenberg, Betsy (Elizabeth Caroline Maria Agatha Felicitas Therese von Furstenberg-Hedringen) (actress); Nelheim-Heusen, Germany, 8/16/35

von Fürstenberg, Diane (Diane Simone Michelle Halfin) (fashion designer); Brussels, 12/31/46

von Hindenburg, Paul (statesman); Posen, Poland (1847–1934)

von Karajan, Herbert (conductor); Salzburg, Austria (1908–1989)

Vonnegut, Kurt, Jr. (novelist); Indianapolis, 11/11/22

Von Stade, Frederica (mezzo-soprano); Somerville, N.J., 6/1/45

Von Stroheim, Erich Oswald Hans Carl Maria von Nordenwall (actor, director); Vienna (1885–1957)

von Zell, Harry (broadcaster); Indianapolis, 7/11/06

Vreeland, Diana (Diana Da Iziel) (fashion journalist, museum consultant); Paris (1903?–1989)

# W

Wagner, Lindsay (actress); Los Angeles, 6/22/49

Wagner, Robert (actor); Detroit, 2/10/30

Wagner, Robert F. (ex-mayor of New York City); New York City (1910–1991)

Wagner, Wilhelm Richard (composer); Leipzig, Germany (1813–1883)

Wahlberg, Mark (actor, model, musician); Dorchester, Mass., 6/5/71

Waits, Tom (blues singer); Pomona, Calif., 12/7/49

Waldheim, Kurt (ex-UN secretary-general); St. Andrae-Wörden, Austria, 12/21/18

Walesa, Lech (Polish labor leader and ex-president); Popowo, Poland, 9/29/43

Walken, Christopher (actor); Queens, N.Y., 3/31/43

Walker, Alice (novelist, poet); Eatonon, Ga., 2/9/44

**Walker,** Nancy (Ann Myrtle Swoyer) (actress, comedienne); Philadelphia **(1922–1992)**
**Walker,** Robert (actor); Salt Lake City **(1918–1951)**
**Walker,** T-Bone (blues singer); Linden, Tex. **(1910–1975)**
**Wallace,** DeWitt (publisher); St. Paul, Minn. **(1889–1981)**
**Wallace,** George C. (ex-governor); Clio, Ala. **(1919–1998)**
**Wallace,** Irving (novelist); Chicago **(1916–1990)**
**Wallace,** Mike (Myron Wallace) (TV interviewer, commentator); Brookline, Mass., 5/9/18
**Wallach,** Eli (actor); Brooklyn, N.Y., 12/7/15
**Wallenberg,** Raoul (diplomat, humanitarian); Stockholm **(1912–1947)**
**Wallenstein,** Alfred (conductor); Chicago **(1898–1983)**
**Waller,** Thomas "Fats" (pianist); New York City **(1904–1943)**
**Wallis,** Hal (film producer); Chicago **(1899–1986)**
**Walpole,** Horace (statesman, novelist); London **(1717–1797)**
**Walsh,** J. T. (actor); San Francisco, Calif. **(1944–1998)**
**Waltari,** Mika (novelist); Helsinki **(1903–1979)**
**Walter,** Bruno (Bruno Walter Schlesinger) (orchestra conductor); Berlin **(1876–1962)**
**Walters,** Barbara (TV commentator); Boston, 9/25/31
**Walton,** Izaak (author); Stafford, England **(1593–1683)**
**Wambaugh,** Joseph (author, screenwriter); East Pittsburgh, 1/22/37
**Wanamaker,** John (merchant); Philadelphia **(1838–1922)**
**Wanamaker,** Sam (actor, director); Chicago **(1919–1993)**
**Ward,** Barbara (economist); York, England **(1914–1981)**
**Ward,** Rachel (actress); Cornwell Manor, England, 9/12/57
**Warhol,** Andy (Warhola) (artist); McKeesport, Pa. **(1928–1987)**
**Waring,** Fred (band leader); Tyrone, Pa. **(1900–1984)**
**Warner,** H. B. (Henry Bryan Warner Lickford) (actor); London **(1876–1958)**
**Warren,** Lesley Ann (actress); New York City, 8/16/46
**Warren,** Robert Penn (novelist); Guthrie, Ky. **(1905–1989)**
**Warrick,** Ruth (actress); St. Joseph, Mo., 6/29/15
**Warwick,** Dionne (singer); East Orange, N.J., 12/12/41
**Washington,** Booker T(aliaferro) (educator); Franklin County, Va. **(1856–1915)**
**Washington,** Denzel (actor); Mt. Vernon, N.Y., 12/28/54
**Washington,** George (1st U.S. president); Westmoreland County, Va. **(1732–1799)**
**Washington,** Harold (ex-mayor of Chicago); Chicago **(1922–1987)**
**Waters,** Ethel (actress, singer); Chester, Pa. **(1896–1977)**
**Waters,** Muddy (McKinley Morganfield) (singer, guitarist); Rolling Fork, Miss. **(1915–1983)**
**Waterston,** Sam (actor); Cambridge, Mass., 11/15/40
**Watson,** James Dewey (scientist, Nobel laureate); Chicago, 4/6/28
**Watson,** Thomas John (industrialist); Campbell, N.Y. **(1874–1956)**
**Watt,** James (inventor); Greenock, Scotland **(1736–1819)**
**Watteau,** Jean-Antoine (painter); Valanciennes, France **(1684–1721)**
**Wattleton,** Faye (family planning advocate); St. Louis, 7/8/43
**Watts,** André (concert pianist); Nuremberg, Germany, 6/20/46
**Waugh,** Alec (Alexander Raban Waugh) (novelist); London **(1898–1981)**
**Waugh,** Evelyn (novelist); London **(1903–1966)**
**Wayans,** Damon (actor, comedian, writer, producer); New York City, 9/4/60
**Wayans,** Keenan Ivory (actor, comedian, writer, director); New York City, 6/8/58
**Wayne,** Anthony (military officer); Waynesboro (family farm), nr. Paoli, Pa. **(1745–1796)**
**Wayne,** David (David McMeekan) (actor); Traverse City, Mich. **(1914–1995)**
**Wayne,** John (Marion Michael Morrison) (actor); Winterset, Iowa **(1907–1979)**
**Weaver,** Dennis (actor); Joplin, Mo., 6/4/25
**Weaver,** Fritz (actor); Pittsburgh, 1/19/26
**Weaver,** Sigourney (actress); New York City, 10/8/49
**Webb,** Clifton (Webb Parmelee Hollenbeck) (actor); Indianapolis **(1893–1966)**
**Webb,** Jack (actor, producer); Santa Monica, Calif. **(1920–1982)**
**Weber,** Karl Maria Friedrich Ernst von (composer); nr. Lübeck, Germany **(1786–1826)**
**Webster,** Daniel (statesman); Salisbury, N.H. **(1782–1852)**
**Webster,** Margaret (producer, director, actress); New York City **(1905–1973)**
**Webster,** Noah (lexicographer); West Hartford, Conn. **(1758–1843)**
**Weill,** Kurt (composer); Dessau, Germany **(1900–1950)**
**Weir,** Peter (director); Sydney, Australia, 8/21/44
**Weissmuller,** Johnny (Peter John Weissmuller) (actor, swimmer); Freidorf, Romania **(1904–1984)**
**Weizmann,** Chaim (statesman); Grodno Province, Russia **(1874–1952)**
**Welch,** Raquel (Raquel Tejada) (actress); Chicago, 9/5/40
**Weld,** Tuesday (Susan Ker Weld) (actress); New York City, 8/27/43

**Welk,** Lawrence (band leader); Strasburg, N.D. **(1903–1992)**
**Welles,** Orson (actor, director, producer); Kenosha, Wis. **(1915–1985)**
**Wellington,** Duke of (Arthur Wellesley) (statesman); Ireland **(1769–1852)**
**Wells,** H(erbert) G(eorge) (author); Bromley, England **(1866–1946)**
**Wells,** Ida Bell (Barnett) (journalist); Holly Springs, Miss. **(1862–1931)**
**Welty,** Eudora (novelist); Jackson, Miss. **(1909–2001)**
**Wenner,** Jann (publisher); New York City, 1/7/46
**Werfel,** Franz (novelist); Prague **(1890–1945)**
**Werner,** Oskar (Josef Schliessmayer) (actor, director); Vienna **(1922–1984)**
**Wertheimer,** Linda (radio journalist); Carlsbad, N.M., 3/19/43
**Wertmueller,** Lina (Arcanguela Felice Assunta W. von Elgg) (director); Rome, 8/14/28
**Wesley,** John (religious leader); Epworth Rectory, Lincolnshire, England **(1703–1791)**
**West,** Benjamin (painter); Springfield, Pa. **(1738–1820)**
**West,** Dame Rebecca (Cicily Fairfield) (novelist); County Kerry, Ireland **(1892–1983)**
**West,** Jessamyn (novelist); nr. North Vernon, Ind. **(1902–1984)**
**West,** Mae (actress); Brooklyn, N.Y. **(1893–1980)**
**West,** Nathanael (Nathan Weinstein) (novelist); New York City **(1902–1940)**
**Westheimer,** Dr. Ruth (Karola Ruth Siegel) (human sexuality expert); Frankfurt, Germany, 1928
**Westinghouse,** George (inventor); Central Bridge, N.Y. **(1846–1914)**
**Westmoreland,** William Childs (ex-Army chief of staff); Saxon, S.C., 3/26/14
**Weyden,** Roger van der (painter); Tournai, Belgium **(c. 1400–1464)**
**Wharton,** Edith Newbold (née Jones) (novelist); New York City **(1862–1937)**
**Wheatley,** Phillis (poet); Senegal **(c. 1753–1784)**
**Wheeler,** Bert (Albert Jerome Wheeler) (comedian); Paterson, N.J. **(1895–1968)**
**Whistler,** James Abbott McNeill (painter, etcher); Lowell, Mass. **(1834–1903)**
**Whitaker,** Forest (actor); Longview, Tex., 7/15/61
**White,** Betty (actress); Oak Park, Ill., 1/17/22
**White,** Edmund (writer); Cincinnati, Ohio, 1/13/40
**White,** E(lwyn) B(rooks) (author); Mt. Vernon, N.Y. **(1899–1985)**
**White,** Pearl (actress); Green Ridge, Mo. **(1889–1938)**
**White,** Stanford (architect); New York City **(1853–1906)**
**White,** Theodore H. (historian); Boston **(1915–1986)**
**White,** Vanna (TV personality); Conway, S.C., 2/18/57
**White,** William Allen (journalist); Emporia, Kans. **(1868–1944)**
**Whitehead,** Alfred North (mathematician, philosopher); Isle of Thanet, England **(1861–1947)**
**Whiteman,** Paul (band leader); Denver **(1891–1967)**
**Whiting,** Margaret (singer, actress); Detroit, 7/22/24
**Whitman,** Walt (Walter) (poet); West Hills, N.Y. **(1819–1892)**
**Whitmore,** James (actor); White Plains, N.Y., 10/1/21
**Whitney,** Cornelius Vanderbilt (sportsman); New York City **(1899–1992)**
**Whitney,** Eli (inventor); Westboro, Mass. **(1765–1825)**
**Whitney,** John Hay (publisher); Ellsworth, Maine **(1904–1982)**
**Whittier,** John Greenleaf (poet); Haverhill, Mass. **(1807–1892)**
**Wideman,** John Edgar (writer); Washington, D.C., 6/14/41
**Widmark,** Richard (actor); Sunrise, Minn., 12/26/14
**Wiesel,** Elie (Eliezer) (author); Signet, Romania, 9/30/28
**Wiesenthal,** Simon (Nazi hunter); Buchach, Ukraine, 12/31/08
**Wilde,** Cornel (film actor, producer); New York City **(1915–1989)**
**Wilde,** Oscar Fingal O'Flahertie Wills (author); Dublin **(1854–1900)**
**Wilder,** Billy (Samuel Wilder) (film producer, director); Vienna **(1906–2002)**
**Wilder,** Gene (Jerome Silberman) (actor, writer, director, producer); Milwaukee, 6/11/35
**Wilder,** Thornton (author); Madison, Wis. **(1897–1975)**
**Wilkins,** Roy (civil rights leader); St. Louis **(1901–1981)**
**William,** Prince (heir to British throne); London, 6/21/82
**Williams,** Andy (singer); Wall Lake, Iowa, 12/3/30
**Williams,** Anson (actor, director); Los Angeles, 9/25/49
**Williams,** Billy Dee (actor); New York City, 4/6/37
**Williams,** Cindy (actress); Van Nuys, Calif., 8/22/47
**Williams,** Edward Bennett (lawyer); Hartford, Conn. **(1920–1988)**
**Williams,** Emlyn (actor, playwright); Mostyn, Wales **(1905–1987)**
**Williams,** Esther (actress, swimmer); Los Angeles, 8/8/23
**Williams,** Gluyas (cartoonist); San Francisco **(1888–1982)**
**Williams,** Hank, Sr. (Hiram King Williams) (singer); Georgiana, Ala. **(1923–1953)**
**Williams,** Joe (singer); Cordele, Ga. **(1918–1999)**
**Williams,** John T. (composer, conductor); Queens, N.Y., 2/8/32
**Williams,** Lucinda (singer, songwriter); Lake Charles, La., 1/26/53

**Williams,** Paul (singer, composer, actor); Omaha, Neb., 9/19/40
**Williams,** Robin (actor, producer); Chicago, 7/21/52
**Williams,** Roger (clergyman); London **(1603?–1683)**
**Williams,** Tennessee (Thomas L. Williams) (playwright); Columbus, Miss. **(1911–1983)**
**Williams,** Treat (Richard Williams) (actor); Rowayton, Conn., 12/1/51
**Williams,** Vanessa (actress, singer); Milwood, N.Y., 3/18/63
**Williams,** William Carlos (physician, poet); Rutherford, N.J. **(1883–1963)**
**Williamson,** Nicol (actor); Hamilton, Scotland, 9/14/38
**Willkie,** Wendell Lewis (lawyer); Elwood, Ind. **(1892–1944)**
**Willis,** Bruce (actor); Germany, 3/19/55
**Willson,** Meredith (composer); Mason City, Iowa **(1902–1984)**
**Wilson,** August (poet, writer, playwright); Pittsburgh, 4/27/45
**Wilson,** Brian (musician); Inglewood, Calif., 6/20/42
**Wilson,** Don (radio and TV announcer); Lincoln, Neb. **(1900–1982)**
**Wilson,** Dooley (actor, musician); Tyler, Tex. **(1894–1953)**
**Wilson,** Edmund (literary critic, author); Red Bank, N.J. **(1895–1972)**
**Wilson,** Flip (Clerow Wilson) (comedian); Jersey City, N.J. **(1933–1998)**
**Wilson,** Harold (ex-prime minister); Huddersfield, England **(1916–1995)**
**Wilson,** Nancy (singer); Chillicothe, Ohio, 2/20/37
**Wilson,** Sloan (novelist); Norwalk, Conn., 5/8/20
**Wilson,** (Thomas) Woodrow (28th U.S. president); Staunton, Va. **(1856–1924)**
**Winchell,** Walter (columnist); New York City **(1897–1972)**
**Windsor,** Duchess of (Bessie Wallis Warfield) Blue Ridge Summit, Pa. **(1896–1986)**
**Windsor,** Duke of (formerly King Edward VIII of England); Richmond Park, England **(1894–1972)**
**Winfrey,** Oprah (TV host, actress, producer); Kosciusko, Miss., 1/29/54
**Winger,** Debra (Mary Debra) (actress); Cleveland, 5/17/55
**Winkler,** Henry (actor, director, producer); New York City, 10/30/45
**Winningham,** Mare (actress); Phoenix, Ariz., 5/16/59
**Winter,** Johnny (guitarist); Leland, Miss., 2/23/44
**Winters,** Jonathan (comedian); Dayton, Ohio, 11/11/25
**Winters,** Shelley (Shirley Schrift) (actress); East St. Louis, Ill., 8/18/22
**Winthrop,** John (first governor, Massachusetts Bay Colony); Suffolk, England **(1588–1649)**
**Wise,** Stephen Samuel (rabbi); Budapest **(1874–1949)**
**Withers,** Jane (actress); Atlanta, 4/12/26
**Witherspoon,** Reese (actress); Nashville, 3/22/76
**Wittig,** Georg F. K. (chemist, Nobel laureate); Berlin, Germany **(1897–1987)**
**Wittgenstein,** Ludwig (Josef Johann) (philosopher); Vienna **(1889–1951)**
**Wodehouse,** P(elham) G(renville) (novelist); Guildford, England **(1881–1975)**
**Wolf,** Scott (actor); Boston, 6/4/68
**Wolfe,** Thomas Clayton (novelist); Asheville, N.C. **(1900–1938)**
**Wolfe,** Tom (journalist); Richmond, Va., 3/2/31
**Wolff,** Tobias (author); Birmingham, Ala., 6/19/45
**Wolsey,** Thomas (prelate, statesman); Ipswich, England **(c. 1475–1530)**
**Wonder,** Stevie (Steveland Judkins, later Steveland Morris) (singer, songwriter); Saginaw, Mich., 5/13/50
**Wong,** Anna May (Lu Tsong Wong) (actress); Los Angeles **(1907–1961)**
**Woo,** John (actor, film director, screenwriter); Guangzhou, Canton, China, 5/1/46
**Wood,** Grant (painter); Anamosa, Iowa **(1892–1942)**
**Wood,** Natalie (Natasha Viparaeff) (actress); San Francisco **(1938–1981)**
**Woods,** James (actor); Vernal, Utah, 4/18/47
**Woodhouse,** Barbara (Blackburn) (dog trainer, author, TV personality); Rathfarnham, Ireland **(1910–1988)**
**Woodruff,** Judy (broadcast journalist); Tulsa, Okla., 11/20/46
**Woodson,** Carter G. (historian); New Canton, Va. **(1875–1950)**
**Woodward,** Edward (actor); Croydon, England, 6/1/30
**Woodward,** Joanne (actress); Thomasville, Ga., 2/27/30
**Woodward,** Robert Burns (chemist, Nobel laureate); Boston **(1917–1979)**
**Woolf,** (Adeline) Virginia (née Stephens) (novelist); London **(1882–1941)**
**Woollcott,** Alexander (author, critic); Phalanx, N.J. **(1887–1943)**
**Woolley,** Monty (Edgar Montillion Woolley) (actor); New York City **(1888–1963)**

**Woolworth,** Frank (merchant); Rodman, N.Y. **(1852–1919)**
**Wopat,** Tom (actor); Lodi, Wis., 9/9/50
**Wordsworth,** William (poet); Cockermouth, England **(1770–1850)**
**Wouk,** Herman (novelist); New York City, 5/27/15
**Wovoka** (Jack Wilson) (Paiute Indian religious leader); (western Nev.) **(c. 1858–1932)**
**Wray,** Fay (actress); nr. Cardston, Alb., Canada, 9/14/07
**Wren,** Sir Christopher (architect); East Knoyle, England **(1632–1723)**
**Wright,** Frank Lloyd (architect); Richland Center, Wis. **(1869–1959)**
**Wright,** Martha (singer); Seattle, 3/23/26
**Wright,** Orville (inventor); Dayton, Ohio **(1871–1948)**
**Wright,** Richard (novelist); nr. Natchez, Miss. **(1908–1960)**
**Wright,** Wilbur (inventor); Millville, Ind. **(1867–1912)**
**Wyatt,** Jane (actress); Campgaw, N.J., 8/12/12
**Wycliffe,** John (church reformer); Hipswell, England **(1320–1384)**
**Wyeth,** Andrew (painter); Chadds Ford, Pa., 7/12/17
**Wyle,** Noah (actor); Hollywood, Calif., 6/4/71
**Wyler,** William (director); Mulhouse, France **(1902–1981)**
**Wyman,** Jane (Sarah Jane Fulks) (actress); St. Joseph, Mo., 1/4/14
**Wynette,** Tammy (Virginia Wynette Pugh) (singer); Tupelo, Miss. **(1942–1998)**
**Wynn,** Ed (Isaiah Edwin Leopold) (comedian); Philadelphia **(1886–1966)**
**Wynn,** Keenan (actor); New York City **(1916–1986)**

# X

**Xavier,** St. Francis (Jesuit missionary); Pamplona, Navarre, Spain **(1506–1552)**
**Xenophon** (soldier, historian, essayist); Athens **(c. 435–c. 355 b.c.)**
**Xerxes,** the Great (king); Persian Empire **(c. 519–465 b.c.)**

# Y

**Yeats,** William Butler (poet); nr. Dublin **(1865–1939)**
**Yeltsin,** Boris (Russian president); Yekaterinburg (then Sverdlovsk), Russia, 2/1/31
**Yevtushenko,** Yevgeny (poet); Zima, Russia, 7/18/33
**York,** Michael (actor); Fulmer, England, 3/27/42
**York,** Susannah (Fletcher) (actress); London, 1/9/42
**Yorty,** Samuel W. (ex-mayor of Los Angeles); Lincoln, Neb. **(1909–1998)**
**Yothers,** Tina (actress); Whittier, Calif., 5/5/73
**Young,** Alan (actor); North Shield, England, 11/19/19
**Young,** Andrew (civil rights leader); New Orleans, 3/12/32
**Young,** Brigham (religious leader); Whitingham, Vt. **(1801–1877)**
**Young,** Gig (Byron Barr) (actor); St. Cloud, Minn. **(1917–1978)**
**Young,** Loretta (Gretchen Young) (actress); Salt Lake City **(1913–2000)**
**Young,** Neil (singer, songwriter); Toronto, 11/12/45
**Young,** Robert (actor); Chicago **(1907–1998)**
**Youngman,** Henny (comedian); Whitechapel, London **(1906–1998)**

# Z

**Zane,** Billy (William George Zane, Jr.) (actor); Chicago, 2/24/66
**Zanuck,** Darryl F. (producer); Wahoo, Neb. **(1902–1979)**
**Zappa,** Frank (Francis Vincent Zappa, Jr.) (singer, songwriter); Baltimore **(1940–1993)**
**Zeffirelli,** Franco (director); Florence, Italy, 2/12/23
**Zellweger,** Renee (actress); Katy, Texas, 4/25/69
**Zemeckis,** Robert (filmmaker); Chicago, 1952
**Ziegfeld,** Florenz (theatrical producer); Chicago **(1869–1932)**
**Ziegler,** Karl (chemist, Nobel laureate); Helsa, Germany **(1898–1973)**
**Zimbalist,** Efrem (concert violinist); Rostov-on-Don, Russia **(1889–1985)**
**Zimbalist,** Efrem, Jr. (actor); New York City, 11/30/23
**Zimbalist,** Stephanie (actress); New York City, 10/8/56
**Zinnemann,** Fred (director); Vienna **(1907–1997)**
**Zola,** Emile (novelist); Paris **(1840–1902)**
**Zoroaster** (religious leader); Persian Empire **(c. 628–c. 551 b.c.)**
**Zucker,** Jerry (film producer, director, screenwriter); Milwaukee, 3/11/50
**Zukerman,** Pinchas (violinist); Tel Aviv, Israel, 7/16/48
**Zukor,** Adolph (movie executive); Risce, Hungary **(1873–1976)**
**Zurbarán,** Francisco de (painter); Fuentes de Cantos, Spain **(1598–1664)**
**Zweig,** Stefan (author); Vienna **(1881–1942)**
**Zwingli,** Huldrych (humanist); Wildaus, Switzerland **(1484–1531)**

# Nobel Prizes

**(For years not listed, no award was made.** *See* **p. 44 for 2002 winners.)**

## PEACE

| | |
|---|---|
| 1901 | Henri Dunant (Switzerland); Frederick Passy (France) |
| 1902 | Elie Ducommun and Albert Gobat (Switzerland) |
| 1903 | Sir William R. Cremer (UK) |
| 1904 | Institut de Droit International (Belgium) |
| 1905 | Bertha von Suttner (Austria) |
| 1906 | Theodore Roosevelt (U.S.) |
| 1907 | Ernesto T. Moneta (Italy) and Louis Renault (France) |
| 1908 | Klas P. Arnoldson (Sweden) and Frederik Bajer (Denmark) |
| 1909 | Auguste M. F. Beernaert (Belgium) and Baron Paul H. B. B. d'Estournelles de Constant de Rebecque (France) |
| 1910 | Bureau International Permanent de la Paix (Switzerland) |
| 1911 | Tobias M. C. Asser (Holland) and Alfred H. Fried (Austria) |
| 1912 | Elihu Root (U.S.) |
| 1913 | Henri La Fontaine (Belgium) |
| 1917 | International Red Cross |
| 1919 | Woodrow Wilson (U.S.) |
| 1920 | Léon Bourgeois (France) |
| 1921 | Karl H. Branting (Sweden) and Christian L. Lange (Norway) |
| 1922 | Fridtjof Nansen (Norway) |
| 1925 | Sir Austen Chamberlain (UK) and Charles G. Dawes (U.S.) |
| 1926 | Aristide Briand (France) and Gustav Stresemann (Germany) |
| 1927 | Ferdinand Buisson (France) and Ludwig Quidde (Germany) |
| 1929 | Frank B. Kellogg (U.S.) |
| 1930 | Lars O. J. Söderblom (Sweden) |
| 1931 | Jane Addams and Nicholas M. Butler (U.S.) |
| 1933 | Sir Norman Angell (UK) |
| 1934 | Arthur Henderson (UK) |
| 1935 | Karl von Ossietzky (Germany) |
| 1936 | Carlos de S. Lamas (Argentina) |
| 1937 | Lord Cecil of Chelwood (UK) |
| 1938 | Office International Nansen pour les Réfugiés (Switzerland) |
| 1944 | International Red Cross |
| 1945 | Cordell Hull (U.S.) |
| 1946 | Emily G. Balch and John R. Mott (U.S.) |
| 1947 | American Friends Service Committee (U.S.) and British Society of Friends' Service Council (UK) |
| 1949 | Lord John Boyd Orr (Scotland) |
| 1950 | Ralph J. Bunche (U.S.) |
| 1951 | Léon Jouhaux (France) |
| 1952 | Albert Schweitzer (French Equatorial Africa) |
| 1953 | George C. Marshall (U.S.) |
| 1954 | Office of U.N. High Commissioner for Refugees |
| 1957 | Lester B. Pearson (Canada) |
| 1958 | Rev. Dominique Georges Henri Pire (Belgium) |
| 1959 | Philip John Noel-Baker (UK) |
| 1960 | Albert John Luthuli (South Africa) |
| 1961 | Dag Hammarskjöld (Sweden) |
| 1962 | Linus Pauling (U.S.) |
| 1963 | Intl. Comm. of Red Cross; League of Red Cross Societies (both Geneva) |
| 1964 | Rev. Dr. Martin Luther King, Jr. (U.S.) |
| 1965 | UNICEF (United Nations Children's Fund) |
| 1968 | René Cassin (France) |
| 1969 | International Labour Organization |
| 1970 | Norman E. Borlaug (U.S.) |
| 1971 | Willy Brandt (West Germany) |
| 1973 | Henry A. Kissinger (U.S.); Le Duc Tho (North Vietnam)[1] |
| 1974 | Eisaku Sato (Japan); Sean MacBride (Ireland) |
| 1975 | Andrei D. Sakharov (USSR) |
| 1976 | Mairead Corrigan and Betty Williams (both Northern Ireland) |
| 1977 | Amnesty International |
| 1978 | Menachem Begin (Israel) and Anwar el-Sadat (Egypt) |
| 1979 | Mother Teresa of Calcutta (India) |
| 1980 | Adolfo Pérez Esquivel (Argentina) |
| 1981 | Office of the United Nations High Commissioner for Refugees |
| 1982 | Alva Myrdal (Sweden) and Alfonso García Robles (Mexico) |
| 1983 | Lech Walesa (Poland) |
| 1984 | Bishop Desmond Tutu (South Africa) |
| 1985 | International Physicians for the Prevention of Nuclear War |
| 1986 | Elie Wiesel (U.S.) |
| 1987 | Oscar Arias Sánchez (Costa Rica) |
| 1988 | UN Peacekeeping Forces |
| 1989 | Dalai Lama (Tibet) |
| 1990 | Mikhail S. Gorbachev (USSR) |
| 1991 | Daw Aung San Suu Kyi (Burma) |
| 1992 | Rigoberta Menchú (Guatemala) |
| 1993 | F. W. de Klerk and Nelson Mandela (both South Africa) |
| 1994 | Yasir Arafat (Palestine), Shimon Peres, and Yitzhak Rabin (both Israel) |
| 1995 | Joseph Rotblat and Pugwash Conference on Science and World Affairs (UK) |
| 1996 | Carlos Filipe Ximenes Belo and José Ramos-Horta (East Timor) |
| 1997 | International Campaign to Ban Landmines and Jody Williams (U.S.) |
| 1998 | John Hume and David Trimble (Northern Ireland) |
| 1999 | Doctors without Borders (France) |
| 2000 | Kim Dae Jung (South Korea) |
| 2001 | United Nations and Kofi Annan |

1. Le Duc Tho refused prize, charging that peace had not yet really been established in South Vietnam.

## LITERATURE

| | |
|---|---|
| 1901 | René F. A. Sully Prudhomme (France) |
| 1902 | Theodor Mommsen (Germany) |
| 1903 | Björnstjerne Björnson (Norway) |

| | |
|---|---|
| 1904 | Frédéric Mistral (France) and José Echegaray (Spain) |
| 1905 | Henryk Sienkiewicz (Poland) |
| 1906 | Giosuè Carducci (Italy) |
| 1907 | Rudyard Kipling (UK) |
| 1908 | Rudolf Eucken (Germany) |
| 1909 | Selma Lagerlöf (Sweden) |
| 1910 | Paul von Heyse (Germany) |
| 1911 | Maurice Maeterlinck (Belgium) |
| 1912 | Gerhart Hauptmann (Germany) |
| 1913 | Rabindranath Tagore (India) |
| 1915 | Romain Rolland (France) |
| 1916 | Verner von Heidenstam (Sweden) |
| 1917 | Karl Gjellerup (Denmark) and Henrik Pontoppidan (Denmark) |
| 1919 | Carl Spitteler (Switzerland) |
| 1920 | Knut Hamsun (Norway) |
| 1921 | Anatole France (France) |
| 1922 | Jacinto Benavente (Spain) |
| 1923 | William B. Yeats (Ireland) |
| 1924 | Wladyslaw Reymont (Poland) |
| 1925 | George Bernard Shaw (Ireland) |
| 1926 | Grazia Deledda (Italy) |
| 1927 | Henri Bergson (France) |
| 1928 | Sigrid Undset (Norway) |
| 1929 | Thomas Mann (Germany) |
| 1930 | Sinclair Lewis (U.S.) |
| 1931 | Erik A. Karlfeldt (Sweden) |
| 1932 | John Galsworthy (UK) |
| 1933 | Ivan G. Bunin (Russia) |
| 1934 | Luigi Pirandello (Italy) |
| 1936 | Eugene O'Neill (U.S.) |
| 1937 | Roger Martin du Gard (France) |
| 1938 | Pearl S. Buck (U.S.) |
| 1939 | Frans Eemil Sillanpää (Finland) |
| 1944 | Johannes V. Jensen (Denmark) |
| 1945 | Gabriela Mistral (Chile) |
| 1946 | Hermann Hesse (Switzerland) |
| 1947 | André Gide (France) |
| 1948 | Thomas Stearns Eliot (UK) |
| 1949 | William Faulkner (U.S.) |
| 1950 | Bertrand Russell (UK) |
| 1951 | Pär Lagerkvist (Sweden) |
| 1952 | François Mauriac (France) |
| 1953 | Sir Winston Churchill (UK) |
| 1954 | Ernest Hemingway (U.S.) |
| 1955 | Halldór Kiljan Laxness (Iceland) |
| 1956 | Juan Ramón Jiménez (Spain) |
| 1957 | Albert Camus (France) |
| 1958 | Boris Pasternak (USSR) (declined) |
| 1959 | Salvatore Quasimodo (Italy) |
| 1960 | St. John Perse (Alexis Léger) (France) |
| 1961 | Ivo Andric (Yugoslavia) |
| 1962 | John Steinbeck (U.S.) |
| 1963 | Giorgos Seferis (Georgiadu) (Greece) |
| 1964 | Jean-Paul Sartre (France) (declined) |
| 1965 | Mikhail Sholokhov (USSR) |
| 1966 | Shmuel Yosef Agnon (Israel) and Nelly Sachs (Sweden) |
| 1967 | Miguel Angel Asturias (Guatemala) |
| 1968 | Yasunari Kawabata (Japan) |
| 1969 | Samuel Beckett (Ireland) |
| 1970 | Aleksandr Solzhenitsyn (USSR) |
| 1971 | Pablo Neruda (Chile) |
| 1972 | Heinrich Böll (Germany) |
| 1973 | Patrick White (Australia) |
| 1974 | Eyvind Johnson and Harry Martinson (both Sweden) |
| 1975 | Eugenio Montale (Italy) |
| 1976 | Saul Bellow (U.S.) |

| | |
|---|---|
| 1977 | Vicente Aleixandre (Spain) |
| 1978 | Isaac Bashevis Singer (U.S.) |
| 1979 | Odysseus Elytis (Greece) |
| 1980 | Czeslaw Milosz (U.S.) |
| 1981 | Elias Canetti (Bulgaria) |
| 1982 | Gabriel García Márquez (Colombia) |
| 1983 | William Golding (UK) |
| 1984 | Jaroslav Seifert (Czechoslovakia) |
| 1985 | Claude Simon (France) |
| 1986 | Wole Soyinka (Nigeria) |
| 1987 | Joseph Brodsky (U.S.) |
| 1988 | Naguib Mahfouz (Egypt) |
| 1989 | Camilo José Cela (Spain) |
| 1990 | Octavio Paz (Mexico) |
| 1991 | Nadine Gordimer (South Africa) |
| 1992 | Derek Walcott (Trinidad) |
| 1993 | Toni Morrison (U.S.) |
| 1994 | Kenzaburo Oe (Japan) |
| 1995 | Seamus Heaney (Ireland) |
| 1996 | Wislawa Szymborska (Poland) |
| 1997 | Dario Fo (Italy) |
| 1998 | José Saramago (Portugal) |
| 1999 | Günter Grass (Germany) |
| 2000 | Gao Xingjian (China) |
| 2001 | V. S. Naipaul (UK) |

## PHYSICS

| | |
|---|---|
| 1901 | Wilhelm K. Roentgen (Germany), for discovery of Roentgen rays |
| 1902 | Hendrik A. Lorentz and Pieter Zeeman (Netherlands), for work on influence of magnetism upon radiation |
| 1903 | A. Henri Becquerel (France), for work on spontaneous radioactivity; and Pierre and Marie Curie (France), for study of radiation |
| 1904 | John Strutt (Lord Rayleigh) (UK), for discovery of argon in investigating gas density |
| 1905 | Philipp Lenard (Germany), for work with cathode rays |
| 1906 | Sir Joseph Thomson (UK), for investigations on passage of electricity through gases |
| 1907 | Albert A. Michelson (U.S.), for spectroscopic and metrologic investigations |
| 1908 | Gabriel Lippmann (France), for method of reproducing colors by photography |
| 1909 | Guglielmo Marconi (Italy) and Ferdinand Braun (Germany), for development of wireless |
| 1910 | Johannes D. van der Waals (Netherlands), for work with the equation of state for gases and liquids |
| 1911 | Wilhelm Wien (Germany), for his laws governing the radiation of heat |
| 1912 | Gustaf Dalén (Sweden), for discovery of automatic regulators used in lighting lighthouses and light buoys |
| 1913 | Heike Kamerlingh-Onnes (Netherlands), for work leading to production of liquid helium |
| 1914 | Max von Laue (Germany), for discovery of diffraction of Roentgen rays passing through crystals |
| 1915 | Sir William Bragg and William L. Bragg (UK), for analysis of crystal structure by X rays |
| 1917 | Charles G. Barkla (UK), for discovery of Roentgen radiation of the elements |
| 1918 | Max Planck (Germany), discoveries in connection with quantum theory |
| 1919 | Johannes Stark (Germany), discovery of Doppler effect in Canal rays and decomposition of spectrum lines by electric fields |

**1920** Charles E. Guillaume (Switzerland), for discoveries of anomalies in nickel-steel alloys

**1921** Albert Einstein (Germany), for discovery of the law of the photoelectric effect

**1922** Niels Bohr (Denmark), for investigation of structure of atoms and radiations emanating from them

**1923** Robert A. Millikan (U.S.), for work on elementary charge of electricity and photoelectric phenomena

**1924** Karl M. G. Siegbahn (Sweden), for investigations in X-ray spectroscopy

**1925** James Franck and Gustav Hertz (Germany), for discovery of laws governing impact of electrons upon atoms

**1926** Jean B. Perrin (France), for work on discontinuous structure of matter and discovery of the equilibrium of sedimentation

**1927** Arthur H. Compton (U.S.), for discovery of Compton phenomenon; and Charles T. R. Wilson (UK), for method of perceiving paths taken by electrically charged particles

**1928** In 1929, the 1928 prize was awarded to Sir Owen Richardson (UK), for work on the phenomenon of thermionics and discovery of the Richardson Law

**1929** Prince Louis Victor de Broglie (France), for discovery of the wave character of electrons

**1930** Sir Chandrasekhara Raman (India), for work on diffusion of light and discovery of the Raman effect

**1932** In 1933, the prize for 1932 was awarded to Werner Heisenberg (Germany), for creation of quantum mechanics

**1933** Erwin Schrödinger (Austria) and Paul A. M. Dirac (UK), for discovery of new fertile forms of the atomic theory

**1935** James Chadwick (UK), for discovery of the neutron

**1936** Victor F. Hess (Austria), for discovery of cosmic radiation; and Carl D. Anderson (U.S.), for discovery of the positron

**1937** Clinton J. Davisson (U.S.) and George P. Thomson (UK), for discovery of diffraction of electrons by crystals

**1938** Enrico Fermi (Italy), for identification of new radioactivity elements and discovery of nuclear reactions effected by slow neutrons

**1939** Ernest Orlando Lawrence (U.S.), for development of the cyclotron

**1943** Otto Stern (U.S.), for detection of magnetic momentum of protons

**1944** Isidor Isaac Rabi (U.S.), for work on magnetic movements of atomic particles

**1945** Wolfgang Pauli (Austria), for work on atomic fissions

**1946** Percy Williams Bridgman (U.S.), for studies and inventions in high-pressure physics

**1947** Sir Edward Appleton (UK), for discovery of layer that reflects radio short waves in the ionosphere

**1948** Patrick M. S. Blackett (UK), for improvement on Wilson chamber and discoveries in cosmic radiation

**1949** Hideki Yukawa (Japan), for mathematical prediction, in 1935, of the meson

**1950** Cecil Frank Powell (UK), for method of photographic study of atom nucleus, and for discoveries about mesons

**1951** Sir John Douglas Cockcroft (UK) and Ernest T. S. Walton (Ireland), for work in 1932 on transmutation of atomic nuclei

**1952** Edward Mills Purcell and Felix Bloch (U.S.), for work in measurement of magnetic fields in atomic nuclei

**1953** Fritz Zernike (Netherlands), for development of "phase contrast" microscope

**1954** Max Born (UK), for work in quantum mechanics; and Walther Bothe (Germany), for work in cosmic radiation

**1955** Polykarp Kusch and Willis E. Lamb, Jr. (U.S.), for atomic measurements

**1956** William Shockley, Walter H. Brattain, and John Bardeen (all U.S.), for developing electronic transistor

**1957** Tsung Dao Lee and Chen Ning Yang (China), for disproving principle of conservation of parity

**1958** Pavel A. Cherenkov, Ilya M. Frank, and Igor E. Tamm (all USSR), for work resulting in development of cosmic-ray counter

**1959** Emilio Segre and Owen Chamberlain (both U.S.), for demonstrating the existence of the anti-proton

**1960** Donald A. Glaser (U.S.), for invention of "bubble chamber" to study subatomic particles

**1961** Robert Hofstadter (U.S.), for determination of shape and size of atomic nucleus; Rudolf Mössbauer (Germany), for method of producing and measuring recoil-free gamma rays

**1962** Lev D. Landau (USSR), for his theories about condensed matter

**1963** Eugene Paul Wigner, Maria Goeppert Mayer (both U.S.), and J. Hans D. Jensen (Germany), for research on structure of atom and its nucleus

**1964** Charles Hard Townes (U.S.), Nikolai G. Basov, and Aleksandr M. Prochorov (both USSR), for developing maser and laser principle of producing high-intensity radiation

**1965** Richard P. Feynman, Julian S. Schwinger (both U.S.), and Shinichiro Tomonaga (Japan), for research in quantum electrodynamics

**1966** Alfred Kastler (France), for work on energy levels inside atom

**1967** Hans A. Bethe (U.S.), for work on energy production of stars

**1968** Luis Walter Alvarez (U.S.), for study of subatomic particles

**1969** Murray Gell-Mann (U.S.), for study of subatomic particles

**1970** Hannes Alfvén (Sweden), for theories in plasma physics; and Louis Néel (France), for discoveries in antiferromagnetism and ferromagnetism

**1971** Dennis Gabor (UK), for invention of holographic method of three-dimensional imagery

**1972** John Bardeen, Leon N. Cooper, and John Robert Schrieffer (all U.S.), for theory of superconductivity, where electrical resistance in certain metals vanishes above absolute zero temperature

**1973** Ivar Giaever (U.S.), Leo Esaki (Japan), and Brian D. Josephson (UK), for theories that have advanced and expanded the field of miniature electronics

**1974** Antony Hewish (UK), for discovery of pulsars; Martin Ryle (UK), for using radiotelescopes to probe outer space with high degree of precision

**1975** James Rainwater (U.S.), Ben Mottelson, and Aage N. Bohr (both Denmark), for showing that the atomic nucleus is asymmetrical

**1976** Burton Richter and Samuel C. C. Ting (both U.S.), for discovery of subatomic particles known as J and psi

**1977** Philip W. Anderson, John H. Van Vleck (both U.S.), and Nevill F. Mott (UK), for work underlying computer memories and electronic devices

**1978** Arno A. Penzias and Robert W. Wilson (both U.S.), for work in cosmic microwave radiation; Piotr L. Kapitsa (USSR), for basic inventions and discoveries in low-temperature physics

**1979** Steven Weinberg, Sheldon L. Glashow (both U.S.), and Abdus Salam (Pakistan), for developing theory that electromagnetism and the "weak" force, which causes radioactive decay in some atomic nuclei, are facets of the same phenomenon

**1980** James W. Cronin and Val L. Fitch (both U.S.), for work concerning the asymmetry of subatomic particles

**1981** Nicolaas Bloembergen, Arthur L. Schawlow (both U.S.), and Kai M. Siegbahn (Sweden), for developing technologies with lasers and other devices to probe the secrets of complex forms of matter

**1982** Kenneth G. Wilson (U.S.), for analysis of changes in matter under pressure and temperature

**1983** Subrahmanyam Chandrasekhar and William A. Fowler (both U.S.), for complementary research on processes involved in the evolution of stars

**1984** Carlo Rubbia (Italy) and Simon van der Meer (Netherlands), for their role in discovering three subatomic particles, a step toward developing a single theory to account for all natural forces

**1985** Klaus von Klitzing (Germany), for developing an exact way of measuring electrical conductivity

**1986** Ernst Ruska, Gerd Binnig (both Germany), and Heinrich Rohrer (Switzerland), for work on microscopes

**1987** K. Alex Müller (Switzerland) and J. Georg Bednorz (Germany), for their discovery of high-temperature superconductors

**1988** Leon M. Lederman, Melvin Schwartz, and Jack Steinberger (all U.S.), for research that improved the understanding of elementary particles and forces

**1989** Norman F. Ramsey (U.S.), for work leading to development of the atomic clock, and Hans G. Dehmelt (U.S.) and Wolfgang Paul (Germany), for developing methods to isolate atoms and subatomic particles

**1990** Richard E. Taylor (Canada), Jerome I. Friedman, and Dr. Henry W. Kendall (both U.S.), for their "breakthrough in our understanding of matter" that confirmed the reality of quarks

**1991** Pierre-Gilles de Gennes (France), for his discoveries about the ordering of molecules in substances ranging from "super" glue to an exotic form of liquid helium

**1992** George Charpak (France), for his inventions of particle detectors

**1993** Joseph H. Taylor and Russell A. Hulse (both U.S.), for their discovery of a binary pulsar

**1994** Clifford G. Shull (U.S.) and Bertram N. Brockhouse (Canada), for adapting beams of neutrons as probes to explore the atomic structure of matter

**1995** Martin L. Perl and Frederick Reines (both U.S.), for their discoveries of "two of nature's most remarkable subatomic particles"—the tau and the neutrino

**1996** David M. Lee, Robert C. Richardson, and Douglas D. Osheroff (all U.S.), for their discovery of superfluity in helium-3

**1997** Steven Chu, William D. Phillips (both U.S.), and Claude Cohen-Tannoudji (France), for developing a method to cool and trap atoms using light from lasers

**1998** Robert B. Laughlin (U.S.), Horst L. Störmer (Germany), and Daniel C. Tsui (U.S.), for their discovery of a new form of quantum fluid with fractionally charged excitations

**1999** Gerardus 't Hooft (Netherlands) and Martinus J. G. Veltman (Netherlands), for their theory concerning the production of the Sun's energy

**2000** Zhores I. Alferov (Russia), Herbert Kroemer, and Jack S. Kilby (both U.S.), for work in the development of transistors and microchip technology

**2001** Wolfgang Ketterle (Germany), Eric A. Cornell, and Carl E. Wieman (both U.S.) for discovering Bose-Einstein condensate, a new state of matter

## CHEMISTRY

**1901** Jacobus H. van't Hoff (Netherlands), for laws of chemical dynamics and osmotic pressure in solutions

**1902** Emil Fischer (Germany), for experiments in sugar and purin groups of substances

**1903** Svante A. Arrhenius (Sweden), for his electrolytic theory of dissociation

**1904** Sir William Ramsay (UK), for discovery and determination of place of inert gaseous elements in air

**1905** Adolf von Baeyer (Germany), for work on organic dyes and hydroaromatic combinations

**1906** Henri Moissan (France), for isolation of fluorine, and introduction of electric furnace

**1907** Eduard Buchner (Germany), for discovery of cell-less fermentation and investigations in biological chemistry

**1908** Sir Ernest Rutherford (UK), for investigations into disintegration of elements

**1909** Wilhelm Ostwald (Germany), for work on catalysis and investigations into chemical equilibrium and reaction rates

**1910** Otto Wallach (Germany), for work in the field of alicyclic compounds

**1911** Marie Curie (France), for discovery of elements radium and polonium

**1912** Victor Grignard (France), for reagent discovered by him; and Paul Sabatier

(France), for methods of hydrogenating organic compounds

**1913** Alfred Werner (Switzerland), for linking up atoms within the molecule

**1914** Theodore W. Richards (U.S.), for determining atomic weight of many chemical elements

**1915** Richard Willstätter (Germany), for research into coloring matter of plants, especially chlorophyll

**1918** Fritz Haber (Germany), for synthetic production of ammonia

**1920** Walther Nernst (Germany), for work in thermochemistry

**1921** Frederick Soddy (UK), for investigations into origin and nature of isotopes

**1922** Francis W. Aston (UK), for discovery of isotopes in nonradioactive elements and for discovery of the whole number rule

**1923** Fritz Pregl (Austria), for method of microanalysis of organic substances discovered by him

**1925** In 1926, the 1925 prize was awarded to Richard Zsigmondy (Germany), for work on the heterogeneous nature of colloid solutions

**1926** Theodor Svedberg (Sweden), for work on disperse systems

**1927** In 1928, the 1927 prize was awarded to Heinrich Wieland (Germany), for investigations of bile acids and kindred substances

**1928** Adolf Windaus (Germany), for investigations on constitution of the sterols and their connection with vitamins

**1929** Sir Arthur Harden (UK) and Hans K. A. S. von Euler-Chelpin (Sweden), for research of fermentation of sugars

**1930** Hans Fischer (Germany), for work on coloring matter of blood and leaves and for his synthesis of hemin

**1931** Karl Bosch and Friedrich Bergius (both Germany), for invention and development of chemical high-pressure methods

**1932** Irving Langmuir (U.S.), for work in realm of surface chemistry

**1934** Harold C. Urey (U.S.), for discovery of heavy hydrogen

**1935** Frédéric and Irène Joliot-Curie (both France), for synthesis of new radioactive elements

**1936** Peter J. W. Debye (Netherlands), for investigations on dipole moments and diffraction of X-rays and electrons in gases

**1937** Walter N. Haworth (UK), for research on carbohydrates and vitamin C; and Paul Karrer (Switzerland), for work on carotenoids, flavins, and vitamins A and B

**1938** Richard Kuhn (Germany), for carotenoid study and vitamin research (declined)

**1939** Adolf Butenandt (Germany), for work on sexual hormones (declined the prize); and Leopold Ruzicka (Switzerland), for work with polymethylenes

**1943** Georg Hevesy De Heves (Hungary), for work on use of isotopes as indicators

**1944** Otto Hahn (Germany), for work on atomic fission

**1945** Arttur Illmari Virtanen (Finland), for research in the field of conservation of fodder

**1946** James B. Sumner (U.S.), for crystallizing enzymes; John H. Northrop and Wendell M. Stanley (both U.S.), for preparing enzymes and virus proteins in pure form

**1947** Sir Robert Robinson (UK), for research in plant substances

**1948** Arne Tiselius (Sweden), for biochemical discoveries and isolation of mouse paralysis virus

**1949** William Francis Giauque (U.S.), for research in thermodynamics, especially effects of low temperature

**1950** Otto Diels and Kurt Alder (both Germany), for discovery of diene synthesis enabling scientists to study structure of organic matter

**1951** Glenn T. Seaborg and Edwin H. McMillan (both U.S.), for discovery of plutonium

**1952** Archer John Porter Martin and Richard Laurence Millington Synge (both UK), for development of partition chromatography

**1953** Hermann Staudinger (Germany), for research in giant molecules

**1954** Linus C. Pauling (U.S.), for study of forces holding together protein and other molecules

**1955** Vincent du Vigneaud (U.S.), for work on pituitary hormones

**1956** Sir Cyril Hinshelwood (UK) and Nikolai N. Semenov (USSR), for parallel research on chemical reaction kinetics

**1957** Sir Alexander Todd (UK), for research with chemical compounds that are factors in heredity

**1958** Frederick Sanger (UK), for determining molecular structure of insulin

**1959** Jaroslav Heyrovsky (Czechoslovakia), for development of polarography, an electrochemical method of analysis

**1960** Willard F. Libby (U.S.), for "atomic time clock" to measure age of objects by measuring their radioactivity

**1961** Melvin Calvin (U.S.), for establishing chemical steps during photosynthesis

**1962** Max F. Perutz and John C. Kendrew (UK), for mapping protein molecules with X-rays

**1963** Karl Ziegler (Germany) and Giulio Natta (Italy), for work in uniting simple hydrocarbons into large molecular substances

**1964** Dorothy Mary Crowfoot Hodgkin (UK), for determining structure of compounds needed in combatting pernicious anemia

**1965** Robert B. Woodward (U.S.), for work in synthesizing complicated organic compounds

**1966** Robert Sanderson Mulliken (U.S.), for research on bond holding atoms together in molecule

**1967** Manfred Eigen (Germany), Ronald G. W. Norrish, and George Porter (both UK), for work in high-speed chemical reactions

**1968** Lars Onsager (U.S.), for development of system of equations in thermodynamics

**1969** Derek H. R. Barton (UK) and Odd Hassel (Norway), for study of organic molecules

**1970** Luis F. Leloir (Argentina), for discovery of sugar nucleotides and their role in biosynthesis of carbohydrates

**1971** Gerhard Herzberg (Canada), for contributions to knowledge of electronic structure and geometry of molecules, particularly free radicals

**1972** Christian Boehmer Anfinsen, Stanford Moore, and William Howard Stein (all U.S.), for pioneering studies in enzymes

1973 Ernst Otto Fischer (W. Germany) and Geoffrey Wilkinson (UK), for work that could solve problem of automobile exhaust pollution

1974 Paul J. Flory (U.S.), for developing analytic methods to study properties and molecular structure of long-chain molecules

1975 John W. Cornforth (Australia) and Vladimir Prelog (Switzerland), for research on structure of biological molecules such as antibiotics and cholesterol

1976 William N. Lipscomb, Jr. (U.S.), for work on the structure and bonding mechanisms of boranes

1977 Ilya Prigogine (Belgium), for contributions to nonequilibrium thermodynamics, particularly the theory of dissipative structures

1978 Peter Mitchell (UK), for contributions to the understanding of biological energy transfer

1979 Herbert C. Brown (U.S.) and Georg Wittig (West Germany), for developing a group of substances that facilitate very difficult chemical reactions

1980 Paul Berg, Walter Gilbert (both U.S.), and Frederick Sanger (UK), for developing methods to map the structure and function of DNA, the substance that controls the activity of the cell

1981 Roald Hoffmann (U.S.) and Kenichi Fukui (Japan), for applying quantum-mechanics theories to predict the course of chemical reactions

1982 Aaron Klug (UK), for research in the detailed structures of viruses and components of life

1983 Henry Taube (U.S.), for research on how electrons transfer between molecules in chemical reactions

1984 R. Bruce Merrifield (U.S.), for research that revolutionized the study of proteins

1985 Herbert A. Hauptman and Jerome Karle (both U.S.), for their outstanding achievements in the development of direct methods for the determination of crystal structures

1986 Dudley R. Herschback, Yuan T. Lee (both U.S.), and John C. Polanyi (Canada), for their work on "reaction dynamics"

1987 Donald J. Cram, Charles J. Pedersen (both U.S.), and Jean-Marie Lehn (France), for wide-ranging research that has included the creation of artificial molecules that can mimic vital chemical reactions of the processes of life

1988 Johann Deisenhofer, Robert Huber, and Hartmut Michel (all West Germany), for ฅฅฅฅฅฅฅฅฅฅฅ ฅฅฅ ฅฅฅฅฅฅฅฅ ฅฅ ฅฅฅฅฅฅฅฅ ฅฅฅฅ ฅฅฅฅ, a crucial role in photosynthesis

1989 Thomas R. Cech and Sidney Altman (both U.S.), for their discovery, independently, that RNA could actively aid chemical reactions in the cells

1990 Elias James Corey (U.S.), for developing new ways to synthesize complex molecules ordinarily found in nature

1991 Richard R. Ernst (Switzerland), for refinements he developed in nuclear magnetic-resonance spectroscopy

1992 Rudolph A. Marcus (U.S.), for his mathematical analysis of how the overall energy in a system of interacting molecules changes and induces an electron to jump from one molecule to another

1993 Kary B. Mullis (U.S.) and Michael Smith (Canada), for their contributions to the science of genetics

1994 George A. Olah (U.S.), University of Southern California in Los Angeles, for research that opened new ways to break apart and rebuild compounds of carbon and hydrogen

1995 F. Sherwood Rowland, Mario Molina (both U.S.), and Paul Crutzen (Netherlands), for their pioneering work in explaining the chemical processes that deplete the earth's ozone shield

1996 Richard E. Smalley, Robert F. Curl, Jr. (both U.S.), and Harold W. Kroto (UK), for discovery of a new class of carbon molecule

1997 Paul D. Boyer (U.S.), Jens C. Skou (Denmark), and John E. Walker (UK), for discoveries about a molecule that allows the human body to store and transfer energy between cells

1998 Walter Kohn (U.S.) and John A. Pople (UK), for their developments in the study of the properties of molecules and the chemical processes in which they are involved

1999 Ahmed H. Zewail (Egypt and U.S.), for creating the world's fastest camera, which captures atoms in motion

2000 Alan J. Heeger, Alan G. MacDiarmid (both U.S.), and Hideki Shirakawa (Japan), for the discovery and development of conductive polymers

2001 William S. Knowles (U.S.) and Ryoji Noyori (Japan), for their work on chirally catalyzed hydrogenation reactions, and K. Barry Sharpless (U.S.), for his work on chirally catalyzed oxidation reactions

## PHYSIOLOGY OR MEDICINE

1901 Emil A. von Behring (Germany), for work on serum therapy against diphtheria

1902 Sir Ronald Ross (UK), for work on malaria

1903 Niels R. Finsen (Denmark), for his treatment of lupus vulgaris with concentrated light rays

1904 Ivan P. Pavlov (USSR), for work on the physiology of digestion

1905 Robert Koch (Germany), for work on tuberculosis

1906 Camillo Golgi (Italy) and Santiago Ramón y Cajal (Spain), for work on structure of the nervous system

1907 Charles L. A. Laveran (France), for work with protozoa in the generation of disease

1908 Paul Ehrlich (Germany) and Elie Metchnikoff (USSR), for work on immunity

1909 Theodor Kocher (Switzerland), for work on the thyroid gland

1910 Albrecht Kossel (Germany), for achievements in the chemistry of the cell

1911 Allvar Gullstrand (Sweden), for work on the dioptrics of the eye

1912 Alexis Carrel (France), for work on vascular ligature and grafting of blood vessels and organs

1913 Charles Richet (France), for work on anaphylaxy

1914 Robert Bárány (Austria), for work on physiology and pathology of the vestibular system

1919 Jules Bordet (Belgium), for discoveries in connection with immunity

**1920** August Krogh (Denmark), for discovery of regulation of capillaries' motor mechanism

**1922** In 1923, the 1922 prize was shared by Archibald V. Hill (UK), for discovery relating to heat-production in muscles; and Otto Meyerhof (Germany), for correlation between consumption of oxygen and production of lactic acid in muscles

**1923** Sir Frederick Banting (Canada) and John J. R. Macleod (Scotland), for discovery of insulin

**1924** Willem Einthoven (Netherlands), for discovery of the mechanism of the electrocardiogram

**1926** Johannes Fibiger (Denmark), for discovery of the Spiroptera carcinoma

**1927** Julius Wagner-Jauregg (Austria), for use of malaria inoculation in treatment of dementia paralytica

**1928** Charles Nicolle (France), for work on typhus exanthematicus

**1929** Christiaan Eijkman (Netherlands), for discovery of the antineuritic vitamins; and Sir Frederick Hopkins (UK), for discovery of growth-promoting vitamins

**1930** Karl Landsteiner (U.S.), for discovery of human blood groups

**1931** Otto H. Warburg (Germany), for discovery of the character and mode of action of the respiratory ferment

**1932** Sir Charles Sherrington (UK) and Edgar D. Adrian (U.S.), for discoveries of the function of the neuron

**1933** Thomas H. Morgan (U.S.), for discoveries on hereditary function of the chromosomes

**1934** George H. Whipple, George R. Minot, and William P. Murphy (U.S.), for discovery of liver therapy against anemias

**1935** Hans Spemann (Germany), for discovery of the organizer effect in embryonic development

**1936** Sir Henry Dale (UK) and Otto Loewi (Germany), for discoveries on chemical transmission of nerve impulses

**1937** Albert Szent-Györgyi von Nagyrapolt (Hungary), for discoveries on biological combustion

**1938** Corneille Heymans (Belgium), for determining importance of sinus and aorta mechanisms in the regulation of respiration

**1939** Gerhard Domagk (Germany), for antibacterial effect of prontocilate

**1943** Henrik Dam (Denmark) and Edward A. Doisy (U.S.), for analysis of vitamin K

**1944** Joseph Erlanger and Herbert Spencer Gasser (both U.S.), for work on functions of the nerve threads

**1945** Sir Alexander Fleming, Ernst Boris Chain, and Sir Howard Florey (all UK), for discovery of penicillin

**1946** Herman J. Muller (U.S.), for hereditary effects of X-rays on genes

**1947** Carl F. and Gerty T. Cori (U.S.), for work on animal starch metabolism; Bernardo A. Houssay (Argentina), for study of pituitary

**1948** Paul Mueller (Switzerland), for discovery of insect-killing properties of DDT

**1949** Walter Rudolf Hess (Switzerland), for research on brain control of body; and Antonio Caetano de Abreu Freire Egas Moniz (Portugal), for development of brain operation

**1950** Philip S. Hench, Edward C. Kendall (both U.S.), and Tadeus Reichstein (Switzerland), for discoveries about hormones of adrenal cortex

**1951** Max Theiler (South Africa), for development of anti-yellow-fever vaccine

**1952** Selman A. Waksman (U.S.), for discovery of streptomycin

**1953** Fritz A. Lipmann (Germany-U.S.) and Hans Adolph Krebs (Germany-UK), for studies of living cells

**1954** John F. Enders, Thomas H. Weller, and Frederick C. Robbins (all U.S.), for work with cultivation of polio virus

**1955** Hugo Theorell (Sweden), for work on oxidation enzymes

**1956** Dickinson W. Richards, Jr., André F. Cournand (both U.S.), and Werner Forssmann (Germany), for new techniques in treating heart disease

**1957** Daniel Bovet (Italy), for development of drugs to relieve allergies and relax muscles during surgery

**1958** Joshua Lederberg (U.S.), for work with genetic mechanisms; George W. Beadle and Edward L. Tatum (both U.S.), for discovering how genes transmit hereditary characteristics

**1959** Severo Ochoa and Arthur Kornberg (both U.S.), for discoveries related to compounds within chromosomes that play a vital role in heredity

**1960** Sir Macfarlane Burnet (Australia) and Peter Brian Medawar (UK), for discovery of acquired immunological tolerance

**1961** Georg von Bekesy (U.S.), for discoveries about physical mechanisms of stimulation within cochlea

**1962** James D. Watson (U.S.), Maurice H. F. Wilkins, and Francis H. C. Crick (both UK), for determining structure of deoxyribonucleic acid (DNA)

**1963** Alan Lloyd Hodgkin, Andrew Fielding Huxley (both UK), and Sir John Carew Eccles (Australia), for research on nerve cells

**1964** Konrad E. Bloch (U.S.) and Feodor Lynen (Germany), for research on mechanism and regulation of cholesterol and fatty-acid metabolism

**1965** François Jacob, André Lwoff, and Jacques Monod (all France), for study of regulatory activities in body cells

**1966** Charles Brenton Huggins (U.S.), for studies in hormone treatment of cancer of prostate; Francis Peyton Rous (U.S.), for discovery of tumor-producing viruses

**1967** Haldan K. Hartline, George Wald, and Ragnar Granit (all U.S.), for work on human eye

**1968** Robert W. Holley, Har Gobind Khorana, and Marshall W. Nirenberg (all U.S.), for studies of genetic code

**1969** Max Delbruck, Alfred D. Hershey, and Salvador E. Luria (all U.S.), for study of mechanism of virus infection in living cells

**1970** Julius Axelrod (U.S.), Ulf S. von Euler (Sweden), and Sir Bernard Katz (UK), for studies of how nerve impulses are transmitted within the body

**1971** Earl W. Sutherland, Jr. (U.S.), for research on how hormones work

**1972** Gerald M. Edelman (U.S.), and Rodney R. Porter (UK), for research on the chemical structure and nature of antibodies

**1973** Karl von Frisch, Konrad Lorenz (both Austria), and Nikolaas Tinbergen (Netherlands), for their studies of individual and social behavior patterns

**1974** George E. Palade, Christian de Duve (both U.S.), and Albert Claude (Belgium), for contributions to understanding inner workings of living cells

**1975** David Baltimore, Howard M. Temin, and Renato Dulbecco (all U.S.), for work in interaction between tumor viruses and genetic material of the cell

**1976** Baruch S. Blumberg and D. Carleton Gajdusek (both U.S.), for discoveries concerning new mechanisms for the origin and dissemination of infectious diseases

**1977** Rosalyn S. Yalow, Roger C. L. Guillemin, and Andrew V. Schally (all U.S.), for research in role of hormones in chemistry of the body

**1978** Daniel Nathans, Hamilton Smith (both U.S.), and Werner Arber (Switzerland), for discovery of restriction enzymes and their application to problems of molecular genetics

**1979** Allan McLeod Cormack (U.S.) and Godfrey Newbold Hounsfield (UK), for developing computed axial tomography (CAT scan) X-ray technique

**1980** Baruj Benacerraf, George D. Snell (both U.S.), and Jean Dausset (France), for discoveries that explain how the structure of cells relates to organ transplants and diseases

**1981** Roger W. Sperry, David H. Hubel (both U.S.), and Torsten N. Wiesel (Sweden), for studies vital to understanding the organization and functioning of the brain

**1982** Sune Bergstrom, Bengt Samuelsson (both Sweden), and John R. Vane (UK), for research in prostaglandins, hormonelike substances involved in a wide range of illnesses

**1983** Barbara McClintock (U.S.), for her discovery of mobile genes in the chromosomes of a plant that change the future generations of plants they produce

**1984** Cesar Milstein (UK/Argentina), Georges J. F. Kohler (West Germany), and Niels K. Jerne (UK/Denmark), for their work in Immunology

**1985** Michael S. Brown and Joseph L. Goldstein (both U.S.), for their work, which has drastically enlightened our understanding of cholesterol metabolism and increased our possibilities to prevent and treat atherosclerosis and heart attacks

**1986** Rita Levi-Montalcini (dual U.S./Italy) and Stanley Cohen (U.S.), for their contributions to the understanding of substances that influence cell growth

**1987** Susumu Tonegawa (Japan), for his discoveries of how the body can suddenly marshal its immunological defenses against millions of different disease agents that it has never encountered before

**1988** Gertrude B. Elion, George H. Hitchings (both U.S.), and Sir James Black (UK), for their discoveries of important principles for drug treatment

**1989** J. Michael Bishop and Harold E. Varmus (both U.S.), for their unifying theory of cancer development

**1990** Joseph E. Murray and E. Donnall Thomas (both U.S.), for their pioneering work in transplants

**1991** Erwin Neher and Bert Sakmann (both Germany), for their research, particularly for the development of a technique called patch clamp

**1992** Edmond H. Fischer and Edwin G. Krebs (both U.S.), for their discovery of a regulatory mechanism affecting almost all cells

**1993** Phillip A. Sharp (U.S.) and Richard J. Roberts (UK), for their independent discovery in 1977 of "split genes"

**1994** Alfred G. Gilman and Martin Rodbell (both U.S.), for discovery of G-proteins that help cells respond to outside signals

**1995** Edward B. Lewis, Eric F. Wieschaus (both U.S.), and Christiane Nüsslein-Volhard (Germany), for studies of the fruit fly that will help explain congenital malformations in humans

**1996** Peter C. Doherty (Australia) and Rolf M. Zinkernagel (Switzerland), for discoveries about how the immune system recognizes virus-infected cells

**1997** Stanley B. Prusiner (U.S.), for discovery of a new type of germ, called prions, that causes degenerative brain disorders

**1998** Robert F. Furchgott, Louis J. Ignarro, and Ferid Murad (all U.S.), for discovering that nitric oxide acts as a signal in the cardiovascular system

**1999** Günter Blobel (U.S.), for discovering that proteins have intrinsic signals that govern their transport and localization in the cell

**2000** Arvid Carlsson (Sweden), Paul Greengard, and Eric R. Kandel (both U.S.), for discoveries concerning signal transduction in the nervous system

**2001** Leland H. Hartwell (U.S.), R. Timothy Hunt, and Paul M. Nurse (both UK), for discoveries concerning control of the cell cycle, which may make new cancer treatments possible

## ECONOMIC SCIENCE

**1969** Ragnar Frisch (Norway) and Jan Tinbergen (Netherlands), for work in econometrics (application of mathematics and statistical methods to economic theories and problems)

**1970** Paul A. Samuelson (U.S.), for raising the level of scientific analysis in economic theory

**1971** Simon Kuznets (U.S.), for developing concept of using a country's gross national product to determine its economic growth

**1972** Kenneth J. Arrow (U.S.) and Sir John R. Hicks (UK), for theories that help to assess business risk and government economic and welfare policies

**1973** Wassily Leontief (U.S.), for devising the input-output technique to determine how different sectors of an economy interact

**1974** Gunnar Myrdal (Sweden) and Friedrich A. von Hayek (UK), for pioneering analysis of the interdependence of economic, social, and institutional phenomena

1975  Leonid V. Kantorovich (USSR) and Tjalling C. Koopmans (U.S.), for work on the theory of optimum allocation of resources

1976  Milton Friedman (U.S.), for work in consumption analysis and monetary history and theory, and for demonstration of complexity of stabilization policy

1977  Bertil Ohlin (Sweden) and James E. Meade (UK), for contributions to theory of international trade and international capital movements

1978  Herbert A. Simon (U.S.), for research into the decision-making process within economic organizations

1979  Sir Arthur Lewis (UK) and Theodore Schultz (U.S.), for work on economic problems of developing nations

1980  Lawrence R. Klein (U.S.), for developing models for forecasting economic trends and shaping policies to deal with them

1981  James Tobin (U.S.), for analyses of financial markets and their influence on spending and saving by families and businesses

1982  George J. Stigler (U.S.), for work on government regulation in the economy and the functioning of industry

1983  Gerard Debreu (U.S.), in recognition of his work on the basic economic problem of how prices operate to balance what producers supply with what buyers want

1984  Sir Richard Stone (UK) for his work to develop the systems widely used to measure the performance of national economics

1985  Franco Modigliani (U.S.), for his pioneering work in analyzing the behavior of household savers and the functioning of financial markets

1986  James M. Buchanan (U.S.), for his development of new methods for analyzing economic and political decision-making

1987  Robert M. Solow (U.S.), for seminal contributions to the theory of economic growth

1988  Maurice Allais (France), for his pioneering development of theories to better understand market behavior and the efficient use of resources

1989  Trygve Haavelmo (Norway), for his pioneering work in methods for testing economic theories

1990  Harry M. Markowitz, William F. Sharpe, and Merton H. Miller (all U.S.), whose work provided new tools for weighing the risks and rewards of different investments and for valuing corporate stocks and bonds

1991  Ronald Coase (U.S.), for his pioneering work in how property rights and the cost of doing business affect the economy

1992  Gary S. Becker (U.S.), for "having extended the domain of economic theory to aspects of human behavior which had previously been dealt with—if at all—by other social science disciplines"

1993  Robert W. Fogel and Douglass C. North (both U.S.), for their work in economic history

1994  John F. Nash, John C. Harsanyi (both U.S.), and Reinhard Selten (Germany), for their pioneering work in game theory

1995  Robert E. Lucas, Jr. (U.S.), for having had the greatest influence on macroeconomic research since 1970

1996  James A. Mirrlees (UK) and William Vickrey (U.S.), for their fundamental contributions to the economic theory of incentives

1997  Robert C. Merton and Myron S. Scholes (both U.S.), for developing a formula that determines the value of stock options and other derivatives

1998  Amartya Sen (India), for his contributions to welfare economics

1999  Robert A. Mundell (Canada), for his work on monetary dynamics and optimum currency areas

2000  James J. Heckman and Daniel L. McFadden (both U.S.), for developing methods used in statistical analysis of individual and household behavior

2001  George A. Akerlof, A. Michael Spence, and Joseph E. Stiglitz (all U.S.), for market analyses with asymmetric information

# Pulitzer Prizes

**For years not listed, no award was made.**

## PULITZER PRIZES IN JOURNALISM

### Meritorious Public Service

1918  *New York Times;* also special award to Minna Lewinson and Henry Beetle Hough
1919  *Milwaukee Journal*
1921  *Boston Post*
1922  *New York World*
1923  *Memphis Commercial Appeal*
1924  *New York World*
1926  *Columbus* (Ga.) *Enquirer Sun*
1927  *Canton* (Ohio) *Daily News*
1928  *Indianapolis Times*
1929  *New York Evening World*
1931  *Atlanta Constitution*
1932  *Indianapolis News*
1933  *New York World-Telegram*
1934  *Medford* (Ore.) *Mail Tribune*
1935  *Sacramento Bee*
1936  *Cedar Rapids* (Iowa) *Gazette*
1937  *St. Louis Post-Dispatch*
1938  *Bismarck* (N.D.) *Tribune*
1939  *Miami Daily News*
1940  *Waterbury* (Conn.) *Republican* and *American*
1941  *St. Louis Post-Dispatch*
1942  *Los Angeles Times*
1943  *Omaha World-Herald*
1944  *New York Times*
1945  *Detroit Free Press*
1946  *Scranton* (Pa.) *Times*
1947  *Baltimore Sun*
1948  *St. Louis Post-Dispatch*
1949  (Lincoln) *Nebraska State Journal*
1950  *Chicago Daily News;* and *St. Louis Post-Dispatch*
1951  *Miami Herald;* and *Brooklyn Eagle*
1952  *St. Louis Post-Dispatch*
1953  *Whiteville* (N.C.) *News Reporter;* and *Tabor City* (N.C.) *Tribune*

1954 *Newsday* (Garden City, N.Y.)
1955 *Columbus* (Ga.) *Ledger* and *Sunday Ledger-Enquirer*
1956 *Watsonville* (Calif.) *Register-Pajaronian*
1957 *Chicago Daily News*
1958 (Little Rock) *Arkansas Gazette*
1959 *Utica* (N.Y.) *Observer Dispatch* and *Utica Daily Press*
1960 *Los Angeles Times*
1961 *Amarillo* (Tex.) *Globe-Times*
1962 *Panama City* (Fla.) *News-Herald*
1963 *Chicago Daily News*
1964 *St. Petersburg* (Fla.) *Times*
1965 *Hutchinson* (Kans.) *News*
1966 *Boston Globe*
1967 *Louisville Courier-Journal* and *Milwaukee Journal*
1968 *Riverside* (Calif.) *Press-Enterprise*
1969 *Los Angeles Times*
1970 *Newsday* (Garden City, N.Y.)
1971 *Winston–Salem* (N.C.) *Journal and Sentinel*
1972 *New York Times*
1973 *Washington Post*
1974 *Newsday* (Garden City, N.Y.)
1975 *Boston Globe*
1976 *Anchorage* (Alaska) *Daily News*
1977 *Lufkin* (Tex.) *News*
1978 *Philadelphia Inquirer*
1979 *Point Reyes* (Calif.) *Light*
1980 *Gannett News Service*
1981 *Charlotte* (N.C.) *Observer*
1982 *Detroit News*
1983 *Jackson* (Miss.) *Clarion-Ledger*
1984 *Los Angeles Times*
1985 *Fort Worth Star-Telegram*
1986 *Denver Post*
1987 *Pittsburgh Press,* reporting by Andrew Schneider and Matthew Brelis
1988 *Charlotte* (N.C.) *Observer*
1989 *Anchorage Daily News*
1990 *Philadelphia Inquirer* and *Washington* (N.C.) *Daily News*
1991 *Des Moines Register,* reporting by Jane Schorer
1992 *Sacramento Bee* for "The Sierra in Peril" series by Tom Knudson
1993 *Miami Herald*
1994 *Akron* (Ohio) *Beacon Journal*
1995 *Virgin Islands Daily News*
1996 *News and Observer* (Raleigh, N.C.)
1997 *Times-Picayune* (New Orleans, La.)
1998 *Grand Forks* (N.D.) *Herald*
1999 *Washington Post*
2000 *Washington Post*
2001 *Oregonian*
2002 *New York Times*

## Editorial

1917 *New York Tribune*
1918 *Louisville Courier-Journal*
1920 Harvey E. Newbranch *(Omaha Evening World-Herald)*
1922 Frank M. O'Brien *(New York Herald)*
1923 William Allen White *(Emporia* [Kan.] *Gazette)*
1924 *Boston Herald;* special prize: Frank I. Cobb *(New York World)*
1925 *Charleston* (S.C.) *News and Courier*
1926 Edward M. Kingsbury *(New York Times)*
1927 F. Lauriston Bullard *(Boston Herald)*
1928 Grover Cleveland Hall *(Montgomery* [Ala.] *Advertiser)*

1929 Louis Isaac Jaffe *(Norfolk Virginian-Pilot)*
1931 Charles S. Ryckman *(Fremont* [Neb.] *Tribune)*
1933 *Kansas City* (Mo.) *Star*
1934 E. P. Chase *(Atlantic* [Iowa] *News Telegraph)*
1936 Felix Morley *(Washington Post);* George B. Parker (Scripps–Howard Newspapers)
1937 John W. Owens *(Baltimore Sun)*
1938 W. W. Waymack *(Des Moines Register and Tribune)*
1939 Ronald G. Callvert *(Portland Oregonian)*
1940 Bart Howard *(St. Louis Post-Dispatch)*
1941 Reuben Maury *(New York Daily News)*
1942 Geoffrey Parsons *(New York Herald Tribune)*
1943 Forrest W. Seymour *(Des Moines Register and Tribune)*
1944 Henry J. Haskell *(Kansas City* [Mo.] *Star)*
1945 George W. Potter *(Providence* [R.I.] *Journal-Bulletin)*
1946 Hodding Carter ([Greenville, Miss.] *Delta Democrat-Times)*
1947 William H. Grimes *(Wall Street Journal)*
1948 Virginius Dabney *(Richmond Times-Dispatch)*
1949 John H. Crider *(Boston Herald);* Herbert Elliston *(Washington Post)*
1950 Carl M. Saunders *(Jackson* [Mich.] *Citizen Patriot)*
1951 William H. Fitzpatrick *(New Orleans States)*
1952 Louis LaCoss *(St. Louis Globe-Democrat)*
1953 Vermont C. Royster *(Wall Street Journal)*
1954 Don Murray *(Boston Herald)*
1955 Royce Howes *(Detroit Free Press)*
1956 Lauren K. Soth *(Des Moines Register and Tribune)*
1957 Buford Boone *(Tuscaloosa* [Ala.] *News)*
1958 Harry S. Ashmore *(Arkansas Gazette)*
1959 Ralph McGill *(Atlanta Constitution)*
1960 Lenoir Chambers *(Virginian-Pilot)*
1961 William J. Dorvillier *(San Juan* [P.R.] *Star)*
1962 Thomas M. Storke *(Santa Barbara* [Calif.] *News-Press)*
1963 Ira B. Harkey, Jr. *(Pascagoula* [Miss.] *Chronicle)*
1964 Hazel Brannon Smith *(Lexington* [Miss.] *Advertiser)*
1965 John R. Harrison *(Gainesville* [Fla.] *Daily Sun)*
1966 Robert Lasch *(St. Louis Post-Dispatch)*
1967 Eugene Patterson *(Atlanta Constitution)*
1968 John S. Knight *(Knight Newspapers)*
1969 Paul Greenberg *(Pine Bluff* [Ark.] *Commercial)*
1970 Phillip L. Geyelin *(Washington Post)*
1971 Horance G. Davis, Jr. *(Gainesville* [Fla.] *Sun)*
1972 John Strohmeyer *(Bethlehem* [Pa.] *Globe Times)*
1973 Roger Bourne Linscott *(Berkshire Eagle* [Pittsfield, Mass.])
1974 F. Gilman Spencer *(Trenton* [N.J.] *Trentonian)*
1975 John Daniell Maurice *(Charleston* [W. Va.] *Daily Mail)*
1976 Philip P. Kerby *(Los Angeles Times)*
1977 Warren L. Lerude, Foster Church, and Norman F. Cardoza *(Reno* [Nev.] *Gazette and Nevada State Journal)*
1978 Meg Greenfield *(Washington Post)*
1979 Edwin M. Yoder, Jr. *(Washington Star)*
1980 Robert L. Bartley *(Wall Street Journal)*
1982 Jack Rosenthal *(New York Times)*
1983 *Miami Herald*
1984 Albert Scardino *(Georgia Gazette)*
1985 Richard Aregood *(Philadelphia Daily News)*

1986 Jack Fuller *(Chicago Tribune)*
1987 Jonathan Freedman *(San Diego Tribune)*
1988 Jane E. Healy *(Orlando Sentinel)*
1989 Lois Wille *(Chicago Tribune)*
1990 Thomas J. Hylton *(Pottstown* [Pa.] *Mercury)*
1991 Ron Casey, Harold Jackson, and Joey Kennedy *(Birmingham* [Ala.] *News)*
1992 Maria Henson *(Lexington* [Ky.] *Herald-Leader)*
1994 R. Bruce Dold *(Chicago Tribune)*
1995 Jeffrey Good *(St. Petersburg* [Fla.] *Times)*
1996 Robert B. Semple, Jr. *(New York Times)*
1997 Michael Gartner *(Daily Tribune* [Ames, Iowa])
1998 Bernard L. Stein *(The Riverdale Press* [Bronx, N.Y.])
1999 Editorial Board *(Daily News* [New York, N.Y.])
2000 John C. Bersia *(The Orlando Sentinel* [Orlando, Fla.])
2001 David Moats *(Rutland Herald* [Rutland, Vt.])
2002 Alex Raksin and Bob Sipchen *(Los Angeles Times)*

**Correspondence**
1929 Paul Scott Mowrer *(Chicago Daily News)*
1930 Leland Stowe *(New York Herald Tribune)*
1931 H. R. Knickerbocker *(Philadelphia Public Ledger* and *New York Evening Post)*
1932 Walter Duranty *(New York Times);* Charles G. Ross *(St. Louis Post-Dispatch)*
1933 Edgar Ansel Mowrer *(Chicago Daily News)*
1934 Frederick T. Birchall *(New York Times)*
1935 Arthur Krock *(New York Times)*
1936 Wilfred C. Barber *(Chicago Tribune)*
1937 Anne O'Hare McCormick *(New York Times)*
1938 Arthur Krock *(New York Times)*
1939 Louis P. Lochner (Associated Press)
1940 Otto D. Tolischus *(New York Times)*
1941 Group award[1]
1942 Carlos P. Romulo *(Philippines Herald)*
1943 Hanson W. Baldwin *(New York Times)*
1944 Ernie Pyle (Scripps–Howard Newspaper Alliance)
1945 Harold V. (Hal) Boyle (Associated Press)
1946 Arnaldo Cortesi *(New York Times)*
1947 Brooks Atkinson *(New York Times)*

1. For the public services and the individual achievements of American news reporters in the war zones.

**Editorial Cartooning**
1922 Rollin Kirby *(New York World)*
1924 Jay Norwood Darling *(New York Tribune)*
1925 Rollin Kirby *(New York World)*
1926 D. R. Fitzpatrick *(St. Louis Post-Dispatch)*
1927 Nelson Harding *(Brooklyn Eagle)*
1928 Nelson Harding *(Brooklyn Eagle)*
1929 Rollin Kirby *(New York World)*
1930 Charles R. Macauley *(Brooklyn Eagle)*
1931 Edmund Duffy *(Baltimore Sun)*
1932 John T. McCutcheon *(Chicago Tribune)*
1933 H. M. Talburt *(Washington Daily News)*
1934 Edmund Duffy *(Baltimore Sun)*
1935 Ross A. Lewis *(Milwaukee Journal)*
1937 C. D. Batchelor *(New York Daily News)*
1938 Vaughn Shoemaker *(Chicago Daily News)*
1939 Charles G. Werner *(Daily Oklahoman* [Oklahoma City])
1940 Edmund Duffy *(Baltimore Sun)*
1941 Jacob Burck *(Chicago Times)*
1942 Herbert L. Block (NEA Service)
1943 Jay Norwood Darling *(New York Herald Tribune)*

1944 Clifford K. Berryman *(Washington Evening Star)*
1945 Bill Mauldin (United Features Syndicate)
1946 Bruce Alexander Russell *(Los Angeles Times)*
1947 Vaughn Shoemaker *(Chicago Daily News)*
1948 Reuben L. Goldberg *(New York Sun)*
1949 Lute Pease *(Newark Evening News)*
1950 James T. Berryman *(Washington Evening Star)*
1951 Reg (Reginald W.) Manning *(Arizona Republic* [Phoenix])
1952 Fred L. Packer *(New York Mirror)*
1953 Edward D. Kuekes *(Cleveland Plain Dealer)*
1954 Herbert L. Block *(Washington Post* and *Times-Herald)*
1955 Daniel R. Fitzpatrick *(St. Louis Post-Dispatch)*
1956 Robert York *(Louisville Times)*
1957 Tom Little *(Nashville Tennessean)*
1958 Bruce M. Shanks *(Buffalo Evening News)*
1959 Bill Mauldin *(St. Louis Post-Dispatch)*
1961 Carey Orr *(Chicago Tribune)*
1962 Edmund S. Valtman *(Hartford Times)*
1963 Frank Miller *(Des Moines Register)*
1964 Paul Conrad (formerly of *Denver Post,* later of *Los Angeles Times)*
1966 Don Wright *(Miami News)*
1967 Patrick B. Oliphant *(Denver Post)*
1968 Eugene Gray Payne *(Charlotte* [N.C.] *Observer)*
1969 John Fischetti *(Chicago Daily News)*
1970 Thomas F. Darcy *(Newsday* [Garden City, N.Y.])
1971 Paul Conrad *(Los Angeles Times)*
1972 Jeffrey K. MacNelly *(Richmond* [Va.] *News Leader)*
1974 Paul Szep *(Boston Globe)*
1975 Garry Trudeau (Universal Press Syndicate)
1976 Tony Auth *(Philadelphia Inquirer)*
1977 Paul Szep *(Boston Globe)*
1978 Jeffrey K. MacNelly *(Richmond* [Va.] *News Leader)*
1979 Herbert L. Block *(Washington Post)*
1980 Don Wright *(Miami News)*
1981 Mike Peters *(Dayton* [Ohio] *Daily News)*
1982 Ben Sargent *(Austin* [Tex.] *American-Statesman)*
1983 Richard Locher *(Chicago Tribune)*
1984 Paul Conrad *(Los Angeles Times)*
1985 Jeff MacNelly *(Chicago Tribune)*
1986 Jules Feiffer *(Village Voice)*
1987 Berke Breathed *(Washington Post* Writers Group)
1988 Doug Marlette *(Atlanta Constitution* and *Charlotte* [N.C.] *Observer)*
1989 Jack Higgins *(Chicago Sun-Times)*
1990 Tom Toles *(Buffalo News)*
1991 Jim Borgman *(Cincinnati Inquirer)*
1992 Signe Wilkinson *(Philadelphia Daily News)*
1993 Stephen R. Benson *(Arizona Republic)*
1994 Michael P. Ramirez *(Commercial Appeal,* Memphis)
1995 Mike Luckovich *(Atlanta Constitution)*
1996 Jim Morin *(Miami Herald)*
1997 Walt Handelsman *(Times-Picayune)*
1998 Stephen P. Breen *(Asbury Park* [N.J.] *Press)*
1999 David Horsey *(Seattle Post-Intelligencer)*
2000 Joel Pett *(Lexington* [Ky.] *Herald-Leader)*
2001 Ann Telnaes (Los Angeles Times Syndicate)
2002 Clay Bennett *(Christian Science Monitor)*

## News Photography

**1942** Milton Brooks *(Detroit News)*
**1943** Frank Noel (Associated Press)
**1944** Frank Filan (Associated Press); Earle L. Bunker *(Omaha World-Herald)*
**1945** Joe Rosenthal (Associated Press)
**1947** Arnold Hardy
**1948** Frank Cushing *(Boston Traveler)*
**1949** Nat Fein *(New York Herald Tribune)*
**1950** Bill Crouch *(Oakland Tribune)*
**1951** Max Desfor (Associated Press)
**1952** John Robinson and Don Ultang *(Des Moines Register & Tribune)*
**1953** William M. Gallagher *(Flint* [Mich.] *Journal)*
**1954** Mrs. Walter M. Schau
**1955** John L. Gaunt, Jr. *(Los Angeles Times)*
**1956** *New York Daily News*
**1957** Harry A. Trask *(Boston Traveler)*
**1958** William C. Beall *(Washington Daily News)*
**1959** William Seaman *(Minneapolis Star)*
**1960** Andrew Lopez (United Press International)
**1961** Yasushi Nagao (Mainichi Newspapers, Tokyo)
**1962** Paul Vathis (Harrisburg [Pa.] bureau of Associated Press)
**1963** Hector Rondon *(La Republica,* Caracas, Venezuela)
**1964** Robert H. Jackson *(Dallas Times Herald)*
**1965** Horst Faas (Associated Press)
**1966** Kyoichi Sawada (United Press International)
**1967** Jack R. Thornell (Associated Press)
**1968** News: Rocco Morabito *(Jacksonville* [Fla.] *Journal);* features: Toshio Sakai (United Press International)
**1969** Spot news: Edward T. Adams (Associated Press); features: Moneta Sleet, Jr.
**1970** Spot news: Steve Starr (Associated Press); features: Dallas Kinney *(Palm Beach Post)*
**1971** Spot news: John Paul Filo *(Valley Daily News* and *Daily Dispatch* [Tarentum and New Kensington, Pa.]); features: Jack Dykinga *(Chicago Sun-Times)*
**1972** Spot news: Horst Faas and Michel Laurent (Associated Press); features: Dave Kennerly (United Press International)
**1973** Spot news: Huynh Cong Ut *(Associated Press);* features: Brian Lanker *(Topeka Capital-Journal)*
**1974** Spot news: Anthony K. Roberts (Associated Press); features: Slava Veder (Associated Press)
**1975** Spot news: Gerald H. Gay *(Seattle Times);* features: Matthew Lewis *(Washington Post)*
**1976** Spot news: Stanley J. Forman *(Boston [unclear]* staff of *Louisville Courier-Journal* and *Times*
**1977** Spot news: Neal Ulevich (Associated Press) and Stanley J. Forman *(Boston Herald-American);* features: Robin Hood *(Chattanooga News-Free Press)*
**1978** Spot news: John Blair, freelance, Evansville, Ind.; features: J. Ross Baughman (Associated Press)
**1979** Spot news: Thomas J. Kelly, 3rd *(Pottstown* [Pa.] *Mercury);* features: photographic staff of *Boston Herald-American*
**1980** Features: Erwin H. Hagler *(Dallas Times Herald)*
**1981** Spot news: Larry C. Price *(Fort Worth Star-Telegram);* features: Taro M. Yamasaki *(Detroit Free Press)*

**1982** Spot news: Ron Edmonds (Associated Press); features: John H. White *(Chicago Sun-Times)*
**1983** Spot news: Bill Foley (Associated Press); features: James B. Dickman *(Dallas Times Herald)*
**1984** Spot news: Stan Grossfeld *(Boston Globe);* features: Anthony Suau *(Denver Post)*
**1985** Spot news: photographic staff of *Register,* Santa Ana, Calif.; features: Stan Grossfeld *(Boston Globe)*
**1986** Spot news: Michel duCille and Carol Guzy *(Miami Herald);* features: Tom Gralish *(Philadelphia Inquirer)*
**1987** Spot news: Kim Komenich *(San Francisco Examiner);* features: David Peterson *(Des Moines Register)*
**1988** Spot news: Scott Shaw *(Odessa* [Texas] *American);* features: Michel duCille *(Miami Herald)*
**1989** Spot news: Ron Olshwanger *(St. Louis Post-Dispatch);* features: Manny Crisostomo *(Detroit Free Press)*
**1990** Spot news: *Oakland Tribune;* features: David C. Turnley *(Detroit Free Press)*
**1991** Spot news: Greg Marinovich (Associated Press); features: William Snyder *(Dallas Morning News)*
**1992** Spot news: Associated Press staff; features: John Kaplan *(Herald* [Monterey, Calif.] and *Pittsburgh Post–Gazette)*
**1993** Spot news: William Snyder and Ken Geiger *(Dallas Morning News);* features: Associated Press
**1994** Spot news: Paul Watson *(Toronto Star);* features: Kevin Carter, freelancer for *New York Times*
**1995** Spot news: Carol Guzy *(Washington Post);* features: Associated Press Staff
**1996** Spot news: Charles Porter IV, freelance photographer for Associated Press; features: Stephanie Walsh, freelance photographer for Newhouse News Service
**1997** Spot news: Annie Wells *(Press Democrat* [Santa Rosa, Calif.]); features: Alexander Zemlianichenko (Associated Press)
**1998** Spot news: Martha Rial *(Pittsburgh Post–Gazette);* features: Clarence Williams *(Los Angeles Times)*
**1999** Spot news: Associated Press photo staff; features: Associated Press photo staff
**2000** Breaking news: photographic staff of *Denver Rocky Mountain News;* features: Carol Guzy, Michael Williamson and Lucian Perkins *(Washington Post)*
**2001** Breaking news: Alan Diaz (Associated Press); features: Matt Rainey *(Star-Ledger* [Newark, N.J.])
**2002** Breaking news: *New York Times* staff; features: *New York Times* staff

## National Telegraphic Reporting

**1942** Louis Stark *(New York Times)*
**1944** Dewey L. Fleming *(Baltimore Sun)*
**1945** James Reston *(New York Times)*
**1946** Edward A. Harris *(St. Louis Post-Dispatch)*
**1947** Edward T. Folliard *(Washington Post)*

## National Reporting

**1948** Bert Andrews *(New York Herald Tribune);* Nat S. Finney *(Minneapolis Tribune)*

1949 C. P. Trussell *(New York Times)*
1950 Edwin O. Guthman *(Seattle Times)*
1952 Anthony Leviero *(New York Times)*
1953 Don Whitehead (Associated Press)
1954 Richard Wilson (Cowles Newspapers)
1955 Anthony Lewis *(Washington Daily News)*
1956 Charles L. Bartlett *(Chattanooga Times)*
1957 James Reston *(New York Times)*
1958 Relman Morin (Associated Press) and Clark Mollenhoff *(Des Moines Register & Tribune)*
1959 Howard Van Smith *(Miami News)*
1960 Vance Trimble (Scripps-Howard Newspaper Alliance)
1961 Edward R. Cony *(Wall Street Journal)*
1962 Nathan G. Caldwell and Gene S. Graham *(Nashville Tennessean)*
1963 Anthony Lewis *(New York Times)*
1964 Merriman Smith (United Press International)
1965 Louis M. Kohlmeier *(Wall Street Journal)*
1966 Haynes Johnson *(Washington Evening Star)*
1967 Stanley Penn and Monroe Karmin *(Wall Street Journal)*
1968 Howard James *(Christian Science Monitor);* Nathan K. (Nick) Kotz *(Des Moines Register* and *Minneapolis Tribune)*
1969 Robert Cahn *(Christian Science Monitor)*
1970 William J. Eaton *(Chicago Daily News)*
1971 Lucinda Franks and Thomas Powers (United Press International)
1972 Jack Anderson *(United Feature Syndicate)*
1973 Robert Boyd and Clark Hoyt *(Knight Newspapers)*
1974 Jack White *(Providence* [R.I.] *Journal-Bulletin);* James R. Polk *(Washington Star-News)*
1975 Donald L. Barlett and James B. Steele *(Philadelphia Inquirer)*
1976 James Risser *(Des Moines Register)*
1977 Walter Mears (Associated Press)
1978 Gaylord D. Shaw *(Los Angeles Times)*
1979 James Risser *(Des Moines Register)*
1980 Bette Swenson Orsini and Charles Stafford *(St. Petersburg Times)*
1981 John M. Crewdson *(New York Times)*
1982 Rick Atkinson *(Kansas City* [Mo.] *Times)*
1983 *Boston Globe*
1984 John N. Wilford *(New York Times)*
1985 Thomas J. Knudson *(Des Moines Register)*
1986 Craig Flournoy and George Rodrigue *(Dallas Morning News)* and Arthur Howe *(Philadelphia Inquirer)*
1987 *Miami Herald,* staff; *New York Times,* staff
1988 Tim Weiner *(Philadelphia Inquirer)*
1989 Donald L. Barlett and James B. Steele *(Philadelphia Inquirer)*
1990 Ross Anderson, Bill Dietrich, Mary Ann Gwinn, and Eric Nalder *(Seattle Times)*
1991 Marjie Lundstrom and Rochelle Sharpe (Gannett News Service)
1992 Jeff Taylor and Mike McGraw *(Kansas City Star)*
1993 David Maraniss *(Washington Post)*
1994 Eileen Welsome *(Albuquerque* [N.M.] *Tribune)*
1995 Tony Horwitz *(Wall Street Journal)*
1996 Alix M. Freedman *(Wall Street Journal)*
1997 *Wall Street Journal* staff
1998 Russell Carollo and Jeff Nesmith *(Dayton* [Ohio] *Daily News)*
1999 *New York Times* staff
2000 *Wall Street Journal* staff

2001 *New York Times* staff
2002 *Washington Post* staff

## International Telegraphic Reporting

1942 Laurence Edmund Allen (Associated Press)
1943 Ira Wolfert (North American Newspaper Alliance, Inc.)
1944 Daniel De Luce (Associated Press)
1945 Mark S. Watson *(Baltimore Sun)*
1946 Homer W. Bigart *(New York Herald Tribune)*
1947 Eddy Gilmore (Associated Press)

## International Reporting

1948 Paul W. Ward *(Baltimore Sun)*
1949 Price Day *(Baltimore Sun)*
1950 Edmund Stevens *(Christian Science Monitor)*
1951 Keyes Beech and Fred Sparks *(Chicago Daily News);* Homer Bigart and Marguerite Higgins *(New York Herald Tribune);* Relman Morin and Don Whitehead (Associated Press)
1952 John M. Hightower (Associated Press)
1953 Austin C. Wehrwein *(Milwaukee Journal)*
1954 Jim G. Lucas (Scripps-Howard Newspapers)
1955 Harrison E. Salisbury *(New York Times)*
1956 William Randolph Hearst, Jr., and Frank Conniff (Hearst Newspapers); Kingsbury Smith (INS)
1957 Russell Jones (United Press)
1958 *New York Times*
1959 Joseph Martin and Philip Santora *(New York Daily News)*
1960 A. M. Rosenthal *(New York Times)*
1961 Lynn Heinzerling (Associated Press)
1962 Walter Lippmann (New York Herald Tribune Syndicate)
1963 Hal Hendrix *(Miami News)*
1964 Malcolm W. Browne (Associated Press); David Halberstam *(New York Times)*
1965 J. A. Livingston *(Philadelphia Bulletin)*
1966 Peter Arnett (Associated Press)
1967 R. John Hughes *(Christian Science Monitor)*
1968 Alfred Friendly *(Washington Post)*
1969 William Tuohy *(Los Angeles Times)*
1970 Seymour M. Hersh (Dispatch News Service)
1971 Jimmie Lee Hoagland *(Washington Post)*
1972 Peter R. Kann *(Wall Street Journal)*
1973 Max Frankel *(New York Times)*
1974 Hedrick Smith *(New York Times)*
1975 William Mullen and Ovie Carter *(Chicago Tribune)*
1976 Sydney H. Schanberg *(New York Times)*
1978 Henry Kamm *(New York Times)*
1979 Richard Ben Cramer *(Philadelphia Inquirer)*
1980 Joel Brinkley and Jay Mather *(Louisville Courier-Journal)*
1981 Shirley Christian *(Miami Herald)*
1982 John Darnton *(New York Times)*
1983 Thomas L. Friedman *(New York Times)*
1984 Karen E. House *(Wall Street Journal)*
1985 Josh Friedman, Dennis Bell, and Ozier Muhammad *(Newsday)*
1986 Lewis M. Simons, Pete Carey, and Katherine Ellison *(San Jose Mercury News)*
1987 Michael Parks *(Los Angeles Times)*
1988 Thomas L. Friedman *(New York Times)*
1989 Bill Keller *(New York Times);* Glenn Frankel *(Washington Post)*
1990 Nicholas D. Kristof and Sheryl WuDunn *(New York Times)*
1991 Caryle Murphy *(Washington Post);* Serge Schmemann *(New York Times)*

**1992** Patrick J. Sloyan (Newsday)
**1993** John F. Burns (New York Times); Roy Gutman (Newsday)
**1994** Dallas Morning News team
**1995** Mark Fritz (Associated Press)
**1996** David Rohde (Christian Science Monitor)
**1997** John F. Burns (New York Times)
**1998** New York Times staff
**1999** Wall Street Journal staff
**2000** Mark Schoofs (Village Voice [New York, N.Y.])
**2001** Ian Johnson (Wall Street Journal) and Paul Salopek (Chicago Tribune)
**2002** Barry Bearak (New York Times)

## Reporting
**1917** Herbert B. Swope (New York World)
**1918** Harold A. Littledale (New York Evening Post)
**1920** John J. Leary, Jr. (New York World)
**1921** Louis Seibold (New York World)
**1922** Kirke L. Simpson (Associated Press)
**1923** Alva Johnston (New York Times)
**1924** Magner White (San Diego Sun)
**1925** James W. Mulroy and Alvin H. Goldstein (Chicago Daily News)
**1926** William Burke Miller (Louisville Courier-Journal)
**1927** John T. Rogers (St. Louis Post-Dispatch)
**1929** Paul Y. Anderson (St. Louis Post-Dispatch)
**1930** Russell D. Owen (New York Times); special award: W. O. Dapping (Auburn [N.Y.] Citizen)
**1931** A. B. MacDonald (Kansas City [Mo.] Star)
**1932** W. C. Richards, D. D. Martin, J. S. Pooler, F. D. Webb, and J. N. W. Sloan (Detroit Free Press)
**1933** Francis A. Jamieson (Associated Press)
**1934** Royce Brier (San Francisco Chronicle)
**1935** William H. Taylor (New York Herald Tribune)
**1936** Lauren D. Lyman (New York Times)
**1937** John J. O'Neill (New York Herald Tribune); William Leonard Laurence (New York Times); Howard W. Blakeslee (Associated Press); Gobind Behari Lal (Universal Service); David Dietz (Scripps–Howard Newspapers)
**1938** Raymond Sprigle (Pittsburg Post-Gazette)
**1939** Thomas L. Stokes (New York World-Telegram)
**1940** S. Burton Heath (New York World-Telegram)
**1941** Westbrook Pegler (New York World-Telegram)
**1942** Stanton Delaplane (San Francisco Chronicle)
**1943** George Weller (Chicago Daily News)
**1944** Paul Schoenstein and associates (New York Journal-American)
**1945** Jack S. McDowall (San Francisco Call-Bulletin)
**1946** William Leonard Laurence (New York Times)
**1947** Frederick Woltman (New York World-Telegram)
**1948** George E. Goodwin (Atlanta Journal)
**1949** Malcolm Johnson (New York Sun)
**1950** Meyer Berger (New York Times)
**1951** Edward S. Montgomery (San Francisco Examiner)
**1952** George de Carvalho (San Francisco Chronicle)
**1953** Editorial staff (Providence Journal and Evening Bulletin);[1] Edward J. Mowery (New York World-Telegram and Sun)[2]
**1954** Vicksburg (Miss.) Sunday Post-Herald;[1] Alvin Scott McCoy (Kansas City [Mo.] Star)[2]

**1955** Mrs. Caro Brown (Alice [Tex.] Daily Echo);[1] Roland Kenneth Towery (Cuero [Tex.] Record)[2]
**1956** Lee Hills (Detroit Free Press);[1] Arthur Daley (New York Times)[2]
**1957** Salt Lake Tribune;[1] Wallace Turner and William Lambert (Portland Oregonian)[2]
**1958** Fargo [N.D.] Forum;[1] George Beveridge (Washington [D.C.] Evening Star)[2]
**1959** Mary Lou Werner (Washington [D.C.] Evening Star);[1] John Harold Brislin (Scranton [Pa.] Tribune & Scrantonian)[2]
**1960** Jack Nelson (Atlanta Constitution);[1] Miriam Ottenberg (Washington Evening Star)[2]
**1961** Sanche de Gramont (New York Herald Tribune);[1] Edgar May (Buffalo Evening News)[2]
**1962** Robert D. Mullins (Deseret News, Salt Lake City);[1] George Bliss (Chicago Tribune)[2]
**1963** Sylvan Fox, Anthony Shannon, and William Longgood (New York World-Telegram and Sun);[1] Oscar Griffin, Jr. (former editor of Pecos [Tex.] Independent and Enterprise, now on staff of Houston Chronicle)[2]

1. Reporting under pressure of edition deadlines.
2. Reporting not under pressure of edition deadlines.

## General Local Reporting
**1964** Norman C. Miller (Wall Street Journal)
**1965** Melvin H. Ruder (Hungry Horse News, Columbia Falls, Mont.)
**1966** Los Angeles Times staff
**1967** Robert V. Cox (Chambersburg [Pa.] Public Opinion)
**1968** Detroit Free Press staff
**1969** John Fetterman (Louisville Times and Courier-Journal)
**1970** Thomas Fitzpatrick (Chicago Sun-Times)
**1971** Akron (Ohio) Beacon staff
**1972** Richard Cooper and John Machacek (Rochester [N.Y.] Times-Union)
**1973** Chicago Tribune
**1974** Arthur M. Petacque and Hugh F. Hough (Chicago Sun-Times)
**1975** Xenia (Ohio) Daily Gazette
**1976** Gene Miller (Miami Herald)
**1977** Margo Huston (Milwaukee Journal)
**1978** Richard Whitt (Louisville Courier-Journal)
**1979** Staff of San Diego (Calif.) Evening Tribune
**1980** Staff of Philadelphia Inquirer
**1981** Longview (Wash.) Daily News
**1982** Kansas City (Mo.) Star and Kansas City (Mo.) Times
**1983** Jackson (Miss.) Clarion-Ledger and Daily News
**1984** Newsday

## General News Reporting
**1985** Thomas Turcol (Virginian-Pilot and Ledger-Star)
**1986** Edna Buchanan (Miami Herald)
**1987** Akron Beacon Journal staff
**1988** Alabama Journal (Montgomery) staff; Lawrence (Mass.) Eagle-Tribune staff
**1989** Louisville Courier-Journal staff
**1990** San Jose (Calif.) Mercury News

## Spot News Reporting
**1991** Miami Herald staff
**1992** New York Newsday staff
**1993** Los Angeles Times staff
**1994** New York Times staff

1995   *Los Angeles Times* staff
1996   Robert D. McFadden *(New York Times)*
1997   *Newsday* staff (Long Island, N.Y.)

## Breaking News Reporting
1998   *Los Angeles Times* staff
1999   *Hartford Courant* staff
2000   *Denver Post* staff
2001   *The Miami Herald* staff
2002   *Wall Street Journal* staff

## Special Local Reporting
1964   James V. Magee, Albert V. Gaudiosi, and Frederick A. Meyer *(Philadelphia Bulletin)*
1965   Gene Goltz *(Houston Post)*
1966   John A. Frasca *(Tampa Tribune)*
1967   Gene Miller *(Miami Herald)*
1968   J. Anthony Lukas *(New York Times)*
1969   Albert L. Delugach and Denny Walsh *(St. Louis Globe-Democrat)*
1970   Harold Eugene Martin *(Montgomery Advertiser)*
1971   William Hugh Jones *(Chicago Tribune)*
1972   Timothy Leland, Gerard N. O'Neill, Stephen A. Kurkjian, and Ann DeSantis *(Boston Globe)*
1973   Sun Newspapers of Omaha, Neb.
1974   William Sherman *(New York Daily News)*
1975   *Indianapolis Star*
1976   *Chicago Tribune*
1977   Acel Moore and Wendell Rawls, Jr. *(Philadelphia Inquirer)*
1978   Anthony R. Dolan *(Stamford* [Conn.] *Advocate)*
1979   Gilbert M. Gaul and Elliot G. Jaspin *(Pottsville* [Pa.] *Republican)*
1980   Nils J. Bruzelius, Alexander B. Hawes, Jr., Stephen A. Kurkjian, Robert M. Porterfield, and Joan Vennochi *(Boston Globe)*
1981   Clark Hallas and Robert B. Lowe *(Arizona Daily Star,* Tucson)
1982   Paul Henderson *(Seattle Times)*
1983   Loretta Tofani *(Washington Post)*
1984   Kenneth Cooper, Joan FitzGerald, Jonathan Kaufman, Norman Lockman, Gary McMillan, Kirk Scharfenberg, and David Wessel *(Boston Globe)*

## Investigative Reporting
1985   Lucy Morgan, Jack Reed *(St. Petersburg* [Fla.] *Times),* and William K. Marimow *(Philadelphia Inquirer)*
1986   Jeffrey A. Marx and Michael M. York *(Lexington* [Ky.] *Herald Leader)*
1987   Daniel R. Biddle, H. G. Bissinger, and Fredric N. Tulsky *(Philadelphia Inquirer)*
1988   Dean Baquet, William C. Gaines, and Ann Marie Lipinski *(Chicago Tribune)*
1989   Bill Dedman *(Atlanta Journal and Constitution)*
1990   Lou Kilzer and Chris Ison *(Minneapolis-St. Paul Star Tribune)*
1991   Joseph T. Hallinan and Susan M. Headden *(Indianapolis Star)*
1992   Lorraine Adams and Dan Malone *(Dallas Morning News)*
1993   Jeff Brazil and Steve Berry *(Orlando* [Fla.] *Sentinel)*
1994   *Providence* (R.I.) *Journal-Bulletin* staff
1995   Stephanie Saul and Brian Donovan *(Newsday)*

1996   *Orange County Register* staff (Santa Ana, Calif.)
1997   Eric Nalder, Deborah Nelson, and Alex Tizon *(Seattle Times)*
1998   Gary Cohn and Will Englund *(Baltimore Sun)*
1999   *The Miami Herald* staff
2000   Sang-Hun Choe, Charles J. Hanley, and Martha Mendoza (Associated Press)
2001   David Willman *(Los Angeles Times)*
2002   Sari Horwitz, Scott Higham, and Sarah Cohen *(Washington Post)*

## Feature Writing
1979   Jon D. Franklin *(Baltimore Evening Sun)*
1980   Madeleine Blais *(Miami Herald)*
1981   Teresa Carpenter (*Village Voice,* New York)
1982   Saul Pett (Associated Press)
1983   Nan Robertson *(New York Times)*
1984   Peter M. Rinearson *(Seattle Times)*
1985   Alice Steinbach *(Baltimore Sun)*
1986   John Camp *(St. Paul Pioneer Press and Dispatch)*
1987   Steve Twomey *(Philadelphia Inquirer)*
1988   Jacqui Banaszynski *(St. Paul Pioneer Press Dispatch)*
1989   David Zucchino *(Philadelphia Inquirer)*
1990   Dave Curtin *(Colorado Springs Gazette Telegraph)*
1991   Sheryl James *(St. Petersburg* [Fla.] *Times)*
1992   Howell Raines *(New York Times)*
1993   George Lardner, Jr. *(Washington Post)*
1994   Isabel Wilkerson *(New York Times)*
1995   Ron Suskind *(Wall Street Journal)*
1996   Rick Bragg *(New York Times)*
1997   Lisa Pollak *(Baltimore Sun)*
1998   Thomas French *(St. Petersburg* [Fla.] *Times)*
1999   Angelo B. Henderson *(Wall Street Journal)*
2000   J. R. Moehringer *(Los Angeles Times)*
2001   Tom Hallman, Jr. *(Oregonian)*
2002   Barry Siegel *(Los Angeles Times)*

## Commentary
1970   Marquis W. Childs *(St. Louis Post-Dispatch)*
1971   William A. Caldwell *(Record* [Hackensack, N.J.])
1972   Mike Royko *(Chicago Daily News)*
1973   David S. Broder *(Washington Post)*
1974   Edwin A. Roberts, Jr. *(National Observer)*
1975   Mary McGrory *(Washington Star)*
1976   Walter W. (Red) Smith *(New York Times)*
1977   George F. Will *(Washington Post* Writers Group)
1978   William Safire *(New York Times)*
1979   Russell Baker *(New York Times)*
1980   Ellen H. Goodman *(Boston Globe)*
1981   Dave Anderson *(New York Times)*
1982   Art Buchwald *(Los Angeles Times* Syndicate)
1983   Claude Sitton *(Raleigh* [N.C.] *News & Observer)*
1984   Vermont Royster *(Wall Street Journal)*
1985   Murray Kempton *(Newsday)*
1986   Jimmy Breslin *(New York Daily News)*
1987   Charles Krauthammer *(Washington Post* Writers Group)
1988   Dave Barry *(Miami Herald)*
1989   Clarence Page *(Chicago Tribune)*
1990   Jim Murray *(Los Angeles Times)*
1991   Jim Hoagland *(Washington Post)*
1992   Anna Quindlen *(New York Times)*
1993   Liz Balmaseda *(Miami Herald)*
1994   William Raspberry *(Washington Post)*
1995   Jim Dwyer *(New York Newsday)*

1996 E. R. Shipp *(New York Daily News)*
1997 Eileen McNamara *(Boston Globe)*
1998 Mike McAlary *(New York Daily News)*
1999 Maureen Dowd *(New York Times)*
2000 Paul A. Gigot *(Wall Street Journal)*
2001 Dorothy Rabinowitz *(Wall Street Journal)*
2002 Thomas Friedman *(New York Times)*

## Criticism
1970 Ada Louise Huxtable *(New York Times)*
1971 Harold C. Schonberg *(New York Times)*
1972 Frank Peters, Jr. *(St. Louis Post-Dispatch)*
1973 Ronald Powers *(Chicago Sun-Times)*
1974 Emily Genauer *(Newsday Syndicate)*
1975 Roger Ebert *(Chicago Sun-Times)*
1976 Alan M. Kriegsman *(Washington Post)*
1977 William McPherson *(Washington Post)*
1978 Walter Kerr *(New York Times)*
1979 Paul Gapp *(Chicago Tribune)*
1980 William A. Henry, 3rd *(Boston Globe)*
1981 Jonathan Yardley *(Washington Star)*
1982 Martin Bernheimer *(Los Angeles Times)*
1983 Manuela Hoelterhoff *(Wall Street Journal)*
1984 Paul Goldberger *(New York Times)*
1985 Howard Rosenberg *(Los Angeles Times)*
1986 Donal Henahan *(New York Times)*
1987 Richard Eder *(Los Angeles Times)*
1988 Tom Shales *(Washington Post)*
1989 Michael Skube *(News and Observer* [Raleigh, N.C.])
1990 Allan Temko *(San Francisco Chronicle)*
1991 David Shaw *(Los Angeles Times)*
1993 Michael Dirda *(Washington Post)*
1994 Lloyd Schwartz *(Boston Phoenix)*
1995 Margo Jefferson *(New York Times)*
1996 Robert Campbell *(Boston Globe)*
1997 Tim Page *(Washington Post)*
1998 Michiko Kakutani *(New York Times)*
1999 Blair Kamin *(Chicago Tribune)*
2000 Henry Allen *(Washington Post)*
2001 Gail Caldwell *(Boston Globe)*
2002 Justin Davidson *(Newsday* [Long Island, N.Y.])

## Explanatory Journalism
1985 Jon Franklin *(Baltimore Evening Sun)*
1986 *New York Times*
1987 Jeff Lyon and Peter Gorner *(Chicago Tribune)*
1988 Daniel Hertzberg and James B. Stewart *(Wall Street Journal)*
1989 David Hanners, William Snyder, and Karen Blessen *(Dallas Morning News)*
1990 David A. Vise and Steve Coll *(Washington Post)*
1991 Susan C. Faludi *(Wall Street Journal)*
1992 Robert S. Capers and Eric Lipton *(Hartford Courant)*
1993 Mike Toner *(Atlanta Journal–Constitution)*
1994 Ronald Kotulak *(Chicago Tribune)*
1995 Leon Dash and Lucian Perkins *(Washington Post)*
1996 Laurie Garrett *(Newsday* [Long Island, N.Y.])
1997 Michael Vitez, Ron Cortes, and April Saul *(Philadelphia Inquirer)*
1998 Paul Salopek *(Chicago Tribune)*
1999 Richard Read *(Oregonian* [Portland, Ore.])
2000 Eric Newhouse *(Great Falls* [Mont.] *Tribune)*
2001 *Chicago Tribune* staff
2002 *New York Times* staff

## Specialized Reporting
1985 Randall Savage and Jackie Crosby *(Macon* [Ga.] *Telegraph and News)*
1986 Andrew Schneider and Mary Pat Flaherty *(Pittsburgh Press)*
1987 Alex S. Jones *(New York Times)*
1988 Walt Bogdanich *(Wall Street Journal)*
1989 Edward Humes *(Orange County Register)*
1990 Tamar Stieber *(Albuquerque* (N.M.) *Journal)*

## Beat Reporting
1991 Natalie Angier *(New York Times)*
1992 Deborah Blum *(Sacramento Bee)*
1993 Paul Ingrassia and Joseph B. White *(Wall Street Journal)*
1994 Eric Freedman and Jim Mitzelfeld *(Detroit News)*
1995 David M. Shribman *(Boston Globe)*
1996 Bob Keeler *(Newsday* [Long Island, N.Y.])
1997 Byron Acohido *(Seattle Times)*
1998 Linda Greenhouse *(New York Times)*
1999 Chuck Philips and Michael A. Hiltzik *(Los Angeles Times)*
2000 George Dohrmann *(St. Paul Pioneer Press)*
2001 David Cay Johnston *(New York Times)*
2002 Gretchen Morgenson *(New York Times)*

## PULITZER PRIZES IN LETTERS

### Fiction[1]
1918 *His Family,* Ernest Poole
1919 *The Magnificent Ambersons,* Booth Tarkington
1921 *The Age of Innocence,* Edith Wharton
1922 *Alice Adams,* Booth Tarkington
1923 *One of Ours,* Willa Cather
1924 *The Able McLaughlins,* Margaret Wilson
1925 *So Big,* Edna Ferber
1926 *Arrowsmith,* Sinclair Lewis
1927 *Early Autumn,* Louis Bromfield
1928 *The Bridge of San Luis Rey,* Thornton Wilder
1929 *Scarlet Sister Mary,* Julia Peterkin
1930 *Laughing Boy,* Oliver La Farge
1931 *Years of Grace,* Margaret Ayer Barnes
1932 *The Good Earth,* Pearl S. Buck
1933 *The Store,* T. S. Stribling
1934 *Lamb in His Bosom,* Caroline Miller
1935 *Now in November,* Josephine Winslow Johnson
1936 *Honey in the Horn,* Harold L. Davis
1937 *Gone With the Wind,* Margaret Mitchell
1938 *The Late George Apley,* John Phillips Marquand
1939 *The Yearling,* Marjorie Kinnan Rawlings
1940 *The Grapes of Wrath,* John Steinbeck
1942 *In This Our Life,* Ellen Glasgow
1943 *Dragon's Teeth,* Upton Sinclair
1944 *Journey in the Dark,* Martin Flavin
1945 *A Bell for Adano,* John Hersey
1947 *All the King's Men,* Robert Penn Warren
1948 *Tales of the South Pacific,* James A. Michener
1949 *Guard of Honor,* James Gould Cozzens
1950 *The Way West,* A. B. Guthrie, Jr.
1951 *The Town,* Conrad Richter
1952 *The Caine Mutiny,* Herman Wouk
1953 *The Old Man and the Sea,* Ernest Hemingway
1955 *A Fable,* William Faulkner
1956 *Andersonville,* MacKinlay Kantor
1958 *A Death in the Family,* James Agee
1959 *The Travels of Jaimie McPheeters,* Robert Lewis Taylor
1960 *Advise and Consent,* Allen Drury

1961   *To Kill a Mockingbird*, Harper Lee
1962   *The Edge of Sadness*, Edwin O'Connor
1963   *The Reivers*, William Faulkner
1965   *The Keepers of the House*, Shirley Ann Grau
1966   *Collected Stories of Katherine Anne Porter*, Katherine Anne Porter
1967   *The Fixer*, Bernard Malamud
1968   *The Confessions of Nat Turner*, William Styron
1969   *House Made of Dawn*, N. Scott Momaday
1970   *Collected Stories*, Jean Stafford
1972   *Angle of Repose*, Wallace Stegner
1973   *The Optimist's Daughter*, Eudora Welty
1975   *The Killer Angels*, Michael Shaara
1976   *Humboldt's Gift*, Saul Bellow
1978   *Elbow Room*, James Alan McPherson
1979   *The Stories of John Cheever*, John Cheever
1980   *The Executioner's Song*, Norman Mailer
1981   *A Confederacy of Dunces*, John Kennedy Toole
1982   *Rabbit Is Rich*, John Updike
1983   *The Color Purple*, Alice Walker
1984   *Ironweed*, William Kennedy
1985   *Foreign Affairs*, Alison Lurie
1986   *Lonesome Dove*, Larry McMurtry
1987   *A Summons to Memphis*, Peter Taylor
1988   *Beloved*, Toni Morrison
1989   *Breathing Lessons*, Anne Tyler
1990   *The Mambo Kings Play Songs of Love*, Oscar Hijuelos
1991   *Rabbit at Rest*, John Updike
1992   *A Thousand Acres*, Jane Smiley
1993   *A Good Scent From a Strange Mountain*, Robert Olen Butler
1994   *The Shipping News*, E. Annie Proulx
1995   *The Stone Diaries*, Carol Shields
1996   *Independence Day*, Richard Ford
1997   *Martin Dressler: The Tale of an American Dreamer*, Steven Millhauser
1998   *American Pastoral*, Philip Roth
1999   *The Hours*, Michael Cunningham
2000   *Interpreter of Maladies*, Jhumpa Lahiri
2001   *The Amazing Adventures of Kavalier & Clay*, Michael Chabon
2002   *Empire Falls*, Richard Russo

1. Before 1948, award was for novels only.

## History of United States

1917   *With Americans of Past and Present Days*, J. J. Jusserand, Ambassador of France to United States
1918   *A History of the Civil War, 1861–1865*, James Ford Rhodes
1920   *The War With Mexico*, Justin H. Smith
1921   *The Victory at Sea*, William Sowden Sims, in collaboration with Burton J. Hendrick
1922   *The Founding of New England*, James Truslow Adams
1923   *The Supreme Court in United States History*, Charles Warren
1924   *The American Revolution—A Constitutional Interpretation*, Charles Howard McIlwain
1925   *A History of the American Frontier*, Frederic L. Paxson
1926   *The History of the United States*, Edward Channing
1927   *Pinckney's Treaty*, Samuel Flagg Bemis
1928   *Main Currents in American Thought*, Vernon Louis Parrington
1929   *The Organization and Administration of the Union Army, 1861–1865*, Fred Albert Shannon

1930   *The War of Independence*, Claude H. Van Tyne
1931   *The Coming of the War: 1914*, Bernadotte E. Schmitt
1932   *My Experiences in the World War*, John J. Pershing
1933   *The Significance of Sections in American History*, Frederick J. Turner
1934   *The People's Choice*, Herbert Agar
1935   *The Colonial Period of American History*, Charles McLean Andrews
1936   *The Constitutional History of the United States*, Andrew C. McLaughlin
1937   *The Flowering of New England*, Van Wyck Brooks
1938   *The Road to Reunion, 1865–1900*, Paul Herman Buck
1939   *A History of American Magazines*, Frank Luther Mott
1940   *Abraham Lincoln: The War Years*, Carl Sandburg
1941   *The Atlantic Migration, 1607–1860*, Marcus Lee Hansen
1942   *Reveille in Washington*, Margaret Leech
1943   *Paul Revere and the World He Lived In*, Esther Forbes
1944   *The Growth of American Thought*, Merle Curti
1945   *Unfinished Business*, Stephen Bonsal
1946   *The Age of Jackson*, Arthur M. Schlesinger, Jr.
1947   *Scientists Against Time*, James Phinney Baxter III
1948   *Across the Wide Missouri*, Bernard DeVoto
1949   *The Disruption of American Democracy*, Roy Franklin Nichols
1950   *Art and Life in America*, Oliver W. Larkin
1951   *The Old Northwest, Pioneer Period 1815–1840*, R. Carlyle Buley
1952   *The Uprooted*, Oscar Handlin
1953   *The Era of Good Feelings*, George Dangerfield
1954   *A Stillness at Appomattox*, Bruce Catton
1955   *Great River: The Rio Grande in North American History*, Paul Horgan
1956   *The Age of Reform*, Richard Hofstadter
1957   *Russia Leaves the War: Soviet–American Relations, 1917–1920*, George F. Kennan
1958   *Banks and Politics in America: From the Revolution to the Civil War*, Bray Hammond
1959   *The Republican Era: 1869–1901*, Leonard D. White, assisted by Jean Schneider
1960   *In the Days of McKinley*, Margaret Leech
1961   *Between War and Peace: The Potsdam Conference*, Herbert Feis
1962   *The Triumphant Empire: Thunder-Clouds Gather in the West*, Lawrence H. Gipson
1963   *Washington, Village and Capital, 1800–1878*, Constance McLaughlin Green
1964   *Puritan Village: The Formation of a New England Town*, Sumner Chilton Powell
1965   *The Greenback Era*, Irwin Unger
1966   *Life of the Mind in America*, Perry Miller
1967   *Exploration and Empire: The Explorer and Scientist in the Winning of the American West*, William H. Goetzmann
1968   *The Ideological Origins of the American Revolution*, Bernard Bailyn
1969   *Origins of the Fifth Amendment*, Leonard W. Levy
1970   *Present at the Creation: My Years in the State Department*, Dean Acheson

1971  *Roosevelt: The Soldier of Freedom*, James McGregor Burns

1972  *Neither Black Nor White: Slavery and Race Relations in Brazil and the United States*, Carl N. Degler

1973  *People of Paradox: An Inquiry Concerning the Origin of American Civilization*, Michael Kammen

1974  *The Americans: The Democratic Experience*, Vol. 3, Daniel J. Boorstin

1975  *Jefferson and His Time*, Dumas Malone

1976  *Lamy of Santa Fe*, Paul Horgan

1977  *The Impending Crisis: 1841–1861*, David M. Potter

1978  *The Invisible Hand: The Managerial Revolution in American Business*, Alfred D. Chandler, Jr.

1979  *The Dred Scott Case: Its Significance in Law and Politics*, Don E. Fehrenbacher

1980  *Been in the Storm So Long*, Leon F. Litwack

1981  *American Education: The National Experience; 1783–1876*, Lawrence A. Cremin

1982  *Mary Chesnut's Civil War*, C. Vann Woodward, editor

1983  *The Transformation of Virginia, 1740–1790*, Rhys L. Isaac

1985  *The Prophets of Regulation*, Thomas K. McCraw

1986  *The Heavens and the Earth: A Political History of the Space Age*, Walter A. McDougall

1987  *Voyagers to the West: A Passage in the Peopling of America on the Eve of the Revolution*, Bernard Bailyn

1988  *The Launching of Modern American Science 1846–1876*, Robert V. Bruce

1989  *Parting the Waters*, Taylor Branch; *Battle Cry of Freedom*, James M. McPherson

1990  *In Our Image: America's Empire in the Philippines*, Stanley Karnow

1991  *A Midwife's Tale: The Life of Martha Ballard, Based on Her Diary 1785–1812*, Laurel Thatcher Ulrich

1992  *The Fate of Liberty: Abraham Lincoln and Civil Liberties*, Mark E. Neely, Jr.

1993  *The Radicalism of the American Revolution*, Gordon S. Wood

1995  *No Ordinary Time: Franklin and Eleanor Roosevelt: The Home Front in World War II*, Doris Kearns Goodwin

1996  *William Cooper's Town: Power and Persuasion on the Frontier of the Early American Republic*, Alan Taylor

1997  *Original Meanings: Politics and Ideas in the Making of the Constitution*, Jack N. Rakove

1998  *Summer for the Gods: The Scopes Trial and America's Continuing Debate Over Science and Religion*, Edward J. Larson

1999  *Gotham: A History of New York City to 1898*, Edwin G. Burrows and Mike Wallace

2000  *Freedom from Fear: The American People in Depression and War, 1929–1945*, David M. Kennedy

2001  *Founding Brothers: The Revolutionary Generation*, Joseph J. Ellis

2002  *The Metaphysical Club: A Story of Ideas in America*, Louis Menand

## Biography or Autobiography

1917  *Julia Ward Howe*, Laura E. Richards and Maude Howe Elliott, assisted by Florence Howe Hall

1918  *Benjamin Franklin, Self-Revealed*, William Cabell Bruce

1919  *The Education of Henry Adams*, Henry Adams

1920  *The Life of John Marshall*, Albert J. Beveridge

1921  *The Americanization of Edward Bok*, Edward Bok

1922  *A Daughter of the Middle Border*, Hamlin Garland

1923  *The Life and Letters of Walter H. Page*, Burton J. Hendrick

1924  *From Immigrant to Inventor*, Michael Idvorsky Pupin

1925  *Barrett Wendell and His Letters*, M. A. DeWolfe Howe

1926  *The Life of Sir William Osler*, Harvey Cushing

1927  *Whitman*, Emory Holloway

1928  *The American Orchestra and Theodore Thomas*, Charles Edward Russell

1929  *The Training of an American: The Earlier Life and Letters of Walter H. Page*, Burton J. Hendrick

1930  *The Raven*, Marquis James

1931  *Charles W. Eliot*, Henry James

1932  *Theodore Roosevelt*, Henry F. Pringle

1933  *Grover Cleveland*, Allan Nevins

1934  *John Hay*, Tyler Dennett

1935  *R. E. Lee*, Douglas S. Freeman

1936  *The Thought and Character of William James*, Ralph Barton Perry

1937  *Hamilton Fish*, Allan Nevins

1938  *Pedlar's Progress*, Odell Shepard; *Andrew Jackson*, Marquis James

1939  *Benjamin Franklin*, Carl Van Doren

1940  *Woodrow Wilson: Life and Letters*, Vols. VII and VIII, Ray Stannard Baker

1941  *Jonathan Edwards*, Ola E. Winslow

1942  *Crusader in Crinoline*, Forrest Wilson

1943  *Admiral of the Ocean Sea*, Samuel Eliot Morison

1944  *The American Leonardo: The Life of Samuel F. B. Morse*, Carleton Mabee

1945  *George Bancroft: Brahmin Rebel*, Russel Blaine Nye

1946  *Son of the Wilderness*, Linnie Marsh Wolfe

1947  *The Autobiography of William Allen White*

1948  *Forgotten First Citizen: John Bigelow*, Margaret Clapp

1949  *Roosevelt and Hopkins*, Robert E. Sherwood

1950  *John Quincy Adams and the Union* or *American Foreign Policy*, Samuel Flagg Bemis

1951  *John C. Calhoun: American Portrait*, Margaret Louise Coit

1952  *Charles Evans Hughes*, Merlo J. Pusey

1953  *Edmund Pendleton, 1721–1803*, David J. Mays

1954  *The Spirit of St. Louis*, Charles A. Lindbergh

1955  *The Taft Story*, William S. White

1956  *Benjamin Henry Latrobe*, Talbot F. Hamlin

1957  *Profiles in Courage*, John F. Kennedy

1958  *George Washington*, Douglas Southall Freeman (Vols. 1–6) and John Alexander Carroll and Mary Wells Ashworth (Vol. 7)

1959  *Woodrow Wilson, American Prophet*, Arthur Walworth

1960  *John Paul Jones*, Samuel Eliot Morison

1961 *Charles Sumner and the Coming of the Civil War*, David Donald
1963 *Henry James: Vol. II, The Conquest of London, 1870–1881; Vol. III, The Middle Years, 1881–1895*, Leon Edel
1964 *John Keats*, Walter Jackson Bate
1965 *Henry Adams* (3 Vols.), Ernest Samuels
1966 *A Thousand Days*, Arthur M. Schlesinger, Jr.
1967 *Mr. Clemens and Mark.Twain*, Justin Kaplan
1968 *Memoirs, 1925–1950*, George F. Kennan
1969 *The Man From New York*, B. L. Reid
1970 *Huey Long*, T. Harry Williams
1971 *Robert Frost: The Years of Triumph, 1915–1938*, Lawrence Thompson
1972 *Eleanor and Franklin: The Story of Their Relationship Based on Eleanor Roosevelt's Private Papers*, Joseph P. Lash
1973 *Luce and His Empire*, W. A. Swanberg
1974 *O'Neill, Son and Artist*, Louis Sheaffer
1975 *The Power Broker: Robert Moses and the Fall of New York*, Robert A. Caro
1976 *Edith Wharton: A Biography*, Richard W. B. Lewis
1977 *A Prince of Our Disorder*, John E. Mack
1978 *Samuel Johnson*, Walter Jackson Bate
1979 *Days of Sorrow and Pain: Leo Baeck and the Berlin Jews*, Leonard Baker
1980 *The Rise of Theodore Roosevelt*, Edmund Morris
1981 *Peter the Great*, Robert K. Massie
1982 *Grant: A Biography*, William S. McFeely
1983 *Growing Up*, Russell Baker
1984 *Booker T. Washington*, Louis R. Harlan
1985 *The Life and Times of Cotton Mather*, Kenneth Silverman
1986 *Louise Bogan: A Portrait*, Elizabeth Frank
1987 *Bearing the Cross: Martin Luther King, Jr., and the Southern Christian Leadership Conference*, David J. Garrow
1988 *Look Homeward: A Life of Thomas Wolfe*, David Herbert Donald
1989 *Oscar Wilde*, Richard Ellmann
1990 *Machiavelli in Hell*, Sebastian de Grazia
1991 *Jackson Pollock: An American Saga*, Steven Naifeh and Gregory White Smith
1992 *Fortunate Son: The Healing of a Vietnam Vet*, Lewis B. Puller, Jr.
1993 *Truman*, David McCullough
1994 *W. E. B. Du Bois: Biography of a Race, 1868–1919*, David Levering Lewis
1995 *Harriet Beecher Stowe: A Life*, Joan D. Hedrick
1996 *God: A Biography*, Jack Miles
1997 *Angela's Ashes: A Memoir*, Frank McCourt
1998 *Personal History*, Katharine Graham
1999 *Lindbergh*, A. Scott Berg
2000 *Vera (Mrs. Vladimir Nabokov)*, Stacy Schiff
2001 *W. E. B. DuBois: The Fight for Equality and the American Century, 1919–1963*, David Levering Lewis
2002 *John Adams*, David McCullough

**Poetry**[1]
1918 *Love Songs*, Sara Teasdale
1919 *Old Road to Paradise*, Margaret Widdemer; *Corn Huskers*, Carl Sandburg
1922 *Collected Poems*, Edwin Arlington Robinson
1923 *The Ballad of the Harp-Weaver; A Few Figs from Thistles; eight sonnets in American Poetry, 1922, A Miscellany*, Edna St. Vincent Millay

1924 *New Hampshire: A Poem With Notes and Grace Notes*, Robert Frost
1925 *The Man Who Died Twice*, Edwin Arlington Robinson
1926 *What's O'Clock*, Amy Lowell
1927 *Fiddler's Farewell*, Leonora Speyer
1928 *Tristram*, Edwin Arlington Robinson
1929 *John Brown's Body*, Stephen Vincent Benét
1930 *Selected Poems*, Conrad Aiken
1931 *Collected Poems*, Robert Frost
1932 *The Flowering Stone*, George Dillon
1933 *Conquistador*, Archibald MacLeish
1934 *Collected Verse*, Robert Hillyer
1935 *Bright Ambush*, Audrey Wurdemann
1936 *Strange Holiness*, Robert P. T. Coffin
1937 *A Further Range*, Robert Frost
1938 *Cold Morning Sky*, Marya Zaturenska
1939 *Selected Poems*, John Gould Fletcher
1940 *Collected Poems*, Mark Van Doren
1941 *Sunderland Capture*, Leonard Bacon
1942 *The Dust Which Is God*, William Rose Benét
1943 *A Witness Tree*, Robert Frost
1944 *Western Star*, Stephen Vincent Benét
1945 *V-Letter and Other Poems*, Karl Shapiro
1947 *Lord Weary's Castle*, Robert Lowell
1948 *The Age of Anxiety*, W. H. Auden
1949 *Terror and Decorum*, Peter Viereck
1950 *Annie Allen*, Gwendolyn Brooks
1951 *Complete Poems*, Carl Sandburg
1952 *Collected Poems*, Marianne Moore
1953 *Collected Poems, 1917–1952*, Archibald MacLeish
1954 *The Waking*, Theodore Roethke
1955 *Collected Poems*, Wallace Stevens
1956 *Poems—North & South*, Elizabeth Bishop
1957 *Things of This World*, Richard Wilbur
1958 *Promises: Poems, 1954–1956*, Robert Penn Warren
1959 *Selected Poems, 1928–1958*, Stanley Kunitz
1960 *Heart's Needle*, William Snodgrass
1961 *Times Three: Selected Verse From Three Decades*, Phyllis McGinley
1962 *Poems*, Alan Dugan
1963 *Pictures From Breughel*, William Carlos Williams
1964 *At the End of the Open Road*, Louis Simpson
1965 *77 Dream Songs*, John Berryman
1966 *Selected Poems*, Richard Eberhart
1967 *Live or Die*, Anne Sexton
1968 *The Hard Hours*, Anthony Hecht
1969 *Of Being Numerous*, George Oppen
1970 *Untitled Subjects*, Richard Howard
1971 *The Carrier of Ladders*, William S. Merwin
1972 *Collected Poems*, James Wright
1973 *Up Country*, Maxine Winokur Kumin
1974 *The Dolphin*, Robert Lowell
1975 *Turtle Island*, Gary Snyder
1976 *Self-Portrait in a Convex Mirror*, John Ashbery
1977 *Divine Comedies*, James Merrill
1978 *Collected Poems*, Howard Nemerov
1979 *Now and Then: Poems, 1976–1978*, Robert Penn Warren
1980 *Selected Poems*, Donald Rodney Justice
1981 *The Morning of the Poem*, James Schuyler
1982 *The Collected Poems*, Sylvia Plath
1983 *Selected Poems*, Galway Kinnell
1984 *American Primitive*, Mary Oliver
1985 *Yin*, Carolyn Kizer
1986 *The Flying Change*, Henry Taylor

1987 *Thomas and Beulah*, Rita Dove
1988 *Partial Accounts: New and Selected Poems*, William Meredith
1989 *New and Collected Poems*, Richard Wilbur
1990 *The World Doesn't End*, Charles Simic
1991 *Near Changes*, Mona Van Duyn
1992 *Selected Poems*, James Tate
1993 *The Wild Iris*, Louise Gluck
1994 *Neon Vernacular*, Yusef Komunyakaa
1995 *Simple Truth*, Philip Levine
1996 *The Dream of the Unified Field*, Jorie Graham
1997 *Alive Together: New and Selected Poems*, Lisel Mueller
1998 *Black Zodiac*, Charles Wright
1999 *Blizzard of One*, Mark Strand
2000 *Repair*, C. K. Williams
2001 *Different Hours*, Stephen Dunn
2002 *Practical Gods*, Carl Dennis

1. The poetry prize was established in 1922. The 1918 and 1919 awards were made from gifts provided by the Poetry Society.

## General Nonfiction

1962 *The Making of the President, 1960*, Theodore H. White
1963 *The Guns of August*, Barbara W. Tuchman
1964 *Anti-Intellectualism in American Life*, Richard Hofstadter
1965 *O Strange New World*, Howard Mumford Jones
1966 *Wandering Through Winter*, Edwin Way Teale
1967 *The Problem of Slavery in Western Culture*, David Brion Davis
1968 *Rousseau and Revolution*, Will and Ariel Durant
1969 *So Human an Animal*, Rene Jules Dubos; *The Armies of the Night*, Norman Mailer
1970 *Gandhi's Truth*, Erik H. Erikson
1971 *The Rising Sun*, John Toland
1972 *Stilwell and the American Experience in China, 1911–1945*, Barbara W. Tuchman
1973 *Fire in the Lake: The Vietnamese and the Americans in Vietnam*, Frances FitzGerald; *Children of Crisis* (Vols. 1 and 2), Robert M. Coles
1974 *The Denial of Death*, Ernest Becker
1975 *Pilgrim at Tinker Creek*, Annie Dillard
1976 *Why Survive? Being Old in America*, Robert N. Butler
1977 *Beautiful Swimmers: Watermen, Crabs and the Chesapeake Bay*, William W. Warner
1978 *The Dragons of Eden*, Carl Sagan
1979 *On Human Nature*, Edward O. Wilson
1980 *Gödel, Escher, Bach: An Eternal Golden Braid*, Douglas R. Hofstadter
1981 *The Soul of a New Machine*, Tracy Kidder (?) Carl E. Schorske
1982 *The Soul of a New Machine*, Tracy Kidder
1983 *Is There No Place on Earth for Me?*, Susan Sheehan
1984 *Social Transformation of American Medicine*, Paul Starr
1985 *The Good War: An Oral History of World War II*, Studs Terkel
1986 *Move Your Shadow: South Africa, Black and White*, Joseph Lelyveld; *Common Ground: A Turbulent Decade in the Lives of Three American Families*, J. Anthony Lukas
1987 *Arab and Jew: Wounded Spirits in a Promised Land*, David K. Shipler
1988 *The Making of the Atomic Bomb*, Richard Rhodes

1989 *A Bright Shining Lie*, Neil Sheehan
1990 *And Their Children After Them*, Dale Maharidge and Michael Williamson
1991 *The Ants*, Bert Holldobler and Edward O. Wilson
1992 *The Prize: The Epic Quest for Oil, Money and Power*, Daniel Yergin
1993 *Lincoln at Gettysburg: The Words That Remade America*, Garry Wills
1994 *Lenin's Tomb: The Last Days of the Soviet Empire*, David Remick
1995 *The Beak of the Finch: A Story of Evolution in Our Time*, Jonathan Weiner
1996 *The Haunted Land: Facing Europe's Ghosts After Communism*, Tina Rosenberg
1997 *Ashes to Ashes: America's Hundred-Year Cigarette War, the Public Health, and the Unabashed Triumph of Philip Morris*, Richard Kluger
1998 *Guns, Germs, and Steel: The Fates of Human Societies*, Jared Diamond
1999 *Annals of the Former World*, John McPhee
2000 *Embracing Defeat: Japan in the Wake of World War II*, John W. Dower
2001 *Hirohito and the Making of Modern Japan*, Herbert P. Bix
2002 *Carry Me Home: Birmingham, Alabama, the Climactic Battle of the Civil Rights Revolution*, Diane McWhorter

## PULITZER PRIZES IN MUSIC

1943 *Secular Cantata No. 2, A Free Song*, William Schuman
1944 *Symphony No. 4 (Op. 34)*, Howard Hanson
1945 *Appalachian Spring*, Aaron Copland
1946 *The Canticle of the Sun*, Leo Sowerby
1947 *Symphony No. 3*, Charles Ives
1948 *Symphony No. 3*, Walter Piston
1949 *Louisiana Story* music, Virgil Thomson
1950 *The Consul*, Gian Carlo Menotti
1951 Music for opera *Giants in the Earth*, Douglas Stuart Moore
1952 *Symphony Concertante*, Gail Kubik
1954 *Concerto for Two Pianos and Orchestra*, Quincy Porter
1955 *The Saint of Bleecker Street*, Gian Carlo Menotti
1956 *Symphony No. 3*, Ernst Toch
1957 *Meditations on Ecclesiastes*, Norman Dello Joio
1958 *Vanessa*, Samuel Barber
1959 *Concerto for Piano and Orchestra*, John La Montaine
1961 *Symphony No. 7*, Walter Piston
1962 *The Crucible*, Robert Ward
1963 *Piano Concerto No. 1*, Samuel Barber
1966 *Variations for Orchestra*, Leslie Bassett
1967 *Quartet No. 3*, Leon Kirchner
1968 *Echoes of Time and the River*, George Crumb
1969 *String Quartet No. 3*, Karel Husa
1970 *Time's Encomium*, Charles Wuorinen
1971 *Synchronisms No. 6 for Piano and Electronic Sound*, Mario Davidovsky
1972 *Windows*, Jacob Druckman
1973 *String Quartet No. 3*, Elliott Carter
1974 *Notturno*, Donald Martino
1975 *From the Diary of Virginia Woolf*, Dominick Argento

1976   *Air Music*, Ned Rorem
1977   *Visions of Terror and Wonder*, Richard Wernick
1978   *Déjà Vu for Percussion Quartet and Orchestra*, Michael Colgrass
1979   *Aftertones of Infinity*, Joseph Schwantner
1980   *In Memory of a Summer Day*, David Del Tredici
1982   *Concerto for Orchestra*, Roger Sessions
1983   *Three Movements for Orchestra*, Ellen T. Zwilich
1984   *Canti del Sole*, Bernard Rands
1985   *Symphony RiverRun*, Stephen Albert
1986   *Wind Quintet IV*, George Perle
1987   *The Flight Into Egypt*, John Harbison
1988   *12 New Etudes for Piano*, William Bolcom
1989   *Whispers Out of Time*, Roger Reynolds
1990   *Duplicates: A Concerto for Two Pianos and Orchestra*, Mel Powell
1991   *Symphony*, Shulamit Ran
1992   *The Face of the Night, The Heart of the Dark*, Wayne Peterson
1993   *Trombone Concerto*, Christopher Rouse
1994   *Of Reminiscences and Reflections*, Gunther Schuller
1995   *Stringmusic*, Morton Gould
1996   *Lilacs*, George Walker
1997   *Blood on the Field*, Wynton Marsalis
1998   *String Quartet No. 2, Musica Instrumentalis*, Aaron Jay Kernis
1999   *Concerto for Flute, Strings and Percussion*, Melinda Wagner
2000   *Life Is a Dream, Opera in Three Acts: Act II, Concert Version*, Lewis Spratlan
2001   *Symphony No. 2 for String Orchestra*, John Corigliano
2002   *Ice Field*, Henry Brant

## PULITZER PRIZES IN DRAMA

1918   *Why Marry?*, Jesse Lynch Williams
1920   *Beyond the Horizon*, Eugene O'Neill
1921   *Miss Lulu Bett*, Zona Gale
1922   *Anna Christie*, Eugene O'Neill
1923   *Icebound*, Owen Davis
1924   *Hell-Bent Fer Heaven*, Hatcher Hughes
1925   *They Knew What They Wanted*, Sidney Howard
1926   *Craig's Wife*, George Kelly
1927   *In Abraham's Bosom*, Paul Green
1928   *Strange Interlude*, Eugene O'Neill
1929   *Street Scene*, Elmer L. Rice
1930   *The Green Pastures*, Marc Connelly
1931   *Alison's House*, Susan Glaspell
1932   *Of Thee I Sing*, George S. Kaufman, Morrie Ryskind, and Ira Gershwin
1933   *Both Your Houses*, Maxwell Anderson
1934   *Men in White*, Sidney Kingsley
1935   *The Old Maid*, Zöe Akins
1936   *Idiot's Delight*, Robert E. Sherwood
1937   *You Can't Take It with You*, Moss Hart and George S. Kaufman
1938   *Our Town*, Thornton Wilder
1939   *Abe Lincoln in Illinois*, Robert E. Sherwood
1940   *The Time of Your Life*, William Saroyan
1941   *There Shall Be No Night*, Robert E. Sherwood
1943   *The Skin of Our Teeth*, Thornton Wilder
1945   *Harvey*, Mary Chase
1946   *State of the Union*, Russel Crouse and Howard Lindsay

1948   *A Streetcar Named Desire*, Tennessee Williams
1949   *Death of a Salesman*, Arthur Miller
1950   *South Pacific*, Richard Rodgers, Oscar Hammerstein II, and Joshua Logan
1952   *The Shrike*, Joseph Kramm
1953   *Picnic*, William Inge
1954   *The Teahouse of the August Moon*, John Patrick
1955   *Cat on a Hot Tin Roof*, Tennessee Williams
1956   *The Diary of Anne Frank*, Frances Goodrich and Albert Hackett
1957   *Long Day's Journey into Night*, Eugene O'Neill
1958   *Look Homeward, Angel*, Ketti Frings
1959   *J. B.*, Archibald MacLeish
1960   *Fiorello!*, George Abbott, Jerome Weidman, Jerry Bock, and Sheldon Harnick
1961   *All the Way Home*, Tad Mosel
1962   *How to Succeed in Business without Really Trying*, Frank Loesser and Abe Burrows
1965   *The Subject Was Roses*, Frank D. Gilroy
1967   *A Delicate Balance*, Edward Albee
1969   *The Great White Hope*, Howard Sackler
1970   *No Place to Be Somebody*, Charles Gordone
1971   *The Effect of Gamma Rays on Man-in-the-Moon Marigolds*, Paul Zindel
1973   *That Championship Season*, Jason Miller
1975   *Seascape*, Edward Albee
1976   *A Chorus Line*, conceived by Michael Bennett
1977   *The Shadow Box*, Michael Cristofer
1978   *The Gin Game*, Donald L. Coburn
1979   *Buried Child*, Sam Shepard
1980   *Talley's Folly*, Lanford Wilson
1981   *Crimes of the Heart*, Beth Henley
1982   *A Soldier's Play*, Charles Fuller
1983   *'Night, Mother*, Marsha Norman
1984   *Glengarry Glen Ross*, David Mamet
1985   *Sunday in the Park with George*, Stephen Sondheim and James Lapine
1987   *Fences*, August Wilson
1988   *Driving Miss Daisy*, Alfred Uhry
1989   *The Heidi Chronicles*, Wendy Wasserstein
1990   *The Piano Lesson*, August Wilson
1991   *Lost in Yonkers*, Neil Simon
1992   *The Kentucky Cycle*, Robert Schenkkan
1993   *Angels in America: Millennium Approaches*, Tony Kushner
1994   *Three Tall Women*, Edward Albee
1995   *The Young Man from Atlanta*, Horton Foote
1996   *Rent*, Jonathan Larson
1998   *How I Learned to Drive*, Paula Vogel
1999   *Wit*, Margaret Edson
2000   *Dinner with Friends*, Donald Margulies
2001   *Proof*, David Auburn
2002   *Topdog/Underdog*, Suzan-Lori Parks

## SPECIAL CITATIONS

1938   *Edmonton* [Alberta] *Journal*, special bronze plaque for editorial leadership in defense of freedom of the press in province of Alberta
1941   *New York Times*, for the public educational value of its foreign news report
1944   Byron Price, director of the Office of Censorship, for the creation and administration of the newspaper and radio codes; Mrs. William Allen White, for her husband's interest and services during the past seven years as a member of the Advisory Board of the Graduate School of Journalism, Columbia University; Richard

Rodgers and Oscar Hammerstein II, for their musical *Oklahoma!*

**1945** The cartographers of the American press, for their war maps

**1947** (Pulitzer centennial year.) Columbia University and the Graduate School of Journalism, for their efforts to maintain and advance the high standards governing the Pulitzer Prize awards; the *St. Louis Post-Dispatch*, for its unswerving adherence to the public and professional ideals of its founder and its leadership in American journalism

**1948** Dr. Frank D. Fackenthal, for his interest and service

**1951** Cyrus L. Sulzberger *(New York Times)*, for his exclusive interview with Archbishop Stepinac in a Yugoslav prison

**1952** *Kansas City Star*, for coverage of 1951 floods; Max Kase *(New York Journal–American)*, for exposures of bribery in basketball

**1953** *New York Times*, for its 17-year publication of "Review of the Week," and Lester Markel, its founder

**1957** Kenneth Roberts, for his historical novels

**1958** Walter Lippmann *(New York Herald Tribune)*, for his "wisdom, perception and high sense of responsibility" in his commentary on national and international affairs

**1960** Garrett Mattingly, for *The Armada*

**1961** *American Heritage Picture History of the Civil War*, as a distinguished example of American book publishing

**1964** Gannett Newspapers, Rochester, N.Y.

**1973** James Thomas Flexner, for his biography *George Washington*

**1974** Roger Sessions, for his "life's work in music"

**1976** John Hohenberg, for "services for 22 years as Administrator of the Pulitzer Prizes"; Scott Joplin, for his contributions to American music

**1977** Alex Haley, for his novel, *Roots*

**1978** E. B. White of *New Yorker* magazine and Richard L. Strout of *The Christian Science Monitor*

**1982** Milton Babbitt, "for his life's work as a distinguished and seminal American composer"

**1984** Theodor Seuss Geisel (Dr. Seuss), for "books full of playful rhymes, nonsense words and strange illustrations"

**1985** William Schuman, for "more than half a century of contribution to American music as a composer and educational leader"

**1987** Joseph Pulitzer, Jr., "for extraordinary services to American journalism and letters during his 31 years as chairman of the Pulitzer Prize Board and for his accomplishments as an editor and publisher"

**1992** *Maus*, Art Spiegelman

**1996** Herb Caen *(San Francisco Chronicle)*, "for his extraordinary and continuing contribution as a voice and conscience of his city"

**1998** George Gershwin

**1999** Edward Kennedy "Duke" Ellington, who "made an indelible contribution to art and culture"

# Academy Awards (Oscars)

**1928**
**Picture:** *Wings,* Paramount
**Director:** Frank Borzage, *Seventh Heaven;* Lewis Milestone, *Two Arabian Nights*
**Actress:** Janet Gaynor, *Seventh Heaven, Street Angel, Sunrise*
**Actor:** Emil Jannings, *The Way of All Flesh, The Last Command*

**1929**
**Picture:** *The Broadway Melody,* MGM
**Director:** Frank Lloyd, *The Divine Lady*
**Actress:** Mary Pickford, *Coquette*
**Actor:** Warner Baxter, *In Old Arizona*

**1930**
**Picture:** *All Quiet on the Western Front,* Universal
**Director:** Lewis Milestone, *All Quiet on the Western Front*
**Actress:** Norma Shearer, *The Divorcee*
**Actor:** George Arliss, *Disraeli*

**1931**
**Picture:** *Cimarron,* RKO Radio
**Director:** Norman Taurog, *Skippy*
**Actress:** Marie Dressler, *Min and Bill*
**Actor:** Lionel Barrymore, *A Free Soul*

**1932**
**Picture:** *Grand Hotel,* MGM
**Director:** Frank Borzage, *Bad Girl*
**Actress:** Helen Hayes, *The Sin of Madelon Claudet*
**Actor:** Fredric March, *Dr. Jekyll and Mr. Hyde,* and Wallace Beery, *The Champ*

**1933**
**Picture:** *Cavalcade,* Fox
**Director:** Frank Lloyd, *Cavalcade*
**Actress:** Katharine Hepburn, *Morning Glory*
**Actor:** Charles Laughton, *The Private Life of Henry VIII*

**1934**
**Picture:** *It Happened One Night,* Columbia
**Director:** Frank Capra, *It Happened One Night*
**Actress:** Claudette Colbert, *It Happened One Night*
**Actor:** Clark Gable, *It Happened One Night*

**1935**
**Picture:** *Mutiny on the Bounty,* MGM
**Director:** John Ford, *The Informer*
**Actress:** Bette Davis, *Dangerous*
**Actor:** Victor McLaglen, *The Informer*

**1936**
**Picture:** *The Great Ziegfeld,* MGM
**Director:** Frank Capra, *Mr. Deeds Goes to Town*
**Actress:** Luise Rainer, *The Great Ziegfeld*
**Actor:** Paul Muni, *The Story of Louis Pasteur*
**Supporting Actress:** Gale Sondergaard, *Anthony Adverse*
**Supporting Actor:** Walter Brennan, *Come and Get It*

**1937**
**Picture:** *The Life of Emile Zola,* Warner Bros.
**Director:** Leo McCarey, *The Awful Truth*
**Actress:** Luise Rainer, *The Good Earth*
**Actor:** Spencer Tracy, *Captains Courageous*
**Supporting Actress:** Alice Brady, *In Old Chicago*
**Supporting Actor:** Joseph Schildkraut, *The Life of Emile Zola*

**1938**
**Picture:** *You Can't Take It with You,* Columbia
**Director:** Frank Capra, *You Can't Take It with You*
**Actress:** Bette Davis, *Jezebel*
**Actor:** Spencer Tracy, *Boys Town*
**Supporting Actress:** Fay Bainter, *Jezebel*
**Supporting Actor:** Walter Brennan, *Kentucky*

**1939**
**Picture:** *Gone with the Wind,* Selznick MGM
**Director:** Victor Fleming, *Gone with the Wind*
**Actress:** Vivien Leigh, *Gone with the Wind*
**Actor:** Robert Donat, *Goodbye, Mr. Chips*
**Supporting Actress:** Hattie McDaniel, *Gone with the Wind*
**Supporting Actor:** Thomas Mitchell, *Stagecoach*

**1940**
**Picture:** *Rebecca,* Selznick-United Artists
**Director:** John Ford, *The Grapes of Wrath*
**Actress:** Ginger Rogers, *Kitty Foyle*
**Actor:** James Stewart, *The Philadelphia Story*
**Supporting Actress:** Jane Darwell, *The Grapes of Wrath*
**Supporting Actor:** Walter Brennan, *The Westerner*

**1941**
**Picture:** *How Green Was My Valley,* 20th Century–Fox
**Director:** John Ford, *How Green Was My Valley*
**Actress:** Joan Fontaine, *Suspicion*
**Actor:** Gary Cooper, *Sergeant York*
**Supporting Actress:** Mary Astor, *The Great Lie*
**Supporting Actor:** Donald Crisp, *How Green Was My Valley*

**1942**
**Picture:** *Mrs. Miniver,* MGM
**Director:** William Wyler, *Mrs. Miniver*
**Actress:** Greer Garson, *Mrs. Miniver*
**Actor:** James Cagney, *Yankee Doodle Dandy*
**Supporting Actress:** Teresa Wright, *Mrs. Miniver*
**Supporting Actor:** Van Heflin, *Johnny Eager*

**1943**
**Picture:** *Casablanca,* Warner Bros.
**Director:** Michael Curtiz, *Casablanca*
**Actress:** Jennifer Jones, *The Song of Bernadette*
**Actor:** Paul Lukas, *Watch on the Rhine*
**Supporting Actress:** Katina Paxinou, *For Whom the Bell Tolls*
**Supporting Actor:** Charles Coburn, *The More the Merrier*

**1944**
**Picture:** *Going My Way,* Paramount
**Director:** Leo McCarey, *Going My Way*
**Actress:** Ingrid Bergman, *Gaslight*
**Actor:** Bing Crosby, *Going My Way*
**Supporting Actress:** Ethel Barrymore, *None but the Lonely Heart*
**Supporting Actor:** Barry Fitzgerald, *Going My Way*

**1945**
**Picture:** *The Lost Weekend,* Paramount
**Director:** Billy Wilder, *The Lost Weekend*
**Actress:** Joan Crawford, *Mildred Pierce*
**Actor:** Ray Milland, *The Lost Weekend*
**Supporting Actress:** Anne Revere, *National Velvet*
**Supporting Actor:** James Dunn, *A Tree Grows in Brooklyn*

**1946**
**Picture:** *The Best Years of Our Lives,* Goldwyn-RKO Radio
**Director:** William Wyler, *The Best Years of Our Lives*
**Actress:** Olivia de Havilland, *To Each His Own*
**Actor:** Fredric March, *The Best Years of Our Lives*
**Supporting Actress:** Anne Baxter, *The Razor's Edge*
**Supporting Actor:** Harold Russell, *The Best Years of Our Lives*

**1947**
**Picture:** *Gentleman's Agreement,* 20th Century–Fox
**Director:** Elia Kazan, *Gentleman's Agreement*
**Actress:** Loretta Young, *The Farmer's Daughter*
**Actor:** Ronald Colman, *A Double Life*
**Supporting Actress:** Celeste Holm, *Gentleman's Agreement*
**Supporting Actor:** Edmund Gwenn, *Miracle on 34th Street*

**1948**
**Picture:** *Hamlet,* Rank-Two Cities-UI
**Director:** John Huston, *Treasure of Sierra Madre*
**Actress:** Jane Wyman, *Johnny Belinda*
**Actor:** Laurence Olivier, *Hamlet*

**Supporting Actress:** Claire Trevor, *Key Largo*
**Supporting Actor:** Walter Huston, *Treasure of Sierra Madre*

**1949**
**Picture:** *All the King's Men,* Rossen-Columbia
**Director:** Joseph L. Mankiewicz, *A Letter to Three Wives*
**Actress:** Olivia de Havilland, *The Heiress*
**Actor:** Broderick Crawford, *All the King's Men*
**Supporting Actress:** Mercedes McCambridge, *All the King's Men*
**Supporting Actor:** Dean Jagger, *Twelve O'Clock High*

**1950**
**Picture:** *All About Eve,* 20th Century–Fox
**Director:** Joseph L. Mankiewicz, *All About Eve*
**Actress:** Judy Holliday, *Born Yesterday*
**Actor:** José Ferrer, *Cyrano de Bergerac*
**Supporting Actress:** Josephine Hull, *Harvey*
**Supporting Actor:** George Sanders, *All About Eve*

**1951**
**Picture:** *An American in Paris,* MGM
**Director:** George Stevens, *A Place in the Sun*
**Actress:** Vivien Leigh, *A Streetcar Named Desire*
**Actor:** Humphrey Bogart, *The African Queen*
**Supporting Actress:** Kim Hunter, *A Streetcar Named Desire*
**Supporting Actor:** Karl Malden, *A Streetcar Named Desire*

**1952**
**Picture:** *The Greatest Show on Earth,* DeMille-Paramount
**Director:** John Ford, *The Quiet Man*
**Actress:** Shirley Booth, *Come Back, Little Sheba*
**Actor:** Gary Cooper, *High Noon*
**Supporting Actress:** Gloria Grahame, *The Bad and the Beautiful*
**Supporting Actor:** Anthony Quinn, *Viva Zapata!*

**1953**
**Picture:** *From Here to Eternity,* Columbia
**Director:** Fred Zinnemann, *From Here to Eternity*
**Actress:** Audrey Hepburn, *Roman Holiday*
**Actor:** William Holden, *Stalag 17*
**Supporting Actress:** Donna Reed, *From Here to Eternity*
**Supporting Actor:** Frank Sinatra, *From Here to Eternity*

**1954**
**Picture:** *On the Waterfront,* Horizon-American Corp., Columbia
**Director:** Elia Kazan, *On the Waterfront*
**Actress:** Grace Kelly, *The Country Girl*
**Actor:** Marlon Brando, *On the Waterfront*
**Supporting Actress:** Eva Marie Saint, *On the Waterfront*
**Supporting Actor:** Edmond O'Brien, *The Barefoot Contessa*

**1955**
**Picture:** *Marty,* Hecht and Lancaster, United Artists
**Director:** Delbert Mann, *Marty*
**Actress:** Anna Magnani, *The Rose Tattoo*
**Actor:** Ernest Borgnine, *Marty*
**Supporting Actress:** Jo Van Fleet, *East of Eden*
**Supporting Actor:** Jack Lemmon, *Mister Roberts*

**1956**
**Picture:** *Around the World in 80 Days,* Michael Todd Co., Inc.-United Artists
**Director:** George Stevens, *Giant*
**Actress:** Ingrid Bergman, *Anastasia*
**Actor:** Yul Brynner, *The King and I*
**Supporting Actress:** Dorothy Malone, *Written on the Wind*
**Supporting Actor:** Anthony Quinn, *Lust for Life*

**1957**
**Picture:** *The Bridge on the River Kwai,* Horizon Films, Columbia
**Director:** David Lean, *The Bridge on the River Kwai*
**Actress:** Joanne Woodward, *The Three Faces of Eve*
**Actor:** Alec Guinness, *The Bridge on the River Kwai*
**Supporting Actress:** Miyoshi Umeki, *Sayonara*
**Supporting Actor:** Red Buttons, *Sayonara*

**1958**
**Picture:** *Gigi,* Arthur Freed Productions, Inc., MGM
**Director:** Vincente Minnelli, *Gigi*
**Actress:** Susan Hayward, *I Want to Live!*
**Actor:** David Niven, *Separate Tables*
**Supporting Actress:** Wendy Hiller, *Separate Tables*
**Supporting Actor:** Burl Ives, *The Big Country*

**1959**
**Picture:** *Ben-Hur,* MGM
**Director:** William Wyler, *Ben-Hur*
**Actress:** Simone Signoret, *Room at the Top*
**Actor:** Charlton Heston, *Ben-Hur*
**Supporting Actress:** Shelley Winters, *The Diary of Anne Frank*
**Supporting Actor:** Hugh Griffith, *Ben-Hur*

**1960**
**Picture:** *The Apartment,* Mirisch Co., Inc., United Artists
**Director:** Billy Wilder, *The Apartment*
**Actress:** Elizabeth Taylor, *Butterfield 8*
**Actor:** Burt Lancaster, *Elmer Gantry*
**Supporting Actress:** Shirley Jones, *Elmer Gantry*
**Supporting Actor:** Peter Ustinov, *Spartacus*

**1961**
**Picture:** *West Side Story,* Mirisch Pictures, Inc., and B and P Enterprises, Inc., United Artists
**Director:** Robert Wise and Jerome Robbins, *West Side Story*
**Actress:** Sophia Loren, *Two Women*
**Actor:** Maximillian Schell, *Judgment at Nuremberg*
**Supporting Actress:** Rita Moreno, *West Side Story*
**Supporting Actor:** George Chakiris, *West Side Story*

**1962**
**Picture:** *Lawrence of Arabia,* Horizon Pictures, Ltd.-Columbia
**Director:** David Lean, *Lawrence of Arabia*
**Actress:** Anne Bancroft, *The Miracle Worker*
**Actor:** Gregory Peck, *To Kill a Mockingbird*
**Supporting Actress:** Patty Duke, *The Miracle Worker*
**Supporting Actor:** Ed Begley, *Sweet Bird of Youth*

**1963**
**Picture:** *Tom Jones,* A Woodfall Production, United Artists-Lopert Pictures
**Director:** Tony Richardson, *Tom Jones*
**Actress:** Patricia Neal, *Hud*
**Actor:** Sidney Poitier, *Lilies of the Field*
**Supporting Actress:** Margaret Rutherford, *The V.I.P.s*
**Supporting Actor:** Melvyn Douglas, *Hud*

**1964**
**Picture:** *My Fair Lady,* Warner Bros.
**Director:** George Cukor, *My Fair Lady*
**Actress:** Julie Andrews, *Mary Poppins*
**Actor:** Rex Harrison, *My Fair Lady*
**Supporting Actress:** Lila Kedrova, *Zorba the Greek*
**Supporting Actor:** Peter Ustinov, *Topkapi*

**1965**
Picture: The Sound of Music, Argyle Enterprises Production, 20th Century–Fox
**Director:** Robert Wise, *The Sound of Music*
**Actress:** Julie Christie, *Darling*
**Actor:** Lee Marvin, *Cat Ballou*
**Supporting Actress:** Shelley Winters, *A Patch of Blue*
**Supporting Actor:** Martin Balsam, *A Thousand Clowns*

**1966**
**Picture:** *A Man for All Seasons,* Highland Films, Ltd., Production, Columbia
**Director:** Fred Zinnemann, *A Man for All Seasons*
**Actress:** Elizabeth Taylor, *Who's Afraid of Virginia Woolf?*
**Actor:** Paul Scofield, *A Man for All Seasons*
**Supporting Actress:** Sandy Dennis, *Who's Afraid of Virginia Woolf?*
**Supporting Actor:** Walter Matthau, *The Fortune Cookie*

**1967**
**Picture:** *In the Heat of the Night,* Mirisch Corp. Productions, United Artists
**Director:** Mike Nichols, *The Graduate*
**Actress:** Katharine Hepburn, *Guess Who's Coming to Dinner*
**Actor:** Rod Steiger, *In the Heat of the Night*
**Supporting Actress:** Estelle Parsons, *Bonnie and Clyde*
**Supporting Actor:** George Kennedy, *Cool Hand Luke*

**1968**
**Picture:** *Oliver!,* Columbia Pictures
**Director:** Sir Carol Reed, *Oliver!*
**Actress:** Katharine Hepburn, *The Lion in Winter* and Barbra Streisand, *Funny Girl*
**Actor:** Cliff Robertson, *Charly*
**Supporting Actress:** Ruth Gordon, *Rosemary's Baby*
**Supporting Actor:** Jack Albertson, *The Subject Was Roses*

**1969**
**Picture:** *Midnight Cowboy,* Jerome Hellman-John Schlesinger Production, United Artists
**Director:** John Schlesinger, *Midnight Cowboy*
**Actress:** Maggie Smith, *The Prime of Miss Jean Brodie*
**Actor:** John Wayne, *True Grit*
**Supporting Actress:** Goldie Hawn, *Cactus Flower*
**Supporting Actor:** Gig Young, *They Shoot Horses, Don't They?*

**1970**
**Picture:** *Patton,* Frank McCarthy-Franklin J. Schaffner Production, 20th Century–Fox
**Director:** Franklin J. Schaffner, *Patton*
**Actress:** Glenda Jackson, *Women in Love*
**Actor:** George C. Scott, *Patton*
**Supporting Actress:** Helen Hayes, *Airport*
**Supporting Actor:** John Mills, *Ryan's Daughter*

**1971**
**Picture:** *The French Connection,* D'Antoni Productions, 20th Century–Fox
**Director:** William Friedkin, *The French Connection*
**Actress:** Jane Fonda, *Klute*
**Actor:** Gene Hackman, *The French Connection*
**Supporting Actress:** Cloris Leachman, *The Last Picture Show*
**Supporting Actor:** Ben Johnson, *The Last Picture Show*

**1972**
**Picture:** *The Godfather,* Albert S. Ruddy Production, Paramount
**Director:** Bob Fosse, *Cabaret*
**Actress:** Liza Minnelli, *Cabaret*
**Actor:** Marlon Brando, *The Godfather*
**Supporting Actress:** Eileen Heckart, *Butterflies Are Free*
**Supporting Actor:** Joel Gray, *Cabaret*

**1973**
**Picture:** *The Sting,* Universal-Bill/Phillips-George Roy Hill Production, Universal
**Director:** George Roy Hill, *The Sting*
**Actress:** Glenda Jackson, *A Touch of Class*
**Actor:** Jack Lemmon, *Save the Tiger*
**Supporting Actress:** Tatum O'Neal, *Paper Moon*
**Supporting Actor:** John Houseman, *The Paper Chase*

**1974**
**Picture:** *The Godfather, Part II,* Coppola Co. Production, Paramount
**Director:** Francis Ford Coppola, *The Godfather, Part II*
**Actress:** Ellen Burstyn, *Alice Doesn't Live Here Anymore*
**Actor:** Art Carney, *Harry and Tonto*
**Supporting Actress:** Ingrid Bergman, *Murder on the Orient Express*
**Supporting Actor:** Robert De Niro, *The Godfather, Part II*

**1975**
**Picture:** *One Flew Over the Cuckoo's Nest,* Fantasy Films Production, United Artists
**Director:** Milos Forman, *One Flew Over the Cuckoo's Nest*

**Actress:** Louise Fletcher, *One Flew Over the Cuckoo's Nest*
**Actor:** Jack Nicholson, *One Flew Over the Cuckoo's Nest*
**Supporting Actress:** Lee Grant, *Shampoo*
**Supporting Actor:** George Burns, *The Sunshine Boys*

**1976**
**Picture:** *Rocky,* Robert Chartoff-Irwin Winkler Production, United Artists
**Director:** John G. Avildsen, *Rocky*
**Actress:** Faye Dunaway, *Network*
**Actor:** Peter Finch, *Network*
**Supporting Actress:** Beatrice Straight, *Network*
**Supporting Actor:** Jason Robards, *All the President's Men*

**1977**
**Picture:** *Annie Hall,* Jack Rollins-Charles H. Joffe Production, United Artists
**Director:** Woody Allen, *Annie Hall*
**Actress:** Diane Keaton, *Annie Hall*
**Actor:** Richard Dreyfuss, *The Goodbye Girl*
**Supporting Actress:** Vanessa Redgrave, *Julia*
**Supporting Actor:** Jason Robards, *Julia*

**1978**
**Picture:** *The Deer Hunter,* Michael Cimino Film Production, Universal
**Director:** Michael Cimino, *The Deer Hunter*
**Actress:** Jane Fonda, *Coming Home*
**Actor:** Jon Voight, *Coming Home*
**Supporting Actress:** Maggie Smith, *California Suite*
**Supporting Actor:** Christopher Walken, *The Deer Hunter*

**1979**
**Picture:** *Kramer vs. Kramer,* Stanley Jaffe Production, Columbia Pictures
**Director:** Robert Benton, *Kramer vs. Kramer*
**Actress:** Sally Field, *Norma Rae*
**Actor:** Dustin Hoffman, *Kramer vs. Kramer*
**Supporting Actress:** Meryl Streep, *Kramer vs. Kramer*
**Supporting Actor:** Melvyn Douglas, *Being There*

**1980**
**Picture:** *Ordinary People,* Wildwood Enterprises Production, Paramount
**Director:** Robert Redford, *Ordinary People*
**Actress:** Sissy Spacek, *Coal Miner's Daughter*
**Actor:** Robert De Niro, *Raging Bull*
**Supporting Actress:** Mary Steenburgen, *Melvin and Howard*
**Supporting Actor:** Timothy Hutton, *Ordinary People*

**1981**
**Picture:** *Chariots of Fire,* Enigma Productions, Ladd Company/Warner Bros.
**Director:** Warren Beatty, *Reds*
**Actress:** Katharine Hepburn, *On Golden Pond*
**Actor:** Henry Fonda, *On Golden Pond*
**Supporting Actress:** Maureen Stapleton, *Reds*
**Supporting Actor:** John Gielgud, *Arthur*

**1982**
**Picture:** *Gandhi,* Indo-British Films Production/Columbia
**Director:** Richard Attenborough, *Gandhi*
**Actress:** Meryl Streep, *Sophie's Choice*
**Actor:** Ben Kingsley, *Gandhi*
**Supporting Actress:** Jessica Lange, *Tootsie*
**Supporting Actor:** Louis Gossett, Jr., *An Officer and a Gentleman*

**1983**
**Picture:** *Terms of Endearment,* Paramount
**Director:** James L. Brooks, *Terms of Endearment*
**Actress:** Shirley MacLaine, *Terms of Endearment*
**Actor:** Robert Duvall, *Tender Mercies*
**Supporting Actress:** Linda Hunt, *The Year of Living Dangerously*
**Supporting Actor:** Jack Nicholson, *Terms of Endearment*

**1984**
**Picture:** *Amadeus,* Orion
**Director:** Milos Forman, *Amadeus*
**Actress:** Sally Field, *Places in the Heart*

**Actor:** F. Murray Abraham, *Amadeus*
**Supporting Actress:** Dame Peggy Ashcroft, *A Passage to India*
**Supporting Actor:** Haing S. Ngor, *The Killing Fields*

**1985**
**Picture:** *Out of Africa,* Universal
**Director:** Sydney Pollack, *Out of Africa*
**Actress:** Geraldine Page, *The Trip to Bountiful*
**Actor:** William Hurt, *Kiss of the Spider Woman*
**Supporting Actress:** Anjelica Huston, *Prizzi's Honor*
**Supporting Actor:** Don Ameche, *Cocoon*

**1986**
**Picture:** *Platoon,* Orion
**Director:** Oliver Stone, *Platoon*
**Actress:** Marlee Matlin, *Children of a Lesser God*
**Actor:** Paul Newman, *The Color of Money*
**Supporting Actress:** Dianne Wiest, *Hannah and Her Sisters*
**Supporting Actor:** Michael Caine, *Hannah and Her Sisters*

**1987**
**Picture:** *The Last Emperor,* Columbia Pictures
**Director:** Bernardo Bertolucci, *The Last Emperor*
**Actress:** Cher, *Moonstruck*
**Actor:** Michael Douglas, *Wall Street*
**Supporting Actress:** Olympia Dukakis, *Moonstruck*
**Supporting Actor:** Sean Connery, *The Untouchables*

**1988**
**Picture:** *Rain Man,* United Artists
**Director:** Barry Levinson, *Rain Man*
**Actress:** Jodie Foster, *The Accused*
**Actor:** Dustin Hoffman, *Rain Man*
**Supporting Actress:** Geena Davis, *The Accidental Tourist*
**Supporting Actor:** Kevin Kline, *A Fish Called Wanda*

**1989**
**Picture:** *Driving Miss Daisy,* Warner Bros.
**Director:** Oliver Stone, *Born on the Fourth of July*
**Actress:** Jessica Tandy, *Driving Miss Daisy*
**Actor:** Daniel Day-Lewis, *My Left Foot*
**Supporting Actress:** Brenda Fricker, *My Left Foot*
**Supporting Actor:** Denzel Washington, *Glory*

**1990**
**Picture:** *Dances With Wolves,* Orion
**Director:** Kevin Costner, *Dances With Wolves*
**Actress:** Kathy Bates, *Misery*
**Actor:** Jeremy Irons, *Reversal of Fortune*
**Supporting Actress:** Whoopi Goldberg, *Ghost*
**Supporting Actor:** Joe Pesci, *Goodfellas*

**1991**
**Picture:** *The Silence of the Lambs,* Orion
**Director:** Jonathan Demme, *The Silence of the Lambs*
**Actress:** Jodie Foster, *The Silence of the Lambs*
**Actor:** Anthony Hopkins, *The Silence of the Lambs*
**Supporting Actress:** Mercedes Ruehl, *The Fisher King*
**Supporting Actor:** Jack Palance, *City Slickers*

**1992**
**Picture:** *Unforgiven,* Warner Bros.
**Director:** Clint Eastwood, *Unforgiven*
**Actress:** Emma Thompson, *Howards End*
**Actor:** Al Pacino, *Scent of a Woman*
**Supporting Actress:** Marisa Tomei, *My Cousin Vinny*
**Supporting Actor:** Gene Hackman, *Unforgiven*

**1993**
**Picture:** *Schindler's List,* Universal
**Director:** Steven Spielberg, *Schindler's List*
**Actress:** Holly Hunter, *The Piano*
**Actor:** Tom Hanks, *Philadelphia*
**Supporting Actress:** Anna Paquin, *The Piano*
**Supporting Actor:** Tommy Lee Jones, *The Fugitive*

**1994**
**Picture:** *Forrest Gump,* Paramount
**Director:** Robert Zemeckis, *Forrest Gump*
**Actress:** Jessica Lange, *Blue Sky*

**Actor:** Tom Hanks, *Forrest Gump*
**Supporting Actress:** Dianne Wiest, *Bullets Over Broadway*
**Supporting Actor:** Martin Landau, *Ed Wood*

**1995**

**Picture:** *Braveheart*, Paramount
**Director:** Mel Gibson, *Braveheart*
**Actress:** Susan Sarandon, *Dead Man Walking*
**Actor:** Nicolas Cage, *Leaving Las Vegas*
**Supporting Actress:** Mira Sorvino, *Mighty Aphrodite*
**Supporting Actor:** Kevin Spacey, *The Usual Suspects*

**1996**

**Picture:** *The English Patient*, Miramax
**Director:** Anthony Minghella, *The English Patient*
**Actress:** Frances McDormand, *Fargo*
**Actor:** Geoffrey Rush, *Shine*
**Supporting Actress:** Juliette Binoche, *The English Patient*
**Supporting Actor:** Cuba Gooding, Jr., *Jerry Maguire*

**1997**

**Picture:** *Titanic*, 20th Century–Fox and Paramount
**Director:** James Cameron, *Titanic*
**Actress:** Helen Hunt, *As Good As It Gets*
**Actor:** Jack Nicholson, *As Good As It Gets*
**Supporting Actress:** Kim Basinger, *L.A. Confidential*
**Supporting Actor:** Robin Williams, *Good Will Hunting*

**1998**

**Picture:** *Shakespeare in Love*, Miramax
**Director:** Steven Spielberg, *Saving Private Ryan*

**Actress:** Gwyneth Paltrow, *Shakespeare in Love*
**Actor:** Roberto Benigni, *Life Is Beautiful*
**Supporting Actress:** Judi Dench, *Shakespeare in Love*
**Supporting Actor:** James Coburn, *Affliction*

**1999**

**Picture:** *American Beauty*, DreamWorks SKG
**Director:** Sam Mendes, *American Beauty*
**Actress:** Hilary Swank, *Boys Don't Cry*
**Actor:** Kevin Spacey, *American Beauty*
**Supporting Actress:** Angelina Jolie, *Girl, Interrupted*
**Supporting Actor:** Michael Caine, *The Cider House Rules*

**2000**

**Picture:** *Gladiator*, DreamWorks and Universal
**Director:** Steven Soderbergh, *Traffic*
**Actress:** Julia Roberts, *Erin Brockovich*
**Actor:** Russell Crowe, *Gladiator*
**Supporting Actress:** Marcia Gay Harden, *Pollock*
**Supporting Actor:** Benicio Del Toro, *Traffic*

**2001**

**Picture:** *A Beautiful Mind*, Brian Grazer and Ron Howard, producers
**Director:** Ron Howard, *A Beautiful Mind*
**Actress:** Halle Berry, *Monster's Ball*
**Actor:** Denzel Washington, *Training Day*
**Supporting Actress:** Jennifer Connelly, *A Beautiful Mind*
**Supporting Actor:** Jim Broadbent, *Iris*

## Other Academy Awards for 2001

**Art Direction:** Catherine Martin, *Moulin Rouge*
**Cinematography:** Andrew Lesnie, *The Lord of the Rings: The Fellowship of the Ring*
**Costume Design:** Catherine Martin and Angus Strathie, *Moulin Rouge*
**Documentary (feature):** *Murder on a Sunday Morning* (Jean-Xavier de Lestrade)
**Editing:** Pietro Scalia, *Black Hawk Down*
**Foreign-Language Film:** *No Man's Land*, Bosnia and Herzegovina
**Makeup:** Peter Owen and Richard Taylor, *The Lord of the Rings: The Fellowship of the Ring*
**Music (original score):** Howard Shore, *The Lord of the Rings: The Fellowship of the Ring*
**Best Original Song:** Randy Newman, "If I Didn't Have You," *Monsters, Inc.*

**Adapted Screenplay:** Akiva Goldsman, *A Beautiful Mind*
**Original Screenplay:** Julian Fellowes, *Gosford Park*
**Short Subject (live action):** *The Accountant* (Ray McKinnon and Lisa Blount)
**Sound:** Michael Minkler, Myron Nettinga, and Chris Munro, *Black Hawk Down*
**Sound Effects Editing:** George Watters II and Christopher Boyes, *Pearl Harbor*
**Visual Effects:** Jim Rygiel, Randall William Cook, Richard Taylor, and Mark Stetson, *The Lord of the Rings: The Fellowship of the Ring*
**Honorary Awards:** Sidney Poitier, actor; Robert Redford, actor, director, producer
**Jean Hersholt Humanitarian Award:** Arthur Hiller

## 2001 National Society of Film Critics Awards

**Best Picture:** *Mulholland Drive*
**Best Actor:** Gene Hackman, *The Royal Tenenbaums*
**Best Actress:** Naomi Watts, *Mulholland Drive*
**Best Supporting Actor:** Steve Buscemi, *Ghost World*
**Best Supporting Actress:** Helen Mirren, *Gosford Park*
**Best Director:** Robert Altman, *Gosford Park*
**Best Screenplay:** Julian Fellowes, *Gosford Park*
**Best Cinematography:** Christopher Doyle, Mark Li Pingbin, *In the Mood for Love*

**Best Foreign Film:** *In the Mood for Love*, Kar-wai Wong (France and Hong Kong)
**Best Documentary:** *The Gleaners and I*, Agnès Varda
**Best Experimental Film:** *Waking Life*, Richard Linklater
**Special Citation:** Faith Hubley, for "a career devoted to exploring animation's art and soul"
**Film Heritage Award:** *My Voyage to Italy*, Martin Scorsese

## 2001 Broadcast Film Critics Association Awards

**Best Picture:** *A Beautiful Mind*
**Best Actor:** Russell Crowe, *A Beautiful Mind*
**Best Actress:** Sissy Spacek, *In the Bedroom*
**Best Supporting Actor:** Ben Kingsley, *Sexy Beast*
**Best Supporting Actress:** Jennifer Connelly, *A Beautiful Mind*
**Best Acting Ensemble:** *Gosford Park*
**Best Director (tie):** Ron Howard, *A Beautiful Mind* and Baz Luhrmann, *Moulin Rouge*
**Best Screenplay:** Christopher Nolan, *Memento*
**Best Young Actor/Actress:** Dakota Fanning, *I Am Sam*
**Best Animated Feature:** *Shrek*
**Best Family Film (live action):** *Harry Potter and the Sorcerer's Stone*

**Best Picture Made for Television:** *Life with Judy Garland: Me and My Shadows*
**Best Actor in a Picture Made for Television:** James Franco, *James Dean*
**Best Actress in a Picture Made for Television:** Judy Davis, *Life with Judy Garland: Me and My Shadows*
**Best Foreign-Language Film:** *Amelie*, Jean-Pierre Jeunet (France)
**Best Song (tie):** "May It Be," Enya, *Lord of the Rings: The Fellowship of the Ring* and "Vanilla Sky," Paul McCartney, *Vanilla Sky*
**Best Composer:** Howard Shore, *The Lord of the Rings: The Fellowship of the Ring*

## 2001 National Board of Review Awards

**Best Picture:** *Moulin Rouge*
**Best Actor:** Billy Bob Thornton, *The Man Who Wasn't There, Monster's Ball,* and *Bandits*
**Best Actress:** Halle Berry, *Monster's Ball*
**Best Supporting Actor:** Jim Broadbent, *Iris* and *Moulin Rouge*
**Best Supporting Actress:** Cate Blanchett, *The Lord of the Rings: The Fellowship of the Ring, The Shipping News,* and *The Man Who Cried*
**Best Director:** Todd Field, *In the Bedroom*
**Best Directorial Debut:** John Cameron Mitchell, *Hedwig & the Angry Inch*
**Best Foreign Film:** *Amores Perros* (Mexico)
**Best Documentary:** *The Endurance*
**Best Screenplay:** Todd Field and Rob Festinger, *In the Bedroom*

**Best Ensemble:** *Last Orders*
**Best Animated Feature:** *Shrek*
**Production Design:** *The Lord of the Rings: The Fellowship of the Ring*
**Breakthrough Performances:** Naomi Watts, *Mulholland Drive* and Hayden Christensen, *Life as a House*
**Career Achievement Awards:** Jon Voight and John Williams
**Special Achievement in Filmmaking:** Peter Jackson, *The Lord of the Rings: The Fellowship of the Ring*
**Billy Wilder Award:** Steven Spielberg
**William Everson Award for Film History:** Martin Scorsese, *Il Mio Viaggo in Italia (My Voyage to Italy)*

## 2001 Golden Globe Awards

**Film Awards**

**Best Motion Picture—Drama:** *A Beautiful Mind*
**Best Actor in a Drama:** Russell Crowe, *A Beautiful Mind*
**Best Actress in a Drama:** Sissy Spacek, *In the Bedroom*
**Best Motion Picture—Musical or Comedy:** *Moulin Rouge*
**Best Actor in a Musical or Comedy:** Gene Hackman, *The Royal Tenenbaums*
**Best Actress in a Musical or Comedy:** Nicole Kidman, *Moulin Rouge*
**Best Supporting Actor:** Jim Broadbent, *Iris*
**Best Supporting Actress:** Jennifer Connelly, *A Beautiful Mind*
**Best Director:** Robert Altman, *Gosford Park*
**Best Screenplay:** Akiva Goldsman, *A Beautiful Mind*
**Best Original Score:** Craig Armstrong, *Moulin Rouge*
**Best Original Song:** "Until . . . ," Sting, *Kate & Leopold*
**Best Foreign Film:** *No Man's Land* (Bosnia and Herzegovina)

**Television Awards**

**Best Series—Drama:** *Six Feet Under* (HBO)
**Best Actor in a Drama:** Kiefer Sutherland, *24*
**Best Actress in a Drama:** Jennifer Garner, *Alias*
**Best Series—Musical or Comedy:** *Sex and the City* (HBO)
**Best Actor in a Musical or Comedy Series:** Charlie Sheen, *Spin City*
**Best Actress in a Musical or Comedy Series:** Sarah Jessica Parker, *Sex and the City*
**Best Miniseries or Movie Made for Television:** *Band of Brothers* (HBO)
**Best Actor in a Miniseries or Movie Made for Television:** James Franco, *James Dean*
**Best Actress in a Miniseries or Movie Made for Television:** Judy Davis, *Life with Judy Garland: Me and My Shadows*
**Best Supporting Actor in a Series, Miniseries, or Movie Made for Television:** Stanley Tucci, *Conspiracy*
**Best Supporting Actress in a Series, Miniseries, or Movie Made for Television:** Rachel Griffiths, *Six Feet Under*

## 2002 Tony (Antoinette Perry) Awards

**Play:** *The Goat or Who Is Sylvia?*
**Musical:** *Thoroughly Modern Millie*
**Revival—Play:** *Private Lives*
**Revival—Musical:** *Into the Woods*
**Actor—Play:** Alan Bates, *Fortune's Fool*
**Actress—Play:** Lindsay Duncan, *Private Lives*
**Actor—Musical:** John Lithgow, *Sweet Smell of Success*
**Actress—Musical:** Sutton Foster, *Thoroughly Modern Millie*
**Featured Actor—Play:** Frank Langella, *Fortune's Fool*
**Featured Actress—Play:** Katie Finneran, *Noises Off*
**Featured Actor—Musical:** Shuler Hensley, *Oklahoma!*
**Featured Actress—Musical:** Harriet Harris, *Thoroughly Modern Millie*
**Director—Play:** Mary Zimmerman, *Metamorphoses*

**Director—Musical:** John Rando, *Urinetown the Musical*
**Book—Musical:** Greg Kotis, *Urinetown the Musical*
**Score—Musical:** Mark Hollmann, music; Mark Hollmann and Greg Kotis, lyrics, *Urinetown the Musical*
**Orchestration:** Doug Besterman and Ralph Burns, *Thoroughly Modern Millie*
**Scenic Designer:** Tim Hatley, *Private Lives*
**Costume Designer:** Martin Pakledinaz, *Thoroughly Modern Millie*
**Choreographer:** Rob Ashford, *Thoroughly Modern Millie*
**Lighting Designer:** Brian MacDevitt, *Into the Woods*
**Special Theatrical Event:** *Elaine Stritch: At Liberty*
**Regional Theater:** Williamstown Theatre Festival
**Special Awards:** Julie Harris and Robert Whitehead, for lifetime achievement

## 2002 Drama Desk Awards

**Outstanding Play (tie):** *The Goat or Who Is Sylvia?* and *Metamorphoses*
**Outstanding Musical:** *Thoroughly Modern Millie*
**Outstanding Musical Revival:** *Into the Woods*
**Outstanding Play Revival:** *Private Lives*
**Best Actor in a Play:** Alan Bates, *Fortune's Fool*
**Best Actress in a Play:** Lindsay Duncan, *Private Lives*
**Best Featured Actor in a Play:** Frank Langella, *Fortune's Fool*
**Best Featured Actress in a Play:** Katie Finneran, *Noises Off*
**Best Actor in a Musical:** John Lithgow, *Sweet Smell of Success*
**Best Actress in a Musical:** Sutton Foster, *Thoroughly Modern Millie*
**Best Featured Actor in a Musical:** Shuler Hensley, *Oklahoma!*

**Best Featured Actress in a Musical:** Harriet Harris, *Thoroughly Modern Millie*
**Best Director of a Play:** Mary Zimmerman, *Metamorphoses*
**Best Director of a Musical:** Michael Mayer, *Thoroughly Modern Millie*
**Best Choreography:** Susan Stroman, *Oklahoma!*
**Best Book of a Musical:** John Lahr and Elaine Stritch, *Elaine Stritch: At Liberty*
**Best Music:** Jason Robert Brown, *The Last 5 Years*
**Best Lyrics:** Jason Robert Brown, *The Last 5 Years*
**Outstanding Orchestrations:** Doug Besterman and Ralph Burns, *Thoroughly Modern Millie*
**Outstanding Music in a Play:** Willy Schwarz, *Metamorphoses*

**Outstanding Set Design of a Play:** Tim Hatley, *Private Lives*

**Outstanding Set Design of a Musical:** Douglas W. Schmidt, *Into the Woods*

**Outstanding Costume Design:** Isaac Mizrahi, *The Women*

**Outstanding Lighting Design:** TJ Gerckens, *Metamorphoses*

**Outstanding Sound Design:** Dan Moses Schreier, *Into the Woods*

**Outstanding Solo Performance:** Elaine Stritch, *Elaine Stritch: At Liberty*

**Special Awards:** Paul Huntley for lifetime achievement; Billy Rosenfield for contributions for preservation of musical theater recordings; The Mint Theatre Company for presenting and preserving little-known classics; The Worth Street Theatre Company for its Stage Door Canteen shows for workers at Ground Zero

## 2001–2002 Obie Awards

The Obie Awards, presented by *The Village Voice*, honor superior off-Broadway theater.

**Playwriting:** Melissa James Gibson, *(sic);* Tony Kushner, *Homebody/Kabul*

**Direction:** George C. Wolfe, *Topdog/Underdog;* Mary Zimmerman, *Metamorphoses*

**Performance:** Bill Camp, *Homebody/Kabul;* Reg E. Cathey, James Himelsbach, Karen Kandel, Anthony Mackie, John Seitz, Marla Tucci (ensemble), *Talk;* Christopher Donahue, *Monster;* Linda Emond, *Homebody/Kabul;* Raul Esparza, *Tick, Tick . . . Boom!;* Juliana Francis, *Maria del Bosco;* Peter Frechette and Reg Rogers, *The Dazzle;* Yvette Ganier, *Breath, Boom;* Martha Plimpton, *Hobson's Choice;* Jeffrey Wright, *Topdog/Underdog*

**Design:** Kevin Adams, sustained excellence of lighting design; Marilys Ernst, video for *Talk;* Angela Moore and

Michael Schmelling, set and lighting design of *Drummer Wanted;* Whit MacLaughlin, sound design for *The Fab 4 Reach the Pearly Gates*

**Special Citations:** A.R.T./NY for support of off-Broadway theater; Daniel Aukin and Louisa Thompson, direction and set design, *(sic);* Ingmar Bergman and the Royal Dramatic Theatre of Sweden, *The Ghost Sonata;* Daniel MacIvor, *In on It;* Charles L. Mee and Les Waters, playwriting and direction, *Big Love;* Elaine Stritch, *Elaine Stritch: At Liberty;* The Wooster Group; *To You, the Birdie!*

**Sustained Achievement:** Caryl Churchill

## Major Grammy Awards for Recording in 2001

**Record:** "Walk On," U2

**Album:** *O Brother, Where Art Thou? Soundtrack,* Various Artists

**Song:** "Fallin'," Alicia Keys, songwriter (Alicia Keys)

**New Artist:** Alicia Keys

**Female Pop Vocal:** "I'm Like a Bird," Nelly Furtado

**Male Pop Vocal:** "Don't Let Me Be Lonely Tonight," James Taylor

**Pop Duo or Group with Vocals:** "Stuck in a Moment You Can't Get Out Of," U2

**Pop Collaboration with Vocals:** "Lady Marmalade," Christina Aguilera, Lil' Kim, Mya, and Pink

**Pop Instrumental:** "Reptile," Eric Clapton

**Dance Recording:** "All for You," Janet Jackson

**Pop Instrumental Album:** *No Substitutions—Live in Osaka,* Larry Carlton and Steve Lukather

**Pop Vocal Album:** *Lovers Rock,* Sade

**Traditional Pop Vocal Album:** *Songs I Heard,* Harry Connick, Jr.

**Female Rock Vocal:** "Get Right with God," Lucinda Williams

**Male Rock Vocal:** "Dig In," Lenny Kravitz

**Rock Duo or Group with Vocals:** "Elevation," U2

**Hard Rock:** " Crawling," Linkin Park

**Metal:** "Schism," Tool

**Rock Instrumental:** "Dirty Mind," Jeff Beck
Hotchkiss, Pat Monahan, Jimmy Stafford, and Scott Underwood, songwriters (Train)

**Rock Album:** *All That You Can't Leave Behind,* U2

**Alternative Music Album:** *Parachutes,* Coldplay

**Female R&B Vocal:** "Fallin'," Alicia Keys

**Male R&B Vocal:** "U Remind Me, " Usher

**R&B Duo or Group with Vocals:** "Survivor," Destiny's Child

**R&B Song:** "Fallin'," Alicia Keys, songwriter (Alicia Keys)

**R&B Album:** *Songs in A Minor,* Alicia Keys

**Traditional R&B Vocal Album:** *At Last,* Gladys Knight

**Rap Solo:** "Get Ur Freak On," Missy "Misdemeanor" Elliott

**Rap Duo or Group:** "Ms. Jackson," Outkast

**Rap Sung/Collaboration:** "Let Me Blow Ya Mind," Eve featuring Gwen Stefani

**Rap Album:** *Stankonia,* Outkast

**Female Country Vocal:** "Shine," Dolly Parton

**Male Country Vocal:** "O Death," Ralph Stanley

**Country Duo or Group with Vocals:** "The Lucky One," Alison Krauss + Union Station

**Country Collaboration with Vocals:** "I Am a Man of Constant Sorrow," Dan Tyminski, Harley Allen, and Pat Enright (The Soggy Bottom Boys)

**Country Instrumental:** "Foggy Mountain Breakdown," Earl Scruggs, Glen Duncan, Randy Scruggs, Steve Martin, Vince Gill, Marty Stuart, Gary Scruggs, Albert Lee, Paul Shaffer, Jerry Douglas, and Leon Russell

**Country Song:** "The Lucky One," Robert Lee Castleman, songwriter (Alison Krauss + Union Station)

**Country Album:** *Timeless—Hank Williams Tribute,* Various Artists

**Bluegrass Album:** *New Favorite,* Alison Krauss + Union Station

**New Age Album:** *A Day Without Rain,* Enya

**Contemporary Jazz Album:** *M²,* Marcus Miller

**Jazz Vocal Album:** *The Calling,* Dianne Reeves

**Jazz Instrumental, Solo:** "Chan's Song," Michael Brecker, soloist

**Jazz Instrumental, Individual or Group:** *This Is What I Do,* Sonny Rollins

**Large Jazz Ensemble Album:** *Homage to Count Basie,* Bob Mintzer Big Band

**Latin Jazz Album:** *Nocturne,* Charlie Haden

**Latin Pop Album:** *Ciclo,* Dú Talk

**Pop/Contemporary Gospel Album:** *CeCe Winans,* CeCe Winans

**Southern, Country, or Bluegrass Gospel Album:** *Bill & Gloria Gaither Present a Billy Graham Music Homecoming,* Bill & Gloria Gaither and the Homecoming Friends

**Traditional Soul Gospel Album:** *Spirit of the Century,* The Blind Boys of Alabama

**Contemporary Soul Gospel Album:** *The Experience,* Yolanda Adams

**Gospel Album by a Choir or Chorus:** *Love Is Live!,* Hezekiah Walker, choir director; LFT Church Choir

**Latin Pop Album:** *La Musica de Baldemar Huerta,* Freddy Fender

**Latin Rock/Alternative Album:** *Embrace the Chaos,* Ozomatli

**Tropical Latin Album:** *Dejame Entrar,* Carlos Vives

**Salsa Album:** *Encore*, Robert Blades
**Merengue Album:** *Yo Por Tí*, Olga Tañón
**Mexican/Mexican-American Album:** *En Vivo...El Hombre y Su Musica*, Ramón Ayala y Sus Bravos Del Norte
**Tejano Album:** *Nadie Como Tu*, Solido
**Traditional Blues Album:** *Do You Get the Blues?*, Jimmie Vaughan
**Contemporary Blues Album:** *Nothing Personal*, Delbert McClinton
**Traditional Folk Album:** *Down from the Mountain*, Various Artists
**Contemporary Folk Album:** *Love and Theft*, Bob Dylan
**Native American Music Album:** *Bless the People—Harmonized Peyote Songs*, Verdell Primeau and Johnny Mike
**Reggae Album:** *Halfway Tree*, Damian Marley
**World Music Album:** *Full Circle/Carnegie Hall 2000*, Ravi Shankar
**Polka Album:** *Gone Polka*, Jimmy Sturr
**Musical Album for Children:** *Elmo and the Orchestra*, Sesame Street Characters
**Spoken Word Album for Children:** *Mama Don't Allow*, Tom Chapin
**Spoken Word Album:** *Q: The Autobiography of Quincy Jones*, Quincy Jones
**Spoken Comedy Album:** *Napalm & Sillyputty*, George Carlin
**Musical Show Album:** *The Producers*
**Best Compilation Soundtrack Album for a Motion Picture, Television, or Other Visual Media:** *O Brother, Where Art Thou?*, Various Artists
**Best Score Soundtrack Album for a Motion Picture, Television, or Other Visual Media:** *Crouching Tiger, Hidden Dragon*, Tan Dun, composer
**Song Written for a Motion Picture, Television, or Other Visual Media:** "Boss of Me" (from *Malcolm In the Middle*), John Flansburgh and John Linnell, songwriters (They Might Be Giants)
**Instrumental Composition:** end credits from *Cast Away*, Alan Silvestri, composer
**Instrumental Arrangement:** "Doctor Gradus Ad Parnassum," Béla Fleck and Edgar Meyer, arrangers
**Instrumental Arrangement with Accompanying Vocals:** "Drops of Jupiter," Paul Buckmaster, arranger

**Historical Album:** *Lady Day: The Complete Billie Holiday on Columbia 1933–1944*
**Producer, Non-Classical:** T Bone Burnett
**Classical Producer:** Manfred Eicher
**Classical Album:** *Berlioz: Les Troyens*, Various Artists; London Symphony Orchestra
**Orchestral Performance:** *Boulez Conducts Varèse (Amériques; Arcana; Déserts; Ionisation)*, Pierre Boulez (Chicago Symphony Orchestra)
**Opera Recording:** *Berlioz: Les Troyens*, Sir Colin Davis, conductor
**Choral Performance:** *Bach: St. Matthew Passion*, Nikolaus Harnoncourt, conductor
**Instrumental Soloist with Orchestra:** *Strauss Wind Concertos (Horn Concerto; Oboe Concerto, Etc.)*, Daniel Barenboim, piano/conductor; Dale Clevenger, horn; Larry Combs, clarinet; Alex Klein, oboe; David McGill, bassoon
**Instrumental Soloist Without Orchestra:** *Britten Cello Suites (1–3)*, Truls Mork, cello
**Chamber Music:** *Haydn: The Complete String Quartets*, The Angeles String Quartet
**Small Ensemble Performance (with or Without Conductor):** *After Mozart (Raskatov, Silvestrov, Schnittke, Etc.)*, Kremerata Baltica
**Classical Vocal:** *Dreams & Fables—Gluck Italian Arias (Tremo Fra' Dubbi Miei; Di Questa Cetra In Seno, Etc.)*, Cecilia Bartoli, mezzo soprano
**Classical Contemporary Composition:** *Rouse: Concert De Gaudí for Guitar and Orch.*, Christopher Rouse, composer
**Classical Crossover Album:** *Perpetual Motion (Scarlatti, Bach, Debussy, Chopin, Etc.)*, Béla Fleck, banjo (Joshua Bell, violin; Evelyn Glennie, marimba; Gary Hoffman, cello; Edgar Meyer, bass and piano; Chris Thile, mandolin; John Williams, guitar)
**Music Video, Short Form:** "Weapon of Choice," (Fatboy Slim Featuring Bootsy Collins), Spike Jonze, video director
**Music Video, Long Form:** *Recording the Producers—A Musical Romp with Mel Brooks* (Mel Brooks), Susan Froemke, video director

## 2001 Country Music Association Awards

**Entertainer of the Year:** Tim McGraw
**Single of the Year:** "I Am a Man of Constant Sorrow," Soggy Bottom Boys
**Album of the Year:** *O Brother, Where Art Thou?* Soundtrack, various artists
**Song of the Year:** "Murder on Music Row," Larry Cordle and Larry Shell
**Male Vocalist of the Year:** Toby Keith
**Female Vocalist of the Year:** Lee Ann Womack

**Vocal Group of the Year:** Lonestar
**Vocal Duo of the Year:** Brooks & Dunn
**Vocal Event of the Year:** "Too Country," Brad Paisley with featured vocals by George Jones, Bill Anderson, and Buck Owens
**Horizon Award:** Keith Urban
**Musician of the Year:** Dann Huff
**Music Video of the Year:** "Born to Fly," Sara Evans

## 2001 National Book Awards

**Fiction:** *The Corrections*, Jonathan Franzen (Farrar, Straus & Giroux)
**Nonfiction:** *The Noonday Demon: An Atlas of Depression*, Andrew Solomon (Scribner)
**Poetry:** *Poems Seven: New and Collected Poetry*, Alan Dugan (Seven Stories Press)

**Young People's Literature:** *True Believer*, Virginia Euwer Wolff (Atheneum Books)
**Medal for Distinguished Contribution to American Literature:** Arthur Miller

## 2001 National Book Critics Circle Awards

**Fiction:** *Austerlitz*, W. G. Sebald (Random House)
**General Nonfiction:** *Double Fold: Libraries and the Assault on Paper*, Nicholson Baker (Random House)
**Biography or Autobiography:** *Boswell's Presumptuous Task: The Making of the Life of Dr. Johnson*, Adam Sisman (Farrar, Straus & Giroux)
**Poetry:** *Saving Lives*, Albert Goldbarth (Ohio State University)

**Criticism:** *The War Against Cliche: Essays and Reviews, 1971–2000*, Martin Amis (Talk Miramax)
**Ivan Sandrof Lifetime Achievement Award:** Jason Epstein
**Nona Balakian Citation for Excellence in Reviewing:** Michael Gorra

# PEN/Faulkner Award

The PEN/Faulkner award is the largest annual juried prize for fiction in the United States. The winner receives $15,000.

**1981** Walter Abish, *How German Is It?*
**1982** David Bradley, *The Chaneysville Incident*
**1983** Toby Olson, *Seaview*
**1984** John Edgar Wideman, *Sent for You Yesterday*
**1985** Tobias Wolff, *The Barracks Thief*
**1986** Peter Taylor, *The Old Forest*
**1987** Richard Wiley, *Soldiers in Hiding*
**1988** T. Coraghessan Boyle, *World's End*
**1989** James Salter, *Dusk*
**1990** E. L. Doctorow, *Billy Bathgate*
**1991** John Edgar Wideman, *Philadelphia Fire*

**1992** Don Delillo, *Mao II*
**1993** E. Annie Proulx, *Postcards*
**1994** Philip Roth, *Operation Shylock*
**1995** David Guterson, *Snow Falling on Cedars*
**1996** Richard Ford, *Independence Day*
**1997** Gina Berriault, *Women in Their Beds*
**1998** Rafi Zabor, *The Bear Comes Home*
**1999** Michael Cunningham, *The Hours*
**2000** Ha Jin, *Waiting*
**2001** Philip Roth, *The Human Stain*
**2002** Ann Patchett, *Bel Canto*

# Booker Prize

Britain's most prestigious literary award, officially the "Booker McConnell Prize," honors the best full-length novel written in English by a citizen of a current or former British Commonwealth country.

**1969** *Something to Answer For*, P. H. Newby
**1970** *The Elected Member*, Bernice Rubens
**1971** *In a Free State*, V. S. Naipaul
**1972** *G.: A Novel*, John Berger
**1973** *The Siege of Krishnapur*, J. G. Farrell
**1974** (tie) *The Conservationist*, Nadine Gordimer *Holiday*, Stanley Middleton
**1975** *Heat and Dust*, Ruth Prawer Jhabvala
**1976** *Saville*, David Storey
**1977** *Staying On*, Paul Scott
**1978** *The Sea, The Sea*, Iris Murdoch
**1979** *Offshore*, Penelope Fitzgerald
**1980** *Rites of Passage*, William Golding
**1981** *Midnight's Children*, Salman Rushdie
**1982** *Schindler's List*, Thomas Keneally
**1983** *Life & Times of Michael K*, J. M. Coetzee
**1984** *Hotel du Lac*, Anita Brookner
**1985** *The Bone People*, Keri Hulme

**1986** *The Old Devils*, Kingsley Amis
**1987** *Moon Tiger*, Penelope Lively
**1988** *Oscar and Lucinda*, Peter Carey
**1989** *The Remains of the Day*, Kazuo Ishiguro
**1990** *Possession: A Romance*, A. S. Byatt
**1991** *The Famished Road*, Ben Okri
**1992** (tie) *The English Patient*, Michael Ondaatje *Sacred Hunger*, Barry Unsworth
**1993** *Paddy Clarke, Ha Ha Ha*, Roddy Doyle
**1994** *How Late It Was, How Late*, James Kelman
**1995** *The Ghost Road*, Pat Barker
**1996** *Last Orders*, Graham Swift
**1997** *The God of Small Things*, Arundhati Roy
**1998** *Amsterdam*, Ian McEwan
**1999** *Disgrace*, J. M. Coetzee
**2000** *The Blind Assassin*, Margaret Atwood
**2001** *True History of the Kelly Gang*, Peter Carey

# Newbery Medal

The Newbery Medal is awarded annually by the American Library Association for the most distinguished contribution to American literature for children.

**2002 Newbery Medal and Honor Books**
Newbery Medal for Best Book: *A Single Shard*, Linda Sue Park (Houghton Mifflin/Clarion Books)
Newbery Honor Books: *Everything on a Waffle*, Polly Horvath (Farrar, Straus & Giroux); *Carver: A Life in Poems*, Marilyn Nelson (Front Street)

**1922–2001**
**1922** *The Story of Mankind*, Hendrick Willem Van Loon
**1923** *The Voyages of Dr. Doolittle*, Hugh A. Lofting
**1924** *The Dark Frigate*, Charles Boardman Hawes
**1925** *Tales from Silver Lands*, Charles Joseph Finger
**1926** *Shen of the Sea*, Arthur Bowie Chrisman
**1927** *Smoky, the Cow Horse*, Will James
**1928** *Gay-Neck, the Story of a Pigeon*, Dhan Gopal Mukerji
**1929** *The Trumpeter of Krakow*, Eric P. Kelly
**1930** *Hitty, Her First Hundred Years*, Rachel Field
**1931** *The Cat Who Went to Heaven*, Elizabeth Jane Coatsworth
**1932** *Waterless Mountain*, Laura Adams Armer
**1933** *Young Fu of the Upper Yangtze*, Elizabeth Foreman Lewis
**1934** *Invincible Louisa*, Cornelia Meigs

**1935** *Dobry*, Monica Shannon
**1936** *Caddie Woodlawn*, Carol Ryrie Brink
**1937** *Roller Skates*, Ruth Sawyer
**1938** *The White Stag*, Kate Seredy
**1939** *Thimble Summer*, Elizabeth Enright
**1940** *Daniel Boone*, James Henry Daugherty
**1941** *Call It Courage*, Armstrong Sperry
**1942** *The Matchlock Gun*, Walter Dumax Edmonds
**1943** *Adam of the Road*, Elizabeth Janet Gray
**1944** *Johnny Tremain*, Esther Forbes
**1945** *Rabbit Hill*, Robert Lawson
**1946** *Strawberry Girl*, Lois Lenski
**1947** *Miss Hickory*, Carolyn Sherwin Bailey
**1948** *The Twenty-One Balloons*, William Pène du Bois
**1949** *King of the Wind*, Marguerite Henry
**1950** *The Door in the Wall*, Marguerite de Angeli
**1951** *Amos Fortune, Free Man*, Elizabeth Yates
**1952** *Ginger Pye*, Eleanor Estes
**1953** *Secret of the Andes*, Ann Nolan Clark
**1954** *. . . And Now Miguel*, Joseph Krumgold
**1955** *The Wheel on the School*, Meindert DeJong
**1956** *Carry On, Mr. Bowditch*, Jean Lee Latham
**1957** *Miracles on Maple Hill*, Virginia Eggertsen Sorensen

1958 *Rifles for Watie,* Harold Keith
1959 *The Witch of Blackbird Pond,* Elizabeth George Speare
1960 *Onion John,* Joseph Krumgold
1961 *Island of the Blue Dolphins,* Scott O'Dell
1962 *The Bronze Bow,* Elizabeth George Speare
1963 *A Wrinkle in Time,* Madeleine L'Engle
1964 *It's Like This, Cat,* Emily Cheney Neville
1965 *Shadow of a Bull,* Maia Wojciechowska
1966 *I, Juan de Pareja,* Elizabeth Borton de Treviño
1967 *Up a Road Slowly,* Irene Hunt
1968 *From the Mixed-Up Files of Mrs. Basil E. Frankweiler,* E. L. Konigsburg
1969 *The High King,* Lloyd Alexander
1970 *Sounder,* William H. Armstrong
1971 *Summer of the Swans,* Betsy Byars
1972 *Mrs. Frisby and the Rats of NIMH,* Robert C. O'Brien
1973 *Julie of the Wolves,* Jean Craighead George
1974 *The Slave Dancer,* Paula Fox
1975 *M. C. Higgins, the Great,* Virginia Hamilton
1976 *The Grey King,* Susan Cooper
1977 *Roll of Thunder, Hear My Cry,* Mildred D. Taylor
1978 *Bridge to Terabithia,* Katherine Paterson
1979 *The Westing Game,* Ellen Raskin

1980 *A Gathering of Days: A New England Girl's Journal, 1830–32,* Joan W. Blos
1981 *Jacob Have I Loved,* Katherine Paterson
1982 *A Visit to William Blake's Inn: Poems for Innocent and Experienced Travelers,* Nancy Willard
1983 *Dicey's Song,* Cynthia Voigt
1984 *Dear Mr. Henshaw,* Beverly Cleary
1985 *The Hero and the Crown,* Robin McKinley
1986 *Sarah, Plain and Tall,* Patricia MacLachlan
1987 *The Whipping Boy,* Sid Fleischman
1988 *Lincoln: A Photobiography,* Russell Freedman
1989 *Joyful Noise: Poems for Two Voices,* Paul Fleischman
1990 *Number the Stars,* Lois Lowry
1991 *Maniac Magee: a Novel,* Jerry Spinelli
1992 *Shiloh,* Phyllis Reynolds Naylor
1993 *Missing May,* Cynthia Rylant
1994 *The Giver,* Lois Lowry
1995 *Walk Two Moons,* Sharon Creech
1996 *The Midwife's Apprentice,* Karen Cushman
1997 *The View from Saturday,* E. L. Konigsburg
1998 *Out of the Dust,* Karen Hesse
1999 *Holes,* Louis Sachar
2000 *Bud, Not Buddy,* Christopher Paul Curtis
2001 *A Year Down Yonder,* Richard Peck

# Caldecott Medal

The Caldecott Medal is awarded annually by the American Library Association for the most distinguished American picture book for children.

**2002 Caldecott Medal and Honor Books**
Caldecott Medal for Best Picture Book: *The Three Little Pigs,* written and illustrated by David Wiesner (Houghton Mifflin/Clarion Books)
Caldecott Honor Books: *Martin's Big Words: The Life of Dr. Martin Luther King, Jr.,* illustrated by Bryan Collier, written by Doreen Rappaport (Hyperion Books for Children/Jump at the Sun); *Dinosaurs of Waterhouse Hawkins: An Illuminating History of Mr. Waterhouse Hawkins, Artist and Lecturer,* illustrated by Brian Selznick, written by Barbara Kerley (Scholastic); *The Stray Dog,* illustrated and written by Marc Simont (HarperCollins)

**1938–2001**
1938 *Animals of the Bible, a Picture Book,* text selected by Helen Dean Fish, illustrated by Dorothy P. Lathrop
1939 *Mei Li,* written and illustrated by Thomas Handforth
1940 *Abraham Lincoln,* written and illustrated by Ingri and Edgar Parin D'Aulaire
1941 *They Were Strong and Good,* written and illustrated by Robert Lawson
1942 *Make Way for Ducklings,* written and illustrated by Robert McCloskey
1943 *The Little House,* written and illustrated by Virginia Lee Burton
1944 *Many Moons,* written by James Thurber, illustrated by Louis Slobodkin
1945 *Prayer for a Child,* written by Elizabeth Orton Jones
1946 *The Rooster Crows,* written and illustrated by Maud and Miska Petersham
1947 *The Little Island,* written by Golden MacDonald, illustrated by Leonard Weisgard
1948 *White Snow, Bright Snow,* written by Alvin Tresselt, illustrated by Roger Duvoisin

1949 *The Big Snow,* written and illustrated by Berta and Elmer Hader
1950 *Song of the Swallows,* written and illustrated by Leo Politi
1951 *The Egg Tree,* written and illustrated by Katherine Milhous
1952 *Finders Keepers,* written by William Lipkind, illustrated by Nicolas Mordivinoff
1953 *The Biggest Bear,* written and illustrated by Lynd Ward
1954 *Madeline's Rescue,* written and illustrated by Ludwig Bemelmans
1955 *Cinderella, or, The Little Glass Slipper,* translated and illustrated by Marcia Brown
1956 *Frog Went A-Courtin',* retold by John Langstaff, illustrated by Feodor Rojankovsky
1957 *A Tree Is Nice,* written by Janice May Udry, illustrated by Marc Simont
1958 *Time of Wonder,* written and illustrated by Robert McCloskey
1959 *Chanticleer and the Fox,* adapted and illustrated by Barbara Cooney
1960 *Nine Days to Christmas,* written by Marie Hall Ets and Aurora Labastida, illustrated by Marie Hall Ets
1961 *Baboushka and the Three Kings,* written by Ruth Robbins, illustrated by Nicolas Sidjakov
1962 *Once a Mouse,* retold and illustrated by Marcia Brown
1963 *The Snowy Day,* written and illustrated by Ezra Jack Keats
1964 *Where the Wild Things Are,* written and illustrated by Maurice Sendak
1965 *May I Bring a Friend?,* written by Beatrice Schenk de Regniers, illustrated by Beni Montresor

1966 *Always Room for One More,* written by Sorche Nic Leodhas, illustrated by Nonny Hogrogian

1967 *Sam, Bangs and Moonshine,* written and illustrated by Evaline Ness

1968 *Drummer Hoff,* written by Barbara Emberley, illustrated by Ed Emberley

1969 *The Fool of the World and the Flying Ship,* retold by Arthur Ransome, illustrated by Uri Shulevitz

1970 *Sylvester and the Magic Pebble,* written and illustrated by William Steig

1971 *A Story, A Story: An African Tale,* retold and illustrated by Gail E. Haley

1972 *One Fine Day,* written and illustrated by Nonny Hogrogian

1973 *The Funny Little Woman,* retold by Arlene Mosel, illustrated by Blair Lent

1974 *Duffy and the Devil,* retold by Harve Zemach, illustrated by Margot Zemach

1975 *Arrow to the Sun: A Pueblo Indian Tale,* adapted and illustrated by Gerald H. McDermott

1976 *Why Mosquitos Buzz in People's Ears (An African Tale),* retold by Verna Aardema, illustrated by Leo and Diane Dillon

1977 *Ashanti to Zulu: African Traditions,* written by Margaret Musgrove, illustrated by Leo and Diane Dillon

1978 *Noah's Ark,* written by Jacob Revius, illustrated by Peter Spier

1979 *The Girl Who Loved Wild Horses,* written and illustrated by Paul Goble

1980 *Ox-Cart Man,* written by Donald Hall, illustrated by Barbara Cooney

1981 *Fables,* written and illustrated by Arnold Lobel

1982 *Jumanji,* written and illustrated by Chris Van Allsburg

1983 *Shadow,* translated and illustrated by Marcia Brown

1984 *The Glorious Flight: Across the Channel with Louis Blériot,* written and illustrated by Alice and Martin Provensen

1985 *St. George and the Dragon,* retold by Margaret Hodges, illustrated by Trina Schart Hyman

1986 *The Polar Express,* written and illustrated by Chris Van Allsburg

1987 *Hey, Al,* written by Arthur Yorinks, illustrated by Richard Egielski

1988 *Owl Moon,* written by Jane Yolen, illustrated by John Schoenherr

1989 *Song and Dance Man,* written by Karen Ackerman, illustrated by Stephen Gammell

1990 *Lon Po Po: A Red-Riding Hood Story from China,* by Ed Young

1991 *Black & White,* written and illustrated by David Macaulay

1992 *Tuesday,* written and illustrated by David Wiesner

1993 *Mirette on the High Wire,* written and illustrated by Emily Arnold McCully

1994 *Grandfather's Journey,* written and illustrated by Allen Say

1995 *Smoky Night,* written by Eve Bunting, illustrated by David Diaz

1996 *Officer Buckle and Gloria,* written and illustrated by Peggy Rathmann

1997 *Golem,* written and illustrated by David Wisniewski

1998 *Rapunzel,* illustrated and retold by Paul O. Zelinsky

1999 *Snowflake Bentley,* written by Jacqueline Briggs Martin, illustrated by Mary Azarian

2000 *Joseph Had a Little Overcoat,* illustrated by Simms Taback

2001 *So You Want to Be President?,* by Judith St. George, illustrated by David Small

# Other American Library Association Awards for Children's Books, 2002

**Coretta Scott King Award, honoring black authors and illustrators: (author):** *The Land,* Mildred D. Taylor (Penguin Putnam/Phyllis Fogelman Books); **(illustrator):** *Goin' Someplace Special,* Jerry Pinkney (Atheneum/Anne Schwartz Books)

**Michael L. Printz Award for excellence in young adult literature:** *A Step from Heaven,* An Na (Front Street)

**2002 Pura Belpré Award, honoring Latino/Latina writers and illustrators (awarded biennially): (author):** *Esperanza Rising,* Pam Muñoz Ryan (Scholastic); **(illustrator):** *Chato and the Party Animals,* illustrated by ~~Quant Quant~~, ~~written by Gary Solo (S. D. Putnam's~~ ~~Sons)~~

**Margaret A. Edwards Award for lifetime contribution in writing for young adults:** Paul Zindel

**Robert F. Sibert Award for informational book:** *Black Potatoes: The Story of the Great Irish Famine 1845–1850,* Susan Campbell Bartoletti (Houghton Mifflin)

**Mildred L. Batchelder Award, for best book originally published in a foreign language in a foreign country:** *How I Became an American,* written by Karin Gündisch in German and translated by James Skofield (Carus Publishing/Cricket Books)

~~May Hill Arbuthnot Honor Lecture Award: Maurice~~ ~~Sendak~~

# 2002 National Magazine Awards

**General Excellence:**
*Print* (circulation less than 200,000)
*National Geographic Adventure* (circulation 200,000 to 500,000)
*Vibe* (circulation 500,000 to 1,000,000)
*Entertainment Weekly* (circulation 1,000,000 to 2,000,000)
*Newsweek* (circulation more than 2,000,000)
**Personal Service:** *National Geographic Adventure*
**Leisure Interests:** *Vogue*
**Reporting:** *The Atlantic Monthly*
**Public Interest:** *The Atlantic Monthly*

**Feature Writing:** *The Atlantic Monthly*
**Columns and Commentary:** *New York*
**Essays:** *The New Yorker*
**Reviews and Criticism:** *Harper's Magazine*
**Profiles:** *The New Yorker*
**Single-topic Issue:** *Time*
**Design:** *Details*
**Photography:** *Vanity Fair*
**Fiction:** *The New Yorker*
**General Excellence Online:** *National Geographic Magazine Online*

# Bollingen Prize in Poetry

The Bollingen Prize in Poetry is administered by the Yale University Library.

| | |
|---|---|
| 1949 Ezra Pound | 1969 John Berryman and Karl Shapiro |
| 1950 Wallace Stevens | 1971 Richard Wilbur and Mona Van Duyn |
| 1951 John Crowe Ransom | 1973 James Merrill |
| 1952 Marianne Moore | 1975 Archie Randolph Ammons |
| 1953 Archibald MacLeish and William Carlos Williams | 1977 David Ignatow |
| 1954 W. H. Auden | 1979 W. S. Merwin |
| 1955 Léonie Adams and Louise Bogan | 1981 Howard Nemerov and May Swenson |
| 1956 Conrad Aiken | 1983 Anthony Hecht and John Hollander |
| 1957 Allen Tate | 1985 John Ashbery and Fred Chappell |
| 1958 e. e. cummings | 1987 Stanley Kunitz |
| 1959 Theodore Roethke | 1989 Edgar Bowers |
| 1960 Delmore Schwartz | 1991 Laura Riding Jackson and Donald Justice |
| 1961 Yvor Winters | 1993 Mark Strand |
| 1962 John Hall Wheelock and Richard Eberhart | 1995 Kenneth Koch |
| 1963 Robert Frost | 1997 Gary Snyder |
| 1965 Horace Gregory | 1999 Robert Creeley |
| 1967 Robert Penn Warren | 2001 Louise Glück |

# Kingsley Tufts Poetry Prize

| | |
|---|---|
| 1993 Susan Mitchell, *Rapture* | 1998 John Koethe, *Falling Water* |
| 1994 Yusef Komunyakaa, *Neon Vernacular* | 1999 B. H. Fairchild, *The Art of the Lathe* |
| 1995 Thomas Lux, *Split Horizon* | 2000 Robert Wrigley, *Reign of Snakes: Poems* |
| 1996 Deborah Digges, *Rough Music* | 2001 Alan Shapiro, *The Dead Alive and Busy* |
| 1997 Campbell McGrath, *Spring Comes to Chicago* | 2002 Carl Phillips, *The Tether* |

# 2002 NAACP Image Awards

## MOTION PICTURE

**Outstanding Motion Picture:** *Ali*

**Outstanding Actress in a Motion Picture:** Halle Berry, *Swordfish*

**Outstanding Actor in a Motion Picture:** Denzel Washington, *Training Day*

**Outstanding Supporting Actress in a Motion Picture:** Angela Bassett, *The Score*

**Outstanding Supporting Actor in a Motion Picture:** Jamie Foxx, *Ali*

## TELEVISION

**Outstanding Comedy Series:** *The Steve Harvey Show* (WB)

**Outstanding Actress in a Comedy Series:** Mo'nique, *The Parkers*

**Outstanding Actor in a Comedy Series:** Steve Harvey, *The Steve Harvey Show*

**Outstanding Supporting Actress in a Comedy Series:** Terri J. Vaughn, *The Steve Harvey Show*

**Outstanding Supporting Actor in a Comedy Series:** Cedric "The Entertainer," *The Steve Harvey Show*

**Outstanding Drama Series:** *Soul Food* (Showtime)

**Outstanding Actress in a Drama Series:** Della Reese, *Touched by an Angel*

**Outstanding Actor in a Drama Series:** Eriq La Salle, *ER*

**Outstanding Supporting Actress in a Drama Series:** Debbi Morgan, *Soul Food*

**Outstanding Supporting Actor in a Drama Series:** Ice-T, *Law & Order: Special Victims Unit*

**Outstanding Television Movie, Miniseries, or Dramatic Special:** *Boycott* (HBO)

**Outstanding Actress in a Television Movie, Miniseries, or Dramatic Special:** Angela Bassett, *Ruby's Bucket of Blood*

**Outstanding Actor in a Television Movie, Miniseries, or Dramatic Special:** Gregory Hines, *Bojangles*

**Outstanding Actress in a Daytime Drama Series:** Tonya Lee Williams, *The Young & the Restless*

**Outstanding Actor in a Daytime Drama Series:** Shemar Moore, *The Young & the Restless*

**Outstanding Variety Series/Special:** Michael Jackson: *30th Anniversary Special* (CBS)

**Outstanding Performance in a Variety Series/Special:** Michael Jackson, *Michael Jackson: 30th Anniversary Special*

**Outstanding News, Talk, or Information Series:** *20/20:* "Birmingham Church Bombing" (ABC)

**Outstanding News, Talk, or Information Special:** *BET Tonight Special:* "Aaliyah"

**Outstanding Youth or Children's Series/Special:** *Teen Summit* (BET)

**Outstanding Performance in a Youth or Children's Series/Special:** Levar Burton, *Reading Rainbow*

**Outstanding Youth Actor/Actress:** Aaron Meeks, *Soul Food*

## RECORDING

**Outstanding New Artist:** Alicia Keys, "Fallin'"

**Outstanding Female Artist:** Aaliyah, *Aaliyah*

**Outstanding Male Artist:** Luther Vandross, "Take You Out"

**Outstanding Duo or Group:** Destiny's Child, *Survivor*

**Outstanding Hip-Hop/Rap Artist:** Ja Rule, "Livin' It Up"

**Outstanding Jazz Artist:** Quincy Jones, *Q: The Musical Biography of Quincy Jones*

**Outstanding Gospel Artist—Traditional:** Shirley Caesar, *Hymns*

**Outstanding Gospel Artist—Contemporary:** Yolanda Adams, *Believe*

**Outstanding Music Video:** Michael Jackson, "You Rock My World"

**Outstanding Song:** Alicia Keys and Erika Rose, songwriters, "A Woman's Worth"

**Outstanding Album:** Alicia Keys, *Songs in A Minor*

## LITERARY WORK

**Outstanding Literary Work, Fiction:** *A Day Late and a Dollar Short,* Terry McMillan

**Outstanding Literary Work, Nonfiction:** *Sally Hemings, An American Scandal: The Struggle to Tell the Controversial True Story,* Tina Andrews

**Outstanding Literary Work, Children's:** *Just the Two of Us,* written by Will Smith, illustrated by Kadir Nelson

# The Spingarn Medal

The Spingarn Medal is awarded annually by the National Association for the Advancement of Colored People for outstanding achievement by a black American.

| | | |
|---|---|---|
| 1915 Ernest E. Just | 1945 Paul Robeson | 1974 Damon Keith |
| 1916 Charles Young | 1946 Thurgood Marshall | 1975 Hank Aaron |
| 1917 Harry T. Burleigh | 1947 Percy Julian | 1976 Alvin Ailey |
| 1918 William Stanley Braithwaite | 1948 Channing H. Tobias | 1977 Alex Haley |
| | 1949 Ralph J. Bunche | 1978 Andrew Young |
| 1919 Archibald H. Grimke | 1950 Charles Hamilton Houston | 1979 Rosa L. Parks |
| 1920 W. E. B. Du Bois | 1951 Mabel Keaton Staupers | 1980 Rayford W. Logan |
| 1921 Charles S. Gilpin | 1952 Harry T. Moore | 1981 Coleman Young |
| 1922 Mary B. Talbert | 1953 Paul R. Williams | 1982 Benjamin E. Mays |
| 1923 George Washington Carver | 1954 Theodore K. Lawless | 1983 Lena Horne |
| | 1955 Carl Murphy | 1984 Tom Bradley |
| 1924 Roland Hayes | 1956 Jackie Robinson | 1985 Bill Cosby |
| 1925 James Weldon Johnson | 1957 Martin Luther King, Jr. | 1986 Benjamin L. Hooks |
| 1926 Carter G. Woodson | 1958 Daisy Bates and the Little Rock Nine | 1987 Percy Ellis Sutton |
| 1927 Anthony Overton | | 1988 Frederick Douglass Patterson |
| 1928 Charles W. Chesnutt | 1959 Edward Kennedy (Duke) Ellington | |
| 1929 Mordecai Wyatt Johnson | | 1989 Jesse Jackson |
| 1930 Henry A. Hunt | 1960 Langston Hughes | 1990 L. Douglas Wilder |
| 1931 Richard Berry Harrison | 1961 Kenneth B. Clark | 1991 Colin T. Powell |
| 1932 Robert Russa Moton | 1962 Robert C. Weaver | 1992 Barbara Jordan |
| 1933 Max Yergan | 1963 Medgar Evers | 1993 Dorothy Irene Height |
| 1934 William T. B. Williams | 1964 Roy Wilkins | 1994 Maya Angelou |
| 1935 Mary McLeod Bethune | 1965 Leontyne Price | 1995 John Hope Franklin |
| 1936 John Hope | 1966 John H. Johnson | 1996 A. Leon Higginbotham, Jr. |
| 1937 Walter White | 1967 Edward W. Brooke III | 1997 Carl Rowan |
| 1938 No award | 1968 Sammy Davis, Jr. | 1998 Myrlie Evers-Williams |
| 1939 Marian Anderson | 1969 Clarence M. Mitchell, Jr. | 1999 Earl G. Graves, Sr. |
| 1940 Louis T. Wright | 1970 Jacob Lawrence | 2000 Oprah Winfrey |
| 1941 Richard Wright | 1971 Leon Howard Sullivan | 2001 Vernon E. Jordan, Jr. |
| 1942 A. Philip Randolph | 1972 Gordon Parks | 2002 John Lewis |
| 1943 William H. Hastie | 1973 Wilson C. Riles | |
| 1944 Charles Drew | | |

# 2001 George Foster Peabody Awards for Broadcasting

**ABC News Coverage of Sept. 11, 2001:** ABC News, New York

**National Public Radio Coverage of Sept. 11, 2001:** National Public Radio, Washington, DC

**CNN Presents:** "Beneath the Veil and Unholy War," CNN Productions (Atlanta), Channel 4 International, and Hard Cash Productions

**Third Watch:** "In Their Own Words," NBC, John Wells Productions

**America: A Tribute to Heroes:** Joel Gallen and U.S. broadcast and cable networks

**Anne Frank:** Touchstone Television, presented on ABC

**American Masters:** "F. Scott Fitzgerald: Winter Dreams," Thirteen/WNET (New York), presented on PBS

**Jazz Profiles:** National Public Radio, Washington, DC The Juniper Hollow an the Edge: Peter Auburn Productions, Inc., and KERA-TV, Dallas/Ft. Worth, Texas

**Mzima—Haunt of the Riverhorse:** Survival Anglia LTD, UK

**ExxonMobil Masterpiece Theatre:** "Talking Heads II: Miss Fozzard Finds Her Feet," Slow Motion Ltd. production for the BBC, presented on PBS

**The Life and Times of Hank Greenberg:** The Chiesla Foundation and Cinemax

**Still Life with Animated Dogs:** Independent Television Service and Paul & Sandra Fierlinger, AR&T Associates, Inc.

**The DNA Files:** SoundVision Productions, presented on National Public Radio

**Visions of Vine Street:** WCPO-TV, Cincinnati, Ohio

**A Murder in the Neighbourhood:** Canadian Broadcasting Corporation

**WTO Challenge:** Television Broadcast Limited, Hong Kong, SAR, People's Republic of China

**Endgame in Ireland:** Brook Lapping Productions for BBC2 in association with WGBH/Boston, RTE (Ireland), La Sept ARTE (France and Germany), SBS (Australia), and YLE (Finland)

**A Huey P. Newton Story:** 40 Acres & A Mule Filmworks, Luna Ray Films, BLACK STARZ!, PBS, and African Heritage Network

**Hell in the Pacific:** A Carlton Production in association with The Learning Channel for Channel Four Television

**Conspiracy:** HBO Films production in association with the British Broadcasting Corporation

**Things Behind the Sun:** Showtime, an Echo Lake Productions/Gidelion Fulmigan Pictures BoyCott: Norman Twain Productions with Shelby Stone Productions in association with HBO Films

**The First Year:** Teachers Documentary Project, presented on PBS

**My Father's Camera:** National Film Board of Canada

**Youth Radio:** Berkeley, Calif.

**Little Bill:** Nickelodeon

**Blue's Clues:** Nickelodeon

**WGBH:** Boston, Mass.

**60 Minutes II:** "Memories of a Massacre," CBS News, New York

**Wit:** Avenue Pictures in association with HBO Films

**The Bernie Mac Show:** Wilmore Films, Regency Television, and 20th Century Fox

**Band of Brothers:** Band of Brothers Ltd. on behalf of DreamWorks and Playtone, presented on HBO

**Nightline:** ABC News, New York

# 2002 Alfred I. du Pont–Columbia University Awards in Television and Radio

**SILVER BATONS**
**Television Awards:**
CBS News *60 Minutes*, Steve Kroft and Leslie Cockburn for "America's Worst Nightmare?"
CBS News, David Martin, and Mary Walsh for reporting on national security on *CBS Evening News* and *60 Minutes II*
WABC-TV, New York, Jim Hoffer, and Daniela Royes for "Caught Off Guard"
CNN, Nic Robertson, and Jonathan Miller for *Northern Ireland: Dying for Peace*
ABC News, Terence Wrong, and Peter Bull for *Hopkins 24/7*
Palfreman Film Group, *Frontline/Nova*, and WGBH-TV, Boston, for "Harvest of Fear" on PBS
*CBS Evening News* and Steve Hartman for *Everybody Has a Story!*

Court TV for *The Interrogation of Michael Crowe*
KIRO-TV, Seattle, for *Why the Orcas of Puget Sound Are Dying*
KCBS-TV, Los Angeles, and Randy Paige for *Poison Paint*
KOLD-TV, Tucson, and Chip Yost, for *Exploding Patrol Cars?*

**Radio Awards:**
National Public Radio and Peter Overby for campaign finance coverage
WNYC Radio, New York, and Beth Fertig for *The Edison Schools Vote*

## 2002 Major Emmy Awards

**Drama Series:** *The West Wing* (NBC)
**Actress:** Allison Janney, *The West Wing*
**Actor:** Michael Chiklis, *The Shield*
**Supporting Actress:** Stockard Channing, *The West Wing*
**Supporting Actor:** John Spencer, *The West Wing*
**Guest Actor:** Charles S. Dutton, *The Practice*
**Guest Actress:** Patricia Clarkson, *Six Feet Under*
**Directing:** Alan Ball, *Six Feet Under:* "Pilot"
**Writing:** Joel Surnow and Robert Cochran, *24:* "Midnight–1:00 A.M."
**Comedy Series:** *Friends* (NBC)
**Actress:** Jennifer Aniston, *Friends*
**Actor:** Ray Romano, *Everybody Loves Raymond*
**Supporting Actress:** Doris Roberts, *Everybody Loves Raymond*
**Supporting Actor:** Brad Garrett, *Everybody Loves Raymond*
**Guest Actress:** Cloris Leachman, *Malcolm in the Middle*
**Guest Actor:** Anthony LaPaglia, *Frasier*
**Directing:** Michael Patrick King, *Sex and the City:* "The Real Me"
**Writing:** Larry Wilmore, *The Bernie Mac Show:* "Pilot"
**Variety, Music, or Comedy Series:** *Late Show with David Letterman* (CBS)
**Variety, Music, or Comedy Special:** *America: A Tribute to Heroes* (broadcast networks)
**Individual Performance, Variety, or Music Program:** Sting, *A&E in Concert: Sting in Tuscany . . . All This Time*

**Directing in a Variety, Music, or Comedy Program:** Ron deMoraes, Kenny Ortega, and Bucky Gunts, *Opening Ceremony Salt Lake 2002 Olympic Winter Games*
**Writing in a Variety, Music, or Comedy Program:** *Saturday Night Live*
**Miniseries or Special:** *Band of Brothers* (HBO)
**Actress:** Laura Linney, *Wild Iris*
**Actor:** Albert Finney, *The Gathering Storm*
**Supporting Actress:** Stockard Channing, *The Matthew Shepard Story*
**Supporting Actor:** Michael Moriarty, *James Dean*
**Directing:** David Frankel, Tom Hanks, David Leland, Richard Loncraine, David Nutter, Phil Alden Robinson, Mikael Salomon, and Tony To, *Band of Brothers*
**Writing:** Larry Ramin and Hugh Whitemore, *The Gathering Storm*
**Made-for-Television Movie:** *The Gathering Storm* (HBO)
**Outstanding Nonfiction Series (informational):** *Biography* (A&E)
**Outstanding Nonfiction Special:** *Inside the Actors Studio: 100th Guest Special* (Bravo)
**Outstanding Nonfiction Program (reality):** *The Osbournes* (MTV)
**Outstanding Special-Class Program:** *The West Wing: Documentary Special* (NBC)
**Outstanding Children's Program:** *Nick News Special Edition: Faces of Hope: The Kids of Afghanistan* (Nickelodeon)
**Outstanding Animated Program (one hour or less):** *Futurama:* "Roswell That Ends Well" (Fox)

## 2001–2002 Daytime Emmy Awards

**Outstanding Drama Series:** *One Life to Live* (ABC)
**Lead Actor in a Drama Series:** Peter Bergman, *The Young and the Restless* (CBS)
**Lead Actress in a Drama Series:** Susan Flannery, *The Bold and the Beautiful* (CBS)
**Supporting Actor in a Drama Series:** Josh Duhamel, *All My Children* (ABC)
**Supporting Actress in a Drama Series:** Crystal Chappell, *Guiding Light* (CBS)
**Younger Actor in a Drama Series:** Jacob Young, *General Hospital* (ABC)
**Younger Actress in a Drama Series:** Jennifer Finnigan, *The Bold and the Beautiful* (CBS)
**Outstanding Pre-School Children's Series:** *Sesame Street* (PBS)
**Outstanding Children's Special:** *My Louisiana Sky* (Showtime)
**Outstanding Children's Animated Program:** *Madeline* (Disney Channel)
**Outstanding Special Class Children's Animated Program:** *Disney's Teacher's Pet* (ABC)
**Performer in a Children's Series:** Levar Burton, *Reading Rainbow* (PBS)

**Performer in a Children's Special:** Kelsey Keel, *My Louisiana Sky* (Showtime)
**Performer in an Animated Program:** Charles Shaughnessy, *Stanley* (Disney Channel)
**Outstanding Children's Series:** *Reading Rainbow* (PBS)
**Outstanding Special Class Series:** *AMC's Behind the Screen with John Burke* (AMC)
**Outstanding Special Class Special:** *Beyond Tara: The Extraordinary Life of Hattie McDaniel* (AMC)
**Outstanding Game/Audience Participation Show:** *Jeopardy!* (syndicated)
**Outstanding Game-Show Host:** Bob Barker, *The Price Is Right* (CBS)
**Outstanding Talk Show:** *The Rosie O'Donnell Show* (syndicated)
**Outstanding Talk-Show Host:** Rosie O'Donnell, *The Rosie O'Donnell Show* (syndicated)
**Outstanding Service Show:** *Wolfgang Puck* (Food Network)
**Outstanding Service-Show Host:** Martha Stewart, *Martha Stewart Living* (syndicated)

# Albany Medical Center Prize in Medicine and Biomedical Research

Each year the Albany Medical Center honors a physician, scientist, or group whose work has led to significant advances in the fields of health care and scientific research. The $500,000 annual award is the largest in the U.S. in medicine.

**2001** Dr. Arnold J. Levine, president of Rockefeller University, for his seminal findings as codiscoverer of the p53 gene and his ongoing research and many other scientific contributions.

**2002** Dr. Anthony S. Fauci, AIDS researcher and director of the National Institute of Allergy and Infectious Diseases, for his seminal research in AIDS and other diseases of the immune system, his overall contributions to the advancement of science, and his distinguished public service.

## Fields Medal Winners

The Fields Medal has been awarded quadrennially since 1936 by the International Congress of Mathematicians in Toronto to recognize outstanding mathematics achievement.

**1936** Lars Valerian Ahlfors (Harvard University) and Jesse Douglas (Massachusetts Institute of Technology)

**(Fields Medals were not awarded during World War II)**

**1950** Laurent Schwarts (University of Nancy) and Atle Selberg (Institute for Advanced Study, Princeton)

**1954** Kunihiko Kodaira (Princeton University) and Jean-Pierre Serre (University of Paris)

**1958** Klaus Friedrich Roth (University of London) and René Thom (University of Strasbourgh)

**1962** Lars V. Hörmander (University of Stockholm) and John Willard Milnor (Princeton University)

**1966** Michael Francis Atiyah (Oxford University), Paul Joseph Cohen (Stanford University), Alexander Grothendieck (University of Paris), and Stephen Smale (University of California, Berkeley)

**1970** Alan Baker (Cambridge University), Heisuke Hironaka (Harvard University), Serge P. Novikov (Moscow University), and John Griggs Thompson (Cambridge University)

**1974** Enrico Bombieri (University of Pisa) and David Bryant Mumford (Harvard University)

**1978** Pierre René Deligne (Institut des Hautes Études Scientifiques), Charles Louis Fefferman (Princeton University), Gregori Alexandrovitch Margulis (Moscow University), and Daniel G. Quillen (Massachusetts Institute of Technology)

**1982** Alain Connes (Institut des Hautes Études Scientifiques), William P. Thurston (Princeton University), and Shing-Tung Yau (Institute for Advanced Study, Princeton)

**1986** Simon Donaldson (Oxford University), Gerd Faltings (Princeton University), and Michael Freedman (University of California, San Diego)

**1990** Vladimir Drinfeld (Phys. Inst. Kharkov), Vaughan Jones (University of California, Berkeley), Shigefumi Mori (University of Kyoto), and Edward Witten (Institute for Advanced Study, Princeton)

**1994** Pierre-Louis Lions (Université de Paris–Dauphine), Jean-Christophe Yoccoz (Université de Paris–Sud), Jean Bourgain (Institute for Advanced Study, Princeton), and Efim Zelmanov (University of Wisconsin)

**1998** Richard E. Borcherds (Cambridge University), William T. Gowers (Cambridge University), Maxim Kontsevich (Institut des Hautes Études Scientifiques and Rutgers University), and Curtis T. McMullen (Harvard University)

**2002** Laurent Lafforgue (Institut des Hautes Études Scientifiques) and Vladimir Voevodsky (Institute for Advanced Study, Princeton)

## Enrico Fermi Award

The $100,000 award is given in recognition of scientific and technical achievement in atomic energy. Awarded by the president, it is the U.S. government's oldest science and technology award.

**1954** Enrico Fermi
**1956** John von Neumann
**1957** Ernest O. Lawrence
**1958** Eugene P. Wigner
**1959** Glenn T. Seaborg
**1961** Hans A. Bethe
**1962** Edward Teller
**1963** J. Robert Oppenheimer
**1964** Hyman G. Rickover
**1966** Otto Hahn, Lise Meitner, and Fritz Strassman
**1968** John A. Wheeler
**1969** Walter H. Zinn
**1970** Norris E. Bradbury
**1971** Shields Warren and Stafford L. Warren
**1972** Manson Benedict
**1976** William L. Russell
**1978** Harold M. Agnew and Wolfgang K. H. Panofsky
**1980** Alvin M. Weinberg and Rudolf E. Peirls

**1981** W. Bennett Lewis
**1982** Herbert Anderson and Seth Neddermeyer
**1983** Alexander Hollaender and John Lawrence
**1984** Hobert R. Wilson and Georges Vendryès
**1985** Norman C. Rasmussen and Marshall N. Rosenblath
**1986** Ernest D. Courant and M. Stanley Livingston
**1987** Luis W. Alvarez and Gerald F. Tape
**1988** Richard B. Setlow and Victor F. Weisskopf
**1990** George A. Cowan and Robley D. Evans
**1992** Leon M. Lederman, Harold Brown, and John S. Foster, Jr.
**1993** Freeman J. Dyson and Liane B. Russell
**1995** Ugo Fano and Martin Kamen
**1996** Richard Garwin, Mortimer Elkind, and H. Rodney Withers
**1998** Maurice Goldhaber and Michael E. Phelps
**2000** Sidney Drell, Sheldon Datz, and Herbert York

# 2002 MacArthur Foundation Awards

The MacArthur Foundation awards $500,000 over five years to each MacArthur Fellow.

Bonnie Bassler, 40, molecular ecobiologist; Princeton, N.J.

Ann Blair, 40, intellectual historian; Cambridge, Mass.

Katharine Boo, 37, journalist; Washington, DC

Paul Ginsparg, 46, physicist and Internet publisher; Ithaca, N.Y.

David Goldstein, 51, energy conservation specialist; San Francisco, Calif.

Karen Hesse, 50, novelist; Brattleboro, Vt.

Janine Jagger, 52, epidemiologist; Charlottesville, Va.

Daniel Jurafsky, 39, computational linguist; Boulder, Colo.

Toba Khedoori, 37, artist; Los Angeles, Calif.

Liz Lerman, 54, choreographer; Takoma Park, Md.

George Lewis, 50, trombonist and composer; La Jolla, Calif.

Liza Lou, 33, glass-bead artist; Los Angeles, Calif.

Edgar Meyer, 41, bassist and composer; Nashville, Tenn.

Jack Miles, 60, literary scholar and critic; Los Angeles, Calif.

Erik Mueggler, 40, anthropologist; Ann Arbor, Mich.

Sendhil Mullainathan, 29, economist; Cambridge, Mass.

Stanley Nelson, 48, documentary filmmaker; New York, N.Y.

Lee Ann Newsom, 45, paleoethnobotanist; University Park, Pa.

Daniela Rus, 39, roboticist; Hanover, N.H.

Charles Steidel, 39, cosmologist; Pasadena, Calif.

Brian Tucker, 56, seismologist and disaster-prevention specialist; Palo Alto, Calif.

Camilo Vergara, 58, urban archivist; New York, N.Y.

Paul Wennberg, 40, atmospheric chemist; Pasadena, Calif.

Colson Whitehead, 32, novelist; Brooklyn, N.Y.

# Presidential Medal of Freedom

The Presidential Medal of Freedom, the nation's highest civilian award, recognizes exceptional meritorious service. The medal was established by President Truman in 1945 to recognize notable service in the war. In 1963, President Kennedy reintroduced it as an honor for distinguished civilian service in peacetime. Shown below are the medals awarded during President Bush's administration.

| | | | |
|---|---|---|---|
| 2002 | Hank Aaron (baseball player) | 2002 | Irving Kristol (author and editor) |
| 2002 | Bill Cosby (comedian and actor) | 2002 | Nelson Mandela (former South African president) |
| 2002 | Plácido Domingo (tenor) | 2002 | Gordon Moore (Intel cofounder) |
| 2002 | Peter Drucker (management theorist) | 2002 | Nancy Reagan (former first lady) |
| 2002* | Katharine Graham (newspaper publisher) | 2002 | Fred Rogers (children's television host) |
| 2002 | Dr. D. A. Henderson (leader in eradication of smallpox) | 2002 | A. M. Rosenthal (editor and columnist) |

NOTE: An asterisk following a year denotes a posthumous award.

# Recipients of Kennedy Center Honors

The Kennedy Center Honors recognize the lifetime achievements of selected American performing artists.

1978   Marian Anderson (contralto), Fred Astaire (dancer-actor), Richard Rodgers (Broadway composer), Arthur Rubinstein (pianist), George Balanchine (choreographer)

1979   Ella Fitzgerald (jazz singer), Henry Fonda (actor), Martha Graham (choreographer), Tennessee Williams (playwright), Aaron Copland (composer)

1980   James Cagney (actor), Leonard Bernstein (composer-conductor), Agnes de Mille (choreographer), Lynn Fontanne (actress), Leontyne Price (soprano)

1981   Count Basie (jazz composer-pianist), Cary Grant (actor), Helen Hayes (actress), Jerome Robbins (choreographer), Rudolf Serkin (pianist)

1982   George Abbott (Broadway producer), Lillian Gish (actress), Benny Goodman (jazz clarinetist), Gene Kelly (dancer-actor), Eugene Ormandy (conductor)

1983   Katherine Dunham (dancer-choreographer), Elia Kazan (director-author), James Stewart (actor), Virgil Thomson (music critic-composer), Frank Sinatra (singer)

1984   Lena Horne (singer), Danny Kaye (comedian-actor), Gian Carlo Menotti (composer), Arthur Miller (playwright), Isaac Stern (violinist)

1985   Merce Cunningham (dancer-choreographer), Irene Dunne (actress), Bob Hope (comedian), Alan Jay Lerner (lyricist-playwright), Frederick Loewe (composer), Beverly Sills (soprano)

1986   Lucille Ball (comedienne), Ray Charles (musician), Yehudi Menuhin (violinist), Antony Tudor (choreographer), Hume Cronyn and Jessica Tandy (husband-and-wife acting team)

1987   Perry Como (singer), Bette Davis (actress), Sammy Davis, Jr., (entertainer), Nathan Milstein (violinist), Alwin Nikolais (choreographer)

1988   Alvin Ailey (choreographer), George Burns (comedian-actor), Myrna Loy (actress), Alexander Schneider (violinist), Roger L. Stevens (theatrical producer and the Kennedy Center's founding chairman)

1989   Harry Belafonte (singer-actor), Claudette Colbert (actress), Alexandra Danilova (ballerina), Mary Martin (actress), William Schuman (composer)

1990   Dizzy Gillespie (jazz trumpeter), Katharine Hepburn (actress), Risë Stevens (mezzo-soprano), Jule Styne (composer), Billy Wilder (director)

1991   Roy Acuff (country songwriter and singer), Betty Comden and Adolph Green (co-authors of books and lyrics of musicals), the brothers

Fayard and Harold Nicholas (dancers), Gregory Peck (actor), Robert Shaw (choral director)

1992 Lionel Hampton (jazz musician), Paul Newman (actor), Joanne Woodward (actress), Ginger Rogers (dancer-actress), Mstislav Rostropovich (cellist-conductor), Paul Taylor (choreographer)

1993 Johnny Carson (talk-show host), Arthur Mitchell (dancer and choreographer), Georg Solti (conductor), Stephen Sondheim (composer and lyricist), Marion Williams (gospel singer)

1994 Kirk Douglas (actor), Aretha Franklin (singer), Morton Gould (composer), Harold Prince (producer and director), Pete Seeger (folk singer)

1995 Jacques d'Amboise (choreographer), Marilyn Horne (mezzo soprano), B. B. King (blues singer), Sidney Poitier (actor), Neil Simon (playwright)

1996 Edward Albee (playwright), Benny Carter (jazz musician), Johnny Cash (musician), Jack Lemmon (actor), Maria Tallchief (ballerina)

1997 Lauren Bacall (actress), Bob Dylan (songwriter and singer), Charlton Heston (actor), Jessye Norman (soprano), Edward Villella (ballet dancer and director)

1998 Bill Cosby (actor and comedian), John Kander and Fred Ebb (Broadway composer and lyricist team), Willie Nelson (singer and songwriter), André Previn (composer and conductor), Shirley Temple Black (actress)

1999 Victor Borge (comedian and pianist), Sean Connery (actor), Judith Jamison (dancer and teacher), Jason Robards (actor), Stevie Wonder (singer and songwriter)

2000 Mikhail Baryshnikov (dancer), Plácido Domingo (tenor), Angela Lansbury (actress), Chuck Berry (rock 'n' roll musician), Clint Eastwood (actor, director, producer)

2001 Julie Andrews (actress), Van Cliburn (pianist), Quincy Jones (music producer and composer), Jack Nicholson (actor), Luciano Pavarotti (singer)

2002 James Earl Jones (actor), James Levine (conductor), Chita Rivera (dancer and actress), Paul Simon (singer), Elizabeth Taylor (actress)

## Miss America Winners

|  |  |
|---|---|
| 1921 | Margaret Gorman, Washington, D.C. |
| 1922–23 | Mary Campbell, Columbus, Ohio |
| 1924 | Ruth Malcolmson, Philadelphia, Pa. |
| 1925 | Fay Lamphier, Oakland, Calif. |
| 1926 | Norma Smallwood, Tulsa, Okla. |
| 1927 | Lois Delaner, Joliet, Ill. |
| 1933 | Marion Bergeron, West Haven, Conn. |
| 1935 | Henrietta Leaver, Pittsburgh, Pa. |
| 1936 | Rose Coyle, Philadelphia, Pa. |
| 1937 | Bette Cooper, Bertrand Island, N.J. |
| 1938 | Marilyn Meseke, Marion, Ohio |
| 1939 | Patricia Donnelly, Detroit, Mich. |
| 1940 | Frances Marie Burke, Philadelphia, Pa. |
| 1941 | Rosemary LaPlanche, Los Angeles, Calif. |
| 1942 | Jo-Caroll Dennison, Tyler, Texas |
| 1943 | Jean Bartel, Los Angeles, Calif. |
| 1944 | Venus Ramey, Washington, D.C. |
| 1945 | Bess Myerson, New York, N.Y. |
| 1946 | Marilyn Buferd, Los Angeles, Calif. |
| 1947 | Barbara Walker, Memphis, Tenn. |
| 1948 | BeBe Shopp, Hopkins, Minn. |
| 1949 | Jacque Mercer, Litchfield, Ariz. |
| 1951 | Yolande Betbeze, Mobile, Ala. |
| 1952 | Coleen Kay Hutchins, Salt Lake City, Utah |
| 1953 | Neva Jane Langley, Macon, Ga. |
| 1954 | Evelyn Margaret Ay, Ephrata, Pa. |
| 1955 | Lee Meriwether, San Francisco, Calif. |
| 1956 | Sharon Ritchie, Denver, Colo. |
| 1957 | Marian McKnight, Manning, S.C. |
| 1958 | Marilyn Van Derbur, Denver, Colo. |
| 1959 | Mary Ann Mobley, Brandon, Miss. |
| 1960 | Lynda Lee Mead, Natchez, Miss. |
| 1961 | Nancy Fleming, Montague, Mich. |
| 1962 | Maria Fletcher, Asheville, N.C. |
| 1963 | Jacquelyn Mayer, Sandusky, Ohio |
| 1964 | Donna Axum, El Dorado, Ark. |
| 1965 | Vonda Kay Van Dyke, Phoenix, Ariz. |
| 1966 | Deborah Irene Bryant, Overland Park, Kan. |
| 1967 | Jane Anne Jayroe, Laverne, Okla. |
| 1968 | Debra Dene Barnes, Moran, Kan. |
| 1969 | Judith Anne Ford, Belvidere, Ill. |
| 1970 | Pamela Anne Eldred, Birmingham, Mich. |
| 1971 | Phyllis Ann George, Denton, Texas |
| 1972 | Laurie Lea Schaefer, Columbus, Ohio |
| 1973 | Terry Anne Meeuwsen, DePere, Wis. |
| 1974 | Rebecca Ann King, Denver, Colo. |
| 1975 | Shirley Cothran, Fort Worth, Texas |
| 1976 | Tawney Elaine Godin, Yonkers, N.Y. |
| 1977 | Dorothy Kathleen Benham, Edina, Minn. |
| 1978 | Susan Perkins, Columbus, Ohio |
| 1979 | Kylene Baker, Galax, Va. |
| 1980 | Cheryl Prewitt, Ackerman, Miss. |
| 1981 | Susan Powell, Elk City, Okla. |
| 1982 | Elizabeth Ward, Russellville, Ark. |
| 1983 | Debra Maffett, Anaheim, Calif. |
| 1984 | Vanessa Williams, Milwood, N.Y.[1] |
| 1984 | Suzette Charles, Mays Landing, N.J. |
| 1985 | Sharlene Wells, Salt Lake City, Utah |
| 1986 | Susan Akin, Meridian, Miss. |
| 1987 | Kellye Cash, Memphis, Tenn. |
| 1988 | Kaye Lani Rae Rafko, Monroe, Mich. |
| 1989 | Gretchen Elizabeth Carlson, Anoka, Minn. |
| 1990 | Debbye Turner, Columbia, Mo. |
| 1991 | Marjorie Judith Vincent, Oak Park, Ill. |
| 1992 | Carolyn Suzanne Sapp, Honolulu, Hawaii |
| 1993 | Leanza Cornell, Jacksonville, Fla. |
| 1994 | Kimberly Clarice Aiken, Columbia, S.C. |
| 1995 | Heather Whitestone, Birmingham, Ala. |
| 1996 | Shawntel Smith, Muldrow, Okla. |
| 1997 | Tara Dawn Holland, Overland Park, Kan. |
| 1998 | Katherine Shindle, Evanston, Ill. |
| 1999 | Nicole Johnson, Roanoke, Va. |
| 2000 | Heather French, Maysville, Ken. |
| 2001 | Angela Perez Baraquio, Honolulu, Hawaii |
| 2002 | Katie Harman, Gresham, Ore. |
| 2003 | Erika Harold, Urbana, Ill. |

1. Resigned July 23, 1984.

# U.S. Symphonies and Their Music Directors

**(with expenses over $1,050,000)**

Akron Symphony Orchestra: Ya-Hui Wang
Alabama Symphony Orchestra: Richard Westerfield
American Composers Orchestra: Steven Sloane
American Symphony Orchestra: Leon Botstein
Arkansas Symphony Orchestra: David Itkin
Aspen Chamber Symphony: David Zinman
Atlanta Symphony Orchestra: Robert Spano
Austin Symphony Orchestra: Peter Bay
Baltimore Symphony Orchestra: Yuri Temirkanov
Baton Rouge Symphony: Timothy Muffitt
Boca Pops (Florida Symphonic Pops): Crafton Beck
Boston Symphony Orchestra: James Levine
Boulder Philharmonic Orchestra: Theodore Kuchar
Brooklyn Philharmonic: Robert Spano
Buffalo Philharmonic Orchestra: JoAnn Falletta
Cedar Rapids Symphony: Christian Tiemeyer
Charleston Symphony Orchestra: David Stahl
Charlotte Symphony: Christof Perick
Chattanooga Symphony & Opera: Robert Bernhardt
Chicago Sinfonietta: Paul Freeman
Chicago Symphony Orchestra: Daniel Barenboim
Cincinnati Symphony Orchestra: Paavo Järvi
Cleveland Orchestra: Christoph von Dohnányi
Colorado Springs Symphony: Lawrence Leighton-Smith
Dallas Symphony Orchestra: Andrew Litton
Dayton Philharmonic Orchestra: Neal Gittleman
Delaware Symphony Orchestra: Stephen Gunzenhauser
Des Moines Symphony: Joseph Giunta
Detroit Symphony Orchestra: Neeme Järvi
Elgin Symphony Orchestra: Robert L. Hanson
El Paso Symphony Orchestra: Gürer Aykal
Erie Philharmonic: Hugh Keelan
Evansville Philharmonic Orchestra: Alfred Savia
Florida Orchestra: Jahja Ling
Florida Philharmonic Orchestra: Joseph Silverstein (acting)
Florida West Coast Symphony: Leif Bjaland[1, 2]
Fort Wayne Philharmonic: Edvard Tchivzhel
Fort Worth Symphony Orchestra: Miguel Harth-Bedoya
Fresno Philharmonic Orchestra: Theodore Kuchar
Grand Rapids Symphony: David Lockington
Grant Park Symphony Orchestra (Chicago): Carlos Kalmar[2]
Greensboro Symphony Orchestra: Stuart Malina
Greenville Symphony Orchestra: Edvard Tchivzhel
Handel & Haydn Society: Grant Llewellyn
Harrisburg Symphony Orchestra: Stuart Malina
Hartford Symphony Orchestra: Edward Cumming
Honolulu Symphony Orchestra: Samuel Wong
Houston Symphony: Hans Graf
Indianapolis Symphony: Mario Venzago
Jacksonville Symphony Orchestra: Fabio Mechetti
Kalamazoo Symphony Orchestra: Raymond Harvey
Kansas City Symphony: Anne Manson
Kennedy Center Opera House Orchestra: Heinz Fricke
Knoxville Symphony Orchestra: Kirk Trevor
Little Orchestra Society of New York: Dino Anagnost[1, 2]
Long Beach Symphony Orchestra: JoAnn Falletta
Long Island Philharmonic: David Wiley
Los Angeles Chamber Orchestra: Jeffrey Kahane
Los Angeles Philharmonic: Esa-Pekka Salonen
Louisiana Philharmonic Orchestra: Klauspeter Seibel
Louisville Orchestra: Uriel Segal
Madison Symphony Orchestra: John DeMain

Memphis Symphony Orchestra: David Loebel
Milwaukee Symphony Orchestra: Andreas Delfs
Minnesota Orchestra: Eiji Oue
Mississippi Symphony Orchestra: Crafton Beck
Monterey Symphony: Kate Tamarkin
Music of the Baroque Chorus & Orchestra: Thomas S. Wikman
Naples Philharmonic Orchestra: Christopher Seaman
Nashville Symphony: Kenneth Schermerhorn
National Sinfonietta: Burton A. Zipser
National Symphony (D.C.): Leonard Slatkin
New Haven Symphony Orchestra: Jung-Ho Pak
New Jersey Symphony Orchestra: Zdenek Macal
New Mexico Symphony: Roger Melone
New West Symphony: Boris Brott
New World Symphony (Fla.): Michael Tilson Thomas[1]
New York Chamber Symphony: Gerard Schwarz
New York Philharmonic: Lorin Maazel
New York Pops: Skitch Henderson
North Carolina Symphony: Gerhardt Zimmermann
Northeastern Pennsylvania Philharmonic: Clyde Mitchell
Ohio Chamber Orchestra: David Lockington
Oklahoma City Philharmonic: Joel Levine
Omaha Symphony: Victor Yampolsky
Omaha Symphony Chamber Orchestra: Victor Yampolsky
Oregon Symphony: James DePreist
Pacific Symphony Orchestra (Calif.): Carl St. Clair
Palm Beach Pops: Bob Lappin
Philadelphia Orchestra: Wolfgang Sawallisch
Philharmonia Baroque Orchestra: Nicholas McGegan
Phoenix Symphony: Hermann Michael
Pittsburgh Symphony: Mariss Jansons
Portland Symphony Orchestra: Toshiyuki Shimada
Quad City Symphony Orchestra: Donald Schleicher
Rhode Island Philharmonic: Larry Rachleff
Richmond Symphony: Mark Russell Smith
River City Brass Band: Denis Colwell
Rochester Philharmonic Orchestra: Christopher Seaman
St. Louis Symphony: Hans Vonk
St. Paul Chamber Orchestra: Andreas Delfs
San Antonio Symphony: Christopher Wilkins
San Francisco Symphony: Michael Tilson Thomas
San Jose Symphony: Leonid Grin
Santa Barbara Symphony Orchestra: Gisèle Ben-Dor
Santa Rosa Symphony: Jeffrey Kahane
Savannah Symphony: Philip Greenberg
Seattle Symphony: Gerard Schwarz
Shreveport Symphony: Dennis Simons
Spokane Symphony: Fabio Mechetti
Springfield Symphony (Mass.): Kevin Rhodes
Stamford Symphony Orchestra: Roger Nierenberg
Syracuse Symphony Orchestra: Daniel Hege
Toledo Symphony: Andrew Massey
Tucson Symphony Orchestra: George Hanson
Tulsa Philharmonic: Bernard Rubenstein
Utah Symphony: Keith Lockhart
Virginia Symphony: JoAnn Falletta
Westchester Philharmonic: Paul Lustig Dunkel
West Virginia Symphony Orchestra: Grant Cooper[1, 2]
Wichita Symphony: Andrew Sewell
Winston-Salem Piedmont Triad Symphony: Peter J. Perret
Youngstown Symphony Orchestra: Isaiah Jackson

1. Artistic Director. 2. Principal Conductor.

## U.S. Opera Companies

(budgets $2,000,000 and over)

**American Musical Theatre of San Jose:** Stewart Slater, exec. prod.
**Arizona Opera Company:** David Speers, gen. dir.
**Aspen Opera Theater Center:** Ed Berkeley, dir.
**Atlanta Opera, The:** William Fred Scott, art. dir.
**Austin Lyric Opera:** Joseph McClain, gen. dir.
**Baltimore Opera Company:** Michael Harrison, gen. dir.
**Boston Lyric Opera Company:** Janice Mancini DelSesto, gen. dir.
**Central City Opera:** Pelham G. Pearce, gen. dir.
**Cincinnati Opera Association:** Nicholas Muni, art. dir.
**Civic Light Opera:** Charles Gray, exec. dir.
**Cleveland Opera:** David Bamberger, gen. dir.
**Dallas Opera, The:** Anthony Whitworth Jones, gen. dir.
**Florentine Opera Company:** Dennis Hanthorn, gen. dir.
**Florida Grand Opera:** Robert M. Heuer, gen. dir.
**Glimmerglass Opera:** Esther Nelson, gen. dir.
**Goodspeed Opera House:** Michael Price, exec. dir.
**Hawaii Opera Theatre:** Henry G. Akina, gen. dir. and art. dir.
**Houston Grand Opera:** R. David Gockley, gen. dir.
**Kentucky Opera:** Thomson Smillie, gen. dir.
**Los Angeles Opera:** Plácido Domingo, art. dir.
**Lyric Opera of Chicago:** William Mason, gen. dir.
**Lyric Opera of Kansas City:** Ardis Krainik, gen. dir.
**Metro Lyric Opera:** Era M. Tognoli, art. dir.
**Metropolitan Opera Association:** James Levine, art. dir.

**Michigan Opera Theatre:** David DiChiera, gen. dir.
**Minnesota Opera, The:** Dale Johnson, art. dir.
**Music Theater of Santa Barbara:** Paul Iannacone, exec. dir.
**New York City Opera:** Paul Kellogg, gen. dir. and art. dir.
**Ohio Light Opera:** Steven Daigle, art. dir.
**Opera Colorado:** Peter Russell, gen. dir.
**Opera Company of Philadelphia:** Robert B. Driver, producing art. dir.
**Opera Pacific:** John DeMain, art. dir.
**Opera Theatre of St. Louis:** Charles MacKay, gen. dir.
**Orlando Opera Company:** Robert Swedberg, gen. dir.
**Palm Beach Opera:** Anton Guadagno, art. dir.
**Pittsburgh Opera:** Christopher Hahn, art. dir.
**Portland Opera Association:** Robert Bailey, gen. dir.
**San Diego Civic Light Opera Association:** Brian Wells, art. dir.
**San Diego Opera:** Ian D. Campbell, gen. dir.
**San Francisco Opera:** Pamela Rosenberg, gen. dir.
**San Francisco Opera Center:** Sheri Greenawald, dir.
**Santa Fe Opera:** Richard Gaddes, gen. dir.
**Sarasota Opera Association:** Victor DeRenzi, art. dir.
**Seattle Opera Association:** Speight Jenkins, gen. dir.
**Utah Opera Company:** Anne Ewers, gen. dir.
**Virginia Opera:** Peter Mark, art. dir.
**Washington (D.C.) Opera, The:** Plácido Domingo, art. dir.

## Most Frequently Produced Operas in North America

(through 2001–2002 season)

| Opera | Composer | Number of productions[1] | Opera | Composer | Number of productions[1] |
|---|---|---|---|---|---|
| **Top works of 2001–2002 season** | | | **Top 5 works over past 10 seasons** | | |
| 1. *The Marriage of Figaro* | Mozart | 17 | 1. *Madama Butterfly* | Puccini | 182 |
| *Rigoletto* | Verdi | 17 | 2. *La Bohème* | Puccini | 180 |
| 3. *La Bohème* | Puccini | 16 | 3. *Carmen* | Bizet | 160 |
| 4. *Carmen* | Bizet | 15 | 4. *La Traviata* | Verdi | 156 |
| *The Magic Flute* | Mozart | 15 | 5. *The Barber of Seville* | Rossini | 146 |
| *Tosca* | Puccini | 15 | | | |

1. Represents the number of productions by professional member companies of Opera America, not the number of performances. *Source:* Opera America. Web: www.operaamerica.org.

## U.S. Dance Companies

(budgets $2,500,000 and over)

**Alvin Ailey American Dance Theatre (1958):** Judith Jamison, art. dir.
**American Ballet Theatre (1940):** Kevin McKenzie, art. dir.
**Atlanta Ballet Company (1929):** John McFall, art. dir.
**Ballet Florida (1986):** Marie Hale, art. dir.
**Ballet San Jose of Silicon Valley (1986):** Dennis Nahat, art. dir.
**BalletMet Columbus (1978):** Gerard Charles, art. dir.
**Ballet West (1968[1]):** Jonas Kåge, art. dir.
**Boston Ballet (1963):** Mikko Nissinen, art. dir.
**Cincinnati Ballet (1958):** Victoria Morgan, art. dir.
**Colorado Ballet (1961):** Martin Fredmann, art. dir. and CEO
**Merce Cunningham Dance Company (1953):** Merce Cunningham, art. dir.
**Dance Theater of Harlem (1969):** Arthur Mitchell, art. dir.
**Eliot Feld's Ballet Tech (1973):** Eliot Feld, dir.
**Fort Worth Dallas Ballet (1993):** David Mallette, exec. dir.
**Martha Graham Dance Company (1926):** Marvin Preston, exec. dir.

**Houston Ballet (1969):** Ben Stevenson, art. dir.
**Joffrey Ballet of Chicago (1956):** Gerald Arpino, art. dir.
**Bill T. Jones/Arnie Zane Dance Company (1982):** Bill T. Jones, art. dir.
**José Limón Dance Company (1946):** Carla Maxwell, art. dir.
**Miami City Ballet (1986):** Edward Villella, art. dir.
**Milwaukee Ballet (1970):** Simon Dow, art. dir.
**Mark Morris Dance Group (1980):** Mark Morris, art. dir.
**New York City Ballet (1948):** Peter Martins, ballet master-in-chief
**Ocheami African Dance Company (1978):** Kofi Anang, art. dir.
**Pacific Northwest Ballet (1972):** Kent Stowell and Francia Russell, art. dirs.
**Pittsburgh Ballet Theater (1970):** Terrence S. Orr, art. dir.
**San Francisco Ballet (1933):** Helgi Tomasson, art. dir.
**Paul Taylor Dance Company (1954):** Paul Taylor, art. dir.
**Washington Ballet (1976):** Septime Webre, art. dir.

NOTE: Year founded appears in parentheses after name. 1. Prior company founded 1963, name changed to Ballet West in 1968.

# Best-Selling Books, 2001

*Source: Publishers Weekly*

## Hardcover Fiction

1. *Desecration,* Jerry B. Jenkins and Tim LaHaye
2. *Skipping Christmas,* John Grisham
3. *A Painted House,* John Grisham
4. *Dreamcatcher,* Stephen King
5. *The Corrections,* Jonathan Franzen
6. *Black House,* Stephen King and Peter Straub
7. *The Kiss,* Danielle Steel
8. *Valhalla Rising,* Clive Cussler
9. *A Day Late and a Dollar Short,* Terry McMillan
10. *Violets Are Blue,* James Patterson
11. *P Is for Peril,* Sue Grafton
12. *He Sees You When You're Sleeping,* Mary and Carol Higgins Clark
13. *A Common Life,* Jan Karon
14. *Isle of Dogs,* Patricia Cornwell
15. *Suzanne's Diary for Nicholas,* James Patterson

## Hardcover Nonfiction

1. *The Prayer of Jabez,* Bruce Wilkinson
2. *Secrets of the Vine,* Bruce Wilkinson
3. *Who Moved My Cheese?,* Spencer Johnson
4. *John Adams,* David McCullough
5. *Guinness World Records 2002,* Guinness World Records Ltd.
6. *Prayer of Jabez Devotional,* Bruce Wilkinson
7. *The No Spin Zone: Confrontations with the Powerful and Famous in America,* Bill O'Reilly
8. *Body for Life: 12 Weeks to Mental and Physical Strength,* Bill Phillips
9. *How I Play Golf,* Tiger Woods
10. *Jack,* Jack Welch
11. *I Hope You Dance,* Mark D. Sanders and Tia Sillers
12. *Self Matters,* Phillip C. McGraw
13. *The Blue Day Book,* Bradley Trevor Greive
14. *The Road to Wealth,* Suze Orman
15. *America's Heroes: Inspiring Stories of Courage, Sacrifice, and Patriotism,* editors at SP LLC

## Trade Paperback

1. *Life Strategies,* Phillip McGraw
2. *We Were the Mulveneys,* Joyce Carol Oates
3. *The Indwelling (Left Behind Series #7),* Jerry B. Jenkins and Tim LaHaye
4. *The Lord of the Rings,* J.R.R. Tolkien
5. *Icy Sparks,* Gwyn Hyman Rubio
6. *The Red Tent,* Anita Diamant
7. *Girl with a Pearl Earring,* Tracy Chevalier
8. *The Fellowship of the Ring,* J.R.R. Tolkien
9. *The Mark (Left Behind Series #8): The Beast Rules the World,* Jerry B. Jenkins and Tim LaHaye
10. *Left Behind (Left Behind Series #1),* Jerry B. Jenkins and Tim LaHaye
11. *Bridget Jones's Diary,* Helen Fielding
12. *The Hobbit,* J.R.R. Tolkien
13. *Band of Brothers,* Stephen E. Ambrose
14. *The Four Agreements,* Don Miguel Ruiz
15. *Tribulation Force (Left Behind Series #2),* Jerry B. Jenkins and Tim LaHaye

## Mass Market Paperback

1. *A Painted House,* John Grisham
2. *Hannibal,* Thomas Harris
3. *Dance Upon Air,* Nora Roberts
4. *Heaven and Earth,* Nora Roberts
5. *Bear and Dragon,* Tom Clancy
6. *Carolina Moon,* Nora Roberts
7. *The Lord of the Rings: The Fellowship of the Ring,* J.R.R. Tolkien
8. *Last Precinct,* Patricia Cornwell
9. *Before I Say Goodbye,* Mary Higgins Clark
10. *Time and Again,* Nora Roberts
11. *Reflections and Dreams,* Nora Roberts
12. *Journey,* Danielle Steel
13. *Stanislavsky Sisters,* Nora Roberts
14. *The Hobbit,* J.R.R. Tolkien
15. *Dreamcatcher,* Stephen King

# Best-Selling Children's Books, 2001

*Source: Publishers Weekly*

## Hardcover

1. *The Prayer of Jabez for Kids,* Bruce Wilkinson and Melody Carlson
2. *The Prayer of Jabez for Little Ones,* Bruce Wilkinson and Melody Carlson; illustrated by Alexi Natchev
3. *The Hostile Hospital (A Series of Unfortunate Events #8),* Lemony Snicket; illustrated by Brett Helquist
4. *The Ersatz Elevator (A Series of Unfortunate Events #6),* Lemony Snicket; illustrated by Brett Helquist
5. *The Vile Village (A Series of Unfortunate Events #7),* Lemony Snicket; illustrated by Brett Helquist
6. *Monsters, Inc.: Read-Aloud Storybook*
7. *Disney's 5-Minute Adventure Stories,* Sarah Heller
8. *Olivia Saves the Circus,* Ian Falconer
9. *Ripley's Believe It or Not*
10. *What's Wrong with Timmy?,* Maria Shriver; illustrated by Sandra Speidel

## Paperback

1. *Harry Potter and the Prisoner of Azkaban,* J. K. Rowling
2. *Harry Potter and the Sorcerer's Stone,* J. K. Rowling
3. *Fantastic Beasts and Where to Find Them,* Newt Scamander (aka J. K. Rowling)
4. *Quidditch Through the Ages,* Kennilworthy Whisp (aka J. K. Rowling)
5. *Captain Underpants and the Wrath of the Wicked Wedgie Woman,* Dav Pilkey
6. *Harry Potter and the Sorcerer's Stone Poster Book*
7. *The Princess Diaries,* Meg Cabot
8. *Chicken Soup for the Teenage Soul: On Tough Stuff,* Jack Canfield, Mark Victor Hansen, and Kimberly Kirberger
9. *Amelia Bedelia 4 Mayor,* Herman Parish; illustrated by Lynn Sweat
10. *Twister on Tuesday (Magic Tree House #23),* Mary Pope Osborne; illustrated by Sal Murdocca

## All-Time Best-Selling Children's Books
*Source: Publishers Weekly*
From the date of publication (in parentheses) through the end of 2000.

### Hardcover

1. *The Poky Little Puppy*, Janette Sebring Lowrey (1942)
2. *The Tale of Peter Rabbit*, Beatrix Potter (1902)
3. *Tootle*, Gertrude Crampton (1945)
4. *Green Eggs and Ham*, Dr. Seuss (1960)
5. *Harry Potter and the Goblet of Fire*, J. K. Rowling (2000)
6. *Pat the Bunny*, Dorothy Kunhardt (1940)
7. *Saggy Baggy Elephant*, Kathryn and Byron Jackson (1947)
8. *Scuffy the Tugboat*, Gertrude Crampton (1955)
9. *The Cat in the Hat*, Dr. Seuss (1957)
10. *Harry Potter and the Chamber of Secrets*, J. K. Rowling (1999)

### Paperback

1. *Charlotte's Web*, E. B. White, illustrated by Garth Williams (1974)
2. *The Outsiders*, S. E. Hinton (1968)
3. *Tales of a Fourth Grade Nothing*, Judy Blume (1976)
4. *Love You Forever*, Robert Munsch, illustrated by Sheila McGraw (1986)
5. *Where the Red Fern Grows*, Wilson Rawls (1973)
6. *Island of the Blue Dolphins*, Scott O'Dell (1971)
7. *Harry Potter and the Sorcerer's Stone*, J. K. Rowling (1999)
8. *Are You There, God? It's Me, Margaret*, Judy Blume (1972)
9. *Shane*, Jack Schaeffer (1972)
10. *The Indian in the Cupboard*, Lynne Reid Banks (1982)

## The 100 Best English-Language Novels of the 20th Century
The Board of the Modern Library, a division of Random House, published its selections in July 1998.

1. *Ulysses*, James Joyce (1922)
2. *The Great Gatsby*, F. Scott Fitzgerald (1925)
3. *A Portrait of the Artist as a Young Man*, James Joyce (1916)
4. *Lolita*, Vladimir Nabokov (1958)
5. *Brave New World*, Aldous Huxley (1932)
6. *The Sound and the Fury*, William Faulkner (1929)
7. *Catch-22*, Joseph Heller (1961)
8. *Darkness at Noon*, Arthur Koestler (1941)
9. *Sons and Lovers*, D. H. Lawrence (1913)
10. *The Grapes of Wrath*, John Steinbeck (1939)
11. *Under the Volcano*, Malcolm Lowry (1947)
12. *The Way of All Flesh*, Samuel Butler (1903)
13. *1984*, George Orwell (1949)
14. *I, Claudius*, Robert Graves (1934)
15. *To the Lighthouse*, Virginia Woolf (1927)
16. *An American Tragedy*, Theodore Dreiser (1925)
17. *The Heart Is a Lonely Hunter*, Carson McCullers (1940)
18. *Slaughterhouse-Five*, Kurt Vonnegut (1969)
19. *Invisible Man*, Ralph Ellison (1952)
20. *Native Son*, Richard Wright (1940)
21. *Henderson the Rain King*, Saul Bellow (1959)
22. *Appointment in Samarra*, John O'Hara (1934)
23. *U.S.A. (trilogy)*, John Dos Passos (1937—trilogy completed)
24. *Winesburg, Ohio*, Sherwood Anderson (1919)
25. *A Passage to India*, E. M. Forster (1924)
26. *The Wings of the Dove*, Henry James (1902)
27. *The Ambassadors*, Henry James (1903)
28. *Tender Is the Night*, F. Scott Fitzgerald (1934)
29. *The Studs Lonigan Trilogy*, James T. Farrell (1935)
30. *The Good Soldier*, Ford Madox Ford (1915)
31. *Animal Farm*, George Orwell (1946)
32. *The Golden Bowl*, Henry James (1904)
33. *Sister Carrie*, Theodore Dreiser (1900)
34. *A Handful of Dust*, Evelyn Waugh (1934)
35. *As I Lay Dying*, William Faulkner (1930)
36. *All the King's Men*, Robert Penn Warren (1946)
37. *The Bridge of San Luis Rey*, Thornton Wilder (1927)
38. *Howards End*, E. M. Forster (1910)
39. *Go Tell It on the Mountain*, James Baldwin (1953)
40. *The Heart of the Matter*, Graham Greene (1948)
41. *Lord of the Flies*, William Golding (1954)
42. *Deliverance*, James Dickey (1969)
43. *A Dance to the Music of Time* (series), Anthony Powell (1975—series completed)
44. *Point Counter Point*, Aldous Huxley (1928)
45. *The Sun Also Rises*, Ernest Hemingway (1926)
46. *The Secret Agent*, Joseph Conrad (1907)
47. *Nostromo*, Joseph Conrad (1904)
48. *The Rainbow*, D. H. Lawrence (1915)
49. *Women in Love*, D. H. Lawrence (1921)
50. *Tropic of Cancer*, Henry Miller (1934)
51. *The Naked and the Dead*, Norman Mailer (1948)
52. *Portnoy's Complaint*, Philip Roth (1969)
53. *Pale Fire*, Vladimir Nabokov (1962)
54. *Light in August*, William Faulkner (1932)
55. *On the Road*, Jack Kerouac (1957)
56. *The Maltese Falcon*, Dashiell Hammett (1930)
57. *Parade's End*, Ford Madox Ford (1950)
58. *The Age of Innocence*, Edith Wharton (1920)
59. *Zuleika Dobson*, Max Beerbohm (1911)
60. *The Moviegoer*, Walker Percy (1961)
61. *Death Comes for the Archbishop*, Willa Cather (1927)
62. *From Here to Eternity*, James Jones (1951)
63. *The Wapshot Chronicles*, John Cheever (1957)
64. *The Catcher in the Rye*, J. D. Salinger (1951)
65. *A Clockwork Orange*, Anthony Burgess (1962)
66. *Of Human Bondage*, W. Somerset Maugham (1915)
67. *Heart of Darkness*, Joseph Conrad (1902)
68. *Main Street*, Sinclair Lewis (1920)
69. *The House of Mirth*, Edith Wharton (1905)
70. *The Alexandria Quartet*, Lawrence Durrell (1960—series completed)
71. *A High Wind in Jamaica*, Richard Hughes (1929)
72. *A House for Mr. Biswas*, V. S. Naipaul (1961)
73. *The Day of the Locust*, Nathanael West (1939)
74. *A Farewell to Arms*, Ernest Hemingway (1929)
75. *Scoop*, Evelyn Waugh (1938)

76. *The Prime of Miss Jean Brodie*, Muriel Spark (1961)
77. *Finnegans Wake*, James Joyce (1939)
78. *Kim*, Rudyard Kipling (1901)
79. *A Room with a View*, E. M. Forster (1908)
80. *Brideshead Revisited*, Evelyn Waugh (1945)
81. *The Adventures of Augie March*, Saul Bellow (1953)
82. *Angle of Repose*, Wallace Stegner (1971)
83. *A Bend in the River*, V. S. Naipaul (1979)
84. *The Death of the Heart*, Elizabeth Bowen (1938)
85. *Lord Jim*, Joseph Conrad (1900)
86. *Ragtime*, E. L. Doctorow (1975)
87. *The Old Wives' Tale*, Arnold Bennett (1908)
88. *The Call of the Wild*, Jack London (1903)
89. *Loving*, Henry Green (1945)
90. *Midnight's Children*, Salman Rushdie (1981)
91. *Tobacco Road*, Erskine Caldwell (1933)
92. *Ironweed*, William Kennedy (1983)
93. *The Magus*, John Fowles (1966)
94. *Wide Sargasso Sea*, Jean Rhys (1966)
95. *Under the Net*, Iris Murdoch (1954)
96. *Sophie's Choice*, William Styron (1979)
97. *The Sheltering Sky*, Paul Bowles (1949)
98. *The Postman Always Rings Twice*, James M. Cain (1934)
99. *The Ginger Man*, J. P. Donleavy (1955)
100. *The Magnificent Ambersons*, Booth Tarkington (1918)

## The 100 Best English-Language Nonfiction Books of the 20th Century

The Board of the Modern Library, a division of Random House, published its selections in April 1999.

1. *The Education of Henry Adams*, Henry Adams (1906)
2. *The Varieties of Religious Experience*, William James (1902)
3. *Up from Slavery*, Booker T. Washington (1901)
4. *A Room of One's Own*, Virginia Woolf (1929)
5. *Silent Spring*, Rachel Carson (1962)
6. *Selected Essays, 1917–1932*, T. S. Eliot (1932)
7. *The Double Helix*, James D. Watson (1968)
8. *Speak, Memory*, Vladimir Nabokov (1967)
9. *The American Language*, H. L. Mencken (1919)
10. *The General Theory of Employment, Interest, and Money*, John Maynard Keynes (1935–1936)
11. *The Lives of a Cell*, Lewis Thomas (1974)
12. *The Frontier in American History*, Frederick Jackson Turner (1920)
13. *Black Boy*, Richard Wright (1945)
14. *Aspects of the Novel*, E. M. Forster (1927)
15. *The Civil War*, Shelby Foote (1958–1974)
16. *The Guns of August*, Barbara Tuchman (1962)
17. *The Proper Study of Mankind*, Isaiah Berlin (1997)
18. *The Nature and Destiny of Man*, Reinhold Niebuhr (1941–1943)
19. *Notes of a Native Son*, James Baldwin (1955)
20. *The Autobiography of Alice B. Toklas*, Gertrude Stein (1933)
21. *The Elements of Style*, William Strunk and E. B. White (1959)
22. *An American Dilemma*, Gunnar Myrdal (1944)
23. *Principia Mathematica*, Alfred North Whitehead and Bertrand Russell (1910–1913)
24. *The Mismeasure of Man*, Stephen Jay Gould (1981)
25. *The Mirror and the Lamp*, Meyer Howard Abrams (1953)
26. *The Art of the Soluble*, Peter B. Medawar (1967)
27. *The Ants*, Bert Hoelldobler and Edward O. Wilson (1990)
28. *A Theory of Justice*, John Rawls (1971)
29. *Art and Illusion*, Ernest H. Gombrich (1961)
30. *The Making of the English Working Class*, E. P. Thompson (1963)
31. *The Souls of Black Folk*, W.E.B. Du Bois (1903)
32. *Principia Ethica*, G. E. Moore (1903)
33. *Philosophy and Civilization*, John Dewey (1927)
34. *On Growth and Form*, D'Arcy Thompson (1917)
35. *Ideas and Opinions*, Albert Einstein (1954)
36. *The Age of Jackson*, Arthur Schlesinger, Jr. (1945)
37. *The Making of the Atomic Bomb*, Richard Rhodes (1986)
38. *Black Lamb and Grey Falcon*, Rebecca West (1942)
39. *Autobiographies*, W. B. Yeats (1926)
40. *Science and Civilization in China*, Joseph Needham (1954–)
41. *Goodbye to All That*, Robert Graves (1929)
42. *Homage to Catalonia*, George Orwell (1938)
43. *The Autobiography of Mark Twain*, Mark Twain (1924)
44. *Children of Crisis*, Robert Coles (1967)
45. *A Study of History*, Arnold J. Toynbee (1934–1961)
46. *The Affluent Society*, John Kenneth Galbraith (1958)
47. *Present at the Creation*, Dean Acheson (1969)
48. *The Great Bridge*, David McCullough (1972)
49. *Patriotic Gore*, Edmund Wilson (1962)
50. *Samuel Johnson*, Walter Jackson Bate (1977)
51. *The Autobiography of Malcolm X*, Alex Haley and Malcolm X (1965)
52. *The Right Stuff*, Tom Wolfe (1979)
53. *Eminent Victorians*, Lytton Strachey (1918)
54. *Working*, Studs Terkel (1974)
55. *Darkness Visible*, William Styron (1990)
56. *The Liberal Imagination*, Lionel Trilling (1950)
57. *The Second World War*, Winston Churchill (1948–1953)
58. *Out of Africa*, Isak Dinesen (1937)
59. *Jefferson and His Time*, Dumas Malone (1948–1981)
60. *In the American Grain*, William Carlos Williams (1925)
61. *Cadillac Desert*, Marc Reisner (1986)
62. *The House of Morgan*, Ron Chernow (1990)
63. *The Sweet Science*, A. J. Liebling (1956)
64. *The Open Society and Its Enemies*, Karl Popper (1945)
65. *The Art of Memory*, Frances A. Yates (1966)
66. *Religion and the Rise of Capitalism*, R. H. Tawney (1926)
67. *A Preface to Morals*, Walter Lippmann (1929)
68. *The Gate of Heavenly Peace*, Jonathan D. Spence (1981)
69. *The Structure of Scientific Revolutions*, Thomas S. Kuhn (1962)
70. *The Strange Career of Jim Crow*, C. Vann Woodward (1955)
71. *The Rise of the West*, William H. McNeill (1963)
72. *The Gnostic Gospels*, Elaine Pagels (1979)
73. *James Joyce*, Richard Ellmann (1959)
74. *Florence Nightingale*, Cecil Woodham-Smith (1950)

75. *The Great War and Modern Memory,* Paul Fussell (1975)
76. *The City in History,* Lewis Mumford (1961)
77. *Battle Cry of Freedom,* James M. McPherson (1988)
78. *Why We Can't Wait,* Martin Luther King, Jr. (1964)
79. *The Rise of Theodore Roosevelt,* Edmund Morris (1979)
80. *Studies in Iconology,* Erwin Panofsky (1939)
81. *The Face of Battle,* John Keegan (1976)
82. *The Strange Death of Liberal England,* George Dangerfield (1935)
83. *Vermeer,* Lawrence Gowing (1952)
84. *A Bright Shining Lie,* Neil Sheehan (1988)
85. *West with the Night,* Beryl Markham (1942)
86. *This Boy's Life,* Tobias Wolff (1989)
87. *A Mathematician's Apology,* G. H. Hardy (1940)
88. *Six Easy Pieces,* Richard P. Feynman (1963)
89. *Pilgrim at Tinker Creek,* Annie Dillard (1974)
90. *The Golden Bough,* James George Frazer (1922) (1 vol. ed.)
91. *Shadow and Act,* Ralph Ellison (1964)
92. *The Power Broker,* Robert A. Caro (1974)
93. *The American Political Tradition,* Richard Hofstadter (1948)
94. *The Contours of American History,* William Appleman Williams (1966)
95. *The Promise of American Life,* Herbert Croly (1909)
96. *In Cold Blood,* Truman Capote (1965)
97. *The Journalist and the Murderer,* Janet Malcolm (1990)
98. *The Taming of Chance,* Ian Hacking (1990)
99. *Operating Instructions,* Anne Lamott (1994)
100. *Melbourne,* Lord David Cecil (1939 & 1954)

## Best American Journalism of the 20th Century

The following works were chosen as the 20th century's best American journalism by a panel of experts assembled by New York University's journalism department.

1. **John Hersey:** "Hiroshima," *The New Yorker,* 1946
2. **Rachel Carson:** *Silent Spring,* book, 1962
3. **Bob Woodward and Carl Bernstein:** Investigation of the Watergate break-in, *The Washington Post,* 1972
4. **Edward R. Murrow:** *Battle of Britain,* CBS radio, 1940
5. **Ida Tarbell:** "The History of the Standard Oil Company," *McClure's,* 1902–1904
6. **Lincoln Steffens:** "The Shame of the Cities," *McClure's,* 1902–1904
7. **John Reed:** *Ten Days That Shook the World,* book, 1919
8. **H. L. Mencken:** Scopes "Monkey" trial, *The Sun* of Baltimore, 1925
9. **Ernie Pyle:** Reports from Europe and the Pacific during World War II, Scripps-Howard newspapers, 1940–45
10. **Edward R. Murrow and Fred Friendly:** Investigation of Sen. Joseph McCarthy, CBS, 1954
11. **Edward R. Murrow, David Lowe, and Fred Friendly:** documentary "Harvest of Shame," CBS television, 1960
12. **Seymour Hersh:** Investigation of massacre by American soldiers at My Lai in Vietnam, Dispatch News Service, 1969
13. *The New York Times:* Publication of the Pentagon Papers, 1971
14. **James Agee and Walker Evans:** *Let Us Now Praise Famous Men,* book, 1941
15. **W. E. B. Du Bois:** *The Souls of Black Folk,* collected articles, 1903
16. **I. F. Stone:** *I. F. Stone's Weekly,* 1953–67
17. **Henry Hampton:** "Eyes on the Prize," documentary, 1987
18. **Tom Wolfe:** *The Electric Kool-Aid Acid Test,* book, 1968
19. **Norman Mailer:** *The Armies of the Night,* book, 1968
20. **Hannah Arendt:** *Eichmann in Jerusalem: A Report on the Banality of Evil,* collected articles, 1963
21. **William Shirer:** *Berlin Diary: The Journal of a Foreign Correspondent, 1939–1941,* collected articles, 1941
22. **Truman Capote:** *In Cold Blood: A True Account of a Multiple Murder and Its Consequences,* book, 1965
23. **Joan Didion:** *Slouching Towards Bethlehem,* collected articles, 1968
24. **Tom Wolfe:** *The Kandy-Kolored Tangerine-Flake Streamline Baby,* collected articles, 1965
25. **Michael Herr:** *Dispatches,* book, 1977
26. **Theodore White:** *The Making of the President: 1960,* book, 1961
27. **Robert Capa:** Ten photographs from D-Day, 1944
28. **J. Anthony Lukas:** *Common Ground: A Turbulent Decade in the Lives of Three American Families,* book, 1985
29. **Richard Harding Davis:** Coverage of German march into Belgium, Wheeler Syndicate and magazines, 1914
30. **Dorothy Thompson:** Reports on the rise of Hitler, *Cosmopolitan* and *Saturday Evening Post,* 1931–1934
31. **John Steinbeck:** Reports on Okie migrant camp life, *The San Francisco News,* 1936
32. **A. J. Liebling:** *The Road Back to Paris,* collected articles, 1944
33. **Ernest Hemingway:** Reports on the Spanish Civil War, *The New Republic,* 1937–1938
34. **Martha Gellhorn:** *The Face of War,* collected articles, 1959
35. **James Baldwin:** *The Fire Next Time,* book, 1963
36. **Joseph Mitchell:** *Up in the Old Hotel and Other Stories,* collected articles, 1992
37. **Betty Friedan:** *The Feminine Mystique,* book, 1963
38. **Ralph Nader:** *Unsafe at Any Speed: The Designed-In Dangers of the American Automobile,* book, 1965
39. **Herblock (Herbert Block):** Cartoons on McCarthyism, *The Washington Post,* 1950
40. **James Baldwin:** "Letter from the South: Nobody Knows My Name," *The Partisan Review,* 1959
41. **Nick Ut:** Photograph of a burning girl running from a napalm attack, The Associated Press, 1972
42. **Pauline Kael:** "Trash, Art, and the Movies," *Harper's,* 1969
43. **Gay Talese:** *Fame and Obscurity: Portraits by Gay Talese,* collected articles, 1970

44. **Randy Shilts:** Reports on AIDS, *The San Francisco Chronicle,* 1981–1985
45. **Janet Flanner (Genet):** *Paris Journals* chronicling Paris' emergence from the Occupation, *The New Yorker,* 1944–1945
46. **Neil Sheehan:** *A Bright Shining Lie: John Paul Vann and America in Vietnam,* book, 1988
47. **A. J. Liebling:** *The Wayward Pressman,* collected articles, 1947
48. **Tom Wolfe:** *The Right Stuff,* book, 1979
49. **Murray Kempton:** *America Comes of Middle Age: Columns 1950–1962,* collected articles, 1963
50. **Murray Kempton:** *Part of Our Time: Some Ruins and Monuments of the Thirties,* book, 1955
51. **Donald L. Barlett and James B. Steele:** "America: What Went Wrong?," *The Philadelphia Inquirer,* 1991
52. **Taylor Branch:** *Parting the Waters: America in the King Years, 1954–63,* book, 1988
53. **Harrison Salisbury:** Reporting from the Soviet Union, *The New York Times,* 1949–1954
54. **John McPhee:** *The John McPhee Reader,* collected articles, 1976
55. **ABC:** Live television broadcast of Army-McCarthy hearings, 1954
56. **Frederick Wiseman:** *Titicut Follies,* documentary, 1967
57. **David Remnick:** *Lenin's Tomb: The Last Days of the Soviet Empire,* book, 1993
58. **Richard Ben Cramer:** *What It Takes: The Way to the White House,* book, 1992
59. **Jonathan Schell:** *The Fate of the Earth,* book, 1982
60. **Russell Baker:** "Francs and Beans," *The New York Times,* 1975
61. **Homer Bigart:** Account of being over Japan in a bomber when World War II came to an end, The New York *Herald-Tribune,* 1945
62. **Ben Hecht:** *1,001 Afternoons in Chicago,* collected articles, 1922
63. **Walter Cronkite:** Documentary on Vietnam, CBS television, 1968
64. **Walter Lippmann:** Early essays, *The New Republic,* 1914
65. **Margaret Bourke-White:** Photographs following the defeat of Germany, *Life* magazine, 1945
66. **Lillian Ross:** *Reporting,* collected articles, 1964
67. **Nicholas Lemann:** *The Promised Land: The Great Black Migration and How It Changed America,* book, 1991
68. **Joe Rosenthal:** Photograph of Marines raising an American flag on Mount Suribachi on the island of Iwo Jima, The Associated Press, 1945
69. **Hodding Carter Jr.:** "Go for Broke," editorial, Carter's *Delta Democrat-Times* (Greenville, Miss.), 1945
70. **The New Yorker:** *The New Yorker Book of War Pieces,* collected articles, 1947

71. **Meyer Berger:** Report on the murderer Howard Unruh, *The New York Times,* 1949
72. **Norman Mailer:** *The Executioner's Song,* book, 1979
73. **Robert Capa:** Spanish Civil War photos, *Life* magazine, 1936
74. **Susan Sontag:** "Notes on 'Camp'," *The Partisan Review,* 1964
75. **Bob Woodward and Carl Bernstein:** *All the President's Men,* book, 1974
76. **John Hersey:** *Here to Stay,* collected articles, 1963
77. **A. J. Liebling:** *The Earl of Louisiana,* book, 1961
78. **Mike Davis:** *City of Quartz: Excavating the Future in Los Angeles,* book, 1990
79. **Melissa Fay Greene:** *Praying for Sheetrock,* book, 1991
80. **J. Anthony Lukas:** "The Two Worlds of Linda Fitzpatrick," *The New York Times,* 1967
81. **Herbert Bayard Swope:** "Klan Exposed," *The New York World,* 1921
82. **William Allen White:** "To an Anxious Friend," *The Emporia* (Kan.) *Gazette,* 1922
83. **Edward R. Murrow:** Report of the liberation of Buchenwald, CBS radio, 1945
84. **Joseph Mitchell:** *McSorley's Wonderful Saloon,* collected articles, 1943
85. **Lillian Ross:** *Picture,* book, 1952
86. **Earl Brown:** Series of articles on race, *Harper's* and *Life* magazines, 1942–1944
87. **Greil Marcus:** *Mystery Train: Images of America in Rock 'n' Roll Music,* book, 1975
88. **Morley Safer:** Atrocities committed by American soldiers on the hamlet of Cam Ne in Vietnam, CBS television, 1965
89. **Ted Poston:** Coverage of the "Little Scottsboro" trial, *The New York Post,* 1949
90. **Leon Dash:** "Rosa Lee's Story," *The Washington Post,* 1994
91. **Jane Kramer:** *Europeans,* collected articles, 1988
92. **Eddie Adams and Vo Suu:** Associated Press photograph and NBC television footage of a Saigon execution, 1968
93. **Grantland Rice:** "Notre Dame's 'Four Horsemen'," The New York *Herald-Tribune,* 1924
94. **Jane Kramer:** *The Politics of Memory: Looking for Germany in the New Germany,* collected articles, 1996
95. **Frank McCourt:** *Angela's Ashes,* book, 1996
96. **Vincent Sheean:** *Personal History,* book, 1935
97. **W.E.B. Du Bois:** Columns on race during his tenure as editor of *The Crisis,* 1910–1934
98. **Damon Runyon:** Crime reporting, *The New York American,* 1926
99. **Joe McGinniss:** *The Selling of the President 1968,* book, 1969
100. **Hunter S. Thompson:** *Fear and Loathing on the Campaign Trail,* book, 1973

## Poets Laureate of the United States

| | | | |
|---|---|---|---|
| Robert Penn Warren | 1986–1987 | Rita Dove | 1993–1995 |
| Richard Wilbur | 1987–1988 | Robert Hass | 1995–1997 |
| Howard Nemerov | 1988–1990 | Robert Pinsky | 1997–2000 |
| Mark Strand | 1990–1991 | Stanley Kunitz | 2000–2001 |
| Joseph Brodsky | 1991–1992 | Billy Collins | 2001– |
| Mona Van Duyn | 1992–1993 | | |

NOTE: The post was established in 1985. Appointment is for a one-year term, but is renewable.

## Poets Laureate of England

| | | | | | |
|---|---|---|---|---|---|
| Edmund Spenser | 1591–1599 | Laurence Eusden | 1718–1730 | Alfred Austin | 1896–1913 |
| Samuel Daniel | 1599–1619 | Colley Cibber | 1730–1757 | Robert Bridges | 1913–1930 |
| Ben Jonson | 1619–1637 | William Whitehead | 1757–1785 | John Masefield | 1930–1967 |
| William Davenant | 1638–1668 | Thomas Warton | 1785–1790 | Cecil Day-Lewis | 1967–1972 |
| John Dryden[1] | 1668–1689 | Henry James Pye | 1790–1813 | Sir John Betjeman | 1972–1984 |
| Thomas Shadwell | 1689–1692 | Robert Southey | 1813–1843 | Ted Hughes | 1984–1998 |
| Nahum Tate | 1692–1715 | William Wordsworth | 1843–1850 | Andrew Motion | 1999– |
| Nicholas Rowe | 1715–1718 | Alfred Lord Tennyson | 1850–1892 | | |

1. First to bear the title officially.

## Longest Broadway Runs

| Show | Dates | Performances[1] | Show | Dates | Performances[1] |
|---|---|---|---|---|---|
| 1. Cats | 10/82–9/2000 | 7,485 | 13. Hello, Dolly! | 1/64–12/70 | 2,844 |
| 2. Les Misérables | 3/87–present | 6,276 | 14. My Fair Lady | 3/56–9/62 | 2,717 |
| 3. A Chorus Line | 7/75–4/90 | 6,137 | 15. Rent | 4/96–present | 2,535 |
| 4. The Phantom of the Opera | 1/88–present | 5,979 | 16. Annie | 4/77–1/83 | 2,377 |
| 5. Oh! Calcutta! (revival) | 9/76–8/89 | 5,959 | 17. Man of La Mancha | 11/65–6/71 | 2,328 |
| 6. Miss Saigon | 4/91–1/2001 | 4,092 | 18. Abie's Irish Rose | 5/22–10/27 | 2,327 |
| 7. 42nd Street | 8/80–1/89 | 3,486 | 19. Chicago (revival) | 11/96–present | 2,306 |
| 8. Grease | 2/72–4/80 | 3,388 | 20. Oklahoma! | 3/43–5/48 | 2,212 |
| 9. Beauty and the Beast | 4/94–present | 3,306 | 21. Smokey Joe's Cafe | 3/95–1/2000 | 2,037 |
| 10. Fiddler on the Roof | 9/64–7/72 | 3,242 | 22. Pippin | 10/72–6/77 | 1,944 |
| 11. Life with Father | 11/39–7/47 | 3,224 | 23. South Pacific | 4/49–1/54 | 1,925 |
| 12. Tobacco Road | 12/33–5/41 | 3,182 | 24. The Magic Show | 5/74–12/78 | 1,920 |
| | | | 25. The Lion King | 11/97–present | 1,896 |

1. As of 5/26/02. Source: League of American Theatres and Producers, Inc.

## Top 15 Concert Grosses of 2001

*Amusement Business* annually ranks domestic and international concert grosses and touring acts. (Headliner, supporting act, dates; gross ticket sales in U.S. dollars; total attendance; venue)

1. **The Concert for New York City (10/20),** $12,269,405; 14,651; Madison Square Garden, New York, N.Y.
2. **Michael Jackson 30th Anniversary Tribute (9/7 and 9/10),** $10,072,105; 70,311; Madison Square Garden, New York, N.Y.
3. **Madonna (7/25–7/31),** $9,297,105; 79,401; Madison Square Garden, New York, N.Y.
4. **Madonna (7/4–7/12),** $8,734,149; 107,415; Earls Court, London
5. **Madonna (9/9–9/15),** $8,303,165; 61,464; Staples Center, Los Angeles, Calif.
6. **'N Sync, BB Mak (6/3–6/5),** $7,364,012; 154,359; Giants Stadium, East Rutherford, N.J.
7. **Backstreet Boys, Krystal (3/23–3/25),** $7,240,702; 154,716; Foro Sol, Mexico City
8. **Madonna (9/1–9/2),** $6,503,950; 9,587; MGM Grand Garden, Las Vegas, Nev.
9. **U2, PJ Harvey (5/12–5/16),** $6,393,525; 78,275; United Center, Chicago, Ill.
10. **Bon Jovi, Sugar Ray, Eve 6 (7/26–7/27),** $6,317,039; 107,248; Giants Stadium, East Rutherford, N.J.
11. **Dave Matthews Band, Macy Gray, Angelique Kidjo (6/11–6/13),** $6,077,066; 124,783; Giants Stadium, East Rutherford, N.J.
12. **Billy Joel and Elton John (5/7–5/11),** $5,784,860; 52,946; Allstate Arena, Rosemont, Ill.
13. **U2, PJ Harvey (6/5–6/9),** $5,620,260; 68,329, Fleet Center, Boston, Mass.
14. **Elton John and Billy Joel (2/17–2/18),** $4,929,450; 27,422; MGM Grand Garden, Las Vegas, Nev.
15. **Billy Joel and Elton John (2/6–2/11),** $4,886,945; 52,861; Great Western Forum, Inglewood, Calif.

## Top 10 Classical Albums, 2001

1. *Verdi,* Andrea Bocelli (Philips/Universal Classics Group)
2. *The Three Tenors Christmas,* Carreras-Domingo-Pavarotti (Sony Classical)
3. *Sacred Arias,* Andrea Bocelli (Philips/Universal Classics Group)
4. *Appalachian Journey,* Yo-Yo Ma/Edgar Meyer/Mark O'Connor (Sony Classical)
5. *Billy Joel: Fantasies & Delusions,* Richard Joo (Columbia/Sony Classical)
6. *Renee Fleming,* Renee Fleming (Decca/Universal Classics Group)
7. *Classic Yo-Yo,* Yo-Yo Ma (Sony Classical)
8. *Fantasia 2000,* Chicago Symphony Orchestra (Walt Disney/Universal Classics Group)
9. *Puccini: La Boheme,* Andrea Boccelli (Decca/Universal Classics Group)
10. *Legend,* Maria Callas (EMI Classics/Angel)

## Top 10 Country Singles, 2001

1. "But I Do Love You/Can't Fight the Moonlight," LeAnn Rimes (Curb)
2. "The Way You Love Me," Faith Hill (Warner Bros./WRN)
3. "Oklahoma/Warm & Fuzzy," Billy Gilman (Epic/Sony)
4. "I Hope You Dance," Lee Ann Womack with Sons of the Desert (MCA Nashville)
5. "Austin," Blake Shelton (Giant/WRN)
6. "God Bless the USA," Lee Greenwood (Curb)
7. "What I Really Meant to Say," Cyndi Thomson (Capitol)
8. "Pour Me," Trick Pony (Warner Bros./WRN)
9. "Where the Stars and Stripes and the Eagle Fly," Aaron Tippin (Lyric Street/Hollywood)
10. "Mrs. Steven Rudy/That's a Plan," Mark McGuinn (VFR)

*Source:* © 2001/2002 VNU Business Media, Inc. The Billboard ® Charts are the exclusive property of VNU Business Media, Inc. and are fully protected by copyright and trademark laws. Any reproduction or copying, in whatever form, now or hereafter requires prior written approval from VNU Business Media, Inc.

## Top 10 Country Albums, 2001

1. *Greatest Hits,* Tim McGraw (Curb)
2. *O Brother, Where Art Thou?* Soundtrack (Mercury)
3. *Coyote Ugly,* Soundtrack (Curb)
4. *Breathe,* Faith Hill (Warner Bros./WRN)
5. *Fly,* Dixie Chicks (Monument/Sony)
6. *I Hope You Dance,* Lee Ann Womack (MCA Nashville)
7. *Greatest Hits,* Kenny Chesney (BNA/RLG)
8. *Set This Circus Down,* Tim McGraw (Curb)
9. *Born to Fly,* Sara Evans (RCA/RLG)
10. *One Voice,* Billy Gilman (Epic/Sony)

*Source:* © 2001/2002 VNU Business Media, Inc. The Billboard ® Charts are the exclusive property of VNU Business Media, Inc. and are fully protected by copyright and trademark laws. Any reproduction or copying, in whatever form, now or hereafter requires prior written approval from VNU Business Media, Inc.

## Top 10 Pop Singles, 2001

1. "Loverboy," Mariah Carey featuring Cameo (Virgin)
2. "Stutter, " Joe featuring Mystikal (Jive)
3. "Get Over Yourself," Eden's Crush (143/London-Sire)
4. "Liquid Dreams," O-Town (J)
5. "My Baby," Lil' Romeo (Soulja/Priority)
6. "All for You," Janet (Virgin)
7. "Could It Be," Jaheim (Divine Mill/Warner Bros.)
8. "What Would You Do?" City High (Booga Basement/Interscope)
9. "He Loves U Not," Dream (Bad Boy/Arista)
10. "Bizounce," Olivia (J)

*Source:* © 2001/2002 VNU Business Media, Inc. The Billboard ® Charts are the exclusive property of VNU Business Media, Inc. and are fully protected by copyright and trademark laws. Any reproduction or copying, in whatever form, now or hereafter requires prior written approval from VNU Business Media, Inc.

## Top 10 Pop Albums, 2001

1. *1,* The Beatles (Apple/Capitol)
2. *Hotshot,* Shaggy (MCA)
3. *Black & Blue,* Backstreet Boys (Jive/Zomba)
4. *Now 5,* Various Artists (Sony/Zomba/Universal/EMI/CRG)
5. *Chocolate Starfish and the Hot Dog Flavored Water,* Limp Bizkit (Flip/Interscope)
6. *[Hybrid Theory],* Linkin Park (Warner Bros.)
7. *Break the Cycle,* Staind (Flip/Elektra/EEG)
8. *A Day Without Rain,* Enya (Reprise/Warner Bros.)
9. *Celebrity,* 'N Sync (Jive/Zomba)
10. *Country Grammar,* Nelly (Fo' Reel/Universal)

*Source:* © 2001/2002 VNU Business Media, Inc. The Billboard ® Charts are the exclusive property of VNU Business Media, Inc. and are fully protected by copyright and trademark laws. Any reproduction or copying, in whatever form, now or hereafter requires prior written approval from VNU Business Media, Inc.

## Top 10 R&B/Hip-Hop Singles, 2001

1. "Could It Be," Jaheim (Divine Mill/Warner Bros.)
2. "All for You," Janet (Virgin)
3. "Loverboy," Mariah Carey featuring Da Brat & Ludacris (Virgin)
4. "My Baby," Lil' Romeo (Soulja/Priority)
5. "Missing You," Case (Def Soul/IDJMG)
6. "Stutter," Joe featuring Mystikal (Jive)
7. "Soul Sista," Bilal (Moyo/Interscope)
8. "Stranger in My House," Tamia (Elektra/EEG)
9. "Bizounce," Olivia (J)
10. "U Remind Me," Usher (Arista)

*Source:* © 2001/2002 VNU Business Media, Inc. The Billboard ® Charts are the exclusive property of VNU Business Media, Inc. and are fully protected by copyright and trademark laws. Any reproduction or copying, in whatever form, now or hereafter requires prior written approval from VNU Business Media, Inc.

## Top 10 R&B/Hip-Hop Albums, 2001

1. *TP-2.com,* R. Kelly (Jive/Zomba)
2. *Hotshot,* Shaggy (MCA)
3. *Songs in A Minor,* Alicia Keys (J)
4. *Aijuswanaseing (I Just Want to Sing),* Musiq Soulchild (Def Soul/IDJMG)
5. *Lovers Rock,* Sade (Epic)
6. *Stankonia,* OutKast (LaFace/Arista)
7. *Tha Last Meal,* Snoop Dogg (No Limit/Priority/Capitol)
8. *Who Is Jill Scott? Words and Sounds Vol 1.,* Jill Scott (Hidden Beach/Epic)
9. *Until the End of Time,* 2Pac (Amaru/Death Row/Interscope)
10. *Rule 3:36,* Ja Rule (Murder Inc./Def Jam/IDJMG)

*Source:* © 2001/2002 VNU Business Media, Inc. The Billboard ® Charts are the exclusive property of VNU Business Media, Inc. and are fully protected by copyright and trademark laws. Any reproduction or copying, in whatever form, now or hereafter requires prior written approval from VNU Business Media, Inc.

## Top 10 Rap Singles, 2001

1. "My Baby," Lil' Romeo (Soulja/Priority)
2. "What Would You Do?," City High (Booga Basement/Interscope)
3. "Ms. Jackson," OutKast (LaFace/Arista)
4. "Bow Wow (That's My Name)," Lil Bow Wow (So So Def/Columbia/CRG)
5. "It Wasn't Me," Shaggy featuring Ricardo "RikRok" Ducent (MCA)
6. "Raise Up," Petey Pablo (Jive Zomba)
7. "Cross the Border," Philly's Most Wanted (Atlantic/AG)
8. "My Projects," Coo Coo Cal (Infinite/Tommy Boy)
9. "Purple Hills," D12 (Shady/Interscope)
10. "Baby If You're Ready," Snoop Dogg presents Doggys Angels featuring LaToya (Doggystyle/TVT)

## The Recording Industry Association of America's Diamond Awards

### Top-Selling Certified Albums of All Time*

The RIAA certifies recordings that sell 10,000,000 or more copies as diamond.

**27 Million**
*Their Greatest Hits 1971–1975*, Eagles (Elektra)

**26 Million**
*Thriller*, Michael Jackson (Epic)

**23 Million**
*The Wall*, Pink Floyd (Columbia)

**22 Million**
*Led Zeppelin IV*, Led Zeppelin (Swan Song)

**21 Million**
*Greatest Hits Volumes I & II*, Billy Joel (Columbia)

**19 Million**
*Back in Black*, AC/DC (Elektra)
*The Beatles*, The Beatles (Capitol)

**18 Million**
*Come On Over*, Shania Twain (Mercury Nashville)
*Rumours*, Fleetwood Mac (Warner Bros.)

**17 Million**
*The Bodyguard* (Soundtrack), Whitney Houston (Arista)

**16 Million**
*Boston*, Boston (Epic)
*Cracked Rear View*, Hootie & the Blowfish (Atlantic)
*Hotel California*, Eagles (Elektra)
*Jagged Little Pill*, Alanis Morissette (Maverick)
*No Fences*, Garth Brooks (Capitol Nashville)
*The Beatles 1967–1970*, The Beatles (Capitol)

**15 Million**
*Appetite for Destruction*, Guns 'N Roses (Geffen)
*Born in the U.S.A.*, Bruce Springsteen (Columbia)
*Dark Side of the Moon*, Pink Floyd (Capitol)
*Greatest Hits*, Elton John (Rocket)
*Physical Graffiti*, Led Zeppelin (Swan Song)
*Saturday Night Fever* (Soundtrack), Bee Gees (Polydor/Atlas)
*The Beatles 1962–1966*, The Beatles (Capitol)

**14 Million**
Cosby?, wait unreadable
*Bat Out of Hell*, Meat Loaf (Epic)

*Double Live*, Garth Brooks (Capitol Nashville)
*Ropin' the Wind*, Garth Brooks (Capitol Nashville)
*Supernatural*, Santana (Arista)

**13 Million**
*. . . Baby One More Time*, Britney Spears (Jive)
*Bruce Springsteen & the E Street Band Live 1975–1985* (Box set), Bruce Springsteen & the E Street Band (Columbia)
*Millennium*, Backstreet Boys (Jive)
*Purple Rain* (Soundtrack), Prince and the Revolution (Warner Bros.)
*Simon & Garfunkel's Greatest Hits*, Simon & Garfunkel (Columbia)
*Whitney Houston*, Whitney Houston (Arista)

**12 Million**
*Abbey Road*, The Beatles (Capitol)
*Breathless*, Kenny G (Arista)
*Forrest Gump* (Soundtrack) (Epic)
*Hysteria*, Def Leppard (Mercury)
*II*, Boyz II Men (Motown)
*Kenny Rogers' Greatest Hits*, Kenny Rogers (Capitol Nashville)
*Led Zeppelin II*, Led Zeppelin (Atlantic)
*Metallica*, Metallica (Elektra)
*No Jacket Required*, Phil Collins (Atlantic)
*Slippery When Wet*, Bon Jovi (Mercury)
*The Woman in Me*, Shania Twain (Mercury Nashville)
*Yourself or Someone Like You*, matchbox twenty (Atlantic)

**11 Million**
*Candle in the Wind 1997/Something About the Way You Look Tonight* (Single), Elton John (Rocket)
*CrazySexyCool*, TLC (LaFace)
*Dirty Dancing* (Soundtrack) (RCA)
*Houses of the Holy*, Led Zeppelin (Atlantic)
*James Taylor's Greatest Hits*, James Taylor (Warner Bros.)
*No Strings Attached*, 'N Sync (Jive)
*Pieces of You*, Jewel (Atlantic)
*Sgt. Pepper's Lonely Hearts Club Band*, The Beatles (Capitol)
*Ten*, Pearl Jam (Epic)
*Titanic* (Soundtrack) (Sony Classical)
*Wide Open Spaces*, Dixie Chicks (Monument)

*Through 11/14/2001.

## Top 10 DVD Sales, 2001

1. *Gladiator* (DreamWorks Home Entertainment)
2. *Crouching Tiger, Hidden Dragon* (Columbia TriStar Home Video)
3. *Cast Away* (FoxVideo)
4. *X-Men* (FoxVideo)
5. *Gone in 60 Seconds* (Touchstone Home Video/Buena Vista Home Entertainment)
6. *Traffic* (USA Home Entertainment)
7. *Star Wars: Episode I—The Phantom Menace* (FoxVideo)
8. *The Matrix* (Warner Home Video)
9. *The Patriot* (Columbia TriStar Home Video)
10. *Meet the Parents* (Universal Studios Home Video)

## Country Music Hall of Fame

**1961**
Jimmie Rodgers
Fred Rose
Hank Williams

**1962**
Roy Acuff

**1963**
No candidate received
enough votes to qualify for
induction.

**1964**
Tex Ritter

**1965**
Ernest Tubb

**1966**
Eddy Arnold
James R. Denny
George D. Hay
Uncle Dave Macon

**1967**
Red Foley
J. L. Frank
Jim Reeves
Stephen H. Sholes

**1968**
Bob Wills

**1969**
Gene Autry

**1970**
Bill Monroe
Original Carter Family

**1971**
Arthur Edward Satherley

**1972**
Jimmie H. Davis

**1973**
Chet Atkins
Patsy Cline

**1974**
Owen Bradley
Frank "Pee Wee" King

**1975**
Minnie Pearl

**1976**
Paul Cohen
Kitty Wells

**1977**
Merle Travis

**1978**
Grandpa Jones

**1979**
Hubert Long
Hank Snow

**1980**
Johnny Cash
Connie B. Gay
Original Sons of the Pioneers

**1981**
Vernon Dalhart
Grant Turner

**1982**
Lefty Frizzell
Roy Horton
Marty Robbins

**1983**
Little Jimmy Dickens

**1984**
Ralph Sylvester Peer
Floyd Tillman

**1985**
Lester Flatt and Earl Scruggs

**1986**
Whitey Ford
Wesley H. Rose

**1987**
Rod Brasfield

**1988**
Loretta Lynn
Roy Rogers

**1989**
Jack Stapp
Cliffie Stone
Hank Thompson

**1990**
Tennessee Ernie Ford

**1991**
Boudleaux and Felice Bryant

**1992**
George Jones
Frances Williams Preston

**1993**
Willie Nelson

**1994**
Merle Haggard

**1995**
Roger Miller
Jo Walker-Meador

**1996**
Patsy Montana
Buck Owens
Ray Price

**1997**
Cindy Walker
Harlan Howard
Brenda Lee

**1998**
Tammy Wynette
Elvis Presley
George Morgan
E. W. "Bud" Wendell

**1999**
Dolly Parton
Conway Twitty
Johnny Bond

**2000**
Faron Young
Charley Pride

**2001**
Bill Anderson
The Delmore Brothers
The Everly Brothers
Don Gibson
Homer & Jethro
Waylon Jennings
The Jordanaires
Don Law
The Louvin Brothers
Ken Nelson
Webb Pierce
Sam Phillips

## Top 10 Video Sales, 2001

1. *The Emperor's New Groove* (Walt Disney Home Video/Buena Vista Home Entertainment)
2. *Chicken Run* (DreamWorks Home Entertainment)
3. *The Silence of the Lambs* (MGM Home Entertainment)
4. *Coyote Ugly* (Touchstone Home Video/Buena Vista Home Entertainment)
5. *Miss Congeniality* (Warner Home Video)
6. *Bring It On* (Universal Studios Home Video)
7. *Gladiator* (DreamWorks Home Entertainment)
8. *102 Dalmatians* (Walt Disney Home Video/Buena Vista Home Entertainment)
9. *Toy Story 2* (Walt Disney Home Video/Buena Vista Home Entertainment)
10. *Meet the Parents* (Universal Studios Home Video)

## Top 10 Video Rentals, 2001

1. *Gladiator* (DreamWorks Home Entertainment)
2. *Meet the Parents* (Universal Studios Home Video)
3. *Almost Famous* (DreamWorks Home Entertainment)
4. *The Family Man* (Universal Studios Home Video)
5. *Wonder Boys* (Paramount Home Video)
6. *Cast Away* (FoxVideo)
7. *O Brother, Where Art Thou?* (Touchstone Home Video/Buena Vista Home Entertainment)
8. *What Lies Beneath* (DreamWorks Home Entertainment)
9. *Erin Brockovich* (Universal Studios Home Video)
10. *Traffic* (USA Home Entertainment)

## Rock and Roll Hall of Fame

**1986**
Chuck Berry
James Brown
Ray Charles
Sam Cooke
Fats Domino
The Everly Brothers
Buddy Holly
Jerry Lee Lewis
Elvis Presley
Little Richard
**Nonperformers**
Alan Freed
Sam Phillips
**Early Influences**
Robert Johnson
Jimmie Rodgers
Jimmy Yancey
**Lifetime Achievement**
John Hammond

**1987**
The Coasters
Eddie Cochran
Bo Diddley
Aretha Franklin
Marvin Gaye
Bill Haley
B.B. King
Clyde McPhatter
Ricky Nelson
Roy Orbison
Carl Perkins
Smokey Robinson
Joe Turner
Muddy Waters
Jackie Wilson
**Nonperformers**
Leonard Chess
Ahmet Ertegun
Jerry Leiber and Mike Stoller
Jerry Wexler
**Early Influences**
Louis Jordan
T-Bone Walker
Hank Williams

**1988**
The Beach Boys
The Beatles
The Drifters
Bob Dylan
The Supremes
**Nonperformer**
Berry Gordy, Jr.
Woody Guthrie
Leadbelly
Les Paul

**1989**
Dion
Otis Redding
The Rolling Stones
The Temptations
Stevie Wonder

**Nonperformer**
Phil Spector
**Early Influences**
The Ink Spots
Bessie Smith
The Soul Stirrers

**1990**
Hank Ballard
Bobby Darin
The Four Seasons
The Four Tops
The Kinks
The Platters
Simon and Garfunkel
The Who
**Nonperformers**
Gerry Goffin and Carole King
Brian Holland, Eddie Holland,
    and Lamont Dozier
**Early Influences**
Louis Armstrong
Charlie Christian
Ma Rainey

**1991**
LaVern Baker
The Byrds
John Lee Hooker
The Impressions
Wilson Pickett
Jimmy Reed
Ike and Tina Turner
**Nonperformers**
Dave Bartholomew
Ralph Bass
**Early Influence**
Howlin' Wolf
**Lifetime Achievement**
Nesuhi Ertegun

**1992**
Bobby "Blue" Bland
Booker T. and the MG's
Johnny Cash
Jimi Hendrix Experience
Isley Brothers
Sam and Dave
The Yardbirds
**Nonperformers**
Leo Fender
Bill Graham
Doc Pomus
**Early Influences**
Elmore James
Professor Longhair

**1993**
Ruth Brown
Cream
Creedence Clearwater
    Revival
The Doors
Etta James
Frankie Lymon and
    the Teenagers
Van Morrison

Sly and the Family Stone
**Nonperformers**
Dick Clark
Milt Gabler
**Early Influence**
Dinah Washington

**1994**
The Animals
The Band
Duane Eddy
The Grateful Dead
Elton John
John Lennon
Bob Marley
Rod Stewart
**Nonperformer**
Johnny Otis
**Early Influence**
Willie Dixon

**1995**
The Allman Brothers Band
Al Green
Janis Joplin
Led Zeppelin
Martha and the Vandellas
Neil Young
Frank Zappa
**Nonperformer**
Paul Ackerman
**Early Influence**
The Orioles

**1996**
David Bowie
Jefferson Airplane
Little Willie John
Gladys Knight and the Pips
Pink Floyd
The Shirelles
The Velvet Underground
**Nonperformer**
Tom Donahue
**Early Influence**
Pete Seeger

**1997**
The Bee Gees
Buffalo Springfield
Crosby, Stills and Nash
The Jackson Five
Joni Mitchell
Parliament-Funkadelic
The (Young) Rascals
Jimi Hendrix
Syd Nathan
**Early Influences**
Mahalia Jackson
Bill Monroe

**1998**
The Eagles
Fleetwood Mac
Mamas and Papas
Lloyd Price
Santana

Gene Vincent
**Nonperformer**
Allen Toussaint
**Early Influence**
"Jelly Roll" Morton

**1999**
Billy Joel
Curtis Mayfield
Paul McCartney
Del Shannon
Dusty Springfield
Bruce Springsteen
The Staple Singers
**Nonperformer**
George Martin
**Early Influences**
Charles Brown
Bob Wills and His Texas
    Playboys

**2000**
Eric Clapton
Earth, Wind, and Fire
Lovin' Spoonful
The Moonglows
Bonnie Raitt
James Taylor
**Nonperformer**
Clive Davis
**Early Influences**
Nat King Cole
Billie Holiday
**Side-Men**
Hal Blaine
King Curtis
James Jamerson
Scotty Moore
Earl Palmer

**2001**
Aerosmith
Solomon Burke
The Flamingos
Michael Jackson
Queen
Paul Simon
Steely Dan
Ritchie Valens
**Nonperformer**
Chris Blackwell
**Side-Men**
James Burton
Johnnie Johnson
**2002**
Isaac Hayes
Brenda Lee
Tom Petty and the
    Heartbreakers
Gene Pitney
Ramones
Talking Heads
**Nonperformer**
Jim Stewart
**Side-Men**
Chet Atkins

## Top Television Specials, 2001–2002[1]

| Rank | Program name (network) | Rating (% of TV households) | Rank | Program name (network) | Rating (% of TV households) |
|---|---|---|---|---|---|
| 1. | Winter Olympics Opening Ceremony (NBC) | 25.5% | 4. | Friends Special (NBC) | 17.2% |
| 2. | Academy Awards (ABC) | 25.4 | 5. | On the Red Carpet: Oscars 2002 (ABC) | 17.1 |
| 3. | Winter Olympics Closing Ceremony (NBC) | 22.3 | 6. | Friends Special (NBC) | 16.6 |
| | | | 7. | Golden Globe Awards (NBC) | 14.9 |

NOTES: Each rating point represents 1,055,000 households using television. Does not include sports telecasts. 1. Through May 22, 2002. *Source:* Nielsen Media Research. © 2002, Nielsen Media Research.

## Top Syndicated TV Programs, 2001–2002[1]

| Rank | Program name | Rating (% of TV households) | Rank | Program name | Rating (% of TV households) |
|---|---|---|---|---|---|
| 1. | Wheel of Fortune | 9.5% | 14. | Live! With Regis and Kelly | 3.8% |
| 2. | Jeopardy | 8.0 | 16. | Buena Vista III | 3.6 |
| 3. | Friends (AT) | 6.9 | 16. | Entertainment Tonight (weekend) | 3.6 |
| 4. | Seinfeld (AT) | 6.3 | 18. | Frasier (AT) | 3.4 |
| 5. | Entertainment Tonight (AT) | 6.1 | 19. | Imagination VI | 3.4 |
| 6. | ESPN NFL Regular Season | 5.9 | 19. | Friends (weekend) | 3.3 |
| 7. | Judge Judy (AT) | 5.8 | 20. | Judge Joe Brown (AT) | 3.3 |
| 7. | Oprah Winfrey Show (AT) | 5.8 | 22. | Everybody Loves Raymond (weekend) | 3.2 |
| 9. | Everybody Loves Raymond (AT) | 5.6 | 22. | Inside Edition | 3.2 |
| 10. | Seinfeld (weekend) (AT) | 5.0 | 22. | King of the Hill | 3.2 |
| 11. | Seinfeld (AT) | 4.3 | 22. | Maury (AT) | 3.2 |
| 12. | Wheel of Fortune (weekend) | 4.2 | | | |
| 13. | Buena Vista VI | 3.9 | | | |
| 14. | ESPN NFL Regular Season 2 | 3.8 | | | |

NOTES: Each rating point represents 1,055,000 households using television. (AT) = Additional Telecasts. 1. Aug. 27, 2001–May 12, 2002. *Source:* Nielsen Media Research. © 2002, Nielsen Media Research.

## Top Regularly Scheduled Network Programs, 2001–2002[1]

| Rank | Program name (network) | Rating (% of TV households) | Rank | Program name (network) | Rating (% of TV households) |
|---|---|---|---|---|---|
| 1. | Friends—8:00 P.M. (NBC) | 15.3% | 14. | Law and Order: SVU (NBC) | 10.4% |
| 2. | CSI (CBS) | 14.6 | 15. | 60 Minutes (CBS) | 10.2 |
| 3. | ER (NBC) | 14.4 | 16. | Frasier (NBC) | 9.9 |
| 4. | Everybody Loves Raymond (CBS) | 12.8 | 16. | JAG (CBS) | 9.9 |
| 5. | Law and Order (NBC) | 12.6 | 18. | Inside Schwartz (NBC) | 9.8 |
| 6. | Friends—8:30 P.M. (NBC) | 12.2 | 18. | Judging Amy (CBS) | 9.8 |
| 7. | Survivor: Africa (CBS) | 11.8 | 20. | NFL Monday Showcase (ABC) | 9.6 |
| 7. | Survivor: Marquesas (CBS) | 11.8 | 21. | Just Shoot Me (NBC) | 9.5 |
| 9. | NFL Monday Night Football (ABC) | 11.5 | 22. | King of Queens (CBS) | 8.9 |
| 10. | West Wing (NBC) | 11.4 | 23. | Crossing Jordan (NBC) | 8.8 |
| 11. | Will & Grace (NBC) | 11.1 | 23. | Yes, Dear (CBS) | 8.8 |
| 12. | Leap of Faith (NBC) | 11.0 | 25. | The Practice (ABC) | 8.5 |
| 13. | Becker (CBS) | 10.7 | | | |

NOTE: Each rating point represents 1,055,000 households using television. 1. Through May 22, 2002. *Source:* Nielsen Media Research. © 2002, Nielsen Media Research.

## Top 10 Sports Telecasts, 2001–2002[1]

| Rank | Program name (network) | Description | Rating (% of TV households) |
|---|---|---|---|
| 1. | Super Bowl XXXVI (Fox) | New England vs. St. Louis | 40.4% |
| 2. | Super Bowl Post-Gun (Fox) | New England vs. St. Louis | 35.2 |
| 3. | Super Bowl Kickoff (Fox) | New England vs. St. Louis | 29.0 |
| 4. | Winter Olympics (NBC) | Thurs., 2/21/02 | 26.8 |
| 5. | Super Bowl Post Game (Fox) | New England vs. St. Louis | 24.7 |
| 6. | World Series Game 7 (Fox) | N.Y. Yankees at Arizona | 23.5 |
| 7. | NFC Championship (Fox) | Philadelphia at St. Louis | 22.7 |
| 8. | Winter Olympics (NBC) | Tues., 2/19/02 | 22.3 |
| 9. | AFC Championship (CBS) | New England at Pittsburgh | 21.2 |
| 10. | Winter Olympics (NBC) | Mon., 2/11/02 | 19.6 |

NOTE: Each rating point represents 1,055,000 households using television. 1. August 27, 2001–May 22, 2002. *Source:* Nielsen Media Research. © 2002, Nielsen Media Research.

## Top-Rated TV Movies, 2001–2002[1]

| Rank | Episode title (network) | Rating (% of TV households) | Rank | Episode title (network) | Rating (% of TV households) |
|---|---|---|---|---|---|
| 1. | 9/11 (CBS) | 22.3% | 10. | Double Jeopardy (CBS) | 10.2% |
| 2. | The Pilot's Wife (CBS) | 12.5 | 11. | Stephen King's Rose Red—Part 3 (ABC) | 9.8 |
| 3. | Stephen King's Rose Red—Part 1 (ABC) | 11.8 | 11. | Star Wars Episode #1 (Fox) | 9.8 |
| 3. | A Town Without Christmas (CBS) | 11.8 | 13. | The Wedding Dress (CBS) | 9.4 |
| 5. | Saving Private Ryan (ABC) | 11.1 | 14. | You've Got Mail (CBS) | 9.1 |
| 5. | Living with the Dead—Part 2 (CBS) | 11.1 | 14. | Deep End of the Ocean (CBS) | 9.1 |
| | | | 14. | Little John (CBS) | 9.1 |
| 7. | Stephen King's Rose Red—Part 2 (ABC) | 11.0 | 14. | Diagnosis Murder: Town Without Pity (CBS) | 9.1 |
| 8. | Living with the Dead—Part 1 (CBS) | 10.4 | 14. | Brian's Song (ABC) | 9.1 |
| | | | 19. | The President's Man (CBS) | 8.7 |
| 9. | My Sister's Keeper (CBS) | 10.3 | 20. | The Santa Clause (ABC) | 8.6 |

NOTE: Each rating point represents 1,055,000 households using television. 1. August 27, 2001–May 22, 2002. *Source:* Nielsen Media Research. © 2002, Nielsen Media Research.

## Weekly TV Viewing by Age
### (in hours and minutes)

| | Time per week | | | | Time per week | | |
|---|---|---|---|---|---|---|---|
| | Nov. 2001 | Nov. 2000 | Nov. 1999 | | Nov. 2001 | Nov. 2000 | Nov. 1999 |
| Women 18–24 | 23 hr 11 min | 23 hr 21 min | 23 hr 21 min | Female teens 12–17 | 21 hr 20 min | 21 hr 20 min | 21 hr 10 min |
| Women 25–54 | 33 hr 56 min | 33 hr 54 min | 32 hr 05 min | Male teens 12–17 | 22 hr 20 min | 22 hr 40 min | 22 hr 51 min |
| Women 55+ | 44 hr 11 min | 44 hr 31 min | 42 hr 20 min | Children 2–5 | 24 hr 01 min | 24 hr 22 min | 23 hr 52 min |
| Men 18–24 | 22 hr 00 min | 23 hr 21 min | 21 hr 30 min | Children 6–11 | 20 hr 40 min | 21 hr 40 min | 20 hr 10 min |
| Men 25–54 | 30 hr 44 min | 31 hr 15 min | 28 hr 34 min | | | | |
| Men 55+ | 39 hr 39 min | 40 hr 40 min | 37 hr 28 min | | | | |

*Source:* Nielsen Media Research. © 2002, Nielsen Media Research.

## Television Set Ownership
### Estimated total number of TV households: 105,500,000[1]

| | 1950 | 1955 | 1960 | 1965 | 1970 | 1975 | 1980 | 1985 | 1990 | 1995 | 2000 | 2001 |
|---|---|---|---|---|---|---|---|---|---|---|---|---|
| **% of total households:** | | | | | | | | | | | | |
| TV households | 10% | 67% | 87% | 94% | 96% | 97% | 98% | 98% | 98% | 98% | 98% | 98% |
| **% of TV households:** | | | | | | | | | | | | |
| Multi-set | — | 4 | 12 | 22 | 35 | 43 | 50 | 57 | 65 | 71 | 76 | 74 |
| Color | — | — | — | 7 | 41 | 74 | 83 | 91 | 98 | 99 | 99 | 100 |
| VCR | — | — | — | — | — | — | — | 14 | 66 | 79 | 86 | 91 |
| Remote control | — | — | — | — | — | — | — | 29 | 77 | 91 | 95 | 95 |
| Wired pay cable | — | — | — | — | — | — | — | 26 | 29 | 28 | 32 | 40 |
| Wired cable | — | — | — | — | 7 | 12 | 20 | 43 | 56 | 63 | 68 | 69 |

*Source:* Nielsen Media Research. © 2002, Nielsen Media Research. 1. As of January 2002.

## Top 100 Daily Newspapers in the United States

| Rank | Newspaper | Circulation | Rank | Newspaper | Circulation |
|---|---|---|---|---|---|
| 1. | USA Today (Arlington, Va.) | 2,149,933 | 15. | Arizona Republic (Phoenix) | 451,288 |
| 2. | Wall Street Journal (New York, N.Y.) | 1,780,605 | 16. | Star-Ledger (Newark, N.J.) | 410,547 |
| 3. | Times (New York, N.Y.) | 1,109,371 | 17. | Journal-Constitution (Atlanta) | 396,464 |
| 4. | Times (Los Angeles) | 944,303 | 18. | Free Press (Detroit) | 371,261 |
| 5. | Post (Washington, D.C.) | 759,864 | 19. | Inquirer (Philadelphia) | 365,154 |
| 6. | Daily News (New York, N.Y.) | 734,473 | 20. | Plain Dealer (Cleveland) | 359,978 |
| 7. | Tribune (Chicago) | 675,847 | 21. | Union-Tribune (San Diego) | 351,762 |
| 8. | Newsday (Long Island, N.Y.) | 577,354 | 22. | Oregonian (Portland) | 351,303 |
| 9. | Chronicle (Houston) | 551,854 | 23. | Star Tribune (Minneapolis) | 340,445 |
| 10. | Post (New York, N.Y.) | 533,860 | 24. | Times (St. Petersburg, Fla.) | 331,903 |
| 11. | Chronicle (San Francisco) | 512,042 | 25. | Register (Orange County, Calif.) | 324,056 |
| 12. | Morning News (Dallas) | 494,890 | 26. | Herald (Miami) | 317,690 |
| 13. | Sun-Times (Chicago) | 480,920 | 27. | Rocky Mountain News (Denver) | 309,938 |
| 14. | Globe (Boston) | 471,199 | 28. | Sun (Baltimore) | 306,341 |

| Rank | Newspaper | Circulation | Rank | Newspaper | Circulation |
|------|-----------|-------------|------|-----------|-------------|
| 29. | Post (Denver) | 305,929 | 65. | Times-Union (Jacksonville, Fla.) | 172,239 |
| 30. | Post-Dispatch (St. Louis) | 290,615 | 66. | Post (W. Palm Beach, Fla.) | 171,572 |
| 31. | Bee (Sacramento, Calif.) | 285,863 | 67. | Asbury Park Press (Neptune, N.J.) | 170,229 |
| 32. | Investor's Business Daily (Los Angeles) | 281,173 | 68. | Post-Intelligencer (Seattle) | 169,105 |
| 33. | Mercury News (San Jose, Calif.) | 268,621 | 69. | Press-Enterprise (Riverside, Calif.) | 168,765 |
| 34. | Star (Kansas City, Mo.) | 259,612 | 70. | Journal (Providence, R.I.) | 165,880 |
| 35. | Herald (Boston) | 259,228 | 71. | Review-Journal (Las Vegas) | 165,754 |
| 36. | Journal Sentinel (Milwaukee) | 255,098 | 72. | News & Observer (Raleigh, N.C.) | 162,869 |
| 37. | Sentinel (Orlando, Fla.) | 254,956 | 73. | Bee (Fresno, Calif.) | 157,820 |
| 38. | Times-Picayune (New Orleans) | 254,897 | 74. | Commercial Appeal (Memphis) | 155,196 |
| 39. | Star (Indianapolis) | 252,349 | 75. | Daily News (Philadelphia) | 152,435 |
| 40. | Sun-Sentinel (Fort Lauderdale, Fla.) | 251,886 | 76. | Register (Des Moines, Iowa) | 152,402 |
| 41. | Dispatch (Columbus, Ohio) | 244,204 | 77. | Advertiser (Honolulu) | 152,098 |
| 42. | News (Detroit) | 242,855 | 78. | Daily Herald (Arlington Heights, Ill.) | 148,375 |
| 43. | Post-Gazette (Pittsburgh, Pa.) | 242,141 | 79. | News (Birmingham, Ala.) | 145,760 |
| 44. | Observer (Charlotte, N.C.) | 235,375 | 80. | Journal News (White Plains, N.Y.) | 144,439 |
| 45. | Courier-Journal (Louisville, Ky.) | 222,332 | 81. | Beacon Journal (Akron, Ohio) | 141,073 |
| 46. | Times (Seattle) | 219,241 | 82. | Blade (Toledo, Ohio) | 140,406 |
| 47. | News (Buffalo, N.Y.) | 218,781 | 83. | Press (Grand Rapids, Mich.) | 139,800 |
| 48. | Star-Telegram (Fort Worth, Tex.) | 213,781 | 84. | World (Tulsa, Okla.) | 139,383 |
| 49. | Tribune (Tampa, Fla.) | 212,983 | 85. | Daily News (Dayton, Ohio) | 135,818 |
| 50. | Express-News (San Antonio, Tex.) | 208,951 | 86. | Tribune (Salt Lake City) | 134,712 |
| 51. | Courant (Hartford, Conn.) | 198,651 | 87. | Morning Call (Allentown, Pa.) | 128,204 |
| 52. | World-Herald (Omaha, Neb.) | 196,326 | 88. | News Tribune (Tacoma, Wash.) | 127,786 |
| 53. | Virginian-Pilot (Norfolk, Va.) | 195,583 | 89. | La Opinion (Los Angeles, Calif.) | 127,576 |
| 54. | Daily Oklahoman (Oklahoma City) | 195,454 | 90. | Post-Standard (Syracuse, N.Y.) | 126,761 |
| 55. | Pioneer Press (St. Paul, Minn.) | 195,042 | 91. | Tribune-Review (Greensburg, Pa.) | 124,851 |
| 56. | Times-Dispatch (Richmond, Va.) | 190,509 | 92. | News Journal (Wilmington, Del.) | 121,640 |
| 57. | Enquirer (Cincinnati) | 188,173 | 93. | State (Columbia, S.C.) | 117,423 |
| 58. | American-Statesman (Austin, Tex.) | 183,873 | 94. | News-Sentinel (Knoxville, Tenn.) | 114,989 |
| 59. | Tennessean (Nashville) | 183,406 | 95. | Journal (Albuquerque) | 108,668 |
| 60. | Contra Costa Times (Walnut Creek, Calif.) | 182,727 | 96. | Herald-Leader (Lexington, Ky.) | 107,670 |
| 61. | Democrat-Gazette (Little Rock, Ark.) | 182,609 | 97. | Herald-Tribune (Sarasota, Fla.) | 106,077 |
| 62. | Daily News (Los Angeles) | 178,156 | 98. | Spokesman-Review (Spokane, Wash.) | 105,911 |
| 63. | Record (Bergen County, N.J.) | 178,029 | 99. | Telegram & Gazette (Worcester, Mass.) | 103,565 |
| 64. | Democrat and Chronicle (Rochester, N.Y.) | 176,040 | 100. | Times (Washington, D.C.) | 103,505 |

NOTE: By circulation, as of Sept. 30, 2001. *Source: Editor & Publisher International Year Book 2002.* Web: www.editorandpublisher.com.

## Top 100 Consumer Magazines, 2001

| Rank | Magazine | Avg. Circulation[1] | Rank | Magazine | Avg. Circulation[1] |
|------|----------|---------------------|------|----------|---------------------|
| 1. | NRTA/AARP Bulletin | 21,465,126 | 23. | O, The Oprah Magazine | 2,641,138 |
| 2. | Modern Maturity | 18,363,840 | 24. | The American Legion Magazine | 2,613,923 |
| 3. | Reader's Digest | 12,558,435 | 25. | Southern Living | 2,547,803 |
| 4. | TV Guide | 9,259,455 | 26. | Maxim | 2,533,521 |
| 5. | National Geographic Magazine | 7,738,611 | 27. | Martha Stewart Living | 2,421,361 |
| 6. | Better Homes and Gardens | 7,603,006 | 28. | Seventeen | 2,351,570 |
| 7. | Family Circle | 4,857,727 | 29. | Redbook | 2,310,430 |
| 8. | Good Housekeeping | 4,531,082 | 30. | YM | 2,241,509 |
| 9. | Woman's Day | 4,150,415 | 31. | Glamour | 2,170,476 |
| 10. | Time—The Weekly Newsmagazine | 4,128,626 | 32. | AAA Going Places | 2,142,601 |
| 11. | Ladies' Home Journal | 4,100,553 | 33. | U.S. News & World Report | 2,075,545 |
| 12. | Rosie | 3,790,421 | 34. | Money | 2,062,246 |
| 13. | People Weekly | 3,714,268 | 35. | Smithsonian | 2,034,137 |
| 14. | Home & Away | 3,310,934 | 36. | Parents | 2,013,163 |
| 15. | Newsweek | 3,254,513 | 37. | National Enquirer | 1,934,706 |
| 16. | Sports Illustrated | 3,223,772 | 38. | Ebony | 1,782,442 |
| 17. | Playboy | 3,154,560 | 39. | Parenting Magazine | 1,759,411 |
| 18. | Westways | 3,150,371 | 40. | Field & Stream | 1,754,385 |
| 19. | Prevention | 3,115,991 | 41. | 'teen | 1,729,433 |
| 20. | Cosmopolitan | 2,701,167 | 42. | V.F.W. Magazine | 1,693,699 |
| 21. | Guideposts | 2,700,475 | 43. | Woman's World | 1,661,260 |
| 22. | Via Magazine | 2,647,933 | 44. | Men's Health | 1,659,505 |

| Rank | Magazine | Avg. Circulation[1] |
|---|---|---|
| 45. | American Rifleman | 1,642,540 |
| 46. | Country Living | 1,635,402 |
| 47. | Shape | 1,633,442 |
| 48. | Teen People | 1,625,343 |
| 49. | In Style | 1,601,549 |
| 50. | Cooking Light | 1,583,399 |
| 51. | Popular Science | 1,569,810 |
| 52. | Golf Digest | 1,563,455 |
| 53. | Entertainment Weekly | 1,534,433 |
| 54. | Star | 1,514,280 |
| 55. | Sunset, the Magazine of Western Living | 1,453,698 |
| 56. | Self | 1,443,300 |
| 57. | Golf Magazine | 1,400,234 |
| 58. | Health | 1,395,072 |
| 59. | First for Women | 1,386,060 |
| 60. | Endless Vacation | 1,381,030 |
| 61. | ESPN the Magazine | 1,380,797 |
| 62. | FamilyFun | 1,377,613 |
| 63. | Car and Driver | 1,368,478 |
| 64. | Outdoor Life | 1,357,351 |
| 65. | Boys' Life | 1,280,320 |
| 66. | Bon Appetit | 1,275,468 |
| 67. | Rolling Stone | 1,267,254 |
| 68. | Motor Trend | 1,262,417 |
| 69. | PC World | 1,256,135 |
| 70. | Scholastic Parent & Child | 1,250,387 |
| 71. | PC Magazine | 1,228,855 |
| 72. | The American Hunter | 1,227,425 |

| Rank | Magazine | Avg. Circulation[1] |
|---|---|---|
| 73. | Popular Mechanics | 1,225,684 |
| 74. | Fitness | 1,175,201 |
| 75. | The Family Handyman | 1,158,306 |
| 76. | Mademoiselle | 1,153,438 |
| 77. | Vogue | 1,148,913 |
| 78. | Kiplinger's Personal Finance Magazine | 1,126,883 |
| 79. | Yahoo! Internet Life | 1,102,939 |
| 80. | Elks Magazine, The | 1,100,563 |
| 81. | Vanity Fair | 1,100,459 |
| 82. | Essence | 1,052,068 |
| 83. | Scouting | 1,040,998 |
| 84. | Stuff | 1,040,065 |
| 85. | Michigan Living | 1,038,292 |
| 86. | Soap Opera Digest | 1,025,869 |
| 87. | Discover | 1,017,664 |
| 88. | Country Home | 1,008,505 |
| 89. | Home | 1,006,600 |
| 90. | Travel + Leisure | 1,004,922 |
| 91. | Victoria | 983,554 |
| 92. | American Homestyle & Gardening | 974,336 |
| 93. | Elle | 971,674 |
| 94. | Businessweek (North America) | 971,599 |
| 95. | Jet | 965,204 |
| 96. | Gourmet | 952,049 |
| 97. | Allure | 944,730 |
| 98. | Food & Wine | 943,097 |
| 99. | Child | 941,745 |
| 100. | This Old House | 939,827 |

1. Figure includes subscriptions and single-copy sales. *Source:* Audit Bureau of Circulations, tabulated by Magazine Publishers of America.

## Movie Revenues

### All-Time Box Office Grosses[1]

| 1. | Titanic (1997) | $600,788,188 |
|---|---|---|
| 2. | Star Wars (1977)[2] | 460,998,007 |
| 3. | Star Wars: Episode One—The Phantom Menace (1999) | 431,088,295 |
| 4. | E.T. the Extra-Terrestrial (1982)[2] | 399,804,539 |
| 5. | Jurassic Park (1993) | 357,067,947 |
| 6. | Forrest Gump (1994)[2] | 329,694,499 |
| 7. | The Lion King (1994)[2] | 312,855,561 |
| 8. | Harry Potter and the Sorcerer's Stone (2001) | 309,659,297[3] |
| 9. | Return of the Jedi (1983)[2] | 309,153,948 |
| 10. | Independence Day (1996) | 306,169,255 |
| 11. | The Sixth Sense (1999) | 293,506,292 |
| 12. | The Empire Strikes Back (1980)[2] | 290,266,497 |
| 13. | Home Alone (1990) | 285,761,243 |
| 14. | Shrek (2001) | 267,990,044 |
| 15. | [Merry] Christmas (2000) | 260,031,035 |
| 16. | Jaws (1975)[2] | 260,000,000 |
| 17. | Batman (1989) | 251,188,924 |
| 18. | Men in Black (1997) | 250,690,539 |
| 19. | Monsters, Inc. (2001) | 249,919,653[3] |
| 20. | The Lord of the Rings: The Fellowship of the Ring (2001) | 248,212,887[3] |
| 21. | Toy Story 2 (1999) | 245,852,179 |
| 22. | Raiders of the Lost Ark (1981)[2] | 245,034,358 |
| 23. | Twister (1996) | 241,708,908 |
| 24. | Ghostbusters (1984)[2] | 238,600,000 |
| 25. | Beverly Hills Cop (1984) | 234,760,478 |

### Top 25 Movies of 2002[1]

| 1. | Harry Potter and the Sorcerer's Stone (Warner Bros.) | $309,659,297[3] |
|---|---|---|
| 2. | Shrek (DreamWorks) | 267,665,011 |
| 3. | Monsters, Inc. (Buena Vista) | 249,919,653[3] |
| 4. | The Lord of the Rings: The Fellowship of the Ring (New Line) | 248,212,887[3] |
| 5. | Rush Hour 2 (New Line) | 226,164,286 |
| 6. | The Mummy Returns (Universal) | 202,007,640 |
| 7. | Pearl Harbor (Buena Vista) | 198,539,855 |
| 8. | Jurassic Park III (Universal) | 181,166,115 |
| 9. | Planet of the Apes (Fox) | 179,996,425[3] |
| 10. | Ocean's 11 (Warner Bros.) | 171,624,204[3] |
| 11. | Hannibal (MGM) | 165,092,266 |
| 12. | American Pie 2 (Universal) | 145,096,820 |
| 13. | The Fast and the Furious (Universal) | 144,533,925 |
| 14. | Rat Race (Paramount) | 131,168,070 |
| 15. | Dr. Dolittle 2 (Fox) | 112,952,899 |
| 16. | Spy Kids (Dimension) | 112,692,062 |
| 17. | The Princess Diaries (Buena Vista) | 108,244,774 |
| 18. | Legally Blonde (MGM) | 96,520,600 |
| 19. | The Others (Dimension) | 96,471,845 |
| 20. | Vanilla Sky (Paramount) | 93,648,572[3] |
| 21. | America's Sweethearts (Sony) | 93,607,673 |
| 22. | Cats & Dogs (Warner Bros.) | 93,375,151 |
| 23. | Save the Last Dance (Paramount) | 91,057,006 |
| 24. | Atlantis: The Lost Empire (Buena Vista) | 84,037,039 |
| 25. | A.I.: Artificial Intelligence (Warner Bros.) | 78,616,689 |

1. As of Jan. 21, 2002. 2. Including reissues. 3. Still tracking. *Source:* Exhibitor Relations Co. Inc.

## American Film Institute's 50 Greatest Screen Legends

### Men

1. Humphrey Bogart
2. Cary Grant
3. James Stewart
4. Marlon Brando
5. Fred Astaire
6. Henry Fonda
7. Clark Gable
8. James Cagney
9. Spencer Tracy
10. Charlie Chaplin
11. Gary Cooper
12. Gregory Peck
13. John Wayne
14. Laurence Olivier
15. Gene Kelly
16. Orson Welles
17. Kirk Douglas
18. James Dean
19. Burt Lancaster
20. The Marx Brothers
21. Buster Keaton
22. Sidney Poitier
23. Robert Mitchum
24. Edward G. Robinson
25. William Holden

### Women

1. Katharine Hepburn
2. Bette Davis
3. Audrey Hepburn
4. Ingrid Bergman
5. Greta Garbo
6. Marilyn Monroe
7. Elizabeth Taylor
8. Judy Garland
9. Marlene Dietrich
10. Joan Crawford
11. Barbara Stanwyck
12. Claudette Colbert
13. Grace Kelly
14. Ginger Rogers
15. Mae West
16. Vivien Leigh
17. Lillian Gish
18. Shirley Temple
19. Rita Hayworth
20. Lauren Bacall
21. Sophia Loren
22. Jean Harlow
23. Carole Lombard
24. Mary Pickford
25. Ava Gardner

## American Film Institute's 100 Greatest Movies of All Time

1. Citizen Kane (1941)
2. Casablanca (1942)
3. The Godfather (1972)
4. Gone with the Wind (1939)
5. Lawrence of Arabia (1962)
6. The Wizard of Oz (1939)
7. The Graduate (1967)
8. On the Waterfront (1954)
9. Schindler's List (1993)
10. Singin' in the Rain (1952)
11. It's a Wonderful Life (1946)
12. Sunset Boulevard (1950)
13. The Bridge on the River Kwai (1957)
14. Some Like It Hot (1959)
15. Star Wars (1977)
16. All About Eve (1950)
17. The African Queen (1951)
18. Psycho (1960)
19. Chinatown (1974)
20. One Flew Over the Cuckoo's Nest (1975)
21. The Grapes of Wrath (1940)
22. 2001: A Space Odyssey (1968)
23. The Maltese Falcon (1941)
24. Raging Bull (1980)
25. E.T. the Extra-Terrestrial (1982)
26. Dr. Strangelove (1964)
27. Bonnie and Clyde (1967)
28. Apocalypse Now (1979)
29. Mr. Smith Goes to Washington (1939)
30. The Treasure of the Sierra Madre (1948)
31. Annie Hall (1977)
32. The Godfather Part II (1974)
33. High Noon (1952)
34. To Kill a Mockingbird (1962)
35. It Happened One Night (1934)
36. Midnight Cowboy (1969)
37. The Best Years of Our Lives (1946)
38. Double Indemnity (1944)
39. Doctor Zhivago (1965)
40. North by Northwest (1959)
41. West Side Story (1961)
42. Rear Window (1954)
43. King Kong (1933)
44. The Birth of a Nation (1915)
45. A Streetcar Named Desire (1951)
46. A Clockwork Orange (1971)
47. Taxi Driver (1976)
48. Jaws (1975)
49. Snow White and the Seven Dwarfs (1937)
50. Butch Cassidy and the Sundance Kid (1969)
51. The Philadelphia Story (1940)
52. From Here to Eternity (1953)
53. Amadeus (1984)
54. All Quiet on the Western Front (1930)
55. The Sound of Music (1965)
56. M*A*S*H (1970)
57. The Third Man (1949)
58. Fantasia (1940)
59. Rebel Without a Cause (1955)
60. Raiders of the Lost Ark (1981)
61. Vertigo (1958)
62. Tootsie (1982)
63. Stagecoach (1939)
64. Close Encounters of the Third Kind (1977)
65. The Silence of the Lambs (1991)
66. Network (1976)
67. The Manchurian Candidate (1962)
68. An American in Paris (1951)
69. Shane (1953)
70. The French Connection (1971)
71. Forrest Gump (1994)
72. Ben-Hur (1959)
73. Wuthering Heights (1939)
74. The Gold Rush (1925)
75. Dances with Wolves (1990)
76. City Lights (1931)
77. American Graffiti (1973)
78. Rocky (1976)
79. The Deer Hunter (1978)
80. The Wild Bunch (1969)
81. Modern Times (1936)
82. Giant (1956)
83. Platoon (1986)
84. Fargo (1996)
85. Duck Soup (1933)
86. Mutiny on the Bounty (1935)
87. Frankenstein (1931)
88. Easy Rider (1969)
89. Patton (1970)
90. The Jazz Singer (1927)
91. My Fair Lady (1964)
92. A Place in the Sun (1951)
93. The Apartment (1960)
94. GoodFellas (1990)
95. Pulp Fiction (1994)
96. The Searchers (1956)
97. Bringing Up Baby (1938)
98. Unforgiven (1992)
99. Guess Who's Coming to Dinner (1967)
100. Yankee Doodle Dandy (1942)

## The National Toy Hall of Fame®

**2002**
jigsaw puzzle
Raggedy Ann™

**2001**
Tonka®
Silly Putty®

**2000**
Slinky®

bicycle
jacks
jump rope
Mr. Potato Head®

**1999**
Hula Hoop
View-Master®
Duncan YoYo®

Red Wagon
Lincoln Logs®
roller skates

**1998**
Barbie®
Tinker Toys®
Crayola Crayons®
Erector Set

Etch a Sketch®
Frisbee®
Monopoly®
Play-Doh®
marbles
teddy bear
Legos®

The National Toy Hall of Fame was opened in 1998 at A. C. Gilbert's Discovery Village in Salem, Ore.

# Test Drive

A new law has made test-prep firms the hottest teacher's aid. But are students really getting better?

**By JODIE MORSE** TIME

By now, state high-stakes exams have become a fact of life in the American classroom. Less noticed is the growing presence—and power—of firms like Kaplan that teach students and their teachers how to master them. The companies, which have spent decades deflating the mystique of the SAT, take a similar tack with the grade-school exams. They maintain that test taking, like telling time or double-knotting a shoelace, is a "life skill" that every child can learn and no youngster should go without. Says Jeff McCullough, Kaplan's director of training and development: "Kids who have done well . . . are suddenly slapped with a challenge that is so foreign to them that they underperform just because of the strangeness of the task."

## Test-Prep Business Is Booming

Schools have needed little convincing. The market for K-12 test-prep services for state exams, which was almost insignificant three years ago, is now a booming $50 million arena dominated by familiar names such as Kaplan, The Princeton Review, and tutoring powerhouse Sylvan Learning Centers, which last year launched a $900 test-prep course for students as young as those in third grade. These testing giants have been joined by hundreds of new, small-time firms that often have little to recommend them beyond their own breathless promises of higher scores.

The demand will only grow with the law signed by President Bush in Jan. 2002 that requires annual testing in reading and math in Grades 3 through 8 by 2005; a provision in the law also pledges up to $1,000 a child in chronically low-scoring schools, for tutoring and test training.

The reach of coaching firms is already long. In the three years since The Princeton Review created its grade-school division, it has signed contracts with schools in 25 states. The company now sells more than 500 [illegible] test-taking tips ("Many problems can be solved without much calculating") throughout 36 different textbooks published by McGraw Hill. In the summer of 2000 it launched Homeroom.com, an online bank of more than 120,000 practice questions, which helps teachers pinpoint their students' strengths and weak spots. Like its competitor Kaplan, The Princeton Review offers workshops to help teachers tailor their daily lessons to state exams. The firm's latest offering: a $1,950 primer for parents on test-taking skills that, among other things, instructs them to serve an extra-large breakfast on test day because "it's better to take an exam bloated than on an empty stomach."

## Tough Choices for Schools

A school's annual tab for teacher and student coaching can easily top $20,000. In the harsh calculus of public-school budgets, that means electives like PE or chorus could be the first to go. In inner-city schools, the cuts can be even less kind. For Deborah Holmes, the principal at Jefferson Junior High School, just a few blocks southwest of the U.S. Capitol, the choice was between buying more computers and doing something to raise her students' scores. In the end, Holmes opted for a $21,000 contract with The Princeton Review, reasoning that her students would become more computer literate by spending much of their time taking online practice exams. "We'll buy the computers another year," she sighs.

## Are Kids Really Learning?

Other sacrifices may not be so easily recouped. Critics, including some classroom teachers, contend that many test-prep activities—such as skimming instead of reading passages or speedily filling in bubble sheets—do nothing to really expand brainpower or knowledge. For example, a Kaplan guide to the writing section of the Texas Assessment of Academic Skills counsels students not to dwell on spelling and punctuation: "If you write a deeply moving essay with atrocious grammar, you might still get a . . . passing score." Says Walt Haney, a testing expert at Boston College: "My main worry is that students will learn how to take tests but not how to think." Maria Aguilar, an eighth-grader at Robert J. Frank Intermediate School in Oxnard, Calif., shares the concern: "It's kind of boring; they go over the same thing so many times."

The complaints boiled over when Kaplan's McCullough visited Robert J. Frank in mid-January 2002 for a teacher-training session. The audience of 50 teachers, many already intimately familiar with the Kaplan regimen, stayed silent throughout his 45-minute spiel. "This [illegible] is [illegible]," grade language arts teacher Charles Manley told him afterward. "When you're doing the language section, you're taught to first eliminate two of the possibilities, leaving two left. That's leverage, not learning." His colleague Jamie French tells of jettisoning Greek and Roman mythology to make room for three weeks of test prep. The teachers draw little sympathy from principal Ron D'Incau, who has fielded angry calls from parents demanding to know why test scores remain so low. "Some teachers want to teach things that are nice to teach but aren't really standards," says D'Incau. "You might teach a tremendous unit on dinosaurs, but nothing in the standards calls for knowledge of dinosaurs, so you have to take it out."

# Benefits Not Clear

It might be easier to give up the stegosaurs if the school were not still falling behind. After one year of Kaplan, its scores have increased 45 points—three times the state-mandated 15-point gain—but it remains dead last in its county. The problem is that there is no solid evidence so far that this kind of preparation makes kids dependable test takers, let alone good learners. One minuscule study of five schools in Houston that used The Princeton Review's Homeroom.com found that fourth-graders who used the online assessments improved their scores twice as much as nonusers—but that study was conducted by the company itself.

Many schools are desperate to try anything. In 2001, Durfee High School in Fall River, Mass., signed a $28,000 deal with TestU, an online test-prep newcomer, to help its students prepare for the Massachusetts Comprehensive Assessment System exam. Though test scores improved only slightly in their short time on the system, Durfee renewed the deal for this year. "It's not an exact science," says the school's assistant principal Jackie Proulx. "But, by golly, every intervention we can use we will." □

## Average SAT Scores[1]

| School year | Verbal score | | | | | Mathematical score | | | | |
|---|---|---|---|---|---|---|---|---|---|---|
| | Total | Male | Female | White | Black | Total | Male | Female | White | Black |
| 1966–1967 | 543 | 540 | 545 | n.a. | n.a. | 516 | 535 | 495 | n.a. | n.a. |
| 1970–1971 | 532 | 531 | 534 | n.a. | n.a. | 513 | 529 | 494 | n.a. | n.a. |
| 1976–1977 | 507 | 509 | 505 | n.a. | n.a. | 496 | 520 | 474 | n.a. | n.a. |
| 1980–1981 | 502 | 508 | 496 | n.a. | n.a. | 492 | 516 | 473 | n.a. | n.a. |
| 1986–1987 | 507 | 512 | 502 | 524 | 428 | 501 | 523 | 481 | 514 | 411 |
| 1990–1991 | 499 | 503 | 495 | 518 | 427 | 500 | 520 | 482 | 513 | 419 |
| 1995–1996 | 505 | 507 | 503 | 526 | 434 | 508 | 527 | 492 | 523 | 422 |
| 1996–1997 | 505 | 507 | 503 | 526 | 434 | 511 | 530 | 494 | 526 | 423 |
| 1997–1998 | 505 | 509 | 502 | 526 | 434 | 512 | 531 | 496 | 528 | 426 |
| 1998–1999 | 505 | 509 | 502 | 527 | 434 | 511 | 531 | 495 | 528 | 422 |
| 1999–2000 | 505 | 507 | 504 | 527 | 434 | 514 | 533 | 498 | 530 | 426 |
| 2000–2001 | 506 | 509 | 502 | 529 | 433 | 514 | 533 | 498 | 531 | 426 |

NOTE: n.a. = not available. 1. Scholastic Assessment Test, formerly known as the Scholastic Aptitude Test. Minimum score 200; maximum score 800. *Source:* U.S. Dept. of Education, National Center for Education Statistics, *Digest of Education Statistics 2001.*

## Funding for Public Elementary and Secondary Schools, 1919–1920 to 1998–1999

### (in thousands except percent)

| School year | Total | Federal | State | Local[1] | % Federal | % State | % Local[1] |
|---|---|---|---|---|---|---|---|
| 1919–1920 | $ 970,121 | $ 2,475 | $ 160,085 | $ 807,561 | 0.3% | 16.5% | 83.2% |
| 1929–1930 | 2,088,557 | 7,334 | 353,670 | 1,727,553 | 0.4 | 16.9 | 82.7 |
| 1939–1940 | 2,260,527 | 39,810 | 684,354 | 1,536,363 | 1.8 | 30.3 | 68.0 |
| 1949–1950 | 5,437,044 | 155,848 | 2,165,689 | 3,115,507 | 2.9 | 39.8 | 57.3 |
| 1959–1960 | 14,746,618 | 651,639 | 5,768,047 | 8,326,932 | 4.4 | 39.1 | 56.5 |
| 1969–1970 | 40,266,923 | 3,219,557 | 16,062,776 | 20,984,589 | 8.0 | 39.9 | 52.1 |
| 1974–1975 | 64,445,239 | 5,811,595 | 27,060,563 | 31,573,079 | 9.0 | 42.0 | 49.0 |
| 1979–1980 | 96,881,165 | 9,503,537 | 45,348,814 | 42,028,813 | 9.8 | 46.8 | 43.4 |
| 1984–1985 | 137,294,678 | 9,105,569 | 67,168,684 | 61,020,425 | 6.6 | 48.9 | 44.4 |
| 1989–1990 | 208,547,573 | 12,700,784 | 98,238,633 | 97,608,157 | 6.1 | 47.1 | 46.8 |
| 1994–1995 | 273,149,449 | 18,582,157 | 127,729,576 | 126,837,717 | 6.8 | 46.8 | 46.4 |
| 1998–1999 | 347,329,664 | 24,521,817 | 169,298,232 | 153,509,615 | 7.1 | 48.7 | 44.2 |

1. Includes a relatively small amount from nongovernmental private sources (gifts and tuition and transportation fees from patrons). These sources accounted for 2.5% of total revenues in 1998–1999. *Source:* U.S. Department of Education, National Center for Education Statistics, *Digest of Education Statistics 2001.*

## Pupil-Teacher Ratios, 1980–1998

### (in thousands)

| Year | Public | | | Private | | |
|---|---|---|---|---|---|---|
| | Total | Elementary | Secondary | Total | Elementary | Secondary |
| 1980 | 18.7 | 20.4 | 16.8 | 17.7 | 18.8 | 15.0 |
| 1985 | 17.9 | 19.5 | 15.8 | 16.2 | 17.1 | 14.0 |
| 1990 | 17.2 | 18.9 | 14.6 | 14.7 | 16.1 | 11.3 |
| 1995 | 17.3 | 19.3 | 14.4 | 14.9 | 16.6 | 10.8 |
| 1998 | 16.5 | 18.0 | 14.2 | 15.2 | 16.6 | 11.6 |

*Source:* U.S. Department of Education, National Center for Education Statistics, *Digest of Education Statistics.* From *Statistical Abstract of the United States, 2001.*

## Educational Attainment by Race and Hispanic Origin, 1960–2000
(percent of population age 25 and older)

| Year | Total[1] | White | Black | Asian and Pacific Islander | Hispanic[2] Total[3] | Mexican | Puerto Rican | Cuban |
|---|---|---|---|---|---|---|---|---|
| **Completed 4 years of high school or more** | | | | | | | | |
| 1960 | 41.1% | 43.2% | 20.1% | — | — | — | — | — |
| 1965 | 49.0 | 51.3 | 27.2 | — | — | — | — | — |
| 1970 | 52.3 | 54.5 | 31.4 | — | 32.1% | 24.2% | 23.4% | 43.9% |
| 1975 | 62.5 | 64.5 | 42.5 | — | 37.9 | 31.0 | 28.7 | 51.7 |
| 1980 | 66.5 | 68.8 | 51.2 | — | 44.0 | 37.6 | 40.1 | 55.3 |
| 1985 | 73.9 | 75.5 | 59.8 | — | 47.9 | 41.9 | 46.3 | 51.1 |
| 1990 | 77.6 | 79.1 | 66.2 | 80.4% | 50.8 | 44.1 | 55.5 | 63.5 |
| 1995 | 81.7 | 83.0 | 73.8 | — | 53.4 | 46.5 | 61.3 | 64.7 |
| 1996 | 81.7 | 82.8 | 74.3 | 83.2 | 53.1 | 46.9 | 60.4 | 63.8 |
| 1997 | 82.1 | 83.0 | 74.9 | 84.9 | 54.7 | 48.6 | 61.1 | 65.2 |
| 1998 | 82.8 | 83.7 | 76.0 | — | 55.5 | 48.3 | 63.8 | 67.8 |
| 1999 | 83.4 | 84.3 | 77.0 | 84.7 | 56.1 | 49.7 | 63.9 | 70.3 |
| 2000 | 84.1 | 84.9 | 78.5 | 85.7 | 57.0 | 51.0 | 64.3 | 73.0 |
| **Completed 4 years of college or more** | | | | | | | | |
| 1960 | 7.7% | 8.1% | 3.1% | — | — | — | — | — |
| 1965 | 9.4 | 9.9 | 4.7 | — | — | — | — | — |
| 1970 | 10.7 | 11.3 | 4.4 | — | 4.5% | 2.5% | 2.2% | 11.1% |
| 1975 | 13.9 | 14.5 | 6.4 | — | — | — | — | — |
| 1980 | 16.2 | 17.1 | 8.4 | — | 7.6 | 4.9 | 5.6 | 16.2 |
| 1985 | 19.4 | 20.0 | 11.1 | — | 8.5 | 5.5 | 7.0 | 13.7 |
| 1990 | 21.3 | 22.0 | 11.3 | 39.9% | 9.2 | 5.4 | 9.7 | 20.2 |
| 1995 | 23.0 | 24.0 | 13.2 | — | 9.3 | 6.5 | 10.7 | 19.4 |
| 1996 | 23.6 | 24.3 | 13.6 | 41.7 | 9.3 | 6.5 | 11.0 | 18.8 |
| 1997 | 23.9 | 24.6 | 13.3 | 42.2 | 10.3 | 7.5 | 10.7 | 19.7 |
| 1998 | 24.4 | 25.0 | 14.7 | — | 11.0 | 7.5 | 11.9 | 22.2 |
| 1999 | 25.2 | 25.9 | 15.4 | 42.4 | 10.9 | 7.1 | 11.1 | 24.8 |
| 2000 | 25.6 | 26.1 | 16.5 | 43.9 | 10.6 | 6.9 | 13.0 | 23.0 |

NOTES: (—) = not available. 1960, 1970, and 1980 as of April 1 and based on sample data from the censuses of population. Other years as of March and based on the Current Population Survey. 1. Includes other races, not shown separately. 2. Persons of Hispanic origin may be of any race. 3. Includes persons of other Hispanic origin, not shown separately. *Source:* U.S. Bureau of the Census, *U.S. Census of Population, U.S. Summary, Current Population Reports,* and unpublished data. From *Statistical Abstract of the United States, 2001.*

## Educational Attainment by Sex, 1910–2000
(percent of population ages 25 and older)

| Year | Both Sexes — Less than 5 years of elementary school | High school completion or higher[1] | 4 or more years of college[2] | Male — Less than 5 years of elementary school | High school completion or higher | 4 or more years of college | Female — Less than 5 years of elementary school | High school completion or higher | 4 or more years of college |
|---|---|---|---|---|---|---|---|---|---|
| 1910[3] | 23.8% | 13.5% | 2.7% | — | — | — | — | — | — |
| 1920[3] | 22.0 | 16.4 | 3.3 | — | — | — | — | — | — |
| 1930[3] | 17.5 | 19.1 | 3.9 | — | — | — | — | — | — |
| April 1940 | 13.7 | 24.5 | 4.6 | 15.1% | 22.7% | 5.5% | 12.4% | 26.3% | 3.8% |
| April 1950 | 11.1 | 34.3 | 6.2 | 12.2 | 32.6 | 7.3 | 10.0 | 36.0 | 5.2 |
| April 1960 | 8.3 | 41.1 | 7.7 | 9.4 | 39.5 | 9.7 | 7.4 | 42.5 | 5.8 |
| March 1970 | 5.3 | 55.2 | 11.0 | 5.0 | 55.0 | 14.1 | 5.6 | 55.4 | 8.2 |
| March 1980 | 3.4 | 68.6 | 17.0 | 3.0 | 69.2 | 20.9 | 3.2 | 68.1 | 13.6 |
| March 1990 | 2.5 | 77.6 | 21.3 | 2.7 | 77.7 | 24.4 | 2.2 | 77.5 | 18.4 |
| March 1994 | 1.9 | 80.9 | 22.2 | 2.1 | 81.1 | 25.1 | 1.7 | 80.8 | 19.0 |
| March 1995 | 1.9 | 81.7 | 23.0 | 2.0 | 81.7 | 26.0 | 1.7 | 81.6 | 20.2 |
| March 1996 | 1.8 | 81.7 | 23.6 | 1.9 | 81.9 | 26.0 | 1.7 | 81.6 | 21.4 |
| March 1997 | 1.7 | 82.1 | 23.9 | 1.8 | 82.0 | 26.2 | 1.6 | 82.2 | 21.7 |
| March 1998 | 1.7 | 82.8 | 24.4 | 1.7 | 82.8 | 26.5 | 1.6 | 82.9 | 22.4 |
| March 1999 | 1.6 | 83.4 | 25.2 | 1.6 | 83.5 | 27.5 | 1.6 | 83.4 | 23.1 |
| March 2000 | 1.6 | 84.1 | 25.6 | 1.6 | 84.2 | 27.8 | 1.5 | 84.0 | 23.6 |

NOTES: (—) = not available. Data for 1980 and subsequent years are for the noninstitutional population. 1. Data for years prior to 1993 include all persons with at least 4 years of high school. 2. Data for 1993 and later years are for persons with a bachelor's degree or higher. 3. Estimates based on Bureau of the Census retrojection of 1940 Census data on education by age. *Source:* Based on data from the U.S. Department of Commerce, Bureau of the Census, *U.S Census of Population, 1960,* Vol. 1, part 1; *Current Population Reports,* Series P-20 and unpublished data; and *1960 Census Monograph,* "Education of the American Population," by John K. Folger and Charles B. Nam. From U.S. Dept. of Education, National Center for Education Statistics, *Digest of Education Statistics 2001.*

## Enrollment in Educational Institutions, 1970–2000

### (in thousands)

| Year | Public elementary and secondary schools | | | Private elementary and secondary schools[1] | | | Degree-granting institutions[2] | | |
|------|-------|-------------------------|------------------------|-------|-------------------------|------------------------|--------|--------|---------|
| | Total | Pre-K through grade 8 | Grades 9 through 12 | Total | K through grade 8 | Grades 9 through 12 | Total | Public | Private |
| Fall 1970 | 45,894 | 32,558 | 13,336 | 5,363 | 4,052 | 1,311 | 8,581 | 6,428 | 2,153 |
| Fall 1980 | 40,877 | 27,647 | 13,231 | 5,331 | 3,992 | 1,339 | 12,097 | 9,457 | 2,640 |
| Fall 1990 | 41,217 | 29,878 | 11,338 | 5,234 | 4,084 | 1,150 | 13,819 | 10,845 | 2,974 |
| Fall 1998 | 46,539 | 33,346 | 13,193 | 5,937[3] | 4,702[3] | 1,235[3] | 14,507 | 11,138 | 3,369 |
| Fall 1999 | 46,857 | 33,488 | 13,369 | 6,018 | 4,765 | 1,254 | 14,791 | 11,309 | 3,482 |
| Fall 2000[4] | 47,160 | 33,622 | 13,537 | 5,944 | 4,678 | 1,266 | 14,979 | 11,535 | 3,444 |

NOTE: Elementary and secondary enrollment excludes home-schooled children. Based on U.S. Department of Education estimates, the home-schooled children numbered approximately 800,000 to 1,000,000 in 1997–1998. Higher education enrollment includes students in colleges, universities, professional schools, and 2-year colleges. 1. Beginning in fall 1980, data include estimates for an expanded universe of private schools. Therefore, direct comparisons with earlier years should be avoided. 2. Two- and four-year institutions eligible to participate in Title IV federal financial aid programs. 3. Estimated. 4. Projected. Source: U.S. Department of Education, National Center for Education Statistics, Digest of Education Statistics 2001.

## High School Dropout Rates by Sex, 1960–2000

| Year | Total | Male | Female |
|------|-------|------|--------|
| 1960 | 27.2% | 27.8% | 26.7% |
| 1970 | 15.0 | 14.2 | 15.7 |
| 1980 | 14.1 | 15.1 | 13.1 |
| 1985 | 12.6 | 13.4 | 11.8 |
| 1990 | 12.1 | 12.3 | 11.8 |
| 1995 | 12.0 | 12.2 | 11.7 |
| 1996 | 11.1 | 11.4 | 10.9 |
| 1997 | 11.0 | 11.9 | 10.1 |
| 1998 | 11.8 | 13.3 | 10.3 |
| 1999 | 11.2 | 11.9 | 10.5 |
| 2000 | 10.9 | 12.0 | 9.9 |

## High School Dropout Rates by Race/Ethnicity, 1960–2000

| Year | White | Black | Hispanic |
|------|-------|-------|----------|
| 1960 | — | — | — |
| 1970 | 13.2% | 27.9% | — |
| 1980 | 11.4 | 19.1 | 35.2% |
| 1985 | 10.4 | 15.2 | 27.6 |
| 1990 | 9.0 | 13.2 | 32.4 |
| 1995 | 8.6 | 12.1 | 30.0 |
| 1996 | 7.3 | 13.0 | 29.4 |
| 1997 | 7.6 | 13.4 | 25.3 |
| 1998 | 7.7 | 13.8 | 29.5 |
| 1999 | 7.3 | 12.6 | 28.6 |
| 2000 | 6.9 | 13.1 | 27.8 |

NOTE: (—) = not available. Data apply to persons ages 16–24. Because of changes in data collection procedures, data for 1992–2000 may not be comparable with figures for earlier years. Source: U.S. Dept. of Education, National Center for Education Statistics, Digest of Education Statistics 2001.

## Students with Disabilities

| Type of disability | Percent of all students served by federally supported programs for students with disabilities[1] | | | | | | |
|--------------------|-----------|-----------|-----------|-----------|-----------|-----------|-----------|
| | 1976–1977 | 1980–1981 | 1990–1991 | 1995–1996 | 1997–1998 | 1998–1999 | 1999–2000 |
| All disabilities | 8.32% | 10.14% | 11.43% | 12.43% | 12.80% | 13.01% | 13.22% |
| Specific learning disabilities | 1.80 | 3.58 | 5.17 | 5.75 | 5.91 | 5.99 | 6.05 |
| Speech or language impairments | 2.94 | 2.86 | 2.39 | 2.28 | 2.30 | 2.29 | 2.30 |
| Mental retardation | 2.17 | 2.03 | 1.30 | 1.27 | 1.28 | 1.28 | 1.28 |
| Serious emotional disturbance | 0.64 | 0.85 | 0.95 | 0.98 | 0.98 | 0.99 | 1.00 |
| Hearing impairments | 0.20 | 0.19 | 0.14 | 0.15 | 0.15 | 0.15 | 0.15 |
| Orthopedic impairments | 0.20 | 0.14 | 0.12 | 0.14 | 0.15 | 0.15 | 0.15 |
| Other health impairments | 0.32 | 0.24 | 0.13 | 0.30 | 0.41 | 0.47 | 0.54 |
| Visual impairments | 0.09 | 0.08 | 0.06 | 0.06 | 0.05 | 0.06 | 0.06 |
| Multiple disabilities | — | 0.17 | 0.23 | 0.21 | 0.23 | 0.23 | 0.24 |
| Deaf–blindness | — | 0.01 | (2) | (2) | (2) | (2) | (2) |
| Developmental delay | — | — | — | — | 0.01 | 0.03 | 0.04 |
| Autism and traumatic brain injury | — | — | — | 0.09 | 0.12 | 0.14 | 0.17 |
| Preschool disabled[3] | .44 | .57 | 0.95 | 1.21 | 1.22 | 1.22 | 1.24 |

NOTES: Counts are based on reports from the 50 states and District of Columbia. Increases since 1987–1988 are due in part to legislation enacted in fall 1986, which mandates public school special education services for all handicapped children ages 3 through 5. Because of rounding, details may not add to totals. 1. Based on the enrollment in public schools, kindergarten through 12th grade, including a relatively small number of prekindergarten students. Includes students ages 0 to 21. 2. Less than .05%. 3. Includes preschool children 3–5 years and 0–5 years served under Chapter I of the Elementary and Secondary Education Act and the Individuals with Disabilities Education Act (IDEA). Prior to 1987–1988, these students were included in the counts by handicapping condition. Beginning in 1987–1988, states were no longer required to report preschool handicapped students (0–5 years) by handicapping condition. Source: U.S. Department of Education, National Center for Education Statistics, Digest of Education Statistics 2001.

## Cost of Higher Education, 1986–2001[1]

| Year | All institutions | 4-year institutions | 2-year institutions | Year | All institutions | 4-year institutions | 2-year institutions |
|---|---|---|---|---|---|---|---|
| Public institutions | | | | Private institutions | | | |
| 1986–1987 | $3,805 | $4,138 | $2,989 | 1986–1987 | $ 9,676 | $10,039 | $ 6,384 |
| 1991–1992 | 5,138 | 5,693 | 3,623 | 1991–1992 | 13,892 | 14,258 | 9,632 |
| 1995–1996 | 6,256 | 7,014 | 4,217 | 1995–1996 | 17,208 | 17,612 | 11,563 |
| 1996–1997 | 6,530 | 7,334 | 4,404 | 1996–1997 | 18,039 | 18,442 | 11,954 |
| 1997–1998 | 6,813 | 7,673 | 4,509 | 1997–1998 | 18,516 | 19,070 | 12,921 |
| 1998–1999 | 7,107 | 8,027 | 4,604 | 1998–1999 | 19,368 | 19,929 | 13,319 |
| 1999–2000 | 7,310 | 8,275 | 4,720 | 1999–2000 | 20,186 | 20,706 | 13,965 |
| 2000–2001[2] | 7,621 | 8,655 | 4,862 | 2000–2001[2] | 21,423 | 21,907 | 14,690 |

1. Average undergraduate tuition, fees, and room and board. 2. Preliminary data based on fall 1999 enrollment weights.
Source: U.S. Department of Education, National Center for Education Statistics, Digest of Education Statistics 2001.

## Mean Annual Earnings by Level of Education, 1999

| | | | | Level of highest degree | | | | | |
|---|---|---|---|---|---|---|---|---|---|
| Characteristic | Total persons | Not a high school graduate | High school graduate only | Some college, no degree | Associate's | Bachelor's | Master's | Professional | Doctorate |
| All persons[1] | 32,356 | 16,121 | 24,572 | 26,958 | 32,152 | 45,678 | 55,641 | 100,987 | 86,833 |
| Age: | | | | | | | | | |
| 25 to 34 | 29,901 | 16,916 | 24,040 | 26,914 | 28,088 | 39,768 | 46,768 | 58,043 | 60,852 |
| 35 to 44 | 36,900 | 18,984 | 27,444 | 34,219 | 35,370 | 50,153 | 56,816 | 100,240 | 94,936 |
| 45 to 54 | 41,465 | 19,707 | 28,883 | 36,935 | 37,508 | 54,922 | 62,158 | 116,327 | 87,659 |
| 55 to 64 | 38,577 | 22,212 | 27,558 | 34,240 | 35,703 | 50,141 | 57,580 | 132,326 | 97,214 |
| 65 and over | 24,263 | 12,121 | 18,704 | 19,052 | 17,609 | 30,624 | 35,639 | 104,055 | 78,333 |
| Sex: | | | | | | | | | |
| Male | 40,257 | 18,855 | 30,414 | 33,614 | 40,047 | 57,706 | 68,367 | 120,352 | 97,357 |
| Female | 23,551 | 12,145 | 18,092 | 20,241 | 25,079 | 32,546 | 42,378 | 59,792 | 61,136 |
| White | 33,326 | 16,623 | 25,270 | 27,674 | 32,686 | 46,894 | 55,622 | 103,450 | 87,746 |
| Male | 41,598 | 19,320 | 31,279 | 34,825 | 41,010 | 59,606 | 68,831 | 123,086 | 97,076 |
| Female | 23,756 | 12,405 | 18,381 | 20,188 | 24,928 | 32,507 | 41,845 | 57,314 | 64,080 |
| Black | 24,979 | 13,569 | 20,991 | 24,101 | 28,772 | 37,422 | 48,777 | 75,509 | — |
| Male | 28,821 | 16,391 | 25,849 | 27,538 | 31,885 | 42,530 | 54,642 | — | — |
| Female | 21,694 | 10,734 | 16,506 | 21,355 | 26,787 | 33,184 | 44,761 | — | — |
| Hispanic[2] | 22,096 | 16,106 | 20,704 | 23,115 | 29,329 | 36,212 | 50,576 | 64,029 | — |
| Male | 24,970 | 18,020 | 23,736 | 27,288 | 36,740 | 42,733 | 60,013 | — | — |
| Female | 18,187 | 12,684 | 16,653 | 18,782 | 22,695 | 29,249 | 41,118 | — | — |

(—) Base figure too small to meet statistical standards for reliability of a derived figure. 1. Includes other races, not shown separately. 2. Persons of Hispanic origin may be of any race. Source: U.S. Census Bureau, Current Population Reports, P20–536. From Statistical Abstract of the United States, 2001.

## College and University Endowments, 2000–2001

(top 50, in millions of dollars)

| Institution | Endowment[1] | Institution | Endowment[1] | Institution | Endowment[1] |
|---|---|---|---|---|---|
| Harvard Univ. | $18,259.2 | Vanderbilt Univ. | $2,159.6 | Univ. of Rochester | $1,234.4 |
| Yale Univ. | 10,738.8 | Univ. of Southern | | Calif. Inst. of Tech. | 1,234.0 |
| Princeton Univ. | 8,359.0 | California | 2,086.2 | Ohio State Univ. | 1,161.1 |
| Stanford Univ. | 8,249.8 | | | | 1,151.3 |
| Univ. of Texas | 8,138.0 | Johns Hopkins Univ. | 1,760.4 | Wellesley Coll. | 1,136.4 |
| Columbia Univ. | 4,323.8 | Univ. of Virginia | 1,742.5 | Univ. of Wisc.-Madison | 1,120.9 |
| Emory Univ. | 4,249.2 | Univ. of Minnesota | 1,095.7 | Univ. of Richmond | 1,110.0 |
| Washington Univ. | 1,017.0 | Mayo Foundation | 1,571.8 | Univ. of N. Carolina at | |
| Univ. of Michigan | 3,689.4 | Univ. of Texas at Austin | 1,463.1 | Chapel Hill | 1,113.5 |
| Univ. of Chicago | 3,491.7 | Brown Univ. | 1,457.2 | Georgia Inst. of Tech. | 1,108.9 |
| Northwestern Univ. | 3,470.1 | Case Western Reserve | | Univ. of Pittsburgh | 1,107.6 |
| Cornell Univ. | 3,436.9 | Univ. | 1,434.0 | Pomona Coll. | 1,105.1 |
| Univ. of Pennsylvania | 3,381.8 | Rockefeller Univ. | 1,411.1 | Boston Coll. | 1,103.7 |
| Rice Univ. | 3,243.0 | Univ. of California, Los | | Baylor Coll. of Medicine | 1,102.4 |
| Texas A&M Univ. | 3,192.9 | Angeles | 1,390.4 | Grinnell Coll. | 1,024.7 |
| Univ. of Notre Dame | 2,884.0 | Williams Coll. | 1,341.3 | Texas Christian Univ. | 1,005.8 |
| Duke Univ. | 2,576.5 | Purdue Univ. | 1,334.5 | Amherst Coll. | 993.2 |
| Dartmouth Coll. | 2,414.2 | Univ. of Washington | 1,247.2 | Penn. State Univ. | 986.3 |

NOTES: List includes only institutions that participated in the 2000–2001 Voluntary Support of Education Survey. State systems that submitted combined endowments above the current cut-off are not included. 1. Endowment is market value at fiscal year-end 2001. Source: 2000–2001 Voluntary Support of Education Survey. Council for Aid to Education, a subsidiary of RAND.

# Accredited U.S. Senior Colleges and Universities

*Source:* Peterson's Database, copyright 2002. Peterson's, a part of the Thomson Corporation. Web: http://petersons.com/.

Schools are listed alphabetically within each state and are accredited four-year institutions offering at least a bachelor's degree. Tuition and room and board listed are average annual figures (including fees) subject to fluctuation, usually covering two semesters, two out of three trimesters, or three out of four quarters, depending on the school calendar.

Note that some schools include room and board expenses within the tuition figures rather than reporting them separately. List includes only schools for which data were provided. For further information, write to the registrar of the school concerned.

(Pr) = private; (Pu) = public.

| Institution name; city (Public/Private) | Students | Percent Accepted | Women | Tuition In-state | Out-of-state | Room and board |
|---|---|---|---|---|---|---|
| **ALABAMA** | | | | | | |
| Alabama Agricultural and Mechanical University; Normal (Pu) | 4,380 | 24% | 52% | $ 2,400 | $ 4,800 | $4,500 |
| Alabama State University; Montgomery (Pu) | 4,348 | 62 | 58 | 2,520 | 5,040 | 3,700 |
| American College of Computer & Information Sciences; Birmingham (Pr) | 1,204 | | | | | |
| Auburn University; Auburn (Pu) | 18,326 | 85 | 48 | 3,050 | 9,150 | 4,640 |
| Auburn University Montgomery; Montgomery (Pu) | 4,098 | | 63 | 3,000 | 9,000 | |
| Birmingham-Southern College; Birmingham (Pr) | 1,395 | 98 | 59 | 15,930 | 15,930 | 5,652 |
| Faulkner University; Montgomery (Pr) | 2,327 | 68 | 59 | 7,800 | 7,800 | 3,950 |
| Huntingdon College; Montgomery (Pr) | 705 | 73 | 62 | 11,000 | 11,000 | 5,740 |
| International Bible College; Florence (Pr) | | 85 | | 5,264 | 5,264 | |
| Jacksonville State University; Jacksonville (Pu) | 6,649 | 50 | 56 | 2,640 | 5,280 | 3,080 |
| Judson College; Marion (Pr) | 321 | 81 | 98 | 7,400 | 7,400 | 4,600 |
| Oakwood College; Huntsville (Pr) | 1,767 | 46 | 57 | 8,820 | 8,820 | 2,646 |
| Samford University; Birmingham (Pr) | 2,870 | 88 | 62 | 10,738 | 10,738 | 4,720 |
| Southeastern Bible College; Birmingham (Pr) | 217 | 52 | | 5,740 | 5,740 | 3,340 |
| Southern Christian University; Montgomery (Pr) | 134 | | 25 | 10,800 | 10,800 | |
| Spring Hill College; Mobile (Pr) | 1,227 | 89 | 62 | 15,254 | 15,254 | 5,768 |
| Talladega College; Talladega (Pr) | 460 | 22 | | 6,752 | 6,752 | 3,260 |
| Troy State University; Troy (Pu) | 4,602 | 64 | 60 | 2,850 | 5,700 | 4,274 |
| Troy State University Dothan; Dothan (Pu) | 1,564 | 76 | 63 | 3,000 | 6,000 | |
| Troy State University Montgomery; Montgomery (Pu) | 2,643 | | 64 | 2,700 | 5,340 | |
| Tuskegee University; Tuskegee (Pr) | 2,467 | 71 | 58 | 9,928 | 9,928 | 5,328 |
| University of Alabama; Tuscaloosa (Pu) | 15,318 | 86 | 52 | 3,014 | 8,162 | 3,800 |
| University of Alabama at Birmingham; Birmingham (Pu) | 10,331 | 90 | 59 | 2,820 | 5,640 | 6,471 |
| University of Alabama in Huntsville; Huntsville (Pu) | 5,220 | 92 | 51 | 3,284 | 6,890 | 4,300 |
| University of West Alabama; Livingston (Pu) | 1,595 | 69 | 55 | 2,504 | 5,008 | 2,822 |
| University of Mobile; Mobile (Pr) | 1,724 | 98 | 68 | 8,160 | 8,160 | 2,550 |
| University of Montevallo; Montevallo (Pu) | 2,557 | 77 | 68 | 3,330 | 6,660 | 3,390 |
| University of North Alabama; Florence (Pu) | 4,944 | 83 | 59 | 2,527 | 5,054 | 3,506 |
| University of South Alabama; Mobile (Pu) | 9,232 | 94 | 58 | 2,670 | 5,340 | 3,114 |
| Virginia College at Birmingham; Birmingham (Pr) | 1,143 | | | 8,000 | 8,000 | |
| **ALASKA** | | | | | | |
| Alaska Bible College; Glennallen (Pr) | 44 | 96 | 30 | 4,750 | 4,750 | 3,900 |
| Alaska Pacific University; Anchorage (Pr) | 480 | 80 | 63 | 14,400 | 14,400 | 5,450 |
| Sheldon Jackson College; Sitka (Pr) | 94 | 100 | | 7,250 | 7,250 | |
| University of Alaska Anchorage; Anchorage (Pu) | 14,235 | | | 1,600 | 6,000 | |
| University of Alaska Fairbanks; Fairbanks (Pu) | 6,358 | 86 | 60 | 2,550 | 7,620 | 4,610 |
| University of Alaska Southeast; Juneau (Pu) | 2,799 | | | 2,602 | 7,194 | |
| **ARIZONA** | | | | | | |
| Arizona State University; Tempe (Pu) | 33,985 | 77 | 52 | 2,272 | 9,728 | 5,240 |
| Arizona State University East; Mesa (Pu) | 1,529 | 83 | 49 | 2,272 | 9,728 | 4,540 |
| Art Institute of Phoenix; Phoenix (Pr) | 1,000 | 100 | 0 | 13,632 | 13,632 | |
| DeVry Institute of Technology; Phoenix (Pr) | 3,705 | 62 | 25 | 8,250 | 8,250 | |
| Grand Canyon University; Phoenix (Pr) | 1,563 | 76 | 64 | 8,960 | 8,960 | 4,286 |
| International Baptist College; Tempe (Pr) | 53 | | | 4,000 | 4,000 | 3,000 |
| Northern Arizona University; Flagstaff (Pu) | 13,905 | 81 | 59 | 2,272 | 8,704 | 4,391 |
| Prescott College; Prescott (Pr) | 757 | | 59 | 12,844 | 12,844 | 9,866 |
| Southwestern College; Phoenix (Pr) | 257 | 59 | 43 | 8,000 | 8,000 | 3,170 |
| University of Advancing Computer Technology; Tempe (Pr) | 1,055 | | 19 | 11,484 | 11,484 | |
| University of Arizona; Tucson (Pu) | 26,404 | 84 | 53 | 2,272 | 9,728 | 5,888 |
| University of Phoenix–Phoenix Campus; Phoenix (Pr) | 46,473 | | | 7,740 | 7,740 | |
| University of Phoenix–Southern Arizona Campus; Tucson (Pr) | 46,473 | | 56 | 7,740 | 7,740 | |
| Western International University; Phoenix (Pr) | 2,004 | | 42 | 7,920 | 7,920 | |
| **ARKANSAS** | | | | | | |
| Arkansas Baptist College; Little Rock (Pr) | 201 | | | 2,200 | 2,200 | |
| Arkansas State University; Jonesboro (Pu) | 9,289 | 65 | 58 | 2,520 | 6,456 | 3,071 |
| Arkansas Tech University; Russellville (Pu) | 4,841 | 54 | 53 | 2,588 | 5,176 | 3,336 |
| Central Baptist College; Conway (Pr) | 381 | 87 | 48 | 5,688 | 5,688 | 3,816 |
| Harding University; Searcy (Pr) | 3,982 | 81 | 55 | 8,175 | 8,175 | 4,336 |
| Henderson State University; Arkadelphia (Pu) | 3,078 | 67 | 55 | 2,520 | 5,040 | 3,152 |
| Hendrix College; Conway (Pr) | 1,130 | 87 | 54 | 12,340 | 12,340 | 4,625 |

| Institution name; city (Public/Private) | Students | Percent Accepted | Women | Tuition In-state | Out-of-state | Room and board |
|---|---|---|---|---|---|---|
| John Brown University; Siloam Springs (Pr) | 1,421 | 80% | 52% | $11,022 | $11,022 | $4,478 |
| Lyon College; Batesville (Pr) | 476 | 85 | 57 | 10,580 | 10,580 | 4,930 |
| Ouachita Baptist University; Arkadelphia (Pr) | 1,714 | 83 | 54 | 9,800 | 9,800 | 4,100 |
| Philander Smith College; Little Rock (Pr) | 932 | 100 | 61 | | | |
| Southern Arkansas University–Magnolia; Magnolia (Pu) | 2,781 | 92 | 57 | 2,304 | 3,552 | 2,930 |
| University of Arkansas; Fayetteville (Pu) | 12,502 | 90 | 49 | 2,968 | 8,260 | 4,358 |
| University of Arkansas at Little Rock; Little Rock (Pu) | 8,383 | 62 | | 2,544 | 6,552 | |
| University of Arkansas at Pine Bluff; Pine Bluff (Pu) | 2,926 | 71 | 55 | 2,400 | 5,550 | 4,100 |
| University of Central Arkansas; Conway (Pu) | 7,453 | 62 | | 2,856 | 5,598 | 3,290 |
| University of the Ozarks; Clarksville (Pr) | 622 | 74 | 52 | 8,830 | 8,830 | 4,080 |
| Williams Baptist College; Walnut Ridge (Pr) | 660 | 75 | 60 | 6,600 | 6,600 | 3,400 |
| **CALIFORNIA** | | | | | | |
| Academy of Art College; San Francisco (Pr) | 5,294 | 45 | 43 | 12,000 | 12,000 | |
| Armstrong University; Oakland (Pr) | 36 | | | 6,192 | 6,192 | |
| Art Center College of Design; Pasadena (Pr) | 1,358 | 63 | 39 | 19,900 | 19,900 | |
| Art Institute of California; San Diego (Pr) | 450 | 85 | 47 | 10,640 | 10,640 | |
| Art Institute of Southern California; Laguna Beach (Pr) | 280 | 93 | 46 | 13,320 | 13,320 | |
| Azusa Pacific University; Azusa (Pr) | 3,453 | 73 | 64 | 15,210 | 15,210 | 4,962 |
| Bethesda Christian University; Anaheim (Pr) | 171 | 91 | 70 | 3,120 | 3,120 | |
| Biola University; La Mirada (Pr) | 2,622 | 82 | 63 | 16,630 | 16,630 | 5,272 |
| California Baptist University; Riverside (Pr) | 1,524 | 80 | 63 | 10,060 | 10,060 | 4,966 |
| California Christian College; Fresno (Pr) | 90 | 100 | 34 | 3,600 | 3,600 | 2,760 |
| California College for Health Sciences; National City (Pr) | 4,093 | | 0 | | | |
| California College of Arts and Crafts; San Francisco (Pr) | 1,116 | 72 | 59 | 19,280 | 19,280 | 6,051 |
| California Institute of Technology; Pasadena (Pr) | 929 | 13 | 32 | 20,904 | 20,904 | 6,543 |
| California Institute of the Arts; Valencia (Pr) | 804 | 40 | 44 | 20,930 | 20,930 | |
| California Lutheran University; Thousand Oaks (Pr) | 1,816 | 79 | 56 | 16,800 | 16,800 | 6,460 |
| California Maritime Academy; Vallejo (Pu) | 583 | 76 | 17 | 0 | 7,380 | 5,900 |
| California Polytechnic State University, San Luis Obispo; San Luis Obispo (Pu) | 15,867 | 45 | 44 | 0 | 5,904 | 6,246 |
| California State Polytechnic University, Pomona; Pomona (Pu) | 16,450 | 70 | 44 | 0 | 5,904 | 6,113 |
| California State University, Chico; Chico (Pu) | 13,904 | 91 | 53 | 1,428 | 8,808 | 6,216 |
| California State University, Dominguez Hills; Carson (Pu) | 7,733 | 77 | 70 | | 7,410 | |
| California State University, Fresno; Fresno (Pu) | 15,414 | 67 | 56 | 1,746 | 7,650 | 5,876 |
| California State University, Fullerton; Fullerton (Pu) | 23,385 | 72 | 59 | 0 | 7,380 | |
| California State University, Hayward; Hayward (Pu) | 9,337 | 62 | 64 | | 7,380 | |
| California State University, Long Beach; Long Beach (Pu) | 25,153 | 86 | 58 | 0 | 7,380 | 5,800 |
| California State University, Los Angeles; Los Angeles (Pu) | 13,476 | 50 | 61 | 1,722 | 7,626 | 6,201 |
| California State University, Northridge; Northridge (Pu) | 22,553 | 78 | 58 | | 7,718 | 6,400 |
| California State University, Sacramento; Sacramento (Pu) | 19,343 | 41 | 56 | 0 | 7,380 | 5,510 |
| California State University, San Bernardino; San Bernardino (Pu) | 10,273 | | | | 5,904 | |
| California State University, San Marcos; San Marcos (Pu) | 5,005 | 66 | 62 | 0 | 5,904 | |
| California State University, Stanislaus; Turlock (Pu) | 5,353 | 73 | 65 | 0 | 9,257 | 6,480 |
| Chapman University; Orange (Pr) | 2,968 | 63 | 55 | 20,724 | 20,724 | 7,246 |
| Charles R. Drew Univ. of Medicine and Science; Los Angeles (Pr) | 210 | 25 | | | | |
| Christian Heritage College; El Cajon (Pr) | 675 | 79 | 65 | 11,924 | 11,924 | |
| Claremont McKenna College; Claremont (Pr) | 1,002 | 28 | 43 | 22,390 | 22,390 | 7,420 |
| Cogswell Polytechnical College; Sunnyvale (Pr) | 500 | 85 | | | | |
| Columbia College–Hollywood; Tarzana (Pr) | 100 | 88 | | 10,500 | 10,500 | |
| Concordia University; Irvine (Pr) | 1,192 | 31 | 69 | 15,700 | 15,700 | 5,600 |
| Design Institute of San Diego; San Diego (Pr) | 350 | | | 10,200 | 10,200 | |
| DeVry Institute of Technology; Fremont (Pr) | 2,149 | 60 | 23 | 9,250 | 9,250 | |
| DeVry Institute of Technology; Long Beach (Pr) | 2,877 | 65 | 29 | 8,250 | 8,250 | |
| DeVry Institute of Technology; Pomona (Pr) | 3,674 | 68 | 27 | 8,250 | 8,250 | |
| DeVry Institute of Technology; West Hills (Pr) | 886 | 58 | 23 | 8,250 | 8,250 | |
| Dominican University of California; San Rafael (Pr) | 946 | 73 | 80 | 17,056 | 17,056 | 7,260 |
| Fresno Pacific University; Fresno (Pr) | 1,149 | 72 | 68 | 13,900 | 13,900 | 4,530 |
| Golden Gate University; San Francisco (Pr) | 1,302 | 97 | 58 | 8,832 | 8,832 | |
| Harvey Mudd College; Claremont (Pr) | 717 | 35 | 29 | 22,663 | 22,663 | 8,418 |
| Holy Names College; Oakland (Pr) | 592 | 71 | 81 | 14,950 | 14,950 | 6,400 |
| Hope International University; Fullerton (Pr) | 703 | 42 | 53 | | | |
| Humboldt State University; Arcata (Pu) | 6,469 | 73 | 54 | 0 | 5,904 | 5,845 |
| John F. Kennedy University; Orinda (Pr) | 196 | | 81 | 10,710 | 10,710 | |
| LIFE Bible College; San Dimas (Pr) | 488 | 94 | 48 | 5,550 | 5,550 | 3,200 |
| Loma Linda University; Loma Linda (Pr) | 967 | | 75 | 14,220 | 14,220 | 8,370 |
| Loyola Marymount University; Los Angeles (Pr) | 4,851 | 62 | 57 | 20,342 | 20,342 | 7,100 |
| Master's College and Seminary; Santa Clarita (Pr) | 1,105 | 79 | 52 | 14,100 | 14,100 | 5,800 |
| Menlo College; Atherton (Pr) | 662 | 73 | 43 | 17,700 | 17,700 | 6,800 |
| Mills College; Oakland (Pr) | 691 | 75 | | 18,000 | 18,000 | 7,588 |
| Mount St. Mary's College; Los Angeles (Pr) | 1,708 | 54 | 95 | 17,036 | 17,036 | 7,070 |
| Mt. Sierra College; Monrovia (Pr) | 1,222 | 73 | 34 | 8,752 | 8,752 | |
| National Hispanic University; San Jose (Pr) | 350 | 82 | | 3,100 | 3,100 | |
| National University; La Jolla (Pr) | 7,040 | 100 | 55 | 7,695 | 7,695 | |
| New College of California; San Francisco (Pr) | 234 | | | 9,190 | 9,190 | |

| Institution name; city (Public/Private) | Students | Percent Accepted | Percent Women | Tuition In-state | Tuition Out-of-state | Room and board |
|---|---|---|---|---|---|---|
| Newschool of Architecture & Design; San Diego (Pr) | 9 | 100% | 22% | $13,500 | $13,500 | |
| Notre Dame de Namur University; Belmont (Pr) | 991 | 79 | | 16,850 | 16,850 | $7,860 |
| Occidental College; Los Angeles (Pr) | 1,697 | 57 | 58 | 23,532 | 23,532 | 6,880 |
| Otis College of Art and Design; Los Angeles (Pr) | 898 | 61 | 62 | 18,894 | 18,894 | |
| Pacific States University; Los Angeles (Pr) | 25 | | 24 | 10,560 | 10,560 | 9,000 |
| Pacific Union College; Angwin (Pr) | 1,453 | | 56 | 14,985 | 14,985 | 4,530 |
| Patten College; Oakland (Pr) | 635 | 68 | 39 | 7,968 | 7,968 | 3,468 |
| Pepperdine University; Malibu (Pr) | 1,849 | 35 | 91 | 23,980 | 23,980 | 7,290 |
| Pitzer College; Claremont (Pr) | 924 | 56 | 62 | 22,572 | 22,572 | 6,458 |
| Point Loma Nazarene University; San Diego (Pr) | 2,312 | 75 | 59 | 13,900 | 13,900 | 5,990 |
| Pomona College; Claremont (Pr) | 1,565 | 30 | 49 | 23,910 | 23,910 | 8,170 |
| Saint Mary's College of California; Moraga (Pr) | 3,038 | 76 | 61 | 18,120 | 18,120 | 7,560 |
| Samuel Merritt College; Oakland (Pr) | 278 | 71 | 92 | 16,360 | 16,360 | |
| San Diego State University; San Diego (Pu) | 25,658 | 65 | 57 | 0 | 6,396 | 7,110 |
| San Francisco Art Institute; San Francisco (Pr) | 493 | 61 | 51 | 20,200 | 20,200 | |
| San Francisco Conservatory of Music; San Francisco (Pr) | 136 | 64 | 55 | 19,300 | 19,300 | |
| San Francisco State University; San Francisco (Pu) | 20,365 | 67 | 60 | 0 | 5,904 | 6,930 |
| San Jose Christian College; San Jose (Pr) | 400 | 42 | | 9,504 | 9,504 | 5,109 |
| San Jose State University; San Jose (Pu) | 21,292 | 72 | 51 | 0 | 5,904 | 6,248 |
| Santa Clara University; Santa Clara (Pr) | 4,308 | 62 | 54 | 20,337 | 20,337 | 8,034 |
| Scripps College; Claremont (Pr) | 787 | 68 | 100 | 22,470 | 22,470 | 7,800 |
| Shasta Bible College; Redding (Pr) | 295 | 100 | 67 | 5,600 | 5,600 | 3,576 |
| Sonoma State University; Rohnert Park (Pu) | 6,211 | 92 | 65 | 0 | 6,006 | 6,471 |
| Southern California Institute of Architecture; Los Angeles (Pr) | 218 | | | 16,026 | 16,026 | |
| St. John's Seminary College; Camarillo (Pr) | 95 | 75 | 1 | 7,400 | 7,400 | 4,500 |
| Stanford University; Stanford (Pr) | 7,886 | 13 | 52 | 24,441 | 24,441 | 8,030 |
| Thomas Aquinas College; Santa Paula (Pr) | 277 | 77 | 47 | 15,400 | 15,400 | 4,400 |
| Touro University International; Los Alamitos (Pr) | 176 | 64 | 31 | 5,760 | 5,760 | |
| United States International University; San Diego (Pr) | 522 | 62 | 56 | 13,200 | 13,200 | 5,775 |
| University of California, Berkeley; Berkeley (Pu) | 22,593 | 27 | 51 | 0 | 10,614 | 8,670 |
| University of California, Davis; Davis (Pu) | 20,418 | 63 | 56 | 0 | 10,245 | 6,800 |
| University of California, Irvine; Irvine (Pu) | 16,223 | 57 | 52 | 0 | 10,244 | 6,724 |
| University of California, Los Angeles; Los Angeles (Pu) | 25,011 | 29 | 55 | 3,698 | 14,312 | 8,565 |
| University of California, Riverside; Riverside (Pu) | 11,436 | 85 | 54 | 0 | 10,613 | 7,200 |
| University of California, San Diego; La Jolla (Pu) | 16,496 | 38 | 52 | 0 | 14,091 | 7,425 |
| University of California, Santa Barbara; Santa Barbara (Pu) | 17,538 | 65 | 54 | 0 | 10,614 | 7,577 |
| University of California, Santa Cruz; Santa Cruz (Pu) | 11,616 | 80 | 57 | | 11,774 | 8,106 |
| University of Judaism; Bel Air (Pr) | 96 | 100 | 67 | 15,000 | 15,000 | 8,100 |
| University of La Verne; La Verne (Pr) | 1,349 | 74 | 58 | 16,940 | 16,940 | 5,400 |
| University of Phoenix–No. Calif. Campus; Pleasanton (Pr) | 46,473 | | 56 | 7,740 | 7,740 | |
| University of Phoenix–Sacramento Campus; Sacramento (Pr) | 46,473 | | 56 | 7,740 | 7,740 | |
| University of Phoenix–San Diego Campus; San Diego (Pr) | 46,473 | | 56 | 7,740 | 7,740 | |
| University of Phoenix–So. Calif. Campus; Fountain Valley (Pr) | 46,473 | | 56 | 7,740 | 7,740 | |
| University of Redlands; Redlands (Pr) | 1,734 | 78 | 56 | 20,260 | 20,260 | 7,590 |
| University of San Diego; San Diego (Pr) | 4,793 | 50 | 59 | 19,020 | 19,020 | 8,440 |
| University of San Francisco; San Francisco (Pr) | 4,084 | | | 18,860 | 18,860 | 8,242 |
| University of Southern California; Los Angeles (Pr) | 15,705 | 34 | 50 | 23,664 | 23,664 | 7,610 |
| University of the Pacific; Stockton (Pr) | 3,093 | 76 | 58 | 20,350 | 20,350 | 6,378 |
| Vanguard University of Southern California; Costa Mesa (Pr) | 1,475 | 88 | 61 | 13,230 | 13,230 | 5,060 |
| Westmont College; Santa Barbara (Pr) | 1,269 | 70 | 62 | 20,378 | 20,378 | 7,068 |
| Whittier College; Whittier (Pr) | 1,296 | 89 | 56 | 20,424 | 20,424 | 6,736 |
| Woodbury University; Burbank (Pr) | 1,135 | 85 | 55 | 17,338 | 17,338 | 6,756 |
| Yeshiva Ohr Elchonon Chabad/West Coast Talmudical Seminary; Los Angeles (Pr) | 62 | | 0 | 7,500 | 7,500 | 4,500 |
| **COLORADO** | | | | | | |
| Adams State College; Alamosa (Pu) | 2,011 | 96 | 57 | 1,574 | 5,970 | 5,185 |
| Art Institute of Colorado; Denver (Pr) | 2,090 | 74 | 44 | 13,824 | 13,824 | 5,994 |
| Colorado Christian University; Lakewood (Pr) | 1,926 | 75 | 54 | 10,400 | 10,400 | 5,330 |
| Colorado College; Colorado Springs (Pr) | 1,919 | 62 | 54 | 22,800 | 22,800 | 5,808 |
| Colorado School of Mines; Golden (Pu) | 2,503 | 81 | 25 | 4,750 | 15,304 | 4,900 |
| Colorado State University; Fort Collins (Pu) | 19,075 | 78 | 52 | 3,133 | 11,153 | 5,280 |
| Colorado Technical University Denver Campus; Greenwood Village (Pr) | 227 | 65 | 28 | 7,875 | 7,875 | |
| Denver Technical College; Denver (Pr) | 864 | | 31 | 10,320 | 10,320 | |
| Fort Lewis College; Durango (Pu) | 4,289 | 88 | 47 | 1,724 | 8,452 | 5,172 |
| Johnson & Wales University; Denver (Pr) | 325 | 81 | 43 | 16,320 | 16,320 | |
| Metropolitan State College of Denver; Denver (Pu) | 17,688 | 84 | 57 | 1,926 | 7,876 | |
| Naropa University; Boulder (Pr) | 434 | 93 | 68 | 13,530 | 13,530 | |
| National American University; Colorado Springs (Pr) | 325 | | | 9,360 | 9,360 | |
| National American University; Denver (Pr) | 380 | | | 9,360 | 9,360 | |
| Nazarene Bible College; Colorado Springs (Pr) | 473 | 60 | 30 | 5,616 | 5,616 | |
| Regis University; Denver (Pr) | 1,022 | 84 | | 17,400 | 17,400 | 6,700 |
| United States Air Force Academy; Colorado Springs (Pu) | 4,319 | 18 | 15 | | | |
| University of Colorado at Boulder; Boulder (Pu) | 23,342 | 86 | 48 | 2,514 | 15,832 | 5,538 |

| Institution name; city (Public/Private) | Students | Percent Accepted | Women | Tuition In-state | Out-of-state | Room and board |
|---|---|---|---|---|---|---|
| University of Colorado at Colorado Springs; Colorado Springs (Pu) | 5,054 | 75% | 61% | $ 2,209 | $10,287 | $5,893 |
| University of Colorado at Denver; Denver (Pu) | 8,478 | 73 | 56 | 2,298 | 16,642 | |
| University of Denver; Denver (Pr) | 3,992 | 78 | 57 | 20,052 | 20,052 | 6,438 |
| University of Northern Colorado; Greeley (Pu) | 10,134 | 79 | 60 | 2,072 | 9,357 | 4,996 |
| University of Phoenix–Colorado Campus; Lone Tree (Pr) | 46,473 | | 56 | 7,740 | 7,740 | |
| University of Phoenix–Southern Colorado Campus; Colorado Springs (Pr) | 46,473 | | 56 | 7,740 | 7,740 | |
| University of Southern Colorado; Pueblo (Pu) | 5,122 | 81 | 57 | 1,860 | 8,786 | 5,164 |
| Western State College of Colorado; Gunnison (Pu) | 2,366 | 66 | 42 | 1,560 | 7,309 | 5,652 |
| **CONNECTICUT** | | | | | | |
| Albertus Magnus College; New Haven (Pr) | 1,873 | 89 | 66 | 14,328 | 14,328 | 6,708 |
| Central Connecticut State University; New Britain (Pu) | 9,443 | 67 | 51 | 2,142 | 6,934 | 5,824 |
| Charter Oak State College; New Britain (Pu) | 1,453 | | 52 | | | |
| Connecticut College; New London (Pr) | 1,814 | 32 | 57 | | | |
| Eastern Connecticut State University; Willimantic (Pu) | 4,821 | 64 | 57 | 2,142 | 6,934 | 5,850 |
| Fairfield University; Fairfield (Pr) | 4,173 | 63 | 55 | 21,000 | 21,000 | 7,630 |
| Hartford College for Women; Hartford (Pr) | 178 | 64 | 98 | | | |
| Holy Apostles College and Seminary; Cromwell (Pr) | | | | | | |
| Lyme Academy of Fine Arts; Old Lyme (Pr) | 191 | 97 | 63 | 11,200 | 11,200 | |
| Paier College of Art, Inc.; Hamden (Pr) | 282 | 78 | 58 | 10,900 | 10,900 | |
| Quinnipiac University; Hamden (Pr) | 4,843 | 75 | 64 | 17,000 | 17,000 | 8,170 |
| Sacred Heart University; Fairfield (Pr) | 4,029 | 74 | 62 | 15,404 | 15,404 | 7,614 |
| Saint Joseph College; West Hartford (Pr) | 1,227 | 83 | 98 | 16,930 | 16,930 | 7,140 |
| Southern Connecticut State University; New Haven (Pu) | 8,080 | 71 | 59 | 2,142 | 7,891 | 6,011 |
| Teikyo Post University; Waterbury (Pr) | 1,356 | 71 | 64 | 13,850 | 13,850 | 6,300 |
| Trinity College; Hartford (Pr) | 2,100 | 30 | 50 | 24,660 | 24,660 | 7,160 |
| United States Coast Guard Academy; New London (Pu) | 879 | 6 | 26 | | | |
| University of Bridgeport; Bridgeport (Pr) | 1,212 | 78 | 53 | 14,150 | 14,150 | 7,070 |
| University of Connecticut; Storrs (Pu) | 13,251 | 67 | 52 | 4,282 | 13,056 | 6,062 |
| University of Hartford; West Hartford (Pr) | 5,369 | 71 | 52 | 18,626 | 18,626 | 7,840 |
| University of New Haven; West Haven (Pr) | 2,536 | 82 | 40 | 15,210 | 15,210 | 6,960 |
| Wesleyan University; Middletown (Pr) | 2,722 | 27 | 52 | 25,380 | 25,380 | 6,630 |
| Western Connecticut State University; Danbury (Pu) | 4,881 | 69 | 55 | 2,142 | 7,895 | 5,668 |
| Yale University; New Haven (Pr) | 5,440 | 16 | 50 | 25,220 | 25,220 | 7,660 |
| **DELAWARE** | | | | | | |
| Delaware State University; Dover (Pu) | 2,855 | 74 | 58 | 3,470 | 7,580 | 5,710 |
| Goldey-Beacom College; Wilmington (Pr) | | 84 | | 9,248 | 9,248 | |
| University of Delaware; Newark (Pu) | 17,314 | 49 | 59 | 4,511 | 13,260 | 5,312 |
| Wesley College; Dover (Pr) | 1,416 | 72 | 54 | 11,314 | 11,314 | 5,266 |
| Wilmington College; New Castle (Pr) | | 99 | | 6,240 | 6,240 | |
| **DISTRICT OF COLUMBIA** | | | | | | |
| American University; Washington (Pr) | 5,705 | 72 | 61 | 21,144 | 21,144 | 8,372 |
| Catholic University of America; Washington (Pr) | 2,609 | 87 | 54 | 19,100 | 19,100 | 8,073 |
| Corcoran College of Art and Design; Washington (Pr) | 341 | 58 | | 15,520 | 15,520 | |
| Gallaudet University; Washington (Pr) | 1,244 | 67 | 54 | 7,350 | 7,350 | 7,340 |
| Georgetown University; Washington (Pr) | 6,418 | 22 | 54 | 23,952 | 23,952 | 9,103 |
| George Washington University; Washington (Pr) | 8,837 | 49 | 57 | 24,005 | 24,005 | 8,538 |
| Southeastern University; Washington (Pr) | 483 | 66 | 68 | 7,740 | 7,740 | |
| Strayer University; Washington (Pr) | 10,279 | | 57 | 8,100 | 8,100 | |
| Trinity College; Washington (Pr) | 910 | 73 | 100 | 14,290 | 14,290 | 6,700 |
| University of the District of Columbia; Washington (Pu) | 5,008 | 86 | 62 | 1,800 | 4,440 | |
| **FLORIDA** | | | | | | |
| American College of Prehospital Medicine; Navarre (Pr) | 200 | 100 | | | | |
| American InterContinental University; Plantation (Pr) | 429 | | | 8,022 | 8,022 | |
| Baptist College of Florida; Graceville (Pr) | 583 | 96 | 36 | 4,520 | 4,520 | 3,150 |
| Barry University; Miami Shores (Pr) | 5,777 | 72 | 65 | 16,600 | 16,600 | 9,100 |
| Bethune Cookman College; Daytona Beach (Pr) | 2,745 | 74 | 57 | 8,988 | 8,988 | 5,782 |
| Clearwater Christian College; Clearwater (Pr) | 652 | 86 | | 8,450 | 8,450 | 4,050 |
| DeVry Institute of Technology; Orlando (Pr) | 349 | 51 | 20 | 9,800 | 9,800 | |
| Eckerd College; St. Petersburg (Pr) | 1,572 | 77 | 55 | 19,500 | 19,500 | 3,110 |
| Embry Riddle Aeronautical University; Daytona Beach (Pr) | 4,525 | 74 | 15 | 11,360 | 11,360 | 5,390 |
| Flagler College; St. Augustine (Pr) | 1,830 | 41 | 63 | 6,320 | 6,320 | 3,910 |
| Florida Agricultural and Mechanical University; Tallahassee (Pu) | 10,707 | 65 | 57 | 2,153 | 9,001 | 4,214 |
| Florida Atlantic University; Boca Raton (Pu) | 17,016 | 72 | 61 | 2,396 | 9,734 | 4,993 |
| Florida Christian College; Kissimmee (Pr) | 223 | 66 | 48 | 5,600 | 5,600 | |
| Florida College; Temple Terrace (Pr) | 555 | 91 | 52 | 7,500 | 7,500 | 5,660 |
| Florida Gulf Coast University; Fort Myers (Pu) | 2,977 | 72 | 65 | 2,150 | 9,488 | 7,000 |
| Florida Institute of Technology; Melbourne (Pr) | 2,033 | 80 | 30 | 18,450 | 18,450 | 5,590 |
| Florida International University; Miami (Pu) | 26,222 | 54 | 56 | 2,242 | 9,580 | |
| Florida Metropolitan Univ.–Brandon Campus; Tampa (Pr) | 680 | | | 6,660 | 6,660 | |
| Florida Metropolitan Univ.–Fort Lauderdale College; Fort Lauderdale (Pr) | 896 | 84 | 54 | 6,660 | 6,660 | |
| Florida Metropolitan Univ.–Melbourne Campus; Melbourne (Pr) | 544 | 68 | 68 | 9,792 | 9,792 | |
| Florida Metropolitan Univ.–Orlando College, North; Orlando (Pr) | 826 | | 66 | 7,200 | 7,200 | |

| Institution name; city (Public/Private) | Students | Percent Accepted | Percent Women | Tuition In-state | Tuition Out-of-state | Room and board |
|---|---|---|---|---|---|---|
| Florida Metropolitan Univ.–Orlando College, South; Orlando (Pr) | 1,250 | | | $ 6,272 | $ 6,272 | |
| Florida Metropolitan Univ.–Tampa College; Tampa (Pr) | 1,125 | | 61% | 7,056 | 7,056 | |
| Florida Southern College; Lakeland (Pr) | 1,755 | 80% | 61 | | | |
| Florida State University; Tallahassee (Pu) | 27,014 | 54 | 56 | 2,379 | 9,716 | $5,150 |
| Hobe Sound Bible College; Hobe Sound (Pr) | 151 | 91 | 48 | 3,940 | 3,940 | 3,005 |
| International Academy of Design & Technology; Tampa (Pr) | 1,359 | | 59 | 10,260 | 10,260 | |
| International College; Naples (Pr) | 961 | 87 | 63 | 6,960 | 6,960 | |
| International Fine Arts College; Miami (Pr) | 1,060 | | | 12,500 | 12,500 | |
| Jacksonville University; Jacksonville (Pr) | 1,817 | 72 | 51 | 15,270 | 15,270 | 5,400 |
| Jones College; Jacksonville (Pr) | 654 | | 73 | 4,440 | 4,440 | |
| Lynn University; Boca Raton (Pr) | 1,823 | 81 | | 18,500 | 18,500 | 6,800 |
| New College of the University of South Florida; Sarasota (Pu) | 649 | 70 | 63 | 2,663 | 11,464 | 4,877 |
| New World School of the Arts; Miami (Pu) | 339 | 62 | 53 | 1,638 | 5,722 | |
| Northwood University, Florida Campus; West Palm Beach (Pr) | 969 | 69 | 47 | 11,763 | 11,763 | 6,216 |
| Nova Southeastern University; Fort Lauderdale (Pr) | 4,110 | 74 | 74 | | | |
| Ringling School of Art and Design; Sarasota (Pr) | 958 | 43 | 45 | 15,220 | 15,220 | 7,718 |
| Rollins College; Winter Park (Pr) | 1,598 | 68 | 60 | 22,206 | 22,206 | 7,000 |
| Saint Leo University; Saint Leo (Pr) | 1,366 | 71 | 57 | 11,990 | 11,990 | 6,300 |
| Schiller International University; Dunedin (Pr) | 190 | | | | | |
| Southeastern College of the Assemblies of God; Lakeland (Pr) | 1,232 | 68 | 53 | 6,500 | 6,500 | 3,850 |
| St. Thomas University; Miami (Pr) | 1,035 | 75 | 55 | 13,390 | 13,390 | 4,400 |
| Stetson University; DeLand (Pr) | 2,155 | 75 | 57 | 17,475 | 17,475 | 6,070 |
| Trinity Baptist College; Jacksonville (Pr) | 362 | 83 | 46 | 3,790 | 3,790 | 3,200 |
| Trinity College of Florida; New Port Richey (Pr) | 157 | 77 | 47 | 4,730 | 4,730 | 2,920 |
| University of Central Florida; Orlando (Pu) | 28,252 | 63 | 55 | 2,279 | 9,617 | 5,436 |
| University of Florida; Gainesville (Pu) | 32,680 | 62 | 53 | 2,256 | 9,594 | 5,440 |
| University of Miami; Coral Gables (Pr) | 8,955 | 53 | 55 | 22,124 | 22,124 | 7,934 |
| University of North Florida; Jacksonville (Pu) | 10,663 | 72 | 58 | 1,941 | 7,812 | 4,990 |
| University of Phoenix–Fort Lauderdale Campus; Plantation (Pr) | 46,473 | | 56 | 7,740 | 7,740 | |
| University of Phoenix–Jacksonville Campus; Jacksonville (Pr) | 46,473 | | 56 | 7,740 | 7,740 | |
| University of Phoenix–Orlando Campus; Maitland (Pr) | 46,473 | | 56 | 7,740 | 7,740 | |
| University of Phoenix–Tampa Campus; Tampa (Pr) | 46,473 | | 56 | 7,740 | 7,740 | |
| University of South Florida; Tampa (Pu) | 27,384 | 58 | 59 | 2,388 | 9,725 | 4,494 |
| University of Tampa; Tampa (Pr) | 2,999 | 76 | 61 | 15,190 | 15,190 | 5,418 |
| University of West Florida; Pensacola (Pu) | 6,753 | 82 | 58 | 1,554 | 8,891 | 4,668 |
| Warner Southern College; Lake Wales (Pr) | 999 | 54 | 59 | 9,390 | 9,390 | 4,640 |
| Webber College; Babson Park (Pr) | 419 | 52 | 50 | 9,900 | 9,900 | 3,395 |
| **GEORGIA** | | | | | | |
| Agnes Scott College; Decatur (Pr) | 892 | 72 | 100 | 16,600 | 16,600 | 6,900 |
| Albany State University; Albany (Pu) | 3,129 | 29 | 67 | 1,876 | 7,504 | 3,366 |
| American InterContinental University; Atlanta (Pr) | 860 | | 60 | 12,000 | 12,000 | |
| Armstrong Atlantic State University; Savannah (Pu) | 5,040 | | 69 | 1,876 | 5,630 | 4,582 |
| Atlanta Christian College; East Point (Pr) | 385 | 73 | 51 | 9,150 | 9,150 | 3,790 |
| Atlanta College of Art; Atlanta (Pr) | 379 | 62 | | 13,800 | 13,800 | |
| Augusta State University; Augusta (Pu) | 4,440 | 72 | 63 | 1,872 | 7,504 | |
| Beacon College; Columbus (Pr) | 57 | 96 | 39 | 2,435 | 2,435 | |
| Berry College; Mount Berry (Pr) | 1,825 | 79 | | 12,500 | 12,500 | 5,488 |
| Beulah Heights Bible College; Atlanta (Pr) | 585 | 90 | | 3,600 | 3,600 | |
| Brenau University; Gainesville (Pr) | 613 | 85 | 100 | 12,180 | 12,180 | 7,170 |
| Clark Atlanta University; Atlanta (Pr) | 3,980 | 72 | 72 | 10,720 | 10,720 | 5,974 |
| Clayton College & State University; Morrow (Pu) | 4,455 | 63 | 64 | 1,876 | 7,506 | |
| Columbus State University; Columbus (Pu) | 4,454 | 69 | 62 | 2,646 | 9,402 | 4,560 |
| Covenant College; Lookout Mountain (Pr) | 1,083 | 98 | 58 | 16,590 | 16,590 | 5,000 |
| Dalton State College; Dalton (Pu) | 3,139 | 67 | | 1,394 | 5,234 | |
| DeVry Institute of Technology; Alpharetta (Pr) | 1,513 | 62 | 32 | 8,250 | 8,250 | |
| DeVry Institute of Technology; Decatur (Pr) | 2,916 | 51 | 42 | 8,250 | 8,250 | |
| Emmanuel College; Franklin Springs (Pr) | 782 | 51 | 55 | 7,766 | 7,766 | 3,776 |
| Emory University; Atlanta (Pr) | 6,215 | 45 | 55 | 24,240 | 24,240 | 7,868 |
| Fort Valley State University; Fort Valley (Pu) | 2,212 | 49 | 57 | 1,206 | 2,820 | 1,801 |
| Georgia Baptist College of Nursing of Mercer Univ.; Atlanta (Pr) | 312 | 46 | 97 | 10,050 | 10,050 | |
| Georgia College and State University; Milledgeville (Pu) | 3,980 | 74 | 62 | 1,876 | 7,506 | 4,312 |
| Georgia Institute of Technology; Atlanta (Pu) | 10,745 | 57 | 29 | 2,506 | 10,024 | 5,234 |
| Georgia Southern University; Statesboro (Pu) | 12,648 | 79 | 53 | 1,876 | 7,504 | 4,154 |
| Georgia Southwestern State University; Americus (Pu) | 1,981 | 65 | 64 | 1,876 | 7,506 | 3,690 |
| Georgia State University; Atlanta (Pu) | 16,439 | 59 | 62 | 2,506 | 10,024 | |
| Kennesaw State University; Kennesaw (Pu) | 11,664 | 73 | | 1,808 | 7,232 | |
| LaGrange College; LaGrange (Pr) | 876 | 83 | 64 | 11,660 | 11,660 | 4,846 |
| Luther Rice Bible College and Seminary; Lithonia (Pr) | 1,300 | | | 2,592 | 2,592 | |
| Macon State College; Macon (Pu) | 4,118 | | 66 | 1,280 | 5,120 | |
| Mercer University; Macon (Pr) | 4,305 | 73 | 64 | 17,028 | 17,028 | 5,378 |
| Morehouse College; Atlanta (Pr) | 2,970 | 75 | 0 | 10,238 | 10,238 | 7,382 |
| Morris Brown College; Atlanta (Pr) | 2,787 | 58 | 58 | 8,368 | 8,368 | 5,262 |
| North Georgia College & State University; Dahlonega (Pu) | 3,144 | 47 | 64 | 1,876 | 7,504 | 3,612 |
| Oglethorpe University; Atlanta (Pr) | 1,169 | 70 | 67 | 18,180 | 18,180 | 5,560 |
| Paine College; Augusta (Pr) | 858 | 54 | 70 | 7,368 | 7,368 | 3,432 |

| Institution name; city (Public/Private) | Students | Percent Accepted | Percent Women | Tuition In-state | Tuition Out-of-state | Room and board |
|---|---|---|---|---|---|---|
| Piedmont College; Demorest (Pr) | 1,026 | 72% | 63% | $ 9,500 | $ 9,500 | $4,400 |
| Roinhardt College; Waleska (Pr) | 1,078 | 89 | 63 | 8,800 | 8,800 | 4,716 |
| Savannah College of Art and Design; Savannah (Pr) | 4,249 | 84 | 43 | 16,200 | 16,200 | 6,750 |
| Savannah State University; Savannah (Pu) | | | | 2,494 | 8,122 | 4,144 |
| Shorter College; Rome (Pr) | 1,889 | 87 | 65 | 9,350 | 9,350 | 4,900 |
| South College; Savannah (Pr) | 483 | | 75 | 10,396 | 14,396 | |
| Southern Polytechnic State University; Marietta (Pu) | 2,943 | 64 | 17 | 1,808 | 7,506 | 4,308 |
| Spelman College; Atlanta (Pr) | 1,952 | 53 | | 9,660 | 9,660 | 6,880 |
| State University of West Georgia; Carrollton (Pu) | 7,109 | 73 | 61 | 1,876 | 7,674 | 3,854 |
| Thomas University; Thomasville (Pr) | 543 | 100 | 66 | 7,500 | 7,500 | |
| Toccoa Falls College; Toccoa Falls (Pr) | 926 | 64 | 56 | 8,888 | 8,888 | 4,012 |
| University of Georgia; Athens (Pu) | 24,213 | 62 | | 2,506 | 10,024 | 5,080 |
| Valdosta State University; Valdosta (Pu) | 7,511 | 65 | 60 | 2,434 | 8,062 | 4,214 |
| Wesleyan College; Macon (Pr) | 583 | 78 | 100 | 15,450 | 15,450 | 7,150 |
| **HAWAII** | | | | | | |
| Brigham Young University–Hawaii Campus; Laie (Pr) | 2,358 | 55 | 60 | 2,988 | 2,988 | 5,275 |
| Chaminade University of Honolulu; Honolulu (Pr) | 1,905 | 69 | 58 | 12,040 | 12,040 | 5,720 |
| Hawaii Pacific University; Honolulu (Pr) | 6,988 | 84 | 52 | 8,920 | 8,920 | 8,350 |
| University of Hawaii at Hilo; Hilo (Pu) | 2,646 | 63 | 60 | 1,416 | 7,032 | 4,989 |
| University of Hawaii at Manoa; Honolulu (Pu) | 11,721 | 71 | 55 | 3,024 | 9,504 | 4,933 |
| University of Phoenix–Hawaii Campus; Honolulu (Pr) | 46,473 | | 56 | 7,740 | 7,740 | |
| **IDAHO** | | | | | | |
| Albertson College of Idaho; Caldwell (Pr) | 812 | 97 | 53 | 16,300 | 16,300 | 4,400 |
| Boise State University; Boise (Pu) | 14,749 | 86 | 55 | 0 | 6,000 | 3,570 |
| Idaho State University; Pocatello (Pu) | 11,768 | 75 | | | 6,240 | 3,920 |
| Lewis-Clark State College; Lewiston (Pu) | 2,702 | 62 | 62 | 2,360 | 7,798 | 3,050 |
| Northwest Nazarene University; Nampa (Pr) | 1,110 | 73 | 55 | 13,700 | 13,700 | 4,140 |
| University of Idaho; Moscow (Pu) | 8,759 | 83 | 46 | 0 | 6,000 | 4,064 |
| **ILLINOIS** | | | | | | |
| American Academy of Art; Chicago (Pr) | 398 | 100 | 32 | 15,080 | 15,080 | |
| Augustana College; Rock Island (Pr) | 2,261 | 72 | 57 | 17,541 | 17,541 | 5,214 |
| Aurora University; Aurora (Pr) | 1,316 | 62 | 59 | 12,918 | 12,918 | 4,914 |
| Barat College; Lake Forest (Pr) | 746 | 62 | 73 | 13,950 | 13,950 | 5,500 |
| Benedictine University; Lisle (Pr) | 2,007 | 81 | 59 | 14,500 | 14,500 | 5,500 |
| Blackburn College; Carlinville (Pr) | 540 | 72 | | 8,190 | 8,190 | 3,670 |
| Blessing-Rieman College of Nursing; Quincy (Pr) | 126 | 100 | 94 | 10,650 | 10,650 | 4,570 |
| Bradley University; Peoria (Pr) | 5,116 | 79 | 54 | 14,500 | 14,500 | 5,460 |
| Columbia College Chicago; Chicago (Pr) | 8,577 | 90 | 50 | 11,600 | 11,600 | |
| Concordia University; River Forest (Pr) | 1,280 | 30 | 68 | 13,760 | 13,760 | 5,365 |
| DePaul University; Chicago (Pr) | 12,436 | 73 | 59 | 15,390 | 15,390 | 6,675 |
| DeVry Institute of Technology; Addison (Pr) | 4,006 | 65 | 23 | 8,250 | 8,250 | |
| DeVry Institute of Technology; Chicago (Pr) | 4,095 | 66 | 36 | 8,250 | 8,250 | |
| DeVry Institute of Technology; Tinley Park (Pr) | 1,010 | 95 | 26 | 8,250 | 8,250 | |
| Dominican University; River Forest (Pr) | 1,127 | 79 | 69 | 14,720 | 14,720 | 5,030 |
| Eastern Illinois University; Charleston (Pu) | 9,344 | 73 | 58 | 2,391 | 7,174 | 5,400 |
| Elmhurst College; Elmhurst (Pr) | 2,484 | 71 | 64 | 15,000 | 15,000 | 5,500 |
| Eureka College; Eureka (Pr) | 441 | 78 | | 15,850 | 15,850 | 5,100 |
| Greenville College; Greenville (Pr) | 1,144 | 97 | 50 | 12,964 | 12,964 | 4,994 |
| Illinois College; Jacksonville (Pr) | 909 | 74 | 55 | 10,735 | 10,735 | 4,725 |
| Illinois Institute of Art; Chicago (Pr) | 1,250 | | | 12,780 | 12,780 | |
| Illinois Institute of Art-Schaumburg; Schaumburg (Pr) | 850 | 100 | | 12,336 | 12,336 | |
| Illinois Institute of Technology; Chicago (Pr) | 1,736 | 65 | 25 | 18,000 | 18,000 | 5,428 |
| Illinois State University; Normal (Pu) | 18,025 | 76 | 58 | 3,332 | 7,275 | 4,544 |
| Illinois Wesleyan University; Bloomington (Pr) | 2,102 | 60 | 57 | 20,284 | 20,284 | 5,150 |
| International Academy of Design & Technology; Chicago (Pr) | 1,739 | 68 | 65 | 10,890 | 10,890 | |
| Judson College; Elgin (Pr) | 1,111 | 76 | 58 | 13,340 | 13,340 | 5,360 |
| Kendall College; Evanston (Pr) | 1,109 | 72 | 57 | 20,940 | 20,940 | 5,436 |
| Lake Forest College; Lake Forest (Pr) | 1,251 | 71 | 60 | 20,900 | 20,900 | 5,000 |
| Lewis University; Romeoville (Pr) | 3,327 | 70 | 56 | 13,320 | 13,320 | 6,000 |
| Lincoln Christian College; Lincoln (Pr) | 653 | 81 | 52 | 6,368 | 6,368 | 3,936 |
| Loyola University Chicago; Chicago (Pr) | 7,141 | 80 | 64 | 18,266 | 18,266 | 7,266 |
| MacMurray College; Jacksonville (Pr) | 727 | 69 | 51 | 13,140 | 13,140 | 4,650 |
| McKendree College; Lebanon (Pr) | 1,993 | 69 | 62 | 12,300 | 12,300 | 4,570 |
| Millikin University; Decatur (Pr) | 2,307 | 99 | 58 | 17,084 | 17,084 | 5,594 |
| Monmouth College; Monmouth (Pr) | 1,069 | 78 | 57 | 16,380 | 16,380 | 4,500 |
| Moody Bible Institute; Chicago (Pr) | 1,294 | 41 | 46 | 0 | 0 | 5,500 |
| National-Louis University; Evanston (Pr) | 3,482 | 77 | | 13,095 | 13,095 | 5,519 |
| North Central College; Naperville (Pr) | 2,117 | 76 | 58 | 15,975 | 15,975 | 5,472 |
| North Park University; Chicago (Pr) | 1,655 | 74 | 62 | 16,910 | 16,910 | 5,870 |
| Northeastern Illinois University; Chicago (Pu) | 8,324 | 70 | 62 | 2,340 | 7,020 | |
| Northern Illinois University; De Kalb (Pu) | 17,151 | 65 | 53 | 3,150 | 6,300 | 5,036 |
| Northwestern University; Evanston (Pr) | 7,724 | 33 | 52 | 24,648 | 24,648 | 7,471 |
| Olivet Nazarene University; Bourbonnais (Pr) | 1,874 | 83 | 59 | 11,928 | 11,928 | 4,696 |
| Principia College; Elsah (Pr) | 560 | 86 | 54 | 15,714 | 15,714 | 5,784 |

| Institution name; city (Public/Private) | Students | Percent Accepted | Percent Women | Tuition In-state | Tuition Out-of-state | Room and board |
|---|---|---|---|---|---|---|
| Quincy University; Quincy (Pr) | 1,041 | 98% | 56% | $14,300 | $14,300 | $4,780 |
| Robert Morris College; Chicago (Pr) | 4,938 | 71 | 67 | 11,550 | 11,550 | |
| Rockford College; Rockford (Pr) | 1,100 | 63 | 65 | 16,800 | 16,800 | 5,430 |
| Roosevelt University; Chicago (Pr) | 4,665 | 51 | 62 | 12,870 | 12,870 | 6,040 |
| Saint Xavier University; Chicago (Pr) | 2,611 | 73 | 73 | 14,400 | 14,400 | 5,744 |
| School of the Art Institute of Chicago; Chicago (Pr) | 2,053 | 76 | 63 | 20,220 | 20,220 | |
| Southern Illinois University Carbondale; Carbondale (Pu) | 17,788 | 71 | 43 | 3,010 | 6,021 | 4,104 |
| Southern Illinois University Edwardsville; Edwardsville (Pu) | 9,576 | 86 | 58 | 2,388 | 4,776 | 4,598 |
| St. Augustine College; Chicago (Pr) | 1,543 | | 79 | 6,420 | 6,420 | |
| Trinity Christian College; Palos Heights (Pr) | 854 | 99 | 63 | 13,240 | 13,240 | 5,190 |
| Trinity International University; Deerfield (Pr) | 1,136 | 86 | 57 | 14,140 | 14,140 | 5,100 |
| University of Chicago; Chicago (Pr) | 4,008 | 44 | 49 | 24,807 | 24,807 | 8,070 |
| University of Illinois at Chicago; Chicago (Pu) | 16,131 | 60 | 55 | 3,232 | 9,696 | 5,856 |
| University of Illinois at Urbana–Champaign; Urbana (Pu) | 27,914 | 64 | 49 | 3,724 | 11,172 | 5,844 |
| University of St. Francis; Joliet (Pr) | 1,471 | 71 | 69 | 13,990 | 13,990 | 5,350 |
| VanderCook College of Music; Chicago (Pr) | 87 | 59 | | 13,440 | 13,440 | 5,600 |
| Western Illinois University; Macomb (Pu) | 10,656 | 65 | 51 | 2,812 | 5,625 | 4,706 |
| Wheaton College; Wheaton (Pr) | 2,418 | 58 | 53 | 15,540 | 15,540 | 5,260 |
| **INDIANA** | | | | | | |
| Anderson University; Anderson (Pr) | 2,090 | 76 | 57 | 14,680 | 14,680 | 4,750 |
| Ball State University; Muncie (Pu) | 16,350 | 79 | 53 | 3,720 | 10,180 | 4,830 |
| Bethel College; Mishawaka (Pr) | 1,534 | 68 | 65 | 12,550 | 12,550 | 4,150 |
| Butler University; Indianapolis (Pr) | 3,313 | 84 | 63 | 18,040 | 18,040 | 6,140 |
| DePauw University; Greencastle (Pr) | 2,225 | 61 | 56 | 20,200 | 20,200 | 6,324 |
| Earlham College; Richmond (Pr) | 1,104 | 85 | 56 | 20,480 | 20,480 | 4,936 |
| Franklin College of Indiana; Franklin (Pr) | 1,020 | 77 | 51 | 14,110 | 14,110 | 4,590 |
| Goshen College; Goshen (Pr) | 1,084 | 68 | 57 | 12,870 | 12,870 | 4,640 |
| Grace College; Winona Lake (Pr) | 923 | 88 | 58 | 10,700 | 10,700 | 4,685 |
| Hanover College; Hanover (Pr) | 1,142 | 83 | 55 | 11,425 | 11,425 | 4,930 |
| Huntington College; Huntington (Pr) | 857 | 93 | 62 | 14,270 | 14,270 | 5,450 |
| Indiana Institute of Technology; Fort Wayne (Pr) | 1,951 | 14 | 51 | | | |
| Indiana State University; Terre Haute (Pu) | 9,537 | 83 | 52 | 3,564 | 8,898 | 4,604 |
| Indiana University Bloomington; Bloomington (Pu) | 29,383 | 82 | 53 | 3,902 | 12,958 | 5,608 |
| Indiana University East; Richmond (Pu) | 2,262 | 64 | 69 | 3,024 | 8,000 | |
| Indiana University Kokomo; Kokomo (Pu) | 2,381 | 91 | 70 | 3,024 | 8,000 | |
| Indiana University Northwest; Gary (Pu) | 4,101 | 75 | 70 | 3,024 | 8,000 | |
| Indiana University South Bend; South Bend (Pu) | 5,897 | 84 | 64 | 3,078 | 8,589 | |
| Indiana University Southeast; New Albany (Pu) | 5,655 | 91 | 62 | 3,024 | 8,000 | |
| Indiana Univ.–Purdue University Fort Wayne; Fort Wayne (Pu) | 9,773 | 94 | 57 | 2,756 | 6,668 | |
| Indiana Univ.–Purdue University Indianapolis; Indianapolis (Pu) | 20,211 | 80 | 59 | 3,570 | 11,108 | 5,098 |
| Indiana Wesleyan University; Marion (Pr) | 5,101 | 78 | 63 | 12,250 | 12,250 | 4,740 |
| Manchester College; North Manchester (Pr) | 1,091 | 81 | 55 | 14,510 | 14,510 | 5,300 |
| Marian College; Indianapolis (Pr) | 1,411 | 89 | 75 | 14,432 | 14,432 | 5,046 |
| Oakland City University; Oakland City (Pr) | 1,492 | 100 | 51 | 10,950 | 10,950 | 4,100 |
| Purdue University; West Lafayette (Pu) | 30,899 | 78 | 43 | 3,872 | 12,904 | 5,800 |
| Purdue University Calumet; Hammond (Pu) | 7,784 | 99 | 56 | 7,143 | | |
| Purdue University North Central; Westville (Pu) | 3,416 | 98 | 60 | 3,043 | 7,710 | |
| Rose-Hulman Institute of Technology; Terre Haute (Pr) | 1,581 | 77 | 17 | 20,694 | 20,694 | 5,175 |
| Saint Joseph's College; Rensselaer (Pr) | 935 | 74 | 56 | 14,920 | 14,920 | 5,380 |
| Saint Mary's College; Notre Dame (Pr) | 1,449 | 83 | 100 | 18,150 | 18,150 | 6,174 |
| Saint Mary-of-the-Woods College; Saint Mary-of-the-Woods (Pr) | 1,385 | 88 | 100 | 14,370 | 14,370 | 5,540 |
| Taylor University; Upland (Pr) | 1,886 | 67 | | 15,600 | 15,600 | 4,740 |
| Taylor University, Fort Wayne Campus; Fort Wayne (Pr) | 477 | 84 | 56 | 13,226 | 13,226 | 4,366 |
| Tri-State University; Angola (Pr) | 1,267 | 81 | 31 | 13,450 | 13,450 | 4,950 |
| University of Evansville; Evansville (Pr) | 2,785 | 91 | 60 | 16,100 | 16,100 | 5,270 |
| University of Indianapolis; Indianapolis (Pr) | 2,856 | 82 | 66 | 14,630 | 14,630 | 5,225 |
| University of Notre Dame; Notre Dame (Pr) | 8,038 | 34 | 46 | 23,180 | 23,180 | 5,920 |
| University of Saint Francis; Fort Wayne (Pr) | 1,390 | 83 | 67 | 12,080 | 12,080 | 4,800 |
| University of Southern Indiana; Evansville (Pu) | 8,539 | 95 | 60 | 3,015 | 7,386 | 5,182 |
| Valparaiso University; Valparaiso (Pr) | 2,980 | 81 | 54 | 17,100 | 17,100 | 4,660 |
| Wabash College; Crawfordsville (Pr) | 852 | 65 | 0 | 17,994 | 17,994 | 5,761 |
| **IOWA** | | | | | | |
| Allen College; Waterloo (Pr) | 248 | 53 | 93 | 8,970 | 8,970 | |
| Briar Cliff College; Sioux City (Pr) | 917 | 80 | 65 | 13,560 | 13,560 | 4,767 |
| Buena Vista University; Storm Lake (Pr) | 1,278 | 86 | 51 | 17,116 | 17,116 | 4,795 |
| Central College; Pella (Pr) | 1,336 | 88 | 57 | 14,638 | 14,638 | 5,242 |
| Clarke College; Dubuque (Pr) | 976 | 73 | 67 | 13,726 | 13,726 | 5,172 |
| Coe College; Cedar Rapids (Pr) | 1,256 | 81 | 55 | 18,240 | 18,240 | 5,200 |
| Cornell College; Mount Vernon (Pr) | 987 | 74 | 59 | 19,410 | 19,410 | 5,410 |
| Dordt College; Sioux Center (Pr) | 1,420 | 95 | 56 | 13,200 | 13,200 | 3,800 |
| Drake University; Des Moines (Pr) | 3,544 | 87 | 61 | 16,980 | 16,980 | 4,870 |
| Emmaus Bible College; Dubuque (Pr) | 293 | 100 | 53 | 5,510 | 5,510 | 2,920 |
| Faith Baptist Bible Coll. and Theological Sem.; Ankeny (Pr) | 382 | 65 | 55 | 7,742 | 7,742 | 3,200 |
| Graceland University; Lamoni (Pr) | 2,952 | 69 | | 12,230 | 12,230 | 4,100 |
| Grand View College; Des Moines (Pr) | 1,380 | 63 | 65 | 12,796 | 12,796 | 4,166 |

| Institution name; city (Public/Private) | Students | Percent Accepted | Women | Tuition In-state | Out-of-state | Room and board |
|---|---|---|---|---|---|---|
| Grinnell College; Grinnell (Pr) | 1,344 | 64% | 56% | $19,982 | $10,982 | $5,820 |
| Hamilton Technical College; Davenport (Pr) | 380 | | | 6,300 | 6,300 | |
| Iowa State University of Science and Technology; Ames (Pu) | 22,087 | 91 | 45 | 2,906 | 9,748 | 4,432 |
| Iowa Wesleyan College; Mount Pleasant (Pr) | 777 | 82 | 60 | 13,200 | 13,200 | 4,250 |
| Loras College; Dubuque (Pr) | 1,626 | 79 | 53 | 15,190 | 15,190 | 5,475 |
| Luther College; Decorah (Pr) | 2,621 | 84 | 60 | 18,080 | 18,080 | 3,914 |
| Maharishi University of Management; Fairfield (Pr) | 239 | | 50 | 15,430 | 15,430 | 5,200 |
| Marycrest International University; Davenport (Pr) | 387 | 68 | 53 | 12,900 | 12,900 | 4,840 |
| Mercy College of Health Sciences; Des Moines (Pr) | 409 | 25 | 92 | 3,900 | 3,900 | |
| Morningside College; Sioux City (Pr) | 968 | 77 | 64 | 13,310 | 13,310 | 4,794 |
| Mount Mercy College; Cedar Rapids (Pr) | 1,363 | 90 | 68 | 13,850 | 13,850 | 4,600 |
| Mount St. Clare College; Clinton (Pr) | 560 | 78 | 55 | 13,200 | 13,200 | 4,630 |
| Northwestern College; Orange City (Pr) | 1,243 | 88 | 61 | 13,000 | 13,000 | 3,650 |
| Palmer College of Chiropractic; Davenport (Pr) | 60 | 100 | 78 | 16,230 | 16,230 | |
| Simpson College; Indianola (Pr) | 1,912 | 86 | 57 | 15,015 | 15,015 | 5,040 |
| St. Ambrose University; Davenport (Pr) | 2,116 | 86 | 60 | 13,890 | 13,890 | 5,160 |
| University of Dubuque; Dubuque (Pr) | 669 | 82 | 41 | 13,990 | 13,990 | 4,820 |
| University of Iowa; Iowa City (Pu) | 19,284 | 83 | 54 | 2,906 | 10,668 | 4,597 |
| University of Northern Iowa; Cedar Falls (Pu) | 12,413 | 82 | 58 | 2,906 | 7,870 | 4,149 |
| Upper Iowa University; Fayette (Pr) | 697 | 75 | 39 | 11,290 | 11,290 | 4,364 |
| Wartburg College; Waverly (Pr) | 1,600 | 89 | 57 | 15,510 | 15,510 | 4,500 |
| William Penn University; Oskaloosa (Pr) | 1,353 | 76 | 42 | 12,400 | 12,400 | 4,140 |
| **KANSAS** | | | | | | |
| Baker University; Baldwin City (Pr) | 923 | 81 | 58 | 12,300 | 12,300 | 4,750 |
| Barclay College; Haviland (Pr) | 193 | 42 | 53 | 6,240 | 6,240 | 3,300 |
| Benedictine College; Atchison (Pr) | 1,323 | 92 | 56 | 12,390 | 12,390 | 4,790 |
| Bethany College; Lindsborg (Pr) | 611 | 63 | 46 | 12,154 | 12,154 | 3,780 |
| Bethel College; North Newton (Pr) | 502 | 79 | 52 | 11,700 | 11,700 | 4,700 |
| Emporia State University; Emporia (Pu) | 4,191 | 100 | 59 | 2,218 | 6,940 | 3,774 |
| Fort Hays State University; Hays (Pu) | 4,427 | 99 | 54 | 2,178 | 6,900 | 2,375 |
| Friends University; Wichita (Pr) | 2,668 | 93 | | 11,660 | 11,660 | 3,540 |
| Haskell Indian Nations University; Lawrence (Pu) | 915 | | | | | |
| Kansas State University; Manhattan (Pu) | 18,252 | 61 | 47 | 2,333 | 9,260 | 4,240 |
| Kansas Wesleyan University; Salina (Pr) | 697 | 70 | | 12,600 | 12,600 | 4,400 |
| Manhattan Christian College; Manhattan (Pr) | 400 | 94 | 56 | 6,870 | 6,870 | 3,610 |
| McPherson College; McPherson (Pr) | 463 | 69 | 51 | 11,500 | 11,500 | 4,900 |
| MidAmerica Nazarene University; Olathe (Pr) | 1,302 | 58 | 52 | 10,150 | 10,150 | 5,074 |
| Newman University; Wichita (Pr) | 1,557 | 98 | 65 | 10,148 | 10,148 | 3,950 |
| Ottawa University; Ottawa (Pr) | 433 | 68 | 45 | 10,750 | 10,750 | 4,642 |
| Pittsburg State University; Pittsburg (Pu) | 5,222 | | 48 | 2,260 | 6,982 | 3,990 |
| Saint Mary College; Leavenworth (Pr) | 506 | 83 | 65 | 12,070 | 12,070 | 4,880 |
| Southwestern College; Winfield (Pr) | 1,114 | 96 | 51 | 11,300 | 11,300 | 4,320 |
| Sterling College; Sterling (Pr) | 439 | 66 | 51 | 11,582 | 11,582 | 4,788 |
| Tabor College; Hillsboro (Pr) | 572 | 68 | 47 | 12,090 | 12,090 | 4,480 |
| University of Kansas; Lawrence (Pu) | 20,157 | 76 | 53 | 2,267 | 9,035 | 4,114 |
| Washburn University of Topeka; Topeka (Pu) | 4,888 | 100 | 62 | 2,996 | 6,748 | 3,410 |
| Wichita State University; Wichita (Pu) | 11,377 | 75 | 56 | 2,149 | 8,764 | 4,120 |
| **KENTUCKY** | | | | | | |
| Alice Lloyd College; Pippa Passes (Pr) | 558 | 66 | | 0 | 0 | |
| Asbury College; Wilmore (Pr) | 1,338 | 82 | 59 | 13,744 | 13,744 | 3,566 |
| Bellarmine University; Louisville (Pr) | 1,682 | 95 | | 13,590 | 13,590 | 4,160 |
| Berea College; Berea (Pr) | 1,590 | 34 | 58 | 0 | 0 | 4,099 |
| Brescia University; Owensboro (Pr) | 688 | | 61 | 9,390 | 9,390 | 4,240 |
| Campbellsville University; Campbellsville (Pr) | 1,502 | 84 | 60 | 8,790 | 8,790 | 4,320 |
| Centre College; Danville (Pr) | 1,057 | 88 | 53 | | | |
| Clear Creek Baptist Bible College; Pineville (Pr) | 190 | 83 | 15 | 3,520 | 3,520 | 2,740 |
| Cumberland College; Williamsburg (Pr) | 1,554 | 71 | 59 | 9,000 | 9,000 | 3,700 |
| Eastern Kentucky University; Richmond (Pu) | 12,878 | | 58 | 2,542 | 6,884 | 3,796 |
| Kentucky Christian College; Grayson (Pr) | 569 | 90 | 55 | 7,360 | 7,360 | 4,070 |
| Kentucky Mountain Bible College; Vancleve (Pr) | 87 | 52 | 43 | 3,750 | 3,750 | 2,800 |
| Kentucky State University; Frankfort (Pu) | 2,129 | 45 | 56 | 2,100 | 6,302 | 3,740 |
| Kentucky Wesleyan College; Owensboro (Pr) | 680 | 79 | 54 | 10,070 | 10,070 | 4,830 |
| Lindsey Wilson College; Columbia (Pr) | 1,366 | 83 | 63 | 9,678 | 9,678 | 4,680 |
| Mid-Continent College; Mayfield (Pr) | 455 | 65 | 46 | 5,440 | 5,440 | 4,000 |
| Midway College; Midway (Pr) | 834 | 92 | 89 | 9,600 | 9,600 | 4,850 |
| Morehead State University; Morehead (Pu) | 6,750 | 74 | 60 | 2,710 | 7,204 | 3,800 |
| Murray State University; Murray (Pu) | 7,487 | 87 | 58 | | | |
| Northern Kentucky University; Highland Heights (Pu) | 10,838 | 98 | 59 | 2,328 | 6,576 | 3,656 |
| Pikeville College; Pikeville (Pr) | 917 | 100 | 59 | 7,800 | 7,800 | 3,340 |
| Spalding University; Louisville (Pr) | 1,014 | 71 | 77 | 11,400 | 11,400 | 2,930 |
| Sullivan University; Louisville (Pr) | | | | 10,080 | 10,080 | |
| Thomas More College; Crestview Hills (Pr) | 1,273 | 79 | 55 | 12,300 | 12,300 | 3,756 |
| Transylvania University; Lexington (Pr) | 1,083 | 91 | 58 | 14,700 | 14,700 | 5,530 |
| Union College; Barbourville (Pr) | 653 | 75 | 48 | 11,070 | 11,070 | 3,650 |
| University of Kentucky; Lexington (Pu) | 16,897 | 61 | 52 | 3,110 | 9,330 | 3,782 |

| Institution name; city (Public/Private) | Students | Percent Accepted | Percent Women | Tuition In-state | Tuition Out-of-state | Room and board |
|---|---|---|---|---|---|---|
| University of Louisville; Louisville (Pu) | 14,464 | 89% | 54% | $ 3,149 | $ 9,448 | $3,500 |
| Western Kentucky University; Bowling Green (Pu) | 13,235 | 87 | 58 | 2,150 | 6,450 | 3,813 |
| **LOUISIANA** | | | | | | |
| Centenary College of Louisiana; Shreveport (Pr) | 858 | 89 | 61 | 14,200 | 14,200 | 4,500 |
| Dillard University; New Orleans (Pr) | 1,953 | 72 | 78 | 9,200 | 9,200 | 5,350 |
| Grantham College of Engineering; Slidell (Pr) | 967 | | | 5,250 | 5,250 | |
| Louisiana State University and Agricultural and Mechanical College; Baton Rouge (Pu) | 26,121 | 78 | 53 | 2,551 | 7,851 | 4,270 |
| Louisiana State Univ. Health Sciences Center; New Orleans (Pu) | 767 | | | 3,659 | 6,784 | |
| Louisiana State University in Shreveport; Shreveport (Pu) | 3,422 | 100 | 61 | 2,050 | 5,982 | |
| Louisiana Tech University; Ruston (Pu) | 8,921 | 93 | 48 | 2,748 | 6,423 | 3,195 |
| Loyola University New Orleans; New Orleans (Pr) | 3,688 | 74 | 64 | 16,188 | 16,188 | 6,806 |
| McNeese State University; Lake Charles (Pu) | 6,703 | 72 | 59 | 1,900 | 8,490 | 2,620 |
| Nicholls State University; Thibodaux (Pu) | 6,556 | 93 | 62 | 1,965 | 7,101 | 3,002 |
| Northwestern State University of Louisiana; Natchitoches (Pu) | 7,972 | 98 | 62 | 2,056 | 7,726 | 2,896 |
| Our Lady of Holy Cross College; New Orleans (Pr) | 1,148 | 45 | 76 | 5,700 | 5,700 | |
| Saint Joseph Seminary College; Saint Benedict (Pr) | | 100 | | 5,225 | 5,225 | 4,550 |
| Southeastern Louisiana University; Hammond (Pu) | 12,916 | 77 | 63 | 2,490 | 7,818 | 3,006 |
| Southern University and Agricultural and Mechanical College; Baton Rouge (Pu) | 7,775 | | 57 | 2,286 | 8,078 | 3,410 |
| Tulane University; New Orleans (Pr) | 7,382 | 73 | 53 | 23,500 | 23,500 | 6,908 |
| University of Louisiana at Lafayette; Lafayette (Pu) | 14,091 | 78 | 56 | 2,275 | 9,225 | 2,726 |
| University of Louisiana at Monroe; Monroe (Pu) | 8,037 | 95 | 62 | 2,307 | 8,259 | 3,660 |
| University of New Orleans; New Orleans (Pu) | 12,260 | 83 | 57 | 2,712 | 9,756 | 3,300 |
| University of Phoenix-Louisiana Campus; Metairie (Pr) | 46,473 | | 56 | 7,740 | 7,740 | |
| **MAINE** | | | | | | |
| Bates College; Lewiston (Pr) | 1,694 | 29 | 52 | | | |
| Bowdoin College; Brunswick (Pr) | 1,609 | 28 | 51 | 25,345 | 25,345 | 6,760 |
| Colby College; Waterville (Pr) | 1,814 | 37 | 54 | | | |
| College of the Atlantic; Bar Harbor (Pr) | 278 | 80 | 64 | 20,124 | 20,124 | 5,343 |
| Husson College; Bangor (Pr) | 1,626 | 97 | 66 | 9,480 | 9,480 | 5,150 |
| Maine College of Art; Portland (Pr) | 413 | 87 | 60 | 17,370 | 17,370 | 6,556 |
| Maine Maritime Academy; Castine (Pu) | 707 | 81 | 15 | 4,739 | 8,774 | 5,327 |
| New England School of Communications; Bangor (Pr) | 135 | 41 | 28 | 7,590 | 7,590 | 5,200 |
| Saint Joseph's College; Standish (Pr) | 832 | 84 | 67 | 13,920 | 13,920 | 6,250 |
| Thomas College; Waterville (Pr) | 598 | 96 | 56 | 12,480 | 12,480 | 5,700 |
| Unity College; Unity (Pr) | 512 | 69 | 34 | 12,330 | 12,330 | 5,300 |
| University of Maine; Orono (Pu) | 8,229 | 83 | 52 | 4,050 | 11,520 | 5,360 |
| University of Maine at Augusta; Augusta (Pu) | 5,617 | 67 | | 3,150 | 7,710 | |
| University of Maine at Farmington; Farmington (Pu) | 2,413 | 66 | 68 | 3,540 | 8,640 | 4,614 |
| University of Maine at Fort Kent; Fort Kent (Pu) | 886 | 89 | 63 | 3,150 | 7,710 | 4,100 |
| University of Maine at Machias; Machias (Pu) | 927 | 87 | 67 | 3,150 | 7,860 | 4,490 |
| University of Maine at Presque Isle; Presque Isle (Pu) | 1,427 | 88 | 63 | 3,150 | 7,710 | 4,140 |
| University of New England; Biddeford (Pr) | 1,869 | 72 | 81 | 15,740 | 15,740 | 6,420 |
| University of Southern Maine; Portland (Pu) | 8,726 | 78 | 60 | 3,720 | 10,410 | 5,202 |
| **MARYLAND** | | | | | | |
| Baltimore International College; Baltimore (Pr) | 456 | 49 | 46 | 11,008 | 11,008 | 5,182 |
| Bowie State University; Bowie (Pu) | 3,109 | 44 | 60 | 2,941 | 8,512 | 4,744 |
| Capitol College; Laurel (Pr) | 684 | 80 | 27 | 13,200 | 13,200 | |
| College of Notre Dame of Maryland; Baltimore (Pr) | 1,930 | 80 | 95 | 15,600 | 15,600 | 6,800 |
| Columbia Union College; Takoma Park (Pr) | 1,030 | 54 | 59 | 12,810 | 12,810 | 4,619 |
| Frostburg State University; Frostburg (Pu) | 4,430 | 73 | 53 | 3,342 | 8,492 | 5,214 |
| Goucher College; Baltimore (Pr) | 1,195 | 82 | 73 | 21,000 | 21,000 | 7,650 |
| Griggs University; Silver Spring (Pr) | 322 | | | 5,400 | 5,400 | |
| Hood College; Frederick (Pr) | 861 | 77 | 88 | 18,295 | 18,295 | 6,900 |
| Johns Hopkins University; Baltimore (Pr) | 3,910 | 32 | 42 | 24,930 | 24,930 | 8,185 |
| Loyola College in Maryland; Baltimore (Pr) | 3,476 | 61 | 56 | 21,230 | 21,230 | 6,040 |
| Maryland Institute, College of Art; Baltimore (Pr) | 1,154 | 45 | 58 | 19,800 | 19,800 | |
| Morgan State University; Baltimore (Pu) | 5,685 | | 59 | 3,030 | 9,000 | 5,780 |
| Mount Saint Mary's College and Seminary; Emmitsburg (Pr) | 1,500 | 87 | 59 | 17,200 | 17,200 | 6,860 |
| Peabody Conservatory of Music of The Johns Hopkins University; Baltimore (Pr) | 332 | 42 | 52 | 22,700 | 22,700 | 8,420 |
| Salisbury State University; Salisbury (Pu) | 5,883 | 21 | 57 | 3,092 | 7,828 | 5,990 |
| Sojourner-Douglass College; Baltimore (Pr) | 844 | | 83 | 4,280 | 4,280 | |
| St. John's College; Annapolis (Pr) | 476 | 79 | 47 | 24,570 | 24,570 | 6,576 |
| St. Mary's College of Maryland; St. Mary's City (Pu) | 1,547 | 74 | 59 | 6,474 | 11,459 | 6,555 |
| Towson University; Towson (Pu) | 13,905 | 62 | 60 | 3,605 | 10,491 | 6,104 |
| United States Naval Academy; Annapolis (Pu) | 4,172 | 15 | 15 | | | |
| University of Maryland Eastern Shore; Princess Anne (Pu) | 2,969 | 66 | 58 | 3,994 | 8,497 | 5,130 |
| University of Maryland University College; Adelphi (Pu) | 13,226 | 100 | 58 | 4,584 | 7,008 | |
| University of Maryland, Baltimore County; Baltimore (Pu) | 9,101 | 66 | 50 | 4,206 | 8,974 | 5,850 |
| University of Maryland, College Park; College Park (Pu) | 24,638 | 51 | 49 | 4,172 | 11,704 | 6,328 |
| University of Phoenix–Maryland Campus; Columbia (Pr) | 46,473 | | 56 | 7,740 | 7,740 | |
| Villa Julie College; Stevenson (Pr) | 2,185 | | 72 | 10,750 | 10,750 | |
| Washington Bible College; Lanham (Pr) | 313 | 56 | 44 | 6,480 | 6,480 | 4,690 |

| Institution name; city (Public/Private) | Students | Percent Accepted | Women | Tuition In-state | Out-of-state | Room and board |
|---|---|---|---|---|---|---|
| Washington College; Chestertown (Pr) | 1,165 | 88% | 60% | $20,750 | $20,750 | $5,740 |
| Western Maryland College; Westminster (Pr) | 1,611 | 77 | 56 | 19,600 | 19,600 | 5,350 |
| **MASSACHUSETTS** | | | | | | |
| American International College; Springfield (Pr) | 1,084 | 79 | 55 | 13,600 | 13,600 | 7,112 |
| Amherst College; Amherst (Pr) | 1,682 | 19 | 48 | 25,600 | 25,600 | 6,800 |
| Anna Maria College; Paxton (Pr) | 797 | 83 | 63 | 13,495 | 13,495 | 6,200 |
| Art Institute of Boston at Lesley University; Boston (Pr) | 791 | 49 | 58 | 13,350 | 13,350 | 7,520 |
| Assumption College; Worcester (Pr) | 2,455 | 71 | 64 | 17,950 | 17,950 | 6,980 |
| Atlantic Union College; South Lancaster (Pr) | 680 | 42 | 61 | 12,260 | 12,260 | 4,552 |
| Babson College; Wellesley (Pr) | 1,751 | 39 | 36 | 21,952 | 21,952 | 8,746 |
| Bay Path College; Longmeadow (Pr) | 764 | 67 | 100 | 13,660 | 13,660 | 6,945 |
| Becker College; Worcester (Pr) | 1,163 | 87 | 77 | 12,300 | 12,300 | 6,420 |
| Bentley College; Waltham (Pr) | 4,316 | 49 | 44 | 18,795 | 18,795 | 8,600 |
| Berklee College of Music; Boston (Pr) | 3,361 | 78 | | 16,590 | 16,590 | 8,890 |
| Boston Architectural Center; Boston (Pr) | 458 | 95 | 27 | 6,682 | 6,682 | |
| Boston College; Chestnut Hill (Pr) | 8,930 | 32 | 52 | 22,680 | 22,680 | 8,510 |
| Boston Conservatory; Boston (Pr) | 350 | 47 | 67 | | | |
| Boston University; Boston (Pr) | 17,819 | 49 | 59 | 24,700 | 24,700 | 8,450 |
| Brandeis University; Waltham (Pr) | 3,169 | 48 | 57 | 25,392 | 25,392 | 7,189 |
| Bridgewater State College; Bridgewater (Pu) | 7,080 | 81 | 61 | 970 | 7,050 | 4,887 |
| Cambridge College; Cambridge (Pr) | 350 | 100 | | 8,400 | 8,400 | |
| Clark University; Worcester (Pr) | 2,124 | 70 | 59 | 24,400 | 24,400 | 4,350 |
| College of Our Lady of the Elms; Chicopee (Pr) | 740 | 85 | 88 | 14,144 | 14,144 | 5,566 |
| College of the Holy Cross; Worcester (Pr) | 2,826 | 41 | 53 | 23,400 | 23,400 | 7,540 |
| Curry College; Milton (Pr) | 2,218 | 76 | 50 | 17,160 | 17,160 | 6,870 |
| Eastern Nazarene College; Quincy (Pr) | 1,209 | 69 | 59 | 13,236 | 13,236 | 4,550 |
| Emerson College; Boston (Pr) | 3,168 | 52 | 58 | 19,520 | 19,520 | 9,020 |
| Emmanuel College; Boston (Pr) | 1,360 | 83 | 89 | 16,112 | 16,112 | 7,390 |
| Endicott College; Beverly (Pr) | 1,553 | 70 | 67 | 14,550 | 14,550 | 7,698 |
| Fitchburg State College; Fitchburg (Pu) | 3,238 | 66 | 58 | 1,030 | 7,050 | 4,680 |
| Framingham State College; Framingham (Pu) | 4,165 | 62 | 65 | 1,030 | 7,050 | 4,154 |
| Gordon College; Wenham (Pr) | 1,528 | 80 | 64 | 16,550 | 16,550 | 5,200 |
| Hampshire College; Amherst (Pr) | 1,172 | 62 | 56 | 25,709 | 25,709 | 6,814 |
| Harvard University; Cambridge (Pr) | 6,660 | 11 | | 22,694 | 22,694 | 7,982 |
| Hebrew College; Brookline (Pr) | | | | 14,850 | 14,850 | |
| Hellenic College; Brookline (Pr) | 47 | 48 | 28 | 9,000 | 9,000 | 7,000 |
| Lasell College; Newton (Pr) | 841 | 79 | 76 | 14,700 | 14,700 | 7,700 |
| Lesley University; Cambridge (Pr) | 553 | 79 | 100 | 16,300 | 16,300 | 7,520 |
| Massachusetts College of Art; Boston (Pu) | 2,214 | 46 | 65 | 1,090 | 9,000 | 7,192 |
| Massachusetts College of Liberal Arts; North Adams (Pu) | 1,392 | 70 | 61 | 1,090 | 8,220 | 4,290 |
| Massachusetts College of Pharmacy and Health Sciences, Boston (Pr) | 446 | 76 | 65 | 16,863 | 16,863 | 8,400 |
| Massachusetts Institute of Technology; Cambridge (Pr) | 4,258 | 16 | 41 | 26,050 | 26,050 | 7,175 |
| Massachusetts Maritime Academy; Buzzards Bay (Pu) | 831 | 72 | 13 | 1,090 | 9,170 | 5,403 |
| Merrimack College; North Andover (Pr) | 2,568 | 70 | 52 | 16,575 | 16,575 | 7,750 |
| Montserrat College of Art; Beverly (Pr) | 402 | 84 | 57 | 13,430 | 13,430 | |
| Mount Holyoke College; South Hadley (Pr) | 2,065 | 55 | 100 | 25,220 | 25,220 | 7,410 |
| Mount Ida College; Newton Centre (Pr) | 1,471 | 80 | 59 | 15,300 | 15,300 | 8,950 |
| New England Conservatory of Music; Boston (Pr) | 407 | 48 | 45 | 20,550 | 20,550 | 8,950 |
| Nichols College; Dudley (Pr) | 1,159 | 85 | 47 | 15,200 | 15,200 | 7,810 |
| Northeastern University; Boston (Pr) | 13,671 | 70 | 50 | 19,395 | 19,395 | 9,135 |
| Pine Manor College; Chestnut Hill (Pr) | 369 | 78 | 100 | 11,894 | 11,894 | 7,450 |
| Regis College; Weston (Pr) | 884 | 89 | 98 | 17,500 | 17,500 | 8,100 |
| Saint John's Seminary College of Liberal Arts; Brighton (Pr) | 32 | 73 | 0 | | | |
| Salem State College; Salem (Pu) | 11,132 | 58 | 63 | 1,455 | 7,050 | 2,860 |
| School of the Museum of Fine Arts; Boston (Pr) | | | | 17,880 | 17,880 | |
| Simmons College; Boston (Pr) | 1,334 | 65 | 100 | 21,740 | 21,740 | 6,700 |
| Smith College; Northampton (Pr) | 2,630 | 53 | 100 | 23,400 | 23,400 | 8,160 |
| Springfield College; Springfield (Pr) | | 58 | | 17,100 | 17,100 | 6,035 |
| Stonehill College; Easton (Pr) | 2,007 | 11 | 59 | 16,080 | 16,080 | 8,166 |
| Suffolk University; Boston (Pr) | 3,355 | 79 | 58 | 16,536 | 16,536 | 9,990 |
| Tufts University; Medford (Pr) | 4,863 | 26 | 53 | 25,062 | 25,062 | 7,680 |
| University of Massachusetts Amherst; Amherst (Pu) | 19,061 | 67 | 51 | 1,714 | 9,967 | 4,895 |
| University of Massachusetts Boston; Boston (Pu) | 10,442 | 59 | 57 | 1,714 | 9,758 | |
| University of Massachusetts Dartmouth; North Dartmouth (Pu) | 6,423 | 73 | 53 | 1,417 | 7,995 | 5,143 |
| University of Massachusetts Lowell; Lowell (Pu) | 9,566 | 67 | | 1,454 | 8,271 | 4,994 |
| Wellesley College; Wellesley (Pr) | 2,267 | 43 | 100 | 23,718 | 23,718 | 7,480 |
| Wentworth Institute of Technology; Boston (Pr) | 3,152 | 67 | 20 | 13,000 | 13,000 | 6,800 |
| Western New England College; Springfield (Pr) | 3,136 | 69 | | 14,354 | 14,354 | 7,050 |
| Westfield State College; Westfield (Pu) | 4,279 | 64 | 55 | 1,030 | 7,050 | 4,556 |
| Wheaton College; Norton (Pr) | 1,474 | 65 | 64 | 24,225 | 24,225 | 6,920 |
| Wheelock College; Boston (Pr) | 637 | 83 | 94 | 17,410 | 17,410 | 6,950 |
| Williams College; Williamstown (Pr) | 2,020 | 24 | 48 | 24,619 | 24,619 | 6,730 |
| Worcester Polytechnic Institute; Worcester (Pr) | 2,817 | 77 | 23 | 23,122 | 23,122 | 7,592 |

| Institution name; city (Public/Private) | Students | Percent Accepted | Percent Women | Tuition In-state | Tuition Out-of-state | Room and board |
|---|---|---|---|---|---|---|
| Worcester State College; Worcester (Pu) | 4,569 | 52% | | $ 1,030 | $ 7,050 | $5,000 |
| **MICHIGAN** | | | | | | |
| Adrian College; Adrian (Pr) | 1,082 | 86 | 54% | 14,150 | 14,150 | 4,990 |
| Albion College; Albion (Pr) | 1,522 | 85 | 58 | 18,690 | 18,690 | 5,404 |
| Alma College; Alma (Pr) | 1,409 | 82 | 59 | 15,734 | 15,734 | 5,726 |
| Andrews University; Berrien Springs (Pr) | 1,736 | 54 | 56 | 12,600 | 12,600 | 4,060 |
| Aquinas College; Grand Rapids (Pr) | 2,021 | 83 | 61 | 14,876 | 14,876 | 5,176 |
| Ave Maria College; Ypsilanti (Pr) | 135 | | 53 | | | |
| Baker College of Auburn Hills; Auburn Hills (Pr) | 1,910 | 100 | 67 | 5,400 | 5,400 | |
| Baker College of Cadillac; Cadillac (Pr) | 864 | 100 | 72 | 5,400 | 5,400 | |
| Baker College of Clinton Township; Clinton Township (Pr) | 2,560 | 46 | 77 | 5,400 | 5,400 | |
| Baker College of Flint; Flint (Pr) | 3,901 | 100 | 67 | 5,580 | 5,580 | |
| Baker College of Jackson; Jackson (Pr) | 1,201 | 100 | 75 | 5,400 | 5,400 | |
| Baker College of Muskegon; Muskegon (Pr) | 2,727 | 75 | 68 | 7,440 | 7,440 | |
| Baker College of Owosso; Owosso (Pr) | 1,905 | 100 | 69 | 7,200 | 7,200 | |
| Baker College of Port Huron; Port Huron (Pr) | 1,230 | 100 | 78 | 7,220 | 7,220 | |
| Calvin College; Grand Rapids (Pr) | 4,263 | 99 | 55 | 14,040 | 14,040 | 4,890 |
| Center for Creative Studies; Detroit (Pr) | 1,086 | 82 | 41 | 15,630 | 15,630 | |
| Central Michigan University; Mount Pleasant (Pu) | 18,550 | 83 | 59 | 3,245 | 8,421 | 4,828 |
| Cleary College; Howell (Pr) | 848 | | 62 | 7,830 | 7,830 | |
| Concordia College; Ann Arbor (Pr) | 590 | 85 | 60 | 13,400 | 13,400 | 5,800 |
| Cornerstone University; Grand Rapids (Pr) | 1,592 | 93 | 60 | 11,250 | 11,250 | 4,830 |
| Davenport University; Dearborn (Pr) | 2,924 | 100 | 74 | 6,984 | 6,984 | |
| Davenport University; Grand Rapids (Pr) | 2,144 | 100 | 65 | 9,408 | 9,408 | |
| Davenport University; Kalamazoo (Pr) | 1,081 | | | 8,865 | 8,865 | |
| Davenport University; Lansing (Pr) | 1,140 | | 71 | 8,364 | 8,364 | |
| Davenport University; Warren (Pr) | 2,465 | 100 | 77 | 6,768 | 6,768 | |
| Eastern Michigan University; Ypsilanti (Pu) | 18,131 | 73 | 61 | 3,200 | 8,990 | 5,016 |
| Ferris State University; Big Rapids (Pu) | 9,235 | 87 | 44 | 4,284 | 9,076 | 5,258 |
| Finlandia University; Hancock (Pr) | 380 | 73 | 67 | 11,700 | 11,700 | 4,340 |
| Grace Bible College; Grand Rapids (Pr) | 140 | 81 | 52 | 7,400 | 7,400 | 4,500 |
| Grand Valley State University; Allendale (Pu) | 15,221 | 77 | 60 | 4,272 | 9,244 | 5,030 |
| Hillsdale College; Hillsdale (Pr) | 1,138 | 84 | 50 | 13,600 | 13,600 | 5,700 |
| Hope College; Holland (Pr) | 3,015 | 89 | 60 | 16,554 | 16,554 | 5,224 |
| Kalamazoo College; Kalamazoo (Pr) | 1,322 | 70 | 57 | 19,764 | 19,764 | 5,961 |
| Kendall College of Art and Design; Grand Rapids (Pr) | 738 | | 57 | | | |
| Kettering University; Flint (Pr) | 2,642 | 72 | 19 | 15,960 | 15,960 | 4,340 |
| Lake Superior State University; Sault Sainte Marie (Pu) | 3,068 | 89 | 53 | 4,014 | 7,701 | 5,078 |
| Lawrence Technological University; Southfield (Pr) | 2,979 | 78 | | 11,100 | 11,100 | |
| Madonna University; Livonia (Pr) | 3,066 | 66 | 78 | 7,020 | 7,020 | 4,852 |
| Marygrove College; Detroit (Pr) | 914 | 58 | | 10,500 | 10,500 | 5,200 |
| Michigan State University; East Lansing (Pu) | 34,342 | 69 | 53 | 5,170 | 12,835 | 4,472 |
| Michigan Technological University; Houghton (Pu) | 5,666 | 94 | 26 | 4,530 | 11,086 | 4,917 |
| Northern Michigan University; Marquette (Pu) | 7,244 | 85 | 54 | 2,850 | 5,376 | 4,976 |
| Northwood University; Midland (Pr) | 3,645 | 96 | 50 | 11,763 | 11,763 | 5,592 |
| Oakland University; Rochester (Pu) | 12,002 | 78 | 64 | 3,849 | 11,113 | 4,833 |
| Olivet College; Olivet (Pr) | 918 | 80 | 48 | 13,382 | 13,382 | 4,452 |
| Reformed Bible College; Grand Rapids (Pr) | 280 | 55 | 48 | 7,650 | 7,650 | 4,200 |
| Rochester College; Rochester Hills (Pr) | 830 | | 54 | 8,448 | 8,448 | 4,768 |
| Sacred Heart Major Seminary; Detroit (Pr) | 275 | 100 | | 6,862 | 6,862 | |
| Saginaw Valley State University; University Center (Pu) | 6,262 | | | 3,289 | 7,092 | 5,015 |
| Saint Mary's College of Ave Maria University; Orchard Lake (Pr) | 479 | 81 | 44 | 6,192 | 6,192 | 5,200 |
| Siena Heights University; Adrian (Pr) | 1,658 | 73 | | 12,100 | 12,100 | 4,502 |
| Spring Arbor University; Spring Arbor (Pr) | 2,125 | 90 | 69 | 12,200 | 12,200 | 4,580 |
| University of Michigan; Ann Arbor (Pu) | 23,904 | 55 | 52 | 6,328 | 20,138 | 5,780 |
| University of Michigan–Dearborn; Dearborn (Pu) | 6,694 | 74 | | 4,275 | 11,343 | |
| University of Michigan–Flint; Flint (Pu) | 5,786 | 82 | 65 | 3,618 | 11,058 | |
| University of Phoenix–Grand Rapids Campus; Grand Rapids (Pr) | 46,473 | | 56 | 7,740 | 7,740 | |
| University of Phoenix–Metro Detroit Campus; Troy (Pr) | 46,473 | | 56 | 7,740 | 7,740 | |
| Wayne State University; Detroit (Pu) | 18,093 | 78 | 60 | 3,567 | 8,175 | |
| Western Michigan University; Kalamazoo (Pu) | 22,756 | 85 | 53 | 3,492 | 8,730 | 5,073 |
| William Tyndale College; Farmington Hills (Pr) | 625 | 99 | 52 | 7,050 | 7,050 | 2,800 |
| **MINNESOTA** | | | | | | |
| Augsburg College; Minneapolis (Pr) | 2,913 | 75 | 60 | 15,974 | 15,974 | 5,320 |
| Bemidji State University; Bemidji (Pu) | 4,368 | 77 | 57 | 2,954 | 6,266 | 3,880 |
| Bethel College; St. Paul (Pr) | 2,652 | 77 | 63 | 15,900 | 15,900 | 5,700 |
| Carleton College; Northfield (Pr) | 1,936 | 44 | 52 | 24,420 | 24,420 | 4,950 |
| College of Saint Benedict; Saint Joseph (Pr) | 2,024 | 80 | 100 | 16,995 | 16,995 | 5,272 |
| College of St. Catherine; St. Paul (Pr) | 3,555 | 85 | 98 | 16,320 | 16,320 | 4,690 |
| College of St. Scholastica; Duluth (Pr) | 1,438 | 36 | | 16,190 | 16,190 | 4,952 |
| College of Visual Arts; St. Paul (Pr) | 278 | 65 | 56 | 11,980 | 11,980 | |
| Concordia College; Moorhead (Pr) | 2,826 | 84 | 66 | 14,020 | 14,020 | 3,900 |
| Concordia University; St. Paul (Pr) | 1,504 | 67 | 59 | 14,752 | 14,752 | 5,160 |
| Crown College; St. Bonifacius (Pr) | 882 | 65 | 58 | 9,840 | 9,840 | 4,420 |
| Gustavus Adolphus College; St. Peter (Pr) | 2,560 | 76 | 57 | 17,970 | 17,970 | 4,605 |

| Institution name; city (Public/Private) | Students | Percent Accepted | Percent Women | Tuition In-state | Tuition Out-of-state | Room and board |
|---|---|---|---|---|---|---|
| Hamline University; St. Paul (Pr) | 1,851 | 81% | 65% | $16,050 | $16,050 | $5,445 |
| Macalester College; St. Paul (Pr) | 1,794 | 53 | 60 | 21,486 | 21,486 | 5,932 |
| Martin Luther College; New Ulm (Pr) | 1,026 | | 50 | 4,610 | 4,610 | 2,340 |
| Metropolitan State University; St. Paul (Pu) | 5,328 | | 60 | 2,752 | 6,272 | |
| Minneapolis College of Art and Design; Minneapolis (Pr) | 598 | 71 | 42 | 19,060 | 19,060 | |
| Minnesota Bible College; Rochester (Pr) | 116 | 68 | 47 | 5,550 | 5,550 | |
| Minnesota State University, Mankato; Mankato (Pu) | 10,442 | | 53 | 3,208 | 6,232 | 3,344 |
| Minnesota State University, Moorhead; Moorhead (Pu) | 7,060 | 91 | | 3,520 | 7,072 | 3,500 |
| North Central University; Minneapolis (Pr) | 1,163 | 77 | | 7,800 | 7,800 | 2,270 |
| Northwestern College; St. Paul (Pr) | 2,084 | 75 | 62 | 14,982 | 14,982 | 4,834 |
| Oak Hills Christian College; Bemidji (Pr) | 155 | 80 | 50 | 7,970 | 7,970 | 3,100 |
| Saint John's University; Collegeville (Pr) | 1,880 | 85 | 1 | 16,995 | 16,995 | 5,129 |
| Saint Mary's University of Minnesota; Winona (Pr) | 1,682 | 91 | 52 | 13,990 | 13,990 | 4,620 |
| Southwest State University; Marshall (Pu) | 4,147 | 48 | 59 | 2,790 | 6,286 | 3,588 |
| St. Cloud State University; St. Cloud (Pu) | 13,942 | 83 | 55 | 2,640 | 5,248 | 3,468 |
| St. Olaf College; Northfield (Pr) | 3,014 | 74 | 57 | 19,400 | 19,400 | 4,500 |
| University of Minnesota, Crookston; Crookston (Pu) | 2,464 | 95 | 55 | 3,800 | 3,800 | 4,100 |
| University of Minnesota, Duluth; Duluth (Pu) | 8,606 | 78 | 51 | 4,462 | 12,660 | 4,338 |
| University of Minnesota, Morris; Morris (Pu) | 1,944 | 87 | 58 | 5,033 | 10,065 | 4,102 |
| University of Minnesota, Twin Cities Campus; Minneapolis (Pu) | 31,824 | 75 | 53 | 4,401 | 12,987 | 4,914 |
| University of St. Thomas; St. Paul (Pr) | 5,469 | 82 | 53 | 17,088 | 17,088 | 5,407 |
| Winona State University; Winona (Pu) | 6,739 | 68 | | 2,800 | 6,300 | 3,600 |
| **MISSISSIPPI** | | | | | | |
| Alcorn State University; Alcorn State (Pu) | 2,398 | | 60 | 2,785 | 6,413 | 2,809 |
| Belhaven College; Jackson (Pr) | 1,467 | 70 | 64 | 10,450 | 10,450 | 4,010 |
| Blue Mountain College; Blue Mountain (Pr) | 371 | 79 | 85 | 5,630 | 5,630 | 3,004 |
| Delta State University; Cleveland (Pu) | 3,356 | | 60 | 2,696 | 6,412 | 2,990 |
| Jackson State University; Jackson (Pu) | 5,471 | 26 | 55 | 2,788 | 3,626 | 3,492 |
| Magnolia Bible College; Kosciusko (Pr) | 37 | 100 | 41 | 4,500 | 4,500 | |
| Millsaps College; Jackson (Pr) | 1,191 | 88 | 54 | 14,900 | 14,900 | 6,339 |
| Mississippi College; Clinton (Pr) | 2,440 | 98 | 58 | 9,150 | 9,150 | 4,176 |
| Mississippi State University; Mississippi State (Pu) | 13,307 | 71 | 46 | 3,117 | 7,065 | 3,990 |
| Mississippi University for Women; Columbus (Pu) | 2,660 | 79 | | 2,656 | 6,412 | 2,790 |
| Mississippi Valley State University; Itta Bena (Pu) | 2,358 | 45 | 64 | 2,746 | 6,413 | 2,825 |
| Rust College; Holly Springs (Pr) | 852 | 40 | 65 | 5,400 | 5,400 | 2,400 |
| Southeastern Baptist College; Laurel (Pr) | | 100 | | 3,520 | 3,520 | |
| Tougaloo College; Tougaloo (Pr) | 1,000 | 99 | 72 | 6,835 | 6,835 | 3,200 |
| University of Mississippi; Oxford (Pu) | 9,608 | 82 | 52 | 3,153 | 7,106 | 3,790 |
| University of Southern Mississippi; Hattiesburg (Pu) | 12,144 | 65 | 61 | 2,970 | 3,928 | 4,212 |
| **MISSOURI** | | | | | | |
| Avila College; Kansas City (Pr) | 1,123 | 97 | 70 | 12,500 | 12,500 | 5,000 |
| Baptist Bible College; Springfield (Pr) | 796 | 100 | | 3,164 | 3,164 | 3,864 |
| Central Bible College; Springfield (Pr) | 849 | 93 | 42 | 5,760 | 5,760 | 3,400 |
| Central Christian College of the Bible; Moberly (Pr) | 133 | | | 4,416 | 4,416 | 1,450 |
| Central Methodist College; Fayette (Pr) | 1,172 | 85 | 61 | 11,390 | 11,390 | 4,330 |
| Central Missouri State University; Warrensburg (Pu) | 9,150 | 82 | 53 | 3,210 | 6,360 | 4,230 |
| College of the Ozarks; Point Lookout (Pr) | 1,404 | 17 | 56 | 0 | 0 | 2,500 |
| Columbia College; Columbia (Pr) | 782 | 97 | 59 | 10,102 | 10,102 | 4,399 |
| Conception Seminary College; Conception (Pr) | 91 | 100 | 3 | 8,650 | 8,650 | 5,068 |
| Culver-Stockton College; Canton (Pr) | 821 | 77 | 55 | 10,650 | 10,650 | 4,750 |
| Deaconess College of Nursing; St. Louis (Pr) | 220 | 37 | 96 | 8,900 | 8,900 | 3,990 |
| DeVry Institute of Technology; Kansas City (Pr) | 2,708 | 70 | 23 | 8,250 | 8,250 | |
| Drury University; Springfield (Pr) | 1,438 | 88 | 56 | 10,950 | 10,950 | 4,304 |
| Evangel University; Springfield (Pr) | 1,488 | 92 | 56 | 9,250 | 9,250 | 3,790 |
| Fontbonne College; St. Louis (Pr) | 1,376 | 81 | 70 | 11,683 | 11,683 | 5,200 |
| Global University of the Assemblies of God; Springfield (Pr) | 2,674 | | 32 | 1,800 | 1,800 | |
| Hannibal-LaGrange College; Hannibal (Pr) | 1,104 | 41 | 60 | 2,100 | | |
| Jewish Hospital Coll. of Nursing and Allied Health; St. Louis (Pr) | 349 | 100 | 86 | 10,560 | 10,560 | |
| Kansas City Art Institute; Kansas City (Pr) | 527 | 77 | 51 | 17,413 | 17,410 | 5,300 |
| Kansas City College of Legal Studies; Kansas City (Pr) | 103 | | | 23,958 | 23,958 | |
| Lester L. Cox College of Nursing and Health Sciences; Springfield (Pr) | 294 | 69 | 93 | 6,288 | 6,288 | |
| Lincoln University; Jefferson City (Pu) | 3,128 | 80 | 58 | 3,314 | 6,628 | 3,790 |
| Lindenwood University; St. Charles (Pr) | 3,991 | | 54 | 10,800 | 10,800 | 5,600 |
| Maryville University of Saint Louis; St. Louis (Pr) | 2,573 | 78 | 73 | 12,880 | 12,880 | 5,600 |
| Messenger College; Joplin (Pr) | 90 | 100 | 46 | 3,750 | 3,750 | 3,100 |
| Missouri Baptist College; St. Louis (Pr) | 2,574 | 75 | 63 | 9,630 | 9,630 | 4,750 |
| Missouri Southern State College; Joplin (Pu) | 5,785 | 91 | 57 | 2,370 | 4,740 | 3,610 |
| Missouri Valley College; Marshall (Pr) | 1,641 | 84 | 41 | 11,500 | 11,500 | 5,000 |
| Missouri Western State College; St. Joseph (Pu) | 5,089 | 100 | 61 | 2,754 | 5,070 | 3,476 |
| National American University; Kansas City (Pr) | 380 | | | 9,120 | 9,120 | |
| Northwest Missouri State University; Maryville (Pu) | 5,568 | 90 | 56 | 3,210 | 5,468 | 4,150 |
| Ozark Christian College; Joplin (Pr) | 750 | 100 | 50 | 4,640 | 4,640 | 3,480 |
| Park University; Parkville (Pr) | 1,242 | 77 | 61 | 4,950 | 4,950 | 4,850 |

| Institution name; city (Public/Private) | Students | Percent Accepted | Women | Tuition In-state | Out-of-state | Room and board |
|---|---|---|---|---|---|---|
| Research College of Nursing; Kansas City (Pr) | 212 | 78% | 96% | $13,500 | $13,500 | $4,850 |
| Rockhurst University; Kansas City (Pr) | 2,034 | 88 | 58 | 13,500 | 13,500 | 4,850 |
| Saint Louis University; St. Louis (Pr) | 9,847 | 67 | 56 | 18,400 | 18,400 | 6,140 |
| Southeast Missouri State University; Cape Girardeau (Pu) | 7,758 | 48 | 58 | 3,099 | 5,799 | 4,718 |
| Southwest Baptist University; Bolivar (Pr) | 1,822 | 86 | | 9,500 | 9,500 | 3,010 |
| Southwest Missouri State University; Springfield (Pu) | 14,699 | 87 | 55 | 3,330 | 6,660 | 4,032 |
| St. Louis Christian College; Florissant (Pr) | 192 | 91 | 43 | 5,190 | 5,190 | 3,180 |
| St. Louis College of Pharmacy; St. Louis (Pr) | 826 | 79 | 65 | 13,250 | 13,250 | 5,375 |
| Stephens College; Columbia (Pr) | 634 | 82 | 93 | 15,770 | 15,770 | 5,870 |
| Truman State University; Kirksville (Pu) | 5,812 | 79 | 58 | 3,680 | 6,664 | 4,552 |
| University of Missouri–Kansas City; Kansas City (Pu) | 8,091 | 71 | 58 | 5,000 | 13,445 | 4,950 |
| University of Missouri–Rolla; Rolla (Pu) | 3,698 | 92 | 23 | 4,104 | 12,273 | 4,838 |
| University of Missouri–St. Louis; St. Louis (Pu) | 12,737 | 57 | 60 | 4,104 | 12,273 | 4,620 |
| University of Phoenix–St. Louis Campus; Maryland Heights (Pr) | 46,473 | | 56 | 7,740 | 7,740 | |
| Washington University in St. Louis; St. Louis (Pr) | 6,695 | 30 | 51 | 24,500 | 24,500 | 7,724 |
| Webster University; St. Louis (Pr) | 4,483 | 63 | 61 | 12,880 | 12,880 | 5,658 |
| Westminster College; Fulton (Pr) | 686 | 86 | 43 | 14,060 | 14,060 | 5,020 |
| William Jewell College; Liberty (Pr) | 1,153 | 87 | 59 | 13,800 | 13,800 | 4,250 |
| William Woods University; Fulton (Pr) | 1,011 | 84 | | 13,200 | 13,200 | 5,600 |
| **MONTANA** | | | | | | |
| Carroll College; Helena (Pr) | 1,251 | 89 | 60 | 12,716 | 12,716 | 5,168 |
| Montana State University–Billings; Billings (Pu) | 3,826 | 88 | 64 | 3,052 | 8,227 | 4,500 |
| Montana State University–Bozeman; Bozeman (Pu) | 10,458 | 84 | 45 | 3,079 | 9,075 | 4,650 |
| Montana State University–Northern; Havre (Pu) | 1,367 | 100 | 52 | 2,692 | 8,078 | 3,800 |
| Montana Tech of The University of Montana; Butte (Pu) | 1,978 | 97 | 45 | 3,006 | 8,530 | 4,278 |
| Rocky Mountain College; Billings (Pr) | 792 | 99 | | 12,088 | 12,088 | 4,147 |
| University of Great Falls; Great Falls (Pr) | 970 | 100 | | 10,000 | 10,000 | |
| University of Montana–Missoula; Missoula (Pu) | 10,666 | 86 | 53 | 2,136 | 7,256 | 4,525 |
| Western Montana College; Dillon (Pu) | 1,160 | 79 | 59 | 2,072 | 7,848 | 3,810 |
| **NEBRASKA** | | | | | | |
| Bellevue University; Bellevue (Pr) | 2,815 | 94 | 50 | 3,168 | 3,168 | |
| Chadron State College; Chadron (Pu) | 2,331 | 100 | 58 | 1,973 | 3,945 | 3,492 |
| Clarkson College; Omaha (Pr) | 274 | 72 | 89 | 8,670 | 8,670 | |
| College of Saint Mary; Omaha (Pr) | 947 | 99 | 97 | 13,350 | 13,350 | 4,784 |
| Concordia University; Seward (Pr) | 1,180 | 92 | 55 | 12,470 | 12,470 | 4,136 |
| Creighton University; Omaha (Pr) | 3,765 | 89 | 59 | 14,312 | 14,312 | 5,782 |
| Dana College; Blair (Pr) | 583 | 97 | 47 | 12,750 | 12,750 | 4,202 |
| Doane College; Crete (Pr) | 1,517 | 89 | 53 | 12,500 | 12,500 | 3,900 |
| Grace University; Omaha (Pr) | 510 | 47 | 55 | 7,800 | 7,800 | 3,700 |
| Hastings College; Hastings (Pr) | 1,090 | 87 | 51 | 13,116 | 13,116 | 4,188 |
| Midland Lutheran College; Fremont (Pr) | 1,025 | 95 | 59 | 13,940 | 13,940 | 3,760 |
| Nebraska Christian College; Norfolk (Pr) | 162 | 65 | 49 | 4,800 | 4,800 | 3,060 |
| Nebraska Methodist College; Omaha (Pr) | 370 | 86 | 92 | 8,550 | 8,550 | |
| Nebraska Wesleyan University; Lincoln (Pr) | 1,675 | 94 | 57 | 13,452 | 13,452 | 4,006 |
| Peru State College; Peru (Pu) | 1,454 | 63 | 55 | 1,972 | 3,945 | 3,526 |
| Union College; Lincoln (Pr) | 801 | 43 | 54 | 10,940 | 10,940 | 3,080 |
| University of Nebraska at Kearney; Kearney (Pu) | 5,502 | 93 | 55 | 2,243 | 4,193 | 3,620 |
| University of Nebraska at Omaha; Omaha (Pu) | 10,694 | 87 | 53 | 2,528 | 6,810 | |
| University of Nebraska–Lincoln; Lincoln (Pu) | 17,968 | 92 | 47 | 2,760 | 7,515 | 4,310 |
| Wayne State College; Wayne (Pu) | 2,982 | 100 | 58 | 1,973 | 3,945 | 3,330 |
| York College; York (Pr) | 497 | 56 | | 8,200 | 8,200 | 2,900 |
| **NEVADA** | | | | | | |
| Sierra Nevada College; Incline Village (Pr) | 354 | 96 | 52 | 12,000 | 12,000 | 5,600 |
| University of Nevada, Las Vegas; Las Vegas (Pu) | 17,327 | 79 | 55 | 2,340 | 9,320 | 5,800 |
| University of Nevada, Reno; Reno (Pu) | 10,134 | 91 | 55 | 2,340 | 9,320 | 5,650 |
| University of Phoenix–Nevada Campus; Las Vegas (Pr) | 46,473 | | 56 | 7,740 | 7,740 | |
| **NEW HAMPSHIRE** | | | | | | |
| Colby-Sawyer College; New London (Pr) | 845 | 84 | 65 | 18,960 | 18,960 | 7,240 |
| Daniel Webster College; Nashua (Pr) | 1,099 | 84 | 31 | 16,250 | 16,250 | 6,340 |
| Dartmouth College; Hanover (Pr) | 4,057 | 21 | 48 | 25,497 | 25,497 | 6,723 |
| Franklin Pierce College; Rindge (Pr) | 1,489 | 75 | 49 | 18,150 | 18,150 | 6,250 |
| Keene State College; Keene (Pu) | 4,297 | 77 | 58 | 4,060 | 9,370 | 5,086 |
| Magdalen College; Warner (Pr) | 75 | 67 | 47 | 6,950 | 6,950 | 5,000 |
| New England College; Henniker (Pr) | 724 | 92 | 51 | 18,382 | 18,382 | 6,538 |
| Notre Dame College; Manchester (Pr) | 685 | 88 | | 15,367 | 15,367 | 6,213 |
| Plymouth State College; Plymouth (Pu) | 3,472 | 79 | 50 | 4,060 | 9,370 | 5,206 |
| Rivier College; Nashua (Pr) | 764 | 70 | | 15,210 | 15,210 | 6,100 |
| Saint Anselm College; Manchester (Pr) | 1,985 | 73 | 56 | 18,350 | 18,350 | 7,000 |
| Southern New Hampshire University; Manchester (Pr) | 3,878 | 80 | 56 | 15,600 | 15,600 | 6,792 |
| Thomas More College of Liberal Arts; Merrimack (Pr) | 72 | 66 | 56 | 10,000 | 10,000 | 7,700 |
| University of New Hampshire; Durham (Pu) | 10,927 | 76 | 58 | 5,770 | 14,840 | 5,154 |
| University of New Hampshire at Manchester; Manchester (Pu) | 1,016 | 73 | 62 | 4,910 | 12,610 | |
| University System College for Lifelong Learning; Concord (Pu) | | | | 4,008 | 4,464 | |
| White Pines College; Chester (Pr) | 129 | 83 | 55 | 10,100 | 10,100 | 5,500 |

| Institution name; city (Public/Private) | Students | Percent Accepted | Percent Women | Tuition In-state | Tuition Out-of-state | Room and board |
|---|---|---|---|---|---|---|
| **NEW JERSEY** | | | | | | |
| Bloomfield College; Bloomfield (Pr) | 1,771 | 55% | 69% | $10,800 | $10,800 | $5,350 |
| Caldwell College; Caldwell (Pr) | 1,844 | 74 | 69 | 13,100 | 13,100 | 6,250 |
| Centenary College; Hackettstown (Pr) | 1,202 | 77 | 81 | 14,500 | 14,500 | 6,250 |
| College of New Jersey; Ewing (Pu) | 6,008 | 50 | 59 | 4,654 | 8,127 | 6,504 |
| College of Saint Elizabeth; Morristown (Pr) | 1,338 | 79 | 91 | 14,000 | 14,000 | 6,850 |
| DeVry College of Technology; North Brunswick (Pr) | 3,779 | 57 | 23 | 8,250 | 8,250 | |
| Drew University; Madison (Pr) | 1,537 | 71 | 60 | 23,472 | 23,472 | 6,782 |
| Fairleigh Dickinson University, Florham-Madison Campus; Madison (Pr) | 2,526 | 76 | 55 | 16,346 | 16,346 | 6,842 |
| Fairleigh Dickinson University, Teaneck–Hackensack Campus; Teaneck (Pr) | 4,034 | 69 | 59 | 16,346 | 16,346 | 6,842 |
| Felician College; Lodi (Pr) | 1,254 | 66 | 73 | 11,010 | 11,010 | 2,980 |
| Georgian Court College; Lakewood (Pr) | 1,621 | 94 | 91 | 12,742 | 12,742 | 4,700 |
| Kean University; Union (Pu) | 9,299 | 62 | 65 | 3,542 | 5,324 | |
| Monmouth University; West Long Branch (Pr) | 4,193 | 84 | 57 | 15,758 | 15,758 | 6,900 |
| Montclair State University; Upper Montclair (Pu) | 10,188 | 23 | 62 | 3,702 | 5,914 | 6,454 |
| New Jersey City University; Jersey City (Pu) | 6,355 | 51 | 62 | 3,540 | 6,900 | 5,600 |
| New Jersey Institute of Technology; Newark (Pu) | 5,270 | 57 | 22 | 5,758 | 10,102 | 7,300 |
| Princeton University; Princeton (Pr) | 4,663 | 12 | 47 | 25,430 | 25,430 | 7,206 |
| Rabbinical College of America; Morristown (Pr) | 250 | 100 | | 7,000 | 7,000 | |
| Ramapo College of New Jersey; Mahwah (Pu) | 4,906 | 48 | 59 | 4,166 | 7,291 | 7,044 |
| Richard Stockton College of New Jersey; Pomona (Pu) | 5,976 | 48 | | 3,600 | 5,840 | 5,516 |
| Rider University; Lawrenceville (Pr) | 4,178 | 81 | 58 | 17,180 | 17,180 | 7,080 |
| Rowan University; Glassboro (Pu) | 8,051 | 30 | 58 | 4,140 | 8,280 | 5,776 |
| Rutgers, The State Univ. of New Jersey, Camden; Camden (Pu) | 3,706 | 59 | 59 | 5,000 | 10,178 | 6,519 |
| Rutgers, The State Univ. of New Jersey, New Brunswick; New Brunswick (Pu) | 27,939 | 58 | 53 | 5,000 | 10,178 | 6,519 |
| Rutgers, The State Univ. of New Jersey, Newark; Newark (Pu) | 5,873 | 52 | 58 | 5,000 | 10,178 | 6,519 |
| Saint Peter's College; Jersey City (Pr) | 2,687 | 84 | | 15,240 | 15,240 | 6,446 |
| Seton Hall University; South Orange (Pr) | 5,403 | 76 | | 17,400 | 17,400 | 8,060 |
| Stevens Institute of Technology; Hoboken (Pr) | 1,564 | 54 | 23 | 21,900 | 21,900 | 7,492 |
| Thomas Edison State College; Trenton (Pu) | 7,975 | | 46 | | | |
| Westminster Choir College of Rider University; Princeton (Pr) | 343 | 68 | 59 | 17,180 | 17,180 | 7,380 |
| William Paterson University of New Jersey; Wayne (Pu) | 8,454 | 51 | 59 | 5,150 | 8,010 | 6,350 |
| **NEW MEXICO** | | | | | | |
| College of Santa Fe; Santa Fe (Pr) | 1,312 | 83 | 61 | 15,750 | 15,750 | 5,072 |
| College of the Southwest; Hobbs (Pr) | 568 | 55 | 69 | 4,800 | 4,800 | 3,766 |
| Eastern New Mexico University; Portales (Pu) | 2,942 | 47 | 60 | 1,386 | 6,570 | 3,690 |
| National American University; Albuquerque (Pr) | | | | 8,880 | 8,880 | |
| New Mexico Highlands University; Las Vegas (Pu) | 1,972 | 79 | | 1,992 | 8,275 | 3,970 |
| New Mexico Institute of Mining and Technology; Socorro (Pu) | 1,236 | 68 | 36 | 1,704 | 7,030 | 3,704 |
| New Mexico State University; Las Cruces (Pu) | 12,453 | 61 | 54 | 2,790 | 9,162 | 3,892 |
| St. John's College; Santa Fe (Pr) | 433 | 81 | 43 | 23,430 | 23,430 | 6,576 |
| University of New Mexico; Albuquerque (Pu) | 15,803 | 85 | | 2,258 | 10,001 | 4,860 |
| University of Phoenix–New Mexico Campus; Albuquerque (Pr) | 46,473 | | 56 | 7,740 | 7,740 | |
| **NEW YORK** | | | | | | |
| Adelphi University; Garden City (Pr) | 3,099 | 70 | 69 | 15,520 | 15,520 | 7,450 |
| Albany College of Pharmacy of Union University; Albany (Pr) | 628 | 80 | 63 | 12,650 | 12,650 | 5,100 |
| Alfred University; Alfred (Pr) | 2,085 | 76 | 52 | 9,316 | 12,844 | 7,450 |
| Audrey Cohen College; New York (Pr) | 1,087 | 68 | 83 | 14,400 | 14,400 | |
| Bard College; Annandale-on-Hudson (Pr) | 1,264 | 48 | 56 | 24,400 | 24,400 | 7,440 |
| Barnard College; New York (Pr) | 2,268 | 37 | 100 | 22,060 | 22,060 | 9,358 |
| Bernard M. Baruch College of the City University of New York; New York (Pu) | 13,025 | 23 | 57 | 3,200 | 6,800 | |
| Boricua College; New York (Pr) | 1,468 | 47 | | | | |
| Briarcliffe College; Bethpage (Pr) | 1,700 | | | | | |
| University of New York, Brooklyn (Pu) | 10,094 | | 61 | 3,200 | 6,800 | |
| Canisius College; Buffalo (Pr) | 3,349 | 83 | 53 | 15,000 | 15,990 | 6,730 |
| Cazenovia College; Cazenovia (Pr) | 000 | 100 | 73 | 13,150 | 13,150 | 6,054 |
| City College of the City University of New York; New York (Pu) | 8,232 | 74 | 52 | 3,200 | 6,800 | |
| Clarkson University; Potsdam (Pr) | 2,539 | 83 | 26 | 20,600 | 20,600 | 7,781 |
| Colgate University; Hamilton (Pr) | 2,773 | 38 | 51 | 25,565 | 25,565 | 6,330 |
| College of Aeronautics; Flushing (Pr) | 1,301 | 88 | 8 | 10,300 | 10,300 | |
| College of Insurance; New York (Pr) | 246 | 52 | 49 | 14,252 | 14,252 | 9,414 |
| College of Mount Saint Vincent; Riverdale (Pr) | 1,202 | 70 | 79 | 16,030 | 16,030 | 7,300 |
| College of New Rochelle; New Rochelle (Pr) | 5,164 | 55 | 87 | 11,900 | 11,900 | 6,250 |
| College of Saint Rose; Albany (Pr) | 2,726 | 75 | 73 | 12,870 | 12,870 | 6,550 |
| College of Staten Island of the City University of New York; Staten Island (Pu) | 9,746 | 100 | 59 | 3,200 | 6,800 | |
| Columbia College; New York (Pr) | 3,913 | 13 | 51 | 25,044 | 25,044 | 7,939 |
| Columbia University, School of General Studies; New York (Pr) | 1,117 | 45 | 55 | 24,240 | 24,240 | 9,000 |
| Concordia College; Bronxville (Pr) | 578 | 83 | 57 | | | |

| Institution name; city (Public/Private) | Students | Percent Accepted | Women | Tuition In-state | Out-of-state | Room and board |
|---|---|---|---|---|---|---|
| Cooper Union for the Advancement of Science and Art; New York (Pr) | 878 | 13% | 36% | $ 0 | $ 0 | |
| Cornell University; Ithaca (Pr) | 13,590 | 31 | 48 | 10,830 | 20,900 | $8,086 |
| Culinary Institute of America; Hyde Park (Pr) | 2,028 | 41 | 32 | 17,850 | 17,850 | |
| D'Youville College; Buffalo (Pr) | 976 | 75 | 75 | 11,580 | 11,580 | 5,720 |
| Daemen College; Amherst (Pr) | 1,704 | 74 | 77 | 12,500 | 12,500 | 6,100 |
| DeVry Institute of Technology; Long Island City (Pr) | 1,652 | 47 | 20 | 9,250 | 9,250 | |
| Dominican College; Orangeburg (Pr) | 1,564 | 86 | 72 | 13,290 | 13,290 | 7,400 |
| Dowling College; Oakdale (Pr) | 3,954 | 89 | 63 | 13,350 | 13,350 | |
| Elmira College; Elmira (Pr) | 1,440 | 78 | 70 | 21,960 | 21,960 | 7,280 |
| Eugene Lang College, New School University; New York (Pr) | 518 | 56 | 68 | 20,800 | 20,800 | 9,083 |
| Excelsior College; Albany (Pr) | 17,886 | 100 | 60 | | | |
| Fashion Institute of Technology; New York (Pu) | 10,708 | 41 | 81 | 3,104 | 7,556 | 7,535 |
| Five Towns College; Dix Hills (Pr) | 907 | 88 | 37 | 9,900 | 9,900 | 6,800 |
| Fordham University; New York (Pr) | 6,989 | 63 | 59 | 20,200 | 20,200 | 8,310 |
| Globe Institute of Technology; New York (Pr) | 662 | 90 | 41 | | | |
| Hamilton College; Clinton (Pr) | 1,767 | 39 | 52 | 26,000 | 26,000 | 6,440 |
| Hartwick College; Oneonta (Pr) | 1,419 | 89 | | 24,760 | 24,760 | 6,530 |
| Hilbert College; Hamburg (Pr) | 893 | 89 | 65 | 11,350 | 11,350 | 4,630 |
| Hobart and William Smith Colleges; Geneva (Pr) | 1,854 | 72 | 53 | 24,700 | 24,700 | 6,808 |
| Hofstra University; Hempstead (Pr) | 9,346 | 80 | 54 | 14,280 | 14,280 | 7,240 |
| Houghton College; Houghton (Pr) | 1,409 | 88 | 63 | 15,180 | 15,180 | 5,400 |
| Hunter College of the City University of New York; New York (Pu) | 15,422 | 53 | 70 | 3,200 | 6,800 | |
| Iona College; New Rochelle (Pr) | 3,422 | 78 | 52 | 15,500 | 15,500 | 8,835 |
| Ithaca College; Ithaca (Pr) | 5,906 | 70 | 56 | 19,192 | 19,192 | 8,284 |
| Jewish Theological Seminary of America; New York (Pr) | 177 | 60 | 63 | 8,820 | 8,820 | |
| John Jay College of Criminal Justice of the City University of New York; New York (Pu) | 9,493 | 73 | | 3,200 | 3,400 | |
| Juilliard School; New York (Pr) | 494 | 8 | 51 | 17,400 | 17,400 | 7,000 |
| Kehilath Yakov Rabbinical Seminary; Brooklyn (Pr) | | 75 | | 4,000 | 4,000 | |
| Keuka College; Keuka Park (Pr) | 952 | 86 | 72 | 13,490 | 13,490 | 6,750 |
| Laboratory Institute of Merchandising; New York (Pr) | 285 | 74 | 98 | 12,800 | 12,800 | |
| Le Moyne College; Syracuse (Pr) | 2,399 | 84 | 59 | 15,370 | 15,370 | 6,760 |
| Lehman College of the City University of New York; Bronx (Pu) | 7,228 | | | 3,200 | 6,800 | |
| Long Island University, Brooklyn Campus; Brooklyn (Pr) | 5,554 | 79 | 71 | 16,100 | 16,100 | 5,730 |
| Long Island University, C.W. Post Campus; Brookville (Pr) | 6,548 | 85 | | 15,340 | 15,340 | 6,790 |
| Long Island University, Southampton College; Southampton (Pr) | 2,528 | 76 | 60 | 16,100 | 16,100 | 7,990 |
| Machzikei Hadath Rabbinical College; Brooklyn (Pr) | | | | 5,200 | 5,200 | |
| Manhattan College; Riverdale (Pr) | 2,593 | 63 | 47 | 18,000 | 18,000 | 7,550 |
| Manhattan School of Music; New York (Pr) | 360 | 32 | 50 | 20,100 | 20,100 | |
| Manhattanville College; Purchase (Pr) | 1,400 | 66 | | 19,620 | 19,620 | 8,320 |
| Mannes College of Music, New School University; New York (Pr) | 134 | 16 | 63 | 18,900 | 18,900 | 9,083 |
| Marist College; Poughkeepsie (Pr) | 4,713 | 53 | 58 | 15,366 | 15,366 | 7,828 |
| Marymount College; Tarrytown (Pr) | 938 | 81 | 96 | 14,700 | 14,700 | 7,800 |
| Marymount Manhattan College; New York (Pr) | 2,497 | 65 | 79 | 13,580 | 13,580 | |
| Medaille College; Buffalo (Pr) | 1,444 | 70 | 70 | 11,700 | 11,700 | 5,500 |
| Medgar Evers College of the City University of New York; Brooklyn (Pu) | 4,700 | | 78 | 3,200 | 6,800 | |
| Mercy College; Dobbs Ferry (Pr) | 6,943 | | | 8,500 | 8,500 | 7,700 |
| Molloy College; Rockville Centre (Pr) | 1,994 | 90 | 77 | 12,500 | 12,500 | |
| Mount Saint Mary College; Newburgh (Pr) | 1,598 | 82 | | 11,550 | 11,550 | 5,980 |
| Nazareth College of Rochester; Rochester (Pr) | 1,810 | 78 | 74 | 14,230 | 14,230 | 6,470 |
| New York Institute of Technology; Old Westbury (Pr) | 5,290 | 75 | 39 | 13,700 | 13,700 | 7,310 |
| New York School of Interior Design; New York (Pr) | 686 | | 86 | 16,000 | 16,000 | |
| New York University; New York (Pr) | 18,628 | 29 | 60 | 23,090 | 23,090 | 9,226 |
| Niagara University; Niagara Falls (Pr) | 2,473 | 84 | 62 | 14,000 | 14,000 | 6,660 |
| Nyack College; Nyack (Pr) | 1,724 | 65 | 59 | 11,990 | 11,990 | 5,800 |
| Pace University, New York City Campus; New York (Pr) | 5,755 | 75 | 62 | 15,870 | 15,870 | 6,900 |
| Pace University, Pleasantville/Briarcliff; Pleasantville (Pr) | 3,394 | 82 | 57 | 15,870 | 15,870 | 6,900 |
| Parsons School of Design, New School Univ.; New York (Pr) | 2,433 | 41 | 73 | 21,550 | 21,550 | 9,083 |
| Plattsburgh State University of New York; Plattsburgh (Pu) | 5,377 | 63 | 57 | 3,400 | 8,300 | 5,116 |
| Polytechnic University, Brooklyn Campus; Brooklyn (Pr) | 1,775 | 66 | 19 | 21,120 | 21,120 | 5,250 |
| Practical Bible College; Bible School Park (Pr) | 252 | 53 | 40 | 6,340 | 6,340 | 4,300 |
| Pratt Institute; Brooklyn (Pr) | 2,922 | 43 | 51 | 19,524 | 19,524 | 7,800 |
| Purchase College, State University of New York; Purchase (Pu) | 3,941 | 33 | 56 | 3,400 | 8,300 | 5,654 |
| Queens College of the City University of New York; Flushing (Pu) | 11,566 | 49 | 63 | 3,200 | 6,800 | |
| Rabbinical Academy Mesivta Rabbi Chaim Berlin; Brooklyn (Pr) | | 100 | | 5,300 | 5,300 | |
| Rabbinical College Bobover Yeshiva B'nei Zion; Brooklyn (Pr) | | 81 | | 4,000 | 4,000 | |
| Rabbinical Seminary Adas Yereim; Brooklyn (Pr) | | | | 4,500 | 4,500 | |
| Rensselaer Polytechnic Institute; Troy (Pr) | 5,167 | 73 | 24 | 24,820 | 24,820 | 8,308 |
| Roberts Wesleyan College; Rochester (Pr) | 1,208 | 92 | 65 | 13,690 | 13,690 | 4,758 |
| Rochester Institute of Technology; Rochester (Pr) | 11,100 | 74 | 33 | 17,934 | 17,934 | 6,996 |
| Russell Sage College; Troy (Pr) | 819 | 76 | 100 | 15,920 | 15,920 | 6,038 |

| Institution name; city (Public/Private) | Students | Percent Accepted | Women | Tuition In-state | Out-of-state | Room and board |
|---|---|---|---|---|---|---|
| Sarah Lawrence College; Bronxville (Pr) | 1,139 | 38% | 75% | $26,040 | $26,040 | $8,460 |
| School of Visual Arts; New York (Pr) | 4,986 | 60 | 54 | 15,750 | 15,750 | |
| Siena College; Loudonville (Pr) | 3,306 | 67 | 52 | 15,330 | 15,330 | 6,680 |
| Skidmore College; Saratoga Springs (Pr) | 2,451 | 43 | 61 | 25,200 | 25,200 | 7,260 |
| St. Bonaventure University; St. Bonaventure (Pr) | 2,203 | 89 | 54 | 14,510 | 14,510 | 5,800 |
| St. Francis College; Brooklyn Heights (Pr) | 2,332 | 75 | 60 | 8,830 | 8,830 | |
| St. John Fisher College; Rochester (Pr) | 2,175 | 73 | 62 | 14,990 | 14,990 | 6,300 |
| St. John's University; Jamaica (Pr) | 14,229 | 80 | 57 | 15,500 | 15,500 | 8,950 |
| St. Joseph's College, New York; Brooklyn (Pr) | 1,256 | 56 | 78 | 9,030 | 9,030 | |
| St. Joseph's College, Suffolk Campus; Patchogue (Pr) | 3,115 | 75 | 78 | 9,290 | 9,290 | |
| St. Lawrence University; Canton (Pr) | 1,969 | 69 | 53 | 23,765 | 23,765 | 7,475 |
| St. Thomas Aquinas College; Sparkill (Pr) | 2,015 | 75 | | 12,500 | 12,500 | 7,350 |
| State University of New York at Albany; Albany (Pu) | 11,780 | 58 | 49 | | | |
| State University of New York at Binghamton; Binghamton (Pu) | 9,858 | 42 | 54 | 3,400 | 8,300 | 5,772 |
| State University of New York at Farmingdale; Farmingdale (Pu) | 5,045 | 69 | 44 | 3,400 | 8,300 | 6,400 |
| State University of New York at New Paltz; New Paltz (Pu) | 6,028 | 46 | 64 | 3,400 | 8,300 | 5,368 |
| State University of New York at Oswego; Oswego (Pu) | 6,999 | 57 | 54 | 3,400 | 8,300 | 6,350 |
| State University of New York College at Brockport; Brockport (Pu) | 6,751 | 54 | 58 | 3,400 | 8,300 | 5,800 |
| State University of New York College at Buffalo; Buffalo (Pu) | 9,386 | 59 | 58 | 3,400 | 8,300 | 5,170 |
| State University of New York College at Cortland; Cortland (Pu) | 5,648 | 62 | 58 | 3,400 | 8,300 | 5,750 |
| State University of New York College at Fredonia; Fredonia (Pu) | 4,743 | 60 | 59 | 3,400 | 8,300 | 5,330 |
| State University of New York College at Geneseo; Geneseo (Pu) | 5,197 | 47 | 66 | 3,400 | 8,300 | 4,890 |
| State University of New York College at Old Westbury; Old Westbury (Pu) | 2,992 | 56 | 60 | 3,400 | 8,300 | 5,345 |
| State University of New York College at Oneonta; Oneonta (Pu) | 5,341 | 71 | 60 | 3,400 | 8,300 | 5,456 |
| State University of New York College at Potsdam; Potsdam (Pu) | 3,580 | 69 | 60 | 3,400 | 8,300 | 6,100 |
| State University of New York College of Agriculture and Technology at Cobleskill; Cobleskill (Pu) | 2,301 | 34 | 46 | 3,200 | 5,000 | 6,100 |
| State University of New York College of Environmental Science and Forestry; Syracuse (Pu) | 1,166 | 57 | 39 | 3,400 | 8,300 | 8,310 |
| State University of New York College of Technology at Canton; Canton (Pu) | 2,126 | 90 | 50 | | 5,000 | 4,800 |
| State University of New York Empire State College; Saratoga Springs (Pu) | 7,672 | | 54 | 3,400 | 8,300 | |
| State University of New York Maritime College; Throggs Neck (Pu) | 623 | 76 | | 3,400 | 8,300 | 5,700 |
| Stony Brook University, State University of New York; Stony Brook (Pu) | 13,257 | 56 | 49 | 3,400 | 8,300 | 6,524 |
| Syracuse University; Syracuse (Pr) | 10,740 | 58 | 54 | 20,380 | 20,380 | 8,750 |
| Talmudical Seminary Oholei Torah; Brooklyn (Pr) | | | | 5,400 | 5,400 | |
| Touro College; New York (Pr) | 6,119 | 74 | 69 | 9,750 | 9,750 | |
| Union College; Schenectady (Pr) | 2,124 | 47 | 48 | 24,750 | 24,750 | 6,639 |
| United States Merchant Marine Academy; Kings Point (Pu) | 921 | 24 | 10 | | | |
| United States Military Academy; West Point (Pu) | 4,088 | 14 | 16 | | | |
| University at Buffalo, The State Univ. of New York; Buffalo (Pu) | 16,683 | 68 | 46 | 3,400 | 8,300 | 6,054 |
| University of Rochester; Rochester (Pr) | 4,528 | 50 | 46 | 23,150 | 23,150 | 7,740 |
| Utica College of Syracuse University; Utica (Pr) | 2,105 | 82 | 62 | 16,844 | 16,844 | 6,660 |
| Vassar College; Poughkeepsie (Pr) | 2,400 | 35 | 61 | 24,610 | 24,610 | 6,940 |
| Wadhams Hall Seminary-College; Ogdensburg (Pr) | 21 | 100 | 0 | 5,300 | 5,300 | 4,970 |
| Wagner College; Staten Island (Pr) | 1,668 | 69 | | 19,200 | 19,200 | 6,800 |
| Webb Institute; Glen Cove (Pr) | 74 | 41 | 19 | 0 | 0 | 6,250 |
| Wells College; Aurora (Pr) | 462 | 89 | 100 | 12,200 | 12,200 | 6,200 |
| Yeshiva Karlin Stolin Rabbinical Institute; Brooklyn (Pr) | 38 | | 0 | 5,200 | 5,200 | 3,200 |
| Yeshiva University; New York (Pr) | 2,529 | 79 | 44 | 16,900 | 16,900 | 5,520 |
| York College of the City University of New York; Jamaica (Pu) | 5,389 | 71 | 70 | 3,200 | 6,800 | |
| **NORTH CAROLINA** | | | | | | |
| Appalachian State University; Boone (Pu) | 12,112 | 70 | 51 | 882 | 8,252 | 3,810 |
| Barber-Scotia College; Concord (Pr) | 543 | 31 | | 12,620 | 12,620 | 3,800 |
| Barton College; Wilson (Pr) | 1,202 | 87 | 69 | 10,812 | 10,812 | 4,270 |
| Belmont Abbey College; Belmont (Pr) | 919 | 81 | 55 | 12,116 | 12,116 | 6,528 |
| Bennett College; Greensboro (Pr) | 619 | 16 | 100 | 7,325 | 7,325 | 4,034 |
| Brevard College; Brevard (Pr) | 710 | 89 | 46 | 10,660 | 10,660 | 4,820 |
| Campbell University; Buies Creek (Pr) | 2,360 | 75 | 53 | 11,350 | 11,350 | 4,122 |
| Catawba College; Salisbury (Pr) | 1,323 | 83 | 51 | 13,330 | 13,330 | 4,980 |
| Chowan College; Murfreesboro (Pr) | 773 | 71 | 45 | 11,870 | 11,870 | 4,780 |
| Davidson College; Davidson (Pr) | 1,679 | 36 | 50 | 22,873 | 22,873 | 6,571 |
| Duke University; Durham (Pr) | 6,325 | 26 | 48 | 24,890 | 24,890 | 7,387 |
| East Carolina University; Greenville (Pu) | 15,018 | 74 | 58 | 1,195 | 9,058 | 4,220 |
| Elizabeth City State University; Elizabeth City (Pu) | 1,920 | 27 | | 820 | 7,240 | 4,008 |
| Elon University; Elon College (Pr) | 3,900 | 61 | 61 | 13,556 | 13,556 | 4,660 |
| Gardner-Webb University; Boiling Springs (Pr) | 2,474 | 81 | 64 | 11,660 | 11,660 | 4,760 |
| Greensboro College; Greensboro (Pr) | 973 | 75 | 52 | 12,500 | 12,500 | 5,100 |
| Guilford College; Greensboro (Pr) | 1,246 | 78 | 53 | 16,400 | 16,400 | 5,610 |
| Heritage Bible College; Dunn (Pr) | 76 | | 25 | 3,600 | 3,600 | 2,236 |

| Institution name; city (Public/Private) | Students | Percent Accepted | Percent Women | Tuition In-state | Tuition Out-of-state | Room and board |
|---|---|---|---|---|---|---|
| High Point University; High Point (Pr) | 2,623 | 86% | 61% | $11,260 | $11,260 | $5,770 |
| John Wesley College; High Point (Pr) | 172 | 64 | 42 | 5,834 | 5,834 | |
| Johnson C. Smith University; Charlotte (Pr) | 1,585 | 33 | 60 | 9,707 | 9,707 | 4,035 |
| Lees-McRae College; Banner Elk (Pr) | 712 | 92 | 54 | 11,200 | 11,200 | 4,100 |
| Lenoir-Rhyne College; Hickory (Pr) | 1,353 | 85 | | 12,870 | 12,870 | 4,920 |
| Livingstone College; Salisbury (Pr) | 917 | 71 | 48 | 7,200 | 7,200 | 3,700 |
| Mars Hill College; Mars Hill (Pr) | 1,224 | 90 | 57 | 12,000 | 12,000 | 4,500 |
| Meredith College; Raleigh (Pr) | 2,432 | 80 | 100 | 9,840 | 9,840 | 4,260 |
| Methodist College; Fayetteville (Pr) | 2,134 | 65 | 46 | 13,300 | 13,300 | 5,080 |
| Montreat College; Montreat (Pr) | 1,064 | 86 | 57 | 11,730 | 11,730 | 4,614 |
| Mount Olive College; Mount Olive (Pr) | 1,713 | 87 | 54 | 9,100 | 9,100 | 4,000 |
| North Carolina Agricultural and Technical State University; Greensboro (Pu) | 6,850 | 93 | 53 | | | |
| North Carolina Central University; Durham (Pu) | 4,057 | 74 | 64 | 982 | 8,252 | 3,837 |
| North Carolina School of the Arts; Winston-Salem (Pu) | 692 | 42 | 41 | 1,527 | 10,155 | 4,686 |
| North Carolina State University; Raleigh (Pu) | 21,990 | 65 | 42 | 1,860 | 11,026 | 5,274 |
| North Carolina Wesleyan College; Rocky Mount (Pr) | 1,956 | 91 | 56 | | | |
| Peace College; Raleigh (Pr) | 604 | 83 | 100 | 9,724 | 9,724 | 5,200 |
| Pfeiffer University; Misenheimer (Pr) | 985 | 84 | 57 | 12,066 | 12,066 | 4,734 |
| Piedmont Baptist College; Winston-Salem (Pr) | 302 | 59 | 40 | 5,490 | 5,490 | 3,700 |
| Queens College; Charlotte (Pr) | 1,156 | 77 | 76 | 11,360 | 11,360 | 5,890 |
| Roanoke Bible College; Elizabeth City (Pr) | 159 | 62 | 43 | 5,280 | 5,280 | 3,860 |
| Saint Augustine's College; Raleigh (Pr) | 1,465 | 45 | | 5,650 | 5,650 | 4,960 |
| Salem College; Winston-Salem (Pr) | 898 | 81 | 98 | 13,730 | 13,730 | 8,240 |
| Shaw University; Raleigh (Pr) | 2,394 | 67 | 66 | 6,712 | 6,712 | 4,648 |
| St. Andrews Presbyterian College; Laurinburg (Pr) | 638 | 81 | 60 | 14,015 | 14,015 | 5,300 |
| University of North Carolina at Asheville; Asheville (Pu) | 3,187 | 64 | 57 | 822 | 7,668 | 4,300 |
| University of North Carolina at Chapel Hill; Chapel Hill (Pu) | 15,608 | 37 | 61 | 1,860 | 11,026 | 5,630 |
| University of North Carolina at Charlotte; Charlotte (Pu) | 14,388 | 71 | 54 | 1,132 | 8,402 | 4,354 |
| University of North Carolina at Greensboro; Greensboro (Pu) | 10,121 | 75 | 67 | 1,108 | 9,562 | 5,422 |
| University of North Carolina at Pembroke; Pembroke (Pu) | 3,076 | 86 | 63 | 982 | 8,252 | 3,680 |
| University of North Carolina at Wilmington; Wilmington (Pu) | 9,138 | 61 | 60 | 1,102 | 8,452 | 4,862 |
| Wake Forest University; Winston-Salem (Pr) | 3,946 | 49 | 51 | 22,410 | 22,410 | 6,340 |
| Warren Wilson College; Asheville (Pr) | 728 | 81 | 63 | 14,125 | 14,125 | 4,644 |
| Western Carolina University; Cullowhee (Pu) | 5,611 | 87 | 52 | 982 | 8,252 | 3,284 |
| Wingate University; Wingate (Pr) | 1,179 | 83 | 49 | 12,300 | 12,300 | 5,200 |
| Winston-Salem State University; Winston-Salem (Pu) | 2,704 | 67 | 67 | 822 | 7,240 | 3,628 |
| **NORTH DAKOTA** | | | | | | |
| Dickinson State University; Dickinson (Pu) | 2,012 | 100 | 58 | 1,982 | 5,292 | 2,716 |
| Jamestown College; Jamestown (Pr) | 1,195 | 99 | 58 | 7,550 | 7,550 | 3,300 |
| Mayville State University; Mayville (Pu) | 776 | 96 | 55 | 1,982 | 5,292 | 3,026 |
| Minot State University; Minot (Pu) | 2,907 | 97 | 63 | 2,144 | 5,724 | 3,080 |
| North Dakota State University; Fargo (Pu) | 8,965 | 78 | 43 | 2,604 | 6,953 | 3,542 |
| Trinity Bible College; Ellendale (Pr) | 360 | 55 | 49 | 5,700 | 5,700 | 3,420 |
| University of Mary; Bismarck (Pr) | 1,908 | | | | | 3,600 |
| University of North Dakota; Grand Forks (Pu) | 9,122 | 59 | 48 | 3,088 | 7,438 | 3,614 |
| Valley City State University; Valley City (Pu) | 1,090 | 94 | 55 | 1,982 | 5,292 | 2,892 |
| **OHIO** | | | | | | |
| Antioch College; Yellow Springs (Pr) | 618 | 80 | 66 | | | |
| Art Academy of Cincinnati; Cincinnati (Pr) | 230 | 83 | 58 | 12,200 | 12,200 | |
| Ashland University; Ashland (Pr) | 2,819 | 90 | 57 | 15,814 | 15,814 | 5,862 |
| Baldwin-Wallace College; Berea (Pr) | 4,043 | 82 | 62 | 15,340 | 15,340 | 5,460 |
| Bluffton College; Bluffton (Pr) | 1,000 | 86 | 54 | 14,056 | 14,056 | 5,122 |
| Bowling Green State University; Bowling Green (Pu) | 15,494 | 88 | 57 | 4,330 | 10,228 | 5,768 |
| Bryant and Stratton College; Cleveland (Pr) | 205 | 93 | 40 | 9,472 | 9,472 | |
| Capital University; Columbus (Pr) | 2,738 | 81 | 63 | 16,880 | 16,880 | 5,170 |
| Case Western Reserve University; Cleveland (Pr) | 3,434 | 71 | 39 | 20,100 | 20,100 | 5,815 |
| Cedarville University; Cedarville (Pr) | 2,849 | 74 | 54 | 11,424 | 11,424 | 4,929 |
| Central State University; Wilberforce (Pu) | 1,101 | 34 | 54 | 1,992 | 6,249 | 5,031 |
| Cincinnati Bible College and Seminary; Cincinnati (Pr) | 639 | 97 | 44 | 7,200 | 7,200 | 4,340 |
| Circleville Bible College; Circleville (Pr) | 216 | 65 | 45 | 7,040 | 7,040 | 4,580 |
| Cleveland College of Jewish Studies; Beachwood (Pr) | 17 | 75 | 88 | 6,300 | 6,300 | |
| Cleveland Institute of Music; Cleveland (Pr) | 221 | 29 | | 18,675 | 18,675 | 5,210 |
| Cleveland State University; Cleveland (Pu) | 10,132 | 86 | 55 | 4,110 | 8,076 | 5,200 |
| College of Mount St. Joseph; Cincinnati (Pr) | 2,056 | 85 | 71 | 13,500 | 13,500 | 5,100 |
| College of Wooster; Wooster (Pr) | 1,837 | 74 | 53 | 21,520 | 21,520 | 5,680 |
| Columbus College of Art and Design; Columbus (Pr) | 1,546 | 70 | 51 | 14,520 | 14,520 | 6,100 |
| David N. Myers College; Cleveland (Pr) | 1,158 | 65 | 70 | 8,760 | 8,760 | |
| Defiance College; Defiance (Pr) | 868 | 78 | 55 | 14,850 | 14,850 | 4,480 |
| Denison University; Granville (Pr) | 2,108 | 68 | 57 | 21,710 | 21,710 | 6,300 |
| DeVry Institute of Technology; Columbus (Pr) | 3,570 | 62 | 25 | 8,250 | 8,250 | |
| Franciscan University of Steubenville; Steubenville (Pr) | 1,701 | 90 | 60 | 12,690 | 12,690 | 5,070 |
| Franklin University; Columbus (Pr) | 4,323 | 100 | | 5,983 | 5,983 | |
| God's Bible School and College; Cincinnati (Pr) | 238 | | | 3,780 | 3,780 | 2,800 |
| Heidelberg College; Tiffin (Pr) | 1,367 | 87 | 53 | 16,998 | 16,998 | 5,974 |

| Institution name; city (Public/Private) | Students | Percent Accepted | Women | Tuition In-state | Out-of-state | Room and board |
|---|---|---|---|---|---|---|
| Hiram College; Hiram (Pr) | 1,199 | 87% | 57% | $17,870 | $17,870 | $6,254 |
| John Carroll University; University Heights (Pr) | 3,525 | 87 | 54 | 17,487 | 17,487 | 6,312 |
| Kent State University; Kent (Pu) | 17,580 | 92 | 60 | 4,234 | 9,410 | 4,764 |
| Kenyon College; Gambier (Pr) | 1,599 | 65 | 55 | 25,370 | 25,370 | 4,370 |
| Lake Erie College; Painesville (Pr) | 560 | 83 | 77 | 15,500 | 15,500 | 5,420 |
| Lourdes College; Sylvania (Pr) | 1,270 | 66 | 81 | 9,024 | 9,024 | |
| Malone College; Canton (Pr) | 1,945 | 84 | 62 | 12,800 | 12,800 | 5,450 |
| Marietta College; Marietta (Pr) | 1,212 | 94 | 52 | 18,010 | 18,010 | 5,196 |
| Miami University; Oxford (Pu) | 14,914 | 69 | 55 | 5,358 | 12,398 | 5,590 |
| Mount Carmel College of Nursing; Columbus (Pr) | 335 | | | 8,700 | 8,700 | |
| Mount Union College; Alliance (Pr) | 2,334 | 84 | 57 | 14,720 | 14,720 | 4,560 |
| Mount Vernon Nazarene College; Mount Vernon (Pr) | 1,888 | 88 | 58 | 11,468 | 11,468 | 4,203 |
| Muskingum College; New Concord (Pr) | 1,562 | 85 | 52 | 12,250 | 12,250 | 5,100 |
| Notre Dame College of Ohio; South Euclid (Pr) | 728 | 55 | | 13,686 | 13,686 | 5,416 |
| Oberlin College; Oberlin (Pr) | 2,932 | 43 | 59 | 25,355 | 25,355 | 6,364 |
| Ohio Dominican College; Columbus (Pr) | 2,085 | 67 | 69 | 10,710 | 10,710 | 5,220 |
| Ohio Northern University; Ada (Pr) | 2,668 | 95 | 50 | 21,435 | 21,435 | 5,265 |
| Ohio State University; Columbus (Pu) | 35,749 | 72 | 49 | 4,383 | 12,732 | 5,807 |
| Ohio State University at Lima; Lima (Pu) | 1,482 | 72 | 63 | 3,351 | 11,700 | |
| Ohio State University–Mansfield Campus; Mansfield (Pu) | 1,583 | 94 | | 3,351 | | |
| Ohio State University–Newark Campus; Newark (Pu) | | 97 | | 3,351 | 3,633 | |
| Ohio University; Athens (Pu) | 16,511 | 77 | 55 | 5,085 | 10,704 | 5,922 |
| Ohio University–Chillicothe; Chillicothe (Pu) | 1,638 | 94 | | 3,033 | 7,782 | |
| Ohio University–Eastern; St. Clairsville (Pu) | 931 | | 68 | 3,033 | 7,782 | |
| Ohio University–Lancaster; Lancaster (Pu) | 1,409 | | | 3,033 | 7,782 | |
| Ohio University–Zanesville; Zanesville (Pu) | 1,188 | 100 | 68 | 3,033 | 7,782 | |
| Ohio Wesleyan University; Delaware (Pr) | 1,880 | 81 | 52 | 21,880 | 21,880 | 6,610 |
| Otterbein College; Westerville (Pr) | 2,525 | 85 | 64 | 16,911 | 16,911 | 5,289 |
| Pontifical College Josephinum; Columbus (Pr) | 50 | 86 | | 8,276 | 8,276 | 5,136 |
| Shawnee State University; Portsmouth (Pu) | 3,280 | 100 | 63 | 2,601 | 5,004 | 4,588 |
| Tiffin University; Tiffin (Pr) | 1,299 | 80 | 52 | 11,130 | 11,130 | 5,100 |
| Union Institute; Cincinnati (Pr) | 690 | 83 | 66 | 6,528 | 6,528 | |
| University of Akron; Akron (Pu) | 18,583 | 90 | 54 | 3,980 | 10,182 | 5,350 |
| University of Cincinnati; Cincinnati (Pu) | 20,039 | 82 | 49 | 4,467 | 12,744 | 6,399 |
| University of Dayton; Dayton (Pr) | 7,122 | 79 | 51 | 15,550 | 15,550 | 5,080 |
| University of Findlay; Findlay (Pr) | 3,459 | 81 | 57 | 15,830 | 15,830 | 5,060 |
| University of Phoenix–Ohio Campus; Independence (Pr) | 46,473 | | 56 | 7,740 | 7,740 | |
| University of Rio Grande; Rio Grande (Pr) | 1,934 | 100 | | 8,421 | 9,090 | 5,169 |
| University of Toledo; Toledo (Pu) | 15,950 | 99 | 52 | 3,828 | 10,579 | 4,798 |
| Urbana University; Urbana (Pr) | 1,310 | 73 | 51 | 11,388 | 11,388 | 5,000 |
| Ursuline College; Pepper Pike (Pr) | 1,016 | 94 | 93 | 13,500 | 13,500 | 4,560 |
| Walsh University; North Canton (Pr) | 1,404 | 82 | 60 | 12,050 | 12,050 | 5,600 |
| Wilberforce University; Wilberforce (Pr) | 908 | 22 | 59 | 8,800 | 8,800 | 5,060 |
| Wilmington College; Wilmington (Pr) | 1,262 | 81 | 54 | 14,230 | 14,230 | 5,220 |
| Wittenberg University; Springfield (Pr) | 2,274 | 88 | 57 | | | |
| Wright State University; Dayton (Pu) | 11,344 | 91 | 57 | 4,335 | 8,670 | 4,700 |
| Xavier University; Cincinnati (Pr) | 4,019 | 88 | 59 | 15,680 | 15,680 | 6,940 |
| Youngstown State University; Youngstown (Pu) | 10,619 | 62 | 53 | 3,048 | 4,992 | 4,800 |
| **OKLAHOMA** | | | | | | |
| American Bible College and Seminary; Oklahoma City (Pr) | 292 | | 45 | 2,800 | 2,800 | |
| Cameron University; Lawton (Pu) | 4,458 | 91 | 56 | 2,030 | 4,820 | 2,746 |
| East Central University; Ada (Pu) | 3,427 | | 60 | 1,919 | 4,439 | 1,167 |
| Hillsdale Free Will Baptist College; Moore (Pr) | 256 | | 37 | 5,400 | 5,400 | 4,040 |
| Langston University; Langston (Pu) | 3,354 | 18 | 58 | 1,176 | 3,192 | 2,964 |
| Mid-America Bible College; Oklahoma City (Pr) | 613 | 100 | 48 | 5,694 | 5,694 | 5,266 |
| Northeastern State University; Tahlequah (Pu) | 7,215 | 74 | 60 | 1,980 | 4,501 | 2,724 |
| ~~Oklahoma Baptist University; Shawnee (Pr)~~ | ~~1,746~~ | ~~100~~ | ~~60~~ | ~~1,970~~ | ~~1,910~~ | ~~▮▮▮▮~~ |
| Oklahoma Baptist University; Shawnee (Pr) | 1,993 | 86 | 56 | 8,800 | 8,800 | 3,510 |
| Oklahoma Christian University; Oklahoma City (Pr) | 1,735 | 90 | | 9,700 | 9,700 | |
| Oklahoma City University; Oklahoma City (Pr) | 2,062 | 82 | 58 | 9,880 | 9,880 | 9,300 |
| Oklahoma Panhandle State University; Goodwell (Pu) | 1,178 | 100 | 53 | 1,470 | 2,355 | 2,580 |
| Oklahoma State University; Stillwater (Pu) | 16,659 | 92 | 48 | 1,830 | 5,910 | 4,716 |
| Oklahoma Wesleyan College; Bartlesville (Pr) | 731 | | | 9,200 | 9,200 | 4,100 |
| Oral Roberts University; Tulsa (Pr) | 3,064 | 81 | 58 | 11,900 | 11,900 | 5,228 |
| Rogers State University; Claremore (Pu) | 2,620 | 100 | 64 | 1,619 | 3,635 | 2,063 |
| Southeastern Oklahoma State University; Durant (Pu) | 3,438 | 77 | 54 | 1,176 | 3,192 | 1,246 |
| Southwestern College of Christian Ministries; Bethany (Pr) | 128 | | 45 | 4,440 | 4,440 | 3,200 |
| Southwestern Oklahoma State University; Weatherford (Pu) | 4,256 | 93 | | 1,920 | 4,440 | 2,506 |
| St. Gregory's University; Shawnee (Pr) | 754 | 77 | 53 | 8,344 | 8,344 | 4,338 |
| University of Central Oklahoma; Edmond (Pu) | 11,752 | 95 | 56 | 1,470 | 3,990 | 2,905 |
| University of Oklahoma; Norman (Pu) | 17,707 | 86 | 48 | 1,890 | 6,225 | 4,610 |
| University of Phoenix–Oklahoma City; Oklahoma City (Pr) | 46,473 | | 56 | 7,740 | 7,740 | |
| University of Phoenix–Tulsa; Tulsa (Pr) | 46,473 | | 56 | 7,740 | 7,740 | |
| University of Science and Arts of Oklahoma; Chickasha (Pu) | 1,409 | 83 | 64 | 1,470 | 3,990 | 2,390 |
| University of Tulsa; Tulsa (Pr) | 2,874 | 75 | 52 | 13,730 | 13,730 | 4,810 |

| Institution name; city (Public/Private) | Students | Percent Accepted | Percent Women | Tuition In-state | Tuition Out-of-state | Room and board |
|---|---|---|---|---|---|---|
| **OREGON** | | | | | | |
| Art Institute of Portland; Portland (Pr) | 668 | | 55% | $12,780 | $12,780 | |
| Cascade College; Portland (Pr) | 321 | 100% | 53 | 9,000 | 9,000 | $4,800 |
| Concordia University; Portland (Pr) | 924 | 67 | 64 | 15,500 | 15,500 | 3,820 |
| Eastern Oregon University; La Grande (Pu) | 2,549 | 92 | 58 | | | |
| Eugene Bible College; Eugene (Pr) | 210 | 60 | 47 | 5,646 | 5,646 | 3,723 |
| George Fox University; Newberg (Pr) | 1,709 | 90 | 59 | 17,300 | 17,300 | 5,550 |
| Lewis & Clark College; Portland (Pr) | 1,709 | 68 | 60 | 21,330 | 21,330 | 6,100 |
| Linfield College; McMinnville (Pr) | 1,534 | 92 | 56 | 18,450 | 18,450 | 5,350 |
| Multnomah Bible College and Biblical Seminary; Portland (Pr) | 590 | 80 | 46 | 8,860 | 8,860 | 3,880 |
| Northwest Christian College; Eugene (Pr) | 463 | 100 | | 13,905 | 13,905 | 5,207 |
| Oregon College of Art and Craft; Portland (Pr) | 95 | 67 | 73 | 11,520 | 11,520 | |
| Oregon Institute of Technology; Klamath Falls (Pu) | 2,831 | 77 | 43 | 2,592 | 11,211 | 4,898 |
| Oregon State University; Corvallis (Pu) | 13,776 | 87 | 46 | 2,694 | 12,144 | 5,508 |
| Pacific Northwest College of Art; Portland (Pr) | 317 | 86 | 61 | 12,420 | 12,420 | |
| Pacific University; Forest Grove (Pr) | 1,094 | 86 | 61 | 17,300 | 17,300 | 4,903 |
| Portland State University; Portland (Pu) | 13,625 | 86 | 56 | 2,694 | 11,460 | 6,150 |
| Reed College; Portland (Pr) | 1,366 | 74 | 53 | 24,820 | 24,820 | 6,820 |
| Southern Oregon University; Ashland (Pu) | 4,879 | 96 | 57 | 2,520 | 9,666 | 5,649 |
| University of Oregon; Eugene (Pu) | 14,076 | 90 | 53 | 2,694 | 12,714 | 5,564 |
| University of Phoenix–Oregon Campus; Portland (Pr) | 46,473 | | 56 | 7,740 | 7,740 | |
| University of Portland; Portland (Pr) | 2,512 | 88 | 57 | 17,860 | 17,860 | 5,398 |
| Warner Pacific College; Portland (Pr) | 634 | 79 | 64 | 14,410 | 14,410 | 4,400 |
| Western Baptist College; Salem (Pr) | 696 | 72 | 58 | 13,490 | 13,490 | 4,940 |
| Western Oregon University; Monmouth (Pu) | 4,201 | 93 | 60 | 2,520 | 9,537 | 5,043 |
| Willamette University; Salem (Pr) | 1,749 | 90 | 55 | 22,700 | 22,700 | 5,930 |
| **PENNSYLVANIA** | | | | | | |
| Albright College; Reading (Pr) | 1,728 | 76 | 57 | 19,760 | 19,760 | 6,040 |
| Allegheny College; Meadville (Pr) | 1,904 | 76 | 52 | 21,290 | 21,290 | 5,100 |
| Alvernia College; Reading (Pr) | 1,506 | 76 | 66 | 12,950 | 12,950 | 5,840 |
| Arcadia University; Glenside (Pr) | 1,628 | 76 | 74 | 17,550 | 17,550 | 7,740 |
| Baptist Bible College of Pennsylvania; Clarks Summit (Pr) | 592 | 79 | 59 | | | |
| Bloomsburg University of Pennsylvania; Bloomsburg (Pu) | 6,843 | 61 | 61 | 3,792 | 9,480 | 4,032 |
| Bryn Athyn College of the New Church; Bryn Athyn (Pr) | 129 | 100 | 58 | 5,100 | 5,100 | 4,581 |
| Bryn Mawr College; Bryn Mawr (Pr) | 1,358 | 61 | 99 | 23,520 | 23,520 | 8,340 |
| Bucknell University; Lewisburg (Pr) | 3,426 | 42 | 48 | 23,698 | 23,698 | 5,596 |
| Cabrini College; Radnor (Pr) | 1,654 | 87 | 66 | 16,150 | 16,150 | 7,560 |
| California University of Pennsylvania; California (Pu) | 5,004 | 78 | 53 | 3,792 | 9,480 | 4,662 |
| Carlow College; Pittsburgh (Pr) | 1,631 | 70 | 93 | 12,950 | 12,950 | 5,280 |
| Carnegie Mellon University; Pittsburgh (Pr) | 5,224 | 36 | 37 | 22,830 | 22,830 | 7,028 |
| Cedar Crest College; Allentown (Pr) | 1,554 | 73 | 95 | 17,790 | 17,790 | 6,465 |
| Chatham College; Pittsburgh (Pr) | 587 | 87 | 99 | 18,080 | 18,080 | 6,246 |
| Chestnut Hill College; Philadelphia (Pr) | 936 | 75 | 85 | 16,200 | 16,200 | 6,834 |
| Cheyney University of Pennsylvania; Cheyney (Pu) | 1,132 | 82 | 56 | 3,792 | 9,480 | 4,983 |
| Clarion University of Pennsylvania; Clarion (Pu) | 5,687 | 86 | 61 | 3,792 | 5,688 | 2,420 |
| College Misericordia; Dallas (Pr) | 1,640 | 84 | 73 | 15,190 | 15,190 | 6,470 |
| Curtis Institute of Music; Philadelphia (Pr) | 148 | 7 | | 0 | 0 | |
| Delaware Valley College; Doylestown (Pr) | 1,838 | 82 | 51 | 16,148 | 16,148 | 6,340 |
| DeSales University; Center Valley (Pr) | 1,869 | 72 | 57 | 14,500 | 14,500 | 6,090 |
| Dickinson College; Carlisle (Pr) | 2,115 | 64 | 61 | 24,050 | 24,050 | 6,450 |
| Duquesne University; Pittsburgh (Pr) | 5,499 | 84 | 58 | 15,169 | 15,169 | 6,504 |
| Eastern College; St. Davids (Pr) | 1,400 | 84 | | 15,150 | 15,150 | 6,490 |
| Edinboro University of Pennsylvania; Edinboro (Pu) | 6,486 | 80 | 57 | 3,792 | 5,688 | 4,104 |
| Elizabethtown College; Elizabethtown (Pr) | 1,825 | 77 | 65 | 19,100 | 19,100 | 5,600 |
| Franklin and Marshall College; Lancaster (Pr) | 1,892 | 56 | 50 | 24,816 | 24,816 | 5,994 |
| Gannon University; Erie (Pr) | 2,470 | 90 | 59 | 13,670 | 13,670 | 5,670 |
| Geneva College; Beaver Falls (Pr) | 2,047 | 78 | 56 | | | |
| Gettysburg College; Gettysburg (Pr) | 2,218 | 68 | 52 | 24,761 | 24,761 | 5,956 |
| Gratz College; Melrose Park (Pr) | 11 | 75 | 64 | 7,560 | 7,560 | |
| Grove City College; Grove City (Pr) | 2,326 | 51 | 50 | 7,710 | 7,710 | 4,206 |
| Gwynedd-Mercy College; Gwynedd Valley (Pr) | 1,665 | 79 | 75 | | | |
| Haverford College; Haverford (Pr) | 1,135 | 32 | 52 | 24,706 | 24,706 | 7,910 |
| Holy Family College; Philadelphia (Pr) | 1,882 | 89 | 77 | 12,300 | 12,300 | |
| Immaculata College; Immaculata (Pr) | 2,587 | 86 | 86 | 13,650 | 13,650 | 6,800 |
| Indiana University of Pennsylvania; Indiana (Pu) | 11,735 | 58 | 56 | 3,792 | 9,480 | 3,966 |
| Juniata College; Huntingdon (Pr) | 1,291 | 81 | 57 | 18,940 | 18,940 | 5,290 |
| King's College; Wilkes-Barre (Pr) | 2,090 | 86 | 52 | 16,000 | 16,000 | 6,890 |
| Kutztown University of Pennsylvania; Kutztown (Pu) | 7,068 | 73 | 60 | 3,792 | 9,480 | 4,522 |
| La Roche College; Pittsburgh (Pr) | 1,627 | 86 | 63 | 11,600 | 11,600 | 6,474 |
| La Salle University; Philadelphia (Pr) | 3,961 | 72 | 57 | 18,020 | 18,020 | 7,676 |
| Lancaster Bible College; Lancaster (Pr) | 686 | 82 | 54 | 9,600 | 9,600 | 4,550 |
| Lebanon Valley College; Annville (Pr) | 1,853 | 73 | 60 | 17,870 | 17,870 | 5,680 |
| Lehigh University; Bethlehem (Pr) | 4,722 | 46 | 41 | 24,000 | 24,000 | 6,440 |
| Lincoln University; Lincoln University (Pu) | 1,454 | 53 | 59 | 5,621 | 8,787 | 5,256 |
| Lock Haven University of Pennsylvania; Lock Haven (Pu) | 3,996 | 77 | 57 | 3,792 | 7,480 | 4,264 |

| Institution name; city (public/private) | Students | Percent Accepted | Women | Tuition In-state | Out-of-state | Room and board |
|---|---|---|---|---|---|---|
| Lycoming College; Williamsport (Pr) | 1,402 | 70% | 56% | $18,240 | $18,240 | $5,145 |
| Mansfield University of Pennsylvania; Mansfield (Pu) | 2,890 | 78 | 59 | 3,792 | 9,480 | 4,198 |
| Marywood University; Scranton (Pr) | 1,609 | 81 | 73 | 15,840 | 15,840 | 6,900 |
| MCP Hahnemann University; Philadelphia (Pr) | 588 | 69 | 65 | 11,030 | 11,030 | 8,526 |
| Mercyhurst College; Erie (Pr) | 3,058 | 80 | 60 | 13,290 | 13,290 | 5,364 |
| Messiah College; Grantham (Pr) | 2,797 | 78 | 61 | 15,830 | 15,830 | 5,770 |
| Millersville University of Pennsylvania; Millersville (Pu) | 6,497 | 71 | 58 | 3,792 | 9,480 | 4,900 |
| Moore College of Art and Design; Philadelphia (Pr) | 530 | 57 | 100 | 15,475 | 15,475 | 6,100 |
| Moravian College; Bethlehem (Pr) | | 69 | | 19,070 | 19,070 | 6,120 |
| Mount Aloysius College; Cresson (Pr) | 1,297 | 53 | 71 | 10,780 | 10,780 | 4,830 |
| Muhlenberg College; Allentown (Pr) | 2,470 | 44 | 58 | 20,865 | 20,865 | 5,650 |
| Neumann College; Aston (Pr) | 1,445 | 87 | 67 | 13,750 | 13,750 | 6,760 |
| Peirce College; Philadelphia (Pr) | 2,334 | 64 | 81 | 8,700 | 8,700 | |
| Pennsylvania College of Technology; Williamsport (Pu) | 5,320 | 57 | 33 | 6,672 | 8,007 | |
| Pennsylvania State University Abington College; Abington (Pu) | 3,048 | 81 | 50 | 6,436 | 9,998 | |
| Pennsylvania State University Altoona College; Altoona (Pu) | 3,749 | 84 | 50 | 6,436 | 9,998 | 4,910 |
| Pennsylvania State University, The Behrend College; Erie (Pu) | 3,606 | 73 | 38 | 6,546 | 12,560 | 4,910 |
| Pennsylvania State University Berks Campus of the Berks–Lehigh Valley College; Reading (Pu) | 2,186 | 85 | 39 | 6,436 | 9,998 | 4,910 |
| Pennsylvania State University Harrisburg Campus of the Capital College; Middletown (Pu) | 1,865 | 100 | 52 | 6,546 | 12,560 | 4,910 |
| Pennsylvania State University Lehigh Valley Campus of the Berks-Lehigh Valley College; Fogelsville (Pu) | 665 | 83 | 38 | 6,340 | 9,812 | |
| Pennsylvania State University Schuylkill Campus of the Capital College; Schuylkill Haven (Pu) | 1,096 | 89 | 54 | 6,340 | 9,812 | 4,910 |
| Pennsylvania State University University Park Campus; State College (Pu) | 34,406 | 48 | 47 | 6,546 | 14,088 | 4,910 |
| Philadelphia Biblical University; Langhorne (Pr) | 1,069 | 67 | 53 | 10,070 | 10,070 | 5,073 |
| Philadelphia University; Philadelphia (Pr) | 2,809 | 79 | 65 | 15,412 | 15,412 | 6,882 |
| Point Park College; Pittsburgh (Pr) | 2,417 | 81 | 54 | 12,596 | 12,596 | 5,718 |
| Robert Morris College; Moon Township (Pr) | 3,814 | 72 | 49 | 8,970 | 8,970 | 6,320 |
| Rosemont College; Rosemont (Pr) | 892 | 97 | 90 | 14,580 | 14,580 | 7,030 |
| Saint Francis University; Loretto (Pr) | 1,174 | 87 | | 16,519 | 16,519 | 7,075 |
| Saint Joseph's University; Philadelphia (Pr) | 4,517 | 60 | 56 | 19,600 | 19,600 | 7,856 |
| Saint Vincent College; Latrobe (Pr) | 1,206 | 84 | 49 | 15,531 | 15,531 | 5,168 |
| Seton Hill College; Greensburg (Pr) | 1,141 | 79 | 83 | 15,225 | 15,225 | 5,200 |
| Shippensburg University of Pennsylvania; Shippensburg (Pu) | 5,990 | 65 | 54 | 3,792 | 9,480 | 4,274 |
| Slippery Rock University of Pennsylvania; Slippery Rock (Pu) | 6,294 | 83 | 57 | 3,792 | 9,480 | 3,988 |
| St. Charles Borromeo Seminary, Overbrook; Wynnewood (Pr) | 298 | 100 | 55 | 8,450 | 8,450 | 5,800 |
| Susquehanna University; Selinsgrove (Pr) | 1,829 | 75 | 58 | 20,140 | 20,140 | 5,770 |
| Swarthmore College; Swarthmore (Pr) | 1,428 | 24 | 53 | 24,950 | 24,950 | 7,804 |
| Temple University; Philadelphia (Pu) | 18,394 | 71 | 58 | 6,648 | 12,022 | 6,482 |
| Thiel College; Greenville (Pr) | 1,039 | 78 | 53 | 10,732 | 10,732 | 5,674 |
| University of Pennsylvania; Philadelphia (Pr) | 9,687 | 23 | 48 | 22,682 | 22,682 | 7,826 |
| University of Phoenix–Philadelphia Campus; Wayne (Pr) | 46,473 | | 56 | 7,740 | 7,740 | |
| University of Phoenix–Pittsburgh Campus; Pittsburgh (Pr) | 46,473 | | 56 | 7,740 | 7,740 | |
| University of Pittsburgh; Pittsburgh (Pu) | 17,424 | 62 | 53 | 6,422 | 14,104 | 5,936 |
| University of Pittsburgh at Bradford; Bradford (Pu) | 1,204 | 82 | 59 | 6,422 | 14,104 | 5,150 |
| University of Pittsburgh at Greensburg; Greensburg (Pu) | 1,587 | 80 | 55 | 6,422 | 14,104 | 5,540 |
| University of Pittsburgh at Johnstown; Johnstown (Pu) | 3,031 | 83 | 55 | 6,422 | 14,104 | 5,400 |
| University of Scranton; Scranton (Pr) | 3,970 | 84 | 58 | 18,460 | 18,460 | 8,112 |
| University of the Arts; Philadelphia (Pr) | 1,919 | 54 | 53 | 17,250 | 17,250 | |
| University of the Sciences in Philadelphia; Philadelphia (Pr) | 2,042 | 82 | 67 | 15,580 | 15,580 | 7,600 |
| Ursinus College; Collegeville (Pr) | 1,290 | 72 | 54 | 23,460 | 23,460 | 6,140 |
| Villanova University; Villanova (Pr) | 7,069 | 52 | 50 | 22,410 | 22,410 | 8,050 |
| Washington & Jefferson College; Washington (Pr) | 1,241 | 79 | 49 | 19,275 | 19,275 | 5,160 |
| Waynesburg College; Waynesburg (Pr) | 1,395 | 81 | | 11,610 | 11,610 | 4,188 |
| West Chester University of Pennsylvania; West Chester (Pu) | 10,320 | 57 | 60 | 3,792 | 9,480 | 4,650 |
| Widener University; Chester (Pr) | 2,235 | 76 | 45 | 17,950 | 17,950 | 7,325 |
| Wilkes University; Wilkes-Barre (Pr) | 1,762 | 84 | 48 | 16,388 | 16,388 | 7,429 |
| Wilson College; Chambersburg (Pr) | 610 | 90 | 79 | 13,570 | 13,570 | 6,310 |
| York College of Pennsylvania; York (Pr) | 5,073 | 67 | 59 | 6,600 | 6,600 | 4,860 |
| **RHODE ISLAND** | | | | | | |
| Brown University; Providence (Pr) | 6,029 | 16 | 53 | 25,600 | 25,600 | 7,346 |
| Bryant College; Smithfield (Pr) | 2,901 | 73 | 41 | 17,330 | 17,330 | 7,250 |
| Johnson & Wales University; Providence (Pr) | 8,533 | 82 | 48 | 13,275 | 13,275 | 5,970 |
| Providence College; Providence (Pr) | 4,405 | 57 | 58 | 18,440 | 18,440 | 7,625 |
| Rhode Island College; Providence (Pu) | 6,917 | 72 | 68 | | | |
| Rhode Island School of Design; Providence (Pr) | 1,829 | 35 | 61 | 21,860 | 21,860 | 6,600 |
| Roger Williams University; Bristol (Pr) | 3,676 | 86 | 51 | 17,300 | 17,300 | 8,200 |
| Salve Regina University; Newport (Pr) | 1,835 | 67 | 69 | 17,200 | 17,200 | 7,750 |
| University of Rhode Island; Kingston (Pu) | 10,647 | 75 | 56 | 3,464 | 11,906 | 6,688 |
| **SOUTH CAROLINA** | | | | | | |
| Allen University; Columbia (Pr) | 466 | 81 | 60 | 4,650 | 4,650 | 4,210 |
| Anderson College; Anderson (Pr) | 1,398 | 78 | 62 | 9,720 | 9,720 | 4,605 |

| Institution name; city (public/private) | Students | Percent | | Tuition | | Room |
| | | Accepted | Women | In-state | Out-of-state | and board |
| --- | --- | --- | --- | --- | --- | --- |
| Charleston Southern University; Charleston (Pr) | 2,315 | 93% | 59% | $11,346 | $11,346 | $4,362 |
| Citadel, The Military College of South Carolina; Charleston (Pu) | 1,995 | 81 | 7 | 3,404 | 9,426 | 4,350 |
| Claflin University; Orangeburg (Pr) | 1,315 | 56 | | 7,538 | 7,538 | 4,116 |
| Clemson University; Clemson (Pu) | 14,066 | 64 | 45 | 3,590 | 9,784 | 4,325 |
| Coastal Carolina University; Conway (Pu) | 4,405 | 72 | 56 | 3,500 | 9,810 | 5,240 |
| Coker College; Hartsville (Pr) | 445 | 88 | 64 | 15,072 | 15,072 | 4,820 |
| College of Charleston; Charleston (Pu) | 9,750 | 67 | 63 | 3,630 | 7,910 | 4,260 |
| Columbia College; Columbia (Pr) | 1,205 | 79 | | 14,760 | 14,760 | 4,990 |
| Columbia International University; Columbia (Pr) | 549 | 61 | 55 | 8,980 | 8,980 | 4,520 |
| Converse College; Spartanburg (Pr) | 725 | 81 | 100 | 15,840 | 15,840 | 4,830 |
| Erskine College; Due West (Pr) | 502 | 78 | 61 | 14,697 | 14,697 | 4,987 |
| Francis Marion University; Florence (Pu) | 2,795 | 77 | 61 | 3,600 | 7,200 | 3,720 |
| Furman University; Greenville (Pr) | 2,789 | 60 | 56 | 18,768 | 18,768 | 5,144 |
| Lander University; Greenwood (Pu) | 2,436 | 81 | 63 | 3,880 | 7,776 | 3,950 |
| Limestone College; Gaffney (Pr) | 1,967 | 70 | 56 | 10,100 | 10,100 | 4,800 |
| Morris College; Sumter (Pr) | 940 | 48 | 66 | 5,894 | 5,894 | 3,051 |
| Newberry College; Newberry (Pr) | 727 | 86 | 46 | 14,282 | 14,282 | 4,230 |
| North Greenville College; Tigerville (Pr) | 1,282 | 66 | 46 | 7,800 | 7,800 | 4,570 |
| Presbyterian College; Clinton (Pr) | 1,147 | 82 | 55 | 15,870 | 15,870 | 5,156 |
| South Carolina State University; Orangeburg (Pu) | 3,639 | 59 | | 3,724 | 7,262 | |
| Southern Methodist College; Orangeburg (Pr) | 82 | | | 3,600 | 3,600 | 3,630 |
| Southern Wesleyan University; Central (Pr) | 1,724 | 66 | 62 | 11,704 | 11,704 | 4,290 |
| University of South Carolina; Columbia (Pu) | 15,266 | 69 | 55 | 3,768 | 10,054 | 4,588 |
| University of South Carolina Aiken; Aiken (Pu) | 3,148 | 64 | 66 | 3,458 | 7,984 | 4,090 |
| University of South Carolina Spartanburg; Spartanburg (Pu) | 3,585 | 62 | 65 | 3,494 | 8,386 | 4,040 |
| Voorhees College; Denmark (Pr) | 677 | 80 | | 6,460 | 6,460 | 3,516 |
| Winthrop University; Rock Hill (Pu) | 4,650 | 72 | 69 | 4,262 | 7,680 | 4,150 |
| Wofford College; Spartanburg (Pr) | 1,087 | 83 | 47 | 17,030 | 17,030 | 5,235 |
| **SOUTH DAKOTA** | | | | | | |
| Augustana College; Sioux Falls (Pr) | 1,728 | 83 | 64 | 14,592 | 14,592 | 4,260 |
| Black Hills State University; Spearfish (Pu) | 3,549 | 66 | 62 | 1,932 | 6,148 | 2,883 |
| Colorado Technical Univ. Sioux Falls Campus; Sioux Falls (Pr) | 773 | 97 | 56 | 7,875 | 7,875 | |
| Dakota State University; Madison (Pu) | 1,632 | 91 | 49 | 3,805 | 8,021 | 2,840 |
| Dakota Wesleyan University; Mitchell (Pr) | 676 | 87 | 61 | 10,611 | 10,611 | 3,640 |
| Huron University; Huron (Pr) | 598 | 39 | 52 | 9,000 | 9,000 | 2,950 |
| Mount Marty College; Yankton (Pr) | 1,044 | 93 | 67 | 9,710 | 9,710 | 4,272 |
| National American University; Rapid City (Pr) | 1,005 | | 47 | 9,600 | 9,600 | 3,675 |
| Northern State University; Aberdeen (Pu) | 2,861 | 91 | 60 | 1,812 | 5,764 | 2,663 |
| Oglala Lakota College; Kyle (Pu) | | | | 1,560 | 1,560 | |
| Presentation College; Aberdeen (Pr) | 462 | 100 | | 7,878 | 7,878 | 4,150 |
| Sinte Gleska University; Rosebud (Pr) | 907 | | | 1,632 | 1,632 | |
| South Dakota School of Mines and Technology; Rapid City (Pu) | 2,023 | 95 | 30 | 1,993 | 6,149 | 3,224 |
| South Dakota State University; Brookings (Pu) | 7,504 | 94 | 51 | 1,932 | 6,148 | 2,922 |
| University of Sioux Falls; Sioux Falls (Pr) | 1,070 | 94 | 56 | 12,100 | 12,100 | 3,790 |
| University of South Dakota; Vermillion (Pu) | 5,148 | | 57 | 1,933 | 6,149 | 3,037 |
| **TENNESSEE** | | | | | | |
| American Baptist College of American Baptist Theological Seminary; Nashville (Pr) | 106 | 100 | | 3,000 | 3,000 | |
| Aquinas College; Nashville (Pr) | 435 | 9 | | 7,800 | 7,800 | |
| Austin Peay State University; Clarksville (Pu) | 6,658 | 48 | 59 | 2,222 | 7,850 | 3,350 |
| Belmont University; Nashville (Pr) | 2,507 | 74 | 62 | 11,990 | 11,990 | 5,437 |
| Bethel College; McKenzie (Pr) | 776 | 62 | 50 | 8,175 | 8,175 | 4,732 |
| Bryan College; Dayton (Pr) | 562 | 37 | | 11,750 | 11,750 | 4,200 |
| Carson-Newman College; Jefferson City (Pr) | 1,994 | 90 | 58 | 11,240 | 11,240 | 3,980 |
| Christian Brothers University; Memphis (Pr) | 1,710 | 82 | 55 | 13,930 | 13,930 | 4,470 |
| Crichton College; Memphis (Pr) | 973 | 63 | 62 | 8,304 | 8,304 | |
| East Tennessee State University; Johnson City (Pu) | 9,125 | 79 | 57 | 2,222 | 7,850 | 3,818 |
| Fisk University; Nashville (Pr) | 839 | 41 | 70 | 8,740 | 8,740 | 5,030 |
| Free Will Baptist Bible College; Nashville (Pr) | 318 | | | 6,688 | 6,688 | 3,788 |
| Freed-Hardeman University; Henderson (Pr) | 1,438 | 71 | 54 | 7,696 | 7,696 | 4,620 |
| Johnson Bible College; Knoxville (Pr) | 548 | 85 | 48 | 4,740 | 4,740 | 3,370 |
| King College; Bristol (Pr) | 602 | 64 | 55 | 11,800 | 11,800 | 4,250 |
| Lambuth University; Jackson (Pr) | 979 | 72 | 57 | 8,498 | 8,498 | 4,482 |
| Lane College; Jackson (Pr) | 702 | 55 | 49 | 5,600 | 5,600 | 3,800 |
| Lee University; Cleveland (Pr) | 3,236 | 91 | 57 | 6,700 | 6,700 | 4,020 |
| LeMoyne-Owen College; Memphis (Pr) | 1,013 | 100 | 66 | 7,500 | 7,500 | 4,200 |
| Lincoln Memorial University; Harrogate (Pr) | 886 | 77 | 69 | 9,600 | 9,600 | 3,900 |
| Lipscomb University; Nashville (Pr) | 2,307 | 83 | 56 | 9,900 | 9,900 | 5,080 |
| Martin Methodist College; Pulaski (Pr) | 582 | 97 | 62 | 9,900 | 9,900 | 3,600 |
| Maryville College; Maryville (Pr) | 982 | 81 | 56 | 16,224 | 16,224 | 5,310 |
| Memphis College of Art; Memphis (Pr) | 255 | 83 | 52 | 12,540 | 12,540 | 5,200 |
| Middle Tennessee State University; Murfreesboro (Pu) | 17,247 | 79 | 54 | 2,222 | 7,850 | 3,436 |
| Milligan College; Milligan College (Pr) | 790 | 69 | 60 | 11,900 | 11,900 | 4,200 |
| Rhodes College; Memphis (Pr) | 1,537 | 70 | 57 | 19,303 | 19,303 | 5,671 |
| Southern Adventist University; Collegedale (Pr) | 1,939 | 72 | 54 | 10,700 | 10,700 | 3,886 |

| Institution name; city (public/private) | Students | Percent Accepted | Percent Women | Tuition In-state | Tuition Out-of-state | Room and board |
|---|---|---|---|---|---|---|
| Tennessee State University; Nashville (Pu) | 7,142 | 54% | 62% | $ 2,672 | $ 8,300 | $3,600 |
| Tennessee Technological University; Cookeville (Pu) | 6,876 | 94 | 47 | 2,704 | 8,070 | 3,650 |
| Tennessee Temple University; Chattanooga (Pr) | 757 | 99 | | 5,500 | 5,500 | 5,120 |
| Tennessee Wesleyan College; Athens (Pr) | 795 | 29 | 63 | 7,900 | 7,900 | 4,150 |
| Trevecca Nazarene University; Nashville (Pr) | 1,021 | 82 | 59 | 10,848 | 10,848 | 4,904 |
| Tusculum College; Greeneville (Pr) | 1,377 | 88 | 55 | 13,100 | 13,100 | 4,300 |
| Union University; Jackson (Pr) | 1,971 | 83 | 61 | 11,550 | 11,550 | 3,830 |
| University of Memphis; Memphis (Pu) | 15,296 | 71 | 58 | 2,999 | 8,785 | 3,908 |
| University of Tennessee; Knoxville (Pu) | 20,009 | 62 | 51 | 2,812 | 9,366 | 4,490 |
| University of Tennessee at Chattanooga; Chattanooga (Pu) | 6,993 | 56 | 57 | 2,834 | 8,514 | |
| University of Tennessee at Martin; Martin (Pu) | 5,478 | 61 | 57 | 2,830 | 8,510 | 3,800 |
| University of the South; Sewanee (Pr) | 1,385 | 68 | 53 | 19,940 | 19,940 | 5,610 |
| Vanderbilt University; Nashville (Pr) | 5,935 | 55 | 53 | 24,080 | 24,080 | 5,364 |
| **TEXAS** | | | | | | |
| Abilene Christian University; Abilene (Pr) | 4,231 | 72 | 55 | 10,410 | 10,410 | 4,420 |
| Angelo State University; San Angelo (Pu) | 5,899 | 76 | 55 | 1,200 | 7,650 | 4,140 |
| Arlington Baptist College; Arlington (Pr) | 220 | 100 | 37 | 3,360 | 3,360 | |
| Austin College; Sherman (Pr) | 1,196 | 84 | 55 | 15,094 | 15,094 | 5,891 |
| Baylor University; Waco (Pr) | 11,806 | 84 | 58 | 10,650 | 10,650 | 5,238 |
| Concordia University at Austin; Austin (Pr) | 785 | 64 | 55 | 12,500 | 12,500 | 5,460 |
| Criswell College; Dallas (Pr) | 336 | | | | | |
| Dallas Baptist University; Dallas (Pr) | 3,190 | 43 | 62 | 9,150 | 9,150 | 3,774 |
| Dallas Christian College; Dallas (Pr) | 254 | 64 | 47 | 6,080 | 6,080 | 3,900 |
| DeVry Institute of Technology; Irving (Pr) | 3,462 | 64 | 29 | 8,250 | 8,250 | |
| East Texas Baptist University; Marshall (Pr) | 1,402 | 92 | 55 | 7,650 | 7,650 | 3,126 |
| Hardin-Simmons University; Abilene (Pr) | 1,910 | 45 | 54 | 9,300 | 9,300 | 3,405 |
| Houston Baptist University; Houston (Pr) | 1,867 | 70 | 70 | 10,362 | 10,362 | 4,080 |
| Howard Payne University; Brownwood (Pr) | 1,480 | 80 | 47 | 8,400 | 8,400 | 3,820 |
| Lamar University; Beaumont (Pu) | 7,215 | 74 | 59 | 2,180 | 7,700 | 3,591 |
| LeTourneau University; Longview (Pr) | 2,708 | 86 | 47 | 12,670 | 12,670 | 5,420 |
| Lubbock Christian University; Lubbock (Pr) | 1,511 | 77 | 58 | 9,198 | 9,198 | 3,588 |
| McMurry University; Abilene (Pr) | 1,344 | 70 | 50 | 9,120 | 9,120 | 4,379 |
| Midwestern State University; Wichita Falls (Pu) | 5,151 | | 57 | 2,516 | 8,966 | 4,024 |
| Northwood University, Texas Campus; Cedar Hill (Pr) | 1,014 | 68 | 56 | 11,763 | 11,763 | 5,160 |
| Our Lady of the Lake Univ. of San Antonio; San Antonio (Pr) | 2,233 | 65 | 77 | 11,708 | 11,708 | 4,466 |
| Paul Quinn College; Dallas (Pr) | | 72 | | 5,250 | 5,250 | 3,800 |
| Prairie View A&M University; Prairie View (Pu) | 5,285 | 97 | 56 | 1,500 | 3,060 | |
| Rice University; Houston (Pr) | 2,658 | 23 | 47 | 15,950 | 15,950 | 6,850 |
| Sam Houston State University; Huntsville (Pu) | 10,882 | 81 | 57 | 1,536 | 6,696 | 3,672 |
| Schreiner University; Kerrville (Pr) | 762 | 72 | 60 | 11,540 | 11,540 | 6,520 |
| Southern Methodist University; Dallas (Pr) | 5,662 | 82 | 55 | 17,406 | 17,406 | 7,177 |
| Southwest Texas State University; San Marcos (Pu) | 19,412 | 64 | 55 | 1,200 | 7,680 | 4,564 |
| Southwestern Adventist University; Keene (Pr) | 1,156 | 62 | 57 | 9,410 | 9,410 | 4,550 |
| Southwestern Assemblies of God University; Waxahachie (Pr) | 1,666 | | | 5,880 | 5,880 | 3,990 |
| Southwestern Christian College; Terrell (Pr) | | 90 | | 4,350 | 4,350 | |
| Southwestern University; Georgetown (Pr) | 1,312 | 59 | 58 | 15,750 | 15,750 | 6,318 |
| St. Edward's University; Austin (Pr) | 3,105 | 78 | 55 | 11,896 | 11,896 | 5,000 |
| Stephen F. Austin State University; Nacogdoches (Pu) | 10,046 | 71 | 57 | 960 | 6,120 | 4,370 |
| Sul Ross State University; Alpine (Pu) | 1,463 | 99 | | 1,200 | 7,650 | 3,690 |
| Tarleton State University; Stephenville (Pu) | 6,345 | 71 | 54 | 2,846 | 8,966 | 3,802 |
| Texas A&M International University; Laredo (Pu) | 2,239 | 92 | 64 | 1,860 | 8,310 | |
| Texas A&M University; College Station (Pu) | 36,229 | 66 | 49 | 2,400 | 8,850 | 5,164 |
| Texas A&M University at Galveston; Galveston (Pu) | 1,363 | 90 | 51 | 1,200 | 7,650 | 3,977 |
| Texas A&M University–Commerce; Commerce (Pu) | 4,314 | 60 | 57 | 2,711 | 9,166 | 4,550 |
| Texas A&M University–Corpus Christi; Corpus Christi (Pu) | 5,329 | 87 | 60 | | | |
| Texas Christian University; Fort Worth (Pr) | 6,675 | 76 | 59 | 11,700 | 11,700 | 4,300 |
| Texas Lutheran University; Seguin (Pr) | 1,500 | 90 | 55 | 12,000 | 12,000 | 4,000 |
| Texas Southern University; Houston (Pu) | 8,124 | 49 | 58 | 960 | 6,120 | 4,016 |
| Texas Tech University; Lubbock (Pu) | 20,518 | 70 | 46 | 2,400 | 8,850 | 5,079 |
| Texas Wesleyan University; Fort Worth (Pr) | 2,015 | 79 | 65 | 9,260 | 9,260 | 8,081 |
| Trinity University; San Antonio (Pr) | 2,330 | 65 | 52 | 15,660 | 15,660 | 6,330 |
| University of Dallas; Irving (Pr) | 1,200 | 76 | | 14,928 | 14,928 | 5,600 |
| University of Houston; Houston (Pu) | 24,350 | 81 | 53 | 960 | 6,120 | 4,513 |
| University of Houston–Downtown; Houston (Pu) | 8,932 | 100 | 59 | 1,200 | 7,650 | |
| University of Mary Hardin-Baylor; Belton (Pr) | 2,401 | 60 | 62 | 8,700 | 8,700 | 3,931 |
| University of North Texas; Denton (Pu) | 21,059 | 75 | 55 | 2,280 | 8,748 | 4,202 |
| University of St. Thomas; Houston (Pr) | 1,904 | 78 | 65 | 12,300 | 12,300 | 5,550 |
| University of Texas at Arlington; Arlington (Pu) | 15,449 | 86 | 53 | | 7,080 | 3,795 |
| University of Texas at Austin; Austin (Pu) | 38,162 | 62 | 50 | 2,400 | 8,850 | 5,113 |
| University of Texas at Dallas; Richardson (Pu) | 6,560 | 49 | 47 | 960 | 6,120 | 5,799 |
| University of Texas at El Paso; El Paso (Pu) | 12,955 | 93 | 54 | 1,776 | 7,152 | 5,165 |
| University of Texas at San Antonio; San Antonio (Pu) | 16,026 | 99 | 55 | 2,520 | 8,850 | 5,904 |
| University of Texas at Tyler; Tyler (Pu) | 2,602 | 45 | 66 | 960 | 6,120 | |
| University of Texas of the Permian Basin; Odessa (Pu) | 1,656 | 89 | 64 | 2,070 | 8,520 | 3,950 |
| University of Texas–Pan American; Edinburg (Pu) | 11,187 | 76 | 58 | 1,860 | 8,210 | 5,531 |

| Institution name; city (public/private) | Students | Percent Accepted | Women | Tuition In-state | Out-of-state | Room and board |
|---|---|---|---|---|---|---|
| University of the Incarnate Word; San Antonio (Pr) | 3,003 | 94% | 68% | $12,470 | $12,470 | $5,010 |
| Wayland Baptist University; Plainview (Pr) | 4,637 | 99 | 42 | 7,500 | 7,500 | 3,121 |
| West Texas A&M University; Canyon (Pu) | 5,623 | 72 | 55 | 1,500 | 6,660 | 3,474 |
| Wiley College; Marshall (Pr) | 552 | 71 | 56 | 4,816 | 4,816 | 3,732 |
| **UTAH** | | | | | | |
| Brigham Young University; Provo (Pr) | 29,688 | 64 | 51 | 2,940 | 2,940 | 4,650 |
| Southern Utah University; Cedar City (Pu) | 5,729 | 84 | 56 | 1,612 | 5,984 | 2,866 |
| University of Phoenix–Utah Campus; Salt Lake City (Pr) | 46,473 | | 56 | 7,740 | 7,740 | |
| University of Utah; Salt Lake City (Pu) | 20,963 | 94 | 46 | 2,371 | 8,302 | 4,669 |
| Utah State University; Logan (Pu) | 17,903 | 98 | 52 | 1,947 | 6,816 | 4,040 |
| Weber State University; Ogden (Pu) | 15,854 | 100 | 52 | 1,670 | 5,846 | 3,878 |
| Western Governors University; Salt Lake City (Pr) | 357 | | | 3,650 | 3,650 | |
| Westminster College; Salt Lake City (Pr) | 1,878 | 86 | 63 | 13,450 | 13,450 | 4,570 |
| **VERMONT** | | | | | | |
| Bennington College; Bennington (Pr) | 545 | 70 | 69 | 23,250 | 23,250 | 6,150 |
| Castleton State College; Castleton (Pu) | 1,507 | 85 | 58 | 4,236 | 9,924 | 5,346 |
| Champlain College; Burlington (Pr) | 2,530 | 77 | 55 | 10,905 | 10,905 | 7,965 |
| College of St. Joseph; Rutland (Pr) | 371 | 95 | 66 | 11,500 | 11,500 | 6,200 |
| Goddard College; Plainfield (Pr) | 335 | 75 | 63 | 17,840 | 17,840 | 1,333 |
| Green Mountain College; Poultney (Pr) | 672 | 65 | 49 | 17,000 | 17,000 | 5,300 |
| Johnson State College; Johnson (Pu) | 1,284 | 83 | 61 | 4,236 | 9,924 | 5,346 |
| Lyndon State College; Lyndonville (Pu) | 1,153 | 93 | 45 | 4,236 | 9,924 | 5,346 |
| Marlboro College; Marlboro (Pr) | 321 | 70 | 59 | 18,800 | 18,800 | 6,750 |
| Middlebury College; Middlebury (Pr) | 2,278 | 25 | 51 | | | |
| Norwich University; Northfield (Pr) | 2,180 | 89 | 39 | 15,450 | 15,450 | 5,890 |
| Saint Michael's College; Colchester (Pr) | 2,073 | 71 | 55 | 18,615 | 18,615 | 7,253 |
| Southern Vermont College; Bennington (Pr) | 479 | 75 | 64 | | | |
| Sterling College; Craftsbury Common (Pr) | 74 | 77 | 49 | 13,230 | 13,230 | 5,670 |
| University of Vermont; Burlington (Pu) | 8,618 | 80 | 56 | 7,692 | 19,236 | 5,806 |
| Vermont Technical College; Randolph Center (Pu) | 1,145 | 71 | 31 | 5,130 | 10,368 | 5,346 |
| **VIRGINIA** | | | | | | |
| American Military University; Manassas Park (Pr) | 802 | 95 | 14 | 9,000 | 9,000 | |
| Art Institute of Washington; Arlington (Pr) | | | | 13,392 | 13,392 | |
| Averett University; Danville (Pr) | 1,707 | 82 | 60 | 13,740 | 13,740 | 4,797 |
| Bridgewater College; Bridgewater (Pr) | 1,223 | 92 | 57 | 14,970 | 14,970 | 6,970 |
| Christendom College; Front Royal (Pr) | 286 | 82 | 57 | 11,300 | 11,300 | 4,570 |
| Christopher Newport University; Newport News (Pu) | 5,101 | 59 | 61 | 1,888 | 7,910 | 5,350 |
| College of William and Mary; Williamsburg (Pu) | 5,585 | 41 | 57 | 4,687 | 16,934 | 5,096 |
| Eastern Mennonite University; Harrisonburg (Pr) | 1,086 | 83 | 58 | 14,150 | 14,150 | 5,120 |
| Emory & Henry College; Emory (Pr) | 975 | 74 | 53 | 12,950 | 12,950 | 5,322 |
| Ferrum College; Ferrum (Pr) | 920 | 81 | 41 | 11,900 | 11,900 | 5,250 |
| George Mason University; Fairfax (Pu) | 15,185 | 61 | 56 | 2,376 | 11,220 | 5,240 |
| Hampden-Sydney College; Hampden-Sydney (Pr) | 976 | 72 | 0 | 17,189 | 17,189 | 6,110 |
| Hampton University; Hampton (Pr) | 4,891 | 48 | 61 | | | |
| Hollins University; Roanoke (Pr) | 796 | 81 | 100 | 16,960 | 16,960 | 6,415 |
| James Madison University; Harrisonburg (Pu) | 14,280 | 64 | 58 | 4,000 | 9,850 | 5,290 |
| Liberty University; Lynchburg (Pr) | 5,403 | 60 | 51 | 8,550 | 8,550 | 4,800 |
| Longwood College; Farmville (Pu) | 3,387 | 77 | 65 | 1,995 | 7,466 | 4,820 |
| Lynchburg College; Lynchburg (Pr) | 1,748 | 82 | | 17,980 | 17,980 | 4,400 |
| Mary Baldwin College; Staunton (Pr) | 1,388 | 93 | 95 | 15,135 | 15,135 | 7,450 |
| Mary Washington College; Fredericksburg (Pu) | 4,103 | 56 | 69 | 1,550 | 7,980 | 5,448 |
| Marymount University; Arlington (Pr) | 2,004 | 78 | 72 | 14,300 | 14,300 | 6,350 |
| Norfolk State University; Norfolk (Pu) | 5,890 | 82 | 64 | 1,326 | 6,526 | 5,267 |
| Old Dominion University; Norfolk (Pu) | 12,786 | 70 | 57 | 3,780 | 11,910 | 5,232 |
| Radford University; Radford (Pu) | 7,622 | 76 | 60 | 1,629 | 7,542 | 4,938 |
| Randolph-Macon College; Ashland (Pr) | 1,171 | 72 | 51 | 17,850 | 17,850 | 4,205 |
| Randolph-Macon Woman's College; Lynchburg (Pr) | 748 | 82 | 100 | 17,300 | 17,300 | 7,160 |
| Roanoke College; Salem (Pr) | 1,677 | 81 | 61 | 17,320 | 17,320 | 5,722 |
| Saint Paul's College; Lawrenceville (Pr) | 531 | 88 | | 7,920 | 7,920 | 4,568 |
| Shenandoah University; Winchester (Pr) | 1,339 | 97 | 57 | 16,300 | 16,300 | 6,000 |
| Sweet Briar College; Sweet Briar (Pr) | 749 | 89 | 95 | 17,174 | 17,174 | 7,016 |
| University of Richmond; Richmond (Pr) | 2,910 | 42 | 51 | 20,140 | 20,140 | 4,530 |
| University of Virginia; Charlottesville (Pu) | 13,712 | 39 | 54 | 3,046 | 16,295 | 4,767 |
| University of Virginia's College at Wise; Wise (Pu) | 1,447 | 73 | 56 | 3,330 | 9,824 | 5,080 |
| Virginia Commonwealth University; Richmond (Pu) | 16,505 | 76 | 60 | 2,492 | 12,185 | 4,955 |
| Virginia Intermont College; Bristol (Pr) | 835 | 69 | 75 | 11,430 | 11,430 | 5,200 |
| Virginia Military Institute; Lexington (Pu) | 1,300 | 66 | 5 | 2,924 | 13,210 | 4,564 |
| Virginia Polytechnic Institute and State Univ.; Blacksburg (Pu) | 21,419 | 63 | 41 | 2,792 | 11,280 | 3,954 |
| Virginia State University; Petersburg (Pu) | 3,473 | 89 | 56 | 1,588 | 7,560 | 5,310 |
| Virginia Union University; Richmond (Pr) | 1,500 | | | 9,580 | 9,580 | 4,250 |
| Virginia Wesleyan College; Norfolk (Pr) | 1,421 | 95 | 68 | 15,035 | 15,035 | 5,750 |
| Washington and Lee University; Lexington (Pr) | 1,736 | 35 | 46 | 17,790 | 17,790 | 5,690 |
| **WASHINGTON** | | | | | | |
| Central Washington University; Ellensburg (Pu) | 7,604 | 85 | 54 | 2,838 | 10,089 | 4,821 |
| Cornish College of the Arts; Seattle (Pr) | 659 | 79 | 61 | 14,900 | 14,900 | |

| Institution name; city (public/private) | Students | Percent Accepted | Women | Tuition In-state | Out-of-state | Room and board |
|---|---|---|---|---|---|---|
| Eastern Washington University; Cheney (Pu) | 7,149 | 89% | 58% | $ 2,790 | $ 9,594 | $4,558 |
| Evergreen State College; Olympia (Pu) | 3,901 | 87 | 57 | 2,856 | 10,110 | 5,244 |
| Gonzaga University; Spokane (Pr) | 2,853 | 82 | 55 | 17,460 | 17,460 | 5,500 |
| Henry Cogswell College; Everett (Pr) | 249 | 100 | 16 | 11,280 | 11,280 | |
| Heritage College; Toppenish (Pr) | 754 | 9 | 80 | 5,400 | 5,400 | |
| Northwest College; Kirkland (Pr) | 1,096 | 53 | 56 | 10,550 | 10,550 | 5,490 |
| Pacific Lutheran University; Tacoma (Pr) | 3,246 | 82 | 61 | 16,800 | 16,800 | 5,300 |
| Saint Martin's College; Lacey (Pr) | 1,197 | 92 | 52 | 14,750 | 14,750 | 4,768 |
| Seattle Pacific University; Seattle (Pr) | 2,692 | 91 | 66 | 15,381 | 15,381 | 5,895 |
| Seattle University; Seattle (Pr) | 3,241 | 80 | 60 | 17,010 | 17,010 | 6,075 |
| Trinity Lutheran College; Issaquah (Pr) | 129 | 77 | 63 | 7,325 | 7,325 | 4,600 |
| University of Phoenix–Washington Campus; Seattle (Pr) | 46,473 | | 56 | 7,740 | 7,740 | |
| University of Puget Sound; Tacoma (Pr) | 2,621 | 72 | 61 | 21,270 | 21,270 | 5,510 |
| University of Washington; Seattle (Pu) | 25,982 | 78 | 52 | 3,761 | 12,453 | 6,060 |
| Walla Walla College; College Place (Pr) | 1,580 | 83 | 49 | 14,427 | 14,427 | 4,176 |
| Washington State University; Pullman (Pu) | 17,469 | 84 | 50 | 3,351 | 10,267 | 4,826 |
| Western Washington University; Bellingham (Pu) | 11,050 | 86 | 56 | 2,832 | 10,086 | 5,100 |
| Whitman College; Walla Walla (Pr) | 1,424 | 50 | 58 | 21,550 | 21,550 | 6,090 |
| Whitworth College; Spokane (Pr) | 1,807 | 90 | 60 | 16,700 | 16,700 | 5,500 |
| **WEST VIRGINIA** | | | | | | |
| Appalachian Bible College; Bradley (Pr) | 302 | | 51 | 5,112 | 5,112 | 3,310 |
| Bethany College; Bethany (Pr) | 750 | 71 | 46 | 19,141 | 19,141 | 6,909 |
| Bluefield State College; Bluefield (Pu) | 2,648 | 99 | 60 | 2,288 | 5,544 | |
| Concord College; Athens (Pu) | 2,955 | 98 | 57 | 2,620 | 5,762 | 4,150 |
| Davis & Elkins College; Elkins (Pr) | 658 | 94 | 56 | 12,624 | 12,624 | 5,570 |
| Fairmont State College; Fairmont (Pu) | 6,496 | 100 | 56 | 2,316 | 5,396 | 4,084 |
| Glenville State College; Glenville (Pu) | 2,198 | 100 | 59 | 2,376 | 5,664 | 3,900 |
| Marshall University; Huntington (Pu) | 9,624 | 74 | 55 | 2,160 | 6,364 | 4,772 |
| Mountain State University; Beckley (Pr) | 2,076 | 50 | | 3,360 | 3,360 | 1,824 |
| Ohio Valley College; Vienna (Pr) | 417 | 45 | 53 | 7,424 | 7,424 | 4,210 |
| Salem International University; Salem (Pr) | 564 | 83 | 44 | 13,040 | 13,040 | 4,430 |
| Shepherd College; Shepherdstown (Pu) | 4,603 | 94 | 58 | 2,508 | 5,938 | 4,112 |
| University of Charleston; Charleston (Pr) | 1,219 | 72 | 64 | 13,200 | 13,200 | 4,637 |
| West Liberty State College; West Liberty (Pu) | 2,606 | 96 | 55 | 2,420 | 5,860 | 3,340 |
| West Virginia State College; Institute (Pu) | 4,823 | 100 | 59 | 2,464 | 5,666 | 3,800 |
| West Virginia University; Morgantown (Pu) | 15,463 | 94 | 46 | 2,836 | 8,362 | 5,152 |
| West Virginia Univ. Institute of Technology; Montgomery (Pu) | 2,313 | 99 | | 3,064 | 6,666 | 4,210 |
| West Virginia Wesleyan College; Buckhannon (Pr) | 1,581 | 82 | 57 | 16,800 | 16,800 | 4,350 |
| Wheeling Jesuit University; Wheeling (Pr) | 1,264 | 86 | 59 | 16,000 | 16,000 | 5,250 |
| **WISCONSIN** | | | | | | |
| Alverno College; Milwaukee (Pr) | 1,754 | 70 | 99 | 11,400 | 11,400 | 4,610 |
| Beloit College; Beloit (Pr) | 1,254 | 67 | 58 | 21,330 | 21,330 | 4,882 |
| Cardinal Stritch University; Milwaukee (Pr) | 3,089 | 77 | 68 | 11,680 | 11,680 | 4,820 |
| Carroll College; Waukesha (Pr) | 2,681 | 85 | 66 | 15,250 | 15,250 | 4,740 |
| Carthage College; Kenosha (Pr) | 2,147 | 89 | 57 | 17,350 | 17,350 | 5,210 |
| Concordia University Wisconsin; Mequon (Pr) | 3,852 | 82 | 64 | 12,900 | 12,900 | 4,820 |
| Edgewood College; Madison (Pr) | 1,535 | 48 | 72 | 12,250 | 12,250 | 4,516 |
| Lakeland College; Sheboygan (Pr) | 3,328 | 76 | 61 | 12,380 | 12,380 | 5,050 |
| Lawrence University; Appleton (Pr) | 1,289 | 73 | 54 | 21,717 | 21,717 | 4,791 |
| Marian College of Fond du Lac; Fond du Lac (Pr) | 1,114 | 79 | 69 | 12,939 | 12,939 | 4,482 |
| Marquette University; Milwaukee (Pr) | 7,496 | 84 | 55 | 17,080 | 17,080 | 6,090 |
| Milwaukee Institute of Art and Design; Milwaukee (Pr) | 656 | 86 | 51 | 16,800 | 16,800 | 6,459 |
| Milwaukee School of Engineering; Milwaukee (Pr) | 2,279 | 82 | 18 | 19,845 | 19,845 | 4,530 |
| Mount Mary College; Milwaukee (Pr) | 1,089 | 63 | 95 | 12,496 | 12,496 | 4,380 |
| Mount Senario College; Ladysmith (Pr) | 830 | 64 | 36 | 12,800 | 12,800 | 4,950 |
| Northland College; Ashland (Pr) | 531 | 87 | 36 | 14,415 | 14,415 | 4,470 |
| Ripon College; Ripon (Pr) | 862 | 90 | 58 | 18,000 | 18,000 | 4,400 |
| Silver Lake College; Manitowoc (Pr) | 727 | 86 | 71 | 12,050 | 12,050 | 4,444 |
| St. Norbert College; De Pere (Pr) | 2,041 | 88 | 59 | 16,570 | 16,570 | 5,162 |
| University of Wisconsin–Eau Claire; Eau Claire (Pu) | 10,101 | 74 | 60 | 3,252 | 10,780 | 3,198 |
| University of Wisconsin–Green Bay; Green Bay (Pu) | 5,991 | 61 | 65 | 2,594 | 10,122 | |
| University of Wisconsin–La Crosse; La Crosse (Pu) | 8,487 | 67 | 30 | 2,594 | 10,526 | 3,360 |
| University of Wisconsin–Madison; Madison (Pu) | 28,493 | 64 | | 3,780 | 13,920 | 4,500 |
| University of Wisconsin–Milwaukee; Milwaukee (Pu) | 19,246 | 69 | 55 | 3,785 | 13,022 | |
| University of Wisconsin–Oshkosh; Oshkosh (Pu) | 9,124 | 78 | 59 | 3,024 | 10,552 | 3,234 |
| University of Wisconsin–Parkside; Kenosha (Pu) | 4,672 | 94 | 59 | 3,094 | 10,622 | 4,230 |
| University of Wisconsin–River Falls; River Falls (Pu) | 6,060 | 43 | 61 | 3,138 | 10,665 | 3,452 |
| University of Wisconsin–Stevens Point; Stevens Point (Pu) | 8,380 | 58 | 57 | 3,165 | 10,693 | 3,616 |
| University of Wisconsin–Stout; Menomonie (Pu) | 7,162 | 81 | 49 | 2,724 | 10,260 | 3,530 |
| University of Wisconsin–Whitewater; Whitewater (Pu) | 9,420 | 79 | 53 | 3,144 | 10,672 | 3,324 |
| Viterbo University; La Crosse (Pr) | 1,686 | 88 | 75 | 12,770 | 12,770 | 4,530 |
| Wisconsin Lutheran College; Milwaukee (Pr) | 634 | 89 | 61 | 12,980 | 12,980 | 4,850 |
| **WYOMING** | | | | | | |
| University of Wyoming; Laramie (Pu) | 8,490 | 97 | 53 | 2,166 | 7,284 | 4,568 |

# The Cost of Starting Families First

For those who choose to have children early in life, the trade-off may involve more than just money

**By JAMES PONIEWOZIK** TIME

Babies cost you dearly. Put aside the romantic images of first steps and bike rides and tearful college graduations, and parenthood is a series of transactions, investments, and calculations of risk vs. reward. And we are not just talking about money. Your children will cost you thousands of dollars, sure, but also chunks of your youth, middle and old age, physical stamina, and, at least for many women, career opportunities.

TIME talked to women across America who began their families early. Many did so by accident (about half of all pregnancies are unplanned), others on purpose. "We wanted to be young parents," says Donna Ballard, 35, of Norwalk, Iowa, who had her first child at 25. "We didn't want to be 60 when they got out of high school." For all these parents, the decision required trade-offs, hard work, and the recognition that having children early usually means giving up something.

## Mortgages and Macaroni

Did we just say that money is not the only trade-off of motherhood? O.K., but don't get us wrong: it's the biggest. Young mothers start off with less of it, and some never catch up. Diane Lowry, 41, of Bloomingdale, Ill., had her first child at 25, having dropped out of college when she married; she and her husband split up after her second baby was born in 1989. Now an administrative assistant, Lowry envies couples who waited to become established. "They built equity in their homes, put some money aside," she says. "We were always behind the eight ball." She advises her 15-year-old daughter to wait until her "late 20s or early 30s" to have children.

For stay-at-home mom Jane Collyer, 33, of Cleveland Heights, Ohio, having her first of three children at 24 meant three words: mac and cheese. Besides getting by on cheap dinners, the Collyers drive a '92 Chevy Cavalier ("There's a lot of life left in it"), and husband Mike, an Ohio assistant attorney general, freelances as a computer consultant. But, says Jane Collyer, they don't feel deprived, because they never had the perks—expensive cars, dinners out, overseas vacations—that some two-income couples get used to before they have to cut back for the children.

Paying the bills is one thing, of course; saving for college and retirement is another, especially on meager beginning-career dollars. Deb Cummings Dunne, 45, of Dallas, postponed her nursing career to have the first of four babies at 19. When college rolled around for the eldest—with three more tuitions to come—she and her husband thought, we'll have to sell the house. They had to cut back on luxuries, but Dunne says the skimping was worth it. "I don't want to be a Pollyanna, but this is great the way it worked out. How much fun to enjoy your children when you're young."

## Growing Up in a Hurry

We live in the age of extended adolescence. Pop culture is full of characters like Bridget Jones and the *Friends* gang, waiting until their 30s to start thinking seriously about marriage and kids. But nature still keeps to the same schedule. Many twentysomething mothers and fathers take to the role easily, but others feel they are still kids themselves, and the sudden responsibility can threaten a relationship. "My husband wanted a softball team," jokes Theresa Mathis, 35. She had scarcely graduated from Virginia Tech when the couple built a six-bedroom farmhouse by hand in southwest Virginia and set out to fill it with children. But her daughter Jessica, now 10, was born prematurely and required special care; son Duncan, now 8, had an underdeveloped heart. The kids thrived but, under the added strain, her marriage didn't. "My ex was more into the idea of family life than the reality," says Mathis. "He never understood the kids' needs came before his."

The extra work hours needed to make ends meet can deprive the family's breadwinner of time with the children and create distance in a marriage. So can the stress of full-time motherhood. The challenge is to make sure that both partners will be comfortable in their roles and maintain their sense of self-esteem. When Donna Ballard quit her job as an office manager at 25 and stayed home with her two children, she was miserable, her marriage suffered, and she separated from her husband Tim. Now she is back at work, and the couple are back together. "In my experience," she says, "you become a lost soul when you are at home. When you start losing respect for yourself, your spouse loses respect for you."

## The Résumé Gap

It's a universal conundrum for mothers in their 20s: the best years for having children coincide with the best years for establishing a career. Leah Halpern, 27, of Hillsdale, N.J., was determined not to end up "a 35-year-old assistant." She took a big pay cut to move from *Vanity Fair* to a smaller magazine before having her baby, so she could get the more elevated job title she will need on her résumé when she goes back to work.

But the isolation and condescension "nonworking" moms face in a career-woman's world ("Oh, you stay at home! And what *else* do you do?") can be especially hard on women who don't have a long list of work accomplishments behind them. And taking an early break is tougher in some fields than in others. Former fashion designer Daisy von Furth, 33, of Northampton, Mass., dropped her X-Girl clothing line after having her son Wolfie when she was 26. Von Furth is enjoying stay-at-home motherhood but says going back into the fashion business probably wouldn't be an option, even if she wanted to. "You've jumped off the career train at a certain point," she says. "How can you come back at 36 or 37 and say, 'I'm here, guys—snap, snap, let me start another line of hip-hop clothing'?"

Some women, however, see a "baby sabbatical" as a chance to define what they want out of work, like Lu Dayment, 46, of Indianapolis, who had three kids in her 20s and at 35 went to graduate school in library science. "It took me a while to figure out what I wanted to do when I grew up," she says.

## Raves to Rattles

In a society that fetishizes fun yet also equates career with identity, young moms are double outsiders. It can be isolating to feel your old cronies are living the *Sex and the City* life while you're stuck on *Yes, Dear.* But if their childless, swinging friends see them as old before their time, older moms— especially in communities where putting children on hold for career is common—can look down on younger women as babies with babies. Single mom Kim Howell, 25, of Oak Park, Ill., finds she can't go clubbing as often now that she has a three-year-old; her friends "can't understand that I can't stay out till 4 A.M. every Monday." Yet Howell, a restaurant server-manager, also has little in common with the older, upper-middle-class moms at her daughter's preschool. "Some of them look at me funny because I'm young," Howell says, "but it doesn't bother me. I'm proud of my daughter." And, she adds, "when my daughter is 18, I'll be only 40."

## The Payoff

Yet for all these costs, many of our young moms believe they did right by themselves and their children. Young parents, they say, have certain intangible advantages money can't buy. They have greater energy to keep up with young kids and can look forward to a longer empty-nest life. In addition to the reduced risk of running into fertility problems, some moms say they're glad they took the physical beating of pregnancy and labor while still in their more resilient 20s.

Babies cost you dearly, no doubt about it. And earlier in life is when you have the least, literally, to spend. But, as Jane Collyer notes, young mothers have more of one important asset in the bank: life itself. "You know what the best part is?" she asks. "I really hope I'll get to see my great-grandchildren. I . . . know I'm thinking way far ahead, but I love my kids so much, and I know they're going to have great kids."                                                 □

## Households,[1] Families, and Married Couples, 1890–2000

| Date | All households | | Families | | Married couples |
|---|---|---|---|---|---|
| | Number | Average population per household | Number | Average population per family | Number |
| June 1890 | 12,690,000 | 4.93 | — | — | — |
| April 1930 | 29,905,000 | 4.11 | — | — | 25,174,000 |
| April 1940 | 34,949,000 | 3.67 | 32,166,000 | 3.76 | 26,571,000 |
| March 1950 | 43,554,000 | 3.37 | 39,303,000 | 3.54 | 34,075,000 |
| April 1955 | 47,874,000 | 3.33 | 41,951,000 | 3.59 | 36,251,000 |
| March 1960[2] | 52,799,000 | 3.35 | 45,111,000 | 3.67 | 39,254,000 |
| March 1965 | 57,436,000 | 3.32 | 47,956,000 | 3.70 | 41,689,000 |
| March 1970 | 63,401,000 | 3.14 | 51,586,000 | 3.58 | 44,728,000 |
| March 1975 | 71,120,000 | 2.94 | 55,712,000 | 3.42 | 46,951,000 |
| March 1980 | 80,776,000 | 2.76 | 59,550,000 | 3.29 | 49,112,000 |
| March 1985 | 86,789,000 | 2.69 | 62,706,000 | 3.23 | 50,350,000 |
| March 1990 | 93,347,000 | 2.63 | 66,090,000 | 3.17 | 52,317,000 |
| March 1995 | 98,990,000 | 2.65 | 69,305,000 | 3.19 | 53,858,000 |
| March 1998 | 102,528,000 | 2.62 | 70,880,000 | 3.18 | 54,317,000 |
| March 1999 | 103,874,000 | 2.61 | 71,535,000 | | |
| March 2000 | 104,705,000 | | | | 56,497,000 |

[1] ... group of persons that live in a housing unit. 2. First year in which figures for Alaska and Hawaii were included
Source: U.S. Census Bureau, *Current Population Reports*. From *Statistical Abstract of the United States, 2001.*

## Unmarried Couples, 1980–1999

| Presence of children and age of householder | 1980 | 1985 | 1990 | 1995 | 1999 |
|---|---|---|---|---|---|
| **Unmarried couples, total** | **1,589,000** | **1,983,000** | **2,856,000** | **3,668,000** | **4,486,000** |
| No children under 15 years old | 1,159,000 | 1,380,000 | 1,966,000 | 2,349,000 | 2,981,000 |
| Some children under 15 years old | 431,000 | 603,000 | 891,000 | 1,319,000 | 1,505,000 |
| Under 25 years old | 411,000 | 425,000 | 596,000 | 742,000 | 824,000 |
| 25 to 44 years old | 837,000 | 1,203,000 | 1,775,000 | 2,188,000 | 2,554,000 |
| 45 to 64 years old | 221,000 | 239,000 | 358,000 | 558,000 | 888,000 |
| 65 years and over | 119,000 | 116,000 | 127,000 | 180,000 | 220,000 |

Source: U.S. Census Bureau, *Current Population Reports.* From *Statistical Abstract of the United States, 2001.*

## Households, 1980–2000

| | Households | | | | |
|---|---|---|---|---|---|
| | Number | | | Percent distribution | |
| Type of household | 1980 | 1990 | 2000 | 1990 | 2000 |
| Total households | 80,776,000 | 93,347,000 | 104,705,000 | 100% | 100% |
| Family households | 59,550,000 | 66,090,000 | 72,025,000 | 71 | 69 |
| Married couple family | 49,112,000 | 52,317,000 | 55,311,000 | 56 | 53 |
| Male householder, no spouse present | 1,733,000 | 2,884,000 | 4,028,000 | 3 | 4 |
| Female householder, no spouse present | 8,705,000 | 10,890,000 | 12,687,000 | 12 | 12 |
| Nonfamily households | 21,226,000 | 27,257,000 | 32,680,000 | 29 | 31 |
| Living alone | 18,296,000 | 22,999,000 | 26,724,000 | 25 | 26 |
| Male householder | 8,807,000 | 11,606,000 | 14,641,000 | 12 | 14 |
| Living alone | 6,966,000 | 9,049,000 | 11,181,000 | 10 | 11 |
| Female householder | 12,419,000 | 15,651,000 | 18,039,000 | 17 | 17 |
| Living alone | 11,330,000 | 13,950,000 | 15,543,000 | 15 | 15 |

*Source:* U.S. Census Bureau, *Current Population Reports.* From *Statistical Abstract of the United States, 2001.*

## Families by Type, Race, and Hispanic Origin, 2000

### (In thousands, except as indicated)

| | | Married couple families | | | | Female family householder[3] | | | | Male family householder,[3] all races |
|---|---|---|---|---|---|---|---|---|---|---|
| Characteristic | All families | All races[1] | White | Black | His-panic[2] | All races[1] | White | Black | His-panic[2] | |
| All families | 72,025 | 55,311 | 48,790 | 4,144 | 5,133 | 12,687 | 8,380 | 3,814 | 1,769 | 4,028 |
| Without own children under 18 | 37,420 | 30,062 | 26,981 | 2,050 | 1,710 | 5,116 | 3,511 | 1,405 | 625 | 2,242 |
| With own children under 18 | 34,605 | 25,248 | 21,809 | 2,093 | 3,423 | 7,571 | 4,869 | 2,409 | 1,145 | 1,786 |
| Average per family with own children under 18 | 1.87 | 1.94 | 1.93 | 1.99 | 2.14 | 1.75 | 1.66 | 1.91 | 1.95 | 1.50 |
| Marital status of householder: | | | | | | | | | | |
| Married, spouse present | 55,311 | 55,311 | 48,790 | 4,144 | 5,133 | — | — | — | — | — |
| Married, spouse absent | 2,434 | — | — | — | — | 1,878 | 1,210 | 567 | 404 | 555 |
| Widowed | 2,797 | — | — | — | — | 2,371 | 1,764 | 522 | 252 | 426 |
| Divorced | 5,820 | — | — | — | — | 4,431 | 3,431 | 874 | 475 | 1,389 |
| Never married | 5,665 | — | — | — | — | 4,007 | 1,974 | 1,851 | 639 | 1,658 |

(—) = not applicable. 1. Includes other races not shown separately. 2. Persons of Hispanic origin may be of any race. 3. No spouse present. *Source:* U.S. Census Bureau, unpublished data. From *Statistical Abstract of the United States, 2001.*

## Young Adults Living at Home, 1960–1998

| | Male | | | Female | | |
|---|---|---|---|---|---|---|
| | Total population, 18–24 years old | Number living at home | Percent | Total population, 18–24 years old | Number living at home | Percent |
| 1960 | 6,842,000 | 3,583,000 | 52% | 7,876,000 | 2,750,000 | 35% |
| 1970 | 10,398,000 | 5,641,000 | 54 | 11,959,000 | 4,941,000 | 41 |
| 1980 | 14,278,000 | 7,755,000 | 54 | 14,844,000 | 6,336,000 | 43 |
| 1985 | 13,695,000 | 8,172,000 | 60 | 14,149,000 | 6,758,000 | 48 |
| 1990 | 12,450,000 | 7,232,000 | 58 | 12,860,000 | 6,135,000 | 48 |
| 1995 | 12,545,000 | 7,328,000 | 58 | 12,613,000 | 5,896,000 | 47 |
| 1998 | 12,633,000 | 7,399,000 | 59 | 12,568,000 | 5,974,000 | 48 |

| | Male | | | Female | | |
|---|---|---|---|---|---|---|
| | Total population, 25–34 years old | Number living at home | Percent | Total population, 25–34 years old | Number living at home | Percent |
| 1960 | 10,896,000 | 1,185,000 | 11% | 11,587,000 | 853,000 | 7% |
| 1970 | 11,929,000 | 1,129,000 | 9 | 12,637,000 | 829,000 | 7 |
| 1980 | 18,107,000 | 1,894,000 | 10 | 18,689,000 | 1,300,000 | 7 |
| 1985 | 20,184,000 | 2,685,000 | 13 | 20,673,000 | 1,661,000 | 8 |
| 1990 | 21,462,000 | 3,213,000 | 15 | 21,779,000 | 1,774,000 | 8 |
| 1995 | 20,589,000 | 3,166,000 | 15 | 20,800,000 | 1,759,000 | 8 |
| 1998 | 19,526,000 | 2,845,000 | 15 | 19,828,000 | 1,680,000 | 8 |

NOTE: Unmarried college students living in dorms are counted as living at home. *Source:* U.S. Bureau of the Census, *Current Population Reports,* March 1998.

# Co-resident Grandparents and Grandchildren

*Source:* U.S. Census Bureau, *Current Population Reports,* P23-198, May 1999

Web: www.census.gov/population/www/socdemo/grandparents.html

Researchers first began to notice an increase in the number of grandchildren living in grandparent-maintained households in the early 1990s. The U.S. Census Bureau's Current Population Report *Marital Status and Living Arrangements: March 1992* noted that the number of children under 18 living in grandparent-maintained households had increased from 2.2 million in 1970, to 2.3 million in 1980, to 3.3 million in 1992. In 1970, a little over 3% of all children under age 18 were living in a home maintained by their grandparents. By 1992, this percentage had increased to nearly 5%. More recent data show that this trend has continued. In 1997, 3.9 million children were living in homes maintained by their grandparents—5.5% of all children under 18.

In most cases (51%), these households have both a grandmother and a grandfather present living with the children. In most other cases (43% of the total), the household is maintained by a grandmother only, with no spouse present. Only 6% of such families are maintained by a grandfather alone. Thus co-resident grandmothers outnumber co-resident grandfathers five to three. The reasons for this discrepancy may have to do with the fact that women in general are longer lived than men, and they are also more likely than men to assume a caregiving role.

Other data show that substantial increases in the number of children living in households maintained by grandparents appear to have occurred regardless of the presence or absence of the grandchildren's parents. Between 1970 and 1992, these increases were greatest among children with only one parent in the household. Between 1992 and 1997, the greatest growth occurred among grandchildren living with grandparents with no parent present.[1] The increase in grandchildren in these "skipped generation" living arrangements has been attributed to a variety of factors, including the growth in drug use among parents, teen pregnancy, divorce, the rapid rise of single-parent households, child abuse and neglect, and incarceration of parents.[2]

---

1. Fuller-Thomson, Minkler, and Driver refer to skipped-generation households as those composed of grandparents and their grandchildren with neither of the child's parents present. Fuller-Thomson, Esme, Meredith Minkler, and Diane Driver. 1997. "A Profile of Grandparents Raising Grandchildren in the United States." *The Gerontologist* 37: 406–411. 2. For a more thorough discussion of these causes see Minkler, M. 1998. "Intergenerational Households Headed by Grandparents: Demographic and Sociological Contexts." In Generations United (eds.) *Grandparents and Other Relatives Raising Children: Background Papers from Generations United's Expert Symposiums.* Washington, D.C.: Generations United.

## Grandchildren Living with Their Grandparents

**Percent of children under 18**

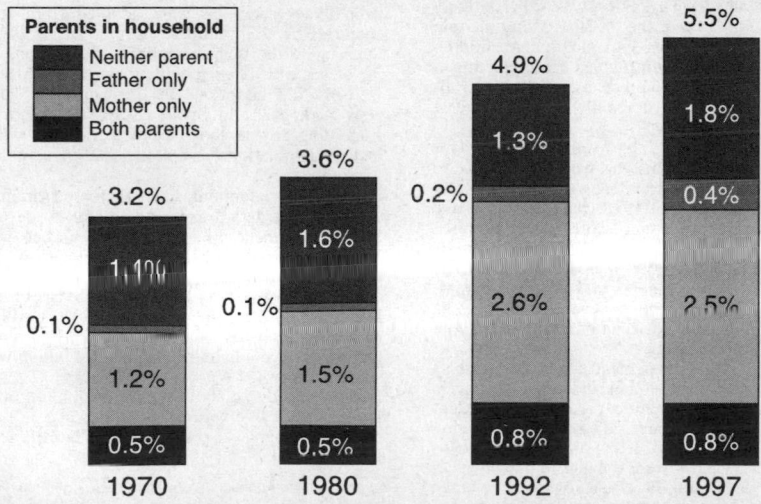

| Parents in household |
| Neither parent |
| Father only |
| Mother only |
| Both parents |

1970 — 3.2%: 0.1%, 1.1%(?), 1.2%, 0.5%
1980 — 3.6%: 1.6%, 0.1%, 1.5%, 0.5%
1992 — 4.9%: 1.3%, 0.2%, 2.6%, 0.8%
1997 — 5.5%: 1.8%, 0.4%, 2.5%, 0.8%

*Source:* U.S. Bureau of the Census, 1970 and 1980 censuses and 1992 and 1997 Current Population Surveys as reported in *Marital Status and Living Arrangements: March 1992* and *Marital Status and Living Arrangements: March 1997.*

# Adoption Trends

## Background

Although adoption is mentioned in the legal codes and writings of many ancient peoples, including the Romans and Hebrews, no such laws existed in England or her colonies prior to the middle of the 19th century. Instead, indigent children were generally sent to public institutions known as almshouses until the age of six or seven, when they could be "put out" as indentured servants or apprentices. Families also sometimes took in children informally, especially in rural areas to help on the farm.

In the United States, these practices worked well enough until the early 19th century, when changes in economic conditions and the size of the population produced numbers of children the system couldn't cope with. At the same time, largely through the efforts of certain social reformers, society's attitude toward adoption began to change. Private agencies were established to place children in homes where they would be treated as members of the family rather than servants. And families who took in children increasingly petitioned state legislatures for private adoption acts to ensure the legal status and inheritance rights of adopted children.

Finally, as a result of pressure from individual families and to provide better care for destitute children, the state legislatures were prompted to take action. Between 1851 and 1873, 17 states enacted adoption legislation, and by 1929 all states had such laws. (England did not enact general adoption laws until 1926.) Under these new statutes, adoptions had to be approved by a judge, after which the adopted child assumed the same rights accorded any natural, legitimate child of the petitioners.

## Adoption in the 20th Century

Despite the legislation, foundling homes continued to exist, and legal adoption was still relatively infrequent until about the 1920s. Many people feared that poor, abandoned, or illegitimate children were doomed to grow into troubled adults. Infants in particular were undesirable because of high mortality rates and the lack of readily available breast milk.

Following World War I, however, the demand for babies began to grow. This was partly a response to the sharp drop in population caused by the war and the influenza epidemic of 1918, and partly also due to the development of a successful feeding formula. The number of adoptions exploded, and "closed" adoptions became the norm. In closed adoptions, the identities of the birth parents and adoptive parents were kept a secret because, it was thought, this helped the child bond to its new family and avoid the stigma of illegitimacy.

By the mid-1950s the demand for healthy infants began to exceed the number available. Agencies began screening prospective parents more selectively, and by 1975 many had stopped accepting applications for nondisabled white children altogether. Other agencies were obliged to put prospective parents on waiting lists, usually for an average of three to five years. Factors contributing to the decline in available infants included the increased availability of effective contraception, a rise in the abortion rate following *Roe* v. *Wade* in 1973, and an increase in the numbers of unmarried women keeping their babies rather than giving them up for adoption.

It was also during the 1970s that "open" adoption, in which adoptive and birth parents were known to each other, became more accepted. A growing number of prospective parents adopted through private placement, contacting a birth mother directly through an advertisement or through the services of a lawyer or other professional specializing in adoption.

## More Recent Trends

Since the end of the 20th century, infertile couples and single people have increasingly turned to transracial and international adoptions, as well as new advanced medical techniques for treating infertility and providing alternative methods of reproduction. Meanwhile, the number of older special needs children waiting adoption has skyrocketed. These children often come from backgrounds of abuse and neglect, and finding appropriate placements for them is one of the most pressing concerns in child welfare today.

*Source:* Columbia Encyclopedia, 6th Edition. Web: www.infoplease.com. Sokoloff, Burton Z., "Antecedents of American Adoption" in *The Future of Children: Adoption,* vol. 3, no. 1. (David and Lucile Packard Foundation: Los Altos, Calif.) Spring 1993. Web: www.futureofchildren.org.

## Some Adoption Statistics:

- In 1992, the last year for which total adoption statistics were available, 127,441 children of all races and nationalities were adopted in the United States.
- Of the adoptions that occurred in 1992, 42% were by a stepparent or relative; 15.5% were adopted from foster care; 5% were adopted from other countries by U.S. families.
- States with the highest number of adoptions are the states with larger populations. In 1992, there were 14,722 adoptions in California, 9,570 in New York, 8,235 in Texas, and 6,839 in Florida.
- According to the most recent estimates, which include international adoptions, 8% of adoptions were transracial.
- International adoptions have increased dramatically over the last decade. According to the U.S. State Department, in 1992, 6,472 children were adopted from abroad. In 1999, the number had increased to 16,396.
- According to the U.S. Department of Health and Human Services, in 1999, 33% of children adopted from foster care were adopted by a single parent, the overwhelming majority of which were single women (31%).
- It is estimated that about 1 million children in the United States live with adoptive parents, and that between 2% and 4% of U.S. families include an adopted child.

*Source:* National Adoption Information Clearinghouse. Web: www.calib.com/naic/. U.S. State Department. Web: http://travel.state.gov/children's_issues.html. U.S. Dept. of Health and Human Services, Administration for Children and Families, Children's Bureau. Web: http://www.acf.dhhs.gov/programs/cb/.

## Child-care Arrangements for Preschool Children, 1999

| | Children | | Type of nonparental arrangement[1] | | | |
|---|---|---|---|---|---|---|
| Characteristic | Number (1,000s) | Percent distribution | Relative care | Nonrelative care | Center-based program[2] | Parental care only |
| **Race/ethnicity** | | | | | | |
| White, non-Hispanic | 5,296 | 61.9 | 18.8 | 19.3 | 59.4 | 23.6 |
| Black, non-Hispanic | 1,258 | 14.7 | 36.0 | 8.0 | 72.5 | 13.1 |
| Hispanic | 1,421 | 16.6 | 25.9 | 12.7 | 44.4 | 33.6 |
| Other | 574 | 6.7 | 31.0 | 9.9 | 66.0 | 17.5 |
| **Household income** | | | | | | |
| Less than $10,001 | 1,126 | 13.2 | 28.9 | 12.8 | 56.6 | 26.6 |
| $10,001 to $20,000 | 1,395 | 16.3 | 29.5 | 12.9 | 51.1 | 28.1 |
| $20,001 to $30,000 | 1,327 | 15.5 | 27.7 | 12.2 | 50.8 | 29.6 |
| $30,001 to $40,000 | 1,050 | 12.3 | 23.3 | 14.9 | 54.5 | 25.3 |
| $40,001 to $50,000 | 792 | 9.3 | 20.9 | 14.2 | 59.7 | 23.1 |
| $50,001 to $75,000 | 1,351 | 15.8 | 17.3 | 20.5 | 65.5 | 19.0 |
| $75,001 or more | 1,509 | 17.7 | 16.2 | 21.9 | 74.0 | 13.4 |
| **Total** | **8,549** | **100.0** | **23.3** | **15.9** | **59.3** | **23.3** |

NOTES: Estimates are based on children three to five years old who have not entered kindergarten. 1. Columns do not add to total because some children participated in more than one type of nonparental arrangement. 2. Center-based programs include day-care centers, head-start programs, preschool, prekindergartens, and nursery schools. *Source: Statistical Abstract of the United States, 2001.*

## Children in Foster Care

| | Percent | Number | | Percent | Number |
|---|---|---|---|---|---|
| **Total** | | **588,000** | **Race/ethnicity** | | |
| | | | White, non-Hispanic | 35% | 207,948 |
| **Ages** | | | Black, non-Hispanic | 38 | 226,363 |
| Under 1 year | 4% | 22,303 | Hispanic[1] | 15 | 88,939 |
| 1–5 years | 24 | 140,980 | American Indian/Alaskan Native | 2 | 9,330 |
| 6–10 years | 25 | 149,357 | Asian/Pacific Islander | 1 | 6,213 |
| 11–15 years | 29 | 168,114 | Unknown/unable to determine | 8 | 49,207 |
| 16–18 years | 16 | 96,349 | **Gender** | | |
| 19 years and over | 2 | 10,897 | Male | 52 | 308,066 |
| | | | Female | 48 | 279,934 |

NOTE: Preliminary estimates as of April 2001. Percentages may not add up to 100% and numbers may not add up to totals due to rounding. 1. Hispanic can be of any race. *Source:* U.S. Dept. of Health and Human Services, Admin. for Children and Families, Adoption and Foster Care Analysis and Reporting System (AFCARS) Report #5. Web: www.acf.dhhs.gov/programs/cb.

## Child Abuse and Neglect

| | 1990 | | 1995 | | 1997 | | 1998 | |
|---|---|---|---|---|---|---|---|---|
| Item | Number | Percent | Number | Percent | Number | Percent | Number | Percent |
| **Types of substantiated maltreatment** | | | | | | | | |
| Victims, total[1, 2] | 690,658 | — | 970,285 | — | 790,157 | — | 861,602 | — |
| Neglect | 338,770 | 49.1% | 507,015 | 52.3% | 431,563 | 54.6% | 461,274 | 53.5% |
| Physical abuse | 186,801 | 27.0 | 237,840 | 24.5 | 192,872 | 24.4 | 195,891 | 22.7 |
| Sexual abuse | 119,506 | 17.3 | 122,964 | 12.7 | 96,070 | 12.2 | 99,278 | 11.5 |
| Emotional maltreatment | 45,621 | 6.6 | 42,051 | 4.3 | 48,407 | 6.1 | 51,618 | 6.0 |
| Medical neglect | n.a. | n.a. | 28,541 | 2.9 | 18,524 | 2.3 | 20,338 | 2.4 |
| **Sex of victim** | | | | | | | | |
| Victims, total[2] | 742,519 | 100.0 | 808,081 | 100.0 | 790,395 | 100.0 | 760,438 | 100.0 |
| Male | 323,339 | 43.5 | 381,075 | 47.1 | 315,045 | 39.9 | 359,568 | 47.3 |
| Female | 369,919 | 49.8 | 425,193 | 52.5 | 348,001 | 44.0 | 388,187 | 51.0 |
| **Age of victim** | | | | | | | | |
| Victims, total[2] | 731,282 | 100.0 | 808,575 | 100.0 | 789,303 | 100.0 | 767,749 | 100.0 |
| 1 year and younger | 97,101 | 13.3 | 103,335 | 12.8 | 83,819 | 10.6 | 105,097 | 13.7 |
| 2 to 5 years old | 172,791 | 23.6 | 215,303 | 26.6 | 166,523 | 21.1 | 187,522 | 24.4 |
| 6 to 9 years old | 157,681 | 21.6 | 195,400 | 24.2 | 165,845 | 21.0 | 193,316 | 25.2 |
| 10 to 13 years old | 135,130 | 18.5 | 154,682 | 19.1 | 130,346 | 16.5 | 151,126 | 19.7 |
| 14 to 17 years old | 103,383 | 14.1 | 121,548 | 15.0 | 97,050 | 12.3 | 111,894 | 14.6 |
| 18 years and over | 4,880 | 0.7 | 7,506 | 0.9 | 2,954 | 0.4 | 4,210 | 0.5 |

NOTE: n.a. = not available. (—) = not applicable. 1. More than one type of maltreatment may be substantiated per child. Therefore, totals for this category will add up to more than 100 percent. Victim totals and maltreatment types are based on subset of states that reported both the number of child victims and maltreatment incidences by type for that year. 2. Includes other and unknown not shown separately. *Source: Statistical Abstract of the United States, 2001.*

# Teen Birth Rates Continue to Decline

*Source:* Centers for Disease Control, National Center for Health Statistics, *National Vital Statistics Reports,* vol. 49, no. 10, Sept. 25, 2001.

Teenage childbearing has been on a long-term decline in the United States since the late 1950s, except for a brief, but steep, upward climb in the late 1980s through 1991. The 2000 rate (49 births per 1,000) is about half the peak rate recorded in 1957 (96 per 1,000). The declining teenage birth rate has had an impressive impact on the number of babies born to teenagers. If the birth rates by age had remained at 1991 levels throughout the 1990s instead of declining as they did, there would have been an additional 546,000 births to teenagers over the decade. Possible factors accounting for the decline include decreased sexual activity reflecting changing attitudes toward premarital sex, an increase in condom use, and the adoption of newly available hormonal contraception, implants, and injectables.

Despite the rates' reaching record lows in 2000, U.S. teenage birth rates remain substantially higher than rates for other developed countries.    □

## Teen Birth Rates in the U.S., Selected Years
### (rates per 1,000 females in specified group)

| Age | 1980 | 1985 | 1990 | 1991 | 1993 | 1995 | 1998 | 2000 |
|---|---|---|---|---|---|---|---|---|
| **All races** | | | | | | | | |
| 10–14 years | 1.1 | 1.2 | 1.4 | 1.4 | 1.4 | 1.3 | 1.0 | 0.9 |
| 15–19 years | 53.0 | 51.0 | 59.9 | 62.1 | 59.6 | 56.8 | 51.1 | 48.7 |
| **White, total** | | | | | | | | |
| 10–14 years | — | — | 0.7 | 0.8 | 0.8 | 0.8 | 0.6 | 0.6 |
| 15–19 years | — | — | 50.8 | 52.8 | 51.1 | 50.1 | 45.4 | 43.9 |
| **White, non-Hispanic** | | | | | | | | |
| 10–14 years | 0.4 | — | 0.5 | 0.5 | 0.5 | 0.4 | 0.3 | 0.3 |
| 15–19 years | 41.2 | — | 42.5 | 43.4 | 40.7 | 39.3 | 35.2 | 32.8 |
| **Black** | | | | | | | | |
| 10–14 years | 4.3 | 4.5 | 4.9 | 4.8 | 4.6 | 4.2 | 2.9 | 2.5 |
| 15–19 years | 97.8 | 95.4 | 112.8 | 115.5 | 108.6 | 96.1 | 85.4 | 79.2 |
| **American Indian[1]** | | | | | | | | |
| 10–14 years | 1.9 | 1.7 | 1.6 | 1.6 | 1.4 | 1.8 | 1.6 | 1.3 |
| 15–19 years | 82.2 | 79.2 | 81.1 | 85.0 | 83.1 | 78.0 | 72.1 | 67.9 |
| **Asian/Pacific Islander** | | | | | | | | |
| 10–14 years | 0.3 | 0.4 | 0.7 | 0.8 | 0.6 | 0.7 | 0.4 | 0.3 |
| 15–19 years | 26.2 | 23.8 | 26.4 | 27.4 | 27.0 | 26.1 | 23.1 | 21.8 |
| **Hispanic[2]** | | | | | | | | |
| 10–14 years | 1.7 | — | 2.4 | 2.4 | 2.7 | 2.7 | 2.1 | 1.9 |
| 15–19 years | 82.2 | — | 100.3 | 106.7 | 106.8 | 106.7 | 93.6 | 94.4 |

1. Includes births to Aleuts and Eskimos. 2. Persons of Hispanic origin may be of any race. *Source:* Centers for Disease Control, National Center for Health Statistics, *National Vital Statistics Reports,* vol. 49, no. 10, Sept. 25, 2001.

## Distribution of Births to Unmarried Women by Age, 1970 and 1999

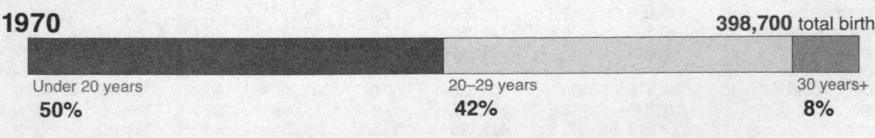

**1970**       **398,700** total births

| Under 20 years | 20–29 years | 30 years+ |
|---|---|---|
| **50%** | **42%** | **8%** |

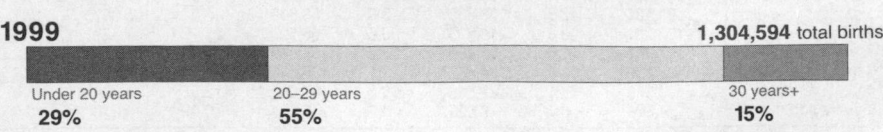

**1999**       **1,304,594** total births

| Under 20 years | 20–29 years | 30 years+ |
|---|---|---|
| **29%** | **55%** | **15%** |

Note: Percentages may not add up to 100 due to rounding. *Source*: National Center for Health Statistics, *National Vital Statistics Reports,* vol. 48, no. 16, Oct. 18, 2000.

# The Gentler Sex?

## Today's young women are drinking as hard as their dates—and studies show an increase in other risky behavior as well

**By Amanda Bower** TIME

Administrators at many U.S. colleges have been alarmed in recent years by an upsurge in binge drinking among female students. (Binge drinking is defined as consuming four or more alcoholic drinks in a row.) Now, experts say, they are measuring an increase in risky behavior by women in other areas, shattering long-established gender differences among young American adults. Young men are still more likely than young women to get arrested, crash their cars, or fight in school. But while men's rates of risky behavior are falling, women's are either holding level or rising.

## Alcohol

Since 1999, some 16,000 men—but more than 19,000 women—have requested screening for alcohol abuse at federally funded day-long clinics held each spring at about 400 colleges. Individual schools have found their own gauges for the trend. At the University of Vermont, for instance, the average blood-alcohol level of drunken women treated at the hospital is now .20, which is 10% higher than that of intoxicated men and more than twice the legal limit of .08. Counselors at Stanford University have observed an uptick in women who had "regretted sex" while drunk. And at Georgetown University there has been a 35% rise in women sanctioned for alcohol violations over the past three years. And the problem is not limited to universities in big cities where Greek life sustains the campus culture. Heavy drinking has also surged at all-women colleges in the past decade, according to a 2002 study in the *Journal of American College Health* that showed a 125% increase in frequent binge drinking between 1993 and 2001 at all-women schools. Another 2002 study found that girls as young as ninth-graders were just as likely as boys to report drinking alcohol.

## Drugs

Today's 15-year-old girls are using illegal drugs as their mothers were. Marijuana is far and away the most popular teen drug. In a national survey, almost 10% of girls ages 12 to 17 said they had used illegal substances in the past month; by the time they're in the 18-to-25 age bracket, it's 16%. For most substances, boys and girls use at similar rates. But girls ages 12 to 17 are more likely to abuse psychotherapeutic drugs such as Valium. They are also more likely to have used inhalants—such as air freshener, glue, paint, or cooking spray—in the past month. A total of 6.2 million American girls and women have risked brain damage and death by "huffing" these common household products to get high.

## Dangerous Driving

Women's fatal traffic accidents have increased 30% since 1982, compared with a decrease for men of 8%. Although drivers ages 15 to 20 have dramatically reduced their alcohol-related fatal traffic accidents, the number of girls involved in other deadly crashes has increased since 1982 while it has fallen for boys. The likelihood that a 16-year-old girl will have an accident has increased almost 10% since 1990—and cars with two or more teens inside are twice as likely to crash as cars in which a teen is driving solo.

## Smoking

Almost 30% of high school senior girls smoked in the past month—an increase since 1992, when 26% said they lighted up. Ten years ago, health officials thought they were winning the war on smoking. The proportion of high school senior girls who smoked had dropped from 40% in 1977 to 26% in 1992. But according to the Surgeon General, it rocketed back up to 35% in five years, undoing much of the progress that had been made. Now almost one-quarter of 10th-grade girls say they have smoked in the past 30 days.

## Fighting

One in ten high school girls was in at least one physical fight at school in the past year. Boys still fight more than girls, but their rate of violence at school has fallen steadily since 1993, while that of girls has stayed virtually the same. Experts say the schools' violence-prevention efforts have been male-focused, concentrating on controlling boys' impulsive behavior and bullying. Girls' fights need a different approach to address their more emotional causes.

## Violent Crime

Since 1991 the number of women arrested for aggravated assault has increased a staggering 46%, to 53,088 in 2000. The number of men arrested decreased 9.5%. More than 2 million women—some 600,000 of them juveniles—commit a violent offense each year, and some three-quarters of their victims are women. Criminal-justice advocates say up to 85% of women convicted of violent crimes are themselves victims of physical and sexual abuse; 43% are drug addicts or alcoholics; 40% suffer from parental absence or neglect; and perhaps 1 in 10 has a mental health problem. □

## Gender of Sexual Partners in the United States

### (sexually active only)

| | Same gender | | Both genders | | Opposite genders | |
|---|---|---|---|---|---|---|
| | Men | Women | Men | Women | Men | Women |
| 1988 | 2.3% | 0.2% | 0.3% | 0.0% | 97.4% | 99.8% |
| 1989 | 1.4 | 1.2 | 0.3 | 0.4 | 98.3 | 98.4 |
| 1990 | 1.1 | 0.5 | 0.9 | 0.0 | 98.0 | 99.5 |
| 1991 | 2.0 | 0.3 | 0.7 | 0.1 | 97.3 | 99.6 |
| 1993 | 1.8 | 1.8 | 0.3 | 0.4 | 97.9 | 97.8 |
| 1994 | 2.1 | 2.1 | 0.5 | 0.4 | 97.5 | 97.5 |
| 1996 | 3.5 | 2.1 | 0.6 | 0.9 | 96.0 | 97.0 |

*Source:* General Social Survey (GSS), National Opinion Research Center, University of Chicago, 1996.

## Key Events in the Women's Rights Movement

**1848** The first women's rights convention is held in Seneca Falls, New York. A Declaration of Sentiments, which outlines grievances and sets the agenda for the women's rights movement, is signed by 68 women and 32 men.

**1850** The first National Women's Rights Convention takes place in Worcester, Mass., attracting more than 1,000 participants. National conventions are held yearly (except for 1857) through 1860.

**1869** In May, Susan B. Anthony and Elizabeth Cady Stanton form the National Woman Suffrage Association. Its primary goal is to achieve voting rights for women by means of a congressional amendment to the Constitution.

In November Lucy Stone, Henry Blackwell, and others form the American Woman Suffrage Association, which focuses exclusively on gaining voting rights for women through amendments to individual state constitutions.

In December the territory of Wyoming passes the first women's suffrage law. The following year, women begin serving on juries in the territory.

**1890** The National Woman Suffrage Association and the American Woman Suffrage Association merge to form the National American Woman Suffrage Association (NAWSA). As the movement's mainstream organization, NAWSA wages state-by-state campaigns to obtain voting rights for women.

**1893** Colorado is the first state to adopt an amendment granting women the right to vote. Utah and Idaho follow suit in 1896, Washington State in 1910, California in 1911, Oregon, Kansas, and Arizona in 1912, Alaska and Illinois in 1913, Montana and Nevada in 1914, New York in 1917, Michigan, South Dakota, and Oklahoma in 1918.

**1896** The National Association of Colored Women is formed, bringing together more than 100 black women's clubs. Leaders in the black women's club movement include Josephine St. Pierre Ruffin, Mary Church Terrell, and Anna Julia Cooper.

**1913** Alice Paul and Lucy Burns form the Congressional Union to work toward the passage of a federal amendment to give women the vote. The group is later renamed the National Women's Party. Members picket the White House and practice other forms of civil disobedience.

**1919** The federal woman suffrage amendment, originally written by Susan B. Anthony and introduced in Congress in 1878, is passed by the House of Representatives and the Senate. It is then sent to the states for ratification.

**1920** On Aug. 26, the 19th Amendment to the Constitution, granting women the right to vote, is signed into law.

**1921** Margaret Sanger founds the American Birth Control League, which evolves into the Planned Parenthood Federation of America in 1942.

**1936** The federal law prohibiting the dissemination of contraceptive information through the mail is modified, and birth control information is no longer classified as obscene. Throughout the 1940s and 1950s, birth control advocates are engaged in numerous legal suits.

**1961** President John F. Kennedy establishes the President's Commission on the Status of Women and appoints Eleanor Roosevelt as chairwoman. The report issued by the commission in 1963 documents substantial discrimination against women in the workplace and urges reform, including fair hiring practices, paid maternity leave, and affordable child care.

**1963** Betty Friedan publishes her highly influential book *The Feminine Mystique,* which becomes a best-seller and galvanizes the modern women's rights movement.

In June Congress passes the Equal Pay Act, making it illegal for employers to pay a woman less than what a man would receive for the same job.

**1964** Title VII of the Civil Rights Act bars discrimination in employment on the basis of race and sex. At the same time it establishes the Equal Employment Opportunity Commission (EEOC) to investigate complaints and impose penalties.

**1965** In *Griswold* v. *Connecticut,* the Supreme Court strikes down the one remaining state law prohibiting the use of contraceptives by married couples.

**1966** The National Organization for Women (NOW) is founded. The largest women's rights group in the United States, NOW seeks to end sexual discrimination by means of legislative lobbying, litigation, and public demonstrations.

**1967** Executive Order 11375 expands President Lyndon Johnson's affirmative action policy of 1965 to cover discrimination based on gender.

**1968** The EEOC rules that sex-segregated help wanted ads in newspapers are illegal. This ruling is upheld in 1973 by the Supreme Court, opening the way for women to apply for higher-paying jobs hitherto open only to men.

**1969** California becomes the first state to adopt a "no fault" divorce law, which allows couples to divorce by mutual consent. By 1985 every state has adopted a similar law. Laws are also passed regarding the equal division of common property.

**1971** *Ms.* magazine is first published as a sample insert in *New York* magazine; 300,000 copies are sold out in 8 days. The first regular issue is published in July 1972. The magazine becomes the major forum for feminist voices and turns cofounder and editor Gloria Steinem into an icon of the modern feminist movement.

In *Eisenstadt* v. *Baird* the Supreme Court rules that the right to privacy includes an unmarried person's right to use contraceptives.

**1972** The Equal Rights Amendment (ERA) is passed by Congress and sent to the states for ratification. Originally drafted by Alice Paul in 1923, the amendment reads: "Equality of rights under the law shall not be denied or abridged by the United States or by any State on account of sex." The amendment died in

1982 when it failed to achieve ratification by a minimum of 38 states.

Title IX of the Education Amendments bans sex discrimination in schools. As a result, the enrollment of women in athletics programs and professional schools increases dramatically.

**1973** As a result of *Roe* v. *Wade,* the Supreme Court establishes a woman's legal right to abortion, overriding the antiabortion laws of many states.

**1974** The Equal Credit Opportunity Act prohibits discrimination in consumer credit practices on the basis of sex, race, marital status, religion, national origin, age, or receipt of public assistance.

**1978** The Pregnancy Discrimination Act bans employment discrimination against pregnant women.

**1984** EMILY's List (Early Money Is Like Yeast) is established as a financial network for pro-choice Democratic women running for national political office. The organization makes a significant impact on the increasing numbers of women elected to Congress.

**1986** In *Meritor Savings Bank* v. *Vinson,* the Supreme Court finds that sexual harassment is a form of illegal job discrimination.

**1994** The Violence Against Women Act tightens federal penalties for sex offenders, funds services for victims of rape and domestic violence, and provides for special training of police officers.

## Domestic Violence

| Type of victimization over lifetime | Percent | | Number | |
|---|---|---|---|---|
| | Women | Men | Women | Men |
| Rape | 7.7% | 0.3% | 7,753,669 | 278,244 |
| Physical assault | 22.1 | 7.4 | 22,254,037 | 6,863,352 |
| Rape and/or physical assault | 24.8 | 7.6 | 24,972,856 | 7,048,848 |
| Stalking | 4.8 | 0.6 | 4,833,456 | 556,488 |
| Total victimized | 25.5 | 7.9 | 25,677,735 | 7,327,092 |

Survey consisted of telephone interviews with a nationally representative sample of 8,000 U.S. women and 8,000 men. **Definitions:** Rape includes completed or attempted forced vaginal, oral, or anal sex. Physical assault includes a range of behaviors from slapping and hitting to using a gun. Stalking involves repeated acts of harassment and intimidation with the victim reporting a high level of fear. *Source:* National Violence Against Women Survey, National Institute of Justice and Centers for Disease Control, July 2000.

## The Wage Gap

*Source:* National Women's Law Center

The wage gap is a statistical indicator often used as an index of the status of women's earnings relative to men's. It is also used to compare the earnings of other races and ethnicities to those of white males, a group generally not subject to race- or sex-based discrimination. The wage gap is expressed as a percentage (e.g., in 2000, women earned 73% as much as men) and is calculated by dividing the median annual earnings for women by the median annual earnings for men.

The Equal Pay Act was signed in 1963, making it illegal for employers to pay unequal wages to men and women who hold the same job and do the same work. At the time of the EPA's passage, women earned just 58 cents for every dollar earned by men. By 2000, nearly 40 years later, that rate has only increased to 73 cents, an improvement of less than

half a penny a year. Minority women fare the worst. African American women earned only 64 cents to the dollar earned by white men, and for Hispanic women that figure drops to merely 52 cents per dollar.

The wage gap between women and men cuts across a wide spectrum of occupations. The Bureau of Labor Statistics reported in 1999 that women physicians earned 62.5% of the median weekly wages of male physicians, and women in sales occupations earned just 59.9% of men's wages in equivalent positions.

If working women earned the same as men (those who work the same number of hours, have the same education, age and union status, and live in the same region of the country), their annual family incomes would rise by $4,000 and poverty rates would be cut in half.

## 2000 Median Annual Earnings by Race and Sex

| Race/gender | Earnings | Wage ratio | Race/gender | Earnings | Wage ratio |
|---|---|---|---|---|---|
| White men | $38,869 | 100% | All men | $37,339 | |
| White women | $28,080 | 72 | All women | $27,355 | |
| Black men | $30,409 | 78 | Wage gap | | 73% |
| Black women | $25,117 | 64 | | | |
| Hispanic men | $24,638 | 63 | | | |
| Hispanic women | $20,527 | 52 | | | |

*Source:* The National Committee on Pay Equity.

## Women's Earnings as a Percentage of Men's, 1951–2000

(for year-round full-time work)

| Year | Percent | Year | Percent | Year | Percent | Year | Percent | Year | Percent |
|---|---|---|---|---|---|---|---|---|---|
| 1951 | 63.9% | 1961 | 59.2% | 1971 | 59.5% | 1981 | 59.2% | 1991 | 69.9% |
| 1952 | 63.9 | 1962 | 59.3 | 1972 | 57.9 | 1982 | 61.7 | 1992 | 70.8 |
| 1953 | 63.9 | 1963 | 58.9 | 1973 | 56.6 | 1983 | 63.6 | 1993 | 71.5 |
| 1954 | 63.9 | 1964 | 59.1 | 1974 | 58.8 | 1984 | 63.7 | 1994 | 72.0 |
| 1955 | 63.9 | 1965 | 59.9 | 1975 | 58.8 | 1985 | 64.6 | 1995 | 71.4 |
| 1956 | 63.3 | 1966 | 57.6 | 1976 | 60.2 | 1986 | 64.3 | 1996 | 73.8 |
| 1957 | 63.8 | 1967 | 57.8 | 1977 | 58.9 | 1987 | 65.2 | 1997 | 74.2 |
| 1958 | 63.0 | 1968 | 58.2 | 1978 | 59.4 | 1988 | 66.0 | 1998 | 73.2 |
| 1959 | 61.3 | 1969 | 58.9 | 1979 | 59.7 | 1989 | 68.7 | 1999 | 72.2 |
| 1960 | 60.7 | 1970 | 59.4 | 1980 | 60.2 | 1990 | 71.6 | 2000 | 73.0 |

*Source:* U.S. Women's Bureau and the National Committee on Pay Equity.

## 20 Leading Occupations of Employed Women

(2001 annual averages)

| Occupations | Total employed (women) (in thousands) | Total employed (men and women) (in thousands) | Percent women | Women's median usual weekly earnings[1] | Ratio of women's earnings to men's earnings |
|---|---|---|---|---|---|
| Total, 16 years and over | 62,992 | 135,073 | 46.6% | $511 | 76.0 |
| Managers and administrators, n.e.c.[2] | 2,486 | 8,018 | 31.0 | 762 | 65.6 |
| Secretaries | 2,366 | 2,404 | 98.4 | 475 | n.a. |
| Cashiers[3] | 2,288 | 2,974 | 76.9 | 292 | 89.3 |
| Sales supervisors and proprietors | 1,990 | 4,836 | 44.1 | 502 | 70.5 |
| Registered nurses | 2,013 | 2,162 | 93.1 | 820 | 87.9 |
| Elementary school teachers | 1,828 | 2,216 | 82.5 | 731 | 94.9 |
| Nursing aides, orderlies, and attendants | 1,874 | 2,081 | 90.0 | 356 | 89.7 |
| Bookkeepers, accounting, and auditing clerks | 1,506 | 1,621 | 92.9 | 474 | 93.7 |
| Waiters and waitresses | 1,029 | 1,347 | 76.4 | 317 | 87.3 |
| Sales workers, retail, and personal services[3] | 1,023 | 2,311 | 44.3 | n.a. | n.a. |
| Receptionists | 1,015 | 1,047 | 96.9 | 401 | n.a. |
| Sales workers, other commodities[3, 4] | 925 | 1,426 | 64.9 | 351 | 82.0 |
| Accountants and auditors | 975 | 1,657 | 58.8 | 687 | 72.0 |
| Cooks | 881 | 2,073 | 42.5 | 305 | 87.9 |
| Investigators and adjusters, excluding insurance | 878 | 1,171 | 75.0 | 487 | 89.4 |
| Janitors and cleaners | 779 | 2,166 | 36.0 | 318 | 81.7 |
| Secondary school teachers | 763 | 1,304 | 58.5 | 759 | 91.9 |
| Hairdressers and cosmetologists | 772 | 854 | 90.4 | 374 | n.a. |
| General office clerks | 756 | 903 | 83.7 | 462 | 96.0 |
| Administrative support occupations | 779 | 1,020 | 76.4 | 512 | 82.3 |

NOTE: n.a. = not available. Median not available where base is less than 50,000 male workers. 1. Wage and salary for full-time workers. 2. Not elsewhere classified. 3. Excludes cashiers and sales workers, other commodities. 4. Includes foods, drugs, health, and other commodities. *Source:* U.S. Dept. of Labor, Bureau of Labor Statistics.

# Foreign-Born Population

According to the 2000 Census, the foreign-born population of the United States reached 31.1 million in 2000, a 57% increase over the foreign-born population in 1990. Over the past 30 years, the foreign-born population rose sharply from 9.6 million (1970 census), to 14.1 million (1980 census), to 19.8 million (1990 census) to the current 31.1 million. The proportion of foreign born versus native born over this 30-year span increased from 4.7% in 1970 to 11.1% in 2000. The 2000 proportion is the highest since 1930, when 11.6% of the population was foreign-born. The proportion of foreign born was at its all-time highest between 1860 and 1920—ranging between 13% and 15%, reflecting large-scale immigration from Europe.

In 2000, 51% of the foreign born population was from Latin America, 25.5% from Asia, and 15.3% from Europe. Together, Latin America and Asia accounted for 76.5% of the foreign-born population, up from 28.3% in 1970. ☐

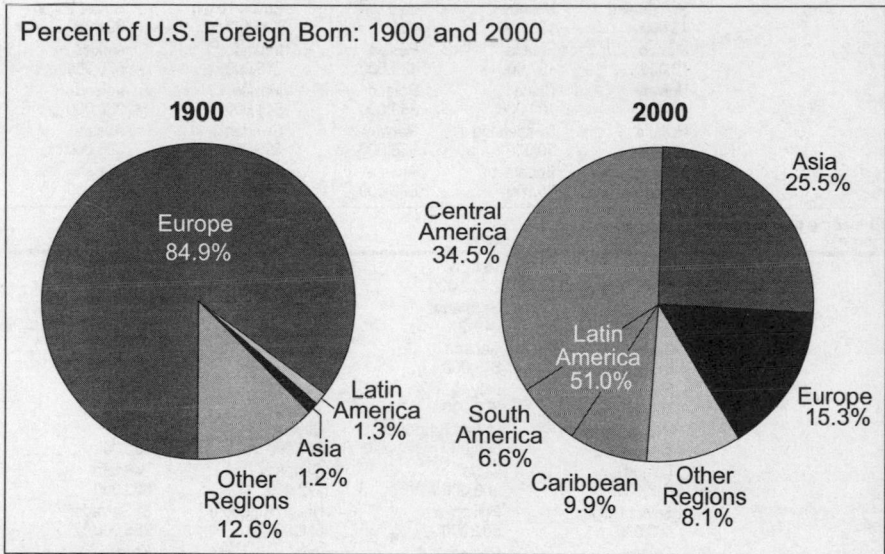

## Percent of U.S. Foreign Born: 1900 and 2000

**1900**
- Europe 84.9%
- Latin America 1.3%
- Asia 1.2%
- Other Regions 12.6%

**2000**
- Asia 25.5%
- Central America 34.5%
- Latin America 51.0%
- South America 6.6%
- Europe 15.3%
- Caribbean 9.9%
- Other Regions 8.1%

*Source:* U.S. Census Bureau

## Ancestry of U.S. Population by Rank

### (1990 U.S. Census figures; groups with populations exceeding one million)

| 1990 Rank | Ancestry group | Percent | 1990 Rank | Ancestry group | Percent | 1990 Rank | Ancestry group | Percent |
|---|---|---|---|---|---|---|---|---|
| 1 | German | 23.2% | 13 | Scottish | 2.2% | 24 | Ukrainian | 0.6 |
| 2 | Irish | 15.6 | 14 | Swedish | 1.9 | 25 | Chinese | 0.6 |
| 3 | English | 13.1 | 15 | Norwegian | 1.6 | 26 | Filipino | 0.6 |
| 4 | African | 9.6 | 16 | Russian | 1.2 | 27 | Czech | 0.5 |
| 5 | Italian | 5.9 | 17 | French Canadian | 0.9 | 28 | Portuguese | 0.5 |
| 6 | American | 5.0 | | | | 29 | British | 0.4 |
| 7 | Mexican | 4.7 | 18 | Welsh | 0.8 | 30 | Hispanic | 0.4 |
| 8 | French | 4.1 | 19 | Spanish | 0.8 | 31 | Greek | 0.4 |
| 9 | Polish | 3.8 | 20 | Puerto Rican | 0.8 | 32 | Swiss | 0.4 |
| 10 | American Indian | 3.5 | 21 | Slovak | 0.8 | 33 | Japanese | 0.4 |
| 11 | Dutch | 2.5 | 22 | White | 0.7 | | | |
| 12 | Scotch-Irish | 2.3 | 23 | Danish | 0.7 | | | |

NOTE: 2000 Census data on ancestry were not available at press time. Data are based on a sample and subject to sampling variability. Since persons who reported multiple ancestries were included in more than one group, the sum of the persons reporting the ancestry is greater than the total; for example, a person reporting "English-French" was tabulated in both the "English" and "French" categories. *Source:* U.S. Census Bureau.

## Countries of Birth of the Foreign-Born Population, 1850–2000
### (resident population)

| 10 leading countries by rank[1] | 1850 | 1880 | 1900 | 1930 | 1960 |
|---|---|---|---|---|---|
| 1. | Ireland 962,000 | Germany 1,967,000 | Germany 2,663,000 | Italy 1,790,000 | Italy 1,257,000 |
| 2. | Germany 584,000 | Ireland 1,855,000 | Ireland 1,615,000 | Germany 1,609,000 | Germany 990,000 |
| 3. | Great Britain 379,000 | Great Britain 918,000 | Canada 1,180,000 | United Kingdom 1,403,000 | Canada 953,000 |
| 4. | Canada 148,000 | Canada 717,000 | Great Britain 1,168,000 | Canada 1,310,000 | United Kingdom 833,000 |
| 5. | France 54,000 | Sweden 194,000 | Sweden 582,000 | Poland 1,269,000 | Poland 748,000 |
| 6. | Switzerland 13,000 | Norway 182,000 | Italy 484 | Soviet Union 1,154,000 | Soviet Union 691,000 |
| 7. | Mexico 13,000 | France 107,000 | Russia 424,000 | Ireland 745,000 | Mexico 576,000 |
| 8. | Norway 13,000 | China 104,000 | Poland 383,000 | Mexico 641,000 | Ireland 339,000 |
| 9. | Holland 10,000 | Switzerland 89,000 | Norway 336,000 | Sweden 595,000 | Austria 305,000 |
| 10. | Italy 4,000 | Bohemia 85,000 | Austria 276,000 | Czechoslovakia 492,000 | Hungary 245,000 |

| 10 leading countries by rank[1] | 1970 | 1980 | 1990 | 2000 |
|---|---|---|---|---|
| 1. | Italy 1,009,000 | Mexico 2,199,000 | Mexico 4,298,000 | Mexico 7,841,000 |
| 2. | Germany 833,000 | Germany 849,000 | China 921,000 | China 1,391,000 |
| 3. | Canada 812,000 | Canada 843,000 | Philippines 913,000 | Philippines 1,222,000 |
| 4. | Mexico 760,000 | Italy 832,000 | Canada 745,000 | India 1,007,000 |
| 5. | United Kingdom 686,000 | United Kingdom 669,000 | Cuba 737,000 | Cuba 952,000 |
| 6. | Poland 548,000 | Cuba 608,000 | Germany 712,000 | Vietnam 863,000 |
| 7. | Soviet Union 463,000 | Philippines 501,000 | United Kingdom 640,000 | El Salvador 765,000 |
| 8. | Cuba 439,000 | Poland 418,000 | Italy 581,000 | Korea 701,000 |
| 9. | Ireland 251,000 | Soviet Union 406,000 | Korea 568,000 | Dominican Republic 692,000 |
| 10. | Austria 214,000 | Korea 290,000 | Vietnam 543,000 | Canada 678,000 |

1. In general, countries as reported at each census. Data are not totally comparable over time due to changes in boundaries for some countries. Great Britain excludes Ireland. United Kingdom includes Northern Ireland. China in 1990 includes Hong Kong and Taiwan. *Source: Profile of the Foreign-Born Population in the United States: 2000*, U.S. Census Bureau, 2001.

## Foreign-Born Population in Metropolitan Areas with 5 Million or More People, 2000

| Metropolitan area | Percent foreign born | Metropolitan area | Percent foreign born |
|---|---|---|---|
| Los Angeles-Riverside-Orange County, Calif. | 29.6% | Boston-Worcester-Lawrence, Mass.-N.H.-Maine-Conn. | 12.5% |
| San Francisco-Oakland- San Jose, Calif. | 28.3 | Chicago-Gary-Kenosha, Ill.-Ind.-Wis. | 12.3 |
| New York-Northern New Jersey-Long Island, N.Y.-N.J.-Conn.-Pa. | 22.8 | Washington-Baltimore, DC-Md.-Va.-W.Va. | 11.9 |
| | | Detroit-Ann Arbor-Flint, Mich. | 7.4 |
| Dallas-Ft. Worth, Tex. | 12.8 | Philadelphia-Wilmington-Atlantic City, Pa.-N.J.-Del.-Md. | 5.1 |

*Source:* U.S. Census Bureau, 2001, Table 5–2A.

## Population of the United States by Race and Hispanic Origin, 2000 Census Results

| | Total population | % of population | | Total population | % of population |
|---|---|---|---|---|---|
| Total population | 281,421,906 | 100.0% | Native Hawaiian and other | | |
| White | 211,460,626 | 75.1 | Pacific Islander | 398,835 | 0.1% |
| Black or African American | 34,658,190 | 12.3 | Some other race | 15,359,073 | 5.5 |
| American Indian and Alaska | | | Two or more races | 6,826,228 | 2.4 |
| Native | 2,475,956 | 0.9 | Hispanic or Latino | 35,305,818 | 12.5 |
| Asian | 10,242,998 | 3.6 | | | |

NOTE: Percentages add up to more than 100% because Hispanics may be of any race and are therefore counted under more than one category. *Source:* U.S. Census Bureau, Census 2000.

### Black or African-American Population for the U.S. by Region, 2000

| | Black or African American | |
|---|---|---|
| Area | Number | Percent of total population |
| **United States** | **34,658,190** | **12.3%** |
| Region | | |
| Northeast | 6,099,881 | 11.4 |
| Midwest | 6,499,733 | 10.1 |
| South | 18,981,692 | 18.9 |
| West | 3,076,884 | 4.9 |

*Source:* U.S. Census Bureau, Census 2000.

### Ten Cities of 100,000 or More with Highest Percentage of Blacks or African Americans, 2000

| City | Percent |
|---|---|
| Gary, Ind. | 84.0% |
| Detroit, Mich. | 81.6 |
| Birmingham, Ala. | 73.5 |
| Jackson, Miss. | 70.6 |
| New Orleans, La. | 67.3 |
| Baltimore, Md. | 64.3 |
| Atlanta, Ga. | 61.4 |
| Memphis, Tenn. | 61.4 |
| Washington, DC | 60.0 |
| Richmond, Va. | 57.2 |

*Source:* U.S. Census Bureau, Census 2000.

## U.S. Hispanic/Latino Population, 2000

| National origin | Population | Percent | National origin | Population | Percent |
|---|---|---|---|---|---|
| **Total** | **35,305,818** | **100.0%** | Other Central American | 103,721 | 0.3% |
| **Mexican** | **20,640,711** | **58.5** | **South American** | **1,353,562** | **3.8** |
| **Puerto Rican** | **3,406,178** | **9.6** | Argentinean | 100,864 | 0.3 |
| **Cuban** | **1,241,685** | **3.5** | Bolivian | 42,068 | 0.1 |
| **Dominican (Dominican Republic)** | **764,945** | **2.2** | Chilean | 68,849 | 0.2 |
| **Central American (excludes Mexican)** | **1,686,937** | **4.8** | Colombian | 470,684 | 1.3 |
| | | | Ecuadorian | 260,559 | 0.7 |
| Costa Rican | 68,588 | 0.2 | Paraguayan | 8,769 | (1) |
| Guatemalan | 372,487 | 1.1 | Peruvian | 233,926 | 0.7 |
| Honduran | 217,569 | 0.6 | Uruguayan | 18,804 | 0.1 |
| Nicaraguan | 177,684 | 0.5 | Venezuelan | 91,507 | 0.3 |
| Panamanian | 91,723 | 0.3 | Other South American | 57,532 | 0.2 |
| Salvadoran | 655,165 | 1.9 | All other Hispanic or Latino | 6,011,000 | 17.0 |

(1)... less than 0.1 ... Source: U.S. Census Bureau, Census 2000.

## Top Ten Places of 100,000 or More Population with the Highest Percent Hispanic, 2000

| Place and state | Total population | Percent Hispanic of total population | Place and state | Total population | Percent Hispanic of total population |
|---|---|---|---|---|---|
| East Los Angeles, Calif. | 124,283 | 96.8% | El Paso, Tex. | 563,662 | 76.6% |
| Laredo, Tex. | 176,576 | 94.1 | Santa Ana, Calif. | 337,977 | 76.1 |
| Brownsville, Tex. | 139,722 | 91.3 | El Monte, Calif. | 115,965 | 72.4 |
| Hialeah, Fla. | 226,419 | 90.3 | Oxnard, Calif. | 170,358 | 66.2 |
| McAllen, Tex. | 106,414 | 80.3 | Miami, Fla. | 362,470 | 65.8 |

*Source:* U.S. Census Bureau, Census 2000, Summary File 1.

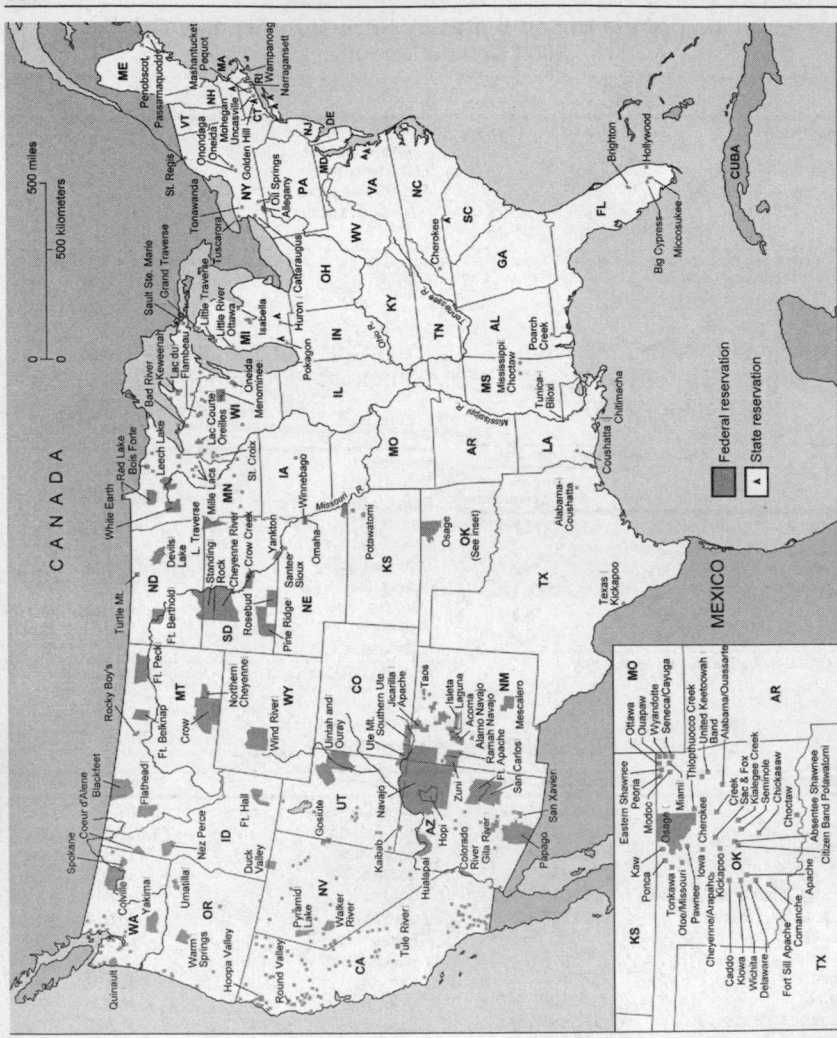

## U.S. Federal and State Reservations

## Populations of the Ten Largest Reservations
### (1990 Census figures)

| Name | Population |
| --- | --- |
| Navajo (Ariz., N.M., Utah) | 143,405 |
| Pine Ridge (Neb., S.D.) | 11,182 |
| Fort Apache (Ariz.) | 9,825 |
| Gila River (Ariz.) | 9,116 |
| Papago (Ariz.) | 8,480 |
| Rosebud (S.D.) | 8,043 |
| San Carlos (Ariz.) | 7,110 |
| Zuni Pueblo (Ariz., N.M.) | 7,073 |
| Hopi (Ariz.) | 7,061 |
| Blackfeet (Mont.) | 7,025 |

The 218,320 American Indians living on these 10 reservations account for about half of all American Indians living on reservations and trust lands. *Source*: 1990, Census Bureau. *Map source*: Frederick E. Hoxie, ed., *Encyclopedia of North American Indians* (Boston: Houghton Mifflin, 1996). Reprinted with permission.

## U.S. Asian Population, 2000

| National origin | Population[1] | Percent | National origin | Population[1] | Percent |
|---|---|---|---|---|---|
| **Total** | **11,898,828** | **100.0%** | Korean | 1,228,427 | 10.3% |
| Asian Indian | 1,899,599 | 16.0 | Laotian | 198,203 | 1.7 |
| Bangladeshi | 57,412 | 0.5 | Malaysian | 18,566 | 0.2 |
| Bhutanese | 212 | ([2]) | Maldivian | 51 | ([2]) |
| Burmese | 16,720 | 0.1 | Nepalese | 9,399 | 0.1 |
| Cambodian | 206,052 | 1.7 | Okinawan | 10,599 | 0.1 |
| Chinese, except Taiwanese | 2,734,841 | 23.0 | Pakistani | 204,309 | 1.7 |
| Filipino | 2,364,815 | 19.9 | Singaporean | 2,394 | ([2]) |
| Hmong | 186,310 | 1.6 | Sri Lankan | 24,587 | 0.2 |
| Indo Chinese | 199 | ([2]) | Taiwanese | 144,795 | 1.2 |
| Indonesian | 63,073 | 0.5 | Thai | 150,283 | 1.3 |
| Iwo Jiman | 78 | ([2]) | Vietnamese | 1,223,736 | 10.3 |
| Japanese | 1,148,932 | 9.7 | Other Asian, not specified | 369,430 | 3.1 |

1. The numbers by national origin do not add up to the total population figure because respondents may have put down more than one country. Respondents reporting several countries are counted several times. 2. Less than 0.1%. *Source:* U.S. Census Bureau, Census 2000.

## Native Hawaiian and Other U.S. Pacific Islander Population, 2000

| National origin | Population[1] | Percent | National origin | Population[1] | Percent |
|---|---|---|---|---|---|
| **Total** | **874,414** | **100.0%** | Kosraean | 226 | ([2]) |
| **Polynesian** | | | Pohnpeian | 700 | 0.1% |
| Native Hawaiian | 401,162 | 45.9 | Chuukese | 654 | 0.1 |
| Samoan | 133,281 | 15.2 | Yapese | 368 | ([2]) |
| Tongan | 36,840 | 4.2 | Marshallese | 6,650 | 0.8 |
| Tahitian | 3,313 | 0.4 | I-Kiribati | 175 | ([2]) |
| Tokelauan | 574 | 0.1 | Micronesian, not specified | 9,940 | 1.1 |
| Polynesian, not specified | 8,796 | 1.0 | **Melanesian** | | |
| **Micronesian** | | | Fijian | 13,581 | 1.6 |
| Guamanian or Chamorro | 92,611 | 10.6 | Papua New Guinean | 224 | ([2]) |
| Mariana Islander | 141 | ([2]) | Solomon Islander | 25 | ([2]) |
| Saipanese | 475 | 0.1 | Ni-Vanuatu | 18 | ([2]) |
| Palauan | 3,469 | 0.4 | Melanesian, not specified | 315 | ([2]) |
| Carolinian | 173 | ([2]) | Other Pacific Islander | 174,912 | 20.0 |

1. The numbers by national origin do not add up to the total population figure because respondents may have put down more than one country. Respondents reporting several countries are counted several times. 2. Less than 0.1%. *Source:* U.S. Census Bureau, Census 2000.

## American Indian and Alaska Native Population by Selected Tribes, 2000

| Tribe | Population[1] | Tribe | Population[1] |
|---|---|---|---|
| **Total** | **4,119,301** | Pima | 11,493 |
| Apache | 96,833 | Potawatomi | 25,595 |
| Blackfeet | 85,750 | Pueblo | 74,085 |
| Cherokee | 729,533 | Puget Sound Salish | 14,631 |
| Cheyenne | 18,204 | Seminole | 27,431 |
| Chickasaw | 38,351 | Shoshone | 12,026 |
| Chippewa | 149,669 | Sioux | 153,360 |
| Choctaw | 158,774 | Tohono O'odham | 20,087 |
| Colville | 9,393 | Ute | 10,385 |
| Comanche | 19,376 | Yakama | 10,171 |
| Cree | 7,161 | Maya | 22,412 |
| Creek | 71,310 | Yuman | 8,976 |
| Crow | 13,394 | Other specified American | |
| Delaware | 10,011 | Indian tribes | 357,658 |
| Houma | 8,713 | American Indian tribe, not specified | 195,902 |
| Iroquois | 80,822 | Alaska Athabascan | 18,838 |
| Kiowa | 12,242 | Aleut | 16,978 |
| Latin American Indian | 180,940 | Eskimo | 54,761 |
| Lumbee | 57,868 | Tlingit-Haida | 22,365 |
| Menominee | 9,840 | Other specified Alaska Native tribes | 3,973 |
| Navajo | 298,197 | Alaska Native tribe, not specified | 8,702 |
| Osage | 15,897 | American Indian or Alaska Native | |
| Ottawa | 10,677 | tribe, not specified | 1,056,457 |
| Paiute | 13,532 | | |

1. The numbers by American Indian and Alaska Native tribe do not add up to the total population figure because respondents may have put down more than one tribe. Respondents reporting several tribes are counted several times. *Source:* U.S. Census Bureau, Census 2000.

# Affirmative Action Timeline

In its tumultuous 30-year history, affirmative action has been both praised and pilloried as an answer to racial inequality. The policy was introduced in 1965 by President Johnson as a method of redressing discrimination that had persisted in spite of civil rights laws and constitutional guarantees. Focusing in particular on education and jobs, affirmative action policies required active measures to ensure that blacks and other minorities enjoyed the same opportunities for promotions, salary increases, career advancement, school admissions, scholarships, and financial aid that had been the nearly exclusive province of whites. From the outset, affirmative action was envisioned as a temporary remedy that would end once there was a "level playing field" for all Americans.

By the late '70s, however, flaws in the policy began to show up amid its good intentions. Reverse discrimination became a passionate issue, epitomized by the famous *Bakke* case in 1978. A backlash against affirmative action mounted, and in the last decade the tide has turned against it in both the courts and on a state level—California and Washington have gone as far as abolishing the policy.

Yet the questions of fairness and racial equality remain troubling for most of those not positioned at the ideological poles of the issue. Even a once-adamant opponent of affirmative action like John Bunzel, president of San Jose State University, has acknowledged that "perhaps the most important lesson I've learned is that there are no airtight, completely coherent, unassailable, and holistic answers on the question of affirmative action. . . . Any intelligent person who wrestles with it is going to be vulnerable and subject to the twists and turns of unintended consequences." Serious advocates both for and against affirmative action could easily share such an estimation.

**March 6, 1961: Executive Order 10925 made the first reference to "affirmative action."** President John F. Kennedy issued Executive Order 10925, which created the Committee on Equal Employment Opportunity and mandated that projects financed with federal funds "take affirmative action" to ensure that hiring and employment practices are free of racial bias.

**July 2, 1964: Civil Rights Act signed by President Lyndon Johnson.** The most sweeping civil rights legislation since Reconstruction, the Civil Rights Act prohibits discrimination of all kinds based on race, color, religion, or national origin.

**June 4, 1965: Speech defining concept of affirmative action.** In a speech to the graduating class at Howard University, President Johnson framed the concept underlying affirmative action, asserting that civil rights laws alone were not enough to remedy discrimination: "You do not wipe away the scars of centuries by saying: 'now, you are free to go where you want, do as you desire, and choose the leaders you please.' You do not take a man who for years has been hobbled by chains, liberate him, bring him to the starting line of a race, saying, 'you are free to compete with all the others,' and still justly believe you have been completely fair. . . . This is the next and more profound stage of the battle for civil rights. We seek not just freedom but opportunity—not just legal equity but human ability—not just equality as a right and a theory, but equality as a fact and as a result."

**Sept. 24, 1965: Executive Order 11246 enforced affirmative action for the first time.** Issued by President Johnson, the executive order required government contractors to "take affirmative action" toward prospective minority employees in all aspects of hiring and employment. Contractors must take specific measures to ensure equality in hiring and must document these efforts. On Oct. 13, 1967, the order was amended to cover discrimination on the basis of gender.

**1969: The Philadelphia Order.** Initiated by President Richard Nixon, the "Philadelphia Order" was the most forceful plan thus far to guarantee fair hiring practices in construction jobs. Philadelphia was selected as the test case because, as Assistant Secretary of Labor Arthur Fletcher explained,

"The craft unions and the construction industry are among the most egregious offenders against equal opportunity laws . . . openly hostile toward letting blacks into their closed circle." The order included definite "goals and timetables." As President Nixon asserted, "We would not impose quotas, but would require federal contractors to show 'affirmative action' to meet the goals of increasing minority employment."

**June 28, 1978: *Regents of the University of California* v. *Bakke*.** This landmark Supreme Court case imposed limitations on affirmative action to ensure that providing greater opportunities for minorities did not come at the expense of the rights of the majority—affirmative action was unfair if it led to reverse discrimination. The case involved the University of California at Davis Medical School, which had two separate admissions pools, one for standard applicants, and another for minority and economically disadvantaged students. The school reserved 16 of its 100 places for this latter group. Allan Bakke, a white applicant, was rejected twice even though there were minority applicants admitted with significantly lower scores than his. Bakke maintained that judging him on the basis of his race was a violation of the Equal Protection Clause of the Fourteenth Amendment. The Supreme Court ruled that while race was a legitimate factor in school admissions, the use of such inflexible quotas as the medical school used set aside was not. The Supreme Court, however, was split 5–4 in its decision on the *Bakke* case and addressed only a minimal number of the many complex issues that had sprung up about affirmative action.

**July 2, 1980: *Fullilove* v. *Klutznick*.** While *Bakke* struck down strict quotas, in *Fullilove* the Supreme Court ruled that some modest quotas were perfectly constitutional. The Court upheld a federal law requiring that 15% of funds for public works be set aside for qualified minority contractors. The "narrowed focus and limited extent" of the affirmative action program did not violate the equal rights of nonminority contractors, according to the Court—there was no "allocation of federal funds according to inflexible percentages solely based on race or ethnicity."

**May 19, 1986:** *Wygant* v. *Jackson Board of Education.* This case challenged a school board's policy of protecting minority employees by laying off nonminority teachers first, even though the nonminority employees had seniority. The Supreme Court ruled against the school board, maintaining that the injury suffered by nonminorities could not justify the benefits to minorities.

**Feb. 25, 1987:** *United States* v. *Paradise.* In July 1970, a federal court found that the State of Alabama Department of Public Safety systematically discriminated against blacks in hiring: "in the thirty-seven-year history of the patrol there has never been a black trooper." The court ordered that the state reform its hiring practices to end "pervasive, systematic, and obstinate discriminatory exclusion of blacks." A full 12 years and several lawsuits later, the department still had not promoted any blacks above entry level. In response, the court ordered specific racial quotas to correct the situation. For every white hired or promoted, one black would also be hired or promoted until at least 25% of the upper ranks of the department were composed of blacks. The case challenged this use of numerical quotas. The Supreme Court, however, upheld the use of strict quotas in this case as one of the only means of combating the department's overt racism.

**Jan. 23, 1989:** *City of Richmond* v. *Croson.* Affirmative action on the state and local level was challenged in this case involving a Richmond, Va., program setting aside 30% of city construction funds for black-owned firms. For the first time, affirmative action was judged as a "highly suspect tool." The Supreme Court ruled that an "amorphous claim that there has been past discrimination in a particular industry cannot justify the use of an unyielding racial quota." It maintained that affirmative action must be subject to "strict scrutiny" and is unconstitutional unless racial discrimination can be proven to be "widespread throughout a particular industry."

**June 12, 1995:** *Adarand Constructors, Inc.* v. *Peña.* What *Croson* was to state- and local-run affirmative action programs, *Adarand* was to federal programs. The Court again called for "strict scrutiny" in determining whether discrimination existed before implementing a federal affirmative action program. "Strict scrutiny" meant that affirmative action programs fulfilled a "compelling governmental interest," and were "narrowly tailored" to fit the particular situation. Although two of the judges (Scalia and Thomas) felt that there should be a complete ban on affirmative action, the majority of judges concluded that the persistence of both the practice and the lingering effects of racial discrimination against minority groups in this country" justified the use of race-based remedial measures in some circumstances.

**July 19, 1995: White House guidelines on affirmative action.** President Clinton asserted in a speech that while *Adarand* set "stricter standards to mandate reform of affirmative action, it actually reaffirmed the need for affirmative action and reaffirmed the continuing existence of systematic discrimination in the United States." In a White House memorandum on the same day, he called for the elimination of any program that "(a) creates a quota; (b) creates preferences for unqualified individuals; (c) creates reverse discrimination; or (d) continues even after its equal opportunity purposes have been achieved."

**March 18, 1996:** *Hopwood* v. *University of Texas Law School.* Four white law-school applicants at the University of Texas challenged the school's affirmative action program, asserting that they were rejected because of unfair preferences toward less qualified minority applicants. As a result, the 5th U.S. Court of Appeals suspended the university's affirmative action admissions program and ruled that the 1978 *Bakke* decision was invalid—while *Bakke* rejected racial quotas, it maintained that race could serve as a factor in admissions. In addition to remedying past discrimination, *Bakke* maintained that the inclusion of minority students would create a diverse student body, and that was beneficial to the educational environment as a whole. *Hopwood,* however, rejected the legitimacy of diversity as a goal, asserting that "educational diversity is not recognized as a compelling state interest." The Supreme Court allowed the ruling to stand.

**Nov. 3, 1997: Proposition 209 enacted in California.** A state ban on all forms of affirmative action was passed in California: "The state shall not discriminate against, or grant preferential treatment to, any individual or group on the basis of race, sex, color, ethnicity, or national origin in the operation of public employment, public education, or public contracting." Proposed in 1996, the controversial ban had been delayed in the courts for almost a year before it went into effect.

**Dec. 3, 1998: Initiative 200 enacted in Washington State.** Washington became the second state to abolish state affirmative action measures when it passed "I 200," which was similar to California's Proposition 209.

**Feb. 22, 2000: Florida banned race as factor in college admissions.** Florida legislature approved education component of Gov. Jeb Bush's "One Florida" initiative, aimed at ending affirmative action in the state.

**Dec. 13, 2000: Univ. of Michigan's undergraduate affirmative action policy.** In *Gratz* v. *Bollinger,* a federal judge ruled that the use of race as a factor in admissions at the university was constitutional. The gist of the university's argument was as follows: just as preference is granted to children of alumni, scholarship athletes, and other groups for reasons associated with the university, so too does the affirmative action program serve "a compelling interest" by providing educational benefits derived from a diverse student body,

**March 27, 2001: Univ. of Michigan Law School's affirmative action policy.** In *Grutter* v. *Bollinger,* a case similar to the University of Michigan undergraduate lawsuit, a different judge drew an opposite conclusion, invalidating the law school's policy and ruling that "intellectual diversity bears no obvious or necessary relationship to racial diversity." But on May 14, 2002, the decision was reversed on appeal, ruling that the admissions policy was, in fact, constitutional.

# Making the World Safer

Four pioneers create new tools for law enforcement
in an age of terrorism

**By the Staff of** TIME

For nations at war, technology has always been an unsteady ally. Yes, the Great Wall kept China's marauders at bay, at least for a while, but all the weaponry America brought to bear on the Vietnamese—from napalm to the B-52s—couldn't win their hearts and minds. In today's war on terror, we will rely more than ever on technology: the clever missiles that target a terrorist leader; the vaccines that protect against biological weapons; the lines of code that render a computer impervious to cyberterrorists. In the aviation system, high-tech innovations promise to do everything from positively identifying passengers at the gate to automatically returning hijacked planes safely to earth.

As part of its ongoing series on Innovators, TIME profiled four people whose work promises to help law enforcement professionals win the war on terror.

## John Daugman: The Iris Scanner

At a time when everyone is worried about airline safety, the work of a little-known Cambridge University scientist could ease the public's fear. John Daugman's mathematical algorithms turn the human eye into a fingerprint. His process uses a camera to photograph the iris—the colored part of the eye—and creates a digital code based on its unique pattern. Daugman's system is extremely accurate; using 255 data points—versus 70 for a fingerprint—it hasn't made a false match yet. Indeed, iris scanners were already enhancing security at airports from Frankfurt, Germany, to Charlotte, N.C., in 2001. Since Dec. 2001, airline passengers from North America who enroll in an iris database don't have to show their passports when arriving at London's Heathrow Airport.

The idea of iris recognition was first proposed by an American opthalmologist in 1936; by the late 1980s, two Boston eye doctors gave it a shot, enlisting the help of Daugman, then a newly minted Harvard Ph.D. "At first I told them I wasn't interested," he recalls. "I told them to go and get one of those clever kids from MIT." But as Daugman thought about the task, he became intrigued.

Born in the U.S. to an immigrant family, Daugman credits his upbringing with opening his mind to off-beat ideas. "I like, for example, the irregularity of the iris," he says. Daugman finally cracked the iris code by embracing randomness. "My system finds what it is looking for by failing to match a pattern," explains Daugman, who rarely mentions that the Queen made him a knight in 2000 for his work. If his iris system makes airports safer, he will have the thanks not only of the British monarchy, but of the world as well.

## Lawrence Farwell: Brain Fingerprinting

He went to Harvard, works in Iowa, and loves swing dancing. That's not the typical profile of an anticrime crusader, but Lawrence Farwell is an unusual guy. While developing technology that would allow the vocally paralyzed to speak, he stumbled across a trove of seemingly extraneous signals stored in the brain. He began looking for a way to put that information to use. Result: a new forensic technology he calls brain fingerprinting.

Here's how it works: Farwell fits a suspect with a sensor-filled headband. By flashing a series of pictures on a screen, he can read the subject's involuntary reactions to them. When there's something familiar about an image, it triggers an electrical response that begins between 300 and 800 milliseconds after the stimulus. Scientists have studied these "p300 bumps" for years. Farwell believes that, combined with other measures—he has patented which ones he looks at—he can determine if a subject is familiar with anything from a phone number to an al-Qaeda code word.

Indeed, the CIA has funded his research with more than $1 million, and a former FBI point man for biological and chemical weapons has joined Farwell's firm. Critics say that p300-type testing needs a lot of refinement before it's a perfect polygraph, but such criticism doesn't deter Farwell. "The fundamental task in law enforcement and espionage and counterespionage is to determine the truth," he says. "My philosophy is that there is a tremendous cost in failing to apply the technology."

## Richard Langlois: The Germ Detector

Lots of little boys ask Santa for a bike or a baseball bat. But when Richard Langlois was growing up in El Cerrito, Calif., all he wanted for Christmas were the test tubes and beakers pictured in his laboratory-supply catalogs. These days, Langlois's equipment is supplied by Lawrence Livermore National Laboratories, where the biologist has been working for several years on a piece of equipment that is suddenly commanding great interest: a continuous air-monitoring system that can detect within an hour the presence of any bacteria or virus in a basketball stadium, shopping mall, or other indoor place. "It's like a smoke alarm" for harmful biological agents, says Langlois.

The benefits of Langlois's Autonomous Pathogen Detection System are obvious. Instead of waiting for someone to come down with anthrax or smallpox—or running a blood test on folks who think they might be infected—the APDS might give public-safety officials sufficient warning to evacuate the area before anyone got exposed. In a world where bioterrorism is no longer unthinkable, the APDS could serve as the first line of defense.

The system works by sucking in an air sample, analyzing its components, then putting out a report at fixed intervals, up to 48 times a day. At its core is a flow cytometer—or cell sorter—that Langlois co-invented in the late 1970s. The device shines laser beams on chromosomes within cells to make a quick genetic ID. A spin-off of early research into mapping the human genome, the cell sorter is now a standard tool for diagnosing AIDS, leukemia, and other cancers. Langlois even took it to Chernobyl to assess workers' genetic damage from radiation exposure after the 1986 nuclear reactor accident.

While other air sniffers are in the works or already in use, the refrigerator-size APDS stands out for its ability to rapidly detect even trace amounts of 100 different germs. To avoid the nuisance of false positives, suspected pathogens undergo a second, DNA-based test before officials are alerted.

## Dorothy Denning: Geo-Encryption

When it comes to cyberwarfare, America has a secret weapon: Georgetown University professor Dorothy Denning. Battles in cyberspace are high-tech brain races: you win by being the first to rec-ognize the weaknesses of a new technology—often hacking it yourself—and then figuring out how to protect it. This is what Denning has been doing for nearly three decades. In the 1970s, when most people thought information security meant locking your file cabinets, Denning devised a way for federal agencies such as the IRS to release vital information while keeping its most sensitive data secure. As computer systems became more complex, she discovered a system now widely used for detecting intruders in real time, rather than combing through log-in records after the fact.

And now she's pioneering a new field she calls geo-encryption. Working with industry, Denning has developed a way to keep information undecipherable until it reaches its location, as determined by GPS satellites. Movie studios, for example, have been afraid to release films digitally for the same reasons record companies hate Napster: once loose on the Internet, there's little to stop someone from posting the latest blockbuster DVD on the web for all to see and download. With Denning's system, however, only subscribers in specified locations—such as movie theaters—would be able to unscramble the data. The technology works as well for national security as it does for *Harry Potter*. Coded messages that the State Department sends its embassies, for example, could only be deciphered in the embassy buildings themselves, greatly reducing the risk of interception.    □

## Murder Victims: by Race and Sex, 2000

| Race and sex | Total no. victims | Percent distribution[1] | Race and sex | Total no. victims | Percent distribution[1] |
|---|---|---|---|---|---|
| **Race** | | | **Sex** | | |
| White | 6,263 | 48.4% | Male | 9,840 | 76.0% |
| Black | 6,193 | 47.8 | Female | 3,076 | 23.8 |
| Other | 319 | 2.5 | Unknown | 27 | 0.2 |
| Unknown | 168 | 1.3 | **Total** | **12,943** | **100.0** |

1. Because of rounding, percentages may not add up to 100. *Source: Crime in the United States, 2000,* FBI, Uniform Crime Reports.

## Murder Victims: Types of Weapon Used, 2000

| Type of weapon | Total no. victims | Percent distribution[1] | Type of weapon | Total no. victims | Percent distribution[1] |
|---|---|---|---|---|---|
| Firearms | 8,493 | 65.6% | Explosives | 9 | 0.1% |
| Knives or cutting instruments | 1,743 | 13.5 | Fire | 128 | 1.0 |
| Blunt objects (clubs, hammers, etc.) | 604 | 4.7 | Narcotics | 20 | 0.2 |
| | | | Strangulation | 166 | 1.3 |
| Personal weapons (hands, fists, feet, etc.)[2] | 900 | 7.0 | Asphyxiation | 89 | 0.7 |
| Poison | 8 | 0.1 | Other weapon or not stated[3] | 811 | 6.3 |
| | | | **Total** | **12,943** | **100.0** |

1. Because of rounding, percentages may not add up to 100. 2. Pushed is included in personal weapons. 3. Includes drowning. *Source: Crime in the United States, 2000,* FBI, Uniform Crime Reports.

### U.S. Prisoners, 1990–2001

| Year | Total inmates | Federal prisoners | State prisoners | Local jails |
|---|---|---|---|---|
| 1990 | 1,148,702 | 58,838 | 684,544 | 405,320 |
| 1995 | 1,585,586 | 89,538 | 989,004 | 507,044 |
| 2000 | 1,934,990 | 131,496 | 1,176,368 | 621,149 |
| 2001 | 1,965,495 | 140,741 | 1,187,322 | 631,240 |

NOTE: Jail counts are for midyear (June 30). State and Federal prisoner counts are for Dec. 31. *Source: Prison and Jail Inmates at Midyear 2001,* U.S. Bureau of Justice Statistics.

### Percent of State and Federal Inmates, by Race

According to a report by the Justice Policy Institute in 2002, the number of black men in prison has grown to five times the rate it was twenty years ago. Today, more African American men are in jail than in college. In 2000 there were 791,600 black men in prison and 603,032 enrolled in college. In 1980, there were 143,000 black men in prison and 463,700 enrolled in college.

| | 1990 | 2000 | | 1990 | 2000 |
|---|---|---|---|---|---|
| White | 35.6% | 35.7% | Hispanic | 17.4% | 16.4% |
| Black | 44.5 | 46.2 | Other | 2.5 | 1.7 |

*Source: Prisoners in 2000,* U.S. Bureau of Justice Statistics.

## Homicide Rate (per 100,000), 1950–2000

| Year | Homicide rate | Year | Homicide rate | Year | Homicide rate | Year | Homicide rate | Year | Homicide rate |
|------|------|------|------|------|------|------|------|------|------|
| 1950 | 4.6 | 1961 | 4.8 | 1972 | 9.0 | 1983 | 8.3 | 1994 | 9.0 |
| 1951 | 4.4 | 1962 | 4.6 | 1973 | 9.4 | 1984 | 7.9 | 1995 | 8.2 |
| 1952 | 4.6 | 1963 | 4.6 | 1974 | 9.8 | 1985 | 7.9 | 1996 | 7.4 |
| 1953 | 4.5 | 1964 | 4.9 | 1975 | 9.6 | 1986 | 8.6 | 1997 | 6.8 |
| 1954 | 4.2 | 1965 | 5.1 | 1976 | 8.8 | 1987 | 8.3 | 1998 | 6.3 |
| 1955 | 4.1 | 1966 | 5.6 | 1977 | 8.8 | 1988 | 8.4 | 1999 | 5.7 |
| 1956 | 4.1 | 1967 | 6.2 | 1978 | 9.0 | 1989 | 8.7 | 2000 | 5.5 |
| 1957 | 4.0 | 1968 | 6.9 | 1979 | 9.7 | 1990 | 9.4 | | |
| 1958 | 4.8 | 1969 | 7.3 | 1980 | 10.2 | 1991 | 9.8 | | |
| 1959 | 4.9 | 1970 | 7.9 | 1981 | 9.8 | 1992 | 9.3 | | |
| 1960 | 5.1 | 1971 | 8.6 | 1982 | 9.1 | 1993 | 9.5 | | |

*Source: Crime in the United States, 2000,* FBI, Uniform Crime Reports.

## Number of Persons Executed,[1] by Jurisdiction, 1930–2000

| State | Number executed since 1930 | 1977[2] | State | Number executed since 1930 | 1977[2] | State | Number executed since 1930 | 1977[2] |
|-------|------|------|-------|------|------|-------|------|------|
| Texas | 536 | 239 | Missouri | 108 | 46 | Delaware | 23 | 11 |
| Georgia | 389 | 23 | Illinois | 102 | 12 | Oregon | 21 | 2 |
| New York | 329 | — | Tennessee | 94 | 1 | Connecticut | 21 | — |
| California | 300 | 8 | Oklahoma | 90 | 30 | Utah | 19 | 6 |
| North Carolina | 279 | 16 | New Jersey | 74 | — | Iowa | 18 | — |
| Florida | 220 | 50 | Maryland | 71 | 3 | Kansas | 15 | — |
| South Carolina | 187 | 25 | Arizona | 60 | 22 | Montana | 8 | 2 |
| Ohio | 173 | 1 | Washington | 50 | 3 | Wyoming | 8 | 1 |
| Virginia | 173 | 81 | Indiana | 48 | 7 | New Mexico | 8 | — |
| Louisiana | 159 | 26 | Colorado | 48 | 1 | Nebraska | 7 | 3 |
| Alabama | 158 | 23 | District of Columbia | 40 | — | Idaho | 4 | 1 |
| Mississippi | 158 | 4 | West Virginia | 40 | — | Vermont | 4 | — |
| Pennsylvania | 155 | 3 | Nevada | 37 | 8 | New Hampshire | 1 | — |
| Arkansas | 141 | 23 | Federal system | 33 | — | South Dakota | 1 | — |
| Kentucky | 105 | 2 | Massachusetts | 27 | — | **U.S. total** | **4,542** | **683** |

1. Executed under civil authority; military authorities carried out an additional 160 executions, 1930–1997. 2. In 1972 the Supreme Court ruled that capital punishment, as it was then administered, was "cruel and unusual" and therefore unconstitutional. On July 1, 1976, however, the Court overturned the ruling by a 7–2 decision, and capital punishment was reinstated. *Source: Capital Punishment, 2000,* U.S. Bureau of Justice Statistics.

## Characteristics of Prisoners Under Sentence of Death

| Characteristic | 1980 | 1990 | 1999 | Characteristic | 1980 | 1990 | 1999 |
|----------------|------|------|------|----------------|------|------|------|
| **Race and age** | | | | **Marital status** | | | |
| White | 418 | 1,368 | 1,948 | Never married | 268 | 998 | 1,689 |
| Black and other | 270 | 978 | 1,579 | Married | 229 | 632 | 731 |
| Under 20 years | 11 | 8 | 16 | Divorced[1] | 217 | 726 | 1,107 |
| 20 to 24 years | 173 | 168 | 251 | **Time elapsed since sentencing** | | | |
| 25 to 34 years | 334 | 1,110 | 1,108 | Less than 12 months | 185 | 231 | 259 |
| 35 to 54 years | 186 | 1,006 | 1,958 | 12 to 47 months | 389 | 753 | 800 |
| 55 years and over | 10 | 64 | 194 | 48 to 71 months | 102 | 438 | 499 |
| **Years of schooling completed** | | | | 72 months and over | 38 | 934 | 1,969 |
| 7 years or less | 68 | 178 | 201 | **Legal status at arrest** | | | |
| 8 years | 74 | 186 | 221 | Not under sentence | 384 | 1,345 | 2,088 |
| 9 to 11 years | 204 | 775 | 1,142 | Parole or probation[2] | 115 | 578 | 886 |
| 12 years | 162 | 729 | 1,157 | Prison or escaped | 45 | 128 | 125 |
| More than 12 years | 43 | 209 | 307 | Unknown | 170 | 305 | 428 |
| Unknown | 163 | 279 | 499 | **Total** | **688** | **2,346** | **3,527** |

1. Includes widows, widowers, and unknown. 2. Includes persons on mandatory conditional release, work release, leave, AWOL, or bail. Excludes prisoners under sentence of death confined in local correctional systems pending appeal or who have not been committed to prison. *Source:* U.S. Bureau of Justice Statistics, *Capital Punishment,* annual, from *Statistical Abstract of the United States, 2001.*

## Methods of Execution

| State | Minimum age | Method | State | Minimum age | Method |
|---|---|---|---|---|---|
| Alabama | 16 | Electrocution | Nebraska | 18 | Electrocution |
| Alaska | — | No death penalty | Nevada | 16 | Lethal injection |
| Arizona[1] | none | Lethal injection or gas | New Hampshire[7] | 17 | Lethal injection or hanging |
| Arkansas[2] | 14 | Lethal injection or electrocution | New Jersey | 18 | Lethal injection |
| California | 18 | Lethal injection or gas | New Mexico | 18 | Lethal injection |
| Colorado | 18 | Lethal injection | New York | 18 | Lethal injection |
| Connecticut | 18 | Lethal injection | North Carolina[8] | 17 | Lethal injection |
| Delaware[3] | 16 | Lethal injection or hanging | North Dakota | — | No death penalty |
| DC | — | No death penalty | Ohio | 18 | Lethal injection or electrocution |
| Florida | 16 | Lethal injection or electrocution | Oklahoma[9] | 16 | Lethal injection, electrocution, or firing squad |
| Georgia | 17 | Lethal injection | | | |
| Hawaii | — | No death penalty | Oregon | 18 | Lethal injection |
| Idaho | none | Lethal injection or firing squad | Pennsylvania | none | Lethal injection |
| Illinois | 18 | Lethal injection | Rhode Island | — | No death penalty |
| Indiana | 16 | Lethal injection | South Carolina | none | Lethal injection or electrocution |
| Iowa | — | No death penalty | South Dakota[10] | none | Lethal injection |
| Kansas | 18 | Lethal injection | Tennessee[11] | 18 | Lethal injection or electrocution |
| Kentucky[4] | 16 | Lethal injection or electrocution | Texas | 17 | Lethal injection |
| Louisiana | none | Lethal injection | Utah | 14 | Lethal injection or firing squad |
| Maine | — | No death penalty | Vermont | — | No death penalty |
| Maryland | 18 | Lethal injection | Virginia[12] | 14 | Lethal injection or electrocution |
| Massachusetts | — | No death penalty | Washington | 18 | Lethal injection or hanging |
| Michigan | — | No death penalty | West Virginia | — | No death penalty |
| Minnesota | — | No death penalty | Wisconsin | — | No death penalty |
| Mississippi[5] | 16 | Lethal injection | Wyoming[13] | 16 | Lethal injection or gas |
| Missouri | 16 | Lethal injection or gas | Federal system[14] | 18 | Lethal injection |
| Montana[6] | none | Lethal injection | | | |

1. Ariz. authorizes lethal injection for those sentenced after 11/15/92; before that date, methods available are lethal injection or lethal gas. 2. Ark. authorizes lethal injection for those whose capital offense occurred on or after 7/4/83; before that date, methods available are lethal injection or electrocution. 3. Del. authorizes lethal injection for those whose capital offense occurred after 6/13/86; before that date, methods available are lethal injection or hanging. 4. Ky. authorizes lethal injection for those sentenced on or after 3/31/98; before that date, methods available are lethal injection or electrocution. 5. Miss. minimum age defined by statute is 13. 6. Montana law specifies that offenders tried under the capital sexual statute be 18 or older. 7. N.H. authorizes hanging only if lethal injection cannot be given. 8. N.C.'s minimum age is 17, unless the person was already incarcerated for murder when the subsequent murder occurred; then the minimum age is 14. 9. Okla. authorizes electrocution if lethal injection is ever held to be unconstitutional and firing squad if both lethal injection and electrocution are held unconstitutional. 10. S.D. authorizes juveniles to possibly be transferred to adult court; age can be a mitigating factor. 11. Tenn. authorizes lethal injection for those whose capital offense occurred after 12/31/98; before that date, methods available are lethal injection or electrocution. 12. Va.'s minimum age for transfer to adult court by statute is 14. 13. Wyo. authorizes lethal gas if lethal injection is ever held to be unconstitutional. 14. The method of execution of federal prisoners is lethal injection. For offenses under the Violent Crime Control and Law Enforcement Act of 1994, the method is that of the state in which the conviction took place. *Source: Capital Punishment, 2000,* U.S. Bureau of Justice Statistics, and the Associated Press.

## Federal Prosecutions of Public Corruption

| Prosecution status | 1999 | 1997 | 1996 | 1995 | 1994 | 1993 | 1992 | 1990 | 1985 | 1980 |
|---|---|---|---|---|---|---|---|---|---|---|
| **Total:** Indicted | 1,134 | 1,057 | 984 | 1,051 | 1,165 | 1,371 | 1,189 | 1,176 | 1,157 | 727 |
| Convicted | 1,065 | 853 | 902 | 878 | 969 | 1,362 | 1,081 | 1,084 | 997 | 602 |
| **Federal officials:** Indicted | 480 | 459 | 456 | 527 | 571 | 627 | 624 | 615 | 563 | 123 |
| Convicted | 460 | 392 | 459 | 438 | 488 | 595 | 532 | 583 | 470 | 131 |
| **State officials:** Indicted | 115 | 51 | 109 | 61 | 99 | 113 | 81 | 96 | 79 | 72 |
| Convicted | 80 | 49 | 83 | 61 | 97 | 133 | 92 | 79 | 66 | 51 |
| **Local officials:** Indicted | 237 | 255 | 219 | 236 | 248 | 309 | 232 | 257 | 248 | 247 |
| Convicted | 319 | 280 | 240 | 231 | 289 | 284 | 211 | 307 | 334 | 139 |

NOTE: Figures are latest available. *Source:* U.S. Department of Justice, *Federal Prosecutions of Corrupt Public Officials, 1970–1980,* and *Report to Congress on the Activities and Operations of the Public Integrity Section,* annual, from *Statistical Abstract of the United States, 2001.*

## Law Enforcement Officers Killed or Assaulted[1]

| | 1999 | 1997 | 1996 | 1995 | 1994 | 1993 | 1992 | 1991 | 1990 | 1989 | 1980 |
|---|---|---|---|---|---|---|---|---|---|---|---|
| **Total officers killed** | 107 | 132 | 112 | 133 | 133 | 129 | 129 | 122 | 132 | 144 | 164 |
| Officers assaulted | | | | | | | | | | | |
| Firearm | 1,783 | 2,110 | 1,878 | 2,354 | 3,168 | 4,002 | 4,455 | 3,532 | 3,662 | 3,154 | 3,295 |
| Knife or cutting instrument | 990 | 971 | 871 | 1,356 | 1,513 | 1,574 | 2,095 | 1,493 | 1,641 | 1,379 | 1,653 |
| Other dangerous weapon | 7,392 | 5,800 | 5,069 | 6,414 | 7,210 | 7,551 | 8,604 | 7,014 | 7,390 | 5,778 | 5,415 |
| Hands, fists, feet, etc. | 44,861 | 43,268 | 38,790 | 47,638 | 53,021 | 53,848 | 66,098 | 50,813 | 59,101 | 51,861 | 47,484 |
| **Total assaulted** | 55,026 | 52,149 | 46,608 | 57,762 | 64,912 | 66,975 | 81,252 | 62,852 | 71,794 | 62,172 | 57,847 |

1. Covers officers killed feloniously and accidentally in line of duty; includes federal officers. NOTE: Data are latest available. *Source: Statistical Abstract of the United States, 2001.*

## A Timeline of Recent U.S. School Shootings

| | |
|---|---|
| **Feb. 2, 1996**<br>**Moses Lake, Wash.** | Two students and one teacher killed, one other wounded when 14-year-old Barry Loukaitis opened fire on his algebra class. |
| **Feb. 19, 1997**<br>**Bethel, Alaska** | Principal and one student killed, two others wounded by Evan Ramsey, 16. |
| **Oct. 1, 1997**<br>**Pearl, Miss.** | Two students killed and seven wounded by Luke Woodham, 16, who was also accused of killing his mother. He and his friends were said to be outcasts who worshiped Satan. |
| **Dec. 1, 1997**<br>**West Paducah, Ky.** | Three students killed, five wounded by Michael Carneal, 14, as they participated in a prayer circle at Heath High School. |
| **Dec. 15, 1997**<br>**Stamps, Ark.** | Two students wounded. Colt Todd, 14, was hiding in the woods when he shot the students as they stood in the parking lot. |
| **March 24, 1998**<br>**Jonesboro, Ark.** | Four students and one teacher killed, ten others wounded outside as Westside Middle School emptied during a false fire alarm. Mitchell Johnson, 13, and Andrew Golden, 11, shot at their classmates and teachers from the woods. |
| **April 24, 1998**<br>**Edinboro, Pa.** | One teacher, John Gillette, killed, two students wounded at a dance at James W. Parker Middle School. Andrew Wurst, 14, was charged. |
| **May 19, 1998**<br>**Fayetteville, Tenn.** | One student killed in the parking lot at Lincoln County High School three days before he was to graduate. The victim was dating the ex-girlfriend of his killer, 18-year-old honor student Jacob Davis. |
| **May 21, 1998**<br>**Springfield, Ore.** | Two students killed, 22 others wounded in the cafeteria at Thurston High School by 15-year-old Kip Kinkel. Kinkel had been arrested and released a day earlier for bringing a gun to school. His parents were later found dead at home. |
| **June 15, 1998**<br>**Richmond, Va.** | One teacher and one guidance counselor wounded by a 14-year-old boy in the school hallway. |
| **April 20, 1999**<br>**Littleton, Colo.** | 14 students (including killers) and one teacher killed, 23 others wounded at Columbine High School in the nation's deadliest school shooting. Eric Harris, 18, and Dylan Klebold, 17, had plotted for a year to kill at least 500 and blow up their school. At the end of their hour-long rampage, they turned their guns on themselves. |
| **May 20, 1999**<br>**Conyers, Ga.** | Six students injured at Heritage High School by Thomas Solomon, 15, who was reportedly depressed after breaking up with his girlfriend. |
| **Nov. 19, 1999**<br>**Deming, N.M.** | Victor Cordova Jr., 12, shot and killed Araceli Tena, 13, in the lobby of Deming Middle School. |
| **Dec. 6, 1999**<br>**Fort Gibson, Okla.** | Four students wounded as Seth Trickey, 13, opened fire with a 9mm semiautomatic handgun at Fort Gibson Middle School. |
| **Feb. 29, 2000**<br>**Mount Morris Township, Mich.** | Six-year-old Kayla Rolland shot dead at Buell Elementary School near Flint, Mich. The assailant was identified as a six-year-old boy with a .32-caliber handgun. |
| **March 10, 2000**<br>**Savannah, Ga.** | Two students killed by Darrell Ingram, 19, while leaving a dance sponsored by Beach High School. |
| **May 26, 2000**<br>**Lake Worth, Fla.** | One teacher, Barry Grunow, shot and killed at Lake Worth Middle School by Nate Brazill, 13, with .25-caliber semiautomatic pistol on the last day of classes. |
| **Sept. 26, 2000**<br>**New Orleans, La.** | Two students wounded with the same gun during a fight at Woodson Middle School. |
| **Jan. 17, 2001**<br>**Baltimore, Md.** | One student shot and killed in front of Lake Clifton Eastern High School. |
| **March 5, 2001**<br>**Santee, Calif.** | Two killed and 13 wounded by Charles Andrew Williams, 15, firing from a bathroom at Santana High School. |
| **March 7, 2001**<br>**Williamsport, Pa.** | Elizabeth Catherine Bush, 14, wounded student Kimberly Marchese in the cafeteria of Bishop Neumann High School; she was depressed and frequently teased. |
| **March 22, 2001**<br>**Granite Hills, Calif.** | One teacher and three students wounded by Jason Hoffman, 18, at Granite Hills High School. A policeman shot and wounded Hoffman. |
| **March 30, 2001**<br>**Gary, Ind.** | One student killed by Donald R. Burt, Jr., a 17-year-old student who had been expelled from Lew Wallace High School. |
| **Nov. 12, 2001**<br>**Caro, Mich.** | Chris Buschbacher, 17, took two hostages at the Caro Learning Center before killing himself. |
| **Jan. 15, 2002**<br>**New York, N.Y.** | A teenager wounded two students at Martin Luther King Jr. High School. |

## Summary of Hate Crime Statistics, 2000

| | Number of incidents | Number of offenses | Number of victims | Number of known offenders |
|---|---|---|---|---|
| **Race** | 4,337 | 5,171 | 5,397 | 4,452 |
| Anti-white | 875 | 1,050 | 1,080 | 1,169 |
| Anti-black | 2,884 | 3,409 | 3,535 | 2,799 |
| Anti-American Indian/Alaskan Native | 57 | 62 | 64 | 58 |
| Anti-Asian/Pacific Islander | 281 | 317 | 339 | 273 |
| Anti-multi-racial group | 240 | 333 | 379 | 153 |
| **Ethnicity/national origin** | 911 | 1,164 | 1,216 | 1,012 |
| Anti-Hispanic | 557 | 735 | 763 | 694 |
| Anti-other ethnicity/national origin | 354 | 429 | 453 | 318 |
| **Religion** | 1,472 | 1,556 | 1,699 | 577 |
| Anti-Jewish | 1,109 | 1,161 | 1,269 | 405 |
| Anti-Catholic | 56 | 61 | 63 | 33 |
| Anti-Protestant | 59 | 62 | 62 | 23 |
| Anti-Islamic | 28 | 33 | 36 | 20 |
| Anti-other religious group | 172 | 187 | 210 | 77 |
| Anti-multi-religious group | 44 | 46 | 52 | 18 |
| Anti-atheism/agnosticism/etc. | 4 | 6 | 7 | 1 |
| **Sexual orientation** | 1,299 | 1,486 | 1,558 | 1,443 |
| Anti-male homosexual | 896 | 1,023 | 1,060 | 1,088 |
| Anti-female homosexual | 179 | 211 | 228 | 169 |
| Anti-homosexual | 182 | 210 | 226 | 153 |
| Anti-heterosexual | 22 | 22 | 24 | 18 |
| Anti-bisexual | 20 | 20 | 20 | 15 |
| **Disability** | 36 | 36 | 36 | 36 |
| Anti-physical | 20 | 20 | 20 | 22 |
| Anti-mental | 16 | 16 | 16 | 14 |
| **Multiple-bias incidents[1]** | 8 | 17 | 18 | 10 |
| **Total** | 8,063 | 9,430 | 9,924 | 7,530 |

1. A *multiple-bias incident* is a hate crime in which two or more offense types were committed as a result of two or more bias motivations. Source: *Crime in the United States, 2000*, FBI, Uniform Crime Reports.

## Index of Crime, United States, 1979–2000

### (rate per 100,000 inhabitants)

| Year | Crime index total | Violent crime[1] | Property crime[2] | Murder and non-negligent manslaughter | Forcible rape | Robbery | Aggravated assault | Burglary | Larceny-theft | Motor vehicle theft |
|---|---|---|---|---|---|---|---|---|---|---|
| 1979 | 5,565.5 | 548.9 | 5,016.6 | 9.7 | 34.7 | 218.4 | 286.0 | 1,511.9 | 2,999.1 | 505.6 |
| 1980 | 5,950.0 | 596.6 | 5,353.3 | 10.2 | 36.8 | 251.1 | 298.5 | 1,684.1 | 3,167.0 | 502.2 |
| 1981 | 5,858.2 | 594.3 | 5,263.9 | 9.8 | 36.0 | 258.7 | 289.7 | 1,649.5 | 3,139.7 | 474.7 |
| 1982 | 5,603.6 | 571.1 | 5,032.5 | 9.1 | 34.0 | 238.9 | 289.2 | 1,488.8 | 3,084.8 | 458.8 |
| 1983 | 5,175.0 | 537.7 | 4,637.4 | 8.3 | 33.7 | 216.5 | 279.2 | 1,337.7 | 2,868.9 | 430.8 |
| 1984 | 5,031.3 | 539.2 | 4,492.1 | 7.9 | 35.7 | 205.4 | 290.2 | 1,263.7 | 2,791.3 | 437.1 |
| 1985 | 5,207.1 | 556.6 | 4,650.5 | 8.0 | 37.1 | 208.5 | 302.9 | 1,287.3 | 2,901.2 | 462.0 |
| 1986 | 5,480.4 | 617.7 | 4,862.6 | 8.6 | 37.9 | 225.1 | 346.1 | 1,344.6 | 3,010.3 | 507.8 |
| 1987 | 5,550.0 | 609.7 | 4,940.3 | 8.3 | 37.4 | 212.7 | 351.3 | 1,329.6 | 3,081.3 | 529.4 |
| 1988 | 5,664.2 | 637.2 | 5,027.1 | 8.4 | 37.6 | 220.9 | 370.2 | 1,309.2 | 3,134.9 | 582.9 |
| 1989 | 5,741.0 | 663.1 | 5,077.9 | 8.7 | 38.1 | 000.0 | | | | |
| 1990 | | | 1,000.0 | | 41.2 | 257.0 | 424.1 | 1,235.9 | 3,194.8 | 657.8 |
| 1991 | 5,897.8 | 758.1 | 5,139.7 | 9.8 | 42.3 | 272.7 | 433.3 | 1,252.0 | 3,228.8 | 659.0 |
| 1992 | 5,660.2 | 757.5 | 4,902.7 | 9.3 | 42.8 | 263.6 | 441.8 | 1,168.0 | 3,103.0 | 631.5 |
| 1993 | 5,484.4 | 746.0 | 1,737.0 | 9.5 | 41.1 | 255.9 | 440.3 | 1,099.2 | 3,032.4 | 606.1 |
| 1994 | 5,070.5 | 713.0 | 4,660.0 | 9.0 | 39.3 | 237.7 | 427.6 | 1,042.0 | 3,026.7 | 591.3 |
| 1995 | 5,275.9 | 684.6 | 4,591.3 | 8.2 | 37.1 | 220.9 | 418.3 | 987.1 | 3,043.8 | 560.4 |
| 1996 | 5,086.6 | 636.5 | 4,450.1 | 7.4 | 36.3 | 201.9 | 390.9 | 944.8 | 2,797.7 | 525.6 |
| 1997 | 4,930.0 | 611.3 | 4,318.7 | 6.8 | 35.9 | 186.3 | 382.3 | 919.4 | 2,893.4 | 506.0 |
| 1998 | 4,619.3 | 567.5 | 4,051.8 | 6.3 | 34.5 | 165.4 | 361.3 | 863.0 | 2,729.0 | 459.8 |
| 1999 | 4,266.8 | 524.7 | 3,742.1 | 5.7 | 32.7 | 150.2 | 336.1 | 770.0 | 2,551.4 | 420.7 |
| 2000 | 4,124.0 | 506.1 | 3,617.9 | 5.5 | 32.0 | 144.9 | 323.6 | 728.4 | 2,475.3 | 414.2 |

1. Violent crimes are offenses of murder, forcible rape, robbery, and aggravated assault. 2. Property crimes are offenses of burglary, larceny-theft, and motor vehicle theft. Data are not included for the property crime of arson. Source: *Crime in the United States*, 2000, FBI, Uniform Crime Reports.

## Arrests by Race, 2000

| Offense charged | Percent distribution[1] | | | | Offense charged | Percent distribution[1] | | | |
|---|---|---|---|---|---|---|---|---|---|
| | White | Black | American Indian or Alaskan Native | Asian or Pacific Islander | | White | Black | American Indian or Alaskan Native | Asian or Pacific Islander |
| Total | 69.7 | 27.9 | 1.2 | 1.2 | Sex offenses, except forcible rape and prostitution | 74.4 | 23.2 | 1.1 | 1.3 |
| Murder[2] | 48.7 | 48.8 | 1.0 | 1.5 | Drug abuse violation | 64.2 | 34.5 | 0.5 | 0.7 |
| Forcible rape | 63.7 | 34.1 | 1.1 | 1.1 | Gambling | 30.7 | 64.4 | 0.4 | 4.4 |
| Robbery | 44.2 | 53.9 | 0.6 | 1.2 | Offenses against family and children | 67.6 | 29.6 | 1.0 | 1.7 |
| Aggravated assault | 63.5 | 34.0 | 1.1 | 1.3 | Driving under the influence | 88.2 | 9.6 | 1.3 | 0.9 |
| Burglary | 69.4 | 28.4 | 0.9 | 1.2 | Liquor laws | 85.6 | 10.6 | 3.0 | 0.8 |
| Larceny-theft | 66.7 | 30.4 | 1.3 | 1.6 | Drunkenness | 84.7 | 13.7 | 1.1 | 0.5 |
| Motor vehicle theft | 55.4 | 41.6 | 1.1 | 1.9 | Disorderly conduct | 65.3 | 32.6 | 1.4 | 0.7 |
| Arson | 76.4 | 21.7 | 0.9 | 1.0 | Vagrancy | 53.6 | 43.4 | 2.6 | 0.5 |
| Other assaults | 66.0 | 31.5 | 1.4 | 1.1 | All other offenses except traffic | 65.8 | 31.6 | 1.3 | 1.3 |
| Forgery and counterfeiting | 68.0 | 30.0 | 0.6 | 1.4 | Suspicion | 69.0 | 29.6 | 0.3 | 1.2 |
| Fraud | 67.3 | 31.5 | 0.6 | 0.7 | Curfew and loitering law violations | 72.2 | 24.7 | 1.1 | 2.0 |
| Embezzlement | 63.6 | 34.1 | 0.4 | 1.9 | Runaways | 76.3 | 17.9 | 1.4 | 4.4 |
| Stolen property—buying, receiving, possessing | 58.9 | 39.1 | 0.7 | 1.2 | | | | | |
| Vandalism | 75.9 | 21.6 | 1.4 | 1.1 | | | | | |
| Weapons—carrying, possessing, etc. | 61.3 | 36.8 | 0.7 | 1.2 | | | | | |
| Prostitution and commercialized vice | 58.0 | 39.5 | 0.8 | 1.7 | | | | | |

1. Because of rounding, the percentages may not add up to total. 2. Includes nonnegligent manslaughter. *Source: Crime in the United States, 2000,* FBI, Uniform Crime Reports.

## Crime Index by State, 2000

| State | Crime index total | | | | | State | Crime index total | | | | |
|---|---|---|---|---|---|---|---|---|---|---|---|
| | Number | Rate per 100,000 | Violent crime | Property crime | Murder[1] | | Number | Rate per 100,000 | Violent crime | Property crime | Murder[1] |
| Ala. | 202,159 | 4,545.9 | 21,620 | 180,539 | 329 | Mont.[2] | 31,878 | 3,533.4 | 2,171 | 29,707 | 16 |
| Alaska | 26,641 | 4,249.4 | 3,554 | 23,087 | 27 | Nebr. | 70,085 | 4,095.5 | 5,606 | 64,479 | 63 |
| Ariz. | 299,092 | 5,829.5 | 27,281 | 271,811 | 359 | Nev. | 85,297 | 4,268.6 | 10,474 | 74,823 | 129 |
| Ark. | 110,019 | 4,115.3 | 11,904 | 98,115 | 168 | N.H. | 30,068 | 2,433.1 | 2,167 | 27,901 | 22 |
| Calif. | 1,266,714 | 3,739.7 | 210,531 | 1,056,183 | 2,079 | N.J. | 265,935 | 3,160.5 | 32,298 | 233,637 | 289 |
| Colo. | 171,304 | 3,982.6 | 14,367 | 156,937 | 134 | N.M. | 100,391 | 5,518.9 | 13,786 | 86,605 | 135 |
| Conn. | 110,091 | 3,232.7 | 11,058 | 99,033 | 98 | N.Y. | 588,189 | 3,099.6 | 105,111 | 483,078 | 952 |
| Del. | 35,090 | 4,478.1 | 5,363 | 29,727 | 25 | N.C. | 395,972 | 4,919.3 | 40,051 | 355,921 | 560 |
| DC | 41,626 | 7,276.5 | 8,626 | 33,000 | 239 | N.D. | 14,694 | 2,288.1 | 523 | 14,171 | 4 |
| Fla. | 910,154 | 5,694.7 | 129,777 | 780,377 | 903 | Ohio | 458,874 | 4,041.8 | 37,935 | 420,939 | 418 |
| Ga. | 388,949 | 4,751.1 | 41,319 | 347,630 | 651 | Okla. | 157,302 | 4,558.6 | 17,177 | 140,125 | 182 |
| Hawaii | 62,987 | 5,198.9 | 2,954 | 60,033 | 35 | Ore. | 165,780 | 4,845.4 | 12,000 | 153,780 | 70 |
| Idaho | 41,228 | 3,186.2 | 3,267 | 37,961 | 16 | Pa. | 367,858 | 2,995.3 | 51,584 | 316,274 | 602 |
| Ill.[2] | 532,315 | 4,286.2 | 81,567 | 450,748 | 891 | P.R. | 75,377 | 1,979.1 | 12,404 | 62,973 | 693 |
| Ind. | 228,135 | 3,751.9 | 21,230 | 206,905 | 352 | R.I. | 36,444 | 3,476.4 | 3,121 | 33,323 | 45 |
| Iowa | 94,630 | 3,233.7 | 7,796 | 86,834 | 46 | S.C. | 209,482 | 5,221.4 | 32,293 | 177,189 | 233 |
| Kans.[2] | 118,527 | 4,408.8 | 10,470 | 108,057 | 169 | S.D. | 17,511 | 2,319.8 | 1,259 | 16,252 | 7 |
| Ky.[2] | 119,626 | 2,959.7 | 11,903 | 107,723 | 193 | Tenn. | 278,218 | 4,890.2 | 40,233 | 237,985 | 410 |
| La. | 242,344 | 5,422.8 | 30,440 | 211,904 | 560 | Tex. | 1,033,311 | 4,955.5 | 113,653 | 919,658 | 1,238 |
| Maine | 33,400 | 2,619.8 | 1,397 | 32,003 | 15 | Utah | 99,958 | 4,476.1 | 5,711 | 94,247 | 43 |
| Md. | 255,085 | 4,816.1 | 41,663 | 213,422 | 430 | Vt. | 18,185 | 2,986.9 | 691 | 17,494 | 9 |
| Mass. | 192,131 | 3,026.1 | 30,230 | 161,901 | 125 | Va. | 214,348 | 3,028.1 | 19,943 | 194,405 | 401 |
| Mich. | 408,456 | 4,109.9 | 55,159 | 353,297 | 669 | Wash. | 300,932 | 5,105.6 | 21,788 | 279,144 | 196 |
| Minn. | 171,611 | 3,488.4 | 13,813 | 157,798 | 151 | W. Va. | 47,067 | 2,602.8 | 5,723 | 41,344 | 46 |
| Miss. | 113,911 | 4,004.4 | 10,267 | 103,644 | 255 | Wisc. | 172,124 | 3,209.1 | 12,700 | 159,424 | 169 |
| Mo. | 253,338 | 4,527.8 | 27,419 | 225,919 | 347 | Wyo. | 16,285 | 3,298.0 | 1,316 | 14,969 | 12 |

NOTE: The Crime Index is composed of the violent and property crime categories. Violent crimes are murder, forcible rape, robbery, and aggravated assault. Property crimes are burglary, larceny-theft, and auto-theft. Data are not included for the property crime of arson. 1. Includes nonnegligent manslaughter. 2. Limited data for 2000 were available for the states of Illinois, Kansas, Kentucky, and Montana; therefore, it was necessary that their crime counts be estimated. *Source: Crime in the United States, 2000,* FBI, Uniform Crime Reports.

## Crime Rates for Selected Large Cities, 1999
### (offenses known to the police per 100,000 population)

| City ranked by population size, 1999[1] | Crime index, total | Violent crime Murder | Forcible rape | Robbery | Aggravated assault | Property crime Burglary | Larceny-theft | Motor vehicle theft |
|---|---|---|---|---|---|---|---|---|
| New York, N.Y. | 4,031.0 | 8.9 | 22.9 | 485.8 | 545.0 | 544.7 | 1,889.4 | 534.3 |
| Los Angeles, Calif. | 4,588.7 | 11.6 | 35.3 | 394.8 | 841.5 | 589.6 | 2,039.8 | 676.1 |
| Chicago, Ill. | (2) | 22.7 | (2) | 716.4 | 993.5 | 1,067.8 | 3,986.3 | 1,278.8 |
| Houston, Tex. | 7,271.2 | 13.3 | 41.3 | 460.7 | 672.0 | 1,365.4 | 3,645.6 | 1,073.0 |
| Philadelphia, Pa. | 7,291.3 | 20.3 | 65.1 | 773.6 | 745.5 | 978.3 | 3,474.6 | 1,233.9 |
| San Diego, Calif. | 4,003.6 | 4.6 | 28.7 | 146.3 | 418.8 | 530.3 | 2,108.7 | 766.3 |
| Phoenix, Ariz. | 7,720.2 | 17.5 | 32.6 | 311.5 | 470.4 | 1,299.2 | 4,124.1 | 1,465.0 |
| San Antonio, Tex. | 6,793.4 | 8.5 | 53.0 | 148.1 | 351.4 | 968.3 | 4,769.0 | 495.1 |
| Dallas, Tex. | 9,615.7 | 17.5 | 60.7 | 582.5 | 753.5 | 1,798.5 | 4,767.0 | 1,635.9 |
| Detroit, Mich. | 10,416.5 | 42.6 | 81.0 | 802.4 | 1,328.0 | 1,874.7 | 3,542.3 | 2,745.6 |
| Las Vegas, Nev. | 5,184.9 | 11.8 | 57.7 | 338.3 | 257.0 | 1,098.2 | 2,362.5 | 1,059.4 |
| San Jose, Calif. | 2,943.9 | 2.9 | 39.6 | 82.9 | 455.6 | 306.6 | 1,729.9 | 326.5 |
| Honolulu, Hawaii | 4,925.0 | 4.3 | 27.1 | 104.7 | 117.6 | 702.4 | 3,507.6 | 461.2 |
| Indianapolis, Ind. | 5,322.1 | 14.9 | 55.9 | 342.3 | 603.2 | 1,313.6 | 2,276.4 | 715.9 |
| San Francisco, Calif. | 5,725.1 | 8.5 | 25.5 | 459.2 | 373.1 | 730.3 | 3,338.7 | 789.9 |
| Jacksonville, Fla. | 7,151.7 | 11.8 | 65.3 | 242.4 | 714.6 | 1,373.9 | 4,049.3 | 694.3 |
| Columbus, Ohio | 9,101.9 | 10.5 | 94.7 | 449.4 | 300.0 | 2,092.4 | 5,141.8 | 1,013.1 |
| Baltimore, Md. | n.a. | n.a. | n.a. | n.a. | n.a. | n.a. | n.a. | n.a. |
| El Paso, Tex. | 5,791.9 | 2.2 | 29.7 | 114.6 | 539.5 | 400.1 | 4,336.0 | 369.8 |
| Memphis, Tenn. | 8,368.1 | 19.3 | 112.8 | 609.2 | 669.2 | 2,132.5 | 3,567.4 | 1,257.7 |
| Charlotte-Mecklenburg, N.C. | 8,829.6 | 13.9 | 43.3 | 416.1 | 872.0 | 1,705.0 | 4,978.4 | 800.9 |
| Milwaukee, Wisc. | 7,929.3 | 21.3 | 46.8 | 539.5 | 435.7 | 1,112.4 | 4,497.2 | 1,276.3 |
| Austin, Tex. | 6,904.1 | 3.7 | 34.4 | 178.8 | 280.9 | 1,204.2 | 4,733.5 | 468.6 |
| Boston, Mass. | 6,288.5 | 5.6 | 60.4 | 442.3 | 793.8 | 612.0 | 3,161.8 | 1,212.6 |
| Seattle, Wash. | 9,164.7 | 8.3 | 34.6 | 302.4 | 422.0 | 1,191.4 | 5,614.7 | 1,591.3 |
| Nashville, Tenn. | 8,883.7 | 13.0 | 88.0 | 374.8 | 1,131.5 | 1,331.3 | 4,991.1 | 954.0 |
| Washington, DC | 8,061.7 | 46.4 | 47.8 | 644.3 | 889.2 | 976.3 | 4,175.9 | 1,281.7 |
| Denver, Colo. | 5,256.0 | 12.4 | 48.9 | 203.7 | 305.9 | 1,061.4 | 2,644.1 | 979.7 |
| Portland, Ore. | 8,133.7 | 6.9 | 66.8 | 278.6 | 884.3 | 1,199.8 | 4,775.8 | 921.4 |
| Fort Worth, Tex. | 7,487.5 | 13.4 | 57.3 | 290.0 | 490.3 | 1,504.6 | 4,350.0 | 781.5 |
| Cleveland, Ohio | 6,743.3 | 15.7 | 101.6 | 610.2 | 487.8 | 1,455.3 | 2,584.4 | 1,488.2 |
| Oklahoma City, Okla. | 9,323.5 | 11.8 | 84.0 | 224.6 | 538.9 | 1,696.6 | 6,001.4 | 766.2 |
| Tucson, Ariz. | 8,992.4 | 7.6 | 52.0 | 271.8 | 582.4 | 1,289.5 | 5,762.3 | 1,026.8 |
| New Orleans, La. | 7,676.9 | 33.9 | 60.1 | 586.7 | 592.5 | 1,207.7 | 3,667.9 | 1,528.0 |
| Kansas City, Mo. | 11,630.8 | 26.4 | 74.3 | 558.3 | 1,090.1 | 1,939.4 | 6,422.0 | 1,520.3 |
| Virginia Beach, Va. | 3,676.1 | 2.7 | 24.4 | 115.8 | 95.5 | 464.7 | 2,808.8 | 164.1 |
| Long Beach, Calif. | 4,152.2 | 10.5 | 27.2 | 358.2 | 349.0 | 767.8 | 1,870.7 | 768.7 |
| Albuquerque, N.M. | 9,766.1 | 11.4 | 52.4 | 396.7 | 790.2 | 1,620.5 | 5,777.9 | 1,116.9 |
| Atlanta, Ga. | 13,488.5 | 34.8 | 78.0 | 990.1 | 1,626.6 | 2,083.9 | 6,893.4 | 1,781.7 |
| Sacramento, Calif. | 6,610.8 | 13.2 | 34.9 | 353.6 | 350.4 | 1,171.7 | 3,599.5 | 1,087.6 |
| Fresno, Calif. | 7,137.5 | 6.4 | 39.6 | 313.9 | 632.2 | 1,093.9 | 3,902.1 | 1,149.4 |
| Tulsa, Okla. | 7,396.1 | 10.7 | 61.4 | 231.8 | 858.2 | 1,713.7 | 3,676.8 | 843.5 |
| Miami, Fla. | 10,723.8 | 16.9 | 30.3 | 823.7 | 1,234.2 | 1,962.5 | 5,123.8 | 1,532.5 |
| Omaha, Neb. | 7,048.2 | 9.1 | 46.7 | 257.8 | 925.2 | 944.2 | 3,902.1 | 963.0 |
| Oakland, Calif. | 8,370.2 | 16.2 | 82.2 | 589.9 | 861.7 | 1,372.2 | 4,158.3 | 1,289.8 |
| Mesa, Ariz. | 6,168.2 | 2.4 | 36.4 | 100.4 | 439.3 | 1,062.6 | 3,753.5 | 773.6 |
| Minneapolis, Minn. | 8,635.2 | 13.2 | 126.7 | 588.8 | 659.9 | 1,562.6 | 4,597.8 | 1,086.1 |
| Colorado Springs, Colo. | 5,189.8 | 6.8 | 64.4 | 141.3 | 312.4 | 811.0 | 3,525.7 | 328.0 |
| Pittsburgh, Pa. | 6,123.5 | 14.1 | 39.8 | 455.5 | 368.2 | 897.5 | 3,427.2 | 921.1 |
| St. Louis, Mo. | 13,998.2 | 38.1 | 42.2 | 819.2 | 1,333.5 | 2,304.9 | 7,510.7 | 1,940.6 |
| Cincinnati, Ohio | 6,431.6 | 8.3 | 73.7 | 957.0 | 747.7 | 1,041.0 | 4,000.0 | 430.0 |
| Wichita, Kan. | 8,888.8 | 9.1 | 110.9 | 210.7 | 948.8 | 310.3 | 1,200.8 | 4,029.1 | 503.2 |
| Toledo, Ohio | 7,409.6 | 4.8 | 49.4 | 290.3 | 343.9 | 1,506.0 | 4,329.0 | 886.2 |
| Arlington, Tex. | 6,242.0 | 3.5 | 35.1 | 175.6 | 413.3 | 1,022.8 | 4,020.5 | 800.2 |
| Santa Ana, Calif. | 3,597.2 | 1.0 | 01.7 | 278.6 | 274.1 | 304.0 | 1,070.7 | 736.7 |
| Buffalo, N.Y. | 6,860.5 | 10.0 | 58.5 | 489.3 | 518.8 | 1,470.8 | 3,327.5 | 993.1 |
| Anaheim, Calif. | 3,373.9 | 5.3 | 28.4 | 156.3 | 357.3 | 547.6 | 1,820.5 | 458.5 |
| Tampa, Fla. | 10,929.2 | 10.6 | 79.5 | 792.3 | 1,371.6 | 2,056.4 | 4,659.3 | 1,959.4 |
| Corpus Christi, Tex. | 7,136.5 | 5.3 | 67.9 | 135.9 | 661.3 | 1,233.2 | 4,503.9 | 528.9 |
| Newark, N.J. | 7,881.2 | 25.7 | 38.4 | 906.3 | 843.3 | 1,150.4 | 2,954.4 | 1,962.7 |
| Riverside, Calif. | 4,385.7 | 11.3 | 28.9 | 236.1 | 499.7 | 845.9 | 2,155.4 | 608.3 |
| Raleigh, N.C. | 7,099.4 | 6.1 | 35.0 | 281.0 | 450.2 | 1,315.2 | 4,504.4 | 507.6 |
| St. Paul, Minn. | 7,064.3 | 5.4 | 76.9 | 297.7 | 469.2 | 1,367.2 | 4,117.1 | 730.7 |
| Anchorage, Alaska | 5,023.2 | 7.4 | 62.1 | 154.4 | 429.1 | 598.6 | 3,286.4 | 485.3 |
| Louisville, Ky. | 5,964.7 | 14.4 | 24.1 | 450.9 | 373.4 | 1,331.0 | 2,991.9 | 778.8 |

1. Resident population estimated by the FBI. 2. The rates for forcible rape and crime index are not shown because the forcible rape figures were not in accordance with national Uniform Crime Reporting guidelines. *Source: Statistical Abstract of the United States, 2001.*

# The War over New Armaments

## Is the Pentagon fighting tomorrow's wars—or yesterday's?

**By the** TIME **staff**

Feb. 2002: A belly-mounted camera inside a U.S. Predator drone sights a potential target—suspected al-Qaeda terrorists—in the mountains of Eastern Afghanistan. After its CIA operator confers with U.S. Central Command officials at their Florida headquarters, the unmanned surveillance plane fires a 100-pound Hellfire missile and scores a direct hit on the terrorists. The surgical strike was a case study in the new American way of waging war: killing foes by remote control, with no risk to U.S. troops, through an extraordinary convergence of intelligence, technology, and high-explosive warheads.

The war in Afghanistan offers a blueprint for fighting future wars—through a mix of agility and lethality, with small groups of special forces on the ground wielding high-tech targeting devices linked to precision-guided munitions in the sky—but the military seems slow to embrace these lessons. On the same day the Predator drone fired in Afghanistan, the Pentagon presented to Congress a five-year, $2 trillion budget plan for 2003 larded with cold war–era weapons.

The budget included the Crusader howitzer, a cannon so cumbersome that in 2000 a presidential candidate named George W. Bush questioned its utility. In hearings on the proposed budget, Bush's Secretary of Defense, Donald Rumsfeld, spoke out against the system; he killed the Crusader program in May. The budget also included the F-22 Raptor, a fighter jet designed to challenge a Soviet air force that no longer exists. There are two other fighter designs in the pipeline as well. Yet the Pentagon plan called for spending $5.3 billion to build 23 Raptors and budgeted only $100 million for 22 new Predator drones. The Raptor stayed in the budget.

Military budgets are always full of riddles and mysteries, but never has the Pentagon appeared so at war with itself. In Afghanistan, it was fighting a new kind of war in remarkably new ways, yet at the same time it was asking the nation to invest heavily in weapons that were created to fight old wars in old ways. The Pentagon's requested budget for 2003 was $379 billion, which included a $48 billion boost over 2002—a sum larger than any other nation's total defense budget.

## Passing the Bucks

The irony is that George W. Bush came into office styling himself a reformer. In a Sept. 2000 speech, he said the military should take advantage of the cold war's end "to skip a generation of technology" and move on to futuristic weapons without necessarily buying all those in development.

Donald Rumsfeld came into office pledging to remake the military. Yet with a surging budget, few

hard choices were being made. The 2003 defense plan allows for some modest transformation: the Navy will spend $1 billion to convert four Trident submarines that now fire nuclear missiles into Tomahawk cruise-missile launchers. The Army will fork out $707 million to develop lighter tanks, and the Air Force will pay $620 million to accelerate development of the Global Hawk unmanned spy plane, which flies farther and higher than the Predator.

But the military stuffed Rumsfeld's most ambitious reforms. His plans to force a transformation by cutting weapons and troop levels alarmed senior officers, who colluded with congressional allies to turn back the changes. The steep rise in defense spending will actually make it more difficult to bring real reform. About a dozen major new weapons systems are just beginning to enter production, and their costs will skyrocket once the assembly lines spool up. Procurement of new weapons, now at $61 billion, is planned to reach $99 billion by 2007. The spigot will only get harder to turn off.

## Deadly Data

Pentagon officials argue it isn't better bullets that will transform the military but better intelligence on where to shoot them. The goal, known as network-centric warfare, is to give pilots a high-resolution picture of the battlefield from sensors on the ground, in the air, and in space, so they can dispatch smart weapons to their targets.

The U.S. military made big strides toward that end in Afghanistan. In the Gulf War, the U.S. had to deploy ten aircraft to be sure of taking out a single target. Now it budgets two targets per aircraft. That's because the share of precision-guided munitions has grown from 7% in 1991 to 60% today. As bombs get smarter, planes can get dumber: for the first time, B-52s are able to drop satellite-guided Joint Direct Attack Munitions from high altitudes, beyond the reach of enemy antiaircraft fire. U.S. commandos on the ground are pinpointing targets with laser spotters and calling in target coordinates. Long-range bombers, some flying from the U.S. mainland, played a key role in the war because Afghanistan's neighbors did not want to be launching pads for American attacks. But the new defense budget contains no funds for new bombers and less than $300 million to improve the B-2 fleet.

Drones have enabled the U.S. military to stare at enemy positions for days, providing far more intelligence than could be gleaned from a reconnaissance flight or satellite flyby. Beyond spying and attacking, the Predator has used its own laser to pinpoint targets for satellite-guided bombs from high-flying bombers. Rumsfeld said early in 2002 that his new budget "substantially" boosted spending on drones, but TIME's review of the budget showed a 13%

increase for Predators, Global Hawks, and other unmanned planes, while spending for fighter jets jumped 37%. Yet U.S. commanders were pleading for drones. "There simply are not enough to go around," Rumsfeld said. "We're building them as rapidly as possible." But the Predator's manufacturer, General Atomics Aeronautics, told TIME it was ready to crank out more.

In 2001 the Pentagon abandoned a decade-old benchmark, the ability to fight two major wars at once. But on Capitol Hill, New York Representative John McHugh, a Republican member of the Armed Services Committee, said the Pentagon should consider bulking up to wage three wars at once in order to face down the "triangle of terror," a reference to Bush's declaration that Iran, Iraq, and North Korea are an "axis of evil." With such talk coming from both ends of Pennsylvania Avenue, the defense budget seems sure to be going up, up, and away, into the wild blue squander. ☐

## The right stuff

### JDAM

• *Price tag:* $5 billion

• *What it does:* The Joint Direct Attack Munition kit bolts onto the tail of a conventional "dumb" bomb, turning it into a satellite-guided smart bomb.

• *Unit cost:* At $24,000 per kit, the Pentagon is retrofitting thousands of bombs.

Reuters

• *Is it worth it?* These all-weather kits work day or night, from low altitudes or high. Cheaper than building whole new bombs, they give the best bang for the buck.

## The right stuff

### GLOBAL HAWK

• *Price tag:* $3.5 billion

• *What it does:* Flying at 65,000 ft—far higher than the Predator—this unmanned drone can scour thousands of square miles on its 36-hour missions and provide high-resolution images through all kinds of weather.

U.S. Air Force

• *Unit cost:* The Air Force plans on buying 51 Global Hawks at $70 million apiece.

• *Is it worth it?* Information is king on the battlefield of the future, and Global Hawk is one way to get plenty of it.

## The wrong stuff?

### CRUSADER

• *Price tag:* $11 billion

• *What it does:* The 155-mm self-propelled howitzer with its resupply vehicle weighs more than 80 tons, making it too heavy for most U.S. military cargo planes.

• *Unit cost:* The Pentagon hoped to spend $475 million on its development in 2003 and ultimately to buy 480 armored-gun systems at $23 million each. The system was killed by Secretary of Defense Rumsfeld in May 2002.

• *Is it worth it?* This behemoth is good for close-in battles with massive armies, just the kind of war that U.S. technological superiority is designed to make obsolete.

U.S. Army

## The wrong stuff?

### F-22 RAPTOR

• *Price tag:* $63 billion

• *What it does:* The stealth fighter was conceived in the early 1980s to combat a growing threat of advanced Soviet planes. The Air Force maintains the U.S. needs to continue with the program because other nations are building ever better warplanes.

USAF-AFP

• *Unit cost:* The Pentagon proposes to buy 295 Raptors at $214 million each.

• *Is it worth it?* Although the Raptor is designed to penetrate enemy airspace and kill anything that gets in its way, critics say upgrades to existing F-15 and F-16 fighters are sufficient.

## The wrong stuff?

### RAH-66 COMANCHE

• *Price tag:* $48 billion

• *What it does:* The Army's next-generation, lightweight, twin-engine helicopter for armed reconnaissance and attack has been under development for nearly two decades.

Boeing

• *Unit cost:* The Pentagon wants to buy 1,213 at $40 million apiece.

• *Is it worth it?* The new armed scout chopper is a costly, stealthy aircraft designed to battle Soviet forces. Plagued by structural-design difficulties, it should be scrapped, opponents suggest.

# Highest-Ranking Officers in U.S. History

### General and Commander-in-Chief[1]

**George Washington** (1732–1799), b. Westmoreland County, Va., unanimously voted by Congress on June 15, 1775, to the rank of general and commander-in-chief (of the Continental army).

### General of the Armies[2]

**John Joseph Pershing** (1860–1948), b. Linn County, Mo., made permanent general of the armies, 1919.

### General of the Army, General of the Air Force, Admiral of the Navy (Five-Stars)

**George Catlett Marshall** (1880–1959), b. Uniontown, Pa., promoted Dec. 1944.

**Douglas MacArthur** (1880–1964), b. Little Rock, Ark., promoted Dec. 1944.

**Dwight David Eisenhower** (1890–1969), b. Denison, Tex., promoted Dec. 1944.

**Henry Harley Arnold** (1866–1950), b. Gladwyne, Pa. Arnold had the unique distinction of being a five-star general twice—in 1944 as general of the army, and in June, 1949 as general of the air force. He is the only air force general to have held the five-star rank.

**Omar Nelson Bradley** (1893–1981), b. Clark, Mo., promoted Sept. 1950.

### Fleet Admiral (Five-Star)

**William Daniel Leahy** (1875–1959), b. Hampton, Iowa, promoted Dec. 1944.

**Ernest Joseph King** (1878–1956), b. Lorain, Ohio, promoted Dec. 1944.

**Chester William Nimitz** (1885–1966), b. Fredericksburg, Tex., promoted Dec. 1944.

**William Frederick Halsey** (1882–1959), b. Elizabeth, N.J., promoted Dec. 1945.

1. On March 15, 1978, George Washington was promoted posthumously to the newly created rank of General of the Armies of the United States. Congress authorized this title to make it clear that Washington was the army's senior general. 2. General Pershing was given the option of five stars but he declined. *Source:* Department of Defense and U.S. Army Historian, Research and Analysis Center.

## The Joint Chiefs of Staff (JCS)

The Joint Chiefs of Staff consist of the chairman, the vice chairman, the chief of staff of the army, the chief of naval operations, the chief of staff of the air force, and the commandant of the Marine Corps.

The collective body of the JCS is headed by the chairman (or vice chairman in the chairman's absence), who sets the agenda and presides over JCS meetings. Their responsibilities take precedence over their duties as the Chiefs of Military Services. The chairman is the principal military adviser to the president, the secretary of defense, and the National Security Council (NSC); however, all JCS members are by law military advisers, and they may respond to a request or voluntarily submit, through the chairman, advice or opinions to the president, the secretary of state, or the NSC. The Joint Chiefs of Staff have no executive authority to commit combatant forces.

In addition to their responsibilities on the JCS, the military service chiefs are responsible to the secretaries of their military departments for management of the services. The service chiefs serve for four years. By custom the vice chiefs of the services act for their chiefs in most matters having to do with day-to-day operation of the services.

### Joint Chiefs of Staff, 2001

Chairman of the Joint Chiefs of Staff, General Richard B. Myers, U.S. Air Force; vice chairman of the Joint Chiefs of Staff, General Peter Pace, Marine Corps; General Eric K. Shinseki, chief of staff of the U.S. Army; Admiral Vern Clark, chief of naval operations; General John P. Jumper, chief of staff of the U.S. Air Force; and General James L. Jones, commandant of the Marine Corps.

### Past Chairmen of the JCS

General of the Army, Omar N. Bradley, 1949–1953
Adm. Arthur W. Radford, U.S. Navy, 1953–1957
Gen. Nathan F. Twining, U.S. Air Force, 1957–1960
Gen. Lyman L. Lemnitzer, U.S. Army, 1960–1962
Gen. Maxwell D. Taylor, U.S. Army, 1962–1964
Gen. Earle G. Wheeler, U.S. Army, 1964–1970
Adm. Thomas H. Moorer, U.S. Navy, 1970–1974
Gen. George S. Brown, U.S. Air Force, 1974–1978
Gen. David C. Jones, U.S. Air Force, 1978–1982
Gen. John W. Vessey, Jr., U.S. Army, 1982–1985
Adm. William J. Crowe, U.S. Navy, 1985–1989
Gen. Colin L. Powell, U.S. Army, 1989–1993
Gen. John M. Shalikashvili, U.S. Army, 1993–1997
Gen. Henry H. Shelton, U.S. Army, 1997–2001

## U.S. Military Spending, 1946–2002

### (billions of 2002 dollars)

| Year | Spending | Year | Spending | Year | Spending | Year | Spending | Year | Spending | Year | Spending |
|---|---|---|---|---|---|---|---|---|---|---|---|
| 1946 | $556.9 | 1956 | $356.2 | 1966 | $356.2 | 1976 | $283.8 | 1986 | $426.6 | 1996 | $307.4 |
| 1947 | 52.4 | 1957 | 360.9 | 1967 | 412.0 | 1977 | 286.2 | 1987 | 427.9 | 1997 | 305.3 |
| 1948 | 103.9 | 1958 | 352.9 | 1968 | 449.3 | 1978 | 286.5 | 1988 | 426.4 | 1998 | 296.7 |
| 1949 | 144.2 | 1959 | 352.5 | 1969 | 438.1 | 1979 | 295.6 | 1989 | 427.7 | 1999 | 298.4 |
| 1950 | 141.2 | 1960 | 344.3 | 1970 | 406.3 | 1980 | 303.4 | 1990 | 409.7 | 2000 | 311.7 |
| 1951 | 224.3 | 1961 | 344.0 | 1971 | 370.6 | 1981 | 317.4 | 1991 | 358.1 | 2001 | 307.8 |
| 1952 | 402.1 | 1962 | 363.4 | 1972 | 343.8 | 1982 | 339.4 | 1992 | 379.5 | 2002 | 328.7 |
| 1953 | 442.3 | 1963 | 368.0 | 1973 | 313.3 | 1983 | 366.7 | 1993 | 358.6 | | |
| 1954 | 420.9 | 1964 | 364.4 | 1974 | 299.7 | 1984 | 381.7 | 1994 | 338.6 | | |
| 1955 | 376.9 | 1965 | 333.1 | 1975 | 293.3 | 1985 | 405.4 | 1995 | 321.6 | | |

*Source:* Center for Defense Information.

## U.S. Military Ranks

*Source:* U.S. Department of Defense

| Pay Grade | Army | Navy and Coast Guard[1] | Marines | Air Force |
|---|---|---|---|---|
| **Commissioned Officers** | | | | |
| O-1 | Second Lieutenant | Ensign | Second Lieutenant | Second Lieutenant |
| O-2 | First Lieutenant | Lieutenant Junior Grade | First Lieutenant | First Lieutenant |
| O-3 | Captain | Lieutenant | Captain | Captain |
| O-4 | Major | Lieutenant Commander | Major | Major |
| O-5 | Lieutenant Colonel | Commander | Lieutenant Colonel | Lieutenant Colonel |
| O-6 | Colonel | Captain | Colonel | Colonel |
| O-7 | Brigadier General | Rear Admiral (L) | Brigadier General | Brigadier General |
| O-8 | Major General | Rear Admiral | Major General | Major General |
| O-9 | Lieutenant General | Vice Admiral | Lieutenant General | Lieutenant General |
| O-10 | General | Admiral | General | General |
| **Special Grades[2]** | | | | |
| (5 stars) | General of the Army | Fleet Admiral | (none) | General of the Air Force |
| **Warrant Officers** | | | | |
| W-1 | Warrant Officer. Grades W-2 to W-5 Chief Warrant Officer | | | |
| **Enlisted Personnel** | | | | |
| E-1 | Private | Seaman Recruit | Private | Airman Basic |
| E-2 | Private | Seaman Apprentice | Private First Class | Airman |
| E-3 | Private First Class | Seaman | Lance Corporal | Airman First Class |
| E-4 | Corporal Specialist 4 | Petty Officer, Third Class | Corporal | Senior Airman |
| E-5 | Sergeant Specialist 5 | Petty Officer, Second Class | Sergeant | Staff Sergeant |
| E-6 | Staff Sergeant Specialist 6 | Petty Officer, First Class | Staff Sergeant | Technical Sergeant |
| E-7 | Sergeant First Class Specialist 7 | Chief Petty Officer | Gunnery Sergeant | Master Sergeant |
| E-8 | First Sergeant Master Sergeant | Senior Chief Petty Officer | First Sergeant Master Sergeant | Senior Master Sergeant |
| E-9 | Command Sergeant Major Sergeant Major | Master Chief Petty Officer | Sergeant Major Master Gunnery Sergeant | Chief Master Sergeant |
| **Special Grades[3]** | | | | |
| | Sergeant Major of the Army | Master Chief Petty Officer of the Navy | Sergeant Major of the Marine Corps | Chief Master Sergeant of the Air Force |

1. During peacetime, the United States Coast Guard operates within the Department of Transportation rather than the Department of Defense. Upon declaration of war or order of the president, the Coast Guard falls under the Department of the Navy. The ranks of the U.S. Coast Guard are identical to those of the U.S. Navy. 2. There are no living five-star commissioned officers. 3. Senior enlisted advisers. There is only one for each branch of service.

## U.S. Military Personnel on Active Duty in Selected Regions/Countries,[1] 2001

| Region/Country | 2001 | Region/Country | 2001 | Region/Country | 2001 |
|---|---|---|---|---|---|
| **United States and Territories** | | Spain* | 1,778 | Qatar | 72 |
| | | Turkey* | 2,170 | Saudi Arabia | 4,802 |
| Continental U.S. | 947,955 | United Kingdom* | 11,361 | United Arab Emirates | 207 |
| Alaska | 15,926 | **East Asia and Pacific** | | **Sub-Saharan Africa** | |
| Hawaii | 33,191 | Australia | 188 | Kenya | 50 |
| Guam | 3,398 | China (includes | 54 | South Africa | 30 |
| Puerto Rico | 2,525 | Hong Kong) | | **Western Hemisphere** | |
| **Europe** | | Indonesia (includes | 48 | Brazil | 10 |
| Belgium* | 1,554 | Timor) | | Canada | 165 |
| Bosnia and Herzegovina | 3,109 | Japan | 39,691 | Chile | 30 |
| France* | 70 | Korea, Rep. of | 37,972 | Colombia | 59 |
| Germany* | 71,434 | Philippines | 31 | Cuba (Quantanamo) | 461 |
| Greece* | 526 | Singapore | 100 | Honduras | 426 |
| Greenland* | 153 | Thailand | 114 | Peru | 40 |
| Iceland* | 1,713 | **North Africa, Near East,** | | Venezuela | 30 |
| Italy* | 11,854 | **and South Asia** | | **Total foreign countries[2]** | 255,065 |
| Macedonia | 346 | Bahrain | 1,280 | Ashore | 212,262 |
| Netherlands* | 696 | Diego Garcia | 537 | Afloat | 42,803 |
| Norway* | 187 | Egypt | 665 | **Total worldwide[2]** | 1,384,812 |
| Portugal* | 992 | Israel | 38 | Ashore | 1,242,524 |
| Russia | 88 | Kuwait | 4,300 | Afloat | 142,288 |
| Serbia (includes Kosovo) | 5,200 | Oman | 560 | | |

*NATO countries. 1. Only countries with 30 or more U.S. military personnel are listed. 2. Includes all regions/countries, not simply those listed. *Source:* U.S. Department of Defense, *Selected Manpower Statistics, Annual.*

## Active Duty Military Personnel, 1940–2000[1]

| Year | Army[2] | Air Force[2, 3] | Navy | Marine Corps | Total |
|---|---|---|---|---|---|
| 1940 | 269,023 | | 160,997 | 28,345 | 458,365 |
| 1945 | 8,266,373 | | 3,319,586 | 469,925 | 12,055,884 |
| 1950 | 593,167 | 411,277 | 380,739 | 74,279 | 1,459,462 |
| 1955 | 1,109,296 | 959,946 | 660,695 | 205,170 | 2,935,107 |
| 1960 | 873,078 | 814,752 | 616,987 | 170,621 | 2,475,438 |
| 1965 | 969,066 | 824,662 | 669,985 | 190,213 | 2,653,926 |
| 1970 | 1,322,548 | 791,349 | 691,126 | 259,737 | 3,064,760 |
| 1975 | 784,333 | 612,751 | 535,085 | 195,951 | 2,128,120 |
| 1980 | 777,036 | 557,969 | 527,153 | 188,469 | 2,050,627 |
| 1985 | 780,787 | 601,515 | 570,705 | 198,025 | 2,151,032 |
| 1990 | 732,403 | 535,233 | 579,417 | 196,652 | 2,043,705 |
| 1991 | 710,821 | 510,432 | 570,262 | 194,040 | 1,985,555 |
| 1992 | 610,450 | 470,315 | 541,883 | 184,529 | 1,807,177 |
| 1993 | 572,423 | 444,351 | 509,950 | 178,379 | 1,705,103 |
| 1994 | 541,343 | 426,327 | 468,662 | 174,158 | 1,610,490 |
| 1995 | 508,559 | 400,409 | 434,617 | 174,639 | 1,518,224 |
| 1996 | 491,103 | 389,001 | 416,735 | 174,883 | 1,471,722 |
| 1997 | 491,707 | 377,385 | 395,564 | 173,906 | 1,438,562 |
| 1998 | 483,880 | 367,470 | 382,338 | 173,142 | 1,406,830 |
| 1999 | 479,426 | 360,590 | 373,046 | 172,641 | 1,385,703 |
| 2000 | 482,170 | 355,654 | 373,193 | 173,321 | 1,384,338 |

NOTE: Figures for 1998 through 2000 include cadets/midshipmen. 1. Military personnel on extended or continuous active duty. Excludes reserves on active duty for training. Prior year totals have been corrected. 2. Represents "Command Strength" prior to June 30, 1956. 3. Army Air Forces and its predecessors for period prior to Sept. 18, 1947. Source: Department of Defense.

# The Medal of Honor

Often called the Congressional Medal of Honor, it is the nation's highest military award for "uncommon valor" by men and women in the armed forces. It is given for actions that are above and beyond the call of duty in combat against an armed enemy. The medal was first awarded by the army on March 25, 1863. More than 3,400 men have been awarded the medal, as well as one woman, Dr. Mary Walker, a surgeon in the Civil War.

Recipients of the medal are awarded $400 per month for life, a right to burial at Arlington National Cemetery, admission for them or their children to a service academy (if they qualify and quotas permit), and free travel on government aircraft to almost anywhere in the world, on a space-available basis. In 2002, there were 145 Medal of Honor recipients living.

## Medal of Honor Recipients

| | Total[1] | Army | Navy | Marines | Coast Guard | Air Force | Civilian |
|---|---|---|---|---|---|---|---|
| Civil War | 1,522 | 1,196 | 305 | 17 | — | — | 4 |
| Noncombat, 1865–1870 | 13 | 1 | 12 | — | — | — | — |
| Indian Wars (1861–1898) | 426 | 422 | — | — | — | — | 4 |
| Korea (1871) | 15 | — | 9 | 6 | — | — | — |
| Noncombat, 1871–1899 | 106 | — | 104 | 2 | — | — | — |
| Spanish-American War | 110 | 31 | 64 | 15 | — | — | — |
| Samoa | 4 | — | 1 | 3 | — | — | — |
| Philippines | 80 | 69 | 5 | 6 | — | — | — |
| China | 59 | 4 | 22 | 33 | — | — | — |
| Noncombat, 1901–1910 | 49 | 1 | 46 | 2 | — | — | — |
| Philippines (1911) | 6 | 1 | 5 | — | — | — | — |
| Mexican Campaign (1914) | 56 | 1 | 46 | 9 | — | — | — |
| Haiti (1915) | 6 | — | — | 6 | — | — | — |
| Noncombat, 1915–1916 | 8 | — | 8 | — | — | — | — |
| Dominican Republic | 3 | — | — | 3 | — | — | — |
| World War I | 119 | 90 | 21 | 8 | — | — | — |
| Haiti (1919–1920) | 2 | — | — | 2 | — | — | — |
| Nicaragua (1927–1933) | 2 | — | — | 2 | — | — | — |
| Noncombat, 1920–1940 | 17 | 1 | 15 | 1 | — | — | — |
| World War II | 464 | 324 | 57 | 82 | 1 | — | — |
| Korean War | 131 | 82 | 7 | 42 | — | — | — |
| Vietnam War | 245 | 159 | 16 | 57 | — | 13 | — |
| Somalia (1993) | 2 | 2 | — | — | — | — | — |
| Unknown Soldiers | 9 | 9 | — | — | — | — | — |
| Total | 3,454 | 2,393 | 743 | 296 | 1 | 13 | 8 |

1. These totals reflect the total number of Medals of Honor awarded through June 2002. Nineteen (19) men received a second award. Sources: The Congressional Medal of Honor Society, Mt. Pleasant, S.C., www.cmohs.org and Home of Heroes, www.homeofheroes.com/moh/history/history_statistics.html.

## U.S. Service Academies

**U.S. Air Force Academy**
Colorado Springs, Colo.
Established 1958
www.usafa.edu

**U.S. Merchant Marine Academy**
Kings Point, N.Y.
Established 1943
www.usmma.edu

**U.S. Coast Guard Academy**
New London, Conn.
Established 1876
www.cga.edu

**U.S. Military Academy**
West Point, N.Y.
Established 1802
www.usma.edu

**U.S. Naval Academy**
Annapolis, Md.
Established 1845
www.usna.edu

## Military & Veterans Websites

**U.S. Air Force:** www.af.mil
**U.S. Army:** www.army.mil
**U.S. Navy:** www.navy.mil
**MarineLINK:** www.usmc.mil
**U.S. Coast Guard:** www.uscg.mil
**DefenseLink (DOD):** www.defenselink.mil
**Military Woman:** www.militarywoman.org
(not a DOD or armed forces site)
**Selective Service System:** www.sss.gov
**Department of Veterans Affairs (VA):** www.va.gov
**BosniaLINK:** www.dtic.mil/bosnia/index.html
**Gulf War Veterans:** www.gulfwarvets.com
**Vietnam Veterans:** www.vva.org
**WWII U.S. Veterans:** ww2.vet.org
**Korean War Veterans Association:** www.kwva.org
**American Legion:** www.legion.org
**Air America:** www.air-america.org/
**North Atlantic Treaty Organization (NATO):**
www.nato.int

## Veterans of U.S. Wars and Their Dependents
### (on the VA Compensation and Pension Rolls as of May 2001)

Veterans' benefits have existed since the origins of the nation. As of May 2001, 3,247,975 veterans, their dependents, and survivors of deceased veterans are receiving VA benefits and services.

The last dependent of a Revolutionary War veteran died in 1911; the War of 1812's last dependent died in 1946; and the last dependent of the Mexican War died in 1962. Some 631 children and widows of Spanish-American War veterans are receiving VA benefits today. There is in fact a surviving widow and 12 children of Civil War veterans who still draw VA benefits.

| | Veterans | Children[1] | Parents | Surviving spouses |
|---|---|---|---|---|
| Civil War | — | 12 | — | 1 |
| Indian Wars | — | 1 | — | — |
| Spanish-American War | — | 245 | — | 386 |
| Mexican Border | 9 | 25 | — | 181 |
| World War I | 144 | 5,810 | 1 | 25,573 |
| World War II | 647,205 | 18,707 | 1,388 | 272,793 |
| Korean Conflict | 249,515 | 4,110 | 1,496 | 63,579 |
| Vietnam Era | 851,143 | 13,465 | 6,118 | 114,514 |
| Gulf War[2] | 344,174 | 8,508 | 338 | 6,261 |
| **Total wartime** | **2,092,190** | **50,883** | **9,341** | **483,288** |
| Nonservice-connected | 352,761 | 27,221 | — | 230,194 |
| Service-connected | 2,306,731 | 30,757 | 11,650 | 288,661 |
| **Total** | **2,659,492** | **57,978** | **11,650** | **518,855** |

1. Children connotes a minor or a helpless adult. 2. For VA benefits purposes, the Gulf War period of service remains open-ended and also includes those discharged from 1991 to date. *Source:* Department of Veterans Affairs and Department of Defense. Web: www.va.gov/pressrel/amwars01.htm.

## Last Living Veterans of America's Wars

**American Revolution (1775–1783)**
• Last veteran, Daniel F. Bakeman, died 4/5/1869, age 109
• Last widow, Catherine S. Damon, died 11/11/06, age 109
• Last dependent, Phoebe M. Palmeter, died 4/25/11, age 90

**War of 1812 (1812–1815)**
• Last veteran, Hiram Cronk, died 5/13/05, age 105
• Last widow, Carolina King, died 6/28/36, age unknown
• Last dependent, Esther A. H. Morgan, died 3/12/46, age 89

**Indian Wars (c. 1861–1898)**
• Last veteran, Fredrak Fraske, died 6/18/73, age 101

**Mexican War (1846–1848)**
• Last veteran, Owen Thomas Edgar, died 9/3/29, age 98
• Last widow, Lena Jones Theobald, died 6/20/63, age 89
• Last dependent, Jesse G. Bivens, died 11/1/62, age 94

**Civil War (1861–1865)**
• Last Union veteran, Albert Woolson, died 8/2/56, age 109
• Last Confederate veteran, John Salling*, died 3/16/58, age 112

**Spanish-American War (1898)**
• Last veteran, Nathan E. Cook, died 9/10/92, age 106

*Disputed. *Source:* Department of Veterans Affairs and Department of Defense. Web: www.va.gov/pressrel/amwars01.htm.

## America's Wars: Casualties and Veterans

**American Revolution (1775–1783)**

| | |
|---|---|
| Total servicemembers | 217,000 |
| Battle deaths | 4,435 |
| Nonmortal woundings | 6,188 |

**War of 1812 (1812–1815)**

| | |
|---|---|
| Total servicemembers | 286,730 |
| Battle deaths | 2,260 |
| Nonmortal woundings | 4,505 |

**Indian Wars (approx. 1817–1898)**

| | |
|---|---|
| Total servicemembers | 106,000[1] |
| Battle deaths | 1,000[1] |

**Mexican War (1846–1848)**

| | |
|---|---|
| Total servicemembers | 78,718 |
| Battle deaths | 1,733 |
| Other deaths in service (nontheater) | 11,550 |
| Nonmortal woundings | 4,152 |

**Civil War (1861–1865)**

| | |
|---|---|
| Total servicemembers (Union) | 2,213,363 |
| Battle deaths (Union) | 140,414 |
| Other deaths in service (nontheater) (Union) | 224,097 |
| Nonmortal woundings (Union) | 281,881 |
| Total servicemembers (Conf.) | 1,050,000 |
| Battle deaths (Conf.) | 74,524 |
| Other deaths in service (nontheater) (Conf.) | 59,297[2] |
| Nonmortal woundings (Conf.) | unknown |

**Spanish-American War (1898–1902)**

| | |
|---|---|
| Total servicemembers | 306,760 |
| Battle deaths | 385 |
| Other deaths in service (nontheater) | 2,061 |
| Nonmortal woundings | 1,662 |

**World War I (1917–1918)**

| | |
|---|---|
| Total servicemembers | 4,734,991 |
| Battle deaths | 53,402 |
| Other deaths in service (nontheater) | 63,114 |
| Nonmortal woundings | 204,002 |
| Living veterans (102)[3] | 2,212 |

**World War II (1940–1945)**

| | |
|---|---|
| Total servicemembers | 16,112,566 |
| Battle deaths | 291,557 |
| Other deaths in service (nontheater) | 113,842 |
| Nonmortal woundings | 671,846 |
| Living veterans (80)[3] | 5,032,591 |

**Korean War (1950–1953)**

| | |
|---|---|
| Total servicemembers | 5,720,000 |
| Battle deaths | 33,686 |
| Other deaths in service (theater) | 2,830 |
| Other deaths in service (nontheater) | 17,730 |
| Nonmortal woundings | 103,284 |
| Living veterans (69)[3] | 2,976,446 |

**Vietnam War (1964–1975)**

| | |
|---|---|
| Total servicemembers | 9,200,000 |
| Deployed to Southeast Asia | 3,100,000 |
| Battle deaths | 47,410 |
| Other deaths in service (theater) | 10,788 |
| Other deaths in service (nontheater) | 32,000 |
| Nonmortal woundings | 153,303 |
| Living veterans (55)[3] | 7,495,029 |

**Gulf War (1990–1991)**

| | |
|---|---|
| Total servicemembers | 2,322,332 |
| Deployed to Gulf | 1,136,658 |
| Battle deaths | 148 |
| Other deaths in service (theater) | 235 |
| Other deaths in service (nontheater) | 914 |
| Nonmortal woundings | 467 |
| Living veterans (35)[3] | 1,753,530[1] |

**America's Wars Total**

| | |
|---|---|
| Military service during war | 42,348,460 |
| Battle deaths | 650,954 |
| Other deaths in service (theater) | 13,853 |
| Other deaths in service (nontheater) | 229,661 |
| Nonmortal woundings | 1,431,290 |
| Living war veterans | 18,865,926 |
| Living veterans | 25,038,459 |

1. Veterans Administration estimate. 2. Estimated figure. Does not include 26,000–31,000 who died in Union prisons. 3. Median ages. *Source:* Department of Defense and Veterans Administration, Sept. 30, 2001.

## Post-Vietnam Combat Casualties[1]

| Place | Dates | Casualties | Place | Dates | Casualties |
|---|---|---|---|---|---|
| Lebanon | Aug. 1982–Feb. 1984 | 254 | Somalia | Dec. 1992–May 1993 | 29 |
| Grenada | Oct.–Nov. 1983 | 18 | Haiti | Sept. 1994–April 1996 | 0 |
| Libya | April 10–16, 1986 | 2 | Yugoslavia | March–June 1999 | 0 |
| Panama | Dec. 1989–Jan. 1990 | 23 | Afghanistan | Oct. 2001–June 2002[2] | 17 |
| Persian Gulf | Aug. 1990–March 1998, Dec. 1998–present | 148 | | | |

1. Defined as battle deaths. Does not include deaths from accidents. 2. Through Aug. 2002. At press time, Operation Enduring Freedom in Afghanistan was ongoing. *Source:* U.S. Department of Defense.

## American Prisoners of War

Congress defines a prisoner of war as a person who, while serving on active military, naval, or air service, is forcibly detained or interned in the line of duty by an enemy government or a hostile force.

| | Total | WWI | WWII | Korea | Vietnam | Persian Gulf | Somalia |
|---|---|---|---|---|---|---|---|
| Captured and interned | 142,233 | 4,120 | 130,201 | 7,140 | 745 | 23 | 1 |
| Returned to U.S. military control | 125,208 | 3,973 | 116,129 | 4,418 | 661 | 23 | 1 |
| Alive on Jan. 1, 1982 | 93,030 | 633 | 87,996 | 3,770 | 631 | n.a. | n.a. |
| Died while POW | 17,004 | 147 | 14,072 | 2,701 | 84 | 0 | 0 |
| Alive on Jan. 1, 2002 | 42,781 | 0 | 39,719 | 2,434 | 601 | 23 | 1 |

NOTES: n.a. = not available. Not included are the more than 92,000 military personnel considered missing in action: WWI, 3,350; WWII, 78,773; Korea, 8,100; Vietnam, 1,912 (as of June 2002); and the Persian Gulf, 1. *Source:* U.S. Department of Veterans Affairs.

For international military affairs, *see* p. 716.

# A Sister Solar System?

## A nearby star and its Jupiter-like planets look a lot like home

By **JEFFREY KLUGER** TIME

Time was, being an earthling was something special. In a universe full of apparently planetless stars, our colorful solar system seemed like one of a cosmic kind. The planet club became a little less elite, however, when astronomers announced in 2002 the discovery of a Jupiter-like world orbiting a not-too-distant star, a star that could well have an Earth-like planet in its brood too.

## Rising Star

The star that's causing all the buzz is 55 Cancri, about the size and age of our Sun, located just 41 light-years away. This is not the first time a planet has been seen orbiting the star. In 1996 Geoffrey Marcy, a professor of astronomy at the University of California, Berkeley, and astrophysicist Paul Butler of the Carnegie Institution of Washington spotted a different Jupiter-size world circling 55 Cancri in a close-up orbit just 10 million miles from the solar fires—closer than little Mercury orbits our own Sun. In fact, this planet is very like most of the 90-odd known exoplanets, so-called hot Jupiters that orbit closer to their stars than Jupiter does to the Sun.

The world revealed by Marcy, Butler, and their team last year, however—yet another around 55 Cancri—is an entirely different beast. About 3.5 to 5 times the mass of Jupiter—close enough by planetary standards to be a sister—it orbits at a distance of 510 million miles, remarkably like Jupiter's 480 million. The new world takes 13 years to complete a single orbit; Jupiter takes almost 12—again, all but identical.

The close similarity to Jupiter has a special significance to astronomers. One of the things that made life on Earth possible in the first place was the looming presence of our Sun's fifth planet, whose massive gravity vacuumed up a lot of incoming comets and asteroids, keeping the small inner worlds relatively safe in the shooting gallery that was the early solar system. The clear lane Jupiter created became a sort of orbital sweet spot, where temperatures could remain moderate and volatile substances such as water could persist, giving life a chance to arise. While plenty of stars beyond 55 Cancri and our sun may have their own Jupiter-size planets, their orbits often carry them through this habitable zone, preventing small Earth-size worlds from gaining a toehold. "An Earth-like planet can't get established when a Jupiter-size wrecking ball is sailing through," explains Butler.

## The Future Is Bright

Whether there's a lush little Earth spinning around 55 Cancri is still anybody's guess. Spotting even a giant planet in the glare of its sun is so hard—astronomers compare it to looking for a firefly next to a searchlight—that no one really sees any of these extra-solar worlds. Instead, investigators look for tiny perturbations in the position of the mother star that may suggest that the gravity of a planet of a certain size and distance is tugging at it.

NASA hopes, however, to launch within the next 20 years two new spacecraft that will study the gravitational wobble of stars and try to filter out some of their light. This, astronomers hope, will allow the hidden planets to pop into view. When the ships go online, 55 Cancri will be one of the first stars to receive a close look—a prospect that has become more tantalizing than ever. □

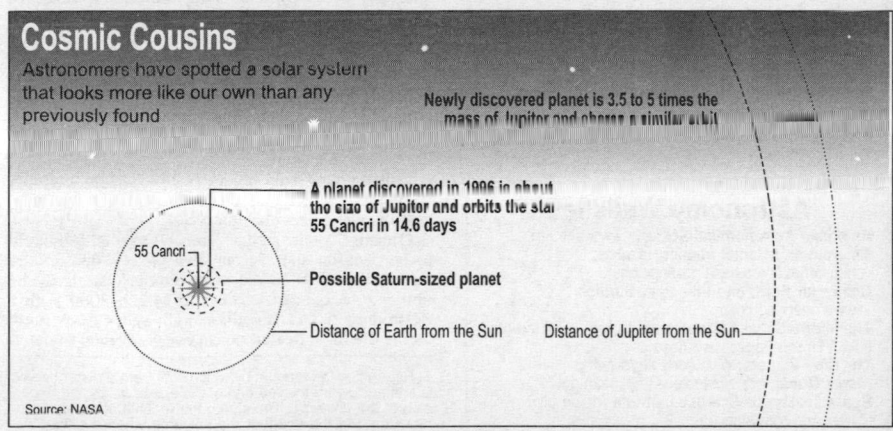

**Cosmic Cousins**

Astronomers have spotted a solar system that looks more like our own than any previously found

Newly discovered planet is 3.5 to 5 times the mass of Jupiter and obeys a similar orbit

A planet discovered in 1996 is about the size of Jupiter and orbits the star 55 Cancri in 14.6 days

55 Cancri

Possible Saturn-sized planet

Distance of Earth from the Sun    Distance of Jupiter from the Sun

Source: NASA

# Astronomical Terms

**Aphelion:** see **Orbit.**

**Apogee:** see **Orbit.**

**Black hole:** the theoretical end-product of the total gravitational collapse of a massive star or group of stars. Crushed even smaller than the incredibly dense neutron star, the black hole may become so dense that not even light can escape its gravitational field. In 1996, astronomers found strong evidence for a massive black hole at the center of the Milky Way. Recent evidence suggests that black holes are so common that they probably exist at the core of nearly all galaxies.

**Conjunction:** the alignment of two celestial objects at the same celestial longitude. Conjunction of the Moon and planets is often determined with reference to the Sun. For example, Saturn is said to be in conjunction with the Sun when Saturn and the Earth are aligned on opposite sides of the Sun.

Mercury and Venus, the two planets with orbits within Earth's orbit, have two positions of conjunction. Mercury, for example, is said to be in *inferior conjunction* when the Sun and the Earth are aligned on opposite sides of Mercury. Mercury is in *superior conjunction* when Mercury and the Earth are aligned on opposite sides of the Sun.

**Elongation:** the angular distance between two points in the sky as measured from a third point. The elongation of Mercury, for example, is the angular distance between Mercury and the Sun as measured from Earth. Planets whose orbits are outside the Earth's can have elongations between 0° and 180°. (When a planet's elongation is 0° it is at conjunction; when it is 180°, it is at opposition.) Because Mercury and Venus are within the Earth's orbit, their greatest elongations measured from the Earth are 28° and 47°, respectively.

**Galaxy:** gas and millions of stars held together by gravity. All that you can see in the sky (with a very few exceptions) belongs to our galaxy—a system of roughly 200 billion stars. The exceptions you can see are other galaxies. Our own galaxy, the rim of which we see as the "Milky Way," is about 100,000 light-years in diameter and about 10,000 light-years in thickness. Its shape is roughly that of a thick lens; more precisely, it is a *spiral nebula,* a term first used for other galaxies when they were discovered and before it was realized that these were separate and distinct galaxies. Astronomers have estimated that the universe could contain 40 to 50 billion galaxies.

**Neutron star:** an extremely dense star with a powerful gravitational pull. Some neutron stars pulse radio waves into space as they spin; these are known as pulsars.

**Occultation:** the eclipse of one celestial object by another. For example, a star is occulted when the Moon passes between it and the Earth.

**Opposition:** the alignment of two celestial objects when their longitude differs by 180°. Opposition of the Moon and planets is often determined with reference to the Sun. For example, Saturn is said to be at opposition when Saturn and the Sun are aligned on opposite sides of the Earth. Only the planets whose orbits lie outside the Earth's can be in opposition to the Sun.

**Orbit:** the path traveled by an object in space. The term comes from the Latin *orbis,* which means "circle" or "disk," and *orbita,* "orbit." Theoretically, there are four mathematical figures, or models, of possible orbits: two are open (hyperbola and parabola) and two are closed (ellipse and circle), but in reality all closed orbits are ellipses. Ellipses can be nearly circular, as are the orbits of most planets, or very elongated, as are the orbits of most comets, but the orbit revolves around a fixed, or *focal,* point. In our solar system, the Sun's gravitational pull keeps the planets in their elliptical orbits; the planets hold their moons in place similarly. For planets, the point of the orbit closest to the Sun is the *perihelion,* and the point farthest from the Sun is the *aphelion.* For orbits around the Earth, the point of closest proximity is the *perigee;* the farthest point is the *apogee.* See also **Retrograde.**

**Perigee:** see **Orbit.**

**Perihelion:** see **Orbit.**

**Planet:** a celestial object in orbit around a star. Even in ancient times, it was known that a number of "stars" did not stay in the same position relative to the others. There were five such restless "stars" known—Mercury, Venus, Mars, Jupiter, and Saturn—and the Greeks referred to them as *planetes,* a word which means "wanderers." That Earth is one of the planets was realized later. The additional planets were discovered after the invention of the telescope.

In 1994, Dr. Alexander Wolszcan, an astronomer at Pennsylvania State University, presented convincing evidence of the first known planets to exist outside our solar system. They circle a pulsar, or exploded star, in the constellation *Virgo.*

In 1995, several of these *extrasolar planets* were discovered orbiting stars similar to our Sun. Swiss astronomers found a planet orbiting star 51 in the constellation *Pegasus,* about 40 light-years away. It is the first planet ever discovered to circle a normal Sun-like star. As of June 2002, more than 90 planets have been discovered.

**Pulsar:** a celestial object, believed to be a rapidly spinning neutron star, that emits intense bursts of radio waves at regular intervals.

**Quasar:** "quasi-stellar" object. Originally thought to be peculiar stars in our own galaxy, quasars are now believed to be the most remote objects in the universe. A quasar detected in March 2000 with a redshift of 5.8 is 12 billion light-years from Earth and is the most distant object ever observed to date.[1]

1. Redshift is the amount by which light from a distant object is shifted toward the red end of the spectrum by the expansion of the universe. The higher the redshift, the greater the distance and the younger the universe when the light was emitted.

Quasars emit tremendous amounts of light and microwave radiation. Although they are not much bigger than Earth's solar system, quasars pour out 100 to 1,000 times as much light as an entire galaxy containing a hundred billion stars. It is believed that quasars are powered by massive black holes that suck up billions of stars.

**Retrograde:** describes the clockwise orbit or rotation of a planet or other celestial object, which is in the direction opposite to the Earth and most celestial bodies. As viewed from a position in space north of the solar system (from some great distance above the Earth's North Pole), all the planets revolve counterclockwise around the Sun, and all but Venus, Uranus, and Pluto rotate counterclockwise on their own axes. These three planets have retrograde motion.

Sometimes *retrograde* is also used to describe apparent backward motion as viewed from Earth. This motion happens when two objects rotate at different speeds around another fixed object. For example, the planet Mars appears to be retrograde when the Earth overtakes and passes by it as they both move around the Sun.

**Satellite** (or **moon**): an object in orbit around a planet. Until the discovery of Jupiter's four main moons by Galileo Galilei, celestial objects in orbit around a planet were called *moons*. However, upon Galilei's discovery, Johannes Kepler (in a letter to Galileo) suggested *satellite* (from the Latin *satelles*, which means "attendant") as a general term for such objects. The word *satellite* is used interchangeably with *moon*, and astronomers speak and write about the moons of Neptune, Saturn, etc. The term *satellite* is also used to describe man-made devices of any size that are launched into orbit.

**Star:** a celestial object consisting of intensely hot gases held together by gravity. Stars derive their energy from nuclear reactions going on in their interiors, generating heat and light. Stars are very large. Our Sun has a diameter of 865,400 mi—a comparatively small star.

A dwarf star is a small star that is of relatively low mass and average or below average luminosity. The Sun is a *yellow dwarf*, which is in its main sequence, or prime of life. This means that nuclear reactions of hydrogen maintain its size and temperature. By contrast, a *white dwarf* is a star at the end of its life, with low luminosity, small size, and very high density.

A *red giant* is a star nearing the end of its life. When a star begins to lose hydrogen and burn helium instead, it gradually collapses, and its outer from these stars is red because of their cooler temperature.

**Supernova:** a celestial phenomenon in which a star explodes, releasing a great burst of light. There are two basic types of supernova. Type Ia happens when a white dwarf star draws large amounts of matter from a nearby star until it can no longer support itself and collapses. The second more well-known kind of supernova, type IIa, is the result of the collapse of a massive star. (Massive is a classification for a star that is at least eight times the size of our Sun.) Once the star's nuclear fuel is exhausted, if its core is heavy enough, the star will collapse in on itself, releasing a huge amount of energy (the supernova), which may be brighter than the star's host galaxy.

The Milky Way, the galaxy containing our solar system, is about 100,000 light-years in diameter and about 10,000 light-years thick.

## Origin of the Universe

Before the universe as we now know it existed, there was no space or time. The Big Bang and its associated theories try to explain or describe the moment of change from nothingness and no time to the existence of the universe filled with space and marked by time. Many physicists describe this event as an explosion, or flash, hence the name *Big Bang*. The Big Bang is a process of expansion in our universe that is still active today.

The universe flashed into existence (according to the Big Bang theory) from a very small agglomeration of matter of extremely high density and temperatures. As a dense, hot globule of gas, containing nothing but hydrogen and a small amount of helium, it began expanding rapidly outward. There were no stars or planets. The first stars probably began to condense out of the primordial hydrogen when the universe was about 100 million years old and continued to form as the universe aged. Recent pictures taken with the Hubble telescope indicate that star births peaked sometime between 500 million and 1 billion years after the Big Bang, but this process continues. Our Sun was formed 4.5 billion years ago, and through telescopes we can now see stars forming out of compressed pockets of hydrogen in outer space.

In 2002, an international team of astronomers studying white dwarf stars was able to confirm that the universe was formed at least 13 billion years ago. The findings support the recent work of other scientists who have calculated the age of the cosmos at between 13 billion and 15 billion years.

## Birth and Death of a Star

Astronomers think that a star begins to form as a dense cloud of gas in the arms of spiral galaxies. Individual hydrogen atoms fall with increasing speed and energy toward the center of the cloud under the force of the star's gravity. The increase in energy heats the gas. When this process has continued for some millions of years, the temperature reaches about 20 million degrees Fahrenheit. At this temperature, the hydrogen within the star ignites and burns in a continuing series of nuclear reactions. The onset of these reactions marks the birth of a star.

When a star begins to exhaust its hydrogen supply, its life nears an end. The first sign of a star's old

## Astronomical Constants

| | |
|---|---|
| Light-year (distance traveled by light in one year) | 5,880,000,000,000 mi |
| Parsec (parallax of one second, or stellar distances) | 3.259 light-years |
| Velocity of light | c. 186,282.4 mi/sec |
| Astronomical unit (A.U.), or mean distance Earth to Sun | ca. 93,000,000 mi[1] |
| Mean distance, Earth to Moon | 238,860 mi |
| General precession | 50′,.26 |
| Obliquity of the ecliptic | 23° 27′8′.26-0′.4684(t-1900)[2] |
| Equatorial radius of Earth | 3963.34 statute mi |
| Polar radius of Earth | 3949.99 statute mi |
| Earth's mean radius | 3958.89 statute mi |
| Oblateness of Earth | 1/297 |
| Equatorial horizontal parallax of the moon | 57′2′.70 |
| Earth's mean velocity in orbit | 18.5 mi/sec |
| Sidereal year | 365d.2564 |
| Tropical year | 365d.2422 |
| Sidereal month | 27d.3217 |
| Synodic month | 29d.5306 |
| Mean sidereal day | 23h56m4s.091 of mean solar time |
| Mean solar day | 24h3m56s.555 of sidereal time |

1. Actual mean distance derived from radar bounces: 92,935,700 mi. The value of 92,897,400 mi (based on parallax of 8″.80) is used in calculations. 2. *t* refers to the year in question, for example, 2003.

age is a swelling and reddening of its outer regions. Such an aging, swollen star is called a *red giant.* The Sun, a middle-aged star, will probably swell to a red giant in 5 billion years, vaporizing Earth and any creatures that may be on its surface. When all its fuel has been exhausted, a star cannot generate sufficient pressure at its center to balance the crushing force of gravity. The star collapses under the force of its own weight; if it is a small star, it collapses gently and remains collapsed. Such a collapsed star, at its life's end, is called a *white dwarf.* The Sun will probably end its life in this way. A different fate awaits a large star. Its final collapse generates a violent explosion, blowing the innards of the star out into space. There, the materials of the exploded star mix with the primeval hydrogen of the universe. Later in the history of the galaxy, other stars are formed out of this mixture. The Sun is one of these stars. It contains the debris of countless other stars that exploded before the Sun was born.

## Formation of the Solar System

Our solar system consists of one star (the Sun), nine planets and all their moons, several thousand minor planets called asteroids or planetoids, and an equally large number of comets. The Sun's age was calculated in 1989 to be 4.49 billion years old, less than the 4.7 billion years previously believed. It was formed from a cloud of hydrogen mixed with small amounts of other substances that had been produced in the bodies of other stars before the Sun was born. This was the parent cloud of the solar system. The dense, hot gas at the center of the cloud gave rise to the Sun; the outer regions of the cloud—cooler and less dense—gave birth to the planets.

## The Sun

All the stars, including our Sun, are gigantic balls of superheated gas, kept hot by atomic reactions in their centers. In our Sun, this atomic reaction is hydrogen fusion: four hydrogen atoms are combined to form one helium atom. The temperature at the core of our Sun is thought to be 36,000,000°F, or about 20,000,000°C, and the surface temperature

averages 11,000°F, or about 6,000°C. The diameter of the Sun is 865,400 mi, and its surface area is approximately 12,000 times that of Earth. Compared with other stars, our Sun is just a bit below average in size and temperature, and is a yellow dwarf star. It is about 4.5 billion years old, and its fuel supply (hydrogen) is estimated to be sufficient for another 5 billion years.

Our Sun is not motionless in space; in fact, it has two kinds of motion. One is a seemingly straight-line motion in the direction of the constellation Hercules at the rate of about 12 miles per second. But since the Sun is a part of the Milky Way system and since the whole system rotates slowly around its own center, the Sun also moves at the rate of 175 miles per second as part of the rotating Milky Way system.

In addition to this motion, the Sun rotates on its axis. Observations of the motion of sunspots (darkish areas that look like enormous whirling storms) and solar flares, which are usually associated with sunspots, have shown that the rotational period of the Sun is just short of 25 days. But this figure is valid for the Sun's equator only; the sections near the Sun's poles seem to have a rotational period of 34 days. Since the Sun generates its own heat and light, there is no temperature difference between poles and equator.

What we call the Sun's "surface" is scientifically known as the *photosphere.* Since the whole Sun is a ball of expanding hot gas, there is really no such thing as a surface; it is a question of visual impression. The layer outside the photosphere is known as the *chromosphere,* which extends several thousand miles beyond the photosphere. It is in steady motion, and often enormous prominences can be seen to burst from it, extending as much as 100,000 mi into space. Outside the chromosphere is the *corona.* The corona consists of very tenuous gases (essentially hydrogen) and makes a magnificent sight when the Sun is eclipsed.

In addition to heat and light, the Sun also generates solar wind, a stream of ionized particles that radiates outward through the solar system at high speeds. One of the effects of solar wind is that it forces the tails of comets to point away from the

# A Star's Magnitude

Magnitude is the degree of brightness of a star. In 1856, British astronomer Norman Pogson proposed a quantitative scale of stellar magnitudes, which was adopted by the astronomical community. He noted that we receive 100 times more light from a first magnitude star as from a sixth; thus with a difference of five magnitudes, there is a 100:1 ratio of incoming light energy, which is called *luminous flux*.

Because of the nature of human perception, equal intervals of brightness are actually equal ratios of luminous flux. Pogson's proposal was that one increment in magnitude be the fifth root

of 100. This means that each increment in magnitude corresponds to an increase in the amount of energy by 2.512, approximately. A fifth magnitude star is 2.512 times as bright as a sixth, and a fourth magnitude star is 6.310 times as bright as a sixth, and so on. The naked eye, upon optimum conditions, can see down to around the sixth magnitude, that is +6. Under Pogson's system, a few of the brighter stars now have negative magnitudes. For example, Sirius is –1.5. The lower the magnitude number, the brighter the object. The full moon has a magnitude of about –12.5, and the sun is a bright –26.51!

## The Brightest Stars

| Star | Constellation | Mag. | Dist (l.-y.) | Star | Constellation | Mag. | Dist (l.-y.) |
|---|---|---|---|---|---|---|---|
| Sirius | Canis Major | -1.6 | 8 | Antares | Scorpius | 1.2 | 170 |
| Canopus | Carina | -0.9 | 650 | Fomalhaut | Piscis Austrinus | 1.3 | 27 |
| Alpha Centauri | Centaurus | +0.1 | 4 | Deneb | Cygnus | 1.3 | 465 |
| Vega | Lyra | 0.1 | 23 | Regulus | Leo | 1.3 | 70 |
| Capella | Auriga | 0.2 | 42 | Beta Crucis | Crux | 1.5 | 465 |
| Arcturus | Boötes | 0.2 | 32 | Eta Carinae | Carina | 1-7 | — |
| Rigel | Orion | 0.3 | 545 | Alpha-one Crucis | Crux | 1.6 | 150 |
| Procyon | Canis Minor | 0.5 | 10 | Castor | Gemini | 1.6 | 44 |
| Achernar | Eridanus | 0.6 | 70 | Gamma Crucis | Crux | 1.6 | — |
| Beta Centauri | Centaurus | 0.9 | 130 | Epsilon Canis Majoris | Canis Major | 1.6 | 325 |
| Altair | Aquila | 0.9 | 18 | Epsilon Ursae Majoris | Ursa Major | 1.7 | 50 |
| Betelgeuse | Orion | 0.9 | 600 | Bellatrix | Orion | 1.7 | 215 |
| Aldebaran | Taurus | 1.1 | 54 | Lambda Scorpii | Scorpius | 1.7 | 205 |
| Spica | Virgo | 1.2 | 190 | Epsilon Carinae | Carina | 1.7 | 325 |
| Pollux | Gemini | 1.2 | 31 | Mira | Cetus | 2-10 | 250 |

Sun. The solar wind also interacts with the Earth's magnetic field, causing the auroras and other phenomena. Solar flares—eruptions of hydrogen gas on the surface of the Sun—can also cause disturbances in the Earth's magnetic field.

As the Sun ages, it gradually expands and heats. It is estimated that the Sun's brilliancy will increase by 10% over the next 1.1 billion years or more, and, in about 6.5 billion years, our aging star will have doubled its present luminosity. The extreme heat generated will be catastrophic for Earth: the oceans will boil away and life as we know it will end. Eight billion years from now, the Sun's radius will extend beyond the present orbit of Venus, causing the total destruction of Earth.

## The Moon

Mercury and Venus do not have any moons. The planet that comes after the Earth, Mars, has two very small moons. Jupiter has four major moons and at least 35 minor ones. Saturn, the ringed planet, has 30 known moons, of which one (Titan) is larger than the planet Mercury. Uranus has at least 21 moons (four of them large) as well as rings, while Neptune has one large and seven small moons. Pluto has one moon, discovered in 1978. Some astronomers still consider Pluto to be a "runaway moon" of Neptune.

Our Moon, with a diameter of 2,160 mi, is one of the larger moons in our solar system and is especially large when compared with the planet that it orbits. In fact, the common center of gravity of the

Earth–Moon system is only about 1,000 mi below Earth's surface. The closest the Moon can come to us (its perigee) is 221,463 mi; the farthest it can go away (its apogee) is 252,710 mi. The period of rotation of the Moon is equal to its period of revolution around Earth, so from Earth we can see only one hemisphere of the Moon. Both periods are 27 days, 7 hours, 43 minutes, and 11.47 seconds. But while the rotation of the Moon is constant, its velocity in its orbit is not, since it moves more slowly in apogee than in perigee. Consequently, some portions near the rim of the Moon that are not normally visible will appear briefly. This phenomenon is called *libration*, and by taking advantage of the librations, astronomers have succeeded in mapping approximately 59% of the lunar surface. The other 41% has since been more fully mapped but has been mapped by American and Russian Moon-orbiting spacecraft.

Though the Moon goes around Earth in the time mentioned, the interval from new moon to new moon is 29 days, 12 hours, 44 minutes, and 2.78 seconds. This delay of nearly two days is due to the fact that Earth is moving around the Sun, so that the Moon needs two extra days to reach a spot in its orbit where no part is illuminated by the Sun, as seen from Earth.

If the plane of Earth's orbit around the Sun (the ecliptic) and the plane of the Moon's orbit around Earth were the same, the Moon would be eclipsed by Earth every time it is full, and the Sun would be eclipsed by the Moon every time the Moon is "new" (it would be better to call it the "black moon" when it is in this position). But because the two orbits do not coincide, the Moon's shadow normally misses Earth and Earth's shadow misses the Moon. The inclination of the two orbital planes to each other is 5°.

The tides are caused by the Moon with the help of the Sun, but in the open ocean they are surprisingly low, amounting to about one yard. The very high tides that can be observed near the shore in some places are due to funneling effects of the shorelines. At new moon and at full moon the tides raised by the Moon are reinforced by the Sun; these are the *spring tides.* If the Sun's tidal power acts at right angles to that of the Moon (quarter moons) we get the low *neap tides.*

The *Lunar Prospector* spacecraft, launched in Jan. 1998, found that as much as three billion metric tons of water ice is hidden in the permanently shaded craters at the poles. The water probably came from interstellar comets that crashed into the Moon. *Lunar Prospector* also confirmed that the Moon has a small core, supporting the theory that the Moon was ripped away from the early Earth when an object the size of Mars collided with the Earth.

At the end of its mission, on July 31, 1999, the spacecraft was intentionally crashed into a permanently shadowed crater at the Moon's south pole in the hope of detecting a rising plume of water ice, but no cloud of water vapor molecules was observed by powerful Earth telescopes.

# Earth

Earth, circling the Sun at an average distance of 93 million miles, is the fifth-largest planet and the third from the Sun. It orbits the Sun at a speed of 67,000 mph, making one revolution in 365 days, 5 hours, 48 minutes, and 45.51 seconds. Earth completes one rotation on its axis every 23 hours, 56 minutes, and 4.09 seconds. Actually a bit pear-shaped rather than a true sphere, Earth has a diameter of 7,927 mi at the equator and a few miles less at the poles. It has an estimated mass of about 6.6 sextillion tons, with an average density of 5.52 grams per cubic centimeter. Earth's surface area encompasses 196,949,970 sq mi of which about three-fourths is water.

## Origin of Earth

Earth, along with the other planets, is believed to have been born 4.5 billion years ago as a solidified cloud of dust and gases left over from the creation of the Sun. For perhaps 500 million years, the interior of Earth stayed solid and relatively cool, perhaps 2,000°F. The main ingredients, according to the best available evidence, were iron and silicates, with small amounts of other elements, some of them radioactive. As millions of years passed, energy released by radioactive decay—mostly of uranium, thorium, and potassium—gradually heated Earth, melting some of its constituents. The iron melted before the silicates, and, being heavier, sank toward the center. This forced up the silicates that it found there. After many years, the iron reached the center, almost 4,000 mi deep, and began to accumulate. No eyes were around at that time to view the turmoil that must have taken place on the face of Earth— gigantic heaves and bubblings on the surface, exploding volcanoes, and flowing lava covering everything in sight. Finally, the iron in the center

accumulated as the core. Around it, a thin but fairly stable crust of solid rock formed as Earth cooled. Depressions in the crust were natural basins in which water, rising from the interior of the planet through volcanoes and fissures, collected to form the oceans. Slowly, Earth acquired its present appearance.

## Earth Today

As a result of radioactive heating over millions of years, Earth's molten *core* is probably fairly hot today, around 11,000°F. By comparison, lead melts at around 800°F. Most of Earth's 2,100-mile-thick core is liquid, but the center of the core is mostly solid iron. The liquid outer portion, about 95% of the core, is constantly in motion. The interaction between the solid inner core and the fluid outer core creates a hydromagnetic dynamo that generates the magnetic field around Earth. The magnetic field protects the Earth from harmful cosmic radiation and makes navigation by compass possible.

Within the last decade, scientists have made some important discoveries about Earth's solid-iron core. In 1996, geophysicists discovered that the core rotates slightly faster than the rest of the planet and gains a quarter-turn every century. This may help explain how Earth's magnetic field periodically reverses its polarity. X-ray images of the inside of the Earth show that the core is not a perfect sphere—there are vast mountains 6 to 7 mi high and deep valleys. These features are in an inverse, or upside-down, relationship to similar features on the Earth's surface.

Outside the core is Earth's *mantle,* 1,800 mi thick and extending nearly to the surface. The mantle is composed of heavy silicate rock, similar to that brought up by volcanic eruptions. It is somewhere between liquid and solid, slightly yielding, and therefore contributing to an active, moving Earth. Most of Earth's radioactive material is in the thin *crust* that covers the mantle, but some is in the mantle and continues to give off heat. The crust's thickness ranges from 5 to 25 mi.

## Continental Drift

A great deal of evidence confirms the theory that the continents of Earth, made mostly of relatively light granite, float in the slightly yielding mantle, like logs in a pond. For many years it had been noticed that if North and South America could be pushed toward western and southern Europe and western Africa, they would fit like pieces in a jigsaw puzzle. Today, there is little question—the continents have drifted widely and continue to do so.

In 10 million years, the world as we know it may be unrecognizable, with California drifting out to sea, Florida joining South America, and Africa moving farther away from Europe and Asia.

## Earth's Atmosphere

The thin blanket of atmosphere that envelops Earth extends several hundred miles into space. From sea level—the very bottom of the ocean of air—to a height of about 60 mi, the air in the atmosphere is made up of the same gases in the same ratio: about 78% nitrogen, 21% oxygen, and the remaining 1% a mixture of argon, carbon dioxide, and tiny amounts of neon, helium, krypton, xenon, and other gases. The atmosphere becomes less dense with increasing altitude: more than three-fourths of Earth's huge envelope is concentrated in the first 5 to 10 mi above the surface. At sea level, a cubic foot of atmosphere weighs about an ounce and a quarter. The entire atmosphere weighs 5,700 trillion tons, and the force with which gravity holds it in place causes it to exert a pressure of nearly 15 psi. Going out from Earth's surface, the atmosphere is divided into five regions. The regions, and the heights to which they extend, are: *troposphere,* 0 to 7 mi (at middle latitudes); *stratosphere,* 7 to 30 mi; *mesosphere,* 30 to 50 mi; *thermosphere,* 50 to 400 mi; and *exosphere,* above 400 mi. The boundaries between each of the regions are known respectively as the *tropopause, stratopause, mesopause,* and *thermopause.* Alternative terms often used for the layers above the troposphere are *ozonosphere* (for stratosphere) and *ionosphere* for the remaining upper layers.

## The Seasons

Seasons are caused by the 23.4° tilt of Earth's axis, which alternately turns the North and South Poles toward the Sun. Times when the Sun's apparent path crosses the equator are known as *equinoxes.* Times when the Sun's apparent path is at the greatest distance from the equator are known as *solstices.* The lengths of the days are most extreme at each solstice. If Earth's axis were perpendicular to the plane of Earth's orbit around the Sun, there would be no seasons, and the days always would be equal in length. Since Earth's axis is at an angle, the Sun strikes Earth directly at the equator only twice a year: in March (vernal equinox) and September (autumnal equinox). In the Northern Hemisphere, spring begins at the vernal equinox, summer at the summer solstice, fall at the autumnal equinox, and winter at the winter solstice. The situation is reversed in the Southern Hemisphere.

## Mercury

Mercury is the planet nearest the Sun. Appropriately named for the wing-footed Roman messenger of the gods, Mercury whizzes around the Sun at a speed of 30 miles per second, completing one circuit in 88 days. The days and nights are long on Mercury. It takes 59 Earth days for Mercury to make a single rotation. It spins at a rate of about 6 mph (about 10 km/h), measured at the equator, as compared to Earth's spin of about 1,000 mph (about 1,600 km/h) at the equator.

The photographs *Mariner 10* (1974–1975) radioed back to Earth revealed an ancient, heavily cratered surface on Mercury, closely resembling our own Moon. The pictures showed huge cliffs, or scarps, crisscrossing the planet. These apparently were created when Mercury's interior cooled and shrank compressing the planet's crust. The cliffs are as high as 1.2 mi (2 km) and as long as 932 mi (1,500 km). Another unique feature is the Caloris Basin, a large impact crater about 808 mi (1,300 km) in diameter.

Mercury, like Earth, appears to have a crust of light silicate rock. Scientists believe it has a heavy iron-rich core that makes up about half of its volume.

Instruments onboard *Mariner 10* discovered that the planet has a weak magnetic field and a trace of atmosphere—a trillionth the density of Earth's and composed chiefly of argon, neon, and helium. The spacecraft reported temperatures ranging from 950°F (510°C) on Mercury's sunlit side to –346°F (–210°C) on the dark side. Mercury literally bakes in daylight and freezes at night.

Until the *Mariner 10* probe, little was known about the planet. Even the best telescopic views from Earth showed Mercury as an indistinct object lacking any surface detail. The planet is so close to the Sun that it is usually lost in the Sun's glare.

Radar images taken by astronomers at Jet Propulsion Laboratories and California Institute of Technology during the summer of 1991 suggest that the polar regions of Mercury may be covered with patches of water ice. Although this seems impossible due to the planet's sizzling heat, the polar regions receive very little sunlight and may get as cold as –235°F (–148°C). The radar images showed bright patterns at the poles that are characteristic of ice reflecting radar signals. Other explanations may be offered for this unexpected discovery.

In March or April 2004, NASA plans to launch a spacecraft, *Messenger,* that will orbit Mercury in April 2009. It will map the planet for one Earth year and search for water, a magnetic field, and other phenomena.

Mercury is visible to the naked eye at morning or evening twilight when it is at its greatest elongation.

## Venus

Although Venus is Earth's closest neighbor, very little is known about the planet because it is permanently covered with thick clouds. In 1962, Soviet and American space probes, coupled with Earth-based radar and infrared spectroscopy, began slowly unraveling some of the mystery surrounding Venus. Twenty-eight years later, the *Magellan* spacecraft, sent by the United States, arrived at Venus in Aug. 1990 and began radar-mapping the planet's surface in greater detail.

According to the latest results, Venus's atmosphere exerts a pressure at the surface 94.5 times greater than Earth's. Walking on Venus would be as difficult as walking a half-mile beneath the ocean. Because of a thick blanket of carbon dioxide, a "greenhouse effect" exists on Venus. Venus intercepts twice as much of the Sun's light as does Earth. The light enters freely through the carbon dioxide gas and is changed to heat radiation in molecular collisions. But carbon dioxide prevents the heat from escaping. Consequently, the temperature of the surface of Venus is over 800°F (427°C), hot enough to melt lead.

The atmospheric composition of Venus is about 96% carbon dioxide, 4% nitrogen, and minor amounts of water, oxygen, and sulfur compounds. There are at least four distinct cloud and haze layers that exist at different altitudes above the planet's surface. The haze layers contain small aerosol particles, possibly droplets of sulfuric acid. A concentration of sulfur dioxide above the cloud tops has been observed to be decreasing since 1978. The source of sulfur dioxide at this altitude is unknown; it may be injected by volcanic explosions or atmospheric overturning.

Measurements of the Venusian atmosphere and its cloud patterns reveal nearly constant high-speed zonal winds, about 220 mph (100 meters per second) at the equator. The winds decrease toward the poles so that the atmosphere at cloud-top level rotates almost like a solid body. The wind speeds at the equator correspond to Venus's rotation period of four to five days at most latitudes. The circulation is always in the same direction—east to west—as

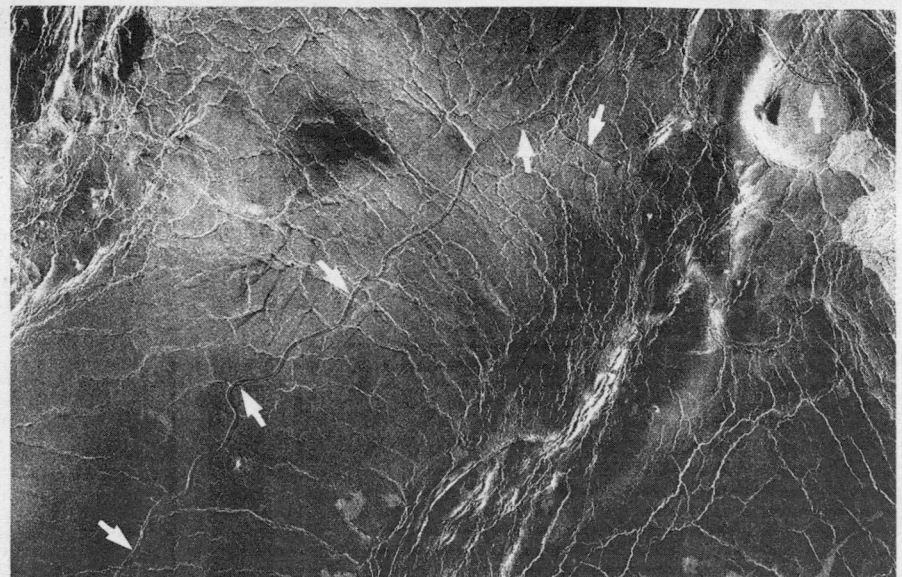

**Largest Channel in Solar System.** *Magellan* took the above image of the largest known channel on Venus. At 4,200 mi (6,800 km) long and an average of 1.1 mi (1.8 km) wide, it is longer than the Nile River, Earth's longest river, making it the longest known channel in the solar system. The channel was originally discovered by the Soviet *Venery 15* and *16* spacecraft orbiters. *Source:* NASA.

Venus's slow retrograde motion. Earth's winds blow from west to east, the same direction as its rotation.

Venus is round, very different from the other planets and from the Moon. Venus has neither polar flattening nor an equatorial bulge. The diameter of Venus is 7,519 mi (12,100 km). Venus has a retrograde axial rotation period of 243.1 Earth days. The surface atmospheric pressure is 1,396 psi (95 Earth atmospheres). The planet's mean distance from the Sun is 67.2 million miles (108.2 million kilometers). The period of its revolution around the Sun is 224.7 days.

The highest point on Venus is the summit of Maxwell Montes, 6.71 mi (10.8 km) above the mean level, more than a mile higher than Mount Everest. There is some evidence that this huge mountain is an active volcano. The lowest point is in the rift valley, Diana Chasma, 1.8 mi (2.9 km) below the mean level. This point is about one-fifth the greatest depth on Earth in the Marianas Trench.

Venus has an extreme lowland basin, Atalanta Planitia, which is about the size of Earth's North Atlantic Ocean basin. The smooth surface of the Atalanta Planitia resembles the mare basins of the Moon.

There are only two highland or continental masses on Venus: Ishtar Terra and Aphrodite Terra. Ishtar Terra is 6.8 mi (11 km) at its highest points (the highest peaks on Venus) and those of Aphrodite Terra rise to about 3.10 mi (5 km) above the planet. Ishtar Terra is about the size of the continental United States and Aphrodite Terra is about the size of Africa.

The unmanned NASA spacecraft *Magellan* was launched on May 4, 1989, from the shuttle *Atlantis* and arrived at Venus Aug. 10, 1990, to map most of

the planet. Despite some problems with its radio transmissions, the results of the radar mapping delighted scientists and provided them with the sharpest images ever taken of the planet's surface. Images taken from *Magellan* show ten times more detail than ever seen before.

The radar images provided scientists with compelling evidence that the planet has been dominated by volcanism on a global scale. The photos also showed that the planet's second-highest mountain, Maat Mons, rising 5 mi (8 km) above the Venusian plains, appears to be covered with fresh lava and is possibly an active volcano.

*Magellan* discovered the longest known channel in the solar system on Venus. It is 4,200 mi (6,800 km) long and averages slightly over a mile (1.8 km) wide. Its origin is puzzling to scientists because high-temperature lava is unlikely to have caused such a long-distance flow on the surface, and there are no known substances that could remain liquid long enough under the planet's atmospheric pressure and temperature to have carved out this snakelike feature. The channel is slightly longer than the Nile River, the longest river on Earth.

*Magellan* ended its radar and emissions mapping in Sept. 1992 after covering 98% of the planet's surface. The spacecraft continued to gather data until Oct. 1994, when it was intentionally crashed into the planet's surface.

Venus is the brightest of all the planets and is often visible in the morning or evening, when it is frequently referred to as the Morning Star or Evening Star. At its brightest, it can sometimes be seen in full daylight with the naked eye, if one knows where to look.

## Mars

Mars, on the other side of Earth from Venus, is Venus's direct opposite in terms of physical properties. Its atmosphere is cold, thin, and transparent, and readily permits observation of the planet's features. We know more about Mars than any other planet except Earth. Mars is a forbidding, rugged planet with huge volcanoes and deep chasms. The largest volcano, Olympus Mons (Olympic Mountain) rises 78,000 ft above the surface, higher than Mount Everest. The plains of Mars are pockmarked by the hits of thousands of meteors over the years.

Until the arrival of *Mars Pathfinder* and *Mars Global Surveyor* in 1997, most of our information about Mars came from the *Mariner* and *Viking* spacecrafts. *Mariner 9* orbited the planet in 1971 and photographed 100% of the planet, uncovering spectacular geological formations, including a Martian "Grand Canyon" that dwarfs the one on Earth. Called Valles Marineris (Mariner Valley), it stretches more than 3,000 mi along the equatorial region of Mars and is over 2.5 mi (4 km) deep in places and 50–62 mi (80 to 100 km) wide. The spacecraft's cameras also recorded what appeared to be dried riverbeds, suggesting the one-time presence of water on the planet. The latter idea gave encouragement to scientists looking for life on Mars, for where there is water, there may be life. However, to date, no evidence of life has been found. Temperatures range from 80°F at the equator during the day to –199°F at the poles at night.

Mars rotates upon its axis in nearly the same period as Earth—24 hours, 37 minutes—so that a Mars day is almost identical to an Earth day. Mars takes 687 days to make one trip around the Sun. Because of its eccentric orbit, Mars's distance from the Sun can vary by about 36 million miles. Its distance from Earth can vary by as much as 200 million miles. The atmosphere of Mars is much thinner than Earth's; atmospheric pressure is about 1% that of our planet. Its gravity is one-third of Earth's. Major constituents are carbon dioxide and nitrogen. Water vapor and oxygen are minor constituents. Mars's polar caps, composed mostly of frozen carbon dioxide (dry ice), recede and advance according to the Martian seasons.

Mars has four seasons like Earth, but they are much longer. For example, in the northern hemisphere, the Martian spring is 198 days, and the winter season lasts 158 days.

The *Mars Pathfinder* lander and its rover, ＶＩＩＩＩＩＩＩＩＩＩＩ ＶＩＩＩ ＩＩＩＩＩＩ ＯＲ ＴＨＡ ＡＡＧＡ ＡＴ Ａ ＲＩＩＩＩＩＩＩＩＩＩＩＩＩ ＶＩＩＩＩＩＩＩＩ outflow channel known as *Ares Vallis* on July 4, 1997, and provided scientists with a wealth of information on the surface, soils, and atmosphere of Mars. The lander sent back the first live pictures of the planet's topography, and its tiny rover explored a variety of rocks and analyzed their mineral composition with its cameras and on-board X-ray spectrometer.

In its three months of operation, the mission returned more than 16,000 images of the Martian landscape from the lander's camera and 550 images from the rover.

Analysis of the reddish surface soil pointed to the presence of oxidized iron, indicating that the planet's surface is rusting. *Sojourner* samples of soil taken from several sites found their composition similar to those analyzed by the two *Viking* landers in 1976, indicating that the Martian winds have distributed the soil evenly over the planet.

Scientists were surprised to learn how rapidly the Martian temperature fluctuates due to atmospheric turbulence. It can change by as much as 30°–40°F (17°–22°C) in a matter of minutes, possibly due to strong, gusty winds bringing warm air from one region or cold air from another.

Pictures and subsequent data from *Pathfinder* give the strongest evidence that Mars had an abundance of water millions of years ago. Scientists have inferred from the variety of rocks and sediments found in the *Ares* basin that the spacecraft landed in a channel that was once awash with torrential floods greater than any known on Earth. The diversity of rocks deposited there suggests their different origins, and it appears that they were washed down from the highlands at a time when great floods moved over the surface of Mars.

Before *Pathfinder*, knowledge of the kinds of rocks present on Mars was based mostly on the Martian meteorites found on Earth. Chemical analysis of the Martian rocks and soil found at Ares Vallis confirmed that these rocks have compositions distinct from those of the Martian meteorites found on Earth.

The *Sojourner* rover traveled a total of about 328 ft (100 m), performed more than 16 chemical analyses of rocks and soil, and explored 820 sq ft (250 sq m) of the planet's surface. Communications were lost with the lander on Sept. 27, 1997, after 83 days of relaying data.

NASA launched the *Mars Global Surveyor* spacecraft on Nov. 7, 1996, to provide detailed maps of the planet's surface, its distribution of minerals, and to monitor its weather. The spacecraft entered Mars's orbit on Sept. 11, 1997, and began mapping operations in mid-March 1999.

*Surveyor* discovered the first clear evidence of an ancient hydrothermal system near the equator. This implies that water was stable at or near the surface and that a thicker atmosphere existed in Mars's early history.

*Surveyor*'s three-dimensional views of the planet's northern polar ice cap showed often striking canyons and spiral troughs in the water and carbon dioxide ice that can reach depths as great as 3,600 ft below the surface. Its data also showed that large areas of the ice cap were extremely smooth, with elevations varying only a few feet over many miles.

NASA's Mars exploration program suffered a setback when the loss of the *Climate Orbiter* as it entered the Martian atmosphere in Sept. 1999. The following December scientists also failed to establish contact with the *Polar Lander* after it reached Mars.

In 2000, NASA announced that the *Mars Global Surveyor* had observed features that looked like gullies carved out by flowing water and deposits of soil and rocks that were transported by the flow. Because gullies had never been seen before on Mars, the *Surveyor* images suggested that there might be current sources of liquid water at or near the surface.

In the spring of 2002, NASA released exciting news that large quantities of water ice had been found just below the surface of Mars. The discovery was made by NASA's *Mars Odyssey* spacecraft, which was launched in April 2001 and has been

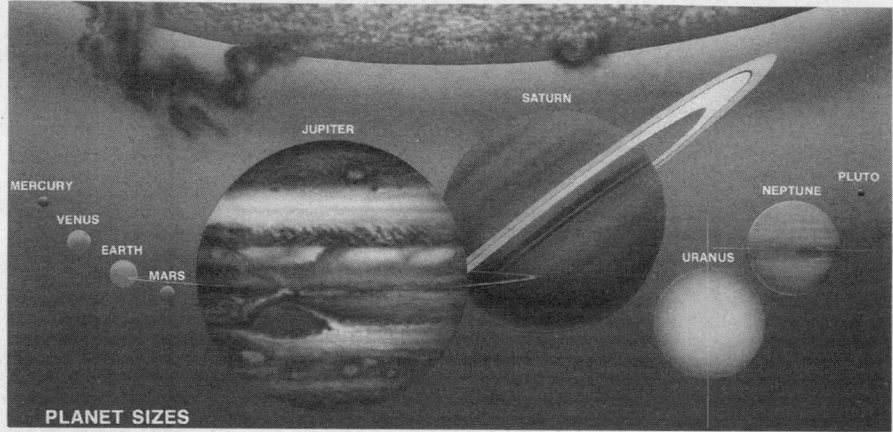

**PLANET SIZES.** Shown from left to right: Mercury, Venus, Earth, Mars, Jupiter, Saturn, Uranus, Neptune, and Pluto. *Copyright 1990 Hansen Planetarium, Salt Lake City, Utah. Reproduced with permission.*

collecting data since late 2001. Because water is necessary for life, the new findings are likely to spur further investigation.

Mars was named for the Roman god of war, because when seen from Earth its distinct red color reminded the ancient people of blood. We know now that the reddish hue reflects the oxidized (rusted) iron in the surface material.

### The Martian Moons

Mars has two very small elliptical-shaped moons, Deimos and Phobos—the Greek names for the companions of the god Mars: Deimos (Terror) and Phobos (Fear). They were discovered in Aug. 1877 by the American astronomer Asaph Hall (1829–1907) of the U.S. Naval Observatory in Washington, DC.

The inner satellite, Phobos, is 16.78 mi (27 km) long, and it revolves around the planet in 7.6 hours. The short orbital period of Phobos means that the satellite travels around Mars three times in a Martian day. The outer moon, Deimos, is 9.32 mi (15 km) long, and it circles the planet in 30.35 hours.

Phobos orbits Mars at a distance of only 5,627 mi (9,378 km) and is closer to its planet than any other moon in the solar system. Observation of Phobos has revealed that the moon's orbit is actually decreasing downward; in about 40 million years it will crash into the planet's surface or break up into a ring.

### Meteorites from Mars

Twenty-six meteorites, almost certainly from Mars, have been discovered as of June 2002. They are known as SNCs[1] (named for the towns where they were found: Shergotty, India, in 1865; Nakhla, Egypt, in 1911; and Chassigny, France, in 1815). This hypothesis was based largely on the composition of noble gases (particularly argon and xenon) trapped in the meteorites, and the shergottites in particular, which resemble measurements of the Martian atmosphere made by the *Viking* spacecraft. Major element compositions of the SNCs are also similar to Martian soil analyses made by *Viking*.

1. Pronounced "snick."

The relatively young isotopic ages of the SNC meteorites (1.3 billion years or less) suggest that Mars has been volcanically active during its recent past.

A 40-pound meteorite that crashed to Earth in Nigeria in 1962 has been classified as coming from Mars. It was named Zagami for the region in which it was found. It is the largest single Martian meteorite ever found.

A 4-pound, 7-ounce (1.9-kilogram) meteorite, ALH 84001, found in the Allen Hills of Antarctica in 1984, was reclassified in 1993 as coming from the Red Planet, making it the tenth meteorite known to have originated from Mars. In 1996, NASA announced that meteorite ALH 84001 contained fossils of ancient Martian microbial life forms.

A 0.38-ounce (12-gram) meteorite (QUE 94201) found in Antarctica in 1995 became the 12th meteorite identified as having a Martian origin.

In 1997, the thirteenth known Martian meteorite, Dar al Gani 476, a 4.8-pound (2.2-kilogram) meteorite, was found in the Sahara Desert.

Two rock specimens weighing 8.6 oz (245.4 g) and 16 oz (452.6 g) that were found in the Mojave Desert about 20 years ago were classified in Feb. 2000 as the fourteenth Mars meteorites. The rocks are known as the Los Angeles meteorites.

It is estimated that some 20,000 meteorites fall to Earth every year, but only a few are from Mars. The most recent finds, mainly in 2000 and 2001, were discovered in Antarctica and the deserts of northern Africa, which have become the favored hunting grounds for meteorite collectors, since there is little or no ground cover to hide the rocks.

### Jupiter

Jupiter is the largest planet in the solar system—a gaseous world as large as 1,300 Earths. Its equatorial diameter is 88,736 mi (142,800 km), while from pole to pole, Jupiter measures only 84,201 mi (133,500 km). For comparison, the diameter of Earth is 7,926.2 mi (12,756 km). The massive planet rotates at a dizzying speed—once every 9 hours and 55 minutes. It takes Jupiter almost 12 Earth years to complete a journey around the Sun.

## Basic Planetary Data

| | Mercury | Venus | Earth | Mars | Jupiter |
|---|---|---|---|---|---|
| Mean distance from Sun (millions of kilometers) | 57.9 | 108.2 | 149.6 | 227.9 | 778.3 |
| Mean distance from Sun (millions of miles) | 36.0 | 67.24 | 92.9 | 141.71 | 483.88 |
| Period of revolution | 88 days | 224.7 days | 365.2 days | 687 days | 11.86 yrs |
| Rotation period | 59 days | 243 days retrograde | 23 hr 56 min 4 sec | 24 hr 37 min | 9 hr 55 min 30 sec |
| Inclination of axis | Near 0° | 3° | 23°27' | 25° 12' | 3° 5' |
| Inclination of orbit to ecliptic | 7° | 3.4° | 0° | 1.9° | 1.3° |
| Eccentricity of orbit | .206 | .007 | .017 | .093 | .048 |
| Equatorial diameter (kilometers) | 4,880 | 12,100 | 12,756 | 6,794 | 142,800 |
| (miles) | 3,032.4 | 7,519 | 7,926.2 | 4,194 | 88,736 |
| Atmosphere (main components) | Virtually none | Carbon dioxide | Nitrogen oxygen | Carbon dioxide | Hydrogen helium |
| Satellites | 0 | 0 | 1 | 2 | 39[1] |
| Rings | 0 | 0 | 0 | 0 | 3 |

| | Saturn | Uranus | Neptune | Pluto |
|---|---|---|---|---|
| Mean distance from Sun (millions of kilometers) | 1,427 | 2,870 | 4,497 | 5,900 |
| Mean distance from Sun (millions of miles) | 887.14 | 1,783.98 | 2,796.46 | 3,666 |
| Period of revolution | 29.46 yrs | 84 yrs | 165 yrs | 248 yrs |
| Rotation period | 10 hr 40 min 24 sec | 16.8 hr (?) retrograde | 16 hr 11 min (?) | 6 days 9 hr 18 mins retrograde |
| Inclination of axis | 26°44' | 97°55' | 28°48' | 60° (?) |
| Inclination of orbit to ecliptic | 2.5° | 0.8° | 1.8° | 17.2° |
| Eccentricity of orbit | .056 | .047 | .009 | .254 |
| Equatorial diameter (kilometers) | 120,660 | 51,810 | 49,528 | 2,290 (?) |
| (miles) | 74,978 | 32,193 | 30,775 | 1,423 (?) |
| Atmosphere (main components) | Hydrogen helium | Helium hydrogen methane | Hydrogen helium methane | None detected |
| Satellites | 30[2] | 21 | 8 | 1 |
| Rings | 1,000 (?) | 11 | 4 | ? |

1. Twenty-one of these moons, designated S/2000 J2 through J11 and S/2001 J1 through J11, were discovered only recently in late 2000 and 2001. 2. Twelve of these moons, designated S/2000 S1 through S12, were discovered in late 2000. *Source:* Basic NASA data and other sources.

The giant planet appears as a banded disk of turbulent clouds with all of its stripes running parallel to its bulging equator. Large dusky gray regions surround each pole. Darker gray or brown stripes called belts intermingle with lighter, yellow-white stripes called zones. The belts are regions of descending air masses and the zones are rising cloudy air masses. The strongest winds—up to 250 mph (400 km)—are found in the equatorial regions of the belts and zones.

This uniquely colorful atmosphere is mainly 89% molecular hydrogen and 11% helium. It contains small amounts of methane, ammonia, ethane, and water.

Cloud-type lightning bolts similar to those on Earth have been found in the Jovian atmosphere. At the polar regions, auroras have been observed. A very thin ring of material less than 0.6 mi (1 km) in thickness and about 4,000 mi (6,000 km) in radial extent has been observed circling the planet about 35,000 mi (55,000 km) above the cloud tops.

The most prominent feature on Jupiter is its "Great Red Spot," an oval larger than the planet Earth. It is a tremendous atmospheric storm that rotates counterclockwise with one revolution every six days at the outer edge, while at the center almost no motion can be seen. The spot is about 16,000 mi (25,000 km) on its long axis, and would cover three Earths. Along the outer rim the winds blow at speeds reaching 225 mph (360 km/h).

Jupiter is circled by faint rings. They are very tenuous and contain many microscopic-sized particles. The rings are formed by dust kicked up as interplanetary micrometeorites smash into the planet's four small inner moons.

Jupiter emits 67% more heat than it absorbs from the Sun. This heat is thought to have been accumulated during the planet's formation several billion years ago.

Twenty-one fragments of comet Shoemaker-Levy 9 bombarded the cloud-covered surface of Jupiter, July 16–22, 1994. It was the most violent event in the recorded history of our solar system. The impact of the comet fragments caused towering plumes of debris and hot gas to rise from the planet's surface.

On Dec. 7, 1995, the *Galileo* spacecraft released a probe into Jupiter's atmosphere to study the planet's physical and chemical properties. The probe lasted 57 minutes and early results indicated a lower abundance of water than was expected. *Galileo* data has shown that Jupiter has both wet and dry regions, just as Earth has tropics and deserts. This could explain why the probe found less water than anticipated. These dry spots cover less than 1% of the Jovian atmosphere.

## Jovian Moons

Jupiter has a total of 39 known satellites. The four great moons of Jupiter were discovered by Galileo Galilei (1564–1642) in Jan. 1610, and are called the Galilean satellites after their discoverer. Their names are Io, Europa, Ganymede, and Callisto. Like our Moon, the satellites always keep the same face turned toward the planet they circle. Jupiter's four largest moons all have thin atmospheres. A carbon dioxide atmosphere envelops Callisto; Europa and Ganymede each have thin oxygen atmospheres; and Io's contains sulfur dioxide.

## Ganymede

Ganymede, 3,275 mi (5,270 km) in diameter, is Jupiter's largest moon, and it is also the largest satellite in the solar system. Ganymede is about one and one-half times the size of our Moon. It is heavily cratered and probably has the greatest variety of geologic process recorded on its surface. Ganymede is half water and half rock, resulting in a density about two-thirds that of Europa, an ice-coated satellite.

The first close-up photos of Ganymede, taken by the *Galileo* spacecraft during its June 1996 flyby, revealed a surface pockmarked with ancient craters and a landscape wrinkled and torn by the same forces that make mountains and move continents on Earth. *Galileo*'s findings also indicated that Ganymede is enveloped in its own magnetic field, possibly created by a molten iron core or even a thin layer of electricity-conducting salty water underneath its icy crust.

Ganymede is the first known moon with its own magnetosphere.

## Europa

Europa, the brightest of Jupiter's satellites, is about 1,950 mi (3,160 km) in diameter or about the size of Earth's Moon. Its density is about three times that of water. The moon is covered with a thin ice crust and is crisscrossed with an amazingly complex network of ridges. Some of the fractures on its crust are more than 1,850 mi (3,000 km) long. Very few impact craters are visible on the surface. In fact, Europa is the smoothest object in the solar system. Its mostly flat surface doesn't exceed 0.62 mi (1 km) in height.

*Galileo* spacecraft photos taken at its closest flyby on Feb. 20, 1997, at a distance of 363 mi (586 km), showed the existence of ice flows on the surface that strongly suggest that the moon has a hidden subsurface ocean of water or ice-slush. The photos revealed chunky ice rafts that appear to be floating, comparable to icebergs on Earth. The presence of water and enough heat to keep water in a liquid state on Europa enhances the possibility that it could provide an environment for some form of extraterrestrial ocean life.

New evidence that a liquid ocean lies beneath Europa's crust was found when *Galileo* visited the moon in Jan. 2000. The spacecraft detected changes in Europa's magnetic field that are best explained by an electrically conducting (salty) body of water.

Definitive answers may not be possible for another decade, however. NASA scientists had proposed sending a spacecraft called the *Europa Ice Clipper* to the moon in 2001, but the mission was scrapped due to lack of funding. The *Europa Orbiter* mission, scheduled for launch in 2008, is currently under consideration. This spacecraft would include instruments such as an ice-penetrating radar that could see through the ice to any ocean below.

## Callisto

Callisto, 2,400 mi (4,800 km) in diameter, is the outermost and, apparently, the least geologically active of Jupiter's four major satellites. Its density is less than twice that of water. Callisto has the oldest body and most cratered face of any body yet observed in the solar system. Like Ganymede, it seems to have a rocky core surrounded by ice. Unlike Ganymede, the surface of Callisto is completely covered with scars left by tens of thousands of meteoric impacts. Scientists estimate that it would take several billion years to accumulate the number of craters found there. So Callisto is believed to be inactive for at least that long. Although it is the darkest of the Galilean satellites, it is twice as bright as Earth's Moon.

Data from the *Galileo* spacecraft in 1998 suggest that Callisto has a salty ocean beneath its crust, similar to Europa's.

## Io

Io, 2,262 mi (3,640 km) in diameter, is the most spectacular of the Galilean moons. Its brilliant colors of red, orange, and yellow set it apart from any other moon or planet. Active volcanoes have been detected on Io, with some plumes extending up to 200 mi (320 km) above the surface. The relative smoothness of Io's surface and its volcanic activity suggest that it has the youngest surface of Jupiter's moons. Its surface is composed of large amounts of sulfur and sulfur-dioxide frost, which account for the primarily yellow-orange surface color.

The volcanoes seem to eject a sufficient amount of sulfur dioxide to form a doughnut-shaped ring (torus) of ionized sulfur and oxygen atoms around Jupiter near Io's orbit. Close-up views taken in 1999 and 2000 showed that Io has more than 100 erupting volcanoes, gigantic lava flows and lava lakes, and towering, collapsing mountains. The eruptions of Loki, the most powerful volcano in the solar system, can be seen by Earth telescopes.

Observations by *Galileo* during 1998 revealed dozens of volcanic vents on Io where lava is hotter than any surface temperatures recorded on any planetary body in our solar system. At one such volcanic vent, known as Pillan Patera, two of the spacecraft's instruments indicated that the lava temperature may have been 3,140°F.

In 1996, the *Galileo* spacecraft detected a huge iron core within Io that occupies half the moon's diameter. *Galileo* also discovered evidence that Io has its own magnetic field.

## Amalthea

Amalthea, Jupiter's innermost satellite, was discovered in 1892. It is so small—165 mi (265 km) long and 90 mi (150 km) wide—that it is extremely difficult to observe from Earth. Amalthea is an elongated, irregularly shaped satellite of reddish color. It orbits the planet every 12 hours and is in synchronous rotation, with its long axis always oriented toward Jupiter.

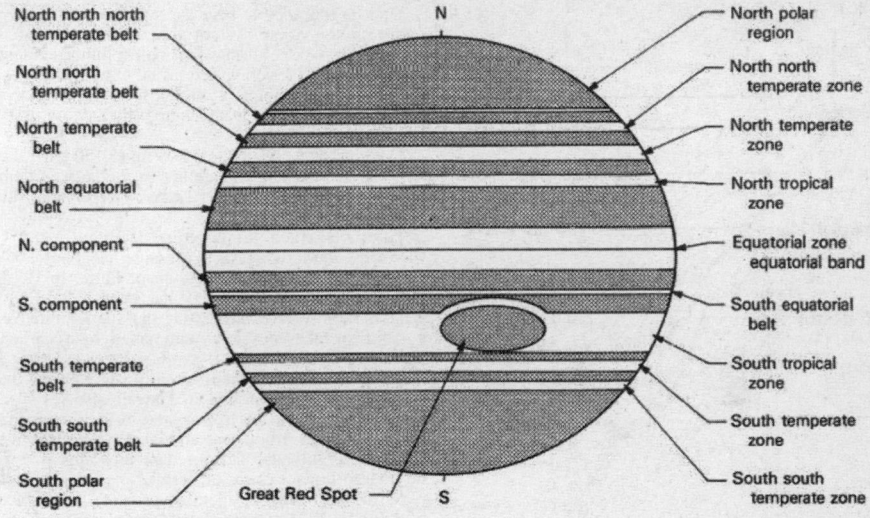

**Schematic diagram of Jupiter's major features.** *Source:* NASA.

Amalthea is heavily cratered, with two that are especially large. The largest crater, Pan, is 56 mi (90 km) long and the other large crater, Gaea, is 47 mi (75 km) in length.

*Galileo* images of the tiny moon taken at the end of 1999 showed that a bright surface feature, previously named Ida, is a linear streak of bright material about 31 mi (50 km) long. The images also revealed a large impact crater about 25 mi (40 km) across.

Jupiter's other named moons are Adrasta, Metis, Thebe, Leda, Himalia, Lysithea, Elara, Ananke, Carne, Pasiphae, and Sinope. *Galileo* images of Thebe taken in Jan. 2000 found a prominent impact crater that is about 25 mi (40 km) across and provisionally named Zethus.

The rest of Jupiter's moons have not been named and carry the temporary designations S/1975 J1 (also S/2000 J1), S/1999 J1, S/2000 J2 through J11, and S/2001 J1 through J11. The 21 most recently discovered moons (S/2000 J2 through J11, announced in Jan. 2001, and S/2001 J1 through J11, announced in May 2002) are thought to be very small—no more than 3 mi (5 km) across. Most of the moons move in retrograde orbits, and all move in distant, ... the ... .

### The Magnetosphere of Jupiter

Perhaps the largest structure in the solar system is the magnetosphere of Jupiter. This is the region of space that is filled with Jupiter's magnetic field and is bounded by the interaction of that magnetic field with the solar wind, which is the Sun's outward flow of charged particles. The plasma of electrically charged particles that exists in the magnetosphere is flattened into a large disk more than 3 million miles (4.8 million kilometers) in diameter, is coupled to the magnetic field, and rotates around Jupiter. The Galilean satellites are located in the inner regions of the magnetosphere and are subjected to intense radiation bombardment.

The intense radiation field that surrounds Jupiter is fatal to humans. If astronauts were able to approach the planet as close as the *Voyager 1* spacecraft did, they would receive a dose of 400,000 rads, or roughly 1,000 times the lethal dose for humans.

Even when nearest Earth, Jupiter is still almost 400 million miles away. However, because of its size, it may rival Venus in brilliance when near. Jupiter's four large moons may be seen through field glasses moving rapidly around Jupiter and changing their positions from night to night.

### Saturn

Saturn, the second-largest planet in the solar system, is the least dense. Its mass is 95 times the mass of Earth and its density is 0.70 gram per cubic centimeter, so that it would float in an ocean if there were one big enough to hold it.

Saturn radiates about 80% more energy than it receives from the Sun. However, the excess thermal energy cannot be primarily attributed to Saturn's primordial heat loss, as is speculated for Jupiter. Saturn's diameter is 71,970 mi (110,000 km) but 10% less at the poles, a consequence of its rapid rotation. Its axis of rotation is tilted by 27° and the length of its day is 10 hours, 39 minutes, and 24 seconds.

Saturn is composed primarily of liquid metallic hydrogen (about 80%) and the second most common element is believed to be helium.

Saturn's atmospheric appearance is very similar to Jupiter's with dark and light cloud markings and swirls, eddies, and curling ribbons; the belts and zones are more numerous and a thick haze mutes the markings. Temperatures recorded by *Voyager II* ranged from 82°K (−312°F) to 143°K (−202°F).

Winds blow at extremely high speeds on Saturn. Near the equator, the *Voyager*s measured winds of

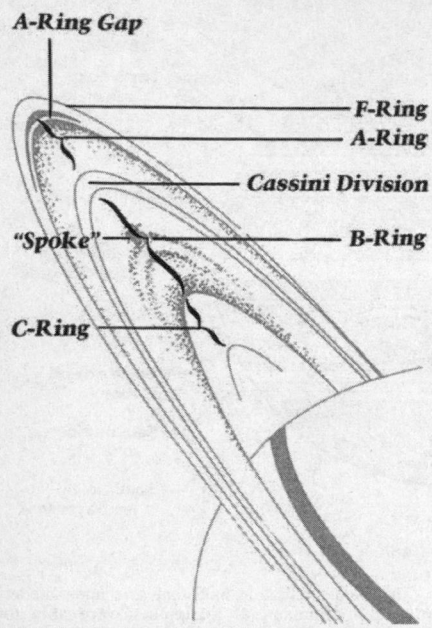

**NASA illustration of the divisions in Saturn's ring system.**

about 1,100 mph (500 meters per second). The winds blow primarily in an eastward direction.

## Saturn's Rings

Saturn's spectacular ring system is unique in the solar system, with uncountable billions of tiny particles of water ice (with traces of other material) in orbit around the planet. The ring particles range in size from smaller than grains of sugar to as large as a house. The main rings stretch out from about 4,350 mi (7,000 km) to above the atmosphere of the planet out to the F ring, a total span of 45,984 mi (74,000 km). Saturn's rings can be likened to a phonograph, rings within rings numbering in the hundreds, and spokes in the B rings, and shepherding satellites controlling the F ring.

The main rings are called the A, B, and C rings moving from outside to inside. The gap between the A and B rings is called Cassini's Division and is named for the Italian-French astronomer Gian Domenico Cassini, who discovered four of Saturn's major moons and the dark, narrow gap, Cassini's Division, splitting the planet's rings.

Saturn's magnetic field has well-defined north and south magnetic poles, and is aligned with Saturn's axis of rotation to within one degree.

## Saturn's Moons

Saturn has 30 known moons, 12 of which were discovered in late 2000 and are known by the temporary designations S/2000 S1 through S12. The five largest moons—Tethys, Dione, Rhea, Titan, and Iapetus—range from 650 to 3,200 mi (1,060 to 5,150 km) in diameter. The planet's outstanding satellite is Titan, first discovered by the Dutch astronomer Christiaan Huygens in 1656.

## Titan

Titan is remarkable because it is the only known moon in the solar system that has a substantial atmosphere—largely nitrogen with a minor amount of methane and a rich variety of other hydrocarbons. Its surface is completely hidden from view (except at infrared and radio wavelengths) by a dense, hazy atmosphere.

The diameter of Titan is 3,200 mi (5,150 km), and it is the second-largest satellite in the solar system after Jupiter's Ganymede. Titan is larger than the planet Mercury.

Titan's surface temperature is about −280°F (−175°C), and its surface pressure is about 50% greater than the surface pressure of Earth. In 1990, radio telescope data showed that Titan reflects and scatters radio waves, suggesting that the satellite has a solid surface, possibly with small hydrocarbon lakes or ponds.

Infrared images of Titan taken in late 1999 by the W. M. Keck II telescope in Hawaii also revealed features that could be frozen land masses separated by frigid hydrocarbon seas and lakes. Other features might be highlands, and one dark area appeared to be a large impact crater or basin.

NASA is sending a scientific probe to the surface of Titan in 2004 as part of its *Cassini* mission. The probe will be provided by the European Space Agency (ESA).

## Other Notable Saturnian Moons

The other four largest moons of Saturn are Tethys, Dione, Rhea, and Iapetus.

**Tethys** is 650 mi (1,060 km) in diameter. Its surface is heavily cratered, and it has a huge, globe-girdling canyon, Ithaca Chasma. Part of the canyon stretches over three-quarters of the satellite's surface. Ithaca Chasma is about 1,550 mi (2,500 km) long. It has an average width of about 62 mi (100 km) and a depth of 1.8 to 3.1 mi (3 to 5 km).

Tethys also has a huge impact crater named Odysseus that is 244 mi (4,400 km) in diameter, or more than one-third of the moon's diameter.

**Dione** is slightly larger than Tethys, 696 mi (1,120 km) in diameter, and is more than half composed of water ice. It has bright, wispy markings resembling thin veils covering its features.

**Rhea**, the largest of the inner satellites, is 951 mi (1,530 km) in diameter. It is composed mainly of water ice, causing its reflective surface to present an almost uniform white appearance.

**Iapetus** is the outermost of Saturn's icy satellites. Its appearance is unique because it has one dark and one bright hemisphere. The origin of the black coating of its dark face is unknown. Iapetus has a diameter of 907 mi (1,460 km).

Other notable moons of Saturn are Mimas, Enceladus, Hyperion, Phoebe, and Pan.

**Mimas** is small, only 244 mi (329 km) in diameter. It has a huge impact crater, Herschel, nearly one-third of its diameter. The crater is about 81 mi (130 km) wide and its icy peak rises almost 6.2 mi (10 km) above the floor.

Mimas is believed to be composed mainly of water and ice and to contain between 20% and 50% rock.

**Enceladus** is remarkable in that its surface shows signs of extensive and recent geological activity. There may be active water volcanism. The surface is extremely bright, reflecting more than 90% of incident sunlight. This suggests that its surface is composed of extremely pure ice without dust or rocks to contaminate it. Enceladus has a diameter of 310 mi (500 km).

**Hyperion** orbits between Iapetus and Titan. It is irregular in shape, measuring about 248 by 155 by 124 mi (400 by 250 by 200 km). It may be a remnant of a much larger object that was shattered by impact with another space body. It appears that Hyperion is composed primarily of water ice.

Hyperion orbits Saturn with an irregular motion ("chaotic tumbling").

**Phoebe** travels in a retrograde orbit at a distance of over 6.2 million miles (10 million kilometers) away from the planet. It is the darkest moon of Saturn and is the planet's only known satellite that does not keep the same face always turned to Saturn. It has been speculated that it is an asteroid that was captured by the planet. Phoebe rotates in about nine hours and orbits Saturn in 406 days. It has a diameter of 124 mi (200 km).

**Pan** was discovered in 1990 from *Voyager 2* photos taken in 1981. The satellite is estimated to be about 12.43 mi (20 km) in diameter, and it orbits within the Encke Gap, a 202-mile (325-kilometer) division in Saturn's A ring. It was identified by Johann Franz Encke (1791–1865) in 1837.

Saturn's other named moons are Atlas, Prometheus, Pandora, Epimetheus, Janus, Telesto, Calypso, and Helene. They are all nonspherical in shape and range from 15 to 120 mi (25 to 190 km) in diameter. In addition, 12 new moons were discovered in late 2000. Designated S/2000 S1 through S12, these new moons are quite small—only about 5 to 30 mi (10 to 50 km) in diameter—and have weak elliptical orbits.

NASA's *Cassini* mission to Saturn, launched in Oct. 1997, will shed more light on the planet's mysteries when it arrives there in 2004.

Saturn is the last of the planets visible to the naked eye. Saturn is never an object of overwhelming brilliance, but it looks like a bright star. The rings can be seen with a small telescope.

# Uranus

Uranus, the first planet discovered in modern times by Sir William Herschel in 1781, is the seventh planet from the Sun, twice as far out as Saturn. Its mean distance from the Sun is 1,783 million miles (2,869 million km). Uranus's equatorial diameter is 32,200 mi (51,810 km). The axis of Uranus is tilted at 97°, so it goes around the Sun nearly lying on its side.

Due to Uranus's unusual inclination, the polar regions receive more sunlight during a Uranus year of 84 Earth years. Scientists had thought that the temperature of its poles would be warmer than that at its equator, but *Voyager 2* discovered that the equatorial temperatures were similar to the temperatures at the poles, −344°F (−209°C), implying that some redistribution of heat toward the equatorial region must occur within the atmosphere. The wind patterns on Uranus are much like Saturn's, flowing parallel to the equator in the direction of the planet's rotation.

Ninety-eight percent of the upper atmosphere is composed of hydrogen and helium; the remaining 2% is methane. Scientists speculate that the bulk of the lower atmosphere is composed of water (perhaps as much as 50%), methane, and ammonia. Methane is responsible for Uranus's blue-green color because it selectively absorbs red sunlight and condenses to form clouds of ice crystals in the cooler, higher regions of Uranus's atmosphere.

It was also discovered that the planet's magnetic field is 60° tilted from the planet's axis of rotation and offset from the planet's center by one-third of Uranus's radius. It may be generated at a depth where water is under sufficient pressure to be electrically conductive.

## The Uranian Rings

*Voyager 2* also expanded the body of information pertaining to the rings and moons of Uranus. *Voyager*'s cameras obtained the first images of 9 previously known narrow rings and discovered at least 2 new rings, one narrow and one broadly diffused, bringing the total known rings to 11. It was found that a highly structured distribution of fine dust exists throughout the ring system.

The outermost (epsilon) ring contains nothing smaller than fist-sized particles. It is flanked by two small moons discovered interior to the orbit of the Uranian moon Miranda. The moons exert a shepherding influence on the epsilon ring and on the outer edges of the gamma and delta rings.

All of the rings lie within one planetary radius[1] of Uranus's cloud tops. Most of Uranus's rings are narrow, ranging in width from 0.6 to 58 mi (1 to 93 km), and are only a few kilometers thick. The Uranian rings are colorless and extremely dark. The dark material may be either irradiated methane ice or organic-rich minerals mixed with water-impregnated, silicon-based compounds. There is evidence that incomplete rings, or "ring arcs," exist at Uranus.

## The Uranian Moons

There are 21 known moons of Uranus. In order of decreasing distance from the planet, the moons are Setebos (1999 U1), Prospero (1999 U3), Sycorax, Stephano (1999 U2), Caliban, Oberon, Titania, Umbriel, Ariel, Miranda, Puck, 1986 U10, Belinda, Rosalind, Portia, Juliet, Desdemona, Cressida, Bianca, Ophelia, and Cordelia. Ten of the moons range in size from 16 to 67 mi (26 to 108 km) in diameter and, being closer to the planet, have faster periods of revolution (8–15 hours) than their more distant relatives.

## Oberon and Titania

The two largest moons, Oberon, 942 mi (1,516 km) in diameter and Titania, 982 mi (1,580 km) in diameter, are less than half the diameter of Earth's Moon. Titania, the reddest of Uranus's moons, may have endured global tectonics as evidenced by complex valleys and fault lines etched into its surface. Smooth sections indicate that volcanic resurfacing has taken place.

## Umbriel and Ariel

Umbriel and Ariel are roughly three-fourths the size of Oberon and Titania. Umbriel is the darkest of the large moons, with huge craters peppering its surface. Umbriel has a paucity of what are known as bright ray craters, which are formed on an older,

1. The equatorial radius of Uranus is 15,880 mi (25,560 km) at a pressure of 1 bar.

darker surface when bright submerged ice is excavated and sprayed by meteoroid impacts.

In contrast, the surface of Ariel, the brightest of the Uranian moons, is relatively free of pockmarks due to volcanism that periodically erases the damage done by foreign projectiles. However, there are several extremely deep cuts on Ariel's surface.

## Miranda

The smallest of Uranus's large moons, Miranda, 293 mi (472 km) in diameter, has been described as "the most bizarre body in the solar system," with the most geologically complex surface. Miranda's remarkable terrain consists of rolling, heavily cratered plains (the oldest known in the Uranian system) adjoined by three huge, 120- to 180-mile (200- to 300-kilometer) oval-to-trapezoidal regions known as coronae, which are characterized by networks of concentric canyons.

## Puck

Puck was the first new moon discovered by *Voyager*. It is 96 mi (154 km) in diameter and makes a trip around Uranus every 18 hours. Puck is shaped somewhat like a potato, with a huge impact crater marring roughly one-fourth of its surface.

## Caliban and Sycorax

In 1997, two new moons, the first with irregular, noncircular orbits, were discovered around Uranus. These far distant satellites were temporarily designated S/1997 U1 and S/1997 U2 and later named Caliban and Sycorax, respectively. Caliban has a diameter of 37 mi (60 km) and orbits Uranus at an average distance of 4.5 million miles (7.2 million kilometers). Sycorax has a diameter of 74.5 mi (120 km) and a much more elliptical orbit than Caliban, bringing it as close as 3.7 million miles (6 million km) to the planet.

## New Uranian Moons Discovered

On May 18, 1999, the International Astronomical Union announced that Erich Karkoschka, a researcher at the Lunar and Planetary Lab of the University of Arizona in Tucson, had discovered the 18th moon orbiting Uranus.

Although the moon was found in 1999, it is designated as satellite S/1986 U10. According to its discoverer, the satellite is approximately 25 mi (40 km) in diameter, about the size of comet Hale-Bopp, and it may have a similar composition to the comet. It orbits 35,000 mi (51,000 km) from Uranus, circling the planet every 15 hours and 18 minutes, similar to the planet's rotational period of about 16.8 hours.

In Sept. 1999, Cornell University astronomers announced the discovery of three more satellites, bringing the total up to 21. The moons, initially designated 1999 U1, 1999 U2, and 1999 U3, have been named Setebos, Stephano, and Prospero. The new satellites are about 12 mi (20 km) in diameter and orbit in distant, elliptical paths.

Uranus can—on rare occasions—become bright enough to be seen with the naked eye, if one knows exactly where to look; normally, a good set of field glasses or a small portable telescope is required.

# Neptune

Little was known about Neptune until Aug. 1989, when NASA's *Voyager 2* became the first spacecraft to observe the planet. Passing about 3,000 mi (4,950 km) above Neptune's north pole, *Voyager 2* made its closest approach to any planet since leaving Earth 12 years prior. The spacecraft passed about 25,000 mi (40,000 km) from Neptune's largest moon, Triton, the last solid body that *Voyager 2* studied before continuing on to the outer boundary of the solar system.

Nearly 3 billion miles (4.5 billion kilometers) from the Sun, Neptune orbits the Sun once in 165 years, and therefore has made not quite a full circle around the Sun since it was discovered.[1]

With an equatorial diameter of 30,775 mi (49,528 km), Neptune is the smallest of our solar system's four gas giants, which also include Jupiter, Saturn, and Uranus.[2] Even so, its volume could hold nearly 60 Earths. Neptune is also denser than the other gas giants and about 64% heavier than if it were composed entirely of water.

Neptune has a blue color as a result of methane in its atmosphere. Methane preferentially absorbs the longer wavelengths of sunlight (those near the red end of the spectrum). What are left to be reflected are colors at the blue end of the spectrum. The atmosphere of Neptune is mainly composed of hydrogen, with helium and traces of methane and ammonia.

Neptune is a dynamic planet even though it receives only 3% as much sunlight as Jupiter does. *Voyager 2* discovered several large, dark spots that were prominent features on the planet. The largest spot was about the size of Earth and was designated the "Great Dark Spot" by its discoverers. It appeared to be an anticyclone similar to Jupiter's Great Red Spot. While Neptune's Great Dark Spot is comparable in size, relative to the planet, and at the same latitude (22°S latitude) as Jupiter's Great Red Spot, it was far more variable in size and shape than its Jovian counterpart. Bright, wispy "cirrus-type" clouds overlaid the Great Dark Spot at its southern and northeast boundaries.

At about 42°S latitude, a bright, irregularly shaped eastward-moving cloud circles much faster than did the Great Dark Spot, "scooting" around Neptune in about 16 hours. This "scooter" may have been a cloud plume rising between cloud decks.

Another spot, designated "D2," was located far to the south of the Great Dark Spot, at 55°S latitude. It is almond-shaped, with a bright central core, and moves eastward around the planet in about 16 hours.

In 1995, images taken by the Hubble Space Telescope showed that the Great Dark Spot has vanished. The great storm center has either dissipated or is obscured by other atmospheric conditions.

The atmosphere above Neptune's clouds is hotter near the equator, cooler in the mid-latitudes, and warm again at the south pole. Temperatures in the stratosphere were measured to be 750°K (900°F),

1. Astronomers have studied Neptune since Sept. 23, 1846, when Johann Gottfried Galle, of the Berlin Observatory, and Louis d'Arrest, an astronomy student, discovered the eighth planet on the basis of mathematical predictions by Urbain Jean Joseph Le Verrier. Similar predictions were made independently by John Couch Adams. Galileo Galilei had seen Neptune during several nights of observing Jupiter, in Jan. 1613, but didn't realize he was seeing a new planet.
2. These four planets are about 4 to 12 times greater in diameter than Earth. They have no solid surfaces, but possess massive atmospheres that contain substantial amounts of hydrogen and helium with traces of other gases.

while at the 100-millibar pressure level they were measured to be 55°K (−360°F).

Long, bright clouds, reminiscent of cirrus clouds on Earth, were seen high in Neptune's atmosphere. They appear to form above most of the methane, and consequently are not blue.

At northern low latitudes (27°N), *Voyager* captured images of cloud streaks casting their shadows on cloud decks estimated to be about 30 to 60 mi (50 to 100 km) below. The widths of these cloud streaks range from 30 to 125 mi (50 to 200 km). Cloud streaks were also seen in the southern polar regions (71°S) where the cloud heights were about 30 mi (50 km).

Most of the winds on Neptune blow in a westward direction, which is retrograde, or opposite to the rotation of the planet.

In Jan. 2000, astronomers announced taking the best Earth-based infrared images of Neptune, captured by the W. M. Keck II telescope in Hawaii. The images revealed giant 600-mph (966-km/hr) storms born of heat generated from the planet's still-contracting core. Storm features are pulled across the face of Neptune as it whirls through its 16-hour day.

### The Magnetic Field of Neptune

Neptune's magnetic field is tilted 47° from the planet's rotation axis and is offset at least 0.55 radii, about 8,500 mi (13,500 km) from the physical center. The dynamo electric currents produced within the planet, therefore, must be relatively closer to the surface than for Earth, Jupiter, or Saturn. Because of its unusual orientation, and the tilt of the planet's rotation axis, Neptune's magnetic field goes through dramatic changes as the planet rotates in the solar wind.

*Voyager*'s planetary radio astronomy instrument measured the periodic radio waves generated by the magnetic field and determined that the rotation rate of the interior of Neptune is 16 hours and 7 minutes. *Voyager* also detected auroras, similar to the northern and southern lights on Earth, in Neptune's atmosphere. Unlike those on Earth, due to Neptune's complex magnetic field, the auroras are extremely complicated processes that occur over wide regions of the planet, not just near the planet's magnetic poles.

### Neptune's Moons

#### Triton

The largest of Neptune's eight known satellites, Triton was discovered in 1846 by British astronomer William Lassell. Triton circles Neptune in a tilted, circular, retrograde orbit, completing an orbit in 5.875 days at an average distance of 205,000 mi (330,000 km) above the planet's cloud tops.

Triton shows evidence of a remarkable geologic history, and *Voyager 2* images show active geyser-like eruptions spewing invisible nitrogen gas and dark dust particles 1 to 5 mi (2 to 8 km) into space.

Triton is about three-quarters the size of Earth's Moon and has a diameter of about 1,680 mi (2,705 km) and a mean density of about 2.066 grams per cubic centimeter. (The density of water is 1.0 grams per cubic centimeter.) This means that Triton contains more rock in its interior than the icy satellites of Saturn and Uranus.

The relatively high density and the retrograde orbit offer strong evidence that Triton did not originate near Neptune, but is a captured object.

An extremely thin atmosphere extends as much as 500 mi (800 km) above the satellite's surface. Tiny nitrogen ice particles may form thin clouds a few kilometers above the surface. Triton is very bright, reflecting 60% to 95% of the sunlight that strikes it. (By comparison, Earth's Moon reflects only 11%.)

The atmospheric pressure at Triton's surface is about 14 microbars, a mere 1/70,000th the surface pressure on Earth. Temperature at the surface is about 38°K (−391°F), making it the coldest surface of any body yet visited in the solar system.

#### Nereid

Nereid was discovered in 1949 through Earth-based telescopes. Little is known about Nereid, which is slightly smaller than Proteus, having a diameter of 211 mi (340 km). The satellite's surface reflects about 14% of the sunlight that strikes it. Nereid's orbit is the most eccentric in the solar system, ranging from about 841,100 mi (1,353,600 km) to 5,980,200 mi (9,623,700 km).

### The Smaller Satellites

In addition to the previously known moons, Triton and Nereid, *Voyager 2* found six more satellites in 1989, making the total eight.

#### Proteus

Like all six of Neptune's more recently discovered small satellites, it is one of the darkest objects in the solar system—"as dark as soot" is a good description. It reflects only 6% of the sunlight that strikes it. Proteus is an ellipsoid about 258 mi (416 km) in diameter, larger than Nereid. It circles Neptune at a distance of about 57,700 mi (92,800 km) above the cloud tops, and completes one orbit in 26 hours and 54 minutes. Scientists say that it is about as large as a satellite can be without being pulled into a spherical shape by its own gravity.

Proteus and its tiny companions are cratered and irregularly shaped—they are not round—and show no signs of any geologic modifications. All circle the planet in the same direction as Neptune rotates and remain close to Neptune's equatorial plane.

#### Larissa

This object is only about 30,300 mi (48,800 km) from Neptune and circles the planet in 13 hours and 18 minutes. Its diameter is 120 mi (190 km).

#### Despina

The satellite is 17,200 mi (27,700 km) from Neptune's clouds and makes one orbit every 8 hours 1 minute. Its diameter is 90 mi (150 km).

#### Galatea

It lies 23,100 mi (37,200 km) from Neptune. Its diameter is 110 mi (180 km), and it completes an orbit in 10 hours and 18 minutes.

#### Thalassa

Thalassa appears to be about 50 mi (80 km) in diameter. It orbits Neptune in 7 hours and 30 minutes some 15,700 mi (25,200 km) above the cloud tops.

#### Naiad

The last satellite discovered, it is about 37 mi (60 km) in diameter and orbits Neptune about 14,400 mi (23,200 km) above the clouds in 7 hours and 6 minutes.

## The First Ten Minor Planets (Asteroids)

| Name | Year of discovery | Mean distance from Sun (millions of mi) | Orbital period (years) | Diameter (mi) | Magnitude |
|------|-------------------|------------------------------------------|------------------------|---------------|-----------|
| 1. Ceres | 1801 | 257.0 | 4.60 | 485 | 7.4 |
| 2. Pallas | 1802 | 257.4 | 4.61 | 304 | 8.0 |
| 3. Juno | 1804 | 247.8 | 4.36 | 118 | 8.7 |
| 4. Vesta | 1807 | 219.3 | 3.63 | 243 | 6.5 |
| 5. Astraea | 1845 | 239.3 | 4.14 | 50 | 9.9 |
| 6. Hebe | 1847 | 225.2 | 3.78 | 121 | 8.5 |
| 7. Iris | 1847 | 221.4 | 3.68 | 121 | 8.4 |
| 8. Flora | 1847 | 204.4 | 3.27 | 56 | 8.9 |
| 9. Metis | 1848 | 221.7 | 3.69 | 78 | 8.9 |
| 10. Hygeia | 1849 | 222.6 | 5.59 | 40(?) | 9.5 |

### Neptune's Rings

*Voyager* found four rings and evidence of ring *arcs* or incomplete rings. The "Main Ring" orbits Neptune at about 23,812.5 mi (38,100 km) above the cloud tops. The "Inner Ring" is about 17,750 mi (28,400 km) from Neptune's cloud tops. An "Inside Diffuse Ring"—a complete ring—is located about 10,687.5 mi (17,100 km) from the planet's cloud tops. Some scientists suspect that this ring may extend all the way down to Neptune's cloud tops. An area called "the Plateau" is a broad, diffuse sheet of fine material just outside the so-called Inner Ring. The fine material is approximately the size of smoke particles. All other rings contain a greater proportion of larger material.

### Pluto

Pluto, the outermost and smallest planet in the solar system, is the only planet not visited by an exploring spacecraft. So little is known about it that it is difficult to classify. Its distance is so great that the Hubble Space Telescope cannot reveal its surface features. Appropriately named for the Roman god of the underworld, it must be frozen, dark, and dead. Pluto's mean distance from the Sun is 3,687.5 million miles (5,900 million kilometers).

In 1978, light-curve studies gave evidence of a moon revolving around Pluto within the same period as Pluto's rotation; therefore, it stays over the same point on Pluto's surface. In addition, it keeps the same face toward the planet. The satellite was later named Charon and is estimated to be about 789 mi (1,262.4 km) in diameter. Recent estimates indicate Pluto's diameter is about 1,441.6 mi (2,306.56 km), making the pair more like a double planet than any other in the solar system. Previously, the Earth–Moon system held this distinction. The density of Pluto is slightly greater than that of water.

There is evidence that Pluto has an atmosphere containing methane and polar ice caps that increase and decrease in size with the planet's seasons. It is not known to have water. The Hubble Space Telescope's faint-object camera revealed light and dark regions on Pluto indicating an ice cap at the planet's north pole. It is not known if there is an ice cap at Pluto's south pole.

Pluto was predicted by calculation when Percival Lowell (1855–1916) noticed irregularities in the orbits of Uranus and Neptune. Clyde Tombaugh (1906–1997) discovered the planet in 1930, precisely where Lowell predicted it would be. The name Pluto was chosen because the first two letters represent the initials of Percival Lowell.

Pluto has the most eccentric orbit in the solar system, bringing it at times closer to the Sun than Neptune. Pluto approached the perihelion of its orbit on Sept. 5, 1989, and until Feb. 1999 was closer to the Sun than Neptune. Even then, it could be seen only with a large telescope.

### The Asteroids

Between the orbits of Mars and Jupiter are an estimated 30,000 pieces of rocky debris, known collectively as the asteroids, or planetoids. The first and, incidentally, the largest (Ceres), was discovered during the New Year's night of 1801 by the Italian astronomer Father Piazzi (1746–1826), and its orbit was calculated by the German mathematician Karl Friedrich Gauss (1777–1855). Gauss invented a new method of calculating orbits on that occasion. A few asteroids do not move in orbits beyond the orbit of Mars, but in orbits that cross the orbit of Mars. The first of them was named Eros because of this peculiar orbit. It had become the rule to bestow female names on the asteroids, but when it was found that Eros crossed the orbit of a major planet, it received a male name. These orbit-crossing asteroids are often referred to as the "male asteroids." A few of them—Albert, Adonis, Apollo, Amor, and Icarus—cross the orbit of Earth, and two of them may come closer than our Moon; but the crossing is like a bridge crossing a highway, not like two highways intersecting. Hence there is very little danger of collision from these bodies. They are all small, 3 to 5 mi (4.8 to 8.0 km) in diameter, and therefore very difficult objects to identify, even when quite close. Some scientists believe the asteroids represent the remains of an exploded planet.

On Oct. 29, 1991, the *Galileo* spacecraft took a historic photograph of asteroid 951 Gaspra from a distance of 10,000 mi (16,000 km) away. It was the first close-up photo ever taken of an asteroid in space. Gaspra is an irregular, potato-shaped object about 12.5 mi (20 km) by 7.5 mi (12 km) by 7 mi (11.2 km) in size. Its surface is covered with a layer of loose rubble and its terrain is marked by several dozen small craters.

NASA's *Near-Earth Asteroid Rendezvous* spacecraft was launched on Feb. 17, 1996. (Near-Earth asteroids come within 121 million miles [195 million kilometers] of the Sun. Their orbits come close enough that one could eventually hit Earth.) It flew within 750 mi (1,200 km) of minor planet 253 Mathilde on June 27, 1997, and took spectacular images of the dark, crater-battered world. The asteroid's mean diameter was found to be 33 mi (52.8 km). The *NEAR* spacecraft discovered that the carbon-rich Mathilde is one of the darkest objects in the solar system, only reflecting about 3% of the Sun's light, making it twice as dark as a chunk of charcoal. The asteroid is almost completely cratered, and at least five of its craters just on the lighted side are larger than 12 mi (19.2 km).

The spacecraft reached asteroid 433 Eros in Dec. 1998, but because of engine problems its original mission to enter into the asteroid's orbit was aborted, and NEAR flew past Eros instead. However, the spacecraft was reset, and on Feb. 14, 2000, NEAR successfully entered into orbit around Eros. NEAR remained in orbit for one year, taking photographs of the asteroid and gathering information about its composition, structure, size, and shape. The spacecraft landed safely on the surface of Eros in a controlled crash on Feb. 12, 2001. Against tremendous odds, it continued to relay information for another two weeks before being shut down.

NEAR measured Eros to be 21 mi (33.6 km) long by 8 mi (12.8 km) wide and 8 mi (12.8 km) deep. It rotates once every 5.27 hours and has no visible moons. NEAR data also showed that the asteroid's ancient surface is covered with craters, ridges, boulders, and other complex features.

NEAR was the first spacecraft to orbit an asteroid and the first craft to operate on solar power so far from the Sun. NEAR gathered about 160,000 images of Eros, about 10 times more than was planned. The spacecraft was renamed *NEAR-Shoemaker* in honor of geologist Dr. Eugene M. Shoemaker (1928–1997), who researched the influence of asteroids and comets in shaping planets.

In June 2002, scientists were caught unaware when an asteroid measuring about 300 ft across hurtled past Earth at a distance of only 75,000 mi—less than a third of the distance to the Moon. The asteroid, which was provisionally named 2002 MN, was only discovered three days after its closest approach. It is the sixth known asteroid to pass within the Moon's orbit.

## Comets

Comets, according to the noted astronomer Fred L. Whipple (1906– ), are enormous "snowballs" of frozen gases (mostly carbon dioxide, methane, and water vapor) and contain very little solid material. The whole behavior of comets can then be [illegible] by the Sun. When the comet Kohoutek made its first appearance to human observers in 1973, its behavior seemed to confirm this theory, and later the international study by five spacecraft that encountered Halley's comet in March 1986 confirmed Whipple's idea of the make-up of comets.

Since comets appear in the sky without any warning, people in classical times and especially during the Middle Ages believed that they had a special meaning, which, of course, was bad. Since a natural catastrophe of some sort or a military conflict occurs every year, it was quite simple to blame the comet that happened to be visible. But even in the past, there were some people who used logical reasoning. When, in Roman times, a comet was blamed for the loss of a battle and hence was called a "bad omen," a Roman writer observed that the victors in the battle probably did not think so.

Up until the middle of the 16th century, comets were believed to be phenomena of the upper atmosphere; they were usually explained as "burning vapors" which had risen from "distant swamps." That nobody had ever actually seen burning vapors rise from a swamp did not matter.

But a large comet that appeared in 1577 was carefully observed by Tycho Brahe (1546–1601), a Danish astronomer who is often, and with the best of reasons, called eccentric, but who insisted on precise measurements for everything. It was Tycho Brahe's accumulation of literally thousands of precise measurements that later enabled his younger collaborator, Johannes Kepler (1571–1630), to discover the laws of planetary motion. Measuring the motion of the comet of 1577, Brahe could show that it had been far beyond the atmosphere, even though he could not give figures for the distance. Brahe's work proved that comets were astronomical and not meteorological phenomena.

In 1682, the second Astronomer Royal of Great Britain, Dr. Edmond Halley (1656–1742), checked the orbit of a bright comet that was in the sky and then compared it with earlier comet orbits that were known in part. Halley found that the comet of 1682 was the third to move through what appeared to be the same orbit, and that the three appearances were roughly 76 years apart. Halley concluded that this was the same comet, moving around the Sun in a closed orbit, like the planets. He predicted that it would reappear in 1758 or 1759. Halley himself died in 1742, but a large comet appeared 16 years after his death as predicted and was immediately referred to as "Halley's comet."

Halley's comet appeared again in 1986, sparking a worldwide effort to study it up close. Five satellites in all took readings from the comet at various distances. Two Soviet craft, *Vega 1* and *Vega 2*, went in close to provide detailed pictures of the comet, including the first of the comet's core. The European Space Agency's craft, *Giotto*, entered the comet itself, coming to within 450 mi of the comet's center and successfully passing through its tail. In addition, two Japanese craft, the *Suisei* and the *Sakigake*, passed at a farther distance and analyzed the cloud and tail of the comet and the effect of solar radiation upon it.

Astronomers refer to comets as *periodic* or *nonperiodic,* but the latter term does not mean that these comets have no period. It usually means that their period is not known. The actual periods of comets run from 3.3 years (the shortest known) to many thousands of years. Their orbits are elliptical, like those of the planets, but they are very eccentric, long, and narrow ellipses. Only comet Schwassmann-Wachmann has an orbit that has such a low eccentricity (for a cometary orbit) that it could be the orbit of a minor planet.

When a comet coming from deep space approaches the Sun, it is at first indistinguishable from a minor planet. Somewhere between the orbits of Mars and Jupiter, its outline becomes fuzzy; it is said to develop a *coma* (the word used here is the Latin word *coma,* which means "hair," not the phonetically identical Greek word that means "deep sleep"). Then, near the orbit of Mars, the comet develops its tail, which at first trails behind. This grows steadily as the comet comes closer and closer to the Sun. As it rounds the Sun (as first noticed by Girolamo Fracastoro, 1483–1553), the tail always points away from the Sun so that the comet, when moving away from the Sun, points its tail ahead like the landing lights of an airplane.

The reason for this behavior is that the tail is pushed in these directions by the radiation pressure of the Sun. It sometimes happens that a comet loses its tail at perihelion; it then grows another one. Although the tail is clearly visible against the black of the sky, it is very tenuous. It has been said that if the tail of Halley's comet could be compressed to the density of iron, it would fit into a small suitcase.

Although very low in mass, comets are among the largest members of the solar system. The nucleus of a comet may be up to 10,000 mi in diameter; its coma between 10,000 and 50,000 mi in diameter; and its tail as long as 28 million miles.

Comet Shoemaker-Levy 9 broke up into 21 fragments in July 1992 and crashed into the surface of Jupiter, July 16–22, 1994, in the most violent event in the recorded history of the solar system.

In 1951, Dutch astronomer Gerard Kuiper first suggested the existence of a disk-shaped swarm of short-period comets that begin beyond the orbit of Neptune and extend past Pluto. In 1995, the Hubble Space Telescope detected the long-sought Kuiper Belt and an estimated 200 million comets were discovered orbiting it.

## Meteors and Meteorites

The term *meteor* for what is usually called a *shooting star* bears an unfortunate resemblance to the term *meteorology*, the science of weather and weather forecasting. This resemblance is due to an ancient misunderstanding that wrongly considered meteors an atmospheric phenomenon. Actually, the streak of light in the sky that scientists call a meteor is essentially an astronomical phenomenon: the entry of a small piece of cosmic matter into our atmosphere.

The distinction between *meteors* and *fireballs* (formerly also called *bolides*) is merely one of convenience; a fireball is an unusually bright meteor than a faint meteor. Incidentally, it also means that a fireball is larger than a faint meteor.

Objects that enter our atmosphere become visible when they are about 60 mi above the ground. The fact that they grow hot enough to emit light is not due to the "friction" of the atmosphere, as one often reads. The phenomenon responsible for the heating is one of compression. Unconfined air cannot move faster than the speed of sound. Since the entering meteorite moves with 30 to 60 times the speed of sound, the air simply cannot get out of the way. Therefore, it is compressed like the air in the cylinder of a diesel engine and is heated by compression. This heat—or part of it—is transferred to the moving object. The details of this process are now fairly well understood as a result of reentry tests with ballistic-missile nose cones.

The average weight of an object producing a faint *shooting star* is only a small fraction of an ounce. Even a bright fireball may not weigh more than 2 or 3 lb. Naturally, the smaller objects are worn to dust by the passage through the atmosphere; only rather large ones reach the ground. Those that are found are called meteorites. (The *meteor*, to repeat, is the

term for the light streak in the sky.) Thousands of meteorites fall to Earth each year.

The largest meteorite known is still embedded in the ground near Grootfontein in southwest Africa and is estimated to weigh 70 tons. The second-largest known is the 34-ton Anighito (on exhibit in the Hayden Planetarium, New York), which was found by Admiral Peary in 1892 at Cape York in Greenland. The largest meteorite found in the United States is the Willamette meteorite (found in Oregon, weight ca. 15 tons), but large portions of this meteorite weathered away before it was found. Its weight as it struck the ground may have been 20 tons.

All these are iron meteorites (an iron meteorite normally contains about 7% nickel), which form one class of meteorites. The other class consists of the stony meteorites, and between them there are the so-called stony irons. Tektites consist of silica-rich glass similar to our volcanic glass obsidian, and because of the similarity, there is doubt in a number of cases whether the glass is of terrestrial or of extraterrestrial origin.

Though no meteorite larger than the Grootfontein is actually known, we do know that Earth has, on occasion, been struck by much larger bodies. Evidence for such hits are the meteorite craters, of which an especially good example is located near the Cañon Diablo in Arizona. Another meteor crater in the United States is a rather old crater near Odessa, Tex. Some scientists theorize that the mass extermination of dinosaurs from the face of Earth 65 million years ago was due to a large meteor that struck our planet at that time.

Meteor showers are caused by multitudes of very small bodies traveling in swarms. Earth travels in its orbit through these swarms like a car driving through falling snow. The point from which the meteors seem to emanate is called the *radiant* and is named for the constellation in that area. The Perseid meteor shower in August is the most spectacular of the year, boasting, at peak, roughly 60 meteors per hour under good atmospheric conditions.

## The Constellations

Constellations are groupings of stars that form easily recognized and remembered patterns, such as Orion and the Big Dipper. The Big Dipper is actually an asterism, not a constellation, because it is only part of the constellation Ursa Major (the Big Bear). Actually, the stars in the majority of all constellations do not "belong together." Usually they are at greatly varying distances from Earth and just happen to lie more or less in the same line of sight as seen from our solar system. But in a few cases, the stars of a constellation are actually associated; most of the bright stars of the Big Dipper travel together and form what astronomers call an *open cluster*.

If you observe a planet, say Mars, for one complete revolution, you will see that it passes successively through 12 constellations. All planets (except Pluto at certain times) can be observed only in these 12 constellations, which form the so-called zodiac, and the Sun also moves through the zodiacal signs, though the Sun's apparent movement is actually caused by the movement of Earth.

Although the constellations are due mainly to the optical accident of line of sight and have no real significance, astronomers have retained them as reference areas. It is much easier to speak of a star in

# The 88 Recognized Constellations

In astronomical works, the Latin names of the constellations are used. The letter N or S following the Latin name indicates whether the constellation is located to the north or south of the Zodiac. The letter Z indicates that the constellation is within the Zodiac.

| Latin name | Letter | English version | Latin name | Letter | English version | Latin name | Letter | English version |
|---|---|---|---|---|---|---|---|---|
| Andromeda | N | Andromeda | Delphinus | N | Dolphin | Pegasus | N | Pegasus |
| Antlia | S | Airpump | Dorado | S | Swordfish (Gold- | Perseus | N | Perseus |
| Apus | S | Bird of Paradise | | | fish) | Phoenix | S | Phoenix |
| Aquarius | Z | Water Bearer | Draco | N | Dragon | Pictor | S | Painter (or his |
| Aquila | N | Eagle | Equuleus | N | Filly | | | Easel) |
| Ara | S | Altar | Eridanus | S | Eridanus (river) | Pisces | Z | Fishes |
| Aries | Z | Ram | Fornax | S | Furnace | Piscis Austrinus | S | Southern Fish |
| Auriga | N | Charioteer | Gemini | Z | Twins | Puppis | S | Poop (of Argo)[1] |
| Boötes | N | Herdsmen | Grus | S | Crane | Pyxis | S | Mariner's Com- |
| Caelum | S | Sculptor's Tool | Hercules | N | Hercules | | | pass |
| Camelopardalis | N | Giraffe | Horologium | S | Clock | Reticulum | S | Net |
| Cancer | Z | Crab | Hydra | N | Sea Serpent | Sagitta | N | Arrow |
| Canes Venatici | N | Hunting Dogs | Hydrus | S | Water Snake | Sagittarius | Z | Archer |
| Canis Major | S | Great Dog | Indus | S | Indian | Scorpius | Z | Scorpion |
| Canis Minor | S | Little Dog | Lacerta | N | Lizard | Sculptor | S | Sculptor |
| Capricornus | Z | Goat (or Sea- | Leo | Z | Lion | Scutum | N | Shield |
| | | Goat) | Leo Minor | N | Little Lion | Serpens | N | Serpent |
| Carina | S | Keel (of Argo)[1] | Lepus | S | Hare | Sextans | S | Sextant |
| Cassiopeia | N | Cassiopeia | Libra | Z | Scales | Taurus | Z | Bull |
| Centaurus | S | Centaur | Lupus | S | Wolf | Telescopium | S | Telescope |
| Cepheus | N | Cepheus | Lynx | N | Lynx | Triangulum | N | Triangle |
| Cetus | S | Whale | Lyra | N | Lyre (Harp) | Triangulum Aus- | S | Southern Triangle |
| Chameleon | S | Chameleon | Mensa | S | Table (mountain) | trale | | |
| Circinus | S | Compasses | Microscopium | S | Microscope | Tucana | S | Toucan |
| Columba | S | Dove | Monoceros | S | Unicorn | Ursa Major | N | Big Dipper[2] |
| Coma Berenices | N | Berenice's Hair | Musca | S | Southern Fly | Ursa Minor | N | Little Dipper[3] |
| Corona Australis | S | Southern Crown | Norma | S | Rule (straight- | Vela | S | Sail (of Argo)[1] |
| Corona Borealis | N | Northern Crown | | | edge) | Virgo | Z | Virgin |
| Corvus | S | Crow (Raven) | Octans | S | Octant | Volans | S | Flying Fish |
| Crater | S | Cup | Ophiuchus | N | Serpent-Bearer | Vulpecula | N | Fox |
| Crux | S | Southern Cross | Orion | S | Orion | | | |
| Cygnus | N | Swan | Pavo | S | Peacock | | | |

1. The original constellation Argo Navis (the Ship Argo) has been divided into Carina, Puppis, and Vela. Normally the brightest star in each constellation is designated by alpha, the first letter of the Greek alphabet, the second brightest by beta, the second letter of the Greek alphabet, and so forth. But the Greek letters run through Carina, Puppis, and Vela as if it were still one constellation. 2. The Big Dipper is only a part of the constellation Ursa Major (Great Bear) and is not a constellation itself. 3. The Little Dipper is called Ursa Minor (Little Bear).

Orion than to give its geometrical position in the sky. During the Astronomical Congress of 1928, it was decided to recognize 88 constellations. A description of their agreed-upon boundaries was published at Cambridge, England, in 1930, under the title *Atlas Céleste*.

## The Auroras

The "northern lights" (*Aurora borealis*) as well as the "southern lights" (*Aurora australis*) are upper-atmosphere phenomena of astronomical origin. The auroras center around the magnetic (not the geographical) poles of Earth, which explains why, in the Western Hemisphere, they have been seen as far to the south as New Orleans and Florida, while the equivalent latitude in the Eastern Hemisphere never sees an aurora. The northern magnetic pole happens to be in the Western Hemisphere.

The lower limit of an aurora is at about 50 mi (80 km). Upper limits have been estimated to be as high as 400 mi (640 km). Since about 1880, a connection between the auroras on Earth and sunspots has been suspected and has gradually come to be accepted. It was said that the sunspots probably eject "particles" (later the word *electrons* was substituted), which on striking Earth's atmosphere cause the auroras. But this explanation suffered from certain difficulties.

Sometimes a very large sunspot group on the Sun, with individual spots bigger than Earth itself, would not cause an aurora. Moreover, even if a sunspot caused an aurora, the time that passed between the appearance of the one and the occurrence of the other was highly unpredictable.

This problem of the time lag is, in all probability, solved by the discovery of the Van Allen layer[1], a double layer of charged subatomic particles around Earth. The inner layer, with its center some 1,500 mi (2,400 km) from the ground, reaches from about 40°N to around 40°S and does not touch the atmosphere. The outer layer, much larger, some several thousand miles from the ground, does touch the atmosphere in the vicinity of the magnetic poles.

It seems probable that the "leakage" of electrons from the outer Van Allen layer causes the auroras. A new burst of electrons from the Sun seems to be caught in the outer layer first. Under the assumption that all electrons are first caught in the outer layer, the time lag can be understood. There has to be an "overflow" from the outer layer to produce an aurora.

1. Named after the American physicist, James Alfred Van Allen (1914– ), who discovered the broad bands of intense radiation surrounding Earth in 1958.

## The Atmosphere

Though reasonably transparent to visible light, the atmosphere may absorb as much as 60% of the visible and near-visible light. It is opaque to most other wavelengths, except certain fairly short radio waves. In addition to absorbing much light, our atmosphere bends light rays entering at a slant (for a given observer) so that the true position of a star close to the horizon is not what it seems to be. One effect is that we see the Sun above the horizon before it actually is. And the unsteady movement of the atmosphere causes the "twinkling" of the stars, which may be romantic, but is a nuisance when it comes to observing.

The composition of our atmosphere near the ground is 78% nitrogen and 21% oxygen, the remaining 1% consisting of other gases, most of it argon. The composition stays the same to an altitude of at least 70 mi (112 km) (except that higher up two impurities, carbon dioxide and water vapor, are missing), but the pressure drops very fast. At 18,000 ft, half of the total mass of the atmosphere is below, and at 100,000 ft, 99% of the mass of the atmosphere is below. The upper limit of the atmosphere is usually given as 120 mi (192 km); no definitive figure is possible, since there is no boundary line between the incredibly attenuated gases 120 mi (192 km) up and space.

## Phenomena, 2003

### Configurations of Sun, Moon, and Planets

NOTE: The hour listings are in Universal Time. For conversion to U.S. time zones, *see* Conversion of Universal Time to Civil Time, p. 399. Terms in boldface can be found on pp. 376–377.

### JANUARY

| Day | Phenomenon | Hour |
|---|---|---|
| 2 | Mercury appears to be motionless in the sky as it goes from direct motion to **retrograde** motion. | 1000 |
| 2 | NEW MOON | 2000 |
| 3 | Mercury is 5° north of the Moon. | 2300 |
| 4 | Earth is at **perihelion**. | 0500 |
| 4 | Neptune is 5° north of the Moon. | 1900 |
| 6 | Uranus is 5° north of the Moon. | 0100 |
| 10 | FIRST QUARTER | 1300 |
| 11 | The Moon is at **apogee**. | 0100 |
| 11 | Venus is at its greatest **elongation**, at 47° west of the Sun. | 0300 |
| 11 | Mercury is in inferior **conjunction**. | 2000 |
| 15 | Saturn is 3° south of the Moon. | 2000 |
| 15 | Venus is 8° north of Antares, the brightest star in the constellation Scorpius. | 2200 |
| 18 | FULL MOON | 1100 |
| 19 | Jupiter is 4° south of the Moon. | 1500 |
| 22 | Mercury appears to be motionless in the sky as it goes from **retrograde** to direct motion. | 2300 |
| 23 | The Moon is at **perigee**. | 2200 |
| 25 | LAST QUARTER | 0900 |
| 27 | Mars is 0° 4' north of the Moon. **Occultation** of Mars by the Moon. | 1500 |
| 28 | Venus is 4° north of the Moon. | 1900 |
| 30 | Mercury is 5° north of the Moon. | 1000 |
| 31 | Neptune is in **conjunction** with the Sun. | 0000 |
| 31 | Mars is 5° north of Antares, the brightest star in the constellation Scorpius. | 0500 |

### FEBRUARY

| Day | Phenomenon | Hour |
|---|---|---|
| 1 | NEW MOON | 1100 |
| 2 | Jupiter is at **opposition**. | 0900 |
| 4 | Mercury is at its greatest **elongation**, at 25° west of the Sun. | 0100 |
| 7 | The Moon is at **apogee**. | 2200 |
| 9 | FIRST QUARTER | 1100 |
| 12 | Saturn is 3° south of the Moon. | 0300 |
| 15 | Jupiter is 4° south of the Moon. | 1800 |
| 16 | Vesta, the third-largest asteroid, appears to be motionless in the sky as it goes from direct motion to **retrograde** motion. | 0600 |
| 17 | FULL MOON | 0000 |
| 17 | Uranus is in **conjunction** with the Sun. | 2200 |
| 19 | The Moon is at **perigee**. | 1600 |

| Day | Phenomenon | Hour |
|---|---|---|
| 21 | Mercury is 1° 6' south of Neptune. | 0000 |
| 22 | Saturn appears to be motionless in the sky as it goes from **retrograde** to direct motion. | 1000 |
| 23 | LAST QUARTER | 1700 |
| 25 | Mars is 1° 9' north of the Moon. | 0500 |
| 27 | Venus is 5° north of the Moon. | 1100 |
| 28 | Neptune is 5° north of the Moon. | 1500 |

### MARCH

| Day | Phenomenon | Hour |
|---|---|---|
| 1 | Mercury is 3° north of the Moon. | 1500 |
| 3 | NEW MOON | 0300 |
| 4 | Mercury is 1° 5' south of Uranus. | 1300 |
| 6 | Pallas, the second-largest asteroid, is in **conjunction** with the Sun. | 2300 |
| 7 | The Moon is at **apogee.** | 1700 |
| 11 | FIRST QUARTER | 0700 |
| 11 | Saturn is 3° south of the Moon. | 1200 |
| 12 | The asteroid Juno appears to be motionless in the sky as it goes from direct motion to **retrograde** motion. | 1000 |
| 12 | Venus is 0° 2' north of Neptune. | 2000 |
| 15 | Jupiter is 4° south of the Moon. | 0000 |
| 18 | FULL MOON | 1100 |
| 19 | The Moon is at **perigee**. | 1900 |
| 21 | Equinox | 0100 |
| 22 | Mercury is in superior **conjunction**. | 0000 |
| 23 | Pluto appears to be motionless in the sky as it goes from direct motion to **retrograde** motion. | 1700 |
| 25 | LAST QUARTER | 0200 |
| 25 | Mars is 3° north of the Moon. | 1800 |
| 26 | Vesta, the third-largest asteroid, is at **opposition**. | 2300 |
| 27 | Neptune is 5° north of the Moon. | 2200 |
| 28 | Venus is 0° 5' north of Uranus. | 1300 |
| 29 | Uranus is 5° north of the Moon. | 0800 |
| 29 | Venus is 5° north of the Moon. | 1000 |

### APRIL

| Day | Phenomenon | Hour |
|---|---|---|
| 1 | NEW MOON | 1900 |
| 4 | The Moon is at **apogee.** | 0400 |
| 4 | Jupiter appears to be motionless in the sky as it goes from **retrograde** to direct motion. | 0500 |

| Day | Phenomenon | Hour |
|---|---|---|
| 7 | Saturn is 3° south of the Moon. | 2200 |
| 10 | FIRST QUARTER | 0000 |
| 11 | Jupiter is 4° south of the Moon. | 0800 |
| 16 | Mercury is at its greatest **elongation,** at 20° east of the Sun. | 1500 |
| 16 | FULL MOON | 2000 |
| 17 | The Moon is at **perigee.** | 0500 |
| 23 | Mars is 3° north of the Moon. | 0700 |
| 23 | LAST QUARTER | 1200 |
| 24 | Neptune is 5° north of the Moon. | 0400 |
| 25 | Uranus is 5° north of the Moon. | 1600 |
| 26 | Mercury appears to be motionless in the sky as it goes from direct motion to **retrograde** motion. | 2200 |
| 28 | Venus is 3° north of the Moon. | 1700 |

## MAY

| Day | Phenomenon | Hour |
|---|---|---|
| 1 | The Moon is at **apogee.** | 0800 |
| 1 | NEW MOON | 1200 |
| 3 | The asteroid Juno is at **opposition.** | 1100 |
| 5 | Saturn is 3° south of the Moon. | 0900 |
| 7 | Mercury is in inferior **conjunction.** Transit of Mercury.[1] | 0700 |
| 8 | Jupiter is 4° south of the Moon. | 1800 |
| 9 | FIRST QUARTER | 1200 |
| 13 | Mars is 2° south of Neptune. | 1400 |
| 15 | Vesta, the third-largest asteroid, appears to be motionless in the sky as it goes from **retrograde** to direct motion. | 0400 |
| 15 | The Moon is at **perigee.** | 1600 |
| 16 | Neptune appears to be motionless in the sky as it goes from direct motion to **retrograde** motion. | 0300 |
| 16 | FULL MOON Total eclipse of the Moon. | 0400 |
| 16 | Ceres, the largest asteroid, is in **conjunction** with the Sun. | 2300 |
| 19 | Mercury appears to be motionless in the sky as it goes from direct motion to **retrograde** motion. | 1400 |
| 21 | Neptune is 5° north of the Moon. | 1200 |
| 21 | Mars is 3° north of the Moon. | 2000 |
| 23 | Uranus is 5° north of the Moon | 0000 |
| 23 | LAST QUARTER | 0100 |
| 28 | Mercury is 2° south of Venus. | 0000 |
| 28 | The Moon is at **apogee.** | 1300 |
| 29 | Mercury is 2° south of the Moon. | 0200 |
| 29 | Venus is 0° 1′ south of the Moon. **Occultation** of Venus by the Moon. | 0400 |
| 31 | NEW MOON Annular eclipse of the Sun. | 0400 |

1. Mercury can be seen (with a specially filtered telescope) moving across the face of the Sun. This is a relatively rare occurrence that happens approximately 13 times a century.

## JUNE

| Day | Phenomenon | Hour |
|---|---|---|
| 1 | Saturn is 4° south of the Moon. | 2100 |
| 3 | Mercury is at its greatest **elongation,** at 24° west of the Sun. | 0600 |
| 5 | Jupiter is 4° south of the Moon. | 0600 |
| 7 | Uranus appears to be motionless in the sky as it goes from direct motion to **retrograde** motion. | 1500 |
| 7 | FIRST QUARTER | 2000 |
| 9 | Pluto is at **opposition.** | 2100 |
| 12 | The Moon is at **perigee.** | 2300 |
| 14 | FULL MOON | 1100 |
| 17 | Neptune is 5° north of the Moon. | 2100 |

| Day | Phenomenon | Hour |
|---|---|---|
| 18 | Venus is 5° north of Aldebaran, the brightest star in the constellation Taurus. | 1900 |
| 19 | Mars is 1° 7′ north of the Moon. | 0600 |
| 19 | Uranus is 5° north of the Moon. | 0800 |
| 19 | Mercury is 4° north of Aldebaran, the brightest star in the constellation Taurus. | 1200 |
| 20 | Mars is 3° south of Uranus. | 2300 |
| 21 | Mercury is 0° 4′ south of Venus. | 0200 |
| 21 | LAST QUARTER | 1500 |
| 21 | Solstice | 1900 |
| 24 | Saturn is in **conjunction** with the Sun. | 1400 |
| 25 | The Moon is at **apogee.** | 0200 |
| 29 | NEW MOON | 1900 |

## JULY

| Day | Phenomenon | Hour |
|---|---|---|
| 2 | The asteroid Juno appears to be motionless in the sky as it goes from **retrograde** to direct motion. | 1600 |
| 2 | Jupiter is 4° south of the Moon. | 2100 |
| 4 | Earth is at **aphelion.** | 0600 |
| 5 | Mercury is in superior **conjunction.** | 1000 |
| 7 | FIRST QUARTER | 0300 |
| 8 | Venus is 0° 8′ north of Saturn. | 0800 |
| 10 | The Moon is at **perigee.** | 2200 |
| 13 | FULL MOON | 1900 |
| 15 | Neptune is 5° north of the Moon. | 0500 |
| 16 | Uranus is 5° north of the Moon. | 1600 |
| 17 | Mars is 0° 3′ south of the Moon. **Occultation** of Mars by the Moon. | 0800 |
| 21 | LAST QUARTER | 0700 |
| 22 | The Moon is at **apogee.** | 2000 |
| 26 | Mercury is 0° 4′ north of Jupiter. | 0100 |
| 27 | Saturn is 4° south of the Moon. | 0000 |
| 29 | NEW MOON | 0700 |
| 30 | Mercury is 0° 2′ north of Regulus, the brightest star in the constellation Leo. | 1100 |
| 30 | Jupiter is 4° south of the Moon. | 1300 |
| 30 | Mars appears to be motionless in the sky as it goes from direct motion to **retrograde** motion. | 2200 |
| 31 | Mercury is 5° south of the Moon. | 0100 |

## AUGUST

| Day | Phenomenon | Hour |
|---|---|---|
| 4 | Neptune is at **opposition.** | 1400 |
| 5 | FIRST QUARTER | 0700 |
| 6 | The Moon is at **perigee.** | 1400 |
| 11 | Neptune is 5° north of the Moon. | 1300 |
| 12 | FULL MOON | 0500 |
| 12 | Uranus is 5° north of the Moon. | 0600 |
| 13 | Mars is 1° 9′ south of the Moon. | 1700 |
| 14 | Mercury is at its greatest **elongation,** at 27° east of the Sun. | 2100 |
| 18 | Venus is in superior **conjunction.** | 1800 |
| 19 | The Moon is at **apogee.** | 1400 |
| 20 | LAST QUARTER | 0100 |
| 22 | Jupiter is in **conjunction** with the Sun. | 1000 |
| 23 | Saturn is 4° south of the Moon. | 1400 |
| 24 | Uranus is at **opposition.** | 1000 |
| 27 | Mars makes its closest approach to Earth in 17 years. | 1000 |
| 27 | NEW MOON | 1700 |
| 28 | Mercury appears to be motionless in the sky as it goes from direct motion to **retrograde** motion. | 0000 |
| 28 | Mars is at **opposition.** | 1800 |

| Day | Phenomenon | Hour |
|---|---|---|
| 29 | Mercury is 9° south of the Moon. | 0100 |
| 30 | Pluto appears to be motionless in the sky as it goes from **retrograde** to direct motion. | 0600 |
| 31 | The Moon is at **perigee.** | 1900 |

## SEPTEMBER

| Day | Phenomenon | Hour |
|---|---|---|
| 3 | FIRST QUARTER | 1300 |
| 5 | Pallas, the second-largest asteroid, appears to be motionless in the sky as it goes from direct motion to **retrograde** motion. | 2100 |
| 7 | Neptune is 5° north of the Moon. | 1900 |
| 9 | Uranus is 5° north of the Moon. | 0600 |
| 9 | Mars is 1° 2′ south of the Moon. **Occultation** of Mars by the Moon. | 1300 |
| 10 | FULL MOON | 1700 |
| 11 | Mercury is in inferior **conjunction.** | 0200 |
| 16 | The Moon is at **apogee.** | 0900 |
| 18 | LAST QUARTER | 1900 |
| 19 | Mercury appears to be motionless in the sky as it goes from direct motion to **retrograde** motion. | 1300 |
| 20 | Saturn is 5° south of the Moon. | 0300 |
| 23 | Equinox | 1100 |
| 24 | Jupiter is 4° south of the Moon. | 0400 |
| 24 | Mercury is 5° south of the Moon. | 1700 |
| 26 | NEW MOON | 0300 |
| 27 | Mercury is at its greatest **elongation,** at 18° west of the Sun. | 0000 |
| 28 | The Moon is at perigee. | 0600 |
| 29 | Mars appears to be motionless in the sky as it goes from **retrograde** to direct motion. | 1400 |

## OCTOBER

| Day | Phenomenon | Hour |
|---|---|---|
| 2 | FIRST QUARTER | 1900 |
| 3 | Venus is 3° north of Spica, the brightest star in the constellation Virgo. | 2200 |
| 5 | Neptune is 5° north of the Moon. | 0000 |
| 6 | Uranus is 5° north of the Moon. | 1000 |
| 6 | Mars is 1° 1′ north of the Moon. **Occultation** of Mars by the Moon. | 1500 |
| 10 | FULL MOON | 0700 |
| 13 | Pallas, the second-largest asteroid, is at **opposition.** | 1500 |
| 14 | The Moon is at **apogee.** | 0200 |
| 17 | Saturn is 5° south of the Moon. | 1300 |
| 18 | LAST QUARTER | 1300 |
| 21 | Jupiter is 4° south of the Moon. | 2300 |
| 23 | Neptune appears to be motionless in the sky as it goes from **retrograde** to direct motion. | 0000 |
| 25 | Mercury is in superior **conjunction.** | 1000 |
| 25 | NEW MOON | 1300 |
| 26 | Saturn appears to be motionless in the sky as it goes from direct motion to **retrograde** motion. | 0000 |
| 26 | The Moon is at **perigee.** | 1200 |
| 26 | Venus is 0° 8′ north of the Moon. **Occultation** of Venus by the Moon. | 2000 |

## NOVEMBER

| Day | Phenomenon | Hour |
|---|---|---|
| 1 | FIRST QUARTER | 0400 |
| 1 | Neptune is 5° north of the Moon. | 0600 |
| 2 | Uranus is 5° north of the Moon. | 1500 |
| 3 | Mars is 3° north of the Moon. | 0900 |
| 8 | Uranus appears to be motionless in the sky as it goes from **retrograde** to direct motion. | 1900 |
| 9 | FULL MOON Total eclipse of the Moon. | 0100 |
| 10 | Venus is 4° north of Antares, the brightest star in the constellation Scorpius. | 0700 |
| 10 | The Moon is at **apogee.** | 1200 |
| 13 | Saturn is 5° south of the Moon. | 1900 |
| 17 | LAST QUARTER | 0400 |
| 18 | Mercury is 3° north of Antares, the brightest star in the constellation Scorpius. | 1200 |
| 18 | Jupiter is 4° south of the Moon. | 1600 |
| 23 | The Moon is at **perigee.** | 2300 |
| 23 | NEW MOON Total eclipse of the Sun. | 2300 |
| 25 | Mercury is 0° 3′ north of the Moon. **Occultation** of Mercury by the Moon. | 0300 |
| 25 | Venus is 2° north of the Moon. | 1800 |
| 26 | Ceres, the largest asteroid, appears to be motionless in the sky as it goes from direct motion to **retrograde** motion. | 0900 |
| 28 | Neptune is 5° north of the Moon. | 1400 |
| 29 | Uranus is 5° north of the Moon. | 2200 |
| 30 | FIRST QUARTER | 1700 |

## DECEMBER

| Day | Phenomenon | Hour |
|---|---|---|
| 1 | Mars is 4° north of the Moon. | 1600 |
| 5 | The asteroid Juno is in **conjunction** with the Sun. | 1900 |
| 7 | The Moon is at **apogee.** | 1200 |
| 8 | Pallas, the second-largest asteroid, appears to be motionless in the sky as it goes from **retrograde** to direct motion. | 1900 |
| 8 | FULL MOON | 2100 |
| 9 | Mercury is at its greatest **elongation,** at 21° east of the Sun. | 0600 |
| 10 | Saturn is 5° south of the Moon. | 2200 |
| 12 | Ceres, the largest asteroid, is 1° 1′ north of the Moon. **Occultation** of Ceres by the Moon. | 0100 |
| 12 | Pluto is in **conjunction** with the Sun. | 0500 |
| 16 | Jupiter is 4° south of the Moon. | 0400 |
| 16 | LAST QUARTER | 1800 |
| 17 | Mercury appears to be motionless in the sky as it goes from direct motion to **retrograde** motion. | 1300 |
| 22 | Solstice | 0700 |
| 22 | The Moon is at **perigee.** | 1200 |
| 23 | NEW MOON | 1000 |
| 24 | Vesta, the third-largest asteroid, is in **conjunction** with the Sun. | 1000 |
| 25 | Venus is 3° north of the Moon. | 1600 |
| 26 | Neptune is 5° north of the Moon. | 0100 |
| 27 | Mercury is in inferior **conjunction.** | 0100 |
| 27 | Uranus is 5° north of the Moon. | 0800 |
| 30 | Mars is 4° north of the Moon. | 0700 |
| 30 | Venus is 1° 9′ south of Neptune. | 0700 |
| 30 | FIRST QUARTER | 1000 |
| 31 | Saturn is at **opposition.** | 2100 |

## Conversion of Universal Time (UT) to Civil Time

| UT | EDT[1] | EST[2] | CST[3] | MST[4] | PST[5] |
|----|--------|--------|--------|--------|--------|
| 00 | *8P | *7P | *6P | *5P | *4P |
| 01 | *9P | *8P | *7P | *6P | *5P |
| 02 | *10P | *9P | *8P | *7P | *6P |
| 03 | *11P | *10P | *9P | *8P | *7P |
| 04 | M | *11P | *10P | *9P | *8P |
| 05 | 1A | M | *11P | *10P | *9P |
| 06 | 2A | 1A | M | *11P | *10P |
| 07 | 3A | 2A | 1A | M | *11P |
| 08 | 4A | 3A | 2A | 1A | M |
| 09 | 5A | 4A | 3A | 2A | 1A |
| 10 | 6A | 5A | 4A | 3A | 2A |
| 11 | 7A | 6A | 5A | 4A | 3A |
| 12 | 8A | 7A | 6A | 5A | 4A |
| 13 | 9A | 8A | 7A | 6A | 5A |
| 14 | 10A | 9A | 8A | 7A | 6A |
| 15 | 11A | 10A | 9A | 8A | 7A |
| 16 | N | 11A | 10A | 9A | 8A |
| 17 | 1P | N | 11A | 10A | 9A |
| 18 | 2P | 1P | N | 11A | 10A |
| 19 | 3P | 2P | 1P | N | 11A |
| 20 | 4P | 3P | 2P | 1P | N |
| 21 | 5P | 4P | 3P | 2P | 1P |
| 22 | 6P | 5P | 4P | 3P | 2P |
| 23 | 7P | 6P | 5P | 4P | 3P |

NOTES: * denotes previous day. N = noon. M = midnight. 1. Eastern Daylight Time. 2. Eastern Standard Time, same as Central Daylight Time. 3. Central Standard Time, same as Mountain Daylight Time. 4. Mountain Standard Time, same as Pacific Daylight Time. 5. Pacific Standard Time.

## Eclipses of the Sun and Moon, 2003

Note: The day of an eclipse is given in Universal Time (U.T.) and may start a day earlier or later depending on your time zone. (*See* Phenomena, 2003, pp. 396–398, to find time of eclipse.)

**May 16.** Total eclipse of the Moon. The beginning of the umbral phase visible in Europe, southern Greenland, eastern North America, Central America, South America, most of Antarctica, Africa, western Middle East, the Atlantic Ocean, the southeast Pacific Ocean, and the western Indian Ocean; the end visible in the southern tip of Greenland, North America except the extreme northwest, Central America, South America, part of New Zealand, most of Antarctica, western Africa, western Iberian Peninsula, the Atlantic Ocean except the extreme northeast, and the eastern Pacific Ocean.

**May 31.** Annular eclipse of the Sun. Visible in northeast Africa, Europe except Iberia (including the British Isles), northern Asia, northern Greenland, northern Canada, and Alaska.

**Nov. 8–9.** Total eclipse of the Moon. The beginning of the umbral phase visible in Africa, Europe, western and central Asia, Greenland, the Arctic region, eastern North America, Central America, South America except the southern tip, coastal Queen Maud Land of Antarctica, the western Indian Ocean, and the Atlantic Ocean; the end visible in Europe, northwest Asia, the Arctic region, Greenland, North America, Central America, South America, Antarctic Peninsula, Africa except extreme eastern part, western Middle East, the Atlantic Ocean, and the eastern Pacific Ocean.

**Nov. 23–24.** Total eclipse of the Sun. Visible in Australia, New Zealand, Antarctica, the South Pacific Ocean, and the southern tip of South America.

## Visibility of Planets in Morning and Evening Twilight, 2003

| | Morning | | Evening |
|---|---------|---|---------|
| Venus | January 1–July 13 | Venus | September 25–December 31 |
| Mars | January 1–August 28 | Mars | August 28–December 31 |
| Jupiter | January 1–February 2 | Jupiter | February 2–August 9 |
| | September 5–December 31 | Saturn | January 1–June 6 |
| Saturn | July 13–December 31 | | December 31 |

# Major Space Explorations

## Ongoing Missions

### Voyager (U.S.)
**Launched:** Aug. 20 *(Voyager 2)* and Sept. 5 *(Voyager 1)*, 1977. **Mission:** To explore Jupiter and the other outer planets. Launched in 1977, *Voyager 1* and *Voyager 2* passed Jupiter in 1979 and sent back surprising color TV images of that planet and its moons. *Voyager 1* passed Saturn in Nov. 1980. *Voyager 2* passed Saturn in Aug. 1981 and Uranus in Jan. 1986. *Voyager 2* encountered Neptune on Aug. 29, 1989, and made many discoveries. It found four rings around the planet, six new moons, a giant spot, and evidence of volcanic-like activity on its largest moon, Triton. The spacecraft sent back over 9,000 pictures of the planet and its system. *Voyager 2* remains the only spacecraft ever to have visited the worlds of Neptune and Uranus. On Feb. 13, 1990, at a distance of 3.7 billion miles, *Voyager 1* took its final pictures of the Sun and six of its planets as seen from deep space. NASA released the extraordinary images to the public on June 6, 1990. Only Mercury, Mars, and Pluto were not seen.

In its quarter century of exploration, the *Voyager* project has returned immense amounts of information. *Voyager 1* is presently the most distant human-made object in the universe, and *Voyager 2* is not far behind. Both spacecraft currently constitute the Voyager Interstellar Mission (VIM), the study of the region of space beyond the Sun's influence (the heliopause), at the outer boundary of the solar system. Both spacecraft continue to relay news of their surroundings through the Deep Space Network (DSN).

### Galileo (U.S.)
**Destination:** Jupiter. **Launched:** Oct. 18, 1989. **Achieved Orbit:** Dec. 7, 1995. **Mission:** To study the chemical composition and physical state of the largest planet in the solar system, its atmosphere, and four of its moons. During its two-year prime mission, *Galileo* made 11 orbits around Jupiter and visited and photographed Jupiter's large moons Io, Callisto, Ganymede, and Europa. Originally slated to end its explorations in Dec. 1997, *Galileo* has been favored with a series of two-year extensions from NASA and Congress. The first extension, dubbed the Galileo Europa Mission (GEM), included eight flybys of Europa, four flybys of Callisto, and two flybys of Io by the end of 1999. The spacecraft also observed the smaller moons Amalthea, Thebe, and Metis on Jan. 3, 2000. After so many successful flybys, *Galileo* was granted another tour, the Galileo Millennium Mission, which collected data on Io and Europa. On Feb. 22, 2000, *Galileo* made the closest pass ever of Io at 124 mi (200 km). Two flybys of Ganymede were conducted May 20 and Dec. 28, 2000. Also in Dec. 2000, *Galileo* embarked on a joint scientific expedition with the Saturn-bound *Cassini* spacecraft to make simultaneous observations of the Jupiter system from two vantage points.

In May of 2002, *Galileo* finished its observations of Io; the results revealed Io—now known as the most active body in the solar system—to be more heavily populated by active volcanoes than had been expected. *Galileo*'s last flyby will be a close brush with Amalthea, an inner satellite of Jupiter, on Nov. 5, 2002. In Sept. 2003, *Galileo* will self-destruct in a final, fatal plunge into Jupiter's atmosphere. *Galileo* was named for the Italian astronomer Galileo Galilei, who discovered the four great moons of Jupiter that were the major targets of this mission.

### Ulysses (U.S. and European Space Agency)
**Destination:** The Sun. **Launched:** Oct. 6, 1990. **Mission:** An international project to study the Sun and map the interstellar space above and below its poles. The spacecraft was put into orbit at right angles to the solar system's ecliptic plane. This special orbit enabled *Ulysses* to examine for the first time the Sun's north and south polar regions. Besides investigating the Sun, the spacecraft is also studying phenomena from the Milky Way and beyond. The spacecraft completed its first full orbit around the Sun on April 17, 1998, and continues to orbit the Sun. Its next major mission milestone will occur in Aug. 2003, when it will observe an eighth conjunction of the Earth and Sun.

### Mars Global Surveyor (U.S.)
**Destination:** Mars. **Launched:** Nov. 7, 1996. **Arrival:** Sept. 11, 1997. **Mission:** An orbiting spacecraft designed to provide detailed maps of the planet's surface and distribution of minerals, and to monitor the Martian weather. Six instruments are studying Martian surface, atmosphere, and gravitational and magnetic fields. *Surveyor*'s cameras are able to distinguish features as small as 10 ft across.

The primary mapping mission was delayed until March 1999, due to problems with the craft's solar panels. *MGS* completed its primary mission in Jan. 2001, and is currently in its second mission extension. Having studied the planet's entire surface, atmosphere, and interior, *MGS* has returned more Mars data than all other Martian missions combined. Its most significant results include photographs of gullies and debris flow that suggest the presence of water at or near the planet's surface.

### Cassini (U.S., the European Space Agency, and the Italian Space Agency)
**Destination:** Saturn. **Launched:** Oct. 15, 1997. **Arrival:** July 1, 2004. **Mission:** Will orbit Saturn for four years. While orbiting Saturn, *Cassini* will send a small probe named *Huygens* (after the Dutch astronomer Christiaan Huygens, who discovered Titan) to the surface of Saturn's largest moon, Titan, to learn more about its dense atmosphere and its surface state and composition. After relaying data to Earth from Titan, *Cassini* will continue with orbits of Saturn and flybys of the planet's moons. The spacecraft will also examine Saturn's equatorial zone and study the planet's polar regions. *Cassini* encountered Jupiter on Dec. 30, 2000, and flew

down the giant planet's magnetotail, performing studies complementing the *Galileo* mission until March 31, 2001. The spacecraft flew by asteroid 2685 Masursky on Jan. 23, 2000. The *Cassini* mission is named for the Italian-French astronomer Gian Domenico Cassini, who discovered four of Saturn's major moons.

### Nozomi ("Hope") (Japan)
**Destination:** Mars. **Launched:** July 4, 1998, from Kagoshima Space Center. **Arrival:** Dec. 2004. Engine problems forced fuel conservation measures and delayed its scheduled 1999 arrival at Mars until 2004. **Mission:** To send an orbiter around Mars to study the effect of the solar wind on the planet's atmosphere for one Martian year (687 days). Its cameras will provide photographic data on cloud distribution, polar haze, dust storms, polar ice, and the planet's surface. After its successful launch, the Planet-B spacecraft was renamed *Nozomi* (hope). Japan's new effort made it the third nation after the United States and Russia to conduct a mission to another planet.

### Stardust (U.S.)
**Destination:** Comet Wild 2. **Launched:** Feb. 7, 1999. **Mission:** To fly through coma of Comet Wild 2 in 2004, capture particles spewing out of comet, and return comet dust samples to Earth in 2006. *Stardust* will be the first mission to return with comet samples. Additionally, the *Stardust* spacecraft will bring back samples of interstellar dust, which is believed to include remnants from the formation of the solar system. On April 18, 2002, *Stardust* reached the farthest distance from the Sun ever traveled by a solar-powered spacecraft, 2.72 AU (253 million mi or 407 million km).

### 2001 Mars Odyssey (U.S.)
**Destination:** Mars. **Launch:** April 7, 2001. **Arrival:** Oct. 24, 2001. **Mission:** To conduct mineralogical mapping of the planet and study the radiation risk to humans over the course of three years. A goal of the program is to determine if Mars's atmosphere could support life.

*Mars Odyssey*'s primary mission will continue through Aug. 2004, mapping the amount and distribution of chemical elements and minerals that form the Martian surface and searching especially for evidence of hydrogen in the subsurface. In addition to its scientific mission, *Mars Odyssey* will provide support to other missions in the Mars Exploration Program, serving as the communications relay for U.S. and international spacecraft scheduled to arrive at Mars in 2003 and later. Imaging data will also be used to identify potential landing sites for future Mars missions.

### MAP (U.S.)
**Launched:** June 30, 2001. **Arrival:** Oct. 1, 2001. **Mission:** To reveal conditions as they existed in the early universe by measuring the properties of cosmic microwave background radiation (CMB), the radiant heat left over from the Big Bang, over the full sky. Each sky scan takes approximately six months, and in April 2002, *MAP* completed its first; the second followed in Oct. 2002. The full sky map will be updated as more data is received and analyzed. The release of data from *MAP*'s first full sky scan is expected in Jan. 2003.

### Genesis (U.S.)
**Destination:** The Sun. **Launch:** Aug. 8, 2001. **Mission:** Gather samples of charged particles of the solar wind and return them to Earth in April 2004 for detailed analysis. The reentry vehicle will separate from the spacecraft and parachute its sample return capsule to a location in the Utah desert. The data to be obtained are crucial for improving theories about the origin of the Sun and planets that formed from the same primordial dust cloud.

### Contour (U.S.)
**Destination:** Comet Nucleus Tour. **Launch:** July 3, 2002. **Mission:** To fly by Comet Encke at 60 mi (100 km) in Nov. 2003, followed by encounters with Comet Schwassmann-Wachmann-3 in June 2006, and Comet d'Arrest in Aug. 2008. The spacecraft will take images and spectral maps of nuclei and analyze dust flowing from them. The mission will help scientists to learn more about the composition and structure of comets, which are believed to be quite individual in their properties.

## Future Missions
(Note: Dates are tentative.)

### Mars Exploration Rovers (MER) 2003 (U.S.)
**Destination:** Mars. **First launch:** June 4, 2003. **Arrival:** Jan. 2004. **Second launch:** 2003. **Arrival:** 2004. **Mission:** To deploy two identical large long-range rovers (larger than *Pathfinder*'s *Sojourner*) in two different locations that can trek up to 300 yards (100 m) across the surface in a Martian day. The rovers' sophisticated instruments will enable them to act as mobile field geologists, taking color pictures, analyzing soil and rocks, and searching for past and present evidence of water. The rovers are designed to operate for 90 days but could continue longer.

### Selene SELenological and Engineering Explorer (Japan)
**Destination:** The Moon. **Launch:** 2003. **Mission:** An orbiting spacecraft to study the origin and evolution of the Moon for one year. It will map the entire surface and gather data on chemical and mineralogical composition, magnetic fields, and interior structure. After a year, the propulsion module of the orbiter will separate from the spacecraft and soft-land on the lunar surface to continue the mission for two more months.

### Space Technology 5 (U.S.)
**Destination:** Earth's magnetosphere. **Launch:** 2003. **Mission:** Fourth deployment mission in NASA's New Millennium program. The Nanosat Constellation Trailblazer, known as Space Technology 5 or ST5, will test methods for operating three miniature spacecraft as a single system. Each of the spacecraft is about the size of a birthday cake, 17 in. (42 cm) across by 8 in. (20 cm) high and weighing about 47 lb.

### SPIDR (2005) (U.S.)
**Launch:** 2005. **Mission:** Of NASA's two most recently announced missions, the Explorer for Spectroscopy and Photometry of the Intergalactic Medium's Diffuse Radiation Orbiter, or *SPIDR*, is hoped to help shed light on how galaxies form and evolve by mapping the distribution of hot gas filaments in the nearby universe.

## AIM (U.S.)

**Launch:** 2006. **Mission:** *AIM*, the Aeronomy of Ice in the Mesosphere mission, will be employed to help scientists investigate the causes of the recent rise in noctilucent (glow-in-the-dark) clouds, wispy swirls that form about 50 mi (80 km) above the surface of the earth. The presence of the clouds over the polar regions has increased markedly in recent decades, and is thought by many scientists to be related to higher concentrations of greenhouse gases in Earth's atmosphere.

## Herschel Space Observatory (European Space Agency)

**Destination:** Earth's magnetosphere. **Launch:** 2007. **Mission:** To study how the first stars and galaxies were formed and to search for water in space. Formerly called the Far Infrared and Submillimetre Telescope (FIRST), Herschel will be equipped with an infrared telescope, a high-resolution spectrograph, and two infrared cameras. Construction of the observatory began in the spring of 2002.

## U.S. Unstaffed Planetary and Lunar Programs

**Lunar Orbiter.** Series of spacecraft designed to orbit the Moon, taking pictures and obtaining data in support of the subsequent staffed *Apollo* landings. The U.S. launched five *Lunar Orbiters* between Aug. 10, 1966 and Aug. 2, 1967.

**Mariner.** Designation for a series of spacecraft designed to fly past or orbit the planets, particularly Mercury, Venus, and Mars. *Mariners* provided the early information on Venus and Mars. *Mariner 9*, orbiting Mars in 1971, returned the most revealing photographs of that planet and helped pave the way for a *Viking* landing in 1976. *Mariner 10* explored Venus and Mercury in 1973 and was the first probe to use a planet's gravity to propel it toward another.

**Pioneer.** Designation for the United States' first series of sophisticated interplanetary spacecraft. *Pioneers 10* and *11* reached Jupiter in 1973 and 1974 and continued on to explore Saturn and the other outer planets. *Pioneer 11*, renamed *Pioneer Saturn*, examined the Saturn system in Sept. 1979. Significant discoveries were the finding of a small new moon and a narrow new ring. In 1986, *Pioneer 10* was the first man-made object to escape the solar system. *Pioneer Venus 1* and *2* reached Venus in 1978 and provided detailed information about that planet's surface and atmosphere.

**Ranger.** NASA's earliest Moon-exploration program. Spacecraft were designed for a crash landing on the Moon, taking pictures and returning scientific data up to the moment of impact. Provided the first close-up views of the lunar surface. The *Rangers* provided more than 17,000 close-up pictures, giving us more information about the Moon in a few years than in all the time that had gone before.

**Surveyor.** Series of unstaffed spacecraft designed to land gently on the Moon and provide information on the surface in preparation for the staffed lunar landings. *Surveyor*'s legs were instrumented to return data on the surface hardness of the Moon. *Surveyor* dispelled the fear that *Apollo* spacecraft might sink several feet or more into the lunar dust.

**Viking.** Designation for two spacecraft designed to conduct detailed scientific examination of the planet Mars, including a search for life. *Viking 1* landed on July 20, 1976; *Viking 2*, Sept. 3, 1976. More was learned about the red planet in a few short months than in all previous missions, but the question of whether there is life on Mars remains unresolved.

## Notable Unstaffed Lunar and Interplanetary Probes

| Spacecraft | Launch date | Destination | Remarks |
|---|---|---|---|
| *Pioneer 3* (U.S.) | Dec. 6, 1958 | Moon | Max. alt.: 66,654 mi. Discovered outer Van Allen layer. |
| *Luna 2* (USSR) | Sept. 12, 1959 | Moon | Impacted on Sept. 14. First space vehicle to reach Moon. |
| *Luna 3* (USSR) | Oct. 4, 1959 | Moon | Flew around Moon and transmitted first pictures of lunar far side, Oct. 7. |
| *Mariner 2* (U.S.) | Aug. 27, 1962 | Venus | Venus probe. Successful mid-course correction. Passed 21,648 mi from Venus Dec. 14, 1962. Reported 800°F surface temp. Contact lost Jan. 3, 1963, at 54 million mi. |
| *Ranger 7* (U.S.) | July 28, 1964 | Moon | Impacted near Crater Guericke 68.5 hr after launch. Sent 4,316 pictures during last 15 min. of flight as close as 1,000 ft above lunar surface. |
| *Mariner 4* (U.S.) | Nov. 28, 1964 | Mars | Transmitted first close-up pictures on June 14, 1965, from altitude of 6,000 mi. |
| *Luna 9* (USSR) | Jan. 31, 1966 | Moon | 3,428 lb instrument capsule of 220 lb soft-landed Feb. 3, 1966. Sent back about 30 pictures. |
| *Surveyor 1* (U.S.) | May 30, 1966 | Moon | Landed June 2, 1966. Sent almost 10,400 pictures, a number after surviving the 14-day lunar night. |
| *Lunar Orbiter 1* (U.S.) | Aug. 10, 1966 | Moon | Orbited Moon Aug. 14. 21 pictures sent. |
| *Surveyor 3* (U.S.) | April 17, 1967 | Moon | Soft-landed on Oceanus Procellarum 65 hr after launch. Scooped and tested lunar soil. |
| *Venera 4* (USSR) | June 12, 1967 | Venus | Arrived Oct. 17. Instrument capsule sent temperature and chemical data. |
| *Surveyor 5* (U.S.) | Sept. 8, 1967 | Moon | Landed near lunar equator Sept. 10. Radiological analysis of lunar soil. Mechanical claw for digging soil. |
| *Surveyor 7* (U.S.) | Jan. 6, 1968 | Moon | Landed near Crater Tycho Jan. 10. Soil analysis. Sent 3,343 pictures. |
| *Pioneer 9* (U.S.) | Nov. 8, 1968 | Sun | Achieved orbit. Six experiments returned solar radiation data. |

| Spacecraft | Launch date | Destination | Remarks |
|---|---|---|---|
| *Venera 5* (USSR) | Jan. 5, 1969 | Venus | Landed May 16, 1969. Returned atmospheric data. |
| *Mariner 6* (U.S.) | Feb. 24, 1969 | Mars | Came within 2000 mi of Mars July 31, 1969. Sent back data and TV pictures. |
| *Luna 16* (USSR) | Sept. 12, 1970 | Moon | Soft-landed Sept. 20, scooped up rock, returned to Earth Sept. 24. |
| *Luna 17* (USSR) | Nov. 10, 1970 | Moon | Soft-landed on Sea of Rains Nov. 17. *Lunokhod 1,* self-propelled vehicle, used for first time. Sent TV photos, made soil analysis, etc. |
| *Mariner 9* (U.S.) | May 30, 1971 | Mars | First craft to orbit Mars, Nov. 13. 7,300 pictures, 1st close-ups of one of Mars's moons. Transmission ended Oct. 27, 1972. |
| *Luna 20* (USSR) | Feb. 14, 1972 | Moon | Soft-landed Feb. 21 in Sea of Fertility. Returned Feb. 25 with rock samples. |
| *Pioneer 10* (U.S.) | March 3, 1972 | Jupiter | 620-million-mi flight path through asteroid belt past Jupiter Dec. 3, 1973, to give man first close-up of planet. In 1986, it became first man-made object to escape solar system. |
| *Luna 21* (USSR) | Jan. 8, 1973 | Moon | Soft-landed Jan. 16. *Lunokhod 2* (moon-car) scooped up soil samples, returned them to Earth Jan. 27. |
| *Mariner 10* (U.S.) | Nov. 3, 1973 | Venus, Mercury | Passed Venus Feb. 5, 1974. Arrived Mercury March 29, 1974, for man's first close-up look at planet. First time gravity of one planet (Venus) used to propel spacecraft toward another (Mercury). |
| *Viking 1* (U.S.) | Aug. 20, 1975 | Mars | Carrying life-detection labs. Landed July 20, 1976, for detailed scientific research, including pictures. Designed to work for only 90 days, it operated for almost 6½ years before it went silent in Nov. 1982. |
| *Viking 2* (U.S.) | Sept. 9, 1975 | Mars | Like Viking 1. Landed Sept. 3, 1976. Functioned 3½ years. |
| *Luna 24* (USSR) | Aug. 9, 1976 | Moon | Soft-landed Aug. 18, 1976. Returned soil samples Aug. 22, 1976. |
| *Voyager 2* (U.S.) | Aug. 20, 1977 | Jupiter, Saturn, Uranus | Launched before *Voyager 1.* Encountered Jupiter in July 1979; flew by Saturn Aug. 1981; passed Uranus Jan. 1986; and passed Neptune in Aug. 1989. |
| *Voyager 1* (U.S.) | Sept. 5, 1977 | Jupiter, Saturn | Flyby mission. Reached Jupiter in March 1979; passed Saturn Nov. 1980; passed Uranus 1986. |
| *Pioneer Venus 1* (U.S.) | May 20, 1978 | Venus | Arrived Dec. 4 and orbited Venus, photographing surface and atmosphere. Crashed into planet's surface mid-Oct. 1992 after circling Venus for 14 years. |
| *Pioneer Venus 2* (U.S.) | Aug. 8, 1978 | Venus | Four-part multiprobe, landed Dec. 9. |
| *Venera 13* (USSR) | Oct. 30, 1981 | Venus | Landed March 1, 1982. Took first X-ray fluorescence analysis of the planet's surface. Transmitted data 2 hours, 7 minutes. |
| *VEGA 1* (USSR) | Deployed on Venus, June 10, 1985 | Halley's Comet | In flyby over Venus while en route to encounter Halley's Comet, *VEGA 1* and *2* dropped scientific capsules onto Venus to study atmosphere and surface material. Encountered Halley's Comet on March 6 and March 9, 1986. Took TV pictures and studied comet's dust particles. |
| *VEGA 2* (USSR) | Deployed on Venus, June 14, 1985 | Halley's Comet | See *VEGA 1* above. |
| *Suisei* (Japan) | Encountered Halley's Comet March 8, 1986 | Halley's Comet | Spacecraft made flyby of comet and studied atmosphere with unPrecedented detail of observed rotation nucleus. |
| *Sakigake* (Japan) | Encountered Halley's Comet March 10, 1986 | Halley's Comet | Spacecraft made flyby to study solar wind and magnetic fields. Detected plasma waves. |
| *Giotto* (E.S.A.) | Encountered Halley's Comet March 13, 1986 | Halley's Comet | European Space Agency spacecraft made closest approach to comet. Studied atmosphere and magnetic fields. Sent back best pictures of nucleus. Flew by comet Grigg-Skjellerup July 10, 1992. Unable to send pictures. |

| Spacecraft | Launch date | Destination | Remarks |
|---|---|---|---|
| Phobos Mission (USSR) | July 7 and July 12, 1988 | Mars and Phobos | Two spacecraft to probe Martian moon Phobos starting April 1989. Were to study orbit and soil chemistry, and send TV pictures and data of planet. Contact was lost with Phobos 1 in Aug. 1988 and with Phobos 2 in March 1989 after it reached the Martian moon. |
| Magellan (U.S.) | May 4, 1989 | Venus | Arrived at Venus on Aug. 10, 1990, and made a geologic map of planet with a powerful radar. Crashed into Venus Oct. 12, 1994. |
| Galileo (U.S.) | Oct. 18, 1989 | Jupiter | To study Jupiter's atmosphere and its moons during 22-month mission. |
| Ulysses (U.S., E.S.A.) | Oct. 6, 1990 | Sun | To study the poles of the Sun and interstellar space above and below the poles. First solar encounter was in 1994, second encounter in 1995. |
| Gamma-Ray Observatory (U.S.) | April 7, 1991 | Earth orbit | To make first survey of gamma-ray sources across the whole sky, studying explosive energy sources such as supernovae, quasars, neutron stars, pulsars, and black holes. Mission ended, it was deorbited and crashed into Pacific Ocean, June 4, 2000. |
| Clementine (U.S.) | Jan. 25, 1994 | Moon and asteroid 1620 Geographos | Entered lunar orbit Feb. 21 and took close-up photos of lunar surface for two months. Computer malfunction prevented planned rendezvous with Geographos. |
| Near-Earth Asteroid Rendezvous (NEAR) (U.S.) | Feb. 17, 1996 | asteroid 433 Eros | Photographed asteroid 253 Mathilde June 27, 1997. Entered into orbit around Eros Feb. 14, 2000, and landed on surface in controlled crash Feb. 12, 2001. Took detailed measurements and generated about 160,000 images of Eros. Renamed NEAR-Shoemaker in honor of geologist Eugene M. Shoemaker. First craft to orbit an asteroid. |
| Mars Pathfinder (U.S.) | Dec. 5, 1996 | Ares Vallis, Mars | Landed July 4, 1997. The spacecraft lander and its rover, Sojourner, provided a wealth of information on the Martian rocks, soil, and atmosphere. Sent back the first live pictures. All Pathfinder's objectives were fulfilled and communications failed on Sept. 27, 1997. |
| Lunar Prospector (U.S.) | Jan. 6, 1998 | Moon | Orbited Moon for one year, mapped chemical composition of lunar surface. Found frozen water at north and south poles. At end of its mission on July 31, 1999, it was intentionally crashed into south polar crater in hope of detecting plume of water ice, but no cloud of molecular water vapor was observed by powerful Earth telescopes. |
| Deep Space 1 (U.S.) | Oct. 24, 1998 | Deep space | The first launch of NASA's New Millennium Program, a series of missions to test new technologies. Famous for its July 1999 photos of the near-Earth Braille asteroid and the first-ever photos of a comet nucleus when it staged a risky flyby of the comet Borelly in Sept. 2001. |

## U.S. Staffed Space Flight Programs

**Mercury.** *Project Mercury,* initiated in 1958 and completed in 1963, was the United States' first human-in-space program. It was designed to further knowledge about humanity's capabilities in space.

In April 1959, seven military-jet test pilots were introduced to the public as America's first astronauts. They were: Lt. M. Scott Carpenter, USN; Capt. L. Gordon Cooper, Jr., USAF; Lt. Col. John H. Glenn, Jr., USMC; Cap. Virgil I. Grissom, USAF; Lt. Cdr. Walter M. Schirra, Jr., USN; Lt. Cdr. Alan B. Shepard, Jr., USN; and Capt. Donald K. Slayton, USAF. Six of the original seven would make a Mercury flight. Slayton was grounded for medical reasons but remained a director of NASA's astronaut office. He returned to flight status in 1975 as Docking Module Pilot on the *Apollo-Soyuz* flight.

### Flight Summary

Each astronaut named his capsule and added the numeral 7 to denote the teamwork of the original astronauts.

**May 5, 1961.** Alan B. Shepard, Jr., made a suborbital flight in *Freedom 7* and became the first American in space. Time: 15 minutes, 22 seconds.

**July 21, 1961.** Virgil I. Grissom made the second successful suborbital flight in *Liberty Bell 7,* but spacecraft sank shortly after splashdown. Time: 15 minutes, 37 seconds. Grissom was later killed in *Apollo 1* fire, Jan. 27, 1967.

**Feb. 20, 1962.** John H. Glenn, Jr., made a three-orbit flight and became the first American in orbit. Time: 4 hours, 55 minutes.

**May 24, 1962.** M. Scott Carpenter duplicated Glenn's flight in *Aurora 7.* Time: 4 hours, 56 minutes.

**Oct. 3, 1962.** Walter M. Schirra, Jr., made a six-orbit engineering test flight in *Sigma 7.* Time: 9 hours, 13 minutes.

**May 15–16, 1963.** L. Gordon Cooper, Jr., performed the last *Mercury* mission and completed 22 orbits in *Faith 7* to evaluate effects of one day in space. Time: 34 hours, 19 minutes.

## The Women in Space Program

In 1960, NASA also tested the first female trainees for astronaut duty in the *Mercury* program. Thirteen out of America's 25 top female civilian pilots (women weren't allowed to be military pilots then) passed the same rigorous testing that male candidates underwent in the *Mercury 7* space program. Although all the pilots proved fit to become *Mercury* astronauts, NASA suddenly canceled its testing of qualified women in July 1961, claiming that they required jet test-pilot training at Edwards Air Force Base. Unfortunately, instruction at Edwards was closed to women. This new requirement ended America's chance to put the first women in space.

It is ironic that unlike her skilled American counterparts, Valentina Tereshkova, the first woman to fly in space, was a textile factory worker when she entered the Soviet space program. She had no experience as a pilot and her only qualification was that of an amateur parachute jumper before being trained as a cosmonaut in 1962.

These outstanding "Mercury 13" candidates deserve much credit for preparing the way for American women in space. They were: Jerrie Cobb, Rhea Allison, Jane Hart, Mary Wallace Funk, Jean Hixson, Myrtle Cagle, Irene Leverton, Sarah Gorelick, twins Jan and Marion Dietrich, Gene Stumbough, Bernice Steadman, and Gerry Sloan Truhill.

**Gemini.** *Gemini* was an extension of *Project Mercury,* to determine the effects of prolonged space flight on humans for two weeks or longer—the time it would take to reach the Moon and return. "Walks in space" provided invaluable information for astronauts' later walks on the Moon. The *Gemini* spacecraft, twice as large as the *Mercury* capsule, accommodated two astronauts. Its crew named the project *Gemini* for the third constellation of the Zodiac and its twin stars, Castor and Pollux. The capsule differed from the *Mercury* spacecrafts in that it had hatches above the capsules so that the astronauts could leave the spacecraft and perform spacewalks or extra-vehicular activities (EVAs).

There were 10 staffed flights in the *Gemini* program, starting with *Gemini 3* on March 23, 1965, and ending with the *Gemini 12* mission on Nov. 15, 1966. *Gemini 1* and *2* were unstaffed test flights of the equipment.

**Apollo.** *Apollo* was the designation for the United States' effort to land a person on the Moon and return him safely to Earth. The goal was successfully accomplished with *Apollo 11* on July 20, 1969, culminating eight years of work and over worth of planning. Astronauts Neil A. Armstrong and Col. Edwin E. Aldrin, Jr., scooped up and brought back the first lunar rocks ever seen on Earth—about 47 pounds.

Tragedy struck Jan. 27, 1967, on the launch pad during a preflight test of what would have become *Apollo 1,* the first staffed mission. Astronauts Lt. Col. Virgil "Gus" Grissom, Lt. Col. Edward H. White, and Lt. Cdr. Roger Chafee lost their lives when a fire swept through the command module.

Six *Apollo* flights followed, ending with *Apollo 17* in December 1972. The last three *Apollos* carried mechanized vehicles called lunar rovers for wide-ranging surface exploration of the Moon by astronauts. The rendezvous and docking of an *Apollo*

spacecraft with a Russian *Soyuz* craft in Earth orbit on July 18, 1975, closed out the *Apollo* program.

During the Apollo project, the following 12 astronauts explored the lunar terrain: Col. Edwin E. "Buzz" Aldrin, Jr., and Neil A. Armstrong, *Apollo 11;* Cdr. Alan L. Bean and Cdr. Charles "Pete" Conrad, Jr., *Apollo 12;* Edgar D. Mitchell and Alan B. Shepard, *Apollo 14;* Lt. Col. James B. Irwin and Col. David R. Scott, *Apollo 15;* Col. Charles M. Duke, Jr., and Capt. John W. Young, *Apollo 16;* and Capt. Eugene A. Cernan and Dr. Harrison H. Schmitt, *Apollo 17.*

*Apollo* was a three-part spacecraft: the command module (CM), the crew's quarters and flight control section; the service modules (SM) for the propulsion and spacecraft support systems (when together, the two modules were called CSM); and the lunar module (LM) that took two of the crew to the lunar surface, supported them on the Moon, and returned them to the CSM in orbit.

The third lunar attempt, *Apollo 13,* April 11–17, 1970, 5 days, 22.9 hours, was aborted after the service module oxygen tank ruptured. The *Apollo 13* crew members were James A. Lovell, Jr., John L. Swigert, Jr., and Fred W. Haise, Jr. The mission was classified as a "successful failure" because the crew was rescued.

**Skylab.** America's first Earth-orbiting space station. *Project Skylab* was designed to demonstrate that men can work and live in space for prolonged periods without ill effects. Originally the spent third stage of a *Saturn 5* Moon rocket, *Skylab* measured 118 ft from stem to stern, and carried the most varied assortment of experimental equipment ever assembled in a single spacecraft. Three three-man crews visited the space stations, spending more than 740 hours observing the Sun and bringing home more than 175,000 solar pictures. These were the first recordings of solar activity above Earth's obscuring atmosphere. *Skylab* also evaluated systems designed to gather information on Earth's resources and environmental conditions. *Skylab's* biomedical findings indicated that humans adapt well to space for at least a period of three months, provided they have a proper diet and adequately programmed exercise, sleep, work, and recreation periods. *Skylab* orbited Earth at a distance of about 300 mi. Five years after the last *Skylab* mission, the 77-ton space station's orbit began to deteriorate faster than expected, owing to unexpectedly high sunspot activity. On July 11, 1979, the parts of *Skylab* that did not burn up in the atmosphere came crashing down on parts of Australia and the Indian Ocean. No one was hurt.

**Space Shuttle.** The space shuttle *Columbia* was successfully launched on April 12, 1981. It made five flights (the first four were test runs), the last completed on Nov. 16, 1982. The second shuttle, *Challenger,* made its maiden flight on April 4, 1983. The third shuttle, *Discovery,* made its first flight on Aug. 30, 1984. The fourth space shuttle, *Atlantis,* made its maiden flight on Oct. 3, 1985.

A tragedy occurred on Jan. 28, 1986, when the shuttle *Challenger* exploded, killing the crew of seven 73 seconds after takeoff. It was the world's worst space flight disaster.

The crew members who were killed were: Francis R. Scobee, shuttle commander; Cdr. Michael J.

Smith, pilot; mission specialists Judith A. Resnik, Lt. Col. Ellison S. Onizuka, and Ronald E. McNair; and payload specialists Gregory B. Jarvis and Christa McAuliffe (who was to be the first civilian schoolteacher in space).

The cause of the explosion was a rupture in a seal on one of the booster rockets that let a jet of flame escape, igniting the fuel. The weakness in the seal was caused by the cold air temperature when the shuttle was launched.

The first U.S. space mission since the *Challenger* disaster was launched 32 months later, on Sept. 29, 1988, with the flight of *Discovery.* It had a crew of five and deployed a communications satellite.

The fifth orbiter, *Endeavour,* was built as a replacement for *Challenger.* It was named after the 16th-century British explorer James Cook's first ship. *Endeavour* was launched on its maiden voyage on May 7, 1992, with a crew of seven astronauts. They made four spacewalks and retrieved a disabled *Intelsat-6* communications satellite. During the mission, Dr. Kathryn Thornton became the second American woman to walk in space.

The shuttle *Columbia* spent a record 17 days, 15 hours in space, Nov. 19–Dec. 7, 1996.

The crew of the 50th mission aboard the *Endeavour,* launched Sept. 12, 1992, included the first black woman astronaut, Dr. Mae C. Jemison, and the first married couple to fly together in space, Air Force Lt. Col. Mark C. Lee and Dr. N. Jan Davis.

Lt. Col. Eileen M. Collins became the first woman to pilot a shuttle, *Discovery,* during the spacecraft's historic rendezvous with the Russian space station *Mir* on Feb. 6, 1995. The shuttle *Atlantis* made the first link-up with the *Mir* on June 29, 1995.

Lt. Col. Collins became the first woman to command a space shuttle when *Columbia* was launched in July 1999 on a mission to deploy the Chandra X-ray Observatory (formerly called AXAF).

Senator John Glenn, 76, the first American to orbit the Earth, flew as a payload specialist on the Oct. 1998 *Discovery* mission. He studied the effects of aging and microgravity on the human body.

In recent years, many of NASA's human spaceflight expeditions have involved improvement of the International Space Station. On May 27, 1999, the

space shuttle *Discovery* began Flight STS-96, the first shuttle docking to the International Space Station. Crewmembers brought new equipment to better operations between the Unity and Zarya modules, including nearly 1,360 kg of equipment for use by future ISS astronauts. In 2000, work on the ISS continued; two successive *Atlantis* missions spent several days making improvements. On Nov. 2, 2001, the ISS celebrated its first full year of continuous international human presence in space. On June 19, 2002, Capt. Daniel Bursch and Col. Carl Walz broke the U.S. record for space flight endurance, having spent 196 days aboard the International Space Station.

## Soviet Staffed Space Flight Programs

**Vostok.** The Soviets' first staffed capsule, roughly spherical, used to place the first six cosmonauts in Earth orbit (1961–1965).

**Voskhod.** Adaptation of the *Vostok* capsule to accommodate two and three cosmonauts. *Voskhod 1* orbited three persons, and *Voskhod 2* orbited two persons, performing the world's first staffed extravehicular activity.

**Soyuz.** Late-model staffed spacecraft with provisions for three cosmonauts and a "working compartment" accessible through a hatch. Soyuz is the Russian word for "union." The *Soyuz* spacecraft can carry three cosmonauts, and routinely brought cosmonauts and their foreign "guests" to the *Mir* space station. *Soyuz 19,* launched July 15, 1975, docked with the American *Apollo* spacecraft.

**Salyut.** Earth-orbiting space station intended for prolonged occupancy and revisitation by cosmonauts. They were usually launched by Soviet Proton rockets. *Salyut 1* was launched April 19, 1971. *Salyut 2,* launched April 3, 1973, malfunctioned in orbit and was never occupied. *Salyut 3* was launched June 25, 1974. *Salyut 4* was launched Dec. 26, 1974. *Salyut 5* was launched June 22, 1976. *Salyut 6* was launched on Sept. 29, 1977. *Salyut 7* was launched on April 19, 1982. A record-breaking Russian endurance flight was set (Feb. 8, 1984–Oct. 2, 1985) when Soviet astronauts spent 237 days in orbit aboard *Salyut 7.* *Salyut 7* reentered the atmosphere and crashed into the Atlantic Ocean on Feb. 6, 1991.

**Mir.** Soviet space station, launched into orbit on Feb. 20, 1986. The Russian government had planned to deorbit the abandoned *Mir* in early 2000 due to lack of funds, but the space station got a new lease on life when private investors provided the cash to keep the craft in orbit. The new Russian partners, MirCorp, a Netherlands-based company, funded cosmonauts Sergei Zaloytin and Alexander Kaleri's return mission to reopen and repair the *Mir,* April 4 to June 15, 2000. However, *Mir* was deorbited on March 23, 2001.

Since the deorbiting of *Mir,* Russia's space program has revolved around projects at the International Space Station. Financial problems continue to curb cosmonaut capabilities, forcing the Russian Space Agency to seek funds elsewhere: in 2001, American businessman Dennis Tito paid a reported $20 million to become the world's first space tourist aboard a Russian spacecraft.

---

### Space Websites

**European Space Agency (ESA):** www.esrin.esa.it
**Liftoff to Space Exploration:** liftoff.msfc.nasa.gov
**Lunar Prospector:** lunar.arc.nasa.gov
**NASA Astronaut Biographies:**
  www.jsc.nasa.gov/Bios/index.html
**NASA homepage:** www.nasa.gov
**NASA Jet Propulsion Laboratory:** www.jpl.nasa.gov
**NASA Spaceflight page:** www.spaceflight.nasa.gov
**National Air & Space Museum:** www.nasm.edu
**National Space Society:** www.nss.org
**The Planetary Society:** www.planetary.org
**SETI Institute:** www.seti-inst.edu
**Skywatch:**
  http://spaceflight.nasa.gov/realdata/sightings
**SpaceViews online magazine:** www.spaceviews.com
**Space Research Institute (Russia):** www.iki.rssi.ru
**Students for the Exploration and Development of Space:** www.seds.org
**Planet Quest:** http://planetquest.jpl.nasa.gov

## China's Unstaffed Spacecraft

China launched its first unstaffed spacecraft from the Jiuquan Space Center in Gansu province on Nov. 19, 1999. The space capsule, named *Shenzhou* ("Divine Ship"), made 14 orbits of Earth in 21 hours before landing in Inner Mongolia.

The *Shenzhou* spacecraft are prototypes for future manned Chinese spacecraft. A small menagerie of passengers on board *Shenzhou II* (launched Jan. 9, 2001), including a rabbit, a dog, and a monkey, survived the shuttle's space-flight unharmed. The subsequent success of *Shenzhou III*, which was equipped with dummy astronauts and human physical monitoring sensors, further enhanced China's hopes of having Chinese *taikonauts* take their place in space next to Russia's cosmonauts and America's astronauts by 2005. *Shenzhou III* was launched from Jiuquan on March 25, 2002, and spent a week in orbit before landing, as had its predecessors, in Inner Mongolia. The next step, the setup of space labs manned by scientists, should set the stage for the eventual construction of a permanent Chinese space station.

## Notable Staffed Space Flights

| Designation and country | Date | Astronauts | Flight time (hr/min) | Remarks |
|---|---|---|---|---|
| *Vostok 1* (USSR) | April 12, 1961 | Yuri A. Gagarin | 1/48 | First person in space. |
| *MR III* (U.S.) | May 5, 1961 | Alan B. Shepard, Jr. | 0/15 | Range 486 km (302 mi), peak 187 km (116.5 mi); capsule recovered. First American in space. |
| *Vostok 2* (USSR) | Aug. 6–7, 1961 | Gherman S. Titov | 25/18 | First long-duration flight. |
| *MA VI* (U.S.) | Feb. 20, 1962 | John H. Glenn, Jr. | 4/55 | First American in orbit. |
| *MA IX* (U.S.) | May 15–16, 1963 | L. Gordon Cooper, Jr. | 34/20 | Longest *Mercury* flight. |
| *Vostok 6* (USSR) | June 16–19, 1963 | Valentina V. Tereshkova | 70/50 | First woman in space. |
| *Voskhod 1* (USSR) | Oct. 12, 1964 | Vladimir M. Komarov, Konstantin P. Feoktistov, Boris G. Yegorov | 24/17 | First 3-person orbital flight; also first flight without space suits. |
| *Voskhod 2* (USSR) | March 18, 1965 | Alexei A. Leonov, Pavel I. Belyayev | 26/2 | First "space walk" (by Leonov), 10 min. |
| *GT III* (U.S.) | March 23, 1965 | Virgil I. Grissom, John W. Young | 4/53 | First American 2-person crew. |
| *GT IV* (U.S.) | June 3–7, 1965 | James A. McDivitt, Edward H. White, II | 97/48 | First American "space walk" (by White), lasting slightly over 20 min. |
| *GT VIII* (U.S.) | March 16–17, 1966 | Neil A. Armstrong, David R. Scott | 10/42 | First docking between staffed spacecraft and an unstaffed space vehicle (an orbiting *Agena* rocket). |
| *Apollo 7* (U.S.) | Oct. 11–22, 1968 | Walter M. Schirra, Jr., Donn F. Eisele, R. Walter Cunningham | 260/9 | First staffed test of *Apollo* command module; first live TV transmissions from orbit. |
| *Soyuz 3* (USSR) | Oct. 26–30, 1968 | Georgi T. Bergeovoi | 94/51 | First staffed rendezvous and possible docking by Soviet cosmonaut. |
| *Apollo 8* (U.S.) | Dec. 21–27, 1968 | Frank Borman, James A. Lovell, Jr., William A. Anders | 147/00 | First spacecraft in circumlunar orbit; TV transmissions from this orbit. The three astronauts were also the first astronauts to view the whole Earth. |
| *Apollo 9* (U.S.) | Mar. 3–13, 1969 | James A. McDivitt, David R. Scott, Russell L. Schweikart | 241/1 | First staffed flight of Lunar Module. |
| *Apollo 10* (U.S.) | May 18–26, 1969 | Thomas P. Stafford, Eugene A. Cernan, John W. Young | 192/3 | First descent to within nine miles of Moon's surface by staffed craft. |
| *Apollo 11* (U.S.) | July 16–24, 1969 | Neil A. Armstrong, Edwin E. Aldrin, Jr., Michael Collins | 195/18 | First staffed landing and EVA on Moon; soil and rock samples collected; experiments left on lunar surface. |
| *Soyuz 6* (USSR) | Oct. 11–16, 1969 | Gorgiy Shonin, Valriy Kabasov | 118/42 | Three spacecraft and seven men put into Earth orbit simultaneously for first time |
| *Apollo 12* (U.S.) | Nov. 11–24, 1969 | Charles Conrad, Jr., Richard F. Gordon, Jr., Alan Bean | 244/36 | Second staffed lunar mission; investigated *Surveyor 3* spacecraft; collected lunar samples. EVA time: 15 hr 30 min. |
| *Apollo 13* (U.S.) | April 11–17, 1970 | James A. Lovell, Jr., Fred W. Haise, Jr., John L. Swigert, Jr. | 142/54 | Third staffed lunar landing attempt, aborted due to pressure loss in liquid oxygen in service module and failure of fuel cells. |
| *Apollo 14* (U.S.) | Jan. 31–Feb. 9, 1971 | Alan B. Shepard, Stuart A. Roosa, Edgar D. Mitchell | 216/42 | Third staffed lunar landing: returned largest amount of lunar material. |
| *Soyuz 11* (USSR) | June 6–30, 1971 | Georgiy Tomofeyevich Dobrovolskiy, Vladislav Nikolayevich Volkov, Viktor Ivanovich Patsyev | 569/40 | Longest stay in space. Linked up with first space station, *Salyut 1*. Astronauts died just before reentry due to loss of pressurization in spacecraft. |
| *Apollo 15* (U.S.) | July 26–Aug. 7, 1971 | David R. Scott, James B. Irwin, Alfred M. Worden | 295/12 | Fourth staffed lunar landing; first use of lunar rover propelled by Scott and Irwin; first live pictures of LM lift-off from Moon; exploration time: 18 hr. |

| Designation and country | Date | Astronauts | Flight time (hr/min) | Remarks |
|---|---|---|---|---|
| Apollo 16 (U.S.) | April 16–27, 1972 | John W. Young, Thomas K. Mattingly, Charles M. Duke, Jr. | 265/51 | Fifth staffed lunar landing; second use of lunar rover vehicle, propelled by Young and Duke. Total exploration time on the Moon was 20 hr., 14 min., setting new record. Mattingly's in-flight "walk in space" was 1 hr., 23 min. Approximately 213 lb of lunar rock returned. |
| Apollo 17 (U.S.) | Dec. 7–19, 1972 | Eugene A. Cernan, Ronald E. Evans, Harrison H. Schmitt | 301/51 | Sixth and last staffed lunar landing; third to carry lunar rover. Cernan and Schmitt, during three EVAs, completed total of 22 hr., 05 min., 3 sec. USS Ticonderoga recovered crew and about 250 lbs of lunar samples. |
| Skylab SL-2 (U.S.) | May 25–June 22, 1973 | Charles Conrad, Jr., Joseph P. Kerwin, Paul J. Weitz | 672/50 | First staffed Skylab launch. Established Skylab Orbital Assembly and conducted scientific and medical experiments. |
| Skylab SL-3 (U.S.) | July 28–Sept. 25, 1973 | Alan L. Bean, Jr., Jack R. Lousma, Owen K. Garriott | 1427/9 | Second staffed Skylab launch. New crew remained in space for 59 days, continuing scientific and medical experiments and Earth observations from orbit. |
| Skylab SL-4 (U.S.) | Nov. 16, 1973– Feb. 8, 1974 | Gerald Carr, Edward Gibson, William Pogue | 2017/16 | Third staffed Skylab launch; obtained medical data on crew for use in extending the duration of staffed space flight; crews "walked in space" 4 times, totaling 44 hr., 40 min. Longest space mission yet: 84 d, 1 hr., 16 min. Splashdown in Pacific, Feb. 9, 1974. |
| Apollo/Soyuz Test Project (U.S. and USSR) | July 15–24, 1975 (U.S.) | U.S.: Brig. Gen. Thomas P. Stafford, Vance D. Brand, Donald K. Slayton | 216/05 | World's first international staffed rendezvous and docking in space; aimed at developing a space rescue capability. |
| Apollo/Soyuz Test Project (U.S. and USSR) | July 15–21, 1975 (USSR) | USSR: Col. A. A. Leonov, V. N. Kubasov | 223/35 | Apollo and Soyuz docked and crewmen exchanged visits on July 17, 1975. Mission duration for Soyuz: 142 hr., 31 min. For Apollo: 217 hr., 28 min. |
| Columbia (U.S.) | April 12–14, 1981 | Capt. Robert L. Crippen, John W. Young | 54/20 | Maiden voyage of space shuttle. |
| Mir (USSR) | Dec. 21, 1987– Dec. 21, 1988 | Col. Vladimir Titov, Musa Manarov | 366 days | Set current record for Soviet team endurance flight in orbiting space station. |
| Endeavour (U.S.) | May 7–16, 1992 | Richard J. Hieb, Maj. Thomas D. Akers, Cdr. Pierre J. Thugt | 8 days, 23 hr., 17 min. | The three mission specialists remained free of the Endeavour for 8 hr., 20 min. on May 13 during the repair of communications satellite, setting an absolute record for extravehicular duration in space. First capture of a satellite using hands only. |
| Endeavour (U.S.) | Dec. 2–13, 1993 | Col. Richard O. Covey, Cdr. Kenneth D. Bowersox, Lt. Col. Tom Akers, Dr. Jeffrey A. Hoffman, Dr. Story Musgrave, Claude Nicollier, Dr. Kathryn C. Thornton | 10 days, 19 hr., 59 min. | Repaired Hubble Space Telescope. Replaced gyroscopes, solar arrays, camera, electronics, and hardware. Installed COSTAR corrective optics to compensate for flaw in Hubble's primary mirror. Record five space walks in a single mission. |
| Mir-17 (Russia) | Jan. 8, 1994– Mar. 22, 1995 | Dr. Valery Polyakov | 439[1] days | Record single endurance flight in orbiting space station. Returned to Earth with crewmates cosmonaut Helena Kondakova and commander Alexander Viktorenko, who spent 169 days each in Mir. |
| Discovery (U.S.) | Feb. 3–11, 1995 | Cdr. James D. Wetherbee, Lt. Col. Eileen M. Collins, Dr. Janice Voss, Dr. Bernard A. Harris, Jr., Dr. C. Michael Foale, Russian cosmonaut Co. Vladimir G. Titov | 8 days, 6 hr., 29 min. | First rendezvous of U.S. spacecraft with a Russian space station (Mir), Feb. 6. Lt. Col. Collins was first female shuttle pilot. Deployed and retrieved solar observatory satellite. Extravehicular activity to test new space suit modifications and practice space station assembly techniques. EVA time: 4 hr., 35 min. |
| Soyuz TM-21 (Russia) | March 14–22, 1995 | Russian cosmonauts Lt. Col. Vladimir N. Dezhurov and Gennady M. Strekalov, and U.S. astronaut Dr. Norman E. Thagard | | Dr. Thagard became the first American astronaut to fly aboard a Soyuz spacecraft with a Russian crew launched from Baikonur Space Center in Kazakhstan. He also became the first American to enter the Mir space station on March 16. |

| Designation and country | Date | Astronauts | Flight time (hr/min) | Remarks |
|---|---|---|---|---|
| Atlantis (U.S.) | June 27–July 7, 1995 | Lt. Col. Charles J. Prescourt, Capt. Robert L. (Hoot) Gibson, Dr. Eileen S. Baker, Gregory J. Harbaugh, Dr. Bonnie Dunbar, Russian cosmonauts: Mir-19 commander Anatoly Y. Solovyev, Nikolai M. Budarin | 10 days | Marked 100th human mission in U.S. space program and first shuttle link-up with Mir: docked June 29, undocked July 4. Joined spacecraft held a record 10 people: 6 Americans and 4 Russians. Three Mir crew (Mir-18 commander Lt. Col. Vladimir N. Dezhurov, cosmonaut Grennady M. Strekalov, and U.S. astronaut Dr. Norman E. Thagard) returned to Earth aboard the Atlantis. Dr. Thagard set a U.S. space record of 112 days in space aboard Mir. Cosmonauts Solovyev and Budarin remained aboard Mir. |
| Atlantis (U.S.) | Nov. 12–20, 1995 | Col. Kenneth D. Cameron, Lt. Col. James D. Halsell, Jr., Col. Jerry L. Ross, Lt. Col. William S. McArthur, Jr., Canadian Major Chris A. Hadfield, who operated the robot arm | 8 days, 4 hr., 31 min. | Second docking with Mir. Carried 15-foot-long Russian-made docking module and attached it to Mir. Brought 2 new solar-powered panels for Mir and also supplies and scientific equipment. U.S. and Russian astronauts spent 3 days together on Mir conducting experiments. |
| Endeavour (U.S.) | Jan. 11–20, 1996 | Col. Brian Duffy, Brent Jett, Dr. Leroy Chiao, Capt. Winston E. Scott, Dr. Daniel T. Berry, and Japanese astronaut Koichi Wakata, who operated robot arm | 8 days, 22 hr., 1 min. | Deployed and retrieved NASA satellite, retrieved Japanese satellite. Two spacewalks performed to test spacesuit components and practice space station construction, tools, and techniques. Total EVA time: 13 hr. |
| Atlantis (U.S.) | March 22–31, 1996 | Col. Kevin P. Chilton, Lt. Col. Richard A. Searfoss, Dr. Ronald M. Sega, Dr. Linda M. Goodwin, Lt. Col. Michael R. Clifford, Shannon W. Lucid | 9 days, 5 hr., 15 min. | Third link-up with Mir (March 22–27). Clifford and Goodwin conducted 6-hour spacewalk in shuttle cargo bay while docked with Mir. Lucid remained on board Mir for scheduled 140-day tour to conduct biomedical and material science experiments. Booster problems delayed her return until mid-September. Lucid was first American woman to live on Mir. On July 15, 1996, she broke the previous record for the longest U.S. manned space flight. |
| Endeavour (U.S.) | May 19–29, 1996 | Col. John H. Casper, Lt. Col. Curtis L. Brown, Jr., Cdr. Daniel W. Bursch, Mario Runco, Jr., Dr. Andrew S.W. Thomas, Canadian astronaut Dr. Marc Garneau | 10 days, 0 hr., 40 min. | Made record of four satellite rendezvous, including three with small PAMS satellite to test the concept of a self-stabilizing satellite in orbit. Deployed and retrieved a Spartan satellite that carried an experimental inflatable antenna. |
| Columbia (U.S.) | June 20–July 7, 1996 | Col. Terence T. Henricks, Kevin R. Kregel, Lt. Col. Susan J. Helms, Richard M. Linnehan, Cdr. Charles E. Brady, Jr., Dr. Jean-Jacques Favier (France), Dr. Robert Brent Thirsk (Canada) | 16 days, 21 hr., 48 min. | Second-longest mission to date. Studied the effects of weightlessness on people, plants, and animals, and material manufacturing in near-zero gravity. |
| Atlantis (U.S.) | Sept. 16–26, 1996 | William F. Readdy, Terrence W. Wilcutt, Thomas D. Akers, John E. Blaha, Jerome Apt, Carl E. Walz. Download: Shannon W. Lucid | 10 days, 3hr., 19 min. | Fourth Mir docking. Carried a Spacelab module. Transferred supplies and equipment to Mir. After breaking all American and women's space endurance records (188 days 5 hr 0 min), Lucid returned with shuttle crew. John E. Blaha remained on Mir for a four-month stay. |
| Columbia (U.S.) | Nov. 19–Dec. 7, 1996 | Kenneth D. Cockrell, Cdr. Kent V. Rominger, Tamara E. Jornigan, Thomas D. Jones, Dr. F. Story Musgrave | 17 days, 18 hr., 50 min. | Deployed and recovered two free-flying satellites, an ultraviolet telescope and Wake Shield (semiconductor processing) Facility. Is longest mission to date. Dr. Musgrave, 61, became first person to fly on all five space shuttles. |
| Atlantis (U.S.) | Jan. 12–22, 1997 | Capt. Michael A. Baker, Cdr. Brent W. Jett, Jr., John M. Grunsfeld, Marsha S. Ivins, Peter J.K. Wiscoff, Dr. Jerry L. Linenger. Download: John E. Blaha | 10 days, 4 hr., 6 min. | Fifth Mir docking (Jan.14–19). Carried Spacehab double module. Transferred supplies to Mir. Conducted experiments in Spacehab and Mir. John E. Blaha returned with Atlantis crew after 128 days in space, 118 aboard Mir. Jerry Linenger remained aboard Mir for 4.5-month stay. |

| Designation and country | Date | Astronauts | Flight time (hr/min) | Remarks |
|---|---|---|---|---|
| *Discovery* (U.S.) | Feb. 11–21, 1997 | Cdr. Kenneth Bowersox, Lt. Col. Scott J. Harowitz, Col. Mark C. Lee, Steven A. Hawley, Gregory J. Harbaugh, Steven L. Smith, Joseph R. Tanner | 9 days, 23 hr., 38 min. | Second space telescope servicing mission. Installed new imaging spectrograph and infrared camera. Also patched torn telescope insulating cover. Deployed telescope at higher altitude: 335 x 321 nautical mile orbit. Mission required five spacewalks totaling 33 hr., 11 min. |
| *Atlantis* (U.S.) | May 15–24, 1997 | Col. Charles J. Precourt, Lt. Col. Eileen M. Collins, Edward T. Lu, Maj. Carlos I. Noriega, Jean-François Clervoy (France), Elena V. Kondakova (Russia), C. Michael Foale. Download: Dr. Jerry M. Linenger | 9 days, 5 hr., 20 min. | Sixth *Mir* docking (May 16–21). Carried a Spacehab double module. Transferred supplies and equipment. Jerry M. Linenger returned with *Atlantis* after 132 days in space. Michael Foale remained on *Mir* for a 4.5-month stay. |
| *Atlantis* (U.S.) | Sept. 25–Oct. 6, 1997 | James T. Wetherbee, Michael J. Boomfield, Col. Vladimir G Titov, Scott E. Parazynski, Jean-Loup J.M. Chretien (France), Wendy B. Lawrence. Up: Dr. David Wolf. Down: C. Michael Foale after 145 days in space, 134 days on *Mir* | 10 days, 19 hr., 22 min. | Seventh Mir docking (Sept. 27–Oct. 3). 5-hr. spacewalks (Oct.1) retrieved U.S. experimental packages from *Mir* for return to Earth. Transferred supplies. Tested emergency jet packs for space station workers. Dr. David Wolf replaced Michael Foale on *Mir* for 4-month stay. |
| *Endeavour* (U.S.) | Jan. 22–31, 1998 | Lt. Col. Terrence W. Wilcutt, Joe F. Edwards, Bonnie J. Dunbar, Maj. Michael P. Anderson, James F. Reilly, II, Salizhan S. Sharipov (Kirghizia), Andrew S.W. Thomas. Down: Dr. David Wol | 8 days, 19 hr., 48 min. | Eighth *Mir* docking (Jan. 24–29). Thomas replaced David Wolf after 128 days in orbit. Thomas is the seventh and last American to live aboard *Mir*. |
| *Discovery* (U.S.) | June 2–12, 1998 | Col. Charles J. Precourt, Cmdr. Dominic L. Gorie, Cmdr. Wendy B. Lawrence, Franklin R. Chang-Diaz, Janet Kavandi, Valeriy Ruymin (Russia) Down: Andrew S.W. Thomas | 9 days, 19 hr., 54 min. | Ninth and final *Mir* docking mission concluded the joint U.S.–Russian program as a precursor to the International Space Station partnership. Thomas returned to Earth after a 4.5-month stay. |
| *Discovery* (U.S.) | Oct. 29–Nov.7, 1998 | Lt. Col. Curtis L. Brown, Maj. Steven W. Lindsey, Stephen K. Robinson, Dr. Scott E. Parazynski, Pedro Duque (Spain), Dr. Chiaki Mukai (Japan), Senator John H. Glenn, Jr. | 8 days, 21 hr., 56 min. | Deployed and retrieved *Spartan* solar observing satellite. Did research with Hubble Telescope Optical Systems Test Platform (HOST). Studied the effects of aging and microgravity in space. |
| *Endeavour* (U.S.) | Dec. 4–15, 1998 | Capt. Robert D. Cabana, Capt. Frederick W. Sturckow, Lt. Col. Nancy Currie, Col. Jerry L. Ross, James H. Newman, Sergei K. Krikalev (Russia) | 11 days, 19 hr., 18 min. | International Space Station assembly mission. Connected Node 1, "Unity," to Functional Cargo Block, "Zarya." Ross and Newman made three spacewalks, total EVA: 21 hr., 22 min. |
| *Discovery* (U.S.) | May 27–June 6, 1999 | Cmdr. Ken V. Rominger, Rick D. Husband, Ellen Ochoa, Tamara E. Jernigan, Daniel T. Barry, Julie Payette (Canada), Valery Tokarev (Russia) | 9 days, 19 hr., 13 min. | Docked 5 days, 18 hr. with uninhabited International Space Station. Readied it for arrival of first resident crew. Jernigan and Barry conducted space walks (7 hr., 55 min.) for assembly work. |
| *Columbia* (U.S.) | July 22–27, 1999 | Lt. Col. Eileen M. Collins, Capt. Jeffrey S. Ashby, Steven A. Hawley, Lt. Col. Catherine G. Coleman, Col. Michel Tognini (France) | 4 days, 22 hr., 50 min. | Deployed Chandra X-ray Observatory (formerly AXAF). Eileen Collins became the first female shuttle commander. |
| *Discovery* (U.S.) | Dec. 19–27, 1999 | Col. Curtis L. Brown Jr., Lt. Cmdr. Scott J. Kelly, Steven L. Smith, C. Michael Foale, John M. Grunsfeld, Claude Nicollier (Switzerland), Jean-François Clervoy (France) | 7 days, 23 hr., 10 min. | Third Hubble Space Telescope servicing mission. Three EVAs totaled 24 hr., 33 min.: Dec. 22, Smith and Grunsfeld, 8 hr., 15 min.; Dec. 23, Foale and Nicollier, 8 hr., 10 min.; Dec. 24, Smith and Grunsfeld, 8 hr., 8 min. |

| Designation and country | Date | Astronauts | Flight time (hr/min) | Remarks |
|---|---|---|---|---|
| *Endeavour* (U.S.) | Feb.11–22, 2000 | Cmdr. Dominic L. Pudwill Gorie, Janet Lynn Kavandi, Janet Voss, Kevin R. Kregel, Mamoru Mohri (Japan), Gerhard P. J. Thiele (Germany) | 11 days, 5 hr., 38 min. | Radar mapping obtained most detailed topographical map of Earth to date. |
| *Atlantis* (U.S.) | Sept. 8–18, 2000 | Lt. Col. Terance Wilcutt, Lt. Cmdr. Scott Altman, Edward Tsang Lu, Richard Mastracchio, Lt. Cmdr. Dan Burbank, Col. Yuri I. Malenchenko (Russia), Boris Morukov (Russia) | 10 days, 18 hr., 41 min. | Prepared International Space Station for arrival of first resident crew. Outfitted *Zvezda* module. |
| *Discovery* (U.S.) | Oct. 11–22, 2000 | Col. Brian Duffy, Lt. Col. Pamela A. Melroy, Koichi Wakata (Japan), Peter J. K. Wisoff, Cmdr. Michael E. Lopez-Alegria, Col. William S. McArthur, Jr. | 10 days, 19 hr., 28 min. | Assembled Integrated Truss Structure on space station to allow solar arrays to be installed. 100th space shuttle flight. |
| *Soyuz* (Russia) | Oct. 31, 2000– March 18, 2001 | William M. Shepherd, Yuri Gidzenko (Russia), Sergei Krikalev (Russia). | 138 days, 18 hr., 39 min. | Expedition One, first crew aboard International Space Station. |
| *Discovery* (U.S.) | March 8–21, 2001 | Capt. James D. Wetherbee, Lt. Col. James M. Kelly, Andrew S.W. Thomas, Paul W. Richards, Yury Usachev (Russia), Jim Voss, Susan Helms. | 12 days, 19 hr., 49 min. | Delivered Expedition Two crew (Usachev, Voss, Helms) to space station and returned Expedition One crew (Shepherd, Krikalev, Gidzenko) to Earth. |
| *Discovery* (U.S.) | Aug. 10–Aug. 22, 2001 | Col. Scott J. Horowitz, Lt. Col. Frederick W. Sturckow, Col. Patrick G. Forrester, Daniel T. Barry, Frank Culbertson, Lt. Col. Vladimir Dezhurov (Russia), Mikhail Tyurin (Russia). | 11 days, 21 hr., 13 min. | Delivered Expedition Three crew (Culbertson, Dezhurov, Tyurin) to space station and returned Expedition Two crew (Usachev, Voss, Helms) to Earth. |
| *Endeavour* (U.S.) | Dec. 5–17, 2001 | Capt. Dominic Gorie, Lt. Cmdr. Mark E. Kelly, Linda M. Godwin, Daniel M. Tani, Col. Yuri Onufrienko (Russia), Col. Carl E. Walz, Capt. Daniel W. Bursch. | 11 days, 19 hr., 36 min. | Delivered Expedition Four crew (Onufrienko, Walz, Bursch) to space station and returned Expedition Three crew (Culbertson, Tyurin, Dezhurov) to Earth. |
| *Columbia* (U.S.) | March 1–12, 2002 | Cmdr. Scott Altman, Lt. Col. Duane Carey, Nancy Currie, John Grunsfield, Richard Linnehan, Michael Massimino, James Newman | 10 days, 22 hr., 10 min. | Fourth Hubble Space Telescope servicing mission. The latest upgrades leave Hubble with a new power unit, camera, and solar arrays. Five EVAs lasted a total of 35 hr. 55 min. |
| *Atlantis* (U.S.) | April 8–19, 2002 | Lt. Col. Michael Bloomfield, Stephen Frick, Rex Walheim, Ellen Ochoa, Lee Morin, Jerry Ross, Steven Smith. | 10 days, 19 hr., 42 min. | Installed S0 (S-Zero) Truss, the backbone for future expansion, onto International Space Station. Prepared Mobile Transporter, first railroad in space, for use. Mission specialist Jerry Ross made two space walks, retaining U.S. record for most space walks (nine) and total space-walking time (58 hr., 18 min.). |
| *Endeavour* (U.S.) | June 5–19, 2002 | Kenneth D. Cockrell, Lt. Col. Paul Lockhart, Philippe Perrin (France), Franklin Chang-Diaz, Col. Valery Korzun (Russia), Peggy Whitson, Sergei Treschev (Russia). | 13 days, 20 hr., 35 min. | Delivered Expedition Five crew (Korzun, Whitson, Treschev) to space station and returned Expedition Four crew (Onufrienko, Walz, Bursch) to Earth. On June 19, Expedition Four flight engineers Carl Walz and Dan Bursch broke the U.S. space flight endurance record (previously held by Shannon Lucid, who spent 188 days in space in 1996). The two spent a total of 196 days in space. |

1. From launch to landing. NOTES: EVA = Extravehicular Activity. The letters MR stand for Mercury (capsule) and Redstone (rocket); MA, for Mercury and Atlas (rocket); GT, for Gemini (capsule) and Titan-II (rocket). The first astronaut listed in the Gemini and Apollo flights is the command pilot. The Mercury capsules had names: MR-III was *Freedom 7*, MR-IV was *Liberty Bell 7*, MA-VI was *Friendship 7*, MA-VII was *Aurora 7*, MA-VIII was *Sigma 7*, and MA-IX was *Faith 7*. The figure 7 referred to the fact that the first group of U.S. astronauts numbered seven men. Only one Gemini capsule had a name: GT-III was called *Molly Brown* (after the Broadway musical *The Unsinkable Molly Brown*); thereafter the practice of naming the capsules was discontinued.

# The Battle for Safer Skies

America's airline security system is vulnerable. Can it be fixed?

**By the** TIME **staff**

How does a plane become a guided missile? The answer to the horrible question raised by the terrorist attacks of 2001 is that the air-security system in the U.S. was so porous that a breach was not surprising—only the incomprehensible dimension of it. For years, countless critics, from government watchdogs and consumer groups to industry officials, had railed against and exposed the nation's lax, inadequate airline-safety net, one they said had broken down in every aspect: policy, personnel, technology, and oversight from the Federal Aviation Administration and Congress. Two weeks before the tragedy, a veteran pilot told TIME: "It's absurd to think we're safe."

In the immediate aftermath of the hijackings, the nation's entire airline system was shut down for the first time—ever. A new set of rules was quickly put into place, rules that many experts had been demanding for years: banning curbside check-in or parking, forbidding family and friends to accompany passengers to the gate, having security personnel check all planes before passengers board, conducting random searches of flight crews and equipment, and prohibiting the transport of cargo or mail on passenger jets. Passengers were prohibited from carrying onboard any kind of cutting devices—metal or plastic knives, razor blades or box cutters, no matter how small. President George W. Bush also deployed National Guard troops to monitor the nation's airports.

Beyond this quick-fix solution, a larger challenge loomed: the government and the airlines had to create new systems that would persuade Americans that the skies were safe—without turning air travel into a nightmare of inconvenience. By July 2002, progress had been made on several fronts, but not without turbulence.

## Screening Passengers

One industry expert called it "the dirty little secret of aviation." Under the old system, in a clear conflict of interest, profit-driven airlines were largely responsible for screening passengers. They farmed the job out to large security agencies, which won business by being low bidders on contract proposals. The security jobs they offered were both thankless and tedious. Many screeners made little more than minimum wage, often without even the meager benefits that airport janitors get, while their counterparts in European countries earn two to three times that, and—surprise, surprise—stay on much longer.

Everyone agreed the screening system was broken, but fixing it turned into a political dilemma. A new federal work force in the airports didn't sit right with conservatives, who saw it as a Big Government solution. Republicans argued it would simply create more bureaucracy, make it harder to fire lackluster employees and, perhaps most important, provide the Democrats with 28,000 brand-new union members just in time for the Nov. 2002 elections.

The Senate, under Democratic leadership, took the opposite view: Only by federalizing security workers and performing high-level background checks, the Democrats maintained, could the government implement truly universal safety standards.

Congress passed a compromise bill just in time for the 2001 Thanksgiving holiday. The bill created a new Transportation Department agency, the Transportation Security Administration, to supervise air security. According to the bill, within a year all airport security screening would be under federal supervision and performed by federal employees (who would be permitted to unionize, but not to strike). That would be the case for at least three years in all commercial airports—except for five airports, chosen for their varying sizes, which would test pilot programs for private screening firms. In a compromise that won Republican support for the measure, those airports that meet federal standards after three years will have the option of using local law enforcement or private firms to maintain their security forces.

Airports were given until the end of 2002 to install explosive detection x-ray systems. However, early in June 2002, 39 managers of the country's largest airports sent a strongly worded joint letter to Secretary of Transportation Norman Mineta, stating that the bomb-detection devices would create crowds of people in terminals, who could be targets for attacks. According to the airport managers, the machines would be installed near terminal entrances and thus create huge congestion there. The letter called on Mineta to stop or slow the process immediately by getting Congress to back off the deadlines. Mineta's office said he had no intention of trying to change the law.

## Safer Cockpits, Air Marshals

The suicidal behavior of the 9/11 hijackers in the air mandated a total revision of emergency procedures in the cabin. In the past, the idea was to try to keep the hijackers calm and get the plane on the ground so negotiations could commence. In the wake of the tragedy, pilot chat sites were burning with a desire to carry weapons, a privilege revoked in 1987.

The Nov. 2001 air-safety bill mandated that flight deck doors must be strengthened and kept locked during flights. In May 2002, Attorney General John Ashcroft declared that the government had decided not to allow pilots to carry arms. But in June, the House of Representatives passed a bill that would arm the pilots, and the Senate overwhelmingly supported the measure as an amendment to the bill creating a Homeland Security Department. But because of the controversy that bill is expected to generate, it is unlikely pilots will bear arms soon.

After Sept. 11, aviation security officials made an easy decision: to rapidly revive the federal air marshal program. Federal air marshals are well-trained armed guards who fly on "high threat" commercial flights. But the program had dwindled so dramatically over its 30 years that there were fewer than 50 of the officers on duty Sept. 11.

The Nov. 2001 bill mandated that more air marshals would travel on planes; their presence would be required on certain flights deemed "high risk." But as of March 2002, many pilots, flight attendants, and airline-operations personnel from carriers across the country were telling TIME they had never had a federal air marshal on any of their flights. A Transportation Security Administration spokesman said the agency had opened a second air-marshal training center. "FAMs will be a significant presence on flights," the spokesman said. But he didn't say when.

## New Technology

A host of plans are now taking shape to advance airport and airplane security. Biometric technology, for instance, uses unique human features to nab potential evildoers. Face-print technology works by instantaneously matching the faces of people passing a camera against a database of faces of known terrorists; when a match occurs, it calls the cops. Other biometric systems, like EyePass, which confirms identity by scanning the iris of the eye, are coming on line. In a program introduced in 2000, nearly 100,000 U.S. citizens have signed up to have their fingerprints and hand geometry digitized to breeze them through immigration controls at seven U.S. airports. Scientists are busy developing even more advanced detection schemes—from digital bomb sniffers to 3-D holographic body scanners.

None of these new laws, new procedures, or new technologies by itself can repulse terrorists. But each is a barrier that makes their tasks more complex, and as is now clear, America's air-security system needs all the complexity we can muster.     ☐

## Famous Firsts in Aviation

**1783**  **First balloon flight.** Jacques and Joseph Montgolfier of Annonay, France, sent up a small smoke-filled balloon about mid-November.

**First hydrogen-filled balloon flight.** Jacques A. C. Charles, Paris physicist, supervised construction by A. J. and M. N. Robert of a 13-foot-diameter balloon that was filled with hydrogen. It got up to about 3,000 ft and traveled about 16 mi in a 45-minute flight (Aug. 27).

**First human balloon flights.** A Frenchman, Jean Pilâtre de Rozier, made the first captive-balloon ascension (Oct. 15). With the Marquis d'Arlandes, Pilâtre de Rozier made the first free flight, reaching a peak altitude of about 500 ft, and traveling about 5½ mi in 20 min. (Nov. 21).

**1784**  **First powered balloon.** Gen. Jean Baptiste Marie Meusnier developed the first propeller-driven and elliptically shaped balloon—the crew cranking three propellers on a common shaft to give the craft a speed of about 3 mph.

**First balloon flight by a woman.** Mme. Thible, a French opera singer (June 4).

**1793**  **First balloon flight in America.** Jean Pierre Blanchard, a French pilot, made it from Philadelphia to near Woodbury, N.J., in just over 45 min. (Jan. 9).

**1794**  **First military use of the balloon.** Jean Marie Coutelle, using a balloon built for the French Army, made two 4-hour observation ascents. The military purpose of the ascents seems to have been to damage the enemy's morale.

**1797**  **First parachute jump.** André-Jacques Garnerin dropped from about 6,500 ft over Monceau Park in Paris in a 23-foot-diameter parachute made of white canvas with a basket attached (Oct. 22).

**1843**  **First air transport company.** In London, William S. Henson and John Stringfellow filed articles of incorporation for the Aerial Transit Company (March 24). It failed.

**1852**  **First dirigible.** Henri Giffard, a French engineer, flew in a controllable (more or less) steam-engine-powered balloon, 144 ft long and 39 ft in diameter, inflated with 88,000 cu ft of coal gas. It reached 6.7 mph on a flight from Paris to Trappe (Sept. 24).

**1860**  **First aerial photographers.** Samuel Archer King and William Black made two photos of Boston, which are still in existence.

**1872**  **First gas-engine-powered dirigible.** Paul Haenlein, a German engineer, flew in a semi-rigid-frame dirigible, powered by a 4-cylinder internal-combustion engine running on coal gas drawn from the supporting bag.

**1873**  **First transatlantic attempt.** *The New York Daily Graphic* sponsored the attempt with a 400,000-cubic-foot balloon carrying a lifeboat. A rip in the bag during inflation brought the collapse of the balloon and the project.

**1897**  **First successful metal dirigible.** An all-metal dirigible, designed by David Schwarz, a Hungarian, took off from Berlin's Tempelhof Field and, powered by a 16-horsepower Daimler engine, got several miles before leaking gas caused it to crash (Nov. 13).

**1900**  **First zeppelin flight.** Germany's Count Ferdinand von Zeppelin flew the first of his long series of rigid-frame airships. It attained a speed of 18 mph and got 3½ mi before its steering gear failed (July 2).

**1903**  **First successful heavier-than-air machine flight.** Aviation was really born on the sand dunes at Kitty Hawk, N.C., when Orville Wright crawled to his prone position between the wings of the biplane he and his brother Wilbur had built, opened the throttle of their home-made 12-horsepower engine, and took to the air. He covered 120 ft in 12 sec. Later that day, in one of four flights, Wilbur stayed up 59 sec. and covered 852 ft (Dec. 17).

**1904**  **First airplane maneuvers.** Orville Wright made the first turn with an airplane (Sept. 15); five days later his brother Wilbur made the first complete circle.

**1905**  **First airplane flight over half an hour.** Orville Wright kept his craft up 33 min., 17 sec. (Oct. 4).

**1906**  **First European airplane flight.** Alberto Santos-Dumont, a Brazilian, flew a heavier-than-air machine at Bagatelle Field, Paris (Sept. 13).

**1908**  **First airplane fatality.** Lt. Thomas E. Selfridge, U.S. Army Signal Corps, was in a group evaluating the Wright plane at Fort Myer, Va. He was up 75 ft with Orville Wright when the propeller hit a bracing wire and was broken, throwing the plane out of control, killing Selfridge and seriously injuring Wright (Sept. 17).

**1909**  **First cross-Channel flight.** Louis Blériot flew in a 25-horsepower Blériot VI monoplane from Les Baraques near Calais, France, to Dover Castle, England, in a 26.61-mile (38-kilometer) 37-minute flight across the English Channel (July 25).

**First International Aviation Competition Meeting.** American Glenn Curtiss narrowly beat France's Louis Blériot in the main event and won the Gordon Bennett Cup. Meet held at Rheims, France (Aug. 22–28).

**1910**  **First licensed woman pilot.** Baroness Raymonde de la Roche of France, who learned to fly in 1909, received ticket No. 36 on March 8.

**First flight from shipboard.** Lt. Eugene Ely, USN, took a Curtiss plane off from the deck of the cruiser *Birmingham* at Hampton Roads, Va., and flew to Norfolk (Nov. 14). The following January he reversed the process, flying from Camp Selfridge to the deck of the armored cruiser *Pennsylvania* in San Francisco Bay (Jan. 18).

**First aircraft to take off from water.** Henri Fabre in a Gnome-powered floatplane, at Martigues, France (March 28).

**1911**  **First U.S. woman pilot.** Harriet Quimby, a magazine writer, got ticket No. 37, making her the second licensed female pilot in the world.

**1912**  **First woman's cross-Channel flight.** Harriet Quimby flew from Dover, England, across the English Channel and landed at Hardelot, France, in a Blériot monoplane loaned to her by Louis Blériot (April 16). She was later killed in a flying accident over Dorchester Bay during a Harvard-Boston aviation meet on July 1, 1912.

**First parachute jump from a powered airplane.** Albert Berry jumped in a test over Jefferson Barracks military post, St. Louis (March 1). Some sources credit Grant Morton as making first jump in 1911.

**1913**  **First multi-engined aircraft.** Built and flown by Igor Ivan Sikorsky while still in his native Russia.

**1914**  **First aerial combat.** In Aug., Allied and German pilots and observers started shooting at each other with pistols and rifles—with negligible results.

**1915**  **First air raids on England.** German zeppelins dropped bombs on four English communities (Jan. 19).

**1918**  **First U.S. air squadron.** The U.S. Army Air Corps made its first independent raids over enemy lines, in DH-4 planes (British-designed) powered with 400-hp American-designed Liberty engines (April 8).

**First regular airmail service.** Operated for the Post Office Department by the Army, the first regular service was inaugurated with one round trip a day (except Sunday) between Washington, DC, and New York City (May 15).

**1919**  **First transatlantic flight.** The NC-4, one of four Curtiss flying boats commanded by Lt. Comdr. Albert C. Read, reached Lisbon, Portugal (May 27), after hops from Trepassy Bay, Newfoundland, to Horta, Azores (May 16–17), to Ponta Delgada (May 20). The Liberty-powered craft was piloted by Walter Hinton.

**First nonstop transatlantic flight.** Capt. John Alcock and Lt. Arthur Whitten Brown, British World War I flyers, made the 1,900-mile trip from St. John's, Newfoundland, to Clifden, Ireland, in 16 hr., 12 min. in a Vickers-Vimy bomber with two 350-horsepower Rolls-Royce engines (June 15–16).

**First lighter-than-air transatlantic flight.** The British dirigible R-34, commanded by Maj. George H. Scott, left Firth of Forth, Scotland (July 2), and touched down at Mineola, L.I., 108 hr. later. The eastbound trip was made in 75 hr. (completed July 13).

**First scheduled London–Paris passenger service (using airplanes).** Aircraft Travel and Transport inaugurated London–Paris service (Aug. 25). Later the company started the first trans-Channel mail service on the same route (Nov. 10).

**First free-fall parachute jump.** Leslie Irvin jumped over McCook Field, Dayton, Ohio, to prove that one won't lose consciousness during a delayed free-fall using a manually operated parachute (April 28).

**1921**  **First U.S. black female pilot.** Bessie Coleman received license June 15. Was killed April 30, 1926, in flying accident.

**First naval vessel sunk by aircraft.** Two battleships being scrapped by treaty were sunk by bombs dropped from Army planes in demonstration put on by Brig. Gen. William S. Mitchell (July 21).

**First helium balloon.** The C-7, nonrigid Navy dirigible was first to use noninflammable helium as lifting gas, making a flight from Hampton Roads, Va., to Washington, D.C. (Dec. 1).

**1922**  **First member of Caterpillar Club.** Lt. (later Maj. Gen.) Harold Harris bailed out of a crippled plane he was testing at McCook Field, Dayton, Ohio (Oct. 20), and became the first man to join the Caterpillar Club—those whose lives have been saved by parachutes.

**1923**  **First nonstop transcontinental flight.** Lts. John A. Macready and Oakley Kelly flew a single-engine Fokker T-2 nonstop from New York to San Diego, a distance of just over 2,500 mi in 26 hr., 50 min. (May 2–3).

**First autogyro flight.** Juan de la Cierva, a brilliant Spanish mathematician, made the first successful flight in a rotary wing aircraft in Madrid (June 9).

**1924**  **First round-the-world flight.** Four Douglas Cruiser biplanes of the U.S. Army Air Corps took off from Seattle under command of Maj. Frederick Martin (April 6). 175 days later, two of the planes (Lt. Lowell Smith's and Lt. Erik Nelson's) landed in Seattle after a circuitous route—one source saying 26,345 mi, another saying 27,553 mi.

**1926**  **First polar flight.** Then–Lt. Cmdr. Richard E. Byrd, acting as navigator, and Floyd Bennett as pilot, flew a Trimotor Fokker from Kings Bay, Spitsbergen, over the North Pole and back in 15½ hr. (May 8–9).

**1927**  **First solo nonstop transatlantic flight.** Charles Augustus Lindbergh lifted his Wright-powered Ryan monoplane, *Spirit of St. Louis,* from Roosevelt Field, N.Y., to stay aloft 33 hr. 39 min. and travel 3,600 mi to Le Bourget Field outside Paris (May 20–21). Although 91 persons in 13 separate flights crossed the Atlantic before him, he flew directly between two great world cities and did it alone.

**First transatlantic passenger.** Charles A. Levine was piloted by Clarence D. Chamberlin from Roosevelt Field, N.Y., to Eisleben, Germany, in a Wright-powered Bellanca (June 4–5).

**1928** **First east–west transatlantic crossing.** Baron Guenther von Huenefeld, piloted by German Capt. Hermann Koehl and Irish Capt. James Fitzmaurice, left Dublin for New York City (April 12) in a single-engine all-metal Junkers-monoplane. Some 37 hr. later, they crashed on Greely Island, Labrador. Rescued.

**First U.S.–Australia flight.** Sir Charles Kingsford-Smith and Capt. Charles T. P. Ulm, Australians, and two American navigators, Harry W. Lyon and James Warner, crossed the Pacific from Oakland to Brisbane. They went via Hawaii and the Fiji Islands in a trimotor Fokker (May 31–June 8).

**First transarctic flight.** Sir Hubert Wilkins, an Australian explorer, and Carl Ben Eielson, who served as pilot, flew from Point Barrow, Alaska, to Spitsbergen (mid-April).

**1929** **First of the endurance records.** With Air Corps Maj. Carl Spaatz in command and Capt. Ira Eaker as chief pilot, an Army Fokker, aided by refueling in the air, remained aloft 150 hr. 40 min. at Los Angeles (Jan. 1–7).

**First round-the-world airship flight.** The LZ-127, known as the *Graf Zeppelin,* flew 21,300 mi in 20 days and 4 hr. Also set distance record (Aug.).

**First blind flight.** James H. Doolittle proved the feasibility of instrument-guided flying when he took off and landed entirely on instruments (Sept. 24).

**First rocket-engine flight.** Fritz von Opel, a German auto maker, stayed aloft in his small rocket-powered craft for 75 sec., covering nearly 2 mi (Sept. 30).

**First South Pole flight.** Comdr. Richard E. Byrd, with Bernt Balchen as pilot, Harold I. June, radio operator, and Capt. A. C. McKinley, photographer, flew a trimotor Fokker from the Bay of Whales, Little America, over the South Pole and back (Nov. 28–29).

**1930** **First Paris–New York nonstop flight.** Dieudonné Costes and Maurice Bellonte, French pilots, flew a Hispano-powered Breguet biplane from Le Bourget Field to Valley Stream, L.I., in 37 hr., 18 min. (Sept. 2–3).

**1931** **First flight into the stratosphere.** Auguste Piccard, a Swiss physicist, and Charles Knipfer ascended in a balloon from Augsburg, Germany, and reached a height of 51,770 ft in 17 hr. The flight that terminated on a glacier near Innsbruck, Austria (May 27).

**First nonstop transpacific flight.** Hugh Herndon and Clyde Pangborn took off from Sabishiro Beach, Japan, dropped their landing gear, and flew 4,860 mi to near Wenatchee, Wash., in 41 hr. 13 min. (Oct. 4–5).

**1932** **First woman's transatlantic solo.** Amelia Earhart, flying a Pratt & Whitney Wasp-powered Lockheed Vega, flew alone from Harbor Grace, Newfoundland, to Ireland in approximately 15 hr. (May 20–21).

**First westbound transatlantic solo.** James A. Mollison, a British pilot, took a de Havilland Puss Moth from Portmarnock, Ireland, to Pennfield, New Brunswick (Aug. 18).

**First woman airline pilot.** Ruth Rowland Nichols, first woman to hold three international records at the same time—speed, distance, and altitude—was employed by N.Y.–New England Airways.

**1933** **First round-the-world solo.** Wiley Post took a Lockheed Vega, *Winnie Mae,* 15,596 mi around the world in 7 days, 18 hr., 49½ min. (July 15–22).

**1937** **First successful helicopter flight.** Hanna Reitsch, a German pilot, flew Dr. Heinrich Focke's FW-61 in free, fully controlled flight at Bremen (July 4). Ms. Reitsch was also the first woman civil and military aviation test pilot.

**First woman known to fly combat.** Sabiha Gokcen, Turkish female army pilot, bombed and strafed Kurdish tribesmen during a rebellion.

**1939** **First turbojet flight.** Just before their invasion of Poland, the Germans flew a Heinkel He-178 plane powered by a Heinkel S3B turbojet (Aug. 27).

**1940** **First wartime use of military gliders.** German commandos made a successful glider assault on Belgium's Fort Eben-Emael during WWII (May 10).

**1941–1945** **Most combat missions flown by a pilot in any war.** Captain Hans-Ulrich Rudel of Germany flew 2,530 combat missions during WWII while flying a JU-87 Stuka dive bomber. He survived the war.

**1942–1945** **Top-scoring fighter pilot of any war.** German Luftwaffe ace Maj. Erich Hartmann scored 352 victories all while flying a Messerschmitt BF 109 during WWII. He was involved in 800 dogfights, and flew 1,425 missions. Maj. Hartmann survived the war.

**1942** **First enemy bombing of U.S. mainland.** During WWII, a floatplane launched from a Japanese submarine off Cape Blanco, Ore., dropped incendiary bombs on the Oregon forest in two attempts to start forest fires and terrorize American civilians, but the bombs did little damage (Sept. 9 and 29).

**First American jet plane flight.** Robert Stanley, chief pilot for Bell Aircraft Corp., flew the Bell XP-59 *Airacomet* at Muroc Army Base, Calif. (Oct. 1).

**First woman fighter pilot to shoot down an enemy aircraft.** Soviet Lieutenant Lilya Litvyak, flying a Yak-1 fighter of the women's 586th Fighter Aviation Regiment, shot down two German planes over Stalingrad on Sept. 13, 1942.

**1944** **First production stage rocket-engine fighter plane.** The German Messerschmitt Me 163B *Komet* (test flown 1941) became operational in 1944 when 300 of these planes were built before WWII in Europe ended.

**1947** **First piloted supersonic flight in an airplane.** Capt. Charles E. Yeager, U.S. Air Force, flew the X-1 rocket-powered research plane built by Bell Aircraft Corp., faster than the speed of sound at Muroc Air Force Base, Calif. (Oct. 14).

**1949** **First round-the-world nonstop flight.** Capt. James Gallagher and USAF crew of 13 flew a Boeing B-50A Superfortress around the world nonstop from Ft. Worth, returning to same point: 23,452 mi in 94 hr., 1 min., with four aerial refuelings en route (Feb. 27–March 2).

**1950** **First nonstop transatlantic jet flight.** Col. David C. Schilling (USAF) flew 3,300 mi from England to Limestone, Maine, in 10 hr., 1 min. (Sept. 22).

## Active Pilot Certificates Held

| Year | Total | Airline transport | Commercial | Private |
|------|-------|-------------------|------------|---------|
| 1970 | 720,028 | 31,442 | 176,585 | 299,491 |
| 1980 | 814,667 | 63,652 | 182,097 | 343,276 |
| 1985 | 722,376 | 79,192 | 155,929 | 320,086 |
| 1990 | 702,659 | 107,732 | 149,666 | 299,111 |
| 1995 | 639,184 | 123,877 | 133,980 | 261,399 |
| 1997 | 616,342 | 130,858 | 125,300 | 247,604 |
| 1998 | 618,298 | 134,612 | 122,053 | 247,226 |
| 1999 | 635,472 | 137,642 | 124,261 | 258,749 |
| 2000 | 625,581 | 141,596 | 121,858 | 251,561 |
| 2001 | 612,274 | 144,702 | 120,502 | 243,823 |

NOTE: Includes student (97,359), glider (9,390), recreational (343), and other pilot categories. Also nonpilot, i.e., mechanic, parachute rigger, etc. *Source:* May 2002 FAA Fact Book.

**1951**   **First solo across North Pole.** Charles F. Blair, Jr., flew a converted P-51 (May 29).

**1952**   **First jetliner service.** The De Havilland Comet flight was inaugurated by BOAC between London and Johannesburg, South Africa (May 2). Flight, including stops, took 23 hr., 38 min.

     **First transatlantic helicopter flight.** Capt. Vincent H. McGovern and 1st Lt. Harold W. Moore piloted two Sikorsky H-19s from Westover, Mass., to Prestwick, Scotland (3,410 mi). Trip was made in five stops, with a flying time of 42 hr., 25 min. (July 15–31).

     **First transatlantic round trip in same day.** A British Canberra twin-jet bomber flew from Aldergrove, Northern Ireland, to Gander, Newfoundland, and back in 7 hr., 59 min. flying time (Aug. 26).

**1955**   **First transcontinental round trip in same day.** Lt. John M. Conroy piloted an F-86 Sabrejet across U.S. (Los Angeles–New York) and back—5,085 mi—in 11 hr., 33 min., 27 sec. (May 21).

**1957**   **First round-the-world nonstop jet plane flight.** Maj. Gen. Archie J. Old, Jr., USAF, led a flight of three Boeing B-52 bombers, powered with eight 10,000-pound-thrust Pratt & Whitney Aircraft J57 engines around the world in 45 hr., 19 min; distance 24,325 mi; average speed 525 mph (completed Jan. 18).

**1958**   **First transatlantic jet passenger service.** BOAC, New York to London (Oct. 4). Pan American started daily service, New York to Paris (Oct. 26).

     **First domestic jet passenger service.** National Airlines inaugurated service between New York and Miami (Dec. 10).

**1968**   **Prototype of world's first supersonic airliner.** The Soviet-designed Tupolev Tu-144 made its first flight, Dec. 31. It first achieved supersonic speed on June 5, 1969.

**1973**   **First female pilot of a major U.S. scheduled airline.** Emily H. Warner became employed by Frontier Airlines on Jan. 29 as second officer on a Boeing 737.

**1976**   **First regularly scheduled commercial supersonic transport (SST) flights begin.** Air France and British Airways inaugurated service (Jan. 21). Air France flew the Paris–Rio de Janeiro route; B.A., the London–Bahrain. Both airlines began SST service to Washington, D.C. (May 24).

**1977**   **First successful human-powered aircraft.** Paul MacCready, an aeronautical engineer from Pasadena, Calif., was awarded the Kremer Prize for creating the world's first successful human-powered aircraft. The *Gossamer Condor* was flown by Bryan Allen over the required 3-mile course on Aug. 23.

**1978**   **First successful transatlantic balloon flight.** Three Albuquerque, N.M., men, Ben Abruzzo, Larry Newman, and Maxie Anderson, completed the crossing (Aug. 16.; landed, Aug. 17) in their helium-filled balloon, *Double Eagle II.*

**1979**   **First man-powered aircraft to fly across the English Channel.** The Kremer Prize for the Channel crossing was won by Bryan Allen, who flew the *Gossamer Albatross* from Folkestone, England, to Cap Gris-Nez, France, in 2 hr., 55 min. (June 12).

**1980**   **First successful balloon flight over the North Pole.** Sidney Conn and his wife, Eleanor, in hot-air balloon *Joy of Sound* (April 11).

     **First nonstop transcontinental balloon flight,** and also record for longest overland voyage in a balloon. Maxie Anderson and his son, Kris, completed four-day flight from Fort Baker, Calif., to successful landing outside Matane, Quebec, in their helium-filled balloon, *Kitty Hawk* (May 12).

     **First long-distance solar-powered flight.** Janice Brown, a 98-pound former teacher, flew a tiny experimental solar-powered aircraft, *Solar Challenger,* 6 mi in 22 min. near Marana, Ariz. (Dec. 3). The craft was powered by a 2.75-horsepower engine.

     **First solar-powered aircraft to fly across the English Channel.** Stephen R. Ptacek flew the 210-pound *Solar Challenger* at an average speed of 30 mph from Cormeilles-en-Vexin near Paris to the Royal Manston Air Force Base in southeast England in 5 hr., 30 min. (July 7).

**1984**   **First solo transatlantic balloon flight.** Joe W. Kittinger landed Sept. 18 near Savona, Italy, in his helium-filled balloon, *Rosie O'Grady's Balloon of Peace,* after a flight of 3,535 mi from Caribou, Maine.

**1986**   **First nonstop flight around the world without refueling.** From Edwards AFB, Calif., Dick Rutan and Jeana Yeager flew in *Voyager* around the world (24,986.727 mi), returning to Edwards in 216 hr., 3 min., 44 sec. (Dec. 14–23).

**1987**   **First transatlantic hot-air balloon flight.** Richard Branson and Per Lindstrand flew 2,789.6 mi from Sugarloaf Mt., Maine, to Ireland in the hot-air balloon *Virgin Atlantic Flyer* (July 2–4).

**1991**   **First transpacific hot-air balloon flight.** Richard Branson and Per Lindstrand flew about 6,700 mi from Miyakonyo, Japan, to 150 mi west of Yellowknife, Northwest Territories, Canada (Jan. 15–17).

**1993**   **First woman to copilot a commercial supersonic plane.** Barbara Harmer, British Airways, flew as first officer on the Concorde from London to New York City (March 25).

**1995**   **First solo transpacific balloon flight.** Steve Fossett made a flight of more than 5,430 mi from Seoul, South Korea, to Leader, Saskatchewan, Canada, in a helium-filled balloon. Also set record for distance (Feb. 18–21, 1995).

**1999**   **First nonstop round-the-world balloon flight.** Bertrand Piccard (Switzerland) and Brian Jones (UK) flew 28,431 mi (45,755 km) from Chateaux d'Oex, Switzerland, to Dakhla, Egypt, in 19 days, 21 hr., and 55 min. (March 1–21).

**2001**   **First solar-powered flight to shatter altitude records.** NASA's solar-powered propeller-driven plane *Helios* reached an altitude of 96,500 ft during a flight over Hawaii, breaking not only the 80,200-foot record for propeller-driven aircraft, but the 85,068-foot mark for all nonrocket aircraft as well (Aug. 13–14).

**2002  First solo nonstop round-the-world balloon flight.** Steve Fossett (U.S.) flew from Northam, West Australia, to Lake Yamma Yamma, Queensland, Australia, landing after 14 days, 19 hrs. He broke three balloon records along the way: fastest time around the world, measured by crossing 117° East longitude (13 days, 3 min.), longest distance flown solo (20,483.25 mi; 32,963.35 km), and longest time flown solo (355 hrs, 50 min.) (June 19–July 3).

## Absolute World Records

### (maximum performance in any class)

*Source:* National Aeronautic Association

**Speed around the World, Nonstop, Nonrefueled**

| Speed (mph) | Date | Plane | Pilots | Place |
|---|---|---|---|---|
| 115.65 | Dec. 14–23, 1986 | *Voyager* | Dick Rutan & Jeana Yeager (U.S.) | Edwards AFB, Calif.—Edwards AFB, Calif. |

**Distance, Great Circle without Landing, also Distance, Closed Circuit without Landing**

| Distance (mi) | Date | Plane | Pilots | Place |
|---|---|---|---|---|
| 24,986.727 | Dec. 14–23, 1986 | *Voyager* | Dick Rutan & Jeana Yeager (U.S.) | Edwards AFB, Calif.—Edwards AFB, Calif. |

**Speed over a Straight Course**

| Speed (mph) | Date | Plane type | Pilot | Place |
|---|---|---|---|---|
| 2,193.16 | July 28, 1976 | Lockheed SR-71A | Capt. Eldon W. Joersz (USAF) | Beale AFB, Calif. |

**Speed over a Closed Circuit**

| Speed (mph) | Date | Plane type | Pilot | Place |
|---|---|---|---|---|
| 2,092.294 | July 27, 1976 | Lockheed SR-71A | Maj. Adolphus H. Bledsoe, Jr. (USAF) | Beale AFB, Calif. |

**Altitude**

| Height (ft) | Date | Plane type | Pilot | Place |
|---|---|---|---|---|
| 123,523.58 | Aug. 31, 1977 | MIG-25, E-266M | Alexander Fedotov (U.S.S.R.) | U.S.S.R. |

**Altitude in Horizontal Flight**

| Height (ft) | Date | | Pilot | Place |
|---|---|---|---|---|
| 85,068.997 | July 28, 1976 | | Capt. Robert C. Helt (USAF) | Beale AFB, Calif. |

**Altitude, Aircraft Launched from a Carrier Airplane**

| Height (ft) | Date | Plane type | Pilot | Place |
|---|---|---|---|---|
| 314,750.00 | July 17, 1962 | N. American X-15-1 | Maj. Robert White (USAF) | Edwards AFB, Calif. |

## World-Class Helicopter Records

Selected records. *Source:* National Aeronautic Association

**Great Circle Distance without Landing**
International: 2,213.04 mi; 3,561.55 km.
Robert G. Ferry (U.S.) in Hughes YOH-6A helicopter powered by Allison T-63-A-5 engine; from Culver City, Calif., to Ormond Beach, Fla., April 6–7, 1966.

~~International: 1,739.96 mi; 2,800.20 km.~~
Jack Schweibold (U.S.) in Hughes YOH-6A helicopter powered by Allison T-63-A-5 engine; Edwards Air Force Base, Calif., March 26, 1966.

**Altitude without Payload**
International: 40,820 ft; 12,442 m.
Jean Boulet (France) in Alouette SA 315-001 *Lama* powered by Artouste IIIB 735 KW engine; Istres, France, June 21, 1972.

**Speed around the World, Eastbound**
40.99 mph; 65.97 kph.
Joe Ronald Bower (U.S.) pilot, in Bell JetRanger III, powered by one Allison 250-C20J (317 shp), covered 23,800 mi in 24 days, 4 hr., 36 min. June 28–July 22, 1994.

**Speed around the World, Westbound**
57.01 mph; 91.75 kph.

Joe Ronald Bower (U.S.) pilot, John W. Williams (U.S.), co-pilot in Bell 430 powered by 2 Allison 250-C40, (811 shp), Aug. 17–Sept. 3, 1996.

## Absolute World Records, Balloons

Selected records. *Source:* National Aeronautic Association

**Altitude**
113,739.9 ft; 34,668 m.
~~Malcolm Ross (U.S.) and Lt. Cmdr. V.A. Prather, Lee~~ Lewis Memorial, Gulf of Mexico, May 4, 1961.

**Distance**
25,000 mi; 40,814 km.
Bertrand Piccard (Switzerland) and Brian Jones (UK), *Cameron Balloons R-650,* Château d'Oex, Switzerland, to Dakhla, Egypt, March 1–21, 1999.

**Duration**
477 hr., 47 min.
Bertrand Piccard (Switzerland) and Brian Jones (UK), *Cameron Balloons R-650,* Château d'Oex, Switzerland, to Dakhla, Egypt, March 1–21, 1999.

**Fastest time around the world**
312 hr., 3 min.
Steve Fossett (U.S.), Spirit of Freedom, Northam, Western Australia to Lake Yamma Yamma, Queensland, Australia. Flight, June 19–July 3; record broken on July 2, 2002.

# 2003

## January

| S | M | T | W | T | F | S |
|---|---|---|---|---|---|---|
|   |   |   | 1 | 2 | 3 | 4 |
| 5 | 6 | 7 | 8 | 9 | 10 | 11 |
| 12 | 13 | 14 | 15 | 16 | 17 | 18 |
| 19 | 20 | 21 | 22 | 23 | 24 | 25 |
| 26 | 27 | 28 | 29 | 30 | 31 |   |

## February

| S | M | T | W | T | F | S |
|---|---|---|---|---|---|---|
|   |   |   |   |   |   | 1 |
| 2 | 3 | 4 | 5 | 6 | 7 | 8 |
| 9 | 10 | 11 | 12 | 13 | 14 | 15 |
| 16 | 17 | 18 | 19 | 20 | 21 | 22 |
| 23 | 24 | 25 | 26 | 27 | 28 |   |

## March

| S | M | T | W | T | F | S |
|---|---|---|---|---|---|---|
|   |   |   |   |   |   | 1 |
| 2 | 3 | 4 | 5 | 6 | 7 | 8 |
| 9 | 10 | 11 | 12 | 13 | 14 | 15 |
| 16 | 17 | 18 | 19 | 20 | 21 | 22 |
| 23 | 24 | 25 | 26 | 27 | 28 | 29 |
| 30 | 31 |   |   |   |   |   |

## April

| S | M | T | W | T | F | S |
|---|---|---|---|---|---|---|
|   |   | 1 | 2 | 3 | 4 | 5 |
| 6 | 7 | 8 | 9 | 10 | 11 | 12 |
| 13 | 14 | 15 | 16 | 17 | 18 | 19 |
| 20 | 21 | 22 | 23 | 24 | 25 | 26 |
| 27 | 28 | 29 | 30 |   |   |   |

1—New Year's Day
6—Epiphany
20—Martin Luther King, Jr.'s Birthday observed

2—Groundhog Day
12—Lincoln's Birthday
14—Valentine's Day
17—Washington's Birthday observed
22—Washington's Birthday

5—Ash Wednesday
17—St. Patrick's Day
18—Purim*

6—Daylight Saving Time begins
13—Palm Sunday
17—1st Day of Passover*
18—Good Friday
20—Easter Sunday
27—Orthodox Easter

## May

| S | M | T | W | T | F | S |
|---|---|---|---|---|---|---|
|   |   |   |   | 1 | 2 | 3 |
| 4 | 5 | 6 | 7 | 8 | 9 | 10 |
| 11 | 12 | 13 | 14 | 15 | 16 | 17 |
| 18 | 19 | 20 | 21 | 22 | 23 | 24 |
| 25 | 26 | 27 | 28 | 29 | 30 | 31 |

## June

| S | M | T | W | T | F | S |
|---|---|---|---|---|---|---|
| 1 | 2 | 3 | 4 | 5 | 6 | 7 |
| 8 | 9 | 10 | 11 | 12 | 13 | 14 |
| 15 | 16 | 17 | 18 | 19 | 20 | 21 |
| 22 | 23 | 24 | 25 | 26 | 27 | 28 |
| 29 | 30 |   |   |   |   |   |

## July

| S | M | T | W | T | F | S |
|---|---|---|---|---|---|---|
|   |   | 1 | 2 | 3 | 4 | 5 |
| 6 | 7 | 8 | 9 | 10 | 11 | 12 |
| 13 | 14 | 15 | 16 | 17 | 18 | 19 |
| 20 | 21 | 22 | 23 | 24 | 25 | 26 |
| 27 | 28 | 29 | 30 | 31 |   |   |

## August

| S | M | T | W | T | F | S |
|---|---|---|---|---|---|---|
|   |   |   |   |   | 1 | 2 |
| 3 | 4 | 5 | 6 | 7 | 8 | 9 |
| 10 | 11 | 12 | 13 | 14 | 15 | 16 |
| 17 | 18 | 19 | 20 | 21 | 22 | 23 |
| 24 | 25 | 26 | 27 | 28 | 29 | 30 |
| 31 |   |   |   |   |   |   |

11—Mother's Day
26—Memorial Day observed

6—1st Day of Shavuot*
8—Pentecost
14—Flag Day
15—Father's Day
15—Orthodox Pentecost

1—Canada Day
4—Independence Day

## September

| S | M | T | W | T | F | S |
|---|---|---|---|---|---|---|
|   | 1 | 2 | 3 | 4 | 5 | 6 |
| 7 | 8 | 9 | 10 | 11 | 12 | 13 |
| 14 | 15 | 16 | 17 | 18 | 19 | 20 |
| 21 | 22 | 23 | 24 | 25 | 26 | 27 |
| 28 | 29 | 30 |   |   |   |   |

## October

| S | M | T | W | T | F | S |
|---|---|---|---|---|---|---|
|   |   |   | 1 | 2 | 3 | 4 |
| 5 | 6 | 7 | 8 | 9 | 10 | 11 |
| 12 | 13 | 14 | 15 | 16 | 17 | 18 |
| 19 | 20 | 21 | 22 | 23 | 24 | 25 |
| 26 | 27 | 28 | 29 | 30 | 31 |   |

## November

| S | M | T | W | T | F | S |
|---|---|---|---|---|---|---|
|   |   |   |   |   |   | 1 |
| 2 | 3 | 4 | 5 | 6 | 7 | 8 |
| 9 | 10 | 11 | 12 | 13 | 14 | 15 |
| 16 | 17 | 18 | 19 | 20 | 21 | 22 |
| 23 | 24 | 25 | 26 | 27 | 28 | 29 |
| 30 |   |   |   |   |   |   |

## December

| S | M | T | W | T | F | S |
|---|---|---|---|---|---|---|
|   | 1 | 2 | 3 | 4 | 5 | 6 |
| 7 | 8 | 9 | 10 | 11 | 12 | 13 |
| 14 | 15 | 16 | 17 | 18 | 19 | 20 |
| 21 | 22 | 23 | 24 | 25 | 26 | 27 |
| 28 | 29 | 30 | 31 |   |   |   |

1—Labor Day
27—Rosh Hashanah*

6—Yom Kippur*
13—Columbus Day observed
13—Thanksgiving Day (Canada)
26—Daylight Saving Time ends
27—Ramadan begins*
31—Halloween

1—All Saints' Day
4—Election Day
11—Veterans Day
26—Ramadan ends (Eid al-Fitr)*
27—Thanksgiving Day
30—1st Sunday of Advent

20—1st Day of Hanukkah*
25—Christmas Day

*All Jewish and Islamic holidays begin at sundown the day before they are listed here.

## Seasons for the Northern Hemisphere, 2003

Mar. 20, 8:00 P.M. EST (March 21, 01:00 UT[1]), Sun enters sign of Aries; spring begins

June 21, 3:10 P.M. EDT (19:10 UT[1]), Sun enters sign of Cancer; summer begins

Sept. 23, 6:47 A.M. EDT (10:47 UT[1]), Sun enters sign of Libra; fall begins

Dec. 22, 2:04 A.M. EST (07:04 UT[1]), Sun enters sign of Capricorn; winter begins

1. Universal Time (UT), also known as Greenwich Mean Time (GMT). *See* p. 399 for a conversion table of Universal Time.

# 2002

| January | February | March | April |
|---|---|---|---|
| S M T W T F S | S M T W T F S | S M T W T F S | S M T W T F S |
|    1 2 3 4 5 |        1 2 |        1 2 |  1 2 3 4 5 6 |
| 6 7 8 9 10 11 12 | 3 4 5 6 7 8 9 | 3 4 5 6 7 8 9 | 7 8 9 10 11 12 13 |
| 13 14 15 16 17 18 19 | 10 11 12 13 14 15 16 | 10 11 12 13 14 15 16 | 14 15 16 17 18 19 20 |
| 20 21 22 23 24 25 26 | 17 18 19 20 21 22 23 | 17 18 19 20 21 22 23 | 21 22 23 24 25 26 27 |
| 27 28 29 30 31 | 24 25 26 27 28 | 24 25 26 27 28 29 30 | 28 29 30 |
| | | 31 | |

| May | June | July | August |
|---|---|---|---|
| S M T W T F S | S M T W T F S | S M T W T F S | S M T W T F S |
|     1 2 3 4 |         1 |  1 2 3 4 5 6 |       1 2 3 |
| 5 6 7 8 9 10 11 | 2 3 4 5 6 7 8 | 7 8 9 10 11 12 13 | 4 5 6 7 8 9 10 |
| 12 13 14 15 16 17 18 | 9 10 11 12 13 14 15 | 14 15 16 17 18 19 20 | 11 12 13 14 15 16 17 |
| 19 20 21 22 23 24 25 | 16 17 18 19 20 21 22 | 21 22 23 24 25 26 27 | 18 19 20 21 22 23 24 |
| 26 27 28 29 30 31 | 23 24 25 26 27 28 29 | 28 29 30 31 | 25 26 27 28 29 30 31 |
| | 30 | | |

| September | October | November | December |
|---|---|---|---|
| S M T W T F S | S M T W T F S | S M T W T F S | S M T W T F S |
| 1 2 3 4 5 6 7 |    1 2 3 4 5 |       1 2 | 1 2 3 4 5 6 7 |
| 8 9 10 11 12 13 14 | 6 7 8 9 10 11 12 | 3 4 5 6 7 8 9 | 8 9 10 11 12 13 14 |
| 15 16 17 18 19 20 21 | 13 14 15 16 17 18 19 | 10 11 12 13 14 15 16 | 15 16 17 18 19 20 21 |
| 22 23 24 25 26 27 28 | 20 21 22 23 24 25 26 | 17 18 19 20 21 22 23 | 22 23 24 25 26 27 28 |
| 29 30 | 27 28 29 30 31 | 24 25 26 27 28 29 30 | 29 30 31 |

# 2004

| January | February | March | April |
|---|---|---|---|
| S M T W T F S | S M T W T F S | S M T W T F S | S M T W T F S |
|      1 2 3 | 1 2 3 4 5 6 7 |  1 2 3 4 5 6 |      1 2 3 |
| 4 5 6 7 8 9 10 | 8 9 10 11 12 13 14 | 7 8 9 10 11 12 13 | 4 5 6 7 8 9 10 |
| 11 12 13 14 15 16 17 | 15 16 17 18 19 20 21 | 14 15 16 17 18 19 20 | 11 12 13 14 15 16 17 |
| 18 19 20 21 22 23 24 | 22 23 24 25 26 27 28 | 21 22 23 24 25 26 27 | 18 19 20 21 22 23 24 |
| 25 26 27 28 29 30 31 | 29 | 28 29 30 31 | 25 26 27 28 29 30 |

| May | June | July | August |
|---|---|---|---|
| S M T W T F S | S M T W T F S | S M T W T F S | S M T W T F S |
|        1 |    1 2 3 4 5 |      1 2 3 | 1 2 3 4 5 6 7 |
| 2 3 4 5 6 7 8 | 6 7 8 9 10 11 12 | 4 5 6 7 8 9 10 | 8 9 10 11 12 13 14 |
| 9 10 11 12 13 14 15 | 13 14 15 16 17 18 19 | 11 12 13 14 15 16 17 | 15 16 17 18 19 20 21 |
| 16 17 18 19 20 21 22 | 20 21 22 23 24 25 26 | 18 19 20 21 22 23 24 | 22 23 24 25 26 27 28 |
| 23 24 25 26 27 28 29 | 27 28 29 30 | 25 26 27 28 29 30 31 | 29 30 31 |
| 30 31 | | | |

| September | October | November | December |
|---|---|---|---|
| S M T W T F S | S M T W T F S | S M T W T F S | S M T W T F S |
|    1 2 3 4 |      1 2 |  1 2 3 4 5 6 |     1 2 3 4 |
| 5 6 7 8 9 10 11 | 3 4 5 6 7 8 9 | 7 8 9 10 11 12 13 | 5 6 7 8 9 10 11 |
| 12 13 14 15 16 17 18 | 10 11 12 13 14 15 16 | 14 15 16 17 18 19 20 | 12 13 14 15 16 17 18 |
| 19 20 21 22 23 24 25 | 17 18 19 20 21 22 23 | 21 22 23 24 25 26 27 | 19 20 21 22 23 24 25 |
| 26 27 28 29 30 | 24 25 26 27 28 29 30 | 28 29 30 | 26 27 28 29 30 31 |
| | 31 | | |

## Astrological Signs

| | | | |
|---|---|---|---|
| ♈ | **Aries (Ram):** March 21–April 19 | ♎ | **Libra (Scales):** Sept. 23–Oct. 22 |
| ♉ | **Taurus (Bull):** April 20–May 20 | ♏ | **Scorpio (Scorpion):** Oct. 23–Nov. 21 |
| ♊ | **Gemini (Twins):** May 21–June 20 | ♐ | **Sagittarius (Archer):** Nov. 22–Dec. 21 |
| ♋ | **Cancer (Crab):** June 21–July 22 | ♑ | **Capricorn (Goat):** Dec. 22–Jan. 19 |
| ♌ | **Leo (Lion):** July 23–Aug. 22 | ♒ | **Aquarius (Water Bearer):** Jan. 20–Feb. 18 |
| ♍ | **Virgo (Virgin):** Aug. 23–Sept. 22 | ♓ | **Pisces (Fish):** Feb. 19–March 20 |

# PERPETUAL CALENDAR

| | | | | | |
|---|---|---|---|---|---|
| 1800...4 | 1844...9 | 1888...8 | 1932.13 | 1976.12 | 2020.11 |
| 1801...5 | 1845...4 | 1889...3 | 1933...1 | 1977...7 | 2021...6 |
| 1802...6 | 1846...5 | 1890...4 | 1934...2 | 1978...1 | 2022...7 |
| 1803...7 | 1847...6 | 1891...5 | 1935...3 | 1979...2 | 2023...1 |
| 1804...8 | 1848.14 | 1892.13 | 1936.11 | 1980.10 | 2024...9 |
| 1805...3 | 1849...2 | 1893...1 | 1937...6 | 1981...5 | 2025...4 |
| 1806...4 | 1850...3 | 1894...2 | 1938...7 | 1982...6 | 2026...5 |
| 1807...5 | 1851...4 | 1895...3 | 1939...1 | 1983...7 | 2027...6 |
| 1808.13 | 1852.12 | 1896.11 | 1940...9 | 1984...8 | 2028.14 |
| 1809..1 | 1853...7 | 1897...6 | 1941...4 | 1985...3 | 2029...2 |
| 1810...2 | 1854...1 | 1898...7 | 1942...5 | 1986...4 | 2030...3 |
| 1811...3 | 1855...2 | 1899...1 | 1943...6 | 1987...5 | 2031...4 |
| 1812.11 | 1856.10 | 1900...2 | 1944.14 | 1988.13 | 2032.12 |
| 1813...6 | 1857...5 | 1901...3 | 1945...2 | 1989...1 | 2033...7 |
| 1814...7 | 1858...6 | 1902...4 | 1946...3 | 1990...2 | 2034...1 |
| 1815...1 | 1859...7 | 1903...5 | 1947...4 | 1991...3 | 2035...2 |
| 1816...9 | 1860...8 | 1904.13 | 1948.12 | 1992.11 | 2036.10 |
| 1817...4 | 1861...3 | 1905...1 | 1949...7 | 1993...6 | 2037...5 |
| 1818...5 | 1862...4 | 1906...2 | 1950...1 | 1994...7 | 2038...6 |
| 1819...6 | 1863...5 | 1907...3 | 1951...2 | 1995...1 | 2039...7 |
| 1820.14 | 1864.13 | 1908.11 | 1952.10 | 1996...9 | 2040...8 |
| 1821...2 | 1865...1 | 1909...6 | 1953...5 | 1997...4 | 2041...3 |
| 1822...3 | 1866...2 | 1910...7 | 1954...6 | 1998...5 | 2042...4 |
| 1823...4 | 1867...3 | 1911...1 | 1955...7 | 1999...6 | 2043...5 |
| 1824.12 | 1868.11 | 1912...9 | 1956...8 | 2000.14 | 2044.13 |
| 1825...7 | 1869...6 | 1913...4 | 1957...3 | 2001...2 | 2045...1 |
| 1826...1 | 1870...7 | 1914...5 | 1958...4 | 2002...3 | 2046...2 |
| 1827...2 | 1871...1 | 1915...6 | 1959...5 | 2003...4 | 2047...3 |
| 1828.10 | 1872...9 | 1916.14 | 1960.13 | 2004.12 | 2048.11 |
| 1829...5 | 1873...4 | 1917...2 | 1961...1 | 2005...7 | 2049...6 |
| 1830...6 | 1874...5 | 1918...3 | 1962...2 | 2006...1 | 2050...7 |
| 1831...7 | 1875...6 | 1919...4 | 1963...3 | 2007...2 | 2051...1 |
| 1832...8 | 1876.14 | 1920.12 | 1964.11 | 2008.10 | 2052...9 |
| 1833...3 | 1877...2 | 1921...7 | 1965...6 | 2009...5 | 2053...4 |
| 1834...4 | 1878...3 | 1922...1 | 1966...7 | 2010...6 | 2054...5 |
| 1835...5 | 1879...4 | 1923...2 | 1967...1 | 2011...7 | 2055...6 |
| 1836.13 | 1880.12 | 1924.10 | 1968...9 | 2012...8 | 2056.14 |
| 1837...1 | 1881...7 | 1925...5 | 1969...4 | 2013...3 | 2057...2 |
| 1838...2 | 1882...1 | 1926...6 | 1970...5 | 2014...4 | 2058...3 |
| 1839...3 | 1883...2 | 1927...7 | 1971...6 | 2015...5 | 2059...4 |
| 1840.11 | 1884.10 | 1928...8 | 1972.14 | 2016.13 | 2060.12 |
| 1841...6 | 1885...5 | 1929...3 | 1973...2 | 2017...1 | 2061...7 |
| 1842...7 | 1886...6 | 1930...4 | 1974...3 | 2018...2 | 2062...1 |
| 1843...1 | 1887...7 | 1931...5 | 1975...4 | 2019...3 | 2063...3 |

**DIRECTIONS:** The number given with each year in the key above is the number of the calendar to use for that year.

## 1

```
JANUARY                FEBRUARY               MARCH                  APRIL
S  M  T  W  T  F  S     S  M  T  W  T  F  S     S  M  T  W  T  F  S     S  M  T  W  T  F  S
 1  2  3  4  5  6  7              1  2  3  4              1  2  3  4                       1
 8  9 10 11 12 13 14     5  6  7  8  9 10 11     5  6  7  8  9 10 11     2  3  4  5  6  7  8
15 16 17 18 19 20 21    12 13 14 15 16 17 18    12 13 14 15 16 17 18     9 10 11 12 13 14 15
22 23 24 25 26 27 28    19 20 21 22 23 24 25    19 20 21 22 23 24 25    16 17 18 19 20 21 22
29 30 31                26 27 28                26 27 28 29 30 31       23 24 25 26 27 28 29
                                                                        30

MAY                    JUNE                   JULY                   AUGUST
S  M  T  W  T  F  S     S  M  T  W  T  F  S     S  M  T  W  T  F  S     S  M  T  W  T  F  S
    1  2  3  4  5  6              1  2  3                       1                 1  2  3  4  5
 7  8  9 10 11 12 13     4  5  6  7  8  9 10     2  3  4  5  6  7  8     6  7  8  9 10 11 12
14 15 16 17 18 19 20    11 12 13 14 15 16 17     9 10 11 12 13 14 15    13 14 15 16 17 18 19
21 22 23 24 25 26 27    18 19 20 21 22 23 24    16 17 18 19 20 21 22    20 21 22 23 24 25 26
28 29 30 31             25 26 27 28 29 30       23 24 25 26 27 28 29    27 28 29 30 31
                                                30 31

SEPTEMBER              OCTOBER                NOVEMBER               DECEMBER
S  M  T  W  T  F  S     S  M  T  W  T  F  S     S  M  T  W  T  F  S     S  M  T  W  T  F  S
             1  2        1  2  3  4  5  6  7              1  2  3  4              1  2
 3  4  5  6  7  8  9     8  9 10 11 12 13 14     5  6  7  8  9 10 11     3  4  5  6  7  8  9
10 11 12 13 14 15 16    15 16 17 18 19 20 21    12 13 14 15 16 17 18    10 11 12 13 14 15 16
17 18 19 20 21 22 23    22 23 24 25 26 27 28    19 20 21 22 23 24 25    17 18 19 20 21 22 23
24 25 26 27 28 29 30    29 30 31                26 27 28 29 30          24 25 26 27 28 29 30
                                                                        31
```

## 2

```
JANUARY                FEBRUARY               MARCH                  APRIL
S  M  T  W  T  F  S     S  M  T  W  T  F  S     S  M  T  W  T  F  S     S  M  T  W  T  F  S
    1  2  3  4  5  6                 1  2  3                 1  2  3     1  2  3  4  5  6  7
 7  8  9 10 11 12 13     4  5  6  7  8  9 10     4  5  6  7  8  9 10     8  9 10 11 12 13 14
14 15 16 17 18 19 20    11 12 13 14 15 16 17    11 12 13 14 15 16 17    15 16 17 18 19 20 21
21 22 23 24 25 26 27    18 19 20 21 22 23 24    18 19 20 21 22 23 24    22 23 24 25 26 27 28
28 29 30 31             25 26 27 28             25 26 27 28 29 30 31    29 30

MAY                    JUNE                   JULY                   AUGUST
S  M  T  W  T  F  S     S  M  T  W  T  F  S     S  M  T  W  T  F  S     S  M  T  W  T  F  S
       1  2  3  4  5                       1  2  1  2  3  4  5  6  7                 1  2  3  4
 6  7  8  9 10 11 12     3  4  5  6  7  8  9     8  9 10 11 12 13 14     5  6  7  8  9 10 11
13 14 15 16 17 18 19    10 11 12 13 14 15 16    15 16 17 18 19 20 21    12 13 14 15 16 17 18
20 21 22 23 24 25 26    17 18 19 20 21 22 23    22 23 24 25 26 27 28    19 20 21 22 23 24 25
27 28 29 30 31          24 25 26 27 28 29 30    29 30 31                26 27 28 29 30 31

SEPTEMBER              OCTOBER                NOVEMBER               DECEMBER
S  M  T  W  T  F  S     S  M  T  W  T  F  S     S  M  T  W  T  F  S     S  M  T  W  T  F  S
                   1        1  2  3  4  5  6                 1  2  3                       1
 2  3  4  5  6  7  8     7  8  9 10 11 12 13     4  5  6  7  8  9 10     2  3  4  5  6  7  8
 9 10 11 12 13 14 15    14 15 16 17 18 19 20    11 12 13 14 15 16 17     9 10 11 12 13 14 15
16 17 18 19 20 21 22    21 22 23 24 25 26 27    18 19 20 21 22 23 24    16 17 18 19 20 21 22
23 24 25 26 27 28 29    28 29 30 31             25 26 27 28 29 30       23 24 25 26 27 28 29
30                                                                      30 31
```

## 3

```
JANUARY                FEBRUARY               MARCH                  APRIL
S  M  T  W  T  F  S     S  M  T  W  T  F  S     S  M  T  W  T  F  S     S  M  T  W  T  F  S
       1  2  3  4  5                    1  2                    1  2        1  2  3  4  5  6
 6  7  8  9 10 11 12     3  4  5  6  7  8  9     3  4  5  6  7  8  9     7  8  9 10 11 12 13
13 14 15 16 17 18 19    10 11 12 13 14 15 16    10 11 12 13 14 15 16    14 15 16 17 18 19 20
20 21 22 23 24 25 26    17 18 19 20 21 22 23    17 18 19 20 21 22 23    21 22 23 24 25 26 27
27 28 29 30 31          24 25 26 27 28          24 25 26 27 28 29 30    28 29 30
                                                31

MAY                    JUNE                   JULY                   AUGUST
S  M  T  W  T  F  S     S  M  T  W  T  F  S     S  M  T  W  T  F  S     S  M  T  W  T  F  S
          1  2  3  4                       1        1  2  3  4  5  6                 1  2  3
 5  6  7  8  9 10 11     2  3  4  5  6  7  8     7  8  9 10 11 12 13     4  5  6  7  8  9 10
12 13 14 15 16 17 18     9 10 11 12 13 14 15    14 15 16 17 18 19 20    11 12 13 14 15 16 17
19 20 21 22 23 24 25    16 17 18 19 20 21 22    21 22 23 24 25 26 27    18 19 20 21 22 23 24
26 27 28 29 30 31       23 24 25 26 27 28 29    28 29 30 31             25 26 27 28 29 30 31
                        30

SEPTEMBER              OCTOBER                NOVEMBER               DECEMBER
S  M  T  W  T  F  S     S  M  T  W  T  F  S     S  M  T  W  T  F  S     S  M  T  W  T  F  S
 1  2  3  4  5  6  7        1  2  3  4  5                    1  2     1  2  3  4  5  6  7
 8  9 10 11 12 13 14     6  7  8  9 10 11 12     3  4  5  6  7  8  9     8  9 10 11 12 13 14
15 16 17 18 19 20 21    13 14 15 16 17 18 19    10 11 12 13 14 15 16    15 16 17 18 19 20 21
22 23 24 25 26 27 28    20 21 22 23 24 25 26    17 18 19 20 21 22 23    22 23 24 25 26 27 28
29 30                   27 28 29 30 31          24 25 26 27 28 29 30    29 30 31
```

## 4

```
JANUARY                FEBRUARY               MARCH                  APRIL
S  M  T  W  T  F  S     S  M  T  W  T  F  S     S  M  T  W  T  F  S     S  M  T  W  T  F  S
          1  2  3  4                       1                       1     1  2  3  4  5
 5  6  7  8  9 10 11     2  3  4  5  6  7  8     2  3  4  5  6  7  8     6  7  8  9 10 11 12
12 13 14 15 16 17 18     9 10 11 12 13 14 15     9 10 11 12 13 14 15    13 14 15 16 17 18 19
19 20 21 22 23 24 25    16 17 18 19 20 21 22    16 17 18 19 20 21 22    20 21 22 23 24 25 26
26 27 28 29 30 31       23 24 25 26 27 28       23 24 25 26 27 28 29    27 28 29 30
                                                30 31

MAY                    JUNE                   JULY                   AUGUST
S  M  T  W  T  F  S     S  M  T  W  T  F  S     S  M  T  W  T  F  S     S  M  T  W  T  F  S
             1  2  3     1  2  3  4  5  6  7        1  2  3  4  5                       1  2
 4  5  6  7  8  9 10     8  9 10 11 12 13 14     6  7  8  9 10 11 12     3  4  5  6  7  8  9
11 12 13 14 15 16 17    15 16 17 18 19 20 21    13 14 15 16 17 18 19    10 11 12 13 14 15 16
18 19 20 21 22 23 24    22 23 24 25 26 27 28    20 21 22 23 24 25 26    17 18 19 20 21 22 23
25 26 27 28 29 30 31    29 30                   27 28 29 30 31          24 25 26 27 28 29 30
                                                                        31

SEPTEMBER              OCTOBER                NOVEMBER               DECEMBER
S  M  T  W  T  F  S     S  M  T  W  T  F  S     S  M  T  W  T  F  S     S  M  T  W  T  F  S
    1  2  3  4  5  6              1  2  3  4                       1        1  2  3  4  5  6
 7  8  9 10 11 12 13     5  6  7  8  9 10 11     2  3  4  5  6  7  8     7  8  9 10 11 12 13
14 15 16 17 18 19 20    12 13 14 15 16 17 18     9 10 11 12 13 14 15    14 15 16 17 18 19 20
21 22 23 24 25 26 27    19 20 21 22 23 24 25    16 17 18 19 20 21 22    21 22 23 24 25 26 27
28 29 30                26 27 28 29 30 31       23 24 25 26 27 28 29    28 29 30 31
                                                30
```

## 5

```
JANUARY                FEBRUARY               MARCH                  APRIL
S  M  T  W  T  F  S     S  M  T  W  T  F  S     S  M  T  W  T  F  S     S  M  T  W  T  F  S
             1  2  3     1  2  3  4  5  6  7     1  2  3  4  5  6  7              1  2  3  4
 4  5  6  7  8  9 10     8  9 10 11 12 13 14     8  9 10 11 12 13 14     5  6  7  8  9 10 11
11 12 13 14 15 16 17    15 16 17 18 19 20 21    15 16 17 18 19 20 21    12 13 14 15 16 17 18
18 19 20 21 22 23 24    22 23 24 25 26 27 28    22 23 24 25 26 27 28    19 20 21 22 23 24 25
25 26 27 28 29 30 31                            29 30 31                26 27 28 29 30

MAY                    JUNE                   JULY                   AUGUST
S  M  T  W  T  F  S     S  M  T  W  T  F  S     S  M  T  W  T  F  S     S  M  T  W  T  F  S
                1  2        1  2  3  4  5  6              1  2  3  4                       1
 3  4  5  6  7  8  9     7  8  9 10 11 12 13     5  6  7  8  9 10 11     2  3  4  5  6  7  8
10 11 12 13 14 15 16    14 15 16 17 18 19 20    12 13 14 15 16 17 18     9 10 11 12 13 14 15
17 18 19 20 21 22 23    21 22 23 24 25 26 27    19 20 21 22 23 24 25    16 17 18 19 20 21 22
24 25 26 27 28 29 30    28 29 30                26 27 28 29 30 31       23 24 25 26 27 28 29
31                                                                      30 31

SEPTEMBER              OCTOBER                NOVEMBER               DECEMBER
S  M  T  W  T  F  S     S  M  T  W  T  F  S     S  M  T  W  T  F  S     S  M  T  W  T  F  S
       1  2  3  4  5              1  2  3     1  2  3  4  5  6  7        1  2  3  4  5
 6  7  8  9 10 11 12     4  5  6  7  8  9 10     8  9 10 11 12 13 14     6  7  8  9 10 11 12
13 14 15 16 17 18 19    11 12 13 14 15 16 17    15 16 17 18 19 20 21    13 14 15 16 17 18 19
20 21 22 23 24 25 26    18 19 20 21 22 23 24    22 23 24 25 26 27 28    20 21 22 23 24 25 26
27 28 29 30             25 26 27 28 29 30 31    29 30                   27 28 29 30 31
```

## 6

```
JANUARY                FEBRUARY               MARCH                  APRIL
S  M  T  W  T  F  S     S  M  T  W  T  F  S     S  M  T  W  T  F  S     S  M  T  W  T  F  S
                1  2        1  2  3  4  5  6        1  2  3  4  5  6              1  2  3
 3  4  5  6  7  8  9     7  8  9 10 11 12 13     7  8  9 10 11 12 13     4  5  6  7  8  9 10
10 11 12 13 14 15 16    14 15 16 17 18 19 20    14 15 16 17 18 19 20    11 12 13 14 15 16 17
17 18 19 20 21 22 23    21 22 23 24 25 26 27    21 22 23 24 25 26 27    18 19 20 21 22 23 24
24 25 26 27 28 29 30    28                      28 29 30 31             25 26 27 28 29 30
31

MAY                    JUNE                   JULY                   AUGUST
S  M  T  W  T  F  S     S  M  T  W  T  F  S     S  M  T  W  T  F  S     S  M  T  W  T  F  S
                   1        1  2  3  4  5              1  2  3     1  2  3  4  5  6  7
 2  3  4  5  6  7  8     6  7  8  9 10 11 12     4  5  6  7  8  9 10     8  9 10 11 12 13 14
 9 10 11 12 13 14 15    13 14 15 16 17 18 19    11 12 13 14 15 16 17    15 16 17 18 19 20 21
16 17 18 19 20 21 22    20 21 22 23 24 25 26    18 19 20 21 22 23 24    22 23 24 25 26 27 28
23 24 25 26 27 28 29    27 28 29 30             25 26 27 28 29 30 31    29 30 31
30 31

SEPTEMBER              OCTOBER                NOVEMBER               DECEMBER
S  M  T  W  T  F  S     S  M  T  W  T  F  S     S  M  T  W  T  F  S     S  M  T  W  T  F  S
          1  2  3  4                 1  2        1  2  3  4  5  6              1  2  3  4
 5  6  7  8  9 10 11     3  4  5  6  7  8  9     7  8  9 10 11 12 13     5  6  7  8  9 10 11
12 13 14 15 16 17 18    10 11 12 13 14 15 16    14 15 16 17 18 19 20    12 13 14 15 16 17 18
19 20 21 22 23 24 25    17 18 19 20 21 22 23    21 22 23 24 25 26 27    19 20 21 22 23 24 25
26 27 28 29 30          24 25 26 27 28 29 30    28 29 30                26 27 28 29 30 31
                        31
```

## 7

```
        JANUARY              FEBRUARY               MARCH                 APRIL
 S  M  T  W  T  F  S   S  M  T  W  T  F  S   S  M  T  W  T  F  S   S  M  T  W  T  F  S
                   1                1  2  3  4  5             1  2  3  4  5                      1  2
 2  3  4  5  6  7  8    6  7  8  9 10 11 12    6  7  8  9 10 11 12    3  4  5  6  7  8  9
 9 10 11 12 13 14 15   13 14 15 16 17 18 19   13 14 15 16 17 18 19   10 11 12 13 14 15 16
16 17 18 19 20 21 22   20 21 22 23 24 25 26   20 21 22 23 24 25 26   17 18 19 20 21 22 23
23 24 25 26 27 28 29   27 28                  27 28 29 30 31         24 25 26 27 28 29 30
30 31

          MAY                  JUNE                  JULY                 AUGUST
 S  M  T  W  T  F  S   S  M  T  W  T  F  S   S  M  T  W  T  F  S   S  M  T  W  T  F  S
 1  2  3  4  5  6  7             1  2  3  4                   1  2       1  2  3  4  5  6
 8  9 10 11 12 13 14    5  6  7  8  9 10 11    3  4  5  6  7  8  9    7  8  9 10 11 12 13
15 16 17 18 19 20 21   12 13 14 15 16 17 18   10 11 12 13 14 15 16   14 15 16 17 18 19 20
22 23 24 25 26 27 28   19 20 21 22 23 24 25   17 18 19 20 21 22 23   21 22 23 24 25 26 27
29 30 31               26 27 28 29 30         24 25 26 27 28 29 30   28 29 30 31
                                              31

        SEPTEMBER             OCTOBER              NOVEMBER              DECEMBER
 S  M  T  W  T  F  S   S  M  T  W  T  F  S   S  M  T  W  T  F  S   S  M  T  W  T  F  S
             1  2  3                      1             1  2  3  4  5                1  2  3
 4  5  6  7  8  9 10    2  3  4  5  6  7  8    6  7  8  9 10 11 12    4  5  6  7  8  9 10
11 12 13 14 15 16 17    9 10 11 12 13 14 15   13 14 15 16 17 18 19   11 12 13 14 15 16 17
18 19 20 21 22 23 24   16 17 18 19 20 21 22   20 21 22 23 24 25 26   18 19 20 21 22 23 24
25 26 27 28 29 30      23 24 25 26 27 28 29   27 28 29 30            25 26 27 28 29 30 31
                       30 31
```

## 8

```
        JANUARY              FEBRUARY               MARCH                 APRIL
 S  M  T  W  T  F  S   S  M  T  W  T  F  S   S  M  T  W  T  F  S   S  M  T  W  T  F  S
 1  2  3  4  5  6  7             1  2  3  4                1  2  3    1  2  3  4  5  6  7
 8  9 10 11 12 13 14    5  6  7  8  9 10 11    4  5  6  7  8  9 10    8  9 10 11 12 13 14
15 16 17 18 19 20 21   12 13 14 15 16 17 18   11 12 13 14 15 16 17   15 16 17 18 19 20 21
22 23 24 25 26 27 28   19 20 21 22 23 24 25   18 19 20 21 22 23 24   22 23 24 25 26 27 28
29 30 31               26 27 28 29            25 26 27 28 29 30 31   29 30

          MAY                  JUNE                  JULY                 AUGUST
 S  M  T  W  T  F  S   S  M  T  W  T  F  S   S  M  T  W  T  F  S   S  M  T  W  T  F  S
       1  2  3  4  5                   1  2    1  2  3  4  5  6  7             1  2  3  4
 6  7  8  9 10 11 12    3  4  5  6  7  8  9    8  9 10 11 12 13 14    5  6  7  8  9 10 11
13 14 15 16 17 18 19   10 11 12 13 14 15 16   15 16 17 18 19 20 21   12 13 14 15 16 17 18
20 21 22 23 24 25 26   17 18 19 20 21 22 23   22 23 24 25 26 27 28   19 20 21 22 23 24 25
27 28 29 30 31         24 25 26 27 28 29 30   29 30 31               26 27 28 29 30 31

        SEPTEMBER             OCTOBER              NOVEMBER              DECEMBER
 S  M  T  W  T  F  S   S  M  T  W  T  F  S   S  M  T  W  T  F  S   S  M  T  W  T  F  S
                   1       1  2  3  4  5  6                1  2  3                      1
 2  3  4  5  6  7  8    7  8  9 10 11 12 13    4  5  6  7  8  9 10    2  3  4  5  6  7  8
 9 10 11 12 13 14 15   14 15 16 17 18 19 20   11 12 13 14 15 16 17    9 10 11 12 13 14 15
16 17 18 19 20 21 22   21 22 23 24 25 26 27   18 19 20 21 22 23 24   16 17 18 19 20 21 22
23 24 25 26 27 28 29   28 29 30 31            25 26 27 28 29 30      23 24 25 26 27 28 29
30                                                                   30 31
```

## 9

```
        JANUARY              FEBRUARY               MARCH                 APRIL
 S  M  T  W  T  F  S   S  M  T  W  T  F  S   S  M  T  W  T  F  S   S  M  T  W  T  F  S
    1  2  3  4  5  6                1  2  3                   1  2    1  2  3  4  5  6  7
 7  8  9 10 11 12 13    4  5  6  7  8  9 10    3  4  5  6  7  8  9    8  9 10 11 12 13 14
14 15 16 17 18 19 20   11 12 13 14 15 16 17   10 11 12 13 14 15 16   15 16 17 18 19 20 21
21 22 23 24 25 26 27   18 19 20 21 22 23 24   17 18 19 20 21 22 23   22 23 24 25 26 27 28
28 29 30 31           25 26 27 28 29         24 25 26 27 28 29 30   29 30
                                              31

          MAY                  JUNE                  JULY                 AUGUST
 S  M  T  W  T  F  S   S  M  T  W  T  F  S   S  M  T  W  T  F  S   S  M  T  W  T  F  S
          1  2  3  4                      1    1  2  3  4  5  6             1  2  3
 5  6  7  8  9 10 11    2  3  4  5  6  7  8    7  8  9 10 11 12 13    4  5  6  7  8  9 10
12 13 14 15 16 17 18    9 10 11 12 13 14 15   14 15 16 17 18 19 20   11 12 13 14 15 16 17
19 20 21 22 23 24 25   16 17 18 19 20 21 22   21 22 23 24 25 26 27   18 19 20 21 22 23 24
26 27 28 29 30 31      23 24 25 26 27 28 29   28 29 30 31            25 26 27 28 29 30 31
                       30

        SEPTEMBER             OCTOBER              NOVEMBER              DECEMBER
 S  M  T  W  T  F  S   S  M  T  W  T  F  S   S  M  T  W  T  F  S   S  M  T  W  T  F  S
 1  2  3  4  5  6  7          1  2  3  4  5                   1  2    1  2  3  4  5  6  7
 8  9 10 11 12 13 14    6  7  8  9 10 11 12    3  4  5  6  7  8  9    8  9 10 11 12 13 14
15 16 17 18 19 20 21   13 14 15 16 17 18 19   10 11 12 13 14 15 16   15 16 17 18 19 20 21
22 23 24 25 26 27 28   20 21 22 23 24 25 26   17 18 19 20 21 22 23   22 23 24 25 26 27 28
29 30                  27 28 29 30 31         24 25 26 27 28 29 30   29 30 31
```

## 10

```
        JANUARY              FEBRUARY               MARCH                 APRIL
 S  M  T  W  T  F  S   S  M  T  W  T  F  S   S  M  T  W  T  F  S   S  M  T  W  T  F  S
       1  2  3  4  5                   1  2                      1                1  2  3  4  5
 6  7  8  9 10 11 12    3  4  5  6  7  8  9    2  3  4  5  6  7  8    6  7  8  9 10 11 12
13 14 15 16 17 18 19   10 11 12 13 14 15 16    9 10 11 12 13 14 15   13 14 15 16 17 18 19
20 21 22 23 24 25 26   17 18 19 20 21 22 23   16 17 18 19 20 21 22   20 21 22 23 24 25 26
27 28 29 30 31         24 25 26 27 28 29      23 24 25 26 27 28 29   27 28 29 30
                                              30 31

          MAY                  JUNE                  JULY                 AUGUST
 S  M  T  W  T  F  S   S  M  T  W  T  F  S   S  M  T  W  T  F  S   S  M  T  W  T  F  S
             1  2  3    1  2  3  4  5  6  7             1  2  3  4                1  2
 4  5  6  7  8  9 10    8  9 10 11 12 13 14    6  7  8  9 10 11 12    3  4  5  6  7  8  9
11 12 13 14 15 16 17   15 16 17 18 19 20 21   13 14 15 16 17 18 19   10 11 12 13 14 15 16
18 19 20 21 22 23 24   22 23 24 25 26 27 28   20 21 22 23 24 25 26   17 18 19 20 21 22 23
25 26 27 28 29 30 31   29 30                  27 28 29 30 31         24 25 26 27 28 29 30
                                                                     31

        SEPTEMBER             OCTOBER              NOVEMBER              DECEMBER
 S  M  T  W  T  F  S   S  M  T  W  T  F  S   S  M  T  W  T  F  S   S  M  T  W  T  F  S
    1  2  3  4  5  6                1  2  3  4                   1                1  2  3  4  5  6
 7  8  9 10 11 12 13    5  6  7  8  9 10 11    2  3  4  5  6  7  8    7  8  9 10 11 12 13
14 15 16 17 18 19 20   12 13 14 15 16 17 18    9 10 11 12 13 14 15   14 15 16 17 18 19 20
21 22 23 24 25 26 27   19 20 21 22 23 24 25   16 17 18 19 20 21 22   21 22 23 24 25 26 27
28 29 30               26 27 28 29 30 31      23 24 25 26 27 28 29   28 29 30 31
                                              30
```

## 11

```
        JANUARY              FEBRUARY               MARCH                 APRIL
 S  M  T  W  T  F  S   S  M  T  W  T  F  S   S  M  T  W  T  F  S   S  M  T  W  T  F  S
          1  2  3  4                      1    1  2  3  4  5  6  7                1  2  3  4
 5  6  7  8  9 10 11    2  3  4  5  6  7  8    8  9 10 11 12 13 14    5  6  7  8  9 10 11
12 13 14 15 16 17 18    9 10 11 12 13 14 15   15 16 17 18 19 20 21   12 13 14 15 16 17 18
19 20 21 22 23 24 25   16 17 18 19 20 21 22   22 23 24 25 26 27 28   19 20 21 22 23 24 25
26 27 28 29 30 31      23 24 25 26 27 28 29   29 30 31               26 27 28 29 30

          MAY                  JUNE                  JULY                 AUGUST
 S  M  T  W  T  F  S   S  M  T  W  T  F  S   S  M  T  W  T  F  S   S  M  T  W  T  F  S
                1  2       1  2  3  4  5  6             1  2  3  4                      1
 3  4  5  6  7  8  9    7  8  9 10 11 12 13    5  6  7  8  9 10 11    2  3  4  5  6  7  8
10 11 12 13 14 15 16   14 15 16 17 18 19 20   12 13 14 15 16 17 18    9 10 11 12 13 14 15
17 18 19 20 21 22 23   21 22 23 24 25 26 27   19 20 21 22 23 24 25   16 17 18 19 20 21 22
24 25 26 27 28 29 30   28 29 30               26 27 28 29 30 31      23 24 25 26 27 28 29
31                                                                   30 31

        SEPTEMBER             OCTOBER              NOVEMBER              DECEMBER
 S  M  T  W  T  F  S   S  M  T  W  T  F  S   S  M  T  W  T  F  S   S  M  T  W  T  F  S
          1  2  3  4                1  2  3    1  2  3  4  5  6  7                1  2  3  4  5
 6  7  8  9 10 11 12    4  5  6  7  8  9 10    8  9 10 11 12 13 14    6  7  8  9 10 11 12
13 14 15 16 17 18 19   11 12 13 14 15 16 17   15 16 17 18 19 20 21   13 14 15 16 17 18 19
20 21 22 23 24 25 26   18 19 20 21 22 23 24   22 23 24 25 26 27 28   20 21 22 23 24 25 26
27 28 29 30            25 26 27 28 29 30 31   29 30                  27 28 29 30 31
```

## 12

```
        JANUARY              FEBRUARY               MARCH                 APRIL
 S  M  T  W  T  F  S   S  M  T  W  T  F  S   S  M  T  W  T  F  S   S  M  T  W  T  F  S
             1  2  3    1  2  3  4  5  6  7       1  2  3  4  5  6                1  2  3
 4  5  6  7  8  9 10    8  9 10 11 12 13 14    7  8  9 10 11 12 13    4  5  6  7  8  9 10
11 12 13 14 15 16 17   15 16 17 18 19 20 21   14 15 16 17 18 19 20   11 12 13 14 15 16 17
18 19 20 21 22 23 24   22 23 24 25 26 27 28   21 22 23 24 25 26 27   18 19 20 21 22 23 24
25 26 27 28 29 30 31   29                     28 29 30 31            25 26 27 28 29 30

          MAY                  JUNE                  JULY                 AUGUST
 S  M  T  W  T  F  S   S  M  T  W  T  F  S   S  M  T  W  T  F  S   S  M  T  W  T  F  S
                   1       1  2  3  4  5                1  2  3    1  2  3  4  5  6  7
 2  3  4  5  6  7  8    6  7  8  9 10 11 12    4  5  6  7  8  9 10    8  9 10 11 12 13 14
 9 10 11 12 13 14 15   13 14 15 16 17 18 19   11 12 13 14 15 16 17   15 16 17 18 19 20 21
16 17 18 19 20 21 22   20 21 22 23 24 25 26   18 19 20 21 22 23 24   22 23 24 25 26 27 28
23 24 25 26 27 28 29   27 28 29 30            25 26 27 28 29 30 31   29 30 31
30 31

        SEPTEMBER             OCTOBER              NOVEMBER              DECEMBER
 S  M  T  W  T  F  S   S  M  T  W  T  F  S   S  M  T  W  T  F  S   S  M  T  W  T  F  S
          1  2  3  4                   1  2    1  2  3  4  5  6             1  2  3  4
 5  6  7  8  9 10 11    3  4  5  6  7  8  9    7  8  9 10 11 12 13    5  6  7  8  9 10 11
12 13 14 15 16 17 18   10 11 12 13 14 15 16   14 15 16 17 18 19 20   12 13 14 15 16 17 18
19 20 21 22 23 24 25   17 18 19 20 21 22 23   21 22 23 24 25 26 27   19 20 21 22 23 24 25
26 27 28 29 30         24 25 26 27 28 29 30   28 29 30               26 27 28 29 30 31
                       31
```

## 13

```
        JANUARY              FEBRUARY               MARCH                 APRIL
 S  M  T  W  T  F  S   S  M  T  W  T  F  S   S  M  T  W  T  F  S   S  M  T  W  T  F  S
                1  2       1  2  3  4  5  6       1  2  3  4  5                1  2
 3  4  5  6  7  8  9    7  8  9 10 11 12 13    6  7  8  9 10 11 12    3  4  5  6  7  8  9
10 11 12 13 14 15 16   14 15 16 17 18 19 20   13 14 15 16 17 18 19   10 11 12 13 14 15 16
17 18 19 20 21 22 23   21 22 23 24 25 26 27   20 21 22 23 24 25 26   17 18 19 20 21 22 23
24 25 26 27 28 29 30   28 29                  27 28 29 30 31         24 25 26 27 28 29 30
31

          MAY                  JUNE                  JULY                 AUGUST
 S  M  T  W  T  F  S   S  M  T  W  T  F  S   S  M  T  W  T  F  S   S  M  T  W  T  F  S
 1  2  3  4  5  6  7             1  2  3  4                1  2       1  2  3  4  5  6
 8  9 10 11 12 13 14    5  6  7  8  9 10 11    3  4  5  6  7  8  9    7  8  9 10 11 12 13
15 16 17 18 19 20 21   12 13 14 15 16 17 18   10 11 12 13 14 15 16   14 15 16 17 18 19 20
22 23 24 25 26 27 28   19 20 21 22 23 24 25   17 18 19 20 21 22 23   21 22 23 24 25 26 27
29 30 31               26 27 28 29 30         24 25 26 27 28 29 30   28 29 30 31
                                              31

        SEPTEMBER             OCTOBER              NOVEMBER              DECEMBER
 S  M  T  W  T  F  S   S  M  T  W  T  F  S   S  M  T  W  T  F  S   S  M  T  W  T  F  S
             1  2  3                      1       1  2  3  4  5                1  2  3
 4  5  6  7  8  9 10    2  3  4  5  6  7  8    6  7  8  9 10 11 12    4  5  6  7  8  9 10
11 12 13 14 15 16 17    9 10 11 12 13 14 15   13 14 15 16 17 18 19   11 12 13 14 15 16 17
18 19 20 21 22 23 24   16 17 18 19 20 21 22   20 21 22 23 24 25 26   18 19 20 21 22 23 24
25 26 27 28 29 30      23 24 25 26 27 28 29   27 28 29 30            25 26 27 28 29 30 31
                       30 31
```

## 14

```
        JANUARY              FEBRUARY               MARCH                 APRIL
 S  M  T  W  T  F  S   S  M  T  W  T  F  S   S  M  T  W  T  F  S   S  M  T  W  T  F  S
                   1       1  2  3  4  5       1  2  3  4                      1
 2  3  4  5  6  7  8    6  7  8  9 10 11 12    5  6  7  8  9 10 11    2  3  4  5  6  7  8
 9 10 11 12 13 14 15   13 14 15 16 17 18 19   12 13 14 15 16 17 18    9 10 11 12 13 14 15
16 17 18 19 20 21 22   20 21 22 23 24 25 26   19 20 21 22 23 24 25   16 17 18 19 20 21 22
23 24 25 26 27 28 29   27 28 29              26 27 28 29 30 31       23 24 25 26 27 28 29
30 31                                                                30

          MAY                  JUNE                  JULY                 AUGUST
 S  M  T  W  T  F  S   S  M  T  W  T  F  S   S  M  T  W  T  F  S   S  M  T  W  T  F  S
    1  2  3  4  5  6                1  2  3                      1       1  2  3  4  5
 7  8  9 10 11 12 13    4  5  6  7  8  9 10    2  3  4  5  6  7  8    6  7  8  9 10 11 12
14 15 16 17 18 19 20   11 12 13 14 15 16 17    9 10 11 12 13 14 15   13 14 15 16 17 18 19
21 22 23 24 25 26 27   18 19 20 21 22 23 24   16 17 18 19 20 21 22   20 21 22 23 24 25 26
28 29 30 31            25 26 27 28 29 30      23 24 25 26 27 28 29   27 28 29 30 31
                                              30 31

        SEPTEMBER             OCTOBER              NOVEMBER              DECEMBER
 S  M  T  W  T  F  S   S  M  T  W  T  F  S   S  M  T  W  T  F  S   S  M  T  W  T  F  S
                1  2    1  2  3  4  5  6  7          1  2  3  4                1  2
 3  4  5  6  7  8  9    8  9 10 11 12 13 14    5  6  7  8  9 10 11    3  4  5  6  7  8  9
10 11 12 13 14 15 16   15 16 17 18 19 20 21   12 13 14 15 16 17 18   10 11 12 13 14 15 16
17 18 19 20 21 22 23   22 23 24 25 26 27 28   19 20 21 22 23 24 25   17 18 19 20 21 22 23
24 25 26 27 28 29 30   29 30 31               26 27 28 29 30         24 25 26 27 28 29 30
                                                                     31
```

# History of the Calendar

The purpose of the calendar is to reckon past or future time, to show how many days until a certain event takes place—the harvest or a religious festival—or how long since something important happened.

The earliest calendars must have been strongly influenced by the geographical location of the people who made them. In colder countries, the concept of the year was determined by the seasons, specifically by the end of winter. But in warmer countries, where the seasons are less pronounced, the Moon became the basic unit for time reckoning; an old Jewish book says that "the Moon was created for the counting of the days."

Most of the oldest calendars for which we have reliable information were lunar calendars, based on the time interval from one new moon to the next—a so-called lunation. But even in a warm climate there are annual events that pay no attention to the phases of the Moon. In some areas it was a rainy season; in Egypt it was the annual flooding of the Nile River. The calendar had to account for these yearly events as well.

## The Egyptian Calendar

The ancient Egyptians used a calendar with 12 months of 30 days each, for a total of 360 days per year. About 4000 B.C. they added five extra days at the end of every year to bring it more into line with the solar year.[1] These five days became a festival because it was thought to be unlucky to work during that time.

The Egyptians had calculated that the solar year was actually closer to 365¼ days, but instead of having a single leap day every four years to account for the fractional day (the way we do now), they let the one-quarter day accumulate. After 1,460 years, or four periods of 365 years, they added an entire leap year of 365 days. This means that as the years passed, the Egyptian months fell out of sync with the seasons, so that the summer months eventually fell during winter. Only once every 1,460 years did their calendar year coincide precisely with the solar year.

In addition to the civic calendar, the Egyptians also had a religious calendar that was based on the 29½-day lunar cycle and was more closely linked with agricultural cycles and the movements of the stars.

## Lunar Calendars

During antiquity the lunar calendar that best approximated a solar-year calendar was based on a 19-year period, with 7 of these 19 years having 13 months. In all, the period contained 235 months. Still using the lunation value of 29½ days, this made a total of 6,932½ days, while 19 solar years added up to 6,939.7 days, a difference of just one week per period and about five weeks per century.

Even the 19-year period required adjustment, but it became the basis of the calendars of the ancient Chinese, Babylonians, Greeks, and Jews. This same calendar was also used by the Arabs, but Muhammad later forbade shifting from 12 months to 13 months, so that the Islamic calendar, even today, has a lunar year of 354 days. As a result, the months of the Islamic calendar, as well as the Islamic religious festivals, migrate through all the seasons of the year.

## The Roman Calendar

When Rome emerged as a world power, the difficulties of making a calendar were well known, but the Romans complicated their lives because of their superstition that even numbers were unlucky. Hence their months were 29 or 31 days long, with the exception of February, which had 28 days. However, four months of 31 days, seven months of 29 days, and one month of 28 days added up to only 355 days. Therefore the Romans invented an extra month called Mercedonius of 22 or 23 days. It was added every second year.

Even with Mercedonius, the Roman calendar eventually became so far off that **Julius Caesar,** advised by the astronomer Sosigenes, ordered a sweeping reform in 45 B.C. One year, made 445 days long by imperial decree, brought the calendar back in step with the seasons. Then the solar year (with the value of 365 days and 6 hours) was made the basis of the calendar. The months were 30 or 31 days in length, and to take care of the 6 hours, every fourth year was made a 366-day year. Moreover, Caesar decreed the year began with the first of January, not with the vernal equinox in late March.

This calendar was named the **Julian calendar,** after Julius Caesar, and it continues to be the calendar of the Eastern Orthodox churches to this day. However, despite the correction, the Julian calendar is still 11½ minutes longer than the actual solar year, and after a number of centuries, even 11½ minutes adds up.

## The Gregorian Reform

By the 15th century the Julian calendar had drifted behind the solar calendar by about a week, so that the vernal equinox was falling around March 12 instead of around March 20. Pope Sixtus IV (who reigned from 1471 to 1484) decided that another reform was needed and called the German astronomer Regiomontanus to Rome to advise him. Regiomontanus arrived in 1475, but unfortunately he died shortly afterward, and the pope's plans for reform died with him.

Then in 1545, the Council of Trent authorized Pope Paul III to reform the calendar once more. Most of the mathematical and astronomical work was done by Father Christopher Clavius, S.J. The immediate correction, advised by Father Clavius and ordered by Pope Gregory XIII, was that Thursday, Oct. 4, 1582, was to be the last day of the Julian calendar. The next day would be Friday, Oct. 15. For long-range accuracy, a formula suggested by the Vatican librarian Aloysius Giglio was adopted: every fourth year is a leap year *unless* it is a century year like 1700 or 1800. Century years can be leap years *only* when they are divisible by 400 (e.g., 1600 and 2000). This rule eliminates three leap years in four centuries, making the calendar sufficiently accurate.

For in spite of the revised leap year rule, an average calendar year is still about 26 seconds longer

---

1. The correct figures are lunation: 29 d, 12 h, 44 min, 2.8 sec (29.530585 d); solar year: 365 d, 5 h, 48 min, 46 sec (365.242216 d); 12 lunations: 354 d, 8 h, 48 min, 34 sec (354.3671 d).

## Drift of the Vernal Equinox in the Julian Calendar

| Date of equinox | Julian year | Date of equinox | Julian year | Date of equinox | Julian year | Date of equinox | Julian year |
|---|---|---|---|---|---|---|---|
| March 21 | A.D. 325 | March 18 | A.D. 709 | March 15 | A.D. 1093 | March 12 | A.D. 1477 |
| March 20 | A.D. 453 | March 17 | A.D. 837 | March 14 | A.D. 1221 | March 11 | A.D. 1605 |
| March 19 | A.D. 581 | March 16 | A.D. 965 | March 13 | A.D. 1349 | | |

than the Earth's orbital period. But this discrepancy will need 3,323 years to build up to a single day.

## Reform Adopted Gradually

The Gregorian reform was not adopted throughout the West immediately. All the Protestant princes in 1582 chose to ignore the papal bull; they continued with the Julian calendar. It was not until 1698 that the German professor Erhard Weigel persuaded the Protestant rulers of Germany and the Netherlands to change to the new calendar. In England the shift took place in 1752, and in Russia it needed the revolution to introduce the Gregorian calendar in 1918. Greece switched over in 1923.

## A Better Calendar?

Despite its widespread use, the Gregorian calendar has a number of weaknesses. It cannot be divided into equal halves or quarters; the number of days per month is haphazard; and months and years may begin on any day of the week. Holidays pegged to specific dates may also fall on any day of the week, and few Americans can predict when Thanksgiving will occur next year.

Since Gregory XIII, many other proposals for calendar reform have been made, but none has been permanently adopted. In the meantime, the Gregorian calendar keeps the calendar dates in reasonable unison with astronomical events. □

## Time and Calendar

The two natural cycles on which time measurements are based are the year and the day. The year is defined as the time required for Earth to complete one revolution around the Sun, while the day is the time required for Earth to complete one turn upon its axis. Earth needs 365 days plus about six hours to go around the Sun once, so a year does not consist of a round number of days; the fractional day has to be taken care of by an extra day every fourth year.

But because Earth, while turning upon its axis, also moves around the Sun, there are two kinds of days. A day may be defined as the interval between the highest point of the Sun in the sky on two successive days. This, averaged out over the year, produces the customary 24-hour day. But one might also define a day as the time interval between the moments when a certain point in the sky, say a conveniently located star, is directly overhead. This is called:

**Sidereal time.** A sidereal day is the time that it takes the Earth to complete one rotation on its axis so that a particular star can be observed twice at the meridian that runs directly overhead. Because the Earth is moving around the Sun as it rotates on its axis, the sidereal day is about four minutes shorter than the solar day, being equivalent to 23 hours, 56 minutes, and 4 seconds in mean solar time. As a result, a star will appear to rise about four minutes

earlier every night, and different stars will be visible at different times of the year. Astronomers use a point that they call the "vernal equinox" to determine local sidereal time.

**Apparent solar time** is the time based directly on the Sun's position in the sky. In ordinary life the day runs from midnight to midnight. It begins when the Sun is invisible by being 12 hours from its zenith.

**Mean solar time,** rather than apparent solar time, is the basis for local civil and standard time. The mean solar time is based on the position of a fictitious "mean sun." The reason why this fictitious sun has to be introduced is the following: Earth turns on its axis regularly; it needs the same number of seconds regardless of the season. But the movement of Earth around the Sun is not regular because Earth's orbit is an ellipse. This has the result (as explained in the section on the seasons below) that Earth moves faster in January and slower in July. Though it is Earth that changes velocity, it looks to us as if the Sun does. In January, when Earth moves faster, the *apparent* movement of the Sun looks faster. The mean sun of time measurements, then, is a sun that moves regularly all year round; the real Sun will be either ahead of or behind the mean sun. The difference between the real Sun and the fictitious mean sun is called the *equation of time.*

**Time zones.** But if all clocks were actually set by mean solar time we would be plagued by a welter of time differences that would be "correct" but a major nuisance. A clock on Long Island, correctly showing mean solar time for its location (this would be *local civil time*), would be slightly ahead of a clock in Newark, N.J. The Newark clock would be slightly ahead of a clock in Trenton, N.J., which, in turn, would be ahead of a clock in Philadelphia. This condition prevailed until 1884, when a system of standard time was adopted by the International Meridian Conference. Earth's surface was divided into 24 zones. The standard time of each zone is the mean astronomical time of one of 24 meridians, 15 degrees apart, beginning at the Greenwich, England, meridian and extending east and west around the globe to the International Date Line. (This system was actually put into use a year earlier by the railroad companies of the U.S. and Canada who, until then, had to contend with some 100 conflicting local sun times observed in terminals across the land.)

For practical purposes, this convention is sometimes altered. For example, Alaska, for a time, consisted of four of the eight U.S. time zones: the Pacific standard time zone (east of Juneau) and the 6th (Juneau), 7th (Anchorage), and 8th (Nome) zones, encompassing the 135°, 150°, and 165° meridians, respectively. In 1983, by act of Congress, the entire state (except the westernmost Aleutians) was united into the 6th zone, Alaska standard time.

## The Names of the Months

**January:** named after Janus, the god of doors and gates
**February:** named after Februalia, a time period when sacrifices were made to atone for sins
**March:** named after Mars, the god of war
**April:** from *aperire*, Latin for "to open" (buds)
**May:** named after Maia, the goddess of growth of plants
**June:** from *junius*, Latin for the goddess Juno

**July:** named after Julius Caesar in 44 B.C.
**August:** named after Augustus Caesar in 8 B.C.
**September:** from *septem*, Latin for "seven"
**October:** from *octo*, Latin for "eight"
**November:** from *novem*, Latin for "nine"
**December:** from *decem*, Latin for "ten"

NOTE: The earliest Latin calendar was a 10-month one, beginning with March; thus, September was the seventh month, October, the eighth, etc. July was originally called Quintilis, meaning fifth; August was originally called Sextilis, meaning sixth.

## The Names of the Days of the Week

| Latin | Old English | English | German | French | Italian | Spanish |
|---|---|---|---|---|---|---|
| Dies Solis | Sunnandaeg | Sunday | Sonntag | dimanche | domenica | domingo |
| Dies Lunae | Monandaeg | Monday | Montag | lundi | lunedì | lunes |
| Dies Martis | Tiwesdaeg | Tuesday | Dienstag | mardi | martedì | martes |
| Dies Mercurii | Wodnesdaeg | Wednesday | Mittwoch | mercredi | mercoledì | miércoles |
| Dies Jovis | Thunresdaeg | Thursday | Donnerstag | jeudi | giovedì | jueves |
| Dies Veneris | Frigedaeg | Friday | Freitag | vendredi | venerdì | viernes |
| Dies Saturni | Saeternesdaeg | Saturday | Samstag | samedi | sabato | sábado |

NOTE: The seven-day week originated in ancient Mesopotamia and became part of the Roman calendar in A.D. 321. The names of the days are based on the seven celestial bodies (the Sun, the Moon, Mars, Mercury, Jupiter, Venus, and Saturn), believed at that time to revolve around Earth and influence its events. Most of Western Europe adopted the Roman nomenclature. The Germanic languages substituted Germanic equivalents for the names of four of the Roman gods: Tiw, the god of war, replaced Mars; Woden, the god of wisdom, replaced Mercury; Thor, the god of thunder, replaced Jupiter; and Frigg, the goddess of love, replaced Venus.

The eight U.S. standard time zones are: Atlantic (includes Puerto Rico and the Virgin Islands), eastern, central, mountain, Pacific, Alaska, Hawaii-Aleutian (includes all of Hawaii and those Aleutians west of the Fox Islands), and Samoa standard time.

**The Date Line.** While the time zones are based on the natural event of the Sun crossing a meridian, the date must be an arbitrary decision. The meridians are traditionally counted from the meridian of the observatory of Greenwich, in England, which is called the zero meridian. The logical place for changing the date is 12 hours, or 180°, from Greenwich. Fortunately, the 180th meridian runs mostly through the open Pacific. The Date Line makes a zigzag in the north to incorporate the eastern tip of Siberia into the Siberian time system and then another one to incorporate a number of islands into the Hawaii-Aleutian time zone. In the south there is a similar zigzag for the purpose of tying a number of British-owned islands to the New Zealand time system. Otherwise, the Date Line is the same as 180° from Greenwich. At points to the east of the Date Line the calendar is one day earlier than at points to the west of it. A traveler going eastward across the Date Line from one island to another would not have to reset his watch because he would stay inside the time zone (provided he does so where the Date Line does *not* coincide with the 180° meridian), but it would be the same time of the *previous* day.

## The Seasons

The seasons are caused by the tilt of Earth's axis (23.4°) and not by the fact that Earth's orbit around the Sun is an ellipse. The average distance of Earth from the Sun is 93 million miles; the difference between aphelion (farthest away from the Sun) and perihelion (closest to the Sun) is 3 million miles, so that perihelion is about 91.4 million miles from the Sun. Earth goes through the perihelion point a few days after New Year's Day, just

when the Northern Hemisphere has winter. Aphelion is passed during the first days of July. This by itself shows that the distance from the Sun is not important within these limits. What is important is that when Earth passes through perihelion, the northern end of Earth's axis happens to tilt away from the Sun, so that the areas beyond the Tropic of Cancer receive only slanting rays from a Sun low in the sky.

The tilt of Earth's axis is responsible for four lines you find on every globe. When, say, the North Pole is tilted away from the Sun as much as possible, the farthest points in the North which can still be reached by the Sun's rays are 23.5° from the pole. This is the Arctic Circle. The Antarctic Circle is the corresponding limit 23.4° from the South Pole; the Sun's rays cannot reach beyond this point when we have midsummer in the North.

When the Sun is vertically above the equator, the day is of equal length all over Earth. This happens twice a year, and these are the "equinoxes" in March and in September. After having been over the equator in March, the Sun will seem to move northward. The northernmost point where the Sun can be straight overhead is 23.4° north of the equator. This is the Tropic of Cancer; the Sun can never be vertically overhead to the north of this line. Similarly the Sun cannot be vertically overhead to the south of a line 23.4° south of the equator—the Tropic of Capricorn.

This explains the climatic zones. In the belt (the Greek word *zone* means "belt") between the Tropic of Cancer and the Tropic of Capricorn, the Sun can be straight overhead; this is the tropical zone. The two zones where the Sun cannot be overhead but will be above the horizon every day of the year are the two temperate zones; the two areas where the Sun will not rise at all for varying lengths of time are the two polar areas, Arctic and Antarctic. □

## The Islamic (Hijri) Calendar

The Islamic calendar is based on the lunar year of 354 days. The number of days each month is adjusted according to the lunar cycle, beginning about two days after the new moon. The months drift backward over the seasons, beginning again on the same day every 32½ years. The Islamic year begins on the first day of Muharram, and is counted from the year of the Hegira (*anno Hegirae*)—the year in which Muhammad emigrated from Mecca to Medina (A.D. 622). The year 2003 translates to A.H. 1423–1424.

| Months | Number of days | Months | Number of days | Months | Number of days | Months | Number of days |
|---|---|---|---|---|---|---|---|
| Muharram | 29 or 30 | Rabi II | 29 or 30 | Rajab | 29 or 30 | Shawwal | 29 or 30 |
| Safar | 29 or 30 | Jumada I | 29 or 30 | Sha'ban | 29 or 30 | Dhu'l-Qa'dah | 29 or 30 |
| Rabi I | 29 or 30 | Jumada II | 29 or 30 | Ramadan | 29 or 30 | Dhu'l-Hijjah | 29 or 30 |

## The Jewish Calendar

The Jewish calendar is based on both solar and lunar years. The average lunar year of 354 days is adjusted to the solar year by the addition of a leap year and an intercalary month. Nisan is considered the first month, although the new year begins with Rosh Hashanah, on the first of Tishri, which is in fact the seventh month—the calendar has different starting points for different purposes. The year 2003 translates to the Jewish year 5763–5764.

| Months | Number of days | Months | Number of days | Months | Number of days |
|---|---|---|---|---|---|
| Nisan (March–April)* | 30 | Tishri (Sept.–Oct.) | 30 | Shevat (Jan.–Feb.) | 30 |
| Iyar (April–May) | 29 | Heshvan (Oct.–Nov.) | 29 | Adar (Feb.–March) | 29 |
| Sivan (May–June) | 30 | in some years | 30 | in some years | 30 |
| Tammuz (June–July) | 29 | Kislev (Nov.–Dec.) | 29 | Adar Sheni | 29 |
| Av (July–Aug.) | 30 | in some years | 30 | (intercalary month | |
| Elul (Aug.–Sept.) | 29 | Tevet (Dec.–Jan.) | 29 | in leap year only) | |

*The months correspond approximately to those of the Gregorian calendar.

## The Hindu (Indian National) Calendar

The Indian National Calendar, often called the "Hindu Calendar," is based on both lunar and solar years. This calendar was introduced in 1957 in a government push for all of India to use the same calendar, but various traditional calendars are also used. The start of the Indian National Calendar year coincides with March 22, except in a leap year, when it coincides with March 21. The year is counted from the first year of the Saka era, in A.D. 78. The year 2003 translates to Saka era 1924–1925.

| Month | Number of days | Month | Number of days | Month | Number of days | Month | Number of days |
|---|---|---|---|---|---|---|---|
| Caitra | 30* | Asadha | 31 | Asvina | 30 | Pausa | 30 |
| Vaisakha | 31 | Sravana | 31 | Kartika | 30 | Magha | 30 |
| Jyaistha | 31 | Bhadra | 31 | Agrahayana | 30 | Phalguna | 30 |

* In a leap year Caitra has 31 days.

## The Chinese Calendar

The Chinese lunar year is divided into 12 months of 29 or 30 days. The calendar is adjusted to the length of the solar year by the addition of extra months at regular intervals. The years are arranged in twelve cycles of years, each year represented by and named after one of 12 animals. These 12-year cycles are continuously repeated. The Chinese New Year is celebrated at the second new moon after the winter solstice and falls between January 21 and February 19 on the Gregorian calendar. The year 2003 translates to the Chinese year 4700–4701.

| Rat | Ox | Tiger | Cat (Rabbit) | Dragon | Snake | Horse | Sheep (Goat) | Monkey | Rooster | Dog | Pig |
|---|---|---|---|---|---|---|---|---|---|---|---|
| 1900 | 1901 | 1902 | 1903 | 1904 | 1905 | 1906 | 1907 | 1908 | 1909 | 1910 | 1911 |
| 1912 | 1913 | 1914 | 1915 | 1916 | 1917 | 1918 | 1919 | 1920 | 1921 | 1922 | 1923 |
| 1924 | 1925 | 1926 | 1927 | 1928 | 1929 | 1930 | 1931 | 1932 | 1933 | 1934 | 1935 |
| 1936 | 1937 | 1938 | 1939 | 1940 | 1941 | 1942 | 1943 | 1944 | 1945 | 1946 | 1947 |
| 1948 | 1949 | 1950 | 1951 | 1952 | 1953 | 1954 | 1955 | 1956 | 1957 | 1958 | 1959 |
| 1960 | 1961 | 1962 | 1963 | 1964 | 1965 | 1966 | 1967 | 1968 | 1969 | 1970 | 1971 |
| 1972 | 1973 | 1974 | 1975 | 1976 | 1977 | 1978 | 1979 | 1980 | 1981 | 1982 | 1983 |
| 1984 | 1985 | 1986 | 1987 | 1988 | 1989 | 1990 | 1991 | 1992 | 1993 | 1994 | 1995 |
| 1996 | 1997 | 1998 | 1999 | 2000 | 2001 | 2002 | 2003 | 2004 | 2005 | 2006 | 2007 |

# Holidays

### Religious and Secular, 2003

In the United States, there are ten federal holidays set by law. Four are set by date (New Year's Day, Independence Day, Veterans Day, and Christmas Day). The other six are set by a day of the week and month: Martin Luther King, Jr.'s Birthday, Washington's Birthday, Memorial Day, Labor Day, Columbus Day, and Thanksgiving. All but the last are celebrated on Mondays to create three-day weekends for federal employees. All Jewish and Islamic holidays begin at sundown the day before they are listed here.

**New Year's Day,** Wed., Jan. 1. A federal holiday in the United States, New Year's Day has its origin in Roman times, when sacrifices were offered to Janus, the two-faced Roman deity who looked back on the past and forward to the future.

**Epiphany** (from Greek *epiphaneia,* "manifestation"), Mon., Jan. 6. Falls on the 12th day after Christmas and commemorates the manifestation of Jesus Christ to the Gentiles, as represented by the Magi, the baptism of Jesus, and the miracle of the wine at the marriage feast at Cana. One of the three major Christian festivals, along with Christmas and Easter. Epiphany originally marked the beginning of the carnival season preceding Lent, and the evening preceding it is known as Twelfth Night.

**Martin Luther King, Jr.'s Birthday,** Mon., Jan. 20. (The actual date of his birthday is Jan. 15.) A federal holiday observed on the third Monday in January that honors the late civil rights leader. It became a federal holiday in 1986. In 1999, New Hampshire became the last state to officially honor the holiday.

**Groundhog Day,** Sun., Feb. 2. Legend has it that if the groundhog sees his shadow, he'll return to his hole, and winter will last another six weeks.

**Lincoln's Birthday,** Wed., Feb. 12. A holiday in many states, this day was first formally observed in Washington, D.C., in 1866, when both houses of Congress gathered for a memorial address in tribute to the assassinated president.

**Eid al-Adha,** Wed., Feb. 12. Eid al-Adha, or the Feast of Sacrifice, commemorates Abraham's willingness to obey God by sacrificing his son. Lasting for three days, it concludes the annual Hajj, or pilgrimage to Mecca. Muslims worldwide sacrifice a lamb or other animal and distribute the meat to relatives or the needy.

**St. Valentine's Day,** Fri., Feb. 14. This day is the festival of two third-century martyrs, both named St. Valentine. It is not known why this day is associated with lovers. It may derive from an old pagan festival about this time of year, or it may have been inspired by the belief that birds mate on this day.

**Washington's Birthday,** Mon., Feb. 17. (The actual date of his birthday is Feb. 22.) A federal holiday observed the third Monday in February. It is a common misperception that the federal holiday was changed to "Presidents' Day" and now celebrates both Washington and Lincoln. Only Washington is commemorated by the federal holiday; 12 states, however, officially celebrate "Presidents' Day."

**Shrove Tuesday,** March 4. Falls the day before Ash Wednesday and marks the end of the carnival season, which once began on Epiphany but is now usually celebrated the last three days before Lent. In France, the day is known as Mardi Gras (Fat Tuesday), and Mardi Gras celebrations are also held in several American cities, particularly in New Orleans. The day is sometimes called Pancake Tuesday by the English because fats, which were prohibited during Lent, had to be used up.

**Ash Wednesday,** March 5. The seventh Wednesday before Easter and the first day of Lent, which lasts 40 days. Having its origin sometime before A.D. 1000, it is a day of public penance and is marked in the Roman Catholic Church by the burning of the palms blessed on the previous year's Palm Sunday. With the ashes from the palms the priest then marks a cross with his thumb upon the forehead of each worshipper. The Anglican Church and a few Protestant groups in the United States also observe the day, but generally without the use of ashes.

**First Day of Muharram,** Wed., March 5. The month of Muharram marks the beginning of the Islamic liturgical year. On the tenth day of the month, many Muslims may observe a day of fasting, known as Ashurah.

**St. Patrick's Day,** Mon., March 17. St. Patrick, patron saint of Ireland, has been honored in America since the first days of the nation. Perhaps the most notable part of the observance is the annual St. Patrick's Day parade in New York City.

**Purim (Feast of Lots),** Tues., March 18. A day of joy and feasting celebrating the deliverance of the Jews from a massacre planned by the Persian minister Haman. According to the Book of Esther, the Jewish queen Esther interceded with her husband, King Ahasuerus, to spare the life of her uncle, Mordecai, and Haman was hanged on the same gallows he had built for Mordecai. The holiday is marked by the reading of the Book of Esther (The Megillah), and by the exchange of gifts, donations to the poor, and the presentation of Purim plays.

**Palm Sunday,** April 13. Observed the Sunday before Easter to commemorate the entry of Jesus into Jerusalem. The procession and the ceremonies introducing the benediction of palms probably had their origins in Jerusalem.

**First Day of Passover (Pesach),** Thurs., April 17. The Feast of the Passover, also called the Feast of Unleavened Bread, commemorates the escape of the Jews from Egypt. As the Jews fled, they ate unleavened bread, and from that time the Jews have allowed no leavening in their houses during Passover, bread being replaced by matzoh.

**Good Friday,** April 18. The Friday before Easter, it commemorates the Crucifixion, which is retold during services from the Gospel according to St. John. A feature in Roman Catholic churches is the Liturgy of the Passion; there is no Consecration, the Host having been consecrated the previous day. The eating of hot-cross buns on this day is said to have started in England.

**Easter Sunday,** April 20. Observed in all Western Christian churches, Easter commemorates the Resurrection of Jesus. It is celebrated on the first Sunday after the full moon that occurs on or next after the vernal equinox (fixed at March 21) and is therefore celebrated between March 22 and April 25 inclusive. This date was fixed by the Council of Nicaea in A.D. 325.

**Orthodox Easter (Pascha),** Sun., April 27. The Orthodox church uses the same formula to calculate Easter as the Western church, but bases it on the traditional Julian calendar instead of the more contemporary Gregorian calendar. For this reason Orthodox Easter generally falls on a different date than the Western Christian Easter.

**Mother's Day,** Sun., May 11. Observed the second Sunday in May, as proposed by Anna Jarvis of Philadelphia in 1907. West Virginia was the first state to recognize the holiday in 1910, and President Woodrow Wilson officially proclaimed Mother's Day a national holiday in 1914.

**Mawlid an-Nabi,** Wed., May 14. This holiday celebrates the birthday of Muhammad, the founder of Islam. It is fixed as the 12th day of the month of Rabi I in the Islamic calendar.

**Memorial Day,** Mon., May 26. Memorial Day became a federal holiday in 1971 that is observed on the last Monday in May. It originated in 1868, when Union General John A. Logan designated a day in which the graves of Civil War soldiers would be decorated. Originally known as Decoration Day, the holiday was changed to Memorial Day within twenty years, becoming a holiday dedicated to the memory of all war dead.

**Ascension Day,** Thurs., May 29. The Ascension of Jesus took place in the presence of His apostles 40 days after the Resurrection. It is traditionally thought to have occurred on Mount Olivet in Bethany.

**First Day of Shavuot (Hebrew Pentecost),** Fri., June 6. This festival, sometimes called the Feast of Weeks, or of Harvest, or of the First Fruits, falls 50 days after Passover and originally celebrated the end of the seven-week grain-harvesting season. In later tradition, it also celebrated the giving of the Law to Moses on Mount Sinai.

**Pentecost (Whitsunday),** June 8. This day commemorates the descent of the Holy Ghost upon the apostles 50 days after the Resurrection. The sermon by the apostle Peter, which led to the baptism of 2,000 who professed belief, originated the ceremonies that have since been followed. "Whitsunday" is believed to have come from "white Sunday" when, among the English, white robes were worn by those baptized on the day.

**Flag Day,** Sat., June 14. This day commemorates the adoption by the Continental Congress on June 14, 1777, of the Stars and Stripes as the U.S. flag. Although it is a legal holiday only in Pennsylvania, President Truman, on Aug. 3, 1949, signed a bill requesting the president to call for its observance each year by proclamation.

**Father's Day,** Sun., June 15. Observed the third Sunday in June. The exact origin of the holiday is not clear, but it was first celebrated June 19, 1910, in Spokane, Wash. In 1966 President Lyndon Johnson signed a proclamation making Father's Day official.

**Independence Day,** Fri., July 4. The day of the adoption of the Declaration of Independence in 1776, celebrated in all states and territories. The observance began the next year in Philadelphia.

**Labor Day,** Mon., Sept. 1. A federal holiday observed the first Monday in September. Labor Day was first celebrated in New York in 1882 under the sponsorship of the Central Labor Union, following the suggestion of Peter J. McGuire, of the Knights of Labor, that the day be set aside in honor of labor.

**First Day of Rosh Hashanah (Jewish New Year),** Sat., Sept. 27. This day marks the beginning of the Jewish year 5764 and opens the Ten Days of Penitence, which close with Yom Kippur.

**Yom Kippur (Day of Atonement),** Mon., Oct. 6. This day marks the end of the Ten Days of Penitence that began with Rosh Hashanah. It is described in Leviticus as a "Sabbath of rest," and synagogue services begin the preceding sundown, resume the following morning, and continue to sundown.

**First Day of Sukkot (Feast of Tabernacles),** Sat., Oct. 11. This festival, also known as the Feast of the Ingathering, originally celebrated the fruit harvest, and the name comes from the booths or tabernacles in which the Jews lived during the harvest, although one tradition traces it to the shelters used by the Jews in their wandering through the wilderness. During the festival many Jews build small huts in their backyards or on the roofs of their houses.

**Columbus Day,** Mon., Oct. 13. A federal holiday, observed the second Monday in October, it commemorates Christopher Columbus's landing in the New World in 1492. Quite likely the first celebration of Columbus Day was that organized in 1792 by the Society of St. Tammany, or the Columbian Order, widely known as Tammany Hall.

**Simchat Torah (Rejoicing of the Law),** Sun., Oct. 19. This joyous holiday falls on the eighth day of Sukkot. It marks the end of the year's reading of the Torah (Five Books of Moses) in the synagogue every Saturday and the beginning of the new cycle of reading.

**First Day of Ramadan,** Mon., Oct. 27. This day marks the beginning of a month-long fast that all Muslims must keep during the daylight hours. It commemorates the first revelation of the Qur'an. Following the last day of Ramadan, **Eid al-Fitr** is celebrated on Wed., Nov. 26.

**Halloween,** Fri., Oct. 31. Eve of All Saints' Day, formerly called All Hallows and Hallowmass. Halloween is traditionally associated in some countries with customs such as bonfires, masquerading, and the telling of ghost stories. These are old Celtic practices marking the beginning of winter.

**All Saints' Day,** Sat., Nov. 1. A Roman Catholic and Anglican holiday celebrating all saints, known and unknown.

**Election Day** (legal holiday in certain states), Tues., Nov. 4. Since 1845, by act of Congress, the first Tuesday after the first Monday in November is the date for choosing presidential electors. State elections are also generally held on this day.

**Veterans Day,** Tues., Nov. 11. Armistice Day, a federal holiday, was established in 1926 to commemorate the signing in 1918 of the armistice ending World War I. On June 1, 1954, the name was changed to Veterans Day to honor all men and women who have served America in its armed forces.

**Thanksgiving,** Thurs., Nov. 27. A federal holiday observed the fourth Thursday in November by act of Congress (1941), it was the first such national proclamation issued by President Lincoln in 1863, on the urging of Mrs. Sarah J. Hale, editor of *Godey's Lady's Book*. Most Americans believe that the holiday dates back to the day of thanks ordered by Governor Bradford of Plymouth Colony in New England in 1621, but scholars point out that days of thanks stem from ancient times.

**First Sunday of Advent,** Nov. 30. Advent is the season in which the faithful must prepare themselves for the coming, or advent, of the Savior on

Christmas. The four Sundays before Christmas are marked by special church services.

**First Day of Hanukkah (Festival of Lights),** Sat., Dec. 20. This festival was instituted by Judas Maccabaeus in 165 B.C. to celebrate the purification of the Temple of Jerusalem, which had been desecrated three years earlier by Antiochus Epiphanes, who set up a pagan altar and offered sacrifices to Zeus Olympius. In Jewish homes, a light is lighted on each night of the eight-day festival.

**Christmas (Feast of the Nativity),** Thurs., Dec. 25. The most widely celebrated holiday of the Christian year, Christmas is observed as the anniversary of the birth of Jesus. Christmas customs are centuries old. The mistletoe, for example, comes from the Druids, who, in hanging the mistletoe, hoped for peace and good fortune. Comparatively recent is the Christmas tree, first set up in Germany in the 17th century. Colonial Manhattan Islanders introduced the name Santa Claus, a corruption of the Dutch name St. Nicholas, who lived in fourth-century Asia Minor.

## Christian and Secular Holidays, 2002–2004

| Year | Ash Wednesday | Easter | Pentecost | Labor Day | Election Day | Thanksgiving | 1st Sun. Advent |
|---|---|---|---|---|---|---|---|
| 2002 | Feb. 13 | March 31 | May 19 | Sept. 2 | Nov. 5 | Nov. 28 | Dec. 1 |
| 2003 | March 5 | April 20 | June 8 | Sept. 1 | Nov. 4 | Nov. 27 | Nov. 30 |
| 2004 | Feb. 25 | April 11 | May 30 | Sept. 6 | Nov. 2 | Nov. 25 | Nov. 28 |

Shrove Tuesday: 1 day before Ash Wednesday. Palm Sunday: 7 days before Easter. Maundy Thursday: 3 days before Easter. Good Friday: 2 days before Easter. Holy Saturday: 1 day before Easter. Ascension Day: 10 days before Pentecost. Trinity Sunday: 7 days after Pentecost. Corpus Christi: 11 days after Pentecost.

## Orthodox Holidays, 2002–2005

| Year | Great Lent Begins | Pascha (Easter) | Ascension | Pentecost | Year | Great Lent Begins | Pascha (Easter) | Ascension | Pentecost |
|---|---|---|---|---|---|---|---|---|---|
| 2002 | March 18 | May 5 | June 13 | June 23 | 2004 | Feb. 23 | April 11 | May 20 | May 30 |
| 2003 | March 10 | April 27 | June 5 | June 15 | 2005 | March 14 | May 1 | June 9 | June 19 |

## Jewish Holidays, 2002–2004

| Year | Purim[1] | 1st day Passover[2] | 1st day Shavuot[3] | 1st day Rosh Hashanah[4] | Yom Kippur[5] | 1st day Sukkot[6] | Simchat Torah[7] | 1st day Hanukkah[8] |
|---|---|---|---|---|---|---|---|---|
| 2002 | Feb. 26 | March 28 | May 17 | Sept. 7 | Sept. 16 | Sept. 21 | Sept. 29 | Nov. 30 |
| 2003 | March 18 | April 17 | June 6 | Sept. 27 | Oct. 6 | Oct. 11 | Oct. 19 | Dec. 20 |
| 2004 | March 7 | April 6 | May 26 | Sept. 16 | Sept. 25 | Sept. 30 | Oct. 8 | Dec. 8 |

1. Feast of Lots. 2. Feast of Unleavened Bread. 3. Hebrew Pentecost; or Feast of Weeks, or of Harvest, or of First Fruits. 4. Jewish New Year. 5. Day of Atonement. 6. Feast of Tabernacles, or of the Ingathering. 7. Rejoicing of the Law. In Israel, Simchat Torah is celebrated on the day before the date given. 8. Festival of Lights.

Length of Jewish holidays (O=Orthodox, C=Conservative, R=Reform): Passover: O & C, 8 days (holy days: first 2 and last 2); R, 7 days (holy days: first and last). Shavuot: O & C, 2 days; R, 1 day. Rosh Hashanah: O & C, 2 days; R, 1 day. Yom Kippur: All groups, 1 day. Sukkot: All groups, 7 days (holy days: first 2; R, first only); O & C observe 2 additional days: Shemini Atseret (Eighth Day of the Feast) and Simchat Torah; R observes Shemini Atseret but not Simchat Torah. Hanukkah: All groups, 8 days. NOTE: All holidays begin at sundown on the evening before the date given.

## Islamic Holidays, 2001–2005 (A.H. 1422–1425)

| In the Year of the Hegira | Muharram (Islamic New Year) | Mawlid al-Nabi (Muhammad's Birthday) | Ramadan begins | Eid al-Fitr (Ramadan ends) | Eid al-Adha (Festival of Sacrifice) |
|---|---|---|---|---|---|
| A.H. 1422 | March 26, 2001 | June 4, 2001 | Nov. 17, 2001 | Dec. 17, 2001 | Feb. 23, 2002 |
| A.H. 1423 | March 15, 2002 | May 24, 2002 | Nov. 6, 2002 | Dec. 6, 2002 | Feb. 12, 2003 |
| A.H. 1424 | March 5, 2003 | May 14, 2003 | Oct. 27, 2003 | Nov. 26, 2003 | Feb. 2, 2004 |
| A.H. 1425 | Feb. 22, 2004 | May 2, 2004 | Oct. 15, 2004 | Nov. 14, 2004 | Jan. 21, 2005 |

NOTE: All holidays begin at sundown on the evening before the date given. Islamic holidays are based on the lunar calendar and thus may vary by one or two days. Dates apply to North America.

## Hindu Festival Dates, 2003

*Source:* Indian Calendars for the 21st Century, by Pal Singh Purewal

| | | | |
|---|---|---|---|
| Jan. 14 | Makar Sankranti | Aug. 12 | Raksha Bandhan |
| Feb. 6 | Vasant Panchami | Aug. 19 | Sri Krishna Jayanti |
| March 1 | Maha Shivaratri Vrat (fast) | Aug. 30 | Ganesh Chaturathi |
| March 18 | Holi (last day) | Sept. 10 | Saradhas begin |
| April 2 | Bikrami Samvat (2060 begins) | Sept. 26 | Asuj Navratras begin |
| April 2 | Chetra Navratras begin | Oct. 4 | Dassehra |
| April 11 | Rama Navmi | Oct. 14 | Karva Chauth Vrat (fast) |
| April 14 | Vaisakhi (solar new year) | Oct. 25 | Diwali (Festival of Lights) |

## Sikh Festival Dates, 2003*

*Source:* Indian Calendars for the 21st Century, by Pal Singh Purewal

| Festival | Nanakshahi (Sikh) | Bikrami (Hindu) | Festival | Nanakshahi (Sikh) | Bikrami (Hindu) |
|---|---|---|---|---|---|
| Birthday of Guru Gobind Singh Sahib | Jan. 5 | Jan. 9 | Installation of Holy Scriptures as Guru Granth Sahib | Oct. 20 | Oct. 27 |
| Maghi | Jan. 13 | Jan. 14 | Bandi Chhor Divas (Diwali) | Oct. 25 | Oct. 25 |
| Nanakshahi Era 535 begins | March 14 | — | Birthday of Guru Nanak Dev Sahib | Nov. 8 | Nov. 8 |
| Hola Mohalla | March 19 | March 19 | | | |
| Vaisakhi | April 14 | April 14 | Martyrdom of Guru Tegh Bahadur Sahib | Nov. 24 | Nov. 28 |
| Martyrdom of Guru Arjan Dev Sahib | June 16 | June 4 | | | |
| First Parkash Guru Granth Sahib | Sept. 1 | Aug. 28 | | | |

*The dates for the Sikh festivals are given according to both the Bikrami (Hindu) calendar, which is based on the sidereal year, and the reformed Nanakshahi (Sikh) calendar, which is based on the tropical year. All Bikrami dates are moveable.
NOTE: Dates for Sikh and Hindu holidays are determined according to the date of their observance in India.

## Chinese New Year

| | | | |
|---|---|---|---|
| **2000** Feb. 5 | **2003** Feb. 1 | **2006** Jan. 29 | **2009** Jan. 26 |
| **2001** Jan. 24 | **2004** Jan. 22 | **2007** Feb. 18 | **2010** Feb. 14 |
| **2002** Feb. 12 | **2005** Feb. 9 | **2008** Feb. 7 | **2011** Feb. 3 |

## State Holidays

**Jan. 6, Three Kings' Day:** P.R.
**Jan. 8, Battle of New Orleans Day:** La.
**Jan. 11, De Hostos's Birthday:** P.R.
**Jan. 19, Robert E. Lee's Birthday:** Ark., Fla., Ky., La., S.C.; **(third Mon.):** Ala., Miss.
**Jan. 19, Confederate Heroes Day:** Tex.
**Jan. (third Mon.), Lee-Jackson-King Day:** Va.
**Jan. 30, F. D. Roosevelt's Birthday:** Ky.
**Feb. 15, Susan B. Anthony's Birthday:** Fla., Minn.
**March (first Tues.), Town Meeting Day:** Vt.
**March 2, Texas Independence Day:** Tex.
**March (first Mon.), Casimir Pulaski's Birthday:** Ill.
**March 17, Evacuation Day:** Mass. (in Suffolk County)
**March 20 (first day of spring), Youth Day:** Okla.
**March 22, Abolition Day:** P.R.
**March 25, Maryland Day:** Md.
**March 26, Prince Jonah Kuhio Kalanianaole Day:** Hawaii
**March (last Mon.), Seward's Day:** Alaska
**April 2, Pascua Florida Day:** Fla.
**April 13, Thomas Jefferson's Birthday:** Ala., Okla.
**April 16, De Diego's Birthday:** P.R.
**April (third Mon.), Patriots' Day:** Maine, Mass.
**April 21, San Jacinto Day:** Tex.
**April 22, Arbor Day:** Nebr.
**April 22, Oklahoma Day:** Okla.
**April 26, Confederate Memorial Day:** Fla., Ga.
**April (fourth Mon.), Fast Day:** N.H.
**April (last Mon.), Confederate Memorial Day:** Ala., Miss.
**May 1, Bird Day:** Okla.
**May 8, Truman Day:** Mo.
**May 11, Minnesota Day:** Minn.
**May 20, Mecklenburg Independence Day:** N.C.

**June (first Mon.), Jefferson Davis's Birthday:** Ala., Miss.
**June 3, Jefferson Davis's Birthday:** Fla., S.C.
**June 3, Confederate Memorial Day:** Ky., La.
**June 9, Senior Citizens Day:** Okla.
**June 11, King Kamehameha I Day:** Hawaii
**June 15, Separation Day:** Del.
**June 17, Bunker Hill Day:** Mass. (in Suffolk County)
**June 19, Emancipation Day:** Tex.
**June 20, West Virginia Day:** W.Va.
**July 17, Muñoz Rivera's Birthday:** P.R.
**July 24, Pioneer Day:** Utah
**July 25, Constitution Day:** P.R.
**July 27, Barbosa's Birthday:** P.R.
**Aug. (first Sun.), American Family Day:** Ariz.
**Aug. (first Mon.), Colorado Day:** Colo.
**Aug. (second Mon.), Victory Day:** R.I.
**Aug. 16, Bennington Battle Day:** Vt.
**Aug. (third Friday), Admission Day:** Hawaii
**Aug. 27, Lyndon B. Johnson's Birthday:** Tex.
**Aug. 30, Huey P. Long Day:** La.
**Sept. 9, Admission Day:** Calif.
**Sept. 12, Defenders' Day:** Md.
**Sept. 16, Cherokee Strip Day:** Okla.
**Sept. (first Sat. after full moon), Indian Day:** Okla.
**Oct. 10, Leif Eriksson Day:** Minn.
**Oct. 10, Oklahoma Historical Day:** Okla.
**Oct. 18, Alaska Day:** Alaska
**Oct. 31, Nevada Day:** Nev.
**Nov. 4, Will Rogers Day:** Okla.
**Nov. (week of the 16th), Oklahoma Heritage Week:** Okla.
**Nov. 19, Discovery Day:** P.R.
**Dec. 7, Delaware Day:** Del.

## Birthstones

| Month | Stone | Month | Stone | Month | Stone |
|---|---|---|---|---|---|
| January | Garnet | June | Pearl, Alexandrite, or | October | Opal or Tourmaline |
| February | Amethyst | | Moonstone | November | Topaz or Citrine |
| March | Aquamarine or Bloodstone | July | Ruby or Star Ruby | December | Turquoise, Lapis Lazuli, |
| April | Diamond | August | Peridot or Sardonyx | | Blue Zircon, or Blue |
| May | Emerald | September | Sapphire or Star Sapphire | | Topaz |

*Source:* Jewelry Industry Council.

## Traditional Wedding Anniversary Gift List

| Anniv. | Gift | Anniv. | Gift | Anniv. | Gift | Anniv. | Gift |
|---|---|---|---|---|---|---|---|
| 1st | Paper | 7th | Copper, wool | 13th | Lace | 35th | Coral |
| 2nd | Cotton | 8th | Bronze, pottery | 14th | Ivory | 40th | Ruby |
| 3rd | Leather | 9th | Pottery, willow | 15th | Crystal | 45th | Sapphire |
| 4th | Fruit, flowers | 10th | Tin | 20th | China | 50th | Gold |
| 5th | Wood | 11th | Steel | 25th | Silver | 55th | Emerald |
| 6th | Sugar | 12th | Silk, linen | 30th | Pearl | 60th | Diamond |

## Modern Wedding Anniversary Gift List

| Anniv. | Gift | Anniv. | Gift | Anniv. | Gift | Anniv. | Gift |
|---|---|---|---|---|---|---|---|
| 1st | Gold jewelry | 8th | Tourmaline | 15th | Ruby | 30th | Pearl jubilee |
| 2nd | Garnet | 9th | Lapis | 16th | Peridot | 35th | Emerald |
| 3rd | Pearls | 10th | Diamond jewelry | 17th | Watch | 40th | Ruby |
| 4th | Blue topaz | 11th | Turquoise | 18th | Cat's-eye | 45th | Sapphire |
| 5th | Sapphire | 12th | Jade | 19th | Aquamarine | 50th | Golden jubilee |
| 6th | Amethyst | 13th | Citrine | 20th | Emerald | 60th | Diamond jubilee |
| 7th | Onyx | 14th | Opal | 25th | Silver jubilee | | |

*Source:* Jewelry Industry Council.

## Selected National Holidays Around the World, 2003

| Country | Date | Country | Date | Country | Date | Country | Date |
|---|---|---|---|---|---|---|---|
| Afghanistan | Aug. 19 | Haiti | Jan. 1 | Pakistan | March 23 | | |
| Albania | Nov. 28 | Hungary | Aug. 20 | Panama | Nov. 3 | | |
| Argentina | May 25 | Iceland | June 17 | Papua New Guinea | Sept. 16 | | |
| Armenia | Sept. 21 | India | Jan. 26 | Paraguay | May 15 | | |
| Australia | Jan. 26 | Indonesia | Aug. 17 | Peru | July 28 | | |
| Austria | Oct. 26 | Iran | Feb. 11 | Philippines | June 12 | | |
| Bahamas | July 10 | Iraq | July 17 | Poland | May 3 | | |
| Bangladesh | March 26 | Ireland | March 17 | Portugal | June 10 | | |
| Barbados | Nov. 30 | Israel | May 7[1] | Romania | Dec. 1 | | |
| Belgium | July 21 | Italy | June 2 | Samoa | June 1 | | |
| Belize | Sept. 21 | Jamaica | Aug. 4[2] | Saudi Arabia | Sept. 23 | | |
| Bolivia | Aug. 6 | Japan | Dec. 23 | Senegal | April 4 | | |
| Brazil | Sept. 7 | Jordan | May 25 | Singapore | Aug. 9 | | |
| Bulgaria | March 3 | Kenya | Dec. 12 | Slovakia | Sept. 1 | | |
| Canada | July 1 | North Korea | Sept. 9 | Slovenia | June 25 | | |
| Chile | Sept. 18 | South Korea | Aug. 15 | Somalia | Oct. 21 | | |
| China | Oct. 1 | Kuwait | Feb. 25 | South Africa | April 27 | | |
| Colombia | July 20 | Lebanon | Nov. 22 | Spain | Oct. 12 | | |
| Congo, Republic of | Aug. 15 | Liberia | July 26 | Sri Lanka | Feb. 4 | | |
| Croatia | May 30 | Lithuania | Feb. 16 | Swaziland | Sept. 6 | | |
| Cuba | Jan. 1 | Luxembourg | June 23 | Sweden | June 6 | | |
| Czech Republic | Oct. 28 | Macedonia | Aug. 2 | Switzerland | Aug. 1 | | |
| Denmark | April 16 | Malaysia | Aug. 31 | Tanzania | April 26 | | |
| Dominican Republic | Feb. 27 | Malta | Sept. 21 | Thailand | Dec. 5 | | |
| Ecuador | Aug. 10 | Mexico | Sept. 16 | Tunisia | March 20 | | |
| Egypt | July 23 | Monaco | Nov. 19 | Turkey | Oct. 29 | | |
| El Salvador | Sept. 15 | Mongolia | July 11 | Uganda | Oct. 9 | | |
| Ethiopia | May 28 | Morocco | March 3 | United Arab Emirates | Dec. 2 | | |
| Finland | Dec. 6 | Mozambique | June 25 | United States | July 4 | | |
| France | July 14 | Nepal | Dec. 28 | Uruguay | Aug. 25 | | |
| Gabon | Aug. 17 | Netherlands | April 30 | Venezuela | July 5 | | |
| Georgia | May 26 | New Zealand | Feb. 6 | Vietnam | Sept. 2 | | |
| Germany | Oct. 3 | Nicaragua | Sept. 15 | Yemen, Republic of | May 22 | | |
| Greece | March 25 | Nigeria | Oct. 1 | Zambia | Oct. 24 | | |
| Guatemala | Sept. 15 | Norway | May 17 | Zimbabwe | April 18 | | |

1. Changes yearly according to Hebrew calendar. 2. Celebrated on first Monday in August.

# Major Religions of the World

There are twelve classical world religions—those religions most often included in history of world religion surveys and studied in world religions classes: Baha'i, Buddhism, Christianity, Confucianism, Hinduism, Islam, Jainism, Judaism, Shinto, Sikhism, Taoism, and Zoroastrianism. Here are overviews of the nine largest of these classical religions.

## Judaism

Judaism is the oldest of the monotheistic faiths. It affirms the existence of one God, Yahweh, who entered into covenant with the descendants of Abraham, God's chosen people. Judaism's holy writings reveal how God has been present with them throughout their history. These writings are known as the Torah, specifically the five books of Moses, but most broadly conceived as the Hebrew Scriptures (traditionally called the Old Testament by Christians) and the compilation of oral tradition known as the Talmud (which includes the Mishnah, the oral law).

According to Scripture, the Hebrew patriarch Abraham (20th century? B.C.) founded the faith that would become known as Judaism. He obeyed the call of God to depart northern Mesopotamia and travel to Canaan. God promised to bless his descendants if they remained faithful in worship. Abraham's line descended through Isaac, then Jacob (also called Israel; his descendants came to be called Israelites). According to Scripture, 12 families that descended from Jacob migrated to Egypt, where they were enslaved. They were led out of bondage (13th century? B.C.) by Moses, who united them in the worship of Yahweh. The Hebrews returned to Canaan after a 40-year sojourn in the desert, conquering from the local peoples the "promised land" that God had provided for them.

The 12 tribes of Israel lived in a covenant association during the period of the judges (1200?–1000? B.C.), leaders known for wisdom and heroism. Saul first established a monarchy (r. 1025?–1005? B.C.); his successor, David (r. 1005?–965? B.C.), unified the land of Israel and made Jerusalem its religious and political center. Under his son, Solomon (r. 968?–928? B.C.), a golden era culminated in the building of a temple, replacing the portable sanctuary in use until that time. Following Solomon's death, the kingdom was split into Israel in the north and Judah in the south. Political conflicts resulted in

the conquest of Israel by Assyria (721 B.C.) and the defeat of Judah by Babylon (586 B.C.). Jerusalem and its temple were destroyed, and many Judeans were exiled to Babylon.

During the era of the kings, the prophets were active in Israel and Judah. Their writings emphasize faith in Yahweh as God of Israel and of the entire universe, and they warn of the dangers of worshiping other gods. They also cry out for social justice.

The Judeans were permitted to return in 539 B.C. to Judea, where they were ruled as a Persian province. Though temple and cult were restored in Jerusalem, during the exile a new class of religious leaders had emerged—the scribes. They became rivals to the temple hierarchy and would eventually evolve into the party known as the Pharisees.

Persian rule ended when Alexander the Great conquered Palestine in 332 B.C. After his death, rule of Judea alternated between Egypt and Syria. When the Syrian ruler Antiochus IV Epiphanes tried to prevent the practice of Judaism, a revolt was led by the Maccabees (a Jewish family), winning Jewish independence in 128 B.C. The Romans conquered Jerusalem in 63 B.C.

During this period the Sadducees (temple priests) and the Pharisees (teachers of the law in the synagogues) offered different interpretations of Judaism. Smaller groups that emerged were the Essenes, a religious order; the Apocalyptists, who expected divine deliverance led by the Messiah; and the Zealots, who were prepared to fight for national independence. Hellenism also influenced Judaism at this time.

When the Zealots revolted, the Roman armies destroyed Jerusalem and its temple (A.D. 70). The Jews were scattered in the Diaspora (dispersion) and experienced much persecution. Rabbinic Judaism, developed according to Pharisaic practice and centered on Torah and synagogue, became the primary expression of faith. The Scriptures became uniform

## Top Ten Organized Religions of the World

Statistics of the world's religions are only very rough approximations. Aside from Christianity, few religions, if any, attempt to keep statistical records, and even Protestants and Catholics employ different methods of counting members.

| Religion | Members | Percentage | Religion | Members | Percentage |
|---|---|---|---|---|---|
| Christianity | 1.9 billion | 33.0% | Judaism | 14 million | 0.2 |
| Islam | 1.1 billion | 20.0 | Baha'ism | 6.1 million | 0.1 |
| Hinduism | 781 million | 13.0 | Confucianism | 5.3 million | 0.1 |
| Buddhism | 324 million | 6.0 | Jainism | 4.9 million | 0.1 |
| Sikhism | 19 million | 0.4 | Shintoism | 2.8 million | 0.0 |

NOTE: This list includes only organized religions and excludes more loosely defined groups such as Chinese or African traditional religions. *Sources:* Encyclopedia Britannica; www.adherents.com.

and the Talmud took shape. In the 12th century Maimonides formulated the influential 13 Articles of Faith, including belief in God, God's oneness and lack of physical or other form, the changelessness of Torah, restoration of the monarchy under the Messiah, and resurrection of the dead.

Two branches of European Judaism developed during the Middle Ages: the Sephardic, based in Spain and with an affinity to Babylonian Jews; and the Ashkenazic, based in Franco-German lands and affiliated with Rome and Palestine. Two forms of Jewish mysticism also arose at this time: medieval Hasidism and attention to the Kabbalah (a mystical interpretation of Scripture).

After a respite during the 18th-century Enlightenment, anti-Semitism again plagued European Jews in the 19th century, sparking the Zionist movement that culminated in the founding of the state of Israel in 1948. The Holocaust of World War II took the lives of more than 6 million Jews.

Jews today continue synagogue worship, which includes readings from the Law and the Prophets and prayers, such as the Shema (Hear, O Israel) and the Amidah (the 18 Benedictions). Religious life is guided by the commandments of the Torah, which include the practice of circumcision and Sabbath observance.

Present-day Judaism has three main expressions: Orthodox, Conservative, and Reform. Reform movements, resulting from the Haskala (Jewish Enlightenment) of the 18th century, began in western Europe but took root in North America. Reform Jews do not hold the oral law (Talmud) to be a divine revelation, and they emphasize ethical and moral teachings. Orthodox Jews follow the traditional faith and practice with great seriousness. They follow a strict kosher diet and keep the Sabbath with care. Conservative Judaism, which developed in the mid-18th century, holds the Talmud to be authoritative and follows most traditional practices, yet tries to make Judaism relevant for each generation, believing that change and tradition can complement each other. Because the Torah assumes belief in God but does not require it, a strong secular movement also exists within Judaism, including atheist and agnostic elements.

In general, Jews do not proselytize, but they do welcome newcomers to their faith.

## Christianity

Christianity is a monotheistic religion founded by the followers of Jesus of Nazareth. Jesus, a Jew, was born in about 7 B.C. and assumed his public life, probably after his 30th year, in Galilee. The New Testament Gospels describe Jesus as a teacher and miracle worker. He proclaimed the kingdom of God, a future reality that is at the same time already present. Jesus set the requirements for participation in the kingdom of God as a change of heart and repentance for sins, love of God and neighbor, and concern for justice. Circa A.D. 30 he was executed on a cross in Jerusalem, a brutal form of punishment for those considered a political threat to the Roman Empire.

After his death his followers came to believe in him as the Christ, the Messiah. The Gospels report his resurrection and how the risen Jesus was witnessed by many of his followers. The apostle Paul helped spread the new faith in his missionary travels. Historically, Christianity arose out of Judaism and claims that Jesus fulfilled many of the promises of the Hebrew Scripture (often referred to as the Old Testament).

The new religion spread rapidly throughout the Roman Empire. In its first two centuries, Christianity began to take shape as an organization, developing distinctive doctrine, liturgy, and ministry. By the fourth century the Christian church had taken root in countries stretching from Spain in the West to Persia and India in the East. Christians had been subject to persecution by the Roman state, but gained tolerance under Constantine the Great (A.D. 313). The church became favored under his successors, and in 380 the emperor Theodosius proclaimed Christianity the state religion. Other religions were suppressed.

Because differences in doctrine threatened to divide the church, a standard Christian creed was formulated by bishops at successive ecumenical councils, the first of which was held in A.D. 325 (Nicaea). Important doctrines were defined concerning the Trinity—in other words, that there is one God in three persons: Father, Son, and Holy Spirit (Constantinople, A.D. 381), and the nature of Christ as both divine and human (Chalcedon, A.D. 541). Christians came to accept both Hebrew Scripture and the New Testament as authoritative. The New Testament comprises four Gospels (narratives of Jesus' life), 21 Epistles, The Acts of the Apostles, and Revelation.

Because of differences between Christians of the East and West, the unity of the church was broken in 1054. The religious center for the Eastern Orthodox Church was Constantinople, and the Roman

### Largest 25 U.S. Churches,[1] 2002

| Denomination name | Members |
| --- | --- |
| The Catholic Church | 63,683,030 |
| Southern Baptist Convention | 15,960,308 |
| The United Methodist Church | 8,340,954 |
| The Church of God in Christ | 5,499,875 |
| The Church of Jesus Christ of Latter-Day Saints | 5,208,827 |
| Evangelical Lutheran Church in America | 5,125,919 |
| National Baptist Convention of America, Inc. | 3,500,000 |
| Presbyterian Church (U.S.A.) | 3,485,332 |
| Assemblies of God | 2,577,560 |
| The Lutheran Church—Missouri Synod (LCMS) | 2,554,088 |
| Progressive National Baptist Convention, Inc. | 2,500,000 |
| African Methodist Episcopal Church | 2,500,000 |
| National Missionary Baptist Convention of America | 2,500,000 |
| Episcopal Church | 2,311,398 |
| Greek Orthodox Archdiocese of America | 1,500,000 |
| Pentecostal Assemblies of the World, Inc. | 1,500,000 |
| Churches of Christ | 1,500,000 |
| American Baptist Churches in the U.S.A. | 1,436,909 |
| United Church of Christ | 1,377,320 |
| African Methodist Episcopal Zion Church | 1,296,662 |
| Baptist Bible Fellowship International | 1,200,000 |
| Christian Churches and Churches of Christ | 1,071,616 |
| The Orthodox Church in America | 1,000,000 |
| Jehovah's Witnesses | 998,166 |
| Church of God (Cleveland, Tenn.) | 895,536 |

1. The National Baptist Convention U.S.A., Inc., one of the ten largest churches in the U.S., is currently at work producing an actual count to be available in subsequent editions. *Source: Yearbook of American & Canadian Churches,* 2002.

Catholic Church defined doctrine and practice for Christians in the West. In 1517 the Reformation began, which ultimately caused a schism in the Western church. Reformers wished to correct certain practices within the Roman church, but they also came to view the Christian faith in a distinctly new way. The major Protestant denominations (Lutheran, Presbyterian, Reformed, and Anglican [Episcopalian]) thus came into being. Over the centuries, numerous denominations have broken with these major traditions, resulting in a spectrum of Christian expression.

In the 21st century, many Christians hope to regain a sense of unity through dialogue and cooperation among different traditions. The ecumenical movement led to the formation of the World Council of Churches in 1948 (Amsterdam), which has since been joined by many denominations.

Through its missionary activity Christianity has spread to most parts of the globe.

### Eastern Orthodoxy

Eastern Orthodoxy comprises the faith and practices stemming from ancient churches in the eastern part of the Roman Empire. It encompasses Orthodox churches in communion with the see of Constantinople.

The Orthodox, Catholic, Apostolic Church is the direct descendant of the Byzantine state church and consists of independent national churches that are united by doctrine, liturgy, and hierarchical organization (church leaders include deacons and priests, who may either be married or be monks before ordination, and bishops, who must be celibates). The heads of these churches are called patriarchs or metropolitans. Rivalry between the pope of Rome and the patriarch of Constantinople, as well as differences that existed for centuries between the eastern and western parts of the empire, led to a schism in 1054. The mutual excommunication pronounced in that year was lifted in 1965, however, and a climate of better understanding has ensued. Orthodox churches belong to the World Council of Churches.

The Eastern Orthodox churches recognize only the canons of the seven ecumenical councils (325–787) as binding for faith, and they reject doctrines that have been added in the West.

The central worship service is called the Liturgy, which is understood as representing God's acts of salvation. Its center is the celebration of the Eucharist, or Lord's Supper. Icons (sacred pictures) have a special place in Orthodox worship. The mother of Christ may also may play a part in it is also greatly venerated. The Orthodox Church and the Western Catholic Church recognize the same number of sacraments.

Orthodox churches are found in Greece, Turkey, Russia, the Balkans, and other parts of the former Soviet Union. In this century Orthodox faith has spread to western Europe and other parts of the world, particularly North America.

### Eastern Rite Churches

These include the Uniate Churches that recognize the authority of the pope but keep their own traditional liturgies and those churches dating back to the fifth century that emancipated themselves from the Byzantine state church. They include the Melchites, Syrian Catholics, Maronites (Arab Christians in Lebanon), Catholic Copts and Ethiopians, the autonomous Nestorian Church, and others.

### Roman Catholicism

Roman Catholicism comprises the beliefs and practices of the Roman Catholic Church. It stands under the authority of the bishop of Rome, the pope, and is led by him and bishops who are held to be, through ordination, successors of Peter and the apostles. Doctrine and sacraments are administered by the hierarchy of archbishops, bishops, priests, and deacons. As successor to Peter, the pope is considered the Vicar of Christ. Roman Catholics believe their church to be the one, holy, catholic, and apostolic church, possessing all the properties of the one, true church of Christ.

The faith of the church is understood to be identical with that taught by Christ and his apostles and contained in the Bible and tradition. New definitions of doctrines, such as the Immaculate Conception of Mary (1854) and the bodily Assumption of Mary (1950), have been declared by popes, however. At Vatican Council I (1870) the pope was proclaimed "endowed with infallibility, *ex cathedra,* in other words, when exercising the office of pastor and teacher of all Christians."

The center of Roman Catholic worship is the celebration of the Mass, the Eucharist, which is the commemoration of Christ's sacrificial death and resurrection. Other sacraments are baptism, confirmation, penance, matrimony, anointing of the sick (formerly known as extreme unction), and holy orders.

## Roman Catholic Church Hierarchy

The Catholic clergy is organized in a strict, sometimes overlapping hierarchy:

**Pope:** Head of the church, he is based at the Vatican. The pope is infallible in defining matters of faith and morals.

**Cardinal:** Appointed by the pope, the 178 cardinals worldwide, including 13 in the U.S., make up the College of Cardinals. As a body, it advises the pope and, on his death, elects a new pope.

**Archbishop:** An archbishop is a bishop of a main or metropolitan diocese, also called an archdiocese. A cardinal can concurrently hold the title. The U.S. has 45 archbishops.

**Bishop:** A bishop, like a priest, is ordained to this station. He is a teacher of church doctrine, a priest of sacred worship, and a minister of church government. The U.S. has 290 active bishops; 194 head dioceses.

**Priest:** An ordained minister who can administer most of the sacraments, including the Eucharist, baptism, and marriage. He can be with a particular religious order or committed to serving a congregation.

**Deacon:** A transitional deacon is a seminarian studying for the priesthood. A permanent deacon can be married and assists a priest by performing some of the sacraments.

*Source: Time Magazine.*

The Virgin Mary and the other saints, and their relics, are venerated, and prayers are made to them to intercede with God, in whose presence they are believed to dwell.

The Roman Catholic Church is the largest Christian organization in the world, found in most countries.

Vatican Council II (1962–1965) sought to "update" the church, bringing about changes in practice and more deeply involving the laity. The immensely popular Pope John Paul II (1978–) has taken a more conservative course and has reached out to Catholics worldwide through his extensive travels.

### Protestantism

Protestantism encompasses the Christian churches that separated from Rome during the Reformation in the 16th century. This movement was initiated by an Augustinian monk, Martin Luther. The term *Protestant* was originally applied to followers of Luther, who protested at the Diet of Spires (1529) against the decree that prohibited all further ecclesiastical reforms. Other influential reformers included John Calvin, Ulrich Zwingli, and John Knox. Protestantism rejected attempts to tie God's revelation to earthly institutions and strictly adhered to the Word of God as sole authority in matters of faith and practice *(sola scriptura)*. Central in the reformers' understanding of the biblical message is the justification of the sinner by faith alone. The church is understood as a fellowship, and the priesthood of all believers is stressed.

The Augsburg Confession (1530) was the principal statement of Lutheran faith and practice. It became a model for other Protestant confessions of faith. Major Protestant denominations include the Lutheran, Reformed (Calvinist), Presbyterian, and Anglican (Episcopalian). Innumerable sects and denominations sprang from these roots, including Quakers, Baptists, Pentecostals, Congregationalists, Methodists, and nondenominational assemblies.

Since the latter part of the 19th century, national councils of churches have been established in many countries, for example, the Federal Council of Churches of Christ in America in 1908. Churches of a particular denomination have joined in federations and world alliances, beginning with the Anglican Lambeth Conference in 1867.

Protestant missionary activity, particularly strong in the 19th century, resulted in the founding of many churches in Asia and Africa. The ecumenical movement, which originated with Protestant missions, aims at unity among Christians and churches.

## Islam

Islam, one of the three major monotheistic faiths, was founded in Arabia by Muhammad between 610 and 632. There are an estimated 5.5 million Muslims in North America and 1 billion Muslims worldwide.

Muhammad was born in A.D. 570 at Mecca and belonged to the Quraysh tribe, which was active in the caravan trade. At the age of 25 he joined the trade from Mecca to Syria in the employment of a rich widow, Khadija, whom he later married. Critical of the lax moral standards and polytheistic practices of the inhabitants of Mecca, he began to lead a contemplative life in the desert. In a dramatic religious vision, the angel Gabriel announced to Muhammad that he was to be a prophet. Encouraged by Khadija, he devoted himself to the reform of religion and society. Polytheism was to be abandoned. But leaders of the Quraysh generally rejected his teaching, and Muhammad gained only a small following and suffered persecution. He eventually fled Mecca.

The Hegira *(Hijra,* meaning "emigration") of Muhammad from Mecca, where he was not honored, to Medina, where he was well received, occurred in 622 and marks the beginning of the Muslim era. After a number of military conflicts with Mecca, in 630 he marched on Mecca and conquered it. Muhammad died at Medina in 632. His grave there has since been a place of pilgrimage.

Muhammad's followers, called Muslims, revered him as the prophet of Allah (God), the only God. Muslims consider Muhammad to be the last in the line of prophets that included Abraham and Jesus. Islam spread quickly, stretching from Spain in the west to India in the east within a century after the prophet's death. Sources of the Islamic faith are the Qur'an (Koran), regarded as the uncreated, eternal Word of God, and tradition *(hadith)* regarding sayings and deeds of the prophet.

*Islam* means "surrender to the will of Allah," the all-powerful, who determines humanity's fate. Good deeds will be rewarded at the Last Judgment in paradise, and evil deeds will be punished in hell.

The Five Pillars, or primary duties, of Islam are profession of faith; prayer, to be performed five times a day; almsgiving to the poor and the mosque (house of worship); fasting during daylight hours in the month of Ramadan; and pilgrimage to Mecca (the *hajj*) at least once in a Muslim's lifetime, if it is physically and financially possible. The pilgrimage includes homage to the ancient shrine of the Ka'aba, the most sacred site in Islam.

Muslims gather for corporate worship on Fridays. Prayers and a sermon take place at the mosque, which is also a center for teaching of the Qur'an. The community leader, the *imam,* is considered a teacher and prayer leader.

Islam succeeded in uniting an Arab world of separate tribes and castes, but disagreements concerning the succession of the prophet caused a division in Islam between two groups, Sunnis and Shi'ites. The Shi'ites rejected the first three successors to Muhammad as usurpers, claiming the fourth, Muhammad's son-in-law Ali, as the rightful leader.

---

### U.S. Protestant Groups

According to the Hartford Institute for Religious Research, U.S. Protestant groups are commonly divided into four broad categories:

**Liberal Protestant:** Episcopal, Presbyterian, Unitarian Universalist, United Church of Christ

**Moderate Protestant:** American Baptist, Disciples of Christ, Evangelical Lutheran, Mennonite, Reformed Church in America, United Methodist

**Evangelical Protestant:** Assemblies of God, Christian Reformed, Nazarene, Churches of Christ, Independent Christian Churches (Instrumental), Mega-churches, Nondenominational Protestant, Seventh-day Adventist, Southern Baptist

**Historically Black Protestant** denominations

The Sunnis (from the word *tradition*), the largest division of Islam (today more than 80%), believe in the legitimacy of the first three successors. Among these, other sects arose (such as the conservative Wahhabi of Saudi Arabia), as well as different schools of theology. Another development within Islam, beginning in the eighth and ninth centuries, was Sufism, a form of mysticism. This movement was influential for many centuries and was instrumental in the spread of Islam in Asia and Africa.

Islam has expanded greatly under Muhammad's successors. It is the principal religion of the Middle East, Asia, and the northern half of Africa.

## Hinduism

Hinduism is the major religion of India, practiced by more than 80% of the population. In contrast to other religions, it has no founder. Considered the oldest religion in the world, it dates back, perhaps, to prehistoric times.

No single creed or doctrine binds Hindus together. Intellectually there is complete freedom of belief, and one can be monotheist, polytheist, or atheist. Hinduism is a syncretic religion, welcoming and incorporating a variety of outside influences.

The most ancient sacred texts of the Hindu religion are written in Sanskrit and called the *Vedas* (*vedah* means "knowledge"). There are four Vedic books, of which the Rig-Veda is the oldest. It discusses multiple gods, the universe, and creation. The dates of these works are unknown (1000 B.C.?). Present-day Hindus rarely refer to these texts but do venerate them.

The Upanishads (dated 1000–300 B.C.), commentaries on the Vedic texts, speculate on the origin of the universe and the nature of deity, and *atman* (the individual soul) and its relationship to *Brahman* (the universal soul). They introduce the doctrine of *karma* and recommend meditation and the practice of yoga.

Further important sacred writings include the Epics, which contain legendary stories about gods and humans. They are the Mahabharata (composed between 200 B.C. and A.D. 200) and the Ramayana. The former includes the Bhagavad-Gita (Song of the Lord), an influential text that describes the three paths to salvation. The Puranas (stories in verse, probably written between the 6th and 13th centuries) detail myths of Hindu gods and heroes and also comment on religious practice and cosmology.

According to Hindu beliefs, Brahman is the principle and source of the universe. This divine intelligence pervades all beings, including the individual soul. Thus the many Hindu deities are manifestations of the one Brahman. Hinduism is based on the concept of reincarnation, in which all living beings, from plants on earth to gods above, are caught in a cosmic cycle of becoming and perishing.

Life is determined by the law of karma—one is reborn to a higher level of existence based on moral behavior in a previous phase of existence. Life on earth is regarded as transient and a burden. The goal of existence is liberation from the cycle of rebirth and death and entrance into the indescribable state of *moksha* (liberation).

The practice of Hinduism consists of rites and ceremonies centering on birth, marriage, and death. There are many Hindu temples, which are considered to be dwelling places of the deities and to which people bring offerings. Places of pilgrimage include Benares on the Ganges, the most sacred river in India. Of the many Hindu deities, the most popular are the cults of Vishnu, Shiva, and Shakti, and their various incarnations. Also important is Brahma, the creator god. Hindus also venerate human saints.

Orthodox Hindu society in India was divided into four major hereditary classes: (1) the Brahmin (priestly and learned class); (2) the Kshatriya (military, professional, ruling, and governing occupations); (3) the Vaishya (landowners, merchants, and business occupations); and (4) the Sudra (artisans, laborers, and peasants). Below the Sudra was a fifth group, the Untouchables (lowest menial occupations and no social standing). The Indian government banned discrimination against the Untouchables in the constitution of India in 1950. Observance of class and caste distinctions varies throughout India.

In modern times work has been done to reform and revive Hinduism. One of the outstanding reformers was Ramakrishna (1836–1886), who inspired many followers, one of whom founded the Ramakrishna mission. The mission is active both in India and in other countries and is known for its scholarly and humanitarian works.

## Buddhism

Buddhism was founded in the fourth or fifth century B.C. in northern India by a man known traditionally as Siddhartha (meaning "he who has reached the goal") Gautama, the son of a warrior prince. Some scholars believe that he lived from 563 to 483 B.C., though his exact life span is uncertain. Troubled by the inevitability of suffering in human life, he left home and a pampered life at the age of 29 to wander as an ascetic, seeking religious insight and a solution to the struggles of human existence. He passed through many trials and practiced extreme self-denial. Finally, while meditating under the bodhi tree ("tree of perfect knowledge"), he reached enlightenment and taught his followers about his new spiritual understanding.

Gautama's teachings differed from the Hindu faith prevalent in India at the time. Whereas in Hinduism the Brahmin caste alone performed religious functions and attained the highest spiritual understanding, Gautama's beliefs were more egalitarian, accessible to all who wished to be enlightened. At the core of his understanding were the Four Noble Truths: (1) all living beings suffer; (2) the origin of this suffering is desire—for material possessions, power, and so on; (3) desire can be overcome; and (4) there is a path that leads to release from desire. This way is called the Noble Eightfold Path: right views, right intention, right speech, right action, right livelihood, right effort, right concentration, and right ecstasy.

Gautama promoted the concept of *anatman* (that a person has no actual self) and the idea that existence is characterized by impermanence. This realization helps one let go of desire for transient things. Still, Gautama did not recommend extreme self-denial but rather a disciplined life called the Middle Way. Like the Hindus, he believed that existence consisted of reincarnation, a cycle of birth and death. He held that it could be broken only by reaching complete detachment from worldly cares. Then the soul could be released into *nirvana* (literally "blowing out")—an indescribable state of total transcendence. Gautama traveled to preach the *dharma* (sacred truth) and was recognized as the Buddha (enlightened one). After his death his followers continued to develop doctrine and practice, which came to center on the Three Jewels: the *dharma* (the sacred teachings of Buddhism), the *sangha* (the community of followers, which now includes nuns, monks, and laity), and the Buddha. Under the patronage of the Mauryan emperor Ashoka (third century B.C.), Buddhism spread throughout India and to other parts of Asia. Monasteries were established, as well as temples dedicated to Buddha; at shrines his relics were venerated. Though by the fourth century A.D. Buddhist presence in India had dwindled, it flourished in other parts of Asia.

Numerous Buddhist sects have emerged. The oldest, called the Theravada (Way of the Elders) tradition, interprets Buddha as a great sage but not a deity. It emphasizes meditation and ritual practices that help the individual become an *arhat*, an enlightened being. Its followers emphasize the authority of the earliest Buddhist scriptures, the Tripitaka (Three Baskets), a compilation of sermons, rules for celibates, and doctrine. This sect is prevalent in Southeast Asia and Sri Lanka. It is sometimes called the Hinayana (Lesser Vehicle) tradition (once considered a pejorative term).

Between the second century B.C. and the second century A.D., the Mahayana (Greater Vehicle) tradition refocused Buddhism to concentrate less on individual attainment of enlightenment and more on concern for humanity. It promotes the ideal of the *bodhisattva* (enlightened being), who shuns entering nirvana until all sentient beings can do so as well, willingly remaining in the painful cycle of birth and death to perform works of compassion. Members of this tradition conceive of Buddha as an eternal being to whom prayers can be made; other Buddhas are revered as well, adding a polytheistic dimension to the religion. Numerous sects have developed from the Mahayana tradition, which has been influential in China, Korea, and Japan.

A third broad tradition, variously called Vajrayana (Diamond Vehicle), Mantrayana (Vehicle of the Mantra), or Tantric Buddhism, offers a quicker, more demanding way to achieve nirvana. Because of its level of challenge—enabling one to reach enlightenment in one lifetime—it requires the guidance of a spiritual leader. It is most prominent in Tibet and Mongolia.

Zen Buddhism encourages individuals to seek the Buddha nature within themselves and to practice a disciplined form of sitting meditation in order to reach *satori*—spiritual enlightenment.

## Sikhism

A major religion of India and the fifth-largest faith in the world, Sikhism emerged in the Punjab under the guidance of the guru Nanak (1469–1539?). This region had been influenced by the Hindu *bhakti* movement, which promoted both the idea that God comprises one reality alone as well as the practice of devotional singing and prayer. The Muslim mystical tradition of Sufism, with its emphasis on meditation, also had some prominence there. Drawing on these resources, Nanak forged a new spiritual path.

In his youth, Nanak began to compose hymns. At the age of 29, he had a mystical experience that led him to proclaim "There is no Hindu; there is no Muslim." A strict monotheist, he rejected Hindu polytheism but accepted the Hindu concept of life as a cycle of birth, death, and rebirth; *moksha,* release from this cycle into unity with God, could be achieved only with the help of a guru, or spiritual teacher. Nanak believed that communion with God could be gained through devotional repetition of the divine name, singing of hymns and praises, and adherence to a demanding ethical code. He rejected idols and the Hindu caste system; it became a custom for Sikhs of all social ranks to take meals together. These beliefs are still central to modern Sikhism.

Nanak was first in a line of ten gurus who shaped and inspired Sikhism. The fifth, Arjun (1563–1606), compiled hymns and other writings by earlier Sikh gurus, as well as medieval Hindu and Muslim saints, in the *Adi Granth* (First Book), or *Guru Granth Sahib* (the Granth Personified). This book became the sacred scripture of Sikhism. In addition to his spiritual leadership, Arjun wielded considerable secular power as he grappled with leaders of the Mughal Empire.

The tenth guru, Gobind Singh (1666–1708), was both a scholar and a military hero. He established the Khalsa (community of pure ones), an order that combined spiritual devotion, personal discipline, and ideals of military valor. Baptism initiates new members into the Khalsa. The *Adi Granth* took its final form under the supervision of Gobind Singh, as did the *Dasam Granth* (Tenth Book), a collection of prayers, poetry, and narrative. After the deaths of his four sons, Gobind Singh declared the line of gurus at an end. The *Adi Granth* would instead be reverenced in houses of worship, taking the place of a living guru.

Today, Sikhs worship at *gurdwaras* (temples), where the *Adi Granth* is the object of devotion. This book is consulted regarding questions of faith and practice. On certain occasions, it is recited in its entirety (requiring more than a day) or carried in procession; offerings may be placed before it. Worshipful singing, meditation, and focus on the divine name remain essential to spiritual life. Some Sikhs undertake pilgrimages to historical *gurdwaras*, such as the Golden Temple of Amritsar, that are associated with the gurus. Some become disciples of living saints. There is no established Sikh priesthood.

## Confucianism

Confucius (K'ung Fu-tzu), born in the state of Lu (northern China), lived from 551 to 479 B.C. He was a brilliant teacher, viewing education not merely as the accumulation of knowledge but as a means of self-transformation. His legacy was a system of thought emphasizing education, proper behavior, and loyalty. His effect on Chinese culture was immense.

The teachings of Confucius are contained in the *Analects*, a collection of his sayings as remembered by his students. They were further developed by philosophers such as Mencius (Meng Tse, fl. 400 B.C.). Confucianism is little concerned with metaphysical discussion of religion or with spiritual attainments. It instead emphasizes moral conduct and right relationships in the human sphere.

Cultivation of virtue is a central tenet of Confucianism. Two important virtues are *jen*, a benevolent and humanitarian attitude, and *li*, maintaining proper relationships and rituals that enhance the life of the individual, the family, and the state. The "five relations," between king and subject, father and son, man and wife, older and younger brother, and friend and friend, are of utmost importance. These relationships are reinforced by participation in rituals, including the formal procedures of court life and religious rituals such as ancestor worship.

Confucius revolutionized educational thought in China. He believed that learning was not to be focused only on attaining the skills for a particular profession, but for growth in moral judgment and self-realization. Confucius's standards for the proper conduct of government shaped the statecraft of China for centuries. Hundreds of temples in honor of Confucius testify to his stature as sage and teacher.

Confucianism was far less dominant in 20th-century China, at least on an official level. The state cult of Confucius was ended in 1911. Still, Confucian traditions and moral standards are part of the cultural essence of China and other East Asian countries.

## Shinto

Shinto comprises the religious ideas and practices indigenous to Japan. Ancient Shinto focused on the worship of the *kami*, a host of supernatural beings that could be known through forms (objects of nature, remarkable people, abstract concepts such as justice) but were ultimately mysterious. Shinto has no formal dogma and no holy writ, though early collections of Japanese religious thought and practice (*Kojiki*, "Records of Ancient Matters," A.D. 712, and *Nihon shoki*, "Chronicles of Japan," A.D. 720) are highly regarded.

Shinto has been influenced by Confucianism and by Buddhism, which was introduced in Japan in the 6th century. Syncretic schools (such as Ryobu Shinto) emerged, as did other sects that rejected Buddhism (such as Ise Shinto).

Under the reign of the emperor Meiji (1868–1912), Shinto became the official state religion. State Shinto, the national cult, emphasized the divinity of the emperor, whose succession was traced back to the first emperor, Jimmu (660 B.C.), and beyond him to the sun goddess Amaterasu-o-mi-kami. State Shinto was disestablished after World War II.

Sect Shinto, deriving from sects that developed during the 19th and 20th centuries, continues to thrive in Japan. Shrines dedicated to particular *kami* are visited by parishioners for prayer and traditional ceremonies, such as presenting a newborn child to the *kami*. Traditional festivals celebrated at the shrines include purification rites, presentation of food offerings, prayer, sacred music and dance, and a feast.

No particular day of the week is set aside for prayer. A person may visit a shrine at will, entering through the *torii* (gateway). It is believed that the *kami* can respond to prayer and can offer protection and guidance.

A variety of Shinto sects and practices exist today. Ten-rikyo emphasizes faith healing. Folk Shinto is characterized by veneration of roadside shrines and rites related to agriculture. Buddhist priests serve at many Shinto shrines, and many families keep a small shrine, or god-shelf, at home. Veneration of ancestors and pilgrimage are also common practices.

## Taoism

Taoism, one of the major religions of China, is based on ancient philosophical works, primarily the Tao Te Ching, "Classic of Tao and Its Virtue." Traditionally, this book was thought to be the work of Lao-tzu, a quasi-historical philosopher of the 6th century B.C.; scholars now believe that the book dates from about the 3rd century B.C. The philosopher Chuang Tzu (4th–3rd centuries B.C.) also contributed to the seminal ideas of Taoism.

Tao, "the Way," is the ultimate reality of the universe, according to Taoism. It is a creative process, and humans can live in harmony with it by clearing the self of obstacles. By cultivating *wu-wei*, a type of inaction characterized by humility and prudence, a person can participate in the simplicity and spontaneity of Tao. Striving to attain virtue or achievement is counterproductive and unnecessary. Taoism values mystical contemplation and balance. The human being is viewed as a microcosm of the universe, and the Chinese principle of *yin-yang*, complementary duality, is a model of harmony.

The religious practices of Taoism emerged from these ancient philosophies and from Chinese shamanistic tradition; by the 2nd century A.D., it constituted an organized religion. Longevity and immortality were sought through regulating the energies of the body through breathing exercises, meditation, and use of medicinal plants, talismans, and magical formulas. A cult of immortals, including the divinized Lao-tzu, also developed. Influenced by Buddhism, Taoists organized monastic orders. Temple worship and forms of divination, including the *I ching*, were practiced.

Since its beginnings, many sects have arisen within Taoism. All subscribe to the philosophical origins of the religion; some have emphasized faith healing, exorcism, the worship of the immortals, meditation, or alchemy. Buddhism and Confucianism influenced some sects; some operated as secret societies.

Though the present Chinese government has tried to suppress it, Taoism is still practiced in mainland China, Taiwan, and Hong Kong. It profoundly influenced Chinese art and literature, and Taoist ideas have become popular in the West.

# U.S. Religious Sects Originating in the 19th Century

The United States was the setting for new developments in religion in the 19th century. Sects and movements of many types arose, inspired variously by new interpretations of the Bible, the teachings of new prophets and thinkers, the expectation of Christ's second coming, and the social, scientific, and philosophical questions of the time. Sects that have thrived for over 100 years include the Christian Scientists, the Mormons, the Seventh-day Adventists, and the Jehovah's Witnesses.

## Christian Scientists

Founded by Mary Baker Eddy (1821–1910) in the 1860s and 1870s, Christian Science views creation as entirely spiritual. The church holds the Bible as authoritative yet interprets it in a distinct way, focusing on the life of Jesus as a model of healing by prayer, a necessary element of spiritual growth. According to the Christian Science concept of Mind-healing, physical illness and injury result from error or wrong belief and can be healed through one's own prayer or the ministrations of a Christian Science practitioner. Worship services focus on readings from the Bible and *Science and Health with Key to the Scriptures,* Eddy's definitive textbook. Christian Science is based at the Mother Church in Boston, Massachusetts. *The Christian Science Monitor,* established under the direction of Eddy, has long been recognized for excellence in journalism.

## Mormons

The Church of Jesus Christ of Latter-day Saints was established by Joseph Smith Jr. (1805–1844) of New York. He described an encounter with an angel who gave him the text that would become the *Book of Mormon,* which, together with the Bible and other texts, forms the Mormon scriptures (Mormon is an ancient American prophet noted in the book). Smith organized a church in 1830; due to persecution, church members searched for a place to practice their faith, finally settling in Utah. Salt Lake City, Utah, is home to institutions such as the Family History Library, the world's largest collection of genealogical information. Mormons believe that the Godhead consists of three separate personages (Father, Son, Holy Spirit), that souls preexist this life, and that the faithful will gain eternal life as gods. These rites can be undertaken by proxy for one's dead forebears. In the Mormon view, the second coming of Christ will lead to a chain of events culminating in a final resurrection, after which earth will become a celestial home for all people.

## Seventh-day Adventists

Seventh-day Adventists trace their beginnings to the preacher William Miller (1782–1849), who expounded the idea that the second coming of Christ would occur between March 21, 1843, and March 21, 1844. His followers, called Adventists, had to rethink their convictions when that event did not occur. Some believed that Miller's dates designated the beginning of God's examination of the Book of Life, which would soon culminate in the final judgment and Christ's reign on earth. In 1863 they established the Seventh-day Adventist denomination, appointing Saturday (the seventh day) for worship and rest. Seventh-day Adventists practice vegetarianism and avoid alcohol and caffeine. They accept the Bible as the word of God and await the second coming. Among their leaders, Ellen Harmon White (1827–1915) was particularly influential; some consider her writings prophetic. Other Adventist groups hold to somewhat different views.

## Jehovah's Witnesses

This sect grew out of the International Bible Students Association, founded in 1872 in Pittsburgh, Pennsylvania, by Charles Taze Russell (1852–1916). After intensive study of the Bible, he concluded that the invisible return of Christ had occurred in 1874, that the Gentile period would cease in 1914, and that, following a war, the kingdom of God would be established on earth. Jehovah's Witnesses no longer set such specific dates but believe that God's kingdom, the Theocracy, will follow Armageddon, the great war described in prophetic books of the Bible. They believe that biblical prophecies are being fulfilled in world events and that Jesus was created by God and acts as his agent. Jehovah's Witnesses worship at meeting places called Kingdom Halls. Because they believe that secular governments are unknowingly entangled with Satan, they do not salute flags or join the military. Jehovah's Witnesses actively seek converts; members are expected to spread the message. Their publishing efforts include the magazines *Watchtower* and *Awake!*

## Roman Catholic Pontiffs

| Name | Birthplace | Reigned From | Reigned To | Name | Birthplace | Reigned From | Reigned To |
|---|---|---|---|---|---|---|---|
| St. Peter | Bethsaida | 42? | 67? | St. Soter | Campania | 166 | 175 |
| St. Linus | Tuscia | c. 67 | 76 | St. Eleutherius | Epirus | 175 | 189 |
| St. Anacletus (Cletus) | Rome | 76 | 88 | St. Victor I | Africa | 189 | 199 |
| | | | | St. Zephyrinus | Rome | 199 | 217 |
| St. Clement | Rome | 88 | 97 | St. Callistus I | Rome | 217 | 222 |
| St. Evaristus | Greece | 97 | 105 | St. Urban I | Rome | 222 | 230 |
| St. Alexander I | Rome | 105 | 115 | St. Pontian | Rome | 230 | 235 |
| St. Sixtus I | Rome | 115 | 125 | St. Anterus | Greece | 235 | 236 |
| St. Telesphorus | Greece | 125 | 136 | St. Fabian | Rome | 236 | 250 |
| St. Hyginus | Greece | 136 | 140 | St. Cornelius | Rome | 251 | 253 |
| St. Pius I | Aquileia | 140 | 155 | St. Lucius I | Rome | 253 | 254 |
| St. Anicetus | Syria | 155 | 166 | St. Stephen I | Rome | 254 | 257 |

| Name | Birthplace | Reigned From | To | Name | Birthplace | Reigned From | To |
|---|---|---|---|---|---|---|---|
| St. Sixtus II | Greece | 257 | 258 | St. Gregory II | Rome | 715 | 731 |
| St. Dionysius | Unknown | 259 | 268 | St. Gregory III | Syria | 731 | 741 |
| St. Felix I | Rome | 269 | 274 | St. Zachary | Greece | 741 | 752 |
| St. Eutychian | Luni | 275 | 283 | Stephen II (III)[4] | Rome | 752 | 757 |
| St. Caius | Dalmatia | 283 | 296 | St. Paul I | Rome | 757 | 767 |
| St. Marcellinus | Rome | 296 | 304 | Stephen III (IV) | Sicily | 768 | 772 |
| St. Marcellus I | Rome | 308 | 309 | Adrian I | Rome | 772 | 795 |
| St. Eusebius | Greece | 309[1] | 309[1] | St. Leo III | Rome | 795 | 816 |
| St. Meltiades | Africa | 311 | 314 | Stephen IV (V) | Rome | 816 | 817 |
| St. Sylvester I | Rome | 314 | 335 | St. Paschal I | Rome | 817 | 824 |
| St. Marcus | Rome | 336 | 336 | Eugene II | Rome | 824 | 827 |
| St. Julius I | Rome | 337 | 352 | Valentine | Rome | 827 | 827 |
| Liberius | Rome | 352 | 366 | Gregory IV | Rome | 827 | 844 |
| St. Damasus I | Spain | 366 | 384 | Sergius II | Rome | 844 | 847 |
| St. Siricius | Rome | 384 | 399 | St. Leo IV | Rome | 847 | 855 |
| St. Anastasius I | Rome | 399 | 401 | Benedict III | Rome | 855 | 858 |
| St. Innocent I | Albano | 401 | 417 | St. Nicholas I (the Great) | Rome | 858 | 867 |
| St. Zozimus | Greece | 417 | 418 | Adrian II | Rome | 867 | 872 |
| St. Boniface I | Rome | 418 | 422 | John VIII | Rome | 872 | 882 |
| St. Celestine I | Campania | 422 | 432 | Marinus I | Gallese | 882 | 884 |
| St. Sixtus III | Rome | 432 | 440 | St. Adrian III | Rome | 884 | 885 |
| St. Leo I (the Great) | Tuscany | 440 | 461 | Stephen V (VI) | Rome | 885 | 891 |
| St. Hilary | Sardinia | 461 | 468 | Formosus | Portus | 891 | 896 |
| St. Simplicius | Tivoli | 468 | 483 | Boniface VI | Rome | 896 | 896 |
| St. Felix III (II)[2] | Rome | 483 | 492 | Stephen VI (VII) | Rome | 896 | 897 |
| St. Gelasius I | Africa | 492 | 496 | Romanus | Gallese | 897 | 897 |
| Anastasius II | Rome | 496 | 498 | Theodore II | Rome | 897 | 897 |
| St. Symmachus | Sardinia | 498 | 514 | John IX | Tivoli | 898 | 900 |
| St. Hormisdas | Frosinone | 514 | 523 | Benedict IV | Rome | 900 | 903 |
| St. John I | Tuscany | 523 | 526 | Leo V | Ardea | 903 | 903 |
| St. Felix IV (III) | Samnium | 526 | 530 | Sergius III | Rome | 904 | 911 |
| Boniface II | Rome | 530 | 532 | Anastasius III | Rome | 911 | 913 |
| John II | Rome | 533 | 535 | Landus | Sabina | 913 | 914 |
| St. Agapitus I | Rome | 535 | 536 | John X | Tossignano | 914 | 928 |
| St. Silverius | Campania | 536 | 537 | Leo VI | Rome | 928 | 928 |
| Vigilius | Rome | 537 | 555 | Stephen VII (VIII) | Rome | 928 | 931 |
| Pelagius I | Rome | 556 | 561 | John XI | Rome | 931 | 935 |
| John III | Rome | 561 | 574 | Leo VII | Rome | 936 | 939 |
| Benedict I | Rome | 575 | 579 | Stephen VIII (IX) | Rome | 939 | 942 |
| Pelagius II | Rome | 579 | 590 | Marinus II | Rome | 942 | 946 |
| St. Gregory I (the Great) | Rome | 590 | 604 | Agapitus II | Rome | 946 | 955 |
| Sabinianus | Tuscany | 604 | 606 | John XII | Tusculum | 955 | 964 |
| Boniface III | Rome | 607 | 607 | Leo VIII[5] | Rome | 963 | 965 |
| St. Boniface IV | Marsi | 608 | 615 | Benedict V[5] | Rome | 964 | 966 |
| St. Deusdedit (Adeodatus I) | Rome | 615 | 618 | John XIII | Rome | 965 | 972 |
| Boniface V | Naples | 619 | 625 | Benedict VI | Rome | 973 | 974 |
| Honorius I | Campania | 625 | 638 | Benedict VII | Rome | 974 | 983 |
| Severinus | Rome | 640 | 640 | John XIV | Pavia | 983 | 984 |
| John IV | Dalmatia | 640 | 642 | John XV | Rome | 985 | 996 |
| Theodore I | Greece | | | Gregory V | Saxony | 996 | 999 |
| St. Martin I | Todi | 649 | 655 | Sylvester II | (illegible) | (illegible) | (illegible) |
| St. Eugene I[3] | Rome | 654 | 657 | John XVII | Rome | 1003 | 1003 |
| St. Vitalian | Segni | 657 | 672 | John XVIII | Rome | 1004 | 1009 |
| Adeodatus II | Rome | 672 | 676 | Sergius IV | Rome | 1009 | 1012 |
| Donus | Rome | 676 | 678 | Benedict VIII | Tusculum | 1012 | 1024 |
| St. Agatho | Sicily | 678 | 681 | John XIX | Tusculum | 1024 | 1032 |
| St. Leo II | Sicily | 682 | 683 | Benedict IX[6] | Tusculum | 1032 | 1044 |
| St. Benedict II | Rome | 684 | 685 | Sylvester III | Rome | 1045 | 1045 |
| John V | Syria | 685 | 686 | Benedict IX (2nd time) | Tusculum | 1045 | 1045 |
| Conon | Unknown | 686 | 687 | Gregory VI | Rome | 1045 | 1046 |
| St. Sergius I | Syria | 687 | 701 | Clement II | Saxony | 1046 | 1047 |
| John VI | Greece | 701 | 705 | Benedict IX (3rd time) | Tusculum | 1047 | 1048 |
| John VII | Greece | 705 | 707 | Damasus II | Bavaria | 1048 | 1048 |
| Sisinnius | Syria | 708 | 708 | St. Leo IX | Alsace | 1049 | 1054 |
| Constantine | Syria | 708 | 715 | Victor II | Germany | 1055 | 1057 |

| Name | Birthplace | Reigned From | To | Name | Birthplace | Reigned From | To |
|---|---|---|---|---|---|---|---|
| Stephen IX (X) | Lorraine | 1057 | 1058 | Pius II | Siena | 1458 | 1464 |
| Nicholas II | Burgundy | 1059 | 1061 | Paul II | Venice | 1464 | 1471 |
| Alexander II | Milan | 1061 | 1073 | Sixtus IV | Savona | 1471 | 1484 |
| St. Gregory VII | Tuscany | 1073 | 1085 | Innocent VIII | Genoa | 1484 | 1492 |
| Bl. Victor III | Benevento | 1086 | 1087 | Alexander VI | Jativa | 1492 | 1503 |
| Bl. Urban II | France | 1088 | 1099 | Pius III | Siena | 1503 | 1503 |
| Paschal II | Ravenna | 1099 | 1118 | Julius II | Savona | 1503 | 1513 |
| Gelasius II | Gaeta | 1118 | 1119 | Leo X | Florence | 1513 | 1521 |
| Callistus II | Burgundy | 1119 | 1124 | Adrian VI | Utrecht | 1522 | 1523 |
| Honorius II | Flagnano | 1124 | 1130 | Clement VII | Florence | 1523 | 1534 |
| Innocent II | Rome | 1130 | 1143 | Paul III | Rome | 1534 | 1549 |
| Celestine II | Città di Castello | 1143 | 1144 | Julius III | Rome | 1550 | 1555 |
| Lucius II | Bologna | 1144 | 1145 | Marcellus II | Montepulciano | 1555 | 1555 |
| Bl. Eugene III | Pisa | 1145 | 1153 | Paul IV | Naples | 1555 | 1559 |
| Anastasius IV | Rome | 1153 | 1154 | Pius IV | Milan | 1559 | 1565 |
| Adrian IV | England | 1154 | 1159 | St. Pius V | Bosco | 1566 | 1572 |
| Alexander III | Siena | 1159 | 1181 | Gregory XIII | Bologna | 1572 | 1585 |
| Lucius III | Lucca | 1181 | 1185 | Sixtus V | Grottammare | 1585 | 1590 |
| Urban III | Milan | 1185 | 1187 | Urban VII | Rome | 1590 | 1590 |
| Gregory VIII | Benevento | 1187 | 1187 | Gregory XIV | Cremona | 1590 | 1591 |
| Clement III | Rome | 1187 | 1191 | Innocent IX | Bologna | 1591 | 1591 |
| Celestine III | Rome | 1191 | 1198 | Clement VIII | Florence | 1592 | 1605 |
| Innocent III | Anagni | 1198 | 1216 | Leo XI | Florence | 1605 | 1605 |
| Honorius III | Rome | 1216 | 1227 | Paul V | Rome | 1605 | 1621 |
| Gregory IX | Anagni | 1227 | 1241 | Gregory XV | Bologna | 1621 | 1623 |
| Celestine IV | Milan | 1241 | 1241 | Urban VIII | Florence | 1623 | 1644 |
| Innocent IV | Genoa | 1243 | 1254 | Innocent X | Rome | 1644 | 1655 |
| Alexander IV | Anagni | 1254 | 1261 | Alexander VII | Siena | 1655 | 1667 |
| Urban IV | Troyes | 1261 | 1264 | Clement IX | Pistoia | 1667 | 1669 |
| Clement IV | France | 1265 | 1268 | Clement X | Rome | 1670 | 1676 |
| Bl. Gregory X | Piacenza | 1271 | 1276 | Bl. Innocent XI | Como | 1676 | 1689 |
| Bl. Innocent V | Savoy | 1276 | 1276 | Alexander VIII | Venice | 1689 | 1691 |
| Adrian V | Genoa | 1276 | 1276 | Innocent XII | Spinazzola | 1691 | 1700 |
| John XXI[7] | Portugal | 1276 | 1277 | Clement XI | Urbino | 1700 | 1721 |
| Nicholas III | Rome | 1277 | 1280 | Innocent XIII | Rome | 1721 | 1724 |
| Martin IV[8] | France | 1281 | 1285 | Benedict XIII | Gravina | 1724 | 1730 |
| Honorius IV | Rome | 1285 | 1287 | Clement XII | Florence | 1730 | 1740 |
| Nicholas IV | Ascoli | 1288 | 1292 | Benedict XIV | Bologna | 1740 | 1758 |
| St. Celestine V | Isernia | 1294 | 1294 | Clement XIII | Venice | 1758 | 1769 |
| Boniface VIII | Anagni | 1294 | 1303 | Clement XIV | Rimini | 1769 | 1774 |
| Bl. Benedict XI | Treviso | 1303 | 1304 | Pius VI | Cesena | 1775 | 1799 |
| Clement V | France | 1305 | 1314 | Pius VII | Cesena | 1800 | 1823 |
| John XXII | Cahors | 1316 | 1334 | Leo XII | Genga | 1823 | 1829 |
| Benedict XII | France | 1334 | 1342 | Pius VIII | Cingoli | 1829 | 1830 |
| Clement VI | France | 1342 | 1352 | Gregory XVI | Belluno | 1831 | 1846 |
| Innocent VI | France | 1352 | 1362 | Pius IX | Senegallia | 1846 | 1878 |
| Bl. Urban V | France | 1362 | 1370 | Leo XIII | Carpineto | 1878 | 1903 |
| Gregory XI | France | 1370 | 1378 | St. Pius X | Riese | 1903 | 1914 |
| Urban VI | Naples | 1378 | 1389 | Benedict XV | Genoa | 1914 | 1922 |
| Boniface IX | Naples | 1389 | 1404 | Pius XI | Desio | 1922 | 1939 |
| Innocent VII | Sulmona | 1404 | 1406 | Pius XII | Rome | 1939 | 1958 |
| Gregory XII | Venice | 1406 | 1415 | John XXIII | Sotto il Monte | 1958 | 1963 |
| Martin V | Rome | 1417 | 1431 | Paul VI | Concesio | 1963 | 1978 |
| Eugene IV | Venice | 1431 | 1447 | John Paul I | Forno di Canale | 1978 | 1978 |
| Nicholas V | Sarzana | 1447 | 1455 | John Paul II | Wadowice, Poland | 1978 | |
| Callistus III | Jativa | 1455 | 1458 | | | | |

1. Or 310. 2. He should be called Felix II, and his successors of the same name should be numbered accordingly. The discrepancy was caused by the erroneous insertion in some lists of the name of St. Felix of Rome, Martyr. 3. He was elected during the exile of St. Martin I, who endorsed him as pope. 4. After St. Zachary died, a Roman priest named Stephen was elected but died before his consecration as bishop of Rome. His name is not included in all lists for this reason. In view of this historical confusion, the *National Catholic Almanac* lists the true Stephen II as Stephen II (III), the true Stephen III as Stephen III (IV), etc. 5. Confusion exists concerning the legitimacy of claims. If the deposition of John was invalid, Leo was an antipope until after the end of Benedict's reign. If the deposition of John was valid, Leo was the legitimate pope and Benedict an antipope. 6. If the triple removal of Benedict IX was not valid, Sylvester III, Gregory VI, and Clement II were antipopes. 7. Elimination was made of the name of John XX in an effort to rectify the numerical designation of popes named John. The error dates back to the time of John XV. 8. The names of Marinus I and Marinus II were construed as Martin. In view of these two pontificates and the earlier reign of St. Martin I, this pontiff was called Martin IV. *Source: National Catholic Almanac,* from *Annuarto Pontificio.*

# The Books of the Bible

Below is the Protestant canon of the Bible (New Revised Standard Version). The Roman Catholic canon also includes the Deuterocanonical books as part of the Old Testament (these are considered apocryphal by most Protestants). The Hebrew Bible recognizes the books referred to as the Old Testament in the Protestant Bible, but not the Apocryphal/Deuterocanonical books or the New Testament.

**The Old Testament with the Apocryphal/ Deuterocanonical Books**

*The Hebrew Scriptures*
Genesis
Exodus
Leviticus
Numbers
Deuteronomy
Joshua
Judges
Ruth
1 Samuel
2 Samuel
1 Kings
2 Kings
1 Chronicles
2 Chronicles
Ezra
Nehemiah
Esther
Job
Psalms

Proverbs
Ecclesiastes
Song of Solomon
Isaiah
Jeremiah
Lamentations
Ezekiel
Daniel
Hosea
Joel
Amos
Obadiah
Jonah
Micah
Nahum
Habakkuk
Zephaniah
Haggai
Zechariah
Malachi

*The Apocryphal/ Deuterocanonical Books*
Tobit
Judith

Additions to the Book of Esther
Wisdom of Solomon
Ecclesiasticus, or the Wisdom of Jesus Son of Sirach
Baruch
The Letter of Jeremiah
The Prayer of Azariah and the Song of the Three Jews
Susanna
Bel and the Dragon
1 Maccabees
2 Maccabees
1 Esdras
Prayer of Manasseh
Psalm 151
3 Maccabees
2 Esdras
4 Maccabees

**The New Testament**
Matthew
Mark
Luke

John
Acts of the Apostles
Romans
1 Corinthians
2 Corinthians
Galatians
Ephesians
Philippians
Colossians
1 Thessalonians
2 Thessalonians
1 Timothy
2 Timothy
Titus
Philemon
Hebrews
James
1 Peter
2 Peter
1 John
2 John
3 John
Jude
Revelation

# The Ten Commandments

The Ten Commandments, also called the Decalogue (Greek, "ten words"), were divine laws revealed to Moses by God on Mt. Sinai. Appearing in both Exodus (Ex. 20: 2–17) and Deuteronomy (Deut. 5:6–21), the commandments are numbered differently depending on whether they appear in a Catholic, Protestant, or Hebrew Bible. The following is the version given in the Revised Standard Version of the Bible.

You shall have no other gods before me.

You shall not make for yourself a graven image, or any likeness of anything that is in heaven above, or that is in the earth beneath, or that is in the water under the earth; you shall not bow down to them or serve them; for I the Lord your God am a jealous God, visiting the iniquity of the fathers upon the children to the third and the fourth generation of those who hate me, but showing steadfast love to thousands of those who love me and keep my commandments.

You shall not take the name of the Lord your God in vain; for the Lord will not hold him guiltless who takes his name in vain.

Remember the Sabbath day, to keep it holy. Six days you shall labor, and do all your work; but the seventh day is a Sabbath to the Lord your God; in it you shall not do any work, you, or your son, or your daughter, your manservant, or your maidservant, or

your cattle, or the sojourner who is within your gates; for in six days the Lord made heaven and earth, the sea, and all that is in them, and rested the seventh day; therefore the Lord blessed the Sabbath day and hallowed it.

Honor your father and your mother, that your days may be long in the land which the Lord your God gives you.

You shall not kill.

You shall not commit adultery.

You shall not steal.

You shall not bear false witness against your neighbor.

You shall not covet your neighbor's house; you shall not covet your neighbor's wife, or his manservant, or his maidservant, or his ox, or his ass, or anything that is your neighbor's.

Source: Revised Standard Version of the Bible (Ex.20: 2–17)

# The Seven Deadly Sins

In Christianity, the seven deadly sins are considered "deadly" because it is believed they can do terrible damage to the soul. The now-famous list does not appear in the Bible and may have been formulated by Gregory the Great (540–604). The deadly sins are sometimes known as "capital" or "cardinal" sins: pride, greed, lust, envy, gluttony, anger, and sloth.

# Selected Worldwide Religious Sites

**Amritsar, India:** Site of the Golden Temple (Sikhism).

**Axum, Ethiopia:** Church of St. Mary of Zion (Ethiopian Orthodox), where the Ark of the Covenant is believed to be kept.

**Bethlehem, Israel:** Birthplace of Jesus.

**Black Hills, South Dakota:** Sacred to the Lakota Indian tribe, who traditionally go on vision quests in the hills.

**Bodhi Gaya, India:** Place where the Buddha reached enlightenment.

**Canterbury, England:** Seat of the archbishop of Canterbury (Anglican).

**Czestochowa, Poland:** Chapel of Our Lady of Czestochowa, the Black Madonna of Poland. This painting is said to have been made by St. Luke.

**Dharamsala, India:** Seat of the Dalai Lama in exile (Tibetan Buddhism).

**Fatima, Portugal:** Site of several visions of the Virgin Mary in 1917. A major pilgrimage site for Catholics.

**Ganges River, India:** Sacred to Hindus (Mother Ganges is a Hindu goddess); immersion in the Ganges symbolizes spiritual purification.

**Haifa, Israel:** World headquarters of the Baha'i faith.

**Istanbul, Turkey:** Seat of the patriarchate of Constantinople (Eastern Orthodox).

**Jerusalem, Israel:** Major holy site for Judaism, Christianity, and Islam. The Temple Mount compound is believed to be both the site of the First and Second Temples of Judaism and the place where redemption will occur when the Messiah arrives. The same area is also called Haram al-Sharif (The Noble Sanctuary) and has great significance to Muslims. Nearby is the Dome of the Rock, the spot from which Muhammad ascended into heaven. Just below Temple Mount is the Western Wall, a remnant of the Second Temple and the holiest site in Judaism, where Jews come to pray. The Wall is part of a larger wall that encloses the Dome of the Rock and the al-Aqsa mosque. The al-Aqsa mosque, one of the holiest mosques in Islam, was originally the site toward which Muslims bowed to pray. The Holy Sepulchre, in which Jesus was buried, and from which he returned from the dead, is in the northwest corner of the Old City.

**Knock, Ireland:** Pilgrimage site for Catholics where 15 people claimed to see a vision of the Virgin Mary, St. Joseph, and St. John the Evangelist in 1879. About 1½ million pilgrims visit the site annually.

**Kusinara, India:** Site of the Buddha's death.

**Lhasa, Tibet:** Potala Palace, historical abode of the Dalai Lama (Tibetan Buddhism).

**Loch Derg, Ireland:** Site of St. Patrick's purgatory, pilgrimage destination; pilgrims walk barefoot around the lake, praying, like St. Patrick did.

**Lourdes, France:** In 1858, the Virgin Mary is said to have appeared to St. Bernadette at Lourdes in seven visions. It is now a Catholic pilgrimage site with a spring that some believe has curative properties.

**Lumbini, Nepal:** Birthplace of the Buddha.

**Mecca, Saudi Arabia:** The center of Islam and the birthplace of Muhammad, Mecca is the place toward which Muslims bow to pray five times a day. Mecca is the destination of the *hajj*, the pilgrimage which all Muslims who are financially and physically able must make in their lifetime. An estimated one million Muslims make the *hajj* annually. The focus of their worship is the Great Mosque at the center of Mecca. It encloses the Ka'aba, a small building that, according to the Qu'ran, was erected by Abraham and his son Ishmael.

**Medina, Saudi Arabia:** Muhammad lived in Medina after escaping Mecca in A.D. 622; it is now a holy city that only Muslims may enter.

**Medjugorje, Bosnia-Herzegovina:** Catholic pilgrimage site where many have claimed visions of the Virgin Mary.

**Mt. Athos, Greece:** Pilgrimage site for Eastern Orthodox males; site of many monasteries.

**Mt. Fuji, Japan:** Sacred to Buddhists and Shintos.

**Mt. Tai Shan, China:** Sacred to Taoists and Buddhists, this mountain with many beautiful temples is thought to be a center of living energy.

**Nazareth, Israel:** Place where Jesus lived and began teaching.

**Palitana, India:** The most important pilgrimage site for Jains, Palitana boasts 863 temples on one mountain, Shatrunjaya Hill.

**Salt Lake City, Utah:** World headquarters of Church of Jesus Christ of Latter-day Saints.

**Santiago de Compostela, Spain:** Medieval pilgrimage site; the pilgrimage route of Santiago de Compostela goes through France and Spain before ending up at the city's cathedral. Santiago is Saint James, who was martyred at Jerusalem c. A.D. 44.

**Sarnath, India:** Place where the Buddha preached his first sermon in the deer park.

**Sea of Galilee, Israel:** Place where Jesus performed the miracle of the loaves and the fishes and preached the Sermon on the Mount.

**Sri Pada (Adam's Peak), Sri Lanka:** Sacred to some Buddhists, Hindus, Muslims, and Christians, the temple on the top of Adam's Peak contains a large footprint believed to belong to either the Buddha, Shiva, Adam, or St. Thomas.

**Tepeyac, Mexico City, Mexico:** Site of the appearance of the Virgin of Guadalupe to Juan Diego in 1531; now home to the Basilica of the Virgin, one of the most-visited churches in the world.

**Turin, Italy:** Place where the Holy Shroud of Turin (linen cloth believed to bear the visage of Jesus Christ) is housed.

**Uluru (Ayer's Rock), Australia:** Sacred site of the aborigines of Australia. Now a major tourist attraction, though the aborigine people ask that tourists not climb the rock.

**Varanasi, India:** City on the banks of the Ganges River; those who die there reach instant enlightenment.

**The Vatican:** Seat of the papacy (Catholicism).

*See* Calendar and Holidays for listings of religious holidays.

# The Seven Wonders of the World

Since ancient times, people have put together many "seven wonders" lists. The content of these lists tends to vary, and none is definitive. The seven wonders that are most widely agreed upon as being in the original list are outlined below. (* indicates photo can be found in the Headline History section.)

The **Pyramids of Egypt**\* are three pyramids at Giza, outside modern Cairo. The largest pyramid, built by Khufu (Cheops), a king of the fourth dynasty, had an original estimated height of 482 ft (now approximately 450 ft). The base has sides 755 ft long. It contains 2,300,000 blocks; the average weight of each is 2.5 tons. Estimated date of completion is 2680 B.C. Of all the Ancient Wonders, the pyramids alone survive.

The **Hanging Gardens of Babylon** were supposedly built by Nebuchadnezzar around 600 B.C. to please his queen, Amuhia. They are also associated with the mythical Assyrian queen, Semiramis. Archeologists surmise that the gardens were laid out atop a vaulted building, with provisions for raising water. The terraces were said to rise from 75 to 300 ft.

The Walls of Babylon, also built by Nebuchadnezzar, are sometimes referred to as the second (or the seventh) wonder instead of the Hanging Gardens.

The **Statue of Zeus (Jupiter) at Olympia** was made of gold and ivory by the Greek sculptor Phidias (5th century B.C.). Reputed to be 40 ft high, the statue has been lost without a trace, except for reproductions on coins.

The **Temple of Artemis (Diana) at Ephesus** was begun about 350 B.C., in honor of a non-Hellenic goddess who later became identified with the Greek goddess of the same name. The temple, with Ionic columns 60 ft high, was destroyed by invading Goths in A.D. 262.

The **Mausoleum at Halicarnassus** was erected by Queen Artemisia in memory of her husband, King Mausolus of Caria in Asia Minor, who died in 353 B.C. Some remains of the structure are in the British Museum. This shrine is the source of the modern word "mausoleum."

The **Colossus at Rhodes** was a bronze statue of Helios (Apollo), about 105 ft high. The work of the sculptor Chares, who reputedly labored for 12 years before completing it in 280 B.C., it was destroyed during an earthquake in 224 B.C.

The **Pharos (Lighthouse) of Alexandria** was built by Sostratus of Cnidus during the 3rd century B.C. on the island of Pharos off the coast of Egypt. It was destroyed by an earthquake in the 13th century.

## Famous Structures

### Ancient

The **Great Sphinx** of Egypt, one of the wonders of ancient Egyptian architecture, adjoins the pyramids of Giza and has a length of 240 ft. Built in the fourth dynasty, it is approximately 4,500 years old. A 10-year $2.5 million restoration project was completed in 1998. Other Egyptian buildings of note include the *Temples of Karnak, Edfu,* and *Abu Simbel,* and the *Tombs at Beni Hassan.*

The **Parthenon**\* of Greece, built on the Acropolis in Athens, was the chief temple to the goddess Athena. It was believed to have been completed by 438 B.C. The present temple remained intact until the 5th century A.D. Today, though the Parthenon is in ruins, its majestic proportions are still discernible.

The **Colosseum** (Flavian Amphitheater) of Rome, the largest and most famous of the Roman amphitheaters, was opened for use A.D. 80. Elliptical in shape, it consisted of three stories and an upper gallery, rebuilt in stone in its present form in the third century A.D. It was principally used for gladiatorial combat and could seat between 40,000 and 50,000 spectators.

The **Pantheon** at Rome, begun by Agrippa in 27 B.C. as a temple, was rebuilt in its present circular form by Hadrian (A.D. 118–128). Literally the Pantheon was intended as a temple of "all the gods." It is remarkable for its perfect preservation today, and it has served continuously for 20 centuries as a place of worship.

Famous Roman triumphal arches, built to commemorate major military victories, include the **Arch of Titus** (c. A.D. 80) and the **Arch of Constantine** (c. A.D. 315).

**Teotihuacán**, located in central Mexico, was the largest city in the Americas at its height between A.D. 300 and 900. Built on a grid plan with a central avenue known as the Street of the Dead, it is the site of two enormous pyramid temples and the temple of the plumed serpent god Quetzalcoatl.

### Later European

**St. Mark's Cathedral** in Venice (1063–1071), one of the great examples of Byzantine architecture, was begun in the 9th century. Partly destroyed by fire in 976, it was later rebuilt as a Byzantine edifice.

The cathedral group at Pisa, one of the most celebrated groups of structures built in Romanesque style, consists of the cathedral, the cathedral's baptistry, and the campanile (**Leaning Tower**\*). The campanile, a form of bell tower, is 180 ft high and now leans 13.5 ft out of the perpendicular.

The **Alhambra** (1248–1354), located in Granada, Spain, is universally esteemed as one of the greatest masterpieces of Muslim architecture. Designed as a palace and fortress for the Moorish monarchs of Granada, it is surrounded by a heavily fortified wall more than a mile in perimeter. The location of the Alhambra in the Sierra Nevada provides a magnificent setting for this jewel of Moorish Spain.

The **Tower of London** is a group of buildings and towers covering 13 acres along the north bank of the Thames. The central *White Tower*, begun in 1078 during the reign of William the Conqueror, was originally a fortress and royal residence, but was later used as a prison. The *Bloody Tower* is associated with Anne Boleyn and other notables.

**Westminster Abbey,** in London, was begun in 1050 and completed in 1065. It was rebuilt and enlarged in several phases, beginning in 1245. With only two exceptions (Edward V and Edward VIII), every British monarch since William the Conqueror has been crowned in the abbey.

**Notre-Dame de Paris** (begun in 1163), one of the great examples of Gothic architecture, is a twin-towered church with a steeple over the crossing and immense flying buttresses supporting the masonry at the rear of the church.

The **Duomo**\* (cathedral) in Florence, with its pink, white, and green marble façade, has become a symbol of the city and the Renaissance. Construction began in 1296, but it was not completed until nearly 200 years later, following the addition of Brunelleschi's massive dome. The adjacent baptistery is famous for its gilded bronze doors by Ghiberti.

The **Vatican** is a group of buildings in Rome comprising the official residence of the pope. The *Basilica of St. Peter,* the largest church in the Christian world, was begun in 1452, and it was rebuilt between 1506 and 1626. The *Sistine Chapel,* begun in 1473, is noted for the art masterpieces of Michelangelo, Botticelli, and others. To the southeast of Vatican City is the *Basilica of the Savior* (known as *St. John Lateran*). As the cathedral of the pope, it is the first-ranking Catholic Church in the world.

The **Palace of Versailles** in France, containing the famous Hall of Mirrors, was built during the reign of Louis XIV in the 17th century and served as the royal palace until 1793. Built on the colossal scale typical of many works of baroque architecture, the palace is also noted for its gardens, which include some 1,400 fountains.

The **Eiffel Tower,** in Paris, was built for the Exposition of 1889 by Alexandre Gustave Eiffel. It is 984 ft high (1,056 ft including the television tower).

## Asian, African, and American

The **Taj Mahal**\* (1632–1650), at Agra, India, built by Shah Jahan as a tomb for his wife, is considered by some as the most perfect example of the Mogul style and by others as the most beautiful building in the world. Four slim white minarets flank the building, which is topped by a white dome; the entire structure is made of marble. Other examples of Indian architecture are the temples at Benares and Tanjore.

The **Dome of the Rock** (687–691) in Jerusalem is considered the first great work of Muslim architecture. It is noted for its beautiful mosaics of scrolling vines and flowers, and for its dome, which was originally covered in pure gold.

Another well-known Muslim edifice is the **Citadel**, located on an outcrop of limestone overlooking Cairo. Begun in 810, it was fortified (1176–1183) by Saladin during the Crusades.

**Angkor Wat,** outside the city of Angkor Thom, Cambodia, is one of the most beautiful examples of

Cambodian or Khmer architecture. The sanctuary was built during the 12th century.

The **Great Wall of China** (begun c. 214 B.C.), designed specifically as a defense against nomadic tribes, has large watch towers that could be called buildings. It was erected by Emperor Ch'in Shih Huang Ti and is 1,400 mi long. Built mainly of earth and stone, it varies in height between 18 and 30 ft.

The **Forbidden City** (1407–1420) in Beijing served as the seat of imperial power during the Ming and Qing dynasties (1368–1911). It is the world's largest palace complex, covering about 183 acres and including 9,999 buildings.

The painted wooden **Torii**, or Gateway, at Miyajima Island, Japan, stands in the tidal flats opposite the historic Itsukushima Shrine. Built in the traditional Shinto style, with two columns supporting a concave crosspiece on top, the gate serves to welcome the spirits of the dead as they come from across the Inland Sea.

Other famous Japanese buildings include the Buddhist temples of **Horyuji** (7th century) and **Todaiji** (8th century) at Nara.

**Machu Picchu** is an ancient Inca fortress in the Andes Mountains of Peru. Thought to have been built and occupied from the mid-15th century, it is surrounded on three sides by stepped agricultural terraces, which are connected to the main plazas and buildings by thousands of stone steps.

## United States

The **Chrysler Building** in New York City is one of the finest examples of Art Deco style high-rise architecture. Built for the automotive magnate Walter P. Chrysler between 1928 and 1930, the building makes use of decorative elements borrowed from automobiles. At 1,046 ft it was briefly the tallest building in the world before the Empire State Building was completed the following year.

The **Empire State Building,** one of the most popular tourist attractions in the heart of Manhattan, was constructed between 1930 and 1931. Features include a tiered structure that recalls ancient Egyptian and Aztec pyramids, and a mast at the top for mooring dirigibles. Rising to 1,250 ft (not including the mast), it remained the tallest building in the world until the 1970s.

The **Cathedral of St. John the Divine,** at 112th St. and Amsterdam Ave. in New York City, was begun in 1892 and is now in the final stages of completion. When completed, it will be the largest cathedral in the world: 601 ft long, 146 ft wide at the nave, 320 ft wide at the transept. The east end is designed in Romanesque-Byzantine style, and the nave and west end are Gothic.

The **Brooklyn Bridge,** built between 1869 and 1883, was the remarkable achievement of engineer John Roebling and his son, Washington Roebling. The first steel-wire suspension bridge in the world, it has a main span of 1,595.5 ft.

The **Statue of Liberty**\* was designed by Frédéric Auguste Bartholdi of Alsace as a gift to Americans from the people of France. The statue of a female figure holding a torch in her raised hand was accepted on Oct. 28, 1886, by President Grover Cleveland. The 225-ton steel-reinforced copper structure stands on Liberty Island in New York Harbor. It is 152 ft tall and stands on a 150-foot pedestal.

The **Sears Tower** in Chicago is, at 1,450 ft, the tallest building in the United States. Constructed between 1974 and 1976 for Sears, Roebuck and Company, the structure is composed of 75-foot square tubes that rise to varying levels.

The **Gateway Arch,** located on the riverfront in St. Louis, Mo., is a tapered curve of stainless steel rising to 630 ft. The tallest manmade memorial in the United States, the Arch was designed by Finnish-born U.S. architect Eero Saarinen and built between 1963 and 1966. Visitors can ride to the top in specially devised capsule-like tram cars.

San Francisco's **Golden Gate Bridge,** completed in 1937, is one of the most recognizable structures in the United States. Designed by Joseph B. Strauss, this elegant suspension bridge has a main span of 4,200 ft.

The Seattle **Space Needle** was planned as the central structure and symbol of the 1962 Seattle World's Fair, the theme of which was "Century 21." The Needle, which is 605 ft tall, is topped by an observation deck and a revolving restaurant.

\* Photos of these structures can be found in the Headline History section.

# World Trade Center History*

The twin towers of the World Trade Center were more than just buildings. They were proof of New York's belief in itself. Built at a time when New York's future seemed uncertain, the towers restored confidence and helped bring a halt to the decline of lower Manhattan. Brash, glitzy, and grand, they quickly became symbols of New York.

## Rockefeller Brainchild

The World Trade Center was conceived in the early 1960s by the Downtown-Lower Manhattan Development Association to revitalize the seedy "radio row" dominated by electronic stores. Chase Manhattan Bank chairman David Rockefeller, founder of the development association, and his brother, New York governor Nelson Rockefeller, pushed hard for the project, insisting it would benefit the entire city.

In 1962, the Port Authority of New York and New Jersey began plans to build the center. Minoru Yamasaki and Associates of Michigan was hired as architect. Eventually, Yamasaki decided on two huge towers. Critics charged that a modern monolith would rob New York of character, ruin the skyline, disrupt television reception, and strain city services. However, the project was approved and construction began in 1966.

In order to create the 16-acre World Trade Center site, five streets were closed off and 164 buildings were demolished. Construction required the excavation of more than 1.2 million cubic yards of earth, which was used to create 23.5 acres of land along the Hudson River in lower Manhattan. During peak construction periods, 3,500 people worked at the site. A total of 10,000 people worked on the towers; 60 died during its construction.

### Instant Landmarks

The north tower was opened in Dec. 1970 and the south tower in Jan. 1972; they were dedicated in April 1973. They were the world's tallest buildings for only a short time, since the Sears Tower in Chicago was completed in May 1973. However, the towers were ranked as the fifth and sixth tallest buildings in the world at the time of their destruction on Sept. 11, 2001. (*See* Disasters, p 625).

Four smaller buildings and a hotel, all built nearby around a central landscaped plaza, completed the complex. The mall at the World Trade Center, which was located immediately below the plaza, was the largest shopping mall in lower Manhattan. The six basements housed two subway stations and a stop on the PATH trains to New Jersey.

Some 50,000 people worked in the buildings, while another 200,000 visited or passed through each day. The complex had its own zip code, 10048.

## Previous Bombing

In 1993 terrorists drove a truck packed with 1,100 lbs of explosives into the basement parking garage at the World Trade Center. Despite the size of the blast—it left a crater 22 ft wide and five stories deep—only six people were killed and 1,000 injured. The towers were repaired, cleaned, and reopened in less than a month.

## Rebuilding Plans

Although the World Trade Center had been leased to New York real-estate developer Larry Silverstein just prior to the attacks, control over what happens now to the site will rest largely with the Port Authority and the Lower Manhattan Development Corporation, which was established by Governor Pataki to coordinate the various agencies and advisory committees involved in the rebuilding efforts.

In July 2002 the development corporation unveiled six possible plans for rebuilding the site, all of which called for 10 million sq ft of office and retail space to replace what was lost on Sept. 11, as well as a transportation hub, cultural facilities, and memorials to the victims of the attacks. However, the public's reaction to the proposals was largely unfavorable, with community groups and others calling for less commercial space and a slower planning process.

Whatever happens, rebuilding will undoubtedly be a complicated process and quite possibly the greatest challenge the city has faced yet.

\*See photo in the Headline History section

---

**Twin Towers Stats**
- —200,000 tons of steel
- —425,000 cubic yards of concrete
- —43,600 windows
- —12,000 miles of electric cables
- —198 miles of heating ducts
- —23,000 fluorescent light bulbs

**Each Tower**
- —110 floors
- —50,000 sq ft (each floor)
- —1,368 ft high (north tower)
- —1,362 ft high (south tower)
- —Weighed 500,000 tons
- —97 elevators for passengers, 6 for freight

## World's Tallest Buildings[1]

| Building, city | Year | Stories | Height m | Height ft. | Building, city | Year | Stories | Height m | Height ft. |
|---|---|---|---|---|---|---|---|---|---|
| Petronas Tower 1, Kuala Lumpur, Malaysia | 1998 | 88 | 452 | 1,483 | Landmark Tower, Yokohama, Japan | 1993 | 70 | 296 | 971 |
| Petronas Tower 2, Kuala Lumpur, Malaysia | 1998 | 88 | 452 | 1,483 | Bank of America Center, Seattle | 1984 | 76 | 295 | 967 |
| Sears Tower, Chicago | 1974 | 110 | 442 | 1,450 | 311 South Wacker Drive, Chicago | 1990 | 65 | 293 | 961 |
| Jin Mao Building, Shanghai | 1999 | 88 | 421 | 1,381 | SEG Plaza, Shenzen | 2000 | 72 | 292 | 957 |
| Citic Plaza, Guangzhou, China | 1996 | 80 | 391 | 1,283 | American International Building, New York | 1932 | 67 | 290 | 952 |
| Shun Hing Square, Shenzhen, China | 1996 | 69 | 384 | 1,260 | Cheung Kong Center, Hong Kong | 1999 | 70 | 290 | 951 |
| Empire State Building, New York | 1931 | 102 | 381 | 1,250 | Key Tower, Cleveland | 1991 | 57 | 290 | 950 |
| Central Plaza, Hong Kong | 1992 | 78 | 374 | 1,227 | One Liberty Place, Philadelphia | 1987 | 61 | 288 | 945 |
| Bank of China Tower, Hong Kong | 1989 | 70 | 369 | 1,209 | Sunjoy Tomorrow Square, Shanghai | 1999 | 59 | 285 | 934 |
| Emirates Tower One, Dubai | 1999 | 55 | 355 | 1,165 | 40 Wall Street, New York | 1930 | 72 | 283 | 927 |
| The Center, Hong Kong | 1998 | 79 | 350 | 1,148 | Plaza 66, Shanghai | 2001 | 62 | 281 | 923 |
| T & C Tower, Kaohsiung, Taiwan | 1997 | 85 | 348 | 1,140 | Bank of America Plaza, Dallas | 1985 | 72 | 281 | 921 |
| Aon Centre, Chicago | 1973 | 80 | 346 | 1,136 | Overseas Union Bank Centre, Singapore | 1986 | 66 | 280 | 919 |
| John Hancock Center, Chicago | 1969 | 100 | 344 | 1,127 | United Overseas Bank Plaza, Singapore | 1992 | 66 | 280 | 919 |
| Burj al Arab Hotel, Dubai | 1999 | 60 | 321 | 1,053 | Republic Plaza, Singapore | 1995 | 66 | 280 | 919 |
| Chrysler Building, New York | 1930 | 77 | 319 | 1,046 | Citicorp Center, New York | 1977 | 59 | 279 | 915 |
| Bank of America Plaza, Atlanta | 1993 | 55 | 312 | 1,023 | Scotia Plaza, Toronto | 1989 | 68 | 275 | 902 |
| Library Tower, Los Angeles | 1990 | 75 | 310 | 1,018 | Williams Tower, Houston | 1983 | 64 | 275 | 901 |
| Telekom Headquarters, Kuala Lumpur | 1999 | 55 | 310 | 1,017 | Renaissance Tower, Dallas | 1975 | 56 | 270 | 886 |
| Emirates Tower Two, Dubai | 2000 | 56 | 309 | 1,014 | Trump World Tower | 2001 | 72 | 267 | 881 |
| AT&T Corporate Center, Chicago | 1989 | 60 | 307 | 1,007 | Al Faisaliah Center, Riyadh | 2000 | 30 | 267 | 876 |
| Chase Tower, Houston | 1982 | 75 | 305 | 1,000 | 900 North Michigan Ave., Chicago | 1989 | 66 | 265 | 871 |
| Baiyoke Tower II, Bangkok | 1997 | 85 | 304 | 997 | NationsBank Corporate Center, Charlotte | 1992 | 60 | 265 | 871 |
| Two Prudential Plaza, Chicago | 1990 | 64 | 303 | 995 | SunTrust Plaza, Atlanta | 1992 | 60 | 265 | 871 |
| Pyongyang Hotel, Pyongyang, N. Korea | 1995 | 105 | 300 | 984 | Hong Kong New World Building, Shanghai | 2001 | 58 | 265 | 871 |
| Commerzbank Tower, Frankfurt | 1997 | 63 | 299 | 981 | Shenzhen Special Zone Daily Tower, Shenzhen | 1998 | 42 | 264 | 866 |
| First Canadian Place, Toronto | 1975 | 72 | 298 | 978 | | | | | |
| Kingdom Centre, Riyadh | 2001 | 72 | 296 | 972 | | | | | |
| Wells Fargo Plaza, Houston | 1983 | 71 | 296 | 972 | | | | | |

NOTE: Height is measured from sidewalk level of main entrance to structural top of building. Antennas and flag poles are not included. 1. World Trade Center twin towers of New York City ranked fifth and sixth (at 1,368 ft and 1,362 ft) on this list until their destruction on Sept. 11, 2001. (*See* Disasters, p. 625.) *Source:* Council on Tall Buildings and Urban Habitat, Lehigh University.

## World's Tallest Towers[1]

| Tower, City | Year | Height (m) | Height (ft) | Tower, City | Year | Height (m) | Height (ft) |
|---|---|---|---|---|---|---|---|
| Canadian National Tower, Toronto, Canada | 1975 | 553 | 1,815 | Liberation Tower, Kuwait City, Kuwait | 1996 | 370 | 1,214 |
| Ostankino Tower, Moscow, Russia | 1967 | 537 | 1,762 | Fernsehturm Tower, Berlin, Germany | 1969 | 365 | 1,198 |
| Oriental Pearl Tower, Shanghai, China | 1995 | 468 | 1,535 | Stratosphere Tower, Las Vegas, United States | 1996 | 350 | 1,149 |
| Menara Kuala Lumpur, Kuala Lumpur, Malaysia | 1996 | 421 | 1,403 | Tokyo Tower, Tokyo, Japan | 1959 | 333 | 1,092 |
| Central Radio & TV Tower, Beijing, China | 1992 | 417 | 1,369 | Skytower, Auckland, New Zealand | 1997 | 328 | 1,076 |
| Tianjin TV Tower, Tianjin, China | 1991 | 415 | 1,362 | AMP Tower Centrepoint, Sydney, Australia | 1981 | 305 | 1,001 |
| Tashkent Tower, Tashkent, Uzbekistan | 1985 | 375 | 1,230 | Eiffel Tower, Paris, France | 1889 | 300 | 984 |

Note: Height is to the structural top of the tower. This includes spires, but does not include television antennas, radio antennas, or flag poles. 1. A tower differs from a building in that the latter is considered to be a structure that is designed for residential, business, or manufacturing purposes. Also, an essential characteristic of a building is that it has floors. The structures listed here are principally telecommunications towers, and while they may have observation decks or restaurants, they do not have floors going all the way up. *Source:* Council on Tall Buildings and Urban Habitat and other sources.

## Notable Modern Bridges

| Name | Location | Length of main span feet | Length of main span meters | Year completed |
|------|----------|------:|-------:|-----------|
| **Suspension** | **United States** | | | |
| Verrazano-Narrows | Lower New York Bay | 4,260 | 1,298 | 1964 |
| Golden Gate | San Francisco Bay | 4,200 | 1,280 | 1937 |
| Mackinac | Mackinac Straits, Mich. | 3,800 | 1,158 | 1957 |
| George Washington | Hudson River at New York City | 3,500 | 1,067 | 1931 |
| Tacoma Narrows II | Puget Sound at Tacoma, Wash. | 2,800 | 853 | 1950 |
| San Francisco–Oakland Bay[1] | San Francisco Bay | 2,310 | 704 | 1936 |
| Bronx-Whitestone | East River, New York City | 2,300 | 701 | 1939 |
| Delaware Memorial[1] | Delaware River near Wilmington, Del. | 2,150 | 655 | 1951, 1968 |
| Seaway Skyway | St. Lawrence River at Ogdensburg, N.Y. | 2,150 | 655 | 1960 |
| Walt Whitman | Delaware River at Philadelphia | 2,000 | 610 | 1957 |
| Ambassador International | Detroit River at Detroit | 1,850 | 564 | 1929 |
| Throgs Neck | East River, New York City | 1,800 | 549 | 1961 |
| Benjamin Franklin | Delaware River at Philadelphia | 1,750 | 533 | 1926 |
| William Preston Lane, Jr.[1] | Chesapeake Bay, Md. | 1,600 | 488 | 1952, 1973 |
| Brooklyn Bridge | East River, New York City | 1,596 | 486 | 1883 |
| Royal Gorge | Arkansas River, Colo. | 1,053 | 321 | 1929 |
| Wheeling Bridge | Ohio River, Wheeling, W.Va. | 1,010 | 308 | 1847 |
| | **International** | | | |
| Akashi Kaikyo | Hyogo, Japan | 6,529 | 1,990 | 1998 |
| Izmit Bay | Marmara Sea, Turkey | 5,472 | 1,668 | UC |
| Storebælt | Denmark | 5,328 | 1,624 | 1998 |
| Humber | Humberside, England | 4,626 | 1,410 | 1981 |
| Jiangyin | Yangtze River, China | 4,543 | 1,385 | 1999 |
| Tsing Ma | Hong Kong | 4,518 | 1,377 | 1997 |
| Höga Kusten (High Coast) | Västernorrland, Sweden | 3,969 | 1,210 | 1997 |
| Minami Bisan-Seto | Japan | 3,609 | 1,100 | 1988 |
| Second Bosporus | Istanbul, Turkey | 3,576 | 1,090 | 1988 |
| First Bosporus | Istanbul, Turkey | 3,524 | 1,074 | 1973 |
| Third Kurushima | Japan | 3,379 | 1,030 | 1999 |
| Second Kurushima | Japan | 3,346 | 1,020 | 1999 |
| Ponte 25 de Abril | Tagus River at Lisbon, Portugal | 3,323 | 1,013 | 1966 |
| Forth Road | Queensferry, Scotland | 3,300 | 1,006 | 1964 |
| Kita Bisan-Seto | Japan | 3,248 | 990 | 1988 |
| Severn | Severn River at Beachley, England | 3,240 | 988 | 1966 |
| Yichang | Yangtze River, Hubei Province, China | 3,150 | 960 | 2001 |
| Shimotsui Straits | Japan | 3,084 | 940 | 1988 |
| Xiling Yangtze | Three Gorges Dam, China | 2,952 | 900 | 1996 |
| Tigergate (Humen) | Pearl River, Guangdong Province, China | 2,913 | 888 | 1997 |
| Ohnaruto | Japan | 2,874 | 876 | 1988 |
| Pierre Laporte | Quebec, Canada | 2,190 | 668 | 1970 |
| **Cantilever** | **United States** | | | |
| Commodore John Barry | Chester, Pa. | 1,644 | 501 | 1974 |
| Crescent City Connection[1] | Mississippi River, New Orleans, La. | 1,576 | 480 | 1958, 1985 |
| Transbay Bridge | San Francisco Bay | 1,400 | 427 | 1936 |
| | **International** | | | |
| Quebec Railway | Quebec, Canada | 1,988 | 171 | 1911 |
| Forth Railway | Queensferry, Scotland | 1,710 | 521 | 1890 |
| Minato Ohashi | Osaka, Japan | 1,673 | 510 | 1974 |
| Howrah | Hooghly River at Calcutta, India | 1,500 | 457 | 1943 |
| **Steel Arch** | **United States** | | | |
| New River Gorge | Fayetteville, W. Va. | 1,700 | 518 | 1977 |
| Bayonne | Kill Van Kull at Bayonne, N.J. | 1,675 | 510 | 1931 |
| Fremont | Portland, Ore. | 1,255 | 383 | 1973 |
| Hell Gate | East River (Hell Gate), New York City | 978 | 298 | 1916 |
| | **International** | | | |
| Sydney Harbor | Sydney, Australia | 1,670 | 509 | 1932 |
| Zdákov | Vltava River, Czech Republic | 1,244 | 380 | 1967 |
| Port Mann | Fraser River at Vancouver, British Columbia | 1,200 | 366 | 1964 |
| **Cable-Stayed** | **United States** | | | |
| Dames Point | Jacksonville, Fla. | 1,300 | 396 | 1988 |
| Houston Ship Channel | Baytown, Tex. | 1,250 | 381 | 1995 |

| Name | Location | Length of main span | | Year completed |
|---|---|---|---|---|
| | | feet | meters | |
| Sidney Lanier | Brunswick River, Ga. | 1,250 | 381 | UC |
| Hale Boggs Memorial | Luling, La. | 1,222 | 373 | 1983 |
| Sunshine Skyway | Tampa, Fla. | 1,200 | 366 | 1987 |
| | **International** | | | |
| Tatara | Honshu-Shikoku, Japan | 2,920 | 890 | 1999 |
| Ponte de Normandie | Le Havre, France | 2,808 | 856 | 1995 |
| Second Nanjing | Yangtze River, Nanjing, China | 2,060 | 628 | 2001 |
| Wuhan Third Yangtze | Wuhan, Hubei Province, China | 2,028 | 618 | 2000 |
| Qingzhou Minjiang | Fuzhou, China | 1,985 | 605 | 1996 |
| Yang Pu | Shanghai, China | 1,975 | 602 | 1993 |
| Xupu | Shanghai, China | 1,936 | 590 | 1997 |
| Meiko Chuo | Aichi, Japan | 1,936 | 590 | 1997 |
| Patras | Greece | 1,837 | 560 | UC |
| Skarnsundet | near Trondheim, Norway | 1,739 | 530 | 1991 |
| Queshi | Guangdong Province, China | 1,700 | 518 | 1999 |
| Tsurumi Tsubasa | Kanagawa, Japan | 1,673 | 510 | 1995 |
| Jingzhou | Yangtze River, Hubei Province, China | 1,640 | 500 | UC |
| Oresund | Denmark/Sweden | 1,614 | 492 | 2000 |
| Ikuchi | Honshu-Shikoku, Japan | 1,608 | 490 | 1991 |
| Higashi Kobe | Hyogo, Japan | 1,591 | 485 | 1994 |
| Zhanjiang Bay | Guangdong Province, China | 1,575 | 480 | 1998 |
| Ting Kau | Hong Kong | 1,558 | 475 | 1997 |
| Seohae Grand | South Korea | 1,542 | 470 | 2000 |
| Alex Fraser | Vancouver, B.C., Canada | 1,525 | 465 | 1986 |
| Yokohama-ko-odan | Kanagawa, Japan | 1,509 | 460 | 1989 |
| Second Hooghly | Calcutta, India | 1,500 | 457 | 1992 |
| Second Severn Crossing | Severn River, England | 1,496 | 456 | 1996 |
| Dartford | Thames River, Dartford, England | 1,476 | 450 | 1992 |
| Dao Kanong | Chao Phraya River, Bangkok, Thailand | 1,476 | 450 | 1987 |
| **Continuous Truss** | **United States** | | | |
| Astoria | Columbia River, Ore. | 1,232 | 376 | 1966 |
| Croton Reservoir | Croton, N.Y. | 1,052 | 321 | 1970 |
| Ravenswood | Ohio River, Ravenswood, W. Va. | 902 | 275 | 1981 |
| Central | Ohio River, Newport, Ky. | 850 | 259 | 1995 |
| Dubuque | Mississippi River at Dubuque, Iowa | 845 | 258 | 1943 |
| | **International** | | | |
| Oshima | Oshima Island, Japan | 1,066 | 325 | 1976 |
| Tenmon | Kumamoto, Japan | 984 | 300 | 1966 |
| Kuronoseto | Nagashima-Kyushu, Japan | 984 | 300 | 1974 |
| Graf Spee | Germany | 839 | 256 | 1936 |
| **Concrete Arch** | **United States** | | | |
| Natchez Trace Pkwy. | Franklin, Tenn. | 582 | 177 | 1994 |
| Westinghouse | Pittsburgh, Pa. | 460 | 140 | 1931 |
| Jack's Run | Pittsburgh, Pa. | 400 | 120 | 1930 |
| Cappelen | Minneapolis, Minn. | 400 | 120 | 1923 |
| | **International** | | | |
| Wanxian | Wanxian, Sichuan Province, China | 1,378 | 420 | 1997 |
| Krk (I) | Krk, Croatia | 1,280 | 390 | 1980 |
| Jiangjiehe | Guizhou Province, China | 1,083 | 330 | 1995 |
| Gladesville | Parramatta River at Sydney, Australia | 1,000 | 305 | 1964 |
| Amizade | Paraná River at Foz do Iguassu, Brazil | 951 | 290 | 1964 |
| Bloukrans | Bloukrans River, South Africa | 892 | 272 | 1983 |
| Arrábida | Porto, Portugal | 886 | 270 | 1963 |
| Sandö | Angerman River at Kramfors, Sweden | 866 | 264 | 1943 |
| Confederation | Northumberland Strait, Canada | 820 | 250 | 1997 |
| Sibenik | Sibenik, Croatia | 808 | 246 | 1966 |
| Krk (II) | Krk, Croatia | 800 | 244 | 1979 |
| Fiumarella | Catanzaro, Italy | 758 | 231 | 1961 |
| Zaporozhe | Old Dnepr River, Ukraine | 748 | 228 | 1952 |
| Esla | Esla River at Zamora, Spain | 645 | 197 | 1940 |
| **Segmental Construction** | **United States** | | | |
| Jesse H. Jones Memorial | Houston Ship Channel, Tex. | 750 | 228 | 1982 |

NOTES: UC = under construction in 2002. 1. Twin span. *Source:* Federal Highway Administration.

## World's Highest Dams

| Name | River, state, and country | Structural height feet | meters | thousands of acre feet | millions of cubic meters | Year completed |
|------|---------------------------|--------:|-------:|-----------------------:|-------------------------:|---------------:|
| Rogun | Vakhsh, Tajikistan | 1099 | 335 | 9,404 | 11,600 | 1985 |
| Nurek | Vakhsh, Tajikistan | 984 | 300 | 8,512 | 10,500 | 1980 |
| Grande Dixence | Dixence, Switzerland | 935 | 285 | 324 | 400 | 1962 |
| Inguri | Inguri, Georgia | 892 | 272 | 801 | 1,100 | 1984 |
| Vaiont | Vaiont, Italy | 859 | 262 | 137 | 169 | 1961 |
| Manuel M. Torres | Grijalva, Mexico | 856 | 261 | 1,346 | 1,660 | 1981 |
| Tehri | Bhagirathi, India | 856 | 261 | 2,869 | 3,540 | UC |
| Alvaro Obregon | Mextiquic, Mexico | 853 | 260 | n.a. | n.a. | 1926 |
| Mauvoisin | Drance de Bagnes, Switzerland | 820 | 250 | 146 | 180 | 1957 |
| Alberto Lleras | Orinoco, Colombia | 797 | 243 | 811 | 1,000 | 1989 |
| Mica | Columbia, Canada | 797 | 243 | 20,000 | 24,670 | 1972 |
| Sayano-Shushensk | Yenisei, Russia | 794 | 242 | 25,353 | 31,300 | 1980 |
| Ertan | Yangtze/Yalong, China | 787 | 240 | 4,702 | 5,800 | 1999 |
| La Esmeralda | Batá, Colombia | 778 | 237 | 661 | 815 | 1975 |
| Kishau | Tons, India | 774 | 236 | 1,946 | 2,400 | 1985 |
| Oroville | Feather, Calif., U.S. | 770 | 235 | 3,538 | 4,299 | 1968 |
| El Cajón | Humuya, Honduras | 768 | 234 | 4,580 | 5,650 | 1984 |
| Chirkey | Sulak, Russia | 764 | 233 | 2,252 | 2,780 | 1977 |
| Bhakra | Sutlej, India | 741 | 226 | 8,002 | 9,870 | 1963 |
| Luzzone | Brenno di Luzzone, Switzerland | 738 | 225 | 71 | 87 | 1963 |
| Hoover | Colorado, Ariz./Nev., U.S. | 732 | 223 | 28,500 | 35,154 | 1936 |
| Contra | Verzasca, Switzerland | 722 | 220 | 70 | 86 | 1965 |
| Mratinje | Piva, Herzegovina | 722 | 220 | 713 | 880 | 1973 |
| Dworshak | N. Fk. Clearwater, Idaho, U.S. | 717 | 219 | 3,453 | 4,259 | 1974 |
| Glen Canyon | Colorado, Ariz., U.S. | 710 | 216 | 27,000 | 33,304 | 1964 |

NOTES: UC = under construction in 2002. n.a. = not available. *Source:* International Commission on Large Dams, *World Register of Dams 1998* and other sources.

## World's Largest Dams

| Dam | Location | Volume (thousands) Cubic meters | Cubic yards | Year completed |
|-----|----------|-------------------:|------------:|---------------:|
| Syncrude Tailings | Canada | 540,000 | 706,320 | UC |
| Chapetón | Argentina | 296,200 | 311,539 | UC |
| Pati | Argentina | 238,180 | 274,026 | UC |
| New Cornelia Tailings | United States | 209,500 | 274,026 | 1973 |
| Tarbela | Pakistan | 121,720 | 159,210 | 1976 |
| Kambaratinsk | Kyrgyzstan | 112,200 | 146,758 | UC |
| Fort Peck | Montana | 96,049 | 125,628 | 1940 |
| Lower Usuma | Nigeria | 93,000 | 121,644 | 1990 |
| Cipasang | Indonesia | 90,000 | 117,720 | UC |
| Atatürk | Turkey | 84,500 | 110,522 | 1990 |
| Yacyretá-Apipe | Paraguay/Argentina | 81,000 | 105,944 | 1998 |
| Guri (Raul Looni) | Venezuela | 78,000 | 100,014 | 1988 |
| Rogun | Tajikistan | 78,800 | 98,750 | 1985 |
| Oahe | South Dakota | 70,339 | 92,000 | 1963 |
| Mangla | Pakistan | 65,651 | 85,872 | 1967 |
| Gardiner | Canada | 65,440 | 85,592 | 1968 |
| Afsluitdijk | Netherlands | 63,400 | 82,927 | 1932 |
| Oroville | California | 59,639 | 78,008 | 1968 |
| San Luis | California | 59,405 | 77,700 | 1967 |
| Nurek | Tajikistan | 58,000 | 75,861 | 1980 |
| Garrison | North Dakota | 50,843 | 66,500 | 1956 |
| Cochiti | New Mexico | 48,052 | 62,850 | 1975 |
| Tabka (Thawra) | Syria | 46,000 | 60,168 | 1976 |
| Bennett W.A.C. | Canada | 43,733 | 57,201 | 1967 |
| Tucuruí | Brazil | 43,000 | 56,242 | 1984 |

NOTE: UC = under construction in 2002. *Source:* Department of the Interior, Bureau of Reclamation and *International Water Power and Dam Construction.*

## Famous Ship Canals

| Name | Location | Length (miles)[1] | Width (feet) | Depth (feet) | Locks | Year opened |
|---|---|---|---|---|---|---|
| Albert | Belgium | 80.0 | 53.0 | 16.5 | 6 | 1939 |
| Amsterdam-Rhine | Netherlands | 45.0 | 164.0 | 41.0 | 3 | 1952 |
| Beaumont-Port Arthur | United States | 40.0 | 200.0 | 34.0 | — | 1916 |
| Canal du Midi | France | 149.0 | n.a. | n.a. | 100 | 1692 |
| Chesapeake and Delaware | United States | 14.0 | 450.0 | 35.0 | — | 1829 |
| Erie Canal | United States | 363.0 | 70 | 7 | 82 | 1825 |
| Grand Canal | China | 1,085.0 | n.a. | n.a. | n.a. | 7th cent. |
| Göta Canal | Sweden | 240.0 | n.a. | n.a. | 58 | 1832 |
| Houston | United States | 50.0 | ([2]) | 40.0 | — | 1914 |
| Kiel (Nord-Ostsee Kanal) | Germany | 61.3 | 144.0 | 36.0 | 4 | 1895 |
| Panama | Panama | 50.7 | 110.0 | 41.0 | 12 | 1914 |
| St. Lawrence Seaway | U.S. and Canada | 2,400.0[3] | ([4]) | — | — | 1959 |
|   Montreal to Prescott | U.S. and Canada | 11.5 | 80.0 | 30.0 | 7 | 1959 |
|   Welland | Canada | 27.5 | 80.0 | 27.0 | 8 | 1931 |
|   Sault Ste. Marie | Canada | 1.2 | 60.0 | 16.8 | 1 | 1895 |
|   Sault Ste. Marie | United States | 1.6 | 80.0 | 25.0 | 4 | 1915 |
| Suez | Egypt | 119.9[5] | 1197.5 | 68.9 | — | 1869 |

1. Statute miles. 2. 300–400 ft. 3. From Montreal to Duluth. 4. 442–550 ft; there are 11.5 mi of locks, 80 ft wide and 30 ft deep. 5. From Port Said lighthouse to entrance channel in Suez roads. *Source:* American Society of Civil Engineers.

## Notable Tunnels

| Name | Location | Length | | Year completed |
|---|---|---|---|---|
| | | mi | km | |
| **Railroad, excluding subways** | | | | |
| Seikan | Tsugaru Strait, Japan | 33.5 | 53.9 | 1988 |
| Channel Tunnel[1] | English Channel, England–France | 31.1 | 50.0 | 1994 |
| Simplon (I and II) | Alps, Switzerland–Italy | 12.3 | 19.8 | 1906 & 1922 |
| Apennine | Bologna–Florence, Italy | 11.5 | 18.5 | 1934 |
| St. Gotthard | Swiss Alps | 9.3 | 15.0 | 1880 |
| Lötschberg | Swiss Alps | 9.1 | 14.6 | 1911 |
| Mont Cénis | French Alps | 8.5[2] | 13.7 | 1871 |
| New Cascade | Cascade Mountains, Washington | 7.8 | 12.6 | 1929 |
| Vosges | Vosges, France | 7.0 | 11.3 | 1940 |
| Flathead | Rocky Mountains, Montana | 7.0 | 11.3 | 1970 |
| Arlberg | Austrian Alps | 6.3 | 10.1 | 1884 |
| Moffat | Rocky Mountains, Colorado | 6.2 | 9.9 | 1928 |
| Shimizu | Shimizu, Japan | 6.1 | 9.8 | 1931 |
| Rimutaka | Wairarapa, New Zealand | 5.5 | 8.9 | 1955 |
| Storebaelt | Great Belt, Denmark | 5.0 | 8.0 | 1995 |
| **Vehicular** | | | | |
| Laerdal | Laerdal–Aurland, Norway | 15.2 | 24.5 | 2000 |
| St. Gotthard | Alps, Switzerland | 10.2 | 16.4 | 1980 |
| Arlberg | Austrian Alps | 8.7 | 14.0 | 1979 |
| Fréjus | French Alps | 8.0 | 12.9 | 1980 |
| Mt. Blanc | Alps, France–Italy | 7.0 | 11.3 | 1965 |
| Aqualine Expressway | Tokyo Bay, Japan | 5.9 | 9.5 | 1997 |
| Mt. Ena | Japan Alps, Japan | 5.3 | 8.5 | 1976[3] |
| Great St. Bernard | Alps, Switzerland–Italy | 3.4 | 5.5 | 1964 |
| Mount Royal | Montreal, Canada | 3.2 | 5.1 | 1918 |
| Queensway | Mersey River, Liverpool, England | 2.2 | 3.5 | 1934 |
| Brooklyn-Battery | East River, New York City | 1.7 | 2.7 | 1950 |
| Fort McHenry | Baltimore, Maryland | 1.7 | 2.7 | 1985 |
| Holland | Hudson River, New York–New Jersey | 1.6 | 2.6 | 1927 |
| Lincoln | Hudson River, New York–New Jersey | 1.6 | 2.6 | 1937 |
| Hampton Roads[4] | Norfolk, Virginia | 1.4 | 2.3 | 1957 |
| Queens-Midtown | East River, New York City | 1.3 | 2.1 | 1940 |
| Liberty Tubes | Pittsburgh, Pennsylvania | 1.2 | 1.9 | 1923 |
| Baltimore Harbor | Baltimore, Maryland | 1.2 | 1.9 | 1957 |
| Allegheny Tunnels | Pennsylvania Turnpike | 1.2 | 1.9 | 1940[5] |
| Yerba | Yerba Buena Island, Calif. | 0.5 | 0.8 | 1936 |

1. Three-tunnel system including two rail tunnels (one carries passengers from England to France, the other from France to England) and a central service tunnel. 2. Lengthened to its present 8.5 miles in 1881. 3. Parallel tunnel begun in 1976. 4. Parallel bridge-tunnel opened in 1976. 5. Parallel tunnel built in 1965, twin tunnel in 1966. *Source:* American Society of Civil Engineers and International Bridge, Tunnel & Turnpike Association, Wittiker's.

# First Aid for Crossword Puzzlers

We cannot begin to list all the odd words you might encounter in your daily and Sunday crossword puzzles, for such words run into the thousands. But we have tried to include those that turn up most frequently, as well as many others that should be of help to you when you are unable to go any further.

We do not guarantee that the definitions in your puzzle will be exactly the same as ours, although we have checked every word with a standard dictionary and have followed its definition.

In nearly every case, we have used as the key word the principal noun of the definition, rather than any adjective, adjective phrase, or noun used as an adjective. And, to simplify your searching, we have grouped the words according to the number of spaces you have to fill.

## Words of Two Letters

Ambary, DA
And (French, Latin), ET
Article (Arabic), AL
  (French), LA, LE, UN
  (Spanish), EL, LA, UN
At the (French), AU
  (Spanish), AL
Behold, LO
Bird: Hawaiian, OO
Birthplace: Abraham's, UR
Bone, OS
Buddha, FO
Butterfly: Peacock, IO
Champagne, AY
Chaos, NU
Chief: Burmese, BO
Coin: Roman, AS
  Siamese, AT
Concerning, RE
Dialect: Chinese, WU
Double (Egy. relig.), KA
Drama: Japanese, NO
Egg (comb. form), OO
Esker, OS

Eye (Scottish), EE
Factor: Amplification, MU
Fifty (Greek), NU
Fish: Carplike, ID
Force, OD
Forty (Greek), MU
From (French, Latin, Spanish),
  DE
  (Latin prefix), AB
From the (French), DU
God: Babylonian, EA, ZU
  Egyptian sun, RA
  Hindu unknown, KA
  Semitic, EL
Goddess: Babylonian, AI
  Greek Earth, GE
Gold (heraldry), OR
Gulf: Arctic, OB
Heart (Egy. relig.), AB
Indian: South American, GE
King: Of Bashan, OG
Language: Artificial, RO
  Assamese, AO
Lava: Hawaiian, AA

Letter: Greek, MU, NU, PI, XI
  Hebrew, HE, PE
Lily: Palm, TI
Measure: Chinese, HO, HU,
  KO, LI, MU, PU, TO, TU
  Japanese, GO, JO, MO, RI,
  SE, TO
  Netherlands, EL
  Portuguese, PE
  Siamese, WA
  Swedish, AM
  Type, EM, EN
  Vietnamese, LY
Monk: Buddhist, BO
Month: Jewish, AB
Mouth, OS
Mulberry: Indian, AL
Native: Burmese, WA
Note: Of scale, DO, FA, MI,
  LA, RE, TI
Of (French, Latin, Spanish), DE
Of the (French), DU

One (Scottish), AE
Pagoda: Chinese, TA
Plant: East Indian fiber, DA
Ridge: Sandy, AS, OS
River: Russian, OB
Sloth: Three-toed, AI
Soul (Egy. relig.), BA
Sound: Hindu mystic, OM
Suffix: Comparative, ER
To the: French, AU
  Spanish, AL
Tree: Buddhist sacred, BO
Tribe: Assamese, AO
Type: Jumbled, PI
Weight: Chinese, LI
  Danish, ES
  Japanese, MO
  Roman, AS
  Vietnamese, TA
Whirlwind: Faeroe Is., OE
Yes (German), JA
  (Italian, Spanish), SI
  (Russian), DA

## Words of Three Letters

**Adherent,** IST
Again, BIS
Age, ERA
Antelope: African, GNU, KOB
Apricot: Japanese, UME
Article (German), DAS, DEM,
  DEN, DER, DES, DIE, EIN
  (French), LES, UNE
  (Spanish), LAS, LOS, UNA
**Banana:** Polynesian, FEI
Barge, HOY
Bass: African, IYO
Beak, NEB, NIB
Beard: Grain, AWN
Beetle: June, DOR
Being, ENS
Berry: Hawthorn, HAW
Beverage: Hawaiian, AVA
Bird: Australian, EMU
  Crowlike, JAY
  ▓▓▓▓, ▓▓ ▓▓
  Fabulous, ROC
  Frigate, IWA
  Parson, POE, TUE, TUI
  ▓▓▓, AWU
Dikalibird, ANI, ANO
Born, NEE
Bronze: Roman, AES
Bugle: Yellow, IVA
By way of, VIA
**Canton:** Swiss, URI
Cap: Turkish, FEZ
Catnip, NEP
Character: In "Faerie Queene,"
  UNA
Coin (Money of account):
  Afghan, PUL
  Albanian, LEK
  Bulgarian, LEV, LEW

French, ECU, SOU
Guyanese, BIT
Indian, PIE
Japanese, SEN, YEN
Korean, WON
Lithuanian, LIT
Macao, Timor, AVO
Palestinian, MIL
Persian, PUL
Peruvian, SOL
Rumanian, BAN, LEU, LEY
Scandinavian, ORE
Siamese, ATT
Collection: Facts, ANA
Commune: Belgian, ANS, ATH
  Netherlands, EDE, EPE
Community: Russian, MIR
Constellation: Southern, ARA
Contraction: Poetic, EEN, EER,
  OER
▓▓▓▓▓▓, Army of, ▓▓▓ PPI
Crab: Fiddler, UCA
Crag: Rocky, TOR
Cry: Crow, rook, raven, CAW
Cup: Wine, AMA
Cymbal, Oriental, TAL, ZEL
**Disease:** Silkworm, UJI
Division: Danish territorial, AMT
  Geologic, EON
Doctrine, ISM
Dowry, DOT
Dry (French), SEC
Dynasty: Chinese, CHI, HAN,
  SUI, WEI, YIN
**Eagle:** Sea, ERN
Earth (comb. form), GEO
Egg: Louse, NIT
Eggs: Fish, ROE
Emmet, ANT

Enzyme, ASE
Equal (comb. form), ISO
Extension: building, ELL
**Far** (comb. form), TEL
Farewell, AVE
Fiber: Palm, TAL
Finial, EPI
Fish: Carplike, IDE
  Pikelike, GAR
Flatfish, DAB
Fleur-de-lis, LIS, LYS
Food: Hawaiian, POI
Formerly, NEE
Friend (French), AMI
**Game:** Card, LOO
Garment: Camel-hair, ABA
Gateway, DAR
Gazelle: Tibetan, GOA
Genus: Ducks, AIX
  ▓▓▓▓, DOL
  ▓▓▓▓▓ (maize), ZEA
  Herbs or shrubs, IVA
  Lizards, UTA
  ▓▓▓▓▓ (incl. ▓▓▓▓ ▓▓▓▓), MUS
  Ruminants (incl. cattle), BOS
  Swine, SUS
Gibbon: Malay, LAR
God: Assyrian, SIN
  Babylonian, ABU, ANU, BEL,
  HEA, SIN, UTU
  Irish sea, LER
  Phrygian, MEN
  Polynesian, ORO
Goddess: Babylonian, AYA
  Etruscan, UNI
  Hindu, SRI, UMA, VAC
  Teutonic, RAN

Governor: Algerian, DEY
  Turkish, BEY
Grampus, ORC
Grape, UVA
Grass: Meadow, POA
Gypsy, ROM
**Hail,** AVE
Hare: Female, DOE
Hawthorn, HAW
Hay: Spread for drying, TED
Herb: Japanese, UDO
  Perennial, PIA
  Used for blue dye, WAD
Herd: Whales, GAM, POD
Hero: Spanish, CID
High (music), ALT
Honey (pharm.), MEL
Humorist: American, ADE
I (Latin), EGO
▓▓▓ (▓▓▓▓) ▓▓▓▓,
Indian: Algonquin, FOX, SAC,
  WEA
Chimakuan, HOH
▓▓▓▓▓▓, UIA
Mayan, MAM
Shoshonean, UTE
Siouan, KAW, OTO
South American, ITE, ONA,
  URO, URU, YAO
Tierra del Fuego, ONA
Wakashan, AHT
Ingot, PIG
Inlet: Narrow, RIA
Island: Cyclades, IOS
  Dodecanese, COS, KOS
  (French), ILE
  River, AIT
**Jackdaw,** DAW

John (Gaelic), IAN
**Keelbill,** ANI, ANO
Kiln, OST
King: British legendary, LUD
Kobold, NIS
**Lace:** To make, TAT
Lamprey, EEL
Language: Artificial, IDO
Bantu, ILA
Siamese, LAO, TAI
Leaf: Palm, OLA, OLE
Leaving, ORT
Left: Cause to turn, HAW
Letter: Greek, CHI, ETA, PHI,
PSI, RHO, TAU
Hebrew, MEM, NUN, SIN,
TAV, VAU
Lettuce, COS
Life (comb. form), BIO
Lily: Palm, TOI
Lizard, EFT
Louse: Young, NIT
Love (Anglo-Irish), GRA
Lute: Oriental, TAR
**Macaw:** Brazilian, ARA
Marble, TAW
Match: Shooting (French), TIR
Meadow, LEA
Measure: Abyssinian, TAT
Algerian, PIK
Arabian, DEN, SAA
Belgian, VAT
Bulgarian, OKA, OKE
Chinese, FEN, TOU, YIN
Cloth, ELL
Cyprus, OKA, OKE, PIK
Czech, LAN, SAH
Danish, FOD, MIL, POT
Dominican Republic, ONA
Dutch, old, AAM
East Indian, KIT
Egyptian, APT, HEN, PIK,
ROB
Electric, MHO, OHM
Energy, ERG
English, PIN
Estonian, TUN
French, POT
German, AAM
Greek, PIK
Hebrew, CAB, HIN, KOR,
LOG
Hungarian, AKO
Icelandic, FET
Indian, GAZ, GUZ, JOW,
KOS
Japanese, BOO, CHO, KEN,
RIN, SHO, SUN, TAN
Malabar, ADY
Metric (land), ARE
Netherlands, KAN, KOP,
MUD, VAT, ZAK
Norwegian, FOT, POT
Persian, GAZ, GUZ, MOU,
ZAR, ZER
Polish, CAL
Rangoon, DHA, LAN
Roman, PES, URN
Russian, FUT, LOF
Scottish, COP

Siamese, KEN, NIU, RAI,
SAT, SEN, SOK, WAH, YOT
Somaliland, TOP
Spanish, PIE
Straits Settlements, PAU,
TUN
Swedish, ALN, FOT, MIL,
REF, TUM
Swiss, POT
Tunisian, SAA
Turkish, OKA, OKE, PIK
Vietnamese, GON, MAU,
NGU, VUO, SAO, TAO, TAT
Wire, MIL
Württemberg, IMI
Yarn, LEA
Yugoslav, OKA, RIF
Milk, LAC
Milkfish, AWA
Moccasin, PAC
Money: Yap stone, FEI
Money of Account (also Coin):
Anglo-Saxon, ORA, ORE
French, SOU
Indian, LAC
Japanese, RIN
Oman, GAJ
Virgin Islands, BIT
Monkey: Capuchin, SAI
Morsel, ORT
Mother: Peer Gynt's, ASE
Mountain: Asia Minor, IDA
Mulberry: Indian, AAL, ACH,
AWL
Muttonbird: New Zealand, OII
**Nahoor,** SNA
Native: Mindanao, ATA
Neckpiece, BOA
Newt, EFT
No (Scottish), NAE
Note: Guido's highest, ELA
Of scale, SOL
Nursemaid: Oriental, AMA, IYA
**Ocher:** Yellow, SIL
One (Scottish), YIN
Ornament: Pagoda, TEE
Oven: Polynesian, UMU
Ox: Tibetan, YAK
**Pagoda:** Chinese, TAA
Parrot: Hawk, HIA
New Zealand, KEA
Part: Footlike, PES
Particle: Electrified, ION
Pasha, DEY
Pass: Mountain, COL
Paste: Rice, AME
Pea: Indian split, DAL
Peasant: Philippine, TAO
Penpoint, NEB, NIB
Piece out, EKE
Pigeon, NUN
Pine: Textile screw, ARA
Pistol (slang), GAT
Pit: Baking, IMU
Plant: Pepper, AVA
Play: By Capek, RUR
Poem: Old French, DIT
Porgy: Japanese, TAI
Priest: Biblical high, ELI
Prince: Ethiopian, RAS

Pseudonym: Dickens', BOZ
**Queen:** Fairy, MAB
Quince: Bengal, BEL
**Record:** Ship's, LOG
Refuse: Flax (Scottish), PAB,
POB
Resin, LAC
Resort, SPA
Revolver (slang), GAT
Right: Cause to turn, GEE
River: Scottish or English, DEE
(Spanish), RIO
Swiss, AAR
Room: Harem, ODA
Rootstock: Fern, ROI
Rose (Persian), GUL
Ruff: Female, REE
Rule: Indian, RAJ
**Sailor,** GOB, TAR
Saint: Female (abbr.), STE
Islamic, PIR
Salt, SAL
Sash: Japanese, OBI
Scrap, ORT
Seed: Poppy, MAW
Small, PIP
Self, EGO
Serpent: Vedic sky, AHI
Sesame, TIL
Sheep: Female, EWE
Indian, SHA
Male, RAM
Sheepfold (Scottish), REE
Shelter, LEE
Shield, ECU
Shooting match (French), TIR
Shrew: European, ERD
Shrub: Evergreen, YEW
Silkworm, ERI
Snake, ASP, BOA
Soak, RET
Son-in-law: Mohammed's, ALI
Sorrel: Wood, OCA
Spade: Long, narrow, LOY
Spirit: Malignant, KER
Spot: Playing-card, PIP
Spread for drying, TED
Spring: Mineral, SPA
Sprite: Water, NIX
Statesman: Japanese, ITO
Stern: Toward, AFT
Stomach: Bird's, MAW
Street (French), RUE
Summer (French), ETE
Sun, SOL
Swamp, BOG, FEN
Swan: Male, COB
**Tea:** Chinese, CHA
Temple: Shinto, SHA
Thing (law), RES
Title: Etruscan, LAR
Monk's, FRA
Portuguese, DOM
Spanish, DON
Turkish, AGA, BEY
Tool: Cutting, ADZ, AXE
Mining, GAD
Piercing, AWL
Tree: Candlenut, AMA
Central American, EBO

East Indian, SAJ, SAL
Evergreen, YEW
Hawaiian, KOA, KOU
Indian, BEL, DAR
Linden, LIN
New Zealand, AKE
Philippine, DAO, TUA, TUI
Rubber, ULE
South American, APA
Tribe: New Zealand, ATI
Turmeric, REA
Twice, BIS
Twin: Siamese, ENG
**Uncle** (dialect), EAM, EME
**Veil:** Chalice, AER, AIR
Vessel: Wine, AMA
Vestment: Ecclesiastical, ALB
Vetch: Bitter, ERS
Victorfish, AKU
Vine: New Zealand, AKA
Philippine, IYO
**Wallaba,** APA
Wapiti, ELK
Water (French), EAU
Waterfall, LIN
Watering place: Prussian, EMS
Weave: Designating plain,
UNI
Weight: Bulgarian, OKA, OKE
Burmese, MOO, VIS
Chinese, FEN, HAO, KIN,
SSU, TAN, YIN
Cyprus, OKA, OKE
Danish, LOD, ORT, VOG
East Indian, TJI
Egyptian, KAT, OKA, OKE
English, for wool, TOD
German, LOT
Greek, MNA, OKA, OKE
Indian, SER
Japanese, FUN, KIN, RIN,
SHI
Korean, KON
Malacca, KIP
Mongolian, LAN
Netherlands, ONS
Norwegian, LOD
Polish, LUT
Rangoon, PAI
Roman, BES
Russian, LOF
Siamese, BAT, HAP, PAI
Swedish, ASS, ORT
Turkish, OKA, OKE
Vietnamese, CAN
Yugoslav, OKA, OKE
Whales: Herd, GAM, POD
Wildebeest, GNU
Wing, ALA
Witticism, MOT
Wolframite, CAL
Worm: African, LOA
Wreath: Hawaiian, LEI
**Yale,** ELI
Yam: Hawaiian, HOI
Yes (French), OUI
Young: Bring forth, EAN
**Z** (letter), ZED

# Words of Four Letters

**Aborigine:** Borneo, DYAK
Agave, ALOE
Animal: Footless, APOD
Ant: White, ANAI, ANAY
Antelope: African, ASSE, BISA, GUIB,
KOBA, KUDU, ORYX, POKU, PUKU,
TOPI, TORA
Apoplexy: Plant, ESCA
Apple, POME
Apricot, ANSU
Ardor, ELAN
Armadillo, APAR, PEBA, PEVA, TATU
Ascetic: Islamic, SUFI
Association: Chinese, TONG

Astronomer: Persian, OMAR
Avatar: Of Vishnu, RAMA
Axillary, ALAR
**Band:** Horizontal (heraldry), FESS
Barracuda, SPET
Bark: Mulberry, TAPA
Base: Column, DADO
Bearing (heraldry), ORLE
Beer: Russian, KVAS
Beige, ECRU
Being, ESSE
Beverage: Japanese rice, SAKE
Bird: Asian, MINA, MYNA
Egyptian sacred, IBIS

Extinct, DODO, MAMO
Flightless, KIWI
Gull-like, TERN
Hawaiian, IIWI, MAMO
Parson, KOKO
Unfledged, EYAS
Birds: As class, AVES
Black, EBON
(French), NOIR
Blackbird: European, MERL
Boat: Flat-bottomed, DORY
Bone: Forearm, ULNA
Bones, OSSA
Box, Japanese, INRO

Bravo (rare), EUGE
Buffalo: Indian wild, ARNA
Bull (Spanish), TORO
Burden, ONUS
**Cabbage:** Sliced, SLAW
Caliph: Islamic, OMAR
Canoe: Malay, PRAU, PROA
Cap: Military, KEPI
Cape, NESS
Capital: Ancient Irish, TARA
Case: Article, ETUI
Cat: Wild, BALU, EYRA
Chalcedony, SARD
Chamber: Indian ceremonial, KIVA
Channel: Brain, ITER
Cheese: Dutch, EDAM
Chest: Sepulchral stone, CIST
Chieftain: Arab, EMIR
Church: Part of, APSE, NAVE
  (Scottish), KIRK
Claim (law), LIEN
Cluster: Flower, CYME
Coin: Chinese, TAEL, YUAN
  German, MARK
  Indian, ANNA
  Iranian, RIAL
  Italian, LIRA
  Moroccan, OKIA
  Siamese, BAHT
  South American, PESO
  Spanish, DURO, PESO
  Turkish, PARA
Commune: Belgian, AATH
Composition: Musical, OPUS
Compound: Chemical, DIOL
Constellation: Southern, PAVO
Council: Russian, DUMA
Counsel, REDE
Covering: Seed, ARIL
Cross: Egyptian, ANKH
Cry: Bacchanalian, EVOE
Cup (Scottish), TASS
Cupbearer, SAKI
**Dagger,** DIRK
  Malay, KRIS
Dam: River, WEIR
Dash, ELAN
Date: Roman, IDES
Dawn: Pertaining to, EOAN
Dean: English, INGE
Decay: In fruit, BLET
Deer: Sambar, MAHA
Disease: Skin, ACNE
Disk: Solar, ATEN
Dog: Hunting, ALAN
Drink: Hindu intoxicating, SOMA
Duck, SMEE, SMEW, TEAL
Dynasty: Chinese, CHEN, CHIN, CHOU,
  CHOW, HSIA, MING, SUNG, TANG,
  TSIN
  Mongol, YUAN
**Eagle:** Biblical, GIER
  Sea, ERNE
Ear: Pertaining to, OTIC
Egyptian: Christian, COPT
Entrance: Mine, ADIT
Envy, EDOM
███████████ ██████, URALE
Eskers, OSAR
Evergreen: New Zealand, TAWA
**Fairy:** Persian, PERI
Family: Italian, ESTE
Far (comb. form), TELE
Farewell, VALE
Father (French), PERE
Fennel: Philippine, ANIS
Fever: Malarial, AGUE
Fiber: East Indian, JUTE
Firn, NEVE
Fish: Carplike, DACE
  Hawaiian, ULUA
  Herringlike, SHAD
  Mackerellike, CERO
  Marine, HAKE
  Sea, LING, MERO, OPAH
  Spiny-finned, GOBY

Food: Tropical, TARO
Foot: Metric, IAMB
Formerly, ERST
Founder: Of Carthage, DIDO
France: Southern, MIDI
Furze, ULEX
**Gaelic,** ERSE
Gaiter, SPAT
Game: Card, FARO, SKAT
Garlic: European wild, MOLY
Garment: Hindu, SARI
  Roman, TOGA
Gazelle, CORA
Gem: JADE, ONYX, OPAL, RUBY
Genus: Amphibians (incl. frogs), RANA
  Amphibians (incl. tree toads), HYLA
  Antelopes, ORYX
  Auks, ALCA, URIA
  Bees, APIS
  Birds (American ostriches), RHEA
  Birds (cranes), CRUS
  Birds (magpies), PICA
  Birds (peacocks), PAVO
  Cetaceans, INIA
  Ducks (incl. mallards), ANAS
  Fishes (burbots), LOTA
  Fishes (incl. bowfins), AMIA
  Geese (snow geese), CHEN
  Gulls, XEMA
  Herbs, ARUM, GEUM
  Insects (water scorpions), NEPA
  Lilies, ALOE
  Mammals (humans), HOMO
  Orchids, DISA
  Owls, ASIO, BUBO, OTUS
  Palms, NIPA
  Sea birds, SULA
  Sheep, OVIS
  Shrubs, Eurasian, ULEX
  Shrubs (hollies), ILEX
  Shrubs (incl. Virginia Willow), ITEA
  Shrubs, tropical, EVEA
  Snakes (sand snakes), ERYX
  Swans, OLOR
  Trees, chocolate, COLA
  Trees (ebony family), MABA
  Trees (incl. maples), ACER
  Trees (olives), OLEA
  Trees, tropical, EVEA
  Turtles, EMYS
Goat: Wild, IBEX, KRAS, TAHR, TAIR,
  THAR
God: Assyrian, ASUR
  Babylonian, ADAD, ADDU, ENKI,
  ENZU, IRRA, NABU, NEBO, UTUG
  Celtic, LLEU, LLEW
  Hindu, AGNI, CIVA, DEVA, DEWA,
  KAMA, RAMA, SIVA, VAYU
  Phrygian, ATYS
  Semitic, BAAL
  Teutonic, HLER
Goddess: Babylonian, ERUA, GULA
  Hawaiian, PELE
  Hindu, DEVI, KALI, SHRI, VACH
Gooseberry: Hawaiian, POHA
Gourd, PEPO
Grandfather ████████, ████
Grandfather (obsolete), AIEL
Grandparents: Pertaining to, AVAL
Grass: Hawaiian, HILO
Gray (French), GRIS
Green (heraldry), VERT
Groom: Indian, SYCE
**Half** (prefix), DEMI, HEMI, SEMI
Hamlet, DORP
Hammerhead: Part of, PEEN
Handle, ANSA
Harp: Japanese, KOTO
Hartebeest, ASSE, TORA
Hautboy, OBOE
Hawk: Taken from nest (falconry), EYAS
Hearing (law), OYER
Heater: For liquids, ETNA
Herb: Aromatic, ANET, DILL
  Fabulous, MOLY
  Perennial, GEUM, SEGO

Pot, WORT
  Used for blue dye, WADE, WOAD
Hill: Flat-topped, MESA
  Sand, DENE, DUNE
Hoarfrost, RIME
Hog: Immature female, GILT
Holly, ILEX
House: Cow, BYRE
  (Spanish), CASA
**Ice:** Floating, FLOE
Image, ICON, IKON
Incarnation: Of Vishnu, RAMA
Indian: Algonquin, CREE, SAUK
  Central American, MAYA
  Iroquoian, ERIE
  Mexican, CORA
  Peruvian, CANA, INCA, MORO
  Shoshonean, HOPI
  Siouan, OTOE
  Southwestern, HOPI, PIMA, YUMA,
  ZUNI
Insect: Immature, PUPA
Instrument: Stringed, LUTE, LYRE
Ireland, EIRE, ERIN
**Jacket:** English, ETON
Jail (British), GAOL
Jar, OLLA
Judge: Islamic, CADI
Juniper: European, CADE
**Kiln,** OAST, OVEN
King: British legendary, LUDD, NUDD
Kiss, BUSS
Knife: Philippine, BOLO
Koran: Section of, SURA
**Laborer:** Spanish American, PEON
Lake: Mountain, TARN
  (Scottish), LOCH
Lamp: Miner's, DAVY
Landing place: Indian, GHAT
Language: Buddhist, PALI
  Japanese, AINU
Latvian, LETT
Layer: Of iris, UVEA
Leaf: Palm, OLAY, OLLA
Legislature: Ukrainian, RADA
Lemur, LORI
Leopard, PARD
Let it stand, STET
Letter: Greek, BETA, IOTA, ZETA
  Hebrew, AYIN, BETH, CAPH, KOPH,
  RESH, SHIN, TETH, YODH
  Papal, BULL
Lily, ALOE
Literature: Hindu sacred, VEDA
Lizard, GILA
  Monitor, URAN
Loquat, BIWA
**Magistrate:** Genoese or Venetian, DOGE
Man (Latin), HOMO
Mark: Omission, DELE
Marmoset: South American, MICO
Meadow: Fertile, VEGA
Measure: Electric, VOLT, WATT
  Force, DYNE
  Hebrew, OMER
  Printing, PICA
  ██████ ██ ████████ ████
  Swiss land, IMMI
Medley, OLIO
Merganser, SMEW
Milk (French), LAIT
Molding, GULA
  Curved, OGEE
Mongoose: Crab-eating, URVA
Monk: Tibetan, LAMA
Monkey: African, MONA, WAAG
  Ceylonese, MAHA
  Cochin-China, DOUC
  South American, SAKI, TITI
Monkshood, ATIS
Month: Jewish, ADAR, ELUL, IYAR
Mother (French), MERE
Mountain: Thessaly, OSSA
Mouse: Meadow, VOLE
Mythology: Norse, EDDA
**Nail** (French), CLOU

Native: Philippine, MORO
Nest: Of pheasants, NIDE
Network, RETE
No (German), NEIN
Noble: Islamic, AMIR
Notice: Death, OBIT
Novel: By Zola, NANA
Nursemaid: Oriental AMAH, AYAH, EYAH
Nut: Philippine, PILI
**Oak:** Holm, ILEX
Oil (comb. form), OLEO
Ostrich: American, RHEA
Oven, KILN, OAST
Owl: Barn, LULU
Ox: Celebes wild, ANOE
   Extinct wild, URUS
**Palm,** ATAP, NIPA, SAGO
Parliament, DIET
Parrot: New Zealand, KAKA
Pass: Indian mountain, GHAT
Passage: Closing (music), CODA
Peach: Clingstone, PAVY
Peasant: Indian, RYOT
   Old English, CARL
Pepper: Australasian, KAVA
Perfume, ATAR
Persia, IRAN
Person: Extraordinary, ONER
Pickerel or pike, ESOX
Pitcher, EWER
Plant: Aromatic, NARD
   Century, ALOE
   Indigo, ANIL
   Pepper, KAVA
Platform: Raised, DAIS
Plum: Wild, SLOE
Pods: Vegetable, OKRA, OKRO
Poem: Epic, EPOS
Poet: Persian, OMAR
   Roman, OVID
Poison, BANE
   Arrow, INEE
Porkfish, SISI
Portico: Greek, STOA
Premium, AGIO
Priest: Islamic, IMAM
Prima donna, DIVA
Prong: Fork, TINE
Pseudonym: Lamb's, ELIA
**Queen:** Carthaginian, DIDO
   Hindu, RANI
**Rabbit,** CONY
Race: Of Japan, AINU
Rail: Ducklike, COOT
   North American, SORA
Redshank, CLEE
Refuse: After pressing, MARC
Regiment: Turkish, ALAI
Reliquary, ARCA
Resort: Italian, LIDO
Ridges: Sandy, ASAR, OSAR
River: German, ELBE, ODER
   Italian, ADDA
   Siberian, LENA
Road: Roman, ITER

Rockfish: California, RENA
Rodent: Mouselike, VOLE
   South American, PACA
Rootstock, TARO
**Salamander,** NEWT
Salmon: Silver, COHO
   Young, PARR
Same (Greek), HOMO
   (Latin), IDEM
Sauce: Fish, ALEC
School: English, ETON
Seaweed, AGAR, ALGA, KELP
Secular, LAIC
Sediment, SILT
Seed: Dill, ANET
   Of vetch, TARE
Serf, ILOT
Sesame, TEEL
Settlement: Eskimo, ETAH
Shark: Atlantic, GATA
   European, TOPE
Sheep: Wild, UDAD
Sheltered, ALEE
Shield, EGIS
Ship: Jason's, ARGO
   Left side of, PORT
   Two-masted, BRIG
Shrine: Buddhist, TOPE
Shrub: New Zealand, TUTU
Sign: Magic, RUNE
Silkworm, ERIA
Skin: Beaver, PLEW
Skink: Egyptian, ADDA
Slave, ESNE
Sloth: Two-toed, UNAU
Smooth, LENE
Snow: Glacial, NEVE
Soapstone, TALC
Society: African secret, EGBO, PORO
Son: Of Seth, ENOS
Song (German), LIED
   Unaccompanied, GLEE
Sound: Lung, RALE
Sour, ACID
Sow: Young, GILT
Spike: Brad-shaped, BROB
Spirit: Buddhist evil, MARA
Stake: Poker, ANTE
Star: Temporary, NOVA
Starch: East Indian, SAGO
Stone: Precious, OPAL
Strap: Bridle, REIN
Strewn (heraldry), SEME
Sweetsop, ATES, ATTA
Sword: Fencing, EPEE, FOIL
**Tambourine:** African, TAAR
Tapir: Brazilian, ANTA
Tax, CESS
Tea: South American, MATE
Therefore (Latin), ERGO
Thing: Extraordinary, ONER
Three (dice, cards, etc.), TREY
Thrush: Hawaiian, OMAO
Tide, NEAP

Tipster: Racing, TOUT
Tissue, TELA
Title: Etruscan, LARS
   Hindu, BABU
   Indian, RAJA
   Islamic, EMIR, IMAM
   Persian, BABA
   Spanish, DONA
   Turkish, AGHA, BABA
Toad: Largest-known, AGUA
   Tree, HYLA
Tool: Cutting, ADZE
Track: Deer, SLOT
Tract: Sandy, DENE
Tree: Apple, SORB
   Central American, EBOE
   East Indian, TEAK
   Eucalyptus, YATE
   Guyanese and Trinidadian, MORA
   Javanese, UPAS
   Linden, LIME, LINN, TEIL, TILL
   Sandarac, ARAR
   Sassafras, AGUE
   Tamarisk salt, ATLE
Tribe: Moro, SULU
Trout, CHAR
**Vessel:** Arab, DHOW
Vestment: Ecclesiastical, COPE
Vetch, TARE
Vine: East Indian, SOMA
Violinist: Famous, AUER
Vortex, EDDY
**Wampum,** PEAG
Wapiti, STAG
Waste: Allowance for, TRET
Watchman: Indian, MINA
Water (Spanish), AGUA
Waterfall, LINN
Wavy (heraldry), ONDE, UNDE
Wax, CERE
   Chinese, PELA
Weed: Biblical, TARE
Weight: Ancient, MINA
   Danish (pl.), ESER
   East Asian, TAEL
   Greek, MINA
   Siamese, BAHT
Well done (rare), EUGE
Whale, CETE
   Killer, ORCA
   White, HUSE, HUSO
Whirlpool, EDDY
Wife: Of Geraint, ENID
Willow: Virginia, ITEA
Wine, PORT
Winged, ALAR
   (Heraldry), AILE
Wings, ALAE
Withered, SERE
Without (French), SANS
Wool: To comb, CARD
Work, OPUS
Wrong: Civil, TORT
**Young:** Bring forth, YEAN

# Words of Five Letters

**Abode of dead:** Babylonian, ARALU
Aborigine: Borneo, DAYAK
Aftersong, EPODE
Aloe, AGAVE
Animal: Footless, APODE
Ant, EMMET
Antelope: African, ADDAX, BEISA,
   CAAMA, ELAND, GUIBA, ORIBI,
   TIANG
   Goat, GORAL, SEROW
   Indian, SASIN
   Siberian, SAIGA
Arch: Pointed, OGIVE
Armadillo, APARA, POYOU, TATOU
Arrowroot, ARARU
Artery: Trunk, AORTA
Association: Russian, ARTEL
   Secret, CABAL
Author: English, READE

Automaton, GOLEM, ROBOT
Award: Motion-picture, OSCAR
**Basket:** Fishing, CREEL
Beer: Russian, KVASS
Bible: Islamic, KORAN, QUR'AN
Bird: Asian, MINAH, MYNAH
   Indian, SHAMA
   Larklike, PIPIT
   Loonlike, GREBE
   Oscine, VIREO
   South American, AGAMI
   Swimming, GREBE
Black: (French), NOIRE
   (Heraldry), SABLE
Blackbird: European, MERLE, OUSEL,
   OUZEL
Block: Glacial, SERAC
Blue (heraldry), AZURE
Boat: Eskimo, BIDAR, UMIAK

Bobwhite, COLIN, QUAIL
Bone (comb. form), OSTEO
   Leg, TIBIA
   Thigh, FEMUR
Broom: Twig, BESOM
Brother (French), FRERE
   Moses, AARON
**Canoe:** Eskimo, BIDAR, KAYAK
Cape: Papal, FANON, ORALE
Caravansary, SERAI
Card: Old playing, TAROT
Caterpillar: New Zealand, AWETO
Catkin, AMENT
Cavity: Stone, GEODE
Cephalopod, SQUID
Cetacean, WHALE
Chariot, ESSED
Cheek: Pertaining to, MALAR
Chieftain: Arab, EMEER

Child (Scottish), BAIRN
Cigar, CLARO
Coating: Seed, TESTA
Cockatoo: Palm, ARARA
Coin: Costa Rican, COLON
 Danish, KRONE
 Ecuadorian, SUCRE
 English, GROAT, PENCE
 French, FRANC
 German, KRONE, TALER
 Hungarian, PENGO
 Icelandic, KRONA
 Indian, RUPEE
 Iraqi, DINAR
 Norwegian, KRONE
 Polish, ZLOTY
 Russian, COPEC, KOPEK, RUBLE
 Swedish, KRONA
 Turkish, ASPER
 Yugoslav, DINAR
Collar: Papal, FANON, ORALE
 Roman, RABAT
Commune: Italian, TREIA
Composition: Choral, MOTET
Compound: Chemical, ESTER
Conceal (law), ELOIN
Council: Ecclesiastical, SYNOD
Court: Anglo-Saxon, GEMOT
 Inner, PATIO
Crest: Mountain, ARETE
Crown: Papal, TIARA
Cuttlefish, SEPIA
**Date:** Roman, NONES
Decree: Islamic, IRADE
 Russian, UKASE
Deposit: Loam, LOESS
Desert: Gobi, SHAMO
Devilfish, MANTA
Disease: Cereals, ERGOT
Disk, PATEN
Dog: Wild, DHOLE, DINGO
Dormouse, LEROT
Drum, TABOR
Duck: Sea, EIDER
Dynasty: Chinese, CHING, LIANG,
 SHANG
**Earthquake,** SEISM
Eel, ELVER, MORAY
Ermine: European, STOAT
Ether: Crystalline, APIOL
**Fabric:** Velvetlike, PANNE
Fabulist, AESOP
Family: Italian, CENCI
Fiber: West Indian, SISAL
Fig: Smyrna, ELEME, ELEMI
Figure: Of speech, TROPE
Finch: European, SERIN
Fish: American small, KILLY
Flower: Garden, ASTER
Friend (Spanish), AMIGO
Fruit: Tropical, MANGO
Fungus: Rye, ERGOT
Furze, GORSE
**Gateway,** TORAN, TORII
Gem, AGATE, BERYL, PEARL, TOPAZ
Genus: Damsels, LEPAS
 Birds, UPUPA
 Birds (loons), GAVIA
 Birds (nuthatches), SITTA
 Cats, FELIS
 Dogs, CANIS
 Fishes (chiros), ELOPS
 Fishes (perch), PERCA
 Geese, ANSER
 Grasses, STIPA
 Grasses (incl. oats), AVENA
 Gulls, LARUS
 Hares, rabbits, LEPUS
 Hawks, BUTEO
 Herbs, old world, INULA
 Herbs, trailing or climbing, APIOS
 Herbs, tropical, TACCA, URENA
 Horses, EQUUS
 Insects (olive flies), DACUS
 Lice, plant, APHIS
 Lichens, USNEA

Lizards, AGAMA
Moles, TAI PA
Mollusks, OLIVA
Monkeys, CEBUS
Palms, ARECA
Pigeons, GOURA
Plants (amaryllis family), AGAVE
Ruminants (goats), CAPRA
Shrubs, Asiatic, SABIA
Shrubs (heath), ERICA
Shrubs (incl. raspberry), RUBUS
Shrubs, tropical, IXORA, TREMA,
 URENA
Ticks, ARGAS
Trees (of elm family), TREMA, ULMUS
Trees, tropical, IXORA, TREMA
Goat: Bezoar, PASAN
God: Assyrian, ASHIR, ASHUR, ASSUR
 Babylonian, DAGAN, SIRIS
 Gaelic, DAGDA
 Hindu, BHAGA, INDRA, SHIVA
 Japanese, EBISU
 Philistine, DAGON
 Phrygian, ATTIS
 Teutonic, AEGIR, GYMIR
 Welsh, DYLAN
Goddess: Babylonian, ISTAR, NANAI
 Hindu, DURGA, GAURI, SHREE
Group: Of six, HEXAD
Grove: Sacred to Diana, NEMUS
Growing out, ENATE
Guitar: Hindu, SITAR
Gull: PEWEE, PEWIT
**Hartebeest,** CAAMA
Headdress: Jewish or Persian, TIARA
 Liturgical, MITER, MITRE
Heath, ERICA
Herb: Grasslike marsh, SEDGE
Heron, EGRET
Hog: Young, SHOAT, SHOTE
**Image,** EIKON
Indian: Cariban, ARARA
 Iroquoian, HURON
 Mexican, AZTEC, OPATA, OTOMI
 Muskhogean, CREEK
 Siouan, OSAGE, TETON
 Spanish American, ARARA, CARIB
Inflorescence: Racemose, AMENT
Insect: Immature, LARVA
Intrigue, CABAL
Iris: Yellow, SEDGE
**Juniper,** GORSE, RETEM
**Kidneys:** Pertaining to, RENAL
King: British legendary, LLUDD
Kite: European, GLEDE
Kobold, NISSE
**Land:** Cultivated, ARADA, ARADO
Landholder (Scottish), LAIRD, THANE
Language: Dravidian, TAMIL
Lariat, LASSO, REATA
Laughing, RIANT
Lawgiver: Athenian, DRACO, SOLON
Leaf: Calyx, SEPAL
 Fern, FROND
Lemur, LORIS
Letter: English, NTBLI
 Greek, ALPHA, DELTA, GAMMA,
 KAPPA, OMEGA, SIGMA, THETA
 Hebrew, ALEPH, CHETH, GIMEL,
 SADHE, ZAYIN
Lichen, USNEA
Lighthouse, PHARE
Lizard: Old World, AGAMA
Loincloth, DHOTI
Louse: Plant, APHID
**Macaw:** Brazilian, ARARA
Mahogany: Philippine, ALMON
Mammal: Badgerlike, RATEL
 Civetlike, GENET
 Giraffelike, OKAPI
 Raccoonlike, COATI
Man (French), HOMME
Marble, AGATE
Mark: Insertion, CARET
Market place: Greek, AGORA
Marsupial: Australian, KOALA

Measure: Electric, FARAD, HENRY
 Energy, JOULE
 Metric, LITER, STERE
 Printing, AGATE
 Russian, VERST
Mixture: Smelting, MATTE
Mohicans: Last of, UNCAS
Molding: Convex, OVOLO, TORUS
Mole, TALPA
Monkey: African, PATAS
 Capuchin, SAJOU
 Howling, ARABA
Monkshood, ATEES
Month: Jewish, NISAN, SIVAN, TEBET
Museum (French), MUSEE
Musketeer, ATHOS
**Native:** Aleutian, ALEUT
 New Zealand, MAORI
Neckpiece: Ecclesiastical, AMICE
Nerve (comb. form), NEURO
Nest: Eagle's or hawk's, AERIE
 Insect's, NIDUS
Net: Fishing, SEINE
Newsstand, KIOSK
Nitrogen, AZOTE
Noble: Islamic, AMEER
Nodule: Stone, GEODE
Nostrils, NARES
Notched irregularly, EROSE
Nymph: Islamic, HOURI
**Official:** Roman, EDILE
Oleoresin, ELEMI
Opening: Mouthlike, STOMA
Oration: Funeral, ELOGE
Ostiole, STOMA
**Page:** Left-hand, VERSO
 Right-hand, RECTO
Palm, ARECA, BETEL
Park: Colorado, ESTES
Perfume, ATTAR
Philosopher: Greek, PLATO
Pillar: Stone, STELA, STELE
Pinnacle: Glacial, SERAC
Plain, LLANO
Plant: Century, AGAVE
 Climbing, LIANA
 Dwarf, CUMIN
 East Asian perennial, RAMIE
 Medicinal, SENNA
 Mustard family, CRESS
Plate: Communion, PATEN
Poem: Lyric, EPODE
Point: Lowest, NADIR
Poplar, ABELE, ALAMO, ASPEN
Porridge: Spanish American, ATOLE
Post: Stair, NEWEL
Priest: Islamic, IMAUM
Protozoan, AMEBA
**Queen:** (French), REINE
 Hindu, RANEE
**Rabbit,** CONEY
Rail, CRAKE
Red (heraldry), GULES
Religion: Moslem, Muslim, ISLAM
Resin, ELEMI
Rich man, MIDAS, NABOB
Ridge: Sandy, ESKAR, ESKER
River: French, LOIRE, SEINE
 Rockfish, Bullfomlu, REINA
Rootstock: Fragrant, ORRIS
Ruff: Female, REEVE
**Sack:** Pack, KYACK
Salt: Ethereal, ESTER
Saltpeter, NITER, NITRE
Salutation: Eastern, SALAM
Sandpiper: Old World, TEREK
Scented, OLENT
School: Fish, SHOAL
 French public, LYCEE
Scriptures: Islamic, KORAN
Seaweeds, ALGAE
Seed: Aromatic, ANISE
Seraglio, HAREM, SERAI
Serf, HELOT
Sheep: Wild, AUDAD

Sheeplike, OVINE
Shield, AEGIS
Shoe: Wooden, SABOT
Shoots: Pickled bamboo, ACHAR
Shot: Billiard, CAROM, MASSE
Shrine: Buddhist, STUPA
Shrub: Burning bush, WAHOO
  Ornamental evergreen, TOYON
  Used in tanning, SUMAC
Silk: Watered, MOIRE
Sister (French), SOEUR
  (Latin), SOROR
Six: Group of, HEXAD
Skeleton: Marine, CORAL
Slave, HELOT
Snake, ABOMA, ADDER, COBRA,
  RACER
Soldier: French, POILU
  Indian, SEPOY
Sour, ACERB
Spirit: Air, ARIEL
Staff: Shepherd's, CROOK
Starwort, ASTER
Steel (German), STAHL
Stockade: Russian, ETAPE

Stop (nautical), AVAST
Storehouse, ETAPE
Subway: Parisian, METRO
**Tapestry,** ARRAS
Tea: Paraguayan, YERBA
Temple: Hawaiian, HEIAU
Terminal: Positive, ANODE
Theater: Greek, ODEON, ODEUM
Then (French), ALORS
Thread: Surgical, SETON
Thrush: Wilson's, VEERY
Title: Hindu, BABOO
  Indian, RAJAH, SAHEB, SAHIB
  Islamic, EMEER, IMAUM
Tree: Buddhist sacred, PIPAL
  East Indian cotton, SIMAL
  Hickory, PECAN
  Light-wooded, BALSA
  Malayan, TERAP
  Mediterranean, CAROB
  Mexican, ABETO
  Mexican pine, OCOTE
  New Zealand, MAIRE
  Philippine, ALMON
  Rain, SAMAN

  South American, UMBRA
  Tamarack, LARCH
  Tamarisk salt, ATLEE
  West Indian, ACANA
Trout, CHARR
Troy, ILION, ILIUM
Twin: Siamese, CHANG
**Vestment:** Ecclesiastical, STOLE
Violin: Famous, AMATI, STRAD
Volcano: Mud, SALSE
**Wampum,** PEAGE
War cry: Greek, ALALA
Wavy (heraldry), UNDEE
Weight: Jewish, GERAH
Wen, TALPA
Wheat, SPELT
Wheel: Persian water, NORIA
Whitefish, CISCO
Willow, OSIER
Window: Bay, ORIEL
Wine, MEDOC, RHINE, TINTA, TOKAY
Winged, ALATE
Woman (French), FEMME
**Year:** Excess of solar over lunar, EPACT
**Zoroastrian,** PARSI

## Words of Six or More Letters

**Agave,** MAGUEY
Alkaloid: Crystalline, ESERIN, ESERINE
Alligator, CAYMAN
Amphibole, EDENITE, URALITE
Ant: White, TERMITE
Antelope: African, DIKDIK, DUIKER,
  GEMSBOK, IMPALA, KOODOO
  European, CHAMOIS
  Indian, NILGAI, NILGAU, NILGHAI,
  NILGHAU
Ape: Asian or East Indian, GIBBON
Appendage: Leaf, STIPEL, STIPULE
Armadillo, PELUDO, TATOUAY
Arrowroot, ARARAO
Ascetic: Jewish, ESSENE
Ass: Asian wild, ONAGER
Avatar: Of Vishnu, KRISHNA
**Babylonian,** ELAMITE
Badge: Shoulder, EPAULET
Baldness, ALOPECIA
Barracuda, SENNET
Bark: Aromatic, SINTOC
Bearlike, URSINE
Beetle, ELATER
Bible: Zoroastrian, AVESTA
Bird: Sea, PETREL
  South American, SERIEMA
  Wading, AVOCET, AVOSET
Bone: Leg, FIBULA
Branched, RAMATE
Brother (Latin), FRATER
Bunting: European, ORTOLAN
**Call:** Trumpet, SENNET
Canoe: Eskimo, BAIDAR, OOMIAK
Caravansary, IMARET
Cat: Asian or African, CHEETAH
  Leopardlike, OCELOT
Cenobite: Jewish, ESSENE
Centerpiece: Table, EPERGNE
Cetacean, DOLPHIN, PORPOISE
Chariot, ESSEDA, ESSEDE
Chief: Seminole, OSCEOLA
Claim: Release as (law), REMISE
Clock: Water, CLEPSYDRA
Cloud, CUMULUS, NIMBUS
Coach: French hackney, FIACRE
Coin: Czech, KORUNA
  Dutch, GUILDER
  Ethiopian, TALARI
  Finnish, MARKKA
  German, THALER
  Greek, DRACHMA
  Haitian, GOURDE
  Honduran, LEMPIRA
  Hungarian, FORINT
  Indo-Chinese, PIASTER
  Panamanian, BALBOA
  Paraguayan, GUARANI
  Portuguese, ESCUDO

  Russian, COPECK, KOPECK,
  ROUBLE
  Spanish, PESETA
  Venezuelan, BOLIVAR
Communion: Last holy, VIATICUM
Conceal (law), ELOIGN
Confection, PRALINE
Construction: Sentence, SYNTAX
Convexity: Shaft of column, ENTASIS
Court: Anglo-Saxon, GEMOTE
Cow: Sea, DUGONG, MANATEE
Cylindrical, TERETE
**Dagger,** STILETTO
  Malay, CREESE, KREESE
Date: Roman, CALENDS, KALENDS
Deer, CARIBOU, WAPITI
Disease: Plant, ERINOSE
Doorkeeper, OSTIARY
Dragonflies: Order of, ODANATA
Drink: Of gods, NECTAR
Drum: TABOUR
  Moorish, ATABAL, ATTABAL
Duck: Fish-eating, MERGANSER
  Sea, SCOTER
Dynasty: Chinese, MANCHU
**Eel,** CONGER
Edit, REDACT
Envelope: Flower, PERIANTH
Eskimo, AMERIND
Ether: Crystalline, APIOLE
Excuse (law), ESSOIN
Eyespots, OCELLI
**Fabric,** ESTAMENE, ESTAMIN,
  ETAMINE
Falcon: European, KESTREL
Figure: Used as column, CARYATID,
  TELAMON
Fine: For punishment, AMERCE
Fish: Asian fresh-water, GOURAMI
  Pikelike, BARRACUDA
Five: Group of, PENTAD
Fly: African, TSETSE
Foot: Metric, ANAPEST, IAMBUS
Foxlike, VULPINE
Frying pan, SPIDER
Fur, KARAKUL
**Galley:** Greek or Roman, BIREME,
  TRIREME
Game: Card, ECARTE
Garment: Greek, CHLAMYS
Gateway, GOPURA, TORANA
Genus: Birds (ravens, crows), CORVUS
  Eels, CONGER
  Fishes, ANABAS
  Foxes, VULPES
  Herbs, ANEMONE
  Insects, CICADA
  Lemurs, GALAGO
  Mints (incl. catnip), NEPETA

  Mollusks, ANOMIA, ASTARTE,
  TEREDO
  Mollusks (incl. oysters), OSTREA
  Monkeys (spider monkeys), ATELES
  Thrushes (incl. robins), TURDUS
  Trees (of elm family), CELTIS
  Trees (inc. dogwood), CORNUS
  Trees, tropical American, SAPOTA
  Wrens, NANNUS
Gibbon, SIAMANG, WOUWOU
Gland: Salivary, RACEMOSE
Goat: Bezoar, PASANG
Goatlike, CAPRINE
God: Assyrian, ASHSHUR, ASSHUR
  Babylonian, BABBAR, MARDUK,
  MERODACH, NANNAR, NERGAL,
  SHAMASH
  Hindu, BRAHMA, KRISHNA, VISHNU
  Tahitian, TAAROA
Goddess: Babylonian, ISHTAR
  Hindu, CHANDI, HAIMAVATI,
  LAKSHMI, PARVATI, SARASVATI,
  SARASWATI
Government, POLITY
Governor: Persian, SATRAP
Grandson (Scottish), NEPOTE
Group: Of five, PENTAD
  Of nine, ENNEAD
  Of seven, HEPTAD
**Hare:** in first year, LEVERET
Harpsichord, SPINET
Herb: Alpine, EDELWEISS
  Chinese, GINSENG
  South African, FREESIA
Hermit, EREMITE
Hero: Legendary, PALADIN
Heron, BITTERN
Horselike, EQUINE
Hound: Short-legged, BEAGLE
House (French), MAISON
**Idiot,** CRETIN
Implement: Stone, NEOLITH
Incarnation: Hindu, AVATAR
Indian, APACHE, COMANCHE, PAIUTE,
  SENECA
Inn: Turkish, IMARET
Insects: Order of, DIPTERA
Instrument: Japanese banjolike,
  SAMISEN
  Musical, CLAVIER, SPINET
Interstice, AREOLA
Ironwood, COLIMA
**Juniper:** Old Testament, RAETAM
**Kettledrum,** ATABAL
King: Fairy, OBERON
Kneecap, PATELLA
Knife, MACHETE
**Langur:** Sumatran, SIMPAI
Legislature: Spanish, CORTES

Lemur: African, GALAGO
  Madagascar, AYEAYE
Letter: Greek, EPSILON, LAMBDA,
  OMICRON, UPSILON
  Hebrew, DALETH, LAMEDH, SAMEKH
Lighthouse, PHAROS
Lizard, IGUANA
Llama, ALPACA
Lockjaw, TETANUS
Locust: CICADA, CICALA
**Macaw:** Brazilian, MARACAN
Maid: Of Astolat, ELAINE
Mammal: Madagascar, TENDRAC,
  TENREC
Man (Spanish), HOMBRE
Marmoset: South American, TAMARIN
Marsupial, BANDICOOT, WOMBAT
Massacre, POGROM
Mayor: Spanish, ALCALDE
Measure: Electric, AMPERE, COULOMB,
  KILOWATT
Medicine: Quack, NOSTRUM
Member: Religious order, CENOBITE
Molasses, TREACLE
Monkey: African, GRIVET, NISNAS
  Asian, LANGUR
  Philippine, MACHIN
  South American, PINCHE, SAIMIRI,
  SAMIRI, SAPAJOU
Monster, CHIMERA, GORGON
  (Comb. form), TERATO
  Cretan, MINOTAUR
Month: Jewish, HESHVAN, KISLEV,
  SHEBAT, TAMMUZ, TISHRI, VEADAR
Mountain: Asia Minor, ARARAT
Mulct, AMERCE
Musketeer, ARAMIS, PORTHOS
**Nearsighted,** MYOPIC
Net, TRAMMEL
New York City, GOTHAM
Nine: Group of, ENNEAD
Nobleman: Spanish, GRANDEE
**Official:** Roman, AEDILE
Onyx: Mexican, TECALI
Order: Dragonflies, ODANATA
  Insects, DIPTERA
Organ: Plant, PISTIL

Ornament: Shoulder, EPAULET
Overcoat: Military, CAPOTE
Ox: Wild, BANTENG
Oxidation: Bronze or copper, PATINA
**Paralysis:** Incomplete, PARESIS
Pear: Alligator, AVOCADO
Persimmon: Mexican, CHAPOTE
Pipe: Peace, CALUMET
Plaid (Scottish), TARTAN
Plain, PAMPAS, STEPPE, TUNDRA
Plant: Buttercup family, ANEMONE
  Century, MAGUEY
  On rocks, LICHEN
Plowing: Fit for, ARABLE
Poem: Heroic, EPOPEE
  Six-lined, SESTET
Point: Highest, ZENITH
Potion: Love, PHILTER, PHILTRE
Protozoan, AMOEBA
Punish, AMERCE
Purple (heraldry), PURPURE
**Queen:** Fairy, TITANIA
**Race:** Skiing, SLALOM
Rat, BANDICOOT, LEMMING
Retort, RIPOST, RIPOSTE
Ring: Harness, TERRET
  Little, ANNULET
Rodent: Jumping, JERBOA
  Spanish American, AGOUTI, AGOUTY
**Sailor:** East Indian, LASCAR
Salmon: Young, GRILSE
Salutation: Eastern, SALAAM
Sandpiper, PLOVER
Sandy, ARENOSE
Sapodilla, SAPOTA, SAPOTE
Saw: Surgical, TREPAN
Seven: Group of, HEPTAD
Sexes: Common to both, EPICENE
Shawl: Mexican, SERAPE
Sheathing: Flower, SPATHE
Sheep: Wild, AOUDAD, ARGALI
Shipworm, TEREDO
Shoes: Mercury's winged, TALARIA
Shortening: Syllable, SYSTOLE
Shrub, SPIRAEA
Sickle-shaped, FALCATE

Silver (heraldry), ARGENT
Snake, ANACONDA
Speech: Loss of, APHASIA
Spiral, HELICAL
Staff: Bishop's, CROSIER, CROZIER
Stalk: Plant, PETIOLE
State: Swiss, CANTON
Studio, ATELIER
Swan: Young, CYGNET
Swimming, NATANT
Sword-shaped, ENSATE
**Terminal:** Negative, CATHODE
Third (music), TIERCE
Thrust: Fencing, RIPOST, RIPOSTE
Tile: Pertaining to, TEGULAR
Tomb: Empty, CENOTAPH
Tooth (comb. form), ODONTO
Tower: Islamic, MINARET
Tree: African timber, BAOBAB
  Black gum, TUPELO
  East Indian, MARGOSA
  Locust, ACACIA
  Malayan, SINTOC
  Marmalade, SAPOTE
**Urn:** Tea, SAMOVAR
**Vehicle,** LANDAU, TROIKA
Verbose, PROLIX
Viceroy: Egyptian, KHEDIVE
Vulture: American, CONDOR
**Warehouse** (French), ENTREPOT
Whale: White, BELUGA
Whirlpool, VORTEX
Will: Addition to, CODICIL
  Having left, TESTATE
Wind, CHINOOK, MONSOON, SIMOOM,
  SIMOON, SIROCCO
Window: In roof, DORMER
Wine, BARBERA, BURGUNDY,
  CABERNET, CHABLIS, CHIANTI,
  CLARET, MUSCATEL, RIESLING,
  SAUTERNE, SHERRY, ZINFANDEL
Wolfish, LUPINE
Woman: Boisterous, TERMAGANT
Woolly, LANATE
Workshop, ATELIER
**Zoroastrian,** PARSEE

# Old Testament Names

We do not pretend that this list is all-inclusive. We list only those names that occur most often in crossword puzzles.

**Aaron:** First high priest of Jews; son of Amram; brother of Miriam and Moses; father of Abihu, Eleazer, Ithamar, and Nadab.
**Abel:** Son of Adam and Eve; slain by Cain.
**Abigail:** Wife of Nabal; later, wife of David.
**Abihu:** Son of Aaron.
**Abimelech:** King of Gerar.
**Abner:** Commander of army of Saul and Ishbosheth; slain by Joab.
**Abraham (or Abram):** Patriarch; forefather of the Jews; son of Terah; husband of Sarah; father of Isaac and Ishmael.
**Absalom:** Son of David and Maacah; revolted against David; slain by Joab.
**Achish:** King of Gath; gave refuge to David.
**Achsa (or Achsah):** Daughter of Caleb; wife of Othniel.
**Adah:** Wife of Lamech.
**Adam:** First man; husband of Eve; father of Cain, Abel, and Seth.
**Adonijah:** Son of David and Haggith.
**Agag:** King of Amalek; spared by Saul; slain by Samuel.
**Ahasuerus:** King of Persia; husband of Vashti and, later, Esther; sometimes identified with Xerxes the Great.
**Ahijah:** Prophet; foretold accession of Jeroboam.
**Ahinoam:** Wife of David.
**Amasa:** Commander of army of David; slain by Joab.
**Amnon:** Son of David and Ahinoam; raped Tamar; slain by Absalom.
**Amram:** Husband of Jochebed; father of Aaron, Miriam and Moses.
**Asenath:** Wife of Joseph.
**Asher:** Son of Jacob and Zilpah.

**Balaam:** Prophet; rebuked by his donkey for cursing God.
**Barak:** Jewish captain; associated with Deborah.
**Baruch:** Secretary to Jeremiah.
**Bathsheba:** Wife of Uriah; later, wife of David.
**Belshazzar:** Crown prince of Babylon.
**Benaiah:** Warrior of David; proclaimed Solomon King.
**Ben-Hadad:** Name of several kings of Damascus.
**Benjamin:** Son of Jacob and Rachel.
**Bezaleel:** Chief architect of Tabernacle.
**Bilhah:** Servant of Rachel; mistress of Jacob.
**Bildad:** Comforter of Job.
**Boaz:** Husband of Ruth; father of Obed.
**Cain:** Son of Adam and Eve; slayer of Abel; father of Enoch.
**Cainan:** Son of Enos.
**Caleb:** Spy sent out by Moses to visit Canaan; father of Achsa.
**Canaan:** Son of Ham.
**Chilion:** Son of Elimelech; husband of Orpah.
**Cush:** Son of Ham; father of Nimrod.
**Dan:** Son of Jacob and Bilhah.
**Daniel:** Prophet; saved from lions by God.
**Deborah:** Hebrew prophetess and judge; helped Israelites conquer Canaanites.
**Delilah:** Mistress and betrayer of Samson.
**Elam:** Son of Shem.
**Eleazar:** Son of Aaron; succeeded him as high priest.
**Eli:** High priest and judge; teacher of Samuel; father of Hophni and Phinehas.
**Eliakim:** Chief minister of Hezekiah.
**Eliezer:** Servant of Abraham.
**Elihu:** Comforter of Job.
**Elijah (or Elias):** Prophet; went to heaven in chariot of fire.

**Elimelech:** Husband of Naomi; father of Chilion and Mahlon.
**Eliphaz:** Comforter of Job.
**Elisha (or Eliseus):** Prophet; successor of Elijah.
**Elkanah:** Husband of Hannah; father of Samuel.
**Enoch:** Son of Cain.
**Enoch:** Father of Methuselah.
**Enos:** Son of Seth; father of Cainan.
**Ephraim:** Son of Joseph.
**Esau:** Son of Isaac and Rebecca; sold his birthright to his twin brother Jacob.
**Esther:** Jewish wife of Ahasuerus; saved Jews from Haman's plotting.
**Eve:** First woman; wife of Adam.
**Ezra (or Esdras):** Hebrew scribe and priest.
**Gad:** Son of Jacob and Zilpah.
**Gehazi:** Servant of Elisha.
**Gideon:** Israelite hero; defeated Midianites.
**Goliath:** Philistine giant; slain by David.
**Hagar:** Handmaid of Sarah; concubine of Abraham; mother of Ishmael.
**Haggith:** Mother of Adonijah.
**Ham:** Son of Noah; father of Cush, Mizraim, Phut, and Canaan.
**Haman:** Chief minister of Ahasuerus; hanged on gallows prepared for Mordecai.
**Hannah:** Wife of Elkanah; mother of Samuel.
**Hanun:** King of Ammonites.
**Haran:** Brother of Abraham; father of Lot.
**Hazael:** King of Damascus.
**Hephzi-Bah:** Wife of Hezekiah; mother of Mannaseh.
**Hiram:** King of Tyre.
**Holofernes:** General of Nebuchadnezzar; slain by Judith.
**Hophni:** Son of Eli.
**Isaac:** Hebrew patriarch; son of Abraham and Sarah; half brother of Ishmael; husband of Rebecca; father of Esau and Jacob.
**Ishmael:** Son of Abraham and Hagar; half brother of Isaac.
**Issachar:** Son of Jacob and Leah.
**Ithamar:** Son of Aaron.
**Jabal:** Son of Lamech and Adah.
**Jabin:** King of Hazor.
**Jacob:** Hebrew patriarch; founder of Israel; son of Isaac and Rebecca; husband of Leah and Rachel; father of sons Asher, Benjamin, Dan, Gad, Issachar, Joseph, Judah, Levi, Naphtali, Reuben, Simeon, and Zebulun, and daughter Dinah.
**Jael:** Slayer of Sisera.
**Japheth:**Son of Noah.
**Jehoiada:** High priest; husband of Jehoshabeath; revolted against Athaliah and made Joash King of Judah.
**Jehoshabeath (or Jehosheba):** Daughter of Jehoram of Judah; wife of Jehoiada.
**Jephthah:** Judge in Israel; sacrificed his only daughter because of vow.
**Jesse:** Son of Obed; father of David.
**Jethro:** Midianite priest; father of Zipporah.
**Jezebel:** Phoenician princess; wife of Ahab; mother of Ahaziah, Athaliah, and Jehoram.
**Joab:** Commander in chief under David; slayer of Abner, Absalom, and Amasa.
**Job:** Patriarch; underwent many afflictions; comforted by Bildad, Elihu, Eliphaz and Zophar.
**Jochebed:** Wife of Amram.
**Jonah:** Prophet; cast into sea and swallowed by great fish.
**Jonathan:** Son of Saul; friend of David.
**Joseph:** Son of Jacob and Rachel; sold into slavery by his brothers; husband of Asenath; father of Ephraim and Manassah.
**Joshua:** Successor of Moses; son of Nun.
**Jubal:** Son of Lamech and Adah.
**Judah:** Son of Jacob and Leah.
**Judith:** Slayer of Holofernes.
**Kish:** Father of Saul.

**Laban:** Father of Leah and Rachel.
**Lamech:** Son of Methuselah; father of Noah.
**Lamech:** Husband of Adah and Zillah; father of Jabal, Jubal, and Tubal-Cain.
**Leah:** Daughter of Laban; wife of Jacob; sister of Rachel.
**Levi:** Son of Jacob and Leah.
**Lot:** Son of Haran; escaped destruction of Sodom.
**Maacah:** Mother of Absalom and Tamar.
**Mahlon:** Son of Elimelech; first husband of Ruth.
**Manasseh:** Son of Joseph.
**Melchizedek:** King of Salem.
**Methuselah:** Patriarch; son of Enoch; father of Lamech.
**Michal:** Daughter of Saul; wife of David.
**Miriam:** Prophetess; daughter of Amram; sister of Aaron and Moses.
**Mizraim:** Son of Ham.
**Mordecai:** Uncle of Esther; with her aid, saved Jews from Haman's plotting.
**Moses:** Prophet and lawgiver; son of Amram; brother of Aaron and Miriam; husband of Zipporah.
**Naaman:** Syrian captain; cured of leprosy by Elisha.
**Nabal:** Husband of Abigail.
**Naboth:** Owner of vineyard; stoned to death because he would not sell it to Ahab.
**Nadab:** Son of Aaron.
**Nahor:** Father of Terah.
**Naomi:** Wife of Elimelech; mother-in-law of Ruth.
**Naphtali:** Son of Jacob and Bilhah.
**Nathan:** Prophet; reproved David for causing Uriah's death.
**Nebuchadnezzar (or Nebuchadrezzar):** King of Babylon; destroyer of Jerusalem.
**Nehemiah:** Jewish leader; empowered by Artaxerxes to rebuild Jerusalem.
**Nimrod:** Mighty hunter; son of Cush.
**Noah:** Patriarch; son of Lamech; escaped Deluge by building Ark; father of Ham, Japheth and Shem.
**Nun (or Non):** Father of Joshua.
**Obed:** Son of Boaz; father of Jesse.
**Og:** King of Bashan.
**Orpah:** Wife of Chilion.
**Othniel:** Kenezite; judge of Israel; husband of Achsa.
**Phinehas:** Son of Eleazer.
**Phinehas:** Son of Eli.
**Phut (or Put):** Son of Ham.
**Potiphar:** Egyptian official; bought Joseph.
**Rachel:** Wife of Jacob; mother of Joseph; sister of Leah.
**Rebecca (or Rebekah):** Wife of Isaac; mother of Esau and Jacob.
**Reuben:** Son of Jacob and Leah.
**Ruth:** Wife of Mahlon, later of Boaz; daughter-in-law of Naomi.
**Samson:** Judge of Israel; famed for strength; betrayed by Delilah.
**Samuel:** Hebrew judge and prophet; son of Elkanah.
**Sarah (or Sara, Sarai):** Wife of Abraham; mother of Isaac.
**Sennacherib:** King of Assyria.
**Seth:** Son of Adam; father of Enos.
**Shem:** Son of Noah; father of Elam.
**Simeon:** Son of Jacob and Leah.
**Sisera:** Canaanite captain; slain by Jael.
**Tamar:** Daughter of David and Maachah; raped by Amnon.
**Terah:** Son of Nahor; father of Abraham.
**Tubal-Cain:** Son of Lamech and Zillah.
**Uriah:** Husband of Bathsheba; sent to death in battle by David.
**Vashti:** Wife of Ahasuerus; set aside by him.
**Zadok:** High priest during David's reign.
**Zebulun (or Zabulon):** Son of Jacob and Leah.
**Zillah:** Wife of Lamech.
**Zilpah:** Servant of Leah; mistress of Jacob.
**Zipporah:** Daughter of Jethro; wife of Moses.
**Zophar:** Comforter of Job.

# Kings of Judah and Israel

## Kings Before Division of Kingdom
**Saul:** First King of Israel; son of Kish; father of Ish-Bosheth, Jonathan and Michal.
**Ish-Bosheth (or Eshbaal):** King of Israel; son of Saul.
**David:** King of Judah; later of Israel; son of Jesse; husband of Abigail, Ahinoam, Bathsheba, Michal, etc.; father of Absalom, Adonijah, Amnon, Solomon, Tamar, etc.
**Solomon:** King of Israel and Judah; son of David; father of Rehoboam.
**Rehoboam:** Son of Solomon; during his reign the kingdom was divided into Judah and Israel.

## Kings of Judah (Southern Kingdom)
**Rehoboam:** First King.
**Abijah (or Abijam or Abia):** Son of Rehoboam.
**Asa:** Probably son of Abijah.
**Jehoshaphat:** Son of Asa.
**Jehoram (or Joram):** Son of Jehoshaphat; husband of Athaliah.
**Ahaziah:** Son of Jehoram and Athaliah.
**Athaliah:** Daughter of King Ahab of Israel and Jezebel; wife of Jehoram; only queen to occupy the throne of Judah.
**Joash (or Jehoash):** Son of Ahaziah.

**Amaziah:** Son of Joash.
**Uzziah (or Azariah):** Son of Amaziah.
**Jotham:** Regent, later King; son of Uzziah.
**Ahaz:** Son of Jotham.
**Hezekiah:** Son of Ahaz; husband of Hephzi-Bah.
**Manasseh:** Son of Hezekiah and Hephzi-Bah.
**Amon:** Son of Manasseh.
**Josiah (or Josias):** Son of Amon.
**Jehoahaz (or Joahaz):** Son of Josiah.
**Jehoiakim:** Son of Josiah.
**Jehoiachin:** Son of Jehoiakim.
**Zedekiah:** Son of Josiah; kingdom overthrown by Babylonians under Nebuchadnezzar.

## Kings of Israel (Northern Kingdom)
**Jeroboam I:** Led secession of Israel.
**Nadab:** Son of Jeroboam I.
**Baasha:** Overthrew Nadab.
**Elah:** Son of Baasha.
**Zimri:** Overthrew Elah.
**Omri:** Overthrew Zimri.

**Ahab:** Son of Omri; husband of Jezebel.
**Ahaziah:** Son of Ahab.
**Jehoram (or Joram):** Son of Ahab.
**Jehu:** Overthrew Jehoram.
**Jehoahaz (or Joahaz):** Son of Jehu.
**Jehoash (or Joash):** Son of Jehoahaz.
**Jeroboam II:** Son of Jehoash.
**Zechariah:** Son of Jeroboam II.
**Shallum:** Overthrew Zechariah.
**Menahem:** Overthrew Shallum.
**Pekahiah:** Son of Menahem.
**Pekah:** Overthrew Pekahiah.
**Hoshea:** Overthrew Pekah; kingdom overthrown by Assyrians under Sargon II.

## Prophets
**Major.** Isaiah, Jeremiah, Ezekiel, Daniel.
**Minor.** Hosea, Obadiah, Nahum, Haggai, Joel, Jonah, Habakkuk, Zechariah, Amos, Micah, Zephaniah, Malachi.

# Greek and Roman Mythology

Most of the Greek deities were adopted by the Romans, although in many cases there was a change of name. In the list below, information is given under the Greek name; the name in parentheses is the Roman equivalent. However, all Latin names are listed with cross-references to the Greek ones. In addition, there are several deities that are exclusively Roman. **Bold** words within entries indicate cross references.

**Acheron:** One of several **Rivers of Underworld.**
**Achilles:** Greek warrior; slew Hector at Troy; slain by Paris, who wounded him in his vulnerable heel.
**Actaeon:** Hunter; surprised Artemis bathing; changed by her to stag; and killed by his dogs.
**Admetus:** King of Thessaly; his wife, Alcestis, offered to die in his place.
**Adonis:** Beautiful youth loved by Aphrodite.
**Aeacus:** One of three judges of dead in Hades; son of Zeus.
**Aeëtes:** King of Colchis; father of Medea; keeper of Golden Fleece.
**Aegeus:** Father of Theseus; believing Theseus killed in Crete, he drowned himself; Aegean Sea named for him.
**Aegisthus:** Son of Thyestes; slew Atreus; with Clytemnestra, his paramour, slew Agamemnon; slain by Orestes.
**Aegyptus:** Brother of Danaus; his sons, except Lynceus, slain by Danaides.
**Aeneas:** Trojan; son of Anchises and Aphrodite; after fall of Troy, led his followers eventually to Italy; loved and deserted Dido.
**Aeolus:** One of several **Winds.**
**Aesculapius:** *See* Asclepius.
**Aeson:** King of Ioclus; father of Jason; overthrown by his brother Pelias; restored to youth by Medea.
**Aether:** Personification of sky.
**Aethra:** Mother of Theseus.
**Agamemnon:** King of Mycenae; son of Atreus; brother of Menelaus; leader of Greeks against Troy; slain on his return home by Clytemnestra and Aegisthus.
**Aglaia:** One of several **Graces.**
**Ajax:** Greek warrior; killed himself at Troy because Achilles's armor was awarded to Odysseus.
**Alcestis:** Wife of Admetus; offered to die in his place but saved from death by Hercules.
**Alcmene:** Wife of Amphitryon; mother by Zeus of Hercules.
**Alcyone:** One of several **Pleiades.**
**Alcithyon:** Youth changed by Ares into cock.
**Althaea:** Wife of Oeneus; mother of Meleager.
**Amazons:** Female warriors in Asia Minor; supported Troy against Greeks.
**Amor:** *See* Eros.
**Amphion:** Musician; husband of Niobe; charmed stones to build fortifications for Thebes.
**Amphitrite:** Sea goddess; wife of Poseidon.
**Amphitryon:** Husband of Alcmene.
**Anchises:** Father of Aeneas.
**Ancile:** Sacred shield that fell from heavens; palladium of Rome.
**Andraemon:** Husband of Dryope.
**Andromache:** Wife of Hector.
**Andromeda:** Daughter of Cepheus; chained to cliff for monster to devour; rescued by Perseus.
**Anteia:** Wife of Proetus; tried to induce Bellerophon to elope with her.
**Anteros:** God who avenged unrequited love.

**Antigone:** Daughter of Oedipus; accompanied him to Colonus; performed burial rite for Polynices and hanged herself.
**Antinoüs:** Leader of suitors of Penelope; slain by Odysseus.
**Aphrodite (Venus):** Goddess of love and beauty; daughter of Zeus and Dione; mother of Eros.
**Apollo:** God of beauty, poetry, music; later identified with Helios as Phoebus Apollo; son of Zeus and Leto.
**Aquilo:** One of several **Winds.**
**Arachne:** Maiden who challenged Athena to weaving contest; changed to spider.
**Ares (Mars):** God of war; son of Zeus and Hera.
**Argo:** Ship in which Jason and followers sailed to Colchis for Golden Fleece.
**Argus:** Monster with hundred eyes; slain by Hermes; his eyes placed by Hera into peacock's tail.
**Ariadne:** Daughter of Minos; aided Theseus in slaying Minotaur; deserted by him on island of Naxos and married to Dionysus.
**Arion:** Musician; thrown overboard by pirates but saved by dolphin.
**Artemis (Diana):** Goddess of moon; huntress; twin sister of Apollo.
**Asclepius (Aesculapius):** Mortal son of Apollo; slain by Zeus for raising dead; later deified as god of medicine. Also known as Asklepios.
**Astarte:** Phoenician goddess of love; variously identified with Aphrodite, Selene, and Artemis.
**Asterope:** *See* Sterope.
**Astraea:** Goddess of Justice; daughter of Zeus and Themis.
**Atalanta:** Princess who challenged her suitors to a foot race; Hippomenes won race and married her.
**Athena (Minerva):** Goddess of wisdom; known poetically as Pallas Athene; sprang fully armed from head of Zeus.
**Atlas:** Titan; held world on his shoulders as punishment for warring against Zeus; son of Iapetus.
**Atreus:** King of Mycenae; father of Menelaus and Agamemnon; brother of Thyestes, three of whose sons he slew and served up to him.
**Atropos:** One of several **Fates.**
**Aurora:** *See* Eos.
**Auster:** One of several **Winds.**
**Avernus:** Internal regions; name derived from small vaporous lake near Vesuvius which was fabled to kill birds and vegetation.
**Bacchus:** *See* Dionysus.
**Bellerophon:** Corinthian hero; killed Chimera with aid of Pegasus; tried to reach Olympus on Pegasus and was thrown to his death.
**Bellona:** Roman goddess of war.
**Boreas:** One of several **Winds.**
**Briareus:** Monster of hundred hands; son of Uranus and Gaea.
**Briseis:** Captive maiden given to Achilles; taken by Agamemnon in exchange for loss of Chryseis, which caused Achilles to cease fighting, until death of Patroclus.
**Cadmus:** Brother of Europa; planter of dragon seeds from which first Thebans sprang.
**Calliope:** One of several **Muses.**

**Calypso:** Sea nymph; kept Odysseus on her island Ogygia for seven years.

**Cassandra:** Daughter of Priam; prophetess who was never believed; slain with Agamemnon.

**Castor:** One of **Dioscuri.**

**Celaeno:** One of several **Pleiades.**

**Centaurs:** Beings half man and half horse; lived in mountains of Thessaly.

**Cephalus:** Hunter; accidentally killed his wife Procris with his spear.

**Cepheus:** King of Ethiopia; father of Andromeda.

**Cerberus:** Three-headed dog guarding entrance to Hades.

**Ceres:** *See* Demeter.

**Chaos:** Formless void; personified as first of gods.

**Charon:** Boatman on Styx who carried souls of dead to Hades; son of Erebus.

**Charybdis:** Female monster; personification of whirlpool.

**Chimera:** Female monster with head of lion, body of goat, tail of serpent; killed by Bellerophon.

**Chiron:** Most famous of centaurs.

**Chronos:** Personification of time.

**Chryseis:** Captive maiden given to Agamemnon; his refusal to accept ransom from her father Chryses caused Apollo to send plague on Greeks besieging Troy.

**Circe:** Sorceress; daughter of Helios; changed Odysseus's men into swine.

**Clio:** One of several **Muses.**

**Clotho:** One of several **Fates.**

**Clytemnestra:** Wife of Agamemnon, whom she slew with aid of her paramour, Aegisthus; slain by her son Orestes.

**Cocytus:** One of several **Rivers of Underworld.**

**Creon:** Father of Jocasta; forbade burial of Polynices; ordered burial alive of Antigone.

**Creüsa:** Princess of Corinth, for whom Jason deserted Medea; slain by Medea, who sent her poisoned robe; also known as Glaüke.

**Creusa:** Wife of Aeneas; died fleeing Troy.

**Cronus (Saturn):** Titan; god of harvests; son of Uranus and Gaea; dethroned by his son Zeus.

**Cupid:** *See* Eros.

**Cybele:** Anatolian nature goddess; adopted by Greeks and identified with Rhea.

**Cyclopes:** Race of one-eyed giants (singular: Cyclops).

**Daedalus:** Athenian artificer; father of Icarus; builder of Labyrinth in Crete; devised wings attached with wax for him and Icarus to escape Crete.

**Danae:** Princess of Argos; mother of Perseus by Zeus, who appeared to her in form of golden shower.

**Danaïdes:** Daughters of Danaüs; at his command, all except Hypermnestra slew their husbands, the sons of Aegyptus.

**Danaüs:** Brother of Aegyptus; father of Danaïdes; slain by Lynceus.

**Daphne:** Nymph; pursued by Apollo; changed to laurel tree.

**Decuma:** One of several **Fates.**

**Deino:** One of several **Graeae.**

**Demeter (Ceres):** Goddess of agriculture; mother of Persephone.

**Diana:** *See* Artemis.

**Dido:** Founder and queen of Carthage; stabbed herself when deserted by Aeneas.

**Diomedes:** Greek hero; with Odysseus, entered Troy and carried off Palladium, sacred statue of Athena.

**Diomedes:** Owner of man-eating horses, which Hercules, as ninth labor, carried off.

**Dione:** Titan goddess; mother by Zeus of Aphrodite.

**Dionysus (Bacchus):** God of wine; son of Zeus and Semele.

**Dioscuri:** Twins Castor and Pollux; sons of Leda by Zeus.

**Dis:** *See* Pluto, Hades.

**Dryads:** Wood nymphs.

**Dryope:** Maiden changed to Hamadryad.

**Echo:** Nymph who fell hopelessly in love with Narcissus; faded away except for her voice.

**Electra:** Daughter of Agamemnon and Clytemnestra; sister of Orestes; urged Orestes to slay Clytemnestra and Aegisthus.

**Electra:** One of several **Pleiades.**

**Elysium:** Abode of blessed dead.

**Endymion:** Mortal loved by Selene.

**Enyo:** One of several **Graeae.**

**Eos (Aurora):** Goddess of dawn.

**Epimetheus:** Brother of Prometheus; husband of Pandora.

**Erato:** One of several **Muses.**

**Erebus:** Spirit of darkness; son of Chaos.

**Erinyes:** One of several **Furies.**

**Eris:** Goddess of discord.

**Eros (Amor or Cupid):** God of love; son of Aphrodite.

**Eteocles:** Son of Oedipus, whom he succeeded to rule alternately with Polynices; refused to give up throne at end of year; he and Polynices slew each other.

**Eumenides:** One of several **Furies.**

**Euphrosyne:** One of several **Graces.**

**Europa:** Mortal loved by Zeus, who, in form of white bull, carried her off to Crete.

**Eurus:** One of several **Winds.**

**Euryale:** One of several **Gorgons.**

**Eurydice:** Nymph; wife of Orpheus.

**Eurystheus:** King of Argos; imposed twelve labors on Hercules.

**Euterpe:** One of several **Muses.**

**Fates:** Goddesses of destiny; Clotho (Spinner of thread of life), Lachesis (Determiner of length), and Atropos (Cutter of thread); also called Moirae. Identified by Romans with their goddesses of fate; Nona, Decuma, and Morta; called Parcae.

**Fauns:** Roman deities of woods and groves.

**Faunus:** *See* Pan.

**Favonius:** One of several **Winds.**

**Flora:** Roman goddess of flowers.

**Fortuna:** Roman goddess of fortune.

**Furies:** Avenging spirits; Alecto, Megaera, and Tisiphone; known also as Erinyes or Eumenides.

**Gaea:** Goddess of earth; daughter of Chaos; mother of Titans; known also as Ge, Gea, Gaia, etc.

**Galatea:** Statue of maiden carved from ivory by Pygmalion; given life by Aphrodite.

**Galatea:** Sea nymph; loved by Polyphemus.

**Ganymede:** Beautiful boy; successor to Hebe as cupbearer of gods.

**Glaucus:** Mortal who became sea divinity by eating magic grass.

**Golden Fleece:** Fleece from ram that flew Phrixos to Colchis; Aeëtes placed it under guard of dragon; carried off by Jason.

**Gorgons.** Female monsters; Euryale, Medusa, and Stheno; had snakes for hair; their glances turned mortals to stone.

**Graces:** Beautiful goddesses: Aglaia (Brilliance), Euphrosyne (Joy), and Thalia (Bloom); daughters of Zeus.

**Graeae.** Sentinels for Gorgons.; Deino, Enyo, and Pephredo; had one eye among them, which passed from one to another.

**Hades (Dis):** Name sometimes given Pluto; also, abode of dead, ruled by Pluto.

**Haemon:** Son of Creon; promised husband of Antigone; killed himself in her tomb.

**Hamadryads:** Tree nymphs.

**Harpies:** Monsters with heads of women and bodies of birds.

**Hebe (Juventas):** Goddess of youth; cupbearer of gods before Ganymede; daughter of Zeus and Hera.

**Hecate:** Goddess of sorcery and witchcraft.

**Hector:** Son of Priam; slayer of Patroclus; slain by Achilles.

**Hecuba:** Wife of Priam.

**Helen:** Fairest woman in world; daughter of Zeus and Leda; wife of Menelaus; carried to Troy by Paris, causing Trojan War.

**Heliades:** Daughters of Helios; mourned for Phaëthon and were changed to poplar trees.

**Helios (Sol):** God of sun; later identified with Apollo.

**Helle:** Sister of Phrixos; fell from ram of Golden Fleece; water where she fell named Hellespont.

**Hephaestus (Vulcan):** God of fire; celestial blacksmith; son of Zeus and Hera; husband of Aphrodite.

**Hera (Juno):** Queen of heaven; wife of Zeus.

**Hercules:** Hero and strong man; son of Zeus and Alcmene; performed twelve labors or deeds to be free from bondage under Eurystheus; after death, his mortal share was destroyed, and he became immortal. Also known as Herakles or Heracles. Labors: (1) killing Nemean lion; (2) killing Lernaean Hydra; (3) capturing Erymanthian boar; (4) capturing Ceryneian hind; (5) killing man-eating Stymphalian birds; (6) procuring girdle of Hippolyte; (7) cleaning Augean stables; (8) capturing Cretan bull; (9) capturing man-eating horses of Diomedes; (10) capturing cattle of Geryon; (11) procuring golden apples of Hesperides; (12) bringing Cerberus up from Hades.

**Hermes (Mercury):** God of physicians and thieves; messenger of gods; son of Zeus and Maia.

**Hero:** Priestess of Aphrodite; Leander swam Hellespont nightly to see her; drowned herself at his death.

**Hesperus:** Evening star.

**Hestia (Vesta):** Goddess of hearth; sister of Zeus.

**Hippolyte:** Queen of Amazons; wife of Theseus.

**Hippolytus:** Son of Theseus and Hippolyte; falsely accused by Phaedra of trying to kidnap her; slain by Poseidon at request of Theseus.

**Hippomenes:** Husband of Atalanta, whom he beat in race by dropping golden apples, which she stopped to pick up.

**Hyacinthus:** Beautiful youth accidentally killed by Apollo, who caused flower to spring up from his blood.

**Hydra:** Nine-headed monster in marsh of Lerna; slain by Hercules.

**Hygeia:** Personification of health.

**Hyman:** God of marriage.

**Hyperion:** Titan; early sun god; father of Helios.

**Hypermnestra:** Daughter of Danaüs; refused to kill her husband Lynceus.

**Hypnos (Somnus):** God of sleep.

**Iapetus:** Titan; father of Atlas, Epimetheus, and Prometheus.

**Icarus:** Son of Daedalus; flew too near sun with wax-attached wings and fell into sea and was drowned.

**Io:** Mortal maiden loved by Zeus; changed by Hera into heifer.

**Iobates:** King of Lycia; sent Bellerophon to slay Chimera.

**Iphigenia:** Daughter of Agamemnon; offered as sacrifice to Artemis at Aulis; carried by Artemis to Tauris where she became priestess; escaped from there with Orestes.

**Iris:** Goddess of rainbow; messenger of Zeus and Hera.

**Ismene:** Daughter of Oedipus; sister of Antigone.

**Iulus:** Son of Aeneas.

**Ixion:** King of Lapithae; for making love to Hera he was bound to endlessly revolving wheel in Tartarus.

**Janus:** Roman god of gates and doors; represented with two opposite faces.

**Jason:** Son of Aeson; to gain throne of Iolcus from Pelias, went to Colchis and brought back Golden Fleece; married Medea; deserted her for Creüsa.

**Jocasta:** Wife of Laius; mother of Oedipus; unwittingly became wife of Oedipus; hanged herself when relationship was discovered.

**Juno:** *See* Hera.

**Jupiter:** *See* Zeus.

**Juventas:** *See* Hebe.

**Lachesis:** One of several **Fates.**

**Laius:** Father of Oedipus, by whom he was slain.

**Laocoön:** Priest of Apollo at Troy; warned against bringing wooden horse into Troy; destroyed with his two sons by serpents sent by Athena.

**Lares:** Roman ancestral spirits protecting descendants and homes.

**Latona:** *See* Leto.

**Lavinia:** Wife of Aeneas after defeat of Turnus.

**Leander:** Swam Hellespont nightly to see Hero; drowned in storm.

**Leda:** Mortal loved by Zeus in form of swan; mother of Helen, Clytemnestra, Dioscuri.

**Lethe:** One of several **Rivers of Underworld.**

**Leto (Latona):** Mother by Zeus of Artemis and Apollo.

**Lucina:** Roman goddess of childbirth; identified with Juno.

**Lynceus:** Son of Aegyptus; husband of Hypermnestra; slew Danaüs.

**Maia:** Daughter of Atlas; mother of Hermes.

**Maia:** One of several **Pleiades.**

**Manes:** Souls of dead Romans, particularly of ancestors.

**Mars:** *See* Ares.

**Marsyas:** Shepherd; challenged Apollo to music contest and lost; flayed alive by Apollo.

**Medea:** Sorceress; daughter of Aeëtes; helped Jason obtain Golden Fleece; when deserted by him for Creüsa, killed her children and Creüsa.

**Medusa:** One of several **Gorgons.** slain by Perseus, who cut off her head.

**Megaera:** One of several **Furies.**

**Meleager:** Son of Althaea; his life would last as long as brand burning on hearth; Althaea quenched and saved it but destroyed it when Meleager slew his uncles.

**Melpomene:** One of several **Muses.**

**Memnon:** Ethiopian king; made immortal by Zeus; son of Tithonus and Eos.

**Menelaus:** King of Sparta; son of Atreus; brother of Agamemnon; husband of Helen.

**Mentor:** Tutor of Telemachus and friend of Odysseus. In the *Odyssey*, on several occasions, Athena assumes form of Mentor to give advice to Telemachus or Odysseus.

**Mercury:** *See* Hermes.

**Merope:** One of several **Pleiades.** Merope is said to have hidden in shame for loving a mortal.

**Mezentius:** Cruel Etruscan king; ally of Turnus against Aeneas; slain by Aeneas.

**Midas:** King of Phrygia; given gift of turning to gold all he touched.

**Minerva:** *See* Athena.

**Minos:** King of Crete; after death, one of three judges of dead in Hades; son of Zeus and Europa.

**Minotaur:** Monster, half man and half beast, kept in Labyrinth in Crete; slain by Theseus.

**Mnemosyne:** Goddess of memory; mother by Zeus of Muses.

**Moirae:** One of several **Fates.**

**Momus:** God of ridicule.

**Morpheus:** God of dreams.

**Mors:** *See* Thanatos.

**Morta:** One of several **Fates.**

**Muses:** Goddesses presiding over arts and sciences: Calliope (epic poetry), Clio (history), Erato (lyric and love poetry), Euterpe (music), Melpomene (tragedy), Polymnia or Polyhymnia (sacred poetry), Terpsichore (choral dance and song), Thalia (comedy and bucolic poetry), Urania (astronomy); daughters of Zeus and Mnemosyne.

**Naiads:** Nymphs of waters, streams, and fountains.

**Napaeae:** Wood nymphs.

**Narcissus:** Beautiful youth loved by Echo; in punishment for not returning her love, he was made to fall in love with his image reflected in pool; pined away and became flower.

**Nemesis:** Goddess of retribution.

**Neoptolemus:** Son of Achilles; slew Priam; also known as Pyrrhus.

**Neptune:** *See* Poseidon.

**Nereids:** Sea nymphs; attendants on Poseidon.

**Nestor:** King of Pylos; noted for wise counsel in expedition against Troy.

**Nike:** Goddess of victory.

**Niobe:** Daughter of Tantalus; wife of Amphion; her children slain by Apollo and Artemis; changed to stone but continued to weep her loss.

**Nona:** One of several **Fates.**

**Notus:** One of several **Winds.**

**Nox:** *See* Nyx.

**Nymphs:** Beautiful maidens; minor deities of nature.

**Nyx (Nox):** Goddess of night.

**Oceanids:** Ocean nymphs; daughters of Oceanus.

**Oceanus:** Eldest of Titans; god of waters.

**Odysseus (Ulysses):** King of Ithaca; husband of Penelope; wandered ten years after fall of Troy before arriving home.

**Oedipus:** King of Thebes; son of Laius and Jocasta; unwittingly murdered Laius and married Jocasta; tore his eyes out when relationship was discovered.

**Oenone:** Nymph of Mount Ida; wife of Paris, who abandoned her; refused to cure him when he was poisoned by arrow of Philoctetes at Troy.

**Ops:** *See* Rhea.

**Oreads:** Mountain nymphs.

**Orestes:** Son of Agamemnon and Clytemnestra; brother of Electra; slew Clytemnestra and Aegisthus; pursued by Furies until his purification by Apollo.

**Orion:** Hunter; slain by Artemis and made heavenly constellation.

**Orpheus:** Famed musician; son of Apollo and Muse Calliope; husband of Eurydice.

**Pales:** Roman goddess of shepherds and herdsmen.

**Palinurus:** Aeneas' pilot; fell overboard in his sleep and was drowned.

**Pan (Faunus):** God of woods and fields; part goat; son of Hermes.

**Pandora:** Opener of box containing human ills; mortal wife of Epimetheus.

**Parcae:** One of several **Fates.**

**Paris:** Son of Priam; gave apple of discord to Aphrodite, for which she enabled him to carry off Helen; slew Achilles at Troy; slain by Philoctetes.

**Patroclus:** Friend of Achilles in Trojan War; wore Achilles' armor and was slain by Hector.

**Pegasus:** Winged horse that sprang from Medusa's body at her death; ridden by Bellerophon when he slew Chimera.

**Pelias:** King of Iolcus; seized throne from his brother Aeson; sent Jason for Golden Fleece; slain unwittingly by his daughters at instigation of Medea.

**Pelops:** Son of Tantalus; his father cooked and served him to gods; restored to life; Peloponnesus named for him.

**Penates:** Roman household gods.

**Penelope:** Wife of Odysseus; waited faithfully for him for many years while putting off numerous suitors.

**Pephredo:** One of several **Graeae.**

**Periphetes:** Giant; son of Hephaestus; slain by Theseus.

**Persephone (Proserpine):** Queen of infernal regions; daughter of Zeus and Demeter; wife of Pluto.

**Perseus:** Son of Zeus and Danaë; slew Medusa; rescued Andromeda from monster and married her.

**Phaedra:** Daughter of Minos; wife of Theseus; caused the death of her stepson, Hippolytus.

**Phaethon:** Son of Helios; drove his father's sun chariot and was struck down by Zeus before he set world on fire.

**Philoctetes:** Greek warrior who possessed Hercules' bow and arrows; slew Paris at Troy with poisoned arrow.

**Phineus:** Betrothed of Andromeda; tried to slay Perseus but turned to stone by Medusa's head.

**Phlegethon:** One of several **Rivers of Underworld.**

**Phosphor:** Morning star.

**Phrixos:** Brother of Helle; carried by ram of Golden Fleece to Colchis.

**Pirithous:** Son of Ixion; friend of Theseus; tried to carry off Persephone from Hades; bound to enchanted rock by Pluto.

**Pleiades:** Alcyone, Celaeno, Electra, Maia, Merope, Sterope or Asterope, Taygeta; seven daughters of Atlas; transformed into heavenly constellation, of which six stars are visible (Merope is said to have hidden in shame for loving a mortal).

**Pluto (Dis):** God of Hades; brother of Zeus.

**Plutus:** God of wealth.

**Pollux:** One of **Dioscuri.**

**Polyhymnia:** *See* Polymnia.

**Polymnia (Polyhymnia):** One of several **Muses.**

**Polynices:** Son of Oedipus; he and his brother Eteocles killed each other; burial rite, forbidden by Creon, performed by his sister Antigone.

**Polyphemus:** Cyclops; devoured six of Odysseus's men; blinded by Odysseus.

**Polyxena:** Daughter of Priam; betrothed to Achilles, whom Paris slew at their betrothal; sacrificed to shade of Achilles.

**Pomona:** Roman goddess of fruits.

**Pontus:** Sea god; son of Gaea.

**Poseidon (Neptune):** God of sea; brother of Zeus.

**Priam:** King of Troy; husband of Hecuba; ransomed Hector's body from Achilles; slain by Neoptolemus.

**Priapus:** God of regeneration.

**Procris:** Wife of Cephalus, who accidentally slew her.

**Procrustes:** Giant; stretched or cut off legs of victims to make them fit iron bed; slain by Theseus.

**Proetus:** Husband of Anteia; sent Bellerophon to Iobates to be put to death.

**Prometheus:** Titan; stole fire from heaven for man. Zeus punished him by chaining him to rock in Caucasus where vultures devoured his liver daily.

**Proserpine:** *See* Persephone.

**Proteus:** Sea god; assumed various shapes when called on to prophesy.

**Psyche:** Beloved of Eros; punished by jealous Aphrodite; made immortal and united with Eros.

**Pygmalion:** King of Cyprus; carved ivory statue of maiden which Aphrodite gave life as Galatea.

**Pyramus:** Babylonian youth; made love to Thisbe through hole in wall; thinking Thisbe slain by lion, killed himself.

**Python:** Serpent born from slime left by Deluge; slain by Apollo.

**Quirinus:** Roman war god.

**Remus:** Brother of Romulus; slain by him.

**Rhadamanthus:** One of three judges of dead in Hades; son of Zeus and Europa.

**Rhea (Ops):** Daughter of Uranus and Gaea; wife of Cronus; mother of Zeus; identified with Cybele.

**Rivers of Underworld.** Acheron (woe), Cocytus (wailing), Lethe (forgetfulness), Phlegethon (fire), Styx (across which souls of dead were ferried by Charon).

**Romulus:** Founder of Rome; he and Remus suckled in infancy by she-wolf; slew Remus; deified by Romans.

**Sarpedon:** King of Lycia; son of Zeus and Europa; slain by Patroclus at Troy.

**Saturn:** *See* Cronus.

**Satyrs:** Hoofed demigods of woods and fields; companions of Dionysus.

**Sciron:** Robber; forced strangers to wash his feet, then hurled them into sea where tortoise devoured them; slain by Theseus.

**Scylla:** Female monster inhabiting rock opposite Charybdis; menaced passing sailors.

**Selene:** Goddess of moon.

**Semele:** Daughter of Cadmus; mother by Zeus of Dionysus; demanded Zeus appear before her in all his splendor and was destroyed by his lightning bolts.

**Sibyls:** Various prophetesses; most famous, Cumaean sibyl, accompanied Aeneas into Hades.

**Sileni:** Minor woodland deities similar to satyrs (singular: silenus). Sometimes Silenus refers to eldest of satyrs, son of Hermes or of Pan.

**Silvanus:** Roman god of woods and fields.

**Sinis:** Giant; bent pines, with which he hurled victims against side of mountain; slain by Theseus.

**Sirens:** Minor deities who lured sailors to destruction with their singing.

**Sisyphus:** King of Corinth; condemned in Tartarus to roll huge stone to top of hill; it always rolled back down again.

**Sol:** *See* Helios.

**Somnus:** *See* Hypnos.

**Sphinx:** Monster of Thebes; killed those who could not answer her riddle; slain by Oedipus. Name also refers to other monsters having body of lion, wings, and head and bust of woman.

**Sterope (Asterope):** One of several **Pleiades.**

**Stheno:** One of several **Gorgons.**

**Styx:** One of several **Rivers of Underworld.** The souls of the dead were ferried across the Styx by Charon.

**Symplegades:** Clashing rocks at entrance to Black Sea; Argo passed through, causing them to become forever fixed.

**Syrinx:** Nymph pursued by Pan; changed to reeds, from which he made his pipes.

**Tantalus:** Cruel king; father of Pelops and Niobe; condemned in Tartarus to stand chin-deep in lake surrounded by fruit branches; as he tried to eat or drink, water or fruit always receded.

**Tartarus:** Underworld below Hades; often refers to Hades.

**Taygeta:** One of several **Pleiades.**

**Telemachus:** Son of Odysseus; made unsuccessful journey to find his father.

**Tellus:** Roman goddess of earth.

**Terminus:** Roman god of boundaries and landmarks.

**Terpsichore:** One of several **Muses.**

**Terra:** Roman earth goddess.

**Thalia:** One of several **Graces.** Also one of several **Muses.**

**Thanatos (Mors):** God of death.

**Themis:** Titan goddess of laws of physical phenomena; daughter of Uranus; mother of Prometheus.

**Theseus:** Son of Aegeus; slew Minotaur; married and deserted Ariadne; later married Phaedra.

**Thisbe:** Beloved of Pyramus; killed herself at his death.

**Thyestes:** Brother of Atreus; Atreus killed three of his sons and served them to him at banquet.

**Tiresias:** Blind soothsayer of Thebes.

**Tisiphone:** One of several **Furies.**

**Titans:** Early gods from which Olympian gods were derived; children of Uranus and Gaea.

**Tithonus:** Mortal loved by Eos; changed into grasshopper.

**Triton:** Demigod of sea; son of Poseidon.

**Turnus:** King of Rutuli in Italy; betrothed to Lavinia; slain by Aeneas.

**Ulysses:** *See* Odysseus.

**Urania:** One of several **Muses.**

**Uranus:** Personification of Heaven; husband of Gaea; father of Titans; dethroned by his son Cronus.

**Venus:** *See* Aphrodite.

**Vertumnus:** Roman god of fruits and vegetables; husband of Pomona.

**Vesta:** *See* Hestia.

**Vulcan:** *See* Hephaestus.

**Winds:** Aeolus (keeper of winds), Boreas (Aquilo) (north wind), Eurus (east wind), Notus (Auster) (south wind), Zephyrus (Favonius) (west wind).

**Zephyrus:** One of several **Winds.**

**Zeus (Jupiter):** Chief of Olympian gods; son of Cronus and Rhea; husband of Hera.

# Norse Mythology

**Aesir:** Chief gods of Asgard.

**Andvari:** Dwarf; robbed of gold and magic ring by Loki.

**Angerbotha (Angrbotha):** Giantess; mother by Loki of Fenrir, Hel, and Midgard serpent.

**Asgard (Asgarth):** Abode of gods.

**Ask (Aske, Askr):** First man; created by Odin, Hoenir, and Lothur.

**Asynjur:** Goddesses of Asgard.

**Atli:** Second husband of Gudrun; invited Gunnar and Hogni to his court, where they were slain; slain by Gudrun.

**Audhumia (Audhumbla):** Cow that nourished Ymir; created Buri by licking ice cliff.

**Balder (Baldr, Baldur):** God of light, spring, peace, joy; son of Odin; slain by Hoth at instigation of Loki.

**Bifrost:** Rainbow bridge connecting Midgard and Asgard.

**Bragi (Brage):** God of poetry; husband of Ithunn.

**Branstock:** Great oak in hall of Volsungs; into it, Odin thrust Gram, which only Sigmund could draw forth.

**Brynhild:** Valkyrie; wakened from magic sleep by Sigurd; married Gunnar; instigated death of Sigurd; killed herself and was burned on pyre beside Sigurd.

**Bur (Bor):** Son of Buri; father of Odin, Hoenir, and Lothur.

**Buri (Bori):** Progenitor of gods; father of Bur; created by Audhumla.

**Embla:** First woman; created by Odin, Hoenir, and Lothur.

**Fafnir:** Son of Rodmar, whom he slew for gold in Otter's skin; in form of dragon, guarded gold; slain by Sigurd.

**Fenrir:** Wolf; offspring of Loki; swallows Odin at Ragnarok and is slain by Vitharr.

**Forseti:** Son of Balder.

**Frey (Freyr):** God of fertility and crops; son of Njorth; originally one of **Vanir.**

**Freya (Freyja):** Goddess of love and beauty; sister of Frey; originally one of **Vanir.**

**Frigg (Frigga):** Goddess of sky; wife of Odin.

**Garm:** Watchdog of Hel; slays, and is slain by, Tyr at Ragnarok.

**Gimle:** Home of blessed after Ragnarok.

**Giuki:** King of Nibelungs; father of Gunnar, Hogni, Guttorm, and Gudrun.

**Glathsehim (Gladsheim):** Hall of gods in Asgard.

**Gram (meaning "Angry"):** Sigmund's sword; rewelded by Regin; used by Sigurd to slay Fafnir.

**Greyfell:** Sigmund's horse; descended from Sleipnir.

**Grimhild:** Mother of Gudrun; administered magic potion to Sigurd which made him forget Brynhild.

**Gudrun:** Daughter of Giuki; wife of Sigurd; later wife of Atli and Jonakr.

**Gunnar:** Son of Giuki; in his semblance Sigurd won Brynhild for him; slain at hall of Atli.

**Guttorm:** Son of Giuki; slew Sigurd at Brynhild's request.

**Heimdall (Heimdallr):** Guardian of Asgard.

**Hel:** Goddess of dead and queen of underworld; daughter of Loki.

**Hiordis:** Wife of Sigmund; mother of Sigurd.

**Hoenir:** One of creators of Ask and Embla; son of Bur.

**Hogni:** Son of Giuki; slain at hall of Atli.

**Hoth (Hoder, Hodur):** Blind god of night and darkness; slayer of Balder at instigation of Loki.

**Ithunn (Ithun, Iduna):** Keeper of golden apples of youth; wife of Bragi.

**Jonakr:** Third husband of Gudrun.

**Jormunrek:** Slayer of Swanhild; slain by sons of Gudrun.

**Jotunnheim (Jotunheim):** Abode of giants.

**Lif and Lifthrasir:** First man and woman after Ragnarok.

**Loki:** God of evil and mischief; instigator of Balder's death.

**Lothur (Lodur):** One of creators of Ask and Embla.

**Midgard (Midgarth):** Abode of mankind; the earth.

**Midgard Serpent:** Sea monster; offspring of Loki; slays, and is slain by, Thor at Ragnarok.

**Mimir:** Giant; guardian of well in Jotunnheim at root of Yggdrasill; knower of past and future.

**Mjollnir:** Magic hammer of Thor.

**Nagifar:** Ship to be used by giants in attacking Asgard at Ragnarok; built from nails of dead men.

**Nanna:** Wife of Balder.

**Nibelungs:** Dwellers in northern kingdom ruled by Giuki.

**Niflheim (Nifelheim):** Outer region of cold and darkness; abode of Hel.

**Njorth:** Father of Frey and Freya; originally one of **Vanir.**

**Norns:** Demigoddesses of fate: Urth (Urdur) (past), Verthandi (Verdandi) (present), Skuld (future).

**Odin (Othin):** Head of **Aesir;** creator of world with Vili and Ve; equivalent to Woden (Wodan, Wotan) in Teutonic mythology.

**Otter:** Son of Rodmar; slain by Loki; his skin filled with gold hoard of Andvari to appease Rodmar.

**Ragnarok:** Final destruction of present world in battle between gods and giants; some minor gods will survive, and Lif and Lifthrasir will repeople world.

**Regin:** Blacksmith; son of Rodmar; foster-father of Sigurd.

**Rerir:** King of Huns; son of Sigi.

**Rodmar:** Father of Regin, Otter, and Fafnir; demanded Otter's skin be filled with gold; slain by Fafnir, who stole gold.

**Sif:** Wife of Thor.

**Siggeir:** King of Goths; husband of Signy; he and his sons slew Volsung and his sons, except Sigmund; slain by Sigmund and Sinflotli.

**Sigi:** King of Huns; son of Odin.

**Sigmund:** Son of Volsung; brother of Signy, who bore him Sinflotli; husband of Hiordis, who bore him Sigurd.

**Signy:** Daughter of Volsung; sister of Sigmund; wife of Siggeir; mother by Sigmund of Sinflotli.

**Sigurd:** Son of Sigmund and Hiordis; wakened Brynhild from magic sleep; married Gudrun; slain by Guttorm at instigation of Brynhild.

**Sigyn:** Wife of Loki.

**Sinflotli:** Son of Sigmund and Signy.

**Skuld:** One of several **Norns.**

**Sleipnir (Sleipner):** Eight-legged horse of Odin.

**Surt (Surtr):** Fire demon; slays Frey at Ragnarok.

**Svartalfaheim:** Abode of dwarfs.

**Swanhild:** Daughter of Sigurd and Gudrun; slain by Jormunrek.

**Thor:** God of thunder; oldest son of Odin; equivalent to Germanic deity Donar.

**Tyr:** God of war; son of Odin; equivalent to Tiu in Teutonic mythology.

**Ull (Ullr):** Son of Sif; stepson of Thor.

**Urth:** One of several **Norns.**

**Valhalla (Valhall):** Great hall in Asgard where Odin received souls of heroes killed in battle.

**Vali:** Odin's son: Ragnarok survivor.

**Valkyries:** Virgins, messengers of Odin, who selected heroes to die in battle and took them to Valhalla; generally considered as nine in number.

**Vanir:** Early race of gods; three survivors, Njorth, Frey, and Freya, are associated with **Aesir.**

**Ve:** Brother of Odin; one of creators of world.

**Verthandi:** One of several **Norns.**

**Vili:** Brother of Odin; one of creators of world.

**Vingolf:** Abode of goddesses in Asgard.

**Vitharr (Vithar):** Son of Odin; survivor of Ragnarok.

**Volsung:** Descendant of Odin, and father of Signy, Sigmund; his descendants were called Volsungs.

**Yggdrasill:** Giant ash tree springing from body of Ymir and supporting universe; its roots extended to Asgard, Jotunnheim, and Niffheim.

**Ymir (Ymer):** Primeval frost giant killed by Odin, Vili, and Ve; world created from his body; also, from his body sprang Yggdrasill.

# Egyptian Mythology

**Amen (Amon, Ammdn):** One of chief Theban deities; united with sun god under form of Amen-Ra; husband of Mut.

**Amenti:** Region of dead where souls were judged by Osiris.

**Anubis:** Guide of souls to Amenti; son of Osiris; jackal-headed.

**Apis:** Sacred bull, an embodiment of Ptah; identified with Osiris as Osiris-Apis or Serapis.

**Geb (Keb, Seb):** Earth god; father of Osiris; represented with goose on head.

**Hathor (Athor):** Goddess of love and mirth; cow-headed.

**Horus:** God of day; son of Osiris and Isis; hawk-headed.

**Isis:** Goddess of motherhood and fertility; sister and wife of Osiris.

**Khepera:** God of morning sun.

**Khnemu (Khnum, Chnuphis, Chnemu, Chnum):** Ram-headed god.

**Khonsu (Khensu, Khuns):** Son of Amen and Mut.

**Mentu (Ment):** Solar deity, sometimes considered god of war; falcon-headed.

**Mut (Maut):** Wife of Amen.

**Nephthys:** Goddess of the dead; sister and wife of Set.

**Nu:** Chaos from which world was created, personified as a god.

**Nut:** Goddess of heavens; consort of Geb.

**Osiris:** God of underworld and judge of dead; son of Geb and Nut; brother and husband of Isis.

**Ptah (Phtha):** Chief deity of Memphis.

**Ra:** God of the Sun, the supreme god; son of Nut; Pharaohs claimed descent from him; represented as lion, cat, or falcon.

**Serapis:** God uniting attributes of Osiris and Apis.

**Set (Seth):** God of darkness or evil; brother and enemy of Osiris; brother and husband of Nephthys.

**Shu:** Solar deity; son of Ra and Hathor.

**Tem (Atmu, Atum, Tum):** Solar deity.

**Thoth (Dhouti):** God of wisdom and magic; scribe of gods; ibis-headed.

# A Concise Guide to Style

This section discusses and illustrates the basic conventions of American capitalization, italicization, and punctuation.

## Capitalization

Capitalize the following:

- **Proper nouns and adjectives derived from proper nouns:**

  Marie Curie China, Chinese
  Smokey Robinson Darwin, Darwinian

  But vocabulary words derived from proper nouns are generally lowercase:

  china cups plaster of paris
  french fries vienna sausage

- **The names of geographic divisions, regions, and localities and topographical features such as rivers, lakes, and mountains:**

  North Pole Gulf States
  Middle East Atlantic Ocean
  Southern Hemisphere Rocky Mountains
  the North Lake Tahoe
  Lower East Side Erie Canal

  Do not capitalize directions: She lives 10 miles north of Boston.

- **The names of nationalities, ethnic groups, tribes, and languages:**

  Spanish Bantu
  Asian American Creole

- **Titles when preceding a name:**

  President Lincoln Aunt Mary
  Queen Victoria Doctor Johnson
  Senator Kennedy Professor Davies

  Do not capitalize such terms elsewhere: a biography of the queen; the senator's speech; my aunt, Mary Wilson; the president's fundraising efforts; the residence of the vice president.

- **Epithets:** Ivan the Terrible; Lincoln is known as The Great Emancipator.

- **The names of political and judicial bodies, social organizations, councils, and departments:**

  U.S. Senate Rotary Club
  Democratic Party United Negro College Fund
  State Department U.S. Supreme Court

- **The names for periods, events, and documents of historical importance:**

  Middle Ages Constitution
  Renaissance Treaty of Versailles
  Battle of Waterloo Magna Carta

- **The names for streets, buildings, and monuments:**

  Fifth Avenue World Trade Center
  Broadway Statue of Liberty

- **The names for the supreme deity and sacred works:**

  God, the Father Almighty Bible
  Yahweh Talmud
  Allah Qu'ran

- **The names for religious denominations and their members:**

  Buddhism, Buddhists
  Catholicism, Catholics
  Judaism, Jews
  Methodist Church, Methodists
  Society of Friends, Quakers

- **The days of the weeks, months of the year, holidays, and holy days:**

  Thursday Labor Day
  December Passover

- **The pronoun I:**

  I told her I didn't want to go.

- **The first word in the salutation and complimentary close of a letter:**

  My dear Carol . . .
  Very truly yours . . .

- **The first word of a sentence:**

  Are you hungry? Lunch will be served soon.

- **The first word of a direct quotation, except when the quotation is split:**

  I asked, "Do you really like bats?"
  "Yes," said Holly, "they're so cute."

- **The first word and all the key words in the title of a literary or other artistic work:**

  *The Bluest Eye* (novel)
  *A Streetcar Named Desire* (play)
  "The Road Not Taken" (poem)
  *Starry Night* (painting)
  "Only the Lonely" (song)

- **The names of ships, aircraft, and space vehicles:**

  USS *Maine*
  *The Spirit of St. Louis*
  space shuttle *Challenger*

- **The names of constellations, planets, and stars:**

  Milky Way Saturn
  the asteroid Juno Little Dipper

- **The names of geologic eras, periods, epochs, and names of prehistoric divisions:**

  *Paleozoic Era* *Pleistocene*
  *Quaternary Period* *Stone Age*

- **The genus but not the species name in binomial nomenclature:**

  *Canis familiaris* (dog)
  *Malus pumila* (apple tree)

## Italicization

Italicize the following:

- **The titles of books, plays, book-length poems, magazines, and newspapers:**

  *War and Peace*          *TIME magazine*
  *Twelfth Night*          *National Geographic*
  *Beowulf*                *Miami Herald*

- **The titles of movies and radio and television programs:**

  *Toy Story*              *The X-Files*
  *Car Talk*               *Masterpiece Theater*

- **The titles of works of art, including paintings, sculptures, and major musical compositions:**

  *Mona Lisa* (painting)
  *The Thinker* (sculpture)
  *Swan Lake* (ballet)
  *Porgy and Bess* (opera)

  Do not italicize musical compositions named by number or key: Symphony No. 4; Quartet in E minor.

- **Words, letters, and numbers used as such:**

  How do you spell *ache*?
  Does your name end with a *c* or a *k*?
  The *6* looked like a *0*.

- **Foreign words and phrases that have not been assimilated into English:**

  Alex's *Weltanschauung* was gloomy.
  Ed made a *tarte au citron* for dessert.

- **Words and phrases that are being emphasized:**

  Paris was *the* place to be in the '20s.

- **The names of the plaintiff and defendant in legal citations:** *Johnson* v. *Smith.*

- **The names of ships, aircraft, and space vehicles:**

  USS *Maine*
  *The Spirit of St. Louis*
  space shuttle *Challenger*

- **The New Latin names of genera, species, subspecies, and varieties in botanical and zoological nomenclature:** *Quercus alba; Homo sapiens.*

## Punctuation

### End Marks

- **Use a period after a declarative or imperative statement:**

  I went to the library.
  Sign your name here.

- **Use a question mark after a direct question or to indicate uncertainty:**

  What is your name?
  Chaucer's dates are 1340?–1400.

  Do not use a question mark after an indirect question: I asked them what time they were leaving.

- **Use an exclamation point after an exclamatory or emphatic sentence or an interjection:**

  Give me a break!
  Hey! Ouch! Wow!

## Comma

Use a comma:

- **To separate words in a list or series:**

  The baby likes grapes, bananas, and cantaloupe.

- **To separate two or more adjectives that come before a noun when *and* can be substituted without changing the meaning:**

  He had a kind, generous nature.
  The dog had thick, soft, shiny fur.

  Do not use the comma if the adjectives together express a single idea or the noun is a compound made up of an adjective and a noun:

  The kitchen had bright yellow curtains.
  A majestic bald eagle soared overhead.

- **To set off words or phrases in apposition to a noun:**

  George Eliot, the great 19th-century novelist, was born in 1819.

  Do not use commas when the appositive word or phrase is essential to the meaning of the sentence:

  The novelist George Eliot was born in 1819.

- **To set off nonessential phrases and clauses:**

  My French professor, who has an odd sense of humor, has been teaching for some 30 years.

  Do not use commas when the phrase or clause is essential to the meaning of the sentence:

  The professor who teaches my French class has an odd sense of humor.

- **To separate the independent clauses joined by a coordinating conjunction in a compound sentence:**

  He lives in New York, and she lives in London.
  Some people like golf, but others prefer tennis.

- **To set off interrupters such as *of course, however, I think,* and *by the way* from the rest of the sentence:**

  She knew, of course, that he was lying.
  By the way, I'll be away next week.

- **To set off an introductory word, phrase, or clause at the beginning of a sentence:**

  Yes, I'd like to go with you.
  After some years, we met again.
  Being tall, she often gets teased.

- **To set off a word in direct address:**

  Thanks, guys, for all your help.
  How was your trip, Kathy?

- **To set off a tag question:**

  You won't do that again, will you?

- **To introduce a short quotation:**

  The queen said, "Let them eat cake!"

- **To close the salutation in a personal letter and the complimentary close in a business or personal letter:**

  Dear Mary, . . . Sincerely, Fred

- **To set off titles and degrees:**

  Sarah Little, Ph.D.          Robert Johnson, Jr.

- **To separate sentence elements that might be read incorrectly without the comma:**

  As they entered, in the shadows you could see a figure lurking.

- **To set off the month and day from the year in full dates:**

  The conference will be held on August 6, 2001.

  Do not use a comma when only the month and year appear:

  The conference will be held in August 2001.

- **To set off the city and state in an address:**

  Sam Green
  10 Joy Street
  Boston, MA 02116

  If the address is inserted into text, add a second comma after the state:

  Cincinnati, Ohio, is their home.

## Colon

Use a colon:

- **To introduce a list, or words, phrases, and clauses that explain, enlarge upon, or summarize what has gone before:**

  Please provide the following: your name, address, and phone number.

  "No honest poet can ever feel quite sure of the permanent value of what he has written: He may have wasted his time and messed up his life for nothing."—T. S. Eliot

- **To introduce a long quotation:**

  In 1780 John Adams wrote: "English is destined to be in the next and succeeding centuries more generally the language of the world than Latin was in the last or French is in the present age . . . "

- **To separate hour and minute(s) in standard time notation:**

  The train arrives at 9:30.

- **To close the salutation in a business letter:**

  Dear Sir or Madam:

## Semicolon

Use a semicolon:

- **To separate the independent clauses in a compound sentence not joined by a conjunction:**

  Only two seats were left; we needed three.

  The situation is hopeful; the storm may lift soon.

- **To separate two independent clauses, the second of which begins with an adverb such as *however, consequently, moreover,* and *therefore*:**

  We waited an hour; however, we couldn't hang around indefinitely.

- **To separate elements already punctuated with commas:**

  Invitations were mailed to the various professors, associate professors, and assistant professors; the secretary of the department; and some of the grad students.

## Dashes & Hyphens

- **Use a dash to indicate a sudden break in continuity or to set off an explanatory, a defining, or an emphatic phrase:**

  The sky grew dark—where were the kids?

  Dairy foods—milk, cheese, yogurt—are a good source of calcium.

- **Use a hyphen to join the elements of a compound word or to join the elements of a compound modifier before a noun:**

  well-wisher                 ice-skating rink
  fifty-three                 college-age students

- **Use a hyphen to divide a word at the end of a line:**

  Rasputin is one of history's most enigmatic and intriguing figures.

## Brackets & Parentheses

- **Use brackets to set off words or letters in quoted matter that have been added by someone other than the author:**

  "She [Willa Cather] is certainly one of the great American writers of the 20th century."

- **Use parentheses to set off nonessential information:**

  We spent an hour (more or less) cleaning up.

## Apostrophe

Use an apostrophe to indicate:

- **The possessive case of singular and plural nouns, indefinite pronouns, and proper nouns:**

  my sister's son             somebody's lunch
  my two sisters' sons        Charles's house
  the children's toys         the Rosses' friends

- **The plural of letters, numbers, symbols, and words used as such:**

  too many *thus*'s           ten 5's in a row
  spelled with two *e*'s      delete some &'s

- **Missing letters in contractions and missing numbers in dates:**

  I'm (I am)                  class of '95
  ma'am (madam)               winter of '97–'98

## Quotation Marks

Use quotation marks:

- **To set off direct quotations:**

  "Let's go to the beach," she suggested.

- **To set off titles of short stories, articles, chapters, essays, songs, poems, and individual radio and television programs:**

  Chapter 9, "The New Englishes"
  sang the "Star-Spangled Banner"
  "The Apparent Trap" episode of *Frasier*

- **To set off words and phrases that are being used in an unusual or questionable way or might be preceded by *so-called*:**

  Mari's "fine" was a day's volunteer work.

  According to the article, bees appear to "remember" landmarks.

## Forms of Address

| Addressee | Address | Salutation |
|---|---|---|
| **Clerical and religious orders** | | |
| Archbishop, Eastern Orthodox | The Most Reverend *First name*, Archbishop of *Place name* | Your Eminence |
| Archbishop, Roman Catholic | The Most Reverend *First name*, Archbishop of *Place name* | Your Excellency |
| Archdeacon, Episcopal | The Venerable *Full name*, Archdeacon of *Place name* | Dear Archdeacon *Last name* |
| Bishop, Episcopal | The Right Reverend *Full name*, Bishop of *Place name* | Right Reverend Sir *or* Dear Bishop *Last name* |
| Bishop, other Protestant | The Reverend *Full name* | Dear Bishop *Last name* |
| Bishop, Roman Catholic | The Most Reverend *Full name*, Bishop of *Place name* | Your Excellency *or* Dear Bishop *Last name* |
| Cardinal | His Eminence *First name* Cardinal *Last name* | Your Eminence |
| Clergyman/woman, Protestant | The Reverend *Full name or* The Reverend *Full name*, D.D. | Dear Mr./Ms. *Last name or* Dear Dr. *Last name* |
| Dean of a Cathedral, Episcopal | The Very Reverend *Full name*, Dean of *Place name* | Dear Dean *Last name* |
| Monsignor | The Right Reverend Monsignor *Full name* | Dear Monsignor |
| Patriarch, Greek Orthodox | His All Holiness the Patriarch of *Place name* | Your All Holiness |
| Patriarch, Russian Orthodox | His Holiness the Patriarch of *Place name* | Your Holiness |
| Pope | His Holiness The Pope | Your Holiness *or* Most Holy Father |
| Priest, Roman Catholic | The Reverend *Full name or* The Reverend *Full name*, S.J. (or other order) | Dear Reverend Father *or* Dear Father |
| Rabbi, man or woman | Rabbi *Full name or Full name*, D.D. | Dear Rabbi *Last name or* Dear Dr. *Last name* |
| **Government officials** | | |
| Assemblyman/woman | The Honorable *Full name* | Dear Mr./Ms. *Last name* |
| Associate Justice, U.S. Supreme Court | The Honorable Justice *Full name* | Dear Sir/Madam *or* Justice *Last name* |
| Cabinet member | The Honorable *Full name*, Secretary of *Department name* | Sir/Madam *or* Dear Mr./Madam Secretary |
| Chief Justice, U.S. Supreme Court | The Honorable *Full name*, Chief Justice of the United States | Dear Mr./Madame Chief Justice |
| Commissioner | The Honorable *Full name* | Dear Mr./Mrs. *Last name* |
| Governor | The Honorable *Full name*, Governor of *State name* | Dear Governor *Last name* |
| Judge, federal | The Honorable *Full name*, Judge, United States District Court | Dear Sir/Madam *or* Judge *Last name* |
| Judge, state or local | The Honorable *Full name*, Judge of the Court of *Place name* | Dear Judge *Last name* |
| Mayor | The Honorable *Full name*, Mayor of *Place name* | Dear Mayor *Last name* |
| President, U.S. | The President | Dear Mr./Madam President |
| President, U.S., former | The Honorable *Full name* | Dear Mr./Madam *Last name* |
| Representative, state | The Honorable *Full name*, House of Representatives, *State name* | Dear Mr./Ms. *or* Dear *Last name* |
| Representative, U.S. | The Honorable *Full name*, United States House of Representatives | Dear Mr./Mrs. *Last name* |
| Senator, state | The Honorable *Full name*, The State Senate, *State Capital* | Dear Senator *Last name* |
| Senator, U.S. | The Honorable *Full name*, United States Senate | Dear Senator *Last name* |
| Speaker, U.S. House of Representatives | The Honorable *Full name*, Speaker of the House of Representatives | Dear Mr./Madam Speaker |
| Vice President, U.S. | The Vice President of the United States | Sir/Madam *or* Dear Mr./Madam Vice President |
| **Military and naval officers** | | |
| All ranks | *Rank Full name*, USA/USN/USCG/USAF/USMC | Dear *Rank Last name* |

# Glossary of Poetry Terms

**accent** The prominence or emphasis given to a syllable or word. In the word *poetry*, the accent (or stress) falls on the first syllable.

**alliteration** The repetition of the same or similar sounds at the beginning of words. Some famous examples of alliteration are tongue twisters such as *She sells seashells by the seashore* and *Peter Piper picked a peck of pickled peppers.*

**anapest** A metrical foot of three syllables, two short (or unstressed) followed by one long (or stressed), as in *seventeen* and *to the moon.* The anapest is the reverse of the dactyl.

**assonance** The repetition or a pattern of similar sounds, especially vowel sounds, as in the tongue twister "Moses supposes his toeses are roses."

**ballad** A poem that tells a story similar to a folk tale or legend and often has a repeated refrain. *The Rime of the Ancient Mariner* by Samuel Taylor Coleridge is an example of a ballad.

**ballade** A type of poem, usually with three stanzas of seven, eight, or ten lines and a shorter final stanza (or envoy) of four or five lines. All stanzas end with the same one-line refrain.

**blank verse** Poetry that is written in unrhymed iambic pentameter. Shakespeare wrote most of his plays in blank verse.

**caesura** A natural pause or break in a line of poetry, usually near the middle of the line. There is a caesura right after the question mark in the first line of this sonnet by Elizabeth Barrett Browning: "How do I love thee? Let me count the ways."

**consonance** The repetition of similar consonant sounds, especially at the ends of words, as in *lost* and *past* or *confess* and *dismiss.*

**couplet** In a poem, a pair of lines that are the same length and usually rhyme and form a complete thought. Shakespearean sonnets usually end in a couplet.

**dactyl** A metrical foot of three syllables, one long (or stressed) followed by two short (or unstressed), as in *happily*. The dactyl is the reverse of the anapest.

**elegy** A poem that laments the death of a person, or one that is simply sad and thoughtful. An example of this type of poem is Thomas Gray's "Elegy Written in a Country Churchyard."

**enjambment** The continuation of a complete idea (a sentence or clause) from one line or couplet of a poem to the next line or couplet without a pause. An example of enjambment can be found in the first line of Joyce Kilmer's poem *Trees:* "I think that I shall never see/A poem as lovely as a tree."

**envoy** The shorter final stanza of a poem, as in a ballade.

**epic** A long, serious poem that tells the story of a heroic figure. Two of the most famous epic poems are the *Iliad* and the *Odyssey* by Homer, which tell about the Trojan War and the adventures of Odysseus on his voyage home after the war.

**epigram** A very short, witty poem: "Sir, I admit your general rule,/That every poet is a fool,/But you yourself may serve to show it,/That every fool is not a poet." (Samuel Taylor Coleridge)

**figure of speech** A verbal expression in which words or sounds are arranged in a particular way to achieve a particular effect. Figures of speech are organized into different categories, such as alliteration, assonance, metaphor, metonymy, onomatopoeia, simile, and synecdoche.

**foot** Two or more syllables that together make up the smallest unit of rhythm in a poem. For example, an iamb is a foot that has two syllables, one unstressed followed by one stressed. An anapest has three syllables, two unstressed followed by one stressed.

**free verse** Poetry composed of either rhymed or unrhymed lines that have no set meter.

**haiku** A Japanese poem composed of three unrhymed lines of five, seven, and five syllables. Haiku often reflect on some aspect of nature.

**heptameter** A line of poetry that has seven metrical feet.

**hexameter** A line of poetry that has six metrical feet.

**iamb** A metrical foot of two syllables, one short (or unstressed) and one long (or stressed). There are four iambs in the line "Come **live**/ with **me**/ and **be**/ my **love**," from a poem by Christopher Marlowe. (The stressed syllables are in bold.) The iamb is the reverse of the trochee.

**iambic pentameter** A type of meter in poetry, in which there are five iambs to a line. (The prefix *penta-* means "five," as in *pentagon*, a geometrical figure with five sides. *Meter* refers to rhythmic units. In a line of iambic pentameter, there are five rhythmic units that are iambs.) Shakespeare's plays were written mostly in iambic pentameter, which is the most common type of meter in English poetry. An example of an iambic pentameter line from Shakespeare's *Romeo and Juliet* is "But **soft!**/ What **light**/ through **yon**/der **win**/dow **breaks**?" (The stressed syllables are in bold.)

**idyll, or idyl** Either a short poem depicting a peaceful, idealized country scene, or a long poem that tells a story about heroic deeds or extraordinary events set in the distant past. *Idylls of the King*, by Alfred Lord Tennyson, is about King Arthur and the Knights of the Round Table.

**limerick** A light, humorous poem of five usually anapestic lines with the rhyme scheme of *aabba*.

**lyric** A poem, such as a sonnet or an ode, that expresses the thoughts and feelings of the poet. A lyric poem may resemble a song in form or style.

**metaphor** A figure of speech in which two things are compared, usually by saying one thing is another, or by substituting a more descriptive word for the more common or usual word that would be expected. Some examples of metaphors: *the world's a stage, he was a lion in battle, drowning in debt,* and *a sea of troubles.*

**meter** The arrangement of a line of poetry by the number of syllables and the rhythm of accented (or stressed) syllables.

**metonymy** A figure of speech in which one word is substituted for another with which it is closely associated. For example, in the expression *The pen* *is mightier than the sword*, the word *pen* is used for "the written word," and *sword* is used for "military power."

**ode** A lyric poem that is serious and thoughtful in tone and has a very precise, formal structure. John Keats's "Ode on a Grecian Urn" is a famous example of this type of poem.

**onomatopoeia** A figure of speech in which words are used to imitate sounds. Examples of onomatopoeic words are *buzz, hiss, zing, clippety-clop, cock-a-doodle-do, pop, splat, thump,* and *tick-tock.*

**pentameter** A line of poetry that has five metrical feet.

**personification** A figure of speech in which things or abstract ideas are given human attributes: *dead leaves dance in the wind, blind justice.*

**quatrain** A stanza or poem of four lines.

**refrain** A line or group of lines that is repeated throughout a poem, usually after every stanza.

**rhyme** The occurrence of the same or similar sounds at the end of two or more words. When the rhyme occurs in a final stressed syllable, it is said to be masculine: *cat/hat, desire/fire, observe/deserve.* When the rhyme occurs in a final unstressed syllable, it is said to be feminine: *longing/yearning.* The pattern of rhyme in a stanza or poem is shown usually by using a different letter for each final sound. In a poem with an *aabba* rhyme scheme, the first, second, and fifth lines end in one sound, and the third and fourth lines end in another.

**scansion** The analysis of a poem's meter. This is usually done by marking the stressed and unstressed syllables in each line and then, based on the pattern of the stresses, dividing the line into feet.

**simile** A figure of speech in which two things are compared using the word "like" or "as." An example of a simile using *like* occurs in Langston Hughes's poem *Harlem*: "What happens to a dream deferred?/ Does it dry up/ like a raisin in the sun?"

**sonnet** A lyric poem that is 14 lines long. Italian (or Petrarchan) sonnets are divided into two quatrains and a six-line "sestet," with the rhyme scheme *abba abba cdecde* (or *cdcdcd*). English (or Shakespearean) sonnets are composed of three quatrains and a final couplet, with a rhyme scheme of *abab cdcd efef gg.* English sonnets are written generally in iambic pentameter.

**spondee** A metrical foot of two syllables, both of which arc long (or stressed).

**stanza** Two or more lines of poetry that together form one of the divisions of a poem. The stanzas of a poem are usually of the same length and follow the same pattern of meter and rhyme.

**stress** The prominence or emphasis given to particular syllables. Stressed syllables usually stand out because they have long, rather than short, vowels, or because they have a different pitch or are louder than other syllables.

**synecdoche** A figure of speech in which a part is used to designate the whole or the whole is used to designate a part. For example, the phrase "all hands on deck" means "all men on deck," not just their hands. The reverse situation, in which the whole is used for a part, occurs in the sentence "The U.S. beat Russia in the final game," where the U.S. and Russia stand for "the U.S. team" and "the Russian team," respectively.

**tetrameter** A line of poetry that has four metrical feet.

**trochee** A metrical foot of two syllables, one long (or stressed) and one short (or unstressed). An easy way to remember the trochee is to memorize the first line of a lighthearted poem by Samuel Taylor Coleridge, which demonstrates the use of various kinds of metrical feet: "**Tro**chee/ **trips** from/ **long** to/ **short**." (The stressed syllables are in bold.) The trochee is the reverse of the iamb.

## Some Basic Phrases in Other Languages

| | The language itself | hello | good bye | please | thank you | English | yes | no | traditional toast |
|---|---|---|---|---|---|---|---|---|---|
| German | Deutsch | hallo | auf Wiedersehen | bitte | danke | Englisch | ja | nein | prosit |
| Dutch | Nederlands | hallo | tot ziens | alstublieft | dankjewel | engels | ja | nee | proost |
| Danish | dansk | hej | farvel | (1) | tak | engelsk | ja | nej | skål |
| Swedish | svenska | hej | hejdå | tack | tack | engelska | ja | nej | skål |
| French | français | bonjour | au revoir | s'il vous plaît | merci | anglais | oui | non | santé |
| Spanish | español | hola | adiós | por favor | gracias | inglés | sí | no | salud |
| | | | | | | | | | |
| Hebrew | ivrit | shalom | lehitraot | bevakasha | toda | anglit | ken | lo | le-chaim |
| Irish | Gaeilge | fáilte | slán | le do thoil | go raibh maith agat | Béarla | sea[2] | ní ha[3] | slainte |
| Swahili | Kiswahili | (4) | kwa heri | tafadhali | asante | Kingereza | ndiyo | siyo | — |
| Japanese | nihongo | konnichiwa | sayonara | kudasai | arigatou | eigo | hai | iie | kanpai |
| Finnish | suomi | päivää | näkemiin | (1) | kiitos | englanti | kyllä | ei | kippis |
| Indonesian | bahasa Indonesia | selamat pagi | selamat tinggal[5] | tolong | terima kasih | bahasa Inggris | ya | tidak | — |

1. There is no single word or expression that directly corresponds to "please." Polite requests are made in different ways.
2. Literally, "it is." This can only be used in answering a question with the verb "to be." In Irish there is no word for "yes" or "no." Instead, the speaker repeats the verb from the question in the affirmative or the negative: Did you sleep well? I did. Are you coming? I am not. 3. Literally, "it is not." See above. 4. There is no single word for "hello." Which greeting is used will depend on the relative ages, number (singular or plural), and/or race of the speakers. For example, "hujambo," reply "sijambo," would be used by two people of similar age and race, whereas "jambo," reply "jambo," would be used by a white person and a black person. 5. Said by the person leaving; "selamat jalan" is said by the person staying.

## Foreign Words and Phrases

The English meanings given below are not necessarily literal translations. Foreign words and phrases should be set in italics (or underlined if written in longhand) if their meanings are likely to be unknown to the reader. Whether the expression is familiar or unfamiliar, however, is a matter of judgment. Below, all foreign words have been italicized for the sake of emphasis.

**ad absurdum**   (ad ab-sir'dum) [Lat.]: to the point of absurdity. "He tediously repeated his argument *ad absurdum.*"

**ad infinitum**   (ad in-fun-eye'tum) [Lat.]: to infinity. "The lecture seemed to drone on *ad infinitum.*"

**ad nauseam**   (ad noz'ee-um) [Lat.]: to a sickening degree. "The politician uttered one platitude after another *ad nauseam.*"

**aficionado**   (uh-fish'ya-nah'doh) [Span.]: an ardent devotee. "I was surprised at what a baseball *aficionado* she had become."

**annus mirabilis**   (an'us muh-ra'buh-lis) [Lat.]: wonderful year. "Last year was the *annus mirabilis* for my company."

**a priori**   (ah pree or'ee) [Lat.]: based on theory rather than observation. "The fact that their house is in such disrepair suggests *a priori* that they are having financial difficulties."

**au courant**   (oh' koo-rahn') [Fr.]: up-to-date. "The shoes, the hair, the clothes—every last detail of her dress, in fact—was utterly *au courant.*"

**beau geste**   (boh zhest') [Fr.]: a fine or noble gesture, often futile. "My fellow writers supported me by writing letters of protest to the publisher, but their *beau geste* could not prevent the inevitable."

**beau monde**   (boh' mond') [Fr.]: high society. "Such elegant decor would impress even the *beau monde.*"

**bête noire**   (bet nwahr') [Fr.]: something or someone particularly disliked. "Talk of the good old college days way back when had become his *bête noire,* and he began to avoid his school friends."

**bona fide**   (boh'na fide) [Lat.]: in good faith; genuine. "For all her reticence and modesty, it was clear that she was a *bona fide* expert in her field."

**bon mot**   (bon moe') [Fr.]: a witty remark or comment. "One *bon mot* after another flew out of his mouth, charming the audience."

**bon vivant**   (bon vee-vahnt') [Fr.]: a person who lives luxuriously and enjoys good food and drink. "It's true he's quite the *bon vivant,* but when he gets down to business he conducts himself like a Spartan."

**carpe diem**   (kar'pay dee'um) [Lat.]: seize the day. "So what if you have an 8:00 a.m. meeting tomorrow and a full day of appointments? *Carpe diem!*"

**carte blanche**   (kart blonsh') [Fr.]: unrestricted power to act on one's own. "I may have *carte blanche* around the office, but at home I'm a slave to my family's demands."

**cause célèbre**   (koz suh-leb'ruh) [Fr.]: a widely known controversial case or issue. "The Sacco and Vanzetti trial became an international *cause célèbre* during the 1920s."

**caveat emptor**   (kav'ee-ot emp'tor) [Lat.]: let the buyer beware. "Before you leap at that real estate deal, *caveat emptor!*"

**comme ci comme ça**   (kom see' kom sah') [Fr.]: so-so. "The plans for the party strike me as *comme ci comme ça.*"

**comme il faut**   (kom eel foe') [Fr.]: as it should be; fitting. "His end was truly *comme il faut.*"

**coup de grâce**   (koo de grahss') [Fr.]: finishing blow. "After an already wildly successful day, the *coup de grâce* came when she won best all-around athlete."

**cri de coeur**   (kree' de kur') [Fr.]: heartfelt appeal. "About to leave the podium, he made a final *cri de coeur* to his people to end the bloodshed."

**de rigueur**   (duh ree-gur') [Fr.]: strictly required, by etiquette, usage, or fashion. "Loudly proclaiming one's support for radical causes had become *de rigueur* among her crowd."

**deus ex machina**   (day'us ex mahk'uh-nuh) [Lat.]: a contrived device to resolve a situation. "Stretching plausibility, the movie concluded with a *deus ex machina* ending in which everyone was rescued at the last minute."

**dolce vita**   (dole'chay vee'tuh) [Ital.]: sweet life; the good life perceived as one of physical pleasure and self-indulgence. "My vacation this year is going to be two uninterrupted weeks of *dolce vita.*"

**Doppelgänger\***   (dop'pul-gang-ur) [Ger.]: a ghostly double or counterpart of a living person. "I could not shake the sense that some shadowy *Doppelgänger* echoed my every move."

**enfant terrible**   (ahn-fahn' tay-reeb'luh) [Fr.]: an incorrigible child; an outrageously outspoken or bold person. "He played the role of *enfant terrible,* jolting us with his blunt assessment."

**entre nous**   (ahn'truh noo') [Fr.]: between ourselves; confidentially. "*Entre nous,* their marriage is on the rocks."

**ex cathedra**   (ex kuh-thee'druh) [Lat.]: with authority; used especially of those pronouncements of the pope that are considered infallible. "I resigned myself to obeying; my father's opinions were *ex cathedra* in our household."

**ex post facto**   (ex' post fak'toh) [Lat.]: retroactively. "I certainly hope that the change in policy will be honored *ex post facto.*"

**fait accompli**   (fate ah-kom-plee') [Fr.]: an accomplished fact, presumably irreversible. "There's no use protesting—it's a *fait accompli.*"

**faux pas**   (foh pah') [Fr.]: a social blunder. "Suddenly, she realized she had unwittingly committed yet another *faux pas.*"

**flagrante delicto**   (fla-grahn'tee di-lik'toh) [Lat.]: in the act. "The detective realized that without hard evidence he had no case; he would have to catch the culprit *flagrante delicto.*"

**glasnost**   (glaz'nohst) [Rus.]: open and frank discussion: initiated by Mikhail Gorbachev in 1985 in the Soviet Union. "Once the old chairman retired, the spirit of *glasnost* pervaded the department."

**hoi polloi**   (hoy' puh-loy') [Gk.]: the common people. "Marie Antoinette recommended cake to the *hoi polloi.*"

**in loco parentis**   (in loh'koh pa-ren'tiss) [Lat.]: in the place of a parent. "The court appointed a guardian for the children, to serve *in loco parentis.*"

**in situ** (in sit′too) [Lat.]: situated in the original or natural position. "I prefer seeing statues *in situ* rather than in the confines of a museum."

**in vino veritas** (in vee′no vare′i-toss) [Lat.]: in wine there is truth. "By the end of the party, several of the guests had made a good deal of their private lives public, prompting the host to murmur to his wife, '*in vino veritas.*'"

**ipso facto** (ip′soh fak′toh) [Lat.]: by the fact itself. "An extremist, *ipso facto,* cannot become part of a coalition."

**je ne sais quoi** (zhun say kwah′) [Fr.]: I know not what; an elusive quality. "She couldn't explain it, but there was something *je ne sais quoi* about him that she found devastatingly attractive."

**mano a mano** (mah′no ah mah′no) [Span.]: directly or face-to-face in a confrontation or conflict. "'Stay out of it,' he admonished his friends, 'I want to handle this guy *mano a mano.*'"

**mea culpa** (may′uh kul′puh) [Lat.]: I am to blame. "His *mea culpa* was so offhand that I hardly think he meant it."

**memento mori** (muh-men′toh more′ee) [Lat.]: a reminder that you must die. "The skull rested on the mantlepiece as a *memento mori.*"

**modus operandi** (moh′dus op-er-an′dee) [Lat.]: a method of operating. "Her *modus operandi* is to sugarcoat the truth so thoroughly that the news almost seems welcome."

**mot juste** (moh zhoost′) [Fr.]: the exact, appropriate word. "'Rats!' screamed the defiant three-year-old, immensely proud of his *mot juste.*"

**ne plus ultra** (nee′ plus ul′truh) [Lat.]: the most intense degree of a quality or state. "Pulling it from the box, he realized he was face to face with the *ne plus ultra* of computers."

**nom de plume** (nom duh ploom′) [Fr.]: pen name. "Deciding it was time to sit down and begin a novel, the would-be writer spent the first several hours deciding upon a suitable *nom de plume.*"

**nota bene** (noh′tuh ben′nee) [Ital.]: note well; take notice. "Her postcard included a reminder, *nota bene,* I'll be returning on the 11 o'clock train."

**persona non grata** (per-soh′nuh non grah′tuh) [Lat.]: unacceptable or unwelcome person. "Once I was cut out of the will, I became *persona non grata* among my relatives."

**pro bono** (pro boh′noh) [Lat.]: done or donated without charge; free. "The lawyer's *pro bono* work gave him a sense of value that his work on behalf of the corporation could not."

**quid pro quo** (kwid′ pro kwoh′) [Lat.]: something for something; an equal exchange. "She vowed that when she had the means, she would return his favors *quid pro quo.*"

**sans souci** (sahn soo-see′) [Fr.]: carefree. "Their mood was definitely *sans souci.*"

**savoir-faire** (sav′wahr fair′) [Fr.]: the ability to say and do the correct thing. "She presided over the gathering with impressive *savoir-faire.*"

**sine qua non** (sin′ay kwah nohn′) [Lat.]: indispensable. "Lemon is the *sine qua non* of this recipe."

**terra incognita** (tare′uh in-kog-nee′tuh) [Lat.]: unknown territory. "When the conversation suddenly switched from contemporary fiction to medieval Albanian playwrights, he felt himself entering *terra incognita.*"

**veni, vidi, vici** (ven′ee vee′dee vee′chee) [Lat.]: I came, I saw, I conquered. "After the takeover the business mogul gloated, '*veni, vidi, vici.*'"

**vox populi** (voks pop′yoo-lie) [Lat.]: the voice of the people. "My sentiments echo those of the *vox populi.*"

**Wanderjahr*** (vahn′der-yahr) [Ger.]: a year or period of travel, especially following one's schooling. "The trio took off on their *Wanderjahr* soon after they graduated, to circle the globe by bicycle."

**Weltschmerz*** (velt′shmerts) [Ger.]: sorrow over the evils of the world. "His poetry expressed a certain *Weltschmerz,* or world-weariness."

**Zeitgeist*** (zite′guyst) [Ger.]: the spirit of the time; general trend of thought or feeling characteristic of a particular period of time. "She blamed it on the *Zeitgeist,* which encouraged hedonistic excess."

---

*German nouns are capitalized. A familiar German expression that is not italicized, however, should be lowercased, following the English conventions of not capitalizing common nouns. "His proclivities leaned more to the occult than to the philosophical: a poltergeist he could understand; the *Zeitgeist* he could not."

## Most Widely Spoken Languages in the World

| Language | Approx. number of speakers |
|---|---|
| 1. Chinese (Mandarin) | 1,075,000,000 |
| 2. English | 514,000,000 |
| 3. Hindustani | 496,000,000 |
| 4. Spanish | 425,000,000 |
| 5. Russian | 275,000,000 |
| 6. Arabic | 256,000,000 |
| 7. Bengali | 215,000,000 |
| 8. Portuguese | 194,000,000 |
| 9. Malay-Indonesian | 176,000,000 |
| 10. French | 129,000,000 |

*Source: Ethnologue,* 13th Edition and other sources.

## Most Studied Foreign Languages in the U.S.[1]

| Language | Number of BA degrees awarded |
|---|---|
| 1. Spanish | 7,031 |
| 2. French | 2,514 |
| 3. German | 1,125 |
| 4. Russian | 340 |
| 5. Japanese | 321 |
| 6. Italian | 237 |
| 7. Chinese | 183 |
| 8. Latin | 79 |
| 9. Portuguese | 33 |
| 10. Ancient Greek | 26 |

1. By number of bachelor degrees awarded in 1999–2000. *Source:* U.S. Dept. of Education, National Center for Education Statistics, *Digest of Education Statistics 2001.*

# American Sign Language

Sign language for the deaf was first systematized in France during the 18th century by Abbot Charles-Michel l'Epée. French Sign Language (FSL) was brought to the United States in 1816 by Thomas Gallaudet, founder of the American School for the Deaf in Hartford, Conn. He developed American Sign Language (ASL), a language of gestures and hand symbols that express words and concepts. It is the fourth most used language in the United States today.

In most respects, sign language is just like any spoken language, with a rich vocabulary and a highly organized, rule-governed grammar. The only difference is that in sign language, information is processed through the eyes rather than the ears. Thus, facial expression and body movement play an important part in conveying information.

In spoken language, the relationship between most words and the objects and concepts they represent is arbitrary—there is nothing about the word "tree" that actually suggests a tree, either in the way it is spelled or pronounced. In the same way, in sign language most signs do not suggest, or imitate, the thing or idea they represent, and must be learned. Sign language may be acquired naturally as a child's first language, or it may be learned through study and practice.

Sign language shares other similarities with spoken languages. Like any living language, ASL grows and changes over time to accommodate native users' needs. ASL also has regional varieties, equivalent to spoken accents, with different signs being used in different parts of the country.

Along with sign language and lip reading, many deaf people also communicate with the manual alphabet, which uses finger positions that correspond to the letters of the alphabet to spell out words and names.

## American Manual Alphabet

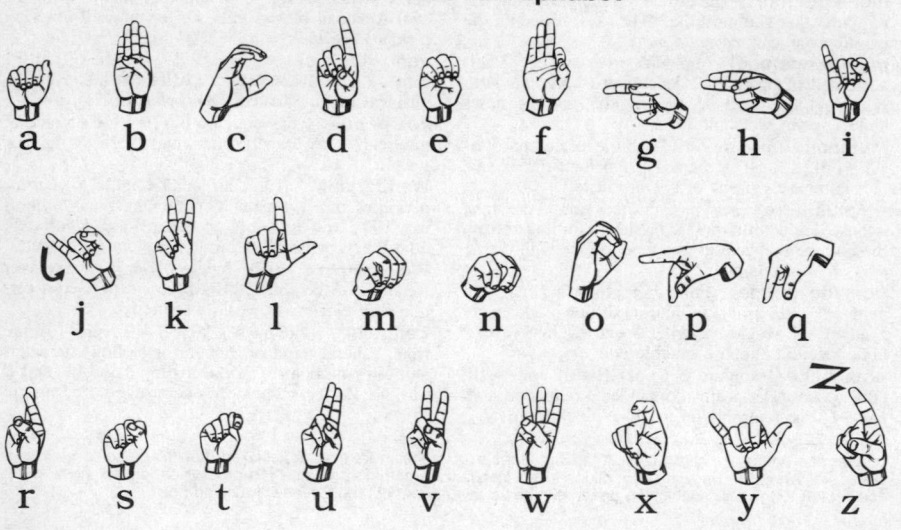

## Frequently Misspelled Words

| | | | | |
|---|---|---|---|---|
| absence | decease | guarantee | miniature | pumpkin |
| address | deceive | harass | miscellaneous | raspberry |
| advice | definite | height | mischievous | receive |
| all right | descent | humorous | misspell | rhythm |
| arctic | desperate | independent | mysterious | sacrilegious |
| beginning | device | jealous | necessary | science |
| believe | disastrous | jewelry | neighbor | scissors |
| bicycle | ecstasy | judgment | nuclear | separate |
| broccoli | embarrass | ketchup | occasion | sincerely |
| bureau | exercise | knowledge | occurrence | special |
| calendar | fascinate | leisure | odyssey | thorough |
| camaraderie | February | library | piece | through |
| ceiling | fiery | license | pigeon | truly |
| cemetery | fluorescent | maintenance | playwright | until |
| changeable | foreign | mathematics | precede | Wednesday |
| conscientious | government | mediocre | prejudice | weird |
| conscious | grateful | millennium | privilege | you're |

## National Spelling Bee

The National Spelling Bee was launched by the Louisville, Kentucky, *Courier-Journal* in 1925. With competitions, cash prizes, and a trip to the nation's capital, it was hoped the Bee would stimulate "general interest among pupils in a dull subject."

The Scripps Howard News Service took over the Bee in 1941. Over the years the national finals have grown from a mere 9 contestants to about 250, and competition week is marked by ice-cream socials, talent shows, and other events. At the end of the 2002 activities, 13-year-old champion Pratyush Buddiga took home $12,000 cash, among other prizes, for correctly spelling *prospicience*. Here are the winning words that made past spellers into national champions.

| | | | | | | | |
|---|---|---|---|---|---|---|---|
| 1925 | gladiolus | 1945 | NO BEE | 1965 | eczema | 1984 | luge |
| 1926 | abrogate | 1946 | semaphore | 1966 | ratoon | 1985 | milieu |
| 1927 | luxuriance | 1947 | chlorophyll | 1967 | chihuahua | 1986 | odontalgia |
| 1928 | albumen | 1948 | psychiatry | 1968 | abalone | 1987 | staphylococci |
| 1929 | asceticism | 1949 | dulcimer | 1969 | interlocutory | 1988 | elegiacal |
| 1930 | fracas | 1950 | haruspex | 1970 | croissant | 1989 | spoliator |
| 1931 | foulard | 1951 | insouciant | 1971 | shalloon | 1990 | fibranne |
| 1932 | knack | 1952 | vignette | 1972 | macerate | 1991 | antipyretic |
| 1933 | propitiatory | 1953 | soubrette | 1973 | vouchsafe | 1992 | lyceum |
| 1934 | deteriorating | 1954 | transept | 1974 | hydrophyte | 1993 | kamikaze |
| 1935 | intelligible | 1955 | custaceology | 1975 | incisor | 1994 | antediluvian |
| 1936 | interning | 1956 | condominium | 1976 | narcolepsy | 1995 | xanthosis |
| 1937 | promiscuous | 1957 | schappe | 1977 | cambist | 1996 | vivisepulture |
| 1938 | sanitarium | 1958 | syllepsis | 1978 | deification | 1997 | euonym |
| 1939 | canonical | 1959 | cacolet | 1979 | maculature | 1998 | chiaroscurist |
| 1940 | therapy | 1960 | troche | 1980 | elucubrate | 1999 | logorrhea |
| 1941 | initials | 1961 | smaragdine | 1981 | sarcophagus | 2000 | demarche |
| 1942 | sacrilegious | 1962 | esquamulose | 1982 | psoriasis | 2001 | succedaneum |
| 1943 | NO BEE | 1963 | equipage | 1983 | Purim | 2002 | prospicience |
| 1944 | NO BEE | 1964 | sycophant | | | | |

## Easily Confused Words

**affect / effect** *Effect* is usually a noun that means a result or the power to produce a result: "The sound of the falling rain had a calming effect, nearly putting me to sleep." *Affect* is usually a verb that means to have an influence on: "His loud humming was affecting my ability to concentrate." Note that *effect* can also be a verb meaning to bring about or execute: "The speaker's somber tone effected a dampening in the general mood of the audience."

**all together / altogether** *All together* is applied to people or things that are being treated as a group. "We put the pots and pans all together on the shelf." *All together* is the form that must be used if the sentence can be reworded so that *all* and *together* are separated by other words: "We put all the pots and pans together on the shelf." *Altogether* is used to mean entirely: "I am altogether pleased to be receiving this award."

**allusion / illusion** *Allusion* is a noun that means an indirect reference: "The speech made allusions to the final report." *Illusion* is a noun that means a misconception. "The policy is nothing but an illusion of reform."

**alternately / alternatively** *Alternately* is an adverb that means in turn, one after the other; we alternately spun the wheel in the game." *Alternatively* is an adverb that means on the other hand; one or the other: "You can choose a large bookcase or, alternatively, you can buy two small ones."

**a.m. / p.m.** The abbreviation *a.m.* (from Latin *ante meridiem,* before noon) is used to refer to any hour between midnight and noon. Similarly, *p.m.* (from Latin *post meridiem,* after noon) is used to refer to any hour between noon and midnight. Midnight is 12 A.M. and noon is 12 P.M.

**beside / besides** *Beside* is a preposition that means next to: "Stand here beside me." *Besides* is an adverb that means also: "Besides, I need to tell you about the new products my company offers."

**bimonthly / semimonthly** *Bimonthly* is an adjective that means every two months: "I brought the cake for the bimonthly office party." *Bimonthly* is also a noun that means a publication issued every two months: "The company publishes several popular bimonthlies." *Semimonthly* is an adjective that means happening twice a month: "We have semimonthly meetings on the 1st and the 15th."

**capital / capitol** The city or town that is the seat of government is called the *capital;* the building in which the legislative assembly meets is the *capitol.* The term *capital* can also refer to an accumulation of wealth or to a capital letter.

**cite / site** *Cite* is a verb that means to quote as an authority or example: "I cited several eminent scholars in my study of water resources." It also means to recognize formally: "The public official was cited for service to the city." It can also mean to summon before a court of law: "Last year the company was cited for pollution violations." *Site* is a noun meaning location: "They chose a new site for the factory just outside town."

**complement / compliment** *Complement* is a noun or verb that means something that completes or makes up a whole: "The red sweater is a perfect complement to the outfit." *Compliment* is a noun or verb that means an expression of praise or admiration: "I received many compliments about my new outfit."

**comprise / compose** According to the traditional rule, the whole comprises the parts, and the parts compose the whole. Thus, the board comprises five members, whereas five members compose (or make up) the board. It is also correct to say that the board is composed (not comprised) of five members.

**concurrent / consecutive** *Concurrent* is an adjective that means simultaneous or happening at the same time as something else: "The concurrent strikes of several unions crippled the economy." *Consecutive* means successive or following one after the other: "The union called three consecutive strikes in one year."

**connote / denote** *Connote* is a verb that means to imply or suggest: "The word 'espionage' connotes mystery and intrigue." *Denote* is a verb that means to indicate or refer to specifically: "The symbol for 'pi' denotes the number 3.14159."

**convince / persuade** Strictly speaking, one convinces a person that something is true but persuades a person to do something. "Pointing out that I was overworked, my friends persuaded [not convinced] me to take a vacation. Now that I'm relaxing on the beach with my book, I am convinced [not persuaded] that they were right." Following this rule, *convince* should not be used with an infinitive.

**council / councilor / counsel / counselor** A *councilor* is a member of a *council,* which is an assembly called together for discussion or deliberation. A *counselor* is one who gives *counsel,* which is advice or guidance. More specifically, a *counselor* can be an attorney or a supervisor at camp.

**discreet / discrete** *Discreet* is an adjective that means prudent, circumspect, or modest: "Their discreet comments about the negotiations led the reporters to expect an early settlement." *Discrete* is an adjective that means separate or individually distinct: "Each company in the conglomerate operates as a discrete entity."

**disinterested / uninterested** *Disinterested* is an adjective that means unbiased or impartial: "We appealed to the disinterested mediator to facilitate the negotiations." *Uninterested* is an adjective that means not interested or indifferent: "They seemed uninterested in our offer."

**emigrant / immigrant** *Emigrant* is a noun that means one who leaves one's native country to settle in another: "The emigrants spent four weeks aboard ship before landing in Los Angeles." *Immigrant* is a noun that means one who enters and settles in a new country: "Most of the immigrants easily found jobs."

**farther / further** *Farther* is an adjective and adverb that means to or at a more distant point: "We drove 50 miles today; tomorrow, we will travel 100 miles farther." *Further* is an adjective and adverb that means to or at a greater extent or degree: "We won't be able to suggest a solution until we are further along in our evaluation of the problem." It can also mean in addition or moreover: "They stated further that they would not change the policy."

**few / less** *Few* is an adjective that means small in number. It is used with countable objects: "This department has few employees." *Less* is an adjective that means small in amount or degree. It is used with objects of indivisible mass: "Which jar holds less water?"

**figuratively / literally** *Figuratively* is an adverb that means metaphorically or symbolically: "Happening upon the shadowy figure, they figuratively jumped out of their shoes." *Literally* is an adverb that means word for word or according to the exact meaning of the words: "I translated the Latin passage literally."

**flammable / inflammable** These two words are actually synonyms, both meaning easily set on fire. "The highly flammable (inflammable) fuel was stored safely in a specially built tank."

**flaunt / flout** To *flaunt* means to show off shamelessly: "Eager to flaunt her knowledge of a wide range of topics, Helene dreamed of appearing on a TV trivia show." To *flout* means to show scorn or contempt for: "Lewis disliked boarding school and took every opportunity to flout the house rules."

**foreword / forward** *Foreword* is a noun that means an introductory note or preface: "In my foreword I explained my reasons for writing the book." *Forward* is an adjective or adverb that means toward the front: "I sat in the forward section of the bus. Please step forward when your name is called." *Forward* is also a verb that means to send on: "Forward the letter to the customer's new address."

**founder / flounder** In its primary sense *founder* means to sink below the surface of the water: "The ship foundered after colliding with an iceberg." By extension, *founder* means to fail utterly. *Flounder* means to move about clumsily, or to act or proceed with confusion. A good synonym for *flounder* is blunder: "After floundering through the first half of the course, Amy finally passed with the help of a tutor."

**hanged / hung** *Hanged* is the past tense and past participle of hang when the meaning is to execute by suspending by the neck: "They hanged the prisoner for treason." "The convicted killer was hanged at dawn." *Hung* is the past tense and participle of hang when the meaning is to suspend from above with no support from below: "I hung the painting on the wall." "The painting was hung at a crooked angle."

**historic / historical** In general usage, *historic* refers to what is important in history, while *historical* applies more broadly to whatever existed in the past whether it was important or not: "A historic summit meeting between the prime ministers; historical buildings torn down in the redevelopment."

**it's / its** *It's* is a contraction for it is, whereas *its* is the possessive form of it: "It's a shame that we cannot talk about its size."

**laid / lain / lay** *Laid* is the past tense and the past participle of the verb lay and not the past tense of lie. *Lay* is the past tense of the verb lie and *lain* is the past participle: "He laid his books down and lay down on the couch, where he has lain for an hour."

**lend / loan** Although some people feel *loan* should only be used as a noun, *lend* and *loan* are both acceptable as verbs in standard English: "Can you lend (loan) me a dollar?" However, only *lend* should be used in figurative senses: "Will you lend me a hand?"

**principal / principle** *Principal* is a noun that means a person who holds a high position or plays an important role: "The school principal has 20 years of teaching experience." It also means a sum of money on which interest accrues: "The investors did not lose their principal." *Principal* is also an adjective that means chief or leading: "The necessity of moving to another city was the principal reason I turned down the job offer." *Principle* is a noun that means a rule or standard: "They refused to compromise their principles."

# U.S. Societies and Associations

Names are listed alphabetically according to key word in title; figure in parentheses is year of founding; other figure is membership.

The following is a partial list selected for general readership interest. A comprehensive listing of approximately 23,000 national and international organizations can be found in the *Encyclopedia of Associations,* 34th ed., 2000, published by Gale Research Company, 835 Penobscot Building, 645 Griswold St., Detroit, Mich. 48226-4049, available in most public libraries.

**AARP (American Association of Retired Persons) (1958):** 601 E. St. N.W., Washington, D.C. 20049. 33,000,000. Phone: (800) 424-3410. www.aarp.org.

**Abortion Federation, National (1977):** 1755 Mass. Ave., Ste. 600, Washington, D.C. 20036. Phone: (202) 667-5881www.prochoice.org.

**Accountants, American Institute of Certified Public (1887):** 1211 Avenue of the Americas, New York, N.Y. 10036-8775. 330,000. Phone: (212) 596-6200. www.aicpa.org.

**ACSM: American Congress on Surveying and Mapping (1941):** 6 Montgomery Village Ave., Ste. 403, Gaithersburg, Md. 20879. 8,000. Phone: (240) 632-9716. www.acsm.net.

**Actors' Equity Association (1913):** 165 W. 46th St., New York, N.Y. 10036. 40,000. Phone: (212) 869-8530. www.actorsequity.org.

**Actuaries, Society of (1949):** 475 N. Martingale Rd., Ste. 800, Schaumburg, Ill. 60173-2226. 16,500. Phone: (847) 706-3500. www.soa.org.

**Adirondack Mountain Club (1922):** 814 Goggins Rd., Lake George, N.Y. 12845-4117. 22,000. Phone: (518) 668-4447. www.adk.org.

**Aeronautic Association, National (1905):** 1815 N. Fort Myer Dr., Ste. 500, Arlington, Va. 22209. 300,000. Phone: (703) 527-0229. www.naa-usa.org.

**Africa-American Institute, The (1953):** 380 Lexington Ave., New York, N.Y. 10168-4298. Phone: (212) 949-5666. http://www.aaionline.org/

**AFS Intercultural Programs—USA (American Field Service) (1947):** 198 Madison Avenue, 8th Flr., New York, N.Y. 10016. 100,000. Phone: (212) 299-9000. www.afs.org.

**Agricultural History Society (1919):** 603 Ross Hall/Dept. of History, Iowa State University, Ames, Iowa 50011. 1,400. Phone: (515) 294-5620. www.iastate.edu/~history_info/aghissoc.htm.

**Agronomy, American Society of (1907):** 677 S. Segoe Rd., Madison, Wis. 53711-1086. 11,400. Phone: (608) 273-8080; fax: (608) 273-2021. www.agronomy.org.

**Air & Waste Management Association (1907):** One Gateway Center, 3rd Flr., Pittsburgh, Pa. 15222. 14,000. Phone: (412) 232-3444. www.awma.org.

**Aircraft Association, Experimental (1953):** FAA Middle Canton, P.B. Box 3083, Oshkosh, Wis. 54903-3086. 170,000. Phone: (920) 426-4800. www.eaa.org.

**Aircraft Owners and Pilots Association (1939):** 421 Aviation Way, Frederick, Md. 21701-4798. 350,000. Phone: (301) 695-2000; fax: (301) 695-2375. www.aopa.org.

**Air Force Association (1946):** 1501 Lee Highway, Arlington, Va. 22209-1198. 150,000. Phone: (703) 247-5800. www.afa.org.

**Air Line Pilots Association (1931):** 1625 Massachusetts Ave. N.W., Washington, D.C. 20036 and 535 Herndon Pkwy., Herndon, Va. 20170. 50,000. Phone: (703) 689-2270. www.alpa.org.

**Al-Anon Family Group Headquarters, Inc. For families and friends of alcoholics. (1951):** 1600 Corporate Landing Pkwy., Virginia Beach, Va.

23454-5617. 33,000 groups worldwide. Phone: (757) 563-1600. www.al-anon.org.

**Alcoholics Anonymous (1935):** A.A. World Services, Inc., P.O. Box 459, New York, N.Y. 10163. 2,160,013. Phone: (212) 870-3400. www.aa.org.

**Alexander Graham Bell Association for the Deaf (1890):** 3417 Volta Place N.W., Washington, D.C. 20007-2778. 6,200. Phone: (202) 337-5220 V, 337-5221 TTY; fax: (202) 337-8314. www.agbell.org.

**Alzheimer's Association (1980):** 919 N. Michigan Ave., Ste. 1100, Chicago, Ill. 60611-1676. 200 chapters. Phone: (312) 335-8700; (800) 272-3900. www.alz.org.

**American Academy of Allergy, Asthma and Immunology (1943):** 611 E. Wells St., Milwaukee, Wis. 53202. 5,000. Phone: (414) 272-6071. www.aaaai.org.

**American Alliance for Health, Physical Education, Recreation and Dance (1885):** 1900 Association Dr., Reston, Va. 20191. 26,000. Phone: (800) 213-7193. www.aahperd.org.

**American Automobile Association (1902):** 1000 AAA Dr., Heathrow, Fla. 32746-5063. Phone: (407) 444-7000. www.aaa.com.

**American Civil Liberties Union (1920):** 125 Broad St., 18th Flr., New York, N.Y. 10004-2400. 275,000. Phone: (212) 549-2500. www.aclu.org.

**American Contract Bridge League (1927):** 2990 Airways Blvd., Memphis, Tenn. 38116-3847. Phone: (800) 467-1623; fax: (901) 398-7754. www.acbl.org.

**American Federation of Labor and Congress of Industrial Organizations (AFL-CIO) (1955):** 815 16th St. N.W., Washington, D.C. 20006. 13,000,000. Phone: (202) 637-5000. www.aflcio.org.

**American Federation of Musicians of the United States and Canada (1896):** 1501 Broadway, Ste. 600, Paramount Bldg., New York, N.Y. 10036. Phone: (212) 869-1330. www.afm.org.

**American Forests (1875):** P.O. Box 2000, Washington, D.C. 20013. 115,000. Phone: (202) 955-4500. www.americanforests.org.

**American Foundrymen's Society, Inc. (1896):** 505 State St., Des Plaines, Ill. 60016-8399. 13,000. Phone: (847) 824-0181; (800) 537-4237. www.afsinc.org.

**American Friends Service Committee (1917):** 1501 Cherry St., Philadelphia, Pa. 19102-1415. Phone: (215) 241-7000. www.afsc.org.

**American Geographical Society, The (1851):** 120 Wall St., Ste. 100, New York, N.Y. 10005-3904. 1,500. Phone: (212) 422-5456; fax: (212) 422-5480. email: amgeosoc@earthlink.net. www.amergeog.org.

**American Geriatrics Society (1942):** 350 Fifth Ave., Ste. 801, New York, N.Y. 10118. 6,000. Phone: (212) 308-1414; fax: (212) 832-8646. www.americangeriatrics.org.

**American Heart Association (1924):** 7272 Greenville Ave., Dallas, Tex. 75231-4596. 4,200,000 volunteers. Phone: (800) AHA-USA1. www.americanheart.org.

**American Historical Association (1884):** 400 A St. S.E., Washington, D.C. 20003-3889. 15,000. Phone: (202) 544-2422. email: aha@theaha.org. www.theaha.org.

**American Indian Affairs, Association on (1923):** Box 268, Sisseton, S.D. 57262. 40,000. Phone: (605) 698-3998. www.indian-affairs.org.

**American Jewish Committee (1906):** Jacob Blaustein Building, 165 East 56th Street, New York, N.Y. 10022. 100,000. Phone: (212) 751-4000. www.ajc.org.

**American Kennel Club (1884):** 260 Madison Ave., New York, N.Y. 10016. 500+ member clubs. Phone: (212) 696-8200; (919) 233-9767 (customer service). www.akc.org.

**American Legion, The (1919):** 700 N. Pennsylvania St., Indianapolis, Ind. 46206. 3,000,000. Phone: (317) 630-1200. www.legion.org.

**American Legion Auxiliary (1919):** 777 N. Meridian St., 3rd Flr., Indianapolis, Ind. 46204. 1,000,000. Phone: (317) 955-3845. www.legion-aux.org.

**American Mensa, Ltd. (1960):** 1229 Corporate Drive West, Arlington, Tex. 76006–6103. 50,000. Phone: (817) 607-0060. www.us.mensa.org.

**American Montessori Society (1960):** 281 Park Avenue South, 6th Flr., New York, N.Y. 10010-6102. Phone: (212) 358-1250; fax: (212) 358-1256. www.amshq.org.

**American Museum of Natural History (1869):** Central Park West at 79th St., New York, N.Y. 10024-5192. 500,000. Phone: (212) 769-5606. www.amnh.org.

**American Planning Association (1917) and American Institute of Certified Planners:** Administrative Offices: 122 S. Michigan Ave., Chicago, Ill. 60603. 30,000. Phone: (312) 431-9100. www.planning.org.

**Americans for Democratic Action, Inc. (1947):** 1625 K St. N.W., Ste. 210, Washington, D.C. 20006. 70,000. Phone: (202) 785-5980. www.adaction.org.

**American Society for Nutritional Sciences (1928):** 9650 Rockville Pike, Ste. 4500, Bethesda, Md. 20814-3990. 3,600. Phone: (301) 530-7050. www.faseb.org/asns.

**American Society for Public Administration (ASPA) (1939):** 1120 G St. N.W., Ste. 700, Washington, D.C. 20005. 12,000. Phone: (202) 393-7878. www.aspanet.org.

**American Universities, Association of (1900):** 1200 New York Avenue NW, Ste. 550, Washington, D.C. 20005. Phone: (202) 408-7500. www.aau.edu.

**American Water Resources Association (1964):** 4 W. Federal St., P.O. Box 1626, Middleburg, Va. 20118-1626. Phone: (540) 687-8390. www.awra.org.

**Amnesty International USA (1961):** 322 Eighth Ave., New York, N.Y. 10001. 300,000. Phone: (212) 807-8400. www.amnesty-usa.org.

**AMVETS (American Veterans of World War II, Korea, and Vietnam) (1943):** 4647 Forbes Blvd., Lanham, Md. 20706-4380. 250,000. Phone: (877) 7AMVETS. www.amvets.org.

**Animals, The American Society for the Prevention of Cruelty to (ASPCA) (1866):** 424 E. 92nd St., New York, N.Y. 10128-6804. 400,000+. Phone: (212) 876-7700. www.aspca.org.

**Animals, The Fund For, Inc. (1967):** 200 W. 57th St., New York, N.Y. 10019. 175,000. Phone: (212) 246-2096. www.fund.org.

**Anthropological Association, American (1902):** 4350 N. Fairfax Dr., Ste. 640, Arlington, Va. 22203-1620. 11,500. Phone: (703) 528-1902. www.aaanet.org.

**Anti-Defamation League (1913):** 823 United Nations Plaza, New York, N.Y. 10017-3560. Phone: (212) 885-7700. www.adl.org.

**Anti-Vivisection Society, The American (1883):** 801 Old York Rd., #204, Jenkintown, Pa. 19046-1685. 15,000. Phone: (215) 887-0816; fax: (215) 887-2088. www.aavs.org.

**Appraisers, American Society of (1936):** 555 Herndon Parkway, Ste. 125, Herndon, VA 20170. 6,500. Phone: (703) 478-2228. www.appraisers.org.

**Arboriculture, International Society of (1924):** P.O. Box 3129, Champaign, Ill. 61826-3129. 8,000. Phone: (217) 355-9411; fax (217) 355-9516. email: isa@isa-arbor.com. www2.champaign.isa-arbor.com.

**Archaeological Institute of America (1879):** 656 Beacon St., Boston, Mass. 02215-2006. 11,000. Phone: (617) 353-9361. email: aia@aai.bu.edu. www.archaeological.org.

**Architects, The American Institute of (1857):** 1735 New York Ave. N.W., Washington, D.C. 20006-5292. 59,000. Phone: (202) 626-7300. www.aia.org.

**Architectural Historians, Society of (1940):** 1365 N. Astor St., Chicago, Ill. 60610-2144. 4,000. Phone: (312) 573-1365; fax: (312) 573-1141. www.sah.org.

**Army, Association of the United States (1950):** 2425 Wilson Blvd., Arlington, Va. 22201-3385. 100,000+. Phone: (703) 841-4300. www.ausa.org.

**Arthritis Foundation (1948):** 1330 West Peachtree St., Atlanta, Ga. 30309. Over 150 local offices. Phone: (404) 872-7100; (800) 283-7800. www.arthritis.org.

**Arts, National Endowment for the (1965):** 1100 Pennsylvania Ave. N.W., Washington, D.C. 20506. Phone: (202) 682-5400. arts.endow.gov.

**ASM International ® (formerly the American Society for Metals) (1913):** 9639 Kinsman Rd., Materials Park, Ohio 44073-0002. 44,000. Phone: (440) 338-5151; fax: (440) 338-4634. www.asm-intl.org.

**Association for Investment Management and Research (1990):** 560 Ray C. Hunt Dr., Charlottesville, Va. 22903-0668. 36,000. Phone: (800) 247-8132. www.aimr.com.

**Astronomical Society, American (1899):** 2000 Florida Ave., Ste. 400, Washington, D.C. 20009. 6,300. Phone: (202) 328-2010. www.aas.org.

**Atheists, American (1963):** P.O. Box 5733, Parsippany, N.J. 07054-6733. 40,000 families. Phone: (908) 276-7300. www.atheists.org.

**Audubon Society, National (1905):** 700 Broadway, New York, N.Y. 10003-9562. 550,000. Phone: (212) 979-3000. www.audubon.org.

**Authors League of America (1912):** 330 W. 42nd St., 29th Flr., New York, N.Y. 10036-6902. 14,000. Phone: (212) 268-1208.

**Autism Society of America (1965):** 7910 Woodmont Ave., Ste. 300, Bethesda, Md. 20814-3015. 18,000+. Phone: (301) 657-0881; (800) 3AUTISM. www.autism-society.org.

**Automobile Club, National (1924):** 1151 East Hillsdale Blvd., Foster City, Calif. 94404. 200,000. Phone: (650) 294-7000. www.nationalautoclub.com.

**Bar Association, American (1878):** 541 N. Fairbanks Court, Chicago, Ill. 60611. 371,000. Phone: (312) 988-5522. www.abanet.org.

**Barber Shop Quartet Singing in America, Society for the Preservation and Encouragement of (SPEBSQSA, Inc.) (1938):** 6315 Harmony Lane, Kenosha, Wis. 53143. 34,000. Phone: (800) 876-SING. www.spebsqsa.org.

**Better Business Bureaus, Council of (1912):** 4200 Wilson Blvd., Ste. 800, Arlington, Va. 22203-1804. Phone: (703) 276-0100; fax: (703) 525-8277. www.bbb.org.

**Bible Society, American (1816):** 1865 Broadway, New York, N.Y. 10023-7505. Phone: (800) 32-BIBLE; (212) 408-1200. www.americanbible.org.

**Biblical Literature, Society of (1880):** 825 Houston Mill Road, Ste. 350, Atlanta, Ga. 30329. 7,000 members, 1,200 subscribers. Phone: (404) 727-3100; fax: (404) 727-3101. www.sbl-site.org.

**Big Brothers Big Sisters of America (1977):** 230 N. 13th St., Philadelphia, Pa. 19107. Phone: (215) 567-7000. www.bbbsa.org.

**Biochemistry and Molecular Biology, American Society for (1906):** 9650 Rockville Pike, Bethesda, Md. 20814. 10,000. Phone: (301) 530-7145. www.faseb.org/asbmb.

**Biological Sciences, American Institute of (1947):** 1444 I St. N.W., Ste. 200, Washington, D.C. 20005. 6,000. Phone: (202) 628-1500. www.aibs.org.

**Blind, American Council of the (1961):** 1155 15th St. N.W., Ste. 1004, Washington, D.C. 20005. 40,000. Phone: (202) 467-5081. www.acb.org.

**Blind, National Federation of the (1940):** 1800 Johnson St., Baltimore, Md. 21230. 50,000. Phone: (410) 659-9314. www.nfb.org.

**B'nai B'rith International (1843):** 1640 Rhode Island Ave. N.W., Washington, D.C. 20036-3278. 500,000. Phone: (202) 857-6589. www.bbinet.org.

**Booksellers Association, American (1900):** 828 So. Broadway, Tarrytown, N.Y. 10591. 4,500. Phone: (914) 591-2665, (800) 637-0037. www.bookweb.org.

**Boys & Girls Clubs of America (1906):** 1230 West Peachtree St. N.W., Atlanta, Ga., 30309. 2,800,000 youth served. Phone: (404) 487-5700. www.bgca.org.

**Boy Scouts of America (1910):** 1325 W. Walnut Hill Lane, P.O. Box 152079, Irving, Tex. 75015-2079. 4.8 mil. www.bsa.scouting.org.

**Brady Campaign, The (1974)** (formerly Handgun Control, Inc.): 1225 Eye St. N.W., Ste. 1100, Washington, D.C. 20005. 380,000. Phone: (202) 898-0792. www.bradycampaign.org.

**Broadcasters, National Association of (1922):** 1771 N St. N.W., Washington, D.C. 20036-2891. Phone: (202) 429-5300. www.nab.org.

**Brookings Institution, The (1916):** 1775 Massachusetts Ave. N.W., Washington, D.C. 20036-2188. Phone: (202) 797-6000. www.brookings.org.

**Business Education Association, National (1946):** 1914 Association Dr., Reston, Va. 20191-1596. 16,000. Phone: (703) 860-8300; fax: (703) 620-4483. email: nbea@nbea.org; www.nbea.org.

**Business Women's Association, American (1949):** 9100 Ward Parkway, P.O. Box 8728, Kansas City, Mo. 64114-0728. 80,000. Phone: (800) 228-0007. fax: (816) 361-4991. email: abwa@abwahq.org. www.abwahq.org.

**Camp Fire USA (1910):** 4601 Madison Ave., Kansas City, Mo. 64112-1278. 629,000. Phone: (816) 756-1950. www.campfire.org.

**Camping Association, The American (1910):** 5000 State Rd. 67 N., Martinsville, Ind. 46151-7902. 5,500, 2,000+ camps. Phone: (765) 342-8456. www.acacamps.org.

**Cancer Society, American (1913):** 1599 Clifton Rd. N.E., Atlanta, Ga. 30329. Over 2 million volunteers. Phone: (800) ACS-2345 or check local listings. www.cancer.org.

**CARE, Inc. (1945):** 151 Ellis St. NE, Atlanta, Ga. 30303-2439. Programs in 62 developing countries. Phone: (404) 681-2552. www.care.org.

**Carnegie Endowment for International Peace (1910):** 1779 Massachusetts Ave., N.W., Washington, D.C. 20036–2103. Phone: (202) 483-7600; fax: (202) 483-1840. www.ceip.org.

**Catholic Charities USA (1910):** 1731 King St., Ste. 200, Alexandria, Va. 22314. 1,400 agencies and institutions. Phone: (703) 549-1390. www.catholiccharitiesusa.org

**Catholic Daughters of the Americas (1903):** 10 W. 71st St., New York, N.Y. 10023. 115,000. Phone: (212) 877-3041. www.catholicdaughters.org.

**Catholic War Veterans of the U.S.A. Inc. (1935):** 441 N. Lee St., Alexandria, Va. 22314. 35,000. Phone: (703) 549-3622. www.cwv.org.

**Cerebral Palsy Associations, Inc., United (1949):** 1660 L St. N.W., Ste. 700, Washington, D.C. 20036. 153 affiliates. Phone: (800) USA-5-UCP, (202) 776-0406, TTY (202) 973-7197. www.ucpa.org.

**Chamber of Commerce of the U.S. (1912):** 1615 H St. N.W., Washington, D.C. 20062. 220,000. Phone: (202) 659-6000. www.uschamber.com.

**Chemical Engineers, American Institute of (1908):** 3 Park Ave., New York, N.Y. 10016-5991. 52,000. Phone: (212) 591-8100; (800) 242-4363. www.aiche.org.

**Chemical Society, American (1876):** 1155 16th St. N.W., Washington, D.C. 20036. 151,024. Phone: (800) 227-5558. www.acs.org.

**Chess Federation, United States (1939):** 3054 NYS Rte. 9W, New Windsor, N.Y. 12553. 50,000+. Phone: (845) 562-8350. www.uschess.org.

**Child Labor Committee, National (1904):** 1501 Broadway, Ste. 403, New York, N.Y. 10036. Phone: (212) 840-1801. www.kapow.org.

**Children's Book Council (1945):** 12 W. 37th St., 2nd Fl., New York, N.Y. 10018-7480. Phone: (212) 966-1990; fax: (212) 966-2073. email: staff@cbcbooks.org. www.cbcbooks.org.

**Child Welfare League of America (1920):** 440 First St. N.W., 3rd Fl., Washington, D.C. 20001-2085. 1,000 agencies. Phone: (202) 638-2952. www.cwla.org.

**Chiropractic Association, American (1963):** 1701 Clarendon Blvd., Arlington, Va. 22209. 22,000. Phone: (800) 986-4636; fax: (703) 243-2593. www.amerchiro.com.

**Cities, National League of (1924):** 1301 Pennsylvania Ave. N.W., Washington, D.C. 20004-1763. 18,000 cities and towns. Phone: (202) 626-3000. www.nlc.org.

**Civil Air Patrol, National Headquarters (1941):** 105 S. Hansell St., Bldg. 714, Maxwell AFB, Ala. 36112-6332. 53,000. Phone: (334) 953-4287. www.capnhq.gov.

**Civil Engineers, American Society of (1852):** 1801 Alexander Bell Dr., Reston, Va. 20191-4400. 123,000. Phone: (800) 548–ASCE (2723); (703) 295-6300. www.asce.org.

**Clinical Pathologists, American Society of (1922):** 2100 W. Harrison St., Chicago, Ill. 60612. 77,200. Phone: (312) 738-1336. www.ascp.org.

**College Fund, United Negro (UNCF) (1944):** 8260 Willow Oaks Corporate Dr., P.O. Box 10444, Fairfax, Va. 22031. 39 member institutions. Phone: (703) 205-3400, (800) 331-2244; fax: (703) 205-3576. www.uncf.org.

**Colleges and Employers, National Association of (formerly College Placement Council) (1956):** 62 E. Highland Ave., Bethlehem, Pa. 18017. 3,200. Phone: (800) 544-5272. www.naceweb.org.

**Common Cause (1970):** 1250 Connecticut Ave. N.W., Washington, D.C. 20036. 250,000. Phone: (800) 926-1064. www.commoncause.org.

**Community Cultural Center Association, American (1978):** 149 Cannongate 3, Nashua, N.H. 03063. Phone: (603) 882-2741. fax: (603) 886-7941.

**Composers/USA, National Association of (1933):** P.O. Box 49256, Barrington Station, Los Angeles, Calif. 90049. 600. Phone: (310) 541-8213. www.music-usa.org/nacusa/

**Congress of Racial Equality (CORE) (1942):** 817 Broadway, 3rd Flr., New York, N.Y. 10003. Nationwide network of chapters. Phone: (212) 598-4000; fax: (212) 598-4141. www.core-online.org.

**Conscientious Objectors, Central Committee for (1948):** 1515 Cherry St., Philadelphia, Pa. 19102. Phone: (215) 563-8787.     630 20th St., Oakland, Calif. 94612. Phone: (510) 465-1617. www.objector.org.

**Conservation Engineers, Association of (1961):**
Attn: Norval Olson, Colorado Division of Wilflife.
Phone: (303) 291-7393; fax: (303) 291-7108.
www.conservation.state.mo.us/engineering/ace.

**Consumer Federation of America (1968):** 1424 16th
St. N.W., Ste. 604, Washington, D.C. 20036. 260
member organizations. Phone: (202) 387-6121.
www.consumerfed.org.

**Consumers League, National (1899):** 1701 K St.
N.W., Ste. 1200, Washington, D.C. 20006. Phone:
(202) 835-3323. www.natlconsumersleague.org.

**Consumers Union (1936):** 101 Truman Ave., Yonkers,
N.Y. 10703-1057. 4.6 million subscribers to
*Consumer Reports Magazine.* Phone: (914)
378-2000. www.consumersunion.org.

**Country Music Association (1958):** One Music Circle
South, Nashville, Tenn. 37203. 6,000. Phone: (615)
244-2840. www.cmaworld.com.

**Credit Management, National Association of (1896):**
8840 Columbia 100 Parkway, Columbia, Md.
21045-2158. 30,000+ members. Phone: (410)
740-5560. www.nacm.org.

**Credit Union National Association (1934):** P.O. Box
431, Madison, Wis. 53701-0431. 51 state leagues
representing 12,400 credit unions. Phone: (800)
356-9655. www.cuna.org.

**Crime and Delinquency, National Council on (1907):**
1970 Broadway, Ste. 500, Oakland, Calif. 94612.
Phone: (510) 208-0500. www.nccd-crc.org.

**CSA/USA, Celiac Sprue Association/United States
of America, Inc., (1978):** P.O. Box 31700, Omaha,
Neb. 68131-0700. 6 regions in U.S., 74 chapters, 36
active resource units. Phone: (402) 558-0600;
fax: (402) 558-1347. www.csaceliacs.org.

**Dairy Council, National (1915):** 10255 W. Higgins Rd.
Ste. 900, Rosemont, Ill. 60018.
www.nationaldairycouncil.org.

**Daughters of the American Revolution, National
Society (1896):** 1776 D St. N.W., Washington, D.C.
20006-5303. 172,000. Phone: (202) 628-1776.
www.dar.org.

**Deaf, National Association of the (1880):** 814 Thayer
Ave., Silver Spring, Md. 20910-4500. 51 state
association affiliates. Phone: (301) 587-1788 V;
(301) 587-1789 TTY. www.nad.org.

**Defenders of Wildlife (1947):** 1101 14th St. N.W.,
#1400, Washington, D.C. 20005. 200,000 members
and supporters. Phone: (202) 682-9400.
www.defenders.org.

**Dental Association, American (1859):** 211 E.
Chicago Ave., Chicago, Ill. 60611. 141,000. Phone:
(312) 440-2500. www.ada.org.

**Diabetes Association, American (1940):** 1701 N.
Beauregard St., Alexandria, Va. 22311. Phone: (703)
549-1500; (800) 342-2383. www.diabetes.org/.

**Dignity (1969):** 1500 Massachusetts Ave. N.W., Ste.
11, Washington, D.C. 20005. 5,000. Phone: (202)
861-0017 and (800) 877-8797. www.dignityusa.org.

**Disabled American Veterans (1920):** 3725 Alexandria
Pike, Cold Spring, Ky. 41076. 1,400,000. Phone:
(859) 441-7300. www.dav.org.

**Dowsers, Inc., The American Society of (1961):** P.O.
Box 24, Danville, Vt. 05828. 5,000. Phone: (800)
711-9530; fax: (802) 748-8565. email:
ASD@dowsers.org. www.dowsers.org.

**Ducks Unlimited, Inc. (1937):** One Waterfowl Way,
Memphis, Tenn. 38120. 600,000. Phone: (800)
45DUCKS. www.ducks.org.

**Earthwatch (1971):** 3 Clock Tower Place, Ste. 100,
Box 75, Maynard, Mass. 01754. 75,000. Phone:
(978) 461-0081. www.earthwatch.org.

**Eastern Star, Order of, General Grand Chapter
(1876):** 1618 New Hampshire Ave. N.W.,
Washington, D.C. 20009-2549. 1,207,301. Phone:
(202) 667-4737. www.easternstar.org.

**Easter Seal Society, The National (1919):** 230 W.
Monroe, Ste. 1800, Chicago, Ill. 60606. 109 state
and local affiliate societies operating 500 service

sites. Phone: (312) 726-6200; (312) 726-4258 TTY.
www.easter-seals.org.

**Economic Association, American (1885):** 2014
Broadway, Ste. 305, Nashville, Tenn. 37203. 22,000.
5,500 inst. subscribers. Phone: (615) 322-2595.
www.vanderbilt.edu/AEA.

**Edison Electric Institute (1933):** 701 Pennsylvania
Ave. N.W., Washington, D.C. 20004-2696. Phone:
(202) 508-5000. www.eei.org.

**Education, American Council on (ACE), (1918):** One
Dupont Circle N.W., Washington, D.C. 20036-1193.
1,600+ colleges and universities and 200+ higher
education associations. Phone: (202) 939-9300.
www.acenet.edu.

**Educational Exchange, Council on International
(1947):** 633 Third Ave., 2nd Fl., New York, N.Y.
10017. Phone: (800) 40-STUDY. www.ciee.org.

**Educational Research Association, American
(1916):** 1230 17th St. N.W., Washington, D.C.
20036-3078. 22,000. Phone: (202) 223-9485.
www.aera.net.

**Education Association, National (1857):** 1201 16th
St. N.W., Washington, D.C. 20036-3290. 2.3 million.
Phone: (202) 833-4000. www.nea.org.

**Electrochemical Society, The (1902):** 65 S. Main St.,
Pennington, N.J. 08534-2839. 7,000. Phone: (609)
737-1902; fax: (609) 737-2743. email:
ecs@electrochem.org. www.electrochem.org.

**Elks of the U.S.A., Benevolent and Protective Order
of the (1868):** 2750 N. Lakeview Ave., Chicago, Ill.
60614-1889. 1,300,000. Phone: (773) 755-4700.
www.elks.org/default.cfm.

**Energy Engineers, Association of (1977):** 4025
Pleasantdale Rd., Ste. 420, Atlanta, Ga. 30340.
8,500. Phone: (770) 447-5083; fax: (770) 446-3969.
email: info@aeecenter.org. www.aeecenter.org.

**English-Speaking Union of the United States
(1920):** 144 E. 39th St., New York, N.Y. 10016.
18,000. Phone: (212) 817-1200.
www.english-speakingunion.org.

**Entomological Society of America (1889):** 9301
Annapolis Rd., Lanham, Md. 20706-3115. 7,400+.
Phone: (301) 731-4535; fax: (301) 731-4538. email:
esa@entsoc.org. www.entsoc.org.

**Esperanto League for North America, The (1952):**
P.O. Box 1129, El Cerrito, Calif. 94530. Over 1,000.
Phone: (800) 377-3726. www.esperanto-usa.org.

**Exceptional Children, The Council for (1922):** 1110
N. Glebe Rd., Ste. 300, Arlington, Va. 22201-5704.
54,000. Phone: (703) 620-3660 V; (703) 264-9446
TTY; fax: (703) 264-9494. email: cec@cec.sped.org.
www.cec.sped.org.

**Exploration Geophysicists, Society of (1930):** 8801
South Yale, Tulsa, Okla. 74137-3575. 16,536.
Phone: (918) 497-5500. www.seg.org.

**Family and Consumer Sciences, American
Association of (1909):** 1555 King St., Alexandria,
Va. 22314. 14,500. Phone: (703) 706-4600.
www.aafcs.org.

**Family Campers & RVers (1949):** 4804 Transit Rd.,
Bldg. 2, Depew, N.Y. 14043. 42,000 families. Phone:
(800) 245-9755; fax: (716) 668-6242. www.fcrv.org.

**Family, Career, and Community Leaders of America
[evolved from Future Homemakers of America,
Inc. (1945)]:** 1910 Association Dr., Reston, Va.
20191-1584. 230,000. Phone: (703) 476-4900.
www.fcclainc.org.

**Family Physicians, American Academy of (1947):**
11400 Tomahawk Creek Pkwy., Leawood, Kans.
66211-2672. 88,000. Phone: (913) 906-6000.
www.aafp.org.

**Family Relations, National Council on (1938):** 3989
Central Ave. N.E., #550, Minneapolis, Minn. 55421.
42,000 families. Phone: (888) 781-9331.
www.ncfr.com.

**Farm Bureau Federation, American (1919):** 225 Touhy Ave., Park Ridge, Ill. 60068. 4.7 million member families. Phone: (847) 685-8600. www.fb.com.

**Federal Bar Association (1920):** 2215 M St. N.W., Washington, D.C. 20037. 15,000. Phone: (202) 785-1614; fax: (202) 785-1568. www.fedbar.org.

**Federal Employees, National Federation of (1917):** 1016 16th St. N.W., Washington, D.C. 20036. 150,000. Phone: (202) 862-4400. www.nffe.org.

**Fellowship of Reconciliation (1915):** 521 N. Broadway, Nyack, N.Y. 10960. 20,000. Phone: (845) 358-4601. www.forusa.org.

**Female Executives, National Association for (1972):** P.O. Box 469031, Escondido, Calif. 92046-9925. 150,000+. Phone: (800) 634-6233. www.nafe.com.

**FFA Organization, National (1928):** P.O. Box 68960, 6060 FFA Dr., Indianapolis, Ind. 46268. 457,278. Phone: (317) 802-6060. www.ffa.org.

**Fire Protection Association, National (1896):** One Batterymarch Park, Quincy, Mass. 02269-9101. 65,000+. Phone: (617) 770-3000. www.nfpa.org.

**Flag Foundation, National (1968):** Flag Plaza, 1275 Bedford Ave, Pittsburgh, Pa. 15219. 3,000+. Phone: (800) 615-1776. www.americanflags.org.

**Fleet Reserve Association (1924):** 125 N. West St., Alexandria, Va. 22314-2754. 162,000. Phone: (703) 683-1400. www.fra.org.

**Foreign Policy Association (1918):** 470 Park Ave. So., New York, N.Y. 10016-6819. Phone: (212) 481-8100. www.fpa.org.

**Foreign Relations, Council on (1921):** 58 E. 68th St., New York, N.Y. 10021. 3,400. Phone: (212) 434-9400. www.cfr.org.

**Foreign Study, American Institute for (1964):** River Plaza, 9 W. Broad St., Stamford, Conn. 06902-3788. Phone: (800) 727-2437. www.aifs.org.

**Forensic Sciences, American Academy of (1948):** 410 N. 21st St., Ste. 203., P.O. Box 669, Colorado Springs, Colo. 80901-0669. 4,315. Phone: (719) 636-1100; fax: (719) 636-1993. www.aafs.org.

**Foresters, Society of American (1900):** 5400 Grosvenor Lane, Bethesda, Md. 20814. 18,000. Phone: (301) 897-8720. www.safnet.org.

**4-H Program (early 1900s):** 1400 Independence Ave., S.W., Washington, D.C. 20250. 5.6 million. Phone: (202) 720-2908. www.4-h.org/.

**Freedom of Information Center (1958):** 127 Neff Annex, Univ. of Missouri, Columbia, Mo. 65211. Phone: (573) 882-4856. www.missouri.edu/~foiwww/

**French Institute/Alliance Française (1898):** 22 E. 60th St., New York, N.Y. 10022. 9,000. Phone: (212) 355-6100. www.fiaf.org.

**Friends of Animals Inc. (1957):** 777 Post Rd., Darien, Conn. 06820. 120,000. Phone: (203) 656-1522. www.friendsofanimals.org/.

**Friends of the Earth (1969):** 1025 Vermont Ave. N.W., Washington, D.C. 20005. 35,000. Phone: (877) 843-8687. www.foe.org.

**Gamblers Anonymous:** P.O. Box 17170, Los Angeles, Calif. 90017. Phone: (213) 386-8789. www.gamblersanonymous.org.

**Gay and Lesbian Task Force, National (1973):** 1700 Kalorama Rd. N.W., Washington, D.C. 20000 2621. 35,000 members. Phone: (202) 332-6483. www.ngltf.org.

**Genealogical Society, National (1903):** 4527 17th St. N., Arlington, Va. 22207-2399. 17,000+. Phone: (703) 525-0050; fax: (703) 525-0052. www.ngsgenealogy.org.

**Geographers, Association of American (1904):** 1710 16th St. N.W., Washington, D.C. 20009-3198. 7,000. Phone: (202) 234-1450; fax: (202) 234-2744. email: gaia@aag.org. www.aag.org.

**Geographic Education, National Council for (1915):** 16A Leonard Hall, Indiana University of Pennsylvania, Indiana, Pa. 15705. 3,700. Phone: (724) 357-6290. www.ncge.org.

**Geographic Society, National (1888):** 1145 17th St. N.W., Washington, D.C. 20036-4688. 9,200,000. Phone: (800) 647-5463. www.nationalgeographic.com.

**Geological Institute, American (1948):** 4220 King St., Alexandria, Va. 22302-1502. 34 geoscience societies representing 100,000 geoscientists. Phone: (703) 379-2480. www.agiweb.org/.

**Geological Society of America, Inc. (1888):** P.O. Box 9140, Boulder, Colo. 80301-9140. 15,000. Phone: (303) 447-2020. www.geosociety.org.

**German American National Congress, The (Deutsch-Amerikanischer National Kongress—D.A.N.K.) (1958):** 4740 N. Western Ave., Executive Office, Chicago, Ill. 60625-2097. Phone: (773) 275-1100. www.dank.org.

**Gideons International, The (1889):** P.O. Box 140800, Nashville, Tenn. 37214-0800. 130,000. Phone: (615) 883-8533. www.gideons.org.

**Gifted, The Association for the (1958):** The Council for Exceptional Children, 1110 Glebe Road, Ste. 300, Arlington, VA. 22201–5704.Phone: (888) 232–7733. www.cectag.org

**Girl Scouts of the U.S.A. (1912):** 420 Fifth Ave., New York, N.Y. 10018-2798. 2,500,000. Phone: (212) 852-8000. www.girlscouts.org.

**Girls Incorporated (1945):** 120 Wall St., 3rd. Flr., New York, N.Y. 10005. 350,000. Phone: (800) 374-4475. www.girlsinc.org.

**Graphoanalysis Society, International (1929):** 111 N. Canal St., Ste. 955, Chicago, Ill. 60606. 10,000. Phone: (312) 930-9446; www.igas.com.

**Gray Panthers (1970):** 733 15th St. N.W., Ste. 437, Washington, D.C. 20005. Over 50 chapters (networks). Phone: (202) 737-1160. www.graypanthers.org.

**Greenpeace (1971):** 702 H St. N.W., Washington, D.C. 20001. 2.5 million. Phone: (800) 326-0959. www.greenpeaceusa.org.

**Guide Dog Foundation for the Blind, Inc.® (1946):** 371 E. Jericho Turnpike, Smithtown, N.Y. 11787-2976. 100,000. Phone: (631) 265-2121; (800) 548-4337; fax: (631) 361-5192. www.guidedog.org.

**Hadassah, The Women's Zionist Organization of America (1912):** 50 W. 58th St., New York, N.Y. 10019. 385,000. Phone: (212) 355-7900. www.hadassah.org.

**Heating, Refrigerating and Air-Conditioning Engineers, Inc., American Society of (1959):** 1791 Tullie Circle N.E., Atlanta, Ga. 30329. 50,000. Phone: (404) 636-8400. www.ashrae.org.www.groupsinc.org.

**Helicopter Association International (1948):** 1635 Prince St., Alexandria, Va. 22314. Phone: (703) 683-4646. www.rotor.com.

**Historians, The Organization of American (1907):** 112 N. Bryan St., Bloomington, Ind. 47408-4199. 12,000. Phone: (812) 855-7311. www.oah.org.

**Historic Preservation, National Trust for (1949):** 1785 Massachusetts Ave. N.W. Washington, D.C. 20036. 275,000. Phone: (202) 588-6000. www.nationaltrust.org.

**Horse Council, Inc., American (1969):** 1700 K St. N.W., #300, Washington, D.C. 20006. More than 180 organizations and 2,400 individuals. Phone: (202) 296-1970. www.horsecouncil.org.

**Horse Shows Association, Inc., American (1917):** 4047 Iron Works Parkway, Lexington, Ky. 40511. 70,000+. Phone: (859) 258-2472. www.ahsa.org.

**Horticultural Association, National Junior (1935):** 15 Railroad Ave., Homer City, Pa. 15748. Phone: (724) 479-3254. www.njha.org.

**Horticultural Society, American (1922):** 7931 East Boulevard Dr., Alexandria, Va. 22308. 22,000. Phone: (703) 768-5700 or (800) 777-7931; fax: (703) 768-8700. www.ahs.org.

**Hostelling International—American Youth Hostels (1934):** 733 15th St. N.W., Ste. 840, Washington,

D.C. 20005. 120,000. Phone: (202) 783-6161 for membership and reservations. www.hiayh.org.

**Humane Association, American (1877):** 63 Inverness Drive East, Englewood, Colo. 80112-5117. Phone: (800) 227-4645. www.americanhumane.org.

**Humane Society of the United States (1954):** 2100 L St. N.W., Washington, D.C. 20037. 5,000,000. Phone: (202) 452-1100. www.hsus.org.

**Humanities, National Endowment for the (1965):** 1100 Pennsylvania Ave. N.W., Washington, D.C. 20506. Phone: (202) 606-8400. www.neh.fed.us.

**Hydrogen Energy, International Association for (1975):** P.O. Box 248266, Coral Gables, Fla. 33124. 2,500. Phone: (305) 284-4666. www.iahe.org.

**Industrial Engineers, Institute of (1948):** 3577 Parkway Lane, Ste. 200, Norcross, Ga. 30092. 17,000+. Phone: (800) 494-0460. www.iienet.org.

**Insurance and Financial Advisors, National Association of (1890):** 2901 Telestar Court, Falls Church, Va. 22042–1205. 108,000. Phone: (877) TO-NAIFA. www.naifa.org..

**Izaak Walton League of America (1922):** 707 Conservation Lane, Gaithersburg, Md. 20878-2983. 50,000+. Phone: (800) 453-5463. www.iwla.org.

**Jewish Community Centers Association (JCC) of North America (1917):** 15 E. 26th St., New York, N.Y. 10010-1579. 275+ affiliated Jewish Community Centers, YM-YWHAs, and camps serving 1 million+ members. Phone: (212) 532-4958; fax: (212) 481-4174. email: info@jcca.org. www.jcca.org.

**Jewish Congress, American (1918):** 1001 Connecticut Ave., N.W., Ste. 407, Washington, D.C., 20036. 50,000. Phone: (202) 466–9661. www.ajcongress.org.

**Jewish Historical Society, American (1892):** 2 Thornton Rd., Waltham, Mass. 02453. 3,500. Phone: (781) 891-8110; fax: (781) 899-9208. email: ajhs@ajhs.org. www.ajhs.org.

**Jewish War Veterans of the U.S.A. (1896):** 1811 R St. N.W., Washington, D.C. 20009-1659. Phone: (202) 265-6280. www.nichecom.com/~vfw/jwv.html.

**Jewish Women, National Council of (1893):** 53 W. 23rd St., New York, N.Y. 10010. 90,000. Phone: (800) 829–NCJW. www.ncjw.org.

**John Birch Society (1958):** P.O. Box 8040, Appleton, Wis. 54912. Under 100,000. Phone: (920) 749-3780; fax: (920) 749-5062. www.jbs.org.

**Journalists, Society of Professional (1909):** 3909 N. Meridian St., Indianapolis, Ind. 46208. 13,500. Phone: (317) 927-8000. www.spj.org.

**Judaism, American Council for (1943):** P.O. Box 9009, Alexandria, Va. 22304. Phone: (703) 836-2546. www.acjna.org.

**Junior Achievement Inc. (1919):** One Education Way, Colorado Springs, Colo. 80906. 5.2 million. Phone: (719) 540-8000; fax: (719) 540-6299. www.ja.org.

**Junior Chamber of Commerce, The United States, Jaycees (1920):** P.O. Box 7, Tulsa, Okla. 74102-0007. 113,000. Phone: (918) 584-2481; fax: (918) 584-4422. www.usjaycees.org.

**Junior Leagues International, Inc., Association of (1921):** 132 W. 31st St., 11th flr.; New York, N.Y. 10001-3406. 295 Leagues, 193,000+ members. Phone: (212) 951–8300. www.ajli.org.

**Junior State of America (1934):** 60 E. Third Ave., Ste. 320, San Mateo, Calif. 94401-4302. 15,000. Phone: (650) 347-1600 or (800) 334-5353. www.jsa.org.

**Kiwanis International (1915):** 3636 Woodview Trace, Indianapolis, Ind. 46268. 316,000. Phone: (317) 875-8755. email: kiwanismail@kiwanis.org. www.kiwanis.org.

**Knights of Columbus (1852):** One Columbus Plaza, New Haven, Conn. 06510. 1,600,000. Phone: (203) 772-2130. www.kofc.org.

**Knights Templar, Grand Encampment of (1816):** 5097 N. Elston Ave., Ste. 101, Chicago, Ill.

60630-2460. 220,000. Phone: (773) 777-3300. www.knightstemplar.org.

**La Leche League International (1956):** 1400 N. Meacham Rd., Schaumburg, Ill. 60173-4808. 50,000. Phone: (847) 519-7730. www.lalecheleague.org.

**Law, American Society of International (1906):** 2223 Massachusetts Ave. N.W., Washington, D.C. 20008. 4,300. Phone: (202) 939-6000. www.asil.org.

**League of Women Voters of the U.S. (1920):** 1730 M St. N.W., Washington, D.C. 20036-4508. Phone: (202) 429-1965; fax: (202) 429-0854. www.lwv.org.

**Legal Aid and Defender Association, National (1911):** 1625 K St. N.W., Ste. 800, Washington, D.C. 20006-1604. 2,400. Phone: (202) 452-0620. www.nlada.org.

**Legal Professionals, National Association of (1949):** 314 East 3rd St., Ste. 210, Tulsa, Okla. 74120-2409. 6,000. Phone: (918) 582-5188. www.nals.org.

**Leukemia & Lymphoma Society (1949):** 1311 Mamaroneck Ave., White Plains, NY 10605. Phone: (914) 949-5213. www.leukemia-lymphoma.org.

**Library Association, American (1876):** 50 E. Huron St., Chicago, Ill. 60611. 57,000. Phone: (800) 545–2433. www.ala.org.

**Lions Clubs International (1917):** 300 22nd St., Oak Brook, Ill. 60523-8842. 1,419,408. Phone: (630) 571-5466. www.lionsclubs.org.

**Lung Association, American (1904):** 1740 Broadway, New York, N.Y. 10019-4374. 99 constituent and affiliate associations. Phone: (212) 315-8700. www.lungusa.org.

**Magazine Editors, American Society of (1963):** 919 Third Ave., 22nd Flr., New York, N.Y. 10022. 900. Phone: (212) 872-3700. www.asme.magazine.org

**Management Accountants, Institute of (1919):** 10 Paragon Dr., Montvale, N.J. 07645-1759. 80,000. Phone: (800) 638-4427 x 265. www.imanet.org.

**Management Association, American (1923):** 1601 Broadway, New York, N.Y. 10019. 700,000. Phone: (212) 586-8100. www.amanet.org.

**Management Consultants, Institute of (1968):** 2025 M St. N.W., Ste. 800, Washington, D.C. 20036–2557. 25 chapters. Phone: (202) 367-2134. www.imcusa.org.

**Manufacturers, National Association of (1895):** 1331 Pennsylvania Ave. N.W., Washington, D.C. 20004-1790. Approx. 14,000. Phone: (202) 637-3000. www.nam.org.

**Manufacturing Engineers, Society of:** One SME Drive, Dearborn, Mich. 48121.Phone: (313) 271–1500 x 1078.Fax: (313) 240–8251.www.sme.org.

**March of Dimes Birth Defects Foundation (1938):** 1275 Mamaroneck Ave., White Plains, N.Y. 10605. 104 chapters. Phone: (888) 663-4637.www.modimes.org.

**Marine Conservation, Center for (1972):**1725 De Sales St., N.W., Ste. 600, Washington, D.C. 20036. 120,000.Phone: (202) 429–5609.www.cmc-ocean.org.

**Marine Corps Association (1913):** 715 Broadway, Quantico, Va. 22134. 100,723. Phone: (703) 640-6161; (800) 336-0291. www.mca-marines.org.

**Marine Technology Society (1963):** 5565 Sterrett Place, Ste. 108, Columbia, Md. 21044. 2,000+. Phone: (410) 884-5330; Fax: (202) 429-9417. www.mtsociety.org.

**Masons, Royal Arch, General Grand Chapter International (1797):** P.O. Box 489, Danville, Ky. 40423-0489. 230,000. Phone: (236) 236-0757. members.aol.com/GGCHAPTER/HomePage.html.

**Mathematical Association of America (1915):** P.O. Box 91112, Washington, D.C. 20090-1112. Phone: (800) 331-1622. www.maa.org.

**Mathematical Society, American (1888):** 201 Charles St., Providence, R.I. 02940-6248. Phone: (401) 455-4000. email: ams@ams.org. www.ams.org.

**Mayflower Descendants, General Society of (1897):** P.O. Box 3297, Plymouth, Mass. 02361. 24,500+. Phone: (508) 746-3188. www.mayflower.org.

**Mechanical Engineers, American Society of (1880):** 3 Park Ave., New York, N.Y. 10016-5990. 125,000. Phone: (800) 843-2763. www.asme.org.

**Medical Association, American (1847):** 515 N. State St., Chicago, Ill. 60610. 300,000 physicians. Phone: (312) 464-5000. www.ama-assn.org.

**Mental Health Association, National (1909):** 1021 Prince St., Alexandria, Va., 22314-2971. 340 affiliates. Phone: (703) 684-7722; (800) 969-NMHA; TTY (800) 433-5959; fax: (703) 684-5968. email: nmhainfo@aol.com. www.nmha.org

**Meteorological Society, American (1919):** 45 Beacon St., Boston, Mass. 02108-3693. 11,000+. Phone: (617) 227-2425. www.mca-usa.org/ams.

**Military Chaplains Association of the U.S.A. (1925):** P.O. Box 7056, Arlington, Va. 22207-7056. 1,500. Phone: (202) 574-2423. www.mca-usa.org

**Mining, Metallurgical, and Petroleum Engineers, The American Institute of (1871):** 3 Park Ave., New York, N.Y. 10016-5998. 4 Member Societies: Society for Mining, Metallurgy and Exploration; The Minerals, Metals & Materials Society; Iron & Steel Society; Society of Petroleum Engineers. Phone: (212) 419-7679; fax: (212) 419-7671. email: AIMENY@aimeny.org. www.aimeny.org.

**Model Aeronautics, Academy of (1936):** 5161 East Memorial Dr., Muncie, Ind. 47302. 150,000. Phone: (765) 287-1256. www.modelaircraft.org/templates/ama/.

**Modern Language Association of America (1883):** 26 Broadway, 3rd Fl., New York, N.Y. 10004-1789. 30,000+. Phone: (646) 576-5000. www.mla.org.

**Moose International, Inc. (1888):** Rte. 31, Mooseheart, Ill. 60539. 1,600,000+. Phone: (630) 859-2000. www.mooseintl.org.

**Mothers Against Drunk Driving (MADD) (1980):** P.O. Box 541688, Dallas, Tex. 75354-1688. 3 million members and supporters. Victim hotline: (800) GET-MADD. www.madd.org

**Motion Picture Arts & Sciences, Academy of (1927):** 8949 Wilshire Blvd., Beverly Hills, Calif. 90211-1972. Phone: (310) 247-3000. www.oscars.org.

**Multiple Sclerosis Society, National (1946):** 733 Third Ave., New York, N.Y. 10017. 350,000. Phone: (800) FIGHT-MS (344-4867). www.nationalmssociety.org.

**Muscular Dystrophy Association (1950):** 3300 East Sunrise Dr., Tucson, Ariz. 85718. 2,300,000 volunteers. Phone: (800) 572-1717. www.mdausa.org.

**Museums, American Association of (1906):** 1575 Eye St. N.W., Ste. 400, Washington, D.C. 20005. 16,000+. Phone: (202) 289-1818; fax: (202) 289-6578, TTY (202) 289-8439. www.aam-us.org.

**[illegible] C Illillily IIIIII. A.cxalIaIIuII l lialIuIIal /1000** P.O. Box 67, Friendship, Ind. 47021-0067. 25,000. Phone: (812) 667-5131. www.nmlra.org.

**NAFSA: Association of International Educators (1948):** 1307 New York Ave. N.W., 8th Flr., Washington, D.C. 20005-4701. 8,000+. Phone: (202) 737-3699. www.nafsa.org.

**National Abortion and Reproductive Rights Action League (NARAL) (1969):** 1156 15th St. N.W., Washington, D.C. 20005. 500,000. Phone: (202) 973-3000. www.naral.org.

**National Association for the Advancement of Colored People (1909):** 4805 Mt. Hope Dr., Baltimore, Md. 21215. 500,000+. Phone: (877) NAACP-98. www.naacp.org.

**National Association of Insurance and Financial Advisors (1890):** 2901 Telestar Court, Falls Church, Va. 22042-1205. 80,000. Phone: (703) 770-8100. www.naifa.org/index.html.

**National Conference for Community and Justice, The (founded as The Natl. Conf. of Christians & Jews) (1927):** 475 Park Avenue South, 19th Flr., New York, N.Y. 10016-6901. Phone: (212) 545-1300. www.nccj.org.

**National Cooperative Business Association (formerly Cooperative League of the U.S.A.) (1916):** 1401 New York Ave. N.W., Ste. 1100, Washington, D.C. 20005. Phone: (202) 638-6222. www.ncba.org.

**National Council of La Raza (1968):** 1111 19th St. N.W., Ste. 1000, Washington, D.C. 20036. 20,000+. Phone: (202) 785-1670. www.nclr.org.

**National Council of the Churches of Christ in the USA (1950):** 475 Riverside Drive, Rm. 850, New York, N.Y. 10115. 35 Protestant and Orthodox communions. Phone: (212) 870-2227. www.ncccusa.org.

**National Grange of the Order of Patrons of Husbandry (1867):** 1616 H St. N.W., Washington, D.C. 20006-4999. 300,000. Phone: (202) 628-3507; fax: (202) 347-1091. www.nationalgrange.org.

**National Press Club (1908):** National Press Bldg., 529 14th St. N.W., 13th Flr., Washington, D.C. 20045. 4,500+. Phone: (202) 662-7500. npc.press.org.

**National PTA (National Congress of Parents and Teachers) (1897):** 330 N. Wabash Ave., Ste. 2100, Chicago, Ill. 60611. 6.5 million. Phone: (800) 307-4782. email: info@pta.org. www.pta.org.

**National Rifle Association of America (1871):** 11250 Waples Mill Rd., Fairfax, Va. 22030. 3,300,000. Phone: (703) 267-1000. www.nra.org.

**National Urban League, Inc. (1910):** 120 Wall St., New York, N.Y. 10005. 115 affiliates in 34 states and D.C. Phone: (212) 558-5300. www.nul.org.

**National Wildlife Federation (1936):** 11100 Wildlife Center Dr., Reston, Va. 20190. 4,000,000+. Phone: (703) 438-6000. www.nwf.org.

**Nature Conservancy, The (1951):** 4245 N. Fairfax Dr., Ste. 100, Arlington, Va. 22203-1606. 900,000. Phone: (800) 628-6860. http://nature.org.

**Naturopathic Physicians, American Association of (1986):** 8201 Greensboro Dr., Ste. 300, McLean, Va. 22102. 1,700. Phone: (800) 628-6860. http://nature.org.

**Naval Architects and Marine Engineers, The Society of (1893):** 601 Pavonia Ave., Jersey City, N.J. 07306. 10,000+. Phone: (800) 798-2188; fax: (201) 798-4975. www.sname.org.

**Naval Engineers, American Society of (1888):** 1452 Duke St., Alexandria, Va. 22314. 6,800. Phone: (703) 836-6727; fax: (703) 836-7491. www.navalengineers.org.

**Naval Institute, United States (1873):** 291 Wood Rd., Annapolis, Md. 21402. 80,000+. Phone: (410) 268-6110. www.usni.org.

**Navigation, The Institute of (1945):** 3975 University Dr., Ste. 390, Fairfax, Va. 22030. 3,800. Phone: (703) 383-9688; fax: (703) 383-9689. email: [illegible]@inst.org. www.ion.org.

**Navy League of the United States (1902):** 2300 Wilson Blvd., Arlington, Va. 22201-3308. 71,500. Phone: (703) 528-1775. www.navyleague.org.

**NDIA (National Defense Industrial Association) (1997):** 2111 Wilson Blvd., Ste. 400, Arlington, Va. 22201. 28,000 individual, 900 companies. Phone: (703) 522-1820. www.ndia.org.

**Neurofibromatosis Foundation, Inc., The National (1978):** 95 Pine St., 16th Flr., New York, N.Y. 10005. 38,000. Phone: (800) 323-7938; in N.Y. State (212) 344-NNFF; fax: (212) 747-0004. email: nnff@aol.com. www.nf.org.

**Newspaper Association of America (1992):** 1921 Gallows Rd., Ste. 600, Vienna, Va. 22182–3900. 70,000+ newspaper executives. Phone (703) 902-1600. www.naa.org.

**Nondestructive Testing, Inc., The American Society for (1941):** 1711 Arlingate Lane, P.O. Box 28518,

Columbus, Ohio 43228-0518. 10,240. Phone: (800) 222-ASNT. www.asnt.org.

**Nuclear Society, American (1954):** 555 N. Kensington Ave., La Grange Park, Ill. 60526. 13,000. Phone: (708) 352-6611. www.ans.org.

**Numismatic Association, American (1891):** 818 N. Cascade Ave., Colorado Springs, Colo. 80903-3279. 28,000. Phone: (719) 632-2646. email: ana@money.org. www.money.org.

**Nurses Association, American (1897):** 600 Maryland Ave. S.W., Ste. 100, Washington, D.C. 20024. 180,000. Phone: (800) 274-4ANA. www.ana.org.

**Ocean Conservancy, The (formerly Center for Marine Conservation) (1972):** 1725 De Sales St. N.W., Ste. 600, Washington, D.C. 20036. 120,000. Phone: (202) 429-5609. www.oceanconservancy.org/

**Odd Fellows, Sovereign Grand Lodge, Independent Order of (1819):** 422 North Trade St., Winston-Salem, N.C. 27101. 460,000. Phone: (336) 725-5955. www.ioof.org.

**Olympic Committee, United States (1921):** One Olympic Plaza, Colorado Springs, Colo. 80909-5760. Phone: (719) 632-5551. www.olympic-usa.org.

**Optimist International (1919):** 4494 Lindell Blvd., St. Louis, Mo. 63108. 130,000+. Phone: (314) 371-6000. www.optimist.org.

**Optometric Association, American (1898):** 243 N. Lindbergh Blvd., St. Louis, Mo. 63141. 32,000. Phone: (314) 991-4100. www.aoanet.org.

**Ornithologists' Union, American (1883):** 1313 Dolley Madison Blvd., Ste. 402, McLean, Va 22101. 4,000. Phone: (202) 357-2051. www.aou.org.

**Overeaters Anonymous, Inc. (1960):** World Service Office, P.O. Box 44020, Rio Rancho, N.M. 87174–4020. 150,000. Phone: (505) 891-2664. www.overeatersanonymous.org.

**Parents, Families and Friends of Lesbians and Gays (1981):** 1726 M St. N.W., Ste. 400, Washington, D.C. 20036. 77,000 households. Phone: (202) 467-8180. www.pflag.org.

**Parents Without Partners (1957):** 1650 South Dixie Hwy., Ste. 510, Boca Raton, Fla. 33432. 50,000+. Phone: (561) 391-8833. www.parentswithoutpartners.org.

**Peace Action (a merger of SANE and the Nuclear Weapons Freeze Campaign) (1957):** 1819 H St. N.W., Ste. 420, Washington D.C. 20006. 55,000. Phone: (202) 862-9740. www.webcom.com/peaceact.

**People For the American Way (1980):** 2000 M St. N.W., Ste. 400, Washington, D.C. 20036. 300,000. Phone: (202) 467-4999. www.pfaw.org.

**Petroleum Geologists, American Association of (1917):** P.O. Box 979, Tulsa, Okla. 74101-0979. 31,500. Phone: (918) 584-2555. www.aapg.org.

**Pharmaceutical Association, American (1852):** 2215 Constitution Ave. N.W., Washington, D.C. 20037-2985. 50,000+. Phone: (202) 628-4410. www.aphanet.org.

**Philatelic Society, American (1886):** 1000 Oakwood Ave., P.O. Box 8000, State College, Pa. 16803. 55,000+. Phone: (814) 237-3803. www.stamps.org.

**Photogrammetry and Remote Sensing, American Society for (1934):** 5410 Grosvenor Lane, Ste. 210, Bethesda, Md. 20814-2160. 7,000+. Phone: (301) 493-0290; fax: (301) 493-0208. email: asprs@asprs.org. www.asprs.org.

**Photographic Society of America (1934):** 3000 United Founders Blvd., Ste. 103, Oklahoma City, Okla. 73112-3940. Phone: (405) 843-1437. www.psa-photo.org.

**Physical Society, The American (1899):** One Physics Ellipse, College Park, Md. 20740-3844. 41,000. Phone: (301) 209-3200. www.aps.org.

**Physical Therapy Association, American (APTA) (1921):** 1111 N. Fairfax St., Alexandria, Va. 22314-1488. 66,000+. Phone: (703) 684-2782. www.apta.org.

**Physics, American Institute of (1931):** One Physics Ellipse, College Park, Md. 20740-3843. 125,000. Phone: (301) 209-3100. www.aip.org.

**Pilot International (1921):** Pilot International Headquarters, 244 College St., P.O. Box 4844, Macon, Ga. 31208-4844. 25,000. Phone: (478) 743-7403. www.pilotinternational.org.

**Planetary Society, The (1980):** 65 N. Catalina Ave., Pasadena, Calif. 91106-2301. 100,000. Phone: (626) 793-5100. www.planetary.org.

**Planned Parenthood® Federation of America, Inc., (1916):** 810 Seventh Ave., New York, N.Y. 10019. 150 affiliates. Phone: (212) 541-7800; fax: (212) 245-1845. www.plannedparenthood.org.

**Plastics Engineers, Society of (1942):** P.O. Box 403, 14 Fairfield Dr., Brookfield, Conn. 06804-0403. 32,000+. Phone: (203) 775-0471. www.4spe.org.

**Police and Concerned Citizens, American Federation of (1966):** Records Center, 3801 Biscayne Blvd., Miami, Fla. 33137. 100,000. Phone: (305) 573-0070. www.aphf.org.

**Police, International Association of Chiefs of (1893):** 515 N. Washington St., Alexandria, Va. 22314-2357. 19,000+. Phone: (703) 836-6767. www.theiacp.org.

**Political and Social Science, American Academy of (1889):** 3814 Walnut St., Philadelphia, Pa. 19104–6197. Phone: (215) 746-6446. www.1891.org.

**Political Science, Academy of (1880):** 475 Riverside Dr., Ste. 1274, New York, N.Y. 10115-1274. 8,500. Phone: (212) 870-2500. www.psqonline.org.

**Prevent Blindness America (1908):** 500 E. Remington Rd., Schaumburg, Ill. 60173. 21 affiliates and divisions. Phone: (800) 331-2020. www.preventblindness.org.

**Professional Engineers, National Society of (1934):** 1420 King St., Alexandria, Va. 22314-2794. 60,000. Phone: (703) 684-2800; fax: (703) 836-4875. www.nspe.org.

**Professional Photographers of America, Inc. (1880):** 299 Peachtree St. N.W., #2200, Atlanta, Ga. 30303-2206. 14,000. Phone: (404) 522-8600. www.ppa.com.

**Psychiatric Association, American (1844):** 1400 K St. N.W., Washington, D.C. 20005. 40,537. Phone: (888) 357-7924. www.psych.org.

**Psychoanalytic Association, The American (1911):** 309 E. 49th St., New York, N.Y. 10017. 3,000+ psychoanalysts. Phone: (212) 752-0450; fax: (212) 593-0571. www.apsa.org.

**Psychological Association, American (1892):** 750 First St. N.E., Washington, D.C. 20002–4242. 159,000. Phone: (202) 336-5510; (202) 336-6123 TTY. www.apa.org.

**Public Health Association, American (1872):** 800 I St. N.W., Washington, D.C. 20001-3710. 50,000+. Phone: (202) 777-2742. www.apha.org.

**Puppeteers of America (1937):** P.O. Box 29417, Parma, Ohio 44129-0417. Phone: (888) 568-6235. www.puppeteers.org.

**Quality, The American Society for (1946):** 600 N. Plankinton Ave., Milwaukee, Wis. 53203. 135,000+. Phone: (414) 272-8575. www.asq.org.

**Railroads, Association of American (1934):** 50 F St. N.W., Washington, D.C. 20001-1564. Phone: (202) 639-2100. www.aar.org.

**Recording Arts & Sciences, Inc., National Academy of (1957):** 3402 Pico Blvd., Santa Monica, Calif. 90405. 13,000. Phone: (310) 392-3777. www.grammy.com.

**Red Cross, American (1881):** 430 17th St. N.W., Washington, D.C. 20006. Approx. 1,650 chapters. Phone: (202) 639-3520. www.redcross.org.

**Rehabilitation Association, National (1925):** 633 S. Washington St., Alexandria, Va. 22314. 12,000. Phone: (703) 836-0850; TDD: (703) 836-0849. www.nationalrehab.org.

**Reserve Officers Association of the United States (1922):** 1 Constitution Ave. N.E., Washington, D.C. 20002-5655. 93,000. Phone: (800) 809-9448. www.roa.org.

**Retired Federal Employees, National Association (1921):** 606 N. Washington St., Alexandria, Va. 22314. 400,000+. Phone: (703) 838-7760. www.narfe.org.

**Reye's Syndrome Foundation, National (1974):** P.O. Box 829, Bryan, Ohio 43506-0829. Phone: (800) 233-7393; fax: (419) 636-9897. email: nsrf@reyessyndrome.org www.reyessyndrome.org.

**RID-USA (Remove Intoxicated Drivers) (1978):** Box 520, Schenectady, N.Y. 12301. Phone: (518) 372-0034/(518) 393-HELP; fax: (518) 370-4917. www.crisny.org/not-for-profit/ridusa/.

**Right to Life, Committee, Inc., National (1973):** 512 10th St. N.W., Washington, D.C. 20004. Phone: (202) 626-8800. www.nrlc.org

**Rotary International (1905):** One Rotary Center, 1560 Sherman Ave., Evanston, Ill. 60201. 1.2 million in 161 countries and 35 geographical regions. Phone: (847) 866-3000. www.rotary.org.

**SAE (Society of Automotive Engineers) (1905):** 400 Commonwealth Dr., Warrendale, Pa. 15096-0001. 80,000. Phone: (724) 776-5760. www.sae.org.

**Safety Council, National (1913):** 1121 Spring Lake Dr., Itasca, Ill. 60143-3201. Phone: (630) 285-1121. www.nsc.org.

**Salvation Army, The (1865):** National Headquarters, P.O. Box 269, Alexandria, Va. 22313. 453,150. Phone: (703) 684-5500. www.salvationarmy.org.

**Save-the-Redwoods League (1918):** 114 Sansome St., Rm 1200, San Francisco, Calif. 94104-3823. 45,000. Phone: (415) 362-2352. www.savetheredwoods.org.

**Science, American Association for the Advancement of (1848):** 1200 New York Ave. N.W., Washington, D.C. 20005. 143,000. Phone: (202) 326-6400. www.aaas.org.

**Science and Health, American Council on (1978):** 1995 Broadway, 2nd Flr., New York, N.Y. 10023-5860. Phone: (212) 362-7044; fax: (212) 362-4919. email: acsh@acsh.org. www.acsh.org.

**Science Fiction Society, World (1939):** P.O. Box 426159, Kendall Square Station, Cambridge, Mass. 02142. email: mpc@wsfs.org www.wsfs.org.

**Scientists, Federation of American (FAS) (1945):** 1717 K St. N.W., Ste. 209, Washington, D.C. 20036. 4,000. Phone: (202) 546-3300. www.fas.org.

**SCRABBLE® Association, National (1978):** P.O. Box 700, 403 Front Street Garden, Greenport, N.Y. 11944. 10,000. Phone: (631) 477-0033. www.scrabble-assoc.com

**Screen Actors Guild (1933):** 5757 Wilshire Blvd., Los Angeles, Calif. 90036-3600. 96,000. Phone: (323) 954-1600. www.sag.com.

**Sculpture Society, National (1893):** 237 Park Ave., New York, N.Y. 10017. 4,000. Phone: (212) 701 5010. nationalsculpture.org

**Seeing Eye Inc., The (1929):** P.O. BOX 375, Morristown, N.J. 07963-0375. Phone: (973) 539-4425. www.seeingeye.org.

**Senior Citizens, National Alliance of (1974):** 2525 Wilson Blvd., Arlington, Va. 22201. 117,000. Fax: (703) 528-4380.

**Shrine of North America and Shriners Hospitals for Children, The (1872 and 1922):** 2900 Rocky Point Drive, Tampa, Fla. 33607-1400. 525,000. Phone: (813) 281-0300. www.shrinershq.org.

**Sierra Club (1892):** 85 2nd Street, San Francisco, Calif. 94105-3441. 700,000+. Phone: (415) 977-5500. www.sierraclub.org

**SIETAR INTERNATIONAL (The International Society for Intercultural Education, Training and Research) (1974):** c/o ICHEC, Blvd. Brand Whitlock 2, 1150 Brussels, Belgium. 12,500. Phone: (+32-2) 739 3843. www.sietarinternational.org.

**Simon Wiesenthal Center (1977):** 1399 South Roxbury, Los Angeles, Calif. 90035. 400,000 member families. Phone: (800) 900-9036. www.wiesenthal.org.

**Small Business United, National (1937):** 1156 15th St. N.W., Washington, D.C. 20005. 65,000+. Phone: (202) 293-8830; fax: (202) 872-8543. email: nsbu@nsbu.org. www.nsbu.org.

**Social Work Education, Council on (1952):** 1725 Duke St., Ste. 500, Alexandria, Va. 22314. Phone: (703) 683-8080; fax: (703) 683-8099. www.cswe.org.

**Social Workers, National Association of (1955):** 750 First St. N.E., Ste. 700, Washington, D.C. 20002-4241. Phone: (202) 408-8600. www.naswdc.org.

**Society for Integrative and Comparative Biology (formerly the American Society of Zoologists) (1890):** 1313 Dolley Madison Blvd. #402, McLean, Va. 22101. 2,100. Phone: (703) 790-1745; (800) 955-1236. email: SICB@BurkInc.com www.sicb.org.

**Soil and Water Conservation Society (1945):** 7515 N.E. Ankeny Rd., Ankeny, Iowa 50021. 10,000. Phone: (515) 289-2331; fax: (515) 289-1227. www.swcs.org.

**Songwriters Guild of America, The (1931):** 1500 Harbor Blvd., Weehawken, N.J. 07087-6732. Phone: (201) 867-7603. www.songwriters.org.

**Sons of Italy in America, Order (1905):** 219 E St. N.E., Washington, D.C. 20002. 500,000. Phone: (202) 547-2900. www.osia.org.

**Sons of the American Revolution, National Society of the (1889):** 1000 S. 4th St., Louisville, Ky. 40203. 26,000. Phone: (502) 589-1776. www.sar.org.

**Soroptimist International of the Americas (1921):** Two Penn Center Plaza, Ste. 1000, Philadelphia, Pa. 19102-1883. 100,000. Phone: (215) 557-9300. www.soroptimist.org/

**Southern Early Childhood Association (formerly SACUS) (1948):** P.O. Box 55930, Little Rock, Ark. 72215-5930. 21,000. Phone: (800) 305-7322; fax: (501) 227-5297. email: seca@aristotle.net. www.seca50.org.

**Space Society, National (1974):** 600 Pennsylvania Ave. S.E., Ste. 201, Washington, D.C. 20003. Phone: (202) 543-1900; fax: (202) 546-4189. www.nss.org/.

**Special Olympics International, Inc. (1968):** 1325 G St. N.W., Ste. 500, Washington, D.C., 20005. 1,000,000. Phone: (202) 628-3630. www.specialolympics.org.

**Speech-Language-Hearing Association, American (1925):** 10801 Rockville Pike, Rockville, Md. 20852. 99,000+. Phone & TTY: (800) 638-8255. www.asha.org.

**Sports Car Club of America Inc. (1944):** 9033 E. Easter Place, Centennial, Colo. 80112. 55,000. Phone: (303) 694-7222. www.scca.org/index.html.

**Statistical Association, American (1839):** 1429 Duke St., Alexandria, Va. 22314-3415. 19,000. Phone: (888) 231-3473. www.amstat.org.

**Student Association, United States (1947):** 1413 K Street N.W., 9th Flr., Washington, D.C. 20005. 350 schools (3.5 million students). Phone: (202) 347-8772. www.usstudents.org.

**Surgeons, American College of (1913):** 633 North Saint Clair, Chicago, Ill. 60611-3211. 56,000+. Phone: (312) 202-5000. www.facs.org.

**Symphony Orchestra League, American (1942):** 33 W. 60th St., 5th Fl., New York, N.Y. 10023. 5,500. Phone: (212) 262-5161. www.symphony.org.

**TASH: The Association for Persons with Severe Handicaps (1974):** 29 W. Susquehanna Ave., Ste. 210, Baltimore, Md. 21204. 8,500. Phone: (410) 828-8274. www.tash.org.

**Teachers, American Federation of (1916):** 555 New Jersey Ave. N.W., Washington, D.C., 20001. 900,000+. Phone: (202) 879-4400. www.aft.org.

**Testing & Materials, American Society for (1898):** 100 Barr Harbor Dr., W. Conshohocken, Pa. 19428-2959. 35,000. Phone: (610) 832-9585. www.astm.org.

**The Arc (1950):** 1010 Wayne Ave., Ste. 650, Silver Spring, Md. 20910. A national organization on mental retardation. 140,000 members, 1,200 state and local chapters. Phone: (301) 565-3842. www.thearc.org.

**Theosophical Society in America, The (1875):** P.O. Box 270, Wheaton, Ill. 60189-0270. 4,400. Phone: (630) 668-1571. www.theosophical.org.

**Tin Can Sailors, Inc. (1976):** P.O. Box 100, Somerset, Mass. 02726. 20,900. Phone: (800) 223-5535. www.destroyers.org.

**Toastmasters International (1924):** P.O. Box 9052, Mission Viejo, Calif. 92690-7052. 170,000. Phone: (949) 858-8255; fax: (949) 858-1207. www.toastmasters.org.

**TOUGHLOVE International (1977):** P.O. Box 1069, Doylestown, Pa. 18901. 500 registered groups. Phone: (215) 348-7090. www.toughlove.org.

**TransAfrica Forum (1981):** 1426 21st St. N.W., Washington, D.C. 20036. Phone: (202) 223-1960; fax: (202) 223-1966. www.transafricaforum.org.

**Travel Agents, American Society of (ASTA) (1931):** 1101 King St., Alexandria, Va. 22314. 26,000. Phone: (703) 739-2782. www.astanet.com.

**Travelers Aid International (1851):** 1612 K St. N.W., Ste. 506, Washington, D.C. 20006. 45 agencies, 500+ corporate representatives. Phone: (202) 546-1127; fax: (202) 546-9112. www.travelersaid.org.

**Tuberous Sclerosis Association, Inc., National (1974):** 801 Roeder Rd., Ste. 750, Silver Spring, Md. 20910. 5,000. Phone: (800) 225-6872; fax: (301) 562-9870. www.tsalliance.org.

**UFOs, National Investigations Committee on (1967):** 14617 Victory Blvd., Ste. 4, Van Nuys, Calif. 91411. Phone: (818) 989-5942. www.nicufo.com.

**UNICEF, U.S. Committee for (1947):** 333 E. 38th St., New York, N.Y. 10016. 20,000 volunteers. Phone: (800) FOR-KIDS. www.unicefusa.org.

**Union of Concerned Scientists (1969):** 2 Brattle Square, Cambridge, Mass. 02238. 70,000. Phone: (617) 547-5552. www.ucsusa.org.

**United Daughters of the Confederacy® (1894):** 328 N. Boulevard, Richmond, Va. 23220-4057. 24,000. Phone: (804) 355-1636. www.hqudc.org.

**United Jewish Communities (formerly United Jewish Appeal) (1939):** Ste. 11E, 111 Eighth Ave., New York, N.Y. 10011. Phone: (212) 284-6500. www.ujc.org.

**United Way of America (1918):** 701 N. Fairfax St., Alexandria, Va. 22314-2045. 1,400 local United Ways. Phone: (703) 836-7100; fax: (703) 683-7840. www.unitedway.org.

**University Women, American Association of (1881):** 1111 16th St. N.W., Washington, D.C. 20036. 150,000. Phone: (800) 326-AAUW (2289); TDD: (202) 785-7777. www.aauw.org.

**USO (United Service Organizations) (1941):** World Headquarters, Washington Navy Yard, 1008 Eberle Place SE, Ste. 301, Washington, D.C. 20374-5096. 120 centers worldwide. Phone: (202) 610–5700. www.uso.org.

**Veterans Committee, American (AVC) (1944):** Bethesda, Md. 20817. 15,000. Phone & fax: (301) 320-6490. www.usmm.net/avc-mast45.html

**Veterans of Foreign Wars of the U.S. (1899):** 406 W. 34th St., Kansas City, Mo. 64111. VFW and Auxiliary, 2.1 million. Phone: (816) 756-3390. www.vfw.org.

**Veterinary Medical Association, American (1863):** 1931 N. Meacham Rd., Ste. 100, Schaumburg, Ill. 60173. 62,000. Phone: (847) 925-8070. www.avma.org.

**Volunteers of America (1896):** 1660 Duke St., Alexandria, Va. 22314-3421. 40,000+ volunteers. Phone: (703) 341-5000; (800) 899-0089. www.voa.org.

**War Resisters League (1923):** 339 Lafayette St., New York, N.Y. 10012. 12,000. Phone: (212) 228-0450; fax: (212) 228-6193. www.warresisters.org.

**Washington Legal Foundation (1977):** 2009 Massachusetts Ave. N.W., Washington, D.C. 20036. 100,000. Phone: (202) 588-0302. www.wlf.org.

**Water Quality Association (1974):** 4151 Naperville Rd., Lisle, Ill. 60532. 2,200. Phone: (630) 929-2509; www.wqa.org.

**Welding Society, American (1919):** 550 N.W. LeJeune Rd., Miami, Fla. 33126. 50,000. Phone: (305) 443-9353; (800) 443-9353. www.aws.org.

**Wildlife Fund (U.S.), World (1961):** 1250 24th St. N.W., Washington, D.C. 20037. 1.2 million. Phone: (800) 225-5993. www.wwf.org.

**Woman's Christian Temperance Union, National (1874):** 1730 Chicago Ave., Evanston, Ill. 60201-4585. Under 20,000. Phone: (847) 864-1397. www.wctu.org.

**Women, National Organization for (NOW) (1966):** 733 15th St. N.W., 2nd fl., Washington, D.C. 20005. 500,000. Phone: (202) 628-8669. www.now.org.

**Women Police, The International Association of (1915):** RR#1, Box 149, Deer Isle, Me. 04627-9700. 3,000. Phone: (207) 348-6976; fax: (207) 348-6171. www.iawp.org.

**Women's American ORT (1927):** 315 Park Ave. South, New York, N.Y. 10010. Chapters throughout the U.S. Phone: (800) 51–WAORT. www.waort.org.

**Women's Educational and Industrial Union (1877):** 356 Boylston St., Boston, Mass. 02116. 1,500. Phone: (617) 536-5651; fax: (617) 247-8826. www.weiu.org.

**Women's International League for Peace and Freedom (1915):** 1213 Race St., Philadelphia, Pa. 19107–1691. 10,000. Phone: (215) 563-7110. www.wilpf.org.

**World Future Society (1966):** 7910 Woodmont Ave., Ste. 450, Bethesda, Md. 20814. 30,000. Phone: (301) 656-8274; fax: (301) 951-0394. www.wfs.org.

**World Health, American Association for (1953):** 1825 K St. N.W., Washington, D.C. 20006. Phone: (202) 466-5883, fax: (202) 466-5896. email: AAWHstaff@aol.com. www.aawhworldhealth.org.

**World Peace, International Association of Educators for (1967):** 2267 Sacramento St. #2, San Francisco, Calif. 94115. 102 countries. Phone: (415) 567-9143. www.homeplanet.org/iaewp.

**World Peace Foundation (1910):** 79 John F. Kennedy St., Cambridge, Mass. 02138. Phone: (617) 496-2258; fax: (617) 491-8588. www.worldpeacefoundation.org

**Worldwatch Institute (1974):** 1776 Massachusetts Ave. N.W., Washington, D.C. 20036-1904. Global environmental research organization. Phone: (202) 452-1999; fax: (202) 296-7365. email: worldwatch@worldwatch.org. www.worldwatch.org.

**Writers Union, National (1981):** 113 University Place, 6th Flr., New York, N.Y. 10003. 6,500. Phone: (212) 254-0279. www.nwu.org.

**YMCA of the USA (1844):** 101 N. Wacker Dr., Chicago, Ill. 60606. 16.9 million. Phone: (312) 977-0031. www.ymca.net.

**Young Women's Christian Association of the U.S.A. (1858 in U.S.A., 1855 in England):** Empire State Building, 350 Fifth Ave., Ste. 301, New York, N.Y. 10118. 2,000,000. Phone: (212) 273-7800. www.ywca.org.

**Zero Population Growth (1968):** 1400 Sixteenth St. N.W., Ste. 320, Washington, D.C. 20036. 55,000. Phone: (202) 332-2200. www.zpg.org.

**Zionist Organization of America (1897):** 4 E. 34th St., New York, N.Y. 10016. 50,000. Phone: (212) 481-1500; fax: (212) 481-1515. www.zoa.org.

# Explorations

| Country or place | Event | Explorer | Date |
|---|---|---|---|
| **AFRICA** | | | |
| Sierra Leone | Explored | Hanno, Carthaginian seaman | c. 520 B.C. |
| Zaire River (Congo) | Mouth visited[1] | Diogo Cão, Portuguese explorer | c. 1484 |
| Cape of Good Hope | Rounded | Bartolomeu Diaz, Portuguese explorer | 1488 |
| Gambia River | Explored | Mungo Park, Scottish explorer | 1795 |
| Sahara | Crossed | Dixon Denham and Hugh Clapperton, English explorers | 1822–1823 |
| Zambezi River | Explored[1] | David Livingstone, Scottish explorer | 1851 |
| Sudan | Explored | Heinrich Barth, German explorer | 1852–1855 |
| Victoria Falls | Explored[1] | David Livingstone, Scottish explorer | 1855 |
| Lake Tanganyika | Explored[1] | Richard Burton and John Speke, British explorers | 1858 |
| Lake Victoria, identified as the source of the Nile | Explored | John Speke, British explorer | 1858 |
| Zaire River (Congo) | Traced | Sir Henry M. Stanley, British explorer | 1877 |
| **ASIA** | | | |
| Punjab (India) | Invaded | Alexander the Great, king of Macedonia | 327 B.C. |
| China | Explored | Marco Polo, Italian traveler | c. 1272 |
| Tibet | Visited | Odoric of Pordenone, Italian monk | c. 1325 |
| Southern China | Explored | Niccolò dei Conti, Venetian traveler | c. 1440 |
| India | Explored (Cape route) | Vasco da Gama, Portuguese navigator | 1498 |
| Japan | Visited | St. Francis Xavier of Spain, missionary | 1549 |
| Arabia | Explored | Carsten Niebuhr, German explorer | 1762 |
| China | Explored | Ferdinand Richthofen, German scientist | 1868 |
| Mongolia | Explored | Nikolai M. Przhevalsky, Russian explorer | 1870–1873 |
| Central Asia | Explored | Sven Hedin, Swedish scientist | 1890–1908 |
| **EUROPE** | | | |
| Shetland Islands | Visited | Pytheas of Massilia (Marseille), Greek navigator and geographer | c. 325 B.C. |
| North Cape | Rounded | Ottar, Norwegian explorer | c. 870 |
| Iceland | Colonized | Norwegian noblemen | c. 890–900 |
| **NORTH AMERICA** | | | |
| Greenland | Colonized | Eric the Red, Norwegian | c. 985 |
| Labrador, Newfoundland, Nova Scotia (?) | Explored[1] | Leif Ericsson, Norse explorer | 1000 |
| West Indies | Explored[1] | Christopher Columbus, Italian | 1492 |
| North America | Coast explored[1] | Giovanni Caboto (John Cabot), for British | 1497 |
| Pacific Ocean | Sighted[1] | Vasco Núñez de Balboa, Spanish explorer | 1513 |
| Florida | Explored | Ponce de León, Spanish explorer | 1513 |
| Mexico | Conquered | Hernando Cortés, Spanish adventurer | 1519–1521 |
| St. Lawrence River | Explored[1] | Jacques Cartier, French navigator | 1534 |
| Southwest United States | Explored | Francisco Coronado, Spanish explorer | 1540–1542 |
| Colorado River | Explored[1] | Hernando de Alarcón, Spanish explorer | 1540 |
| Mississippi River | Explored[1] | Hernando de Soto, Spanish explorer | 1541 |
| Frobisher Bay | Explored[1] | Martin Frobisher, English seaman | 1576 |
| Maine Coast | Explored | Samuel de Champlain, French explorer | 1604 |
| Jamestown, Va. | Settled | John Smith, English colonist | 1607 |
| Hudson River | Explored | Henry Hudson, English navigator | 1609 |
| Hudson Bay (Canada) | Explored[1] | Henry Hudson | 1610 |
| Baffin Bay | Explored | William Baffin, English navigator | 1616 |
| Lake Michigan | Navigated | Jean Nicolet, French explorer | 1634 |
| Arkansas River | Explored[1] | Jacques Marquette and Louis Jolliet, French explorers | 1673 |
| Mississippi River | Explored | Sieur de La Salle, French explorer | 1682 |
| Bering Strait | Explored[1] | Vitus Bering, Danish explorer | 1728 |
| Alaska | Explored[1] | Vitus Bering | 1741 |
| Mackenzie River (Canada) | Explored[1] | Sir Alexander Mackenzie, Scottish-Canadian explorer | 1789 |
| Northwest United States | Explored | Meriwether Lewis and William Clark, American explorers | 1804–1806 |
| Northeast Passage (Arctic Ocean) | Navigated | Nils Nordenskjöld, Swedish explorer | 1879 |
| Greenland | Explored | Robert E. Peary, American explorer | 1892 |
| Northwest Passage | Navigated | Roald Amundsen, Norwegian explorer | 1906 |

| Country or place | Event | Explorer | Date |
|---|---|---|---|
| **SOUTH AMERICA** | | | |
| Continent | Explored | Christopher Columbus, Italian | 1498 |
| Brazil | Explored[1] | Pedro Alvarez Cabral, Portuguese | 1500 |
| Peru | Conquered | Francisco Pizarro, Spanish explorer | 1532–1533 |
| Amazon River | Explored | Francisco Orellana, Spanish explorer | 1541 |
| Cape Horn | Explored[1] | Willem C. Schouten, Dutch navigator | 1615 |
| **OCEANIA** | | | |
| Papua New Guinea | Explored | Jorge de Menezes, Portuguese explorer | 1526 |
| Australia | Explored | Abel Janszoon Tasman, Dutch navigator | 1642 |
| Tasmania | Explored[1] | Abel Janszoon Tasman | 1642 |
| Australia | Crossed | John McDouall Stuart, English explorer | 1862 |
| Australia | Explored | Robert Burke and William Wills, Australian explorers | 1861 |
| New Zealand | Sighted (and named) | Abel Janszoon Tasman, Dutch navigator | 1642 |
| New Zealand | Explored | James Cook, English navigator | 1769 |
| **ARCTIC, ANTARCTIC, AND MISCELLANEOUS** | | | |
| Africa, Middle East, Asia, and Europe | Explored | Ibn Batuta, greatest Arab traveler | 1325–1349 |
| Ocean exploration | Expedition | Ferdinand Magellan's ships circled globe for Spain | 1519–1522 |
| Galápagos Islands | Explored | Diego de Rivadeneira, Spanish captain | 1535 |
| Spitsbergen | Explored | Willem Barents, Dutch navigator | 1596 |
| Antarctic Circle | Crossed | James Cook, English navigator | 1773 |
| Antarctica | Explored[1] | Nathaniel Palmer, American whaler (archipelago), and Fabian Gottlieb von Bellingshausen, Russian admiral (mainland) | 1820–1821 |
| Antarctica | Explored | Charles Wilkes, American explorer | 1840 |
| North Pole | Reached[2] | Robert E. Peary, American explorer | 1909 |
| South Pole | Reached | Roald Amundsen, Norwegian explorer | 1911 |

1. First European to reach the area. 2. Admiral Peary's claim to have reached the Pole has been disputed from the beginning—as was the claim made by his former colleague, Dr. Frederick Cook, who has been generally dismissed as a charlatan. The credit ultimately went to Peary, a claim officially backed by the U.S. Congress. But recent scholarship, including evidence culled from the journals and diaries of both Cook and Peary, has cast doubt on both explorers' veracity. If it is the case that neither reached the Pole, then the credit goes to Joseph Fletcher, who landed a U.S. Air Force C-47 plane there in 1952.

## The Continents

A continent is defined as a large unbroken land mass completely surrounded by water, although in some cases continents are (or were in part) connected by land bridges. The seven continents are North America, South America, Europe, Asia, Africa, Australia, and Antarctica. The island groups in the Pacific are often called Oceania but this name does *not* imply that scientists consider them the remains of a continent.

Political considerations have often overridden geographical facts when it came to naming continents. Geographically, Europe, including the British Isles, is a large western peninsula of the continent of Asia; and many geographers, when referring to Europe and Asia, speak of the Eurasian continent. But traditionally, Europe is counted as a separate continent, with the Ural and the Caucasus mountains forming the line of demarcation between Europe and Asia. To the south of Europe, Asia has an odd-shaped peninsula jutting westward, which has a large number of political subdivisions. The northern section is taken up by Turkey; to the south of Turkey there are Syria, Iraq, Israel, Jordan, Saudi Arabia, and a number of smaller Arab countries. All these are part of Asia. Traditionally, the island of Cyprus in the Mediterranean is also considered to be part of Asia.

## Continental Drift and Plate-Tectonics Theory

*Source:* U.S. Dept. of the Interior, Geological Survey

According to the theory of continental drift, the world was made up of a single continent through most of geologic time. That continent eventually separated and drifted apart, forming into the seven continents we have today. The first comprehensive theory of continental drift was suggested by the German meteorologist Alfred Wegener in 1912. The hypothesis asserts that the continents consist of lighter rocks that rest on heavier crustal material—similar to the manner in which icebergs float on water. Wegener contended that the relative positions of the continents are not rigidly fixed but are slowly moving—at a rate of about one yard per century.

According to the generally accepted plate-tectonics theory, scientists believe that Earth's surface is broken into a number of shifting slabs or plates, which average about 50 miles in thickness. These plates move relative to one another above a hotter, deeper, more mobile zone at average rates as great as a few inches per year. Most of the world's active volcanoes are located along or near the boundaries between shifting plates and are called plate-boundary volcanoes.

The peripheral areas of the Pacific Ocean Basin, containing the boundaries of several plates, are dotted with many active volcanoes that form the so-called Ring of Fire.

## World Land Areas and Elevations

| Area | Approximate land area sq. km | Approximate land area sq. mi. | Percentage of total land area | Elevation, feet and meters | |
| --- | --- | --- | --- | --- | --- |
| | | | | Highest | Lowest |
| **WORLD** | 148,429,545 | 57,308,738 | 100.0% | Mt. Everest, Tibet-Nepal, 29,035 ft. (8,850 m)[1] | Dead Sea, Israel-Jordan, 1,349 ft. below sea level (−411 m) |
| **ASIA** (includes the Middle East) | 44,579,160 | 17,212,041 | 30.0 | Mt. Everest, Tibet-Nepal, 29,035 ft. (8,850 m) | Dead Sea, Israel-Jordan, 1,349 ft. below sea level (−411 m) |
| **AFRICA** | 30,065,107 | 11,608,156 | 20.3 | Mt. Kilimanjaro, Tanzania, 19,340 ft. (5,895 m) | Lake Assal, Djibouti, 512 ft. below sea level (−156 m) |
| **NORTH AMERICA** | 24,256,087 | 9,365,290 | 16.3 | Mt. McKinley, Alaska, 20,320 ft. (6,194 m) | Death Valley, Calif., 282 ft. below sea level (−86 m) |
| **SOUTH AMERICA** (includes Central America and the Caribbean) | 17,819,065 | 6,879,952 | 12.0 | Mt. Aconcagua, Argentina, 22,834 ft. (6,960 m) | Valdes Peninsula, Argentina 131 ft. below sea level (−40 m) |
| **ANTARCTICA** | 13,209,047 | 5,100,021 | 8.9 | Vinson Massif, Ellsworth Mts., 16,066 ft. (4,897 m) | Bentley Subglacial Trench, 8,327 ft. below sea level (−2,538 m) |
| **EUROPE** (includes the recently independent states of the former Soviet Union) | 9,938,037 | 3,837,082 | 6.7 | Mt. Elbrus, Russia/Georgia, 18,510 ft. (5,642 m) | Caspian Sea, Russia/Kazakhstan 92 ft. below sea level (−28 m) |
| **AUSTRALIA** (includes Oceania) | 7,687,027 | 2,967,966 | 5.2 | Mt. Kosciusko, Australia, 7,310 ft. (2,228 m) | Lake Eyre, Australia, 52 ft. below sea level (−12 m) |

1. The 1954 elevation of Everest, 29,028 ft (8,848 m) was revised on Nov. 11, 1999, and now stands at 29,035 ft. (8,850 m). *Source:* National Geographic Society.

# Volcanoes of the World

*Source:* U.S. Dept. of the Interior, Geological Survey

About 550 volcanoes have erupted on Earth's surface since recorded history; about 60 are active each year. Far more have erupted unobserved on the ocean floor. Most volcanoes exist at the boundaries of Earth's crustal plates, such as the famous Ring of Fire that surrounds the Pacific Ocean plate. Fifty volcanoes have erupted in the United States since recorded history, and the United States ranks third, behind Indonesia and Japan, in the number of historically active volcanoes.

### The Nature of Volcanoes

Volcanoes are built by the accumulation of their own eruptive products—lava, bombs (crusted over ash flows), and tephra (airborne ash and dust). A volcano is most commonly a conical hill or mountain built around a vent that connects with reservoirs of molten rock below the surface of Earth. The term *volcano* also refers to the opening or vent through which molten rock and gases are expelled.

Driven by buoyancy and gas pressure, the molten rock, which is lighter than the surrounding solid rock, forces its way upward and may ultimately break though zones of weaknesses in Earth's crust. If so, an eruption begins, and the molten rock may pour from the vent as nonexplosive lava flows, or it may shoot violently into the air as dense clouds of lava fragments. Larger fragments fall back around the vent, and accumulations of fall-back fragments may move downslope as ash flows under the force of gravity. Some of the finer ejected materials may be carried by the wind and fall to the ground many miles away. The finest ash particles may be injected miles into the atmosphere and carried many times around the world by stratospheric winds before settling out.

### Magma, Lava, and Pumice

Molten rock below the surface of Earth that rises in volcanic vents is known as magma, but after it erupts from a volcano it is called lava. Originating many tens of miles beneath the ground, the ascending magma commonly contains some crystals, fragments of surrounding (unmelted) rocks, and dissolved gases, but it is primarily a liquid composed of oxygen, silicon, aluminum, iron, magnesium, calcium, sodium, potassium, titanium, and manganese. Magmas also contain many other chemical elements in trace quantities. Upon cooling, the liquid magma may precipitate crystals of various minerals until solidification is complete to form an igneous or magmatic rock.

Lava is red-hot when it pours or blasts out of a vent but soon changes to dark red, gray, black, or some other color as it cools and solidifies. Very hot, gas-rich lava containing abundant iron and magnesium is fluid and flows like hot tar, whereas cooler, gas-poor lava high in silicon, sodium, and potassium flows sluggishly, like thick honey, or in other cases, like pasty, blocky masses.

All magmas contain dissolved gases, and as they rise to the surface to erupt, the confining pressures are reduced and the dissolved gases are liberated either quietly or explosively. If the lava is a thin fluid (not viscous), the gases may escape easily. But if the lava is thick and pasty (highly viscous), the gases will not move freely but will build up tremendous pressure and ultimately escape with explosive violence, throwing out great masses of solid rock as well as lava, dust, and ashes.

The violent separation of gas from lava may produce rock froth called pumice. Some of this froth is so light—because of the many gas bubbles—that it floats on water. In many eruptions the froth is shattered explosively into small fragments that are hurled high into the air in the form of volcanic cinders (red or black), volcanic ash (commonly tan or gray), and volcanic dust. ☐

## Recent Volcanic Activity

(**Bold** indicates activity in 2002)

| Volcano | Date of last eruption or activity | Volcano | Date of last eruption or activity |
|---|---|---|---|
| Adatara, Honshu, Japan | Sept. 15, 1997 | Maroa, New Zealand | March 30, 2001 |
| Akutan, Alaska | March 10, 1996 | Masaya, Nicaragua | April 23, 2001 |
| Amukta, Alaska | Sept. 17, 1996 | Mayon, Philippines | July 26, 2001 |
| Arenal, Costa Rica | April 4, 2001 | McDonald Island, Australia | Dec. 1996 |
| Axial Seamount | Jan. 25–28, 1998 | **Merapi, Indonesia** | **March 3, 2002** |
| Bandai, Honshu, Japan | Aug. 16, 2000 | Metis Shoal, Tonga | June 6, 1995 |
| Barren Island, Indian Ocean | Dec. 20, 1994 | Momotombo, Nicaragua | April 4, 1996 |
| Bezymianny, Kamchatka, Russia | March 15, 2000 | Monowai Seamount, Kermadec Islands | Dec. 5, 1997 |
| Bromo, Java, Indonesia | Nov. 30, 2000 | | |
| Mount Cameroon, Cameroon | June 7, 2000 | Nyamuragira, Congo (Dem. Rep.) | Feb. 6, 2001 |
| Canlaon, Philippines | Jan. 2001 | **Nyiragongo, Congo (Dem. Rep.)** | **Jan. 18, 2002** |
| Cerro Azul, Galápagos Islands, Ecuador | Oct. 5, 1998 | Okmok, Alaska | May 2, 1997 |
| | | **Mount Oyama, Japan** | **April 2, 2002** |
| Cerro Negro, Nicaragua | Aug. 6, 1999 | Pacaya, Guatemala | Feb. 21, 2001 |
| Chiginagak, Alaska | Nov. 7, 1997 | Papandayan, Java, Indonesia | July 1, 1998 |
| Mt. Cleveland, Chuginadak, Alaska | March 20, 2001 | Pavlof, Alaska | June 3, 1997 |
| **Colima, Mexico** | **March 25, 2002** | Peuet Sague, Indonesia | April 27, 1998 |
| Copahue, Argentina and Chile | July 16, 2000 | Piparo, Trinidad | Feb. 22, 1997 |
| Eastern Gemini Seamount, Vanuatu | Feb. 23, 1996 | **Piton de la Fournaise, Réunion, Indian Ocean** | **Jan. 16, 2002** |
| **Etna, Sicily, Italy** | **June 23, 2002** | **Popocatepetl, Mexico** | **July 9, 2002** |
| Fernandina, Galápagos | Jan. 25, 1995 | Rabaul, Papua New Guinea | May 28, 1997 |
| Fogo, Cape Verde | April 2, 1995 | Rincon de la Vieja, Costa Rica | Feb. 16, 1998 |
| **Fuego, Guatemala** | **Feb. 12, 2002** | Rotorua, New Zealand | Jan. 26, 2001 |
| Grimsvotn, Iceland | Dec. 18–28, 1998 | Ruapehu, New Zealand | Sept. 13, 1999 |
| Guagua Pichincha, Ecuador | July 12, 2000 | Ruby Seamount, Mariana Islands | Oct. 25, 1995 |
| Hakkoda, Japan | July 12, 1997 | Mount St. Helens, Washington | July 1, 1998 |
| Hekla, Iceland | Feb. 26, 2000 | Sakura-Jima, Japan | Oct. 9, 2000 |
| Mount Hili Aludo, Indonesia | May 13, 1997 | San Cristobal, Nicaragua | May 10, 2001 |
| Hosho, Kyushu, Japan | Oct. 12, 1995 | **Semeru, Java, Indonesia** | **April 30, 2002** |
| Ijen, Java, Indonesia | Feb. 5, 2001 | **Sheveluch, Kamchatka, Russia** | **July 9, 2002** |
| Iwate-san, Honshu, Japan | July 10, 1998 | Shin-dake, Kuchinoerabujima Island, Japan | Aug. 26, 1999 |
| Jackson Segment, N. Gorda Ridge (nr. Oregon) | April 3, 2001 | | |
| Kaba, Sumatra, Indonesia | Aug. 17, 2000 | Shishaldin, Unimak Island, Alaska | May 15, 2000 |
| **Mount Karangetang, Indonesia** | **July 1, 2002** | **Soufriere Hills, Montserrat, West Indies** | **Jan. 5, 2002– continuing** |
| **Karymsky, Kamchatka, Russia** | **July 9, 2002** | South Sister, Oregon | May 8, 2001 |
| **Kavachi Seamount, Solomon Islands** | **Jan. 13, 2002** | **Stromboli, Italy** | **Jan. 23, 2002** |
| | | Tavurvur, Papua New Guinea | Sept. 6, 2000 |
| Kelut, Java, Indonesia | Jan. 29, 2001 | Taal, Philippines | Sept. 30, 1999 |
| **Kilauea, Hawaii** | **1983–ongoing** | Telica, Nicaragua | Aug. 11, 1999 |
| **Kliuchevskoi, Kamchatka, Russia** | **Feb. 27, 2002** | Terceira, Azores | Jan. 8, 1999 |
| Komagatake, Hokkaido, Japan | Nov. 8, 2000 | Tonga (unnamed volcano) | Jan. 18, 1999 |
| Korovin, Alaska | June 30, 1998 | **Tungurahua, Ecuador** | **July 12, 2002** |
| Krakatau, Indonesia | March 27, 2001 | **Ulawun, New Britain, Papua New Guinea** | **Feb. 21, 2002** |
| **Langila, New Britain** | **July 11, 2002** | | |
| Lascar, Chile | July 20, 2000 | Usu, Japan | April 17, 2000 |
| Mount Lewotobi, Indonesia | July 1, 1999 | Villarrica, Chile | Jan. 20–May 30, 2000 |
| Loihi Seamount, Hawaii | July 26, 1996 | | |
| **Lokon, Sulawesi, Indonesia** | **April 14, 2002** | **White Island, New Zealand** | **July 27, 2000– ongoing** |
| Long Valley caldera, California | April 2, 1996 | | |
| Lopevi, Central Islands, Vanuatu | June 8, 2001 | Yellowstone, Wyoming | Jan. 9, 1998 |
| La Madera, Nicaragua | Sept. 27, 1996 | Zacatecas, Mexico | June 1997 |
| **Manam, Papua New Guinea** | **May 20, 2002** | | |

*Source:* Volcano World, University of North Dakota (http://volcano.und.nodak.edu) and the European Volcanological Society (www.sveurop.org).

## The Deadliest Volcanic Eruptions

| Volcano | Year | Deaths | Major cause of deaths |
|---|---|---|---|
| Tambora, Indonesia | 1815 | 92,000 | Starvation |
| Krakatau, Indonesia | 1883 | 36,417 | Tsunami |
| Mount Pelee, Martinique | 1902 | 29,025 | Ash flows |
| Ruiz, Colombia | 1985 | 25,000 | Mudflows |
| Unzen, Japan | 1792 | 14,300 | Volcano collapse, tsunami |
| Laki, Iceland | 1783 | 9,350 | Starvation |
| Kelut, Indonesia | 1919 | 5,110 | Mudflows |
| Galunggung, Indonesia | 1882 | 4,011 | Mudflows |
| Vesuvius, Italy | 1631 | 3,500 | Mudflows, lava flows |
| Vesuvius, Italy | 79 | 3,360 | Ash flows and falls |
| Papandayan, Indonesia | 1772 | 2,957 | Ash flows |
| Lamington, Papua New Guinea | 1951 | 2,942 | Ash flows |
| El Chichon, Mexico | 1982 | 2,000 | Ash flows |
| Soufriere, St. Vincent | 1902 | 1,680 | Ash flows |
| Oshima, Japan | 1741 | 1,475 | Tsunami |
| Asama, Japan | 1783 | 1,377 | Ash flows, mudflows |
| Taal, Philippines | 1911 | 1,335 | Ash flows |
| Mayon, Philippines | 1814 | 1,200 | Mudflows |
| Agung, Indonesia | 1963 | 1,184 | Ash flows |
| Cotopaxi, Ecuador | 1877 | 1,000 | Mudflows |
| Pinatubo, Philippines | 1991 | 800 | Disease |
| Komagatake, Japan | 1640 | 700 | Tsunami |
| Ruiz, Colombia | 1845 | 700 | Mudflows |
| Hibok-Hibok, Philippines | 1951 | 500 | Ash flows |

NOTE: All eruptions with more than 500 known human fatalities. Based on data in *Volcanic Hazards: A Sourcebook on the Effects of Eruptions* by Russell J. Blong (Academic Press, 1984). *Source:* Volcano World, University of North Dakota (http://volcano.und.nodak.edu).

## Principal Types of Volcanoes
*Source:* U.S. Dept. of the Interior, Geological Survey

Geologists generally group volcanoes into four main kinds—cinder cones, composite volcanoes, shield volcanoes, and lava domes.

### Cinder Cones

Cinder cones are the simplest type of volcano. They are built from particles and blobs of congealed lava ejected from a single vent. As the gas-charged lava is blown violently into the air, it breaks into small fragments that solidify and fall as cinders around the vent to form a circular or oval cone. Most cinder cones have a bowl-shaped crater at the summit and rarely rise more than a thousand feet or so above their surroundings. Cinder cones are numerous in western North America as well as throughout other volcanic terrains of the world.

### Composite Volcanoes

Composite volcanoes, sometimes called *stratovolcanoes*, are typically deep-sided, symmetrical cones of large dimension built of alternating layers of lava flows, volcanic ash, cinders, blocks, and bombs and may rise as much as 8,000 ft above their bases. Some of the most beautiful mountains in the world are composite volcanoes, including Mount Fuji in Japan, Mount Cotopaxi in Ecuador, Mount Shasta in California, Mount Hood in Oregon, and Mount St. Helens and Mount Rainier in Washington.

Most composite volcanoes have a crater at the summit that contains a central vent or a clustered group of vents. Lavas either flow through breaks in the crater wall or issue from fissures on the flanks of the cone. Lava, solidified within the fissures, forms *dikes* that act as ribs which greatly strengthen the cone.

The essential feature of a composite volcano is a conduit system through which magma from a reservoir deep in Earth's crust rises to the surface. The volcano is built up by the accumulation of material erupted through the conduit and increases in size as lava, cinders, and ash are added to its slopes.

### Shield Volcanoes

Shield volcanoes are built almost entirely of fluid lava flows. Flow after flow pours out in all directions from a central summit vent, or group of vents, building a broad, gently sloping cone of flat, domical shape, with a profile much like that of a warrior's shield. They are built up slowly by the accretion of thousands of flows of highly fluid basaltic (from *basalt*, a hard, dense dark volcanic rock) lava that spread widely over great distances, and then cool as thin, gently dipping sheets. Lavas also commonly erupt from vents along fractures (rift zones) that develop on the flanks of the cone. Some of the largest volcanoes in the world are shield volcanoes. In northern California and Oregon, many shield volcanoes have diameters of 3 or 4 mi and heights of 1,500 to 2,000 ft. The Hawaiian Islands are composed of linear chains of these volcanoes including Kilauea and Mauna Loa on the island of Hawaii.

In some shield volcano eruptions, basaltic lava pours out quietly from long fissures instead of central vents and floods the surrounding countryside, forming broad plateaus. Lava plateaus of this type can be seen in Iceland, southeast Washington, eastern Oregon, and southern Idaho.

### Lava Domes

Volcanic or lava domes are formed by relatively small, bulbous masses of lava too viscous to flow any great distance; consequently, on extrusion, the lava piles over and around its vent. A dome grows largely by expansion from within. As it grows, its outer surface cools and hardens, then shatters, spilling loose fragments down its sides. Some domes form craggy knobs or spines over the volcanic vent, whereas others form short, steep-sided lava flows known as *coulees*. Volcanic domes commonly occur within the craters or on the flanks of large composite volcanoes. The nearly circular Novarupta Dome that formed during the 1912 eruption of Katmai Volcano, Alaska, measures 800 ft across and 200 ft high. The internal structure of this dome—defined by layering of lava fanning upward and outward from the center—indicates that it grew largely by expansion from within. Mount Pelée in Martinique, West Indies, and Lassen Peak and Mono domes in California are examples of lava domes.

## Submarine Volcanoes

Submarine volcanoes and volcanic vents are common features on certain zones of the ocean floor. Some are active at the present time and, in shallow water, disclose their presence by blasting steam and rock-debris high above the surface of the sea.

Many others lie at such great depths that the tremendous weight of the water above them results in high, confining pressure and prevents the formation and release of steam and gases. Even very large, deepwater eruptions may not disturb the ocean floor.

The famous black sand beaches of Hawaii were created virtually instantaneously by the violent interaction between hot lava and seawater.

# Earthquakes

## The Severity of an Earthquake

*Source:* National Earthquake Information Center, U.S. Geological Survey

Earthquakes are the result of forces deep within Earth's interior that continuously affect its surface. The energy from these forces is stored in a variety of ways within the rocks. When this energy is released suddenly—by shearing movements along faults in the crust of Earth, for example—an earthquake results. The area of the fault where the sudden rupture takes place is called the focus or hypocenter of the earthquake. The point on Earth's surface directly above the focus is called the epicenter of the earthquake.

The severity of an earthquake can be expressed in terms of both intensity and magnitude. The two terms are quite different, however, and they are often confused. Intensity is based on the observed effects of ground shaking on people, buildings, and natural features. It varies from place to place within the disturbed region depending on the location of the observer with respect to the earthquake epicenter. Magnitude is related to the amount of seismic energy released at the hypocenter of the earthquake. It is based on the amplitude of the earthquake waves recorded on instruments, which have a common calibration. Magnitude is thus represented by a single, instrumentally determined value.

## The Richter Magnitude Scale

Seismic waves are the vibrations from earthquakes that travel through Earth; they are recorded on instruments called seismographs. Seismographs record a zigzag trace that shows the varying amplitude of ground oscillations beneath the instrument. Sensitive seismographs, which greatly magnify these ground motions, can detect strong earthquakes from sources anywhere in the world. The time, location, and magnitude of an earthquake can be determined from the data recorded by seismograph stations.

The Richter magnitude scale was developed in 1935 by Charles F. Richter of the California Institute of Technology as a mathematical device to compare the size of earthquakes. The magnitude of an earthquake is determined from the logarithm of the amplitude of waves recorded by seismographs. Adjustments are included in the magnitude formula to compensate for the variation in the distance between the various seismographs and the epicenter of the earthquakes. On the Richter Scale, magnitude is expressed in whole numbers and decimal fractions. For example, a magnitude of 5.3 might be computed for a moderate earthquake, and a strong earthquake might be rated as magnitude 6.3. Because of the logarithmic basis of the scale, each whole number increase in magnitude represents a tenfold increase in measured amplitude; as an estimate of energy, each whole number step in the magnitude scale corresponds to the release of about 31 times more energy than the amount associated with the preceding whole number value. Although the Richter Scale has no upper limit, the largest known shocks have had magnitudes in the 8.8 to 8.9 range.

## Why Are There So Many Earthquake Magnitude Scales?

Earthquake size, as measured by the Richter Scale, is a well-known, but not well understood, concept. What is even less well understood is the proliferation of magnitude scales and their relation to Richter's original magnitude scale. Richter's magnitude scale was first created for measuring the size of earthquakes occurring in southern California, using relatively high-frequency data from nearby seismograph stations. This magnitude scale was referred to as ML, with the L standing for local.

As more seismograph stations were installed around the world, it became apparent that the method developed by Richter was strictly valid only for certain frequency and distance ranges. In order to take advantage of the growing number of globally distributed seismograph stations, new magnitude scales that are an extension of Richter's original idea were developed. These include body-wave magnitude, "mb," and surface-wave magnitude, "MS." Each is valid for a particular frequency range and type of seismic signal. In its range of validity each is equivalent to the Richter magnitude.

Because of the limitations of all three magnitude scales—ML, mb, and MS—a new, more uniformly applicable extension of the magnitude scale, known as moment magnitude, or "MW," was developed. In particular, for very large earthquakes moment magnitude gives the most reliable estimate of earthquake size. New techniques that take advantage of modern telecommunications have recently been implemented, allowing reporting agencies to obtain rapid estimates of moment magnitude for significant earthquakes. So nowadays, when most seismologists announce a magnitude number, they are rarely referring to the Richter Scale.

## The Modified Mercalli Intensity Scale

The effect of an earthquake on Earth's surface is called the intensity. The intensity scale consists of a series of certain key responses, such as people awakening, movement of furniture, damage to chimneys, and finally—total destruction. Although numerous intensity scales have been developed over the past several hundred years to evaluate the effects of earthquakes, the one currently used in the United States is the Modified Mercalli (MM) Intensity Scale. It was developed in 1931 by the American seismologists Harry Wood and Frank Neumann. This scale, composed of 12 increasing levels of intensity that range from imperceptible shaking to catastrophic destruction, is designated by Roman numerals. It does not have a mathematical basis; instead it is an arbitrary ranking based on observed effects. The Modified Mercalli Intensity value assigned to a specific site after an earthquake has a more meaningful measure of severity to the nonscientist than the magnitude because intensity refers to the effects actually experienced at that place.

## Frequency of Earthquakes Worldwide[1]

| Descriptor | Magnitude | Annual average | Descriptor | Magnitude | Annual average |
|---|---|---|---|---|---|
| Great | 8 or higher | 1 | Light | 4–4.9 | c. 6,200 |
| Major | 7–7.9 | 18 | Minor | 3–3.9 | c. 49,000 |
| Strong | 6–6.9 | 120 | Very minor | 2–3 | c. 1,000[2] |
| Moderate | 5–5.9 | 800 | Very minor | 1–2 | c. 8,000[2] |

1. Since 1900. 2. Per day. *Source:* National Earthquake Information Center, U.S. Geological Survey.

## Number of Earthquakes Worldwide, 1990–2002, and Mortality Figures[1]

| Magnitude | 1990 | 1993 | 1994 | 1995 | 1996 | 1997 | 1998 | 1999 | 2000 | 2001 | 2002 |
|---|---|---|---|---|---|---|---|---|---|---|---|
| 8.0–9.9 | 0 | 1 | 2 | 3 | 1 | 0 | 2 | 0 | 4 | 1 | 0 |
| 7.0–7.9 | 12 | 15 | 13 | 22 | 21 | 20 | 14 | 23 | 16 | 14 | 9 |
| 6.0–6.9 | 115 | 141 | 161 | 185 | 160 | 125 | 113 | 123 | 153 | 127 | 83 |
| 5.0–5.9 | 1,635 | 1,449 | 1,542 | 1,327 | 1,223 | 1,118 | 979 | 1,106 | 1,345 | 1,199 | 682 |
| 4.0–4.9 | 4,493 | 5,034 | 4,544 | 8,140 | 8,794 | 7,938 | 7,303 | 7,042 | 8,045 | 8,143 | 5,313 |
| 3.0–3.9 | 2,457 | 4,263 | 5,000 | 5,002 | 4,869 | 4,467 | 5,945 | 5,521 | 4,784 | 6,137 | 4,076 |
| 2.0–2.9 | 2,364 | 5,390 | 5,369 | 3,838 | 2,388 | 2,397 | 4,091 | 4,201 | 3,758 | 4,140 | 3,405 |
| 1.0–1.9 | 474 | 1,177 | 779 | 645 | 295 | 388 | 805 | 715 | 1,028 | 948 | 687 |
| 0.1–0.9 | 0 | 9 | 17 | 19 | 1 | 4 | 10 | 5 | 5 | 1 | 3 |
| No magnitude | 5,062 | 3,997 | 1,944 | 1,826 | 2,186 | 3,415 | 2,426 | 2,096 | 3,120 | 2,871 | 1,849 |
| Total | 16,612 | 21,476 | 19,371 | 21,007 | 19,938 | 19,872 | 21,688 | 20,832 | 22,256 | 23,581[1] | 16,107[1] |
| Estimated deaths | 51,916 | 10,036 | 1,038 | 7,949 | 419 | 2,907 | 8,928 | 22,711 | 231 | 21,357 | 1,595 |

1. As of Sept. 20, 2002. *Source:* National Earthquake Information Center, U.S. Geological Survey.

## Major Earthquakes around the World, 2002[1]

| Date | Location | Magnitude[1] | Date | Location | Magnitude[1] |
|---|---|---|---|---|---|
| Jan. 2 | Vanuatu Islands | 7.3 | June 28 | E. Russia-N.E. China Border Region | 7.3 |
| March 3 | Hindu Kush region, Afghanistan | 7.4 | | | |
| March 5 | Mindanao, Philippines | 7.5 | Aug. 19 | Fiji Islands | 7.6 |
| March 31 | Taiwan region | 7.1 | Aug. 19 | South of Fiji Islands | 7.7 |
| April 26 | Mariana Islands | 7.1 | Sept. 8 | Papua New Guinea | 7.6 |

NOTE: A major earthquake is defined here as having a magnitude of 7.0 or more. 1. As of Sept. 2002. 2. Unless otherwise indicated, magnitudes listed are moment magnitudes, the newest, most uniformly applicable magnitude scale. *Source:* National Earthquake Information Center, U.S. Geological Survey.

## Estimated Deaths from Earthquakes, 2002[1]

| Date | Region | Magnitude | Number killed[2] | Date | Region | Magnitude | Number killed[2] |
|---|---|---|---|---|---|---|---|
| Jan. 9 | Tajikistan | 5.2 | 3 | April 12 | Hindu Kush region, Afghanistan | 5.9 | 50 |
| Jan. 10 | Papua New Guinea | 6.7 | 1 | | | | |
| Jan. 20 | Dem. Rep. of Congo | 4.7 | Several | April 22 | Near coast of Peru | 4.4 | 1 |
| Jan. 22 | Crete, Greece | 6.3 | 1 | April 24 | Northwestern Balkan region | 5.7 | 1 |
| Feb. 3 | Turkey | 6.5 | 44 | | | | |
| Feb. 17 | Southern Iran | 5.4 | 1 | April 24 | Western Iran | 4.9 | 2 |
| March 3 | Hindu Kush region, Afghanistan | 7.4 | 166 | April 25 | Northwestern Caucasus | 4.7 | 5 |
| March 5 | Mindanao, Philippines | 7.5 | 15 | May 15 | Taiwan | 6.2 | 1 |
| March 25 | Hindu Kush region, Afghanistan | 6.1 | 1,000 | May 18 | Lake Victoria Region | 5.5 | 2 |
| | | | | June 22 | Western Iran | 6.5 | 261 |
| March 31 | Taiwan | 7.1 | 5 | | | | |
| April 1 | Papua New Guinea | 5.9 | 36 | **Total** | | | **1,595** |

1. As of Sept. 2002. 2. Includes "missing and presumed dead." *Source:* National Earthquake Information Center, U.S. Geological Survey.

## The Ten Largest[1] Earthquakes of the 20th Century

| Location | Date | Magnitude[2] | Location | Date | Magnitude[2] |
|---|---|---|---|---|---|
| 1. Chile | May 22, 1960 | 9.5 | 6. Rat Islands, Aleutian Islands | Feb. 4, 1965 | 8.7 |
| 2. Prince William Sound, Alaska | March 28, 1964 | 9.2 | 7. India-China border | Aug. 15, 1950 | 8.6 |
| 3. Andreanof Islands, Aleutian Islands | March 9, 1957 | 9.1 | 8. Kamchatka | Feb. 3, 1923 | 8.5 |
| 4. Kamchatka | Nov. 4, 1952 | 9.0 | 9. Banda Sea, Indonesia | Feb. 1, 1938 | 8.5 |
| 5. Off the coast of Ecuador | Jan. 31, 1906 | 8.8 | 10. Kuril Islands | Oct. 13, 1963 | 8.5 |

1. In terms of magnitude. 2. Moment magnitude. *Source:* National Earthquake Information Center, U.S. Geological Survey.

## Deadliest Earthquakes on Record

(50,000 deaths or more)

| Date | Location | Deaths | Magnitude | Date | Location | Deaths | Magnitude |
|---|---|---|---|---|---|---|---|
| Jan. 23, 1556 | Shansi, China | 830,000 | n.a. | Sept. 1290 | Chihli, China | 100,000 | n.a. |
| July 27, 1976 | Tangshan China | 255,000[1] | 8.0 | Nov. 1667 | Shemakha, Caucasia | 80,000 | n.a. |
| Aug. 9, 1138 | Aleppo, Syria | 230,000 | n.a. | Nov. 18, 1727 | Tabriz, Iran | 77,000 | n.a. |
| May 22, 1927 | near Xining, China | 200,000 | 8.3 | Nov. 1, 1755 | Lisbon, Portugal | 70,000 | 8.7 |
| Dec. 22, 856[2] | Damghan, Iran | 200,000 | n.a. | Dec. 25, 1932 | Gansu, China | 70,000 | 7.6 |
| Dec. 16, 1920 | Gansu, China | 200,000 | 8.6 | May 31, 1970 | Peru | 66,000 | 7.8 |
| March 23, 893[2] | Ardabil, Iran | 150,000 | n.a. | 1268[4] | Silicia, Asia Minor | 60,000 | n.a. |
| Sept. 1, 1923 | Kwanto, Japan | 143,000 | 8.3 | Jan. 11, 1693 | Sicily, Italy | 60,000 | n.a. |
| Oct. 5, 1948 | Ashgabat, Turkmenistan, USSR | 110,000 | 7.3 | May 30, 1935 | Quetta, Pakistan | 30,000– 60,000 | 7.5 |
| Dec. 28, 1908 | Messina, Italy | 70,000– 100,000[3] | 7.5 | Feb. 4, 1783 | Calabria, Italy | 50,000 | n.a. |
| | | | | June 20, 1990 | Iran | 50,000 | 7.7 |

1. Official. Estimated death toll as high as 655,000. 2. Note that these dates are prior to A.D. 1000. No digit is missing. 3. Estimated. 4. No date available. *Source:* National Earthquake Information Center, U.S. Geological Survey. Data compiled from several sources.

## The World's 14 Highest Mountain Peaks (above 8,000 meters)

All 14 of the world's 8,000-meter peaks are located in the Himalaya or the Karakoram ranges in Asia. According to Everestnews.com, only ten climbers have reached the summits of all 14: Reinhold Messner (Italy) was first, followed by Jerzy Kukuczka (Poland), Ehardt Loretan (Switzerland), Carlos Carsolio (Mexico), Krzysztof Wielicki (Poland), Juan Oiarzabal (Spain), Sergio Martini (Italy), Park Young Seok (Korea), Hang-Gil Um (Korea), and Alberto Inurrategui (Spain).

| Mountain | Location | Height Meters | Height Feet | First to summit (nationality) | Date |
|---|---|---|---|---|---|
| 1. Everest[1] | Nepal/Tibet | 8,850 | 29,035 | Edmund Hillary (New Zealander, UK), Tenzing Norgay (Nepalese) | May 29, 1953 |
| 2. K2 (Godwin Austen) | Pakistan/China | 8,611 | 28,250 | A. Compagnoni, L. Lacedelli (Italian) | July 31, 1954 |
| 3. Kangchenjunga | Nepal/India | 8,586 | 28,169 | G. Band, J. Brown, N. Hardie, S. Streather (UK) | May 25, 1955 |
| 4. Lhotse | Nepal/Tibet | 8,516 | 27,940 | F. Luchsinger, E. Reiss (Swiss) | May 18, 1956 |
| 5. Makalu | Nepal/Tibet | 8,463 | 27,766 | J. Couzy, L. Terray, J. Franco, G. Magnone-Gialtsen, J. Bouier, S. Coupé, P. Leroux, A. Vialatte (French) | May 15, 1955 |
| 6. Cho Oyu | Nepal/Tibet | 8,201 | 26,906 | H. Tichy, S. Jöchler (Austrian), Pasang Dawa Lama (Nepalese) | Oct. 19, 1954 |
| 7. Dhaulagiri | Nepal | 8,167 | 26,795 | A. Schelbert, E. Forrer, K. Diemberger, P. Diener (Swiss), Nyima Dorji, Nawang Dorji (Nepalese) | May 13, 1960 |
| 8. Manaslu | Nepal | 8,163 | 26,781 | T. Imamishi, K. Kato, M. Higeta, (Japanese) G. Norbu (Nepalese) | May 9, 1956 |
| 9. Nanga Parbat | Pakistan | 8,125 | 26,660 | Hermann Buhl (Austrian) | July 3, 1953 |
| 10. Annapurna | Nepal | 8,091 | 26,545 | M. Herzog, L. Lachenal (French) | June 3, 1950 |
| 11. Gasherbrum I | Pakistan/China | 8,068 | 26,470 | P. K. Schoeing, A. J. Kauffman | July 4, 1958 |
| 12. Broad Peak | Pakistan/China | 8,047 | 26,400 | M. Schmuck, F. Wintersteller, K. Diemberger, H. Buhl (Austrian) | June 9, 1957 |
| 13. Gasherbrum II | Pakistan/China | 8,035 | 26,360 | F. Moravec, S. Larch, H. Willenpart (Austrian) | July 7, 1956 |
| 14. Shisha Pangma | Tibet | 8,013 | 26,289 | Hsu Ching and team of 9 (Chinese) | May 2, 1964 |

1. The 1955 elevation of Everest, 29,028 ft. (8,848 m), was revised on Nov. 11, 1999, and now stands at 29,035 ft. (8,850 m).

# Highest Mountain Peaks of the World (continued from p. 492)

(*See* p. 502 for U.S. peaks.)

| Mountain peak | Range | Location | Height ft | Height m | Mountain peak | Range | Location | Height ft | Height m |
|---|---|---|---|---|---|---|---|---|---|
| Annapurna II | Himalayas | Nepal | 26,041 | 7,937 | Gauri Sankar | Himalayas | Nepal/Tibet | 23,440 | 7,145 |
| Gyachung Kang | Himalayas | Nepal | 25,910 | 7,897 | Badrinath | Himalayas | India | 23,420 | 7,138 |
| | | | | | Nunkun | Himalayas | Kashmir | 23,410 | 7,135 |
| Disteghil Sar | Karakoram | Pakistan | 25,858 | 7,882 | Lenin Peak | Pamirs | Tajikistan/ Kyr- gyzstan | 23,405 | 7,134 |
| Himalchuli | Himalayas | Nepal | 25,801 | 7,864 | | | | | |
| Nuptse | Himalayas | Nepal | 25,726 | 7,841 | | | | | |
| Nanda Devi | Himalayas | India | 25,663 | 7,824 | Pyramid | Himalayas | Nepal | 23,400 | 7,132 |
| Masherbrum | Karakoram | Kashmir[1] | 25,660 | 7,821 | Api | Himalayas | Nepal | 23,399 | 7,132 |
| Rakaposhi | Karakoram | Pakistan | 25,551 | 7,788 | Pauhunri | Himalayas | India/China | 23,385 | 7,128 |
| Kanjut Sar | Karakoram | Pakistan | 25,461 | 7,761 | Trisul | Himalayas | India | 23,360 | 7,120 |
| Kamet | Himalayas | India/Tibet | 25,446 | 7,756 | Korzhenevski Peak | Pamirs | Tajikistan | 23,310 | 7,105 |
| Namcha Barwa | Himalayas | Tibet | 25,445 | 7,756 | Kangto | Himalayas | Tibet | 23,260 | 7,090 |
| Gurla Mandhata | Himalayas | Tibet | 25,355 | 7,728 | Nyainqen- tanglha | Nyainqen- tanglha Shan | China | 23,255 | 7,088 |
| Ulugh Muz- tagh | Kunlun | Tibet | 25,340 | 7,723 | | | | | |
| | | | | | Trisuli | Himalayas | India | 23,210 | 7,074 |
| Kungur | Muztagh Ata | China | 25,325 | 7,719 | Dunagiri | Himalayas | India | 23,184 | 7,066 |
| Tirich Mir | Hindu Kush | Pakistan | 25,230 | 7,690 | Revolution Peak | Pamirs | Tajikistan | 22,880 | 6,974 |
| Saser Kangri | Karakoram | India | 25,172 | 7,672 | | | | | |
| Makalu II | Himalayas | Nepal | 25,120 | 7,657 | Aconcagua | Andes | Argentina | 22,834 | 6,960 |
| Minya Konka (Gongga Shan) | Daxue Shan | China | 24,900 | 7,590 | Ojos del Salado | Andes | Argentina/ Chile | 22,664 | 6,908 |
| | | | | | Bonete | Andes | Argentina/ Chile | 22,546 | 6,872 |
| Kula Kangri | Himalayas | Bhutan | 24,783 | 7,554 | | | | | |
| Chang-tzu | Himalayas | Tibet | 24,780 | 7,553 | Ama Dablam | Himalayas | Nepal | 22,494 | 6,856 |
| Muztagh Ata | Muztagh Ata | China | 24,757 | 7,546 | Tupungato | Andes | Argentina/ Chile | 22,310 | 6,800 |
| Skyang Kangri | Himalayas | Kashmir | 24,750 | 7,544 | | | | | |
| Ismail Samani Peak (for- merly Com- munism Peak) | Pamirs | Tajikistan | 24,590 | 7,495 | Moscow Peak | Pamirs | Tajikistan | 22,260 | 6,785 |
| | | | | | Pissis | Andes | Argentina | 22,241 | 6,779 |
| | | | | | Mercedario | Andes | Argentina/ Chile | 22,211 | 6,770 |
| | | | | | Huascarán | Andes | Peru | 22,205 | 6,768 |
| Jongsong Peak | Himalayas | Nepal | 24,472 | 7,459 | Llullaillaco | Andes | Argentina/ Chile | 22,057 | 6,723 |
| Pobeda Peak | Tien Shan | Kyrgyzstan | 24,406 | 7,439 | El Libertador | Andes | Argentina | 22,047 | 6,720 |
| Sia Kangri | Himalayas | Kashmir | 24,350 | 7,422 | Cachi | Andes | Argentina | 22,047 | 6,720 |
| Haramosh Peak | Karakoram | Pakistan | 24,270 | 7,397 | Kailas | Himalayas | Tibet | 22,027 | 6,714 |
| | | | | | Incahuasi | Andes | Argentina/ Chile | 21,720 | 6,620 |
| Istoro Nal | Hindu Kush | Pakistan | 24,240 | 7,388 | Yerupaja | Andes | Peru | 21,709 | 6,617 |
| Tent Peak | Himalayas | Nepal | 24,165 | 7,365 | Kurumda | Pamirs | Tajikistan | 21,686 | 6,610 |
| Chomo Lhari | Himalayas | Tibet/Bhutan | 24,040 | 7,327 | Galan | Andes | Argentina | 21,654 | 6,600 |
| Chamlang | Himalayas | Nepal | 24,012 | 7,319 | El Muerto | Andes | Argentina/ Chile | 21,463 | 6,542 |
| Kabru | Himalayas | Nepal | 24,002 | 7,316 | | | | | |
| Alung Gangri | Himalayas | Tibet | 24,000 | 7,315 | Sajama | Andes | Bolivia | 21,391 | 6,520 |
| Baltoro Kangri | Himalayas | Kashmir | 23,990 | 7,312 | Nacimiento | Andes | Argentina | 21,302 | 6,493 |
| Muztagh Ata (K 5) | Kunlun | China | 23,890 | 7,282 | Illampu | Andes | Bolivia | 21,276 | 6,485 |
| Mana | Himalayas | India | 23,860 | 7,270 | Illimani | Andes | Bolivia | 21,201 | 6,462 |
| | | | | | Ooropuna | Andes | Peru | 21,000 | 6,400 |
| Baruntse | Himalayas | Nepal | 23,688 | 7,220 | Laudo | Andes | Argentina | 20,997 | 6,400 |
| Nepal Peak | Himalayas | Nepal | 23,500 | 7,163 | Ancohuma | Andes | Bolivia | 20,958 | 6,388 |
| Amne Machin | Kunlun | China | 23,490 | 7,160 | Cuzco (Ausangate) | Andes | Peru | 20,945 | 6,384 |

1. Kashmir is divided between India, Pakistan, and China, and the three countries dispute the boundaries. *Source:* National Geographic Society.

## Climbing the Seven Summits

About 70 mountaineers have climbed all "Seven Summits"—the highest peak on each of the seven continents. The first was Dick Bass, an American businessman, on April 30, 1985. The seven summits are Mt. Everest (Asia) 29,035 ft., Mt. Aconcagua (South America) 22,834 ft., Mt. McKinley (North America) 20,320 ft., Mt. Kilimanjaro (Africa) 19,340 ft., Mt. Elbrus (Europe) 18,510 ft., Vinson Massif (Antarctica) 16,066 ft., and Kosciusko (Australia) 7,310 ft.

## Oceans and Seas

| Name | Area sq. mi. | Area sq. km | Average depth ft. | Average depth m | Greatest known depth ft. | Greatest known depth m | Place of greatest known depth |
|---|---|---|---|---|---|---|---|
| Pacific Ocean | 155,557,000 | 60,060,900 | 13,215 | 4,028 | 36,198 | 11,033 | Mariana Trench |
| Atlantic Ocean | 76,762,000 | 29,638,000 | 12,880 | 3,926 | 30,246 | 9,219 | Puerto Rico Trench |
| Indian Ocean | 68,556,000 | 26,469,600 | 13,002 | 3,963 | 24,460 | 7,455 | Sunda Trench |
| Southern Ocean[1] | 20,327,000 | 7,848,300 | 13,100–16,400 | 4,000–5,000 | 23,736 | 7,235 | South Sandwich Trench |
| Arctic Ocean | 14,056,000 | 5,427,050 | 3,953 | 1,205 | 18,456 | 5,625 | 77°45′N; 175°W |
| Mediterranean Sea[2] | 1,145,100 | 2,965,800 | 4,688 | 1,429 | 15,197 | 4,632 | Off Cape Matapan, Greece |
| Caribbean Sea | 1,049,500 | 2,718,200 | 8,685 | 2,647 | 22,788 | 6,946 | Off Cayman Islands |
| South China Sea | 895,400 | 2,319,000 | 5,419 | 1,652 | 16,456 | 5,016 | West of Luzon |
| Bering Sea | 884,900 | 2,291,900 | 5,075 | 1,547 | 15,659 | 4,773 | Off Buldir Island |
| Gulf of Mexico | 615,000 | 1,592,800 | 4,874 | 1,486 | 12,425 | 3,787 | Sigsbee Deep |
| Okhotsk Sea | 613,800 | 1,589,700 | 2,749 | 838 | 12,001 | 3,658 | 146°10′E; 46°50′N |
| East China Sea | 482,300 | 1,249,200 | 617 | 188 | 9,126 | 2,782 | 25°16′N; 125°E |
| Hudson Bay | 475,800 | 1,232,300 | 420 | 128 | 600 | 183 | Near entrance |
| Japan Sea | 389,100 | 1,007,800 | 4,429 | 1,350 | 12,276 | 3,742 | Central Basin |
| Andaman Sea | 308,100 | 797,700 | 2,854 | 870 | 12,392 | 3,777 | Off Car Nicobar Island |
| North Sea | 222,100 | 575,200 | 308 | 94 | 2,165 | 660 | Skagerrak |
| Red Sea | 169,100 | 438,000 | 1,611 | 491 | 7,254 | 2,211 | Off Port Sudan |
| Baltic Sea | 163,000 | 422,200 | 180 | 55 | 1,380 | 421 | Off Gotland |

1. A decision by the International Hydrographic Organization in spring 2000 delimited a fifth world ocean. 2. Includes Black Sea and Sea of Azov. NOTE: For Caspian Sea, *see* Large Lakes of the World.

## Large Lakes of the World

| Name and location | Area sq. mi. | Area km | Length mi. | Length km | Maximum depth ft. | Maximum depth m |
|---|---|---|---|---|---|---|
| Caspian Sea, Azerbaijan-Russia-Kazakhstan-Turkmenistan-Iran[1] | 152,239 | 394,299 | 745 | 1,199 | 3,104 | 946 |
| Superior, U.S.-Canada | 31,820 | 82,414 | 383 | 616 | 1,333 | 406 |
| Victoria, Tanzania-Uganda | 26,828 | 69,485 | 200 | 322 | 270 | 82 |
| Huron, U.S.-Canada | 23,010 | 59,596 | 247 | 397 | 750 | 229 |
| Michigan, U.S. | 22,400 | 58,016 | 321 | 517 | 923 | 281 |
| Aral, Kazakhstan-Uzbekistan | 13,000 | 33,800 | 266 | 428 | 223 | 68 |
| Tanganyika, Tanzania-Congo | 12,700 | 32,893 | 420 | 676 | 4,708 | 1,435 |
| Baikal, Russia | 12,162 | 31,500 | 395 | 636 | 5,712 | 1,741 |
| Great Bear, Canada | 12,000 | 31,080 | 232 | 373 | 270 | 82 |
| Nyasa, Malawi-Mozambique-Tanzania | 11,600 | 30,044 | 360 | 579 | 2,316 | 706 |
| Great Slave, Canada | 11,170 | 28,930 | 298 | 480 | 2,015 | 614 |
| Chad,[2] Chad-Niger-Nigeria | 9,946 | 25,760 | — | — | 23 | 7 |
| Erie, U.S.-Canada | 9,930 | 25,719 | 241 | 388 | 210 | 64 |
| Winnipeg, Canada | 9,094 | 23,553 | 264 | 425 | 204 | 62 |
| Ontario, U.S.-Canada | 7,520 | 19,477 | 193 | 311 | 778 | 237 |
| Balkhash, Kazakhstan | 7,115 | 18,428 | 376 | 605 | 87 | 27 |
| Ladoga, Russia | 7,000 | 18,130 | 124 | 200 | 738 | 225 |
| Onega, Russia | 3,819 | 9,891 | 154 | 248 | 361 | 110 |
| Titicaca, Bolivia-Peru | 3,141 | 8,135 | 110 | 177 | 1,214 | 370 |
| Nicaragua, Nicaragua | 3,089 | 8,001 | 110 | 177 | 230 | 70 |
| Athabaska, Canada | 3,058 | 7,920 | 208 | 335 | 407 | 124 |
| Rudolf, Kenya | 2,473 | 6,405 | 154 | 248 | — | — |
| Reindeer, Canada | 2,444 | 6,330 | 152 | 245 | — | — |
| Eyre, South Australia | 2,400[3] | 6,216 | 130 | 209 | varies | varies |
| Issyk-Kul, Kyrgyzstan | 2,394 | 6,200 | 113 | 182 | 2,297 | 700 |
| Urmia,[2] Iran | 2,317 | 6,001 | 81 | 130 | 49 | 15 |
| Torrens, South Australia | 2,200 | 5,698 | 130 | 209 | — | — |
| Vänern, Sweden | 2,141 | 5,545 | 87 | 140 | 322 | 98 |
| Winnipegosis, Canada | 2,086 | 5,403 | 152 | 245 | 59 | 18 |
| Mobutu Sese Seko, Uganda | 2,046 | 5,299 | 100 | 161 | 180 | 55 |
| Nettilling, Baffin Island, Canada | 1,950 | 5,051 | 70 | 113 | — | — |
| Nipigon, Canada | 1,870 | 4,843 | 72 | 116 | — | — |
| Manitoba, Canada | 1,817 | 4,706 | 140 | 225 | 22 | 7 |
| Great Salt, U.S. | 1,800 | 4,662 | 75 | 121 | 15–25 | 5–8 |
| Kioga, Uganda | 1,700 | 4,403 | 50 | 80 | about 30 | 9 |

NOTE: area more than 1,700 sq. mi. 1. The Caspian Sea is called "sea" because the Romans, finding it salty, named it *Mare Caspium*. Many geographers, however, consider it a lake because it is land-locked. 2. Figures represent high-water data. 3. Varies with the rainfall of the wet season. It has been reported to dry up almost completely on occasion.

## Principal Rivers of the World

(*See* pp. 500–501 for other U.S. rivers.)

| River | Source | Outflow | Approx. length mi. | km |
|---|---|---|---|---|
| Nile | Tributaries of Lake Victoria, Africa | Mediterranean Sea | 4,180 | 6,690 |
| Amazon | Glacier-fed lakes, Peru | Atlantic Ocean | 3,912 | 6,296 |
| Mississippi-Missouri-Red Rock | Source of Red Rock, Montana | Gulf of Mexico | 3,710 | 5,970 |
| Chang Jiang (Yangtze) | Tibetan plateau, China | China Sea | 3,602 | 5,797 |
| Ob | Altai Mts., Russia | Gulf of Ob | 3,459 | 5,567 |
| Huang Ho (Yellow) | Eastern part of Kunlan Mts., West China | Gulf of Chihli | 2,900 | 4,667 |
| Yenisei | Tannu-Ola Mts., western Tuva, Russia | Arctic Ocean | 2,800 | 4,506 |
| Paraná | Confluence of Paranaiba and Grande rivers | Río de la Plata | 2,795 | 4,498 |
| Irtish | Altai Mts., Russia | Ob River | 2,758 | 4,438 |
| Zaire (Congo) | Confluence of Lualab and Luapula rivers, Congo | Atlantic Ocean | 2,716 | 4,371 |
| Heilong (Amur) | Confluence of Shilka (Russia) and Argun (Manchuria) rivers | Tatar Strait | 2,704 | 4,352 |
| Lena | Baikal Mts., Russia | Arctic Ocean | 2,652 | 4,268 |
| Mackenzie | Head of Finlay River, British Columbia, Canada | Beaufort Sea (Arctic Ocean) | 2,635 | 4,241 |
| Niger | Guinea | Gulf of Guinea | 2,600 | 4,184 |
| Mekong | Tibetan highlands | South China Sea | 2,500 | 4,023 |
| Mississippi | Lake Itasca, Minnesota | Gulf of Mexico | 2,348 | 3,779 |
| Missouri | Confluence of Jefferson, Gallatin, and Madison rivers, Montana | Mississippi River | 2,315 | 3,726 |
| Volga | Valdai plateau, Russia | Caspian Sea | 2,291 | 3,687 |
| Madeira | Confluence of Beni and Maumoré rivers, Bolivia–Brazil boundary | Amazon River | 2,012 | 3,238 |
| Purus | Peruvian Andes | Amazon River | 1,993 | 3,207 |
| São Francisco | Southwest Minas Gerais, Brazil | Atlantic Ocean | 1,987 | 3,198 |
| Yukon | Junction of Lewes and Pelly rivers, Yukon Territory, Canada | Bering Sea | 1,979 | 3,185 |
| St. Lawrence | Lake Ontario | Gulf of St. Lawrence | 1,900 | 3,058 |
| Rio Grande | San Juan Mts., Colorado | Gulf of Mexico | 1,885 | 3,034 |
| Brahmaputra | Himalayas | Ganges River | 1,800 | 2,897 |
| Indus | Himalayas | Arabian Sea | 1,800 | 2,897 |
| Danube | Black Forest, Germany | Black Sea | 1,766 | 2,842 |
| Euphrates | Confluence of Murat Nehri and Kara Su rivers, Turkey | Shatt-al-Arab | 1,739 | 2,799 |
| Darling | Central part of Eastern Highlands, Australia | Murray River | 1,702 | 2,739 |
| Zambezi | 11°21′S, 24°22′E, Zambia | Mozambique Channel | 1,700 | 2,736 |
| Tocantins | Goiás, Brazil | Pará River | 1,677 | 2,699 |
| Murray | Australian Alps, New South Wales | Indian Ocean | 1,609 | 2,589 |
| Nelson | Head of Bow River, western Alberta, Canada | Hudson Bay | 1,600 | 2,575 |
| Paraguay | Mato Grosso, Brazil | Paraná River | 1,584 | 2,549 |
| Ural | Southern Ural Mts., Russia | Caspian Sea | 1,574 | 2,533 |
| Ganges | Himalayas | Bay of Bengal | 1,557 | 2,506 |
| Amu Darya (Oxus) | Nicholas Range, Pamir Mts., Turkmenistan | Aral Sea | 1,500 | 2,414 |
| Japurá | Andes, Colombia | Amazon River | 1,500 | 2,414 |
| Salween | Tibet, south of Kunlun Mts. | Gulf of Martaban | 1,500 | 2,414 |
| Arkansas | Central Colorado | Mississippi River | 1,459 | 2,348 |
| Colorado | Grand County, Colorado | Gulf of California | 1,450 | 2,333 |
| Ohio-Allegheny | Potter County, Pennsylvania | Mississippi River | 1,306 | 2,102 |
| Irrawaddy | Confluence of Nmai and Mali rivers, northeast Burma | Bay of Bengal | 1,300 | 2,092 |
| Orange | Lesotho | Atlantic Ocean | 1,300 | 2,092 |
| Orinoco | Serra Parima Mts., Venezuela | Atlantic Ocean | 1,281 | 2,062 |
| Pilcomayo | Andes Mts., Bolivia | Paraguay River | 1,242 | 1,999 |
| Xi Jiang (Si Kiang) | Eastern Yunnan Province, China | China Sea | 1,236 | 1,989 |
| Columbia | Columbia Lake, British Columbia, Canada | Pacific Ocean | 1,232 | 1,983 |
| Don | Tula, Russia | Sea of Azov | 1,223 | 1,968 |
| Sungari | China–North Korea boundary | Amur River | 1,215 | 1,955 |
| Saskatchewan | Canadian Rocky Mts. | Lake Winnipeg | 1,205 | 1,939 |
| Peace | Stikine Mts., British Columbia, Canada | Great Slave River | 1,195 | 1,923 |
| Tigris | Taurus Mts., Turkey | Shatt-al-Arab | 1,180 | 1,899 |

## Large Islands of the World

| Island | Location and political affiliation | Area sq. mi. | Area sq. km |
|---|---|---|---|
| Greenland | North Atlantic (Danish) | 839,999 | 2,175,597 |
| New Guinea | Southwest Pacific (West Papua [Irian Jaya], Indonesia, western part; Papua New Guinea, eastern part) | 316,615 | 820,033 |
| Borneo | West mid-Pacific (Indonesian, south part; Brunei and Malaysian, north part) | 286,914 | 743,107 |
| Madagascar | Indian Ocean (Malagasy Republic) | 226,657 | 587,042 |
| Baffin | North Atlantic (Canadian) | 183,810 | 476,068 |
| Sumatra | Northeast Indian Ocean (Indonesian) | 182,859 | 473,605 |
| Honshu | Sea of Japan–Pacific (Japanese) | 88,925 | 230,316 |
| Great Britain | Off coast of NW Europe (England, Scotland, and Wales) | 88,758 | 229,883 |
| Ellesmere | Arctic Ocean (Canadian) | 82,119 | 212,688 |
| Victoria | Arctic Ocean (Canadian) | 81,930 | 212,199 |
| Sulawesi (Celebes) | West mid-Pacific (Indonesian) | 72,986 | 189,034 |
| South Island | South Pacific (New Zealand) | 58,093 | 150,461 |
| Java | Indian Ocean (Indonesian) | 48,990 | 126,884 |
| North Island | South Pacific (New Zealand) | 44,281 | 114,688 |
| Cuba | Caribbean Sea (republic) | 44,218 | 114,525 |
| Newfoundland | North Atlantic (Canadian) | 42,734 | 110,681 |
| Luzon | West mid-Pacific (Philippines) | 40,420 | 104,688 |
| Iceland | North Atlantic (republic) | 39,768 | 102,999 |
| Mindanao | West mid-Pacific (Philippines) | 36,537 | 94,631 |
| Ireland | West of Great Britain (republic, south part; United Kingdom, north part) | 32,597 | 84,426 |
| Hokkaido | Sea of Japan–Pacific (Japanese) | 30,372 | 78,663 |
| Hispaniola | Caribbean Sea (Dominican Republic, east part; Haiti, west part) | 29,355 | 76,029 |
| Tasmania | South of Australia (Australian) | 26,215 | 67,897 |
| Sri Lanka (Ceylon) | Indian Ocean (republic) | 25,332 | 65,610 |
| Sakhalin (Karafuto) | North of Japan (Russian) | 24,560 | 63,610 |
| Banks | Arctic Ocean (Canadian) | 23,230 | 60,166 |
| Devon | Arctic Ocean (Canadian) | 20,861 | 54,030 |

NOTE: Australia is not included in this list because it is defined as a continent rather than an island.

## Highest Waterfalls of the World

| Name(s) (foreign) | Location | Height Feet | Height Meters |
|---|---|---|---|
| Angel (Salto Angel) | Canaima Nat'l Park, Venezuela | 3,212 | 979 |
| Tugela | Natal Nat'l Park, South Africa | 2,800 | 850 |
| Utigord (Utigordsfoss) | Norway | 2,625 | 800 |
| Monge (Mongefoss) | Marstein, Norway | 2,540 | 774 |
| Mutarazi (Mtarazi) | Nyanga Nat'l Park, Zimbabwe | 2,499 | 762 |
| Yosemite | Yosemite Nat'l Park, California, U.S. | 2,425 | 739 |
| Espelands (Espelandsfoss) | Hardanger Fjord, Norway | 2,307 | 703[1] |
| Lower Mar Valley (Østra Mardolafoss) | Eikesdal, Norway | 2,151 | 655[2] |
| Tyssestrengene | Odda, Norway | 2,123 | 647[2] |
| Cuquenan (Salto Kukenan) | Kukenan Tepuy, Venezuela | 2,000 | 610 |
| Sutherland | Milford Sound, New Zealand | 1,904 | 580 |
| Kjell (Kjellfossen) | Gudvanger, Norway | 1,841 | 561 |
| Takkakaw | Yoho Nat'l Park, B.C., Canada | 1,650 | 503 |
| Ribbon | Yosemite Nat'l Park, California, U.S. | 1,612 | 491 |
| Upper Mar Valley (Mardalsfossen) | nr. Eikesdal, Norway | 1,536 | 468 |
| Gavarnie | nr. Lourdes, France | 1,388 | 423 |
| Vettis (Vettisfoss) | Jotunheimen, Norway | 1,215 | 370 |
| Hunlen | British Columbia, Canada | 1,198 | 365 |
| Tin Mine | Kosciusko Nat'l Park, Australia | 1,182 | 360[1] |
| Silver Strand (Widows' Tears) | Yosemite Nat'l Park, California, U.S. | 1,170 | 357 |
| Basaseachic (Salto Basaseachic) | Barance del Cobre, Mexico | 1,120 | 311 |
| Spray Stream (Staubbachfalle) | Lauterburnnental, Switzerland | 985 | 300 |
| Fachoda (Cascade de Fachoda) | Tahiti, Fr. Polynesia | 985 | 300[1] |
| King Edward VIII | Guyana | 850 | 259 |
| Wallaman | nr. Ingham, Australia | 844 | 257[3] |
| Gersoppa (Jog) | Western Ghats, India | 829 | 253 |
| Kaieteur | Guyana | 822 | 251 |
| Montezuma | nr. Rosebery, Tasmania, Australia | 800 | 240[1] |
| Wollomombi | nr. Armidale, Australia | 722 | 220[3] |

1. Unofficial (estimated) height. Subject to revision. 2. Incorporated in hydroelectric scheme. Greatly diminished flow. 3. Official heights established in April 2000. *Source:* Fifth Continent Australia Pty Limited.

# Polar Regions

## Antarctica

The second smallest continent, mostly south of the Antarctic Circle.

**Area:** 14.2 million sq. km (5.5 million sq. mi.).

**Geographic South Pole:** Earth's southernmost point, at latitude 90°S, where all lines of longitude meet.

**Magnetic South Pole:** The magnetic South Pole shifts about 5 miles (km) a year and is now located at about 66°S and 139°E on the Adélie Coast of Antarctica.

**Terrain:** About 98% thick ice sheet and 2% barren rock; glaciers form ice shelves along about half of the coastline, and floating ice shelves constitute 11% of the area of the continent. **Ice sheet:** The continental ice sheet contains approximately 7 million cubic miles (30 million cu km) of ice, representing about 90% of the world's total. **Major ice shelves:** Amery, Filchner, Larsen, Ronne, Ross. Ice shelves make up about 10% of Antarctica's ice, and are floating sheets of ice attached to land that project out into coastal waters.

**Climate:** The coldest, windiest, driest continent.

**Regions:** East Antarctica (c. 3,000,000 sq. mi./7,770,000 sq. km), the largest portion of the continent, is a high, ice-covered plateau. West Antarctica (c. 2,500,000 sq. mi./6,475,000 sq. km), is an archipelago of mountainous islands connected by ice. A mountain range divides them.

**Elevation extremes:** *Lowest point:* Bentley Subglacial Trench –8,327 ft. below sea level (–2,538 m). *Highest point:* Vinson Massif 16,066 ft. (4,897 m), Ellsworth Mountains.

## The Arctic

Region, primarily made up of the frozen Arctic Ocean, that surrounds the North Pole. Land masses include islands and the northern parts of the European, Asian, and North American continents.

**Area:** 14.056 million sq. km (5.4 million sq. mi.), largely frozen ocean.

**Geographic North Pole:** Northern end of Earth's axis, located at about latitude 90°N.

**Magnetic North Pole:** Continues to shift and is located at about 78°N and 104°W in the Queen Elizabeth Islands of northern Canada.

**Terrain:** Central surface covered by a perennial drifting polar icepack that averages about 3 meters in thickness; the icepack is surrounded by open seas during the summer, but more than doubles in size during the winter and extends to the encircling landmasses.

**Climate:** Polar climate characterized by persistent cold and relatively narrow annual temperature ranges; winters characterized by continuous darkness, cold and stable weather conditions, and clear skies; summers characterized by continuous daylight, damp and foggy weather, and weak cyclones with rain or snow.

**Regions:** The Arctic is divided by the summer isotherm, a climatic boundary between regions with summer temperatures averaging 50°F (or 10°C)—the subarctic—and colder regions (the true Arctic).

**Elevation extremes:** *Lowest point:* Fram Basin –4,665 m. *Highest point:* sea level 0 m.

# Interesting Caves and Caverns of the World

**Aggtelek.** In village of same name, northern Hungary. Large stalactitic cavern about 5 mi. long.

**Altamira Cave.** Near Santander, Spain. Contains Stone Age animal paintings on roof and walls.

**Antiparos.** On island of same name in the Grecian Archipelago. Some stalactites are 20 ft. long. Brilliant colors and fantastic shapes.

**Blue Grotto.** On island of Capri, Italy. Sea cavern hollowed out in limestone by constant wave action. Now half filled with water because of sinking coast. Name derived from unusual blue light permeating the cave. Source of light is a submerged opening allowing light to pass through the water.

**Carlsbad Caverns.** Southeast New Mexico. Contains some of the largest and most impressive stalactites and stalagmites, particularly in the Lechuguilla Cave.

**Fingal's Cave.** On island of Staffa off coast of western Scotland. Penetrates about 200 ft. inland. Contains basaltic columns almost 40 ft. high.

**Jenolan Caves.** In Blue Mountain plateau, New South Wales, Australia. Beautiful stalactitic formations.

**Kent's Cavern.** Near Torquay, England. Source of much information on Paleolithic humans.

**Lascaux Cave.** Southwestern France. Features prehistoric cave paintings estimated to be tens of thousands of years old. Closed to the public.

**Lubang Nasib Bagus.** Sarawak, Malaysia. World's largest cave chamber; 2,300 ft. long, 1,480 ft. wide, and everywhere at least 230 ft. high.

**Luray Caverns.** Near Luray, Va. Has large stalactitic and stalagmitic columns of many colors.

**Mogao Caves.** Located along the old Silk Route in China, Mogao is composed of 492 cells and cave sanctuaries that are famous for their statues and wall paintings, spanning a thousand years of Buddhist art.

**Mammoth Cave.** This limestone cavern in central Kentucky is the longest cave system in the world. Cave area is about 10 mi. in diameter but has 345 mi. of irregular subterranean passageways at various levels, plus underground lakes and rivers.

**Peak Cavern or Devil's Hole.** Derbyshire, England. About 2,250 ft. into a mountain. Lowest part is about 600 ft. below the surface.

**Postojna Grotto.** Postojna, Slovenia. Largest cavern in Europe; numerous beautiful stalactites. Famous example of a karst cave—grooved and irregularly eroded limestone formations carved out by underground streams. Pivka River flows through part of it.

**Singing Cave.** Iceland. A lava cave; name derived from sounds of people singing in it.

**Waitomo Cave.** North Island, New Zealand. Glowworms on cave ceiling look like thousands of stars in the night sky.

**Wind Cave.** In Black Hills of South Dakota. Limestone caverns with stalactites and stalagmites almost entirely missing. Variety of crystal formations called "boxwork."

**Wyandotte Cave.** In Crawford County, southern Indiana. A limestone cavern with five levels of passages; one of the largest in North America. "Monumental Mountain," approximately 135 ft. high, is believed to be one of the world's largest underground "mountains."

## Principal Deserts of the World

Deserts are arid regions, generally receiving less than ten inches of precipitation a year, or regions where the potential evaporation rate is twice as great as the precipitation.

The world's deserts are divided into four categories. **Subtropical deserts** are the hottest, with parched terrain and rapid evaporation. Although **cool coastal deserts** are located within the same latitudes as subtropical deserts, the average temperature is much cooler because of frigid offshore ocean currents. **Cold winter deserts** are marked by stark temperature differences from season to season, ranging from 100° F (38° C) in the summer to 10° F (−12° C) in the winter. **Polar regions** are also considered to be deserts because nearly all moisture in these areas is locked up in the form of ice.

| Desert | Location | Size | Topography |
|---|---|---|---|
| **SUBTROPICAL DESERTS** | | | |
| Sahara | Morocco, Western Sahara, Algeria, Tunisia, Libya, Egypt, Mauritania, Mali, Niger, Chad, Ethiopia, Eritrea, Somalia | 3.5 million sq. mi. | 70% gravel plains, sand, and dunes. Contrary to popular belief, the desert is only 30% sand. The world's largest nonpolar desert gets its name from the Arabic word *Sahra'*, meaning desert |
| Arabian | Saudi Arabia, Kuwait, Qatar, United Arab Emirates, Oman, Yemen | 1 million sq. mi. | Gravel plains, rocky highlands; one-fourth is the Rub al-Khali ("Empty Quarter"), the world's largest expanse of unbroken sand |
| Kalahari | Botswana, South Africa, Namibia | 220,000 sq. mi. | Sand sheets, longitudinal dunes |
| Australian Desert | | | |
|   Gibson | Australia (southern portion of the Western Desert) | 120,000 sq. mi. | Sandhills, gravel, grass. These three regions of desert are collectively referred to as the Great Western Desert— otherwise known as "the Outback." Contains Ayers Rock, or Uluru, one of the world's largest monoliths |
|   Great Sandy | Australia (northern portion of the Western Desert) | 150,000 sq. mi. | |
|   Great Victoria | Australia (southernmost portion of the Western Desert) | 250,000 sq. mi. | |
|   Simpson and Sturt Stony | Australia (eastern half of the continent) | 56,000 sq. mi. | Simpson's straight, parallel sand dunes are the longest in the world—up to 125 mi. Encompasses the Stewart Stony Desert, named for the Australian explorer |
| Mojave | U.S.: Arizona, Colorado, Nevada, Utah, California | 54,000 sq. mi. | Mountain chains, dry alkaline lake beds, calcium carbonate dunes |
| Sonoran | U.S.: Arizona, California; Mexico | 120,000 sq. mi. | Basins and plains bordered by mountain ridges; home to the Saguaro cactus |
| Chihuahuan | Mexico; southwestern U.S. | 175,000 sq. mi. | Shrub desert; largest in North America |
| Thar | India, Pakistan | 175,000 sq. mi. | Rocky sand and sand dunes |
| **COOL COASTAL DESERTS** | | | |
| Namib | Angola, Namibia, South Africa | 13,000 sq. mi. | Gravel plains |
| Atacama | Chile | 54,000 sq. mi. | Salt basins, sand, lava; world's driest desert |
| **COLD WINTER DESERTS** | | | |
| Great Basin | U.S.: Nevada, Oregon, Utah | 190,000 sq. mi. | Mountain ridges, valleys, 1% sand dunes |
| Colorado Plateau | U.S.: Arizona, Colorado, New Mexico, Utah, Wyoming | 130,000 sq. mi. | Sedimentary rock, mesas, and plateaus— includes the Grand Canyon and is also called the "Painted Desert" because of the spectacular colors in its rocks and canyons |
| Patagonian | Argentina | 260,000 sq. mi. | Gravel plains, plateaus, basalt sheets |
| Kara-Kum | Uzbekistan, Turkmenistan | 135,000 sq. mi. | 90% gray layered sand—name means "black sand" |
| Kyzyl-Kum | Uzbekistan, Turkmenistan, Kazakhstan | 115,000 sq. mi. | Sands, rock—name means "red sand" |
| Iranian | Iran | 100,000 sq. mi. | Salt, gravel, rock |
| Taklamakan | China | 105,000 sq. mi. | Sand, dunes, gravel |
| Gobi | China, Mongolia | 500,000 sq. mi. | Stony, sandy soil, steppes (dry grasslands) |
| **POLAR** | | | |
| Arctic | U.S., Canada, Greenland, Iceland, Norway, Sweden, Finland, Russia | | Snow, glaciers, tundra |
| Antarctic | Antarctica | 5.4 million sq. mi. | Ice, snow, bedrock |

## Latitude and Longitude of World Cities
### (and time corresponding to 12:00 noon, Eastern Standard Time)

| City | Latitude ° ' | Longitude ° ' | Time |
|------|--------------|---------------|------|
| Aberdeen, Scotland | 57 9 N | 2 9 W | 5:00 p.m. |
| Adelaide, Australia | 34 55 S | 138 36 E | 2:30 a.m.[1] |
| Algiers, Algeria | 36 50 N | 3 0 E | 6:00 p.m. |
| Amsterdam, Netherlands | 52 22 N | 4 53 E | 6:00 p.m. |
| Ankara, Turkey | 39 55 N | 32 55 E | 7:00 p.m. |
| Asunción, Paraguay | 25 15 S | 57 40 W | 1:00 p.m. |
| Athens, Greece | 37 58 N | 23 43 E | 7:00 p.m. |
| Auckland, New Zealand | 36 52 S | 174 45 E | 5:00 a.m.[1] |
| Bangkok, Thailand | 13 45 N | 100 30 E | midnight |
| Barcelona, Spain | 41 23 N | 2 9 E | 6:00 p.m. |
| Beijing, China | 39 55 N | 116 25 E | 1:00 a.m.[1] |
| Belém, Brazil | 1 28 S | 48 29 W | 2:00 p.m. |
| Belfast, Northern Ireland | 54 37 N | 5 56 W | 5:00 p.m. |
| Belgrade, Yugoslavia | 44 52 N | 20 32 E | 6:00 p.m. |
| Berlin, Germany | 52 30 N | 13 25 E | 6:00 p.m. |
| Birmingham, England | 52 25 N | 1 55 W | 5:00 p.m. |
| Bogotá, Colombia | 4 32 N | 74 15 W | 12:00 noon |
| Bombay, India | 19 0 N | 72 48 E | 10:30 p.m. |
| Bordeaux, France | 44 50 N | 0 31 W | 6:00 p.m. |
| Bremen, Germany | 53 5 N | 8 49 E | 6:00 p.m. |
| Brisbane, Australia | 27 29 S | 153 8 E | 3:00 a.m.[1] |
| Bristol, England | 51 28 N | 2 35 W | 5:00 p.m. |
| Brussels, Belgium | 50 52 N | 4 22 E | 6:00 p.m. |
| Bucharest, Romania | 44 25 N | 26 7 E | 7:00 p.m. |
| Budapest, Hungary | 47 30 N | 19 5 E | 6:00 p.m. |
| Buenos Aires, Argentina | 34 35 S | 58 22 W | 2:00 p.m. |
| Cairo, Egypt | 30 2 N | 31 21 E | 7:00 p.m. |
| Calcutta, India | 22 34 N | 88 24 E | 10:30 p.m. |
| Canton, China | 23 7 N | 113 15 E | 1:00 a.m.[1] |
| Cape Town, South Africa | 33 55 S | 18 22 E | 7:00 p.m. |
| Caracas, Venezuela | 10 28 N | 67 2 W | 1:00 p.m. |
| Cayenne, French Guiana | 4 49 N | 52 18 W | 1:00 p.m. |
| Chihuahua, Mexico | 28 37 N | 106 5 W | 11:00 a.m. |
| Chongqing, China | 29 46 N | 106 34 E | 1:00 a.m.[1] |
| Copenhagen, Denmark | 55 40 N | 12 34 E | 6:00 p.m. |
| Córdoba, Argentina | 31 28 S | 64 10 W | 2:00 p.m. |
| Dakar, Senegal | 14 40 N | 17 28 W | 5:00 p.m. |
| Darwin, Australia | 12 28 S | 130 51 E | 2:30 a.m.[1] |
| Djibouti, Djibouti | 11 30 N | 43 3 E | 8:00 p.m. |
| Dublin, Ireland | 53 20 N | 6 15 W | 5:00 p.m. |
| Durban, South Africa | 29 53 S | 30 53 E | 7:00 p.m. |
| Edinburgh, Scotland | 55 55 N | 3 10 W | 5:00 p.m. |
| Frankfurt, Germany | 50 7 N | 8 41 E | 6:00 p.m. |
| Georgetown, Guyana | 6 45 N | 58 15 W | 1:15 p.m. |
| Glasgow, Scotland | 55 50 N | 4 15 W | 5:00 p.m. |
| Guatemala City, Guatemala | 14 37 N | 90 31 W | 11:00 a.m. |
| Guayaquil, Ecuador | 2 10 S | 79 50 W | 12:00 noon |
| Hamburg, Germany | 53 33 N | 10 2 E | 6:00 p.m. |
| Hammerfest, Norway | 70 38 N | 23 38 E | 6:00 p.m. |
| Havana, Cuba | 23 8 N | 82 23 W | 12:00 noon |
| Helsinki, Finland | 60 10 N | 25 0 E | 7:00 p.m. |
| Hobart, Tasmania | 42 52 S | 147 19 E | 3:00 a.m.[1] |
| Iquique, Chile | 20 10 S | 70 7 W | 1:00 p.m. |
| Irkutsk, Russia | 52 30 N | 104 20 E | 1:00 a.m. |
| Jakarta, Indonesia | 6 16 S | 106 48 E | 0:30 a.m.[1] |
| Johannesburg, South Africa | 26 12 S | 28 4 E | 7:00 p.m. |
| Kingston, Jamaica | 17 59 N | 76 49 W | 12:00 noon |
| Kinshasa, Congo | 4 18 S | 15 17 E | 6:00 p.m. |
| La Paz, Bolivia | 16 27 S | 68 22 W | 1:00 p.m. |
| Leeds, England | 53 45 N | 1 30 W | 5:00 p.m. |
| Lima, Peru | 12 0 S | 77 2 W | 12:00 noon |
| Lisbon, Portugal | 38 44 N | 9 9 W | 5:00 p.m. |
| Liverpool, England | 53 25 N | 3 0 W | 5:00 p.m. |
| London, England | 51 32 N | 0 5 W | 5:00 p.m. |
| Lyons, France | 45 45 N | 4 50 E | 6:00 p.m. |
| Madrid, Spain | 40 26 N | 3 42 W | 6:00 p.m. |
| Manchester, England | 53 30 N | 2 15 W | 5:00 p.m. |
| Manila, Philippines | 14 35 N | 120 57 E | 1:00 a.m.[1] |
| Marseilles, France | 43 20 N | 5 20 E | 6:00 p.m. |
| Mazatlán, Mexico | 23 12 N | 106 25 W | 10:00 a.m. |
| Mecca, Saudi Arabia | 21 29 N | 39 45 E | 8:00 p.m. |
| Melbourne, Australia | 37 47 S | 144 58 E | 3:00 a.m.[1] |
| Mexico City, Mexico | 19 26 N | 99 7 W | 11:00 a.m. |
| Milan, Italy | 45 27 N | 9 10 E | 6:00 p.m. |
| Montevideo, Uruguay | 34 53 S | 56 10 W | 2:00 p.m. |
| Moscow, Russia | 55 45 N | 37 36 E | 8:00 p.m. |
| Munich, Germany | 48 8 N | 11 35 E | 6:00 p.m. |
| Nagasaki, Japan | 32 48 N | 129 57 E | 2:00 a.m.[1] |
| Nagoya, Japan | 35 7 N | 136 56 E | 2:00 a.m.[1] |
| Nairobi, Kenya | 1 25 S | 36 55 E | 8:00 p.m. |
| Nanjing (Nanking), China | 32 3 N | 118 53 E | 1:00 a.m.[1] |
| Naples, Italy | 40 50 N | 14 15 E | 6:00 p.m. |
| Newcastle-on-Tyne, England | 54 58 N | 1 37 W | 5:00 p.m. |
| Odessa, Ukraine | 46 27 N | 30 48 E | 8:00 p.m. |
| Osaka, Japan | 34 32 N | 135 30 E | 2:00 a.m.[1] |
| Oslo, Norway | 59 57 N | 10 42 E | 6:00 p.m. |
| Panama City, Panama | 8 58 N | 79 32 W | 12:00 noon |
| Paramaribo, Suriname | 5 45 N | 55 15 W | 1:30 p.m. |
| Paris, France | 48 48 N | 2 20 E | 6:00 p.m. |
| Perth, Australia | 31 57 S | 115 52 E | 1:00 a.m.[1] |
| Plymouth, England | 50 25 N | 4 5 W | 5:00 p.m. |
| Port Moresby, Papua New Guinea | 9 25 S | 147 8 E | 3:00 a.m.[1] |
| Prague, Czech Republic | 50 5 N | 14 26 E | 6:00 p.m. |
| Rangoon, Myanmar | 16 50 N | 96 0 E | 11:30 p.m. |
| Reykjavík, Iceland | 64 4 N | 21 58 W | 4:00 p.m. |
| Rio de Janeiro, Brazil | 22 57 S | 43 12 W | 2:00 p.m. |
| Rome, Italy | 41 54 N | 12 27 E | 6:00 p.m. |
| Salvador, Brazil | 12 56 S | 38 27 W | 2:00 p.m. |
| Santiago, Chile | 33 28 S | 70 45 W | 1:00 p.m. |
| St. Petersburg, Russia | 59 56 N | 30 18 E | 8:00 p.m. |
| São Paulo, Brazil | 23 31 S | 46 31 W | 2:00 p.m. |
| Shanghai, China | 31 10 N | 121 28 E | 1:00 a.m.[1] |
| Singapore, Singapore | 1 14 N | 103 55 E | 0:30 a.m.[1] |
| Sofia, Bulgaria | 42 40 N | 23 20 E | 7:00 p.m. |
| Stockholm, Sweden | 59 17 N | 18 3 E | 6:00 p.m. |
| Sydney, Australia | 34 0 S | 151 0 E | 3:00 a.m.[1] |
| Tananarive, Madagascar | 18 50 S | 47 33 E | 8:00 p.m. |
| Teheran, Iran | 35 45 N | 51 45 E | 8:30 p.m. |
| Tokyo, Japan | 35 40 N | 139 45 E | 2:00 a.m.[1] |
| Tripoli, Libya | 32 57 N | 13 12 E | 7:00 p.m. |
| Venice, Italy | 45 26 N | 12 20 E | 6:00 p.m. |
| Veracruz, Mexico | 19 10 N | 96 10 W | 11:00 a.m. |
| Vienna, Austria | 48 14 N | 16 20 E | 6:00 p.m. |
| Vladivostok, Russia | 43 10 N | 132 0 E | 3:00 a.m.[1] |
| Warsaw, Poland | 52 14 N | 21 0 E | 6:00 p.m. |
| Wellington, New Zealand | 41 17 S | 174 47 E | 5:00 a.m.[1] |
| Zürich, Switzerland | 47 21 N | 8 31 E | 6:00 p.m. |

1. On the following day.

## Miscellaneous Data for the United States

**Highest point:** Mount McKinley, Alaska — 20,320 ft. (6,198 m)
**Lowest point:** Death Valley, Calif. — 282 ft. (86 m) below sea level
**Approximate mean elevation** — 2,500 ft. (763 m)
**Points farthest apart** (50 states): Log Point, Elliot Key, Fla., and Kure Island, Hawaii — 5,859 mi. (9,429 km)
**Geographic center** (50 states): in Butte County, S.D. (west of Castle Rock) — 44°58′N lat.103°46′W long.
**Geographic center** (48 conterminous states): in Smith County, Kan. (near Lebanon) — 39°50′N lat. 98°35′W long.
**Boundaries:**
  Between Alaska and Canada — 1,538 mi. (2,475 km)
  Between the 48 conterminous states and Canada (incl. the Great Lakes) — 3,987 mi. (6,416 km)
  Between the United States and Mexico — 1,933 mi. (3,111 km)

*Source:* U.S. Geological Survey.

## Extreme Points of the United States (50 States)

| Extreme point | Latitude | Longitude | Distance[1] mi. | km |
|---|---|---|---|---|
| Northernmost point: Point Barrow, Alaska | 71°23′ N | 156°29′ W | 2,507 | 4,034 |
| Easternmost point: West Quoddy Head, Maine | 44°49′ N | 66°57′ W | 1,788 | 2,997 |
| Southernmost point: Ka Lae (South Cape), Hawaii | 18°55′ N | 155°41′ W | 3,463 | 5,573 |
| Westernmost point: Cape Wrangell, Alaska (Attu Island) | 52°55′ N | 172°27′ E | 3,625 | 5,833 |

1. From geographic center of United States (incl. Alaska and Hawaii), west of Castle Rock, S.D., 44°58′ lat., 103°46′ W long. If measured from the prime meridian in Greenwich, England, Cape Wrangell, Attu Island, Alaska, would be the easternmost point.

## The Continental Divide

The Continental Divide is a ridge of high ground that runs irregularly north and south through the Rocky Mountains and separates eastward-flowing from westward-flowing streams. The waters that flow eastward empty into the Atlantic Ocean, chiefly by way of the Gulf of Mexico; those that flow westward empty into the Pacific. Every continent with the exception of Antarctica has a continental divide.

## Rivers of the United States
### (350 or more miles long)

**Alabama-Coosa** (600 mi.; 966 km): From junction of Oostanula and Etowah R. in Georgia to Mobile R.

**Altamaha-Ocmulgee** (392 mi.; 631 km): From junction of Yellow R. and South R., Newton Co. in Georgia to Atlantic Ocean.

**Apalachicola-Chattahoochee** (524 mi.; 843 km): From Towns Co. in Georgia to Gulf of Mexico in Florida.

**Arkansas** (1,459 mi.; 2,348 km): From Lake Co. in Colorado to Mississippi R. in Arkansas.

**Brazos** (923 mi.; 1,490 km): From junction of Salt Fork and Double Mountain Fork in Texas to Gulf of Mexico.

**Canadian** (906 mi.; 1,458 km): From Las Animas Co. in Colorado to Arkansas R. in Oklahoma.

**Cimarron** (600 mi.; 966 km): From Colfax Co. in New Mexico to Arkansas R. in Oklahoma.

**Colorado** (1,450 mi.; 2,333 km): From Rocky Mountain National Park in Colorado to Gulf of California in Mexico.

**Colorado** (862 mi.; 1,387 km): From Dawson Co. in Texas to Matagorda Bay.

**Columbia** (1,243 mi.; 2,000 km): From Columbia Lake in British Columbia to Pacific Ocean (entering between Oregon and Washington).

**Colville** (350 mi.; 563 km): From Brooks Range in Alaska to Beaufort Sea.

**Connecticut** (407 mi.; 655 km): From Third Connecticut Lake in New Hampshire to Long Island Sound in Connecticut.

**Cumberland** (720 mi.; 1,159 km): From junction of Poor and Clover Forks in Harlan Co. in Kentucky to Ohio R.

**Delaware** (390 mi.; 628 km): From Schoharie Co. in New York to Liston Point, Delaware Bay.

**Gila** (649 mi.; 1,044 km): From Catron Co. in New Mexico to Colorado R. in Arizona.

**Green** (360 mi.; 579 km): From Lincoln Co. in Kentucky to Ohio R. in Kentucky.

**Green** (730 mi.; 1,175 km): From Sublette Co. in Wyoming to Colorado R. in Utah.

**Illinois** (420 mi.; 676 km): From St. Joseph Co. in Indiana to Mississippi R. at Grafton in Illinois.

**James** (sometimes called *Dakota*) (710 mi.; 1,143 km): From Wells Co. in North Dakota to Missouri R. in South Dakota.

**Kanawha-New** (352 mi.; 566 km): From junction of North and South Forks of New R. in North Carolina, through Virginia and West Virginia (New R. becoming Kanawha R.), to Ohio R.

**Kansas** (743 mi.; 1,196 km): From source of Arikaree R. in Elbert Co., Colorado, to Missouri R. at Kansas City, Kansas.

**Koyukuk** (470 mi.; 756 km): From Brooks Range in Alaska to Yukon R.

**Kuskokwim** (724 mi.; 1,165 km): From Alaska Range in Alaska to Kuskokwim Bay.

**Licking** (350 mi.; 563 km): From Magoffin Co. in Kentucky to Ohio R. at Cincinnati in Ohio.

**Little Missouri** (560 mi.; 901 km): From Crook Co. in Wyoming to Missouri R. in North Dakota.

**Milk** (625 mi.; 1,006 km): From junction of forks in Alberta Province to Missouri R.

**Mississippi** (2,348 mi.; 3,779 km): From Lake Itasca in Minnesota to mouth of Southwest Pass in Louisiana.

**Mississippi-Missouri-Red Rock** (3,710 mi.; 5,970 km): From source of Red Rock R. in Montana to mouth of Southwest Pass in Louisiana.

**Missouri** (2,315 mi.; 3,726 km): From junction of Jefferson R., Gallatin R., and Madison R. in Montana to Mississippi R. near St. Louis.

**Missouri-Red Rock** (2,540 mi.; 4,090 km): From source of Red Rock R. in Montana to Mississippi R. near St. Louis.

**Mobile-Alabama-Coosa** (645 mi.; 1,040 km): From junction of Etowah R. and Oostanula R. in Georgia to Mobile Bay.

**Neosho** (460 mi.; 740 km): From Morris Co. in Kansas to Arkansas R. in Oklahoma.

**Niobrara** (431 mi.; 694 km): From Niobrara Co. in Wyoming to Missouri R. in Nebraska.

**Noatak** (350 mi.; 563 km): From Brooks Range in Alaska to Kotzebue Sound.

**North Canadian** (800 mi.; 1,290 km): From Union Co. in New Mexico to Canadian R. in Oklahoma.

**North Platte** (618 mi.; 995 km): From Jackson Co. in Colorado to junction with South Platte R. in Nebraska to form Platte R.

**Ohio** (981 mi.; 1,579 km): From junction of Allegheny R. and Monongahela R. at Pittsburgh to Mississippi R. between Illinois and Kentucky.

**Ohio-Allegheny** (1,306 mi.; 2,102 km): From Potter Co. in Pennsylvania to Mississippi R. at Cairo in Illinois.

**Osage** (500 mi.; 805 km): From east-central Kansas to Missouri R. near Jefferson City in Missouri.

**Ouachita** (605 mi.; 974 km): From Polk Co. in Arkansas to Red R. in Louisiana.

**Pearl** (411 mi.; 661 km): From Neshoba County in Mississippi to Gulf of Mexico (Mississippi-Louisiana).

**Pecos** (926 mi.; 1,490 km): From Mora Co. in New Mexico to Rio Grande in Texas.

**Pee Dee-Yadkin** (435 mi.; 700 km): From Watauga Co. in North Carolina to Winyah Bay in South Carolina.

**Pend Oreille–Clark Fork** (531 mi.; 855 km): Near Butte in Montana to Columbia R. on Washington-Canada border.

**Platte** (990 mi.; 1593 km): From source of Grizzly Creek in Jackson Co., Colorado, to Missouri R. south of Omaha, Nebraska.

**Porcupine** (569 mi.; 916 km): From Yukon Territory, Canada, to Yukon R. in Alaska.

**Potomac** (383 mi.; 616 km): From Garrett Co. in Maryland to Chesapeake Bay at Point Lookout in Maryland.

**Powder** (375 mi.; 603 km): From junction of forks in Johnson Co. in Wyoming to Yellowstone R. in Montana.

**Red** (1,290 mi.; 2,080 km): From source of Tierra Blanca Creek in Curry County, New Mexico, to Mississippi R. in Louisiana.

**Red** (also called *Red River of the North*) (545 mi.; 877 km): From junction of Otter Tail R. and Bois de Sioux R. in Minnesota to Lake Winnipeg in Manitoba, Canada.

**Republican** (445 mi.; 716 km): From junction of North Fork and Arikaree R. in Nebraska to junction with Smoky Hill R. in Kansas to form the Kansas R.

**Rio Grande** (1,900 mi.; 3,060 km): From San Juan Co. in Colorado to Gulf of Mexico.

**Roanoke** (380 mi.; 612 km): From junction of forks in Montgomery Co. in Virginia to Albemarle Sound in North Carolina.

**Sabine** (380 mi.; 612 km): From junction of forks in Hunt Co. in Texas to Sabine Lake between Texas and Louisiana.

**Sacramento** (377 mi.; 607 km): From Siskiyou Co. in California to Suisun Bay.

**Saint Francis** (425 mi.; 684 km): From Iron Co. in Missouri to Mississippi R. in Arkansas.

**Salmon** (420 mi.; 676 km): From Custer Co. in Idaho to Snake R.

**San Joaquin** (350 mi.; 563 km): From junction of forks in Madera Co. in California to Suisun Bay.

**San Juan** (360 mi.; 579 km): From Archuleta Co. in Colorado to Colorado R. in Utah.

**Santee-Wateree-Catawba** (538 mi.; 866 km): From McDowell Co. in North Carolina to Atlantic Ocean in South Carolina.

**Smoky Hill** (540 mi.; 869 km): From Cheyenne Co. in Colorado to junction with Republican R. in Kansas to form Kansas R.

**Snake** (1,038 mi.; 1,670 km): From Ocean Plateau in Wyoming to Columbia R. in Washington.

**South Platte** (424 mi.; 682 km): From Park Co. in Colorado to junction with North Platte R. in Nebraska to form Platte R.

**Stikine** (379 mi.; 610 km): From British Columbia in Canada to Stikine Strait near Wrangell, Alaska.

**Susquehanna** (444 mi.; 715 km): From Otsego Lake in New York to Chesapeake Bay in Maryland.

**Tanana** (659 mi.; 1,060 km): From Wrangell Mts. in Yukon Territory, Canada, to Yukon R. in Alaska.

**Tennessee** (652 mi.; 1,049 km): From junction of Holston R. and French Broad R. in Tennessee to Ohio R. in Kentucky.

**Tennessee–French Broad** (886 mi.; 1,417 km): From Transylvania Co. in North Carolina to Ohio R. at Paducah in Kentucky.

**Tombigbee** (525 mi.; 845 km): From junction of forks in Itawamba Co. in Mississippi to Mobile R. in Alabama.

**Trinity** (360 mi.; 579 km): From junction of forks in Dallas Co. in Texas to Galveston Bay.

**Wabash** (512 mi.; 824 km): From Darke Co. in Ohio to Ohio R. between Illinois and Indiana.

**Washita** (500 mi.; 805 km): From Hemphill Co. in Texas to Red R. in Oklahoma.

**White** (722 mi.; 1,160 km): From Madison Co. in Arkansas to Mississippi R.

**Wisconsin** (430 mi.; 692 km): From Vilas Co. in Wisconsin to Mississippi R.

**Yellowstone** (692 mi.; 1,110 km): From Park Co. in Wyoming to Missouri R. in North Dakota.

**Yukon** (1,979 mi.; 3,185 km): From source of McNeil R. in Yukon Territory, Canada, to Bering Sea in Alaska.

## Coastline of the United States

| State | Lengths, statute miles General coastline[1] | Lengths, statute miles Tidal shoreline[2] | State | Lengths, statute miles General coastline[1] | Lengths, statute miles Tidal shoreline[2] |
|---|---|---|---|---|---|
| **Atlantic Coast:** | | | **Gulf Coast:** | | |
| Maine | 228 | 3,478 | Florida (Gulf) | 770 | 5,095 |
| New Hampshire | 13 | 131 | Alabama | 53 | 607 |
| Massachusetts | 192 | 1,519 | Mississippi | 44 | 359 |
| Rhode Island | 40 | 384 | Louisiana | 397 | 7,721 |
| Connecticut | — | 618 | Texas | 367 | 3,359 |
| New York | 127 | 1,850 | Total Gulf Coast | 1,631 | 17,141 |
| New Jersey | 130 | 1,792 | **Pacific Coast:** | | |
| Pennsylvania | — | 89 | California | 840 | 3,427 |
| Delaware | 28 | 381 | Oregon | 296 | 1,410 |
| Maryland | 31 | 3,190 | Washington | 157 | 3,026 |
| Virginia | 112 | 3,315 | Hawaii | 750 | 1,052 |
| North Carolina | 301 | 3,375 | Alaska (Pacific) | 5,580 | 31,383 |
| South Carolina | 187 | 2,876 | Total Pacific Coast | 7,623 | 40,298 |
| Georgia | 100 | 2,344 | **Arctic Coast:** | | |
| Florida (Atlantic) | 580 | 3,331 | Alaska (Arctic) | 1,060 | 2,521 |
| Total Atlantic Coast | 2,069 | 28,673 | Total Arctic Coast | 1,060 | 2,521 |
| | | | **States Total** | **12,383** | **88,633** |

1. Figures are lengths of general outline of seacoast. Measurements are made with unit measure of 30 minutes of latitude on charts as near scale of 1:1,200,000 as possible. Coastline of bays and sounds is included to point where they narrow to width of unit measure, and distance across at such point is included. 2. Figures were obtained in 1939–1940 with recording instrument on the largest-scale maps and charts then available. Shoreline of outer coast, offshore islands, sounds, bays, rivers, and creeks is included to head of tidewater, or to point where tidal waters narrow to width of 100 feet. *Source:* Department of Commerce, National Oceanic and Atmospheric Administration, National Ocean Service.

## Mountain Peaks in the United States Higher Than 14,000 Feet

| Name | State | Height (ft.) | Name | State | Height (ft.) | Name | State | Height (ft.) |
|---|---|---|---|---|---|---|---|---|
| Mt. McKinley | Alaska | 20,320 | Castle Peak | Colo. | 14,265 | Windom Peak | Colo. | 14,082 |
| Mt. St. Elias | Alaska | 18,008 | Quandary Peak | Colo. | 14,265 | Mt. Columbia | Colo. | 14,073 |
| Mt. Foraker | Alaska | 17,400 | Mt. Evans | Colo. | 14,264 | Mt. Augusta | Alaska | 14,070 |
| Mt. Bona | Alaska | 16,500 | Longs Peak | Colo. | 14,255 | Missouri Mtn. | Colo. | 14,067 |
| Mt. Blackburn | Alaska | 16,390 | Mt. Wilson | Colo. | 14,246 | Humboldt Peak | Colo. | 14,064 |
| Mt. Sanford | Alaska | 16,237 | White Mtn. | Calif. | 14,246 | Mt. Bierstadt | Colo. | 14,060 |
| Mt. Vancouver | Alaska | 15,979 | North Palisade | Calif. | 14,242 | Sunlight Peak | Colo. | 14,059 |
| South Buttress | Alaska | 15,885 | Mt. Cameron | Colo. | 14,238 | Split Mtn. | Calif. | 14,058 |
| Mt. Churchill | Alaska | 15,638 | Mt. Shavano | Colo. | 14,229 | Handies Peak | Colo. | 14,048 |
| Mt. Fairweather | Alaska | 15,300 | Crestone Needle | Colo. | 14,197 | Culebra Peak | Colo. | 14,047 |
| Mt. Hubbard | Alaska | 14,950 | Mt. Belford | Colo. | 14,197 | Mt. Lindsey | Colo. | 14,042 |
| Mt. Bear | Alaska | 14,831 | Mt. Princeton | Colo. | 14,197 | Ellingwood Point | Colo. | 14,042 |
| East Buttress | Alaska | 14,730 | Mt. Yale | Colo. | 14,196 | Middle Palisade | Calif. | 14,040 |
| Mt. Hunter | Alaska | 14,573 | Mt. Bross | Colo. | 14,172 | Little Bear Peak | Colo. | 14,037 |
| Browne Tower | Alaska | 14,530 | Kit Carson Mtn. | Colo. | 14,165 | Mt. Sherman | Colo. | 14,036 |
| Mt. Alverstone | Alaska | 14,500 | Mt. Wrangell | Alaska | 14,163 | Redcloud Peak | Colo. | 14,034 |
| Mt. Whitney | Calif. | 14,494[1] | Mt. Sill | Calif. | 14,162 | Mt. Langley | Calif. | 14,027 |
| University Peak | Alaska | 14,470 | Mt. Shasta | Calif. | 14,162 | Conundrum Peak | Colo. | 14,022 |
| Mt. Elbert | Colo. | 14,433 | El Diente Peak | Colo. | 14,159 | Mt. Tyndall | Calif. | 14,019 |
| Mt. Massive | Colo. | 14,421 | Point Success | Wash. | 14,158 | Pyramid Peak | Colo. | 14,018 |
| Mt. Harvard | Colo. | 14,420 | Maroon Peak | Colo. | 14,156 | Wilson Peak | Colo. | 14,017 |
| Mt. Rainier | Wash. | 14,410 | Tabeguache Mtn. | Colo. | 14,155 | Wetterhorn Peak | Colo. | 14,015 |
| Mt. Williamson | Calif. | 14,370 | Mt. Oxford | Colo. | 14,153 | North Maroon Peak | Colo. | 14,014 |
| La Plata Peak | Colo. | 14,361 | Mt. Sneffels | Colo. | 14,150 | San Luis Peak | Colo. | 14,014 |
| Blanca Peak | Colo. | 14,345 | Mt. Democrat | Colo. | 14,148 | Middle Palisade | Calif. | 14,012 |
| Uncompahgre Peak | Colo. | 14,309 | Capitol Peak | Colo. | 14,130 | Mt. Muir | Calif. | 14,012 |
| Crestone Peak | Colo. | 14,294 | Liberty Cap | Wash. | 14,112 | Mt. of the Holy Cross | Colo. | 14,005 |
| Mt. Lincoln | Colo. | 14,286 | Pikes Peak | Colo. | 14,110 | Huron Peak | Colo. | 14,003 |
| Grays Peak | Colo. | 14,270 | Snowmass Mtn. | Colo. | 14,092 | Thunderbolt Peak | Calif. | 14,003 |
| Mt. Antero | Colo. | 14,269 | Mt. Russell | Calif. | 14,088 | Sunshine Peak | Colo. | 14,001 |
| Torreys Peak | Colo. | 14,267 | Mt. Eolus | Colo. | 14,083 | | | |

1. National Geodetic Survey. *Source:* U.S. Dept. of the Interior, Geological Survey.

## Highest, Lowest, and Mean Elevations in the United States

| State | Elevation (ft.)[1] | Highest point | Elevation (ft.) | Lowest point | Elevation (ft.) |
|---|---|---|---|---|---|
| Alabama | 500 | Cheaha Mountain | 2,405 | Gulf of Mexico | Sea level |
| Alaska | 1,900 | Mt. McKinley | 20,320 | Pacific Ocean | Sea level |
| Arizona | 4,100 | Humphreys Peak | 12,633 | Colorado River | 70 |
| Arkansas | 650 | Magazine Mountain | 2,753 | Ouachita River | 55 |
| California | 2,900 | Mt. Whitney | 14,494 | Death Valley | −282[2] |
| Colorado | 6,800 | Mt. Elbert | 14,433 | Arkansas River | 3,350 |
| Connecticut | 500 | Mt. Frissell, on south slope | 2,380 | Long Island Sound | Sea level |
| Delaware | 60 | Ebright Road, Del.–Pa. state line | 448 | Atlantic Ocean | Sea level |
| D.C. | 150 | Tenleytown, at Reno Reservoir | 410 | Potomac River | 1 |
| Florida | 100 | Sec. 30, T6N, R20W, Walton County | 345 | Atlantic Ocean | Sea level |
| Georgia | 600 | Brasstown Bald | 4,784 | Atlantic Ocean | Sea level |
| Hawaii | 3,030 | Puu Wekiu, Mauna Kea | 13,796 | Pacific Ocean | Sea level |
| Idaho | 5,000 | Borah Peak | 12,662 | Snake River | 710 |
| Illinois | 600 | Charles Mound | 1,235 | Mississippi River | 279 |
| Indiana | 700 | Franklin Township, Wayne County | 1,257 | Ohio River | 320 |
| Iowa | 1,100 | Sec. 29, T100N, R41W, Osceola County | 1,670 | Mississippi River | 480 |
| Kansas | 2,000 | Mt. Sunflower | 4,039 | Verdigris River | 679 |
| Kentucky | 750 | Black Mountain | 4,139 | Mississippi River | 257 |
| Louisiana | 100 | Driskill Mountain | 535 | New Orleans | −8[2] |
| Maine | 600 | Mt. Katahdin | 5,267 | Atlantic Ocean | Sea level |
| Maryland | 350 | Backbone Mountain | 3,360 | Atlantic Ocean | Sea level |
| Massachusetts | 500 | Mt. Greylock | 3,487 | Atlantic Ocean | Sea level |
| Michigan | 900 | Mt. Arvon | 1,979 | Lake Erie | 572 |
| Minnesota | 1,200 | Eagle Mountain | 2,301 | Lake Superior | 600 |
| Mississippi | 300 | Woodall Mountain | 806 | Gulf of Mexico | Sea level |
| Missouri | 800 | Taum Sauk Mountain | 1,772 | St. Francis River | 230 |
| Montana | 3,400 | Granite Peak | 12,799 | Kootenai River | 1,800 |
| Nebraska | 2,600 | Johnson Township, Kimball County | 5,424 | Missouri River | 840 |
| Nevada | 5,500 | Boundary Peak | 13,140 | Colorado River | 479 |
| New Hampshire | 1,000 | Mt. Washington | 6,288 | Atlantic Ocean | Sea level |
| New Jersey | 250 | High Point | 1,803 | Atlantic Ocean | Sea level |
| New Mexico | 5,700 | Wheeler Peak | 13,161 | Red Bluff Reservoir | 2,842 |
| New York | 1,000 | Mt. Marcy | 5,344 | Atlantic Ocean | Sea level |
| North Carolina | 700 | Mt. Mitchell | 6,684 | Atlantic Ocean | Sea level |
| North Dakota | 1,900 | White Butte | 3,506 | Red River | 750 |
| Ohio | 850 | Campbell Hill | 1,549 | Ohio River | 455 |
| Oklahoma | 1,300 | Black Mesa | 4,973 | Little River | 289 |
| Oregon | 3,300 | Mt. Hood | 11,239 | Pacific Ocean | Sea level |
| Pennsylvania | 1,100 | Mt. Davis | 3,213 | Delaware River | Sea level |
| Rhode Island | 200 | Jerimoth Hill | 812 | Atlantic Ocean | Sea level |
| South Carolina | 350 | Sassafras Mountain | 3,560 | Atlantic Ocean | Sea level |
| South Dakota | 2,200 | Harney Peak | 7,242 | Big Stone Lake | 966 |
| Tennessee | 900 | Clingmans Dome | 6,640 | Mississippi River | 178 |
| Texas | 1,700 | Guadalupe Peak | 8,749 | Gulf of Mexico | Sea level |
| Utah | 6,100 | Kings Peak | 13,528 | Beaverdam Wash | 2,000 |
| Vermont | 1,000 | Mt. Mansfield | 4,393 | Lake Champlain | 95 |
| Virginia | 950 | Mt. Rogers | 5,729 | Atlantic Ocean | Sea level |
| Washington | 1,700 | Mt. Rainier | 14,410 | Pacific Ocean | Sea level |
| West Virginia | 1,500 | Spruce Knob | 4,861 | Potomac River | 240 |
| Wisconsin | 1,050 | Timms Hill | 1,951 | Lake Michigan | 579 |
| Wyoming | 6,700 | Gannett Peak | 13,804 | Belle Fourche River | 3,099 |
| **United States** | **2,500** | **Mt. McKinley (Alaska)** | **20,320** | **Death Valley (California)** | **−282[2]** |

1. Approximate mean elevation. 2. Below sea level. *Source:* U.S. Geological Survey.

## Latitude and Longitude of U.S. and Canadian Cities
### (and time corresponding to 12:00 noon, Eastern Standard Time)

| City | Lat. ° | Lat. ′ | Long. ° | Long. ′ | Time | City | Lat. ° | Lat. ′ | Long. ° | Long. ′ | Time |
|---|---|---|---|---|---|---|---|---|---|---|---|
| Albany, N.Y. | 42 | 40 | 73 | 45 | 12:00 noon | Miami, Fla. | 25 | 46 | 80 | 12 | 12:00 noon |
| Albuquerque, N.M. | 35 | 05 | 106 | 39 | 10:00 a.m. | Milwaukee, Wis. | 43 | 2 | 87 | 55 | 11:00 a.m. |
| Amarillo, Tex. | 35 | 11 | 101 | 50 | 11:00 a.m. | Minneapolis, Minn. | 44 | 59 | 93 | 14 | 11:00 a.m. |
| Anchorage, Alaska | 61 | 13 | 149 | 54 | 8:00 a.m. | Mobile, Ala. | 30 | 42 | 88 | 3 | 11:00 a.m. |
| Atlanta, Ga. | 33 | 45 | 84 | 23 | 12:00 noon | Montgomery, Ala. | 32 | 21 | 86 | 18 | 11:00 a.m. |
| Austin, Tex. | 30 | 16 | 97 | 44 | 11:00 a.m. | Montpelier, Vt. | 44 | 15 | 72 | 32 | 12:00 noon |
| Baker, Ore. | 44 | 47 | 117 | 50 | 9:00 a.m. | Montreal, Que., Can. | 45 | 30 | 73 | 35 | 12:00 noon |
| Baltimore, Md. | 39 | 18 | 76 | 38 | 12:00 noon | Moose Jaw, Sask., Can. | 50 | 37 | 105 | 31 | 10:00 a.m. |
| Bangor, Maine | 44 | 48 | 68 | 47 | 12:00 noon | | | | | | |
| Birmingham, Ala. | 33 | 30 | 86 | 50 | 11:00 a.m. | Nashville, Tenn. | 36 | 10 | 86 | 47 | 11:00 a.m. |
| Bismarck, N.D. | 46 | 48 | 100 | 47 | 11:00 a.m. | Nelson, B.C., Can. | 49 | 30 | 117 | 17 | 9:00 a.m. |
| Boise, Idaho | 43 | 36 | 116 | 13 | 10:00 a.m. | Newark, N.J. | 40 | 44 | 74 | 10 | 12:00 noon |
| Boston, Mass. | 42 | 21 | 71 | 5 | 12:00 noon | New Haven, Conn. | 41 | 19 | 72 | 55 | 12:00 noon |
| Buffalo, N.Y. | 42 | 55 | 78 | 50 | 12:00 noon | New Orleans, La. | 29 | 57 | 90 | 4 | 11:00 a.m. |
| Calgary, Alba., Can. | 51 | 1 | 114 | 1 | 10:00 a.m. | New York, N.Y. | 40 | 47 | 73 | 58 | 12:00 noon |
| Carlsbad, N.M. | 32 | 26 | 104 | 15 | 10:00 a.m. | Nome, Alaska | 64 | 25 | 165 | 30 | 8:00 a.m. |
| Charleston, S.C. | 32 | 47 | 79 | 56 | 12:00 noon | Oakland, Calif. | 37 | 48 | 122 | 16 | 9:00 a.m. |
| Charleston, W. Va. | 38 | 21 | 81 | 38 | 12:00 noon | Oklahoma City, Okla. | 35 | 26 | 97 | 28 | 11:00 a.m. |
| Charlotte, N.C. | 35 | 14 | 80 | 50 | 12:00 noon | Omaha, Neb. | 41 | 15 | 95 | 56 | 11:00 a.m. |
| Cheyenne, Wyo. | 41 | 9 | 104 | 52 | 10:00 a.m. | Ottawa, Ont., Can. | 45 | 24 | 75 | 43 | 12:00 noon |
| Chicago, Ill. | 41 | 50 | 87 | 37 | 11:00 a.m. | Philadelphia, Pa. | 39 | 57 | 75 | 10 | 12:00 noon |
| Cincinnati, Ohio | 39 | 8 | 84 | 30 | 12:00 noon | Phoenix, Ariz. | 33 | 29 | 112 | 4 | 10:00 a.m. |
| Cleveland, Ohio | 41 | 28 | 81 | 37 | 12:00 noon | Pierre, S.D. | 44 | 22 | 100 | 21 | 11:00 a.m. |
| Columbia, S.C. | 34 | 0 | 81 | 2 | 12:00 noon | Pittsburgh, Pa. | 40 | 27 | 79 | 57 | 12:00 noon |
| Columbus, Ohio | 40 | 0 | 83 | 1 | 12:00 noon | Port Arthur, Ont., Can. | 48 | 30 | 89 | 17 | 12:00 noon |
| Dallas, Tex. | 32 | 46 | 96 | 46 | 11:00 a.m. | Portland, Maine | 43 | 40 | 70 | 15 | 12:00 noon |
| Denver, Colo. | 39 | 45 | 105 | 0 | 10:00 a.m. | Portland, Ore. | 45 | 31 | 122 | 41 | 9:00 a.m. |
| Des Moines, Iowa | 41 | 35 | 93 | 37 | 11:00 a.m. | Providence, R.I. | 41 | 50 | 71 | 24 | 12:00 noon |
| Detroit, Mich. | 42 | 20 | 83 | 3 | 12:00 noon | Quebec, Que., Can. | 46 | 49 | 71 | 11 | 12:00 noon |
| Dubuque, Iowa | 42 | 31 | 90 | 40 | 11:00 a.m. | Raleigh, N.C. | 35 | 46 | 78 | 39 | 12:00 noon |
| Duluth, Minn. | 46 | 49 | 92 | 5 | 11:00 a.m. | Reno, Nev. | 39 | 30 | 119 | 49 | 9:00 a.m. |
| Eastport, Maine | 44 | 54 | 67 | 0 | 12:00 noon | Richfield, Utah | 38 | 46 | 112 | 5 | 10:00 a.m. |
| El Centro, Calif. | 32 | 38 | 115 | 33 | 9:00 a.m. | Richmond, Va. | 37 | 33 | 77 | 29 | 12:00 noon |
| El Paso, Tex. | 31 | 46 | 106 | 29 | 10:00 a.m. | Roanoke, Va. | 37 | 17 | 79 | 57 | 12:00 noon |
| Eugene, Ore. | 44 | 3 | 123 | 5 | 9:00 a.m. | Sacramento, Calif. | 38 | 35 | 121 | 30 | 9:00 a.m. |
| Fargo, N.D. | 46 | 52 | 96 | 48 | 11:00 a.m. | St. John, N.B., Can. | 45 | 18 | 66 | 10 | 1:00 p.m. |
| Flagstaff, Ariz. | 35 | 13 | 111 | 41 | 10:00 a.m. | St. Louis, Mo. | 38 | 35 | 90 | 12 | 11:00 a.m. |
| Fort Worth, Tex. | 32 | 43 | 97 | 19 | 11:00 a.m. | Salt Lake City, Utah | 40 | 46 | 111 | 54 | 10:00 a.m. |
| Fresno, Calif. | 36 | 44 | 119 | 48 | 9:00 a.m. | San Antonio, Tex. | 29 | 23 | 98 | 33 | 11:00 a.m. |
| Grand Junction, Colo. | 39 | 5 | 108 | 33 | 10:00 a.m. | San Diego, Calif. | 32 | 42 | 117 | 10 | 9:00 a.m. |
| Grand Rapids, Mich. | 42 | 58 | 85 | 40 | 12:00 noon | San Francisco, Calif. | 37 | 47 | 122 | 26 | 9:00 a.m. |
| Havre, Mont. | 48 | 33 | 109 | 43 | 10:00 a.m. | San Jose, Calif. | 37 | 20 | 121 | 53 | 9:00 a.m. |
| Helena, Mont. | 46 | 35 | 112 | 2 | 10:00 a.m. | San Juan, P.R. | 18 | 30 | 66 | 10 | 1:00 p.m. |
| Honolulu, Hawaii | 21 | 18 | 157 | 50 | 7:00 a.m. | Santa Fe, N.M. | 35 | 41 | 105 | 57 | 10:00 a.m. |
| Hot Springs, Ark. | 34 | 31 | 93 | 3 | 11:00 a.m. | Savannah, Ga. | 32 | 5 | 81 | 5 | 12:00 noon |
| Houston, Tex. | 29 | 45 | 95 | 21 | 11:00 a.m. | Seattle, Wash. | 47 | 37 | 122 | 20 | 9:00 a.m. |
| Idaho Falls, Idaho | 43 | 30 | 112 | 1 | 10:00 a.m. | Shreveport, La. | 32 | 28 | 93 | 42 | 11:00 a.m. |
| Indianapolis, Ind. | 39 | 46 | 86 | 10 | 12:00 noon | Sioux Falls, S.D. | 43 | 33 | 96 | 44 | 11:00 a.m. |
| Jackson, Miss. | 32 | 20 | 90 | 12 | 11:00 a.m. | Sitka, Alaska | 57 | 10 | 135 | 15 | 8:00 a.m. |
| Jacksonville, Fla. | 30 | 22 | 81 | 40 | 12:00 noon | Spokane, Wash. | 47 | 40 | 117 | 26 | 9:00 a.m. |
| Juneau, Alaska | 58 | 18 | 134 | 24 | 8:00 a.m. | Springfield, Ill. | 39 | 48 | 89 | 38 | 11:00 a.m. |
| Kansas City, Mo. | 39 | 6 | 94 | 35 | 11:00 a.m. | Springfield, Mass. | 42 | 6 | 72 | 34 | 12:00 noon |
| Key West, Fla. | 24 | 33 | 81 | 48 | 12:00 noon | Springfield, Mo. | 37 | 13 | 93 | 17 | 11:00 a.m. |
| Kingston, Ont., Can. | 44 | 15 | 76 | 30 | 12:00 noon | Syracuse, N.Y. | 43 | 2 | 76 | 8 | 12:00 noon |
| Klamath Falls, Ore. | 42 | 10 | 121 | 44 | 9:00 a.m. | Tampa, Fla. | 27 | 57 | 82 | 27 | 12:00 noon |
| Knoxville, Tenn. | 35 | 57 | 83 | 56 | 12:00 noon | Toledo, Ohio | 41 | 39 | 83 | 33 | 12:00 noon |
| Las Vegas, Nev. | 36 | 10 | 115 | 12 | 9:00 a.m. | Toronto, Ont., Can. | 43 | 40 | 79 | 24 | 12:00 noon |
| Lewiston, Idaho | 46 | 24 | 117 | 2 | 9:00 a.m. | Tulsa, Okla. | 36 | 09 | 95 | 59 | 11:00 a.m. |
| Lincoln, Neb. | 40 | 50 | 96 | 40 | 11:00 a.m. | Victoria, B.C., Can. | 48 | 25 | 123 | 21 | 9:00 a.m. |
| London, Ont., Can. | 43 | 2 | 81 | 34 | 12:00 noon | Virginia Beach, Va. | 36 | 51 | 75 | 58 | 12:00 noon |
| Long Beach, Calif. | 33 | 46 | 118 | 11 | 9:00 a.m. | Washington, D.C. | 38 | 53 | 77 | 02 | 12:00 noon |
| Los Angeles, Calif. | 34 | 3 | 118 | 15 | 9:00 a.m. | Wichita, Kan. | 37 | 43 | 97 | 17 | 11:00 a.m. |
| Louisville, Ky. | 38 | 15 | 85 | 46 | 12:00 noon | Wilmington, N.C. | 34 | 14 | 77 | 57 | 12:00 noon |
| Manchester, N.H. | 43 | 0 | 71 | 30 | 12:00 noon | Winnipeg, Man., Can. | 49 | 54 | 97 | 7 | 11:00 a.m. |
| Memphis, Tenn. | 35 | 9 | 90 | 3 | 11:00 a.m. | | | | | | |

For more on U.S. geography, *see* National Parks, pp. 598–602.

ALL PHOTOS: AP—IDE WCRLD

**FIRE!** A wall of flames threatens a house north of Durango, Colo., on June 25. This fire along Missionary Ridge in the Rocky Mountains was one of a host of wildfires that plagued America's western states in the summer of 2002. But the wildfires were not confined to the West: in a summer struck by drought, big blazes burned in every state. By mid-August, some 56,000 individual wildfires had burned a total of some 6 million acres of forest.

**ALLIES:** The U.S. relied on the aid of regional leaders to pursue the war on the al-Qaeda terror network in Asia. Above, President George W. Bush meets with Pakistan's President Pervez Musharraf in Washington in February.

**NEW BOSS:** Hamid Karzai, who was strongly backed by the U.S., was sworn in as the leader of Afghanistan in June.

**DIRTY WORK:** With Afghanistan's Taliban government toppled, the search for terrorists became a manhunt. Above, U.S. soldiers scout a cave in eastern Afghanistan in April.

**REID:** Richard Reid, right, a British citizen, was charged with attempting to light a bomb in his shoe on an American Airlines transatlantic flight in late December 2001.

**MOUSSAOUI:** Zacarias Moussaoui, a French Moroccan who was detained in August 2001, will be tried in 2003 for being an accomplice in the 9/11 terrorist attacks.

**LINDH:** John Walker Lindh, 21, an American Taliban fighter, reached a plea bargain with the U.S. and may serve 20 years in prison.

**PEARL:** *Wall Street Journal* reporter Daniel Pearl, 38, was kidnapped in January and murdered (on tape) by Pakistani terrorists.

**SOLEMN MOMENT:** A May 30 ceremony marked the end of the clean-up of the World Trade Center site in New York City. The giant effort continued 24 hours a day, seven days a week, for 262 days; required 3.1 million man-hours of labor; and moved 1,642,698 tons of material. The cost—$750 million—was far below initial estimates of $7 billion.

**ACCUSER:** Minneapolis FBI agent Coleen Rowley tells a Senate committee that the bureau deliberately obstructed steps that might have disrupted the 9/11 attacks.

**DEFENDER:** FBI Director Robert Mueller rejected Rowley's charges. The failure of U.S. security agencies to detect and avert the attacks tarnished their reputations.

**SAFE!** Americans cheered when nine mine workers in Pennsylvania were rescued after 77 hours trapped deep underground. The miners braved hunger, damp and cold; they were isolated when a drill breached a flooded mine that faulty maps showed to be 300 ft. away. Above, the third miner rescued, Thomas Foy, 51, reaches the surface on July 28.

**WEST BANK INCURSION:** Trapped in an escalating cycle of terror and retaliation, Israeli and Palestinian civilians endured the most violent year in the recent history of the Middle East. Above, Palestinian youths stone an Israeli tank that had taken up a position outside Yasir Arafat's compound as Israel occupied the West Bank city of Ramallah in February.

**TERROR IN ISRAEL:** On April 12, a device set off by a Palestinian suicide bomber devastated a crowded market in Jerusalem, above, killing 6 and injuring 84. By summer's end, more than 1,500 Palestinians and 550 Israelis had been killed in the nearly two-year-old intifada.

**CRISIS IN KASHMIR:** India and Pakistan's long-running dispute over Kashmir—a region split between the two nations since 1949, despite its majority Muslim population—almost erupted in war before the two nuclear powers cooled down in June. Tensions remain: above, Indian soldiers in the Gurez region scramble in July, awaiting orders to fire on Pakistani positions.

**INDEPENDENCE DAY:** East Timorese outside the city of Dili celebrate their nation's new independence following a 24-year insurrection against Indonesia. East Timor officially joined the community of nations at the stroke of midnight on Monday, May 20, 2002.

**JUBILEE:** Britons cheered Queen Elizabeth II's 50-year reign with a Golden Jubilee in June, top. But the Queen, 76, lost both her mother the Queen Mum, bottom left, who died in March at 101, and her younger sister Princess Margaret, right, who died in February at 71.

**ENRON:** Corruption and failure tarnished U.S. business in 2002. Kenneth Lay, above, resigned as CEO of power giant Enron; its collapse devastated its workers' savings.

**ADELPHIA:** John Rigas, the founder of the bankrupt cable-TV firm, was arraigned on charges of securities and bank fraud on July 24; his two sons were also charged.

**TYCO:** Dennis Kozlowski, the flamboyant CEO of the conglomerate, was charged with evading some $1 million in sales taxes.

**WORLDCOM:** CEO Bernard Ebbers resigned from the telecom giant, which admitted it had claimed $7 billion in false earnings.

**SUMMIT TALK:** Pope John Paul II summoned America's Roman Catholic cardinals to an emergency session in Rome in April as the church struggled to respond to a series of scandals in which high officials admitted to sheltering sexual predators in the priesthood.

**NEW VIEW:** After a tune-up by astronauts, the revived NICMOS (Near Infrared Camera and Multi-Object Spectrometer) on NASA's Hubble telescope captured this view of four galaxies colliding a billion light years away.

**OLD VIEW:** French paleontologist Michel Brunet holds a hominid skull, left, found in Chad. *Sahelanthropus tchadensis* may extend the roots of man's family tree back by a million years, to 7 million years B.C.

**SOLO MAGELLAN:** Wealthy adventurer Steve Fossett, 58, launches his sixth attempt at becoming the first balloonist to circumnavigate the globe solo. Fossett achieved his dream when the *Spirit of Freedom* touched down in Australia in June after a 14-day flight.

**WINTER OLYMPICS:** Salt Lake City played host to a memorable (and peaceful) series of Games in February. American Sarah Hughes, 15, took first in figure skating.

**JUSTICE!** After a judging scandal, Canadian pairs team Jamie Salé and David Pelletier, in maroon, shared first place with Russians Elena Berezhnaya and Anton Sikharulidze.

**OH, YES:** Popular American short-track speed skater Apolo Anton Ohno garnered a gold and a silver medal at the Games.

**CLEAN SWEEP:** Serena Williams, right, topped sister Venus at the French Open, at Wimbledon, above, and at the U.S. Open.

**WORLD CUP:** Japan and South Korea were the site of the world's favorite sporting event, soccer's World Cup. In a surprise turn, favorites France and Italy fell early, while upstarts Senegal, South Korea, and the U.S. survived. In the final, the dazzling Brazilians, led by Ronaldo and Ronaldinho, above, beat Germany to win the Cup for an unequaled fifth time.

**SYMBOLIC MOMENT:** In a triumph for Hollywood's African-American actors, stars Denzel Washington and Halle Berry received the Oscars for Best Actor and Actress at the 74th Academy Awards presentation. Washington won for *Training Day*, Berry for *Monster's Ball*.

WALLY McNAMEE—CORBIS

**TED WILLIAMS:** The "Splendid Splinter" of the Boston Red Sox takes a swing in 1950. Baseball's last player to hit .400 died at 83.

**STEPHEN JAY GOULD:** The respected paleontologist, also an essayist, critic of creationism and baseball fan, died at 60.

**ANN LANDERS:** The queen of advice columnists, born Esther Friedman, died at 83, while still dispensing good sense daily.

**MILTON BERLE:** The veteran stand-up comic, 93, was TV's first great comedy star. Above, he hams it up in 1963.

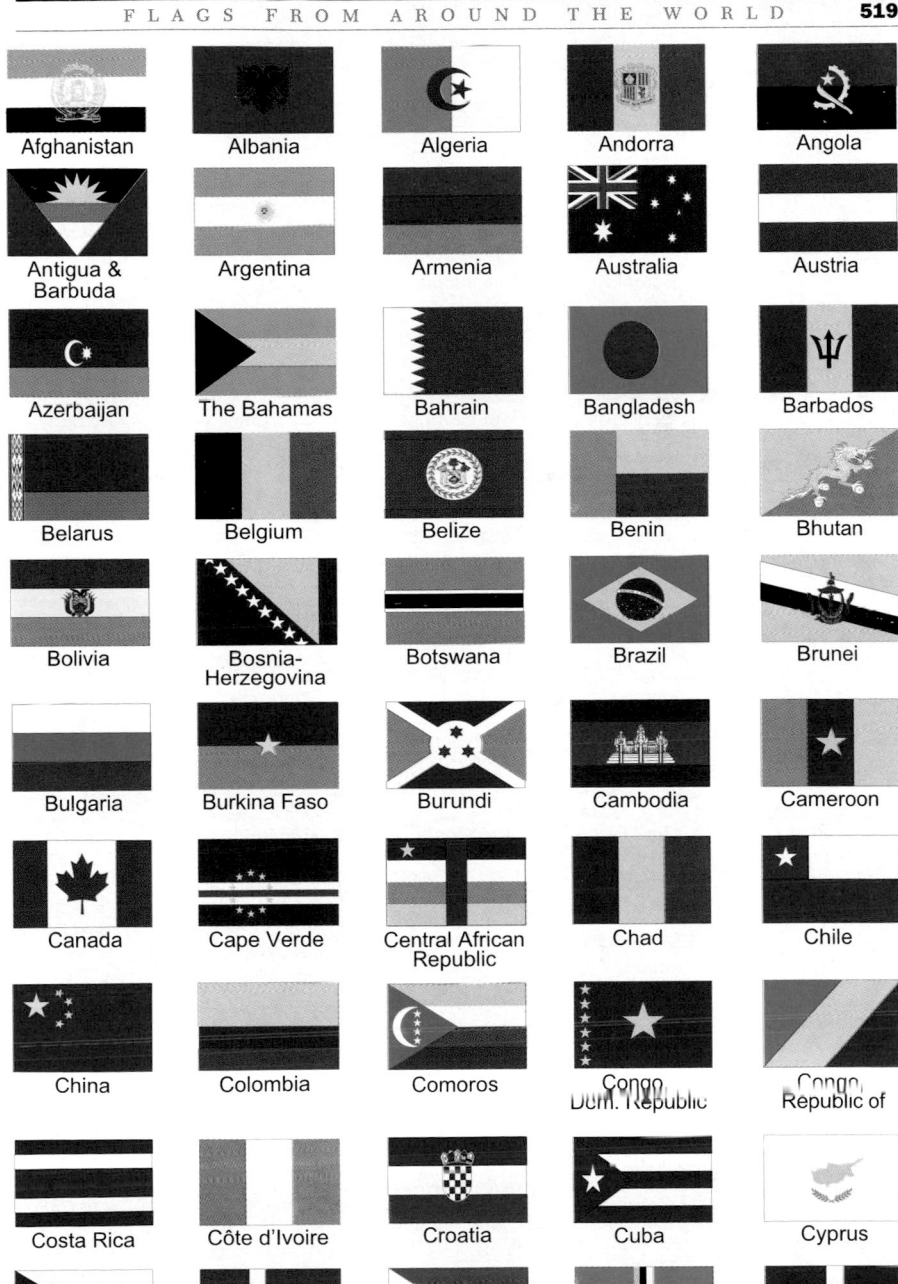

| | | | | |
|---|---|---|---|---|
| Afghanistan | Albania | Algeria | Andorra | Angola |
| Antigua & Barbuda | Argentina | Armenia | Australia | Austria |
| Azerbaijan | The Bahamas | Bahrain | Bangladesh | Barbados |
| Belarus | Belgium | Belize | Benin | Bhutan |
| Bolivia | Bosnia-Herzegovina | Botswana | Brazil | Brunei |
| Bulgaria | Burkina Faso | Burundi | Cambodia | Cameroon |
| Canada | Cape Verde | Central African Republic | Chad | Chile |
| China | Colombia | Comoros | Congo Dem. Republic | Congo Republic of |
| Costa Rica | Côte d'Ivoire | Croatia | Cuba | Cyprus |
| Czech Republic | Denmark | Djibouti | Dominica | Dominican Rep. |

East Timor

Ecuador

Egypt

El Salvador

Equatorial Guinea

Eritrea

Estonia

Ethiopia

Fiji

Finland

France

Gabon

The Gambia

Georgia

Germany

Ghana

Greece

Grenada

Guatemala

Guinea

Guinea-Bissau

Guyana

Haiti

Honduras

Hungary

Iceland

India

Indonesia

Iran

Iraq

Ireland

Israel

Italy

Jamaica

Japan

Jordan

Kazakhstan

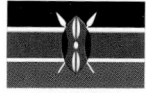
Kenya

Kiribati

Korea, North

Korea, South

Kuwait

Kyrgyzstan

Laos

Latvia

Lebanon

Lesotho

Liberia

Libya

Liechtenstein

| | | | | |
|---|---|---|---|---|
| Lithuania | Luxembourg | Macedonia | Madagascar | Malawi |
| Malaysia | Maldives | Mali | Malta | Marshall Is. |
| Mauritania | Mauritius | Mexico | Micronesia | Moldova |
| Monaco | Mongolia | Morocco | Mozambique | Myanmar |
| Namibia | Nauru | Nepal | The Netherlands | New Zealand |
| Nicaragua | Niger | Nigeria | Norway | Oman |
| Pakistan | Palau | Panama | Papua New Guinea | Paraguay |
| Peru | The Philippines | Poland | Portugal | Qatar |
| Romania | Russia | Rwanda | St. Kitts & Nevis | St. Lucia |
| St. Vincent & The Grenadines | Samoa | San Marino | São Tomé & Príncipe | Saudi Arabia |

Senegal

Seychelles

Sierra Leone

Singapore

Slovakia

Slovenia

Solomon Is.

Somalia

South Africa

Spain

Sri Lanka

The Sudan

Suriname

Swaziland

Sweden

Switzerland

Syria

Taiwan

Tajikistan

Tanzania

Thailand

Togo

Tonga

Trinidad &
Tobago

Tunisia

Turkey

Turkmenistan

Tuvalu

Uganda

Ukraine

United Arab
Emirates

United Kingdom

United States

Uruguay

Uzbekistan

Vanuatu

Vatican City

Venezuela

Vietnam

Yemen

Yugoslavia

Zambia

Zimbabwe

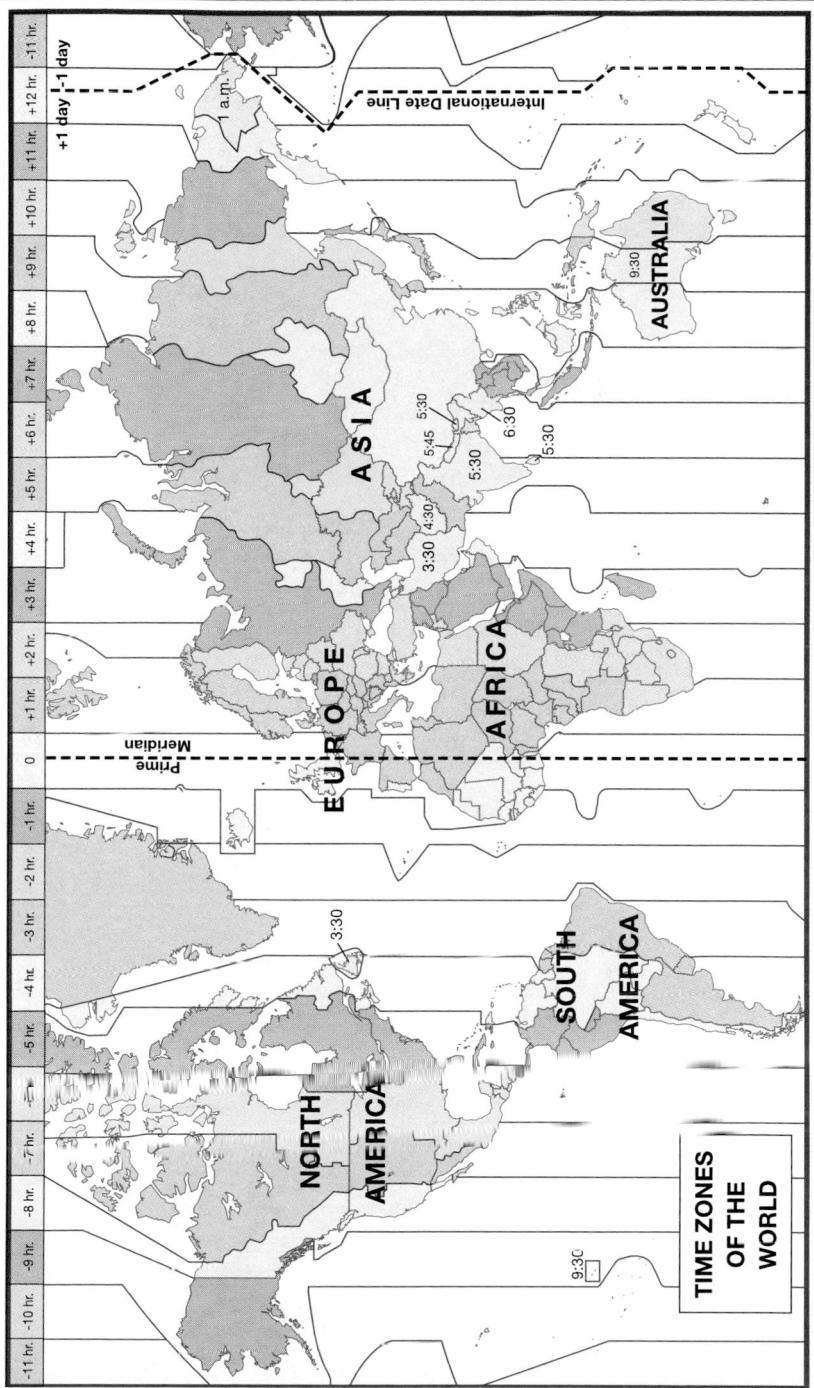

TIME ZONES
OF THE
WORLD

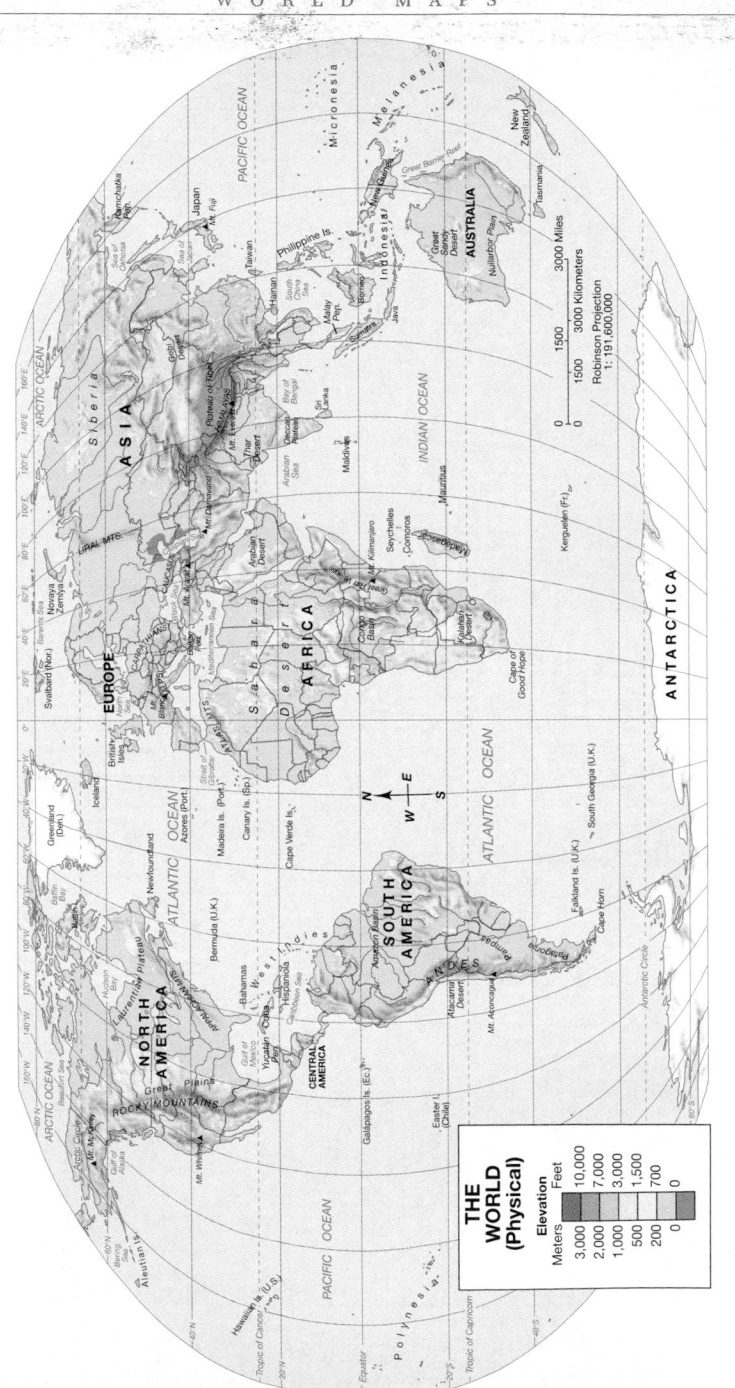

THE WORLD (Physical)

Elevation

| Meters | Feet |
|--------|--------|
| 3,000 | 10,000 |
| 2,000 | 7,000 |
| 1,000 | 3,000 |
| 500 | 1,500 |
| 200 | 700 |
| 0 | 0 |

Robinson Projection
1: 191,600,000

0   1500   3000 Kilometers
0   1500   3000 Miles

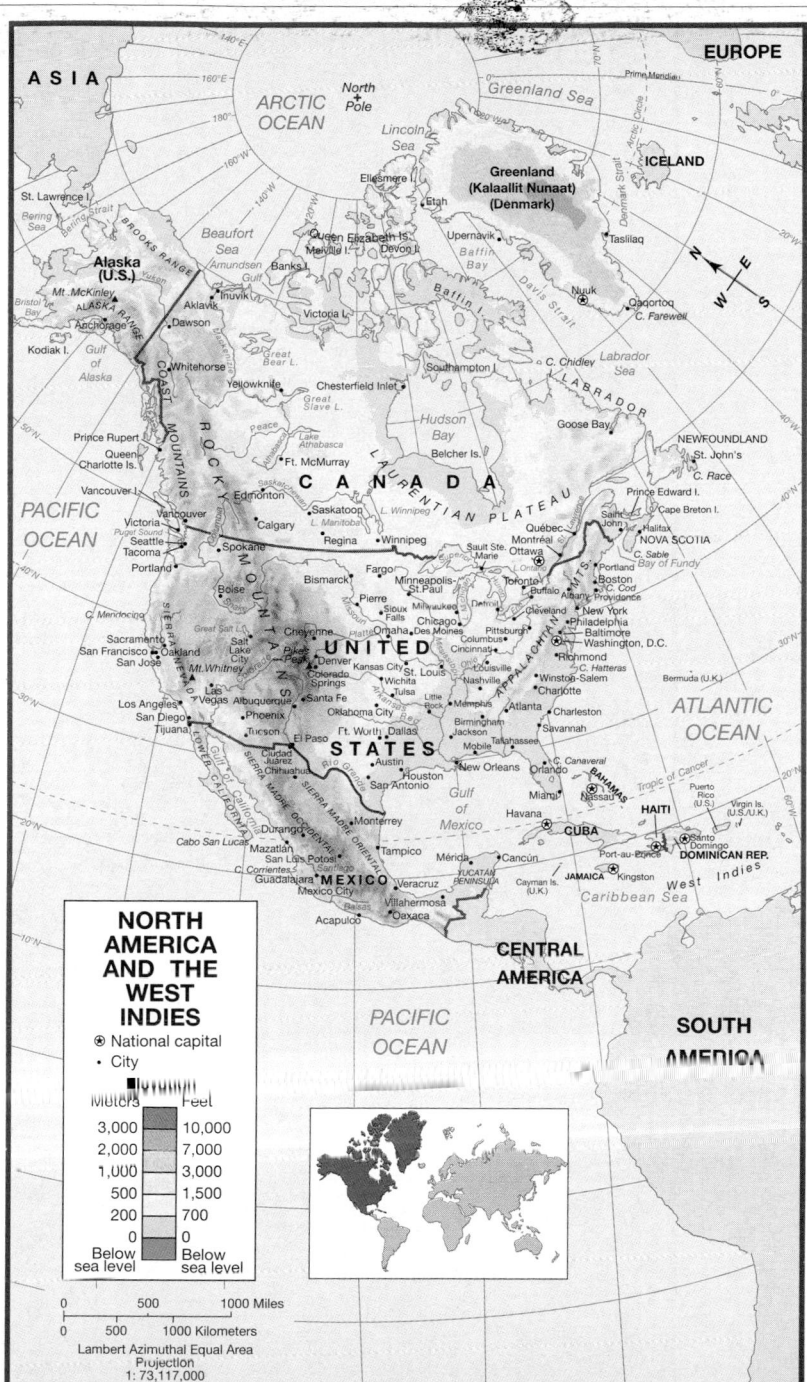

ASIA

ARCTIC
OCEAN

North
Pole

Lincoln
Sea

Greenland Sea

EUROPE

Prime Meridian

ICELAND

Greenland
(Kalaallit Nunaat)
(Denmark)

St. Lawrence I.

Bering
Sea

Beaufort
Sea

Queen Elizabeth Is.
Melville I.
Banks I.
Devon I.
Ellesmere I.

Upernavik

Tasiilaq

Alaska
(U.S.)

Mt. McKinley
ALASKA RANGE
Anchorage

BROOKS RANGE
Amundsen
Gulf
Inuvik
Aklavik

Etah

Baffin
Bay

Nuyk
Qaqortoq
C. Farewell

Bristol
Bay

Dawson

Victoria I.

Baffin I.

Davis Strait

Labrador
Sea

Kodiak I.
Gulf
of
Alaska

Whitehorse

Great
Bear L.

Chesterfield Inlet

C. Chidley

LABRADOR

Goose Bay

NEWFOUNDLAND
St. John's
C. Race

PACIFIC
OCEAN

Prince Rupert
Queen
Charlotte Is.
Vancouver I.

COAST MOUNTAINS

Yellowknife
Great
Slave L.

Hudson
Bay

Belcher Is.

Prince Edward I.
C. Breton I.

Victoria
Seattle
Tacoma
Portland

Vancouver
Puget Sound
Spokane

Peace
Lake
Athabasca
Ft. McMurray
Edmonton

CANADA

Southampton I.

Saskatoon
Calgary

ROCKY MOUNTAINS

L. Manitoba
Regina

Saint
John
Montréal
Ottawa

Québec
Sault Ste.
Marie

C. Sable Bay of Fundy
NOVA SCOTIA
Halifax

C. Mendocino

Boise

M
O
U
N
T
A
I
N
S

Bismarck

Fargo

Winnipeg

L. Winnipeg

Toronto
Buffalo
Detroit
Cleveland

Portland
C. Cod
Boston
Providence
Albany
New York

Sacramento
San Francisco
San Jose
Oakland

Great Salt L.

Cheyenne
Salt
Lake
City

Pierre

Sioux
Falls

Minneapolis-
St. Paul

Milwaukee
Chicago

Pittsburgh
Columbus
Cincinnati

Philadelphia
Baltimore
Washington, D.C.

Bermuda (U.K.)

Mt. Whitney
SIERRA NEVADA

Pikes
Peak

Denver
Colorado
Springs

Platte

Omaha

UNITED

Des Moines

Kansas City
St. Louis
Wichita
Tulsa

Louisville
Nashville

Richmond
C. Hatteras
Winston-Salem
Charlotte

Los Angeles
San Diego
Tijuana

Las Vegas
Phoenix
Tucson

Albuquerque
Santa Fe

Little
Rock
Memphis

Birmingham

Atlanta
Charleston
Savannah

ATLANTIC
OCEAN

Oklahoma City

STATES

Jackson

Mobile
Tallahassee

Ciudad
Juárez
Chihuahua

El Paso

Ft. Worth
Dallas
Austin

New Orleans

Orlando

C. Canaveral

Tropic of Cancer

SIERRA MADRE OCCIDENTAL

Rio Grande

Houston
San Antonio

Gulf
of
Mexico

Miami
Nassau

BAHAMAS

Puerto
Rico
(U.S.)

Virgin Is.
(U.S./U.K.)

Cabo San Lucas
Mazatlán

Durango
San Luis Potosí

Monterrey

Havana

CUBA

HAITI

Santo
Domingo

C. Corrientes
Santiago

Tampico

Mérida

Cancún

Port-au-Prince
JAMAICA
Kingston

DOMINICAN REP.

West Indies

Guadalajara
Mexico City

MEXICO

Veracruz

Balsas

Villahermosa

Acapulco

YUCATAN
PENINSULA

Cayman Is.
(U.K.)

Oaxaca

Caribbean Sea

CENTRAL
AMERICA

PACIFIC
OCEAN

SOUTH
AMERICA

## NORTH
## AMERICA
## AND THE
## WEST
## INDIES

⊕ National capital
· City

| Meters | Feet |
|--------|------|
| 3,000 | 10,000 |
| 2,000 | 7,000 |
| 1,000 | 3,000 |
| 500 | 1,500 |
| 200 | 700 |
| 0 | 0 |
| Below sea level | Below sea level |

0        500        1000 Miles
0        500        1000 Kilometers

Lambert Azimuthal Equal Area
Projection
1: 73,117,000

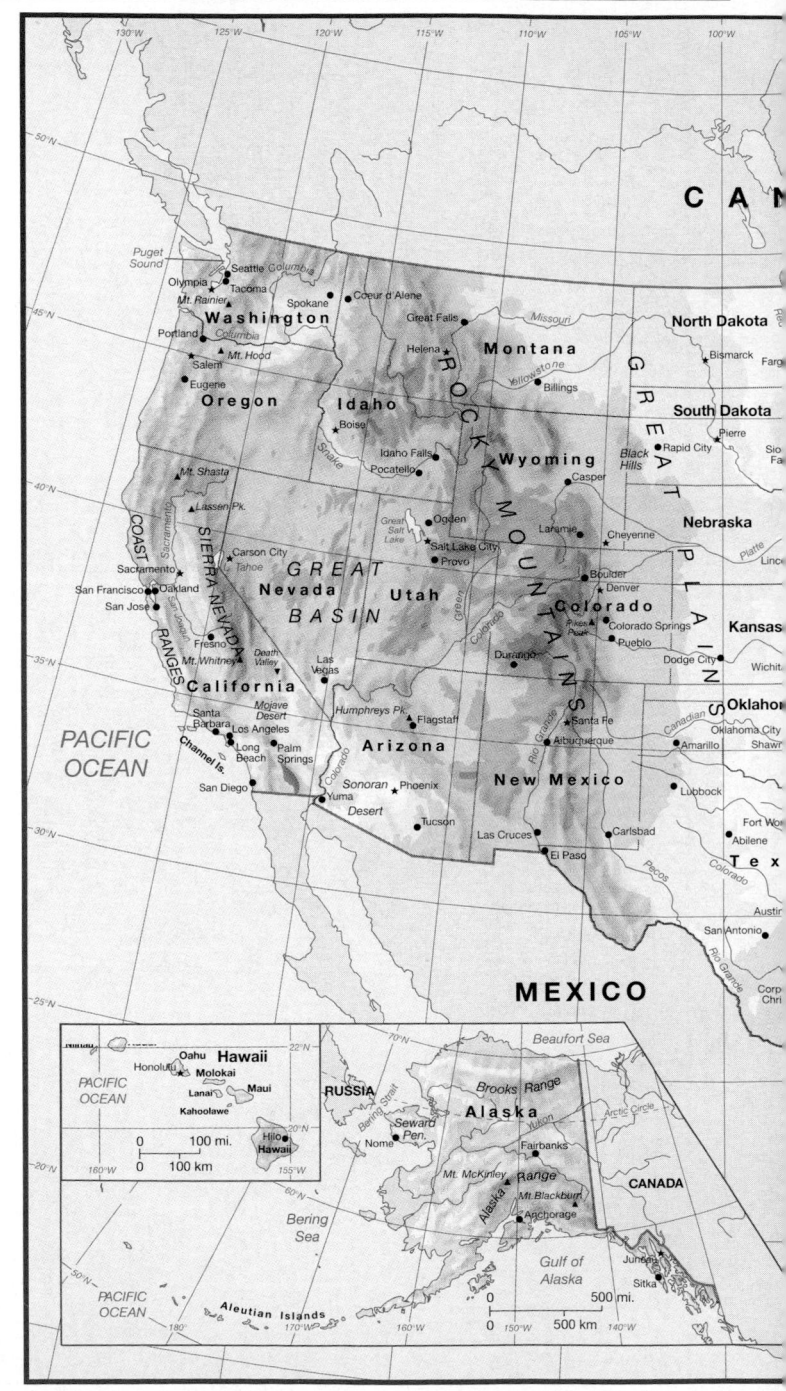

130°W    125°W    120°W    115°W    110°W    105°W    100°W

50°N

C A N

45°N

Puget
Sound
Seattle Columbia
Olympia    Tacoma
Mt. Rainier    Spokane        Coeur d'Alene
Washington                Great Falls        North Dakota
Portland        Columbia            Helena        Montana            Bismarck    Fargo
Salem    Mt. Hood                        Yellowstone
Eugene                                Billings
Oregon            Idaho                        South Dakota
Boise                                    Pierre
Missouri
R
Idaho Falls        O                    Rapid City    Sioux
Mt. Shasta            Pocatello        C    Wyoming    Black    Falls
K                Casper    Hills
40°N
Lassen Pk.                        Great    Ogden        Y        Laramie    Cheyenne    Nebraska
Salt        Salt Lake City        M            Platte
Carson City    Lake    Provo        O            Lincoln
Sacramento    Tahoe    G R E A T                U                Boulder
San Francisco    Oakland    Nevada        Denver
San Jose            BASIN    Utah        N    Colorado
Fresno                            T            Colorado Springs    Kansas
Mt. Whitney    Death            A            Pueblo
35°N    Valley    Las                    Durango    I        Dodge City    Wichita
California    Vegas                    N
Santa    Mojave        Humphreys Pk.    Flagstaff        S    Santa Fe    Oklahoma
Barbara    Desert                        Oklahoma City    Shawnee
PACIFIC        Los Angeles            Albuquerque    Amarillo
OCEAN    Channel Is.    Long    Palm                Arizona
Beach    Springs        Colorado    New Mexico    Lubbock
San Diego                Phoenix            Fort Worth
Sonoran                            Carlsbad    Abilene
Yuma    Desert        Tucson                        Tex
Las Cruces                    Pecos
30°N                        El Paso            Colorado    Austin
                                    San Antonio
                                    Corpus
MEXICO                                Christi
25°N

PACIFIC
OCEAN        Oahu    Hawaii    22°N        70°W    Beaufort Sea
Honolulu    Molokai
PACIFIC        Lanai    Maui    RUSSIA    Brooks Range    Arctic Circle
OCEAN    Kahoolawe        Seward        Alaska    Yukon
Hilo    20°N    Pen.    Fairbanks    CANADA
0    100 mi.    Hawaii    Nome
0    100 km    155°W            Mt. McKinley    Range
160°W    20°N                    Mt. Blackburn
                        Alaska    Anchorage
Bering
Sea                    Gulf of        Juneau
Alaska    Sitka
PACIFIC            0    500 mi.
OCEAN    Aleutian Islands        0    500 km    140°W
180°    170°W    160°W    150°W

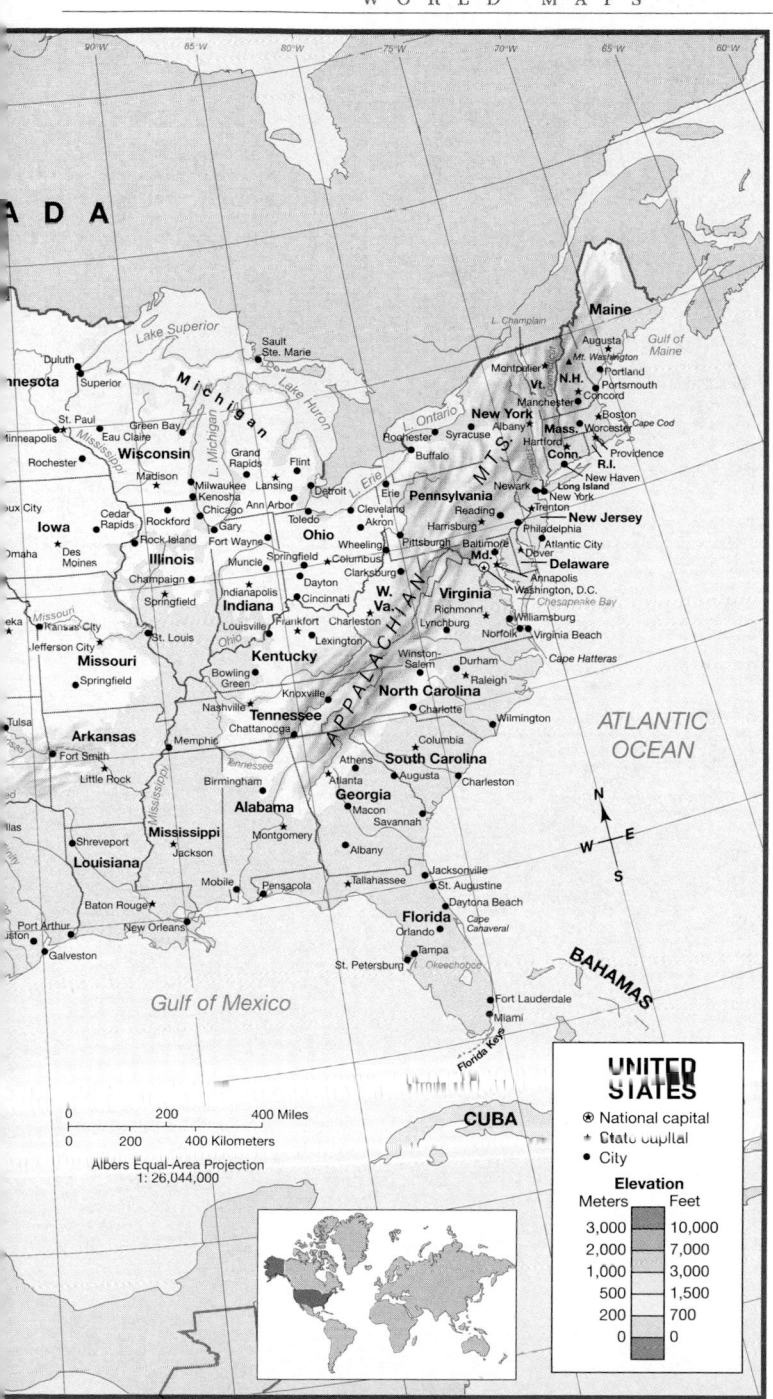

ATLANTIC
OCEAN

Gulf of Mexico

BAHAMAS

CUBA

| 0 | 200 | 400 Miles |
| 0 | 200 | 400 Kilometers |

Albers Equal-Area Projection
1: 26,044,000

**UNITED STATES**

⊛ National capital
★ State capital
● City

**Elevation**

| Meters | | Feet |
|--------|--|------|
| 3,000 | | 10,000 |
| 2,000 | | 7,000 |
| 1,000 | | 3,000 |
| 500 | | 1,500 |
| 200 | | 700 |
| 0 | | 0 |

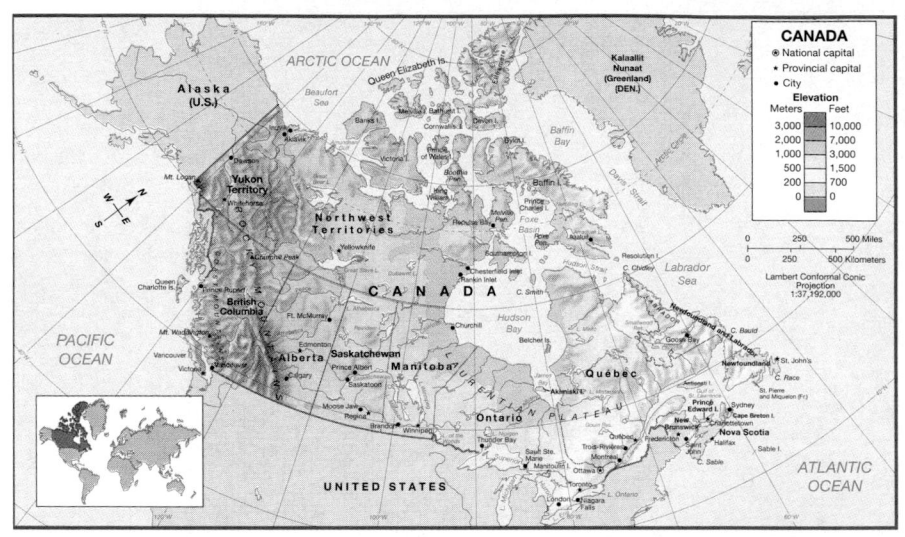

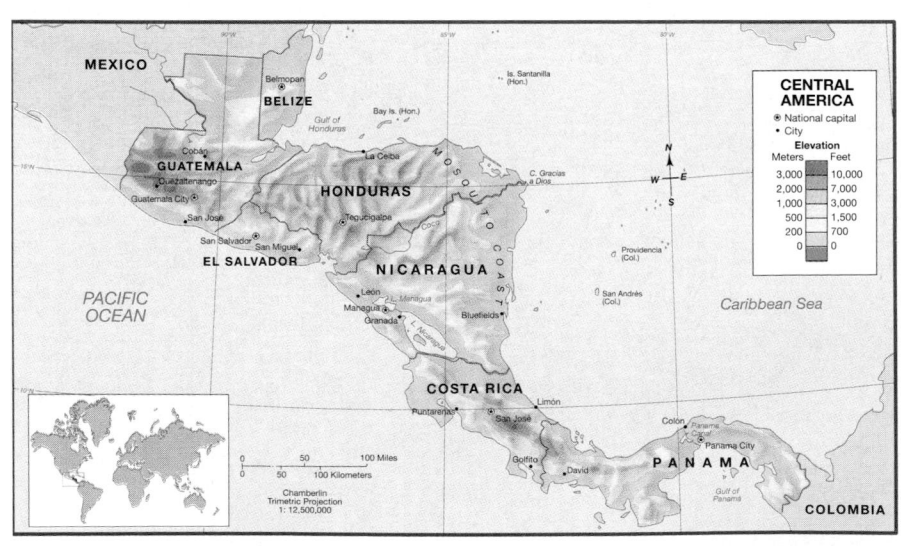

**SOUTH AMERICA**

⊛ National capital
• City

**Elevation**

| Meters | Feet |
| --- | --- |
| 3,000 | 10,000 |
| 2,000 | 7,000 |
| 1,000 | 3,000 |
| 500 | 1,500 |
| 200 | 700 |
| 0 | 0 |

Galápagos Is. (Ecuador)

I. Marchena
I. San Salvador
Santa Cruz
I. San Cristóbal
I. Fernandina
I. Sta. María
I. Española
I. Isabela

N
W   E
S

0    300    600 Miles
0    300    600 Kilometers

Lambert Azimuthal
Equal-Area Projection
1: 43,697,000

ARCTIC OCEAN

Barents Sea

Denmark Strait

Arctic Circle

Jan Mayen (Norway)

North Cape

Hammerfest

Vardø

70°N

60°N

50°N

40°N

30°W

20°W

10°W

0°

10°E

20°E

30°E

Norwegian Sea

Akureyri

Reykjavik ⊛ ICELAND

Seydhisfjordhur

Faroe Is. (Den.)

LAPLAND

Kiruna

SWEDEN

NORWAY

Inari

Oulu

L. Oulu

FINLAND

Vaasa

Kuopio

Trondheimsfjorden

Trondheim

Kristiansund

Ålesund

Sundsvall

Tampere

Helsinki ⊛

Turku

Espoo ⊛

Kotka

Shetland Is. (U.K.)

Sognefjorden

Bergen

Hardanger-fjorden

Lillehammer

Gävle

Ahvenanmaa (Finland)

G. of Finland

Hebrides

C. Wrath

Orkney Is.

Moray Firth

Stavanger

Drammen ⊛ Oslo

Arendal

Stockholm ⊛

Varnern

Gulf of Bothnia

ATLANTIC OCEAN

UNITED KINGDOM

Inverness

SCOTLAND

Kristiansand

Visby

Gotland (Sw.)

North Channel

Glasgow

Edinburgh

North Sea

Ålborg

Öland

Baltic Sea

Donegal Bay

N. IRELAND

Belfast

Newcastle-upon-Tyne

JUTLAND

Århus

Odense

Bornholm (Den.)

IRELAND

Galway

Irish Sea

Bradford

Leeds

DENMARK

Copenhagen ⊛

Malmö

Limerick

Cork

Dublin ⊛

Manchester

Liverpool

Sheffield

ENGLAND

The Wash

Kiel

Lübeck

Hamburg

Bremen

C. Clear

St. George's Channel

WALES

Birmingham

Frisian Is.

NETHERLANDS

Amsterdam

Hannover

Berlin

Cardiff

London

The Hague

Utrecht

Dortmund

Magdeburg

Land's End

Bristol

Southampton

Rotterdam

Antwerp

Essen

Düsseldorf

Leipzig

Dresden

Portsmouth

Calais

Lille

Brussels ⊛

BELGIUM

Cologne

Bonn

GERMANY

EASTERN EUROPE

Channel Is. (U.K.)

Cherbourg

Le Havre

Rouen

Liège

LUX.

Frankfurt

Mannheim

Brest

Versailles

Paris ⊛

Reims

Nuremberg

Nantes

Orléans

Strasbourg

Freiburg

Stuttgart

Munich

Linz

Vienna ⊛

Bay of Biscay

FRANCE

Loire

Vichy

Basel

Bern ⊛

LIECHTENSTEIN

Salzburg

Graz

MASSIF CENTRAL

Lyon

SWITZ.

Innsbruck

AUSTRIA

Bordeaux

Dordogne

Geneva

ALPS

Mt. Blanc

Milan

Venice

Trieste

Biarritz

Grenoble

Turin

Genoa

Bologna

Adriatic Sea

CANTABRIAN MTS.

Toulouse

Nîmes

MONACO

Nice

Ravenna

SAN MARINO

PYRENEES

Marseille

G. of Lions

Ligurian Sea

Pisa

Florence

APENNINES

Porto

Braga

ANDORRA

Saragossa

C. Creus

Corsica (Fr.)

Siena

Perugia

ITALY

Duero

Coimbra

SIERRA DE GUADARRAMA

Madrid ⊛

Barcelona

Ajaccio

VATICAN CITY

Rome ⊛

Naples

Bari

Lisbon ⊛

Tegus

Toledo

Majorca

Minorca

Sardinia (It.)

Brindisi

Setúbal

PORTUGAL

SIERRA MORENA

SPAIN

Valencia

Palma

Balearic Is.

Mt. Vesuvius

Évora

Guadiana

Ibiza

Cagliari

Tyrrhenian Sea

G. of Taranto

C. St. Vincent

Seville

Córdoba

Granada

C. Nao

Reggio di Calabria

Gulf of Cádiz

Cádiz

Málaga

Almería

C. Palos

Palermo

Messina

G. of Squillace

Strait of Gibraltar

Gibraltar (U.K.)

Cueta (Sp.)

C. Gata

Catania

Mt. Etna

Sicily

Ionian Sea

C. Passero

Valletta ⊛ MALTA

Mediterranean Sea

AFRICA

N

W   E

S

Rockall (U.K.)

## WESTERN EUROPE

⊛ National capital

• City

**Elevation**

| Meters | | Feet |
|---|---|---|
| 3,000 | | 10,000 |
| 2,000 | | 7,000 |
| 1,000 | | 3,000 |
| 500 | | 1,500 |
| 200 | | 700 |
| 0 | | 0 |

0    200    400 Miles

0    200    400 Kilometers

Azimuthal Equal-Area Projection

1: 31,019,000

10°E

20°E

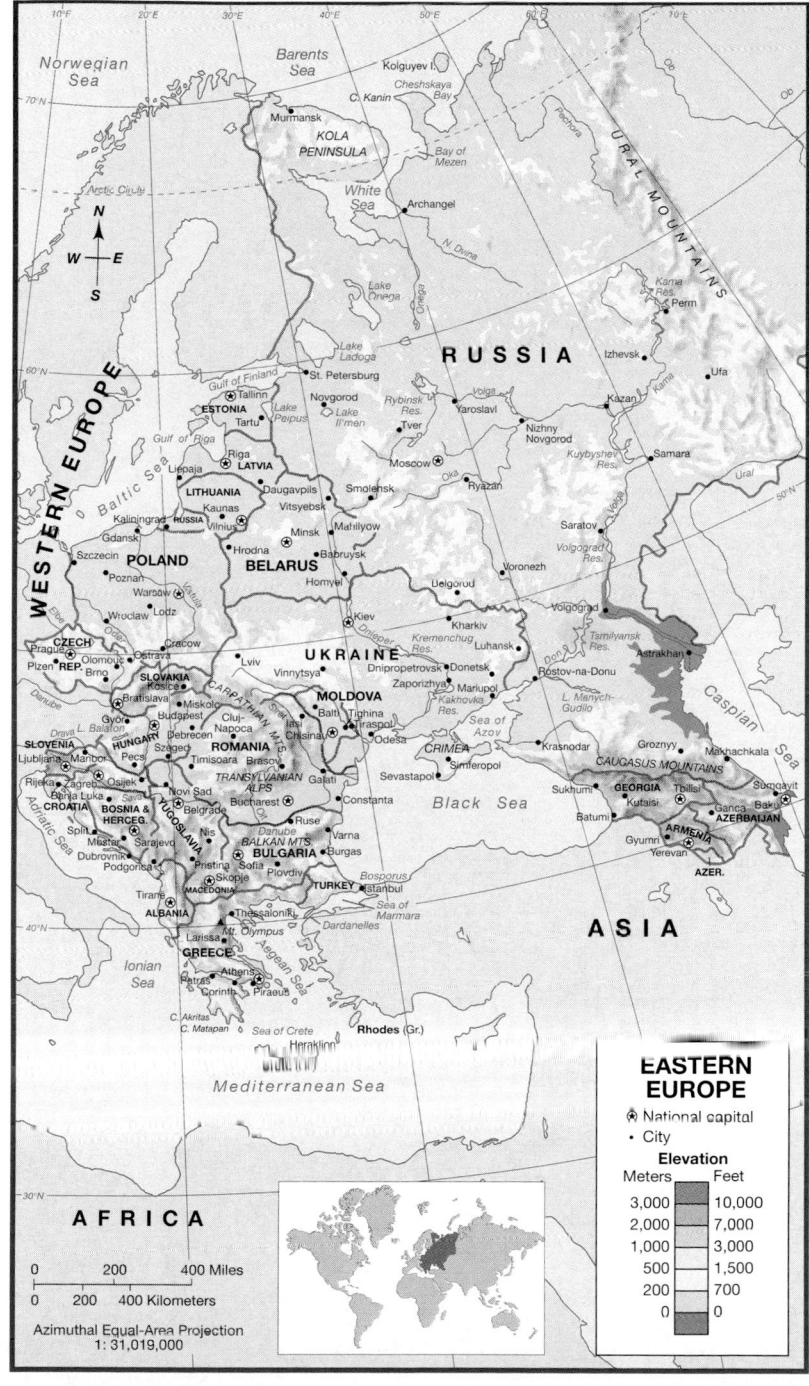

**EASTERN EUROPE**

⊛ National capital

• City

**Elevation**

| Meters | | Feet |
|---|---|---|
| 3,000 | | 10,000 |
| 2,000 | | 7,000 |
| 1,000 | | 3,000 |
| 500 | | 1,500 |
| 200 | | 700 |
| 0 | | 0 |

0    200    400 Miles

0    200    400 Kilometers

Azimuthal Equal-Area Projection
1 : 31,019,000

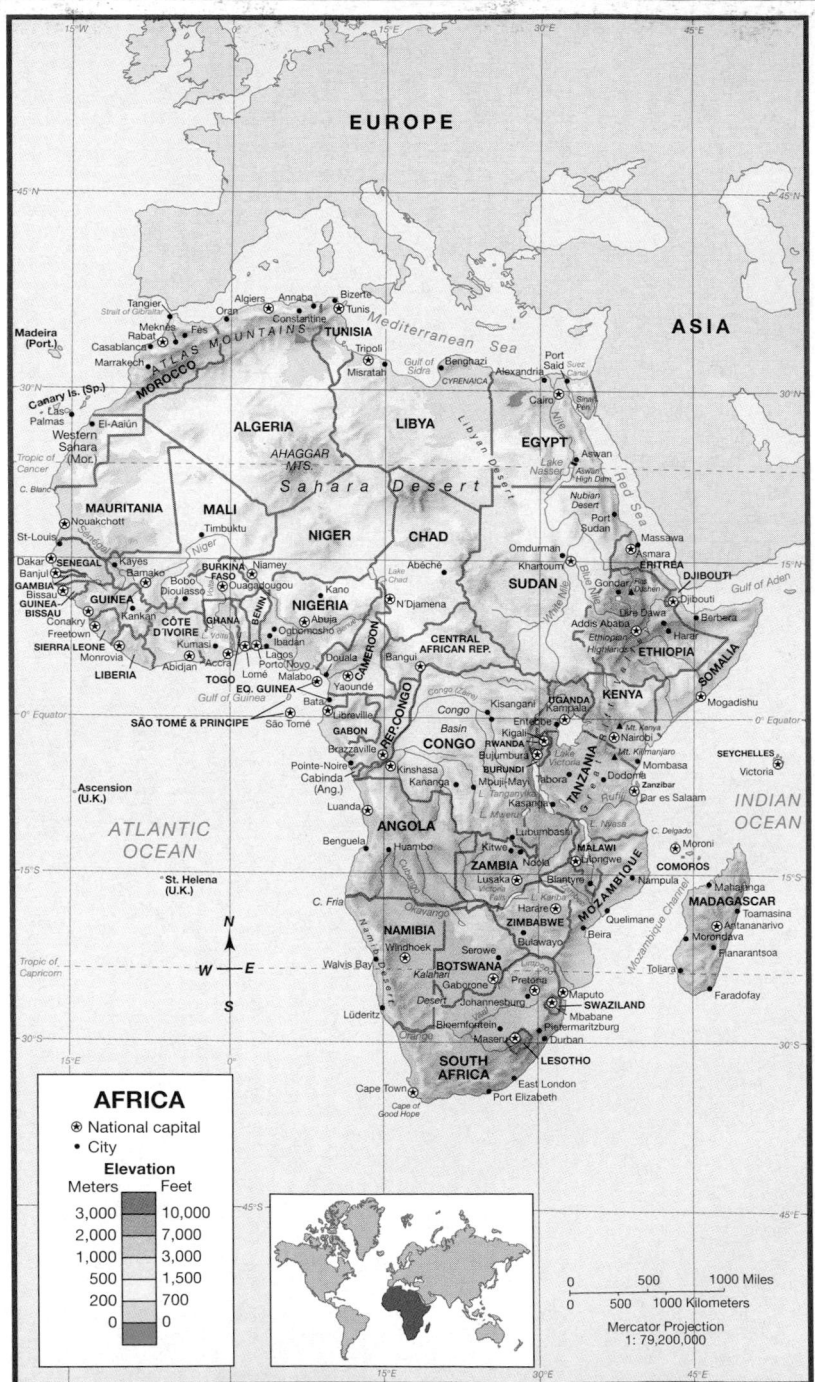

# AFRICA

⊛ National capital
• City

**Elevation**

| Meters | | Feet |
|---|---|---|
| 3,000 | | 10,000 |
| 2,000 | | 7,000 |
| 1,000 | | 3,000 |
| 500 | | 1,500 |
| 200 | | 700 |
| 0 | | 0 |

0        500        1000 Miles
0    500    1000 Kilometers

Mercator Projection
1: 79,200,000

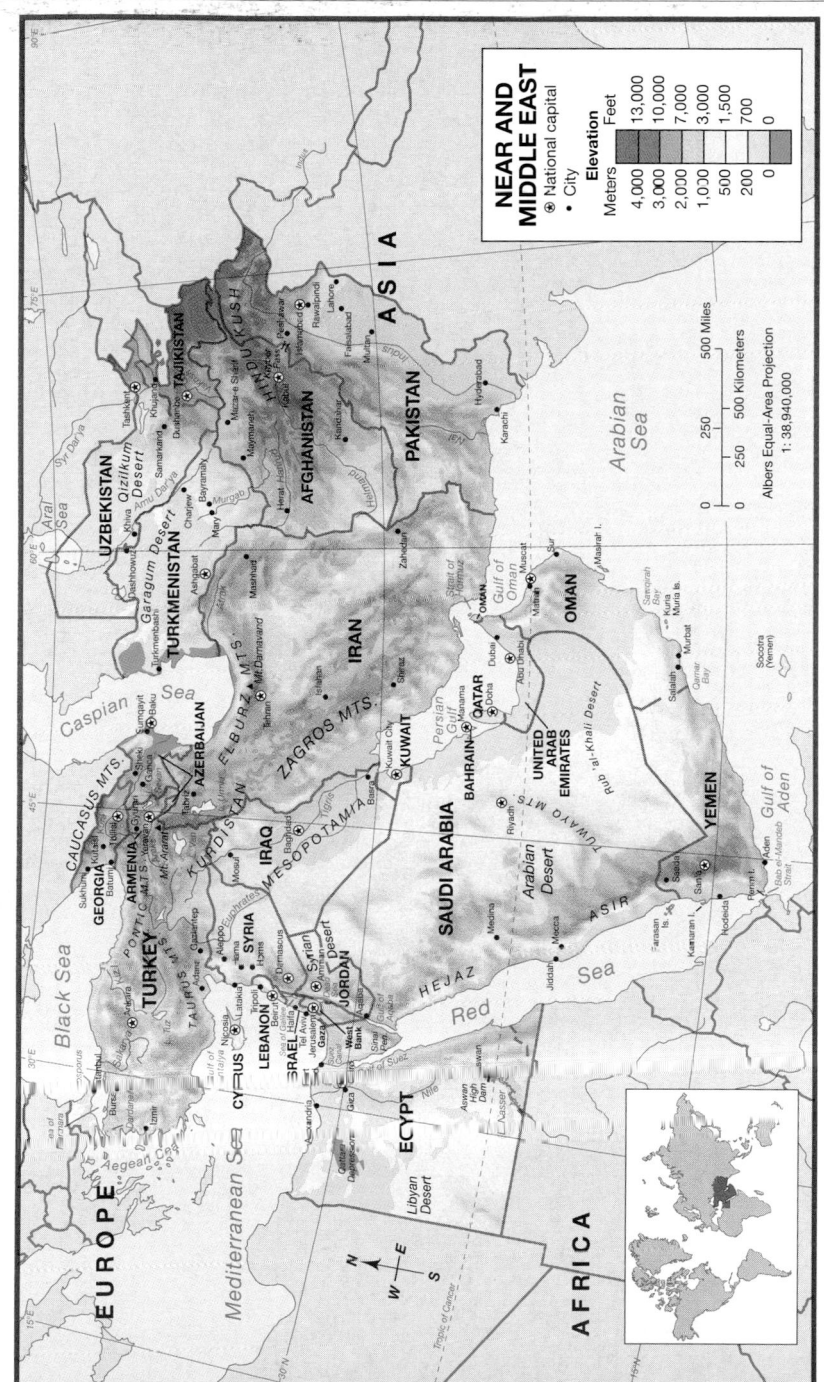

**NEAR AND
MIDDLE EAST**

⊕ National capital
• City

**Elevation**

| Meters | Feet |
| --- | --- |
| 4,000 | 13,000 |
| 3,000 | 10,000 |
| 2,000 | 7,000 |
| 1,000 | 3,000 |
| 500 | 1,500 |
| 200 | 700 |
| 0 | 0 |

Albers Equal-Area Projection
1:38,940,000

0   250   500 Miles

0   250   500 Kilometers

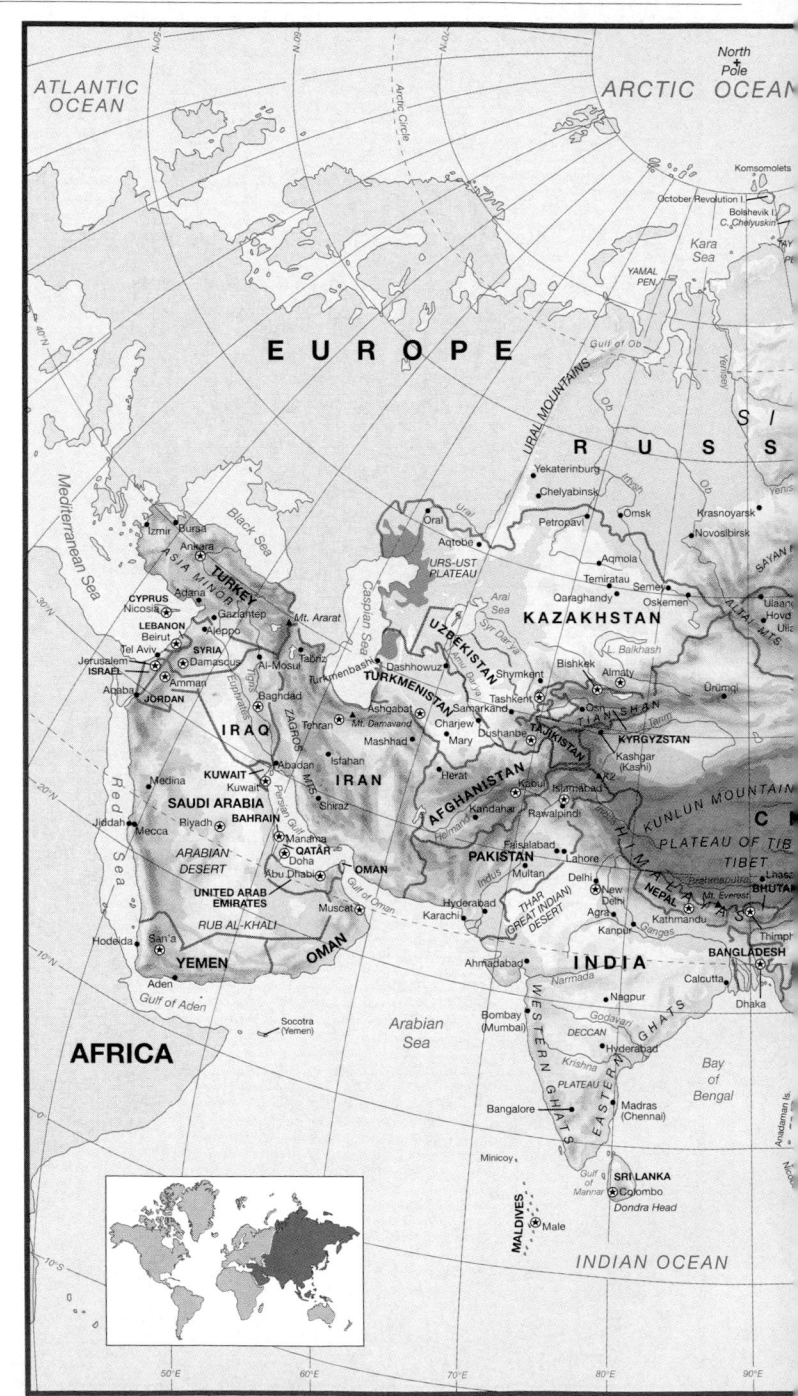

ATLANTIC
OCEAN

North
Pole

ARCTIC OCEAN

Komsomolets

October Revolution I

Bolshevik I.
C. Chelyuskin

Kara
Sea

YAMAL
PEN.

Arctic Circle

Gulf of Ob

E U R O P E

URAL MOUNTAINS

S I

R U S S

Yekaterinburg

Chelyabinsk

Omsk

Krasnoyarsk

Novosibirsk

Mediterranean Sea

Black Sea

Izmir
Bursa
Ankara

ASIA MINOR

TURKEY

CYPRUS
Nicosia

Adana

Gaziantep

Mt. Ararat

LEBANON
Beirut
Aleppo

Tel Aviv
Damascus
SYRIA

Jerusalem
ISRAEL

Amman

Abadan

JORDAN

Al-Mosul

Baghdad

ZAGROS MTS.

Tigris

Euphrates

IRAQ

Caspian Sea

Ural

URS-UST
PLATEAU

Aral
Sea

Syr Darya

Oral

Aqtobe

Aqmola

Temiratau

Qaraghandy

UZBEKISTAN

Dashhowuz

Turkmenbashi

TURKMENISTAN

Ashgabat

Mt. Damavand

Tehran

Charjew

Mary

Mashhad

Amu Darya

Samarkand

Petropavl

Ishim

Balkhash

Bishkek

Shymkent

Tashkent

Dushanbe

TAJIKISTAN

Herat

KAZAKHSTAN

Semey

Oskemen

Almaty

Osh

KYRGYZSTAN

Ürümqi

Kashgar
(Kashi)

TIAN SHAN

SAYAN

ALTAI MTS.

Ulaan
Hovd
Ula

Yenis

Ob

Irtysh

Ili

Tarim

KUWAIT
Kuwait

SAUDI ARABIA

Medina

Jiddah
Mecca

Riyadh

ARABIAN
DESERT

BAHRAIN

Manama
QATAR
Doha

Abu Dhabi

UNITED ARAB
EMIRATES

RUB AL-KHALI

Isfahan

Shiraz

IRAN

Persian Gulf

Gulf of Oman

Muscat

OMAN

AFGHANISTAN

Kabul

Kandahar

Helmand

Islamabad

Rawalpindi

PAKISTAN

Faisalabad

Multan

Indus

Lahore

Delhi
New
Delhi

KUNLUN MOUNTAIN

HIMALAYA

PLATEAU OF TIB

TIBET

Brahmaputra

Mt. Everest

NEPAL

Kathmandu

BHUTAN

Thimp

C

Lhas

Red Sea

Hodeida

San'a

YEMEN

Aden

Gulf of Aden

Socotra
(Yemen)

Arabian
Sea

AFRICA

Hyderabad

Karachi

THAR
(GREAT INDIAN)
DESERT

Ahmadabad

Narmada

Bombay
(Mumbai)

WESTERN GHATS

DECCAN

PLATEAU

Krishna

Bangalore

Agra

Kanpur

Ganges

INDIA

Nagpur

Godavari

Hyderabad

EASTERN GHATS

Madras
(Chennai)

Minicoy

MALDIVES

Male

Gulf of
Mannar

SRI LANKA
Colombo

Dondra Head

Kanpur

BANGLADESH

Calcutta

Dhaka

Bay
of
Bengal

Andaman Is.

INDIAN OCEAN

### ASIA

⊗ National capital
• City
〜 Great Wall of China

**Elevation**

| Meters | | Feet |
|---|---|---|
| 6,000 | | 19,000 |
| 3,000 | | 10,000 |
| 2,000 | | 7,000 |
| 1,000 | | 3,000 |
| 500 | | 1,500 |
| 200 | | 700 |
| 0 | | 0 |

0          500          1000 Miles
0     500     1000 Kilometers
Lambert Azimuthal Equal-Area
Projection
1:61,016,000

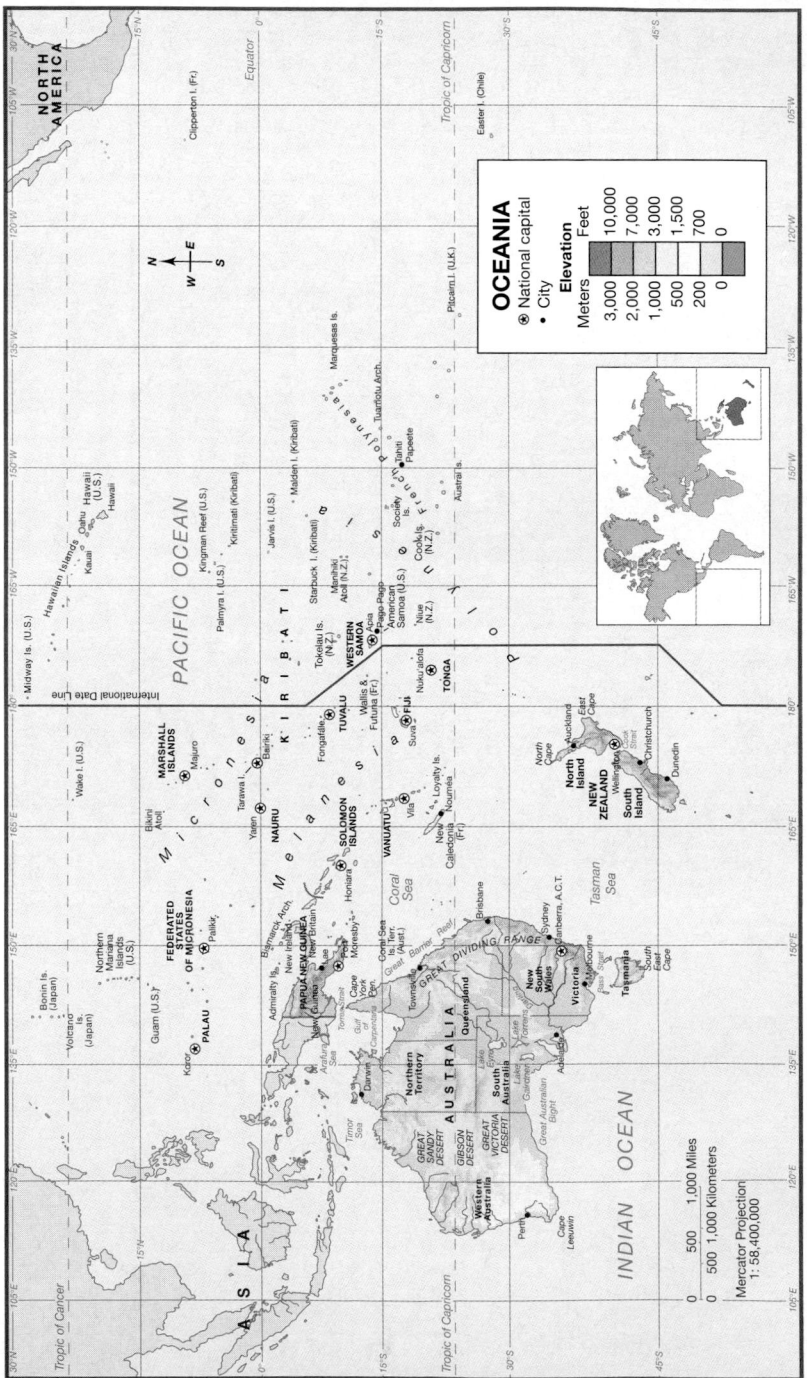

OCEANIA

⊛ National capital
• City

Elevation

| Meters | Feet |
|--------|------|
| 3,000 | 10,000 |
| 2,000 | 7,000 |
| 1,000 | 3,000 |
| 500 | 1,500 |
| 200 | 700 |
| 0 | 0 |

Mercator Projection
1:58,400,000

0    500    1,000 Miles
0    500  1,000 Kilometers

# Conversion Factors

| To change | To | Multiply by | To change | To | Multiply by |
|---|---|---|---|---|---|
| acres | square feet | 43,560 | liters | quarts (liquid) | 1.0567 |
| acres | square miles | .001562 | meters | feet | 3.2808 |
| atmospheres | cms. of mercury | 76 | meters | miles | .0006214 |
| Btu | kilowatt-hour | .0002931 | meters | yards | 1.0936 |
| Btu/hour | watts | .2931 | metric tons | tons (long) | .9842 |
| bushels | cubic inches | 2150.4 | metric tons | tons (short) | 1.1023 |
| centimeters | inches | .3937 | miles | kilometers | 1.6093 |
| centimeters | feet | .03281 | miles | feet | 5280 |
| cubic feet | cubic meters | .0283 | miles (nautical) | miles (statute) | 1.1516 |
| cubic meters | cubic feet | 35.3145 | miles (statute) | miles (nautical) | .8684 |
| cubic meters | cubic yards | 1.3079 | miles/hour | feet/minute | 88 |
| cubic yards | cubic meters | .7646 | millimeters | inches | .0394 |
| fathoms | feet | 6.0 | ounces (avdp) | grams | 28.3495 |
| feet | meters | .3048 | ounces | pounds | .0625 |
| feet | miles (nautical) | .0001645 | ounces (troy) | ounces (avdp) | 1.09714 |
| feet | miles (statute) | .0001894 | pecks | liters | 8.8096 |
| feet/second | miles/hour | .6818 | pints (dry) | liters | .5506 |
| furlongs | feet | 660.0 | pints (liquid) | liters | .4732 |
| furlongs | miles | .125 | pounds (ap or troy) | kilograms | .3782 |
| gallons (U.S.) | liters | 3.7853 | pounds (avdp) | kilograms | .4536 |
| grains | grams | .0648 | pounds | ounces | 16 |
| grams | ounces (avdp) | .0353 | quarts (dry) | liters | 1.1012 |
| grams | pounds | .002205 | quarts (liquid) | liters | .9463 |
| hectares | acres | 2.4710 | radians | degrees | 57.30 |
| hectoliters | bushels (U.S.) | 2.8378 | rods | meters | 5.029 |
| horsepower | watts | 745.7 | rods | feet | 16.5 |
| horsepower | Btu/hour | .001341 | square feet | square meters | .0929 |
| hours | days | .04167 | square kilometers | square miles | .3861 |
| inches | millimeters | 25.4000 | square meters | square feet | 10.7639 |
| inches | centimeters | 2.5400 | square miles | square kilometers | 2.5900 |
| kilograms | pounds (avdp or troy) | 2.2046 | square yards | square meters | .8361 |
| kilometers | miles | .6214 | tons (long) | metric tons | 1.016 |
| kilowatt-hour | Btu | 3412 | tons (short) | metric tons | .9072 |
| knots | nautical miles/hour | 1.0 | tons (long) | pounds | 2240 |
| knots | statute miles/hour | 1.151 | tons (short) | pounds | 2000 |
| liters | gallons (U.S.) | .2642 | watts | Btu/hour | 3.4121 |
| liters | pints (dry) | 1.8162 | watts | horsepower | .001341 |
| liters | pints (liquid) | 2.1134 | yards | meters | .9144 |
| liters | quarts (dry) | .9081 | yards | miles | .0005682 |

NOTE: avdp = avoirdupois weight, ap = apothecaries' weight. *See also* p.539.

## Fahrenheit and Celsius (Centigrade) Scales

| °Celsius | °Fahrenheit | °Celsius | °Fahrenheit |
|---|---|---|---|
| −273.15 | −459.67 | 30 | 86 |
| −250 | −418 | 35 | 95 |
| −200 | −328 | 40 | 104 |
| −150 | −238 | 45 | 113 |
| −100 | −148 | 50 | 122 |
| −50 | −58 | 55 | 131 |
| −40 | −40 | 60 | 140 |
| −30 | −22 | 65 | 149 |
| −20 | −4 | 70 | 158 |
| −10 | 14 | 75 | 167 |
| 0 | 32 | 80 | 176 |
| 5 | 41 | 85 | 185 |
| 10 | 50 | 90 | 194 |
| 15 | 59 | 95 | 203 |
| 20 | 68 | 100 | 212 |
| 25 | 77 | | |

Zero on the Fahrenheit scale represents the temperature produced by the mixing of equal weights of snow and common salt.

| | °Fahrenheit | °Celsius |
|---|---|---|
| Boiling point of water | 212° | 100° |
| Freezing point of water | 32° | 0° |
| Absolute zero | −459.6° | −273.1° |

Absolute zero is theoretically the lowest possible temperature, the point at which all molecular motion would cease.

To convert Fahrenheit to Celsius (Centigrade), subtract 32 and divide by 1.8.

To convert Celsius (Centigrade) to Fahrenheit, multiply by 1.8 and add 32.

## Kelvin Scale

Absolute zero, −273.15° on the Celsius (Centigrade) scale, is 0 Kelvin. Thus, Kelvin is equivalent to Celsius plus 273.15. The freezing point of water, 0°C and 32°F, is 273.15K. The conversion formula is K = C° + 273.15.

## Cardinal, Ordinal, and Nominal Numbers

**Cardinal numbers,** known as the "counting numbers," indicate quantity. **Ordinal numbers** indicate the order or rank of things in a set (e.g., sixth in line; fourth place). **Nominal numbers** name or identify something (e.g., a zip code or a player on a team.) They do not show quantity or rank.

## Roman Numerals

Roman numerals are expressed by letters of the alphabet and are rarely used today except for formality or variety. There are four basic principles for reading Roman numerals:

1. A letter repeated once or twice repeats its value that many times (XXX = 30, CC = 200, etc.).
2. One or more letters placed after another letter of greater value increases the greater value by the amount of the smaller (VI = 6, LXX = 70, MCC = 1200, etc.).
3. A letter placed before another letter of greater value decreases the greater value by the amount of the smaller (IV = 4, XC = 90, CM = 900, etc.).
4. A bar placed on top of a letter or string of letters increases the numeral's value by 1,000 times (XV = 15, $\overline{XV}$ = 15,000).

| Letter | Value | Letter | Value | Letter | Value | Letter | Value | Letter | Value |
|---|---|---|---|---|---|---|---|---|---|
| I | 1 | VII | 7 | XL | 40 | C | 100 | $\overline{C}$ | 100,000 |
| II | 2 | VIII | 8 | L | 50 | D | 500 | $\overline{D}$ | 500,000 |
| III | 3 | IX | 9 | LX | 60 | M | 1,000 | $\overline{M}$ | 1,000,000 |
| IV | 4 | X | 10 | LXX | 70 | $\overline{V}$ | 5,000 | | |
| V | 5 | XX | 20 | LXXX | 80 | $\overline{X}$ | 10,000 | | |
| VI | 6 | XXX | 30 | XC | 90 | $\overline{L}$ | 50,000 | | |

## Mean and Median

The arithmetic mean, also called the average, of a series of quantities is obtained by finding the sum of the quantities and dividing it by the number of quantities. In the series 1, 3, 5, 18, 19, 20, 25, the mean or average is 13—in other words, 91 divided by 7.

The median of a series is that point which so divides it that half the quantities are on one side, half on the other. In the above series, the median is 18.

The median often better expresses the common-run, since it is not, as is the mean, affected by an excessively high or low figure. In the series 1, 3, 4, 7, 55, the median of 4 is a truer expression of the common-run than is the mean of 14.

### Prime Numbers between 1 and 1,000

| | | | | | | | | |
|---|---|---|---|---|---|---|---|---|
| | 2 | 3 | 5 | 7 | 11 | 13 | 17 | 19 | 23 |
| 29 | 31 | 37 | 41 | 43 | 47 | 53 | 59 | 61 | 67 |
| 71 | 73 | 79 | 83 | 89 | 97 | 101 | 103 | 107 | 109 |
| 113 | 127 | 131 | 137 | 139 | 149 | 151 | 157 | 163 | 167 |
| 173 | 179 | 181 | 191 | 193 | 197 | 199 | 211 | 223 | 227 |
| 229 | 233 | 239 | 241 | 251 | 257 | 263 | 269 | 271 | 277 |
| 281 | 283 | 293 | 307 | 311 | 313 | 317 | 331 | 337 | 347 |
| 349 | 353 | 359 | 367 | 373 | 379 | 383 | 389 | 397 | 401 |
| 409 | 419 | 421 | 431 | 433 | 439 | 443 | 449 | 457 | 461 |
| 463 | 467 | 479 | 487 | 491 | 499 | 503 | 509 | 521 | 523 |
| 541 | 547 | 557 | 563 | 569 | 571 | 577 | 587 | 593 | 599 |
| 601 | 607 | 613 | 617 | 619 | 631 | 641 | 643 | 647 | 653 |
| 659 | 661 | 673 | 677 | 683 | 691 | 701 | 709 | 719 | 727 |
| 733 | 739 | 743 | 751 | 757 | 761 | 769 | 773 | 787 | 797 |
| 809 | 811 | 821 | 823 | 827 | 829 | 839 | 853 | 857 | 859 |
| 863 | 877 | 881 | 883 | 887 | 907 | 911 | 919 | 929 | 937 |
| 941 | 947 | 953 | 967 | 971 | 977 | 983 | 991 | 997 | (1009) |

## Portraits and Designs of U.S. Paper Currency

| Currency[1] | Portrait | Design on back | Currency[1] | Portrait | Design on back |
|---|---|---|---|---|---|
| $1 | Washington | ONE between obverse and reverse of Great Seal of U.S. | $50[6] | Grant | U.S. Capitol |
| $2[2] | Jefferson | Monticello | $100[7] | Franklin | Independence Hall |
| $2[3] | Jefferson | "The Signing of the Declaration of Independence" | $500 | McKinley | Ornate FIVE HUNDRED |
| | | | $1,000 | Cleveland | Ornate ONE THOUSAND |
| $5[4] | Lincoln | Lincoln Memorial | $5,000 | Madison | Ornate FIVE THOUSAND |
| $10[4] | Hamilton | U.S. Treasury Building | $10,000 | Chase | Ornate TEN THOUSAND |
| $20[5] | Jackson | White House | $100,000[8] | Wilson | Ornate ONE HUNDRED THOUSAND |

1. Denominations of $500 and higher were discontinued in 1969. 2. Discontinued in 1966. 3. New issue, April 1976. 4. New issue, May 2000. 5. New issue, Sept. 1998. 6. New issue, fall 1997. 7. New issue, March 1996. 8. For use only in transactions between Federal Reserve System and Treasury Department.

## New Quarters and Dollar Coin

The 50 State Quarters Program Act began in 1999 and is expected to run until 2008, with five new quarters released every year over ten years. The quarters are being released in the order that the states joined the union. 700 million copies of each quarter will be produced. Each quarter will feature a different state design on the back

In 2000, a new dollar coin, featuring the Shoshone guide Sacagawea, replaced the Susan B. Anthony coin, whose reserves are running low.

| State | Date of Statehood | Year of Issue | Design |
|---|---|---|---|
| Delaware | Dec. 7, 1787 | 1999 | Caesar Rodney's horseback ride |
| Pennsylvania | Dec. 12, 1787 | 1999 | Commonwealth statue, keystone, and outline of state |
| New Jersey | Dec. 18, 1787 | 1999 | Washington crossing the Delaware River |
| Georgia | Jan. 2, 1788 | 1999 | Peach, Live Oak, and outline of state |
| Connecticut | Jan. 9, 1788 | 1999 | The Charter Oak |
| Massachusetts | Feb. 6, 1788 | 2000 | Minuteman statue and outline of state |
| Maryland | April 28, 1788 | 2000 | Maryland Statehouse and White Oak |
| South Carolina | May 23, 1788 | 2000 | Palmetto tree, Carolina wren, and Yellow Jessamine |
| New Hampshire | June 21, 1788 | 2000 | Old Man of the Mountain rock formation |
| Virginia | June 25, 1788 | 2000 | First three ships to Jamestown |
| New York | July 26, 1788 | 2001 | Statue of Liberty, state outline, the words, "Gateway to Freedom," 11 stars |
| North Carolina | Nov. 21, 1789 | 2001 | First flight at Kitty Hawk |
| Rhode Island | May 29, 1790 | 2001 | A sailboat on the open sea, commemorating the "Ocean State" |
| Vermont | March 4, 1791 | 2001 | Camel's Hump Mountain, maple trees with sap buckets |
| Kentucky | June 1, 1792 | 2001 | Federal Hill, or "My Old Kentucky Home," race horse behind a fence |
| Tennessee | June 1, 1796 | 2002 | Fiddle, trumpet, guitar, and musical score |
| Ohio | March 1, 1803 | 2002 | Early airplane, astronaut, and state outline |
| Louisiana | April 30, 1812 | 2002 | Pelican, horn with musical notes, and outline of Louisiana Purchase |
| Indiana | Dec. 11, 1816 | 2002 | Race car and state outline |
| Mississippi | Dec. 10, 1817 | 2002 | Blossoms and leaves of two magnolias |

# Customary U.S. Weights and Measures

### Linear Measure

12 inches (in.) = 1 foot (ft.)
3 feet = 1 yard (yd)
5½ yards = 1 rod (rd), pole, or perch (16½ ft.)
40 rods = 1 furlong (fur) = 220 yds = 660 ft.
8 furlongs = 1 statute mile (mi.) = 1,760 yds
= 5,280 ft.
3 land miles = 1 league
5,280 feet = 1 statute or land mile
6,076.11549 feet = 1 international nautical mile

### Area Measure

144 square inches = 1 sq ft.
9 square feet = 1 sq yd = 1,296 sq in.
30¼ square yards = 1 sq rd = 272¼ sq ft.
160 square rods = 1 acre = 4,840 sq yds
= 43,560 sq ft.
640 acres = 1 sq mi.
1 mile square = 1 section (of land)
6 miles square = 1 township = 36 sections
= 36 sq mi.

### Cubic Measure

1,728 cubic inches = 1 cu ft.
27 cubic feet = 1 cu yd

### Liquid Measure

When necessary to distinguish the liquid pint or quart from the dry pint or quart, the word "liquid" or the abbreviation "liq" should be used in combination with the name or abbreviation of the liquid unit.

4 gills (gi) = 1 pint (pt) (= 28.875 cu in.)
2 pints = 1 quart (qt) (= 57.75 cu in.)
4 quarts = 1 gallon (gal) (= 231 cu in.)
= 8 pts = 32 gills

### Apothecaries' Fluid Measure

60 minims (min.) = 1 fluid dram (fl dr) (= 0.2256 cu in.)
8 fluid drams = 1 fluid ounce (fl oz) (= 1.8047 cu in.)
16 fluid ounces = 1 pt (= 28.875 cu in.) = 128 fl drs
2 pints = 1 qt (= 57.75 cu in.) = 32 fl oz
= 256 fl drs
4 quarts = 1 gal (= 231 cu in.) = 128 fl oz
= 1,024 fl drs

### Avoirdupois Weight

When necessary to distinguish the avoirdupois dram from the apothecaries' dram, or to distinguish the avoirdupois dram or ounce from the fluid dram or ounce, or to distinguish the avoirdupois ounce or pound from the troy or apothecaries' ounce or pound, the word "avoirdupois" or the abbreviation "avdp" should be used in combination with the name or abbreviation of the avoirdupois unit. (The "grain" is the same in avoirdupois, troy, and apothecaries' weights.)

27 11⁄32 grains = 1 dram
16 drams = 1 oz = 437½ grains
16 ounces = 1 lb = 256 drams = 7,000 grains
100 pounds = 1 hundredweight (cwt)[1]
20 hundredweights = 1 ton (tn) = 2,000 lbs[1]

In "gross" or "long" measure, the following values are recognized:

112 pounds = 1 gross or long cwt[1]
20 gross or long hundredweights = 1 gross or long ton
= 2,240 lbs[1]

1. When the terms "hundredweight" and "ton" are used unmodified, they are commonly understood to mean the 100-pound hundredweight and the 2,000-pound ton, respectively; these units may be designated "net" or "short" when necessary to distinguish them from the corresponding units in gross or long measure.

### Dry Measure

When necessary to distinguish the dry pint or quart from the liquid pint or quart, the word "dry" should be used in combination with the name or abbreviation of the dry unit.

2 pints = 1 qt (= 67.2006 cu in.)
8 quarts = 1 peck (pk) (= 537.605 cu in.) = 16 pts
4 pecks = 1 bushel (bu) (= 2,150.42 cu in.) = 32 qts

### Apothecaries' Weight

20 grains = 1 scruple (s ap)
3 scruples = 1 dram apothecaries' (dr ap)
= 60 grains
8 drams apothecaries' = 1 ounce apothecaries' (oz ap)
= 24 scruples = 480 grains
12 ounces apothecaries' = 1 pound apothecaries' (lb ap)
= 96 drams apothecaries'
= 288 scruples
= 5,760 grains

### Units of Circular Measure

Second ('') = —
Minute (') = 60 seconds
Degree (°) = 60 minutes
Right angle = 90 degrees
Straight angle = 180 degrees
Circle = 360 degrees

### Troy Weight

24 grains = 1 pennyweight (dwt)
20 pennyweights = 1 ounce troy (oz t) = 480 grains
12 ounces troy = 1 pound troy (lb t)
= 240 pennyweights
= 5,760 grains

### Gunter's or Surveyor's Chain Measure

7.92 inches = 1 link (li)
100 links = 1 chain (ch) = 4 rods = 66 ft.
80 chains = 1 statute mile = 320 rods = 5,280 ft.

# The International System (Metric)

*Source:* Department of Commerce, National Bureau of Standards.

The International System of Units is a modernized version of the metric system, established by international agreement, that provides a logical and interconnected framework for all measurements in science, industry, and commerce. The system is built on a foundation of seven basic units, and all other units are derived from them. (Use of metric weights and measures was legalized in the United States in 1866, and our customary units of weights and measures are defined in terms of the meter and kilogram.)

**Length.** Meter. Up until 1983, the meter was defined as 1,650,763.73 wavelengths in a vacuum of the orange-red line of the spectrum of krypton-86. Since then, it is equal to the distance traveled by light in a vacuum in 1/299,792,45 of a second.

**Time.** Second. The second is defined as the duration of 9,192,631,770 cycles of the radiation associated with a specified transition of the cesium-133 atom.

**Mass.** Kilogram. The standard for the kilogram is a cylinder of platinum-iridium alloy kept by the International Bureau of Weights and Measures at Paris. A duplicate at the National Bureau of Standards serves as the mass standard for the United States. The kilogram is the only base unit still defined by a physical object.

**Temperature.** Kelvin. The Kelvin is defined as the fraction 1/273.16 of the thermodynamic temperature of the triple point of water; that is, the point at which water forms an interface of solid, liquid, and vapor. This is defined as 0.01°C on the Centigrade or Celsius scale and 32.02°F on the Fahrenheit scale. The temperature 0°K is called "absolute zero."

**Electric Current.** Ampere. The ampere is defined as that current that, if maintained in each of two long parallel wires separated by one meter in free space, would produce a force between the two wires (due to their magnetic fields) of $2 \times 10^{-7}$ newton for each meter of length. (A newton is the unit of force that when applied to one kilogram mass would experience an acceleration of one meter per second per second.)

**Luminous Intensity.** Candela. The candela is defined as the luminous intensity of 1/600,000 of a square meter of a cavity at the temperature of freezing platinum (2,042°K).

**Amount of Substance.** Mole. The mole is the amount of substance of a system that contains as many elementary entities as there are atoms in 0.012 kilogram of carbon-12.

# Tables of Metric Weights and Measures

### Linear Measure

10 millimeters (mm) = 1 centimeter (cm)
10 centimeters = 1 decimeter (dm) = 100 millimeters
10 decimeters = 1 meter (m) = 1,000 millimeters
10 meters = 1 dekameter (dam)
10 dekameters = 1 hectometer (hm) = 100 meters
10 hectometers = 1 kilometer (km) = 1,000 meters

### Area Measure

100 square millimeters (mm²) = 1 sq centimeter (cm²)
10,000 square centimeters = 1 sq meter (m²) =
1,000,000 sq millimeters
100 square meters = 1 are (a)
100 ares = 1 hectare (ha) =
10,000 sq meters
100 hectares = 1 sq kilometer (km²) =
1,000,000 sq meters

## Volume Measure

10 milliliters (ml) = 1 centiliter (cl)
10 centiliters = 1 deciliter (dl) = 100 milliliters
10 deciliters = 1 liter (l) = 1,000 milliliters
10 liters = 1 dekaliter (dal)
10 dekaliters = 1 hectoliter (hl) = 100 liters
10 hectoliters = 1 kiloliter (kl) = 1,000 liters

## Cubic Measure

1,000 cubic millimeters ($mm^3$) = 1 cu centimeter ($cm^3$)
1,000 cubic centimeters = 1 cu decimeter ($dm^3$) = 1,000,000 cu millimeters
1,000 cubic decimeters = 1 cu meter ($m^3$) = 1 stere = 1,000,000 cu centimeters = 1,000,000,000 cu millimeters

## Weight

10 milligrams (mg) = 1 centigram (cg)
10 centigrams = 1 decigram (dg) = 100 milligrams
10 decigrams = 1 gram (g) = 1,000 milligrams
10 grams = 1 dekagram (dag)

10 dekagrams = 1 hectogram (hg) = 100 grams
10 hectograms = 1 kilogram (kg) = 1,000 grams
1,000 kilograms = 1 metric ton (t)

# Metric and U.S. Equivalents

| | | | |
|---|---|---|---|
| 1 angstrom[1](light wave measurement) | 0.1 millimicron<br>0.000 1 micron<br>0.000 000 1 millimeter<br>0.000 000 004 inch | 1 meter | 39.37 inches<br>1.094 yards |
| | | 1 micron | 0.001 millimeter<br>0.000 039 37 inch |
| 1 cable's length | 120 fathoms<br>720 feet<br>219.456 meters | 1 mil | 0.001 inch<br>0.025 4 millimeter |
| 1 centimeter | 0.3937 inch | 1 mile (statute or land) | 5,280 feet<br>1.609 kilometers |
| 1 decimeter | 3.937 inches | 1 mile (nautical international) | 1.852 kilometers<br>1.151 statute miles<br>0.999 U.S. nautical miles |
| 1 dekameter | 32.808 feet | | |
| 1 fathom | 6 feet<br>1.8288 meters | 1 millimeter | 0.03937 inch |
| 1 foot | 0.3048 meter | 1 millimicron (m+GRKm) | 0.001 micron<br>0.000 000 039 37 inch |
| 1 furlong | 10 chains (surveyor's)<br>660 feet<br>220 yards<br>⅛ statute mile<br>201.168 meters | 1 nanometer | 0.001 micrometer or<br>0.000 000 039 37 inch |
| | | 1 point (typography) | 0.013 837 inch<br>1/72 inch (approximately)<br>0.351 millimeter |
| 1 inch | 2.54 centimeters | | |
| 1 kilometer | 0.621 mile | 1 rod, pole, or perch | 16½ feet<br>5.0292 meters |
| 1 league (land) | 3 statute miles<br>4.828 kilometers | 1 yard | 0.9144 meter |

## Areas or Surfaces

| | | | |
|---|---|---|---|
| 1 acre | 43,560 square feet<br>4,840 square yards<br>0.405 hectare | 1 square kilometer | 0.386 square mile<br>247.105 acres |
| | | 1 square meter | 1.196 square yards<br>10.764 square feet |
| 1 are | 119.599 square yards<br>0.025 acre | 1 square mile | 258.999 hectares |
| 1 hectare | 2.471 acres | 1 square millimeter | 0.002 square inch |
| 1 square centimeter | 0.155 square inch | 1 square rod, square pole or square perch | 25.293 square meters |
| 1 square decimeter | 15.5 square inches | | |
| 1 square foot | 929.030 square centimeters | 1 square yard | 0.836 square meters |
| 1 square inch | 6.4516 square centimeters | | |

# Capacities or Volumes

| | | | | |
|---|---|---|---|---|
| 1 barrel, liquid | 31 to 42 gallons[2] | | 1 quart, liquid (U.S.) | 57.75 cubic inches<br>0.946 liter<br>0.833 British quart |
| 1 bushel (U.S.) struck measure[3] | 2,150.42 cubic inches<br>35.238 liters | | 1 quart (British) | 69.354 cubic inches<br>1.032 U.S. dry quarts<br>1.201 U.S. liquid quarts |
| 1 bushel, heaped (U.S.) | 2,747.715 cubic inches<br>1.278 bushels, struck measure[4] | | 1 tablespoon, measuring | 3 teaspoons<br>4 fluid drams<br>½ fluid ounce |
| 1 cord (firewood) | 128 cubic feet | | 1 teaspoon, measuring | ⅓ tablespoon<br>1⅓ fluid drams |
| 1 cubic centimeter | 0.061 cubic inch | | 1 carat | 200 milligrams<br>3.086 grains |
| 1 cubic decimeter | 61.024 cubic inches | | 1 dram, apothecaries' | 60 grains<br>3.888 grams |
| 1 cubic foot | 7.481 gallons<br>28.316 cubic decimeters | | 1 dram, avoirdupois | 27 1½2 (=27.344) grains<br>1.772 grams |
| 1 cubic inch | 0.554 fluid ounce<br>4.433 fluid drams<br>16.387 cubic centimeters | | 1 grain | 64.798 91 milligrams |
| 1 cubic meter | 1.308 cubic yards | | 1 gram | 15.432 grains<br>0.035 avoirdupois ounce |
| 1 cubic yard | 0.765 cubic meter | | 1 kilogram | 2.205 pounds |
| 1 cup, measuring | 8 fluid ounces<br>½ liquid pint | | 1 microgram (µg—the Greek letter mu in combination with the letter g) | 0.000 001 gram |
| 1 dram, fluid or liquid (U.S.) | ⅛ fluid ounces<br>0.226 cubic inch<br>3.697 milliliters<br>1.041 British fluid drachms | | 1 milligram | 0.015 grain |
| 1 dekaliter | 2.642 gallons<br>1.135 pecks | | 1 ounce, avoirdupois | 437.5 grains<br>0.911 troy or apothecaries' ounce<br>28.350 grams |
| 1 gallon (U.S.) | 231 cubic inches<br>3.785 liters<br>0.833 British gallon<br>128 U.S. fluid ounces | | 1 ounce, troy or apothecaries' | 480 grains<br>1.097 avoirdupois ounces<br>31.103 grams |
| 1 gallon (British Imperial) | 277.42 cubic inches<br>1.201 U.S. gallons<br>4.546 liters<br>160 British fluid ounces | | 1 pennyweight | 1.555 grams |
| | | | 1 point | 0.01 carat<br>2 milligrams |
| 1 hectoliter | 26.418 gallons<br>2.838 bushels | | 1 pound, avoirdupois | 7,000 grains<br>1.215 troy or apothecaries' pounds<br>453.592 37 grams |
| 1 liter | 1.057 liquid quarts<br>0.908 dry quart<br>61.024 cubic inches | | 1 pound, troy or apothecaries' | 5,760 grains<br>0.823 avoirdupois pound<br>373.242 grams |
| 1 milliliter | 0.271 fluid dram<br>16.231 minims<br>0.061 cubic inch | | 1 ton, gross or long[5] | 2,240 pounds<br>1.12 net tons<br>1.016 metric tons |
| 1 ounce, fluid or liquid (U.S.) | 1.805 cubic inch<br>29.574 milliliters<br>1.041 British fluid ounces | | 1 ton, metric | 2,204.623 pounds<br>0.984 gross ton<br>1.102 net tons |
| 1 peck | 8.810 liters | | 1 ton, net or short | 2,000 pounds<br>0.893 gross ton<br>0.907 metric ton |
| 1 pint, dry | 33.600 cubic inches<br>0.551 liter | | | |
| 1 pint, liquid | 28.875 cubic inches<br>0.473 liter | | | |
| 1 quart, dry (U.S.) | 67.201 cubic inches<br>1.101 liters<br>0.969 British quart | | | |

1. The angstrom is basically defined as $10^{-10}$ meter. 2. There is a variety of "barrels" established by law or usage. For example, federal taxes on fermented liquors are based on a barrel of 31 gallons; many state laws fix the "barrel for liquids" at 31½ gallons; one state fixes a 36-gallon barrel for cistern measurement; federal law recognizes a 40-gallon barrel for "proof spirits"; by custom, 42 gallons compose a barrel of crude oil or petroleum products for statistical purposes, and this equivalent is recognized "for liquids" by four states. 3. "Struck measure" refers to a struck, or level, bushel. It is the only official bushel measure in the UK. 4. Frequently recognized as 1¼ bushels, struck measure. 5. The gross or long ton is used commercially in the United States to only a limited extent, usually in restricted industrial fields. These units are the same as the British "ton."

## Definitions of Gold Terminology

The term "fineness" defines a gold content in parts per thousand. For example, a gold nugget containing 885 parts of pure gold, 100 parts of silver, and 15 parts of copper would be considered 885-fine.

The word "karat" indicates the proportion of solid gold in an alloy based on a total of 24 parts. Thus, 14-karat (14K) gold indicates a composition of 14 parts of gold and 10 parts of other metals.

The term "gold-filled" is used to describe articles of jewelry made of base metal that are covered on one or more surfaces with a layer of gold alloy. No article having a gold alloy portion of less than one twentieth by weight may be marked "gold-filled." Articles may be marked "rolled gold plate" provided the proportional fraction and fineness designations are also shown.

Electroplated jewelry items carrying at least 7 millionths of an inch of gold on significant surfaces may be labeled "electroplate." Plate thicknesses less than this may be marked "gold-flashed" or "gold-washed."

## Bolts and Screws: Conversion from Fractions of an Inch to Millimeters

| Inch | mm | Inch | mm | Inch | mm | Inch | mm |
|------|------|------|------|------|------|------|------|
| 1/64 | 0.40 | 17/64 | 6.75 | 33/64 | 13.10 | 49/64 | 19.45 |
| 1/32 | 0.79 | 9/32 | 7.14 | 17/32 | 13.50 | 25/32 | 19.84 |
| 3/64 | 1.19 | 19/64 | 7.54 | 35/64 | 13.90 | 51/64 | 20.24 |
| 1/16 | 1.59 | 5/16 | 7.94 | 9/16 | 14.29 | 13/16 | 20.64 |
| 5/64 | 1.98 | 21/64 | 8.33 | 37/64 | 14.69 | 53/64 | 21.03 |
| 3/32 | 2.38 | 11/32 | 8.73 | 19/32 | 15.08 | 27/32 | 21.43 |
| 7/64 | 2.78 | 23/64 | 9.13 | 39/64 | 15.48 | 55/64 | 21.83 |
| 1/8 | 3.18 | 3/8 | 9.53 | 5/8 | 15.88 | 7/8 | 22.23 |
| 9/64 | 3.57 | 25/64 | 9.92 | 41/64 | 16.27 | 57/64 | 22.62 |
| 5/32 | 3.97 | 13/32 | 10.32 | 21/32 | 16.67 | 29/32 | 23.02 |
| 11/64 | 4.37 | 27/64 | 10.72 | 43/64 | 17.06 | 59/64 | 23.42 |
| 3/16 | 4.76 | 7/16 | 11.11 | 11/16 | 17.46 | 15/16 | 23.81 |
| 13/64 | 5.16 | 29/64 | 11.51 | 45/64 | 17.86 | 61/64 | 24.21 |
| 7/32 | 5.56 | 15/32 | 11.91 | 23/32 | 18.26 | 31/32 | 24.61 |
| 15/64 | 5.95 | 31/64 | 12.30 | 47/64 | 18.65 | 63/64 | 25.00 |
| 1/4 | 6.35 | 1/2 | 12.70 | 3/4 | 19.05 | 1 | 25.40 |

## Cooking Measurement Equivalents

1 tablespoon (tbsp) = 3 teaspoons (tsp)

1/16 cup = 1 tablespoon

1/8 cup = 2 tablespoons

1/6 cup = 2 tablespoons + 2 teaspoons

1/4 cup = 4 tablespoons

1/3 cup = 5 tablespoons + 1 teaspoon

3/8 cup = 6 tablespoons

1/2 cup = 8 tablespoons

2/3 cup = 10 tablespoons + 2 teaspoons

3/4 cup = 12 tablespoons

1 cup = 48 teaspoons

1 cup = 16 tablespoons

8 fluid ounces (fl oz) = 1 cup

1 pint (pt) = 2 cups

1 quart (qt) = 2 pints

4 cups = 1 quart

1 gallon (gal) = 4 quarts

16 ounces (oz) = 1 pound (lb)

1 milliliter (ml) = 1 cubic centimeter (cc)

1 inch (in) = 2.54 centimeters (cm)

*Source:* United States Dept. of Agriculture (USDA).

## U.S.–Metric Cooking Conversions

### U.S. to Metric

| Capacity | | Weight | |
|----------|------|--------|----------|
| 1/5 teaspoon | 1 milliliter | 1 oz | 28 grams |
| 1 teaspoon | 5 ml | 1 pound | 454 grams |
| 1 tablespoon | 15 ml | | |
| 1 fluid oz | 30 ml | | |
| 1/5 cup | 47 ml | | |
| 1 cup | 237 ml | | |
| 2 cups (1 pint) | 473 ml | | |
| 4 cups (1 quart) | .95 liter | | |
| 4 quarts (1 gal.) | 3.8 liters | | |

### Metric to U.S.

| Capacity | | Weight | |
|----------|------|--------|----------|
| 1 milliliter | 1/5 teaspoon | 1 gram | .035 ounce |
| 5 ml | 1 teaspoon | 100 grams | 3.5 ounces |
| 15 ml | 1 tablespoon | 500 grams | 1.10 pounds |
| 100 ml | 3.4 fluid oz | 1 kilogram | 2.205 pounds |
| 240 ml | 1 cup | | 35 oz |
| 1 liter | 34 fluid oz | | |
| | 4.2 cups | | |
| | 2.1 pints | | |
| | 1.06 quarts | | |
| | 0.26 gallon | | |

## Prefixes and Multiples

| Prefix | Suffix | Equivalent | Multiple/submultiple | Prefix | Suffix | Equivalent | Multiple/submultiple |
|--------|--------|------------|----------------------|--------|--------|------------|----------------------|
| atto | a | quintillionth part | $10^{-18}$ | deci | d | tenth part | $10^{-1}$ |
| femto | f | quadrillionth part | $10^{-15}$ | deka | da | tenfold | $10$ |
| pico | p | trillionth part | $10^{-12}$ | hecto | h | hundredfold | $10^2$ |
| nano | n | billionth part | $10^{-9}$ | kilo | k | thousandfold | $10^3$ |
| micro | μ | millionth part | $10^{-6}$ | mega | M | millionfold | $10^6$ |
| milli | m | thousandth part | $10^{-3}$ | giga | G | billionfold | $10^9$ |
| centi | c | hundredth part | $10^{-2}$ | tera | T | trillionfold | $10^{12}$ |

# Common Formulas

## CIRCUMFERENCE
**Circle:** $C = \pi d$, in which $\pi$ is 3.1416 and $d$ the diameter.

## AREA
**Triangle:** $A = \dfrac{ab}{2}$, in which $a$ is the base and $b$ the height.

**Square:** $A = a^2$, in which $a$ is one of the sides.

**Rectangle:** $A = ab$, in which $a$ is the base and $b$ the height.

**Trapezoid:** $A = \dfrac{h(a+b)}{2}$, in which $h$ is the height, $a$ the longer parallel side, and $b$ the shorter.

**Regular pentagon:** $A = 1.720a^2$, in which $a$ is one of the sides.

**Regular hexagon:** $A = 2.598a^2$, in which $a$ is one of the sides.

**Regular octagon:** $A = 4.828a^2$, in which $a$ is one of the sides.

**Circle:** $A = \pi r^2$, in which $\pi$ is 3.1416 and $r$ the radius.

## VOLUME
**Cube:** $V = a^3$, in which $a$ is one of the edges.

**Rectangular prism:** $V = abc$, in which $a$ is the length, $b$ is the width, and $c$ the depth.

**Pyramid:** $V = \dfrac{Ah}{3}$, in which $A$ is the area of the base and $h$ the height.

**Cylinder:** $V = \pi r^2 h$, in which $\pi$ is 3.1416, $r$ the radius of the base, and $h$ the height.

**Cone:** $V = \dfrac{\pi r^2 h}{3}$, in which $\pi$ is 3.1416, $r$ the radius of the base, and $h$ the height.

**Sphere:** $V = \dfrac{4 \pi r^3}{3}$, in which $\pi$ is 3.1416 and $r$ the radius.

## TEMPERATURE SCALES
**Degrees Fahrenheit to Degrees Celsius:**
$$T_C = \frac{5}{9} (T_F - 32)$$

**Degrees Celsius to Degrees Fahrenheit:**
$$T_F = \frac{9}{5} T_C + 32$$

**Degrees Celsius to Kelvin:**
$$T_K = T_C + 273.15$$

## MISCELLANEOUS
**Distance in feet traveled by falling body:**
$d = 16t^2$, in which $t$ is the time in seconds.

**Speed of sound in feet per second through any given temperature of air:**
$$V = \frac{1087 \sqrt{273 + t}}{16.52}$$, in which $t$ is the temperature Celsius.

**Cost in cents of operation of electrical device:**
$$C = \frac{Wtc}{1000}$$, in which $W$ is the number of watts, $t$ the time in hours, and $c$ the cost in cents per kilowatt-hour.

**Conversion of matter into energy (Einstein's Theorem):** $E = mc^2$, in which $E$ is the energy in ergs, $m$ the mass of the matter in grams, and $c$ the speed of light in centimeters per second:
$$(c^2 = 9 \times 10^{20})$$

## Decimal Equivalents of Common Fractions

| | | | | | | | | | | | | | | | |
|---|---|---|---|---|---|---|---|---|---|---|---|---|---|---|---|
| 1/2 | .5000 | 1/10 | .1000 | 2/7 | .2857 | 3/11 | .2727 | 5/9 | .5556 | 7/11 | .6364 |
| 1/3 | .3333 | 1/11 | .0909 | 2/9 | .2222 | 4/5 | .8000 | 5/11 | .4545 | 7/12 | .5833 |
| 1/4 | .2500 | 1/12 | .0833 | 2/11 | .1818 | 4/7 | .5714 | 5/12 | .4167 | 8/9 | .8889 |
| 1/5 | .2000 | 1/16 | .0625 | 3/4 | .7500 | 4/9 | .4444 | 6/7 | .8571 | 8/11 | .7273 |
| 1/6 | .1667 | 1/32 | .0313 | 3/5 | .6000 | 4/11 | .3636 | 6/11 | .5455 | 9/10 | .9000 |
| 1/7 | .1429 | 1/64 | .0156 | 3/7 | .4286 | 5/6 | .8333 | 7/8 | .8750 | 9/11 | .8182 |
| 1/8 | .1250 | 2/3 | .6667 | 3/8 | .3750 | 5/7 | .7143 | 7/9 | .7778 | 10/11 | .9091 |
| 1/9 | .1111 | 2/5 | .4000 | 3/10 | .3000 | 5/8 | .6250 | 7/10 | .7000 | 11/12 | .9167 |

# Life-Saving Skills Summary

| Skill | Adult (9 years and older) | Child (1 to 8 years) | Infant (birth to 1 year) |
|---|---|---|---|
| Rescue breathing (used when victim is not breathing) | Give 1 slow breath about every 5 seconds; about 1½ seconds per breath; 1 minute = about 10 to 12 breaths | Give 1 slow breath about every 3 seconds; about 1½ seconds per breath; 1 minute = about 20 breaths | Give 1 slow breath about every 3 seconds; about 1½ seconds per breath; 1 minute = about 20 breaths |
| CPR (used if victim is not breathing *and* does not have a heart-beat) | Depth of compression is about 2 inches; compressions are performed with both hands; complete 15 compressions in about 10 seconds; do cycles of 15 compressions and 2 breaths | Depth of compression is about 1½ inches; compressions are performed with 1 hand; complete 5 compressions in about 3 seconds; do cycles of 5 compressions and 1 breath | Depth of compression is about 1 inch; compressions are performed with 2 fingers; complete 5 compressions in about 3 seconds; do cycles of 5 compressions and 1 breath |
| Choking (conscious) | Determine if person is choking; stand behind person and deliver abdominal thrusts; repeat until object is expelled or victim loses consciousness | Determine if child is choking; stand or kneel behind child and deliver abdominal thrusts; repeat until object is expelled or child loses consciousness | Determine if infant is choking; give 5 back blows; give 5 chest thrusts; repeat until object is expelled or infant loses consciousness |
| Choking (unconscious) | Give 2 slow breaths; retilt head and give 2 slow breaths; give up to 5 abdominal thrusts; do finger sweep; give 2 slow breaths; repeat abdominal thrusts, finger sweep, and 2 slow breaths | Give 2 slow breaths; retilt head and give 2 slow breaths; give up to 5 abdominal thrusts; check for object in throat; do finger sweep if object is visible; give 2 slow breaths; repeat abdominal thrusts, foreign-body check/finger sweep, and 2 slow breaths | Give 2 slow breaths; retilt head and give 2 slow breaths; give 5 back blows; give 5 chest thrusts; check for object in throat; do finger sweep if object is visible; repeat back blows, chest thrusts, foreign-body check/finger sweep, and 2 slow breaths |

## Rescue Breathing

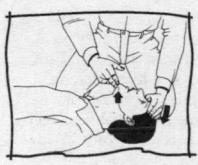

1. With head tilted back, pinch nose shut.

2. ADULT: Give 1 slow breath about every 5 seconds.

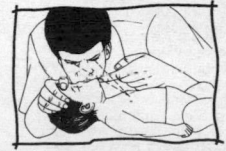

CHILD/INFANT: Give 1 slow breath about every 3 seconds.

## CPR (Adult)

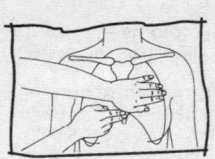

1. Find hand position.

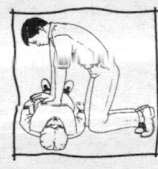

2. Position shoulders over hands. Compress chest 15 times.

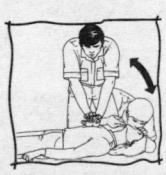

3. Give 2 slow breaths. Recheck pulse and breathing. If no pulse, continue sets of 15 compressions and 2 breaths.

## Choking

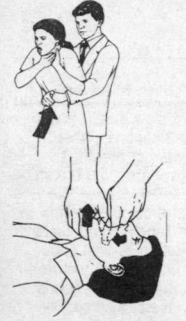

**If conscious but choking, give abdominal thrusts until object comes out.**

**If a person becomes unconscious:**

**Step 1. Clear any object from mouth.**

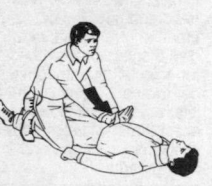

**Step 2. Give 2 slow breaths.**

**If air won't go in, give up to 5 abdominal thrusts.**

## Other Emergencies

### Burns

**First Degree: Signs/Symptoms**—reddened skin. **Treatment**—Immerse quickly in cold water or apply ice until pain stops.

**Second Degree: Signs/Symptoms**—reddened skin, blisters. **Treatment**—(1) Cut away loose clothing. (2) Cover with several layers of cold moist dressings or, if limb is involved, immerse in cold water for relief of pain. (3) Treat for shock.

**Third Degree: Signs/Symptoms**—skin destroyed, tissues damaged, charring. **Treatment**—(1) Cut away loose clothing (do not remove clothing adhered to skin). (2) Cover with several layers of sterile, cold, moist dressings for relief of pain and to stop burning action. (3) Treat for shock.

### Poisons

**Treatment**—(1) Dilute by drinking large quantities of water. (2) Induce vomiting except when poison is corrosive or a petroleum product. (3) Call the poison-control center or a doctor.

### Shock

Shock may accompany any serious injury: blood loss, breathing impairment, heart failure, burns. Shock can kill—treat as soon as possible and continue until medical aid is available.

**Signs/Symptoms**—(1) Shallow breathing. (2) Rapid and weak pulse. (3) Nausea, collapse, vomit-ing. (4) Shivering. (5) Pale, moist skin. (6) Mental confusion. (7) Drooping eyelids, dilated pupils.

**Treatment**—(1) Establish and maintain an open airway. (2) Control bleeding. (3) Keep victim lying down. Exception: Head and chest injuries, heart attack, stroke, sun stroke. If no spine injury, victim may be more comfortable and breathe better in a semi-reclining position. If in doubt, keep the victim flat. Elevate the feet unless injury would be aggravated. Maintain normal body temperature. Place blankets under and over victim.

### Frostbite

Most frequently frostbitten: toes, fingers, nose, and ears. It is caused by exposure to cold.

**Signs/Symptoms**—(1) Skin becomes pale or a grayish-yellow color. (2) Parts feel cold and numb. (3) Frozen parts feel doughy.

**Treatment**—(1) Victim should be wrapped in woolen cloth and kept dry. (2) Do not rub, chafe, or manipulate frostbitten parts. (3) Bring victim indoors. (4) Place affected parts in warm water (102°F to 105°F) and make sure water remains warm. Never thaw if the victim has to go back out into the cold, which may cause the affected area to be refrozen. (5) Do not use hot water bottles or a heat lamp, and do not place victim near a hot stove. (6) For serious frostbite, seek medical aid for thawing because pain will be intense and tissue damage extensive.

### Heat Cramps

Affects people who work or do strenuous exercises in a hot environment. To prevent it, such people should drink large amounts of cool water and add a pinch of salt to each glass of water.

**Signs/Symptoms**—(1) Painful muscle cramps in legs and abdomen. (2) Faintness. (3) Profuse perspiration.

**Treatment**—(1) Move victim to a cool place. (2) Give victim sips of salted drinking water (one teaspoon of salt to one quart of water). (3) Apply manual pressure to the cramped muscle.

### Heat Exhaustion

**Signs/Symptoms**—(1) Pale and clammy skin. (2) Profuse perspiration. (3) Rapid and shallow breathing. (4) Weakness, dizziness, and headache.

**Treatment**—(1) Care for victim as if he or she were in shock. (2) Remove victim to a cool area, do not allow chilling. (3) If body gets too cold, cover victim.

### Heat Stroke

**Signs/Symptoms**—(1) Face is red and flushed. (2) Victim becomes rapidly unconscious. (3) Skin is hot and dry with no perspiration.

**Treatment**—(1) Lay victim down with head and shoulders raised. (2) Reduce the high body temperature as quickly as possible. (3) Apply cold applications to the body and head. (4) Use ice and fan if available. (5) Watch for signs of shock and treat accordingly. (6) Get medical aid as soon as possible.

# A to Z Guide to Advances in Medicine

From artificial hearts to the Zone diet, here is TIME's guide to the latest key developments in medical science

**By ALICE PARK and
DAVID BJERKLIE** TIME

## A

**Alzheimer's** A nunnery might seem an odd place to conduct medical research, but some of the most intriguing advances in Alzheimer's in 2001 came from studying a group of nuns who agreed six years before to give their brains to science. A long-term study of 678 School Sisters of Notre Dame showed—surprisingly—that something as simple and nonmedical as a handwritten missive, penned in youth, may be able to predict a person's chances of getting Alzheimer's later in life. That link is still quite controversial; less so are some of the study's other findings, such as the protection the brain apparently gets from higher education pursued in young adulthood or from engaging in constant mental activity like playing card games or teaching during one's golden years.

**Artificial Heart** Almost 20 years after the bulky Jarvik artificial heart failed so miserably, AbioMed, a Massachusetts-based bioengineering company, developed a new, miniaturized version called the AbioCor. The device, totally self-contained (except for a belt-worn battery pack), was implanted in six terminally ill patients; the first, Robert Tools, survived for five months, many months longer than his doctors dared hope. Doctors have had even more success with a small pump that takes over just one of the heart's chambers. (*See* LVAD.)

**ALS** Amyotrophic lateral sclerosis, the paralyzing disease that took the life of Yankees great Lou Gehrig, is showing up in Gulf War veterans at twice the rate it occurs in other military personnel. That's the conclusion of the Defense Department and the Veterans Administration after reviewing the medical records of 2.5 million servicemen and women. ALS, which destroys nerve connections in the brain and spinal cord and causes muscles to atrophy, is the first disease directly linked to the generalized symptoms of Gulf War syndrome.

**Aspirin** It's a painkiller, a blood thinner, and a heart saver as well. But taking aspirin in combination with ibuprofen (in the form of Advil or Motrin) can render the multipurpose pill powerless. Ibuprofen, it turns out, blocks aspirin's blood-thinning ability 98%; more studies are needed to determine whether people who take both drugs need to worry about a higher heart-attack risk. In the meantime, doctors note that aspirin does not cancel the effects of other major painkillers, including rofecoxib and acetaminophen.

**Asthma** In July 2001, a Maryland woman participating in a Johns Hopkins Hospital study designed to better understand asthma inhaled an experimental chemical, developed a severe reaction, and died. The government reacted swiftly: it shut down all federally funded human research at the hospital for four days. The death was only the latest in a series of mortalities in clinical trials and prompted Hopkins and hundreds of other institutions where human trials are conducted to scrutinize their procedures. Since then, hospital review boards have tightened their protocols for clinical trials, requiring that doctors be closely monitored and patients fully informed of the risks.

## B

**Baycol** Among the best-selling prescription drugs in the U.S. today are the statins—powerful medications that can lower cholesterol levels by as much as 30 points. A fix that quick comes at a price, however, as Baycol users learned. The popular statin was pulled off the market after health officials discovered that a disturbing number of users were suffering from muscle disorders. Other statins, including atorvastatin, lovastatin, and pravastatin, remain safe, according to the FDA.

**Botox** In April 2002, the Food and Drug Administration approved the use of botox—botulinum toxin—to remove facial frown lines. The toxin that causes botulism, a form of food poisoning, was initially used to treat spasmodic eye muscles. Then doctors saw it also smoothed skin, and began employing it to remove wrinkles and smooth the face—a so-called "off-label use" of a drug. The FDA approval makes the use of botox for cosmetic effect legal. The price: $300 or more per injection—and the shots must be repeated every few months.

**BSE** The panic over bovine spongiform encephalopathy, commonly known as "mad cow" disease, has spread all the way to Japan, where a handful of cases caused beef sales to plummet. The good news was that researchers using a mathematical model estimated that the brain-wasting BSE variant in humans may max out at 100 cases per year in Britain, ground zero for mad cow, and kill no more than a few thousand people in the coming decade. Feel any better?

**Bypass Surgery** More than 500,000 bypass operations are performed in the U.S. each year, but what is good for the heart may not be good for the head. About a third of surgery patients, particularly those who are older and less educated, are at higher risk of cognitive decline after bypass surgery, according to a Duke University study. Doctors stress, however, that heart patients should not take this as an excuse to avoid needed surgery; it's not clear exactly how much of the mental fogginess is a direct result of the bypass operation and how much is a function of aging, medication, or pre-existing cognitive problems.

# C

**Cipro** Cipro was just another antibiotic used mostly for treating stubborn infections when it was catapulted to pharmaceutical stardom by the anthrax attacks. Cipro, it turned out, was the only antibiotic specifically approved by the FDA to treat anthrax, and suddenly it was the hottest drug in town. Doctors were besieged by patients demanding prescriptions "just in case," and pharmacies, particularly in New York, Washington, and Florida, couldn't keep up. Other antibiotics, including doxycycline and that old standby penicillin, are just as effective against the particular strain that was showing up in tainted letters, and a few weeks later, when the CDC recommended that doctors switch to those, Cipro's days in the spotlight were over.

**Cloning** Nobody has cloned a human yet (at least so far as we know), but a Massachusetts biotech firm managed to create a stir nonetheless just by making a six-celled embryo from a human cell. The goal was to achieve what the company called therapeutic cloning, by which cells are coaxed into generating whatever replacement tissues or organs a patient might need. The House of Representatives, however, voted to ban all human-cloning research—including therapeutic cloning—out of concern that it might be the first step down a slippery slope to a world of Mini-Me's. The Senate put off debating the issue until later.

**C.T. Scans** Computed tomography is an invaluable tool for doctors, giving them an inside view of the body that can help spot appendicitis as well as cancer, pneumonia, and other dangerous diseases before they become untreatable. But young children, whose growing cells are still dividing rapidly, may be at higher risk of developing brain cancer when exposed to the radiation of C.T. scans, according to a new study. The risk is small, but it can be reduced even further if technicians lower the dose for kids.

# D

**Defibrillators** "A portable E.R. in the chest" is how Dick Cheney's doctor described the device he installed—along with a pacemaker, to keep the Veep's heart beating regularly—in July 2001. Cheney, who suffered his fourth heart attack that year, may have to wear the business card-size device for the rest of his life. But should his heart ever act up again, the thing will automatically deliver a small jolt of electricity (enough to light a 30-watt bulb for one second) and snap it back into line.

**Diabetes** Daily injections of insulin are not simply a pain in the butt. For diabetics, they are taxing and inconvenient reminders of their disease. Studies of inhaled insulins, in the form of oral and powdered sprays, suggest that they may be nearly as effective as injections are in quickly normalizing blood-sugar levels. While no injection-free insulins have yet been approved by the FDA, doctors—and their diabetic patients—are looking forward to the day when those hated needles can be replaced by inhalers.

# F

**Fish Oil** You've seen the "heart healthy" menu logo next to the fish entrees. Well, supersize that. Studies have shown that eating fish rich in omega-3 fatty acids (such as sardines, salmon, and herring) not only protects you against heart disease but also cuts your risk of stroke. The more you eat, the greater the protection. And if that isn't enough to steer you to seafood, a 30-year study of 6,000 Swedish twins found that non-fish eaters are two to three times as likely to get prostate cancer. Go fish!

**Flu** Flu season is a scary time for asthmatics. They believe—correctly—that the disease can be especially dangerous for them. But many also believe—incorrectly—that the flu shot itself can trigger an asthma attack, which is one of the reasons 9 out of 10 asthmatics pass on getting an annual flu shot. Those fears are misplaced, according to researchers who studied the risks and determined that the vaccine is safe for both children and adults—and who strongly recommend that America's 25 million asthmatics get a flu shot every year.

# G

**Gaur** Once scientists cloned run-of-the-mill livestock like Dolly the sheep, could exotic endangered species have been far behind? Meet Noah the gaur, the first endangered clone. The gaur is a species of wild ox that is fast disappearing from its native India and Burma. Noah started out as a skin cell on an adult gaur that was fused with an empty egg from an ordinary cow and then brought to term by another cow named Bessie. Scientists hope that similar operations will someday be a practical way to keep endangered species alive. Too late for Noah, however. He died from an infection two days after he was born.

**Gleevec** There is still no cure for cancer, but drugs against the disease are getting a lot smarter. Instead of killing cells indiscriminately, as standard chemotherapy and radiation do, designer drugs such as Gleevec are engineered to block specific biological reactions that tumor cells—and not healthy ones—need to grow and thrive. Gleevec is currently approved to treat a form of leukemia and a rare stomach cancer. Close behind it in clinical trials is a string of experimental drugs that promise to do the same for other cancers, all with fewer side effects, so far, than current therapies.

**Genetic Engineering** You wouldn't normally expect to find a jellyfish gene in a rhesus monkey, but ANDi is not just any monkey. He's the first primate to carry an artificially introduced snippet of DNA in every one of his cells. Scientists have been splicing genes in and out of lesser species for years, but this is the first time they've done it to such a close cousin of Homo sapiens. Their success with ANDi (whose name is a backward acronym for inserted DNA) suggests that they are closer to manipulating human cells to treat disease or—to choose a more controversial application—genetically enhancing individual humans and all their offspring.

# H

**Heart Disease** About half of heart attacks occur in people with normal cholesterol levels. So is that a reason to stop holding back on fatty foods? Before you reach for those French fries, better ask your doctor about your CRPs. There's growing evidence that in some people, inflammation (measured by the levels of so-called C-reactive protein present in the blood) is as important as cholesterol in determining the risk of heart attacks. The theory holds that the same aggravation by the immune system that seizes joints in arthritis may irritate heart arteries, making them more hospitable environments for fatty plaque deposits. Fortunately, the statins that work so well to lower cholesterol levels are also extremely effective at reducing CRP levels and, doctors hope, cutting the risk of heart attacks. More and more heart doctors routinely test levels of both cholesterol and CRP in their patients.

**Hormone Replacement Therapy** More than 40% of all women in the U.S. start some form of hormone replacement therapy (HRT) in their menopause years. In July 2002, a large, federally funded clinical trial, part of a group of studies called the Women's Health Initiative, definitively showed for the first time that the hormones in question— estrogen and progestin—are not the age-defying drugs everyone thought they were. The results of the study proved that taking these hormones together for more than a few years actually increases a woman's risk of developing potentially deadly cardiovascular problems and invasive breast cancer, among other things. The findings were so striking that the study was stopped three years short of its scheduled completion so the news could be released.

# L

**Low-Tar Cigarettes** If you can't kick the habit, you can at least minimize the damage by switching to an ultralight, low-tar brand, right? Sorry. A comprehensive National Cancer Institute study concluded that "light" smokes are every bit as bad for you as regular cigarettes. The report blasted the tobacco industry for deceptive marketing and called for a ban on the terms light, ultralight, and low-tar.

**LVAD** For desperately ill heart-disease patients, the implantable pump called the LVAD (left ventricular assist device) buys precious time while they wait for a donor with a heart to spare to turn up in a morgue. A kind of poor man's artificial heart that gives a boost to the heart's main pumping chamber, the LVAD can lengthen and improve the quality of life even in a patient with no prospect of a transplant. Once thought of as only a temporary solution, the LVAD may soon be playing a bigger role in long-term management of heart disease.

# M

**Mammography** The logic of early detection seems hard to argue against; after all, the sooner you catch a cancer, the better your chances of nipping it in the bud. That's why for decades doctors have been recommending annual mammograms for women over 40. But an analysis of several large studies cast doubt on the conventional wisdom suggesting that the presumed benefits of early detection were based on flawed studies. The American Cancer Society, however, was quick to point to other studies indicating that mammographic screening reduces mortality even more than previously thought.

**Memory Loss** Lost keys, confusion in the parking lot, and more and more stories that start "Did I ever tell you . . . ?" They may be harbingers of something serious like Alzheimer's. Or maybe not. What clinicians call "mild cognitive impairment" can be caused by trauma, depression, or the side effects of medication. While not all cases of MCI lead inexorably to dementia, new studies suggest that a substantial number do. There are no drugs to prevent Alzheimer's, but there are treatments for MCI that can slow deterioration and preserve mental function a little longer.

**Mousepox Virus** It was an accidental discovery, but it could hardly be called serendipitous. By adding a single gene to its DNA, Australian researchers turned a mousepox virus that normally causes only mild symptoms in rodents into a virulent killer that wiped out all their lab mice in less than 10 days. Alarms were sounded, not over the prospect of mouse plague but out of concern that rogue scientists might use the technique to create human pathogens even more lethal than anthrax or smallpox.

# O

**OxyContin** It seemed like the perfect drug, a time-released synthetic opiate that killed pain without making users high. But soon after OxyContin hit the market, sales became suspiciously brisk. Drug abusers had discovered that they could get a heroin-like buzz by crushing the pills and snorting or injecting them intravenously. Almost overnight, OxyContin became the drug of choice on city streets and in the suburbs; it has now been linked to 300 deaths. As the drug skates between success and excess, the manufacturer has come under increased scrutiny for its aggressive marketing campaign.

**Ovarian Cancer** Aspirin, which can prevent everything from heart attacks to headaches, may also protect against cancer of the ovaries. A new study shows that women who took aspirin three or more times a week for at least six months had a 40% lower incidence of the most common type of ovarian cancer. The authors caution that the results are not yet conclusive. Aspirin also increases the risk of stroke and can cause gastrointestinal bleeding. Further studies will be needed to determine whether the benefits outweigh the risks.

# R

**Ritalin** Hailed as a wonder drug for the treatment of hyperactive children, Ritalin has also come under increased scrutiny from health professionals who are worried it is being overprescribed. New research suggests the drug may cause long-lasting changes in brain-cell structure and function similar to those seen with cocaine use. "Ritalin does appear to be safe when used properly," conclude researchers, "but it is still important to take a look at its impact on the brain."

# S

**Stem Cells** Taken from embryos only days old, stem cells are nature's blank slates, capable of developing into any one of the more than 200 cell types found in the human body. Scientists hope these cells may someday be used to treat a range of degenerative diseases, including Alzheimer's, Parkinson's, and diabetes. But using human embryos for research poses ethical problems, and until recently federal funding for such work was blocked. After much soul searching, President Bush decided to allow federal grants for research that used only the 60 or so stem-cell lines that have already been established. Some scientists fear those 60 lines will not be adequate. Meanwhile, other scientists are making headway in turning adult cells into functional equivalents of embryonic stem cells, which, if successful, would neatly sidestep the controversy.

**Smallpox** Just two decades after it was declared gone for good, this deadly scourge is back—in our fears if not in fact. Anthrax was bad enough, but smallpox in the hands of terrorists could make a far more devastating bioweapon. There is no effective treatment for the disease, and because routine vaccination was halted in 1972, even a single case could spread like wildfire. Officially, the only remaining sources of the virus are small quantities kept at two secure labs in the U.S. and Russia. Experts believe, however, that Iraq, North Korea, and Russia may have secretly pursued weapons research that involved smallpox. Erring on the side of caution, the White House has ordered 300 million doses of the vaccine, enough for every man, woman, and child in the U.S.

**Secondhand Smoke** Banishing smokers from offices, restaurants, malls, and airplanes has been a big success—for nonsmokers anyway. The Centers for Disease Control reports that the levels of toxic chemicals produced in nonsmokers' blood by secondhand smoke have plunged more than 75% since they were last measured about ten years ago. That's great news, considering that secondhand smoke is blamed for thousands of cancer and heart-disease deaths each year.

# T

**Tamoxifen** Although a new class of drugs called aromatase inhibitors shows signs of being even more effective than tamoxifen at treating breast cancer, don't count the old drug out yet. Women who take tamoxifen might also be doing their hearts a favor. Though it's not clear what the mechanism is, tamoxifen appears to lower the incidence of cardiovascular disease, which kills 500,000 women each year, more than ten times as many as breast cancer.

# Z

**Zone Diet** The lure of fast and easy weight loss is as enduring as young love. It is no surprise, then, that high-protein diets like the Zone, Atkins, Protein Power, and Sugar Busters have seduced many a problem eater. Alas, there's no hard evidence that these diets deliver on their promise of sustained, long-term weight loss. In fact, the American Heart Association cautions, such regimens may do more damage than good by increasing fat consumption and reducing important sources of vitamins, minerals, and fiber. Better to stick with the tried and true: exercise, portion control, and a balanced diet. Not very sexy, but it may just work.  □

## Status of the World AIDS Epidemic, End of 2001

| | Total | Adults | Women | Children under 15 years |
|---|---|---|---|---|
| People newly infected with HIV in 2001 | 5 million | 4.3 million | 1.8 million | 800,000 |
| Number of people living with HIV/AIDS | 40 million | 37.2 million | 17.6 million | 2.7 million |
| AIDS deaths in 2001 | 3 million | 2.4 million | 1.1 million | 580,000 |
| Total number of AIDS deaths since beginning of epidemic | 24.8 million | 19.9 million | 10.1 million | 4.9 million |

Source: World Health Organization; UNAIDS. Web: www.unaids.org.

## HIV/AIDS Statistics and Features by World Region

### (as of Dec. 2001)

| World region | Epidemic started | Adults & children living with HIV/AIDS | Adults & children newly infected with HIV | Adult prevalence rate[1] | Percent of HIV-positive adults who are women | Main mode(s) of transmission for adults[2] |
|---|---|---|---|---|---|---|
| Sub-Saharan Africa | late '70s–early '80s | 28.1 million | 3.4 million | 8.4% | 55% | Hetero |
| North Africa & Middle East | late '80s | 440,000 | 80,000 | 0.2% | 40% | Hetero, IDU |
| South & Southeast Asia | late '80s | 6.1 million | 800,000 | 0.6% | 35% | Hetero, IDU |
| East Asia & Pacific | late '80s | 1 million | 270,000 | 0.1% | 20% | IDU, Hetero, MSM |
| Latin America | late '70s–early '80s | 1.4 milion | 130,000 | 0.5% | 30% | MSM, IDU, Hetero |
| Caribbean | late '70s–early '80s | 420,000 | 60,000 | 2.2% | 50% | Hetero, MSM |
| Eastern Europe & Central Asia | early '90s | 1 million | 250,000 | 1% | 25% | IDU |
| Western Europe | late '70s–early '80s | 560,000 | 30,000 | 0.3% | 25% | MSM, IDU |
| North America | late '70s–early '80s | 940,000 | 45,000 | 0.6% | 20% | MSM, IDU, Hetero |
| Australia & New Zealand | late '70s–early '80s | 15,000 | 500 | 0.1% | 10% | MSM |
| **Total** | | **40 million** | **5 million** | **1.2%** | **48%** | |

1. The proportion of adults (15 to 49 years of age) living with HIV/AIDS in 2001, using 2001 population numbers. 2. Hetero (heterosexual transmission), IDU (transmission through injecting drug use), MSM (sexual transmission among men who have sex with men). *Source:* World Health Organization, UNAID. Web: www.unaids.org.

**Global Estimates[1] of the HIV/AIDS Epidemic as of End 2001**

| Region | Number |
| --- | --- |
| Western Europe | 560,000 |
| Eastern Europe & Central Asia | 1 million |
| North America | 940,000 |
| East Asia & Pacific | 1 million |
| North Africa & Middle East | 440,000 |
| Caribbean | 420,000 |
| South & Southeast Asia | 6.1 million |
| Latin America | 1.4 million |
| Sub-Saharan Africa | 28.1 million |
| Australia & New Zealand | 15,000 |
| Global Total | 40 million |

1. Number of people currently infected with HIV/AIDS.
*Source*: World Health Organization, UNAIDS.

# Understanding AIDS

Acquired Immune Deficiency Syndrome, or AIDS, was first reported in mid-1981 in the United States; it is believed to have originated in Sub-Saharan Africa. The human immunodeficiency virus (HIV) that causes AIDS was identified in 1983, and by 1985 tests to detect the virus were available. The credit for discovering the AIDS virus is jointly shared by Dr. Robert Gallo, a researcher at the National Cancer Institute, and Luc Montagnier of the Pasteur Institute, France.

## Destruction of Immune System

A fatal and incurable disease caused by HIV, AIDS attacks and destroys the immune system, gradually leaving the individual defenseless against illnesses that lead to death. These illnesses are referred to as "opportunistic" infections or diseases: in AIDS patients the most common are Pneumocystis carinii pneumonia (PCP), a parasitic infection of the lungs, and a type of cancer known as Kaposi's sarcoma (KS). Other opportunistic infections include unusually severe infections with yeast, cytomegalovirus, herpes virus, and parasites such as Toxoplasma or Cryptosporidia. Milder infections with these organisms do not suggest immune deficiencies. Symptoms of full-blown AIDS include a persistent cough, fever, and difficulty in breathing. Multiple purplish blotches and bumps on the skin may indicate Kaposi's sarcoma. The virus can also cause brain damage.

People infected with the virus can have a wide range of symptoms—from none to mild to severe. At least a fourth to a half of those infected will develop AIDS within four to ten years. Many experts think the percentage will be much higher.

## Transmission

Although the first reported cases involved homosexual men in Los Angeles who were infected through sexual contact, the principal mode of transmission throughout the world is through the exchange of bodily fluids during heterosexual intercourse. According to the World Health Organization, extensive spread of HIV appears to have begun in the late 1970s and early 1980s. It spread in men and

women with multiple sexual partners in East and Central Africa and among homosexual and bisexual men in certain urban areas of the Americas, Australasia, and Western Europe.

In addition to sexual contact, AIDS has been spread by intravenous drug users sharing infected hypodermic needles. The virus can also be passed on through transfused blood or its components. It may also be transmitted from infected mother to infant before, during, or shortly after birth.

Two major types of HIV have been recognized, HIV-1 and HIV-2. HIV-1 is the dominant type worldwide. HIV-2 is found principally in West Africa but cases have been reported in East Africa, Europe, Asia, and Latin America. There are at least ten different genetic subtypes of HIV-1, but their biological and epidemiological significance is unclear at present. Both HIV-1 and HIV-2 are transmitted in the same ways.

## Pandemic

With no cure at present, prudence could save thousands of people who have yet to be exposed to the virus. Use of condoms lessens the possibility of transmission as does the elimination of sharing hypodermic needles. The fate of many will depend less on science than on the ability of large numbers of human beings to change their behavior in the face of growing danger.

New drugs used in AIDS have given physicians renewed optimism in treating AIDS. Powerful drug combinations, called "cocktails," are able to decrease the amount of HIV in the blood to undetectable levels. However, not everyone can tolerate the potent medications, which can have devastating side effects—including diabetes, anemia, and high cholesterol. In addition, doctors are reporting a significant increase of patients with drug-resistant HIV strains, prompting research to produce different drugs. As of June 2001, some 100 separate drugs were either in use or being tested for use against AIDS. Meanwhile, HIV has been spreading, with rising rates of infection in Eastern Europe, Russia, China, and Southeast Asia, prompting some scientists to grimly warn that the epidemic has only just begun.

## Leading Causes of Mortality throughout the World

| Deaths | All countries rank | All countries % of total | Africa rank | Africa % of total | The Americas rank | The Americas % of total | Eastern Mediterranean rank | Eastern Mediterranean % of total | Europe rank | Europe % of total | Southeast Asia rank | Southeast Asia % of total | Western Pacific rank | Western Pacific % of total |
|---|---|---|---|---|---|---|---|---|---|---|---|---|---|---|
| Ischematic heart disease | 1 | 13.7% | 9 | 2.9% | 1 | 17.9% | 1 | 13.6% | 1 | 25.5% | 1 | 13.8% | 3 | 11.1% |
| Cerebrovascular disease | 2 | 9.5 | 7 | 4.7 | 2 | 10.3 | 5 | 5.3 | 2 | 13.7 | 4 | 6.5 | 1 | 14.3 |
| Acute lower respiratory infections | 3 | 6.4 | 3 | 8.2 | 3 | 4.2 | 2 | 9.1 | 4 | 3.6 | 2 | 9.3 | 4 | 4.0 |
| HIV/AIDS | 4 | 4.2 | 1 | 19.0 | 13 | 1.8 | 27 | 0.4 | 42 | 0.2 | 8 | 2.2 | 42 | 0.2 |
| Chronic obstructive pulmonary disease | 5 | 4.2 | 14 | 1.1 | 6 | 2.8 | 10 | 1.7 | 5 | 2.7 | 11 | 1.6 | 2 | 12.0 |
| Diarrheal diseases | 6 | 4.1 | 4 | 7.6 | 10 | 2.0 | 3 | 7.4 | 22 | 0.7 | 3 | 6.6 | 17 | 1.2 |
| Perinatal conditions | 7 | 4.0 | 5 | 5.5 | 7 | 2.6 | 4 | 7.3 | 13 | 1.2 | 5 | 6.0 | 10 | 2.2 |
| Tuberculosis | 8 | 2.8 | 11 | 2.2 | 19 | 1.0 | 7 | 3.7 | 23 | 0.6 | 6 | 5.1 | 9 | 2.9 |
| Cancer of trachea/ bronchus/lung | 9 | 2.3 | 38 | 0.3 | 4 | 3.2 | 20 | 1.0 | 3 | 4.2 | 15 | 1.2 | 6 | 3.6 |
| Road traffic accidents | 10 | 2.2 | 12 | 1.8 | 5 | 3.1 | 9 | 1.9 | 8 | 1.9 | 7 | 2.5 | 12 | 2.0 |

*Source: The World Health Report, 1999,* The World Health Organization (WHO).

# Common Infectious Diseases Worldwide

*Sources:* The Centers for Disease Control (CDC); The World Health Organization (WHO).

The following is a list of the most common infectious diseases throughout the world today. Accurate caseload numbers are difficult to determine, especially because so many of these diseases are endemic to developing countries, where many people do not have access to modern medical care. Approximately half of all deaths caused by infectious diseases each year can be attributed to just three diseases: tuberculosis, malaria, and AIDS. Together, these diseases cause over 300 million illnesses and more than 5 million deaths each year.

**African Trypanosomiasis ("sleeping sickness"):** African trypanosomiasis is spread by the tsetse fly, which is common to many African countries. The World Health Organization (WHO) estimates that nearly 450,000 cases occur each year, although the number of reported cases was only 45,000 in 1999. Symptoms of the disease include fever, headaches, joint pains, and itching in the early stage, and confusion, sensory disturbances, poor coordination, and disrupted sleep cycles in the second stage. If the disease goes untreated in its first stage, it causes irreparable neurological damage; if it goes untreated in its second stage, it is fatal.

**Cholera:** Cholera is a disease spread mostly through contaminated drinking water and unsanitary conditions. It is endemic in the Indian subcontinent, Russia, and sub-Saharan Africa. It is an acute infection of the intestines with the bacterium *Vibrio cholerae*. Its main symptom is copious diarrhea. Between 5% and 10% of those infected with the disease will develop severe symptoms, which also include vomiting and leg cramps. In its severe form, cholera can cause death by dehydration. An estimated 200,000 cases are reported to WHO annually.

**Cryptosporidiosis:** Cryptosporidiosis has become one of the most common causes of waterborne disease in the United States in recent years; it is also found throughout the rest of the world. It is caused by a parasite that spreads when a water source is contaminated, usually with the feces of infected animals or humans. Symptoms include diarrhea, stomach cramps, an upset stomach, and slight fever. Some people do not exhibit any symptoms.

**Dengue:** WHO estimates that 50 million cases of dengue fever appear each year. It is spread through the bite of the *Aedes aegypti* mosquito. Recent years have seen dengue outbreaks all over Asia and Africa. Dengue fever can be mild to moderate, and occasionally severe, though it is rarely fatal. Mild cases, which usually affect infants and young children, involve a nonspecific febrile illness, while moderate cases, seen in older children and adults, display high fever, severe headaches, muscle and joint pains, and rash. Severe cases develop into dengue hemorrhagic fever, which involves high fever, hemorrhaging, and sometimes circulatory failure.

**Hepatitis A:** Hepatitis A is a highly contagious liver disease caused by the hepatitis A virus. Spread primarily by the fecal-oral route or by ingestion of contaminated water or food, the number of annual infections worldwide is estimated at 1.4 million. Although milder than Hepatitis B, its effects can nonetheless be debilitating; symptoms include fever, fatigue, jaundice, and dark urine. Most common where crowding and poor sanitation facilitate transmission. Although those exposed usually develop lifelong immunity, the best protection against Hepatitis A is vaccination.

**Hepatitis B:** Approximately 2 billion people are infected with the hepatitis B virus (HBV), making it the most common infectious disease in the world today. Over 350 million of those infected never rid themselves of the infection. Hepatitis is an inflammation of the liver that causes symptoms such as jaundice, extreme fatigue, nausea, vomiting, and stomach pain; hepatitis B is the most serious form of the disease. Chronic infections can cause cirrhosis of the liver or liver cancer in later years.

**Hepatitis C:** Hepatitis C is a less common, and less severe, form of hepatitis. An estimated 170 million people worldwide are infected with hepatitis C virus (HCV); 3–4 million more are infected every year. The majority of HCV cases are asymptomatic, even in people who develop chronic infection.

**HIV/AIDS::** *See* pp. 550–551.

**Influenza:** Several influenza epidemics in the 20th century caused millions of deaths worldwide, including the worst epidemic in American history, the Spanish influenza outbreak that killed more than 600,000 in 1918. Today influenza is less of a public health threat, though it continues to be a serious disease that affects many people. Approximately 20,000 people die of the flu in the United States every year. The influenza virus attacks the human respiratory tract, causing symptoms such as fever, headaches, fatigue, coughing, sore throat, nasal congestion, and body aches.

**Japanese Encephalitis:** Japanese encephalitis is a mosquito-borne disease endemic in Asia. Around 50,000 cases occur each year; 25% to 30% of all cases are fatal. The major symptom is acute encephalitis, which can develop into paralysis, seizures, and coma before ending in death.

**Leishmaniasis:** Leishmaniasis is a disease spread by the bite of the sandfly. It is found mostly in tropical countries. There are several types of leishmaniasis, and they vary in symptoms and severity. Visceral leishmaniasis (VL, or *kala azar*) is the most severe; left untreated, it is always fatal. Its symptoms include fever, weight loss, anemia, and a swelling of the spleen and liver. Mucocutaneous leishmaniasis (MCL, or *espundia*) produces lesions that affect the nose, mouth, and throat and can destroy their mucous membranes. Cutaneous leishmaniasis (CL) produces skin ulcers, sometimes as many as 200, that cause disability and extensive scarring. Diffuse cutaneous leishmaniasis (DCL) is similar to CL, and infected people are prone to relapses. Approximately 12 million cases of leishmaniasis exist today.

**Malaria:** Malaria is a mosquito-borne disease that affects 300–500 million people annually, causing over 1 million deaths per year. It is most common in tropical and subtropical climates and is found in over 100 countries, including many parts of Central and South America, Africa, Southeast Asia and the Indian subcontinent, and the Middle East. Symptoms include several stages of illness. The first stage consists of shaking and chills, the next stage involves high fever and severe headache, and in the final stage the infected person's temperature drops and he or she sweats profusely. Infected people also often suffer from anemia, weakness, and a swelling of the spleen. Some strains of the disease—including most strains of *plasmodium falciparum*, the most severe form—have become resistant to the drugs used to treat them. Malaria was almost eradicated 30 years ago; now it is on the rise again.

**Measles:** Measles is a disease that has seen a drastic reduction in countries where a vaccine is readily available, but it is still prevalent in developing countries, where most of the 777,000 deaths (out of 30 million cases) it caused in 2001 occurred. Symptoms include high fever, coughing, and a maculo-papular rash; common complications include diarrhea, pneumonia, and ear infections.

**Meningitis:** Meningitis, often known as spinal meningitis, is an infection of the spinal cord. It is usually the result of a viral or bacterial infection. Bacterial meningitis is more severe than viral meningitis and may cause brain damage, hearing loss, and learning disabilities. An estimated 1.2 million cases of bacterial meningitis occur every year, over a tenth of which are fatal. Symptoms include severe headache, fever, nausea, vomiting, lethargy, delirium, photophobia, and a stiff neck.

**Onchocerciasis ("river blindness"):** Onchocerciasis is caused by the larvae of *Onchocerca volvulus*, a parasitic worm that lives in the human body for years. It is endemic in Africa, where nearly all of the 18 million people infected with the disease live. Of those infected, over 6.5 million have developed dermatitis and 270,000 have gone blind. Symptoms include visual impairment, rashes, lesions, intense itching, skin depigmentation, and lymphadenitis.

**Pneumonia:** Pneumonia has many possible causes, but it is usually an infection of the streptococcus or mycoplasma bacteria. These bacteria can live in the human body without causing infection for years, and only surface when another illness has lowered the person's immunity to disease. *Streptococcus pneumoniae* causes streptococcal pneumonia, the most common kind, which is more severe than mycoplasmal pneumonia. *S. pneumoniae* is responsible for more than 100,000 hospitalizations for pneumonia annually, as well as 6 million cases of otitis media and over 60,000 cases of invasive diseases such as meningitis.

**Rotavirus:** Rotavirus is the most common cause of viral gastroenteritis worldwide. It kills more than 600,000 children each year, mostly in developing countries. Symptoms include vomiting, watery diarrhea, fever, and abdominal pain.

**Schistosomiasis:** Schistosomiasis is a parasitic disease that is endemic in many developing countries. Roughly 200 million people worldwide are infected with the flukeworm, whose eggs cause the symptoms of the disease. Some 120 million of those infected are symptomatic, and 20 million suffer severely from the infection. Symptoms include rash and itchiness soon after becoming infected, followed by fever, chills, coughing, and muscle aches.

**Shigellosis:** Shigella infection causes an estimated 600,000 deaths worldwide every year. It is most common in developing countries with poor sanitation. Shigella bacteria cause bacillary dysentery, or shigellosis. Symptoms include diarrhea with frequent bloody stool, vomiting, and abdominal cramps.

**Strep Throat:** Strep throat is caused by the streptococcus bacteria. Several million cases of strep throat occur every year. If left untreated, it can develop into rheumatic fever. Symptoms include a sore throat, fever, headache, fatigue, and nausea.

**Tuberculosis:** Tuberculosis causes nearly 2 million deaths every year, and WHO estimates that nearly 1 billion people will be infected between 2000 and 2020 if more effective preventive procedures are not adopted. The combination of HIV and TB has contributed to its spread, and incomplete treatment has created new, tougher strains of TB. The TB bacteria are most often found in the lungs, where they can cause chest pain and a bad cough that brings up bloody phlegm. Other symptoms include fatigue, weight loss, appetite loss, chills, fever, and night sweats.

**Typhoid:** Typhoid fever causes an estimated 600,000 deaths annually, out of 12–17 million cases. It is usually spread through infected food or water. Symptoms include a sudden and sustained fever, severe headache, nausea, severe appetite loss, constipation, and sometimes diarrhea. Severe cases can develop meningitis as well.

**Yellow Fever:** Yellow fever causes an estimated 30,000 deaths each year, out of 200,000 cases. The disease has two phases. In the "acute phase," symptoms include fever, muscle pain, headache, shivers, appetite loss, nausea, and vomiting. This lasts for 3–4 days, after which most patients recover. But 15% will enter the "toxic phase," in which fever reappears, along with other symptoms, including jaundice; abdominal pain; vomiting; bleeding from the mouth, nose, eyes, and stomach; and deterioration of kidney function (sometimes complete kidney failure). Half of all patients in the toxic phase die within two weeks; the other half recover with no significant organ damage.

## Is It a Cold or the Flu?

| Symptoms | Cold | Flu |
|---|---|---|
| fever | rare | characteristic, high (102°–104° F); lasts 3–4 days |
| headache | rare | prominent |
| general aches, pains | slight | usual; often severe |
| fatigue, weakness | quite mild | can last up to 2–3 weeks |
| extreme exhaustion | never | early and prominent |
| stuffy nose, sore throat | common | sometimes |
| **Complications** | sinus congestion or earache | bronchitis, pneumonia; can be life-threatening |
| **Prevention** | none | annual vaccination; antiviral medicines—see your doctor |
| **Treatment** | only temporary relief of symptoms | antiviral medicines—see your doctor |

*Source:* National Institute of Allergy and Infectious Diseases.

# The Common Cold

*Source:* National Institute of Allergy and Infectious Diseases, National Institutes of Health.

**The problem.** Adults average about two to four colds a year, although the range varies widely. Women, especially those aged 20–30 years, have more colds than men, possibly because of their closer contact with children. On average, individuals older than 60 have fewer than one cold a year. Colds are most prevalent among children, and seem to be related to youngsters' relative lack of resistance to infection and to contacts with other children in day-care centers and schools. Children have about six to ten colds a year.

**The causes: viruses.** More than 200 different viruses are known to cause the symptoms of the common cold. **Rhinoviruses** (from the Greek *rhin,* meaning nose) cause an estimated 30% to 35% of all adult colds, and are most active in early fall, spring, and summer. **Coronaviruses** are believed to cause a large percentage of all adult colds. They induce colds primarily in the winter and early spring. Of the more than 30 isolated strains, three or four infect humans.

**Does cold weather cause a cold?** Although many people are convinced that a cold results from exposure to cold weather, or from getting chilled or overheated, these conditions in fact have little or no effect on the development or severity of a cold.

**How cold viruses cause disease.** Viruses cause infection by overcoming the body's complex defense system. The body's first line of defense is mucus, produced by the membranes in the nose and throat. Mucus traps the material we inhale: pollen, dust, bacteria, and viruses. When a virus penetrates the mucus and enters a cell, it commandeers the protein-making machinery to manufacture new viruses, which, in turn, attack surrounding cells.

**How colds are spread.** Depending on the virus type, any or all of the following routes of transmission may be common:

• Touching infectious respiratory secretions on the skin and on environmental surfaces and then touching the eyes or nose.
• Inhaling relatively large particles of respiratory secretions transported briefly in the air.
• Inhaling droplet nuclei, smaller infectious particles suspended in the air for long periods of time.

**Prevention.** Handwashing is the simplest and most effective way to keep from getting rhinovirus colds. Not touching the nose or eyes is another. Individuals with colds should always sneeze or cough into a facial tissue, and promptly throw it away. Rhinoviruses can survive up to three hours outside the nasal passages on inanimate objects and skin.

**Treatment.** Only symptomatic treatment is available for uncomplicated cases of the common cold: bed rest, plenty of fluids, gargling with warm salt water, applying petroleum jelly to a raw nose, and taking aspirin or acetaminophen to relieve headache or fever. Nonprescription cold remedies, including decongestants and cough suppressants, may relieve some cold symptoms but will not prevent, cure, or even shorten the duration of illness.

Antibiotics do not kill viruses. These prescription drugs should be used only for rare bacterial complications, such as sinusitis or ear infections, that can develop as secondary infections. (The flu, also caused by a virus, should also not be treated by antibiotics.)

**Does vitamin C have a role?** Many people are convinced that taking large quantities of vitamin C will prevent colds or relieve symptoms. To test this theory, several large-scale, controlled studies involving children and adults have been conducted. To date, no conclusive data have shown that large doses of vitamin C prevent colds. The vitamin may reduce the severity or duration of symptoms, but there is no definitive evidence.

# National Transplant Data

## Registered U.S. Patients Waiting for Transplants
### (as of June 28, 2002)

| | | | | | |
|---|---|---|---|---|---|
| Kidney | 55,496 | Lung | 3,833 | Heart-Lung | 212 |
| Liver | 17,797 | Kidney-Pancreas | 2,618 | Intestine | 196 |
| Heart | 4,190 | Pancreas | 1,338 | **Total patients** | **85,680**[1] |

NOTE: Patients can be listed with more than one transplant center, thus the number of registrations is greater than the actual number of patients. 1. Some patients are waiting for more than one organ; therefore the total number of patients is less than the sum of patients waiting for each organ. *Source:* National Organ Procurement and Transplantation Network.

## Number of U.S. Transplants Per Year, 1988–2001

| | 1988 | 1990 | 1995 | 2000 | 2001 | | 1988 | 1990 | 1995 | 2000 | 2001 |
|---|---|---|---|---|---|---|---|---|---|---|---|
| Heart | 1,676 | 2,107 | 2,355 | 2,194 | 2,201 | Liver | 1,713 | 2,690 | 3,931 | 4,961 | 5,179 |
| Heart-Lung | 74 | 52 | 69 | 48 | 27 | Lung | 33 | 203 | 872 | 956 | 1,054 |
| Intestine | — | 5 | 46 | 79 | 111 | Pancreas | 79 | 69 | 107 | 436 | 469 |
| Kidney | 8,873 | 9,416 | 11,054 | 13,402 | 14,167 | **Total:** | | | | | |
| Kidney-Pancreas | 170 | 459 | 919 | 913 | 886 | All organs | 12,618 | 15,001 | 19,353 | 22,989 | 24,094 |

NOTE: Kidney-pancreas transplants are counted apart from kidney transplants and pancreas transplants and do not show up in the totals for the individual organs. Double kidney, double lung, and heart-lung transplants are each counted as one transplant. All other multi-organ transplants are included in the total for each individual organ. *Source:* National Organ Procurement and Transplantation Network.

## Americans Without Health Insurance[1] by Characteristic, 2000

| Characteristic | Percent | Characteristic | Percent |
|---|---|---|---|
| **Total** | **14.0%** | **Age** | |
| **Race and ethnicity** | | Under 18 years | 11.6% |
| White | 12.9 | 18 to 24 years | 27.3 |
| Non-Hispanic | 9.7 | 25 to 34 years | 21.2 |
| Black | 18.5 | 35 to 44 years | 15.5 |
| Asian and Pacific Islander | 18.0 | 45 to 64 years | 12.6 |
| Hispanic[2] | 32.0 | 65 years and over | 0.7 |
| **Household income** | | **Nativity** | |
| Less than $25,000 | 22.7 | Native | 11.9 |
| $25,000 to $49,999 | 17.0 | Foreign born | 31.6 |
| $50,000 to $74,999 | 11.0 | **Work experience (18 to 64 years old)** | |
| $75,000 or more | 6.9 | Worked during year | 16.2 |
| | | Did not work | 23.6 |

1. For the entire year. 2. Hispanics may be of any race. *Source:* U.S. Census Bureau, *Current Population Survey, March 2001.*

## Percent of Americans Without Health Insurance by State, 2000

| State | Percent | State | Percent | State | Percent |
|---|---|---|---|---|---|
| Alabama | 13.6% | Louisiana | 18.9% | Oklahoma | 19.3% |
| Alaska | 19.3 | Maine | 11.8 | Oregon | 13.8 |
| Arizona | 16.0 | Maryland | 9.9 | Pennsylvania | 7.5 |
| Arkansas | 13.7 | Massachusetts | 9.5 | Rhode Island | 6.3 |
| California | 17.9 | Michigan | 9.0 | South Carolina | 12.0 |
| Colorado | 13.3 | Minnesota | 9.0 | South Dakota | 11.7 |
| Connecticut | 8.5 | Mississippi | 12.9 | Tennessee | 10.3 |
| Delaware | 10.6 | Missouri | 10.8 | Texas | 21.4 |
| DC | 14.5 | Montana | 18.4 | Utah | 13.4 |
| Florida | 17.2 | Nebraska | 10.0 | Vermont | 11.0 |
| Georgia | 14.4 | Nevada | 15.7 | Virginia | 12.7 |
| Hawaii | 10.2 | New Hampshire | 6.8 | Washington | 13.7 |
| Idaho | 15.5 | New Jersey | 12.5 | West Virginia | 14.3 |
| Illinois | 13.4 | New Mexico | 23.8 | Wisconsin | 7.4 |
| Indiana | 11.9 | New York | 15.1 | Wyoming | 14.4 |
| Iowa | 8.8 | North Carolina | 12.9 | | |
| Kansas | 11.7 | North Dakota | 11.5 | **Total U.S.** | **14.0** |
| Kentucky | 13.0 | Ohio | 10.8 | | |

NOTE: These estimates should not be used to rank the states. Results from different samplings could easily show different estimates and rankings because of small sampling sizes. For example, the high noncoverage for Texas is not statistically different from that of New Mexico. *Source:* U.S. Census Bureau, *March 2001 Current Population Survey.*

## Human Carcinogens

The *Ninth Report on Carcinogens,* published May 15, 2000, lists 218 substances known or suspected to cause cancer. The *Ninth Report* added (or upgraded) 14 substances, including secondhand smoke, alcoholic beverages, excessive sun, sun lamps, and tanning beds. Saccharin, the artificial sweetener, was removed from the list of suspected carcinogens.

## Substances Known to Be Human Carcinogens

Aflatoxins
Alcoholic Beverage Consumption
4-Aminobiphenyl (4-Aminodiphenyl)
Analgesic Mixtures Containing Phenacetin
Arsenic and certain Arsenic Compounds
Asbestos
Azathioprine
Benzene
Benzidine
bis(Chloromethyl) Ether
1,3-Butadiene
1,4-Butanediol Dimethylsulfonate
Cadmium and Cadmium Compounds
Chlorambucil
Chromium Hexavalent Compounds

Coke Oven Emissions
Conjugated Estrogens
Cyclophosphamide
Cyclosporin A
Diethylstilbestrol
Dyes that Metabolize to Benzidine
   Direct Black 38
   Direct Blue 6
Environmental Tobacco Smoke
Erionite
Ethylene Oxide
Melphalan
Mustard Gas
2-Naphthylamine
Radon
Silica, Crystalline (Respirable Size)
   Quartz

Cristobalite
   Tridymite
Smokeless Tobacco
Solar Radiation and Exposure to Sun Lamps or Sunbeds
Soots
Strong Inorganic Acid Mists Containing Sulfuric Acid
Tamoxifen
Tars and Mineral Oils
2,3,7,8-Tetrachlorodibenzo-*p*-Dioxin (TCDD)
Thiotepa
Thorium Dioxide
Tobacco Smoking
Vinyl Chloride

Source: *Ninth Report on Carcinogens,* The National Institute for Environmental Health Sciences.

## Cancer: Estimated New Cases (2001) and Survival Rates

| Site | Estimated new cases, 2001 (cancer per 1,000) | | | Five-year relative survival rates[1] (percent) | | | |
|---|---|---|---|---|---|---|---|
| | | | | White | | Black | |
| | Total | Male | Female | 1980–1982 | 1989–1996 | 1980–1982 | 1989–1996 |
| All sites[2] | 1,268 | 643 | 625 | 52.1% | 61.5% | 39.7% | 48.9% |
| Lung | 170 | 91 | 79 | 13.5 | 14.4 | 12.2 | 11.3 |
| Breast[3] | 194 | 2 | 192 | 77.1 | 86.3 | 65.8 | 71.4 |
| Colon and rectum | 135 | 67 | 68 | 54.8 | 62.1 | 46.4 | 52.2 |
| Colon | 98 | 46 | 52 | 55.7 | 62.6 | 49.1 | 52.2 |
| Rectum | 37 | 21 | 16 | 52.9 | 60.7 | 38.0 | 52.3 |
| Prostate | 198 | 198 | n.a. | 74.5 | 94.1 | 64.7 | 86.7 |
| Bladder | 54 | 39 | 15 | 79.0 | 81.9 | 58.9 | 63.7 |
| Corpus uteri | 38 | n.a. | 38 | 82.8 | 85.6 | 54.5 | 56.9 |
| Non-Hodgkin's lymphoma[4] | 56 | 31 | 25 | 51.9 | 52.6 | 50.0 | 41.9 |
| Oral cavity and pharynx | 30 | 20 | 10 | 55.5 | 56.2 | 30.8 | 34.6 |
| Leukemia[4] | 32 | 18 | 14 | 39.6 | 45.4 | 33.2 | 34.0 |
| Melanoma of skin | 51 | 29 | 22 | 83.1 | 88.5 | 60.9 | 70.0 |
| Pancreas | 29 | 14 | 15 | 2.8 | 4.2 | 4.7 | 3.8 |
| Kidney | 31 | 19 | 12 | 51.2 | 61.5 | 56.1 | 58.0 |
| Stomach | 22 | 13 | 8 | 16.4 | 19.5 | 19.4 | 21.6 |
| Ovary | 23 | n.a. | 23 | 38.8 | 50.1 | 38.3 | 47.5 |
| Cervix uteri[5] | 13 | n.a. | 13 | 68.0 | 71.6 | 61.2 | 58.6 |

NOTE: n.a. = not applicable. 1. The 5-year relative survival rate indicates that a person will not die from causes directly related to their cancer within 5 years. 2. Includes other sites not shown separately. 3. Survival rates for female only. 4. All types combined. 5. Invasive cancer only. *Source:* U.S. National Institutes of Health, National Cancer Institute.

## What Is Cancer?

*Source:* National Cancer Institute.

Cancer is a group of many different diseases that have some important things in common. Cancer affects our cells, the body's basic unit of life.

To understand cancer, it is helpful to know what happens when normal cells become cancerous. Usually, cells grow, divide, and produce more cells as they are needed to keep the body healthy. Sometimes, however, the process goes astray—cells keep dividing when new cells are not needed. The mass of extra cells forms a growth or tumor.

**Benign tumors** are not cancer. They often can be removed and, in most cases, they do not come back. Cells in benign tumors do not spread to other parts of the body. Most important, benign tumors are rarely a threat to life.

**Malignant tumors** are cancer. Cells in malignant tumors are abnormal and divide without control or order. These cancer cells can invade and destroy the tissue around them. Cancer cells can also break away from a malignant tumor and enter the bloodstream or lymphatic system (these two networks of vessels carry blood and lymph throughout the body). The process by which cancer spreads from the original tumor to form new tumors in other parts of the body is called metastasis.

## Sexually Transmitted Diseases (STDs)

More than 25 diseases are spread primarily through sexual activity. The latest estimates (1999) indicate that there are 15 million new sexually transmitted disease cases in the United States each year. Approximately one-fourth of these new infections are in teenagers. Nearly two-thirds of all STD cases occur in people younger than 25 years.

While some sexually transmitted diseases, such as syphilis, have been brought to all-time lows, others, like genital herpes, gonorrhea, and chlamydia, continue to resurge and spread through the population.

Not including HIV, the most common sexually transmitted diseases in the U.S. are chlamydia, gonorrhea, syphilis, genital herpes, human papillomavirus, hepatitis B, trichomoniasis, and bacterial vaginosis.

| Sexually transmitted disease | Incidence (estimated number of new cases every year) | Prevalence[1] (estimated number of people currently infected) |
|---|---|---|
| Chlamydia | 3 million | 2 million |
| Gonorrhea | 650,000 | n.a. |
| Syphilis | 70,000 | n.a. |
| Herpes | 1 million | 45 million |
| Human papillomavirus (hpv) | 5.5 million | 20 million |
| Hepatitis B | 120,000 | 417,000 |
| Trichomoniasis | 5 million | n.a. |
| Bacterial vaginosis[2] | n.a. | n.a. |

NOTE: n.a. = not available. 1. No recent surveys on national prevalence for gonorrhea, syphilis, trichomoniasis, or bacterial vaginosis have been conducted. 2. Bacterial vaginosis is a genital infection that is not sexually transmitted but is associated with sexual intercourse. *Source:* Centers for Disease Control, 1999.

## Abortion in the United States

### Incidence of Abortion

- 48% of pregnancies among American women are unintended; half of these are terminated by abortion.
- In 1997, 1.33 million abortions took place, down from an estimated 1.61 million in 1990. From 1973 through 1997, more than 35 million legal abortions occurred.
- Each year, two out of every 100 women aged 15–44 have an abortion; 47% of them have had at least one previous abortion and 55% have had a previous birth.
- An estimated 43% of women will have at least one abortion by the time they are 45 years old.
- Each year, an estimated 46 million abortions occur worldwide. Of these, 20 million procedures are obtained illegally.

### Who Has Abortions

- 52% of U.S. women obtaining abortions are younger than 25: women aged 20–24 obtain 32% of all abortions, and teenagers obtain 20%.
- Black women are more than three times as likely as white women to have an abortion, and Hispanic women are roughly twice as likely.
- Catholic women are 29% more likely than Protestants to have an abortion, but are about as likely as all women nationally to do so.
- Two-thirds of all abortions are among never-married women.
- On average, women give at least three reasons for choosing abortion: three-fourths say that having a baby would interfere with work, school, or other responsibilities; about two-thirds say they cannot afford a child; and half say they do not want to be a single parent or are having problems with their husband or partner.
- About 13,000 women have abortions each year following rape or incest.

### Contraceptive Use

- 58% of women having abortions in 1995 had used a contraceptive method during the month they became pregnant.
- 11% of women having abortions have never used a method of birth control; nonuse is greatest among those who are young, unmarried, poor, black, Hispanic, or poorly educated.
- Nine in ten women at risk of unintended pregnancy are using a contraceptive method.

### Providers and Services

- 93% of U.S. abortions are performed in clinics or doctors' offices.
- The number of abortion providers declined by 14% between 1992 and 1996 (from 2,380 to 2,042). 86% of all U.S. counties lacked an abortion provider in 1996. These counties were home to 32% of all 15–44-year-old women.
- 43% of all abortion facilities provide services only through the 12th week of pregnancy.
- 42% of nonhospital facilities provided abortions to women less than six weeks pregnant in 1996, a 27% increase since 1992, when only one-third (33%) provided such early abortions.
- In 1997, the cost of a nonhospital abortion with local anesthesia at ten weeks of gestation ranged from about $100 to $1,100 and the average was $316.
- In nonhospital facilities offering both surgical and medical abortion in 1997, the cost of medical abortion ranged from $100 to $1,230, and the average was $401; the average cost of a surgical abortion was $355.
- About 4,200 medical abortions were performed in 1996 and 4,300 in the first half of 1997; these procedures involved the use of mifepristone and methotrexate (in clinical trials or off-label use).

*Source:* Alan Guttmacher Institute, *Induced Abortion, Facts in Brief*, 2002. www.guttmacher.org. Reprinted with permission.

For U.S. contraception and abortion statistics, *see* p. 131.

# Overview of Mental Illness

*Source: Mental Health: A Report of the Surgeon General, 1999*

Mental illness is a term rooted in history that refers collectively to all of the diagnosable mental disorders. Mental disorders are characterized by abnormalities in cognition, emotion or mood, or the highest integrative aspects of behavior, such as social interactions or planning of future activities.

This overview of mental illness focuses on the most common of these disorders.

## Anxiety

Anxiety is one of the most readily accessible and easily understood of the major symptoms of mental disorders. Each of us encounters anxiety in many forms throughout the course of our routine activities. Anxiety has evolved as a vitally important physiological response to dangerous situations that prepares one to evade or confront a threat in the environment. However, the mechanisms that regulate anxiety may break down in a wide variety of circumstances, leading to excessive or inappropriate expression of anxiety. Specific examples include phobias, panic attacks, and generalized anxiety. In phobias, high-level anxiety is aroused by specific situations or objects that may range from concrete entities such as snakes, to complex circumstances such as social interactions or public speaking. Panic attacks are brief and very intense episodes of anxiety that often occur without a precipitating event or stimulus. Generalized anxiety represents a more diffuse and nonspecific kind of anxiety that is most often experienced as excessive worrying, restlessness, and tension occurring with a chronic and sustained pattern. In each case, an anxiety disorder may be said to exist if the anxiety experienced is disproportionate to the circumstance, is difficult for the individual to control, or interferes with normal functioning.

In addition to these common manifestations of anxiety, obsessive-compulsive disorder and post-traumatic stress disorder are generally believed to be related to the anxiety disorders. In the case of obsessive-compulsive disorder, individuals experience a high level of anxiety that drives their obsessional thinking or compulsive behaviors. When such an individual fails to carry out a repetitive behavior such as hand washing or checking, there is an experience of severe anxiety. Post-traumatic stress disorder is produced by an intense and overwhelmingly fearful event that is often life-threatening in nature. The characteristic symptoms that result from such a traumatic event include the persistent reexperience of the event in dreams and memories, persistent avoidance of stimuli associated with the event, and increased arousal.

## Psychosis

Disturbances of perception and thought process fall into a broad category of symptoms referred to as psychosis. The threshold for determining whether thought is impaired varies somewhat with the cultural context. Like anxiety, psychotic symptoms may occur in a wide variety of mental disorders. They are most characteristically associated with schizophrenia, but psychotic symptoms can also occur in severe mood disorders.

One of the most common groups of symptoms that result from disordered processing and interpretation of sensory information are hallucinations. Hallucinations are said to occur when an individual experiences a sensory impression that has no basis in reality. Hallucinations may be auditory, olfactory, gustatory, kinesthetic, tactile, or visual. For example, auditory hallucinations frequently involve the impression that one is hearing a voice. In each case, the sensory impression is falsely experienced as real.

A more complex group of symptoms resulting from disordered interpretation of information consists of delusions. A delusion is a false belief that an individual holds despite evidence to the contrary. A common example is paranoia, in which a person has delusional beliefs that others are trying to harm him or her. Attempts to convince the person that these beliefs are unfounded typically fail and may even result in the further entrenchment of the beliefs.

Hallucinations and delusions are among the most commonly observed psychotic symptoms. Symptoms of schizophrenia are divided into two broad classes: positive symptoms and negative symptoms. Positive symptoms generally involve the experience of something in consciousness that should not normally be present. For example, hallucinations and delusions represent perceptions or beliefs that should not normally be experienced. In addition to hallucinations and delusions, patients with psychotic disorders such as schizophrenia frequently have marked disturbances in the logical process of their thoughts. Specifically, psychotic thought processes are characteristically loose, disorganized, illogical, or bizarre. The severe disturbances of thought content and process that comprise the positive symptoms often are the most recognizable and striking features of psychotic disorders such as schizophrenia or manic depressive illness.

---

### Common signs of acute anxiety

- Feelings of fear or dread
- Trembling, restlessness, and muscle tension
- Rapid heart rate
- Lightheadedness or dizziness
- Perspiration
- Cold hands/feet
- Shortness of breath

---

### Common manifestations of schizophrenia

**Positive symptoms**
- Hallucinations
- Delusions
- Disorganized thoughts and behaviors
- Loose or illogical thoughts
- Agitation

**Negative symptoms**
- Flat or blunted affect
- Concrete thoughts
- Anhedonia (inability to experience pleasure)
- Poor motivation, spontaneity, and initiative

However, in addition to positive symptoms, patients with schizophrenia and other psychoses have been noted to exhibit major deficits in motivation and spontaneity that are referred to as negative symptoms. While positive symptoms represent the presence of something not normally experienced, negative symptoms reflect the absence of thoughts and behaviors that would otherwise be expected. Concreteness of thought represents impairment in the ability to think abstractly. Blunting of affect refers to a general reduction in the ability to express emotion. Motivational failure and inability to initiate activities represent a major source of long-term disability in schizophrenia. Anhedonia reflects a deficit in the ability to experience pleasure and to react appropriately to pleasurable situations. Positive symptoms such as hallucinations are responsible for much of the acute distress associated with schizophrenia, but negative symptoms appear to be responsible for much of the chronic and long-term disability associated with the disorder.

## Disturbances of Mood

Most of us have an immediate and intuitive understanding of the notion of mood. We readily comprehend what it means to feel sad or happy. These concepts are nonetheless very difficult to formulate in a scientifically precise and quantifiable way; the challenge is greater given the cultural differences that are associated with the expression of mood. Nevertheless, dysregulation of mood and the expression of mood, or affect, represent a major category among mental disorders.

Disturbances of mood characteristically manifest themselves as a sustained feeling of sadness or sustained elevation of mood. As with anxiety and psychosis, disturbances of mood may occur in a variety of patterns associated with different mental disorders. The disorder most closely associated with persistent sadness is major depression, while that associated with sustained elevation or fluctuation of mood is bipolar disorder. Along with the prevailing feelings of sadness or elation, disorders of mood are associated with a host of related symptoms that include disturbances in appetite, sleep patterns, energy level, concentration, and memory.

## Disturbances of Cognition

Cognitive function refers to the general ability to organize, process, and recall information. Progressive deterioration of cognitive function is referred to as dementia. Dementia may be caused by a number of specific conditions including Alzheimer's disease. It is not uncommon to find profound disturbances of

---

### Common signs of mood disorders

**Symptoms commonly associated with depression**

- Persistent sadness or despair
- Insomnia (sometimes hypersomnia)
- Decreased appetite
- Psychomotor retardation
- Anhedonia (inability to experience pleasure)
- Irritability
- Apathy, poor motivation, social withdrawal
- Hopelessness
- Poor self-esteem, feelings of helplessness
- Suicidal ideation

**Symptoms commonly associated with mania**

- Persistently elevated or euphoric mood
- Grandiosity (inappropriately high self-esteem)
- Psychomotor agitation
- Decreased sleep
- Racing thoughts and distractibility
- Poor judgment and impaired impulse control
- Rapid or pressured speech

---

cognition in patients suffering from severe mood disturbances. More recently, cognitive deficits have been reported in schizophrenia and now have become a major new topic of research. Last, cognitive impairment frequently occurs in a host of chemical, metabolic, and infectious diseases that exert an impact on the brain.

## Other Symptoms

Anxiety, psychosis, mood disturbances, and cognitive impairments are among the most common and disabling manifestations of mental disorders. It is important, however, to appreciate that mental disorders leave no aspect of human experience untouched. Other common manifestations include, for example, somatic or other physical symptoms and impairment of impulse control.

## Diagnosis of Mental Illness

The standard manual used for diagnosis of mental disorders in the United States is the *Diagnostic and Statistical Manual of Mental Disorders*. Most recently revised in 1994, this manual, first published in 1952, is now in its fourth edition. *DSM-IV* organizes mental disorders into 16 major diagnostic classes. *DSM-IV* is descriptive in its listing of symptoms and does not take a position about underlying causation.

---

### Major diagnostic classes of mental disorders *(DSM-IV)*

- Delirium, dementia, and amnestic and other cognitive disorders
- Mental disorders due to a general medical condition
- Substance-related disorders
- Schizophrenia and other psychotic disorders
- Mood disorders
- Anxiety disorders
- Somatoform disorders
- Factitious disorders
- Dissociative disorders
- Sexual and gender identity disorders
- Eating disorders
- Sleep disorders
- Impulse-control disorders
- Adjustment disorders
- Personality disorders
- Disorders of childhood and adolescence

# Overview of Drug Use in the United States

*Source:* SAMHSA.

The *National Household Survey on Drug Abuse,* an annual survey conducted by the Substance Abuse and Mental Health Services Administration, estimates the prevalence of illicit drug use in the United States. Some of the more notable statistics from the 2000 study follow.

• An estimated 14 million Americans were current users of illicit drugs in 1999, meaning they used an illicit drug at least once during the 30 days prior to being interviewed. By comparison, the number of current illicit drug users was at its highest level in 1979, when the estimate was 25.4 million.

• Among youths aged 12–17 in 2000, 9.7% had used an illicit drug within the 30 days prior to being interviewed. The rate was highest in 1979 (16.3%), declined to 5.3% in 1992, then increased to 10.9% in 1995. The percentage of youths reporting current use of illicit drugs has fluctuated since 1995 (9% in 1996; 11.4% in 1997, 9.8% in 1998). Interestingly, among youths defined as heavy drinkers in 2000, 65.5% were also current illicit drug users, while among nondrinkers, only 4.2% were. Youth smokers showed similar tendencies: among youths who smoked cigarettes, 42.7% had used illicit drugs in the past month, whereas only 4.6% of nonsmokers had.

• Results from the most recent NHSDA on the nonmedical use of OxyContin, whose abuse by celebrities made headlines in 2002, showed evidence of an emerging problem: estimated numbers of lifetime nonmedical OxyContin users increased from 221,000 in 1999 to 399,000 in 2000.

• Drug-related deaths reported by medical examiners in 2000 most often included heroin, cocaine, and alcohol in combination with other drugs. Narcotic analgesics like methadone, codeine, hydrocodone, and oxycodone also frequently ranked in the top ten drugs mentioned by medical examiners participating in the survey. 137 medical examiner jurisdictions from 43 metropolitan areas reported on drug-related deaths to the NHSDA's Drug Abuse Warning Network in 2000.

## Drug Use by Americans, 12 Years and Older

| Type of drug | Ever used | | | Current user | | |
|---|---|---|---|---|---|---|
| | 1979 | 1990 | 2000 | 1979 | 1990 | 2000 |
| Any illicit drug[1] | n.a. | n.a. | 38.9% | n.a. | n.a. | 6.3% |
| Marijuana and hashish | 27.9% | 30.5% | 34.2 | 13.2% | 5.4% | 4.8 |
| Cocaine | 8.6 | 11.2 | 11.2 | 2.6 | 0.9 | 0.5 |
| Crack | n.a. | n.a. | 2.4 | n.a. | n.a. | 0.1 |
| Hallucinogens | 8.9 | 7.9 | 11.7 | 1.9 | 0.4 | 0.4 |
| LSD | n.a. | n.a. | 8.8 | n.a. | n.a. | 0.2 |
| PCP | n.a. | n.a. | 2.6 | n.a. | n.a. | 0.0 |
| Heroin | 1.3 | 0.8 | 1.2 | 0.1 | n.a. | 0.1 |
| Stimulants[2] | n.a. | 5.5 | 6.6 | n.a. | 0.6 | 0.4 |
| Methamphetamine | n.a. | n.a. | 4.0 | n.a. | n.a. | 0.2 |
| Sedatives[2] | n.a. | 2.8 | 3.2 | n.a. | 0.2 | 0.1 |
| Tranquilizers[2] | n.a. | 4.0 | 5.8 | n.a. | 0.6 | 0.4 |

NOTE: Current users are those who used drugs at least once within month prior to this study. n.a. = not available. 1. Any illicit drug indicates use at least once of marijuana/hashish, cocaine (including crack), heroin, hallucinogens (including LSD and PCP), inhalants, or any prescription-type psychotherapeutic used nonmedically. 2. Nonmedical use; does not include over-the-counter drugs. *Source:* U.S. Substance Abuse and Mental Health Services Administration (SAMHSA), Office of Applied Studies, *National Household Survey on Drug Abuse.*

## Marijuana Use

### (over a lifetime)

| Characteristic | 1979 | 1982 | 1985 | 1988 | 1991 | 1992 | 1993 | 1994 | 1995 | 1996 | 1999 | 2000 |
|---|---|---|---|---|---|---|---|---|---|---|---|---|
| **Total** | 28.0% | 28.6% | 29.4% | 30.6% | 30.5% | 30.2% | 31.0% | 31.1% | 31.0% | 32.0% | 34.6% | 34.2% |
| **Age** | | | | | | | | | | | | |
| 12–17 years | 27.0 | 23.2 | 20.1 | 15.0 | 11.1 | 9.1 | 9.9 | 13.6 | 16.2 | 16.8 | 18.7 | 18.3 |
| 18–25 years | 66.0 | 61.3 | 57.6 | 54.6 | 48.8 | 46.6 | 45.7 | 41.9 | 41.4 | 44.0 | 46.8 | 45.7 |
| 26–34 years | 45.0 | 51.5 | 54.1 | 57.6 | 55.2 | 54.3 | 54.9 | 52.7 | 51.8 | 50.5 | 47.7 | 46.0 |
| 35 years or more | 9.0 | 10.4 | 13.9 | 17.6 | 21.1 | 22.2 | 23.8 | 25.4 | 25.3 | 27.0 | 31.5 | 31.6 |
| **Race** | | | | | | | | | | | | |
| White | 28.0 | 29.3 | 31.1 | 32.0 | 32.0 | 32.4 | 33.6 | 33.5 | 33.5 | 34.4 | 37.1 | 37.0 |
| Black | 28.0 | 28.2 | 26.6 | 26.8 | 28.7 | 25.0 | 24.6 | 27.5 | 28.2 | 29.6 | 32.1 | 30.8 |
| Hispanic | 21.0 | 23.7 | 18.4 | 21.7 | 21.0 | 20.0 | 21.8 | 21.6 | 20.2 | 22.0 | 25.3 | 24.2 |
| **Sex** | | | | | | | | | | | | |
| Male | 34.0 | 34.0 | 34.7 | 33.9 | 34.6 | 34.8 | 35.9 | 35.9 | 35.6 | 37.0 | 38.7 | 38.7 |
| Female | 22.0 | 23.6 | 24.5 | 27.6 | 26.8 | 25.9 | 26.4 | 26.8 | 26.8 | 27.5 | 30.7 | 30.0 |

*Source:* Substance Abuse and Mental Health Services Administration (SAMHSA).

## Smoking Prevalence Among U.S. Adults, 1965–1999

### (as a percent of population, 18 years of age and older)

| Year | Overall population | Males | Females | White male | Black male | White female | Black female |
|---|---|---|---|---|---|---|---|
| 1965 | 41.9% | 51.2% | 33.7% | 50.4% | 58.8% | 33.9% | 31.8% |
| 1974 | 37.0 | 42.8 | 32.2 | 41.7 | 53.6 | 32.0 | 35.6 |
| 1983 | 31.9 | 34.8 | 29.4 | 34.2 | 41.7 | 29.6 | 31.3 |
| 1985 | 29.9 | 32.2 | 27.9 | 31.3 | 40.2 | 27.9 | 30.9 |
| 1990 | 25.3 | 28.0 | 22.9 | 27.6 | 32.8 | 23.5 | 20.8 |
| 1992 | 26.3 | 28.1 | 24.6 | 27.7 | 33.3 | 25.3 | 24.5 |
| 1994 | 25.3 | 27.6 | 23.1 | 27.1 | 34.3 | 24.0 | 21.6 |
| 1995 | 24.6 | 26.5 | 22.7 | 26.2 | 29.4 | 23.4 | 23.5 |
| 1997 | 24.6 | 27.1 | 22.2 | 26.8 | 32.4 | 22.8 | 22.5 |
| 1998 | 24.0 | 25.9 | 22.1 | 26.0 | 29.0 | 23.0 | 21.1 |
| 1999 | 23.3 | 25.2 | 21.6 | 25.0 | 28.5 | 22.5 | 20.7 |

*Source: Health, United States, 2001,* Centers for Disease Control and Prevention.

## Alcohol Consumption, 1999

### (persons 18 years of age and over)

| | Both sexes | Male | Female |
|---|---|---|---|
| **Drinking status[1]** | | | |
| All | 100.0% | 100.0% | 100.0% |
| **Lifetime abstainer** | 22.4 | 14.7 | 29.4 |
| **Former drinker** | 14.9 | 15.3 | 14.5 |
| Infrequent | 8.1 | 6.9 | 9.3 |
| Regular | 6.7 | 8.4 | 5.2 |
| **Current drinker** | 62.7 | 70.0 | 56.1 |
| Infrequent | 14.3 | 11.0 | 17.3 |
| Regular | 48.4 | 59.0 | 38.8 |

| | Both sexes | Male | Female |
|---|---|---|---|
| **Level of alcohol consumption in past year for current drinkers[2]** | | | |
| All drinking levels | 100.0% | 100.0% | 100.0% |
| Light | 69.2 | 58.9 | 80.7 |
| Moderate | 23.1 | 32.3 | 12.5 |
| Heavier | 7.8 | 8.7 | 6.7 |
| **Number of days in the past year with 5 or more drinks** | | | |
| All current drinkers | 100.0% | 100.0% | 100.0% |
| No days | 67.2 | 56.7 | 78.9 |
| At least 1 day | 32.8 | 43.3 | 21.1 |
| 1–11 days | 17.4 | 20.8 | 13.6 |
| 12 or more days | 15.4 | 22.5 | 7.5 |

1. Lifetime abstainers had fewer than 12 drinks in their lifetime. Former drinkers had at least 12 drinks in their lifetime and none in the past year. Former infrequent drinkers are former drinkers who had fewer than 12 drinks in any one year. Former regular drinkers are former drinkers who had at least 12 drinks in any one year. Current drinkers had 12 drinks in their lifetime and at least one drink in the past year. Current infrequent drinkers are current drinkers who had fewer than 12 drinks in the past year. Current regular drinkers are current drinkers who had at least 12 drinks in the past year. 2. Level of alcohol consumption categories are defined as follows: light drinkers, up to 3 drinks per week; moderate drinkers, 4–14 drinks per week for men and 4–7 drinks per week for women; heavier drinkers, more than 14 drinks per week for men and more than 7 drinks per week for women. *Source:* Centers for Disease Control and Prevention, *Health, United States, 2001.*

## Caffeine Content of Selected Foods and Drugs

| Product | Serving size[1] | Caffeine (mg) | Product | Serving size[1] | Caffeine (mg) |
|---|---|---|---|---|---|
| **Over-the-counter drugs** | | | **Soft drinks** | | |
| Excedrin | 2 tablets | 130 | Mountain Dew | 12 ounces | 55 |
| Anacin | 2 tablets | 64 | Diet Coke | 12 ounces | 47 |
| **Coffees** | | | Coca-Cola | 12 ounces | 45 |
| Coffee, brewed | 8 ounces | 135 | Dr. Pepper | 12 ounces | 41 |
| Coffee, instant | 8 ounces | 95 | Sunkist Orange | | |
| Coffee, decaffeinated | 8 ounces | 5 | Soda | 12 ounces | 40 |
| **Teas** | | | Pepsi-Cola | 12 ounces | 37 |
| Tea, leaf or bag | 8 ounces | 50 | **Chocolates or candies** | | |
| Snapple Iced Tea | 16-ounce bottle | 48 | Hershey Bar, 1 bar | 1.5 ounces | 10 |
| Tea, green | 8 ounces | 30 | Cocoa or hot | | |
| Tea, instant | 8 ounces | 15 | chocolate | 8 ounces | 5 |

1. Serving sizes are based on commonly eaten portions, pharmaceutical instructions, or the amount of the leading-selling container size. *Source:* Center for Science in the Public Interest. Reprinted/Adapted from *Nutrition Action Healthletter* (1875 Connecticut Ave., NW., Suite 300, Washington, DC 20009–5728.)

## Measuring Body Mass

Body mass index (BMI) is measure of body fat based on height and weight that applies to both adult men and women. To determine BMI, weight in kilograms is divided by height in meters, squared. To calculate your body mass index from the table below, locate your height in inches in the left-hand column, then follow it across until you locate your weight; the number at the very top is your body mass index. A BMI of less than 18.5 is considered underweight, 18.5 to 24.9 is considered normal weight, 25 to 29.9 is considered overweight, and one of 30 or above is considered obese.

### Body Mass Index Chart

| | 19 | 20 | 21 | 22 | 23 | 24 | 25 | 26 | 27 | 28 | 29 | 30 | 31 | 32 | 33 | 34 | 35 |
|---|---|---|---|---|---|---|---|---|---|---|---|---|---|---|---|---|---|
| Height (inches) | | | | | | | | Body weight (pounds) | | | | | | | | | |
| 58 | 91 | 96 | 100 | 105 | 110 | 115 | 119 | 124 | 129 | 134 | 138 | 143 | 148 | 153 | 158 | 162 | 167 |
| 59 | 94 | 99 | 104 | 109 | 114 | 119 | 124 | 128 | 133 | 138 | 143 | 148 | 153 | 158 | 163 | 168 | 173 |
| 60 | 97 | 102 | 107 | 112 | 118 | 123 | 128 | 133 | 138 | 143 | 148 | 153 | 158 | 163 | 168 | 174 | 179 |
| 61 | 100 | 106 | 111 | 116 | 122 | 127 | 132 | 137 | 143 | 148 | 153 | 158 | 164 | 169 | 174 | 180 | 185 |
| 62 | 104 | 109 | 115 | 120 | 126 | 131 | 136 | 142 | 147 | 153 | 158 | 164 | 169 | 175 | 180 | 186 | 191 |
| 63 | 107 | 113 | 118 | 124 | 130 | 135 | 141 | 146 | 152 | 158 | 163 | 169 | 175 | 180 | 186 | 191 | 197 |
| 64 | 110 | 116 | 122 | 128 | 134 | 140 | 145 | 151 | 157 | 163 | 169 | 174 | 180 | 186 | 192 | 197 | 204 |
| 65 | 114 | 120 | 126 | 132 | 138 | 144 | 150 | 156 | 162 | 168 | 174 | 180 | 186 | 192 | 198 | 204 | 210 |
| 66 | 118 | 124 | 130 | 136 | 142 | 148 | 155 | 161 | 167 | 173 | 179 | 186 | 192 | 198 | 204 | 210 | 216 |
| 67 | 121 | 127 | 134 | 140 | 146 | 153 | 159 | 166 | 172 | 178 | 185 | 191 | 198 | 204 | 211 | 217 | 223 |
| 68 | 125 | 131 | 138 | 144 | 151 | 158 | 164 | 171 | 177 | 184 | 190 | 197 | 203 | 210 | 216 | 223 | 230 |
| 69 | 128 | 135 | 142 | 149 | 155 | 162 | 169 | 176 | 182 | 189 | 196 | 203 | 209 | 216 | 223 | 230 | 236 |
| 70 | 132 | 139 | 146 | 153 | 160 | 167 | 174 | 181 | 188 | 195 | 202 | 209 | 216 | 222 | 229 | 236 | 243 |
| 71 | 136 | 143 | 150 | 157 | 165 | 172 | 179 | 186 | 193 | 200 | 208 | 215 | 222 | 229 | 236 | 243 | 250 |
| 72 | 140 | 147 | 154 | 162 | 169 | 177 | 184 | 191 | 199 | 206 | 213 | 221 | 228 | 235 | 242 | 250 | 258 |
| 73 | 144 | 151 | 159 | 166 | 174 | 182 | 189 | 197 | 204 | 212 | 219 | 227 | 235 | 242 | 250 | 257 | 265 |
| 74 | 148 | 155 | 163 | 171 | 179 | 186 | 194 | 202 | 210 | 218 | 225 | 233 | 241 | 249 | 256 | 264 | 272 |
| 75 | 152 | 160 | 168 | 176 | 184 | 192 | 200 | 208 | 216 | 224 | 232 | 240 | 248 | 256 | 264 | 272 | 279 |
| 76 | 156 | 164 | 172 | 180 | 189 | 197 | 205 | 213 | 221 | 230 | 238 | 246 | 254 | 263 | 271 | 279 | 287 |

Source: National Heart, Lung, and Blood Institute.

## First Federal Obesity Guidelines: More Than Half of All Americans Are Too Fat

Overweight and obesity continue to be an alarming public-health problem in the United States, affecting an astonishing 55% of the population. Between 1960 and 1994, the prevalence of obesity in adults increased from nearly 13% to 22.5% of the U.S. population, with most of the increase occurring in the 1990s. These findings are recorded in the first federal guidelines on the identification, evaluation, and treatment of overweight and obesity in adults, which was released by the National Heart, Lung, and Blood Institute (NHLBI) in June 1998.

According to the guidelines, assessment of overweight involves evaluation of three key measures—body mass index (BMI), waist circumference, and a patient's risk factors for diseases and conditions associated with obesity. Overweight is defined as having a BMI of 25 to 29.9 and obesity as a BMI of 30 and above, which is consistent with the definitions used in many other countries. BMI describes body weight relative to height and is strongly correlated with total body-fat content in adults.

### Overweight and Obesity in the United States, 1960–1994

| | Overweight[1] and obesity | | Obesity[2] | | | Overweight[1] and obesity | | Obesity[2] | |
|---|---|---|---|---|---|---|---|---|---|
| | 1960–1962 | 1988–1994 | 1960–1962 | 1988–1994 | | 1960–1962 | 1988–1994 | 1960–1962 | 1988–1994 |
| Both sexes | 43.3% | 54.9% | 12.8% | 22.3% | 50–59 | 54.1% | 73.0% | 13.4% | 28.9% |
| Men | 48.2 | 59.4 | 10.4 | 19.5 | 60–69 | 52.9 | 70.3 | 7.7 | 24.8 |
| Women | 38.7 | 50.7 | 15.1 | 25.0 | 70–79 | 36.0 | 63.1 | 8.6 | 20.0 |
| White men | 48.8 | 61.0 | 10.1 | 20.0 | Women | | | | |
| White women | 36.1 | 49.2 | 13.7 | 23.5 | 20–29 | 17.0 | 33.1 | 6.1 | 14.6 |
| Black men | 43.1 | 56.5 | 13.9 | 20.6 | 30–39 | 32.8 | 47.0 | 12.1 | 25.8 |
| Black women | 57.0 | 65.8 | 25.0 | 36.5 | 40–49 | 42.3 | 52.7 | 17.1 | 26.9 |
| Men | | | | | 50–59 | 55.0 | 64.4 | 20.4 | 35.6 |
| 20–29 | 39.9 | 43.1 | 9.0 | 12.5 | 60–69 | 63.1 | 64.0 | 27.2 | 29.8 |
| 30–39 | 49.6 | 58.1 | 10.4 | 17.2 | 70–79 | 57.4 | 57.9 | 21.9 | 25.0 |
| 40–49 | 53.6 | 65.5 | 11.9 | 23.1 | | | | | |

1. BMI greater than or equal to 25. 2. BMI greater than or equal to 30. Source: Health, United States, 2000, Centers for Disease Control and Prevention.

## Self-Perception of Being Overweight

Not only do many Americans struggle with weight problems, but they often harbor misperceptions about their weight—considering themselves in the correct weight range when they are actually unhealthily overweight, or the reverse, considering themselves overweight when in fact they are not.

- Almost twice as many women as men who are not overweight think that they are. 25.3% of men and 47.9% of women defined as within their normal weight range think they weigh too much.
- Overweight women are more realistic than overweight men in recognizing themselves as overweight. 91.8% of women defined as overweight perceive themselves as such, whereas only 83.4% of overweight men consider themselves to be so.
- The group least forgiving of itself consists of white women between 40 and 59 years who are within their target weight range—a full 59.6% of these women are convinced that they are overweight when they actually aren't.
- Least concerned about their weight are overweight black men 60 years and older—36.3% of these overweight men don't accept being labeled overweight.

| | Percent of overweight people who think they are overweight | | | | | |
| | Total[1] | | Non-Hispanic white | | Non-Hispanic black | |
| Age | Male | Female | Male | Female | Male | Female |
|---|---|---|---|---|---|---|
| Total | 83.4% | 91.8% | 86.2% | 94.2% | 71.9% | 87.4% |
| 20 to 39 years old | 84.5 | 94.5 | 88.8 | 97.4 | 73.4 | 90.9 |
| 40 to 59 years old | 89.0 | 95.4 | 92.1 | 98.0 | 74.0 | 93.4 |
| 60 years old and over | 73.0 | 83.6 | 74.6 | 86.5 | 63.7 | 71.7 |

| | Percent of population not overweight who think they are overweight | | | | | |
| | Total[1] | | Non-Hispanic white | | Non-Hispanic black | |
| Age | Male | Female | Male | Female | Male | Female |
|---|---|---|---|---|---|---|
| Total | 25.3% | 47.9% | 28.1% | 50.2% | 13.1% | 37.5% |
| 20 to 39 years old | 24.8 | 49.5 | 28.1 | 51.4 | 10.1 | 41.1 |
| 40 to 59 years old | 27.6 | 56.5 | 30.7 | 59.6 | 19.6 | 46.5 |
| 60 years old and over | 23.2 | 35.3 | 24.7 | 38.6 | 12.6 | 13.5 |

1. Includes other races and persons of Hispanic origin not shown separately. *Source:* U.S. National Center for Health Statistics, unpublished data covering 1988–1994.

## Physical Activity and Cardiovascular Health

- Cardiovascular disease (CVD) is the No. 1 killer in America. About 950,000 Americans died last year of CVD, accounting for over 40% of all deaths.
- Lack of physical activity is clearly shown to be a risk factor for coronary heart disease.
- Estimates are that up to 250,000 deaths per year in the U.S.—about 12% of total deaths—are due to a lack of regular physical activity.
- The relative risk of coronary heart disease associated with physical inactivity ranges from 1.5 to 2.4, an increase in risk comparable with that observed for high cholesterol, high blood pressure, and cigarette smoking.
- Less active, less fit persons have a 30–50% greater risk of developing high blood pressure.
- Participation in regular physical activity gradually increased during the 1960s, 70s, and early 80s but decreased in the recent years.
- Surveys show that 28% of Americans age 18 or older aren't active at all. 44% of adults get some

exercise, but they don't do it regularly or intensely enough to protect their hearts. Only 27% of American adults get enough leisure-time exercise to achieve cardiovascular fitness.
- People with lower incomes and less than a 12th grade education are more likely to be physically inactive.
- Of people age 55 and older, 38% report essentially sedentary lifestyles.
- Even low-to-moderate intensity activities, when done for as little as 30 minutes a day, can bring benefits. These activities include pleasure walking, climbing stairs, gardening, yard work, moderate-to-heavy housework, dancing, and home exercise.
- More vigorous aerobic activities, such as brisk walking, running, swimming, bicycling, roller skating, and jumping rope—done most days of the week for at least 30 minutes—are best for improving the fitness of the heart and lungs.

## America's Best Hospitals, 2002

The annual *U.S. News & World Report* list of the United States' best hospitals is prepared by the National Opinion Research Center at the University of Chicago. The list recognizes hospitals that excel in many specialties.

1. Johns Hopkins Hospital, Baltimore, Md.
2. Mayo Clinic, Rochester, Minn.
3. Cleveland Clinic, Ohio
4. Massachusetts General Hospital, Boston
5. University of California, Los Angeles Medical Center
6. Duke University Medical Center, Durham, N.C.
7. University of California, San Francisco Medical Center
8. University of Michigan Medical Center, Ann Arbor
9. Barnes-Jewish Hospital, St. Louis, Mo.
10. Brigham and Women's Hospital, Boston, Mass.

## Percentage of Adults Engaging in Leisure Time Physical Activity, 1998

| Characteristic | No participation in physical activity | Participates in regular, sustained activity[1] | Participates in regular, vigorous activity[2] | Characteristic | No participation in physical activity | Participates in regular, sustained activity[1] | Participates in regular, vigorous activity[2] |
|---|---|---|---|---|---|---|---|
| **Total** | **28.7%** | **20.8%** | **13.6%** | 30 to 44 years old | 28.2% | 19.9% | 14.8% |
| Male | 26.2 | 21.9 | 13.3 | 45 to 64 years old | 31.5 | 19.8 | 13.2 |
| Female | 31.0 | 19.7 | 13.8 | 65 to 74 years old | 35.9 | 20.3 | 13.0 |
| White, non-Hispanic | 26.7 | 21.6 | 14.0 | 75 years old and over | 47.1 | 14.9 | 12.3 |
| Black, non-Hispanic | 33.8 | 17.8 | 12.3 | **School years completed** | | | |
| Hispanic | 38.4 | 17.4 | 11.4 | Less than 12 years | 49.7 | 14.3 | 8.2 |
| Other | 28.8 | 21.8 | 14.3 | 12 years | 33.9 | 18.2 | 10.7 |
| **Males** | | | | Some college | 23.9 | 22.3 | 13.9 |
| 18 to 29 years old | 17.6 | 26.5 | 12.2 | College | 16.3 | 25.7 | 19.7 |
| 30 to 44 years old | 24.9 | 19.0 | 11.8 | **Household income** | | | |
| 45 to 64 years old | 30.6 | 20.5 | 14.1 | Less than $10,000 | 42.4 | 17.8 | 10.7 |
| 65 to 74 years old | 31.1 | 24.8 | 14.2 | $10,000 to $19,999 | 39.8 | 16.9 | 10.5 |
| 75 years old and over | 39.1 | 22.2 | 22.0 | $20,000 to $34,999 | 31.3 | 19.4 | 12.1 |
| **Females** | | | | $35,000 to $49,999 | 24.4 | 21.4 | 14.0 |
| 18 to 29 years old | 25.1 | 20.9 | 14.2 | $50,000 and over | 16.9 | 25.5 | 17.6 |

NOTE: Covers persons 18 years old and over. 1. Any type or intensity of activity that occurs 5 times or more per week and 30 minutes or more per occasion. 2. Rhythmic contraction of large muscle groups performed at 50% or more of estimated age- and sex-specific maximum cardio-respiratory capacity, 3 times per week or more for at least 20 minutes per occasion. *Source:* U.S. National Center for Chronic Disease Prevention and Health Promotion, unpublished data; *Statistical Abstract of the United States, 2000.*

## Blood Types

Human blood is grouped into four types: A, B, AB, and O. Each letter refers to a kind of antigen, or protein, on the surface of red blood cells. For example, the surface of red blood cells in Type A blood has antigens known as A-antigens.

Each blood type is also grouped by its Rhesus factor, or Rh factor. Blood is either Rh positive (Rh+) or Rh negative (Rh-). About 85% of Americans have Rh+ blood.

Rhesus refers to another type of antigen, or protein, on the surface of red blood cells. The name Rhesus comes from Rhesus monkeys, in which the protein was discovered.

Blood types become very important when a blood transfusion is necessary. In a blood transfusion, a patient must receive a blood type that is compatible with his or her own blood type—that is, the donated blood must be accepted by the patient's own blood. If the blood types are not compatible, red blood cells will clump together, making clots that can block blood vessels and cause death.

Type O- blood is considered the "universal donor" because it can be donated to people of any blood type. Type AB+ blood is considered the "universal recipient" because people with this type can receive any blood type.

| Blood Type | Percent of Americans with this type | Who can receive this type |
|---|---|---|
| O+ | 37% | O+, A+, B+, AB+ |
| O- | 6% | All blood types |
| A+ | 34% | A+, AB+ |
| A- | 6% | A+, A-, AB+, AB- |
| B+ | 10% | B+, AB+ |
| B- | 2% | B+, B-, AB+, AB- |
| AB+ | 4% | AB+ |
| AB- | 1% | AB+, AB- |

## Blood Pressure Explained

Blood pressure is the force of blood against the walls of arteries. Blood pressure is recorded as two numbers—the systolic pressure (as the heart beats) over the diastolic pressure (as the heart relaxes between beats). The measurement is written one above or before the other, with the systolic number on top and the diastolic number on the bottom. For example, a blood pressure measurement of 120/80 mm Hg (millimeters of mercury) is expressed verbally as "120 over 80."

Normal blood pressure is less than 130 mm Hg systolic and less than 85 mm Hg diastolic. Optimal blood pressure is less than 120 mm Hg systolic and less than 80 mm Hg diastolic.

When systolic and diastolic blood pressures fall into different categories, the higher category should be used to classify blood pressure level. For example, 160/80 mm Hg would be stage 2 hypertension (high blood pressure).

| Category | Blood pressure level (mm Hg) | |
|---|---|---|
| | Systolic | Diastolic |
| Optimal[1] | < 120 | < 80 |
| Normal | < 130 | < 85 |
| High Normal | 130–139 | 85–89 |
| **High Blood Pressure** | | |
| Stage 1 | 140–159 | 90–99 |
| Stage 2 | 160–179 | 100–109 |
| Stage 3 | ≥180 | ≥110 |

NOTE: < means less than; ≥ means greater than or equal to. 1. Optimal blood pressure with respect to heart disease risk is below 120/80 mm Hg. However, unusually low readings should be evaluated for clinical significance. *Source:* National Heart, Lung, and Blood Institute.

# 12 Steps for Email Addicts

## Can't stop working your messages? Experts say it may be as addictive as gambling. Here's how to quit

**By CHRIS TAYLOR** TIME

I used to think I could quit checking my email any time I wanted to, but I stopped kidding myself years ago. My email program is up and running 24 hours a day, and once I submit to its siren call, whole hours can go missing. I have a friend who recently found herself stuck on a cruise ship near Panama that didn't offer email, so she chartered a helicopter to take her to the nearest Internet cafe. There was nothing in her queue but junk mail and other spam, but she thought the trip was worth it.

I know how she felt. You never know when you're going to get that note from Uncle Eric about your inheritance. Or that White House dinner invitation with a time-sensitive R.S.V.P.

My friend and I are not alone. According to a Gartner Group study, 42% of American email users—and there are more than 100 million of us—check email on vacation. Nearly 1 in 4 look for messages every weekend.

## Email High

Dr. David Greenfield, founder of the Center for Internet Studies in West Hartford, Conn., believes that at least 6% of us are what he would classify as compulsive email checkers. "It sounds silly, but people report withdrawal symptoms when they're away from it," he says. "It's very likely the brain gets the same kind of hit from email as it does from gambling."

If email is really as addictive as gambling, there must be a 12-step program somewhere to treat it. Sure enough, a Web search turns up an email recovery program created back in 1997 by a pair of Florida State University administrators, Perry Crowell and Larry Conrad. It's pretty crude, Crowell admits, and because it was written before the explosion in users, traffic, and email viruses, it seems almost naive. "If we were to update it today, we might very well declare defeat," says Crowell.

## Stop by Step Recovery

Unwilling to give up all hope, we consulted a few experts and pieced together our own 12-step program for breaking the email habit (or at least getting it under control). It goes like this:

### Step 1: Admit You Have a Problem

Mark Ellwood, author of *Cut the Glut of Email*, calculates that white-collar workers waste an average of three hours a week just on sorting through junk mail. If you spend any more than that, you had better read on.

### Step 2: Recognize the Symptoms

Dry eyes, back aches, wrist cramping, and numb fingers are signs that you are spending too much time at the keyboard.

### Step 3: Take Responsibility

If you didn't send so much email, maybe you wouldn't get so much.

### Step 4: Practice the Rule of Three

If an email thread has gone back and forth three times, it is time to pick up the phone.

### Step 5: Don't Copy the World

Think twice about the people you put on your cc: list. If they all respond, then where will you be?

### Step 6: Turn Off the Chime

Nothing triggers a Pavlovian response faster than a ringing bell, but a flashing icon in the task bar comes close. Turn both off, and your urge to check will diminish over time.

### Step 7: Slow Down

Answering messages the moment you get them creates an expectation that you will always respond as quickly. Let it be known that you won't. Train people to call if it's really urgent.

### Step 8: Touch Each Message Only Once

If it isn't relevant, hit the delete key. If it is, set it aside, and plan to spend some time at the end of the day to reply.

### Step 9: Let Your Software Do the Work

The more you filter out spam and divert email lists to their own folders, the more manageable your inbox becomes.

### Step 10: Get Help from Humans

And I don't mean your therapist. Senior managers: let your assistant wade through your inbox for you. Ordinary mortals: ask friends to stop by or phone in from time to time to interrupt your email reveries.

### Step 11: Don't Check Your Email at Home

This may seem extreme, but forcing yourself to go to a library or Internet cafe will at least allow the possibility of some face-to-face human interaction in your life.

### Step 12: Take Time Off

Designate one day a week that is utterly email free. That goes double for cruise-ship vacations. □

# Online Activities by Age, 2001

## Adults | Teens

| Online activities | 18–34 | 35-54 | 55+ | Online Activities | 13–17 |
|---|---|---|---|---|---|
| Received and sent email | 92% | 95% | 97% | Received and sent email | 86% |
| Used a search engine | 77 | 76 | 78 | Did homework/research for school | 78 |
| Participated in contests or sweepstakes | 62 | 64 | 61 | Used AOL Instant Messenger, Yahoo Messenger, MSN Messenger, or a similar instant message service | 63 |
| Gathered information on local events, restaurants, maps, or traffic | 62 | 57 | 56 | Visited music sites | 61 |
| Sent electronic greeting/post cards | 60 | 66 | 67 | Downloaded music files online to playback on the computer (Napster.com or MP3.com) | 48 |
| Researched products and services | 58 | 66 | 67 | Participated in a chat room | 45 |
| Used AOL Instant Messenger, ICQ, Yahoo Messenger, or similar instant message services | 56 | 50 | 34 | Viewed personal Web pages created by other individuals | 42 |
| Visited an online directory site to find addresses or phone numbers | 47 | 47 | 47 | Played games online such as action games, fantasy games, flight simulators, etc. | 39 |
| Chatted online | 45 | 35 | 27 | Watched a music video, movie clip, or other video clip online | 39 |
| Used the Internet to get the daily news | 45 | 51 | 55 | Downloaded free software | 31 |

Source: Jupiter Media Metrix. Web: www.mediametrix.com.

# Percent of Households with a Computer, 2001

| | U.S. | Rural | Urban | Central cities | | U.S. | Rural | Urban | Central cities |
|---|---|---|---|---|---|---|---|---|---|
| Total | 56.5% | 55.6% | 56.7% | 51.5% | $50,000–$74,999 | 77.7% | 78.1% | 77.6% | 75.8% |
| Income | | | | | $75,000+ | 89.0 | 89.0 | 88.9 | 86.4 |
| Under $5,000 | 25.9 | 17.9 | 28.2 | 24.5 | Race/Hispanic Origin | | | | |
| $5,000–$9,999 | 19.2 | 16.4 | 20.1 | 20.6 | White | 61.1 | 58.0 | 62.4 | 60.0 |
| $10,000–$14,999 | 25.7 | 24.3 | 26.3 | 24.3 | Black | 37.1 | 31.5 | 37.7 | 33.9 |
| $15,000–$19,999 | 31.8 | 29.4 | 32.6 | 33.9 | Asian Amer. and Pac. Isl. | 72.7 | 69.4 | 72.8 | 67.4 |
| $20,000–$24,999 | 40.1 | 40.0 | 40.1 | 36.4 | Hispanic | 40.0 | 36.6 | 40.3 | 38.1 |
| $25,000–$34,999 | 49.7 | 49.4 | 49.9 | 49.9 | | | | | |
| $35,000–$49,999 | 64.3 | 64.7 | 64.2 | 64.4 | | | | | |

Source: NTIA and ESA, U.S. Dept. of Commerce, using U.S. Bureau of the Census Current Population Survey supplements.

# Percent of Households with Internet Access, 2001

| | U.S. | Rural | Urban | Central cities | | U.S. | Rural | Urban | Central cities |
|---|---|---|---|---|---|---|---|---|---|
| Total | 50.5% | 48.7% | 51.1% | 45.7% | $50,000–$74,999 | 71.4% | 70.6% | 71.7% | 70.5% |
| Income | | | | | $75,000+ | 85.4 | 84.8 | 85.5 | 83.8 |
| Under $5,000 | 20.5 | 12.5 | 22.7 | 20.2 | Race/Hispanic Origin | | | | |
| $5,000–$9,999 | 14.4 | 11.0 | 15.5 | 14.5 | White | 55.4 | 51.0 | 57.2 | 54.8 |
| $10,000–$14,999 | 19.4 | 18.1 | 19.8 | 19.3 | Black | 30.8 | 24.4 | 31.6 | 27.4 |
| $15,000–$19,999 | 23.6 | 21.0 | 24.4 | 24.6 | Asian Amer. and Pac. Isl. | 68.1 | 68.2 | 68.1 | 63.1 |
| $20,000–$24,999 | 31.8 | 31.7 | 31.9 | 28.7 | Hispanic | 32.0 | 29.9 | 32.2 | 29.8 |
| $25,000–$34,999 | 42.2 | 40.5 | 42.8 | 41.3 | | | | | |
| $35,000–$49,999 | 56.4 | 55.0 | 56.8 | 56.2 | | | | | |

Source: NTIA and ESA, U.S. Dept. of Commerce, using U.S. Bureau of the Census Current Population Survey supplements.

# Share of Total Online Sales by Category

## Total 2001 sales of domestic online retailers: $53 billion

| Category | Q1 2001 | Q2 2001 | Q3 2001 | Q4 2001 | 2001 | Category | Q1 2001 | Q2 2001 | Q3 2001 | Q4 2001 | 2001 |
|---|---|---|---|---|---|---|---|---|---|---|---|
| Travel | 32% | 39% | 43% | 32% | 36% | Event tickets | 2% | 4% | 3% | 2% | 3% |
| Computer hardware | 14 | 12 | 15 | 17 | 15 | Home & garden | 2 | 2 | 3 | 3 | 2 |
| Apparel & accessories | 11 | 9 | 8 | 11 | 10 | Music | 2 | 2 | 1 | 2 | 2 |
| Office | 11 | 7 | 7 | 7 | 8 | Health & beauty | 2 | 2 | 2 | 2 | 2 |
| Consumer electronics | 5 | 6 | 5 | 7 | 6 | All other categories | 14 | 13 | 9 | 13 | 12 |
| Books | 5 | 4 | 4 | 4 | 4 | Total | 100 | 100 | 100 | 100 | 100 |

NOTE: comScore data are based on the buying activity at U.S. websites (excluding auctions) of more than 1.5 million representative Internet-using individuals, who have given comScore permission to confidentially monitor their browsing and actual buying behavior using comScore's patent-pending technology. Source: comScore Networks.

## Internet Use from Any Location by Individuals Age 3 and Older

| | Internet use (percent of total U.S. population) | | | | | Internet use (percent of total U.S. population) | | | |
|---|---|---|---|---|---|---|---|---|---|
| | Oct. 1997 | Dec. 1998 | Aug. 2000 | Sept. 2001 | | Oct. 1997 | Dec. 1998 | Aug. 2000 | Sept. 2001 |
| Total[1] | 22.2% | 32.7% | 44.4% | 53.9% | Some college | 24.8% | 38.6% | 54.2% | 62.4% |
| **Gender** | | | | | Bachelors degree | 41.4 | 58.4 | 72.5 | 80.8 |
| Male | 24.3 | 34.2 | 44.6 | 53.9 | Beyond bachelors degree | 51.9 | 66.4 | 78.5 | 83.7 |
| Female | 20.2 | 31.4 | 44.2 | 53.8 | **Age group** | | | | |
| **Race/origin** | | | | | Age 3–8 | 7.2 | 11.0 | 15.3 | 27.9 |
| White | 25.3 | 37.6 | 50.3 | 59.9 | Age 9–17 | 33.2 | 43.0 | 53.4 | 68.6 |
| Black | 13.2 | 19.0 | 29.3 | 39.8 | Age 18–24 | 31.6 | 44.3 | 56.8 | 65.0 |
| Asian Amer. & Pac. Isl. | 26.4 | 35.8 | 49.4 | 60.4 | Age 25–49 | 27.1 | 40.9 | 55.4 | 63.9 |
| Hispanic | 11.0 | 16.6 | 23.7 | 31.6 | Male | 29.3 | 41.7 | 54.1 | 61.8 |
| **Employment status** | | | | | Female | 25.1 | 40.2 | 56.5 | 66.0 |
| Employed[2] | 28.5 | 42.5 | 56.6 | 65.4 | Age 50+ | 11.2 | 19.3 | 29.6 | 37.1 |
| Not employed[2, 3] | 12.4 | 19.5 | 28.9 | 36.9 | Male | 14.6 | 22.8 | 32.7 | 39.9 |
| **Family income** | | | | | Female | 8.4 | 16.4 | 26.9 | 34.6 |
| Less than $15,000 | 9.2 | 13.7 | 18.9 | 25.0 | **Geographic location of household in which the individual lives** | | | | |
| $15,000–$24,999 | 11.6 | 18.4 | 25.5 | 33.4 | | | | | |
| $25,000–$34,999 | 17.1 | 25.3 | 35.7 | 44.1 | Rural | n.a. | 29.3 | 42.5 | 52.9 |
| $35,000–$49,999 | 22.8 | 34.7 | 46.5 | 57.1 | Urban | n.a. | 33.9 | 45.0 | 54.2 |
| $50,000–$74,999 | 32.3 | 45.5 | 57.7 | 67.3 | Urban not central city | n.a. | 36.1 | 47.9 | 57.4 |
| $75,000 & above | 44.5 | 58.9 | 70.1 | 78.9 | Urban central city | n.a. | 30.6 | 40.6 | 49.1 |
| **Educational attainment[4]** | | | | | | | | | |
| Less than high school | 1.8 | 4.2 | 8.8 | 12.8 | | | | | |
| High school diploma /GED | 9.7 | 19.2 | 30.6 | 39.8 | | | | | |

1. U.S. population: 1997: 255,689,000; 1998: 258,453,000; 2000: 262,620,000; 2001: 265,180,000. 2. Age 16 and older. 3. Both people who are unemployed and people not in the labor force. 4. Age 25 and older. *Source:* U.S. Bureau of the Census, Current Population Survey supplements, Oct. 1997, Dec. 1998, Aug. 2000, and Sept. 2001.

## Computer Use from Any Location by Individuals Age 3 and Older

| | Percent of total U.S. population who are computer users | | Growth in use rate (annual rate) | | Percent of total U.S. population who are computer users | | Growth in use rate (annual rate) |
|---|---|---|---|---|---|---|---|
| | Oct. 1997 | Sept. 2001 | Oct. 1997 to Sept. 2001 | | Oct. 1997 | Sept. 2001 | Oct. 1997 to Sept. 2001 |
| Total[1] | 53.5% | 65.6% | 5.3% | $50,000–$74,999 | 71.7% | 79.4% | 2.6% |
| **Gender** | | | | $75,000 & above | 80.8 | 88.0 | 2.2 |
| Male | 53.8 | 65.5 | 5.2 | **Educational attainment[4]** | | | |
| Female | 53.3 | 65.8 | 5.5 | Less than high school | 7.9 | 17.0 | 21.5 |
| **Race/origin** | | | | High school diploma/GED | 33.5 | 47.3 | 9.2 |
| White | 57.5 | 70.0 | 5.2 | Some college | 51.1 | 69.5 | 7.0 |
| Black | 41.1 | 55.7 | 8.0 | Bachelors degree | 74.3 | 84.9 | 3.5 |
| Asian Amer. & Pac. Isl. | 57.5 | 71.2 | 5.6 | Beyond bachelors degree | 79.1 | 86.9 | 2.4 |
| Hispanic | 38.0 | 48.8 | 6.6 | **Age group** | | | |
| **Employment status** | | | | Age 3–8 | 59.0 | 71.0 | 4.9 |
| Employed[2] | 61.7 | 73.2 | 4.5 | Age 9–17 | 85.1 | 92.6 | 2.2 |
| Not employed[2, 3] | 24.8 | 40.8 | 13.5 | Age 18–24 | 58.2 | 71.3 | 5.3 |
| **Family income** | | | | Age 25–49 | 57.7 | 70.2 | 5.1 |
| Less than $15,000 | 29.8 | 37.3 | 5.9 | Male | 55.0 | 67.3 | 5.3 |
| $15,000–$24,999 | 37.4 | 46.8 | 5.9 | Female | 60.3 | 73.0 | 5.0 |
| $25,000–$34,999 | 49.3 | 57.7 | 4.1 | Age 50+ | 27.6 | 42.5 | 11.6 |
| $35,000–$49,999 | 60.4 | 70.0 | 3.8 | Male | 30.9 | 45.1 | 10.2 |
| | | | | Female | 24.9 | 40.2 | 13.1 |

1. U.S. population: 1997: 255,689,000; 2001: 265,180,000. 2. Age 16 and older. 3. Unemployed and not in the labor force. 4. Age 25 and older. *Source:* U.S. Bureau of the Census, Current Population Survey supplements, Oct. 1997, Sept. 2001.

## Internet Use by Location as a Percent of U.S. Population, 1998 and 2001

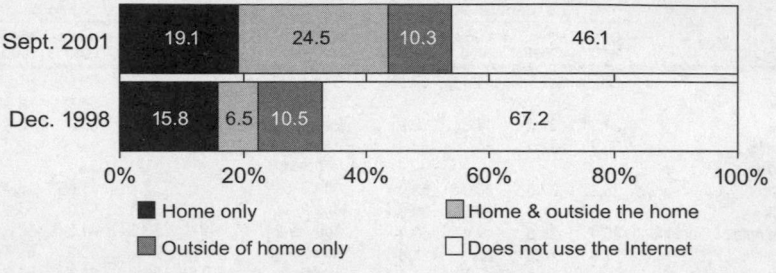

| | | | | |
|---|---|---|---|---|
| Sept. 2001 | 19.1 | 24.5 | 10.3 | 46.1 |
| Dec. 1998 | 15.8 | 6.5 | 10.5 | 67.2 |

0%     20%     40%     60%     80%     100%

■ Home only          ■ Home & outside the home

■ Outside of home only     □ Does not use the Internet

*Source:* NTIA and ESA, U.S. Department of Commerce, using U.S. Census Bureau Current Population Survey supplements

## How Many Online Worldwide?

| | | | |
|---|---|---|---|
| **World total** | **544.2 million** | Middle East | 4.65 million |
| Africa | 4.15 million | Canada & U.S. | 181.23 million |
| Asia/Pacific | 157.49 million | Latin America | 25.33 million |
| Europe | 171.35 million | | |

NOTE: These are estimated figures, as of Feb. 2002, based on several surveys. *Source:* Nua Internet Surveys.

## Top 15 Countries by Computers-in-Use at Year-End 2000 and 2001

| Rank | Country | Year-end 2000 (millions) | 2000 % share of total | Year-end 2001 projected* (millions) | Rank | Country | Year-end 2000 (millions) | 2000 % share of total | Year-end 2001 projected* (millions) |
|---|---|---|---|---|---|---|---|---|---|
| 1. | United States (.us) | 168.84 | 30.64% | 182.24 | 10. | Brazil (.br) | 11.23 | 2.04% | 13.48 |
| 2. | Japan (.jp) | 48.00 | 8.71 | 54.65 | 11. | Australia (.au) | 10.43 | 1.89 | 11.41 |
| 3. | Germany (.de) | 31.59 | 5.73 | 35.84 | 12. | Russia (.ru) | 9.33 | 1.69 | 11.15 |
| 4. | United Kingdom (.uk) | 25.91 | 4.70 | 29.33 | 13. | Spain (.es) | 7.80 | 1.41 | 9.21 |
| 5. | France (.fr) | 21.81 | 3.96 | 24.97 | 14. | Taiwan (.tw) | 7.39 | 1.34 | 8.88 |
| 6. | China (.cn) | 21.31 | 3.87 | 25.87 | 15. | Netherlands (.nl) | 7.33 | 1.33 | 8.17 |
| 7. | Canada (.ca) | 17.20 | 3.12 | 19.10 | | **Total Top 15 Countries** | **420.20** | **76.24** | **472.52** |
| 8. | Italy (.it) | 17.17 | 3.11 | 20.02 | | **Total Worldwide** | **551.10** | **100.00%** | **625.90** |
| 9. | South Korea (.kr) | 14.86 | 2.70 | 18.20 | | | | | |

*As of July 15, 2001. *Source:* Computer Industry Almanac Inc. Web: www.c-i-a.com. Reprinted with permission.

## Home Internet Connection Type as a Percent of Individuals Using the Internet at Home, 2001

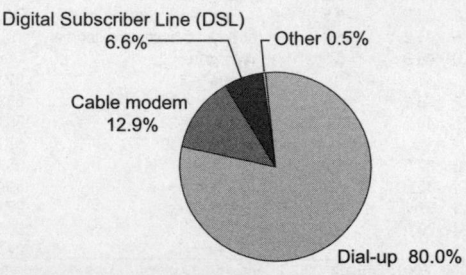

Digital Subscriber Line (DSL)
6.6% ── ┌ Other 0.5%

Cable modem
12.9%

Dial-up 80.0%

*Source:* NTIA and ESA, U.S. Department of Commerce, using U.S. Census Bureau Current Population Survey supplements

# Top Domains/Websites, March 2002

| Rank | Website | Unique visitors (thousands) | Rank | Website | Unique visitors (thousands) |
|---|---|---|---|---|---|
| 1. | AOL Time Warner Network— Proprietary & WWW | 91,899 | 13. | Viacom Online | 21,266 |
| 2. | MSN-Microsoft Sites | 83,010 | 14. | Vivendi-Universal Sites | 20,766 |
| 3. | Yahoo! Sites | 78,647 | 15. | Real.com Network | 20,479 |
| 4. | Terra Lycos | 40,954 | 16. | Classmates.com Sites | 20,244 |
| 5. | About/Primedia | 36,016 | 17. | eUniverse Network | 18,402 |
| 6. | Google Sites | 33,000 | 18. | Ask Jeeves | 17,955 |
| 7. | Gator Network | 32,154 | 19. | Ticketmaster Sites | 17,625 |
| 8. | eBay | 29,334 | 20. | Excite Network | 17,435 |
| 9. | Amazon Sites | 29,259 | 21. | American Greetings Property | 16,655 |
| 10. | CNET Networks | 26,232 | 22. | AT&T Properties | 16,646 |
| 11. | InfoSpace Network | 24,991 | 23. | Monster.com Property | 15,373 |
| 12. | Walt Disney Internet Group (WDIG) | 23,588 | 24. | Weather Channel, The | 15,321 |
|  |  |  | 25. | SBC Communications | 14,633 |

NOTES: "Unique visitors" refers to the estimated number of total users who visited the website once in the given month. All unique visitors are unduplicated (only counted once). *Source:* Jupiter Media Metrix. Web: www.mediametrix.com.

# Top Entertainment Sites, March 2002

| Rank | Website | Unique visitors (thousands) Total | Rank | Website | Unique visitors (thousands) Total |
|---|---|---|---|---|---|
| 1. | Viacom Online | 21,266 | 9. | AOL Prop Music | 10,548 |
| 2. | Real.com Network | 20,479 | 10. | ABC News Digital | 9,861 |
| 3. | eUniverse Network | 18,402 | 11. | Shockwave.com Sites | 9,240 |
| 4. | Ticketmaster Sites | 17,625 | 12. | AOL Media Player | 8,803 |
| 5. | AOL Prop Entertainment | 14,039 | 13. | MSN Entertainment | 8,322 |
| 6. | Disney Online | 13,716 | 14. | WindowsMedia | 7,738 |
| 7. | Sony Online | 12,238 | 15. | Eonline.com | 7,722 |
| 8. | UGO Networks | 10,560 |  |  |  |

NOTES: "Unique visitors" refers to the estimated number of total users who visited the website once in the given month. All unique visitors are unduplicated (only counted once). *Source:* Jupiter Media Metrix. Web: www.mediametrix.com.

# Top General News Sites, March 2002

| Rank | Website | Unique visitors (thousands) Total | Rank | Website | Unique visitors (thousands) Total |
|---|---|---|---|---|---|
| 1. | CNN.COM | 18,095 | 9. | Knight Ridder Digital | 6,521 |
| 2. | MSNBC | 16,334 | 10. | CBS Sites | 6,271 |
| 3. | Yahoo! News | 15,490 | 11. | Time.com Sites | 6,269 |
| 4. | AOL Prop News | 15,351 | 12. | Washingtonpost.com | 4,986 |
| 5. | ABC News Digital | 9,861 | 13. | Discovery.com Sites | 4,940 |
| 6. | Tribune Interactive | 9,430 | 14. | Hearst Newspaper Digital | 4,231 |
| 7. | USATODAY Sites | 7,028 | 15. | BBC.co.uk | 4,143 |
| 8. | NYTimes.com* | 6,670 |  |  |  |

NOTES: "Unique visitors" refers to the estimated number of total users who visited the website once in the given month. All unique visitors are unduplicated (only counted once). *Represents an aggregation of commonly owned/branded domain names. *Source:* Jupiter Media Metrix. Web: www.mediametrix.com.

# Top Travel Sites, March 2002

| Rank | Website | Unique visitors (thousands) Total | Rank | Website | Unique visitors (thousands) Total |
|---|---|---|---|---|---|
| 1. | MAPQUEST.com | 18,071 | 9. | AA.com | 4,769 |
| 2. | Expedia Travel | 12,022 | 10. | Hotwire.com | 4,671 |
| 3. | Travelocity | 11,686 | 11. | Priceline.com | 4,639 |
| 4. | Trip Network Inc. | 8,523 | 12. | Yahoo! Travel | 4,427 |
| 5. | AmericanExpress.com | 8,497 | 13. | Delta.com | 4,416 |
| 6. | ORBITZ.com | 7,968 | 14. | TravelZoom.com | 4,157 |
| 7. | AOL Prop Travel | 6,391 | 15. | UAL.com | 3,652 |
| 8. | Southwest.com | 5,295 |  |  |  |

NOTES: "Unique visitors" refers to the estimated number of total users who visited the website once in the given month. All unique visitors are unduplicated (only counted once). *Source:* Jupiter Media Metrix. Web: www.mediametrix.com.

## Search Services, February 2002

| Rank | Service | Unique visitors (millions) | Avg. min. used a month | Rank | Service | Unique visitors (millions) | Avg. min. used a month |
|---|---|---|---|---|---|---|---|
| 1. | MSN Search | 40.5 | 6.0 | 6. | LookSmart | 9.8 | 7.6 |
| 2. | Yahoo Search[1] | 36.2 | 10.7 | 7. | InfoSpace Search | 9.0 | 6.9 |
| 3. | Google sites | 29.0 | 24.1 | 8. | Netscape Search | 8.8 | 7.3 |
| 4. | AOL.com Search | 25.2 | 6.9 | 9. | Overture.com | 7.4 | 3.4 |
| 5. | Ask Jeeves | 17.7 | 16.2 | 10. | AltaVista Search | 6.4 | 18.0 |

1. Includes 24.6 million visitors to Google.Yahoo.com. *Source:* Jupiter Media Metrix.

## Internet Timeline

**1969**  ARPA (Advanced Research Projects Agency) goes online in December, connecting four major U.S. universities. Designed for research, education, and government organizations, it provides a communications network linking the country in the event that a military attack destroys conventional communications systems.

**1972**  Electronic mail is introduced by Ray Tomlinson, a Cambridge, Mass., computer scientist. He uses the @ to distinguish between the sender's name and network name in the email address.

**1973**  Transmission Control Protocol/Internet Protocol (TCP/IP) is designed and in 1983 it becomes the standard for communicating between computers over the Internet. One of these protocols, FTP (File Transfer Protocol), allows users to log onto a remote computer, list the files on that computer, and download files from that computer.

**1976**  Presidential candidate Jimmy Carter and running mate Walter Mondale use email to plan campaign events.

Queen Elizabeth sends her first email. She's the first state leader to do so.

**1984**  Domain Name System (DNS) is established, with network addresses identified by extensions such as .com, .org, and .edu.

**1989**  The first effort to index the Internet is created by Peter Deutsch at McGill University in Montreal, who devises Archie, an archive of FTP sites. Another indexing system, WAIS (Wide Area Information Server), is developed by Brewster Kahle of Thinking Machines Corp. Tim Berners-Lee of CERN (European Laboratory for Particle Physics) develops a new technique for distributing information on the Internet, which eventually is called the World Wide Web. The Web is based on hypertext, which permits the user to connect from one document to another at different sites on the Internet via hyperlinks (specially programmed words, phrases, buttons, or graphics). Unlike other Internet protocols, such as FTP and email, the Web is accessible through a graphical user interface.

**1991**  Gopher, the first userfriendly interface, is created at the University of Minnesota and named after the school mascot. Gopher becomes the most popular interface for several years.

**1993**  Mosaic is developed by Marc Andreeson at the National Center for Supercomputing Applications (NCSA). It becomes the dominant navigating system for the World Wide Web, which at this time accounts for merely 1% of all Internet traffic.

**1994**  The White House launches its website, www.whitehouse.gov. Initial commerce sites are established and mass marketing campaigns are launched via email, introducing the term "spamming" to the Internet vocabulary.

**1996**  Approximately 45 million people are using the Internet, with roughly 30 million of those in North America (United States and Canada), 9 million in Europe, and 6 million in Asia/Pacific (Australia, Japan, etc.). 43.2 million (44%) U.S. households own a personal computer, and 14 million of them are online.

**1997**  On July 8, 1997, Internet traffic records are broken as the NASA website broadcasts images taken by *Pathfinder* on Mars. The broadcast generates 46 million hits in one day.

**1999**  The number of Internet users worldwide reaches 150 million by the beginning of 1999. More than 50% are from the United States. "E-commerce" becomes the new buzzword as Internet shopping rapidly spreads.

**2000**  To the chagrin of the Internet population, deviant computer programmers begin designing and circulating viruses with greater frequency. "Love Bug" and "Stages" are two examples of self-replicating viruses that send themselves to people listed in a computer user's email address book. The heavy volume of email messages being sent and received forces many infected companies to temporarily shut down their clogged networks.

The Internet bubble bursts, as the fountain of investment capital dries up and the Nasdaq stock index plunges, causing the initial public offering (IPO) window to slam shut and many dotcoms to shutter their doors.

**2001**  Napster is dealt a potentially fatal blow when the 9th U.S. Circuit Court of Appeals in San Francisco rules that the company is violating copyright laws and orders it to stop distributing copyrighted music. The file-swapping company says it is developing a subscription-based service.

About 9.8 billion electronic messages are sent daily.

**2002**  As of January, 58.5% of the U.S. population (164.14 million people) uses the Internet. Worldwide there are 544.2 million users.

The death knell tolls for Napster after a bankruptcy judge ruled in September that German media giant Bertelsmann cannot buy the assets of troubled Napster Inc. The ruling prompts Konrad Hilbers, Napster CEO, to resign and lay off his staff.

Sources for this timeline include International Data Corporation, the W3C Consortium, Nielsen/NetRatings, and the Internet Society.

## Top-Selling Software, 2001

| Rank | Title | Publisher | Average price | Rank | Title | Publisher | Average price |
|---|---|---|---|---|---|---|---|
| 1. | TurboTax Deluxe | Intuit | $37.95 | 7. | Harry Potter & the Sorcerer's Stone | Electronic Arts | $28.47 |
| 2. | TurboTax | Intuit | 19.31 | | | | |
| 3. | The Sims | Electronic Arts | 40.82 | 8. | Norton Antivirus 2002 8.0 | Symantec | 44.85 |
| 4. | Norton Antivirus 2001 7.0 | Symantec | 33.33 | 9. | Diablo 2 Expansion Set: Lord of Destruction | Vivendi Universal Publishing | 34.05 |
| 5. | Taxcut 2000 Deluxe | Block Financial | 19.84 | | | | |
| 6. | Roller Coaster Tycoon | Infogrames Entertainment | 22.99 | 10. | VirusScan 5.0 | Network Associates | 25.98 |

*Source:* NPDTechworld. Web: www.npd.com.

## Top-Selling Education Software, 2001

| Rank | Title | Publisher | Average price | Rank | Title | Publisher | Average price |
|---|---|---|---|---|---|---|---|
| 1. | Adventure Workshop 1st–3rd Grade | The Learning Company | $19.52 | 6. | Mickey's Preschool Ages 2–4 | Disney | $18.36 |
| 2. | Instant Immersion Spanish | Topics Entertainment | 19.06 | 7. | Adventure Workshop Preschool–1st Grade | The Learning Company | 20.17 |
| 3. | Blue's ABC Time Activities (jewel case) | Infogrames Entertainment | 9.96 | 8. | Lego Creator: Harry Potter | Lego Media | 27.69 |
| 4. | Clifford's Reading Adventure | Scholastic | 19.57 | 9. | Clifford's Thinking Adventure | Scholastic | 19.86 |
| 5. | Adventure Workshop 4th–6th Grade | The Learning Company | 20.34 | 10. | Jumpstart Phonics (jewel case) | Vivendi Universal Publishing | 8.34 |

*Source:* NPDTechworld. Web: www.npd.com.

## Top-Selling Business Software, 2001

| Rank | Title | Publisher | Average price | Rank | Title | Publisher | Average price |
|---|---|---|---|---|---|---|---|
| 1. | Norton Antivirus 2001 7.0 | Symantec | $33.33 | 7. | MS Windows 98 2nd Ed. Upgr. | Microsoft | $91.35 |
| 2. | Norton Antivirus 2002 8.0 | Symantec | 44.85 | 8. | Norton Antivirus 7.5 Corp. Ed. PVP Lic. | Symantec | 23.87 |
| 3. | VirusScan 5.0 | Network Associates | 25.98 | | | | |
| 4. | MS Windows XP Home Ed. Upgr. | Microsoft | 98.52 | 9. | Norton Antivirus 7.5 Corp. Ed. Mnt PVP Lic. | Symantec | 9.88 |
| 5. | Norton System Works 2001 4.0 | Symantec | 54.34 | | | | |
| 6. | MS Windows 2000 Svr. Clnt. Acc. OPEN Lic. | Microsoft | 28.99 | 10. | MS Windows ME Upgr. | Microsoft | 90.06 |

*Source:* NPDTechworld. Web: www.npd.com.

## Top-Selling Game Software, 2001

| Rank | Title | Publisher | Average price | Rank | Title | Publisher | Average price |
|---|---|---|---|---|---|---|---|
| 1. | The Sims | Electronic Arts | $40.82 | 6. | The Sims: Livin' Large Expansion Pack | Electronic Arts | $28.10 |
| 2. | Roller Coaster Tycoon | Infogrames Entertainment | 22.99 | 7. | The Sims: Hot Date Expansion Pack | Electronic Arts | 26.50 |
| 3. | Harry Potter & the Sorcerer's Stone | Electronic Arts | 28.47 | 8. | Diablo 2 | Vivendi Universal Publishing | 37.51 |
| 4. | Diablo 2 Expansion Set: Lord of Destruction | Vivendi Universal Publishing | 34.05 | 9. | Sim Theme Park | Electronic Arts | 19.30 |
| 5. | The Sims: House Party Expansion Pack | Electronic Arts | 27.95 | 10. | MS Age Of Empires 2: Age of Kings | Microsoft | 40.61 |

*Source:* NPDTechworld. Web: www.npd.com.

# The Periodic Table

Although some elements, such as gold and iron, have been known to humans since prehistoric times, it wasn't until the 17th century that the first scientific discovery of an element (phosphorus) was made. Only 12 elements were known prior to 1700, but as more and more elements were discovered—by 1900 there were more than 80—scientists tried to find a way to organize them systematically, according to their physical and chemical properties.

Today, the periodic table (see opposite) organizes the elements in horizontal rows, or periods, by order of increasing atomic number, which equals the number of protons in the atomic nucleus of each element. The elements are also organized in vertical columns, or groups, based on similar physical characteristics and chemical behavior. This arrangement developed side by side with atomic theory over about 200 years, and it continues to evolve as new elements are discovered.

## Early Attempts

One of the earliest attempts to organize the elements based on their chemical and physical properties was made by German chemist Johann Dobereiner. In 1817 Dobereiner noticed that certain elements that were chemically similar could be grouped together in threes, for example, calcium, strontium, and barium; lithium, sodium, and potassium; chlorine, bromine, and iodine. In each group of three, the atomic weight of one element fell halfway between the atomic weights of the other two elements. The pattern seemed too remarkable to be a coincidence. Based on his findings, Dobereiner proposed the Law of Triads in 1829. His work soon prompted other scientists to find patterns among even larger groups of elements.

Another attempt to systematically organize the elements based on their properties was made by the French geologist Alexandre-Émile Beguyer de Chancourtois in 1862. He devised a kind of spiral graph that was arranged on a cylinder, with the elements ordered by increasing atomic weight and with similar elements lined up vertically. De Chancourtois was the first to notice the periodicity of the elements, that is, when the elements were arranged according to their atomic weights, similar elements seemed to occur at regular intervals.

A year later, the English chemist John Newlands also attempted to classify the known elements of his day based on their atomic weight. Like de Chancourtois, he noticed a repeating pattern—every eighth element had similar properties. Newlands called this the Law of Octaves. Although the tables worked out by both de Chancourtois and Newlands were important precursors to the periodic table, neither received much attention at the time.

## Mendeleev

The next milestone in the development of the periodic table was set by the Russian chemist Dmitri Mendeleev, who is generally acknowledged as the "father" of the modern periodic table. Men-

deleev wrote out the names of the elements, along with their atomic weights and other properties, on cards, which he then laid out in rows and columns much like a game of solitaire. When the elements were ordered according to atomic weight, Mendeleev, like de Chancourtois and Newlands, could see that certain chemical properties were repeated periodically; however, not all the elements fit this pattern neatly. Mendeleev's solution was to move certain elements to new positions, despite their accepted weight, in order to group them with other elements sharing similar properties. (Nearly half a century later, after the periodic table was revised according to atomic number rather than atomic weight, these elements fell into place.)

Mendeleev's work on periodic law—which states that the properties of elements recur periodically as their atomic weights increase—was announced in 1869. At about the same time, a German chemist named Julius Lothar Meyer independently arrived at a periodic table that was remarkably similar to Mendeleev's. Unfortunately for Meyer, Mendeleev presented his work to the scientific community first. However, Mendeleev's table was also superior to Meyer's because he left a number of empty spaces to account for elements that were yet to be discovered.

## 20th-Century Revisions

The first major change to the periodic table occurred following the discovery of an entirely new group of elements, the noble gases, between 1895 and 1901. They were called the noble gases because they were believed to be inert—incapable of reacting with other elements to form compounds. (Today it is known that they do enter into chemical combinations, only reluctantly.) These elements were simply added on in a separate column under helium.

The first major revision of the entire periodic table was carried out by Henry Gwyn-Jeffries Moseley, an English physicist who began his research under Ernest Rutherford. In 1914, Moseley showed that each atomic nucleus could be assigned a number that was equal to the number of units of positive charge (later identified as "protons") associated with it. Once the periodic table was reorganized according to this atomic number instead of atomic weight, the few discrepancies in Mendeleev's system disappeared.

Over the years other revisions of the table have been made, including the incorporation of the rare-earth elements (lanthanide series) and the synthetic elements (technetium, promethium, and all the elements with atomic number 93 or higher). The actinides, which are radioactive and mainly synthetic, and the lanthanides do not fit into the same pattern of repeated properties as the other elements, so they are generally shown below the periodic table in separate rows. Most of these changes were the work of American chemist Glenn Seaborg, who codiscovered elements 94 (plutonium) through 102 (nobelium) between 1940 and 1958. Seaborg also suggested a superactinide series of elements, with atomic numbers 122 through 153, but so far none of these has been synthesized or detected. □

# Periodic Table of Elements

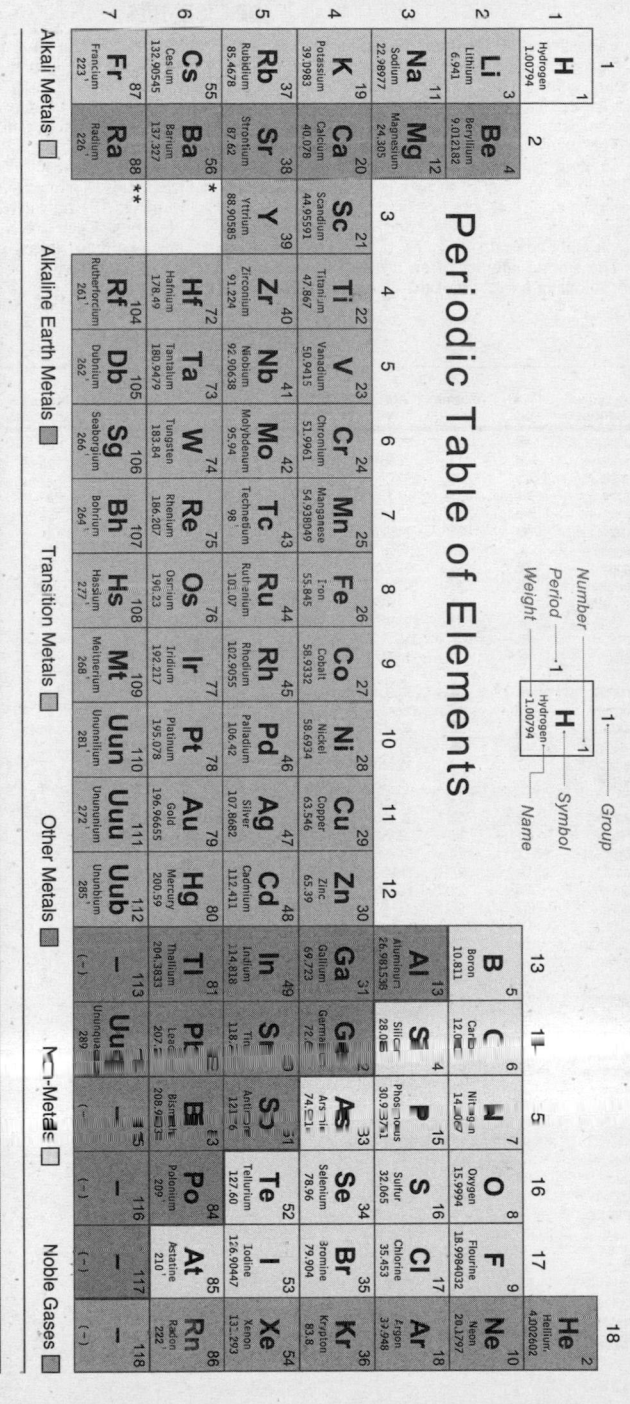

Notes: Elements 110, 111, 112, and 114 are under review. A temporary system of naming recommended by J. Chatt has been used above. 1. Mass number is the longest-lived isotope that is known. Source: International Union of Pure and Applied Chemistry (IUPAC). Web: http://www.chem.qmw.ac.uk/iupac/AtWt/

# The Elements

Elements are the building blocks of nature. Water, for example, is a compound consisting of the elements hydrogen and oxygen. Each element is a pure substance that cannot be split up into any simpler pure substance.

The smallest particle of an element that can exist is an atom. An atom consists of subatomic particles. The most important of these are protons, which have positive electrical charges; electrons, which have negative electrical charges; and neutrons, which are electrically neutral.

The atomic number of an element is the number of protons in one atom of the element. Each element has a different atomic number. For example, the atomic numbers of hydrogen and oxygen are 1 and 8, respectively.

Elements with atomic numbers 1 (hydrogen) to 94 (plutonium) occur naturally on Earth. The remaining artificial elements have been created since 1940 by using nuclear reactors and particle accelerators. Element 100 is named fermium. Elements with atomic numbers 101 onward are known as the transfermium elements. They are also known as heavy elements because their atoms have very large masses compared with atoms of hydrogen, the lightest of all elements.

## Chemical Elements

| Element | Symbol | Atomic no. | Atomic wt. | Specific gravity | Melting point °C | Boiling point °C | No. of isotopes[1] | Discoverer | Year |
|---|---|---|---|---|---|---|---|---|---|
| Actinium | Ac | 89 | $227^2$ | $10.07^3$ | 1051 | 3198 | 11 | Debierne/Giesel | 1899/1902 |
| Aluminum | Al | 13 | 26.981538 | 2.6989 | 660.32 | 2519 | 8 | Wöhler | 1827 |
| Americium | Am | 95 | $243^2$ | 13.67 | 1176 | 2011 | $13^4$ | Seaborg et al. | 1944 |
| Antimony | Sb | 51 | 121.76 | 6.61 | 630.63 | 1587 | 29 | Early historic times | — |
| Argon | Ar | 18 | 39.948 | $1.7837^5$ | −189.35 | −185.85 | 8 | Rayleigh and Ramsay | 1894 |
| Arsenic (gray) | As | 33 | 74.9216 | 5.73 | 817 | 603 | 14 | Albertus Magnus | 1250 |
| Astatine | At | 85 | $210^2$ | — | 302 | — | 21 | Corson et al. | 1940 |
| Barium | Ba | 56 | 137.327 | 3.5 | 727 | 1897 | 25 | Davy | 1808 |
| Berkelium | Bk | 97 | $247^2$ | $14.00^6$ | 1050 (α form) | — | $8^4$ | Seaborg et al. | 1949 |
| Beryllium | Be | 4 | 9.012182 | 1.848 | 1287 | 2471 | 6 | Vauquelin | 1798 |
| Bismuth | Bi | 83 | 208.98038 | 9.747 | 271.40 | 1564 | 19 | Geoffroy the Younger | 1753 |
| Bohrium | Bh | 107 | $264^2$ | — | — | — | — | Armbruster and Münzenberg | 1981 |
| Boron | B | 5 | 10.811 | $2.37^7$ | 2075 | 4000 | 6 | Gay-Lussac and Thénard; Davy | 1808 |
| Bromine | Br | 35 | 79.904 | $3.12^5$ | −7.2 | 58.8 | 19 | Balard | 1826 |
| Cadmium | Cd | 48 | 112.411 | 8.65 | 321.07 | 767 | 22 | Stromeyer | 1817 |
| Calcium | Ca | 20 | 40.078 | 1.55 | 842 | 1484 | 14 | Davy | 1808 |
| Californium | Cf | 98 | $251^2$ | — | 900 | — | $12^4$ | Seaborg et al. | 1950 |
| Carbon | C | 6 | 12.0107 | $1.8–3.5^8$ | 4492 (graphite) | 3825 | 7 | Prehistoric | — |
| Cerium | Ce | 58 | 140.116 | 6.771 | 798 | 3443 | 19 | Berzelius and Hisinger; Klaproth | 1803 |
| Cesium | Cs | 55 | 132.90545 | 1.873 | 28.5 | 671 | 22 | Bunsen and Kirchoff | 1860 |
| Chlorine | Cl | 17 | 35.453 | $1.56^5$ | −101.5 | −34.04 | 11 | Scheele | 1774 |
| Chromium | Cr | 24 | 51.9961 | 7.18–7.20 | 1907 | 2671 | 9 | Vauquelin | 1797 |
| Cobalt | Co | 27 | 58.9332 | 8.9 | 1495 | 2927 | 14 | Brandt | c.1735 |
| Copper | Cu | 29 | 63.546 | 8.96 | 1084.62 | 2562 | 11 | Prehistoric | — |
| Curium | Cm | 96 | $247^2$ | $13.51^3$ | 1345 | 3100 | $13^4$ | Seaborg et al. | 1944 |
| Dubnium | Db | 105 | $262^2$ | — | — | — | — | Ghiorso et al. | 1970 |
| Dysprosium | Dy | 66 | 162.5 | 8.540 | 1412 | 2567 | 21 | de Boisbaudran | 1886 |
| Einsteinium | Es | 99 | $252^2$ | — | 860 | — | $12^4$ | Ghiorso et al. | 1952 |
| Erbium | Er | 68 | 167.259 | 9.045 | 1529 | 2868 | 16 | Mosander | 1843 |
| Europium | Eu | 63 | 151.964 | 5.283 | 822 | 1529 | 21 | Demarcay | 1901 |
| Fermium | Fm | 100 | $257^2$ | — | 1527 | — | $10^4$ | Ghiorso et al. | 1953 |
| Fluorine | F | 9 | 18.9984032 | $1.108^5$ | −219.67 | −188.12 | 6 | Moissan | 1886 |
| Francium | Fr | 87 | $223^2$ | — | 27 | — | 21 | Perey | 1939 |
| Gadolinium | Gd | 64 | 157.25 | 7.898 | 1313 | 3273 | 17 | de Marignac | 1880 |
| Gallium | Ga | 31 | 69.723 | 5.904 | 29.76 | 2204 | 14 | de Boisbaudran | 1875 |
| Germanium | Ge | 32 | 72.64 | 5.323 | 938.25 | 2833 | 17 | Winkler | 1886 |
| Gold | Au | 79 | 196.96655 | 19.32 | 1064.18 | 2856 | 21 | Prehistoric | — |
| Hafnium | Hf | 72 | 178.49 | 13.31 | 2233 | 4603 | 17 | Coster and von Hevesy | 1923 |
| Hassium | Hs | 108 | $277^2$ | — | — | — | — | Armbruster and Münzenberg | 1983 |
| Helium | He | 2 | 4.002602 | $0.1785^5$ | −272.2 | −268.934 | 5 | Janssen | 1868 |
| Holmium | Ho | 67 | 164.93032 | 8.781 | 1474 | 2700 | 29 | Delafontaine and Soret | 1878 |
| Hydrogen | H | 1 | 1.00794 | $0.070^5$ | −259.34 | −252.87 | 3 | Cavendish | 1766 |
| Indium | In | 49 | 114.818 | 7.31 | 156.60 | 2072 | 34 | Reich and Richter | 1863 |
| Iodine | I | 53 | 126.90447 | 4.93 | 113.7 | 184.4 | 24 | Courtois | 1811 |
| Iridium | Ir | 77 | 192.217 | 22.42 | 2446 | 4428 | 25 | Tennant | 1804 |
| Iron | Fe | 26 | 55.845 | 7.894 | 1538 | 2861 | 10 | Prehistoric | — |
| Krypton | Kr | 36 | 83.8 | $3.733^5$ | −157.38 | −153.22 | 23 | Ramsay and Travers | 1898 |
| Lanthanum | La | 57 | 138.9055 | 6.166 | 918 | 3464 | 19 | Mosander | 1839 |
| Lawrencium | Lr | 103 | $262^2$ | — | 1627 | — | $20^4$ | Ghiorso et al. | 1961 |
| Lead | Pb | 82 | 207.2 | 11.35 | 327.46 | 1749 | 29 | Prehistoric | — |

| Element | Symbol | Atomic no. | Atomic wt. | Specific gravity | Melting point °C | Boiling point °C | No. of isotopes[1] | Discoverer | Year |
|---|---|---|---|---|---|---|---|---|---|
| Lithium | Li | 3 | 6.941 | 0.534 | 180.50 | 1342 | 5 | Arfvedson | 1817 |
| Lutetium | Lu | 71 | 174.967 | 9.835 | 1663 | 3402 | 22 | Urbain/ von Welsbach | 1907 |
| Magnesium | Mg | 12 | 24.305 | 1.738 | 650 | 1090 | 8 | Black | 1755 |
| Manganese | Mn | 25 | 54.938049 | 7.21–7.44[9] | 1246 | 2061 | 11 | Gahn, Scheele, and Bergman | 1774 |
| Meitnerium | Mt | 109 | 268[2] | — | — | — | — | GSI, Darmstadt, West Germany | 1982 |
| Mendelevium | Md | 101 | 258[2] | – | 827 | — | 3[4] | Ghiorso et al. | 1955 |
| Mercury | Hg | 80 | 200.59 | 13.546 | –38.83 | 356.73 | 26 | Prehistoric | |
| Molybdenum | Mo | 42 | 95.94 | 10.22 | 2623 | 4639 | 20 | Scheele | 1778 |
| Neodymium | Nd | 60 | 144.24 | 6.80 & 7.004[9] | 1021 | 3074 | 16 | von Welsbach | 1885 |
| Neon | Ne | 10 | 20.1797 | 0.89990 (g/10°C/1 atm) | –248.59 | –246.08 | 8 | Ramsay and Travers | 1898 |
| Neptunium | Np | 93 | 237[2] | 20.25 | 644 | — | 15[4] | McMillan and Abelson | 1940 |
| Nickel | Ni | 28 | 58.6934 | 8.902 | 1455 | 2913 | 11 | Cronstedt | 1751 |
| Niobium (Columbium) | Nb | 41 | 92.90638 | 8.57 | 2477 | 4744 | 24 | Hatchett | 1801 |
| Nitrogen | N | 7 | 14.0067 | 0.808[5] | –210.00 | –195.79 | 8 | Rutherford | 1772 |
| Nobelium | No | 102 | 259[2] | — | 827 | — | 7[4] | Ghiorso et al. | 1958 |
| Osmium | Os | 76 | 190.23 | 22.57 | 3033 | 5012 | 19 | Tennant | 1803 |
| Oxygen | O | 8 | 15.9994 | 1.14[5] | –218.79 | –182.95 | 8 | Priestley/Scheele | 1774 |
| Palladium | Pd | 46 | 106.42 | 12.02 | 1554.9 | 2963 | 21 | Wollaston | 1803 |
| Phosphorous (white) | P | 15 | 30.973761 | 1.82 | 44.15 | 280.5 | 7 | Brand | 1669 |
| Platinum | Pt | 78 | 195.078 | 21.45 | 1768.4 | 3825 | 32 | Ulloa/Wood | 1735/1741 |
| Plutonium | Pu | 94 | 244[2] | 19.84 | 640 | 3228 | 16[4] | Seaborg et al. | 1940 |
| Polonium | Po | 84 | 209[2] | 9.32 | 254 | 962 | 34 | Curie | 1898 |
| Potassium | K | 19 | 39.0983 | 0.862 | 63.5 | 759 | 10 | Davy | 1807 |
| Praseodymium | Pr | 59 | 140.90765 | 6.772 | 931 | 3520 | 15 | von Welsbach | 1885 |
| Promethium | Pm | 61 | 145[2] | — | 1042 | 3000 | 14 | Marinsky et al. | 1945 |
| Protactinium | Pa | 91 | 231.03588 | 15.37[3] | 1572 | — | 14 | Hahn and Meitner | 1917 |
| Radium | Ra | 88 | 226[2] | 5.0? | 700 | — | 15 | Pierre and Marie Curie | 1898 |
| Radon | Rn | 86 | 222[2] | 4.4[5] | –71 | –61.7 | 20 | Dorn | 1900 |
| Rhenium | Re | 75 | 186.207 | 21.02 | 3186 | 5596 | 21 | Noddack, Berg, and Tacke | 1925 |
| Rhodium | Rh | 45 | 102.9055 | 12.41 | 1964 | 3695 | 20 | Wollaston | 1803 |
| Rubidium | Rb | 37 | 85.4678 | 1.532 | 39.30 | 688 | 20 | Bunsen and Kirchoff | 1861 |
| Ruthenium | Ru | 44 | 101.07 | 12.44 | 2334 | 4150 | 16 | Klaus | 1844 |
| Rutherfordium | Rf | 104 | 261[2] | — | — | — | — | Ghiorso et al. | 1969 |
| Samarium | Sm | 62 | 150.36 | 7.536 | 1074 | 1794 | 17 | Boisbaudran | 1879 |
| Scandium | Sc | 21 | 44.95591 | 2.989 | 1541 | 2836 | 15 | Nilson | 1878 |
| Seaborgium | Sg | 106 | 266[2] | — | — | — | — | Ghiorso et al. | 1974 |
| Selenium (gray) | Se | 34 | 78.96 | 4.79 | 220.5 | 685 | 20 | Berzelius | 1817 |
| Silicon | Si | 14 | 28.0855 | 2.33 | 1414 | 3265 | 8 | Berzelius | 1824 |
| Silver | Ag | 47 | 107.8682 | 10.5 | 961.78 | 2162 | 27 | Prehistoric | — |
| Sodium | Na | 11 | 22.98977 | 0.971 | 97.80 | 883 | 7 | Davy | 1807 |
| Strontium | Sr | 38 | 87.62 | 2.54 | 777 | 1382 | 18 | Davy | 1808 |
| Sulfur | S | 16 | 32.065 | 2.07[9] | 95.3 (rhombic) | 444.60 | 10 | Prehistoric | — |
| Tantalum | Ta | 73 | 180.9479 | 16.654 | 3017 | 5458 | 19 | Ekeberg | 1801 |
| Technetium | Tc | 43 | 98[2] | 11.50[3] | 2157 | 4265 | 23 | Perrier and Segré | 1937 |
| Tellurium | Te | 52 | 127.60 | 6.24 | 449.51 | 988 | 29 | von Reichenstein | 1782 |
| Terbium | Tb | 65 | 158.92534 | 8.234 | 1356 | 3230 | 24 | Mosander | 1843 |
| Thallium | Tl | 81 | 204.3833 | 11.85 | 304 | 1473 | 28 | Crookes | 1828 |
| Thulium | Tm | 69 | 168.93421 | 9.314 | 1545 | 1950 | 18 | Cleve | 1879 |
| Tin (white) | Sn | 50 | 118.71 | 7.31 | 231.93 | 2602 | 28 | Prehistoric | — |
| Titanium | Ti | 22 | 47.867 | 4.55 | 1668 | 3287 | 0 | Gregor | 1791 |
| Tungsten | W | 74 | 183.84 | 19.3 | 3422 | 5555 | 22 | J. and F. d'Elhuyar | 1783 |
| Uranium | U | 92 | 238.02891 | 19.05 | 1135 | 4131 | 15 | Peligot | 1841 |
| Vanadium | V | 23 | 50.9415 | 6.11 | 1910 | 3407 | 9 | del Rio | 1801 |
| Xenon | Xe | 54 | 131.293 | 3.52[5] | –111.79 | –108.12 | 31 | Ramsay and Travers | 1898 |
| Ytterbium | Yb | 70 | 173.04 | 6.972 | 819 | 1196 | 16 | Marignac | 1878 |
| Yttrium | Y | 39 | 88.90585 | 4.457 | 1522 | 3345 | 21 | Gadolin | 1794 |
| Zinc | Zn | 30 | 65.39 | 7.133 | 419.5 | 907 | 15 | Prehistoric | — |
| Zirconium | Zr | 40 | 91.224 | 6.506[3] | 1855 | 4409 | 20 | Klaproth | 1789 |

NOTES: Elements 110, 111, 112, and 114 are under review and are thus not included. ≈ means "approximately." < means "less than." 1. Isotopes are different forms of the same element having the same atomic number but different atomic weights. 2. Mass number of the longest-lived isotope that is known. 3. Calculated figure. 4. Artificially produced. 5. Liquid. 6. Estimated. 7. Amorphous. 8. Depending on whether amorphous, graphite, or diamond. 9. Depending on allotropic form.

# Major Discoveries About Human Ancestors

Living and extinct human beings and their near human ancestors are called "hominids" and belong to the *Hominidae* family of primates. They should not be confused with "hominoids," which belong to the *Hominoidea* superfamily of primates and include apes and humans. Scientists theorize that the human and ape lines branched off from a common ancestor 8 million to 6 million years ago.

| Years ago | Species | Discovered | Remarks |
|---|---|---|---|
| 5.8–5.2 million | *Ardipithecus ramidus kadabba* | 1997–1998 in Alayla, Ethiopia | Oldest known human ancestor. About the size of modern chimpanzees, or 4 ft tall standing. Walked upright |
| c. 4.4 million | *Ardipithecus ramidus ramidus* | 1994 in Aramis, Ethiopia | Similar to *A. ramidus kadabba* |
| c. 4.2 million | *Australopithecus anamensis* | 1995, two sites at Lake Turkana in Kenya: Kanapoi and Allia Bay | Possible ancestor of *A. afarensis* (Lucy). Walked upright |
| c. 3.2 million | *Australopithecus afarensis* | 1974 at Hadar in the Afar triangle of eastern Ethiopia; Laetoli, Tanzania | Nicknamed "Lucy." Her skeleton was 3.5 ft (100 cm) tall. Had apelike skull. Walked fully upright. Lived in family groups throughout eastern Africa |
| c. 2.5 million | *Australopithecus africanus* | 1924 at Taung, northern Cape Province, South Africa | Descendant of "Lucy." Lived in social groups |
| c. 2 million | *Australopithecus robustus* | 1938 in Kromdraai, South Africa | Was related to *A. africanus* |
| c. 2 million | *Homo habilis* ("skillful" or "handy man") | 1960 in Olduvai Gorge, Tanzania | First brain enlargement; is believed to have used stone tools |
| c. 1.8 million | *Homo erectus* ("upright man") | 1891 at Trinil, Java, Indonesia | Brain size twice that of *australopithecine* species. "Java Man" may have been a direct ancestor of *Homo sapiens* or instead developed on a separate evolutionary track. He is the first hominid to use fire and the hand ax, and to live in caves |
| c. 100,000(?) | *Homo sapiens* ("knowing or wise man") | 1868, Cro-Magnon, France | Anatomically modern humans |

## Scientific Classification

Classification, or taxonomy, is a system of categorizing living things. There are seven divisions in the system: (1) Kingdom; (2) Phylum or Division; (3) Class; (4) Order; (5) Family; (6) Genus; (7) Species.

Kingdom is the broadest division. There is no consensus about the number of kingdoms, though most scientists support a four-kingdom (Animalia, Plantae, Protista, and Monera) or five-kingdom (Animalia, Plantae, Protista, Monera, and Fungi) system. The lowest, most basic division is species, which consists of organisms that resemble each other and are capable of interbreeding to produce fertile offspring. Species are identified by two names (binomial nomenclature). The first name is the genus, the second is the species.

For example, a lion is *Panthera leo,* a tiger is *Panthera tigris.* The first word is always capitalized, the second is not, and both should be italicized. Humans, of course, are *Homo sapiens.* The full classification for a lion would be: Kingdom, Animalia (animals); Phylum, Chordata (vertebrate animals); Class, Mammalia (mammals); Order, Carnivora (meat eaters); Family, Felidae (all cats); Genus, Panthera (great cats); Species, leo (lions).

## Table of Geological Periods

It is generally assumed that planets are formed by the accretion of gas and dust in a cosmic cloud, but there is no way of estimating the length of this process. Our Earth acquired its present size, more or less, between 4 billion and 5 billion years ago. Life on Earth originated about 2 billion years ago, but there are no good fossil remains from periods earlier than the Cambrian, which began about 550 million years ago. The largely unknown past before the Cambrian Period is referred to as the Pre-Cambrian and is subdivided into the Lower (or older) and Upper (or younger) Pre-Cambrian—also called the Archaeozoic and Proterozoic Eras.

The known geological history of Earth since the beginning of the Cambrian Period is subdivided into three eras, each of which includes a number of periods. They, in turn, are subdivided into subperiods. In a subperiod, a certain section may be especially well known because of rich fossil finds. Such a section is called a formation, and it is usually identified by a place name.

## Paleozoic Era

This era began 570 million years ago and lasted for 325 million years. The name was compounded from Greek *palaios* (old) and *zoön* (animal).

| Period | Duration[1] | Subperiods | Events |
|---|---|---|---|
| Cambrian (from *Cambria*, Latin name for Wales) | 60 | Lower Cambrian<br>Middle Cambrian<br>Upper Cambrian | Invertebrate sea life of many types, proliferating during this and the following period |
| Ordovician (from Latin *Ordovices*, people of early Britain) | 70 | Lower Ordovician<br>Upper Ordovician | First known fishes |
| Silurian (from Latin *Silures*, people of early Wales) | 30 | Lower Silurian<br>Upper Silurian | Gigantic sea scorpions |
| Devonian (from Devonshire in England) | 50 | Lower Devonian<br>Upper Devonian | Proliferation of fishes and other forms of sea life; land still largely lifeless |
| Carboniferous (from Latin *carbo* = coal + *fero* = to bear) | 70 | Lower or Mississippian<br>Upper or Pennsylvanian | Period of maximum coal formation in swampy forests; early insects and first known amphibians |
| Permian (from district of Perm in Russia) | 45 | Lower Permian<br>Upper Permian | Early reptiles and mammals; earliest form of turtles |

1. In millions of years.

## Mesozoic Era

This era began 245 million years ago and lasted for 180 million years. The name was compounded from Greek *mesos* (middle) and *zoön* (animal). Popular name: Age of Reptiles.

| Period | Duration[1] | Subperiods | Events |
|---|---|---|---|
| Triassic (from *trias* = triad) | 37 | Lower or Buntsandstein (from German *bunt* = colorful + *sandstein* = sandstone). Middle or Muschelkalk (from German *muschel* = shell + *kalk* = limestone). Upper or Keuper (old miner's term) | Early saurians (reptiles that resemble lizards) |
| Jurassic (from Jura Mountains) | 62 | Lower or Black Jurassic, or Lias (from French *liais* = hard stone)<br>Middle or Brown Jurassic, or Dogger (old provincial English for ironstone)<br>Upper or White Jurassic, or Malm (Middle English for sand) | Many seagoing reptiles; early large dinosaurs; somewhat later, flying reptiles (pterosaurs), earliest known birds |
| Cretaceous (from Latin *creta* = chalk) | 81 | Lower Cretaceous<br>Upper Cretaceous | Maximum development of dinosaurs; birds proliferating; opossumlike mammals |

1. In millions of years.

## Cenozoic Era

This era began 65 million years ago and includes the geological present. The name was compounded from Greek *kainos* (new) and *zoön* (animal). Popular name: Age of Mammals.

| Period | Duration[1] | Subperiods | Events |
|---|---|---|---|
| Tertiary (originally thought to be the third of only three periods) | c. 65 | Paleocene (from Greek *palaios* = old + *kainos* = new). Eocene (from Greek *au* = ... + *kainos* = new). Oligocene (from Greek *oligos* = few + *kainos* = new). Miocene (from Greek *meios* = less + *kainos* = new). Pliocene (from Greek *pleios* = more + *kainos* = new) | First mammals other than ... amber, rich insect fauna, early bats, steady increase of large mammals. Mammals closely resembling present types; protohumans |
| Pleistocene (from Greek *pleistos* = most + *kainos* = new) (popular name: Ice Age) | 2.0 | Four major glaciations, named Günz, Mindel, Riss, and Würm, originally the names of rivers. Last glaciation ended 10,000 to 15,000 years ago | Various forms of early humans |
| Holocene (from Greek *holos* = entire + *kainos* = new) | 0.01 | The last 10,000 years to the present | Earliest written documents c. 3200 B.C., Sumer |

1. In millions of years.

# The Nation's Highest Science and Technology Honors

## The National Medal of Science

The National Medal of Science, established by Congress in 1959, is administered by the National Science Foundation. The medal honors the contributions made by outstanding individuals who have significantly advanced knowledge in the following fields: physics, biology, chemistry, mathematics, engineering, and sociology and other behavioral sciences.

The 2001 National Medal of Science recipients were awarded their medals by President George W. Bush on June 12, 2002.

### 2001 National Medal of Science Recipients

**Andreas Acrivos,** Albert Einstein Professor of Science and Engineering, City College of the City University of New York, for his pioneering research in fluid mechanics and leadership in the fluid mechanics and chemical engineering communities.

**Francisco J. Ayala,** Donald Bren Professor of Biological Sciences, University of California at Irvine, for his theoretical and experimental discoveries on the origin of species, genetic diversity, and population dynamics that led to a new understanding of biological evolution, and for his distinguished contributions to education and the promotion of public understanding of science.

**George F. Bass,** Distinguished Professor Emeritus of Nautical Archaeology and Founder, The Institute of Nautical Archaeology, Texas A&M University, for pioneering ocean technology and creating a new branch of scholarship, nautical archaeology, which has furthered understanding of the histories of economics, technology, and literacy.

**Mario R. Capecchi,** Professor of Human Genetics, University of Utah School of Medicine, for his groundbreaking biomedical research, which has provided a powerful tool for understanding disease mechanisms and gene functions.

**Marvin L. Cohen,** University Professor of Physics, University of California at Berkeley, for his creation and application of a quantum theory for explaining and predicting properties of real materials, which formed the basis for semiconductor physics and nanoscience.

**Ernest R. Davidson,** Distinguished Professor and the Robert and Marjorie Mann Chair of Computational Quantum Chemistry, Indiana University, for his innovative leadership and numerous conceptual and algorithmic developments that led to the field of computational quantum chemistry and made possible the accurate modeling of chemical reactions and molecular response to radiation.

**Raymond Davis,** Research Professor, Brookhaven National Laboratory, for creating the first experiment to measure solar neutrino flux, continuing research on tracking the time dependence of the solar neutrino flux, and creating the new field of neutrino astronomy.

**Ann M. Graybiel,** Walter A. Rosenblith Professor of Neuroscience, Massachusetts Institute of Technology, for her pioneering contributions to the understanding of the anatomy and physiology of the brain, including the structure, chemistry, and function of the pathways involved in thought and movement.

**Charles D. Keeling,** Professor of Oceanography, Scripps Institution of Oceanography, for his pioneering and fundamental research on atmospheric and oceanic carbon dioxide, the basis for understanding the global carbon cycle and global warming.

**Gene E. Likens,** Director and President and G. Evelyn Hutchinson Chair in Ecology, Institute of Ecosystem Studies, for his discovery of acid rain in North America and his sustained leadership in developing the fields of ecology and ecosystem science.

**Victor A. McKusick,** University Professor of Medical Genetics, Professor of Biology, Professor of Epidemiology, and Professor of Medicine, Johns Hopkins University School of Medicine, for his contributions to the founding of medical genetics and the human genome project.

**Calyampudi R. Rao,** Eberly Professor in Statistics, Pennsylvania State University, for his pioneering contributions to statistical theory and methodology, which have enriched the physical, biological, mathematical, economic, and engineering sciences.

**Gabor A. Somorjai,** Professor of Chemistry and University Professor, University of California at Berkeley, for his innovative study of surfaces at the molecular level, which has revolutionized the way scientists think about chemical reactions and has contributed to the development of many useful products, including high-octane gasoline and plastic polymers.

**Elias M. Stein,** Albert Baldwin Dod Professor of Mathematics, Princeton University, for his contributions to mathematical analysis, especially harmonic analysis, partial differential equations, several complex variables, and representation theory.

**Harold Varmus,** President and Chief Executive Officer, Memorial Sloan-Kettering Cancer Center, for his codiscovery of the cellular origins of retroviral oncogenes, which heralded a new era in the control of human cancer, and for reinvigorating the nation's medical research enterprise.

## The National Medal of Technology

The National Medal of Technology, established by Congress in 1980, is administered by the U.S. Department of Commerce. The medal is awarded for technological innovation and the advancement of U.S. global competitiveness. The medal also recognizes groundbreaking contributions that commercialize a technology, create jobs, improve productivity, or stimulate the nation's growth and development in other ways.

The 2001 National Medal of Technology recipients were awarded their medals by President George W. Bush on June 12, 2002.

### 2001 National Medal of Technology Recipients

**John A. Ewen,** President, Catalyst Research Corporation, for his discoveries in the field of metallocene catalysis, which have revolutionized the production of polyethylene and polypropylene plastics and stimulated the growth of the entire industry.

**Arun N. Netravali,** Chief Scientist, Lucent Technologies, and Past President of Bell Labs, for pioneering contributions to the technology involved in compressing images for digital and high-definition television, video conferencing systems, streaming video over the Internet, and multimedia computers; and for technical expertise and leadership that have kept Bell Labs at the forefront in communications technology.

**Sidney Pestka, M.D.,** University of Medicine & Dentistry of New Jersey, Robert Wood Johnson Medical School, for pioneering achievements that led to the development of interferons—substances produced by cells that act to prevent viral replication—for the treatment of cancers, viral diseases such as hepatitis B and C, and multiple sclerosis; for fundamental technologies leading to other biotherapeutics; and for his basic, overall contribution to the development of the biotechnology industry.

**Jerry M. Woodall,** C. Baldwin Sawyer Professor of Electrical Engineering, Yale University, for the invention and development of compound semiconductor materials and devices, such as light-emitting diodes, lasers, ultra-fast transistors, and solar cells. His inventions include the infrared LED (light-emitting diode), which is used in CD players, TV remote controls, computer networks, cell phones, and satellites.

**The Dow Chemical Company,** a leading science and technology company, "for the vision to create great science and innovative technology in the chemical industry and the positive impact that commercialization of this technology has had on society."

# Branches of Science

Science describes an area of knowledge, typically about something in the physical world, that can be explained in terms of scientific observation or the scientific method. The scientific method is a discovery process that has evolved over several hundred years and can be summarized as follows:

- a phenomenon in the physical world is observed
- an explanation, or hypothesis, for the phenomenon is formed
- the hypothesis is tested by means of objective, reproducible experiments

If the results of the experiments support the hypothesis, it becomes accepted as scientific theory. Later, if new information is found to contradict the hypothesis, it may be revised or abandoned in favor of a new hypothesis, which is then subjected to additional experiments.

The sciences that describe the physical universe are categorized in different ways. The largest distinction in science is whether a science is pure, or theoretical, or whether it is applied, or practical. Pure science explains a phenomenon, while applied science determines how a particular phenomenon

may be put to use. In general, pure science is divided into the following categories:

- Physical sciences, which deal with matter and energy and allow us to describe the material universe in terms of weight, mass, volume, and other standard, objective measures.
- Earth sciences, which explain the phenomena of the Earth, its atmosphere, and the solar system to which it belongs.
- Life sciences, which describe living organisms, their internal processes, and their relationship to each other and the environment.

However, these three categories of pure science have areas of overlap, where one type of phenomenon may be associated with another. For example, light (studied in physics) is the energy source behind the (chemical) process of photosynthesis, or food production, in plants (studied in biology). For this reason, distinctions between pure sciences, and even between pure and applied sciences, can blur, and a new compound science can develop. An example of this is biochemistry, in which the chemical processes of living things (such as photosynthesis) are observed and explained.

| Physical Sciences | Life Sciences | Earth Sciences |
|---|---|---|
| Physics<br>Kinetics<br>Mechanics<br>Electromagnetics<br>Thermodynamics | Biology<br>Botany<br>Zoology | Geology<br>Meteorology<br>Astronomy |
| Chemistry<br>Inorganic Chemistry<br>Electrochemistry<br>Analytical Chemistry | | |
| **Examples of Overlapping Sciences** | | |
| Physics + Chemistry =<br>Physical Chemistry | Biology + Chemistry =<br>Biochemistry<br>Organic Chemistry | Geology + Chemistry =<br>Geochemistry |
| Astronomy + Physics =<br>Astrophysics | Biology + Geology =<br>Paleontology | Geology + Astronomy =<br>Astrogeology |
| | Biology + Astronomy + Physics =<br>Astronautics | |

# Roundup of Recent Discoveries

## Mystery Skull

In July 2002, an international team led by French paleontologist Michel Brunet announced the discovery of a humanlike skull that may be up to seven million years old, twice as old as any others found. The previously unknown ape species, named *Sahelanthropus tchadensis,* was found in Chad, in central Africa. The remarkably complete skull was nicknamed "Toumai," which means "hope of life" in the Goran language. Compared to the famous four-million-year-old "Lucy," Toumai looks more modern and less chimplike, with a shorter, flatter face and smaller canine teeth.

Is Toumai a direct ancestor of later hominids, perhaps even modern humans? While some scientists support this theory, others believe that Toumai was one of various hominids that once walked, perhaps upright, on the African continent. In this model, evolution looks less like a tree, with humans and apes branching from a single common ancestor, than a bush in which various hominids evolved and became extinct. Meanwhile, some rival anthropologists think the skull is that of an ancient female "proto-gorilla."

## First Synthetic Virus

U.S. scientists at the State University of New York at Stony Brook have created the first synthetic virus. Using directions downloaded from the Internet and chemicals obtained from a mail-order company, they built an apparently identical copy of the poliovirus. When injected into lab mice, the synthetic virus caused paralysis and then death. The scientists, who published their findings in the online journal *Science Express* in July 2002, said that they undertook the experiment to prove the alarming fact that a functional pathogenic virus could be constructed without access to a natural virus.

Is this small step for biochemistry a great leap for bioterrorism? Scientists say that few people now have the skill to build a synthetic virus, much less one that could be an efficient bioweapon. The genome of the highly contagious smallpox virus is about 25 times as long as that of the poliovirus and has a more complex process of replication. But its synthesis may one day be possible. This being so, the experiment raises questions about the wisdom of ceasing vaccination when a natural virus has been eradicated.

## More Moons for Jupiter

In May 2002 astronomers announced the discovery of 11 new moons orbiting Jupiter. This means that Jupiter is not only the largest planet in our solar system but the one with the most moons—a total of 39. The newly discovered moons are relatively small and have irregular orbits. Researchers say they are probably rocky, like asteroids, and were likely trapped in Jupiter's orbit during the first million years of our solar system.

The moons were first detected in images taken by the Canada-France-Hawaii Telescope in Mauna Kea, Hawaii. Their orbits were verified at the University of Hawaii. Improved technology has been a factor in the discovery of dozens of moons in recent years, including ten Jovian moons in late 2000.

## Very Personal Computer

In Jan. 2002 the Virginia-based Xybernaut company debuted the Poma ("personal multimedia appliance"), the first wearable personal computer for consumers. An 11-ounce unit clips onto a belt, a 2-ounce handheld knob takes the place of a mouse, and an inch-wide 3-ounce screen slips over one eye—an innovation the company had developed to let on-duty soldiers safely read commands.

But at $1,499, it's no bargain. The Poma is not only awkward—the screen is difficult to position, and wearers must tap at a virtual keyboard on its edge—but low on power. It may, however, foreshadow a time when instead of lugging a laptop and a cellular phone, a commuter can don office equipment as easily as sunglasses.

## Elusive Element

The heyday of element 118 was short-lived. Just three years after a group of Berkeley scientists announced the discovery of the heaviest known element—element 118, or ununoctium—they officially retracted the news, saying they had been in error. Like the other heavy elements following element 100, ununoctium is not found in nature and would be expected to decay a fraction of a second after synthesis in a laboratory. However, follow-up experiments failed to duplicate the element's synthesis, and reanalysis of the original data could not confirm its decay sequence.

## Cloning a Rare Breed . . .

A team of European scientists led by Pasqualino Loi of the University of Teramo, Italy, announced in Oct. 2001 that they had produced the first surviving clone of an endangered animal. A baby mouflon—a wild sheep found in Sardinia, Corsica, and Cyprus—was created by extracting DNA from the eggs of two mouflon ewes found dead and injecting it into emptied egg cells from domestic ewes. The resulting embryos were implanted in four domestic ewes, one of which delivered the mouflon.

The cloned mouflon lamb appears normal and is living at a wildlife center in Sardinia. This success came on the heels of failed attempts to clone an argali sheep and a gaur ox, both of which are endangered. Some researchers hope that cloning may one day help preserve endangered animal populations.

## . . . and the Common Cat

After hundreds of cell-transfer procedures and the loss of 86 embryos, a team of scientists at Texas A&M University found their grail: a calico kitten.

The first cloned pet, "CC" (for "Copy Cat") was born in Dec. 2001 by C-section and appears healthy. Although she is a genetic clone, CC is not identical with either her genetic calico mother or her surrogate tabby mother; a cat's markings are determined partly by genetics and partly by the process of fetal development.

Scientists hope their findings may aid endocrinology research as well as endangered wildcats. However, animal welfare groups concerned with pet overpopulation have decried the project. The work was funded by Arizona millionaire John Sperling, who dreams of cloning his dog. Sperling is also the founder of Genetic Savings and Clone, a Texas company that hopes to clone pets for profit.

## Dashing Dino

British scientists believe they have proof that a *Tyrannosaurus rex* ancestor sprinted across Oxfordshire, England, more than 160 million years ago. The well-preserved footprints, which extend nearly 600 ft, probably belonged to a two-ton Megalosaurus. At first, the giant beast seemed to be waddling at about 4 mph. But suddenly, the spacing between its footprints doubled as it broke into a run of 18 mph. Why the change in speed? Perhaps the massive meat-eater laid eyes on a tasty herbivore.

Although scientists had evidence that smaller dinosaurs could run, many thought that large dinosaurs were too heavy and clumsy to move quickly. These tracks may be the best proof yet that the big guys could gather speed.

## Green Ham and Eggs?

What do you get when you cross a pig with some spinach? Healthier pork—or so hopes a research team that has implanted spinach genes into pigs. In Jan. 2002, after three years of experiments, the team at Kinki University in Osaka, Japan, announced that it has two generations of pigs that sport the spinach gene. This is the first time that plant genes have functioned normally in living animals.

The implanted spinach gene, known as FAD2, transforms about 20% of the pigs' saturated fats into unsaturated fats, making for less fatty meat. But don't expect to see lean green bacon at a store near you—only about 1% of the pigs in the experiment inherited the spinach gene.

## Mars Meteorites

Scientists confirmed in Jan. 2002 that five recently discovered meteorites had fallen from the red planet. Like most of the other 19 known Mars meteorites, these were found in Antarctica and in the deserts of Oman and the Sahara areas with little plant cover that could hide space rocks. Scientists hope the meteorites will offer clues about whether primitive life once existed on Mars.

Each year about 20,000 meteorites reach Earth, but few are from Mars. The new meteorites probably broke off from Mars billions of years ago, after an asteroid collision, and floated through space until landing on Earth.

## A New New Yorker

A centipede of a new genus and species was discovered in a pile of leaf litter in New York's Central Park. At 10.3 mm (about .4 in.) long, the pale yellow creature may be the world's smallest centipede. Nevertheless, it has an above-average 41 pairs of legs. Formally known as *Nannarrup hoffmani,* it appears to be more closely related to Asian centipedes than native ones, suggesting that, like many denizens of Manhattan, it is an immigrant, perhaps having arrived in potted soil.

## Plants in Space?

In spring 2002 the European Space Agency (ESA) and NASA began testing a machine that could make it possible to cultivate plants in outer space. Developed by the Denmark-based Rovsing company, the European Modular Cultivation System (EMCS) centers on a climate chamber in which temperature, humidity, air, light, and water can be computer-controlled. The EMCS will be tested at the International Space Station in 2003.

The extraterrestrial hothouse isn't just a high-tech gardening gadget—it may yield new evidence about the effect of gravity on plant growth. And more importantly, it could someday provide astronauts on long missions a means of producing their own food crops.

## Tropical Colorado

Although Colorado is ravaged by drought today, 64 million years ago it may have been home to a lush rainforest. Excavations at Castle Rock, a site south of Denver, have yielded fossils of tropical-looking blooms, giant fronds, and trees 6 ft across—more than 100 kinds of flora in all, double the variety found in many Brazilian rainforests today. Scientists believe the plants were nurtured in a hot, humid climate with an annual rainfall of some 100 in. A vast inland sea may have provided some of the moisture.

This rainforest flourished only a million years after the dinosaurs and most other life on Earth died out, probably as the result of an asteroid collision. Scientists had previously thought that it took plant life about 10 million years to recover from the devastation. The Castle Rock fossils suggest that recovery, at least in some areas, may have been astonishingly quick.

## Robo-Rats

Other rats have navigated obstacle courses, but five at the State University of New York did so by remote control—and, reportedly, enjoyed it. A research team implanted electrodes into pleasure-sensing zones of the rats' brains, as well as the zones that register obstacles near their whiskers. Using radio signals transmitted by computer, the scientists guided the rats by stimulating "touch" signals near their whiskers and rewarding them with electrical pulses, which team leader Sanjiv Talwar described as producing a "burst of happiness." The whiskery robots skirted ledges, climbed ladders, and explored rubble via commands issued up to 1,640 ft away.

Researchers believe that the rats, by accessing areas humans and machines cannot reach, could someday aid search-and-rescue missions, minefield clearing, and, ironically, pest control. The project was inspired in part by rescue efforts following the Sept. 11 terrorist attacks and received funding from the U.S. military.

## Segway Human Transporter

In Dec. 2001 U.S. engineer Dean Kamen unveiled the Segway Human Transporter, a scooterlike "superinvention" he hopes will transform short-distance travel while reducing traffic and pollution. Also known as "the people-mover," the two-wheeled, battery-powered Segway is self-balancing, thanks to aviation-grade gyroscopes, and can travel up to 15 mph. "Tilt sensors" permit riders to guide the Segway simply by leaning. The problem of where Segway riders might fit among cars, bicyclists, and pedestrians has yet to be resolved.

The U.S. Postal Service and the National Park Service are exploring the Segway's possibilities, as are some corporations and police forces. Field testing by the Atlanta police in May 2002 led to the first Segway-related accident, when the machine hit a bump on the sidewalk and spilled its rider. A consumer version of the Segway will be available by the end of 2002 for about $3,000.

## Ancient Chocoholics

Yet one more way the ancient Maya were ahead of their time: love of hot chocolate. In July 2002 scientists at Hershey Foods confirmed that brown stains on a 2,600-year-old Mayan pot found in northern Belize were traces of a cocoa beverage. Spanish accounts from the 1500s described the widespread use of liquid chocolate among the Maya, who consumed it with most meals. The ancient residue offers proof that they had been enjoying cocoa drinks for at least a millennium before the conquest. Mayan hot chocolate was served thick, with a foamy top, and might contain honey, maize, or chili.

# Inventions & Discoveries

*See also* Famous Firsts in Aviation, Nobel Prizes.

**Adrenaline:** (isolation of) John Jacob Abel, U.S., 1897.

**Aerosol can:** Erik Rotheim, Norway, 1926.

**Air brake:** George Westinghouse, U.S., 1868.

**Air conditioning:** Willis Carrier, U.S., 1911.

**Airship:** (non-rigid) Henri Giffard, France, 1852; (rigid) Ferdinand von Zeppelin, Germany, 1900.

**Aluminum manufacture:** (by electrolytic action) Charles M. Hall, U.S., 1866.

**Anatomy, human:** (*De fabrica corporis humani,* an illustrated systematic study of the human body) Andreas Vesalius, Belgium, 1543; (comparative: parts of an organism are correlated to the functioning whole) Georges Cuvier, France, 1799–1805.

**Anesthetic:** (first use of anesthetic—ether—on humans) Crawford W. Long, U.S., 1842.

**Antibiotics:** (first demonstration of antibiotic effect) Louis Pasteur, Jules-François Joubert, France, 1887; (discovery of penicillin, first modern antibiotic) Alexander Fleming, Scotland, 1928; (penicillin's infection-fighting properties) Howard Florey, Ernst Chain, England, 1940.

**Antiseptic:** (surgery) Joseph Lister, England, 1867.

**Antitoxin, diphtheria:** Emil von Behring, Germany, 1890.

**Appliances, electric:** (fan) Schuyler Wheeler, U.S., 1882; (flatiron) Henry W. Seely, U.S., 1882; (stove) Hadaway, U.S., 1896; (washing machine) Alva Fisher, U.S., 1906.

**Aqualung:** Jacques-Yves Cousteau, Emile Gagnan, France, 1943.

**Aspirin:** Dr. Felix Hoffman, Germany, 1899.

**Astronomical calculator:** The Antikythera device, first century B.C., Greece. Found off island of Antikythera in 1900.

**Atom:** (nuclear model of) Ernest Rutherford, England, 1911.

**Atomic theory:** (ancient) Leucippus, Democritus, Greece, c. 500 B.C.; Lucretius, Rome c.100 B.C.; (modern) John Dalton, England, 1808.

**Atomic structure:** (formulated nuclear model of atom, Rutherford model) Ernest Rutherford, England, 1911; (proposed current concept of atomic structure, the Bohr model) Niels Bohr, Denmark, 1913.

**Automobile:** (first with internal combustion engine, 250 rpm) Karl Benz, Germany, 1885; (first with practical high-speed internal combustion engine, 900 rpm) Gottlieb Daimler, Germany, 1885; (first true automobile, not carriage with motor) René Panhard, Emile Lavassor, France, 1891; (carburetor, spray) Charles E. Duryea, U.S., 1892.

**Autopilot:** (for aircraft) Elmer A. Sperry, U.S., c.1910, first successful test, 1912, in a Curtiss flying boat.

**Avogadro's law:** (equal volumes of all gases at the same temperature and pressure contain equal number of molecules) Amedeo Avogadro, Italy, 1811.

**Bacteria:** Anton van Leeuwenhoek, The Netherlands, 1683.

**Balloon, hot-air:** Joseph and Jacques Montgolfier, France, 1783.

**Barbed wire:** (most popular) Joseph E. Glidden, U.S., 1873.

**Bar codes (computer-scanned binary signal code):** (retail trade use) Monarch Marking, U.S. 1970; (industrial use) Plessey Telecommunications, England, 1970.

**Barometer:** Evangelista Torricelli, Italy, 1643.

**Bicycle:** Karl D. von Sauerbronn, Germany, 1816; (first modern model) James Starley, England, 1884.

**Big Bang theory:** (the universe originated with a huge explosion) George LeMaitre, Belgium, 1927; (modified LeMaitre theory labeled "Big Bang") George A. Gamow, U.S., 1948; (cosmic microwave background radiation discovered, confirms theory) Arno A. Penzias and Robert W. Wilson, U.S., 1965.

---

### Science Websites

**National Science Foundation:** www.nsf.gov

**National Academy of Sciences:** www.nas.edu

**American Association for the Advancement of Science:** www.aaas.org/

**Federation of American Scientists:** www.fas.org

**The Franklin Institute:** www.fi.edu/tfi/welcome.html

**Science News Online:** www.sciencenews.org

**Popular Science:** www.popsci.com

**Periodic Table of Elements:** WebElements Periodic Table: www.webelements.com

**Dinosauria Online:** www.dinosauria.com/

**Discovery Channel Online:** www.discovery.com

**Fermi National Accelerator Lab:** www.fnal.gov/

**Argonne National Laboratory:** www.anl.gov/

**American Geophysical Union:** http://earth.agu.org/homepage.html

**American Museum of Natural History:** www.amnh.org

**Newton** (for K–12 teachers and students): www.newton.dep.anl.gov

**Field Museum** (Chicago): www.fmnh.org

**Santa Barbara Museum of Natural History:** www.sbnature.org

**Inventors Hall of Fame:** www.invent.org/

**The Smithsonian Web:** www.si.edu

**Blood, circulation of:** William Harvey, England, 1628.

**Boyle's law:** (relation between pressure and volume in gases) Robert Boyle, Ireland, 1662.

**Braille:** Louis Braille, France, 1829.

**Bridges:** (suspension, iron chains) James Finley, Pa., 1800; (wire suspension) Marc Seguin, Lyons, 1825; (truss) Ithiel Town, U.S., 1820.

**Bullet:** (conical) Claude Minié, France, 1849.

**Calculating machine:** (logarithms: made multiplying easier and thus calculators practical) John Napier, Scotland, 1614; (slide rule) William Oughtred, England, 1632; (digital calculator) Blaise Pascal, 1642; (multiplication machine) Gottfried Leibniz, Germany, 1671; (important 19th-century contributors to modern machine) Frank S. Baldwin, Jay R. Monroe, Dorr E. Felt, W. T. Ohdner, William Burroughs, all U.S.; ("analytical engine" design, included concepts of programming, taping) Charles Babbage, England, 1835.

**Calculus:** Isaac Newton, England, 1669; (differential calculus) Gottfried Leibniz, Germany, 1684.

**Camera:** (hand-held) George Eastman, U.S., 1888; (Polaroid Land) Edwin Land, U.S., 1948.

**"Canals" of Mars:** Giovanni Schiaparelli, Italy, 1877.

**Carpet sweeper:** Melville R. Bissell, U.S., 1876.

**Car radio:** William Lear, Elmer Wavering, U.S., 1929, manufactured by Galvin Manufacturing Co., "Motorola."

**Cells:** (word used to describe microscopic examination of cork) Robert Hooke, England, 1665; (theory: cells are common structural and functional unit of all living organisms) Theodor Schwann, Matthias Schleiden, 1838–1839.

**Cement, Portland:** Joseph Aspdin, England, 1824.

**Chewing gum:** (spruce-based) John Curtis, U.S., 1848; (chicle-based) Thomas Adams, U.S., 1870.

**Cholera bacterium:** Robert Koch, Germany, 1883.

**Circuit, integrated:** (theoretical) G.W.A. Dummer, England, 1952; (phase-shift oscillator) Jack S. Kilby, Texas Instruments, U.S., 1959.

**Classification of plants:** (first modern, based on comparative study of forms) Andrea Cesalpino, Italy, 1583; (classification of plants and animals by genera and species) Carolus Linnaeus, Sweden, 1737–1753.

**Clock, pendulum:** Christian Huygens, The Netherlands, 1656.

**Coca-Cola:** John Pemberton, U.S., 1886.

**Combustion:** (nature of) Antoine Lavoisier, France, 1777.

**Compact disk:** RCA, U.S., 1972.

**Computers:** (first design of analytical engine) Charles Babbage, 1830s; (ENIAC, Electronic Numerical Integrator and Calculator, first all-electronic, completed) John Presper Eckert, Jr., John Mauchly, U.S., 1945; (dedicated at University of Pennsylvania) 1946; (UNIVAC, Universal Automatic Computer, handled both numeric and alphabetic data) 1951; (personal computer) Steve Wozniak, U.S., 1976.

**Concrete:** (reinforced) Joseph Monier, France, 1877.

Conditioned reflex: Ivan Pavlov, Russia, c.1910.

**Conservation of electric charge:** (the total electric charge of the universe or any closed system is constant) Benjamin Franklin, U.S., 1751–1754.

**Contagion theory:** (infectious diseases caused by living agent transmitted from person to person) Girolamo Fracastoro, Italy, 1546.

**Continental drift theory:** (geographer who pieced together continents into a single landmass on maps) Antonio Snider-Pellegrini, France, 1858; (first proposed in lecture) Frank Taylor, U.S.; (first comprehensive detailed theory) Alfred Wegener, Germany, 1912.

**Contraceptive, oral:** Gregory Pincus, Min Chuch Chang, John Rock, Carl Djerassi, U.S., 1951.

**Converter, Bessemer:** William Kelly, U.S., 1851.

**Cosmetics:** Egypt, c. 4000 B.C.

**Cosmic string theory:** (first postulated) Thomas Kibble, 1976.

**Cotton gin:** Eli Whitney, U.S., 1793.

**Crossbow:** China, c. 300 B.C.

**Cyclotron:** Ernest O. Lawrence, U.S., 1931.

**Defibrillator:** Dr. William Bennett Kouwenhoven, U.S., 1932; (implantable) M. Stephen Heilman, MD, Dr. Alois Langer, Morton Mower, MD, Michel Mirowski, MD, 1980.

**Deuterium:** (heavy hydrogen) Harold Urey, U.S., 1931.

**Disease:** (chemicals in treatment of) crusaded by Philippus Paracelsus, 1527–1541; (germ theory) Louis Pasteur, France, 1862–1877.

**DNA:** (deoxyribonucleic acid) Friedrich Meischer, Germany, 1869; (determination of double-helical structure) Rosalind Elsie Franklin, F. H. Crick, England, James D. Watson, U.S., 1953.

**Dye:** (aniline, start of synthetic dye industry) William H. Perkin, England, 1856.

**Dynamite:** Alfred Nobel, Sweden, 1867.

**Electric cooking utensil:** (first) patented by St. George Lane-Fox, England, 1874.

**Electric generator (dynamo):** (laboratory model) Michael Faraday, England, 1832; Joseph Henry, U.S., c.1832; (hand-driven model) Hippolyte Pixii, France, 1833; (alternating-current generator) Nikola Tesla, U.S., 1892.

**Thomas Alva Edison**
**(1847–1931)** *Library of Congress*

**Electric lamp:** (arc lamp) Sir Humphrey Davy, England, 1801; (fluorescent lamp) A.E. Becquerel, France, 1867; (incandescent lamp) Sir Joseph Swann, England, Thomas A. Edison, U.S., contemporaneously, 1870s; (carbon arc street lamp) Charles F. Brush, U.S., 1879; (first widely marketed incandescent lamp) Thomas A. Edison, U.S., 1879; (mercury vapor lamp) Peter Cooper Hewitt, U.S., 1903; (neon lamp) Georges Claude, France, 1911; (tungsten filament) Irving Langmuir, U.S., 1915.

**Electrocardiography:** Demonstrated by Augustus Waller, 1887; (first practical device for recording activity of heart) Willem Einthoven, 1903, Dutch physiologist.

**Electromagnet:** William Sturgeon, England, 1823.

**Electron:** Sir Joseph J. Thompson, England, 1897.

**Elevator, passenger:** (safety device permitting use by passengers) Elisha G. Otis, U.S., 1852; (elevator utilizing safety device) 1857.

**E = mc²:** (equivalence of mass and energy) Albert Einstein, Switzerland, 1907.

**Engine, internal combustion:** No single inventor. Fundamental theory established by Sadi Carnot, France, 1824; (two-stroke) Etienne Lenoir, France, 1860; (ideal operating cycle for four-stroke) Alphonse Beau de Roche, France, 1862; (operating four-stroke) Nikolaus Otto, Germany, 1876; (diesel) Rudolf Diesel, Germany, 1892; (rotary) Felix Wankel, Germany, 1956.

**Evolution:** (organic) Jean-Baptiste Lamarck, France, 1809; (by natural selection) Charles Darwin, England, 1859.

**Exclusion principle:** (no two electrons in an atom can occupy the same energy level) Wolfgang Pauli, Germany, 1925.

**Expanding universe theory:** (first proposed) George LeMaitre, Belgium, 1927; (discovered first direct evidence that the universe is expanding) Edwin P. Hubble, U.S., 1929; (Hubble constant: a measure of the rate at which the universe is expanding) Edwin P. Hubble, U.S., 1929.

**Falling bodies, law of:** Galileo Galilei, Italy, 1590.

**Fermentation:** (microorganisms as cause of) Louis Pasteur, France, c.1860.

**Fiber optics:** Narinder Kapany, England, 1955.

**Fibers, man-made:** (nitrocellulose fibers treated to change flammable nitrocellulose to harmless cellulose, precursor of rayon) Sir Joseph Swann, England, 1883; (rayon) Count Hilaire de Chardonnet, France, 1889; (Celanese) Henry and Camille Dreyfuss, U.S., England, 1921; (research on polyesters and polyamides, basis for modern man-made fibers) U.S., England, Germany, 1930s; (nylon) Wallace H. Carothers, U.S., 1935.

**Frozen food:** Clarence Birdseye, U.S., 1924.

**Gene transfer:** (recombinant DNA organism) Herbert Boyer, Stanley Cohen, U.S., 1973; (human) Steven Rosenberg, R. Michael Blaese, W. French Anderson, U.S., 1989.

**Geometry, elements of:** Euclid, Alexandria, Egypt, c. 300 B.C.; (analytic) René Descartes, France; and Pierre de Fermat, Switzerland, 1637.

**Gravitation, law of:** Sir Isaac Newton, England, c.1665 (published 1687).

**Gunpowder:** China, c.700.

**Gyrocompass:** Elmer A. Sperry, U.S., 1905.

**Gyroscope:** Jean Léon Foucault, France, 1852.

**Halley's Comet:** Edmund Halley, England, 1705.

**Heart implanted in human, permanent artificial:** Dr. Robert Jarvik, U.S., 1982.

**Heart, temporary artificial:** Willem Kolft, 1957.

**Helicopter:** (double rotor) Heinrich Focke, Germany, 1936; (single rotor) Igor Sikorsky, U.S., 1939.

**Helium first observed on sun:** Sir Joseph Lockyer, England, 1868.

**Heredity, laws of:** Gregor Mendel, Austria, 1865.

**Holograph:** Dennis Gabor, England, 1947.

**Home videotape systems (VCR):** (Betamax) Sony, Japan, 1975; (VHS) Matsushita, Japan, 1975.

**Ice age theory:** Louis Agassiz, Swiss-American, 1840.

**Induction, electric:** Joseph Henry, U.S., 1828.

**Insulin:** (first isolated) Sir Frederick G. Banting and Charles H. Best, Canada, 1921; (discovery first published) Banting and Best, 1922; (Nobel Prize awarded for purification for use in humans) John Macleod and Banting, 1923; (first synthesized), China, 1966.

**Intelligence testing:** Alfred Binet, Theodore Simon, France, 1905.

**Interferon:** Alick Isaacs, Jean Lindemann, England, Switzerland, 1957.

**Isotopes:** (concept of) Frederick Soddy, England, 1912; (stable isotopes) J. J. Thompson, England, 1913; (existence demonstrated by mass spectrography) Francis W. Ashton, 1919.

**Jet propulsion:** (engine) Sir Frank Whittle, England, Hans von Ohain, Germany, 1936; (aircraft) *Heinkel He 178,* 1939.

**Kinetic theory of gases:** (molecules of a gas are in a state of rapid motion) Daniel Bernoulli, Switzerland, 1738.

**Laser:** (theoretical work on) Charles H. Townes, Arthur L. Schawlow, U.S., N. Basov, A. Prokhorov, U.S.S.R., 1958; (first working model) T. H. Maiman, U.S., 1960.

**Lawn mower:** Edwin Budding, John Ferrabee, England, 1830–1831.

**LCD (liquid crystal display):** Hoffmann-La Roche, Switzerland, 1970.

**Lens, bifocal:** Benjamin Franklin, U.S., c.1760.

**Leyden jar:** (prototype electrical condenser) Canon E. G. von Kleist of Kamin, Pomerania, 1745; independently evolved by Cunaeus and P. van Musschenbroek, University of Leyden, Holland, 1746, from where name originated.

**Light, nature of:** (wave theory) Christian Huygens, The Netherlands, 1678; (electromagnetic theory) James Clerk Maxwell, England, 1873.

**Light, speed of:** (theory that light has finite velocity) Olaus Roemer, Denmark, 1675.

**Lightning rod:** Benjamin Franklin, U.S., 1752.

**Locomotive:** (steam powered) Richard Trevithick, England, 1804; (first practical, due to multiple-fire-tube boiler) George Stephenson, England, 1829; (largest steam-powered) Union Pacific's "Big Boy," U.S., 1941.

**Benjamin Franklin (1706–1790)**

**Lock, cylinder:** Linus Yale, U.S., 1851.

**Loom:** (horizontal, two-beamed) Egypt, c. 4400 B.C.; (Jacquard drawloom, pattern controlled by punch cards) Jacques de Vaucanson, France, 1745, Joseph-Marie Jacquard, 1801; (flying shuttle) John Kay, England, 1733; (power-driven loom) Edmund Cartwright, England, 1785.

**Machine gun:** (hand-cranked multibarrel) Richard J. Gatling, U.S., 1862; (practical single barrel, belt-fed) Hiram S. Maxim, Anglo-American, 1884.

**Magnet, Earth is:** William Gilbert, England, 1600.

**Match:** (phosphorus) François Derosne, France, 1816; (friction) Charles Sauria, France, 1831; (safety) J. E. Lundstrom, Sweden, 1855.

**Measles vaccine:** John F. Enders, Thomas Peebles, U.S., 1953.

**Metric system:** revolutionary government of France, 1790–1801.

**Microphone:** Charles Wheatstone, England, 1827.

**Microscope:** (compound) Zacharias Janssen, The Netherlands, 1590; (electron) Vladimir Zworykin et al., U.S., Canada, Germany, 1932–1939.

**Microwave oven:** Percy Spencer, U.S., 1947.

**Motion, laws of:** Isaac Newton, England, 1687.

**Motion pictures:** Thomas A. Edison, U.S., 1893.

**Motion pictures, sound:** Product of various inventions. First picture with synchronized musical score: *Don Juan,* 1926; with spoken dialogue: *The Jazz Singer,* 1927; both Warner Bros.

**Motor, electric:** Michael Faraday, England, 1822; (alternating-current) Nikola Tesla, U.S., 1892.

**Motorcycle:** (motor tricycle) Edward Butler, England, 1884; (gasoline-engine motorcycle) Gottlieb Daimler, Germany, 1885.

**Moving assembly line:** Henry Ford, U.S., 1913.

**Neptune:** (discovery of) Johann Galle, Germany, 1846.

**Neptunium:** (first transuranic element, synthesis of) Edward M. McMillan, Philip H. Abelson, U.S., 1940.

**Neutron:** James Chadwick, England, 1932.

**Neutron-induced radiation:** Enrico Fermi et al., Italy, 1934.

**Nitroglycerin:** Ascanio Sobrero, Italy, 1846.

**Nuclear fission:** Otto Hahn, Fritz Strassmann, Germany, 1938.

**Nuclear reactor:** Enrico Fermi, Italy, et al., 1942.

**Ohm's law:** (relationship between strength of electric current, electromotive force, and circuit resistance) Georg S. Ohm, Germany, 1827.

**Oil well:** Edwin L. Drake, U.S., 1859.

**Oxygen:** (isolation of) Joseph Priestley, 1774; Karl Scheele, 1773.

**Ozone:** Christian Schönbein, Germany, 1839.

**Pacemaker:** (internal) Clarence W. Lillehie, Earl Bakk, U.S., 1957.

**Paper:** China, c.100 A.D.

**Parachute:** Louis S. Lenormand, France, 1783.

**Pen:** (fountain) Lewis E. Waterman, U.S., 1884; (ball-point, for marking on rough surfaces) John H. Loud, U.S., 1888; (ball-point, for handwriting) Lazlo Biro, Argentina, 1944.

**Periodic law:** (that properties of elements are functions of their atomic weights) Dmitri Mendeleev, Russia, 1869.

**Periodic table:** (arrangement of chemical elements based on periodic law) Dmitri Mendeleev, Russia, 1869.

**Phonograph:** Thomas A. Edison, U.S., 1877.

**Photography:** (first paper negative, first photograph, on metal) Joseph Nicéphore Niepce, France, 1816–1827; (discovery of fixative powers of hyposulfite of soda) Sir John Herschel, England, 1819; (first direct positive image on silver plate, the daguerreotype) Louis Daguerre, based on work with Niepce, France, 1839; (first paper negative from which a number of positive prints could be made) William Talbot, England, 1841. Work of these four men, taken together, forms basis for all modern photography. (First color images) Alexandre Becquerel, Claude Niepce de Saint-Victor, France, 1848–1860; (commercial color film with three emulsion layers, Kodachrome) U.S., 1935.

**Photovoltaic effect:** (light falling on certain materials can produce electricity) Edmund Becquerel, France, 1839.

**Piano:** (Hammerklavier) Bartolommeo Cristofori, Italy, 1709; (pianoforte with sustaining and damper pedals) John Broadwood, England, 1873.

**Planetary motion, laws of:** Johannes Kepler, Germany, 1609, 1619.

**Plant respiration and photosynthesis:** Jan Ingenhousz, Holland, 1779.

**Plastics:** (first material, nitrocellulose softened by vegetable oil, camphor, precursor to Celluloid) Alexander Parkes, England, 1855; (Celluloid, involving recognition of vital effect of camphor) John W. Hyatt, U.S., 1869; (Bakelite, first completely synthetic plastic) Leo H. Baekeland, U.S., 1910; (theoretical background of macromolecules and process of polymerization on which modern plastics industry rests) Hermann Staudinger, Germany, 1922; (polypropylene and low-pressure method for producing high-density polyethylene) Robert Banks, Paul Hogan, U.S., 1958.

**Plate tectonics:** Alfred Wegener, Germany, 1912–1915.

**Plow, forked: Mesopotamia, before 3000 B.C.**

**Plutonium, synthesis of:** Glenn T. Seaborg, Edwin M. McMillan, Arthur C. Wahl, Joseph W. Kennedy, U.S., 1941.

**Polio, vaccine:** (experimentally safe dead-virus vaccine) Jonas E. Salk, U.S., 1952; (effective large-scale field trials) 1954; (officially approved) 1955; (safe oral live-virus vaccine developed) Albert B. Sabin, U.S., 1954; (available in the U.S.) 1960.

**Positron:** Carl D. Anderson, U.S., 1932.

**Pressure cooker:** (early version) Denis Papin, France, 1679.

**Printing:** (block) Japan, c.700; (movable type) Korea, c.1400; Johann Gutenberg, Germany, c.1450 (lithography, offset) Aloys Senefelder, Germany, 1796; (rotary press) Richard Hoe, U.S., 1844; (linotype) Ottmar Mergenthaler, U.S., 1884.

**Johann Gutenberg**
**(c. 1400–1468)**

**Probability theory:** René Descartes, France; and Pierre de Fermat, Switzerland, 1654.

**Proton:** Ernest Rutherford, England, 1919.

**Prozac:** (antidepressant fluoxetine) Bryan B. Malloy, Scotland, and Klaus K. Schmiegel, U.S., 1972; (released for use in U.S.) Eli Lilly & Company, 1987.

**Psychoanalysis:** Sigmund Freud, Austria, c.1904.

**Pulsars:** Antony Hewish and Jocelyn Bell Burnel, England, 1967.

**Quantum theory:** (general) Max Planck, Germany, 1900; (sub-atomic) Niels Bohr, Denmark, 1913; (quantum mechanics) Werner Heisenberg, Erwin Schrödinger, Germany, 1925.

**Quarks:** Jerome Friedman, Henry Kendall, Richard Taylor, U.S., 1967.

**Quasars:** Marten Schmidt, U.S., 1963.

**Rabies immunization:** Louis Pasteur, France, 1885.

**Radar:** (limited to one-mile range) Christian Hulsmeyer, Germany, 1904; (pulse modulation, used for measuring height of ionosphere) Gregory Breit, Merle Tuve, U.S., 1925; (first practical radar—radio detection and ranging) Sir Robert Watson-Watt, England, 1934–1935.

**Radio:** (electromagnetism, theory of) James Clerk Maxwell, England, 1873; (spark coil, generator of electromagnetic waves) Heinrich Hertz, Germany, 1886; (first practical system of wireless telegraphy) Guglielmo Marconi, Italy, 1895; (first long-distance telegraphic radio signal sent across the Atlantic) Marconi, 1901; (vacuum electron tube, basis for radio telephony) Sir John Fleming, England, 1904; (triode amplifying tube) Lee de Forest, U.S., 1906; (regenerative circuit, allowing long-distance sound reception) Edwin H. Armstrong, U.S., 1912; (frequency modulation—FM) Edwin H. Armstrong, U.S., 1933.

**Radioactivity:** (X-rays) Wilhelm K. Roentgen, Germany, 1895; (radioactivity of uranium) Henri Becquerel, France, 1896; (radioactive elements, radium and polonium in uranium ore) Marie Sklodowska-Curie, Pierre Curie, France, 1898; (classification of alpha and beta particle radiation) Pierre Curie, France, 1900; (gamma radiation) Paul-Ulrich Villard, France, 1900.

**Radiocarbon dating, carbon-14 method:** (discovered) Willard F. Libby, U.S., (first demonstrated) U.S., 1950.

**Radio signals, extraterrestrial:** first known radio noise signals were received by U.S. engineer, Karl Jansky, originating from the Galactic Center, 1931.

**Radio waves:** (cosmic sources, led to radio astronomy) Karl Jansky, U.S., 1932.

**Razor:** (safety, successfully marketed) King Gillette, U.S., 1901; (electric) Jacob Schick, U.S., 1928, 1931.

**Reaper:** Cyrus McCormick, U.S., 1834.

**Refrigerator:** Alexander Twining, U.S., James Harrison, Australia, 1850; (first with a compressor device) the Domelse, Chicago, U.S., 1913.

**Refrigerator ship:** (first) the *Frigorifique*, cooling unit designed by Charles Teller, France, 1877.

**Relativity:** (special and general theories of) Albert Einstein, Switzerland, Germany, U.S., 1905–1953.

**Revolver:** Samuel Colt, U.S., 1835.

**Richter scale:** Charles F. Richter, U.S., 1935.

**Rifle:** (muzzle-loaded) Italy, Germany, c.1475; (breech-loaded) England, France, Germany, U.S., c.1866; (bolt-action) Paul von Mauser, Germany, 1889; (automatic) John Browning, U.S., 1918.

**Rocket:** (liquid-fueled) Robert Goddard, U.S., 1926.

**Roller bearing:** (wooden for cartwheel) Germany or France, c.100 B.C.

**Rotation of Earth:** Jean Bernard Foucault, France, 1851.

**Royal Observatory, Greenwich:** established in 1675 by Charles II of England; John Flamsteed first Astronomer Royal.

**Rubber:** (vulcanization process) Charles Goodyear, U.S., 1839.

**Saccharin:** Constantine Fuhlberg, Ira Remsen, U.S., 1879.

**Safety pin:** Walter Hunt, U.S., 1849.

**Saturn, ring around:** Christian Huygens, The Netherlands, 1659.

**"Scotch" tape:** Richard Drew, U.S., 1929.

**Screw propeller:** Sir Francis P. Smith, England, 1836; John Ericsson, England, worked independently of and simultaneously with Smith, 1837.

**Seat belt:** (three point) Nils Bohlin, Sweden, 1962.

**Seismograph:** (first accurate) John Milne, England, 1880.

**Sewing machine:** Elias Howe, U.S., 1846; (continuous stitch) Isaac Singer, U.S., 1851.

**Solar energy:** First realistic application of solar energy using parabolic solar reflector to drive caloric engine on steam boiler, John Ericsson, U.S., 1860s.

**Solar system, universe:** (Sun-centered universe) Nicolaus Copernicus, Warsaw, 1543; (establishment of planetary orbits as elliptical) Johannes Kepler, Germany, 1609; (infinity of universe) Giordano Bruno, Italian monk, 1584.

**Spectrum:** (heterogeneity of light) Sir Isaac Newton, England, 1665–1666.

**Spectrum analysis:** Gustav Kirchhoff, Robert Bunsen, Germany, 1859.

**Spermatozoa:** Anton van Leeuwenhoek, The Netherlands, 1683.

**Spinning:** (spinning wheel) India, introduced to Europe in Middle Ages; (Saxony wheel, continuous spinning of wool or cotton yarn) England, c.1500–1600; (spinning jenny) James Hargreaves, England, 1764; (spinning frame) Sir Richard Arkwright, England, 1769; (spinning mule, completed mechanization of spinning, permitting production of yarn to keep up with demands of modern looms) Samuel Crompton, England, 1779.

**Star catalog:** (first modern) Tycho Brahe, Denmark, 1572.

**Steam engine:** (first commercial version based on principles of French physicist Denis Papin) Thomas Savery, England, 1639; (atmospheric steam engine) Thomas Newcomen, England, 1705; (steam engine for pumping water from collieries) Savery, Newcomen, 1725; (modern condensing, double acting) James Watt, England, 1782; (high-pressure) Oliver Evans, U.S., 1804.

**Steamship:** Claude de Jouffroy d'Abbans, France, 1783; James Rumsey, U.S., 1787; John Fitch, U.S., 1790; (high-pressure) Oliver Evans, U.S., 1804. All preceded Robert Fulton, U.S., 1807, credited with launching first commercially successful steamship.

**Stethoscope:** René Laënnec, France, 1819.

**Sulfa drugs:** (parent compound, para-aminobenzenesulfanomide) Paul Gelmo, Austria, 1908; (antibacterial activity) Gerhard Domagk, Germany, 1935.

**Superconductivity:** (theory) John Bardeen, Leon Cooper, John Scheiffer, U.S., 1957.

**Symbolic logic:** George Boule, 1854; (modern) Bertrand Russell, Alfred North Whitehead, England, 1910–1913.

**Tank, military:** Sir Ernest Swinton, England, 1914.

**Tape recorder:** (magnetic steel tape) Valdemar Poulsen, Denmark, 1899.

**Teflon:** DuPont, U.S., 1943.

**Telegraph:** Samuel F. B. Morse, U.S., 1837.

**Telephone:** Alexander Graham Bell, U.S., 1876.

**Telescope:** Hans Lippershey, The Netherlands, 1608; (astronomical) Galileo Galilei, Italy, 1609; (reflecting) Isaac Newton, England, 1668.

**Samuel F. B. Morse (1791–1872)**
*Library of Congress*

**Television:** (Iconoscope–T.V. camera table) Vladimir Zworkin, U.S., 1923, and also kinescope (cathode ray tube) 1928; (mechanical disk-scanning method) successfully demonstrated by J.L. Baird, Scotland, C.F. Jenkins, U.S., 1926; (first all-electric television image) 1927, Philo T. Farnsworth, U.S; (color, mechanical disk) Baird, 1928; (color, compatible with black and white) George Valensi, France, 1938; (color, sequential rotating filter) Peter Goldmark, U.S., first introduced, 1951; (color, compatible with black and white) commercially introduced in U.S., National Television Systems Committee, 1953.

**Thermodynamics:** (first law: energy cannot be created or destroyed, only converted from one form to another) Julius von Mayer, Germany, 1842; James Joule, England, 1843; (second law: heat cannot of itself pass from a colder to a warmer body) Rudolph Clausius, Germany, 1850; (third law: the entropy of ordered solids reaches zero at the absolute zero of temperature) Walter Nernst, Germany, 1918.

**Thermometer:** (open-column) Galileo Galilei, c.1593; (clinical) Santorio Santorio, Padua, c.1615; (mercury, also Fahrenheit scale) Gabriel D. Fahrenheit, Germany, 1714; (centigrade scale) Anders Celsius, Sweden, 1742; (absolute-temperature, or Kelvin, scale) William Thompson, Lord Kelvin, England, 1848.

**Tire, pneumatic:** Robert W. Thompson, England, 1845; (bicycle tire) John B. Dunlop, Northern Ireland, 1888.

**Toilet, flush:** Product of Minoan civilization, Crete, c. 2000 B.C. Alleged invention by "Thomas Crapper" is untrue.

**Tractor:** Benjamin Holt, U.S., 1900.

**Transformer, electric:** William Stanley, U.S., 1885.

**Transistor:** John Bardeen, Walter H. Brattain, William B. Shockley, U.S., 1947.

**Tuberculosis bacterium:** Robert Koch, Germany, 1882.

**Typewriter:** Christopher Sholes, Carlos Glidden, U.S., 1867.

**Uncertainty principle:** (that position and velocity of an object cannot both be measured exactly, at the same time) Werner Heisenberg, Germany, 1927.

**Uranus:** (first planet discovered in recorded history) William Herschel, England, 1781.

**Vaccination:** Edward Jenner, England, 1796.

**Vacuum cleaner:** (manually operated) Ives W. McGaffey, 1869; (electric) Hubert C. Booth, England, 1901; (upright) J. Murray Spangler, U.S., 1907.

**Van Allen (radiation) Belt:** (around Earth) James Van Allen, U.S., 1958.

**Video disk:** Philips Co., The Netherlands, 1972.

**Vitamins:** (hypothesis of disease deficiency) Sir F. G. Hopkins, Casimir Funk, England, 1912; (vitamin A) Elmer V. McCollum, M. Davis, U.S., 1912–1914; (vitamin B) McCollum, U.S., 1915–1916; (thiamin, $B_1$) Casimir Funk, England, 1912; (riboflavin, $B_2$) D. T. Smith, E. G. Hendrick, U.S., 1926; (niacin) Conrad Elvehjem, U.S., 1937; ($B_6$) Paul Gyorgy, U.S., 1934; (vitamin C) C. A. Hoist, T. Froelich, Norway, 1912; (vitamin D) McCollum, U.S., 1922; (folic acid) Lucy Wills, England, 1933.

**Voltaic pile:** (forerunner of modern battery, first source of continuous electric current) Alessandro Volta, Italy, 1800.

**Wallpaper:** Europe, 16th and 17th century.

**Wassermann test:** (for syphilis) August von Wassermann, Germany, 1906.

**Wheel:** (cart, solid wood) Mesopotamia, c.3800–3600 B.C.

**Windmill:** Persia, c.600.

**World Wide Web:** (developed while working at CERN) Tim Berners-Lee, England, 1989; (development of Mosaic browser makes WWW available for general use) Marc Andreeson, U.S., 1993.

**Xerography:** Chester Carlson, U.S., 1938.

**Yellow Fever:** (transmission of) Walter Reed, U.S., 1900.

**Zero:** India, c.600; (absolute zero temperature, cessation of all molecular energy) William Thompson, Lord Kelvin, England, 1848.

**Zipper:** W. L. Judson, U.S., 1891.

# The National Inventors Hall of Fame

The Inventors Hall of Fame, located in Akron, Ohio, was established in 1973 by the National Council of Patent Law Associations, now the National Council of Intellectual Property Law Associations, and the Patent and Trademark Office of the U.S. Department of Commerce.

## The 2002 Class of Inductees

**Raymond Kurzweil,** 1948–, KURZWEIL READING MACHINE. When entrepreneur Kurzweil introduced the Kurzweil Reading Machine in 1976, it was hailed as the most important advance in reading for the blind since Braille. The machine scans ordinary printed materials, which are then read aloud by computer. Its text-to-speech process was considered a landmark in the use of artificial intelligence, and has provided the basis for numerous information technologies since.

**Nils Bohlin,** 1920–, THREE-POINT SAFETY BELT. The now-standard three-point safety belt, with a strap for the upper body and a strap for the lower body joined at a single buckle, was developed by Swedish engineer Bohlin in 1962. A tireless advocate for seatbelt use, Bohlin is considered a force behind the seatbelt safety legislation that has been adopted in 49 states. Bohlin has been a safety engineer for Volvo since 1958.

**Rangaswamy Srinivasan,** 1929–, **James Wynne,** 1943–, and **Samuel Blum,** 1920–, EXCIMER EYE SURGERY. IBM researchers Srinivasan, Wynne, and Blum developed this technique used in LASIK (Laser-Assisted In Situ Keratomileusis) eye surgery, which has improved the eyesight of more than 5 million people and allowed many to give up their glasses and contact lenses. The procedure uses an ultraviolet excimer laser to reshape the cornea without damaging the surrounding tissue.

**M. Stephen Heilman,** 1933–, **Alois Langer,** 1945–, **Morton Mower,** 1933–, and **Michel Mirowski,** 1924–1990, IMPLANTABLE DEFIBRILLATOR. This team of doctors developed the implantable defibrillator, an internal electronic device that continuously monitors and regulates heart rhythms. By correcting irregular rhythms it helps ensure that sufficient blood is pumped through the heart to the body and brain, thus preventing cardiac arrest. Since its first successful use in 1980 more than 300,000 people worldwide have received an implantable defibrillator, including Vice President Dick Cheney.

**Rodney Bagley,** 1934–, **Irwin Lachman,** 1930–, and **Ronald Lewis,** 1936–, CERAMIC SUBSTRATE FOR CATALYTIC CONVERTORS. In response to the Clean Air Act of 1970, engineers Bagley and Lachman and geologist Lewis, all of Corning Glass, created a ceramic substrate for use in automotive technology that converts 95% of exhaust pollutants into water vapor and carbon dioxide. Thirty years later, their invention is credited with reducing automotive pollutants by more than 3 billion tons worldwide. Ceramic substrate technology is now used by every automotive manufacturer in the world.

**Felix Hoffmann,** 1868–1946, ASPIRIN. Hoffman, a young German chemist, sought to relieve his father's arthritis pain with a chemical derivative of salicylic acid, a natural painkiller obtained from willow bark. Convinced of its promise, Hoffman urged Germany's Bayer Company to sell the drug, which was marketed under the name Aspirin. Aspirin is one of the world's most widely used painkillers and has been notably effective in preventing heart attacks and strokes.

**John Presper Eckert, Jr.,** 1919–1995, and **John Mauchly,** 1907–1980, ENIAC DATA TRANSLATING DEVICE. Engineers Eckert and Mauchly invented ENIAC (Electronic Numerical Integrator and Calculator), the first multipurpose computer, whose completion in 1945 heralded the dawn of the electronic era and provided a prototype for later computers. Although far less powerful than handheld calculators today, in its time ENIAC set speed records with more than 5,000 additions per second. ENIAC weighed about 30 tons, filled an 1,800-square-foot room, and included 6,000 manual switches.

**Henry Bessemer,** 1813–1898, BESSEMER STEEL PROCESS. In 1855 Bessemer, an English industrialist, patented the "Bessemer converter," an early blast furnace that allowed quick and cheap production of steel in larger amounts than ever before. Previously, steel production had been a laborious process requiring skilled workers. By making possible the mass manufacture of steel, the Bessemer Process transformed production of firearms and railways and helped fuel the Industrial Revolution.

# Why Hybrids Are Hot

Cars that run on both gas and electricity are finally catching on

**By ANITA HAMILTON**   TIME

With their oddball designs—critics dubbed them "clown cars"—the first generation of hybrid cars, which alternately guzzle climate-heating gasoline and sip environmentally friendly electricity, barely dented the consciousness of car-buying Americans. According to one survey, most Americans still think the batteries in hybrids have to be plugged in to get recharged. (Wrong. They are rejuiced automatically as you drive.) No wonder only 20,000 of the 17 million automobiles sold in the U.S. in 2001 were hybrids.

But now the auto industry wants to take another crack at it. A hybrid version of the Honda Civic, the best-selling compact car in America, started rolling into dealerships nationwide in April 2002. In 2003 Ford, which has produced a string of electric cars, is expected to be the first U.S. manufacturer to introduce a hybrid vehicle. Meanwhile, Toyota, General Motors, and Chrysler have all promised a new crop of hybrid vehicles by 2004. J.D. Power & Associates, which tracks consumer tastes for the auto industry, expects that by 2006, American consumers will be buying half a million hybrids a year.

Why all the excitement? "Hybrids are the first viable alternative to the gasoline engine," says Prabhakar Patil, the chief engineer for Ford's hybrid program, who notes that cars that run on fuel cells—widely expected to be the next technological advance in automotive power—are at least ten years off. Hybrids still have a major hurdle to overcome: sticker shock (more on that later). But for car buyers who want to do their part for the environment and are willing to pay a few grand extra to do it, hybrids are the only game in Motown.

## Fun to Drive

The first thing you notice when you drive one is how quiet it is. The engine goes blissfully silent every time you stop at an intersection. That's because the gas engine shuts off to allow the electric motor to take over. Gas engines are at their least efficient—and produce the most emissions—when idling, so that's when it makes the most sense to make the switch. The cars are chock-full of clever tricks like this. Every time you touch the brakes, for example, kinetic energy that would normally be lost in the braking system is recaptured by the electric motor, which in turn recharges the battery—a process known as regenerative braking. Some hybrids use their electric motors to control the power steering or to give the car extra oomph at higher speeds.

Hybrids are surprisingly fun to drive. The electric motor on the Toyota Prius can keep the car cruising at speeds up to 42 mph without any help, although it needs power from the gas engine to accelerate to that speed. A panel on the dashboard displays average fuel efficiency, calculated on the fly, and tells you when the electric motor is being used to charge the batteries or to assist the gas engine.

## Electricity Guzzlers

The new hybrid Civic uses a smaller electric motor and a more powerful gas engine than the Prius, so it's always burning gas, except when it's braking or standing still. Even so, it gets 47 mpg in the city and 51 mpg on the freeway, approximately a 25% improvement over the gas-only version. Aside from a small HYBRID logo on the trunk, it looks just like a regular Civic. About the only drawbacks are the higher sticker price ($19,550, roughly $2,500 more than a similarly equipped standard Civic) and slightly slower acceleration.

Ford, for its part, claims that when its hybrid Escape SUV goes on sale in 2003, it will have all the zip of the regular Escape, even though it will run off a smaller four-cylinder engine. The extra horsepower is supposed to come from a state-of-the-art electric motor. The company is promising an impressive 40 mpg in city driving, versus the 23 mpg the gas-only version gets.

I got behind the wheel of a hybrid Escape when I visited Ford's product-development center in Dearborn, Mich., in 2002. Ford would not let me drive the prototype up the steepest hills or around the sharpest curves, but I was impressed by the gentle, seamless shifting between the gas engine and electric power at low speeds. The car went silent every time I released the gas pedal or drove it slowly in reverse.

For all their benefits, however, hybrids do cost a few thousand dollars more than their gas-only counterparts. While you may be able to recoup that money in fuel savings within ten years, it's still a big initial investment. And the batteries are guaranteed under warranty for only eight years, at which point customers may have to shell out as much as $2,000 for a replacement. "People are not willing to pay extra money for fuel economy in the U.S.," says Rich Marsh, who heads GM's hybrid-truck program. That's why GM plans to market its hybrid GMC Sierra and Chevrolet Silverado pickups, due out in 2004, not on their tiny 2-miles-per-gallon improvement in fuel consumption but on the benefits of their onboard electric generators and standard outlets for plugging in power tools.

It's still hard to tell whether Detroit is really serious about the hybrid-car business. After all, the same companies touting their hybrids have also lobbied successfully to put the brakes on legislation that would have mandated tougher fuel-efficiency standards. President Bush has proposed tax credits of $2,000 to $3,000 for hybrid-car buyers, but those funds aren't likely to kick in until 2004, if ever. Until then, if you want your fancy hybrid car, you'll have to pay a premium.  □

# International Energy Annual 2000

*Source:* Energy Information Administration, Dept. of Energy. Web: www.eia.doe.gov/emeu/iea/overview.html.

## World Primary Energy Production Trends

Between 1991 and 2000, the world's output of primary energy—petroleum, natural gas, coal, and electric power (hydro, nuclear, geothermal, solar, wind, and wood and waste)—increased at an average annual rate of 1.4%. World production increased from 351 quadrillion Btu (British thermal units) in 1991 to 397 quadrillion Btu in 2000.

In 2000, petroleum (crude oil and natural gas plant liquids) continued to be the most important energy source, accounting for 39.1%, or 155 quadrillion Btu, of world primary energy production. Between 1991 and 2000, petroleum production increased by 9.3 million barrels per day, or 14.3%, rising from 65 to 74.3 million barrels per day. Production grew most in the Middle East, followed by Central and South America and Western Europe. Their combined gains from 1991 to 2000 were 10 million barrels per day. In the Eastern Europe and former USSR region, average daily production fell 2.3 million barrels per day.

Coal was the second primary energy source in 2000, accounting for 23.3% of world primary energy production. World coal production totaled 5.06 billion short tons—93 quadrillion Btu—in 2000, down 1.1% from 5.12 billion short tons in 1991.

Dry natural gas ranked third, accounting for 22.9% of world primary energy production in 2000. Production of dry natural gas was 88 trillion cu ft, or 91 quadrillion Btu, in 2000. Production increased by 13.3 trillion cu ft from 74.8 trillion cu ft in 1991, a gain of 17.7%.

Hydro, nuclear, and other (geothermal, solar, wind, and wood and waste) electric power generation ranked fourth, fifth, and sixth, as primary energy sources in 2000, accounting for 6.9%, 6.5%, and 0.8%, respectively, of world primary energy production. Together they accounted for 5.3 trillion kilowatthours—56 quadrillion Btu—in 2000. Nuclear electric power generation increased from 2 trillion kilowatthours to 2.4 trillion kilowatthours, a 22.2% increase, between 1991 and 2000. Geothermal, solar, wind, and wood and waste electric power generation increased from 138 billion kilowatthours to 240 billion kilowatthours, a 74% increase. Hydro-

mary electric power generation, 2.6 trillion kilowatthours in 2000, up 19.9% from 2.2 trillion kilowatthours in 1991.

## Major Energy Producers and Consumers

In 2000, the United States, Russia, and China were the leading energy producers and consumers, producing 38% and consuming 41% of the world's total energy.

The United States, Russia, China, Saudi Arabia, and Canada were the largest producers of energy in 2000, supplying 47.6% of the world's total. The

United States supplied 71.6 quadrillion Btu of primary energy; Russia, 43.3 quadrillion Btu; and China, 34.9 quadrillion Btu. The United Kingdom, Iran, Norway, Australia, and India together supplied an additional 12.8% of the world's total energy.

The United States, China, Russia, Japan, and Germany were the largest primary energy consumers in 2000, accounting for 50.1% of world energy consumption. The United States consumed 98.8 quadrillion Btu; China, 36.7 quadrillion Btu; and Russia 28.1 quadrillion Btu. Canada, India, France, the United Kingdom, and Brazil together used an additional 13.9% of the world's energy.

## Regional Energy Production and Consumption

Between 1991 and 2000, energy production and consumption increased in every world region except Eastern Europe and the former Soviet bloc. The largest increases were in Asia and Oceania, where production increased by 17.3 quadrillion Btu and consumption grew by 28.8 quadrillion Btu. Energy production in the Middle East rose 16.8 quadrillion Btu, the second-largest regional increase. Consumption increased 5.5 quadrillion Btu.

In North America, energy production rose by 6.6 quadrillion Btu, and consumption grew by 17.8 quadrillion Btu, the second-largest regional consumption increase. Production in Central and South America rose 8.2 quadrillion, with consumption increasing 6 quadrillion Btu. Energy production in Western Europe was 5.7 quadrillion Btu higher than in 1991, while consumption increased by 6.2 quadrillion Btu. Energy production in Africa rose 5.5 quadrillion Btu, and consumption increased 2.1 quadrillion Btu. In Eastern Europe and the former USSR, energy production declined 13.2 million Btu and consumption fell by 18.3 quadrillion Btu.

### Petroleum

Global production of petroleum (crude oil and natural gas plant liquids) increased by 9.3 million barrels per day between 1991 and 2000, an average annual growth rate of 1.5%. Saudi Arabia, the United States, and Russia were the three largest producers in 2000. Together, they produced 31.7% of the world's petroleum. Iran and Mexico accounted for 13.8%.

In 2000, the United States consumed 19.7 million barrels per day of petroleum, 26% of world consumption. Japan used 5.5 million barrels per day, followed by China, Germany, and Russia.

### Natural Gas

Production of dry natural gas increased by 13.3 trillion cu ft, an average annual rate of 1.8%, from 1991 to 2000. Russia and the United States produced 45% of the world total, followed by Canada, the United Kingdom, and Algeria. In 2000, the United States and Russia accounted for 42% of world consumption, followed by the United Kingdom, Canada, and Germany.

## Coal

Coal production declined by 57 million short tons from 1991 to 2000. China, the United States, India, Australia, and South Africa produced 67% of the world total in 2000. China, the United States, India, Russia, and Germany accounted for 64% of world coal consumption.

## Hydroelectric Power

Hydroelectric power generation increased by 440 billion kilowatthours between 1991 and 2000, an average annual rate of 2%. Canada, Brazil, the United States, China, and Russia produced 49% of the world total.

## Nuclear Electric Power

Nuclear electric power generation increased by 442 billion kilowatthours between 1991 and 2000, an average annual rate of 2.3%. The United States, France, and Japan generated 59% of the world total.

## Geothermal, Solar, Wind, and Wood and Waste Electric Power

The generation of geothermal, solar, wind, and wood and waste electric power increased by 102 billion kilowatthours between 1991 and 2000, an average annual rate of 6.3%. The United States, Japan, Germany, Brazil, and the Philippines accounted for 59% of the world total.

## World Net Electricity Consumption by Selected Countries, 1990–2020

### (billion kilowatt-hours)

| Region | History | | | Projections | | | | Average annual percent change, 1999–2020 |
|---|---|---|---|---|---|---|---|---|
| | 1990 | 1998 | 1999 | 2005 | 2010 | 2015 | 2020 | |
| United States | 2,817 | 3,400 | 3,236 | 3,793 | 4,170 | 4,556 | 4,916 | 2.0% |
| France | 326 | 394 | 399 | 450 | 486 | 523 | 572 | 1.7 |
| Japan | 765 | 932 | 947 | 1,036 | 1,117 | 1,194 | 1,275 | 1.4 |
| Eastern Europe/ Former Soviet Union | 1,906 | 1,459 | 1,452 | 1,651 | 1,807 | 2,006 | 2,173 | 1.9 |
| China | 551 | 1,013 | 1,084 | 1,523 | 2,031 | 2,631 | 3,349 | 5.5 |
| India | 257 | 396 | 424 | 537 | 649 | 784 | 923 | 3.8 |
| Africa | 287 | 361 | 367 | 460 | 550 | 671 | 776 | 3.6 |
| Central and South America | 449 | 656 | 684 | 788 | 988 | 1,249 | 1,517 | 3.9 |
| **Total industralized countries** | **6,385** | **7,604** | **7,517** | **8,620** | **9,446** | **10,281** | **11,151** | **1.9** |
| **Total developing countries** | **2,258** | **3,663** | **3,863** | **4,912** | **6,127** | **7,548** | **9,082** | **4.2** |
| **Total world** | **10,549** | **12,725** | **12,833** | **15,182** | **17,380** | **19,835** | **22,407** | **2.7** |

*Sources:* Energy Information Administration (EIA): *International Energy Outlook 2002.*

## Greatest Oil Reserves by Country, 2001

| 2001 rank | Country | 2001 proved reserves (billion barrels) | 2001 rank | Country | 2001 proved reserves (billion barrels) |
|---|---|---|---|---|---|
| 1. | Saudi Arabia | 261.7 | 6. | Venezuela | 76.9 |
| 2. | Iraq | 112.5 | 7. | Russia | 48.6 |
| 3. | United Arab Emirates | 97.8 | 8. | Libya | 29.5 |
| 4. | Kuwait | 96.5 | 9. | Mexico | 28.3 |
| 5. | Iran | 89.7 | 10. | China | 24.0 |

NOTES: Figures for Russia are "explored reserves," which are understood to be proved plus some probable. All other figures are proved reserves recoverable with present technology and prices. *Source:* U.S. Energy Information Administration, *International Energy Annual 2000* (May 2002).

## Greatest Gas Reserves by Country, 2001

| 2001 rank | Country | 2001 proved reserves (trillion cu ft) | 2001 rank | Country | 2001 proved reserves (trillion cu ft) |
|---|---|---|---|---|---|
| 1. | Russia | 1,700.0 | 6. | United States | 177.4 |
| 2. | Iran | 812.3 | 7. | Algeria | 159.7 |
| 3. | Qatar | 393.8 | 8. | Venezuela | 146.8 |
| 4. | Saudi Arabia | 213.3 | 9. | Nigeria | 124.0 |
| 5. | United Arab Emirates | 212.1 | 10. | Iraq | 109.8 |

NOTES: Figures for Russia are "explored reserves," which are understood to be proved plus some probable. All other figures are proved reserves recoverable with present technology and prices. *Source:* U.S. Energy Information Administration, *International Energy Annual 2000* (May 2002).

## World Energy Consumption and Carbon Dioxide Emissions, 1990–2020

| Region | Energy consumption (quadrillion btu) | | | | Carbon dioxide emissions (million metric tons) | | | |
|---|---|---|---|---|---|---|---|---|
| | 1990 | 1999 | 2010[5] | 2020[5] | 1990 | 1999 | 2010[5] | 2020[5] |
| Industrialized nations[1] | 182.7 | 209.7 | 246.6 | 277.8 | 2,849 | 3,129 | 3,692 | 4,169 |
| Eastern Europe/Former Soviet Union | 76.3 | 50.4 | 61.8 | 73.4 | 1,337 | 810 | 978 | 1,139 |
| Developing nations | | | | | | | | |
| Asia[2] | 51.0 | 70.9 | 113.9 | 162.2 | 1,053 | 1,361 | 2,139 | 3,017 |
| Middle East[3] | 13.1 | 19.3 | 26.3 | 34.8 | 231 | 330 | 439 | 566 |
| Africa | 9.3 | 11.8 | 15.7 | 20.3 | 179 | 218 | 287 | 365 |
| Central and South America[4] | 13.7 | 19.8 | 28.3 | 43.1 | 178 | 249 | 377 | 595 |
| Total developing | 87.2 | 121.8 | 184.1 | 260.3 | 1,641 | 2,158 | 3,241 | 4,542 |
| Total world | 346.2 | 381.9 | 492.6 | 611.5 | 5,827 | 6,097 | 7,910 | 9,850 |

1. Includes the U.S., Canada, Mexico, Japan, France, Germany, Italy, the Netherlands, and the United Kingdom. 2. China, India, and South Korea are represented in developing Asia. 3. Turkey is represented in the Middle East. 4. Brazil is represented in Central and South America. 5. Projections. *Source:* U.S. Energy Information Administration, *International Energy Outlook 2002.* Web: www.eia.doe.gov/oiaf/ieo/tbl_1.html.

## Renewable Energy Consumption in the U.S. by Source, 1989–2002

### (quadrillion btu)

| Year | Wood and waste[1] | Geothermal[2] | Conventional hydroelectric power[3, 4] | Solar[5] | Wind[6] | Total |
|---|---|---|---|---|---|---|
| 1989 | 2.635e | 0.334 | 3.014 | 0.059 | 0.024 | 6.492 |
| 1990 | 2.188e | 0.355 | 3.146 | 0.063 | 0.032 | 6.254 |
| 1995 | 2.418 | 0.333 | 3.481 | 0.073 | 0.033 | 6.987 |
| 1996 | 2.465 | 0.346 | 3.892 | 0.075 | 0.035 | 7.473 |
| 1997 | 2.348 | 0.322 | 3.961 | 0.074 | 0.033 | 7.395 |
| 1998 | 2.326 | 0.328 | 3.569 | 0.074 | 0.031 | 6.977 |
| 1999 | 2.566 | 0.335 | 3.512 | 0.073 | 0.046 | 7.226 |
| 2000 | 2.596e | 0.319e | 3.152e | 0.070e | 0.051 | 6.868 |
| 2001 | 2.571 | 0.312 | 2.404 | 0.070e | 0.060 | 6.189 |
| 2002[7] | 0.845 | 0.101e | 1.125e | 0.021e | 0.010 | 2.332 |

NOTES: Totals may not equal sum of components due to independent rounding. 1. Wood, wood waste and various other waste, including some medical and municipal waste and agricultural byproducts. 2. Includes electricity imports from Mexico that are derived from geothermal energy. Includes grid-connected electricity, and geothermal heat pump and direct use energy. Excludes shaft power and remote electrical power. 3. Hydroelectricity generated by pumped storage is not included in renewable energy. 4. Includes electricity net imports from Canada that are derived from hydroelectric power. 5. Includes solar thermal and photovoltaic energy. 6. Includes only grid-connected electricity. 7. Estimate through April 2002 or first quarter. e = estimated. *Source:* Energy Information Administration (EIA). Web: www.eia.doe.gov.

## Motor Vehicle Fuel Consumption and Travel in the U.S., 1960–1999

| | 1960 | 1970 | 1980 | 1990 | 1995 | 1996 | 1997 | 1998 | 1999 |
|---|---|---|---|---|---|---|---|---|---|
| **Number registered (thousands)** | | | | | | | | | |
| Passenger car | 61,671 | 89,244 | 121,601 | 133,700 | 136,066 | 129,728 | 129,749 | 131,839 | 132,432 |
| Total[1] | 73,858 | 111,242 | 161,490 | 193,057 | 201,530 | 206,365 | 207,754 | 211,617 | 216,309 |
| **Vehicle-miles traveled (millions)** | | | | | | | | | |
| Passenger car | 587,000 | 917,000 | 1,112,000 | 1,408,000 | 1,438,294 | 1,469,854 | 1,501,820 | 1,549,577 | 1,569,270 |
| Total[1] | | | | | | | | | |
| **Fuel consumed (million gallons)** | | | | | | | | | |
| Passenger car | 41,171 | 67,819 | 69,982 | 69,568 | 68,072 | 69,221 | 69,867 | 71,695 | 73,160 |
| Total[1] | 57,880 | 92,329 | 114,960 | 130,755 | 143,834 | 147,365 | 150,386 | 154,884 | 160,441 |
| **Average miles traveled per vehicle (thousands)** | | | | | | | | | |
| Passenger car | 9.5 | 10.3 | 9.1 | 10.5 | 11.2 | 11.3 | 11.6 | 11.8 | 11.8 |
| Total[1] | 9.7 | 10.0 | 9.5 | 11.1 | 14.8 | 14.7 | 15.1 | 14.8 | 15.1 |
| **Average miles traveled per gallon** | | | | | | | | | |
| Passenger car | 14.3 | 13.5 | 15.9 | 20.2 | 21.1 | 21.2 | 21.5 | 21.6 | 21.4 |
| Total[1] | 12.4 | 12.0 | 13.3 | 16.4 | 12.3 | 12.8 | 13.0 | 12.9 | 12.8 |
| **Average annual fuel consumed per vehicle (gallons)** | | | | | | | | | |
| Passenger car | 668 | 760 | 576 | 520 | 530 | 534 | 538 | 544 | 552 |
| Total[1] | 784 | 830 | 712 | 677 | 1,738 | 1,716 | 1,732 | 1,710 | 1,777 |

1. Includes personal passenger vehicles, buses, and trucks. *Source:* U.S. Department of Transportation. Web: www.dot.gov.

## U.S. Emissions of Greenhouse Gases, 1990–2000
### (million metric tons of gas)

| Gas | 1990 | 1993 | 1994 | 1995 | 1996 | 1997 | 1998 | 1999 | 2000[1] |
|---|---|---|---|---|---|---|---|---|---|
| Carbon dioxide | 4,969.4 | 5,130.4 | 5,224.4 | 5,273.5 | 5,454.8 | 5,533.0 | 5,540.0 | 5,630.7 | 5,805.5 |
| Methane | 31.7 | 31.0 | 31.0 | 31.1 | 29.9 | 29.6 | 28.9 | 28.7 | 28.2 |
| Nitrous oxide | 1.2 | 1.2 | 1.3 | 1.3 | 1.2 | 1.2 | 1.2 | 1.2 | 1.2 |
| HFCs, PFCs, and SF$_6$ | — | — | — | — | — | — | — | — | — |

NOTES: (—) Less than 0.05 million metric tons of gas. 1. Preliminary data. *Source:* Compiled by the U.S. Energy Information Administration. Web: www.eia.doe.gov/.

## Air Quality in Selected U.S. Cities, 1990–1999
### (number of days with AQI values greater than 100)[1]

| Metropolitan statistical area | 1990 | 1991 | 1992 | 1993 | 1994 | 1995 | 1996 | 1997 | 1998 | 1999 |
|---|---|---|---|---|---|---|---|---|---|---|
| Atlanta, Ga. | 42 | 23 | 20 | 36 | 15 | 35 | 25 | 31 | 50 | 61 |
| Baltimore, Md. | 29 | 50 | 23 | 48 | 41 | 36 | 28 | 30 | 51 | 40 |
| Boston, Mass.-N.H. | 7 | 13 | 9 | 6 | 10 | 8 | 2 | 8 | 7 | 5 |
| Chicago, Ill. | 4 | 22 | 4 | 3 | 8 | 21 | 6 | 9 | 7 | 12 |
| Cleveland/Lorain/Elyria, Ohio | 10 | 23 | 11 | 13 | 23 | 24 | 18 | 11 | 20 | 18 |
| Dallas, Tex. | 24 | 2 | 12 | 14 | 27 | 36 | 12 | 20 | 28 | 23 |
| Denver, Colo. | 9 | 6 | 11 | 3 | 1 | 2 | 0 | 0 | 5 | 1 |
| Detroit, Mich. | 11 | 28 | 8 | 5 | 11 | 14 | 13 | 12 | 17 | 15 |
| El Paso, Tex. | 19 | 7 | 10 | 7 | 11 | 8 | 7 | 4 | 6 | 6 |
| Houston, Tex. | 51 | 36 | 32 | 28 | 38 | 66 | 26 | 47 | 38 | 50 |
| Kansas City, Mo.-Kans. | 2 | 11 | 1 | 4 | 10 | 22 | 10 | 18 | 15 | 5 |
| Los Angeles/Long Beach, Calif. | 173 | 168 | 175 | 134 | 139 | 113 | 94 | 60 | 56 | 27 |
| Miami, Fla. | 1 | 1 | 3 | 6 | 1 | 2 | 1 | 3 | 8 | 5 |
| Minneapolis/St. Paul, Minn.-Wis. | 4 | 2 | 1 | 0 | 2 | 5 | 0 | 0 | 1 | 0 |
| New York, N.Y. | 36 | 49 | 10 | 19 | 21 | 19 | 15 | 23 | 17 | 24 |
| Philadelphia, Pa.-N.J. | 39 | 49 | 24 | 51 | 26 | 30 | 22 | 32 | 37 | 32 |
| Phoenix/Mesa, Ariz. | 12 | 11 | 13 | 16 | 10 | 22 | 17 | 12 | 17 | 12 |
| Pittsburgh, Pa. | 19 | 21 | 9 | 13 | 19 | 25 | 11 | 21 | 39 | 23 |
| St. Louis, Mo.-Ill. | 23 | 32 | 15 | 9 | 32 | 34 | 20 | 15 | 23 | 29 |
| San Diego, Calif. | 96 | 67 | 66 | 58 | 46 | 48 | 31 | 14 | 33 | 16 |
| San Francisco, Calif. | 0 | 0 | 0 | 0 | 0 | 2 | 0 | 0 | 0 | 0 |
| Seattle/Bellevue/Everett, Wash. | 9 | 4 | 3 | 0 | 3 | 0 | 6 | 1 | 3 | 1 |
| Washington, D.C.-Md.-Va.-W.Va. | 25 | 48 | 14 | 52 | 20 | 29 | 18 | 29 | 47 | 39 |

1. AQI—Air Quality Index. AQI measures how polluted air is by measuring five major pollutants: ground-level ozone, particulate matter, carbon monoxide, sulfur dioxide, and nitrogen oxide. Based on the amount of each pollutant in the air, the AQI assigns a numerical value to air quality as follows: 0 to 50 (good); 51 to 100 (moderate); 101 to 150 (unhealthy for sensitive groups); 151 to 200 (unhealthy); 201 to 300 (very unhealthy); 301 to 500 (hazardous). *Source:* U.S. Environmental Protection Agency, Office of Air Quality Planning & Standards.

## Major Air Pollutants

| Pollutant | Sources | Effects |
|---|---|---|
| **Ozone.** A gas that can be found in two places. Near the ground (the troposphere), it is a major part of smog. Higher in the air (the stratosphere), it helps block radiation from the sun. | Ozone is not created directly, but is formed when nitrogen oxides and volatile organic compounds mix in sunlight. That is why ozone is mostly found in the summer. Nitrogen oxides come from burning gasoline, coal, or other fossil fuels. There are many types of volatile organic compounds, and they come from sources ranging from factories to trees. | Ozone near the ground can cause a number of health problems. Ozone can lead to more frequent asthma attacks in people who have asthma and can cause sore throats, coughs, and breathing difficulty. It may even lead to premature death. Ozone can also hurt plants and crops. |
| **Carbon monoxide.** A gas that comes from the burning of fossil fuels, mostly in cars. It cannot be seen or smelled. | Carbon monoxide is released when engines burn fossil fuels. Emissions are higher when engines are not tuned properly, and when fuel is not completely burned. Cars emit a lot of the carbon monoxide found outdoors. Furnaces and heaters in the home can emit high concentrations of carbon monoxide, too, if they are not properly maintained. | Carbon monoxide makes it hard for body parts to get the oxygen they need to run correctly. Exposure to carbon monoxide makes people feel dizzy and tired and gives them headaches. Elderly people with heart disease are hospitalized more often when they are exposed to higher amounts of carbon monoxide. |

| Pollutant | Sources | Effects |
|---|---|---|
| **Nitrogen dioxide.** A reddish-brown gas that comes from the burning of fossil fuels. It has a strong smell at high levels. | Nitrogen dioxide mostly comes from power plants and cars. Nitrogen dioxide is formed in two ways—when nitrogen in the fuel is burned, or when nitrogen in the air reacts with oxygen at very high temperatures. Nitrogen dioxide can also react in the atmosphere to form ozone, acid rain, and particles. | High levels of nitrogen dioxide exposure can give people coughs and can make them feel short of breath. People who are exposed to nitrogen dioxide for a long time have a higher chance of getting respiratory infections. Acid rain can hurt plants and animals and can make lakes dangerous to swim or fish in. |
| **Particulate matter.** Solid or liquid matter that is suspended in the air. To remain in the air, particles are usually less than 0.1 mm wide and can be as small as 0.00005 mm. | Particulate matter can be divided into two types—coarse particles and fine particles. Coarse particles are bigger than 0.002 mm and are formed from sources like road dust, sea spray, and construction. Fine particles are smaller than 0.002 mm and are formed when fuel is burned in automobiles and power plants. | Particulate matter that is small enough can enter the lungs and cause health problems. Some of these problems include more frequent asthma attacks, respiratory problems, and premature death. Particulate matter can also make clothes and other materials dirty. |
| **Sulfur dioxide.** A corrosive gas that cannot be seen or smelled at low levels but can have a "rotten egg" smell at high levels. | Sulfur dioxide mostly comes from the burning of coal or oil in power plants. It also comes from factories that make chemicals, paper, or fuel. Like nitrogen dioxide, sulfur dioxide also reacts in the atmosphere to form acid rain and particles. | Sulfur dioxide exposure can affect people who have asthma or emphysema by making it more difficult for them to breathe. It can also irritate people's eyes, noses, and throats. Sulfur dioxide can harm trees and crops, damage buildings, and make it harder for people to see long distances. |
| **Lead.** A blue-gray metal that is very toxic and is found in a number of forms and locations. | Outside, lead comes from cars in areas where unleaded gasoline is not used. Lead can also come from power plants and other industrial sources. Inside, lead paint is an important source of lead, especially in houses where paint is peeling. Lead in old pipes can also be a source of lead in drinking water. | High amounts of lead can be dangerous for small children and can lead to lower IQs and kidney problems. For adults, exposure to lead can increase the chance of having heart attacks or strokes. |
| **Toxic air pollutants.** A large number of chemicals that are known or suspected to cause cancer. Some important pollutants in this category include arsenic, asbestos, benzene, and dioxin. | Each toxic air pollutant comes from a slightly different source, but many are created in chemical plants or are emitted when fossil fuels are burned. Some toxic air pollutants, like asbestos and formaldehyde, can be found in building materials and can lead to indoor air problems. Many toxic air pollutants can also enter the food and water supply, and people can be exposed when they eat or drink. | Toxic air pollutants can cause cancer. Some toxic air pollutants can also cause birth defects. Other effects depend on the pollutant, but can include skin and eye irritation and breathing problems. |
| **Stratospheric ozone depleters.** Chemicals that can destroy the ozone in the stratosphere. These chemicals include chlorofluorocarbons (CFCs), halons, and other compounds that include chlorine or bromine. | CFCs are used in air conditioners and refrigerators, since they work well as coolants. They can also be found in aerosol cans and fire extinguishers. Other stratospheric ozone depleters are used as solvents in industry. | If the ozone in the stratosphere is destroyed, people are exposed to more radiation from the sun (ultraviolet radiation). This can lead to skin cancer and eye problems. Higher ultraviolet radiation can also harm plants and animals. |
| **Greenhouse gases.** Gases that stay in the air for a long time and warm up the planet by trapping sunlight. This is called the "greenhouse effect" because the gases act like the glass in a greenhouse. Some of the important greenhouse gases are carbon dioxide, methane, and nitrous oxide. | Carbon dioxide is the most important greenhouse gas, and it comes from the burning of fossil fuels in cars, power plants, houses, and industry. Methane is released during the processing of fossil fuels, and also comes from natural sources like cows and rice paddies. Nitrous oxide comes from industrial sources and decaying plants. | The greenhouse effect can lead to changes in the climate of the planet. Some of these changes might include more temperature extremes, higher sea levels, changes in forest composition, and damage to land near the coast. Human health might be affected by diseases that are related to temperature or by damage to land and water. |

*Source:* Jonathan Levy, Harvard School of Public Health. Based on information provided by the Environmental Protection Agency.

## Largest Nuclear Power Plants in the U.S.

| Plant | Operating utility | Capacity (net MW[e]) | Year operative |
|---|---|---|---|
| South Texas 1, Tex. | STP Nuclear Operating Co. | 1250 | 1988 |
| South Texas 2, Tex. | STP Nuclear Operating Co. | 1250 | 1989 |
| Palo Verde 3, Ariz. | Arizona Nuclear Power Project | 1247 | 1987 |
| Palo Verde 1, Ariz. | Arizona Nuclear Power Project | 1243 | 1985 |
| Palo Verde 2, Ariz. | Arizona Nuclear Power Project | 1243 | 1986 |
| Grand Gulf 1, Miss. | Entergy Nuclear | 1204 | 1984 |
| Wolf Creek, Kans. | Wolf Creek Nuclear Operating | 1170 | 1985 |
| Perry 1, Ohio | FirstEnergy Nuclear Operating Co. | 1169 | 1986 |
| Seabrook 1, N.H. | North Atlantic Energy Service Corp. | 1161 | 1990 |
| Millstone 3, Conn. | Dominion Generation | 1155 | 1986 |
| Comanche Peak 1, Tex. | Texas Utilities Electric Co. | 1150 | 1990 |
| Comanche Peak 2, Tex. | Texas Utilities Electric Co. | 1150 | 1993 |
| Limerick 2, Pa. | Exelon | 1150 | 1989 |
| Vogtle 2, Ga. | Southern Nuclear Operating Co. | 1149 | 1989 |
| Vogtle 1, Ga. | Southern Nuclear Operating Co. | 1148 | 1987 |
| Nine Mile Point 2, N.Y. | Constellation Nuclear | 1142 | 1987 |
| Limerick 1, Pa. | Exelon | 1134 | 1985 |
| Catawba 1, S.C. | Duke Power Co. | 1129 | 1985 |
| Catawba 2, S.C. | Duke Power Co. | 1129 | 1986 |
| Callaway 1, Mo. | AmerenUE | 1127 | 1984 |
| Sequoyah 1, Tenn. | Tennessee Valley Authority | 1122 | 1980 |
| Browns Ferry 2, Tenn. | Tennessee Valley Authority | 1118 | 1975 |
| Browns Ferry 3, Tenn. | Tennessee Valley Authority | 1118 | 1977 |
| Watts Bar 1, Tenn. | Tennessee Valley Authority | 1118 | 1996 |
| Columbia 2, Wash. | Energy NW | 1117 | 1984 |
| Sequoyah 2, Tenn. | Tennessee Valley Authority | 1117 | 1981 |
| Braidwood 1, Ill. | Exelon | 1116 | 1988 |
| Braidwood 2, Ill. | Exelon | 1116 | 1988 |

*Source:* Department of Energy, Energy Information Administration. Web: www.eia.doe.gov/.

# Animals and Nature

## Animal Names: Male, Female, and Young

| Animal | Male | Female | Young | Animal | Male | Female | Young | Animal | Male | Female | Young |
|---|---|---|---|---|---|---|---|---|---|---|---|
| Ass | Jack | Jenny | Foal | Duck | Drake | Duck | Duckling | Sheep | Ram | Ewe | Lamb |
| Bear | Boar | Sow | Cub | Elephant | Bull | Cow | Calf | Swan | Cob | Pen | Cygnet |
| Cat | Tom | Queen | Kitten | Fox | Dog | Vixen | Cub | Swine | Boar | Sow | Piglet |
| Cattle | Bull | Cow | Calf | Goose | Gander | Goose | Gosling | Tiger | Tiger | Tigress | Cub |
| Chicken | Rooster | Hen | Chick | Horse | Stallion | Mare | Foal | Whale | Bull | Cow | Calf |
| Deer | Buck | Doe | Fawn | Lion | Lion | Lioness | Cub | Wolf | Dog | Bitch | Pup |
| Dog | Dog | Bitch | Pup | Rabbit | Buck | Doe | Bunny | | | | |

*Source:* James G. Doherty, General Curator, The Wildlife Conservation Society.

## Gestation, Incubation, and Longevity of Certain Animals

| Animal | Gestation or incubation, in days (average) | Longevity, in years (record exceptions) | Animal | Gestation or incubation, in days (average) | Longevity, in years (record exceptions) |
|---|---|---|---|---|---|
| Ass | 365 | 18–20 (63) | Horse | 329–345 (336) | 20–25 (50+) |
| Bear | 180–240[1] | 15–30 (47) | Human | 253–303 | [2] |
| Cat | 52–69 (63) | 10–12 (26+) | Kangaroo | 32–39[1] | 4–6 (23) |
| Chicken | 22 | 7–8 (14) | Lion | 105–113 (108) | 10 (29) |
| Cow | 280 | 9–12 (39) | Monkey | 139–270[1] | 12–15[1] (29) |
| Deer | 197–300[1] | 10–15 (26) | Mouse | 19–31[1] | 1–3 (4) |
| Dog | 53–71 (63) | 10–12 (24) | Parakeet (Budgerigar) | 17–20 (18) | 8 (12+) |
| Duck | 21–35[1] (28) | 10 (15) | Pig | 101–130 (115) | 10 (22) |
| Elephant | 510–730[1] (624) | 30–40 (71) | Pigeon | 11–19 | 10–12 (39) |
| Fox | 51–63[1] | 8–10 (14) | Rabbit | 30–35 (31) | 6–8 (15) |
| Goat | 136–160 (151) | 12 (17) | Rat | 21 | 3 (5) |
| Groundhog | 31–32 | 4–9 | Sheep | 144–152[1] (151) | 12 (16) |
| Guinea pig | 58–75 (68) | 3 (6) | Squirrel | 44 | 8–9 (15) |
| Hamster, golden | 15–17 | 2 (8) | Whale | 365–547[1] | — |
| Hippopotamus | 220–255 (240) | 30 (49+) | Wolf | 60–63 | 10–12 (16) |

1. Depending on kind. 2. For life expectancy charts, *see* Life Expectancy at Birth by Race and Sex, p. 132. *Source:* James G. Doherty, General Curator, The Wildlife Conservation Society.

## Animal Group Terminology

*Source:* James G. Doherty, General Curator, The Wildlife Conservation Society.

**ants:** colony
**bears:** sleuth, sloth
**bees:** grist, hive, swarm
**birds:** flight, volery
**cats:** clutter, clowder
**cattle:** drove
**chicks:** brood, clutch
**clams:** bed
**cranes:** sedge, seige
**crows:** murder
**doves:** dule
**ducks:** brace, team
**elephants:** herd
**elks:** gang
**finches:** charm

**fish:** school, shoal, draught
**foxes:** leash, skulk
**geese:** flock, gaggle, skein
**gnats:** cloud, horde
**goats:** trip
**gorillas:** band
**hares:** down, husk
**hawks:** cast
**hens:** brood
**hogs:** drift
**horses:** pair, team
**hounds:** cry, mute, pack
**kangaroos:** troop
**kittens:** kindle, litter
**larks:** exaltation

**lions:** pride
**locusts:** plague
**magpies:** tidings
**mules:** span
**nightingales:** watch
**oxen:** yoke
**oysters:** bed
**parrots:** company
**partridges:** covey
**peacocks:** muster, ostentation
**pheasants:** nest, bouquet
**pigs:** litter
**ponies:** string
**quail:** bevy, covey

**rabbits:** nest
**seals:** pod
**sheep:** drove, flock
**sparrows:** host
**storks:** mustering
**swans:** bevy, wedge
**swine:** sounder
**toads:** knot
**turkeys:** rafter
**turtles:** bale
**vipers:** nest
**whales:** gam, pod
**wolves:** pack, route
**woodcocks:** fall

## Speed of Animals

Most of the following measurements are for maximum speeds over approximate quarter-mile distances. Exceptions—which are included to give a wide range of animals—are the lion and elephant, whose speeds were clocked in the act of charging; the whippet, which was timed over a 200-yard course; the cheetah over a 100-yard distance; humans for a 15-yard segment of a 100-yard run; and the black mamba snake, six-lined race runner, spider, giant tortoise, three-toed sloth, and garden snail, which were measured over various small distances.

| Animal | Speed (mph) | Animal | Speed (mph) | Animal | Speed (mph) |
|---|---|---|---|---|---|
| Peregrine falcon | 200.00+ | Zebra | 40.00 | Cat (domestic) | 30.00 |
| Cheetah | 70.00 | Mongolian wild ass | 40.00 | Human | 27.89 |
| Pronghorn antelope | 61.00 | Greyhound | 39.35 | Elephant | 25.00 |
| Wildebeest | 50.00 | Whippet | 35.50 | Black mamba snake | 20.00 |
| Lion | 50.00 | Rabbit (domestic) | 35.00 | Six-lined race runner | 18.00 |
| Thomson's gazelle | 50.00 | Mule deer | 35.00 | Squirrel | 12.00 |
| Quarter horse | 47.50 | Jackal | 35.00 | Pig (domestic) | 11.00 |
| Elk | 45.00 | Reindeer | 32.00 | Chicken | 9.00 |
| Cape hunting dog | 45.00 | Giraffe | 32.00 | House mouse | 8.00 |
| Coyote | 43.00 | Kangaroo | 30.00 | Spider (Tegenearia atrica) | 1.17 |
| Gray fox | 42.00 | White-tailed deer | 30.00 | Giant tortoise | 0.17 |
| Ostrich | 40.00 | Wart hog | 30.00 | Three-toed sloth | 0.15 |
| Hyena | 40.00 | Grizzly bear | 30.00 | Garden snail | 0.03 |

*Source: Natural History* Magazine, March 1974, copyright 1974. The American Museum of Natural History; and James G. Doherty, General Curator, The Wildlife Conservation Society.

## Threatened and Endangered Species

| Group | Endangered[1] U.S. | Endangered[1] Foreign | Threatened[2] U.S. | Threatened[2] Foreign | Total species | Species with recovery plans |
|---|---|---|---|---|---|---|
| Mammals | 65 | 251 | 9 | 17 | 342 | 53 |
| Birds | 78 | 175 | 14 | 6 | 273 | 75 |
| Reptiles | 14 | 64 | 22 | 15 | 115 | 32 |
| Amphibians | 12 | 8 | 9 | 1 | 30 | 13 |
| Fishes | 71 | 11 | 44 | 1 | 127 | 97 |
| Clams | 62 | 2 | 8 | 0 | 72 | 56 |
| Snails | 21 | 1 | 11 | 0 | 33 | 21 |
| Insects | 35 | 4 | 9 | 0 | 48 | 29 |
| Arachnids | 12 | 0 | 0 | 0 | 12 | 5 |
| Crustaceans | 18 | 0 | 3 | 0 | 21 | 12 |
| **Animal subtotal** | **388** | **516** | **129** | **39** | **1,072** | **390** |
| Flowering plants | 569 | 1 | 144 | 0 | 714 | 566 |
| Conifers and cycads | 2 | 0 | 1 | 2 | 5 | 2 |
| Ferns and allies | 24 | 0 | 2 | 0 | 26 | 26 |
| Lichens | 2 | 0 | 0 | 0 | 2 | 2 |
| **Plant subtotal** | **597** | **1** | **147** | **2** | **747** | **596** |
| **Total** | **985** | **517** | **276** | **41** | **1,819[3]** | **986** |

NOTE: As of July 31, 2002. 1. *Endangered species* are those in danger of extinction. 2. *Threatened species* are those likely to become an endangered species within the foreseeable future. 3. Nine U.S. species have dual status. *Source:* U.S. Fish and Wildlife Service. Web: http://ecos.fws.gov/tess/html/boxscore.html.

# Sharks!

## Myths and statistics about the oceans' most fearsome creature

While *Jaws* and other movies and TV shows portray sharks as ferocious predators aggressively devouring innocent swimmers, nothing could be further from the truth. Considering that tens of thousands of people come in close contact with sharks each year while swimming, surfing, or boating, the numbers of shark attacks are negligible. In 2001, there were 76 unprovoked shark attacks in the world, resulting in 5 deaths.

However, the actual number of attacks is hard to determine because of poor reporting in many areas. News about shark attacks is often repressed so tourists will not be driven away.

Most shark attacks occur on the inshore side of a sandbar or between sandbars because fish congregate there and because sharks can become trapped at low tide. Sharp drop-offs also attract lots of fish and, therefore, sharks.

## Hit and Run

The most common type of attack is the so-called "hit and run" assault. The shark bites and then quickly releases the person and disappears. These attacks usually involve injuries to the leg below the knee and usually are not fatal. Humans are probably too bony to be a good meal for a shark.

Hit-and-run attacks are probably most often cases of mistaken identity. They usually happen near the surface and in poor visibility. Breaking surf, heavy currents, and other factors may make it hard for the shark to see its victim clearly.

Seen from below, swimmers or surfboarders are often mistaken for seals or sea lions, whose fatty bodies are a favorite treat for sharks. Human splashing creates irregular ripples in the water below, which to a shark may indicate an injured seal or fish that is likely be an easy meal.

Shiny jewelry that gleams like fish scales, multicolor swimsuits, and irregular tanning, especially on the bottom of the feet, could also confuse a shark into thinking a person was an animal.

In some hit-and-run attacks, sharks could be displaying dominance behavior, perhaps warning a human that it is intruding in its territory.

When attacks are reported, it is often difficult to determine what type of shark was involved since even experts can have trouble distinguishing them in the water. In Florida waters, black tip, black nose, and spinner sharks are probably responsible for most of the hit-and-run attacks.

## Bump and Bite

"Bump and bite" and sneak attacks are much more rare and more apt to result in serious injury or fatality. In bump-and-bite attacks, the shark circles its victim then bumps into it before attacking. Sneak attacks occur without warning. Often, these attacks are repeated several times. These incidents usually take place in deeper water and are not believed to be cases of mistaken identity. Rather, sharks are angry or want to eat.

White, tiger, and bull sharks are believed responsible for most bump-and-bite and sneak attacks on humans. These are the largest species that eat human-size prey, including marine mammals, sea turtles, and large fish. Other species believed to attack in this manner, but more rarely, include the hammerhead, short fin mako, oceanic whitetip, Galapagos, and some reef sharks such as the Caribbean. Gray reef, lemon, dusky, blue, sand tiger, nurse, and Ganges River sharks will also attack humans.

Still, most of the more than 250 species in the world do not attack humans. In fact the largest species, the whale and basking sharks, eat only plankton. Even so, experts warn that any shark 6 ft long or more is large and powerful enough to kill a person and should be treated with caution.

Provoked attacks are most common when a person touches a shark, including helping untangle it from fishing nets. Divers who touch or feed a shark risk attack.

## World Shark Attacks, 1580–2001

**According to the International Shark Attack File, between 1580 and 2001 there were 2,111 confirmed shark attacks around the world.**

| Region | Confirmed attacks | Deaths | Region | Confirmed attacks | Deaths |
|---|---|---|---|---|---|
| United States | 754 | 48 | Antilles and the Bahamas | 78 | 15 |
| Hawaii | 101 | 20 | Bermuda | 6 | 0 |
| Australia | 323 | 149 | Mexico and Central America | 65 | 35 |
| Africa | 293 | 76 | Pacific Islands, Oceania | 156 | 59 |
| Asia | 120 | 57 | New Zealand | 53 | 8 |
| Europe | 37 | 19 | Canada | 3 | 0 |
| South America | 93 | 24 | Other | 29 | 7 |

*Source:* International Shark Attack File, maintained by the Florida Museum of Natural History at the University of Florida, Gainesville, and the American Elasmobranch Society. Web: www.flmnh.ufl.edu/fish/sharks/isaf/isaf.htm.

## America's Eleven Most Endangered Rivers, 2002

Each year the organization American Rivers analyzes the condition of the nation's rivers to determine which are the most "endangered." Threats to these rivers include dams and channelizations that are harmful to fish or wildlife populations; depletion due to the rivers' use as a water supply for human populations; and coal mining operations that fill streams with coal and dirt. For more information, refer to the American Rivers website: www.amrivers.org.

| Rank | River | State(s) | Threat(s) |
|---|---|---|---|
| 1. | Missouri River | Mont., N.D., S.D., Neb., Kans., Iowa, Mo. | Dam operations |
| 2. | Big Sunflower River | Miss. | Flood control projects |
| 3. | Klamath River | Ore./Calif. | Water withdrawal and pollution |
| 4. | Kansas River | Kans. | Pollution; removal of Clean Water Act protections |
| 5. | White River | Ark. | Navigation and irrigation projects |
| 6. | Powder River | Wyo. | Coal bed methane extraction |
| 7. | Altamaha River | Ga. | Reservoir and power plant construction |
| 8. | Allagash Wilderness Waterway | Maine | Removal from the Wild and Scenic Rivers System; loss of wilderness values |
| 9. | Canning River | Alaska | Oil and gas exploration and development |
| 10. | Guadalupe River | Tex. | Water diversion |
| 11. | Apalachicola River | Fla. | Navigation and water withdrawals |

## Water Supply of the World

The Antarctic Icecap is the largest supply of fresh water, nearly 2% of the world's total of fresh and salt water. As can be seen from the table below, the amount of water in our atmosphere is over ten times as much as the water in all the rivers taken together. The fresh water actually available for human use in lakes and rivers and the accessible ground water amounts to only about one-third of 1% of the world's total water supply.

| | Surface area (sq mi) | Volume (cu mi) | Percentage of total[1] |
|---|---|---|---|
| **Salt water** | | | |
| The oceans | 139,500,000 | 317,000,000 | 97.2% |
| Inland seas and saline lakes | 270,000 | 25,000 | 0.008 |
| **Fresh water** | | | |
| Freshwater lakes | 330,000 | 30,000 | 0.009 |
| All rivers (average level) | — | 300 | 0.0001 |
| Antarctic Icecap | 6,000,000 | 6,300,000 | 1.9 |
| Arctic Icecap and glaciers | 900,000 | 680,000 | 0.21 |
| Water in the atmosphere | 197,000,000 | 3,100 | 0.001 |
| Ground water within half a mile from surface | — | 1,000,000 | 0.31 |
| Deep-lying ground water | — | 1,000,000 | 0.31 |
| **Total (rounded)** | — | **326,000,000** | **100.00** |

1. All figures are estimated. *Source:* Department of the Interior, Geological Survey.

## Human Access to Water Supplies, by Region, 2000

| | Percent served | | | | Percent served | | |
|---|---|---|---|---|---|---|---|
| Region | Urban water supply | Rural water supply | Total water supply | Region | Urban water supply | Rural water supply | Total water supply |
| Global | 94% | 71% | 82% | Oceania | 98% | 63% | 88% |
| Africa | 85 | 47 | 81 | Europe | 100 | 87 | 96 |
| Asia | 94 | 75 | 81 | North America | 100 | 100 | 100 |
| Latin America and the Caribbean | 93 | 62 | 85 | | | | |

*Source: Global Water Supply and Sanitation Assessment 2000 Report, World Health Organization (WHO). Web: www.who.int.*

## State of the World's Forests

*Source: FAO; Natural Resources Defense Council; World Resources Institute.*

- Half of the forests that originally covered 46% of the Earth's land surface are gone. Only one-fifth of the Earth's original forests remain pristine and undisturbed.
- In the 1990s, the world's forested area declined by about 2.4% (90,000 sq km) per year.
- Tropical deforestation rates, the world's highest, are estimated at over 130,000 sq km per year.

- The U.S. consumes 27% of the wood commercially harvested worldwide.
- In North America, 56% of coastal temperate rainforests have been destroyed.
- 430,000 mi of roads cut through U.S. National Forests, primarily for logging purposes.
- Global wood consumption is projected to double over the next 30 years.

# The National Park System

*Source:* Department of the Interior, National Park Service.

The National Park System of the United States is administered by the National Park Service, a bureau of the Department of the Interior. Started with the establishment of Yellowstone National Park on March 1, 1872, the system includes not only the most extraordinary and spectacular scenic exhibits in the United States, but also a large number of sites distinguished either for their historic or prehistoric importance or scientific interest, or for their superior recreational assets. The National Park System is made up of 375 areas covering more than 83 million acres in every state except Delaware. It also includes areas in the District of Columbia, American Samoa, Guam, Puerto Rico, and the Virgin Islands. A list of the areas follows. Note that the National Park System does not include the Affiliated Areas, National Heritage Areas, Wild and Scenic Rivers System, and the National Trails System. See also the excellent website of the Park Service: www.nps.gov.

## NATIONAL PARKS

| Name, location, and year authorized | Acreage | Outstanding characteristics |
|---|---|---|
| Acadia (Maine), 1919 | 47,498.27 | Rugged seashore on Mt. Desert Island and adjacent mainland |
| Arches (Utah), 1971 | 76,518.98 | Unusual stone arches, windows, pedestals caused by erosion (park was a National Monument 1929–1971) |
| Badlands (S.D.), 1978 | 242,755.94 | Arid land of fossils, prairie, bison, deer, bighorn sheep, antelope (park was a National Monument 1929–1978) |
| Big Bend (Tex.), 1935 | 801,163.21 | Mountains and desert bordering the Rio Grande |
| Biscayne (Fla.), 1980 | 172,924.07 | Aquatic, coral reef park south of Miami (park was a National Monument, 1968–1980) |
| Bryce Canyon (Utah), 1924 | 35,835.08 | Area of grotesque eroded rocks brilliantly colored |
| Canyonlands (Utah), 1964 | 337,597.83 | Colorful wilderness with impressive red-rock canyons, spires, arches |
| Capitol Reef (Utah), 1971 | 241,904.26 | Highly colored sedimentary rock formations in high, narrow gorges (park was a National Monument 1937–1971) |
| Carlsbad Caverns (N.M.), 1930 | 46,766.45 | One of the world's largest known caves |
| Channel Islands (Calif.), 1980 | 249,561.00 | Area is rich in marine mammals, sea birds, endangered species, and archeology (park was a National Monument 1938–1980) |
| Crater Lake (Ore.), 1902 | 183,224.05 | Deep blue lake in heart of inactive volcano |
| Cuyahoga Valley (Ohio) | 32,859.09 | Wilderness area offering recreational, historic, and cultural attractions, including scenic rail journeys (park was a National Recreation Area 1974–2000) |
| Death Valley (Calif.-Nev.), 1994 | 3,340,409.65 | Largest desert, surrounded by high mountains, containing the lowest point in the Western Hemisphere (park was a National Monument 1933–1994) |
| Denali (Alaska), 1917 | 4,740,911.72 | Contains Mt. McKinley, N. America's highest mountain (20,320 ft) (formerly Mt. McKinley National Park, 1917–1980) |
| Dry Tortugas (Fla.), 1992 | 64,701.22 | Located 70 mi off Key West. Features an underwater nature trail (formerly Ft. Jefferson National Monument 1935–1992) |
| Everglades (Fla.), 1934 | 1,398,902.95 | Subtropical area with abundant bird and animal life |
| Gates of the Arctic (Alaska), 1980 | 7,523,897.77 | Diverse north central wilderness contains part of Brooks Range |
| Glacier (Mont.), 1910 | 1,013,572.42 | Rocky Mountain scenery with many glaciers and lakes |
| Glacier Bay (Alaska), 1980 | 3,224,840.31 | Popular for wildlife, whale-watching, glacier-calving, and scenery (park was a National Monument 1925–1980) |
| Grand Canyon (Ariz.), 1919 | 1,217,403.32 | Mile-deep gorge, 4 to 18 mi wide, 217 mi long |
| Grand Teton (Wyo.), 1929 | 309,994.93 | Picturesque range of high mountain peaks |
| Great Basin (Nev.), 1986 | 77,180.00 | Exceptional scenic, biologic, and geologic attractions (formerly Lehman Caves National Monument 1922–1986) |
| Great Smoky Mts. (N.C.-Tenn.), 1926 | 521,490.18 | Highest mountain range east of Black Hills; luxuriant plant life |
| Guadalupe Mountains (Tex.), 1966 | 86,415.97 | Contains highest point in Texas: Guadalupe Peak (8,751 ft) |
| Haleakala (Hawaii), 1916 | 29,830.15 | World-famous 10,023-foot Haleakala volcano (dormant) (formerly part of Hawaii National Park. Renamed in 1960) |
| Hawaii Volcanoes (Hawaii), 1916 | 209,695.38 | Spectacular volcanic area; luxuriant vegetation at lower levels (formerly Hawaii National Park. Renamed in 1961) |
| Hot Springs (Ark.), 1921 | 5,549.78 | 47 mineral hot springs said to have therapeutic value |
| Isle Royale (Mich.), 1931 | 571,790.11 | Largest wilderness island in Lake Superior; moose, wolves, lakes |
| Joshua Tree (Calif.), 1994 | 1,018,121.62 | Desert region featuring Joshua trees and a great variety of plants and animals (park was a National Monument 1936–1994) |
| Katmai (Alaska), 1980 | 3,674,529.68 | Expansion may assure brown bear's preservation. Park is known for fishing, 1912 eruption of Novarupta, bears (park was a National Monument 1918–1980) |
| Kenai Fjords (Alaska), 1980 | 669,982.99 | Mountain goats, marine mammals, birdlife are features at this seacoast park near Seward (park was a National Monument 1978–1980) |

| Name, location, and year authorized | Acreage | Outstanding characteristics |
|---|---|---|
| Kings Canyon (Calif.), 1890 | 461,901.20 | Huge canyons; high mountains; giant sequoias (formerly General Grant National Park 1890–1940) |
| Kobuk Valley (Alaska), 1980 | 1,750,736.86 | Native culture and anthropology center around the broad Kobuk River in northwest Alaska (park was a National Monument 1978–1980) |
| Lake Clark (Alaska), 1980 | 2,619,733.21 | Park provides scenic and wilderness recreation across Cook Inlet from Anchorage (park was a National Monument 1978–1980) |
| Lassen Volcanic (Calif.), 1916 | 106,372.36 | Exhibits of impressive volcanic phenomena |
| Mammoth Cave (Ky.), 1926 | 52,830.19 | Vast limestone labyrinth with underground river |
| Mesa Verde (Colo.), 1906 | 52,121.93 | Best-preserved prehistoric cliff dwellings in United States |
| Mount Rainier (Wash.), 1899 | 235,625.00 | Single-peak glacial system; dense forests, flowered meadows |
| National Park of American Samoa, 1988 | 9,000.00 | Samoa National Park, American Samoa: two rain forest preserves and a coral reef on the island of Ofu are home to unique tropical animals. The park also includes several thousand acres on the islands of Tutuila and Ta'u |
| North Cascades (Wash.), 1968 | 504,780.94 | Roadless Alpine landscape; jagged peaks; mountain lakes; glaciers |
| Olympic (Wash.), 1938 | 922,650.94 | Finest Pacific Northwest rain forest; scenic mountain park |
| Petrified Forest (Ariz.), 1962 | 93,532.57 | Extensive natural exhibit of petrified wood (park was a National Monument 1906–1962) |
| Redwood (Calif.), 1968 | 112,612.98 | Coastal redwood forests; contains world's tallest known tree (369.2 ft) |
| Rocky Mountain (Colo.), 1915 | 265,769.14 | Section of the Rocky Mountains; 107 named peaks over 10,000 ft |
| Saguaro (Ariz.), 1994 | 91,445.46 | Giant saguaro cacti, unique to the Sonoran Desert, sometimes reach a height of 50 ft in this cactus forest (park was a National Monument 1933–1994) |
| Sequoia (Calif.), 1890 | 402,510.05 | Giant sequoias; magnificent High Sierra scenery, including Mt. Whitney |
| Shenandoah (Va.), 1926 | 199,016.61 | Tree-covered mountains; scenic Skyline Drive |
| Theodore Roosevelt (N.D.), 1978 | 70,446.89 | Scenic valley of Little Missouri River; T.R. Ranch; wildlife (Theodore Roosevelt National Memorial Park 1947–1978) |
| Virgin Islands (U.S. V.I.), 1956 | 14,688.87 | Beaches; lush hills; prehistoric Carib Indian relics |
| Voyageurs (Minn.), 1971 | 218,200.17 | Wildlife, canoeing, fishing, and hiking |
| Wind Cave (S.D.), 1903 | 28,295.03 | Limestone caverns in Black Hills; buffalo herd |
| Wrangell-St. Elias (Alaska), 1980 | 8,323,147.59 | Largest Park System area has abundant wildlife, second highest peak in U.S. (Mt. St. Elias); adjoins Canadian park (park was a National Monument 1978–1980) |
| Yellowstone (Wyo.-Mont.-Idaho), 1872 | 2,219,790.71 | World's greatest geyser area; abundant falls, wildlife, and canyons |
| Yosemite (Calif.), 1890 | 761,266.28 | Mountains; inspiring gorges and waterfalls; giant sequoias |
| Zion (Utah), 1919 | 146,592.31 | Multicolored gorge in heart of southern Utah desert |

| Name and location | Total acreage | Name and location | Total acreage |
|---|---|---|---|
| **National Historical Parks** | | Minuteman (Mass.) | 965.03 |
| Appomattox Court House (Va.) | 1,772.35 | Morristown (N.J.) | 1,706.11 |
| Boston (Mass.) | 43.32 | Natchez (Miss.) | 108.26 |
| Cane River Creole (La.) | 207.38 | New Bedford Whaling (Mass.) | 34.00 |
| Chaco Culture (N.M.) | 33,974.29 | New Orleans Jazz (La.) | 5.13 |
| Chesapeake and Ohio Canal (Md.-W.Va.-D.C.) | 19,592.98 | Nez Perce (Idaho) | 2,133.65 |
| Colonial (Va.) | 9,401.07 | Pecos (N.M.) | 6,666.79 |
| Cumberland Gap (Ky.-Tenn.-Va.) | 20,463.15 | Puʻuhonua o Hōnaunau (Hawaii) | 181.80 |
| Dayton Aviation Heritage (Ohio) | 86.46 | Rosie the Riveter/WW II Home Front (Calif.) | 145.19 |
| George Rogers Clark (Ind.) | 26.17 | Salt River Bay and Ecological Preserve (U.S. V.I.) | 947.75 |
| Harpers Ferry (W.Va.-Md.) | 2,502.54 | San Antonio Missions (Tex.) | 816.34 |
| Hopewell Culture (Ohio) | 1,164.96 | San Francisco Maritime (Calif.) | 49.86 |
| Independence (Pa.) | 44.91 | San Juan Island (Wash.) | 1,751.99 |
| Jean Lafitte (La.) | 20,035.09 | Saratoga (N.Y.) | 3,392.42 |
| Kalaupapa (Hawaii) | 10,778.88 | Sitka (Alaska) | 113.17 |
| Kaloko Honokohau (Hawaii) | 1,160.91 | Tumacacori (Ariz.) | 46.28 |
| Keweenaw (Mich.) | 1,869.40 | Valley Forge (Pa.) | 3,464.25 |
| Klondike Goldrush (Alaska-Wash.) | 13,191.35 | War in the Pacific (Guam) | 2,036.98 |
| Lowell (Mass.) | 141.34 | Women's Rights (N.Y.) | 7.44 |
| Lyndon B. Johnson (Tex.) | 1,570.15 | | |
| Marsh-Billings-Rockefeller (Vt.) | 643.07 | | |

| Name and location | Total acreage |
|---|---|
| **National Monuments** | |
| Agate Fossil Beds (Neb.) | 3,055.22 |
| Alibates Flint Quarries (Tex.) | 1,370.97 |
| Aniakchak (Alaska) | 137,176.00 |
| Aztec Ruins (N.M.) | 317.80 |
| Bandelier (N.M.) | 33,676.67 |
| Black Canyon of the Gunnison (Colo.) | 29,926.60 |
| Booker T. Washington (Va.) | 223.92 |
| Buck Island Reef (U.S. V.I.) | 19,015.47 |
| Cabrillo (Calif.) | 159.94 |
| Canyon de Chelly (Ariz.) | 83,840.00 |
| Cape Krusenstern (Alaska) | 649,182.18 |
| Capulin Volcano (N.M.) | 792.84 |
| Casa Grande Ruins (Ariz.) | 472.50 |
| Castillo de San Marcos (Fla.) | 20.21 |
| Castle Clinton (N.Y.) | 1.00 |
| Cedar Breaks (Utah) | 6,154.60 |
| Chiricahua (Ariz.) | 11,984.73 |
| Colorado (Colo.) | 20,533.93 |
| Congaree Swamp (S.C.) | 21,887.53 |
| Craters of the Moon (Idaho) | 714,727.05 |
| Devils Postpile (Calif.) | 798.46 |
| Devils Tower (Wyo.) | 1,346.91 |
| Dinosaur (Utah-Colo.) | 210,277.55 |
| Effigy Mounds (Iowa) | 2,526.39 |
| El Malpais (N.M.) | 114,276.95 |
| El Morro (N.M.) | 1,278.72 |
| Florissant Fossil Beds (Colo.) | 5,998.09 |
| Fort Frederica (Ga.) | 241.42 |
| Fort Matanzas (Fla.) | 300.11 |
| Fort McHenry (Md.) | 43.26 |
| Fort Pulaski (Ga.) | 5,623.10 |
| Fort Stanwix (N.Y.) | 15.52 |
| Fort Sumter (S.C.) | 199.57 |
| Fort Union (N.M.) | 720.60 |
| Fossil Butte (Wyo.) | 8,198.00 |
| George Washington Birthplace (Va.) | 550.23 |
| George Washington Carver (Mo.) | 210.00 |
| Gila Cliff Dwellings (N.M.) | 533.13 |
| Governor's Island (N.Y.) | 20.00 |
| Grand Canyon–Parashant (Ariz.) | 1,217,403.32 |
| Grand Portage (Minn.) | 709.97 |
| Great Sand Dunes (N.M.) | 42,272.18 |
| Hagerman Fossil Beds (Idaho) | 4,351.15 |
| Hohokam Pima (Ariz.) | 1,690.00 |
| Homestead (Neb.) | 195.11 |
| Hovenweep (Utah-Colo.) | 784.93 |
| Jewel Cave (S.D.) | 1,273.51 |
| John Day Fossil Beds (Ore.) | 14,056.73 |
| Lava Beds (Calif.) | 46,559.87 |
| Little Big Horn Battlefield (Mont.) | 765.34 |
| Montezuma Castle (Ariz.) | 857.69 |
| Muir Woods (Calif.) | 553.55 |
| Natural Bridges (Utah) | 7,636.49 |
| Navajo (Ariz.) | 360.00 |
| Ocmulgee (Ga.) | 701.54 |
| Oregon Caves (Ore.) | 487.98 |
| Organ Pipe Cactus (Ariz.) | 330,688.50 |
| Petroglyph (N.M.) | 7,231.63 |
| Pinnacles (Calif.) | 16,265.44 |
| Pipe Spring (Ariz.) | 40.00 |
| Pipestone (Minn.) | 281.78 |
| Poverty Point (La.) | 910.85 |
| Rainbow Bridge (Utah) | 160.00 |
| Russell Cave (Ala.) | 310.45 |
| Salinas Pueblo Missions (N.M.) | 1,071.42 |

| Name and location | Total acreage |
|---|---|
| Scotts Bluff (Neb.) | 3,003.30 |
| Statue of Liberty (N.Y.-N.J.) | 58.38 |
| Sunset Crater Volcano (Ariz.) | 3,040.00 |
| Timpanogos Cave (Utah) | 250.00 |
| Tonto (Ariz.) | 1,120.00 |
| Tuzigoot (Ariz.) | 800.62 |
| U.S. Virgin Islands Coral Reef (V.I.) | 13,892.78 |
| Walnut Canyon (Ariz.) | 3,579.46 |
| White Sands (N.M.) | 143,732.92 |
| Wupatki (Ariz.) | 35,422.13 |
| Yucca House (Colo.) | 33.97 |
| **National Preserves** | |
| Aniakchak (Alaska) | 465,603.00 |
| Bering Land Bridge (Alaska) | 2,697,405.72 |
| Big Cypress (Fla.) | 720,565.67 |
| Big Thicket (Tex.) | 97,168.03 |
| Denali (Alaska) | 1,334,117.99 |
| Gates of the Arctic (Alaska) | 948,628.90 |
| Glacier Bay (Alaska) | 58,406.00 |
| Great Sand Dunes (Colo.) | 41,686.00 |
| Katmai (Alaska) | 418,699.22 |
| Lake Clark (Alaska) | 1,410,291.99 |
| Little River Canyon (Ala.) | 13,632.96 |
| Mojave (Calif.) | 1,494,665.51 |
| Noatak (Alaska) | 6,569,904.43 |
| Tallgrass Prairie (Kans.) | 10,894.00 |
| Timucuan Ecological and Historic Preserve (Fla.) | 46,288.82 |
| Wrangell-St. Elias (Alaska) | 4,852,753.10 |
| Yukon-Charley (Alaska) | 2,526,512.31 |
| **National Reserves** | |
| City of Rocks (Idaho) | 14,107.19 |
| Ebey's Landing (Wash.) | 19,018.64 |
| **National Military Parks** | |
| Chickamauga and Chattanooga (Ga.-Tenn.) | 8,227.82 |
| Fredericksburg and Spotsylvania (Va.) | 8,362.34 |
| Gettysburg Nat. Mil. Park (Pa.) | 5,990.91 |
| Guilford Courthouse (N.C.) | 220.69 |
| Horseshoe Bend (Ala.) | 2,040.00 |
| Kings Mountain (S.C.) | 3,945.29 |
| Pea Ridge (Ark.) | 4,300.35 |
| Shiloh Nat. Park (Tenn.) | 4,015.81 |
| Vicksburg Nat. Mil. Park (Miss.) | 1,737.65 |
| **National Battlefields** | |
| Antietam (Md.) | 3,376.53 |
| Big Hole (Mont.) | 655.61 |
| Cowpens (S.C.) | 841.56 |
| Fort Donelson (Tenn.) | 551.69 |
| Fort Necessity (Pa.) | 902.80 |
| Little Big Horn (Mont.) | 765.34 |
| Monocacy (Md.) | 1,647.01 |
| Moores Creek (N.C.) | 87.75 |
| Petersburg (Va.) | 2,659.19 |
| Stones River (Tenn.) | 713.63 |
| Tupelo (Miss.) | 1.00 |
| Wilson's Creek (Mo.) | 1,749.91 |
| **National Battlefield Parks** | |
| Kennesaw Mountain (Ga.) | 2,884.14 |
| Manassas (Va.) | 5,067.23 |
| Richmond (Va.) | 1,718.08 |

| Name and location | Total acreage |
|---|---|
| **National Battlefield Site** | |
| Brices Cross Roads (Miss.) | 1.00 |

| Name and location | Total acreage |
|---|---|
| **National Historic Sites** | |
| Abraham Lincoln Birthplace (Ky.) | 116.50 |
| Adams (Mass.) | 23.82 |
| Allegheny Portage Railroad (Pa.) | 1,249.20 |
| Andersonville (Ga.) | 494.61 |
| Andrew Johnson (Tenn.) | 16.68 |
| Bent's Old Fort (Colo.) | 798.80 |
| Boston African-American (Mass.) | 0.59 |
| Brown v. Board of Education (Kans.) | 1.85 |
| Carl Sandburg Home (N.C.) | 263.65 |
| Charles Pinckney (S.C.) | 28.45 |
| Christiansted (U.S. V.I.) | 27.15 |
| Clara Barton (Md.) | 8.59 |
| Edgar Allan Poe (Pa.) | 0.52 |
| Edison (N.J.) | 21.25 |
| Eisenhower (Pa.) | 690.46 |
| Eleanor Roosevelt (N.Y.) | 180.50 |
| Eugene O'Neill (Calif.) | 13.19 |
| First Ladies (Ohio) | 0.33 |
| Ford's Theatre (Lincoln Museum) (D.C.) | 0.29 |
| Fort Bowie (Ariz.) | 999.45 |
| Fort Davis (Tex.) | 473.87 |
| Fort Laramie (Wyo.) | 832.85 |
| Fort Larned (Kan.) | 718.39 |
| Fort Point (Calif.) | 29.00 |
| Fort Raleigh (N.C.) | 512.93 |
| Fort Scott (Kan.) | 16.69 |
| Fort Smith (Ark.-Okla.) | 75.05 |
| Fort Union Trading Post (N.D.-Mont.) | 443.81 |
| Fort Vancouver (Wash.) | 208.89 |
| Frederick Douglass Home (D.C.) | 8.53 |
| Frederick Law Olmsted (Mass.) | 7.21 |
| Friendship Hill (Pa.) | 674.56 |
| Golden Spike (Utah) | 2,735.28 |
| Grant-Kohrs Ranch (Mont.) | 1,618.38 |
| Hampton (Md.) | 62.04 |
| Harry S. Truman (Mo.) | 6.67 |
| Herbert Hoover (Iowa) | 186.80 |
| Home of F. D. Roosevelt (N.Y.) | 799.98 |
| Hopewell Furnace (Pa.) | 848.06 |
| Hubbell Trading Post (Ariz.) | 160.09 |
| James A. Garfield (Ohio) | 7.82 |
| Jimmy Carter (Ga.) | 70.86 |
| John F. Kennedy (Mass.) | 0.09 |
| John Muir (Calif.) | 344.73 |
| Knife River Indian Villages (N.D.) | 1,758.35 |
| Lincoln Home (Ill.) | 12.24 |
| Little Rock Central High School (Ark.) | 27.56 |
| Longfellow (Mass.) | 1.98 |
| Maggie L. Walker (Va.) | 1.29 |
| Manzanar (Calif.) | 813.81 |
| Martin Luther King, Jr. (Ga.) | 38.73 |
| Martin Van Buren (N.Y.) | 39.55 |
| Mary McLeod Bethune Council House (D.C.) | 0.07 |
| Minuteman Missile (S.D.) | 15.00 |
| Nicodemus (Kans.) | 161.35 |
| Ninety Six (S.C.) | 989.14 |
| Palo Alto Battlefield (Tex.) | 3,357.42 |
| Pennsylvania Avenue (D.C.) | 0.00 |
| Puukohola Heiau (Hawaii) | 86.24 |
| Sagamore Hill (N.Y.) | 83.02 |
| Saint-Gaudens (N.H.) | 148.15 |

| Name and location | Total acreage |
|---|---|
| Saint Paul's Church (N.Y.) | 6.13 |
| Salem Maritime (Mass.) | 9.02 |
| San Juan (P.R.) | 75.13 |
| Saugus Iron Works (Mass.) | 8.51 |
| Springfield Armory (Mass.) | 54.93 |
| Steamtown (Pa.) | 62.48 |
| Theodore Roosevelt Birthplace (N.Y.) | 0.11 |
| Theodore Roosevelt Inaugural (N.Y.) | 1.03 |
| Thomas Stone (Md.) | 328.25 |
| Tuskegee Airmen (Ala.) | 86.69 |
| Tuskegee Institute (Ala.) | 57.92 |
| Ulysses S. Grant (Mo.) | 9.60 |
| Vanderbilt Mansion (N.Y.) | 211.65 |
| Washita Battlefield (Okla.) | 315.20 |
| Weir Farms (Conn.) | 74.30 |
| Whitman Mission (Wash.) | 98.15 |
| William Howard Taft (Ohio) | 3.10 |

| Name and location | Total acreage |
|---|---|
| **National Memorials** | |
| Arkansas Post (Ark.) | 746.88 |
| Arlington House, the Robert E. Lee Memorial (Va.) | 27.91 |
| Chamizal (Tex.) | 54.90 |
| Coronado (Ariz.) | 4,750.22 |
| De Soto (Fla.) | 26.84 |
| Federal Hall (N.Y.) | 0.45 |
| Fort Caroline (Fla.) | 138.39 |
| Fort Clatsop (Ore.) | 125.20 |
| Franklin Delano Roosevelt Memorial (D.C.) | 7.50 |
| General Grant (N.Y.) | 0.76 |
| Hamilton Grange (N.Y.) | 1.04 |
| Jefferson National Expansion Memorial (Mo.) | 192.83 |
| Johnstown Flood (Pa.) | 164.12 |
| Korean War Veterans (D.C.) | 2.20 |
| Lincoln Boyhood (Ind.) | 199.65 |
| Lincoln Memorial (D.C.) | 107.43 |
| Lyndon Baines Johnson Memorial Grove on the Potomac (D.C.) | 17.00 |
| Mount Rushmore (S.D.) | 1,278.45 |
| Oklahoma City (Okla.) | 6.24 |
| Perry's Victory and International Peace Memorial (Ohio) | 25.39 |
| Roger Williams (R.I.) | 4.56 |
| Thaddeus Kosciuszko (Pa.) | 0.02 |
| Theodore Roosevelt Island (D.C.) | 88.50 |
| Thomas Jefferson Memorial (D.C.) | 18.36 |
| USS Arizona Memorial (Hawaii) | 10.50 |
| Vietnam Veterans Memorial (D.C.) | 2.00 |
| Washington Monument (D.C.) | 106.01 |
| Wright Brothers (N.C.) | 428.44 |

| Name and location | Total acreage |
|---|---|
| **National Seashores** | |
| Assateague Island (Md.-Va.) | 39,733.43 |
| Canaveral (Fla.) | 57,661.69 |
| Cape Cod (Mass.) | 43,604.94 |
| Cape Hatteras (N.C.) | 30,321.46 |
| Cape Lookout (N.C.) | 28,243.36 |
| Cumberland Island (Ga.) | 36,415.13 |
| Fire Island (N.Y.) | 19,579.47 |
| Gulf Islands (Fla.-Miss.) | 137,457.89 |
| Padre Island (Tex.) | 130,434.27 |
| Point Reyes (Calif.) | 71,067.70 |

| Name and location | Total acreage |
|---|---|
| **National Parkways** | |
| Blue Ridge (Va.-N.C.) | 91,966.37 |
| George Washington Memorial (Va.-Md.) | 7,333.02 |
| John D. Rockefeller, Jr., Memorial (Wyo.) | 23,777.22 |
| Natchez Trace (Miss.-Tenn.-Ala.) | 51,981.90 |
| **National Lakeshores** | |
| Apostle Islands (Wis.) | 69,371.89 |
| Indiana Dunes (Ind.) | 15,062.82 |
| Pictured Rocks (Mich.) | 73,228.37 |
| Sleeping Bear Dunes (Mich.) | 71,176.17 |
| **National Park System Rivers** | |
| Alagnak Wild River (Alaska) | 30,665.45 |
| Big South Fork National River and Recreation Area (Ky.-Tenn.) | 125,310.34 |
| Bluestone National Scenic River (W. Va.) | 4,309.51 |
| Buffalo National River (Ark.) | 94,294,06 |
| Delaware National Scenic River (Pa.) | 1,973.33 |
| Great Egg Harbor Scenic and Recreational River (N.J.-Pa.) | 43,311.42 |
| Mississippi National River and Recreation Area (Minn.) | 53,775.00 |
| Missouri National Recreational River (Neb.) | 45,350.00 |
| New River Gorge National River (W.Va.) | 70,075.35 |
| Niobrara National Scenic Riverway (Neb.) | 5,962.00 |
| Obed Wild and Scenic River (Tenn.) | 5,173.69 |
| Ozark National Scenic Riverways (Mo.) | 80,800.04 |
| Rio Grande Wild and Scenic River (Tex.) | 9,600.00 |
| St. Croix National Scenic River (Minn.-Wis.) | 67,478.18 |
| Upper Delaware Scenic and Recreational River (Pa.) | 75,000.28 |
| **National Recreation Areas** | |
| Amistad (Tex.) | 58,500.00 |
| Bighorn Canyon (Wyo.-Mont.) | 120,296.22 |
| Boston Harbor Islands (Mass.) | 1,482.25 |
| Chattahoochee River (Ga.) | 9,111.35 |
| Chickasaw (Okla.) | 9,888.83 |
| Curecanti (Colo.) | 41,972.42 |
| Delaware Water Gap (Pa.-N.J.) | 66,741.81 |
| Gateway (N.Y.-N.J.) | 26,606.63 |
| Gauley River (W. Va.) | 11,497.70 |
| Glen Canyon (Ariz.-Utah) | 1,254,306.19 |
| Golden Gate (Calif.) | 74,815.85 |
| Lake Chelan (Wash.) | 61,957.92 |

| Name and location | Total acreage |
|---|---|
| Lake Mead (Ariz.-Nev.) | 1,495,665.69 |
| Lake Meredith (Tex.) | 44,977.63 |
| Lake Roosevelt (Wash.) | 100,390.31 |
| Ross Lake (Wash.) | 117,574.59 |
| Santa Monica Mountains (Calif.) | 153,686.66 |
| Whiskeytown-Shasta-Trinity (Calif.) | 42,503.46 |
| **National Scenic Trails** | |
| Appalachian (Maine-N.H.-Vt.-Mass.-Conn.-N.Y.-N.J.- Pa.-Md.-W.Va.-Va.-N.C.-Tenn., Ga.) | 222,650.69 |
| Natchez Trace (Ala.-Miss.-Tenn.) | 10,995.00 |
| Potomac Heritage (D.C.-Md.-Va.-Pa.) | n.a. |
| **International Historic Site** | |
| Saint Croix Island (Maine) | 44.90 |
| **National Cemeteries**[1] | |
| Antietam (Md.) | 11.36 |
| Battleground (D.C.) | 1.03 |
| Chalmette Cemetery (La.) | 17.5 |
| Fort Donelson (Tenn.) | 15.30 |
| Fredericksburg (Va.) | 12.00 |
| Gettysburg (Pa.) | 20.58 |
| Poplar Grove (Va.) | 8.72 |
| Shiloh (Tenn.) | 10.05 |
| Stones River (Tenn.) | 719.81 |
| Vicksburg (Miss.) | 116.28 |
| Yorktown (Va.) | 2.91 |

1. The National Cemeteries are not independent areas of the National Park System; each is part of a military park, battlefield, etc., except Battleground. Their acreage is kept separately. Arlington National Cemetery is under the Department of the Army.

| Name and location | Total acreage |
|---|---|
| **Other Parks** | |
| Catoctin Mountain (Md.) | 5,809.87 |
| Constitution Gardens (D.C.) | 52.00 |
| Fort Washington Park (Md.) | 341.00 |
| Greenbelt (Md.) | 1,175.99 |
| National Capital Parks (D.C.) | 6,637.67 |
| National Mall (D.C.) | 146.35 |
| Piscataway (Md.) | 4,626.52 |
| Prince William Forest (Va.) | 18,729.01 |
| Rock Creek Park (D.C.) | 1,754.70 |
| White House (D.C.) | 18.07 |
| Wolf Trap Farm Park for the Performing Arts (Va.) | 130.28 |

## Ten Most Visited National Park Sites, 2001

| Rank | Name and location | Number of visitors |
|---|---|---|
| 1. | Blue Ridge Parkway, Va.-N.C. | 19,661,621 |
| 2. | Golden Gate National Recreation Area, Calif. | 13,394,614 |
| 3. | Great Smoky Mountains National Park, Tenn. | 9,457,323 |
| 4. | Lake Mead National Recreation Area, Nev.-Ariz. | 8,803,754 |
| 5. | Gateway National Recreation Area, N.Y.-N.J. | 8,160,879 |
| 6. | George Washington Memorial Parkway, Va.-Md.-D.C. | 7,829,818 |
| 7. | Natchez Trace Parkway, Miss.-Ala.-Tenn. | 5,538,255 |
| 8. | Statue of Liberty National Monument, N.Y.-N.J. | 5,382,315 |
| 9. | Delaware Water Gap National Recreation Area, Pa.-N.J. | 4,796,824 |
| 10. | Castle Clinton, N.Y. | 4,636,526 |

*Source:* Based on data from the National Park Service. Web: www.nps.gov.

# Worst Weather of the Twentieth Century

Climatologists, meteorologists, and hydrologists at the National Oceanic and Atmospheric Administration (NOAA) compiled a list of the world's most notable weather, water, and climate events in the twentieth century. Criteria for selection included an event's magnitude, meteorological uniqueness, as well as its economic impact and death toll. Events are listed in chronological order.

## United States

| Date(s) | Event |
|---|---|
| 1900 | Galveston Hurricane |
| 1925 | Tri-state Tornado |
| 1928 | Great Okeechobee Hurricane and Flood |
| 1930s | Dust Bowl |
| 1935 | Florida Keys Hurricane |
| 1938 | New England Hurricane |
| 1950 | "Storm of the Century" |
| 1969 | Hurricane Camille |
| 1974 | Super Tornado Outbreak |
| 1978 | New England Blizzard |
| 1982–83 & 1997–98 | El Niño Episodes |
| 1992 | Hurricane Andrew |
| 1993 | Great Midwest Flood |
| 1993 | "Superstorm" |
| 1999 | Okla./Kan. Tornado Outbreak |

Source: [...] of climate and weather experts at the National [...] d Atmospheric Administration (NOAA). For backgrou[...] w.noaanews.noaa.gov/stories/s334c.htm.

## World

| Date(s) | Event |
|---|---|
| 1910–1914, 1940–44, 1970–85 | Sahel Drought, Africa |
| India: 1900, 1907, 1965–67; China: 1907, 1928–30, 1936, 1941–42; Soviet Union: 1921–22 | Asian Droughts |
| 1912, 1922 | China Typhoons |
| 1931 | Yangtze River Flood, China |
| 1952 | Great Smog of London |
| 1953 | Europe Storm Surge |
| 1954 | Great Iran Flood |
| 1958 | Typhoon Vera, Japan |
| 1970 | Bangladesh Cyclone |
| 1971 | North Vietnam Flood |
| 1972 | Iran Blizzard |
| 1982–83 | El Niño |
| 1991 | Typhoon Thelma, Philippines |
| 1991 | Bangladesh Cyclone |
| 1998 | Hurricane Mitch, Honduras and Nicaragua |

## Atlantic Hurricane Names

Becaus[...] es often occur at the same time, officials assign short, distinctive names to the storms to avoid con[...] ng weather stations, coastal bases, and ships at sea. Since 1953, Atlantic tropical storms have been [...] m lists created by the National Hurricane Center and now maintained and updated by an internat[...] mittee of the World Meteorological Organization. The lists featured only women's names until [...] en men's and women's names were alternated. Six lists are used in rotation. Thus, the 2002 list wi[...] again in 2008. A storm is given a name once its winds reach an intensity of 39 mph. In addition t[...] ntic list of names, there are ten other lists corresponding to other storm-prone regions of the world.

| 2002 | 2003 | 2004 | 2005 | 2006 | 2007 |
|---|---|---|---|---|---|
| Arthur | Ana | Alex | Arlene | Alberto | Andrea |
| Bertha | Bill | Bonnie | Bret | Beryl | Barry |
| Cristobal | Claudette | Charley | Cindy | Chris | Chantal |
| Dolly | Danny | Danielle | Dennis | Debby | Dean |
| Edouard | Erika | Earl | Emily | Ernesto | Erin |
| Fay | Fabian | Frances | Franklin | Florence | Felix |
| Gustav | Grace | Gaston | Gert | Gordon | Gabrielle |
| Hanna | Henri | Hermine | Harvey | Helene | Humberto |
| Isidore | Isabel | Ivan | Irene | Isaac | Ingrid |
| Josephine | Juan | Jeanne | Jose | Joyce | Jerry |
| Kyle | Kate | Karl | Katrina | Kirk | Karen |
| Lili | Larry | Lisa | Lee | Leslie | Lorenzo |
| Maroo | Mindy | Matthew | Marla | Michael | Melissa |
| Nana | Nicholas | Nicole | Nate | Nadine | Noel |
| Omar | Odette | Otto | Ophelia | Oscar | Olga |
| Paloma | Peter | Paula | Philippe | Patty | Pablo |
| Rene | Rose | Richard | Rita | Rafael | Rebekah |
| Sally | Sam | Shary | Stan | Sandy | Sebastien |
| Teddy | Teresa | Tomas | Tammy | Tony | Tanya |
| Vicky | Victor | Virginie | Vince | Valerie | Van |
| Wilfred | Wanda | Walter | Wilma | William | Wendy |

Source: National Hurricane Center, National Oceanic and Atmospheric Administration (NOAA).

# Retired Hurricane Names

When hurricanes are particularly destructive, their names are retired from the list of usable names. Any country affected by a particularly terrible storm can request that the name be retired by petitioning the World Meteorological Organization. Below is a list of infamous hurricanes that have settled into retirement.

| Name | Year | Location(s) affected | Name | Year | Location(s) affected |
|---|---|---|---|---|---|
| Agnes | 1972 | Florida, Northeast U.S. | Elena | 1985 | Mississippi, Alabama, Western Florida |
| Alicia | 1983 | North Texas | Ekiuse | 1975 | Antilles, Northwest Florida, Alabama |
| Allen | 1980 | Antilles, Mexico, South Texas | Flora | 1963 | Haiti, Cuba |
| Andrew | 1992 | Bahamas, South Florida, and Louisiana | Frederic | 1979 | Alabama and Mississippi |
| Anita | 1977 | Mexico | Gilbert | 1988 | Lesser Antilles, Jamaica, Yucatan |
| Audrey | 1957 | Louisiana, North Texas | | | Peninsula, Mexico |
| Betsy | 1965 | Bahamas, Southeast Florida, Southeast Louisiana | Gloria | 1985 | North Carolina, Northeast U.S. |
| | | | Hattie | 1961 | Belize, Guatemala |
| Beulah | 1967 | Antilles, Mexico, South Texas | Hazel | 1954 | Antilles, North and South Carolina |
| Bob | 1991 | North Carolina, Northeast U.S. | Hilda | 1964 | Louisiana |
| Camille | 1969 | Louisiana, Mississippi, and Alabama | Hugo | 1989 | Antilles, South Carolina |
| Carla | 1961 | Texas | Ione | 1955 | North Carolina |
| Carmen | 1974 | Mexico | Inez | 1966 | Lesser Antilles, Hispanola, Cuba, |
| Carol | 1954 | Northeast U.S. | | | Florida Keys, Mexico |
| Celia | 1970 | South Texas | Janet | 1955 | Lesser Antilles, Belize, Mexico |
| Cleo | 1964 | Lesser Antilles, Haiti, Cuba, Southeast Florida | Joan | 1988 | Curacao, Venezuela, Colombia, Nicaragua (crossed Pacific and became |
| Connie | 1955 | North Carolina | | | Miriam) |
| David | 1979 | Lesser Antilles, Hispanola, Florida, and Eastern U.S. | Klaus | 1990 | Martinique |
| | | | Luis | 1995 | Lesser Antilles |
| Diana | 1990 | Mexico | Marilyn | 1995 | Lesser Antilles, Puerto Rico |
| Diane | 1955 | Mid-Atlantic U.S. and Northeast U.S. | Mitch | 1998 | Central America, Nicaragua, Honduras |
| Donna | 1960 | Bahamas, Florida, and Eastern U.S. | Opal | 1995 | Central America, Mexico, Florida |
| Dora | 1964 | Northeast Florida | Roxanne | 1995 | Mexico |

Source: National Hurricane Center, National Oceanic and Atmospheric Administration (NOAA).

## Costliest Hurricanes in the United States[1]
### (U.S. Mainland)

| Rank | Hurricane | Location | Year | Category[2] | Damage (in billions) | Rank | Hurricane | Location | Year | Category[2] | Damage (in billions) |
|---|---|---|---|---|---|---|---|---|---|---|---|
| 1. | Andrew | Fla./La. | 1992 | 5[3] | $26.5 | 6. | Georges | Fla./Miss./Ala. | 1998 | 2 | 2.31 |
| 2. | Hugo | S.C. | 1989 | 4 | 7.0 | | | | | | |
| 3. | Floyd | Mid Atlantic/NE U.S. | 1999 | 2 | 4.5 | 7. | Frederic | Ala./Miss. | 1979 | 3 | 2.3 |
| | | | | | | 8. | Agnes | Fla./NE U.S. | 1972 | 1 | 2.1 |
| 4. | Fran | N.C. | 1996 | 3 | 3.2 | 9. | Alicia | Tex. | 1983 | 3 | 2.0 |
| 5. | Opal | Fla./Ala. | 1995 | 3 | 3.0 | 10. | Bob | N.C./NE U.S. | 1991 | 2 | 1.5 |
| | | | | | | 10. | Juan | La. | 1985 | 1 | 1.5 |

1. 1900–2000. 2. Saffir-Simpson Hurricane scale: Cat. 1 = weak; Cat. 5 = devastating. 3. Hurricane Andrew was upgraded in Aug. 2002 from Cat. 4 to 5. Source: National Oceanic and Atmospheric Administration (NOAA).

## Deadliest Hurricanes in the United States[1]
### (U.S. Mainland)

| Rank | Hurricane | Year | Category[2] | Deaths | Rank | Hurricane | Year | Category[2] | Deaths |
|---|---|---|---|---|---|---|---|---|---|
| 1. | Galveston, Tex. | 1900 | 4 | 8,000[3] | 6. | Audrey (SW La./N. Tex.) | 1957 | 4 | 390 |
| 2. | Lake Okeechobee, Fla. | 1928 | 4 | 1,836 | | NE U.S. | 1944 | 3[5] | 390[6] |
| 3. | Florida Keys/S. Tex. | 1919 | 4 | 600[4] | 8. | Grand Isle, La. | 1909 | 4 | 350 |
| 4. | New England | 1938 | 3[5] | 600 | 9. | New Orleans, La. | 1915 | 4 | 275 |
| 5. | Florida Keys | 1935 | 5 | 408 | 10. | Galveston, Tex. | 1915 | 4 | 275 |

1. 1900–2000. 2. Saffir-Simpson Hurricane scale: Cat. 1 = weak; Cat. 5 = devastating. 3. May actually have been as high as 10,000 to 12,000. 4. Over 500 of these lost on ships at sea; 600–900 estimated deaths. 5. Moving more than 30 mph. 6. Some 344 of these lost on ships at sea. Source: National Oceanic and Atmospheric Administration (NOAA).

## Most Intense[1] Hurricanes in the United States[2]
### (U.S. Mainland)

| Rank | Hurricane | Year | Category[3] | Rank | Hurricane | Year | Category[3] |
|---|---|---|---|---|---|---|---|
| 1. | Florida Keys | 1935 | 5 | 6. | Donna (Fla./Eastern U.S.) | 1960 | 4 |
| 2. | Camille (Miss./La./Va.) | 1969 | 5 | 7. | Galveston, Tex. | 1900 | 4 |
| 3. | Andrew (Fla./La.) | 1992 | 5[4] | 8. | Grand Isle, La. | 1909 | 4 |
| 4. | Florida Keys/Tex. | 1919 | 4 | 9. | New Orleans, La. | 1915 | 4 |
| 5. | Lake Okeechobee, Fla. | 1928 | 4 | 10. | Carla (Tex.) | 1961 | 4 |

1. Intensity is for time of landfall. May have been stronger at other times. 2. 1900–2000. 3. Saffir-Simpson Hurricane scale: Cat. 1 = weak; Cat. 5 = devastating. 4. Hurricane Andrew was upgraded in Aug. 2002 from Cat. 4 to 5. Source: National Oceanic and Atmospheric Administration (NOAA).

## The 25 Deadliest Tornadoes

| Date | Location(s) | Deaths | Date | Location(s) | Deaths |
|---|---|---|---|---|---|
| 1. March 18, 1925 | Tri-State (Mo., Ill., Ind.) | 689 | 14. June 23, 1944 | Shinnston, W. Va. | 100 |
| 2. May 6, 1840 | Natchez, Miss. | 317 | 15. April 18, 1880 | Marshfield, Mo. | 99 |
| 3. May 27, 1896 | St. Louis, Mo. | 255 | 16. June 1, 1903 | Gainesville, Holland, Ga. | 98 |
| 4. April 5, 1936 | Tupelo, Miss. | 216 | 16. May 9, 1927 | Poplar Bluff, Mo. | 98 |
| 5. April 6, 1936 | Gainesville, Ga. | 203 | 18. May 10, 1905 | Snyder, Okla. | 97 |
| 6. April 9, 1947 | Woodward, Okla. | 181 | 19. April 24, 1908 | Natchez, Miss. | 91 |
| 7. April 24, 1908 | Amite La.; Purvis, Miss. | 143 | 20. June 9, 1953 | Worcester, Mass. | 90 |
| 8. June 12, 1899 | New Richmond, Wis. | 117 | 21. April 20, 1920 | Starkville, Miss.; Waco, Ala. | 88 |
| 9. June 8, 1953 | Flint, Mich. | 115 | 22. June 28, 1924 | Lorain, Sandusky, Ohio | 85 |
| 10. May 11, 1953 | Waco, Tex. | 114 | 23. May 25, 1955 | Udall, Kans. | 80 |
| 10. May 18, 1902 | Goliad, Tex. | 114 | 24. Sept. 29, 1927 | St. Louis, Mo. | 79 |
| 12. March 23, 1913 | Omaha, Neb. | 103 | 25. March 27, 1890 | Louisville, Ky. | 76 |
| 13. May 26, 1917 | Mattoon, Ill. | 101 | | | |

*Source:* Storm Prediction Center at the National Weather Service, National Oceanographic and Atmospheric Administration (NOAA). Web. www.spc.noaa.gov/archive/tornadoes/t-deadly.html.

# Lightning Dangers

The National Weather Service publication *Storm Data* recorded a total of 3,239 deaths and 9,818 injuries from lightning strikes between 1959 and 1994. In 2000, lightning caused 51 deaths, up from 46 in 1999.

During a thunderstorm, avoid open spaces, trees, telephone booths, and ballparks. The safest place to be is in a building, preferably one with a lightning rod. The rod offers protection by intercepting lightning—an electrical charge—and transmitting its current into the ground. The other safe place is a car with the windows rolled up, as long as you don't touch any of the metal parts. If lightning strikes, the car's metal body will conduct the charge down to the ground—contrary to popular belief, the rubber of the wheels offers no protection.

## Ten States with Most Lightning Deaths, 1959–1994

| Rank | State | Number of deaths | Number of injuries |
|---|---|---|---|
| 1. | Florida | 345 | 1,178 |
| 2. | North Carolina | 165 | 464 |
| 3. | Texas | 164 | 334 |
| 4. | New York | 128 | 449 |
| 5. | Tennessee | 124 | 349 |
| 6. | Louisiana | 116 | 231 |
| 7. | Maryland | 116 | 134 |
| 8. | Ohio | 115 | 430 |
| 9. | Arkansas | 110 | 245 |
| 10. | Pennsylvania | 109 | 535 |

*Source:* National Severe Storms Laboratory, National Oceanic and Atmospheric Administration (NOAA).

## Greatest Snowfalls in North America

| | Place | Date | Inches | Centimeters |
|---|---|---|---|---|
| 1 month (U.S.) | Tamarack, Calif. | Jan. 1911 | 390 | 991 |
| 24 hours (N. America) | Silver Lake, Colo. | April 14–15, 1921 | 76 | 195.6 |
| 24 hours (Alaska) | Thompson Pass | Dec. 29, 1955 | 62 | 157.5 |
| 19 hours (France) | Bessans | April 5–6, 1969 | 68 | 173 |
| 1 storm (N. America) | Mt. Shasta Ski Bowl, Calif. | Feb. 13–19, 1959 | 189 | 480 |
| 1 storm (Alaska) | Thompson Pass | Dec. 26–31, 1955 | 175 | 445.5 |
| 1 season (N. America) | Mount Baker, Wash. | 1998–1999 | 1,140 | 2,895.6 |
| 1 season (Alaska) | Thompson Pass | 1952–1953 | 974.5 | 2,475 |
| 1 season (Canada) | Revelstoke Mt. Copeland, British Columbia | 1971–1972 | 964 | 2,446.5 |

*Source:* U.S. Army Corps of Engineers, Engineer Topographic Laboratories.

## Recorded Weather Extremes

**Highest average annual mean temperature (world):** Dallol, Ethiopia (Oct. 1960–Dec. 1966), 94° F (34.4° C). **(U.S.):** Key West, Fla. (30-year normal), 78.2° F (25.7° C).

**Lowest average annual mean temperature (world):** Plateau Station, Antarctica, –70° F (–56.7° C). **(U.S.):** Barrow, Alaska (30-year normal), 9.3° F (–12.6° C).

**Greatest average yearly rainfall (world):** Cherrapunji, India (74-year avg), 450 in. (1,143 cm). **(U.S.):** Mt. Waialeale, Kauai, Hawaii (32-year avg), 460 in. (1,168 cm).

**Minimum average yearly rainfall (world):** Arica, Chile (59-year avg), 0.03 in. (0.08 cm) (no rainfall for 14 consecutive years). **(U.S.):** Death Valley, Calif. (42-year avg), 1.63 in. (4.14 cm). Bagdad, Calif., holds the U.S. record for the longest period with no measurable rain, 767 days, from Oct. 3, 1912 to Nov. 8, 1914.

**Hottest summer average in Western Hemisphere (U.S.):** Death Valley, Calif., 98° F (36.7° C).

**Longest hot spell (world):** Marble Bar, W. Australia, 100° F (37.8° C) (or above) for 162 consecutive days, Oct. 30, 1923 to Apr. 7, 1924.

**Largest hailstone (U.S.):** Coffeyville, Kans., 17.5 in. (44.5 cm), Sept. 3, 1970.

# World and U.S. Extremes of Climate

## Highest Recorded Temperatures

| | Place | Date | Degrees Fahrenheit | Degrees Celsius |
|---|---|---|---|---|
| World (Africa) | El Azizia, Libya | Sept. 13, 1922 | 136 | 58 |
| North America (U.S.) | Death Valley, Calif. | July 10, 1913 | 134 | 57 |
| Asia | Tirat Tsvi, Israel | June 21, 1942 | 129 | 54 |
| Australia | Cloncurry, Queensland | Jan. 16, 1889 | 128 | 53 |
| Europe | Seville, Spain | Aug. 4, 1881 | 122 | 50 |
| South America | Rivadavia, Argentina | Dec. 11, 1905 | 120 | 49 |
| Canada | Midale and Yellow Grass, Saskatchewan, Canada | July 5, 1937 | 113 | 45 |
| Oceania | Tuguegarao, Philippines | April 29, 1912 | 108 | 45.6 |
| Persian Gulf (sea-surface) | | Aug. 5, 1924 | 96 | 36 |
| Antarctica | Vanda Station, Scott Coast | Jan. 5, 1974 | 59 | 15 |
| South Pole | | Dec. 27, 1978 | 7.5 | −14 |

## Lowest Recorded Temperatures

| | Place | Date | Degrees Fahrenheit | Degrees Celsius |
|---|---|---|---|---|
| World (Antarctica) | Vostok | July 21, 1983 | −129 | −89 |
| Asia | Oimekon, Russia | Feb. 6, 1933 | −90 | −68 |
| | Verkhoyansk, Russia | Feb. 7, 1892 | −90 | −68 |
| Greenland | Northice | Jan. 9, 1954 | −87 | −66 |
| North America (excl. Greenland) | Snag, Yukon, Canada | Feb. 3, 1947 | −81 | −63 |
| United States | Prospect Creek, Alaska | Jan. 23, 1971 | −80 | −62 |
| U.S. (excl. Alaska) | Rogers Pass, Mont. | Jan. 20, 1954 | −70 | −56.5 |
| Europe | Ust 'Shchugor, Russia | Jan.[1] | −67 | −55 |
| South America | Sarmiento, Argentina | June 1, 1907 | −27 | −33 |
| Africa | Ifrane, Morocco | Feb. 11, 1935 | −11 | −24 |
| Australia | Charlotte Pass, N.S.W. | June 29, 1994 | −9 | −22 |
| Oceania | Haleakala Summit, Maui, Hawaii | Jan. 2, 1961 | 14 | −10.8 |

1. Exact date unknown; lowest in 15-year period.

## Greatest Rainfalls

| | Place | Date | Inches | Centimeters |
|---|---|---|---|---|
| 1 minute (World) | Unionville, Md. | July 4, 1956 | 1.23 | 3.1 |
| 20 minutes (World) | Curtea-de-Arges, Romania | July 7, 1889 | 8.1 | 20.5 |
| 42 minutes (World) | Holt, Mo. | June 22, 1947 | 12 | 30.5 |
| 12 hours (World) | Grand Ilet, La Réunion | Jan. 26, 1980 | 46 | 114 |
| 24 hours (World) | Foc-Foc, La Réunion | Jan. 7–8, 1966 | 72 | 182.5 |
| 24 hours (N. Hemisphere) | Paishih, Taiwan | Sept. 10–11, 1963 | 49 | 125 |
| 24 hours (Australia) | Bellenden Ker, Queensland | Jan. 4, 1979 | 44 | 114 |
| 24 hours (U.S.) | Alvin, Tex. | July 25–26, 1979 | 43 | 109 |
| 24 hours (Canada) | Ucluelet Brynnor Mines, British Columbia | Oct. 6, 1967 | 19 | 49 |
| 5 days (World) | Commerson, La Réunion | Jan. 23–28, 1980 | 156 | 395 |
| 1 month (World) | Cherrapunji, India | July 1861 | 366 | 930 |
| 12 months (World) | Cherrapunji, India | Aug. 1860–Aug. 1861 | 1,042 | 2,647 |
| 12 months (U.S.) | Kukui, Maui, Hawaii | Dec. 1981–Dec. 1982 | 739 | 1878 |

## Lowest Average Annual Precipitation Extremes

| Continent | Place | Lowest avg. (in.) | Elevation (ft) | Years of record |
|---|---|---|---|---|
| World (South America) | Arica, Chile | 0.03 | 95 | 59 |
| Africa | Wadi Halfa, Sudan | <0.10[1] | 410 | 39 |
| Antarctica | Amundsen-Scott South Pole Station | 0.80[1] | 9,186 | 10 |
| North America | Batagues, Mexico | 1.20 | 16 | 14 |
| Asia | Aden, Yemen | 1.80 | 22 | 50 |
| Australia | Mulka (Troudaninna), South Australia | 4.05 | 160[2] | 42 |
| Europe | Astrakhan, Russia | 6.40 | 45 | 25 |
| Oceania | Puako, Hawaii, Hawaii | 8.93 | 5 | 13 |

1. The value given is the average amount of solid snow accumulating in one year as indicated by snow markers. The liquid content of the snow is undetermined. 2. Approximate elevation. Source: U.S. Army Corps of Engineers, Engineer Topographic Laboratories.

# Record Highest Temperatures by State

| State | Temp. °F | Temp. °C | Date | Station | Elevation in feet |
|---|---|---|---|---|---|
| Alabama | 112 | 44 | Sept. 5, 1925 | Centerville | 345 |
| Alaska | 100 | 38 | June 27, 1915 | Fort Yukon | est. 420 |
| Arizona | 128 | 53 | June 29, 1994 | Lake Havasu City | 505 |
| Arkansas | 120 | 49 | Aug. 10, 1936 | Ozark | 396 |
| California | 134 | 57 | July 10, 1913 | Greenland Ranch | -178 |
| Colorado | 118 | 48 | July 11, 1888 | Bennett | 5,484 |
| Connecticut | 106 | 41 | July 15, 1995 | Danbury | 450 |
| Delaware | 110 | 43 | July 21, 1930 | Millsboro | 20 |
| D.C. | 106 | 41 | July 20, 1930 | Washington | 410 |
| Florida | 109 | 43 | June 29, 1931 | Monticello | 207 |
| Georgia | 112 | 44 | Aug. 20, 1983 | Greenville | 860 |
| Hawaii | 100 | 38 | Apr. 27, 1931 | Pahala | 850 |
| Idaho | 118 | 48 | July 28, 1934 | Orofino | 1,027 |
| Illinois | 117 | 47 | July 14, 1954 | E. St. Louis | 410 |
| Indiana | 116 | 47 | July 14, 1936 | Collegeville | 672 |
| Iowa | 118 | 48 | July 20, 1934 | Keokuk | 614 |
| Kansas | 121 | 49 | July 24, 1936[1] | Alton (near) | 1,651 |
| Kentucky | 114 | 46 | July 28, 1930 | Greensburg | 581 |
| Louisiana | 114 | 46 | Aug. 10, 1936[1] | Plain Dealing | 268 |
| Maine | 105 | 41 | July 10, 1911[1] | North Bridgton | 450 |
| Maryland | 109 | 43 | July 10, 1936[1] | Cumberland & Frederick | 623; 325 |
| Massachusetts | 107 | 42 | Aug. 2, 1975 | New Bedford & Chester | 120; 640 |
| Michigan | 112 | 44 | July 13, 1936 | Mio | 963 |
| Minnesota | 114 | 46 | July 6, 1936[1] | Moorhead | 904 |
| Mississippi | 115 | 46 | July 29, 1930 | Holly Springs | 600 |
| Missouri | 118 | 48 | July 14, 1954[1] | Warsaw & Union | 705; 560 |
| Montana | 117 | 47 | July 5, 1937 | Medicine Lake | 1,950 |
| Nebraska | 118 | 48 | July 24, 1936[1] | Minden | 2,169 |
| Nevada | 125 | 52 | June 29, 1994 | Laughlin | 605 |
| New Hampshire | 106 | 41 | July 4, 1911 | Nashua | 125 |
| New Jersey | 110 | 43 | July 10, 1936 | Runyon | 18 |
| New Mexico | 122 | 50 | June 27, 1994 | Waste Isolat. Pilot Pit | 3,418 |
| New York | 108 | 42 | July 22, 1926 | Troy | 35 |
| North Carolina | 110 | 43 | Aug. 21, 1983 | Fayetteville | 213 |
| North Dakota | 121 | 49 | July 6, 1936 | Steele | 1,857 |
| Ohio | 113 | 45 | July 21, 1934[1] | Gallipolis (near) | 673 |
| Oklahoma | 120 | 49 | June 27, 1994[1] | Tipton | 1,350 |
| Oregon | 119 | 48 | Aug. 10, 1898 | Pendleton | 1,074 |
| Pennsylvania | 111 | 44 | July 10, 1936[1] | Phoenixville | 100 |
| Rhode Island | 104 | 40 | Aug. 2, 1975 | Providence | 51 |
| South Carolina | 111 | 44 | June 28, 1954[1] | Camden | 170 |
| South Dakota | 120 | 49 | July 5, 1936 | Gannvalley | 1,750 |
| Tennessee | 113 | 45 | Aug. 9, 1930[1] | Perryville | 377 |
| Texas | 120 | 49 | Aug. 12, 1936 | Seymour | 1,291 |
| Utah | 117 | 47 | July 5, 1895 | Saint George | 2,880 |
| Vermont | 105 | 41 | July 4, 1911 | Vernon | 310 |
| Virginia | 110 | 43 | July 15, 1954 | Balcony Falls | 725 |
| Washington | 118 | 48 | Aug. 5, 1961[1] | Ice Harbor Dam | 475 |
| West Virginia | 112 | 44 | July 10, 1936[1] | Martinsburg | 435 |
| Wisconsin | 114 | 46 | July 13, 1936 | Wisconsin Dells | 900 |
| Wyoming | 114 | 46 | July 12, 1900 | Basin | 3,500 |

1. Also on earlier dates at the same or other places. *Source:* National Climatic Data Center, Asheville, N.C., and Storm Phillips, STORMFAX, INC.

# Record Lowest Temperatures by State

| State | Temp. °F | Temp. °C | Date | Station | Elevation in feet |
|---|---|---|---|---|---|
| Alabama | -27 | -33 | Jan. 30, 1966 | New Market | 760 |
| Alaska | -80 | -62 | Jan. 23, 1971 | Prospect Creek Camp | 1,100 |
| Arizona | -40 | -40 | Jan. 7, 1971 | Hawley Lake | 8,180 |
| Arkansas | -29 | -34 | Feb. 13, 1905 | Pond | 1,250 |
| California | -45 | -43 | Jan. 20, 1937 | Boca | 5,532 |
| Colorado | -61 | -52 | Feb. 1, 1985 | Maybell | 5,920 |
| Connecticut | -32 | -36 | Feb. 16, 1943 | Falls Village | 585 |
| Delaware | -17 | -27 | Jan. 17, 1893 | Millsboro | 20 |
| D.C. | -15 | -26 | Feb. 11, 1899 | Washington | 410 |
| Florida | -2 | -19 | Feb. 13, 1899 | Tallahassee | 193 |
| Georgia | -17 | -27 | Jan. 27, 1940 | CCC Camp F-16 | est. 1,000 |
| Hawaii | 12 | -11 | May 17, 1979 | Mauna Kea | 13,770 |
| Idaho | -60 | -51 | Jan. 18, 1943 | Island Park Dam | 6,285 |
| Illinois | -36 | -38 | Jan. 5, 1999 | Congerville | 635 |
| Indiana | -36 | -38 | Jan. 19, 1994 | New Whiteland | 785 |
| Iowa | -47 | -44 | Feb. 3, 1996 | Elkader | 770 |
| Kansas | -40 | -40 | Feb. 13, 1905 | Lebanon | 1,812 |
| Kentucky | -37 | -38 | Jan. 19, 1994 | Shelbyville | 730 |
| Louisiana | -16 | -27 | Feb. 13, 1899 | Minden | 194 |
| Maine | -48 | -44 | Jan. 19, 1925 | Van Buren | 510 |
| Maryland | -40 | -40 | Jan. 13, 1912 | Oakland | 2,461 |
| Massachusetts | -35 | -37 | Jan. 12, 1981 | Chester | 640 |
| Michigan | -51 | -46 | Feb. 9, 1934 | Vanderbilt | 785 |
| Minnesota | -60 | -51 | Feb. 2, 1996 | Tower | 1,460 |
| Mississippi | -19 | -28 | Jan. 30, 1966 | Corinth | 420 |
| Missouri | -40 | -40 | Feb. 13, 1905 | Warsaw | 700 |
| Montana | -70 | -57 | Jan. 20, 1954 | Rogers Pass | 5,470 |
| Nebraska | -47 | -44 | Feb. 12, 1899 | Camp Clarke | 3,700 |
| Nevada | -50 | -46 | Jan. 8, 1937 | San Jacinto | 5,200 |
| New Hampshire | -47 | -44 | Jan. 29, 1934 | Mt. Washington | 6,262 |
| New Jersey | -34 | -37 | Jan. 5, 1904 | River Vale | 70 |
| New Mexico | -50 | -46 | Feb. 1, 1951 | Gavilan | 7,350 |
| New York | -52 | -47 | Feb. 18, 1979[1] | Old Forge | 1,720 |
| North Carolina | -34 | -37 | Jan. 21, 1985 | Mt. Mitchell | 6,525 |
| North Dakota | -60 | -51 | Feb. 15, 1936 | Parshall | 1,929 |
| Ohio | -39 | -39 | Feb. 10, 1899 | Milligan | 800 |
| Oklahoma | -27 | -33 | Jan. 18, 1930 | Watts | 958 |
| Oregon | -54 | -48 | Feb. 10, 1933[1] | Seneca | 4,700 |
| Pennsylvania | -42 | -41 | Jan. 5, 1904 | Smethport | est. 1,500 |
| Rhode Island | -23 | -31 | Jan. 11, 1942 | Kingston | 100 |
| South Carolina | -19 | -28 | Jan. 21, 1985 | Caesars Head | 3,115 |
| South Dakota | -58 | -50 | Feb. 17, 1936 | McIntosh | 2,277 |
| Tennessee | -32 | -36 | Dec. 30, 1917 | Mountain City | 2,471 |
| Texas | -23 | -31 | Feb. 8, 1933[1] | Seminole | 3,275 |
| Utah | -69 | -56 | Feb. 1, 1985 | Peter's Sink | 8,092 |
| Vermont | -50 | -46 | Dec. 30, 1933 | Bloomfield | 915 |
| Virginia | -30 | -34 | Jan. 22, 1985 | Mountain Lake | 3,870 |
| Washington | -48 | -44 | Dec. 30, 1968 | Mazama & Winthrop | 2,120; 1,765 |
| West Virginia | -37 | -38 | Dec. 30, 1917 | Lewisburg | 2,200 |
| Wisconsin | -55 | -48 | Feb. 4, 1996 | Couderay | 1,300 |
| Wyoming | -66 | -54 | Feb. 9, 1933 | Riverside R.S. | 6,500 |

1. Also on earlier dates at the same or other places. *Source:* National Climatic Data Center, Asheville, N.C., and Storm Phillips, STORMFAX, INC.

# Record Monthly High and Low Temperatures in the United States

*Source:* National Climatic Data Center, Asheville, N.C., and Storm Phillips, STORMFAX, Inc.

## January

The highest temperature ever recorded for the month of January occurred on January 17, 1936, and again in 1954, in Laredo, Tex. (elevation 421 ft), where the temperature reached 98°F.

The lowest temperature ever recorded for the month of January occurred on January 20, 1954, in Rogers Pass, Mont. (elevation 5,470 ft), where the temperature fell to –70°F.

## February

The highest temperature ever recorded for the month of February occurred on February 3, 1963, in Montezuma, Ariz. (elevation 735 ft), where the temperature reached 105°F.

The lowest temperature ever recorded for the month of February occurred on February 1, 1985, at the Peters Sink station in Utah (elevation 8,095 ft), where the temperature fell to –69°F.

## March

The highest temperature ever recorded for the month of March occurred on March 31, 1954, in Rio Grande City, Tex. (elevation 168 ft), where the temperature reached 108°F.

The lowest temperature ever recorded for the month of March occurred on March 17, 1906, in Snake River, Wyo. (elevation 6,862 ft), where the temperature dropped to –50°F.

## April

The highest temperature ever recorded for the month of April occurred on April 25, 1898, at Volcano Springs, Calif. (elevation –220 ft), where temperature reached 118°F.

The lowest temperature ever recorded for the month of April occurred on April 5, 1945, in Eagle Nest, N.M. (elevation 8,250 ft), where the temperature dropped to –36°F.

## May

The highest temperature ever recorded for the month of May occurred on May 27, 1896, in Salton, Calif. (elevation –263 ft), where the temperature reached 124°F.

The lowest temperature ever recorded for the month of May occurred on May 7, 1964, in White Mountain 2, Calif. (elevation 12,470 ft), where temperature dropped to –15°F.

## June

The highest temperature ever recorded for the month of June occurred on June 23, 1902, at Volcano Springs, Calif. (elevation –220 ft), where temperature reached 129°F.

The lowest temperature ever recorded for the month of June occurred on June 13, 1907, in Tamarack, Calif. (elevation 8,000 ft), where the temperature dropped to 2°F.

## July

The highest temperature ever recorded for the month of July occurred on July 10, 1913, at Greenland Ranch, Calif. (elevation –178 ft), where temperature reached 134°F.

The lowest temperature ever recorded for the month of July occurred on July 21, 1911, at Painter, Wyo. (elevation 6,800 ft), where the temperature fell to 10°F.

## August

The highest temperature ever recorded for the month of August occurred on August 12, 1933, at Greenland Ranch, Calif. (elevation –178 ft), where the temperature reached 127°F.

The lowest temperature ever recorded for the month of August occurred on August 25, 1910, in Bowen, Mont. (elevation 6,080 ft), where the temperature fell to 5°F.

## September

The highest temperature ever recorded for the month of September occurred on September 2, 1950, in Mecca, Calif. (elevation –175 ft), where temperature reached 126°F.

The lowest temperature ever recorded for the month of September occurred on September 24, 1926, at Riverside Ranger Station, Mont. (elevation 6,700 ft), where the temperature fell to –9°F.

## October

The highest temperature ever recorded for the month of October occurred on October 5, 1917, in Sentinel, Ariz. (elevation 685 ft), where the temperature reached 116°F.

The lowest temperature ever recorded for the month of October occurred on October 29, 1917, in Soda Butte, Wyo. (elevation 6,600 ft), where the temperature fell to –33°F.

## November

The highest temperature ever recorded for the month of November occurred on November 12, 1906, in Craftonville, Calif. (elevation 1,759 ft), where the temperature reached 105°F.

The lowest temperature ever recorded for the month of November occurred on November 16, 1959, at Lincoln, Mont. (elevation 5,130 ft), where the temperature fell to –53°F.

## December

The highest temperature ever recorded for the month of December occurred on December 8, 1938, in La Mesa, Calif. (elevation 539 ft), where the temperature reached 100°F.

The lowest temperature ever recorded for the month of December occurred on December 19, 1924, at Riverside Ranger Station, Mont. (elevation 6,700 ft), where the temperature fell to –59°F.

## Climate of 100 Selected U.S. Cities

(For world cities, *see* p. 214)

(For world cities, *see* p. 214)

| City | Average monthly temperature (°F)[1] Jan. | April | July | Oct. | Precipitation Average annual (in.)[1] | (days)[2] | Snowfall Average annual (in.)[2] | Years[2] |
|---|---|---|---|---|---|---|---|---|
| Albany, N.Y. | 21.1 | 46.6 | 71.4 | 50.5 | 35.74 | 134 | 65.5 | 38 |
| Albuquerque, N.M. | 34.8 | 55.1 | 78.8 | 57.4 | 8.12 | 59 | 10.6 | 45 |
| Anchorage, Alaska | 13.0 | 35.4 | 58.1 | 34.6 | 15.20 | 115 | 69.2 | 41[3] |
| Asheville, N.C. | 36.8 | 55.7 | 73.2 | 56.0 | 47.71 | 124 | 17.5 | 20 |
| Atlanta, Ga. | 41.9 | 61.8 | 78.6 | 62.2 | 48.61 | 115 | 1.9 | 50 |
| Atlantic City, N.J. | 31.8 | 51.0 | 74.4 | 55.5 | 41.93 | 112 | 16.4 | 40[3] |
| Austin, Texas | 49.1 | 68.7 | 84.7 | 69.8 | 31.50 | 83 | 0.9 | 43 |
| Baltimore, Md. | 32.7 | 54.0 | 76.8 | 56.9 | 41.84 | 113 | 21.8 | 34 |
| Baton Rouge, La. | 50.8 | 68.4 | 82.1 | 68.2 | 55.77 | 108 | 0.1 | 34[3] |
| Billings, Mont. | 20.9 | 44.6 | 72.3 | 49.3 | 15.09 | 96 | 57.2 | 50 |
| Birmingham, Ala. | 42.9 | 62.8 | 80.1 | 62.6 | 54.52 | 117 | 1.3 | 41 |
| Bismarck, N.D. | 6.7 | 42.5 | 70.4 | 46.1 | 15.36 | 96 | 40.3 | 45 |
| Boise, Idaho | 29.9 | 48.6 | 74.6 | 51.9 | 11.71 | 92 | 21.4 | 45 |
| Boston, Mass. | 29.6 | 48.7 | 73.5 | 54.8 | 43.81 | 127 | 41.8 | 49[3] |
| Bridgeport, Conn. | 29.5 | 48.6 | 74.0 | 56.0 | 41.56 | 117 | 26.0 | 36 |
| Buffalo, N.Y. | 23.5 | 45.4 | 70.7 | 51.5 | 37.52 | 169 | 92.2 | 41 |
| Burlington, Vt. | 16.6 | 42.7 | 69.6 | 47.9 | 33.69 | 153 | 78.2 | 41 |
| Caribou, Maine | 10.7 | 37.3 | 65.1 | 43.1 | 36.59 | 160 | 113.3 | 45 |
| Casper, Wyo. | 22.2 | 42.1 | 70.9 | 47.1 | 11.43 | 95 | 80.5 | 34 |
| Charleston, S.C. | 47.9 | 64.3 | 80.5 | 65.8 | 51.59 | 113 | 0.6 | 42 |
| Charleston, W.Va. | 32.9 | 55.3 | 74.5 | 55.9 | 42.43 | 151 | 31.5 | 37 |
| Charlotte, N.C. | 40.5 | 60.3 | 78.5 | 60.7 | 43.16 | 111 | 6.1 | 45 |
| Cheyenne, Wyo. | 26.1 | 41.8 | 68.9 | 47.5 | 13.31 | 98 | 54.1 | 49 |
| Chicago, Ill. | 21.4 | 48.8 | 73.0 | 53.5 | 33.34 | 127 | 40.3 | 26 |
| Cleveland, Ohio | 25.5 | 48.1 | 71.6 | 53.2 | 35.40 | 156 | 53.6 | 43 |
| Columbia, S.C. | 44.7 | 63.8 | 81.0 | 63.4 | 49.12 | 109 | 1.9 | 37 |
| Columbus, Ohio | 27.1 | 51.4 | 73.8 | 53.9 | 36.97 | 137 | 28.3 | 37[3] |
| Concord, N.H. | 19.9 | 44.1 | 69.5 | 48.3 | 36.53 | 125 | 64.5 | 43 |
| Dallas-Ft. Worth, Texas | 44.0 | 65.9 | 86.3 | 67.9 | 29.46 | 78 | 3.1 | 31 |
| Denver, Colo. | 29.5 | 47.4 | 73.4 | 51.9 | 15.31 | 88 | 59.8 | 50 |
| Des Moines, Iowa | 18.6 | 50.5 | 76.3 | 54.2 | 30.83 | 107 | 34.7 | 45 |
| Detroit, Mich. | 23.4 | 47.3 | 71.9 | 51.9 | 30.97 | 133 | 40.4 | 26 |
| Dodge City, Kan. | 29.5 | 54.3 | 80.0 | 57.7 | 20.66 | 78 | 19.5 | 42 |
| Duluth, Minn. | 6.3 | 38.3 | 65.4 | 44.2 | 29.68 | 135 | 77.4 | 41[3] |
| El Paso, Texas | 44.2 | 63.6 | 82.5 | 63.6 | 7.82 | 47 | 5.2 | 45 |
| Fairbanks, Alaska | −12.7 | 30.2 | 61.5 | 25.1 | 10.37 | 106 | 67.5 | 33 |
| Fargo, N.D. | 4.3 | 42.1 | 70.6 | 46.3 | 19.59 | 100 | 35.9 | 42 |
| Grand Junction, Colo. | 25.5 | 51.7 | 78.9 | 54.9 | 8.00 | 72 | 26.1 | 38 |
| Grand Rapids, Mich. | 22.0 | 46.3 | 71.4 | 50.9 | 34.35 | 143 | 72.4 | 21 |
| Hartford, Conn. | 25.2 | 48.8 | 73.4 | 52.4 | 44.39 | 127 | 50.0 | 30 |
| Helena, Mont. | 18.1 | 42.3 | 67.9 | 45.1 | 11.37 | 96 | 47.9 | 44 |
| Honolulu, Hawaii | 72.6 | 75.7 | 80.1 | 79.5 | 23.47 | 100 | 0.0 | 38[3] |
| Houston, Texas | 51.4 | 68.7 | 83.1 | 69.7 | 44.76 | 105 | 0.4 | 50 |
| Indianapolis, Ind. | 26.0 | 52.4 | 75.1 | 54.8 | 39.12 | 125 | 23.1 | 53[3] |
| Jackson, Miss. | 45.7 | 65.1 | 81.9 | 65.0 | 52.82 | 109 | 1.2 | 21 |
| Jacksonville, Fla. | 53.2 | 67.7 | 81.3 | 69.5 | 52.76 | 116 | T | 43 |
| Juneau, Alaska | 21.8 | 39.1 | 55.7 | 41.8 | 53.15 | 220 | 102.8 | 41 |
| Kansas City, Mo. | 28.4 | 56.9 | 80.9 | 59.6 | 29.27 | 98 | 20.0 | 43 |
| Knoxville, Tenn. | 38.2 | 59.6 | 77.6 | 59.5 | 47.29 | 127 | 12.3 | 42 |
| Las Vegas, Nev. | 44.5 | 63.5 | 90.2 | 67.5 | 4.19 | 26 | 1.4 | 36 |
| Lexington, Ky. | 31.5 | 55.1 | 75.9 | 56.8 | 45.68 | 131 | 16.3 | 40 |
| Little Rock, Ark. | 39.9 | 62.4 | 82.1 | 63.1 | 49.20 | 104 | 5.4 | 42 |
| Long Beach, Calif. | 55.2 | 60.9 | 72.8 | 67.5 | 11.54 | 32 | T | 41[3] |
| Los Angeles, Calif. | 56.0 | 59.5 | 69.0 | 66.3 | 12.08 | 36 | T | 49 |
| Louisville, Ky. | 32.5 | 56.6 | 77.6 | 57.7 | 43.56 | 125 | 17.5 | 37 |
| Madison, Wisc. | 15.6 | 45.8 | 70.6 | 49.5 | 30.84 | 118 | 40.8 | 36 |
| Memphis, Tenn. | 39.6 | 62.6 | 82.1 | 62.9 | 51.57 | 107 | 5.5 | 34 |
| Miami, Fla. | 67.1 | 75.3 | 82.5 | 77.9 | 57.55 | 129 | 0.0 | 42 |
| Milwaukee, Wisc. | 18.7 | 44.6 | 70.5 | 50.9 | 30.94 | 125 | 47.0 | 44 |
| Minneapolis–St. Paul, Minn. | 11.2 | 46.0 | 73.1 | 49.6 | 26.36 | 115 | 48.9 | 46 |
| Mobile, Ala. | 50.8 | 68.0 | 82.2 | 68.5 | 64.64 | 123 | 0.3 | 43 |
| Montgomery, Ala. | 46.7 | 65.2 | 81.7 | 65.3 | 49.16 | 108 | 0.3 | 40 |
| Mt. Washington, N.H. | 5.1 | 22.4 | 48.7 | 30.5 | 89.92 | 209 | 246.8 | 52 |
| Nashville, Tenn. | 37.1 | 59.7 | 79.4 | 60.2 | 48.49 | 119 | 11.1 | 43 |
| Newark, N.J. | 31.2 | 52.1 | 76.8 | 57.2 | 42.34 | 122 | 28.2 | 43 |
| New Orleans, La. | 52.4 | 68.7 | 82.1 | 69.2 | 59.74 | 114 | 0.2 | 38[3] |
| New York, N.Y. | 31.8 | 51.9 | 76.4 | 57.5 | 42.82 | 119 | 26.1 | 40[3] |
| Norfolk, Va. | 39.9 | 58.2 | 78.4 | 61.3 | 45.22 | 115 | 7.9 | 36 |

| City | Average monthly temperature (°F)[1] | | | | Precipitation | | Snowfall | |
|---|---|---|---|---|---|---|---|---|
| | Jan. | April | July | Oct. | Average annual (in.)[1] | (days)[2] | Average annual (in.)[2] | Years[2] |
| Oklahoma City, Okla. | 35.9 | 60.2 | 82.1 | 62.3 | 30.89 | 82 | 9.0 | 45 |
| Olympia, Wash. | 37.2 | 47.3 | 63.0 | 50.1 | 50.96 | 164 | 18.0 | 43 |
| Omaha, Neb. | 20.2 | 52.2 | 77.7 | 54.5 | 30.34 | 98 | 31.1 | 49[3] |
| Philadelphia, Pa. | 31.2 | 52.9 | 76.5 | 56.5 | 41.42 | 117 | 21.9 | 42[3] |
| Phoenix, Ariz. | 52.3 | 68.1 | 92.3 | 73.4 | 7.11 | 36 | T | 47[3] |
| Pittsburgh, Pa. | 26.7 | 50.1 | 72.0 | 52.5 | 36.30 | 154 | 44.6 | 32 |
| Portland, Maine | 21.5 | 42.8 | 68.1 | 48.5 | 43.52 | 128 | 72.4 | 44 |
| Portland, Ore. | 38.9 | 50.4 | 67.7 | 54.3 | 37.39 | 154 | 6.8 | 44 |
| Providence, R.I. | 28.2 | 47.9 | 72.5 | 53.2 | 45.32 | 124 | 37.1 | 31 |
| Raleigh, N.C. | 39.6 | 59.4 | 77.7 | 59.7 | 41.76 | 112 | 7.7 | 40 |
| Reno, Nev. | 32.2 | 46.4 | 69.5 | 50.3 | 7.49 | 51 | 25.3 | 42 |
| Richmond, Va. | 36.6 | 57.9 | 77.8 | 58.6 | 44.07 | 113 | 14.6 | 47 |
| Roswell, N.M. | 41.4 | 61.9 | 81.4 | 61.7 | 9.70 | 52 | 11.4 | 37[3] |
| Sacramento, Calif. | 45.3 | 58.2 | 75.6 | 63.9 | 17.10 | 58 | 0.1 | 36[3] |
| Salt Lake City, Utah | 28.6 | 49.2 | 77.5 | 53.0 | 15.31 | 90 | 59.1 | 56 |
| San Antonio, Texas | 50.4 | 69.6 | 84.6 | 70.2 | 29.13 | 81 | 0.4 | 42 |
| San Diego, Calif. | 56.8 | 61.2 | 70.3 | 67.5 | 9.32 | 43 | T | 44 |
| San Francisco, Calif. | 48.5 | 54.8 | 62.2 | 60.6 | 19.71 | 63 | T | 57 |
| Savannah, Ga. | 49.1 | 66.0 | 81.2 | 66.9 | 49.70 | 111 | 0.3 | 34 |
| Seattle-Tacoma, Wash. | 39.1 | 48.7 | 64.8 | 52.4 | 38.60 | 158 | 12.8 | 40 |
| Sioux Falls, S.D. | 12.4 | 46.4 | 74.0 | 49.4 | 24.12 | 96 | 39.9 | 39 |
| Spokane, Wash. | 25.7 | 45.8 | 69.7 | 47.5 | 16.71 | 114 | 51.5 | 37 |
| Springfield, Ill. | 24.6 | 53.3 | 76.5 | 56.0 | 33.78 | 114 | 24.5 | 37 |
| St. Louis, Mo. | 28.8 | 56.1 | 78.9 | 57.9 | 33.91 | 111 | 19.8 | 48[3] |
| Tampa, Fla. | 59.8 | 71.5 | 82.1 | 74.4 | 46.73 | 107 | T | 38 |
| Toledo, Ohio | 23.1 | 47.8 | 71.8 | 51.7 | 31.78 | 137 | 38.3 | 29 |
| Tucson, Ariz. | 51.1 | 64.9 | 86.2 | 70.4 | 11.14 | 52 | 1.2 | 44 |
| Tulsa, Okla. | 35.2 | 61.0 | 83.2 | 62.6 | 38.77 | 89 | 9.0 | 46 |
| Vero Beach, Fla. | 61.9 | 71.7 | 81.1 | 75.2 | 51.41 | n.a. | n.a. | 0 |
| Washington, D.C. | 35.2 | 56.7 | 78.9 | 59.3 | 39.00 | 112 | 17.0 | 41[3] |
| Wichita, Kan. | 29.6 | 56.3 | 81.4 | 59.1 | 28.61 | 85 | 16.4 | 31 |
| Wilmington, Del. | 31.2 | 52.4 | 76.0 | 56.3 | 41.38 | 117 | 20.9 | 37 |

1. Based on 30-year period 1951–1980. Data latest available. 2. Data through 1984 based on number of years as indicated in Years column. 3. For snowfall data where number of years differs from that for precipitation data. T = trace. n.a. = not available. *Source:* National Oceanic and Atmospheric Administration (NOAA).

## Revised Wind Chill Index

*Source:* The National Weather Service

The wind chill temperature index measures how cold people feel when outside. Wind chill is based on the rate of heat loss from exposed skin caused by wind and cold. As the wind increases, it draws heat from the body, driving down skin temperature and eventually the internal body temperature. The wind therefore makes it feel much colder. If the temperature is 0°F and the wind is blowing at 15 mph, the wind chill is –19°F. At this wind chill temperature, exposed skin can freeze in 30 minutes.

A revised wind chill table was introduced by the National Weather Service on Nov. 1, 2001. The new index was tested on human subjects and is based on heat loss from exposed skin. The old index, formulated in 1945 by Antarctic explorers, measured the cooling rate of water.

| Wind speed (mph) | Temperature (°F) | | | | | | | | | | | | | | | | | |
|---|---|---|---|---|---|---|---|---|---|---|---|---|---|---|---|---|---|---|
| | 40 | 35 | 30 | 25 | 20 | 15 | 10 | 5 | 0 | –5 | –10 | –15 | –20 | –25 | –30 | –35 | –40 | –45 |
| 5 | 36 | 31 | 25 | 19 | 13 | 7 | 1 | –5 | –11 | –16 | –22 | –28 | –34 | –40 | –46 | –52 | –57 | –63 |
| 10 | 34 | 27 | 21 | 15 | 9 | 3 | –4 | –10 | –16 | –22 | –28 | –35 | –41 | –47 | –53 | –59 | –66 | –72 |
| 15 | 32 | 25 | 19 | 13 | 6 | 0 | –7 | –13 | –19 | –26 | –32 | –39 | –45 | –51 | –58 | –64 | –71 | –77 |
| 20 | 30 | 24 | 17 | 11 | 4 | –2 | –9 | –15 | –22 | –29 | –35 | –42 | –48 | –55 | –61 | –68 | –74 | –81 |
| 25 | 29 | 23 | 16 | 9 | 3 | –4 | –11 | –17 | –24 | –31 | –37 | –44 | –51 | –58 | –64 | –71 | –78 | –84 |
| 30 | 28 | 22 | 15 | 8 | 1 | –5 | –12 | –19 | –26 | –33 | –39 | –46 | –53 | –60 | –67 | –73 | –80 | –87 |
| 35 | 28 | 21 | 14 | 7 | 0 | –7 | –14 | –21 | –27 | –34 | –41 | –48 | –55 | –62 | –69 | –76 | –82 | –89 |
| 40 | 27 | 20 | 13 | 6 | –1 | –8 | –15 | –22 | –29 | –36 | –43 | –50 | –57 | –64 | –71 | –78 | –84 | –91 |
| 45 | 26 | 19 | 12 | 5 | –2 | –9 | –16 | –23 | –30 | –37 | –44 | –51 | –58 | –65 | –72 | –79 | –86 | –93 |
| 50 | 26 | 19 | 12 | 4 | –3 | –10 | –17 | –24 | –31 | –38 | –45 | –52 | –60 | –67 | –74 | –81 | –88 | –95 |
| 55 | 25 | 18 | 11 | 4 | –3 | –11 | –18 | –25 | –32 | –39 | –46 | –54 | –61 | –68 | –75 | –82 | –89 | –97 |
| 60 | 25 | 17 | 10 | 3 | –4 | –11 | –19 | –26 | –33 | –40 | –48 | –55 | –62 | –69 | –76 | –84 | –91 | –98 |

Frostbite Times: **Bold = 30 minutes**  *Italic = 10 Minutes*  ***Bold italic = 5 minutes***

Formula: Wind Chill (°F) = 35.74 + 0.6215T – 35.75(V^{0.16}) + 0.4275T(V^{0.16})

Where, T = Air Temperature (°F)  V = Wind Speed (mph)

# GREAT DISASTERS

The following lists are not all-inclusive due to space limitations. Only disasters involving great loss of life and/or property, historical interest, or unusual circumstances are listed. Data as of mid–September 2002. For other disasters *see* Current Events: What Happened in 2002, pp. 36–44.

## WORST UNITED STATES DISASTERS

**AIRCRAFT**

1979  **May 25, Chicago:** American Airlines DC-10 crashed seconds after takeoff, killing all 272 persons aboard and three on the ground.

**AVALANCHE**

1910  **March 1, Wellington, Wash.:** two trains snowbound in Stevens Pass in Cascade Range swept off tracks into canyon 150 ft below, killing 96.

**DROUGHT**

1930s  **Many states:** longest drought of 20th century. Peak periods were 1930, 1934, 1936, 1939, and 1940. During 1934, dry regions stretched solidly from N.Y. and Pa. across the Great Plains to the Calif. coast. A great "dust bowl" covered 50 million acres in south-central plains during winter of 1935–1936.

**EARTHQUAKE**

1906  **April 18, San Francisco:** earthquake accompanied by fire razed more than 4 sq mi; more than 500 dead or missing.

**EPIDEMIC**

1918  **Nationwide:** Spanish influenza killed over 500,000 Americans.

**EXPLOSION**

1947  **April 16–18, Texas City, Tex.:** a fire and subsequent explosion on the French freighter *Grandcamp* destroyed most of the city; 516 killed.

**FIRE**

1871  **Oct. 8, Peshtigo, Wis.:** over 1,500 lives lost and 3.8 million acres burned in forest fire.

**FLOOD**

1889  **May 31, Johnstown, Pa.:** collapse of South Fork Dam left more than 2,200 dead.

**HURRICANE**

1900  **Sept. 8, Galveston, Tex.:** an estimated 6,000–8,000 dead, mostly from devastation due to tidal surge.

**MARINE**

1865  **April 27, Mississippi River, nr. Memphis, Tenn.:** explosion on steamboat *Sultana* killed 1,547.

**MINE**

1907  **Dec. 6, Monongha, W. Va.:** coal mine explosion killed 361.

**OIL SPILL**

1989  **March 24, Prince William Sound, Alaska:** tanker *Exxon Valdez* hit an undersea reef and released 10 million plus gallons of oil into the waters.

**RAILROAD**

1918  **July 9, Nashville, Tenn.:** 101 killed in a two-train collision near Nashville.

**SUBMARINE**

1963  **April 10, North Atlantic:** atomic-powered submarine *Thresher* sank; 129 dead.

**TERRORIST ATTACK**

2001  **Sept. 11, New York City, Arlington, Va., and Shanksville, Pa.:** hijackers crashed two commercial jets into twin towers of World Trade Center; two more hijacked jets were crashed into the Pentagon and a field in rural Pa. Total dead numbered 3,044, including the 19 hijackers. Islamic al-Qaeda terrorist group blamed.

**TORNADO**

1925  **March 18, Mo., Ill., and Ind.:** great "Tri-State Tornado"; 689 dead; over 2,000 injured. Property damage estimated at $16.5 million.

**WINTER STORM**

1888  **March 11–14, East Coast:** the "Blizzard of 1888." 400 people died; as much as 5 ft of snow. Damage was estimated at $20 million.

## EARTHQUAKES AND VOLCANIC ERUPTIONS

**A.D. 79**  **Aug. 24, Italy:** eruption of Mt. Vesuvius buried cities of Pompeii and Herculaneum, killing thousands.

856  **Dec. 22, Damghan, Iran:** 200,000 were killed in one of the deadliest earthquakes on record.

893  **March 23, Ardabil, Iran:** earthquake killed about 150,000 people.

1138  **Aug. 9, Aleppo, Syria:** deadly earthquake claimed lives of 230,000 people.

1290  **Sept., Chihli, China:** earthquake killed about 100,000 people.

1556  **Jan. 23, Shaanxi (Shensi) province, China:** most deadly earthquake in history; 830,000 killed.

1667  **Nov., Shemakha, Caucasia:** earthquake killed about 80,000 people.

1727  **Nov. 18, Tabriz, Iran:** about 77,000 victims killed in deadly earthquake.

1755  **Nov. 1, Portugal:** earthquake leveled Lisbon and was felt as far away as southern France and North Africa; 70,000 killed.

1783  **June 8, Iceland:** eruption of Laki volcano lasted until Feb. 1784. Haze from eruption resulted in loss of island's livestock (from eating contaminated grass) and widespread crop failure (from acid rain); 9,350 deaths, mostly due to starvation.

1792  **May 21, Kyushu Island, Japan:** collapse of old lava dome during eruption of Unzen volcano caused avalanche and tsunami that killed an estimated 14,300 people. (Most of the people were killed by the tsunami.) Japan's greatest volcano disaster.

1811  **Dec. 16, Mississippi Valley nr. New Madrid, Mo.:** earthquake reversed the course of the Mississippi River. Fatalities unknown due to sparse population in area. Aftershocks and tremors continued into 1812. It has been estimated that three of the series of earthquakes had surface-wave magnitudes of 8.6, 8.4, and 8.8 on the Richter scale. It is the largest series of earthquakes known to have occurred in North America.

1815  **April 5, 10–11, Netherlands Indies (Sumbawa, Indonesia):** eruption of Tambora largest in historic times. An estimated 92,000 people were killed, about 10,000 directly as a result of explosions and ash fall and about 82,000 indirectly by starvation and disease.

**1877 June 26, north-central Ecuador:** eruption of Mt. Cotopaxi caused severe mudflows that wiped out surrounding cities and valleys; 1,000 deaths.

**1883 Aug. 26–28, Netherlands Indies (Krakatau, Indonesia):** eruption of Krakatau; violent explosions destroyed two-thirds of island, leaving an estimated 36,000 dead. Sea waves occurred as far away as Cape Horn and possibly England.

**1886 Aug. 31, Charleston, S.C.:** 60 persons killed and extensive damage to city. Earthquake's magnitude was 7.7 on the Richter scale.

**1902 May 7, St. Vincent, West Indies:** Soufrière volcano erupted, devastating one-third of the island and killing some 1,680 people.

**May 8, Martinique, West Indies:** Mt. Pelée erupted and wiped out city of St. Pierre; 40,000 dead.

**1906 April 18, San Francisco:** earthquake accompanied by fire razed more than 4 sq mi; more than 500 dead or missing.

**1908 Dec. 28, Messina, Sicily:** city totally destroyed by earthquake. Death toll 70,000–100,000 in Sicily and southern Italy.

**1915 Jan. 13, Avezzano, Italy:** earthquake left 29,980 dead.

**1920 Dec. 16, Gansu province, China:** magnitude 8.6 earthquake killed 200,000 in northwest China.

**1923 Sept. 1, Japan:** magnitude 8.3 earthquake destroyed one third of Tokyo and most of Yokohama. More than 140,000 killed.

**1927 May 22, nr. Xining, China:** magnitude 8.3 earthquake claimed approximately 200,000 victims.

**1932 Dec. 25, Gansu, China:** magnitude 7.6 earthquake rattled China, killing approximately 70,000.

**1935 May 30, Pakistan:** earthquake at Quetta killed 30,000–60,000.

**1939 Jan. 24, Chile:** earthquake razed 50,000 sq mi; about 30,000 killed.

**Dec. 27, northern Turkey:** severe quakes destroyed city of Erzingan; about 100,000 casualties.

**1950 Aug. 15, India:** earthquake affected 30,000 sq mi in Assam; 20,000–30,000 believed killed.

**1960 Feb. 29, Agadir, Morocco:** 10,000–12,000 dead as earthquake set off tidal wave and fire, destroying most of city.

**1964 March 28, Alaska:** strongest earthquake ever to strike North America hit 80 mi east of Anchorage; followed by seismic wave 50 ft high that traveled 8,445 mi at 450 mph; 117 killed.

**1970 Jan. 5, Yunnan province, China:** magnitude 7.7 quake killed 15,621.

**May 31, Peru:** earthquake left more than 50,000 killed; 17,000 missing.

**1972 Dec. 22, Managua, Nicaragua:** earthquake devastated city, leaving up to 6,000 dead.

**1976 Feb. 4, Guatemala:** quake left over 23,000 dead.

**July 28, Tangshan, China:** worst earthquake to hit China in 20th century; devastated 20 sq mi of city, leaving 242,000 dead (official). Estimated death toll as high as 655,000.

**Aug. 17, Mindanao, Philippines:** earthquake and tidal wave left up to 8,000 dead or missing.

**1978 Sept. 16, Tabas, Iran:** earthquake destroyed city in eastern Iran, leaving 25,000 dead.

**1985 Sept. 19–20, Mexico:** magnitude 8.1 earthquake struck central and southwest regions, devastating part of Mexico City and three coastal states; estimated 25,000 killed.

**Nov. 14–16, Colombia:** eruption of Nevada del Ruiz, 85 mi northwest of Bogotá. Mudslides buried most of the town of Armero and devastated Chinchiná; estimated 25,000 killed.

**1988 Dec. 7, Armenia:** earthquake measuring 6.9 in magnitude killed nearly 25,000, injured 15,000, and left at least 400,000 homeless.

**1989 Oct. 17, San Francisco Bay area:** earthquake measuring 7.1 in magnitude killed 67 and injured over 3,000. Over 100,000 buildings damaged or destroyed. Damage cost city billions of dollars.

**1990 June 21, northwest Iran:** earthquake measuring 7.7 in magnitude destroyed cities and villages in Caspian Sea area. At least 50,000 dead, over 60,000 injured, and 400,000 homeless.

**July 16, northern Philippines:** magnitude 7.7 quake killed nearly 2,000.

**1991 July 15, Luzon Island, Philippines:** eruption of Mt. Pinatubo buried over 300 sq mi under volcanic ash and resulted in more than 800 deaths.

**1993 Aug. 8, Guam:** earthquake measuring 8.1 in magnitude caused severe damage to many structures but no fatalities. Damages were estimated at nearly $300 million.

**1994 Jan. 17, San Fernando Valley, Calif.:** earthquake measuring 6.6 in magnitude killed 61 and injured over 8,000. Damage estimated at $13–20 billion.

**1995 Jan.17, Osaka, Kyoto, and Kobe, Japan:** 5,100 killed and 26,800 injured; estimated damage $100 billion. Magnitude: 7.2.

**1997 May 12, northeast Iran:** severe earthquake measuring 7.1 in magnitude left more than 1,500 people dead and at least 4,460 injured.

**June–Sept., southern Montserrat:** ongoing eruption of Soufrière Hills volcano since July 1995; killed 20 persons in major eruption on June 25, 1997, rendered southern two-thirds of Montserrat uninhabitable, and forced some 8,000 of the island's 12,000 residents to abandon the island.

**1998 May 30, northern Afghanistan:** magnitude 7.1 earthquake and aftershocks killed an estimated 5,000 and injured at least 1,500. A quake on Feb. 4 in same area had killed about 2,300.

**1999 Jan. 25, Armenia, Colombia:** 1,124 dead and 4,000 injured in magnitude 6 earthquake. More than 200,000 left homeless.

**Aug. 17, northwest Turkey:** magnitude 7.4 quake centered near Izmit killed over 17,000 and injured over 44,000. Damage estimated at $8.5 billion. Another severe 7.2 temblor killed more than 700 in Ducze and surrounding towns in Nov.

**Sept. 21, central Taiwan:** major quake and aftershocks killed 2,295 and injured 8,729.

**2001 Jan. 13, El Salvador:** magnitude 7.7 earthquake set off some 185 landslides across El Salvador; at least 844 died and nearly 100,000 houses were destroyed.

**Jan. 26, Bhuj, India:** magnitude 7.7 earthquake rocked western Indian state of Gujarat, killing more than 20,000 people and leaving 600,000 homeless. Total cost was estimated at $1.3 billion.

**2002 March 25, northeast Afghanistan:** series of earthquakes—the largest measuring 6.1 in magnitude—rattled an area 100 mi north of Kabul. Estimated 1,000 people killed and 7,000 families homeless. The city of Nahrin, a densely populated district capital, was completely razed.

## MAJOR U.S. EPIDEMICS

**1793** **Philadelphia:** more than 4,000 residents died from yellow fever.

**1832** **July–Aug., New York City:** over 3,000 people killed in a cholera epidemic.
**Oct., New Orleans:** cholera took the lives of 4,340 people.

**1848** **New York City:** more than 5,000 deaths caused by cholera.

**1853** **New Orleans:** yellow fever killed 7,790.

**1867** **New Orleans:** 3,093 perished from yellow fever.

**1878** **Southern states:** over 13,000 people died from yellow fever in lower Mississippi Valley.

**1916** **Nationwide:** over 7,000 deaths occurred and 27,363 cases were reported of polio (infantile paralysis) in America's worst polio epidemic.

**1918** **March–Nov., nationwide:** outbreak of Spanish influenza killed over 500,000 people in the worst single U.S. epidemic.

**1949** **Nationwide:** 2,720 deaths occurred from polio, and 42,173 cases were reported.

**1952** **Nationwide:** polio killed 3,300; 57,628 cases reported; worst epidemic since 1916.

**1981** **1981 to June 2001:** total U.S. AIDS cases reported to Centers for Disease Control: 793,026; total AIDS deaths reported: 457,667.

## FLOODS, AVALANCHES, AND TIDAL WAVES

**1228** **Holland:** 100,000 people reputedly drowned by sea flood in Friesland.

**1642** **China:** rebels destroyed Kaifeng seawall; 300,000 drowned.

**1889** **May 31, Johnstown, Pa.:** more than 2,200 died in flood after South Fork Dam collapsed.

**1896** **June 15, Sanriku, Japan:** earthquake and tidal wave killed 27,000.

**1910** **March 1, Wellington, Wash.:** avalanche in Cascade Range swept two trains into canyon, killing 96. Worst U.S. avalanche.

**1928** **March 12, Santa Paula, Calif.:** collapse of St. Francis Dam left 450 dead.

**1931** **July–Aug., China:** flood along Yangtze River left 3.7 million people dead from disease, starvation, or drowning.

**1953** **Jan. 31–Feb. 5, northwest Europe:** storm followed by floods devastated North Sea coastal areas. Netherlands was hardest hit with 1,794 dead.

**1954** **Aug., Teheran, Iran:** flood rains resulted in some 10,000 deaths.

**1959** **Dec. 2, Fréjus, France:** flood caused by collapse of Malpasset Dam left 412 dead.

**1962** **Jan. 10, Peru:** avalanche down extinct Huascaran volcano killed more than 3,000.

**1963** **Oct. 9, Italy:** landslide into the Vaiont Dam; flood killed about 2,000.

**1966** **Oct. 21, Aberfan, Wales:** avalanche of coal, waste, mud, and rocks killed 144 people, including 116 children in school.

**1969** **Jan. 18–26, southern Calif.:** floods and mudslides from heavy rains caused widespread property damage; at least 100 dead. Another downpour (Feb. 23–26) caused further floods and mudslides; at least 18 dead.

**1970** **Nov. 13, East Pakistan:** 200,000 killed by cyclone-driven tidal wave from Bay of Bengal. Over 100,000 missing.

**1971** **Aug., Hanoi, North Vietnam:** heavy rains caused severe flooding in the Red River Delta, killing 100,000.

**1972** **Feb. 26, Man, W. Va.:** more than 118 died when slag-pile dam collapsed under pressure of torrential rains and flooded 17-mile valley.
**June 9–10, Rapid City, S.D.:** flash flood caused 237 deaths and $160 million in damage.
**June 20, Eastern Seaboard:** tropical storm Agnes, in ten-day rampage, caused widespread flash floods. Death toll 129; 115,000 left homeless; damage estimated at $3.5 billion.

**1988** **Aug.–Sept., Bangladesh:** heaviest monsoon in 70 years inundated three-fourths of country, killing more than 1,300 and leaving 30 million homeless. Damage estimated at over $1 billion.

**1993** **June–Aug., Ill., Iowa, Kan., Ky., Minn., Mo., Neb., N.D., S.D., Wis.:** two months of heavy rain caused Mississippi River and tributaries to flood; almost 50 deaths and about $12 billion in damage. Almost 70,000 left homeless.

**1997** **Dec. 1996–Jan. 1997, U.S. West Coast:** torrential rains and snowmelt produced severe floods in parts of Calif., Ore., Wash., Idaho, Nev., and Mont., causing 36 deaths and about $2–3 billion in damage.
**March, Ohio and Mississippi Valleys:** flooding and tornadoes plagued Ark., Mo., Miss., Tenn., Ill., Ind., Ky., Ohio, and W.Va. 67 were killed and damage totaled approximately $1 billion.
**April, N.D., S.D., and Minn.:** Grand Forks, N.D., and surrounding area devastated as the Red River swelled 13 ft above flood level.

**1998** **July 17, Papua New Guinea:** three tsunamis, possibly spurred by an undersea landslide following an earthquake, wiped out entire villages in the northwest province of Sepik. At least 2,000 found or presumed dead.
**Summer, central and northeast China:** heaviest flooding of Yangtze and other rivers since 1954. More than 3,000 killed and 14 million left homeless. Estimated damages exceeded $20 billion.

**1999** **Summer, Asia:** torrential downpours and flooding left more than 950 dead and millions homeless in S. Korea, China, Japan, the Philippines, and Thailand.
**Oct., southwest Mexico:** over a week of heavy rains killed at least 360 people in mudslides and flood waters.
**Nov. and Dec., Vietnam:** devastating floods caused $285 million in damage and killed more than 700 people.
**Dec. 15–16, northern Venezuela:** heavy rains caused catastrophic flooding and mudslides, killing an estimated 5,000 to 20,000 people. Is country's worst modern-day natural disaster.

**2000** **Feb., southeast Africa:** weeks of rain resulted in deadly floods in Mozambique and Zimbabwe. About 700 people were killed and more than 280,000 were left homeless.

# MAJOR STORMS

Cyclones, hurricanes, and typhoons are the same kind of tropical storm but are called by different names in different areas of the world.

## CYCLONES

**1864** Oct. 5, Calcutta, India: 70,000 killed.

**1942** Oct. 16, Bengal, India: about 40,000 lives lost.

**1960** Oct. 10, East Pakistan: cyclone and tidal wave killed about 6,000.

**1963** May 28–29, East Pakistan: cyclone killed about 22,000 along coast.

**1965** May 11–12 and June 1–2, East Pakistan: cyclones killed about 47,000.

Dec. 15, Karachi, Pakistan: cyclone killed about 10,000.

**1970** Nov. 12–13, East Pakistan: cyclone and tidal waves killed 200,000 and another 100,000 were reported missing.

**1971** Sept. 29, Orissa state, India: cyclone and tidal wave off the Bay of Bengal killed as many as 10,000.

**1974** Dec. 25, Darwin, Australia: cyclone destroyed nearly the entire city; 50 reported dead.

**1977** Nov. 19, Andhra Pradesh, India: cyclone and tidal wave claimed lives of 20,000.

**1991** April 30, southeast Bangladesh: cyclone killed over 131,000 and left as many as 9 million homeless. Thousands of survivors died from hunger and water-borne disease.

**1999** Oct. 29, Orissa state, India: supercyclone swept in from Bay of Bengal, killing at least 9,573 and leaving over 10 million homeless.

## U.S. HURRICANES

(U.S. deaths only, except where noted. Damages are given in 1998 dollars, except where noted.)

**1776** Sept. 2–Sept. 9, N.C. to Nova Scotia: called the "Hurricane of Independence," it is believed that 4,170 in the U.S. and Canada died in the storm.

**1856** Aug. 11, Last Island, La.: 400 died.

**1893** Aug. 28, Savannah, Ga., Charleston, S.C., Sea Islands, S.C.: at least 1,000 died.

**1900** Sept. 8, Galveston, Tex.: an estimated 6,000–8,000 died in hurricane and tidal surge. The "Galveston Hurricane" is considered the deadliest in U.S. history.

**1909** Sept. 10–21, La. and Miss.: 350 deaths.

**1915** Aug. 5–23, Galveston,Tex., and New Orleans, La.: 275 killed.

**1919** Sept. 2–15, Fla. keys, La., and southern Tex.: more than 600 killed, mostly lost on ships at sea.

**1926** Sept. 11–22, southeast Fla. and Ala.: 243 deaths. Costliest hurricane in U.S. history, with damages estimated at nearly $84 billion.

**1928** Sept. 6-19, Lake Okeechobee, southeast Fla.: 1,836 deaths. Second-deadliest U.S. hurricane on record.

**1935** Aug. 29-Sept. 10, Fla. keys: Labor Day Hurricane", 408 deaths.

**1938** Sept. 10–22, Long Island, N.Y., and southern New England: "New England Hurricane"; 600 deaths.

**1944** Sept. 9–16, N.C. to New England: 390 deaths, 344 of which were at sea.

**1947** Sept. 4–21, southeast Fla., La., Miss., Ala.: 51 killed.

**1954** Aug. 25–31, N.C. to New England: "Carol" killed 60 in Long Island–New England area.

Oct. 5–18, S.C. to N.Y.: "Hazel" killed 95 in U.S.; about 400–1,000 in Haiti; 78 in Canada.

**1955** Aug. 7–21, N.C. to New England: "Diane" took 184 lives.

**1957** June 25–28. southwest La. and northern Tex.: "Audrey" wiped out Cameron, La., causing 390 deaths.

**1960** Aug. 29–Sept. 13, Fla. to New England: "Donna" killed 50 in the U.S.; 115 deaths in Antilles, mostly from flash floods in Puerto Rico.

**1961** Sept. 3–15, Tex. coast: "Carla" devastated Tex. gulf cities, taking 46 lives.

**1965** Aug. 27–Sept. 12, southern Fla. and La.: "Betsy" killed 75 people and cost more than $14 billion.

**1969** Aug. 14–22, Miss., La., Ala., Va., and W. Va.: 256 killed as a result of "Camille." Damages estimated at nearly $13 billion.

**1972** June 14–23, northwest Fla. to N.Y.: "Agnes" caused 117 deaths (50 in Pa.). Damages estimated at over $12 billion. Still the worst natural disaster ever in Pa.

**1979** Aug. 29–Sept. 15, Ala. and Miss.: "Frederic" devastated Mobile, Ala., and caused $7.2 billion in damage overall. One of the costliest U.S. hurricanes ever.

**1985** Oct. 6–Nov. 1: "Juan" struck La. and the Southeast. Though only a category 1 hurricane, it caused severe flooding and $1.5 billion (actual cost) in damages; 63 lives were lost.

**1989** Sept. 10–22, Caribbean Sea, S.C., and N.C.: "Hugo" claimed 86 lives (57 U.S. mainland). With damages estimated at over $12.6 billion, it is one of the most costly U.S. hurricanes.

**1992** Aug. 22–26, Bahamas, southern Fla., and La.: Hurricane "Andrew" left 26 dead and more than 100,000 homes destroyed or damaged. With total U.S. damages estimated at $26.5 billion, it is the most costly hurricane in U.S. history.

**1994** Nov. 8–21, Caribbean and southern Fla.: "Gordon" led to an estimated 1,122 deaths in Haiti. Eight died in Fla.; estimated U.S. damage $400 million (actual cost).

**1995** Nov. 29, Fla. panhandle and Ala.: storm surge during "Opal" caused extensive damage to coastal areas. In U.S. death toll reached nine and damages more than $3 billion.

**1996** Sept. 5, N.C. and Va.: "Fran" took 37 lives and caused more than $3.2 billion in damage.

**1999** Sept. 14–18, Bahamas to New England: "Floyd" and associated flooding caused at least 57 deaths including one in the Bahamas. Hardest-hit N.C. suffered 35 "Floyd" related deaths. Deadliest U.S. hurricane since "Agnes" in 1972. Damage estimated at $4.5 billion (in 1999 dollars).

**2001** June 5–15, Gulf Coast to southern New England: Tropical Storm "Allison" caused severe flooding, especially in and around Houston, where 20,000 residents were evacuated from their homes. Damage estimated at $5 billion (actual cost); 41 deaths, including 23 in Tex.

## OTHER HURRICANES

**1780** Oct. 10–16, Barbados, West Indies: "The Great Hurricane of 1780" killed 20,000–22,000 persons and completely flattened the islands of Barbados, Martinique, and St. Eustatius; is the deadliest western hemisphere hurricane on record.

**1926** Oct. 20, Cuba: powerful hurricane killed 650.

**1930** Sept. 3, Dominican Republic: hurricane killed about 8,000 people.

**1955** Sept. 19, Mexico: "Hilda" took 200 lives.

**Sept. 22–28, Caribbean:** "Janet" killed 200 in Honduras and 300 in Mexico.

**1961 Oct. 31, British Honduras:** "Hattie" devastated capital Belize, killed at least 400.

**1963 Oct. 2–7, Caribbean:** "Flora" killed about 7,200 in Haiti and Cuba.

**1966 Sept. 24–30, Caribbean area:** "Inez" killed 293.

**1974 Sept. 14–19, Honduras:** "Fifi" struck northern part of country, leaving 8,000 dead and 100,000 homeless.

**1988 Sept. 12–17, Caribbean Sea and Gulf of Mexico:** "Gilbert" took at least 260 lives and caused some 39 tornadoes in Tex.

**1997 Oct. 8–10, southern Mexico:** "Pauline" devastated resort city of Acapulco and villages along the coast in states of Oaxaca and Guerrero, leaving 217 dead and 20,000 homeless.

**1998 Sept. 20–29, Caribbean, Fla. Keys, and Gulf Coast:** "Georges" killed about 600 people, mostly in Dominican Republic. Damage estimated to be $5 billion, including $2 billion in Puerto Rico.
**Oct. 26–Nov. 4, Honduras, Nicaragua, Guatemala:** "Mitch" killed more than 11,000 people, becoming the deadliest Atlantic storm in 200 years. Two to three million people were left homeless; damages were more than $5 billion.

## TYPHOONS

**1906 Sept. 18, Hong Kong:** typhoon with tsunami killed an estimated 10,000 persons.

**1934 Sept. 21, Japan:** typhoon killed more than 4,000 on Honshu.

**1949 Dec. 5, off Korea:** typhoon struck fishing fleet; several thousand men reported dead.

**1958 Sept. 27, Honshu, Japan:** "Vera" left nearly 5,000 dead and 1.5 million homeless.

**1959 Aug. 20, Fukien province, China:** "Iris" killed 2,334.

**1960 June 9, Fukien province, China:** "Mary" caused at least 1,600 deaths.

**1984 Sept. 2–3, Philippines:** "Ike" hit seven major islands, leaving 1,300 dead.

**1991 Nov. 5, central Philippines:** flash floods triggered by tropical storm "Thelma" killed about 3,000 people. City of Ormoc on Leyte was worst hit.

## RECENT HURRICANE-LIKE STORMS

**1999 Dec. 26–28, northern and western Europe:** two back-to-back hurricane-force storms left 97 people dead. Winds reaching 120 mph uprooted trees, disrupted transportation, and left millions of homes without power.

## BLIZZARDS

**1888 Jan. 12, Dakota and Montana territories, Minn., Nebr., Kans., and Tex.:** "Schoolchildren's Blizzard" resulted in 235 deaths, many of which were children on their way home from school.

**March 11–14, East Coast:** "Blizzard of 1888" resulted in 400 deaths and as much as 5 ft of snow. Damage was estimated at $20 million.

**1949 Jan. 2–4, Nebr., Wyo., S.D., Utah, Colo., and Nev.:** Actually one of a series of winter storms between Jan. 1 and Feb. 22. Although only 1 ft to 30 in. of snow fell, fierce winds of up to 72 mph created drifts as high as 30 ft. Tens of thousands of cattle and sheep perished.

**1950 Nov. 25–27, eastern U.S.:** "Storm of the Century" generated heavy snow and hurricane-force winds across 22 states and claimed 383 lives. Damages estimated at $70 million.

**1978 Feb. 6–8, eastern U.S.:** "Blizzard of 1978" battered the East Coast, particularly the Northeast; claimed 54 lives and caused $1 billion in damage. Snowfall ranged from 2–4 ft in New England, plus nearly 2 ft of snow already on the ground from an earlier storm.

**1993 March 12–14, eastern U.S.:** "Superstorm" paralyzed the eastern seaboard, causing the deaths of some 270 people. Record snowfalls (with rates of 2–3 in. per hour) and high winds caused $3–6 billion in damage.

**1996 Jan. 6–8, eastern U.S.:** heavy snow paralyzed the Appalachians, the mid-Atlantic, and the Northeast. 187 were killed in the blizzard and in the floods that resulted after a sudden warm-up. Damages reached $3 billion.

# U.S. TORNADOES

**1840 May 6, Natchez, Miss.:** tornado struck heart of the city, killing 317 and injuring over 1,000.

**1880 April 18, Marshfield, Mo.:** series of 24 tornadoes demolished city, killing 99 people.

**1884 Feb. 19, Miss., Ala., N.C., S.C., Tenn., Ky., Ind.:** series of 60 tornadoes caused estimated 800 deaths.

**1896 May 27, eastern Mo. and southern Ill.:** series of 18 tornadoes; one tornado destroyed large section of St. Louis, Mo., killing 255.

**1899 June 12, New Richmond, Wis.:** tornado struck while circus was in town, causing 117 deaths.

**1902 May 18, Goliad, Tex.:** tornado killed 114.

**1903 June 1, Gainesville, Holland, Ga.:** twister caused 98 deaths.

**1905 May 10, Snyder, Okla.:** tornado killed 97.

**1908 April 24–25, La., Miss., Ala., Ga.:** 18 tornadoes resulted in 310 deaths (143 of these caused by one tornado that moved from Amite, La., to Purvis, Miss.).
**April 24, Natchez, Miss.:** twister struck, causing 91 deaths.

**1913 March 23, eastern Nebr. and western Iowa:** Easter Sunday, 8 tornadoes resulted in 181 deaths (94 in Omaha, Nebr.).

**1917 May 26, Mattoon, Ill.:** tornado smashed area, causing 101 deaths.

**1925 March 18, Mo., Ill., Ind.:** the "Tri-State Tornado" was the most violent single twister in U.S. history. It caused the deaths of 689 people and injured over 2,000. Property damage was estimated at $16.5 million.

**1927 May 9, Poplar Bluff, Mo.:** twister killed 98.
**Sept. 29, St. Louis, Mo.:** a five-minute tornado ripped through the city and caused 79 deaths.

**1932 March 21–22, Ala., Miss., Ga., Tenn.:** outbreak of 33 tornadoes killed 334 (268 in Ala.).

**1936 April 5–6, Deep South:** series of 17 tornadoes; 216 killed in Tupelo, Miss., and 203 killed in Gainesville, Ga., a small mill town that was obliterated.

**1944 June 23, W.Va., Pa., Md.:** 4 tornadoes caused 153 deaths.

**1947 April 9, Woodward, Okla.:** tornado demolished town, killing 181.

1952  March 21–22, Ark. and Tenn.: 28 tornadoes caused 204 deaths.

1953  May 11, Waco, Tex.: a single tornado struck, killing 114.

June 8, Flint, Mich.: tornado killed 116.

June 9, Worcester, Mass.: tornado hit town, causing 90 deaths.

1955  May 25, Udall, Kans.: tornado killed 80.

1965  April 11–12, Midwest–Great Lakes region: tornadoes in Iowa, Ill., Ind., Ohio, Mich., and Wis. caused 256 deaths.

1967  April 21, northern Ill., also Mo., Iowa, lower Mich.: series of 52 tornadoes caused 58 deaths.

1971  Feb. 21, Miss., La., Ark., Tenn.: series of 10 tornadoes resulted in 121 deaths.

1974  April 3–4: a series of 148 twisters comprised the deadly "Super Tornado Outbreak" that struck 13 states in the East, South, and Midwest. Before it was over, 330 died and 5,484 were injured in a damage path covering more than 2,500 mi. It was the worst tornado outbreak in U.S. history.

1979  April 10, northern Tex. and southern Okla.: 11 tornadoes caused 59 deaths.

1984  March 28, N.C. and S.C.: 22 tornadoes caused 57 deaths.

1985  May 31, Pa. and Ohio: 27 tornadoes resulted in 75 deaths. Damages were estimated at $450 million.

1990  Aug. 28, northern Ill.: fast-moving tornado struck the southwest suburbs of Chicago, killing 29 and injuring more than 300.

1992  Nov. 21–23, southeast Tex. to Mid-Atlantic and Ohio Valley: total of 94 tornadoes caused 26 deaths and $291 million in damage.

1994  March 27, Ala., Ga., and N.C.: Palm Sunday tornado outbreak resulted in 42 deaths, 320 injuries, and $107 million in property damage. Twenty people died and 90 were injured when a tornado caused the roof of a church near Piedmont, Ala., to collapse.

1999  May 3, Okla. and Kans.: unusually large twister, thought to have been a mile wide at times, killed 41 people and injured at least 748 others in Okla. A separate tornado killed another 5 and injured about 150 in Kans. Damages totaled at least $1 billion.

## DROUGHTS AND HEAT WAVES

1930s  Many states: longest drought of the 20th century. Peak periods were 1930, 1934, 1936, 1939, and 1940. A great "dust bowl" covered some 50 million acres in the south-central plains during the winter of 1935–1936.

1955  Aug. 31–Sept. 7, Los Angeles: 8-day run of 100°-plus heat left 946 people dead.

1972  July 14–26, New York City: 891 people died in 14-day heat wave.

1980  June–Sept., central and eastern U.S.: an estimated 10,000 people were killed during the summer in a long heat wave and drought. Damages totaled about $20 billion.

1982–1983  worldwide: El Niño caused wildly unusual weather in the U.S. and elsewhere throughout 1983. Drought in the western Pacific region led to disastrous forest fires in Indonesia and Australia. Overall loss to world economy was over $8 billion. Similar event in 1997–1998 resulted in estimated loss of $25–33 billion.

1988  Summer, central and eastern U.S.: a severe drought and heat wave killed an estimated 5,000–10,000 people, including heat stress-related deaths. Damages reached $40 billion.

1995  July 12–17, Chicago: 739 people died in record heat wave.

Fall–summer 1996, Tex. and Okla.: severe drought in southern plains region caused $4 billion in agricultural losses; no deaths.

1998  Summer, southern U.S.: severe heat and drought spread across Tex. and Okla., all the way to North and South Carolina. At least 200 were left dead and $6–9 billion of damage was estimated.

1999  Summer, eastern U.S.: rainfall shortages resulted in worst drought on record for Md., Del., N.J., and R.I. The state of W.Va. was declared a disaster area. 3.81 million acres were consumed by fire as of mid-Aug. Crops were severely damaged in many states, putting losses in the mid-Atlantic region at at least $800 million. Record heat throughout the country resulted in 282 deaths nationwide.

## NUCLEAR POWER PLANT ACCIDENTS

1952  Dec. 12, Chalk River, nr. Ottawa, Canada: a partial meltdown of the reactor's uranium fuel core resulted after the accidental removal of four control rods. Although millions of gallons of radioactive water accumulated inside the reactor, there were no injuries.

1957  Oct. 7, Windscale Pile No. 1, north of Liverpool, England: fire in a graphite-cooled reactor spewed radiation over the countryside, contaminating a 200-square-mile area.

South Ural Mountains: explosion of radioactive wastes at Soviet nuclear weapons factory 12 mi from city of Kyshtym forced the evacuation of over 10,000 people from a contaminated area. No casualties were reported by Soviet officials.

1976  nr. Greifswald, East Germany: radioactive core of reactor in the Lubmin nuclear power plant nearly melted down due to the failure of safety systems during a fire.

1979  March 28, Three Mile Island, nr. Harrisburg, Pa.: one of two reactors lost its coolant, which caused overheating and partial meltdown of the uranium core. Some radioactive water and gases were released.

1986  April 26, Chernobyl, nr. Kiev, Ukraine: explosion and fire in the graphite core of one of four reactors released radioactive material that spread over part of the Soviet Union, eastern Europe, Scandinavia, and later western Europe. 31 claimed dead. Total casualties are unknown. Worst such accident to date.

1999  Sept. 30, Tokaimura, Japan: uncontrolled chain reaction in a uranium-processing nuclear fuel plant spewed high levels of radioactive gas into the air killing one worker and seriously injuring two others. Japan's worst nuclear accident.

# FIRES AND EXPLOSIONS

**1666**  **Sept. 2, England:** "Great Fire of London" destroyed St. Paul's Cathedral, etc. Damage £10 million.

**1835**  **Dec. 16, New York City:** 530 buildings destroyed by fire.

**1871**  **Oct. 8, Chicago:** the "Chicago Fire" burned 17,450 buildings and killed 250 persons; $196 million in damage.

**1872**  **Nov. 9, Boston:** fire destroyed 800 buildings; $75 million in damage.

**1876**  **Dec. 5, New York City:** fire in Brooklyn Theater killed more than 300.

**1881**  **Dec. 8, Vienna:** at least 620 died in fire at Ring Theatre.

**1900**  **June 30, Hoboken, N.J.:** piers of North German Lloyd Steamship line burned; 326 dead.

**1903**  **Dec. 30, Chicago:** Iroquois Theatre fire killed 602.

**1904**  **Feb. 7, Baltimore, Md.:** blaze spread through downtown Baltimore. More than 1,500 buildings were destroyed. Damages $150 million, but no lives lost.

**1906**  **March 10, France:** explosion in coal mine in Courrières killed 1,060.

**1907**  **Dec. 6, Monongha, W. Va.:** coal mine explosion killed 361.
  **Dec. 19, Jacobs Creek, Pa.:** explosion in coal mine left 239 dead.

**1908**  **Jan. 13, Boyertown, Pa.:** fire in Rhoads Opera House killed 170 people who were attending church-sponsored stage performance.

**1909**  **Nov. 13, Cherry, Ill.:** explosion in coal mine killed 259.

**1911**  **March 25, New York City:** fire in Triangle Shirtwaist Factory fatal to 145.

**1913**  **Oct. 22, Dawson, N.M.:** coal mine explosion left 263 dead.

**1917**  **Dec. 6, Halifax Harbor, Nova Scotia:** Belgian steamer collided with ammunition ship *Mont Blanc*, which was carrying over 2,500 tons of explosives. Explosion leveled part of Halifax and left about 1,600 people dead.

**1930**  **April 21, Columbus, Ohio:** fire in Ohio State Penitentiary killed 320 convicts.

**1937**  **March 18, New London, Tex.:** explosion destroyed schoolhouse; 294 killed.

**1942**  **April 26, Manchuria:** explosion in Honkeiko Colliery killed 1,549.
  **Nov. 28, Boston, Mass.:** Coconut Grove nightclub fire killed 491.

**1944**  **July 6, Hartford, Conn.:** fire and ensuing stampede in main tent of Ringling Brothers Circus killed 168, injured 487.
  **July 17, Port Chicago, Calif.:** 322 killed when ammunition ships exploded.

**1946**  **Dec. 7, Atlanta:** fire in Winecoff Hotel killed 119.

**1947**  **April 16–18, Texas City, Tex.:** most of the city destroyed by a fire and subsequent explosion on the French freighter *Grandcamp*, which was carrying a cargo of ammonium nitrate. At least 516 were killed and over 3,000 injured.

**1949**  **Sept. 2, China:** fire on Chongqing (Chungking) waterfront killed 1,700.

**1954**  **May 26, off Quonset Point, R.I.:** explosion and fire aboard aircraft carrier *Bennington* killed 103 crewmen.

**1956**  **Aug. 7, Colombia:** about 1,100 reported killed when seven army ammunition trucks exploded at Cali.
  **Aug. 8, Belgium:** 262 died in coal mine fire at Marcinelle.

**1960**  **Jan. 21, Coalbrook, South Africa:** coal mine explosion killed 437.

**Nov. 13, Syria:** 152 children killed in moviehouse fire.

**1961**  **Dec. 17, Niteroi, Brazil:** circus fire fatal to 323.

**1962**  **Feb. 7, Saarland, West Germany:** coal mine gas explosion killed 298.

**1963**  **Nov. 9, Japan:** explosion in coal mine at Omuta killed 447.

**1965**  **May 28, India:** coal mine fire in state of Bihar killed 375.
  **June 1, nr. Fukuoka, Japan:** coal mine explosion killed 236.

**1967**  **May 22, Brussels, Belgium:** fire in L'Innovation department store left 322 dead.
  **July 29, off North Vietnam:** fire on U.S. carrier *Forrestal* killed 134.

**1972**  **June 6, Wankie, Rhodesia:** explosion in coal mine killed 427.

**1973**  **Nov. 29, Kumamoto, Japan:** fire in Taiyo department store killed 101.

**1974**  **Feb. 1, São Paulo, Brazil:** fire in upper stories of bank building killed 189 persons, many of whom leaped to their deaths.

**1975**  **Dec. 27, Dhanbad, India:** explosion in coal mine followed by flooding from nearby reservoir left 372 dead.

**1977**  **May 28, Southgate, Ky.:** fire in Beverly Hills Supper Club; 167 dead.

**1978**  **Aug. 20, Abadan, Iran:** nearly 400 killed when arsonists set fire to crowded theater.

**1986**  **Dec. 31, San Juan, P.R.:** fire in Dupont Plaza Hotel set by three employees, killing 96 people.

**1989**  **June 3, Ural Mountains:** liquefied petroleum gas leaking from a pipeline running alongside the Trans-Siberian railway near Uta, 72 mi east of Moscow, exploded and destroyed two passing passenger trains. About 500 travelers were killed and 723 injured of an estimated 1,200 passengers on both trains.

**1990**  **March 25, New York City:** arson fire in the illegal Happy Land Social Club, in the Bronx, killed 87 people.

**1993**  **May 10, nr. Bangkok, Thailand:** fire in doll factory killed at least 187 persons and injured 500 others. World's deadliest factory fire.

**1999**  **March 24, Chamonix, France:** Belgian truck carrying margarine and flour broke out in flames in the Mont Blanc tunnel, trapping dozens of cars. Death toll was at least 42.

**2000**  **Nov. 11, nr. Kaprun, Austria:** cable car transporting skiers to the Kitzsteinhorn glacier broke into flames while moving through mountain tunnel. Final death toll reached 156 in what was termed Austria's worst Alpine disaster.
  **Dec. 25, Luoyang, China:** at least 309 people were killed in fire at shopping center. Most of the victims had been attending Christmas party at unlicensed disco in building.

**2002**  **Jan. 27, Lagos, Nigeria:** series of explosions at military depot triggered a stampede from the surrounding neighborhoods. More than 1,000 killed; many of the victims drowned in two muddy canals as they tried to flee.
  **June 20, Jixi, Heilongjiang Province, China:** gas explosion at the Chengzihe coal mine killed 111 people. China's mining industry is one of the deadliest; it is estimated that more than 5,000 mining-related deaths occurred in 2001.

## WORST U.S. FOREST FIRES

**1871 Oct. 8–14, Peshtigo, Wis:** over 1,500 lives lost and 3.8 million acres burned in nation's worst forest fire.

**1889 June 6, Seattle, Wash.:** fire destroyed 64 acres of the city and killed 2 persons. Damage was estimated at $15 million.

**1894 Sept. 1, Minn.:** forest fires ravaged over 160,000 acres and destroyed six towns; 600 killed, including 413 in town of Hinckley.

**1902 Sept., Wash. and Ore.:** Yacoult fire destroyed 1 million acres and left 38 dead.

**1910 Aug. 10, Idaho and Mont.:** fires burned 3 million acres of woods and killed 85 people.

**1918 Oct. 13–15, Minn. and Wis.:** forest fire struck towns in both states; 1,000 died, including 400 in town of Cloquet, Minn. About $1 million in losses.

**1947 Oct. 25–27, Maine:** forest fire destroyed part of Bar Harbor and damaged Acadia National Park. In all, 205,678 acres burned and 16 lives were lost.

**1949 Aug. 5, Mann Gulch, Mont.:** 12 smokejumpers—firefighters who parachuted near the fire—and one forest ranger died after being overtaken by a 200-ft wall of fire at the top of a gulch near Helena, Mont. Three smokejumpers survived.

**1970 Sept. 26, Laguna, Calif.:** large-scale brush fire burned 175,425 acres and 382 structures.

**1988 Aug.–Sept., western U.S.:** fires destroyed over 1.2 million acres in Yellowstone National Park and damaged Alaska woodlands.

**1990 June, Santa Barbara, Calif.:** Painted Cave fire consumed 4,900 acres and destroyed 641 structures.

**1991 Oct. 20–23, Oakland–Berkeley, Calif.:** brush fire in drought-stricken area destroyed over 3,000 homes and apartments. At least 24 persons died; damage estimated at $1.5 billion.

**1994 July 2–11, South Canyon, Colo.:** relatively small fire (2,000 acres) resulted in deaths of 14 firefighters.

**2000 April–May, northern N.M.:** prescribed fire started by National Park Service raged out of control, destroying 235 structures and forcing evacuation of more than 20,000 people. Blaze consumed an estimated 47,000 acres and threatened Los Alamos National Laboratory.

**Nov. 3, western U.S.:** combination of hot, dry weather and plenty of dry vegetation led to one of the most destructive forest fire seasons in U.S. history. As of Nov. 3 about 7.2 million acres had burned nationwide, nearly double the ten-year average. States hardest hit included Alaska, Idaho, Mont., N.M., Nev., and Ore.

**2002 June–early July, mainly western U.S.:** Hayman fire in Pike National Forest destroyed 137,760 acres and 600 structures, making it the worst wildfire in Colorado history. In central Ariz., the 85,000-acre Rodeo fire, which had already been declared the worst in Arizona's history, merged with the Chediski fire to form an inferno that destroyed 468,638 acres and more than 400 structures. Large wildfires also burned in Alaska, southern Calif., N.M., Utah, Oregon, and Ga.

# SHIPWRECKS

**1833 May 11, *Lady of the Lake:*** bound from England to Quebec, struck iceberg; 215 perished.

**1853 Sept. 29, *Annie Jane:*** emigrant vessel off coast of Scotland; 348 died.

**1865 April 27, *Sultana:*** boiler explosion on Mississippi River steamboat, near Memphis; 1,547 killed. Most of the dead were Union POWs finally heading home at the end of the Civil War.

**1898 Feb. 15, *Maine:*** U.S. battleship destroyed in Havana harbor by an explosion that killed 260 men. The incident led to the outbreak of the Spanish-American War in April 1898.

**Nov. 26, *City of Portland:*** 157 died nr. Cape Cod.

**1904 June 15, *General Slocum:*** excursion steamer burned in East River, N.Y.; 1,021 perished.

**1912 March 5, *Principe de Asturias:*** Spanish steamer struck rock off Sebastien Point; 500 drowned.

**April 15, *Titanic:*** supposedly unsinkable British ocean liner went down on maiden voyage after colliding with an iceberg. More than 1,500 people died.

**1914 May 29, *Empress of Ireland:*** sank after collision in St. Lawrence River; 1,024 perished.

**1915 July 24, *Eastland:*** Great Lakes excursion steamer overturned in Chicago River; 812 died.

**1934 Sept. 8, *Morro Castle:*** 134 killed in fire off Asbury Park, N.J.

**1945 Jan. 30, *Wilhelm Gustloff:*** cruise ship carrying German refugees and soldiers sunk by Soviet submarine in Baltic. It is thought that as many as 10,000 people were aboard, of which only about 900 survived.

**1949 Sept. 17, *Noronic:*** Canadian Great Lakes cruise ship burned at Toronto dock; about 130 died.

**1952 April 26, *Hobson:*** minesweeper collided with aircraft carrier *Wasp* and sank during night maneuvers in mid-Atlantic; 176 persons lost.

**1953 Jan. 9, *Chang Tyong-Ho:*** South Korean ferry foundered off Pusan; 249 reported dead.

**1954 Sept. 26, *Toya Maru:*** more than 1,000 killed when commercial ferry sank in Tsugaru Strait, Japan.

**1956 July 25, *Andrea Doria:*** Italian liner collided with Swedish liner *Stockholm* off Nantucket Island, Mass., and sank the next day. At least 52 died or were unaccounted for.

**1962 April 8, *Dara:*** British liner exploded and sank in Persian Gulf; 236 dead. Caused by time bomb.

**1963 April 10, *Thresher:*** atomic-powered U.S. submarine sank in North Atlantic; 129 dead.

**1968 Late May, *Scorpion:*** U.S. nuclear submarine sank in Atlantic 400 mi southwest of Azores; 99 dead.

**1975 Nov. 10, *Edmund Fitzgerald:*** cargo vessel carrying 10,000 long tons of iron ore pellets sank in eastern Lake Superior; all 29 crew lost.

**1983 May 25, *10th of Ramadan:*** Nile steamer caught fire and sank in Lake Nasser, near Aswan, Egypt; 272 dead and 75 missing.

**1987 March 9:** British ferry capsized after leaving Belgian port of Zeebrugge with 500 aboard; 134 drowned.

**Dec. 20:** over 4,000 killed when passenger ferry *Dona Paz* collided with oil tanker *Victor* off Mindoro Is., 110 mi south of Manila.

**1990 April 7, *Scandinavian Star:*** suspected arson fire aboard Danish-owned North Sea ferry killed at least 110 passengers in Skagerrak Strait off Norway.

**1991 Dec. 14:** ferry carrying 569 passengers sank in Red Sea off coast of Safaga, Egypt, after hitting a coral reef. Over 460 people believed drowned.

**1993** **Feb. 17, _Neptune:_** triple-deck ferry capsized off southern peninsula of Haiti during a squall. Over 1,000 passengers believed drowned. About 300 survived the sinking.

**1994** **Sept. 28, _Estonia:_** passenger ferry capsized off coast of southwest Finland and sank in a stormy Baltic Sea. Only about 140 of the estimated 1,040 passengers aboard survived.

**1996** **Jan. 21, _Gurita:_** overloaded ferry sank off the coast of northern Sumatra, killing 340.

**1999** **Feb., _Harta Rimba:_** ship sank in the South China Sea, killing about 325 people. The ship had not been licensed for passenger use.

**2000** **June 29, _Cahaya Bahari:_** ferry carrying refugees sank about 40 mi off the coast of Sulawesi. None of the 492 persons aboard survived.

**Aug. 12, _Kursk:_** Russian nuclear submarine sank to bottom of Barents Sea following an explosion; 118 dead.

**2001** **Feb. 9, _Ehime Maru:_** U.S. submarine _Greeneville_ collided with Japanese fishing boat near Pearl Harbor, Hawaii. Twenty-six people aboard the _Ehime Maru_ were rescued; nine others, including four students, were presumed dead.

**2002** **May 3, _Salahuddin 2:_** overloaded ferry capsized in storm on Meghna River in southern Bangladesh; estimated death toll 300.

**MYSTERIOUS DISAPPEARANCES**

**1872** **_Mary Celeste:_** the brigantine set sail from New York harbor for Genoa, Italy, on Nov. 5. A British brigantine, the _DeGratia,_ discovered the ship derelict on Dec. 5 and boarded her. Everyone aboard the _Mary Celeste_ had vanished—her captain, his family, and its 14-man crew. The ship was in perfect order with ample supplies and there was no sign of violence or trouble. The fate of the crew remains unknown.

**1918** **USS _Cyclops:_** the navy coal ship, used to deliver fuel and other supplies to U.S. battlefleet during World War I, disappeared while en route from Brazil to Baltimore. The ship docked briefly at Barbados on March 3–4. When it failed to arrive in Baltimore on March 13, a search was made, but neither her wreck nor any of the 309 people aboard were ever found, and the cause of her loss remains unknown.

**1928** **_Köbenhavn:_** five-masted Danish steel barque, a sail-training ship with a crew of 75 including 45 boy cadets, sailed from the River Plate for Melbourne, Australia, on Dec. 14. The last radio contact with the ship was made on Dec. 22 and all was well. The _Köbenhavn_ and its crew disappeared without a trace and no one knows what happened to it.

---

# AIRCRAFT CRASHES

(150 deaths or more, with exceptions. _See also_ Terrorist Attacks, p. 624.)

**1921** **Aug. 24, England:** British dirigible _AR-2_ broke in two on trial trip near Hull; 62 died.

**1925** **Sept. 3, Caldwell, Ohio:** U.S. dirigible _Shenandoah_ broke apart; 14 dead.

**1930** **Oct. 5, Beauvais, France:** British dirigible _R 101_ crashed, killing 47.

**1933** **April 4, N.J.:** U.S. dirigible _Akron_ crashed; 73 died.

**1937** **May 6, Lakehurst, N.J.:** German zeppelin _Hindenburg_ destroyed by fire at tower mooring; 36 killed.

**1945** **July 28, New York City:** U.S. Army bomber B-25 crashed into Empire State Building; 13 dead.

**1960** **Dec. 16, New York City:** United DC-8 and Trans World Super Constellation collided then crashed in two boroughs, killing 134 in air and on ground.

**1961** **Feb. 15, nr. Brussels, Belgium:** 72 on board and farmer on ground killed in crash of Sabena plane; U.S. figure skating team wiped out.

**1966** **Dec. 24, Binh Thai, South Vietnam:** crash of military-chartered CL-44 into village killed 129.

**1971** **July 30, Morioka, Japan:** Japanese Boeing 727 and F-86 fighter collided in midair; 162 died.

**1973** **Jan. 22, Kano, Nigeria:** 171 Nigerian Muslims returning from Mecca and five crewmen died in crash.

**Feb. 21, Sinai:** civilian Libyan Arab Airlines Boeing 727 shot down by Israeli fighters after it had strayed off course; 108 died, five survived. Officials claimed that the pilot had ignored fighters' warnings to land.

**1974** **March 3, Paris:** Turkish DC-10 jumbo jet crashed in forest shortly after takeoff; all 346 passengers and crew killed.

**Dec. 4, Colombo, Sri Lanka:** Dutch DC-8 carrying Muslims to Mecca crashed on landing approach, killing all 191 persons aboard.

**1975** **April 4, nr. Saigon, Vietnam:** Air Force Galaxy C-5A crashed after takeoff, killing 172, mostly Vietnamese children.

**Aug. 3, Agadir, Morocco:** chartered Boeing 707, returning Moroccan workers home after vacation in France, plunged into mountainside; all 188 aboard killed.

**1976** **Sept. 10, Zagreb, Yugoslavia:** midair collision between British Airways Trident and Yugoslav charter DC-9 fatal to all 176 persons aboard.

**1977** **March 27, Santa Cruz de Tenerife, Canary Islands:** Pan American and KLM Boeing 747s collided on runway. All 249 on KLM plane and 333 of 394 aboard Pan Am jet killed. Total of 582 is highest for any type of aviation disaster.

**1978** **Jan. 1, Bombay:** Air India 747 with 213 aboard exploded and plunged into sea minutes after takeoff.

**Nov. 15, Colombo, Sri Lanka:** chartered Icelandic Airlines DC-8, carrying 249 Muslim pilgrims from Mecca, crashed in thunderstorm during landing approach; 183 killed.

**1979** **May 25, Chicago:** American Airlines DC-10 lost left engine upon takeoff and crashed seconds later, killing all 272 persons aboard and three on the ground in worst U.S. air disaster.

**Nov. 26, Jidda, Saudi Arabia:** Pakistan International Airlines 707 carrying pilgrims returning from Mecca crashed on takeoff; all 156 aboard killed.

**Nov. 28, Mt. Erebus, Antarctica:** Air New Zealand DC-10 crashed on sightseeing flight; 257 killed.

**1980** **Aug. 19, Riyadh, Saudi Arabia:** all 301 aboard Saudi Arabian jet killed when burning plane made safe landing but passengers were unable to escape.

**1981** **Dec. 1, Ajaccio, Corsica:** Yugoslav DC-9 Super 80 carrying tourists crashed into mountain on landing approach, killing all 178 aboard.

**1983** **Aug. 30, nr. island of Sakhalin off Siberia:** Korean Air Lines Boeing 747 shot down by Soviet fighter after it strayed off course into Soviet airspace. All 269 aboard killed. Secret Soviet documents released in Oct. 1992 reveal that the plane was flying a straight course for two hours with its navigational lights on and did not take evasive action. The Soviet fighter did not give a warning by firing tracer bullets as originally claimed. Recorded conversations indicated that the crew members did not know what hit them.

**1985 Aug. 12, Japan:** Japan Air Lines Boeing 747 crashed into a mountain, killing 520 of the 524 aboard. Highest death toll in a single-plane crash in aviation history.

**Dec. 12, Gander, Newfoundland:** a chartered Arrow Air DC-8 bringing American soldiers home for Christmas crashed on takeoff. All 256 aboard died.

**1987 Aug. 16, Romulus, Mich.:** Northwest Airlines McDonnell Douglas MD-80 crashed into a highway shortly after takeoff from Detroit Metropolitan Airport, killing 156 (including 2 on the ground). Girl, 4, only survivor.

**Nov. 29, Burma:** Korean Air Boeing 747 jetliner exploded from bomb planted by North Korean agents and crashed into sea, killing all 115 aboard.

**1988 July 3, Persian Gulf:** U.S. Navy cruiser *Vincennes* shot down Iran Air Airbus A-300 after mistaking it for an attacking jet fighter; 290 killed.

**Aug. 28, Ramstein Air Force Base, West Germany:** three jets from Italian Air Force acrobatic team collided in midair during air show and crashed, killing 70 persons, including the pilots and spectators on the ground.

**1989 June 7, Paramaribo, Suriname:** a Surinam Airways DC-8 carrying 174 passengers and 9 crew members crashed into the jungle while making a third attempt to land in a thick fog, killing 168 aboard.

**1991 July 11, Jedda, Saudi Arabia:** Canadian-chartered DC-8 carrying pilgrims returning to Nigeria crashed after takeoff, killing 261 persons.

**1994 April 14, northern Iraq:** two American F-15C fighter aircraft mistook two U.S. Army blackhawk helicopters for Russian-made Iraqi MI-24 helicopters and shot them down over no-fly zone, killing all 26 on board.

**April 26, Nagoya, Japan:** China Airlines Airbus A-300 from Taiwan crash-landed and exploded on the tarmac. Only 7 of the 271 passengers aboard survived.

**1995 Dec. 20, nr. Cali, Colombia:** 160 people killed when American Airlines Boeing 757 crashed in Andean Mountains.

**1996 Jan. 8, Kinshasa, Zaire:** Russian-built Antonov-32 cargo plane crashed after takeoff from Kinshasa into the center of the city, killing over 350 people and injuring at least 470.

**Feb. 6, off coast of Puerto Plata, Dominican Republic:** Dominican AMA Air Turkish Boeing 737 crashed into Atlantic Ocean after takeoff, killing 189.

**May 11, Everglades, Fla.:** ValuJet DC-9 went down in swamp, killing 110. Cargo fire caused by oxygen generators missing safety caps.

**July 17, off coast of Long Island, N.Y.:** TWA Boeing 747-100 bound for Paris from N.Y. exploded over waters of eastern L.I. and crashed into Atlantic Ocean, killing all 230 aboard.

**Nov. 12, nr. New Delhi, India:** shortly after takeoff, Saudi Arabian Airlines Boeing 747 collided in midair with Kazak Airlines Ilyushin 76 plane approaching the New Delhi airport. All 349 passengers and crew were killed; the world's worst midair collision.

**1997 Aug. 6, Guam:** Korean Air Boeing 747-300 from Seoul crashed into jungle near Agana International Airport, killing 228 persons; 26 survived.

**Sept. 26, nr. northern Indonesia:** Indonesian Garuda Airlines A-300 Airbus jetliner crashed while approaching Medan Airport, Sumatra, killing all 234 persons aboard.

**1998 Feb. 16, Taipei, Taiwan:** China Airlines Airbus A-300 jumbo jet crashed while trying to land in fog at Chiang Kai-shek International Airport, killing all 196 passengers and crew and at least 6 persons on the ground.

**Sept. 2, off Nova Scotia, Canada:** Swissair flight from New York to Geneva crashed off Canadian coast, killing all 229 aboard. 136 Americans were on the McDonnell Douglas MD-11.

**1999 Oct. 31, southeast of Nantucket Island:** Egypt Air Boeing 767-300 on flight from N.Y. to Cairo crashed into the Atlantic Ocean, killing all 217 aboard.

**2000 Jan. 30, off the Ivory Coast:** Kenya Airways Airbus A-310, carrying 179 passengers and crew, crashed after takeoff from Abidjan into the Atlantic Ocean. Ten persons survived.

**July 25, Gonesse, France:** Air France Concorde jet en route to New York crashed into a hotel just after taking off from Charles de Gaulle airport near Paris; all 109 aboard and 4 on the ground were killed; first Concorde jet to crash since the plane went into commercial service in 1976.

**Aug. 23, off Bahrain:** Gulf Air jet crashed into the Persian Gulf, killing all 143 aboard.

**2001 Sept. 11, New York City, Arlington, Va., and Shanksville, Pa.:** For the attacks on the World Trade Center and the Pentagon, *see* p. 625.

**Nov. 12, Queens, N. Y.:** American Airlines Airbus A-300 bound for Santo Domingo, Dominican Republic, crashed into residential neighborhood minutes after taking off from JFK International Airport. All 260 people aboard and 5 on the ground were killed.

**2002 April 15, nr. Pusan, South Korea:** Air China Boeing 767 en route from Beijing crashed into a forested hillside near airport, killing at least 115 people. Miraculously, 39 passengers survived. Poor weather conditions were blamed for the crash.

**May 4, Kano, Nigeria:** EAS Airline BAC 1-11 bound for Lagos ploughed into a poor, densely populated suburb of Kano shortly after takeoff, killing 148. Dead included all 76 aboard and dozens on the ground.

**May 7, Dalian Bay, northeast China:** China Northern Airlines MD-82 jet crashed into the bay shortly after captain reported a fire in the cabin. Out of 103 passengers and 9 crew aboard, none survived.

**May 25, nr. Pescadores off western Taiwan:** China Airlines Boeing 747, bound for Hong Kong with 225 people aboard, broke apart in midair and plunged into sea 20 minutes after takeoff from Taipei. There were no survivors.

**July 27, nr. Lviv, Ukraine:** Russian-built Sukhoi-27 fighter jet crashed while performing an acrobatic maneuver during an air show. Eighty-three people were killed, including 23 children; the two pilots ejected to safety. It is the worst air show disaster in history.

## SPACE ACCIDENTS

**1967**  **Jan. 27, *Apollo 1*:** a fire aboard the space capsule on the ground at Cape Kennedy, Fla., killed astronauts Virgil I. Grissom, Edward H. White, and Roger Chaffee.

**April 23–24, *Soyuz 1*:** Vladimir M. Komarov was killed when his craft crashed after its parachute lines, released at 23,000 ft for reentry, became snarled.

**1971**  **June 6–30, *Soyuz 11*:** three cosmonauts, Georgi T. Dolrovolsky, Vladislav N. Volkov, and Viktor I. Patsayev, found dead in the craft after its automatic landing. Apparent cause of death was loss of pressurization in the space craft during reentry into the earth's atmosphere.

**1980**  **March 18, USSR:** a Vostok rocket exploded on its launch pad while being refueled, killing 50 at the Plesetsk Space Center.

**1986**  **Jan. 28, *Challenger* Space Shuttle:** exploded 73 seconds after liftoff, killing all seven crew members. They were: Francis R. Scobee, Michael J. Smith, Judith A. Resnick, Ronald E. McNair, Ellison S. Onizuka, Gregory B. Jarvis, and schoolteacher Christa McAuliffe. A booster leak ignited the fuel, causing the explosion.

## RAILROAD ACCIDENTS

**NOTE:** Very few passengers were killed in a single U.S. train wreck up until 1853. These early trains ran slowly and made short trips, night travel was rare, and there were not many of them in operation.

**1831**  **June 17, nr. Charleston, S.C.:** boiler exploded on America's first passenger locomotive, *The Best Friend of Charleston,* injuring the fireman and the engineer.

**1833**  **Nov. 8, nr. Heightstown, N.J.:** world's first train wreck and first passenger fatalities recorded. A 24-passenger Camden & Amboy train derailed due to a broken axle, killing two passengers and injuring all others. Former President John Quincy Adams and Cornelius Vanderbilt, who later made a fortune in railroads, were aboard the train.

**1853**  **May 6, Norwalk, Conn.:** New Haven Railroad train ran through an open drawbridge and plunged into the Norwalk River. Forty-six passengers were crushed to death or drowned. This was the first major drawbridge accident.

**1856**  **July 17, Camp Hill, nr. Ft. Washington, Pa.:** two Northern Penn trains crashed head-on. Approximately 50–60 people died, mostly children on their way to a Sunday school picnic.

**1876**  **Dec. 29, Ashtabula, Ohio:** Lake Shore train fell into the Ashtabula River when the bridge it was crossing collapsed; 92 people were killed.

**1887**  **Aug. 10, nr. Chatsworth, Ill.:** a burning railroad trestle collapsed while a Toledo, Peoria & Western train was crossing, killing 81 and injuring 372.

**1904**  **Aug. 7, Eden, Colo.:** train derailed on bridge during flash flood; 96 killed.

**1910**  **March 1, Wellington, Wash.:** two trains swept into canyon by avalanche; 96 dead.

**1915**  **May 22, Gretna, Scotland:** two passenger trains and troop train collided; 227 killed.

**1917**  **Dec. 12, Modane, France:** nearly 550 killed in derailment of troop train near mouth of Mt. Cenis tunnel.

**1918**  **July 9, Nashville, Tenn.:** 101 killed in a two-train collision near Nashville.

**Nov. 1, New York City:** derailment of subway train in Malbone St. tunnel in Brooklyn left 92 dead.

**1926**  **March 14, Virilla River Canyon, Costa Rica:** an overcrowded train carrying pilgrims derailed while crossing the Colima Bridge, killing over 300 people and injuring hundreds more.

**1939**  **Dec. 22, nr. Magdeburg, Germany:** more than 125 killed in collision; 99 killed in another wreck near Friedrichshafen.

**1943**  **Dec. 16, nr. Rennert, N.C.:** 72 killed in derailment and collision of two Atlantic Coast Line trains.

**1944**  **March 2, nr. Salerno, Italy:** 521 suffocated when Italian train stalled in tunnel.

**1949**  **Oct. 22, nr. Nowy Dwor, Poland:** more than 200 reported killed in derailment of Danzig-Warsaw express.

**1950**  **Nov. 22, Richmond Hill, N.Y.:** 79 died when one Long Island Railroad commuter train crashed into rear of another.

**1951**  **Feb. 6, Woodbridge, N.J.:** 85 died when Pennsylvania Railroad commuter train plunged through temporary overpass.

**1952**  **Oct. 8, Harrow-Wealdstone, England:** two express trains crashed into commuter train; 112 dead.

**1957**  **Sept. 1, nr. Kendal, Jamaica:** about 175 killed when train plunged into ravine.

**Sept. 29, nr. Montgomery, West Pakistan:** express train crashed into standing oil train; nearly 300 killed.

**Dec. 4, St. John's, England:** 92 killed and 187 injured as one commuter train crashed into another in fog.

**1960**  **Nov. 14, Pardubice, Czechoslovakia:** two trains collided; 110 dead, 106 injured.

**1962**  **May 3, nr. Tokyo:** 163 killed and 400 injured when train crashed into wreckage of collision between inbound freight train and outbound commuter train.

**1963**  **Nov. 9, nr. Yokohama, Japan:** two passenger trains crashed into derailed freight train, killing 162.

**1964**  **July 26, Custoias, Portugal:** passenger train derailed; 94 dead.

**1970**  **Feb. 4, nr. Buenos Aires:** 236 killed when express train crashed into standing commuter train.

**1972**  **Oct. 6, nr. Saltillo, Mexico:** train carrying religious pilgrims derailed and caught fire, killing 204 and injuring over 1,000.

**Oct. 30, Chicago:** two Illinois Central commuter trains collided during morning rush hour; 45 dead and over 200 injured.

**1974**  **Aug. 30, Zagreb, Yugoslavia:** train entering station derailed, killing 153 and injuring 60.

**1981**  **June 6, nr. Mansi, India:** driver of train carrying over 500 passengers braked to avoid hitting a cow, causing train to plunge off a bridge into the Baghmati River; 268 passengers were reported killed, but at least 300 more were missing.

**1982**  **July 11, Tepic, Mexico:** Nogales-Guadalajara train plunged down mountain gorge, killing 120.

**1989**  **Jan. 15, Maizdi Khan, Bangladesh:** train carrying Muslim pilgrims crashed head-on with a mail train, killing at least 110 persons and injuring as many as 1,000.

**Aug. 10, nr. Los Mochis, Mexico:** a second-class passenger train traveling from Mazatlán to Mexicali, plunged off a bridge at Puente del Rio Bamoa into the river and killed an estimated 85 people and injured 107.

**1990 Jan. 4, Sangi village, Sindh province, Pakistan:** overcrowded 16-car passenger train rammed into a standing freight train. At least 210 persons were killed and 700 were believed injured in what is said to be Pakistan's worst train disaster.

**1993 Sept. 22, nr. Mobile, Ala.:** Amtrak's *Sunset Limited,* en route to Miami, jumped rails on weakened bridge and plunged in Big Bayou Canot, killing 47 persons.

**1995 Aug. 20, Firozabad, northern India:** a speeding passenger train rammed another train that was stalled after hitting a cow. About 300 persons were killed and over 400 injured.

**1997 March 3, Punjab province, Pakistan:** passenger train crashed due to failed brakes, killing 119 and injuring at least 80 persons.

**1998 June 3, nr. Eschede, Germany:** Inter City Express passenger train traveling at 125 mph crashed into support pier of overpass, killing 98. Is nation's worst postwar train accident.

**1999 Oct. 5, London:** out-bound Thames commuter train passed a red signal near Paddington Station and collided with London-bound Great Western express, killing 30 persons and injuring 245.

**2002 Feb. 20, nr. Ayyat, Egypt:** 361 killed in fire after gas cylinder used for cooking exploded aboard crowded passenger train. Egypt's worst train disaster.

**May 25, Muamba, Mozambique:** 192 died and dozens more injured when passenger cars rolled for several miles at top speed into freight cars from which they had been disconnected because of mechanical problems.

**June 24, nr. Msagali, central Tanzania:** runaway passenger train collided with freight train on same track, leaving 200 dead.

## OIL SPILLS

**1976 Dec. 15, Buzzards Bay, Mass.:** *Argo Merchant* ran aground and broke apart southeast of Nantucket Island, spilling its entire cargo of 7.7 million gallons of fuel oil.

**1978 March 16, off Portsall, France:** wrecked supertanker *Amoco Cadiz* spilled 68 million gallons, causing widespread environmental damage over 100 mi of Brittany coast—world's largest tanker disaster.

**1979 June 3, Gulf of Mexico:** exploratory oil well Ixtoc 1 blew out, spilling an estimated 140 million gallons of crude oil into the open sea. Although it is the largest known oil spill, it had a low environmental impact.

**1989 Mar. 24, Prince William Sound, Alaska:** tanker *Exxon Valdez* hit an undersea reef and spilled 10 million plus gallons of oil into the waters, causing the worst oil spill in U.S. history.

**Dec. 19, off Las Palmas, the Canary Islands:** explosion in Iranian supertanker, the *Kharg-5,*

caused 19 million gallons of crude oil to spill into Atlantic Ocean about 400 mi north of Las Palmas, forming a 100-square-mile oil slick.

**1991 Jan. 25, southern Kuwait:** during the Persian Gulf War, Iraq deliberately released an estimated 460 million gallons of crude oil into the Persian Gulf from tankers 10 mi off Kuwait. Spill had little military significance. On Jan. 27, U.S. warplanes bombed pipe systems to stop the flow of oil.

**1994 Sept. 8, Russia:** dam built to contain oil burst and spilled oil into Kolva River tributary. U.S. Energy Department estimated spill at 2 million barrels. Russian state-owned oil company claimed spill was only 102,000 barrels.

**1996 Feb. 15, off Welsh coast:** supertanker *Sea Empress* ran aground at port of Milford Haven, Wales, spewed out 70,000 tons of crude oil, and created a 25-mile slick.

## SPORTS DISASTERS

**1955 June 11, Le Mans, France:** racing car in Grand Prix hurtled into grandstand, killing 82 spectators.

**1964 May 24, Lima, Peru:** more than 300 soccer fans killed and over 500 injured during riot and panic following unpopular ruling by referee in Peru vs. Argentina soccer game. It is worst soccer disaster on record.

**1971 Jan. 2 Glasgow, Scotland:** 66 killed in crush in Glasgow Rangers home stadium when soccer fans trying to leave encountered fans trying to return to stadium after hearing that a late goal had been scored.

**1982 Oct. 20, Moscow:** according to *Sovietsky Sport,* as many as 340 died at Lenin Stadium when exiting soccer fans collided with returning fans after final goal was scored. All the fans had been crowded into one section of stadium by police.

**1985 May 11, Bradford, England:** 56 burned to death and over 200 injured when fire engulfed main grandstand at Bradford's soccer stadium.

**May 29, Brussels, Belgium:** group of drunken British soccer fans supporting Liverpool club stormed stand filled with Italian supporters of Juventus team before European Champion's Cup

final. While British fans attacked rival spectators at the Heysel Stadium, concrete retaining wall collapsed and 39 persons were crushed or trampled to death, 32 of them Italians. More than 400 persons were injured.

**1988 March 12, Katmandu, Nepal:** some 80 soccer fans seeking cover during a violent hail storm at the stadium stadium were trampled to death in a stampede because the stadium doors were locked.

**1989 April 15, Sheffield, England:** 96 people were killed at Hillsborough stadium during a semifinal match between Liverpool and Nottingham Forest. Most of the victims, who were Liverpool fans, were crushed when a barrier collapsed on an overcrowded pen behind one of the goals. It is Britain's worst soccer disaster.

**1996 Oct. 16, Guatemala City:** at least 84 killed and 147 injured by stampeding soccer fans before a 1998 World Cup qualifying match between Guatemala and Peru held at Mateo Flores National Stadium.

**2001 May 9, Accra, Ghana:** at least 120 people were killed in a stampede at a soccer match. It was Africa's worst soccer-related disaster ever.

# TERRORIST ATTACKS

### (within the United States or against Americans abroad)

**1920**  **Sept. 16, New York City:** TNT bomb planted in unattended horse-drawn wagon exploded on Wall Street opposite House of Morgan, killing 35 persons and injuring hundreds more. Bolshevist or anarchist terrorists believed responsible, but crime never solved.

**1975**  **Jan. 24, New York City:** bomb set off in historical Fraunces Tavern killed four and injured more than 50 persons. Puerto Rican nationalist group (FALN) claimed responsibility and police tied 13 other bombings to it.

**1983**  **April 18, Beirut, Lebanon:** U.S. embassy is destroyed in suicide car-bomb attack; 63 dead.

  **Oct. 23, Beirut, Lebanon:** Shi'ite suicide bombers exploded truck near U.S. military barracks at Beirut airport, killing 241 Marines. Minutes later a second bomb killed 58 French paratroopers in their barracks in West Beirut.

**1988**  **Dec. 21, Lockerbie, Scotland:** N.Y.-bound Pan-Am Boeing 747 exploded in flight from a terrorist bomb and crashed into Scottish village, killing all 259 aboard and 11 on the ground. Passengers included 35 Syracuse University students and many U.S. military personnel. Two Libyan intelligence officers were tried under Scottish law in The Hague; only one, Abdelbaset Ali Mohmed Al Megrahi, was found guilty, in Jan. 2001.

**1993**  **Feb. 26, New York City:** bomb exploded in basement garage of World Trade Center; killing six and injuring at least 1,040 others. In 1995, militant Islamist Sheik Omar Abdel Rahman and nine others were convicted of conspiracy charges, and in 1998, Ramzi Yousef, believed to have been the mastermind, was convicted of the bombing. Al-Qaeda involvement is suspected.

**1995**  **April 19, Oklahoma City:** car bomb exploded outside federal office building, collapsing wall and floors. 168 persons were killed, including 19

children and one person who died in rescue effort. Over 220 buildings sustained damage. Timothy McVeigh and Terry Nichols later convicted in the antigovernment plot to avenge the Branch Davidian standoff in Waco, Tex., exactly two years earlier. (*See* Miscellaneous Disasters.)

**1996**  **June 25, Dhahran, Saudi Arabia:** truck bomb exploded outside Khobar Towers military complex, killing 19 American servicemen and injuring hundreds of others. Thirteen Saudis and a Lebanese, all alleged members of Islamic militant group Hezbollah, were indicted on charges relating to the attack in June 2001.

**1998**  **Aug. 7, Nairobi, Kenya, and Dar es Salaam, Tanzania:** truck bombs exploded almost simultaneously near two U.S. embassies, killing 224 (213 in Kenya and 11 in Tanzania) and injuring about 4,500. Four men, two of whom had received training at al-Qaeda camps inside Afghanistan, were convicted of the killings in May 2001 and later sentenced to life in prison. A federal grand jury had indicted 22 men in connection with the attacks, including Saudi dissident Osama bin Laden, who remained at large.

**2000**  **Oct. 12, Aden, Yemen:** U.S. Navy destroyer USS *Cole* was heavily damaged when a small boat loaded with explosives blew up alongside it. Seventeen sailors were killed in what was apparently a deliberate terrorist attack. Prime suspect thought to be Osama bin Laden, or members of his al-Qaeda terrorist network.

**2001**  **Sept. 11, New York City, Arlington, Va., and Shanksville, Pa.:** hijackers crashed two commercial jets into twin towers of World Trade Center; two more hijacked jets were crashed into the Pentagon and a field in rural Pa. Total dead and missing numbered 3,044, including the 19 hijackers. Islamic al-Qaeda terrorist group blamed. (*See* p. 625.)

---

# MISCELLANEOUS DISASTERS

**1952**  **Dec. 4–7, London, England:** high-pressure system settled over London, trapping pollution near the ground. Some 4,000 people died in "Great Smog," mostly from respiratory and cardiac distress.

**1981**  **July 18, Kansas City, Mo.:** suspended walkway in Hyatt Regency Hotel collapsed; 113 dead, 186 injured.

**1982–1983  worldwide:** El Niño caused wildly unusual weather in the U.S. throughout 1983, including severe winter storms in southern Calif., widespread flooding across the South, and unusually mild winter weather in the central and northern parts of the country. Warming ocean currents resulted in failed fishing harvests in Peru and Ecuador, and drought in the western Pacific region led to disastrous forest fires in Indonesia and Australia. Overall loss to world economy was over $8 billion. Similar event in 1997–1998 resulted in estimated loss of $25–33 billion.

**1984**  **Dec. 3, Bhopal, India:** toxic gas, methyl isocyanate, seeped from Union Carbide insecticide plant, killed more than 2,000, injured about 150,000.

**1987**  **Sept. 18, Goiânia, Brazil:** 244 people contaminated with cesium-137 that was removed from a steel

cylinder taken from a cancer-therapy machine in an abandoned clinic and sold as scrap. Four people died in worst radiation disaster in Western Hemisphere.

**1988**  **July 6, North Sea off Scotland:** 166 workers killed in explosion and fire on Occidental Petroleum's *Piper Alpha* rig in North Sea; 64 survivors. It is the world's worst offshore oil disaster.

**1993**  **April 19, Waco, Tex.:** 51-day stalemate between federal agents and members of Christian Branch Davidian cult ended in a fiery tragedy after federal agents botched their assault on the sect's compound. About 80 Branch Davidians, including at least 17 children, died when the compound burned to the ground in a suspicious blaze. Earlier, on Feb. 28, four agents were shot to death in failed attack on heavily armed compound. Jurors in the criminal trial of surviving cult members were unable to determine who fired the first shot. The incident was reopened for investigation in Aug. 1999.

**1996**  **May 10–11, Mt. Everest, Nepal:** eight climbers died near summit during storm on mountain. Is worst single loss of lives to occur in a season on Mt. Everest. Another four died over the remaining course of the month.

## SEPTEMBER 11, 2001: TIMELINE OF TERRORISM

### (all times are eastern daylight time)

An American Airlines Boeing 767 and a United Airlines Boeing 767, both en route from Boston to Los Angeles, were hijacked and flown only minutes apart into the north and south towers of the World Trade Center in New York City. Shortly afterward, an American Airlines Boeing 757, en route from Washington, DC, to Los Angeles, crashed into the Pentagon. A fourth hijacked plane, operated by United and headed from Newark to San Francisco, crashed in a field near Shanksville, Pa. Both World Trade Center towers collapsed, and a section of the Pentagon was destroyed. All 266 persons aboard the planes were killed; the total number of dead and missing was 3,044 (including the 19 hijackers). The names of the hijackers, Islamic radicals part of the al-Qaeda terrorist organization, were released a few days after the attacks.

**8:45 A.M.**—American Airlines Flight 11, Boston to Los Angeles, with 92 people aboard, crashes into the north tower of the World Trade Center in New York City.

**9:03 A.M.**—United Airlines Flight 175, Boston to Los Angeles, with 65 people aboard, flies into the south tower of the World Trade Center.

**9:40 A.M.**—American Flight 77, Washington, DC, to Los Angeles, with 64 people aboard, crashes into the Pentagon.

**9:48 A.M.**—The U.S. Capitol and the West Wing of the White House are evacuated.

**9:49 A.M.**—The Federal Aviation Administration orders all aircraft grounded in the United States.

**9:50 A.M.**—South tower of the World Trade Center collapses.

**9:58 A.M.**—Emergency operator in Pennsylvania receives a call from a passenger on United Flight 93, Newark to San Francisco, with 45 people aboard, stating the plane was being hijacked.

**10:00 A.M.**—United Flight 93 crashes about 80 mi southeast of Pittsburgh. Passengers apparently attempted to overpower the hijackers, who were heading the plane toward Washington, DC.

**10:29 A.M.**—North tower of the World Trade Center collapses.

**5:20 P.M.**—Another World Trade Center building collapses.

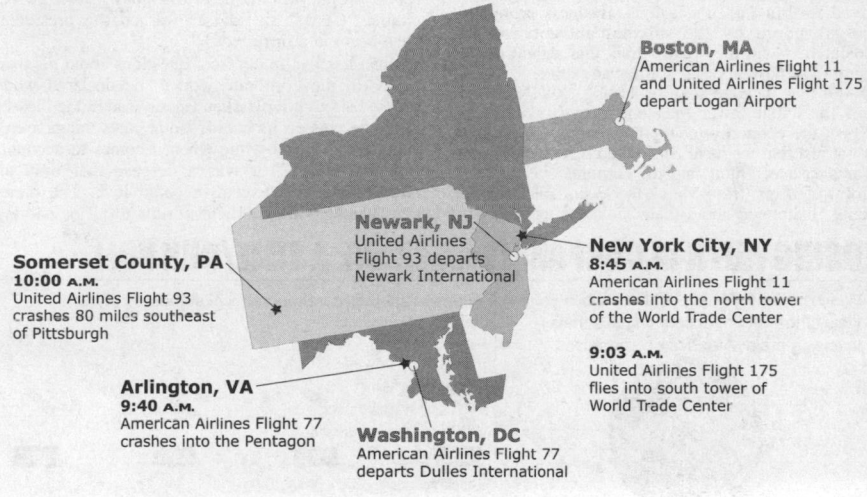

**Boston, MA**
American Airlines Flight 11 and United Airlines Flight 175 depart Logan Airport

**Somerset County, PA**
**10:00 A.M.**
United Airlines Flight 93 crashes 80 miles southeast of Pittsburgh

**Newark, NJ**
United Airlines Flight 93 departs Newark International

**New York City, NY**
**8:45 A.M.**
American Airlines Flight 11 crashes into the north tower of the World Trade Center

**9:03 A.M.**
United Airlines Flight 175 flies into south tower of World Trade Center

**Arlington, VA**
**9:40 A.M.**
American Airlines Flight 77 crashes into the Pentagon

**Washington, DC**
American Airlines Flight 77 departs Dulles International

Map by Sean M. Dessureau, Information Please

### Other Suspected al-Qaeda Acts

**1993**—Bombing of World Trade Center; 6 killed.

**1993**—Killing of U.S. soldiers in Somalia.

**1994**—Investigation of the WTC bombing reveals that it was only a small part of a massive attack plan that included hijacking a plane and crashing it into CIA headquarters.

**1998**—Bombing of U.S. embassies in East Africa; 224 killed, including 12 Americans.

**1999**—Jordanian police arrested members of a cell planning attacks against Western tourists.

**1999**—Plot to bomb millennium celebrations in Seattle foiled when customs agents arrest an Algerian smuggling explosives into the U.S.

**2000**—Bombing of the USS *Cole* in port in Yemen; 17 U.S. sailors killed.

**2001**—Destruction of WTC, Pentagon attack.

**2002**—Explosion at historic synagogue in Tunisia left 17 dead, including 11 German tourists.

# Summer of Mistrust

Scamming CEOs have accomplished what Osama bin Laden could not—denting our spirit. Can anything restore our faith in the markets?

**By NANCY GIBBS**   TIME

American confidence is more than a state of mind; it is a muscle, a westward-ho-ing, atom-splitting, moon-landing muscle, and Osama bin Laden's autumn 2001 ambush, designed to break it, seemed only to make it stronger. The markets reopened within a week after Sept. 11, swooned and then revived, and even as the fires still burned downtown and the soldiers headed off to war, many Americans said they believed the country was on the right track. But that wasn't the case during 2002's summer of corporate scandals. Is it possible we could do to ourselves what our worst enemies did not manage?

The corporate criminals among us, the swindlers and profiteers, are now described in language once saved for bin Laden's legions. Business professors are staggered by the suicidal audacity of top executives—did they really think they would not be caught?—and marvel at the damage done.

And that damage may be lasting. A TIME/CNN poll finds that fewer than one-third of Americans expect the economy to improve in the next year. It is not just that we have confronted in WorldCom the worst case of fraud in U.S. corporate history; the bluest of chips, from Merck to General Electric, are being challenged about their bookkeeping. The per-ception of deception is so widespread, the stakes so high, and the costs so great that investors are choosing to forfeit a game they now think is rigged.

## Presidential Profiteer

President Bush has worked hard to show that he feels the country's pain and shares its outrage. No matter how stern Bush looks when he declares that bad guys should go to jail, he has not erased charges that as an oilman in the '80s, he profited from the same kind of sweetheart deals he now decries. Public opinion is focused not on the Beltway but on the boardroom, and the president's career, lineage, and aspect all put him in one of the fancy leather swivel chairs. "CEO," an adviser warned the president, "has become a dirty word."

Bush has had to confront questions about his own past. "In the corporate world," he declared when pressed about how Harken Energy had hidden losses while he was on its board, "sometimes things aren't exactly black and white when it comes to accounting procedures." It was a defense that only an Arthur Andersen executive could love. The president whose wartime rhetoric runs to all or nothing

# LOSING FAITH IN CORPORATE AMERICA: A TIME/CNN POLL

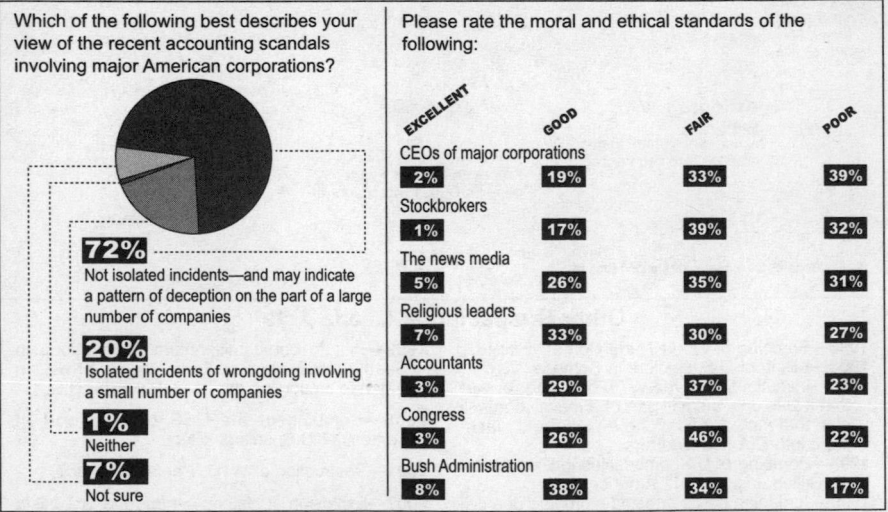

Which of the following best describes your view of the recent accounting scandals involving major American corporations?

**72%**
Not isolated incidents—and may indicate a pattern of deception on the part of a large number of companies

**20%**
Isolated incidents of wrongdoing involving a small number of companies

**1%**
Neither

**7%**
Not sure

Please rate the moral and ethical standards of the following:

| | EXCELLENT | GOOD | FAIR | POOR |
|---|---|---|---|---|
| CEOs of major corporations | 2% | 19% | 33% | 39% |
| Stockbrokers | 1% | 17% | 39% | 32% |
| The news media | 5% | 26% | 35% | 31% |
| Religious leaders | 7% | 33% | 30% | 27% |
| Accountants | 3% | 29% | 37% | 23% |
| Congress | 3% | 26% | 46% | 22% |
| Bush Administration | 8% | 38% | 34% | 17% |

From a telephone poll of 1,003 adult Americans taken for TIME/CNN on July 10–11, 2002, by HarrisInteractive. Margin of error is ±3.1%.

was making a case for relativism; his business experience was being channeled not into a call for probity but into an excuse for conduct he would later declare unethical.

# Smoke and Mirrors

By now people know that capitalism is a spectacle of hope and greed and guts and guile, all racing toward the bottom line. That is its genius, but without guardrails, the whole contraption can take us over a cliff. CEOs have raided company coffers to pay off margin calls or build new mansions. Awash in options, they manage the stock price instead of the company; as their business falls into bankruptcy and the layoffs pile up, they float away on golden parachutes—or yachts bought with company loans. Each week seemed to bring a new shudder and crack—first Enron and Arthur Andersen, then WorldCom, Adelphia, Xerox, and the trials of Martha Stewart.

Most Americans—72% in the TIME/CNN poll—fear that they see not a few isolated cases but a pattern of deception by a large number of companies. In one survey, more than half of corporate chief financial officers said they had been pressured by their bosses to cook the books, if not to a full boil then at least to a simmer. People now know that this crisis was years in the making. Stocks kept climbing because executives kept finding creative new ways to hide the truth and fake a profit, to pretend they were investing money rather than just spending it. The revelations make for some dark magic now. When Xerox overstates revenue by $1.4 billion over five years and $4 billion disappears from World-Com's balance sheets, it makes people feel poorer even if they personally lost nothing. If people stop investing and capital becomes tight, then how exactly does a recovery happen? If they feel poor and stop spending, how does the economy grow?

# A Bump in the Road?

People say they have stopped investing and play poker instead; it's a safer bet. Fully one-third of Americans between 50 and 64 said they had decided to delay their retirement because their assets had shrunk in the market—and that was in early 2002.

For Democrats, the political beauty of the corporate scandals is that they "play into what people already believe" about Republicans—"that these guys are in the tank with corporate special interests," says Steve Elmendorf, chief of staff to House minority leader Dick Gephardt. But when the interests of voters clash with the interests of donors, the Democrats too put on the brakes, helping to kill a proposal that companies list stock options as expenses.

America's gilded ages have reliably ended in scandal, followed by soul-searching and reform. But investors are divided over what needs to be done. The gentle, self-policing era touted by SEC chairman Harvey Pitt is dead and gone, but even some battered investors don't trust grandstanding lawmakers to distinguish between reforms that are needed and those that will cramp the recovery even more. That was the argument Dick Cheney and others made to the president—that in the long run, Bush will suffer more if he gets a quick political boost from reforms that strangle the economy. While more Americans now see Big Business as a threat, polls show they think Big Government is more dangerous yet.

There are still plenty of cool-headed investors out there who have seen these bumps before and are confident the market will come back. But that has a way of taking years, even without a crisis of ethical confidence. Stocks didn't return to their 1929 levels until 1940; they took 30 years, till 1996, to return to the peak reached in 1966. Many stocks still aren't cheap, third quarters are often painful, and the bears think there's more bad news to come. □

| Do you have less trust in any of the following than you did before the scandals? | | Compared with the average person, do you think the typical CEO is more honest and ethical or less honest and ethical? | | Do you think the policy changes called for by George Bush to ensure that corporate executives behave responsibly go far enough? | |
|---|---|---|---|---|---|
| CEOs of major American corporations | 69% | More honest and ethical | 14% | Go far enough | 27% |
| Major American corporations | 59% | Less honest and ethical | 71% | Don't go far enough | 49% |
| The stock market | 52% | No difference | 7% | Do you think George Bush pays too much attention to Big Business? | |
| Stockbrokers | 50% | In your opinion, are most CEOs of major corporations paid too much? | | July 10–11, 2002: | |
| The federal government | 36% | | | Yes | 45% |
| Republicans in Congress | 35% | Too much | 70% | No | 44% |
| George Bush | 32% | About right | 16% | March 21–22, 2001: | |
| | | | | Yes | 53% |
| Democrats in Congress | 25% | Not enough | 11% | No | 36% |

# Corporations Under the Microscope: Accounting Irregularities, Tax Fraud, and Other Shady Dealings

## (as of August 2002)

**Adelphia Communications:** The SEC and two federal grand juries are investigating allegations that the cable television operator overstated earnings. The inquiry began when Adelphia acknowledged that the company gave $3.1 billion in off-the-book loans to members of the Rigas family, which founded Adelphia. In Sept. 2002 John Rigas, founder and former CEO of the company, and two of his sons were indicted on charges of bank, wire, and securities fraud. The company filed for bankruptcy protection in June 2002.

**AOL Time Warner:** The country's biggest media company announced in July 2002 that the SEC and the Justice Department are investigating AOL's accounting procedures to determine if it burnished revenue over a span of two years, ending in March 2002.

**Arthur Andersen:** The accounting firm was convicted in June 2002 of obstruction of justice for destroying documents relating to Enron Corp., a former client. The verdict, along with the steady stream of clients that defected during the investigation into Enron's collapse, hastened the fall of the firm. Andersen also audited Halliburton, Global Crossing, and Merck, companies whose accounting practices are under investigation by the government.

**Bristol-Myers Squibb** The SEC is investigating the pharmaceutical giant to determine if it inflated revenues by as much as $1 billion in 2001. The drug maker disclosed that in April 2002 it had oversold inventory by offering price incentives to wholesalers, thereby boosting profits.

**Computer Associates International Inc.** In Feb. 2002 the SEC and the Justice Department launched an investigation to find out if the software company burnished the books by more than $500 million in 1998, effecting a rise in the stock price and thus activating a lucrative $1 billion bonus package for senior managers. Restatements of revenue reduced the company's profits by 11%.

**Dynegy** Federal investigators are probing allegations that the energy trader engaged in sham trades to artificially inflate revenue and volume. Late in 2001, Dynegy was poised to take over Enron. CEO Chuck Watson resigned in May 2002.

**Enron** First there was Enron. The headline-grabbing scandal rocked the nation in late 2001 and into 2002, and seemed to have opened a floodgate of corporate malfeasance. Enron, previously the country's largest energy trader, filed for bankruptcy on Dec. 2, 2001, while under federal investigation for hiding debt and pumping up profits. The company used complicated off-the-balance-sheet partnerships to inflate profits by as much as $600 million.

**Global Crossing** The SEC and the FBI are looking into the accounting methods of this telecommunications company to determine if it artificially inflated revenue by such means as swapping fiber-optic network capacity with other telecoms. Global Crossing filed for bankruptcy in Jan. 2002, shortly after CEO Gary Winnick sold $734 million in company stock.

**Halliburton** In May 2002 the SEC began a probe to determine how the oil-services company accounted for cost overruns on construction projects. In July, Judicial Watch, a watchdog organization, filed suit against the company; Vice President Dick Cheney, who served as Halliburton's CEO from 1995 to 2000; several board members; and its auditor, Arthur Andersen, accusing them of accounting fraud and misleading investors. The accounting irregularities allegedly occurred during Cheney's tenure as CEO.

**ImClone Systems** A House committee is investigating the Dec. 3–27, 2001, sale of ImClone stock by executives of the biotech firm. On Dec. 28, the Food and Drug Administration announced it had declined to review ImClone's experimental cancer drug, Erbitux. The announcement sent shares tumbling. ImClone's founder and former CEO Samuel Waksal was indicted in Aug. 2002 on charges of insider trading and perjury. Martha Stewart, a friend of Waksal's, has also been scrutinized for selling about 4,000 ImClone shares a day before the FDA made its announcement.

**Merck** In a July 2002 filing to the SEC, Merck, a pharmaceutical company, revealed that since 1999 its pharmacy-benefits division, Medco, had reported as revenue $14 billion in drug copayments that Medco members paid to pharmacies when filling prescriptions. The pharmacies kept the copayments, but Medco, Merck's pharmacy-benefits unit, recorded the copayments as their own profit.

**Merrill Lynch** In May 2002 Merrill Lynch agreed to pay $100 million to settle a conflict-of-interest case brought by New York Attorney General Eliot Spitzer. The suit alleged that Merrill Lynch, the country's largest securities firm, urged investors to buy shaky Internet stocks simply to earn hefty transaction fees. CEO David Komansky announced his resignation in July 2002.

**Qwest Communications International** In March 2002 the SEC began an investigation to determine if the embattled phone company used improper accounting methods in booking about $1.4 billion in sales, which resulted from swapping fiber-optic network capacity with other firms. CEO Joseph Nacchio resigned in June 2002. In July 2002, Qwest admitted to incorrectly accounting for $1.1 billion in transactions related to sales of fiber-optic capacity and communications equipment from 1999 to 2001. The firm also faces a criminal probe by the Justice Department.

**Tyco International** Dennis Kozlowski, former CEO of Tyco, a manufacturing and services company, was indicted in June 2002 on charges that he avoided paying more than $1 million in sales tax on six pieces of art he purchased in 2001 for $13.1 million. He was indicted later in the month on charges that he tampered with evidence in the first indictment. Prosecutors are investigating Tyco to determine if Kozlowski used corporate funds for personal purchases.

**WorldCom** The nation's second-largest telecommunications company filed for bankruptcy in July 2002. It was the largest claim in U.S. history. The move followed the company's June 2002 announcement that by hiding $3.85 billion in expenses over five quarters, the company was able to show net income of $1.38 billion in 2001, rather than a loss. In addition, WorldCom CEO and founder Bernie Ebbers resigned in April 2002 following the disclosure that he borrowed hundreds of millions of dollars from the company.

**Xerox** Xerox announced in June 2002 that over the past five years it had misstated revenue by almost $2 billion. The company restated earnings, reporting $1.4 billion less in profits. In April, Xerox agreed to pay a $10 million fine to settle a civil fraud case brought by the SEC, which alleged the company boosted revenue by prematurely booking equipment sales.

## Largest Bankruptcies, 1980–Present

| Company | Bankruptcy date | Total assets pre-bankruptcy (in millions) | Company | Bankruptcy date | Total assets pre-bankruptcy (in millions) |
|---|---|---|---|---|---|
| Worldcom, Inc.[1] | 7/21/2002 | $103,914 | Gibraltar Financial Corp. | 2/8/90 | $15,011 |
| Enron Corp.[2] | 12/2/2001 | 63,392 | FINOVA Group, Inc. (The) | 3/7/2001 | 14,050 |
| Texaco, Inc. | 4/12/87 | 35,892 | HomeFed Corp. | 10/22/92 | 13,885 |
| Financial Corp. of America | 9/9/88 | 33,864 | Southeast Banking Corp. | 9/20/91 | 13,390 |
| Global Crossing Ltd. | 1/28/2002 | 25,511 | Reliance Group Holdings, Inc. | 6/12/2001 | 12,598 |
| Adelphia Communcations | 6/25/2002 | 24,410 | | | |
| Pacific Gas and Electric Co. | 4/6/2001 | 21,470 | Imperial Corp. of America | 2/28/90 | 12,263 |
| | | | Federal-Mogul Corp. | 10/1/2001 | 10,150 |
| MCorp | 3/31/89 | 20,228 | First City Bancorp. of Texas | 10/31/92 | 9,943 |
| Kmart Corp. | 1/22/2002 | 17,007 | | | |
| NTL, Inc. | 5/8/2002 | 16,834 | First Capital Holdings | 5/30/91 | 9,675 |
| First Executive Corp. | 5/13/91 | 15,193 | Baldwin-United | 9/26/83 | 9,383 |

1. Worldcom, Inc. assets taken from the audited annual report dated 12/31/2001. 2. The Enron assets were taken from the tax documents filed on 11/19/2001. The company has announced that the financials were under review at the time of filing for Chapter 11. *Source:* New Generation Research, Inc. Web: www.bankruptcydata.com.

## Extended Mass Layoff Events and Number of Workers Laid Off by Industry, 1998–2000

| Industry | Number of mass layoffs | | | Number of workers laid off | | |
|---|---|---|---|---|---|---|
| | 1998 | 1999 | 2000 | 1998 | 1999 | 2000 |
| Total[1] | 5,851 | 5,675 | 5,622 | 1,227,573 | 1,149,267 | 1,169,438 |
| Total, private | 5,602 | 5,480 | 5,432 | 1,160,418 | 1,098,216 | 1,107,497 |
| Agriculture | 751 | 932 | 860 | 169,823 | 197,734 | 194,789 |
| Nonagriculture | 4,837 | 4,525 | 4,543 | 988,767 | 897,986 | 907,902 |
| Manufacturing | 2,056 | 1,758 | 1,825 | 475,200 | 360,806 | 363,630 |
| Nonmanufacturing | 2,781 | 2,767 | 2,718 | 513,567 | 537,180 | 544,272 |
| Mining | 89 | 88 | 48 | 13,434 | 15,931 | 6,215 |
| Construction | 736 | 799 | 750 | 106,768 | 117,764 | 109,017 |
| Transportation and public utilities | 289 | 266 | 322 | 66,729 | 55,937 | 57,350 |
| Wholesale and retail trade | 532 | 547 | 507 | 105,540 | 140,343 | 132,656 |
| Wholesale trade | 124 | 146 | 147 | 18,898 | 23,541 | 23,872 |
| Retail trade | 408 | 401 | 360 | 86,642 | 116,802 | 108,784 |
| Finance, insurance, and real estate | 122 | 129 | 131 | 25,627 | 25,412 | 33,617 |
| Services | 1,013 | 938 | 960 | 195,469 | 181,793 | 205,417 |
| Not identified | 14 | 23 | 29 | 1,828 | 2,496 | 4,806 |
| Government | 249 | 195 | 190 | 67,155 | 51,051 | 61,941 |
| Federal | 50 | 38 | 51 | 12,641 | 9,372 | 18,242 |
| State | 54 | 42 | 35 | 11,174 | 14,472 | 9,164 |
| Local | 145 | 115 | 104 | 43,340 | 27,207 | 34,535 |
| **Selected industry groupings** | | | | | | |
| High-technology-intensive industries | 239 | 218 | 180 | 48,253 | 59,662 | 41,846 |
| Food production, processing, and distribution | 1,309 | 1,493 | 1,342 | 279,845 | 325,243 | 303,858 |

NOTE: A mass layoff is the laying off of 50 or more employees for more than 31 days. 1. Data on layoffs were reported by employers in all states and the District of Columbia. *Source:* Bureau of Labor Statistics. Web: www.bls.gov/mls/mls00ext.pdf.

## Economic Outlook Through 2010

Source: Bureau of Labor Statistics, *Monthly Labor Review*, Nov. 2001, www.bls.gov/opub/mlr/2001/11/art1abs.htm

Every two years the Bureau of Labor Statistics (BLS) publishes its latest projections on the structure of the economy, labor force demographics, and future job growth. The following is a summary of the most recent BLS projections that were released at the end of 2001.

### Continued Growth

BLS projections for the U.S. economy during the 2000–10 decade reflect continued growth. Gross domestic product (GDP) is expected to reach $12.8 trillion in chained 1996 dollars by the end of the decade, an increase of $3.6 trillion over the period. Rising by an average annual rate of 3.4%, GDP is projected to grow faster than the 3.2% annual rate of growth over the preceding 10-year period.

Slower growth of civilian household employment, from 1.3% a year during the 1990–2000 period to 1.1% from 2000–2010, is expected to result in an increase of 16.2 million employees over the latter period, slightly less than the increase of 16.4 million employees between 1990 and 2000. The report assumes an unemployment rate of 4.0% in 2010, the same as in 2000.

## Consumer Spending to Grow

Personal consumption spending, which makes up two-thirds of economic activity, is expected to grow at an average annual rate of 3.5% from 2000 to 2010, versus 3.4% from 1990 to 2000.

Consumer spending on long-lasting items, such as motor vehicles, personal computers, and household furnishings, is highly cyclical. Over the coming decade, with a projected rise in family income—a key in determining future spending trends—durable goods are still expected to be the fastest growth sector, increasing at an annual average rate of 5.0% in the 2000–2010 period.

During the past several decades, expenditures on non-durable goods, such as food and clothing, have increased at a significantly slower pace than spending on durable goods. As family income increases, spending on these short-term consumable necessities also rises, up to a point, after which spending tends to increase less rapidly than rises in income, although the latter increases do enhance demand for higher quality products.

### Continued Trade Deficit

Globalization and international competition have played an important role in U.S. economic activity. With the world assumed to become more open to trade, the share of GDP accounted for by both exports and imports is expected to grow apace, and the dollar is expected to remain moderately strong throughout the projection period, but not so strong as to significantly weaken anticipated export growth.

Exports are expected to grow at a 7.8% annual rate between 2000 and 2010, compared with 7.0% per year during the 1990–2000 period. Exports of goods are expected to lead the way with an 8.1% annual rate of growth during the coming 10-year period, while exports of services are anticipated to grow at a rate of 7.1%.

Imports are expected to grow at 7.9% annually over the 2000–2010 projection period, 0.1 percentage point higher than the projected growth rate for exports, but lower than the 9.3% annual growth rate for imports over the 1990–2000 span. Imports of goods are expected to grow at 8.4% per year, and a 4.9 annual rate of growth is projected for imports of services during the 2000–2010 period.

As a result, net exports (exports minus imports) are projected to continue to make a negative contribution to the aggregate demand, reaching $889.1 billion in real terms by 2010. Both exports and imports are expected to increase their share of GDP by 2010, to 18.6% and 25.6%, respectively.

## Disposable Income on the Rise

On a per capita basis, nominal disposable income is projected to increase at an annual average rate of 4.8% from 2000 to 2010, reaching a level of $40,768 in the latter year, a gain of more than $15,000 over the projection span. In real terms—chained 1996 dollars—per capita income is projected to grow 2.6% per year from 2000 to 2010, up from a 1.7% rate of growth between 1990 and 2000. Thus, the bureau expects its projections to be characterized by a long-term improvement in the real standard of living, at least as measured on the basis of growth of disposable personal income.

## Employment Outlook

Civilian household employment is projected to increase by 1.1% per year from 2000 to 2010, or 1.62 million persons per year. The result is that more than 16 million employed persons will be added to the economy over the 10–year projection period. The civilian labor force is projected to grow at a rate of 1.1% per year from 2000 to 2010, the same rate of increase as that attained over the preceding 10–year period. This translates into an increase of almost 17 million over the projection span.

## Characteristics of the Civilian Labor Force, 1990–2010

### (in thousands)

| Group | Level | | | Percent change | | | Percent distribution | | |
|---|---|---|---|---|---|---|---|---|---|
| | 1990 | 2000 | 2010* | 1990 | 2000 | 2010* | 1990 | 2000 | 2010* |
| **Total** | 125,840 | 140,863 | 157,721 | 17.7% | 11.9% | 12.0% | 100.0% | 100.0% | 100.0% |
| **Age** | | | | | | | | | |
| 16 to 24 | 22,492 | 22,715 | 26,081 | −11.1 | 1.0 | 14.8 | 17.9 | 16.1 | 16.5 |
| 25 to 54 | 88,322 | 99,974 | 104,994 | 32.6 | 13.2 | 5.0 | 70.2 | 71.0 | 66.6 |
| 55 and older | 15,026 | 18,175 | 26,646 | −0.1 | 21.0 | 46.6 | 11.9 | 12.9 | 16.9 |
| **Sex** | | | | | | | | | |
| Men | 69,011 | 75,247 | 82,221 | 12.3 | 9.0 | 9.3 | 54.8 | 53.4 | 52.1 |
| Women | 56,829 | 65,616 | 75,500 | 24.9 | 15.5 | 15.1 | 45.2 | 46.6 | 47.9 |
| **Race** | | | | | | | | | |
| White | 107,447 | 117,574 | 128,043 | 14.8 | 9.4 | 8.9 | 85.4 | 83.5 | 81.2 |
| Black | 13,740 | 16,603 | 20,041 | 26.5 | 20.8 | 20.7 | 10.9 | 11.8 | 12.7 |
| Asian and other[1] | 4,653 | 6,687 | 9,636 | 87.9 | 43.7 | 44.1 | 3.7 | 4.7 | 6.1 |
| Hispanic origin | 10,720 | 15,368 | 20,947 | 74.4 | 43.4 | 36.3 | 8.5 | 10.9 | 13.3 |
| Other than Hispanic origin | 115,120 | 125,495 | 136,774 | 14.2 | 9.0 | 9.0 | 91.5 | 89.1 | 86.7 |
| White non-Hispanic | 97,818 | 102,963 | 109,118 | 11.6 | 5.3 | 6.0 | 77.0 | 73.1 | 69.2 |

* Projected. NOTE: Data apply to workers age 16 and older. 1. The "Asian and other" group includes (1) Asians and Pacific Islanders and (2) American Indians and Alaska Natives. The historical data are derived by subtracting "black" and "white" from the total; projections are made directly, not by subtraction. *Source: Monthly Labor Review,* Nov. 2001.

## Persons in the Labor Force, 1840–2001

| Year | Labor force[1] Number (thousands) | Percent of working-age population | Year | Labor force[1] Number (thousands) | Percent of working-age population |
|---|---|---|---|---|---|
| 1840 | 5,420 | 46.6% | 1930 | 48,830 | 49.5% |
| 1850 | 7,697 | 46.8 | 1940 | 52,789 | 52.2 |
| 1860 | 10,533 | 47.0 | 1950 | 60,054 | 53.5 |
| 1870 | 12,925 | 45.8 | 1960 | 69,877 | 55.3 |
| 1880 | 17,392 | 47.3 | 1970 | 82,049 | 58.2 |
| 1890 | 23,318 | 49.2 | 1980 | 106,085 | 62.0 |
| 1900 | 29,073 | 50.2 | 1990 | 125,182 | 65.3 |
| 1910 | 37,371 | 52.2 | 2000 | 140,863 | 67.2 |
| 1920 | 42,434 | 51.3 | 2001 | 141,815 | 66.9 |

1. For 1830 to 1930, the data relate to the population and gainful workers at age 10 and over. For 1940 to 1960, the data relate to the population and labor force at age 14 and over; for 1970 and 1980, the data relate to the population and labor force at age 16 and over. For 1940 to 1980, the data include the Armed Forces. *Source:* U.S. Bureau of the Census and *Monthly Labor Review,* March 2002. Web: www.census.gov.

## Farm and Non-Farm Labor Force, 1940–2000

### (number in thousands)

| Year | Civilian labor force employed Total | Agriculture | Nonagricultural industries | Year | Civilian labor force employed Total | Agriculture | Nonagricultural industries |
|---|---|---|---|---|---|---|---|
| 1940 | 47,520 | 9,540 | 37,980 | 1975 | 85,846 | 3,408 | 82,438 |
| 1945 | 52,820 | 8,580 | 44,240 | 1980 | 99,303 | 3,364 | 95,938 |
| 1950 | 58,918 | 7,160 | 51,758 | 1985 | 107,150 | 3,179 | 103,971 |
| 1955 | 62,170 | 6,450 | 55,722 | 1990[1] | 118,793 | 3,223 | 115,570 |
| 1960[1] | 65,778 | 5,458 | 60,318 | 1995 | 124,900 | 3,440 | 121,460 |
| 1965 | 71,088 | 4,361 | 66,726 | 2000[2] | 135,208 | 3,305 | 131,903 |
| 1970 | 78,678 | 3,463 | 75,215 | | | | |

1. Not strictly comparable with data for prior years. 2. Beginning in Jan. 2000, data are not strictly comparable with data for 1999 and earlier years because of the revisions in the population controls used in the household survey. *Source:* U.S. Department of Labor, Bureau of Labor Statistics. Web: stats.bls.gov.

## Fastest-Growing Occupations, 2000–2010

### (by percentage; numbers in thousands of jobs)

| Occupation | Employment 2000 | 2010* | Percent change | Occupation | Employment 2000 | 2010* | Percent change |
|---|---|---|---|---|---|---|---|
| Computer software engineers, applications | 380 | 760 | 100% | Physical therapist aides | 36 | 53 | 46% |
| Computer support specialists | 506 | 996 | 97 | Occupational therapist aides | 9 | 12 | 45 |
| Computer software engineers, systems software | 317 | 601 | 90 | Physical therapist assistants | 44 | 64 | 45 |
| Network and computer systems administrators | 229 | 416 | 82 | Audiologists | 13 | 19 | 45 |
| Network systems/data communications analysts | 119 | 211 | 77 | Fitness trainers/aerobics instructors | 158 | 222 | 40 |
| Desktop publishers | 38 | 63 | 67 | Computer/information scientists, research | 28 | 39 | 40 |
| Database administrators | 106 | 176 | 66 | Veterinary assistants/laboratory animal caretakers | 71 | 77 | 40 |
| Personal/home-care aides | 414 | 672 | 62 | Occupational therapist assistants | 17 | 23 | 40 |
| Computer systems analysts | 431 | 689 | 60 | Veterinary technologists/ technicians | 49 | 68 | 39 |
| Medical assistants | 329 | 516 | 57 | Speech-language pathologists | 88 | 122 | 39 |
| Social/human service assistants | 271 | 418 | 54 | Mental health/substance abuse social workers | 83 | 116 | 39 |
| Physician assistants | 58 | 89 | 53 | Dental assistants | 247 | 339 | 37 |
| Medical records/health information technicians | 136 | 202 | 49 | Dental hygienists | 147 | 201 | 37 |
| Computer/information systems managers | 313 | 463 | 48 | Special ed., preschool, kindergarten, elementary teachers | 234 | 320 | 37 |
| Home health aides | 615 | 907 | 47 | | | | |

*Projected. *Source:* U.S. Department of Labor, Bureau of Labor Statistics, *Monthly Labor Review,* Nov. 2001. Web: stats.bls.gov.

## Employed Persons by Occupation and Sex
### (in thousands; 16 years and over)

| Occupation | Total | | Men | | Women | |
|---|---|---|---|---|---|---|
| | 2000 | 2001 | 2000 | 2001 | 2000 | 2001 |
| Total | 135,208 | 135,073 | 72,293 | 72,080 | 62,915 | 62,992 |
| Managerial and professional specialty | 40,887 | 41,894 | 20,543 | 20,966 | 20,345 | 20,928 |
|   Executive, administrative, and managerial | 19,774 | 20,338 | 10,814 | 10,990 | 8,960 | 9,348 |
|   Professional specialty | 21,113 | 21,556 | 9,728 | 9,976 | 11,385 | 11,580 |
| Technical, sales, and administrative support | 39,442 | 39,044 | 14,288 | 14,167 | 25,154 | 24,877 |
|   Technicians and related support | 4,385 | 4,497 | 2,118 | 2,097 | 2,267 | 2,400 |
|   Sales occupations | 16,340 | 16,044 | 8,231 | 8,120 | 8,110 | 7,924 |
|   Administrative support, including clerical | 18,717 | 18,503 | 3,939 | 3,950 | 14,778 | 14,553 |
| Service occupations | 18,278 | 18,359 | 7,245 | 7,263 | 11,034 | 11,096 |
|   Private household | 792 | 715 | 35 | 27 | 757 | 688 |
|   Protective service | 2,399 | 2,478 | 1,944 | 1,972 | 455 | 507 |
|   Service, except private household and protective | 15,087 | 15,166 | 5,265 | 5,264 | 9,822 | 9,902 |
| Precision production, craft, and repair | 14,882 | 14,833 | 13,532 | 13,545 | 1,351 | 1,287 |
| Operators, fabricators, and laborers | 18,319 | 17,698 | 13,988 | 13,569 | 4,331 | 4,129 |
|   Machine operators, assemblers, and inspectors | 7,319 | 6,734 | 4,622 | 4,286 | 2,697 | 2,448 |
|   Transportation and material moving occupations | 5,557 | 5,638 | 5,003 | 5,049 | 554 | 589 |
|   Handlers, equipment cleaners, helpers, and laborers | 5,443 | 5,326 | 4,363 | 4,234 | 1,080 | 1,092 |
| Farming, forestry, and fishing | 3,399 | 3,245 | 2,698 | 2,570 | 701 | 675 |

Source: U.S. Department of Labor, Bureau of Labor Statistics. Web: www.bls.gov/cps/cpsaat9.pdf.

## Number of Employed and Unemployed Workers by Sex and Age, 1970–2000
### (in thousands)

| | 2000[1] | 1999[1] | 1998[1] | 1997[1] | 1995[1] | 1990[2] | 1985 | 1980 | 1970 |
|---|---|---|---|---|---|---|---|---|---|
| **Men, 20 years and over** | | | | | | | | | |
|   Employed | 68,580 | 67,761 | 67,134 | 66,524 | 64,085 | 61,678 | 56,562 | 53,101 | 45,581 |
|   Unemployed | 2,350 | 2,433 | 2,580 | 2,826 | 3,239 | 3,239 | 3,715 | 3,353 | 1,638 |
| **Women, 20 years and over** | | | | | | | | | |
|   Employed | 59,352 | 58,655 | 57,278 | 57,647 | 54,396 | 50,535 | 44,154 | 38,492 | 26,952 |
|   Unemployed | 2,212 | 2,285 | 2,424 | 2,187 | 2,819 | 2,596 | 3,129 | 2,615 | 1,349 |
| **Total, 16 years and over** | | | | | | | | | |
|   Employed | 135,208 | 133,488 | 131,463 | 130,785 | 124,900 | 118,793 | 107,150 | 99,303 | 78,678 |
|   Unemployed | 5,655 | 5,880 | 6,209 | 5,957 | 7,404 | 7,047 | 8,312 | 7,637 | 4,093 |
| **Total, 16–19 years** | | | | | | | | | |
|   Employed | 7,276 | 7,172 | 7,051 | 6,614 | 6,419 | 6,581 | 6,434 | 7,710 | 6,144 |
|   Unemployed | 1,093 | 1,162 | 1,205 | 944 | 1,346 | 1,212 | 1,468 | 1,669 | 1,106 |

1. Data beginning in 1994 are not directly comparable with earlier years due to the introduction of a major redesign of the Current Population Survey. 2. Revised; data beginning in 1990 are not directly comparable with earlier years due to the introduction of 1990 census-based population controls, adjusted for the estimated undercount. Source: U.S. Department of Labor, Bureau of Labor Statistics. Current Population Survey. Web: stats.bls.gov.

## Overall Unemployment Rate in the Civilian Labor Force, 1920–2002

| Year | Rate | Year | Rate | Year | Rate | Year | Rate | Year | Rate | Year | Rate |
|---|---|---|---|---|---|---|---|---|---|---|---|
| 1920 | 5.2% | 1944 | 1.2% | 1962 | 5.5% | 1980 | 7.1% | 1992 | 7.5% | 2001 | 4.8% |
| 1928 | 4.2 | 1946 | 3.9 | 1964 | 5.2 | 1982 | 9.7 | 1993 | 6.9 | 2002 | |
| 1930 | 8.7 | 1948 | 3.8 | 1966 | 3.8 | 1984 | 7.5 | 1994 | 6.1 |   Jan. | 5.6 |
| 1932 | 23.6 | 1950 | 5.3 | 1968 | 3.6 | 1986 | 7.0 | 1995 | 5.6 |   Feb. | 5.5 |
| 1934 | 21.7 | 1952 | 3.0 | 1970 | 4.9 | 1987 | 6.2 | 1996 | 5.4 |   March | 5.7 |
| 1936 | 16.9 | 1954 | 5.5 | 1972 | 5.6 | 1988 | 5.5 | 1997 | 4.9 |   April | 6.0 |
| 1938 | 19.0 | 1956 | 4.1 | 1974 | 5.6 | 1989 | 5.3 | 1998 | 4.5 |   May | 5.8 |
| 1940 | 14.6 | 1958 | 6.8 | 1976 | 7.7 | 1990 | 5.6 | 1999 | 4.2 |   June | 5.9 |
| 1942 | 4.7 | 1960 | 5.5 | 1978 | 6.1 | 1991 | 6.8 | 2000 | 4.0 |   July | 5.9 |

NOTES: Estimates prior to 1940 are based on sources other than direct enumeration. Data prior to 1948 are for persons age 14 and over. Data beginning in 1948 are for persons age 16 and over. Source: U.S. Department of Labor, Bureau of Labor Statistics. Web: stats.bls.gov.

## Employment Status by Race, 1975–2001

### (numbers in thousands)

| Year | Employment rate | Unemployment rate | Year | Employment rate | Unemployment rate |
|---|---|---|---|---|---|
| **White** | | | 1990 | 56.7% | 11.4% |
| 1975 | 56.7% | 7.8% | 1995 | 57.1 | 10.4 |
| 1980 | 60.0 | 6.3 | 2000 | 60.8 | 7.6 |
| 1985 | 61.0 | 6.2 | 2001 | 59.7 | 8.7 |
| 1990 | 63.7 | 4.8 | **Hispanic[1]** | | |
| 1995 | 63.8 | 4.9 | 1975 | 53.4 | 12.2 |
| 2000 | 65.1 | 3.5 | 1980 | 57.6 | 10.1 |
| 2001 | 64.4 | 4.2 | 1985 | 57.8 | 10.5 |
| **Black** | | | 1990 | 61.9 | 8.2 |
| 1975 | 50.1 | 14.8 | 1995 | 59.7 | 9.3 |
| 1980 | 52.3 | 14.3 | 2000 | 64.7 | 5.7 |
| 1985 | 53.4 | 15.1 | 2001 | 63.6 | 6.6 |

NOTE: Data apply to workers age 16 and older. 1. Hispanic persons may be of any race. *Source:* U.S. Department of Labor, Bureau of Labor Statistics. Web: data.bls.gov.

## Unemployment Rate by Race, Age, and Sex, 2000–2001

| Age and sex | Men | | Women | |
|---|---|---|---|---|
| | 2000 | 2001 | 2000 | 2001 |
| Total, 16 years and over | 3.9% | 4.8% | 4.1% | 4.7% |
| White, 16 years and over | 3.4 | 4.3 | 3.6 | 4.1 |
| Black, 16 years and over | 8.1 | 9.3 | 7.2 | 8.1 |
| Total, 25 years and over | 2.8 | 3.6 | 3.2 | 3.7 |
| White, 25 years and over | 2.5 | 3.2 | 2.8 | 3.3 |
| Black, 25 years and over | 5.6 | 6.7 | 5.2 | 5.9 |

*Source:* U.S. Department of Labor, Bureau of Labor Statistics. Web: stats.bls.gov.

# Youth Employment Trends

*Source:* U.S. Department of Labor. *Report on the Youth Labor Force,* November 2000. Based on Current Population Survey data. Web: stats.bls.gov/opub/rylf/rylfhome.htm.

## How Many Youths Work?

During the 1996–1998 period, 2.9 million youths age 15 to 17 worked during school months, and 4.0 million worked during the summer months.

Among youths, employment increased markedly with age. During the school months of 1996–1998, only 9% of 15-year-olds were employed in an average month, compared with 26% of those a year older and 39% of 17-year-olds. Youths in each age group were more likely to work in the summer, during which employment rates increased to 18%, 36%, and 48% at each age, respectively.

Despite popular perceptions that youths work more than they did in the past, the proportion of 15- to 17-year-olds who work has declined over time. Employment-population ratios declined with economic downturns in the early 1980s and 1990s. After the decline in the early 1990s, however, the rates did not return to earlier levels. During the 1996–1998 period, a quarter of youths worked during the school months, down from 30% in 1977–1979. Just over a third worked during the summer, down from 43% during the late 1970s.

## How Much Do Youths Earn?

The minimum wage often is associated with young workers first entering the labor force. CPS data indicate that earnings were above the minimum wage for most youths, with hourly earnings in the school and summer months about the same. The minimum wage was $5.15 in 1998.

In 1998, median earnings of 15- to 17-year-olds combined were $5.57 per hour. In 1998, the earnings increased with age: 15-year-olds earned a median of $5.38 per hour, 16-year-olds earned $5.52, and 17-year-olds earned $5.65 per hour. Earnings varied slightly across sex and race groups. Hispanic and white males had the highest median hourly earnings; Hispanic and black females had the lowest.

## Where Do Youths Work?

About 62% of youths age 15 to 17 employed during the school months of the 1996–1998 period worked in retail trade, more than in any other major industry. Within retail trade, eating and drinking places accounted for the greatest share of employed youths, about one-third of all employed 15- to 17-year-olds. Another 1 in 4 youths was employed in service industries. In the summer, youth employment was less concentrated in retail trade and youths were employed in a wider variety of industries than during the school months. Retail trade still accounted for about half, services increased to 30%, and employment in agriculture and goods-producing industries (mining, construction, and manufacturing) increased. This seasonal pattern of employment also was present in earlier periods.

## Industries that Employ Largest Share of Youths Age 15–17

| Industry | Percent of total employed youths | Industry | Percent of total employed youths |
|---|---|---|---|
| **Male** | | **Female** | |
| Eating and drinking places | 31.3% | Eating and drinking places | 32.6% |
| Grocery stores | 13.6 | Grocery stores | 9.9 |
| Miscellaneous entertainment and recreation services | 4.5 | Private households | 5.7 |
| Agricultural production, livestock | 3.6 | Department stores | 4.4 |
| Construction | 3.6 | Miscellaneous entertainment and recreation services | 4.0 |
| Department stores | 3.1 | Stores, apparel and accessory, except shoe | 3.6 |
| Landscape and horticultural services | 2.2 | Drug stores | 1.9 |
| Newspaper publishing and printing | 1.9 | Nursing and personal care facilities | 1.7 |
| Agricultural production, crops | 1.5 | Retail bakeries | 1.5 |
| Gasoline service stations | 1.3 | Child day-care services | 1.4 |

NOTE: Figures based on youths working during school months, which are January to May and September to December. *Source:* U.S. Department of Labor. *Report on the Youth Labor Force,* Nov. 2000. Web: www.bls.gov/opub/rylf/pdf/chapter4.pdf.

## Mothers Participating in Labor Force, 1955–2001

| Year | Percentage of mothers with children | | |
|---|---|---|---|
| | Under 18 years | 6 to 17 years | Under 6 years[1] |
| 1955 | 27.0% | 38.4% | 18.2% |
| 1965 | 35.0 | 45.7 | 25.3 |
| 1975 | 47.3 | 54.8 | 38.8 |
| 1980 | 56.6 | 64.3 | 46.8 |
| 1985 | 62.1 | 69.9 | 53.5 |
| 1986 | 62.8 | 70.4 | 54.4 |
| 1987 | 64.7 | 72.0 | 56.7 |
| 1988 | 65.1 | 73.3 | 56.1 |
| 1989 | 65.7 | 74.2 | 56.7 |
| 1990 | 66.7 | 74.7 | 58.2 |
| 1991 | 66.6 | 74.4 | 58.4 |
| 1992 | 67.2 | 75.9 | 58.0 |
| 1993 | 67.0 | 75.4 | 57.9 |
| 1994 | 68.4 | 76.0 | 60.3 |
| 1995 | 69.7 | 76.4 | 62.3 |
| 1996 | 70.2 | 77.2 | 62.3 |
| 1997 | 72.1 | 78.1 | 65.0 |
| 1998 | 71.8 | 77.6 | 64.9 |
| 1999 | 72.2 | 78.2 | 64.8 |
| 2000 | 72.3 | 78.7 | 64.6 |
| 2001 | 72.1 | 78.3 | 64.3 |

1. May also have older children. NOTE: 1955 data are for April; 1965 and 1975–1994 data are for March. Data for 1994 and subsequent years are not directly comparable to previous years because of major revisions to the survey questionnaire and the data collection methodology, and the introduction of 1990 census-based population controls into the estimation process. *Source:* U.S. Department of Labor, Bureau of Labor Statistics. Web: stats.bls.gov.

## Women in the Civilian Labor Force, 1900–2001

| Year | Number[1] (thousands) | % female population aged 16 and over[1] | % of labor force population aged 16 and over[1] |
|---|---|---|---|
| 1900 | 5,319 | 18.8% | 18.3% |
| 1910 | 7,445 | 21.5 | 19.9 |
| 1920 | 8,637 | 21.4 | 20.4 |
| 1930 | 10,752 | 22.0 | 22.0 |
| 1940 | 12,845 | 25.4 | 24.3 |
| 1950 | 18,389 | 33.9 | 29.6 |
| 1960 | 23,240 | 37.7 | 33.4 |
| 1970 | 31,543 | 43.3 | 38.1 |
| 1980 | 45,487 | 51.5 | 42.5 |
| 1990[2] | 56,829 | 57.5 | 45.2 |
| 1993 | 58,795 | 57.9 | 45.5 |
| 1994[3] | 60,239 | 58.8 | 46.0 |
| 1996 | 61,857 | 59.3 | 46.2 |
| 1997 | 63,036 | 59.8 | 46.2 |
| 1998 | 63,714 | 59.8 | 46.3 |
| 1999 | 64,855 | 60.0 | 46.5 |
| 2000 | 65,616 | 60.2 | 46.6 |
| 2001 | 62,992 | 60.1 | 44.4 |

1. For 1900–1930, data relate to population and labor force aged 10 and over; for 1940, to population and labor force aged 14 and over; beginning 1950, to civilian population and labor force aged 16 and over. 2. Data beginning in 1990 are not strictly comparable with data for prior years because population controls were adjusted. 3. Data beginning 1994 are not strictly comparable with data for prior years because of a major redesign of the Current Population Survey (household survey) questionnaire and collection methodology. *Source:* U.S. Department of Labor, Women's Bureau.

## Employed Wage and Salary Workers Represented by Unions, 2000

| Occupation | Percent of workers | Industry | Percent of workers |
|---|---|---|---|
| Precision production, craft, and repair | 22.5% | Government workers | 42.0% |
| Operators, fabricators, and laborers | 20.9 | Transportation and public utilities | 25.6 |
| Managerial and professional specialty | 14.9 | Manufacturing | 15.6 |
| Service occupations | 14.4 | Private wage and salary workers | 9.8 |
| Technical, sales, and administrative support | 9.7 | Wholesale and retail trade | 5.2 |
| Farming, forestry, and fishing | 5.5 | Agriculture | 2.5 |
| | | Finance, insurance, and real estate | 2.1 |

*Source:* U.S. Bureau of Labor Statistics.

## Work Stoppages (Strikes) Involving 1,000 Workers or More

| Year | Work stoppages | Workers involved (thousands) | Days idle (thousands) | Year | Work stoppages | Workers involved (thousands) | Days idle (thousands) |
|------|------|------|------|------|------|------|------|
| 1950 | 424 | 1,698 | 30,390 | 1990 | 44 | 185 | 5,926 |
| 1960 | 222 | 896 | 13,260 | 1991 | 40 | 392 | 4,584 |
| 1970 | 381 | 2,468 | 52,761 | 1992 | 35 | 364 | 3,989 |
| 1975 | 235 | 965 | 17,563 | 1993 | 35 | 182 | 3,981 |
| 1980 | 187 | 795 | 20,844 | 1994 | 45 | 322 | 5,020 |
| 1983 | 81 | 909 | 17,461 | 1995 | 31 | 192 | 5,771 |
| 1984 | 62 | 376 | 8,499 | 1996 | 37 | 273 | 4,889 |
| 1985 | 54 | 324 | 7,079 | 1997 | 29 | 339 | 4,497 |
| 1986 | 69 | 533 | 11,861 | 1998 | 34 | 387 | 5,116 |
| 1987 | 46 | 174 | 4,481 | 1999 | 17 | 73 | 1,996 |
| 1988 | 40 | 118 | 4,381 | 2000 | 39 | 394 | 20,419 |
| 1989 | 51 | 452 | 16,996 | 2001 | 29 | 99 | 1,151 |

NOTE: Refers to stoppages that began in the year. Days idle is total for all stoppages in effect. Workers are counted more than once if they were involved in more than one stoppage during the year. *Source:* U.S. Department of Labor, Bureau of Labor Statistics. Web: stats.bls.gov.

## Union Membership, by States

*Source: Monthly Labor Review Online,* Bureau of Labor Statistics, http://www.bls.gov.

Roughly 14% of nonagricultural wage-and-salary workers are union members. Union membership among wage and salary workers shows a distinct geographic pattern, according to the Current Population Survey. Union membership is highest in the Northeast, Midwest, and Pacific regions, and lowest in the South.

New York, Hawaii, and Michigan have the highest rates of union membership, all more than 21.0% of workers. These states, along with Alaska and New Jersey, have been among the most unionized since at least 1995. North Carolina and South Carolina have the lowest rates, 3.2% and 3.5%, respectively. New York has a union membership rate eight times that of North Carolina (25.3% vs. 3.2% of workers).

California (2.3 million), New York (1.9 million), and Illinois and Michigan (both 1 million) have the greatest number of union members. More than half (53%) of the 16.5 million union members in the United States live in seven states, although these states accounted for only 38% of wage and salary employment nationally. Interestingly, Washington has slightly more union members than Texas, despite having less than one-third as much employment.

## Union Membership Rates by State, 2000 Annual Average
### (U.S. Rate = 13.5%)

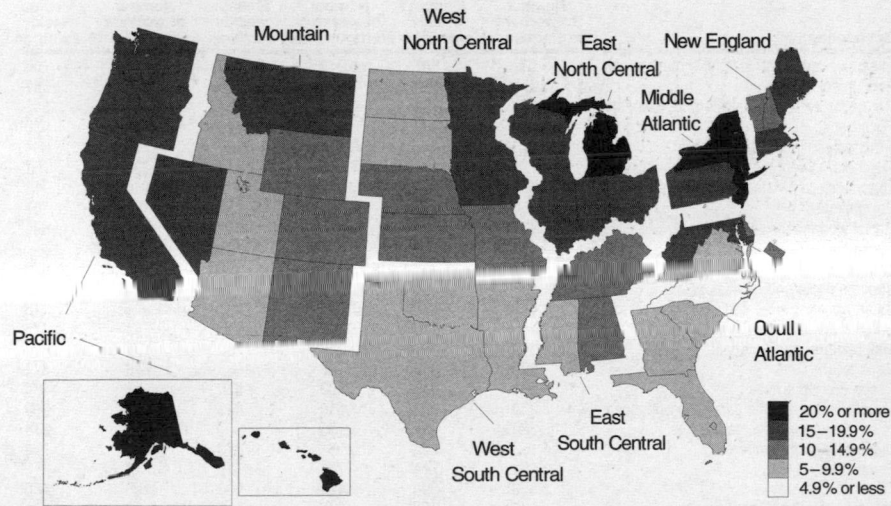

*Source:* Current Population Survey, Bureau of Labor Statistics; Web: www.bls.gov.

## National Labor Organizations with Membership over 100,000

| Members | Union[1] |
|---|---|
| 2,530,000 | National Education Association |
| 1,402,000 | International Brotherhood of Teamsters |
| 1,380,722 | United Food and Commercial Workers International Union |
| 1,374,300 | Service Employees International Union |
| 1,300,000 | American Federation of State, County, and Municipal Employees |
| 818,412 | Laborers' International Union of North America |
| 730,763 | International Association of Machinists and Aerospace Workers |
| 727,836 | International Brotherhood of Electrical Workers |
| 706,973 | American Federation of Teachers |
| 671,853 | International Union, United Automobile, Aerospace, and Agricultural Implement Workers of America |
| 612,157 | United Steelworkers of America |
| 534,023 | United Brotherhood of Carpenters and Joiners of America |
| 499,557 | Communications Workers of America |
| 410,364 | National Postal Mail Handlers Union |
| 379,309 | International Union of Operating Engineers |
| 315,582 | American Postal Workers Union |
| 311,406 | Paper, Allied-Industrial, and Chemical International Union |
| 307,454 | United Association of Journeymen and Apprentices of the Plumbing and Pipe-Fitting Industry of the U.S. and Canada |
| 304,335 | National Association of Letter Carriers |
| 248,669 | Hotel Employees and Restaurant Employees International Union |
| 235,527 | International Association of Fire Fighters |
| 219,968 | Union of Needletrades, Industrial, and Textile Employees |
| 197,196 | American Federation of Government Employees |
| 170,466 | Amalgamated Transit Union |
| 146,400 | Sheet Metal Workers International Association |
| 130,439 | International Association of Bridge, Structural, Ornamental, and Reinforcing Iron Workers |
| 117,997 | Office and Professional Employees International Union |
| 117,083 | Bakery, Confectionery, Tobacco Workers, and Grain Millers International Union |
| 112,481 | United Mine Workers of America |
| 112,342 | Transportation Communications Workers International Union |
| 109,000 | Transport Workers Union of America |
| 105,000 | American Federation of Musicians of the U.S. and Canada |
| 102,402 | International Brotherhood of Painters and Allied Trades |
| 100,000 | International Alliance of Theatrical Stage Employees, Moving Picture Technicians, Artists, and Allied Crafts of the U.S. and Canada |

1. Unless otherwise noted, unions are AFL-CIO affiliated. *Source:* U.S. Department of Labor. From *Directory of U.S. Labor Organizations, 2001.*

## Median Weekly Earnings of Selected Occupations, 2001

| Occupation | Both sexes | | Men | | Women | |
|---|---|---|---|---|---|---|
| | Number of workers (in thousands) | Median weekly earnings | Number of workers (in thousands) | Median weekly earnings | Number of workers (in thousands) | Median weekly earnings |
| Executive, administrative, and managerial | 15,795 | $ 867 | 8,349 | $1,060 | 7,446 | $ 706 |
| Accountants and auditors | 1,374 | 773 | 581 | 954 | 793 | 687 |
| Computer systems analysts and scientists | 1,603 | 1,100 | 1,173 | 1,161 | 430 | 918 |
| Physicians | 494 | 1,258 | 333 | 1,410 | 161 | 958 |
| Teachers, college and university | 663 | 1,009 | 420 | 1,126 | 244 | 844 |
| Teachers, except college and university | 4,421 | 730 | 1,189 | 780 | 3,232 | 707 |
| Librarians, archivists, and curators | 181 | 724 | 33 | — | 148 | 713 |
| Psychologists | 151 | 818 | 64 | 914 | 87 | 757 |
| Social workers | 711 | 644 | 211 | 677 | 500 | 630 |
| Clergy | 303 | 699 | 269 | 723 | 34 | — |
| Lawyers | 572 | 1,398 | 377 | 1,547 | 195 | 1,073 |
| Airplane pilots and navigators | 101 | 1,150 | 98 | 1,145 | 3 | — |
| Sales workers, retail and personal services | 3,474 | 363 | 1,504 | 460 | 1,971 | 313 |
| Secretaries, stenographers, and typists | 2,333 | 479 | 48 | — | 2,285 | 478 |
| Mail carriers, postal service | 317 | 721 | 225 | 753 | 91 | 641 |
| Bank tellers | 303 | 376 | 33 | — | 270 | 372 |
| Police and detectives | 111 | 949 | 100 | 970 | 11 | — |
| Food preparation and service occupations | 3,285 | 322 | 1,648 | 343 | 1,638 | 309 |
| Hairdressers and cosmetologists | 326 | 381 | 35 | — | 291 | 374 |
| Mechanics and repairers | 4,153 | 665 | 3,951 | 670 | 201 | 594 |
| Electricians | 752 | 714 | 739 | 716 | 14 | — |
| Truck drivers | 2,530 | 593 | 2,421 | 600 | 108 | 456 |
| Taxicab drivers and chauffeurs | 162 | 487 | 143 | 509 | 19 | — |
| Farm operators and managers | 77 | 510 | 59 | 560 | 18 | — |

NOTES: Dash indicates base is less than 50,000 workers, so no data are provided. *Source:* U.S. Department of Labor, Bureau of Labor Statistics. Web: stats.bls.gov.

## Federal Minimum Wage Rates, 1955–2002

| Year | Value of the minimum wage Current dollars | Constant (1996) dollars[1] | Year | Value of the minimum wage Current dollars | Constant (1996) dollars[1] | Year | Value of the minimum wage Current dollars | Constant (1996) dollars[1] | Year | Value of the minimum wage Current dollars | Constant (1996) dollars[1] |
|---|---|---|---|---|---|---|---|---|---|---|---|
| 1955 | $0.75 | $4.39 | 1967 | $1.40 | $6.58 | 1979 | $2.90 | $6.27 | 1991 | $4.25 | $4.90 |
| 1956 | 1.00 | 5.77 | 1968 | 1.60 | 7.21 | 1980 | 3.10 | 5.90 | 1992 | 4.25 | 4.75 |
| 1957 | 1.00 | 5.58 | 1969 | 1.60 | 6.84 | 1981 | 3.35 | 5.78 | 1993 | 4.25 | 4.61 |
| 1958 | 1.00 | 5.43 | 1970 | 1.60 | 6.47 | 1982 | 3.35 | 5.45 | 1994 | 4.25 | 4.50 |
| 1959 | 1.00 | 5.39 | 1971 | 1.60 | 6.20 | 1983 | 3.35 | 5.28 | 1995 | 4.25 | 4.38 |
| 1960 | 1.00 | 5.30 | 1972 | 1.60 | 6.01 | 1984 | 3.35 | 5.06 | 1996 | 4.75 | 4.75 |
| 1961 | 1.15 | 6.03 | 1973 | 1.60 | 5.65 | 1985 | 3.35 | 4.88 | 1997 | 5.15 | 5.03 |
| 1962 | 1.15 | 5.97 | 1974 | 2.00 | 6.37 | 1986 | 3.35 | 4.80 | 1998 | 5.15 | 4.96 |
| 1963 | 1.25 | 6.41 | 1975 | 2.10 | 6.12 | 1987 | 3.35 | 4.63 | 1999 | 5.15 | 4.85 |
| 1964 | 1.25 | 6.33 | 1976 | 2.30 | 6.34 | 1988 | 3.35 | 4.44 | 2000 | 5.15 | 4.72 |
| 1965 | 1.25 | 6.23 | 1977 | 2.30 | 5.95 | 1989 | 3.35 | 4.24 | 2001 | 5.15 | 4.56 |
| 1966 | 1.25 | 6.05 | 1978 | 2.65 | 6.38 | 1990 | 3.80 | 4.56 | 2002 | 5.15 | n.a. |

NOTE: n.a. = not available. 1. Adjusted for inflation using the CPI-U (Consumer Price Index for All Urban Consumers). *Source:* Web: www.dol.gov/esa/public/minwage.

## Median Income of Households by Selected Characteristics, 2000

| Characteristic | Number (thousands) | Median income | Characteristic | Number (thousands) | Median income |
|---|---|---|---|---|---|
| **All households** | **106,417** | **$42,148** | 35 to 44 | 23,904 | $53,240 |
| **Type of household** | | | 45 to 54 | 21,797 | 58,218 |
| Family households | 72,375 | 51,751 | 55 to 64 | 13,943 | 44,992 |
| Married-couple families | 55,598 | 59,346 | 65 and over | 21,828 | 23,048 |
| Female householder, no husband present | 12,525 | 28,116 | **Region** | | |
| | | | Northeast | 20,212 | 45,106 |
| Male householder, no wife present | 4,252 | 42,128 | Midwest | 24,497 | 44,646 |
| Nonfamily households | 34,042 | 25,438 | South | 38,525 | 38,410 |
| Female householder | 18,824 | 20,929 | West | 23,183 | 44,744 |
| Male householder | 15,218 | 31,267 | **Earnings of full-time, year-round workers** | | |
| **Race and Hispanic origin of householder** | | | Male | 58,731 | 37,339 |
| White | 88,545 | 44,226 | Female | 41,567 | 27,355 |
| Non-Hispanic | 79,376 | 45,904 | **Per capita income** | | |
| Black | 13,352 | 30,439 | All races[1] | 276,540 | 22,199 |
| Asian and Pacific Islander | 3,527 | 55,521 | White | 226,401 | 23,415 |
| Hispanic origin[2] | 9,663 | 33,447 | Non-Hispanic | 194,161 | 25,278 |
| **Age of householder** | | | Black | 35,919 | 15,197 |
| 15 to 24 | 6,392 | 27,689 | Asian and Pacific Islander | 11,384 | 22,352 |
| 25 to 34 | 18,554 | 44,473 | Hispanic origin[2] | 33,863 | 12,306 |

1. Data for American Indians and Alaska Natives are not shown separately in this table. 2. Persons of Hispanic origin may be of any race. *Source:* U.S. Bureau of the Census, *Money Income in the United States: 2000.* Web: www.census.gov.

## Median Four-Person Family Income
### (in current dollars)

| Year | Income | Percent change | Year | Income | Percent change | Year | Income | Percent change |
|---|---|---|---|---|---|---|---|---|
| 2000 | $65,381 | 5.2% | 1991 | $43,056 | 0.0% | 1982 | $27,619 | 5.1% |
| 1999 | 59,981 | 4.7 | 1990 | 41,151 | 1.7 | 1981 | 26,274 | 8.0 |
| 1998 | 56,061 | 3.5 | 1989 | 40,763 | 4.4 | 1980 | 24,332 | 8.6 |
| 1997 | 53,350 | 3.6 | 1988 | 39,051 | 6.1 | 1979 | 22,395 | 9.6 |
| 1996 | 51,518 | 3.7 | 1987 | 36,812 | 6.0 | 1978 | 20,428 | 9.1 |
| 1995 | 49,687 | 5.7 | 1986 | 34,716 | 5.9 | 1977 | 18,723 | 8.1 |
| 1994 | 47,012 | 4.1 | 1985 | 32,777 | 5.4 | 1976 | 17,315 | 9.3 |
| 1993 | 45,161 | 2.1 | 1984 | 31,097 | 6.6 | 1975 | 15,848 | 7.5 |
| 1992 | 44,251 | 2.8 | 1983 | 29,184 | 5.7 | | | |

*Source:* Income Statistics Branch/HHES Division, U.S. Bureau of the Census. Web: www.census.gov.

## Per Capita Personal Income

| Year | Amount | Year | Amount | Year | Amount | Year | Amount | Year | Amount | Year | Amount |
|------|--------|------|--------|------|--------|------|--------|------|--------|------|--------|
| 1935 | $ 474 | 1965 | $2,773 | 1981 | $10,949 | 1986 | $15,122 | 1991 | $19,652 | 1996 | $24,651 |
| 1945 | 1,223 | 1970 | 3,893 | 1982 | 11,731 | 1987 | 15,968 | 1992 | 20,576 | 1997 | 25,924 |
| 1950 | 1,501 | 1975 | 5,851 | 1983 | 12,352 | 1988 | 17,052 | 1993 | 21,231 | 1998 | 27,203 |
| 1955 | 1,881 | 1979 | 8,638 | 1984 | 13,585 | 1989 | 18,176 | 1994 | 22,086 | 1999 | 28,546 |
| 1960 | 2,219 | 1980 | 9,910 | 1985 | 14,427 | 1990 | 19,188 | 1995 | 23,562 | 2000 | 29,469 |

*Source:* U.S. Department of Commerce, Bureau of Economic Analysis, *Survey of Current Business.* Web: www.bea.doc.gov/bea/regional/spi/.

## Distribution of Household Income by Race

| Income range | White | | | Black | | | Hispanic origin[1] | | |
|---|---|---|---|---|---|---|---|---|---|
| | 1972 | 1985 | 2000 | 1972 | 1985 | 2000 | 1972 | 1985 | 2000 |
| Number of households (thousands) | 60,618 | 76,576 | 88,545 | 6,809 | 9,797 | 13,352 | 2,655 | 5,213 | 9,663 |
| **Percent distribution** | | | | | | | | | |
| Under $5,000 | 3.6% | 2.9% | 2.3% | 8.3% | 7.7% | 6.1% | 3.8% | 4.9% | 3.3% |
| $5,000 to $9,999 | 7.9 | 7.4 | 5.5 | 15.4 | 17.0 | 10.4 | 8.6 | 11.8 | 7.3 |
| $10,000 to $14,999 | 7.5 | 7.3 | 6.6 | 13.0 | 11.2 | 9.5 | 12.1 | 11.4 | 8.3 |
| $15,000 to $24,999 | 14.1 | 14.7 | 13.0 | 20.0 | 18.7 | 16.5 | 20.7 | 18.8 | 18.3 |
| $25,000 to $34,999 | 15.0 | 13.8 | 12.6 | 15.6 | 13.4 | 12.9 | 20.5 | 15.4 | 14.7 |
| $35,000 to $49,999 | 20.9 | 18.2 | 15.4 | 13.7 | 14.1 | 16.8 | 18.9 | 16.8 | 17.7 |
| $50,000 to $74,999 | 19.7 | 19.2 | 19.4 | 10.9 | 11.4 | 15.2 | 11.4 | 13.1 | 17.4 |
| $75,000 to $99,999 | 6.8 | 9.2 | 11.0 | 2.2 | 4.5 | 6.5 | 2.6 | 5.3 | 7.4 |
| $100,000 and over | 4.6 | 7.4 | 14.2 | 1.0 | 1.9 | 6.1 | 1.5 | 2.5 | 5.8 |
| Median income | $36,510 | $38,226 | $44,226 | $21,311 | $22,742 | $30,439 | $27,552 | $26,803 | $33,447 |

1. Persons of Hispanic origin may be of any race. *Source:* U.S. Bureau of the Census. *Current Population Reports,* P60-206. Sept. 2001. Web: www.census.gov/hhes/www/income.html.

## Per Capita Personal Income by State

| State | 1980 | 1990 | 1995 | 2000 | State | 1980 | 1990 | 1995 | 2000 |
|---|---|---|---|---|---|---|---|---|---|
| Alabama | $ 7,465 | $14,899 | $19,683 | $23,521 | Montana | $ 8,342 | $14,743 | $18,764 | $22,518 |
| Alaska | 13,007 | 20,887 | 25,798 | 29,642 | Nebraska | 8,895 | 17,379 | 22,196 | 27,630 |
| Arizona | 8,854 | 16,262 | 20,634 | 24,988 | Nevada | 10,848 | 20,248 | 25,808 | 29,506 |
| Arkansas | 7,113 | 13,779 | 18,546 | 21,995 | New Hampshire | 9,150 | 20,231 | 25,008 | 33,169 |
| California | 11,021 | 20,656 | 24,496 | 32,149 | New Jersey | 10,966 | 24,182 | 29,277 | 37,118 |
| Colorado | 10,143 | 18,818 | 24,865 | 32,434 | New Mexico | 7,940 | 14,213 | 18,852 | 21,931 |
| Connecticut | 11,532 | 25,426 | 31,947 | 40,702 | New York | 10,179 | 22,322 | 27,721 | 34,689 |
| Delaware | 10,059 | 19,719 | 25,391 | 31,012 | North Carolina | 7,780 | 16,284 | 21,938 | 26,882 |
| DC | 12,251 | 24,643 | 33,045 | 38,838 | North Dakota | 8,642 | 15,320 | 19,084 | 24,708 |
| Florida | 9,246 | 18,785 | 23,512 | 27,764 | Ohio | 9,399 | 17,547 | 22,887 | 27,977 |
| Georgia | 8,021 | 17,121 | 22,230 | 27,794 | Oklahoma | 9,018 | 15,117 | 19,394 | 23,650 |
| Hawaii | 10,129 | 20,905 | 25,584 | 27,851 | Oregon | 9,309 | 17,201 | 22,668 | 27,660 |
| Idaho | 8,105 | 15,304 | 19,630 | 23,727 | Pennsylvania | 9,353 | 18,884 | 23,738 | 29,504 |
| Illinois | 10,454 | 20,159 | 25,643 | 31,856 | Rhode Island | 9,227 | 19,035 | 24,046 | 29,113 |
| Indiana | 8,914 | 16,815 | 21,845 | 26,933 | South Carolina | 7,392 | 15,101 | 19,473 | 24,000 |
| Iowa | 9,226 | 16,683 | 21,181 | 26,431 | South Dakota | 7,800 | 15,628 | 19,848 | 25,958 |
| Kansas | 9,880 | 17,639 | 21,889 | 27,374 | Tennessee | 7,711 | 15,903 | 21,800 | 25,946 |
| Kentucky | 7,679 | 14,751 | 19,215 | 24,085 | Texas | 9,439 | 16,747 | 21,526 | 27,752 |
| Louisiana | 8,412 | 14,279 | 19,541 | 23,090 | Utah | 7,671 | 14,063 | 18,858 | 23,436 |
| Maine | 7,760 | 17,041 | 20,240 | 25,380 | Vermont | 7,957 | 17,444 | 21,359 | 26,848 |
| Maryland | 10,394 | 22,088 | 26,896 | 33,482 | Virginia | 9,413 | 19,543 | 24,456 | 31,120 |
| Massachusetts | 10,103 | 22,248 | 28,051 | 37,704 | Washington | 10,256 | 19,268 | 23,878 | 31,230 |
| Michigan | 9,801 | 18,239 | 23,975 | 29,127 | West Virginia | 7,764 | 13,964 | 17,913 | 21,738 |
| Minnesota | 9,673 | 18,784 | 24,583 | 31,935 | Wisconsin | 9,364 | 17,399 | 22,573 | 28,100 |
| Mississippi | 6,573 | 12,578 | 17,185 | 20,900 | Wyoming | 11,018 | 16,905 | 21,514 | 27,372 |
| Missouri | 8,812 | 17,407 | 22,094 | 27,206 | **United States** | **9,494** | **18,667** | **23,562** | **29,469** |

NOTE: Per capita personal income was computed using midyear population estimates of the Bureau of the Census. *Source:* U.S. Department of Commerce, Bureau of Economic Analysis, *Survey of Current Business.* Web: www.bea.doc.gov/bea/regional/spi/.

## Consumer Credit Outstanding[1]
### (in billions of dollars)

| | Total | Commercial banks | Finance companies | Credit unions | Savings institutions | Nonfinancial business | Pools of securitized assets[2] |
|---|---|---|---|---|---|---|---|
| 1975 | $ 168.7 | $ 82.9 | $ 32.7 | $ 25.7 | n.a. | n.a. | n.a. |
| 1980 | 302.1 | 147.0 | 62.3 | 44.0 | n.a. | n.a. | n.a. |
| 1985 | 526.3 | 245.1 | 111.7 | 72.7 | n.a. | n.a. | n.a. |
| 1990 | 751.9 | 347.1 | 133.3 | 93.1 | n.a. | n.a. | n.a. |
| 1995 | 1,122.8 | 502.0 | 152.1 | 131.9 | $40.1 | $85.1 | $211.6 |
| 1999 | 1,426.2 | 499.8 | 181.6 | 167.9 | 61.5 | 80.3 | 435.1 |
| 2000 | 1,566.5 | 541.5 | 193.2 | 184.4 | 64.6 | 82.7 | 500.1 |
| 2001 | 1,702.8 | 558.0 | 236.5 | 189.6 | 69.1 | 67.9 | 581.7 |

1. Covers most short- and intermediate-term credit extended to individuals, excluding loans secured by real estate. 2. Outstanding balances of pools upon which securities have been issued; these balances are no longer carried on the balance sheets of the loan originators. n.a. = not available. *Source:* Federal Reserve Board. Web http://www.federalreserve.gov/default.htm.

# Poverty in the United States

*Source:* U.S. Bureau of the Census March 2001 supplement to the Current Population Survey (CPS). Web: www.census.gov.

The poverty rate in 2000 dropped to 11.3%, down half a percentage point from 1999. This rate was not statistically different from the record low of 11.1% set in 1973. About 31.1 million people were poor in 2000, 1.1 million fewer than in 1999.

The decrease in poverty between 1999 and 2000 was not concentrated in any one region of the United States, although the poverty rate did fall significantly for those living in metropolitan areas but outside of central cities (7.8% in 2000, down from 8.3% in 1999).

Compared with the most recent poverty-rate peak in 1993, a greater percentage of people in 2000 lived in families with at least one worker, and the poverty rate for people in these families fell since 1993; however, poor family members in 2000 were more likely to be living with at least one worker.

Several groups set record-low poverty rates in 2000, while others tied their record-lows:

• The poverty rate for people under 18 years old dropped to 16.2% in 2000 (down from 16.9% in 1999)—their lowest poverty rate since 1979. The poverty rate declined more for 18- to 24-year-olds than for any other age group.

• Blacks (22.1%) and female-householder families (24.7%) had their lowest measured poverty rates in 2000.

• People 65 years old and over (10.2%), Asians and Pacific Islanders (10.8%), Hispanics (21.2%), white non-Hispanics (7.5%), married-couple families (4.7%), and people living in the South (12.5%) had poverty rates in 2000 that were not statistically different from their measured lows.

• Poverty rates fell for blacks (from 23.6% to 22.1%) and Hispanics (from 22.8% to 21.2%) between 1999 and 2000.

• While blacks remained disproportionately poor, the difference in poverty rates between blacks and white non-Hispanics narrowed since the most recent poverty-rate peak. In 1993, the black poverty rate was 23.2 percentage points higher than that for white non-Hispanics; by 2000 this difference had fallen to 14.6 percentage points.

## Weighted Average Poverty Thresholds[1] for Families of Specified Size, 1960–2000

| Calendar year | Individual | Families of 2 persons or more | | | | | |
|---|---|---|---|---|---|---|---|
| | | 2 persons[2] | 3 persons | 4 persons | 5 persons | 6 persons | 7 persons |
| 1960 | $1,490 | $ 1,924 | $ 2,359 | $ 3,022 | $ 3,560 | $ 4,002 | $ 4,921[3] |
| 1965 | 1,582 | 2,048 | 2,514 | 3,223 | 3,797 | 4,091 | 5,741 |
| 1970 | 1,954 | 2,525 | 3,099 | 3,968 | 4,680 | 5,260 | 6,468[3] |
| 1975 | 2,724 | 3,506 | 4,293 | 5,500 | 6,499 | 7,316 | 9,022[3] |
| 1980 | 4,190 | 5,363 | 6,565 | 8,414 | 9,966 | 11,269 | 12,761 |
| 1985 | 5,469 | 6,998 | 8,573 | 10,989 | 13,007 | 14,696 | 16,656 |
| 1990 | 6,652 | 8,509 | 10,419 | 13,359 | 15,792 | 17,839 | 20,241 |
| 1995 | 7,763 | 9,933 | 12,158 | 15,569 | 18,408 | 20,804 | 23,552 |
| 1996 | 7,995 | 10,223 | 12,516 | 16,036 | 18,952 | 21,389 | 24,268 |
| 1997 | 8,183 | 10,473 | 12,802 | 16,400 | 19,380 | 21,886 | 24,802 |
| 1998 | 8,316 | 10,634 | 13,003 | 16,660 | 19,680 | 22,228 | 25,257 |
| 1999 | 8,501 | 10,869 | 13,290 | 17,029 | 20,127 | 22,727 | 25,912 |
| 2000 | 8,959 | 11,531 | 13,470 | 17,761 | 21,419 | 24,636 | 28,347 |
| 2001 | 9,214 | 11,859 | 13,853 | 18,267 | 22,029 | 25,337 | 29,154 |

1. Annual income. 2. Householder under 65 years. 3. For years before 1980, data are for families with seven persons or more. *Source:* U.S. Bureau of the Census. Web: www.census.gov.

## Persons Below Poverty Level, 1975–2000
### (in thousands)

| Year | All persons | Percent | White | Percent | Black | Percent | Hispanic origin[1] | Percent | Asian and Pac. Isl. | Percent |
|---|---|---|---|---|---|---|---|---|---|---|
| 1975 | 25,877 | 12.3% | 17,770 | 9.7% | 7,545 | 31.3% | 2,991 | 26.9% | n.a. | n.a. |
| 1976 | 24,975 | 11.8 | 16,713 | 9.1 | 7,595 | 31.1 | 2,783 | 24.7 | n.a. | n.a. |
| 1977 | 24,720 | 11.6 | 16,416 | 8.9 | 7,726 | 31.3 | 2,700 | 22.4 | n.a. | n.a. |
| 1978 | 24,497 | 11.4 | 16,259 | 8.7 | 7,625 | 30.6 | 2,607 | 21.6 | n.a. | n.a. |
| 1979 | 26,072 | 11.7 | 17,214 | 9.0 | 8,050 | 31.0 | 2,921 | 21.8 | n.a. | n.a. |
| 1980 | 29,272 | 13.0 | 19,699 | 10.2 | 8,579 | 32.5 | 3,491 | 25.7 | n.a. | n.a. |
| 1981 | 31,822 | 14.0 | 21,553 | 11.1 | 9,173 | 34.2 | 3,713 | 26.5 | n.a. | n.a. |
| 1982 | 34,398 | 15.0 | 23,517 | 12.0 | 9,697 | 35.6 | 4,301 | 29.9 | n.a. | n.a. |
| 1983 | 35,303 | 15.2 | 23,984 | 12.1 | 9,882 | 35.7 | 4,633 | 28.0 | n.a. | n.a. |
| 1984 | 33,700 | 14.4 | 22,955 | 11.5 | 9,490 | 33.8 | 4,806 | 28.4 | n.a. | n.a. |
| 1985 | 33,064 | 14.0 | 22,860 | 11.4 | 8,926 | 31.3 | 5,236 | 29.0 | n.a. | n.a. |
| 1986 | 32,370 | 13.6 | 22,183 | 11.0 | 8,983 | 31.1 | 5,117 | 27.3 | n.a. | n.a. |
| 1987 | 32,221 | 13.4 | 21,195 | 10.4 | 9,520 | 32.4 | 5,422 | 28.0 | 1,021 | 16.1% |
| 1988 | 31,745 | 13.0 | 20,715 | 10.1 | 9,356 | 31.3 | 5,357 | 26.7 | 1,117 | 17.3 |
| 1989 | 31,528 | 12.8 | 20,785 | 10.0 | 9,525 | 30.7 | 6,086 | 26.2 | 939 | 14.1 |
| 1990 | 33,585 | 13.5 | 22,326 | 10.7 | 9,837 | 31.9 | 6,006 | 28.1 | 858 | 12.2 |
| 1991 | 35,708 | 14.2 | 23,747 | 11.3 | 10,242 | 32.7 | 6,339 | 28.7 | 996 | 13.8 |
| 1992 | 38,014 | 14.8 | 25,259 | 11.9 | 10,827 | 33.4 | 7,592 | 29.6 | 985 | 12.7 |
| 1993 | 39,265 | 15.1 | 26,226 | 12.2 | 10,877 | 33.1 | 8,126 | 30.6 | 1,134 | 15.3 |
| 1994 | 38,059 | 14.5 | 25,379 | 11.7 | 10,196 | 30.6 | 8,416 | 30.7 | 974 | 14.6 |
| 1995 | 36,425 | 13.8 | 24,423 | 11.2 | 9,872 | 29.3 | 8,574 | 30.3 | 1,411 | 14.6 |
| 1996 | 36,529 | 13.7 | 24,650 | 11.2 | 9,694 | 28.4 | 8,697 | 29.4 | 1,454 | 14.5 |
| 1997 | 35,574 | 13.3 | 24,396 | 11.0 | 9,116 | 26.5 | 8,308 | 27.1 | 1,468 | 14.0 |
| 1998 | 34,476 | 12.7 | 23,454 | 10.5 | 9,091 | 26.1 | 8,070 | 25.6 | 1,360 | 12.5 |
| 1999 | 32,258 | 11.8 | 21,922 | 9.8 | 8,360 | 23.6 | 7,439 | 22.8 | 1,163 | 10.7 |
| 2000 | 31,139 | 11.3 | 21,291 | 9.4 | 7,901 | 22.1 | 7,155 | 21.2 | 1,226 | 10.8 |

n.a. = not available. 1. Persons of Hispanic origin may be of any race. *Source:* U.S. Bureau of the Census. Web: www.census.gov.

## Percent of People in Poverty by State, 1998–2000

| State | 3-year average 1998–2000 | Average 1999–2000 | Average 1998–1999 | State | 3-year average 1998–2000 | Average 1999–2000 | Average 1998–1999 |
|---|---|---|---|---|---|---|---|
| United States | 11.9% | 11.5% | 12.3% | Missouri | 9.7% | 9.7% | 10.7% |
| Alabama | 14.6 | 14.6 | 14.8 | Montana | 16.0 | 15.8 | 16.1 |
| Alaska | 8.3 | 7.8 | 8.5 | Nebraska | 10.6 | 9.8 | 11.6 |
| Arizona | 13.6 | 12.0 | 14.3 | Nevada | 10.0 | 9.7 | 10.9 |
| Arkansas | 15.8 | 16.4 | 14.7 | New Hampshire | 7.4 | 6.3 | 8.8 |
| California | 14.0 | 13.3 | 14.6 | New Jersey | 8.1 | 7.9 | 8.2 |
| Colorado | 8.5 | 8.1 | 8.7 | New Mexico | 19.3 | 18.7 | 20.5 |
| Connecticut | 7.6 | 6.7 | 8.3 | New York | 14.7 | 13.8 | 15.4 |
| Delaware | 9.8 | 9.5 | 10.3 | North Carolina | 13.2 | 12.9 | 13.8 |
| DC | 17.3 | 14.8 | 18.6 | North Dakota | 12.7 | 11.5 | 14.1 |
| Florida | 12.1 | 11.5 | 12.8 | Ohio | 11.1 | 11.1 | 11.6 |
| Georgia | 12.6 | 12.1 | 13.2 | Oklahoma | 14.1 | 14.0 | 13.4 |
| Hawaii | 10.5 | 10.3 | 10.9 | Oregon | 12.8 | 11.6 | 13.8 |
| Idaho | 13.3 | 13.5 | 13.5 | Pennsylvania | 9.9 | 9.2 | 10.3 |
| Illinois | 10.5 | 10.8 | 10.0 | Rhode Island | 10.0 | 9.2 | 10.7 |
| Indiana | 8.2 | 7.6 | 8.0 | South Carolina | 11.9 | 11.0 | 12.7 |
| Iowa | 7.9 | 7.3 | 8.3 | South Dakota | 9.3 | 8.6 | 9.3 |
| Kansas | 10.4 | 10.8 | 10.9 | Tennessee | 13.3 | 13.3 | 12.7 |
| Kentucky | 12.5 | 11.9 | 12.8 | Texas | 14.9 | 14.9 | 15.0 |
| Louisiana | 18.6 | 18.3 | 19.1 | Utah | 8.1 | 7.6 | 7.3 |
| Maine | 9.8 | 9.5 | 10.5 | Vermont | 10.1 | 10.2 | 9.8 |
| Maryland | 7.3 | 7.4 | 7.2 | Virginia | 8.1 | 7.8 | 8.4 |
| Massachusetts | 10.2 | 10.9 | 10.2 | Washington | 9.4 | 9.6 | 9.2 |
| Michigan | 10.2 | 9.9 | 10.3 | West Virginia | 15.8 | 14.8 | 16.8 |
| Minnesota | 7.8 | 6.6 | 8.8 | Wisconsin | 8.8 | 8.9 | 8.7 |
| Mississippi | 15.5 | 14.5 | 16.9 | Wyoming | 11.0 | 11.2 | 11.1 |

*Source:* U.S. Census Bureau, *Poverty in the United States, 2000.* Web: www.census.gov.

## People and Families in Poverty by Selected Characteristics, 1999 and 2000

| Characteristic | 2000 | | 1999 | |
| --- | --- | --- | --- | --- |
| | Number (thousands) | Percent[1] | Number (thousands) | Percent |
| **PEOPLE** | | | | |
| **Total** | **31,139** | **11.3%** | **32,258** | **11.8%** |
| Race[2] and Hispanic origin | | | | |
| White | 21,291 | 9.4 | 21,922 | 9.8 |
| Non-Hispanic | 14,572 | 7.5 | 14,875 | 7.7 |
| Black | 7,901 | 22.1 | 8,360 | 23.6 |
| Asian and Pacific Islander | 1,226 | 10.8 | 1,163 | 10.7 |
| Hispanic[3] | 7,155 | 21.2 | 7,439 | 22.8 |
| Age | | | | |
| Under 18 | 11,633 | 16.2 | 12,109 | 16.9 |
| 18 to 64 | 16,146 | 9.4 | 16,982 | 10.0 |
| 18 to 24 | 3,893 | 14.4 | 4,603 | 17.3 |
| 25 to 34 | 3,892 | 10.4 | 3,968 | 10.5 |
| 35 to 44 | 3,678 | 8.2 | 3,733 | 8.3 |
| 45 to 54 | 2,441 | 6.4 | 2,466 | 6.7 |
| 55 to 59 | 1,175 | 8.8 | 1,179 | 9.2 |
| 60 to 64 | 1,066 | 10.2 | 1,033 | 9.8 |
| 65 and over | 3,360 | 10.2 | 3,167 | 9.7 |
| Region | | | | |
| Northeast | 5,433 | 10.3 | 5,678 | 10.9 |
| Midwest | 5,971 | 9.5 | 6,210 | 9.8 |
| South | 12,205 | 12.5 | 12,538 | 13.1 |
| West | 7,530 | 11.9 | 7,833 | 12.6 |
| **FAMILIES** | | | | |
| **Total** | **6,226** | **8.6** | **6,676** | **9.3** |
| White | 4,153 | 6.9 | 4,377 | 7.3 |
| Non-Hispanic | 2,820 | 5.3 | 2,942 | 5.5 |
| Black | 1,686 | 19.1 | 1,898 | 21.9 |
| Asian and Pacific Islander | 235 | 8.8 | 258 | 10.3 |
| Hispanic[3] | 1,431 | 18.5 | 1,525 | 20.2 |

1. Percentage of total population. 2. Data for American Indians and Alaska Natives are not shown separately. 3. Hispanics may be of any race. *Source:* U.S. Census Bureau, *Current Population Survey,* March 2000 and 2001.

## Social Welfare Expenditures Under Public Programs
### (in millions of dollars)

| Item | 1965 | 1970 | 1975 | 1980 | 1985 | 1990 | 1995 |
| --- | --- | --- | --- | --- | --- | --- | --- |
| **Amount** | | | | | | | |
| Gross domestic product | $701,000 | $1,023,100 | $1,590,800 | $2,718,900 | $4,108,000 | $5,682,900 | $7,186,900 |
| Total social welfare expenditures[1] | 77,084 | 145,979 | 288,967 | 492,213 | 731,840 | 1,048,951 | 1,505,136 |
| Social insurance | 28,123 | 54,691 | 123,013 | 229,754 | 369,595 | 513,822 | 705,483 |
| Public aid | 6,283 | 16,488 | 41,447 | 72,703 | 98,362 | 146,811 | 253,530 |
| Health and medical programs | 6,155 | 10,030 | 16,535 | 26,762 | 38,643 | 61,684 | 85,507 |
| Veterans' programs | 6,031 | 9,078 | 17,019 | 21,466 | 27,042 | 30,916 | 39,072 |
| Education | 28,108 | 50,846 | 80,834 | 121,050 | 172,048 | 258,332 | 365,625 |
| Housing | 318 | 701 | 3,172 | 6,879 | 12,598 | 19,468 | 29,361 |
| Other social welfare | 2,066 | 4,145 | 6,947 | 13,599 | 13,552 | 17,918 | 26,558 |
| All health and medical care[2] | 9,302 | 24,801 | 51,022 | 99,145 | 170,665 | 274,472 | 435,075 |
| **As percent of gross domestic product** | | | | | | | |
| Gross domestic product | 100.0% | 100.0% | 100.0% | 100.0% | 100.0% | 100.0% | 100.0% |
| Total social welfare expenditures | 11.0 | 14.3 | 18.2 | 18.1 | 17.8 | 18.5 | 20.9 |
| Social insurance | 4.0 | 5.3 | 7.7 | 8.5 | 9.0 | 9.0 | 9.8 |
| Public aid | .9 | 1.6 | 2.6 | 2.7 | 2.4 | 2.6 | 3.5 |
| Health and medical programs | .0 | 1.0 | 1.0 | 1.0 | .9 | 1.1 | 1.2 |
| Veterans' programs | .9 | .9 | 1.1 | .8 | .7 | .5 | .5 |
| Education | 4.0 | 5.0 | 5.1 | 4.5 | 4.2 | 4.5 | 5.1 |
| Housing | (3) | .1 | .2 | .3 | .3 | .3 | .4 |
| Other social welfare | .3 | .4 | .4 | .5 | .3 | .3 | .4 |
| All health and medical care | 1.3 | 2.4 | 3.2 | 3.6 | 4.2 | 4.8 | 6.1 |

NOTES: Through 1976, fiscal year ended June 30 for federal government, most states, and some localities. Beginning in 1977, federal fiscal year ended Sept. 30. 1. Represents program and administrative expenditures from federal, state, and local public revenues and trust funds under public law. Includes workers' compensation and temporary disability insurance payments made through private carriers and self-insurers. Includes capital outlay and some expenditures abroad. 2. Combines "health and medical programs" with medical services provided in connection with social insurance, public aid, veterans', and "other social welfare" categories. 3. Less than 0.05%. *Source:* Social Security Administration. Web: www.ssa.gov/statistics/Supplement/1999/tables/index.html.

## Drop in Welfare Rolls, 1993–2000

| | Number of families on welfare Jan. 1993 | Number of families on welfare June 2000 | Percent reduction 1993–2000 | | Number of families on welfare Jan. 1993 | Number of families on welfare June 2000 | Percent reduction 1993–2000 |
|---|---|---|---|---|---|---|---|
| Alabama | 51,910 | 18,677 | –64% | Nebraska | 16,637 | 10,088 | –39% |
| Alaska | 11,626 | 7,542 | –35 | Nevada | 12,892 | 6,916 | –46 |
| Arizona | 68,982 | 31,897 | –54 | New Hampshire | 10,805 | 5,791 | –46 |
| Arkansas | 26,897 | 12,046 | –55 | New Jersey | 126,179 | 50,126 | –60 |
| California | 844,494 | 489,054 | –42 | New Mexico | 31,103 | 22,701 | –27 |
| Colorado | 42,445 | 10,772 | –75 | New York | 428,191 | 248,148 | –42 |
| Connecticut | 56,759 | 27,149 | –52 | North Carolina | 128,946 | 44,731 | –65 |
| Delaware | 11,315 | 5,819 | –49 | North Dakota | 6,577 | 2,887 | –56 |
| DC | 24,628 | 22,397 | –09 | Ohio | 257,665 | 95,835 | –63 |
| Florida | 256,145 | 62,805 | –75 | Oklahoma | 50,955 | 7,251 | –86 |
| Georgia | 142,040 | 51,215 | –64 | Oregon | 42,409 | 17,121 | –60 |
| Guam | 1,406 | 2,760 | 96 | Pennsylvania | 204,216 | 87,972 | –57 |
| Hawaii | 17,869 | 14,942 | –16 | Puerto Rico | 60,950 | 31,273 | –49 |
| Idaho | 7,838 | 1,382 | –82 | Rhode Island | 21,900 | 16,324 | –25 |
| Illinois | 229,308 | 85,807 | –63 | South Carolina | 54,599 | 15,496 | –72 |
| Indiana | 73,115 | 35,068 | –52 | South Dakota | 7,262 | 2,789 | –62 |
| Iowa | 36,515 | 20,082 | –45 | Tennessee | 112,159 | 55,491 | –51 |
| Kansas | 29,818 | 12,404 | –58 | Texas | 279,002 | 128,289 | –54 |
| Kentucky | 83,320 | 37,471 | –55 | Utah | 18,606 | 8,157 | –56 |
| Louisiana | 89,931 | 25,521 | –72 | Vermont | 10,081 | 5,858 | –42 |
| Maine | 23,903 | 10,654 | –55 | Virgin Islands | 1,073 | 778 | –27 |
| Maryland | 80,256 | 28,895 | –64 | Virginia | 73,446 | 30,078 | –59 |
| Massachusetts | 113,571 | 41,682 | –63 | Washington | 100,568 | 54,768 | –46 |
| Michigan | 228,377 | 70,897 | –69 | West Virginia | 41,525 | 10,661 | –74 |
| Minnesota | 63,995 | 39,295 | –39 | Wisconsin | 81,291 | 16,410 | –80 |
| Mississippi | 60,520 | 14,979 | –75 | Wyoming | 6,493 | 565 | –91 |
| Missouri | 88,744 | 45,912 | –48 | **U.S. total** | **4,963,050** | **2,208,095** | **–56** |
| Montana | 11,793 | 4,467 | –62 | | | | |

*Source:* U.S. Dept. of Health and Human Services, Administration for Children and Families. Web: www.acf.dhhs.gov.

# Social Security

*Source:* Social Security Administration

The original Social Security Act was passed in 1935 and is administered by the Social Security Administration and other agencies within the Department of Health and Human Services.

## What Does Social Security Offer?

The Social Security contribution you pay gives you four different kinds of protection: (1) retirement benefits, (2) survivors' benefits, (3) disability benefits, and (4) Medicare hospital insurance benefits.

### Retirement Benefits

Currently, as a worker you become eligible for the full amount of your retirement benefits at age 65. You may retire at age 62 and get 80% of your full benefit. The closer you are to age 65 when you start collecting your benefit, the larger the fraction of your full benefit you will get.

The amount of the retirement benefit you are entitled to at age 65 is the key to all other benefits under the program. The retirement benefit is based on covered earnings, which will be updated (indexed) to reflect the increases in average wages that have occurred since the earnings were paid. Your largest 35 years of adjusted earnings are averaged together and a formula is applied to the adjusted average to figure the benefit rate.

In general, the highest retirement check that can be paid to a worker who retired at 65 in Jan. 2002 is

about $1,660 a month. Maximum payment to the family of this retired worker was about $2,324.40 as of Jan. 1997.

### Survivor Benefits

This feature of the Social Security program gives your family valuable life-insurance protection. The amount of protection is again geared to what the worker would be entitled to if he had been age 65 when he died. Total family survivor benefits were estimated to be as high as $2,534.00 a month if the worker died in 1995. Your survivors could get:

1. A one-time cash payment of $255 for your spouse or minor children if you have enough work credits.
2. A benefit for each child until he or she reaches 18 (or 19, if the child is in full-time attendance at an elementary or secondary school), or at any age if disabled before 22. "Child" includes biological or legally adopted children, or dependent stepchildren or grandchildren.
3. A benefit for your widow(er), at any age, if she/he has your entitled children under 16 or disabled in care.
4. Your spouse or divorced spouse can get a widow's, widower's, or surviving divorced spouse's benefit starting at age 60. A widow, or widower, who first becomes entitled at 65 or later will get 100% of his or her deceased spouse's basic amount (or the amount of the deceased spouse's reduced benefits).

5. Dependent parents can sometimes collect survivors' benefits. They are usually eligible if: (a) they were getting at least half their support from the deceased worker; (b) they have reached 62; (c) they are not eligible for a greater retirement benefit based on their own earnings; and (d) they have not married since the worker's death.

### Disability Benefits

Disability benefits can be paid to several groups of people:

• Disabled workers under age 65 and their families.

• Persons disabled before age 22 who continue to be disabled. These benefits are payable as early as age 18 when a parent (or step-parent or grandparent under certain circumstances) receives Social Security retirement or disability benefits or when an insured parent dies.

• Disabled widows and widowers and (under certain conditions) disabled, surviving, and divorced spouses of workers who were insured at death. These benefits are payable as early as 50. Consult your local Social Security office for the latest disability information.

The SSA determines whether or not you qualify for disability benefits based on criteria including the severity of your condition and the earnings you continue to receive after you become disabled. To be considered for disability benefits, you should file a claim with a Social Security office as soon as you become disabled. However, even if you are approved, benefits will not begin until after a waiting period of six months after the beginning of your disability.

### Medicare Program

Medicare is the nation's largest health insurance program. Generally, you are eligible for Medicare if you or your spouse worked for at least ten years in Medicare-covered employment and you are 65 years old and a citizen or permanent resident of the United States. You might also qualify for coverage if you are a younger person with a disability or with chronic kidney disease.

Medicare-covered services include:

• **Hospital insurance.** Financial assistance is available for necessary medical care and services furnished by Medicare-certified hospitals, skilled nursing facilities, home health agencies, and hospices.

• **Inpatient hospital care.** Medicare helps pay for up to 90 days of inpatient hospital care in each benefit period. Covered services include your semi-private room and meals, general nursing services, operating and recovery room costs, intensive care, drugs, laboratory tests, X rays, and all other necessary medical services and supplies.

• **Skilled nursing facility care.** You may need inpatient skilled nursing or rehabilitation services after a hospital stay. If you meet certain conditions, Medicare will help pay for up to 100 days in a participating skilled nursing facility in each benefit period.

• **Home health care.** If you meet certain conditions, Medicare pays the full approved cost of covered home health care services. This includes part-time or intermittent skilled nursing services prescribed by a physician for treatment or rehabilitation of homebound patients.

• **Hospice care.** Medicare helps pay for hospice care for terminally ill beneficiaries who select the hospice care benefit.

• **Medical insurance (Part B).** Medicare Part B helps pay for doctor's services, outpatient hospital services (including emergency room visits), ambulance transportation, diagnostic tests, laboratory services, some preventive care like mammography and Pap smear screening, outpatient therapy services, durable medical equipment and supplies, and a variety of other health services.

Additional benefits are available through the Medicare program. For further information contact the Social Security Administration at 1-800-772-1213.

## Average Monthly Social Security Benefits, 1940–2000

| | Retired workers | | | Disabled workers | | | Non-disabled widows |
|---|---|---|---|---|---|---|---|
| Year | Total | Men | Women | Total | Men | Women | |
| 1940 | $ 22.71 | $ 23.26 | $ 18.38 | — | — | — | $ 20.36 |
| 1945 | 25.11 | 25.71 | 19.00 | — | — | — | 20.19 |
| 1950 | 90.00 | 90.10 | 44.08 | — | — | — | 21.65 |
| 1955 | 69.74 | 75.86 | 56.05 | — | — | — | 49.68 |
| 1960 | 81.73 | 92.03 | 63.26 | $ 91.16 | $ 94.02 | $ 78.91 | 60.10 |
| 1965 | 90.00 | 90.05 | 68.78 | 98.26 | 97.80 | 80.27 | 73.81 |
| 1970 | 123.82 | 136.80 | 103.67 | 139.79 | 148.39 | 115.74 | 106.95 |
| 1975[2] | 196.42 | 220.35 | 160.50 | 220.60 | 241.48 | 175.27 | 185.34 |
| 1980[2] | 321.10 | 374.00 | 244.90 | 352.10 | 388.80 | 269.70 | 277.50 |
| 1985[3] | 432.00 | 509.60 | 322.20 | 459.20 | 514.00 | 345.00 | 431.10 |
| 1990[3] | 550.50 | 654.60 | 403.30 | 566.90 | 637.80 | 438.90 | 541.10 |
| 1995[3] | 671.70 | 794.30 | 505.80 | 675.70 | 767.30 | 546.00 | 662.50 |
| 1998[3] | 744.70 | 882.10 | 577.10 | 737.00 | 841.50 | 610.60 | 716.70 |
| 1999 | 757.71 | 904.62 | 697.50 | 754.12 | 846.48 | 629.63 | 776.07 |
| 2000 | 844.60 | 951.50 | 729.60 | 787.00 | 883.00 | 661.10 | 811.80 |

1. Jan.–Aug. 2. Jan.–May. 3. Jan.–Nov. *Source:* Social Security Administration, *Social Security Bulletin: Annual Statistical Supplement, 2001.*

## The Federal Budget, 2000–2004

### (in billions of dollars)

| Description | Actual 2000 | Estimates 2001 | 2002 | 2003 | 2004 |
|---|---|---|---|---|---|
| **Receipts by source** | | | | | |
| Individual income taxes | $1,004.5 | $1,072.9 | $1,078.8 | $1,092.3 | $1,117.9 |
| Corporate income taxes | 207.3 | 213.1 | 218.8 | 227.3 | 235.5 |
| Social insurance and retirement receipts | 652.9 | 689.7 | 725.8 | 766.0 | 806.0 |
| Excise taxes | 68.9 | 71.1 | 74.0 | 76.3 | 78.3 |
| Estate and gift taxes | 29.0 | 31.1 | 28.7 | 26.6 | 28.3 |
| Customs duties and fees | 19.9 | 21.4 | 22.5 | 24.3 | 25.0 |
| Miscellaneous receipts: | 42.8 | 37.6 | 43.1 | 45.4 | 47.8 |
| **Total receipts** | **2,052.2** | **2,136.9** | **2,191.7** | **2,258.2** | **2,338.8** |
| **Outlays by function** | | | | | |
| National defense | 294.5 | 299.1 | 319.2 | 322.1 | 333.1 |
| International affairs | 17.2 | 17.5 | 21.0 | 21.3 | 21.5 |
| General science, space, and technology | 18.6 | 19.7 | 20.8 | 21.4 | 22.2 |
| Energy | −1.1 | −0.7 | −0.3 | −0.1 | −0.6 |
| Natural resources and environment | 25.0 | 27.4 | 27.5 | 27.7 | 28.0 |
| Agriculture | 36.6 | 25.9 | 18.6 | 15.0 | 14.0 |
| Commerce and housing credit | 3.2 | −0.8 | 6.9 | 4.7 | 3.6 |
| Transportation | 46.9 | 51.1 | 55.0 | 57.5 | 59.7 |
| Community and regional development | 10.6 | 10.6 | 11.7 | 11.3 | 10.8 |
| Education, training, employment, and social services | 59.2 | 65.3 | 76.6 | 81.3 | 82.6 |
| Health | 154.5 | 175.3 | 201.5 | 224.4 | 243.3 |
| Medicare | 197.1 | 219.3 | 229.9 | 242.1 | 255.9 |
| Income security | 247.9 | 262.6 | 275.7 | 285.9 | 295.9 |
| Social security | 409.4 | 433.6 | 455.1 | 477.1 | 501.6 |
| Veterans' benefits and services | 47.1 | 45.4 | 51.6 | 53.6 | 55.8 |
| Administration of justice | 27.8 | 29.4 | 32.3 | 35.4 | 35.5 |
| General government | 13.5 | 16.8 | 16.3 | 16.7 | 18.4 |
| Net interest | 223.2 | 206.4 | 188.1 | 175.2 | 161.5 |
| Allowances | — | — | 2.4 | 3.9 | 4.7 |
| Undistributed offsetting receipts | −42.6 | −47.7 | −49.4 | −60.4 | −70.6 |
| **Total outlays** | **1,788.8** | **1,856.2** | **1,960.6** | **2,016.2** | **2,076.7** |

*Source:* Department of the Treasury and Office of Management and Budget.

## Gross Domestic Product or Expenditure, 1930–2001

### (in billions of dollars)

| Item | 1930 | 1940 | 1950 | 1960 | 1970 | 1980 | 1990 | 2000 | 2001[1] |
|---|---|---|---|---|---|---|---|---|---|
| Gross domestic product | $91.3 | $101.3 | $294.3 | $527.4 | $1,039.7 | $2,795.6 | $5,803.2 | $9,872.9 | $10,208.1 |
| Personal consumption expenditures | 70.2 | 71.2 | 192.7 | 332.2 | 648.9 | 1,762.9 | 3,831.5 | 6,728.4 | 7,064.5 |
| Gross private domestic investment | 10.8 | 13.6 | 54.1 | 75.7 | 150.4 | 484.2 | 847.2 | 1,767.5 | 1,633.9 |
| Exports of goods and services | 4.4 | 4.8 | 12.3 | 25.3 | 57.0 | 278.9 | 557.2 | 1,102.9 | 1,050.4 |
| Imports of goods and services | 4.1 | 3.4 | 11.6 | 22.8 | 55.8 | 293.8 | 628.6 | 1,466.9 | 1,380.1 |
| Government | 10.0 | 15.1 | 46.9 | 113.8 | 237.1 | 569.7 | 1,181.4 | 1,741.0 | 1,839.5 |

NOTE: Government consumption expenditures and gross investment. 1. Preliminary data. *Source:* U.S. Bureau of Economic Analysis. Web: www.bea.doc.gov.

## The Public Debt

| Year | Gross debt amount | Year | Gross debt amount | Year | Gross debt amount | Year | Gross debt amount |
|---|---|---|---|---|---|---|---|
| 1800 | $82,976,294 | 1855 | $ 35,586,957 | 1910 | $ 2,652,665,838 | 1965 | $ 320,904,110,042 |
| 1805 | 82,312,151 | 1860 | 64,842,288 | 1915 | 3,058,136,873 | 1970 | 389,158,403,690 |
| 1810 | 53,173,218 | 1865 | 2,680,647,870 | 1920 | 25,952,456,406 | 1975 | 576,649,000,000[1] |
| 1815 | 99,833,660 | 1870 | 2,480,672,428 | 1925 | 20,516,193,888 | 1980 | 930,210,000,000[1] |
| 1820 | 91,015,566 | 1875 | 2,232,284,532 | 1930 | 16,185,309,831 | 1985 | 1,945,941,616,460 |
| 1825 | 83,788,433 | 1880 | 2,120,415,371 | 1935 | 28,700,892,625 | 1990 | 3,233,313,451,777 |
| 1830 | 48,565,407 | 1885 | 1,863,964,873 | 1940 | 42,967,531,038 | 1995 | 4,973,982,900,709 |
| 1835 | 33,733 | 1890 | 1,552,140,205 | 1945 | 258,682,187,410 | 1999 | 5,656,270,901,615 |
| 1840 | 3,573,344 | 1895 | 1,676,120,983 | 1950 | 257,357,352,351 | 2000 | 5,674,178,209,887 |
| 1845 | 15,925,303 | 1900 | 2,136,961,092 | 1955 | 280,768,553,189 | 2001 | 5,807,463,412,200 |
| 1850 | 63,452,774 | 1905 | 2,274,615,064 | 1960 | 290,216,815,242 | | |

NOTE: Figures as of Jan. 1 for years 1800–1840; as of July 1 for years 1845–1920; as of June 30 for years 1925–1950; as of Dec. 31 for years 1955–1985; as of Sept. 30 for years 1990–present. 1. Rounded to millions. *Source:* U.S. Department of the Treasury, The Public Debt Online. Web: www.publicdebt.treas.gov/opd/opd.htm.

## Receipts and Outlays of the Federal Government, 1789–2006
### (in millions of dollars)

From 1789 to 1842, the federal fiscal year ended on Dec. 31; from 1844 to 1976, on June 30; and beginning in 1977, on Sept. 30.

| Year | Total | | | On-budget[1] | | |
|---|---|---|---|---|---|---|
| | Receipts | Outlays | Surplus or deficit (–) | Receipts | Outlays | Surplus or deficit (–) |
| 1789–1849 | $ 1,160 | $ 1,090 | $ 70 | $ 1,160 | $ 1,090 | $ 70 |
| 1850–1900 | 14,462 | 15,453 | –991 | 14,462 | 15,453 | –991 |
| 1905 | 544 | 567 | –23 | 544 | 567 | –23 |
| 1910 | 676 | 694 | –18 | 676 | 694 | –18 |
| 1915 | 683 | 746 | –63 | 683 | 746 | –63 |
| 1920 | 6,649 | 6,358 | 291 | 6,649 | 6,358 | 291 |
| 1925 | 3,641 | 2,924 | 717 | 3,641 | 2,924 | 717 |
| 1930 | 4,058 | 3,320 | 738 | 4,058 | 3,320 | 738 |
| 1935 | 3,609 | 6,412 | –2,803 | 3,609 | 6,412 | –2,803 |
| 1940 | 6,548 | 9,468 | –2,920 | 5,998 | 9,482 | –3,484 |
| 1945 | 45,159 | 92,712 | –47,553 | 43,849 | 92,569 | –48,720 |
| 1950 | 39,443 | 42,562 | –3,119 | 37,336 | 42,038 | –4,702 |
| 1955 | 65,451 | 68,444 | –2,933 | 60,370 | 64,461 | –4,091 |
| 1960 | 92,492 | 92,191 | 301 | 81,851 | 81,341 | 510 |
| 1965 | 116,817 | 118,228 | –1,411 | 100,094 | 101,699 | –1,605 |
| 1970 | 192,807 | 195,649 | –2,842 | 159,348 | 168,042 | –8,694 |
| 1975 | 279,090 | 332,332 | –53,242 | 216,633 | 271,892 | –55,260 |
| 1980 | 517,112 | 590,947 | –73,835 | 403,903 | 476,618 | –72,715 |
| 1985 | 734,088 | 946,423 | –212,334 | 547,918 | 769,615 | –221,698 |
| 1990 | 1,031,969 | 1,253,198 | –221,229 | 750,314 | 1,028,133 | –277,819 |
| 1995 | 1,351,830 | 1,515,837 | –164,007 | 1,000,751 | 1,227,173 | –226,422 |
| 2000 | 2,025,218 | 1,788,826 | 236,392 | 1,544,634 | 1,458,061 | 86,573 |
| 2005[2] | 2,437,783 | 2,168,745 | 269,038 | 1,808,786 | 1,776,379 | 32,407 |
| 2006[2] | 2,528,711 | 2,223,902 | 304,809 | 1,870,204 | 1,817,759 | 52,445 |

1. Excludes the Social Security surplus. For years prior to 1933, on-budget surplus was not calculated separately. 2. Estimated. *Source:* The Budget for Fiscal Year 2002.

## Summary of Federal Government Expenditure, by State and Territory, Fiscal Year 2001
### (in millions of dollars)

| State and outlying area | Total | Retirement and disability | Other direct payments | Grants | Procurement | Salaries and wages |
|---|---|---|---|---|---|---|
| **United States total** | **$1,778,884** | **$600,014** | **$405,599** | **$338,977** | **$246,219** | **$188,075** |
| Alabama | 31,700 | 11,460 | 6,843 | 5,298 | 5,204 | 2,895 |
| Alaska | 6,403 | 936 | 610 | 2,314 | 1,130 | 1,414 |
| Arizona | 30,376 | 11,075 | 5,934 | 5,190 | 5,260 | 2,917 |
| Arkansas | 16,632 | 6,666 | 4,648 | 3,448 | 692 | 1,178 |
| California | 188,517 | 58,306 | 43,608 | 39,797 | 28,949 | 17,858 |
| Colorado | 24,345 | 7,856 | 4,238 | 3,916 | 4,468 | 3,868 |
| Connecticut | 22,742 | 7,228 | 5,041 | 4,364 | 4,734 | 1,375 |
| Delaware | 4,246 | 1,796 | 983 | 892 | 110 | 411 |
| District of Columbia | 41,811 | 1,116 | 2,770 | 4,620 | 10,203 | 12,646 |
| Florida | 99,998 | 42,718 | 26,340 | 13,666 | 8,859 | 8,415 |
| Georgia | 47,320 | 15,578 | 9,500 | 7,929 | 7,382 | 6,931 |
| Hawaii | 9,722 | 2,798 | 1,419 | 1,514 | 1,467 | 2,525 |
| Idaho | 7,529 | 2,609 | 1,465 | 1,505 | 1,197 | 753 |
| Illinois | 65,036 | 23,675 | 19,090 | 11,883 | 4,135 | 6,252 |
| Indiana | 32,166 | 12,589 | 8,873 | 5,850 | 2,734 | 2,121 |
| Iowa | 17,401 | 6,437 | 5,959 | 3,079 | 897 | 1,029 |
| Kansas | 16,699 | 5,860 | 4,868 | 2,721 | 1,383 | 1,866 |
| Kentucky | 25,835 | 9,729 | 5,443 | 5,100 | 2,759 | 2,805 |
| Louisiana | 27,816 | 9,091 | 7,617 | 6,173 | 2,625 | 2,310 |
| Maine | 8,180 | 3,195 | 1,598 | 1,905 | 674 | 808 |
| Maryland | 48,164 | 12,378 | 8,542 | 7,586 | 10,736 | 8,921 |
| Massachusetts | 44,179 | 13,328 | 11,067 | 9,718 | 6,851 | 3,214 |
| Michigan | 51,632 | 20,846 | 13,371 | 10,887 | 3,378 | 3,150 |

| State and outlying area | Total | Retirement and disability | Other direct payments | Grants | Procurement | Salaries and wages |
|---|---|---|---|---|---|---|
| Minnesota | $ 24,395 | $ 8,969 | $ 6,752 | $ 5,260 | $ 2,049 | $ 1,904 |
| Mississippi | 20,212 | 6,621 | 5,756 | 4,246 | 1,863 | 1,725 |
| Missouri | 39,191 | 12,795 | 9,327 | 6,865 | 6,741 | 3,463 |
| Montana | 6,618 | 2,134 | 1,737 | 1,665 | 371 | 711 |
| Nebraska | 10,771 | 3,684 | 3,532 | 2,054 | 447 | 1,053 |
| Nevada | 9,624 | 4,206 | 1,915 | 1,442 | 1,041 | 1,019 |
| New Hampshire | 6,314 | 2,654 | 1,201 | 1,288 | 655 | 516 |
| New Jersey | 46,240 | 17,590 | 12,232 | 8,478 | 4,158 | 3,782 |
| New Mexico | 16,587 | 4,052 | 2,079 | 3,586 | 5,122 | 1,747 |
| New York | 116,366 | 38,772 | 30,408 | 32,897 | 6,168 | 8,122 |
| North Carolina | 44,557 | 17,514 | 9,265 | 9,122 | 3,154 | 5,502 |
| North Dakota | 5,948 | 1,352 | 2,398 | 1,284 | 280 | 634 |
| Ohio | 61,705 | 24,262 | 15,706 | 11,762 | 5,124 | 4,851 |
| Oklahoma | 22,672 | 8,201 | 5,089 | 4,119 | 2,212 | 3,050 |
| Oregon | 18,401 | 7,450 | 4,091 | 4,308 | 959 | 1,592 |
| Pennsylvania | 79,310 | 30,386 | 21,526 | 14,847 | 6,788 | 5,763 |
| Rhode Island | 6,989 | 2,455 | 1,786 | 1,607 | 392 | 747 |
| South Carolina | 24,675 | 9,502 | 4,763 | 4,730 | 3,155 | 2,526 |
| South Dakota | 5,807 | 1,657 | 1,995 | 1,254 | 301 | 600 |
| Tennessee | 36,758 | 12,954 | 8,031 | 7,027 | 5,811 | 2,935 |
| Texas | 112,530 | 36,323 | 26,870 | 21,675 | 15,649 | 12,104 |
| Utah | 11,377 | 3,605 | 1,679 | 2,244 | 2,084 | 1,765 |
| Vermont | 3,734 | 1,274 | 680 | 1,069 | 391 | 319 |
| Virginia | 71,257 | 18,071 | 7,998 | 5,908 | 26,935 | 12,345 |
| Washington | 36,903 | 12,696 | 6,988 | 6,794 | 5,480 | 4,945 |
| West Virginia | 12,541 | 5,359 | 2,679 | 2,971 | 527 | 1,005 |
| Wisconsin | 26,645 | 10,884 | 6,475 | 5,843 | 1,817 | 1,626 |
| Wyoming | 3,584 | 1,066 | 528 | 1,213 | 341 | 435 |
| American Samoa | 116 | 40 | 1 | 58 | 12 | 5 |
| Micronesia | 98 | — | 3 | 94 | 1 | — |
| Guam | 908 | 191 | 75 | 176 | 219 | 247 |
| Marshall Islands | 150 | 1 | — | 48 | 101 | — |
| Northern Marianas | 96 | 21 | 4 | 60 | 9 | 3 |
| Palau | 36 | — | — | 35 | — | — |
| Puerto Rico | 13,181 | 5,242 | 2,697 | 3,899 | 477 | 866 |
| Virgin Islands | 404 | 132 | 102 | 111 | 15 | 45 |
| Undistributed | 24,066 | — | — | 183 | 19,443 | 4,440 |

NOTE: Detail may not add to total due to rounding. *Source: Consolidated Federal Funds Report for Fiscal Year 2001.* www.census.gov.

## U.S. Direct Investment in Other Countries, 2001
### (in millions of dollars)

| | All industries | Petro-leum | Manu-facturing | Wholesale trade | Banking | Finance, insurance, real estate | Services | Other industries |
|---|---|---|---|---|---|---|---|---|
| All countries | $113,977 | $12,668 | $36,381 | $9,289 | $9,925 | $34,983 | $7,513 | $3,217 |
| Canada | 14,440 | 8,088 | 3,877 | 682 | −100 | 1,076 | 241 | 576 |
| Europe | 56,133 | 1,217 | 25,036 | 4,522 | −31 | 20,648 | 4,216 | 524 |
| Austria | 766 | (D) | 524 | 127 | 33 | 139 | 40 | (D) |
| Belgium | 1,279 | −19 | 169 | 214 | 53 | 366 | 468 | 27 |
| Denmark | −369 | −216 | 43 | −219 | 0 | (D) | −11 | (D) |
| Finland | 137 | −11 | 131 | 35 | 0 | (D) | 1 | (D) |
| France | 655 | (D) | 218 | 12 | −140 | −142 | 98 | (D) |
| Germany | 11,360 | 191 | 11,257 | −479 | −26 | −453 | 746 | 124 |
| Greece | 41 | (D) | 34 | 66 | −33 | (D) | 6 | 21 |
| Ireland | 581 | (D) | 1,551 | 176 | 20 | −1,513 | 1,008 | (D) |
| Italy | 1,609 | (D) | 749 | −61 | 29 | 351 | 60 | (D) |
| Luxembourg | 4,848 | −1 | 199 | 267 | 73 | 4,208 | 101 | 1 |
| Netherlands | 16,058 | 1,263 | 5,644 | 1,844 | (D) | 6,198 | 608 | (D) |
| Norway | 970 | 113 | −4 | 78 | (D) | 773 | −84 | (D) |
| Portugal | 9 | (D) | 44 | 83 | −1 | 1 | −98 | (D) |

| | All industries | Petro-leum | Manu-facturing | Wholesale trade | Banking | Finance, insurance, real estate | Services | Other industries |
|---|---|---|---|---|---|---|---|---|
| Spain | $496 | (D) | $214 | $–305 | $87 | $551 | $–15 | (D) |
| Sweden | –4,106 | $–27 | –4,723 | 101 | (D) | 665 | –100 | (D) |
| Switzerland | 6,629 | –4 | 1,031 | 2,446 | –72 | 3,550 | 329 | $–651 |
| Turkey | 29 | –29 | 8 | 22 | 45 | 2 | 22 | –42 |
| United Kingdom | 13,231 | –1,278 | 7,757 | 56 | 161 | 4,812 | 1,011 | 713 |
| Other | 1,909 | 849 | 192 | 57 | (D) | 1,082 | 27 | (D) |
| **Latin America and other Western Hemisphere** | 26,510 | 718 | 1,668 | 1,403 | 10,462 | 8,016 | 1,295 | 2,948 |
| South America | 3,887 | –12 | 61 | –49 | 235 | 1,485 | 244 | 1,924 |
| Argentina | –421 | –90 | –826 | –134 | 60 | 708 | 21 | –161 |
| Brazil | –17 | –45 | –31 | –14 | 120 | 347 | –11 | –384 |
| Chile | 2,834 | 8 | 610 | 13 | 58 | 361 | –13 | 1,795 |
| Colombia | –104 | –71 | 116 | 2 | (D) | –22 | (D) | (D) |
| Ecuador | –66 | –35 | –37 | 12 | (D) | 20 | (D) | (D) |
| Peru | 120 | 62 | 18 | 5 | (D) | 15 | (*) | (D) |
| Venezuela | 1,360 | 100 | 108 | 51 | –14 | 56 | 264 | 795 |
| Other | 181 | 59 | 101 | 14 | 13 | –1 | –25 | 18 |
| **Central America** | (D) | –376 | 1,115 | 48 | (D) | 1,748 | 227 | (D) |
| Costa Rica | –16 | 10 | 48 | (D) | 0 | 4 | (*) | (D) |
| Guatemala | –372 | –383 | 1 | –4 | (D) | 7 | (*) | (D) |
| Honduras | –163 | (D) | –118 | 4 | (D) | –4 | 0 | (D) |
| Mexico | (D) | 123 | 1,118 | 98 | (D) | 1,303 | –66 | (D) |
| Panama | 753 | –23 | 21 | (D) | (D) | 422 | 293 | (D) |
| Other | –53 | (D) | –24 | 10 | (D) | 16 | 0 | (D) |
| **Other Western Hemisphere** | (D) | 1,106 | 492 | 1,405 | (D) | 4,784 | 824 | (D) |
| Bahamas | –122 | (D) | (D) | (D) | –552 | 362 | 5 | (D) |
| Barbados | 56 | (D) | 2 | 75 | (D) | (D) | 157 | (D) |
| Bermuda | 5,865 | (D) | (D) | 1,196 | 0 | 2,951 | 460 | (D) |
| Dominican Republic | (D) | (D) | 21 | 13 | (D) | (*) | (D) | (D) |
| Jamaica | –44 | (D) | –20 | (D) | (D) | 5 | 7 | (D) |
| Netherlands Antilles | 131 | (*) | (D) | 2 | 0 | 131 | (D) | 0 |
| Trinidad and Tobago | (D) | 397 | 60 | 2 | (D) | (D) | (*) | (D) |
| United Kingdom Islands, Caribbean | 697 | –76 | 123 | 87 | –1,284 | 1,530 | 222 | 94 |
| Other | (D) | (D) | (D) | (D) | (D) | (D) | (D) | (D) |
| **Africa** | 798 | 1,750 | –166 | 67 | –22 | –778 | –192 | 139 |
| Egypt | 762 | 1,088 | –330 | –12 | (D) | 2 | 31 | (D) |
| Nigeria | 221 | 955 | –2 | (D) | (D) | (D) | 0 | 0 |
| South Africa | –4 | 61 | 269 | 10 | (D) | (D) | –243 | (D) |
| Other | –181 | –354 | –103 | (D) | 16 | 93 | 20 | (D) |
| **Middle East** | 1,269 | 501 | 466 | 63 | –72 | 221 | 21 | 68 |
| Israel | 493 | (*) | 421 | –2 | –9 | 10 | –5 | 77 |
| Saudi Arabia | –75 | –2 | 32 | (*) | (D) | –22 | 36 | (D) |
| United Arab Emirates | 196 | 25 | (D) | 66 | (D) | (D) | 16 | 16 |
| Other | 655 | 478 | (D) | (*) | –24 | (D) | –26 | (D) |
| **Asia and Pacific** | 15,012 | 507 | 5,501 | 2,552 | –313 | 5,800 | 1,932 | –967 |
| Australia | –423 | 987 | –1,039 | 10 | 55 | 736 | –477 | –696 |
| China | 1,336 | 220 | 1,199 | 281 | 111 | –116 | 67 | 1 |
| Hong Kong | 2,992 | –39 | –457 | 1,913 | –593 | 1,713 | 149 | 306 |
| India | 289 | –6 | 187 | –93 | 37 | 43 | 26 | 95 |
| Indonesia | 291 | –14 | –12 | (D) | 10 | (D) | (D) | 408 |
| Japan | 5,474 | –135 | 1,626 | 456 | –140 | 2,606 | 2,047 | –985 |
| Korea, Republic of | 953 | 2 | 669 | –42 | 92 | 137 | 21 | 74 |
| Malaysia | –549 | –305 | –292 | 32 | (D) | 51 | –38 | (D) |
| New Zealand | 235 | 36 | 51 | 104 | (D) | –17 | (D) | (D) |
| Philippines | 47 | –152 | 264 | 19 | 6 | 89 | (*) | –178 |
| Singapore | 2,970 | 58 | 2,782 | –145 | 30 | 48 | 203 | –6 |
| Taiwan | 955 | 4 | 166 | 90 | 123 | 437 | 25 | 111 |
| Thailand | 668 | 328 | 137 | (*) | 67 | 231 | 19 | –114 |
| Other | –126 | –26 | 17 | (D) | (D) | (D) | –2 | (D) |

NOTES: Only countries receiving more than ten trillion dollars in 2001 are listed separately. * Less than $500,000 (+/–). (D) Suppressed to avoid disclosure of data of individual companies. *Source:* U.S. Department of Commerce, Bureau of Economic Analysis. Web: www.bea.doc.gov/bea/di/diapos_01.htm.

## U.S. Contributions to International Organizations
### (in millions of dollars)

| Organization | 2001 | 2002 (est.) | 2003 (est.) | Organization | 2001 | 2002 (est.) | 2003 (est.) |
|---|---|---|---|---|---|---|---|
| **UN and affiliated agencies:** | | | | *Subtotal* | *$ 89* | *$ 94* | *$107* |
| Food and Agriculture Organization | $ 82 | $ 73 | $ 73 | **Other international organizations:** | | | |
| International Atomic Energy Agency | 45 | 47 | 52 | Org. for Prohibition of Chemical Weapons | 11 | 11 | 13 |
| International Civil Aviation Organization | 12 | 12 | 13 | OPCW—Title IV & V | 3 | 2 | 4 |
| International Labor Organization | 56 | 55 | 50 | World Trade Org./GATT | 11 | 13 | 14 |
| International Maritime Organization | 1 | 1 | 1 | Other international organizations | 8 | 8 | 8 |
| International Telecommunications Union | 6 | 6 | 6 | *Subtotal* | *33* | *34* | *39* |
| United Nations—Regular | 267 | 251 | 279 | UN Buydown | 15 | — | — |
| UN War Crimes Tribunals | 20 | 24 | 27 | **Total** | **869** | **850** | **891** |
| Cambodia War Crimes Commission | — | 3 | — | **International peacekeeping activities:** | | | |
| Iraq War Crimes Commission | — | 4 | 4 | UN Disengagement Observer Force | 8 | 11 | 8 |
| UN Capital Master Plan | — | — | 8 | UN Interim Force in Lebanon | 60 | 31 | 34 |
| UN Capital Master Plan Task Force | — | — | 1 | UN Iraq-Kuwait Observer Mission | 5 | 6 | 4 |
| Universal Postal Union | 1 | 1 | 1 | UN Mission for the Referendum in Western Sahara | 12 | 15 | 12 |
| World Health Organization | 108 | 108 | 94 | UN Mission in Bosnia and Herzegovina | 48 | 35 | — |
| World Intellectual Property Org. | 1 | 1 | 1 | UN Mission in Kosovo | 145 | 139 | 97 |
| World Meteorological Org. | 9 | 8 | 8 | UN Mission in Cyprus | 6 | 7 | 5 |
| *Subtotal* | *608* | *595* | *618* | UN Observer Mission in Georgia | 6 | 9 | 6 |
| **Inter-American organizations:** | | | | War Crimes Tribunal—Yugoslavia | 12 | 18 | 15 |
| Inter-American Institute for Cooperation on Agriculture | 17 | 17 | 17 | War Crimes Tribunal—Rwanda | 11 | 17 | 12 |
| Organization of American States | 54 | 54 | 54 | UN Mission in Sierra Leone | 97 | 382 | 146 |
| Pan American Health Org. | 52 | 55 | 56 | UN Transitional Administration Mission in East Timor | 151 | 146 | 58 |
| *Subtotal* | *123* | *126* | *127* | UN Organization Mission in the Dem. Rep. of the Congo | 74 | 92 | 273 |
| **Regional organizations:** | | | | UN Mission in Ethiopia and Eritrea | 71 | 63 | 56 |
| Asia-Pacific Economic Coop. | 1 | 1 | 1 | Payment of outstanding FY 2000 MONUC Assessments | 12 | — | — |
| North Atlantic Assembly | 1 | 1 | 1 | **Total new obligations** | **718** | **971** | **726** |
| North Atlantic Treaty Org. | 41 | 42 | 45 | | | | |
| Org. for Economic Coop. and Development | 45 | 49 | 59 | | | | |
| South Pacific Commission | 1 | 1 | 1 | | | | |

NOTE: All years are fiscal years. *Source:* Budget of the United States Government Fiscal Year 2003.

## National Income by Type
### (in billions of dollars)

| Type of income | 1930 | 1940 | 1950 | 1960 | 1970 | 1980 | 1990 | 1995 | 2000 | 2001 |
|---|---|---|---|---|---|---|---|---|---|---|
| **National income** | **$75.6** | **$81.1** | **$241.0** | **$427.5** | **$837.5** | **$2,243.0** | **$4,642.1** | **$5,876.7** | **$7,980.9** | **$8,217.5** |
| Compensation of employees | 46.9 | 52.2 | 155.4 | 296.4 | 617.2 | 1,651.7 | 3,351.0 | 4,202.5 | 5,715.2 | 6,010.0 |
| Wage and salary accruals | 46.2 | 49.9 | 147.2 | 272.8 | 551.5 | 1,377.4 | 2,754.6 | 3,441.1 | 4,837.2 | 5,098.2 |
| Supplements to wages and salaries | 0.7 | 2.3 | 8.1 | 23.6 | 65.7 | 274.3 | 596.4 | 761.4 | 878.0 | 911.8 |
| Proprietors' income[1],[2] | | | | | | | | | | |
| Farm | 4.4 | 4.5 | 13.5 | 11.4 | 14.3 | 13.1 | 31.1 | 22.2 | 30.6 | 27.6 |
| Nonfarm | 7.3 | 8.4 | 25.1 | 40.4 | 65.5 | 164.5 | 349.9 | 475.5 | 684.4 | 715.9 |
| Rental income[1] | 4.9 | 3.4 | 8.7 | 16.2 | 20.3 | 31.3 | 49.1 | 117.9 | 141.6 | 142.6 |
| Corporate profits[1],[2] | 7.3 | 9.5 | 35.4 | 52.3 | 81.6 | 198.5 | 408.6 | 668.8 | 876.4 | 767.1 |
| Net interest | 4.8 | 3.2 | 3.0 | 10.7 | 38.4 | 183.9 | 452.4 | 389.8 | 532.7 | 554.3 |
| Personal income | 76.5 | 78.6 | 229.9 | 412.7 | 841.1 | 2,323.9 | 4,903.2 | 6,200.9 | 8,319.2 | 8,723.5 |
| Disposable personal income | 74.6 | 76.7 | 210.6 | 366.2 | 736.5 | 2,019.8 | 4,293.6 | 5,422.6 | 7,031.0 | 7,417.3 |
| Personal savings | 3.2 | 4.5 | 15.2 | 26.4 | 69.5 | 205.6 | 334.3 | 302.4 | 67.7 | 118.4 |

1. Includes capital consumption adjustment. 2. Includes inventory valuation adjustment. *Source:* U.S. Department of Commerce, Bureau of Economic Analysis, *Survey of Current Business,* May 2002. Web: www.bea.doc.gov.

## Exports and Imports of Goods and Services, 1980–2010

| Category | Billions of chained 1996 dollars | | | | Average annual rate of change | | |
|---|---|---|---|---|---|---|---|
| | 1980 | 1990 | 2000 | 2010[1] | 1980–1990 | 1990–2000 | 2000–2010[1] |
| **Exports of goods and services** | **$333.4** | **$575.7** | **$1,133.2** | **$2,393.7** | **5.6%** | **7.0%** | **7.8%** |
| Goods | 238.9 | 393.2 | 836.1 | 1,821.2 | 5.1 | 7.8 | 8.1 |
| Foods, feeds, and beverages | 44.7 | 44.4 | 60.0 | 91.4 | –0.1 | 3.1 | 4.3 |
| Industrial supplies and materials | 86.9 | 111.7 | 168.2 | 228.4 | 2.5 | 4.2 | 3.1 |
| Capital goods, except autos | 56.0 | 124.8 | 394.9 | 1,123.1 | 8.3 | 12.2 | 11.0 |
| Computers | 1.0 | 12.3 | 85.6 | 406.0 | 28.5 | 21.4 | 16.8 |
| Civilian aircraft and parts | 26.9 | 40.9 | 43.1 | 78.2 | 4.3 | 0.5 | 6.1 |
| Other | 48.5 | 79.1 | 271.5 | 740.4 | 5.0 | 13.1 | 10.6 |
| Autos and parts | 28.3 | 39.8 | 78.3 | 154.5 | 3.5 | 7.0 | 7.0 |
| Consumer goods | 25.1 | 48.1 | 89.8 | 182.7 | 6.7 | 6.4 | 7.4 |
| Other merchandise exports | 14.8 | 32.4 | 45.9 | 103.3 | 8.1 | 3.6 | 8.4 |
| Services | 89.0 | 183.4 | 299.3 | 591.7 | 7.5 | 5.0 | 7.1 |
| Residual[2] | –31.8 | –16.5 | –8.6 | –182.9 | — | — | — |
| **Imports of goods and services** | **$326.3** | **$632.2** | **$1,532.3** | **$3,282.7** | **6.8%** | **9.3%** | **7.9%** |
| Goods | 260.6 | 497.9 | 1,315.6 | 2,954.5 | 6.7 | 10.2 | 8.4 |
| Foods, foods, and beverages | 20.9 | 30.4 | 49.4 | 61.9 | 3.8 | 5.0 | 2.3 |
| Industrial supplies and materials | 118.1 | 142.4 | 254.5 | 331.6 | 1.9 | 6.0 | 2.7 |
| Petroleum and products | 51.5 | 59.5 | 86.0 | 96.6 | 1.4 | 3.8 | 1.2 |
| Other | 55.0 | 83.6 | 167.9 | 234.8 | 4.3 | 7.2 | 3.4 |
| Capital goods, except autos | 18.5 | 88.8 | 451.7 | 1,428.6 | 17.0 | 17.7 | 12.2 |
| Computers | 0.2 | 11.6 | 152.6 | 670.2 | 50.1 | 29.4 | 15.9 |
| Civilian aircraft and parts | 6.0 | 13.5 | 23.9 | 36.7 | 8.5 | 5.8 | 4.4 |
| Other | 19.1 | 68.9 | 279.3 | 824.0 | 13.7 | 15.0 | 11.4 |
| Autos and parts | 52.5 | 101.6 | 192.5 | 322.8 | 6.8 | 6.6 | 5.3 |
| Consumer goods | 49.8 | 112.8 | 293.5 | 858.9 | 8.5 | 10.0 | 11.3 |
| Other merchandise imports | 12.4 | 35.2 | 80.9 | 148.0 | 11.0 | 8.7 | 6.2 |
| Services | 65.6 | 136.6 | 218.7 | 352.8 | 7.6 | 4.8 | 4.9 |
| Residual[3] | –6.7 | –21.5 | –12.6 | –323.9 | — | — | — |
| **Trade Deficit** | **$ 7.1** | **$–56.5** | **$ –399.1** | **$ –889.1** | — | **21.6%** | **8.3%** |

1. Projected. 2. The residual following the detailed categories for exports is the difference between the aggregate of "exports of goods and services" and the sum of the figures for those separate categories for exports of goods and services. 3. The residual following the detailed categories for imports is the difference between the aggregate of "imports of goods and services" and the sum of the figures for those separate categories for imports of goods and services. *Source:* Bureau of Labor Statistics, *Monthly Labor Review,* Nov. 2001.

## Producer Price Indexes by Major Commodity Groups

| Commodity | 2001 | 2000 | 1995 | 1990 | 1985 | 1980 | 1975 | 1970 |
|---|---|---|---|---|---|---|---|---|
| All commodities | 134.2 | 132.7 | 124.7 | 116.3 | 103.2 | 89.8 | 58.4 | 38.1 |
| Farm products | 103.8 | 99.5 | 107.4 | 112.2 | 95.1 | 102.9 | 77.0 | 45.8 |
| Processed foods and feeds | 137.3 | 133.1 | 127.0 | 121.9 | 103.5 | 95.9 | 72.6 | 44.6 |
| Textile products and apparel | 121.3 | 121.4 | 120.8 | 114.9 | 102.9 | 89.7 | 67.4 | 52.4 |
| Hides, skins, and leather products | 158.4 | 151.5 | 153.7 | 141.7 | 108.9 | 94.7 | 56.5 | 42.0 |
| Fuels and related products and power | 105.3 | 103.5 | 78.0 | 82.2 | 91.4 | 82.8 | 35.4 | 15.3 |
| Chemicals and allied products | 151.8 | 151.0 | 142.5 | 123.6 | 103.7 | 89.0 | 62.0 | 35.0 |
| Rubber and plastic products | 127.2 | 125.5 | 124.3 | 113.6 | 101.9 | 90.1 | 62.2 | 44.9 |
| Lumber and wood products | 174.4 | 178.2 | 178.1 | 129.7 | 106.6 | 101.5 | 62.1 | 39.9 |
| Pulp, paper, and allied products | 184.8 | 183.7 | 172.2 | 141.3 | 113.3 | 86.3 | 59.0 | 37.5 |
| Metals and metal products | 125.4 | 128.1 | 134.5 | 123.0 | 104.4 | 95.0 | 61.5 | 38.7 |
| Machinery and equipment | 123.7 | 124.0 | 126.6 | 120.7 | 107.2 | 86.0 | 57.9 | 40.0 |
| Furniture and household durables | 133.2 | 132.6 | 128.2 | 119.1 | 107.1 | 90.7 | 67.5 | 01.0 |
| Nonmetallic mineral products | 144.3 | 140.5 | 100.0 | 114.7 | 100.1 | 88.1 | 54.4 | 35.3 |
| Transportation equipment | 116.0 | 143.8 | 139.7 | 121.5 | 107.9 | 82.9 | 56.7 | 41.9 |

NOTES: 1982 = 100. *Source:* U.S. Department of Labor, Bureau of Labor Statistics, Division of Industrial Prices and Price Indexes. Web: stats.bls.gov.

## Consumer Price Index for All Urban Consumers

| Group | 2001 | 2000 | 1999 | 1995 | 1990 | 1985 | 1980 | 1975 | 1970 | 1965 | 1960 | 1950 |
|---|---|---|---|---|---|---|---|---|---|---|---|---|
| All items | 177.1 | 172.2 | 166.6 | 152.4 | 130.7 | 107.6 | 82.4 | 53.8 | 38.8 | 31.5 | 29.6 | 24.1 |
| Food and beverages | 173.6 | 168.4 | 164.6 | 148.9 | 132.1 | 105.6 | 86.7 | 60.2 | 40.1 | n.a. | n.a. | n.a. |
| Housing | 176.4 | 169.6 | 163.9 | 148.5 | 128.5 | 107.7 | 81.1 | 50.7 | 36.4 | n.a. | n.a. | n.a. |
| Apparel | 127.3 | 129.6 | 131.3 | 132.0 | 124.1 | 105.0 | 90.9 | 72.5 | 59.2 | 47.8 | 45.7 | 40.3 |
| Transportation | 154.3 | 153.3 | 144.4 | 139.1 | 120.5 | 106.4 | 83.1 | 50.1 | 37.5 | 31.9 | 29.8 | 22.7 |
| Medical care | 272.8 | 260.8 | 250.6 | 220.5 | 162.8 | 113.5 | 74.9 | 47.5 | 34.0 | 25.2 | 22.3 | 15.1 |

NOTES: 1982–1984 = 100. n.a. = not available. *Source:* U.S. Department of Labor, Bureau of Labor Statistics. Web: www.bls.gov.

## Imports and Exports of Leading Commodities
### by Principal SITC Groupings (in millions of dollars)

| Item | 2001 Cumulative Exports | Imports | Item | 2001 Cumulative Exports | Imports |
|---|---|---|---|---|---|
| **Selected commodities** | | | Liquefied propane/butane | $ 137 | $ 968 |
| Total Balance of Payment Basis | $254,236 | $395,633 | Live animals | 195 | 770 |
| Net Adjustments | –3,040 | 2,324 | Meat and preparations | 2,297 | 1,351 |
| ADP equipment; office machines | 14,744 | 26,615 | Metal manufactures, n.e.s. | 4,000 | 5,202 |
| Airplane parts | 5,328 | 2,090 | Metal ores; scrap | 1,336 | 1,108 |
| Airplanes | 9,175 | 4,800 | Metalworking machinery | 1,874 | 2,635 |
| Alcoholic bev.,distilled | 139 | 906 | Mineral fuels, other | 1,250 | 680 |
| Aluminum | 1,152 | 2,209 | Natural gas | 203 | 8,230 |
| Animal feeds | 1,545 | 206 | Nickel | 165 | 412 |
| Basketware, etc. | 1,183 | 1,734 | Oils/fats, vegetable | 227 | 332 |
| Cereal flour | 447 | 541 | Optical goods | 1,156 | 1,381 |
| Chemicals—medicinal | 4,626 | 5,437 | Paper and paperboard | 3,448 | 4,953 |
| Chemicals—organic | 5,832 | 10,801 | Petroleum preparations | 1,576 | 10,510 |
| Chemicals—plastics | 6,403 | 3,530 | Photographic equipment | 1,114 | 1,921 |
| Cigarettes | 965 | 64 | Platinum | 557 | 2,782 |
| Clothing | 2,398 | 20,169 | Pottery | 35 | 528 |
| Coal | 624 | 292 | Power generating mach. | 10,841 | 12,247 |
| Coffee | 3 | 502 | Printed materials | 1,643 | 1,155 |
| Copper | 403 | 1,588 | Pulp and waste paper | 1,305 | 1,100 |
| Cork, wood, lumber | 1,329 | 2,422 | Records/magnetic media | 1,611 | 1,484 |
| Corn | 1,623 | 109 | Rice | 262 | 59 |
| Cotton, raw and linters | 733 | 10 | Rubber tires and tubes | 734 | 1,347 |
| Crude fertilizers | 571 | 428 | Scientific instruments | 10,415 | 7,387 |
| Crude oil | 62 | 25,894 | Ships, boats | 337 | 516 |
| Electrical machinery | 27,717 | 31,594 | Silver and bullion | 70 | 178 |
| Fish and preparations | 1,045 | 2,709 | Soybeans | 2,201 | 12 |
| Footwear | 213 | 5,196 | Specialized ind. mach. | 9,918 | 7,499 |
| Furniture and bedding | 1,443 | 6,341 | Sugar | 1 | 138 |
| Gem diamonds | 684 | 3,455 | Television, VCR, etc. | 8,465 | 20,021 |
| General industrial machinery | 11,413 | 11,966 | Textile yarn, fabric | 3,521 | 4,863 |
| Glass | 872 | 716 | Tobacco, unmanufactured | 479 | 242 |
| Glassware | 318 | 584 | Toys/games/sporting goods | 1,100 | 5,245 |
| Gold, nonmonetary | 2,318 | 651 | Vegetables and fruits | 2,331 | 3,706 |
| Hides and skins | 582 | 36 | Vehicles | 18,050 | 53,059 |
| Iron and steel mill products | 1,875 | 4,121 | Watches/clocks/parts | 100 | 932 |
| Jewelry | 760 | 1,891 | Wheat | 1,076 | 73 |
| Lighting, plumbing | 431 | 1,439 | Wood manufactures | 548 | 2,156 |

NOTES: SITC = Standard International Trade Classification. Details may not equal totals due to rounding. Data not seasonally adjusted. *Source:* U.S. Census Bureau, Foreign Trade Division. Web: http://www.census.gov/foreign-trade/PressRelease/current_press_release/exh15.txt.

## Retail Prices of Selected Foods in U.S. Cities, 1890–1970
### (in cents per unit indicated)

| Year | Flour (5 lbs) | Bread (lb) | Round steak (lb) | Bacon (lb) | Butter (lb) | Eggs (doz.) | Milk (½ gal.) | Oranges (doz.) | Potatoes (10 lbs) | Coffee (lb) | Sugar (5 lb) |
|---|---|---|---|---|---|---|---|---|---|---|---|
| 1970 | 58.9 | 24.3 | 130.2 | 94.9 | 86.6 | 61.4 | 65.9 | 86.4 | 89.7 | 91.1 | 64.8 |
| 1965 | 58.1 | 20.9 | 108.4 | 81.3 | 75.4 | 52.7 | 52.6 | 77.8 | 93.7 | 83.3 | 59.0 |
| 1960 | 55.4 | 20.3 | 105.5 | 65.5 | 74.9 | 57.3 | 52.0 | 74.8 | 71.8 | 75.3 | 58.2 |
| 1955 | 53.8 | 17.7 | 90.3 | 65.9 | 70.9 | 60.6 | 46.2 | 52.8 | 56.4 | 93.0 | 52.1 |
| 1950 | 49.1 | 14.3 | 93.6 | 63.7 | 72.9 | 60.4 | 41.2 | 49.3 | 46.1 | 79.4 | 48.7 |
| 1945 | 32.1 | 8.8 | 40.6 | 41.1 | 50.7 | 58.1 | 31.2 | 48.5 | 49.3 | 30.5 | 33.4 |
| 1940 | 21.5 | 8.0 | 36.4 | 27.3 | 36.0 | 33.1 | 25.6 | 29.1 | 23.9 | 21.2 | 26.0 |
| 1935 | 25.3 | 8.3 | 36.0 | 41.3 | 36.0 | 37.6 | 23.4 | 22.0 | 19.1 | 25.7 | 28.2 |
| 1930 | 23.0 | 8.6 | 42.6 | 42.5 | 46.4 | 44.5 | 28.2 | 57.1 | 36.0 | 39.5 | 30.5 |
| 1925 | 30.5 | 9.3 | 36.2 | 47.1 | 55.2 | 55.4 | 27.8 | 57.1 | 36.0 | 50.4 | 35.0 |
| 1920 | 40.5 | 11.5 | 39.5 | 52.3 | 70.1 | 68.1 | 33.4 | 63.2 | 63.0 | 47.0 | 97.0 |
| 1915 | 21.0 | 7.0 | 23.0 | 26.9 | 35.8 | 34.1 | 17.6 | n.a. | 15.0 | 30.0 | 33.0 |
| 1910 | 18.0 | n.a. | 17.4 | 25.5 | 35.9 | 33.7 | 16.8 | n.a. | 17.0 | n.a. | 30.0 |
| 1905 | 16.0 | n.a. | 14.0 | 18.1 | 29.0 | 27.2 | 14.4 | n.a. | 17.0 | n.a. | 30.0 |
| 1900 | 12.5 | n.a. | 13.2 | 14.3 | 26.1 | 20.7 | 13.6 | n.a. | 14.0 | n.a. | 30.5 |
| 1895 | 12.0 | n.a. | 12.3 | 13.0 | 24.9 | 20.6 | 13.6 | n.a. | 14.0 | n.a. | 26.5 |
| 1890 | 14.5 | n.a. | 12.3 | 12.5 | 25.5 | 20.8 | 13.6 | n.a. | 16.0 | n.a. | 34.5 |

NOTE: n.a. = not available. *Source:* U.S. Bureau of the Census, *Historical Statistics of the United States, Colonial Times to 1970, Bicentennial Edition, Part 2.*

## Output by Major Industry Division, 1990–2010

| Industry | Billions of chained 1992 dollars | | | Percent distribution | | | Percent change | |
|---|---|---|---|---|---|---|---|---|
| | 1990 | 2000 | 2010* | 1990 | 2000 | 2010* | 1990–2000 | 2000–2010* |
| Total | $11,472.2 | $16,180.2 | $22,286.1 | 100.0% | 100.0% | 100.0% | 3.5% | 3.3% |
| Goods producing | 3,947.5 | 5,724.4 | 7,681.0 | 34.4 | 35.4 | 34.5 | 3.8 | 3.0 |
| Mining | 205.4 | 212.1 | 229.9 | 1.8 | 1.3 | 1.0 | 0.3 | 0.8 |
| Construction | 730.0 | 910.1 | 1,182.1 | 6.4 | 5.6 | 5.3 | 2.2 | 2.6 |
| Manufacturing | 3,022.0 | 4,601.4 | 6,278.6 | 26.3 | 28.4 | 28.2 | 4.3 | 3.2 |
| Durable | 1,480.8 | 2,785.2 | 4,136.4 | 12.9 | 17.2 | 18.6 | 6.5 | 4.0 |
| Nondurable | 1,553.0 | 1,834.5 | 2,219.7 | 13.5 | 11.3 | 10.0 | 1.7 | 1.9 |
| Service producing | 6,732.3 | 9,421.9 | 13,079.1 | 58.7 | 58.2 | 58.7 | 3.4 | 3.3 |
| Transportation, communications, and utilities | 931.1 | 1,278.0 | 1,961.9 | 8.1 | 7.9 | 8.8 | 3.2 | 4.4 |
| Wholesale trade | 607.7 | 920.4 | 1,409.6 | 5.3 | 5.7 | 6.3 | 4.2 | 4.4 |
| Retail trade | 896.8 | 1,222.4 | 1,627.9 | 7.8 | 7.6 | 7.3 | 3.1 | 2.9 |
| Finance, insurance, and real estate | 1,198.1 | 1,806.4 | 2,429.1 | 10.4 | 11.2 | 10.9 | 4.2 | 3.0 |
| Services | 2,056.7 | 3,031.5 | 4,377.9 | 17.9 | 18.7 | 19.6 | 4.0 | 3.7 |
| Government | 1,043.4 | 1,161.6 | 1,287.5 | 9.1 | 7.2 | 5.8 | 1.1 | 1.0 |
| Federal government | 388.9 | 353.3 | 359.8 | 3.4 | 2.2 | 1.6 | −1.0 | 0.2 |
| State and local government | 654.5 | 808.3 | 927.7 | 5.7 | 5.0 | 4.2 | 2.1 | 1.4 |
| Agriculture | 257.2 | 333.7 | 404.5 | 2.2 | 2.1 | 1.8 | 2.6 | 1.9 |
| Private households | 12.6 | 14.7 | 13.3 | 0.1 | 0.1 | 0.1 | 1.5 | −1.0 |
| Special industries[1] | 529.9 | 706.8 | 1,102.2 | 4.6 | 4.4 | 4.9 | 2.9 | 4.5 |
| Residual[2] | −7.4 | −21.3 | 5.9 | −0.1 | −0.1 | 0.0 | — | — |

*Projected. 1. Consists of nonproducing accounting categories to reconcile input-output system with NIPA accounts. 2. Residual is shown for the first level only. Subcategories do not necessarily add to higher categories as a byproduct of chain-weighting. *Source:* U.S. Department of Labor, Bureau of Labor Statistics, *Monthly Labor Review,* Nov. 2001.

## Per Capita Consumption of Principal Foods[1]

### (in pounds)

| Food | 1990 | 1995 | 1997 | 1998 | 1999 | Food | 1990 | 1995 | 1997 | 1998 | 1999 |
|---|---|---|---|---|---|---|---|---|---|---|---|
| Red meats[2,3,4] | 112.3 | 115.1 | 111.0 | 115.6 | 117.7 | Fats and oils | 63.0 | 66.3 | 64.9 | 65.6 | 68.5 |
| Beef | 63.9 | 64.4 | 63.8 | 64.9 | 65.8 | Butter and margarine (product weight) | 15.3 | 13.7 | 12.8 | 12.8 | 12.9 |
| Veal | 0.9 | 0.8 | 0.9 | 0.7 | 0.6 | | | | | | |
| Lamb & mutton | 1.0 | 0.9 | 0.8 | 0.9 | 0.9 | | | | | | |
| Pork | 46.4 | 49.0 | 45.5 | 49.2 | 50.5 | Shortening | 22.2 | 22.5 | 20.9 | 21.0 | 21.6 |
| Poultry[2,3,4] | 56.3 | 62.9 | 64.2 | 65.0 | 68.3 | Lard | 2.2 | 4.3 | 4.1 | 5.2 | 5.7 |
| Chicken | 42.4 | 48.8 | 50.3 | 50.8 | 54.2 | Salad and cooking oils | 25.3 | 26.9 | 28.6 | 27.9 | 29.4 |
| Turkey | 13.8 | 14.1 | 13.9 | 14.2 | 14.1 | | | | | | |
| Fish and shellfish[3] | 15.0 | 14.9 | 14.5 | 14.8 | 15.2 | Fruits and vegetables | 656.0 | 694.3 | 717.9 | 702.4 | 719.0 |
| Eggs[4] | 30.2 | 30.2 | 30.7 | 31.8 | 32.8 | Fruit | 272.6 | 284.9 | 296.9 | 284.4 | 297.9 |
| Cheese [2,5] | 24.6 | 27.3 | 28.0 | 28.3 | 29.8 | Vegetables | 383.5 | 409.4 | 421.0 | 418.0 | 421.2 |
| Cottage cheese | 3.4 | 2.7 | 2.7 | 2.7 | 2.7 | Peanuts (shelled) | 6.0 | 5.7 | 5.9 | 5.9 | 6.4 |
| Beverage milks[2] | 221.8 | 209.8 | 206.8 | 204.6 | 203.8 | Tree nuts (shelled) | 2.4 | 1.9 | 2.1 | 2.3 | 2.7 |
| Fluid cream products[5] | 7.6 | 8.4 | 9.0 | 9.2 | 9.7 | Flour and cereal products[8] | 181.0 | 192.8 | 200.9 | 198.4 | 201.9 |
| Yogurt (excluding frozen) | 4.0 | 5.1 | 5.1 | 5.1 | 5.0 | Wheat flour | 100.0 | 141.0 | 140.8 | 146.0 | 148.4 |
| Ice cream | 15.8 | 15.7 | 16.4 | 16.6 | 16.8 | Rice (milled basis) | 15.8 | 18.9 | 18.4 | 18.9 | 19.4 |
| Lowfat ice cream[6] | 7.7 | 7.5 | 7.9 | 8.3 | 7.9 | Caloric sweeteners[9] | 136.9 | 149.8 | 154.0 | 155.1 | 158.4 |
| Frozen yogurt | 3.0 | 0.5 | 1.1 | 2.2 | 2.1 | Coffee (green bean equiv.) | 10.3 | 8.0 | 9.3 | 9.5 | 10.0 |
| All dairy products, milk equivalent, milkfat basis[7] | 568.3 | 583.8 | 577.6 | 581.7 | 597.9 | Cocoa (chocolate liquor equiv.) | 4.3 | 3.6 | 4.1 | 4.4 | 4.6 |

1. In pounds, retail weight unless otherwise stated. Consumption normally represents total supply minus exports, nonfood use, and ending stocks. Calendar-year data, except fresh citrus fruits, peanuts, tree nuts, and rice, which are on crop year basis. 2. Totals may not add due to rounding. 3. Boneless, trimmed weight. Chicken series revised to exclude amount of ready-to-cook chicken going to pet food as well as some water leakage that occurs when chicken is cut up before packaging. 4. Excludes shipments to the U.S. territories. 5. Heavy cream, light cream, half and half, eggnog, sour cream, and dip. 6. Formerly known as ice milk. 7. Includes condensed and evaporated milk and dry milk products. 8. Includes rye, corn, oats, and barley products. Excludes quantities used in alcoholic beverages, corn sweeteners, and fuel. 9. Dry weight equivalent. *Source:* U.S. Department of Agriculture, Economic Research Service. Web: www.usda.gov.

## Farm Income
(in millions of dollars)

| Year | Cash receipts from marketings Crops[1] | Livestock, livestock products | Government payments | Gross cash income | Year | Cash receipts from marketings Crops[1] | Livestock, livestock products | Government payments | Gross cash income |
|---|---|---|---|---|---|---|---|---|---|
| 1930 | $ 3,868 | $ 5,187 | — | $ 9,055 | 1990 | $80,131 | $89,843 | $ 9,298 | $186,824 |
| 1935 | 2,977 | 4,143 | $ 573 | 7,693 | 1991 | 82,060 | 86,735 | 8,214 | 184,858 |
| 1940 | 3,469 | 4,913 | 723 | 9,105 | 1992 | 84,853 | 86,350 | 9,169 | 188,160 |
| 1945 | 9,655 | 12,008 | 742 | 22,405 | 1993 | 87,500 | 90,200 | 13,402 | 200,100 |
| 1950 | 12,356 | 16,105 | 283 | 28,764 | 1994 | 93,100 | 88,200 | 7,900 | 198,300 |
| 1955 | 13,523 | 15,967 | 229 | 29,842 | 1995 | 101,000 | 87,100 | 7,300 | 205,900 |
| 1960 | 15,023 | 18,989 | 703 | 34,958 | 1996 | 106,200 | 93,000 | 7,300 | 217,400 |
| 1965 | 17,479 | 21,886 | 2,463 | 42,215 | 1997 | 111,100 | 96,500 | 7,500 | 227,500 |
| 1970 | 20,977 | 29,532 | 3,717 | 54,768 | 1998 | 102,200 | 94,500 | 12,200 | 225,000 |
| 1975 | 45,813 | 43,089 | 807 | 90,707 | 1999 | 93,100 | 95,500 | 20,600 | 225,000 |
| 1980 | 71,746 | 67,991 | 1,285 | 143,295 | 2000 | 94,100 | 99,500 | 22,900 | 230,100 |
| 1985 | 74,293 | 69,822 | 7,705 | 157,854 | 2001[2] | 97,000 | 108,500 | 20,000 | 239,300 |

1. Includes items not listed. 2. Forecast. *Source:* U.S. Department of Agriculture, Economic Research Service. *Agricultural Income and Finance.* Web: www.usda.gov.

## Farm Indexes
(1990–1992 = 100)

| Year | Prices paid by farmers[1] | Prices rec'd by farmers[2] | Ratio[3] | Year | Prices paid by farmers[1] | Prices rec'd by farmers[2] | Ratio[3] |
|---|---|---|---|---|---|---|---|
| 1975 | 47 | 73 | 155 | 1994 | 106 | 100 | 94 |
| 1980 | 75 | 98 | 137 | 1995 | 109 | 102 | 93 |
| 1985 | 86 | 91 | 106 | 1996 | 115 | 112 | 98 |
| 1990 | 99 | 104 | 105 | 1997 | 118 | 107 | 91 |
| 1991 | 100 | 100 | 99 | 1998 | 115 | 101 | 88 |
| 1992 | 101 | 98 | 97 | 1999 | 115 | 96 | 83 |
| 1993 | 104 | 101 | 97 | 2000 | 120 | 96 | 80 |

1. Commodities and services, interest, taxes, and wage rates. 2. All farm products. 3. Ratio of index of prices received by farmers to index of prices paid by farmers. May not compute directly due to rounding. *Source:* U.S. Department of Agriculture, National Agricultural Statistics Service. Web: www.usda.gov.

## Number of Farms by State, 1999–2001

| State | 1999 | 2000 | 2001 | State | 1999 | 2000 | 2001 |
|---|---|---|---|---|---|---|---|
| Alabama | 48,000 | 47,000 | 47,000 | Nebraska | 55,000 | 54,000 | 53,000 |
| Alaska | 570 | 580 | 580 | Nevada | 3,000 | 3,000 | 3,000 |
| Arizona | 7,700 | 7,500 | 7,300 | New Hampshire | 3,100 | 3,100 | 3,100 |
| Arkansas | 48,500 | 48,000 | 48,000 | New Jersey | 9,600 | 9,600 | 9,600 |
| California | 89,000 | 87,500 | 88,000 | New Mexico | 15,500 | 15,200 | 15,000 |
| Colorado | 29,000 | 29,000 | 30,000 | New York | 39,000 | 38,000 | 37,500 |
| Connecticut | 4,000 | 3,900 | 3,900 | North Carolina | 58,000 | 57,000 | 56,000 |
| Delaware | 2,600 | 2,600 | 2,500 | North Dakota | 30,500 | 30,300 | 30,300 |
| Florida | 45,000 | 44,000 | 44,000 | Ohio | 80,000 | 80,000 | 78,000 |
| Georgia | 50,000 | 50,000 | 50,000 | Oklahoma | 84,000 | 85,000 | 86,000 |
| Hawaii | 5,500 | 5,700 | 5,300 | Oregon | 40,500 | 40,000 | 40,000 |
| Idaho | 24,500 | 24,500 | 24,000 | Pennsylvania | 59,000 | 59,000 | 59,000 |
| Illinois | 79,000 | 78,000 | 76,000 | Rhode Island | 700 | 700 | 700 |
| Indiana | 65,000 | 64,000 | 63,000 | South Carolina | 25,000 | 24,000 | 24,000 |
| Iowa | 96,000 | 95,000 | 93,500 | South Dakota | 32,500 | 32,500 | 32,500 |
| Kansas | 65,000 | 64,000 | 63,000 | Tennessee | 91,000 | 90,000 | 91,000 |
| Kentucky | 91,000 | 90,000 | 88,000 | Texas | 227,000 | 226,000 | 227,000 |
| Louisiana | 30,000 | 29,500 | 29,000 | Utah | 15,500 | 15,500 | 15,000 |
| Maine | 6,900 | 6,800 | 6,700 | Vermont | 6,700 | 6,800 | 6,600 |
| Maryland | 12,400 | 12,400 | 12,400 | Virginia | 49,000 | 49,000 | 49,000 |
| Massachusetts | 6,100 | 6,100 | 6,000 | Washington | 40,000 | 40,000 | 39,000 |
| Michigan | 53,000 | 52,000 | 52,000 | West Virginia | 20,500 | 20,500 | 20,500 |
| Minnesota | 80,000 | 79,000 | 79,000 | Wisconsin | 78,000 | 77,000 | 77,000 |
| Mississippi | 43,000 | 43,000 | 42,000 | Wyoming | 9,200 | 9,200 | 9,200 |
| Missouri | 110,000 | 109,000 | 108,000 | **U.S. total** | **2,192,070** | **2,172,080** | **2,157,780** |
| Montana | 28,000 | 27,600 | 26,600 | | | | |

NOTE: A farm is any establishment from which $1,000 or more of agricultural products were sold or would normally be sold during the year. *Source:* U.S. Department of Agriculture. Web: www.usda.gov.

## Agricultural Output by State, 2001 Crops

| State | Corn (1,000 bu) | Wheat (1,000 bu) | Cotton, ginned (1,000 ba) | Potatoes (1,000 cwt) | Rice (1,000 cwt) | Cattle[1] (1,000 head) | Hogs and pigs[2] (1,000 head) |
|---|---|---|---|---|---|---|---|
| Alabama | 16,050 | 3,360 | 890 | 624 | | 1,360 | 195 |
| Alaska | | | | | | 10.5 | 1 |
| Arizona | 5,824 | 8,517 | 705 | 2,214 | | 840 | 133 |
| Arkansas | 26,825 | 50,440 | 1,825 | | 101,312 | 1,800 | 570 |
| California | 27,200 | 35,105 | 2,420 | 12,788 | 38,490 | 5,150 | 110 |
| Colorado | 149,800 | 69,168 | | 23,274 | | 3,150 | 780 |
| Connecticut | | | | | | 63 | 3.5 |
| Delaware | 23,652 | 3,477 | | 1,161 | | 27 | 26 |
| Florida | 2,262 | 369 | 169 | 9,295 | | 1,800 | 35 |
| Georgia | 29,480 | 10,600 | 2,200 | | | 1,270 | 310 |
| Hawaii | | | | | | 150 | 27 |
| Idaho | 6,750 | 85,150 | | 127,980 | | 1,960 | 24 |
| Illinois | 1,649,200 | 43,920 | | 1,855 | | 1,470 | 4,250 |
| Indiana | 884,520 | 25,080 | | 928 | | 880 | 3,150 |
| Iowa | 1,664,400 | 972 | | | | 3,650 | 15,00 |
| Kansas | 387,350 | 328,000 | 23 | 720 | | 6,700 | 1,560 |
| Kentucky | 156,200 | 23,760 | | | | 2,260 | 405 |
| Louisiana | 45,436 | 8,000 | 1,030 | | 30,014 | 860 | 26 |
| Maine | | | | 16,120 | | 97 | 6.5 |
| Maryland | 55,760 | 11,025 | | 1,175 | | 235 | 52 |
| Massachusetts | | | | 742 | | 48 | 18 |
| Michigan | 199,500 | 35,840 | | 14,030 | | 980 | 960 |
| Minnesota | 806,000 | 79,655 | | 18,425 | | 2,550 | 5,600 |
| Mississippi | 50,050 | 11,700 | 2,360 | | 16,445 | 1,070 | 285 |
| Missouri | 345,800 | 41,040 | 720 | 1,904 | 12,317 | 4,250 | 3,000 |
| Montana | 1,924 | 96,570 | | 3,040 | | 2,550 | 170 |
| Nebraska | 1,139,250 | 59,200 | | 8,512 | | 6,600 | 2,900 |
| Nevada | | 270 | | 2,340 | | 520 | 7 |
| New Hampshire | | | | | | 42 | 3.5 |
| New Jersey | 7,392 | 1,215 | | 638 | | 48 | 13 |
| New Mexico | 8,280 | 8,160 | 130 | 2,198 | | 1,580 | 3 |
| New York | 56,700 | 6,360 | | 5,942 | | 1,380 | 75 |
| North Carolina | 78,125 | 18,330 | 1,620 | 3,515 | | 950 | 9,500 |
| North Dakota | 81,075 | 292,400 | | 26,400 | | 1,980 | 154 |
| Ohio | 437,460 | 60,300 | | 984 | | 1,240 | 1,420 |
| Oklahoma | 26,250 | 122,100 | 210 | | | 5,050 | 2,470 |
| Oregon | 2,520 | 33,250 | | 20,730 | | 1,360 | 29 |
| Pennsylvania | 97,020 | 8,320 | | 3,173 | | 1,640 | 1,060 |
| Rhode Island | | | | 135 | | 6 | 2.5 |
| South Carolina | 25,920 | 9,030 | 425 | | | 445 | 320 |
| South Dakota | 370,600 | 76,766 | | 648 | | 4,050 | 1,280 |
| Tennessee | 81,840 | 18,360 | 975 | | | 2,170 | 225 |
| Texas | 167,560 | 108,800 | 4,183 | 5,190 | 14,467 | 13,700 | 900 |
| Utah | 2,130 | 6,034 | | 345 | | 910 | 610 |
| Vermont | | | | | | 295 | 2.5 |
| Virginia | 40,590 | 10,200 | 199 | 1,386 | | 1,650 | 410 |
| Washington | 10,450 | 132,580 | | 94,400 | | 1,180 | 24 |
| West Virginia | 3,120 | 464 | | | | 400 | 11 |
| Wisconsin | 330,200 | 10,708 | | 31,955 | | 3,350 | 540 |
| Wyoming | 6,375 | 3,048 | | | | 1,550 | 117 |
| **Total U.S.** | **9,506,840** | **1,957,643** | **20,084** | **444,766** | **213,045** | **97,276.5** | **58,774** |

NOTE: All figures are for th— ... ███ 1. grapaa ██████████, 1. Inventory as of Jan. 1, 2002. 2. Inventory as of Dec. 1, 2001. *Source:* U.S. Department of Agriculture, National Agricultural Statistics Service. Web: www.usda.gov.

## Number of Farms, Land in Farms, and Average-Size Farm: United States, 1990–2001

| Year | Number of farms | Land in farms (1,000 acres) | Average farm size (acres) | Year | Number of farms | Land in farms (1,000 acres) | Average farm size (acres) |
|---|---|---|---|---|---|---|---|
| 1990 | 2,145,820 | 986,850 | 460 | 1996 | 2,190,500 | 958,675 | 438 |
| 1991 | 2,116,760 | 981,736 | 464 | 1997 | 2,190,510 | 956,010 | 436 |
| 1992 | 2,107,840 | 978,503 | 464 | 1998 | 2,191,360 | 953,500 | 435 |
| 1993 | 2,201,590 | 968,845 | 440 | 1999 | 2,192,070 | 947,440 | 432 |
| 1994 | 2,197,690 | 965,935 | 440 | 2000 | 2,172,080 | 942,990 | 434 |
| 1995 | 2,196,400 | 962,515 | 438 | 2001 | 2,157,780 | 941,210 | 436 |

NOTE: A farm is any establishment from which $1,000 or more of agricultural products were sold or would normally be sold during the year. *Source:* U.S. Department of Agriculture. Web: www.usda.gov.

## Top Advertising Categories

| Rank | Category | 2001 spending | Change vs. 2000 | Rank | Category | 2001 spending | Change vs. 2000 |
|---|---|---|---|---|---|---|---|
| 1 | Automotive | $1,675,861,966 | −2.1% | 12 | Liquor | $307,270,267 | 7.3% |
| 2 | Direct response companies | 1,095,578,705 | 6.0 | 13 | Audio and video equipment and supplies | 304,091,970 | 7.0 |
| 3 | Medicines and proprietary remedies | 1,011,291,447 | 4.8 | 14 | Jewelry and watches | 293,439,525 | 4.2 |
| 4 | Media and advertising | 965,577,684 | −15.7 | 15 | Misc. services and amusements | 287,134,345 | −7.4 |
| 5 | Computers, software, and the internet | 816,528,705 | −32.2 | 16 | Personal hygiene and health | 283,593,128 | 4.5 |
| 6 | Cosmetics and beauty aids | 758,879,605 | 18.6 | 17 | Sporting goods | 279,434,297 | 6.1 |
| 7 | Public transportation, hotels, and resorts | 745,210,320 | 0.3 | 18 | Insurance and real estate | 268,056,447 | 3.2 |
| 8 | Financial | 693,603,026 | −22.4 | 19 | Hair products and accessories | 264,242,087 | 21.8 |
| 9 | Retail | 692,498,320 | −19.7 | 20 | Household furnishings and accessories | 263,986,068 | −3.1 |
| 10 | Ready-to-wear | 560,328,271 | −4.3 | | | | |
| 11 | Dairy, produce, meat, and bakery goods | 377,698,735 | 20.0 | | | | |

*Source:* Magazine Publishers of America.

## Leading National Advertisers

### (in millions; ranked by total U.S. advertising spending)

| Rank | Advertiser | 2001 ad dollars | Rank | Advertiser | 2001 ad dollars |
|---|---|---|---|---|---|
| 1 | General Motors Corp. | $3,374.4 | 14 | Toyota Motor Corp. | $1,399.1 |
| 2 | Procter & Gamble Co. | 2,540.6 | 15 | AT&T Corp. | 1,371.9 |
| 3 | Ford Motor Co. | 2,408.2 | 16 | Sony Corp. | 1,310.1 |
| 4 | PepsiCo | 2,210.4 | 17 | Viacom | 1,282.8 |
| 5 | Pfizer | 2,189.5 | 18 | McDonald's Corp. | 1,194.7 |
| 6 | DaimlerChrysler | 1,985.3 | 19 | Diageo | 1,180.8 |
| 7 | AOL Time Warner | 1,885.3 | 20 | Sprint Corp. | 1,160.1 |
| 8 | Philip Morris Cos. | 1,815.7 | 21 | Merck & Co. | 1,136.6 |
| 9 | Walt Disney Co. | 1,757.3 | 22 | Honda Motor Co. | 1,102.9 |
| 10 | Johnson & Johnson | 1,618.1 | 23 | J.C. Penney Corp. | 1,085.7 |
| 11 | Unilever | 1,483.6 | 24 | U.S. Government | 1,056.8 |
| 12 | Sears, Roebuck & Co. | 1,480.1 | 25 | L'Oreal | 1,040.7 |
| 13 | Verizon Communications | 1,461.6 | | | |

*Source:* AdAge. Web: adage.com.

## World Port Ranking, 1999

| Total cargo volume, metric tons (000s) | | | | Container traffic (TEUs) | | | |
|---|---|---|---|---|---|---|---|
| Rank | Port | Country | Tons | Rank | Port | Country | TEUs |
| 1 | Singapore | Singapore | 325,902 | 1 | Hong Kong | China | 16,211,000 |
| 2 | Rotterdam | Netherlands | 303,520 | 2 | Singapore | Singapore | 15,945,000 |
| 3 | South Louisiana | United States | 194,448 | 3 | Kaohsiung | Taiwan | 6,985,361 |
| 4 | Shanghai | China | 187,000 | 4 | Rotterdam | Netherlands | 6,400,000 |
| 5 | Hong Kong | China | 168,838 | 5 | Busan | South Korea | 6,310,664 |
| 6 | Chiba | Japan | 164,741 | 6 | Long Beach | United States | 4,408,480 |
| 7 | Ulsan | South Korea | 148,332 | 7 | Shanghai | China | 4,210,000 |
| 8 | Houston | United States | 144,184 | 8 | Los Angeles | United States | 3,828,851 |
| 9 | Nagoya | Japan | 133,038 | 9 | Hamburg | Germany | 3,738,307 |
| 10 | Kwangyang | South Korea | 131,059 | 10 | Antwerp | Belgium | 3,614,246 |
| 11 | New York/New Jersey | United States | 121,387 | 11 | Dubai | UAE | 2,844,634 |
| 12 | Antwerp | Belgium | 115,654 | 12 | New York/New Jersey | United States | 2,828,878 |
| 13 | Yokohama | Japan | 114,538 | 13 | Felixstowe | UK | 2,610,000 |
| 14 | Kaohsiung | Taiwan | 110,722 | 14 | Tokyo | Japan | 2,595,000 |
| 15 | Inchon | South Korea | 108,227 | 15 | Port Kelang | Malaysia | 2,550,419 |
| 16 | Busan | South Korea | 107,757 | 16 | Gioia Tauro | Italy | 2,253,401 |
| 17 | Kobe | Japan | 102,527 | 17 | Bremen Ports | Germany | 2,201,220 |
| 18 | Marseilles | France | 90,258 | 18 | Yokohama | Japan | 2,172,919 |
| 19 | Kitayushu | Japan | 87,346 | 19 | Manila | Philippines | 2,147,422 |
| 20 | Richards Bay | South Africa | 86,120 | 20 | San Juan | United States | 2,084,711 |
| 21 | Tokyo | Japan | 85,415 | 21 | Algeciras | Spain | 1,832,557 |
| 22 | Osaka | Japan | 85,391 | 22 | Laem Chabang | Thailand | 1,828,460 |
| 23 | Dampier | Australia | 82,528 | 23 | Colombo | Sri Lanka | 1,704,389 |
| 24 | Hamburg | Germany | 81,037 | 24 | Keelung | Taiwan | 1,665,618 |

| | Total cargo volume, metric tons (000s) | | | | Container traffic (TEUs) | | |
|---|---|---|---|---|---|---|---|
| Rank | Port | Country | Tons | Rank | Port | Country | TEUs |
| 25 | New Orleans | United States | 79,443 | 25 | Oakland | United States | 1,663,756 |
| 26 | Dalian | China | 75,150 | 26 | Yantian | China | 1,580,000 |
| 27 | Newcastle | Australia | 72,711 | 27 | Nagoya | Japan | 1,566,961 |
| 28 | Vancouver (BC) | Canada | 71,213 | 28 | Quindao | China | 1,540,000 |
| 29 | Corpus Christi | United States | 70,796 | 29 | Seattle | United States | 1,490,048 |
| 30 | Qindao | China | 70,180 | 30 | Charleston | United States | 1,482,995 |
| 31 | Tubarao | Brazil | 67,069 | 31 | LeHavre | France | 1,378,379 |
| 32 | Port Hedland | Australia | 65,431 | 32 | Hampton Roads | United States | 1,306,537 |
| 33 | LeHavre | France | 63,922 | 33 | Xingang/Tientijin | China | 1,300,000 |
| 34 | Beaumont | United States | 63,007 | 34 | Tacoma | United States | 1,271,011 |
| 35 | Port Kelang | Malaysia | 60,970 | 35 | Barcelona | Spain | 1,234,987 |
| 36 | Manila | Philippines | 59,133 | 36 | Genoa | Italy | 1,233,817 |
| 37 | Baton Rouge | United States | 57,853 | 37 | Cristobal | Panama | 1,153,000 |
| 38 | Plaquemines | United States | 56,702 | 38 | Valencia | Spain | 1,152,780 |
| 39 | Amsterdam | Netherlands | 55,725 | 39 | Melbourne | Australia | 1,125,748 |
| 40 | Long Beach | United States | 55,269 | 40 | Taichung | Taiwan | 1,106,668 |

*Source:* American Association of Port Authorities. Web: www.aapa-ports.org.

## Largest U.S. Businesses

| 2001 rank | Company | Revenues ($ millions) | 2001 rank | Company | Revenues ($ millions) |
|---|---|---|---|---|---|
| 1 | Wal-Mart Stores | $219,812.0 | 47 | Johnson & Johnson | 33,004.0 |
| 2 | Exxon Mobil | 191,581.0 | 48 | Conoco | 32,795.0 |
| 3 | General Motors | 177,260.0 | 49 | Pfizer | 32,259.0 |
| 4 | Ford Motor | 162,412.0 | 50 | J.C. Penney | 32,004.0 |
| 5 | Enron | 138,718.0 | 51 | MetLife | 31,928.0 |
| 6 | General Electric | 125,913.0 | 52 | Mirant | 31,502.0 |
| 7 | Citigroup | 112,022.0 | 53 | Dell Computer | 31,168.0 |
| 8 | ChevronTexaco | 99,699.0 | 54 | Goldman Sachs Group | 31,138.0 |
| 9 | Intl. Business Machines | 85,866.0 | 55 | United Parcel Service | 30,646.0 |
| 10 | Philip Morris | 72,944.0 | 56 | Motorola | 30,004.0 |
| 11 | Verizon Communications | 67,190.0 | 57 | Allstate | 28,865.0 |
| 12 | American Intl. Group | 62,402.0 | 58 | TXU | 27,927.0 |
| 13 | American Electric Power | 61,257.0 | 59 | United Technologies | 27,897.0 |
| 14 | Duke Energy | 59,503.0 | 60 | Dow Chemical | 27,805.0 |
| 15 | AT&T | 59,142.0 | 61 | ConAgra | 27,194.2 |
| 16 | Boeing | 58,198.0 | 62 | Prudential Financial | 27,177.0 |
| 17 | El Paso | 57,475.0 | 63 | PepsiCo | 26,935.0 |
| 18 | Home Depot | 53,553.0 | 64 | Wells Fargo | 26,891.0 |
| 19 | Bank of America Corp. | 52,641.0 | 65 | Intel | 26,539.0 |
| 20 | Fannie Mae | 50,803.0 | 66 | International Paper | 26,363.0 |
| 21 | J.P. Morgan Chase | 50,429.0 | 67 | Delphi | 26,088.0 |
| 22 | Kroger | 50,098.0 | 68 | Sprint | 26,071.0 |
| 23 | Cardinal Health | 47,947.6 | 69 | New York Life Insurance | 25,678.2 |
| 24 | Merck | 47,715.7 | 70 | DuPont de Nemours (E.I.) | 25,370.0 |
| 25 | State Farm Insurance | 46,705.2 | 71 | Georgia-Pacific | 25,309.0 |
| 26 | Reliant Energy | 46,225.8 | 72 | Microsoft | 25,296.0 |
| 27 | SBC Communications | 45,908.0 | 73 | Walt Disney | 25,269.0 |
| 28 | Hewlett-Packard | 45,226.0 | 74 | Aetna | 25,190.8 |
| 29 | Morgan Stanley | 43,727.0 | 75 | Ingram Micro | 25,186.9 |
| 30 | Dynegy | 42,242.0 | 76 | Lucent Technologies | 25,132.0 |
| 31 | MirKisson | 42,010.0 | 77 | I Annran Mann | 24,700.0 |
| 32 | Sears Roebuck | 41,078.0 | 78 | Walgreen | 24,623.0 |
| 33 | Aquila | 40,376.8 | 79 | Bank One Corp. | 24,527.0 |
| 34 | Target | 39,000.0 | 80 | TIAA-CREF | 24,230.6 |
| 35 | Procter & Gamble | 39,244.0 | 81 | Phillips Petroleum | 24,189.0 |
| 36 | Merrill Lynch | 38,793.0 | 82 | BellSouth | 24,130.0 |
| 37 | AOL Time Warner | 38,234.0 | 83 | Honeywell Intl. | 23,652.0 |
| 38 | Albertson's | 37,931.0 | 84 | UnitedHealth Group | 23,454.0 |
| 39 | Berkshire Hathaway | 37,668.0 | 85 | Viacom | 23,222.8 |
| 40 | Kmart | 36,910.0 | 86 | Supervalu | 23,194.3 |
| 41 | Freddie Mac | 35,523.0 | 87 | PG&E Corp. | 22,959.0 |
| 42 | WorldCom | 35,179.0 | 88 | Alcoa | 22,859.0 |
| 43 | Marathon Oil | 35,041.0 | 89 | American Express | 22,582.0 |
| 44 | Costco Wholesale | 34,797.0 | 90 | Wachovia Corp. | 22,396.0 |
| 45 | Safeway | 34,301.0 | 91 | Lehman Brothers Hldgs. | 22,392.0 |
| 46 | Compaq Computer | 33,554.0 | 92 | Cisco Systems | 22,293.0 |

| 2001 rank | Company | Revenues ($ millions) | 2001 rank | Company | Revenues ($ millions) |
|---|---|---|---|---|---|
| 93 | CVS | 22,241.4 | 97 | Electronic Data Systems | 21,543.0 |
| 94 | Lowe's | 22,111.1 | 98 | Caterpillar | 20,450.0 |
| 95 | Sysco | 21,784.5 | 99 | Coca-Cola | 20,092.0 |
| 96 | Bristol-Myers Squibb | 21,717.0 | 100 | Archer Daniels Midland | 20,051.4 |

*Source:* Fortune 500, © 2002 Time, Inc. All rights reserved. For more detailed information, visit *Fortune* on the Web, www.fortune.com/lists/F500/index.html.

## United States' Largest Banks
### (in thousands of U.S. dollars)

| Rank | Name (city, state) | Total assets | Rank | Name (city, state) | Total assets |
|---|---|---|---|---|---|
| 1 | Citigroup Inc. (New York, N.Y.) | $1,057,657,000 | 17 | State Street Corp. (Boston, Mass.) | 73,299,137 |
| 2 | J. P. Morgan Chase & Company (New York, N.Y.) | 712,508,000 | 18 | Fifth Third Bancorp (Cincinnati, Ohio) | 70,618,618 |
| 3 | Bank of America Corp. (Charlotte, N.C.) | 619,921,000 | 19 | PNC Financial Services Group, Inc., The (Pittsburgh, Pa.) | 66,582,915 |
| 4 | Wachovia Corp. (Charlotte, N.C.) | 319,853,000 | 20 | Citizens Financial Group, Inc. (Providence, R.I.) | 52,972,492 |
| 5 | Wells Fargo & Company (San Francisco, Calif.) | 311,509,000 | 21 | Comerica Inc. (Detroit, Mich.) | 50,322,058 |
| 6 | Bank One Corp. (Chicago, Ill.) | 262,947,000 | 22 | Southtrust Corp. (Birmingham, Ala.) | 48,458,485 |
| 7 | Taunus Corp. (New York, N.Y.) | 235,867,000 | 23 | MBNA Corp. (Wilmington, Del.) | 46,511,939 |
| 8 | FleetBoston Financial Corp. (Boston, Mass.) | 192,032,000 | 24 | Regions Financial Corp. (Birmingham, Ala.) | 44,304,788 |
| 9 | ABN Amro North America Holding Company (Chicago, Ill.) | 174,451,001 | 25 | Charles Schwab Corp., The (San Francisco, Calif.) | 38,821,020 |
| 10 | U.S. Bancorp (Minneapolis, Minn.) | 164,745,000 | 26 | Amsouth Bancorporation (Birmingham, Ala.) | 38,275,540 |
| 11 | HSBC North America Inc. (Buffalo, N.Y.) | 110,468,140 | 27 | Northern Trust Corp. (Chicago, Ill.) | 37,961,610 |
| 12 | Suntrust Banks, Inc. (Atlanta, Ga.) | 106,244,822 | 28 | Charter One Financial, Inc. (Cleveland, Ohio) | 37,818,302 |
| 13 | National City Corp. (Cleveland, Ohio) | 100,196,346 | 29 | Unionbancal Corp. (San Francisco, Calif.) | 36,224,237 |
| 14 | Keycorp (Cleveland, Ohio) | 80,726,567 | 30 | Bankmont Financial Corp. (Wilmington, Del.) | 34,811,350 |
| 15 | Bank of New York Company, Inc., The (New York, N.Y.) | 76,823,850 | | | |
| 16 | BB&T Corp. (Winston-Salem, N.C.) | 74,949,720 | | | |

NOTE: As of March 31, 2002. *Source:* Federal Reserve System, National Information Center.

## Top-Selling Light Trucks in the U.S., 1999–2001

| Rank | 1999 | Number | 2000 | Number | 2001 | Number |
|---|---|---|---|---|---|---|
| 1 | Ford F Series | 806,579 | Ford F Series | 820,248 | Ford F Series | 1,330,230 |
| 2 | Chevy Silverado | 533,177 | Chevy Silverado | 634,118 | Ford Explorer | 611,766 |
| 3 | Dodge Ram Pickup | 428,930 | Ford Explorer | 445,157 | Dodge Ram Pickup | 539,877 |
| 4 | Ford Explorer | 428,772 | Dodge Ram Pickup | 380,874 | Ford Ranger | 386,274 |
| 5 | Ford Ranger | 348,358 | Ford Ranger | 330,125 | Dodge Caravan | 386,174 |
| 6 | Jeep Grand Cherokee | 300,031 | Dodge Caravan | 285,739 | Jeep Grand Cherokee | 326,910 |
| 7 | Dodge Caravan | 293,100 | Jeep Grand Cherokee | 271,723 | GMC Sierra | 306,580 |
| 8 | Chevrolet S10 Pickup | 233,669 | Chevrolet S Blazer | 225,948 | Chevy Tahoe | 301,777 |
| 9 | Ford Expedition | 233,125 | Ford Windstar | 222,298 | Ford Windstar | 257,247 |
| 10 | Chevrolet S Blazer | 232,140 | Ford Expedition | 213,483 | Ford Expedition | 253,200 |

*Source:* Ward's AutoInfoBank. Web: www.wardsauto.com.

## Top-Selling Passenger Cars in the U.S., 1999–2001

| Rank | 1999 | Number | 2000 | Number | 2001 | Number |
|---|---|---|---|---|---|---|
| 1 | Toyota Camry | 448,162 | Toyota Camry | 422,961 | Toyota Camry | 616,054 |
| 2 | Honda Accord | 404,192 | Honda Accord | 404,515 | Honda Accord | 596,321 |
| 3 | Ford Taurus | 368,327 | Ford Taurus | 382,035 | Ford Taurus | 517,523 |
| 4 | Honda Civic | 318,308 | Honda Civic | 324,528 | Honda Civic | 487,336 |
| 5 | Chevrolet Cavalier | 272,122 | Ford Focus | 286,166 | Ford Focus | 381,748 |
| 6 | Ford Escort | 260,486 | Chevrolet Cavalier | 236,803 | Chevy Cavalier | 372,909 |
| 7 | Toyota Corolla | 249,128 | Toyota Corolla | 230,156 | Toyota Corolla | 338,534 |
| 8 | Pontiac Grand Am | 234,936 | Pontiac Grand Am | 214,923 | Chevy Impala | 302,953 |
| 9 | Chevrolet Malibu | 218,540 | Chevrolet Malibu | 207,376 | Pontiac Grand Am | 267,070 |
| 10 | Saturn S | 207,977 | Saturn S | 177,355 | Chevy Malibu | 264,841 |

*Source:* Ward's AutoInfoBank. Web: www.wardsauto.com.

## Top NYSE Stocks by Dollar Value

| Rank 2001 | Rank 2000 | Company name (symbol) | 2001 dollar volume (in millions) | Rank 2001 | Rank 2000 | Company name (symbol) | 2001 dollar volume (in millions) |
|---|---|---|---|---|---|---|---|
| 1 | 5 | Int'l Business Machines (IBM) | $189,407 | 26 | 34 | Lilly (Eli) Co. (LLY) | $59,707 |
| 2 | 3 | General Electric (GE) | 187,414 | 27 | 45 | Viacom Inc. (VIA.B) | 58,822 |
| 3 | 2 | AOL Time Warner (AOL) | 143,769 | 28 | — | Verizon Communications (VZ) | 55,539 |
| 4 | 8 | Citigroup Inc. (C) | 136,829 | 29 | 44 | Schering-Plough (SGP) | 55,532 |
| 5 | 14 | Pfizer Inc. (PFE) | 114,141 | 30 | 49 | Pharmacia Corp. (PHΛ) | 54,471 |
| 6 | 6 | EMC Corp. (EMC) | 111,481 | 31 | 11 | AT&T Corp. (T) | 53,741 |
| 7 | 22 | Tyco International Ltd. (TYC) | 106,576 | 32 | 1 | Nortel Networks Corp. (NT) | 53,631 |
| 8 | 23 | American Int'l Group Inc. (AIG) | 99,890 | 33 | 38 | Schlumberger Limited (SLB) | 51,217 |
| 9 | 15 | Exxon Mobil Corp. (XOM) | 98,421 | 34 | — | Enron Corp. (ENE) | 50,434 |
| 10 | 28 | Johnson & Johnson (JNJ) | 95,479 | 35 | 29 | Procter & Gamble (PG) | 50,339 |
| 11 | 18 | Merck & Co. (MRK) | 88,359 | 36 | 7 | Corning Inc. (GLW) | 49,854 |
| 12 | 20 | Wal-Mart Stores (WMT) | 79,856 | 37 | 35 | American Express (AXP) | 49,452 |
| 13 | 39 | J.P. Morgan Chase & Co. (JPM) | 76,451 | 38 | — | Freddie Mac (FRE) | 49,281 |
| 14 | 9 | Texas Instruments (TXN) | 76,221 | 39 | — | Minnesota Mining and Manufacturing Co. (MMM) | 49,266 |
| 15 | 33 | Bank of America Corp. (BAC) | 75,011 | 40 | 36 | Coca-Cola Co. (KO) | 47,639 |
| 16 | 24 | Morgan Stanley Dean Witter (MWD) | 74,763 | 41 | 48 | American Home Products (AHP) | 47,457 |
| 17 | 10 | Nokia Corp. (NOK) | 73,222 | 42 | — | PepsiCo, Inc. (PEP) | 47,244 |
| 18 | 26 | Merrill Lynch & Co., Inc. (MER) | 72,251 | 43 | — | Wells Fargo & Company (WFC) | 46,093 |
| 19 | 37 | Philip Morris Cos. (MO) | 71,275 | 44 | 32 | Qwest Communications Int'l (Q) | 45,280 |
| 20 | 42 | Fannie Mae (FNM) | 69,416 | 45 | 50 | Honeywell Int'l Inc. (HON) | 45,264 |
| 21 | 27 | Home Depot Inc. (HD) | 69,073 | 46 | 17 | Hewlett-Packard (HWP) | 42,663 |
| 22 | 25 | Bristol-Myers Squibb (BMY) | 66,460 | 47 | — | The Boeing Company (BA) | 42,146 |
| 23 | 13 | Micron Technology Inc. (MU) | 65,867 | 48 | 12 | Motorola, Inc. (MOT) | 41,244 |
| 24 | 30 | SBC Communications Inc. (SBC) | 63,073 | 49 | — | Medtronic, Inc. (MDT) | 40,923 |
| 25 | — | The Goldman Sachs Group, Inc. (GS) | 60,780 | 50 | — | Washington Mutual, Inc. (WM) | 39,470 |

Source: New York Stock Exchange.

## 50 Most Active Stocks on NYSE

| Rank 2001 | Rank 2000 | Company name (symbol) | 2001 share volume (in millions) | Rank 2001 | Rank 2000 | Company name (symbol) | 2001 share volume (in millions) |
|---|---|---|---|---|---|---|---|
| 1 | 8 | General Electric (GE) | 4,363.4 | 27 | 16 | Wal-Mart Stores (WMT) | 1,542.7 |
| 2 | 1 | Lucent Technologies, Inc. (LU) | 4,264.1 | 28 | 24 | Disney (Walt) Co. (DIS) | 1,520.4 |
| 3 | 13 | EMC Corp. (EMC) | 3,864.1 | 29 | 11 | Philip Morris Cos. (MO) | 1,515.0 |
| 4 | 5 | Nortel Networks Corp. (NT) | 3,541.8 | 30 | 19 | SBC Communications Inc. (SBC) | 1,468.0 |
| 5 | 4 | AOL Time Warner (AOL) | 3,444.8 | 31 | — | Johnson & Johnson (JNJ) | 1,415.2 |
| 6 | 9 | Nokia Corp. (NOK) | 2,950.8 | 32 | 31 | Schering-Plough (SGP) | 1,410.4 |
| 7 | 7 | Citigroup Inc. (C) | 2,836.6 | 33 | 32 | Advanced Micro Devices (AMD) | 1,399.7 |
| 8 | 6 | Pfizer Inc. (PFE) | 2,759.3 | 34 | — | Solectron Corp. (SLR) | 1,346.5 |
| 9 | 2 | Compaq Computer (CPQ) | 2,743.6 | 35 | 23 | Bank of America Corp. (BAC) | 1,325.0 |
| 10 | 3 | AT&T Corp. (T) | 2,649.4 | 36 | — | American Express (AXP) | 1,299.3 |
| 11 | — | Enron Corp. (ENE) | 2,647.7 | 37 | — | Merrill Lynch & Co., Inc. (MER) | 1,294.7 |
| 12 | 10 | Motorola Inc. (MOT) | 2,460.7 | 38 | — | Viacom Inc. (VIA.B) | 1,255.7 |
| 13 | 12 | Texas Instruments Inc. (TXN) | 2,255.2 | 39 | 25 | Merck & Co. (MRK) | 1,249.3 |
| 14 | 33 | Corning Inc. (GLW) | 2,181.6 | 40 | — | American Int'l Group Inc. (AIG) | 1,237.3 |
| 15 | 14 | Tyco International Ltd. (TYC) | 2,011.9 | 41 | 45 | Morgan Stanley Dean Witter (MWD) | 1,227.4 |
| 16 | — | AOL Time Warner Ltd. (UX) | 1,989.8 | 42 | — | Agere Systems Inc. (AGR.A) | 1,222.6 |
| 17 | 15 | Micron Technology Inc. (MU) | 1,809.9 | 43 | — | Pharmacia Corp. (PHA) | 1,182.6 |
| 18 | 21 | Qwest Communications Int'l (Q) | 1,792.4 | 44 | 38 | Honeywell Int'l Inc. (HON) | 1,180.7 |
| 19 | 17 | Int'l Business Machines (IBM) | 1,790.2 | 45 | 22 | Bristol-Myers Squibb (BMY) | 1,166.0 |
| 20 | 19 | J.P. Morgan Chase & Co. (JPM) | 1,782.2 | 46 | 27 | Vodafone Group Plc (VOD) | 1,146.4 |
| 21 | 35 | Hewlett-Packard Co. (HWP) | 1,719.7 | 47 | — | Calpine Corp. (CPN) | 1,145.8 |
| 22 | — | AT&T Wireless Services, Inc. (AWE) | 1,689.6 | 48 | 39 | Ford Motor Co. (F) | 1,142.3 |
| 23 | 26 | Exxon Mobil Corp. (XOM) | 1,685.7 | 49 | 41 | Gap Inc. (GPS) | 1,141.9 |
| 24 | 42 | Sprint Corp. (PCS) | 1,578.8 | 50 | — | Verizon Communications (VZ) | 1,069.0 |
| 25 | 40 | Cendant Corp. (CD) | 1,571.0 | | | | |
| 26 | 20 | Home Depot Inc. (HD) | 1,542.9 | | | | |

Source: New York Stock Exchange.

## Most Active NASDAQ Stocks, 2001

| Rank | Name | Symbol | Total volume (in thousands) | Rank | Name | Symbol | Total volume (in thousands) |
|---|---|---|---|---|---|---|---|
| 1 | Cisco Systems, Inc. | CSCO | 21,295,701 | 25 | Yahoo! Inc. | YHOO | 2,865,702 |
| 2 | Intel Corporation | INTC | 13,427,869 | 26 | ADC Telecommunications, Inc. | ADCT | 2,821,116 |
| 3 | Sun Microsystems, Inc. | SUNW | 12,831,940 | 27 | Network Appliance, Inc. | NTAP | 2,798,883 |
| 4 | Oracle Corporation | ORCL | 11,870,793 | 28 | Ariba, Inc. | ARBA | 2,772,047 |
| 5 | Microsoft Corporation | MSFT | 9,607,375 | 29 | Check Point Software Technologies Ltd. | CHKP | 2,733,579 |
| 6 | JDS Uniphase Corporation | JDSU | 8,977,780 | 30 | Flextronics International Ltd. | FLEX | 2,616,711 |
| 7 | Dell Computer Corporation | DELL | 7,890,830 | 31 | PMC-Sierra, Inc. | PMCS | 2,606,767 |
| 8 | WorldCom, Inc. | WCOM | 7,628,937 | 32 | Amgen Inc. | AMGN | 2,484,015 |
| 9 | Juniper Networks, Inc. | JNPR | 5,744,064 | 33 | NVIDIA Corporation | NVDA | 2,324,663 |
| 10 | CIENA Corporation | CIEN | 5,469,941 | 34 | VeriSign, Inc. | VRSN | 2,306,223 |
| 11 | Applied Materials, Inc. | AMAT | 5,063,247 | 35 | Sanmina-SCI Corporation | SANM | 2,257,353 |
| 12 | LM Ericsson Telephone Company | ERICY | 4,547,278 | 36 | Xilinx, Inc. | XLNX | 2,194,650 |
| 13 | Siebel Systems, Inc. | SEBL | 4,195,755 | 37 | Immunex Corporation | IMNX | 2,182,024 |
| 14 | Applied Micro Circuits Corporation | AMCC | 3,949,945 | 38 | KLA-Tencor Corporation | KLAC | 2,175,154 |
| 15 | QUALCOMM Incorporated | QCOM | 3,898,502 | 39 | Amazon.com, Inc. | AMZN | 2,130,222 |
| 16 | Brocade Communications Systems, Inc. | BRCD | 3,869,002 | 40 | Altera Corporation | ALTR | 2,092,974 |
| 17 | Palm, Inc. | PALM | 3,819,993 | 41 | PeopleSoft, Inc. | PSFT | 2,052,010 |
| 18 | BEA Systems, Inc. | BEAS | 3,680,815 | 42 | QLogic Corporation | QLGC | 2,033,308 |
| 19 | VERITAS Software Corporation | VRTS | 3,617,039 | 43 | Comcast Corporation | CMCSK | 2,000,625 |
| 20 | i2 Technologies, Inc. | ITWO | 3,452,795 | 44 | Novellus Systems, Inc. | NVLS | 1,998,876 |
| 21 | Broadcom Corporation | BRCM | 3,314,392 | 45 | RF Micro Devices, Inc. | RFMD | 1,948,722 |
| 22 | Metromedia Fiber Network, Inc. | MFNX | 3,267,968 | 46 | Level 3 Communications, Inc. | LVLT | 1,818,798 |
| 23 | Nextel Communications, Inc. | NXTL | 3,189,873 | 47 | Tellabs, Inc. | TLAB | 1,783,244 |
| 24 | McLeodUSA Incorporated | MCLD | 2,952,136 | 48 | Vitesse Semiconductor Corporation | VTSS | 1,741,064 |
|  |  |  |  | 49 | Emulex Corporation | EMLX | 1,736,148 |
|  |  |  |  | 50 | Apple Computer, Inc. | AAPL | 1,714,756 |

*Source:* The NASDAQ Stock Market, Inc.

## Top NASDAQ Stocks by Market Value, 2001

| Rank | Name | Symbol | Market value (in thousands) | Rank | Name | Symbol | Market value (in thousands) |
|---|---|---|---|---|---|---|---|
| 1 | Microsoft Corporation | MSFT | $356,806,203 | 27 | Gemstar-TV Guide International Inc. | GMST | $11,478,271 |
| 2 | Intel Corporation | INTC | 211,092,400 | 28 | IDEC Pharmaceuticals Corporation | IDPH | 10,512,376 |
| 3 | Cisco Systems, Inc. | CSCO | 132,835,256 | 29 | Sanmina-SCI Corporation | SANM | 10,384,656 |
| 4 | Oracle Corporation | ORCL | 76,806,649 | 30 | JDS Uniphase Corporation | JDSU | 10,191,587 |
| 5 | Dell Computer Corporation | DELL | 70,858,260 | 31 | Yahoo! Inc. | YHOO | 10,104,917 |
| 6 | Amgen Inc. | AMGN | 59,008,641 | 32 | MedImmune, Inc. | MEDI | 9,931,878 |
| 7 | WorldCom, Inc. | WCOM | 41,668,380 | 33 | Bed Bath & Beyond Inc. | BBBY | 9,832,254 |
| 8 | Sun Microsystems, Inc. | SUNW | 39,871,655 | 34 | NVIDIA Corporation | NVDA | 9,672,001 |
| 9 | QUALCOMM Incorporated | QCOM | 38,603,160 | 35 | Check Point Software Technologies Ltd. | CHKP | 9,607,467 |
| 10 | Fifth Third Bancorp | FITB | 35,437,026 | 36 | KLA-Tencor Corporation | KLAC | 9,184,410 |
| 11 | Comcast Corporation | CMCSK | 32,891,580 | 37 | Intuit Inc. | INTU | 9,072,089 |
| 12 | Applied Materials, Inc. | AMAT | 32,732,387 | 38 | VeriSign, Inc. | VRSN | 8,891,165 |
| 13 | Costco Wholesale Corporation | COST | 20,077,778 | 39 | Staples, Inc. | SPLS | 8,632,219 |
| 14 | eBay Inc. | EBAY | 18,405,595 | 40 | USA Networks, Inc. | USAI | 8,575,258 |
| 15 | VERITAS Software Corporation | VRTS | 17,971,271 | 41 | Biogen, Inc. | BGEN | 8,482,180 |
| 16 | Maxim Integrated Products, Inc. | MXIM | 16,958,315 | 42 | SouthTrust Corporation | SOTR | 8,454,039 |
| 17 | Concord EFS, Inc. | CEFT | 16,512,696 | 43 | Nextel Communications, Inc. | NXTL | 8,358,611 |
| 18 | Immunex Corporation | IMNX | 15,091,670 | 44 | Biomet, Inc. | BMET | 8,331,320 |
| 19 | Northern Trust Corporation | NTRS | 13,375,765 | 45 | Chiron Corporation | CHIR | 8,292,380 |
| 20 | Paychex, Inc. | PAYX | 13,059,689 | 46 | Electronic Arts Inc. | ERTS | 8,218,006 |
| 21 | Xilinx, Inc. | XLNX | 13,043,715 | 47 | Altera Corporation | ALTR | 8,173,498 |
| 22 | Siebel Systems, Inc. | SEBL | 12,936,917 | 48 | Cintas Corporation | CTAS | 8,146,224 |
| 23 | Genzyme Corporation | GENZ | 12,701,634 | 49 | Fiserv, Inc. | FISV | 7,920,569 |
| 24 | Linear Technology Corporation | LLTC | 12,359,088 | 50 | Apple Computer, Inc. | AAPL | 7,682,783 |
| 25 | PeopleSoft, Inc. | PSFT | 12,175,575 |  |  |  |  |
| 26 | Flextronics International Ltd. | FLEX | 11,678,068 |  |  |  |  |

*Source:* The NASDAQ Stock Market, Inc.

# What's Behind the Debit Card

## This popular piece of plastic helps some shoppers avoid overspending—but beware of its hidden costs and risks

**By JEAN CHATZKY** TIME

Americans are carrying record amounts of debt—and seem determined to do something about it. Two recent studies from Dove Consulting and the American Bankers Association show that credit cards have been overtaken by debit cards as the plastic of choice. Some 26% of consumers now pay for most purchases with debit cards, which draw money directly and immediately from their checking accounts, while 21% mainly use credit cards and pay some portion of the bill when it arrives.

Why is this happening? Consumers, feeling less flush than they did in recent years, say using a debit card helps them manage their money better. "It doesn't allow them to overspend," says Richard Crone, a Dove vice president. And while writing checks serves the same purpose, it's a much bigger hassle for you—and it's much less profitable for the banks. They make 60¢ in merchant fees, on average, every time you sign for a debit-card purchase. And they don't face the risk of nonpayment posed by credit-card transactions. That's why they're giving debit the hard sell.

## Doubts About the Debit

In particular, banks are trying to push debit cards onto those credit-card customers who avoid interest payments by clearing their balances every month—the so-called convenience users. But it's precisely these customers for whom debit cards make the least sense. Why?

• **You lose the float.** Use a credit card, and you will generally have 20 to 30 days to pay the bill. During that time, the earning power of your money is yours, not the merchant's or the bank's. That cushion also gives you time to return defective merchandise or dispute a transaction before you have to pay for it. Not so with debit cards, though issuers are so eager for consumers to embrace them that they routinely "give the customer the benefit of the doubt on a bad transaction," says George Albright of Speer & Associates, an Atlanta financial consulting.

• **You lose the miles.** These days, points or miles collected on a credit card can be used to pay for everything from round-trip plane tickets to college tuition (on Citibank's Upromise card) to your teen's braces (on Diner's Club, which lets you choose a reward once you hit 100,000 points). Chase allows you to earn Continental Airline miles by using your debit card, but at a rate of half a mile per dollar spent—versus one mile on the typical credit card.

• **You lose some security.** If your credit cards fall into the wrong hands, you're liable only for the first $50 of expenditures, and many issuers waive that. While the ultimate liability with a debit card is the same, a thief could clean out your checking account before you realize what's happening. (Some 42% of debit cards can be used without a personal identification number, or PIN.) Yes, your bank will give you back the money—Visa requires its issuers to grant you credit within five days, and many do so within 24 hours—but it's a much bigger hassle than losing a credit card.

That said, if you are the type of customer who

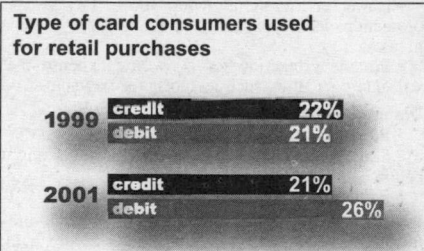

**Type of card consumers used for retail purchases**

| | | |
|---|---|---|
| 1999 | credit | 22% |
| | debit | 21% |
| 2001 | credit | 21% |
| | debit | 26% |

*Source:* Dove Consulting

charges one day and regrets it the next, a debit card probably does make sense. Rudy Cavazos, director of corporate relations for **moneymanagement.org**, says there's no doubt that debit cards help keep consumers within their spending limits. "If you use a debit card, you know the money's coming directly from checking," he says. "You know you're not going to accumulate late finance charges or fees. If every minimum payment has you feeling like you're spinning your wheels, debit cards are the way to go." □

## Six Warning Signs of a Financial Problem

The Federal Deposit Insurance Corporation offers the following guidelines to evaluate whether you are facing significant financial difficulties.

• Loan payments, excluding mortgages, but including credit card charges, take up more than 20% of your monthly net income.
• You are close to, or surpass, your credit card limit.
• You must borrow to make payments on existing loans.
• You only pay the minimum amount on your bill.
• Lack of money is forcing you to pay bills late or postpone doctor's visits.
• You must work overtime, or take a second job, to cover basic living expenses.

# How to Buy Life Insurance

*Source:* The American Council of Life Insurers. Web: www.acli.com/public/media/mainframe_med.htm.

Life insurance is intended to provide for your dependents after you die. There is no federal income tax on life insurance benefits.

## Evaluate the Need

To determine how much insurance you need, consider ongoing obligations (mortgage payments, school tuition, monthly bills), costs associated with your death (medical bills, burial fees, estate taxes), and your family's readjustment (moving, job hunting expenses).

Generally, you will need a life insurance policy with a **face amount** worth from five to seven times your gross annual income. The face amount is what is paid at your death.

The **cash value** of a policy is what it is worth at any given time, based on how much you have paid in premiums, how long you have had the policy, and your insurance company's financial situation. A policy may have no cash value in its early years.

## Types of Life Insurance

**TERM LIFE INSURANCE:** provides coverage for a specific period of time. Policies can often be renewed at the end of the term, which can last from one to 30 years.
**Advantages:**
• Lower premiums, allowing you to buy greater protection when you are younger and the need is greatest.
• Provide protection for a specific expense that will end over time, such as mortgage payments.

**Disadvantages:**
• Premiums usually increase as you age.
• Some policies cannot be renewed; others might become too expensive to keep.
• Policies generally don't offer a cash value.

**PERMANENT LIFE INSURANCE:** offers lifetime protection as long as the premiums are paid. There are several types of permanent life offering various features. For instance, premiums can either be fixed or flexible. Some permanent life premiums can be invested in stocks or bonds.
**Advantages:**
• Premiums can be fixed or flexible.
• Policy accumulates a cash value against which you can borrow. (To avoid reduced death benefits for your survivors, you must repay loans with interest.)
• You can surrender part, or all, of the policy and receive the cash value, or convert it into an income-producing annuity.
• You may be able to buy added insurance without taking a medical exam.

**Disadvantages:**
• Premiums may be expensive.
• It may cost more than term insurance if you don't keep the policy long enough.

## Finding an Agent

Most people buy policies through an insurance agent. Get the names of several agents from business associates or family members. Find out what companies they represent, what types of policy they sell, and what licenses they hold.

## Choosing a Policy

Your agent's role is to find a policy that is right for you. Be prepared to discuss your financial situation, personal goals, family background, and health. You may have to take a physical exam. Tell the truth. Lying on your application could result in a denial of benefits for your survivors.

The agent should be able to explain various insurance policies. Get a step-by-step explanation. Many companies offer buyer's guides. Consider:
• When does the policy take effect?
• Can you afford the premiums?
• Will the premiums increase?
• What happens if you fail to pay a premium?
• What amounts in the policy are guaranteed?
• Will death benefits be affected by interest rates or other factors?
• Does the policy pay dividends?
• What provisions in the policy could change?
• Will you be notified if there are changes?

## Consider Other Provisions

**Riders** are additional provisions that can be added to a policy. Riders might include additional benefits for accidental death; suspending premium payments if you become disabled; or provisions for "accelerated" or "living benefits," which pay for long-term care for catastrophic or terminal illnesses.

## Research the Company

Some 1,700 U.S. companies sell life insurance. Make sure you choose a company in sound financial shape and licensed in your state. Contact your state's insurance department. A number of organizations rate the financial health of insurance companies. Many libraries have publications listing these ratings.

**Points to Remember:**
• Take your time. Make sure you understand what the policy offers and that you are comfortable with the product, agent, and company.
• Make your check payable to the company issuing the policy, not the agent. Get a receipt.
• When you receive your policy, there is often a cancellation period.
• Notify the company or the agent of any errors in your policy.
• It can be expensive to surrender one policy and buy another.
• Contact the company's customer service department with complaints. If you remain unsatisfied, contact your state insurance commission.
• Review your policy periodically, especially when your situation changes, to ensure adequate coverage.

**For More Information**
• American Council of Life Insurers, Web: www.acli.com/public/media/mainframe_med.htm
• National Insurance Consumer Helpline (NICH) 1 (800) 942-2424
• Books and periodicals on personal finance and insurance in your local library
• Consumer affairs division of your state insurance commission

# How to Measure the Shrinking Value of the Dollar

The CPI inflation calculator uses the average Consumer Price Index for a given calendar year. This data represents changes in prices of all goods and services purchased for consumption by urban households. This index value has been calculated every year since 1913. For the current year, the latest monthly index value is used. In 2002, for example, it took $17.89 to buy what $1 bought in 1913. Note that in 1920, it cost $2.02, and declined in 1925 and through the 1930s, illustrating the effect of the Great Depression, when prices slumped. Prices only passed $2 again in 1950.

| Year | Amount it took to equal $1 in 1913 | Year | Amount it took to equal $1 in 1913 | Year | Amount it took to equal $1 in 1913 | Year | Amount it took to equal $1 in 1913 |
|---|---|---|---|---|---|---|---|
| 1913 | $1.00 | 1940 | 1.41 | 1965 | 3.18 | 1990 | 13.20 |
| 1920 | 2.02 | 1945 | 1.82 | 1970 | 3.92 | 1995 | 15.39 |
| 1925 | 1.77 | 1950 | 2.43 | 1975 | 5.43 | 2000 | 17.39 |
| 1930 | 1.69 | 1955 | 2.71 | 1980 | 8.32 | 2001 | 17.89 |
| 1935 | 1.38 | 1960 | 2.99 | 1985 | 10.87 | 2002 | 17.89 |

*Source:* Bureau of Labor Statistics, Web: http://stats.bls.gov/.

# Top 10 Ways to Prepare for Retirement

*Source:* Department of Labor, Web: http://www.dol.gov/dol/pwba/public/pubs/topten/top10txt.htm

### 1. Know your retirement needs.

Retirement is expensive. Experts estimate that you'll need about 70% of your pre-retirement income—lower earners, 90% or more—to maintain your standard of living when you stop working.

### 2. Find out about Social Security.

Social Security pays the average retiree about 40% of pre-retirement earnings. Call the Social Security Administration at 1-800-772-1213 for a free Personal Earnings and Benefit Estimate Statement (PEBES).

### 3. Learn about your employer's pension or profit sharing plan.

If your employer offers a plan, check to see what your benefit is worth. Most employers will provide an individual benefit statement. Before you change jobs, find out what will happen to your pension. Learn what benefits you may have from previous employment. Find out if you will be entitled to benefits from your spouse's plan. For a free booklet on private pensions, call the U.S. Department of Labor at 1-800-998-7542.

### 4. Contribute to a tax-sheltered plan.

If your employer offers a tax-sheltered savings plan, such as a 401(k), sign up and contribute all you can. Your taxes will be lower, your company may kick in more, and automatic deductions make it easy.

### 5. Ask your employer to start a plan.

If your employer doesn't offer a retirement plan, suggest that he/she start one. Simplified plans can be set up by certain employers. For information on simplified employee pensions, order Internal Revenue Service Publication 590 by calling 1-800-829-3676.

### 6. Put money into an IRA.

You can put $2,000 a year into an Individual Retirement Account (IRA) and delay paying taxes on investment earnings until retirement age. If you don't have a retirement plan (or are in a plan and earn less than a certain amount), you can also take a tax deduction for your IRA contributions. IRS Publication 590 contains information about IRAs.

### 7. Don't touch your savings.

Don't dip into your retirement savings. You'll lose principal and interest, and you may lose tax benefits. If you change jobs, roll over your savings directly into an IRA or your new employer's retirement plan.

### 8. Start now, set goals, and stick to them.

Start early. The sooner you start saving, the more time your money has to grow.

### 9. Consider basic investment principles.

How you save can be as important as how much you save. Inflation and the type of investments you make play important roles in how much you'll have saved at retirement. Know how your pension or savings plan is invested.

### 10. Ask questions.

Talk to your employer, your bank, your union, or a financial advisor.

## Retirement Information

The following government organizations offer retirement planning information:

**Administration on Aging**
www.aoa.dhhs.gov/default.htm
Variety of information

**Department of Veteran Affairs**
www.va.gov/
Material for veterans

**FirstGov for Seniors**
www.seniors.gov/index.htm
Federal clearinghouse

**Internal Revenue Service**
www.irs.gov/
Tax-oriented information

**Pension and Welfare Benefits Administration**
www.dol.gov/pwba/welcome.html
Pension plan information

**Pension Benefit Guaranty Corporation**
www.pbgc.gov/default.htm
Private pension plan information

**Railroad Retirement Board** www.rrb.gov/
Retirement programs for railroad workers

**Social Security Administration**
www.ssa.gov/retirement/
Range of material

# Glossary of Financial Terms

**Adjusted gross income** Amount of income that is subject to federal income tax. In addition to any other tax credits, contributions to IRAs and 401(k) plans are subtracted from the total.

**Aggressive** Relating or referring to an investment philosophy that seeks above-average returns by accepting above-average risk.

**American Stock Exchange (AMEX)** Specializes in small-to-medium-size companies.

**Annual percentage rate (APR)** A standardized method of calculating interest rates. It permits the comparison of different interest rates just as unit pricing enables comparison shopping at the supermarket.

**Annuity** Contract issued by a life insurance company that promises to make periodic payments to the buyer over a set period of time. Payments are made to individuals, referred to as annuitants.

**Appreciation** An increase in value of an asset.

**Arbitrage** The purchase of assets, such as securities, on one market for immediate resale on another market to take advantage of price differences.

**Balanced fund** A type of mutual fund that spreads its investments among stocks and bonds. Essentially, a balanced fund is a middle-of-the-road fund that balances its portfolio to achieve both moderate income and moderate capital growth.

**Bear market** An extended period of general price declines in the securities market.

**Bellwether** A stock whose performance is indicative of the overall market direction.

**Blue chip** A very high-quality investment involving a lower-than-average risk of loss of principal or reduction in income.

**Bond** A long-term promissory note that obligates the borrower to make specified payments over a set period of time.

**Bull market** An extended period of general price increases in the securities market.

**Capital gain** The excess by which proceeds from the sale of a capital asset exceeds the cost.

**Capitalization** The company's stock price per share multiplied by the total number of shares outstanding. **Small-cap:** less than $1.5 billion. **Mid-cap:** between $1.5 billion and $10 billion. **Large-cap:** over $10 billion.

**Certificate of deposit (CD)** A receipt for a deposit of funds in a financial institution that permits the holder to receive interest plus the deposit at maturity.

**Collateral** Assets used as security for a loan.

**Commercial paper** A short-term unsecured promissory note issued by a finance company or a large industrial firm. Commonly found in money-market funds.

**Common stock** A class of stock that has no preference as to dividends or any distribution of assets.

**Compound interest** Interest paid on interest from previous periods in addition to principal.

**Consumer price index (CPI)** A measure of the average change over time in the prices paid by urban consumers for a fixed "market basket" of day-to-day expenses.

**Correction** Reverse movement in the price of an individual stock, bond, commodity, or index after any long-term move. Can be a movement up or down, but usually refers to a fall in the price.

**Depreciation** The decrease in value of a tangible asset because of age, wear, or market conditions. Corporations can choose between several types of depreciation, which affects the value of assets and corporate earnings.

**Diversification** Minimizing risk by investing in a wide range of securities invested in many industries.

**Dividend** A share of a company's net profits distributed to a class of its stockholders.

**Dividend Reinvestment Plan (DRIP)** Automatic plan allowing stockholders to use their dividends to buy additional shares of stock.

**Dollar-cost averaging** Investment of an equal amount of money at regular intervals resulting in the purchase of more shares during market downturns and fewer shares during market upturns.

**Dow Jones Industrial Average (DJIA)** A widely quoted measure of stock market price movements of 30 large, seasoned industrial firms.

**Earnings per share** The amount a stock will pay in income or dividends.

**Emerging growth stock** The common stock of a relatively young firm operating in an industry with very good growth prospects. This kind of stock offers unusually high returns and a high risk.

**Emerging market** Market in a country that does not have a fully developed economy. Investments in these markets are usually characterized by a high level of risk and possibility of a high return.

**Federal funds** Reserve balances above those required that are maintained by commercial banks in the Federal Reserve System.

**Federal Reserve Board** The seven governing members of the Federal Reserve System who determine the country's monetary policy.

**Fixed annuity** Annuity that guarantees fixed payments to the annuitant, either for life or for a set period of time.

**401(k) plan** Plan in which employees elect to contribute pretax dollars to a qualified, tax-deferred investment plan.

**Futures contract** A pact in which a buyer and seller agree to exchange a specific commodity on a certain date.

**Futures market** The place where futures contracts are traded, such as the Commodity Exchange in New York, which handles metals, and the Chicago Board of Trade, which deals in grain futures. Other exchanges handle sugar, cotton, and other commodities.

**Global fund** A mutual fund that includes at least 25% foreign securities in its portfolio.

**Gross national product (GNP)** The dollar output of final goods and services in the economy during a period of time.

**Growth stock** The stock of a firm that is expected to have above-average increases in revenues and earnings. These firms normally retain most of their earnings for reinvestment and therefore pay small dividends.

**Hedge fund** A very specialized, volatile investment company (mutual fund) that permits the manager to use a variety of investment techniques normally prohibited in other types of funds.

**Income fund** An investment company (mutual fund) whose main objective is to achieve current income for its owners; typically, the fund purchases bonds, preferred stocks, and common stocks paying high dividends.

**Index** Statistical composite that measures changes in the economy or in financial markets and that can be expressed in percent changes from a base year or from the previous month. Most common are the S&P and the Dow Jones Industrial Average.

**Index fund** A mutual fund that keeps a portfolio of securities designed to match the performance of a certain market as a whole.

**Individual Retirement Account (IRA)** A custodial account or trust in which individuals may set aside earned income in a tax-deferred retirement plan.

**Initial Public Offering (IPO)** The first sale of a corporation's stock to the investing public.

**International fund** A mutual fund that invests only outside the country in which it is located.

**Junk bonds** Debt issued by a company whose credit rating is below investment grade (BBB for S&P and Baa for Moody's). Because there is a considerable risk, the company must offer a high coupon to make the bond attractive to an investor.

**Keogh plan** A federally approved retirement program that permits self-employed people to set aside for savings up to $30,000 or 25% of their income, whichever is lower.

**Large-capitalization stock** The stock of a big company that has considerable retained earnings and a large amount of common stock outstanding, typically a market capitalization of over $3 billion.

**Liquid asset** A security that can easily be sold for cash.

**Load** The sales fee that the buyer pays in order to acquire a security, typically a mutual fund.

**Long-term bonds** Debt securities with maturities of 10 to 30 years. The benchmark for this asset class is the Lehman Government Long Bond Index.

**Money market fund** A mutual fund that purchases short-term, high-quality securities, such as treasury bills, negotiable CDs, and commercial paper.

**Money market securities** Low-risk, very liquid securities with maturities of one year or less. Other short-term debt that is scheduled to mature within one year may also be classified as money-market securities.

**Moody's** A company rating service issuing ratings denoting the relative investment quality of corporate and municipal bonds.

**Mutual fund** An investment company that continually offers new shares and stands ready to redeem existing shares from the owners. Also an investment company.

**NASDAQ** The National Association of Securities Dealers' Automated Quotation marketplace, which trades shares electronically. Companies traded on the NASDAQ include many small-to-medium-size firms and many technology companies.

**Net Asset Value (NAV)** The market value of an investment company's (mutual fund) asset less any liabilities divided by the number of shares outstanding. This is the value of each share if the fund sold all of its assets at their current market value and paid off any outstanding debts.

**Net income** Income after all expenses and taxes have been deducted.

**New York Stock Exchange** The oldest stock exchange in the U.S., located at 11 Wall Street in New York City. Companies traded on the NYSE are typically the largest in the U.S.

**Nikkei Stock Average** Compilation of prices of 225 companies listed on the Tokyo Stock Exchange.

**No-load fund** An open-end investment company (mutual fund), shares of which are sold without a sales charge.

**Option** A contract that permits the owner, depending on the contract, to purchase or sell a security at a fixed price until a specific date.

**Over-the-counter stock** Stock that is traded outside of an organized exchange, usually through telephone or electronic connections.

**Round lot** Standard unit for trading a particular security, generally 100 shares for stock, $1,000 or $5,000 par value for bonds.

**Preferred stock** A security that shows ownership in a corporation and gives the holder a claim prior to the claim of common stockholders on earnings and also generally on assets in the event of liquidation.

**Price/earnings ratio** Price of a stock divided by its earnings per share.

**Prime rate** The interest rate banks charge on loans to their biggest and best customers.

**Profit-sharing plan** An agreement that allows employees to share in the corporation's profit.

**Real estate investment trust (REIT)** A trust that either finances or owns and manages income-producing real estate, passing profits on to shareholders.

**Security** An instrument indicating ownership, in the case of stocks, or representing the debt of a corporation or government agency, in the case of bonds.

**Securities and Exchange Commission (SEC)** Federal agency that administers U.S. securities law; created in 1934.

**Small-cap stocks** The stock of a relatively small firm with little equity and few shares of common stock outstanding. Small capitalization stocks tend to be subject to large fluctuations; therefore, the potential for short-term gains and losses is great.

**Standard & Poor's 500 (S&P 500)** An inclusive index of 500 stocks, including 400 Industrial stocks, 40 utilities, 20 transportation stocks, and 40 financial stocks.

**Stock** An ownership share(s) in a corporation; also equity, common stock. *See also* **Preferred stock.**

**Treasuries** All bonds backed by the U.S. government that are issued through the Department of the Treasury.

**Yield to maturity** The total return an investor will get by holding a long-term, interest-bearing instrument (usually a bond) until it matures.

# Credit Card Use, 1989–1998

General-purpose credit cards include Mastercard, Visa, Optima, and Discover. All dollar figures are given in constant 1998 dollars based on consumer price index data as published by the U.S. Bureau of Labor Statistics.

| Age of family head and family income[1] | Percent having a general-purpose credit card | Percent having a balance after last month's bills | Median balance[2] | Percent of cardholding families who: | | |
|---|---|---|---|---|---|---|
| | | | | Almost always pay off the balance | Sometimes pay off the balance | Hardly ever pay off the balance |
| 1989, total | 56.0% | 52.1% | $1,300 | 52.9% | 21.2% | 25.8% |
| 1992, total | 62.4 | 52.6 | 1,100 | 53.0 | 19.6 | 27.4 |
| 1995, total | 66.4 | 56.0 | 1,600 | 52.4 | 20.1 | 27.5 |
| **1998 total** | **67.5** | **54.7** | **1,900** | **53.6** | **19.3** | **26.9** |
| Under 35 years old | 58.3 | 71.6 | 1,500 | 39.0 | 22.5 | 38.5 |
| 35 to 44 years old | 71.3 | 62.5 | 2,000 | 46.5 | 19.1 | 34.4 |
| 45 to 54 years old | 75.3 | 59.2 | 2,000 | 48.2 | 22.7 | 29.1 |
| 55 to 64 years old | 76.0 | 48.8 | 2,300 | 61.0 | 20.1 | 18.9 |
| 65 to 74 years old | 71.2 | 33.9 | 1,000 | 74.0 | 14.9 | 11.1 |
| 75 years old and over | 50.8 | 16.7 | 700 | 86.3 | 7.8 | 5.9 |
| Less than $10,000 | 23.2 | 64.0 | 900 | 46.4 | 19.9 | 33.8 |
| $10,000 to $24,999 | 50.8 | 56.9 | 1,200 | 52.3 | 19.3 | 28.4 |
| $25,000 to $49,999 | 73.2 | 58.2 | 1,700 | 48.3 | 20.5 | 31.2 |
| $50,000 to $99,999 | 89.6 | 55.9 | 2,400 | 53.9 | 20.2 | 25.9 |
| $100,000 and more | 97.9 | 36.4 | 3,100 | 72.0 | 13.8 | 14.1 |

1. Families include one-person units. 2. Among families having a balance. *Source:* Board of Governors of the Federal Reserve System, unpublished data. From *Statistical Abstract of the U.S., 2001.*

# Credit Reports

## Understanding Credit Reports

Source: Federal Reserve Bank of Philadelphia. Web: www.phil.frb.org/consumers/creditreport.html

Just about everyone uses credit, whether it is for car, student, or bank loans; mortgages; or credit cards. Banks and other businesses rely on credit reports, which contain:

• Social Security numbers, current and previous addresses, nicknames, spouse's name, year of birth, plus current and previous employers;

• records of loans, credit cards, bank accounts, and retail store accounts;

• public information on bankruptcy, tax liens, or legal judgments against you;

• names of people who have obtained copies of your credit report within the last six months (two years for employment purposes).

Consumer reporting agencies (credit bureaus) obtain the information from various sources, including retail stores or banks.

The report can only be shown to:

• businesses thinking of extending you credit;

• current or potential employers;

• insurance companies;

• government agencies considering granting you certain licenses or benefits;

• anyone with a legitimate business reason initiated by the consumer.

The decision to grant you a loan or issue you a credit card is made by the business that requested the report, not the credit bureau.

If you are denied credit, the lender must give you the name, address, and telephone number of the company that provided the report.

Even if you have never been denied credit, you have the right to see your report. In making the request include your name, telephone number, addresses for the last five years, Social Security number, and birth date. The agency may charge you for the report, depending on what state you live in.

You should tell the reporting agency if you disagree with anything in your report. Mistakes must be removed. If the reporting agency stands by its original report, however, you have the right to present your side of the story in a short statement that gets attached to your credit report.

Material stays on your report for seven years—ten years if a bankruptcy is involved; it is automatically deleted thereafter. Exceptions are cases of transactions of $150,000 or more (including life insurance), or employment with an annual salary of $75,000 or more.

## To obtain your credit report

The three main credit bureaus are:
**Equifax Information Services, LLC**
P.O. Box 740241
Atlanta, GA 30374
(800) 685-1111
www.equifax.com
**Experian National Consumer Assistance Center**
P.O. Box 2002
Allen, TX 75013
(888) 397-3742
www.experian.com
**TransUnion Consumer Disclosure Center**
P.O. Box 1000
Chester, PA 19022
(800) 888-4213
www.tuc.com

# Know Your Telemarketing Rights

*Source:* Federal Trade Commission. Web: www.ftc.gov/bcp/conline/pubs/tmarkg/ditch.htm.

In "Ditch the Pitch: Hanging Up on Telephone Hucksters," the Federal Trade Commission (FTC) outlines your rights in dealing with telephone solicitation. The following is a synopsis.

Telemarketing fraud costs Americans more than $40 billion a year. The FTC warns consumers to be alert to such common telephone marketing schemes:

• **Credit card protection offers:** Consumers are only liable for $50 in unauthorized credit card charges. Do not buy "insurance" to protect against greater loss. Do not give out personal information, such as credit card or bank account numbers, unless you know whom you are dealing with, and understand why the information is requested. Thieves sometimes claim to be bank security officials and ask for personal information so they can activate "protection features" on your credit card.

• **Advance-fees for "guaranteed" loans:** It is illegal for companies doing business by phone to promise you a loan and ask you for money in advance. Legitimate lenders may charge fees, but these are seldom required before the loan is approved. In addition, banks also consider a loan applicant's credit history. Legitimate lenders do not "guarantee" loans in advance. Legitimate fees are usually paid to the lending institution, not the person who handled the paperwork.

• **International sweepstakes and lotteries:** It is illegal for U.S. citizens to participate in foreign sweepstakes or lotteries whether it is over the phone,

by mail, or on the Internet. Mail about foreign lotteries should be turned over to the post office.

## FTC Telemarketing Rules:

• Calls are restricted to between 8 A.M. and 9 P.M.
• Telemarketers must tell you it is a sales call, the name of the seller, and what they are selling.
• It is illegal for telemarketers to lie about their products or services.
• Telemarketers must tell you the total cost of whatever they are selling, any restrictions, and if a sale is nonrefundable.
• Callers promoting prizes must tell you the odds of winning, that no purchase or payment is necessary to win, and any restrictions on receiving the prize.
• It is illegal for telemarketers to withdraw money from your bank account without your express, verifiable authorization.
• You do not have to pay for credit services until those services are delivered.
• It is illegal for a telemarketer to call you if you have asked not to be called.

Do not be pressured into making an immediate payment. You can take time to evaluate the offer. If you suspect fraud, contact your local police, state Attorney General's office, or consumer protection agency.

Remember, if an offer seems too good to be true, it probably is.

## Catching the Facts on Identity Theft

*Source:* Federal Trade Commission. Web: www.consumer.gov/idtheft/index.html.

Identity theft occurs when someone uses your bank account number, Social Security number, credit card, or other personal information for his or her own ends. It can be months before the theft has been discovered.

### Minimize Risk

Sign your credit cards upon receipt. Only carry cards that you need. Do not carry your Social Security card. Never write your PIN or Social Security number on anything, and bring in mind that. Shred documents containing your Social Security number.

Do not release personal information such as your Social Security or bank account number over the phone unless you made the phone call and understand why the information is necessary.

Obtain an annual copy of your credit report from the three main credit bureaus and ensure the material is correct.

Be aware of credit card billing cycles. If you do not receive a bill on time, contact the company. A thief charging purchases to your account would likely change your billing address, so it takes you longer to discover the fraud.

### If You are Victimized

If a credit card is stolen, close the account immediately. Notify the three main credit bureaus. Put passwords (not your mother's maiden name) on any new accounts. File a report with the police in the community where the theft occurred. Keep a copy of the report in case it is needed later. If your Social Security number is being used fraudulently, notify the Social Security Administration.

**Federal Trade Commission:** Identity Theft Clearinghouse, 600 Pennsylvania Ave, NW, Washington, DC 20580, 1-877-ID-THEFT (438-4338).

**To report identity theft online:** See the FTC consumer information page at www.ftc.gov/ftc/consumer.htm.

**Main Credit Reporting Bureaus:** Equifax, P.O. Box 740241, Atlanta, GA 30374-0241, (800) 525-6285; Experian, P.O. Box 9530, Allen, TX 75013, (888) 397-3742; Trans Union, 760 Sproul Road, P.O. Box 390, Springfield, PA, 19064-0390, (800) 680-7289.

**Social Security Administration's Office of the Inspector General:** SSA Fraud Hotline, PO Box 17768, Baltimore MD 21235, 1-800-269-0271, Fax: 410-597-0118, Email: oig.hotline@ssa.gov.

## Better Business Bureaus

Better Business Bureaus (BBBs) are nonprofit organizations supported primarily by local business members. BBBs offer a variety of consumer services including educational materials, information on charities and other organizations seeking public donations, and mediation and arbitration services. If you need help with a consumer question or complaint, call your local BBB to ask about its services, or contact the BBB online at www.bbb.org.

## National Consumer Organizations

NOTE: For other organizations, *see* Societies & Associations, pp. 475–484

**Alliance Against Fraud In Telemarketing & Electronic Commerce (AAFTEC),** c/o National Consumers League, 1701 K St. N.W., Suite 1200, Washington, DC 20006; 202-835-3323; 202-835-0747 (fax); Web: www.nclnet.org.

Combats telemarketing and Internet fraud through consumer education.

**American Association of Retired Persons (AARP),** Consumer Affairs Section, 601 E St. N.W., Washington, DC 20049; 800-424-3410; Web: www.aarp.org.

Offers information on housing, insurance, funeral practices, eligibility for public benefits, financial security, transportation, and consumer protection issues on behalf of midlife and older consumers.

**American Council on Consumer Interests (ACCI),** 240 Stanley Hall, University of Missouri, Columbia, MO 65211-0001; 573-882-3817; 573-884-6571 (fax); Web: http://consumerinterests.org.

Provides research-based information on topics of consumer interest. Provides information about consumer publications, policies, and resources.

**American Council on Science and Health (ACSH),** 1995 Broadway, 2nd Fl., New York, NY 10023-5860; 212-362-7044; 212-362-4919 (fax); Web: www.acsh.org.

A consumer education consortium concerned with issues related to food, nutrition, chemicals, pharmaceuticals, lifestyle, the environment, and health.

**American Savings Education Council,** 2121 K Street N.W., Suite 600, Washington, DC 20037-1896; 202-659-0670; Web: www.asec.org.

Raises public awareness about what is needed to ensure long-term personal financial independence.

**Center for Auto Safety (CAS),** 1825 Connecticut Ave. N.W., Suite 330, Washington, DC 20009-5708; 202-328-7700; Web: www.autosafety.org.

Founded by Consumers Union and Ralph Nader in 1970 to advocate for auto safety and quality.

**Center for Science in the Public Interest (CSPI),** 1875 Connecticut Ave. N.W., Suite 300, Washington, DC 20009; 202-332-9110; 202-265-4954 (fax); Web: www.cspinet.org.

Provides research, education, and advocacy on nutrition, health, food safety, and related issues.

**Center for the Study of Services/Consumers' Checkbook,** 733 15th Street N.W., Suite 820, Washington, DC 20005; 202-347-7283; Web: www.checkbook.org.

Aids consumers in selecting doctors, hospitals, and health plans, cars, and finding bargains.

**Coalition Against Insurance Fraud,** 1012 14th St. N.W., Washington, DC 20005; 202-393-7330; 202-293-7329 (fax); Web: www.insurancefraud.org.

Organization of consumers, government agencies, and insurers dedicated to combating all forms of insurance fraud.

**Congress Watch,** 215 Pennsylvania Avenue, SE, Washington, DC 20003; 202-546-4996; 202-547-7392 (fax); Web: www.citizen.org .

An arm of Public Citizen, Congress Watch works for consumer-related legislation, regulation, and policies in such areas as health and safety, and campaign financing.

**Consumer Action (CA),** 717 Market St., Suite 310, San Francisco, CA 94103-2109; 415-777-9635 (multilingual consumer complaint hotline); 415-777-9456 (voice/ttd); Web: www.consumer-action.org.

Advocate for credit, finance, HMOs, and telecommunications issues.

**Consumer Federation of America (CFA),** 1424 16th St. N.W., Suite 604, Washington, DC 20036; 202-387-6121; Web: www.consumerfed.org.

Composed of more than 260 organizations, CFA is a consumer advocacy and education organization. CFA focuses much of its advocacy in the areas of financial service, utilities, product safety, transportation, health care, and food safety.

**Consumers Union of U.S., Inc. (CU),** 101 Truman Ave., Yonkers, NY 10703-1057; 914-378-2000; Web: www.consumersunion.org.

Publisher of *Consumer Reports.* Researches and tests consumer goods and services.

**Families USA Foundation,** 1334 G St. N.W., Washington, DC 20005; 202-628-3030; 202-347-2417 (fax); Web: www.familiesusa.org.

Advocates for high-quality, affordable healthcare.

## The Consumer Action Handbook

*Source:* U.S. Office of Consumer Affairs

The *2002 Consumer Action Handbook,* published by the Federal Consumer Information Center, is 160 pages of valuable information that no consumer should be without. It provides advice on car repair, purchase and leasing, shopping from home, avoiding consumer and investment fraud, home improvement and financing, and much more. Also included is the *Consumer Assistance Directory* with thousands of useful names, addresses, phone numbers, and websites.

Single copies of the *Consumer Action Handbook* are available free ($2.00 service fee) by writing to: Handbook, Federal Consumer Information Center, Pueblo, CO 81009, or by calling 1-800-688-9889. The handbook can also be viewed on the FCIC website: www.pueblo.gsa.gov.

**Federal Trade Commission (FTC),** CRC-240, Washington, DC 20580; 1-877-FTC-HELP or 202-326-2222; Web: www.ftc.gov.

Enforces a variety of federal antitrust and consumer protection laws.

**HALT: An Organization of Americans for Legal Reform,** 1612 K Street N.W., Suite 510, Washington, DC 20006; 202-887-8255, toll-free: 1-888-367-4258; 202-887-9699 (fax); Web: www.halt.org

Helps consumers handle their legal affairs.

**National Community Reinvestment Coalition (NCRC),** 733 15th Street N.W., Suite 540, Washington, DC 20005; 202-628-8866; 202-628-9800 (fax); Web: www.ncrc.org.

Works toward ending discriminatory banking practices, and increasing the flow of private capital and credit into underserved communities.

**National Consumer Law Center (NCLC),** 77 Summer Street, 10th Fl., Boston, MA 02110-1006; 617-542-8010; 617-542-8028 (fax); Web: www.consumerlaw.org.

Focuses on the interests of low-income consumers in court, before administrative agencies, and before legislatures.

**National Consumers League (NCL),** 1701 K St. N.W., Suite 1200, Washington, DC 20006; 202-835-3323; 202-835-0747 (fax); Web: nclnet.org.

Founded in 1899, NCL is America's pioneer consumer advocacy organization, and focuses on consumer health and safety protection as well as fairness in the marketplace and workplace.

**National Foundation for Credit Counseling, Inc. (NFCC),** 801 Roeder Rd., Suite 900, Silver Spring, MD 20910; 301-589-5600; 301-405-5620 (fax); Web: www.ntcc.org.

Provides assistance with stressful financial situations.

**National Fraud Information Center/Internet Fraud Watch (NFIC/IFW),** P.O. Box 65868, Washington, DC 20035; 800-876-7060, TDD/TTY: 202-835-0778; Web: www.fraud.org.

Help on avoiding telemarketing fraud and online and Internet fraud, and assistance in filing complaints.

**National Senior Citizens Law Center,** 1101 14th St. N.W., Suite 400, Washington, DC 20005; 202-289-6976; 202-289-7224 (fax); Web: www.nsclc.org.

Helps low-income and older Americans with legal services.

**Public Citizen, Inc.,** 1600 20th St. N.W., Washington, DC 20009; 202-885-1000; Web: www.citizen.org.

Represents consumer interests in Congress, the courts, government agencies, and the media. Its divisions include Auto Safety, Congress Watch, Critical Mass (Energy & Environment Program), Global Trade Watch, Health Research group, and the Litigation Group.

**Public Voice for Food and Health Policy,** 1101 14th St. N.W., Washington, DC 20005; 202-371-1840; 202-371-1910 (fax)

Promotes a safer, healthier, and more affordable food supply.

**United Seniors Health Cooperative (USHC),** 409 Third Street S.W., Suite 200, Washington, DC 20024; 202-479-6973; 202-479-6660 (fax); Web: www.unitedseniors health.org.

Helps seniors achieve good health, independence, and financial security.

**U.S. Public Interest Research Group (U.S. PIRG),** 218 D St. S.E., Washington, DC 20003; 202-546-9707; 202-546-2461 (fax); Web: www.uspirg.org.

Advocates on issues such as the environment, product safety, financial privacy, and identity theft.

**Women's Bureau, Dept. of Labor,** 200 Constitution Ave., N.W., Room S-3002, Washington, DC 20210; 202-219-5529; 1-800-827-5335; 202-693-6710; 202-693-6725 (fax); Web: www.dol.gov/wb/

Advocates for work issues such as sexual harassment, pregnancy discrimination, and child care.

# Recalls

Several federal government agencies enforce product safety regulations and provide recall information. Recalls are also posted regularly on the FCIC website: www.pueblo.gsa.gov.

**Cars:** National Highway Traffic Safety Administration; Phone: 1-800-DASH-2-DOT; Web: www.nhtsa.dot.gov

**Drugs, medical devices, food:** Food and Drug Administration (FDA); Phone: 1-888-INFO-FDA; Web: www.fda.gov

**Seafood:** FDA; U.S. Department of Commerce; Web: www.doc.gov

**Toy, baby, and play equipment, household products:** U.S. Consumer Product Safety Commission; Web: www.cpsc.gov

# Copyrights

Source: Excerpted from Copyright Basics (Circular 1), U.S. Copyright Office

Copyright is a form of protection provided by the laws of the United States to the creators of "original works of authorship," including literary, dramatic, musical, artistic, and certain other intellectual works. This protection is available to both published and unpublished works. The 1976 Copyright Act generally gives the owner of copyright the exclusive right to do and to authorize others to do the following:

• to reproduce the copyrighted work in copies or phonorecords;

• to prepare derivative works based upon the copyrighted work;

• to distribute copies or phonorecords of the copyrighted work to the public by sale or other transfer of ownership, or by rental, lease, or lending;

• to perform and/or display the copyrighted work publicly; and

• in the case of sound recordings, to perform the work publicly by means of a digital audio transmission.

It is illegal for anyone to violate these rights. However, these rights are not unlimited in scope. In some cases they are limited by the doctrine of "fair use," or by a "compulsory license" under which certain limited uses of copyrighted works are permitted in exchange for payment.

## What Works Are Protected

Copyright protects "original works of authorship" that are fixed in a tangible form of expression. The fixation need not be directly perceptible so long as it may be communicated with the aid of a machine or device. Categories include:
- literary works;
- musical works, including any accompanying words;
- dramatic works, including any accompanying music;
- pantomimes and choreographic works;
- pictorial, graphic, and sculptural works;
- motion pictures and other audiovisual works;
- sound recordings; and
- architectural works.

These categories should be viewed quite broadly. For example, computer programs and most "compilations" are registrable as "literary works." Maps and architectural plans are registrable as "pictorial, graphic, and sculptural works."

## What Is Not Protected

Several categories of material are generally not eligible for federal copyright protection. These include, among others:
- works that have not been fixed in a tangible form of expression. For example, choreographic works that have not been notated or recorded, or improvisational speeches or performances that have not been written or recorded;
- titles, names, short phrases, and slogans; familiar symbols or designs; mere variations of typographic ornamentation, lettering, or coloring; mere listings of ingredients or contents;
- ideas, procedures, methods, systems, processes, concepts, principles, discoveries, or devices, as distinguished from a description, explanation, or illustration;
- works consisting entirely of information that is common property and containing no original authorship. For example, standard calendars, height and weight charts, tape measures and rulers, and lists or tables taken from public documents or other common sources.

## General Principles

"Copies" are material objects from which a work can be read or visually perceived, such as books, manuscripts, sheet music, film, videotape, or microfilm. "Phonorecords" are material objects embodying fixations of sounds (excluding, by statutory definition, motion picture soundtracks), such as cassette tapes, CDs, or LPs. Thus, for example, a song (the "work") can be fixed in sheet music ("copies") or in phonograph disks ("phonorecords"), or both. If a work is prepared over a period of time, the part of the work that is fixed on a particular date constitutes the created work as of that date.

Copyright protection is available for all unpublished works, regardless of the nationality or domicile of the author. Published works are eligible for copyright protection in the United States if any one of the several conditions regarding the nationality of the authors or place of publication is met. Check with the Copyright Office for details.

Copyright protection exists from the time the work is created in fixed form. The copyright in the work of authorship immediately becomes the property of the author who created it. Only the property of the author, or those deriving their rights through the author, can rightfully claim copyright.

In the case of works made for hire, the employer and not the employee is considered the author.

The authors of a joint work are co-owners of the copyright in the work, unless there is an agreement to the contrary.

Copyright in each separate contribution to a periodical or other collective work is distinct from copyright in the collective work as a whole and vests initially with the author of the contribution.

- Mere ownership of a book, manuscript, painting, or any other copy or phonorecord does not give the possessor the copyright. The law provides that transfer of ownership of any material object that embodies a protected work does not of itself convey any rights in the copyright.
- Minors may claim copyright, but state laws may regulate the business dealings involving copyrights owned by minors. For information on relevant state laws, consult an attorney.

Copyright is secured automatically when the work is created, and a work is "created" when it is fixed in a copy or phonorecord for the first time.

For further information about the limitations of any of these rights, consult the Copyright Law or write to the Copyright Office.

## Notice of Copyright

The use of a copyright notice is no longer required under U.S. law, although it is often beneficial. Because prior law did contain such a requirement, however, the use of notice is still relevant to the copyright status of older works. Use of the notice may be important because it informs the public that the work is protected by copyright, identifies the copyright owners, and shows the year of first publication.

Furthermore, in the event that a work is infringed, if a proper notice of copyright appears on the published copy or copies to which a defendant in a copyright infringement suit had access, then no weight shall be given to such a defendant's interposition of a defense based on innocent infringement in mitigation of actual or statutory damages, except as provided in section 504(c)(2) of the Copyright Code. Innocent infringement occurs when the infringer did not realize that the work was protected.

The use of the copyright notice is the responsibility of the copyright owner and does not require advance permission from, or registration with, the Copyright Office.

### Position of Notice

The notice should be positioned so as to "give reasonable notice of the claim of copyright." The Copyright Office has issued regulations concerning the form and position of the copyright notice. For more information, contact them directly.

## Form of Notice for Visually Perceptible Copies

The notice for visually perceptible copies should contain all of the following three elements:

1. the symbol © (the letter C in a circle), or the word "Copyright," or the abbreviation "Copr.";
2. the year of first publication of the work; and
3. the name of the owner of copyright in the work, or an abbreviation by which the name can be recognized, or a generally known alternative designation of the owner.

Example: © 2001 John Doe

## Form of Notice for Sound Recordings

The copyright notice for phonorecords of sound recordings should contain the following three elements:

1. the symbol ℗ (the letter P in a circle);
2. the year of first publication of the sound recording; and
3. the name of the owner of copyright in the sound recording, or an abbreviation by which the name can be recognized, or a generally known alternative designation of the owner. If the producer of the sound recording is named on the phonorecord labels or containers, and if no other name appears in conjunction with the notice, the producer's name shall be considered a part of the notice.

Example: ℗ 2001 A.B.C., Inc.

## Publications Incorporating United States Government Works

Works by the U.S. government are not eligible for copyright protection. For works published on or after March 1, 1989, the previous notice requirement for works that consist primarily of one or more works of the U.S. government has been eliminated. Copies of works published before March 1, 1989, that consist mostly of one or more works of the U.S. government should have a notice and the accompanying statement. Example:

© 2001 Jane Brown. Copyright claimed in Chapters 7–10, exclusive of U.S. government maps.

## Unpublished Works

The author or other owner of copyright may wish to place a copyright notice on any unpublished copies or phonorecords that leave his or her control. An appropriate notice for an unpublished work is "Unpublished work © 2001 Jane Doe."

NOTE: Since questions may arise from the use of variant forms of the notice, you may wish to seek legal advice before using any form of the notice other than those given here.

# Copyright Registration

Copyright registration makes a public record of the basic facts of a particular copyright. Even though registration is not a requirement for protection, the copyright law provides several incentives to encourage copyright owners to register. They include the following:

• Registration establishes a public record of the copyright claim;
• Before an infringement suit may be filed in court, registration is necessary for works of U.S. origin;
• If made before or within five years of publication, registration will establish *prima facie* evidence

in court of the validity of the copyright and of the facts stated in the certificate;

• If registration is made within three months after publication of the work or prior to an infringement of the work, statutory damages and attorney's fees will be available to the copyright owner in court actions. Otherwise, only an award of actual damages and profits is available to the copyright owner; and
• Copyright registration allows the owner of the copyright to record the registration with the U.S. Customs Service for protection against the importation of infringing copies.

Registration may be made at any time within the life of the copyright. When a work has been registered in unpublished form, it is not necessary to make another registration when the work becomes published (although the copyright owner may register the published edition, if desired).

To register a work, send the following three elements in the same envelope or package to the Registrar of Copyrights, Copyright Office, Library of Congress, 101 Independence Ave. S.E., Washington, DC 20559-6000:

1. a properly completed application form;
2. a nonrefundable filing fee of $30 (effective through June 30, 2002) for each application; and
3. a nonreturnable deposit of the work that is being registered. The deposit requirements vary in particular situations. Contact the Copyright Office for current information on fees and special requirements.

A copyright registration is effective on the date the Copyright Office receives all of the required elements in acceptable form, regardless of how long it takes to process the application and mail the certificate of registration. The time the Copyright Office requires to process an application varies, depending on the amount of material the office is receiving. If you apply for copyright registration, you will not receive an acknowledgment that your application has been received, but you can expect a letter or telephone call from a Copyright Office staff member if further information is needed.

# Copyright Protection Endurance

## Works Originally Created on or after Jan. 1, 1978

A work that is created on or after Jan. 1, 1978, is automatically protected from the moment of its creation, and is ordinarily given a term of the author's life, plus an additional 70 years after the author's death. In the case of a joint work prepared by two or more authors who did not work for hire, the term lasts for 70 years after the last surviving author's death. For works made for hire, and for anonymous and pseudonymous works (unless the author's identity is revealed in Copyright Office records), the duration of copyright will be 95 years from publication or 120 years from creation, whichever is shorter.

## Works Originally Created before Jan. 1, 1978

Works that were created but not published or registered for copyright before Jan. 1, 1978, have been automatically brought under the statute and are now given federal copyright protection. The duration of copyright in these works will generally be computed in the same way as for works created on or after Jan.

1, 1978: the life-plus-70 or 95/120-year terms will apply to them as well. The law provides that in no case will the term of copyright for works in this category expire before Dec. 31, 2002, and for works published on or before Dec. 31, 2002, the term of copyright will not expire before Dec. 31, 2047. Works that were created and published or registered before Jan. 1, 1978, generally enjoy a copyright term of 75 years from the date of publication or registration. Check with the Copyright Office for details.

## International Copyright Protection

There is no "international copyright" that will automatically protect an author's work throughout the entire world. Protection against unauthorized use in a particular country depends basically on the national laws of that country. However, most countries do offer protection to foreign works under certain conditions, and these conditions have been greatly simplified by international copyright treaties and conventions. For a list of countries that maintain copyright relations with the United States, request Circular 38a from the Copyright Office.

### For More Information

Information on registration and application forms may be obtained free of charge by writing or calling the Copyright Office. Address inquiries to the Copyright Office, Publications Section, LM-455, Library of Congress, 101 Independence Ave. S.E., Washington, DC 20559-6000. To speak with an information specialist, call 202-707-3000. Copyright information is also available on the Web, www.loc.gov/copyright.

# Trademarks
*Source:* Department of Commerce, Patent and Trademark Office

A trademark may be defined as a word, letter, device, or symbol, as well as any combination of these, that is used in connection with merchandise and that points distinctly to the origin of the goods.

Certificates of registration of trademarks are issued under the seal of the Patent and Trademark Office and may be registered by the owner if he or she is engaged in interstate or foreign commerce. Federal jurisdiction over trademarks arises under the commerce clause of the Constitution. Effective Nov. 16, 1989, applications to register may also be based on a "bona fide intention to use the mark in commerce." Trademarks may be registered by foreign owners who comply with U.S. law, as well as by citizens of foreign countries with which the United States has treaties relating to trademarks. American citizens may register trademarks in foreign countries by complying with the laws of those countries. The right to registration and protection of trademarks in many foreign countries is guaranteed by treaties.

General jurisdiction in trademark cases involving Federal Registrations is given to federal courts. Adverse decisions of examiners on applications for registration are appealable to the Trademark Trial and Appeal Board, whose affirmances and decisions in *inter partes* proceedings are subject to court review. Before adopting a trademark, a person should make a search of prior marks to avoid unwittingly infringing upon them.

The duration of a trademark registration is ten years, but it may be renewed indefinitely for 10-year periods, provided the trademark is still in use at the time of expiration.

The application fee for registering is $325 per class.

# Patents
*Source:* Department of Commerce, Patent and Trademark Office

A patent, in the most general sense, is a document issued by a government, conferring some special right or privilege. The term is now restricted mainly to patents for inventions, and occasionally, land patents.

The grant of a patent for an invention gives the inventor the privilege, for a limited period of time, of excluding others from making, using, or selling a certain article.

In the United States, the law provides that a patent may be granted, for a term of 20 years from the date of application, to any person who has invented or discovered any new and useful art, machine, manufacture, or composition of matter, as well as any new and useful improvements thereof. A patent may also be granted to a person who has invented or discovered and asexually reproduced a new and distinct variety of plant (other than a tuber-propagated one) or has invented a new, original, and ornamental design for an article of manufacture, for a term of 20 years and 14 years, respectively.

A patent is granted only upon receipt of a complete, regularly filed application and the appropriate fees, and upon determination that the invention is new, useful, and, in view of the prior art, unobvious to one skilled in the art. The disclosure must be of such nature as to enable others to reproduce the invention.

Patents are not granted for printed matter, for methods of doing business, or for devices for which claims contrary to natural laws are made. Applications for a perpetual-motion machine have been made from time to time, but until a working model is presented that actually fulfills the claim, no patent will be issued.

A complete application, which must be addressed to the Commissioner of Patents and Trademarks, Washington, DC 20231, consists of a specification with one or more claims; oath or declaration; drawing (whenever the nature of the case admits of it); and a basic filing fee of $380. The filing fee is not returned to the applicant if the patent is refused. If the patent is allowed, another fee of $660 is required before the patent is issued. The fee for design patent application is $155; the issue fee is $215. The fee for a plant patent application is $240; the issue fee is $290. Maintenance fees are required on utility patents at stipulated intervals. Phone 1-800-786-9119 for the latest fees.

I n any broad overview of history, arbitrary compartmentalization of facts is self-defeating (and makes locating interrelated people, places, and things that much harder). Therefore, Headline History is designed as a "timeline"—a chronology that highlights both the march of time and interesting, sometimes surprising, juxtapositions.

*See also* related sections of the almanac, particularly Inventions and Discoveries, U.S. Government and History, and Countries of the World.

# B.C.

## Before Christ (B.C.) or Before the Common Era (B.C.E.)

**4.5 billion B.C.** Planet Earth formed.

**3 billion B.C.** First signs of primeval life (bacteria and blue-green algae) appear in oceans.

**600 million B.C.** Earliest date to which fossils can be traced.

**4.4 million B.C.** Earliest known hominid fossils (*Ardipithecus ramidus*) found in Aramis, Ethiopia, 1994.

**4.2 million B.C.** *Australopithecus anamensis* found in Lake Turkana, Kenya, 1995.

**3.2 million B.C.** *Australopithecus afarenis* (nicknamed "Lucy") found in Ethiopia, 1974.

**2.5 million B.C.** *Homo habilis* ("Skillful Man"). First brain expansion; is believed to have used stone tools.

**1.8 million B.C.** *Homo erectus* ("Upright Man"). Brain size twice that of *Australopithecine* species.

**1.7 million B.C.** *Homo erectus* leaves Africa.

**100,000 B.C.** First modern *Homo sapiens* in South Africa.

**70,000 B.C.** Neanderthal man (use of fire and advanced tools).

**35,000 B.C.** Neanderthal man replaced by later groups of *Homo sapiens* (i.e., Cro-Magnon man, etc.).

**18,000 B.C.** Cro-Magnons replaced by later cultures.

**15,000 B.C.** Migrations across Bering Straits into the Americas.

**10,000 B.C.** Semi-permanent agricultural settlements in Old World.

**10,000–4,000 B.C.** Development of settlements into cities and development of skills such as the wheel, pottery, and improved methods of cultivation in Mesopotamia and elsewhere.

**5500–3000 B.C.** Predynastic Egyptian cultures develop (5500–3100 B.C.); begin using agriculture (c. 5000 B.C.). Earliest known civilization arises in Sumer (4500–4000 B.C.). Earliest recorded date in Egyptian calendar (4241 B.C.). First year of Jewish calendar (3760 B.C.). First phonetic writing appears (c. 3500 B.C.). Sumerians develop a city-state civilization (c. 3000 B.C.). Copper used by Egyptians and Sumerians. Western Europe is neolithic, without metals or written records.

**3000–2000 B.C.** Pharaonic rule begins in Egypt. King Khufu (Cheops), 4th dynasty (2700–2675 B.C.), completes construction of the Great Pyramid at Giza (c. 2680 B.C.). The Great Sphinx of Giza (c. 2540 B.C.) is built by King Khafre. Earliest Egyptian mummies. Papyrus. Phoenician settlements on coast of what is now Syria and Lebanon. Semitic tribes settle in Assyria. Sargon, first Akkadian king, builds Mesopotamian empire. The *Gilgamesh* epic (c. 3000 B.C.). Abraham leaves Ur (c. 2000 B.C.). Systematic astronomy in Egypt, Babylon, India, China.

**3000–1500 B.C.** The most ancient civilization on the Indian subcontinent, the sophisticated and extensive Indus Valley civilization, flourishes in what is today Pakistan. In Britain, Stonehenge erected according to some unknown astronomical rationale. Its three main phases of construction are thought to span c. 3000–1500 B.C.

**2000–1500 B.C.** Hyksos invaders drive Egyptians from Lower Egypt (17th century B.C.). Amosis I frees Egypt from Hyksos (c. 1600 B.C.). Assyrians rise to power—cities of Ashur and Nineveh. Twenty-four-character alphabet in Egypt. Israelites enslaved in Egypt. Cuneiform inscriptions used by Hittites. Peak of Minoan culture on Isle of Crete—earliest form of written Greek. Hammurabi, king of Babylon, develops oldest existing code of laws (18th century B.C.).

Ra, Egyptian
Sun God
(3000–2000 B.C.)

The Great Pyramid
at Giza
(c. 2680 B.C.)

Stonehenge
(c. 3000–1500 B.C.)

**Pythagoras
(582?–507? B.C.)**

**Buddha
(563?–483? B.C.)**

**1500–1000 B.C.** Ikhnaton develops monotheistic religion in Egypt (c. 1375 B.C.). His successor, Tutankhamen, returns to earlier gods. Moses leads Israelites out of Egypt into Canaan—Ten Commandments. Greeks destroy Troy (c. 1193 B.C.). End of Greek civilization in Mycenae with invasion of Dorians. Chinese civilization develops under Shang Dynasty. Olmec civilization in Mexico—stone monuments; picture writing.

**1000–900 B.C.** Solomon succeeds King David, builds Jerusalem temple. After Solomon's death, kingdom divided into Israel and Judah. Hebrew elders begin to write Old Testament books of Bible. Phoenicians colonize Spain with settlement at Cadiz.

**900–800 B.C.** Phoenicians establish Carthage (c. 810 B.C.). The *Iliad* and the *Odyssey,* perhaps composed by Greek poet Homer.

**800–700 B.C.** Prophets Amos, Hosea, Isaiah. First recorded Olympic games (776 B.C.). Legendary founding of Rome by Romulus (753 B.C.). Assyrian king Sargon II conquers Hittites, Chaldeans, Samaria (end of Kingdom of Israel). Earliest written music. Chariots introduced into Italy by Etruscans.

**700–600 B.C.** End of Assyrian Empire (616 B.C.)—Nineveh destroyed by Chaldeans (Neo-Babylonians) and Medes (612 B.C.). Founding of Byzantium by Greeks (c. 660 B.C.). Building of the Acropolis in Athens. Solon, Greek lawgiver (640–560 B.C.). Sappho of Lesbos, Greek poet (fl. c. 610–580 B.C.). Lao-tse, Chinese philosopher and founder of Taoism (born c. 604 B.C.).

**600–500 B.C.** Babylonian King Nebuchadnezzar builds empire, destroys Jerusalem (586 B.C.). Babylonian Captivity of the Jews (starting 587 B.C.). Hanging Gardens of Babylon. Cyrus the Great of Persia creates great empire, conquers Babylon (539 B.C.), frees the Jews. Athenian democracy develops. Aeschylus, Greek dramatist (525–465 B.C.). Pythagoras, Greek philosopher and mathematician (582?–507? B.C.). Confucius (551–479 B.C.) develops ethical and social philosophy in China. The *Analects* or Lun-yü ("collected sayings") are compiled by the second generation of Confucian disciples. Buddha (563?–483? B.C.) founds Buddhism in India.

## SOME ANCIENT CIVILIZATIONS

| Name | Approximate dates | Location | Major cities |
|---|---|---|---|
| Akkadian | 2350–2230 B.C. | Mesopotamia, parts of Syria, Asia Minor, Iran | Akkad, Ur, Erich |
| Assyrian | 1800–889 B.C. | Mesopotamia, Syria | Assur, Nineveh, Calah |
| Babylonian | 1728–1686 B.C. (old) 625–539 B.C. (new) | Mesopotamia, Syria, Palestine | Babylon |
| Cimmerian | 750–500 B.C. | Caucasus, northern Asia Minor | — |
| Egyptian | 2850–715 B.C. | Nile valley | Thebes, Memphis, Tanis |
| Etruscan | 900–396 B.C. | Northern Italy | — |
| Greek | 900–200 B.C. | Greece | Athens, Sparta, Thebes, Mycenae, Corinth |
| Hittite | 1640–1200 B.C. | Asia Minor, Syria | Hattusas, Nesa |
| Indus Valley | 3000–1500 B.C. | Pakistan, Northwestern India | — |
| Lydian | 700–547 B.C. | Western Asia Minor | Sardis, Miletus |
| Mede | 835–550 B.C. | Iran | Media |
| Minoan | 3000–1100 B.C. | Crete | Knossos |
| Persian | 559–330 B.C. | Iran, Asia Minor, Syria | Persepolis, Pasargadae |
| Phoenician | 1100–332 B.C. | Palestine (colonies: Gibraltar, Carthage, Sardinia) | Tyre, Sidon, Byblos |
| Phrygian | 1000–547 B.C. | Central Asia Minor | Gordion |
| Roman | 500 B.C.–A.D. 300 | Italy, Mediterranean region, Asia Minor, western Europe | Rome, Byzantium |
| Scythian | 800–300 B.C. | Caucasus | — |
| Sumerian | 3200–2360 B.C. | Mesopotamia | Ur, Nippur |

**500–400 b.c.** Greeks defeat Persians: battles of Marathon (490 b.c.), Thermopylae (480 b.c.), Salamis (480 b.c.). Peloponnesian Wars between Athens and Sparta (431–404 b.c.)—Sparta victorious. Pericles comes to power in Athens (462 b.c.). Flowering of Greek culture during the Age of Pericles (450–400 b.c.). The Parthenon is built in Athens as a temple of the goddess Athena (447–432 b.c.). Ictinus and Callicrates are the architects and Phidias is responsible for the sculpture. Sophocles, Greek dramatist (496?–406 b.c.). Hippocrates, Greek "Father of Medicine" (born 460 b.c.). Xerxes I, king of Persia (rules 485–465 b.c.).

**400–300 b.c.** Pentateuch—first five books of the Old Testament evolve in final form. Philip of Macedon, who believed himself to be a descendant of the Greek people, assassinated (336 b.c.) after subduing the Greek city-states; succeeded by son, Alexander the Great (356–323 b.c.), who destroys Thebes (335 b.c.), conquers Tyre and Jerusalem (332 b.c.), occupies Babylon (330 b.c.), invades India, and dies in Babylon. His empire is divided among his generals; one of them, Seleucis I, establishes Middle East empire with capitals at Antioch (Syria) and Seleucia (in Iraq). Trial and execution of Greek philosopher Socrates (399 b.c.). Dialogues recorded by his student, Plato (c. 427–348 or 347 b.c.). Euclid's work on geometry (323 b.c.). Aristotle, Greek philosopher (384–322 b.c.). Demosthenes, Greek orator (384–322 b.c.). Praxiteles, Greek sculptor (400–330 b.c.).

**300–251 b.c.** First Punic War (264–241 b.c.): Rome defeats the Carthaginians and begins its domination of the Mediterranean. Temple of the Sun at Teotihuacan, Mexico (c. 300 b.c.). Invention of Mayan calendar in Yucatán—more exact than older calendars. First Roman gladiatorial games (264 b.c.). Archimedes, Greek mathematician (287–212 b.c.).

**250–201 b.c.** Second Punic War (219–201 b.c.): Hannibal, Carthaginian general (246–142 b.c.), crosses the Alps (218 b.c.), reaches gates of Rome (211 b.c.), retreats, and is defeated by Scipio Africanus at Zama (202 b.c.). Great Wall of China built (c. 215 b.c.).

**200–151 b.c.** Romans defeat Seleucid King Antiochus III at Thermopylae (191 b.c.)—beginning of Roman world domination. Maccabean revolt against Seleucids (167 b.c.).

**150–101 b.c.** Third Punic War (149–146 b.c.): Rome destroys Carthage, killing 450,000 and enslaving the remaining 50,000 inhabitants. Roman armies conquer Macedonia, Greece, Anatolia, Balearic Islands, and southern France. Venus de Milo (c. 140 b.c.). Cicero, Roman orator (106–43 b.c.).

**100–51 b.c.** Julius Caesar (100–44 b.c.) invades Britain (55 b.c.) and conquers Gaul (France) (c. 50 b.c.). Spartacus leads slave revolt against Rome (71 b.c.). Romans conquer Seleucid empire. Roman general Pompey conquers Jerusalem (63 b.c.). Cleopatra on Egyptian throne (51–31 b.c.). Chinese develop use of paper (c. 100 b.c.). Virgil, Roman poet (70–19 b.c.). Horace, Roman poet (65–8 b.c.).

**50–1 b.c.** Caesar crosses Rubicon to fight Pompey (50 b.c.). Herod made Roman governor of Judea (37 b.c.). Caesar murdered (44 b.c.). Caesar's nephew, Octavian, defeats Mark Antony and Cleopatra at Battle of Actium (31 b.c.), and establishes Roman empire as Emperor Augustus—rules 27 b.c.–a.d. 14. Pantheon built for the first time under Agrippa, 27 b.c. Ovid, Roman poet (43 b.c.–a.d. 18).

Confucius
(551–479 b.c.)

Parthenon
(447–432 b.c.)

Plato
(427?–348 or 347 b.c.)

# A.D.

## Christian Era (a.d.) or the Common Era (c.e.)

**1–49** Birth of Jesus Christ (variously given from 4 b.c. to a.d. 7). After Augustus, Tiberius becomes emperor (dies, a.d. 37), succeeded by Caligula (assassinated, a.d. 41), who is followed by Claudius. Crucifixion of Jesus (probably a.d. 30). Han dynasty in China founded by Emperor Kuang Wu Ti. Buddhism introduced to China.

**50–99** Claudius poisoned (a.d. 54), succeeded by Nero (commits suicide, a.d. 68). Missionary journeys of Paul the Apostle (a.d. 34–60). Jews revolt against Rome; Jerusalem destroyed (a.d. 70). Roman persecutions of Christians begin (a.d. 64). Colosseum built in Rome (a.d. 71–80). Trajan (rules a.d. 98–116); Roman empire extends to Mesopotamia, Arabia, Balkans. First Gospels of St. Mark, St. John, St. Matthew.

Roman Aqueduct
Montpellier, France

**Mayan Pyramid at Chichén Itzá**

**Celtic Cross**

**Japanese Pagoda**

**Viking Ship (c. 900)**

**100–149**  Hadrian rules Rome (A.D. 117–138); codifies Roman law, rebuilds Pantheon, establishes postal system, builds wall between England and Scotland. Jews revolt under Bar Kokhba (A.D. 122–135); final Diaspora (dispersion) of Jews begins.

**150–199**  Marcus Aurelius rules Rome (A.D. 161–180). Oldest Mayan temples in Central America (c. A.D. 200).

**200–249**  Goths invade Asia Minor (c. A.D. 220). Roman persecutions of Christians increase. Persian (Sassanid) empire re-established. End of Chinese Han dynasty.

**250–299**  Increasing invasions of the Roman empire by Franks and Goths. Buddhism spreads in China. Classic period of Mayan civilization (A.D. 250–900); develop hieroglyphic writing, advances in art, architecture, science.

**300–349**  Constantine the Great (rules A.D. 312–337) reunites eastern and western Roman empires, with new capital (Constantinople) on site of Byzantium (A.D. 330); issues Edict of Milan legalizing Christianity (A.D. 313); becomes a Christian on his deathbed (A.D. 337). Council of Nicaea (A.D. 325) defines orthodox Christian doctrine. First Gupta dynasty in India (c. A.D. 320).

**350–399**  Huns (Mongols) invade Europe (c. A.D. 360). Theodosius the Great (rules A.D. 392–395)—last emperor of a united Roman empire. Roman empire permanently divided in A.D. 395: western empire ruled from Rome; eastern empire ruled from Constantinople.

**400–449**  Western Roman empire disintegrates under weak emperors. Alaric, king of the Visigoths, sacks Rome (A.D. 410). Attila, Hun chieftain, attacks Roman provinces (A.D. 433). St. Patrick returns to Ireland (A.D. 432) and brings Christianity to the island. St. Augustine's *City of God* (A.D. 411).

**450–499**  Vandals destroy Rome (A.D. 455). Western Roman empire ends as Odoacer, German chieftain, overthrows last Roman emperor, Romulus Augustulus, and becomes king of Italy (A.D. 476). Ostrogothic kingdom of Italy established by Theodoric the Great (A.D. 493). Clovis, ruler of the Franks, is converted to Christianity (A.D. 496). First schism between western and eastern churches (A.D. 484).

**500–549**  Eastern and western churches reconciled (519). Justinian I, the Great (483–565), becomes Byzantine emperor (527), issues his first code of civil laws (529), conquers North Africa, Italy, and part of Spain. Plague spreads through Europe (542 *et seq.*). Arthur, semi-legendary king of the Britons (killed, c. 537). Boëthius, Roman scholar (executed, 524).

**550–599**  Beginnings of European silk industry after Justinian's missionaries smuggle silkworms out of China (553). Mohammed, founder of Islam (570–632). Buddhism in Japan (c. 560). St. Augustine of Canterbury brings Christianity to Britain (597). After killing about half the population, plague in Europe subsides (594).

**600–649**  Mohammed flees from Mecca to Medina (the *Hegira*); first year of the Muslim calendar (622). Muslim empire grows (634). Arabs conquer Jerusalem (637), destroy Alexandrian library (641), conquer Persians (641). Fatima, Mohammed's daughter (606–632).

**650–699**  Arabs attack North Africa (670), destroy Carthage (697). Venerable Bede, English monk (672–735).

**700–749**  Arab empire extends from Lisbon to China (by 716). Charles Martel, Frankish leader, defeats Arabs at Tours/Poitiers, halting Arab advance in Europe (732). Charlemagne (742–814). Introduction of pagodas in Japan from China.

**750–799**  Charlemagne becomes king of the Franks (771). Caliph Harun al-Rashid rules Arab empire (786–809): the "golden age" of Arab culture. Vikings begin attacks on Britain (790), land in Ireland (795). City of Machu Picchu flourishes in Peru.

**800–849**  Charlemagne crowned first Holy Roman Emperor in Rome (800). Charlemagne dies (814), succeeded by his son, Louis the Pious, who divides France among his sons (817). Arabs conquer Crete, Sicily, and Sardinia (826–827).

**850–899**  Norsemen attack as far south as the Mediterranean but are thwarted (859), discover Iceland (861). Alfred the Great becomes king of Britain (871), defeats Danish invaders (878). Russian nation founded by Vikings under Prince Rurik, establishing capital at Novgorod (855–879).

**900–949**  Beginning of Mayan Post-Classical period (900–1519). Vikings discover Greenland (c. 900). Arab Spain under Abd ar-Rahman III becomes center of learning (912–961). Otto I becomes King of Germany (936).

**950–999**  Mieczyslaw I becomes first ruler of Poland (960). Eric the Red establishes first Viking colony in Greenland (982). Hugh Capet elected King of France in 987; Capetian dynasty to rule until 1328. Musical notation systematized (c.

990). Vikings and Danes attack Britain (988–999). Otto I crowned Holy Roman Emperor by Pope John XII (962).

## 1000–1099 (A.D.)

**c. 1000–1300** Classic Pueblo period of Anasazi culture; cliff dwellings.

**c. 1000** Hungary and Scandinavia converted to Christianity. Viking raider Leif Eriksson discovers North America, calls it Vinland. *Beowulf,* Old English epic.

**c. 1008** Murasaki Shikibu finishes *The Tale of Genji,* the world's first novel.

**1009** Muslims destroy Holy Sepulchre in Jerusalem.

**1013** Danes control England. Canute takes throne (1016), conquers Norway (1028), dies (1035); kingdom divided among his sons: Harold Harefoot (England), Sweyn (Norway), Hardecanute (Denmark).

**Mesa Verde
Cliff Dwellings
(c. 1000–1300)**

**1040** Macbeth murders Duncan, king of Scotland.

**1053** Robert Guiscard, Norman invader, establishes kingdom in Italy, conquers Sicily (1072).

**1054** Final separation between Eastern (Orthodox) and Western (Roman) churches.

**1055** Seljuk Turks, Asian nomads, move west, capture Baghdad, Armenia (1064), Syria, and Palestine (1075).

**1066** William of Normandy invades England, defeats last Saxon king, Harold II, at Battle of Hastings, crowned William I of England ("the Conqueror").

**1068** Construction on the cathedral in Pisa, Italy, begins.

**1073** Emergence of strong papacy when Gregory VII is elected. Conflict with English and French kings and German emperors will continue throughout medieval period.

**Cathedral and Tower
at Pisa**

**1095** At Council of Clermont, Pope Urban II calls for a holy war to wrest control of Jerusalem from Muslims, which launches the First Crusade (1096), one of at least 8 European military campaigns between 1095 and 1291 to regain the Holy Land.

## 1100–1199 (A.D.)

**1100–1300** Construction of Cathedral at Chartres, France.

**1144** Second Crusade begins.

**c. 1150** Angkor Wat is completed.

**1150–1167** Universities of Paris and Oxford founded in France and England.

**1162** Thomas á Becket named Archbishop of Canterbury, murdered by Henry II's men (1170). Troubadours (wandering minstrels) glorify romantic concepts of feudalism.

**1169** Ibn-Rushd begins translating Aristotle's works.

**1189** Richard I ("the Lionhearted") succeeds Henry II in England, killed in France (1199), succeeded by King John. Third Crusade.

**Chartres Cathedral**

## 1200–1299 (A.D.)

**1200–1204** Fourth Crusade.

**1211** Genghis Khan invades China, captures Peking (1214), conquers Persia (1218), invades Russia (1223), dies (1227).

**1212** Children's Crusade.

**1215** King John forced by barons to sign Magna Carta at Runneymede, limiting royal power.

**1228** Sixth Crusade.

**King John
(1167–1216)**

### THE CRUSADES (1096–1291)

In 1095 at Council of Clermont, Pope Urban II calls for war to rescue Holy Land from Muslim infidels. The *First Crusade* (1096) is assembled in response to Emperor Alexius I. The Christians capture Antioch (1098) and Jerusalem (1099). They establish the Crusader States, ruled by Europeans. It is the only successful crusade. The *Second Crusade* begins after the Seljuk Turks recapture Edessa, one of the Crusader States, in 1144. It is led by King Louis VIII of France and Holy Roman Emperor Conrad III. Crusaders perish in Asia Minor (1147).

Saladin controls Egypt (1171), unites Islam in holy war *(jihad)* against Christians, recaptures Jerusalem

(1187). *Third Crusade* (1189) under kings of France, England, and Germany falls to reduce Saladin's power. *Fourth Crusade* (1200–1204)—French knights sack Greek Christian Constantinople, establish Latin empire in Byzantium. Greeks reestablish Orthodox faith (1262).

*Children's Crusade* (1212)—only one of 30,000 French children and about 200 of 20,000 German children survive to return home. Other Crusades—*Fifth,* against Egypt (1217), *Sixth* (1228), *Seventh* (1248), *Eighth* (1270). Mamelukes conquer Acre; end of the Crusades (1291).

**Thomas Aquinas
(1225–1274)**

**The Duomo in
Florence**

**Joan of Arc
(1412–1431)**

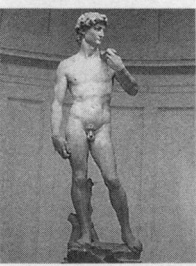

**Michelangelo's David
(1504)**

**Balboa
(1475–1517)**

**1231** The Inquisition begins as Pope Gregory IX assigns Dominicans responsibility for combating heresy. Torture used (1252). Ferdinand and Isabella establish Spanish Inquisition (1478). Tourquemada, Grand Inquisitor, forces conversion or expulsion of Spanish Jews (1492). Forced conversion of Moors (1499). Inquisition in Portugal (1531). First Protestants burned at the stake in Spain (1543). Spanish Inquisition abolished (1834).

**1241** Mongols defeat Germans in Silesia, invade Poland and Hungary, withdraw from Europe after Ughetai, Mongol leader, dies.

**1248** Seventh Crusade.

**1251** Kublai Khan governs China, becomes ruler of Mongols (1259), establishes Yuan dynasty in China (1280), invades Burma (1287), dies (1294).

**1260** Chartres cathedral consecrated.

**1270** Eighth Crusade.

**1271** Marco Polo of Venice travels to China, in court of Kublai Khan (1275–1292), returns to Genoa (1295) and writes *Travels*.

**1273** Thomas Aquinas stops work on *Summa Theologica*, the basis of all Catholic theological teaching; never completes it.

**1295** English King Edward I summons the Model Parliament.

### 1300–1399 (A.D.)

**1312–1337** Mali Empire reaches its height in Africa under King Mansa Musa.

**c. 1325** The beginning of the Renaissance in Italy: writers Dante, Petrarch, Boccaccio; painter Giotto. Development of *Noh* drama in Japan. Aztecs establish Tenochtitlán on site of modern Mexico City. Peak of Muslim culture in Spain. Small cannon in use.

**1337–1453** Hundred Years' War—English and French kings fight for control of France.

**1347–1351** At least 25 million people die in Europe's "Black Death" (bubonic plague).

**1368** Ming Dynasty begins in China.

**1376–1382** John Wycliffe, pre-Reformation religious reformer, and followers translate Latin Bible into English.

**1378** The Great Schism (to 1417)—rival popes in Rome and Avignon, France, fight for control of Roman Catholic Church.

**c. 1387** Chaucer's *Canterbury Tales*.

**1399** Tamerlane begins last great conquest.

### 1400–1499 (A.D.)

**1407** Casa di San Giorgio, one of the first public banks, founded in Genoa.

**1415** Henry V defeats French at Agincourt. Jan Hus, Bohemian preacher and follower of Wycliffe, burned at stake in Constance as heretic.

**1418–1460** Portugal's Prince Henry the Navigator sponsors exploration of Africa's coast.

**1420** Brunelleschi begins work on the Duomo in Florence.

**1428** Joan of Arc leads French against English, captured by Burgundians (1430) and turned over to the English, burned at the stake as a witch after ecclesiastical trial (1431).

**1438** Incas rule in Peru.

**1450** Florence becomes center of Renaissance arts and learning under the Medicis.

**1453** Turks conquer Constantinople, end of the Byzantine empire, beginning of the Ottoman empire.

**1455** The Wars of the Roses, civil wars between rival noble factions, begin in England (to 1485). Having invented printing with movable type at Mainz, Germany, Johann Gutenberg completes first Bible.

**1462** Ivan the Great rules Russia until 1505 as first czar; ends payment of tribute to Mongols.

**1492** Moors conquered in Spain by troops of Ferdinand and Isabella. Columbus becomes first European to encounter Caribbean islands, returns to Spain (1493). Second voyage to Dominica, Jamaica, Puerto Rico (1493–1496). Third voyage to Orinoco (1498). Fourth voyage to Honduras and Panama (1502–1504).

**1497** Vasco da Gama sails around Africa and discovers sea route to India (1498). Establishes Portuguese colony in India (1502). John Cabot, employed by England, reaches and explores Canadian coast. Michelangelo's *Bacchus* sculpture.

### 1500–1599 (A.D.)

**1501** First black slaves in America brought to Spanish colony of Santo Domingo.

**c. 1503** Leonardo da Vinci paints the *Mona Lisa*. Michelangelo sculpts the *David* (1504).

**1506** St. Peter's Church started in Rome; designed and decorated by such artists and architects as Bramante, Michelangelo, da Vinci, Raphael, and
Bernini before its completion in 1626.

**1509** Henry VIII ascends English throne. Michelangelo paints the ceiling of
the Sistine Chapel.

**1513** Balboa becomes the first European to encounter the Pacific Ocean.
Machiavelli's *The Prince*.

**1517** Turks conquer Egypt, control Arabia. Martin Luther posts his 95 theses
denouncing church abuses on church door in Wittenberg—start of the
Reformation in Germany.

**1519** Ulrich Zwingli begins Reformation in Switzerland. Hernando Cortes
conquers Mexico for Spain. Charles I of Spain is chosen Holy Roman
Emperor Charles V. Portuguese explorer Ferdinand Magellan sets out to
circumnavigate the globe.

Martin Luther
(1483–1546)

**1520** Luther excommunicated by Pope Leo X. Suleiman I ("the Magnificent")
becomes Sultan of Turkey, invades Hungary (1521), Rhodes (1522),
attacks Austria (1529), annexes Hungary (1541), Tripoli (1551), makes
peace with Persia (1553), destroys Spanish fleet (1560), dies (1566).
Magellan reaches the Pacific, is killed by Philippine natives (1521). One
of his ships under Juan Sebastián del Cano continues around the world,
reaches Spain (1522).

**1524** Verrazano, sailing under the French flag, explores the New England coast
and New York Bay.

**1527** Troops of the Holy Roman Empire attack Rome, imprison Pope Clement
VII—the end of the Italian Renaissance. Castiglione writes *The Courtier*. The Medici family expelled from Florence.

Henry VIII
(1491–1547)

**1532** Pizarro marches from Panama to Peru, kills the Inca chieftain, Atahual-
pa, of Peru (1533). Machiavelli's *The Prince* published posthumously.

**1535** Reformation begins as Henry VIII makes himself head of English
Church after being excommunicated by Pope. Sir Thomas More
executed as traitor for refusal to acknowledge king's religious authority.
Jacques Cartier sails up the St. Lawrence River, basis of French claims
to Canada.

**1536** Henry VIII executes second wife, Anne Boleyn. John Calvin establishes
Reformed and Presbyterian form of Protestantism in Switzerland, writes
*Institutes of the Christian Religion*. Danish and Norwegian Reforma-
tions. Michelangelo's *Last Judgment*.

**1541** John Knox leads Reformation in Scotland, establishes Presbyterian
church there (1560).

Queen Elizabeth I
(1533–1603)

**1543** Publication of *On the Revolution of Heavenly Bodies* by Polish scholar
Nicolaus Copernicus—giving his theory that the earth revolves around
the sun.

**1545** Council of Trent to meet intermittently until 1563 to define Catholic
dogma and doctrine, reiterate papal authority.

**1547** Ivan IV ("the Terrible") crowned as czar of Russia, begins conquest of
Astrakhan and Kazan (1552), battles nobles (boyars) for power (1564),
kills his son (1580), dies, and is succeeded by his weak and feeble-
minded son, Fyodor I.

**1553** Roman Catholicism restored in England by Queen Mary I.

**1556** Akbar the Great becomes Mogul emperor of India, conquers Afghanistan
(1581), continues wars of conquest (until 1605).

**1558** Queen Elizabeth I ascends the throne (rules to 1603). Restores Protestantism, establishes state Church of England (Anglicanism). Renaissance
will reach height in England—Shakespeare, Marlowe, Spenser.

William Shakespeare
(1564–1616)

**1561** Persecution of Huguenots in France stopped by Edict of Orleans. French
religious wars begin again with massacre of Huguenots at Vassy. St.
Bartholomew's Day Massacre—thousands of Huguenots murdered
(1572). Amnesty granted (1573). Persecution continues periodically until
Edict of Nantes (1598) gives Huguenots religious freedom (until 1685).

**1568** Protestant Netherlands revolts against Catholic Spain; independence will
be acknowledged by Spain in 1648. High point of Dutch Renaissance—
painters Rubens, Van Dyck, Hals, and Rembrandt.

**1570** Japan permits visits of foreign ships. Queen Elizabeth I excommunicated
by Pope. Turks attack Cyprus and war on Venice. Turkish fleet defeated
at Battle of Lepanto by Spanish and Italian fleets (1571). Peace of Constantinople (1572) ends Turkish attacks on Europe.

Rembrandt van Rijn
(1606–1669)

**1580** Francis Drake returns to England after circumnavigating the globe;
knighted by Queen Elizabeth I (1581). Montaigne's *Essays* published.

**1582** Pope Gregory XIII implements the Gregorian calendar.

Catherine de Medici
(1519–1589)

Galileo
(1564–1642)

Pocahontas
(c. 1595–1617)

Taj Mahal

John Milton
(1608–1674)

**1583** William of Orange rules the Netherlands; assassinated on orders of Philip II of Spain (1584).

**1587** Mary, Queen of Scots, executed for treason by order of Queen Elizabeth I. Monteverdi's *First Book of Madrigals.*

**1588** Defeat of the Spanish Armada by English. Henry, King of Navarre and Protestant leader, recognized as Henry IV, first Bourbon king of France. Converts to Roman Catholicism in 1593 in attempt to end religious wars.

**1590** Henry IV enters Paris, wars on Spain (1595), marries Marie de Medici (1600), assassinated (1610). Spenser's *The Faerie Queen.* El Greco's *St. Jerome.* Galileo's experiments with falling objects.

**1598** Boris Godunov becomes Russian czar. Tycho Brahe describes his astronomical experiments.

### 1600–1699 (A.D.)

**1600** Giordano Bruno burned as a heretic. English East India Company established.

**1603** Ieyasu rules Japan, moves capital to Edo (Tokyo). Shakespeare's *Hamlet.*

**1605** Cervantes's *Don Quixote de la Mancha,* the first modern novel.

**1607** Jamestown, Virginia, established—first permanent English colony on American mainland. Pocahontas, daughter of Chief Powhatan, saves life of John Smith.

**1609** Samuel de Champlain establishes French colony of Quebec. The *Relation,* the first newspaper, debuts in Germany.

**1610** Galileo sees the moons of Jupiter through his telescope.

**1611** Gustavus Adolphus elected King of Sweden. King James Version of the Bible published in England. Rubens paints his *Descent from the Cross.*

**1614** John Napier discovers logarithms.

**1618** Start of the Thirty Years' War—Protestants revolt against Catholic oppression; Denmark, Sweden, and France will invade Germany in later phases of war. Kepler proposes last of three laws of planetary motion.

**1619** A Dutch ship brings the first African slaves to British North America.

**1620** Pilgrims, after three-month voyage in *Mayflower,* land at Plymouth Rock. Francis Bacon's *Novum Organum.*

**1623** New Netherland founded by Dutch West India Company.

**1630** Massachusetts Bay Colony.

**1632** Maryland founded by Lord Baltimore.

**1633** Inquisition forces Galileo to recant his belief in Copernican theory.

**1642** English Civil War. Cavaliers, supporters of Charles I, against Roundheads, parliamentary forces. Oliver Cromwell defeats Royalists (1646). Parliament demands reforms. Charles I offers concessions, brought to trial (1648), beheaded (1649). Cromwell becomes Lord Protector (1653). Rembrandt paints his *Night Watch.*

**1643** Taj Mahal completed.

**1644** End of Ming Dynasty in China—Manchus come to power. Descartes's *Principles of Philosophy.*

**1648** End of the Thirty Years' War. German population about half of what it was in 1618 because of war and pestilence.

**1658** Cromwell dies; son Richard resigns and Puritan government collapses.

**1660** English Parliament calls for the restoration of the monarchy; invites Charles II to return from France.

**1661** Charles II is crowned King of England. Louis XIV begins personal rule as absolute monarch; starts to build Versailles.

**1664** British take New Amsterdam from the Dutch. English limit "Nonconformity" with reestablished Anglican Church. Isaac Newton's experiments with gravity.

**1665** Great Plague in London kills 75,000.

**1666** Great Fire of London. Molière's *Misanthrope.*

**1667** Milton's *Paradise Lost,* widely considered the greatest epic poem in English.

**1682** Pennsylvania founded by William Penn.

**1683** War of European powers against the Turks (to 1699). Vienna withstands three-month Turkish siege; high point of Turkish advance in Europe.

**1684** Gottfried Wilhelm Leibniz's calculus published.

**1685** James II succeeds Charles II in England, calls for freedom of conscience (1687). Protestants fear restoration of Catholicism and demand "Glorious Revolution." William of Orange invited to England and James II escapes to France (1688). William III and his wife, Mary, crowned. In France, Edict of Nantes of 1598, granting freedom of worship to Huguenots, is revoked by Louis XIV; thousands of Protestants flee.

**1689** Peter the Great becomes Czar of Russia—attempts to westernize nation and build Russia as a military power. Defeats Charles XII of Sweden at Poltava (1709). Beginning of the French and Indian Wars (to 1763), campaigns in America linked to a series of wars between France and England for domination of Europe.

**1690** William III of England defeats former king James II and Irish rebels at Battle of the Boyne in Ireland. John Locke's *Human Understanding*.

### 1700–1799 (A.D.)

**1701** War of the Spanish Succession begins—the last of Louis XIV's wars for domination of the continent. The Peace of Utrecht (1714) will end the conflict and mark the rise of the British Empire. Called Queen Anne's War in America, it ends with the British taking New Foundland, Acadia, and Hudson's Bay Territory from France, and Gibraltar and Minorca from Spain.

Sir Isaac Newton
(1642–1727)

**1704** Deerfield (Mass.) Massacre of English colonists by French and Indians. Bach's first cantata. Jonathan Swift's *Tale of a Tub*. *Boston News Letter*—first newspaper in America.

**1707** United Kingdom of Great Britain formed—England, Wales, and Scotland joined by parliamentary Act of Union.

**1729** Bach's *St. Matthew Passion*. Isaac Newton's *Principia* translated from Latin into English.

**1732** Benjamin Franklin begins publishing *Poor Richard's Almanack*. James Oglethorpe and others found Georgia.

**1735** John Peter Zenger, New York editor, acquitted of libel in New York, establishing press freedom.

Frederick the Great
(1712–1786)

**1740** Capt. Vitus Bering, Dane employed by Russia, discovers Alaska. Frederick II "the Great" crowned king of Prussia.

**1746** British defeat Scots under Stuart Pretender Prince Charles at Culloden Moor. Last battle fought on British soil.

**1751** Publication of the *Encyclopédie* begins in France, the "bible" of the Enlightenment.

**1755** Samuel Johnson's *Dictionary* first published. Great earthquake in Lisbon, Portugal—over 60,000 die. U.S. postal service established.

**1756** Seven Years' War (French and Indian Wars in America) (to 1763), in which Britain and Prussia defeat France, Spain, Austria, and Russia. France loses North American colonies; Spain cedes Florida to Britain in exchange for Cuba. In India, over 100 British prisoners die in "Black Hole of Calcutta."

Samuel Johnson
(1709–1784)

**1757** Beginning of British Empire in India as Robert Clive, British commander, defeats Nawab of Bengal at Plassey.

**1759** British capture Quebec from French. Voltaire's *Candide*. Haydn's *Symphony No. 1*.

**1762** Catherine II ("the Great") becomes czarina of Russia. Jean Jacques Rousseau's *Social Contract*. Mozart tours Europe as six-year-old prodigy.

**1765** James Watt invents the steam engine. Britain imposes the Stamp Act on the American colonists.

---

## THE REVOLUTIONARY WAR

Conflicts increase between colonists and Britain on western frontier because of royal edict limiting western expansion (1763) and regulation of colonial trade and increased taxation of colonies (Writs of Assistance to allow search for illegal shipments, 1761; Sugar Act, 1764; Currency Act, 1764; Stamp Act, 1765; Quartering Act, 1765; Duty Act, 1767), Boston Massacre (1770), Lord North attempts conciliation (1770). Boston Tea Party (1773), followed by punitive measures passed by Parliament—the "Intolerable Acts."

First Continental Congress (1774) sends "Declaration of Rights and Grievances" to King George III, urges colonies to form Continental Association. Paul Revere's ride and Lexington and Concord battle between Massachusetts Minutemen and British (1775).

Second Continental Congress (1775), while sending "olive branch" to the king, begins to raise army, appoints Washington commander-in-chief, and seeks alliance with France. Some colonial legislatures urge their delegates to vote for independence. Declaration

of Independence **(July 4, 1776).**

Major Battles of the Revolutionary War: *Long Island*: Howe defeats Putnam's division of Washington's Army in Brooklyn Heights, but Americans escape across East River (1776). *Trenton and Princeton*: Washington defeats Hessians at Trenton. British at Princeton. Winters at Morristown (1776–1777). Howe winters in Philadelphia; Washington at Valley Forge (1777–1778). Burgoyne surrenders British army to General Gates at *Saratoga* (1777).

France recognizes American independence (1778). The War moves south: Savannah captured by British (1778); Charleston occupied (1780); Americans fight successful guerrilla actions under Marion, Pickens, and Sumter. In the West, George Rogers Clark attacks Forts Kaskaskia and Vincennes (1778–1779), defeating British in the region. Cornwallis surrenders at *Yorktown*, Virginia **(Oct. 19, 1781).** By 1782, Britain is eager for peace because of conflicts with European nations. *Peace of Paris* (1783): Britain recognizes American independence.

**Benjamin Franklin**
**(1706–1790)**

**George Washington**
**(1732–1799)**

**Alexander Hamilton**
**(1755–1804)**

**Ludwig van Beethoven**
**(1770–1827)**

**1769** Sir William Arkwright patents a spinning machine—an early step in the Industrial Revolution.

**1770** The Boston Massacre.

**1772** Joseph Priestley and Daniel Rutherford independently discover nitrogen. Partition of Poland—in 1772, 1793, and 1795, Austria, Prussia, and Russia divide land and people of Poland, end its independence.

**1773** The Boston Tea Party.

**1774** First Continental Congress drafts "Declaration of Rights and Grievances."

**1775** The American Revolution begins with battle of Lexington and Concord. Second Continental Congress. Priestley discovers hydrochloric and sulfuric acids.

**1776** Declaration of Independence. Gen. George Washington crosses the Delaware Christmas night. Adam Smith's *Wealth of Nations.* Edward Gibbon's *Decline and Fall of the Roman Empire.* Thomas Paine's *Common Sense.* Fragonard's *Washerwoman.* Mozart's *Haffner Serenade.*

**1778** Capt. James Cook discovers Hawaii. Franz Mesmer uses hypnotism.

**1781** Immanuel Kant's *Critique of Pure Reason.* Herschel discovers Uranus.

**1783** Revolutionary War ends with Treaty of Paris. William Blake's poems. Beethoven's first printed works.

**1784** Crimea annexed by Russia. John Wesley's *Deed of Declaration,* the basic work of Methodism.

**1785** Russians settle Aleutian Islands.

**1787** The Constitution of the United States signed. Lavoisier's work on chemical nomenclature. Mozart's *Don Giovanni.*

**1788** French *Parlement* presents grievances to Louis XVI who agrees to convening of Estates-General in 1789—not called since 1613. Goethe's *Egmont.* Laplace's *Laws of the Planetary System.*

**1789** French Revolution begins with the storming of the Bastille. In U.S., Washington elected president with all 69 votes of the Electoral College, takes oath of office in New York City. Vice President: John Adams. Secretary of State: Thomas Jefferson. Secretary of Treasury: Alexander Hamilton.

**1790** H.M.S. *Bounty* mutineers settle on Pitcairn Island. Aloisio Galvani experiments on electrical stimulation of the muscles. Philadelphia temporary capital of U.S. as Congress votes to establish new capital on Potomac. U.S. population about 3,929,000, including 698,000 slaves. Lavoisier formulates *Table of 31 chemical elements.*

**1791** U.S. Bill of Rights ratified. Boswell's *Life of Johnson.*

**1792** Mary Wollstonecraft's *Vindication of the Rights of Woman.*

**1793** Louis XVI and Marie Antoinette executed. Reign of Terror begins in France. Eli Whitney invents the cotton gin, spurring the growth of the cotton industry and helping to institutionalize slavery in the U.S. South.

**1794** Kosciusko's uprising in Poland quelled by the Russians. In U.S., Whiskey Rebellion in Pennsylvania as farmers object to liquor taxes. Reign of Terror ends with execution of Robespierre.

**1796** Napoléon Bonaparte, French general, defeats Austrians. In the U.S., Washington's Farewell Address **(Sept. 17);** John Adams elected president; Thomas Jefferson, vice president. Edward Jenner introduces smallpox vaccination.

**1798** Napoleon extends French conquests to Rome and Egypt. U.S. Navy Department established.

---

**FRENCH REVOLUTION (1789–1799)**

Revolution begins when Third Estate (Commons) delegates swear not to disband until France has a constitution. Paris mob storms Bastille, symbol of royal power **(July 14, 1789).** National Assembly votes for Constitution, Declaration of the Rights of Man, a limited monarchy, and other reforms (1789–1790). Legislative Assembly elected, Revolutionary Commune formed, and French Republic proclaimed (1792). War of the First Coalition—Austria, Prussia, Britain, Netherlands, and Spain fight to restore French nobility (1792–1797).

Start of series of wars between France and European powers that will last, almost without interruption, for 23 years. Louis XVI and Marie Antoinette executed. Committee of Public Safety begins Reign of Terror as political control measure. Interfactional rivalry leads to mass killings. Danton and Robespierre executed. Third French Constitution sets up Directory government (1795). Napoleon abolishes the Directory, establishes the Consulate, becomes the First Consul of France (1799).

**1799** Rosetta Stone discovered in Egypt. Napoleon leads coup that overthrows Directory, establishes the Consulate, becomes First Consul—one of three who rule France together.

## 1800–1899 (A.D.)

**1800** Napoleon conquers Italy, firmly establishes himself as First Consul in France. In the U.S., federal government moves to Washington, D.C. Robert Owen's social reforms in England. William Herschel discovers infrared rays. Alessandro Volta produces electricity.

**1801** Austria makes temporary peace with France. United Kingdom of Great Britain and Ireland established with one monarch and one parliament; Catholics excluded from voting.

**Napoléon Bonaparte (1769–1821)**

**1803** U.S. negotiates Louisiana Purchase from France: for $15 million, U.S. doubles its domain, increasing its territory by 827,000 sq. mi. (2,144,500 sq km), from Mississippi River to Rockies and from Gulf of Mexico to British North America.

**1804** Haiti declares independence from France; first black nation to gain freedom from European colonial rule. Napoleon transforms the Consulate of France into an empire, proclaims himself emperor of France, systematizes French law under *Code Napoleon.* In the U.S., Alexander Hamilton is mortally wounded in duel with Aaron Burr. Lewis and Clark expedition begins exploration of what is now northwest U.S.

**Edgar Allan Poe (1809–1849)**

**1805** Lord Nelson defeats the French-Spanish fleets in the Battle of Trafalgar. Napoleon victorious over Austrian and Russian forces at the Battle of Austerlitz.

**1807** Robert Fulton makes first successful steamboat trip on *Clermont* between New York City and Albany.

**1808** French armies occupy Rome and Spain, extending Napoleon's empire. Britain begins aiding Spanish guerrillas against Napoleon in Peninsular War. In the U.S., Congress bars importation of slaves. Beethoven's *Fifth* and *Sixth Symphonies* performed.

**1812** Napoleon's Grand Army invades Russia in June. Forced to retreat in winter, most of Napoleon's 600,000 men are lost. In the U.S., war with Britain declared over freedom of the seas for U.S. vessels (War of 1812). USS *Constitution* sinks British frigate.

**Richard Wagner (1813–1883)**

**1814** French defeated by allies (Britain, Austria, Russia, Prussia, Sweden, and Portugal) in War of Liberation. Napoleon exiled to Elba, off Italian coast. Bourbon king Louis XVIII takes French throne. George Stephenson builds first practical steam locomotive.

**1815** Napoleon returns: "Hundred Days" begin. Napoleon defeated by Wellington at Waterloo, banished again to St. Helena in South Atlantic. Congress of Vienna: victorious allies change the map of Europe. War of 1812 ends with Treaty of Ghent.

**1819** Simón Bolívar liberates New Granada (now Colombia, Venezuela, and Ecuador) as Spain loses hold on South American countries; named president of Colombia.

**Harriet Beecher Stowe (1811–1896)**

**1820** Missouri Compromise—Missouri admitted as slave state but slavery barred in rest of Louisiana Purchase north of 36°30′ N.

**1821** Guatemala, Panama, and Santo Domingo proclaim independence from Spain.

**1822** Greeks proclaim a republic and independence from Turkey. Turks invade Greece. Russia declares war on Turkey (1828). Greece also aided by France and Britain. War ends and Turks recognize Greek independence (1829). Brazil becomes independent of Portugal. Schubert's *Eighth Symphony* ("The Unfinished").

**1823** U.S. Monroe Doctrine warns European nations not to interfere in Western Hemisphere.

**1824** Mexico becomes a republic, three years after declaring independence from Spain. Bolívar liberates Peru, becomes its president. Beethoven's *Ninth Symphony.*

**1825** First passenger-carrying railroad in England.

**1826** Joseph-Nicéphore Niepce takes the world's first photograph.

**Walt Whitman (1819–1892)**

---

**WAR OF 1812**

British interference with American trade, impressment of American seamen, and "War Hawks" drive for western expansion lead to war. American attacks on Canada foiled; U.S. Commodore Perry wins battle of Lake Erie (1813). British capture and burn Washington (1814) but fail to take Fort McHenry at Baltimore. Andrew Jackson repulses assault on New Orleans after Treaty of Ghent ends war (1815). War settles little but strengthens U.S. as independent nation.

**Dred Scott
(1795?–1858)**

**Charles Darwin
(1809–1882)**

**Frederick Douglass
(1817–1895)**

**Harriet Tubman
(c. 1820–1913)**

**Samuel Clemens
(Mark Twain)
(1835–1910)**

**1830**   French invade Algeria. Louis Philippe becomes "Citizen King" as revolution forces Charles X to abdicate. Mormon church formed in U.S. by Joseph Smith.

**1831**   Polish revolt against Russia fails. Belgium separates from the Netherlands. In U.S., Nat Turner leads unsuccessful slave rebellion.

**1833**   Slavery abolished in British Empire.

**1834**   Charles Babbage invents "analytical engine," precursor of computer. McCormick patents reaper.

**1836**   Boer farmers start "Great Trek"—Natal, Transvaal, and Orange Free State founded in South Africa. Mexican army besieges Texans in Alamo. Entire garrison, including Davy Crockett and Jim Bowie, wiped out. Texans gain independence from Mexico after winning Battle of San Jacinto. Dickens's *Pickwick Papers.*

**1837**   Victoria becomes queen of Great Britain. Mob kills Elijah P. Lovejoy, Illinois abolitionist publisher.

**1839**   First Opium War (to 1842) between Britain and China, over importation of drug into China.

**1840**   Lower and Upper Canada united.

**1841**   U.S. President Harrison dies (**April 4**) one month after inauguration; John Tyler becomes first vice president to succeed to presidency.

**1842**   Crawford Long uses first anesthetic (ether).

**1843**   Wagner's opera *The Flying Dutchman.*

**1844**   Democratic convention calls for annexation of Texas and acquisition of Oregon ("Fifty-four-forty-or-fight"). Five Chinese ports opened to U.S. ships. Samuel F. B. Morse patents telegraph.

**1845**   Congress adopts joint resolution for annexation of Texas. Edgar Allan Poe publishes *The Raven and Other Poems.*

**1846**   U.S. declares war on Mexico. California and New Mexico annexed by U.S. Brigham Young leads Mormons to Great Salt Lake. W. T. Morton uses ether as anesthetic. Sewing machine patented by Elias Howe. Frederick Douglass launches abolitionist newspaper *The North Star.* Failure of potato crop causes famine in Ireland.

**1848**   Revolt in Paris: Louis Philippe abdicates; Louis Napoleon elected president of French Republic. Revolutions in Vienna, Venice, Berlin, Milan, Rome, and Warsaw. Put down by royal troops in 1848–1849. U.S.-Mexico War ends; Mexico cedes claims to Texas, California, Arizona, New Mexico, Utah, Nevada. U.S. treaty with Britain sets Oregon Territory boundary at 49th parallel. Karl Marx and Friedrich Engels's *Communist Manifesto.* Harriet Tubman escapes from slavery and joins the Underground Railroad. Women's Rights Convention in Seneca Falls, N.Y.

**1849**   California gold rush begins.

**1850**   Henry Clay opens great debate on slavery, warns South against secession.

**1851**   Herman Melville's *Moby-Dick.*

**1852**   South African Republic established. Louis Napoleon proclaims himself Napoleon III ("Second Empire"). Harriet Beecher Stowe's *Uncle Tom's Cabin.*

**1853**   Crimean War begins as Turkey declares war on Russia. Commodore Perry reaches Tokyo.

**1854**   Britain and France join Turkey in war on Russia. In U.S., Kansas-Nebraska Act permits local option on slavery; rioting and bloodshed. Japanese allow American trade. Antislavery men in Michigan form Republican Party. Tennyson's *Charge of the Light Brigade.* Thoreau's *Walden.*

**1855**   Armed clashes in Kansas between pro- and anti-slavery forces. Florence Nightingale nurses wounded in Crimea. Walt Whitman's *Leaves of Grass.*

**1856**   Flaubert's *Madame Bovary.*

**1857**   Supreme Court, in Dred Scott decision, rules that a slave is not a citizen. Financial crisis in Europe and U.S. Great Mutiny (Sepoy Rebellion) begins in India. India placed under crown rule as a result.

**1858**   Pro-slavery constitution rejected in Kansas. Abraham Lincoln makes strong antislavery speech in Springfield, Ill.: "This Government cannot endure permanently half slave and half free." Lincoln-Douglas debates. First trans-Atlantic telegraph cable completed by Cyrus W. Field.

**1859**   John Brown raids Harpers Ferry; is captured and hanged. Work begins on Suez Canal. Unification of Italy starts under leadership of Count Cavour, Sardinian premier. Joined by France in war against Austria. Jean-Joseph-Étienne Lenoir builds first practical internal-combustion engine. Edward Fitzgerald's translation of *The Rubaiyat of Omar Khayyam.* Charles Darwin's *Origin of Species.* J. S. Mill's *On Liberty.*

**1860** South Carolina secedes from the Union.

**1861** U.S. Civil War begins as attempts at compromise fail. Mississippi, Florida, Alabama, Georgia, Louisiana, and Texas secede; with South Carolina, they form the Confederate States of America, with Jefferson Davis as president. Virginia, Arkansas, Tennessee, North Carolina secede and join Confederacy. First Battle of Bull Run (Manassas). Congress creates Colorado, Dakota, and Nevada territories; adopts income tax; Lincoln inaugurated. Serfs emancipated in Russia. Pasteur's theory of germs. Independent Kingdom of Italy proclaimed under Sardinian king Victor Emmanuel II.

**1862** Several major Civil War battles: Battle of Shiloh, Second Battle of Bull Run (Manassas), Battle of Antietam. Salon des Refusés introduces impressionism.

**Abraham Lincoln**
**(1809–1865)**

**1863** French capture Mexico City; proclaim Archduke Maximilian of Austria emperor. Battle of Gettysburg.

**1864** Gen. Sherman's Atlanta campaign and "march to the sea."

**1865** Gen. Lee surrenders to Grant at Appomattox; the Civil War is over. Lincoln fatally shot at Ford's Theater by John Wilkes Booth. Vice President Johnson sworn as successor. Booth caught and dies of gunshot wounds; four conspirators are hanged. Joseph Lister begins antiseptic surgery. Gregor Mendel's *Law of Heredity.* Lewis Carroll's *Alice's Adventures in Wonderland.*

**1866** Alfred Nobel invents dynamite (patented in Britain, 1867). Seven Weeks' War: Austria defeated by Prussia and Italy.

**1867** Austria-Hungary Dual Monarchy established. French leave Mexico; Maximilian executed. Dominion of Canada established. U.S. buys Alaska from Russia for $7,200,000. South African diamond field discovered. Japan ends 675-year shogun rule. Volume I of Marx's *Das Kapital.* Strauss's *Blue Danube.*

**Robert E. Lee**
**(1807–1870)**

**1868** Revolution in Spain; Queen Isabella deposed, flees to France. In U.S., Fourteenth Amendment giving civil rights to blacks is ratified. Georgia under military government after legislature expels blacks.

**1869** First U.S. transcontinental rail route completed. James Fisk and Jay Gould's attempt to control gold market causes Black Friday panic. Suez Canal opens. Mendeleev's periodic table of elements.

**1870** Franco-Prussian War (to 1871): Napoleon III capitulates at Sedan. Revolt in Paris; Third Republic proclaimed.

**William Tecumseh**
**Sherman**
**(1820–1891)**

**1871** France surrenders Alsace-Lorraine to Germany; war ends. German Empire proclaimed with Prussian King as Kaiser Wilhelm I. Fighting with Apaches begins in American West. Boss Tweed corruption exposed in New York. The Chicago Fire, with 250 deaths and $196-million damage. Stanley meets Livingstone in Africa.

**1872** Congress gives amnesty to most Confederates. Jules Verne's *Around the World in 80 Days.*

---

### THE CIVIL WAR

Apart from the matter of slavery, the Civil War arose out of both the economic and political rivalry between an agrarian South and an industrial North and the issue of the right of states to secede from the Union.

**1861** After South Carolina secedes **(Dec. 20, 1860),** Mississippi, Florida, Alabama, Georgia, Louisiana, and Texas follow, forming the Confederate States of America, with Jefferson Davis as president **(Jan.–March).** War begins as Confederates fire on Fort Sumter **(April 12).** Lincoln calls for 75,000 volunteers; institution of blockade closed by superior Union naval forces. Virginia, Arkansas, Tennessee, and North Carolina secede to complete 11-state Confederacy. Union army advancing on Richmond repulsed at first Battle of Bull Run (Manassas) **(July).**

**1862** Edwin M. Stanton named secretary of war **(Jan.).** Grant wins first important Union victory in West, at Fort Donelson; Nashville falls **(Feb.).** Ironclads, Union's *Monitor* and Confederate's *Virginia (Merrimac)* duel at Hampton Roads **(March).** New Orleans falls to Union fleet under Farragut; city occupied **(April).** Grant's army escapes defeat at Shiloh. Memphis falls as Union gunboats control upper Mississippi **(June).** Confederate general Robert E. Lee victorious at second Battle of Bull Run (Manassas) **(Aug.).** Union army under McClellan halts Lee's attack on Washington in the Battle of Antietam **(Sept.).** Lincoln removes McClellan for lack of aggressiveness. Burnside's drive on Richmond fails at Fredericksburg **(Dec.).** Union forces under Rosecrans chase Bragg through Tennessee; battle of Murfreesboro **(Oct.–Jan. 1863).**

**1863** Lee defeats Hooker at Chancellorsville; "Stonewall" Jackson, Confederate general, dies **(May).** Confederate invasion of Pennsylvania stopped at Gettysburg by George Meade—Lee loses 20,000 men—the greatest battle of the war **(July).** It and the Union victory at Vicksburg mark the war's turning point. Union general George H. Thomas, the "Rock of Chickamauga," holds Bragg's forces on Georgia-Tennessee border **(Sept.).** Sherman, Hooker, and Thomas drive Bragg back to Georgia. Tennessee restored to the Union **(Nov.).**

**1864** Ulysses S. Grant named commander-in-chief of Union forces **(March).** In the Wilderness campaign, Grant forces Lee's Army of Northern Virginia back toward Richmond **(May–June).** Sherman's Atlanta campaign and "march to the sea" **(May–Sept.).** Farragut's victory at Mobile Bay **(Aug.).** Hood's Confederate army defeated at Nashville. Sherman takes Savannah **(Dec.).**

**1865** Sheridan defeats Confederates at Five Forks; Confederates evacuate Richmond **(April).** On **April 9,** Lee surrenders to Grant at Appomattox.

**Johannes Brahms
(1833–1897)**

**Chief Joseph
(c. 1840–1904)**

**Statue of Liberty**

**Marie Curie
(1867–1934)**

**1873** Economic crisis in Europe. U.S. establishes gold standard.

**1875** First Kentucky Derby.

**1876** Sioux kill Gen. George A. Custer and 264 troopers at Little Big Horn River. Alexander Graham Bell patents the telephone.

**1877** After presidential election of 1876, electoral commission gives disputed electoral college votes to Rutherford B. Hayes despite Tilden's popular majority. Russo-Turkish war (ends in 1878 with power of Turkey in Europe broken). Reconstruction ends in the American South. Thomas Edison patents phonograph. The Nez Perce leader Chief Joseph is forced to surrender. Tchaikovsky's *Swan Lake.*

**1878** Congress of Berlin revises Treaty of San Stefano, ending Russo-Turkish War; makes extensive redivision of southeast Europe. First commercial telephone exchange opened in New Haven, Conn.

**1879** Thomas A. Edison invents electric light.

**1880** U.S.-China treaty allows U.S. to restrict immigration of Chinese labor.

**1881** President Garfield fatally shot by assassin; Vice President Arthur succeeds him. Charles J. Guiteau convicted and executed (1882).

**1882** Terrorism in Ireland after land evictions. Britain invades and conquers Egypt. Germany, Austria, and Italy form Triple Alliance. In U.S., Congress adopts Chinese Exclusion Act. Rockefeller's Standard Oil Trust is first industrial monopoly. In Berlin, Robert Koch announces discovery of tuberculosis germ.

**1883** Congress creates Civil Service Commission. Brooklyn Bridge and Metropolitan Opera House completed.

**1884** Berlin West Africa Conference held in Berlin (lasting until **Feb. 1885**), at which the major European nations discuss expansion in Africa.

**1885** British general Charles G. "Chinese" Gordon killed at Khartoum in Egyptian Sudan. World's first skyscraper built in Chicago.

**1886** Bombing at Haymarket Square, Chicago, kills seven policemen and injures many others. Eight alleged anarchists accused—three imprisoned, one commits suicide, four hanged. (In 1893, Illinois governor Altgeld, critical of trial, pardons three survivors.) Statue of Liberty dedicated. Geronimo, Apache Indian chief, surrenders.

**1887** Queen Victoria's Golden Jubilee. Sir Arthur Conan Doyle's first Sherlock Holmes story, *A Study in Scarlet.*

**1888** Historic March blizzard in northeast U.S.—many perish, property damage exceeds $25 million. George Eastman's box camera (the Kodak). J. B. Dunlop invents pneumatic tire. Jack the Ripper murders in London.

**1889** Second (Socialist) International founded in Paris. Indian Territory in Oklahoma opened to settlement. Thousands die in Johnstown, Pa. flood. Eiffel Tower built for the Paris exposition. Mark Twain's *A Connecticut Yankee in King Arthur's Court.*

**1890** Congress votes to pass Sherman Antitrust Act. Sioux chief Sitting Bull arrested and killed by police on Pine Ridge reservation; two weeks later, U.S. troops kill over 200 Sioux at Battle of Wounded Knee.

**1892** Battle between steel strikers and Pinkerton guards at Homestead, Pa.; union defeated after militia intervenes. Silver mine strikers in Idaho fight non-union workers; U.S. troops dispatched. Diesel engine patented.

**1893** New Zealand becomes first country in the world to grant women the vote.

**1894** Sino-Japanese War begins (ends in 1895 with China's defeat). In France, Capt. Alfred Dreyfus convicted on false treason charge (pardoned in 1906). In U.S., Jacob S. Coxey of Ohio leads "Coxey's Army" of unemployed on Washington. Eugene V. Debs calls general strike of rail workers to support Pullman Company strikers; strike broken, Debs jailed for six months. Edison's kinetoscope given first public showing in New York City.

**1895** X-rays discovered by German physicist Wilhelm Roentgen. Auguste and Louis Lumière premiere motion pictures at a café in Paris.

---

**SPANISH-AMERICAN WAR (1898–1899)**

War fires stoked by "jingo journalism" as American people support Cuban rebels against Spain. American business sees economic gain in Cuban trade and resources and American power zones in Latin America. Outstanding events: Submarine mine sinks U.S. battleship *Maine* in Havana Harbor (**Feb. 15**); 260 killed; responsibility never fixed. Congress declares independence of Cuba (**April 19**). Spain declares war on U.S. (**April 24**); Congress (**April 25**) formally declares nation has been at war with Spain since **April 21**. Commodore George Dewey wins seven-hour battle of Manila Bay (**May 1**). Spanish fleet destroyed off Santiago, Cuba (**July 3**); city surrenders (**July 17**). Treaty of Paris (ratified by Senate 1899) ends war. U.S. given Guam and Puerto Rico and agrees to pay Spain $20 million for Philippines. Cuba independent of Spain; under U.S. military control for three years until **May 20, 1902.** Yellow fever is eradicated and political reforms achieved.

**1896** Supreme Court's *Plessy v. Ferguson* decision—"separate but equal" doctrine. Alfred Nobel's will establishes prizes for peace, science, and literature. Marconi receives first wireless patent in Britain. William Jennings Bryan delivers "Cross of Gold" speech at Democratic Convention in Chicago. First modern Olympic games held in Athens, Greece.

**1897** Theodor Herzl launches Zionist movement.

**1898** Chinese "Boxers," anti-foreign organization, established. They stage uprisings against Europeans in 1900; U.S. and other Western troops relieve Peking legations. U.S. Battleship *Maine* is sunk in Havana Harbor. Spanish-American War begins. U.S. destroys Spanish fleet near Santiago, Cuba. Pierre and Marie Curie discover radium and polonium.

**1899** Boer War (or South African War): conflict between British and Boers (descendants of Dutch settlers of South Africa). Causes rooted in long-standing territorial disputes and in friction over political rights for English and other "uitlanders" following 1886 discovery of vast gold deposits in Transvaal. (British victorious as war ends in 1902.) Casualties: 5,774 British dead, about 4,000 Boers. Union of South Africa established in 1908 as confederation of colonies; becomes British dominion in 1910.

Sigmund Freud
(1856–1939)

### 1900–2000 (A.D.)

**1900** Hurricane ravages Galveston, Tex.; 6,000–8,000 dead. Fauvist movement in painting begins, led by Henri Matisse. Sigmund Freud's *The Interpretation of Dreams*. Carrie Chapman Catt succeeds Susan B. Anthony as president of National Woman Suffrage Association.

**1901** Queen Victoria dies, and is succeeded by her son, Edward VII. As President McKinley begins second term, he is shot fatally by anarchist Leon Czolgosz. Theodore Roosevelt sworn in as successor.

**1902** Enrico Caruso's first gramophone recording. Aswan Dam completed.

**1903** Wright brothers, Orville and Wilbur, fly first powered, controlled, heavier-than-air plane at Kitty Hawk, N.C. Henry Ford organizes Ford Motor Company. The Boston Red Sox win the first World Series against the Pittsburgh Pirates. W. E. B. Du Bois publishes *The Souls of Black Folk*.

Carrie Chapman Catt
(1859–1947)

**1904** Russo-Japanese War begins—competition for Korea and Manchuria. *Entente Cordiale:* Britain and France settle their international differences. General theory of radioactivity by Rutherford and Soddy. New York City subway opens.

**1905** In Russo-Japanese War, Port Arthur surrenders to Japanese; Russia suffers other defeats. President Roosevelt mediates Treaty of Portsmouth, N.H., which recognizes Japan's control of Korea and restores southern Manchuria to China. The Russian Revolution of 1905 begins on "Bloody Sunday" when troops fire onto a defenseless group of demonstrators in St. Petersburg. Strikes and riots follow. Sailors on battleship *Potemkin* mutiny; reforms, including first Duma (parliament), established by Czar Nicholas II's "October Manifesto." Albert Einstein's special theory of relativity and other key theories in physics. Franz Lehar's *Merry Widow.*

Albert Einstein
(1879–1955)

**1906** San Francisco earthquake and three-day fire; more than 500 dead. Roald Amundsen, Norwegian explorer, fixes magnetic North Pole.

**1907** Second Hague Peace Conference, of 46 nations, adopts 10 conventions on rules of war. Financial panic of 1907 in U.S. Mahler begins work on "Song of the Earth." Oklahoma becomes 46th state. Picasso's *Les Demoiselles d'Avignon* introduces cubism.

Vladimir Lenin
(1870–1924)

**1908** Earthquake kills 150,000 in southern Italy and Sicily. U.S. Supreme Court, in Danbury Hatters' case, outlaws secondary union boycott. Model T produced by Ford Motor Company.

**1909** North Pole reportedly reached by American explorers Robert E. Peary and Matthew Henson. The National Association for the Advancement of Colored People is founded in New York by prominent black and white intellectuals and led by W. E. B. Du Bois.

**1910** Boy Scouts of America incorporated. Angel Island, in San Francisco Bay, becomes immigration center for Asians entering U.S.

**1911** First use of aircraft as offensive weapon in Turkish-Italian War. Italy defeats Turks and annexes Tripoli and Libya. Chinese Republic proclaimed after revolution overthrows Manchu dynasty. Sun Yat-sen named president. Mexican Revolution: Porfirio Diaz, president since 1877, replaced by Francisco Madero. Triangle Shirtwaist Company fire in New York; 146 killed. Amundsen reaches South Pole. Ernest Rutherford discovers the structure of the atom. Richard Strauss's *Der Rosenkavalier.* Irving Berlin's *Alexander's Ragtime Band.*

Robert Peary
(1856–1920)

**W. E. B. Du Bois**
**(1868–1963)**

**Woodrow Wilson**
**(1856–1924)**

**Bessie Smith**
**(1894–1937)**

**1912** Balkan Wars (1912–1913) resulting from territorial disputes: Turkey defeated by alliance of Bulgaria, Serbia, Greece, and Montenegro; London peace treaty (1913) partitions most of European Turkey among the victors. In second war (1913), Bulgaria attacks Serbia and Greece and is defeated after Romania intervenes and Turks recapture Adrianople. *Titanic* sinks on maiden voyage; over 1,500 drown. New Mexico and Arizona admitted as states.

**1913** Suffragists demonstrate in London. Garment workers strike in New York and Boston; win pay raise and shorter hours. Henry Ford develops first moving assembly line. 16th Amendment (income tax) and 17th (popular election of U.S. senators) adopted. Bill creating U.S. Federal Reserve System becomes law. Stravinsky's *The Rite of Spring*. Woodrow Wilson becomes 28th U.S. president. Armory Show introduces modern art to U.S.; Duchamp's *Nude Descending a Staircase* shocks public.

**1914** World War I begins: Austrian Archduke Francis Ferdinand and wife Sophie are assassinated; Austria declares war on Serbia, Germany on Russia and France, Britain on Germany. Panama Canal officially opened. Congress sets up Federal Trade Commission, passes Clayton Antitrust Act. U.S. Marines occupy Veracruz, Mexico, intervening in civil war to protect American interests.

**1915** *Lusitania* sunk by German submarine. Second Battle of Ypres. U.S. banks lend $500 million to France and Britain. Genocide of estimated 600,000 to 1 million Armenians by Turkish soldiers. D. W. Griffith's film *Birth of a Nation*. Albert Einstein's *General Theory of Relativity*.

**1916** Congress expands armed forces. Battle of Verdun. Battle of the Somme. Tom Mooney arrested for San Francisco bombing (pardoned in 1939). Pershing fails in raid into Mexico in quest of rebel Pancho Villa. U.S. buys Virgin Islands from Denmark for $25 million. President Wilson re-elected with "he kept us out of war" slogan. "Black Tom" explosion at munitions dock in Jersey City, N.J., $40,000,000 damages; traced to German saboteurs. Margaret Sanger opens first birth control clinic. Easter Rebellion in Ireland put down by British troops. Jeannette Rankin becomes first woman elected to Congress.

**1917** First U.S. combat troops in France as U.S. declares war on Germany **(April 6)**. Third Battle of Ypres. Russian Revolution of 1917—climax of long unrest under czars. February Revolution—Nicholas II forced to abdicate, liberal government created. Kerensky becomes prime minister and forms provisional government **(July)**. In October Revolution, Bolsheviks seize power in armed coup d'état led by Lenin and Trotsky. Kerensky flees. Balfour Declaration promises Jewish homeland in Palestine. U.S. declares war on Austria-Hungary **(Dec. 7)**. Armistice between

---

**WORLD WAR I (1914–1918)**

Imperial, territorial, and economic rivalries led to the "Great War" between the Central Powers (Austria-Hungary, Germany, Bulgaria, and Turkey) and the Allies (U.S., Britain, France, Russia, Belgium, Serbia, Greece, Romania, Montenegro, Portugal, Italy, Japan). About 10 million combatants killed, 20 million wounded.

**1914** Austrian Archduke Francis Ferdinand and wife assassinated in Sarajevo by Serbian nationalist, Gavrilo Princip **(June 28)**. Austria declares war on Serbia **(July 28)**. Germany declares war on Russia **(Aug. 1)**, on France **(Aug. 3)**, invades Belgium **(Aug. 4)**. Britain declares war on Germany **(Aug. 4)**. Germans defeat Russians in Battle of Tannenberg on Eastern Front **(Aug.)**. First Battle of the Marne **(Sept.)**. German drive stopped 25 miles from Paris. By end of year, war on the Western Front is "positional" in the trenches.

**1915** German submarine blockade of Great Britain begins **(Feb.)**. Dardanelles Campaign—British land in Turkey **(April)**, withdraw from Gallipoli **(Dec.–Jan. 1916)**. Germans use gas at second Battle of Ypres **(April–May)**. *Lusitania* sunk by German submarine—1,198 lost, including 128 Americans **(May 7)**. On Eastern Front, German and Austrian "great offensive" conquers all of Poland and Lithuania; Russians lose 1 million men (by **Sept. 6**). "Great Fall Offensive" by Allies results in little change from 1914 **(Sept.–Oct.)**. Britain and France declare war on Bulgaria **(Oct. 14)**.

**1916** Battle of Verdun—Germans and French each lose about 350,000 men **(Feb.)**. Extended submarine warfare begins **(March)**. British-German sea battle of Jutland **(May)**; British lose more ships, but German fleet never ventures forth again. On Eastern Front, the Brusilov offensive demoralizes Russians, costs them 1 million men **(June–Sept.)**. Battle of the Somme—British lose over 400,000; French, 200,000; Germans, about 450,000; all with no strategic results **(July–Nov.)**. Romania declares war on Austria-Hungary **(Aug. 27)**. Bucharest captured **(Dec.)**.

**1917** U.S. declares war on Germany **(April 6)**. Submarine warfare at peak **(April)**. On Italian Front, Battle of Caporetto—Italians retreat, losing 600,000 prisoners and deserters **(Oct.–Dec.)**. On Western Front, Battles of Arras, Champagne, Ypres (third battle), etc. First large British tank attack **(Nov.)**. U.S. declares war on Austria-Hungary **(Dec. 7)**. Armistice between new Russian Bolshevik government and Germans **(Dec. 15)**.

**1918** Great offensive by Germans **(March–June)**. Americans' first important battle role at Château-Thierry—as they and French stop German advance **(June)**. Second Battle of the Marne **(July–Aug.)**—start of Allied offensive at Amiens, St. Mihiel, etc. Battles of the Argonne and Ypres panic German leadership **(Sept.–Oct.)**. British offensive in Palestine **(Sept.)**. Germans ask for armistice **(Oct. 4)**. British armistice with Turkey **(Oct.)**. German Kaiser abdicates **(Nov.)**. Hostilities cease on Western Front **(Nov. 11)**.

new Russian Bolshevik government and Germans (**Dec. 15**). Sigmund Freud's *Introduction to Psychoanalysis.*

**1918** Russian revolutionaries execute the former czar and his family. Russian Civil War between Reds (Bolsheviks) and Whites (anti-Bolsheviks); Reds win in 1920. Allied troops (U.S., British, French) intervene (**March**); leave in 1919. Second Battle of the Marne (**July–Aug.**) German Kaiser abdicates (**Nov.**); hostilities cease on the Western Front. Japanese hold Vladivostok until 1922. Worldwide influenza epidemic strikes; by 1920, nearly 20 million are dead. In U.S. alone, 500,000 perish.

**1919** Third International (Comintern) establishes Soviet control over international Communist movements. Paris peace conference. Versailles Treaty, incorporating Woodrow Wilson's draft Covenant of League of Nations, signed by Allies and Germany; rejected by U.S. Senate. Congress formally ends war in 1921. 18th (Prohibition) Amendment adopted. Alcock and Brown make first trans-Atlantic nonstop flight. Mahatma Gandhi initiates satyagraha ("truth force") campaigns, beginning his nonviolent resistance movement against British rule in India.

Mahatma Gandhi
(1869–1948)

**1920** League of Nations holds first meeting at Geneva, Switzerland. U.S. Dept. of Justice "red hunt" nets thousands of radicals; aliens deported. Women's suffrage (19th) amendment ratified. Treaty of Sèvres dissolves Ottoman Empire. First Agatha Christie mystery. Sinclair Lewis's *Main Street.*

**1921** Reparations Commission fixes German liability at 132 billion gold marks. German inflation begins. Major treaties signed at Washington Disarmament Conference limit naval tonnage and pledge to respect territorial integrity of China. In U.S., Nicola Sacco and Bartolomeo Vanzetti, Italian-born anarchists, convicted of armed robbery murder; case stirs worldwide protests; they are executed in 1927.

William Butler Yeats
(1865–1939)

**1922** Mussolini marches on Rome; forms Fascist government. Irish Free State, a self-governing dominion of British Empire, officially proclaimed. Kemal Atatürk, founder of modern Turkey, overthrows last sultan. James Joyce's *Ulysses.*

**1923** Adolf Hitler's "Beer Hall Putsch" in Munich fails; in 1924 he is sentenced to five years in prison where he writes *Mein Kampf;* released after eight months. Occupation of Ruhr by French and Belgian troops to enforce reparations payments. Widespread Ku Klux Klan violence in U.S. Earthquake destroys third of Tokyo. George Gershwin's *Rhapsody in Blue.* Bessie Smith, known as "the Empress of the Blues," makes her first record. Irish poet William Butler Yeats wins Nobel Prize in Literature.

Robert Frost
(1874–1963)

**1924** Death of Lenin; Stalin wins power struggle, rules as Soviet dictator until death in 1953. Italian Fascists murder Socialist leader Giacomo Matteotti. Interior Secretary Albert B. Fall and oilmen Harry Sinclair and Edward L. Doheny are charged with conspiracy and bribery in the Teapot Dome scandal, involving fraudulent leases of naval oil reserves. In 1931, Fall is sentenced to year in prison; Doheny and Sinclair acquitted of bribery. Nathan Leopold and Richard Loeb convicted in "thrill killing" of Bobby Franks in Chicago; defended by Clarence Darrow; sentenced to life imprisonment. (Loeb killed by fellow convict in 1936; Leopold paroled in 1958, dies in 1971.) Robert Frost wins first of four Pulitzers.

Pablo Picasso
(1881–1973)

**1925** Nellie Tayloe Ross elected governor of Wyoming; first woman governor elected in U.S. Locarno conferences seek to secure European peace by mutual guarantees. John T. Scopes convicted and fined for teaching evolution in a public school in Tennessee. Monkey Trial; evidence not aside. John Logie Baird, Scottish inventor, transmits human features by television. Hitler publishes Volume I of *Mein Kampf.*

**1926** General strike in Britain brings nation's activities to standstill. U.S. marines dispatched to Nicaragua during revolt; they remain until 1933. Gertrude Ederle of U.S. is first woman to swim English Channel. Ernest Hemingway's *The Sun Also Rises.*

**1927** German economy collapses. Socialists riot in Vienna; general strike follows acquittal of Nazis for political murder. Trotsky expelled from Russian Communist Party. Charles A. Lindbergh flies first successful solo nonstop flight from New York to Paris. Ruth Snyder and Judd Gray convicted of murder of Albert Snyder; they are executed at Sing Sing prison in 1928. Philo T. Farnsworth demonstrates working television model. Georges Lemaître proposes Big Bang Theory. Babe Ruth hits 60 home runs in the season; record stands for next 34 years. *The Jazz Singer,* with Al Jolson, first part-talking motion picture.

Babe Ruth
(George Herman Ruth)
(1895–1948)

**Benito Mussolini**
**(1883–1945)**

**Joseph Stalin**
**(1879–1953)**

**Adolf Hitler**
**(1889–1945)**

**1928** Kellogg-Briand Pact, outlawing war, signed in Paris by 65 nations. Alexander Fleming discovers penicillin. Richard E. Byrd starts expedition to Antarctic; returns in 1930. Anthropologist Margaret Mead publishes *Coming of Age in Samoa*. *Oxford English Dictionary* published after 44 years of research.

**1929** Trotsky expelled from USSR Lateran Treaty establishes independent Vatican City. In U.S., stock market prices collapse, with U.S. securities losing $26 billion—first phase of Depression and world economic crisis. St. Valentine's Day gangland massacre in Chicago. Edwin Powell Hubble proposes theory of expanding universe.

**1930** Britain, U.S., Japan, France, and Italy sign naval disarmament treaty. Nazis gain in German elections. Cyclotron developed by Ernest O. Lawrence, U.S. physicist. Pluto discovered by astronomers.

**1931** Spain becomes a republic with overthrow of King Alfonso XIII. German industrialists finance 800,000-strong Nazi party. British parliament enacts statute of Westminster, legalizing dominion equality with Britain. Mukden Incident begins Japanese occupation of Manchuria. In U.S., Hoover proposes one-year moratorium of war debts. Harold C. Urey discovers heavy hydrogen. Gangster Al Capone sentenced to 11 years in prison for tax evasion (freed in 1939; dies in 1947). Notorious Scottsboro trial begins, exposing depth of Southern racism. "The Star Spangled Banner" officially becomes national anthem.

**1932** Nazis lead in German elections with 230 Reichstag seats. Famine in USSR. In U.S., Congress sets up Reconstruction Finance Corporation to stimulate economy. Veterans march on Washington—most leave after Senate rejects payment of cash bonuses; others removed by troops under Douglas MacArthur. U.S. protests Japanese aggression in Manchuria. Amelia Earhart is first woman to fly Atlantic solo. Charles A. Lindbergh's baby son kidnapped, killed. (Bruno Richard Hauptmann arrested in 1934, convicted in 1935, executed in 1936.)

**1933** Hitler appointed German chancellor, gets dictatorial powers. Reichstag fire in Berlin; Nazi terror begins. Germany and Japan withdraw from League of Nations. Giuseppe Zangara executed for attempted assassination of president-elect Roosevelt in which Chicago mayor Cermak is fatally shot. Roosevelt inaugurated ("the only thing we have to fear is fear itself"); launches New Deal. Prohibition repealed. USSR recognized by U.S.

**1934** Chancellor Dollfuss of Austria assassinated by Nazis. Hitler becomes führer. USSR admitted to League of Nations. Dionne sisters, first quintuplets to survive beyond infancy, born in Canada. Mao Zedong begins the Long March north with 100,000 soldiers.

**1935** Saar incorporated into Germany after plebiscite. Nazis repudiate Versailles Treaty, introduce compulsory military service. Mussolini invades Ethiopia; League of Nations invokes sanctions. Roosevelt opens second phase of

---

## THE HOLOCAUST (1933–1945)

"Holocaust" is the term describing the Nazi annihilation of about 6 million Jews (two thirds of the pre-World War II European Jewish population), including 4,500,000 from Russia, Poland, and the Baltic; 750,000 from Hungary and Romania; 290,000 from Germany and Austria; 105,000 from The Netherlands; 90,000 from France; 54,000 from Greece.

The Holocaust was unique in its being *genocide*—the systematic destruction of a people solely because of religion, race, ethnicity, nationality, or sexual preference—on an unmatched scale. Along with the Jews, another 9 to 10 million people—Gypsies, Slavs (Poles, Ukrainians, and Belarussians), homosexuals, and the disabled—were exterminated.

**1933** Hitler named German Chancellor **(Jan.)**. Dachau, first concentration camp, established **(March)**. Boycotts against Jews begin **(April)**.

**1935** Anti-Semitic Nuremberg Laws passed by Reichstag; Jews lose citizenship and civil rights **(Sept.)**.

**1937** Buchenwald concentration camp opens **(July)**.

**1938** Extension of anti-Semitic laws to Austria after annexation **(March)**. *Kristallnacht* (Night of Broken Glass)—anti-Semitic riots and destruction of Jewish institutions in Germany and Austria **(Nov. 9)**. 26,000 Jews sent to concentration camps; Jewish children expelled from schools **(Nov. 9–10)**. Expropriation of Jewish property and businesses **(Dec.)**.

**1940** As war continues, Einsatzgruppen (mobile killing squads) follow German army into conquered lands, rounding up and massacring Jews and other "undesirables."

**1941** Goering instructs Heydrich to carry out the "final solution to the Jewish question" **(July 31)**. Deportation of German Jews begins; massacres of Jews in Odessa and Kiev **(Nov.)**; and in Riga and Vilna **(Dec.)**.

**1942** Mass killings using Zyklon-B begin at Auschwitz-Birkenau **(Jan.)**. Nazi leaders attend Wannsee Conference to coordinate the "final solution" **(Jan. 20)**. 100,000 Jews from Warsaw Ghetto deported to Treblinka death camp **(July)**.

**1943** Warsaw Ghetto uprisings **(Jan.** and **April)**; Ghetto exterminated **(May)**.

**1944** 476,000 Hungarian Jews sent to Auschwitz **(May–June)**. D-day **(June 6)**. Soviet Army liberates Maidanek death camp **(July)**. Nazis try to hide evidence of death camps **(Nov.)**.

**1945** As Allies advance, Nazis force concentration camp inmates on death marches. Americans liberate Buchenwald and British liberate Bergen-Belsen camps **(April)**. Nuremberg War Crimes Trial **(Nov. 1945–Oct. 1946)**.

New Deal in U.S., calling for social security, better housing, equitable taxation, and farm assistance. Huey Long assassinated in Louisiana.

**1936** Germans occupy Rhineland. Italy annexes Ethiopia. Rome-Berlin Axis proclaimed (Japan to join in 1940). Trotsky exiled to Mexico. King George V dies; succeeded by son, Edward VIII, who soon abdicates to marry an American-born divorcée, and is succeeded by brother, George VI. Spanish civil war begins. Hundreds of Americans join the "Lincoln Brigades." (Franco's fascist forces defeat Loyalist forces by 1939, when Madrid falls.) War between China and Japan begins, to continue through World War II. Japan and Germany sign anti-Comintern pact; joined by Italy in 1937.

**1937** Hitler repudiates war guilt clause of Versailles Treaty; continues to build German power. Italy withdraws from League of Nations. U.S. gunboat *Panay* sunk by Japanese in Yangtze River. Japan invades China, conquers most of coastal area. Amelia Earhart lost somewhere in Pacific on round-the-world flight. Picasso's *Guernica* mural.

**1938** Hitler marches into Austria; political and geographical union of Germany and Austria proclaimed. Munich Pact—Britain, France, and Italy agree to let Germany partition Czechoslovakia. Douglas "Wrong-Way" Corrigan flies from New York to Dublin. Fair Labor Standards Act establishes minimum wage. Orson Welles's radio broadcast *War of the Worlds*.

**1939** Germany invades Poland; occupies Bohemia and Moravia; renounces pact with England and concludes 10-year non-aggression pact with USSR. Russo-Finnish War begins; Finns to lose one-tenth of territory in 1940 peace treaty. World War II begins. In U.S., Roosevelt submits $1,319-million defense budget, proclaims U.S. neutrality, and declares limited emergency. Einstein writes FDR about feasibility of atomic bomb. New York World's Fair opens. DAR refuses to allow Marian Anderson to perform. *Gone with the Wind* premieres.

Dorothea Lange's photo "Migrant Mother" (1936) documented the Great Depression (1929–1940)

Amelia Earhart (1897–1937)

## WORLD WAR II (1939–1945)

Axis powers (Germany, Italy, Japan, Hungary, Romania, Bulgaria) *versus* Allies (U.S., Britain, France, USSR, Australia, Belgium, Brazil, Canada, China, Denmark, Greece, Netherlands, New Zealand, Norway, Poland, South Africa, Yugoslavia).

**1939** Germany invades Poland and annexes Danzig; Britain and France give Hitler ultimatum (**Sept. 1**), declare war (**Sept. 3**). Disabled German pocket battleship *Admiral Graf Spee* blown up off Montevideo, Uruguay, on Hitler's orders (**Dec. 17**). Limited activity ("Sitzkrieg") on Western Front.

**1940** Nazis invade Netherlands, Belgium, and Luxembourg (**May 10**). Chamberlain resigns as Britain's prime minister; Churchill takes over (**May 10**). Germans cross French frontier (**May 12**) using air/tank/infantry "Blitzkrieg" tactics. Dunkerque evacuation—about 335,000 out of 400,000 Allied soldiers rescued from Belgium by British civilian and naval craft (**May 26–June 3**). Italy declares war on France and Britain; invades France (**June 10**). Germans enter Paris; city undefended (**June 14**). France and Germany sign armistice at Compiègne (**June 22**). Nazis bomb Coventry, England (**Nov. 14**).

**1941** Germans launch attack in Balkans; Yugoslavia surrenders; General Mihajlovic continues guerrilla warfare; Tito leads left-wing guerrillas (**April 17**). Nazi tanks enter Athens; remnants of British Army quit Greece (**April 27**). Hitler attacks Russia (**June 22**). Atlantic Charter—FDR and Churchill agree on war aims (**Aug. 14**). Japanese attacks on Pearl Harbor, Philippines, Guam force U.S. into war; U.S. Pacific fleet crippled (**Dec. 7**). U.S. and Britain declare war on Japan. Germany and Italy declare war on U.S.; Congress declares war on those countries (**Dec. 11**).

**1942** British surrender Singapore to Japanese (**Feb. 15**). Roosevelt orders Japanese and Japanese Americans in western U.S. to be exiled to "relocation centers," many for the remainder of the war (**Feb. 19**). U.S. forces on Bataan peninsula in Philippines surrender (**April 9**). U.S. and Filipino troops on Corregidor island in Manila Bay surrender to Japanese (**May 6**). Village of Lidice in Czechoslovakia razed by Nazis

(**June 10**). U.S. and Britain land in French North Africa (**Nov. 8**).

**1943** Casablanca Conference—Churchill and FDR agree on unconditional surrender goal (**Jan. 14–24**). German 6th Army surrenders at Stalingrad—turning point of war in Russia (**Feb. 1–2**). Remnants of Nazis trapped on Cape Bon, ending war in Africa (**May 12**). Mussolini deposed; Badoglio named premier (**July 25**). Allied troops land on Italian mainland after conquest of Sicily (**Sept. 3**). Italy surrenders (**Sept. 8**). Nazis seize Rome (**Sept. 10**). Cairo Conference: FDR, Churchill, Chiang Kai-shek pledge defeat of Japan, free Korea (**Nov. 22–26**). Teheran Conference: FDR, Churchill, Stalin agree on invasion plans (**Nov. 28–Dec. 1**).

**1944** U.S. and British troops land at Anzio on west Italian coast and hold beachhead (**Jan. 22**). U.S. and British troops enter Rome (**June 4**). D-Day—Allies launch Normandy invasion (**June 6**). Hitler wounded in bomb plot (**July 20**). Paris liberated (**Aug. 25**). Athens freed by Allies (**Oct. 13**). Americans invade Philippines (**Oct. 20**). Germans launch counteroffensive in Belgium—Battle of the Bulge (**Dec. 16**).

**1945** Yalta Conference: agreement by FDR, Churchill, Stalin—establishes basis for occupation of Germany, returns to Soviet Union lands taken by Germany and Japan; USSR agrees to friendship pact with China (**Feb. 11**). Mussolini killed at Lake Como (**April 28**). Admiral Doenitz takes command in Germany; suicide of Hitler announced (**May 1**). Berlin falls (**May 2**). Germany signs unconditional surrender terms at Rheims (**May 7**). Allies declare V-E Day (**May 8**). Potsdam Conference—Truman, Churchill, Atlee (after **July 28**), Stalin establish council of foreign ministers to prepare peace treaties; plan German postwar government and reparations (**July 17–Aug. 2**). A-bomb dropped on Hiroshima by U.S. (**Aug. 6**). USSR declares war on Japan (**Aug. 8**). Nagasaki hit by A-bomb (**Aug. 9**). Japan agrees to surrender (**Aug. 14**). V-J Day—Japanese sign surrender terms aboard battleship *Missouri* (**Sept. 2**).

**Franklin Delano
Roosevelt
(1882–1945)**

**Winston Churchill
(1874–1965)**

**Harry S. Truman
(1884–1972)**

**Atomic Bomb**

**Anne Frank
(1929–1945)**

**1940** Hitler invades Norway, Denmark (**April 9**), the Netherlands, Belgium, Luxembourg (**May 10**), and France (**May 12**). Churchill becomes Britain's prime minister. Trotsky assassinated in Mexico (**Aug. 20**). Estonia, Latvia, and Lithuania annexed by USSR. U.S. trades 50 destroyers for leases on British bases in Western Hemisphere. Selective Service Act signed. The first official network television broadcast is put out by NBC.

**1941** Germany attacks the Balkans and Russia. Japanese surprise attack on U.S. fleet at Pearl Harbor brings U.S. into World War II; U.S. and Britain declare war on Japan. Manhattan Project (atomic bomb research) begins. Roosevelt enunciates "four freedoms," signs Lend-Lease Act, declares national emergency, promises aid to USSR. Orson Welles's *Citizen Kane.*

**1942** Declaration of United Nations signed in Washington (**Jan. 1**). Nazi leaders attend Wannsee Conference to coordinate the "final solution to the Jewish question," the systematic genocide of Jews known as the Holocaust. Women's military services established. Enrico Fermi achieves nuclear chain reaction. More than 120,000 Japanese and persons of Japanese ancestry living in western U.S. moved to "relocation centers," some for the duration of the war (Executive Order 9066). Coconut Grove nightclub fire in Boston kills 492 (**Nov. 28**).

**1943** Churchill and Roosevelt hold Casablanca Conference (**Jan. 14–23**). Mussolini deposed. President freezes prices, salaries, and wages to prevent inflation. Income tax withholding introduced.

**1944** Allies invade Normandy on D-Day (**June 6**). G.I. Bill of Rights enacted. Bretton Woods Conference creates International Monetary Fund and World Bank (**July 1–22**). Dumbarton Oaks Conference—U.S., British Commonwealth, and USSR propose establishment of United Nations (**Aug. 21–Oct. 7**). Battle of the Bulge (**Dec. 16**). Gunnar Myrdal's *An American Dilemma.*

**1945** Yalta Conference (Roosevelt, Churchill, Stalin) plans final defeat of Germany (**Feb. 4–11**). FDR dies (**April 12**). Hitler commits suicide (**April 30**); Germany surrenders (**May 7**); **May 8** is declared V-E Day. Potsdam Conference (Truman, Churchill, Stalin) establishes basis of German reconstruction (**July–Aug.**). U.S. drops atomic bombs on Japanese cities of Hiroshima (**Aug. 6**) and Nagasaki (**Aug. 9**). Japan signs official surrender on V-J Day (**Sept. 2**). United Nations established (**Oct. 24**). First electronic computer, ENIAC, built.

**1946** First meeting of UN General Assembly opens in London (**Jan. 10**). Winston Churchill's "Iron Curtain" speech warns of Soviet expansion (**March 5**). League of Nations dissolved (**April**). Italy abolishes monarchy (**June**). Verdict in Nuremberg war trial: 12 Nazi leaders (including 1 tried in absentia) sentenced to hang; 7 imprisoned; 3 acquitted (**Oct. 1**). Goering commits suicide a few hours before 10 other Nazis are executed (**Oct. 15**). Juan Perón becomes president of Argentina. Benjamin Spock's childcare classic published.

**1947** Britain nationalizes coal mines (**Jan. 1**). Peace treaties for Italy, Romania, Bulgaria, Hungary, Finland signed in Paris (**Feb. 10**). Soviet Union rejects U.S. plan for UN atomic-energy control (**March 4**). Truman proposes Truman Doctrine, which was to aid Greece and Turkey in resisting communist expansion (**March 12**). Marshall Plan for European recovery proposed—a coordinated program to help European nations recover from ravages of war (**June**). (By the time it ended in 1951, this "European Recovery Program" had cost $13 billion.) India and Pakistan gain independence from Britain (**Aug. 15**). U.S. Air Force pilot Chuck Yeager becomes first person to break the sound barrier (**Oct. 14**). Jackie Robinson joins the Brooklyn Dodgers. Anne Frank's *The Diary of a Young Girl* published.

**1948** Gandhi assassinated in New Delhi by Hindu fanatic (**Jan. 30**). Burma (**Jan. 4**) and Ceylon (**Feb. 4**) granted independence by Britain. Communists seize power in Czechoslovakia (**Feb. 23–25**). Organization of American States (OAS) Charter signed at Bogotá, Colombia (**April 30**). Nation of Israel proclaimed; British end mandate at midnight; Arab armies attack (**May 14**). Berlin blockade begins (**June 24**), prompting Allied airlift (**June 26**). (Blockade ends **May 12, 1949**; airlift continues until **Sept. 30, 1949**.) Stalin and Tito break (**June 28**). Independent Republic of Korea is proclaimed, following election supervised by UN (**Aug. 15**). Verdict in Japanese war trial: 18 imprisoned (**Nov. 12**); Tojo and six others hanged (**Dec. 23**). United States of Indonesia established as Dutch and Indonesians settle conflict (**Dec. 27**). Alger Hiss, former

U.S. State Department official, indicted on perjury charges after denying passing secret documents to communist spy ring; convicted in second trial (1950) and sentenced to five-year prison term. Truman ends racial segregation in military. Alfred Kinsey publishes *Sexual Behavior in the American Male.* Tennessee Williams's *A Streetcar Named Desire* wins Pulitzer.

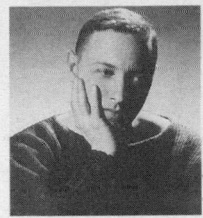

**Tennessee Williams**
**(1911–1983)**

**1949** Cease-fire in Palestine (**Jan. 7**). Truman proposes Point Four Program to help world's less developed areas (**Jan. 20**). Israel signs armistice with Egypt (**Feb. 24**). Start of North Atlantic Treaty Organization (NATO)—treaty signed by 12 nations (**April 4**). Federal Republic of Germany (West Germany) established (**May 23**). First successful Soviet atomic test (**July 14**). Communist People's Republic of China formally proclaimed by Chairman Mao Zedong (**Oct. 1**). German Democratic Republic (East Germany) established under Soviet rule (**Oct. 7**). South Africa institutionalizes apartheid.

**1950** Brink's robbery in Boston; almost $3 million stolen (**Jan. 17**). Truman orders development of hydrogen bomb (**Jan. 31**). Robert Schuman proposes Schuman Plan to pool European coal and steel (**May 9**). Korean War begins when North Korean Communist forces invade South Korea (**June 25**). Assassination attempt on President Truman by Puerto Rican nationalists (**Nov. 1**). McCarthyism begins.

**Woody Guthrie**
**(1912–1967)**

**1951** Julius and Ethel Rosenberg sentenced to death for passing atomic secrets to Russians (**March**). Spurred by Schuman Plan, six nations form European Coal and Steel Community (**April**); effective 1952. Japanese peace treaty signed in San Francisco by 49 nations (**Sept. 8**). Color television introduced in U.S. Libya gains independence (**Dec. 24**).

**1952** George VI dies; his daughter becomes Elizabeth II (**Feb. 6**). AEC announces "satisfactory" experiments in hydrogen-weapons research; eyewitnesses tell of blasts near Enewetak (**Nov.**). Ralph Ellison's *The Invisible Man.*

**1953** Gen. Dwight D. Eisenhower inaugurated president of United States (**Jan. 20**). Stalin dies (**March 5**). Malenkov becomes Soviet premier; Beria, minister of interior; Molotov, foreign minister (**March 6**). Dag Hammarskjöld begins term as UN secretary-general (**April 10**). James Watson and Francis Crick publish their discovery of the molecular model of DNA (**April–May**). Edmund Hillary of New Zealand and Tenzing Norgay of Nepal reach top of Mt. Everest (**May 29**). East Berliners rise against Communist rule; quelled by tanks (**June 17**). Egypt becomes republic ruled by military junta (**June 18**). Julius and Ethel Rosenberg executed in Sing Sing prison (**June 19**). Korean armistice signed (**July 27**). Moscow announces explosion of hydrogen bomb (**Aug. 20**). Tito becomes president of Yugoslavia. James Watson, Francis Crick, and Rosalind Franklin discover structure of DNA. Ernest Hemingway wins Pulitzer for *The Old Man and the Sea.*

**Dwight D. Eisenhower**
**(1890–1969)**

**1954** First atomic submarine *Nautilus* launched (**Jan. 21**). Five U.S. congressmen shot on floor of House as Puerto Rican nationalists fire from spectators' gallery; all five recover (**March 1**). Soviet Union grants sovereignty to East Germany (**March 23**). *Army* v. *McCarthy* inquiry—Senate subcommittee report blames both sides (**April 22–June 17**). Dien Bien Phu, French military outpost in Vietnam, falls to Vietminh army (**May 7**). U.S. Supreme Court (in *Brown* v. *Board of Education of Topeka*) unanimously bans racial segregation in public schools (**May 17**). Eisenhower launches world atomic pool without Soviet Union (Sept. 6). Eight-nation Southeast Asia defense treaty (SEATO) signed at Manila (**Sept. 8**). Dr. Jonas Salk starts inoculating children against polio. Algerian War of Independence against France begins (Nov.). France struggles to maintain colonial rule until 1962 when it agrees to Algeria's independence. William Faulkner's *A Fable* wins Pulitzer.

**Dag Hammarskjöld**
**(1905–1961)**

---

**KOREAN WAR (1950–1953)**

**1950** North Korean Communist forces invade South Korea (**June 25**). UN calls for cease-fire and asks UN members to assist South Korea (**June 27**). Truman orders U.S. forces into Korea (**June 27**). North Koreans capture Seoul (**June 28**). Gen. Douglas MacArthur designated commander of unified UN forces (**July 8**). Pusan Beachhead—UN forces counterattack and capture Seoul (**Aug.–Sept.**), capture Pyongyang, North Korean capital (**Oct.**). Chinese Communists enter war

(**Oct. 26**), force UN retreat toward 39th parallel (**Dec.**).

**1951** Gen. Matthew B. Ridgeway replaces MacArthur after he threatens Chinese with massive retaliation (**April 11**). Armistice negotiations (**July**) continue with interruptions until **June 1953**.

**1953** Armistice signed (**July 27**). Chinese troops withdraw from North Korea (**Oct. 26, 1958**), but over 200 violations of armistice noted to **1959**.

**Fidel Castro
(1926– )**

**John H. Glenn, Jr.
(1921– )**

**Martin Luther King, Jr.
(1929–1968)**

**John F. Kennedy
(1917–1963)**

**1955** Nikolai A. Bulganin becomes Soviet premier, replacing Malenkov (**Feb. 8**). Churchill resigns; Anthony Eden succeeds him (**April 6**). West Germany becomes a sovereign state (**May 5**). Western European Union (WEU) comes into being (**May 6**). Warsaw Pact, east European mutual defense agreement, signed (**May 14**). Argentina ousts Perón (**Sept. 19**). President Eisenhower suffers coronary thrombosis in Denver (**Sept. 24**). Rosa Parks refuses to sit at the back of the bus. Martin Luther King, Jr., leads black boycott of Montgomery, Ala., bus system (**Dec. 1**); desegregated service begins **Dec. 21, 1956.** AFL and CIO become one organization—AFL-CIO (**Dec. 5**). Tennessee Williams's *Cat on a Hot Tin Roof* wins Pulitzer.

**1956** Nikita Khrushchev, First Secretary of USSR Communist Party, denounces Stalin's excesses (**Feb. 24**). First aerial H-bomb tested over Namu islet, Bikini Atoll—10 million tons TNT equivalent (**May 21**). Workers' uprising against Communist rule in Poznan, Poland, is crushed (**June 28–30**); rebellion inspires Hungarian students to stage a protest against Communism in Budapest (**Oct. 23**). Egypt takes control of Suez Canal (**July 26**). Hungarian rebellion forces Soviet troops to withdraw from Budapest (**Oct.**). Israel launches attack on Egypt's Sinai peninsula and drives toward Suez Canal (**Oct. 29**). Imre Nagy announces Hungary's withdrawal from Warsaw Pact (**Nov. 1**); Soviet troops enter and reclaim Budapest (**Nov. 4**). British and French invade Port Said on the Suez Canal (**Nov. 5**). Cease-fire forced by U.S. pressure stops British, French, and Israeli advance (**Nov. 6**). Morocco gains independence. Ingmar Bergman's *The Seventh Seal.* Woody Guthrie composes "This Land is Your Land." Allen Ginsberg's *Howl.*

**1957** Eisenhower Doctrine calls for aid to Mideast countries which resist armed aggression from Communist-controlled nations (**Jan. 5**). The "Little Rock Nine" integrate Arkansas high school. Eisenhower sends troops to quell mob and protect school integration (**Sept. 24**). Russians launch *Sputnik I,* first Earth-orbiting satellite—the Space Age begins (**Oct. 4**).

**1958** European Economic Community (Common Market) becomes effective (**Jan. 1**). Army's Jupiter-C rocket fires first U.S. Earth satellite, *Explorer I,* into orbit (**Jan. 31**). Egypt and Syria merge into United Arab Republic (**Feb. 1**). Khrushchev becomes premier of Soviet Union as Bulganin resigns (**Mar. 27**). Gen. Charles de Gaulle becomes French premier (**June 1**), remaining in power until 1969. Eisenhower orders U.S. Marines into Lebanon at request of President Chamoun, who fears overthrow (**July 15**). New French constitution adopted (**Sept. 28**), de Gaulle elected president of 5th Republic (**Dec. 21**).

**1959** Cuban President Batista resigns and flees—Castro takes over (**Jan. 1**). Tibet's Dalai Lama escapes to India (**Mar. 31**). St. Lawrence Seaway opens, allowing ocean ships to reach Midwest (**April 25**). Alaska and Hawaii become states. Leakeys discover hominid fossils.

**1960** American U-2 spy plane, piloted by Francis Gary Powers, shot down over Russia (**May 1**). Khrushchev kills Paris summit conference because of U-2 (**May 16**). Top Nazi murderer of Jews, Adolf Eichmann, captured by Israelis in Argentina (**May 23**)—executed in Israel in 1962. Powers sentenced to prison for 10 years (**Aug. 19**)—freed in **February 1962** in exchange for Soviet spy. Communist China and Soviet Union split in conflict over Communist ideology. Senegal, Ghana, Nigeria, Madagascar, and Zaire (Belgian Congo) gain independence. Cuba begins confiscation of $770 million of U.S. property (**Aug. 7**). There are 900 U.S. military advisers in South Vietnam.

**1961** U.S. breaks diplomatic relations with Cuba (**Jan. 3**). Robert Frost recites "The Gift Outright" at John F. Kennedy's inauguration as president of U.S. (**Jan. 20**). Moscow announces putting first man in orbit around Earth, Maj. Yuri A. Gagarin (**April 12**). Cuba invaded at Bay of Pigs by an estimated 1,200 anti-Castro exiles aided by U.S.; invasion crushed (**April 17**). First U.S. spaceman, Navy Cmdr. Alan B. Shepard, Jr., rockets 116.5 miles up in 302-mile trip (**May 5**). Virgil Grissom becomes second American astronaut, making 118-mile-high, 303-mile-long rocket flight over Atlantic (**July 21**). Gherman Stepanovich Titov is launched in Soviet spaceship *Vostok II:* makes 17½ orbits in 25 hours, covering 434,960 miles before landing safely (**Aug. 6**). East Germans erect Berlin Wall between East and West Berlin to halt flood of refugees (**Aug. 13**). USSR fires 50-megaton hydrogen bomb, biggest explosion in history (**Oct. 29**). There are 2,000 U.S. military advisers in South Vietnam.

**1962** Lt. Col. John H. Glenn, Jr., is first American to orbit Earth—three times in 4 hr 55 min **(Feb. 20).** France transfers sovereignty to new republic of Algeria **(July 3).** Cuban missile crisis—USSR to build missile bases in Cuba; Kennedy orders Cuban blockade, lifts blockade after Russians back down **(Aug.–Nov.).** James H. Meredith, escorted by federal marshals, registers at University of Mississippi **(Oct. 1).** Pope John XXIII opens Second Vatican Council **(Oct. 11)**—Council holds four sessions, finally closing **Dec. 8, 1965.** Cuba releases 1,113 prisoners of 1961 invasion attempt **(Dec. 24).** Burundi, Jamaica, Western Samoa, Uganda, and Trinidad and Tobago become independent. William Faulkner wins Pulitzer for *The Reivers.* Rachel Carson's *Silent Spring.*

James H. Meredith
(1933–)

**1963** France and West Germany sign treaty of cooperation ending four centuries of conflict **(Jan. 22).** Michael E. De Bakey implants artificial heart in human for first time at Houston hospital; plastic device functions and patient lives for four days **(April 21).** Pope John XXIII dies **(June 3)**—succeeded **June 21** by Cardinal Montini, who becomes Paul VI. U.S. Supreme Court rules no locality may require recitation of Lord's Prayer or Bible verses in public schools **(June 17).** U.K.'s Profumo scandal **(June).** Civil rights rally held by 200,000 blacks and whites in Washington, D.C.; Martin Luther King delivers "I have a dream" speech **(Aug. 28).** Washington-to-Moscow "hot line" communications link opens, designed to reduce risk of accidental war **(Aug. 30).** President Kennedy shot and killed by sniper in Dallas, Tex. Lyndon B. Johnson becomes president same day **(Nov. 22).** Lee Harvey Oswald, accused assassin of President Kennedy, is shot and killed by Jack Ruby, Dallas nightclub owner **(Nov. 24).** Kenya achieves independence. Betty Friedan publishes *The Feminine Mystique.* There are 15,000 U.S. military advisers in South Vietnam.

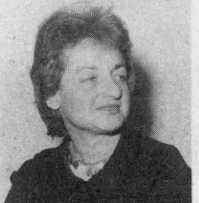

Betty Friedan
(1921–)

## VIETNAM WAR (1950–1975)

U.S., South Vietnam, and Allies versus North Vietnam and National Liberation Front (Viet Cong).

**1950** President Truman sends 35-man military advisory group to aid French fighting to maintain colonial power in Vietnam.

**1954** After defeat of French at Dien Bien Phu, Geneva Agreements **(July)** provide for withdrawal of French and Vietminh to either side of demarcation zone (DMZ) pending reunification elections, which are never held. Presidents Eisenhower and Kennedy (from 1954 onward) send civilian advisers and, later, military personnel to train South Vietnamese.

**1960** Communists form National Liberation Front in South.

**1960–1963** U.S. military advisers in South Vietnam rise from 900 to 15,000.

**1963** Ngo Dinh Diem, South Vietnam's premier, slain in coup **(Nov. 1).**

**1964** North Vietnamese torpedo boats reportedly attack U.S. destroyers in Gulf of Tonkin **(Aug. 2).** President Johnson orders retaliatory air strikes. Congress approves Gulf of Tonkin resolution **(Aug. 7)** authorizing president to take "all necessary measures" in war in Vietnam, allowing for the war's expansion.

**1965** U.S. planes begin combat missions over South Vietnam. In **June,** 23,000 American advisers committed to combat. By end of year over 184,000 U.S. troops in area.

**1966** B-52s bomb DMZ, reportedly used by North Vietnam for entry into South **(July 31).**

**1967** South Vietnam National Assembly approves election of Nguyen Van Thieu as president **(Oct. 21).**

**1968** U.S. has almost 525,000 men in Vietnam. In Tet offensive **(Jan.–Feb.),** Viet Cong guerrillas attack Saigon, Hue, and some provincial capitals. In My Lai massacre, American soldiers kill 300 Vietnamese villagers **(March 16).** President Johnson orders halt to U.S. bombardment of North Vietnam **(Oct. 31).** Saigon and N.L.F. join U.S. and North Vietnam in Paris peace talks.

**1969** President Nixon announces Vietnam peace offer **(May 14)**—begins troop withdrawals **(June).** Viet Cong forms Provisional Revolutionary Government. U.S. Senate calls for curb on commitments **(June 25).** Ho Chi Minh, 79, North Vietnam president, dies **(Sept. 3);** collective leadership chosen. Some 6,000 U.S. troops pulled back from Thailand and 1,000 marines from Vietnam (announced **Sept. 30).** Massive demonstrations in U.S. protest or support war policies **(Oct. 15).**

**1970** U.S. troops invade Cambodia in order to destroy North Vietnamese sanctuaries **(May 1).**

**1971** Congress bars use of combat troops, but not air power, in Laos and Cambodia **(Jan. 1).** South Vietnamese troops, with U.S. air cover, fail in Laos thrust. Many American ground forces withdrawn from Vietnam combat. *New York Times* publishes Pentagon papers, classified material on expansion of war **(June).**

**1972** Nixon responds to North Vietnamese drive across DMZ by ordering mining of North Vietnam ports and heavy bombing of Hanoi-Haiphong area **(April 1).** Nixon orders "Christmas bombing" of North to get North Vietnamese back to conference table **(Dec.).**

**1973** President orders halt to offensive operations in North Vietnam **(Jan. 15).** Representatives of North and South Vietnam, U.S., and N.L.F. sign peace pacts in Paris, ending longest war in U.S. history **(Jan. 27).** Last American troops departed in their entirety **(March 29)**

**1974** Both sides accuse each other of frequent violations of cease-fire agreement.

**1975** Full-scale warfare resumes. South Vietnam premier Nguyen Van Thieu resigns **(April 21).** South Vietnamese government surrenders to North Vietnam; U.S. Marine embassy guards and U.S. civilians and dependents evacuated **(April 30).** More than 140,000 Vietnamese refugees leave by air and sea, many to settle in U.S. Provisional Revolutionary Government takes control **(June 6).**

**1976** Election of National Assembly paves way for reunification of North and South.

**The Beatles**

**Malcolm X
(1925–1965)**

**Thurgood Marshall
(1908–1993)**

**Lyndon B. Johnson
(1908–1973)**

**Richard Nixon
(1913–1994)**

**1964** U.S. Supreme Court rules that congressional districts should be roughly equal in population (**Feb. 17**). Jack Ruby convicted of murder in slaying of Lee Harvey Oswald; sentenced to death by Dallas jury (**March 14**)— conviction reversed **Oct. 5, 1966**; Ruby dies **Jan. 3, 1967**, before second trial can be held. Three civil rights workers—Schwerner, Goodman, and Cheney—murdered in Mississippi (**June**). Twenty-one arrests result in trial and conviction of seven by federal jury. Nelson Mandela sentenced to life imprisonment (**June 11**). Congress approves Gulf of Tonkin resolution (**Aug. 7**). President's Commission on the Assassination of President Kennedy issues Warren Report concluding that Lee Harvey Oswald acted alone. The Beatles appear on *The Ed Sullivan Show.*

**1965** Rev. Dr. Martin Luther King, Jr., and more than 2,600 other blacks arrested in Selma, Ala., during three-day demonstrations against voter-registration rules (**Feb. 1**). Malcolm X, black-nationalist leader, shot to death at Harlem rally in New York City (**Feb. 21**). U.S. Marines land in Dominican Republic as fighting persists between rebels and Dominican army (**April 28**). Medicare, senior citizens' government medical assistance program, begins (**July 1**). Blacks riot for six days in Watts section of Los Angeles: 34 dead, over 1,000 injured, nearly 4,000 arrested, fire damage put at $175 million (**Aug. 11–16**). Power failure in Ontario plant blacks out parts of eight states of northeast U.S. and two provinces of southeast Canada (**Nov. 9**). Ralph Nader's *Unsafe at Any Speed.*

**1966** Black teenagers riot in Watts, Los Angeles; two men killed and at least 25 injured (**March 15**). Supreme Court decides *Miranda* v. *Arizona.*

**1967** Three Apollo astronauts—Col. Virgil I. Grissom, Col. Edward White II, and Lt. Cmdr. Roger B. Chaffee—killed in spacecraft fire during simulated launch (**Jan. 27**). Biafra secedes from Nigeria (**May 30**). Israeli and Arab forces battle; six-day war ends with Israel occupying Sinai Peninsula, Golan Heights, Gaza Strip, and east bank of Suez Canal (**June 5**). Red China announces explosion of its first hydrogen bomb (**June 17**). Racial violence in Detroit; 7,000 National Guardsmen aid police after night of rioting. Similar outbreaks occur in New York City's Spanish Harlem, Rochester, N.Y., Birmingham, Ala., and New Britain, Conn. (**July 23**). Thurgood Marshall sworn in as first black U.S. Supreme Court justice (**Oct. 2**). Dr. Christiaan N. Barnard and team of South African surgeons perform world's first successful human heart transplant (**Dec. 3**)—patient dies 18 days later.

**1968** North Korea seizes U.S. Navy ship *Pueblo;* holds 83 on board as spies (**Jan. 23**). Tet offensive, turning point in Vietnam war (**Jan.–Feb.**). My Lai massacre (**March 16**). President Johnson announces he will not seek or accept presidential renomination (**March 31**). Martin Luther King, Jr., civil rights leader, is slain in Memphis (**April 4**)—James Earl Ray, indicted in murder, captured in London on **June 8**. In 1969 Ray pleads guilty and is sentenced to 99 years. Sen. Robert F. Kennedy is shot and critically wounded in Los Angeles hotel after winning California primary (**June 5**)—dies **June 6**. Sirhan B. Sirhan convicted 1969. Czechoslovakia is invaded by Russians and Warsaw Pact forces to crush liberal regime (**Aug. 20**).

**1969** Richard M. Nixon is inaugurated 37th president of the U.S. (**Jan. 20**). Stonewall riot in New York City marks beginning of gay rights movement (**June 28**). Apollo 11 astronauts—Neil A. Armstrong, Edwin E. Aldrin, Jr., and Michael Collins—take man's first walk on moon (**July 20**). Sen. Edward M. Kennedy pleads guilty to leaving scene of fatal accident at Chappaquiddick, Mass. (**July 18**), in which Mary Jo Kopechne was drowned—gets two-month suspended sentence (**July 25**). Woodstock Festival (**Aug. 15–17**). *Sesame Street* debuts. Internet (ARPA) goes online.

**1970** Biafra surrenders after 32-month fight for independence from Nigeria (**Jan. 15**). Rhodesia severs last tie with British crown and declares itself a racially segregated republic (**March 1**). U.S. troops invade Cambodia (**May 1**). Four students at Kent State University in Ohio slain by National Guardsmen at demonstration protesting incursion into Cambodia (**May 4**). Senate repeals Gulf of Tonkin resolution (**June 24**).

**1971** Supreme Court rules unanimously that busing of students may be ordered to achieve racial desegregation (**April 20**). Anti-war militants attempt to disrupt government business in Washington (**May 3**)—police and military units arrest as many as 12,000; most are later released. *Pentagon Papers* published (**June**). Twenty-sixth Amendment to U.S. Constitution lowers voting age to 18. UN seats Communist China and expels Nationalist China (**Oct. 25**).

**1972** President Nixon makes unprecedented eight-day visit to Communist China and meets with Mao Zedong (**Feb. 21–27**). Britain takes over direct rule of Northern Ireland in bid for peace (**March 24**). Gov. George C. Wallace of Alabama is shot by Arthur H. Bremer at Laurel, Md., political rally (**May 15**). Five men are apprehended by police in attempt to bug Democratic National Committee headquarters in Washington, D.C.'s Watergate complex—start of the Watergate scandal (**June 17**). Supreme Court rules that death penalty is unconstitutional (**June 29**). Eleven Israeli athletes at Olympic Games in Munich are killed after eight members of an Arab terrorist group invade Olympic Village; five guerrillas and one policeman are also killed (**Sept. 5**). "Christmas bombing" of North Vietnam (**Dec. 25**).

Mao Zedong
(1893–1976)

**1973** Great Britain, Ireland, and Denmark enter European Economic Community (**Jan. 1**). Supreme Court rules on *Roe* v. *Wade* (**Jan. 22**). Vietnam War ends with signing of peace pacts (**Jan. 27**). Nixon, on national TV, accepts responsibility, but not blame, for Watergate; accepts resignations of advisers H. R. Haldeman and John D. Ehrlichman, fires John W. Dean III as counsel (**April 30**). Greek military junta abolishes monarchy and proclaims republic (**June 1**). U.S. bombing of Cambodia ends, marking official halt to 12 years of combat activity in Southeast Asia (**Aug. 15**). Chile's Marxist president, Salvadore Allende, is overthrown (**Sept. 11**). Fourth and biggest Arab-Israeli conflict begins as Egyptian and Syrian forces attack Israel as Jews mark Yom Kippur, holiest day in their calendar (**Oct. 6**). Spiro T. Agnew resigns as vice president and then, in federal court in Baltimore, pleads no contest to charges of evasion of income taxes on $29,500 he received in 1967, while governor of Maryland. He is fined $10,000 and put on three years' probation (**Oct. 10**). In the "Saturday Night Massacre," Nixon fires special Watergate prosecutor Archibald Cox and Deputy Attorney General William D. Ruckelshaus; Attorney General Elliot L. Richardson resigns (**Oct. 20**). Egypt and Israel sign U.S.-sponsored cease-fire accord (**Nov. 11**). Duke Ellington's autobiography, *Music Is My Mistress,* is published.

Duke Ellington
(1899–1974)

**1974** Patricia Hearst, 19-year-old daughter of publisher Randolph Hearst, kidnapped by Symbionese Liberation Army (**Feb. 5**). House Judiciary Committee adopts three articles of impeachment charging President Nixon with obstruction of justice, failure to uphold laws, and refusal to produce material subpoenaed by the committee (**July 30**). Richard M. Nixon announces he will resign the next day, the first president to do so (**Aug. 8**). Vice President Gerald R. Ford of Michigan is sworn in as 38th president of the U.S. (**Aug. 9**). Ford grants "full, free, and absolute pardon" to ex-president Nixon (**Sept. 8**).

Gerald R. Ford
(1913– )

**1975** John N. Mitchell, H. R. Haldeman, John D. Ehrlichman found guilty of Watergate cover-up (**Jan. 1**); sentenced to 30 months to 8 years in jail (**Feb. 21**). Pol Pot and Khmer Rouge take over Cambodia (**April**). American merchant ship *Mayaguez,* seized by Cambodian forces, is rescued in operation by U.S. Navy and Marines, 38 of whom are killed (**May 15**). *Apollo* and *Soyuz* spacecraft take off for U.S.-Soviet link-up in space (**July 15**). President Ford escapes assassination attempt in Sacramento, Calif. (**Sept. 5**). President Ford escapes second assassination attempt in 17 days (**Sept. 22**).

**1976** Supreme Court rules that blacks and other minorities are entitled to retroactive job seniority (**March 24**). Ford signs Federal Election Campaign Act (May 11); Supreme Court rules that death penalty is not inherently cruel or unusual and is a constitutionally acceptable form of punishment (**July 3**). Nation celebrates bicentennial (**July 4**). Israeli airborne commandos attack Uganda's Entebbe Airport and free 103 hostages held by pro-Palestinian hijackers of Air France plane; one Israeli and several Ugandan soldiers killed in raid (**July 4**). Mysterious disease that eventually claims 29 lives strikes American Legion convention in Philadelphia (**Aug. 4**). Jimmy Carter elected U.S. president (**Nov. 2**).

Jimmy Carter
(1924– )

**1977** First woman Episcopal priest ordained (**Jan. 1**). Scientists identify previously unknown bacterium as cause of mysterious "legionnaire's disease" (**Jan. 18**). Carter pardons Vietnam draft evaders (**Jan. 21**). Scientists report using bacteria in lab to make insulin (**May 23**). Supreme Court rules that states are not required to spend Medicaid funds on elective abortions (**June 20**). Deng Xiaoping, purged Chinese leader, restored to power as "Gang of Four" is expelled from Communist Party (**July 22**). South African activist Stephen Biko dies in police custody

**Pope John Paul II
(1920– )**

**Anwar Sadat
(1918–1981)**

**Ayatollah Ruhollah
Khomeini
(1900–1989)**

**Ronald Reagan
(1911– )**

**Sandra Day O'Connor
(1930– )**

(Sept. 12). Nuclear-proliferation pact, curbing spread of nuclear weapons, signed by 15 countries, including U.S. and USSR (Sept. 21).

**1978** President chooses Federal Appeals Court Judge William H. Webster as F.B.I. Director (Jan. 19). Rhodesia's prime minister Ian D. Smith and three black leaders agree on transfer to black majority rule (Feb. 15). U.S. Senate approves Panama Canal neutrality treaty (March 16); votes treaty to turn canal over to Panama by year 2000 (April 18). Former Italian premier Aldo Moro kidnapped by left wing terrorists, who kill five bodyguards (March 16); he is found slain (May 9). Californians in referendum approve Proposition 13 for nearly 60% slash in property tax revenues (June 6). Supreme Court, in Bakke case, bars quota systems in college admissions but affirms constitutionality of programs giving advantage to minorities (June 28). Pope Paul VI, dead at 80, mourned (Aug. 6); new Pope, John Paul I, 65, dies unexpectedly after 34 days in office (Sept. 28); succeeded by Karol Cardinal Wojtyla of Poland as John Paul II (Oct. 16). "Framework for Peace" in Middle East signed by Egypt's president Anwar Sadat and Israeli premier Menachem Begin after 13-day conference at Camp David led by President Carter (Sept. 17). Jim Jones's followers commit mass suicide in Jonestown, Guyana (Nov. 18).

**1979** Oil spills pollute ocean waters in Atlantic and Gulf of Mexico (Jan. 1, June 8, July 21). Ohio agrees to pay $675,000 to families of dead and injured in Kent State University shootings (Jan. 4). Vietnam and Vietnam-backed Cambodian insurgents announce fall of Phnom Penh, Cambodian capital, and collapse of Pol Pot regime (Jan. 7). Shah leaves Iran after year of turmoil (Jan. 16); revolutionary forces under Muslim leader, Ayatollah Ruhollah Khomeini, take over (Feb. 1 et seq.). Conservatives win British election; Margaret Thatcher new prime minister (March 28). Nuclear power plant accident at Three Mile Island, Pa., releases radiation (March 28). Carter and Brezhnev sign SALT II agreement (June 14). Nicaraguan president Gen. Anastasio Somoza Debayle resigns and flees to Miami (July 17); Sandinistas form government (July 19). Earl Mountbatten of Burma, 79, British World War II hero, and three others killed by blast on fishing boat off Irish coast (Aug. 27); two I.R.A. members accused (Aug. 30). Iranian militants seize U.S. embassy in Teheran and hold hostages (Nov. 4). Soviet invasion of Afghanistan stirs world protests (Dec. 27).

**1980** Six U.S. embassy aides escape from Iran with Canadian help (Jan. 29). F.B.I.'s undercover operation "Abscam" (for Arab scam) implicates public officials (Feb. 2). U.S. breaks diplomatic ties with Iran (April 7). Eight U.S. servicemen are killed and five are injured as helicopter and cargo plane collide in abortive desert raid to rescue American hostages in Teheran (April 25). Supreme Court upholds limits on federal aid for abortions (June 30). Shah of Iran dies at 60 (July 27). Anastasio Somoza Debayle, ousted Nicaragua ruler, and two aides assassinated in Asunción, Paraguay capital (Sept. 17). Iraq troops hold 90 square miles of Iran after invasion; 8-year Iran-Iraq war begins (Sept. 19). Ronald Reagan elected president in Republican sweep (Nov. 4). Three U.S. nuns and lay worker found shot in El Salvador (Dec. 4). John Lennon of the Beatles shot dead in New York City (Dec. 8). Smallpox eradicated.

**1981** Ronald Reagan takes oath as 40th president (Jan. 20). U.S.-Iran agreement frees 52 hostages held in Teheran since 1979 (Jan. 20); hostages welcomed back in U.S. (Jan. 25). President Reagan wounded by gunman, with press secretary and two law-enforcement officers (March 30). Pope John Paul II wounded by gunman (May 14). Supreme Court rules, 4–4, that former president Nixon and three top aides may be required to pay monetary damages for unconstitutional wiretap of home telephone of former national security aide (June 22). Reagan nominates Judge Sandra Day O'Connor, 51, of Arizona, as first woman on Supreme Court (July 7). More than 110 die in collapse of aerial walkways in lobby of Hyatt Regency Hotel in Kansas City; 188 injured (July 18). Air controllers strike, disrupting flights (Aug. 3); government dismisses strikers (Aug. 11). AIDS is first identified.

**1982** British overcome Argentina in Falklands war (April 2–June 15). Israel invades Lebanon in attack on P.L.O. (June 4). John W. Hinckley, Jr., found not guilty because of insanity in shooting of President Reagan (June 21). Alexander M. Haig, Jr., resigns as secretary of state (June 25). Equal Rights Amendment fails ratification (June 30). Princess

Grace, 52, dies of injuries when car plunges off mountain road; daughter Stephanie, 17, suffers serious injuries (Sept. 14). Lebanese Christian Phalangists kill hundreds of people in two Palestinian refugee camps in West Beirut (Sept. 15). Leonid Brezhnev, Soviet leader, dies at 75 (Nov. 10). Yuri V. Andropov, 68, chosen as successor (Nov. 15). Permanent artificial heart implanted in human for first time in Dr. Barney B. Clark, 61, at University of Utah Medical Center in Salt Lake City (Dec. 2).

1983 Pope John Paul II signs new Roman Catholic code incorporating changes brought about by Second Vatican Council (Jan. 25). Second space shuttle, Challenger, makes successful maiden voyage, which includes the first U.S. space walk in nine years (April 4). U.S. Supreme Court declares many local abortion restrictions unconstitutional (June 15). Sally K. Ride, 32, first U.S. woman astronaut in space as a crew member aboard space shuttle Challenger (June 18). U.S. admits shielding former Nazi Gestapo chief Klaus Barbie, the "butcher of Lyon," wanted in France for war crimes (Aug. 15). Benigno S. Aquino, Jr., 50, political rival of Philippines president Marcos, slain in Manila (Aug. 21). South Korean Boeing 747 jetliner bound for Seoul apparently strays into Soviet airspace and is shot down by a Soviet SU-15 fighter after it had tracked the airliner for two hours; all 269 aboard are killed, including 61 Americans (Aug. 30). Terrorist explosion kills 237 U.S. Marines in Beirut (Oct. 23). U.S. and Caribbean allies invade Grenada (Oct. 25).

1984 Bell System broken up (Jan. 1). France gets first deliveries of Soviet natural gas (Jan. 1). Syria frees captured U.S. Navy pilot, Lieut. Robert C. Goodman, Jr. (Jan. 3). U.S. and Vatican exchange diplomats after 116-year hiatus (Jan. 10). Reagan orders U.S. Marines withdrawn from Beirut international peacekeeping force (Feb. 7). Yuri V. Andropov dies at 69; Konstantin U. Chernenko, 72, named Soviet Union leader (Feb. 9). Italy and Vatican agree to end Roman Catholicism as state religion (Feb. 18). Reagan ends U.S. role in Beirut by relieving Sixth Fleet from peacekeeping force (March 30). Congress rebukes President Reagan on use of federal funds for mining Nicaraguan harbors (April 10). Soviet Union withdraws from summer Olympic games in U.S., and other bloc nations follow (May 7 et seq.). José Napoleón Duarte, moderate, elected president of El Salvador (May 11). Three hundred slain as Indian Army occupies Sikh Golden Temple in Amritsar (June 6). Thirty-ninth Democratic National Convention, in San Francisco, nominates Walter F. Mondale and Geraldine A. Ferraro (July 16–19). Thirty-third Republican National Convention, at Dallas, renominates President Reagan and Vice President Bush (Aug. 20–25). Brian Mulroney and Conservative party win Canadian election in landslide (Sept. 4). Indian prime minister Indira Gandhi assassinated by two Sikh bodyguards; 1,000 killed in anti-Sikh riots; son Rajiv succeeds her (Oct. 31). President Reagan re-elected in landslide with 59% of vote (Nov. 7). Toxic gas leaks from Union Carbide plant in Bhopal, India, killing 2,000 and injuring 150,000 (Dec. 3).

1985 Ronald Reagan, 73, takes oath for second term as 40th president (Jan. 20). General Westmoreland settles libel action against CBS (Feb. 18). Prime Minister Margaret Thatcher addresses Congress, endorsing Reagan's policies (Feb. 20). USSR leader Chernenko dies at 73 and is replaced by Mikhail Gorbachev, 54 (March 11). Two Shi'ite Muslim gunmen capture TWA airliner with 133 aboard, 104 of them Americans (June 14); 39 remaining hostages freed in Beirut (June 30). Supreme Court, 5–4, bars public school teachers from parochial schools (July 1). Arthur James Walker, 50, retired naval officer, convicted by federal judge of participating in Soviet spy ring operated by his brother, John Walker (Aug. 9). P.L.O. terrorists hijack Achille Lauro, Italian cruise ship with 80 passengers, plus crew (Oct. 7); American, Leon Klinghoffer, killed (Oct. 8); Italian government toppled by political crisis over hijacking (Oct. 16). John A. Walker and son, Michael I. Walker, 22, sentenced in Navy espionage case (Oct. 28). Reagan and Gorbachev meet at summit (Nov. 19); agree to step up arms control talks and renew cultural contacts (Nov. 21). Terrorists seize Egyptian Boeing 737 airliner after takeoff from Athens (Nov. 23); 59 dead as Egyptian forces storm plane on Malta (Nov. 24). U.S. budget-balancing bill enacted (Dec. 12).

1986 Spain and Portugal join European Economic Community (Jan. 1). President freezes Libyan assets in U.S. (Jan. 8). Supreme Court bars racial bias in trial jury selection (Jan. 14). Voyager 2 spacecraft reports secrets of Uranus (Jan. 26). Space shuttle Challenger explodes after launch at Cape Canaveral, Fla., killing all seven aboard (Jan. 28). Haiti president

Indira Gandhi
(1917–1984)

Corazon Aquino
(1933– )

Mikhail S. Gorbachev
(1931– )

Margaret Thatcher
(1925– )

Sally K. Ride
(1951– )

**William Rehnquist**
**(1924– )**

**George Bush**
**(1924– )**

**Benazir Bhutto**
**(1953– )**

Jean-Claude Duvalier flees to France **(Feb. 7)**. President Marcos flees Philippines after ruling 20 years, as newly elected Corazon Aquino succeeds him **(Feb. 26)**. Prime Minister Olof Palme of Sweden shot dead **(Feb. 28)**. Austrian president Kurt Waldheim's service as Nazi army officer revealed **(March 3)**. Union Carbide agrees to settlement with victims of Bhopal gas leak in India **(March 22)**. Halley's comet yields information on return visit **(April 10)**. U.S. planes attack Libyan "terrorist centers" **(April 14)**. Desmond Tutu elected archbishop in South Africa **(April 14)**. Major nuclear accident at Soviet Union's Chernobyl power station alarms world **(April 26** *et seq.*). Ex-Navy analyst, Jonathan Jay Pollard, 31, guilty as spy for Israel **(June 4)**. Supreme Court reaffirms abortion rights **(June 11)**. World Court rules U.S. broke international law in mining Nicaraguan waters **(June 27)**. Supreme Court voids automatic provisions of budget-balancing law **(July 7)**. Jerry A. Whitworth, ex-Navy radioman, convicted as spy **(July 24)**; he is also part of Walker family spy ring. Muslim captors release Rev. Lawrence Martin Jenco **(July 26)**. Senate Judiciary Committee approves William H. Rehnquist as chief justice of U.S. **(Aug. 14)**. House votes arms appropriations bill rejecting administration's "star wars" policy **(Aug. 15)**. Three Lutheran church groups in U.S. set to merge **(Aug. 29)**. Congress overrides Reagan veto of stiff sanctions against South Africa **(Sept. 29** and **Oct. 2)**. Congress approves immigration bill barring hiring of illegal aliens, with amnesty provision **(Oct. 17)**. Reagan signs $11.7-billion budget reduction measure **(Oct. 21)**. He approves sweeping revision of U.S. tax code **(Oct. 22)**. Democrats triumph in elections, gaining eight seats to win Senate majority **(Nov. 4)**. Secret initiative to send arms to Iran revealed **(Nov. 6** *et seq.*); Reagan denies exchanging arms for hostages and halts arms sales **(Nov. 19)**; diversion of funds from arms sales to Nicaraguan Contras revealed **(Nov. 25)**.

**1987**  William Buckley, U.S. hostage in Lebanon, reported slain **(Jan. 20)**. Supreme Court rules Rotary Clubs must admit women **(May 4)**. Iraqi missiles kill 37 in attack on U.S. frigate *Stark* in Persian Gulf **(May 17)**; Iraqi president apologizes **(May 18)**. Prime Minister Thatcher wins rare third term in Britain **(June 11)**. Supreme Court justice Lewis F. Powell, Jr., retires **(June 26)**. Klaus Barbie, 73, Gestapo wartime chief in Lyon, sentenced to life by French court for war crimes **(July 4)**. Oliver North, Jr., tells congressional inquiry higher officials approved his secret Iran-Contra operations **(July 7–10)**. Admiral John M. Poindexter, former National Security Adviser, testifies he authorized use of Iran arms sale profits to aid Contras **(July 15–22)**. Secretary of State George P. Shultz testifies he was deceived repeatedly on Iran-Contra affair **(July 23–24)**. Defense Secretary Caspar W. Weinberger tells inquiry of official deception and intrigue **(July 31, Aug. 3)**. Reagan says Iran arms-Contra policy went astray and accepts responsibility **(Aug. 12)**. Severe earthquake strikes Los Angeles, leaving 100 injured and six dead **(Oct. 1)**. Senate, 58–42, rejects Robert H. Bork as Supreme Court justice **(Oct. 23)**.

**1988**  U.S. and Canada reach free trade agreement **(Jan. 2)**. Robert C. McFarlane, former National Security Adviser, pleads guilty in Iran-Contra case **(March 11)**. U.S. Navy ship shoots down Iranian airliner in Persian Gulf, mistaking it for jet fighter; 290 killed **(July 3)**. Terrorists kill nine tourists on Aegean cruise **(July 11)**. Democratic convention nominates Gov. Michael Dukakis of Massachusetts for president and Texas senator Lloyd Bentsen for vice president **(July 17** *et seq.*). Republicans nominate George Bush for president and Indiana senator Dan Quayle for vice president **(Aug. 15** *et seq.*). Plane blast kills Pakistani president Mohammad Zia ul-Haq **(Aug. 17)**. Republicans sweep 40 states in election. Bush beats Dukakis **(Nov. 8)**. Benazir Bhutto, first Islamic woman prime minister, chosen to lead Pakistan **(Dec. 1)**. Pan-Am 747 explodes from terrorist bomb and crashes in Lockerbie, Scotland, killing all 259 aboard and 11 on ground **(Dec. 21)**.

**1989**  U.S. planes shoot down two Libyan fighters over international waters in Mediterranean **(Jan. 4)**. Emperor Hirohito of Japan dead at 87 **(Jan. 7)**. George Herbert Walker Bush inaugurated as 41st U.S. president **(Jan. 20)**. Iran's Ayatollah Khomeini declares author Salman Rushdie's book *The Satanic Verses* offensive and sentences him to death **(Feb. 14)**. Ruptured tanker *Exxon Valdez* sends 11 million gallons of crude oil into Alaska's Prince William Sound **(March 24)**. Tens of thousands of Chinese students take over Beijing's Tiananmen Square in rally for democracy **(April 19** *et seq.*). U.S. jury convicts Oliver North in Iran-Contra affair (**May 4**). More than one million in Beijing demonstrate for democracy; chaos spreads across nation (**mid-May** *et seq.*). Mikhail S. Gorbachev named Soviet president (**May 25**). Thousands killed in Tiananmen Square as Chinese leaders take hard line toward demonstrators (**June 4** *et seq.*). Army general Colin R. Powell is first black chairman of Joint Chiefs of Staff (**Aug. 9**). P. W. Botha quits as South Africa's president (**Aug. 14**). *Voyager 2* spacecraft speeds by Neptune after making startling discoveries about the planet and its moons (**Aug. 29**). Deng Xiaoping resigns from China's leadership (**Nov. 9**). After 28 years, Berlin Wall is open to West (**Nov. 11**). Czech Parliament ends Communists' dominant role (**Nov. 30**). Romanian uprising overthrows Communist government (**Dec. 15** *et seq.*); President Ceausescu and wife executed (**Dec. 25**). U.S. troops invade Panama, seeking capture of Gen. Manuel Noriega (**Dec. 20**); resistance to U.S. collapses (**Dec. 24**). Dalai Lama wins Nobel Peace Prize.

François Mitterrand
(1916–1996)

**1990** World Wide Web debuts, popularizes Internet. Gen. Manuel Noriega surrenders in Panama (**Jan. 3**). Yugoslav Communists end 45-year monopoly of power (**Jan. 22**). Soviet Communists relinquish sole power (**Feb. 7**). South Africa frees Nelson Mandela, imprisoned 27½ years (**Feb. 11**). Violeta Barrios de Chamorro inaugurated as Nicaraguan president. Hubble Space Telescope launched (**April 25**). U.S.-Soviet summit reaches accord on armaments (**June 1**). Western Alliance ends cold war and proposes joint action with Soviet Union and Eastern Europe (**July 6**). U.S. Appeals Court overturns Oliver North's Iran-Contra conviction (**July 20**). Iraqi troops invade Kuwait and seize petroleum reserves, setting off Persian Gulf War (**Aug. 2** *et seq.*). East and West Germany reunited (**Oct. 3**). Republicans set back in midterm elections (**Nov. 8**). Gorbachev assumes emergency powers (**Nov. 17**). Leaders of 34 nations in Europe and North America proclaim a united Europe (**Nov. 21**). Margaret Thatcher resigns as British prime minister (**Nov. 22**); John Major succeeds her (**Nov. 28**). Lech Walesa wins Poland's runoff presidential election (**Dec. 9**). Haiti elects leftist priest as president in first democratic election (**Dec. 17**).

General Colin Powell
(1937– )

**1991** U.S. and Allies at war with Iraq (**Jan. 15**). Warsaw Pact dissolves military alliance (**Feb. 25**). Cease-fire ends Persian Gulf War; UN forces are victorious (**April 3**). Europeans end sanctions on South Africa (**April 15**). Supreme Court limits death row appeals (**April 16**). Winnie Mandela sentenced in kidnapping (**May 13**). William H. Webster retires as director of CIA; Robert H. Gates succeeds him (**May 14**). France agrees to sign 1968 treaty banning spread of atomic weapons (**June 3**). Communist government of Albania resigns (**June 4**). Jiang Qing, widow of Mao, commits suicide (**June 4**). South African Parliament repeals apartheid laws (**June 5**). Warsaw Pact dissolved (**July 1**). Boris N. Yeltsin inaugurated as first freely elected president of Russian Republic (**July 10**). Bush-Gorbachev summit negotiates strategic arms reduction treaty (**July 31**). China accepts nuclear nonproliferation treaty (**Aug. 10**). Lithuania, Estonia, and Latvia win independence (**Aug. 25**); Bush recognizes them (**Sept. 2**). Haitian

Saddam Hussein
(1937– )

---

**THE PERSIAN GULF WAR (Aug. 2, 1990–April 6, 1991)**

**1990** Iraq invades its tiny neighbor, Kuwait, after talks break down over oil production and debt repayment. Iraqi president Saddam Hussein later annexes Kuwait and declares it a 19th province of Iraq (**Aug. 2**). President Bush, alleging that Iraq may invade Saudi Arabia and take control of the region's oil supplies. He begins organizing a multinational coalition to seek Kuwait's freedom and restoration of its legitimate government. The UN Security Council authorizes economic sanctions against Iraq. Bush orders U.S. troops to protect Saudi Arabia at the Saudis' request and "Operation Desert Shield" begins (**Aug. 6**). 230,000 American troops arrive in Saudi Arabia to take defensive action, but when Iraq continues a huge military buildup in Kuwait, the President orders an additional 200,000 troops deployed to prepare for a possible offensive action by the U.S.-led coalition forces. He subsequently obtains a UN Security Council resolution setting a **Jan. 15, 1991** deadline for Iraq to withdraw unconditionally from Kuwait (**Nov. 8**).

**1991** Bush wins congressional approval for his position with the most devastating air assault in history

against military targets in Iraq and Kuwait (**Jan. 16**). He rejects a Soviet-Iraq peace plan for a gradual withdrawal that does not comply with all the UN resolutions and gives Iraq an ultimatum to withdraw from Kuwait by noon Feb. 23 (**Feb. 22**). The president orders the ground war to begin (**Feb. 24**). In a brilliant and lightning-fast campaign, U.S. and coalition forces smash through Iraq's defenses and defeat Saddam Hussein's troops in only four days of combat. Allies enter Kuwait City (**Feb. 26**). Iraqi army sets fire to over 500 of Kuwait's oil wells as final act of destruction to Kuwait's infrastructure. Bush orders a unilateral cease-fire 100 hours after the ground offensive started (**Feb. 27**). Allied and Iraqi military leaders meet on battlefield to discuss terms for a formal cease-fire to end the Gulf War. Iraq agrees to abide by all of the UN resolutions (**Mar. 3**). The first Allied prisoners of war are released (**Mar. 4**). Official cease-fire accepted and signed (**April 6**). 532,000 U.S. forces served in Operation Desert Storm. There were a total of 148 U.S. battle deaths during the Gulf War, 145 nonbattle deaths, and 467 wounded in action.

Hubble Space Telescope

Lech Walesa
(1943– )

Toni Morrison
(1931– )

Ruth Bader Ginsburg
(1933– )

troops seize president in uprising (**Sept. 30**). U.S. suspends assistance to Haiti (**Oct. 1**). Professor Anita Hill accuses Judge Clarence Thomas of sexual harassment (**Oct. 6**); Senate, 52–48, confirms Thomas for Supreme Court after stormy hearings (**Oct. 15**). Israel and Soviet Union resume relations after 24 years (**Oct. 18**). U.S. indicts two Libyans in 1988 bombing of Pan Am Flight 103 over Lockerbie, Scotland (**Nov. 15**). Anglican envoy Terry Waite and U.S. Prof. Thomas M. Sutherland freed by Lebanese (**Nov. 18**). Last three U.S. hostages freed in Lebanon (**Dec. 2–4**). Soviet Union breaks up after President Gorbachev's resignation; constituent republics form Commonwealth of Independent States (**Dec. 25**).

**1992** Yugoslav Federation broken up (**Jan. 15**). Bush and Yeltsin proclaim formal end to cold war (**Feb. 1**). U.S. lifts trade sanctions against China (**Feb. 21**). U.S. recognizes three former Yugoslav republics (**April 7**). Gen. Noriega, former Panama leader, convicted in U.S. court (**April 9**). Four police officers acquitted in Los Angeles beating of Rodney King; rioting erupts in South-Central Los Angeles (**April 29** *et seq.*). Caspar W. Weinberger indicted in Iran-Contra affair (**June 16**). Last Western hostages freed in Lebanon (**June 17**). Supreme Court reaffirms right to abortion (**June 29**). Democrats nominate Bill Clinton and Al Gore (**July 1**). Gen. Noriega sentenced to 40 years on drug charges (**July 10**). Court clears *Exxon Valdez* skipper (**July 10**). Israeli Parliament approves Yitzhak Rabin's coalition government, dominated by Labor Party (**July 13**). Police officers acquitted in April on criminal charges in Rodney King beating are indicted on federal civil rights charges (**Aug. 5**). North American trade compact announced (**Aug. 12**). Republicans renominate Bush and Quayle (**Aug. 20**). UN expels Serbian-dominated Yugoslavia (**Sept. 22**). Senate ratifies second Strategic Arms Limitation Treaty (**Oct. 1**). Top Japanese leader, Shin Kanemaru, resigns in scandal (**Oct. 14**). Bill Clinton elected president, Al Gore vice president; Democrats keep control of Congress (**Nov. 3**). Russian Parliament approves START treaty (**Nov. 4**). U.S. forces leave Philippines, ending nearly a century of American military presence (**Nov. 24**). Czechoslovak Parliament approves separation into two nations (**Nov. 25**). UN approves U.S.-led force to guard food for Somalia (**Dec. 3**). Prince and Princess of Wales agree to separate (**Dec. 9**). Bush pardons former Reagan administration officials involved in Iran-Contra affair (**Dec. 24**).

**1993** Vaclav Havel elected as Czech president (**Jan. 26**). Clinton agrees to compromise on military's ban on homosexuals (**Jan. 29**). U.S. begins airlift of supplies to besieged Bosnia towns (**Feb. 28**). Federal agents besiege Texas Branch Davidian religious cult after six are killed in raid (**March 1** *et seq.*). Five arrested, sixth sought in bombing of World Trade Center in New York (**March 29**). Two police officers convicted on federal civil rights charges in Rodney King beating (**April 17**); sentenced **Aug. 4**. Fire kills 72 as cult standoff in Texas ends with federal assault (**April 19**). President of Sri Lanka assassinated (**May 1**). British Commons approves European unity pact (**May 20**). Twenty-two UN troops killed in Somalia (**June 5**). Ruth Bader Ginsburg appointed to Supreme Court (**June 14**). Iraq accepts UN weapons monitoring (**July 19**). Vincent W. Foster, Jr., senior White House lawyer, commits suicide (**July 22**). Midwest flood damage expected to exceed $10 billion (**July 24**). Israeli-Palestinian accord reached (**Aug. 28**). U.S. agents blamed in Waco, Tex., siege (**Oct. 1**). Yeltsin's forces crush revolt in Russian Parliament (**Oct. 4** *et seq.*). China breaks nuclear test moratorium (**Oct. 5**). Canada's opposition Liberal Party regains power in landslide (**Oct. 25**). Europe's Maastricht Treaty takes effect, creating European Union (**Nov. 1**). Jean Chretien sworn in as Canada's 20th prime minister (**Nov. 4**). House of Representatives approves North American Free Trade Agreement (**Nov. 17**); Senate follows (**Nov. 21**). South Africa adopts majority rule constitution (**Nov. 18**). Clinton signs Brady bill regulating firearms purchases (**Nov. 30**). Toni Morrison wins Nobel prize for literature.

**1994** Serbs' heavy weapons pound Sarajevo (**Jan. 5–6**). Olympic figure skater Nancy Kerrigan attacked (**Jan. 6**); three arrested in attack (**Jan. 13**). Major earthquake jolts Los Angeles; 51 dead (**Jan. 17** *et seq.*). Clinton ends trade embargo on Vietnam (**Feb. 9**). Aldrich Ames, high C.I.A. official, charged with spying for Soviets (**Feb. 22**). Four convicted in World Trade Center bombing (**March 4**). Mexican presidential candidate assassinated (**March 23**). Rwandan genocide of Tutsis by Hutus begins; estimated 800,000 slaughtered in c. 100 days (**April 6**). South Africa holds first interracial national election (**April 29**);

Nelson Mandela elected president. Israel and Palestinians sign accord **(May 4)**. Clinton accused of sexual harassment while governor of Arkansas **(May 6)**. Congress votes protection for women's health clinics **(May 12)**. O. J. Simpson arrested in killings of wife, Nicole Brown Simpson, and friend, Ronald Goldman **(June 18)**. Supreme Court approves limit on abortion protests **(June 30)**. Senate confirms Stephen G. Breyer for Supreme Court **(July 29)**. Women's health clinic doctor shot dead outside Florida clinic **(July 29)**. Major league baseball players strike **(Aug. 13)**. "Carlos the Jackal," international terrorist, captured **(Aug. 15)**. IRA declares cease-fire in Northern Ireland **(Aug. 31)**. Small plane crashes into White House **(Sept. 12)**. Baseball owners end season and cancel World Series **(Sept. 14)**. Powerful earthquake strikes Japan **(Oct. 4)**. Aristide returns to joyous Haiti **(Oct. 4)**. U.S. sends forces to Persian Gulf **(Oct. 7)**. Ulster Protestants declare cease-fire **(Oct. 13)**. Israel and Jordan sign peace treaty **(Oct. 17)**. Reagan, 83, reveals he has Alzheimer's disease **(Nov. 6)**. G.O.P. wins control of House and Senate **(Nov. 8)**. Aristide forms Haitian government with prime minister and full cabinet **(Nov. 9)**. Clinton orders Bosnian arms embargo ended **(Nov. 10)**. Newt Gingrich named House Speaker **(Dec. 5)**. Bentsen resigns as Treasury Secretary **(Dec. 6)**. Russians attack secessionist Republic of Chechnya **(Dec. 11** *et seq.***)**. John Salvi kills two at Massachusetts Planned Parenthood clinic **(Dec. 30)**.

Nelson Mandela
(1918– )

**1995**   Republicans take control of Congress **(Jan. 4)**. More than 5,000 dead in Japanese earthquake **(Jan. 17** *et seq.***)**. Criminal trial of O. J. Simpson opens in California **(Jan. 24)**. U.S. rescues Mexico's economy with $20-billion aid program **(Feb. 21)**. Senate rejects balanced-budget amendment **(March 2)**. Nerve gas attack in Tokyo subway kills eight and injures thousands. The Aum Shinrikyo ("Supreme Truth") cult is to blame **(March 20)**. Major League Baseball strike ends **(April 2)**. Appeals court upholds woman's plea to enter Citadel military academy **(April 13)**. UN Council votes easier sanctions for Iraq **(April 14)**. Scores killed as terrorist's car bomb blows up block-long Oklahoma City federal building **(April 19)**; Timothy McVeigh, 27, Army veteran, arrested as suspect **(April 21)**; authorities seek second suspect, link right-wing paramilitary groups to bombing **(April 22)**. Death toll 2,000 in Rwanda massacre **(April 22)**. Fighting escalates in Bosnia and Croatia **(May 1)**. U.S. shuttle docks with Russian space station **(June 27)**. F.B.I. suspends four in Idaho siege inquiry **(Aug. 11)**. France explodes nuclear device in Pacific; wide protests ensue **(Sept. 5)**. Senator Bob Packwood of Oregon resigns under pressure for sexual and official misconduct **(Sept. 6)**. Israelis and Palestinians agree on transferring West Bank to Arabs **(Sept. 24)**. Los Angeles jury finds O. J. Simpson not guilty of murder charges **(Oct. 3)**. Pope John Paul II visits U.S. on whirlwind tour **(Oct. 4–8)**. Warring parties agree on cease-fire in Bosnia **(Oct. 5)**. Million Man March draws hundreds of thousands of black men to capital **(Oct. 16)**. Quebec narrowly rejects independence from Canada **(Oct. 30)**. Israeli prime minister Yitzhak Rabin slain by Jewish extremist at peace rally **(Nov. 4)**. U.S. servicemen admit rape of Japanese schoolgirl in Okinawa **(Nov. 7)**. Nigeria hangs writer Ken Saro-Wiwa and eight other minority rights advocates **(Nov. 10)**. Irish voters approve end to constitutional ban on divorce **(Nov. 24)**. Combatants sign Bosnia peace treaty **(Dec. 14)**. House move stalls Congress while Clinton negotiations to avert government shutdown **(Dec. 20)**. Seamus Heaney wins Nobel prize for literature.

Jean-Bertrand Aristide
(1953– )

Dalai Lama
(1935– )

Yitzhak Rabin
(1922–1995)

**1996**   U.S. budget crisis in fourth month **(Jan. 3)**. Clinton approves resumption of many government operations **(Jan. 6)**. Senate ratifies major arms reduction treaty **(Jan. 26)**. France announces end to nuclear tests **(Jan. 29)**. At least 73 dead in Sri Lankan suicide bombing **(Feb. 1)**. Suicide bombers kill 59 in Israel **(March 4)**. Bob Dole sweeps Republican primaries **(March 5)**. Britain alarmed by deadly cow disease **(March 20** *et seq.***)**. UN tribunal charges war crimes by Bosnian Muslims and Croats **(March 22)**. Commerce Secretary Ronald H. Brown killed in plane crash **(April 3)**. FBI arrests suspected Unabomber **(April 3)**. Clinton signs line-item veto bill **(April 9)**. President blocks ban on late-term abortions **(April 10)**. ValuJet crashes in Everglades; all 110 aboard killed **(May 11)**. Chechnya peace treaty signed **(May 27)**. Israel elects Benjamin Netanyahu as prime minister **(May 31)**. China agrees to world ban

Seamus Heaney
(1939– )

**Ella Fitzgerald
(1918–1996)**

**Madeleine Albright
(1937– )**

**Kofi Annan
(1938– )**

**Hale-Bopp Comet**

**Princess Diana
(1961–1997)**

on atomic testing **(June 6)**. Leaders in Balkans sign accord on arms limits **(June 14)**. Jazz great Ella Fitzgerald dies **(June 15)**. Truck bomb kills 19 at U.S. base in Saudi Arabia **(June 25)**. Boris Yeltsin is reelected in Russian election **(July 3)**. Prince Charles and Princess Diana agree on divorce **(July 12)**. 747 airliner crashes in Atlantic off Long Island; all 230 aboard perish **(July 17)**. Bomb mars Summer Olympic games in Atlanta **(July 25)**. Clinton signs bill to raise minimum wage **(Aug. 2)**. Congress passes welfare reform bill **(Aug. 2)**; approved by Clinton **(Aug. 22)**. Republican convention opens in San Diego **(Aug. 12)**; Bob Dole and Jack Kemp nominated **(Aug. 14)**. Democrats convene in Chicago **(Aug. 26)**. Iraqis strike at Kurdish enclave **(Aug. 31)**; after warning, U.S. attacks Iraq's southern air defenses **(Sept. 2–3)**; Iraq halts attacks on U.S. planes enforcing flight exclusion zones in north and south **(Sept. 13)**. Violence flares in Jerusalem over Israel opening tourist tunnel **(Sept. 24)**. Taliban Muslim fundamentalists capture Afghan capital **(Sept. 27)**. Ethnic violence breaks out in Zairian refugee camps **(Oct. 13)**; thousands of refugees from Rwanda and Burundi abandon camps **(Oct. 21)**. Clinton-Gore ticket wins national election; Republicans retain control of Congress **(Nov. 5)**. Mid-air collision in India kills 342 **(Nov. 12)**. Texaco settles racial bias suit **(Nov. 15)**. Hundreds of thousands of Hutu refugees return to Rwanda **(Nov. 15–18)**. Clinton appoints Madeleine Albright as first female U.S. secretary of state **(Dec. 5)**. Kofi Annan named UN secretary-general **(Dec. 13)**. FBI agent charged with spying for Moscow **(Dec. 18)**. Thousands march in Belgrade in continuing protest against president's annulment of election results **(Dec. 26)**.

**1997**    Two Hutu sentenced to death in Rwandan genocide **(Jan. 3)**. Floods cause wide damage in U.S. West **(Jan. 5)**. Newt Gingrich reelected as House Speaker **(Jan. 7)**. Hebron agreement signed; Israel gives up large part of West Bank city of Hebron **(Jan. 16)**. U.S. shuttle joins Russian space station **(Jan. 17)**. Gingrich found guilty of ethics violations **(Jan. 17)**. President Clinton starts second term **(Jan. 20)**. U.S., U.K., and France agree to freeze Nazis' gold loot **(Feb. 3)**. O. J. Simpson found liable in civil suit **(Feb. 5)**. Deng Xiaoping, Chinese leader, dead at 92 **(Feb. 19)**. Israeli government approves establishment of Jewish settlement in East Jerusalem, a setback in Middle East peace process **(Feb. 26)**. Tornadoes wreak havoc in Arkansas, Ohio, and Kentucky **(March 3)**. State of anarchy in Albania when third of population loses savings because of pyramid schemes **(March 13)**. Hale-Bopp comet is the closest it will be to Earth until 4397 **(March 22)**. Heaven's Gate cult members commit mass suicide in California **(March 27)**. U.S. Appeals Court upholds California ban on affirmative action **(April 8)**. U.S. judge upholds California marijuana law **(April 11)**. Tiger Woods breaks multiple records in Masters golf tournament **(April 13)**. Fire kills 300 pilgrims outside Mecca **(April 15)**. Senate, 74–26, approves chemical-weapons treaty **(April 24)**. Thousands flee North Dakota flood **(April 27)**. Sergeant Major of the Army, Gene C. McKinney, charged in sex cases **(May 7)**. Russian president Yeltsin signs Chechnya peace treaty **(May 12)**. U.S.-Russian spaceship linkup in orbit ends **(May 21)**. U.S. jobless rate for May reported 4.8%, lowest since 1973 **(June 6)**. European Union bolsters currency merger **(June 16)**. Congress votes major tax cuts **(June 26)**. Hong Kong returns to Chinese rule **(June 30)**. U.S. spacecraft begins exploration of Mars **(July 4)**. Andrew Cunanan murders fashion designer Gianni Versace **(July 15)**. Khmer Rouge hold trial of longtime leader Pol Pot **(July 25)**. White House and GOP agree on measure to balance budget **(July 28)**. U.S. spacecraft transmits thousands of pictures from Mars **(Aug. 8)**. Clinton exercises new line-item veto **(Aug. 11)**. Timothy J. McVeigh sentenced to death for Oklahoma City bombing **(Aug. 14)**. Princess Diana, 36, killed with two others in Paris car crash **(Aug. 31)**. Three Islamic suicide bombers kill four persons in Jerusalem **(Sept. 4)**. Mother Teresa dead at 87 **(Sept. 5)**. Swiss plan first payment to Holocaust victims **(Sept. 17)**. Militant Taliban leaders seize Kabul **(Sept. 27)**. Iraq expels all U.S. members of UN arms-inspection team **(Oct. 29)**. GOP victorious in off-year elections **(Nov. 4)**. Pakistani convicted in 1993 CIA killings **(Nov. 10)**. Two convicted in New York World Trade Center bombing **(Nov. 12)**. Egyptian Islamic militants kill 62 at Luxor tourist site **(Nov. 17)**. FBI ends 16-month investigation of crash of Flight 800 off Long Island; denies sabotage **(Nov. 18)**. European Union plans to admit six nations **(Dec. 13)**. U.S. company launches first commercial spy satellite **(Dec. 24)**. Paris court convicts "Carlos the Jackal" of murder **(Dec. 24)**.

**1998** Ramzi Ahmed Yousef sentenced to life for 1993 World Trade Center bombing **(Jan. 9).** Pope John Paul II visits Cuba **(Jan. 21–25).** President accused in White House sex scandal; denies allegations of affair with White House intern, Monica Lewinsky **(Jan. 21** *et seq.***).** President outlines first balanced budget in 30 years **(Feb. 3).** U.S. plane cuts ski cable in Italy and sends car plunging; 20 killed **(Feb. 3).** Thousands dead in Afghanistan quake **(Feb. 4** *et seq.***).** U.S. court rules line-item veto unconstitutional **(Feb. 12).** Serbs battle ethnic Albanians in Kosovo **(March 5** *et seq.***).** U.S. drops condemnation of China's human rights record **(March 13).** Hindu nationalist Vajpayee becomes India's prime minister **(March 19).** FDA approves Viagra, male impotence drug **(March 27).** Federal judge in Arkansas throws out Paula Jones case **(April 1).** Landmark peace settlement, the Good Friday Accord, reached in Northern Ireland **(April 10).** U.S. trade deficit biggest in decade **(April 17).** Europeans agree on single currency, the euro **(May 3).** Unabomber, Theodore Kaczynski, sentenced to four life terms **(May 4).** India conducts three atomic tests despite worldwide disapproval **(May 11, 13).** Indonesian dictator Suharto steps down after 32 years in power **(May 21).** Pakistan stages five nuclear tests in response to India's **(May 29, 30).** Serbs renew attack on Kosovo rebels **(June 1).** Life sentence meted out to Terry Nichols, convicted in Oklahoma City bombing fatal to 168 **(June 4).** Nigerian dictator Sani Abacha dies **(June 8).** Congress votes to overhaul IRS **(July 9).** Iraq ends cooperation with UN arms inspectors **(Aug. 5).** U.S. embassies in Kenya and Tanzania bombed **(Aug. 7).** Clinton admits to affair with White House intern in televised address to nation **(Aug. 17).** Russia fights to avert financial collapse **(Aug. 17).** U.S. cruise missiles hit suspected terrorist bases in Sudan and Afghanistan **(Aug. 20).** North Korea fires missile across Japan **(Aug. 31).** Swissair jet crashes; kills 229 **(Sept. 2).** Starr Report by independent counsel outlines case for impeachment proceedings against president **(Sept. 11).** Senate sustains veto of bill to outlaw late-term abortions **(Sept. 18).** Iran lifts death threat against Salman Rushdie **(Sept. 24).** German chancellor Helmut Kohl defeated by Gerhard Schröder **(Sept. 27).** U.S. budget surplus largest in three decades **(Oct. 5).** Matthew Shepard, gay Wyoming student, fatally beaten in hate crime **(Oct. 6).** NATO, on verge of air strikes, reaches settlement with Milosevic on Kosovo **(Oct. 12).** Former Chilean dictator Pinochet arrested in London **(Oct. 16).** Wye Mills Agreement between Netanyahu and Arafat moves Middle East peace talks forward **(Oct. 23).** More than 10,000 die in Central American hurricane, Mitch **(Nov. 1).** Democrats unexpectedly gain five House seats in national election; Republicans keep control of House and Senate **(Nov. 3).** House Speaker Gingrich to step down **(Nov. 9).** House panel drafts impeachment charges; votes along party lines to approve four articles **(Dec. 11–12).** Clinton orders air strikes on Iraq **(Dec. 16–19).** House impeaches President Clinton along party lines on two charges, perjury and obstruction of justice **(Dec. 19).**

**1999** U.S. agrees to ease restrictions on Cuba **(Jan. 4).** Dennis Hastert elected to replace Newt Gingrich as Speaker of the House **(Jan. 6).** NBA ends 191-day labor dispute **(Jan. 6).** Michael Jordan retires from the Chicago Bulls **(Jan. 13).** International Olympic Committee expels six members as bribery scandal widens **(Jan. 24).** King Hussein of Jordan dies **(Feb. 7).** Senate acquits President Clinton of impeachment charges **(Feb. 12).** Gen. Olusegun Obasanjo elected president of Nigeria **(Feb. 28).** First nonstop balloon flight around world completed in 20 days by Bertrand Piccard [?????????] and Brian Jones (??) (??????? 1–20). Marine pilot acquitted in killing of 20 in 1998 Italian ski gondola accident; Italians outraged **(March 4).** U.S. accuses China of stealing nuclear secrets **(March 5).** Joe DiMaggio dies at age 81 **(March 8).** Czech Republic, Poland, and Hungary join NATO **(March 12).** NATO launches air strikes on Serbia to end attacks against ethnic Albanians in Kosovo **(March 24).** Dr. Jack Kevorkian convicted of second-degree murder in assisted-suicide case **(March 26).** "Melissa" computer virus spreads through the Internet **(March 27).** Libya hands over two suspects in 1988 Pan Am jet bombing **(April 5).** Two Colo. students go on shooting spree in Columbine High School, killing 15, including themselves **(April 20).** NATO bombs mistakenly hit Chinese embassy in Belgrade **(May 7).** Citadel graduates its first woman **(May 8).** Crime rate in U.S. falls for seventh consecutive year **(May 16).** Ehud Barak defeats Benjamin Netanyahu in Israeli prime minister election **(May 17).** U.S. inspects suspected nuclear weapons site in North Korea, finds nothing **(May 20–24).** Serbs sign agreement to pull

Mother Teresa
(1910–1997)

Euro 100

Mars Sojourner Rover

William J. Clinton
(1946– )

**Boris Yeltsin
(1931– )**

**Eileen Collins
(1956– )**

**George W. Bush
(1946– )**

troops out of Kosovo after 11 weeks of NATO air attacks (**June 9**). Nelson Mandela retires as president of South Africa; succeeded by Thabo Mbeki (**June 16**). Britain's Prince Edward marries Sophie Rhys-Jones (**June 19**). Kurd leader Abdullah Ocalan sentenced to death for treason in Turkey (**June 29**). White supremacist goes on shooting spree in Midwest, killing three including self and wounding eight (**July 2–5**). U.S. soccer team tops China for women's World Cup (**July 10**). Taiwanese leader Lee Teng-hui challenges "One China" policy (**July 11**). Serial killer Rafael Reséndez-Ramirez surrenders himself to U.S. authorities (**July 13**). John F. Kennedy, Jr., wife Carolyn Bessette Kennedy, and sister-in-law Lauren Bessette killed in plane crash off coast of Martha's Vineyard (**July 16**). Col. Eileen Collins becomes first female to head a space shuttle mission (**July 16**). Falun Gong meditation sect banned by Chinese government (**July 22**). Day-trader kills 9 and wounds 13 in two Atlanta brokerage offices before committing suicide (**July 29**). Yeltsin replaces Prime Minister Stepashin with Vladimir Putin in fourth government shakeup in 17 months (**Aug. 9**). Islamic militants declare independence for Dagestan and announce holy war against Russia (**Aug. 10**). White supremacist opens fire at Jewish community center in LA, wounding five and killing one as he flees (**Aug. 10**). More than 17,000 people die in 7.4 earthquake in Turkey (**Aug. 17**). Attorney General Janet Reno reopens investigation of 1993 Waco, Tex., stand-off (**Aug. 25**). People of East Timor vote for independence from Indonesia (**Aug. 31**). Israeli prime minister Ehud Barak and PLO leader Yasir Arafat announce peace accord (**Sept. 4**). Larry Gene Ashbrook goes on rampage in Tex. church, killing seven and himself (**Sept. 15**). NASA accidentally loses $125 million spacecraft as it orbits Mars (**Sept. 23**). Dozens of people exposed to radiation in Japan's worst nuclear accident (**Sept. 30**). Russia sends ground troops to Chechnya as conflict with Islamic militants intensifies (**Oct. 1**). World population reaches six billion milestone (**Oct. 11**). Military coup led by Gen. Pervez Musharraf overthrows Pakistani government (**Oct. 12**). Tobacco companies admit to harm caused by cigarette smoking (**Oct. 13**). Senate rejects 1996 nuclear test-ban treaty; international leaders upset by U.S. stand (**Oct. 13**). Indonesia elects Muslim leader Abdurrahman Wahid president (**Oct. 20**). Pro golfer Payne Stewart and five others killed in plane crash (**Oct. 25**). EgyptAir flight crashes over Atlantic, killing all 217 on board (**Oct. 31**). Judge finds Microsoft to be a monopoly (**Nov. 5**). U.S. and China reach landmark trade agreement (**Nov. 15**). China launches first spacecraft (**Nov. 21**). Five-year-old Cuban refugee Elián González gets caught in politically charged custody battle (**Nov. 25**). World Trade Organization conference disrupted by violent protests in Seattle (**Nov. 29** *et seq.*). New Northern Ireland government begins self-rule for first time in 25 years (**Dec. 2**). Muslim terrorists hijack Indian Airlines jet with 189 on board (**Dec. 24**).

**2000** Socialist president, Ricardo Lagos, elected in Chile (**Jan. 16**). George W. Bush and Al Gore take Iowa caucuses in U.S. presidential race (**Jan. 22**). Austria at center of European dispute after conservative People's Party forms coalition with the far-right Freedom Party, headed by xenophobe Jörg Haider (**Feb. 3**). First Lady Hillary Clinton officially enters N.Y. Senate race (**Feb. 6**). Hijackers seize Afghan plane; release hostages in Stansted, England (**Feb. 6–12**). Britain ends self-rule in Northern Ireland after Irish Republican Army misses disarmament deadline (**Feb. 11**). NEAR spacecraft becomes first to orbit an asteroid (**Feb. 14**). Wary investors cause stock plunge; beginning of the end of the Internet stock boom (**Feb. 25**). Reformists win control of Iranian parliament for first time since 1979 Islamic revolution (**Feb. 26**). Gun maker Smith & Wesson limits the manufacture and distribution of handguns in light of lawsuits (**March 17**). Mass murder or suicide of hundreds in Ugandan doomsday cult (**March 18**). Acting Russian president Vladimir V. Putin formally chosen for post (**March 25**). Microsoft loses antitrust suit; appeal expected (**April 3**). Controversial Osprey plane crash kills 19 marines (**April 8**). Cuban boy Elián González reunited with father after federal raid of Miami relatives' home (**April 22**). Vermont approves same-sex unions (**April 25**). "I love you" virus disrupts computers worldwide (**May 4**). South Carolina removes Confederate battle flag from capitol dome (**May 18**). Chile ends Augusto Pinochet's immunity, clearing way for trial on murder and torture charges during years as dictator (**May 24**). Israeli troops withdraw from Lebanese security zone after 22 years of occupation (**May 24**). Former Indonesian president Suharto under house arrest, charged with corruption and abuse of power (**May 29**). Britain restores parliamentary powers to Northern Ireland after Sinn Fein agrees to disarm (**June 4**). Presidents of North and South Korea sign peace accord, ending half-century of antagonism (**June 15**). British find 58 bodies of illegal Asian immigrants suffocated in Dutch truck that transported them (**June 20**). Elián González returns to Cuba with father (**June 23**). U.S. navy resumes shelling exercises of Puerto Rico's Vieques Island, used as a training site (**June 25**). Human genome deciphered; expected to revolutionize the practice of medicine (**June 26**). Iraq believed to resume missile program (**June 30**). Vicente Fox Quesada elected president of Mexico (**July 2**). Bashar al-Assad succeeds late father, Hafez al-Assad, as Syrian president (**July 10**). Concorde crash kills 113 near Paris (**July 25**). Republican convention picks Texas governor George W. Bush as presidential candidate; Dick Cheney for vice presidential spot (**Aug. 2**). Democratic convention selects Vice President Al Gore and Sen. Joseph I. Lieberman to head ticket (**Aug. 14**). Los Alamos scientist Wen Ho Lee, accused of stealing sensitive nuclear weapons data, freed after serving nine months in prison (**Sept. 13**). Olympic Games open in Australia (**Sept. 15**). Six-year Whitewater investigation of the Clintons ends without indictments (**Sept. 20**). Yugoslav opposition claims victory; incumbent Slobodan Milosevic denies results (**Sept. 25**). Danish voters reject euro (**Sept. 26**). Abortion pill, RU-486, wins U.S. approval (**Sept. 28**). Palestinians and Israelis clash, spurred by visit of right-wing Israeli leader Ariel Sharon to a joint Jewish/Muslim holy site; "Al Aksa intifada" continues unabated (**Sept. 30** *et seq.*). Nationwide uprising overthrows Yugoslavian president Milosevic (**Oct. 5**). Vojislav Kostunica sworn in as Yugoslav president (**Oct. 7**). 17 U.S. sailors on navy destroyer *Cole* die in Yemen terrorist explosion (**Oct. 12**). U.S. presidential election closest in decades; Bush's slim lead in Florida leads to automatic recount in that state (**Nov. 7–8**). Republicans file federal suit to block manual recount of Florida presidential election ballots sought by Democrats (**Nov. 11**). Philippine president Joseph Estrada impeached after receiving gambling payoffs (**Nov. 13**). Florida Supreme Court rules hand count of presidential ballots may continue (**Nov. 21**). Global warming talks collapse at Hague conference (**Nov. 25**). Florida Secretary of State Katherine Harris certifies Bush as winner by 537 votes (**Nov. 26**). Mad Cow disease alarms Europe (**Nov. 30** *et seq.*). Israeli prime minister Ehud Barak resigns (**Dec. 9**). U.S. Supreme Court orders halt to manual recount of presidential votes in Florida (**Dec. 9**). Supreme Court seals Bush victory by 5–4; rules there can be no further recounting (**Dec. 12**).

**2001** Congo president Laurent Kabila assassinated by bodyguard (**Jan. 16**). In final days of presidency, Bill Clinton issues controversial pardons, including one for Marc Rich, billionaire fugitive financier (**Jan. 20**). George W. Bush is sworn in as 43rd president (**Jan. 20**). Earthquake kills thousands in India (**Jan. 26** *et seq.*). Libyan convicted in Flight 103 bombing over Lockerbie, Scotland (**Jan. 31**). Right-winger Ariel Sharon wins election in Israel (**Feb. 6**). U.S. submarine *Greeneville* sinks Japanese fishing boat, killing 9 (**Feb. 9**). FBI agent Robert Hanssen is charged with spying for Russia for 15 years (**Feb. 20**). The long-simmering resentment of Macedonia's ethnic Albanians erupts into violence (**March 15** *et seq.*). British livestock epidemic, foot-and-mouth disease, reaches crisis levels (**March 23**). Bush abandons global-warming treaty (Kyoto Protocol), angering European leaders (March 30; *et seq.*). A spy plane and a Chinese jet collide. The 24 crew members of the U.S. plane are detained for 11 days; U.S. issues a formal statement of regret (**April 2** *et seq.*). Race riots in Cincinnati continue for several days following a shooting of an unarmed black man by a white police officer (**April 7** *et seq.*). U.S. millionaire Dennis Tito becomes first space tourist, visiting the International Space Station aboard a Russian booster (**April 28**). Former Klansman Thomas E. Blanton convicted of 1963 murder of four black girls in Birmingham, Ala. (**May 1**). After a Palestinian suicide bomber kills 5 and wounds more than 100 in a Netanya shopping mall, Israeli warplanes retaliate by bombing West Bank and Gaza strip (**May 18**). Four are declared guilty in 1998 terrorist bombings of U.S. embassies in Kenya and Tanzania (**May 29**). Balance of the Senate shifts after Jim Jeffords of Vermont changes his party affiliation from Republican to Independent. The move strips Republicans of control of the Senate and gives Democrats the narrowest of majorities (50–49–1) (**June 5**). Bush signs new tax-cut law, cutting taxes by $1.35 trillion over

Vojislav Kostunica
(1944– )

Yasir Arafat
(1929– )

Ariel Sharon
(1928– )

**World Trade Center**

**Hamid Karzai
(1957– )**

11 years, the largest tax cut in 2 decades **(June 7)**. Mohammad Khatami, Iran's moderate president, is reelected in a landslide **(June 9)**. Oklahoma City bomber Timothy McVeigh executed **(June 11)**. Syrian forces evacuate Beirut area after decades of occupation **(June 19)**. Former Yugoslav president Slobodan Milosevic is delivered to UN tribunal in The Hague to await war-crimes trial **(June 29)**. Without U.S., 178 nations reach agreement on climate accord, which rescues, though dilutes, 1997 Kyoto Protocol **(July 23)**. Bush allows stem cell research, approving federal funds for studies using existing strains of stem cells **(Aug. 9)**. After six months of fighting, a peace agreement is signed between rebels and the Macedonian government **(Aug. 13)**. Budget surplus dwindles; some blame the slowing economy and the Bush tax cut **(Aug. 22)**. Terrorists attack United States. Hijackers ram jetliners into twin towers of New York City's World Trade Center and the Pentagon. A fourth hijacked plane crashes 80 mi outside of Pittsburgh. Toll of dead and injured in the thousands. Within days, Islamic militant Osama bin Laden and the al-Qaeda terrorist network are identified as the parties behind the attacks **(Sept. 11)**. Anthrax scare rivets nation, as anthrax-laced letters are sent to various media and government officials. Several die after handling the letters **(October 5 et seq.)**. In response to Sept. 11 terrorist attacks, U.S. and British forces launch bombing campaign against Taliban government and al-Qaeda terrorist camps in Afghanistan. Bombings continue on a daily basis **(Oct. 7 et seq.)**. Irish Republican Army announces that it has begun to dismantle its weapons arsenal, marking a dramatic leap forward in Northern Ireland peace process **(Oct. 23)**. Plane crash kills 260 in Queens, N.Y. **(Nov. 12)**. Afghani factions create a post-Taliban government **(Nov. 27)**. Enron Corp, one of world's largest energy companies, files bankruptcy **(Dec. 2)**. Israel condemns the Palestinian Authority as a "terror-supporting entity" and severs ties with leader Yasir Arafat following mounting violence against Israelis. The Israeli Army begins bombing Palestinian areas **(Dec. 4 et seq.)**. Taliban regime in Afghanistan collapses after two months of bombing by American warplanes and fighting by Northern Alliance ground troops **(Dec. 9)**. Hamid Karzai, new interim Afghan leader, is sworn in **(Dec. 22)**.

For 2002 chronology, *see* Current Events pp. 33-44.

## PICTURE CREDITS

The editors wish to thank the following organizations and individuals who have contributed illustrations to Headline History.
Agence France Press/Archive Photos: **Mao Zedong;** AIP Niels Bohr Library: **Marie Curie, Albert Einstein;** AMW Pressedienst/Archive Photos: **Nelson Mandela;** Archive Photos: **Richard Wagner, William Butler Yeats, Pablo Picasso, Anne Frank, Woody Guthrie, Robert Frost, William Faulkner, The Beatles, Mahatma Gandhi, Duke Ellington, Tennessee Williams, Toni Morrison, Seamus Heaney, Ella Fitzgerald, Lech Walesa, Princess Diana, Pope John Paul, Mother Teresa, Yitzhak Rabin, Malcolm X, William Rehnquist, Anwar Sadat;** Linda J. Barnes: **the Duomo in Florence;** British Information Services: **Margaret Thatcher;** Consolidated News/Archive Photos: **Jean-Bertrand Aristide;** Tina Diodati: **Aqueduct, Parthenon;** Embassy of the Philippines: **Corazon Aquino;** Embassy of Yugoslavia: **Vojislav Kostunica;** The French Consulate, Boston: **François Mitterrand;** Gerald R. Ford Library: **Gerald Ford;** Peter F. Harrington: **Stonehenge;** Erik Hjortshoj: **Pagoda;** Imapress/Archive Photos: **Boris Yeltsin;** INA/Reuters/Archive Photos: **Saddam Hussein;** John Fitzgerald Kennedy Library, Boston: **John F. Kennedy;** Priscilla Lee: **Dalai Lama;** Leo Baeck Inst./Archive Photos: **Sigmund Freud;** Jimmy Carter Library: **Jimmy Carter;** The Library of Congress Picture Collection: **Pocahontas, Taj Mahal, Edgar Allan Poe, Harriet Tubman, Walt Whitman, Dred Scott, Samuel Clemens (Mark Twain), Henri Matisse, W.E.B. Du Bois, Woodrow Wilson, Bessie** **Smith, Dorothea Lange, Amelia Earhart, Harry S. Truman, John H. Glenn, Jr., James H. Meredith, Betty Friedan, Richard Nixon, Lyndon B. Johnson;** Pete Maio: **Mesa Verde;** Muzammil Paha/Reuters/ Archive Photos: **Benazir Bhutto;** National Archives and Records Admin.: **Frederick Douglass, Harriet Beecher Stowe, Abraham Lincoln, Robert E. Lee, William Tecumseh Sherman, Chief Joseph, Benito Mussolini, Franklin Delano Roosevelt, Adolf Hitler, Winston Churchill, Atomic Bomb, Dwight D. Eisenhower, Rev. Martin Luther King, Jr.;** NASA: **Eileen Collins, Hubble Space Telescope;** NASA/JPL/Caltech: **Mars Sojourner Rover;** NOAA: **World Trade Center;** Novosti Photos: **Vladimir Lenin, Mikhail S. Gorbachev;** Elaine Ouellette: **Pantheon in Rome;** The Permanent Mission of India to the UN: **Indira Gandhi;** Permanent Mission of Islamic Republic of Iran to the UN: **Ayatollah Ruhollah Khomeini;** Renée Scott: **Celtic Cross, Mayan Pyramid;** The Republican National Committee: **Ronald Reagan, George Bush;** Kim Storm: **Egyptian Pyramid;** United Nations: **Dag Hammarskjöld, Fidel Castro, Kofi Annan, Hamid Karzai, Yasir Arafat, Ariel Sharon;** U.S. Army Photos: **Joseph Stalin, Yalta Conference, General Colin Powell;** U.S. State Department: **Madeleine Albright;** U.S. Supreme Court: **Ruth Bader Ginsburg, Thurgood Marshall, Sandra Day O'Connor;** Tasha Vincent: **Cathedral and Tower at Pisa, Chartres Cathedral, Michelangelo's David, Statue of Liberty;** The White House: **William J. Clinton, George W. Bush.**

# Their Modern Majesties

As a new millennium begins, Europe's ten surviving monarchies are more secure—and more popular—than ever before

**By Aisha Labi** TIME

In the 1950s, Egypt's King Farouk, on the verge of losing his throne, famously predicted that only five royal houses would survive the 20th century: Spades, Hearts, Diamonds, Clubs, and Windsor. His pessimism was understandable. Eastern Europe lay imprisoned behind the Iron Curtain, swaths of Western Europe were infatuated with socialism, fascism held sway in Spain under Franco, and, while some of Europe's monarchies continued to bask in the residual popularity they had earned as symbols of national resistance during World War II, their modern relevance seemed increasingly dubious. The Windsors, to be sure, remained paragons of popularity. At the very least they managed to keep busy, with even junior members of the family trekking off to distant reaches of the globe to represent the queen. But not every monarch had a growing Commonwealth over which to preside and, with Europe increasingly focused on integration and supranational cooperation, the long-term prognosis for a hereditary institution rooted in feudal society did not seem good.

Were he to set foot in Europe today, Farouk would be astounded by the robustness of the institution whose very survival he doubted. Europe has ten reigning monarchs—a clutch of kings, queens, princes, and a grand duke. Failed marriages and relentless tabloid scrutiny have eroded popular regard for the British royal family, but according to a 2002 poll, 70% of Britons still prefer a monarchy to a republic. Europe's two other female sovereigns command even higher approval ratings: around 80% for the Netherlands' Beatrix and her family and above 90% for Denmark's Margrethe II.

## Jubilant Jubilee

As Britain's Elizabeth marked the golden anniversary of her reign, there may have been less enthusiasm for British royalty than 50 years ago, when the accession of the glamorous young queen was heralded as the harbinger of a new Elizabethan Age than the enthusiastic outpouring of affection for the queen and her family during the jubilee celebrations surprised observers with their fervor—and the important thing is that both monarch and monarchy have endured.

In the Netherlands, the marriage in Feb. of the heir to the throne, Willem-Alexander, and his Argentinian girlfriend Maxima Zorreguieta prompted a frenzy reminiscent of the excitement that surrounded the 1981 wedding of Elizabeth's son Charles to Lady Diana Spencer. The May 2002 wedding of Norway's Princess Märtha Louise, though less grand than her brother Crown Prince Haakon's nuptials in August 2001, generated almost as much coverage. Even Europe's smallest monarchy, Monaco, whose scandal-prone royals are also among the most high-profile, has taken steps to guarantee its reigning family's future. An April 2, 2002, change to the constitution clarifies that the throne can pass from a reigning prince who dies without children to his siblings. This ensures that if 78-year-old Prince Rainier III's bachelor son Albert, 44, remains childless the Grimaldi clan will retain the throne through Albert's sisters, Caroline and Stephanie, and their seven children.

Even in countries that long ago relinquished royalty, the institution of monarchy is enjoying something of a comeback, and once-banished royals are flocking home. In 2001 ex-king Simeon of Bulgaria became prime minister of the country he had reigned over as a child, and the son of the last king of Yugoslavia returned to Belgrade to take up residence in the royal palace. In May 2002, the Italian Senate voted to overturn a constitutional provision barring male members of that country's exiled royal family, who fled in 1943 as the Mussolini regime they had supported was crumbling, from setting foot on Italian soil. The Savoys' chances of reclaiming their throne are remote, but given that Italy is one of the few European countries that actually have monarchist political parties, anything is possible.

## A Unifying Force

At the start of the 21st century, monarchs consistently outscore their nations' politicians in popularity polls. A new generation of photogenic young royals has come of age and is primed for the spotlight. The institution of monarchy, far from being an anachronistic relic, is finding new justifications: as a unifying force for increasingly diverse populations and as a national symbol at a time when other representations of identity—like border controls and currencies—are being subsumed in the larger unit of Europe. In many ways the Continent is in the midst of a royal revival.

Even as Europe has assumed some of the characteristics of a giant federal state—the euro has displaced the currencies of Belgium, Luxembourg, the Netherlands, and Spain, although the royal profile continues to be embossed on each country's version of the euro coin—the national monarchies have taken on an enhanced significance. "In step with economic and political integration and giving up passports, we Europeans will become more conscious about our origin and national characteristics," says University of Copenhagen historian Claus Bjorn. "In this context the monarchies are prime symbols."

British constitutional historian David Starkey believes that in an increasingly integrated Europe the concept of national identity assumes greater importance. "On the one hand there's this realization that you're disappearing into a rather weak Franco-German bouillabaisse called Europe, and on the other hand, passionate senses of local differences and identity remain." And, says Starkey, the very concept of national identity is itself in flux. "There's been a redefinition of nationhood, away from political self-assertion and conquest, toward a form of cultural and historical nationalism." As West European nationalism is reconceived as a nonbellicose, benign amalgam of history and culture, what better institution to serve as the incarnation of national identity than a symbolically powerful, substantively emasculated monarchy?

In 2002, Farouk's bet on the future of royalty appears to be a bust: In today's republican age, monarchy is not only surviving, it is thriving, through a deft combination of popular appeal, symbolic role playing, and occasional statecraft.    □

## Kingdoms and Monarchs of the World

| Country | Monarch | Type of monarchy |
|---|---|---|
| Bahrain | Sheik Hamad bin Isa al-Khalifa | Constitutional |
| Belgium | King Albert II | Constitutional |
| Bhutan | King Jigme Singye Wangchuck | Constitutional |
| Brunei | Sultan Haji Hassanal Bolkiah | Constitutional |
| Cambodia | King Norodom Sihanouk | Constitutional |
| Denmark | Queen Margrethe II | Constitutional |
| Japan | Emperor Akihito | Constitutional |
| Jordan | King Abdullah II | Constitutional |
| Kuwait | Sheik Jaber al-Ahmad al-Sabah | Constitutional |
| Lesotho | King Letsie III | Constitutional |
| Liechtenstein | Prince Hans Adam II | Constitutional |
| Luxembourg | Grand Duke Henri | Constitutional |
| Malaysia | King Syed Sirajuddin Syed Putra Jamalullail | Constitutional |

| Country | Monarch | Type of monarchy |
|---|---|---|
| Monaco | Prince Rainier III | Constitutional principality |
| Morocco | King Muhammad VI | Constitutional |
| Nepal | King Gyandendra Bir Bikram Shah Deva | Constitutional |
| Netherlands | Queen Beatrix | Constitutional |
| Norway | King Harald V | Constitutional |
| Oman | Sultan Qabus ibn Sa'id | Absolute |
| Qatar | Emir Sheik Hamad ibn Khalifa al-Thani | Traditional |
| Saudi Arabia | King Fahd bin 'Abdulaziz | Absolute |
| Spain | King Juan Carlos I | Parliamentary |
| Swaziland | King Mswati III | Absolute |
| Sweden | King Carl XVI Gustaf | Constitutional |
| Thailand | King Bhumibol Adulyadej | Constitutional |
| Tonga | King Taufa'ahau Tupou IV | Constitutional |
| United Kingdom | Queen Elizabeth II[1] | Constitutional[2] |

1. Queen Elizabeth II is also the Sovereign of 15 countries in the Commonwealth of Nations: Antigua and Barbuda, Australia, the Bahamas, Barbados, Belize, Canada, Grenada, Jamaica, New Zealand, Papua New Guinea, St. Kitts and Nevis, St. Lucia, St. Vincent and the Grenadines, the Solomon Islands, and Tuvalu. 2. Also parliamentary democracy.

## Territories, Colonies, and Dependencies
*Source: The World Factbook, 2001*

The following is a list of dependencies—territories under the jurisdiction of another country.

**Under Australian Jurisdiction (6)**
Ashmore and Cartier Islands
Christmas Island
Cocos (Keeling) Islands
Coral Sea Islands
Heard Island and McDonald Islands
Norfolk Island

**Under Danish Jurisdiction (2)**
Faeroe Islands
Greenland

**Under Dutch Jurisdiction (2)**
Aruba
Netherlands Antilles

**Under French Jurisdiction (16)**
Bassas da India
Clipperton Island
Europa Island
French Guiana
French Polynesia
French Southern and Antarctic Lands
Glorioso Islands
Guadeloupe
Juan de Nova Island

Martinique
Mayotte
New Caledonia
Réunion
Saint Pierre and Miquelon
Tromelin Island
Wallis and Futuna

**Under New Zealand Jurisdiction (3)**
Cook Islands
Niue
Tokelau

**Under Norwegian Jurisdiction (3)**
Bouvet Island
Jan Mayen
Svalbard

**Under UK Jurisdiction (15)**
Anguilla
Bermuda
British Indian Ocean Territory
British Virgin Islands
Cayman Islands
Falkland Islands

Gibraltar
Guernsey
Jersey
Isle of Man
Montserrat
Pitcairn Islands
Saint Helena
South Georgia and the South Sandwich Islands
Turks and Caicos Islands

**Under U.S. Jurisdiction (14)**
American Samoa
Baker Island
Guam
Howland Island
Jarvis Island
Johnston Atoll
Kingman Reef
Midway Islands
Navassa Island
Northern Mariana Islands
Palmyra Atoll
Puerto Rico
Virgin Islands
Wake Island

**Disputed Territories (6):** Antarctica, Gaza Strip, Paracel Islands, Spratly Islands, West Bank, Western Sahara

# A Profile of the World

*Source: The World Factbook, 2001*

## Geography

**Total area:** 510.072 million sq km (316.96 million sq mi).
**Land area:** 148.94 million sq km (92.55 million sq mi).
**Water area:** 361.132 million sq km (224.41 million sq mi).
**Coastline:** 356,000 km (221,208 mi) **Note:** 70.8% of the world is water, 29.2% is land.
**Terrain:** Highest elevation is Mt. Everest at 8,850 m (29,035 ft) and lowest land depression is the Dead Sea at –411 m (–1,349 ft) below sea level. The greatest ocean depth is the Mariana Trench at 10,924 m in the Pacific Ocean.
**Land use:** *Arable land:* 10%. *Permanent crops:* 1%. *Meadows and pastures:* 26%. *Forests and woodlands:* 32%. *Other:* 31% (1993 est.). *Irrigated land:* 2,481,250 sq km (1,541,849 sq mi).

## People

**Population:** 6,243,990,877 (Aug. 16, 2002, est. from U.S. Census Bureau)
**Growth rate:** 1.25% (2001 est.)
**Birth rate:** 21 births/1,000 population (2001 est.)
**Death rate:** 9 deaths/1,000 population (2001 est.)
**Sex ratio (at birth):** 1.05 male(s)/female (2001 est.)
**Infant mortality rate:** 53 deaths/1,000 live births (2001 est.)
**Life expectancy at birth:** *Total population:* 64 years. *Male:* 62 years. *Female:* 65 years (2001 est.)
**Total fertility rate:** 2.7 children born/woman (2001 est.)
**Literacy:** Age 15 and over who can read and write (1999 est., UN figs.) *Combined:* 79.4%. *Male:* 85.2%. *Female:* 73.6%.

## Government and Economy

**Political divisions:** 193 sovereign nations, 61 dependent areas, and 6 disputed territories.
**Economy:** Growth in global output (gross world product, GWP) rose to 4.8% in 2000 from 3.5% in 1999, despite continued low growth in Japan, severe financial difficulties in other East Asian countries, and widespread dislocations in several transition economies. The U.S. economy continued its remarkable sustained prosperity, growing at 5% in 2000, although growth slowed in fourth quarter 2000; the U.S. accounted for 23% of GWP. The EU economies grew at 3.3% and produced 20% of GWP. China, the second largest economy in the world, continued its strong growth and accounted for 10% of GWP. Japan grew at only 1.3% in 2000; its share in GWP is 7%.
**GWP:** (gross world product/purchasing power parity)— $43.6 trillion (2000 est.)
**GWP—real growth rate:** 4.8% (2000 est.)
**GWP/PPP—per capita:** $7,200 (2000 est.)
**Inflation rate (consumer price index):** *All countries:* 25%; developed countries 1% to 3% typically; developing countries 5% to 60% typically (2000 est.). *Note: National inflation rates vary widely.*
**Unemployment rate:** 30% combined unemployment and underemployment in many non-industrialized countries; developed countries typically 4%–12% unemployment (2000 est.)
**Exports:** $6 trillion (f.o.b., 2000 est.)
**Imports:** $6 trillion (c.i.f., 2000 est.)
**External debt:** $2 trillion for less developed nations (2000 est.)
**Military expenditures:** roughly 2% of GWP (2000 est.)

# Global Political, Economic, and Social Facts

From the UN's *Human Development Report 2002*

- In the last two decades, **political and civil rights** have improved substantially throughout the world: since 1980, 81 countries have taken significant steps in democratization, with 33 military regimes replaced by civilian governments. But of these fledgling democracies, only 47 are considered full democracies today.

- Only 82 countries, representing 57% of the world's population, are **fully democratic.**

- **Multiparty elections** are now held in 140 of the world's 193 countries.

- Countri governments 4b elected governments in the second half of the twentieth century.

- The proportion of the world's extremely poor fell from 29% in 1990 to 23% in 1999.

- In 1999, **2.8 billion people lived on less than $2 a day,** with 1.2 billion of them surviving on the margins of subsistence with less than $1 a day.

- In 2000, 1.1 billion people lacked access to **safe water,** and 2.4 billion did not have access to any form of improved sanitation services.

- Between 1970 and 2000 the under-5 **mortality rate** worldwide fell from 96 to 56 per 1,000 live births.

- Just 125 countries, with 62% of the world's population, have a free or partly **free press.**

- In 2001, **37 journalists died in the line of duty.** Another 118 were imprisoned. Worldwide, more than 600 journalists or their news organizations were intimidated or physically attacked.

- In 103 countries the proportion of **women in parliament** increased between 1995 and 2000, but around the world it still averages just 14%.

- Of the world's estimated 864 million illiterate adults, 544 million are women.

- Armed conflict continues to blight the lives of millions; since 1990, 3.6 million people have died as a result of **civil wars and ethnic violence,** more than 16 times the number killed in wars between states.

- **Civilians** have accounted for more than **90% of the casualties**—either injured or killed—in post-cold war conflicts.

- Ninety countries are affected by **landmines** and unexploded ordinance, with rough estimates of 15,000 to 20,000 mine victims each year.

# Country Statistics at a Glance

Country rankings of the type presented below cannot pretend to be definitive; instead they aspire only to provide the reader with an approximation of the high and low ends on a particular scale. Country data vary enormously depending on the sources, and the absence of reliable data on some countries requires their omission, which further skews the results.

| LARGEST COUNTRIES[1] (in sq mi)*: 2001 | | |
|---|---|---|
| (1) | Russia | 6,592,735 |
| (2) | Canada | 3,851,788 |
| (3) | United States | 3,794,083 |
| (4) | China | 3,705,386 |
| (5) | Brazil | 3,286,470 |
| (6) | Australia | 2,967,893 |
| (7) | India | 1,269,338 |
| (8) | Argentina | 1,068,296 |
| (9) | Kazakhstan | 1,049,150 |
| (10) | Sudan | 967,493 |

| SMALLEST COUNTRIES[1] (in sq mi): 2001 | | |
|---|---|---|
| (1) | Vatican City | 0.17 |
| (2) | Monaco | 0.75 |
| (3) | Nauru | 8.11 |
| (4) | Tuvalu | 10.0 |
| (5) | San Marino | 23.6 |
| (6) | Liechtenstein | 62.0 |
| (7) | Marshall Islands | 70.0 |
| (8) | St. Kitts & Nevis | 101.0 |
| (9) | Maldives | 116.0 |
| (10) | Malta | 122.0 |

| HIGHEST POPULATION DENSITY[2] (per sq mi): 2001 | | |
|---|---|---|
| (1) | Monaco | 42,485 |
| (2) | Singapore | 17,797 |
| (3) | Vatican City | 5,239 |
| (4) | Malta | 3,258 |
| (5) | Maldives | 2,764 |
| (6) | Bahrain | 2,742 |
| (7) | Bangladesh | 2,399 |
| (8) | Mauritius | 1,671 |
| (9) | Barbados | 1,666 |
| (10) | Taiwan | 1,623 |

| LOWEST POPULATION DENSITY[2] (per sq mi): 2001 | | |
|---|---|---|
| (1) | Western Sahara | 2.5 |
| (2) | Mongolia | 4.5 |
| (3) | Namibia | 5.7 |
| (4) | Australia | 6.6 |
| (5) | Suriname | 6.9 |
| | Botswana | 6.9 |
| (7) | Iceland | 7.0 |
| (8) | Mauritania | 7.1 |
| (9) | Libya | 7.9 |
| (10) | Canada | 8.3 |

| HIGHEST GDP PER CAPITA[3] (PPP in U.S. dollars): 2000 | | |
|---|---|---|
| (1) | Luxembourg | $36,400 |
| (2) | United States | 36,200 |
| (3) | San Marino | 32,000 |
| (4) | Switzerland | 28,600 |
| (5) | Norway | 27,700 |
| (6) | Monaco | 27,000 |
| (7) | Singapore | 26,500 |
| (8) | Denmark | 25,500 |
| (9) | Belgium | 25,300 |
| (10) | Austria | 25,000 |

| LOWEST GDP PER CAPITA[3] (PPP in U.S. dollars): 2000 | | |
|---|---|---|
| (1) | Sierra Leone | $510 |
| (2) | Congo, Dem. Rep. of | 600 |
| | Ethiopia | 600 |
| | Somalia | 600 |
| (5) | Eritrea | 710 |
| | Tanzania | 710 |
| (7) | Burundi | 720 |
| | Comoros | 720 |
| (9) | Afghanistan | 800 |
| | Madagascar | 800 |

| HIGHEST INFLATION:[3] 2000 | | |
|---|---|---|
| (1) | Congo Dem. Rep. of | 540.0% |
| (2) | Angola | 325.0 |
| (3) | Belarus | 200.0 |
| (4) | Iraq | 100.0 |
| (5) | Ecuador | 96.0 |
| (6) | Suriname | 78.0 |
| (7) | Zimbabwe | 60.0 |
| (8) | Romania | 45.7 |
| (9) | Yugoslavia | 42.0 |
| (10) | Uzbekistan | 40.0 |

| LOWEST INFLATION:[3] 2000 | | |
|---|---|---|
| (1) | Nauru | −6.0% |
| (2) | Oman | −0.8 |
| (3) | Japan | −0.7 |
| (4) | Vietnam | −0.6 |
| (5) | Fiji | 0.0 |
| | Lebanon | 0.0 |
| (7) | Israel | 0.1 |
| (8) | Cuba | 0.3 |
| (9) | China | 0.4 |
| (10) | Liechtenstein | 0.5 |
| | Saudi Arabia | 0.5 |

| HIGHEST INFANT MORTALITY RATE:[2] 2001 (deaths per 1,000 births) | | |
|---|---|---|
| (1) | Angola | 191.7 |
| (2) | Afghanistan | 144.8 |
| (3) | Sierra Leone | 144.4 |
| (4) | Mozambique | 138.6 |
| (5) | Liberia | 130.2 |
| (6) | Guinea | 127.0 |
| (7) | Somalia | 122.2 |
| | Niger | 122.2 |
| (9) | Malawi | 120.0 |
| (10) | Mali | 119.6 |

| LOWEST INFANT MORTALITY RATE:[2] 2001 (deaths per 1,000 births) | | |
|---|---|---|
| (1) | Sweden | 3.4 |
| (2) | Iceland | 3.5 |
| (3) | Singapore | 3.6 |
| (4) | Finland | 3.8 |
| | Japan | 3.8 |
| (6) | Norway | 3.9 |
| (7) | Andorra | 4.1 |
| (8) | Netherlands | 4.3 |
| (9) | Austria | 4.4 |
| | France | 4.4 |
| | Switzerland | 4.4 |

| HIGHEST LIFE EXPECTANCY[2] (in years): 2001 | | |
|---|---|---|
| (1) | Andorra | 83.5 |
| (2) | San Marino | 81.3 |
| (3) | Japan | 80.9 |
| (4) | Singapore | 80.3 |
| (5) | Australia | 80.0 |
| (6) | Switzerland | 79.9 |
| (7) | Sweden | 79.8 |
| (8) | Canada | 79.7 |
| | Iceland | 79.7 |
| (10) | Italy | 79.2 |

| LOWEST LIFE EXPECTANCY[2] (in years): 2001 | | |
|---|---|---|
| (1) | Botswana | 35.3 |
| (2) | Mozambique | 35.5 |
| (3) | Zimbabwe | 36.5 |
| (4) | Malawi | 36.6 |
| (5) | Swaziland | 37.0 |
| (6) | Zambia | 37.4 |
| (7) | Rwanda | 38.7 |
| (8) | Angola | 38.9 |
| (9) | Namibia | 39.0 |
| (10) | Niger | 41.9 |

NOTE: Only countries for which statistics were available in sources 1, 2, or 3 figure in these lists. *Sources:* 1. Information Please Database. 2. U.S. Census Bureau, International Database. 3. *The World Factbook, 2001.* *Size refers to the total area of a country, which includes the land area plus bodies of water.

## Total Population of the World by Decade, 1950–2040

### (historical and projected)

| Year | Total world population (mid-year figures) | Ten-year growth rate (%) | Year | Total world population (mid-year figures) | Ten-year growth rate (%) |
|------|-------------------------------------------|--------------------------|------|-------------------------------------------|--------------------------|
| 1950 | 2,556,000,053 | 18.9% | 2000 | 6,082,966,429 | 12.6% |
| 1960 | 3,039,451,023 | 22.0 | 2010* | 6,848,932,929 | 10.7 |
| 1970 | 3,706,618,163 | 20.2 | 2020* | 7,584,821,144 | 8.7 |
| 1980 | 4,453,831,714 | 18.5 | 2030* | 8,246,619,341 | 7.3 |
| 1990 | 5,278,639,789 | 15.2 | 2040* | 8,850,045,889 | 5.6 |

* Projected. *Source:* U.S. Census Bureau, International Database.

## World's 50 Most Populous Countries: 2002

| Rank | Country | Population | Rank | Country | Population | Rank | Country | Population |
|------|---------|-----------|------|---------|-----------|------|---------|-----------|
| 1. | China | 1,284,303,705 | 19. | Thailand | 62,354,402 | 35. | Canada | 31,902,268 |
| 2. | India | 1,045,845,226 | 20. | United Kingdom | 59,778,002 | 36. | Morocco | 31,167,783 |
| 3. | United States | 280,562,489 | 21. | France | 59,765,983 | 37. | Kenya | 31,138,735 |
| 4. | Indonesia | 232,073,071 | 22. | Italy | 57,715,625 | 38. | Peru | 27,949,639 |
| 5. | Brazil | 176,029,560 | 23. | Congo, Dem. | | 39. | Afghanistan | 27,755,775 |
| 6. | Pakistan | 147,663,429 | | Rep. of | 55,225,478 | 40. | Nepal | 25,873,917 |
| 7. | Russia | 144,978,573 | 24. | Ukraine | 48,396,470 | 41. | Uzbekistan | 25,563,441 |
| 8. | Bangladesh | 133,376,684 | 25. | Korea, South | 48,324,000 | 42. | Uganda | 24,699,073 |
| 9. | Nigeria | 129,934,911 | 26. | South Africa | 43,647,658 | 43. | Venezuela | 24,287,670 |
| 10. | Japan | 126,974,628 | 27. | Burma | | 44. | Iraq | 24,001,816 |
| 11. | Mexico | 103,400,165 | | (Myanmar) | 42,238,224 | 45. | Saudi Arabia | 23,513,330 |
| 12. | Philippines | 84,525,639 | 28. | Colombia | 41,008,227 | 46. | Malaysia | 22,662,365 |
| 13. | Germany | 83,251,851 | 29. | Spain | 40,077,100 | 47. | Taiwan | 22,548,009 |
| 14. | Vietnam | 81,098,416 | 30. | Poland | 38,625,478 | 48. | Romania | 22,317,730 |
| 15. | Egypt | 70,712,345 | 31. | Argentina | 37,812,817 | 49. | Korea, North | 22,224,195 |
| 16. | Ethiopia | 67,673,031 | 32. | Tanzania | 37,187,939 | 50. | Ghana | 20,244,154 |
| 17. | Turkey | 67,308,928 | 33. | Sudan | 37,090,298 | | | |
| 18. | Iran | 66,622,704 | 34. | Algeria | 32,277,942 | | | |

*Source:* U.S. Census Bureau, International Database.

## Most Populous Cities of the World

| Rank | City[1] | Population | Year[2] | Rank | City[1] | Population | Year[2] |
|------|---------|-----------|---------|------|---------|-----------|---------|
| 1. | Mumbai (Bombay), India | 11,914,398 | 2001c | 11. | Tokyo, Japan | 8,130,000 | 2000e |
| 2. | São Paulo, Brazil | 10,406,166 | 2000c | 12. | New York City, U.S. | 8,008,278 | 2000c |
| 3. | Seoul, South Korea | 9,981,649 | 2000e | 13. | London, United Kingdom | 7,285,000 | 1997e |
| 4. | Karachi, Pakistan | 9,863,000 | 1995e | 14. | Beijing, China | 6,970,000 | 1995e |
| 5. | Delhi, India | 9,817,439 | 2001c | 15. | Cairo, Egypt | 6,955,000 | 1995e |
| 6. | Shanghai, China | 9,220,000 | 1995c | 16. | Teheran, Iran | 6,758,845 | 1996c |
| 7. | Jakarta, Indonesia | 9,122,700 | 1995c | 17. | Bogotá, Colombia | 6,712,247 | 2001e |
| 8. | Mexico City, Mexico | 8,591,309 | 2000c | 18. | Bangkok, Thailand | 6,320,174 | 2000c |
| 9. | Moscow, Russia | 8,434,000 | 1996e | 19. | Lima, Peru | 6,214,100 | 1996e |
| 10. | Istanbul, Turkey | 8,141,163 | 1997c | 20. | Rio de Janeiro, Brazil | 5,850,544 | 2000c |

1. Refers to the city proper, as opposed to an urban agglomeration, which would also count the surrounding urban areas in the total. 2. Year of population count: "e" = estimated; "c" = census figure. *Source:* © Johan van der Heyden, GeoHive, 2002. Reprinted with permission. Web: www.geohive.com.

## Most Populous Urban Agglomerations[1]

| Name | Country | Est. population (in millions) | Name | Country | Est. population (in millions) |
|------|---------|-------------------------------|------|---------|-------------------------------|
| 1. Tokyo | Japan | 34.9 | 11. Cairo | Egypt | 15.1 |
| 2. New York | USA | 21.6 | 12. Calcutta | India | 14.3 |
| 3. Seoul | South Korea | 21.1 | 13. Buenos Aires | Argentina | 13.7 |
| 4. Mexico City | Mexico | 20.7 | 14. Manila | Philippines | 13.4 |
| 5. São Paulo | Brazil | 20.2 | 15. Moscow | Russia | 13.2 |
| 6. Mumbai (Bombay) | India | 18.1 | 16. Karachi | Pakistan | 12.3 |
| 7. Osaka | Japan | 18.0 | 17. Rio de Janeiro | Brazil | 12.2 |
| 8. Delhi | India | 17.1 | 18. Shanghai | China | 12.2 |
| 9. Los Angeles | USA | 16.8 | 19. London | UK | 11.8 |
| 10. Jakarta | Indonesia | 15.8 | 20. Teheran | Iran | 11.0 |

NOTE: The definitions of agglomerations vary significantly from city to city, hence the difficulty of compiling an accurate, comparative list of the world's most populous urban areas. 1. Includes metropolitan areas and surrounding urban agglomerations. Agglomerations include a central city and bordering urban areas. Some agglomerations have more than one central city (e.g., Washington, DC, includes Baltimore; Tokyo includes Yokohama and Kawasaki; New York includes Newark and Paterson, N.J.) *Source:* Thomas Brinkhoff, *Principal Agglomerations and Cities of the World.* Web: www.citypopulation.de, May 11, 2002.

# Area and Population of Countries

## (mid-2002 estimates)

| Country | Area (in sq km) | Population | Country | Area (in sq km) | Population |
|---|---|---|---|---|---|
| Afghanistan | 647,500 | 27,755,775 | Greece | 131,940 | 10,645,343 |
| Albania | 28,748 | 3,544,841 | Grenada | 340 | 89,227 |
| Algeria | 2,381,740 | 32,277,942 | Guatemala | 108,890 | 13,314,079 |
| Andorra | 468 | 68,403 | Guinea | 245,857 | 7,775,065 |
| Angola | 1,246,700 | 10,593,171 | Guinea-Bissau | 36,120 | 1,345,479 |
| Antigua and Barbuda | 442 | 67,448 | Guyana | 214,970 | 698,209 |
| Argentina | 2,766,890 | 37,812,817 | Haiti | 27,750 | 7,063,722 |
| Armenia | 29,800 | 3,330,099 | Honduras | 112,090 | 6,560,608 |
| Australia | 7,686,850 | 19,546,792 | Hungary | 93,030 | 10,075,034 |
| Austria | 83,858 | 8,169,929 | Iceland | 103,000 | 279,384 |
| Azerbaijan | 86,600 | 7,798,497 | India | 3,287,590 | 1,045,845,226 |
| Bahamas, The | 13,940 | 300,529 | Indonesia | 1,919,440 | 232,073,071 |
| Bahrain | 620 | 656,397 | Iran | 1,648,000 | 66,622,704 |
| Bangladesh | 144,000 | 133,376,684 | Iraq | 437,072 | 24,001,816 |
| Barbados | 430 | 276,607 | Ireland | 70,280 | 3,883,159 |
| Belarus | 207,600 | 10,335,382 | Israel | 20,770 | 6,029,529 |
| Belgium | 30,510 | 10,274,595 | Italy | 301,230 | 57,715,625 |
| Belize | 22,966 | 262,999 | Jamaica | 10,990 | 2,680,029 |
| Benin | 112,620 | 6,787,625 | Japan | 377,835 | 126,974,628 |
| Bhutan | 47,000 | 2,094,176 | Jordan | 92,300 | 5,307,470 |
| Bolivia | 1,098,580 | 8,445,134 | Kazakhstan | 2,717,300 | 16,741,519 |
| Bosnia and Herzegovina | 51,129 | 3,964,388 | Kenya | 582,650 | 31,138,735 |
| Botswana | 600,370 | 1,591,232 | Kiribati | 717 | 96,335 |
| Brazil | 8,511,965 | 176,029,560 | Korea, North | 120,540 | 22,224,195 |
| Brunei | 5,770 | 350,898 | Korea, South | 98,480 | 48,324,000 |
| Bulgaria | 110,910 | 7,621,337 | Kuwait | 17,820 | 2,111,561 |
| Burkina Faso | 274,200 | 12,603,185 | Kyrgyzstan | 198,500 | 4,822,166 |
| Burma (Myanmar) | 678,500 | 42,238,224 | Laos | 236,800 | 5,777,180 |
| Burundi | 27,830 | 6,373,002 | Latvia | 64,589 | 2,366,515 |
| Cambodia | 181,040 | 12,775,324 | Lebanon | 10,400 | 3,677,780 |
| Cameroon | 475,440 | 16,184,748 | Lesotho | 30,355 | 2,207,954 |
| Canada | 9,976,140 | 31,902,268 | Liberia | 111,370 | 3,288,198 |
| Cape Verde | 4,033 | 408,760 | Libya | 1,759,540 | 5,368,585 |
| Central African Republic | 622,984 | 3,642,739 | Liechtenstein | 160 | 32,842 |
| Chad | 1,284,000 | 8,997,237 | Lithuania | 65,200 | 3,601,138 |
| Chile | 756,950 | 15,498,930 | Luxembourg | 2,586 | 448,569 |
| China | 9,596,960 | 1,284,303,705 | Macedonia | 25,333 | 2,054,800 |
| Colombia | 1,138,910 | 41,008,227 | Madagascar | 587,040 | 16,473,477 |
| Comoros | 2,170 | 614,382 | Malawi | 118,480 | 10,701,824 |
| Congo, Democratic Republic of the (formerly Zaire) | 2,345,410 | 55,225,478 | Malaysia | 329,750 | 22,662,365 |
| Congo, Republic of the | 342,000 | 2,958,448 | Maldives | 300 | 320,165 |
| Costa Rica | 51,100 | 3,834,934 | Mali | 1,240,000 | 11,340,480 |
| Côte d'Ivoire | 322,460 | 16,804,784 | Malta | 316 | 397,499 |
| Croatia | 56,542 | 4,390,751 | Marshall Islands | 181 | 73,630 |
| Cuba | 110,860 | 11,224,321 | Mauritania | 1,030,700 | 2,828,858 |
| Cyprus | 9,250 | 767,314 | Mauritius | 1,860 | 1,200,206 |
| Czech Republic | 78,866 | 10,256,760 | Mexico | 1,972,550 | 103,400,165 |
| Denmark | 43,094 | 5,368,854 | Micronesia, Federated States of | 702 | 135,869 |
| Djibouti | 22,000 | 472,810 | Moldova | 33,843 | 4,434,547 |
| Dominica | 754 | 70,158 | Monaco | 1.95 | 31,987 |
| Dominican Republic | 48,730 | 8,721,594 | Mongolia | 1,565,000 | 2,694,432 |
| East Timor | 14,874 | 800,000 | Morocco | 446,550 | 31,167,783 |
| Ecuador | 283,560 | 13,447,494 | Mozambique | 801,590 | 19,607,519 |
| Egypt | 1,001,450 | 70,712,345 | Namibia | 825,418 | 1,820,916 |
| El Salvador | 21,040 | 6,353,681 | Nauru | 21 | 12,329 |
| Equatorial Guinea | 28,051 | 498,144 | Nepal | 140,800 | 25,873,917 |
| Eritrea | 121,320 | 4,465,651 | Netherlands | 41,526 | 16,067,754 |
| Estonia | 45,226 | 1,415,681 | New Zealand | 268,680 | 3,908,037 |
| Ethiopia | 1,127,127 | 67,673,031 | Nicaragua | 129,494 | 5,023,818 |
| Fiji | 18,270 | 856,346 | Niger | 1,267,000 | 10,639,744 |
| Finland | 337,030 | 5,183,545 | Nigeria | 923,768 | 129,934,911 |
| France | 547,030 | 59,765,983 | Norway | 324,220 | 4,525,116 |
| Gabon | 267,667 | 1,233,353 | Oman | 212,460 | 2,713,462 |
| Gambia, The | 11,300 | 1,455,842 | Pakistan | 803,940 | 147,663,429 |
| Georgia | 69,700 | 4,960,951 | Palau | 458 | 19,409 |
| Germany | 357,021 | 83,251,851 | Panama | 78,200 | 2,882,329 |
| Ghana | 238,540 | 20,244,154 | Papua New Guinea | 462,840 | 5,172,033 |

| Country | Area (in sq km) | Population | Country | Area (in sq km) | Population |
|---|---|---|---|---|---|
| Paraguay | 406,750 | 5,884,491 | Sweden | 449,964 | 8,876,744 |
| Peru | 1,285,220 | 27,949,639 | Switzerland | 41,290 | 7,301,994 |
| Philippines | 300,000 | 84,525,639 | Syria | 185,180 | 17,155,814 |
| Poland | 312,685 | 38,625,478 | Taiwan | 35,980 | 22,548,009 |
| Portugal | 92,391 | 10,084,245 | Tajikistan | 143,100 | 6,719,567 |
| Qatar | 11,437 | 793,341 | Tanzania | 945,087 | 37,187,939 |
| Romania | 237,500 | 22,317,730 | Thailand | 514,000 | 62,354,402 |
| Russia | 17,075,200 | 144,978,573 | Togo | 56,785 | 5,285,501 |
| Rwanda | 26,338 | 7,398,074 | Tonga | 748 | 106,137 |
| Saint Kitts and Nevis | 261 | 38,736 | Trinidad and Tobago | 5,128 | 1,163,724 |
| Saint Lucia | 620 | 160,145 | Tunisia | 163,610 | 9,815,644 |
| Saint Vincent and the | | | Turkey | 780,580 | 67,308,928 |
| Grenadines | 389 | 116,394 | Turkmenistan | 488,100 | 4,688,963 |
| Samoa | 2,860 | 178,631 | Tuvalu | 26 | 11,146 |
| San Marino | 61.20 | 27,730 | Uganda | 236,040 | 24,699,073 |
| São Tomé and Príncipe | 1,001 | 170,372 | Ukraine | 603,700 | 48,396,470 |
| Saudi Arabia | 1,960,582 | 23,513,330 | United Arab Emirates | 82,880 | 2,445,989 |
| Senegal | 196,190 | 9,979,752 | United Kingdom | 244,820 | 59,778,002 |
| Seychelles | 455 | 80,098 | United States | 9,629,091 | 280,562,489 |
| Sierra Leone | 71,740 | 5,614,743 | Uruguay | 176,220 | 3,386,575 |
| Singapore | 648 | 4,452,732 | Uzbekistan | 447,400 | 25,563,441 |
| Slovakia | 48,845 | 5,422,366 | Vanuatu | 12,200 | 196,178 |
| Slovenia | 20,253 | 1,932,917 | Vatican City | 0.44 | 890 |
| Solomon Islands | 28,450 | 494,786 | Venezuela | 912,050 | 24,287,670 |
| Somalia | 637,657 | 7,753,310 | Vietnam | 329,560 | 81,098,416 |
| South Africa | 1,219,912 | 43,647,658 | Western Sahara | 266,000 | 256,177 |
| Spain | 504,782 | 40,077,100 | Yemen | 527,970 | 18,701,257 |
| Sri Lanka | 65,610 | 19,576,783 | Yugoslavia | 102,350 | 10,589,571 |
| Sudan | 2,505,810 | 37,090,298 | Zambia | 752,614 | 9,959,037 |
| Suriname | 163,270 | 436,494 | Zimbabwe | 390,580 | 11,376,676 |
| Swaziland | 17,363 | 1,123,605 | | | |

*Source:* U.S. Census Bureau, International Database and *The World Factbook, 2001.*

## The Death Penalty Worldwide

**Death Penalty Outlawed (year)**
Andorra (1990)
Angola (1992)
Australia (1985)
Austria (1968)
Azerbaijan (1998)
Belgium (1996)
Bermuda (1999)
Bulgaria (1998)
Cambodia (1989)
Canada (1998)
Cape Verde (1981)
Colombia (1910)
Costa Rica (1877)
Côte d'Ivoire (2000)
Croatia (1990)
Czech Republic (1990)
Denmark (1978)
Djibouti (1995)
Dominican Republic (1966)
East Timor (1999)
Ecuador (1906)
Estonia (1998)
Finland (1972)
France (1981)
Georgia (1997)
Germany (1987)
Guinea-Bissau (1993)
Haiti (1987)
Honduras (1956)
Hungary (1990)

Iceland (1928)
Ireland (1990)
Italy (1994)
Kiribati (1979)
Liechtenstein (1987)
Lithuania (1998)
Luxembourg (1979)
Macedonia (n.a.)
Malta (2000)
Marshall Islands (1986)
Mauritius (1995)
Micronesia (1986)
Moldova (1995)
Monaco (1962)
Mozambique (1990)
Namibia (1990)
Nepal (1997)
Netherlands (1982)
New Zealand (1989)
Nicaragua (1979)
Norway (1979)
Palau (n.a.)
Panama (1903)
Paraguay (1992)
Poland (1997)
Portugal (1976)
Romania (1989)
San Marino (1865)
São Tomé and Príncipe (1990)
Seychelles (1993)
Slovak Republic (1990)
Slovenia (1989)

Solomon Islands (1966)
South Africa (1997)
Spain (1995)
Sweden (1972)
Switzerland (1992)
Turkmenistan (1999)
Tuvalu (1978)
Ukraine (1999)
United Kingdom (1965)
Uruguay (1907)
Vanuatu (1980)
Vatican City State (1969)
Venezuela (1863)
Yugoslavia (2001)

**Death Penalty Permitted in Exceptional Cases[1]**
Albania
Argentina
Bolivia
Bosnia-Herzegovina
Brazil
Chile
Cook Islands
Cyprus
El Salvador
Fiji
Greece
Israel
Latvia

Mexico
Peru
Turkey

**De Facto Ban on Death Penalty[2]**
Bhutan (1964)
Brunei Darussalam (1957)
Burkina Faso (1988)
Central African Republic (1981)
Congo (Republic) (1982)
Gambia (1981)
Grenada (1978)
Madagascar (1958)
Maldives (1952)
Mali (1980)
Nauru (1968)
Niger (1976)
Papua New Guinea (1950)
Russian Federation (1996)
Samoa (1962)
Senegal (1967)
Sri Lanka (1976)
Suriname (1982)
Togo (n.a.)
Tonga (1982)

**Death Penalty Permitted**
Afghanistan

Algeria
Antigua and Barbuda
Armenia
Bahamas
Bahrain
Bangladesh
Barbados
Belarus
Belize
Benin
Botswana
Burundi
Cameroon
Chad
China (People's Republic)
(illegible)
Congo (Democratic Republic)
Cuba
Dominica
Egypt
Equatorial Guinea
Eritrea
Ethiopia
Gabon
Ghana
Guatemala
Guinea
Guyana
India
Indonesia
Iran
Iraq

| | | | | |
|---|---|---|---|---|
| Jamaica | Lesotho | Pakistan | Singapore | Uganda |
| Japan | Liberia | Palestinian Authority | Somalia | United Arab |
| Jordan | Libya | Philippines | Sudan | Emirates |
| Kazakhstan | Malawi | Qatar | Swaziland | United States of |
| Kenya | Malaysia | Rwanda | Syria | America |
| Korea, North | Mauritania | St. Kitts and Nevis | Taiwan | Uzbekistan |
| Korea, South | Mongolia | St. Lucia | Tajikistan | Vietnam |
| Kuwait | Morocco | St. Vincent and the | Tanzania | Yemen |
| Kyrgyzstan | Myanmar | Grenadines | Thailand | Zambia |
| Laos | Nigeria | Saudi Arabia | Trinidad and Tobago | Zimbabwe |
| Lebanon | Oman | Sierra Leone | Tunisia | |

NOTE: n.a. = date not available. 1. Exceptional crimes include some committed under military law or crimes committed in wartime. 2. Death penalty is sanctioned by law but has not been the practice for 10 or more years (year of last execution). *Source:* Amnesty International, June 2002.

## Infant Mortality and Life Expectancy for Selected Countries, 2002

| Country | Infant mortality[1] | Life expectancy[2] | Country | Infant mortality[1] | Life expectancy[2] | Country | Infant mortality[1] | Life expectancy[2] |
|---|---|---|---|---|---|---|---|---|
| Albania | 38.6 | 72.1 | Germany | 4.7 | 77.8 | Panama | 19.6 | 75.9 |
| Angola | 191.7 | 38.9 | Greece | 6.3 | 78.7 | Peru | 38.2 | 70.6 |
| Australia | 4.9 | 80.0 | Guatemala | 44.5 | 66.8 | Poland | 9.2 | 73.7 |
| Austria | 4.4 | 78.0 | Hungary | 8.8 | 71.9 | Portugal | 5.8 | 76.1 |
| Bangladesh | 68.0 | 60.9 | India | 61.5 | 63.2 | Russia | 19.8 | 67.5 |
| Brazil | 35.9 | 63.5 | Iran | 28.1 | 70.2 | Slovakia | 8.8 | 74.2 |
| Canada | 5.0 | 79.7 | Ireland | 5.4 | 77.2 | South Africa | 61.8 | 45.4 |
| Chile | 9.1 | 76.1 | Israel | 7.5 | 78.9 | Spain | 4.8 | 79.1 |
| China | 27.3 | 71.9 | Italy | 5.8 | 79.2 | Sri Lanka | 15.7 | 72.3 |
| Costa Rica | 10.9 | 76.2 | Japan | 3.8 | 80.9 | Sweden | 3.4 | 79.8 |
| Cyprus | 7.7 | 77.1 | Kenya | 67.2 | 47.0 | Switzerland | 4.4 | 79.9 |
| Czech Republic | 5.5 | 75.0 | Korea, South | 7.6 | 74.9 | Syria | 32.7 | 69.1 |
| Denmark | 5.0 | 76.9 | Mexico | 24.5 | 72.0 | United Kingdom | 5.5 | 78.0 |
| Ecuador | 33.0 | 71.6 | Mozambique | 138.5 | 35.5 | United States | 6.7 | 77.4 |
| Egypt | 58.6 | 64.0 | New Zealand | 6.2 | 78.2 | Venezuela | 24.6 | 73.6 |
| Finland | 3.8 | 77.8 | Norway | 3.9 | 78.9 | Zimbabwe | 63.0 | 36.5 |
| France | 4.4 | 79.0 | Pakistan | 78.5 | 61.8 | | | |

1. Infant deaths per 1,000 live births. 2. Life expectancy at birth, in years, both sexes. *Source:* U.S. Census Bureau, International Database.

## Crude Birth and Death Rates for Selected Countries
### (per 1,000 population)

| Country | Birth rate | | | | | | Death rate | | | | | |
|---|---|---|---|---|---|---|---|---|---|---|---|---|
| | 2002 | 2001 | 1990 | 1985 | 1980 | 1975 | 2002 | 2001 | 1990 | 1985 | 1980 | 1975 |
| Australia | 12.71 | 12.86 | 15.4 | 15.7 | 15.3 | 16.9 | 7.25 | 7.18 | 7.0 | 7.5 | 7.4 | 7.9 |
| Austria | 9.58 | 9.74 | 11.6 | 11.6 | 12.0 | 12.5 | 9.73 | 9.80 | 10.6 | 11.9 | 12.2 | 12.8 |
| Belgium | 10.58 | 10.74 | 12.6 | 11.5 | 12.7 | 12.2 | 10.08 | 10.10 | 10.6 | 11.2 | 11.6 | 12.2 |
| Czech Republic[1] | 9.08 | 9.11 | 13.4 | 14.5 | 16.4 | 19.6 | 10.76 | 10.81 | 11.7 | 11.8 | 12.1 | 11.5 |
| France | 11.94 | 12.10 | 13.5 | 13.9 | 14.8 | 14.1 | 9.04 | 9.09 | 9.3 | 10.1 | 10.2 | 10.6 |
| Germany[2] | 8.99 | 9.16 | 11.4 | 9.6 | 10.0 | 9.7 | 10.36 | 10.42 | 11.2 | 11.5 | 11.6 | 12.1 |
| Greece | 9.82 | 9.83 | 10.2 | 11.7 | 15.4 | 15.7 | 9.79 | 9.73 | 9.3 | 9.4 | 9.1 | 8.9 |
| Ireland | 14.62 | 14.57 | 15.1 | 17.6 | 21.9 | 21.5 | 8.01 | 8.07 | 9.1 | 9.4 | 9.7 | 10.6 |
| Israel | 18.91 | 19.12 | 22.2 | 23.5 | 24.1 | 28.2 | 6.21 | 6.22 | 6.2 | 6.6 | 6.7 | 7.1 |
| Italy | 8.93 | 9.05 | 9.8 | 10.1 | 11.2 | 14.8 | 10.13 | 10.07 | 9.4 | 9.5 | 9.7 | 9.9 |
| Japan | 10.03 | 10.04 | 9.9 | 11.9 | 13.7 | 17.2 | 8.53 | 8.34 | 6.7 | 6.2 | 6.2 | 6.4 |
| Mauritius | 16.34 | 16.50 | 21.0 | 18.8 | 27.0 | 25.1 | 6.81 | 6.82 | 6.5 | 6.8 | 7.2 | 8.1 |
| Netherlands | 11.58 | 11.85 | 13.3 | 12.3 | 12.8 | 13.0 | 8.67 | 8.69 | 8.6 | 8.5 | 8.1 | 8.3 |
| New Zealand | 14.23 | 14.28 | 18.0 | 15.6 | — | 18.4 | 7.55 | 7.56 | 7.9 | 8.4 | — | 8.1 |
| Norway | 12.39 | 12.60 | 14.3 | 12.3 | 12.5 | 14.1 | 9.78 | 9.83 | 10.7 | 10.7 | 10.1 | 9.9 |
| Panama | 18.60 | 19.06 | 23.9 | 26.6 | 26.8 | 32.3 | 4.96 | 4.95 | — | — | — | — |
| Poland | 10.29 | 10.20 | 14.3 | 18.2 | 19.5 | 18.9 | 9.97 | 9.98 | 10.2 | 10.3 | 9.8 | 8.7 |
| Portugal | 11.50 | 11.51 | 11.8 | 12.8 | 16.4 | 19.1 | 10.21 | 10.21 | 10.4 | 9.6 | 9.9 | 10.4 |
| Romania | 10.81 | 10.80 | 13.6 | 15.8 | — | — | 12.27 | 12.28 | 10.6 | 10.9 | — | — |
| Switzerland | 9.84 | 10.12 | 12.5 | 11.6 | 11.3 | 12.3 | 8.79 | 8.77 | 9.5 | 9.2 | 9.2 | 8.7 |
| Tunisia | 16.83 | 17.11 | 25.8 | 31.3 | 35.2 | 36.6 | 5.00 | 4.99 | — | — | — | — |
| United Kingdom | 11.34 | 11.54 | 13.9 | 13.3 | 13.5 | 12.5 | 10.30 | 10.35 | 11.2 | 11.8 | 11.8 | 11.9 |
| United States | 14.10 | 14.20 | 16.7 | 15.7 | 16.2 | 14.0 | 8.70 | 8.70 | 8.6 | 8.7 | 8.9 | 8.9 |

1. Data prior to 1994 pertain to the former Czechoslovakia. 2. All data pertaining to Germany prior to 1990 are for West Germany. NOTE: (—) = not available. *Source:* United Nations, *Monthly Bulletin of Statistics, June 1997.* Data for 2001, 2002 from the U.S. Census Bureau, International Database.

# The 2002 Transparency International Corruption Perceptions Index

According to the annual survey by the Berlin-based organization Transparency International, the world's least corrupt country is Finland and its most corrupt is Bangladesh. The index defines corruption as the abuse of public office for private gain, and measures the degree to which corruption is perceived to exist among a country's public officials and politicians. It is a composite index, drawing on 15 surveys from 9 independent institutions, which gathered the opinions of business people and country analysts. Because of the absence of reliable data, only 102 of the world's countries are included in the survey. The scores range from 10 (squeaky clean) to zero (highly corrupt). A score of 5.5 is the number Transparency International considers the borderline figure distinguishing countries that do and do not have a serious corruption problem.

| Country rank | Country | 2002 CPI Score | Country rank | Country | 2002 CPI Score | Country rank | Country | 2002 CPI Score |
|---|---|---|---|---|---|---|---|---|
| 1. | Finland | 9.7 | | Trinidad & Tobago | 4.9 | | Uzbekistan | 2.9 |
| 2. | Denmark | 9.5 | 36. | Belarus | 4.8 | 70. | Argentina | 2.8 |
| | New Zealand | 9.5 | | Lithuania | 4.8 | 71. | Côte d'Ivoire | 2.7 |
| 4. | Iceland | 9.4 | | South Africa | 4.8 | | Honduras | 2.7 |
| 5. | Singapore | 9.3 | | Tunisia | 4.8 | | India | 2.7 |
| | Sweden | 9.3 | 40. | Costa Rica | 4.5 | | Russia | 2.7 |
| 7. | Canada | 9.0 | | Jordan | 4.5 | | Tanzania | 2.7 |
| | Luxembourg | 9.0 | | Mauritius | 4.5 | | Zimbabwe | 2.7 |
| | Netherlands | 9.0 | | South Korea | 4.5 | 77. | Pakistan | 2.6 |
| 10. | United Kingdom | 8.7 | 44. | Greece | 4.2 | | Philippines | 2.6 |
| 11. | Australia | 8.6 | 45. | Brazil | 4.0 | | Romania | 2.6 |
| 12. | Norway | 8.5 | | Bulgaria | 4.0 | | Zambia | 2.6 |
| | Switzerland | 8.5 | | Jamaica | 4.0 | 81. | Albania | 2.5 |
| 14. | Hong Kong | 8.2 | | Peru | 4.0 | | Guatemala | 2.5 |
| 15. | Austria | 7.8 | | Poland | 4.0 | | Nicaragua | 2.5 |
| 16. | United States | 7.7 | 50. | Ghana | 3.9 | | Venezuela | 2.5 |
| 17. | Chile | 7.5 | 51. | Croatia | 3.8 | 85. | Georgia | 2.4 |
| 18. | Germany | 7.3 | 52. | Czech Republic | 3.7 | | Ukraine | 2.4 |
| | Israel | 7.3 | | Latvia | 3.7 | | Vietnam | 2.4 |
| 20. | Belgium | 7.1 | | Morocco | 3.7 | 88. | Kazakhstan | 2.3 |
| | Japan | 7.1 | | Slovak Republic | 3.7 | 89. | Bolivia | 2.2 |
| | Spain | 7.1 | | Sri Lanka | 3.7 | | Cameroon | 2.2 |
| 23. | Ireland | 6.9 | 57. | Colombia | 3.6 | | Ecuador | 2.2 |
| 24. | Botswana | 6.4 | | Mexico | 3.6 | | Haiti | 2.2 |
| 25. | France | 6.3 | 59. | China | 3.5 | 93. | Moldova | 2.1 |
| | Portugal | 6.3 | | Dominican Rep. | 3.5 | | Uganda | 2.1 |
| 27. | Slovenia | 6.0 | | Ethiopia | 3.5 | 95. | Azerbaijan | 2.0 |
| 28. | Namibia | 5.7 | 62. | Egypt | 3.4 | 96. | Indonesia | 1.9 |
| 29. | Estonia | 5.6 | | El Salvador | 3.4 | | Kenya | 1.9 |
| | Taiwan | 5.6 | 64. | Thailand | 3.2 | 98. | Angola | 1.7 |
| 31. | Italy | 5.2 | | Turkey | 3.2 | | Madagascar | 1.7 |
| 32. | Uruguay | 5.1 | 66. | Senegal | 3.1 | | Paraguay | 1.7 |
| 33. | Hungary | 4.9 | 67. | Panama | 3.0 | 101. | Nigeria | 1.6 |
| | Malaysia | 4.9 | 68. | Malawi | 2.9 | 102. | Bangladesh[1] | 1.2 |

1. The Bangladesh score was based on only three available independent survey sources, which varied greatly. Transparency International stresses that these results need to be viewed with caution. Source: Transparency International, 2002. Web: www.transparency.org.

# Most and Least Livable Countries: UN Human Development Index, 2002

The Human Development Index (HDI), published annually by the UN, ranks nations according to their citizens' quality of life rather than strictly by a nation's traditional economic figures. The criteria for calculating rankings include life expectancy, educational attainment, and adjusted real income.

| Most Livable Countries, 2002 | | Least Livable Countries, 2002 | |
|---|---|---|---|
| 1. Norway | 14. Denmark | 1. Sierra Leone | 14. Gambia |
| 2. Sweden | 15. Austria | 2. Niger | 15. Guinea |
| 3. Canada | 16. Luxembourg | 3. Burundi | 16. Benin |
| 4. Belgium | 17. Germany | 4. Mozambique | 17. Eritrea |
| 5. Australia | 18. Ireland | 5. Burkina Faso | 18. Côte d'Ivoire |
| 6. United States | 19. New Zealand | 6. Ethiopia | 19. Congo, Dem. Rep. of |
| 7. Iceland | 20. Italy | 7. Guinea-Bissau | 20. Senegal |
| 8. Netherlands | 21. Spain | 8. Chad | 21. Zambia |
| 9. Japan | 22. Israel | 9. Central African Republic | 22. Mauritania |
| 10. Finland | 23. Hong Kong, China | 10. Mali | 23. Tanzania |
| 11. Switzerland | 24. Greece | 11. Malawi | 24. Uganda |
| 12. France | 25. Singapore | 12. Rwanda | 25. Djibouti |
| 13. United Kingdom | | 13. Angola | |

Source: Human Development Report, 2002, United Nations; www.undp.org/hdr2002.

## Military Budgets of Selected Countries, 2001

### (in billions of dollars)

| Country | Military budget | Country | Military budget | Country | Military budget | Country | Military budget |
|---|---|---|---|---|---|---|---|
| United States | $396.1 | Iran | $9.1 | Poland | $3.7 | North Korea | $1.3 |
| Russia[1] | 60.0 | Israel | 9.0 | Greece | 3.3 | Portugal | 1.3 |
| China[1] | 42.0 | Taiwan | 8.2 | Argentina[1] | 3.1 | Libya | 1.2 |
| Japan | 40.4 | Canada | 7.7 | Pakistan | 2.6 | Czech Republic | 1.1 |
| United Kingdom | 34.0 | Spain | 6.9 | Norway | 2.8 | Philippines | 1.1 |
| Saudi Arabia | 27.2 | Australia | 6.6 | Kuwait | 2.6 | Luxembourg | 0.9 |
| France | 25.3 | Netherlands | 5.6 | Denmark | 2.4 | Hungary | 0.8 |
| Germany | 21.0 | Turkey | 5.1 | Belgium | 2.2 | Syria | 0.8 |
| Brazil[1] | 17.9 | Singapore | 4.3 | Colombia | 2.1 | Cuba | 0.7 |
| India | 15.6 | Sweden | 4.2 | Egypt | 2.1 | Sudan | 0.6 |
| Italy | 15.5 | United Arab | | Vietnam | 1.8 | Yugoslavia | 0.5 |
| South Korea | 11.8 | Emirates[1] | 3.9 | Iraq | 1.4 | | |

1. 2000 budget. *Sources:* Center for Defense Information and International Institute for Strategic Studies, Department of Defense.

## Significant Armed Conflicts, 2002

| Main warring parties | Year began[1] | Main warring parties | Year began[1] |
|---|---|---|---|
| **Middle East** | | **Africa** | |
| Iran vs. Mujahideen Khalq Organization (MKO) | 1979 | Algeria vs. Armed Islamic Group (GIA) | 1991 |
| | | Burundi: Tutsi vs. Hutu | 1988 |
| Iraq vs. Desert Storm Coalition (U.S. & U.K.) | 1991 | Democratic Republic of Congo and allies vs. Rwanda, Uganda, and indigenous rebels[2] | 1997 |
| Iraqi government (Sunni) vs. Shi'a (Supreme Council for Islamic Revolution in Iraq) | 1991 | Liberia vs. LURD rebels | 2000 |
| Iraq vs. Kurds | 1961 | Somalia vs. rival clans | 1991 |
| Israel vs. Palestinian Authority/Hamas/ Hezbollah/Palestinian separatists | 1948 | Sudan vs. Sudanese People's Liberation Army[2] | 1983 |
| **Asia** | | Uganda vs. Lord's Resistance Army (LRA) | 1986 |
| Afghanistan: U.S., U.K., Northern Alliance, and Coalition Forces vs. al-Qaeda | 2001 | **Europe** | |
| | | Russia vs. Chechen separatists | 1994 |
| India vs. Kashmiri separatist groups/Pakistan | 1948 | **Latin America** | |
| India vs. Assam insurgents (various) | 1979 | Colombia vs. National Liberation Army (ELN) | 1978 |
| Indonesia vs. Aceh separatists | 1969 | Colombia vs. Revolutionary Armed Forces of Colombia (FARC) | 1978 |
| Indonesia vs. Irian Jaya separatists | 1969 | | |
| Philippines vs. Mindanaoan separatists (MILF/ASG) | 1971 | Colombia vs. Autodefensas Unidas de Colombia (AUC) | 1990 |

As of August 2002. 1. Where multiple parties and long-standing but sporadic conflict are concerned, date of first combat deaths is given. 2. Cease-fire agreements signed in 2002; violence may resume. *Source:* Center for Defense Information, www.cdi.org and Project Ploughshares, www.ploughshares.ca.

## Recently Suspended Armed Conflicts

| Main warring parties | Year began– year ceasefire declared | Main warring parties | Year began– year ceasefire declared |
|---|---|---|---|
| Angola vs. UNITA | 1975–2002 | Tajikistan vs. United Tajik Opposition (UTO) | 1992–2000 |
| Sri Lanka vs. Tamil Eelan | 1978–2002 | | |
| Chad vs. Muslim separatists (MDJT) | 1998–2002 | Indonesia vs. East Timor | 1975–2000 |
| Sierra Leone vs. RUF | 1991–2002 | Ethiopia vs. Eritrea | 1998–2000 |
| Taliban vs. Northern Alliance | 1995–2001 | Fiji vs. insurgents | 2000 |

*Source:* Center for Defense Information, www.cdi.org and Project Ploughshares, www.ploughshares.ca.

## Countries with Nuclear Weapons Capability

**Acknowledged Nuclear Weapons Capability**
Britain    France    Pakistan    United States
China    India    Russia

**Unacknowledged Nuclear Weapons Capability**
Israel

**Seeking Nuclear Weapons Capability**
Iran      Iraq

**Abandoned Nuclear Weapons Development**
North Korea—An accord was reached with the North Korean government in 1994 to freeze and dismantle nuclear weapons development.
South Africa—Constructed but then voluntarily dismantled 6 uranium bombs.
Belarus, Kazakhstan, Ukraine—When Soviet Union broke up, these former states possessed nuclear warheads that they have since given up.

*Source:* U.S. State Department and *Time* magazine.

*See also* UN peacekeeping missions, p. 900.

# International Terrorist Organizations

*Source:* U.S. Department of State

On March 27, 2002, the State Department's list of Foreign Terrorist Organizations (FTOs) was updated to include 33 groups. This partial list focuses on groups recently engaged in terrorist attacks.

**Abu Sayyaf Group (ASG)** The smallest and most radical of the Islamic separatist groups operating in the southern Philippines. Some ASG members developed ties to the *mujahideen* while fighting in Afghanistan but the group is largely profit-driven. **Activities:** Kidnappings, extortion, murder—in 2001–2002 the group held an American missionary couple and other hostages, several of whom were killed in a shoot-out with Philippine troops.

**Al-Gama'a al-Islamiyya (Islamic Group, IG)** Egypt's largest militant group, IG's primary goal is to replace Egyptian government with an Islamic state. **Activities:** Armed attacks against Egyptian government officials and Coptic Christians. Launched the 1997 attack at Luxor that killed 58 foreign tourists. Attempted to assassinate Egyptian president Hosni Mubarak in 1995.

**Al-Jihad/Islamic Egyptian Jihad** Active since the late 1970s, al-Jihad was established to overthrow the Egyptian government and create an Islamic state. Vehemently anti-U.S. and anti-Israel. **Activities:** Armed attacks and car bombings aimed at U.S. and Egyptian facilities. Carried out the 1981 assassination of President Anwar Sadat. Merged with al-Qaeda in June 2001; its leader, Ayman al-Zawahiri, is Osama bin Laden's closest adviser.

**Al-Qaeda** Established in the late 1980s by Osama bin Laden, al-Qaeda's current stated goals are to drive Americans and American influence out of all Muslim nations, especially Saudi Arabia; destroy Israel; and topple pro-Western dictatorships around the Middle East. Al-Qaeda also aims to unite all Muslims and establish, by force, a global Islamic caliphate. **Activities:** Include the Aug. 1998 bombings of two U.S. embassies in Africa, the Oct. 2000 suicide attack on the U.S.S. *Cole,* the Sept. 2001 attacks on the World Trade Center and Pentagon. (*See* p. 625 for detailed list.)

**Armed Islamic Group (GIA)/Salafi Group for Call and Combat (GSPC)** Extremist group that aims to replace the secular Algerian regime with an Islamic state. **Activities:** Between 1992 and 1998 the group massacred an estimated 100,000 civilians; violence resumed again in 2001.

**Hamas** Formed in late 1987 to establish an Islamic Palestinian state in place of Israel. Some elements may deal through legitimate social and political institutions. Militant elements advocate and use violence. **Activities:** Many attacks, including suicide bombings, against Israeli civilian and military targets; major force in both intifadas.

**Harakat ul-Mujahidin (HUM)** Islamic militant group based in Pakistan that operates primarily in Kashmir. The group has been linked to Osama bin Laden and in 1998 called for attacks on the U.S. and Western interests. **Activities:** Attacks against Indian troops, Western tourists, and civilian targets in Kashmir. Hijacked Indian airliner in Dec. 1999 to bargain for release of a number of Indian-held prisoners, including Ahmad Omar Sheikh, who in July 2002 was sentenced to death for the abduction and murder of U.S. journalist Daniel Pearl.

**Hezbollah** Extremist Shi'ite group that aims for the creation of Iranian-style Islamic republic in Lebanon. Formed in 1982 after the Israeli invasion of Lebanon, the group is strongly anti-West and anti-Israel. **Activities:** Anti-Israeli and anti-U.S. attacks, including the suicide truck bombing of the U.S. Marine barracks and embassy in Beirut in 1983.

**Jaish-e-Mohammed (JEM)** Islamic extremist group formed in early 2000 by Masood Azhar, whose release from prison was a condition for the freeing of hostages from an Indian airliner hijacked in Dec. 1999. JEM's overriding objective is Pakistani control of Kashmir. **Activities:** Claimed responsibility for the Oct. 2001 suicide attack on the Kashmir legislative assembly building; implicated, along with Lashkar-e-Tayyiba, in the Dec. 2001 attack on the Indian parliament.

**Lashkar-e-Tayyiba (LT)** One of the largest militant groups seeking Pakistani control of Kashmir. **Activities:** Responsible for numerous attacks on Indian military and civilian targets in Kashmir since 1993. Implicated in the Dec. 2001 attack on the Indian Parliament.

**Mujahedin-e Khalq Organization (MEK/MKO)** An Iranian Marxist-Islamic organization founded in the 1960s. MEK, both anti-Western and against Iran's clerical regime, is bankrolled by Saddam Hussein of Iraq. **Activities:** Murdered dozens of top-level Iranian officials since 1981. Aided Iraqi government in suppression of anti-Hussein Shia and Kurdish uprisings in 1991.

**The Palestine Islamic Jihad (PIJ)** Loosely affiliated factions committed to the creation of an Islamic Palestinian state and the destruction of Israel through holy war. **Activities:** Suicide bombing attacks against Israeli targets.

**Popular Front for the Liberation of Palestine (PFLP)** Marxist-Leninist group founded in 1967 by a former PLO member. **Activities:** International terrorist attacks in the 1970s since diminished; attacks against Israelis and moderate Arabs; assassination of right-wing Israeli cabinet minister Rehavam Ze'evi in Oct. 2001,

**Revolutionary Armed Forces of Colombia (FARC)** Best-trained and best-equipped guerrilla organization in Colombia. Established in 1964 as military wing of Colombian Communist Party, seeks to overthrow the government. Anti-U.S. since its inception. **Activities:** Armed attacks against Colombian political and military targets. Traffics in drugs.

## State-Sponsored Terrorism

The U.S. State Department has designated the following countries state sponsors of international terrorism: Cuba, Iran, Iraq, Libya, North Korea, Sudan, and Syria. Though most no longer engage directly in terrorist activity themselves, they may support terrorist groups by providing funding or arms. In 2002, President Bush singled out Iran, Iraq, and North Korea for special condemnation, labeling them "an axis of evil."

## Worldwide Refugees and Asylum Seekers, 2001

| Group or country of origin | Number | Group or country of origin | Number | Group or country of origin | Number |
|---|---|---|---|---|---|
| Palestinians | 3,800,000[1] | Western Sahara | 166,000 | Ukraine | 27,000 |
| Afghanistan | 3,800,000 | Yugoslavia | 134,000 | Congo, Rep. of | 24,000 |
| Burundi | 554,000 | Sri Lanka | 123,000 | Tibet | 21,000 |
| Iraq | 528,000 | China | 117,000 | Cuba | 19,000 |
| Sudan | 490,000 | Bhutan | 111,000 | Colombia | 18,000 |
| Angola | 470,000 | Rwanda | 105,000 | Georgia | 17,000 |
| Somalia | 440,000 | Iran | 91,000 | Guatemala | 17,000 |
| Bosnia and Herzegovina | 426,000 | East Timor | 73,000 | Ghana | 15,000 |
| Congo, Dem. Rep. of | 392,000 | Ethiopia | 59,000 | Laos | 13,000 |
| Vietnam | 353,000 | Russian Federation | 57,000 | Pakistan | 12,000 |
| Palestinian Territories | 350,000[2] | Chad | 46,000 | Macedonia | 12,000 |
| Eritrea | 333,000 | Turkey | 46,000 | India | 12,000 |
| Croatia | 289,000 | Tajikistan | 44,000 | Indonesia | 9,000 |
| Azerbaijan | 269,000 | Uganda | 40,000 | Lebanon | 9,000 |
| Liberia | 245,000 | Cambodia | 35,000 | Senegal | 9,000 |
| Myanmar (Burma) | 191,000 | Mauritania | 30,000 | Algeria | 8,000 |
| Sierra Leone | 179,000 | Central African Republic | 29,000 | | |

NOTE: All figures rounded. This table shows the countries that have produced the greatest numbers of refugees and asylum seekers. Statistics on refugees and other uprooted people are often inexact and controversial. One country's refugee is another's illegal alien. Government tallies cannot always be trusted to give full and unbiased accounts of refugee movements. As of May 2002, the UN High Commissioner for Refugees (UNHCR) estimated that there were 22 million refugees worldwide. 1. Not UNHCR administered. Figure comes from United Nations Relief and Works Agency for Palestine Refugees in the Near East (UNRWA). 2. UNHCR administered. *Source:* UN High Commissioner for Refugees (UNHCR), Geneva, May 2002.

## Economic Statistics by Country, 2000

| Country | GDP/PPP | GDP/PPP per capita | Real growth rate (%) | Inflation (%) | Country | GDP/PPP | GDP/PPP per capita | Real growth rate (%) | Inflation (%) |
|---|---|---|---|---|---|---|---|---|---|
| Afghanistan | $21 billion | $ 800 | n.a. | n.a. | Comoros | $419 million | $ 720 | 0.5% | 3.5[3]% |
| Albania | 10.5 billion | 3,000 | 7.5% | 1.0% | Congo, Rep. of | 3.1 billion | 1,100 | 3.8 | 3.5 |
| Algeria | 171 billion | 5,500 | 5.0 | 2.0 | Congo, Dem. | | | | |
| Andorra | 1.2 billion[1] | 18,000 | n.a. | 1.6[2] | Rep. of | 31 billion | 600 | −15.0 | 540.0 |
| Angola | 10.1 billion | 1,000 | 4.9 | 325.0 | Costa Rica | 25 billion | 6,700 | 3.0 | 11.0 |
| Antigua and | | | | | Côte d'Ivoire | 26.2 billion | 1,600 | −0.3 | 2.5 |
| Barbuda | 533 million[3] | 8,200 | 4.6 | 1.6 | Croatia | 24.9 billion | 5,800 | 3.2 | 6.0 |
| Argentina | 476 billion | 12,900 | 0.8 | −0.9 | Cuba | 19.2 billion | 1,700 | 5.6 | 0.3[3] |
| Armenia | 10 billion | 3,000 | 5.0 | 1.0[3] | Cyprus* | 9.7 billion | 16,000 | 4.2 | 4.2 |
| Australia | 445.8 billion | 23,200 | 4.7 | 1.4 | | 830 million[3] | 5,300 | 4.9[3] | 58.0[3] |
| Austria | 203 billion | 25,000 | 3.1 | 2.0 | Czech Rep. | 132.4 billion | 12,900 | 2.5 | 3.8 |
| Azerbaijan | 23.5 billion | 3,000 | 11.4 | 1.8 | Denmark | 136.2 billion | 25,500 | 2.8 | 2.9 |
| Bahamas | 4.5 billion | 15,000 | 4.5 | 1.9 | Djibouti | 574 million | 1,300 | 2.0 | 2.0 |
| Bahrain | 10.1 billion | 15,900 | 5.0 | 2.0 | Dominica | 290 million | 4,000 | 0.5 | 2.5 |
| Bangladesh | 203 billion | 1,570 | 5.3 | 5.8 | Dominican | | | | |
| Barbados | 4 billion | 14,500 | 2.8 | 2.0 | Rep. | 48.3 billion | 5,700 | 8.0 | 7.9 |
| Belarus | 78.8 billion | 7,500 | 4.0 | 200.0 | East Timor | n.a. | n.a. | n.a. | n.a. |
| Belgium | 259.2 billion | 25,300 | 4.1 | 2.2 | Ecuador | 37.2 billion | 2,900 | 0.8 | 96.0 |
| Belize | 790 million | 3,200 | 4.0 | 2.0 | Egypt | 247 billion | 3,600 | 5.0 | 3.0 |
| Benin | 6.6 billion | 1,030 | 5.0 | 3.0 | El Salvador | 24 billion | 4,000 | 2.5 | 2.5 |
| Bhutan | 2.3 billion | 1,100 | 6.0 | 7.0 | Eq. Guinea | 960 million | 2,000 | 12.0 | 6.0[3] |
| Bolivia | 20.9 billion | 2,600 | 2.5 | 4.4 | Eritrea | 2.9 billion | 710 | −1.0 | 14.0 |
| Bosnia and | | | | | Estonia | 14.7 billion | 10,000 | 6.4 | 4.1[3] |
| Herzegovina | 6.5 billion | 1,700 | 8.0 | 8.0 | Ethiopia | 39.2 billion | 600 | 2.0 | 5.0 |
| Botswana | 10.4 billion | 6,600 | 6.0 | 8.6 | Fiji | 5.9 billion[3] | 7,300 | −8.0 | 0.0 |
| Brazil | 1.13 trillion | 6,500 | 4.2 | 6.0 | Finland | 118.3 billion | 22,900 | 5.6 | 3.4 |
| Brunei | 5.9 billion | 17,600 | 3.0 | 1.0[3] | France | 1.448 trillion | 24,400 | 3.1 | 1.7 |
| Bulgaria | 48 billion | 6,200 | 5.0 | 10.4 | Gabon | 7.7 billion | 6,300 | 1.2 | 1.5 |
| Burkina Faso | 12 billion | 1,000 | 5.0 | 1.5 | Gambia, The | 1.5 billion | 1,100 | 4.9 | 3.4 |
| Burundi | 4.4 billion | 720 | 1.8 | 22.0 | Georgia | 22.8 billion | 4,600 | 1.9 | 4.1 |
| Cambodia | 16.1 billion | 1,300 | 4.0 | 1.6 | Germany | 1.936 trillion | 23,400 | 3.0 | 2.0 |
| Cameroon | 26 billion | 1,700 | 4.4 | 2.0 | Ghana | 37.4 billion | 1,900 | 3.0 | 22.8 |
| Canada | 774.7 billion | 24,800 | 4.3 | 2.6 | Greece | 181.9 billion | 17,200 | 3.8 | 3.1 |
| Cape Verde | 670 million | 1,700 | 6.0 | 4.0 | Grenada | 394 million | 4,400 | 7.0 | 2.5 |
| Central African | | | | | Guatemala | 46.2 billion | 3,700 | 3.0 | 6.0 |
| Republic | 6.1 billion | 1,700 | 3.5 | 3.0 | Guinea | 10 billion | 1,300 | 5.0 | 6.0 |
| Chad | 8.1 billion | 1,000 | 4.0 | 3.0 | Guinea-Bissau | 1.1 billion | 850 | 7.6 | 3.0 |
| Chile | 153.1 billion | 10,100 | 5.5 | 4.5 | Guyana | 3.4 billion | 4,800 | 3.0 | 5.9 |
| China | 4.5 trillion | 3,600 | 8.0 | 0.4 | Haiti | 12.7 billion | 1,800 | 1.2 | 19.0 |
| Colombia | 250 billion | 6,200 | 3.0 | 9.0 | Honduras | 17 billion | 2,700 | 5.0 | 11.0 |

| Country | GDP/PPP | GDP/PPP per capita | Real growth rate (%) | Inflation (%) | Country | GDP/PPP | GDP/PPP per capita | Real growth rate (%) | Inflation (%) |
|---|---|---|---|---|---|---|---|---|---|
| Hungary | $113.9 billion | $11,200 | 5.5 % | 9.8[3]% | Paraguay | $26.2 billion | $ 4,750 | 1.0% | 8.0 % |
| Iceland | 6.85 billion | 24,800 | 4.3 | 3.5 | Peru | 123 billion | 4,550 | 3.6 | 3.7 |
| India | 2.2 trillion | 2,200 | 6.0 | 5.4 | The Philip- | | | | |
| Indonesia | 654 billion | 2,900 | 4.8 | 9.0 | pines | 310 billion | 3,800 | 3.6 | 5.0 |
| Iran | 413 billion | 6,300 | 3.0 | 16.0 | Poland | 327.5 billion | 8,500 | 4.8 | 10.2 |
| Iraq | 57 billion | 2,500 | 15.0 | 100.0 | Portugal | 159 billion | 15,800 | 2.7 | 2.8 |
| Ireland | 81.9 billion | 21,600 | 9.9 | 5.6 | Qatar | 15.1 billion | 20,300 | 4.0 | 2.5 |
| Israel | 110.2 billion | 18,900 | 5.9 | 0.1 | Romania | 132.5 billion | 5,900 | 2.2 | 45.7 |
| Italy | 1.273 trillion | 22,100 | 2.7 | 2.5 | Russia | 1.12 trillion | 7,700 | 6.3 | 20.6 |
| Jamaica | 9.7 billion | 3,700 | 0.2 | 8.8 | Rwanda | 6.4 billion | 900 | 5.8 | 4.0 |
| Japan | 3.15 trillion | 24,900 | 1.3 | –0.7 | St. Kitts | 274 million | 7,000 | 5.0 | 2.5 |
| Jordan | 17.3 billion | 3,500 | 2.0 | 0.7 | St. Lucia | 700 million | 4,500 | 0.5 | 2.5 |
| Kazakhstan | 85.6 billion | 5,000 | 10.5 | 13.4 | St. Vincent | 322 million | 2,800 | 2.0 | 2.0 [3] |
| Kenya | 45.6 billion | 1,500 | 0.4 | 7.0 | Samoa | 571 million | 3,200 | 6.8 | 0.8 |
| Kiribati | 76 million | 850 | 1.0 | 2.0[3] | San Marino | 860 million | 32,000 | 8.0 | 2.2 |
| Korea, North | 22 billion | 1,000 | –3.0 | n.a. | São Tomé | 178 million | 1,100 | 3.0 | 5.0 |
| Korea, South | 764.6 billion | 16,100 | 9.0 | 2.3 | Saudi Arabia | 232 billion | 10,500 | 4.0 | 0.5 |
| Kuwait | 29.3 billion | 15,000 | 6.0 | 3.0 | Senegal | 16 billion | 1,600 | 5.7 | 1.5 |
| Kyrgyzstan | 12.6 billion | 2,700 | 5.7 | 18.7 | Seychelles | 610 million | 7,700 | 1.5 | 6.0 [3] |
| Laos | 9 billion | 1,700 | 4.0 | 33.0 | Sierra Leone | 2.7 billion | 510 | 4.2 | 15.0 |
| Latvia | 17.3 billion | 7,200 | 5.5 | 2.7 | Singapore | 109.8 billion | 26,500 | 10.1 | 1.4 |
| Lebanon | 18.2 billion | 5,000 | 1.0 | 0.0 | Slovakia | 55.3 billion | 10,200 | 2.2 | 12.2 |
| Lesotho | 5.1 billion | 2,400 | 2.5 | 6.0 | Slovenia | 22.9 billion | 12,000 | 4.5 | 8.9 |
| Liberia | 3.35 billion | 1,100 | 15.0 | 5.0 | Solomon Is. | 900 million | 2,000 | 1.0 | 10.0 [3] |
| Libya | 45.4 billion | 8,900 | 6.5 | 18.5 | Somalia | 4.3 billion | 600 | n.a. | +100.0 |
| Liechtenstein | 730 million[2] | 23,000 | n.a. | 0.5[4] | South Africa | 369 billion | 8,500 | 3.0 | 5.3 |
| Lithuania | 26.4 billion | 7,300 | 2.9 | 1.0 | Spain | 720.8 billion | 18,000 | 4.0 | 3.4 |
| Luxembourg | 15.9 billion | 36,400 | 5.7 | 7.8 | Sri Lanka | 62.7 billion | 3,250 | 5.6 | 8.5 |
| Macedonia | 9 billion | 4,400 | 5.0 | 11.0 | Sudan | 35.7 billion | 1,000 | 7.0 | 10.0 |
| Madagascar | 12.3 billion | 800 | 4.8 | 10.0[3] | Suriname | 1.48 billion[3] | 3,400 | –1.0 | 78.0 |
| Malawi | 9.4 billion | 900 | 3.0 | 29.5 | Swaziland | 4.4 billion | 4,000 | 2.4 | 6.4 |
| Malaysia | 223.7 billion | 10,300 | 8.6 | 1.7 | Sweden | 197 billion | 22,200 | 4.3 | 1.2 |
| Maldives | 594 million | 2,000 | 7.6 | 3.0 | Switzerland | 207 billion | 28,600 | 3.0 | 1.5 |
| Mali | 9.1 billion | 850 | 4.8 | 0.8 | Syria | 50.9 billion | 3,100 | 3.5 | 1.5 |
| Malta | 5.6 billion | 14,300 | 3.4 | 2.5 | Taiwan | 386 billion | 17,400 | 6.0 | 1.0 |
| Marshall Is | 105 million[2] | 1,070 | –5.0 | 5.0[4] | Tajikistan | 7.3 billion | 1,140 | 5.1 | 33.0 |
| Mauritania | 5.4 billion | 2,000 | 5.0 | 4.5 | Tanzania | 25.1 billion | 710 | 5.2 | 6.0 |
| Mauritius | 12.3 billion | 10,400 | 7.5 | 5.3 | Thailand | 413 billion | 6,700 | 4.2 | 2.1 |
| Mexico | 915 billion | 9,100 | 7.1 | 9.0 | Togo | 7.3 billion | 1,500 | 3.4 | 2.5 |
| Micronesia | 263 million[3] | 2,000 | 0.3 | 2.6[5] | Tonga | 225 million | 2,200 | 5.0 | 7.0 |
| Moldova | 11.3 billion | 2,500 | –1.5 | 32.0 | Trinidad | 11.2 billion | 9,500 | 5.0 | 3.2 |
| Monaco | 870 million[3] | 27,000 | n.a. | n.a. | Tunisia | 62.8 billion | 6,500 | 5.0 | 3.0 |
| Mongolia | 4.7 billion | 1,780 | –1.0 | 7.6[3] | Turkey | 444 billion | 6,800 | 6.0 | 39.0 |
| Morocco | 105 billion | 3,500 | 0.8 | 2.0 | Turkmenistan | 19.6 billion | 4,300 | 16.0 | 14.0 |
| Mozambique | 19.1 billion | 1,000 | 3.8 | 11.4 | Tuvalu | 11.6 million[3] | 1,100 | 3.0 | 7.0 [3] |
| Myanmar | 63.7 billion | 1,500 | 4.9 | n.a. | Uganda | 26.2 billion | 1,100 | 6.0 | 6.5 |
| Namibia | 7.6 billion | 4,300 | 4.0 | 9.1 | Ukraine | 189.4 billion | 3,850 | 6.0 | 25.8 |
| Nauru | 59 million | 5,000 | n.a. | –6.0[6] | UAE | 54 billion | 22,800 | 4.0 | 4.5 |
| Nepal | 33.7 billion | 1,360 | 3.7 | 3.3[7] | UK | 1.36 trillion | 22,800 | 3.0 | 2.4 |
| The Nether- | | | | | U.S. | 9.963 trillion | 36,200 | 5.0 | 3.4 |
| lands | 388.4 billion | 24,400 | 4.0 | 2.6 | Uruguay | 31 billion | 9,300 | –1.1 | 4.8 |
| New Zealand | 67.6 billion | 17,700 | 3.6 | 2.4 | Uzbekistan | 60 billion | 2,500 | 2.1 | 40.0 |
| Nicaragua | 11.7 billion | 2,700 | 6.0 | 11.8 | Vanuatu | 245 million[3] | 1,300 | –2.5 | 2.5 |
| Niger | 10 billion | 1,000 | 3.5 | 2.8 | Venezuela | 146.2 billion | 6,200 | 3.2 | 13.0 |
| Nigeria | 117 billion | 950 | 3.5 | 6.5 | Vietnam | 154.4 billion | 1,950 | 5.5 | 0.0 |
| Norway | 124.1 billion | 27,700 | 2.7 | 2.9 | Yemen | 14.4 billion | 820 | 6.0 | 10.0 |
| Oman | 19.6 billion | 7,700 | 4.6 | –0.8 | Yugoslavia | 24.2 billion | 2,300 | 15.0 | 42.0 [3] |
| Pakistan | 282 billion | 2,000 | 4.8 | 5.2 | Zambia | 8.5 billion | 880 | 4.0 | 27.3 |
| Palau | 129 million[2] | 7,100 | –1.4 | n.a. | Zimbabwe | 28.2 billion | 2,500 | –6.1 | 60.0 |
| Panama | 16.6 billion | 6,000 | 2.5 | 1.8 | | | | | |
| Papua New Guinea | 12.2 billion | 2,500 | 2.9 | 17.0 | | | | | |

Definitions: Gross domestic product (GDP): The value of all goods and services produced domestically. Purchasing power parity (PPP): The PPP method involves the use of standardized international dollar price weights, which are applied to the GDP produced in a given economy. The data derived from the 1998 method provide a better comparison of economic well-being between countries than conversions at official currency exchange rates. n.a. = not available. *First line of figures for Greek Cyprus, second for Turkish Cyprus. 1. 1996 est. 2. 1998 est. 3. 1999 est. 4. 1997 est. 5. FY 1998/1999. 6. 1993. 7. FY 1999/2000 est. Source: U.S. Census Bureau, International Database and The World Factbook, 2001.

*Major sources: The World Factbook 2001;* Center for International Research, U.S. Bureau of the Census; *The Columbia Encyclopedia; The World Book Encyclopedia; Encyclopædia Britannica;* U.S. State Dept., and various newspapers.
(information as of Sept. 2002)

Definitions: Gross domestic product (GDP): The value of all goods and services produced domestically; purchasing power parity (PPP): The PPP method involves the use of standardized international dollar price weights, which are applied to the GDP produced in a given economy. The data derived from the PPP method provide a better comparison of economic well-being between countries than conversions at official currency exchange rates. Literacy rates and population figures are supplied by the U.S. Census Bureau.

# Afghanistan

### ISLAMIC EMIRATE OF AFGHANISTAN

**National name:** Dowlat-e Eslami-ye Afghanestan
**President:** Hamid Karzai (2002)
**Area:** 250,000 sq mi (647,500 sq km)
**Population (2002 est.):** 27,755,775 (growth rate: 2.4%); birth rate: 41.0/1000; infant mortality rate: 144.8/1000; density per sq mi: 111
**Capital (2000 est.):** Kabul, 2,450,000. **Largest cities (2000 est.):** Mazar-i-Sharif, 2,500,000; Kandahar, 225,500; Herat, 177,300. **Monetary unit:** Afghani.
**Languages:** Pushtu, Dari Persian, other Turkic and minor languages. **Ethnicity/race:** Pashtun 38%, Tajik 25%, Uzbek 6%, Hazara 19%, minor ethnic groups (Chahar Aimaks, Turkmen, Baloch, and others).
**Religion:** Islam (Sunni 84%, Shi'ite 15%, other 1%).
**Literacy rate:** 29% (1990)
**Economic summary: GDP/PPP** (2000 est.): $21 billion; per capita $800. **Real growth rate:** n.a. **Inflation:** n.a. **Unemployment:** n.a. **Arable land:** 12%. **Agriculture:** opium poppies, wheat, fruits, nuts; wool, mutton, karakul pelts. **Labor force** (2000 est): 10 million; agriculture 70%, industry 15%, services 15% (1990 est.). **Natural resources:** natural gas, petroleum, coal, copper, chromite, talc, barites, sulfur, lead, zinc, iron ore, salt, precious and semiprecious stones. **Industries:** small-scale production of textiles, soap, furniture, shoes, fertilizer, and cement; handwoven carpets; natural gas, oil, coal, copper. **Exports:** $80 million (does not include opium) (1996 est.): opium, fruits and nuts, handwoven carpets, wool, cotton, hides and pelts, precious and semiprecious gems. **Imports:** $150 million (1996 est.): capital goods, food and petroleum products; most consumer goods. **Major trading partners:** Former Soviet Union, Pakistan, Iran, Germany, India, UK, Belgium, Luxembourg, Czech Republic, Japan, Singapore, South Korea.

**Geography** Afghanistan, approximately the size of Texas, is bordered on the north by Turkmenistan, Uzbekistan, and Tajikistan, on the extreme northeast by China, on the east and south by Pakistan, and by Iran on the west. The country is split east to west by the Hindu Kush mountain range, rising in the east to heights of 24,000 ft (7,315 m). With the exception of the southwest, most of the country is covered by high snow-capped mountains and is traversed by deep valleys.

**Government** In June 2002 a multiparty republic replaced an interim government that had been established in Dec. 2001, following the fall of the Islamic Taliban government.

**History** Darius I and Alexander the Great were the first to use Afghanistan as the gateway to India. Islamic conquerors arrived in the 7th century, and Genghis Khan and Tamerlane followed in the 13th and 14th centuries.

In the 19th century, Afghanistan became a battleground in the rivalry between imperial Britain and czarist Russia for control of Central Asia. Three Anglo-Afghan wars (1839–42, 1878–80, and 1919) ended inconclusively. In 1893 Britain established an unofficial border, the Durand Line, separating Afghanistan from British India, and London granted full independence in 1919. Emir Amanullah founded an Afghan monarchy in 1926.

During the cold war, King Mohammed Zahir Shah developed close ties with the Soviet Union, accepting extensive economic assistance from Moscow. He was overthrown in 1973 by his cousin Mohammed Daoud, who was himself ousted in a 1978 coup by Noor Taraki. Taraki and his successor, Babrak Karmal, attempted to create a Marxist state. However, the new leadership was criticized by armed insurgents who bitterly opposed communism and hoped to create an Islamic state in Afghanistan. Fearing his government was on the verge of collapse, Karmal called for Soviet troops. Moscow responded with a full-scale invasion of the country in Dec. 1979.

The Soviets were met with fierce resistance from groups already energized by opposition to the Karmal government. The guerrilla forces, calling themselves *mujahideen*, pledged a jihad, or holy war, to expel the invaders. Initially armed with outdated weapons, the mujahideen became a focus of U.S. cold war strategy against the Soviet Union, and with Pakistan's help, Washington began funneling sophisticated arms to the resistance. Moscow's troops were soon bogged down in a no-win conflict with determined Afghan fighters. In April 1988 the USSR, U.S., Afghanistan, and Pakistan signed accords calling for an end to outside aid to the warring factions. In return, a Soviet withdrawal took place in Feb. 1989, but the pro-Soviet government of President Najibullah was left in the capital, Kabul.

By mid-April 1992 Najibullah was ousted as Islamic rebels advanced on the capital. Almost immediately, the various rebel groups began fighting one another for control. Amid the chaos of competing factions, a group calling itself the Taliban—consisting of Islamic students—seized control of Kabul in Sept. 1996. It imposed harsh fundamentalist laws, including stoning for adultery and severing hands for theft. Women were prohibited from work and school, and they were required to cover themselves from head to foot in public. By fall 1998 the Taliban controlled about 90% of the country and, with its scorched-earth tactics and human rights abuses, had turned itself into an international pariah. Only three countries, Pakistan, Saudi Arabia, and the UAR, recognized the Taliban as Afghanistan's legitimate government

On Aug. 20, 1998, U.S. cruise missiles struck a terrorist training complex in Afghanistan believed to have been financed by Osama bin Laden, a wealthy Islamic radical sheltered by the Taliban. The U.S. asked for the deportation of bin Laden, whom they believed was involved in the bombing of the U.S.

embassies in Kenya and Tanzania on Aug. 7, 1998. The United Nations Security Council passed resolutions in 1999 and 2000 demanding that the Taliban cease their support for terrorism and hand over bin Laden for trial.

In Sept. 2001, legendary guerrilla leader Ahmed Shah Masoud was killed by suicide bombers, a seeming death knell for the anti-Taliban forces, a loosely connected group referred to as the Northern Alliance. Days later, terrorists attacked New York's World Trade Center Towers and the Pentagon, and bin Laden emerged as the primary suspect in the tragedy.

On Oct. 7, after the Taliban repeatedly and defiantly refused to turn over bin Laden, the U.S. and its allies began daily air strikes against Afghan military installations and terrorist training camps. Five weeks later, with the help of U.S. air support, the Northern Alliance managed with breathtaking speed to take the key cities of Mazar-i-Sharif and Kabul, the capital. On Dec. 7, the Taliban regime collapsed entirely when its troops fled their last stronghold, Kandahar. However, al-Qaeda members and other mujahideen from various parts of the Islamic world who had earlier fought alongside the Taliban persisted in pockets of fierce resistance, forcing U.S. and allied troops to maintain a presence in Afghanistan. Taliban leader, Mullah Muhammad Omar, remained at large. In the meantime, Osama bin Laden was believed to be hiding somewhere in a cave complex in the mountains of Tora Bora.

The U.S. and the international community have vowed to assist Afghanistan in forming a stable government and have pledged $25 billion for reconstruction. But intricate political, ideological, and ethnic differences, deepened by decades of war, complicated the formation of a broad-based representative government. In Dec. 2001, Hamid Karzai, a Pashtun (the dominant ethnic group in the country), and the leader of the powerful 500,000-strong Populzai clan, was named head of Afghanistan's interim government. In June 2002, 1,500 delegates gathered for a *loya jirga,* or grand council, and formally elected Karzai president. His term expires in 2004, when general elections will be held. Karzai, a popular figure in the West, has not yet solidified power within the country, as warlords maintain tight regional control. Haji Abdul Qadir, one of Karzai's newly appointed vice presidents, was gunned down in Kabul in July, and an assassination attempt on Karzai himself was narrowly averted in Sept.

The U.S. and its Afghan allies continued the assault through the summer of 2002 on the remaining positions held by al-Qaeda fighters. Some of the war's heaviest fighting occurred in March's Operation Anaconda, a ground offensive in Paktia Province intended to root out remaining soldiers. The U.S. war strategy met stinging criticism in Afghanistan when the number of civilian casualties hovered near 400 by mid-July. In one particularly bloody assault, more than 50 members of a wedding party were killed after an Air Force fighter jet dropped a 2,000-pound bomb in Oruzgan Province.

# Albania

**THE REPUBLIC OF ALBANIA**
**National name:** Republika E Shqiperise
**President:** Alfred Moisiu (2002)
**Prime Minister:** Fatos Nano (2002)
**Area:** 11,100 sq mi (28,748 sq km)
**Population (2002 est.):** 3,544,841 (growth rate: 1.2%); birth rate: 18.6/1000; infant mortality rate: 38.6/1000; density per sq mi: 319

**Capital and largest city (1991 est.):** Tirana, 300,000.
**Monetary unit:** Lek. **Languages:** Albanian (Tosk is the official dialect), Greek. **Ethnicity/race:** Albanian 95%, Greeks 3%, other 2%: Vlachs, Gypsies, Serbs, and Bulgarians (1989 est.). **Religions (1980):** Muslim 70%, Albanian Orthodox 20%, Roman Catholic 10%. **Literacy rate:** 72% (1955)
**Economic summary: GDP/PPP** (2000 est.): $10.5 billion; per capita $3,000. **Real growth rate:** 7.5%. **Inflation:** 1%. **Unemployment:** 16% (2000 est.) officially, but may be as high as 25%. **Arable land:** 21%. **Agriculture:** wheat, corn, potatoes, vegetables, fruits, sugar beets, grapes; meat, dairy products. **Labor force:** 1.692 million (including 352,000 emigrant workers and 261,000 domestically unemployed) (1994 est.); agriculture 50%, industry and services 50%. **Industries:** food processing, textiles and clothing; lumber, oil, cement, chemicals, mining, basic metals, hydropower. **Natural resources:** petroleum, natural gas, coal, chromium, copper, timber, nickel, hydropower. **Exports:** $310 million (f.o.b., 2000 est.): textiles and footwear; asphalt, metals and metallic ores, crude oil; vegetables, fruits, tobacco. **Imports:** $1 billion (f.o.b., 2000 est.): machinery and equipment, foodstuffs, textiles, chemicals. **Major trading partners:** Italy, Greece, Germany, Austria, Macedonia, Turkey, Bulgaria.

**Geography** Albania is situated on the eastern shore of the Adriatic Sea, with Montenegro and Serbia to the north, Macedonia to the east, and Greece to the south. Slightly larger than Maryland, Albania may be divided into two major regions: a mountainous highland region (north, east, and south) constituting 70% of the land area, and a western coastal lowland region that contains nearly all of the country's agricultural lands and is the most densely populated part of Albania.

**Government** Emerging democracy.

**History** A part of Illyria in ancient times and later of the Roman Empire, Albania was ruled by the Byzantine Empire from 535 to 1204. An alliance (1444–66) of Albanian chiefs failed to halt the advance of the Ottoman Turks, and the country remained under at least nominal Turkish rule for more than four centuries, until it proclaimed its independence on Nov. 28, 1912.

Largely agricultural, Albania is one of the poorest countries in Europe. A battlefield in World War I, after the war it became a republic in which a conservative Muslim landlord, Ahmed Zogu, proclaimed himself president in 1925, and king (Zog I) in 1928. He ruled until Italy annexed Albania in 1939. Communist guerrillas under Enver Hoxha seized power in 1944, near the end of World War II. Hoxha was a devotee of Stalin, emulating the Soviet leader's repressive tactics, imprisoning or executing landowners and others who did not conform to the socialist ideal. Hoxha eventually broke with Soviet communism in 1961 because of differences with Khrushchev and then aligned himself with Chinese communism, which he also abandoned in 1978 after the death of Mao. From then on Albania went its own way to forge its individual version of the socialist state and became one of the most isolated—and economically underdeveloped—countries in the world. Hoxha was succeeded by Ramiz Alia in 1982.

Elections in March 1991 gave the Communists a decisive majority. But a general strike and street demonstrations soon forced the all-Communist cabinet to resign. In June 1991 the Communist Party of Labor renamed itself the Socialist Party and renounced its past ideology. The opposition Democratic Party won a landslide victory in the 1992 elections, and Sali Berisha, a former cardiologist, became Albania's first elected president. The following year, ex-Communists, including Ramiz Alia and former prime minister Fatos Nano, were imprisoned on corruption charges.

But Albania's experiment with democratic reform and a free-market economy went disastrously awry in March 1997, when large numbers of its citizens invested in shady get-rich-quick pyramid schemes. When five of these schemes collapsed in the beginning of the year, robbing Albanians of an estimated $1.2 billion in savings, their rage turned against the government, which appeared to have sanctioned the nationwide swindle. Rioting broke out, the country's fragile infrastructure collapsed, and gangsters and rebels overran the country, plunging it into virtual anarchy. A multinational protection force eventually restored order and set up the elections that formally ousted President Sali Berisha.

In spring 1999, Albania was heavily involved in the affairs of its fellow ethnic Albanians to the north, in Kosovo. Albania served as an outpost for NATO troops and took in approximately 440,000 Kosovar refugees, about half the total number of ethnic Albanians who were driven from their homes in Kosovo.

Ilir Meta, elected prime minister in 1999, rapidly moved forward in his first years to modernize the economy, privatize business, fight crime, and reform the judiciary and tax systems. In 2001, after the outbreak of an ethnic Albanian separatist movement in neighboring Macedonia, Meta supported greater rights for Macedonia's Albanian minority but condemned the rebels' violence. Meta, however, resigned in Jan. 2002, frustrated by political infighting.

In June 2002, former general Alfred Moisiu was elected president, endorsed by both the Socialists (headed by Fatos Nano) and the Democrats (led by Sali Berisha) in an effort to end the unproductive political fractiousness that has stalemated the government.

# Algeria

**DEMOCRATIC AND POPULAR REPUBLIC OF ALGERIA**

**National name:** Al Jumhuriyah al Jaza'iriyah ad Dimuqratiyah ash Shabiyah
**President:** Abdel-Aziz Bouteflika (1999)
**Prime Minister:** Ali Benflis (2000)
**Area:** 919,590 sq mi (2,381,740 sq km)
**Population (2002 est.):** 32,277,942 (growth rate: 1.7%); birth rate: 22.3/1000; infant mortality rate: 39.1/1000; density per sq mi: 35
**Capital:** Algiers. **Largest cities (1987):** Algiers, 1,507,241; Oran, 628,558; Constantine, 440,842; Annaba, 305,526.
**Monetary unit:** Dinar. **Languages:** Arabic (official), French, Berber dialects. **Ethnicity/race:** Arab-Berber 99%, European less than 1%. **Religion:** 99% Islam (Sunni). **Literacy rate:** 57% (1990)
**Economic summary: GDP/PPP** (2000 est.): $171 billion; per capita $5,500. **Real growth rate:** 5%. **Inflation:** 2%. **Unemployment:** 30% (1999 est.). **Arable land:** 3%. **Agriculture:** wheat, barley, oats, grapes, olives, citrus, fruits; sheep, cattle. **Labor force:** 9.1 million (2000 est.); government 29%, agriculture 25%, construction and public works 15%, industry 11%, other 20% (1996 est.). **Industries:** petroleum, natural gas, light industries, mining, electrical, petrochemical, food processing. **Natural resources:** petroleum, natural gas, iron ore, phosphates, uranium, lead, zinc. **Exports:** $19.6 billion (f.o.b., 2000 est.): petroleum, natural gas, and petroleum products 97%. **Imports:** $9.2 billion (f.o.b., 2000 est.): capital goods, food and beverages, consumer goods. **Major trading partners:** Italy, U.S., France, Spain, Brazil, Netherlands, Germany, Turkey.

**Geography** Nearly four times the size of Texas, Algeria is bordered on the west by Morocco and Western Sahara and on the east by Tunisia and Libya. To the south are Mauritania, Mali, and Niger. The Saharan region, which is 85% of the country, is almost completely uninhabited. The highest point is Mount Tahat in the Sahara, which rises 9,850 ft (3,000 m).

**Government** Parliamentary republic.

**History** Excavations in Algeria have indicated that *Homo erectus* resided there between 500,000 and 700,000 years ago. Phoenician traders settled on the coast in the 1st millennium B.C. As ancient Numidia, Algeria became a Roman colony, part of what was called Mauretania Caesariensis, at the close of the Punic Wars (145 B.C.). Conquered by the Vandals about A.D. 440, it fell from a high state of civilization to virtual barbarism, from which it partly recovered after an invasion by Arabs about 650. Christian during its Roman period, the indigenous Berbers were then converted to Islam. Falling under the control of the Ottoman Empire by 1536, Algiers served for three centuries as the headquarters of the Barbary pirates. Ostensibly to rid the region of the pirates, the French occupied Algeria in 1830 and made it a part of France in 1848.

Algerian independence movements led to the uprisings of 1954–55, which developed into full-scale war. In 1962, French president Charles de Gaulle began the peace negotiations, and on July 5, 1962, Algeria was proclaimed independent. In Oct. 1963, Ahmed Ben Bella was elected president, and the country became socialist. He began to nationalize foreign holdings and aroused opposition. He was overthrown in a military coup on June 19, 1965, by Col. Houari Boumediène, who suspended the constitution and sought to restore economic stability.

In Dec. 1991 in the first parliamentary elections ever held in Algeria, the fundamentalist Islamic Salvation Front (Front Islamique du Salut; FIS) won the largest number of votes. To thwart the electoral results, the army cancelled the general election, which plunged the country into a bloody civil war. An estimated 100,000 people have been massacred by Islamic terrorists since war began in Jan. 1992. The undeclared civil war escalated in its brutality and senselessness in 1997–98. Islamic extremists, who had originally focused their attacks on government officials and then shifted to intellectuals and journalists, abandoned political motivations entirely and targeted defenseless villagers. The mass slaughters were as savage as they were random, and the government was markedly ineffectual in stemming the violence. There is some evidence that the army in fact looked the other way while its civilians were slaughtered. Algeria refused international mediation and kept the outside world largely in the dark about the war within its borders.

Abdel-Aziz Bouteflika's ascension to the presidency in April 1999 was initially expected to bring peace and some economic improvement to this desperate wartorn country. Bouteflika, however, has been locked in power struggles with the military, whose support is crucial. Despite the appearance of democracy, Algeria remains in essence a military dictatorship. Bouteflika's plan of national reconciliation, which included an amnesty for Islamic militants not convicted of murder or rape, has done little to heal wounds. In 2001 violence by Islamic militants was again on the rise, and the long-disaffected Berber minority engaged in several large-scale protests. The Berber-speaking region of Kabylia and other regions continued large protests against the government in 2002.

# Andorra

### PRINCIPALITY OF ANDORRA

**National name:** Valls d'Andorra
**Head of Government:** Marc Forné Molné (1994)
**Area:** 181 sq mi (468 sq km)
**Population (2002 est.):** 68,403 (growth rate: 0.4%); birth rate: 10.0/1000; infant mortality rate: 4.1/1000; density per sq mi: 379
**Capital and largest city (1993 est.):** Andorra la Vella, 22,390. **Monetary units:** Euro. **Languages:** Catalán (official), French, Spanish. **Ethnicity/race:** Spanish 61%, Andorran 30%, French 6%, other 3%. **Religion:** Roman Catholic. **Literacy rate:** 100%
**Economic summary: GDP/PPP** (1996 est.): $1.2 billion; per capita $18,000. **Real growth rate:** n.a. **Inflation:** 1.62% (1998). **Unemployment:** 0%. **Arable land:** 4%. **Agriculture:** small quantities of tobacco, rye, wheat, barley, oats, vegetables; sheep. **Labor force:** 30,787 salaried employees (1998); agriculture 1%, industry 21%, services 72%, other 6% (1998). **Industries:** tourism (particularly skiing), cattle raising, timber, tobacco, banking. **Natural resources:** hydropower, mineral water, timber, iron ore, lead. **Exports:** $58 million (f.o.b., 1998): tobacco products, furniture. **Imports:** $1.077 billion (c.i.f., 1998): consumer goods, food, electricity. **Major trading partners:** France, Spain, U.S.

**Geography** Andorra is nestled high in the Pyrenees Mountains on the French-Spanish border.

**Government** A parliamentary coprincipality composed of the bishop of Urgel (Spain) and the president of France. The principality was internationally recognized as a sovereign state in 1993.

**History** An autonomous and semi-independent coprincipality, Andorra has been under the joint suzerainty of the French state and the Spanish bishops of Urgel since 1278. It maintains closer ties to Spain, however, and Catalán is its official language. In the late 20th century, Andorra became a popular tourist and winter sports destination and a wealthy international commercial center because of its banking facilities, low taxes, and lack of customs duties. In 1990 Andorra approved a customs union treaty with the EU permitting free movement of industrial goods between the two, but with Andorra applying the EU's external tariffs to third countries. Andorra became a member of the UN in 1993 and a member of the Council of Europe in 1994.

# Angola

### REPUBLIC OF ANGOLA

**President:** José Eduardo dos Santos (1979)
**Area:** 481,351 sq mi (1,246,700 sq km)
**Population (2002 est.):** 10,593,171 (growth rate: 0.0%); infant mortality rate: 191.7/1000; density per sq mi: 22
**Capital and largest city (1993):** Luanda, 2,000,000. **Other large cities (1993 est.):** Huambo, 400,000, Lubango, 105,000. **Monetary unit:** New Kwanza. **Languages:** Bantu, Portuguese (official). **Ethnicity/race:** Ovimbundu 37%, Kimbundu 25%, Bakongo 13%, mestico (mixed European and Native African) 2%, European 1%, other 22%. **Religions:** Roman Catholic 47%, Protestant 38%, Indigenous 15%. **Literacy rate:** 42% (1990)
**Economic summary: GDP/PPP** (2000 est.): $10.1 billion; per capita $1,000. **Real growth rate:** 4.9%. **Inflation:** 325%. **Unemployment:** extensive unemployment and underemployment affecting more than half the population. **Arable land:** 2%. **Agriculture:** bananas, sugarcane, coffee, sisal, corn, cotton, manioc (tapioca), tobacco, vegetables, plantains; livestock; forest products; fish. **Labor force:** 5 million (1997 est.); agriculture 85%, industry and services 15%. **Industries:** petroleum; diamonds, iron ore, phosphates, feldspar, bauxite, uranium, and gold; cement; basic metal products; fish processing; food processing; brewing; tobacco products; sugar; textiles. **Natural resources:** petroleum, diamonds, iron ore, phosphates, copper, feldspar, gold, bauxite, uranium. **Exports:** $7.8 billion (f.o.b., 2000 est.): crude oil, diamonds, refined petroleum products, gas, coffee, sisal, fish and fish products, timber, cotton. **Imports:** $2.5 billion (f.o.b., 2000 est.): machinery and electrical equipment, vehicles and spare parts; medicines, food, textiles, military goods. **Major trading partners:** U.S., South Korea, Benelux, China, Taiwan, Portugal, South Africa, France.

**Geography** Angola, more than three times the size of California, extends for more than 1,000 mi (1,609 km) along the South Atlantic in southwest Africa. The Democratic Republic of the Congo and the Republic of Congo are to the north and east, Zambia is to the east, and Namibia is to the south. A plateau averaging 6,000 ft (1,829 m) above sea level rises abruptly from the coastal lowlands. Nearly all the land is desert or savanna, with hardwood forests in the northeast.

**Government** Angola underwent a transition from a one-party socialist state to a nominally multiparty democracy in 1992.

**History** The original inhabitants of Angola are thought to have been Khoisan speakers. After 1000, large numbers of Bantu speakers migrated to the region and became the dominant group. Angola derives its name from the Bantu kingdom of Ndongo, whose name for its king is *ngola*.

Explored by the Portuguese navigator Diego Cão in 1482, Angola became a link in trade with India and Southeast Asia. Later it was a major source of slaves for Portugal's New World colony of Brazil. Development of the interior began after the Berlin Conference in 1885 fixed the colony's borders, and British and Portuguese investment fostered mining, railways, and agriculture.

Following World War II, independence movements began but were sternly suppressed by Portuguese military force. The major nationalist organizations were the Popular Movement for the Liberation of Angola (MPLA), a Marxist party, National Front for the Liberation of Angola (FNLA), and the National Union for the Total Independence of Angola (UNITA). After 14 years of war, Portugal finally granted independence to Angola in 1975. The MPLA, which had led the independence movement, has controlled the government ever since. But after its long war for independence, the country confronted no promise of peace. UNITA disputed the MPLA's ascendancy, and civil war broke out almost immediately. With the Soviet Union and Cuba supporting the Marxist MPLA, and the United States and South Africa supporting the anticommunist UNITA, the country became a cold war battleground.

With the waning of the cold war and the withdrawal of Cuban troops in 1989, the MPLA began to make the transition to a multiparty democracy. Despite shifting ideologies, the civil war continued, with UNITA's charismatic rebel leader, Jonas Savimbi, armed and sustained by his control of approximately 80% of the country's diamond trade. Free elections took place in 1992, with incumbent president José Eduardo dos Santos and the MPLA winning the UN-certified election over Savimbi and UNITA. Savimbi then withdrew, charging election fraud, and the civil war resumed.

In 1997 Angola played a crucial role in the civil wars of both the Republic of Congo and the Democratic Republic of the Congo. By aiding in the overthrow of these countries' leaders, Pascal Lissouba and Mobutu Sese Seko, the Angolan government was also able to destroy the UNITA strongholds within their borders. Angola again came to the aid of the Democratic Republic of the Congo's new leader, Laurent Kabila, in 1998, helping to fight the rebellion against his shaky year-old administration.

Four years of relative peace took place between 1994 and 1998, when the UN, at a cost of $1.6 billion, oversaw the 1994 Lusaka peace accord. In 1997 it was agreed that a coalition government with UNITA would be implemented. But Savimbi violated the accord repeatedly by refusing to give up his strongholds, failing to demobilize his army, and retaking territory. As a result, the government suspended coalition rule in Sept. 1998, and the country again plunged into civil war. Angola's citizens continued to suffer. The hostilities affected an estimated four million people, about a third of the total population, and there were almost two million refugees.

On Feb. 22, 2002, government troops killed Jonas Savimbi, and his exhausted troops were ready to lay down their arms. Six weeks later, on April 4, rebel leaders signed a cease-fire deal with the government, signalling the end of 30 years of civil war. Within another five weeks, 80% of the rebels had been disarmed. While peace finally seemed secure, more than a half-million Angolans were faced with starvation.

# Antigua and Barbuda

**Sovereign:** Queen Elizabeth II (1952)
**Governor-General:** James Beethoven Carlisle (1993)
**Prime Minister:** Lester Bryant Bird (1994)
**Land area:** 171 sq mi (442 sq km)
**Population (2002 est.):** 67,448 (growth rate: 1.3%); birth rate: 18.8/1000; infant mortality rate: 21.6/1000; density per sq mi: 395
**Capital and largest city (1991):** St. John's, 21,514; Codrington (capital of Barbuda), est. pop. 1,000.
**Monetary unit:** East Caribbean dollar. **Language:** English. **Ethnicity/race:** black, British, Portuguese, Lebanese, Syrian. **Religions:** Anglican and Roman Catholic. **Literacy rate:** 89% (1960)
**Economic summary: GDP/PPP** (1999 est.): $533 million; per capita $8,200. **Real growth rate:** 4.6%. **Inflation:** 1.6%. **Unemployment:** 7%. **Arable land:** 18%. **Agriculture:** cotton, fruits, vegetables, bananas, coconuts, cucumbers, mangoes, sugarcane; livestock. **Labor force:** 30,000; commerce and services 82%, agriculture 11%, industry 7% (1983). **Industries:** tourism, construction, light manufacturing (clothing, alcohol, household appliances). **Natural resources:** negl; pleasant climate fosters tourism. **Exports:** $38 million (1998): petroleum products, manufactures, machinery and transport equipment, food and live animals. **Imports:** $330 million (1998): food and live animals, machinery and transport equipment, manufactures, chemicals, oil. **Major trading partners:** OECS, Barbados, Guyana, Trinidad and Tobago, U.S., UK, Canada. **Member of Commonwealth of Nations**

**Geography** Antigua, the larger of the two main islands, is 108 sq mi (280 sq km). The island dependencies of Redonda (an uninhabited rocky islet) and Barbuda (a coral island formerly known as Dulcina) are 0.5 sq mi (1.30 sq km) and 62 sq mi (161 sq km), respectively.

**Government** Constitutional monarchy.

**History** Antigua was explored by Christopher Columbus in 1493 and named for the Church of Santa Maria de la Antigua in Seville. Antigua was colonized by Britain in 1632; Barbuda was first colonized in 1678. The country joined the West Indies Federation in 1958. With the breakup of the federation, it became one of the West Indies Associated States in 1967, self-governing its internal affairs. Full independence was granted Nov. 1, 1981.

The Bird family has controlled the islands since Vere C. Bird founded the Antigua Labor Party in the mid-1940s. While tourism and financial services have turned the country into one of the more prosperous in the Caribbean, law enforcement officials have charged that Antigua and Barbuda is a major center of money laundering, drug trafficking, and arms smuggling. Several scandals have tainted the Bird family, especially the 1995 conviction of Lester Bird's brother, Ivor, for cocaine smuggling.

# Argentina

### ARGENTINE REPUBLIC

**National name:** República Argentina.
**President:** Eduardo Duhalde (2002)
**Area:** 1,068,296 sq mi (2,766,890 sq km)
**Population (2002 est.):** 37,812,817 (growth rate: 1.1%); birth rate: 18.2/1000; infant mortality rate: 17.2/1000; density per sq mi: 35
**Capital and largest city (2000 est.):** Buenos Aires, 13,250,000 (metro. area). **Other large cities (1999 est.):** Córdoba, 1,200,000; Rosario, 950,000; Mar del Plata, 900,000; Mendoza, 400,000. **Monetary unit:** Peso. **Languages:** Spanish (official), English, Italian, German, French. **Ethnicity/race:** European 97% (mostly of Spanish and Italian descent), 3% other (mostly Indian or mestizo). **Religions:** Roman Catholic 92%, Protestant 2%, Jewish 2%, other 4%. **Literacy rate:** 96% (1991)
**Economic summary: GDP/PPP** (2000 est.): $476 billion; per capita $12,900. **Real growth rate:** 0.8%. **Inflation:** –0.9%. **Unemployment:** 15% (Dec. 2000). **Arable land:** 9%. **Agriculture:** sunflower seeds, lemons, soybeans, grapes, corn, tobacco, peanuts, tea, wheat; livestock. **Labor force:** 15 million (1999); agriculture n.a., industry n.a., services n.a. **Industries:** food processing, motor vehicles, consumer durables, textiles, chemicals and petrochemicals, printing, metallurgy, steel. **Natural resources:** fertile plains of the pampas, lead, zinc, tin, copper, iron ore, manganese, petroleum, uranium. **Exports:** $26.5 billion (f.o.b., 2000 est.): edible oils, fuels and energy, cereals, feed, motor vehicles. **Imports:** $25.2 billion (f.o.b., 2000 est.): machinery and equipment, motor vehicles, chemicals, metal manufactures, plastics. **Major trading partners:** Brazil, EU, U.S.

**Geography** Second in South America only to Brazil in size and population, Argentina is a plain, rising from the Atlantic to the Chilean border and the towering Andes peaks. Aconcagua (23,034 ft; 7,021 m) is the highest peak in the world outside Asia. Argentina is also bordered by Bolivia and Paraguay on the north, and by Uruguay and Brazil on the east. The northern area is the swampy and partly wooded Gran Chaco, bordering on Bolivia and Paraguay. South of that are the rolling, fertile Pampas, which are rich in agriculture and sheep- and cattle-grazing and support most of the population. Next southward is Patagonia, a region of cool, arid steppes with some wooded and fertile sections.

**Government** Republic.

**History** First explored in 1516 by Juan Díaz de Solis, Argentina developed slowly under Spanish colonial rule. Buenos Aires was settled in 1580; the cattle industry was thriving as early as 1600. Invading British forces were expelled in 1806–07, and after Napoléon conquered Spain (1808), the Argentinians set up their own government in 1810. On July 9, 1816, independence was formally declared.

As it had in World War I, Argentina proclaimed neutrality at the outbreak of World War II, but in the closing phase declared war on the Axis powers on March 27, 1945. Juan D. Perón, an army colonel, emerged as the strongman of the postwar era, winning the presidential elections of 1946 and 1951. Perón's political strength was reinforced by his second wife— Eva Duarte de Perón (Evita)—and her popularity with the working classes. Although she never held a government post, Evita acted as de facto minister of health and labor, establishing a national charitable organization, and awarding generous wage increases to the unions, who responded with political support for Perón. Opposition to Perón's increasing authoritarianism led to a coup by the armed forces, which sent Perón into exile in 1955, three years after Evita's death. Argentina entered a long period of military dictatorships with brief intervals of constitutional government.

The former dictator returned to power in 1973 and his third wife, Isabel Martínez de Perón, was elected vice president. After Perón's death in 1974, she became the hemisphere's first woman chief of state, assuming control of a nation teetering on economic and political collapse. In 1975, terrorist acts by left- and right-wing groups killed some 700 people. The cost of living rose 355%, while strikes and demonstrations were constant. On March 24, 1976, a military junta led by army commander Lt. Gen. Jorge Rafael Videla seized power and imposed martial law.

The military began the "dirty war" to restore order and eradicate its opponents. The Argentine Commission for Human Rights, in Geneva, has charged the junta with 2,300 political murders, over 10,000 political arrests, and the disappearances of 20,000 to 30,000 people. While violence declined, the economy remained in chaos. In March 1981 Videla was deposed by Field Marshal Roberto Viola, who in turn was succeeded by Lt. Gen. Leopoldo Galtieri.

On April 2, 1982, Galtieri invaded the British-held Falkland Islands, known as Las Islas Malvinas (Malvinas Islands) in Spanish, in what was seen as an attempt to increase his popularity. Great Britain, however, won a decisive victory, and Galtieri resigned in disgrace three days after Argentina's surrender. Maj. Gen. Reynaldo Bignone took over June 14, amid increasing public humiliation. As the 1983 elections approached, inflation hit 900% and Argentina's crippling foreign debt reached unprecedented levels.

In the presidential election of Oct. 1983, Raúl Alfonsín, leader of the Radical Civic Union, handed the Peronist Party its first defeat since its founding. Growing unemployment and quadruple-digit inflation, however, led to a Peronist victory in the elections of May 1989. Alfonsín resigned a month later in the wake of riots over high food prices, in favor of the new Peronist president, Carlos Menem. In 1991, Menem promoted economic austerity measures that deregulated businesses and privatized state-owned industries. But beginning in Sept. 1998, eight years into Menem's two-term presidency, Argentina entered its worst recession in a decade. Menem's economic policies, tolerance of corruption, and pardoning of military leaders involved in the dirty war eventually lost him the support of the poor and the working class who had elected him.

In Dec. 1999 Fernando de la Rua became president. Despite the introduction of several tough economic austerity plans, by 2001 the recession slid into its third year. In March 2001, de la Rua brought back former Peronist economy minister Domingo Cavallo, who had rescued the country from hyperinflation in 1991. The IMF gave Argentina $13.7 billion in emergency aid in Jan. 2001 and $8 billion in Aug. 2001.

The international help was not enough, however, and by the end of 2001, Argentina neared economic collapse. Rioters protesting government austerity measures forced de la Rua to resign in Dec. 2001. Argentina then defaulted on its $155 billion foreign debt payments, the largest such default in history. After a period of instability, Congress named Eduardo Duhalde president on Jan. 1, 2002. Duhalde soon announced an economic plan devaluing the Argentine peso, which had been pegged to the dollar for a decade. The devaluation plunged the banking industry into crisis and wiped out much of the savings of the middle class.

In July 2002, former junta leader Galtieri and 42 other military officers were arrested and charged with the torture and execution of 22 leftist guerrillas during Argentina's 7-year military dictatorship. In recent years, judges have found legal loopholes allowing them to circumvent the blanket amnesty laws passed in 1986 and 1987, which have allowed many accused of atrocities during the dirty war to walk free.

# Armenia

**President:** Robert Kocharian (1998)
**Prime Minister:** Andranik Markarian (2000)
**Area:** 11,506 sq mi (29,800 sq km)
**Population (2002 est.):** 3,330,099 (growth rate: 0.2%) (Armenian, 93%; others, Kurds, Ukrainians, and Russians); birth rate: 12.0/1000; infant mortality rate: 41.1/1000, density per sq mi: 289
**Capital and largest city (1998 est.):** Yerevan, 1,226,000. **Other large cities (1998 est.):** Gyumri (Leninakan), 121,000; Vanadzor, 74,000; Abovian, 54,000. **Monetary unit:** Dram. **Language:** Armenian. **Ethnicity/race:** Armenian 93%, Azeri 3%, Russian 2%, other (mostly Yezidi Kurds) 2% (1989). Note: as of the end of 1993, virtually all Azeris had emigrated from Armenia. **Religion:** Armenian Orthodox 94%. **Literacy rate:** 99% (1989)
**Economic summary: GDP/PPP** (2000 est.): $10 billion; per capita $3,000. **Real growth rate:** 5%. **Inflation:** 1% (1999 est.). **Unemployment:** 20% (1999 est.). Note: official rate is 9.0% for 1998. **Arable land:** 17%. **Agriculture:** fruit (especially grapes), vegetables; livestock. **Labor force:** 1.5 million (1999); agriculture 55%, services 25%, industry 20% (1999 est.). **Industries:** metal-cutting machine tools, forging-pressing machines, electric motors, tires, knitted wear, hosiery, shoes, silk fabric, chemicals, trucks, instruments, microelectronics, gem cutting, jewelry manufacturing, software development, brandy. **Natural resources:** small deposits of gold, copper, molybdenum, zinc, alumina. **Exports:** $284 million (f.o.b., 2000 est.): diamonds, scrap metal, machinery and equipment, brandy, copper ore. **Imports:** $913 million (f.o.b., 2000 est.): natural gas, petroleum, tobacco products, foodstuffs, diamonds. **Major trading partners:** Belgium, Iran, Russia, U.S., Turkmenistan, Georgia, UK, Turkey.

**Geography** Armenia is located in the southern Caucasus and is the smallest of the former Soviet republics. It is bounded by Georgia on the north, Azerbaijan on the east, Iran on the south, and Turkey on the west. Contemporary Armenia is a fraction of the size of ancient Armenia. A land of rugged mountains and extinct volcanoes, its highest point is Mount Aragats, 13,435 ft (4,095 m).

**Government** Republic.

**History** One of the world's oldest civilizations, Armenia once included Mount Ararat, which biblical tradition identifies as the mountain that Noah's ark rested on after the flood. It was the first country in the world to officially embrace Christianity as its religion (c. A.D. 300).

In the 6th century B.C., Armenians settled in the kingdom of Urartu (the Assyrian name for Ararat), which was in decline. Under Tigrane the Great (fl. 95–55 B.C.) the Armenian empire reached its height and became one of the most powerful in Asia, stretching from the Caspian to the Mediterranean Seas. Throughout most of its long history, however, Armenia has been invaded by a succession of empires. Under constant threat of domination by foreign forces, Armenians became both cosmopolitan as well as fierce protectors of their culture and tradition.

Over the centuries Armenia was conquered by Greeks, Romans, Persians, Byzantines, Mongols, Arabs, Ottoman Turks, and Russians. From the 16th century through World War I major portions of Armenia were controlled by their most brutal invader, the Ottoman Turks, under whom the Armenians experienced discrimination, religious persecution, heavy taxation, and armed attacks. In response to Armenian nationalist stirrings, the Turks massacred thousands of Armenians in 1894 and 1896. The most horrific massacre took place in April 1915 during World War I, when the Turks ordered the deportation of the Armenian population to the deserts of Syria and Mesopotamia. According to the majority of historians, between 600,000 and 1.5 million Armenians were murdered or died of starvation. The Armenian massacre is considered the first genocide in the 20th century. Turkey denies that a genocide took place, and claims that a much smaller number died in a civil war.

After the Turkish defeat in World War I, the independent Republic of Armenia was established on May 28, 1918, but survived only until Nov. 29, 1920, when it was annexed by the Soviet Army. On March 12, 1922, the Soviets joined Georgia, Armenia, and Azerbaijan to form the Transcaucasian Soviet Socialist Republic, which became part of the USSR. In 1936, after a reorganization, Armenia became a separate constituent republic of the USSR. Since 1988, Armenia has been involved in a territorial dispute with Azerbaijan over the enclave of Nagorno-Karabakh, to which both lay claim. Also in 1988, a devastating earthquake killed thousands and wreaked economic havoc.

Armenia declared its independence from the collapsing Soviet Union on Sept. 23, 1991. In the years that followed, Armenia successfully fought Azerbaijan for control of Nagorno-Karabakh. The majority population of the enclave are Armenian Christians who want to secede from Azerbaijan and either become part of Armenia or gain full independence. A cease-fire agreement was reached between the two countries in 1994, but the fate of Nagorno-Karabakh remained unresolved. Real progress finally began in April 2001, when Azerbaijani president Heidar Aliev and Armenian president Robert Kocharian met with American,

French, and Russian negotiators, and began to hammer out the details regarding the future of the enclave.

An Armenian diaspora has existed throughout the nation's history, and Armenian emigration has been particularly heavy since independence from the Soviet Union. An estimated 60% of the total eight million Armenians worldwide live outside the country, with one million each in the U.S. and Russia. Significant Armenian communities are located in Georgia, France, Iran, Lebanon, Syria, Argentina, and Canada.

Prime Minister Vazgen Sarkisian and six others were assassinated Oct. 27, 1999, when gunmen broke into Parliament and began firing. The prime minister's brother, Aras Sarkisian, was appointed to succeed him, but in May 2000, President Kocharian replaced Sarkisian, a political rival, with a new prime minister, Andranik Markarian.

# Australia

### COMMONWEALTH OF AUSTRALIA

**Sovereign:** Queen Elizabeth II (1952)
**Governor-General:** Peter Hollingworth (2001)
**Prime Minister:** John Howard (1996)
**Area:** 2,967,893 sq mi (7,686,850 sq km)
**Population (2002 est.):** 19,546,792 (growth rate: 0.6%); birth rate: 12.7/1000; infant mortality rate: 4.9/1000; density per sq mi: 7
**Capital (1996 est.):** Canberra, 307,700. **Largest cities (1993 est.):** Sydney, 3,713,500; Melbourne, 3,189,200; Brisbane, 1,520,600; Perth, 1,295,100; Adelaide, 1,079,200. **Monetary unit:** Australian dollar.
**Language:** English. **Ethnicity/race:** Caucasian 95%, Asian 4%, aboriginal (353,000) and other 1%.
**Religions:** Anglican 26.1%, Roman Catholic 26.0%, other Christian 24.3%. **Literacy rate:** 100% (1980)
**Economic summary:** GDP/PPP (2000 est.): $445.8 billion; per capita $23,200. **Real growth rate:** 4.7%. **Inflation:** 1.4%. **Unemployment:** 6.4%. **Arable land:** 6%. **Agriculture:** wheat, barley, sugarcane, fruits; cattle, sheep, poultry. **Labor force:** 9.5 million (Dec. 1999); services 73%, industry 22%, agriculture 5% (1997 est.). **Industries:** mining, industrial and transportation equipment, food processing, chemicals, steel. **Natural resources:** bauxite, coal, iron ore, copper, tin, silver, uranium, nickel, tungsten, mineral sands, lead, zinc, diamonds, natural gas, petroleum. **Exports:** $69 billion (f.o.b., 2000 est.): coal, gold, meat, wool, alumina, iron ore, wheat, machinery and transport equipment. **Imports:** $77 billion (f.o.b., 2000 est.): machinery and transport equipment, computers and office machines, telecommunication equipment and parts; crude oil and petroleum products. **Major trading partners:** Japan, EU, ASEAN, U.S., South Korea, New Zealand, Taiwan, Hong Kong, China.
**Member of Commonwealth of Nations**

**Geography** The continent of Australia, with the island state of Tasmania, is approximately equal in area to the United States (excluding Alaska and Hawaii). Mountain ranges run from north to south along the east coast, reaching their highest point in Mount Kosciusko (7,308 ft; 2,228 m). The western half of the continent is occupied by a desert plateau that rises into barren, rolling hills near the west coast. It includes the Great Victoria Desert to the south and the Great Sandy Desert to the north. The Great Barrier Reef, extending about 1,245 mi (2,000 km), lies along the northeast coast. The island of Tasmania (26,178 sq mi; 67,800 sq km) is off the southeast coast.

**Government** Democracy. Symbolic executive power is vested in the British monarch, who is represented throughout Australia by the governor-general.

**History** The first inhabitants of Australia were the Aborigines, who migrated there at least 40,000 years ago from Southeast Asia. There may have been between a half million to a full million Aborigines at the time of European settlement; today there are about 350,000.

Dutch, Portuguese, and Spanish ships sighted Australia in the 17th century; the Dutch landed at the Gulf of Carpentaria in 1606. In 1616 the territory became known as New Holland. The British arrived in 1688, but it was not until Captain James Cook's voyage in 1770 that Great Britain claimed possession of the vast island, calling it New South Wales. A British penal colony was set up at Port Jackson (what is now Sydney) in 1788, and about 161,000 transported English convicts were settled there until the system was suspended in 1839.

Free settlers established six colonies: New South Wales (1786), Tasmania (then Van Diemen's Land) (1825), Western Australia (1829), South Australia (1834), Victoria (1851), and Queensland (1859). Various gold rushes attracted settlers, as did the mining of other minerals. Sheep farming and grain soon became important economic enterprises. The six colonies became states and in 1901 federated into the Commonwealth of Australia with a constitution that incorporated British parliamentary and U.S. federal traditions. Australia became known for its liberal legislation: free compulsory education, protected trade unionism with industrial conciliation and arbitration, the secret ballot, women's suffrage, maternity allowances, and sickness and old-age pensions.

Australia fought alongside Britain in World War I, notably with the Australia and New Zealand Army Corps (ANZAC) in the Dardanelles campaign (1915). Participation in World War II brought Australia closer to the United States. Parliamentary power in the second half of the 20th century shifted between three political parties: the Australian Labour Party, the Liberal Party, and the National Party. Australia relaxed its discriminatory immigration laws in the 1960s and 1970s, which favored Northern Europeans. Thereafter, about 40% of its immigrants came from Asia, diversifying a population that was predominantly of English and Irish heritage.

In March 1996 the opposition Liberal Party–National Party coalition easily won the national elections, removing the Labour Party after 13 years in power. Pressure from the new, conservative One Nation Party threatened to reduce the gains made by Aborigines and to limit immigration. An Aboriginal movement had grown in the 1960s that gained full citizenship and improved education for the country's poorest socioeconomic group.

In Sept. 1999, Australia led the international peace-keeping force in to restore order in East Timor, Indonesia. Pro-Indonesian militias had begun massacring civilians following a UN-sponsored referendum that overwhelmingly called for East Timor's independence.

In Nov. 1999, Australia's 11.6 million voters rejected a referendum that would have ended Australia's formal allegiance to the British Crown. The referendum would have replaced the British governor-general with an Australian president chosen by Parliament. Although the vast majority of Australians do not consider themselves monarchists, they rejected the referendum because it did not provide for direct, popular elections but gave Parliament the power to select the president.

In 2000, Prime Minister Howard instituted a new tax system, lowering income and corporate taxes, and adding sales taxes on goods and services. Sydney hosted the 2000 Summer Olympic games.

John Howard won a third term of office in Nov. 2001, primarily as the result of his policy against illegal immigration, which some have condemned as xenophobic. Howard has dealt with refugees attempting to enter Australia—most of them from Afghanistan, Iran, and Iraq, and numbering about 5,000 annually—by imprisoning them in bleak detention camps and subjecting them to a lengthy immigration process. The asylum-seekers have staged riots and hunger strikes. Howard has also dealt with immigrants through the "Pacific solution," which re-routes boat people from Australian shores to camps in Papua New Guinea and Nauru.

## Australian External Territories

**Norfolk Island** (13.36 sq mi; 34.6 sq km) was placed under Australian administration in 1914. Population 1,879 (July 2001 est.). A former penal colony, Norfolk Island became home to the entire population of Pitcairn Island in 1856. The 194 residents of tiny Pitcairn—all of whom were the descendants of the mutineers from the HMS *Bounty* and their Tahitian wives—embarked on the 3,700-mile journey to Norfolk because of overpopulation. Many Norfolk residents can trace their genealogy directly to the adventurers from *Bounty*.

**The Ashmore and Cartier Islands** (1.93 sq mi), situated in the Indian Ocean off the northwest coast of Australia, came under Australian administration in 1934.

**Heard Island and the McDonald Islands** (159 sq mi; 412 sq km), lying in the sub-Antarctic, were placed under Australian administration in 1947. The islands are uninhabited.

**Christmas Island** (52 sq mi; 135 sq km) is situated in the Indian Ocean. It came under Australian administration in 1958. Most of the island's residents had been phosphate miners until the 1990s, when the Australian-based Casinos Austria International Ltd. built a $45 million casino on Christmas Island. As a result, the population has more than doubled, to 2,771 (July 2001 est.).

**Coral Sea Islands** (400,000 sq mi; 1,036,000 sq km, but only a few sq mi of land) became a territory of Australia in 1969. There is no permanent population on the islands.

**Cocos (Keeling) Islands** are made up of a group of 27 small coral islands in two separate atolls in the Indian Ocean, 1,721 mi (2,768 km) northwest of Perth. West Island is the largest, about 6.2 mi (10 km) long. The islands became an Australian territory in 1955. In April 1984 the residents voted to merge with Australia. The population of the Cocos is 633 (July 2001 est.)

---

# Austria

**REPUBLIC OF AUSTRIA**

**National name:** Republik Österreich
**President:** Thomas Klestil (1992)
**Chancellor:** Wolfgang Schüssel (2000)
**Area:** 32,378 sq mi (83,858 sq km)
**Population (2002 est.):** 8,169,929 (growth rate: 0.0%); birth rate 9.6/1000; infant mortality rate: 4.4/1000; density per sq mi: 252
**Capital and largest city (1991 est.):** Vienna, 1,600,000.
**Other large cities (1995 est.):** Graz, 237,150; Linz, 203,000; Salzburg, 144,000; Innsbruck, 118,000.
**Monetary units:** Euro (formerly schilling).
**Languages:** German 98% (small Slovene, Croatian, and Hungarian-speaking minorities). **Ethnicity/race:**

German 99.4%, Croatian 0.3%, Slovene 0.2%.
**Religions:** Roman Catholic 85%, Protestant 6%, other 9%. **Literacy rate:** 99% (1974)
**Economic summary: GDP/PPP** (2000 est.): $203 billion; per capita $25,000. **Real growth rate:** 3.1%. **Inflation:** 2%. **Unemployment:** 5.4%. **Arable land:** 17%. **Agriculture:** grains, potatoes, sugar beets, wine, fruit; dairy products, cattle, pigs, poultry; lumber. **Labor force:** 3.7 million (1999); services 68%, industry and crafts 29%, agriculture and forestry 3% (1999 est.). **Industries:** construction, machinery, vehicles and parts, food, chemicals, lumber and wood processing, paper and paperboard, communications equipment, tourism. **Natural resources:** iron ore, oil, timber, magnesite, lead, coal, lignite, copper, hydropower. **Exports:** $63.2 billion (2000 est.): machinery and equipment, paper and paperboard, metal goods, chemicals, iron and steel; textiles, foodstuffs. **Imports:** $65.6 billion (2000 est.): machinery and equipment, chemicals, metal goods, oil and oil products; foodstuffs. **Major trading partners:** EU, Switzerland, U.S., Hungary.

**Geography** Slightly smaller than Maine, Austria includes much of the mountainous territory of the eastern Alps (about 75% of the area). The country contains many snowfields, glaciers, and snowcapped peaks, the highest being the Grossglockner (12,530 ft; 3,819 m). The Danube is the principal river. Forests and woodlands cover about 40% of the land.

**Government** Federal republic.

**History** Settled in prehistoric times, the central European land that is now Austria was overrun in pre-Roman times by various tribes, including the Celts. After the fall of the Roman Empire, of which Austria was part, the area was invaded by Bavarians and Slavic Avars. Charlemagne conquered the area in 788 and encouraged colonization and Christianity. In 1252, Ottokar, king of Bohemia, gained possession, only to lose the territories to Rudolf of Hapsburg in 1278. Thereafter, until World War I, Austria's history was largely that of its ruling house, the Hapsburgs. Austria emerged from the Congress of Vienna in 1815 as the continent's dominant power. The *Ausgleich* of 1867 provided for a dual sovereignty, the empire of Austria and the kingdom of Hungary, under Franz Joseph I, who ruled until his death on Nov. 21, 1916. The Austrian-Hungarian minority rule of this immensely diverse empire became increasingly difficult in an age of emerging nationalist movements. When Archduke Francis Ferdinand was assassinated by a Serbian nationalist in Sarajevo in 1914, World War I, as well as the destruction of the Austro-Hungarian Empire, began.

During World War I, Austria-Hungary was one of the Central powers with Germany, Bulgaria, and Turkey, and the conflict left the country in political chaos and economic ruin. Austria, shorn of Hungary, was proclaimed a republic in 1918, and the monarchy was dissolved in 1919. A parliamentary democracy was set up by the constitution of Nov. 10, 1920. To check the power of Nazis advocating union with Germany, Chancellor Engelbert Dolfuss in 1933 established a dictatorship, but was assassinated by the Nazis on July 25, 1934. Kurt von Schuschnigg, his successor, struggled to keep Austria independent, but on March 12, 1938, German troops occupied the country, and Hitler proclaimed its *Anschluss* (union) with Germany, annexing it to the Third Reich.

After World War II, the U.S. and Britain declared the Austrians a "liberated" people. But the Russians prolonged the occupation. Finally Austria concluded a state treaty with the USSR and the other occupying powers and regained its independence on May 15, 1955. The second Austrian republic, established Dec. 19, 1945, on the basis of the 1920 constitution (amended in 1929), was declared by the federal Parliament to be permanently neutral.

On June 8, 1986, former UN secretary-general Kurt Waldheim was elected to the ceremonial office of president in a campaign marked by controversy over his alleged links to Nazi war crimes in Yugoslavia. Austria became a member of the European Union in 1995, but it retained its strict constitutional neutrality and forbade the stationing of foreign troops on its soil.

In Feb. 2000 the conservative People's Party formed a coalition with the far-right Freedom Party, headed by Jörg Haider. A nationalist against immigration, Haider had made several controversial remarks praising some Nazi policies, which he has since recanted. His gradual rise to power—from 5% in 1983 to 28% in the October 1999 election—was credited to voters weary of decades of stasis under the rule of the Social Democrats. The European Union condemned Austria's new coalition, froze diplomatic contacts, and imposed sanctions, accusing Haider of being a racist, xenophobe, and Nazi-sympathizer. Austria responded angrily by criticizing the EU for interfering in the affairs of a democratically elected government. Given the controversy, Haider chose not to join the government and resigned from the party in May 2000, but he continued to wield influence from the sidelines. In Sept. 2000, the EU lifted sanctions against Austria. The Freedom Party's popularity began to decline markedly in 2001.

In Sept. 2002, the coalition between the People's Party and the Freedom Party dissolved after a shake-up in the Freedom Party, instigated by Haider. Haider then quit his party altogether. New elections are expected in Nov.

# Azerbaijan

### REPUBLIC OF AZERBAIJAN

**President:** Heydar Aliyev (1993)
**Prime Minister:** Artur Rasizade (1996)
**Area:** 33,436 sq mi (86,600 sq km)
**Population (2002 est.):** 7,798,497 (growth rate: 0.9%).
  Birth rate: 18.8/1000; infant mortality rate: 82.7/1000; density per sq mi: 233
**Capital and largest city (1991):** Baku, 1,713,300, a port on the Caspian Sea. **Other large cities:** Ganja (1989), 278,000; Sumgait, 231,000. **Monetary unit:** Manat. **Languages:** Azerbaijani Turkic, 82%; Russian, 7%; Armenian, 2%. **Ethnicity/race:** Azeri 90%, Dagestani 3.2%, Russian 2.5%, Armenian 2.3%, other 2% (1995 est.). Note: almost all Armenians live in the separatist Nagorno-Karabakh region. **Religions:** Muslim 87%, Russian Orthodox 5.6%, Armenian Orthodox 2%. **Literacy rate:** 97% (1989)
**Economic summary: GDP/PPP** (2000 est.): $23.5 billion; per capita $3,000. **Real growth rate:** 11.4%. **Inflation:** 1.8%. **Unemployment:** 20% (1999 est.). **Arable land:** 18%. **Agriculture:** cotton, grain, rice, grapes, fruit, vegetables, tea, tobacco; cattle, pigs, sheep, goats. **Labor force:** 2.9 million (1997); agriculture and forestry 32%, industry and construction 15%, services 53% (1997). **Industries:** petroleum and natural gas, petroleum products, oilfield equipment; steel, iron ore, cement; chemicals and petrochemicals; textiles. **Natural resources:** petroleum, natural gas, iron ore, nonferrous metals, alumina. **Exports:** $1.9 billion (f.o.b., 2000 est.): oil and gas 75%, machinery, cotton, foodstuffs. **Imports:** $1.4 billion (f.o.b., 2000 est.): machinery and equipment, foodstuffs, metals, chemicals. **Major trading partners:** Italy, Turkey, Russia, Georgia, Iran, Ukraine, UAE.

**Geography** Azerbaijan is located on the western shore of the Caspian Sea at the southeast extremity of the Caucasus. The region is a mountainous country. About 7% of it is arable land. The Kura River Valley is the area's major agricultural zone.

**Government** Constitutional republic.

**History** Northern Azerbaijan was known as Caucasian Albania in ancient times. The area was the site of many conflicts involving Arabs, Kazars, and Turks. After the 11th century, the territory became dominated by Turks and eventually a stronghold of the Shi'ite Muslim religion and Islamic culture. The territory of Soviet Azerbaijan was acquired by Russia from Persia through the Treaty of Gulistan in 1813 and the Treaty of Turkamanchai in 1828.

After the Bolshevik Revolution, Azerbaijan declared its independence from Russia in May 1918. The republic was reconquered by the Red Army in 1920, and was annexed into the Transcaucasian Soviet Socialist Republic in 1922. It was later reestablished as a separate Soviet Republic on Dec. 5, 1936. Azerbaijan declared independence from the collapsing Soviet Union on Aug. 30, 1991.

Since 1988, Azerbaijan and Armenia have been feuding over the enclave of Nagorno-Karabakh. The majority of the enclave's inhabitants are Armenian Christians agitating to secede from the predominantly Muslim Azerbaijan and join with Armenia. War broke out in 1988 when Nagorno-Karabakh tried to break away and annex itself to Armenia, and 30,000 died before a cease-fire agreement was reached in 1994, with Armenia retaining its hold over the disputed enclave. Final plans on the status of Nagorno-Karabakh have yet to be determined; in April 2001, however, Azerbaijani president Heydar Aliev and Armenian president Robert Kocharian met with American, French, and Russian negotiators, and made significant progress toward a settlement.

The country's economic troubles are expected to be transformed through Western investment in Azerbaijan's oil resources, an untapped reserve whose estimated worth is trillions of dollars. Since 1994, the Azerbaijan state oil company (SOCAR) has signed several billion-dollar agreements with international oil companies. A total of 15 production-sharing agreements have been signed; only one, run by BP led Azerbaijan International Operating Company (AIOC) is thus far producing crude oil. Azerbaijan's pro-Western stance and its careful economic management have made it the most attractive of the oil-rich Caspian countries for foreign investment. In the years since its independence, the country has undergone political pain the IMF has given it high marks as one of the most successful economic overhauls ever.

But difficult negotiations over the route of the pipeline have stalled Azerbaijan's potential oil boom. Routes through Russia, Turkey, Georgia, and Iran have been proposed, and U.S., Russian, British, Iranian, and Chinese contenders in the "pipeline war" are all vying for dominance. In the volatile Caucasus region the options are complex, since all the proposed routes must pass through an unstable field of political, ethnic, religious, and environmental land mines.

In July 2001 an Iranian warship chased two Azerbaijani oil-exploration ships out of disputed waters in the Caspian, intensifying the hostilities between the two countries over oil rights.

# Bahamas

### COMMONWEALTH OF THE BAHAMAS

**Sovereign:** Queen Elizabeth II (1952)
**Governor-General:** Ivy Dumont (2001)
**Prime Minister:** Perry Christie (2002)
**Area:** 5,382 sq mi (13,940 sq km)
**Population (2002 est.):** 300,529 (growth rate: 1.1%); birth rate: 18.7/1000; infant mortality rate: 17.1/1000; density per sq mi: 56
**Capital and largest city (1991 census):** Nassau, 171,542. **Monetary unit:** Bahamian dollar. **Language:** English. **Ethnicity/race:** black 85%, white 15%. **Religions:** Baptist 29%, Anglican 23%, Roman Catholic 22%, others. **Literacy rate:** 90% (1963)
**Economic summary: GDP/PPP** (2000 est.): $4.5 billion; per capita $15,000. **Real growth rate:** 4.5%. **Inflation:** 1.9%. **Unemployment:** 9% (1998 est.). **Arable land:** 1%. **Agriculture:** citrus, vegetables; poultry. **Labor force:** 156,000 (1999); tourism 40%, other services 50%, industry 5%, agriculture 5% (1995 est.). **Industries:** tourism, banking, cement, oil refining and transshipment, salt, rum, aragonite, pharmaceuticals, spiral-welded steel pipe . **Natural resources:** salt, aragonite, timber, arable land. **Exports:** $376.8 million (2000 est.): pharmaceuticals, cement, rum, crawfish, refined petroleum products. **Imports:** $1.73 billion (2000 est.): foodstuffs, manufactured goods, crude oil, vehicles, electronics. **Major trading partners:** U.S., Switzerland, UK, Denmark, Italy, Japan. **Member of Commonwealth of Nations**

**Geography** The Bahamas are an archipelago of about 700 islands and 2,400 uninhabited islets and cays lying 50 mi off the east coast of Florida. They extend for about 760 mi (1,223 km). Only about 30 of the islands are inhabited; the most important is New Providence (80 sq mi; 207 sq km), on which the capital, Nassau, is situated. Other islands include Grand Bahama, Abaco, Eleuthera, Andros, Cat Island, and San Salvador (or Watling's Island).

**Government** Constitutional parliamentary democracy.

**History** The Arawak Indians were the first inhabitants of the Bahamas. Columbus's first encounter with the New World was on Oct. 12, 1492, when he landed on the Bahamian island of San Salvador. The British first built settlements on the islands in the 17th century. In the early 18th century, the Bahamas were a favorite pirate haunt.

The Bahamas were a crown colony from 1717 until they were granted internal self-government in 1964. The islands moved toward greater autonomy in 1968 after the overwhelming victory in general elections of the Progressive Liberal Party, led by Prime Minister Lynden O. Pindling, over the predominantly white United Bahamians Party. With its mandate from the black population, Pindling's government negotiated a new constitution with Britain under which the colony became the Commonwealth of the Bahama Islands in 1969. On July 10, 1973, the Bahamas became an independent nation.

Hubert A. Ingraham, of the Free National Movement Party, was sworn in as prime minister on Aug. 20, 1992, ending 25 years of rule by the Progressive Liberal Party. Once heavily reliant on agriculture and fishing, the Bahamas has diversified its economy into tourism, financial services, and international shipping. While it enjoys a per capita income that is among the top 30 in the world, there is a big gap between the urban middle class and poor farmers. In addition, the nation is vulnerable to hurricanes, which regularly inflict serious damage.

In May 2002, the Progressive Liberal Party won 29 out of 40 seats in Parliamentary elections, unseating the ruling Free National Movement party. Perry Christie became prime minister.

# Bahrain

### STATE OF BAHRAIN

**Emir:** Sheik Hamad ibn Isa al-Khalifah (1999)
**Prime Minister:** Sheik Khalifah ibn Sulman al-Khalifah (1970)
**Area:** 239 sq mi (620 sq km)
**Population (2002 est.):** 656,397 (growth rate: 1.6%); birth rate: 19.5/1000; infant mortality rate: 19.2/1000; density per sq mi: 2,742
**Capital (1992 est.):** Al-Manámah, 140,401. **Monetary unit:** Bahrain dinar. **Languages:** Arabic (official), English, Farsi, Urdu. **Ethnicity/race:** Bahraini 63%, Asian 13%, other Arab 10%, Iranian 8%, other 6%. **Religion:** Islam. **Literacy rate:** 77% (1990)
**Economic summary: GDP/PPP** (2000 est): $10.1 billion; per capita $15,900. **Real growth rate:** 5%. **Inflation:** 2%. **Unemployment:** 15% (1998 est.). **Arable land:** 1%. **Agriculture:** fruit, vegetables; poultry, dairy products; shrimp, fish. **Labor force:** 295,000 (1998 est.); industry, commerce, and service 79%, government 20%, agriculture 1% (1997 est.). **Industries:** petroleum processing and refining, aluminum smelting, offshore banking, ship repairing; tourism. **Natural resources:** oil, associated and nonassociated natural gas, fish, pearls. **Exports:** $5.8 billion (f.o.b., 2000): petroleum and petroleum products, aluminum. **Imports:** $4.2 billion (f.o.b., 2000): nonoil, crude oil. **Major trading partners:** India, Saudi Arabia, U.S., UAE, Japan, South Korea, France.

**Geography** Bahrain is an archipelago in the Persian Gulf off the coast of Saudi Arabia. The islands for the most part are level expanses of sand and rock. A causeway connects Bahrain to Saudi Arabia.

**Government** Constitutional monarchy.

**History** Known in ancient times as Dilmun, Bahrain was an important center of trade by the 3rd millennium B.C. The islands were ruled by the Persians in the 4th century A.D., and then by Arabs until 1541, when the Portuguese invaded them. Persia again claimed Bahrain in 1602. In 1783 Ahmad ibn al-Khalifah took over, and the al-Khalifahs remain the ruling family today. Bahrain became a British protectorate in 1820. It did not gain full independence until Aug. 14, 1971.

Although oil was discovered in Bahrain in the 1930s, it was relatively little compared to other Gulf states, and the wells are expected to be the first in the region to dry up. Sheik Isa ibn-Sulman al-Khalifah, who became emir in 1961, was determined to diversify his country's economy, and set about establishing Bahrain as a major financial center. The country provides its people with free medical care, education, and old-age pensions.

Conflicts between the Shi'ites and Sunnis are a continuing problem in Bahrain. The Sunni minority, to which the ruling al-Khalifah family belongs, controls nearly all the power and wealth in the country. Shi'ite Muslims have continued to agitate for more representation in government, and minor violent clashes have led to about two dozen deaths since 1994.

Bahrain has been an important Western ally, serving as a Western air base during the Persian Gulf War in 1991, and continuing to serve as the base of the United States' Fifth Fleet, which patrols the Gulf.

Sheik Isa ibn-Sulman al-Khalifah died in 1999 after four decades of rule. He was succeeded by his son, Sheik Hamad ibn Isa al-Khalifah, who immediately began a sweeping democratization of the country: censorship has been relaxed and draconian laws repealed, exiles have been repatriated, and the stateless Bidoons have been granted citizenship. In a Feb. 2001 referendum, which permitted women to vote for the first time, Bahrainis overwhelmingly supported the transformation of the traditional monarchy into a constitutional one.

# Bangladesh

### PEOPLE'S REPUBLIC OF BANGLADESH

**President:** Iajuddin Ahmed (2002)
**Prime Minister:** Khaleda Zia (2001)
**Area:** 55,598 sq mi (144,000 sq km)
**Population (2002 est.):** 133,376,684 (growth rate: 1.7%); birth rate: 25.1/1000; infant mortality rate: 68.0/1000; density per sq mi: 2,399
**Capital and largest city (2000 est.):** Dhaka, 9,600,000 (metro. area). **Other large cities (est. mid-1994):** Chittagong, 3,000,000; Khulna, 2,000,000. **Monetary unit:** Taka. **Principal languages:** Bangla (official), English. **Ethnicity/race:** Bengali 98%, Biharis 250,000, tribals less than 1 million. **Religions:** Muslim 83%, Hindu 16%, Buddhist, Christian, other. **Literacy rate:** 36% (1991)
**Economic summary: GDP/PPP** (2000 est.): $203 billion; per capita $1,570. **Real growth rate:** 5.3%. **Inflation:** 5.8%. **Unemployment:** 35.2% (1996). **Arable land:** 73%. **Agriculture:** rice, jute, tea, wheat, sugarcane, potatoes, tobacco, pulses, oilseeds, spices, fruit; beef, milk, poultry. **Labor force:** 64.1 million (1998); note: extensive export of labor to Saudi Arabia, Kuwait, UAE, Oman, Qatar, and Malaysia; agriculture, 63%, services 26%, industry 11% (FY95/96). **Industries:** cotton textiles, jute, garments, tea processing, paper newsprint, cement, chemical fertilizer, light engineering, sugar. **Natural resources:** natural gas, arable land, timber, coal. **Exports:** $5.9 billion (2000): garments, jute and jute goods, leather, frozen fish and seafood. **Imports:** $8.1 billion (2000): machinery and equipment, chemicals, iron and steel, textiles, raw cotton, food, crude oil and petroleum products, cement. **Major trading partners:** U.S., Germany, UK, France, Italy, India, Singapore, Japan, China. **Member of Commonwealth of Nations**

**Geography** Bangladesh, on the northern coast of the Bay of Bengal, is surrounded by India, with a small common border with Myanmar in the southeast. The country is low-lying riverine land traversed by the many branches and tributaries of the Ganges and Brahmaputra Rivers. Tropical monsoons and frequent floods and cyclones inflict heavy damage in the delta region.

**Government** Parliamentary democratic republic within the British Commonwealth.

**History** What is now called Bangladesh is part of the historic region of Bengal, the northeast portion of the Indian subcontinent. The earliest reference to the region was to a kingdom called Vanga, or Banga (c. 1000 B.C.). Buddhists ruled for centuries, but by the 10th century Bengal was primarily Hindu. In 1576, Bengal became part of the Mogul Empire, and the majority of East Bengalis converted to Islam. Bengal was ruled by British India from 1757 until Britain withdrew in 1947, and Pakistan was founded out of the two predominantly Muslim regions of the Indian subcontinent. West Pakistan and East Pakistan were united by religion (Islam), but their peoples were separated by culture, physical features, and 1,000 miles of Indian territory. Bangladesh consists primarily of East Bengal (West Bengal is part of India and its people are primarily Hindu) plus the Sylhet district of the Indian state of Assam. For almost 25 years after independence from Britain, its history was part of Pakistan's (*see* Pakistan).

Tension between East and West Pakistan developed from the outset because of their vast geographic, economic, and cultural differences. East Pakistan's Awami League, a political party founded by the Bengali nationalist Sheik Mujibur Rahman in 1949, sought independence from West Pakistan. Although 56% of the population resided in East Pakistan, the West held the lion's share of political and economic power. In 1970 East Pakistanis secured a majority of the seats in the National Assembly. President Yahya Khan postponed the opening of the National Assembly in an attempt to circumvent East Pakistan's demand for greater autonomy. As a consequence East Pakistan seceded, and the independent state of Bangladesh, or Bengali nation, was proclaimed on March 26, 1971. Civil war broke out, and with the help of Indian troops in the last few weeks of the war, East Pakistan defeated West Pakistan on Dec. 16, 1971. An estimated one million Bengalis were killed in the fighting or later slaughtered. Ten million more took refuge in India. In Feb. 1974, Pakistan agreed to recognize the independent state of Bangladesh.

Founding president Sheikh Mujibur was assassinated in 1975, as was the next president, Zia ur-Rahman. On March 24, 1982, Gen. Hossain Mohammad Ershad, army chief of staff, took control in a bloodless coup but was forced to resign on Dec. 6, 1990, amid violent protests and numerous allegations of corruption. A succession of prime ministers governed in the 1990s, including Khaleda Zia, wife of the assassinated president Zia ur-Rahman and Sheikh Hasina Wazed, the daughter of Sheik Mujibur.

Prime Minister Sheikh Hasina completed her five-year term as prime minister in July 2000—the first leader to do so since the country gained independence from Pakistan in 1974. In Oct. 2001 elections, Khaleda Zia again won the prime ministership.

Bangladesh is facing a catastrophic public-health crisis. Dangerous levels of arsenic have been found in groundwater, the result of a safe-water program sponsored by UNICEF, the government, and other aid organizations almost 30 years ago. To save people from drinking contaminated river and pond water, between 3 and 4 million wells were built throughout the country. But arsenic naturally occurring in the ground has seeped into well water, causing slow poisoning. The World Bank has estimated that an many as 85 million people may have been affected, with ailments ranging from cancer to diabetes to skin lesions. The International Development Association, a branch of the World Bank announced in August 2003 that beginning in 2003 it would fund a $40 million program to monitor arsenic levels.

# Barbados

**Sovereign:** Queen Elizabeth II (1952)
**Governor-General:** Sir Clifford Husbands (1996)
**Prime Minister:** Owen Arthur (1994)
**Area:** 166 sq mi (430 sq km)
**Population (2002 est.):** 276,607 (growth rate: 0.5%); birth rate: 13.3/1000; infant mortality rate: 11.7/1000; density per sq mi: 1,666
**Capital and largest city (1990):** Bridgetown, 6,700.

**Monetary unit:** Barbados dollar. **Language:** English.
**Ethnicity/race:** African 80%, European 4%, other 16%. **Religions:** Anglican 40%, Methodist 7%, Pentecostal 8%, Roman Catholic 4%. **Literacy rate:** 99% (1970)
**Economic summary: GDP/PPP** (2000 est.): $4 billion; per capita: $14,500. **Real growth rate:** 2.8%. **Inflation:** 2%. **Unemployment:** 11% (1999 est.). **Arable land:** 37%. **Agriculture:** sugarcane, vegetables, cotton. **Labor force:** 136,000 (1998 est.); services 75%, industry 15%, agriculture 10% (1996 est.). **Industries:** tourism, sugar, light manufacturing, component assembly for export. **Natural resources:** petroleum, fish, natural gas. **Exports:** $260 million (2000 est.): sugar and molasses, rum, other foods and beverages, chemicals, electrical components, clothing. **Imports:** $800.3 million (2000 est.): consumer goods, machinery, foodstuffs, construction materials, chemicals, fuel, electrical components. **Major trading partners:** UK, U.S., Trinidad and Tobago, Venezuela, Jamaica, Japan, Canada. **Member of Commonwealth of Nations**

**Geography** An island in the Atlantic about 300 mi (483 km) north of Venezuela, Barbados is only 21 mi long (34 km) and 14 mi across (23 km) at its widest point. It is circled by fine beaches and narrow coastal plains. The highest point is Mount Hillaby (1,105 ft; 337 m) in the north-central area.

**Government** Parliamentary democracy.

**History** Barbados is thought to have been originally inhabited by Arawak Indians. By the time Europeans explored the island, however, it was uninhabited. The Portuguese were the first Europeans to set foot on the island, but it was the British who first established a colony there in 1627. Colonists first cultivated tobacco and cotton, but by the 1640s they had switched to sugar, which was enormously profitable. Slaves were brought in from Africa to work sugar plantations, and eventually the population was about 90% black. A slave revolt took place in 1816; slavery was abolished in the British Empire in 1834.

Barbados was the administrative headquarters of the Windward Islands until it became a separate colony in 1885. Barbados was a member of the Federation of the West Indies from 1958 to 1962. Britain granted the colony independence on Nov. 30, 1966, and it became a parliamentary democracy within the Commonwealth.

Since independence, Barbados has been politically stable. However, local anger over rulings by the final appeals court, appointed by Queen Elizabeth, led to the creation in 1997 of a constitutional commission to consider abandoning all ties to Great Britain.

Prime minister Arthur, who has seen Barbados's unemployment fall from 22% to 11%, was reelected in 1999 by a landslide. With one of the highest literacy rates in the world, 98%, Barbados has expanded its financial services and tourist industries, reducing reliance on sugar cane exports.

# Belarus

**REPUBLIC OF BELARUS**

**President:** Alyaksandr Lukashenka (1994)
**Prime Minister:** Henadz Navitski (2001)
**Area:** 80,154 sq mi (207,600 sq km)
**Population (2002 est.):** 10,335,382 (growth rate: –0.4%); birth rate: 9.9/1000; infant mortality rate: 14.1/1000; density per sq mi: 129
**Capital (1992 est.):** Mensk (Minsk), 1,666,000. **Other**

**large cities (1992 est.):** Gomel, 517,300; Vitebsk, 373,000; Mogilyov, 364,000; Grodno, 291,800; Brest, 284,000; Bobruysk, 224,000. **Monetary unit:** Belorussian ruble. **Language:** Belorussian (White Russian). **Ethnicity/race:** Belorussian 77.9%, Russian 13.2%, Polish 4.1%, Ukrainian 2.9%, other 1.9%. **Religion:** Orthodoxy is predominant. **Literacy rate:** 100% (1979)
**Economic summary: GDP/PPP** (2000 est.): $78.8 billion; per capita $7,500. **Real growth rate:** 4%. **Inflation:** 200%. **Unemployment:** 2.1% officially registered unemployed (Dec. 2000); large number of underemployed workers. **Arable land:** 29%. **Agriculture:** grain, potatoes, vegetables, sugar beets, flax; beef, milk. **Labor force:** 4.8 million (2000); industry and construction n.a., agriculture and forestry n.a., services n.a. **Industries:** metal-cutting machine tools, tractors, trucks, earth movers, motorcycles, television sets, chemical fibers, fertilizer, textiles, radios, refrigerators. **Natural resources:** forests, peat deposits, small quantities of oil and natural gas. **Exports:** $7.4 billion (f.o.b., 2000): machinery and equipment, chemicals, metals, textiles, foodstuffs. **Imports:** $8.3 billion (f.o.b., 2000): mineral products, machinery and equipment, metals, chemicals, foodstuffs. **Major trading partners:** Russia, Ukraine, Poland, Germany, Lithuania.

**Geography** Much of Belarus (formerly the Belorussian Soviet Socialist Republic of the USSR, and then Byelorussia) is a hilly lowland with forests, swamps, and numerous rivers and lakes. There are wide rivers emptying into the Baltic and Black Seas. Its forests cover over one-third of the land and its peat marshes are a valuable natural resource. The largest lake is Narach, 31 sq mi (79.6 sq km).

**Government** Republic.

**History** In the 5th century A.D., Belarus (also known as White Russia) was colonized by east Slavic tribes. Kiev dominated it from the 9th to 12th centuries. After the destruction of Kiev by the Mongols in the 13th century, the territory was conquered by the dukes of Lithuania, although it retained a degree of autonomy. Belarus became part of the Grand Duchy of Lithuania, which merged with Poland in 1569. Following the partitions of Poland in 1772, 1793, and 1795, in which Poland was divided among Russia, Prussia, and Austria, Belarus became part of the Russian empire.

Following World War I, Belarus proclaimed itself a republic, only to find itself occupied by the Red Army soon after its March 1918 announcement. The Polish-Soviet War of 1918–21 was fought to decide the fate of Belarus. West Belarus was ceded to Poland; the larger eastern part formed the Belorussian SSR, and was then joined to the USSR in 1922. In 1939, the Soviet Union took back West Belarus from Poland under the secret protocol of the Nazi-Soviet Nonaggression Pact and incorporated it into the Belorussian Soviet Socialist Republic. Occupied by the Nazis in World War II, Belarus was one of the most devastated battlefields.

When the Chernobyl nuclear power plant in Ukraine exploded in 1986, 70% of its radioactivity fell on Belarus. Cancer and other illnesses have multiplied as a result.

Belarus declared its sovereignty in July 1990 and its independence in Aug. 1991. It became a cofounder of the Commonwealth of Independent States (CIS) in Dec. 1991. In Jan. 1994, the country's Parliament ousted its reform-minded leader, Stanislav Shushkevich, in protest against his support for market economics. He was replaced by Alyaksandr Lukashenka, who over the next two years greatly expanded the powers of the presidency. Lukashenka sought to renew ties with Russia, and, with much fanfare, Belarus and Russia signed a treaty in April 1997 aimed at significantly increasing cooperation between the two states, stopping just short of union.

The Russian financial crisis that began in fall 1998 severely affected Belarus's Soviet-style planned economy. Belarus is almost completely dependent on Russia, which buys 70% of its exports.

Critics continue to denounce the increasingly oppressive political atmosphere and human rights violations in Belarus under the Soviet-style authoritarianism of President Lukashenka. In 1999, the year Lukashenka was to step down, he rigged a national referendum allowing him to cancel the elections and remain president. Lukashenka's government has been accused of running a death squad that has killed dozens, including opposition party members and underworld figures.

After harassing the opposition and curtailing their campaign activities, Lukashenka won reelection in the Sept. 9, 2001, presidential race.

# Belgium

**KINGDOM OF BELGIUM**

**National name:** Royaume de Belgique—Koninkrijk België
**Sovereign:** King Albert II (1993)
**Prime Minister:** Guy Verhofstadt (1999)
**Area:** 11,780 sq mi (30,510 sq km)
**Population (2002 est.):** 10,274,595 (growth rate: 0.1%); birth rate: 10.6/1000; infant mortality rate: 4.6/1000; density per sq mi: 872
**Capital and largest city (1994):** Brussels, 949,070 (metro area). **Other large cities (1994):** Antwerp, 476,044; Ghent, 229,900; Liège, 207,496; Charleroi, 206,898; Bruges, 116,724. **Monetary units:** Euro (formerly Belgian franc). **Languages:** Dutch (Flemish), 57%; French, 32%; bilingual (Brussels), 10%; German, 0.7%. **Ethnicity/race:** Fleming 55%, Walloon 33%, mixed or other 12%. **Religion:** Roman Catholic 75%. **Literacy rate:** 99% (1980)
**Economic summary: GDP/PPP** (2000 est.): $259.2 billion; per capita $25,300. **Real growth rate:** 4.1%. **Inflation:** 2.2%. **Unemployment:** 8.4%. **Arable land:** 24%. **Agriculture:** sugar beets, fresh vegetables, fruits, grain, tobacco; beef, veal, pork, milk. **Labor force:** 4.34 million (1999); services 73%, industry 25%, agriculture 2% (1999 est.). **Industries:** engineering and metal products, motor vehicle assembly, processed food and beverages, chemicals, basic metals, textiles, glass, petroleum, coal . **Natural resources:** coal, natural gas. **Exports:** $181.4 billion (f.o.b., 2000): machinery and equipment, chemicals, diamonds, metals and metal products. **Imports:** $166 billion (c.i.f., 2000): machinery and equipment, chemicals, metals and metal products. **Major trading partners:** EU.

**Geography** Located in western Europe, Belgium has about 40 mi of seacoast on the North Sea, at the Strait of Dover, and is approximately the size of Maryland. The Meuse and the Schelde, Belgium's principal rivers, are important commercial arteries.

**Government** Parliamentary democracy under a constitutional monarch. Under the 1994 constitution, autonomy was granted to the Walloon region (Wallonia), the Flemish region (Flanders), and the bilingual Brussels-Capital region; autonomy was also guaranteed for the Flemish-, French-, and German-speaking "communities." The central government retains responsibility for foreign policy, defense, taxation, and social security.

**History** Belgium occupied part of the Roman province of Belgica, named after the Belgae, a people of ancient Gaul. The area was conquered by Julius Caesar in 57–50 B.C., then was overrun by the Franks in the 5th century A.D. It was part of Charlemagne's empire in the 8th century, then in the next century was absorbed into Lotharingia and later into the duchy of Lower Lorraine. In the 12th century it was partitioned into the duchies of Brabant and Luxembourg, the bishopric of Liège, and the domain of the count of Hainaut, which included Flanders. In the 16th century, Belgium, with most of the area of the low countries, passed to the duchy of Burgundy and was inherited by Charles V, who incorporated it into his Holy Roman Empire. Then, in 1555, the low countries were united with Spain. By the Treaty of Utrecht in 1713, the country's sovereignty passed to Austria. During the wars that followed the French Revolution, Belgium was occupied and later annexed to France. But with the downfall of Napoléon, the Congress of Vienna in 1815 gave the country to the Netherlands. The Belgians revolted in 1830 and declared their independence.

Germany's invasion of Belgium in 1914 set off World War I. The Treaty of Versailles (1919) gave the areas of Eupen, Malmédy, and Moresnet to Belgium. Leopold III succeeded Albert, king during World War I, in 1934. In World War II, Belgium was overwhelmed by Nazi Germany, and Leopold III was held prisoner. When he attempted to return in 1950, socialists and liberals revolted. He abdicated July 16, 1951, and his son, Baudouin, became king. Because of growing opposition to Belgian rule in its African colonies, Belgium granted independence to the Congo (now Democratic Republic of the Congo) in 1960 and to Ruanda-Urundi (now the nations of Rwanda and Burundi) in 1962.

Divisions between Flemings and Walloons grew, and linguistic regionalization increased, culminating in the revised constitution of 1994, which granted more autonomy to Belgium's three regions and language "communities."

In the 1990s the Belgian government was involved in numerous scandals that tainted it with a reputation for incompetence and corruption. In 1991, a deputy prime minister was murdered in a contract killing that remained unsolved. In 1998, Belgian statesman and former NATO secretary-general Willy Claes was convicted of bribery. International relations fared no better. Belgian peacekeeping troops abandoned Rwanda, a former colony, at the height of the 1994 genocide against the Tutsis. The discovery of the Dutroux child-sex-and-murder ring in 1996 led to further national outrage that was compounded by disclosures that official negligence and corruption had resulted in even more children's deaths. As the scandal continued into 1997, it fueled pressure for reform of the political, judicial, and police systems.

It was evident that little had changed, however, when Belgium stumbled into its next crisis in spring 1999. Dioxin, a cancer-causing chemical, was leaked into batches of chicken feed, contaminating the country's poultry and dairy products. Government ministers admitted to keeping the public in the dark for months after they realized the public health danger. Prime Minister Jean-Luc Dehaene resigned under the weight of the scandal. Dehaene has been credited with having reduced the budget deficit from 7% in 1993 to 1% in 1999, and for reducing the public debt by 20% during the same period.

The new prime minister, Guy Verhofstadt of the Liberal Party, cobbled together a coalition of six political parties in June 1999. Verhofstadt has promised a series of reforms aimed at the legal system and the civil service.

Under "universal jurisdiction," Belgian prosecutors may try anyone accused of war crimes, whatever their nationality and wherever the crimes took place. In 2001, Belgian courts convicted four Rwandans, including two nuns, for their role in the massacre of the Tutsi people in Rwanda.

# Belize

**Sovereign:** Queen Elizabeth II (1952)
**Governor-General:** Sir Colville Young (1993)
**Prime Minister:** Said Musa (1998)
**Area:** 8,867 sq mi (22,966 sq km)
**Population (2002 est.):** 262,999 (growth rate: 2.7%); birth rate: 31.1/1000; infant mortality rate: 24.3/1000.; density per sq mi: 30
**Capital (1997 est.):** Belmopan, 5,845. **Largest city (1997 est.):** Belize City, 52,500. **Monetary unit:** Belize dollar. **Languages:** English (official), Creole, Spanish, Garifuna, Mayan. **Ethnicity/race:** mestizo 44%, Creole 30%, Maya 11%, Garifuna 7%, other 8%. **Religions:** Roman Catholic 62%, Protestant 30%. **Literacy rate:** 91% (1970)
**Economic summary: GDP/PPP** (2000 est.): $790 million; per capita $3,200. **Real growth rate:** 4%. **Inflation:** 2%. **Unemployment:** 12.8% (1999). **Arable land:** 10%. **Agriculture:** bananas, coca, citrus, sugarcane; lumber; fish, cultured shrimp. **Labor force:** 71,000; note: shortage of skilled labor and all types of technical personnel (1997 est.); agriculture 38%, industry 32%, services 30% (1994). **Industries:** garment production, food processing, tourism, construction. **Natural resources:** arable land potential, timber, fish, hydropower. **Exports:** $235.7 million (f.o.b., 2000 est.): sugar, bananas, citrus, clothing, fish products, molasses, wood. **Imports:** $413 million (c.i.f., 2000 est.): machinery and transportation equipment, manufactured goods; food, beverages, tobacco; fuels, chemicals, pharmaceuticals. **Major trading partners:** U.S., UK, EU, Caricom, Canada, Mexico, Central America. **Member of Commonwealth of Nations**

**Geography** Belize is situated on the Caribbean Sea, south of Mexico and east and north of Guatemala in Central America. In area, it is about the size of New Hampshire. Most of the country is heavily forested with various hardwoods. Mangrove swamps and cays along the coast give way to hills and mountains in the interior. The highest point is Victoria Peak, 3,681 ft (1,122 m).

**Government** Parliamentary democracy within the British Commonwealth.

**History** The Mayan civilization spread into the area of Belize between 1500 B.C. and A.D. 300 and flourished until about 1200. Several major archeological sites—notably Caracol, Lamanai, Lubaantun, Altun Ha, and Xunantunich—reflect the advanced civilization and much denser population of that period. European contact began in 1502 when Columbus sailed along the coast. The first recorded European settlement was begun by shipwrecked English seamen in 1638. Over the next 150 years, more English settlements were established. This period was also marked by piracy, indiscriminate logging, and sporadic attacks by Indians and neighboring Spanish settlements. Great Britain first sent an official representative to the area in the late 18th century, but Belize was not formally termed the Colony of British Honduras until 1840. It became a Crown colony in 1862. Subsequently, several constitutional changes were enacted to expand representative government. Full internal self-government under a ministerial system was granted in Jan. 1964.

Guatemala had long made claims on Honduran territory. Although the dispute between Guatemala and Great Britain remained unresolved, Belize became independent on Sept. 21, 1981, after having been self-governing since 1964. Guatemala recognized Belize's sovereignty in Sept. 1991. However, Guatemala still claims more than half of Belize's territory. At talks held at the Organization of American States' conference in July 2000, Belize and Guatemala agreed to an agenda for formal negotiations to resolve the dispute.

# Benin

### REPUBLIC OF BENIN

**National name:** Republique du Benin
**President:** Mathieu Kérékou (1996)
**Area:** 43,483 sq mi (112,620 sq km)
**Population (2002 est.):** 6,787,625 (growth rate: 2.9%); birth rate: 43.7/1000; infant mortality rate: 88.5/1000; density per sq mi: 156
**Capital and largest city (1996):** Porto-Novo (official), 177,660; Cotonou (de facto capital) 33,212. **Other large city (1992):** Djougou, 132,192. **Monetary unit:** CFA Franc. **Languages:** French (official), African languages. **Ethnicity/race:** African 99% (42 ethnic groups, most important being Fon, Adja, Yoruba, Bariba), Europeans 5,500. **Religions:** indigenous 70%, Christian 15%, Islam 15%. **Literacy rate:** 23% (1990)
**Economic summary: GDP/PPP** (2000 est.): $6.6 billion; per capita $1,030. **Real growth rate:** 5%. **Inflation:** 3%. **Unemployment:** n.a. **Arable land:** 13%. **Agriculture:** corn, sorghum, cassava (tapioca), yams, beans, rice, cotton, palm oil, peanuts; poultry, livestock. **Labor force:** n.a. **Industries:** textiles, cigarettes; beverages, food; construction materials, petroleum. **Natural resources:** small offshore oil deposits, limestone, marble, timber. **Exports:** $396 million (f.o.b., 1999): cotton, crude oil, palm products, cocoa. **Imports:** $566 million (f.o.b., 1999): foodstuffs, tobacco, petroleum products, capital goods. **Major trading partners:** Brazil, Libya, Indonesia, Italy, France, China, UK, Côte d'Ivoire.

**Geography** This West African nation on the Gulf of Guinea, between Togo on the west and Nigeria on the east, is about the size of Tennessee. It is bounded also by Burkina Faso and Niger on the north. The land consists of a narrow coastal strip that rises to a swampy, forested plateau and then to highlands in the north. A hot and humid climate blankets the entire country.

**Government** Republic under a multiparty democratic rule.

**History** The Abomey kingdom of the Dahomey, or Fon, peoples was established in 1625. A rich cultural life flourished, and Benin's wooden masks, bronze statues, tapestries, and pottery are world renowned. One of the smallest and most densely populated regions in Africa, Benin was annexed by the French in 1893 and incorporated into French West Africa in 1904. It became an autonomous republic within the French Community in 1958, and on Aug. 1, 1960, Dahomey was granted its independence within the Community.

Gen. Christophe Soglo deposed the first president, Hubert Maga, in an army coup in 1963. He dismissed the civilian government in 1965, proclaiming himself chief of state. A group of young army officers seized

power in Dec. 1967, deposing Soglo. In Dec. 1969, Benin had its fifth coup of the decade, with the army again taking power. In May 1970, a three-man presidential commission with a six-year term was created to take over the government. In May 1972, yet another army coup ousted the triumvirate and installed Lt. Col. Mathieu Kérékou as president. Between 1974 and 1989 Dahomey embraced socialism, and changed its name to the People's Republic of Benin. The name *Benin* commemorates an African kingdom that flourished from the 15th to the 17th century in what is now southwest Nigeria. In 1990, Benin abandoned Marxist ideology, began moving toward multiparty democracy, and changed its name again, to the Republic of Benin.

By the end of the 1980s, Benin's economy was near collapse. As its oil boom ended, Nigeria expelled 100,000 Beninese migrant workers and closed the border with Benin. Kérékou's socialist collectivization of Benin's agriculture and the ballooning bureaucracy further damaged the economy. By 1988, international financial institutions feared Benin would default on its loans and pressured Kérékou to make financial reforms.

Kérékou subsequently embarked on a major privatization campaign, cut the government payroll, and reduced social services, prompting student and labor union unrest. Fearing a revolution, Kérékou agreed to a new constitution and free elections. In 1991, Nicéphore Soglo, an economist and former director of the International Bank for Reconstruction and Development, was elected president with 67% of the vote.

Although he enjoyed widespread support at first, Soglo gradually became unpopular as austerity measures reduced living standards and a 50% currency devaluation in 1994 caused inflation. Kérékou defeated Soglo in the 1996 elections, with 52.5% of the vote. In March 2001, Kérékou was easily reelected after two of his main opponents, charging fraud, withdrew from the race.

# Bhutan

### KINGDOM OF BHUTAN

**National name:** Druk-yul
**Ruler:** King Jigme Singye Wangchuck (1972)
**Prime Minister:** Lyonpo Kinzang Dorji (2002)
**Area:** 18,147 sq mi (47,000 sq km)
**Population (2002 est.):** 2,094,176 (growth rate: 2.2%); birth rate: 35.3/1000; infant mortality rate: 106.8/1000; density per sq mi: 115
**Capital and largest city (1993):** Thimphu (official), 30,340. **Monetary unit:** Ngultrum. **Language:** Dzongkha (official). **Ethnicity/race:** Bhote 50%, ethnic Nepali 35%, indigenous or migrant tribes 15%. **Religions:** Buddhist 75%, Hindu 25%. **Literacy rate:** 42% (1995)
**Economic summary: GDP/PPP** (2000 est.): $2.3 billion; per capita $1,100. **Real growth rate:** 6%. **Inflation:** 7%. **Unemployment:** n.a. **Arable land:** 2%. **Agriculture:** rice, corn, root crops, citrus, foodgrains; dairy products, eggs. **Labor force:** n.a.; note: massive lack of skilled labor; agriculture 93%, services 5%, industry and commerce 2%. **Industries:** cement, wood products, processed fruits, alcoholic beverages, calcium carbide. **Natural resources:** timber, hydropower, gypsum, calcium carbide. **Exports:** $154 million (f.o.b., 2000 est.): cardamom, gypsum, timber, handicrafts, cement, fruit, electricity (to India), precious stones, spices. **Imports:** $269 million (c.i.f., 2000 est.): fuel and lubricants, grain, machinery and parts, vehicles, fabrics, rice. **Major trading partners:** India, Bangladesh, Japan, UK, Germany, U.S.

**Geography** Mountainous Bhutan, half the size of Indiana, is situated on the southeast slope of the Himalayas, bordered on the north and east by Tibet and on the south and west and east by India. The landscape consists of a succession of lofty and rugged mountains running generally from north to south and separated by deep valleys. In the north, towering peaks reach a height of 24,000 ft (7,315 m).

**Government** In the 1990s, the king gradually gave up absolute rule, transforming his kingdom into a constitutional monarchy.

**History** Although archeological exploration of Bhutan has been limited, evidence of civilization in the region dates back to at least 2000 B.C. Aboriginal Bhutanese, known as Monpa, are believed to have migrated from Tibet. The traditional name of the country since the 17th century has been Drukyul, Land of the Drokpa (Dragon People), a reference to the dominant branch of Tibetan Buddhism that is still practiced in the Himalayan kingdom.

British troops invaded the region in 1865 and negotiated an agreement under which Britain agreed to pay an annual allowance to the Bhutanese monarchy on condition of good behavior. A treaty between India and the seat of government, Thimphu, in 1949 increased this subsidy and placed Bhutan's foreign affairs under Indian control. Until the 1960s Bhutan was largely isolated from the rest of the world, and its people carried on a tranquil, traditional way of life, farming and trading, which had remained intact for centuries. After China invaded Tibet, however, Bhutan strengthened its ties and contact with India in an effort to avoid Tibet's fate. New roads and other connections to India began to end its isolation. In the 1960s Bhutan also undertook social modernization, abolishing slavery and the caste system, emancipating women, and enacting land reform. In 1985, Bhutan made its first diplomatic links with non-Asian countries.

A pro-democracy campaign emerged in 1991, which the government claimed was composed largely of Nepali immigrants. As a result of the campaign, some 100,000 Nepali civil servants were either evicted or encouraged to emigrate. Most of them crossed the border back into Nepal, where they were housed in UN-administered refugee camps. Several rounds of talks aimed at deciding which country should claim the refugees have yielded few results, and the refugees have continued to languish in the camps for more than a decade.

In 1998, King Jigme Singye Wangchuck voluntarily curtailed his powerful monarchy by yielding to the formerly rubber-stamp legislature, giving it the right to remove him from leadership and appoint his cabinet. The move was the largest step in what is a gradual program to dilute the monarchy after nearly a century of absolute rule. Income tax was introduced, with tax forms due for the first time in Feb. 2000.

Nepal and Bhutan reached a significant breakthrough on the refugee issue in Dec. 2000's 10th round of bilateral talks. Both sides agreed to begin a joint verification process in the Nepali refugee camps, with repatriation to Bhutan the intended goal. Verification began in 2001, though at a snail's pace.

The United Liberation Front of Assam (ULFA), a group of separatist rebels fighting for independence from India, has maintained nine well-fortified bases in southern Bhutan since 1990. Bhutanese officials have pressured the group to shut down the camps, but the militants remained through the summer of 2002.

# Bolivia

## REPUBLIC OF BOLIVIA

**National name:** República de Bolivia
**President:** Gonzalo Sánchez de Lozada (2002)
**Area:** 424,162 sq mi (1,098,580 sq km)
**Population (2002 est.):** 8,445,134 (growth rate: 1.8%); birth rate: 26.4/1000; infant mortality rate: 57.5/1000; density per sq mi: 20
**Historic and judicial capital (1997 est.):** Sucre, 131,800; **Administrative capital and largest city (1997 est.):** La Paz, 713,400. **Other large cities (1997 est.):** Santa Cruz, 697,000; Cochabamba, 407,800; El Alto, 405,500; Oruro, 184,000. **Monetary unit:** Boliviano. **Languages:** Spanish (official), Quechua, Aymara, Guarani. **Ethnicity/race:** Quechua 30%, Aymara 25%, mestizo (mixed European and Indian ancestry) 25%–30%, European 5%–15%. **Religion:** Roman Catholic 85%. **Literacy rate:** 82% (1992)
**Economic summary: GDP/PPP** (2000 est.): $20.9 billion; per capita $2,600. **Real growth rate:** 2.5%. **Inflation:** 4.4%. **Unemployment:** 11.4% (1997) with widespread underemployment. **Arable land:** 2%. **Agriculture:** soybeans, coffee, coca, cotton, corn, sugarcane, rice, potatoes; timber. **Labor force:** 2.5 million; agriculture n.a., industry n.a., services n.a. **Industries:** mining, smelting, petroleum, food and beverages, tobacco, handicrafts, clothing. **Natural resources:** tin, natural gas, petroleum, zinc, tungsten, antimony, silver, iron, lead, gold, timber, hydropower. **Exports:** $1.26 billion (f.o.b., 2000 est.): soybeans, natural gas, zinc, gold, wood. **Imports:** $1.86 billion (f.o.b., 2000 est.): capital goods, raw materials and semi-manufactures, chemicals, petroleum, food. **Major trading partners:** UK, U.S., Peru, Argentina, Colombia, Japan, Brazil, Chile, Germany.

**Geography** Landlocked Bolivia is equal in size to California and Texas combined. Brazil forms its eastern border; its other neighbors are Peru and Chile on the west and Argentina and Paraguay on the south. The western part, enclosed by two chains of the Andes, is a great plateau—the Altiplano, with an average altitude of 12,000 ft (3,658 m). Almost half the population lives on the plateau, which contains Oruro, Potosí, and La Paz. At an altitude of 11,910 ft (3,630 m), La Paz is the highest administrative capital city in the world. The Oriente, a lowland region ranging from rain forests to grasslands, comprises the northern and eastern two-thirds of the country. Lake Titicaca, at an altitude of 12,507 ft (3,812 m), is the highest commercially navigable body of water in the world.

**Government** Republic.

**History** Famous since Spanish colonial days for its mineral wealth, modern Bolivia was once a part of the ancient Inca empire. After the Spaniards defeated the Incas in the 16th century, Bolivia's predominantly Indian population was reduced to slavery. The remoteness of the Andes helped protect the Bolivian Indians from the European diseases that decimated other South American Indians. But the existence of a large indigenous group forced to live under the thumb of their colonizers created a stratified society of haves and have-nots that continues to this day.

By the end of the 17th century the mineral wealth had begun to dry up. The country won its independence in 1825 and was named after Simón Bolívar, the famous liberator. Hampered by internal strife, Bolivia lost great slices of territory to three neighboring nations. Several thousand square miles and its outlet to the Pacific were taken by Chile after the War of the Pacific (1879–84). In 1903, a piece of Bolivia's Acre

Province, rich in rubber, was ceded to Brazil. And in 1938, after losing the Chaco War of 1932–35 to Paraguay, Bolivia gave up its claim to nearly 100,000 square mi of the Gran Chaco. Political instability ensued.

In 1965, a guerrilla movement mounted from Cuba and headed by Maj. Ernesto (Ché) Guevara began a revolutionary war. With the aid of U.S. military advisers, the Bolivian army smashed the guerrilla movement, capturing and killing Guevara on Oct. 8, 1967. Faltering steps toward restoration of civilian government were halted abruptly on July 17, 1980, when Gen. Luis Garcia Meza Tejada seized power. A series of military leaders followed before the military returned the government to civilian rule in 1982, when Hernán Siles Zuazo became president. Under Siles's left-of-center government, the country was regularly shut down by work stoppages, and the bulk of Bolivia's natural resources—natural gas, gold, lithium, potassium, and tungsten—were either sold on the black market or left in the ground. The country also had the lowest per capita income in South America, and inflation approached 3000%. In 1985, Siles decided he was unable to carry on and quit a year early.

Since 1985, Bolivia has implemented economic changes that have been phenomenally successful. Still at the bottom of the South American economic ladder, its economy has steadily improved over the past fifteen years. Political stability has helped.

In June 1993, free-market advocate Gonzalo Sánchez de Lozada was elected president. He was succeeded by former general Hugo Bánzer, an ex-dictator cum democrat who became president for the second time in Aug. 1997. Bánzer made significant progress in wiping out illicit coca production and drug trafficking, which has pleased the United States. However, the eradication of coca, a major crop in Bolivia since Incan times, has plunged many Bolivian farmers into abject poverty.

Bánzer, battling lung cancer, resigned as president in Aug. 2001 after serving four years out of his five-year term. In Aug. 2002, Gonzalo Sánchez de Lozada again became president, pledging to continue economic reforms and to create jobs.

# Bosnia and Herzegovina

**THE FEDERATION OF BOSNIA AND HERZEGOVINA**
**President:** Beriz Belkic (2002)
**Chairman, Council of Ministers:** Dragan Mikerevic (2002)
**Area:** 19,741 sq mi (51,129 sq km)
**Population (2002 est.):** 3,964,388 (all data dealing with population is subject to considerable error because of the dislocations caused by military action and ethnic cleansing) (growth rate: 0.5%); birth rate: 12.8/1000; infant mortality rate: 23.5/1000; density per sq mi: 201
**Capital and largest city (1998 est.):** Sarajevo, 387,876 (unofficial). **Other large cities:** Banja Luka, 220,407; Mostar, 208,904; Tuzla 118,500. **Monetary unit:** Marka. **Language:** The language that used to be known as Serbo-Croatian but is now known as Serbian, Croatian, or Bosnian, depending on the speaker's ethnic and political affiliation. It is written in Latin and Cyrillic. **Ethnicity/race:** Serb 31%, Bosniak 44%, Croat 17%, Yugoslav 5.5%, other 2.5% (1991) . **Religions:** Slavic Muslim 44%, Orthodox 31%, Catholic 15%, Protestant 4%, other 6%. **Literacy rate:** 93% (1999)
**Economic summary:** GDP/PPP (2000 est.): $6.5 billion; per capita $1,700. **Real growth rate:** 8%. **Inflation:** 8%. **Unemployment:** 35%-40% (1999 est.). **Arable land:** 14%. **Agriculture:** wheat, corn, fruits, vegetables; livestock. **Labor force:** 1.026 million; agriculture n.a.,

industry n.a., services n.a. **Industries:** steel, coal, iron ore, lead, zinc, manganese, bauxite, vehicle assembly, textiles, tobacco products, wooden furniture, tank and aircraft assembly, domestic appliances, oil refining. **Natural resources:** coal, iron, bauxite, manganese, forests, copper, chromium, lead, zinc, hydropower. **Exports:** $950 million (f.o.b., 2000 est.): n.a. **Imports:** $2.45 billion (f.o.b., 2000 est.): n.a. **Major trading partners:** Croatia, Switzerland, Italy, Germany, Slovenia.

**Geography** Bosnia and Herzegovina make up a triangular-shaped republic, about half the size of Kentucky, on the Balkan peninsula. The Bosnian region in the north is mountainous and covered with thick forests. The Herzegovina region in the south is largely rugged, flat farmland. It has a narrow coastline without natural harbors stretching 13 mi (20 km) along the Adriatic Sea.

**Government** Emerging democracy.

**History** Since the time of the Roman Empire, the Balkans has been a crossroads of religions and civilizations. The ethnic groups now known as Bosnians, Croats, and Serbs are largely the result of different religious and cultural identities created by contact with neighboring empires that expanded and contracted in the Balkans over centuries. With minor differences, they speak the same language, called Serbo-Croatian or sometimes Bosnian.

Called Illyricum in ancient times, the Romans conquered the area now called Bosnia and Herzegovina in the 2nd and 1st centuries B.C. and folded it into the Roman province of Dalmatia. In the 4th and 5th centuries A.D. Goths overran that portion of the declining Roman Empire and occupied the area until the 6th century, when the Byzantine Empire claimed it. Slavs began settling the region during the 7th century. Around 1200, Bosnia won independence from Hungary and endured as an independent Christian state for some 260 years.

The expansion of the Ottoman Empire into the Balkans introduced another cultural, political, and religious framework. The Turks defeated the Serbs at the famous battle of Kosovo in 1389. They conquered Bosnia in 1463. During the roughly 450 years Bosnia and Herzegovina were under Ottoman rule, many Christian Slavs became Muslim. A Bosnian Islamic elite gradually developed and ruled the country on behalf of the Turkish overlords. As the borders of the Ottoman Empire began to shrink in the 19th century, Muslims from elsewhere in the Balkans migrated to Bosnia. Bosnia also developed a sizable Jewish population, with many Jews settling in Sarajevo after their expulsion from Spain in 1492. However, through the 19th century the term *Bosnian* commonly included residents of all faiths. A relatively secular society, intermarriage among religious groups was not unknown.

Neighboring Serbia and Montenegro fought against the Ottoman Empire in 1876, and were aided by the Russians, their fellow Slavs. At the Congress of Berlin in 1878, following the end of the Russo-Turkish War (1877–78), Austria-Hungary was given a mandate to occupy and govern Bosnia and Herzegovina, in an effort by Europe to ensure that Russia did not dominate the Balkans. Although the provinces were still officially part of the Ottoman Empire, they were annexed by the Austro-Hungarian Empire on Oct. 7, 1908. As a result, relations with Serbia, which had claims on Bosnia and Herzegovina, became embittered. The hostility between the two countries climaxed in the assassination of Austrian Archduke Franz Ferdinand in Sarajevo on June 28, 1914, by a

Serbian nationalist. This event precipitated the start of World War I (1914–18). Bosnia and Herzegovina were annexed to Serbia as part of the newly formed Kingdom of Serbs, Croats, and Slovenes on Oct. 26, 1918. The name was later changed to Yugoslavia in 1929.

When Germany invaded Yugoslavia in 1941, Bosnia and Herzegovina were made part of Nazi-controlled Croatia. During the German and Italian occupation, Bosnian and Herzegovinian resistance fighters fought a fierce guerrilla war against the Ustachi, the Croatian Fascist troops. At the end of World War II, Bosnia and Herzegovina were reunited into a single state as one of the six republics of the newly reestablished Communist Yugoslavia under Marshall Tito. His authoritarian control kept the ethnic enmities of his patchwork nation in check. Tito died in 1980, and with growing economic dissatisfaction and the fall of the iron curtain over the next decade, Yugoslavia began to splinter.

In Dec. 1991, Bosnia and Herzegovina declared independence from Yugoslavia and asked for recognition by the European Union (EU). In a March 1992 referendum, Bosnian voters chose independence, and President Izetbegovic declared the nation an independent state. Unlike the other former Yugoslav states, which were generally composed of a dominant ethnic group, Bosnia was an ethnic tangle of Muslims (44%), Serbs (31%), and Croats (17%), and this mix contributed to the duration and savagery of its fight for independence.

Both the Croatian and Serbian presidents had planned to partition Bosnia between themselves. Attempting to carve out their own enclaves, the Serbian minority, with the help of the Serbian Yugoslav army, took the offensive and laid siege, particularly on Sarajevo, and began its ruthless campaigns of ethnic cleansing, which involved the expulsion or massacre of Muslims. Croats also began carving out their own communities. By the end of Aug. 1992, rebel Bosnian Serbs had conquered over 60% of Bosnia. The war did not begin to wane until NATO stepped in, bombing Serb positions in Bosnia in Aug. and Sept. 1995. This was followed by a joint offensive by Bosnian Muslim and Croatian forces that took back a significant amount of critical Bosnian territory.

U.S.-sponsored peace talks in Dayton, Ohio, led to an agreement in 1995 that called for a Muslim-Croat federation and a Serb entity within the larger federation of Bosnia. Sixty thousand NATO troops were to supervise its implementation. Fighting abated and orderly elections were held in Sept. 1996. President Alija Izetbegovic, a Bosnian Muslim, or Bosniac, won the majority of votes to become the leader of the three-member presidency, each representing one of the three ethnic groups.

But this alliance of unreconstructed enemies had little success in meeting a lasting commitment or curbing violent clashes in check. The terms of the Dec. 1995 Dayton Peace Accord were largely ignored by Bosnian Serbs, with its former president, archnationalist Radovan Karadzic, still in de facto control of the Serbian enclave. Many indicted war criminals, including Karadzic, remain at large. Despite NATO's pledge in Oct. 1997 to remain in Bosnia beyond the 1998 mandate, the largely ineffective peacekeeping force was characterized by chronic ambivalence.

The crucial priorities facing postwar Bosnian leaders were rebuilding the economy, resettling the estimated one million refugees still displaced, and establishing a working government. Progress on these goals has been minimal, and a massive corruption scandal uncovered in 1999 severely tested the goodwill of the international community. Millions of dollars from international aid projects earmarked for reconstruction and humanitarian purposes had been pilfered by Bosnian officials, according to an American-led international antifraud unit.

In 1994, the UN's International Criminal Tribunal for the former Yugoslavia adjourned in The Hague, Netherlands. As of 2001, more than 100 individuals had been indicted. The first genocide conviction was handed down in Aug. 2001. Radislav Drstic, a Bosnian Serb general, was found guilty of genocide in the killing of up to 8,000 Bosnian Muslims in Srebrenica in 1995. It was the first genocide conviction in Europe since the UN genocide treaty was drawn up in 1951. In 2001, the trial of former Serbian president Slobodan Milosevic began. He was charged with crimes against humanity.

In July 2002, the presidents of Bosnia, Croatia, and Yugoslavia met for the first time since war broke out in the Balkans more than a decade ago. The countries pledged to cooperate on the repatriation of refugees, fight organized crime, and assist each other in economic development.

# Botswana

## REPUBLIC OF BOTSWANA

**President:** Festus Mogae (1998)
**Area:** 231,803 sq mi (600,370 sq km)
**Population (2002 est.):** 1,591,232 (growth rate: 0.2%); birth rate: 28.0/1000; infant mortality rate: 64.7/1000; density per sq mi: 7
**Capital and largest city (1992 est.):** Gaborone, 138,000. **Monetary unit:** Pula. **Languages:** English (official), Setswana. **Ethnicity/race:** Batswana 95%, Kalanga, Basarwa, and Kgalagadi 4%, white 1%. **Religions:** indigenous beliefs 50%, Christian 50%. **Literacy rate:** 69% (1993)
**Economic summary: GDP/PPP** (2000 est.): $10.4 billion; per capita $6,600. **Real growth rate:** 6%. **Inflation:** 8.6%. **Unemployment:** 40%. **Arable land:** 1%. **Agriculture:** sorghum, corn, millet, pulses, groundnuts (peanuts), beans, cowpeas, sunflower seed; livestock. **Labor force:** 235,000 formal sector employees (1995); 100,000, public sector; 135,000, private sector; including 14,300 who are employed in various mines in South Africa; most others engaged in cattle raising and subsistence agriculture (1995 est.). **Industries:** diamonds, copper, nickel, coal, salt, soda ash, potash; livestock processing. **Natural resources:** diamonds, copper, nickel, salt, soda ash, potash, coal, iron ore, silver. **Exports:** $2.6 billion (f.o.b., 2000 est.): diamonds 72%, vehicles, copper, nickel, meat (1998). **Imports:** $2.2 billion (f.o.b., 2000 est.): foodstuffs, machinery and transport equipment, textiles, petroleum products. **Major trading partners:** EU, Southern African Customs Union (SACU), EFTA/EDWU, Europe, South Korea. **Member of Commonwealth of Nations**

**Geography** Twice the size of Arizona, Botswana is in south-central Africa, bounded by Namibia, Zambia, Zimbabwe, and South Africa. Most of the country is near-desert, with the Kalahari occupying the western part of the country. The eastern part is hilly, with salt lakes in the north.

**Government** Parliamentary republic.

**History** The earliest inhabitants of the region were the San, who were followed by the Tswana. About half the country today is ethnic Tswana. The term for the country's people, *Batswana*, refers to national rather than ethnic origin.

Encroachment by the Zulu in the 1820s and by Boers from Transvaal in the 1870s and 1880s threatened the peace of the region. In 1885, Britain established the area as a protectorate, then known as Bechuanaland. In 1961, Britain granted a constitution to the country. Self-government began in 1965, and on Sept. 30, 1966, the country became independent. Botswana is Africa's oldest democracy.

The new country maintained good relations with its white-ruled neighbors, but gradually changed its policies, harboring rebel groups from South Rhodesia as well as some from South Africa.

Although Botswana is rich in diamonds, it has high unemployment and stratified socioeconomic classes. In 1999 it suffered its first budget deficit in 16 years because of a slump in the international diamond market. Yet it remains one of the wealthiest as well as most stable countries on the continent.

After 17 years in power, President Ketumile Masire retired in 1997, and Festus Mogae, an Oxford-educated economist, became the new president. Mogae has won high marks from the international financial community for continuing to privatize Botswana's mining and industrial operations.

Although Botswana's economic outlook remains strong, the devastation that AIDS is causing threatens to destroy the country's future. In 2001, Botswana had the highest rate of HIV infection in the world: 350,000 of its 1.6 million people were infected, and half the population between 25 and 29 are dying of the disease. In 2002, however, Botswana, with the help of international donors, launched an ambitious national campaign against AIDS that promises that there will be no new HIV cases by 2016, the 50th anniversary of the country's independence.

# Brazil

### FEDERATIVE REPUBLIC OF BRAZIL

**National name:** República Federativa do Brasil
**President:** Fernando Henrique Cardoso (1995)
**Area:** 3,286,470 sq mi (8,511,965 sq km)
**Population (2002 est.):** 176,029,560 (growth rate: 0.9%); birth rate: 18.1/1000; infant mortality rate: 35.9/1000; density per sq mi: 54
**Capital (1997 est.):** Brasília, 1,800,000. **Largest cities:** São Paulo (2000 est.), 17,900,000 (metro. area); Rio de Janeiro (2000 est.), 10,650,000 (metro. area); Porto Alegre, 3,000,000; Recife, 2,900,999; Salvador, 2,600,000; Belo Horizonte, 2,600,000. **Monetary unit:** Real. **Language:** Portuguese. **Ethnicity/race:** white (includes Portuguese, German, Italian, Spanish, Polish) 55%, mixed white and African 38%, African 6%, other (includes Japanese, Arab, Amerindian) 1%. **Religion:** Roman Catholic 90% (nominal). **Literacy rate:** 81% (1990)
**Economic summary: GDP/PPP** (2000 est.): $1.13 trillion; per capita $6,500. **Real growth rate:** 4.2%. **Inflation:** 6%. **Unemployment:** 7.1%. **Arable land:** 5%. **Agriculture:** coffee, soybeans, wheat, rice, corn, sugarcane, cocoa, citrus; beef. **Labor force:** 79 million (1999 est.); services 53.2%, agriculture 23.1%, industry 23.7%. **Industries:** textiles, shoes, chemicals, cement, lumber, iron ore, tin, steel, aircraft, motor vehicles and parts, other machinery and equipment. **Natural resources:** bauxite, gold, iron ore, manganese, nickel, phosphates, platinum, tin, uranium, petroleum, hydropower, timber. **Exports:** $55.1 billion (f.o.b., 2000): manufactures, iron ore, soybeans, footwear, coffee. **Imports:** $55.8 billion (f.o.b., 2000): machinery and equipment, chemical products, oil, electricity. **Major trading partners:** U.S., Argentina, Germany, Netherlands, Japan, Italy.

**Geography** Brazil covers nearly half of South America and is the continent's largest nation. It extends 2,965 mi (4,772 km) north-south, 2,691 mi (4,331 km) east-west, and borders every nation on the continent except Chile and Ecuador. Brazil may be divided into the Brazilian Highlands, or plateau, in the south and the Amazon River Basin in the north. More than a third of Brazil is drained by the Amazon and its more than 200 tributaries. The Amazon is navigable for ocean steamers to Iquitos, Peru, 2,300 mi (3,700 km) upstream. Southern Brazil is drained by the Plata system—the Paraguay, Uruguay, and Paraná Rivers.

**Government** Federal republic.

**History** Brazil is the only Latin American nation that derives its language and culture from Portugal. The native inhabitants mostly consisted of the nomadic Tupí-Guaraní Indians. Adm. Pedro Alvares Cabral claimed the territory for Portugal in 1500. The early explorers brought back a wood that produced a red dye, *pau-brasil,* from which the land received its name. Portugal began colonization in 1532 and made the area a royal colony in 1549.

During the Napoleonic Wars, King João VI, fearing the advancing French armies, fled the country in 1808 and set up his court in Rio de Janeiro. João was drawn home in 1820 by a revolution, leaving his son as regent. When Portugal tried to reimpose colonial rule, the prince declared Brazil's independence on Sept. 7, 1822, becoming Pedro I, emperor of Brazil. Harassed by his Parliament, Pedro I abdicated in 1831 in favor of his five-year-old son, who became emperor in 1840 (Pedro II). The son was a popular monarch, but discontent built up and, in 1889, following a military revolt, he abdicated. Although a republic was proclaimed, Brazil was ruled by military dictatorships until a revolt permitted a gradual return to stability under civilian presidents.

President Wenceslau Braz cooperated with the Allies and declared war on Germany during World War I. In World War II, Brazil again cooperated with the Allies, welcoming Allied air bases, patrolling the South Atlantic, and joining the invasion of Italy after declaring war on the Axis powers.

After a military coup in 1964, Brazil had a series of military governments. Gen. João Baptista de Oliveira Figueiredo became president in 1979 and pledged a return to democracy in 1985. The election of Tancredo Neves on Jan. 15, 1985, the first civilian president since 1964, brought a nationwide wave of optimism, but when Neves died several months later, Vice President José Sarney became president. Collor de Mello won the election of late 1989, pledging to lower hyperinflation with free-market economics. When Collor faced impeachment by Congress because of a corruption scandal in Dec. 1992 and resigned, Vice President Itamar Franco assumed the presidency.

A former finance minister, Fernando Cardoso, won the presidency in the Oct. 1994 election with 54% of the vote. Cardoso has sold off inefficient government-owned monopolies in the telecommunication, electrical power, port, mining, railway, and banking industries. In his short time in office Cardoso's economic acumen has made a measurable dent in Brazil's poverty level.

In Jan. 1999, the Asian economic crisis spread to Brazil. Rather than prop up the currency through financial markets, Brazil opted to let the currency float, which sent the real plummeting—at one time as much as 40%. Cardoso has been highly praised by the international community for quickly turning around his country's economic crisis. He has shown strong political courage in forcing belt-tightening measures on the economy, causing short-term misery and discontent in an effort to reap long-term stability and growth. Despite Cardoso's efforts, however, the economy continued to slow throughout 2001, and the country also faced an energy crisis. The IMF offered Brazil an additional aid package in Aug. 2001. And in Aug. 2002, to ensure that Brazil would not be dragged down by neighboring Argentina's catastrophic economic problems, the IMF agreed to lend Brazil a phenomenal $30 billion over fifteen months.

In 2002, Brazil won the World Cup soccer match for the fifth time.

# Brunei Darussalam

### STATE OF BRUNEI DARUSSALAM

**Sultan:** Haji Hassanal Bolkiah (1967)
**Area:** 2,228 sq mi (5,770 sq km)
**Population (2002 est.):** 350,898 (growth rate: 1.7%); birth rate: 20.1/1000; infant mortality rate: 13.9/1000; density per sq mi: 158
**Capital and largest city (1991 est.):** Bandar Seri Begawan, 52,300. **Other large cities:** Seria 23,511, Kuala Belait 19,335. **Monetary unit:** Brunei dollar. **Languages:** Malay (official), Chinese, English. **Ethnicity/race:** Malay 64%, Chinese 20%, other 16%. **Religions:** Islam (official religion) 67%, Buddhist 12%, Christian 9%, indigenous beliefs and other 12%. **Literacy rate:** 80% (1981)
**Economic summary: GDP/PPP** (2000 est.): $5.9 billion; per capita $17,600. **Real growth rate:** 3%. **Inflation:** 1% (1999 est.). **Unemployment:** 4.9% (1995 est.). **Arable land:** 1%. **Agriculture:** rice, vegetables, fruits, chickens, water buffalo. **Labor force:** 144,000 (1995 est.); note: includes foreign workers and military personnel; government 48%, production of oil, natural gas, services, and construction 42%, agriculture, forestry, and fishing 10% (1999 est.). **Industries:** petroleum, petroleum refining, liquefied natural gas, construction. **Natural resources:** petroleum, natural gas, timber. **Exports:** $2.55 billion (f.o.b., 1999 est.): crude oil, natural gas, refined products. **Imports:** $1.3 billion (c.i.f., 1999 est.): machinery and transport equipment, manufactured goods, food, chemicals. **Major trading partners:** Japan, U.S., South Korea, Thailand, Singapore, UK, Malaysia.

**Geography** About the size of Delaware, Brunei is an independent sultanate on the northwest coast of the island of Borneo in the South China Sea, wedged between the Malaysian states of Sabah and Sarawak. Three-quarters of the thinly populated country is covered with tropical rain forest; there are rich oil and gas deposits.

**Government** Constitutional sultanate.

**History** Brunei was trading with China during the 6th century, and, through allegiance to the Javanese Majapahit kingdom (13th to 15th century), it came under Hindu influence. In the early 15th century, with the decline of the Majapahit kingdom and widespread conversion to Islam, Brunei became an independent sultanate. It was a powerful state from the 16th to the 19th century, ruling over the northern part of Borneo and adjacent island chains. But it fell into decay and lost Sarawak in 1841, becoming a British protectorate in 1888 and a British dependency in 1905. Japan occupied Brunei during World War II; it was liberated by Australia in 1945.

The sultan regained control over internal affairs in 1959, but Britain retained responsibility for the state's defense and foreign affairs until 1984, when the sultanate became fully independent. Sultan Bolkiah was crowned in 1967 at the age of 22, succeeding his father, Sir Omar Ali Saifuddin, who had abdicated. During his reign, exploitation of the rich Seria oilfield had made the sultanate wealthy. Brunei has one of the highest per capita incomes in Asia, and the sultan is believed to be one of the richest men in the world. In Aug. 1998, Oxford-educated Prince Al-Muhtadee Billah was inaugurated as heir to the 500-year-old monarchy.

Brunei hosted July 2002's Association of Southeast Asian Nations (ASEAN) Regional Forum, at which the group's 10 members and the United States signed a pact, vowing to "prevent, disrupt, and combat" global terrorism.

# Bulgaria

### REPUBLIC OF BULGARIA

**National name:** Republika Bulgariya
**President:** Georgi Purvanov (2002)
**Prime Minister:** Simeon Saxe-Coburg Gotha (2001)
**Area:** 42,822 sq mi (110,910 sq km)
**Population (2002 est.):** 7,621,337 (growth rate: −0.6%); birth rate: 8.1/1000; infant mortality rate: 14.2/1000; density per sq mi: 178
**Capital and largest city (1994 est.):** Sofia, 1,113,674. **Largest cities (1994 est.):** Plovdiv, 345,205; Varna, 307,200; Burgas, 198,439; Ruse, 170,209. **Monetary unit:** Lev. **Language:** Bulgarian. **Ethnicity/race:** Bulgarian 85.3%, Turk 8.5%, Gypsy 2.6%, Macedonian 2.5%, Armenian 0.3%, Russian 0.2%, other 0.6%. **Religions:** Bulgarian Orthodox 85%, Muslim 13%, Jewish 0.8%, Roman Catholic 0.5%, Uniate Catholic 0.2%, Protestant, Gregorian-Armenian, and other 0.5%. **Literacy rate:** 93% (1970)
**Economic summary: GDP/PPP** (2000 est.): $48 billion; per capita $6,200. **Real growth rate:** 5%. **Inflation:** 10.4%. **Unemployment:** 17.7%. **Arable land:** 43%. **Agriculture:** vegetables, fruits, tobacco, livestock, wine, wheat, barley, sunflowers, sugar beets. **Labor force:** 3.83 million; agriculture 26%, industry 31%, services 43% (1998 est.). **Industries:** electricity, gas and water; food, beverages and tobacco; machinery and equipment, base metals, chemical products, coke, refined petroleum, nuclear fuel. **Natural resources:** bauxite, copper, lead, zinc, coal, timber, arable land. **Exports:** $4.8 billion (f.o.b., 2000 est.): clothing, footwear, iron and steel, machinery and equipment, fuels. **Imports:** $5.9 billion (f.o.b., 2000 est.): fuels, minerals, and raw materials; machinery and equipment; metals and ores; chemicals and plastics; food, textiles. **Major trading partners:** Italy, Turkey, Germany, Greece, Yugoslavia, Belgium, France, Russia, Romania, U.S.

**Geography** Two mountain ranges and two great valleys mark the topography of Bulgaria, a country the size of Tennessee and situated on the Black Sea. The Maritsa is Bulgaria's principal river, and the Danube also flows through the country.

**Government** Parliamentary democracy.

**History** The Thracians lived in what is now known as Bulgaria from about 3500 B.C. They were incorporated into the Roman Empire by the first century A.D. At the decline of the empire, the Goths, Huns, Bulgars, and Avars invaded. The Bulgars, who crossed the Danube from the north in 679, took control of the region. Although the country bears the name of the Bulgars, the Bulgar language and culture died out, replaced by a Slavic language, writing, and religion. In 865, Boris I adopted Orthodox Christianity. The Bulgars twice conquered most of the Balkan peninsula between 893 and 1280. But in 1396 they were invaded by the Ottoman Empire, which made Bulgaria a Turkish province until 1878. Ottoman rule was harsh and inescapable, given Bulgaria's proximity to its oppressor. In 1878, Russia forced Turkey to give Bulgaria its independence after the Russo-Turkish War (1877–78), but the European powers, fearing Russia's and Bulgaria's dominance in the Balkans, intervened at the Congress of Berlin (1878), limited Bulgaria's territory, and fashioned it into a small principality ruled by the nephew of the Russian czar, Alexander of Battenburg.

Alexander was succeeded in 1887 by Prince Ferdinand of Saxe-Coburg-Gotha, who declared a kingdom independent of Russia on Oct. 5, 1908. In the First Balkan War (1912–13), Bulgaria and the other members of the Balkan League fought against Turkey to regain Balkan territory. Angered by the small portion of Macedonia it received after the battle—it considered Macedonia an integral part of Bulgaria—the country instigated the Second Balkan War (June–Aug. 1913) against Turkey as well as its former allies. Bulgaria lost the war and all the territory it had gained in the First Balkan War. Bulgaria joined Germany in World War I in the hope of again gaining Macedonia. After this second failure, Ferdinand abdicated in favor of his son in 1918. Boris III squandered Bulgaria's resources and assumed dictatorial powers in 1934–35. Bulgaria fought on the side of the Nazis in World War II, but after Russia declared war on Bulgaria on Sept. 5, 1944, Bulgaria switched sides. Three days later, on Sept. 9, 1944, a Communist coalition took control of the country and set up a government under Kimon Georgiev.

A Soviet-style People's Republic was established in 1947 and Bulgaria acquired the reputation of being the most slavishly loyal to Moscow of all the East European Communist countries. The general secretary of the Bulgarian Communist Party, Todor Zhikov, resigned in 1989 after 35 years in power. His successor, Peter Mladenov, purged the Politburo, ended the Communist monopoly on power, and held free elections in May 1990 that led to a surprising victory for the Communist Party, renamed the Bulgarian Socialist Party (BSP). Mladenov was forced to resign in July 1990.

In Oct. 1991, the Union of Democratic Forces won, forming Bulgaria's first non-Communist government since 1946. Power has shifted back and forth between the pro-Western Union of Democratic Forces (UDF) and the BSP during the 1990s. The economy continued to deteriorate amid growing concern over the spread of organized crime. The new UDF government, led by Prime Minister Ivan Kostov, was elected in 1997 to overhaul the economic system and institute reforms aimed at stopping the rise of public corruption. Progress on both fronts remained slow. As a result, the UDF lost the July 2001 election to the former king of Bulgaria, leader of the recently founded Simeon II National Movement (SNM). The new prime minister, Simeon Saxe-Coburg Gotha (Simeon II), had been dethroned 55 years earlier (at age nine) during the Communist take-over of the country.

# Burkina Faso

**National name:** Burkina Faso
**President:** Blaise Compaoré (1987)
**Prime Minister:** Paramanga Ernest Yonli (2000)
**Area:** 105,869 sq mi (274,200 sq km)
**Population (2002 est.):** 12,603,185 (growth rate: 2.7%); birth rate: 44.3/1000; infant mortality rate: 105.3/1000; density per sq mi: 119

**Capital and largest city (1994 est.):** Ouagadougou, 500,000. **Monetary unit:** CFA Franc. **Languages:** French (official), tribal languages. **Ethnicity/race:** Mossi (about 24%), Gurunsi, Senufo, Lobi, Bobo, Mande, Fulani. **Religions:** Muslim 50%, Christian (mainly Roman Catholic) 10%, indigenous beliefs 40%. **Literacy rate:** 18% (1990)
**Economic summary: GDP/PPP (2000 est.):** $12 billion; per capita $1,000. **Real growth rate:** 5%. **Inflation:** 1.5%. **Unemployment:** n.a. **Arable land:** 13%. **Agriculture:** peanuts, shea nuts, sesame, cotton, sorghum, millet, corn, rice; livestock. **Labor force:** 5 million (1999); note: a large part of the male labor force migrates annually to neighboring countries for seasonal employment; agriculture 90% (2000 est.) **Industries:** cotton lint, beverages, agricultural processing, soap, cigarettes, textiles, gold. **Natural resources:** manganese, limestone, marble; small deposits of gold, antimony, copper, nickel, bauxite, lead, phosphates, zinc, silver. **Exports:** $220 million (f.o.b., 2000 est.): cotton, animal products, gold. **Imports:** $610 million (f.o.b., 2000 est.): machinery, food products, petroleum. **Major trading partners:** Italy, France, Indonesia, Thailand, Côte d'Ivoire, Spain, Benelux.

**Geography** Slightly larger than Colorado, Burkina Faso, formerly known as Upper Volta, is a landlocked country in West Africa. Its neighbors are Côte d'Ivoire, Mali, Niger, Benin, Togo, and Ghana. The country consists of extensive plains, low hills, high savannas, and a desert area in the north.

**Government** Parliamentary.

**History** Burkina Faso was originally inhabited by the Bobo, Lobi, and Gurunsi peoples, with the Mossi and Gurma peoples immigrating to the region in the 14th century. The lands of the Mossi empire became a French protectorate in 1897, and by 1903 France had subjugated the other ethnic groups. Called Upper Volta by the French, it became a separate colony in 1919, was partitioned among Niger, the Sudan, and Côte d'Ivoire in 1932, and was reconstituted in 1947. An autonomous republic within the French Community, Upper Volta became independent on Aug. 5, 1960.

President Maurice Yameogo was deposed on Jan. 3, 1966, by a military coup led by Col. Sangoulé Lamizana, who dissolved the National Assembly and suspended the constitution. Constitutional rule returned in 1978 with the election of an Assembly and a presidential vote in June in which Gen. Lamizana won by a narrow margin over three other candidates.

On Nov. 25, 1980, Col. Sayé Zerbo led a bloodless coup that toppled Lamizana. In turn, Maj. Jean-Baptist Ouedraogo ousted Zerbo on Nov. 7, 1982. But the real revolutionary change occurred the following year when a 33-year-old flight commander, Thomas Sankara, took control. A Marxist-Leninist, he challenged the traditional Mossi chiefs, advocated women's liberation, and allied the country with North Korea, Libya, and Cuba. To sever ties to the colonial past, Sankara changed the name of the country in 1984 to Burkina Faso, which combines two of the nation's languages and means "the land of upright men."

While Sankara's investments in schools, food production, and clinics brought some improvement in living standards, foreign investment declined, many businesses left the country, and unhappy labor unions began strikes. On Oct. 15, 1987, formerly loyal soldiers assassinated Sankara. His best friend and ally Blaise Compaoré became president. Compaoré immediately set about "rectifying" Sankara's revolution. In 1991 he agreed to economic reforms proposed by the

World Bank. A new constitution paved the way for elections in 1991, which Compaoré won easily, although opposition parties boycotted.

In 2000, the UN accused Burkina Faso's president of being a chief player in Africa's illicit diamond trade. Compaoré, the reports claim, has traded weapons for diamonds with UNITA rebels in Angola, Sierra Leone's Revolutionary United Front (RUF), and Liberia, ignoring the international arms embargo and fueling the continuing violence plaguing western Africa.

# Burma (Myanmar)

*SEE* MYANMAR.

# Burundi

### REPUBLIC OF BURUNDI

**National name:** Republika Y'Uburundi
**President:** Pierre Buyoya (2001)
**Area:** 10,745 sq mi (27,830 sq km)
**Population (2002 est.):** 6,373,002 (growth rate: 2.4%); birth rate: 39.9/1000; infant mortality rate: 70.0/1000; density per sq mi: 593
**Capital and largest city (1994 est.):** Bujumbura, 300,000. **Other large city (est. 1982):** Gitega, 101,827. **Monetary unit:** Burundi franc. **Languages:** Kirundi and French (official), Swahili. **Ethnicity/race:** Hutu (Bantu) 85%, Tutsi (Hamitic) 14%, Twa (Pygmy) 1%. **Religions:** Roman Catholic 62%, Protestant 5%, indigenous 32%. **Literacy rate:** 41% (1990)
**Economic summary: GDP/PPP** (2000 est.): $4.4 billion; per capita $720. **Real growth rate:** 1.8%. **Inflation:** 22%. **Unemployment:** n.a. **Arable land:** 44%. **Agriculture:** coffee, cotton, tea, corn, sorghum, sweet potatoes, bananas, manioc (tapioca); beef, milk, hides. **Labor force:** 1.9 million. **Industries:** light consumer goods such as blankets, shoes, soap; assembly of imported components; public works construction, food processing. **Natural resources:** nickel, uranium, rare earth oxides, peat, cobalt, copper, platinum (not yet exploited), vanadium, arable land, hydropower. **Exports:** $32 million (f.o.b., 2000): coffee, tea, sugar, cotton, hides. **Imports:** $110 million (f.o.b., 2000): capital goods, petroleum products, foodstuffs. **Major trading partners:** Germany, Belgium, U.S., France, Switzerland, Zambia, Kenya, South Africa.

**Geography** Wedged between Tanzania, the Democratic Republic of the Congo, and Rwanda in east-central Africa, Burundi occupies a high plateau divided by several deep valleys. It is equal in size to Maryland.

**Government** Republic.

**History** Th[...]l [...] [...], a Pygmy people who now make up only 1% of the population. Today the population is divided between the Hutu (approximately 85%) and the Tutsi, approximately 14%. While the Hutu and Tutsi are considered to be two separate ethnic groups, scholars point out that they speak the same language, have a history of intermarriage, and share many cultural characteristics. Traditionally, the differences between the two groups were occupational rather than ethnic. Agricultural people were considered Hutu, while the cattle-owning elite were identified as Tutsi. Supposedly Tutsi were tall and thin, while Hutu were short and square, but in fact it is often impossible to tell one from the other. The 1933 requirement by the Belgians that everyone carry an identity card indicating tribal ethnicity as Tutsi or Hutu increased the distinction. Since independence, the land-owning Tutsi aristocracy has dominated Burundi.

Burundi was once part of German East Africa. Belgium won a League of Nations mandate in 1923, and subsequently Burundi, with Rwanda, was transferred to the status of a United Nations trust territory. In 1962, Burundi gained independence and became a kingdom under Mwami Mwambutsa IV, a Tutsi. A Hutu rebellion took place in 1965, leading to brutal Tutsi retaliations. Mwambutsa was deposed by his son, Ntaré V, in 1966. Ntaré in turn was overthrown the same year in a military coup by Premier Michel Micombero, also a Tutsi. In 1970–71, a civil war erupted, leaving more than 100,000 Hutu dead.

On Nov. 1, 1976, Lt. Col. Jean-Baptiste Bagaza led a coup and assumed the presidency. He suspended the constitution and announced that a 30-member Supreme Revolutionary Council would be the governing body. In Sept. 1987 Bagaza was overthrown by Maj. Pierre Buyoya, who became president. Ethnic hatred again flared in Aug. 1988, and about 20,000 Hutu were slaughtered. Buyoya, however, began reforms to heal the country's ethnic rift. The Burundi Democracy Front's candidate, Melchior Ndadaye, won the country's first democratic presidential elections, held on June 2, 1993. Ndadaye, the first Hutu to assume power in Burundi, was killed within months during a coup. The second Hutu president, Cyprien Ntaryamira, was killed on April 6, 1994, when a plane carrying him and the Rwandan president was shot down. As a result, Hutu youth gangs began massacring Tutsi; the Tutsi-controlled army retaliated by killing Hutus.

The frequency of ethnic clashes increased, developing into a low-intensity civil war. A six-nation regional proposal to send troops into Burundi to maintain peace and order was devised in July 1996. Distrustful of the scheme, the Tutsi-dominated army led a coup deposing the Hutu president and installed Maj. Pierre Buyoya that month. More than 200,000 people have been killed since the conflict began, and both the Tutsi-dominated army and the Hutu rebel forces are responsible for the continuing slaughter. Nelson Mandela was appointed the new mediator for the civil war in early 2000. In July 2001 a fragile peace accord and power-sharing agreement was signed by the government and 18 political groups, but Hutu rebels fighting against the government did not participate, which essentially rendered the accord meaningless. The civil war continued in 2002, with various unsuccessful attempts to reach a cease-fire agreement.

# Cambodia

**King:** Norodom Sihanouk (1993)
**Prime Minister:** Hun Sen (1998)
**Area:** 69,900 sq mi (181,040 sq km)
**Population (2002 est.):** 12,775,324 (growth rate: 2.2%); birth rate: 32.9/1000; infant mortality rate: 61.0/1000, density per sq mi: 183
**Capital and largest city (1991 est.):** Phnom Penh, 900,000. **Monetary unit:** Riel. **Languages:** Khmer (official), French, English. **Ethnicity/race:** Khmer 90%, Vietnamese 5%, Chinese 1%, other 4%. **Religions:** Theravada Buddhist 95%, others 5%. **Literacy rate:** 69% (1996)
**Economic summary: GDP/PPP** (2000 est.): $16.1 billion; per capita $1,300. **Real growth rate:** 4%. **Inflation:** 1.6%. **Unemployment:** 2.8% (1999 est.). **Arable land:** 13%. **Agriculture:** rice, rubber, corn, vegetables. **Labor force:** 6 million (1998 est.); agriculture 80% (1999 est.). **Industries:** garments, tourism, rice milling, fishing, wood and wood products,

rubber, cement, gem mining, textiles. **Natural resources:** timber, gemstones, some iron ore, manganese, phosphates, hydropower potential. **Exports:** $942 million (f.o.b., 2000 est.): timber, garments, rubber, rice, fish. **Imports:** $1.3 billion (f.o.b., 2000 est.): cigarettes, gold, construction materials, petroleum products, machinery, motor vehicles. **Major trading partners:** Vietnam, Thailand, U.S., Singapore, China, Japan, Hong Kong.

**Geography** Situated on the Indochinese peninsula, Cambodia is bordered by Thailand and Laos on the north and Vietnam on the east and south. The Gulf of Thailand is off the western coast. The country, the size of Missouri, consists chiefly of a large alluvial plain ringed by mountains and on the east by the Mekong River. The plain is centered on Lake Tonle Sap, which is a natural storage basin of the Mekong.

**Government** Multiparty liberal democracy under a constitutional monarchy.

**History** The area that is present-day Cambodia came under Khmer rule about 600, when the region was at the center of a vast empire that stretched over most of Southeast Asia. Under the Khmers, who were Hindus, a magnificent temple complex was constructed at Angkor. Buddhism was introduced in the 12th century during the rule of Jayavaram VII. However, the kingdom, then known as Kambuja, fell into decline after Jayavaram's reign and was nearly annihilated by Thai and Vietnamese invaders. Its power steadily diminished until 1863, when France colonized the region, joining Cambodia, Laos, and Vietnam into a single protectorate known as French Indochina.

The French quickly usurped all but ceremonial powers from the monarch, Norodom. When he died in 1904, the French passed over his sons and handed the throne to his brother, Sisowath. Sisowath and his son ruled until 1941, when Norodom Sihanouk was elevated to power. Sihanouk's coronation, along with the Japanese occupation during the war, worked to reinforce a sentiment among Cambodians that the region should be free from outside control. After World War II, Cambodians sought independence, but France was reluctant to part with its colony. Cambodia was granted independence within the French Union in 1949. But the French-Indochinese War provided an opportunity for Sihanouk to gain full military control of the country. He abdicated in 1955 in favor of his parents, remaining head of the government, and when his father died in 1960, became chief of state without returning to the throne. In 1963, he sought a guarantee of Cambodia's neutrality from all parties to the Vietnam War.

However, North Vietnamese and Vietcong troops had begun using eastern Cambodia as a safe haven from which to launch attacks into South Vietnam, making it increasingly difficult to stay out of the war. An indigenous Communist guerrilla movement known as the Khmer Rouge also began to put pressure on the government in Phnom Penh. On March 18, 1970, while Sihanouk was abroad, anti-Vietnamese riots broke out and Sihanouk was overthrown by Gen. Lon Nol. The Vietnam peace agreement of 1973 stipulated withdrawal of foreign forces from Cambodia, but fighting continued between Hanoi-backed insurgents and U.S.-supplied government troops.

Combat climaxed in April 1975 when the Lon Nol regime was overthrown by Pol Pot, leader of the Khmer Rouge forces. The four years of nightmarish Khmer Rouge rule led to the state-sponsored extermination of citizens by its own government. Between 1 million and 2 million people were massacred on the "killing fields" of Cambodia or worked to death through forced labor. Pol Pot's radical vision of transforming the country into a Marxist agrarian society led to the virtual extermination of the country's professional and technical class.

Pol Pot was ousted by Vietnamese forces on Jan. 8, 1979, and a new pro-Hanoi government led by Heng Samrin was installed. Pol Pot and 35,000 Khmer Rouge fighters fled into the hills of western Cambodia, where they were joined by forces loyal to the ousted Sihanouk in a guerrilla movement aimed at overthrowing the Heng Samrin government. The Vietnamese plan originally called for a withdrawal by early 1990 and a negotiated political settlement. The talks became protracted, however, and a UN agreement was not signed until 1992, when Sihanouk was appointed leader of an interim Supreme National Council convened to run the country until elections could be held in 1993.

Free elections in May 1993 saw the defeat of Heng Samrin's successor, Hun Sen, who refused to accept the outcome of the vote and insisted instead on a power-sharing agreement. Under the arrangement, Hun Sen and Sihanouk's son, Prince Norodom Ranariddh, would act as co–prime ministers.

The Khmer Rouge stronghold in the western jungles splintered in 1997, with factions either battling each other or defecting. Ranariddh and Hun Sen both courted Khmer Rouge factions in an effort to shore up their power. In early July, Hun Sen took advantage of the charged political atmosphere to depose Ranariddh, the country's only popularly elected leader. Hun Sen later launched a brutal purge, executing more than 40 political opponents. Meanwhile, King Norodom Sihanouk was unable to broker peace between Hun Sen and his son, Prince Ranariddh.

Shortly after the July coup, the Khmer Rouge organized a show trial of their notorious leader, Pol Pot, who had not been seen by the West in more than two decades. He was sentenced to house arrest for his crimes against humanity. He died on April 15, 1998.

In the July 1998 election, Hun Sen defeated opposition leaders Sam Rainsy and Prince Ranariddh, but the opposition parties accused him of voter fraud. Although Hun Sen's CCP Party won the most seats, it needed a coalition with Ranariddh's FUNCINPEC Party to reach the two-thirds majority needed to form a government. A coalition government was formed in Nov. 1998, with Hun Sen as sole prime minister and Ranariddh accepting the lesser role of president of the National Assembly. Cambodia was able to regain its UN seat, lost nearly a year earlier as a result of Hun Sen's coup.

In Feb. 2002 the United Nations announced that after five years of negotiations it had abandoned its joint effort with the Cambodian government to set up an international war crimes tribunal to try senior Khmer Rouge officials on charges of genocide. The UN said the trials as planned "would not guarantee the independence, objectivity, and impartiality that a court established with the support of the United Nations must have." Cambodian officials said they would continue without the UN, though few in the international community believe the trials will be more than a sham. Among those expected to stand trial are Ta Mok, alias "the butcher," and Kang Kech Iev, alias Duch, who ran the notorious Tuol Sleng prison. Prime Minister Hun Sen, once a member of the Khmer Rouge himself, has been decidedly unenthusiastic about bringing former Khmer Rouge to justice.

# Cameroon

**REPUBLIC OF CAMEROON**

**National name:** République du Cameroun
**President:** Paul Biya (1982)
**Prime Minister:** Peter Mafany Musonge (1996)
**Area:** 183,567 sq mi (475,440 sq km)
**Population (2002 est.):** 16,184,748 (growth rate: 2.4%);
birth rate: 35.7/1000; infant mortality rate: 68.8/1000;
density per sq mi: 88
**Capital:** Yaoundé. **Largest cities (1991 est.):** Douala,
908,000; Yaoundé, 730,000. **Monetary unit:** CFA
Franc. **Languages:** French and English (both official);
24 major African language groups. **Ethnicity/race:**
Cameroon Highlanders 31%, Equatorial Bantu 19%,
Kirdi 11%, Fulani 10%, Northwest Bantu 8%, Eastern
Nigritic 7%, other African 13%, non-African less than
1%. **Religions:** 51% indigenous beliefs, 33%
Christian, 16% Muslim. **Literacy rate:** 54% (1990)
**Economic summary: GDP/PPP** (2000 est.): $26 billion;
per capita $1,700. **Real growth rate:** 4.4%. **Inflation:**
2%. **Unemployment:** 30% (1998 est.). **Arable land:**
13%. **Agriculture:** coffee, cocoa, cotton, rubber,
bananas, oilseed, grains, root starches; livestock;
timber. **Labor force:** n.a.; agriculture 70%, industry
and commerce 13%, other 17%. **Industries:**
petroleum production and refining, food processing,
light consumer goods, textiles, lumber. **Natural
resources:** petroleum, bauxite, iron ore, timber,
hydropower. **Exports:** $2.1 billion (f.o.b., 2000 est.):
crude oil and petroleum products, lumber, cocoa
beans, aluminum, coffee, cotton. **Imports:** $1.6 billion
(f.o.b., 2000 est.): machines and electrical equipment,
transport equipment, fuel, food. **Major trading
partners:** Italy, France, Netherlands, Germany, U.S.,
Japan.

**Geography** Cameroon is a Central African nation
on the Gulf of Guinea, bordered by Nigeria, Chad, the
Central African Republic, the Republic of Congo,
Equatorial Guinea, and Gabon. It is nearly twice the
size of Oregon. Mount Cameroon (13,350 ft; 4,069
m), near the coast, is the highest elevation in the country. The main rivers are the Benue, Nyong, and
Sanaga.

**Government** After a 1972 plebiscite, a unitary
republic was formed out of East and West Cameroon
to replace the former federal republic.

**History** Bantu speakers were among the first groups
to settle Cameroon, followed by the Muslim Fulani in
the 18th and 19th centuries. The land escaped colonial
rule until 1884, when treaties with tribal chiefs
brought the area under German domination. After
World War I, the League of Nations gave the French a
mandate over 80% of the area, and the British 20%
adjacent to Nigeria. After World War II, when the
country came under a UN trusteeship in 1946, self-
government was granted, and the Cameroon People's
Union emerged as the dominant party by campaigning
for reunification of French and British Cameroon and
for independence. Accused of being under Communist
control, the party waged a campaign of revolutionary
terror from 1955 to 1958, when it was crushed. In
British Cameroon, unification was also promoted by
the leading party, the Kamerun National Democratic
Party, led by John Foncha.

France set up Cameroon as an autonomous state in
1957, and the next year its legislative assembly voted
for independence by 1960. In 1959 a fully autonomous
government of Cameroon was formed under Ahmadou
Ahidjo. Cameroon became an independent republic on
Jan. 1, 1960. In 1961 the southern part of the British

territory joined the new Federal Republic of Cameroon and the northern section voted for unification
with Nigeria. The president of Cameroon since independence, Ahmadou Ahidjo, was replaced in 1982 by
the prime minister, Paul Biya. Both administrations
have been authoritarian.

With the expansion of oil, timber, and coffee
exports, the economy has continued to improve,
although corruption is prevalent, and environmental
degradation remains a concern. In June 2000 the
World Bank agreed to provide more than $200 million
to build a $3.7 billion pipeline connecting the oil fields
in neighboring Chad with the Cameroon coast.

Fifteen opposition parties filed complaints of fraud
in Cameroon's June 2002 parliamentary and municipal
elections, and the country's supreme court annulled
the results in nine districts. President Paul Biya's
Cameroon People's Democratic Movement holds the
vast majority of parliamentary seats.

# Canada

**Sovereign:** Queen Elizabeth II (1952)
**Governor-General:** Adrienne Clarkson (1999)
**Prime Minister:** Jean Chrétien (1993)
**Area:** 3,851,788 sq mi (9,976,140 sq km)
**Population (2002 est.):** 31,902,268 (growth rate: 0.4%);
birth rate: 11.1/1000; infant mortality rate: 5.0/1000;
density per sq mi: 8
**Capital:** Ottawa, Ontario. **Largest cities (1996 census;
metropolitan areas):** Toronto, 4,263,757; Montreal,
3,326,510; Vancouver, 1,831,665; Ottawa/Hull,
1,010,498; Edmonton, 862,597; Calgary, 821,628;
Quebec, 671,889; Winnipeg, 667,209; Hamilton,
624,360; London, 398,616. **Monetary unit:** Canadian
dollar. **Languages:** English, French (both official).
**Ethnicity/race:** British Isles origin 40%, French origin
27%, other European 20%, indigenous Indian and Inuit
1.5%, other, mostly Asian 11.5%. **Religions:** Roman
Catholic 46%, United Church 16%, Anglican 10%.
**Literacy rate:** 96% (1986)
**Economic summary: GDP/PPP** (2000 est.): $774.7
billion; per capita $24,800. **Real growth rate:** 4.3%.
**Inflation:** 2.6%. **Unemployment:** 6.8%. **Arable land:**
5%. **Agriculture:** wheat, barley, oilseed, tobacco,
fruits, vegetables; dairy products; forest products; fish.
**Labor force:** 16.1 million (2000); services 74%,
manufacturing 15%, construction 5%, agriculture 3%,
other 3% (2000). **Industries:** processed and
unprocessed minerals, food products, wood and paper
products, transportation equipment, chemicals, fish
products, petroleum and natural gas. **Natural
resources:** iron ore, nickel, zinc, copper, gold, lead,
molybdenum, potash, silver, fish, timber, wildlife, coal,
petroleum, natural gas, hydropower. **Exports:** $272.3
billion (f.o.b., 2000 est.): motor vehicles and parts,
newsprint, wood pulp, timber, crude petroleum,
machinery, natural gas, aluminum, telecommunications
equipment, electricity. **Imports:** $238.2 billion (f.o.b.,
2000 est.): machinery and equipment, crude oil,
chemicals, motor vehicles and parts, durable
consumer goods, electricity. **Major trading partners:**
U.S., Japan, UK, Germany, South Korea, Netherlands,
China, France, Mexico, Taiwan.

**Geography** Covering most of the northern part of
the North American continent and with an area larger
than that of the United States, Canada has an
extremely varied topography. In the east the mountainous maritime provinces have an irregular coastline on
the Gulf of St. Lawrence and the Atlantic. The St.
Lawrence plain, covering most of southern Quebec
and Ontario, and the interior continental plain, covering southern Manitoba and Saskatchewan and most of

## Canadian Prime Ministers Since 1867

| Term | Prime Minister | Party | Term | Prime Minister | Party |
|------|----------------|-------|------|----------------|-------|
| 1867–1873 | Sir John A. Macdonald | Conservative | 1926–1930 | W. L. Mackenzie King | Liberal |
| 1873–1878 | Alexander Mackenzie | Liberal | 1930–1935 | Richard B. Bennett | Conservative |
| 1878–1891 | Sir John A. Macdonald | Conservative | 1935–1948 | W. L. Mackenzie King | Liberal |
| 1891–1892 | Sir John J. C. Abbott | Conservative | 1948–1957 | Louis S. St. Laurent | Liberal |
| 1892–1894 | Sir John S. D. Thompson | Conservative | 1957–1963 | John G. Diefenbaker | Conservative |
| 1894–1896 | Sir Mackenzie Bowell | Conservative | 1963–1968 | Lester B. Pearson | Liberal |
| 1896 | Sir Charles Tupper | Conservative | 1968–1979 | Pierre Elliott Trudeau | Liberal |
| 1896–1911 | Sir Wilfrid Laurier | Liberal | 1979–1980 | Charles Joseph Clark | Conservative |
| 1911–1917 | Sir Robert L. Borden | Conservative | 1980–1984 | Pierre Elliott Trudeau | Liberal |
| 1917–1920 | Sir Robert L. Borden | Unionist | 1984 | John Turner | Liberal |
| 1920–1921 | Arthur Meighen | Unionist | 1984–1993 | Brian Mulroney | Conservative |
| 1921–1926 | W. L. Mackenzie King | Liberal | 1993 | Kim Campbell | Conservative |
| 1926 | Arthur Meighen | Conservative | 1993– | Jean Chrétien | Liberal |

Alberta, are the principal cultivable areas. They are separated by a forested plateau rising from Lakes Superior and Huron.

Westward toward the Pacific, most of British Columbia, Yukon, and part of western Alberta are covered by parallel mountain ranges, including the Rockies. The Pacific border of the coast range is ragged with fjords and channels. The highest point in Canada is Mount Logan (19,850 ft; 6,050 m), which is in the Yukon. The two principal river systems are the Mackenzie and the St. Lawrence. The St. Lawrence, with its tributaries, is navigable for over 1,900 mi (3,058 km).

**Government** Canada is a federation of 10 provinces (Alberta, British Columbia, Manitoba, New Brunswick, Newfoundland, Nova Scotia, Ontario, Prince Edward Island, Quebec, and Saskatchewan) and three territories (Northwest Territories, Yukon, and as of April 1, 1999, Nunavut). Formally considered a constitutional monarchy, Canada is governed by its own House of Commons. While the governor-general is officially the representative of Queen Elizabeth II, in reality the governor-general acts only upon the advice of the Canadian prime minister.

**History** The first inhabitants of Canada were native Indian peoples, primarily the Inuit (Eskimo). The Norse explorer Leif Eriksson probably reached the shores of Canada (Labrador or Nova Scotia) in 1000, but the history of the white man in the country actually began in 1497, when John Cabot, an Italian in the service of Henry VII of England, reached New-

## Population by Provinces and Territories

| Province | 2000 | 2001 |
|----------|------|------|
| | (in thousands) | |
| Alberta | 2,997.2 | 3,064.2 |
| British Columbia | 4,063.8 | 4,095.9 |
| Manitoba | 1,147.9 | 1,150.0 |
| New Brunswick | 756.6 | 757.0 |
| Newfoundland | 538.8 | 533.7 |
| Nova Scotia | 941.0 | 942.6 |
| Ontario | 11,669.3 | 11,874.4 |
| Prince Edward Island | 138.9 | 138.5 |
| Quebec | 7,372.4 | 7,410.5 |
| Saskatchewan | 1,023.6 | 1,015.7 |
| Northwest Territories | 42.1 | 40.8 |
| Yukon Territory | 30.7 | 29.8 |
| Nunavut | 27.7 | 28.1 |

*Source: Statistics Canada.*

foundland or Nova Scotia. Canada was taken for France in 1534 by Jacques Cartier. The actual settlement of New France, as it was then called, began in 1604 at Port Royal in what is now Nova Scotia; in 1608, Quebec was founded. France's colonization efforts were not very successful, but French explorers by the end of the 17th century had penetrated beyond the Great Lakes to the western prairies and south along the Mississippi to the Gulf of Mexico. Meanwhile, the English Hudson's Bay Company had been established in 1670. Because of the valuable fisheries and fur trade, a conflict developed between the French and English; in 1713, Newfoundland, Hudson Bay, and Nova Scotia (Acadia) were lost to England. During the Seven Years' War (1756–63), England extended its conquest, and the British general James Wolfe won his famous victory over Gen. Louis Montcalm outside Quebec on Sept. 13, 1759. The Treaty of Paris in 1763 gave England control.

At that time the population of Canada was almost entirely French, but in the next few decades, thousands of British colonists emigrated to Canada from the British Isles and from the American colonies. In 1849, the right of Canada to self-government was recognized. By the British North America Act of 1867, the dominion of Canada was created through the confederation of Upper and Lower Canada, Nova Scotia, and New Brunswick. In 1869, Canada purchased from the Hudson's Bay Company the vast middle west (Rupert's Land) from which the provinces of Manitoba (1870), Alberta (1905), and Saskatchewan (1905) were later formed. In 1871, British Columbia joined the dominion, and in 1873, Prince Edward Island followed. The country was linked from coast to coast in 1885 by the Canadian Pacific Railway.

During the formative years between 1866 and 1896, the Conservative Party, led by Sir John A. Macdonald, governed the country, except during the years 1873–1878. In 1896 the Liberal Party took over and, under Sir Wilfrid Laurier, an eminent French Canadian, ruled until 1911. By the Statute of Westminster in 1931 the British dominions, including Canada, were formally declared to be partner nations with Britain, "equal in status, in no way subordinate to each other," and bound together only by allegiance to a common Crown.

Newfoundland became Canada's 10th province on March 31, 1949, following a plebiscite. Canada also includes three territories—the Yukon Territory, the Northwest Territories, and the newest territory, Nunavut. This new territory includes all of the Arctic north of the mainland, Norway having recognized Canadian sovereignty over the Sverdrup Islands in the Arctic in 1931.

The Liberal Party, led by William Lyon Mackenzie King, dominated Canadian politics from 1921 until 1957, when it was succeeded by the Progressive Conservatives. The Liberals, under the leadership of Lester B. Pearson, returned to power in 1963. Pearson remained prime minister until 1968, when he retired and was replaced by a former law professor, Pierre Elliott Trudeau. Trudeau maintained Canada's defensive alliance with the United States but began moving toward a more independent policy in world affairs.

Trudeau's election was considered in part a response to the most serious problem confronting the country, the division between French- and English-speaking Canadians, which had led to a separatist movement in the predominantly French province of Quebec. In 1974, the provincial government, the Parti Québécois (PQ) passed a law making French the official language of Quebec, but in Dec. 1979, the law was voided by the Canadian Supreme Court. In May 1980, Quebec held a referendum on whether the province should seek independence from Canada; it was defeated by 60% of the voters.

Resolving a dispute that had occupied Trudeau since the beginning of his tenure, Queen Elizabeth II signed the Constitution Act (also called the Canada Act) in Ottawa on April 17, 1982, thereby cutting the last legal tie between Canada and Britain. The constitution retains Queen Elizabeth as queen of Canada and keeps Canada's membership in the Commonwealth.

In the national election on Sept. 4, 1984, the Progressive Conservative Party scored an overwhelming victory, fundamentally changing the country's political landscape. The Conservatives, led by Brian Mulroney, won the highest political majority in Canadian history. The dominant foreign issue was a free-trade pact with the U.S., a treaty bitterly opposed by the Liberal and New Democratic Parties. The conflict led to elections in Nov. 1988 that solidly reelected Mulroney and gave him a mandate to proceed with the agreement.

The issue of separatist sentiments in French-speaking Quebec flared up again in 1990 with the failure of the Meech Lake Accord. The accord was designed to ease the Quebecers' fear of losing their identity within the English-speaking majority by giving Quebec constitutional status as a "distinct society." In an attempt to keep Canada united, the three major political parties came to an agreement in Feb. 1992 on constitutional reforms. Voters in the Northwest Territories authorized the division of their region in two, creating a homeland for Canadian Eskimos, the Inuits, which in April 1999 became the territory of Nunavut. Also in 1999, Canada announced its decision to withdraw its combat units from NATO command. The economy continued to be mired in a long recession that many blamed on the free trade agreement. A national referendum was held in Oct. 1992 on the proposal to change the constitution to ensure greater representation in Parliament for the more populous regions and thereby the French-speaking Quebecers. The referendum, however, was defeated.

Brian Mulroney's popularity continued to decline, causing him to resign before the next election. In June 1993 the governing Progressive Conservative Party chose Defense Minister Kim Campbell as its leader, making her the first female prime minister in Canadian history. The national election in Oct. 1993 resulted in the reemergence of the Liberal Party and the installation of Jean Chrétien as prime minister.

The Quebec referendum on secession in Oct. 1995 yielded a narrow rejection of the proposal. But separatists vowed to try again. Since then, however, the Reform Party has replaced the Bloc Québécois as the official opposition.

On April 1, 1999, the Northwest Territories were officially divided to create a new territory in the east that would be governed by Canada's Inuits, who make up 85% of the area's population. Composed of 770,000 sq mi of mostly snow and ice reaching well to the north of the Arctic Circle, the 25,700 residents of Nunavut are governed from the new capital, Iqaluit.

In July 2000, Stockwell Day of the new conservative Canadian Alliance Party unexpectedly emerged as the leader of Canada's opposition. In elections held in Nov. 2000, however, Prime Minister Jean Chrétien of the Liberal Party won a landslide victory of a third five-year term. After the election, the conservatives rapidly lost steam.

Chrétien announced in Aug. 2002 that he would not seek a fourth term and instead retire from politics in 2004. Conflict between Chrétien and his former finance minister, Paul Martin, has divided and weakened the Liberal Party.

## Cape Verde

### REPUBLIC OF CAPE VERDE

**National name:** República de Cabo Verde
**President:** Pedro Pires (2001)
**Prime Minister:** José Maria Neves (2001)
**Area:** 1,557 sq mi (4,033 sq km)
**Population (2002 est.):** 408,760 (growth rate: 2.1%); birth rate: 27.8/1000; infant mortality rate: 51.9/1000; density per sq mi: 263
**Capital (1990):** Praia, 61,797. **Other large city (est. 1982):** Mindelo, 50,000. **Monetary unit:** Cape Verdean escudo. **Languages:** Portuguese, Criuolo. **Ethnicity/race:** Creole (mulatto) /1%, African 28%, European 1%. **Religion:** Roman Catholic fused with indigenous beliefs. **Literacy rate:** 67% (1989)
**Economic summary:** GDP/PPP (2000 est.): $670 million; per capita $1,700. **Real growth rate:** 6%. **Inflation:** 4%. **Unemployment:** 24% (1999 est.). **Arable land:** 11%. **Agriculture:** bananas, corn, beans, sweet potatoes, sugarcane, coffee, peanuts; fish. **Labor force:** n.a. **Industries:** food and beverages, fish processing, shoes and garments, salt mining, ship repair. **Natural resources:** salt, basalt rock, pozzuolana (a siliceous volcanic ash used to produce hydraulic cement), limestone, kaolin, fish. **Exports:** $40 million (f.o.b., 2000 est.): fuel, shoes, garments, fish, bananas, hides. **Imports:** $250 million (f.o.b., 2000 est.): foodstuffs, industrial products, transport equipment, fuels. **Major trading partners:** Portugal, U.S., Germany, Spain, France, Malaysia, Netherlands, U.S.

**Geography** Cape Verde, only slightly larger than Rhode Island, is an archipelago in the Atlantic 385 mi (500 km) west of Senegal.

The islands are divided into two groups: Barlavento in the north, composed of Santo Antão (291 sq mi; 754 sq km), Boa Vista (240 sq mi; 622 sq km), São Nicolau (132 sq mi; 342 sq km), São Vicente (88 sq mi; 246 sq km), Sal (83 sq mi; 298 sq km), and Santa Luzia (13 sq mi; 34 sq km); and Sotavento in the south, consisting of São Tiago (383 sq mi; 992 sq km), Fogo (184 sq mi; 477 sq km), Maio (103 sq mi; 267 sq km), and Brava (25 sq mi; 65 sq km). The islands are mostly mountainous, with the land deeply scarred by erosion. There is an active volcano on Fogo.

**Government** Republic.

**History** Uninhabited upon their discovery in 1456, the Cape Verde islands became part of the Portuguese empire in 1495. A majority of today's inhabitants are of mixed Portuguese and African ancestry.

Positioned on the great trade routes between Africa, Europe, and the New World, the islands became a prosperous center for the slave trade but suffered economic decline after the slave trade was abolished in 1876. In the 20th century, Cape Verde served as a shipping port.

In 1951, Cape Verde's status changed from a Portuguese colony to an overseas province, and in 1961 the inhabitants became full Portuguese citizens. An independence movement led by the African Party for the Independence of Guinea-Bissau (another former Portuguese colony) and Cape Verde (PAIGC) was founded in 1956. Following the 1974 coup in Portugal, after which Portugal began abandoning its colonial empire, the islands became independent (July 5, 1975).

The first multiparty elections since independence on Jan. 13, 1991, resulted in the ruling African Party for the Independence of Cape Verde (PAICV) losing its majority to the Movement for Democracy Party (MPD). The MPD candidate, Antonio Monteiro, won the subsequent presidential election. Monteiro was easily reelected in 1996.

In an effort to take advantage of its proximity to cross-Atlantic sea and air lanes, the government has embarked on a major expansion of its port and airport capacities. It is also modernizing the fishing fleet and enhancing its fish processing industry. These projects are being partly paid for by the EU and the World Bank, making Cape Verde one of the largest per capita aid recipients in the world. Disenchantment with the government's privatization program, continued high unemployment, and widespread poverty helped defeat the MPD in elections held in Jan. 2001. The PAICV swept back into power and José Maria Neves became prime minister.

# Central African Republic

**National name:** République Centrafricaine
**President:** Ange-Félix Patassé (1993)
**Prime Minister:** Martin Ziguélé (2001)
**Area:** 240,534 sq mi (622,984 sq km)
**Population (2002 est.):** 3,642,739 (growth rate: 1.8%); birth rate: 36.6/1000; infant mortality rate: 103.8/1000; density per sq mi: 15
**Capital and largest city (1990 est.):** Bangui, 706,000.
**Monetary unit:** CFA Franc. **Languages:** French (official), Sangho, Arabic, Hansa, Swahili. **Ethnicity/ race:** Baya 34%, Banda 27%, Sara 10%, Mandjia 21%, Mboum 4%, M'Baka 4%, Yakoma, Ubangi, Europeans 6,500 (including 3,600 French). **Religions:** indigenous beliefs 24%, Protestant and Roman Catholic with animist influence 50%, Muslim 15%, other 11%. **Literacy rate:** 38% (1990)
**Economic summary:** GDP/PPP (2000 est.): $6.1 billion; per capita $1,700. **Real growth rate:** 3.5%. **Inflation:** 3%. **Unemployment:** 6% (1993). **Arable land:** 3%. **Agriculture:** cotton, coffee, tobacco, manioc (tapioca), yams, millet, corn, bananas; timber. **Labor force:** n.a. **Industries:** diamond mining, sawmills, breweries, textiles, footwear, assembly of bicycles and motorcycles. **Natural resources:** diamonds, uranium, timber, gold, oil, hydropower. **Exports:** $166 million (f.o.b., 2000): food, textiles, petroleum products, machinery, electrical equipment, motor vehicles, chemicals, pharmaceuticals, consumer goods, industrial products. **Imports:** $154 million (f.o.b., 2000): food, textiles, petroleum products, machinery,

electrical equipment, motor vehicles, chemicals, pharmaceuticals, consumer goods, industrial products. **Major trading partners:** Benelux, Côte d'Ivoire, Spain, Egypt, France, Cameroon, Germany, Japan.

**Geography** Situated about 500 mi (805 km) north of the equator, the Central African Republic is a landlocked nation bordered by Cameroon, Chad, the Sudan, the Democratic Republic of the Congo, and the Republic of Congo. The Ubangi and the Shari are the largest of many rivers.

**Government** Multiparty republic since 1991.

**History** From the 16th to 19th century, the people of this region were ravaged by slave traders. The Banda, Baya, Ngbandi, and Azande make up the largest ethnic groups.

The French occupied the region in 1894. As the colony of Ubangi-Shari, what is now the Central African Republic was united with Chad in 1905. In 1910 it was joined with Gabon and the Middle Congo to become French Equatorial Africa. After World War II a rebellion in 1946 forced the French to grant self-government. In 1958 the territory voted to become an autonomous republic within the French Community, and on Aug. 13, 1960, President David Dacko proclaimed the republic's independence from France. Dacko moved the country into Beijing's orbit, but was overthrown in a coup on Dec. 31, 1965, by Col. Jean-Bédel Bokassa, army chief of staff.

On Dec. 4, 1976, the Central African Republic became the Central African Empire. Marshal Jean-Bédel Bokassa, who had ruled the republic since he took power in 1965, was declared Emperor Bokassa I. Brutality and excess characterized his regime. He was overthrown in a coup on Sept. 20, 1979. Former president David Dacko returned to power and changed the country's name back to the Central African Republic. An army coup on Sept. 1, 1981, deposed President Dacko again.

In 1991, President André Kolingba, under pressure, announced a move toward parliamentary democracy. In elections held in Aug. 1993, Prime Minister Ange-Félix Patassé defeated Kolingba. Part of Patassé's popularity rested on his pledge to pay the back salaries of the military and civil servants.

A 1994 economic upturn was too small to effectively improve the catastrophic financial condition of the nation. Patassé was unable to pay the salaries due government workers, and the military revolted in 1996. At Patassé's request, French troops suppressed the uprising. In 1998 the United Nations sent an all-African peacekeeping force to the country. In elections held in Sept. 1999, amid widespread charges of massive fraud, Patassé easily defeated Kolingba.

President Ange-Félix Patassé survived a failed coup attempt in May 2001 with the help of Libya and Congolese rebels. Former president André Kolingba was thought to be behind it. Reprisals against Kolingba's ethnic group, the Yakomas, followed the coup attempt.

# Chad

### REPUBLIC OF CHAD

**National name:** République du Tchad
**President:** Idriss Déby (1990)
**Prime Minister:** Nagoum Yamassoum (1999)
**Area:** 495,752 sq mi (1,284,000 sq km)
**Population (2002 est.):** 8,997,237 (growth rate: 3.3%); birth rate: 47.7/1000; infant mortality rate: 93.5/1000; density per sq mi: 18
**Capital and largest city (1993):** N'Djamena, 529,555.

**Monetary unit:** CFA Franc. **Languages:** French and Arabic (official), more than 100 tribal languages. **Ethnicity/race:** North and center: Muslims (Arabs, Toubou, Hadjerai, Fulbe, Kotoko, Kanembou, Baguirmi, Boulala, Zaghawa, and Maba); South: non-Muslims (Sara [the largest ethnic group, 25% of the population], Ngambaye, Mbaye, Goulaye, Moundang, Moussei, Massa). **Religions:** Islam 44%, Christian 33%, traditional 23%. **Literacy rate:** 30% (1990)
**Economic summary:** GDP/PPP (2000 est.): $8.1 billion; per capita $1,000. **Real growth rate:** 4%. **Inflation:** 3%. **Unemployment:** n.a. **Arable land:** 3%. **Agriculture:** cotton, sorghum, millet, peanuts, rice, potatoes, manioc (tapioca); cattle, sheep, goats, camels. **Labor force:** n.a.; agriculture 85% (subsistence farming, herding, and fishing). **Industries:** cotton textiles, meatpacking, beer brewing, natron (sodium carbonate), soap, cigarettes, construction materials. **Natural resources:** petroleum (unexploited but exploration under way), uranium, natron, kaolin, fish (Lake Chad). **Exports:** $172 million (f.o.b., 2000 est.): cotton, cattle, textiles. **Imports:** $223 million (f.o.b., 2000 est.): machinery and transportation equipment, industrial goods, petroleum products, foodstuffs, textiles. **Major trading partners:** Portugal, Germany, Thailand, Costa Rica, South Africa, France, Cameroon, Nigeria, India.

**Geography** A landlocked country in north-central Africa, Chad is about 85% the size of Alaska. Its neighbors are Niger, Libya, the Sudan, the Central African Republic, Cameroon, and Nigeria. Lake Chad, from which the country gets its name, lies on the western border with Niger and Nigeria. In the north is a desert that runs into the Sahara.

**Government** Republic.

**History** The area around Lake Chad has been inhabited since at least 500 B.C. In the 8th century A.D. Berbers began migrating to the area. Islam arrived in 1085, and by the 16th century a trio of rival kingdoms flourished: the Kanem-Bornu, the Baguirmi, and Ouaddaï. In 1883–1893, all three kingdoms came under the rule of the Sudanese conqueror Rabih al-Zubayr. In 1900, Rabih was overthrown by the French, who absorbed these kingdoms into the colony of French Equatorial Africa, as part of Ubangi-Shari, in 1910.

France began the country's development after 1920, when it became a separate colony. In 1946, French Equatorial Africa was admitted to the French Community, and in 1958 the Chad territory became an autonomous republic within the French Community. An independence movement led by the first premier and president, François (later Ngarta) Tombalbaye, achieved complete independence on Aug. 11, 1960. Tombalbaye was killed in the 1975 coup and succeeded by Gen. Félix Malloum, who faced a Libyan-financed civil war throughout his tenure in office. In 1977, Libya seized a strip of Chadian land and launched an invasion two years later.

Nine rival groups meeting in Lagos, Nigeria, in March 1979 agreed to form a provisional government headed by Goukouni Oueddei, a former rebel leader. Fighting broke out again in Chad in March 1980, when Defense Minister Hissen Habré challenged Goukouni and seized the capital. Libyan president Muammar al-Qaddafi, in Jan. 1981, proposed a merger of Chad with Libya. The Libyan proposal was rejected and Libyan troops withdrew from Chad that year, but in 1983 they poured back into the northern part of the country in support of Goukouni. France, in turn, sent troops into southern Chad in support of Habré. Government troops then launched an offensive in early 1987 that drove the Libyans out of most of the country.

In 1990, Idriss Déby, a former defense minister and head of a rebel group, the Patriotic Salvation Movement, overthrew Habré, suspended the constitution, and dissolved the legislature. In 1994 a new constitution was drafted and an amnesty for political prisoners was declared. Déby won multiparty elections in 1996 and was reelected in 2001.

The Movement for Democracy and Justice in Chad (MDJC), led by Déby's former defense minister, Youssouf Togoimi, began fighting against the government in 1998. In Jan. 2002 a ceasefire was declared, but some clashes between the rebels and the government have persisted.

In June 2000 the World Bank agreed to provide more than $200 million to build a $3.7 billion pipeline connecting the oil fields in Chad to those in Cameroon. Oil revenues are estimated to earn $2.5 billion over the next 30 years. But environmentalists fear the giant project will harm rain forests, and human rights groups are concerned it will only benefit the oil companies and the political elite in Cameroon and Chad. The World Bank, however, has forced Chad to agree to spend 80% of the resulting oil revenues on education, health, infrastructure, and other social welfare projects desperately needed by this impoverished country.

# Chile

### REPUBLIC OF CHILE

**National name:** República de Chile
**President:** Ricardo Lagos (2000)
**Area:** 292,258 sq mi (756,950 sq km)
**Population (2002 est.):** 15,498,930 (growth rate: 1.1%); birth rate: 16.5/1000; infant mortality rate: 9.1/1000; density per sq mi: 53
**Capital and largest city (2000 est.):** Santiago, 5,400,000 (metro. area). **Other large cities (1996 est.):** Concepción, 356,371; Viña del Mar, 326,448; Valparaíso, 282,850; Talcahuano, 265,060; Temuco, 246,304. **Monetary unit:** Chilean Peso. **Language:** Spanish. **Ethnicity/race:** European and European-Indian 95%, Indian 3%, other 2%. **Religions:** Roman Catholic 89%, Protestant 11%, small Jewish and Muslim populations. **Literacy rate:** 95% (1992)
**Economic summary:** GDP/PPP (2000 est.): $153.1 billion; per capita $10,100. **Real growth rate:** 5.5%. **Inflation:** 4.5%. **Unemployment:** 9% (Dec. 2000). **Arable land:** 5%. **Agriculture:** wheat, corn, grapes, beans, sugar beets, potatoes, fruit; beef, poultry, wool; fish; timber. **Labor force:** 5.8 million (1999 est.); agriculture 14%, industry 27%, services 59% (1997 est.). **Industries:** copper, other minerals, foodstuffs, fish processing, iron and steel, wood and wood products, transport equipment, cement, textiles. **Natural resources:** copper, timber, iron ore, nitrates, precious metals, molybdenum, hydropower. **Exports:** $18 billion (f.o.b., 2000): copper, fish, fruits, paper and pulp, chemicals. **Imports:** $17 billion (f.o.b., 2000): consumer goods, chemicals, motor vehicles, fuels, electrical machinery, heavy industrial machinery, food. **Major trading partners:** EU, U.S., Japan, Brazil, Argentina, Mexico.

**Geography** Situated south of Peru and west of Bolivia and Argentina, Chile fills a narrow 1,800-mile (2,897 km) strip between the Andes and the Pacific. One-third of Chile is covered by the towering ranges of the Andes. In the north is the driest place on Earth, the Atacama Desert, and in the center is a 700-mile-long (1,127 km), thickly populated valley with most of Chile's arable land. At the southern tip of Chile's mainland is Punta Arenas, the southernmost city in the world, and beyond that lies the Strait of Magellan and Tierra del Fuego, an island divided between Chile and Argentina. The southernmost point of South America is Cape Horn, a 1,390-foot (424 m) rock on Horn Island in the Wollaston group, which belongs to Chile. Chile also claims sovereignty over 482,628 sq mi (1,250,000 sq km) of Antarctic territory, the Juan Fernández Islands, about 400 mi (644 km) west of the mainland, and Easter Island, about 2,000 mi (3,219 km) west.

**Government** Republic.

**History** Chile was originally under the control of the Incas in the north and the nomadic Araucanos in the south. In 1541, a Spaniard, Pedro de Valdivia, founded Santiago. Chile won its independence from Spain in 1818 under Bernardo O'Higgins and an Argentinian, José de San Martin. O'Higgins, dictator until 1823, laid the foundations of the modern state with a two-party system and a centralized government.

The dictator from 1830 to 1837, Diego Portales, fought a war with Peru in 1836–39 that expanded Chilean territory. Chile fought the War of the Pacific with Peru and Bolivia from 1879 to 1883, winning Antofagasta, Bolivia's only outlet to the sea, and extensive areas from Peru. Pedro Montt led a revolt that overthrew José Balmaceda in 1891 and established a parliamentary dictatorship lasting until a new constitution was adopted in 1925. Industrialization began before World War I and led to the formation of Marxist groups. Juan Antonio Ríos, president during World War II, was originally pro-Nazi but in 1944 led his country into the war on the side of the Allies.

A small abortive army uprising in 1969 raised the fear of military intervention in preventing a Marxist, Salvador Allende Gossens, from taking office after his election to the presidency on Sept. 4, 1970. Allende was the first president in a non-Communist country freely elected on a Marxist-Leninist program. Allende quickly established relations with Cuba and the People's Republic of China and nationalized several American companies. Allende's overthrow and death in an army assault on the presidential palace in Sept. 1973 ended a 46-year era of constitutional government in Chile.

The takeover was led by a four-man junta headed by Army Chief of Staff Augusto Pinochet Ugarte, who assumed the office of president. Committed to "exterminat[ing] Marxism," the junta suspended Parliament, banned political activity, and broke relations with Cuba. It also abolished DINA, the secret police, and decreed an amnesty for political prisoners, while free-market reforms improved the economy. In 1977, Pinochet promised elections by 1985 if conditions warranted. After losing the plebiscite, Pinochet stepped down in Jan. 1990 in favor of Patricio Aylwin, who was elected in Dec. 1989 as the head of a 17-party coalition. In Dec. 1993, Eduardo Frei Ruiz-Tagle, the candidate of a center-left coalition and son of a previous president, was elected president.

In March 1998, Pinochet retired as army commander in chief. In Oct. 1998, he was arrested and detained in England on an extradition request issued by a Spanish judge who sought Pinochet in connection with the disappearance of Spanish citizens during his rule. British courts ultimately denied his extradition, and Pinochet returned to Chile in March 2000. The Chilean Supreme Court stripped Pinochet of his immunity from prosecution in June 2000, but in July 2001, Chilean courts ruled that he was mentally unfit to stand trial.

Ricardo Lagos became president in March 2000, the first socialist to run the country since Allende. Chile's economic growth slowed to 3% for 2001, partly the result of a drop in international copper prices and the economic turmoil in neighboring Argentina. The country's economic outlook, however, remained generally good in 2002.

# China

### PEOPLE'S REPUBLIC OF CHINA

**National name:** Zhonghua Renmin Gongheguo
**President:** Jiang Zemin (1993)
**Prime Minister:** Zhu Rongji (1998)
**Area:** 3,705,386 sq mi (9,596,960 sq km)[1]
**Population (2002 est.):** 1,284,303,705 (growth rate: 0.9%); birth rate: 15.8/1000; infant mortality rate: 27.2/1000; density per sq mi: 347.
**Capital (2000 est.):** Beijing, 8,450,000 (metro. area). **Largest cities (1990 est.):** Shanghai (2000 est.), 11,800,000 (metro. area); Hong Kong (Xianggang) (2000 est.), 6,750,000 (metro. area); Tianjin (Tientsin) (2000 est.), 5,350,000 (metro. area); Shenyang (Mukden), 4,669,737; Wuhan, 4,040,113; Guangzhou, 3,935,193; Chungking (Chongqing) 3,127,178; Haerbin, 2,990,921; Chengdu, 2,954,872; Xian, 2,872,539. **Monetary unit:** Yuan/Renminbi.
**Languages:** Chinese, Mandarin, also local dialects. **Ethnicity/race:** Han Chinese 91.9%, Zhuang, Uygur, Hui, Yi, Tibetan, Miao, Manchu, Mongol, Buyi, Korean, and other nationalities 8.1%. China has 56 ethnic groups. **Religions:** Officially atheist but traditional religion contains elements of Confucianism, Taoism, Buddhism. **Literacy rate:** 84% (1995)
**Economic summary:** GDP/PPP (2000 est.): $4.5 trillion; per capita $3,600. **Real growth rate:** 8%. **Inflation:** 0.4%. **Unemployment:** urban unemployment roughly 10%; substantial unemployment and underemployment in rural areas. **Arable land:** 10%. **Agriculture:** rice, wheat, potatoes, sorghum, peanuts, tea, millet, barley, cotton, oilseed; pork; fish. **Labor force:** 700 million (1998 est.); agriculture 50%, industry 24%, services 26% (1998). **Industries:** iron and steel, coal, machine building, armaments, textiles and apparel, petroleum, cement, chemical fertilizers, footwear, toys, food processing, automobiles, consumer electronics, telecommunications. **Natural resources:** coal, iron ore, petroleum, natural gas, mercury, tin, tungsten, antimony, manganese, molybdenum, vanadium, magnetite, aluminum, lead, zinc, uranium, hydropower potential (world's largest). **Exports:** $232 billion (f.o.b., 2000): machinery and equipment; textiles and clothing, footwear, toys and sporting goods; mineral fuels. **Imports:** $197 billion (f.o.b., 2000): machinery and equipment, mineral fuels, plastics, iron and steel, chemicals. **Major trading partners:** U.S., Hong Kong, Japan, South Korea, Germany, Netherlands, UK, Singapore, Taiwan, Russia, Malaysia.

1. Including Manchuria and Tibet.

**Geography** The greater part of the country is mountainous. Its principal ranges are the Tien Shan, the Kunlun chain, and the Trans-Himalaya. In the southwest is Tibet, which China annexed in 1950. The Gobi Desert lies to the north. China proper consists of three great river systems: the Yellow River (Huang He),

2,109 mi (5,464 km) long; the Yangtze River (Chang Jiang), the third-longest river in the world at 2,432 mi (6,300 km); and the Pearl River (Zhu Jiang), 848 mi (2,197 km) long.

**Government** Communist state.

**History** The earliest recorded human settlements in what is today called China were discovered in the Huang Ho basin and date from about 5000 B.C. During the Shang dynasty (1500–1000 B.C.), the precursor of modern China's ideographic writing system developed, allowing the emerging feudal states of the era to achieve an advanced stage of civilization, rivaling in sophistication anything found at the time in Europe, the Middle East, or the Americas. It was following this initial flourishing of civilization, in a period known as the Chou dynasty (1122–249 B.C.), that Lao-tse, Confucius, Mo Ti, and Mencius laid the foundation of Chinese philosophical thought.

The feudal states, often at war with one another, were first united under Emperor Ch'in Shih Huang Ti, during whose reign (246–210 B.C.) work was begun on the Great Wall of China, a monumental bulwark against invasion from the West. Although the Great Wall symbolized China's desire to protect itself from the outside world, under the Han dynasty (206 B.C.–A.D. 220), the civilization conducted extensive commercial trading with the West.

In the T'ang dynasty (618–907)—often called the golden age of Chinese history—painting, sculpture, and poetry flourished, and woodblock printing, which enabled the mass production of books, made its earliest known appearance. The Mings, last of the native rulers (1368–1644), overthrew the Mongol, or Yuan, dynasty (1271–1368) established by Kublai Khan. The Mings in turn were overthrown in 1644 by invaders from the north, the Manchus.

China remained largely isolated from the rest of the world's civilizations, closely restricting foreign activities. By the end of the 18th century only Canton (location of modern-day Hong Kong) and the Portuguese port of Macao were open to European merchants. But with the first Anglo-Chinese War in 1839–42, a long period of instability and concessions to Western colonial powers began. Following the war, several ports were opened up for trading, and Hong Kong was ceded to Britain. Treaties signed after further hostilities (1856–60) weakened Chinese sovereignty and gave foreigners immunity from Chinese jurisdiction. European powers took advantage of the disastrous Sino-Japanese War of 1894–95 to gain further trading concessions from China. Peking's response, the Boxer Rebellion (1900), was suppressed by an international force.

The death of Empress Dowager Tzu Hsi in 1908 and the accession of the infant emperor Hsüan T'ung (Pu-Yi) were followed by a nationwide rebellion led by Dr. Sun Yat-sen, who overthrew the Manchus and became the first president of the Provisional Chinese Republic in 1911. Dr. Sun resigned in favor of Yuan Shih-k'ai, who suppressed the Republicans in a bid to consolidate his power. Yuan's death in June 1916 was followed by years of civil war between rival militarists and Dr. Sun's Republicans. Nationalist forces, led by General Chiang Kai-shek and with the advice of Communist experts, soon occupied most of China, setting up a Kuomintang regime in 1928. Internal strife continued, however, and Chiang eventually broke with the Communists.

On Sept. 18, 1931, Japan launched an invasion of Manchuria, capturing the province. Tokyo set up a puppet state dubbed Manchukuo and installed the last Manchu emperor, Henry Pu-Yi (Hsüan T'ung), as its nominal leader. Japanese troops moved to seize China's northern provinces in July 1937 but were resisted by Chiang, who had been able to use the Japanese invasion to unite most of China behind him. Within two years, however, Japan had seized most of the nation's eastern ports and railways. The Kuomintang government retreated first to Hankow and then to Chungking, while the Japanese set up a puppet government at Nanking, headed by Wang Jingwei.

Japan's surrender to the Western Allies in 1945 touched off civil war between the Kuomintang forces under Chiang and Communists led by Mao Zedong, who had been battling since the 1930s for control of China. Despite U.S. aid, the Kuomintang were overcome by the Soviet-supported Communists, and Chiang and his followers were forced to flee the mainland, establishing a government-in-exile on the island of Formosa (Taiwan). The Mao regime proclaimed the People's Republic of China on Oct. 1, 1949, with Beijing as the new capital and Zhou Enlai as premier.

After the Korean War began in June 1950, China led the Communist bloc in supporting North Korea, and on Nov. 26, 1950, the Mao regime sent troops to assist the North in its efforts to capture the South.

In an attempt to restructure China's primarily agrarian economy, Mao undertook the "Great Leap Forward" campaign in 1958, a disastrous program that aimed to combine the establishment of rural communes with a crash program of village industrialization. The Great Leap forced the abandonment of farming activities, leading to widespread famine in which more than 20 million people died of malnutrition.

In 1959, a failed uprising against China's invasion and occupation of Tibet forced Tibetan Buddhism's spiritual leader, the Dalai Lama, and 100,000 of his followers to flee to India. The invasion of Tibet, as well as border disputes between China and India—with whom Moscow had warm relations—and a perceived rivalry for the leadership of the world Communist movement caused a serious souring of relations between China and the USSR, former allies.

The failure of the Great Leap Forward touched off a power struggle within the Chinese Communist Party between Mao and his supporters and a reformist faction including future premier Deng Xiaoping. Mao moved to Shanghai, and from that base he and his supporters waged what they called the Cultural Revolution. Beginning in the spring of 1966, Mao ordered the closing of schools and the formation of ideologically pure Red Guard units, dominated by youths and students. The Red Guards campaigned against "old ideas, old culture, old habits, and old customs." Millions died as a series of violent purges were carried out. By early 1967, the Cultural Revolution had succeeded in bolstering Mao's position as China's paramount leader.

Anxious to exploit the Sino-Soviet rift, the Nixon administration made a dramatic announcement in July 1971 that National Security Adviser Henry Kissinger had secretly visited Beijing and reached an agreement whereby Nixon would visit China. The movement toward reconciliation, which signaled the end of the U.S. containment policy toward China, provided momentum for China's admission to the UN. Despite U.S. opposition to expelling Taiwan (Nationalist China), the world body overwhelmingly voted to oust Taiwan in favor of Beijing's Communist government.

President Nixon went to Beijing for a week early in 1972, meeting Mao as well as Zhou. The summit ended with a historic communiqué on Feb. 28, in which both nations promised to work toward improved relations. Full diplomatic relations were barred by China as long as the U.S. continued to recognize the legitimacy of Nationalist China.

Following Zhou's death on Jan. 8, 1976, his successor, Vice Premier Deng Xiaoping, was supplanted within a month by Hua Guofeng, former minister of public security. Hua became permanent premier in April. In Oct. he was named successor to Mao as chairman of the Communist Party. But Mao's death on Sept. 10 unleashed the bitter intraparty rivalries that had been suppressed since the Cultural Revolution. Old opponents of Mao launched a campaign against his widow, Jiang Qing, and three of her "radical" colleagues. The so-called Gang of Four was denounced for having undermined the party, the government, and the economy. They were tried and convicted in 1981. Meanwhile, in 1977, Deng Xiaoping was reinstated as deputy premier, chief of staff of the army, and member of the Central Committee of the Politburo.

Beijing and Washington announced full diplomatic relations on Jan. 1, 1979, and the Carter administration abrogated the Taiwan defense treaty. Deputy Premier Deng sealed the agreement with a visit to the U.S. that coincided with the opening of embassies in both capitals on March 1. On Deng's return from the U.S., Chinese troops invaded and briefly occupied an area along Vietnam's northern border. The action was seen as a response to Vietnam's invasion of Cambodia and ouster of the Khmer Rouge government, which China had supported.

In 1981, Deng protégé Hu Yaobang replaced Hua Guofeng as party chairman. Deng became chairman of the committee's military commission, giving him control over the army. The body's 215 members concluded the session with a statement holding Mao Zedong responsible for the "grave blunder" of the Cultural Revolution.

Under Deng Xiaoping's leadership, meanwhile, China's Communist ideology went through a massive reinterpretation, and sweeping economic changes were set in motion in the early 1980s. The Chinese scrapped the personality cult that idolized Mao Zedong, muted Mao's old call for class struggle and exportation of the Communist revolution, and imported Western technology and management techniques to replace the Marxist tenets that had slowed modernization. Deng concluded an agreement for the return of Hong Kong following the expiration of Britain's 99-year lease on the territory on July 1, 1997.

The removal of Hu Yaobang as party chairman in Jan. 1987 signaled a hard-line resurgence within the party. Hu—who had become a hero to many reform-minded Chinese—was replaced by former premier Zhao Ziyang. With the death of Hu in April 1989, the ideological struggle spilled into the streets of the capital, as student demonstrators occupied Beijing's Tiananmen Square in May, calling for democratic reforms. Less than a month later, the demonstrations were crushed in a bloody crackdown as troops and tanks moved onto the square and fired on protesters, killing several hundred.

In annual sessions of the rubber-stamp National People's Congress in 1992 and 1993, the government called for accelerating the drive for economic reform, but the sessions were widely seen as an effort to maintain China's moves toward a market economy while retaining political authoritarianism. At the session in 1993, Communist Party leader Jiang Zemin was elected president, while hard-liner Li Peng was reelected to another five-year term as prime minister. Since 1993, the Chinese economy has continued to grow rapidly. In Nov. 1993 the Central Committee adopted a resolution envisaging the conversion of state-owned enterprises into joint-stock companies, and the creation of a central bank and modern tax system.

Deng Xiaoping's death in Feb. 1997 left a younger generation in charge of managing the enormous country. In 1998, Prime Minister Zhu Rongji introduced a sweeping program to privatize state-run businesses and further liberalize the nation's economy, a move lauded by Western economists.

On July 1, 1997, when Britain's lease on the New Territories expired, Hong Kong returned to Chinese sovereignty, and in 1999, the Portuguese colony of Macao also was returned to Chinese rule.

Chinese-U.S. relations in May 1999 were severely strained when Congress accused China of stealing U.S. nuclear secrets over the past two decades. Relations eroded even further when a month later the U.S. mistakenly bombed the Chinese embassy in Belgrade during Operation Allied Force in Yugoslavia, killing three Chinese journalists and wounding 20 others.

In Aug. 1999, China rounded up thousands of members of the Falun Gong sect, a highly popular religious movement that combines elements of Buddhism, Taoism, and martial arts. China, which has now outlawed the sect, was thought to consider the apolitical spiritual group threatening because its numbers exceeded the membership of the Chinese Communist Party.

In March 2000, relations with Taiwan nearly reached a boiling point when Chen Shui-bian was elected president of Taiwan. Chen and his Democratic Progressive Party had previously called for recognition of Taiwan's independence from mainland China, but he softened his stance days before the election. The move stabilized the growing threat of armed conflict, and China adapted a "wait and see" attitude and signaled it was open to talks with Chen.

Tensions between the U.S. and China reached crisis levels in April 2001, when a U.S. Navy EP-3 surveillance plane and a Chinese fighter F-8 jet collided near the Chinese coast. The crew members of the U.S. plane were detained for 11 days and released after the U.S. issued a formal statement of regret.

The International Olympic Committee (IOC) in July 2001 awarded Beijing the 2008 Summer Games, despite some criticism of China's human rights practices and its environmental record.

In Nov. 2001 China was admitted to the World Trade Organization, ending a 15-year debate over whether the country is entitled to the full trading rights of capitalist countries.

Vice President Hu Jintao is poised to become general secretary of the Communist Party at the 16th Party Congress in fall 2002, succeeding President Jiang, who is expected to retire.

## Hong Kong

**Status:** Special Administrative Region of China
**Chief Executive:** Tung Chee Hwa (1997)
**Area:** 422 sq mi (1,092 sq km)
**Population (2002 est.):** 7,303,334 (growth rate: 0.5%); birth rate: 10.9/1000; infant mortality rate: 5.7/1000; density per sq mi: 17,322

Hong Kong consists of the island of Hong Kong (32 sq mi; 83 sq km), Stonecutters' Island, Kowloon Peninsula, and the New Territories on the adjoining mainland. The island of Hong Kong was ceded to Britain in 1841. Stonecutters' Island and Kowloon were annexed in 1860, and the New Territories, which are mainly agricultural lands, were leased from China in 1898 for 99 years. On July 1, 1997, Hong Kong was returned to China. The vibrant capitalist enclave retains its status as a free port, with its laws to remain unchanged for 50 years. Chief Executive Tung Chee Hwa formulated a policy agenda based upon the concept of "one country, two systems," thus preserving Hong Kong's economic independence.

## Macao

**Status:** Special Administrative Region of China
**Chief Executive:** Edmund Ho (1999)
**Area:** 8 sq mi (21 sq km)
**Population (2002 est.):** 461,833 (average annual growth rate: 0.8%); birth rate: 12.2/1000; infant mortality rate: 4.4/1000; density per sq mi: 56,959

Colonized by the Portuguese in 1557, Macao was the oldest European outpost in China. In 1987, Portugal and China reached an agreement to return Macao to Chinese rule on Dec. 20, 1999. They agreed upon provisions to insure the autonomy of Macao, including its right to elect local leaders, the right of its residents to travel freely, and the right to maintain its way of life for 50 years after the start of Chinese rule.

# Colombia

### REPUBLIC OF COLOMBIA

**National name:** República de Colombia
**President:** Alvaro Uribe (2002)
**Area:** 439,733 sq mi (1,138,910 sq km)
**Population (2002 est.):** 41,008,227 (growth rate: 1.6%); birth rate: 22.0/1000; infant mortality rate: 23.2/1000; density per sq mi: 93
**Capital and largest city (2000 est.):** Santafé de Bogotá, 7,350,000 (metro. area). **Largest cities (1995 est.):** Cali, 1,718,871; Medellín, 1,621,356; Barranquilla, 1,064,255; Cartagena, 745,689.
**Monetary unit:** Colombian Peso. **Language:** Spanish.
**Ethnicity/race:** mestizo 58%, white 20%, mulatto 14%, black 4%, mixed black-Indian 3%, Indian 1%.
**Religion:** Roman Catholic 95%. **Literacy rate:** 87% (1990)
**Economic summary:** GDP/PPP (2000 est.): $250 billion; per capita $6,200. **Real growth rate:** 3%. **Inflation:** 9%. **Unemployment:** 20%. **Arable land:** 4%. **Agriculture:** coffee, cut flowers, bananas, rice, tobacco, corn, sugarcane, cocoa beans, oilseed, vegetables; forest products; shrimp. **Labor force:** 18.3 million (1999 est.); services 46%, agriculture 30%, industry 24% (1990). **Industries:** textiles, food processing, oil, clothing and footwear, beverages, chemicals, cement, gold, coal, emeralds. **Natural resources:** petroleum, natural gas, coal, iron ore, nickel, gold, copper, emeralds, hydropower. **Exports:** $14.5 billion (f.o.b., 2000 est.): petroleum, coffee, coal, apparel, bananas, cut flowers. **Imports:** $12.4 billion (f.o.b., 2000 est.): industrial equipment, transportation equipment, consumer goods, chemicals, paper products, fuels, electricity. **Major trading partners:** U.S., EU, Andean Community of Nations, Japan.

**Geography** Colombia, in the northwest part of South America, is the only country on that continent that borders both the Atlantic and Pacific Oceans. It is nearly equal in size to the combined areas of California and Texas. Colombia is bordered by Panama on the northwest, on the east by Venezuela and Brazil, and on the southwest by Peru and Ecuador. Through the western half of the country, three Andean ranges run north and south, merging into one at the Ecuadorian border. The eastern half is a low, jungle-covered plain, drained by spurs of the Amazon and Orinoco Rivers, inhabited mostly by isolated tropical-forest Indian tribes. The fertile plateau and valley of the eastern range are the most densely populated parts of the country.

**Government** Republic.

**History** Little is known about the various Indian tribes who inhabited Colombia before the Spanish arrived. In 1510 Spaniards founded Darien, the first permanent European settlement on the American mainland. In 1538 they established the colony of New Granada, the area's name until 1861.

After a 14-year struggle, in which Simón Bolívar's Venezuelan troops won the battle of Boyacá in Colombia on Aug. 7, 1819, independence was attained in 1824. Bolívar united Colombia, Venezuela, Panama, and Ecuador in the Republic of Greater Colombia (1819–1830), but lost Venezuela and Ecuador to separatists. Two political parties dominated the region: the Conservatives believed in a strong central government and a powerful church; the Liberals believed in a decentralized government, strong regional power, and a less influential role for the church. Bolívar was himself a Conservative, while his vice president, Francisco de Paula Santander, was the founder of the Liberal Party.

Santander served as president between 1832 and 1836, a period of relative stability, but by 1840 civil war erupted. Other periods of Liberal dominance (1849–1857 and 1861–1880), which sought to disestablish the Roman Catholic Church, were marked by insurrection. Nine different governments followed, each rewriting the constitution. In 1861 the country was called the United States of New Granada; in 1863 it became the United States of Colombia; and in 1885, it became the Republic of Colombia.

In 1899 a brutal civil war broke out, the War of a Thousand Days, that lasted until 1902. The following year, Colombia lost its claims to Panama because it refused to ratify the lease to the U.S. of the Canal Zone. Panama declared its independence in 1903.

The Conservatives held power until 1930, when revolutionary pressure put the Liberals back in power. The Liberal administrations of Enrique Olaya Herrera and Alfonso López (1930–1938) were marked by social reforms that failed to solve the country's problems, and in 1946, a period of insurrection and banditry broke out, referred to as La Violencia, which claimed hundreds of thousands of lives by 1958. Laureano Gómez (1950–1953); the army chief of staff, Gen. Gustavo Rojas Pinilla (1953–1956); and a military junta (1956–1957) sought to curb disorder by repression.

Marxist guerrilla groups organized in the 1960s and 1970s, most notably the May 19th Movement (M-19), the National Liberation Army (ELN), and the Revolutionary Armed Forces of Colombia (FARC), plunging the country into violence and instability. In the 1970s and 1980s, Colombia became one of the international centers for illegal drug production and trafficking, and at times the drug cartels (the Medellin and Cali cartels were the most notorious) virtually controlled the country.

In the 1990s, numerous right-wing paramilitary groups also formed, made up of drug traffickers and landowners. The umbrella group for these paramilitaries is the United Self-Defense Forces of Colombia (AUC).

Belisario Betancur Cuartas, a Conservative who assumed the presidency in 1982, unsuccessfully attempted to stem the guerrilla violence. In an official war against drug trafficking, Colombia became a public battleground with bombs, killings, and kidnappings. By 1989, homicide had become the leading cause of death in the nation. Elected president in 1990, César Gaviria Trujillo proposed lenient punishment in exchange for surrender by the leading drug dealers. Ernesto Samper of the Liberal Party became president in 1994. In 1996 he was accused of accepting campaign contributions from drug traffickers, but the House of Representatives absolved him of the charges.

Andrés Pastrana Arango was elected president in 1998, pledging to clean up corruption. In Dec. 1999 the Colombian military reported that 2,787 people were kidnapped that year—the largest number in the world—and blamed rebels. The murder rate soared in 1999, with some 23,000 people reported killed by leftist guerrillas, right-wing paramilitaries, drug traffickers, and common criminals. The violence has created more than 100,000 refugees, while 2 million Colombians have fled the country in recent years.

In Aug. 2000, the U.S. government approved "Plan Colombia," a $1.3 billion in antidrug trafficking aid that Pastrana used to undercut drug production and prevent guerrilla groups from benefiting from drug sales. In Aug. 2001, Pastrana signed "war legislation," which expands the rights of the military in dealing with rebels. In Jan. 2002, peace talks, which had been underway between the government and FARC rebels since 1998, broke down.

Alvaro Uribe of the Liberal party easily won the presidential election in May 2002. He took office in Aug., pledging to get tough on the rebels and drug traffickers by increasing military spending and seeking U.S. military cooperation. An upsurge in violence accompanied his inauguration, and Uribe declared a state of emergency within a week.

# Comoros

### UNION OF COMOROS ISLANDS

**President:** Azali Assoumani (2002)
**Area:** 838 sq mi (2,170 sq km)
**Population (2002 est.):** 614,382 (growth rate: 3.0%); birth rate: 39.0/1000; infant mortality rate: 81.8/1000; density per sq mi: 733
**Capital and largest city (1990 est.):** Moroni (on Grande Comoro), 23,432. **Monetary unit:** Franc. **Languages:** French and Arab (both official), Shaafi Islam (Swahili dialect), Malagasu. **Ethnicity/race:** Antalote, Cafre, Makoa, Oimatsaha, Sakalava. **Religions:** Sunni Muslim 86%, Roman Catholic 14%. **Literacy rate:** 48% (1980)
**Economic summary:** GDP/PPP: (2000 est.) $419 million; per capita $720. **Real growth rate:** 0.5%. **Inflation:** 3.5% (1999). **Unemployment:** 20% (1996 est.). **Arable land:** 35%. **Agriculture:** vanilla, cloves, perfume essences, copra, coconuts, bananas, cassava (tapioca). **Labor force:** 144,500 (1996 est.): agriculture 80%. **Industries:** tourism, perfume distillation, textiles, furniture, jewelry, construction materials, soft drinks. **Natural resources:** negl. **Exports:** $7.9 million (f.o.b., 1999 est.): vanilla, ylang-ylang, cloves, perfume oil, copra. **Imports:** $55.1 million (f.o.b., 1999 est.): rice and other foodstuffs, consumer goods; petroleum products, cement, transport equipment. **Major trading partners:** France, U.S., Germany, Pakistan, South Africa, Kenya.

**Geography** The Comoros Islands—Grande Comoro (Ngazidja), Anjouan, Mohéli, and Mayotte (which is not part of the country and retains ties to France)—are an archipelago of volcanic origin in the Indian Ocean, 190 mi off the coast of Mozambique.

**Government** Emerging republic. Under a new constitution ratified in March 2002, each island will have its own president with a federal president assuming overall authority. The federal presidency will rotate every four years between the three islands.

**History** Comoros was frequented by travelers from Africa, Madagascar, Indonesia, and Arabia before the first Europeans encountered the islands. Arabic influence has been the strongest.

France colonized Mayotte in 1843 and by 1904 had annexed the remainder of the archipelago. In a 1974 referendum, 95% of the population voted for independence. The exception was Mayotte, which, with its Christian majority, voted against joining the other mainly Islamic islands in independence. Today it remains a French overseas territory. The remaining Comoros islands declared themselves independent on July 6, 1975.

A month after independence, Justice Minister Ali Soilih staged a coup with the help of a group of white mercenaries known as Les Affreux (The Terrible Ones), overthrowing the new nation's first president, Ahmed Abdallah. Soilih was himself overthrown on May 13, 1978. This was only the beginning of Comoros's chronic instability: the country has gone through more than 20 coups since independence and has experienced several attempts at secession.

The island of Anjouan declared independence on Aug. 3, 1997, after months of protests and clashes with security forces. The secessionists wanted a return to French rule, contending that independence from France has brought economic disaster and political chaos. Mohéli, the smallest island, also seceded. But France refused to support the secession of either island.

In Sept. 1997, President Mohamed Taki's forces attempted to retake Anjouan but failed. Taki then declared a state of emergency. Peace talks in spring 1999 ended inconclusively when all other Anjouan representatives failed to sign a peace agreement that the other two islands had agreed to. Anti-Anjouan riots took place on Grande Comoros, and on April 30, 1999, Col. Azali Assoumani led a coup, overthrowing interim president Tadjidine. He promised interim military rule would end in a year. This was the first of Comoros's four coups to be carried out by the Comorian army itself rather than mercenaries. The other three were led by the notorious French mercenary leader "Colonel" Bob Denard. The island of Anjouan continued to fight against the government on Grande Comoros throughout 1999.

In March 2000 the Organization of African Unity cut communications with Anjouan in an effort to end the rebellion. The OAU demanded that President Assoumani impose a trade embargo and return Comoros to civilian rule. In Feb. 2001 the president signed an OAU-brokered reconciliation agreement with various political leaders from the three islands, including the secessionist leader of Anjouan, Col. Said Abeid. But in Aug. 2001, the peace process was again disrupted when soldiers on Anjouan led a coup against its separatist leader, Abeid.

Finally, in March 2002, a new constitution was approved, and the three islands were reunited. Each island elected its own president, and in May a federal president was elected from Grand Comoros, former military coup leader Assoumani.

# Congo

REPUBLIC OF CONGO

**National name:** République Populaire du Congo
**President:** Denis Sassou-Nguesso (1997)
**Area:** 132,046 sq mi (342,000 sq km)
**Population (2002 est.):** 2,958,448 (growth rate: 2.2%); birth rate: 37.9/1000; infant mortality rate: 97.9/1000; density per sq mi: 22
**Capital and largest city (1992 est.):** Brazzaville, 937,580. **Other large city (1992 est.):** Pointe-Noire, 576,206. **Monetary unit:** CFA Franc. **Languages:** French (official), Lingala, Kikongo, others. **Ethnicity/race:** south: Kongo 48%; north: Sangha 20%, M'Bochi 12%; center: Teke 17%, Europeans 8,500 (mostly French). **Religions:** Christian 50%, animist 48%, Muslim 2%. **Literacy rate:** 57% (1990)
**Economic summary: GDP/PPP** (2000 est.): $3.1 billion; per capita $1,100. **Real growth rate:** 3.8%. **Inflation:** 3.5%. **Unemployment:** n.a. **Arable land:** 0%. **Agriculture:** cassava (tapioca), sugar, rice, corn, peanuts, vegetables, coffee, cocoa; forest products. **Labor force:** n.a. **Industries:** petroleum extraction, cement kilning, lumbering, brewing, sugar milling, palm oil, soap, flour, cigarette making. **Natural resources:** petroleum, timber, potash, lead, zinc, uranium, copper, phosphates, natural gas, hydropower. **Exports:** $2.6 billion (f.o.b., 2000): petroleum 50%, lumber, plywood, sugar, cocoa, coffee, diamonds. **Imports:** $870 million (f.o.b., 2000): petroleum products, capital equipment, construction materials, foodstuffs. **Major trading partners:** U.S., Benelux, Germany, Italy, Taiwan, China, France, Belgium, UK.

**Geography** The Congo is situated in west-central Africa astride the equator. It borders Gabon, Cameroon, the Central African Republic, the Democratic Republic of the Congo, and the Angola exclave of Cabinda, with a short stretch of coast on the South Atlantic. Its area is nearly three times that of Pennsylvania. Most of the inland is tropical rain forest, drained by tributaries of the Congo River, which flows south along the eastern border with the Democratic Republic of the Congo to Stanley Pool. The narrow coastal plain rises to highlands separated from the inland plateaus by the 200-mile-wide Niari River valley, which gives passage to the coast.

**Government** Republic.

**History** In precolonial times, the region now called the Republic of Congo was dominated by three kingdoms: Kongo (originating about 1000), the Loango (flourishing in the 17th century), and Tio. After the Portuguese located the Congo River in 1482, commerce was carried on with the tribes, especially the slave trade.

The Frenchman Pierre S... ... ...... ......  .. ..... .... ... ... ... Makoko, ruler of the Bateke people, in 1880, thus establishing French control. It was first called French Congo, and after 1905 Middle Congo. With Gabon and Ubangi-Shari, it became the colony of French Equatorial Africa in 1910. Abuse of laborers led to public outcry against the French colonialists as well as rebellions among the Congolese, but the exploitation of the native workers continued until 1930. During World War II the colony joined Chad in supporting the Free French cause against the Vichy government. The Congo proclaimed its independence without leaving the French Community in 1960, calling itself the Republic of Congo.

Congo's second president, Alphonse Massemba Débat, instituted a Marxist-Leninist government. In 1968, Maj. Marien Ngouabi overthrew him but kept Congo on a socialist course. He was sworn in for a second five-year term in 1975. A four-man commando squad assassinated Ngouabi on March 18, 1977. Col. Joachim Yhombi-Opango, army chief of staff, assumed the presidency on April 4. Yhombi-Opango resigned on Feb. 4, 1979, and was replaced by Col. Denis Sassou-Nguesso.

In July 1990 the leaders of the ruling party voted to end the one-party system. A national political conference, hailed as a model for sub-Saharan Africa, renounced Marxism in 1991, and scheduled the country's first free elections for 1992.

Political and ethnic tensions intensified in 1993 after legislative elections, when the opposition's rejection of the results developed into violence. A peace agreement was signed between the government and the opposition in Aug. 1994. A four-month civil war (June 5–Oct. 15, 1997) devastated Brazzaville, the capital. Buttressed by military aid from Angola, former Marxist dictator Denis Sassou-Nguesso overthrew President Pascal Lissouba, the country's first democratically elected president. In late 1999 a peace agreement was signed between Sassou-Nguesso, who comes from the north, and the rebels representing the populous south. The postwar period has been traumatic: a recurrence of sleeping sickness and other diseases have swept the country, yet 60% of its health centers are out of commission.

In March 2002, President Denis Sassou-Nguesso was reelected with 89.4% of the vote. His opponents were either barred from the country or withdrew from the election.

The so-called Ninja rebels continue to battle government forces, each attempting to gain or maintain control of the country's rich oil reserves and each seemingly unconcerned about the toll this new outbreak of violence is taking on civilians.

# Congo, Democratic Republic of the

DEMOCRATIC REPUBLIC OF THE CONGO

**President:** Joseph Kabila (2001)
**Area:** 905,563 sq mi (2,345,410 sq km)
**Population (2002 est.):** 55,225,478 (growth rate: 3.1%); birth rate: 45.5/1000; infant mortality rate: 98.0/1000; density per sq mi: 61
**Capital and largest city (2000 est.):** Kinshasa, 6,050,000 (metro. area). **Other large cities:** Lubumbashi, 851,381; Mbuji-Mayi, 806,475; Kisangani, 417,517; Kolwezi, 417,810. **Monetary unit:** Congolese franc. **Languages:** French (official), Swahili, Lingala, Ishiluba, and Kikongo, others. **Ethnicity/race:** over 200 African ethnic groups, the majority are Bantu; the four largest tribes—Mongo, Luba, Kongo (all Bantu), and the Mangbetu-Azande (Hamitic)—make up about 45% of the population. **Religions:** Roman Catholic 50%, Protestant 20%, Kimbanguist 10%, Islam 10%; syncretic and traditional, 10%. **Literacy rate:** 72% (1990)
**Economic summary: GDP/PPP** (2000 est.): $31 billion; per capita $600. **Real growth rate:** –15%. **Inflation:** 540%. **Unemployment:** n.a. **Arable land:** 3%. **Agriculture:** coffee, sugar, palm oil, rubber, tea, quinine, cassava (tapioca), palm oil, bananas, root crops, corn, fruits; wood products. **Labor force:** 14.51 million (1993 est.); agriculture 65%, industry 16%, services 19% (1991 est.). **Industries:** mining (diamonds, copper, zinc), mineral processing, consumer products (including textiles, footwear, cigarettes, processed foods and beverages), cement. **Natural resources:** cobalt, copper, cadmium,

petroleum, industrial and gem diamonds, gold, silver, zinc, manganese, tin, germanium, uranium, radium, bauxite, iron ore, coal, hydropower, timber. **Exports**: $960 million (f.o.b., 2000 est.): diamonds, copper, coffee, cobalt, crude oil. **Imports**: $660 million (c.i.f., 2000 est.): foodstuffs, mining and other machinery, transport equipment, fuels. **Major trading partners:** Benelux, U.S., South Africa, Finland, Italy, Nigeria, Kenya, China.

**Geography** The Congo, in west-central Africa, is bordered by the Congo Republic, the Central African Republic, the Sudan, Uganda, Rwanda, Burundi, Tanzania, Zambia, Angola, and the Atlantic Ocean. It is one-quarter the size of the U.S. The principal rivers are the Ubangi and Bomu in the north and the Congo in the west, which flows into the Atlantic. The entire length of Lake Tanganyika lies along the eastern border with Tanzania and Burundi.

**Government** Dictatorship.

**History** Formerly the Belgian Congo, this territory was inhabited by ancient Negrito peoples (Pygmies), who were pushed into the mountains by Bantu and Nilotic invaders. The American correspondent Henry M. Stanley navigated the Congo River in 1877 and opened the interior to exploration. Commissioned by King Leopold II of the Belgians, Stanley made treaties with native chiefs that enabled the king to obtain personal title to the territory at the Berlin Conference of 1885.

Leopold accumulated a vast personal fortune from ivory and rubber through Congolese slave labor; 10 million people are estimated to have died from forced labor, starvation, and outright extermination during Leopold's colonial rule. His brutal exploitation of the Congo eventually became an international cause célèbre, prompting Belgium to take over administration of the Congo, which remained a colony until agitation for independence forced Brussels to grant freedom on June 30, 1960. The Katanga Province, led by Moise Tshombe, seceded from the new republic on July 11, and another mining province, South Kasai, followed. Belgium sent paratroopers to quell the civil war, and with President Joseph Kasavubu and Prime Minister Patrice Lumumba of the national government in conflict, the United Nations flew in a peacekeeping force.

Kasavubu staged an army coup in 1960 and handed Lumumba over to the Katangan forces. A UN investigating commission found that Lumumba had been killed by a Belgian mercenary in the presence of Tshombe, who was then the president of Katanga. Dag Hammarskjold, UN secretary-general, died in a plane crash en route to a peace conference with Tshombe on Sept. 17, 1961.

Tshombe rejected a national reconciliation plan in 1962 submitted by the UN. Tshombe's troops fired on the UN force in Dec., and in the ensuing conflict he capitulated on Jan. 14, 1963. The peacekeeping force withdrew, and, in a complete about-face, Kasavubu named Tshombe premier in order to fight a spreading rebellion. Tshombe used foreign mercenaries, and with the help of Belgian paratroops airlifted by U.S. planes, defeated the most serious opposition, a Communist-backed regime in the northeast.

Kasavubu abruptly dismissed Tshombe in 1965 and was himself ousted by Gen. Joseph-Desiré Mobutu, army chief of staff. The new president nationalized the Union Minière, the Belgian copper mining enterprise that had been a dominant force in the Congo since colonial days.

Mobutu eliminated opposition to win the election in 1970. In 1975, he nationalized much of the economy, barred religious instruction in schools, and decreed the adoption of African names. On March 8, 1977, invaders from Angola calling themselves the Congolese National Liberation Front pushed into Shaba and threatened the important mining center of Kolwezi. France and Belgium responded to Mobutu's pleas for help with weapons, but the U.S. gave only nonmilitary supplies. In April, France flew 1,500 Moroccan troops to Shaba to defeat the invaders, who were, Mobutu charged, Soviet-inspired and Cuban-led. U.S. intelligence sources, however, confirmed Soviet and Cuban denials of any participation and identified the rebels as former Katanga gendarmes who had fled to Angola after their 1963 defeat.

In April 1990, Mobutu announced he intended to introduce multiparty democracy but that elections in Jan. 1991 would reduce the number of political parties to two besides his own. Opposition leaders denounced the scheme as giving Mobutu's party an unfair advantage.

In early 1993, Mobutu rejected Western demands that he yield power and announced plans to regroup his one-party Parliament, dismissing the main opposition leader, Prime Minister Tshisekedi. In Jan. 1994, Mobutu dissolved Parliament and dismissed his prime minister, which led to a general strike in the capital.

Mobutu Sese Seko was overthrown in May 1997, ending one of the world's most corrupt and megalomaniacal regimes. The last of the CIA-nurtured cold war despots, Mobutu deftly courted France and the U.S., which used Zaire as a launching pad for covert operations against bordering countries, particularly Marxist Angola. Mobutu's disastrous policies drove his country to economic collapse while he siphoned off millions of dollars for himself.

Laurent Kabila and his long-standing but little-known guerrilla movement launched a seven-month campaign that ousted Mobutu. The country was renamed the Democratic Republic of the Congo, its name before Mobutu changed it to Zaire in 1971. Mobutu's downfall began in Oct. 1996, when he planned to banish the Zairian Tutsi who had lived for centuries in eastern Zaire. Neighboring Rwanda's Tutsi-led government came to their aid, as did other rebel groups, one of which was led by Kabila. After conquering eastern Zaire, Kabila earned the support of a host of Mobutu's enemies, including Uganda, Burundi, Tanzania, Zambia, Zimbabwe, and Angola. His troops swept through the country, encountering little resistance. Mobutu fled in exile to Morocco on May 16, 1997, where he died of cancer in Sept.

Elation over Mobutu's downfall faded as Kabila's own autocratic style emerged, and he seemed devoid of a clear plan for reconstructing the country. He stymied UN human rights investigations into the alleged massacres of Hutu refugees and continued to depend on foreign troops for border skirmishes rather than establish a strong national army. Many Congolese dismissed him as a puppet ruler who allowed his country to be overrun by outsiders, particularly the Rwandans. At the same time, he alienated many of his former supporters, including Rwanda and Uganda.

In Aug. 1998, Congolese rebel forces, led by ethnic Tutsi in eastern Congo, who were backed by Rwanda and Uganda, began attacking Kabila's forces. The rebels gained control of a large portion of the country until Angolan, Namibian, and Zimbabwean troops came to Kabila's aid and pushed the rebels back. In 1999, the Lusaka Accord was signed by all six of the countries involved, as well as by most, but not all, of the various rebel groups. The UN's small peace-keeping force had minimal influence in implementing the accord, which unravelled within months. The warring parties have been looting the Congo of its natural resources and have little incentive to end the war.

In Jan. 2001, Kabila was assassinated, allegedly by one of his bodyguards. His young and inexperienced son Joseph became the new president, and demonstrated a willingness to engage in talks to end the civil war. In April 2002, the government agreed to a power-sharing arrangement with Ugandan-supported rebels, and in July, the presidents of the Congo and Rwanda signed an accord: Rwanda promised to withdraw its 35,000 troops from the eastern Congolese border; the Congo would in turn disarm the thousands of Hutu militiamen in its territory, who threaten Rwandan security—many of them supported or participated in the 1994 genocide against Rwandan Tutsis. In Sept. 2002, Uganda also signed a peace accord with the nation. More than 2.5 million people are estimated to have died in the Congo's complex four-year civil war, which has involved 7 foreign armies and numerous rebel groups that often fought among themselves.

# Costa Rica

### REPUBLIC OF COSTA RICA

**National name:** República de Costa Rica
**President:** Abel Pacheco (2002)
**Area:** 19,730 sq mi (51,100 sq km)
**Population (2002 est.):** 3,834,934 (growth rate: 1.6%); birth rate: 19.8/1000; infant mortality rate: 10.9/1000; density per sq mi: 194
**Capital and largest city (1994 est.):** San José, 315,909. **Monetary unit:** Colón. **Language:** Spanish. **Ethnicity/race:** white (including mestizo) 96%, black 2%, Indian 1%, Chinese 1%. **Religion:** Roman Catholic 95%. **Literacy rate:** 93% (1990)
**Economic summary: GDP/PPP** (2000 est.) $25 billion; per capita $6,700. **Real growth rate:** 3%. **Inflation:** 11%. **Unemployment:** 5.2%. **Arable land:** 6%. **Agriculture:** coffee, pineapples, bananas, sugar, corn, rice, beans, potatoes; beef; timber. **Labor force:** 1.9 million (1999); agriculture 20%, industry 22%, services 58% (1999 est.). **Industries:** microprocessors, food processing, textiles and clothing, construction materials, fertilizer, plastic products. **Natural resources:** hydropower. **Exports:** $6.1 billion (f.o.b., 2000 est.): coffee, bananas, sugar; pineapples; textiles, electronic components, medical equipment. **Imports:** $5.9 billion (f.o.b., 2000 est.): raw materials, consumer goods, capital equipment, petroleum. **Major trading partners:** U.S., EU, Central America, Mexico, Japan.

**Geography** This Central American country lies between Nicaragua to the north and Panama to the south. Its area slightly exceeds that of Vermont and New Hampshire combined. It has a narrow Pacific coastal region. Cocos Island (10 sq mi; 26 sq km), about 300 mi (483 km) off the Pacific Coast, is under Costa Rican sovereignty.

**Government** Democratic republic.

**History** Costa Rica was inhabited by an estimated 25,000 Indians when Columbus explored it in 1502. Few of the Indians survived the Spanish conquest, which began in 1563. The region grew slowly and was administered as a Spanish province. Costa Rica achieved independence in 1821 but was absorbed for two years by Agustín de Iturbide in his Mexican empire. It became a republic in 1848. Except for the military dictatorship of Tomás Guardia from 1870 to 1882, Costa Rica has enjoyed one of the most democratic governments in Latin America.

In the 1970s, rising oil prices, falling international commodity prices, and inflation hurt the economy. Efforts have since been made to reduce reliance on coffee, banana, and beef exports. Tourism is now a major business. Oscar Arias Sanchez, who became president in 1986, was awarded the Nobel Peace Prize in 1987 for his role in negotiating settlements to both the Nicaraguan and the Salvadoran civil wars.

José Maria Figueres Olsen of the National Liberation Party became president in 1994. He opposed economic suggestions made by the International Monetary Fund, instead favoring greater government intervention in the economy. The World Bank subsequently withheld $100 million of financing. In 1998, Miguel Angel Rodríguez of the Social Christian Unity Party became president, pledging economic reforms, such as privatization. In 2000, Costa Rica and Nicaragua resolved a long-standing dispute over navigation of the San Juan River, which forms their border. A psychiatrist, Abel Pacheco, also of the Social Christian Unity Party, won the presidency in elections held in April 2002.

# Côte d'Ivoire

### REPUBLIC OF CÔTE D'IVOIRE

**National name:** République de la Côte d'Ivoire
**President:** Laurent Gbagbo (2000)
**Prime Minister:** Affi N'Guessan (2000)
**Area:** 124,502 sq mi (322,460 sq km)
**Population (2002 est.):** 16,804,784 (growth rate: 2.3%); birth rate: 40.0/1000; infant mortality rate: 92.2/1000; density per sq mi: 135
**Capital (1984):** Yamoussoukro (official), 120,000; Abidjan (administrative). **Largest city (est. 1988):** Abidjan, 2,797,000. **Monetary unit:** CFA Franc. **Languages:** French (official) and African languages (Diaula esp.). **Ethnicity/race:** Baoule 23%, Bete 18%, Senoufou 15%, Malinke 11%, Agni, foreign Africans (mostly Burkinabe and Malians, about 3 million). **Religions:** indigenous 60%, Islam 23%, Christian 17%. **Literacy rate:** 54% (1990)
**Economic summary:GDP/PPP** (2000 est.): $26.2 billion; per capita $1,600. **Real growth rate:** –0.3%. **Inflation:** 2.5%. **Unemployment:** 13% in urban areas (1998 est.). **Arable land:** 8%. **Agriculture:** coffee, cocoa beans, bananas, palm kernels, corn, rice, manioc (tapioca), sweet potatoes, sugar, cotton, rubber; timber. **Labor force:** 68% agricultural (2000 est.). **Industries:** foodstuffs, beverages; wood products, oil refining, truck and bus assembly, textiles, fertilizer, building materials, electricity. **Natural resources:** petroleum, natural gas, diamonds, manganese, iron ore, cobalt, bauxite, copper, hydropower. **Exports:** $3.8 billion (f.o.b., 2000 est.): cocoa 33%, coffee, tropical woods, petroleum, bananas, pineapples, palm oil, cotton, fish (1999). **Imports:** $2.5 billion (f.o.b., 2000 est.): food, consumer goods; capital goods, fuel, transport equipment. **Major trading partners:** France, U.S., Netherlands, Germany, Italy, Nigeria, China.

**Geography** Côte d'Ivoire (also known as the Ivory Coast), in western Africa on the Gulf of Guinea is a little larger than New Mexico. Its neighbors are Liberia, Guinea, Mali, Burkina Faso, and Ghana. The country consists of a coastal strip in the south, dense forests in the interior, and savannas in the north.

**Government** Presidential/parliamentary democracy until Dec. 1999, when a coup installed a military dictatorship.

**History** Côte d'Ivoire was originally made up of numerous isolated settlements; today it represents more than sixty distinct tribes, including the Baoule, Bete, Senoufou, Agni, Malinke, Dan, and Lobi. Côte d'Ivoire attracted both French and Portuguese merchants in the 15th century who were in search of ivory and slaves. French traders set up establishments early in the 19th century, and in 1842, the French obtained territorial concessions from local tribes, gradually extending their influence along the coast and inland. The area was organized as a territory in 1893, became an autonomous republic in the French Union after World War II, and achieved independence on Aug. 7, 1960. Côte d'Ivoire formed a customs union in 1959 with Dahomey (Benin), Niger, and Burkina Faso. The nation's economy is one of the most developed in sub-Saharan Africa. It is the world's largest exporter of cocoa and one of the largest exporters of coffee.

From independence until his death in 1993, Felix Houphouët-Boigny served as president. Massive protests by students, farmers, and professionals forced the president to legalize opposition parties and hold the first contested presidential election in Oct. 1990, which Houphouët-Boigny won with 81% of the vote. Beginning in Sept. 1998, thousands of demonstrators protested a constitutional revision that granted President Henri Konan Bédié greatly enhanced powers. Bédié has also promoted the concept of *ivoirité*, which, roughly translated, means "pure Ivoirian pride." Although its defenders describe *ivoirité* as a term of positive national pride, it has led to a dangerous xenophobia, with numerous ethnic Malians and Burkinans being driven out of the country in 1999.

President Bédié was overthrown in the country's first military coup in Dec. 1999, and Gen. Robert Guei assumed control of the country. As a result, the majority of foreign aid to the country has ceased.

Presidential elections were held in Oct. 2000, between Gen. Guei and a civilian opposition candidate, Laurent Gbagbo. Each declared victory in an election most believe to have been rife with fraud. Popular outcry against Guei soon turned violent, forcing him to leave the country, and Gbagbo assumed the presidency. Many observers questioned his mandate, however, since the opposition leader Alassane Ouattara had been excluded from the election on the specious grounds that he was not a pure-blooded Ivoirian. Parliamentary elections in March 2001 were considered an important indication of genuine political support because each of the three main political parties—those affiliated with Gbagbo, Ouattara, and Guei—were permitted to participate. Ouattara's party in fact trounced Gbagbo's party, weakening the president's authority. It was not until June 2002 that Ouattara was finally granted full Ivoirian citizenship, which will allow him to run in the next presidential election in 2005. Hundreds have died in violence sparked by the dispute.

Mutineering soldiers attempted a coup in Sept. 2002. Guei and Interior Minister Doudou were killed in fighting between government soldiers and rebels. President Gbagbo accused Guei of staging the coup. Fighting continued into October.

# Croatia

### REPUBLIC OF CROATIA
**President:** Stipe Mesic (2000)
**Prime Minister:** Ivica Racan (2000)
**Area:** 21,831 sq mi (56,542 sq km)
**Population (2002 est.):** 4,390,751 (growth rate: 0.2%); birth rate: 12.8/1000; infant mortality rate: 7.1/1000; density per sq mi: 201

**Capital (1991):** Zagreb, 930,753. **Other large cities (1991):** Split, 189,444; Rijeka, 167,757; Osijek, 129,792. **Monetary unit:** Kuna. **Language:** What was once known as Serbo-Croatian is now known as Serbian, Croatian, or Bosnian, depending on the speaker's political and ethnic affiliation. **Ethnicity/race:** Croat 78%, Serb 12%, Muslim 0.9%, Hungarian 0.5%, Slovenian 0.5%, others 8.1% (1991). **Religions:** Catholic 76.5%, Orthodox 11.1%, Slavic Muslim 1.2%, Protestant 0.4%, others 10.8%. **Literacy rate:** 97% (1991)
**Economic summary:** GDP/PPP (2000 est.): $24.9 billion; per capita $5,800. **Real growth rate:** 3.2%. **Inflation:** 6%. **Unemployment:** 22% (Oct. 2000). **Arable land:** 21%. **Agriculture:** wheat, corn, sugar beets, sunflower seed, alfalfa, clover, olives, citrus, grapes, soy beans, potatoes; livestock, dairy products. **Labor force:** 1.68 million (Oct. 2000); agriculture n.a., industry n.a., services n.a. **Industries:** chemicals and plastics, machine tools, fabricated metal, electronics, pig iron and rolled steel products, aluminum, paper, wood products, construction materials, textiles, shipbuilding, petroleum and petroleum refining, food and beverages; tourism. **Natural resources:** oil, some coal, bauxite, low-grade iron ore, calcium, natural asphalt, silica, mica, clays, salt, hydropower. **Exports:** $4.3 billion (f.o.b., 1999): transport equipment, textiles, chemicals, foodstuffs, fuels. **Imports:** $7.8 billion (c.i.f., 1999): machinery, transport and electrical equipment, chemicals, fuels and lubricants, foodstuffs. **Major trading partners:** Italy, Germany, Bosnia and Herzegovina, Slovenia, Austria, Russia.

**Geography** Croatia is a former Yugoslav republic on the Adriatic Sea; it is about the size of West Virginia. Part of Croatia is a barren, rocky region lying in the Dinaric Alps. The Zagorje region north of the capital, Zagreb, is a land of rolling hills, and the fertile agricultural region of the Pannonian Plain is bordered by the Drava, Danube, and Sava Rivers in the east. Over one-third of Croatia is forested.

**Government** Presidential/parliamentary democracy.

**History** Croatia, at one time the Roman province of Pannonia, was settled in the 7th century by the Croats. They converted to Christianity between the 7th and 9th centuries and adopted the Roman alphabet under the suzerainty of Charlemagne. In 925, the Croats defeated Byzantine and Frankish invaders and established their own independent kingdom, which reached its peak during the 11th century. A civil war ensued in 1089, which later led to the country being conquered by the Hungarians in 1091. The signing of the *Pacta Conventa* by Croatian tribal chiefs and the Hungarian king in 1102 united the two nations politically under the Hungarian monarch, but Croatia retained its autonomy.

Following the defeat of the Hungarians by the Turks at the battle of Mohács in 1526, Croatia (along with Hungary) elected Austrian Archduke Ferdinand of Hapsburg as their king. After the establishment of the Austro-Hungarian kingdom in 1867, Croatia became part of Hungary until the collapse of Austria-Hungary in 1918 following its defeat in World War I. On Oct. 29, 1918, Croatia proclaimed its independence and joined in union with Montenegro, Serbia, and Slovenia to form the Kingdom of Serbs, Croats, and Slovenes. The name was changed to Yugoslavia in 1929.

When Germany invaded Yugoslavia in 1941, Croatia became a Nazi puppet state. Croatian Fascists, the Ustachi, slaughtered countless Serbs and Jews during the war. After Germany was defeated in 1945, Croatia was made into a republic of the newly reestablished Communist nation of Yugoslavia. In June 1991, the Croatian Parliament passed a declaration of independence from Yugoslavia. A six-month civil war followed with the Serbian-dominated Yugoslavian army. The war claimed thousands of lives and wrought mass destruction.

A UN cease-fire was arranged on Jan. 2, 1992. The Security Council in Feb. approved sending a 14,000-member peacekeeping force to monitor the cease-fire and protect the minority Serbs in Croatia. In a 1993 referendum the Serb-occupied portion of Croatia (Krajina) resoundingly voted for integration with Serbs in Bosnia and Serbia proper. Although the Zagreb government and representatives of Krajina signed a cease-fire in March 1994, further negotiations broke down. In a lightning-quick operation, the Croatian army retook western Slavonia in May 1995. Similarly, in Aug., the central Croatian region of Krajina, held by Serbs, was returned to Zagreb's control.

Announcing on television in 1999 that "national issues are more important than democracy," President Tudjman continued to alienate Croatians with his authoritarian rule, out-of-touch nationalism, and disastrous handling of the war-shattered economy. In Dec. 1999, Tudjman died and was succeeded by Stipe Mesic, a reformer. One of his first acts in office was to invite back the 300,000 ethnic Serbs who had been banished from the country under Tudjman.

In July 2002, Mesic met with the presidents of Bosnia and Yugoslavia for the first time since war broke out between Croatia and Yugoslavia more than a decade ago. The three countries pledged to cooperate on the repatriation of refugees, to fight organized crime, and to assist each other economically.

# Cuba

### REPUBLIC OF CUDA

**National name:** República de Cuba
**President:** Fidel Castro (1976)
**Area:** 42,803 sq mi (110,860 sq km)
**Population (2002 est.):** 11,224,321 (growth rate: 0.5%); birth rate: 12.1/1000; infant mortality rate: 7.3/1000; density per sq mi: 262
**Capital and largest city (1994 est.):** Havana, 2,241,000. **Other large cities (1994 est.):** Santiago de Cuba, 440,084; Camagüey, 293,961; Holguin, 242,085; Guantánamo, 207,796; Santa Clara, 205,400. **Monetary unit:** Cuban Peso. **Language:** Spanish. **Ethnicity/race:** mulatto 51%, white 37%, black 11%, Chinese 1%. **Religion:** at least 85% nominally Roman Catholic before Castro assumed power. **Literacy rate:** 94% (1990)
**Economic summary: GDP/PPP** (2000 est.): $19.2 billion; per capita $1,700. **Real growth rate:** 5.6%. **Inflation:** 0.3% (1999 est.). **Unemployment:** 5.5% (2000 est.). **Arable land:** 24%. **Agriculture:** sugar, tobacco, citrus, coffee, rice, potatoes, beans, livestock. **Labor force:** 4.3 million (2000 est.); agriculture 25%, industry 24%, services 51% (1998). **Industries:** sugar, petroleum, tobacco, chemicals, construction, services, nickel, steel, cement, agricultural machinery. **Natural resources:** cobalt, nickel, iron ore, copper, manganese, salt, timber, silica, petroleum, arable land. **Exports:** $1.8 billion (f.o.b., 2000 est.): sugar, nickel, tobacco, fish, medical products, citrus, coffee. **Imports:** $3.4 billion (f.o.b., 2000 est.): petroleum, food, machinery, chemicals, semifinished goods, transport equipment, consumer goods. **Major trading partners:** Russia, Netherlands, Canada, Spain, Venezuela.

**Geography** The largest island of the West Indies group (equal in area to Pennsylvania), Cuba is also the westernmost—just west of Hispaniola (Haiti and the Dominican Republic), and 90 mi (145 km) south of Key West, Fla., at the entrance to the Gulf of Mexico. The island is mountainous in the southeast and south-central area (Sierra Maestra). It is flat or rolling elsewhere. Cuba also includes numerous smaller islands, islets, and cays.

**Government** Communist state.

**History** Arawak (or Taino) Indians inhabiting Cuba when Columbus landed on the island in 1492 died from diseases brought by sailors and settlers. By 1511, Spaniards under Diego Velásquez had established settlements. Havana's superb harbor made it a common transit point to and from Spain.

In the early 1800s, Cuba's sugarcane industry boomed, requiring massive numbers of black slaves. A simmering independence movement turned into open warfare from 1867 to 1878. Slavery was abolished in 1886. In 1895, the poet José Marti led the struggle that finally ended Spanish rule, thanks largely to U.S. intervention in 1898 after the sinking of the battleship *Maine* in Havana harbor.

An 1899 treaty made Cuba an independent republic under U.S. protection. The U.S. occupation, which ended in 1902, suppressed yellow fever and brought large American investments. The 1901 Platt Amendment allowed the U.S. to intervene in Cuba's affairs, which it did four times from 1906 to 1920. Cuba terminated the amendment in 1934.

In 1933 a group of army officers, including army sergeant Fulgencio Batista, overthrew President Gerado Machado. Batista became president in 1940, running a corrupt police state.

In 1956, Fidel Castro Ruz launched a revolution from his camp in the Sierra Maestra mountains. Castro's brother Raul, and Ernesto (Ché) Guevara, an Argentine physician, were his top lieutenants. Many anti-Batista landowners supported the rebels. The U.S. ended military aid to Cuba in 1958, and on New Year's Day 1959, Batista fled into exile and Castro took over the government.

The U.S. initially welcomed what looked like a democratic Cuba, but a rude awakening came within a few months when Castro established military tribunals for political opponents and jailed hundreds. Castro disavowed Cuba's 1952 military pact with the U.S., confiscated U.S. assets, and established Soviet-style collective farms. The U.S. broke relations with Cuba on Jan. 3, 1961, and Castro formalized his alliance with the Soviet Union. Thousands of Cubans fled the country.

In 1961 a U.S.-backed group of Cuban exiles invaded Cuba. Planned during the Eisenhower administration, the invasion was given the go-ahead by President John Kennedy, although he refused to give U.S. air support. The landing at the Bay of Pigs on April 17, 1961, was a fiasco. The invaders did not receive popular Cuban support and were easily repulsed by the Cuban military.

A Soviet attempt to install medium-range missiles in Cuba—capable of striking targets in the United States with nuclear warheads—provoked a crisis in 1962. Denouncing the Soviets for "deliberate deception," on Oct. 22 Kennedy said that the U.S. would blockade Cuba so the missiles could not be delivered. Six days later Soviet premier Nikita Khrushchev ordered the missile sites dismantled and returned to the USSR, in return for a U.S. pledge not to attack Cuba.

Cuba fomented Communist revolution around the world, especially in Angola, where thousands of

Cuban troops were sent in the 1980s. The U.S. established limited diplomatic ties with Cuba on Sept. 1, 1977, making it easier for Cuban-Americans to visit the island. Contact with the more affluent Cuban Americans prompted a wave of discontent in Cuba, producing a flood of asylum seekers. In response, Castro opened the port of Mariel to a "freedom flotilla" of boats from the U.S., allowing 125,000 to flee to Miami. After the refugees arrived, it was discovered their ranks were swelled with prisoners, mental patients, homosexuals, and others unwanted by the Cuban government.

Russian aid, which had long supported Cuba's failing economy, ended when communism collapsed in eastern Europe in 1990. Cuba's foreign trade also plummeted, producing a severe economic crisis. In 1993, Castro permitted limited private enterprise, allowed Cubans to possess convertible currencies, and encouraged foreign investment in its tourist industry. In March 1996, the U.S. tightened its embargo with the Helms-Burton Act.

Christmas became an official holiday in 1997, for the first time since the revolution, in response to Pope John Paul II's 1998 visit to Cuba, which raised hopes for greater religious freedom.

In June 2000, Castro won a publicity bonanza when the Clinton administration sent Elian Gonzalez, a young boy found clinging to an inner tube, back to Cuba. The U.S. Cuban community had demanded that the boy remain in Miami rather than be returned to his father in Cuba. By many accounts, the influential Cuban-Americans lost public sympathy by pitting political ideology against familial bonds.

In June 2002, Castro claimed to have secured signatures from 99% of the electorate calling for a constitutional amendment that would declare the country's socialist system "untouchable."

# Cyprus

### REPUBLIC OF CYPRUS

**National name:** Kypriaki Dimokratia—Kibris Cumhuriyeti
**President:** Glafcos Klerides (1993)
**Area:** 3,571 sq mi (9,250 sq km)
**Population (2002 est.):** 767,314 (growth rate: 0.5%); birth rate: 12.9/1000; infant mortality rate: 7.7/1000; density per sq mi: 215
**Capital and largest city (1993):** Lefkosia (Nicosia) (in government-controlled area), 186,400. **Monetary unit:** Cyprus pound. **Languages:** Greek, Turkish (official), English is widely spoken. **Ethnicity/race:** total: Greek 78% (99.5% of the Greeks live in the Greek area, 0.5% live in the Turkish area), Turkish 18% (1.3% live in the Greek area, 98.7% live in the Turkish area), other 4%. **Religions (1993 est.):** Greek Orthodox 78%, Sunni Muslim 18%, Maronite, Armenian, Apostolic, Latin, and others 4%. **Literacy rate:** 94% (1987)
**Economic summary: GDP/PPP:** Greek Cypriot area (2000 est.): $9.7 billion; $16,000 per capita; Turkish Cypriot area (1999 est.): $830 million; $5,300 per capita. **Real growth rate:** Greek Cypriot area: 4.2% (2000 est.); Turkish Cypriot area: 4.9% (1999 est.). **Inflation:** Greek Cypriot area: 4.2% (2000 est.); Turkish Cypriot area: 58% (1999 est.). **Unemployment:** Greek Cypriot area: 3.6% (2000 est.); Turkish Cypriot area: 6% (1998 est.). **Arable land:** 12%. **Agriculture:** potatoes, citrus, vegetables, barley, grapes, olives, vegetables. **Labor force** (2000): Greek Cypriot area: 291,000; Turkish Cypriot area: 86,300; Greek Cypriot area: services 73%, industry 22%, agriculture 5% (2000); Turkish Cypriot area: services 56.4%, industry 22.8%, agriculture 20.8%

(1998). **Industries:** food, beverages, textiles, chemicals, metal products, tourism, wood products. **Natural resources:** copper, pyrites, asbestos, gypsum, timber, salt, marble, clay earth pigment. **Exports:** Greek Cypriot area: $1 billion (f.o.b., 1999 est.); Turkish Cypriot area: $51.1 million (f.o.b., 1999): Greek Cypriot area: citrus, potatoes, grapes, wine, cement, clothing and shoes; Turkish Cypriot area: citrus, potatoes, textiles. **Imports:** Greek Cypriot area: $3.6 billion (f.o.b., 1999 est.); Turkish Cypriot area: $402 million (f.o.b., 1999): Greek Cypriot area: consumer goods, petroleum and lubricants, food and feed grains, machinery; Turkish Cypriot area: food, minerals, chemicals, machinery. **Major trading partners:** Greek Cypriot area: UK, Greece, Russia, U.S., Italy, Germany; Turkish Cypriot area: Turkey, UK, other EU. **Member of Commonwealth of Nations**

**Geography** The third-largest island in the Mediterranean (one and one-half times the size of Delaware), Cyprus lies off the southern coast of Turkey and the western shore of Syria. The highest peak is Mount Olympus at 6,406 ft (1,953 m).

**Government** Republic. Mediation efforts by the UN seek to achieve reunification of the island under one federated system of government.

**History** Cyprus was the site of early Phoenician and Greek colonies. For centuries its rule passed through many hands. It fell to the Turks in 1571, and a large Turkish colony settled on the island.

In World War I, at the outbreak of hostilities with Turkey, Britain annexed the island. It was declared a Crown colony in 1925. For centuries the Greek population, regarding Greece as its mother country, has sought self-determination and reunion with Greece *(enosis)*. The resulting quarrel with Turkey threatened NATO. Cyprus became an independent nation on Aug. 16, 1960, with Britain, Greece, and Turkey as guarantor powers.

Archbishop Makarios, president since 1959, was overthrown on July 15, 1974, by a military coup led by the Cypriot National Guard. The new regime named Nikos Giorgiades Sampson as president and Bishop Gennadios as head of the Cypriot Church to replace Makarios. Diplomacy failed to resolve the crisis. Turkey invaded Cyprus by sea and air on July 20, 1974, asserting its right to protect the Turkish Cypriot minority. Geneva talks involving Greece, Turkey, Britain, and the two Cypriot factions failed in mid-Aug., and the Turks subsequently gained control of 40% of the island. Some 180,000 Greek Cypriots were uprooted by the Turkish troops. Greece made no armed response to the superior Turkish force but bitterly suspended military participation in the NATO alliance. The tension continued after Makarios returned to become president on Dec. 7, 1974. He offered self-government to the Turkish minority, but rejected any solution "involving transfer of populations and amounting to partition of Cyprus."

Turkish Cypriots proclaimed a separate state under Rauf Denktash in the northern part of the island on Nov. 15, 1983, naming it the "Turkish Republic of Northern Cyprus." The UN Security Council, in its Resolution 541 of Nov. 18, 1983, declared this action illegal and called for withdrawal. No country except Turkey has recognized this illegal entity.

In 1988, George Vassiliou, a conservative and critic of UN proposals to reunify Cyprus, became president. The purchase of missiles capable of reaching the Turkish coast evoked threats of retaliation from Turkey in 1997, and Cyprus's plans to deploy more missiles in Aug. 1999 again raised Turkey's ire.

Cyprus has a good chance at joining the European Union; it has in fact met all the economic standards. But the continued strife between Greek Cypriots and Turkish Cypriots threatens Cyprus's potential EU membership.

UN-sponsored talks between the Greek and Turkish leaders, Kleridas and Denktash, continued intensively in 2002, but no resolution was reached by their self-imposed deadline of June 30.

# Czech Republic

**President:** Vaclav Havel (1993)
**Prime Minister:** Vladimír Spidla (2002)
**Area:** 30,450 sq mi (78,866 sq km)
**Population (2002 est.):** 10,256,760 (growth rate: –0.2%); birth rate: 9.1/1000; infant mortality rate: 5.5/1000; density per sq mi: 337
**Capital and largest city (Jan. 1, 1994):** Prague, 1,215,771. **Other large cities:** Brno, 389,727; Ostrava, 326,396; Plzen, 172,402; Olomouc, 106,003. **Monetary unit:** Koruna. **Languages:** Czech; Slovak minority. **Ethnicity/race:** Czech 94.4%, Slovak 3%, Polish 0.6%, German 0.5%, Roma (Gypsy) 0.3%, Hungarian 0.2%, other 1%. **Religions:** atheist 39.8%, Roman Catholic 39.2%, Protestant 4.6%, Orthodox 3%, other 13.4%. **Literacy rate:** 99%
**Economic summary: GDP/PPP** (2000 est.): $132.4 billion; per capita $12,900. **Real growth rate:** 2.5%. **Inflation:** 3.8%. **Unemployment:** 8.7%. **Arable land:** 41%. **Agriculture:** wheat, potatoes, sugar beets, hops, fruit; pigs, poultry. **Labor force:** 5.203 million (1999 est.); agriculture 5%, industry 40%, services 55% (2000 est.). **Industries:** metallurgy, machinery and equipment, motor vehicles, glass, armaments. **Natural resources:** hard coal, soft coal, kaolin, clay, graphite, timber. **Exports:** $28.3 billion (f.o.b., 2000): machinery and transport equipment 44%, other manufactured goods 40%, chemicals 7%, raw materials and fuel 7% (1999). **Imports:** $31.4 billion (f.o.b., 2000): machinery and transport equipment 42%, other manufactured goods 33%, chemicals 12%, raw materials and fuels 10% (1999). **Major trading partners:** Germany, Slovakia, Austria, Poland, France, Italy.

**Geography** The Czech Republic's central European landscape is dominated by the Bohemian Massif, which rises to heights of 3,000 ft (900 m) above sea level. This ring of mountains encircles a large elevated basin, the Bohemian Plateau. The principal rivers are the Elbe and the Vltava.

**Government** Parliamentary democracy.

**History** Probably about the 5th century A.D., Slavic tribes from the Vistula basin settled in the region of Bohemia, Moravia, and Silesia. The Czechs founded the kingdom of Bohemia and the Premyslide dynasty, which ruled Bohemia and Moravia from the 10th to the 16th century. One of the Bohemian kings, Charles IV, Holy Roman emperor, made Prague an imperial capital and a center of Latin scholarship. The Hussite movement founded by Jan Hus (1369?–1415) linked the Slavs to the Reformation and revived Czech nationalism, previously under German domination. A Hapsburg, Ferdinand I, ascended the throne in 1526. The Czechs rebelled in 1618, precipitating the Thirty Years' War (1618–1648). Defeated in 1620, they were ruled for the next 300 years as part of the Austrian empire. Full independence from the Hapsburgs was not achieved until the end of World War I, following the collapse of the Austrian-Hungarian Empire.

A union of the Czech lands and Slovakia was proclaimed in Prague on Nov. 14, 1918, and the Czech nation became one of the two component parts of the newly formed Czechoslovakian state. In March 1939, German troops occupied Czechoslovakia, and Czech Bohemia and Moravia became German protectorates for the duration of World War II. The former government returned in April 1945 when the war ended and the country's pre-1938 boundaries were restored. When elections were held in 1946, Communists became the dominant political party and gained control of the Czechoslovakian government in 1948. Thereafter, the former democracy was turned into a Soviet-style state.

Nearly 42 years of Communist rule ended when Vaclav Havel, a highly respected writer and dissident, was elected president of Czechoslovakia in 1989. The return of democratic political reform saw a strong Slovak nationalist movement emerge by the end of 1991, which sought independence for Slovakia. When the general elections of June 1992 failed to resolve the continuing coexistence of the two republics within the federation, Czech and Slovak political leaders agreed to separate their states into two fully independent nations. On Jan. 1, 1993, the Czechoslovakian federation was dissolved and two separate independent countries were established—the Czech Republic and Slovakia.

In March 1999, the Czech Republic joined NATO. The country's next goal in international relations is to gain entrance into the European Union.

In parliamentary elections in June 2002, the Czech Social Democratic Party won 30% of the vote, and Vladimír Spidla became prime minister. The Communist party did surprisingly well, garnering 19% of the vote, their best showing since the collapse of communism in 1989.

Scandal rocked the Czech Republic in 2002 when Karol Srba, a senior foreign-ministry official, was arrested for allegedly hiring a hit man to attempt to murder a muckraking journalist, Sabina Slonkova.

In Aug. 2002, severe flooding caused 70,000 people in Prague and 200,000 nationwide to be evacuated.

# Denmark

**KINGDOM OF DENMARK**

**National name:** Kongeriget Danmark
**Sovereign:** Queen Margrethe II (1972)
**Prime Minister:** Anders Fogh Rasmussen (2001)
**Area:** 16,639 sq mi (43,094 sq km)[1]
**Population (2002 est.):** 5,368,854 (growth rate: 0.1%); birth rate: 11.7/1000; infant mortality rate: 5.0/1000; density per sq mi: 323
**Capital and largest city (1992):** Copenhagen, 1,339,395. **Other large cities (1992):** Århus, 204,139; Odense, 140,886; Ålborg, 114,970. **Monetary unit:** Krone. **Languages:** Danish, Faroese, Greenlandic (an Inuit dialect), small German-speaking minority. **Ethnicity/race:** Scandinavian, Eskimo, Faeroese, German. **Religions:** Evangelical Lutheran 91%, other Protestant and Roman Catholic 2%, other 7%. **Literacy rate:** 99% (1980)
**Economic summary: GDP/PPP** (2000 est.): $136.2 billion; per capita $25,500. **Real growth rate:** 2.8%. **Inflation:** 2.9%. **Unemployment:** 5.3%. **Arable land:** 60%. **Agriculture:** grain, potatoes, rape, sugar beets; pork and beef, dairy products; fish. **Labor:** 2.856 million; services 79%, industry 17%, agriculture 4%. **Industries:** food processing, machinery and equipment, textiles and clothing, chemical products, electronics, construction, furniture, and other wood products, shipbuilding, windmills. **Natural resources:** petroleum, natural gas, fish, salt, limestone, stone, gravel and sand. **Exports:** $50.8 billion (f.o.b., 2000):

machinery and instruments, meat and meat products, dairy products, fish, chemicals, furniture, ships, windmills. **Imports:** $43.6 billion (f.o.b., 2000): machinery and equipment, raw materials and semimanufactures for industry, chemicals, grain and foodstuffs, consumer goods. **Major trading partners:** EU, Norway, U.S.

1. Excluding Faeroe Islands and Greenland.

**Geography**  Smallest of the Scandinavian countries (half the size of Maine), Denmark occupies the Jutland peninsula, a lowland area. The country also consists of several islands in the Baltic Sea; the two largest are Sjælland, the site of Copenhagen, and Fyn.

**Government**  Constitutional monarchy.

**History**  From 10,000 to 1500 B.C., the population of present-day Denmark evolved from a society of hunters and fishers into an agricultural one. Called Jutland by the end of the 8th century, its mariners were among the Vikings, or Norsemen, who raided western Europe and the British Isles from the 9th to 11th century.

The country was Christianized by Saint Ansgar and Harald Blaatand (Bluetooth)—the first Christian king—in the 10th century. Harald's son, Sweyn, conquered England in 1013. His son, Canute the Great, who reigned from 1014 to 1035, united Denmark, England, and Norway under his rule; the southern tip of Sweden was part of Denmark until the 17th century. On Canute's death, civil war tore apart the country until Waldemar I (1157–1182) reestablished Danish hegemony over the north.

In 1282, the nobles won the Great Charter, and Eric V was forced to share power with Parliament and a Council of Nobles. Waldemar IV (1340–1375) restored Danish power, checked only by the Hanseatic League of north German cities allied with ports from Holland to Poland. Denmark, Norway, and Sweden united under the rule of his daughter Margrethe in 1397. But Sweden later achieved autonomy and in 1523, under Gustavus I, independence.

Denmark supported Napoléon, for which it was punished at the Congress of Vienna in 1815 by the loss of Norway to Sweden. In 1864, the Prussians under Bismarck and the Austrians made war on Denmark as an initial step in the unification of Germany. Denmark was neutral in World War I.

In 1940, Denmark was invaded by the Nazis. King Christian X reluctantly cautioned his fellow Danes to accept the occupation, but there was widespread resistance against the Nazis. Denmark was the only occupied country in World War II to save all its Jews from extermination, by smuggling them out of the country.

Beginning in 1944, Denmark's relationship with its territories changed substantially. In that year, Iceland declared its independence from Denmark, ending a union that had existed since 1380. In 1948, the Faeroe Islands, which had also belonged to Denmark since 1380, were granted home rule, and in 1953, Greenland officially became a territory of Denmark.

Immigration to Denmark fell dramatically in 2002, after Denmark's center-right government instituted more restrictive laws for asylum-seekers. Because of Denmark's social welfare benefits, it had become a much sought-after haven for refugees.

## Outlying Territories of Denmark

### Faeroe Islands

**Status:** Autonomous part of Denmark
**Chief of State:** Queen Margrethe II (1972)
**High Commissioner:** Birgit Kleis (2001)

**Prime Minister:** Anfinn Kallsberg (1998)
**Area:** 540 sq mi (1,399 sq km)
**Population (2002 est.):** 46,011 (average annual growth rate: 0.5%); birth rate: 13.7/1000; infant mortality rate: 6.7/1000; density per sq mi: 85
**Capital and largest city (1993 est.):** Tórshavn, 16,100.
**Monetary unit:** Faeroese krone. **Languages:** Faeroese, Danish (both official). **Ethnicity/race:** Scandinavian. **Literacy rate:** 99%

This group of 18 islands, of which 17 are inhabited, is located in the North Atlantic about 200 mi (322 km) northwest of the Shetland Islands. They were settled by the Vikings, the ancestors of the modern-day Faeroese, in the 8th century. The Faeroese language is derived from Old Norse. The islands joined Denmark in 1386 and have been part of the Danish kingdom ever since. The Faeroes have had home rule, under Danish authority, since 1948.

### Greenland

**Status:** Autonomous part of Denmark
**Chief of State:** Queen Margrethe II (1972)
**High Commissioner:** Gunnar Martens (1995)
**Premier:** Jonathan Motzfeldt (1997)
**Area:** 839,999 sq mi (incl. 708,069 sq mi covered by icecap) (2,175,600 sq km)
**Population (2002 est.):** 56,376 (average annual growth rate: 0.9%); birth rate: 16.3/1000; infant mortality rate: 17.3/1000; density per sq mi: 0.07
**Capital and largest city (1995 est.):** Godthaab, 12,723.
**Monetary unit:** Krone. **Ethnicity/race:** Greenlander 87% (Eskimos and Greenland-born whites), Danish and other 13%. **Literacy rate:** 99%

The Inuit are believed to have crossed from North America to northwest Greenland, the world's largest island, between 4000 B.C. and A.D. 1000. Greenland was colonized in A.D. 985–986 by Eric the Red. The Norse settlements declined in the 14th century, however, mainly as a result of a cooling in Greenland's climate, and in the 15th century they became extinct. In 1721, Greenland was recolonized by the Royal Greenland Trading Company of Denmark.

Greenland was under U.S. protection during World War II, but maintained Danish sovereignty. A definitive agreement for the joint defense of Greenland within the framework of NATO was signed in 1951. A large U.S. air base at Thule in the far north was completed in 1953.

Under 1953 amendments to the Danish constitution, Greenland became part of Denmark, with two representatives in the Danish Folketing. On May 1, 1979, Greenland gained home rule, with its own local Parliament (Landsting). In Feb. 1982, Greenlanders voted to withdraw from the European Union, which they had joined as part of Denmark in 1973.

## Djibouti

### REPUBLIC OF DJIBOUTI

**National name:** Jumhouriyya Djibouti
**President:** Ismail Omar Guelleh (1999)
**Prime Minister:** Dileita Mohamed Dileita (2001)
**Area:** 8,494 sq mi (22,000 sq km)
**Population (2002 est.):** 472,810 (growth rate: 2.6%); birth rate: 40.3/1000; infant mortality rate: 99.7/1000; density per sq mi: 56
**Capital (1992 est.):** Djibouti, 395,000. **Monetary unit:** Djibouti franc. **Languages:** Arabic and French (both official), Afar, Somali. **Ethnicity/race:** Somali 60%, Afar 35%, French, Arab, Ethiopian, and Italian 5%. **Religions:** Muslim 94%, Christian 6%. **Literacy rate:** 46% (1995)
**Economic summary:** GDP/PPP (2000 est.): $574

million; per capita $1,300. **Real growth rate:** 2%. **Inflation:** 2%. **Unemployment:** 50%. **Arable land:** 0%. **Agriculture:** ruits, vegetables; goats, sheep, camels. **Labor:** 282,000; agriculture, 75%; industry, 11%; services, 14% (1991 est.). **Industries:** limited to a few small-scale enterprises, such as dairy products and mineral-water bottling. **Natural resources:** geothermal areas. **Exports:** $260 million (f.o.b., 1999 est.): reexports, hides and skins, coffee (in transit). **Imports:** $440 million (f.o.b., 1999 est.): foods, beverages, transport equipment, chemicals, petroleum products. **Major trading partners:** Somalia, Yemen, Ethiopia, France, Italy, Saudi Arabia, UK.

**Geography** Djibouti lies in northeast Africa on the Gulf of Aden at the southern entrance to the Red Sea. It borders on Ethiopia, Eritrea, and Somalia. The country, the size of Massachusetts, is mainly a stony desert, with scattered plateaus and highlands.

**Government** Republic with a unicameral legislature.

**History** Ablé immigrants from Arabia migrated to what is now Djibouti in about the 3rd century B.C. Their descendants are the Afars, one of the two main ethnic groups that make up Djibouti today. Somali Issas arrived thereafter. Islam came to the region in A.D. 825.

Djibouti was acquired by France between 1843 and 1886 by treaties with the Somali sultans. Small, arid, and sparsely populated, it is important chiefly because of the capital city's port, the terminal of the Djibouti–Addis Ababa railway that carries 60% of Ethiopia's foreign trade. Originally known as French Somaliland, the colony voted in 1958 and 1967 to remain under French rule. It was renamed the Territory of the Afars and Issas in 1967 and took the name of its capital city on June 27, 1977, when France transferred sovereignty to the new independent nation of Djibouti. On Sept. 4, 1992, voters approved in referendum a new multiparty constitution. In 1991, conflict between the Afars and the Issa-dominated government erupted and the continued warfare has ravaged the country.

The dictatorial president, Hassan Gouled Aptidon, who had run the country since its independence, finally stepped aside in 1999, and Ismail Omar Guelleh was elected president. In March 2000, the main Afars rebel group signed a peace accord with the government. The fighting, severe drought, and the presence of tens of thousands of refugees from its war-torn neighbors, Ethiopia and Somalia, have severely strained Djibouti's agricultural capacity.

# Dominica

**COMMONWEALTH OF DOMINICA**
**President:** Vernon Shaw (1998)
Prima Minister: Pierre Charles (2000)
**Area:** 291 sq mi (754 sq km)
**Population (2002 est.):** 70,158 (growth rate: 1.0%); birth rate: 17.3/1000; infant mortality rate: 15.9/1000; density per sq mi: 241
**Capital and largest city (1991):** Roseau, 15,853.
**Monetary unit:** East Caribbean dollar. **Languages:** English (official) and French patois. **Ethnicity/race:** black, Carib Indians. **Religions:** Roman Catholic 77%, Protestant 15%. **Literacy rate:** 94% (1970)
**Economic summary:** GDP/PPP (2000 est.): $290 million; per capita $4,000. **Real growth rate:** 0.5%. **Inflation:** 2.5%. **Unemployment:** 20% (1999 est.). **Labor force:** 25,000; agriculture 40%, industry and commerce 32%, services 28%. **Arable land:** 9%. **Agriculture:** bananas, citrus, mangoes, root crops, coconuts, cocoa; forest and fishery potential not exploited. **Industries:** soap, coconut oil, tourism,

copra, furniture, cement blocks, shoes. **Natural resources:** timber, hydropower, arable land. **Exports:** $60.7 million (2000 est.): bananas, soap, bay oil, vegetables, grapefruit, oranges. **Imports:** $126 million (2000 est.): manufactured goods, machinery and equipment, food, chemicals. **Major trading partners:** Caricom countries, UK, U.S., Netherlands, Canada. **Member of Commonwealth of Nations**

**Geography** Dominica (pronounced Dom-in-EEK-a) is a mountainous island of volcanic origin of the Lesser Antilles in the Caribbean, south of Guadeloupe and north of Martinique.

**Government** Parliamentary democracy.

**History** Explored by Columbus in 1493, Dominica was claimed by Britain and France until 1763, when it was formally ceded to Britain. Along with other Windward Isles, it became a self-governing member of the West Indies Associated States in free association with Britain in 1967.

Dissatisfaction over the slow pace of reconstruction after Hurricane David devastated the island in Sept. 1979 brought a landslide victory to Mary Eugenia Charles of the Freedom Party in July 1980. The Freedom Party won again in 1985 and 1990, and the government sold state enterprises. The opposition United Workers' Party won in June 1995. In 1997 Dominica became the first Caribbean country to participate in the work of Green Globe, aiming to make Dominica a model ecotourism destination. Although the island is poorer than some of its Caribbean neighbors, Dominica has a relatively low crime rate and does not have the extremes of wealth and poverty evident on other islands. On Oct. 3, 2000, Pierre Charles, previously Communications and Works Minister, became the country's sixth prime minister.

Economic austerity measures, including higher taxes, were introduced in 2002. Massive protests followed.

# Dominican Republic

**National name:** República Dominicana
**President:** Hipólito Mejía (2000)
**Area:** 18,815 sq mi (48,730 sq km)
**Population (2002 est.):** 8,721,594 (growth rate: 2.0%); birth rate: 24.4/1000; infant mortality rate: 33.4/1000; density per sq mi: 464
**Capital and largest city (1993):** Santo Domingo, 2,100,000. **Other large city (1993):** Santiago de los Caballeros, 690,000. **Monetary unit:** Dominican Peso. **Languages:** Spanish, English widely spoken. **Ethnicity/race:** white 16%, black 11%, mixed 73%. **Religion:** Roman Catholic 90%. **Literacy rate:** 84% (1990)
**Economic summary:** GDP/PPP (2000 est.): $48.3 billion; per capita $5,700. **Real growth rate:** 8%. **Inflation:** 7.9%. **Unemployment:** 13.8% (1999 est.). **Arable land:** 21%. **Agriculture:** sugarcane, coffee, cotton, cocoa, tobacco, rice, beans, potatoes, corn, bananas; cattle, pigs, dairy products, beef, eggs. **Labor force:** 2.3 million to 2.6 million; services and government 58.7%, industry 24.3%, agriculture 17% (1998 est.). **Industries:** tourism, sugar processing, ferronickel and gold mining, textiles, cement, tobacco. **Natural resources:** nickel, bauxite, gold, silver. **Exports:** $5.8 billion (f.o.b., 2000): ferronickel, sugar, gold, silver, coffee, cocoa, tobacco, meats. **Imports:** $9.6 billion (f.o.b., 2000 est.): foodstuffs, petroleum, cotton and fabrics, chemicals and pharmaceuticals. **Major trading partners:** U.S., Netherlands, Canada, Russia, UK, Venezuela, Mexico, Japan, Panama.

**Geography** The Dominican Republic in the West Indies occupies the eastern two-thirds of the island of Hispaniola, which it shares with Haiti. Its area equals that of Vermont and New Hampshire combined. Duarte Peak, at 10,417 ft (3,175 m), is the highest point in the West Indies.

**Government** Representative democracy.

**History** The Dominican Republic was explored by Columbus on his first voyage in 1492. He named it La Española, and his son, Diego, was its first viceroy. The capital, Santo Domingo, founded in 1496, is the oldest European settlement in the Western Hemisphere.

Spain ceded the colony to France in 1795, and Haitian blacks under Toussaint L'Ouverture conquered it in 1801. In 1808 the people revolted and captured Santo Domingo the next year, setting up the first republic. Spain regained title to the colony in 1814. In 1821 Spanish rule was overthrown, but in 1822 the colony was reconquered by the Haitians. In 1844 the Haitians were thrown out, and the Dominican Republic was established, headed by Pedro Santana. Uprisings and Haitian attacks led Santana to make the country a province of Spain from 1861 to 1865.

President Buenaventura Báez, faced with an economy in shambles, attempted to have the country annexed to the U.S. in 1870, but the U.S. Senate refused to ratify a treaty of annexation. Disorder continued until the dictatorship of Ulíses Heureaux; in 1916, when chaos broke out again, the U.S. sent in a contingent of marines, who remained until 1934.

A sergeant in the Dominican army trained by the marines, Rafaél Leonides Trujillo Molina overthrew Horacio Vásquez in 1930 and established a dictatorship that lasted until his assassination 31 years later.

Leftists rebelled on April 24, 1965, and U.S. president Lyndon Johnson sent in marines and troops. After a cease-fire on May 6, a compromise installed Hector Garcia-Godoy as provisional president. Joaquin Balaguer won in free elections in 1966 against Bosch, and U.S. and other foreign troops withdrew. Balaguer restored political and economic stability.

In 1978 the army suspended the counting of ballots when Balaguer trailed in a fourth-term bid. After a warning from President Jimmy Carter, however, Balaguer accepted the victory of Antonio Guzmán of the Dominican Revolutionary Party. Salvador Jorge Blanco of the Dominican Revolutionary Party was elected president on May 16, 1982, defeating Balaguer and Bosch. Balaguer was again elected president in May 1986 and remained in office for the next ten years.

In 1996, U.S.-raised Leonel Fernandez secured more than 51% of the vote through an alliance with Balaguer. The first item on the president's agenda was the partial sale of some state-owned enterprises. Fernandez was praised for ending decades of isolationism and improving ties with other Caribbean countries, but he was criticized for not fighting corruption and alleviating the poverty that affects 60% of the population.

In Aug. 2000 the center-left Hipólito Mejía was elected president amid popular discontent over power outages in the recently privatized electric industry. In 2001 the army was deployed in major cities to fight rising crime.

A UNICEF report in 2002 claimed that about 2,500 Haitian children are smuggled illegally into the Dominican Republic annually to work as manual laborers or beggars.

# East Timor

**EAST TIMOR**
**President:** José Alexandre Gusmão (2002)
**Prime Minister:** Mari Alkatiri (2002)
**Area:** 5,743 sq mi (14,874 sq km)
**Population (2002 est.):** 800,000
**Capital and largest city (1999 est.):** Dili (65,000).
**Monetary unit:** U.S. dollar. **Languages:** Tetum, Portuguese (official), Bahasa Indonesia, English.
**Ethnicity/race:** Malay and Papuan descent.
**Religions:** Roman Catholic (91.4%), Protestant (2.6%), Muslim (1.7%), Hindu (0.3%), Buddhist (0.1%).
**Literary rate:** 48%
**Economy:** primarily subsistence farming and fishing.
**Unemployment:** 70%. **Natural resources:** off-shore gas and oil, not yet tapped. **Exports:** Coffee, oil and natural gas, logging, fisheries, spices, coconuts, cacao. **Major trading partners:** Australia, Portugal

**Geography** East Timor is located in the eastern part of Timor, an island in the Indonesian archipelago that lies between the South China Sea and the Indian Ocean. East Timor includes the enclave of Oecussi, which is located within West Timor (Indonesia). After Indonesia, East Timor's closest neighbor is Australia, 400 mi to the south. It is semi-arid and mountainous.

**Government** In a 1999 referendum East Timor voted to secede from Indonesia. The UN Transitional Authority in East Timor (UNTAET) governed the territory from 1999 until nationhood was declared on May 20, 2002. The president has a largely symbolic role; real power rests with the prime minister and the 88-member parliament.

**History** Timor was first colonized by the Portuguese in 1520. The Dutch, who claimed many of the surrounding islands, took control of the western portion of the island in 1613. Portugal and the Netherlands fought over the island until an 1860 treaty divided Timor, granting Portugal the eastern half of the island as well as the western enclave of Oecussi (the first Portuguese settlement on the island). Australia and Japan fought each other on the island during World War II; nearly 50,000 East Timorese died during the subsequent Japanese occupation.

In 1949, the Netherlands gave up its colonies in the Dutch West Indies, including West Timor, and the nation of Indonesia was born. East Timor remained under Portuguese control until 1975, when the Portuguese abruptly pulled out after 400 years of colonization. The sudden Portuguese withdrawal left the island vulnerable. Nine days after the Democratic Republic of East Timor was declared an independent nation, it was invaded by Indonesia and annexed on July 16, 1976. Although no country except Australia officially recognized the annexation, Indonesia's invasion was sanctioned by the United States and other western countries, who had cultivated Indonesia as a trading partner and cold-war ally (Fretilin, the East Timorese political party spearheading independence, was Marxist at the time).

Indonesia's invasion and its brutal occupation of East Timor—small, remote, and poor—largely escaped international attention. East Timor's resistance movement was violently suppressed by Indonesian military forces, and more than 200,000 Timorese were reported to have died from famine, disease, and fighting since the annexation. Indonesia's human rights abuses finally began receiving international notice in the 1990s, and in 1996 two East Timorese activists, Bishop Carlos Filipe Ximenes Belo and José

Ramos-Horta, received the Nobel Peace Prize for their efforts to gain freedom peacefully for East Timor.

After Indonesia's hard-line president Suharto left office in 1998, his successor, B. J. Habibie, unexpectedly announced his willingness to hold a referendum on East Timorese independence, reversing 25 years of Indonesian intransigence. As the referendum on self-rule drew closer, fighting between separatist guerrillas and pro-Indonesian paramilitary forces in East Timor intensified. The UN-sponsored referendum had to be rescheduled twice because of violence. On Aug. 30, 1999, 78.5% of the population voted to secede from Indonesia. In the days following the referendum, pro-Indonesian militias and Indonesian soldiers retaliated by razing towns, slaughtering civilians, and forcing a third of the population out of the province. After enormous international pressure, Indonesia finally agreed to allow UN forces into East Timor on Sept. 12. Led by Australia, an international peacekeeping force began restoring order to the ravaged region.

The UN Transitional Authority in East Timor (UNTAET) then governed the territory for nearly three years. A parliament was elected in 2001 and a constitution assembled, and on May 20, 2002, nationhood was declared. Charismatic rebel leader José Alexandre Gusmão, who was imprisoned by Indonesia from 1992 to 1999, was overwhelmingly elected the nation's first president on April 14, 2002. The president has a largely symbolic role; real power rests with the parliament and Prime Minister Mari Alkatiri, also a former guerrilla leader.

The first new country of the millennium, East Timor is also one of the world's poorest. Its meager infrastructure was destroyed by the Indonesian militias in 1999 and the economy, primarily made up of subsistence farming and fishing, is in shambles. As-of-yet-untapped off-shore gas and oil reserves, however, promise to bolster the economy in the next few years.

In Aug. 2002, Abilio Soares, the former governor of East Timor, was convicted by an Indonesian court of crimes against humanity for failing to control the deadly rampage after the 1999 independence referendum. But six other military and police leaders were acquitted of the charges; human rights groups expressed outrage at the sham trials.

# Ecuador

### REPUBLIC OF ECUADOR

**National name:** República del Ecuador
**President:** Gustavo Noboa (2000)
**Area:** 109,483 sq mi (283,560 sq km)
**Population (2002 est.):** 13,447,494 (growth rate: 2.0%); birth rate: 25.5/1000; infant mortality rate: 33.0/1000; density per sq mi: 123
**Capital (1000 est.):** Quito, 1,300,000. **Other large cities (1998 est.):** Guayaquil, 2,000,000; Cuenca, 200,000.
**Monetary unit:** U.S. dollar. **Languages:** Spanish (official), Quechua. **Ethnicity/race:** mestizo (mixed Indian and Spanish) 65%, Indian 25%, Spanish 7%, black 3%. **Religion:** Roman Catholic 95%. **Literacy rate:** 90% (1990)
**Economic summary:** GDP/PPP (2000 est.): $37.2 billion; per capita $2,900. **Real growth rate:** 0.8%. **Inflation:** 96%. **Unemployment:** 13% with widespread underemployment (2000 est.). **Arable land:** 6%. **Agriculture:** bananas, coffee, cocoa, rice, potatoes, manioc (tapioca), plantains, sugarcane; cattle, sheep, pigs, beef, pork, dairy products; balsa wood; fish, shrimp. **Labor force:** 4.2 million; agriculture 30%, industry 25%, services 45% (1999 est.). **Industries:** petroleum, food processing, textiles, metal work, paper products, wood products, chemicals, plastics, fishing,

lumber. **Natural resources:** petroleum, fish, timber, hydropower. **Exports:** $5.6 billion (f.o.b., 2000 est.): petroleum, bananas, shrimp, coffee, cocoa, cut flowers, fish. **Imports:** $3.4 billion (f.o.b., 2000 est.): machinery and equipment, raw materials, fuels; consumer goods. **Major trading partners:** U.S., Colombia, Italy, Chile, Peru, Venezuela, Japan, Mexico.

**Geography** Ecuador, about equal in area to Nevada, is in the northwest part of South America fronting on the Pacific. To the north is Colombia and to the east and south is Peru. Two high and parallel ranges of the Andes, traversing the country from north to south, are topped by tall volcanic peaks. The highest is Chimborazo at 20,577 ft (6,272 m). The Galápagos Islands (or Colón Archipelago; 3,029 sq mi; 7,845 sq km), in the Pacific Ocean about 600 mi (966 km) west of the South American mainland, became part of Ecuador in 1832.

**Government** Republic.

**History** The tribes in the northern highlands of Ecuador formed the Kingdom of Quito around 1000. It was absorbed, by conquest and marriage, into the Inca empire. Spanish conquistador Francisco Pizarro conquered the land in 1532, and through the 17th century a Spanish colony thrived by exploitation of the Indians. The first revolt against Spain occurred in 1809. Ecuador then joined Venezuela, Colombia, and Panama in a confederacy known as Greater Colombia.

When Greater Colombia collapsed in 1830, Ecuador became independent. Revolts and dictatorships followed; it had 48 presidents during the first 131 years of the republic. Conservatives ruled until the revolution of 1895 ushered in nearly a half century of Radical Liberal rule, during which the church was disestablished and freedom of worship, speech, and press was introduced. Although it was under military rule in the 1970s, the country did not experience the violence and repression characteristic of other Latin American military regimes. Its last 20 years of democracy, however, have been largely ineffectual because of a weak executive branch and a strong, fractious Congress.

Peru invaded Ecuador in 1941 and seized a large tract of Ecuadorian territory in the disputed Amazon. In 1981 and 1995 war broke out again. In May 1999, Ecuador and Peru signed a treaty ending a nearly 60-year border dispute involving the stretch of Amazon jungle.

In 1998, Ecuador experienced one of its worst economic crises. El Niño caused $3 billion in damage, the price of its principal export, oil, plunged, and its inflation rate, 43%, was the highest in Latin America. In 1999, the government was near bankruptcy, the currency lost 100% of its value against the dollar, and the poverty rate soared to 70%, doubling in five years. The president's economic austerity plan was protested with massive strikes in March 1999.

President Jamil Mahuad was overthrown in Jan. 2000, in the first military coup in Latin America in a decade. The junta gave power to the vice president, Gustavo Noboa. Faced with the worst economic crisis in Ecuador's history, Noboa restructured Ecuador's foreign debt, adopted the U.S. dollar as the national currency, and continued privatization of state-owned industries, generating enormous opposition. In Feb. 2001, the government cut fuel prices after violent protests by Indians, who are among Ecuador's most disadvantaged people.

Within two years, Ecuador's economy had rebounded from the brink of collapse. The economy grew by 5.4% for 2001, the highest rate in Latin

America. Inflation was 22%, down from 91% in 2000, and the budget was balanced. But chronic corruption among senior government officials, as well as among the courts and the judiciary, has continued. According to Quito's chamber of commerce, Ecuador annually loses $2 billion (11.2% of the GDP) a year to corruption.

# Egypt

**ARAB REPUBLIC OF EGYPT**

**President:** Hosni Mubarak (1981)
**Prime Minister:** Atef Ebeid (1999)
**Area:** 386,660 sq mi (1,001,450 sq km)
**Population (2002 est.):** 70,712,345 (growth rate: 1.7%); birth rate: 24.4/1000; infant mortality rate: 58.6/1000; density per sq mi: 183
**Capital and largest city (2000 est.):** Cairo, 14,350,000 (metro. area). **Other large cities (1992 est.):** Alexandria, 3,380,000; Giza, 2,144,000 (part of Cairo metro. area); Shubra el Khema, 834,000 (part of Cairo metro. area); El Mahalla el Kubra, 408,000. **Monetary unit:** Egyptian pound. **Language:** Arabic. **Ethnicity/ race:** Eastern Hamitic stock (Egyptians, Bedouins, and Berbers) 99%, Greek, Nubian, Armenian, other European (primarily Italian and French) 1%. **Religions:** Islam 94%, Christian (mostly Coptic) 6%. **Literacy rate:** 48% (1990)
**Economic summary: GDP/PPP** (2000 est.): $247 billion; per capita $3,600. **Real growth rate:** 5%. **Inflation:** 3%. **Unemployment:** 11.5%. **Arable land:** 2%. **Agriculture:** cotton, rice, corn, wheat, beans, fruits, vegetables; cattle, water buffalo, sheep, goats. **Labor force:** 19.9 million; agriculture 29%, services 49%, industry 22% (FY99). **Industries:** textiles, food processing, tourism, chemicals, hydrocarbons, construction, cement, metals. **Natural resources:** petroleum, natural gas, iron ore, phosphates, manganese, limestone, gypsum, talc, asbestos, lead, zinc. **Exports:** $7.3 billion (f.o.b., 2000 est.): crude oil and petroleum products, cotton, textiles, metal products, chemicals. **Imports:** $17 billion (f.o.b., 2000 est.): machinery and equipment, foodstuffs, chemicals, wood products, fuels. **Major trading partners:** EU, Middle East, Afro-Asian countries, U.S.

**Geography** Egypt, at the northeast corner of Africa on the Mediterranean Sea, is bordered on the west by Libya, on the south by the Sudan, and on the east by the Red Sea and Israel. It is nearly one and one-half times the size of Texas. Egypt is divided into two unequal, extremely arid regions by the landscape's dominant feature, the northward-flowing Nile River. The Nile starts 100 mi (161 km) south of the Mediterranean and fans out to a sea front of 155 mi between the cities of Alexandria and Port Said.

**Government** Republic.

**History** Egyptian history dates back to about 4000 B.C., when the kingdoms of upper and lower Egypt, already highly sophisticated, were united. Egypt's golden age coincided with the 18th and 19th dynasties (16th to 13th century B.C.), during which the empire was established. Persia conquered Egypt in 525 B.C., Alexander the Great subdued it in 332 B.C., and then the dynasty of the Ptolemies ruled the land until 30 B.C., when Cleopatra, last of the line, committed suicide and Egypt became a Roman, then Byzantine, province. Arab caliphs ruled Egypt from 641 until 1517, when the Turks took it for their Ottoman Empire.

Napoléon's armies occupied the country from 1798 to 1801. In 1805, Mohammed Ali, leader of a band of Albanian soldiers, became pasha of Egypt. After completion of the Suez Canal in 1869, the French and British took increasing interest in Egypt. British troops occupied Egypt in 1882, and British resident agents became its actual administrators, though it remained under nominal Turkish sovereignty. In 1914, this fiction was ended, and Egypt became a protectorate of Britain.

Egyptian nationalism forced Britain to declare Egypt an independent sovereign state on Feb. 28, 1922, although the British reserved rights for the protection of the Suez Canal and the defense of Egypt. In 1936, by an Anglo-Egyptian treaty of alliance, all British troops and officials were to be withdrawn, except from the Suez Canal Zone. When World War II started, Egypt remained neutral. British imperial troops finally ended the Nazi threat to Suez in 1942 in the battle of El Alamein, west of Alexandria. In 1951, Egypt abrogated the 1936 treaty and the 1899 Anglo-Egyptian condominium of the Sudan. Rioting and attacks on British troops in the Suez Canal Zone followed, reaching a climax in Jan. 1952. The army, led by Gen. Mohammed Naguib, seized power on July 23, 1952. Three days later, King Farouk abdicated in favor of his infant son. The monarchy was abolished and a republic proclaimed on June 18, 1953, with Naguib holding the posts of provisional president and premier. He relinquished the latter in 1954 to Gamal Abdel Nasser, leader of the ruling military junta, who was confirmed as president in a referendum on June 23, 1956.

Nasser's policies embroiled his country in continual conflict. In 1956, the U.S. and Britain withdrew their pledges of financial aid for the building of the Aswan High Dam. In response, Nasser nationalized the Suez Canal and expelled British oil and embassy officials. Israel, barred from the canal and exasperated by terrorist raids, invaded the Gaza Strip and the Sinai Peninsula. Britain and France, after demanding Egyptian evacuation of the canal zone, attacked Egypt on Oct. 31, 1956. Worldwide pressure forced Britain, France, and Israel to halt the hostilities. A UN emergency force occupied the canal zone, and all troops were evacuated in the spring of 1957.

From 1956 to 1961, Egypt and Syria united to form a single country called the United Arab Republic (UAR). Syria ended this relationship in 1961 after a military coup, but Egypt continued to call itself the UAR until 1971.

On June 5, 1967, Israel invaded the Sinai Peninsula, the East Bank of the Jordan River, and the zone around the Gulf of Aqaba. A UN cease-fire on June 10 saved the Arabs from complete rout. Nasser declared the 1967 cease-fire void along the canal in April 1969 and began a war of attrition. The U.S. peace plan of June 19, 1970, resulted in Egypt's agreement to reinstate the cease-fire for at least three months (from Aug.) and to accept Israel's existence within "recognized and secure" frontiers that might emerge from UN-mediated talks. In return, Israel accepted the principle of withdrawing from occupied territories. On Sept. 28, 1970, Nasser died of a heart attack. Anwar el-Sadat, an associate of Nasser and a former newspaper editor, became the next president.

In July 1972, Sadat ordered the expulsion of Soviet "advisers and experts" from Egypt because the Russians had not provided the sophisticated weapons he felt were needed to retake territory lost to Israel in 1967. The fourth Arab-Israeli War broke out on Oct. 6, 1973, during the Jewish holiday of Yom Kippur. Egypt swept deep into the Sinai, while Syria strove to throw Israel off the Golan Heights. A UN-sponsored truce was accepted on Oct. 22. In

Jan. 1974, both sides agreed to a settlement negotiated by U.S. secretary of state Henry A. Kissinger that gave Egypt a narrow strip along the entire Sinai bank of the Suez Canal. In June, President Nixon made the first visit by a U.S. president to Egypt and full diplomatic relations were established. The Suez Canal was cleared and reopened on June 5, 1975.

In the most audacious act of his career, Sadat flew to Jerusalem at the invitation of Prime Minister Menachem Begin and pleaded before Israel's Knesset on Nov. 20, 1977, for a permanent peace settlement. The Arab world reacted with fury—only Morocco, Tunisia, Sudan, and Oman approved. Egypt and Israel signed a formal peace treaty on March 26, 1979. The pact ended 30 years of war and established diplomatic and commercial relations.

Egyptian and Israeli officials met in the Sinai desert on April 26, 1979, to implement the peace treaty calling for the phased withdrawal of occupation forces from the peninsula. By mid-1980, two-thirds of the Sinai was transferred, but progress was not matched elsewhere—the negotiation of Arab autonomy in the Gaza Strip and the West Bank remained stymied. Sadat halted further talks in Aug. 1980 because of continued Israeli settlement of the West Bank. On Oct. 6, 1981, Sadat was assassinated by extremist Muslim soldiers at a parade in Cairo. Vice President Hosni Mubarak, a former air force chief of staff, succeeded him. Israel completed the return of the Sinai to Egyptian control on April 25, 1982. Israel's invasion of Lebanon in June brought a marked cooling in Egyptian-Israeli relations, but not a disavowal of the peace treaty.

The government has concentrated much of its time and attention in recent years on combating Islamic extremism, particularly attacks against Copts (Egyptian Christians).

# El Salvador

**REPUBLIC OF EL SALVADOR**

**National name:** República de El Salvador
**President:** Francisco Flores (1999)
**Area:** 8,124 sq mi (21,040 sq km)
**Population (2002 est.):** 6,353,681 (growth rate: 2.2%); birth rate: 28.3/1000; infant mortality rate: 27.6/1000; density per sq mi: 782
**Capital and largest city (1993 est.):** San Salvador, 972,810. **Other large cities (1993 est.):** Santa Ana, 208,322; San Miguel, 161,156; Zacatecoluca, 81,035. **Monetary unit:** Colón. **Language:** Spanish. **Ethnicity/race:** mestizo 94%, Indian 5%, white 1%. **Religion:** Roman Catholic. **Literacy rate:** 73% (1000).

**National summary:** GDP/PPP (2000 est.): 524 billion, per capita $4,000. **Real growth rate:** 2.5%. **Inflation:** 2.5%. **Unemployment:** 10%. **Arable land:** 27%. **Agriculture:** coffee, sugar, corn, rice, beans, oilseed, cotton, sorghum; shrimp; beef, dairy products. **Labor force:** 2.35 million (1999); agriculture 30%, industry 15%, services 55% (1999 est.). **Industries:** food processing, beverages, petroleum, chemicals, fertilizer, textiles, furniture, light metals. **Natural resources:** hydropower, geothermal power, petroleum, arable land. **Exports:** $2.8 billion (f.o.b., 2000): offshore assembly exports, coffee, sugar, shrimp, textiles, chemicals, electricity. **Imports:** $4.6 billion (f.o.b., 2000): raw materials, consumer goods, capital goods, fuels, foodstuffs, petroleum, electricity. **Major trading partners:** U.S., Guatemala, Honduras, Costa Rica, Mexico.

**Geography** Situated on the Pacific coast of Central America, El Salvador has Guatemala to the west and Honduras to the north and east. It is the smallest of the Central American countries, its area equal to that of Massachusetts, and the only one without an Atlantic coastline. Most of the country is on a fertile volcanic plateau about 2,000 ft (607 m) high.

**Government** Republic.

**History** The Pipil Indians, descendants of the Aztecs, likely migrated to the region in the 11th century. In 1525, Pedro de Alvarado, a lieutenant of Cortés, conquered El Salvador.

El Salvador, with the other countries of Central America, declared its independence from Spain on Sept. 15, 1821, and was part of a federation of Central American states until that union dissolved in 1838. For decades after its independence, El Salvador experienced numerous revolutions and wars against other Central American republics. From 1931 to 1979 El Salvador was ruled by a series of military dictatorships.

In 1969, El Salvador invaded Honduras after Honduran landowners deported several thousand Salvadorans. Five thousand people ultimately died in what became known as the "football war" because it broke out during a soccer game between the two countries.

In the 1970s discontent with societal inequalities, a poor economy, and the repressive measures of dictatorship led to civil war between the government, the right-wing Nationalist Republican Alliance (ARENA) party, and leftist antigovernment guerrilla units, whose leading group was the Farabundo Martí National Liberation Front (FMLN). The U.S. intervened on the side of the military, despite its scores of human rights violations. The presidency of José Napoleón Duarte, a moderate civilian, from 1984–1989, offered an alternative to the political extremes of right and left, but Duarte was unable to end the war and in 1989, Alfredo Cristiani of ARENA was elected.

On Jan. 16, 1992, the government signed a peace treaty with the guerrilla forces, formally ending the 12-year civil war that had killed 75,000. El Salvador's subsequent presidents have all belonged to ARENA, including the current president, Francisco Flores, who took office in 1999. In 1998, Hurricane Mitch devastated the country, leaving 200 dead and over 30,000 homeless.

Along with Guatemala and Honduras, El Salvador signed a free trade agreement with Mexico in June 2000. Flores also won parliamentary approval for a U.S. military base in El Salvador over opposition by former Marxist rebels, who feared U.S. intervention in the country's internal affairs. The base will fight drug trafficking, and replaces facilities that were shut down when the U.S. withdrew from the Panama Canal.

# Equatorial Guinea

**REPUBLIC OF EQUATORIAL GUINEA**

**National name:** República de Guinea Ecuatorial
**President:** Col. Teodoro Obiang Nguema Mbasogo (1979)
**Prime Minister:** Cándido Muatetema Rivas (2001)
**Area:** 10,830 sq mi (28,051 sq km)
**Population (2002 est.):** 498,144 (growth rate: 2.5%); birth rate: 37.3/1000; infant mortality rate: 91.0/1000; density per sq mi: 46
**Capital and largest city (1983):** Malabo, 30,418.
**Monetary unit:** CFA Franc. **Languages:** Spanish (official), French (2nd official), pidgin English, Fang,

Bubi, Creole. **Ethnicity/race:** Bioko (primarily Bubi, some Fernandinos), Río Muni (primarily Fang), Europeans less than 1,000, mostly Spanish. **Religions:** Roman Catholic, Protestant, traditional. **Literacy rate:** 50% (1990)
**Economic summary: GDP/PPP** (2000 est.): $960 million; per capita $2,000. **Real growth rate:** 12%. **Inflation:** 6% (1999 est.). **Unemployment:** 30% (1998 est.). **Arable land:** 5%. **Agriculture:** coffee, cocoa, rice, yams, cassava (tapioca), bananas, palm oil nuts; livestock; timber. **Labor force:** n.a. **Industries:** petroleum, fishing, sawmilling, natural gas. **Natural resources:** oil, petroleum, timber, small unexploited deposits of gold, manganese, uranium. **Exports:** $860 million (f.o.b., 2000 est.): petroleum, timber, cocoa. **Imports:** $300 million (f.o.b., 1999): manufactured goods and equipment. **Major trading partners:** U.S., Spain, China, France, Japan, Cameroon, UK.

**Geography** Equatorial Guinea, formerly Spanish Guinea, consists of Río Muni (10,045 sq mi; 26,117 sq km), on the western coast of Africa, and several islands in the Gulf of Guinea, the largest of which is Bioko (formerly Fernando Po) (785 sq mi; 2,033 sq km). The other islands are Annobón, Corisco, Elobey Grande, and Elobey Chico. The total area is twice that of Connecticut.

**Government** Presidential republic with a 17-member Supreme Military Council since a 1979 coup.

**History** The mainland was originally inhabited by Pygmies. The Fang and Bubi migrated there in the 17th century and to the main island of Fernando Po (now called Bioko) in the 19th century. In the 18th century, the Portuguese ceded land to the Spanish that included Equatorial Guinea. From 1827 to 1844, Britain administered Fernando Po, but it was then reclaimed by Spain. Río Muni, the mainland, was not occupied by the Spanish until 1926. Spanish Guinea, as it was then called, gained independence from Spain on Oct. 12, 1968. It is Africa's only Spanish-speaking country.

From the outset, President Francisco Macías Nguema, considered the father of independence, began a brutal reign, destroying the economy of the fledgling country and abusing human rights. Calling himself the "Unique Miracle," Nguema is considered one of the worst despots in African history. In 1971, the U.S. State Department reported that his regime was "characterized by abandonment of all government functions except internal security, which was accomplished by terror; this led to the death or exile of up to one-third of the population."

On Aug. 3, 1979, Nguema was overthrown and executed by his nephew, Lieut. Col. Teodoro Obiang Nguema Mbasogo. Obiang has been gradually modernizing the country but has retained many of his uncle's dictatorial practices, including the amassing of personal wealth by siphoning it from the public coffers.

A recent off-shore oil boom has filled the country's coffers. Equatorial Guinea's economy grew by 71.2% in 1997, the first year of the petroleum bonanza, and has sustained this phenomenal rate of growth. It is unlikely, however, that the country's new wealth will benefit the average citizen—the president's family and cronies control the industry.

In 2002, 68 political opponents of the government were given stiff prison sentences in sham trials for plotting against the government.

# Eritrea

**President:** Isaias Afwerki (1993)
**Area:** 46,842 sq mi (121,320 sq km)
**Population (2002 est.):** 4,465,651 (of which 0.5 million are refugees awaiting repatriation) (growth rate: 3.0%); birth rate: 42.2/1000; infant mortality rate: 73.6/1000; density per sq mi: 95
**Capital and largest city (1993):** Asmara, 400,000.
**Other major cities:** the ports of Massawa and Assab. **Monetary unit:** Nakfa. **Languages:** Afar, Bilen, Kunama, Nara, Arabic, Tobedawi, Saho, Tigre, Tigrinya. **Ethnicity/race:** ethnic Tigrinya 50%, Tigre and Kunama 40%, Afar 4%, Saho (Red Sea coast dwellers) 3%. **Religions:** Islam and Eritrean Orthodox Christianity. **Literacy rate:** 25%
**Economic summary: GDP/PPP** (2000 est.): $2.9 billion; per capita $710. **Real growth rate:** –1%. **Inflation:** 14%. **Unemployment:** n.a. **Arable land:** 12%. **Agriculture:** sorghum, lentils, vegetables, corn, cotton, tobacco, coffee, sisal; livestock, goats; fish. **Labor force:** n.a.; agriculture 80%, industry and services 20%. **Industries:** food processing, beverages, clothing and textiles. **Natural resources:** gold, potash, zinc, copper, salt, possibly oil and natural gas, fish. **Exports:** $26 million (f.o.b., 1999): livestock, sorghum, textiles, food, small manufactures. **Imports:** $560 million (c.i.f., 1999): machinery, petroleum products, food, manufactured goods. **Major trading partners:** Sudan, Ethiopia, Japan, UAE, Italy, Germany, UK, Korea.

**Geography** Eritrea was formerly the northernmost province of Ethiopia and is about the size of Indiana. Much of the country is mountainous. Its narrow Red Sea coastal plain is one of the hottest and driest places in Africa. The cooler central highlands have fertile valleys that support agriculture. Eritrea is bordered by the Sudan on the north and west, the Red Sea on the north and east, and Ethiopia and Djibouti on the south.

**Government** A transitional government committed to a democratic system.

**History** Eritrea was part of the first Ethiopian kingdom of Aksum until its decline in the 8th century. It came under the control of the Ottoman Empire in the 16th century, and later of the Egyptians. The Italians captured the coastal areas in 1885, and the Treaty of Uccialli (May 2, 1889) gave Italy sovereignty over part of Eritrea. The Italians named their colony after the Roman name for the Red Sea, *Mare Erythraeum,* and ruled it up until World War II. The British captured Eritrea in 1941 and later administered it as a UN Trust Territory until it became federated with Ethiopia on Sept. 15, 1952. It was made an Ethiopian province on Nov. 14, 1962. A civil war broke out against the Ethiopian government, led by rebel groups who opposed the union and wanted independence for Eritrea. Fighting continued over the next 32 years.

In 1991, the Ethiopian People's Revolutionary Democratic Front deposed the country's hardline communist dictator Mengistu. Without Mengistu's troops to battle, the Eritrean People's Liberation Front was able to gain control of Asmara, the Eritrean capital, and form a provisional government. In 1993, a referendum on Eritrean independence was held, supported by the UN and the new Ethiopian government. Eritrean voters almost unanimously opted for an independent republic. Ethiopia recognized Eritrea's sovereignty on May 3, 1993, and sought a new era of cooperation between the two countries.

The cooperation did not last long. Following Eritrea's independence, Eritrea and Ethiopia disagreed about the exact demarcation of their borders, and in May 1998 border clashes broke out. After an eight-month lull that both sides used to reinforce their 600-mile common border, war broke out in earnest. Both impoverished countries spent millions of dollars on warplanes and weapons, about 80,000 people were killed, and refugees were legion. Eritrea eventually lost the war against its more populous and powerful neighbor, and a formal peace agreement was signed in Dec. 2000. The United Nations has supplied more than four-thousand troops to continue patrolling the buffer zone between the two nations. An international boundary commission ruled on the disputed border between the two countries on April 13, 2002.

# Estonia

### REPUBLIC OF ESTONIA

**National name:** Eesti
**President:** Arnold Rüütel (2001)
**Prime Minister:** Siim Kallas (2002)
**Area:** 17,462 sq mi (45,226 sq km)
**Population (2002 est.):** 1,415,681 (growth rate: –0.5%); birth rate: 9.0/1000; infant mortality rate: 12.3/1000; density per sq mi: 81
**Capital and largest city (1992 est.):** Tallinn, 471,608.
**Other large city (1992 est.):** Tartu, 113,400.
**Monetary unit:** Kroon. **Languages:** Estonian (official), Russian, Finnish, English. **Ethnicity/race:** Estonian 61.5%, Russian 30.3%, Ukrainian 3.2%, Belorussian 1.8%, Finn 1.1%, other 2.1% (1989). **Religions:** Lutheran 78%, Orthodox 19%. **Literacy:** 100% (1989)
**Economic summary: GDP/PPP** (2000 est.): $14.7 billion; per capita $10,000. **Real growth rate:** 6.4%. **Inflation:** 4.1% (1999 est.). **Unemployment:** 11.7% (1999 est.). **Arable land:** 25%. **Agriculture:** potatoes, fruits, vegetables; livestock and dairy products; fish. **Labor force:** 785,500; industry 20%, agriculture 11%, services 69% (1999 est.). **Industries:** oil shale, shipbuilding, phosphates, electric motors, excavators, cement, furniture, clothing, textiles, paper, shoes, apparel. **Natural resources:** shale oil (kukersite), peat, phosphorite, amber, cambrian blue clay, limestone, dolomite, arable land. **Exports:** $3.1 billion (f.o.b., 2000): machinery and equipment, wood products, textiles, food products, metals, chemical products (1999). **Imports:** $4 billion (f.o.b., 2000): machinery and equipment, chemical products, foodstuffs, metal product, textiles (1999). **Major trading partners:** Finland, Sweden, Russia, Latvia, Germany, U.S., Japan.

**Geography**  Estonia is mainly a lowland country that borders on the Baltic Sea. It has numerous lakes and forests and many rivers, most draining northward into the Gulf of Finland or eastward into Lake Peipus. Lake Peipus is Estonia's largest lake and is important to the fishing and shipping industries.

**Government**  Parliamentary democracy

**History**  Estonians resisted the assaults of Vikings, Danes, Swedes, and Russians before the 13th century. In 1346, the Danes, who possessed northern Estonia, sold the land to the Teutonic Knights of Germany, who already possessed Livonia (southern Estonia and Latvia). The Teutonic Knights reduced the Estonians to serfdom. In 1526, the Swedes took over, and the power of the German (Balt) landowning class was reduced. But after 1721, when Russia succeeded Sweden as the ruling power under the Peace of Nystad, the Estonians were subject to a double bondage—the Balts and the czarist officials. The oppression lasted until the closing months of World War I, when Esto-

nia finally achieved independence after a victorious war (1918–20). But shortly after the start of World War II, the nation was occupied by Russian troops and incorporated as the 16th republic of the USSR in 1940. Germany occupied the nation from 1941 to 1944, when it was retaken by the Soviets.

Estonia declared independence from the Soviet Union in March 1990. Soviet resistance ensued, but after recognition by European and other countries, the Soviet Union acknowledged Estonian nationhood on Sept. 6, 1991. UN membership followed on Sept. 17, 1991. The newly independent nation embraced free-market reforms. Fueled by foreign investments, economic advances continued unabated in 1997. This prompted the European Commission (EC) to recommend that Estonia begin accession talks for membership in the European Union.

At the end of 1998, Estonia relaxed the strict citizenship requirements that kept the country's Russian speakers—about one-third of the population—from gaining citizenship. This reform eased the way for Estonia's bid for entry into the European Union.

# Ethiopia

### FEDERAL DEMOCRATIC REPUBLIC OF ETHIOPIA

**President:** Girma Woldegiorgis (2001)
**Prime Minister:** Meles Zenawi (1995)
**Area:** 435,184 sq mi (1,127,127 sq km)
**Population (2002 est.):** 67,673,031 (growth rate: 2.6%); birth rate: 44.3/1000; infant mortality rate: 98.6/1000; density per sq mi: 156
**Capital and largest city (1993 est.):** Addis Ababa, 2,200,186. **Monetary unit:** Birr. **Languages:** Amharic (official), English, Orominga, Tigrigna, over 70 languages spoken. **Ethnicity/race:** Oromo 40%, Amhara and Tigrean 32%, Sidamo 9%, Shankella 6%, Somali 6%, Afar 4%, Gurage 2%, other 1%. **Religions:** Ethiopian Orthodox 35%–40%, Islam 40%–45%, animist 15%–20%, other 5%. **Literacy rate:** 28% (1984)
**Economic summary: GDP/PPP** (2000 est.): $39.2 billion; per capita $600. **Real growth rate:** 2%. **Inflation:** 5%. **Unemployment:** n.a. **Arable land:** 12%. **Agriculture:** cereals, pulses, coffee, oilseed, sugarcane, potatoes, qat; hides, cattle, sheep, goats. **Labor force:** n.a; agriculture and animal husbandry 80%, government and services 12%, industry and construction 8% (1985). **Industries:** food processing, beverages, textiles, chemicals, metals processing, cement. **Natural resources:** small reserves of gold, platinum, copper, potash, natural gas, hydropower. **Exports:** $460 million (f.o.b., 1999): coffee, gold, leather products, oilseeds, qat. **Imports:** $1.25 billion (f.o.b., 1999): food and live animals, petroleum and petroleum products, chemicals, machinery, motor vehicles. **Major trading partners:** Germany, Japan, Djibouti, Saudi Arabia, Italy, Russia, U.S.

**Geography**  Ethiopia is in east-central Africa, bordered on the west by the Sudan, the east by Somalia and Djibouti, the south by Kenya, and the northeast by Eritrea. It is nearly three times the size of California. Over its main plateau land, Ethiopia has several high mountains, the highest of which is Ras Dashan at 15,158 ft (4,620 m). The Blue Nile, or Abbai, rises in the northwest and flows in a great semicircle east, south, and northwest before entering the Sudan. Its chief reservoir, Lake Tana, lies in the northwest part of the plateau.

**Government**  Federal republic.

**History** Archeologists have found the oldest known human ancestors in Ethiopia, including *Ardipithecus ramidus kadabba* (c. 5.8–5.2 million years old) and *Australopithecus anamensis* (c. 4.2 million years old). Originally called Abyssinia, Ethiopia is sub-Saharan Africa's oldest state, and its Solomonic dynasty claims descent from King Menelik I, traditionally believed to have been the son of the queen of Sheba and King Solomon. The current nation is a consolidation of smaller kingdoms that owed feudal allegiance to the Ethiopian emperor.

Hamitic peoples migrated to Ethiopia from Asia Minor in prehistoric times. Semitic traders from Arabia penetrated the region in the 7th century B.C. Its Red Sea ports were important to the Roman and Byzantine Empires. Coptic Christianity was brought to the region in A.D. 341, and a variant of it became Ethiopia's state religion. Ancient Ethiopia reached its peak in the 5th century, then was isolated by the rise of Islam and weakened by feudal wars.

Modern Ethiopia emerged under Emperor Menelik II, who established its independence by routing an Italian invasion in 1896. He expanded Ethiopia by conquest. Disorders that followed Menelik's death brought his daughter to the throne in 1917, with his cousin, Tafari Makonnen, as regent and heir apparent. When the empress died in 1930, Tafari was crowned Emperor Haile Selassie I.

Haile Selassie, called the "Lion of Judah," outlawed slavery and tried to centralize his scattered realm, in which 70 languages were spoken. In 1931, he created a constitution, revised in 1955, that called for a Parliament with an appointed senate and an elected chamber of deputies, and a system of courts. But basic power remained with the emperor.

Fascist Italy invaded Ethiopia on Oct. 3, 1935, forcing Haile Selassie into exile in May 1936. Ethiopia was annexed to Eritrea, then an Italian colony, and to Italian Somaliland, forming Italian East Africa. In 1941, British troops routed the Italians, and Haile Selassie returned to Addis Ababa. In 1952, Eritrea was incorporated into Ethiopia.

On Sept. 12, 1974, Haile Selassie was deposed, the constitution suspended, and Ethiopia proclaimed a socialist state under a collective military dictatorship called the Provisional Military Administrative Council (PMAC), also known as the Derg. U.S. aid stopped, and Cuban and Soviet aid began. Lt. Col. Mengistu Haile Mariam became head of state in 1977. During this period Ethiopia fought against Eritrean secessionists as well as Somali rebels, and the government fought against its own people in a campaign called the "red terror." Thousands of political opponents were killed. Mengistu remained leader until 1991, when his greatest supporter, the Soviet Union, dismantled itself.

A group called the Ethiopian People's Revolutionary Democratic Front seized the capital in 1991, and in May a separatist guerrilla organization, the Eritrean People's Liberation Front, took control of the province of Eritrea. The two groups agreed that Eritrea would have an internationally supervised referendum on independence. This election took place in April 1993 with almost unanimous support for Eritrean independence. Ethiopia accepted and recognized Eritrea as an independent state within a few days. Sixty-eight leaders of the former military government were put on trial in April 1996 on charges that included genocide and crimes against humanity.

Since Eritrea's independence, Eritrea and Ethiopia had disagreed about the exact demarcation of their borders, and in May 1998 Eritrea initiated border clashes that developed into a full-scale war that left more than 80,000 dead and further destroyed both countries' ailing economies. After a costly and bloody two-year war, a permanent cease-fire was reached in June 2000—Ethiopia had the upper hand when the fighting ceased—and a formal peace agreement was signed in Dec. 2000. The United Nations has provided more than four thousand peacekeeping forces to patrol the buffer zone between the two nations. An international commission defined a new border between the two countries in April 2002.

# Fiji

**REPUBLIC OF THE FIJI ISLANDS**

**President:** Ratu Josefa Iloilo (2000)
**Prime Minister:** Laisenia Qarase (2001)
**Area:** 7,054 sq mi (18,270 sq km)
**Population (2002 est.):** 856,346 (growth rate: 1.8%); birth rate: 23.2/1000; infant mortality rate: 13.7/1000; density per sq mi: 121
**Capital (1990 est.):** Suva (on Viti Levu), 200,000.
**Monetary unit:** Fiji dollar. **Languages:** Fijian, Hindustani, English (official). **Ethnicity/race:** Fijian 49%, Indian 46%, European, other Pacific Islanders, overseas Chinese, and other 5%. **Religions:** Christian 52%, Hindu 38%, Islam 8%, other 2%. **Literacy rate:** 79% (1976)
**Economic summary: GDP/PPP** (1999 est.): $5.9 billion; per capita $7,300. **Real growth rate:** –8%. **Inflation:** 0%. **Unemployment:** 6% (1997 est.). **Arable land:** 10%. **Agriculture:** sugarcane, coconuts, cassava (tapioca), rice, sweet potatoes, bananas; cattle, pigs, horses, goats; fish. **Labor force:** 235,000; subsistence agriculture 67%, wage earners 18%, salary earners 15% (1987). **Industries:** tourism, sugar, clothing, copra, gold, silver, lumber, small cottage industries. **Natural resources:** timber, fish, gold, copper, offshore oil potential, hydropower. **Exports:** $537 million (f.o.b., 1999): sugar, garments, gold, timber, fish. **Imports:** $653 million (f.o.b., 1999): manufactured goods, machinery and transport equipment, petroleum products, food, chemicals. **Major trading partners:** Australia, U.S., UK, other Pacific island countries, New Zealand, Japan, Taiwan.

**Geography** Fiji consists of 332 islands in the southwest Pacific Ocean about 1,960 mi (3,152 km) from Sydney, Australia. About 110 of these islands are inhabited. The two largest are Viti Levu (4,109 sq mi; 10,642 sq km) and Vanua Levu (2,242 sq mi; 5,807 sq km).

**Government** Republic until May 2000, when coup installed interim military dictatorship.

**History** Fiji, which had been inhabited since the second millennium B.C., was explored by the Dutch and the British in the 17th and 18th centuries. In 1874, an offer of cession by the Fijian chiefs was accepted, and Fiji was proclaimed a possession and dependency of the British Crown. In the 1880s large-scale cultivation of sugarcane began. Over the next 40 years, more than 60,000 indentured laborers from India were brought to the island to work the plantations. By 1920, all indentured servitude had ended. Racial conflict between Indians and the indigenous Fijians has been central to the small island's history.

Fiji became independent on Oct. 10, 1970. In Oct. 1987, Brig. Gen. Sitiveni Rabuka staged a coup to prevent an Indian-dominated coalition party from taking power. The military coup caused an exodus of thousands of Fijians of Indian origin who suffered ethnic discrimination at the hands of the government.

A new constitution, which took effect in July 1998, provided for a multiracial cabinet and raised the prospect of a coalition government. The previous constitution had guaranteed dominance to ethnic Fijians. In 1999, Fiji's first ethnic Indian prime minister, Mahendra Chaudhry, took office.

Continuing ethnic tensions, partly fueled by economic problems, plunged Fiji into a national nightmare in 2000. On May 19, a group of armed soldiers entered the Parliament and took three dozen people hostage, including the country's ethnic Indian prime minister. George Speight, a part-Fijian businessman, led the insurrection, and demanded that the 1997 constitution be rewritten to allow dominance of ethnic Fijians. The standoff lasted two months. In July 2000, Speight and other coup leaders were taken into custody and charged with treason.

But when the attempted coup ended, deposed prime minister Chaudry and his democratically elected government were not restored to power. Instead, the military and the Great Council of Chiefs, a group of 50 traditional Fijian leaders, appointed an interim government dominated by ethnic Fijians. Elections were held in Aug.-Sept. 2001, but no party achieved a majority. Interim prime minister Laisenia Qarase's Fijian United Party won 31 of 71 seats, and Qarase was sworn in as prime minister in September. His cabinet consists entirely of ethnic Fijians, but a court ruled in 2002 that ethnic Indians must be included. In Feb. 2002, Speight was sentenced to death, but Qarase commuted his sentence.

# Finland

### REPUBLIC OF FINLAND

**National name:** Suomen Tasavalta—Republiken Finland
**President:** Tarja Halonen (2000)
**Prime Minister:** Paavo Lipponen (1995)
**Area:** 130,127 sq mi (337,030 sq km)
**Population (2002 est.):** 5,183,545 (growth rate: 0.1%); birth rate: 10.6/1000; infant mortality rate: 3.8/1000; density per sq mi: 40
**Capital and largest city (1995 est.):** Helsinki, 515,765.
**Other large cities (1995 est.):** Espoo, 186,507; Tampere, 179,251; Vantaa, 164,376; Turku, 162,370.
**Monetary units:** Euro (formerly markka). **Languages:** Finnish, Swedish (both official); small Sami- (Lapp) and Russian-speaking minorities. **Ethnicity/race:** Finn 93%, Swede 6%, Sami (Lapp) 0.11%, Romany (Gypsy) 0.12%, Tatar 0.02%. **Religions:** Evangelical Lutheran 90%, Greek Orthodox 1.2%, none 9%, other 1%. **Literacy rate:** 100% (1980)
**Economic summary: GDP/PPP** (2000 est.): $118.3 billion; per capita $22,900. **Real growth rate:** 5.6%. **Inflation:** 3.4%. **Unemployment:** 9.8%. **Arable land:** 8%. **Agriculture:** cereals, sugar beets, potatoes, dairy cattle; fish. **Labor force:** 2.6 million; public services 32%, industry 22%, commerce 14%, finance, insurance, and business services 10%, agriculture and forestry 8%, transport and communications 8%, construction 6%. **Industries:** metal products, shipbuilding, pulp and paper, copper refining, foodstuffs, chemicals, textiles, clothing. **Natural resources:** timber, copper, zinc, iron ore, silver. **Exports:** $44.4 billion (f.o.b., 2000): machinery and equipment, chemicals, metals; timber, paper, pulp. **Imports:** $32.7 billion (f.o.b., 2000): foodstuffs, petroleum and petroleum products, chemicals, transport equipment, iron and steel, machinery, textile yarn and fabrics, grains. **Major trading partners:** EU, U.S., Russia, Japan.

**Geography** Finland is three times the size of Ohio. It is heavily forested and contains thousands of lakes, numerous rivers, and extensive areas of marshland. Except for a small highland region in the extreme northwest, the country is a lowland less than 600 ft (180 m) above sea level. Off the southwest coast are the Swedish-populated Åland Islands (581 sq mi; 1,505 sq km), which have had an autonomous status since 1921.

**Government** Republic.

**History** The first inhabitants of Finland were the Sami (Lapp) people. When Finnish speakers migrated to Finland in the first millennium B.C., the Sami were forced to move northward to the arctic regions, with which they are traditionally associated. The Finns' repeated raids on the Scandinavian coast impelled Eric IX, the Swedish king, to conquer the country in 1157. It was made a part of the Swedish kingdom and converted to Christianity.

By 1809 the whole of Finland was conquered by Alexander I of Russia, who set up Finland as a grand duchy. The period of Russification (1809–1914) sapped Finnish political power and made Russian the country's official language. When Russia became engulfed by the March Revolution of 1917, Finland seized the opportunity to declare independence on Dec. 6, 1917.

The USSR attacked Finland on Nov. 30, 1939, after Finland refused to give into Soviet territorial demands. The Finns staged a strong defense for three months before capitulating. They were forced to cede the Soviets 16,000 sq mi (41,440 sq km). Under German pressure, the Finns joined the Nazis against Russia in 1941, but were defeated again and forced to cede the Petsamo area to the USSR. In 1948, a treaty of friendship and mutual assistance was signed by the two nations. Finland continued to pursue a foreign policy of nonalignment throughout the cold war era.

Running on a platform to revitalize the economy, Ahtisaari, a Social Democrat, won the country's first direct presidential election in a runoff in Feb. 1994. Previously, presidents had been chosen by electors. Finland became a member of the European Union in Jan. 1995. Showing concern over NATO expansion eastward, Russian president Yeltsin in March 1997 iterated his view that Finnish membership in the military alliance was unacceptable. On Jan. 1, 1999, Finland, along with ten other European countries, adopted the euro as its currency. In 2000, Tarja Halonen, who had been Finland's foreign minister, became its first woman president.

In 2000, 2001, and 2002, Finland was judged to be the world's least corrupt country, according to the annual corruption survey by the Berlin-based organization Transparency International.

# France

### FRENCH REPUBLIC

**National name:** République Française
**President:** Jacques Chirac (1995)
**Prime Minister:** Jean-Pierre Raffarin (2002)
**Area:** 211,208 sq mi (547,030 sq km)
**Population (2002 est.):** 59,765,983 (growth rate: 0.3%); birth rate: 11.9/1000; infant mortality rate: 4.4/1000; density per sq mi: 283
**Capital and largest city (2000 est.):** Paris, 10,150,000 (metro. area). **Other large cities:** Marseille, 801,000; Lyon, 415,000; Toulouse, 359,000; Nice, 342,000; Strasbourg, 252,000; Nantes, 245,000; Bordeaux, 201,000. **Monetary units:** Euro (formerly French franc). **Languages:** French, declining regional dialects (Provençal, Breton, Alsatian, Corsican). **Ethnicity/**

**race:** Celtic and Latin with Teutonic, Slavic, North African, Southeast Asian, and Basque minorities. **Religions:** Roman Catholic 81%, Protestant 1.7%, Muslim 6.9%, Jewish 1.3%. **Literacy rate:** 99% (1980) **Economic summary: GDP/PPP** (2000 est.): $1.448 trillion; per capita $24,400. **Real growth rate:** 3.1%. **Inflation:** 1.7%. **Unemployment:** 9.7%. **Arable land:** 33%. **Agriculture:** wheat, cereals, sugar beets, potatoes, wine grapes; beef, dairy products; fish. **Labor force:** 25 million (2000); services 71%, industry 25%, agriculture 4% (1997). **Industries:** machinery, chemicals, automobiles, metallurgy, aircraft, electronics; textiles, food processing; tourism. **Natural resources:** coal, iron ore, bauxite, zinc, potash, timber, fish. **Exports:** $325 billion (f.o.b., 2000 est.): machinery and transportation equipment, aircraft, plastics, chemicals, pharmaceutical products, iron and steel, beverages. **Imports:** $320 billion (f.o.b., 2000 est.): machinery and equipment, vehicles, crude oil, aircraft, plastics, chemicals. **Major trading partners:** EU, U.S.

**Geography** France is about 80% the size of Texas. In the Alps near the Italian and Swiss borders is western Europe's highest point—Mont Blanc (15,781 ft; 4,810 m). The forest-covered Vosges Mountains are in the northeast, and the Pyrénées are along the Spanish border. Except for extreme northern France, the country may be described as four river basins and a plateau. Three of the streams flow west—the Seine into the English Channel, the Loire into the Atlantic, and the Garonne into the Bay of Biscay. The Rhône flows south into the Mediterranean. For about 100 mi (161 km), the Rhine is France's eastern border. In the Mediterranean, about 115 mi (185 km) east-southeast of Nice, is the island of Corsica (3,367 sq mi; 8,721 sq km).

**Government** Fifth republic.

**History** Archeological excavations indicate that France has been continuously settled since Paleolithic times. The Celts, who were later called *Gauls* by the Romans, migrated from the Rhine valley into what is now France. In about 600 B.C. Greeks and Phoenicians established settlements along the Mediterranean, most notably at Marseille. Julius Caesar conquered part of Gaul in 57–52 B.C., and it remained Roman until Franks invaded in the 5th century A.D.

The Treaty of Verdun (843) divided the territories corresponding roughly to France, Germany, and Italy among the three grandsons of Charlemagne. Charles the Bald inherited *Francia Occidentalis,* which became an increasingly feudalized kingdom. By 987, the crown passed to Hugh Capet, a princeling who controlled only the Ile-de-France, the region surrounding Paris. For 350 years, an unbroken Capetian line added to its domain and consolidated royal authority until the accession in 1328 of Philip VI, first of the Valois line. France was then the most powerful nation in Europe, with a population of 15 million.

The missing pieces in Philip Valois's domain were the French provinces still held by the Plantagenet kings of England, who also claimed the French crown. Beginning in 1338, the Hundred Years' War eventually settled the contest. After France's victory in the final battle, Castillon (1453), the Valois were the ruling family, and the English had no French possessions left except Calais. Once Burgundy and Brittany were added, the Valois dynasty's holdings resembled modern France. Protestantism spread throughout France in the 16th century and led to civil wars. Henry IV, of the Bourbon dynasty, issued the Edict of Nantes (1598), granting religious tolerance to the Huguenots (French Protestants). Absolute monarchy reached its apogee in the reign of Louis XIV (1643–1715), the Sun King, whose brilliant court was the center of the Western world.

After a series of costly foreign wars that weakened the government, the French Revolution plunged France into a bloodbath beginning in 1789 with the establishment of the First Republic and ending with a new authoritarianism under Napoléon Bonaparte, who had successfully defended the infant republic from foreign attack and then made himself first consul in 1799 and emperor in 1804. The Congress of Vienna (1815) sought to restore the pre-Napoléonic order in the person of Louis XVIII, but industrialization and the middle class, both fostered under Napoléon, built pressure for change, and a revolution in 1848 drove Louis Philippe, last of the Bourbons, into exile. Prince Louis Napoléon, a nephew of Napoléon I, declared the Second Empire in 1852 and took the throne as Napoléon III. His opposition to the rising power of Prussia ignited the Franco-Prussian War (1870–1871), which ended in his defeat, his abdication, and the creation of the Third Republic.

A new France emerged from World War I as the continent's dominant power. But four years of hostile occupation had reduced northeast France to ruins. Beginning in 1919, French foreign policy aimed at keeping Germany weak through a system of alliances, but it failed to halt the rise of Adolf Hitler and the Nazi war machine. On May 10, 1940, Nazi troops attacked, and, as they approached Paris, Italy joined with Germany. The Germans marched into an undefended Paris and Marshal Henri Philippe Pétain signed an armistice on June 22. France was split into an occupied north and an unoccupied south, Vichy France, the latter becoming a totalitarian German puppet state with Pétain as its chief. Allied armies liberated France in Aug. 1944, and a provisional government in Paris headed by Gen. Charles de Gaulle was established. The Fourth Republic was born on Dec. 24, 1946. The empire became the French Union; the National Assembly was strengthened and the presidency weakened; and France joined NATO. A war against Communist insurgents in French Indochina, now Vietnam, was abandoned after the defeat of French forces at Dien Bien Phu in 1954. A new rebellion in Algeria threatened a military coup, and on June 1, 1958, the Assembly invited de Gaulle to return as premier with extraordinary powers. He drafted a new constitution for a Fifth Republic, adopted on Sept. 28, which strengthened the presidency and reduced legislative power. He was elected president on Dec. 21, 1958.

France next turned its attention to decolonization in Africa; the French protectorates of Morocco and Tunisia had received independence in 1956. French West Africa was partitioned and the new nations were granted independence in 1960. Algeria, after a long civil war, finally became independent in 1962. Relations with most of the former colonies remained amicable. De Gaulle took France out of the NATO military command in 1967 and expelled all foreign-controlled troops from the country. De Gaulle's government was weakened by massive protests in May 1968 when student rallies became violent and millions of factory workers engaged in wildcat strikes across France. After normalcy was reestablished in 1969, de Gaulle's successor, Georges Pompidou, modified Gaullist policies to include a classical laissez-faire attitude toward domestic economic affairs. The conservative, pro-business climate contributed to the election of Valéry Giscard d'Estaing as president in 1974.

Socialist François Mitterrand attained a stunning victory in the May 10, 1981, presidential election.

## Rulers of France

| Name | Born | Ruled[1] | Name | Born | Ruled[1] |
|------|------|---------|------|------|---------|
| **Carolingian Dynasty** | | | Louis XV the Well-Beloved | 1710 | 1715–1774 |
| Pepin the Short | c. 714 | 751–768 | Louis XVI | 1754 | 1774–1792[13] |
| Charlemagne[2] | 742 | 768–814 | Louis XVII (Louis Charles de | 1785 | 1793–1795 |
| Louis I the Pious[3] | 778 | 814–840 | France)[14] | | |
| Charles I the Bald[4] | 823 | 840–877 | **First Republic** | | |
| Louis II the Stammerer | 846 | 877–879 | National Convention | — | 1792–1795 |
| Louis III[5] | c. 863 | 879–882 | Directory (Directoire) | — | 1795–1799 |
| Carloman[5] | ? | 879–884 | **Consulate** | | |
| Charles II the Fat[6] | 839 | 884–887[7] | Napoléon Bonaparte[15] | 1769 | 1799–1804 |
| Eudes (Odo), count of Paris | ? | 888–898 | **First Empire** | | |
| Charles III the Simple[8] | 879 | 893–923[9] | Napoléon I | 1769 | 1804–1815[16] |
| Robert I[10] | c. 865 | 922–923 | **Restoration of House of Bourbon** | | |
| Rudolf (Raoul), duke of Burgundy | ? | 923–936 | Louis XVIII le Désiré | 1755 | 1814–1824 |
| Louis IV d'Outremer | c. 921 | 936–954 | Charles X | 1757 | 1824–1830[17] |
| Lothair | 941 | 954–986 | **Bourbon-Orleans Line** | | |
| Louis V the Sluggard | c. 967 | 986–987 | Louis Philippe ("Citizen King") | 1773 | 1830–1848[18] |
| **Capetian Dynasty** | | | **Second Republic** | | |
| Hugh Capet | c. 940 | 987–996 | Louis Napoléon[19] | 1808 | 1848–1852 |
| Robert II the Pious[11] | c. 970 | 996–1031 | **Second Empire** | | |
| Henry I | 1008 | 1031–1060 | Napoléon III (Louis Napoléon) | 1808 | 1852–1870[20] |
| Philip I | 1052 | 1060–1108 | **Third Republic (Presidents)** | | |
| Louis VI the Fat | 1081 | 1108–1137 | Louis Adolphe Thiers | 1797 | 1871–1873 |
| Louis VII the Young | c.1121 | 1137–1180 | Marie E. P. M. de MacMahon | 1808 | 1873–1879 |
| Philip II (Philip Augustus) | 1165 | 1180–1223 | François P. J. Grévy | 1807 | 1879–1887 |
| Louis VIII the Lion | 1187 | 1223–1226 | Sadi Carnot | 1837 | 1887–1894 |
| Louis IX (St. Louis) | 1214 | 1226–1270 | Jean Casimir-Périer | 1847 | 1894–1895 |
| Philip III the Bold | 1245 | 1270–1285 | François Félix Faure | 1841 | 1895–1899 |
| Philip IV the Fair | 1268 | 1285–1314 | Émile Loubet | 1838 | 1899–1906 |
| Louis X the Quarreler | 1289 | 1314–1316 | Clement Armand Fallières | 1841 | 1906–1913 |
| John I[12] | 1316 | 1316 | Raymond Poincaré | 1860 | 1913–1920 |
| Philip V the Tall | 1294 | 1316–1322 | Paul E. L. Deschanel | 1856 | 1920–1920 |
| Charles IV the Fair | 1294 | 1322–1328 | Alexandre Millerand | 1859 | 1920–1924 |
| **House of Valois** | | | Gaston Doumergue | 1863 | 1924–1931 |
| Philip VI | 1293 | 1328–1350 | Paul Doumer | 1857 | 1931–1932 |
| John II the Good | 1319 | 1350–1364 | Albert Lebrun | 1871 | 1932–1940 |
| Charles V the Wise | 1337 | 1364–1380 | **Vichy Government (Chief of State)** | | |
| Charles VI the Well-Beloved | 1368 | 1380–1422 | Henri Philippe Pétain | 1856 | 1940–1944 |
| Charles VII | 1403 | 1422–1461 | **Provisional Government (Presidents)** | | |
| Louis XI | 1423 | 1461–1483 | Charles de Gaulle | 1890 | 1944–1946 |
| Charles VIII | 1470 | 1483–1498 | Félix Gouin | 1884 | 1946–1946 |
| Louis XII the Father of the People | 1462 | 1498–1515 | Georges Bidault | 1899 | 1946–1947 |
| Francis I | 1494 | 1515–1547 | **Fourth Republic (Presidents)** | | |
| Henry II | 1519 | 1547–1559 | Vincent Auriol | 1884 | 1947–1954 |
| Francis II | 1544 | 1559–1560 | René Coty | 1882 | 1954–1959 |
| Charles IX | 1550 | 1560–1574 | **Fifth Republic (Presidents)** | | |
| Henry III | 1551 | 1574–1589 | Charles de Gaulle | 1890 | 1959–1969 |
| **House of Bourbon** | | | Georges Pompidou | 1911 | 1969–1974 |
| Henry IV of Navarre | 1553 | 1589–1610 | Valéry Giscard d'Estaing | 1926 | 1974–1981 |
| Louis XIII | 1601 | 1610–1643 | François Mitterrand | 1916 | 1981–1995 |
| Louis XIV the Great | 1638 | 1643–1715 | Jacques Chirac | 1932 | 1995– |

1. For those and important through the first reign, year of end of rule is also that of death. Unless otherwise indicated. 2. Crowned Emperor of the West in 800. His brother, Carloman, ruled as king of the Eastern Franks from 768 until his death in 771. 3. Holy Roman Emperor, 814–840. 4. Holy Roman Emperor, 875–877 as Charles II. 5. Ruled jointly, 879–882. 6. Holy Roman Emperor, 881–887, as Charles III. 7. Died 888. 8. King, 893–898, in opposition to Eudes. 9. Died 929. 10. Not counted in regular line of kings of France by some authorities. Elected by nobles but killed in Battle of Soissons. 11. Sometimes called Robert I. 12. Posthumous son of Louis X; lived for only five days. 13. Executed 1793. 14. Titular king only. He died in prison according to official reports, but many pretenders appeared during the Bourbon restoration. 15. As first consul, Napoléon held the power of government. In 1804, he became emperor. 16. Abdicated first time, June 1814. Reentered Paris, March 1815, after escape from Elba; Louis XVIII fled to Ghent. Abdicated second time, June 1815. He named as his successor his son, Napoléon II, who was not acceptable to the Allies. He died 1821. 17. Died 1836. 18. Died 1850. 19. President; became emperor in 1852. 20. Died 1873.

The victors immediately moved to carry out campaign pledges to nationalize major industries, halt nuclear testing, suspend nuclear power plant construction, and impose new taxes on the rich. The Socialists' policies during Mitterrand's first two years created a 12% inflation rate, a huge trade deficit, and devaluations of the franc. In March 1986, a center-right coalition led by Jacques Chirac won a slim majority in legislative elections. Chirac became prime minister, initiating a period of "cohabitation" between him and the Socialist president, Mitterrand. Mitterrand's decisive reelection in 1988 led to Chirac being replaced as premier by Michel Rocard, a Socialist. Relations, however, cooled with Rocard, and in May

1991 he was replaced with Edith Cresson, France's first female prime minister and, like Mitterrand, a Socialist. But Cresson's unpopularity forced Mitterrand to replace Cresson with a more well-liked Socialist, Pierre Bérégovoy, who eventually was embroiled in a scandal and committed suicide. Mitterrand did succeed in helping draft the Maastricht Treaty and, after winning a slim victory in a referendum, confirming close economic and security ties between France and the European Union (EU).

On his third try Chirac won the presidency in May 1995, campaigning vigorously on a platform to reduce unemployment. Elections for the National Assembly in 1997 gave the Socialist coalition a majority. Shortly after becoming president, Chirac resumed France's nuclear testing in the South Pacific, despite widespread international protests as well as rioting in the countries affected by it. Socialist leader Lionel Jospin became prime minister in 1997. In the spring of 1999, the country took part in the NATO airstrikes in Kosovo, despite some internal opposition.

In the fall of 1999, Britain and France argued heatedly about France's refusal to allow the importation of British beef. France remained leery of the possibility of infection from bovine spongiform encephalopathy (BSE), commonly known as mad cow disease, despite the fact that the EU had lifted the three-year ban on British beef in Aug. 1999.

Jean-Marie Le Pen, leader of the right-wing, anti-immigrant National Front party, shocked France in April 2002 with his second-place finish in the first round of France's presidential election. He took 17% of the vote, eliminating Lionel Jospin, the Socialist prime minister, who tallied 16%. Jospin, stunned by the result, announced that he was retiring from politics and threw his support behind incumbent President Jacques Chirac, who led the group of 16 candidates with 20% of the vote. Jospin was replaced with center-right prime minister Jean-Pierre Raffarin. In the presidential election runoff Chirac won with an overwhelming 82.2% of the vote, and his center-right coalition won an absolute majority in Parliament. Le Pen's party did not win any seats. In July 2002, Chirac survived an assassination attempt by a right-wing extremist.

## Overseas Departments

Overseas Departments elect representatives to the National Assembly, and the same administrative organization as that of continental France applies to them.

### French Guiana (including Inini)
**Status:** Overseas Department
**Prefect:** Henri Masse (1999)
**Area:** 35,135 sq mi (91,000 sq km)
**Population (2002 est.):** 182,333 (growth rate: 1.7%); birth rate 21.7/1000; infant mortality rate 13.2/1000; density per sq mi: 5
**Capital and largest city (1995 est.):** Cayenne, 41,659. **Monetary unit:** Franc. **Language:** French. **Ethnicity/race:** black or mulatto 66%, white 12%, East Indian, Chinese, Amerindian 12%, other 10%. **Religion:** Roman Catholic. **Literacy rate:** 80% (1982)
**Economic summary: GDP/PPP** (1998 est.): $1 billion; per capita $6,000. **Real growth rate:** n.a. **Inflation:** 2.5% (1992). **Unemployment:** 21.4% (1998). **Arable land:** 0%. **Agriculture:** rice, manioc (tapioca), sugar, cocoa, vegetables, bananas; cattle, pigs, poultry. **Labor force:** 58,800 (1997); services, government, and commerce 60.6%, industry 21.2%, agriculture 18.2% (1980). **Industries:** construction, shrimp processing, forestry products, rum, gold mining.

**Natural resources:** bauxite, timber, gold (widely scattered), cinnabar, kaolin, fish. **Exports:** $155 million (f.o.b., 1997): shrimp, timber, gold, rum, rosewood essence, clothing. **Imports:** $625 million (c.i.f., 1997): food (grains, processed meat), machinery and transport equipment, fuels and chemicals. **Major trading partners:** France, Switzerland, U.S., Trinidad and Tobago.

French Guiana, lying north of Brazil and east of Suriname on the northeast coast of South America, was variously settled by the Spanish, Dutch, and French. The Treaty of Breda awarded France the territory in 1667. The French used it as a penal colony between 1852 and 1939, which included the infamous Devil's Island. In 1947 it became an overseas department of France. Since then, many indigenous French Guianians have called for increased autonomy, although only around 5% favor independence from France, partly due to the vast subsidies from the French government. The European Space Center at Kourou has brought a corner of French Guiana into the modern world and attracted a sizable expatriate workforce.

### Guadeloupe
**Status:** Overseas Department
**Prefect:** Dominique Vian (2002)
**Area:** 687 sq mi (1,780 sq km)
**Population (2002 est.):** 435,739 (growth rate: 1.1%); birth rate: 16.5/1000; infant mortality rate: 9.3/1000; density per sq mi: 634
**Capital (1990):** Basse-Terre, 14,000. **Largest city (1990):** Pointe-à-Pitre, over 26,029. **Monetary unit:** Franc. **Languages:** French, Creole patois. **Ethnicity/race:** black or mulatto 90%, white 5%, East Indian, Lebanese, Chinese less than 5%. **Religion:** Roman Catholic. **Literacy rate:** 91% (1982)
**Economic summary: GDP/PPP** (1996 est.): $3.7 billion; per capita $9,000. **Real growth rate:** n.a. **Inflation:** n.a. **Unemployment:** 27.8% (1998). **Arable land:** 14%. **Agriculture:** bananas, sugarcane, tropical fruits and vegetables; cattle, pigs, goats. **Labor force:** 125,900 (1997). **Industries:** construction, cement, rum, sugar, tourism. **Natural resources:** cultivable land, beaches and climate that foster tourism. **Exports:** $140 million (f.o.b., 1997): bananas, sugar, rum. **Imports:** $1.7 billion (c.i.f., 1997): foodstuffs, fuels, vehicles, clothing and other consumer goods, construction materials. **Major trading partners:** France, Martinique, U.S., Germany, Japan, Netherlands Antilles.

Guadeloupe, in the West Indies about 300 mi (483 km) southeast of Puerto Rico, was explored by Columbus in 1493. It consists of the twin islands of Basse-Terre and Grande-Terre and five dependencies—Marie-Galante, Les Saintes, La Désirade, St. Barthélemy, and the northern three-fifths of St. Martin. The volcano Soufrière (4,813 ft; 1,467 m), also called La Grande Soufrière, is the highest point on Guadeloupe. Violent activity in 1976 and 1977 caused thousands to flee their homes.

French colonization began in 1635, and in 1674 Guadeloupe became part of the domain of France. In 1946, it became an overseas department of France.

### Martinique
**Status:** Overseas Department
**Prefect:** Michel Cadot (2000)
**Area:** 425 sq mi (1,100 sq km)
**Population (2002 est.):** 422,277 (growth rate: 0.9%); birth rate: 15.4/1000; infant mortality rate: 7.6/1000; density per sq mi: 994

**Capital and largest city (1990):** Fort-de-France, 100,072. **Other cities (1990):** Le Lamentin, 30,026; Schoelcher, 19,683; Sainte-Marie, 19,683. **Monetary unit:** Franc. **Languages:** French, Creole patois. **Ethnicity/race:** African and African-white-Indian mixture 90%, white 5%, East Indian, Lebanese, Chinese less than 5%. **Religion:** Roman Catholic. **Literacy rate:** 100% (1983)
**Economic summary: GDP/PPP** (1997 est.): $4.39 billion; per capita $11,000. **Real growth rate:** n.a. **Inflation:** 3.9% (1990). **Unemployment:** 27.2% (1998). **Arable land:** 8%. **Agriculture:** pineapples, avocados, bananas, flowers, vegetables, sugarcane. **Labor force:** 170,000 (1997); agriculture 10%, industry 17%, services 73% (1997). **Industries:** construction, rum, cement, oil refining, sugar, tourism. **Natural resources:** coastal scenery and beaches, cultivable land. **Exports:** $250 million (f.o.b., 1997): refined petroleum products, bananas, rum, pineapples. **Imports:** $2 billion (c.i.f., 1997): petroleum products, crude oil, foodstuffs, construction materials, vehicles, clothing and other consumer goods. **Major trading partners:** France, Guadeloupe, Venezuela, Germany, Italy, U.S.

Martinique, a mountainous island lying in the Lesser Antilles about 300 mi (483 km) northeast of Venezuela, was probably explored by Columbus in 1502 and was taken for France in 1635. Martinique became a domain of the French crown in 1674. It became an overseas department of France in 1946.

## Réunion

**Status:** Overseas Department
**Prefect:** Jean Doubigny (1998)
**Area:** 970 sq mi (2,512 sq km)
**Population (2002 est.):** 743,981 (growth rate: 1.5%); birth rate: 20.7/1000; infant mortality rate: 8.3/1000; density per sq mi: 767
**Capital and largest city (1993):** Saint-Denis, 121,999 **Other cities (est. 1993):** Saint-Paul, 71,667; Saint-Pierre, 58,846; Le Tampon, 47,598. **Monetary unit:** Franc. **Languages:** French, Creole. **Ethnicity/ race:** French, African, Malagasy, Chinese, Pakistani, Indian. **Religion:** Roman Catholic 70%. **Literacy rate:** 70% (1982)
**Economic summary: GDP/PPP** (1998 est.): $3.4 billion; per capita $4,800. **Real growth rate:** 3.8%. **Inflation:** n.a. **Unemployment:** 42.8%. **Arable land:** 17%. **Agriculture:** sugarcane, vanilla, tobacco, tropical fruits, vegetables, corn. **Labor force:** 261,000 (1995); agriculture 8%, industry 19%, services 73% (1990). **Industries:** sugar, rum, cigarettes, handicraft items, flower oil extraction. **Natural resources:** fish, arable land, hydropower. **Exports:** $214.162 million (f.o.b., 1997): sugar, rum and molasses, perfume essences. Imports: $2.892 billion (c.i.f., 1997): manufactured goods, food, beverages, tobacco, machinery and transportation equipment, raw materials, and petroleum products. Major trading partners. France, Japan, Comoros, Bahrain, Germany, Italy.

Of volcanic origin, Réunion consists mostly of rugged mountains and short torrential rivers. It is located about 450 mi (724 km) east of Madagascar, in the Indian Ocean. First explored by Portuguese navigators in the 16th century, the island of Réunion, then uninhabited, was taken as a French possession in 1642. African slaves were imported first to work coffee and then sugar plantations; with the abolition of slavery in 1848, indentured laborers from Indochina, India, and East Africa were brought in. In 1947, Réunion became an overseas department of France.

## Overseas Territories

Overseas Territories are comparable to Departments except that their administrative organization includes a locally elected government.

## French Polynesia

**Status:** Overseas Territory
**High Commissioner:** Jean Aribaud (1999)
**Area:** 1,609 sq mi (4,167 sq km)
**Population (2002 est.):** 257,847 (growth rate: 1.4%); birth rate: 18.2/1000; infant mortality rate: 8.9/1000; density per sq mi: 160
**Capital (1988):** Papeete (on Tahiti), 23,555. **Monetary unit:** Pacific financial community franc. **Language:** French. **Ethnicity/race:** Polynesian 78%, Chinese 12%, local French 6%, metropolitan French 4%. **Religions:** Protestant 55%, Roman Catholic 30%, other 16%. **Literacy rate:** 98% (1977)
**Economic summary: GDP/PPP** (1997 est.): $2.6 billion; per capita $10,800. **Real growth rate:** 2.5%. **Inflation:** 1.5% (1994). **Unemployment:** 15% (1992 est.). **Arable land:** 1%. **Agriculture:** coconuts, vanilla, vegetables, fruits; poultry, beef, dairy products. **Labor force:** 70,000 (1996); agriculture 13%, industry 19%, services 68% (1997). **Industries:** tourism, pearls, agricultural processing, handicrafts. **Natural resources:** timber, fish, cobalt, hydropower. **Exports:** $205 million (f.o.b., 1999): cultured pearls, coconut products, mother-of-pearl, vanilla, shark meat (1997). **Imports:** $749 million (f.o.b., 1999): fuels, foodstuffs, equipment. **Major trading partners:** Japan, U.S., France, Australia.

The term *French Polynesia* is applied to the scattered French possessions in the South Pacific— Mangareva (Gambier), Makatea, the Marquesas Islands, Rapa, Rurutu, Rimatara, the Society Islands, the Tuamotu Archipelago, Tubuai, Raivavae, and the island of Clipperton—which were organized into a single colony in 1903. There are 120 islands, of which 25 are uninhabited. The principal and most populous island—Tahiti, in the Society group—was claimed by the French in 1768. The indigenous people are mostly Maoris.

The Pacific Nuclear Test Center on the atoll of Mururoa, 744 mi (1,200 km) from Tahiti, was completed in 1966. In 1975 worldwide opposition forced the French to move the testing underground on Fangataufa. To compensate the residents for the nuclear weapons tests in 1995–96, France offered a 10-year $194-million annual compensation package. An independence movement continues to flourish in French Polynesia.

## New Caledonia and Dependencies

**Status:** Overseas Territory
**President:** Pierre Frogier (2001)
**High Commissioner:** Thierry Lataste (1998)
**Area:** 7,360 sq mi (19,060 sq km)
**Population (2002 est.):** 207,858 (growth rate: 1.4%); birth rate: 19.9/1000; infant mortality rate: 8.2/1000; density per sq mi: 28
**Capital (1989):** Nouméa, 65,110. **Monetary unit:** Pacific financial community franc. **Languages:** French, Melanesian and Polynesian dialects. **Ethnicity/race:** Kanak (Melanesian) 42.5%, European 37.1%, Wallisian 8.4%, Polynesian 3.8%, Indonesian 3.6%, Vietnamese 1.6%, other 3%. **Religions:** Roman Catholic 60%, Protestant 30%. **Literacy rate:** 91% (1976)
**Economic summary: GDP/PPP** (1998 est.): $3 billion; per capita $15,000. **Real growth rate:** 3.5%. **Inflation:** 1.5%. **Unemployment:** 19% (1996). **Arable**

land: 0%. **Agriculture:** vegetables; beef, deer, other livestock products. **Labor force:** 79,395 (including 15,018 unemployed, 1996); agriculture 7%, industry 23%, services 70% (1999 est.). **Industries:** nickel mining and smelting. **Natural resources:** nickel, chrome, iron, cobalt, manganese, silver, gold, lead, copper. **Exports:** $411 million (f.o.b.; 1999): ferronickels, nickel ore, fish. **Imports:** $843 million (f.o.b., 1999): transport equipment, machinery and electrical equipment, fuels, minerals, wine, sugar, rice. **Major trading partners:** Japan, France, Taiwan, South Korea, Australia, Singapore, New Zealand, U.S.

New Caledonia (6,466 sq mi; 16,747 sq km), about 1,070 mi (1,722 km) northeast of Sydney, Australia, was explored by Capt. James Cook in 1774 and annexed by France in 1853. The government also administers the Isle of Pines, the Loyalty Islands (Uvéa, Lifu, and Maré), the Belep Islands, the Huon Island group, and Chesterfield Islands. The native people are Melanesians called the Kanak. In 1984, the French National Assembly passed a law that granted internal autonomy to New Caledonia. In 1998 the Nouméa Accords postponed discussions about independence for the territory until at least 2013.

## Southern and Antarctic Lands

**Status:** Overseas Territory
**Administrator:** François Garde (2000)
**Area:** 3,004 sq mi (7,781 sq km, excluding Adélie Land)
**Capital:** Port-au-Français

This territory is uninhabited except for the personnel of scientific bases. It consists of Adélie Land (166,752 sq mi; 431,888 sq km) on the Antarctic mainland (which the U.S. does not recognize) and the following islands in the southern Indian Ocean: the Kerguelen and Crozet archipelagos and the islands of Saint-Paul and New Amsterdam.

## Wallis and Futuna Islands

**Status:** Overseas Territory
**Administrator:** Christian Job (2002)
**Area:** 106 sq mi (274 sq km)
**Population (2002 est.):** 15,585 (growth rate n.a.); birth rate n.a./1000; infant mortality rate n.a./1000; density per sq mi: 147
**Capital (1983):** Mata-Utu. **Languages:** French, Wallisian. **Ethnicity/race:** Polynesian. **Religion:** Roman Catholic. **Literacy rate:** 50% (1969)
**Economic summary: GDP/PPP** (1997 est.): $30 million; per capita $2,000. **Real growth rate:** n.a. **Inflation:** n.a. **Unemployment:** n.a. **Arable land:** 5%. **Agriculture:** breadfruit, yams, taro, bananas; pigs, goats. **Labor force:** n.a.; agriculture, livestock, and fishing 80%, government 4% (est.). **Industries:** copra, handicrafts, fishing, lumber. **Natural resources:** negl. **Exports:** $250,000 (f.o.b., 1999): copra, chemicals, construction materials. **Imports:** $300,000 (f.o.b., 1999): chemicals, machinery, passenger ships, consumer goods. **Major trading partners:** Italy, Croatia, U.S., Denmark, France, Australia, New Zealand.

The two island groups in the South Pacific between Fiji and Samoa were settled by French missionaries at the beginning of the 19th century. A protectorate was established in the 1880s. There is a French-appointed high administrator, a 20-member Territorial Assembly, and a deputy and a senator to the French national Parliament. The three traditional Polynesian kings also help decide internal policy matters. Following a referendum by the Polynesian inhabitants, the status was changed to that of an Overseas Territory in 1961.

## Territorial Collectivities

The Territorial Collectivity status was created in 1976 for Mayotte; it was conceived as being midway between an Overseas Territory and an Overseas Department.

## Saint Pierre and Miquelon

**Status:** Territorial Collectivity
**Prefect:** Jean-François Tallec (2001)
**Area:** 93 sq mi (242 sq km)
**Population (2002 est.):** 6,954 (growth rate 0.8%); birth rate 15.0/1000; infant mortality rate 8.2/1000; density per sq mi: 74
**Capital (1990):** Saint Pierre, 5,683. **Ethnicity/race:** Basques and Bretons (French fishermen). **Literacy rate:** 99% (1982)
**Economic summary: GDP/PPP** (1996 est.): $74 million, supplemented by annual payments from France of about $60 million; per capita $11,000. **Real growth rate:** n.a. **Inflation:** 2.1% (1991–96 average). **Unemployment:** 9.8% (1997). **Arable land:** 13%. **Agriculture:** vegetables; poultry, cattle, sheep, pigs; fish. **Labor force:** 3,000 (1997); fishing 18%, industry (mainly fish processing) 41%, services 41% (1996 est.). **Industries:** fish processing and supply base for fishing fleets; tourism. **Natural resources:** fish, deepwater ports. **Exports:** $12 million (f.o.b., 1999): fish and fish products, soybeans, animal feed, mollusks and crustaceans, fox and mink pelts. **Imports:** $55 million (f.o.b., 1999): meat, clothing, fuel, electrical equipment, machinery, building materials. **Major trading partners:** U.S., Egypt, Japan, Colombia, France, Canada.

The sole remnant of the French colonial empire in North America, these islands were first occupied by the French in 1604. Their importance arises from their proximity to the Grand Banks, located 10 mi south of Newfoundland, making them the center of the French Atlantic cod fisheries.

## Mayotte

**Status:** Territorial Collectivity
**Prefect:** Pierre Bayle (1998)
**Area:** 144 sq mi (374 sq km)
**Population (2002 est.):** 170,879 (growth rate: 3.5%); birth rate 43.6/1000; infant mortality rate 67.8/1000; density per sq mi: 1,183
**Capital and largest city (1991):** Mamoudzou (Dzaoudzi), 20,450
**Economic summary: GDP/PPP** (1998 est.): $85 million; per capita $600. **Real growth rate:** n.a. **Inflation:** n.a. **Unemployment:** 45% (1997). **Arable land:** n.a. **Agriculture:** vanilla, ylang-ylang (perfume essence), coffee, copra. **Labor force:** n.a. **Industries:** newly created lobster and shrimp industry, construction. **Natural resources:** negl. **Exports:** $3.44 million (f.o.b., 1997): ylang-ylang (perfume essence), vanilla, copra, coconuts, coffee, cinnamon. **Imports:** $141.3 million (f.o.b., 1997): food, machinery and equipment, transportation equipment, metals, chemicals. **Major trading partners:** France, Comoros, Réunion, Africa, Southeast Asia.

France gained colonial control over Mayotte in 1843. It is the most populous of the four Comoros Islands in the Indian Ocean off Mozambique in Africa. Mayotte chose to remain a French dependency rather than join the other Comoran islands in declaring independence in 1975. Comoros laid claim to Mayotte shortly after independence and continues to do so. In July 2000, 70% of voters opted to accept greater autonomy but remain a part of France.

# Gabon

**GABONESE REPUBLIC**

**National name:** République Gabonaise
**President:** Omar Bongo (1967)
**Premier:** Jean-François Ntoutoume (1999)
**Area:** 103,346 sq mi (267,667 sq km)
**Population (2002 est.):** 1,233,353 (growth rate: 1.0%); birth rate: 27.2/1000; infant mortality rate: 93.5/1000; density per sq mi: 12
**Capital and largest city (1994):** Libreville, 419,596. **Other cities (1994):** Port-Gentil, 80,000; Franceville, 42,000. **Monetary unit:** CFA Franc. **Languages:** French (official), Fang, Myene, Bateke, Bapounou/Eschira, Bandjabi. **Ethnicity/race:** (1993) Bantu tribes, including six major tribal groupings: Fang 25%, Punu 23%, Nzeiby 13%, Mbede (Obamba/Bateke) 9%, Kota 7%, and Myene 5%; Pygmies 0.7%, naturalized population 0.3%, foreigners 15%. **Religions:** Catholic 75%, Protestant 20%, Animist 4%. **Literacy rate:** 61% (1990)
**Economic summary: GDP/PPP** (2000 est.): $7.7 billion; per capita $6,300. **Real growth rate:** 1.2%. **Inflation:** 1.5%. **Unemployment:** 21% (1997 est.). **Arable land:** 1%. **Agriculture:** cocoa, coffee, sugar, palm oil, rubber; cattle; okoume (a tropical softwood); fish. **Labor force:** 600,000; agriculture 60%, services and government 25%, industry and commerce 15%. **Industries:** food and beverage; textile; lumbering and plywood; cement; petroleum extraction and refining; manganese, uranium, and gold mining; chemicals; ship repair. **Natural resources:** petroleum, manganese, uranium, gold, timber, iron ore, hydropower. **Exports:** $3.4 billion (f.o.b., 2000 est.): crude oil 75%, timber, manganese, uranium (1998). **Imports:** $1 billion (f.o.b., 2000 est.): machinery and equipment, foodstuffs, chemicals, petroleum products, construction materials. **Major trading partners:** U.S., France, China, Japan, UK, Netherlands. **Member of French Community**

**Geography** This West African country with the Atlantic as its western border is also bounded by Equatorial Guinea, Cameroon, and the Congo. Its area is slightly less than Colorado's. Most of the country is covered by a dense tropical forest.

**Government** Republic.

**History** The earliest humans in Gabon were believed to be the Babinga, or Pygmies, dating back to 7000 B.C., who were later followed by Bantu groups from southern and eastern Africa. Now there are many tribal groups in the country, the largest being the Fang peoples, who constitute 25% of the population.

Gabon was first explored by the Portuguese navigator Diego Cam in the 15th century. In 1472, the Portuguese explorers encountered the mouth of the Como River, and named it "Rio de Gabao," river of Gabon, which later became the name of the country. The Dutch began arriving in 1593, and the French in 1630. In 1839, the French founded their first settlement on the left bank of the Gabon estuary and gradually occupied the hinterland during the second half of the 19th century. The land became a French territory in 1888, an autonomous republic within the French Union after World War II, and an independent republic on Aug. 17, 1960.

After his conversion to Islam in 1973, President Bongo changed his given name, Albert Bernard, to Omar. He has been reelected every five years since 1967. Strikes and riots led to a transitional constitution in May 1990 legalizing political parties and calling for free elections. In its first multiparty election in Dec. 1993, the incumbent president received just over 51%

of the vote, while the opposition candidate refused to accept defeat; he alleged fraud and tried to establish a rival government.

In Dec. 1998, President Bongo, who had ruled the country for 31 years, was elected for an additional seven. Gabon lacks roads, schools, and adequate health care, yet the oil-rich country has lined the pockets of its ruler, who, according to the French weekly *L'Autre Afrique*, is said to own more real estate in Paris than any other foreign leader. Despite his reputation for corruption and authoritarianism, however, Bongo has a strong national following.

# Gambia, The

**REPUBLIC OF THE GAMBIA**

**President:** Yahya Jammeh (1997)
**Area:** 4,363 sq mi (11,300 sq km)
**Population (2002 est.):** 1,455,842 (growth rate: 2.9%); birth rate: 41.2/1000; infant mortality rate: 76.4/1000; density per sq mi: 334
**Capital (1986):** Banjul, 44,188. **Monetary unit:** Dalasi. **Languages:** Native tongues, English (official). **Ethnicity/race:** African 99% (Mandinka 42%, Fula 18%, Wolof 16%, Jola 10%, Serahuli 9%, other 4%), non-Gambian 1%. **Religions:** Islam 90%, Christian 9%, traditional 1%. **Literacy rate:** 27% (1990)
**Economic summary: GDP/PPP** (2000 est.): $1.5 billion; per capita $1,100. **Real growth rate:** 4.9%. **Inflation:** 3.4%. **Unemployment:** n.a. **Arable land:** 18%. **Agriculture:** peanuts, millet, sorghum, rice, corn, sesame, cassava (tapioca), palm kernels; cattle, sheep, goats; forest and fishery resources not fully exploited. **Labor force:** 400,000; agriculture 75%, industry, commerce, and services 19%, government 6%. **Industries:** processing peanuts, fish, and hides; tourism; beverages; agricultural machinery assembly, woodworking, metalworking; clothing. **Natural resources:** fish. **Exports:** $125.8 million (f.o.b., 1999): peanuts and peanut products, fish, cotton lint, palm kernels. **Imports:** $202.5 million (f.o.b., 1999): foodstuffs, manufactures, fuel, machinery and transport equipment. **Major trading partners:** Benelux, Japan, UK, Spain, China, Netherlands, Brazil, Senegal. **Member of Commonwealth of Nations**

**Geography** Situated on the Atlantic coast in westernmost Africa and surrounded on three sides by Senegal, Gambia is twice the size of Delaware. The Gambia River flows for 200 mi (322 km) through Gambia on its way to the Atlantic. The country, the smallest on the continent, averages only 20 mi (32 km) in width.

**Government** Republic.

**History** Since the 13th century, the Wolof, Malinke, and Fulani peoples settled in what is now The Gambia. The Portuguese were the first European explorers, encountering the Gambia River in 1455, and in 1681 the French founded an enclave at Albredabut. During the 17th century, Gambia was settled by various companies of English merchants. Slavery was the chief source of revenue before it was abolished in 1807. Gambia became a Crown colony in 1843 and an independent nation within the Commonwealth of Nations on Feb. 18, 1965. Full independence was approved in a 1970 referendum, and on April 24 of that year Gambia proclaimed itself a republic.

Elections on April 29, 1992, returned President Jawara for a fifth term. His People's Progressive Party won 25 of the 36 seats in the House of Representatives. A military coup led by Capt. Yahya Jammeh deposed the president in July 1994, suspended the constitution, and banned existing political parties. Jammeh promised new elections, which were held in Sept. 1996, and he won 55% of the vote against his nearest rival, Ousseynou Darboe. In April 1997, he completed the promised return to civilian rule. Censorship of the press and other repressive measures continue to mar the country's transition to democracy.

Unrest plagued Gambia throughout much of 2000. In January Jammeh crushed a coup attempt staged by some of his own bodyguards, and in April violent student protests rocked the country. The peanut export system collapsed in the same year from mismanagement, leaving farmers unpaid and unable to sell a bumper crop of the country's main commodity. In 2001, Jammeh lifted the ban against various opposition parties he had outlawed after his 1994 coup. He was reelected in Oct. 2001 with 53% of the vote.

# Georgia

GEORGIA

**National Name:** Sakartvelo
**President:** Eduard Shevardnadze (1992)
**Minister of State:** Avtandil Jorbenadze (2001)
**Area:** 26,911 sq mi (69,700 sq km)
**Population (2002 est.):** 4,960,951 (growth rate: –0.3%); birth rate: 11.5/1000; infant mortality rate: 51.8/1000; density per sq mi: 184
**Capital and largest city (1991):** Tbilisi, 1,279,000.
**Other cities (1989):** Kutaisi, 235,000; Batoumi, 136,000; and Sokhumi, 121,000. **Monetary unit:** Lari.
**Languages:** Georgian (official), 71%; Russian, 9%; Armenian, 7%; Azerbaijani, 6%. **Ethnicity/race:** Georgian 70.1%, Armenian 8.1%, Russian 6.3%, Azeri 5.7%, Ossetian 3%, Abkhaz 1.8%, other 5%.
**Religions:** Georgian Orthodox 65%, Russian Orthodox 10%, Armenian Orthodox 8%, Muslim 11%.
**Literacy rate:** 99% (1989)
**Economic summary: GDP/PPP** (2000 est.): $22.8 billion; per capita $4,600. **Real growth rate:** 1.9%. **Inflation:** 4.1%. **Unemployment:** 14.9% (1999 est.). **Arable land:** 9%. **Agriculture:** citrus, grapes, tea, vegetables, potatoes; livestock. **Labor force:** 3.08 million (1997); industry 20%, agriculture 40%, services 40% (1999 est.). **Industries:** steel, aircraft, machine tools, electric locomotives, trucks, tractors, textiles, shoes, chemicals, wood products, wine. **Natural resources:** forests, hydropower, manganese deposits, iron ore, copper, minor coal and oil deposits; coastal climate and soils allow for important tea and citrus growth. **Exports:** $372 million (2000 est.): citrus fruits, tea, wine, other agricultural products; diverse types of machinery and metals; chemicals; fuel reexports; textiles. **Imports:** $898 million (2000 est.): fuel, grain and other foods, machinery and parts, transport equipment. **Major trading partners:** Russia, Turkey, Azerbaijan, Armenia, EU, U.S.

**Geography**   Georgia is bordered by the Black Sea in the west, by Turkey and Armenia in the south, by Azerbaijan in the east, and Russia in the north. The republic also includes the Abkhaz and Adzhar autonomous republics and the Yugo-Ossetian Autonomous Oblast. Mount Elbrus (Lalbuzi in Georgian) at 18,841 ft is the highest peak in Europe.

**Government**   Republic.

**History**   Georgia became a kingdom about 4 B.C. and Christianity was introduced in A.D. 337. During the reign of Queen Tamara (1184–1213), its territory included the whole of Transcaucasia. During the 13th century, Tamerlane and the Mongols decimated its population. From the 16th century on, the country was the scene of a struggle between Persia and Turkey. In

the 18th century it became a vassal to Russia in exchange for protection from the Turks and Persians.

Georgia joined Azerbaijan and Armenia in 1917 to establish the anti-Bolshevik Transcaucasian Federation, and upon its dissolution, proclaimed its independence in 1918. In 1922, Georgia, Armenia, and Azerbaijan were annexed by the USSR and formed the Transcaucasian Soviet Socialist Republic. In 1936, it became a separate Soviet republic. Under Soviet rule Georgia was transformed from an agrarian country to a largely industrial, urban society.

Georgia proclaimed its independence from the USSR on April 6, 1991. In Jan. 1992, its leader Zviad Gamsakhurdia was sacked and later accused of dictatorial policies, the jailing of opposition leaders, human rights abuses, and clamping down on the media. A ruling military council was established by the opposition until a civilian authority could be restored. In 1992, Eduard Shevardnadze, the Soviet Union's foreign minister under Gorbachev, became president.

In 1992–93, the government engaged in armed conflict with separatists in the breakaway province of Abkhazia. In 1994, Russia and Georgia signed a cooperation treaty that authorized Russia to keep three military bases in Georgia and allowed Russians to train and equip the Georgian army. In 1996, Georgia and its breakaway region of South Ossetia agreed to a cessation of hostilities in their six-year conflict. With little progress in resolving the Abkhazia situation, however, Parliament in April 1997 voted overwhelmingly to threaten Russia with loss of its military bases should it fail to extend Russian military control over the separatist region. In 1998, the U.S. and Britain began an operation to remove nuclear material from Georgia, dangerous remains from its Soviet years. A darling of the West since his days as the Soviet Union's foreign minister, Shevardnadze is viewed far less favorably by his own people, who are frustrated by unemployment, poverty, cronyism, and rampant corruption. In the 2000 presidential elections, Shevardnadze was reelected with 80% of the vote, though international observers have determined the election was marred by irregularities.

In 2002, U.S. troops trained Georgia's military in antiterrorism measures. The U.S. hopes that Georgian troops will subdue Muslim rebels fighting in the country, who are believed to be linked to al-Qaeda.

Tensions between Georgia and Russia have increased over the Pankisi Gorge, a lawless region of Georgia that Russia says has become a haven for Islamic militants and Chechen rebels.

# Germany

FEDERAL REPUBLIC OF GERMANY

**National name:** Bundesrepublik Deutschland
**President:** Johannes Rau (1999)
**Chancellor:** Gerhard Schröder (1998)
**Area:** 137,846 sq mi (357,021 sq km)
**Population (2002 est.):** 83,251,851 (growth rate: –0.1%); birth rate: 9.0/1000; infant mortality rate: 4.7/1000; density per sq mi: 604
**Capital and largest city (1995 est.):** Berlin (capital since Oct. 3, 1990), 3,471,418. **Other large cities (1997):** Hamburg, 1,703,800; Munich, 1,251,100; Cologne, 963,300; Frankfurt, 656,200; Essen, 619,600; Dortmund, 601,500; Stuttgart, 592,000; Düsseldorf, 573,100; Bremen, 551,000; Hanover, 526,400; Duisberg, 536,500. **Monetary units:** Euro (formerly Deutsche mark). **Language:** German.
**Ethnicity/race:** German 91.5%, Turkish 2.4%, Italians 0.7%, Greeks 0.4%, Poles 0.4%, other 4.6%.
**Religions:** Protestant 38%, Roman Catholic 34%,

Muslim 1.7%, Unaffiliated or other 26.3%. **Literacy rate:** 99% (1977)
**Economic summary GDP/PPP** (2000 est.): $1.936 trillion; per capita $23,400. **Real growth rate:** 3%. **Inflation:** 2%. **Unemployment:** 9.9%. **Arable land:** 33%. **Agriculture:** potatoes, wheat, barley, sugar beets, fruit, cabbages; cattle, pigs, poultry. **Labor force:** 40.5 million (1999 est.); industry 33.4%, agriculture 2.8%, services 63.8% (1999). **Industries:** among the world's largest and most technologically advanced producers of iron, steel, coal, cement, chemicals, machinery, vehicles, machine tools, electronics, food and beverages; shipbuilding; textiles. **Natural resources:** iron ore, coal, potash, timber, lignite, uranium, copper, natural gas, salt, nickel, arable land. **Exports:** $578 billion (f.o.b., 2000 est.): machinery, vehicles, chemicals, metals and manufactures, foodstuffs, textiles. **Imports:** $505 billion (f.o.b., 2000 est.): machinery, vehicles, chemicals, foodstuffs, textiles, metals. **Major trading partners:** EU, U.S., Japan.

**Geography** Located in central Europe, Germany is made up of the North German Plain, the Central German Uplands (Mittelgebirge), and the Southern German Highlands. The Bavarian plateau in the southwest averages 1,600 ft (488 m) above sea level, but it reaches 9,721 ft (2,962 m) in the Zugspitze Mountains, the highest point in the country. Germany's major rivers are the Danube, the Elbe, the Oder, the Weser, and the Rhine. Germany is about the size of Montana.

**Government** Federal republic.

**History** The Celts are believed to have been the first inhabitants of Germany. They were followed by German tribes at the end of the 2nd century B.C. German invasions destroyed the declining Roman Empire in the 4th and 5th centuries A.D. One of the tribes, the Franks, attained supremacy in western Europe under Charlemagne, who was crowned Holy Roman Emperor in 800. By the Treaty of Verdun (843), Charlemagne's lands east of the Rhine were ceded to the German Prince Louis. Additional territory acquired by the Treaty of Mersen (870) gave Germany approximately the area it maintained throughout the Middle Ages. For several centuries after Otto the Great was crowned king in 936, German rulers were also usually heads of the Holy Roman Empire.

By the 14th century, the Holy Roman Empire was little more than a loose federation of the German princes who elected the Holy Roman emperor. In 1438, Albert of Hapsburg became emperor, and for the next several centuries the Hapsburg line ruled the Holy Roman Empire until its decline in 1806. Relations between state and church were changed by the Reformation, which began with Martin Luther's 95 theses nailed to a door in 1517, when Luther scattered the forces of the Protestant League at Mühlberg. The Counter Reformation followed. A dispute over the succession to the Bohemian throne brought on the Thirty Years' War (1618–48), which devastated Germany and left the empire divided into hundreds of small principalities virtually independent of the emperor.

Meanwhile, Prussia was developing into a state of considerable strength. Frederick the Great (1740–86) reorganized the Prussian army and defeated Maria Theresa of Austria in a struggle over Silesia. After the defeat of Napoléon at Waterloo (1815), the struggle between Austria and Prussia for supremacy in Germany continued, reaching its climax in the defeat of Austria in the Seven Weeks' War (1866) and the formation of the Prussian-dominated North German Confederation (1867). The architect of this new German unity was Otto von Bismarck, a conservative, monarchist, and militaristic Prussian prime minister. He unified all of Germany in a series of three wars against Denmark (1864), Austria (1866), and France (1870–71). On Jan. 18, 1871, King Wilhelm I of Prussia was proclaimed German emperor in the Hall of Mirrors at Versailles. The North German Confederation, created in 1867, was abolished, and the Second German Reich, consisting of the North and South German states, was born. With a powerful army, an efficient bureaucracy, and a loyal bourgeoisie, Chancellor Bismarck consolidated a powerful centralized state.

Wilhelm II dismissed Bismarck in 1890 and embarked upon a "New Course," stressing an intensified colonialism and a powerful navy. His chaotic foreign policy culminated in the diplomatic isolation of Germany and the disastrous defeat in World War I (1914–18). The Second German Empire collapsed following the defeat of the German armies in 1918, the naval mutiny at Kiel, and the flight of the kaiser to the Netherlands. The Social Democrats, led by Friedrich Ebert and Philipp Scheidemann, crushed the Communists and established a moderate state, known as the Weimar Republic, with Ebert as president. President Ebert died on Feb. 28, 1925, and on April 26, Field Marshal Paul von Hindenburg was elected president. The mass of Germans regarded the Weimar Republic as a child of defeat, imposed upon a Germany whose legitimate aspirations to world leadership had been thwarted by a world conspiracy. Added to this were a crippling currency debacle, a tremendous burden of reparations, and acute economic distress.

Adolf Hitler, an Austrian war veteran and a fanatical nationalist, fanned discontent by promising a Greater Germany, abrogation of the Treaty of Versailles, restoration of Germany's lost colonies, and the destruction of the Jews, whom he scapegoated as the reason for Germany's downfall and depressed economy. When the Social Democrats and the Communists refused to combine against the Nazi threat, President von Hindenburg made Hitler the chancellor on Jan. 30, 1933. With the death of von Hindenburg on Aug. 2, 1934, Hitler repudiated the Treaty of Versailles and began full-scale rearmament. In 1935, he withdrew Germany from the League of Nations, and the next year he reoccupied the Rhineland and signed the Anti-Comintern pact with Japan, at the same time strengthening relations with Italy. Austria was annexed in March 1938. By the Munich agreement in Sept. 1938, he gained the Czech Sudetenland, and in violation of this agreement he completed the dismemberment of Czechoslovakia in March 1939. His invasion of Poland on Sept. 1, 1939, precipitated World War II.

Hitler established death camps to carry out "the final solution to the Jewish question." By the end of the war, Hitler's Holocaust had killed 6 million Jews, as well as Gypsies, homosexuals, Communists, the handicapped, and others not fitting the Aryan ideal. After some dazzling initial successes in 1939–42, Germany surrendered unconditionally to Allied and Soviet military commanders on May 8, 1945. On June 5 the four-nation Allied Control Council became the de facto government of Germany.

(For details of World War II and of the Holocaust, see Headline History, World War II.)

At the Berlin (or Potsdam) Conference (July 17–Aug. 2, 1945) President Truman, Premier Stalin, and Prime Minister Clement Attlee of Britain set forth the guiding principles of the Allied Control Council: Germany's complete disarmament and demilitarization, destruction of its war potential, rigid control of industry, and decentralization of the political and economic structure. Pending final determination of territorial questions at a peace conference, the three victors agreed to the ultimate transfer of the city of Königsberg (now Kaliningrad) and its adjacent area to the USSR and to the administration by Poland of former German territories lying generally east of the Oder-Neisse Line. For purposes of control, Germany was divided into four national occupation zones.

The Western powers were unable to agree with the USSR on any fundamental issues. Work of the Allied Control Council was hamstrung by repeated Soviet vetoes; and finally, on March 20, 1948, Russia walked out of the Council. Meanwhile, the U.S. and Britain had taken steps to merge their zones economically (Bizone); on May 31, 1948, the U.S., Britain, France, and the Benelux countries agreed to set up a German state comprising the three Western zones. The USSR reacted by clamping a blockade on all ground communications between the Western zones and West Berlin, an enclave in the Soviet zone. The Western Allies countered by organizing a gigantic airlift to fly supplies into the beleaguered city. The USSR was finally forced to lift the blockade on May 12, 1949.

The Federal Republic of Germany was proclaimed on May 23, 1949, with its capital at Bonn. In free elections, West German voters gave a majority in the Constituent Assembly to the Christian Democrats, with the Social Democrats largely making up the opposition. Konrad Adenauer became chancellor, and Theodor Heuss of the Free Democrats was elected first president.

The East German states adopted a more centralized constitution for the Democratic Republic of Germany, put into effect on Oct. 7, 1949. The USSR thereupon dissolved its occupation zone but Soviet troops remained. The Western Allies declared that the East German Republic was a Soviet creation undertaken without self-determination and refused to recognize it. Soviet forces created a state controlled by the secret police with a single party, the Socialist Unity (Communist) Party.

Agreements in Paris in 1954 giving the Federal Republic full independence and complete sovereignty came into force on May 5, 1955. Under the agreement, West Germany and Italy became members of the Brussels treaty organization created in 1948 and renamed the Western European Union. West Germany also became a member of NATO. In 1955, the USSR recognized the Federal Republic. The Saar territory, under an agreement between France and West Germany, held a plebiscite and despite economic links to France, elected to rejoin West Germany on Jan. 1, 1957.

The division between West Germany and East Germany was intensified when the Communists erected the Berlin Wall in 1961. In 1968, the East German Communist leader, Walter Ulbricht, imposed restrictions on West German movements into West Berlin. The Soviet-bloc invasion of Czechoslovakia in Aug. 1968 added to the tension. West Germany signed a treaty with Poland in 1970, renouncing force and setting Poland's western border as the Oder-Neisse Line. It subsequently resumed formal relations with Czechoslovakia in a pact that "voided" the Munich treaty that gave Nazi Germany the Sudetenland. By 1973, normal relations were established between East and West Germany and the two states entered the United Nations.

West German chancellor Willy Brandt, winner of a Nobel Peace Prize for his foreign policies, was forced to resign in 1974 when an East German spy was discovered to be one of his top staff members. Succeeding him was a moderate Social Democrat, Helmut Schmidt. Schmidt staunchly backed U.S. military strategy in Europe, staking his political fate on placing U.S. nuclear missiles in Germany unless the Soviet Union reduced its arsenal of intermediate missiles. He also strongly opposed nuclear freeze proposals.

Helmut Kohl of the Christian Democrat Party became chancellor in 1982. An economic upswing in 1986 led to Kohl's reelection. The fall of the Communist government in East Germany left only Soviet objections to German reunification to be dealt with. On the night of Nov. 9, 1989, the Berlin Wall was opened, making reunification all but inevitable. In July 1990, Kohl asked Soviet leader Gorbachev to drop his objections in exchange for financial aid from (West) Germany. Gorbachev agreed, and on Oct. 3, 1990, the German Democratic Republic acceded to the Federal Republic and Germany became a united and sovereign state for the first time since 1945.

A reunited Berlin serves as the official capital of unified Germany, although the government would continue to have administrative functions in Bonn during the 12-year transition period. The issue of the cost of reunification and the modernization of the former East Germany were serious considerations facing the reunified nation.

In its most important election in decades, on Sept. 27, 1998, Germans chose Social Democrat Gerhard Schröder as chancellor over Christian Democrat incumbent Helmut Kohl, ending a 16-year-long rule that oversaw the reunification of Germany and symbolized the end of the cold war in Europe. A centrist, Schröder campaigned for "the new middle" and promised to rectify Germany's high unemployment rate of 10.6%.

Tension between the old-style left-wing and the more probusiness pragmatists within Schröder's government came to a head with the abrupt resignation of Finance Minister Oskar Lafontaine in March 1999, who was also chairman of the ruling Social Democratic Party. Lafontaine's plans to raise taxes on industry and raise German wages—already nearly the highest in the world—went against the more centrist policies of Schröder. Hans Eichel was chosen to become the next finance minister.

Germany joined the other NATO allies in the military conflict in Kosovo in 1999. Before the Kosovo crisis, Germans had not participated in an armed conflict since World War II. Germany agreed to take 40,000 Kosovar refugees, the most of any NATO country.

In Dec. 1999, former chancellor Helmut Kohl and other high officials in the Christian Democrat Party admitted accepting tens of millions of dollars in illegal donations during the 1980s and 1990s. The enormity of the scandal led to the virtual dismemberment of the CDU in early 2000, a party that had long been a stable conservative force in German politics.

In July 2000, Schröder managed to pass significant tax reforms that would lower the top income-tax rate from 51% to 42% by 2005. He also eliminated the capital gains tax on companies selling shares in other companies, a measure that was expected to spur mergers. In May 2001, the German Parliament authorized the payment of $4.4 billion in compensation to 1.2 million surviving Nazi-era slave laborers.

Schröder was narrowly reelected in Sept. 2002, defeating conservative businessman Edmund Stoiber. Schröder's Social Democrats and coalition partner, the Greens, won a razor-thin majority in parliament. Stoiber held an early lead in the polls, but Schröder's deft handling of Germany's catastrophic floods in Aug. and his tough stance against U.S. plans for a preemptive attack on Iraq buoyed him in the weeks leading up to the election.

# Ghana

**REPUBLIC OF GHANA**

**President:** John Agyekum Kufuor (2001)
**Area:** 92,100 sq mi (238,540 sq km)
**Population (2002 est.):** 20,244,154 (growth rate: 1.8%);
birth rate: 28.1/1000; infant mortality rate: 55.6/1000;
density per sq mi: 220
**Capital:** Accra. **Largest cities (est. 1988):** Accra,
949,100; Kumasi, 385,200; Tamale, 151,100.
**Monetary unit:** Cedi. **Languages:** English (official),
Native tongues (Brong Ahafo, Twi, Fanti, Ga, Ewe,
Dagbani). **Ethnicity/race:** black African 99.8% (major
tribes: Akan 44%, Moshi-Dagomba 16%, Ewe 13%,
Ga 8%), European and other 0.2%. **Religions:**
indigenous beliefs 38%, Islam 30%, Christian 24%.
**Literacy rate:** 60% (1990)
**Economic summary: GDP/PPP** (2000 est.): $37.4
billion; per capita $1,900. **Real growth rate:** 3%.
**Inflation:** 22.8%. **Unemployment:** 20% (1997 est.).
**Arable land:** 12%. **Agriculture:** cocoa, rice, coffee,
cassava (tapioca), peanuts, corn, shea nuts, bananas;
timber. **Labor force:** 9 million (2000 est.); agriculture
60%, industry 15%, services 25% (1999 est.).
**Industries:** mining, lumbering, light manufacturing,
aluminum smelting, food processing. **Natural
resources:** gold, timber, industrial diamonds, bauxite,
manganese, fish, rubber, hydropower. **Exports:** $1.6
billion (f.o.b., 2000): gold, cocoa, timber, tuna, bauxite,
aluminum, manganese ore, diamonds. **Imports:** $2.2
billion (f.o.b., 2000): capital equipment, petroleum,
foodstuffs. **Major trading partners:** Togo, UK, Italy,
Netherlands, Germany, U.S., France, Nigeria, Spain.
**Member of Commonwealth of Nations**

**Geography** A West African country bordering on the
Gulf of Guinea, Ghana is bounded by Côte d'Ivoire to
the west, Burkina Faso to the north, Togo to the east,
and the Atlantic Ocean to the south. It compares in size
to Oregon, and its largest river is the Volta.

**Government** Constitutional democracy.

**History** Several major civilizations flourished in the
general region of what is now Ghana. The ancient
empire of Ghana (located 500 mi northwest of the contemporary state) reigned until the 13th century. The
Akan peoples established the next major civilization,
beginning in the 13th century, and then the Ashanti
empire flourished in the 18th and 19th centuries.

Called the Gold Coast, the area was first seen by
Portuguese traders in 1470. They were followed by the
English (1553), the Dutch (1595), and the Swedes
(1640). British rule over the Gold Coast began in
1820, but it was not until after quelling the severe
resistance of the Ashanti in 1901 that it was firmly
established. British Togoland, formerly a colony of
Germany, was incorporated into Ghana by referendum
in 1956. Created as an independent country on March
6, 1957, Ghana, as the result of a plebiscite, became a
republic on July 1, 1960.

Premier Kwame Nkrumah attempted to take leadership of the Pan-African Movement, holding the All-
African People's Congress in his capital, Accra, in
1958 and organizing the Union of African States with
Guinea and Mali in 1961. But he oriented his country
toward the Soviet Union and China and built an autocratic rule over all aspects of Ghanaian life. In Feb.
1966, while Nkrumah was visiting Beijing and Hanoi,
he was deposed by a military coup led by Gen.
Emmanuel K. Kotoka.

A series of military coups followed and on June 4,
1979, Flight Lt. Jerry Rawlings overthrew Lt. Gen.
Frederick Akuffo's military rule. Rawlings permitted
the election of a civilian president to go ahead as
scheduled the following month, and Hilla Limann,
candidate of the People's National Party, took office.
Charging the civilian government with corruption and
repression, Rawlings staged another coup on Dec. 31,
1981. As chairman of the Provisional National
Defense Council, Rawlings instituted an austerity program and reduced budget deficits. Rawlings was
reelected in 1982 and again in 1996.

A major cocoa producer, Ghana has been hurt by
several year-long slumps in cocoa prices. In July 2000,
Ghana and neighboring countries began destroying
massive amounts of cocoa to drive up the price.
Together they produce 70% of the world's cocoa.
Since gold is Ghana's largest source of foreign
exchange, fluctuating prices have hammered the
economy, and mining companies cut 10,000 jobs in
1999. Saudi Arabian investors rescued Ashanti Gold-
fields, the largest company in sub-Saharan Africa,
from near collapse in Feb. 2000.

In Jan. 2001, John Agyekum Kufuor took office,
becoming Ghana's first democratically elected president since independence.

# Greece

**HELLENIC REPUBLIC**

**National name:** Elliniki Dimokratia
**President:** Kostis Stephanopoulos (1995)
**Prime Minister:** Kostas Simitis (1996)
**Area:** 50,942 sq mi (131,940 sq km)
**Population (2002 est.):** 10,645,343 (growth rate: 0.0%);
birth rate: 9.8/1000; infant mortality rate: 5.4/1000;
density per sq mi: 209
**Capital:** Athens. **Largest cities (1991 est.):** Athens,
3,000,000; Thessaloníki, 720,000; Piraeus, 170,000;
Patras, 155,000. **Monetary unit:** Euro (formerly
drachma). **Language:** Greek. **Ethnicity/race:** Greek
98%, other 2%; note: the Greek government states
there are no ethnic divisions in Greece. **Religions:**
Greek Orthodox 98%, Muslim 1.3%, other 0.7%.
**Literacy rate:** 93% (1990)
**Economic summary: GDP/PPP** (2000 est.): $181.9
billion; per capita $17,200. **Real growth rate:** 3.8%.
**Inflation:** 3.1%. **Unemployment:** 11.3%. **Arable land:**
19%. **Agriculture:** wheat, corn, barley, sugar beets,
olives, tomatoes, wine, tobacco, potatoes; beef, dairy
products. **Labor force:** 4.32 million (1999 est.);
industry 21%, agriculture 20%, services 59% (2000
est.). **Natural resources:** bauxite, lignite, magnesite,
petroleum, marble, hydropower potential. **Industries:**
tourism; food and tobacco processing, textiles;
chemicals, metal products; mining, petroleum.
**Exports:** $15.8 billion (f.o.b., 2000): manufactured
goods, food and beverages, petroleum products.
**Imports:** $29.9 billion (c.i.f., 2000): manufactured
goods, foodstuffs, fuels, chemicals. **Major trading
partners:** EU, U.S.

**Geography** Located in southern Europe, Greece
forms an irregular-shaped peninsula in the Mediterranean with two additional large peninsulas projecting
from it: the Chalcidice and the Peloponnese. The
Greek Islands are generally subdivided into two
groups, according to location: the Ionian Islands
(including Corfu, Cephalonia, and Leucas) west of the
mainland and the Aegean Islands (including Euboea,
Samos, Chios, Lesbos, and Crete) to the east and
south. North-central Greece, Epirus, and western
Macedonia are all mountainous. The main chain of the
Pindus Mountains extends from northwest Greece to
the Peloponnese. Mount Olympus, rising to 9,570 ft
(2,909 m), is the highest point in the country.

**Government** Ceremonial executive power is held by the president; the prime minister heads the government and is responsible to a 300-member unicameral Parliament.

**History** Indo-European peoples, including the Mycenaeans, began entering Greece about 2000 B.C. and set up sophisticated civilizations. About 1200 B.C., the Dorians, another Indo-European people, invaded Greece, and a dark age followed, known mostly through the Homeric epics. At the end of this time, classical Greece began to emerge (c. 750 B.C.) as a loose composite of city-states with a heavy involvement in maritime trade and a devotion to art, literature, politics, and philosophy. Greece reached the peak of its glory in the 5th century B.C., but the Peloponnesian War (431–404 B.C.) weakened the nation, and it was conquered by Philip II and his son Alexander the Great of Macedonia, who considered themselves Greek. By the middle of the 2nd century B.C., Greece had declined to the status of a Roman province. It remained within the eastern Roman Empire until Constantinople fell to the Crusaders in 1204. In 1453, the Turks took Constantinople and by 1460, Greece was a Turkish province with its Orthodox Church intact. The insurrection made famous by the poet Lord Byron broke out in 1821, and in 1827, Greece won independence with sovereignty guaranteed by Britain, France, and Russia.

The protecting powers chose Prince Otto of Bavaria as the first king of modern Greece in 1832 to reign over an area only slightly larger than the Peloponnese peninsula. Chiefly under the next king, George I, chosen by the protecting powers in 1863, Greece acquired much of its present territory. During his 57-year reign, a period in which he encouraged parliamentary democracy, Thessaly, Epirus, Macedonia, Crete, and most of the Aegean islands were added from the disintegrating Turkish empire. Unfavorable economic conditions forced about one-sixth of the entire Greek population to emigrate (mostly to the U.S.) in the late 19th and early 20th centuries. An unsuccessful war against Turkey after World War I brought down the monarchy, which was replaced by a republic in 1923.

Two military dictatorships and a financial crisis brought George II back from exile, but only until 1941, when Italian and German invaders defeated tough Greek resistance. After British and Greek troops liberated the country in Oct. 1944, Communist guerrillas staged a long military campaign against the government; the Greek civil war, infamous for its brutality, began in Dec. 1944 and continued until Oct. 16, 1949, when the Communist guerrillas conceded defeat. The Greek government received U.S. aid under the Truman Doctrine, the predecessor of the Marshall Plan, to fight against the Communists.

Greece was a charter member of the UN, and became a member of the North Atlantic Treaty Organization (NATO) in 1951. A military junta seized power in April 1967, sending young King Constantine II into exile. Col. George Papadopoulos, a leader of the junta, gradually attempted to revamp his hardline, right-wing image: first, by giving up his military post for that of prime minister in 1973, and later, as president, by ending martial law. A coup ousted Papadopoulos in Nov. 1973. The seven-year regime of the "colonels," infamous for torturing and exiling opponents and scoffing at human rights, collapsed entirely a year later, after having bungled an attempt to seize Cyprus.

A referendum in Dec. 1974, five months after the demise of the military dictatorship, ended the Greek monarchy and established a republic. Former premier Karamanlis returned from exile to become premier of Greece's first civilian government since 1967. Greece has continued to be ruled by freely elected civilian governments ever since. On Jan. 1, 1981, Greece became the 10th member of the European Union. Andreas Papandreou, son of former premier George Papandreou, founded the Panhellenic Socialist Movement (PASOK) and became Greece's first socialist premier (1981–1989).

The Greeks were the most vocal dissenters within the NATO alliance regarding the 1999 intervention in Kosovo. They were both wary of the economic and political instability that would accompany a large influx of refugees and reluctant to ignore an Eastern Orthodox religious history shared with the Serbs.

Greece continued to experience tensions with Turkey over a disputed, unpopulated 10-acre island and over Cyprus, which is divided into Greek and Turkish sectors.

The pro-Western socialist prime minister Kostas Simitis is credited with reviving the Greek economy. Still, *The Economist* magazine estimates it will be at least 15 years before the per capita GDP in Greece comes close to the current EU average.

In the summer of 2002, the government was finally able to crack down on the 17 November (17N) terrorist organization, which had entirely eluded the Greek authorities for the past 27 years. The radical leftist group is responsible for more than 20 assassinations of American, British, and Greek diplomats, military personnel, and businessmen. Greece has been criticized for decades by the international community for being soft on terrorism, and confidence in its ability to provide adequate security when it hosts the 2004 Olympics has never been strong.

# Grenada

### STATE OF GRENADA

**Sovereign:** Queen Elizabeth II (1952)
**Governor-General:** Sir Daniel Williams (1996)
**Prime Minister:** Keith C. Mitchell (1995)
**Area:** 131 sq mi (340 sq km)
**Population (2002 est.):** 89,227 (growth rate 1.5%); birth rate: 23.1/1000; infant mortality rate: 14.6/1000; density per sq mi: 680
**Capital and largest city (1991):** St. George's, 4,439.
**Monetary unit:** East Caribbean dollar. **Language:** English. **Ethnicity/race:** black African descent 85%, mixed 11%, white, other 0.3%. **Religions:** Roman Catholic 64%, Anglican 21%. **Literacy rate:** 98% (1970)
**Economic summary:** GDP/PPP (2000 est.): $394 million; per capita $4,400. **Real growth rate:** 7%. **Inflation:** 2.5%. **Unemployment:** 15% (1997). **Arable land:** 15%. **Agriculture:** bananas, cocoa, nutmeg, mace, citrus, avocados, root crops, sugarcane, corn, vegetables. **Labor force:** 42,300 (1996); services 62%, agriculture 24%, industry 14% (1999 est.). **Industries:** food and beverages, textiles, light assembly operations, tourism, construction. **Natural resources:** timber, tropical fruit, deepwater harbors. **Exports:** $62.3 million (2000 est.): bananas, cocoa, nutmeg, fruit and vegetables, clothing, mace. **Imports:** $217.5 million (2000 est.): food, manufactured goods, machinery, chemicals, fuel (1989). **Major trading partners:** Caricom, UK, U.S., Netherlands, Japan. **Member of Commonwealth of Nations**

**Geography** Grenada (the first "a" is a long vowel) is the most southerly of the Windward Islands, about 100 mi (161 km) from the Venezuelan coast. It is a volcanic island traversed by a mountain range, the highest peak of which is Mount St. Catherine (2,756 ft; 840 m).

**Government** Constitutional monarchy. A governor-general represents the sovereign, Elizabeth II.

**History** The Arawak Indians were the first to inhabit Grenada, but they were all eventually massacred by the belligerent Carib Indians. When Columbus arrived in 1498 he encountered the Caribs, who continued to rule over the island for another 150 years. The French gained control of the island in 1672 and held on to it until 1762, when the British invaded. Black slaves were granted freedom in 1833. After more than 200 years of British rule, most recently as part of the West Indies Associated States, Grenada became independent on Feb. 7, 1974, with Eric M. Gairy as prime minister.

In 1979, the Marxist New Jewel Movement staged a coup, and its leader, Maurice Bishop, became prime minister. Bishop, a protégé of Cuba's President Castro, was killed in a military coup on Oct. 19, 1983.

In an effort to establish order on the island and eliminate the Cuban military presence, U.S. president Ronald Reagan ordered an invasion of Grenada on Oct. 25 involving over 1,900 U.S. troops and a small military force from Barbados, Dominica, Jamaica, St. Lucia, and St. Vincent. The troops met strong resistance from Cuban military personnel on the island but soon occupied it. After a gradual withdrawal of peacekeeping forces, a centrist coalition led by Herbert A. Blaize won a parliamentary majority in 1984. The New National Party (NNP), led by Dr. Keith C. Mitchell, won a majority in the 1995 parliamentary elections; in 1999 general elections, the NNP won all 15 seats in Parliament.

# Guatemala

### REPUBLIC OF GUATEMALA

**National name:** República de Guatemala
**President:** Alfonso Portillo Cabrera (2000)
**Area:** 42,042 sq mi (108,890 sq km)
**Population (2002 est.):** 13,314,079 (growth rate: 2.8%); birth rate: 34.2/1000; infant mortality rate: 44.5/1000; density per sq mi: 317
**Capital and largest city (1994 est.):** Guatemala City, 1,150,452. **Other large cities (1994 est.):** Mixco, 413,002; Villa Nueva, 154,508. **Monetary unit:** Quetzal. **Languages:** Spanish, Indian languages. **Ethnicity/race:** Mestizo—mixed Amerindian-Spanish ancestry (in local Spanish called Ladino) 56%, Amerindian or predominantly Amerindian 44%. **Religions:** Roman Catholic, Protestant, Mayan. **Literacy rate:** 55% (1990)
**Economic summary: GDP/PPP** (2000 est.): $46.2 billion; per capita $3,700. **Real growth rate:** 3%. **Inflation:** 6%. **Unemployment:** 7.5% (1999 est.). **Arable land:** 12%. **Agriculture:** sugarcane, corn, bananas, coffee, beans, cardamom; cattle, sheep, pigs, chickens. **Labor force:** 4.2 million (1999 est.); agriculture 50%, industry 15%, services 35% (1999 est.). **Industries:** sugar, textiles and clothing, furniture, chemicals, petroleum, metals, rubber, tourism. **Natural resources:** petroleum, nickel, rare woods, fish, chicle, hydropower. **Exports:** $2.9 billion (f.o.b., 2000): coffee, sugar, bananas, fruits and vegetables, cardamom, meat, apparel, petroleum, electricity. **Imports:** $4.4 billion (f.o.b., 2000): fuels, machinery and transport equipment, construction materials, grain, fertilizers, electricity. **Major trading partners:** U.S., El Salvador, Honduras, Costa Rica, Germany, Mexico, Japan, Venezuela.

**Geography** The northernmost of the Central American nations, Guatemala is the size of Tennessee. Its neighbors are Mexico on the north and west, and Belize, Honduras, and El Salvador on the east. The country consists of three main regions—the cool highlands with the heaviest population, the tropical area along the Pacific and Caribbean coasts, and the tropical jungle in the northern lowlands (known as the Petén).

**Government** Constitutional democratic republic.

**History** Once the site of the impressive ancient Mayan civilization, Guatemala was conquered by Spanish conquistador Pedro de Alvarado in 1524 and became a republic in 1839 after the United Provinces of Central America collapsed. From 1898 to 1920, dictator Manuel Estrada Cabrera ran the country, and from 1931 to 1944, Gen. Jorge Ubico Castaneda served as strongman.

After Ubico's overthrow in 1944, liberal-democratic coalitions led by Juan José Arévalo (1945–51) and Jacobo Arbenz Guzmán (1951–54) instituted social and political reforms that strengthened the peasantry and urban workers at the expense of the military and big landowners like the U.S.-owned United Fruit Company. With covert U.S. backing, Col. Carlos Castillo Armas led a coup in 1954, and Arbenz took refuge in Mexico.

A series of repressive regimes followed, and the country was plunged into a 36-year civil war between military governments and leftist rebels. Death squads murdered an estimated 50,000 leftists and political opponents during the 1970s. The U.S. ended military aid in 1978.

After several other military governments, civilian Marco Vinicio Cerezo Arévalo took office in 1986. He was followed by Jorge Serrano Elías in 1991. In 1993, Serrano moved to dissolve Congress and the Supreme Court and suspend constitutional rights, but the military deposed Serrano and allowed the inauguration of de Leon Carpio, the former attorney general for human rights. A peace agreement was signed in Dec. 1996, ending the longest civil war in Latin American history, which had left some 200,000 dead. In June 1997, the new president Álvaro Arzú Irigoyen and the guerrilla movement leader Ricardo Ramirez received the UNESCO Houphouet-Boigny Peace Prize.

In 1999, a Guatemalan truth commission blamed the army for 93% of the atrocities and the rebels (the Guatemalan National Revolutionary Unit) for 3%. The former guerrillas apologized for their crimes, and President Clinton apologized for U.S. support of the right-wing military governments. The army has not acknowledged its guilt.

Alfonso Portillo Cabrera became president in Jan. 2000. In Aug. 2000 Portillo apologized for the former government's human rights abuses and pledged to prosecute those responsible and compensate victims.

# Guinea

### REPUBLIC OF GUINEA

**National name:** République de Guinée
**President:** Lansana Conté (1984)
**Premier:** Lamine Sidimé (1999)
**Area:** 94,925 sq mi (245,857 sq km)
**Population (2002 est.):** 7,775,065 (growth rate: 2.2%); birth rate: 39.5/1000; infant mortality rate: 127.0/1000; density per sq mi: 82
**Capital and largest city (1995 est.):** Conakry, 1,508,000. **Monetary unit:** Guinean franc. **Languages:** French (official), native tongues (Malinké,

Susu, Fulani). **Ethnicity/race:** Peuhl 40%, Malinke 30%, Susu 20%, smaller tribes 10%. **Religions:** Islam 85%, indigenous 7%, Christian 8%. **Literacy rate:** 24% in French; 48% in local languages (1990) **Economic summary: GDP/PPP** (2000 est.): $10 billion; per capita $1,300. **Real growth rate:** 5%. **Inflation:** 6%. **Unemployment:** n.a. **Arable land:** 2%. **Agriculture:** rice, coffee, pineapples, palm kernels, cassava (tapioca), bananas, sweet potatoes; cattle, sheep, goats; timber. **Labor force:** 3 million (1999); agriculture 80%, industry and services 20% (2000 est.). **Industries:** bauxite, gold, diamonds; alumina refining; light manufacturing and agricultural processing industries. **Natural resources:** bauxite, iron ore, diamonds, gold, uranium, hydropower, fish. **Exports:** $820 million (f.o.b., 2000 est.): bauxite, alumina, gold, diamonds, coffee, fish, agricultural products. **Imports:** $634 million (f.o.b., 2000 est.): petroleum products, metals, machinery, transport equipment, textiles, grain and other foodstuffs. **Major trading partners:** Russia, U.S., Benelux, Ukraine, Ireland, France, Côte d'Ivoire.

**Geography** Guinea, in West Africa on the Atlantic, is also bordered by Guinea-Bissau, Senegal, Mali, Côte d'Ivoire, Liberia, and Sierra Leone. Slightly smaller than Oregon, the country consists of a coastal plain, a mountainous region, a savanna interior, and a forest area in the Guinea Highlands. The highest peak is Mount Nimba at 5,748 ft (1,752 m).

**Government** Republic.

**History** Beginning in 900, the Susu migrated from the north and began settling in the area that is now Guinea. The Susu civilization reached its height in the 13th century. Today the Susu make up about 20% of Guinea's population. From the 16th to the 19th century, the Fulani empire dominated the region. In 1849, the French claimed it as a protectorate. First called Rivières du Sud, the protectorate was rechristened French Guinea, and finally, in 1895, it became part of French West Africa.

Guinea achieved independence on Oct. 2, 1958, and became an independent state with Sékou Touré as president. Under Touré, the country became the first avowedly Marxist state in Africa. Diplomatic relations with France were suspended in 1965, with the Soviet Union replacing France as the country's chief source of economic and technical assistance.

Prosperity came in 1960 after the start of exploitation of bauxite deposits. Touré was reelected to a seven-year term in 1974 and again in 1981. Touré died after 26 years as president in March 1984. A week later, a military regime headed by Col. Lansana Conté took power.

In 1989, President Conté announced that Guinea would move to a multiparty democracy, and in 1991, voters approved a new constitution. In Dec. 1993 elections, the president's Unity and Progress Party took almost 51% of the vote. In 2001, a government referendum was passed doing away with presidential term limits, which would allow Conté to run for a third term in 2003. Despite the trappings of multiparty rule, Conté has ruled the country with an iron fist.

Guinea has had ongoing difficulties with its neighbor Liberia, which was embroiled in a long civil war during the 1990s. The fighting in Liberia spilled over the border into Guinea on several occasions, and border skirmishes continued after the civil war subsided. Guinea had taken sides against rebel leader Charles Taylor in Liberia's civil war and was part of the Nigerian-led ECOMOG forces that intervened in the crisis. As a consequence, President Conté's relations with Taylor remained sour after Taylor became Liberia's president in 1997.

Since Sept. 2000, fighting at the junction of Guinea's border with Sierra Leone and Liberia has increased. Guinea's army has been battling a variety of factions, including rebel Guineans and Liberians, and Sierra Leone's Revolutionary United Front (RUF). Already burdened by an inadequate infrastructure and a weak economy, nearly 300,000 refugees from the civil war in Sierra Leone have overwhelmed Guinea.

# Guinea-Bissau

### REPUBLIC OF GUINEA-BISSAU

**National name:** Républica da Guiné-Bissau **President:** Kumba Yalá (2000) **Prime Minister:** Alamara Nhassé (2001) **Area:** 13,946 sq mi (36,120 sq km) **Population (2002 est.):** 1,345,479 (growth rate: 2.4%); birth rate: 39.0/1000; infant mortality rate: 108.5/1000; density per sq mi: 96 **Capital and largest city (1991 est.):** Bissau, 200,000. **Monetary unit:** CFA Franc. **Languages:** Portuguese Criolo, African languages. **Ethnicity/race:** African 99% (Balanta 30%, Fula 20%, Manjaca 14%, Mandinga 13%, Papel 7%), European and mulatto less than 1%. **Religions:** traditional 65%, Islam 30%, Christian 5%. **Literacy rate:** 37% (1990) **Economic summary: GDP/PPP** (2000 est.): $1.1 billion; per capita $850. **Real growth rate:** 7.6%. **Inflation:** 3%. **Unemployment:** n.a. **Arable land:** 11%. **Agriculture:** rice, corn, beans, cassava (tapioca), cashew nuts, peanuts, palm kernels, cotton; timber; fish. **Labor force:** 480,000; agriculture 78%. **Industries:** agricultural products processing, beer, soft drinks. **Natural resources:** fish, timber, phosphates, bauxite, unexploited deposits of petroleum. **Exports:** $80 million (f.o.b., 2000 est.): cashew nuts, shrimp, peanuts, palm kernels, sawn lumber (1996). **Imports:** $55.2 million (f.o.b., 2000 est.): foodstuffs, machinery and transport equipment, petroleum products (1996). **Major trading partners:** India, Singapore, Italy, Portugal, France, Senegal, Netherlands.

**Geography** A neighbor of Senegal and Guinea in West Africa, on the Atlantic coast, Guinea-Bissau is about half the size of South Carolina. The country is a low-lying coastal region of swamps, rain forests, and mangrove-covered wetlands, with about 25 islands off the coast. The Bijagos archipelago extends 30 mi (48 km) out to sea.

**Government** Republic.

**History** The land now known as Guinea-Bissau was once the kingdom of Gabú, which was part of the larger Mali empire. After 1546 Gabú became more autonomous, and at least portions of the kingdom existed until 1867. The first European to encounter Guinea-Bissau was the Portuguese explorer Nuño Tristão in 1446; colonists in the Cape Verde Islands obtained trading rights in the territory, and it became a center of the Portuguese slave trade. In 1879, the connection with the islands was broken.

The African Party for the Independence of Guinea-Bissau and Cape Verde (another Portuguese colony) was founded in 1956, and guerrilla warfare by nationalists grew increasingly effective. By 1974 the rebels controlled most of the countryside, where they formed a government that was soon recognized by scores of countries. The military coup in Portugal in April 1974 brightened the prospects for freedom, and in Aug. the Lisbon government signed an agreement granting independence to the province. The new republic took the name Guinea-Bissau.

In Nov. 1980, Premier João Bernardo Vieira headed a military coup that deposed Luis Cabral, president since 1974. In his 19 years of rule, Vieira was criticized for crony capitalism and corruption and for failing to alleviate the poverty of Guinea-Bissau, one of the world's poorest countries. Vieira also brought in troops from Senegal and the Republic of Guinea to help fight against an insurgency movement, a highly unpopular move. The rebels managed to gain control of most of the country and part of the capital in 1998 before a Nov. peace deal halted the fighting. But in May 1999, after the presidential guard refused to disarm, the rebels deposed Vieira.

Following a period of military rule, Kumba Yalá, a former teacher and popular leader of Guinea-Bissau's independence movement, was elected president in 2000.

# Guyana

### COOPERATIVE REPUBLIC OF GUYANA

**President:** Bharrat Jagdeo (1999)
**Prime Minister:** Samuel Hinds (1999)
**Area:** 83,000 sq mi (214,970 sq km)
**Population (2002 est.):** 698,209 (growth rate: 0.9%); birth rate: 17.9/1000; infant mortality rate: 38.4/1000; density per sq mi: 8
**Capital and largest city (1992 est.):** Georgetown, 248,500. **Monetary unit:** Guyanese dollar.
**Languages:** English (official), Amerindian dialects.
**Ethnicity/race:** East Indian 51%, black and mixed 43%, Amerindian 4%, European and Chinese 2%.
**Religions:** Hindu 34%, Protestant 18%, Islam 9%, Roman Catholic 18%, Anglican 16%. **Literacy rate:** 96% (1990)
**Economic summary: GDP/PPP** (2000 est.): $3.4 billion; per capita $4,800. **Real growth rate:** 3%. **Inflation:** 5.9%. **Unemployment:** 12% (1992 est.). **Labor force:** 245,492 (1992); agriculture n.a., industry n.a., services n.a. **Arable land:** 2%. **Agriculture:** sugar, rice, wheat, vegetable oils; beef, pork, poultry, dairy products; forest and fishery potential not exploited. **Industries:** bauxite, sugar, rice milling, timber, fishing (shrimp), textiles, gold mining. **Natural resources:** bauxite, gold, diamonds, hardwood timber, shrimp, fish. **Exports:** $570 million (f.o.b., 2000 est.): sugar, gold, bauxite/alumina, rice, shrimp, molasses, rum, timber. **Imports:** $660 million (c.i.f., 2000 est.): manufactures, machinery, petroleum, food. **Major trading partners:** U.S., Canada, UK, Netherlands Antilles, Jamaica, Trinidad and Tobago, Japan. **Member of Commonwealth of Nations**

**Geography** Guyana is the size of Idaho and is situated on the northern coast of South America east of Venezuela, west of Suriname, and north of Brazil. The country consists of a low coastal area and the Guyana Highlands, a tropical forest zone covering more than 80% of the country, in the south. There is an extensive north-south network of rivers.

**Government** Republic.

**History** The Dutch, English, and French established colonies in what is now known as Guyana, but by the early 17th century the majority of the settlements were Dutch. During the Napoleonic wars Britain took over the Dutch colonies of Berbice, Demerara, and Essequibo, which became British Guiana in 1831.

Slavery was outlawed in 1834, and the great need for plantation workers led to a large wave of immigration, primarily of East Indians. Today, about half of the population is of East Indian descent and about 43% are of African descent.

British Guiana was made a Crown colony in 1928, and in 1953 it was granted home rule. In 1950, Forbes Burnham, who was Afro-Guyanese, and Cheddi Jagan, who was Indian-Guyanese, created the colony's first political party, which was dedicated to gaining the colony's independence. The two leaders split in 1955, creating separate parties. The leftist Jagan and the more moderate Burnham were to dominate Guyanan politics for decades to come. On May 26, 1966, the country gained independence, and resumed its traditional name, Guyana.

Burnham and his People's National Congress ruled Guyana for 21 years, until Burnham's death in 1985. In 1992, Jagan's People's Progressive Party won a majority in the general election. Jagan, who had served as prime minister in the 1960s while Guyana was still a colony, became president. Former finance minister Bharrat Jagdeo assumed the presidency in Aug. 1999.

Guyana's potential economic development was hurt in 2000 as border disputes with both Venezuela to the west and Suriname to the east heated up. Suriname and Guyana have been unable to resolve the border dispute in an oil-rich coastal area. Venezuela's president Hugo Chavez has revived a 19th-century claim to more than half of Guyana's territory.

In March 2001, Bharrat Jagdeo won a second term in elections that underscored Guyana's bitter racial tensions. The reelection of Jagdeo, an ethnic East Indian, caused rioting among Afro-Guyanese, who claimed widespread election fraud.

# Haiti

### REPUBLIC OF HAITI

**National name:** République d'Haïti
**President:** Jean-Bertrand Aristide (2000)
**Prime Minister:** Yvon Neptune (2002)
**Area:** 10,714 sq mi (27,750 sq km)
**Population (2002 est.):** 7,063,722 (growth rate: 1.7%); birth rate: 31.4/1000; infant mortality rate: 93.3/1000; density per sq mi: 659
**Capital and largest city (1993 est.):** Port-au-Prince, 1.5 million. **Monetary unit:** Gourde. **Languages:** Creole and French (both official). **Ethnicity/race:** black 95%, mulatto and European 5%. **Religions:** Roman Catholic 80%, Protestant 16%, Vaudou 95%. **Literacy rate:** 53% (1990)
**Economic summary: GDP/PPP** (2000 est.): $12.7 billion; per capita $1,800. **Real growth rate:** 1.2%. **Inflation:** 19%. **Unemployment:** widespread unemployment and underemployment; more than two-thirds of the labor force do not have formal jobs (1999). **Arable land:** 20%. **Agriculture:** coffee, mangoes, sugarcane, rice, corn, sorghum; wood. **Labor force:** 3.6 million (1995); note: shortage of skilled labor, unskilled labor abundant (1998); agriculture 66%, services 25%, industry 9%. **Industries:** sugar refining, flour milling, textiles, cement, tourism, light assembly industries based on imported parts. **Natural resources:** bauxite, copper, calcium carbonate, gold, marble, hydropower. **Exports:** $186 million (f.o.b., 1999): manufactures, coffee, oils, mangoes. **Imports:** $1.2 billion (c.i.f., 1999): food, machinery and transport equipment, fuels, raw materials. **Major trading partners:** U.S., EU.

**Geography** Haiti, in the West Indies, occupies the western third of the island of Hispaniola, which it shares with the Dominican Republic. About the size of

Maryland, Haiti is two-thirds mountainous, with the rest of the country marked by great valleys, extensive plateaus, and small plains.

**Government** Republic with an elected government.

**History** Explored by Columbus on Dec. 6, 1492, Haiti's native Arawaks fell victim to Spanish rule. In 1697, Haiti became the French colony of Saint-Dominique, which became a leading sugarcane producer dependent on slaves. In 1791, an insurrection erupted among the slave population of 480,000, resulting in a declaration of independence by Pierre-Dominique Toussaint l'Ouverture in 1801. Napoléon Bonaparte suppressed the independence movement, but it eventually triumphed in 1804 under Jean-Jacques Dessalines, who gave the new nation the Arawak name *Haiti*.

The revolution wrecked Haiti's economy. Years of strife between the light-skinned mulattos who dominated the economy and the majority black population, plus disputes with neighboring Santo Domingo, continued to hurt the nation's development. After a succession of dictatorships a bankrupt Haiti accepted a U.S. customs receivership from 1905 to 1941. Occupation by U.S. Marines from 1915 to 1934 brought stability. Haiti's high population growth made it the most densely populated nation in the hemisphere.

In 1949, after four years of democratic rule by President Dumarsais Estimé, dictatorship returned under Gen. Paul Magloire, who was succeeded by François Duvalier, nicknamed "Papa Doc," in 1957. Duvalier's secret police, the "Tontons Macoutes," ensured political stability with brutal efficiency. Duvalier's son, Jean-Claude, or "Baby Doc," succeeded his father in 1971 as ruler of the poorest nation in the Western Hemisphere. In the early 1980s, Haiti became one of the first countries to face an AIDS epidemic. Fear of the disease caused tourists to stay away, and the tourist industry collapsed, causing rising unemployment. Unrest generated by the economic crisis forced Duvalier to flee the country in 1986.

Throughout the 1990s the international community tried to establish democracy in Haiti. The country's first elected chief executive, Jean-Bertrand Aristide, a Roman Catholic priest, took office on Feb. 7, 1991. The military, however, soon took control. A UN peacekeeping force, led by the U.S.—Operation Uphold Democracy—arrived in 1994. Aristide was restored to office and René Preval became his successor in 1996 elections.

U.S. soldiers left in 2000, but UN peacekeepers remain. Haiti's government is ineffectual and the economy is in ruins. Haiti has become a major drug shipment point. With 50% unemployment, Haiti produces a steady flow of refugees to the U.S.

In 2000, former president Aristide was reelected president in elections boycotted by the opposition and questioned by many foreign observers. The government charged opposition leaders with masterminding an attempted coup in July 2001, while opposition leaders claimed the government arranged the attack itself as an excuse to crack down on critics. Another coup attempt was thwarted in Dec. 2001. The U.S. and other countries have threatened Haiti, already one of the world's poorest countries, with sanctions unless democratic procedures are strengthened. In Jan. 2002, Prime Minister Jean-Marie Chérestal resigned amid allegations of corruption. Aristide named Senate President Yvon Neptune to the post in March 2002.

# Honduras
## REPUBLIC OF HONDURAS

**National name:** República de Honduras
**President:** Ricardo Maduro (2002)
**Area:** 43,278 sq mi (112,090 sq km)
**Population (2002 est.):** 6,560,608 (growth rate: 2.6%); birth rate: 31.2/1000; infant mortality rate: 30.5/1000; density per sq mi: 152
**Capital and largest city (1995):** Tegucigalpa, 1,500,000.
**Monetary unit:** Lempira. **Languages:** Spanish (official), English widely spoken in business. **Ethnicity/race:** mestizo (mixed Indian and European) 90%, Indian 7%, black 2%, white 1%. **Religions:** Roman Catholic 94%, Protestant minority. **Literacy rate:** 73% (1990)
**Economic summary:** GDP/PPP (2000 est.): $17 billion; per capita $2,700. **Real growth rate:** 5%. **Inflation:** 11%. **Unemployment:** 28%. **Arable land:** 15%. **Agriculture:** bananas, coffee, citrus; beef; timber; shrimp. **Labor force:** 2.3 million (1997 est.); agriculture 29%, industry 21%, services 60% (1998 est.). **Industries:** sugar, coffee, textiles, clothing, wood products. **Natural resources:** timber, gold, silver, copper, lead, zinc, iron ore, antimony, coal, fish, hydropower. **Exports:** $2 billion (f.o.b., 2000 est.): coffee, bananas, shrimp, lobster, meat; zinc, lumber. **Imports:** $2.8 billion (f.o.b., 2000 est.): machinery and transport equipment, industrial raw materials, chemical products, fuels, foodstuffs. **Major trading partners:** U.S., Germany, El Salvador, Guatemala, Nicaragua, Mexico, Japan.

**Geography** Honduras, in the north-central part of Central America, has a 400-mile (644-km) Caribbean coastline and a 40-mile (64-km) Pacific frontage. Its neighbors are Guatemala to the west, El Salvador to the south, and Nicaragua to the east. The second-largest country in Central America, Honduras is slightly larger than Tennessee. Generally mountainous, the country is marked by fertile plateaus, river valleys, and narrow coastal plains.

**Government** Democratic constitutional republic.

**History** During the first millennium, Honduras was inhabited by the Maya. Columbus explored the country in 1502. Honduras, with four other Central American nations, declared its independence from Spain in 1821 to form a federation of Central American states. In 1838, Honduras left the federation and became independent. Political unrest rocked Honduras in the early 1900s, resulting in an occupation by U.S. Marines. Dictator Gen. Tiburcio Carias Andino established a strong government in 1932.

In 1969, El Salvador invaded Honduras after Honduran landowners deported several thousand Salvadorans. Five thousand people ultimately died in what is called "the football war," because it broke out during a soccer game between the two countries. By threatening economic sanctions and military intervention, the OAS induced El Salvador to withdraw. After a decade of military rule, parliamentary democracy returned with the election of Roberto Suazo Córdova as president in 1982. However, Honduras faced severe economic problems and tensions along its border with Nicaragua. "Contra" rebels, waging a guerrilla war against the Sandinista regime in Nicaragua, used Honduras as a training and staging area. The U.S. also used Honduras for military exercises and built bases to train Honduran and Salvadoran troops.

In 1997, Carlos Flores Facussé of the Liberal Party was elected president. He began to reform the economy and modernize the government. In recent years, Honduras has faced high unemployment, inflation, and over-dependence on coffee and bananas. In Oct. 1998, Hurricane Mitch killed some 13,000 Hondurans, left 2 million homeless, and caused more than $5 billion in damage.

The UN sent food aid to southern Honduras in the summer of 2000 because of severe drought.

In 2002, Ricardo Maduro became president, promising to lessen crime and corruption. He increased the number of police and armed forces to stem the violence and crime that has plagued the cities. But his hardline efforts, growing increasingly more repressive, have not improved the problem.

# Hungary

### REPUBLIC OF HUNGARY

**National name:** Magyar Köztársaság
**President:** Ferenc Mádl (2000)
**Prime Minister:** Péter Medgyessy (2002)
**Area:** 35,919 sq mi (93,030 sq km)
**Population (2002 est.):** 10,075,034 (growth rate: -0.4%); birth rate: 9.3/1000; infant mortality rate: 8.8/1000; density per sq mi: 280
**Capital and largest city (1995 est.):** Budapest, 2,008,546. **Other large cities (1995 est.):** Debrecen, 210,000; Miskolc, 182,000; Szeged, 169,000; Pécs, 163,000. **Monetary unit:** Forint. **Languages:** Magyar (Hungarian), 98.2%; other, 1.8%. **Ethnicity/race:** Hungarian 89.9%, Gypsy 4%, German 2.6%, Serb 2%, Slovak 0.8%, Romanian 0.7%. **Religions:** Roman Catholic 67.5%, Protestant 25%, atheist and others 7.5%. **Literacy rate:** 98% (1980)
**Economic summary:** GDP/PPP (2000 est.): $113.9 billion; per capita $11,200. **Real growth rate:** 5.5%. **Inflation:** 9.8% (1999 est.). **Unemployment:** 9.4% (2000 est.). **Arable land:** 51%. **Agriculture:** wheat, corn, sunflower seed, potatoes, sugar beets; pigs, cattle, poultry, dairy products. **Labor force:** 4.2 million (1997); services 65%, industry 27%, agriculture 8% (1996). **Industries:** mining, metallurgy, construction materials, processed foods, textiles, chemicals (especially pharmaceuticals), motor vehicles. **Natural resources:** bauxite, coal, natural gas, fertile soils, arable land. **Exports:** $25.2 billion (f.o.b., 2000): machinery and equipment, other manufactures, agriculture and food products, raw materials, fuels and electricity. **Imports:** $27.6 billion (f.o.b., 2000): machinery and equipment, other manufactures, fuels and electricity, food products, raw materials. **Major trading partners:** Germany, Austria, Italy, Netherlands, Russia.

**Geography** This central European country is the size of Indiana. Most of Hungary is a fertile, rolling plain lying east of the Danube River and drained by the Danube and Tisza Rivers. In the extreme northwest is the Little Hungarian Plain. South of that area is Lake Balaton (250 sq mi; 648 sq km).

**Government** Parliamentary democracy.

**History** By 14 B.C., western Hungary was part of the Roman Empire's provinces of Pannonia and Dacia. The area east of the Danube was never a part of the Roman Empire and was largely occupied by various Germanic and Asiatic peoples. In 896 all of Hungary was invaded by the Magyars, who founded a kingdom. Christianity was accepted during the reign of Stephen I (Saint Stephen), 977–1038. A devastating invasion by the Mongols killed half of Hungary's population in 1241. The peak of Hungary's great period of medieval power came during the reign of Louis I the Great (1342–82), whose dominions touched the Baltic, Black, and Medi-

terranean seas. War with the Turks broke out in 1389, and for more than 100 years the Turks advanced through the Balkans. When the Turks smashed a Hungarian army in 1526, western and northern Hungary accepted Hapsburg rule to escape Turkish occupation. Transylvania became independent under Hungarian princes. Intermittent war with the Turks was waged until a peace treaty was signed in 1699.

After the suppression of the 1848 revolt against Hapsburg rule, led by Louis Kossuth, the dual monarchy of Austria-Hungary was set up in 1867. The dual monarchy was defeated with the other Central Powers in World War I. After a short-lived republic in 1918, the chaotic Communist rule of 1919 under Béla Kun ended with the Romanians occupying Budapest on Aug. 4, 1919. When the Romanians left, Adm. Nicholas Horthy entered the capital with a national army. The Treaty of Trianon of June 4, 1920, by which the Allies parceled out Hungarian territories, cost Hungary 68% of its land and 58% of its population. Meanwhile, the National Assembly had restored the legal continuity of the old monarchy and, on March 1, 1920, Horthy was elected regent.

In World War II, Hungary allied with Germany, which aided the country in recovering lost territories. Following the German invasion of Russia on June 22, 1941, Hungary joined the attack against the Soviet Union, but the war was not popular and Hungarian troops were almost entirely withdrawn from the eastern front by May 1943. Germany occupied the country for the remainder of the war. German occupation troops set up a puppet government after Horthy's appeal for an armistice with advancing Soviet troops on Oct. 15, 1944, had resulted in his overthrow. The German regime soon fled the capital, however, and on Dec. 23 a provisional government was formed in Soviet-occupied eastern Hungary. On Jan. 20, 1945, the government signed an armistice in Moscow. Early the next year, the National Assembly approved a constitutional law abolishing the thousand-year-old monarchy and establishing a republic.

By the Treaty of Paris (1947), Hungary had to give up all territory it had acquired since 1937 and to pay $300 million reparations to the USSR, Czechoslovakia, and Yugoslavia. In 1948, the Communist Party, with the support of Soviet troops, seized control. Hungary was proclaimed a People's Republic and one-party state in 1949. Industry was nationalized, the land collectivized into state farms, and the opposition terrorized by the secret police. The terror, modeled after that of the USSR, reached its height with the trial and life imprisonment of József Cardinal Mindszenty, the leader of Hungary's Roman Catholics, in 1948. On Oct. 23, 1956, an anti-Communist revolution broke out in Budapest. To cope with it, the Communists set up a coalition government and called former premier Imre Nagy back to head the government. But he and most of his ministers were swept by the logic of events into the anti-Communist opposition, and he declared Hungary a neutral power, withdrawing from the Warsaw Treaty and appealing to the United Nations for help. One of his ministers, János Kádár, established a counterregime and asked the USSR to send in military power. Soviet troops and tanks suppressed the revolution in bloody fighting after 190,000 people had fled the country. Under Kádár (1956–88), Communist Hungary henceforth maintained more liberal policies in the economic and cultural spheres, and Hungary became the most liberal of the Soviet-bloc nations of eastern Europe. Continuing his program of national reconciliation, Kádár emptied prisons, reformed the secret police, and eased travel restrictions.

Hungary's Communists abandoned their monopoly on power in 1989 voluntarily, and the constitution was amended in Oct. 1989 to allow for a multiparty state. The last Soviet troops left Hungary in June 1991, thereby ending almost 47 years of military presence. The transition to a market economy proved difficult.

In April 1999, Hungary became part of NATO, along with the Czech Republic and Poland. Hungary's hopes to join the EU in 2004 appear promising.

In May 2002, the Socialist party's Péter Medgyessy became prime minister; the following month it was revealed that he had been a communist-era spy. But investigations did not uncover any untoward behavior on the part of the prime minister while he served as a counterintelligence agent.

# Iceland

### REPUBLIC OF ICELAND

**National name:** Lydveldid Island
**President:** Ólafur Ragnar Grímsson (1996)
**Prime Minister:** David Oddsson (1991)
**Area:** 39,768 sq mi (103,000 sq km)[1]
**Population (2002 est.):** 279,384 (growth rate: 0.7%); birth rate: 14.4/1000; infant mortality rate: 3.5/1000; density per sq mi: 7
**Capital and largest city (1994 est.):** Reykjavik, 103,036. **Monetary unit:** Icelandic króna. **Language:** Icelandic. **Ethnicity/race:** homogeneous mixture of descendants of Norwegians and Celts. **Religions:** Church of Iceland (Evangelical Lutheran) 96%, other Protestant and Roman Catholic 3%, none 1%. **Literacy rate:** 100% (1976)
**Economic summary: GDP/PPP (2000 est.):** $6.85 billion; per capita $24,800. **Real growth rate:** 4.3%. **Inflation:** 3.5%. **Unemployment:** 2.7% (Jan. 2001). **Arable land:** 0%. **Agriculture:** potatoes, turnips; cattle, sheep; fish. **Labor force:** 159,000 (2000); agriculture 5.1%, fishing and fish processing 11.8%, manufacturing 12.9%, construction 10.7%, other services 59.5% (1999). **Industries:** fish processing; aluminum smelting, ferrosilicon production, geothermal power; tourism. **Natural resources:** fish, hydropower, geothermal power, diatomite. **Exports:** $2 billion (f.o.b., 2000): fish and fish products 70%, animal products, aluminum, diatomite and ferrosilicon. **Imports:** $2.2 billion (f.o.b., 2000): machinery and equipment, petroleum products; foodstuffs, textiles. **Major trading partners:** EU, U.S., Japan.

1. Including some offshore islands.

**Geography** Iceland, an island about the size of Kentucky, lies in the north Atlantic Ocean east of Greenland and just touches the Arctic Circle. It is one of the most volcanic regions in the world. More than 13% is covered by snowfields and glaciers, and most of the people live in the 7% of the island that is made up of fertile coastland. The Gulf Stream keeps Iceland's climate milder than one would expect from an island near the Arctic Circle.

**Government** Constitutional republic.

**History** The earliest inhabitants of Iceland were Irish hermits, who left the island upon the arrival of the pagan Norse people in the late 9th century. A constitution drawn up c. 930 created a form of democracy and provided for an *Althing*, the world's oldest practicing legislative assembly. The island's early history was preserved in the Icelandic sagas of the 13th century.

In 1262–64, Iceland came under Norwegian rule and passed to ultimate Danish control through the unification of the kingdoms of Norway, Sweden, and Denmark (the Kalmar Union) in 1397.

In 1874, Icelanders obtained their own constitution, and in 1918, Denmark recognized Iceland, via the Act of Union, as a separate state with unlimited sovereignty. It remained, however, nominally under the Danish monarchy.

During the German occupation of Denmark in World War II, British, then American, troops occupied Iceland and used it for a strategic air base. While officially neutral, Iceland cooperated with the Allies throughout the conflict. On June 17, 1944, after a popular referendum, the Althing proclaimed Iceland an independent republic.

The country joined the North Atlantic Treaty Organization in 1949, and subsequently received an American air force base in 1951. In 1970, it was admitted to the European Free Trade Association. Iceland unilaterally extended its territorial fishing limit from 3 to 200 nautical mi in 1972, precipitating a dispute with the UK known as the "cod wars," which ended in 1976, when the UK recognized the new limits. In 1980, the Icelanders elected a woman to the office of the presidency, the first elected female chief of state (i.e., president as distinct from prime minister) in the world. After the recession of the early 1990s, Iceland's economy rebounded.

# India

### REPUBLIC OF INDIA

**National name:** Bharat
**President:** A.P.J. Abdul Kalam (2002)
**Prime Minister:** Atal Bihari Vajpayee (1998)
**Area:** 1,269,338 sq mi (3,287,590 sq km)
**Population (2002 est.):** 1,045,845,226 (growth rate: 1.5%); birth rate: 23.8/1000; infant mortality rate: 61.5/1000; density per sq mi: 824
**Capital (2000 est.):** Delhi, 11,500,000 (metro. area). **Largest cities:** Bombay (Mumbai) (2000 est.), 17,850,000 (metro. area); Calcutta (Kolkata) (2000 est.), 12,900,000 (metro. area); Madras (Chennai) (2000 est.), 6,600,000 (metro. area); Hyderabad (2000 est.), 6,650,000 (metro. area); Bangalore (2000 est.), 5,500,000 (metro. area); Ahmedabad, 4,150,000; Kanpur, 1,874,409. **Monetary unit:** Rupee. **Principal languages:** Hindi (official), English (official), Bengali, Gujarati, Kashmiri, Malayalam, Marathi, Oriya, Punjabi, Tamil, Telugu, Urdu, Kannada, Assamese, Sanskrit, Sindhi (all recognized by the constitution). Dialects, 1,652. **Ethnicity/race:** Indo-Aryan 72%, Dravidian 25%, Mongoloid and other 3%. **Religions:** Hindu 82.6%, Islam 11.3%, Christian 2.4%, Sikh 2%, Buddhists 0.71%, Jains 0.48%. **Literacy rate:** 52% (1991)
**Economic summary: GDP/PPP (2000 est.):** $2.2 trillion; per capita $2,200. **Real growth rate:** 6%. **Inflation:** 5.4%. **Unemployment:** n.a. **Arable land:** 56%. **Agriculture:** rice, wheat, oilseed, cotton, jute, tea, sugarcane, potatoes; cattle, water buffalo, sheep, goats, poultry; fish. **Labor force:** n.a.; agriculture 67%, services 18%, industry 15% (1995 est.). **Industries:** textiles, chemicals, food processing, steel, transportation equipment, cement, mining, petroleum, machinery, software. **Natural resources:** coal (fourth-largest reserves in the world), iron ore, manganese, mica, bauxite, titanium ore, chromite, natural gas, diamonds, petroleum, limestone, arable land. **Exports:** $43.1 billion (f.o.b., 2000): textile goods, gems and jewelry, engineering goods, chemicals, leather manufactures. **Imports:** $60.8 billion (f.o.b., 2000): crude oil, machinery, gems, fertilizer, chemicals. **Major trading partners:** U.S., UK, Germany, Japan, Hong Kong, UAE, Benelux, Saudi Arabia. **Member of Commonwealth of Nations**

**Geography** One-third the area of the United States, the Republic of India occupies most of the subcontinent of India in south Asia. It borders on China in the northeast. Other neighbors are Pakistan on the west, Nepal and Bhutan on the north, and Burma and Bangladesh on the east.

The country can be divided into three distinct geographic regions: the Himalayan region in the north, which contains some of the highest mountains in the world, the Gangetic Plain, and the plateau region in the south and central part. Its three great river systems have extensive deltas and all rise in the Himalayas: the Ganges, 1,540 mi (2,478 km), the Indus, and the Brahmaputra.

India includes several groups of islands—the Laccadives (14 islands) in the Arabian Sea and the Andamans (204 islands) and the Nicobars (19 islands) in the Bay of Bengal.

**Government** Federal republic.

**History** One of the earliest civilizations, the Indus Valley civilization flourished on the Indian subcontinent from c. 2600 B.C. to c. 2000 B.C. The Aryans who invaded India c. 1500 B.C. from the northwest found a land that was already home to an advanced civilization. They introduced Sanskrit and the Vedic religion, a forerunner of Hinduism, to the area. Buddhism was founded in the 6th century B.C. and was spread throughout northern India, most notably by one of the great ancient kings of the Mauryan dynasty, Asoka (c. 269–232 B.C.), who also unified most of the Indian subcontinent for the first time.

In 1526, Muslim invaders founded the great Mogul empire, centered on Delhi, which lasted, at least in name, until 1857. Akbar the Great (1542–1605) strengthened and consolidated this empire. The long reign of his great-grandson, Aurangzeb (1618–1707), represents both the greatest extent of the Mogul empire and the beginning of its decay.

Vasco da Gama, the Portuguese explorer, visited India first in 1498, and for the next 100 years the Portuguese had a virtual monopoly on trade with the subcontinent. Meanwhile, the English founded the East India Company, which set up its first factory at Surat in 1612 and began expanding its influence, fighting the Indian rulers and the French, Dutch, and Portuguese traders simultaneously.

Bombay, taken from the Portuguese, became the seat of English rule in 1687. The defeat of French and Mogul armies by Lord Clive in 1757 laid the foundation of the British Empire in India. The East India Company continued to suppress native uprisings and extend British rule until 1858, when the administration of India was formally transferred to the British Crown following the Sepoy Mutiny of native troops in 1857–58.

After World War I, in which the Indian states sent more than 6 million troops to fight beside the Allies, Indian nationalist unrest rose to new heights under the leadership of a Hindu lawyer, Mohandas K. Gandhi, called Mahatma Gandhi. His philosophy of civil disobedience called for nonviolent noncooperation against British authority. He soon became the leading spirit of the Indian National Congress Party, which was the spearhead of revolt. In 1919, the British gave added responsibility to Indian officials, and in 1935, India was given a federal form of government and a measure of self-rule.

In 1942, with the Japanese pressing hard on the eastern borders of India, the British War Cabinet tried and failed to reach a political settlement with nationalist leaders. The Congress Party took the position that the British must quit India. In 1942, fearing mass civil disobedience, the government of India carried out widespread arrests of Congress leaders, including Gandhi.

Gandhi was released in 1944 and negotiations for a settlement were resumed. Finally, in Aug. 1947, India gained full independence. The victory was soured, however, by the partitioning of the predominantly Muslim regions of the north into the separate nation of Pakistan. The Muslim League, led by Mohammed Ali Jinnah, demanded a separate nation for the Muslim minority to prevent Hindu political and social domination. Indian Hindus, however, had hoped for a unified rather than balkanized Indian subcontinent. Lord Mountbatten as viceroy partitioned India along religious lines and split the provinces of Bengal and the Punjab, which both nations claimed. The partition of Pakistan and India led to the largest migration in human history, with 17 million people fleeing across the borders in both directions to escape the bloody riots occurring among sectarian groups. Armed conflict also broke out over rival claims to the princely states of Jammu and Kashmir.

Jawaharlal Nehru, nationalist leader and head of the Congress Party, was made prime minister. In 1949, a constitution was approved, making India a sovereign republic. Under a federal structure the states were organized on linguistic lines. The dominance of the Congress Party contributed to stability. In 1956, the republic absorbed former French settlements. Five years later, the republic forcibly annexed the Portuguese enclaves of Goa, Damao, and Diu.

Nehru died in 1964. His successor, Lal Bahadur Shastri, died on Jan. 10, 1966. Nehru's daughter, Indira Gandhi, became prime minister, and she continued his policy of nonalignment.

In 1971, the Pakistani army moved in to quash the independence movement in East Pakistan that was supported by India, and some 10 million Bengali refugees poured across the border into India, creating social, economic, and health problems. After numerous border incidents, India invaded East Pakistan and in two weeks forced the surrender of the Pakistani army. East Pakistan was established as an independent state and renamed Bangladesh.

In May 1975, the 300-year-old kingdom of Sikkim became a full-fledged Indian state. Situated in the Himalayas, Sikkim was a virtual dependency of Tibet until the early 19th century. Under an 1890 treaty between China and Great Britain, it became a British protectorate, and was made an Indian protectorate after Britain quit the subcontinent.

In the summer of 1975, the world's largest democracy veered suddenly toward authoritarianism when a judge in Allahabad, India, found a wrongdoing conviction ... Gandhi's landslide victory in the 1971 elections invalid because civil servants had illegally aided her campaign. Amid demands for her resignation, Gandhi decreed a state of emergency on June 26 and ordered mass arrests of her critics, including all opposition party leaders except the Communists.

Despite strong opposition to her repressive measures, particularly resentment against compulsory birth control programs, Gandhi, in 1977, announced parliamentary elections for March. At the same time, she freed most political prisoners. The landslide victory of Morarji R. Desai unseated Gandhi, but she staged a spectacular comeback in the elections of Jan. 1980.

In 1984, Gandhi ordered the Indian army to root out a band of Sikh holy men and gunmen who were using the most sacred shrine of the Sikh religion, the Golden Temple in Amritsar, as a base for terrorist raids in a violent campaign for greater political autonomy in the strategic Punjab border state. The perceived sacrilege to the Golden Temple kindled outrage among many of India's 14 million Sikhs and brought a spasm of mutinies and desertions by Sikh officers and soldiers in the army.

On Oct. 31, 1984, Indira Gandhi was assassinated by two men identified by police as Sikh members of her bodyguard. The ruling Congress Party chose her older son, Rajiv Gandhi, to succeed her as prime minister for four years. While running for reelection, former prime minister Rajiv Gandhi was assassinated on May 22, 1991, by Tamil militants who objected to India's mediation of the civil war in Sri Lanka.

The ruling Congress Party lost the parliamentary elections of May 1996, and its waning resulted in a period of political instability. The Hindu nationalist Bharatiya Janata Party (BJP) then became the dominant force in politics, with Atal Bihari Vajpayee becoming prime minister twice in two years.

In May 1998, India set off five nuclear tests, surprising the international community, which widely condemned India's pronuclear stance. Despite international urging for restraint, Pakistan responded by conducting several nuclear tests of its own two weeks later. India has resisted signing the Comprehensive Test Ban Treaty for nuclear weapons and has been slapped with sanctions by the U.S. and other countries. Less than a year later, in April 1999, both India and Pakistan tested nuclear-capable ballistic missiles.

India and Pakistan have held various talks about the disputed territory of Kashmir, which is the issue at the base of their chronic antagonism and their displays of nuclear strength. India controls two-thirds of this Himalayan region, which is the only Indian state that is predominantly Muslim.

The Indian Air Force launched air strikes on May 26, 1999, and later sent in ground troops against Islamic guerrilla forces in Kashmir. India blamed Pakistan for orchestrating violence in Kashmir by sending soldiers and mercenaries across the so-called Line of Control that divides Kashmir between India and Pakistan. Pakistan countered that the guerrillas were independent Kashmiri freedom fighters struggling for India's ouster from the region. Most international sources agreed with India's assumption that Pakistan was arming the soldiers. In Aug. 1999, Pakistan was forced to withdraw, but fighting continued sporadically during the coming year.

In Oct. 2001, violence again broke out in the region when a suicide bombing by a Pakistan-based militant organization killed 38 in India-controlled Kashmir. India retaliated with heavy shelling across the Line of Control. India, angered by Washington's sudden coziness to Pakistan following Sept. 11, took the opportunity to point out that while Pakistan might be helping the U.S. fight terrorism on the Afghan front, it was simultaneously supporting terrorism on its own borders with India. On Dec. 13, 2001, suicide bombers attacked the Indian parliament, killing 14 people. Indian officials blamed the deadly attack on Islamic militants supported by Pakistan.

After six months of steadily escalating tensions that brought the two countries to the brink of war—the threat of nuclear confrontation loomed large—India and Pakistan made modest gestures in the summer of 2002 to thwart disaster. More than 1 million troops, however, remained stationed along the Line of Control, and any resolution in the conflict over the disputed territory remained elusive.

Violent clashes between Muslims and Hindus rocked the state of Gujarat in late Feb. and early March 2002 after a Muslim mob fire-bombed a train, killing 58 Hindu activists who were returning from Ayodhya, where the Hindu World Congress plans to build a temple on the ruins of a Muslim mosque. Hindus retaliated, and more than 500 people died in the bloodshed. The ruling Hindu nationalist BJP was criticized for not stemming the gruesome attacks on Muslims.

In July 2002, A.P.J. Abdul Kalam, a Muslim nuclear scientist, was elected president of India.

# Indonesia

### REPUBLIC OF INDONESIA

**National name:** Republik Indonesia
**President:** Megawati Sukarnoputri (2001)
**Area:** 741,096 sq mi (1,919,440 sq km)
**Population (2002 est.):** 232,073,071 (growth rate: 1.6%); birth rate: 21.9/1000; infant mortality rate: 39.6/1000; density per sq mi: 313
**Capital and largest city (2000 est.):** Jakarta, 12,300,000 (metro. area). **Other large cities (1995 est.):** Surabaya, 2,701,300; Bandung, 2,368,200; Medan, 1,909,700; Semarang, 1,366,500. **Monetary unit:** Rupiah. **Languages:** Bahasa Indonesia (official), Dutch, English, and more than 583 languages and dialects. **Ethnicity/race:** Javanese 45%, Sundanese 14%, Madurese 7.5%, coastal Malays 7.5%, other 26%. **Religions:** Islam 87%, Christian 9%, Hindu 2%, other 2%. **Literacy rate:** 84% (1990)
**Economic summary: GDP/PPP** (2000 est.): $654 billion; per capita $2,900. **Real growth rate:** 4.8%. **Inflation:** 9%. **Unemployment:** 15%–20% (1998 est.). **Arable land:** 10%. **Agriculture:** rice, cassava (tapioca), peanuts, rubber, cocoa, coffee, palm oil, copra; poultry, beef, pork, eggs. **Labor force:** 99 million (1999); agriculture 45%, industry 16%, services 39% (1999 est.) **Industries:** petroleum and natural gas; textiles, apparel, and footwear; mining, cement, chemical fertilizers, plywood; rubber; food; tourism. **Natural resources:** petroleum, tin, natural gas, nickel, timber, bauxite, copper, fertile soils, coal, gold, silver. **Exports:** $64.7 billion (f.o.b., 2000 est.): oil and gas, plywood, textiles, rubber. **Imports:** $40.4 billion (c.i.f., 2000 est.): machinery and equipment; chemicals, fuels, foodstuffs. **Major trading partners:** Japan, EU, U.S., Singapore, South Korea, Netherlands, Australia, Hong Kong, China, Taiwan, Germany.

**Geography** Indonesia is an archipelago in Southeast Asia consisting of 17,000 islands (6,000 inhabited) and straddling the equator. The largest islands are Sumatra, Java (the most populous), Bali, Kalimantan (Indonesia's part of Borneo), Sulawesi (Celebes), the Nusa Tenggara islands, the Moluccas Islands, and Irian Jaya (also called West Papua), the western part of New Guinea. Its neighbor to the north is Malaysia and to the east is Papua New Guinea.

Indonesia, part of the "ring of fire," has the largest number of active volcanoes in the world. Earthquakes are frequent. The "Wallace Line," a zoological demarcation between Asian and Australian flora and fauna, divides Indonesia.

**Government** Republic.

**History** The 17,000 islands that make up Indonesia were home to a diversity of cultures and indigenous beliefs when the islands came under the influence of Hindu priests and traders in the first and second centuries A.D. Muslim invasions began in the 13th century, and most of the archipelago had converted to Islam by the 15th. Portuguese traders arrived early in the next century but were ousted by the Dutch around 1595.

The Dutch United East India Company established posts on the island of Java, in an effort to control the spice trade.

After Napoléon subjugated the Netherlands in 1811, the British seized the islands but returned them to the Dutch in 1816. In 1922, Indonesia was made an integral part of the Dutch kingdom. During World War II, Japan seized the islands. Tokyo was primarily interested in Indonesia's oil, which was vital to the war effort, and tolerated fledgling nationalists such as Sukarno and Mohammed Hatta. After Japan's surrender, Sukarno and Hatta proclaimed Indonesian independence on Aug. 17, 1945. Allied troops, mostly British Indian forces, fought nationalist militia to reassert the prewar status quo until the arrival of Dutch troops.

In Nov. 1946, a draft agreement on forming a Netherlands-Indonesian Union was reached, but differences in interpretation resulted in more fighting between Dutch and nationalist forces. Following a bitter war for independence, leaders on both sides agreed to terms of a union on Nov. 2, 1949. The transfer of sovereignty took place in Amsterdam on Dec. 27, 1949. In Feb. 1956, Indonesia abrogated the union, and began seizing Dutch property in the islands.

In 1963, Netherlands New Guinea (the Dutch portion of the island of New Guinea) was transferred to Indonesia and renamed West Irian, which became Irian Jaya in 1973 and West Papua in 2000. Hatta and Sukarno, the cofathers of Indonesian independence, split over Sukarno's concept of "guided democracy," and under Sukarno's rule the Indonesian Communist Party (PKI) steadily increased its influence.

Three years later, Sukarno was named president for life. Sukarno enjoyed mass support for his policies, but a growing power struggle between the military and the PKI loomed over his government. After an attempted military coup was put down by army chief of staff General Suharto and officers loyal to him, Suharto's forces killed hundreds of thousands of suspected Communists in a massive purge aimed at undermining Sukarno's rule.

Suharto took over the reins of government and gradually eased Sukarno out of office, completing his consolidation of power in 1967. Under Suharto the military assumed an overarching role in national affairs, and relations with the West were enhanced. Indonesia's economy improved dramatically and national elections were permitted, although the opposition was so tightly controlled as to virtually choke off dissent.

In 1975, Indonesia invaded the former Portuguese half of the island of Timor and seized the territory in 1976. A separatist movement developed at once. Unlike the rest of Indonesia, which had been a Dutch colony, East Timor was controlled by the Portuguese for 400 years, and while 90% of Indonesians are Muslim, the East Timorese are primarily Catholic. More than 200,000 Timorese are reported to have died from famine, disease, and fighting since the annexation. East Timor has received international attention for human rights abuses, and, in 1996, two East Timorese resistance activists, Bishop Carlos Filipe Ximenes Belo and José Ramos-Horta, received the Nobel Peace Prize.

In the summer of 1997, Indonesia suffered a major economic setback along with most other Asian economies. Banks failed and the value of Indonesia's currency, the rupiah, plummeted. Antigovernment demonstrations and riots broke out, directed mainly at the country's prosperous ethnic Chinese. As the economic crisis deepened, student demonstrators occupied the national Parliament, demanding Suharto's ouster. On May 21, 1998, Suharto stepped down, ending 32 years of rule, and handed over power to Vice President B. J. Habibie.

June 7, 1999, marked Indonesia's first free parliamentary election since 1955. The ruling Golkar Party took a backseat to the Indonesian Democratic Party-Struggle (PDI-P), led by Megawati Sukarnoputri, the daughter of Sukarno, Indonesia's first president.

The ethnic, religious, and political tensions kept in check during former President Suharto's 32 years of authoritarian rule ruptured in the months following his downfall. Rioting and violence shook the provinces of Aceh, Ambon (in the Moluccas), Borneo, and Irian Jaya. But nowhere was the violence more brutal and unjust than in East Timor. Habibie unexpectedly ended 25 years of Indonesian intransigence by announcing in Feb. 1999 that he was willing to hold a referendum on East Timorese independence. Twice rescheduled because of violence, a UN-organized referendum took place on Aug. 30, 1999, with 79% of the population voting to secede from Indonesia. In the days following the election, pro-Indonesian militias and Indonesian soldiers massacred civilians and forced a third of the population out of the region. Despite repeated assurances that order would be restored to the region, Habibie and the head of the military, General Wiranto, were either unwilling or unable to stop the violent rampage. After enormous international pressure, Indonesia finally agreed to allow UN forces into East Timor on Sept. 12. Led by Australia, an international peacekeeping force began restoring order to the ravaged region.

In a surprising upset, the Indonesian parliament elected Abdurrahman Wahid as the new president of Indonesia on October 20, 1999, defeating Megawati Sukarnoputri, the popular leader of the Indonesian Democratic Party-Struggle. Wahid, commonly known as Gus Dur, was a Sufi cleric as well as an adept politician with a reputation for honesty and moderation.

In fall 2000, Suharto failed twice to show up in court to face corruption charges of embezzling $570 million in state funds, but his lawyers insisted he was too ill to stand trial.

In the fall of 2000 and winter of 2001, Wahid himself came under increasing criticism for corruption and incompetence. He was blamed for not stopping the continuing ethnic clashes and loss of life in Aceh, Irian Jaya, the Moluccas Islands, and especially in Borneo, where the Dayak people turned against Madurese immigrants, slaughtering hundreds.

He was forced from power in July 2001, and Vice President Megawati Sukarnoputri assumed the helm. Popular among the poor, Megawati's retiring nature and lack of political experience led many to question her abilities to govern this fledgling democracy beleaguered by separatist movements and continuous violence.

In Aug. 2002, Abilio Soares, the former governor of East Timor, was convicted of crimes against humanity and sentenced to three years in prison for failing to control the deadly rampage by pro-Indonesian militias and soldiers after the 1999 independence referendum. But six other military and police leaders were acquitted of the charges; human rights groups have expressed outrage.

The U.S. announced in Aug. plans to give Indonesia $50 million over the next two years to train troops and modernize the police force. The aid, the first such package to the country since the early 1990s, is intended to help Indonesia fight terrorism.

# Iran

**ISLAMIC REPUBLIC OF IRAN**

**Chief of State:** Ayatollah Khamenei (1989)
**President:** Mohammad Khatami (1997)
**Area:** 636,293 sq mi (1,648,000 sq km)
**Population (2002 est.):** 66,622,704 (growth rate: 1.2%);
birth rate: 17.5/1000; infant mortality rate: 28.1/1000;
density per sq mi: 105
**Capital and largest city (1994 est.):** Teheran,
10,400,000 (metro. area). **Largest cities (1994 est.):**
Mashad, 1,964,489; Isfahan, 1,220,595; Tabriz,
1,166,203. **Monetary unit:** Rial. **Languages:** Farsi
(Persian), Azari, Kurdish, Arabic. **Ethnicity/race:**
Persian 51%, Azerbaijani 24%, Gilaki and Mazandarani
8%, Kurd 7%, Arab 3%, Lur 2%, Baloch 2%, Turkmen
2%, other 1%. **Religions:** Shi'ite Muslim 95%, Sunni
Muslim 4%. **Literacy rate:** 54% (1990)
**Economic summary: GDP/PPP** (2000 est.): $413 billion;
per capita $6,300. **Real growth rate:** 3%. **Inflation:**
16%. **Unemployment:** 14% (1999 est.). **Arable land:**
10%. **Agriculture:** wheat, rice, other grains, sugar
beets, fruits, nuts, cotton; dairy products, wool; caviar.
**Labor force:** 17.3 million; note: shortage of skilled
labor (1998); agriculture 33%, industry 25%, services
42% (1999 est.). **Industries:** petroleum,
petrochemicals, textiles, cement and other construction
materials, food processing (particularly sugar refining
and vegetable oil production), metal fabricating,
armaments. **Natural resources:** petroleum, natural
gas, coal, chromium, copper, iron ore, lead,
manganese, zinc, sulfur. **Exports:** $25 billion (f.o.b.,
2000 est.): petroleum 85%, carpets, fruits and nuts, iron
and steel, chemicals. **Imports:** $15 billion (f.o.b., 2000
est.): industrial raw materials and intermediate goods,
capital goods, foodstuffs and other consumer goods,
technical services, military supplies. **Major trading
partners:** Japan, Italy, UAE, South Korea, France,
China, Germany.

**Geography** Iran, a Middle Eastern country south of
the Caspian Sea and north of the Persian Gulf, is three
times the size of Arizona. It shares borders with Iraq,
Turkey, Azerbaijan, Turkmenistan, Armenia, Afghanistan, and Pakistan.

The Elburz Mountains in the north rise to 18,603 ft
(5,670 m) at Mount Damavend. From northwest to
southeast, the country is crossed by a desert 800 mi
(1,287 km) long.

**Government** Iran has been an Islamic theocracy
since the Pahlavi monarchy regime was overthrown on
Feb. 11, 1979.

**History** The region now called Iran was occupied by
the Medes and the Persians in the 1500s B.C., until the
Persian king Cyrus the Great overthrew the Medes and
became ruler of the Achaemenid (Persian) Empire,
which reached from the Indus to the Nile at its zenith
in 525 B.C. Persia fell to Alexander in 331–330 B.C.,
and a succession of other rulers: the Seleucids (312–
302 B.C.), the Greek-speaking Parthians (247 B.C.–A.D.
226), the Sasanians, and the Arab Muslims (in 641).
By the mid-800s Persia had become an international
scientific and cultural center. In the 12th century it was
invaded by the Mongols. The Safavid dynasty (1501–
1722), under whom the dominant religion became
Shi'ite Islam, followed, and was then replaced by the
Qajar dynasty (1794–1925).

During the Qajar dynasty, the Russians and the British fought for economic control of the area, and during World War I, Iran's neutrality did not stop it from
becoming a battlefield for Russian and British troops.
A coup in 1921 brought Reza Kahn to power. In 1925,
he became shah and changed his name to Reza Shah
Pahlavi. He subsequently did much to modernize the
country and abolished all foreign extraterritorial
rights.

The country's pro-Axis allegiance in World War II
led to Anglo-Russian occupation of Iran in 1941 and
deposition of the shah in favor of his son, Mohammed
Reza Pahlavi. Pahlavi's Westernization programs
alienated the clergy, and his authoritarian rule led to
massive demonstrations during the 1970s, to which the
shah responded with the imposition of martial law in
Sept. 1978. The shah and his family fled Iran on Jan.
16, 1979, and the exiled cleric Ayatollah Ruhollah
Khomeini returned to establish an Islamic theocracy.
Khomeini proceeded with his plans for revitalizing
Islamic traditions. He urged women to return to the
veil; banned alcohol, Western music, and mixed bathing; shut down the media; closed universities, and
eliminated political parties.

Revolutionary militants invaded the U.S. embassy
in Teheran on Nov. 4, 1979, seized staff members as
hostages, and precipitated an international crisis.
Khomeini refused all appeals, even a unanimous vote
by the UN Security Council demanding immediate
release of the hostages. Iranian hostility toward Washington was reinforced by the Carter administration's
economic boycott and deportation order against Iranian students in the U.S., the break in diplomatic relations, and ultimately an aborted U.S. raid in April
aimed at rescuing the hostages.

As the first anniversary of the embassy seizure
neared, Khomeini and his followers insisted on their
original conditions: guarantee by the U.S. not to interfere in Iran's affairs, cancellation of U.S. damage
claims against Iran, release of $8 billion in frozen Ira-
nian assets, an apology, and the return of the assets
held by the former imperial family. These conditions
were largely met and the 52 American hostages were
released on Jan. 20, 1980, ending 444 days in captivity.

The sporadic war with Iraq regained momentum in
1982, as Iran launched an offensive in March and
regained much of the border area occupied by Iraq in
late 1980. The stalemated war with Iraq dragged on
well into 1988. Although Iraq expressed its willingness to cease fighting, Iran stated that it would not
stop the war until Iraq agreed to pay for war damages
and to punish the Iraqi government leaders involved in
the conflict. On July 20, 1988, Khomeini, after a series
of Iranian military reverses, agreed to cease-fire negotiations with Iraq. A cease-fire went into effect on Aug.
20, 1988. Khomeini died in June 1989 and Ayatollah
Khamenei succeeded him as the supreme leader.

By early 1991 the Islamic revolution appeared to
have lost much of its militancy. Attempting to revive a
stagnant economy, President Rafsanjani took measures
to decentralize the command system and introduce
free-market mechanisms.

Mohammad Khatami, a little-known moderate
cleric, former newspaperman, and national librarian,
won the presidential election with 70% of the vote on
May 23, 1997, a stunning victory over the conservative ruling elite. Khatami has supported greater social
and political freedoms, and has made overtures for
friendlier relations with the West. But his steps toward
liberalizing the strict clerical rule governing the country have put him at odds with the supreme leader,
Ayatollah Khamenei.

Signaling a seismic change in Iran's political environment, reform candidates won the overwhelming
majority of seats in Feb. 2000 parliamentary elections,
thereby wresting control from hard-liners, who had

dominated the Parliament since the 1979 Islamic revolution. The Parliament's reformist transformation greatly buttressed the efforts of Khatami in constructing a nation of "lasting pluralism and Islamic democracy." Khatami has walked a jittery tightrope between student groups and other liberals pressuring him to introduce bolder freedoms, and Iran's military and conservative clerical elite (including Iran's supreme leader, Ayatollah Khamenei), who have expressed growing impatience with the president's liberalizing measures.

In June 2001 elections, Mohammad Khatami demonstrated the overwhelming popularity of his reforms by winning reelection with 77% of the vote. Khatami's new cabinet, composed of 20 moderates, disappointed liberals who hoped he would step up the pace of reform. Friction between Iran's reformers and conservatives increased in 2002.

Iran cooperated in the fight against global terrorism after the Sept. 11 bombings, capturing and turning over al-Qaeda suspects and assisting its war-torn neighbor Afghanistan in restoring peace. Yet U.S. President Bush, who announced in Jan. 2002 that Iran was part of an "axis of evil," virtually ignored Iran's efforts, exacerbating Iran's existing antipathy toward the United States.

# Iraq

### REPUBLIC OF IRAQ

**National name:** Jumhouriyat Al Iraq
**President:** Saddam Hussein (1979)
**Area:** 168,753 sq mi (437,072 sq km)
**Population (2002 est.):** 24,001,816 (growth rate: 2.8%); birth rate: 34.2/1000; infant mortality rate: 57.6/1000; density per sq mi: 142
**Capital and largest city (2000 est.):** Baghdad, 4,850,000 (metro. area). **Largest cities (est. 1987):** Mosul, 664,221; Irbil, 485,968; Karkuk (Kirkuk), 418,624; Basra, 406,296. **Monetary unit:** Iraqi dinar. **Languages:** Arabic (official) and Kurdish. **Ethnicity/ race:** Arab 75%–80%, Kurdish 15%–20%, Turkoman, Assyrian, or other 5%. **Religions:** Muslim 97% (Shi'ite 60%–65%, Sunni 32%–37%), Christian or other 3%. **Literacy rate:** 60% (1990)
**Economic summary:** GDP/PPP (2000 est.): $57 billion; per capita $2,500. **Real growth rate:** 15%. **Inflation:** 100%. **Unemployment:** n.a. **Arable land:** 12%. **Agriculture:** wheat, barley, rice, vegetables, dates, cotton; cattle, sheep. **Labor force:** 4.4 million (1989); agriculture n.a., industry n.a., services n.a. **Industries:** petroleum, chemicals, textiles, construction materials, food processing. **Natural resources:** petroleum, natural gas, phosphates, sulfur. **Exports:** $21.8 billion (2000 est.): crude oil. **Imports:** $13.8 billion (2000 est.): food, medicine, manufactures. **Major trading partners:** Russia, France, Switzerland, China, Egypt, Vietnam.

**Geography** Iraq, a triangle of mountains, desert, and fertile river valley, is bounded on the east by Iran, on the north by Turkey, on the west by Syria and Jordan, and on the south by Saudi Arabia and Kuwait. It is twice the size of Idaho. The country has arid desert land west of the Euphrates, a broad central valley between the Euphrates and Tigris, and mountains in the northeast.

**Government** One-party republic.

**History** From earliest times Iraq was known as Mesopotamia—the land between the rivers—for it embraces a large part of the alluvial plains of the Tigris and Euphrates Rivers.

An advanced civilization existed by 4000 B.C. Sometime after 2000 B.C. the land became the center of the ancient Babylonian and Assyrian Empires. Mesopotamia was conquered by Cyrus the Great of Persia in 538 B.C., and by Alexander in 331 B.C. After an Arab conquest in 637–40, Baghdad became capital of the ruling caliphate. The country was cruelly pillaged by the Mongols in 1258, and during the 16th, 17th, and 18th centuries was the object of repeated Turkish-Persian competition.

Nominal Turkish suzerainty imposed in 1638 was replaced by direct Turkish rule in 1831. In World War I, Britain occupied most of Mesopotamia and was given a mandate over the area in 1920. The British renamed the area Iraq and recognized it as a kingdom in 1922. In 1932, the monarchy achieved full independence. Britain again occupied Iraq during World War II because of its pro-Axis stance in the initial years of the war.

Iraq became a charter member of the Arab League in 1945, and Iraqi troops took part in the Arab invasion of Palestine in 1948.

King Faisal II, born on May 2, 1935, succeeded his father, Ghazi I, who was killed in an automobile accident on April 4, 1939. Faisal and his uncle, Crown Prince Abdul-Illah, were assassinated in July 1958 in a swift revolutionary coup that ended the monarchy and brought to power a military junta headed by Abdul Karem Kassim. Kassim reversed the monarchy's pro-Western policies, attempted to rectify the economic disparities between rich and poor, and began to form alliances with Communist countries.

Kassim was overthrown and killed in a coup staged on March 8, 1963, by the Ba'ath Socialist Party. Abdel Salam Arif, a leader in the 1958 coup, staged another coup in Nov. 1963, driving the Ba'ath members of the revolutionary council from power. He adopted a new constitution in 1964. In 1966, he, two cabinet members, and other supporters died in a helicopter crash. His brother, Gen. Abdel Rahman Arif, assumed the presidency, crushed the opposition, and won an indefinite extension of his term in 1967.

His regime was ousted in July 1968 by a junta led by Maj. Gen. Ahmed Hassan al-Bakr of the Ba'ath Party. Bakr and his second-in-command, Saddam Hussein, imposed authoritarian rule in an effort to end the decades of political instability that followed World War II.

One of the world's leading producers of oil, Iraq's oil revenues were used to develop one of the strongest military forces in the region. On July 16, 1979, President Bakr was succeeded by Saddam Hussein, whose regime steadily developed an international reputation for repression, human rights abuses, and terrorism.

A long-standing territorial dispute over control of the Shatt-al-Arab waterway between Iraq and Iran broke into full-scale war on Sept. 20, 1980, when Iraq invaded western Iran. The eight-year war cost the lives of an estimated 1.5 million people, and finally ended in a UN-brokered ceasefire in 1988. Poison gas was used by both Iran and Iraq. Iraq also used poison gas against its own Kurdish population in 1988.

In July 1990, President Hussein asserted spurious territorial claims on Kuwaiti land. A mediation attempt by Arab leaders failed, and on Aug. 2, 1990, Iraqi troops invaded Kuwait and set up a puppet government. The UN unsuccessfully imposed trade sanctions against Iraq to pressure it to withdraw. On Jan. 18, 1991, UN forces, under the leadership of U.S. general Norman Schwarzkopf, launched Operation Desert Storm, liberating Kuwait in less than a week. In 1991, the UN set up a northern no-fly zone to protect Iraq's Kurdish population; in 1992 a southern no-fly zone was established as a buffer between Iraq and Kuwait.

The war did little to dwarf Iraq's resilient dictator. Despite rebellions by both Shi'ites and Kurds following Iraq's crushing defeat in the Gulf War, Saddam Hussein maintained his draconian grip on Iraq. The UN Security Council imposed sanctions beginning in 1990, which barred Iraq from selling oil except in exchange for food and medicine. Despite the debilitating effects of UN sanctions, Hussein continued to defy the terms of the cease-fire agreement. He waged a propaganda campaign that blamed the U.S. for the starvation and poverty suffered by the Iraqi people rather than his own refusal to meet the terms required to remove sanctions.

On Nov. 13, 1997, Iraq expelled the American members of the UN inspections team mandated to ascertain that Iraq had destroyed all its nuclear, chemical, biological, and ballistic arms. Under the 1991 cease-fire resolution, the UN would not lift sanctions until Iraq fully complied. The standoff stretched on over months, and as tensions rose, the U.S. began a military buildup in the Gulf. In Feb. 1998, UN secretary-general Kofi Annan brokered a peaceful solution to the standoff. Over the next months Baghdad continued to impede the UN inspection team, demanding that sanctions be lifted. Finally, in Aug. 1998, Hussein put a complete halt to the inspections. This time, the U.S. opted for diplomatic arm-twisting rather than military threats, and in Sept., the UN Security Council voted unanimously that the lifting of sanctions would not be discussed until cooperation with UN arms inspectors resumed. In Oct. 1998, the United States and Britain threatened Iraq with the possibility of a military strike if it did not begin cooperating. On Nov. 14, Iraq agreed to unconditional cooperation with the UN inspectors, but by Dec. 15, chief UN weapons inspector Richard Butler reported that Iraq had not lived up to its promise. The United States and Britain began four days of intensive air strikes. Since then, the U.S. and Britain have waged a steady war of attrition against Iraq, conducting hundreds of air strikes on Iraqi targets within the no-fly zones. The sustained, low-level warfare continued unabated into 2002.

In 2000, the original UN inspections team, UNSCOM, was replaced with UNMOVIC, after the Clinton administration admitted that it had received intelligence reports from UNSCOM's weapons inspectors. In fall 2000, however, Baghdad was still refusing to let the new inspections team into the country. The sanctions against Iraq have failed to crush its leader but have caused catastrophic suffering among its people—the country's infrastructure is in ruins, and disease, malnutrition, and the infant mortality rate have skyrocketed.

After the Sept. 11 terrorist attacks, President Bush began calling for a "regime change" in Iraq, describing it as part of an "axis of evil." The alleged existence of weapons of mass destruction, the stymying of UN weapons inspections, Iraq's links to terrorism, and Saddam Hussein's despotism and human rights abuses were the major reasons cited for necessitating a preemptive strike against the country. Foreign and domestic critics expressed skepticism about the Bush administration's allegations and whether military means were the only way to resolve them. The Bush administration originally presented action against Iraq as part of the U.S. war on terrorism, but it failed to link Iraq to al-Qaeda. Critics warned that a focus on Iraq would deflect attention away from the real threat of terrorism and thwart the chance for a resolution in the Israeli-Palestinian conflict. Bush then cited Iraq's development of chemical, biological, and nuclear weapons as the prime justification for a preemptive attack. The Arab world and much of Europe condemned the hawkish and unilateral U.S. stance, contending that the U.S. must enlist the approval of the UN in any action it takes or it is otherwise violating international law. Only the UK declared its intention to support the U.S. in military action. In response to the U.S. threats, Hussein continued to refuse UN weapons inspections and engaged in his characteristic defiant bluster. On Sept. 12, 2002, Bush addressed the UN, challenging the organization to swiftly enforce its own resolutions against Iraq, or else the U.S. would have no choice but to act on its own. Bush's multilateral gesture began drawing modest support from the international community. Surprising much of the world, Hussein agreed within days to allow United Nations weapons inspectors to return to his country unconditionally. While the U.S. was openly skeptical of the notoriously disingenuous Iraqis, the involvement of the UN at least united parts of the world in efforts to find a political, if not a military solution to Iraq.

# Ireland

**National name:** Ireland, or Eire in the Irish language
**President:** Mary McAleese (1997)
**Taoiseach (Prime Minister):** Bertie Ahern (1997)
**Area:** 27,135 sq mi (70,280 sq km)
**Population (2002 est.):** 3,883,159 (growth rate: 0.7%); birth rate: 14.6/1000; infant mortality rate: 5.4/1000; density per sq mi: 143
**Capital:** Dublin. **Largest cities (1996):** Dublin, 953,000; Cork, 180,000; Limerick, 79,000; Galway, 57,000. **Monetary units:** Euro (formerly Irish pound [punt]). **Languages:** English, Irish Gaelic. **Ethnicity/race:** Celtic, English. **Religions:** Roman Catholic 93%, Anglican 3%, none 1%, unknown 2%, other 1%. **Literacy rate:** 98% (1981)
**Economic summary:** GDP/PPP (2000 est.): $81.9 billion; per capita $21,600. **Real growth rate:** 9.9%. **Inflation:** 5.6%. **Unemployment:** 4.1% (2000). **Arable land:** 13%. **Agriculture:** turnips, barley, potatoes, sugar beets, wheat; beef, dairy products. **Labor force:** 1.82 million (2000 est.); services 64%, industry 28%, agriculture 8%. **Industries:** food products, brewing, textiles, clothing; chemicals, pharmaceuticals, machinery, transportation equipment, glass and crystal; software. **Natural resources:** zinc, lead, natural gas, barite, copper, gypsum, limestone, dolomite, peat, silver. **Exports:** $73.5 billion (f.o.b., 2000): machinery and equipment, computers, chemicals, pharmaceuticals; live animals, animal products. **Imports:** $45.7 billion (f.o.b., 2000 est.): data processing equipment, other machinery and equipment, chemicals; petroleum and petroleum products, textiles, clothing. **Major trading partners:** EU, U.S., Japan, Singapore.

**Geography** Ireland is situated in the Atlantic Ocean and separated from Great Britain by the Irish Sea. Half the size of Arkansas, it occupies the entire island except for the six counties that make up Northern Ireland. Ireland resembles a basin—a central plain rimmed with mountains, except in the Dublin region. The mountains are low, with the highest peak, Carrantuohill in County Kerry, rising to 3,415 ft (1,041 m). The principal river is the Shannon, which begins in the north-central area, flows south and southwest for about 240 mi (386 km), and empties into the Atlantic.

**Government** Republic.

**History** In the Stone and Bronze Ages, Ireland was inhabited by Picts in the north and a people called the Erainn in the south, the same stock, apparently, as in all the isles before the Anglo-Saxon invasion of Britain. About the 4th century B.C., tall, red-haired Celts arrived from Gaul or Galicia. They subdued and assimilated the inhabitants and established a Gaelic civilization. By the beginning of the Christian Era, Ireland was divided into five kingdoms—Ulster, Connacht, Leinster, Meath, and Munster. Saint Patrick introduced Christianity in 432, and the country developed into a center of Gaelic and Latin learning. Irish monasteries, the equivalent of universities, attracted intellectuals as well as the pious and sent out missionaries to many parts of Europe and, some believe, to North America.

Norse depredations along the coasts, starting in 795, ended in 1014 with Norse defeat at the Battle of Clontarf by forces under Brian Boru. In the 12th century, the pope gave all of Ireland to the English Crown as a papal fief. In 1171, Henry II of England was acknowledged "Lord of Ireland," but local sectional rule continued for centuries, and English control over the whole island was not reasonably absolute until the 17th century. In the Battle of the Boyne (1690), the Catholic King James II and his French supporters were defeated by the Protestant King William III (of Orange). An era of Protestant political and economic supremacy began.

By the Act of Union (1801), Great Britain and Ireland became the "United Kingdom of Great Britain and Ireland." A steady decline in the Irish economy followed in the next decades. The population had reached 8.25 million when the great potato famine of 1846–48 took many lives and drove more than 2 million people to immigrate to North America.

In the meantime, anti-British agitation continued along with demands for Irish home rule. The advent of World War I delayed the institution of home rule and resulted in the Easter Rebellion in Dublin (April 24–29, 1916), in which Irish nationalists unsuccessfully attempted to throw off British rule. Guerrilla warfare against British forces followed proclamation of a republic by the rebels in 1919. The Irish Free State was established as a dominion on Dec. 6, 1922, with six northern counties remaining as part of the United Kingdom. A civil war ensued between those supporting the Anglo-Irish Treaty that established the Irish Free State and those repudiating it because it led to the partitioning of the island. The Irish Republican Army (IRA), led by Eamon de Valera, fought against the partition but lost. De Valera joined the government in 1927 and became prime minister in 1932. In 1937 a new constitution changed the nation's name to Éire. Ireland remained neutral in World War II.

In 1948, the Valera was defeated by John A. Costello, who demanded final independence from Britain. The Republic of Ireland was proclaimed on April 18, 1949, and withdrew from the Commonwealth. From the 1960s onwards, two antagonistic currents dominated Irish politics. One sought to bind the wounds of the rebellion and civil war. The other was the effort of the outlawed Irish Republican Army and more moderate groups to bring Northern Ireland into the republic. The "troubles"—the violence and terrorist acts between Republicans and Unionists in both the Republic of Ireland and Northern Ireland—would plague the island for the remainder of the century.

Under the First Programme for Economic Expansion (1958–63), economic protection was dismantled and foreign investment encouraged. This prosperity brought profound social and cultural changes to what had been one of the poorest and least technologically advanced countries in Europe. Ireland joined the European Economic Community (now the EU) in 1973. In the 1990 presidential election, Mary Robinson was elected the republic's first woman president. The election of a candidate with socialist and feminist sympathies was regarded as a watershed in Irish political life, reflecting the changes taking place in Irish society. Irish voters approved the Maastricht Treaty, which paved the way for the establishment of the EU, by a large majority in a referendum held in 1992. In 1993, the Irish and British governments signed a joint peace initiative (the Downing Street Declaration), in which they pledged to seek mutually agreeable political structures in Northern Ireland and between the two islands. A referendum on allowing divorce under certain conditions—hitherto constitutionally forbidden—was held in Nov. 1995 and narrowly passed.

In 1998 hope for a solution to the troubles in Northern Ireland seemed palpable. A landmark settlement, the Good Friday Agreement of April 10, 1998, called for Protestants to share political power with the minority Catholics, and gave the Republic of Ireland a voice in Northern Irish affairs. The resounding commitment to the settlement was demonstrated in a dual referendum on May 22: the North approved the accord by a vote of 71% to 29%, and in the Irish Republic 94% favored it. After numerous stops and starts, the new government in Northern Ireland was formed on Dec. 2, 2000, when the British government formally transferred governing powers over to the Northern Irish Parliament. But the Good Friday Accord stipulated that the IRA and other paramilitary groups disarm; it wasn't until Oct. 2001 that the IRA finally began to comply. In July 2002 the IRA publicly apologized for killing civilians.

In June 2001, Ireland voted against expansion of the EU to include other countries. Ireland's rejection of the Nice Treaty came as a shock to the 14 other EU members as well as to the numerous countries aspiring to EU membership—the vote had to be unanimous among the EU partners to move ahead with the expansion.

Despite a number of recent corruption and bribery scandals, most of which involved the centrist Fianna Fáil party of Prime Minister Bertie Ahern, the party won 81 of 166 seats in May 2002. Ahern became the first Irish prime minister in 33 years to be elected to a second successive term.

*See also* Northern Ireland, under United Kingdom.

# Israel

**STATE OF ISRAEL**

**National name:** Medinat Yisra'el
**President:** Moshe Katzav (2000)
**Prime Minister:** Ariel Sharon (2001)
**Area:** 8,019 sq mi (20,770 sq km)
**Population (2002 est.):** 6,029,529 (growth rate: 1.3%); birth rate: 18.9/1000; infant mortality rate: 7.5/1000; density per sq mi: 752
**Capital (1995):**[1] Tel Aviv, 355,900. **Largest city (1995 est.):** Jerusalem, 591,400. **Other large city (1995 est.):** Haifa, 250,000. **Monetary unit:** Shekel.
**Languages:** Hebrew (official), Arabic, English.
**Ethnicity/race:** Jewish 82% (Israel-born 50%, Europe/Americas/Oceania-born 20%, Africa-born 7%, Asia-born 5%), non-Jewish 18% (mostly Arab) (1993 est.). **Religions:** Judaism 82%, Islam 14%, Christian 2%, others 2%. **Literacy rate:** 92% (1983)
**Economic summary:** GDP/PPP (2000 est.): $110.2 billion; per capita $18,900. **Real growth rate:** 5.9%. **Inflation:** 0.1%. **Unemployment:** 9%. **Arable land:** 17%. **Agriculture:** citrus, vegetables, cotton; beef,

poultry, dairy products. **Labor force:** 2.4 million (2000 est.); public services 31.2%, manufacturing 20.2%, finance and business 13.1%, commerce 12.8%, construction 7.5%, personal and other services 6.4%, transport, storage, and communications 6.2%, agriculture, forestry, and fishing 2.6% (1996). **Industries:** high-technology projects (including aviation, communications, computer-aided design and manufactures, medical electronics), wood and paper products, potash and phosphates, food, beverages, and tobacco, caustic soda, cement, diamond cutting. **Natural resources:** timber, potash, copper ore, natural gas, phosphate rock, magnesium bromide, clays, sand, oil. **Exports:** $31.5 billion (f.o.b., 2000): machinery and equipment, software, cut diamonds, agricultural products, chemicals, textiles and apparel. **Imports:** $35.1 billion (f.o.b., 2000): raw materials, military equipment, investment goods, rough diamonds, fuels, consumer goods. **Major trading partners:** U.S., UK, Benelux, Hong Kong, Netherlands, Germany, Switzerland, Italy.

1. Israel proclaimed Jerusalem as its capital in 1950, but the U.S., like nearly all other countries, maintains its embassy in Tel Aviv.

**Geography** Israel, slightly larger than Massachusetts, lies at the eastern end of the Mediterranean Sea. It is bordered by Egypt on the west, Syria and Jordan on the east, and Lebanon on the north. Northern Israel is largely a plateau traversed from north to south by mountains and broken by great depressions, also running from north to south.

The maritime plain of Israel is remarkably fertile. The southern Negev region, which comprises almost half the total area, is largely a wide desert steppe area. Parts of it have been irrigated and cultivated. The Jordan, the only important river, flows from the north through Lake Hule (Waters of Merom) and Lake Kinneret (Sea of Galilee or Sea of Tiberias), finally entering the Dead Sea, 1,312 ft (400 m) below sea level. This "sea," which is actually a salt lake (394 sq mi; 1,020 sq km), has no outlet, its water balance being maintained by evaporation.

**Government** Parliamentary democracy.

**History** Palestine, considered a holy land by Jews, Muslims, and Christians, and homeland of the modern state of Israel, was known as Canaan to the ancient Hebrews. Palestine's name derives from the Philistines, a people who occupied the southern coastal part of the country in the 12th century B.C.

A Hebrew kingdom established in 1000 B.C. was later split into the kingdoms of Judah and Israel; they were subsequently invaded by Assyrians, Babylonians, Egyptians, Persians, Romans, and Alexander the Great of Macedonia. By A.D. 135, few Jews were left in Palestine; most lived in the scattered and tenacious communities of the Diaspora. Palestine became a center of Christian pilgrimage after the emperor Constantine converted to that faith. The Arabs took Palestine from the Byzantine empire in 634–40. Interrupted only by Christian Crusaders, Muslims ruled Palestine until the 20th century. During World War I, British forces defeated the Turks in Palestine and governed the area under a League of Nations mandate from 1923.

As part of the 19th-century Zionist movement, Jews had begun settling in Palestine as early as 1820. This effort to establish a Jewish homeland received British approval in the Balfour Declaration of 1917. During the 1930s, Jews persecuted by the Hitler regime poured into Palestine. The postwar acknowledgment of the Holocaust—Hitler's genocide of 6 million Jews—increased international interest in and sympathy for the cause of Zionism. However, Arabs in Palestine and surrounding countries bitterly opposed prewar and postwar proposals to partition Palestine into Arab and Jewish sectors. The British mandate to govern Palestine ended after the war, and, in 1947, the UN voted to partition Palestine. When the British officially withdrew on May 14, 1948, the Jewish National Council proclaimed the State of Israel.

U.S. recognition came within hours. The next day, Arab forces from Egypt, Jordan, Syria, Lebanon, and Iraq invaded the new nation. By the cease-fire on Jan. 7, 1949, Israel had increased its original territory by 50%, taking western Galilee, a broad corridor through central Palestine to Jerusalem, and part of modern Jerusalem. Chaim Weizmann and David Ben-Gurion became Israel's first president and prime minister. The new government was admitted to the UN on May 11, 1949.

The next clash with Arab neighbors came when Egypt nationalized the Suez Canal in 1956 and barred Israeli shipping. Coordinating with an Anglo-French force, Israeli troops seized the Gaza Strip and drove through the Sinai to the east bank of the Suez Canal, but withdrew under U.S. and UN pressure. In the Six-Day War of 1967, Israel made simultaneous air attacks against Syrian, Jordanian, and Egyptian air bases, totally defeating the Arabs. Expanding its territory by 200%, Israel at the cease-fire held the Golan Heights, the West Bank of the Jordan River, Jerusalem's Old City, and all of the Sinai and the east bank of the Suez Canal.

In the face of Israeli reluctance even to discuss the return of occupied territories, the fourth Arab-Israeli War erupted on Oct. 6, 1973, with a surprise Egyptian and Syrian assault on the Jewish high holy day of Yom Kippur. Initial Arab gains were reversed when a cease-fire took effect two weeks later, but Israel suffered heavy losses.

A dramatic breakthrough in the tortuous history of Mideast peace efforts occurred on Nov. 9, 1977, when Egypt's president Anwar Sadat declared his willingness to talk peace. Prime Minister Menachem Begin, on Nov. 15, extended an invitation to the Egyptian leader to address the Knesset in Jerusalem. Sadat's arrival in Israel four days later raised worldwide hopes, but a peace agreement between Egypt and Israel was long in coming. On March 14, 1979, the Knesset approved a final peace treaty, and 12 days later, Begin and Sadat signed the document, together with President Jimmy Carter, in a White House ceremony. Israel began its withdrawal from the Sinai, which it had annexed from Egypt, on May 25.

Although Israel withdrew its last settlers from the Sinai in April 1982, the fragile Mideast peace was shattered on June 9, 1982, by a massive Israeli assault on southern Lebanon, where the Palestinian Liberation Organization was entrenched. The PLO had long plagued Israelis with terrorist actions. Israel destroyed PLO strongholds in Tyre and Sidon and reached the suburbs of Beirut on June 10. A U.S.-mediated accord between Lebanon and Israel, signed on May 17, 1983, provided for Israeli withdrawal from Lebanon. Israel eventually withdrew its troops from the Beirut area but kept them in southern Lebanon, where occasional skirmishes would continue. Lebanon, under pressure from Syria, canceled the accord in March 1984.

A continual source of tension has been the relationship between the Jews and the Palestinians living within Israeli territories. Most Arabs fled the region when the state of Israel was declared, but those who remain now make up almost one-fifth of the population of Israel. They are about two-thirds Muslim, as well as Christian and Druze. Palestinians living on the West Bank and the Gaza Strip fomented the riots begun in 1987, known as the *intifada*. Violence heightened as Israeli police cracked down and Palestinians retaliated. Continuing Jewish settlement of lands designated for Palestinians has added to the unrest.

In 1989, the leader of the PLO, Yasir Arafat, reversed decades of PLO polemic by acknowledging Israel's right to exist. He stated his willingness to enter negotiations to create a Palestinian political entity that would coexist with the Israeli state.

In 1991, Israel was struck by Iraqi missiles during the Persian Gulf War. The Israelis did not retaliate in order to preserve the international coalition against Iraq. In 1992, Yitzhak Rabin became prime minister. He halted the disputed Israeli settlement of the occupied territories.

Highly secretive talks in Norway resulted the landmark Oslo Accord between the PLO and the Israeli government in 1993. The accord stipulated a five-year plan in which Palestinians of the West Bank and the Gaza Strip would gradually become self-governing. Arafat becomes president of the new Palestinian Authority. In 1994, Israel signed a peace treaty with Jordan; Israel still has no formal peace agreement with Syria or Lebanon.

On Nov. 4, 1995, Prime Minister Rabin was slain by a Jewish extremist, jeopardizing the tenuous progress toward peace. Shimon Peres succeeded him until May 1996 elections for the Knesset gave Israel a new hardline prime minister, Benjamin Netanyahu, by a razorthin margin. Netanyahu reversed or stymied much of the Oslo Agreement, contending that it offered too many concessions too fast and jeopardized Israelis' safety.

Israeli-Palestinian peace negotiations in 1997 were repeatedly undermined by both sides. Although the Hebron Accord was signed in Jan., calling for the withdrawal of Israeli troops from the city, the construction of new Jewish settlements on the West Bank in March profoundly upset progress toward peace. Terrorism erupted again in 1997 when radical Hamas suicide bombers claimed the lives of more than 20 Israeli civilians. Netanyahu, accusing Palestinian Authority president Arafat of lax security, retaliated with draconian sanctions against Palestinians working in Israel, including the withholding of millions of dollars in tax revenue, a blatant violation of the Oslo Agreement. Netanyahu also persisted in authorizing right-wing Israelis to build new settlements in mostly Arab East Jerusalem. Arafat, meanwhile, seemed unwilling or unable to curb the violence of extremist Arabs.

An Oct. 1998 summit at Wye Mills, Md., generated the first real progress in the stalled Middle East peace talks. In 19 months, with Israeli prime minister Benjamin Netanyahu and Palestinian president Yasir Arafat settling several important interim issues called for by the 1993 Oslo Peace Agreement. The Palestinians agreed to remove language from their founding charter that called for the dismantling of the Jewish state; Israelis agreed to cede an additional 13% of the West Bank. Although Israel completed the first of three withdrawals from the West Bank on Nov. 20, the peace accord began unraveling almost immediately.

By the end of April 1999, Israel had made 41 air raids on Hezbollah guerrillas in Lebanon. The guerrillas were fighting against Israeli troops and their allies, the South Lebanon Army militia, who occupied a security zone set up in 1985 to guard Israel's borders.

Public pressure in Israel to withdraw the troops grew, and the issue dominated the Israeli election campaign in spring 1999.

Ehud Barak of the Labour Party won the 1999 election with 56% of the vote, against 44% for incumbent Benjamin Netanyahu of Likud. Barak created a broad coalition government and announced that his primary goal was "putting an end to the 100-year conflict in the Middle East." By this he meant not only pursuing peace with the Palestinians but establishing relations with Syria and ending the low-grade war in Southern Lebanon with the Iranian-armed Hezbollah guerrillas.

In Dec. 1999, Israeli-Syrian talks resumed after a nearly four-year hiatus. By Jan. 2000, however, talks had broken down when Syria demanded a detailed discussion of the return of all of the Golan Heights.

In Feb., new Hezbollah attacks on Israeli troops in southern Lebanon led to Israel's retaliatory bombing as well as Barak's decision to pull out of Lebanon. Israeli troops pulled out of Lebanon on May 24, 2000, after 22 years of occupation.

Peace talks in July 2000 at Camp David between Ehud Barak and Yasir Arafat ended unsuccessfully, despite President Clinton's strongest efforts—the status of Jerusalem the primary sticking point. Clinton blamed Arafat's intransigence, but Palestinian supporters praised their president's strong stand.

In Sept., Likud leader Ariel Sharon visited the compound called Temple Mount by Jews and Haram al Sharif by Muslims, a fiercely contested site that is sacred to both Jews and Muslims. The visit set off the worst violence in years, killing around 400 people, mostly Palestinians. The violence (dubbed the Al Aksa intifada after the mosque that is part of the complex) and the stalled peace process fueled growing concerns about Israeli security, paving the way for Sharon's stunning landslide victory over Barak in Feb. 2001. With the Barak-brokered peace negotiations in shambles and Palestinian-Israeli relations deteriorating, Sharon's uncompromising stance on Israeli security became a powerful draw. Violence on both sides continued at an alarming rate throughout 2001, intensifying in the fall and escalating further in 2002. Palestinians carried out some of the most horrific suicide bombings and terrorist attacks in years, killing Israeli civilians in cafes, bus stops, and supermarkets. In retaliation, Israel unleashed bombing raids on Palestinian territory and sent troops and tanks to occupy West Bank and Gaza cities.

An olive branch was extended by an unlikely source in March 2002. Crown Prince Abdullah of Saudi Arabia offered a Middle East peace plan at the annual Arab summit: all Arab governments would offer "normal relations and the security of Israel in exchange for a full Israeli withdrawal from all occupied Arab lands, recognition of an independent Palestinian state with noble Jerusalem as its capital and the return of the Palestinian refugees." An extraordinary offer because it promised the backing of the entire Arab world, the Saudi plan nevertheless seemed unrealistic in the concessions it expected from Israel. And without a ceasefire, much less an agreement to negotiate between the Israelis and Palestinians, the plan languished.

In late March, Israeli troops stepped up their occupation of Palestinian-controlled territories in the West Bank in response to the escalating number of suicide bombers. Israeli troops also surrounded Yasir Arafat at the Palestinian Authority headquarters in Ramallah, and Prime Minister Sharon called for his expulsion from the territories. Arafat, unable or unwilling to prevent a wave of suicide bombings in 2002, managed to hold onto power despite his growing political irrelevance. Neither Sharon nor Arafat seemed willing to entertain a political solution. Throughout the summer, Palestinian suicide bombings (Hamas and the Al-Aksa Martyr Brigade claimed responsibility for the majority of them) and Israeli reprisals continued. By Sept. 2002, the second anniversary of the intifada, more than 1,500 Palestinians and 550 Israelis had been killed.

# Italy

### ITALIAN REPUBLIC

**National name:** Repubblica Italiana
**President:** Carlo Azeglio Ciampi (1999)
**Prime Minister:** Silvio Berlusconi (2001)
**Area:** 116,305 sq mi (301,230 sq km)
**Population (2002 est.):** 57,715,625 (growth rate: –0.1%); birth rate: 8.9/1000; infant mortality rate: 5.8/1000; density per sq mi: 496
**Capital and largest city (1994 est.):** Rome, 2,693,383.
**Other large cities:** Milan, 1,561,438; Naples, 1,204,149; Turin, 952,736; Genoa, 706,754; Palermo, 694,749; Florence, 460,924; Bologna, 394,969; Catania, 372,212; Bari, 355,352; Venice, 306,439.
**Monetary units:** Euro (formerly lira). **Languages:** Italian; small German-, French-, and Slovene-speaking minorities. **Ethnicity/race:** Italian (includes small clusters of German-, French-, and Slovene-Italians in the north and Albanian-Italians and Greek-Italians in the south), Sicilians, Sardinians. **Religions:** Roman Catholic 98%, other 2%. **Literacy rate:** 97% (1990)
**Economic summary: GDP/PPP** (2000 est.): $1.273 trillion; per capita $22,100. **Real growth rate:** 2.7%. **Inflation:** 2.5%. **Unemployment:** 10.4%. **Arable land:** 31%. **Agriculture:** fruits, vegetables, grapes, potatoes, sugar beets, soybeans, grain, olives; beef, dairy products; fish. **Labor force:** 23.4 million (2000); services 61.9%, industry 32.6%, agriculture 5.5% (1999). **Industries:** tourism, machinery, iron and steel, chemicals, food processing, textiles, motor vehicles, clothing, footwear, ceramics. **Natural resources:** mercury, potash, marble, sulfur, dwindling natural gas and crude oil reserves, fish, coal, arable land. **Exports:** $241.1 billion (f.o.b., 2000): engineering products, textiles and clothing, production machinery, motor vehicles, transport equipment, chemicals; food, beverages and tobacco; minerals and nonferrous metals. **Imports:** $231.4 billion (f.o.b., 2000): engineering products, chemicals, transport equipment, energy products, minerals and nonferrous metals, textiles and clothing; food, beverages and tobacco. **Major trading partners:** EU, U.S.

**Geography** Italy, slightly larger than Arizona, is a long peninsula shaped like a boot bounded on the west by the Tyrrhenian Sea and on the east by the Adriatic. Approximately 600 of Italy's 708 mi (1,139 km) of length are in the long peninsula that projects into the Mediterranean from the fertile basin of the Po River. The Apennine Mountains, branching off from the Alps between Nice and Genoa, form the peninsula's backbone, and rise to a maximum height of 9,560 ft (2,912 m) at the Gran Sasso d'Italia (Corno). The Alps form Italy's northern boundary.

Italy has many northern lakes, lying below the snow-covered peaks of the Alps. The largest are Garda (143 sq mi; 370 sq km), Maggiore (83 sq mi; 215 sq km), and Como (55 sq mi; 142 sq km). The Po, the principal river, flows from the Alps on Italy's western border and crosses the Lombard plain to the Adriatic Sea.

Several islands form part of Italy. Sicily (9,926 sq mi; 25,708 sq km) lies off the toe of the boot, across the Strait of Messina, with a steep and rockbound northern coast and gentler slopes to the sea in the west and south. Mount Etna, an active volcano, rises to 10,741 ft (3,274 m), and most of Sicily is more than 500 ft (3,274 m) in elevation. Sixty-two mi (100 km) southwest of Sicily lies Pantelleria (45 sq mi; 117 sq km), and south of that are Lampedusa and Linosa. Sardinia (9,301 sq mi; 24,090 sq km), which is just south of Corsica and about 125 mi (200 km) west of the mainland, is mountainous, stony, and unproductive.

**Government** Republic.

**History** The migrations of Indo-European peoples into Italy probably began about 2000 B.C. and continued down to 1000 B.C. From about the 9th century B.C. until it was overthrown by the Romans in the 3rd century B.C., the Etruscan civilization dominated the area. By 264 B.C. all Italy south of Cisalpine Gaul was under the leadership of Rome. For the next seven centuries, until the barbarian invasions destroyed the western Roman Empire in the 4th and 5th centuries A.D., the history of Italy is largely the history of Rome. From 800 on, the Holy Roman Emperors, Roman Catholic popes, Normans, and Saracens all vied for control over various segments of the Italian peninsula. Numerous city-states, such as Venice and Genoa, whose political and commercial rivalries were intense, and many small principalities flourished in the late Middle Ages. Although Italy remained politically fragmented for centuries, it became the cultural center of the Western world from the 13th to the 16th century.

In 1713, after the War of the Spanish Succession, Milan, Naples, and Sardinia were handed over to the Hapsburgs of Austria, which lost some of its Italian territories in 1735. After 1800, Italy was unified by Napoléon, who crowned himself king of Italy in 1805; but with the Congress of Vienna in 1815, Austria once again became the dominant power in a disunited Italy. Austrian armies crushed Italian uprisings in 1820–21 and 1831. In the 1830s, Giuseppe Mazzini, brilliant liberal nationalist, organized the Risorgimento (Resurrection), which laid the foundation for Italian unity. Disappointed Italian patriots looked to the House of Savoy for leadership. Count Camille di Cavour (1810–61), premier of Sardinia in 1852 and the architect of a united Italy, joined England and France in the Crimean War (1853–56), and in 1859, helped France in a war against Austria, thereby obtaining Lombardy. By plebiscite in 1860, Modena, Parma, Tuscany, and the Romagna voted to join Sardinia. In 1860, Giuseppe Garibaldi conquered Sicily and Naples and turned them over to Sardinia. Victor Emmanuel II, king of Sardinia, was proclaimed king of Italy in 1861. The annexation of Venetia in 1866 and of papal Rome in 1870 marked the complete unification of peninsular Italy into one nation under a constitutional monarchy.

Italy declared its neutrality upon the outbreak of World War I on the ground that Germany had embarked upon an offensive war. In 1915, Italy entered the war on the side of the Allies but obtained less territory than it expected in the postwar settlement. Benito ("Il Duce") Mussolini, a former socialist, organized discontented Italians in 1919 into the Fascist Party to "rescue Italy from Bolshevism." He led his Black Shirts in a march on Rome and, on Oct. 28, 1922, became premier. He transformed Italy into a dictatorship, embarking on an expansionist foreign policy with the invasion and annexation of Ethiopia in 1935 and allying himself with Adolf Hitler in the Rome-Berlin Axis in 1936. When the Allies invaded Italy in 1943, Mussolini's dictatorship collapsed; he was executed by Partisans on April 28, 1945, at Dongo on Lake Como. Following the armistice with the Allies (Sept. 3, 1943), Italy joined the war against

Germany as a cobelligerent. A June 1946 plebiscite rejected monarchy and a republic was proclaimed. The peace treaty of Sept. 15, 1947, required Italian renunciation of all claims in Ethiopia and Greece and the cession of the Dodecanese to Greece and of five small Alpine areas to France. The Trieste area west of the new Yugoslav territory was made a free territory (until 1954, when the city and a 90-square-mile zone were transferred to Italy and the rest to Yugoslavia).

Italy became an integral member of NATO and the European Economic Community (later the EU) as it successfully rebuilt its postwar economy. A prolonged outbreak of terrorist activities by the left-wing Red Brigades threatened domestic stability in the 1970s, but by the early 1980s the terrorist groups had been suppressed. "Revolving door" governments, political instability, scandal, and corruption characterized Italian politics in 1980s and 1990s.

Italy adopted the euro as its currency in Jan. 1999. Treasury Secretary Carlo Ciampi, who is credited with the economic reforms that permitted Italy to enter the European Monetary Union, was elected president in May 1999.

Italy joined its NATO partners in the Kosovo crisis. Aviano Air Base in northern Italy was a crucial base for launching air strikes into Kosovo and Yugoslavia.

In June 2001, Silvio Berlusconi, the conservative billionaire, was sworn in as prime minister. He pledged to reduce unemployment, cut taxes, revamp the educational system, and reform the bureaucracy. His critics are alarmed by the apparent massive conflict of interest of a prime minister who also owns his country's media empire. He has also been accused of Mafia connections and was under indictment for tax fraud and bribery, though he was acquitted of most of these charges in 2002.

# Jamaica

**Sovereign:** Queen Elizabeth II (1952)
**Governor-General:** Sir Howard Cooke (1991)
**Prime Minister:** Percival J. Patterson (1992)
**Area:** 4,243 sq mi (10,990 sq km)
**Population (2002 est.):** 2,680,029 (growth rate: 1.2%); birth rate: 17.7/1000; infant mortality rate: 13.7/1000; density per sq mi: 632
**Capital and largest city (1991 est.):** Kingston, 104,000. **Monetary unit:** Jamaican dollar. **Languages:** English, Jamaican Creole. **Ethnicity/race:** African 76.3%, Afro-European 15.1%, East Indian and Afro-East Indian 3%, white 3.2%, Chinese and Afro-Chinese 1.2%, other 1.2%. **Religions:** Protestant 55.9%, Roman Catholic 5%, other 39.1%. **Literacy rate:** 98% (1990)
**Economic summary: GDP/PPP** (2000 est.): $9.7 billion; per capita $3,700. **Real growth rate:** 0.2%. **Inflation:** 8.8%. **Unemployment:** 16% **Arable land:** 14%. **Agriculture:** sugarcane, bananas, coffee, citrus, potatoes, vegetables; poultry, goats, milk. **Labor force:** 1.13 million (1998); services 60%, agriculture 21%, industry 19% (1998). **Industries:** tourism, bauxite, textiles, food processing, light manufactures, rum, cement, metal, paper, chemical products. **Natural resources:** bauxite, gypsum, limestone. **Exports:** $1.7 billion (f.o.b., 2000 est.): alumina, bauxite; sugar, bananas, rum. **Imports:** $3 billion (f.o.b., 2000 est.): machinery and transport equipment, construction materials, fuel, food, chemicals, fertilizers. **Major trading partners:** U.S., EU, UK, Canada, Caricom countries, Latin America. **Member of Commonwealth of Nations**

**Geography** Jamaica is an island in the West Indies, 90 mi (145 km) south of Cuba and 100 mi (161 km) west of Haiti. It is a little smaller than Connecticut. The island is made up of coastal lowlands, a limestone plateau, and the Blue Mountains, a group of volcanic hills, in the east. Blue Mountain (7,402 ft; 2,256 m) is the tallest peak.

**Government** Constitutional parliamentary democracy.

**History** Jamaica was inhabited by Arawak Indians when Columbus explored it in 1494 and named it St. Iago. It remained under Spanish rule until 1655, when it became a British possession. Buccaneers operated from Port Royal, also the capital, until it fell into the sea in an earthquake in 1692. Disease decimated the Arawaks, so black slaves were imported to work on the sugar plantations. During the 17th and 18th centuries the British were consistently harassed by the Maroons, armed bands of freed slaves roaming the countryside. Abolition of the slave trade (1807), emancipation of the slaves (1833), and a drop in sugar prices eventually led to a depression that resulted in an uprising in 1865. The following year Jamaica became a Crown colony, and conditions improved considerably. Introduction of bananas reduced dependence on sugar.

On May 5, 1953, Jamaica gained internal autonomy, and, in 1958, it led in organizing the West Indies Federation. A nationalist labor leader, Sir Alexander Bustamente, later campaigned to withdraw from the federation. After a referendum, Jamaica became independent on Aug. 6, 1962. Michael Manley, of the socialist People's National Party, became prime minister in 1972.

The Labour Party defeated Manley in 1980 and its capitalist-oriented leader, Edward P. G. Seaga, became prime minister. He encouraged private investment and began an austerity program. Like other Caribbean countries, Jamaica was hard-hit by the 1981–82 recession. Devaluation of the Jamaican dollar made Jamaican products more competitive on the world market and the country achieved record growth in tourism and agriculture. While manufacturing also grew, food prices rose as much as 75% and thousands of Jamaicans fell deeper into poverty.

In 1989, Manley was reelected, but he resigned in 1992 and was replaced by P. J. Patterson. In May 1997, the government signed a "Ship-Rider Agreement," allowing U.S. authorities to enter Jamaican waters and search vessels with the Jamaican government's permission, to fight drug trafficking. In 2001, violence between politically connected gangs escalated in Kingston, promoting fears that the tourist industry could suffer.

# Japan

**National name:** Nippon
**Emperor:** Akihito (1989)
**Prime Minister:** Junichiro Koizumi (2001)
**Area:** 145,882 sq mi (377,835 sq km)
**Population (2002 est.):** 126,974,628 (growth rate: 0.2%); birth rate: 10.0/1000; infant mortality rate: 3.8/1000; density per sq mi: 870
**Capital and largest city (2000 est.):** Tokyo, 34,750,000 (metro. area). **Other large cities:** Osaka (2000 est.), 17,800,000 (metro. area); Yokohama, 3,307,136 (part of Tokyo metro. area); Nagoya (2000 est.), 5,100,000 (metro. area); Sapporo, 1,719,000; Kobe, 1,501,000 (part of Osaka metro. area); Kyoto, 1,456,000 (part of Osaka metro. area); Fukuoka, 1,263,000; Kawasaki, 1,196,000 (part of Tokyo metro. area); Hiroshima, 1,099,000. **Monetary unit:** Yen. **Language:** Japanese. **Ethnicity/race:** Japanese 99.4%, other 0.6% (mostly

Korean). **Religions:** Shintoist, Buddhist, Christian. **Literacy rate:** 99% (1970)
**Economic summary: GDP/PPP** (2000 est.): $3.15 trillion; per capita $24,900. **Real growth rate:** 1.3%. **Inflation:** −0.7%. **Unemployment:** 4.7% (2000). **Arable land:** 11%. **Agriculture:** rice, sugar beets, vegetables, fruit; pork, poultry, dairy products, eggs; fish. **Labor force:** 67.7 million (Dec. 2000); services 65%, industry 30%, agriculture 5%. **Industries:** among world's largest and technologically advanced producers of motor vehicles, electronic equipment, machine tools, steel and nonferrous metals, ships, chemicals; textiles, processed foods. **Natural resources:** negligible mineral resources, fish. **Exports:** $450 billion (f.o.b., 2000): motor vehicles, semiconductors, office machinery, chemicals. **Imports:** $355 billion (c.i.f., 2000): fuels, foodstuffs, chemicals, textiles, office machinery. **Major trading partners:** U.S., Taiwan, South Korea, China, Hong Kong, Indonesia, Australia.

**Geography** An archipelago extending in an arc more than 1,744 mi (2,790 km) from northeast to southwest in the Pacific, Japan is separated from the east coast of Asia by the Sea of Japan. It is approximately the size of Montana. Japan's four main islands are Honshu, Hokkaido, Kyushu, and Shikoku. The Ryukyu chain to the southwest was U.S.-occupied from 1945 to 1972, when it reverted to Japanese control, and the Kurils to the northeast are Russian-occupied. The surface of the main islands consists largely of mountains separated by narrow valleys.

**Government** Constitutional monarchy with a parliamentary government.

**History** Legend attributes creation of Japan to the sun goddess, from whom the emperors were descended. The first of them was Jimmu, supposed to have ascended the throne in 660 B.C., a tradition that constituted official doctrine until 1945.

Recorded Japanese history begins in approximately A.D. 400, when the Yamato clan, eventually based in Kyoto, managed to gain control of other family groups in central and western Japan. Contact with Korea introduced Buddhism to Japan at about this time. Through the 700s Japan was much influenced by China, and the Yamato clan set up an imperial court similar to that of China. In the ensuing centuries, the authority of the imperial court was undermined as powerful gentry families vied for control.

At the same time, warrior clans were rising to prominence as a distinct class known as samurai. In 1192, the Minamoto clan set up a military government under their leader, Yoritomo. He was designated shogun (military dictator). For the following 700 years, shoguns from a succession of clans ruled in Japan, while the imperial court existed in relative obscurity.

First contact with the West came in about 1542, when a Portuguese ship off course arrived in Japanese waters. Portuguese traders, Jesuit missionaries, and Spanish, Dutch, and English traders followed. Suspicious of Christianity and of Portuguese support of a local Japanese revolt, the shoguns of the Tokugawa period (1603–1867) prohibited all trade with foreign countries; only a Dutch trading post at Nagasaki was permitted. Western attempts to renew trading relations failed until 1853, when Commodore Matthew Perry sailed an American fleet into Tokyo Bay. Trade with the West was forced upon Japan under terms less than favorable to the Japanese. Strife caused by these actions brought down the feudal world of the shoguns. In 1868, the emperor Meiji came to the throne, and the shogun system was abolished.

Japan quickly made the transition from a medieval to a modern power. An imperial army was established with conscription, and parliamentary government was formed in 1889. The Japanese began to take steps to extend their empire. After a brief war with China in 1894–95, Japan acquired Formosa (Taiwan), the Pescadores Islands, and part of southern Manchuria. China also recognized the independence of Korea (Chosen), which Japan later annexed (1910).

In 1904–05, Japan defeated Russia in the Russo-Japanese War, gaining the territory of southern Sakhalin (Karafuto) and Russia's port and rail rights in Manchuria. In World War I, Japan seized Germany's Pacific islands and leased areas in China. The Treaty of Versailles then awarded Japan a mandate over the islands.

At the Washington Conference of 1921–22, Japan agreed to respect Chinese national integrity, but, in 1931, invaded Manchuria. The following year, Japan set up this area as a puppet state, "Manchukuo," under Emperor Henry Pu-Yi, the last of China's Manchu dynasty. On Nov. 25, 1936, Japan joined the Axis. The invasion of China came the next year, followed by the Pearl Harbor attack on the U.S. on Dec. 7, 1941. Japan won its first military engagements during the war, extending its power over a vast area of the Pacific. Yet, after 1942, the Japanese were forced to retreat, island by island, to their own country. The dropping of atomic bombs on the cities of Hiroshima and Nagasaki in 1945 by the United States finally brought the government to admit defeat. Japan surrendered formally on Sept. 2, 1945, aboard the battleship *Missouri* in Tokyo Bay. Southern Sakhalin and the Kuril Islands reverted to the USSR, and Formosa (Taiwan) and Manchuria to China. The Pacific islands remained under U.S. occupation.

Gen. Douglas MacArthur was appointed supreme commander of the U.S. occupation of postwar Japan (1945–52). In 1947, a new constitution took effect. The emperor became largely a symbolic head of state. The U.S. and Japan signed a security treaty in 1951, allowing for U.S. troops to be stationed in Japan. In 1952, Japan regained full sovereignty, and, in 1972, the U.S. returned to Japan the Ryuku Islands, including Okinawa.

Japan's postwar economic recovery was nothing short of remarkable. New technologies and manufacturing were undertaken with great success. A shrewd trade policy gave Japan larger shares in many Western markets, an imbalance that caused some tensions with the U.S. The close involvement of Japanese government in the country's banking and industry produced accusations of protectionism. Yet economic growth continued through the 1970s and 1980s, eventually making Japan the world's second-largest economy (after the U.S.).

During the 1990s, Japan suffered an economic downturn prompted by scandals involving government officials, bankers, and leaders of industry. Japan succumbed to the Asian economic crisis in 1998, experiencing its worst recession since World War II. These setbacks led to the resignation of Prime Minister Ryutaro Hashimoto in July 1998. He was replaced by Keizo Obuchi. In 1999, Japan seemed to make slight progress in an economic recovery.

Prime Minister Obuchi died of a stroke in May 2000 and was succeeded by Yoshiro Mori, whose administration was dogged by scandal and blunders from the get-go.

Despite attempts to revive the economy, fears that Japan would slide back into recession increased in early 2001. The embattled Mori resigned in April 2001 and was replaced by Liberal Democrat Junichiro

Koizumi—the country's 11th prime minister in 13 years. Koizumi's plans to revitalize the country's tattered economy with painful reforms were buoyed in July elections, when his coalition dominated parliamentary elections. Koizumi's popularity was fleeting, however, and after a year in office the economy remained in a slump and his attempts at reform have been thwarted.

At an unprecedented summit meeting in North Korea in Sept. 2002, President Kim Jong Il apologized to Koizumi for North Korea's kidnapping of Japanese citizens during the 1970s and 1980s, and Koizumi pledged a generous aid package—both significant steps toward normalizing relations.

# Jordan

### THE HASHEMITE KINGDOM OF JORDAN

**National name:** Al Mamlaka al Urduniya al Hashemiyah
**Ruler:** King Abdullah II (1999)
**Prime Minister:** Ali Abu al-Ragheb (2000)
**Area:** 35,637 sq mi (92,300 sq km) excludes West Bank
**Population (2002 est.):** 5,307,470 (growth rate: 2.2%); birth rate: 24.6/1000; infant mortality rate: 19.6/1000; density per sq mi: 149
**Capital and largest city (1994 est.):** Amman, 963,490.
**Largest cities (1994 est.):** Zarka, 420,900 (1990); Irbid, 208,201; As-Salt, 187,014. **Monetary unit:** Jordanian dinar. **Languages:** Arabic (official), English. **Ethnicity/race:** Arab 98%, Circassian 1%, Armenian 1%. **Religions:** Islam 92%, Christian 6%, other 2%. **Literacy rate:** 86% (1994)
**Economic summary: GDP/PPP (2000 est.):** $17.3 billion; per capita $3,500. **Real growth rate:** 2%. **Inflation:** 0.7%. **Unemployment:** 15% official rate; actual rate is 25%–30% (1999 est.). **Arable land:** 4%. **Agriculture:** wheat, barley, citrus, tomatoes, melons, olives; sheep, goats, poultry. **Labor force:** 1.15 million; note: in addition, at least 300,000 workers are employed abroad (1997 est.); industry 11.4%, commerce, restaurants, and hotels 10.5%, construction 10%, transport and communications 8.7%, agriculture 7.4%, other services 52% (1992). **Industries:** phosphate mining, petroleum refining, cement, potash, light manufacturing, tourism. **Natural resources:** phosphates, potash, shale oil. **Exports:** $2 billion (f.o.b., 2000 est.): phosphates, fertilizers, potash, agricultural products, manufactures. **Imports:** $4 billion (f.o.b., 2000 est.): crude oil, machinery, transport equipment, food, live animals, manufactured goods. **Major trading partners:** India, Iraq, Saudi Arabia, EU, Indonesia, UAE, Lebanon, Kuwait, Syria, Ethiopia, Germany, U.S., Japan, UK, Italy, Turkey, Malaysia, China.

**Geography** The Middle East kingdom of Jordan is bordered on the west by Israel and the Dead Sea, on the north by Syria, on the east by Iraq, and on the south by Saudi Arabia. It is comparable in size to Indiana. Arid hills and mountains make up most of the country. The southern section of the Jordan River flows through the country.

**Government** Constitutional hereditary monarchy.

**History** In biblical times, the country that is now Jordan contained the lands of Edom, Moab, Ammon, and Bashan. Together with other Middle Eastern territories, Jordan passed in turn to the Assyrians, the Babylonians, the Persians, and, about 330 B.C., the Seleucids. Conflict between the Seleucids and the Ptolemies enabled the Arabic-speaking Nabataeans to create a kingdom in southeast Jordan. In A.D. 106 it became part of the Roman province of Arabia and in 633–36 was conquered by the Arabs. In the 16th century, Jordan submitted to Ottoman Turkish rule and was administered from Damascus. Taken from the Turks by the British in World War I, Jordan (formerly known as Transjordan) was separated from the Palestine mandate in 1920, and in 1921, placed under the rule of Abdullah ibn Hussein.

In 1923, Britain recognized Jordan's independence, subject to the mandate. In 1946, grateful for Jordan's loyalty in World War II, Britain abolished the mandate. That part of Palestine occupied by Jordanian troops was formally incorporated by action of the Jordanian Parliament in 1950. King Abdullah was assassinated in 1951. His son Talal, who was mentally ill, was deposed the next year. Talal's son Hussein, born on Nov. 14, 1935, succeeded him.

From the beginning of his reign, Hussein had to steer a careful course between his powerful neighbor to the west, Israel, and rising Arab nationalism, frequently a direct threat to his throne. Riots erupted when he joined the Central Treaty Organization (the Baghdad Pact) in 1955, and he incurred further unpopularity when Britain, France, and Israel attacked the Suez Canal in 1956, forcing him to place his army under nominal command of the United Arab Republic of Egypt and Syria. The 1961 breakup of the UAR eased Arab national pressure on Hussein, who was the first to recognize Syria after it reclaimed its independence. Jordan was swept into the 1967 Arab-Israeli War, however, and lost the old city of Jerusalem and all of its territory west of the Jordan River, the West Bank. Embittered Palestinian guerrilla forces virtually took over sections of Jordan in the aftermath of defeat, and open warfare broke out between the Palestinians and government forces in 1970.

Despite intervention of Syrian tanks, Hussein's Bedouin army defeated the Palestinians. The Jordanians drove out the Syrians and 12,000 Iraqi troops who had been in the country since the 1967 war. Ignoring protests from other Arab states, Hussein, by mid-1971, crushed Palestinian strength in Jordan and shifted the problem to Lebanon, where many of the guerrillas had fled. As Egypt and Israel neared final agreement on a peace treaty early in 1979, Hussein met with Yasir Arafat, the PLO leader, on March 17, and issued a joint statement of opposition. Although the U.S. pressed Jordan to break Arab ranks on the issue, Hussein elected to side with the great majority, cutting ties with Cairo and joining the boycott against Egypt.

Jordan's stance during the Persian Gulf War strained relations with the U.S. and led to the termination of U.S. aid. The signing of a national charter by King Hussein and leaders of the main political groups in June 1991 meant political parties were permitted in exchange for acceptance of the constitution and the monarchy. King Hussein's decision to join the Middle East peace talks in mid-1991 helped restore his country's relations with the U.S.

In July 1994, King Hussein and the Israeli prime minister signed a declaration ending the state of belligerency between the two countries. A peace agreement between the two countries was signed on Oct. 26, 1994, although a clause in it calling the king the "custodian" of Islamic holy shrines in Jerusalem angered the PLO. In the wake of the agreement Jordan's relations with the U.S. and with the moderate Arab states, including Saudi Arabia, warmed. In 1997, Jordan began negotiating with the United States about membership in the World Trade Organization, determined to attract foreign investment. On Feb. 7, 1999, King Hussein died of cancer after 46 years on the throne, sending the Middle East and much of the world into mourning for the influential Middle East statesman. Just weeks earlier, on Jan. 26, King Hussein unexpectedly deposed his brother, Prince Hassan, who had been heir apparent for 34 years, and named his eldest son, Abdullah, 37, as the new crown prince. King Abdullah II, a popular military leader with little political experience, became king on Feb. 7, 2000. In June, King Abdullah dismissed conservative prime minister Abdul Raouf al-Rawabdeh and replaced him with Ali Abu al-Ragheb, a liberal with strong business ties. But the Jordanian economy has continued to stagnate and unemployment remains high.

In fall 2002, Jordan found itself caught in the middle of the mounting hostility between the U.S. and Iraq; much of Jordan's oil is imported from its neighbor, and a war next door could ignite political instability in the country—many of Jordan's 5 million Palestinians are Iraqi supporters. But at the same time, Jordan does not want to anger its superpower benefactor—the U.S. is its largest aid donor.

# Kazakhstan

### REPUBLIC OF KAZAKHSTAN

**President:** Nursultan A. Nazarbayev (1990)
**Prime Minister:** Imangali Tasmagambetov (2002)
**Area:** 1,049,150 sq mi (2,717,300 sq km)
**Population (2002 est.):** 16,741,519 (growth rate: 0.7%); birth rate: 17.8/1000; infant mortality rate: 59.0/1000; density per sq mi: 16
**Capital (1995 est.):** Astana, 280,200 (formerly Aqmola; capital since 1997). **Largest cities (1991):** Almaty (former capital), 1,200,000; Karaganda, 608,600; Shymkent, 438,000; Ust-Kamenogorsk, 332,900; Taraz, 312,300; Astana, 287,000; Aqtöbe, 266,600.
**Monetary unit:** Tenge. **Languages:** Kazak (Qazaq), official language spoken by over 40% of population; Russian, official language spoken by two-thirds of population and used in everyday business. **Ethnicity/race:** Kazak (Qazaq) 46%, Russian 34.7%, Ukrainian 4.9%, German 3.1%, Uzbek 2.3%, Tatar 1.9%, other 7.1% (1996). **Religions:** Muslim, 47%; Russian Orthodox, 44%; Protestant, 2%; other, 7%. **Literacy rate:** 98% (1989)
**Economic summary: GDP/PPP** (2000 est.): $85.6 billion; per capita $5,000. **Real growth rate:** 10.5%. **Inflation:** 13.4%. **Unemployment:** 13.7% (1998 est.). **Arable land:** 12%. **Agriculture:** grain (mostly spring wheat), cotton; wool, livestock. **Labor force:** 8.8 million (1997); industry 27%, agriculture and forestry 23%, other 50% (1996). **Industries:** oil, coal, iron ore, manganese, chromite, lead, zinc, copper, titanium, bauxite, gold, silver, phosphates, sulfur, iron and steel, nonferrous metal, tractors and other agricultural machinery, electric motors, construction materials. **Natural resources:** major deposits of petroleum, natural gas, coal, iron ore, manganese, chrome ore, nickel, cobalt, copper, molybdenum, lead, zinc, bauxite, gold, uranium. **Exports:** $8.8 billion (f.o.b., 2000 est.): oil accounts for 40%, ferrous and nonferrous metals, machinery, chemicals, grain, wool, meat, coal. **Imports:** $6.9 billion (f.o.b., 2000 est.): machinery and parts, industrial materials, oil and gas, vehicles. **Major trading partners:** EU, Russia, China, U.S., Uzbekistan, Turkey, UK, Germany, Ukraine, South Korea.

**Geography** Kazakhstan lies in the north of the central Asian republics and is bounded by Russia in the north, China in the east, the Kyrgyzstan and Uzbekistan in the south, and the Caspian Sea and part of Turkmenistan in the west. It has almost 1,177 mi (1,894 km) of coastline on the Caspian Sea. Kazakhstan is slightly more than twice the size of Texas. The territory is mostly steppe land with hilly plains and plateaus.

**Government** Republic.

**History** The indigenous Kazakhs were a nomadic Turkic people who belonged to several divisions of Kazakh hordes. They grouped together in settlements and lived in dome-shaped tents made of felt called "yurts." Their tribes migrated seasonally to find pastures for their herds of sheep, horses, and goats. Although they had chiefs, the Kazakhs were rarely united as a single nation under one great leader. Their tribes fell under Mongol rule in the 13th century and they were dominated by Tartar khanates until the area was conquered by Russia in the 18th century.

The area became part of the Kirgiz Autonomous Republic formed by the Soviet authorities in 1920, and in 1925 this entity's name was changed to the Kazakh Autonomous Soviet Socialist Republic (Kazakh ASSR). After 1927, the Soviet government began forcing the nomadic Kazakhs to settle on collective and state farms, and the Soviets continued the czarist policy of encouraging large numbers of Russians and other Slavs to settle in the region.

Owing to the region's intensive agricultural development and its use as a testing ground for nuclear weapons by the Soviet government, serious environmental problems developed by the late 20th century. Along with the other central Asian republics, Kazakhstan obtained its independence from the collapsing Soviet Union in 1991. Kazakhstan proclaimed its membership in the Commonwealth of Independent States on Dec. 21, 1991, along with ten other former Soviet republics. In 1993, the country overwhelmingly approved the Nuclear Non-Proliferation Treaty. The president restructured and consolidated many operations of the government in 1997, eliminating a third of the government ministries and agencies. In 1997, the national capital was changed from Almaty, the largest city, to Astana (formerly Aqmola).

In Jan. 1999, Nursultan Nazarbayev was sworn into office for another seven years, although the election was widely criticized because an opposition leader was disqualified from running on a technicality. Despite his authoritarianism, Nazarbayev, who has ruled Kazakhstan since 1989 when it was still part of the Soviet Union, is a widely popular leader. Kazakhstan has the potential for becoming one of central Asia's richest countries because of its huge mineral and oil resources and its liberalized economy, which encourages Western investment. In 2000, oil was discovered in Kazakhstan's portion of the Caspian Sea—it is believed to be the largest oil find in 30 years. In March 2001, a pipeline opened to transport oil from the Tengiz fields to the Russian Black Sea port of Novorossiysk. The 950-mile pipeline has an initial capacity of 560,000 barrels of oil per day. In 2001, Kazakhstan and the governments of Azerbaijan, Georgia, and Turkey signed a memorandum of agreement for an even more ambitious pipeline, which would extend 1,075 mi from Baku, Azerbaijan, to Ceyhan, Turkey, on the Mediterranean.

But as its economic outlook blossoms, Kazakhstan's scarce democratic principles continued to wither. In 2002, the president harassed the independent media, arrested opposition leaders, and passed a law making it virtually impossible for new political parties to form.

# Kenya

**REPUBLIC OF KENYA**

**National name:** Jamhuri ya Kenya
**President:** Daniel arap Moi (1978)
**Area:** 224,961 sq mi (582,650 sq km)
**Population (2002 est.):** 31,138,735 (growth rate: 1.3%); birth rate: 27.6/1000; infant mortality rate: 67.2/1000; density per sq mi: 138
**Capital and largest city (1991 est.):** Nairobi, 2,000,000. **Other large city:** Mombasa, 600,000. **Monetary unit:** Kenya shilling. **Languages:** English (official), Swahili (national), and several other languages spoken by 25 ethnic groups. **Ethnicity/race:** Kikuyu 22%, Luhya 14%, Luo 13%, Kalenjin 12%, Kamba 11%, Kisii 6%, Meru 6%, Asian, European, and Arab 1%, other 15%. **Religions:** Protestant, 40%; Roman Catholic, 36%; traditional, 6%; Islam, 16%; others, 2%. **Literacy rate:** 69% (1990)
**Economic summary: GDP/PPP** (2000 est.): $45.6 billion; per capita $1,500. **Real growth rate:** 0.4%. **Inflation:** 7%. **Unemployment:** 50% (1998 est.). **Arable land:** 7%. **Agriculture:** coffee, tea, corn, wheat, sugarcane, fruit, vegetables; dairy products, beef, pork, poultry, eggs. **Labor force:** 9.2 million (1998 est.); agriculture 75%–80%. **Industries:** small-scale consumer goods (plastic, furniture, batteries, textiles, soap, cigarettes, flour), agricultural products processing; oil refining, cement; tourism. **Natural resources:** gold, limestone, soda ash, salt barites, rubies, fluorspar, garnets, wildlife, hydropower. **Exports:** $1.7 billion (f.o.b., 2000 est.): tea, coffee, horticultural products, petroleum products, fish, cement. **Imports:** $3 billion (f.o.b., 2000 est.): machinery and transportation equipment, petroleum products, iron and steel. **Major trading partners:** Uganda, UK, Tanzania, Pakistan, UAE, Japan, U.S. **Member of Commonwealth of Nations**

**Geography** Kenya lies across the equator in east-central Africa on the coast of the Indian Ocean. It is twice the size of Nevada. Kenya borders Somalia to the east, Ethiopia to the north, Tanzania to the south, Uganda to the west, and Sudan to the northwest. In the north, the land is arid; the southwest corner is in the fertile Lake Victoria Basin; and a length of the eastern depression of the Great Rift Valley separates western highlands from those that rise from the lowland coastal strip. Large game reserves have been developed.

**Government** Republic.

**History** Paleontologists believe people may first have inhabited Kenya about 2 million years ago. In the 700s, Arab seafarers established settlements along the coast, and the Portuguese took control of the area in the early 1500s. More than 40 ethnic groups reside in Kenya. Its largest group, the Kikuyu, migrated to the region at the beginning of the 18th century.

The land became a British protectorate in 1890 and a Crown colony in 1920, with it being by the name British East Africa. Nationalist stirrings began in 1940s, and, in 1952, the Mau Mau movement, made up of Kikuyu militants, rebelled against the government. The fighting lasted until 1956.

On Dec. 12, 1963, Kenya became fully independent. Jomo Kenyatta, a nationalist leader during the independence struggle who had been jailed by the British, became its first president. From 1964 to 1992, the country was ruled as a one-party state by the Kenya African National Union (KANU), first under Kenyatta and then under Daniel arap Moi. Demonstrations and riots pressured Moi to allow for multiparty elections in 1992.

The economy has not flourished under Daniel arap Moi's rule. In the 1990s, Kenya's infrastructure began disintegrating and official graft was rampant, contributing to the withdrawal of much foreign aid. In early 1995, President Moi moved against the opposition, and ordered the arrest of anyone who insulted him.

A series of disasters plagued Kenya in 1997 and 1998: severe flooding destroyed roads, bridges, and crops; epidemics of malaria and cholera overwhelmed the ineffectual health care system; and ethnic clashes erupted between the Kikuyu and Kalenjin ethnic groups in the Rift Valley.

On Aug. 7, 1998, the U.S. embassy in Nairobi was bombed by terrorists, killing 243 and injuring more than 1,000. The embassy in neighboring Tanzania was bombed the same day, killing ten.

In a successful effort to win back IMF and World Bank funding, which had been suspended because of Kenya's corruption and poor economic practices, President Moi appointed his high-profile critic and political opponent, Richard Leakey, as head of the civil service in 1999. The third-generation white Kenyan, son of paleontologists Louis and Mary Leakey, had been highly effective as head of the Kenya Wildlife Service, introducing a greater amount of efficiency and fairness into the Kenyan government. In his new position as head of the civil service, Leakey made a promising start at cleaning up Kenya's corrupt bureaucracy. But it soon became apparent that the president was not serious about reform, and, after 20 months, Moi sacked Leakey. Kenya is regularly ranked among the ten most corrupt countries in the world, according to the watchdog group Transparency International.

An anticorruption law, sponsored by the ruling party, failed to pass in Parliament in Aug. 2001, and imperiled Kenya's chances for international aid. Opposition leaders called the law a cynical ploy meant to give the appearance of reform — the proposed law, they contended, was in fact too weak and full of loopholes to make a dent in corruption.

# Kiribati

**REPUBLIC OF KIRIBATI**

**President:** Teburoro Tito (1994)
**Area:** 277 sq mi (717 sq km)
**Population (2002 est.):** 96,335 (growth rate: 2.3%); birth rate: 31.6/1000; infant mortality rate: 52.6/1000; density per sq mi: 348
**Capital (1990):** Tarawa, 25,154. **Monetary unit:** Australian dollar. **Languages:** English (official), I-Kiribati (Gilbertese). **Ethnicity/race:** Micronesian. **Religions:** Roman Catholic 52.6%, Protestant 40.9%. **Literacy rate:** 90%
**Economic summary: GDP/PPP** (2000 est.): $76 million, supplemented by a nearly equal amount from external sources; per capita $850. **Real growth rate:** 1%. **Inflation:** 2% (1999 est.). **Unemployment:** 2%; underemployment 70% (1992 est.) **Arable land:** 0%. **Agriculture:** copra, taro, breadfruit, sweet potatoes, vegetables; fish. **Labor force:** 7,870 economically active, not including subsistence farmers (1985 est.) **Industries:** fishing, handicrafts. **Natural resources:** phosphate (production discontinued in 1979). **Exports:** $6 million (f.o.b., 1998): copra 62%, seaweed, fish. **Imports:** $44 million (c.i.f., 1999): foodstuffs, machinery and equipment, miscellaneous manufactured goods, fuel. **Major trading partners:** Bangladesh, Australia, U.S., Hong Kong, Fiji, Japan, New Zealand, China. **Member of Commonwealth of Nations**

**Geography** Kiribati, formerly the Gilbert Islands, consists of three widely separated main groups of southwest Pacific islands, the Gilberts on the equator, the Phoenix Islands to the east, and the Line Islands farther east. Ocean Island, producer of phosphates until it was mined out in 1981, is also included in the

2 million square miles of ocean. Most of the islands of Kiribati are low-lying coral atolls built on a submerged volcanic chain and encircled by reefs.

**Government**  Republic.

**History**  Kiribati was first settled by early Austronesian-speaking peoples long before the 1st century A.D. Fijians and Tongans arrived about the 14th century and subsequently merged with the older groups to form the traditional I-Kiribati Micronesian society and culture. The islands were first sighted by British and American ships in the late 18th and early 19th centuries, and the first British settlers arrived in 1837. A British protectorate since 1892, the Gilbert and Ellice Islands became a Crown colony in 1915–16. Kiritimati (Christmas) Atoll became a part of the colony in 1919, the Phoenix Islands in 1937.

Tarawa and others of the Gilbert group were occupied by Japan during World War II. Tarawa was the site of one of the bloodiest battles in U.S. Marine Corps history when Marines landed in Nov. 1943 to dislodge the Japanese defenders. The Gilbert Islands and Ellice Islands (now Tuvalu) were separated in 1975 and granted internal self-government by Britain. Kiribati became independent on July 12, 1979.

Kiribati's 1995 act of moving the international date line far to the east, so that it encompassed Kiribati's Line Islands group, courted controversy. The move, which fulfilled one of President Tito's campaign promises, was intended to enable Kiribati to become the first country to see the dawn on Jan. 1, 2000, and welcome the new millennium—an event of significance for tourism. In 1999, Kiribati gained UN membership.

In 2002, Kiribati passed a controversial law enabling it to shut down newspapers. The legislation followed the launching of Kiribati's first successful nongovernment-run newspaper.

# Korea, North

### DEMOCRATIC PEOPLE'S REPUBLIC OF KOREA

**National name:** Choson Minjujuui Inmin Konghwaguk
**Head of State:** Kim Jong Il (1994)
**Premier:** Hong Song Nam (1997)
**Area:** 46,540 sq mi (120,540 sq km)
**Population (2002 est.):** 22,224,195 (growth rate: 1.1%); birth rate: 17.9/1000; infant mortality rate: 22.8/1000; density per sq mi: 478
**Capital and largest city (1993):** Pyongyang, 2,741,260.
**Monetary unit:** Won. **Language:** Korean. **Ethnicity/race:** racially homogeneous. **Religions:** Buddhism and Confucianism; religious activities almost nonexistent. **Literacy rate:** 100% (1979)
**Economic summary: GDP/PPP** (2000 est.): $22 billion; per capita $1,000. **Real growth rate:** –3%. **Inflation:** n.a. **Unemployment:** n.a. **Arable land:** 14%. **Agriculture:** rice, corn, potatoes, soybeans, pulses; cattle, pigs, pork, eggs. **Labor force:** 9.6 million; agricultural 36%, nonagricultural 64%. **Industries:** military products; machine building, electric power, chemicals; mining (coal, iron ore, magnesite, graphite, copper, zinc, lead, and precious metals); metallurgy; textiles, food processing; tourism. **Natural resources:** coal, lead, tungsten, zinc, graphite, magnesite, iron ore, copper, gold, pyrites, salt, fluorspar, hydropower. **Exports:** $520 million (f.o.b., 1999 est.): minerals, metallurgical products, manufactures (including armaments); agricultural and fishery products. **Imports:** $960 million (c.i.f., 1999 est.): petroleum, coking coal, machinery and equipment; consumer goods, grain. **Major trading partners:** Japan, South Korea, China, Germany, Russia.

**Geography**  Korea is a 600-mile (966 km) peninsula jutting out from Manchuria and China (and a small portion of the USSR) into the Sea of Japan and the Yellow Sea off eastern Asia. North Korea occupies an area slightly smaller than Pennsylvania north of the 38th parallel.

The country is almost completely covered by a series of north-south mountain ranges separated by narrow valleys. The Yalu River forms part of the northern border with Manchuria.

**Government**  Authoritarian socialist; one-man dictatorship.

**History**  The ancient history of the Korean peninsula can be traced to the Neolithic Age, when Turkic-Manchurian-Mongol peoples migrated into the region from China. The first agriculturally based settlements appeared around 6000 B.C. Some of the larger communities of this era were established along the Han-gang River near modern-day Seoul, others near Pyongyang and Pusan. According to ancient lore, Korea's earliest civilization, known as Choson, was founded in 2333 B.C. by Tan-gun.

In the 17th century, Korea became a vassal state of China and was cut off from outside contact until the Sino-Japanese War of 1894–95. Following Japan's victory, Korea was granted independence. By 1910, Korea had been annexed by Japan, which developed the country but never won over the Korean nationalists, who continued to agitate for independence.

After Japan's surrender at the conclusion of World War II, the Korean peninsula was partitioned into two occupation zones, divided at the 38th parallel. The USSR controlled the north, with the U.S. taking charge of the south. In 1948, the division was made permanent with the establishment of the separate regimes of North and South Korea. The Democratic People's Republic of Korea (North Korea) was established on May 1, 1948, with Kim Il Sung as president.

Hoping to unify the Koreas under a single Communist government, the North launched a surprise invasion of South Korea on June 25, 1950. In the following days, the UN Security Council condemned the attack and demanded an immediate withdrawal.

President Harry S. Truman ordered U.S. air and naval units into action to enforce the UN order. The British government followed suit, and soon a UN multinational command was set up to aid the South Koreans.

The North Korean invaders swiftly seized Seoul and surrounded the allied forces in the peninsula's southeast corner near Pusan. In a desperate bid to reverse the military situation, UN Commander Gen. Douglas MacArthur ordered an amphibious landing at Inchon on Sept. 15 and routed the North Korean army. MacArthur's forces pushed north across the 38th parallel, approaching the Yalu River.

Prompted by this successful counteroffensive, Communist China entered the war, forcing the UN troops into a headlong retreat. Seoul was lost again, then regained. Ultimately, the war stabilized near the 38th parallel, but dragged on for two years while negotiations took place. An armistice was agreed to on July 27, 1953.

By early 1994, tensions had mounted over international inspection of North Korea's nuclear sites. Kim Il Sung's death on July 8, 1994, introduced a period of uncertainty, as his son, Kim Jong Il, assumed the leadership mantle. Negotiations over the country's suspected atomic weapons dragged on, but an agreement was reached in June 1995 that included a provision for providing the North with a South Korean nuclear reactor.

The nuclear crises that characterized the mid-1990s were overshadowed when famine struck the nation's 24 million inhabitants in 1998 and 1999. Two years of floods were followed by severe droughts in 1997 and 1998, causing devastating crop failures. Because of lack of fuel and machinery parts, and weather conditions that have encouraged parasites, only 10% of North Korea's rice fields could be worked. Despite the staggering food crisis that necessitated foreign aid, North Korea remains one of the world's few remaining hermetic hard-line Communist regimes.

In Sept. 1998, North Korea launched a test missile over Japan, claiming it was simply a scientific satellite. This launch alarmed Japan, and much of the rest of the world about North Korea's intentions regarding reentry into the nuclear arms race. In 1999, North Korea agreed to allow the United States to conduct ongoing inspections of a suspected nuclear development site, Kumchangri, which North Korea admitted had been devised for "a sensitive military purpose." In exchange, the U.S. would increase food aid and initiate a program for bringing potato production to the country.

Antagonism between North and South Korea erupted into open aggression twice within six months in late 1998 and 1999, with South Korea hitting one North Korean vessel and sinking two others that were discovered trespassing in South Korean waters. In late summer 1999, there were signs that North Korea might test a new version of the long-range rocket it launched over Japan a year earlier.

In the fall of 1999, North Korea's four years of severe famine, which claimed an estimated 2 million to 3 million lives between 1995 and 1998, had begun to wane. Tension with South Korea eased dramatically in June 2000, when South Korea's president, Kim Dae Jung, met with North Korea's President Kim Jong Il in Pyongyang. The summit marked the first ever meeting of the two countries' leaders. The officials signed a hopeful, yet vague, agreement that outlined plans for unification and peace. Reconciliation between the North and South eroded in January, when President Bush described North Korea as part of an "axis of evil."

Five South Koreans and as many as 30 North Koreans died during a deadly naval clash in the Yellow Sea in June 2002. The exchange began when patrol boats from the North, reportedly in South Korean waters, fired on South Korean vessels.

In July 2002, North Korea began a series of radical economic initiatives aimed at reforming the devastated economy and introducing free-market policies. The country devalued its currency, raised food prices by as much as 50%, and increased wages.

At an unprecedented summit meeting in Sept. 2002 in Pyongyang with Japanese prime minster Junichiro Koizumi, Kim apologized for the abduction of 12 Japanese citizens during the 1970s and 1980s and Koizumi pledged a generous aid package to North Korea—both significant steps toward normalizing relations.

Kim stunned the world again in Sept. when he announced plans to build a free-trade zone near North Korea's northwest border with China. Yang Bin, a wealthy Chinese businessman, will run the special economic zone with full autonomy. North Korea is expected to turn to China, Japan, South Korea, and Western nations for investment capital.

# Korea, South

**REPUBLIC OF KOREA**

**National name:** Taehan Min'guk
**President:** Kim Dae Jung (1998)
**Prime Minister:** Kim Suk Soo (2002)
**Area:** 38,023 sq mi (98,480 sq km)
**Population (2002 est.):** 48,324,000 (growth rate: 0.9%); birth rate: 14.6/1000; infant mortality rate: 7.6/1000; density per sq mi: 1,271
**Capital and largest city (2000 est.):** Seoul, 19,850,000 (metro. area). **Other large cities:** Pusan, 3,814,235; Taegu, 2,449,000; Inchon, 2,308,000 (part of Seoul metro. area). **Monetary unit:** Won. **Language:** Korean. **Ethnicity/race:** homogeneous (except for about 20,000 Chinese). **Religions (est. mid-1996):** Christian, 48.2%; Buddhist, 48.8%; Confucianist, 0.8%; Chondogyo (religion of the Heavenly Way), 0.2%; other, 2%. **Literacy rate:** 98% (1995)
**Economic summary:** GDP/PPP (2000 est.): $764.6 billion; per capita $16,100. **Real growth rate:** 9%. **Inflation:** 2.3% (2000). **Unemployment:** 4.1% (2000 est.). **Arable land:** 19%. **Agriculture:** rice, root crops, barley, vegetables, fruit; cattle, pigs, chickens, milk, eggs; fish. **Labor force:** 22 million (2000); services 68%, industry 20%, agriculture 12% (1999). **Industries:** electronics, automobile production, chemicals, shipbuilding, steel, textiles, clothing, footwear, food processing. **Natural resources:** coal, tungsten, graphite, molybdenum, lead, hydropower potential. **Exports:** $172.6 billion (f.o.b., 2000): electronic products, machinery and equipment, motor vehicles, steel, ships; textiles, clothing, footwear; fish. **Imports:** $160.5 billion (f.o.b., 2000): machinery, electronics and electronic equipment, oil, steel, transport equipment, textiles, organic chemicals, grains. **Major trading partners:** U.S., Japan, China, Hong Kong, Taiwan, Saudi Arabia, Australia.

**Geography** Slightly larger than Indiana, South Korea lies below the 38th parallel on the Korean peninsula, bordering the East Sea and the Yellow Sea. It is mountainous in the east; in the west and south are many harbors on the mainland and offshore islands.

**Government** Republic.

**History** South Korea came into being after World War II, the result of a 1945 agreement reached by the Allies at the Potsdam Conference, making the 38th parallel the boundary between a northern zone of the Korean peninsula to be occupied by the USSR and southern zone to be controlled by U.S. forces. (For details, see Korea, North.)

Elections were held in the U.S. zone in 1948 for a national assembly, which adopted a republican constitution and elected Syngman Rhee as the nation's president. The new republic was proclaimed on Aug. 15 and was recognized as the legal government of Korea by the UN on Dec. 12, 1948.

On June 25, 1950, North Korean Communist forces launched a massive surprise attack on South Korea, quickly overrunning the capital, Seoul. U.S. armed intervention was ordered on June 27 by President Harry S. Truman, and on the same day the UN invoked military sanctions against North Korea. Gen. Douglas MacArthur was named commander of the UN forces. U.S. and South Korean troops fought a heroic holding action, but by the first week of Aug. were forced back to a 4,000-square-mile beachhead in southeast Korea. There they stood off superior North Korean forces until Sept. 15, when a major UN amphibious assault was launched deep behind Communist lines at Inchon, the port of Seoul.

By Sept. 30, UN forces were in complete control of South Korea. They then crossed the 38th parallel and pursued retreating Communist forces into North Korea. In late October, as UN forces neared the Sino-Korean border, several hundred thousand Chinese Communist troops entered the conflict, pushing Mac-Arthur's forces back to the border between North and South Korea. By the time truce talks began on July 10, 1951, UN forces had crossed over the parallel again and were driving back into North Korea. Cease-fire negotiations dragged on for two years before an armistice was finally signed at Panmunjom on July 27, 1953, leaving a devastated Korea in need of large-scale rehabilitation. No official peace treaty has ever been signed between the former combatants.

Rhee, after 12 years in office, was forced to resign in 1960 amid rising discontent with his autocratic leadership. Po Sun Yun was elected to succeed him, but political instability continued. In 1961, Gen. Park Chung Hee seized power and subsequently began a program of economic reforms designed to stimulate the nation's economy. The U.S. stepped up military aid, strengthening South Korea's armed forces to 600,000 men. Park's assassination on Oct. 26, 1979, by Kim Jae Kyu, head of the Korean Central Intelligence Agency, brought a liberalizing trend as new president Choi Kyu Hah freed imprisoned dissidents.

The release of opposition leader Kim Dae Jung in Feb. 1980 sparked antigovernment demonstrations that turned into riots, which were brutally suppressed by authorities. Kim, the most visible leader of the opposition, was imprisoned again. Choi resigned on Aug. 16. Chun Doo Hwan, head of a military Special Committee for National Security Measures, was the sole candidate as the electoral college confirmed him as president on Aug. 27. In 1986–87, South Korea's opposition demanded the president be selected by direct popular vote. After weeks of protest and rioting, Chun agreed to the demand. A split in the opposition led to Roh Tae Woo's election on Dec. 16, 1987.

In Aug. of 1996 Roh was convicted on bribery charges and Chun was convicted for bribery as well as his role in the 1979 coup and the 1980 crackdown on rioters. In 1997, an accumulation of corrupt business practices and bad loans led to a series of bankruptcies and a massive devaluation of South Korea's currency. The political instability that followed helped former dissident Kim Dae Jung become the first South Korean president ever to be elected from the political opposition.

In 1998 the Asian economic crisis bottomed out in South Korea, and it began rebounding in 1999—the only sizable Asian economy to do so.

Antagonism between North and South Korea erupted into open aggression twice in six months in late 1998 and 1999, with South Korea hitting one North Korean vessel and sinking two others that were discovered trespassing in South Korean waters. Tensions eased dramatically in June 2000, when President Kim Dae Jung met with the North's president, Kim Jong Il, in Pyongyang. The summit marked the first ever meeting of the countries' leaders.

President Kim Dae Jung won the Nobel Peace Prize in Oct. 2000, for his "Sunshine Policy," which included initiating peace and reconciliation with North Korea. Cross-border discussions stalled after President George W. Bush told President Kim Dae Jung in a March 2001 meeting that he will not discuss missile negotiations any time soon with North Korea, shelving President Clinton's efforts toward normalizing relations.

Five South Koreans and as many as 30 North Koreans died during a deadly naval clash in the Yellow Sea in June 2002. The exchange began when patrol boats from the North, reportedly in South Korean waters, fired on South Korean vessels.

# Kuwait

**STATE OF KUWAIT**

**National name:** Dawlat al Kuwayt
**Emir:** Sheik Jaber al-Ahmad al-Sabah (1977)
**Prime Minister:** Sheik Saad al-Abdullah Al-Sabah (1978)
**Area:** 6,880 sq mi (17,820 sq km)
**Population (2002 est.):** 2,111,561 (growth rate: 1.9%); birth rate: 21.8/1000; infant mortality rate: 10.9/1000; density per sq mi: 307
**Capital (1990 est.):** Kuwait, 151,060. **Other large city (1993 est.):** as-Salimiyah, 116,104. **Monetary unit:** Kuwaiti dinar. **Languages:** Arabic (official), English.
**Ethnicity/race:** Kuwaiti 45%, other Arab 35%, South Asian 9%, Iranian 4%, other 7%. **Religions:** Islam, 85% (Shi'ite 30%, Sunni 45%, other 10%); Christian, Hindu, Parsi, and other, 15%. **Literacy rate:** 73% (1990)
**Economic summary: GDP/PPP** (2000 est.): $29.3 billion; per capita $15,000. **Real growth rate:** 6%. **Inflation:** 3% (2000). **Unemployment:** 1.8% (official 1996 est.). **Arable land:** 0%. **Agriculture:** practically no crops; fish. **Labor force:** 1.3 million (1998 est.); note: 68% of the population in the 15–64 age group is non-national (July 1998 est.); agriculture n.a., industry n.a., services n.a. **Industries:** petroleum, petrochemicals, desalination, food processing, construction materials. **Natural resources:** petroleum, fish, shrimp, natural gas. **Exports:** $23.2 billion (f.o.b., 2000 est.): oil and refined products, fertilizers. **Imports:** $7.6 billion (f.o.b., 2000 est.): food, construction materials, vehicles and parts, clothing. **Major trading partners:** Japan, U.S., Singapore, Netherlands, Germany.

**Geography** Kuwait is situated northeast of Saudi Arabia at the northern end of the Persian Gulf, south of Iraq. It is slightly larger than Hawaii. The low-lying desert land is mainly sandy and barren.

**Government** Kuwait is a constitutional monarchy, governed by the al-Sabah family.

**History** Kuwait is believed to have been part of an early civilization in the 3rd millennium B.C. and to have traded with Mesopotamian cities. Archeological and historical traces disappeared around the first millennium B.C. At the beginning of the 18th century A.D., the 'Anizah tribe of central Arabia founded Kuwait City, which became an autonomous sheikdom by 1756. 'Abd Rahim of the al-Sabah became the first sheik, and his descendants continue to rule Kuwait today. In the late 18th and early 19th centuries, the sheikdom belonged to the fringes of the Ottoman Empire. Kuwait obtained British protection in 1897 when the sheik feared that the Turks would expand their hold over the area. In 1961, Britain ended the protectorate, giving Kuwait independence, and agreed to give military aid on request. Iraq immediately threatened to occupy the area, and the British sent troops to defend Kuwait. Soon afterward the Arab League sent in troops, replacing the British. Iraq's claim was dropped when the Arab League recognized Kuwait's independence on July 20, 1961. Kuwait typically followed a neutral and mediatory policy among Arab states.

Oil was discovered there in the 1930s, and Kuwait proved to have 20% of the world's known oil resources. Since 1946 it has been the world's second-largest oil exporter. The sheik, who receives half the profits, devotes most of them to the education, welfare, and modernization of his kingdom. In 1966, Sheik Sabah designated a relative, Jaber al-Ahmad al-Sabah, as his successor. By 1968, the sheikdom had established a model welfare state, and it sought to establish dominance among the sheikdoms and emirates of the Persian Gulf.

In July 1990, Iraqi president Hussein blamed Kuwait for falling oil prices. After a failed Arab mediation attempt to solve the dispute peacefully, Iraq invaded Kuwait on Aug. 2, 1990, set up a pro-Iraqi provisional government, and drained Kuwait of its economic resources. A coalition of Arab and Western military forces drove Iraqi troops from Kuwait in a mere four days, from Feb. 23–27, ending the Persian Gulf War. The emir returned to his country from Saudi Arabia in mid-March. Martial law, in effect since the end of the Gulf War, ended in late June. The U.S. sent 2,400 troops to the country in Aug. 1992 as part of a training exercise but this was widely interpreted as a show of strength to Saddam Hussein.

The general election of Oct. 1992 was a success for supporters of a return to Islamic law. A political independent was named speaker of the Parliament, and the opposition held 31 of the 50 seats. Iraqi "training" maneuvers near the Kuwaiti border in Oct. 1994 renewed fears of aggression in the country. A Kuwaiti appeal brought the quick deployment of U.S. and British troops and equipment. In 1999, the emir gave women the right to vote and run for Parliament. Later in 1999, however, Parliament defeated the ruler's decree. Kuwaiti society has grown increasingly conservative under the influence of Islamic fundamentalists. In 2002, coeducation was banned in Kuwait's only university.

# Kyrgyzstan

### THE KYRGYZ REPUBLIC

**President:** Askar Akayev (1990)
**Prime Minister:** Nikolay Tanayev (2002)
**Area:** 76,641 sq mi (198,500 sq km)
**Population (2002 est.):** 4,822,166; (Kyrgyz, 52%; Russian, 21%; Uzbek, 13%; other, 14%) (growth rate: 1.7%); birth rate: 26.1/1000; infant mortality rate: 75.9/1000; density per sq mi: 63
**Capital and largest city (1994):** Bishkek (formerly Frunze), 631,000. **Other large city (1994):** Osh 213,000. **Monetary unit:** Som. **Languages:** Kyrgyz (official); Russian is de facto second language of communication. **Ethnicity/race:** Kyrgyz 52.4%, Russian 18%, Uzbek 12.9%, Ukrainian 2.5%, German 2.4%, other 11.8%. **Religions:** Muslim, 75%; Russian Orthodox, 20%; other, 5%. **Literacy rate:** 97% (1989)
**Economic summary:** GDP/PPP (2000 est.): $12.6 billion; per capita $2,700 . **Real growth rate:** 5.7%. **Inflation:** 18.7%. **Unemployment:** 6% (1998 est.). **Arable land:** 7%. **Agriculture:** tobacco, cotton, potatoes, vegetables, grapes, fruits and berries; sheep, goats, cattle, wool. **Labor force:** 1.7 million; agriculture and forestry 55%, industry and services 30% (1999 est.). **Industries:** small machinery, textiles, food processing, cement, shoes, sawn logs, refrigerators, furniture, electric motors, gold, rare earth metals. **Natural resources:** abundant hydropower; significant deposits of gold and rare earth metals; locally exploitable coal, oil, and natural gas; other deposits of nepheline, mercury, bismuth, lead, and zinc. **Exports:** $482 million (f.o.b., 2000 est.): cotton, wool, meat, tobacco; gold, mercury, uranium, hydropower; machinery; shoes. **Imports:** $579 million (f.o.b., 2000 est.): oil and gas, machinery and equipment, foodstuffs. **Major trading partners:** Germany, Russia, Kazakhstan, Uzbekistan, China, U.S.

**Geography** Kyrgyzstan (formerly Kirghizia) is a rugged country with the Tien Shan mountain range covering approximately 95% of the whole territory. The mountaintops are covered with perennial snow and glaciers. Kyrgyzstan borders Kazakhstan on the north and northwest, Uzbekistan in the southwest, Tajikistan in the south, and China in the southeast. The republic is the same size in area as the state of Nebraska.

**Government** Constitutional republic.

**History** The native Kyrgyz are a Turkic people who in ancient times first settled in the Tien Shan mountains. They were traditionally pastoral nomads. There was extensive Russian colonization in the 1900s and Russian settlers were given much of the best agricultural land. This led to an unsuccessful and disastrous revolt by the Kyrgyz people in 1916. Kyrgyzstan became part of the Soviet Federated Socialist Republic in 1924, and was made an autonomous republic in 1926. It became a constituent republic of the USSR in 1936. The Soviets forced the Kyrgyz to abandon their nomadic culture and brought modern farming and industrial production techniques into their society. It has greatly changed their traditional way of life.

Kyrgyzstan proclaimed its independence from the Soviet Union on Aug. 31, 1991. On Dec. 21, 1991, Kyrgyzstan joined the Commonwealth of Independent States. The country joined the UN and the IMF in 1992 and adopted a shock-therapy economic program. Voters endorsed market reforms in a referendum held in Jan. 1994, and in 1996, referendum voters overwhelmingly endorsed proposed constitutional changes that enhanced the power of the president. Representatives of the country along with those of Russia, China, Kazakhstan, and Tajikistan signed a nonaggression agreement in April 1996. In March 1997, Russian border control was extended until the end of the year as authorities in Kyrgyzstan grew increasingly concerned about the growth of the illegal narcotics trade in the country.

Since 1999, several groups of radical Islamic gunmen, believed to be from Uzbekistan or Tajikistan, have led raids and kidnappings from camps in Kyrgyzstan's mountains.

In elections held Oct. 30, 2000, President Askar Akayev easily won reelection with nearly 75% of the vote. The election, however, was marred by allegations of fraud, diminishing Kyrgyzstan's claim to be the centerpiece of Central Asian democracy.

In 2001, Kyrgyzstan permitted troops from the U.S. and seven other nations to be stationed in the country in support of efforts to fight against the Taliban and al-Qaeda in neighboring Afghanistan. In 2002, construction of a large U.S. airbase began outside of Bishkek.

# Laos

### LAO PEOPLE'S DEMOCRATIC REPUBLIC

**President:** Khamtai Siphandon (2001)
**Prime Minister:** Boungnang Vorachith (2001)
**Area:** 91,428 sq mi (236,800 sq km)
**Population (2002 est.):** 5,777,180 (growth rate: 2.5%); birth rate: 37.4/1000; infant mortality rate: 91.0/1000; density per sq mi: 63
**Capital and largest city (1990):** Vientiane, 442,000. **Monetary unit:** New Kip. **Languages:** Lao (official), French, English. **Ethnicity/race:** Lao Loum (lowland) 68%, Lao Theung (upland) 22%, Lao Soung (highland) including the Hmong ("Meo") and the Yao (Mien) 9%, ethnic Vietnamese/Chinese 1%. **Religions:** Buddhist 85%, animist and other 15%. **Literacy rate:** 45% (1988)

**Economic summary: GDP/PPP** (2000 est.): $9 billion; per capita $1,700 . **Real growth rate:** 4%. **Inflation:** 33%. **Unemployment:** 5.7% (1997 est.). **Arable land:** 3%. **Agriculture:** sweet potatoes, vegetables, corn, coffee, sugarcane, tobacco, cotton; tea, peanuts, rice; water buffalo, pigs, cattle, poultry. **Labor force:** 1 million–1.5 million; agriculture 80% (1997 est.). **Industries:** tin and gypsum mining, timber, electric power, agricultural processing, construction, garments, tourism. **Natural resources:** timber, hydropower, gypsum, tin, gold, gemstones. **Exports:** $323 million (f.o.b., 2000 est.): wood products, garments, electricity, coffee, tin. **Imports:** $540 million (f.o.b., 2000 est.): machinery and equipment, vehicles, fuel. **Major trading partners:** Vietnam, Thailand, Germany, France, Belgium, Japan, China, Singapore, Hong Kong.

**Geography** A landlocked nation in Southeast Asia occupying the northwest portion of the Indochinese peninsula, Laos is surrounded by China, Vietnam, Cambodia, Thailand, and Burma. It is twice the size of Pennsylvania. Laos is a mountainous country, especially in the north, where peaks rise above 9,000 ft (2,800 m). Dense forests cover the northern and eastern areas. The Mekong River, which forms the boundary with Burma and Thailand, flows entirely through the country for 932 mi (1,500 km) of its course.

**Government** Communist state.

**History** The Lao people migrated into Laos from southern China from the 8th century onward. In the 14th century, the first Laotian state was founded, the Lan Xang kingdom, which ruled Laos until it split into three separate kingdoms in 1713. During the 18th century the three kingdoms came under Siamese (Thai) rule, and, in 1893, became a French protectorate. Its territory was incorporated into the union of Indochina. A strong nationalist movement developed during World War II, but France reestablished control in 1946 and made the king of Luang Prabang constitutional monarch of all Laos. France granted semiautonomy in 1949 and then, spurred by the Viet Minh rebellion in Vietnam, full independence within the French Union in 1950.

In 1951, Prince Souphanouvong organized the Pathet Lao, a Communist independence movement, in North Vietnam. Viet Minh and Pathet Lao forces invaded central Laos, and civil war resulted. By the Geneva agreements of 1954 and an armistice of 1955, two northern provinces were given to the Pathet Lao: the rest went to the royal regime. Full sovereignty was given to the kingdom by the Paris agreements of Dec. 29, 1954. In 1957, Prince Souvanna Phouma, the royal premier, and the Pathet Lao leader, Prince Souphanouvong, the premier's half-brother, agreed to reestablishment of a unified government, with Pathet Lao participation and integration of Pathet Lao forces into the royal army. The agreement broke down in 1959, and armed conflict began anew.

In 1960, the struggle became three-way as Gen. Phoumi Nosavan, controlling the bulk of the royal army, set up in the south a pro-Western revolutionary government headed by Prince Boun Oum. General Phoumi took Vientiane in December, driving Souvanna Phouma into exile in Cambodia. The Soviet bloc supported Souvanna Phouma. In 1961, a cease-fire was arranged and the three princes agreed to a coalition government headed by Souvanna Phouma.

But North Vietnam, the U.S. (in the form of CIA personnel), and China remained active in Laos after the settlement. North Vietnam used a supply line (Ho Chi Minh Trail) running down the mountain valleys of eastern Laos into Cambodia and South Vietnam, particularly after the U.S.–South Vietnamese incursion into Cambodia in 1970 stopped supplies via Cambodian seaports.

An agreement reached in 1973 revived the coalition government. The Communist Pathet Lao seized complete power in 1975, installing Souphanouvong as president and Kaysone Phomvihane as premier. Since then other parties and political groups have been moribund and most of their leaders have fled the country. The monarchy was abolished on Dec. 2, 1975, when the Pathet Lao ousted a coalition government and King Sisavang Vatthana abdicated.

The Supreme People's Assembly in Aug. 1991 adopted a new constitution that dropped all references to socialism but retained the one-party state. In addition to implementing market-oriented policies, the country has passed laws governing property, inheritance, and contracts.

During the 1990s, the country began making more diplomatic overtures toward its neighbors. In 1995, the U.S. announced a lifting of its ban on aid to the nation.

Since March 2000, Vientiane has been rocked by a series of unexplained blasts. The activity has been widely attributed to a group of Hmong tribesmen based in the north. The anti-Communist rebel group has been protesting the government's reluctance to embrace democratic reforms. Others attribute the bombs to rival factions in the government or military.

By most international estimates, Laos is one of the ten poorest countries in the world. The subsistence farmers who make up more than 80% of the population have been plagued with bad agricultural conditions—alternately flood or drought—since 1993. In April 2001, the IMF approved a three-year, $40 million loan for Laos.

# Latvia

## THE REPUBLIC OF LATVIA

**National name:** Latvija
**President:** Vaira Vike-Freiberga (1999)
**Prime Minister:** Andris Berzins (2000)
**Area:** 24,938 sq mi (64,589 sq km)
**Population (2002 est.):** 2,366,515 (growth rate: –0.7%); birth rate: 8.3/1000; infant mortality rate: 15.0/1000; density per sq mi: 95
**Capital and largest city (1993 est.):** Riga, 874,000.
**Other large cities:** Daugavpils, 125,000; Liepaja, 108,000. **Monetary unit:** Lats. **Language:** Latvian. **Ethnicity/race:** Latvian 51.8%, Russian 33.8%, Belorussian 4.5%, Ukrainian 3.4%, Polish 2.3%, other 4.2%. **Religions:** Lutheran, Catholic, and Baptist. **Literacy:** 99% (1989)
**Economic summary: GDP/PPP** (2000 est.): $17.3 billion; per capita $7,200. **Real growth rate:** 5.5%. **Inflation:** 2.7%. **Unemployment:** 7.8%. **Arable land:** 27%. **Agriculture:** grain, sugar beets, potatoes, vegetables; beef, milk, eggs; fish. **Labor force:** 1.4 million; agriculture 10%, industry 25%, services 65%. **Industries:** buses, vans, street and railroad cars, synthetic fibers, agricultural machinery, fertilizers, washing machines, radios, electronics, pharmaceuticals, processed foods, textiles; note - dependent on imports for energy, raw materials, and intermediate products. **Natural resources:** minimal; amber, peat, limestone, dolomite, hydropower, arable land. **Exports:** $2.1 billion (f.o.b., 2000): wood and wood products, machinery and equipment, metals, textiles, foodstuffs. **Imports:** $3.2 billion (f.o.b., 2000): machinery and equipment, chemicals, fuels. **Major trading partners:** Germany, UK, Sweden, Russia, Finland.

**Geography** Latvia borders Estonia on the north, Lithuania in the south, the Baltic Sea with the Gulf of Riga in the west, Russia in the east, and Belarus in the southeast. Latvia is largely a fertile lowland with numerous lakes and hills to the east.

**Government** Parliamentary democracy.

**History** Baltic tribespeople settled along the Baltic Sea, and lacking a centralized government, fell prey to more powerful peoples. In the 13th century they were overcome by the Livonian Brothers of the Sword, a German order of knights whose mission was to conquer and Christianize the Baltic region. The land became part of the state of Livonia until 1561. Germans made up the ruling class of Livonia and Baltic tribes made up the peasantry. German became the official language of the region.

Poland conquered the territory in 1562, until Sweden took over the land in 1629, and ruled over it until 1721. Then the land passed to Russia. From that time until 1918, the Latvians remained Russian subjects, although they preserved their language, customs, and folklore.

The Russian Revolution of 1917 gave them their opportunity for freedom, and the Latvian republic was proclaimed on Nov. 18, 1918. The republic lasted little more than 20 years. Plagued by political instability, Latvia essentially became a dictatorship under President Karlis Ulmanis. It was occupied by Russian troops in 1939 and incorporated into the Soviet Union in 1940. Latvia allied itself with Germany in World War II, and German armies occupied the nation from 1941 to 1943–44. Of the 70,000 Jews living in Latvia during the war, 95% were massacred. In 1944, Russia again took control of Latvia.

Latvia was one of the most economically well-off and industrialized parts of the Soviet Union. When a coup against Soviet president Mikhail Gorbachev failed in 1991, the Baltic nations saw an opportunity to free themselves from Soviet domination and, following the actions of Lithuania and Estonia, Latvia declared its independence on Aug. 21, 1991. European and most other nations quickly recognized their independence, and on Sept. 2, 1991, President Bush announced full diplomatic recognition for Latvia, Estonia, and Lithuania. The Soviet Union recognized Latvia's independence on Sept. 6, and UN membership followed on Sept. 17, 1991.

Because Latvians' ethnic identity had been quashed throughout its history by foreign rulers, the new Latvian republic set up strict citizenship laws, limiting citizenship to ethnic Latvians and to those who had lived in the region before Soviet rule in 1940. This denied about 452,000 of the country's 740,000 ethnic Russians of citizenship.

Latvia's bid to join the European Union was not accepted in talks that began in 1997. In addition to improving its administrative systems, Latvia was told that it had to speed up naturalization of minorities, in particular its large number of Russians. In 1998, a referendum passed easing the citizenship rules, although it was still necessary to be competent in the Latvian language, which many believe is unreasonable to expect of older or poorly educated ethnic Russians. The EU began negotiations for the admission of Latvia in 1999.

In May 2001, Latvia and eight other central and eastern European countries declared their wish to join NATO. To aid in admission to NATO, Parliament in 2002 passed a law no longer requiring parliamentary candidates to speak Latvian.

# Lebanon

### REPUBLIC OF LEBANON

**National name:** Al-Joumhouriya al-Lubnaniya
**President:** Émile Lahoud (1998)
**Premier:** Rafiq al-Hariri (2000)
**Area:** 4,015 sq mi (10,400 sq km)
**Population (2002 est.):** 3,677,780 (growth rate: 1.4%); birth rate: 20.0/1000; infant mortality rate: 27.4/1000; density per sq mi: 916
**Capital and largest city (1991 est.):** Beirut, 1,100,000. **Other large cities:** Tripoli, 240,000; Sidon, 100,000. **Monetary unit:** Lebanese pound. **Languages:** Arabic (official), French, English. **Ethnicity/race:** Arab 95%, Armenian 4%, other 1%. **Religions:** Islam, 60%; Christian, 40% (17 recognized sects); Judaism, negl. (1 sect). **Literacy rate:** 80% (1990)
**Economic summary: GDP/PPP** (2000 est.): $18.2 billion; per capita $5,000. **Real growth rate:** 1%. **Inflation:** 0%. **Unemployment:** 18% (1997 est.). **Arable land:** 18%. **Agriculture:** citrus, grapes, tomatoes, apples, vegetables, potatoes, olives, tobacco; sheep, goats. **Labor force:** 1.3 million (1999 est.); note: in addition, there are as many as 1 million foreign workers (1997 est.); services n.a., industry n.a., agriculture n.a. **Industries:** banking; food processing; jewelry; cement; textiles; mineral and chemical products; wood and furniture products; oil refining; metal fabricating. **Natural resources:** limestone, iron ore, salt, water-surplus state in a water-deficit region, arable land. **Exports:** $700 million (f.o.b., 2000 est.): foodstuffs and tobacco, textiles, chemicals, precious stones, metal and metal products, electrical equipment and products, jewelry, paper and paper products. **Imports:** $6.2 billion (f.o.b., 2000 est.): foodstuffs, machinery and transport equipment, consumer goods, chemicals, textiles, metals, fuels, agricultural foods. **Major trading partners:** UAE, Saudi Arabia, Syria, U.S., Kuwait, France, Belgium, Jordan, Italy, Germany, U.S., Switzerland, Japan, UK.

**Geography** Lebanon lies at the eastern end of the Mediterranean Sea north of Israel and west of Syria. It is four-fifths the size of Connecticut.

The Lebanon Mountains, which parallel the coast on the west, cover most of the country, while on the eastern border is the Anti-Lebanon range. Between the two lies the Bekaa Valley, the principal agricultural area.

**Government** Republic.

**History** After World War I, France was given a League of Nations mandate over Lebanon and its neighbor Syria, which together had previously been a single political unit in the Ottoman Empire. France divided them in 1920 into separate colonial administrations, drawing a border that separated predominantly Muslim Syria from the kaleidoscope of religious communities in Lebanon where Maronite Christians were then dominant. After 20 years of French mandate regime, Lebanon's independence was proclaimed on Nov. 26, 1941, but full independence came in stages. Under an agreement between representatives of Lebanon and the French National Committee of Liberation, most of the powers exercised by France were transferred to the Lebanese government on Jan. 1, 1944. The evacuation of French troops was completed in 1946.

According to the National Pact, different religious communities are represented in the government by having a Maronite Christian president, a Sunni Muslim prime minister, and a Shi'ite National Assembly speaker. The arrangement worked for two decades. Civil war broke out in 1958, with Muslim factions led by Kamal Jumblat and Saeb Salam rising in insurrection against the Lebanese government headed by President Camille Chamoun, a Maronite Christian favoring close ties to the West. At Chamoun's request, President Eisenhower, on July 15, sent U.S. troops to reestablish the government's authority.

Clan warfare between various religious factions in Lebanon goes back centuries. The hodgepodge includes Maronite Christians, who since independence have dominated the government; Sunni Muslims, who have prospered in business and shared political power; the Druze, who hold a faith incorporating aspects of Islam and Gnosticism; and Shi'ite Muslims.

A new—and bloodier—Lebanese civil war that broke out in 1975 resulted in the addition of still another ingredient in the brew—the Syrians. In the fighting between Lebanese factions, 40,000 Lebanese were estimated to have been killed and 100,000 wounded between March 1975 and Nov. 1976. At that point, a Syrian-dominated Arab Deterrent Force intervened and brought large-scale fighting to a halt.

Palestinian guerrillas staging raids on Israel from Lebanese territory drew punitive Israeli raids on Lebanon and two large-scale Israeli invasions, in 1978 and again in 1982. The Israelis withdrew in June 1978 after the UN Security Council created a 6,000-man peacekeeping force for the area, called UNIFIL. As they departed, the Israelis turned their strongholds over to a Christian militia that they had organized, instead of to the UN force.

The second Israeli invasion came on June 6, 1982, after an assassination attempt by Palestinian terrorists on the Israeli ambassador in London. As a base of the PLO, Lebanon became the Israelis' target. Nearly 7,000 Palestinians were dispersed to other Arab nations, and Israel pulled back some of its forces. The violence seemed to have come to an end when, on Sept. 14, Bashir Gemayel, the 34-year-old president-elect, was killed by a bomb that destroyed the headquarters of his Christian Phalangist Party.

The day after Gemayel's assassination, Israeli troops moved into West Beirut in force. On Sept. 17, it was revealed that Christian militiamen had massacred hundreds of Palestinians in two refugee camps, but Israel denied responsibility. On Sept. 20, Amin Gemayel, older brother of Bashir Gemayel, was elected president by the Parliament.

The massacre in the refugee camps prompted the return of a multinational peacekeeping force. Its mandate was to support the central Lebanese government, but it soon found itself drawn into the struggle for power between different Lebanese factions. During their stay in Lebanon, 260 U.S. Marines and about 60 French soldiers were killed, most of them in suicide bombings of the Marine and French army compounds on Oct. 23, 1983. The multinational force left in the spring of 1984.

In July 1986, Syrian observers took a position in Beirut to monitor a peacekeeping agreement. The agreement broke down and fighting between Shi'ite and Druze militia in West Beirut became so intense that Syrian troops mobilized in Feb. 1987, suppressing militia resistance.

In early 1991, the Lebanese government, backed by Syria, attempted to regain control over the south and disband all private militias, thereby ending the 16-year civil war. These conflicts destroyed much of the infrastructure and industry of Lebanon.

In the general elections of Aug. 1992 most Christians abstained from voting, demanding that Syrian forces first leave the country. The new legislature consisted of mostly pro-Syrian members. The largest

Christian party was further weakened when in Jan. 1993 it appeared to split into two factions.

In June 1999, just before Israeli prime minister Benjamin Netanyahu left office, Israel bombed Southern Lebanon, its most severe attack on the country since 1996. In May 2000, the new prime minister, Ehud Barak, withdrew Israeli troops after 22 years of occupation.

In Sept. 2000, opposition party candidates allied with former prime minister Rafiq al-Hariri won a landslide victory in parliamentary elections, in which Lebanon's severe recession was a major issue. Hariri became prime minister a month later.

In the summer of 2001, Syria withdrew nearly all of its 25,000 troops from Beirut and surrounding areas. Troops, however, remain in the countryside. With the continuation of Israeli-Palestinian violence in 2002, Hezbollah began again building up forces along the Lebanese-Israeli border.

# Lesotho

### KINGDOM OF LESOTHO

**Sovereign:** King Letsie III (1996)
**Prime Minister:** Pakalitha Mosisili (1998)
**Area:** 11,720 sq mi (30,355 sq km)
**Population (2002 est.):** 2,207,954 (growth rate: 1.4%); birth rate: 30.7/1000; infant mortality rate: 82.6/1000; density per sq mi: 188
**Capital and largest city (1992):** Maseru (1992), 170,000. **Monetary unit:** Maluti. **Languages:** English and Sesotho (official); also Zulu and Xhosa. **Ethnicity/ race:** Sotho 99.7%, Europeans 1,600, Asians 800. **Religions:** Christian, 80%; indigenous beliefs, Muslim, and Bahai. **Literacy rate:** 56% (1966)
**Economic summary:** GDP/PPP (2000 est.): $5.1 billion; per capita $2,400. **Real growth rate:** 2.5%. **Inflation:** 6%. **Unemployment:** 45%. **Arable land:** 11%. **Agriculture:** corn, wheat, pulses, sorghum, barley; livestock. **Labor force:** 700,000 economically active; 86% of resident population engaged in subsistence agriculture; roughly 35% of the active male wage earners work in South Africa. **Industries:** food, beverages, textiles, handicrafts; construction; tourism. **Natural resources:** water, agricultural and grazing land, some diamonds and other minerals. **Exports:** $175 million (f.o.b., 2000 est.): manufactures 75% (clothing, footwear, road vehicles), wool and mohair, food and live animals (1998). **Imports:** $700 million (f.o.b., 2000 est.): food; building materials, vehicles, machinery, medicines, petroleum products (1995). **Major trading partners:** South African Customs Union, North America, Asia. **Member of Commonwealth of Nations**

**Geography** Mountainous Lesotho, the size of Maryland, is surrounded by the Republic of South Africa in the east-central part of that country except for short borders on the east and south with two discontinuous units of the Republic of Transkei. The Drakensberg Mountains in the east are Lesotho's principal chain. Elsewhere the region consists of rocky tableland.

**Government** Parliamentary constitutional monarchy.

**History** Lesotho (formerly Basutoland) was constituted a native state under British protection by a treaty signed with the native chief Moshoeshoe in 1843. It was annexed to Cape Colony in 1871, but in 1884 it was restored to direct control by the Crown. The colony of Basutoland became the independent nation of Lesotho on Oct. 4, 1966, with King Moshoeshoe II as sovereign.

In the 1970 elections, Ntsu Mokhehle, head of the Basutoland Congress Party, claimed a victory, but Prime Minister Leabua Jonathan declared a state of emergency, suspended the constitution, and arrested Mokhehle. King Moshoeshoe II returned after a compromise with Jonathan in which the new constitution would name him head of state but forbid his participation in politics.

After the king refused to approve the replacement in Feb. 1990 of individuals dismissed by Justin Metsino Lekhanya, the chairman of the Military Council, the latter stripped the king of his executive power. Then in early March, Lekhanya sent the king into exile. In Nov., the king was dethroned, and his son was sworn in as King Letsie III.

Lekhanya was himself forced to resign in April 1991, and Col. Ramaema became the new chairman in May. In Jan. 1995, the crown reverted to the father of Letsie III, Moshoeshoe II. Letsie again became crown prince. In 1996, however, King Moshoeshoe died in an automobile accident, and Letsie again assumed the throne.

In fall 1998, hundreds of demonstrators protested for weeks in front of the king's palace, claiming voting fraud in the May elections that put Prime Minister Pakalitha Mosisili in power. They demanded that the government step down and hold new elections. Troops from South Africa and Botswana entered the country to stop the riots and put down an army mutiny.

In parliamentary elections in 2002, the ruling Lesotho Congress for Democracy won 54% of the vote.

# Liberia

### REPUBLIC OF LIBERIA

**President:** Charles Taylor (1997)
**Area:** 43,000 sq mi (111,370 sq km)
**Population (2002 est.):** 3,288,198 (growth rate: 3.0%); birth rate: 46.0/1000; infant mortality rate: 130.2/1000; density per sq mi: 76
**Capital and largest city (1993 est.):** Monrovia, 1,000,000. **Monetary unit:** Liberian dollar.
**Languages:** English (official) and tribal dialects.
**Ethnicity/race:** indigenous African tribes 95% (including Kpelle, Bassa, Gio, Kru, Grebo, Mano, Krahn, Gola, Gbandi, Loma, Kissi, Vai, and Bella), Americo-Liberians 5% (descendants of former slaves).
**Religions:** traditional 40%, Christian 40%, Islam 20%.
**Literacy rate:** 40% (1990)
**Economic summary:** GDP/PPP (2000 est.): $3.35 billion; per capita $1,100. **Real growth rate:** 15%. **Inflation:** 5%. **Unemployment:** 70%. **Arable land:** 1%. **Agriculture:** rubber, coffee, cocoa, rice, cassava (tapioca), palm oil, sugarcane, bananas; sheep, goats; timber. **Labor force:** agriculture 70%, industry 8%, services 22% (1999 est.). **Industries:** rubber processing, palm oil processing, diamonds. **Natural resources:** iron ore, timber, diamonds, gold, hydropower. **Exports:** $55 million (f.o.b. 2000 est.): diamonds, iron ore, rubber, timber, coffee, cocoa. **Imports:** $170 million (f.o.b. 2000 est.): fuels, chemicals, machinery, transportation equipment, manufactured goods; rice and other foodstuffs. **Major trading partners:** Belgium, Switzerland, France, South Korea, Italy, Japan, Germany.

**Geography** Lying on the Atlantic in the southern part of West Africa, Liberia is bordered by Sierra Leone, Guinea, and Côte d'Ivoire. It is comparable in size to Tennessee. Most of the country is a plateau covered by dense tropical forests, which thrive under an annual rainfall of about 160 in. a year.

**Government** Republic.

**History** Africa's first republic, Liberia was founded in 1822 as a result of the efforts of the American Colonization Society to settle freed American slaves in West Africa. The society contended that the immigration of blacks to Africa was an answer to the problem of slavery as well as to what it felt was the incompatibility of the races. Over the course of forty years, about 12,000 slaves were voluntarily relocated. Originally called Monrovia, the colony became the Free and Independent Republic of Liberia in 1847.

The English-speaking Americo-Liberians, descendants of former American slaves, make up only 5% of the population, but have historically dominated the intellectual and ruling class. Liberia's indigenous population is composed of 16 different ethnic groups.

The government of Africa's first republic was modeled after that of the United States, and Joseph Jenkins Roberts of Virginia was elected the first president. Ironically, Liberia's constitution denied indigenous Liberians equal rights with the lighter-skinned American emigrants and their descendants.

After 1920, considerable progress was made toward opening up the interior, a process that was spurred in 1951 by the establishment of a 43-mile (69-km) railroad to the Bomi Hills from Monrovia. In July 1971, while serving his sixth term as president, William V. S. Tubman died following surgery and was succeeded by his long-time associate, Vice President William R. Tolbert, Jr.

Tolbert was ousted in a military coup on April 12, 1980, by Master Sgt. Samuel K. Doe, backed by the U.S. government. Doe's rule was characterized by corruption and brutality. A rebellion led by Charles Taylor, a former Doe aide, and the National Patriotic Front of Liberia (NPFL), started in Dec. 1989. The following year, Doe was assassinated. The Economic Community of West African States (ECOWAS) negotiated with the government and the rebel factions and attempted to restore order, but the civil war raged on. By April 1996, factional fighting by the country's warlords had destroyed any last vestige of normalcy and civil society. The civil war finally ended in 1997.

In what was considered by international observers to be a free election, Charles Taylor won 75% of the presidential vote in July 1997. Taylor's government has focused more on armed security rather than reconstruction of the country after its long civil war. While Taylor attempts to fashion himself into a democratic political leader, his behavior remains that of a militia rebel. The country has next to no health care system, and the capital is without electricity and running water. Taylor supported Sierra Leone's brutal Revolutionary United Front (RUF) in the hopes of toppling his neighbor's government, and in exchange for diamonds, which enriched his personal coffers. As a consequence, the UN issued sanctions.

Between 2000 and 2002, fighting at the junction of the border between Liberia, Sierra Leone, and Guinea occurred between a jumble of warring factions, including the armies of Liberia and Guinea, rebel Guineans and Liberians, and the RUF. Taylor charged neighboring Guinea with aiding the rebels, who were operating from within Guinean territory. In 2002, rebels—Liberians United for Reconciliation and Democracy (LURD)—intensified their attacks on Taylor's government.

# Libya

### SOCIALIST PEOPLE'S LIBYAN ARAB JAMAHIRIYA

**National name:** Socialist People's Libyan Arab Jamahiriya
**Chief of State:** Col. Muammar al-Qaddafi (1969)
**Prime Minister:** Mubarak Abdallah al-Shamikh (2000)
**Area:** 679,358 sq mi (1,759,540 sq km)
**Population (2002 est.):** 5,368,585 (growth rate: 2.4%); birth rate: 27.6/1000; infant mortality rate: 27.9/1000; density per sq mi: 8
**Capital:** Tripoli. **Largest cities (est. 1988):** Tripoli, 591,062; Benghazi, 446,250. **Monetary unit:** Libyan dinar. **Languages:** Arabic, Italian and English widely understood in major cities. **Ethnicity/race:** Berber and Arab 97%, Greeks, Maltese, Italians, Egyptians, Pakistanis, Turks, Indians, Tunisians. **Religion:** Islam. **Literacy rate:** 64% (1990)
**Economic summary: GDP/PPP** (2000 est.): $45.4 billion; per capita $8,900. **Real growth rate:** 6.5%. **Inflation:** 18.5%. **Unemployment:** 30%. **Arable land:** 1%. **Agriculture:** wheat, barley, olives, dates, citrus, vegetables, peanuts, soybeans; cattle. **Labor force:** 1.5 million (2000 est.); services and government 54%, industry 29%, agriculture 17% (1997 est.). **Industries:** petroleum, food processing, textiles, handicrafts, cement. **Natural resources:** petroleum, natural gas, gypsum. **Exports:** $13.9 billion (f.o.b., 2000 est.): crude oil, refined petroleum products. **Imports:** $7.6 billion (f.o.b., 2000 est.): machinery, transport equipment, food, manufactured goods. **Major trading partners:** Italy, Germany, Spain, France, Turkey, Tunisia, UK, South Korea.

**Geography**　Libya stretches along the northeast coast of Africa between Tunisia and Algeria on the west and Egypt on the east; to the south are the Sudan, Chad, and Niger. It is one-sixth larger than Alaska. A greater part of the country lies within the Sahara. Along the Mediterranean coast and farther inland is arable plateau land.

**Government**　Military dictatorship.

**History**　The first inhabitants of Libya were Berber tribes. In the 7th century, B.C., Phoenicians colonized the eastern section of Libya, called Cyrenaica, and Greeks colonized the western portion, called Tripolitania. Tripolitania was for a time under Carthaginian control. It became part of the Roman Empire from 46 B.C. to A.D. 436, after which it was sacked by the Vandals. Cyrenaica belonged to the Roman Empire from the 1st century B.C. until its decline, after which it was invaded by Arab forces in 642. Beginning in the 16th century, both Tripolitania and Cyrenaica nominally became part of the Ottoman Empire.

Tripolitania was one of the outposts for the Barbary pirates who raided Mediterranean merchant ships or required them to pay tribute. In 1801, the pasha of Tripoli raised the price of tribute, which led to the Tripolitan war with the United States. When the peace treaty was signed on June 4, 1805, U.S. ships no longer had to pay tribute to Tripoli.

Following the outbreak of hostilities between Italy and Turkey in 1911, Italian troops occupied Tripoli. Italian sovereignty was recognized in 1912. Libyans continued to fight the Italians until 1914, by which time Italy controlled most of the land. Italy formally united Tripolitania and Cyrenaica in 1934 as the colony of Libya.

Libya was the scene of much desert fighting during World War II. After the fall of Tripoli on Jan. 23, 1943, it came under Allied administration. In 1949, the UN voted that Libya should become independent, and in 1951 it became the United Kingdom of Libya. Oil was discovered in the impoverished country in 1958, and eventually transformed its economy.

On Sept. 1, 1969, 27-year-old Col. Muammar al-Qaddafi deposed the king and revolutionized the country, making it a pro-Arabic, anti-Western, Islamic republic with socialist leanings. It was also rabidly anti-Israeli. A notorious firebrand, Qaddafi aligned himself with dictators, such as Uganda's Idi Amin, and fostered anti-Western terrorism.

On Aug. 19, 1981, two U.S. Navy F-14s shot down two Soviet-made SU-22s of the Libyan air force that had attacked them in air space above the Gulf of Sidra. On March 24, 1986, U.S. and Libyan forces skirmished in the Gulf of Sidra, and two Libyan patrol boats were sunk. Qaddafi's troops also supported rebels in Chad but suffered major military reverses in 1987. A two-year-old U.S. covert policy to destabilize the Libyan government ended in failure in Dec. 1990.

On Dec. 21, 1988, a Boeing 747 exploded in flight over Lockerbie, Scotland, the result of a terrorist bomb, killing all 259 people aboard and 11 on the ground. Two Libyan intelligence agents were indicted, but Qaddafi refused to hand them over, leading to UN-approved trade and air traffic embargoes in 1992. On April 5, 1999, after years of negotiations, Libya surrendered the two men. The suspects, Abdel Basset Ali al-Megrahi and Lamen Khalifa Fhimah, were tried in the Netherlands in 2000–2001. Megrahi was found guilty of mass murder; the other defendant was found innocent. As a result of Libya's cooperation, the United Nations suspended sanctions against the nation, which had severely affected the Libyan economy. European companies almost immediately began to court the oil-rich nation once again. The U.S. and Britain both stipulated that before they lifted sanctions, Libya would have to admit responsibility for the Lockerbie bombing, renounce terrorism, and compensate the victims' families. Negotiations were underway in 2002.

Qaddafi has also sought to play a leading role in African affairs, promoting a united Africa. The policy suffered a severe setback, however, in Sept. 2000, when Libyan resentment over the 1 million black Africans living in the country of 6 million people erupted into violence. Rampaging mobs killed hundreds of blacks, prompting several African nations to launch airlifts to repatriate thousands of citizens.

# Liechtenstein

### PRINCIPALITY OF LIECHTENSTEIN

**Ruler:** Prince Hans Adam II (1989)
**Head of Government:** Otmar Hasler (2001)
**Area:** 62 sq mi (160 sq km)
**Population (2002 est.):** 32,842 (growth rate: 0.5%); birth rate: 11.2/1000; infant mortality rate: 4.9/1000; density per sq mi: 532
**Capital and largest city (1994):** Vaduz, 5,067.
**Monetary unit:** Swiss franc. **Languages:** German (official), Alemmanic dialect. **Ethnicity/race:** Alemannic 87.5%; Italian, Turkish, and other 12.5%. **Religions:** Roman Catholic, 80%; Protestant, 6.9%; unknown, 5.6%; other, 7.5%. **Literacy rate:** 100% (1981)
**Economic summary: GDP/PPP** (1998 est.): $730 million; per capita $23,000. **Real growth rate:** n.a. **Inflation:** 0.5% (1997 est.). **Unemployment:** 1.8% (Feb. 1999). **Arable land:** 24%. **Agriculture:** wheat, barley, corn, potatoes; livestock, dairy products. **Labor force:** 22,891 of which 13,847 are foreigners; 8,231 commute from Austria and Switzerland to work each day; industry, trade, and building 45%, services 53%, agriculture, fishing, forestry, and horticulture 2% (1997 est.).

**Industries:** electronics, metal manufacturing, textiles, ceramics, pharmaceuticals, food products, precision instruments, tourism. **Natural resources:** hydroelectric potential, arable land. **Exports:** $2.47 billion (1996): small specialty machinery, dental products, stamps, hardware, pottery. **Imports:** $917.3 million (1996): machinery, metal goods, textiles, foodstuffs, motor vehicles. **Major trading partners:** EU and EFTA countries.

**Geography** Tiny Liechtenstein, not quite as large as Washington, D.C., lies on the east bank of the Rhine River south of Lake Constance between Austria and Switzerland. It consists of low valley land and Alpine peaks. Falknis (8,401 ft; 2,561 m) and Naafkopf (8,432 ft; 2,570 m) are the tallest.

**Government** Hereditary constitutional monarchy.

**History** The Liechtensteiners are descended from the Alemanni tribe that came into the region after A.D. 500. Founded in 1719, Liechtenstein was a member of the German Confederation from 1815 to 1866, when it became an independent principality. It abolished its army in 1868 and has managed to stay neutral and undamaged in all European wars since then. Liechtenstein still claims 1,600 sq km of Czech territory (the royal family's ancestral home) confiscated in 1918; the Czech Republic insists that restitution does not go back before Feb. 1948, when the Communists seized power. In a referendum on July 1, 1984, male voters granted women the right to vote in national (but not local) elections—a victory for Prince Hans Adam. A treaty negotiated between EFTA (European Free Trade Association) and the EU linking the two as the European Economic Area was ratified by Liechtenstein in a Dec. 1993 vote, but Switzerland rejected it. After renegotiation the treaty was again subjected to a referendum in April 1995 and approved. Liechtenstein won a special concession limiting immigration.

Blacklisted in 2000 as a center for money laundering, Liechtenstein toughened its laws and made major efforts to clean up its financial practices. In 2002, the country was removed from the OECD's (Organization of Economic Cooperation and Development's) money-laundering blacklist.

# Lithuania

**REPUBLIC OF LITHUANIA**

**National name:** Lietuva
**President:** Valdas Adamkus (1998)
**Prime Minister:** Algirdas Brazauskas (2001)
**Area:** 25,174 sq mi (65,200 sq km)
**Population (2002 est.):** 3,601,138 (growth rate: –0.3%); birth rate: 10.2/1000; infant mortality rate: 14.3/1000; density per sq mi: 143
**Capital and largest city (1993 est.):** Vilnius, 590,100. **Other large cities:** Kaunas, 429,000; Klaipeda, 206,400. **Monetary unit:** Litas. **Languages:** Lithuanian (official), Polish, Russian. **Ethnicity/race:** Lithuanian 80.1%, Russian 8.6%, Polish 7 7%, Belorussian 1.5%, other 2.1%. **Religions:** Catholic 85%, others include Lutheran, Russian Orthodox, Protestant, evangelical Christian Baptist, Islam, Judaism. **Literacy:** 98% (1989)
**Economic summary: GDP/PPP** (2000 est.): $26.4 billion; per capita $7,300. **Real growth rate:** 2.9%. **Inflation:** 1%. **Unemployment:** 10.8% (2000). **Arable land:** 39%. **Agriculture:** grain, potatoes, sugar beets, flax, vegetables; beef, milk, eggs; fish. **Labor force:** 2 million; industry 30%, agriculture 20%, services 50% (1997 est.). **Industries:** metal-cutting machine tools, electric motors, television sets, refrigerators and freezers, petroleum refining, shipbuilding (small ships),

furniture making, textiles, food processing, fertilizers, agricultural machinery, optical equipment, electronic components, computers, amber. **Natural resources:** peat, arable land. **Exports:** $3.7 billion (f.o.b., 2000). machinery and equipment 22%, mineral products 15%, chemicals 12%, textiles and clothing, foodstuffs (1999). **Imports:** $4.9 billion (f.o.b., 2000): machinery and equipment 18%, mineral products 16%, chemicals 10%, textiles and clothing 10%, transport equipment 7% (1999). **Major trading partners:** Germany, Latvia, Russia, Belarus, Denmark.

**Geography** Lithuania is situated on the eastern shore of the Baltic Sea and borders Latvia on the north, Belarus on the east and south, Poland and the Kaliningrad region of Russia on the southwest. It is a country of gently rolling hills, many forests, rivers and streams, and lakes. Its principal natural resource is agricultural land.

**Government** Parliamentary democracy.

**History** The Liths, or Lithuanians, united in the 12th century under the rule of Mindaugas, who became king in 1251. Through marriage, one of the later Lithuanian rulers became the king of Poland (Ladislaus II) in 1386, uniting the countries. In 1410, the Poles and Lithuanians defeated the powerful Teutonic Knights at Tannenberg. From the 14th to the 16th century, Poland and Lithuania made up one of medieval Europe's largest empires, stretching from the Black Sea almost to Moscow. The two countries formed a confederation for almost 200 years, and in 1569 they formally united. Russia, Prussia, and Austria partitioned Poland in 1772, 1792, and 1795. As a consequence, Lithuania came under Russian rule after the last partition. Russia attempted to immerse Lithuania in Russian culture and language, but anti-Russian sentiment continued to grow. Following World War I and the collapse of Russia, Lithuania declared independence (1918), under German protection.

The republic was then annexed by the Soviet Union in 1940. From June 1941 to 1944, it was occupied by German troops, with whom Lithuania served in World War II. Some 240,000 Jews were massacred in Lithuania during the Nazi years. In 1944, the Soviets again annexed Lithuania.

The Lithuanian independence movement reemerged in 1988. In 1990, Vytautas Landsbergis, the non-Communist head of the largest Lithuanian popular movement (Sajudis), was elected president. On the same day, the Supreme Council rejected Soviet rule and declared the restoration of Lithuania's independence, the first Baltic republic to take this action. Confrontation with the Soviet Union ensued along with economic sanctions, but they were lifted after both sides agreed to a face-saving compromise.

Lithuania's independence was quickly recognized by major European and other nations, including the United States. The Soviet Union finally recognized the independence of the Baltic states on Sept. 6, 1991. UN admittance followed on Sept. 17, 1991. Successful implementation of structural and legislative reforms in Lithuania attracted greater foreign direct investments by the mid-1990s.

The EU began negotiations for the admission of Lithuania in 1999. In May 2001, Lithuania and eight other central and eastern European countries declared their wish to join NATO. To help secure EU membership, Lithuania agreed in 2002 to shut down Ignalina nuclear power station, similar in design to the disastrous Chernobyl plant.

# Luxembourg

## GRAND DUCHY OF LUXEMBOURG

**National name:** Grand-Duché de Luxembourg
**Ruler:** Grand Duke Henri (2000)
**Premier:** Jean-Claude Juncker (1995)
**Area:** 998 sq mi (2,586 sq km)
**Population (2002 est.):** 448,569 (growth rate: 0.3%); birth rate: 12.1/1000; infant mortality rate: 4.7/1000; density per sq mi: 449
**Capital and largest city (1991):** Luxembourg, 75,622.
**Monetary units:** Euro (formerly Luxembourg franc).
**Languages:** Luxembourgish, French, German.
**Ethnicity/race:** Celtic base (with French and German blend), Portuguese, Italian, and European (guest and worker residents). **Religions:** Roman Catholic 97%, Protestant and Jewish 3%. **Literacy rate:** 100% (1980)
**Economic summary: GDP/PPP** (2000 est.): $15.9 billion; per capita $36,400. **Real growth rate:** 5.7%. **Inflation:** 7.8%. **Unemployment:** 2.7%. **Arable land:** 24%. **Agriculture:** barley, oats, potatoes, wheat, fruits, wine grapes; livestock products. **Labor force:** 248,000 (of whom 70,200 are foreign cross-border workers primarily from France, Belgium, and Germany) (2000); services 83.2%, industry 14.3%, agriculture 2.5% (1998 est.). **Industries:** banking, iron and steel, food processing, chemicals, metal products, engineering, tires, glass, aluminum. **Natural resources:** iron ore (no longer exploited), arable land. **Exports:** $7.6 billion (f.o.b., 2000): machinery and equipment, steel products, chemicals, rubber products, glass. **Imports:** $10 billion (c.i.f., 2000): minerals, metals, foodstuffs, quality consumer goods. **Major trading partners:** EU, U.S.

**Geography** Luxembourg is about half the size of Delaware. The Ardennes Mountains extend from Belgium into the northern section of Luxembourg. The rolling plateau of the fertile Bon Pays is in the south.

**Government** Constitutional monarchy.

**History** Luxembourg, once part of Charlemagne's empire, became an independent state in 963, when Siegfried, count of Ardennes, became sovereign of Lucilinburhuc ("Little Fortress"). In 1060, Conrad, a descendant of Siegfried, took the title count of Luxembourg. From the 15th to the 18th century, Spain, France, and Austria held the duchy in turn. The Congress of Vienna in 1815 made it a Grand Duchy and gave it to William I, king of the Netherlands. In 1839, the Treaty of London ceded the western part of Luxembourg to Belgium. The eastern part, continuing in personal union with the Netherlands and a member of the German Confederation, became autonomous in 1848 and a neutral territory by decision of the London Conference of 1867, governed by its grand duke. Germany occupied the duchy in World Wars I and II. Allied troops liberated the enclave in 1944.

Luxembourg joined NATO in 1949, the Benelux Economic Union (with Belgium and the Netherlands) in 1948, and the European Economic Community (later the EU) in 1957. In 1961, Prince Jean, son and heir of Grand Duchess Charlotte, was made head of state, acting for his mother. She abdicated in 1964, and Prince Jean became grand duke. Grand Duchess Charlotte died in 1985. Luxembourg's Parliament approved the Maastricht Accord, paving the way for the economic unity of the EU in July 1992. Crown Prince Henri was sworn in as grand duke in Oct. 2000, replacing his father, Jean, who had been head of state for 26 years. In 2002, the euro became the country's new currency.

# Macedonia

## REPUBLIC OF MACEDONIA[1]

**National Name:** Republica Makedonija
**President:** Boris Trajkovski (1999)
**Prime Minister:** Branko Crvenkovski (2002)
**Area:** 9,781 sq mi (25,333 sq km)
**Population (2002 est.):** 2,054,800 (growth rate: 0.6%); birth rate: 13.3/1000; infant mortality rate: 12.5/1000; density per sq mi: 210
**Capital and largest city (1994 est.):** Skopje, 444,229.
**Other large cities:** Bitola, 84,002; Prelep, 70,152; Kumanovo, 68,148. **Monetary unit:** Denar.
**Languages:** Macedonian (official), which uses the Cyrillic alphabet, 70%; Albanian (official), 21%; Turkish, 3%; other, 6%. **Ethnicity/race:** Macedonian 65%, Albanian 22%, Turkish 4%, Serb 2%, Rom (Gypsy) 3%, other 4%. **Religions (1994):** Eastern Orthodox 67%, Muslim 30%
**Economic summary: GDP/PPP** (2000 est.): $9 billion; per capita $4,400. **Real growth rate:** 5%. **Inflation:** 11%. **Unemployment:** 32% (2000). **Arable land:** 24%. **Agriculture:** rice, tobacco, wheat, corn, millet, cotton, sesame, mulberry leaves, citrus, vegetables; beef, pork, poultry, mutton. **Labor force:** 1 million (1999 est.); agriculture n.a., industry n.a., services n.a. **Industries:** coal, metallic chromium, lead, zinc, ferronickel, textiles, wood products, tobacco. **Natural resources:** chromium, lead, zinc, manganese, tungsten, nickel, low-grade iron ore, asbestos, sulfur, timber, arable land. **Exports:** $1.4 billion (f.o.b., 2000 est.): food, beverages, tobacco; miscellaneous manufactures, iron and steel. **Imports:** $2 billion (f.o.b., 2000 est.): machinery and equipment, chemicals, fuels; food products. **Major trading partners:** Germany, Yugoslavia, U.S., Greece, Italy, Ukraine, Russia.

1. The UN recognized the Republic of Macedonia on April 8, 1993, under the temporary name the Former Yugoslav Republic of Macedonia. The U.S. recognized Macedonia as a state in Feb. 1994.

**Geography** Macedonia is a landlocked state in the heart of the Balkans and is slightly smaller than the state of Vermont. It is a mountainous country with small basins of agricultural land linked by rivers. The three major rivers are the Aliakmon, the Vardar, and the Strymon. The Vardar is the largest and most important river.

**Government** Emerging democracy.

**History** The Republic of Macedonia occupies the western half of the ancient Kingdom of Macedonia. Historic Macedonia was defeated by Rome and became a Roman province in 148 B.C. After the Roman Empire was divided in A.D. 395, Macedonia was intermittently ruled by the Byzantine Empire until Turkey took possession of the land in 1389. The Ottoman Turks dominated Macedonia for the next five centuries, up until 1913. During the 19th and 20th centuries, there was a constant struggle by the Balkan powers to possess Macedonia for its economic wealth and its strategic military corridors. The Treaty of San Stefano in 1878 ending the Russo-Turkish War gave the largest part of Macedonia to Bulgaria. Bulgaria lost much of its Macedonian territory when it was defeated by the Greeks and Serbs in the Second Balkan War of 1913. Most of Macedonia went to Serbia and the remainder was divided among Greece and Bulgaria.

In 1914, Serbia, which included Macedonia, joined in union with Croatia, Slovenia, and Montenegro to form the Kingdom of Serbs, Croats, and Slovenes, which was renamed Yugoslavia in 1929. Bulgaria joined the Axis powers in World War II and occupied parts of Yugoslavia including Macedonia in 1941. During the occupation of their country, Macedonian resistance fighters fought a guerrilla war against the invading troops. The Yugoslavian republic was reestablished after the defeat of Germany in 1945, and in 1946, the government removed Macedonia from Serbian control and made it an autonomous Yugoslavian republic. Later, when President Tito recognized the Macedonian people as a separate nation, the Macedonians strove to develop their own culture and language separate from Bulgaria and Serbia.

In Jan. 1992, Macedonia declared its independence from Yugoslavia and asked for recognition from the European Union nations. It became a member of the UN in 1993 under the provisional name of the Former Yugoslav Republic of Macedonia (FYROM) because Greece vociferously protested Macedonia's right to the name, which is also the name of a large northern province of Greece. To Greece, the use of the name implies Macedonia's interest in territorial expansion into the Greek province. Greece has imposed two trade embargoes against the country as a result.

The Macedonian government, in 1997, urged NATO to extend its peacekeeping role in the Balkans beyond its mid-1998 mandate, saying NATO troops provided a stabilizing role. Ethnic tensions between ethnic Albanians and Macedonians continued to rise during the Kosovo crisis, during which more than 140,000 refugees streamed into the country from neighboring Kosovo. Most of the refugees returned to Kosovo in 2000.

The long-simmering resentment of Macedonia's ethnic Albanians erupted into violence in March 2000, prompting the government to send troops into the heavily Albanian western section of the country. The rebels sought greater autonomy within Macedonia. The more radical aspired to create a greater Albania, one that would unite the ethnic Albanians of Macedonia, Kosovo, and Albania proper, but there was little enthusiasm for pan-Albanianism among Macedonia's war-weary neighbors. On Aug. 13, after six months of fighting, the rebels and the Macedonian government signed a peace agreement that allowed a British-led NATO force to enter the country and disarm the guerrillas.

In Nov. 2001, Macedonia's Parliament agreed to constitutional amendments giving broader rights to its Albanian minority. Albanian became one of the country's two official languages. NATO extended its peacekeeping mission in the country through Oct. 2002.

In Sept. 2002 elections, a center-left coalition ousted the governing coalition, which had been embroiled in previous years' guerrilla insurgency. Branko Crvenkovski of the Together for Macedonia coalition became the new prime minister.

# Madagascar

## REPUBLIC OF MADAGASCAR

**National name:** Repoblikan'i Madagasikara
**President:** Marc Ravalomanana (2002)
**Prime Minister:** Jacques Sylla(2002)
**Area:** 226,656 sq mi (587,040 sq km)
**Population (2002 est.):** 16,473,477 (growth rate: 3.0%); birth rate: 42.4/1000; infant mortality rate: 81.9/1000; density per sq mi: 73
**Capital and largest city (1993 est.):** Antananarivo, 1,000,000. **Monetary unit:** Malagasy franc.
**Languages:** Malagasy and French (both official).
**Ethnicity/race:** Malayo-Indonesian (Merina and related Betsileo), Cotiers (mixed African, Malayo-Indonesian, and Arab ancestry—

Betsimisaraka, Tsimihety, Antaisaka, Sakalava), French, Indian, Creole, Comoran. **Religions:** traditional 52%, Christian 41%, Islam 7%. **Literacy rate:** 80% (1990)
**Economic summary: GDP/PPP** (2000 est.): $12.3 billion; per capita $800. **Real growth rate:** 4.8%. **Inflation:** 10% (1999 est.). **Unemployment:** n.a. **Arable land:** 4%. **Agriculture:** coffee, vanilla, sugarcane, cloves, cocoa, rice, cassava (tapioca), beans, bananas, peanuts; livestock products. **Labor force:** 7 million (1999). **Industries:** meat processing, soap, breweries, tanneries, sugar, textiles, glassware, cement, automobile assembly plant, paper, petroleum, tourism. **Natural resources:** graphite, chromite, coal, bauxite, salt, quartz, tar sands, semiprecious stones, mica, fish, hydropower. **Exports:** $538 million (f.o.b., 1998): coffee, vanilla, shellfish, sugar; cotton cloth, chromite, petroleum products. **Imports:** $693 million (f.o.b., 1998): intermediate manufactures, capital goods, petroleum, consumer goods, food. **Major trading partners:** France, U.S., Germany, UK, Japan, Hong Kong, China, Singapore.

**Geography** Madagascar lies in the Indian Ocean off the southeast coast of Africa opposite Mozambique. The world's fourth-largest island, it is twice the size of Arizona. The country's low-lying coastal area gives way to a central plateau. The once densely wooded interior has largely been cut down.

**Government** Multiparty republic.

**History** The Malagasy are of mixed Malayo-Indonesian and African-Arab ancestry. Indonesians are believed to have migrated to the island about 700. King Andrianampoinimerina (1787–1810) ruled the major kingdom on the island, and his son, Radama I (1810–28) unified much of the island. The French made the island a protectorate in 1885, and then, in 1894–95, ended the monarchy, exiling Queen Rànavàlona III to Algiers. A colonial administration was set up, to which the Comoro Islands were attached in 1908, and other territories later. In World War II, the British occupied Madagascar, which retained ties to Vichy France.

An autonomous republic within the French community since 1958, Madagascar became an independent member of the community in 1960. In May 1973, an army coup led by Maj. Gen. Gabriel Ramanantsoa ousted Philibert Tsiranana, president since 1959. Comdr. Didier Ratsiraka, named president on June 15, 1975, announced that he would follow a socialist course and, after nationalizing banks and insurance companies, declared all mineral resources nationalized. Repression and censorship characterized his regime. Ratsiraka was reelected in 1989 in a suspicious election that led to riots as the formation of a multiparty system in 1990. In 1991, Ratsiraka agreed to share power with the democratically minded opposition leader, Albert Zafy, who then overwhelmingly won the presidential elections in Feb. 1993. But Zafy was impeached by Parliament for abusing his constitutional powers during an economic crisis and lost the 1996 presidential election to Ratsiraka, who became president in Feb. 1997.

The Dec. 2001 presidential election between incumbent president Didier Ratsiraka and Marc Ravalomanana, the mayor of Antananarivo, proved inconclusive and a run-off vote was scheduled. But Ravalomanana claimed the election was rigged, and on Feb. 22, 2002, declared himself president. In response, Ratsiraka declared martial law and set up a rival capital in Toamasina, and Madagascar in effect found itself with two presidents and two capitals. After a recount in April, the High Constitutional Court declared Ravalomanana was the winner with 51.5% of the vote. Ratsiraka, however, refused to accept the outcome. Finally, after some minor skirmishes between rival army factions, Ratsiraka fled to France on July 5, and Madagascar's six-month civil war ended.

# Malawi

**REPUBLIC OF MALAWI**

**President:** Bakili Muluzi (1994)
**Area:** 45,745 sq mi (118,480 sq km)
**Population (2002 est.):** 10,701,824 (growth rate: 1.4%); birth rate: 37.1/1000; infant mortality rate: 120.0/1000; density per sq mi: 234
**Capital (1993 est.):** Lilongwe, 260,000. **Largest city (1993 est.):** Blantyre, 399,000. **Monetary unit:** Kwacha. **Languages:** English and Chichewa (both official). **Ethnicity/race:** Chewa, Nyanja, Tumbuko, Yao, Lomwe, Sena, Tonga, Ngoni, Ngonde, Asian, European. **Religions:** Christian 75%, Islam 20%. **Literacy rate:** 49% (1987)
**Economic summary: GDP/PPP** (2000 est.): $9.4 billion; per capita $900. **Real growth rate:** 3%. **Inflation:** 29.5%. **Unemployment:** n.a. **Arable land:** 34%. **Agriculture:** tobacco, sugarcane, cotton, tea, corn, potatoes, cassava (tapioca), sorghum, pulses; cattle, goats. **Labor force:** 3.5 million; agriculture 86% (1997 est.). **Industries:** tobacco, tea, sugar, sawmill products, cement, consumer goods. **Natural resources:** limestone, arable land, hydropower, unexploited deposits of uranium, coal, and bauxite. **Exports:** $416 million (f.o.b., 2000): tobacco, tea, sugar, cotton, coffee, peanuts, wood products. **Imports:** $435 million (f.o.b., 2000): food, petroleum products, semimanufactures, consumer goods, transportation equipment. **Major trading partners:** South Africa, Germany, U.S., Netherlands, Japan, Zimbabwe, UK, Zambia. **Member of Commonwealth of Nations**

**Geography** Malawi is a landlocked country the size of Pennsylvania in southeast Africa, surrounded by Mozambique, Zambia, and Tanzania. Lake Malawi, formerly Lake Nyasa, occupies most of the country's eastern border. The north-south Rift Valley is flanked by mountain ranges and high plateau areas.

**Government** Multiparty democracy.

**History** Early human inhabitants of what is now Malawi date to 8000–2000 B.C. Bantu-speaking peoples migrated there between the 1st and 4th centuries A.D. A large slave trade took place in the 18th and 19th centuries and brought Islam to the region. At the same time, missionaries introduced Christianity. Several major kingdoms were established in the precolonial period: the Maravi in 1480, the Ngonde in 1600, and the Chikulamayembe in the 18th century.

The first European to make extensive explorations in the area was David Livingstone in the 1850s and 1860s. In 1884, Cecil Rhodes's British South African Company received a charter to develop the country. The company came into conflict with the Arab slavers in 1887–89. Britain annexed what was then called the Nyasaland territory in 1891 and made it a protectorate in 1892. Sir Harry Johnstone, the first high commissioner, used Royal Navy gunboats to wipe out the slavers.

Between 1951 and 1953, Britain combined Nyasaland with the colonies of Northern and Southern Rhodesia to form a federation, a move protested by black Africans who were wary of alignment with the ultra conservative white-minority rule in South Rhodesia. On July 6, 1964, Nyasaland became the independent nation of Malawi. Two years later, it became a republic within the Commonwealth of Nations. Dr. Hastings K. Banda became Malawi's first prime minister (a title later changed to president). In his first month as ruler, he declared, "one party, one leader, one government, and no nonsense about it." In 1971, he became president for life, further consolidating his authoritarian rule. In addition to allowing former colonialists to retain considerable power in the country, he maintained warm relations with the white-minority government of South Africa. These policies drew heavy criticism from Malawian citizens and other African nations. In 1992, Banda faced violent protests.

Bakili Muluzi of the United Democratic Front (UDF) won the country's first free election in May 1994, ending Banda's 30-year rule. In 1999, Muluzi was reelected. While Malawi is no longer the repressive society it was under Banda, Muluzi's government has been tainted by corruption scandals. Senior officials are believed to have sold off 160,000 tons of reserve maize in 2000, despite the signs of a coming famine. In 2002, the country faced severe food shortages, with more than 3 million people close to starvation. Corruption and mismanagement in the Malawian government have caused western donors to withhold assistance just when Malawi most desperately needs it.

# Malaysia

**Head of State:** King Syed Sirajuddin Syed Putra Jamalullail
**Prime Minister:** Mahathir bin Mohamad (1981)
**Area:** 127,316 sq mi (329,750 sq km)
**Population (2002 est.):** 22,662,365 (growth rate: 1.9%); birth rate: 24.2/1000; infant mortality rate: 19.71000; density per sq mi: 178
**Capital and largest city (1991 est.):** Kuala Lumpur, 1,145,000. **Largest cities (1991 est.):** Georgetown (Pinang), 220,000; Ipoh, 382,600. **Monetary unit:** Ringgit. **Languages:** Malay (official), Chinese, Tamil, English. **Ethnicity/race:** Malay and other indigenous 59%, Chinese 32%, Indian 9%. **Religions:** Malays (all Muslims), Chinese (predominantly Buddhists), Indians (predominantly Hindus). **Literacy rate:** 78% (1990)
**Economic summary: GDP/PPP** (2000 est.): $223.7 billion; per capita $10,300. **Real growth rate:** 8.6%. **Inflation:** 1.7%. **Unemployment:** 2.8%. **Arable land:** 3%. **Agriculture:** Peninsular Malaysia—rubber, palm oil, cocoa, rice; Sabah—subsistence crops, rubber, timber, coconuts, rice; Sarawak—rubber, pepper; timber. **Labor force:** 9.6 million; local trade and tourism 28%, manufacturing 27%, agriculture, forestry, and fisheries 16%, services 10%, government 10%, construction 9% (2000 est.). **Industries:** Peninsular Malaysia—rubber and oil palm processing and manufacturing, light manufacturing industry, electronics, tin mining and smelting, logging and processing timber; Sabah—logging, petroleum production; Sarawak—agriculture processing, petroleum production and refining, logging. **Natural resources:** tin, petroleum, timber, copper, iron ore, natural gas, bauxite. **Exports:** $97.9 billion (2000 est.): electronic equipment, petroleum and liquefied natural gas, chemicals, palm oil, wood and wood products, rubber, textiles. **Imports:** $82.6 billion (2000 est.): machinery and transport equipment, chemicals, food, fuel and lubricants. **Major trading partners:** U.S., Singapore, Japan, Hong Kong, Netherlands, Taiwan, Thailand, South Korea, China. **Member of Commonwealth of Nations**

**Geography** Malaysia is on the Malay Peninsula in southeast Asia. The nation also includes Sabah and Sarawak on the island of Borneo to the east. Its area slightly exceeds that of New Mexico.

Most of Malaysia is covered by forest, with a mountain range running the length of the peninsula. Extensive forests provide ebony, sandalwood, teak, and other woods.

**Government** Constitutional monarchy.

**History** The ancestors of the people that now inhabit the Malaysian peninsula first migrated to the area between 2500 and 1500 B.C. Those living in the coastal regions had early contact with Chinese and Indians; seafaring traders from India brought with them Hinduism, which was blended with the local animist beliefs. As Muslims conquered India, they spread the religion of Islam to Malaysia. In the 15th century A.D., Islam acquired a firm hold on the region when the Hindu ruler of the powerful city-state of Malacca, Parameswara Dewa Shah, was overthrown by his Muslim half-brother, Mudzaffar Shah.

British and Dutch interest in the region grew in the 1800s, with the British East India Company establishing a trading settlement on the island of Singapore. Trade soared, with Singapore's population growing from only 5,000 in 1820 to nearly 100,000 in just 50 years. In the 1880s, Britain formally established protectorates in Malaysia. At about the same time, rubber trees were introduced from Brazil. With the mass production of automobiles, rubber became a valuable export, and laborers were brought in from India to work the rubber plantations.

Following the Japanese occupation of Malaysia during World War II, a growing nationalist movement prompted the British to establish the semi-autonomous Federation of Malaya in 1948. But Communist guerrillas took to the jungles to begin a war of national liberation against the British, who declared a state of emergency to quell the insurgency, which lasted until 1960.

The independent state of Malaysia came into existence on Sept. 16, 1963, as a federation of Malaya, Singapore, Sabah (North Borneo), and Sarawak. In 1965, Singapore withdrew from the federation to become a separate nation. Since 1966, the 11 states of former Malaya have been known as West Malaysia, and Sabah and Sarawak have been known as East Malaysia.

By the late 1960s Malaysia was torn by communal rioting directed against Chinese and Indians, who controlled a disproportionate share of the country's wealth. Beginning in 1968, the government moved to achieve greater economic balance through a national economic policy.

Malaysia was significantly affected in 1978 by the "boat people" fleeing Vietnam. Because the refugees were mostly ethnic Chinese, the government was apprehensive that any increase in a minority that previously had been the source of internal conflict in the country. In April 1988, it announced that within the year it would cease accepting refugees.

In the 1980s, Dr. Mohamad Mahathir succeeded Datuk Hussein as prime minister. Mahathir instituted economic reforms that would transform Malaysia into one of the so-called Asian Tigers. Throughout the 1990s, Mahathir embarked on a massive project to build a new capital from scratch in an attempt to bypass congested Kuala Lumpur.

Beginning in 1997 and continuing through the next year, Malaysia suffered from the Asian currency crisis. Instead of following the economic prescriptions of the International Monetary Fund and World Bank, the prime minister opted for fixed exchange rates and capital controls. In late 1999, Malyasia was on the road to economic recovery, and it appeared Mahathir's measures were working.

In Sept. 1998, Mahathir sacked his heir apparent, Anwar Ibrahim, from his posts as deputy prime minister and finance minister, after a disagreement over how to deal with the country's economic problems. In defiance, Anwar launched a reform movement attacking the government. The prime minister then jailed Anwar, who was beaten and convicted of trumped-up corruption and sex crimes.

In July 2002, the prime minister announced plans to retire in late 2003, ending his two-decade reign. He named Abdullah Ahmad Badawi, deputy prime minister, as his successor.

In early 2002, Malaysia passed stringent immigration laws that called for stiff fines, imprisonment, or caning for foreigners caught working in the country without proper permits. By the time the law was enacted at the end of July, more than 300,000 domestic, farm, and factory workers had left the country. There had been about 600,000 foreign laborers in Malaysia, mostly from Indonesia and the Philippines, who performed primarily menial tasks. Malaysian officials blame the country's crime problems on the foreigners.

# Maldives

### REPUBLIC OF MALDIVES

**President:** Maumoon Abdul Gayoom (1978)
**Area:** 116 sq mi (300 sq km)
**Population (2002 est.):** 320,165 (growth rate: 3.0%); birth rate: 37.4/1000; infant mortality rate: 61.9/1000; density per sq mi: 2,764
**Capital and largest city (1995 census):** Malé, 62,973. **Monetary unit:** Rufiya. **Languages:** Dhivehi (official); Arabic, Hindi, and English are also spoken. **Ethnicity/race:** Sinhalese, Dravidian, Arab, African. **Religion:** Islam (Sunni Muslim). **Literacy rate:** 91% (1985)
**Economic summary:** GDP/PPP (2000 est.): $594 million; per capita $2,000. **Real growth rate:** 7.6%. **Inflation:** 3%. **Unemployment:** negl. **Arable land:** 10%. **Agriculture:** coconuts, corn, sweet potatoes; fish. **Labor force:** 67,000 (1995); agriculture 22%, industry 18%, services 60% (1995). **Industries:** fish processing, tourism, shipping, boat building, coconut processing, garments, woven mats, rope, handicrafts, coral and sand mining. **Natural resources:** fish. **Exports:** $88 million (f.o.b., 2000 est.): fish, clothing. **Imports:** $372 million (f.o.b., 2000 est.): consumer goods, intermediate and capital goods, petroleum products. **Major trading partners:** U.S., UK, Sri Lanka, Japan, Singapore, India, Canada.

**Geography** The Republic of Maldives is a group of atolls in the Indian Ocean about 417 mi (671 km) southwest of Sri Lanka. Its 1,190 coral islets stretch over an area of 35,200 square mi (90,000 sq km). With concerns over global warming and the shrinking of the polar ice caps, Maldives feels directly threatened, as none of its islands rises more than six feet above sea level.

**Government** Republic.

**History** The Maldives (formerly called the Maldive Islands) were first settled in the 5th century B.C. by Buddhist seafarers from India and Sri Lanka. According to tradition, Islam was adopted in A.D. 1153. Originally the islands were under the suzerainty of Ceylon (now Sri Lanka). They came under British protection in 1887 and were a dependency of the then-colony of Ceylon until 1948. The independence agreement with Britain was signed July 26,

1965. For centuries a sultanate, the islands adopted a republican form of government in 1952, but the sultanate was restored in 1954. In 1968, however, as the result of a referendum, a republic was again established in the recently independent country. Ibrahim Nasir, the authoritarian president since 1968, was removed from office and replaced by the more progressive Maumoon Abdul Gayoom in 1978.

# Mali

**REPUBLIC OF MALI**

**National name:** République de Mali
**President:** Amadou Toumani Touré (2002)
**Prime Minister:** Ahmed Mohamed Ag Hamani (2002)
**Area:** 478,764 sq mi (1,240,000 sq km)
**Population (2002 est.):** 11,340,480 (growth rate: 3.0%); birth rate: 48.4/1000; infant mortality rate: 119.6/1000; density per sq mi: 24
**Capital and largest city (1992 est.):** Bamako, 746,000.
**Monetary unit:** CFA Franc. **Languages:** French (official), African languages. **Ethnicity/race:** Mande 50% (Bambara, Malinke, Sarakole), Peul 17%, Voltaic 12%, Songhai 6%, Tuareg and Moor 10%, other 5%.
**Religions:** Islam 90%, traditional 9%, Christian 1%.
**Literacy rate:** 32% (1990)
**Economic summary: GDP/PPP** (2000 est.): $9.1 billion; per capita $850. **Real growth rate:** 4.8%. **Inflation:** 0.8%. **Unemployment:** n.a. **Arable land:** 2%.
**Agriculture:** cotton, millet, rice, corn, vegetables, peanuts; cattle, sheep, goats. **Labor force:** n.a.; agriculture and fishing 80% (1998 est.). **Industries:** minor local consumer goods production and food processing; construction; phosphate and gold mining.
**Natural resources:** gold, phosphates, kaolin, salt, limestone, uranium, hydropower; note: bauxite, iron ore, manganese, tin, and copper deposits are known but not exploited. **Exports:** $480 million (f.o.b. 2000 est.): cotton 50%, gold, livestock (1999 est.). **Imports:** $575 million (f.o.b., 2000 est.): machinery and equipment, construction materials, petroleum, foodstuffs, textiles. **Major trading partners:** Italy, Thailand, Germany, Portugal, Côte d'Ivoire, France, Senegal, Benelux.

**Geography**   Most of Mali, in West Africa, lies in the Sahara. A landlocked country four-fifths the size of Alaska, it is bordered by Guinea, Senegal, Mauritania, Algeria, Niger, Burkina Faso, and the Côte d'Ivoire. The only fertile area is in the south, where the Niger and Senegal Rivers provide irrigation.

**Government**   Republic.

**History**   Caravan routes have passed through Mali since A.D. 300. The Malinke empire ruled regions of Mali from the 12th to 16th centuries, and the Songhai empire reigned over the Timbuktu-Gao region in the 15th century. Morocco conquered Timbuktu in 1591, and ruled over it for two centuries. Subjugated by France by the end of the 19th century, the land became a colony in 1904 (named French Sudan in 1920) and in 1946 became part of the French Union. On June 20, 1960, it became independent and, under the name of Sudanese Republic, was federated with the Republic of Senegal in the Mali federation. However, Senegal seceded from the federation on Aug. 20, 1960, and the Sudanese Republic then changed its name to the Republic of Mali on Sept. 22.

In the 1960s, Mali concentrated on economic development, continuing to accept aid from both Soviet bloc and Western nations, as well as international agencies. In the late 1960s, it began retreating from close ties with China. But a purge of conservative opponents brought greater power to President Modibo

Keita, and in 1968, the influence of the Chinese and their Malian sympathizers increased. The army overthrew the government on Nov. 19, 1968, and for the next than 20 years, Mali was under military rule. Mali and Burkina Faso fought a brief border war from Dec. 25th to 29th, 1985. In 1991, dictator Moussa Traoré was overthrown, and Mali made a peaceful transition to democracy. In 1992, Alpha Konaré became Mali's first democratically elected president.

Mali's second multiparty national elections took place in May 1997, with President Konaré winning reelection.

Konaré has won international praise for his efforts to revive Mali's faltering economy. His adherence to International Monetary Fund guidelines has increased foreign investment and helped make Mali the second-largest cotton producer in Africa. He is also the chairman of the 15-nation ECOWAS (the Economic Community of West African States), which in recent years has concentrated on brokering peace in Sierra Leone, Liberia, and Guinea. Konaré retired after serving the two five-year terms permitted by the constitution.

In June 2002, Amadou Toumani Touré became president. A highly popular and respected public figure, he engineered the 1991 coup that freed the country from military rule.

# Malta

**MALTA**

**President:** Guido de Marco (1999)
**Prime Minister:** Eddie Fenech Adami (1998)
**Area:** 122 sq mi (316 sq km)
**Population (2002 est.):** 397,499 (growth rate: 0.5%); birth rate: 12.8/1000; infant mortality rate: 5.7/1000; density per sq mi: 3,258
**Capital (1992 est.):** Valletta, 9,183. **Largest city (est. 1990):** Sliema, 13,541. **Monetary unit:** Maltese lira.
**Languages:** Maltese and English (both official).
**Ethnicity/race:** Maltese (descendants of ancient Carthaginians and Phoenicians, with strong elements of Italian and other Mediterranean stock), Spanish, English, Arab. **Religion:** Roman Catholic 98%.
**Literacy rate:** 88% (1985)
**Economic summary: GDP/PPP** (2000 est.): $5.6 billion; per capita $14,300. **Real growth rate:** 3.4%.
**Inflation:** 2.5%. **Unemployment:** 4.5% (3rd quarter 2000). **Arable land:** 32%. **Agriculture:** potatoes, cauliflower, grapes, wheat, barley, tomatoes, citrus, cut flowers, green peppers; pork, milk, poultry, eggs.
**Labor force:** 145,901 (1999); industry 24%, services 71%, agriculture 5% (1999 est.). **Industries:** tourism; electronics, ship building and repair, construction; food and beverages, textiles, footwear, clothing, tobacco.
**Natural resources:** limestone, salt, arable land.
**Exports:** $2 billion (f.o.b., 1999): machinery and transport equipment, manufactures. **Imports:** $2.6 billion (f.o.b., 1999): machinery and transport equipment, manufactured and semi-manufactured goods; food, drink, and tobacco. **Major trading partners:** U.S., France, Germany, UK, Italy. **Member of Commonwealth of Nations**

**Geography**   The five Maltese islands—Malta, Gozo, Comino, Comminotto, and Filflawith—have a combined land area smaller than Philadelphia. Malta is located in the Mediterranean Sea, about 60 mi (97 km) south of the southeast tip of Sicily.

**Government**   Republic.

**History**   The strategic importance of Malta was recognized by the Phoenicians, who occupied it, as did, in turn, the Greeks, Carthaginians, and Romans. The apostle Paul was shipwrecked there in A.D. 60. With the division of the Roman Empire in A.D. 395, Malta was assigned to the eastern portion dominated by Constantinople. Between 870 and 1090, it came under Arab rule. In 1091, the Norman noble Roger I, then ruler of Sicily, came to Malta with a small retinue and defeated the Arabs. The Knights of St. John (Malta), who obtained the three habitable Maltese islands of Malta, Gozo, and Comino from Charles V in 1530, reached their highest fame when they withstood an attack by superior Turkish forces in 1565. Napoléon seized Malta in 1798, but the French forces were ousted by British troops the next year, and British rule was confirmed by the Treaty of Paris in 1814.

Malta was heavily attacked by German and Italian aircraft during World War II but was never invaded by the Axis powers. It became an independent nation on Sept. 21, 1964, and a republic on Dec. 13, 1974, but remained in the British Commonwealth. In 1979, when its alliance with Great Britain ended, Malta sought to guarantee its neutrality through agreements with other countries. Although Malta applied for membership in the European Union, when the Labour Party won the election in Oct. 1996, it froze Malta's EU application and withdrew from the NATO Partnership for Peace program in an effort to maintain its neutrality. When the Nationalist Party won the Sept. 1998 elections, however, it revived the EU accession bid. Malta plans to hold a referendum in 2003 to decide whether the country will accept EU membership if it is offered.

# Marshall Islands
### REPUBLIC OF THE MARSHALL ISLANDS
**President:** Kessai H. Note (2000)
**Total land area:** 70 sq mi (181 sq km), includes the atolls of Bikini, Eniwetok, and Kwajalein
**Population (2002 est.):** 73,630 (growth rate: 3.9%); birth rate 45.0/1000; infant mortality rate 38.7/1000; density per sq mi: 1,052
**Capital and largest city (1990 est.):** Majuro, 20,000.
**Languages:** Both Marshallese and English are official languages. Marshallese is a language in the Malayo-Polynesian family. **Ethnicity/race:** Micronesian. **Religions:** predominantly Christian, mostly Protestant. **Literacy rate:** 91% (1980)
**Economic summary: GDP/PPP** (1998 est.): $105 million, supplemented by approximately $65 million annual U.S. aid; per capita $1,670. **Real growth rate:** –5%. **Inflation:** 5% (1997). **Unemployment:** 16% (1991 est.). **Arable land:** 0%. **Agriculture:** coconuts, cacao, taro, breadfruit, fruits; pigs, chickens. **Labor force:** n.a. **Industries:** copra, fish, tourism, craft items from shell, wood, and pearls, offshore banking (financial services), tourism, household deposits, marine products, deep seabed minerals. **Exports:** $28 million (f.o.b., 1997 est.): fish, coconut oil, fish, trochus shells. **Imports:** $58 million (f.o.b., 1997 est.): foodstuffs, machinery and equipment, fuels, beverages, and tobacco. **Major trading partners:** U.S., Japan, Australia, New Zealand, Guam, Singapore.

**Geography** The Marshall Islands, east of the Carolines, are divided into two chains: the western, or Ralik, group, including the atolls Jaluit, Kwajalein, Wotho, Bikini, and Eniwetok; and the eastern, or Ratak, group, including the atolls Mili, Majuro, Maloelap, Wotje, and Likiep. The islands are of the coral-reef type and rise only a few feet above sea level. The Marshall Islands comprise an area slightly larger than Washington, D.C.

**Government** Constitutional government in free association with the U.S.

**History** Micronesian peoples were the first inhabitants of the archipelago. The islands were explored by the Spanish in the 16th century and were named for a British captain in 1788. Germany unsuccessfully attempted to colonize the islands in 1885. Japan claimed them in 1914, but after several battles during World War II, the U.S. seized them from the Japanese. In 1947, the UN made the island group, along with the Mariana and Caroline archipelagos, a U.S. trust territory.

U.S. nuclear testing took place between 1946 and 1958 on the islands of Bikini and Enewetak. The people of Bikini were removed to another island, and a total of 23 U.S. atomic and hydrogen bomb tests were conducted. Despite clean-up attempts, the islands remain uninhabited today because of nuclear contamination. The U.S. paid the islands $183.7 million in damages in 1983, and in 1999, the U.S. approved a one-time $3.8-million payment to the relocated people of Bikini atoll.

The United States and the Marshall Islands signed a Compact of Free Association in 1986, which meant the islands became self-governing but would receive U.S. military and economic aid, roughly $65 million a year. The Marshall Islands were admitted to the UN on Sept. 17, 1991.

Kwajalein atoll is the site of an American military base, and has been used for missile defense testing since the 1960s.

In 2000, Kessai Note became the first commoner to become president—his predecessors had been island chiefs. He ran on an anticorruption ticket and is attempting to make his small nation more self-sufficient. The U.S. and the Marshall Islands are currently negotiating an extension of the lease to use the Kwajalein military base.

# Mauritania
### ISLAMIC REPUBLIC OF MAURITANIA
**National name:** République Islamique de Mauritanie
**President:** Col. Maaouye Ould Sidi Ahmed Taya (1992)
**Prime Minister:** Cheikh El Afia Ould Mohamed Khouna (1998)
**Area:** 397,953 sq mi (1,030,700 sq km)
**Population (2002 est.):** 2,828,858 (growth rate: 2.9%); birth rate: 42.5/1000; infant mortality rate: 75.2/1000; density per sq mi: 7
**Capital and largest city (1992 est.):** Nouakchott, 480,000. **Monetary unit:** Ouguiya. **Languages:** Arabic (official) and French. **Ethnicity/race:** mixed Maur/black 40%, Maur 30%, black 30%. **Religion:** Islam. **Literacy rate:** 34% (1990)
**Economic summary: GDP/PPP** (2000 est.): $5.4 billion, per capita $2,000. **Real growth rate:** 5%. **Inflation:** 4.5%. **Unemployment:** 23% (1995 est.). **Arable land:** 0%. **Agriculture:** dates, millet, sorghum, rice, corn, dates; cattle, sheep. **Labor force:** 750,000 (1999); agriculture 47%, services 39%, industry 14%. **Industries:** fish processing, mining of iron ore and gypsum. **Natural resources:** iron ore, gypsum, fish, copper, phosphate, diamonds, gold. **Exports:** $333 million (f.o.b., 1999): iron ore, fish and fish products, gold. **Imports:** $305 million (f.o.b., 1999): machinery and equipment, petroleum products, capital goods, foodstuffs, consumer goods. **Major trading partners:** Japan, Italy, France, Spain, Benelux, Germany.

**Geography** Mauritania, three times the size of Arizona, is situated in northwest Africa with about 350 mi (592 km) of coastline on the Atlantic Ocean. It is bordered by Morocco on the north, Algeria and Mali on the east, and Senegal on the south. The country is mostly desert, with the exception of the fertile Senegal River valley in the south and grazing land in the north.

**Government** Republic under military government. The legal system is based on Islam.

**History** Mauritania was first inhabited by blacks and Berbers, and it became a center for the Berber Almoravid movement in the 11th century, which sought to spread Islam through western Africa. It was first explored by the Portuguese in the 15th century, but by the 19th century the French gained control. They organized the area into a territory in 1904, and in 1920 it became one of the colonies that comprised French West Africa. In 1946, it became a French Overseas territory.

Mauritania became an independent nation on Nov. 28, 1960, and was admitted to the United Nations in 1961 over the strenuous opposition of Morocco, which claimed the territory. In the late 1960s, the government sought to make Arab culture dominant. Racial and ethnic tensions between Moors, Arabs, Berbers, and blacks were frequent.

Mauritania and Morocco divided the territory of Spanish Sahara (later called Western Sahara) between them after the Spanish departed in 1975, with Mauritania controlling the southern third. The Polisario Front, indigenous Saharawi rebels, fought for the territory against both Mauritania and Morocco. Increased military spending and rising casualties in the region helped bring down the civilian government of Ould Daddah in 1978. A succession of military rulers followed. In 1979, Mauritania withdrew from Western Sahara.

In 1984, Col. Maaouye Ould Sidi Ahmed Taya took control of the government. He relaxed Islamic law, fought corruption, instituted economic reforms urged by the International Monetary Fund, and held the country's first multiparty parliamentary elections in 1986. Although the 1991 constitution set up a multiparty democracy, politics remains based on ethnic and racial lines. The primary conflict is between blacks that dominate southern regions, and the Moorish-Arabic north, which runs the country. Racial tensions reached a peak in 1989 when Mauritania went to war with Senegal in a dispute over the border. As each country repatriated citizens of the other, critics accused Mauritania of taking the opportunity to expel thousands of blacks.

Although Mauritania officially abolished slavery in 1980, the nation continues to tolerate the enslavement of blacks by North African Arabs. In 1993, the U.S. State Department estimated that there were more than 90,000 chattel slaves in the country.

In 1992, Taya won the nation's first multiparty presidential election, which opponents charged was rigged. Taya's attempts to restructure the economy provoke periodic protests, the most serious of which were the bread riots in Nouakchott in 1995.

In 2002, the government banned a political party, Action for Change (AC), which has campaigned for greater rights for blacks, calling it racist and violent. Two other opposition parties have been banned in the past few years. The IMF granted Mauritania debt relief in June 2002, wiping out $1.1 billion, half of Mauritania's overall debt.

# Mauritius

**President:** Karl Offman (2002)
**Prime Minister:** Sir Anerood Jugnauth (2000)
**Area:** 718 sq mi (1,860 sq km)
**Population (2002 est.):** 1,200,206 (growth rate: 1.0%); birth rate: 16.3/1000; infant mortality rate: 16.6/1000; density per sq mi: 1,671
**Capital and largest city (1993 est.):** Port Louis, 134,516. **Monetary unit:** Mauritian rupee.
  **Languages:** English (official), French, Creole, Hindi, Urdu, Hakka, Bojpoori. **Ethnicity/race:** Indo-Mauritian 68%, Creole 27%, Sino-Mauritian 3%, Franco-Mauritian 2%. **Religions:** Hindu 52%, Christian 28.3%, Islam 16.6%, other 3.1%. **Literacy rate:** 81% (1990)
**Economic summary: GDP/PPP** (2000 est.): $12.3 billion; per capita $10,400. **Real growth rate:** 7.5%. **Inflation:** 5.3%. **Unemployment:** 6.4% (1999 est.). **Arable land:** 49%. **Agriculture:** sugarcane, tea, corn, potatoes, bananas, pulses; cattle, goats; fish. **Labor force:** 514,000 (1995); construction and industry 36%, services 24%, agriculture and fishing 14%, trade, restaurants, hotels 16%, transportation and communication 7%, finance 3% (1995). **Industries:** food processing (largely sugar milling), textiles, clothing; chemicals, metal products, transport equipment, nonelectrical machinery; tourism. **Natural resources:** arable land, fish. **Exports:** $1.6 billion (f.o.b., 1999): clothing and textiles, sugar, cut flowers, molasses. **Imports:** $2.3 billion (f.o.b., 1999): manufactured goods, capital equipment, foodstuffs, petroleum products, chemicals (1996). **Major trading partners:** UK, France, U.S., Germany, Italy, South Africa, India. **Member of Commonwealth of Nations**

**Geography** Mauritius is a mountainous island in the Indian Ocean east of Madagascar.

**Government** Parliamentary democracy within the British Commonwealth.

**History** After a brief Dutch settlement, French immigrants who came in 1715 named the island Île de France and established the first road and harbor infrastructure, as well as the sugar industry, under the leadership of Gov. Mahe de Labourdonnais. Blacks from Africa and Madagascar came as slaves to work in the cane fields. In 1810, the British captured the island and in 1814, by the Treaty of Paris, it was ceded to Great Britain along with its dependencies.

Indian immigration, which followed the abolition of slavery in 1835, rapidly changed the fabric of Mauritian society, and the country flourished with the increased cultivation of sugarcane. The opening of the Suez Canal in 1869 heralded the decline of Mauritius as a port of call for ships rounding the southern tip of Africa, bound for South and East Asia. The economic instability of the price of sugar, the main crop, in the first half of the 20th century brought civil unrest, then economic, administrative, and political reforms. Mauritius became independent on March 12, 1968.

The effects of Cyclone Claudette in 1979, and of falling world sugar prices in the early 1980s, led the government to initiate a vigorous program of agricultural diversification and to develop the processing of imported goods for the export market. The country formally broke ties with the British Crown in March 1992, becoming a republic within the Commonwealth.

In addition to sugarcane, textile production and tourism are the leading industries. Primary education is free, and Mauritius boasts one of the highest literacy rates in sub-Saharan Africa.

With a complicated ethnic mix—about 30% of the population is of African descent, the remainder is of

Indian descent, both Hindu and Muslim—racial unrest continually gnaws at the country.

In Feb. 2002, Mauritius went through four successive presidents. Two resigned within days of each other, each after refusing to sign a controversial antiterrorism law that severely curtails the rights of suspects. The law, supported by the prime minister, was ultimately signed by a third, interim president. At the end of February, a fourth president, Karl Offman, was elected by Parliament.

# Mexico

### UNITED MEXICAN STATES

**Official name:** Estados Unidos Mexicanos
**President:** Vicente Fox Quesada (2000)
**Area:** 761,602 sq mi (1,972,550 sq km)
**Population (2002 est.):** 103,400,165 (growth rate: 1.7%); birth rate: 22.4/1000; infant mortality rate: 24.5/1000; density per sq mi: 136
**Capital and largest city (2000 est.):** Mexico City, 19,750,000 (metro. area). **Other large cities (1995):** Guadalajara, 2,178,000; Monterrey, 1,702,000; Ecatepec, 1,456,438 (part of Mexico City metro. area); Nezahualcóyotl, 1,259,543 (part of Mexico City metro. area); Puebla, 1,222,177. **Monetary unit:** Mexican peso. **Languages:** Spanish, Indian languages. **Ethnicity/race:** mestizo (Indian-Spanish) 60%, Amerindian or predominantly Amerindian 30%, Caucasian or predominantly Caucasian 9%, other 1%. **Religions:** nominally Roman Catholic 97%, Protestant 3%. **Literacy rate:** 87% (1990)
**Economic summary: GDP/PPP** (2000 est.): $915 billion; per capita $9,100. **Real growth rate:** 7.1%. **Inflation:** 9%. **Unemployment:** urban—2.2% (2000); plus considerable underemployment. **Arable land:** 12%. **Agriculture:** corn, wheat, soybeans, rice, beans, cotton, coffee, fruit, tomatoes; beef, poultry, dairy products; wood products. **Labor force:** 39.8 million (2000); agriculture 20%, industry 24%, services 56% (1998). **Industries:** food and beverages, tobacco, chemicals, iron and steel, petroleum, mining, textiles, clothing, motor vehicles, consumer durables, tourism. **Natural resources:** petroleum, silver, copper, gold, lead, zinc, natural gas, timber. **Exports:** $168 billion (f.o.b., 2000), includes in-bond industries (assembly plant operations): manufactured goods, oil and oil products, silver, fruits, vegetables, coffee, cotton. **Imports:** $176 billion (f.o.b., 2000), includes in-bond industries (assembly plant operations): metal-working machines, steel mill products, agricultural machinery, electrical equipment, car parts for assembly, repair parts for motor vehicles, aircraft, and aircraft parts. **Major trading partners:** U.S., Canada, Spain, Germany, Japan, UK, Netherlands Antilles, Switzerland, Venezuela, Chile, South Korea, China, Taiwan, Italy, Brazil.

**Geography** Mexico is bordered by the United States on the north, and by Belize and Guatemala to the southeast. Mexico is about one-fifth the size of the United States. Baja California in the west is an 800-mile (1,287-km) peninsula and forms the Gulf of California. In the east are the Gulf of Mexico and the Bay of Campeche, which is formed by Mexico's other peninsula, the Yucatán. The center of Mexico is a great, high plateau, open to the north, with mountain chains on the east and west and with ocean-front lowlands lying outside of them.

**Government** Federal republic.

**History** At least three great civilizations—the Mayas, the Olmecs, and later the Toltecs—preceded the wealthy Aztec empire, conquered in 1519–21 by the Spanish under Hernando Cortés. Spain ruled Mexico as part of the viceroyalty of New Spain for the next 300 years until Sept. 16, 1810, when the Mexicans first revolted. They won independence in 1821.

From 1821 to 1877, there were two emperors, several dictators, and enough presidents and provisional executives to make a new government on the average of every nine months. Mexico lost Texas (1836), and after defeat in the war with the U.S. (1846–48) it lost the area that is now California, Nevada, and Utah, most of Arizona and New Mexico, and parts of Wyoming and Colorado under the Treaty of Guadalupe Hidalgo. In 1855, the Indian patriot Benito Juárez began a series of reforms, including the disestablishment of the Catholic Church, which owned vast property. The subsequent civil war was interrupted by the French invasion of Mexico (1861) and the crowning of Maximilian of Austria as emperor (1864). He was overthrown and executed by forces under Juárez, who again became president in 1867.

The years after the fall of the dictator Porfirio Diaz (1877–80 and 1884–1911) were marked by bloody political-military strife and trouble with the U.S., culminating in the punitive U.S. expedition into northern Mexico (1916–17) in unsuccessful pursuit of the revolutionary Pancho Villa. Since a brief civil war in 1920, Mexico has enjoyed a period of gradual agricultural, political, and social reforms. The Partido Nacional Revolucionario (PNR; National Revolutionary Party), dominated by revolutionary and reformist politicians from northern Mexico, was established in 1929; it continued to control Mexico throughout the 20th century and was renamed the Partido Revolucionario Institucional (PRI; Institutional Revolutionary Party) in 1946. Relations with the U.S. were disturbed in 1938 when all foreign oil wells were expropriated, but a compensation agreement was reached in 1941.

Following World War II, the government emphasized economic growth. During the mid-1970s, under the leadership of President José López Portillo, Mexico became a major petroleum-producer. By the end of Portillo's term, however, Mexico had accumulated a huge external debt because of the government's unrestrained borrowing on the strength of its petroleum revenues. The collapse of oil prices in 1986 cut Mexico's export earnings. In Jan. 1994, Mexico joined Canada and the United States in the North American Free Trade Agreement (NAFTA), which will phase out all tariffs over a 15-year period, and in Jan. 1996, it became a founding member of the World Trade Organization (WTO).

In 1995, the U.S. agreed to prevent the collapse of Mexico's private banks. In return, the U.S. won virtual veto power over much of Mexico's economic policy. In 1997, in what observers called the freest elections in Mexico's history, the PRI lost control of the lower legislative house and the mayoralty of Mexico City in a stunning upset. To increase democracy, President Ernesto Zedillo said in 1999 that he would break precedent and not personally choose the next PRI presidential nominee. Several months later, Mexico held its first presidential primary, which was won by former interior secretary Francisco Labastida, Zedillo's closest ally among the candidates.

In elections held July 2, 2000, the PRI lost the presidency, ending 71 years of one-party rule. Vicente Fox Quesada, of the center-right National Action Party (PAN), took 43% of the vote to Labastida's 36%. Fox vowed tax reform, an overhaul of the legal system, and a reduction in power of the central government. By 2002, however, Fox had made little headway on his ambitious reform agenda. Congress, dominated by PRI, has blocked most of the legislation he has supported.

# Micronesia

**FEDERATED STATES OF MICRONESIA**

**President:** Leo A. Falcam (1999)
**Total area:** 271 sq mi (702 sq km). Land area, same (includes islands of Pohnpei, Yap, Chuuk, and Kosrae)
**Population (2002 est.):** 135,869 (growth rate: n.a.); birth rate: n.a./1000; infant mortality rate: n.a./1000; density per sq mi: 501
**Capital:** Palikir. **Languages:** English is the official and common language; major indigenous languages are Chukese, Pohnpeian, Yapase, and Kosrean.
**Ethnicity/race:** nine ethnic Micronesian and Polynesian groups. **Literacy rate:** 85% (1980)
**Economic summary: GDP/PPP** (1999 est.): $263 million; note: GDP is supplemented by grant aid, averaging perhaps $100 million annually; per capita $2,000. **Real growth rate:** 0.3%. **Inflation:** 2.6% (FY98/99). **Unemployment:** 16% (1999 est.). **Arable land:** n.a. **Agriculture:** black pepper, tropical fruits and vegetables, coconuts, cassava (tapioca), sweet potatoes; pigs, chickens. **Labor force:** n.a.; two-thirds are government employees. **Industries:** tourism, construction, fish processing, craft items from shell, wood, and pearls. **Natural resources:** forests, marine products, deep-seabed minerals. **Exports:** $73 million (f.o.b., 1996 est.): fish, garments, bananas, black pepper. **Imports:** $168 million (c.i.f., 1996 est.): food, manufactured goods, machinery and equipment, beverages. **Major trading partners:** Japan, U.S., Guam, Australia.

**Geography**  The Federated States of Micronesia is composed of the island states of Yap, Chuuk (Truk), Pohnpei (Ponape), and Kosrae, all in the Caroline Islands. The islands vary geologically from high mountainous islands to low coral atolls, with volcanic outcroppings on Pohnpei, Kosrae, and Chuuk. They are located 3,200 mi (5,150 km) west-southwest of Hawaii, in the north Pacific Ocean.

**Government**  Constitutional government in free association with the United States since Nov. 1986.

**History**  The islands, inhabited by Micronesian and Polynesian peoples, were colonized by Spain in the 17th century. Germany purchased them from Spain in 1898. They were occupied by the Japanese in 1914, but American forces seized them from the Japanese during World War II. On April 2, 1947, the United Nations Security Council created the Trust Territory of the Pacific Islands. The trust placed the Northern Mariana, Caroline, and Marshall Islands under the administration of the United States.

The Micronesian Federation (FMA) became self-governing in 1979. In 1983, the FMA. voted to accept a Compact of Free Association with the U.S., and in Nov. 1986, the U.S. government declared the Trust Territory agreements no longer in effect—thereby granting the Federated States of Micronesia full independence.

The FMA was admitted to the United Nations on Sept. 17, 1991. In July 1993, the country became a member of the International Monetary Fund. Micronesia, as well as many other South Pacific countries, is alarmed by the effect continued global warming will have on their islands—the consequent rise in the level of the oceans threatens low-lying islands with flooding and, eventually, with submergence.

# Moldova

**REPUBLIC OF MOLDOVA**

**President:** Vladimir Voronin (2001)
**Prime Minister:** Vasile Tarlev (2001)
**Area:** 13,067 sq mi (33,843 sq km)
**Population (2002 est.):** 4,434,547 (growth rate: 0.1%); birth rate: 13.8/1000; infant mortality rate: 42.2/1000, density per sq mi: 339
**Capital and largest city (1991):** Chisinau, 676,700.
**Other large cities (1991 est.):** Tiraspol, 186,000; Beltsy, 165,000; Bendery (Tighina), 141,500.
**Monetary unit:** Leu. **Languages:** Moldovan (official; virtually the same as Romanian), Russian, Gagauz (a Turkish dialect). **Ethnicity/race:** Moldavian/Romanian 64.5%, Ukrainian 13.8%, Russian 13%, Gagauz 3.5%, Jewish 1.5%, Bulgarian 2%, other 1.7% (1989 figures). **Religions (1991):** Eastern Orthodox 98.5%, Jewish 1.5%, Baptist (only about 1,000 members). **Literacy rate:** 97% (1989)
**Economic summary: GDP/PPP** (2000 est.): $11.3 billion; per capita $2,500. **Real growth rate:** –1.5%. **Inflation:** 32%. **Unemployment:** 1.9% (includes only officially registered unemployed; large numbers of underemployed workers) (Nov. 2000). **Arable land:** 53%. **Agriculture:** vegetables, fruits, wine, grain, sugar beets, sunflower seed, tobacco; beef, milk. **Labor force:** 1.7 million (1998); agriculture 40%, industry 14%, other 46% (1998). **Industries:** food processing, agricultural machinery, foundry equipment, refrigerators and freezers, washing machines, hosiery, sugar, vegetable oil, shoes, textiles. **Natural resources:** lignite, phosphorites, gypsum, arable land. **Exports:** $500 million (f.o.b., 2000): foodstuffs 57%, wine, tobacco; textiles and footwear, machinery (1999). **Imports:** $761 million (f.o.b., 2000): mineral products and fuel 38%, machinery and equipment, chemicals, textiles (1999). **Major trading partners:** Russia, Romania, Germany, Ukraine, Italy, Belarus.

**Geography**  Moldova (formerly Moldavia) is a landlocked republic of hilly plains lying west of the Carpathian Mountains between the Prut and Dneister (Dnestr) Rivers. The country is sandwiched between Romania and Ukraine. The area is a very fertile region with rich black soil (chernozem) covering three-quarters of the territory.

**Government**  Democratic republic.

**History**  Most of what is now Moldova was the independent principality of Moldavia in the 14th century. In the 16th century it came under Ottoman Turkish rule. Russia acquired Moldavian territory in 1791, and again in 1812 (the Treaty of Bucharest) when Turkey gave up the province of Bessarabia[1] to Russia. Turkey held the rest of Moldavia but it was passed to Romania in 1918. Russia did not recognize the cession of this territory.

In 1924, the USSR established Moldavia as an Autonomous Soviet Socialist Republic. As a result of the Nazi-Soviet Nonaggression Pact of 1939, Romania was forced to cede all of Bessarabia to the Soviet Union in 1940. The Soviets merged the Moldavia ASSR with the Romanian-speaking districts of Bessarabia to form the Moldavian Soviet Socialist Republic. During World War II, Romania joined Germany in the attack on the Soviet Union and reconquered Bessarabia. But Soviet troops retook the territory in 1944 and reestablished the Moldavian SSR.

For many years, Romania and the USSR disputed each other's territorial claims over Bessarabia. Following the aborted coup against Soviet president

Mikhail Gorbachev, Moldavia proclaimed its independence in Sept. 1991, and changed its name to the Romanian spelling, Moldova.

Conflict between ethnic Romanians and the Russian Ukrainian majority in Trans-Dniester erupted upon independence. Trans-Dniester separatists (primarily ethnic Russians and Ukrainians) fought for independence from Moldova in 1992; progress on resolving the conflict has been slow. In the south, Gagauz, which is composed mostly of Turkic Christians, has also attempted secession.

The Russian financial crisis in fall 1998 severely affected Moldova, which relies on Russia for 60% of its foreign trade. Economic disaster caused an exodus of an estimated 600,000 Moldovans since then—Moldova is considered the poorest country in Europe. In Feb. 2001, the Communist Party won an overwhelming victory in parliamentary elections, and their leader, Vladimir Voronin, became prime minister. Voronin has attempted to forge closer relations with Moscow, which has sparked protests among those who advocate for closer cultural and ethnic ties to Romania.

1. The area between the Prut and Dniester Rivers.

# Monaco

PRINCIPALITY OF MONACO
**National name:** Principauté de Monaco
**Ruler:** Prince Rainier III (1949)
**Minister of State:** Patrick Leclercq (2000)
**Area:** 0.75 sq mi (465 acres) (1.95 sq km)
**Population (2002 est.):** 31,987 (growth rate: –0.3%); birth rate 9.6/1000; infant mortality rate: 5.7/1000; density per sq mi: 42,485
**Capital and largest city (1995 est.):** Monaco, 30,400.
　**Monetary unit:** Euro. **Languages:** French (official), English, Italian, Monégasque. **Ethnicity/race:** French 47%, Monegasque 16%, Italian 16%, other 21%.
　**Religion:** Roman Catholic 95%. **Literacy rate:** 99%
**Economic summary: GDP/PPP** (1999 est.): $870 million; $27,000 per capita. **Real growth rate:** n.a. **Inflation:** n.a. **Unemployment:** 3.1% (1998). **Arable land:** 0%. **Agriculture:** none. **Labor force:** 30,540 (Jan. 1994). **Natural resources:** none. **Exports:** n.a. **Imports:** n.a. Full customs integration with France, which collects and rebates Monegasque trade duties; also participates in EU.

**Geography** Monaco is a tiny, hilly wedge driven into the French Mediterranean coast; it is 9 mi east of Nice, France.

**Government** Constitutional monarchy.

**History** The Phoenicians, and after them the Greeks, had a temple on the Monaco headland. Their ruler. From Monoikos, the Greek surname for this mythological strong man, the principality took its name. After being independent for 800 years, Monaco was annexed to France in 1793 and was placed under Sardinia's protection in 1815. By the Franco-Monegasque treaty of 1861, Monaco went under French guardianship but continued to be independent. A treaty made with France in 1918 contained a clause providing that, in the event that the male Grimaldi dynasty should die out, Monaco would become an autonomous state under French protection.

Monaco has a tourist business that runs as high as 1.5 million visitors a year and is famous for its beaches and casinos. It had gaming tables as early as 1856. Five years later, a 50-year concession to operate the games was granted to François Blanc, of Bad Homburg. This concession passed into the hands of a private company in 1898.

Prince Rainier III, born on May 31, 1923, succeeded his grandfather, Louis II, on the latter's death, May 9, 1949. Rainier was married, in 1956, to U.S. actress Grace Kelly and they subsequently had three children. Their son, Prince Albert Louis Pierre (b. 1958) is heir to the throne. Immensely popular, Princess Grace died on Sept. 14, 1982, of injuries received in a car accident near Monte Carlo. She was 52.

Monaco's practice of providing a tax shelter for French businessmen resulted in a 1962 dispute between the countries. A compromise was reached by which French citizens with less than five years' residence in Monaco were taxed at French rates, and taxes were imposed on Monegasque companies doing more than 25% of their business outside the principality. In 1967, Rainier took control of the Société des Bains de Mer, operator of the famous Monte Carlo gambling casino, in a program to increase hotel and convention space. The country was admitted to the UN in May 1993, making it the smallest country represented there. The country celebrated the 700th anniversary of the Grimaldi reign during 1997.

# Mongolia

MONGOLIA
**President:** Natsagiyn Bagabandi (1997)
**Prime Minister:** Nambaryn Enkhbayar (2000)
**Area:** 604,247 sq mi (1,565,000 sq km)
**Population (2002 est.):** 2,694,432 (growth rate: 1.5%); birth rate: 21.8/1000; infant mortality rate: 52.0/1000; density per sq mi: 4
**Capital and largest city (1993 est.):** Ulaan Baatar, 619,000. **Monetary unit:** Tugrik. **Languages:** Mongolian, 90%; also Turkic, Russian, and Chinese. **Ethnicity/race:** Mongol 90%, Kazak 4%, Chinese 2%, Russian 2%, other 2%. **Religions:** predominantly Tibetan Buddhist; Islam about 4%. **Literacy rate:** 97% (1989)
**Economic summary: GDP/PPP** (2000 est.): $4.7 billion; per capita $1,780. **Real growth rate:** –1%. **Inflation:** 7.6% (1999). **Unemployment:** n.a. **Arable land:** 5.7%. **Agriculture:** wheat, barley, potatoes, forage crops; sheep, goats, cattle, camels, horses. **Labor force:** 1.3 million (1999); primarily herding/agricultural. **Industries:** construction materials, mining (particularly coal and copper); food and beverages, processing of animal products. **Natural resources:** oil, coal, copper, molybdenum, tungsten, phosphates, tin, nickel, zinc, wolfram, fluorspar, gold, silver, iron, phosphate. **Exports:** $454.3 million (f.o.b., 1999): copper, livestock, animal products, wool, hides, fluorspar, other nonferrous metals. **Imports:** $510.7 million (c.i.f., 1999): machinery and equipment, fuels, food products, industrial consumer goods, chemicals, building materials, sugar, tea. **Major trading partners:** China, U.S., Russia, Japan, South Korea.

**Geography** Mongolia lies in central Asia between Siberia on the north and China on the south. It is slightly larger than Alaska.

The productive regions of Mongolia—a tableland ranging from 3,000 to 5,000 ft (914 to 1,524 m) in elevation—are in the north, which is well drained by numerous rivers, including the Hovd, Onon, Selenga, and Tula. Much of the Gobi Desert falls within Mongolia.

**Government** Parliamentary republic now in transition from Communism.

**History** Nomadic tribes that periodically plundered agriculturally based China from the west are recorded in Chinese history dating back more than 2,000 years. It was to protect China from these marauding peoples that the Great Wall was constructed around 200 B.C. The name *Mongol* comes from a small tribe whose leader, Ghengis Khan, began a conquest that would eventually encompass an enormous empire stretching from Asia to Europe, as far west as the Black Sea and as far south as India and the Himalayas. However, by the 14th century, the kingdom was in serious decline, with invasions from a resurgent China and internecine warfare.

The State of Mongolia was formerly known as Outer Mongolia. It contains the original homeland of the historic Mongols, whose power reached its zenith during the 13th century under Kublai Khan. The area accepted Manchu rule in 1689, but after the Chinese Revolution of 1911 and the fall of the Manchus in 1912, the northern Mongol princes expelled the Chinese officials and declared independence under the Khutukhtu, or "Living Buddha."

In 1921, Soviet troops entered the country, and facilitated the establishment of a republic by Mongolian revolutionaries in 1924. China also made a claim to the region, but was too weak to assert it. Under the 1945 Chinese-Russian Treaty, China agreed to give up Outer Mongolia, which, after a plebiscite, became a nominally independent country.

Allied with the USSR in its dispute with China, Mongolia began mobilizing troops along its borders in 1968 when the two powers became involved in border clashes on the Kazakh-Sinkiang frontier to the west and at the Amur and Ussuri Rivers. A 20-year treaty of friendship and cooperation, signed in 1966, entitled Mongolia to call upon the USSR for military aid in the event of invasion.

In 1989, the Mongolian democratic revolution began, led by Sanjaasurengiyn Zorig. Free elections held in Aug. 1990 produced a multiparty government, though it was still largely Communist. As a result, Mongolia has moved only gradually toward a market economy. With the collapse of the USSR, however, Mongolia was deprived of Soviet aid. Many of the country's factories were forced to shut down, and unemployment rose to 30%. Primarily in reaction to the economic turmoil, the Communist Mongolian People's Revolutionary Party (MPRP) won a significant majority in parliamentary elections in 1992. In 1996, however, the Democratic Alliance, an electoral coalition, defeated the MPRP, breaking with Communist rule for the first time since 1921. But in 1997, a former Communist and chairman of the People's Revolutionary Party, Natsagiyn Bagabandi, was elected president, further strengthening the hand of the antireformers.

Disagreement within Mongolia's ruling coalition over the pace and direction of market reforms in April 1998 caused a shakeup that thrust Tsakhiagiyn Elbegdorj, a proreform politician, into the prime minister's position. But parliamentary cross-purposes led to his resignation, and a succession of prime ministers followed.

In July 2000, and again in May 2001, the Mongolian People's Revolutionary Party (formerly the Communist Party) nearly swept parliamentary elections, winning 72 out of 76 seats. Natsagiyn Bagabandi was reelected in the 2001 elections, giving the MPRP control of both the presidency and Parliament, as well as a mandate to bolster the sluggish economy and dismal living standards. Former Communists, Bagabandi and the MPRP now support radical reform.

# Morocco

### KINGDOM OF MOROCCO

**National name:** al-Mamlaka al-Maghrebia
**Ruler:** King Muhammad VI (1999)
**Prime Minister:** Driss Jettou (2002)
**Area:** 172,413 sq mi (446,550 sq km)
**Population (2002 est.):** 31,167,783 (growth rate: 1.8%); birth rate: 23.7/1000; infant mortality rate: 46.5/1000; density per sq mi: 181
**Capital (1993 est.):** Rabat, 1,220,000. **Largest cities:** Casablanca, 2,943,000; Marrakech, 602,000; Fez, 564,000; Salé, 521,000. **Monetary unit:** Dirham.
**Languages:** Arabic (official), French, Berber dialects, Spanish. **Ethnicity/race:** Arab-Berber 99.1%, other 0.7%, Jewish 0.2%. **Religions:** Islam 98.7%, Christian 1.1%, Jewish 0.2%. **Literacy rate:** 50% (1990)
**Economic summary:** GDP/PPP (2000 est.): $105 billion; per capita $3,500. **Real growth rate:** 0.8%. **Inflation:** 2%. **Unemployment:** 23% (1999 est.). **Arable land:** 21%. **Agriculture:** barley, wheat, citrus, wine, vegetables, olives; livestock. **Labor force:** 11 million (1997 est.); agriculture 50%, services 35%, industry 15% (1999 est.). **Industries:** phosphate rock mining and processing, food processing, leather goods, textiles, construction, tourism. **Natural resources:** phosphates, iron ore, manganese, lead, zinc, fish, salt. **Exports:** $7.6 billion (f.o.b., 2000 est.): phosphates and fertilizers, food and beverages, minerals. **Imports:** $12.2 billion (f.o.b., 1999 est.): semiprocessed goods, machinery and equipment, food and beverages, consumer goods, fuel. **Major trading partners:** France, Spain, UK, Germany, U.S., Italy.

**Geography** Morocco, about one-tenth larger than California, lies across the Strait of Gibraltar on the Mediterranean and looks out on the Atlantic from the northwest shoulder of Africa. Algeria is to the east and Mauritania to the south. On the Atlantic coast there is a fertile plain. The Mediterranean coast is mountainous. The Atlas Mountains, running northeastward from the south to the Algerian frontier, average 11,000 ft (3,353 m) in elevation.

**Government** Constitutional monarchy.

**History** Morocco has been the home of the Berbers since the second millennium B.C. In A.D. 46, Morocco was annexed by Rome as part of the province of Mauritania until the Vandals overran this portion of the declining empire in the 5th century. The Arabs invaded circa 685, bringing Islam. The Berbers joined them in invading Spain in 711, but then revolted against the Arabs, resenting their secondary status. In 1086, Berbers took control of large areas of Moorish Spain until they were expelled in the 13th century.

The land was rarely unified and was usually ruled by small tribal states. Conflicts between Berbers and Arabs were chronic. Portugal and Spain began invading Morocco, which helped to unify the land in defense. In 1660, Morocco came under the control of the Alawite dynasty. It is a sherif dynasty—descended from the prophet Muhammad—and rules Morocco to this day.

During the 17th and 18th centuries Morocco was one of the Barbary states, the headquarters of pirates who pillaged Mediterranean traders. European powers became interested in colonizing the country beginning in 1840, and there were frequent clashes with the French and Spanish. Finally, in 1904, France and Spain concluded a secret agreement that divided Morocco into zones of French and Spanish influence, with France controlling almost all of Morocco and Spain controlling the small southwest portion, which became known as Spanish Sahara. Morocco became an even greater object of European rivalry by the turn of the century, leading almost to a European war in 1905 when Germany attempted to gain a foothold in the mineral-rich country. By the terms of the Algeciras Conference (1906), the sultan of Morocco maintained control of his lands and France's privileges were curtailed. The conference was a telling indication of what was to come in World War I, with Germany and Austria-Hungary lining up on one side of the territorial dispute, and France, Britain, and the United States on the other.

In 1912, the sultan of Morocco, Moulay Abd al-Hafid, permitted the French protectorate status. Nationalism began to grow during World War II. Sultan Mohammed V was deposed by the French in 1953 and replaced by his uncle, but nationalist agitation forced his return in 1955. On his death on Feb. 26, 1961, his son, Hassan, became king. France and Spain recognized the independence and sovereignty of Morocco in 1956. Sultan Sidi Muhammad formed a constitutional government, and in 1961 Moulay Hassan succeeded his father as Hassan II.

Maintaining excellent relations with the West, King Hassan became the second Arab leader to meet with an Israeli leader when, on July 21, 1986, Prime Minister Shimon Peres came to Morocco. Morocco was also the first Arab state to condemn the 1990 Iraqi invasion of Kuwait. In the 1990s, King Hassan promulgated "Hassanian democracy," which allowed for significant political freedom while at the same time retaining ultimate power for the monarch. In Aug. 1999, King Hassan II died after 38 years on the throne and his son, Prince Sidi Muhammad, was crowned King Muhammad VI. Since then Muhammad VI has pledged to make the political system more open, to allow freedom of expression, and to support economic reform. He has also advocated giving more rights to women, which has been opposed by Islamic fundamentalists. The entrenched political elite and the military have also been leery of some reform proposals. With about 20% of the population living in dire poverty, economic expansion is a prime goal.

Morocco's occupation of Western Sahara (formerly Spanish Sahara) has been repeatedly criticized by the international community. In the 1970s, tens of thousands of Moroccans crossed the border into Spanish Sahara to back their government's contention that the northern part of the territory was historically part of Morocco. Spain, which had controlled the territory since 1912, withdrew in 1976, creating a power vacuum that was filled by Morocco in the north and Mauritania in the south. When Mauritania withdrew in Aug. 1979 Morocco ~~~~~~~~ the remainder of the territory. A rebel group, the Polisario Front, has fought against Morocco since 1976 for the independence of Western Sahara on behalf of the indigenous Saharawis. The Polisario and Morocco agreed in Sept. 1991 to a UN-negotiated cease-fire, which was contingent on a referendum regarding independence. For the past decade, however, the UN has failed to hold the referendum; disputes over voter eligibility have been the major stumbling block, as well as Morocco's opposition to the referendum. In 2002, King Mohammed VI reasserted that he "will not renounce an inch of" Western Sahara.

In July 2002, Morocco invaded a tiny, uninhabited island claimed by Spain off its Mediterranean coast. Spain promptly seized back the island.

# Mozambique

### REPUBLIC OF MOZAMBIQUE

**National name:** República de Moçambique
**President:** Joaquim Chissanó (1986)
**Prime Minister:** Pascoal Mocumbi (1994)
**Area:** 309,494 sq mi (801,590 sq km)
**Population (2002 est.):** 19,607,519 (growth rate: 1.1%); birth rate: 36.4/1000; infant mortality rate: 138.6/1000; density per sq mi: 63
**Capital and largest city (1996 est.):** Maputo, 1,095,300. **Monetary unit:** Metical. **Languages:** Portuguese (official), Bantu languages. **Ethnicity/race:** indigenous tribal groups 99.6% (Shangaan, Chokwe, Manyika, Sena, Makua, and others), Europeans 0.06%, Euro-Africans 0.2%, Indians 0.08%. **Religions:** traditional 60%, Christian 30%, Islam 10%. **Literacy rate:** 33% (1990)
**Economic summary: GDP/PPP** (2000 est.): $$19.1 billion; per capita $1,000. **Real growth rate:** 3.8%. **Inflation:** 11.4%. **Unemployment:** 21% (1997 est.). **Arable land:** 4%. **Agriculture:** cotton, cashew nuts, sugarcane, tea, cassava (tapioca), corn, rice, coconuts, sisal, tropical fruits; beef, poultry. **Labor force:** 7.4 million (1997 est.); agriculture 81%, industry 6%, services 13% (1997 est.). **Industries:** food, beverages, chemicals (fertilizer, soap, paints), petroleum products, textiles, cement, glass, asbestos, tobacco. **Natural resources:** coal, titanium, natural gas, hydropower, tantalum, graphite. **Exports:** $390 million (f.o.b., 2000 est.): prawns 40%, cashews, cotton, sugar, citrus, timber; bulk electricity (2000). **Imports:** $1.4 billion (c.i.f., 2000 est.): machinery and equipment, mineral products, chemicals, metals, foodstuffs, textiles (2000). **Major trading partners:** EU, South Africa, Zimbabwe, India, U.S., Japan, Pakistan.

**Geography** Mozambique stretches for 1,535 mi (2,470 km) along Africa's southeast coast. It is nearly twice the size of California. Tanzania is to the north; Malawi, Zambia, and Zimbabwe to the west; and South Africa and Swaziland to the south.

The country is generally a low-lying plateau broken up by 25 sizable rivers that flow into the Indian Ocean. The largest is the Zambezi, which provides access to central Africa. The principal ports are Maputo, Beira, and Nacala.

**Government** Multiparty republic.

**History** Bantu-speakers migrated to Mozambique in the first millennium, and Arab and Swahili traders settled the region thereafter. It was explored by Vasco da Gama in 1498, and first colonized by Portugal in 1505. By 1510, the Portuguese had ~~~~~~ ~~ ~~~~ ~~~ ~~ ~~~ former Arab sultanates on the east African coast. Mozambique was administered as part of Goa, in India, until 1752, when it received its own captain-general. Portuguese colonial rule was repressive.

Guerrilla activity began in 1963 and became so effective by 1973 that Portugal was forced to dispatch 40,000 troops to fight the rebels. A cease-fire was signed in Sept. 1974, and after having been under Portuguese colonial rule for 470 years, Mozambique became independent on June 25, 1975. The first president, Samora Moises Machel, had been the head of the National Front for the Liberation of Mozambique (FRELIMO) in its 10-year guerrilla war for independence. He died in a plane crash on Oct. 19, 1986, and was succeeded by his foreign minister, Joaquim Chissanó.

On Jan. 25, 1985, after a decade of independence, the government was locked in a paralyzing war with antigovernment guerrillas, the Mozambique National Resistance (MNR or Renamo), who were backed by the white minority government in South Africa. The guerrilla movement weakened President Chissanó's attempts to institute socialism, which he then decided to abandon in 1989. A new constitution was drafted calling for three branches of government and granting civil liberties. A cease-fire agreement was signed in Oct. 1992 between the government and the MNR, ending 16 years of civil war.

In multiparty elections in 1994 President Chissanó won. In Nov. 1995 the country was the first non-former British colony to become a member of the British Commonwealth. The president's disciplined economic plan has been extremely successful, winning the country foreign confidence and aid. While Mozambique posted some of the world's largest economic growth rates in the late 1990s, it has suffered enormous setbacks because of natural disaster—the enormous damage caused by severe flooding in the winters of 2000 and 2001. Hundreds have died and thousands were displaced by the flooding.

In 2002 Chissanó announced he would not seek a third term in the 2004 presidential elections. FRELIMO selected independence hero Armando Guebuza as their new candidate.

# Myanmar

### UNION OF MYANMAR

**National name:** Pyidaungsu Myanmar Naingngandau
**Prime Minister:** Senior Gen. Than Shwe (1992)
**Area:** 261,969 sq mi (678,500 sq km)
**Population (2002 est.):** 42,238,224 (growth rate: 0.7%); birth rate: 19.6/1000; infant mortality rate:73.7/1000; density per sq mi: 161
**Capital:** Rangoon (Yangon). **Largest cities (est. 1983):** Rangoon (Yangon), 2,458,712; Mandalay, 532,895.
**Monetary unit:** Kyat. **Languages:** Burmese, minority languages. **Ethnicity/race:** Burman 68%, Shan 9%, Karen 7%, Rakhine 4%, Chinese 3%, Mon 2%, Indian 2%, other 5%. **Religions:** Buddhist 89.5%, Christian 4.9%, Muslim 3.8%, Hindu 0.05%, Animist 1.3%.
**Literacy rate:** 81% (1990)
**Economic summary: GDP/PPP** (2000 est.): $63.7 billion; per capita $1,500. **Real growth rate:** 4.9%. **Inflation:** 18% (1999). **Unemployment:** 7.1% (official FY97/98 est.). **Arable land:** 15%. **Agriculture:** paddy rice, corn, oilseed, sugarcane, pulses; hardwood. **Labor force:** 19.7 million (FY98/99 est.); agriculture 65%, industry 10%, services 25% (1999 est.). **Industries:** agricultural processing; textiles and footwear; wood and wood products; copper, tin, tungsten, iron; construction materials; pharmaceuticals; fertilizer. **Natural resources:** petroleum, timber, tin, antimony, zinc, copper, tungsten, lead, coal, some marble, limestone, precious stones, natural gas, hydropower. **Exports:** $1.3 billion (f.o.b., 1999): apparel 36%, foodstuffs 22%, wood products 21%, precious stones 5% (1999). **Imports:** $2.5 billion (f.o.b., 1999): machinery, transport equipment, construction materials, food products. **Major trading partners:** India, Singapore, China, U.S., Thailand, Japan, South Korea.

**Geography** Slightly smaller than Texas, Myanmar occupies the northwest portion of the Indochinese peninsula. India lies to the northwest and China to the northeast. Bangladesh, Laos, and Thailand are also neighbors. The Bay of Bengal touches the southwest coast. The fertile delta of the Irrawaddy River in the south contains a network of intercommunicating canals and nine principal river mouths.

**Government** Military regime. In 1989, the military government changed the name of Burma to Myanmar. The U.S. State Department does not recognize the name Myanmar or the military regime that represents it.

**History** The ethnic origins of modern Myanmar (known historically as Burma) are a mixture of Indo-Aryans, who began pushing into the area around 700 B.C., and the Mongolian invaders under Kublai Khan who penetrated the region in the 13th century. Anawrahta (1044–77) was the first great unifier of Myanmar.

In 1612, the British East India Company sent agents to Burma, but the Burmese doggedly resisted efforts of British, Dutch, and Portuguese traders to establish posts along the Bay of Bengal. Through the Anglo-Burmese War in 1824–26 and two subsequent wars, the British East India Company expanded to the whole of Burma. By 1886, Myanmar was annexed to India, then became a separate colony in 1937.

During World War II, Burma was a key battleground; the 800-mile Burma Road was the Allies' vital supply line to China. The Japanese invaded the country in Dec. 1941, and by May 1942 had occupied most of it, cutting off the Burma Road. After one of the most difficult campaigns of the war, Allied forces liberated most of Burma prior to the Japanese surrender in Aug. 1945.

Burma became independent on Jan. 4, 1948. In 1962, left-wing general Ne Win staged a coup, banned political opposition, suspended the constitution, and introduced the "Burmese way of socialism." After 25 years of economic hardship and repression, the Burmese people held massive demonstrations in 1987 and 1988. These were brutally quashed by the State Law and Order Council (SLORC). In 1989, the military government officially changed the name of the country to Myanmar.

In May 1990 elections, the opposition National League for Democracy (NLD) won in a landslide. But the military, or SLORC, refused to recognize the election results. The leader of the opposition, Aung San Suu Kyi, was awarded the Nobel Peace Prize in 1991, which focused world attention on SLORC's repressive policies. Daughter of the assassinated general Aung San, who was revered as the father of Burmese independence, Suu Kyi remained under house arrest from 1989 until 1995. A new constitution was drafted in 1994 that called for an elected executive branch but appeared designed specifically to forbid Suu Kyi from becoming president. Suu Kyi continued to protest against the government, but almost every move she made was answered with a counterblow from SLORC.

Although the ruling junta has maintained a tight grip on Myanmar since 1988, it has not been able to subdue an insurgency in the country's south that has gone on for decades. The ethnic Karen movement has sought an independent homeland along Myanmar's southern border with Thailand. The economy has been in a state of collapse except for the junta-controlled heroin trade, the universities have remained closed, and the AIDS epidemic, unrecognized by the junta, has gripped the country.

From 2000 to 2002, Suu Kyi was again placed under house arrest. But during this time the military regime and Suu Kyi began unprecedented talks, though signs of democratic reforms remain elusive.

# Namibia

**REPUBLIC OF NAMIBIA**

**President:** Sam Nujoma (1990)
**Prime Minister:** Theo-Ben Gurirab (2002)
**Status:** Independent Country
**Area:** 318,694 sq mi (825,418 sq km)
**Population (2002 est.):** 1,820,916 (growth rate: 1.2%); birth rate: 34.2/1000; infant mortality rate: 72.4/1000; density per sq mi: 6
**Capital and largest city (1992 est.):** Windhoek, 161,000
**Summer capital (est. 1980):** Swakopmund, 17,500.
**Monetary unit:** Namibian dollar. **Languages:** Afrikaans, German, English (official), several indigenous. **Ethnicity/race:** black 86%, white 6.6%, mixed 7.4%. Note: about 50% of the population belong to the Ovambo tribe and 9% to the Kavangos tribe; other ethnic groups are: Herero 7%, Damara 7%, Nama 5%, Caprivian 4%, Bushmen 3%, Baster 2%, Tswana 0.5%. **Religion:** Predominantly Christian. **Literacy rate:** 38% (1960)
**Economic summary: GDP/PPP** (2000 est.): $7.6 billion; per capita $4,300. **Real growth rate:** 4%. **Inflation:** 9.1%. **Unemployment:** 30% to 40%, including underemployment (1997 est.). **Arable land:** 1%. **Agriculture:** millet, sorghum, peanuts; livestock; fish. **Labor force:** 500,000; agriculture 47%, industry 25%, services, 28% (1999 est.). **Industries:** meatpacking, fish processing, dairy products; mining (diamond, lead, zinc, tin, silver, tungsten, uranium, copper). **Natural resources:** diamonds, copper, uranium, gold, lead, tin, lithium, cadmium, zinc, salt, vanadium, natural gas, hydropower, fish; note: suspected deposits of oil, coal, and iron ore. **Exports:** $1.4 billion (f.o.b., 2000 est.): diamonds, copper, gold, zinc, lead, uranium; cattle, processed fish, karakul skins. **Imports:** $1.6 billion (f.o.b., 2000 est.): foodstuffs; petroleum products and fuel, machinery and equipment, chemicals. **Major trading partners:** UK, South Africa, Spain, France, Japan, U.S., Germany.

**Geography** Namibia, bounded on the north by Angola and Zambia and on the east by Botswana and South Africa in the south. It is for the most part a portion of the high plateau of southern Africa with a general elevation of from 3,000 to 4,000 ft.

**Government** Republic.

**History** The San peoples may have inhabited what is now Namibia more than 2000 years ago. The Bantu-speaking Herero migrated there in the 1600s. The Ovambo, the largest ethnic group today, migrated there in the 1800s.

In the late 15th century, the Portuguese explorer Bartolomeu Dias became the first European to visit Namibia. Formerly called South-West Africa, the territory became a German colony in 1884. In 1908, German troops massacred the majority of the Herero population. The land was taken by South African forces in 1915, becoming a South African mandate by the terms of the Treaty of Versailles in 1920.

South Africa's application for incorporation of the territory was rejected by the UN General Assembly in 1946, and South Africa was invited to prepare a trusteeship agreement instead. By a law passed in 1949, however, the territory was brought into much closer association with South Africa—including representation in its Parliament.

In 1968, the UN called for South Africa's withdrawal from the territory, which was given the name *Namibia*. When South Africa refused, the UN Security Council and the International Court of Justice condemned it. Under a 1974 Security Council resolution, South Africa was required to begin the transfer of power to the Namibians by May 30, 1975, or face UN action. Prime Minister Balthazar J. Vorster rejected UN supervision, claiming that his government was prepared to negotiate Namibian independence, but not with the South-West African People's Organization (SWAPO), the principal black separatist group. Meanwhile, the all-white legislature of South-West Africa eased several laws on apartheid in public places.

Despite international opposition, the Turnhalle Conference in Windhoek drafted a constitution to organize an interim government based on racial divisions, a proposal overwhelmingly endorsed by white voters in the territory in 1977. At the urging of ambassadors of the five Western members of the Security Council, South Africa on June 11 announced rejection of the Turnhalle constitution and acceptance of the Western proposal to include the South-West African People's Organization in negotiations.

As policemen wielding riot sticks charged demonstrators in a black South-West Africa township, South Africa handed over limited powers to a new, multiracial administration in the former German colony on June 17, 1985. Installation of the new government ended South Africa's direct rule, but South Africa retained an effective veto over the new government's decisions along with responsibility for the territory's defense and foreign policy.

An agreement between South Africa, Angola, and Cuba arranged for elections for a constituent assembly in Nov. 1989 to establish a new government. SWAPO won 57% of the vote, a majority but not enough to dictate a constitution unilaterally. In Feb. 1990, SWAPO leader Sam Nujoma was elected president and took office when Namibia became independent on March 21, 1990.

Nujoma was reelected in 1994, and again in 1999, after the constitution was amended to allow him to seek a third term. In Sept. 1999, fighting took place between Namibian troops and separatists from the Caprivi Strip, a narrow corridor jutting out of Namibia that provides the country with access to the Zambezi River.

In Jan. 2001, Nujoma ordered police to arrest, deport, and imprison gays. Home Affairs Minister Jerry Ekandjo had made similar remarks in 2000, telling new police officers to "eliminate gays and lesbians from the face of Namibia."

Nujoma announced in Nov. 2001 that he would not seek reelection when his term expires in 2004.

# Nauru

**REPUBLIC OF NAURU**

**President:** René Harris (2001)
**Area:** 8.11 sq mi (21 sq km)
**Population (2002 est.):** 12,329 (growth rate: 2.0%); birth rate 26.6/1000; infant mortality rate 10.5/1000; density per sq mi: 1,521
**Capital (1983):** Yaren, 559. **Monetary unit:** Australian dollar. **Languages:** Nauruan (official) and English. **Ethnicity/race:** Nauruan 58%, other Pacific Islander 26%, Chinese 8%, European 8%. **Religions:** Protestant 58%, Roman Catholic 24%, Confucian and Taoist 8%. **Literacy rate:** 99%
**Economic summary: GDP/PPP** (2000 est.): $59 million; per capita $5,000. **Real growth rate:** n.a. **Inflation:** -3.6% (1993). **Unemployment:** 0%. **Arable land:** 0%. **Agriculture:** coconuts. **Labor force:** employed in mining phosphates, public administration, education, and transportation. **Industries:** phosphate mining,

financial services, coconut products. **Natural resources:** phosphates. **Exports:** $25.3 million (f.o.b., 1991): phosphates. **Imports:** $21.1 million (c.i.f., 1991): food, fuel, manufactures, building materials, machinery. **Major trading partners:** Australia, New Zealand, UK, Japan. **Special relationship within the Commonwealth of Nations**

**Geography** Nauru (pronounced NAH-oo-roo) is an island in the Pacific just south of the equator, about 2,500 mi (4,023 km) southwest of Honolulu. Phosphate mining has virtually destroyed the tiny nation's ecology, turning its tropical vegetation into a barren, rocky wasteland.

**Government** Republic.

**History** In 1798, a British navigator became the first European to visit the island. Germany annexed it in 1888, and by the turn of the century, phosphate, a lucrative fertilizer, began to be mined. The island was placed under joint Australian, New Zealand, and British mandate after World War I. The Japanese occupied the island during World War II, and forced 1,200 Nauruans—roughly two-thirds of the population—to relocate. In 1947, it became a UN trusteeship administered by Australia. By 1967, the phosphate mining industry finally came under control of the islanders, and on Jan. 31, 1968, Nauru became one of the world's smallest independent republics.

Devastated by almost a century of phosphate stripmining by foreign companies, Nauru appealed to the International Court of Justice. In 1993, Australia offered Nauru an out-of-court settlement for damages, agreeing to pay $2.5 million Australian dollars annually for 20 years. New Zealand and the UK additionally agreed to pay a one-time settlement of $12 million each. Declining phosphate prices, the high cost of maintaining an international airline, and the government's financial mismanagement combined to make the economy flounder in the late 1990s.

In 2000, the G7 nations put pressure on the country to review its banking system, which is used by Russian criminals for money laundering.

Since Sept. 2001, Nauru has accepted three boatloads of Asian refugees destined for Australia. Australia compensated the island with $20 million and other financial incentives for taking this refugee problem off their hands.

# Nepal

### KINGDOM OF NEPAL

**Ruler:** King Gyanendra Bir Bikram Shah Deva (2001)
**Prime Minister:** vacant (Oct. 2002)
**Area:** 54,363 sq mi (140,800 sq km)
**Population (2002 est.):** 25,873,917 (growth rate: 2.3%); birth rate: 32.9/1000; infant mortality rate: 72.4/1000; density per sq mi: 476
**Capital and largest city (1993):** Kathmandu, 535,000.
**Other large cities:** Lalitpur, 190,000; Biratnagar, 132,000. **Monetary unit:** Nepalese rupee.
**Languages:** Nepali (official), Newari, Bhutia, Maithali.
**Ethnicity/race:** Newars, Indians, Tibetans, Gurungs, Magars, Tamangs, Bhotias, Rais, Limbus, Sherpas.
**Religions:** Hindu 90%, Buddhist 5%, Islam 3%.
**Literacy rate:** 38% (1993)
**Economic summary:** GDP/PPP (2000 est.): $33.7 billion; per capita $1,360. **Real growth rate:** 3.7%. **Inflation:** 3.3% (FY99/00 est.). **Unemployment:** n.a.; substantial underemployment (1999). **Arable land:** 17%. **Agriculture:** rice, corn, wheat, sugarcane, root crops; milk, water buffalo meat. **Labor force:** 10 million (1996 est.); note: severe lack of skilled labor;

agriculture 81%, services 16%, industry 3%. **Industries:** tourism, carpets, textiles; small rice, jute, sugar, and oilseed mills; cigarettes; cement and brick production. **Natural resources:** quartz, water, timber, hydropower, scenic beauty, small deposits of lignite, copper, cobalt, iron ore. **Exports:** $485 million (f.o.b., 1998), but does not include unrecorded border trade with India: carpets, clothing, leather goods, jute goods, grain. **Imports:** $1.2 billion (f.o.b., 1998): gold, machinery and equipment, petroleum products, fertilizer. **Major trading partners:** India, U.S., Germany, China/Hong Kong, Singapore.

**Geography** A landlocked country the size of Arkansas, lying between India and the Tibetan Autonomous Region of China, Nepal contains Mount Everest (29,035 ft; 8,850 m), the tallest mountain in the world. Along its southern border, Nepal has a strip of level land that is partly forested, partly cultivated. North of that is the slope of the main section of the Himalayan range, including Everest and many other peaks higher than 8,000 m.

**Government** In Nov. 1990, King Birendra promulgated a new constitution and introduced a multiparty parliamentary democracy in Nepal.

**History** The first civilizations in Nepal, which flourished around the 6th century B.C., were confined to the fertile Kathmandu Valley where the present-day capital of the same name is located. It was in this region that Prince Siddhartha Gautama was born circa 563 B.C. Gautama achieved enlightenment as Buddha, and spawned Buddhist belief.

Nepali rulers' early patronage of Buddhism largely gave way to Hinduism, reflecting the increased influence of India, around the 12th century. Though the successive dynasties of the Gopalas, the Kiratis, and the Licchavis expanded their rule, it was not until the reign of the Malla kings from 1200–1769 that Nepal assumed the approximate dimensions of the modern state.

The kingdom of Nepal was unified in 1768 by King Prithvi Narayan Shah, who had fled India following the Moghul conquests of the subcontinent. Under Shah and his successors Nepal's borders expanded as far west as Kashmir and as far east as Sikkim (now part of India). A commercial treaty was signed with Britain in 1792, and again in 1816 after more than a year of hostilities with the British East India Company.

In 1923, Britain recognized the absolute independence of Nepal. Between 1846 and 1951, the country was ruled by the Rana family, which always held the office of prime minister. In 1951, however, the king took over all power and proclaimed a constitutional monarchy. Mahendra Bir Bikram Shah became king in 1955. After Mahendra died of a heart attack in 1972, Prince Birendra, at 26, succeeded to the throne.

In 1990, a prodemocracy movement forced King Birendra to lift the ban on political parties. The first free election in three decades provided a victory for the liberal Nepali Congress Party in 1991, although the Communists made a strong showing. A small but growing Maoist guerrilla movement, seeking to overthrow the constitutional monarchy and install a Communist government, began operating in the countryside in 1996.

On June 1, 2001, King Birendra was shot and killed by his equally popular son, Dipendra. Crown Prince Dipendra, angered by his family's disapproval of his choice of a bride, also killed his mother and several other members of the royal family before shooting himself. Dipendra was crowned king while in a coma;

upon his death on June 4, Prince Gyanendra, the younger brother of Birendra, succeeded him.

The Maoist guerrillas agreed to a cease-fire with the government in July. Peace talks broke down, however, when the government refused to abolish the constitutional monarchy and establish an assembly. The rebels launched a deadly offensive against security targets, and King Gyanendra declared a state of emergency in November and ordered the army to crack down on the group. The rebels stepped up their campaign in western Nepal in April and May 2002, and the government responded with equal intensity, killing hundreds of Maoists, the largest toll since the insurgency began in 1996.

Continued rebel attacks prompted Gyanendra to sack his prime minister in Oct. 2002, citing incompetence. The king also postponed elections.

# The Netherlands

### KINGDOM OF THE NETHERLANDS

**National name:** Koninkrijk der Nederlanden
**Sovereign:** Queen Beatrix (1980)
**Prime Minister:** Jan Peter Balkenende (2002)
**Area:** 16,033 sq mi (41,526 sq km)
**Population (2002 est.):** 16,067,754 (growth rate: 0.3%); birth rate: 11.6/1000; infant mortality rate: 4.3/1000; density per sq mi: 1,002
**Capital and largest city (1994 est.):** Amsterdam (official), 724,096; The Hague (administrative capital), 445,279. **Other large cities (1994 est.):** Rotterdam, 598,521; Utrecht, 234,106; Eindhoven, 196,130.
**Monetary units:** Euro (formerly guilder). **Language:** Dutch, Frisian. **Ethnicity/race:** Dutch 96%, Moroccans, Turks, and other 4% (1988). **Religions:** Roman Catholic 34%, Protestant 25%, Muslim 3%, other 2%, unaffiliated 36%. **Literacy rate:** 99% (1979)
**Economic summary: GDP/PPP** (2000 est.): $388.4 billion; per capita $24,400. **Real growth rate:** 4%. **Inflation:** 2.6%. **Unemployment:** 2.6%. **Arable land:** 25%. **Agriculture:** grains, potatoes, sugar beets, fruits, vegetables; livestock. **Labor force:** 7.2 million (2000); services 73%, industry 23%, agriculture 4% (1998 est.). **Industries:** agroindustries, metal and engineering products, electrical machinery and equipment, chemicals, petroleum, construction, microelectronics, fishing. **Natural resources:** natural gas, petroleum, arable land. **Exports:** $210.3 billion (f.o.b., 2000): machinery and equipment, chemicals, fuels; foodstuffs. **Imports:** $201.2 billion (c.i.f., 2000 est.): machinery and equipment, chemicals, fuels; foodstuffs. **Major trading partners:** EU, Central and Eastern Europe, U.S.

**Geography** The Netherlands, on the coast of the North Sea, is twice the size of New Jersey. Part of the great plain of north and west Europe, the Netherlands has continuous dimensions of 190 by 160 mi (360 by 257 km) and is low and flat except in Limburg in the southeast, where some hills rise to 300 ft (92 m). About half the country's area is below sea level, making the famous Dutch dikes a requisite for the use of much land. Reclamation of land from the sea through dikes has continued through recent times. All drainage reaches the North Sea, and the principal rivers—Rhine, Maas (Meuse), and Schelde—have their sources outside the country.

**Government** Constitutional monarchy.

**History** Julius Caesar found the low-lying Netherlands inhabited by Germanic tribes—the Nervii, Frisii, and Batavi. The Batavi on the Roman frontier did not submit to Rome's rule until 13 B.C., and then only as allies.

The Franks controlled the region from the 4th to the 8th century, and it became part of Charlemagne's empire in the 8th and 9th centuries. The area later passed into the hands of Burgundy and the Austrian Hapsburgs, and finally in the 16th century came under Spanish rule.

When Philip II of Spain suppressed political liberties and the growing Protestant movement in the Netherlands, a revolt led by William of Orange broke out in 1568. Under the Union of Utrecht (1579), the seven northern provinces became the United Provinces of the Netherlands. War between the United Provinces and Spain continued into the 17th century, but in 1648 Spain finally recognized Dutch independence.

The Dutch East India Company was established in 1602, and by the end of the 17th century Holland was one of the great sea and colonial powers of Europe.

The nation's independence was not completely established until after the Thirty Years' War (1618–48), when the country's rise as a commercial and maritime power began. In 1688, the English Parliament invited William of Orange, stadtholder, and his wife, Mary Stuart, to rule England as William III and Mary II. William then used the combined resources of England and the Netherlands to wage war on Louis XIV's France. In 1814, all the provinces of Holland and Belgium were merged into one kingdom, but in 1830 the southern provinces broke away to form the kingdom of Belgium. A liberal constitution was adopted by the Netherlands in 1848. The country remained neutral during World War I.

In spite of its neutrality in World War II, the Netherlands was invaded by the Nazis in May 1940, and the Dutch East Indies were later taken by the Japanese. The nation was liberated in May 1945. In 1948, after a reign of 50 years, Queen Wilhelmina abdicated and was succeeded by her daughter Juliana.

In 1949, after a four-year war, the Netherlands granted independence to the Dutch East Indies, which became the Republic of Indonesia. The Netherlands also joined NATO that year. The Netherlands joined the European Economic Community (later, the EU) in 1958. In 1999, it adopted the single European currency, the euro.

In 1963, it turned over the western half of New Guinea to Indonesia, ending 300 years of Dutch presence in Asia. Attainment of independence by Suriname on Nov. 25, 1975, left the Netherlands Antilles and Aruba as the country's only overseas territories.

Although prostitution is legal, the government moved in July 1997 to permit the operation of brothels as a means of regulating the former. Only those with a valid resident's permit would be permitted to be employed in the brothels. In 1999, the Netherlands again defied convention by preparing to legalize euthanasia. In Sept. 2000, the Netherlands became the first nation in the world to legalize same-sex marriages.

The Hague is currently host to the UN War Crimes Tribunal for Yugoslavia, which in 2001 began prosecuting former Yugoslavian dictator Slobodan Milosevic, among others.

Wim Kok's government resigned in April 2002 after a report concluded that Dutch UN troops failed to prevent a massacre of Bosnian Muslims by Bosnian Serbs in a UN safe haven near Srebrenica in 1995. Explaining his action, the popular prime minister said, "The international community is big and anonymous. We are taking the consequences of the international community's failure in Srebrenica."

The country's normally bland political scene was further rocked with the May 2002 assassination of Pim Fortuyn, a right-wing, anti-immigrant politician. Days later, his party, Lijst Pim Fortuyn, placed second in national elections, behind Jan Peter Balkenende's Christian Democrats. Leading the country into a marked shift to the right, Balkenende formed a three-way center-right coalition government with his Christian Democrats, Pim Fortuyn List, and the People's Party for Freedom and Democracy. He was sworn in as prime minister in July.

## Netherlands Autonomous Countries

### Netherlands Antilles
**Status:** Part of the Kingdom of the Netherlands
**Governor:** Frits Goedgedrag (2002)
**Prime Minister:** Miguel A. Pourier (2000)
**Area:** 371 sq mi (960 sq km)
**Population (2002 est.):** 214,258 (growth rate: 1.0%); birth rate: 16.2/1000; infant mortality rate: 11.1/1000; density per sq mi: 578. **Ethnicity/race:** mixed African 85%, Carib Indian, European, Latin, Asian
**Capital and largest city (1993 est.):** Willemstad, 197,019. **Literacy rate:** 94% (1981)
**Economic summary: GDP/PPP** (2000 est.): $2.4 billion; per capita $11,400. **Real growth rate:** –3.5%. **Inflation:** 6.4%. **Unemployment:** 14.9% (1998 est.). **Arable land:** 10%. **Agriculture:** aloes, sorghum, peanuts, vegetables, tropical fruit. **Labor force:** 89,000; agriculture 1%, industry 13%, services 86% (1994 est.). **Industries:** tourism (Curaçao, Sint Maarten, and Bonaire), petroleum refining (Curaçao), petroleum transshipment facilities (Curaçao and Bonaire), light manufacturing (Curaçao). **Natural resources:** phosphates (Curaçao only), salt (Bonaire only). **Exports:** $276 million (f.o.b., 2000): petroleum products. **Imports:** $1.5 billion (f.o.b., 2000): crude petroleum, food, manufactures. **Major trading partners:** U.S., Guatemala, Costa Rica, the Bahamas, Jamaica, Chile, Venezuela, Mexico, Italy, Netherlands, Brazil.

The Netherlands Antilles are composed of two groups of Caribbean islands 500 mi (805 km) apart: Curaçao (173 sq mi; 448 sq km) and Bonaire (95 sq mi; 246 sq km) are located about 40 mi (64 km) off the Venezuelan coast.

Originally inhabited by Arawak Indians, these two islands as well as Aruba were claimed by Spain in 1527, and then by the Dutch in 1643. The Dutch Lesser Antilles to the north—Sint Eustatius, the southern part of Saint Martin (Dutch: Sint Maarten), and Saba—make up the remainder of the island federation. First inhabited by the Carib Indians, Saint Martin was explored by Columbus in 1493. In 1845, the six islands (then including Aruba) officially formed the Netherlands Antilles. In 1994, the islands voted to preserve their federation with the Netherlands.

### Aruba
**Status:** Part of the Kingdom of the Netherlands
**Governor:** Olindo Koolman (1992)
**Prime Minister:** Nelson O. Oduber (2001)
**Area:** 75 sq mi (193 sq km)
**Population (2002 est.):** 70,441 (growth rate: 0.6%); birth rate: 12.2/1000; infant mortality rate: 6.3/1000; density per sq mi: 945
**Capital and largest city (1991 est.):** Oranjestad, 20,050. **Ethnicity/race:** mixed European/Caribbean Indian 80%. **Literacy rate:** 95%
**Economic summary: GDP/PPP** (2000 est.): $2 billion; per capita $28,000. **Real growth rate:** 3.5%.

**Inflation:** 4.2%. **Unemployment:** 0.6% (1999 est.). **Arable land:** 7% aloe plantations included (0.01%). **Agriculture:** aloes; livestock; fish. **Labor force:** 41,501 (1997 est.); most employment is in wholesale and retail trade and repair, followed by hotels and restaurants (1997 est.). **Industries:** tourism, transshipment facilities, oil refining. **Natural resources:** negl.; white sandy beaches. **Exports:** $2.2 billion (including oil reexports) (2000 est.): live animals and animal products, art and collectibles, machinery and electrical equipment, transport equipment. **Imports:** $2.5 billion (2000 est.): machinery and electrical equipment, crude oil for refining and reexport, chemicals; foodstuff. **Major trading partners:** U.S., Colombia, Netherlands, Netherlands Antilles, Japan.

Aruba, an island slightly larger than Washington, D.C., lies 18 mi (28.9 km) off the coast of Venezuela in the southern Caribbean.

The Arawak Indians were the first inhabitants of Aruba. Spain explored the island in 1499, and more than a century later the Netherlands (1636) claimed the island. After a brief rule by the British, the Dutch again took control of the island in 1816, and it officially became part of the Netherlands Antilles in 1846.

On Jan. 1, 1986, Aruba seceded from the federation, but decided in 1994 to indefinitely postpone the transition to full independence. The Netherlands controls Aruba's defense and foreign affairs, but all internal affairs are handled by an island government directing its own civil service, judiciary, revenue, and currency.

## New Zealand
**Sovereign:** Queen Elizabeth II (1952)
**Governor-General:** Dame Silvia Cartwright (2001)
**Prime Minister:** Helen Clark (1999)
**Area:** 103,737 sq mi (268,680 sq km) (excluding dependencies)
**Population (2002 est.):** 3,908,037 (growth rate: 0.7%); birth rate: 14.2/1000; infant mortality rate: 6.2/1000; density per sq mi: 38
**Capital:** Wellington. **Largest cities (est. 1995):** Auckland, 952,600; Wellington, 331,100; Christchurch, 324,400. **Monetary unit:** New Zealand dollar. **Languages:** English (official), Maori. **Ethnicity/race:** European 88%, Maori 8.9%, Pacific Islander 2.9%, other 0.2%. **Religions:** Christian 81%, none or unspecified 18%, Hindu, Confucian, and other 1%. **Literacy rate:** 99% (1980)
**Economic summary: GDP/PPP** (2000 est.): $67.6 billion; per capita $17,700. **Real growth rate:** 3.6%. **Inflation:** 2.4%. **Unemployment:** 6.3%. **Arable land:** 9%. **Agriculture:** wheat, barley, potatoes, pulses, fruits, vegetables; wool, beef, dairy products; fish. **Labor force:** 1.88 million (2000): services 65%, industry 25%, agriculture 10% (1995). **Industries:** food processing, wood and paper products, textiles, machinery, transportation equipment, banking and insurance, tourism, mining. **Natural resources:** natural gas, iron ore, sand, coal, timber, hydropower, gold, limestone. **Exports:** $14.6 billion (f.o.b., 2000 est.): dairy products, meat, fish, wool, forestry products, manufactures. **Imports:** $14.3 billion (f.o.b., 2000 est.): machinery and equipment, vehicles and aircraft, petroleum, consumer goods, plastics. **Major trading partners:** Australia, Japan, U.S., UK. **Member of Commonwealth of Nations**

**Geography**  New Zealand, about 1,250 mi (2,012 km) southeast of Australia, consists of two main islands and a number of smaller, outlying islands so scattered that they range from the tropical to the antarctic. The country is the size of Colorado. New Zealand's two main components are the North Island

and the South Island, separated by Cook Strait, which varies from 16 to 190 mi (26 to 396 km) in width. The North Island (44,281 sq mi; 115,777 sq km) is 515 mi (829 km) long and volcanic in its south-central part. This area contains many hot springs and beautiful geysers. South Island (58,093 sq mi; 151,215 sq km) has the Southern Alps along its west coast, with Mount Cook (12,283.3 ft; 3,754 m) the highest point. Other inhabited islands include Stewart Island, the Chatham Islands, and Great Barrier Island. The largest of the uninhabited outlying islands are the Auckland Islands (234 sq mi; 606 sq km), Campbell Island (44 sq mi; 114 sq km), the Antipodes Islands (24 sq mi; 62 sq km), and the Kermadec Islands (13 sq mi; 34 sq km).

**Government** Parliamentary democracy.

**History** Maoris were the first inhabitants of New Zealand, arriving on the islands in about 1000. Maori oral history maintains the Maoris came to the island in seven canoes from other parts of Polynesia. In 1642, New Zealand was explored by Abel Tasman, a Dutch navigator. British captain James Cook made three voyages to the islands, beginning in 1769. Britain formally annexed the islands in 1840.

The Treaty of Waitangi (Feb. 6, 1840) between the British and several Maori tribes promised to protect Maori land if the Maoris recognized British rule. Encroachment upon the land by European settlers was relentless, however, and skirmishes between the two groups intensified.

From the outset, the country has been in the forefront in instituting social welfare legislation. New Zealand was the world's first country to give women the right to vote (1893). It adopted old age pensions (1898); a national child welfare program (1907); social security for the aged, widows, and orphans, along with family benefit payments; minimum wages; a 40-hour workweek and unemployment and health insurance (1938); and socialized medicine (1941).

New Zealand fought with the Allies in both world wars as well as in Korea. In 1999, it became part of the UN peacekeeping force sent to East Timor.

In June 2002, Prime Minister Helen Clark apologized to Samoans for the unfair treatment they received during colonial rule. The Labor Party's Clark was elected to a second term as prime minister in July 2002.

## Cook Islands and Overseas Territories

The **Cook Islands** (93 sq mi; 241 sq km) were placed under New Zealand administration in 1901. They achieved self-governing status in association with New Zealand in 1965. **Population (2002 est.):** 20,811.

**Niue** (100 sq mi; 259 sq km) was formerly administered as part of the Cook Islands. It was placed under separate New Zealand administration in 1901 and achieved self-governing status in association with New Zealand in 1974. The capital is Alofi. **Population (July 2001 est.):** 2,124.

**Tokelau** (3.86 sq mi; 10 sq km) was formerly administered as part of the Gilbert and Ellice Islands colony. It was placed under New Zealand administration in 1925. **Population (July 2001 est.):** 1,445.

# Nicaragua

**REPUBLIC OF NICARAGUA**

**National name:** República de Nicaragua
**President:** Enrique Bolaños (2002)
**Area:** 49,998 sq mi (129,494 sq km)
**Population (2002 est.):** 5,023,818 (growth rate: 2.2%);

birth rate: 27.0/1000; infant mortality rate: 32.5/1000; density per sq mi: 100
**Capital and largest city (1992 est.):** Managua, 974,000. **Monetary unit:** Gold cordoba. **Language:** Spanish. **Ethnicity/race:** mestizo (mixed Amerindian and white) 69%, white 17%, black 9%, Indian 5%. **Religions:** Roman Catholic 95%, Protestant 5%. **Literacy rate:** 57% (1971)
**Economic summary: GDP/PPP** (2000 est.): $13.1 billion; per capita $2,700. **Real growth rate:** 5%. **Inflation:** 11%. **Unemployment:** 20% plus considerable underemployment (1999 est.). **Arable land:** 9%. **Agriculture:** coffee, bananas, sugarcane, cotton, rice, corn, tobacco, sesame, soya, beans; beef, veal, pork, poultry, dairy products. **Labor force:** 1.7 million (1999); services 43%, agriculture 42%, industry 15% (1999 est.). **Industries:** food processing, chemicals, machinery and metal products, textiles, clothing, petroleum refining and distribution, beverages, footwear, wood. **Natural resources:** gold, silver, copper, tungsten, lead, zinc, timber, fish. **Exports:** $631 million (f.o.b., 2000 est.): coffee, shrimp and lobster, cotton, tobacco, beef, sugar, bananas; gold. **Imports:** $1.6 billion (f.o.b., 2000 est.): machinery and equipment, raw materials, petroleum products, consumer goods. **Major trading partners:** U.S., El Salvador, Germany, Costa Rica, Spain, France, Guatemala, Panama, Venezuela.

**Geography** Largest but most sparsely populated of the Central American nations, Nicaragua borders on Honduras to the north and Costa Rica to the south. It is slightly larger than New York State. Nicaragua is mountainous in the west, with fertile valleys. A plateau slopes eastward toward the Caribbean. Two big lakes—Nicaragua, about 100 mi long (161 km), and Managua, about 38 mi long (61 km)—are connected by the Tipitapa River. The Pacific coast is volcanic and very fertile. The Caribbean coast, swampy and indented, is aptly called the "Mosquito Coast."

**Government** Republic.

**History** Nicaragua, which derives its name from the chief of the area's leading Indian tribe at the time of the Spanish Conquest, was first settled by the Spanish in 1522. The country won independence in 1838. For the next century, Nicaragua's politics were dominated by the competition for power between the Liberals, who were centered in the city of León, and the Conservatives, centered in Granada.

To back up its support of the new Conservative government in 1909, the U.S. sent a small detachment of Marines to Nicaragua from 1912 to 1925. The Bryan-Chamorro Treaty of 1916 (terminated in 1970) gave the U.S. an option on a canal route through Nicaragua and naval bases. U.S. Marines were sent again to quell disorder after the 1924 elections. A guerrilla leader, César Augusto Sandino, fought the U.S. troops from 1927 until their withdrawal in 1933.

After ordering Sandino's assassination, Gen. Anastasio Somoza García was dictator from 1936 until his own assassination in 1956. He was succeeded by his son Luis, who alternated with trusted family friends in the presidency until his death in 1967. He was succeeded by his brother, Maj. Gen. Anastasio Somoza Debayle. The Somozas ruled Nicaragua with an iron fist, reducing its dependence on banana exports, exiling political foes, and amassing a family fortune.

Sandinista guerrillas, leftists who took their name from Sandino, launched an offensive in 1979. After seven weeks of fighting, Somoza fled the country on July 17, 1979. The Sandinistas assumed power two days later. On Jan. 23, 1981, the Reagan administration suspended U.S. aid, charging that Nicaragua, with the aid of Cuba and the Soviet Union, was supplying arms to rebels in El Salvador. The Sandinistas denied the charges. Later that year, Nicaraguan guerrillas known as "Contras," began a war to overthrow the Sandinistas. Elections were finally held on Nov. 4, 1984, with Daniel Ortega, the Sandinista junta coordinator, winning the presidency. The war intensified in 1986–87. Negotiations sponsored by the Contadora (neutral Latin American) nations foundered, but Costa Rican president Oscar Arias promoted a treaty signed by Central American leaders in Aug. 1987.

Violetta Barrios de Chamorro, owner of the opposition paper *La Prensa,* led a broad anti-Sandinista coalition to victory in the 1990 election, ending 11 years of Sandinista rule. Enthusiasm for Chamorro gradually faded. Business groups were dissatisfied with the pace of reforms; Sandinistas, upset with what they regarded as the dismantling of their earlier achievements, threatened to take up arms again; and many people were disillusioned over governmental corruption and the continuing influence of the Sandinistas on the government and the army. Former Managua mayor and Conservative candidate Arnoldo Alemán won the 1996 election. Ortega was his closest rival.

In 1998, Hurricane Mitch killed more than 9,000 people, left 2 million people homeless, and caused $10 billion in damages. Many people fled to the U.S., which offered Nicaraguans an immigration amnesty program until July 1999.

Nicaragua remains one of the poorest countries in the Western Hemisphere. Property is often caught in a three-way battle between those who owned it before the Sandinistas came to power; cooperatives set up by the Sandinistas; and former Contras who claim they were promised land for joining the anti-Sandinista forces.

In June 2000, Nicaragua did resolve its border dispute with Costa Rica. On Nov. 6, 2000, the Sandinista Party candidate was elected mayor of Managua, defeating the Liberal Party incumbent. Observers said the election indicated disillusionment with the scandal-ridden national government.

In Nov. 2001 presidential elections, Enrique Bolaños, the ruling Liberal party leader, defeated Daniel Ortega, the Sandinista leader who had attempted a comeback after his defeat in 1990. The Sandinistas elected Ortega as party head in March 2002, despite his series of losses in recent presidential elections.

Former president Arnoldo Aleman was charged with corruption in Aug. 2002. Prosecutors allege that during his presidential term in the late 1990s, he stole up to $10 million in state funds.

# Niger

### REPUBLIC OF NIGER

**National name:** République du Niger
**President:** Tandja Mamadou (1999)
**Prime Minister:** Hama Amadou (1999)
**Area:** 489,189 sq mi (1,267,000 sq km)
**Population (2002 est.):** 10,639,744 (growth rate: 2.8%); birth rate: 50.0/1000; infant mortality rate: 122.2/1000; density per sq mi: 22
**Capital and largest city (1988):** Niamey, 398,265.
**Other large cities:** Zinder, 120,900; Maradi, 112,970.
**Monetary unit:** CFA Franc. **Languages:** French (official); Hausa; Songhai; Arabic. **Ethnicity/race:** Hausa 56%, Djerma 22%, Fula 8.5%, Tuareg 8%, Beri Beri (Kanouri) 4.3%, Arab, Toubou, and Gourmantche 1.2%, about 4,000 French expatriates. **Religions:**

Islam 80%, Animist and Christian 20%. **Literacy rate:** 28% (1990)
**Economic summary: GDP/PPP** (2000 est.): $10 billion; per capita $1,000. **Real growth rate:** 3.5%. **Inflation:** 2.8%. **Unemployment:** n.a. **Arable land:** 3%. **Agriculture:** cowpeas, cotton, peanuts, millet, sorghum, cassava (tapioca), rice; cattle, sheep, goats, camels, donkeys, horses, poultry. **Labor force:** 70,000 receive regular wages or salaries; agriculture 90%, industry and commerce 6%, government 4%. **Industries:** uranium mining, cement, brick, textiles, food processing, chemicals, slaughterhouses. **Natural resources:** uranium, coal, iron ore, tin, phosphates, gold, petroleum. **Exports:** $385 million (f.o.b., 1999): uranium ore 65%, livestock products, cowpeas, onions (1998 est.). **Imports:** $317 million (f.o.b., 1999): consumer goods, primary materials, machinery, vehicles and parts, petroleum, cereals. **Major trading partners:** France, Nigeria, UK, Côte d'Ivoire, U.S.

**Geography**   Niger, in West Africa's Sahara region, is four-fifths the size of Alaska. It is surrounded by Mali, Algeria, Libya, Chad, Nigeria, Benin, and Burkina Faso. The Niger River in the southwest flows through the country's only fertile area. Elsewhere the land is semiarid.

**Government**   Republic, emerging from military rule.

**History**   The nomadic Tuaregs were the first inhabitants in the Sahara region. The Hausa (14th century), the Zerma (17th century), the Gobir (18th century), and Fulani (19th century) also established themselves in the region now called Niger.

Niger was incorporated into French West Africa in 1896. There were frequent rebellions, but when order was restored in 1922, the French made the area a colony. In 1958, the voters approved the French constitution and voted to make the territory an autonomous republic within the French Community. The republic adopted a constitution in 1959 but the next year withdrew from the Community, proclaiming its independence.

During the 1970s, the country's economy flourished from uranium production, but when uranium prices fell in the 1980s, its brief period of prosperity ended. The 1974 army coup ousted President Hamani Diori, who had held office since 1960. An estimated 2 million people were starving in Niger, but 200,000 tons of imported food, half U.S.-supplied, substantially ended famine conditions by the year's end. The new president, Lt. Col. Seyni Kountché, chief of staff of the army, installed a 12-man military government. A predominantly civilian government was formed by Kountché in 1976.

In 1993, the country's first multiparty election resulted in the presidency of Ousmane Mahamane, who was then deposed in a Jan. 1996 coup. In July, the military leader of the coup, Ibrahim Baré Maïnassara, was declared president in a rigged election. Considered a corrupt and ineffectual president, Maïnassara was assassinated in April 1999 by his own guards. The National Reconciliation Council, responsible for the coup, kept its promise and held democratic elections; in Nov. 1999, Tandja Mamadou was elected president. As a result, foreign aid, primarily from France, was restored.

The nomadic Tuaregs of the north, of Berber and Arab descent, have a fiercely insular culture and share little affinity with the black African majority of Niger. Conflict between the Tuaregs and the other tribes of

Niger first surfaced in the early 20th century. A cease-fire between the government and Tuareg rebels (Revolutionary Armed Forces of the Sahara) went into effect in 1995, and in June 1997, the Democratic Renewal Front, a holdout Tuareg rebel group, also agreed to sign a peace accord. The impoverished Tuaregs have received little of the economic aid they were promised, which is not surprising given Niger's political instability and desperate poverty.

In July 2002, a group of mutinous soldiers seized several army garrisons in N'Gourti, Diffa, N'Guigmi, and the capital Niamey, demanding better work conditions and months of back pay. Nearly 220 renegade soldiers were arrested and three were killed in the mutiny.

# Nigeria

### FEDERAL REPUBLIC OF NIGERIA

**President:** Olusegun Obasanjo (1999)
**Area:** 356,667 sq mi (923,768 sq km)
**Population (2002 est.):** 129,934,911 (growth rate: 2.5%); birth rate: 39.2/1000; infant mortality rate: 72.5/1000; density per sq mi: 364
**Capital (1995 est.):** Abuja, 339,000. **Largest cities:** Lagos (2000 est.), 13,050,000 (metro. area); Ibadan, 1,365,000; Ogbomosho, 711,900; Kano, 657,300.
**Monetary unit:** Naira. **Languages:** English (official), Hausa, Yoruba, Ibo, and more than 200 others.
**Ethnicity/race:** Hausa, Fulani, Yoruba, Ibo, Kanuri, Ibibio, Tiv, Ijaw. **Religions:** Islam 50%, Christian 40%, indigenous 10%. **Literacy rate:** 51% (1990)
**Economic summary:** GDP/PPP (2000 est.): $117 billion; per capita $950. **Real growth rate:** 3.5%. **Inflation:** 6.5%. **Unemployment:** 28% (1992 est.). **Arable land:** 33%. **Agriculture:** cocoa, peanuts, palm oil, corn, rice, sorghum, millet, cassava (tapioca), yams, rubber; cattle, sheep, goats, pigs; timber; fish. **Labor force:** 66 million; agriculture 70%, industry 10%, services 20% (1999 est.). **Industries:** crude oil, coal, tin, columbite, palm oil, peanuts, cotton, rubber, wood, hides and skins, textiles, cement and other construction materials, food products, footwear, chemicals, fertilizer, printing, ceramics, steel. **Natural resources:** natural gas, petroleum, tin, columbite, iron ore, coal, limestone, lead, zinc, arable land. **Exports:** $22.2 billion (f.o.b., 2000 est.): petroleum and petroleum products 95%, cocoa, rubber. **Imports:** $10.7 billion (f.o.b., 2000 est.): machinery, chemicals, transport equipment, manufactured goods, food and live animals. **Major trading partners:** U.S., India, Spain, Brazil, France, UK, Germany, China. **Member of Commonwealth of Nations**

**Geography** Nigeria, one-third larger than Texas and the most populous country in Africa, is situated on the Gulf of Guinea in West Africa. Its neighbors are Benin, Niger, Cameroon, and Chad. The lower course of the Niger River flows south through the western part of the country into the Gulf of Guinea. Swamps and mangrove forests border the southern coast, inland are hardwood forests.

**Government** Multiparty government transitioning from military to civilian rule.

**History** The first inhabitants of what is now Nigeria were thought to have been the Nok people (500 B.C.–circa A.D. 200). The Kanuri, Hausa, and Fulani peoples subsequently migrated there. Islam was introduced in the 13th century, and the empire of Kanem controlled the area from the end of the 11th century to the 14th. The Fulani empire ruled the region from the beginning of the 19th century until the British annexed

Lagos in 1851 and seized control of the rest of the region by 1886. It formally became the Colony and Protectorate of Nigeria in 1914. During World War I, native troops of the West African frontier force joined with French forces to defeat the German garrison in the Cameroons.

On Oct. 1, 1960, Nigeria gained independence, becoming a member of the Commonwealth of Nations and joining the United Nations. Organized as a loose federation of self-governing states, the independent nation faced an overwhelming task of unifying a country with 250 ethnic and linguistic groups.

Rioting broke out in 1966, and military leaders, primarily of Ibo ethnicity, seized control. In July, a second military coup put Col. Yakubu Gowon in power, a choice unacceptable to the Ibos. Also in that year, the Muslim Hausas in the north massacred the predominantly Christian Ibos in the east, many of whom had been driven from the north. Thousands of Ibos took refuge in the eastern region, which declared its independence as the Republic of Biafra on May 30, 1967. Civil war broke out. In Jan. 1970, after 31 months of civil war, Biafra surrendered to the federal government.

Gowon's nine-year rule was ended in 1975 by a bloodless coup that made Army Brig. Muritala Rufai Mohammed the new chief of state. The return of civilian leadership was established with the election of Alhaji Shehu Shagari as president in 1979. An oil boom in the 1970s buoyed the economy and by the 1980s Nigeria was considered an exemplar of African democracy and economic well-being.

The military again seized power in 1984, only to be followed by another military coup the following year. Maj. Gen. Ibrahim Babangida announced that the country would be returned to civilian rule, but after the presidential election of June 12, 1993, he voided the results. Nevertheless, Babangida resigned as president in Aug. In Nov. the military, headed by defense minister Sani Abacha, seized power again.

Corruption and notorious governmental inefficiency as well as a harshly repressive military regime characterized Abacha's reign over this oil-rich country. A UN fact-finding mission in 1996 reported that Nigeria's "problems of human rights are terrible and the political problems are terrifying." During the 1970s, Nigeria had the 33rd highest per-capita income in the world, but by 1997 it had dropped to the 13th poorest.

As leader of the multination peacekeeping force, ECOMOG, Nigeria has established itself as West Africa's superpower, intervening militarily in the civil wars of Liberia and Sierra Leone. But Nigeria's costly war efforts have been unpopular with its own people, who feel Nigeria's limited economic resources are being unnecessarily drained.

Under military rule for all but ten years since independence from Britain, the military has reneged on its promises to give up power eight times. Despite international pressure to institute democratic rule, the notoriously authoritarian Gen. Sani Abacha, whose formidable security forces kept a tight rein over the country, refused to loosen his absolute grip on political and military power. Abacha's repressive rule turned Nigeria into an international pariah. The hanging of writer Ken Saro-Wiwa in 1995 because he protested against the government was condemned around the world.

Abacha died of a heart attack on June 8, 1998, and was succeeded by another military ruler, Gen. Abdulsalam Abubakar, who pledged to step aside for an elected leader by May 1999. Abubakar's freeing of political prisoners and other gestures of easing the military's iron-clad rule were signs of hope, but the suspicious death of opposition leader Mashood Abiola, who had been imprisoned by the military ever since he legally won the 1993 presidential election, was a crushing blow to democratic proponents. In Feb. 1999, free presidential elections led to an overwhelming victory for Gen. Olusegun Obasanjo, a former member of the military elite who was imprisoned for three years for criticizing the military rule, and released just eight months before his election. Obasanjo's commitment to democracy, his anticorruption drives, and his desire to recover billions allegedly stolen by the family and cronies of Abacha initially gained him high praise from the populace as well as the international community. But within two years, the hope of reform seemed doomed as economic mismanagement and rampant corruption persisted. Obasanjo's priorities in 2001 were symbolized by his plans to build a $330 million national soccer stadium, an extravagance that exceeded the combined budget for both health and education.

Nigeria's stability has been repeatedly threatened by fighting between fundamentalist Muslims and Christians over the spread of Islamic law (sharia) across the heavily Muslim north. More than 10,000 people have died in religious clashes since military rule ended in 1999. In Feb. 2002, about 100 people were killed in Lagos during battles between the Islamic Hausas from the north and Yorubas from the Christian-dominated southwest. Christian and Muslim leaders in Kaduna state signed a peace accord in August, promising to crack down on violence.

# Norway

### KINGDOM OF NORWAY

**National name:** Kongeriket Norge
**Sovereign:** King Harald V (1991)
**Prime Minister:** Kjell Magne Bondevik (2001)
**Area:** 125,181 sq mi (324,220 sq km)
**Population (2002 est.):** 4,525,116 (growth rate: 0.3%); birth rate: 12.4/1000; infant mortality rate: 3.9/1000; density per sq mi: 36
**Capital and largest city (1995):** Oslo, 483,401. **Other large cities:** Bergen, 221,717; Trondheim, 142,927; Stavanger, 103,496. **Monetary unit:** Norwegian krone. **Languages:** Two official forms of Norwegian: Bokmål and Nynorsk. **Ethnicity/race:** Germanic (Nordic, Alpine, Baltic), Lapps (Sami). **Religions:** Evangelical Lutheran 87.8% (state church), other Protestant and Roman Catholic 3.8%, none 3.2%, unknown 5.2%. **Literacy rate:** 99% (1976)
**Economic summary: GDP/PPP** (1999 est.): $124.1 billion; per capita $27,700 (2000 est.). **Real growth rate:** 2.7%. **Inflation:** 2.9%. **Unemployment:** 3%. **Arable land:** 3%. **Agriculture:** barley, other grains, potatoes; beef, milk; fish. **Labor force:** 2.4 million (2000 est.); services 74%, industry 22%, agriculture, forestry, and fishing 4% (1995). **Industries:** petroleum and gas, food processing, shipbuilding, pulp and paper products, metals, chemicals, timber, mining, textiles, fishing. **Natural resources:** petroleum, copper, natural gas, pyrites, nickel, iron ore, zinc, lead, fish, timber, hydropower. **Exports:** $59.2 billion (f.o.b., 2000 est.): petroleum and petroleum products, machinery and equipment, metals, chemicals, ships, fish. **Imports:** $35.2 billion (f.o.b., 2000 est.): machinery and equipment, chemicals, metals, foodstuffs. **Major trading partners:** EU, U.S., Japan.

**Geography** Norway is situated in the western part of the Scandinavian peninsula. It extends about 1,100 mi (1,770 km) from the North Sea along the Norwegian Sea to more than 300 mi (483 km) above the Arctic Circle, the farthest north of any European country. It is slightly larger than New Mexico. Nearly 70% of Norway is uninhabitable and covered by mountains, glaciers, moors, and rivers. The hundreds of deep fjords that cut into the coastline give Norway an overall oceanfront of more than 12,000 mi (19,312 km). Galdhø Peak, at 8,100 ft (2,469 m), is Norway's highest point and the Glåma (Glomma) is the principal river, at 372 mi (598 km) long.

**Government** Constitutional monarchy.

**History** Norwegians, like the Danes and Swedes, are of Teutonic origin. The Norsemen, also known as Vikings, ravaged the coasts of northwest Europe from the 8th to the 11th century and were ruled by local chieftains. Olaf II Haraldsson became the first effective king of all Norway in 1015 and began converting the Norwegians to Christianity. After 1442, Norway was ruled by Danish kings until 1814, when it was united with Sweden—although retaining a degree of independence and receiving a new constitution—in an uneasy partnership. In 1905, the Norwegian Parliament arranged a peaceful separation and invited a Danish prince to the Norwegian throne—King Haakon VII. A treaty with Sweden provided that all disputes be settled by arbitration and that no fortifications be erected on the common frontier.

When World War I broke out, Norway joined with Sweden and Denmark in a decision to remain neutral and to cooperate in the joint interest of the three countries. In World War II, Norway was invaded by the Germans on April 9, 1940. It resisted for two months before the Nazis took complete control. King Haakon and his government fled to London, where they established a government-in-exile. Maj. Vidkun Quisling, who served as Norway's premier during the war, was the most notorious of the Nazi collaborators. The word for traitor, *quisling*, bears his name. He was executed by the Norwegians on Oct. 24, 1945.

Despite severe losses in the war, Norway recovered quickly as its economy expanded. The country led the world in social experimentation. It entered the North Atlantic Treaty Organization in 1949. In the late 20th century, the Labor Party and the Conservative Party seesawed for control, each sometimes having to lead minority governments. An important debate has been over Norway's membership in the European Union. In an advisory referendum held in Nov. 1994, voters rejected seeking membership for their nation in the EU. The country became the second-largest net oil exporter after Saudi Arabia in 1995. Norway continued to experience rapid economic growth into the new millennium.

In March 2000, Prime Minister Kjell Magne Bondevik resigned after parliament voted to build the country's first gas-fired power stations. Bondevik had objected to the project, asserting that the plants would emit too much carbon dioxide. Labor Party leader Jens Stoltenberg succeeded Bondevik. Stoltenberg and the Labor Party were soundly defeated in Sept. 2001 elections, and no party emerged with a clear majority. After a month of talks, the Conservatives, the Christian People's Party, and the Liberals formed a coalition with Bondevik as prime minister. The governing coalition was backed by the far-right Progress Party.

Tension mounted between Norway and Australia in Aug. 2001, when Australia refused to allow a Norwegian ship, the *Tampa*, which had rescued 460 mainly Afghan refugees from a sinking ferry off Indonesia, to dock on Australia's Christmas Island. New Zealand and Nauru stepped in and offered to process the refugees' asylum claims.

## Dependencies of Norway

**Svalbard** (23,957 sq mi; 62,049 sq km), in the Arctic Ocean about 360 mi north of Norway, consists of the Spitsbergen group and several smaller islands, including Bear Island, Hope Island, King Charles Land, and White Island (or Gillis Land). The capital is Longyearbyen. It came under Norwegian administration in 1925. **Population:** 2,332 (July 2001 est.). 62% of the population is Russian and Ukrainian; 38% are Norwegian. Coal mining is the major economic activity. **Bouvet Island** (23 sq mi; 59 sq km), an island nature reserve in the South Atlantic about 1,600 mi south-southwest of the Cape of Good Hope, came under Norwegian administration in 1928. It is uninhabited.

**Jan Mayen Island** (144 sq mi; 373 sq km), in the Arctic Ocean between Norway and Greenland, came under Norwegian administration in 1929. There are no permanent inhabitants, just workers at the navigation base and weather/radio station.

# Oman

SULTANATE OF OMAN

**National name:** Saltonat Uman
**Sultan:** Qabus ibn Sa'id (1970)
**Area:** 82,031 sq mi (212,460 sq km)[1]
**Population (2002 est.):** 2,713,462 (growth rate: 3.4%); birth rate: 37.8/1000; infant mortality rate: 21.8/1000; density per sq mi: 33
**Capital and largest city (1991 est.):** Muscat, 350,000.
**Monetary unit:** Omani rial. **Languages:** Arabic (official); also English and Indian languages. **Ethnicity/race:** Arab, Baluchi, South Asian (Indian, Pakistani, Sri Lankan, Bangladeshi), African. **Religion:** Islam 95%.
**Literacy rate:** 80%
**Economic summary: GDP/PPP** (2000 est.): $19.6 billion; per capita $7,700. **Real growth rate:** 4.6%. **Inflation:** –0.8%. **Unemployment:** n.a. **Arable land:** 0%. **Agriculture:** dates, limes, bananas, alfalfa, vegetables; camels, cattle; fish. **Labor force:** 850,000 (1997 est.); agriculture n.a., industry n.a., services n.a. **Industries:** crude oil production and refining, natural gas production, construction, cement, copper. **Natural resources:** petroleum, copper, asbestos, some marble, limestone, chromium, gypsum, natural gas. **Exports:** $11.1 billion (f.o.b., 2000 est.): petroleum, reexports, fish, metals, textiles. **Imports:** $4.5 billion (f.o.b., 2000 est.): machinery and transport equipment, manufactured goods, food, livestock, lubricants. **Major trading partners:** Japan, China, Thailand, UAE, South Korea, U.S., UK, Italy, Germany.

1. Excluding the Kuria Muria Islands.

**Geography** Oman is a 1,000-mile-long (1,700-km) coastal plain at the southeast tip of the Arabian peninsula lying on the Arabian Sea and the Gulf of Oman. The interior is a plateau. The country is the size of Kansas.

**Government** Absolute monarchy.

**History** Arabs migrated to Oman from the 9th century B.C. onward, and conversion to Islam occurred in the 7th century A.D. Muscat, the capital of the geographical area known as Oman, was occupied by the Portuguese from 1508 to 1648. Then it fell to Ottoman Turks, but in 1741 Ahmad ibn Sa'id forced them out. The descendants of Sultan Ahmad rule Oman today.

Ahmad expanded his empire to East Africa, and for a time the Omani capital was in Zanzibar. After 1861, however, Zanzibar fell from Omani control.

The sultans and imams of Oman clashed continuously throughout the 20th century until 1959, when the last Ibadi imam was evicted from the country. In a

palace coup on July 23, 1970, the sultan, Sa'id bin Taimur, who had ruled since 1932, was overthrown by his son, who promised to establish a modern government and use newfound oil wealth to aid the people of this very isolated state. Oman joined the Arab League and the United Nations in 1971.

A long border dispute with Yemen ended in late Oct. 1992 when the sultan signed an agreement with the Yemeni president. In 1997, Oman and Yemen signed maps defining the border between the two countries.

In 1997, Sultan Qabus granted women the right to be elected to the country's consultative body, the Shura Council (Majlis al-Shura). The council has no formal powers, but it advises the sultan on economic matters and public policy. Two women were elected to the council in 1997 as well as in 2000.

The British military used Oman as a training ground for more than 20,000 troops in 2001. It was the largest such exercise in Oman in 15 years.

# Pakistan

ISLAMIC REPUBLIC OF PAKISTAN

**President:** Gen. Pervez Musharraf (2001)
**Area:** 310,401 sq mi (803,940 sq km)[1]
**Population (2002 est.):** 147,663,429 (growth rate: 2.1%); birth rate: 30.4/1000; infant mortality rate: 78.5/1000; density per sq mi: 476
**Capital (1981 census):** Islamabad, 201,000. **Largest cities:** Karachi (2000 est.), 12,100,000 (metro. area); Lahore (2000 est.), 6,350,000 (metro. area); Faisalabad (Lyallpur), 1,920,000; Rawalpindi, 920,000; Hyderabad, 795,000. **Monetary unit:** Pakistan rupee.
**Principal languages:** Punjabi 48%, Sindhi 12%, Siraiki (a Punjabi variant) 10%, Pashtu 8%, Urdu (official) 8%, Balochi 3%, Hindko 2%, Brahui 1%, English, Burushaski, and others. **Ethnicity/race:** Punjabi, Sindhi, Pashtun (Pathan), Baloch, Muhajir (immigrants from India and their descendants).
**Religions:** Islam 97%, Hindu, Christian, Buddhist, Parsi. **Literacy rate:** 35% (1990)
**Economic summary GDP/PPP** (2000 est.): $282 billion; per capita $2,000. **Real growth rate:** 4.8%. **Inflation:** 5.2%. **Unemployment:** 6% (FY99/00 est.). **Arable land:** 27%. **Agriculture:** cotton, wheat, rice, sugarcane, fruits, vegetables; milk, beef, mutton, eggs. **Labor force:** 40 million; note: extensive export of labor, mostly to the Middle East, and use of child labor (2000 est.); agriculture 44%, industry 17%, services 39% (1999 est.). **Industries:** textiles, food processing, beverages, construction materials, clothing, paper products, shrimp. **Natural resources:** land, extensive natural gas reserves, limited petroleum, poor quality coal, iron ore, copper, salt, limestone. **Exports:** $8.6 billion (f.o.b., FY99/00): textiles (garments, cotton cloth, and yarn), rice, other agricultural products. **Imports:** $9.6 billion (f.o.b., FY99/00): machinery, petroleum, petroleum products, chemicals, transportation equipment, edible oils, grains, pulses, flour. **Major trading partners:** U.S., Hong Kong, UK, Germany, UAE, Saudi Arabia, Japan, Malaysia.

1. Excluding Kashmir and Jammu.

**Geography** Pakistan is situated in the western part of the Indian subcontinent, with Afghanistan and Iran on the west, India on the east, and the Arabian Sea on the south. The name *Pakistan* is derived from the Urdu words *Pak* (meaning pure) and *stan* (meaning country). It is nearly twice the size of California.

The northern and western highlands of Pakistan contain the towering Karakoram and Pamir mountain ranges, which include some of the world's highest peaks: K2 (28,250 ft [8,611 m]) and Nanga Parbat

(26,660 ft [8,126 m]). The Baluchistan Plateau lies to the west, and the Thar Desert and an expanse of alluvial plains, the Punjab and Sind, lie to the east. The 1,000-mile-long (1,609 km) Indus River and its tributaries flow through the country from the Kashmir region to the Arabian Sea.

**Government** Military rule was instituted Oct. 1999; a nominal democracy was declared in June 2001 by the ruling military leader, Pervez Musharraf.

**History** Pakistan was one of the two original successor states to British India, which was partitioned along religious lines in 1947. For almost 25 years following independence, it consisted of two separate regions, East and West Pakistan, but now is made up only of the western sector. Both India and Pakistan have laid claim to the Kashmir region, and this territorial dispute led to war in 1949, and again in 1965, 1971, and 1999, and remains unresolved today.

What is now Pakistan was in prehistoric times the Indus Valley civilization (c. 2500–1700 B.C.). A series of invaders—Aryans, Persians, Greeks, Arabs, Turks, and others—controlled the region for the next several thousand years. Islam, the dominant religion, was introduced in 711. In 1526, the land became part of the Mogul Empire, which ruled most of the Indian subcontinent from the 16th to the mid-18th century. By 1857, the British became the dominant power in the region. With Hindus holding most of the economic, social, and political advantages, the Muslim minority's dissatisfaction grew, leading to the formation of the nationalist Muslim League in 1906 by Mohammed Ali Jinnah (1876–1949). The league supported Britain in the Second World War while the Hindu nationalist leaders, Nehru and Gandhi, refused. In return for the league's support of Britain, Jinnah expected British backing for Muslim autonomy. Britain agreed to the formation of Pakistan as a separate dominion within the Commonwealth in Aug. 1947, a bitter disappointment to India's dream of a unified subcontinent. Jinnah became governor-general. The partition of Pakistan and India along religious lines resulted in the largest migration in human history, with 17 million people fleeing across the borders in both directions to escape the sectarian violence accompanying the partition.

Pakistan became a republic on March 23, 1956, with Maj. Gen. Iskander Mirza becoming the first president. Military rule prevailed for the next two decades. Tensions between East and West Pakistan existed from the outset. Separated by more than a thousand miles, the two regions shared few cultural and social traditions other than religion. To the growing resentment of East Pakistan, the West monopolized the country's political and economic power. In 1970, East Pakistan's Awami League, led by the Bengali leader Sheik Mujibur Rahman, secured a majority of the seats in the National Assembly. President Yahya Khan postponed the opening of the National Assembly to skirt East Pakistan's demand for greater autonomy, provoking civil war. The independent state of Bangladesh, or Bengali nation, was proclaimed on March 26, 1971. Indian troops entered the war in its last weeks fighting on the side of the new state. Pakistan was defeated on Dec. 16, 1971, and President Yahya Khan stepped down. Zulfikar Ali Bhutto took over Pakistan and accepted Bangladesh as an independent entity. In 1976, formal relations between India and Pakistan resumed.

Pakistan's first elections under civilian rule took place in March 1977, and the overwhelming victory of Bhutto's Pakistan People's Party (PPP) was denounced as fraudulent. A rising tide of violent protest and political deadlock led to a military takeover on July 5 by Gen. Mohammed Zia ul-Haq. Bhutto was tried and convicted for the 1974 murder of a political opponent, and despite worldwide protests was executed on April 4, 1979, touching off riots by his supporters. Zia declared himself president on Sept. 16, 1978, and ruled by martial law until Dec. 30, 1985, when a measure of representative government was restored. On Aug. 19, 1988, President Zia was killed in a midair explosion of a Pakistani Air Force plane. Elections at the end of 1988 brought longtime Zia opponent Benazir Bhutto, daughter of Zulfikar Bhutto, into office as prime minister.

In the 1990s, Pakistan saw a shaky succession of governments—Benazir Bhutto was prime minister twice and Nawaz Sharif three times, until he was deposed in a coup on Oct. 12, 1999, by Gen. Pervez Musharraf. The Pakistani public, familiar with military rule for 25 of the nation's 52-year history, generally viewed the coup as a positive step, and hoped it would bring a badly needed economic upswing.

Former prime minister Sharif was convicted in April 2000 of hijacking and terrorism and sentenced to two life terms in prison. The charges stemmed from the Oct. 1999 incident in which Sharif refused to allow a passenger plane, which was carrying 198 passengers, including Musharraf, to land in Karachi.

India went ahead with five nuclear tests in May 1998 near Pakistan's borders, which further deteriorated fragile relations between Pakistan and India. In an act of nuclear brinkmanship, Pakistan conducted its own nuclear tests in late May. Fighting with India again broke out in the disputed territory of Kashmir in May 1999.

Close ties with Afghanistan's Taliban government thrust Pakistan into a difficult position following the Sept. 11 terrorist attacks on the U.S. Under U.S. pressure, Pakistan broke with its neighbor to become the United States' chief ally in the region. In return, President Bush ended sanctions (instituted after Pakistan's testing of nuclear weapons in 1998), rescheduled its debt, and helped to bolster the legitimacy of Pervez Musharraf's rule—the general, who came to power in a military coup, had appointed himself president in 2001.

In Oct. 2001, violence again broke out in the Kashmir region when a suicide bombing by a Pakistan-based militant organization killed 38 in India-controlled Kashmir.

On Dec. 13, 2001, suicide bombers attacked the Indian parliament, killing 14 people, including 5 assailants. Indian officials blamed the attack on Islamic militants supported by Pakistan. Both sides assembled hundreds of thousands of troops along the Indian-Pakistani border, bringing the two nuclear powers to the brink of war.

Pakistan and India took small steps in June 2002 to thwart nuclear confrontation. Bowing to international pressure, Musharraf halted the infiltration of Muslim militants and weapons into India-controlled Kashmir. More than one million troops, however, remained stationed along the Line of Control, and any resolution in the conflict over the disputed territory remained elusive through the summer.

In April 2002, voters overwhelmingly approved a referendum to extend Musharraf's presidency for another five years. The vote, however, outraged opposing political parties and human rights groups that said the process was rigged to ensure a landslide victory for Musharraf. In Aug. 2002, Musharraf unveiled 29 constitutional amendments that strengthened his grip on the country.

# Palau

**REPUBLIC OF PALAU**

**President:** Tommy Remengesau (2001)
**Total area:** 177 sq mi (458 sq km)
**Population (2002 est.):** 19,409 (growth rate: 1.2%); birth rate: 19.3/1000; infant mortality rate: 16.2/1000; density per sq mi: 110
**Capital and largest city (1995):** Koror, 12,299.
**Monetary unit:** U.S. dollar used. **Languages:** Palauan, English (official). **Ethnicity/race:** Palauans are a composite of Polynesian, Malayan, and Melanesian races. **Religions:** Christian. About one-third of the islanders observe Modekngei religion, indigenous to Palau. **Literacy rate:** 86% (1980)
**Economic summary:** GDP/PPP (1998 est.): $129 million; note: GDP numbers reflect U.S. spending; per capita $7,100. **Real growth rate:** −1.4%. **Inflation:** n.a. **Unemployment:** 2.3% (2000 est.). **Arable land:** n.a. **Agriculture:** coconuts, copra, cassava (tapioca), sweet potatoes. **Labor force:** 8,300 (1999); agriculture n.a., industry n.a., services n.a. **Industries:** tourism, craft items (from shell, wood, pearls), construction, garment making. **Natural resources:** forests, minerals (especially gold), marine products, deep-seabed minerals. **Exports:** $14.3 million (f.o.b., 1996): trochus (type of shellfish), tuna, copra, handicrafts. **Imports:** $126 million (f.o.b., FY99/00): machinery and equipment, fuels, metals; foodstuffs. **Major trading partners:** U.S., Japan.

**Geography** The Palau island chain consists of about 200 islands located in the western Pacific Ocean 528 mi (650 km) southeast of the Philippines. Only eight of the islands are permanently inhabited.

**Government** Constitutional republic.

**History** The original settlers of Palau are believed to have arrived from Indonesia as early as 2500 B.C. The Palau islands' position on the western threshold of Oceania and their proximity to Southeast Asia have led to the population being a mixture of Malay, Melanesian, Filipino, and Polynesian ancestry.

Explored by the Spanish navigator Ruy López de Villalobos in 1543, the islands remained under nominal Spanish ownership for more than 300 years before Spain sold them to Germany in 1899. Japan occupied Palau during World War I and received a mandate over them from the League of Nations in 1920. They remained in Japanese control and served as an important naval base until the U.S. seized them during World War II. After the war they became a UN trusteeship (1947), administered by the United States. Palau signed a Compact of Free Association with the U.S. in 1992, requiring the United States to provide economic aid in exchange for the right to build and maintain U.S. military facilities in Palau. Palau became a sovereign state in 1994.

# Palestinian State (proposed)

**WEST BANK AND GAZA STRIP**

**President:** Yasir Arafat (1996)
**Area:** West Bank: 2,263 sq mi (5,860 sq km); Gaza Strip: 139 sq mi (360 sq km)
**Population (2002 est.):** West Bank: 2,163,667, Gaza Strip: 1,225,911 (growth rate: West Bank: 3.1%, Gaza Strip: 3.8%); birth rate: West Bank: 34.9/1000, Gaza Strip: 41.9/1000; infant mortality rate: West Bank: 21.2/1,000, Gaza Strip: 24.0/1000; density per sq mi: West Bank: 956, Gaza Strip: 8,820
**Capital:** Undetermined. **Largest cities (1996 est.):**

Hebron, 294,116; Nablus, 217,935. **Monetary units:** New Israeli shekels, Jordanian dinars, U.S. dollars. **Languages:** Arabic, Hebrew, English, French. **Ethnicity/race:** West Bank: Palestinian Arab and other 83%, Jewish 17%; Gaza Strip: Palestinian Arab and other 99.4%, Jewish 0.6%. **Religions:** West Bank: Muslim 75%, Jewish 17%, Christian and other 8%; Gaza Strip: Muslim 98.7%, Christian 0.7%, Jewish 0.6%
**Economic summary:** Gaza Strip: GDP/PPP (2000 est.): $1.11 billion; $1,000 per capita. **Real growth rate:** −7.5%. **Inflation:** 3% (includes West Bank). **Unemployment:** 40% (includes West Bank) (yearend 2000). **Arable land:** 24%. **Agriculture:** olives, citrus, vegetables; beef, dairy products. **Labor force:** n.a.; services 66%, industry 21%, agriculture 13% (1996). **Industries:** generally small family businesses that produce textiles, soap, olive-wood carvings, and mother-of-pearl souvenirs; the Israelis have established some small-scale modern industries in an industrial center. **Natural resources:** arable land. **Exports:** $682 million (f.o.b., 1998 est.) (includes West Bank): citrus, flowers. **Imports:** $2.5 billion (c.i.f., 1998 est.) (includes West Bank): food, consumer goods, construction materials. **Major trading partners:** Israel, Egypt, West Bank. **West Bank:** GDP/PPP (2000 est.): $3.1 billion; $1,500 per capita. **Real growth rate:** −7.5%. **Arable land:** 27%. **Agriculture:** olives, citrus, vegetables; beef, dairy products. **Labor force:** n.a.; agriculture 13%; industry 13%, commerce, restaurants, and hotels 12%, construction 8%, other services 54% (1996). **Natural resources:** arable land. **Major trading partners:** Israel, Jordan, Gaza Strip.

**Geography** The West Bank is mostly composed of limestone hills (conventionally called the Samarian Hills north of Jerusalem and the Judaean Hills south of Jerusalem) having an average height of 2,300 to 3,000 ft (700 to 900 m). The Gaza Strip is located between Israel and Egypt on the Mediterranean coast. It is a flat to rolling sand- and dune-covered coastal plain.

**Government** The Palestinian Authority (PA), with Arafat its elected leader, took control of the newly non-Israeli occupied areas, assuming all governmental duties in 1994. Permanent peace talks and implementation of Palestinian self-rule in the West Bank and Gaza Strip are ongoing.

**History** The history of the proposed modern Palestinian state, which is expected to be formed from the territories of the West Bank and Gaza Strip, began with the British Mandate of Palestine. From Sept. 29, 1923, until May 14, 1948, Britain controlled the region, but by 1947, Britain had appealed to the UN to solve the complex problem of competing Palestinian and Jewish claims to the land. In Aug. 1947, the UN proposed dividing Palestine into a Jewish state, an Arab state, and a small international zone. Arabs rejected the idea. As soon as Britain pulled out of Palestine in 1948, neighboring Arab nations invaded, intent on crushing the newly declared State of Israel. Israel emerged victorious, affirming its sovereignty. The remaining areas of Palestine were divided between Transjordan (now Jordan), which annexed the West Bank, and Egypt, which gained control of the Gaza Strip.

Through a series of political and social policies, Jordan sought to consolidate its control over the political future of Palestinians and to become their speaker. Jordan even extended citizenship to Palestinians in 1949—Palestinians constituted about two-thirds of the country's population. In the Gaza Strip, administered by Egypt from 1948–67, poverty and unemployment were high, and most of the Palestinians lived in refugee camps.

In the Arab-Israeli war of 1967, Israel, over a period of six days, defeated the military forces of Egypt, Syria, and Jordan, and annexed the territories of East Jerusalem, the Golan Heights, the West Bank, the Gaza Strip, and all of the Sinai peninsula. The Palestinian Liberation Organization (PLO), formed in 1964, was a terrorist organization bent on Israel's annihilation. Palestinian rioting, demonstrations, and terrorist acts against Israelis became chronic. In 1974, PLO leader Yasir Arafat addressed the UN General Assembly, the first stateless government to do so. Violence again escalated in 1987 during the *intifada* ("shaking off"), a new era in Palestinian mass mobilization. In 1988, Yasir Arafat publicly eschewed terrorism and officially recognized the state of Israel.

In 1993, highly secretive talks in Norway between the PLO and the Israeli government resulted in the Oslo Agreement. The accord stipulated a five-year plan in which Palestinians of the West Bank and the Gaza Strip would gradually become self-governing. On Sept. 13, 1993, Arafat and Israeli prime minister Yitzak Rabin signed the historic "Declaration of Principles." As part of the agreement, Israel pulled out of the Gaza Strip and Jericho in the West Bank in 1994.

The Palestinian Authority (PA), with Arafat as its elected leader, took control of the newly non-Israeli-occupied areas, assuming all governmental duties. The election in 1999 of Israeli prime minister Ehud Barak was viewed by moderate Palestinians as a positive step toward peace.

But despite intensive negotiations between Barak and Arafat in the summer and fall of 2000, the two leaders remained deadlocked over Israeli-occupied East Jerusalem, which Arafat insists must be the capital of the future Palestinian state. Arafat, however, allowed his Sept. 13 deadline for declaring a Palestinian state to pass in the interest of continued negotiations with Israel. At the end of Sept., however, the stalemate disintegrated into the worst violence between Israelis and Palestinians in years, provoked by Likud hardliner Ariel Sharon's visit to the compound called Temple Mount by Jews and Haram al Sharif by Muslims, a fiercely contested site that is sacred to both Jews and Muslims. The continuing violence, dubbed the Al Aksa intifada, fueled growing concerns about Israeli security, paving the way for the right-wing Sharon's stunning landslide victory over Barak in Feb. 2001, which outraged Palestinians and much of the Arab world.

Violence on both sides continued at an alarming rate throughout 2001 and escalated further in 2002. In late March 2002, Israeli troops invaded Palestinian-controlled territories in the West Bank in response to the growing number of suicide bombers. Israeli troops razed several major Palestinian cities and refugee camps, vowing to destroy the "terrorist infrastructure."

For five months in the first part of 2002, Israeli troops surrounded Yasir Arafat at the Palestinian Authority headquarters in Ramallah, and Prime Minister Sharon, blaming Arafat directly for inciting terror, called for his expulsion from the territories. Arafat, unable or unwilling to prevent the wave of suicide bombings, claimed he would welcome martyrdom at the hands of the Israelis.

Neither leader seemed willing to entertain a political solution. But Arafat outlined a series of reforms for the PA that included setting presidential and legislative elections for early 2003 and streamlining police and intelligence agencies. He made the announcement shortly after President Bush said that the U.S. will not recognize an independent Palestinian state until Arafat is replaced.

Throughout the summer, Palestinian suicide bombings (Hamas and the Al-Aksa Martyr Brigade claimed responsibility for the majority of them) and Israeli reprisals continued. Israeli troops killed two top Hamas leaders. Muhanad Taher, a Palestinian bomb maker, died in a June attack in Nablus, and Sheik Salah Shehada, the leader of the group's military wing, died in a missile attack on his Gaza home. Israel also imposed strict 24-hour curfews on West Bank towns, allowing residents only brief windows of time to shop and seek medical treatment. The move created a humanitarian crisis and coincided with the release of a U.S. Agency for International Development report that found that 30% of Palestinian children under age 5 suffer chronic malnutrition.

In August, the PA and Israel agreed on a tentative plan, "Gaza, Bethlehem first," in which Israeli troops would begin to withdraw from the areas if Palestinians made an effort to reign in militants. Hamas and Islamic Jihad, however, rejected the agreement from the get-go, and hopes quickly faded that the accord would move beyond the first phase.

By Sept. 2002, the second anniversary of the intifada, more than 1,500 Palestinians and 550 Israelis had been killed.

# Panama

### REPUBLIC OF PANAMA

**National name:** República de Panamá
**President:** Mireya Moscoso (1999)
**Area:** 30,193 sq mi (78,200 sq km)
**Population (2002 est.):** 2,882,329 (growth rate: 1.4%); birth rate: 18.6/1000; infant mortality rate: 19.6/1000; density per sq mi: 95
**Capital and largest city (1993 est.):** Panama City, 450,668. **Other large cities:** San Miguelito, 293,564; Colón, 137,825. **Monetary unit:** Balboa. **Languages:** Spanish (official); many bilingual in English. **Ethnicity/race:** mestizo (mixed Indian and European ancestry) 70%, West Indian 14%, white 10%, Indian 6%.
**Religions:** Roman Catholic over 93%, Protestant 6%.
**Literacy rate:** 89% (1990)
**Economic summary: GDP/PPP** (2000 est.): $16.6 billion; per capita $6,000. **Real growth rate:** 2.5%. **Inflation:** 1.8%. **Unemployment:** 13%. **Arable land:** 7%. **Agriculture:** bananas, rice, corn, coffee, sugarcane, vegetables; livestock; shrimp. **Labor force:** 1.1 million (2000 est.); note: shortage of skilled labor, but an oversupply of unskilled labor; agriculture 20.8%, industry 18%, services 61.2% (1995 est.). **Industries:** construction, petroleum refining, brewing, cement and other construction materials, sugar milling. **Natural resources:** copper, mahogany forests, shrimp, hydropower. **Exports:** $5.7 billion (f.o.b., 2000 est.): bananas, shrimp, sugar, coffee, clothing. **Imports:** $6.9 billion (f.o.b., 2000 est.): capital goods, crude oil, foodstuffs, consumer goods, chemicals. **Major trading partners:** U.S., Germany, Costa Rica, Benelux, Italy, Colon Free Zone, Japan, Ecuador, Mexico.

**Geography** The southernmost of the Central American nations, Panama is south of Costa Rica and north of Colombia. The Panama Canal bisects the isthmus at its narrowest and lowest point, allowing passage from the Caribbean Sea to the Pacific Ocean. Panama is slightly smaller than South Carolina. It is marked by a chain of mountains in the west, moderate hills in the interior, and a low range on the east coast. There are extensive forests in the fertile Caribbean area.

**Government** Constitutional democracy.

**History** Explored by Columbus in 1502 and by Balboa in 1513, Panama was the principal shipping point to and from South and Central America in colonial days. In 1821, when Central America revolted against Spain, Panama joined Colombia, which had already declared its independence. For the next 82 years, Panama attempted unsuccessfully to break away from Colombia. Between 1850 and 1900 Panama had 40 administrations, 50 riots, 5 attempted secessions, and 13 U.S. interventions. After a U.S. proposal for canal rights over the narrow isthmus was rejected by Colombia, Panama proclaimed its independence with U.S. backing in 1903.

For canal rights in perpetuity, the U.S. paid Panama $10 million and agreed to pay $250,000 each year, which was increased to $430,000 in 1933. It was increased again in 1955. In exchange, the U.S. got the Canal Zone—a 10-mile-wide strip across the isthmus—and considerable influence in Panama's affairs. On Sept. 7, 1977, President Omar Torrijos Herrera and President Jimmy Carter signed treaties giving Panama gradual control of the canal, phasing out U.S. military bases, and guaranteeing the canal's neutrality.

Nicolas Ardito Barletta, Panama's first directly elected president in 16 years, was inaugurated on Oct. 11, 1984, for a five-year term. He was a puppet of strongman Gen. Manuel Noriega, a former CIA operative and head of the secret police. Noriega replaced Barletta with vice president Eric Arturo Delvalle a year later. In 1988, Noriega was indicted in the U.S. for drug trafficking, but when Delvalle attempted to fire him, Noriega forced the National Assembly to replace Delvalle with Manuel Solis Palma. In Dec. 1989, the assembly named Noriega "maximum leader" and declared the U.S. and Panama to be in a state of war. In Dec. 1989, 24,000 U.S. troops seized control of Panama City in an attempt to capture Noriega after a U.S. soldier was killed in Panama. On Jan. 3, 1990, Noriega surrendered himself to U.S. custody and was transported to Miami, where he was later convicted of drug trafficking. Guillermo Endara, who probably would have won an election suppressed earlier by Noriega, was installed as president.

On Dec. 31, 1999, the U.S. formally handed over control of the Panama Canal to Panama. Meanwhile, Colombian rebels and paramilitary forces have made periodic incursions into Panamanian territory, raising security concerns. Panama has also faced increased drug and arms smuggling.

**Panama Canal.** In 1524, King Charles V of Spain ordered a survey of a waterway across the isthmus in consideration of building a canal. In 1878, the Colombian government gave a construction concession to the French Canal Company. The firm ended in bankruptcy nine years later, and the United States ultimately paid the French $40 million for their rights and assets. The U.S. project, built on territory controlled by the United States, began in 1904 and was completed in 1914.

# Papua New Guinea

**Sovereign:** Queen Elizabeth II (1952)
**Governor-General:** Sir Silas Atopare (1997)
**Prime Minister:** Sir Michael Somare (2002)
**Area:** 178,703 sq mi (462,840 sq km)
**Population (2002 est.):** 5,172,033 (growth rate: 2.4%); birth rate: 31.6/1000; infant mortality rate: 56.5/1000; density per sq mi: 29
**Capital and largest city (1994 est.):** Port Moresby, 250,000. **Monetary unit:** Kina. **Languages:** English,

Tok Pisin (a Melanesian Creole English), Hiri Motu, and 717 distinct native languages. **Ethnicity/race:** Papuan, Melanesian, Negrito, Micronesian, Polynesian. **Religions:** over half are Christian, remainder indigenous. **Literacy rate:** 50% (1990)
**Economic summary: GDP/PPP** (2000 est.): $12.2 billion; per capita $2,500. **Real growth rate:** 2.9%. **Inflation:** 17%. **Unemployment:** n.a. **Arable land:** 0.1%. **Agriculture:** coffee, cocoa, coconuts, palm kernels, tea, rubber, sweet potatoes, fruit, vegetables; poultry, pork. **Labor force:** 1.941 million; agriculture n.a., industry n.a., services n.a. **Industries:** copra crushing, palm oil processing, plywood production, wood chip production; mining of gold, silver, and copper; crude oil production; construction, tourism. **Natural resources:** gold, copper, silver, natural gas, timber, oil, fisheries. **Exports:** $2.1 billion (f.o.b., 2000 est.): oil, gold, copper ore, logs, palm oil, coffee, cocoa, crayfish, prawns. **Imports:** $1 billion (f.o.b., 2000 est.): machinery and transport equipment, manufactured goods, food, fuels, chemicals. **Major trading partners:** Australia, Japan, Germany, South Korea, Philippines, UK, Singapore, U.S., New Zealand, Malaysia. **Member of Commonwealth of Nations**

**Geography** Papua New Guinea occupies the eastern half of the island of New Guinea, just north of Australia, and many outlying islands. The Indonesian province of West Papua (Irian Jaya) is to the west. To the north and east are the islands of Manus, New Britain, New Ireland, and Bougainville, all part of Papua New Guinea. About one-tenth larger than California, its mountainous interior has only recently been explored. Two major rivers, the Sepik and the Fly, are navigable for shallow-draft vessels.

**Government** Constitutional monarchy with parliamentary democracy.

**History** The first inhabitants of the island New Guinea were Papuan, Melanesian, and Negrito tribes, who altogether spoke more than 700 distinct languages. The eastern half of New Guinea was first explored by Spanish and Portuguese explorers in the 16th century. In 1828, the Dutch formally took possession of the western half of the island (now the province of West Papua [Irian Jaya], Indonesia). In 1885, Germany formally annexed the northern coast and Britain took similar action in the south. In 1906, Britain transferred its rights to British New Guinea to a newly independent Australia, and the name of the territory was changed to the Territory of Papua. Australian troops invaded German New Guinea (called Kaiser-Wilhelmsland) in World War I and gained control of the territory under a League of Nations mandate. New Guinea and some of Papua were invaded by Japanese forces in 1942. After being liberated by the Australians in 1945, it became a United Nations trusteeship, administered by Australia. The territories were combined and called the Territory of Papua and New Guinea.

Australia granted limited home rule in 1951. Autonomy in internal affairs came nine years later, and in Sept. 1975, Papua New Guinea achieved complete independence from Britain.

A violent nine-year secessionist movement took place on the island of Bougainville. In 1989, guerrillas of the Bougainville Revolutionary Army (BRA) shut down the island's Australian-owned copper mine, a major source of revenue for the country. The rebels believed that Bougainville deserved a greater share of the earnings for its copper. In 1990, the BRA declared Bougainville's independence, whereupon the government blockaded the island until Jan. 1991, when a peace treaty was signed. In 1997, Papua New Guinea's government hired South African mercenary soldiers to fight on Bougainville in order to end the long-running crisis, but this action led to massive demonstrations and the mercenary contract was rescinded. In April 1998, a cease-fire was declared.

On July 17, 1998, an earthquake-triggered tsunami (tidal wave) off the northern coast of Papua New Guinea killed at least 1,500 people and left thousands more injured and homeless.

# Paraguay

### REPUBLIC OF PARAGUAY

**National name:** República del Paraguay
**President:** Luis Ángel González Macchi (1999)
**Area:** 157,046 sq mi (406,750 sq km)
**Population (2002 est.):** 5,884,491 (growth rate: 2.6%); birth rate: 30.5/1000; infant mortality rate: 28.8/1000; density per sq mi: 37
**Capital and largest city (1992):** Asunción, 502,426. **Other large cities (1992):** Ciudad del Este, 133,893; San Lorenzo, 133,311. **Monetary unit:** Guaraní.
**Languages:** Spanish (official), Guaraní. **Ethnicity/race:** mestizo (mixed Spanish and Indian) 95%, whites plus Amerindians 5%. **Religion:** Roman Catholic 90%. **Literacy rate:** 90% (1990)
**Economic summary: GDP/PPP** (2000 est.): $26.2 billion; per capita $4,750. **Real growth rate:** 1%. **Inflation:** 8%. **Unemployment:** 16%. **Arable land:** 6%. **Agriculture:** cotton, sugarcane, soybeans, corn, wheat, tobacco, cassava (yucca), fruits, vegetables; beef, pork, eggs, milk; timber. **Labor force:** 2 million; agriculture 45%. **Industries:** sugar, cement, textiles, beverages, wood products. **Natural resources:** hydropower, timber, iron ore, manganese, limestone. **Exports:** $3.5 billion (f.o.b., 2000 est.): electricity, soybeans, feed, cotton, meat, edible oils. **Imports:** $3.3 billion (f.o.b., 2000 est.): road vehicles, consumer goods, tobacco, petroleum products, electrical machinery. **Major trading partners:** Brazil, Argentina, EU, U.S., Uruguay, Hong Kong.

**Geography** California-size Paraguay is surrounded by Brazil, Bolivia, and Argentina in south-central South America. Eastern Paraguay, between the Paraná and Paraguay Rivers, is upland country with the thickest population settled on the grassy slope that inclines toward the Paraguay River. The greater part of the Chaco region to the west is covered with marshes, lagoons, dense forests, and jungles.

**Government** Constitutional republic.

**History** Indians speaking Guaraní—the most common language in Paraguay today, after Spanish—were the country's first inhabitants. In 1526 and again in 1529, Sebastian Cabot explored Paraguay when he sailed up the Paraná and Paraguay Rivers. From 1608 until their expulsion from the Spanish dominions in 1767, the Jesuits maintained an extensive establishment in the south and east of Paraguay. In 1811, Paraguay revolted against Spanish rule and became a nominal republic under two consuls.

Paraguay was governed by three dictators during the first 60 years of independence. The third, Francisco López, waged war against Uruguay, Brazil, and Argentina in 1865–70, a conflict in which half the male population was killed. A new constitution in 1870, designed to prevent dictatorships and internal strife, failed to do so, and not until 1912 did a period of comparative economic and political stability begin. The Chaco War (1932–35) with Bolivia won Paraguay more western territory.

After World War II, politics became particularly unstable. Alfredo Stroessner was dictator from 1954 until 1989, during which he was accused of the torture and murder of thousands of political opponents. Despite Paraguay's human rights record, the U.S. continuously supported Stroessner.

Stroessner was overthrown by army leader, Gen. Andres Rodriguez, in 1989. Rodriguez went on to win Paraguay's first multicandidate election in decades. Paraguay's new constitution went into effect in 1992. In 1993, Juan Carlos Wasmosy, a wealthy businessman and the candidate of the governing Colorado Party, won a five-year term in free elections. Raúl Cubas Grau was elected president in May 1998.

In 1999, Cubas was forced from office for his alleged involvement in the assassination of Vice President Luis María Argaña. The vice president had criticized Cubas for refusing to jail his mentor, Gen. Lino Oviedo, who had been convicted of leading a failed 1996 coup against Wasmosy.

The new president, Luis Ángel González Macchi, has undertaken a governmental overhaul, and for the first time since Stroessner was overthrown, political and economic power is no longer entirely within the hands of the corrupt and military-backed Colorado Party. The U.S. has accused the Colorado Party of smuggling, money laundering, trafficking Bolivian cocaine, and supporting international terrorist organizations.

In Aug. 2000, the opposition Liberal Party won its first major victory in more than 50 years with the election of Julio Cesar Franco as vice president. He narrowly defeated the son of the previous vice president, Argaña. Paraguay's government has sought to clean up the political system by bringing to trial political and military figures suspected of human rights violations, corruption, or other crimes.

The government briefly imposed a state of emergency in July 2002, after two people were killed and several were injured in street protests. Anti-government rioters demanded that President Macchi resign, blaming him for Paraguay's protracted recession. Macchi accused former general Lino Oviedo of organizing the protests from exile in Brazil.

In August, the IMF proposed $200 million in loans to bail out Paraguay.

# Peru

### REPUBLIC OF PERU

**National name:** República del Perú
**President:** Alejandro Toledo (2001)
**Prime Minister:** Luis Solari (2002)
**Area:** 496,223 sq mi (1,285,220 sq km)
**Population (2002 est.):** 27,949,639 (growth rate: 1.8%); birth rate: 23.4/1000; infant mortality rate: 38.2/1000; density per sq mi: 56
**Capital and largest city (2000 est.):** Lima, 7,450,000 (metro. area). **Other large cities:** Arequipa, 939,800; Callao, 648,000; Trujillo, 1,287,000; Chiclayo, 951,000. **Monetary unit:** Nuevo sol (1991). **Languages:** Spanish and Quéchua (both official), Aymara, and other native languages. **Ethnicity/race:** Indian 45%, mestizo (mixed Indian and European ancestry) 37%, white 15%, black, Japanese, Chinese, and other 3%. **Religion:** Roman Catholic. **Literacy rate:** 85% (1990)
**Economic summary: GDP/PPP** (2000 est.): $123 billion; per capita $4,550. **Real growth:** 3.6%. **Inflation:** 3.7%. **Unemployment:** 7.7%; extensive underemployment (1997). **Arable land:** 3%. **Agriculture:** coffee, cotton, sugarcane, rice, wheat, potatoes, plantains, coca; poultry, beef, dairy products, wool; fish. **Labor force:** 7.6 million (1996 est.); agriculture, mining and quarrying,

manufacturing, construction, transport, services.
**Industries:** mining of metals, petroleum, fishing, textiles, clothing, food processing, cement, auto assembly, steel, shipbuilding, metal fabrication. **Natural resources:** copper, silver, gold, petroleum, timber, fish, iron ore, coal, phosphate, potash, hydropower. **Exports:** $7 billion (f.o.b., 2000 est.): fish and fish products, copper, zinc, gold, crude petroleum and byproducts, lead, coffee, sugar, cotton. **Imports:** $7.4 billion (f.o.b., 2000 est.): machinery, transport equipment, foodstuffs, petroleum, iron and steel, chemicals, pharmaceuticals. **Major trading partners:** U.S., EU, Andean Community, Japan, Mercosur.

**Geography** Peru, in western South America, extends for nearly 1,500 mi (2,414 km) along the Pacific Ocean. Colombia and Ecuador are to the north, Brazil and Bolivia to the east, and Chile to the south. Five-sixths the size of Alaska, Peru is divided by the Andes Mountains into three sharply differentiated zones. To the west is the coastline, much of it arid, extending 50 to 100 mi (80 to 160 km) inland. The mountain area, with peaks over 20,000 ft (6,096 m), lofty plateaus, and deep valleys, lies centrally. Beyond the mountains to the east is the heavily forested slope leading to the Amazonian plains.

**Government** Constitutional republic.

**History** Peru was once part of the great Incan empire and later the major vice-royalty of Spanish South America. It was conquered in 1531–33 by Francisco Pizarro. On July 28, 1821, Peru proclaimed its independence, but the Spanish were not finally defeated until 1824. For a hundred years thereafter, revolutions were frequent; a new war was fought with Spain in 1864–66, and an unsuccessful war was fought with Chile from 1879 to 1883 (the War of the Pacific).

Peru emerged from 20 years of dictatorship in 1945 with the inauguration of President José Luis Bustamente y Rivero after the first free election in many decades. But he served for only three years and was succeeded in turn by Gen. Manual A. Odria, Manuel Prado y Ugarteche, and Fernando Belaúnde Terry. On Oct. 3, 1968, Belaúnde was overthrown by Gen. Juan Velasco Alvarado. Velasco nationalized the nation's second-biggest bank and turned two large newspapers over to Marxists in 1970, but he also allowed a new agreement with a copper-mining consortium of four American firms. In 1975, Velasco was replaced in a bloodless coup by his premier, Gen. Francisco Morales Bermudez, who promised to restore civilian government. In elections held on May 18, 1980, Belaúnde Terry, the last previous civilian president and the candidate of the conservative parties that have traditionally governed Peru, was elected president again.

Belaúnde Terry was the first elected president to turn over power to a constitutionally elected successor since 1945. Alberto Fujimori won the 1990 elections. Citing continuing terrorism, drug trafficking, and corruption, Fujimori dissolved Congress, suspended the constitution, and imposed censorship in April 1992. A new constitution was approved in 1993. In Jan. 1995, fighting flared along the disputed border with Ecuador, as it had in 1941 and 1981. In April, Fujimori was reelected, and his party (Change 90–New Majority) won a legislative majority.

In 1997, the disastrous effects of El Niño caused the failure of the fish harvest and a severe drought in Peru. In May 1999, Ecuador and Peru signed a treaty ending the nearly 60-year dispute over a stretch of Amazon jungle.

Fujimori was easily reelected in May 2000 to a third five-year term, after his opponent, Alejandro Toledo, withdrew from the contest, charging fraud. In Sept. 2000, after Fujimori's intelligence chief, Vladimiro Montesinos, was videotaped bribing a congressman, Fujimori called for new elections, declared he would step down, and announced he would dismantle the powerful National Intelligence Service, which has been accused of human rights violations. Two months later, he stunned his nation by resigning during a trip to Japan. Revelations that Fujimori secretly held Japanese citizenship—and could not be extradited to face corruption charges—enraged the populace.

In 2001, the centrist Alejandro Toledo was elected president with 53.1% of the vote, narrowly defeating former president Alan García. His rags-to-riches story and mixed Indian and Latino heritage made him popular among the poor. Inheriting a country wracked by economic troubles and corruption, Toledo did little, however, to restore confidence in the government. In June 2002, a popular revolt took place in the cities of Arequipa, Tacna, and other areas of southern Peru after the sale of two state-run electricity firms to a Belgian company Tractebel—Toledo had specifically promised during his campaign not to sell these firms. Opinion polls have revealed that more than 60% of Peruvians are adamantly opposed to privatization and foreign investment, which in the past has led to price increases, mass layoffs, corruption, and few discernible benefits for the populace. To quell the rioting, Toledo suspended the decision to privatize, apologized publicly, and reshuffled his government.

# The Philippines
### REPUBLIC OF THE PHILIPPINES

**National name:** Republika ng Pilipinas
**President:** Gloria Macapagal-Arroyo (2001)
**Area:** 115,830 sq mi (300,000 sq km)
**Population (2002 est.):** 84,525,639 (growth rate: 2.1%); birth rate: 26.9/1000; infant mortality rate: 27.9/1000; density per sq mi: 730
**Capital and largest city (2000 est.):** Manila, 13,450,000 (metro. area). **Other large cities:** Quezon City, 1,669,776 (part of Manila metro. area); Cebu, 610,415.
**Monetary unit:** Peso. **Languages:** Filipino (based on Tagalog) and English (both official); regional languages: Tagalog, Ilocano, Cebuano, others.
**Ethnicity/race:** Christian Malay 91.5%, Muslim Malay 4%, Chinese 1.5%, other 3%. **Religions:** Roman Catholic 84%, Protestant 10%, Islam 5%, Buddhist and other 3%. **Literacy rate:** 94% (1990)
**Economic summary: GDP/PPP** (2000 est.): $310 billion; per capita $3,800. **Real growth rate:** 3.6%. **Inflation:** 5%. **Unemployment:** 10% (2000). **Arable land:** 19%. **Agriculture:** rice, coconuts, corn, sugarcane, bananas, pineapples, mangoes; pork, eggs, beef; fish. **Labor force:** 48.1 million (2000 est.); agriculture 39.8%, government and social services 19.4%, services 17.7%, manufacturing 9.8%, construction 5.8%, other 7.5% (1998 est.). **Industries:** textiles, pharmaceuticals, chemicals, wood products, food processing, electronics assembly, petroleum refining, fishing. **Natural resources:** timber, petroleum, nickel, cobalt, silver, gold, salt, copper. **Exports:** $38 billion (f.o.b., 2000 est.): electronic equipment, machinery and transport equipment, garments, coconut products. **Imports:** $35 billion (f.o.b., 2000 est.): raw materials and intermediate goods, capital goods, consumer goods, fuels. **Major trading partners:** U.S., Japan, Netherlands, Singapore, UK, Hong Kong, South Korea, Taiwan.

**Geography** The Philippine Islands are an archipelago of over 7,000 islands lying about 500 mi (805 km) off the southeast coast of Asia. The overall land area is comparable to that of Arizona. Only about 7% of the islands are larger than one square mile, and only one-third have names. The largest are Luzon in the north (40,420 sq mi; 104,687 sq km), Mindanao in the south (36,537 sq mi; 94,631 sq km), and Samar (5,124 sq mi; 13,271 sq km). The islands are of volcanic origin, with the larger ones crossed by mountain ranges. The highest peak is Mount Apo (9,690 ft; 2,954 m) on Mindanao.

**Government** Republic.

**History** Ferdinand Magellan, the Portuguese navigator in the service of Spain, explored the Philippines in 1521. Twenty-one years later, a Spanish exploration party named the group of islands in honor of Prince Philip, who was later to become Philip II of Spain. Spain retained possession of the islands for the next 350 years.

The Philippines were ceded to the U.S. in 1899 by the Treaty of Paris after the Spanish-American War. Meanwhile, the Filipinos, led by Emilio Aguinaldo, had declared their independence. They initiated guerrilla warfare against U.S. troops that persisted until the capture of Aguinaldo in 1901. By 1902, peace was established except among the Islamic Moros on the southern island of Mindanao.

The first U.S. civilian governor-general was William Howard Taft (1901–04). The Jones Law (1916) provided for the establishment of a Philippine Legislature composed of an elective Senate and House of Representatives. The Tydings-McDuffie Act (1934) provided for a transitional period until 1946, at which time the Philippines would become completely independent. Under a constitution approved by the people of the Philippines in 1935, the Commonwealth of the Philippines came into being with Manuel Quezon y Molina as president.

On Dec. 8, 1941, the islands were invaded by Japanese troops. Following the fall of Gen. Douglas MacArthur's forces at Bataan and Corregidor, Quezon established a government-in-exile that he headed until his death in 1944. He was succeeded by Vice President Sergio Osmeña. U.S. forces under MacArthur reinvaded the Philippines in Oct. 1944 and, after the liberation of Manila in Feb. 1945, Osmeña reestablished the government.

The Philippines achieved full independence on July 4, 1946. Manual A. Roxas y Acuña was elected its first president, succeeded by Elpidio Quirino (1948–53), Ramón Magsaysay (1953–57). Carlos P. García (1957–61), Diosdado Macapagal (1961–65), and Ferdinand E. Marcos (1965–86).

Under Marcos, civil unrest broke out in opposition to the leader's despotic rule. Martial law was declared on Sept. 21, 1972, and Marcos proclaimed a new constitution that ensconced himself as president. Martial law was officially lifted on Jan. 17, 1981, but Marcos and his wife, Imelda, retained broad powers.

Despite warnings that his life would be endangered, opposition leader Benigno S. Aquino returned to the Philippines from self-exile on Aug. 21, 1983. He was shot to death as he was being escorted from his plane by military police at Manila International Airport. There was widespread suspicion that Marcos had ordered Aquino's assassination. The event became a watershed in modern Filipino political history, acting as a catalyst for opposition groups and the "People Power" movement, led by the late leader's widow, Corazon Aquino.

In an attempt to resecure American support, Marcos set presidential elections for Feb. 7, 1986. With the support of the Catholic Church, Corazon Aquino declared her candidacy. Marcos was declared the official winner, but independent observers reported widespread election fraud and vote-rigging. Anti-Marcos protests exploded in the capital Manila, Defense Minister Juan Enrile and Lt. Gen. Fidel Ramos defected to the opposition, and Marcos lost virtually all support; he was forced to flee into exile and entered the U.S. on Feb. 25, 1986.

The Aquino government survived coup attempts by Marcos supporters and other right-wing elements, including one in November by Enrile. Legislative elections on May 11, 1987, gave pro-Aquino candidates a large majority. Negotiations on renewal of leases for U.S. military bases threatened to sour relations between the two countries. Volcanic eruptions from Mount Pinatubo, however, severely damaged Clark Air Base, and in July 1991, the U.S. decided simply to abandon it.

In elections in May 1992, Gen. Fidel Ramos, who had the support of outgoing Aquino, won the presidency in a seven-way race. In September of that year, the U.S. Navy turned over the Subic Bay naval base to the Philippines, ending a long-standing U.S. military presence. Meanwhile, the separatist Moro National Liberation Front was fighting a protracted war for an Islamic homeland on Mindanao, the southernmost of the two main islands. In 1996, the group agreed to a government plan designed to grant it a greater degree of political autonomy. Frequent and violent clashes continued into mid-2001, however. The army also battled another rebel group, the Moro Islamic Liberation Front. In Aug. 2001, the Moro Islamic Liberation Front and the Moro National Liberation Front signed unity agreements with the Philippine government.

Even as the Philippines experienced a somewhat lower rate of growth than many of its Asian neighbors throughout the 1990s, it was spared the brunt of the region's financial crisis following a wave of currency devaluations sparked in July 1997.

In May 1998, 61-year-old former action film star Joseph Estrada was elected president of the Philippines. Within two years, however, the Philippine Senate began to impeach Estrada on corruption charges. Massive street demonstrations and the loss of political support eventually forced Estrada from office. Vice President Gloria Macapagal-Arroyo, daughter of former president Diosdado Macapagal, became president in Jan. 2001.

Abu Sayyaf, a small group of guerrillas that has been fighting since the 1970s for an independent Islamic state and reportedly has links to Osama bin Laden, gained international notoriety throughout 2000 and 2001 with its spree of kidnappings that has resulted in dozens of deaths. Hostages have included several Americans vacationing at beach resorts.

In late Jan. 2002, American troops arrived in the Philippines, where for six months they trained Filipino soldiers to eliminate Abu Sayyaf. The group's leader, Abu Sabaya, was killed in June during a clash with government troops. The Philippine military then began to focus on eliminating the New People's Army, a group of communist guerrillas that has targeted Philippine security forces since 1969 and opposes any U.S. presence in the Philippines.

# Poland

**REPUBLIC OF POLAND**

**National name:** Rzeczpospolita Polska
**President:** Aleksander Kwasniewski (1995)
**Premier:** Leszek Miller (2001)
**Area:** 120,728 sq mi (312,685 sq km)
**Population (2002 est.):** 38,625,478 (growth rate: 0.0%);
birth rate: 10.3/1000; infant mortality rate: 9.2/1000;
density per sq mi: 320
**Capital and largest city (1994 est.):** Warsaw,
1,642,700. **Other large cities:** Lodz, 833,700; Krakow,
745,100; Wroclaw, 642,300; Poznan, 582,800;
Gdansk, 463,100; Szczecin, 417,700. **Monetary unit:**
Zloty. **Language:** Polish. **Ethnicity/race:** Polish
97.6%, German 1.3%, Ukrainian 0.6%, Belorussian
0.5% (1990 est.). **Religions:** Roman Catholic 95%
(about 75% practicing), Russian Orthodox, Protestant,
and other 5%. **Literacy rate:** 98% (1978)
**Economic summary: GDP/PPP** (2000 est.): $327.5
billion; per capita $8,500. **Real growth rate:** 4.8%.
**Inflation:** 10.2%. **Unemployment:** 12% (1999).
**Arable land:** 47%. **Agriculture:** potatoes, fruits,
vegetables, wheat; poultry, eggs, pork. **Labor force:**
17.2 million (1999 est.); industry 22.1%, agriculture
27.5%, services 50.4% (1999). **Industries:** machine
building, iron and steel, coal mining, chemicals,
shipbuilding, food processing, glass, beverages,
textiles. **Natural resources:** coal, sulfur, copper,
natural gas, silver, lead, salt, arable land. **Exports:**
$28.4 billion (f.o.b., 2000): machinery and transport
equipment 30.2%, intermediate manufactured goods
25.5%, miscellaneous manufactured goods 20.9%,
food and live animals 8.5% (1999). **Imports:** $42.7
billion (f.o.b., 2000): machinery and transport
equipment 38.2%, intermediate manufactured goods
20.8%, chemicals 14.3%, miscellaneous manufactured
goods 9.5% (1999). **Major trading partners:**
Germany, Italy, Netherlands, France, UK, Czech
Republic, Russia.

**Geography** Poland, a country the size of New
Mexico, is in north-central Europe. Most of the coun-
try is a plain with no natural boundaries except the
Carpathian Mountains in the south and the Oder and
Neisse Rivers in the west. Other major rivers, which
are important to commerce, are the Vistula, Warta, and
Bug.

**Government** Democratic republic.

**History** Great (north) Poland was founded in 966 by
Mieszko I, who belonged to the Piast dynasty. The
tribes of southern Poland then united to form Little
Poland. In 1047, both Great Poland and Little Poland
united under the rule of Casimir I the Restorer. Poland
merged with Lithuania by royal marriage in 1386. The
Polish-Lithuanian state reached the peak of its power
between the 14th and 16th century, scoring military
successes against the (Germanic) Knights of the Teutonic Order, the Russians, and the Ottoman Turks.

Lack of a strong monarchy enabled Russia, Prussia,
and Austria to carry out a first partition of the country
in 1772, a second in 1792, and a third in 1795. For
more than a century thereafter, there was no Polish
state, just Austrian, Prussian, and Russian sectors, but
the Poles never ceased their efforts to regain their
independence. The Polish people revolted against Russian, Prussian, and Austrian dominance throughout the
19th century. Poland was formally reconstituted in
Nov. 1918, with Marshal Josef Pilsudski as chief of
state. In 1919, Ignace Paderewski, the famous pianist
and patriot, became the first premier. In 1926, Pilsudski seized complete power in a coup and ruled dicta-
torially until his death on May 12, 1935.

Despite a ten-year nonaggression pact signed in
1934, Hitler attacked Poland on Sept. 1, 1939. Soviet
troops invaded from the east on Sept. 17, and on Sept.
28, a German-Soviet agreement divided Poland
between the USSR and Germany. Wladyslaw Racz-
kiewicz formed a government-in-exile in France,
which moved to London after France's defeat in 1940.
All of Poland was occupied by Germany after the Nazi
attack on the USSR in June 1941. Nazi Germany's
occupation policy in Poland was designed to eradicate
Polish culture through mass executions and to exter-
minate the country's large Jewish minority.

The Polish government-in-exile was replaced with
the Communist-dominated Polish Committee of
National Liberation by the Soviet Union in 1944.
Moving to Lublin after that city's liberation, it pro-
claimed itself the Provisional Government of Poland.
Some former members of the Polish government in
London joined with the Lublin government to form
the Polish Government of National Unity, which Britain and the U.S. recognized. On Aug. 2, 1945, in
Berlin, President Harry S. Truman, Joseph Stalin, and
Prime Minister Clement Attlee of Britain established
a new de facto western frontier for Poland along the
Oder and Neisse Rivers. (The border was finally
agreed to by West Germany in a nonaggression pact
signed on Dec. 7, 1970.) On Aug. 16, 1945, the USSR
and Poland signed a treaty delimiting the Soviet-
Polish frontier. Under these agreements, Poland was
shifted westward. In the east, it lost 69,860 sq mi
(180,934 sq km); in the west, it gained (subject to
final peace-conference approval) 38,986 sq mi
(100,973 sq km).

A new constitution in 1952 made Poland a "people's democracy" of the Soviet type. In 1955, Poland
became a member of the Warsaw Treaty Organization,
and its foreign policy became identical to that of the
USSR. The government undertook persecution of the
Roman Catholic Church as a remaining source of
opposition. Wladyslaw Gomulka was elected leader of
the United Workers (Communist) Party in 1956. He
denounced the Stalinist terror, ousted many Stalinists,
and improved relations with the church. Most collective farms were dissolved, and the press became freer.
A strike that began in shipyards and spread to other
industries in Aug. 1980 produced a stunning victory
for workers when the economically hard-pressed government accepted for the first time in a Marxist state
the right of workers to organize in independent unions.

Led by Solidarity, a free union founded by an electrician, Lech Walesa, workers launched a drive for liberty and improved conditions. A national strike for a
five-day workweek in Jan. 1981 led to the dismissal of
Premier Pinkowski and the naming of the fourth premier in less than a year, Gen. Wojciech Jaruzelski.
Martial law was declared on Dec. 13, when Walesa
and other Solidarity leaders were arrested. It formally
ended in 1984 but the government retained emergency
powers. Increasing opposition to the government
because of the failing economy led to a new wave of
strikes in 1988. Unable to totally quell the dissent, the
government relegalized Solidarity and allowed it to
compete in elections.

Solidarity members won a stunning victory in 1989,
taking almost all the seats in the Senate and all of the
169 seats they were allowed to contest in the Sejm.
This gave them substantial influence in the new government. Tadeusz Mazowiecki was appointed prime
minister. Lech Walesa won the presidential election of
1990 with 74% of the vote. In 1991, the first fully free
parliamentary election since World War II resulted in
representation for 29 political parties. In the second

democratic parliamentary election of Sept. 1993, voters returned power to ex-Communists and their allies.

Solidarity's popularity and influence, however, began to wane. In 1995, Aleksander Kwasniewski, leader of the successor to the Communist Party, the Democratic Left, won the presidency over Walesa in a landslide.

In 1999, Poland became part of NATO, along with the Czech Republic and Hungary. Poland is expected to become the next country accepted into the European Union (EU), though membership is not anticipated before 2004.

In Sept. 2001 parliamentary elections, former Communists, reconstituted as the center-left Democratic Left Alliance, won 41% of the vote. The election seemed to mark the demise of Solidarity, which did not win a single seat.

Russian president Vladimir Putin visited Poland in Jan. 2002, becoming the first Russian head of state to do so since 1993. The meeting between Putin and President Kwasniewski marked a thawing in relations that have been cool since Poland joined NATO in 1999.

# Portugal

### REPUBLIC OF PORTUGAL

**National name:** República Portuguesa
**President:** Jorge Sampaio (1996)
**Prime Minister:** José Manuel Durão Barroso (2002)
**Area:** 35,672 sq mi (92,391 sq km)
**Population (2002 est.):** 10,084,245 (growth rate: 0.1%); birth rate: 11.5/1000; infant mortality rate: 5.8/1000; density per sq mi: 283
**Capital and largest city (1991):** Lisbon, 677,790. **Other large city (1991):** Oporto, 350,000. **Monetary units:** Euro (formerly escudo). **Language:** Portuguese. **Ethnicity/race:** Homogeneous Mediterranean stock in mainland, Azores, Madeira Islands; citizens of black African descent who immigrated to mainland during decolonization number less than 100,000. **Religions:** Roman Catholic 97%, 1% Protestant, 2% other. **Literacy rate:** 85% (1991)
**Economic summary: GDP/PPP** (2000 est.): $159 billion; per capita $15,800. **Real growth rate:** 2.7%. **Inflation:** 2.8%. **Unemployment:** 4.3%. **Arable land:** 26%. **Agriculture:** grain, potatoes, olives, grapes; sheep, cattle, goats, poultry, beef, dairy products. **Labor force:** 5 million (1999); services 60%, industry 30%, agriculture 10% (1999 est.). **Industries:** textiles and footwear; wood pulp, paper, and cork; metalworking; oil refining; chemicals; fish canning; wine; tourism. **Natural resources:** fish, forests (cork), tungsten, iron ore, uranium ore, marble, arable land, hydropower. **Exports:** $26.1 billion (f.o.b., 2000 est.): clothing and footwear, machinery, chemicals, cork and paper products, hides. **Imports:** $41 billion (f.o.b., 2000 est.): machinery and transport equipment, chemicals, petroleum, textiles, agricultural products. **Major trading partners:** EU, U.S., Japan.

**Geography** Portugal occupies the western part of the Iberian Peninsula and is slightly smaller than Indiana. The country is crossed by three large rivers that rise in Spain, flow into the Atlantic, and divide the country into three geographic areas. The Minho River, part of the northern boundary, cuts through a mountainous area that extends south to the vicinity of the Douro River. South of the Douro, the mountains slope to the plains around the Tejo River. The remaining division is the southern one of Alentejo. The Azores stretch over 340 mi (547 km) in the Atlantic, and consist of nine islands with a total area of 902 square mi (2,335 sq km). Madeira, consisting of two inhabited islands, Madeira and Porto Santo, and two groups of uninhabited islands, lies in the Atlantic about 535 mi (861 km) southwest of Lisbon.

**Government** Parliamentary democracy.

**History** An early Celtic tribe, the Lusitanians, are believed to have been the first inhabitants of Portugal. The Roman Empire conquered the region in about 140 B.C. Toward the end of the Roman Empire, the Visigoths had invaded the entire Iberian peninsula.

Portugal won its independence from Moorish Spain in 1143. King John I (1385–1433) unified his country at the expense of the Castilians and the Moors of Morocco. The expansion of Portugal was brilliantly coordinated by John's son, Prince Henry the Navigator. In 1488, Bartolomeu Dias reached the Cape of Good Hope, proving that Asia was accessible by sea. In 1498, Vasco da Gama reached the west coast of India. By the middle of the 16th century, the Portuguese Empire extended to West and East Africa, Brazil, Persia, Indochina, and Malaya.

In 1581, Philip II of Spain invaded Portugal and held it for 60 years, precipitating a catastrophic decline in Portuguese commerce. Courageous and shrewd explorers, the Portuguese proved to be inefficient and corrupt colonizers. By the time the Portuguese monarchy was restored in 1640, Dutch, English, and French competitors began to seize the lion's share of the world's colonies and commerce. Portugal retained Angola and Mozambique in Africa, and Brazil (until 1822).

The corrupt King Carlos, who ascended the throne in 1889, made Joao Franco the premier with dictatorial power in 1906. In 1908, Carlos and his heir were shot dead on the streets of Lisbon. The new king, Manoel II, was driven from the throne in the revolution of 1910, and Portugal became a French-style republic. Traditionally friendly to Britain, Portugal fought in World War I on the Allied side in Africa as well as on the Western Front. Weak postwar governments and a revolution in 1926 brought Antonio Oliveira Salazar to power. As minister of finance (1928–40) and premier (1932–68), Salazar ruled Portugal as a virtual dictator. He kept Portugal neutral in World War II but gave the Allies naval and air bases after 1943. Portugal joined NATO as a founding member in 1949 but did not gain admission to the United Nations until 1955.

Portugal's foreign and colonial policies met with increasing difficulty both at home and abroad beginning in the 1950s—the bloodiest and most protracted wars against colonialism in Africa were fought against the Portuguese. Portugal lost the tiny remnants of its Indian empire—Goa, Daman, and Diu—to Indian military occupation in 1961, the year an insurrection broke out in Angola. For the next 13 years, Salazar, who died in 1970, and his successor, Marcello Caetano, fought independence movements amid growing world criticism. Leftists in the armed forces, weary of a losing battle, launched a successful revolution on April 25, 1974. After the 1974 revolution, the new military junta gave up its territories, beginning with Portuguese Guinea in Sept. 1974, which became the Republic of Guinea-Bissau. The decolonization of the Cape Verde Islands and Mozambique was effected in July 1975. Angola achieved independence later that same year, thus ending a colonial involvement in that continent that had begun in 1415. Full-scale, internationalized civil war, however, followed Portugal's departure from Angola, and Indonesia forcibly annexed independent East Timor. Also in that year, the government nationalized banking, transport, heavy industries, and the media. Portugal continued to experience social, economic, and political upheavals for the next decade.

Portugal was admitted to the European Economic Community (now European Union) on Jan. 1, 1986, and on Feb. 16, Mario Soares became the country's first civilian president in 60 years. Aníbal Cavaço Silva, an advocate of free-market economics and the Social Democratic candidate, was elected as prime minister in 1985, signaling a more politically stable era. General elections in Oct. 1995 went to the Socialist Party, which fell just short of an absolute majority in the assembly. Lisbon mayor Jorge Sampaio, a Socialist, won the race for president in Jan. 1996. Portugal's Socialist government continued to take advantage of rosy economic conditions in 1997, and in 1999, it became a founding member of the European Economic and Monetary Union (EMU). After Portugal's former territory, East Timor, was plunged into violence when its people voted to separate from Indonesia in Aug. 1999, Portugal was in the forefront of urging the UN to send in an armed, international peacekeeping force to protect the East Timorese from pro-Indonesian militia groups.

Portugal gave up its last colony, Macao, on Dec. 20, 1999, turning the small Asian seaport over to China.

In Jan. 2001 presidential elections, incumbent Jorge Sampaio was reelected with 55.8% of the vote. Prime Minister Antonio Guterres resigned in Dec. 2001, after his Socialist Party suffered major losses in local elections. In March 2002, Social Democrats won 102 parliamentary seats in national elections. Center-right Social Democrat leader José Manuel Durão Barroso formed a coalition with the Popular Party, thus gaining a slight majority in Parliament, and became prime minister.

## Qatar

### STATE OF QATAR

**Emir:** Sheik Hamad bin Khalifa al-Thani (1995)
**Prime Minister:** Abdullah bin Khalifa al-Thani (1996)
**Area:** 4,416 sq mi (11,437 sq km)
**Population (2002 est.):** 793,341 (growth rate: 1.1%); birth rate: 15.8/1000; infant mortality rate: 20.7/1000; density per sq mi: 180
**Capital (1990 est.):** Doha, 300,000. **Monetary unit:** Qatari riyal. **Languages:** Arabic (official); English is also widely spoken. **Ethnicity/race:** Arab 40%, Pakistani 18%, Indian 18%, Iranian 10%, other 14%. **Religion:** Islam 95%. **Literacy rate:** 76% (1986)
**Economic summary: GDP/PPP** (2000 est.): $15.1 billion; per capita $20,300. **Real growth rate:** 4%. **Inflation:** 2.5%. **Unemployment:** n.a. **Arable land:** 1%. **Agriculture:** fruits, vegetables; poultry, dairy ⏐⏐⏐⏐⏐⏐, ⏐⏐⏐⏐, ⏐⏐⏐, ⏐⏐⏐⏐⏐ ⏐⏐⏐⏐⏐⏐⏐⏐ (⏐⏐⏐⏐ ⏐⏐⏐ )
**Industries:** crude oil production and refining, fertilizers, petrochemicals, steel reinforcing bars, cement. **Natural resources:** petroleum, natural gas, fish. **Exports:** $9.8 billion (f.o.b., 2000 est.): petroleum products 80%, fertilizers, steel. **Imports:** $3.8 billion (f.o.b., 2000 est.): machinery and transport equipment, food, chemicals. **Major trading partners:** Japan, Singapore, South Korea, U.S., UAE, UK, Italy.

**Geography** Qatar (pronounced KA-tar) occupies a small peninsula that extends into the Persian Gulf from the east side of the Arabian Peninsula. Saudi Arabia is to the west and the United Arab Emirates to the south. The country is mainly barren.

**Government** Traditional monarchy.

**History** Qatar was once controlled by the sheikhs of Bahrain, but in 1867, war broke out between the people and their absentee rulers. To keep the peace in the Gulf, the British installed Muhammad ibn Thani Al Thani, head of a leading Qatari family, as the region's ruler. In 1893, the Ottoman Turks made incursions into Qatar, but the emir successfully deflected them. In 1916, the emir agreed to allow Qatar to become a British protectorate.

Oil was discovered in the 1940s, bringing wealth to the country in the 1950s and 1960s. About 85% of Qatar's income from exports comes from oil. Its people have one of the highest per capita incomes in the world. In 1971, Qatar was to join the other emirates of the Trucial Coast to become part of the United Arab Emirates. But both Qatar and Bahrain decided against the merger and instead became independent nations.

Qatar permitted the international forces to use Qatar as a base during the 1991 Persian Gulf War. A border dispute erupted with Saudi Arabia that was settled in Dec. 1992. A territorial dispute with Bahrain over the Hawar Islands remains unresolved, however. In 1994, Qatar signed a defense pact with the U.S., becoming the third Gulf state to do so.

In June 1995, Crown Prince Hamad bin Khalifa al-Thani deposed his father, primarily because the king was out of step with the country's economic reforms. The emir was not stripped of his title, and much of the power was already in his son's hands. The new emir has lifted press censorship and instituted other liberal reforms, including the first democratic election in its history. Although the 1999 election—for the 29-member municipal council—was a minor election, it involved major political change: women were permitted to vote in the election as well as run for office.

Qatar is the home of Al Jazeera, the Arabic satellite television network that has broadcast exclusive video footage of and statements by Osama bin Laden. The independent station is immensely popular in the Middle East, but has been criticized by many Arab countries for running interviews with controversial and opposition figures.

## Romania

### REPUBLIC OF ROMANIA

**President:** Ion Iliescu (2000)
**Prime Minister:** Adrian Nastase (2000)
**Area:** 91,699 sq mi (237,500 sq km)
**Population (2002 est.):** 22,317,730 (growth rate: –0.2%); birth rate: 10.8/1000; infant mortality rate: 18.9/1000; density per sq mi: 243
**Capital and largest city (1992):** Bucharest, 2,351,000. **Largest cities (1992):** Constanta, 350,476; Iasi, 342,994; Timisoara, 334,278; Cluj-Napoca, 328,008; ⏐⏐⏐⏐⏐ ⏐⏐⏐,⏐⏐⏐ ⏐⏐⏐⏐⏐⏐, ⏐⏐⏐,⏐⏐⏐. **Monetary unit: Leu.** **Languages:** Romanian (official); Hungarian- and German-speaking minorities. **Ethnicity/race:** Romanian 89.1%, Hungarian 8.9%, German 0.4%, Ukrainian, Serb, Croat, Russian, Turk, and Gypsy 1.6%. **Religions:** Romanian Orthodox 70%, Roman Catholic 6% (of which 3% are Uniate), Protestant 6%, unaffiliated 18%. **Literacy rate:** 96% (1992)
**Economic summary: GDP/PPP** (2000 est.): $132.5 billion; per capita $5,900. **Real growth rate:** 2.2%. **Inflation:** 45.7%. **Unemployment:** 11.5% (1999). **Arable land:** 41%. **Agriculture:** wheat, corn, sugar beets, sunflower seed, potatoes, grapes; eggs, sheep. **Labor force:** 9.9 million (1999 est.); agriculture 40%, industry 25%, services 35% (1998). **Industries:** textiles and footwear, light machinery and auto assembly, mining, timber, construction materials, metallurgy, chemicals, food processing, petroleum

refining. **Natural resources:** petroleum (reserves declining), timber, natural gas, coal, iron ore, salt, arable land, hydropower. **Exports:** $11.2 billion (f.o.b., 2000 est.): textiles and footwear 26%, metals and metal products 15%, machinery and equipment 11%, minerals and fuels 6% (1999). **Imports:** $11.9 billion (f.o.b., 2000 est.): machinery and equipment 23%, fuels and minerals 12%, chemicals 9%, textile and products 19% (1999). **Major trading partners:** Italy, Germany, France, Turkey, U.S., Russia.

**Geography** Romania is in southeast Europe and is slightly smaller than Oregon. The Carpathian Mountains divide Romania's upper half from north to south and connect near the center of the country with the Transylvanian Alps, running east and west. North and west of these ranges lies the Transylvanian plateau, and to the south and east are the plains of Moldavia and Walachia. In its last 190 mi (306 km), the Danube River flows through Romania only. It enters the Black Sea in northern Dobruja, just south of the border with the Ukraine.

**Government** Republic.

**History** Most of Romania was the Roman province of Dacia from about A.D. 100 to 271. From the 3rd to the 12th century, wave after wave of barbarian conquerors overran the native Daco-Roman population. Subjection to the first Bulgarian empire (8th–10th century) brought Eastern Orthodox Christianity to the Romanians. In the 11th century, Transylvania was absorbed into the Hungarian empire. By the 16th century, the main Romanian principalities of Moldavia and Walachia had become satellites within the Ottoman Empire, although they retained much independence. After the Russo-Turkish War of 1828–29, they became Russian protectorates. The nation became a kingdom in 1881 after the Congress of Berlin.

At the start of World War I, Romania proclaimed its neutrality, but later joined the Allied side and in 1916 declared war on the Central Powers. The armistice of Nov. 11, 1918, gave Romania vast territories from Russia and the Austro-Hungarian Empire, doubling its size. The areas acquired included Bessarabia, Transylvania, and Bukovina. The Banat, a Hungarian area, was divided with Yugoslavia. King Carol II was crowned in 1930 and transformed the throne into a royal dictatorship. In 1938, he abolished the democratic constitution of 1923. In 1940, the country was reorganized along Fascist lines, and the Fascist Iron Guard became the nucleus of the new totalitarian party. On June 27, the Soviet Union occupied Bessarabia and northern Bukovina. King Carol II dissolved Parliament, granted the new premier, Ion Antonescu, full power, abdicated his throne, and went into exile.

Romania subsequently signed the Axis Pact on Nov. 23, 1940, and the following June joined in Germany's attack on the Soviet Union, reoccupying Bessarabia. About 270,000 Jews were massacred in Fascist Romania. Following the invasion of Romania by the Red Army in Aug. 1944, King Michael led a coup that ousted the Antonescu government. An armistice with the Soviet Union was signed in Moscow on Sept. 12, 1944. A Communist-dominated government bloc won elections in 1946, Michael abdicated on Dec. 30, 1947, and in 1955 Romania joined the Warsaw Treaty Organization and the United Nations.

Running a neo-Stalinist police state from 1967–89, Nicolae Ceausescu wound the iron curtain tightly around Romania, turning a moderately prosperous country into one at the brink of starvation. To repay his $10 billion foreign debt in 1982, he ransacked the Romanian economy of everything that could be exported, leaving the country with desperate shortages of food, fuel, and other essentials. An army-assisted rebellion in Dec. 1989 led to Ceausescu's overthrow, trial, and execution.

An ex-Communist, Ion Iliescu of the National Salvation Front, served as president from 1990–95. Emil Constantinescu of the Democratic Convention Party served as president from 1996–2000. The post-Communist governments' conflicted and half-hearted attempts to change to a free-market economy have been largely unrealized. In 2000 former president Iliescu returned to power with a landslide victory, easily defeating a xenophobic nationalist opponent. Discrimination against the Magyars (ethnic Hungarians), and the Roma (gypsies) continues, fueled by several ultra-nationalist political parties.

The country applied for membership in the EU in June 1995, but it is doubtful that Romania will be able to join the Union before at least 2007. Economic reform has proceeded at a glacial pace, and growing dissatisfaction with the government's inefficiencies and economic policies led to a wave of protests by workers, students, and others that peaked in 1997, and again in 1999, when coal miners striked.

# Russia

### RUSSIAN FEDERATION

**President:** Vladimir Putin (2000)
**Prime Minister:** Mikhail Kasyanov (2000)
**Area:** 6,592,735 sq mi (17,075,200 sq km)
**Population (2002 est.):** 144,978,573 (growth rate: –0.4%); birth rate: 9.7/1000; infant mortality rate: 19.8/1000; density per sq mi: 22
**Capital and largest city (2000 est.):** Moscow, 13,200,000 (metro. area). **Other large cities:** St. Petersburg (2000 est.), 5,550,000 (metro. area); Novosibirsk, 1,418,200; Samara, 1,222,500; Chelyabinsk, 1,124,500; Yekaterinburg, 1,347,000; Nizhny Novgorod, 1,424,600; Kazan, 1,092,300; Perm, 1,086,100; Ufa, 1,091,800; Volgograd, 1,000,400.
**Monetary unit:** Ruble. **Languages:** Russian, others.
**Ethnicity/race:** Russian 81.5%, Tatar 3.8%, Ukrainian 3%, Chuvash 1.2%, Bashkir 0.9%, Byelorussian 0.8%, Moldavian 0.7%, other 8.1%. **Religions:** Russian Orthodox, Muslim, others. **Literacy rate:** 98% (1989)
**Economic summary:** GDP/PPP (2000 est.): $1.12 trillion; per capita $7,700. **Real growth rate:** 6.3%. **Inflation:** 20.6%. **Unemployment:** 10.5%, plus considerable underemployment. **Arable land:** 8%. **Agriculture:** grain, sugar beets, sunflower seed, vegetables, fruits; beef, milk. **Labor force:** 66 million (1997); agriculture 15%, industry 30%, services 55% (1999 est.). **Industries:** complete range of mining and extractive industries producing coal, oil, gas, chemicals, and metals; all forms of machine building from rolling mills to high-performance aircraft and space vehicles; shipbuilding; road and rail transportation equipment; communications equipment; agricultural machinery, tractors, and construction equipment; electric power generating and transmitting equipment; medical and scientific instruments; consumer durables, textiles, foodstuffs, handicrafts. **Natural resources:** wide natural resource base including major deposits of oil, natural gas, coal, and many strategic minerals, timber. **Exports:** $105.1 billion (2000 est.): petroleum and petroleum products, natural gas, wood and wood products, metals, chemicals, and a wide variety of civilian and military manufactures. **Imports:** $44.2 billion (2000 est.): machinery and equipment, consumer goods, medicines, meat, grain, sugar, semifinished metal products. **Major trading partners:** U.S., Germany, Ukraine, Belarus, Italy, Netherlands, Kazakhstan.

**Geography** The Russian Federation is the largest republic of the Commonwealth of Independent States. It occupies an area about one and four-fifths of the size of the United States and occupies most of eastern Europe and north Asia. Russia stretches from the Baltic Sea in the west to the Pacific Ocean in the east and from the Arctic Ocean in the north to the Black Sea and the Caucasus, the Altai, and Sayan Mountains, and the Amur and Ussuri Rivers in the south. It is bordered by Norway and Finland in the northwest, Estonia, Latvia, Belarus, Poland, and Lithuania in the west, Georgia and Azerbaijan in the southwest, and Kazakhstan, Mongolia, China, and North Korea along the southern border. The federation is composed of 21 republics.

**Government** Constitutional federation.

**History** Tradition says the Viking Rurik came to Russia in 862 and founded the first Russian dynasty in Novgorod. The various tribes were united by the spread of Christianity in the 10th and 11th centuries; Vladimir "the Saint" was converted in 988. During the 11th century, the grand dukes of Kiev held such centralizing power as existed. In 1240, Kiev was destroyed by the Mongols, and the Russian territory was split into numerous smaller dukedoms. Early dukes of Moscow extended their dominion over other Russian cities through their office of tribute collector for the Mongols and because of Moscow's role as an administrative and trade center.

In the late 15th century, Duke Ivan III acquired Novgorod and Tver and threw off the Mongol yoke. Ivan IV, the Terrible (1533–84), first Muscovite czar, is considered to have founded the Russian state. He crushed the power of rival princes and boyars (great landowners), but Russia remained largely medieval until the reign of Peter the Great (1689–1725), grandson of the first Romanov czar, Michael (1613–45). Peter made extensive reforms aimed at westernization and, through his defeat of Charles XII of Sweden at the Battle of Poltava in 1709, he extended Russia's boundaries to the west. Catherine the Great (1762–96) continued Peter's westernization program and also expanded Russian territory, acquiring the Crimea, Ukraine, and part of Poland. During the reign of Alexander I (1801–25), Napoléon's attempt to subdue Russia was defeated (1812–13), and new territory was gained, including Finland (1809) and Bessarabia (1812). Alexander originated the Holy Alliance, which for a time crushed Europe's rising liberal movement.

Alexander II (1855–81) pushed Russia's borders to the Pacific and into central Asia. Serfdom was abolished in 1861, but heavy restrictions were imposed on the emancipated class. Revolutionary strikes, following Russia's defeat in the war with Japan, forced Nicholas II (1894–1917) to grant a representative national body (Duma), elected by narrowly limited suffrage. It met for the first time in 1906, little influencing Nicholas in his reactionary course.

World War I demonstrated czarist corruption and inefficiency, and only patriotism held the poorly equipped army together for a time. Disorders broke out in Petrograd (renamed Leningrad and now St. Petersburg) in March 1917, and defection of the Petrograd garrison launched the revolution. Nicholas II was forced to abdicate on March 15, 1917, and he and his family were killed by revolutionists on July 16, 1918. A provisional government under the successive premierships of Prince Lvov and a moderate, Alexander Kerensky, lost ground to the radical, or Bolshevik, wing of the Socialist Democratic Labor Party. On Nov. 7, 1917, the Bolshevik Revolution, engineered by N.

Lenin[1] and Leon Trotsky, overthrew the Kerensky government and authority was vested in a Council of People's Commissars, with Lenin as premier.

The humiliating Treaty of Brest-Litovsk (March 3, 1918) concluded the war with Germany, but civil war and foreign intervention delayed Communist control of all Russia until 1920. A brief war with Poland in 1920 resulted in Russian defeat.

**Emergence of the USSR** The Union of Soviet Socialist Republics was established as a federation on Dec. 30, 1922. The death of Lenin on Jan. 21, 1924, precipitated an intraparty struggle between Joseph Stalin, general secretary of the party, and Trotsky, who favored swifter socialization at home and fomentation of revolution abroad. Trotsky was dismissed as commissar of war in 1925 and banished from the Soviet Union in 1929. He was murdered in Mexico City on Aug. 21, 1940, by a political agent. Stalin further consolidated his power by a series of purges in the late 1930s, liquidating prominent party leaders and military officers. Stalin assumed the premiership on May 6, 1941.

Soviet foreign policy, at first friendly toward Germany and antagonistic toward Britain and France and then, after Hitler's rise to power in 1933, becoming anti-Fascist and pro–League of Nations, took an abrupt turn on Aug. 24, 1939, with the signing of a nonaggression pact with Nazi Germany. The next month, Moscow joined in the German attack on Poland, seizing territory later incorporated into the Ukrainian and Belorussian SSRs. The Russo-Finnish War (1939–40) added territory to the Karelian SSR set up on March 31, 1940; the annexation of Bessarabia and Bukovina from Romania became part of the new Moldavian SSR on Aug. 2, 1940; and the annexation of the Baltic republics of Estonia, Latvia, and Lithuania in June 1940 created the 14th, 15th, and 16th Soviet republics. The illegal annexation of the Baltic republics was never acknowledged by the U.S. for the 51 years leading up to Soviet recognition of Estonia, Latvia, and Lithuania's independence on Sept. 6, 1991. The Soviet-German collaboration ended abruptly with a lightning attack by Hitler on June 22, 1941, which seized 500,000 sq mi of Russian territory before Soviet defenses, aided by U.S. and British arms, could halt it. The Soviet resurgence at Stalingrad from Nov. 1942 to Feb. 1943 marked the turning point in a long battle, ending in the final offensive of Jan. 1945. Then, after denouncing a 1941 nonaggression pact with Japan in April 1945, when Allied forces were nearing victory in the Pacific, the Soviet Union declared war on Japan on Aug. 8, 1945, and quickly occupied Manchuria, Karafuto, and the Kuril Islands.

The USSR built a cordon of Communist states running from Poland in the north to Albania and Bulgaria in the south, including East Germany, Czechoslovakia, Hungary, and Romania, which composed the territories the Soviet troops occupied at the war's end. With its eastern front solidified, the Soviet Union launched a political offensive against the non-Communist West, moving first to block the Western access to Berlin. The Western powers countered with an airlift, completed unification of West Germany, and organized the defense of western Europe in the North Atlantic Treaty Organization (NATO). Stalin died on March 6, 1953, and was succeeded the next day by G. M. Malenkov as premier.

---

1. N. Lenin was the pseudonym taken by Vladimir Ilich Ulyanov. It is sometimes given as Nikolai Lenin or V. Lenin.

## Rulers of Russia Since 1533

| Name | Born | Ruled[1] | Name | Born | Ruled[1] |
|---|---|---|---|---|---|
| Ivan IV the Terrible | 1530 | 1533–1584 | Alexander II | 1818 | 1855–1881 |
| Theodore I | 1557 | 1584–1598 | Alexander III | 1845 | 1881–1894 |
| Boris Godunov | c.1551 | 1598–1605 | Nicholas II | 1868 | 1894–1917[7] |
| Theodore II | 1589 | 1605–1605 | **PROVISIONAL GOVERNMENT (PREMIERS)** | | |
| Demetrius I[2] | ? | 1605–1606 | Prince Georgi Lvov | 1861 | 1917–1917 |
| Basil IV Shuiski | ? | 1606–1610[3] | Alexander Kerensky | 1881 | 1917–1917 |
| "Time of Troubles" | — | 1610–1613 | **POLITICAL LEADERS OF USSR** | | |
| Michael Romanov | 1596 | 1613–1645 | Vladimir Ilyich Lenin | 1870 | 1917–1924 |
| Alexis I | 1629 | 1645–1676 | Aleksei Rykov | 1881 | 1924–1930 |
| Theodore III | 1656 | 1676–1682 | Vyacheslav Molotov | 1890 | 1930–1941 |
| Ivan V[4] | 1666 | 1682–1689[5] | Joseph Stalin[8] | 1879 | 1941–1953 |
| Peter I the Great[4] | 1672 | 1682–1725 | Georgi M. Malenkov | 1902 | 1953–1955 |
| Catherine I | c.1684 | 1725–1727 | Nikolai A. Bulganin | 1895 | 1955–1958 |
| Peter II | 1715 | 1727–1730 | Nikita S. Khrushchev | 1894 | 1958–1964 |
| Anna | 1693 | 1730–1740 | Leonid I. Brezhnev | 1906 | 1964–1982 |
| Ivan VI | 1740 | 1740–1741[6] | Yuri V. Andropov | 1914 | 1982–1984 |
| Elizabeth | 1709 | 1741–1762 | Konstantin U. Chernenko | 1912 | 1984–1985 |
| Peter III | 1728 | 1762–1762 | Mikhail S. Gorbachev | 1931 | 1985–1991 |
| Catherine II the Great | 1729 | 1762–1796 | **PRESIDENT OF RUSSIA** | | |
| Paul I | 1754 | 1796–1801 | Boris Yeltsin | 1931 | 1991–1999 |
| Alexander I | 1777 | 1801–1825 | Vladimir Putin | 1952 | 2000– |
| Nicholas I | 1796 | 1825–1855 | | | |

1. For czars through Nicholas II, year of end of rule is also that of death, unless otherwise indicated. 2. Also known as Pseudo-Demetrius. 3. Died 1612. 4. Ruled jointly until 1689, when Ivan was deposed. 5. Died 1696. 6. Died 1764. 7. Killed 1918. 8. General secretary of Communist Party, 1924–53.

The new power in the Kremlin was Nikita S. Khrushchev, first secretary of the party. Khrushchev formalized the eastern European system into a Council for Mutual Economic Assistance (Comecon) and a Warsaw Pact Treaty Organization as a counterweight to NATO. The Soviet Union exploded a hydrogen bomb in 1953, developed an intercontinental ballistic missile by 1957, sent the first satellite into space (Sputnik I) in 1957, and put Yuri Gagarin in the first orbital flight around Earth in 1961. Khrushchev's downfall stemmed from his decision to place Soviet nuclear missiles in Cuba and then, when challenged by the U.S., backing down and removing the weapons. He was also blamed for the ideological break with China after 1963. Khrushchev was forced into retirement on Oct. 15, 1964, and was replaced by Leonid I. Brezhnev as first secretary of the party and Aleksei N. Kosygin as premier.

U.S. president Jimmy Carter and Brezhnev signed the SALT II treaty in Vienna on June 18, 1979, setting ceilings on each nation's arsenal of intercontinental ballistic missiles. The U.S. Senate refused to ratify the treaty because of the invasion of Afghanistan by Soviet troops on Dec. 27, 1979. On Nov. 10, 1982, Soviet radio and television announced the death of Leonid Brezhnev. Yuri V. Andropov, who had formerly headed the KGB, became his successor, but died less than two years later, in Feb. 1984. Konstantin U. Chernenko, a 72-year-old party stalwart who had been close to Brezhnev, succeeded him.

In the months following Chernenko's assumption of power, the Kremlin took on a hostile attitude toward the West of a kind rarely seen since the height of the cold war 30 years before. Led by Moscow, all the Soviet bloc countries except Romania boycotted the 1984 Summer Olympic Games in Los Angeles—tit-for-tat for the U.S.-led boycott of the 1980 Moscow Games, in the view of most observers. After 13 months in office, Chernenko died on March 10, 1985. He had been ill much of the time and left only a minor imprint on Soviet history. Chosen to succeed him as Soviet leader was Mikhail S. Gorbachev, who led the Soviet

Union in its long-awaited shift to a new generation of leadership. Unlike his immediate predecessors, Gorbachev did not also assume the title of president but wielded power from the post of party general secretary.

The Soviet Union took much criticism in early 1986 over the April 24 meltdown at the Chernobyl nuclear plant and its reluctance to give out any information on the accident.

In June 1987, Gorbachev obtained the support of the Central Committee for proposals that would loosen some government controls over the economy and in June 1988, an unusually open party conference approved several resolutions reforming the Soviet system. These included a shift of some power from the party to local soviets, and a ten-year limit on the terms of elected government and party officials. Gorbachev was elected president in 1989. The elections to the Duma were the first competitive elections in the Soviet Union since 1917. Dissident candidates won a surprisingly large minority although pro-government deputies maintained a strong lock on the Supreme Soviet.

**Dissolution of the USSR** The possible beginning of the fragmentation of the Communist Party took place when Boris Yeltsin, leader of the Russian SSR who urged faster reform, left the Communist Party along with other radicals. In March 1991, the Soviet people were asked to vote in a referendum on national unity engineered by Gorbachev. The resultant victory for the federal government was tempered by the separate approval in Russia for the creation of a popularly elected presidency of the Russian republics. The bitter election contest for the Russian presidency, principally between Yeltsin and a Communist loyalist, resulted in a major victory for Yeltsin. He took the oath of office for the new position on July 10, 1991.

Reversing his relative hard-line position, Gorbachev together with leaders of nine Soviet republics signed an accord called the Union Treaty, which was meant to preserve the unity of the nation. In exchange the federal government would have turned over control of industrial and natural resources to the individual republics. An attempted coup d'état took place on Aug. 19, 1991, orchestrated by a group of eight senior officials calling itself the State Committee on the State of Emergency. Boris Yeltsin, barricaded in the Russian Parliament building, defiantly called for a general strike. The next day huge crowds demonstrated in Leningrad, and Yeltsin supporters fortified barricades surrounding the Parliament building. On Aug. 21 the coup committee disbanded, and at least some of its members attempted to flee Moscow. The Soviet Parliament formally reinstated Gorbachev as president. Two days later he resigned from his position as general-secretary of the Communist Party and recommended that its Central Committee be disbanded. On Aug. 29 the Parliament approved the suspension of all Communist Party activities pending an investigation of its role in the failed coup. At the time of the attempted coup, the republic's president, Boris Yeltsin, was the most popular political figure in the former Soviet Union. A leading reformer, he became the first directly elected leader in Russian history and received 60% of the vote for president of the Russian Republic.

Yeltsin championed the cause for national reconstruction and the adoption of a Union Treaty with the other republics to create a free-market economic association. On Dec. 12, 1991, the Russian Parliament ratified Yeltsin's plea to establish a new commonwealth of independent nations open to all former members of the Soviet Union. The new union was created with the governments of Ukraine and Belarus who along with Russia were the three original cofounders of the Soviet Union in 1922. After the end of the Soviet Union, Russia and ten other Soviet republics joined in a Commonwealth of Independent States on Dec. 21, 1991.

At the start of 1992, Russia embarked on a series of dramatic economic reforms, including the freeing of prices on most goods, which led to an immediate downturn. A national referendum on confidence in Yeltsin and his economic program took place in April 1993. To the surprise of many, the president and his shock-therapy program won by a resounding margin. In September, Yeltsin dissolved the legislative bodies left over from the Soviet era. The impasse between the executive and the legislature resulted in an armed conflict on Oct. 3. Yeltsin prevailed largely through the support of the military and other forces.

The southern republic of Chechnya's president accelerated his region's drive for independence in 1994. In December, Russian troops closed the borders and sought to squelch the independence drive. The Russian military forces met firm and costly resistance. In May 1997, the two-year war formally ended with the signing of a peace treaty that adroitly avoided the issue of Chechen independence.

In March 1998 Yeltsin dismissed his entire government and replaced Prime Minister Viktor Chernomyrdin with the young and little known fuel and energy minister Sergei Kiriyenko. On Aug. 28, 1998, amid the Russian stock market's free fall, the Russian government halted trading of the ruble on international currency markets. This financial crisis led to a long-term economic downturn and to political upheaval. President Boris Yeltsin then sacked Prime Minister Kiriyenko and reappointed Chernomyrdin. The Duma rejected Chernomyrdin and on Sept. 11 elected foreign minister Yevgeny Primakov as prime minister. The repercussions of Russia's financial emergency were felt throughout the Commonwealth of Independent States.

Impatient with Yeltsin's chronic illnesses and increasingly erratic behavior, the Duma attempted to impeach him in May 1999 on five charges: provoking the 1991 fall of the Soviet Union, using force to dissolve the Parliament in 1993, starting the ill-conceived 1994–96 war in Chechnya, ruining the nation's military, and impoverishing the Russian people through ruinous economic policies—the charge regarding Chechnya was considered the only one with a chance of approval. But the impeachment motion was quickly quashed and soon Yeltsin was on the ascendancy again. In keeping with his capricious style, Yeltsin dismissed Prime Minister Yevgeny Primakov and replaced him with Interior Minister Sergei Stepashin. Just three months later, however, Yeltsin ousted Stepashin and replaced him with Vladimir Putin on Aug. 9, 1999, announcing that in addition to serving as prime minister, the former KGB agent was his choice as a successor in the 2000 presidential election.

In a decision that took Russia and the world by surprise, Boris Yeltsin resigned on Dec. 31, 1999, and Vladimir Putin became the acting president. One of Putin's first acts was to grant Yeltsin immunity from prosecution (Yeltsin and family members had been accused of corruption and financial misconduct). On March 26, 2000, Putin won the presidential election with about 53% of the vote. Since then Putin has moved to centralize power in Moscow and has attempted to limit the power and influence of both the regional governors and wealthy business leaders. Although Russia remains economically stagnant, Putin has brought his nation a measure of political stability it never had under the mercurial and erratic Yeltsin.

Just three years after the bloody 1994–96 Chechen-Russian war ended in devastation and stalemate, the fighting started again in 1999, with Russia launching air strikes and following up with ground troops. By the end of November, Russian troops had surrounded Chechnya's capital, Grozny, and about 215,000 Chechen refugees had fled to neighboring Ingushetia. Russia maintained that a political solution was impossible until Islamic militants in Chechnya had been vanquished. In Feb. 2000, after almost five months of fighting, Russian troops captured Grozny, the Chechen capital. The control of Grozny was a political as well as a military victory for Putin, whose hard-line stance against Chechnya has greatly contributed to his political popularity. Despite repeated Russian claims of victory, the war continued to drag on in 2002.

In 1999, the former Russian satellites of Poland, Hungary, and the Czech Republic joined NATO, raising Russia's hackles. The desire of Lithuania, Latvia, and Estonia, all of which were once part of the Soviet Union, to join the organization in the future has further alarmed Russia.

In Aug. 2000 the Russian government was severely criticized for its handling of the Kursk disaster, a nuclear submarine accident that left 118 sailors dead.

Russia was initially alarmed in 2001 when the U.S. announced its rejection of the Anti-Ballistic Missile Treaty of 1972, which for 30 years had been viewed as a crucial force in keeping the nuclear arms race at bay. But Putin was eventually placated by Bush's reassurances, and in May 2002, the U.S. and Russian leaders announced a landmark pact to cut both countries' nuclear arsenals by up to two-thirds over the next ten years.

# Rwanda

**RWANDESE REPUBLIC**

**National name:** Repubulika y'u Rwanda
**President:** Paul Kagame (2000)
**Prime Minister:** Bernard Makuza (2000)
**Area:** 10,169 sq mi (26,338 sq km)
**Population (2002 est.):** 7,398,074 (growth rate: 1.2%);
birth rate: 33.3/1000; infant mortality rate: 117.8/1000;
density per sq mi: 728
**Capital and largest city (1991):** Kigali, 232,733.
**Monetary unit:** Rwanda franc. **Languages:**
Kinyarwanda, French, and English (all official).
**Ethnicity/race:** Hutu 80%, Tutsi 19%, Twa (Pygmoid)
1%. **Religions:** Roman Catholic 56%, Protestant 18%,
Islam 1%, Animist 25%. **Literacy rate:** 50% (1990)
**Economic summary: GDP/PPP** (2000 est.): $6.4 billion;
per capita $900. **Real growth rate:** 5.8%. **Inflation:**
4% (2000). **Unemployment:** n.a. **Arable land:** 35%.
**Agriculture:** coffee, tea, pyrethrum (insecticide made
from chrysanthemums), bananas, beans, sorghum,
potatoes; livestock. **Labor force:** 3.6 million;
agriculture 90%. **Industries:** cement, agricultural
products, small-scale beverages, soap, furniture,
shoes, plastic goods, textiles, cigarettes. **Natural
resources:** gold, cassiterite (tin ore), wolframite
(tungsten ore), methane, hydropower, arable land.
**Exports:** $68.4 million (f.o.b., 2000 est.): coffee, tea,
hides, tin ore. **Imports:** $245.9 million (f.o.b., 2000
est.): foodstuffs, machinery and equipment, steel,
petroleum products, cement and construction material.
**Major trading partners:** Germany, Belgium, Pakistan,
Italy, Kenya, Tanzania, U.S., Benelux, France, India.

**Geography** Rwanda, in east-central Africa, is surrounded by Congo, Uganda, Tanzania, and Burundi. It
is slightly smaller than Maryland. Steep mountains
and deep valleys cover most of the country. Lake Kivu
in the northwest, at an altitude of 4,829 ft (1,472 m) is
the highest lake in Africa. Extending north of it are the
Virunga Mountains, which include the volcano
Karisimbi (14,187 ft; 4,324 m), Rwanda's highest
point.

**Government** Republic.

**History** The original inhabitants of Rwanda were the
Twa, a Pygmy people who now make up only 1% of
the population. While the Hutu and Tutsi are often
considered to be two separate ethnic groups, scholars
point out that they speak the same language, have a
history of intermarriage, and share many cultural characteristics. Traditionally, the differences between the
two groups were occupational rather than ethnic. Agricultural people were considered Hutu, while the cattle-
owning elite were identified as Tutsi. Supposedly Tutsi
were tall and thin, while Hutu were short and square,
but it is often impossible to tell one from the other.
The 1933 requirement by the Belgians that everyone
carry an identity card indicating tribal ethnicity as
Tutsi or Hutu increased the distinction. Since independence, repeated violence in both Rwanda and Burundi
has increased ethnic differentiation between the
groups.

Rwanda, which became a part of German East
Africa in 1890, was first visited by European explor-
ers in 1854. During World War I, it was occupied in
1916 by Belgian troops. After the war, it became a
Belgian League of Nations mandate, along with
Burundi, under the name of Ruanda-Urundi. The man-
date was made a UN trust territory in 1946. Until the
Belgian Congo achieved independence in 1960,
Ruanda-Urundi was administered as part of that
colony. Belgium at first maintained Tutsi dominance

but eventually encouraged power sharing between
Hutu and Tutsi. Ethnic tensions led to civil war, forcing many Tutsi into exile. When Ruanda became the
independent nation of Rwanda on July 1, 1962, it was
under Hutu rule.

In Oct. 1990, the Rwandan Patriotic Front (RPF),
Tutsi rebels in exile in Uganda, invaded in an attempt
to overthrow the Hutu-led Rwandan government.
Peace accords were signed in Aug. 1993, calling for a
coalition government. But after the downing of a plane
in April 1994 that killed the presidents of both
Rwanda and Burundi, deep-seated ethnic violence
erupted. (It is now believed that the plane was shot
down by Hutu extremists who rejected the Hutu-Tutsi
power-sharing plan proposed by President Juvénal
Habyarimana, a Hutu moderate.)

The presidential guard began murdering Tutsi opposition leaders, and soon policeman and soldiers began
attempting to murder the entire Tutsi population. In
100 days, beginning in April 1994, Hutus rampaged
through the country, slaughtered an estimated 800,000
Tutsi and Hutu sympathizers. A 30,000-member militia group, the Interahamwe, led much of the murderous spree, but, goaded by radio propaganda, ordinary
Hutus joined in massacring their Tutsi neighbors.
Although the genocidal slaughter seemed a spontane-
ous eruption of hatred, it has in fact been shown to
have been carefully orchestrated by the Hutu government.

In response, the Tutsi rebel force, the Rwandan
Patriotic Front, swept across the country in a 14-week
civil war, routing the largely Hutu government.
Despite horrific reports of genocide, no country came
to the Tutsi's assistance. The UN, already stationed in
Rwanda at the time of the killing, withdrew entirely
after ten of its soldiers were killed.

In the aftermath of the genocide, an estimated 1.7
million Hutus fled across the border into neighboring
Zaire (now the Democratic Republic of the Congo).
Although Tutsi rebels took control of the government,
they permitted a Hutu to serve as president, attempting
to deflect accusations of a resurgence in Tutsi elitism
and to foster national unity. Paul Kagame, the Tutsi
rebel leader, became vice president and minister of
defense.

Amid the legitimate refugees from the genocide
were Hutu militiamen who began waging guerrilla
warfare from Zaire. The Hutu guerrillas in Zaire, as
well as Zaire's threat to exile their own ethnic Tutsi,
led to Rwanda's support of rebel forces bent on overthrowing Zaire's Mobutu Sese Seko. But Rwanda
soon grew disenchanted with the new regime of Laurent Kabila. The Kabila government was not able to
prevent the raids from Hutu guerrillas that continued
to traumatize the country and destabilize the region. In
Aug. 1998, a little more than a year after Kabila took
over, a rebellion began against his reign, instigated by
Rwanda and Uganda.

Refugee problems, continued massacres, and the
horrific legacy of genocide continued to haunt the
national psyche. In Sept. 1998, a UN tribunal sentenced Jean Kambanda, a former prime minister of
Rwanda, to life in prison for his part in the 1994 genocide. He became the first person in history to be convicted for the crime of genocide, first defined in the
1948 Genocide Convention after World War II. By
2001, eight others had also been convicted of the same
charge. The UN tribunal, however, has been criticized
for its inefficiency and slow pace. In Dec. 1999, an
independent report, commissioned by the UN, took
Kofi Annan and other UN officials to task for not intervening effectively in the genocide.

In April 2000, President Bizimungu resigned and Vice President Paul Kagame became the first Tutsi president of the nation. It was Kagame's rebel force that seized Rwanda's capital and put an end to the genocide in 1994.

Rwanda continued fighting against Congo throughout its 4-year civil war. Finally, in July 2002, Kagame and Joseph Kabila, who became president of Congo after his father was assassinated in 1999, signed a peace accord: Rwanda promised to withdraw its 35,000 troops from the eastern Congolese border; Congo would in turn disarm the thousands of Hutu militiamen in its territory, who threaten Rwandan security—many of them supported or participated in the Rwandan genocide.

# St. Kitts and Nevis

### FEDERATION OF ST. KITTS AND NEVIS

**Sovereign:** Queen Elizabeth II (1952)
**Governor-General:** Sir Cuthbert Sebastian (1996)
**Prime Minister:** Denzil Douglas (1995)
**Area:** St. Kitts 65 sq mi (168 sq km); Nevis 36 sq mi (93 sq km)
**Population (2002 est.):** 38,736 (growth rate: 1.0%); birth rate: 18.6/1000; infant mortality rate: 15.8/1000; density per sq mi: 384
**Capital:** Basseterre (on St. Kitts), 19,000. **Largest town on Nevis:** Charlestown, 1,771. **Monetary unit:** East Caribbean dollar. **Ethnicity/race:** black African. **Literacy rate:** 98% (1970)
**Economic summary: GDP/PPP** (2000 est.): $274 million; per capita $7,000. **Real growth rate:** 5%. **Inflation:** 2.5%. **Unemployment:** 4.5% (1997). **Arable land:** 22%. **Agriculture:** sugarcane, rice, yams, vegetables, bananas; fish. **Labor force:** 18,172 (June 1995). **Industries:** sugar processing, tourism, cotton, salt, copra, clothing, footwear, beverages. **Natural resources:** arable land. **Exports:** $53.2 million (2000 est.): machinery, food, electronics, beverages, tobacco. **Imports:** $151.5 million (2000 est.): machinery, manufactures, food, fuels. **Major trading partners:** U.S., UK, Caricom countries.

**Geography** St. Kitts, the larger of the two islands, is roughly oval in shape except for a long, narrow peninsula to the southeast. Its highest point is Mount Liamuiga (3,792 ft [1,156 m]). The Narrows, a 2-mile- (3-km-) wide channel, separates the two islands. The circularly shaped Nevis is surrounded by coral reefs and the island is almost entirely a single mountain, Nevis Peak (3,232 ft [985 m]). A volcanic mountain chain dominates the center of both islands.

**Government** Constitutional monarchy.

**History** When Christopher Columbus explored the island in 1493, it was inhabited by the Carib people. Today, most of the inhabitants are the descendants of African slaves. St. Kitts, formerly St. Christopher, was settled by the British in 1623; Nevis in 1628. The French settled on St. Kitts in 1627, and an Anglo-French rivalry lasted for more than 100 years. After a decisive British victory over the French at Brimstone Hill in 1782, the islands came under permanent British control. The islands, including nearby Anguilla, were united in 1882. They joined the West Indies federation in 1958 and remained in that association until its dissolution in 1962. St. Kitts-Nevis-Anguilla became an associated state of the United Kingdom in 1967. Anguilla seceded in 1980, and St. Kitts and Nevis became independent on Sept. 19, 1983.

A drop in world sugar prices hurt the nation's economy through the mid-1980s, and the government sought to reduce the islands' dependence on sugar production and to diversify the economy, promoting tourism and financial services. In 1990, the premier of Nevis announced that he intended to seek an end to the federation with St. Kitts by 1992, but a local election in June 1992 postponed the idea. In Aug. 1998, 62% of the population voted for Nevis to secede, but the vote fell short of the two-thirds majority required.

The country had been blacklisted by various international financial agencies for improprieties in its offshore financial services industry, but by 2002 it had been removed from all such lists.

# St. Lucia

**Sovereign:** Queen Elizabeth II (1952)
**Governor-General:** Dame Pearlette Louisy (1997)
**Prime Minister:** Kenny D. Anthony (1997)
**Area:** 239 sq mi (620 sq km)
**Population (2002 est.):** 160,145 (growth rate: 1.6%); birth rate: 21.4/1000; infant mortality rate: 14.8/1000; density per sq mi: 669
**Capital and largest city (1992 est.):** Castries, 13,600. **Monetary unit:** East Caribbean dollar. **Languages:** English (official) and patois. **Ethnicity/race:** African descent 90.3%, mixed 5.5%, East Indian 3.2%, white 0.8%. **Religions:** Roman Catholic 90%, Protestant 7%, Anglican 3%. **Literacy rate:** 67% (1980)
**Economic summary: GDP/PPP** (2000 est.): $700 million; per capita $4,500. **Real growth rate:** 0.5%. **Inflation:** 2.5%. **Unemployment:** 15% (1996 est.). **Arable land:** 8%. **Agriculture:** bananas, coconuts, vegetables, citrus, root crops, cocoa. **Labor force:** 43,800; agriculture 43.4%, services 38.9%, industry and commerce 17.7% (1983 est.). **Industries:** clothing, assembly of electronic components, beverages, corrugated cardboard boxes, tourism, lime processing, coconut processing. **Natural resources:** forests, sandy beaches, minerals (pumice), mineral springs, geothermal potential. **Exports:** $68.3 million (2000 est.): bananas 41%, clothing, cocoa, vegetables, fruits, coconut oil. **Imports:** $319.4 million (2000 est.): food 23%, manufactured goods 21%, machinery and transportation equipment 19%, chemicals, fuels. **Major trading partners:** UK, U.S., Caricom countries, Japan, Canada. **Member of Commonwealth of Nations**

**Geography** One of the Windward Islands of the eastern Caribbean, St. Lucia lies just south of Martinique. It is of volcanic origin. A chain of wooded mountains runs from north to south, and from them flow many streams into fertile valleys.

**Government** Parliamentary democracy. A governor-general represents the sovereign, Queen Elizabeth II.

**History** The first inhabitants of the island were the Arawak Indians, who were forced off the island by the Caribs. Explored by Spain and then France, St. Lucia became a British territory in 1814 and one of the Windward Islands in 1871. With other Windward Islands, St. Lucia was granted home rule in 1967 as one of the West Indies Associated States. On Feb. 22, 1979, St. Lucia achieved full independence in ceremonies boycotted by the opposition St. Lucia Labour Party, which had advocated a referendum before cutting ties with Britain. The United Workers Party (UWP), then in power, called for new elections and was defeated by the St. Lucia Labour Party (SLP). The UWP was returned to power in the elections of 1982, 1987, and 1992.

Kenny Anthony became prime minister in 1997, when his St. Lucia Labour Party won 16 of the 17 parliamentary seats.

The 1999 European Union decision to end its preferential treatment of bananas imported from former colonies has led St. Lucia to try to diversify its agricultural crops.

# St. Vincent and the Grenadines

**Sovereign:** Queen Elizabeth II (1952)
**Acting Governor-General:** Monica Dacon (2002)
**Prime Minister:** Dr. Ralph Gonsalves (2001)
**Area:** 150 sq mi (389 sq km)
**Population (2002 est.):** 116,394 (growth rate: 1.1%); birth rate: 17.5/1000; infant mortality rate: 16.1/1000; density per sq mi: 775
**Capital and largest city (1992 est.):** Kingstown, 15,466.
**Monetary unit:** East Caribbean dollar. **Languages:** English (official), French patois. **Ethnicity/race:** African descent, white, East Indian, Carib Indian. **Religions:** Anglican 47%, Methodist 28%, Roman Catholic 13%. **Literacy rate:** 96% (1970)
**Economic summary: GDP/PPP** (2000 est.): $322 million; per capita $2,800. **Real growth rate:** 2%. **Inflation:** 2% (1999 est.). **Unemployment:** 22% (1997 est.). **Arable land:** 10%. **Agriculture:** bananas, coconuts, sweet potatoes, spices; small numbers of cattle, sheep, pigs, goats; fish. **Labor force:** 67,000 (1984 est.); agriculture 26%, industry 17%, services 57% (1980 est.). **Industries:** food processing, cement, furniture, clothing, starch. **Natural resources:** hydropower, cropland. **Exports:** $53.7 million (2000 est.): bananas 39%, eddoes and dasheen (taro), arrowroot starch, tennis racquets. **Imports:** $185.6 million (2000 est.): foodstuffs, machinery and equipment, chemicals and fertilizers, minerals and fuels. **Major trading partners:** Caricom countries, UK, U.S. **Member of Commonwealth of Nations**

**Geography** St. Vincent, chief island of the chain, is 18 mi (29 km) long and 11 mi (18 km) wide, and is located 100 mi (161 km) west of Barbados. The island is mountainous and well forested. St. Vincent is dominated by the volcano Mount Soufrière, which rises to 4,048 ft (1,234 m). The Grenadines, a chain of nearly 600 islets with a total area of only 17 sq mi (27 sq km), extend for 60 mi (96 km) between St. Vincent and Grenada. The main islands in the Grenadines are Bequia, Balliceau, Canouan, Mayreau, Mustique, Isle D'Quatre, Petit Saint Vincent, and Union Island.

**Government** Parliamentary democracy.

**History** The Carib Indians inhabited St. Vincent before the Europeans arrived, and the island still sports a sizable number of Carib artifacts. Explored by Columbus in 1498, and alternately claimed by Britain and France, St. Vincent became a British colony by the Treaty of Paris in 1763. In 1773, the island was divided between the Caribs and the British, but conflicts between the groups persisted. In 1776, the Caribs revolted and were subdued. Thereafter the British deported most of them to islands in the Gulf of Honduras. Sugarcane cultivation brought thousands of African slaves and, later, Portuguese and East Indian laborers.

The islands belonged to the West Indies Federation from 1958 until its dissolution in 1962, won home rule in 1969 as part of the West Indies Associated States, and achieved full independence Oct. 26, 1979. Prime Minister Milton Cato's government quelled a brief rebellion on Dec. 8, 1979, attributed to economic problems following the eruption of La Soufrière in April 1979 (which had caused the evacuation of the northern two-thirds of the island). The eruption, followed by Hurricane Allen in 1980, seriously damaged the nation's economy, particularly the important banana crop, in the 1980s. But by the 1990s the economy had begun to rebound, and the small tourism industry began to grow. In 1996, St. Vincent and the Grenadines signed agreements with the U.S. that allowed U.S. Coast Guard personnel to pursue suspected drug smugglers into their territorial waters and provided for extradition of criminals. In 1997, the country's permanent representative to the Organization of American States assumed the chairmanship of that body's Permanent Council.

With the 1999 decision by the European Union to end its preferential treatment of bananas imported from former colonies, St. Vincent and the Grenadines has sought to diversify its economy, primarily through expanding tourism. In March 2001 elections, the Unity Labour Party (ULP) won a landslide upset, capturing 12 of the 15 contested parliamentary seats. The incumbent New Democrat Party (NDP) won only three seats. Dr. Ralph Gonsalves, a lawyer, became the new prime minister.

# Samoa

INDEPENDENT STATE OF SAMOA

**Head of State:** Malietoa Tanumafili II (1963)
**Prime Minister:** Tuilaepa Sailele Malielegaoi (1998)
**Area:** 1,104 sq mi (2,860 sq km)
**Population (2002 est.):** 178,631 (growth rate: 0.9%); birth rate: 15.5/1000; infant mortality rate: 30.7/1000; density per sq mi: 162
**Capital and largest city (1991):** Apia, 32,859.
**Monetary unit:** Tala. **Languages:** Samoan and English. **Ethnicity/race:** Samoan 92.6%, Euronesians 7% (persons of European and Polynesian blood), Europeans 0.4%. **Religion:** Christian 99.7%. **Literacy rate:** 98% (1971)
**Economic summary: GDP/PPP** (2000 est.): $571 million; per capita $3,200. **Real growth rate:** 6.8%. **Inflation:** 0.8%. **Unemployment:** n.a.; note: substantial underemployment. **Arable land:** 19%. **Agriculture:** coconuts, bananas, taro, yams. **Labor force:** 90,000 (2000 est.); agriculture 65%, services 30%, industry 5% (1995 est.). **Industries:** food processing, building materials, auto parts. **Natural resources:** hardwood forests, fish, hydropower. **Exports:** $17 million (f.o.b., 2000): coconut oil and cream, copra, fish, beer. **Imports:** $90 million (f.o.b., 2000): machinery and equipment, industrial supplies, foodstuffs. **Major trading partners:** American Samoa, U.S., Germany, New Zealand, Australia, Fiji.

**Geography** Samoa, formerly Western Samoa, is in the South Pacific Ocean about 2,200 mi (3,540 km) south of Hawaii. The larger islands in the Samoan chain, Upolu and Savai'i, are mountainous and of volcanic origin. There is little level land except in the coastal areas, where most cultivation takes place.

**Government** Constitutional monarchy under a native chief.

**History** Polynesians, possibly from Tonga, first settled in the Samoan islands about 1000 B.C. The Samoa was explored by Dutch and French traders in the 18th century. Toward the end of the 19th century, conflicting interests of the U.S., Britain, and Germany resulted in an 1899 treaty that recognized the paramount interests of the U.S. in those islands west of 171°W (American Samoa) and Germany's interests in the other islands (Western Samoa).

New Zealand seized Western Samoa from Germany in 1914, and in 1946 it became a UN trust territory administered by New Zealand. A resistance movement to both German and New Zealand rule, known as the *Mau* ("strongly held view") movement, helped to edge the islands toward independence on Jan. 1, 1962. A constitutional monarchy, Samoa has a legislative assembly whose members are from the *matai,* or titled class.

Barraged regularly by cyclones that have wreaked havoc on the country's primarily agrarian economy, Samoa has begun stepping up its tourism industry—not such a difficult undertaking in this archetypical South Pacific paradise.

A referendum in 1990 gave most women the right to vote for the first time. In 1997, a new constitutional amendment changed the country's name to Samoa. In 2002, the prime minister of New Zealand apologized to Samoa for the injustices that occurred under New Zealand rule.

# San Marino

### MOST SERENE REPUBLIC OF SAN MARINO
**National name:** Repubblica di San Marino
**Captains Regent:** Giuseppe Maria Morganti and Mauro Chiaruzzi (2002)
**Area:** 24 sq mi (61.2 sq km)
**Population (2002 est.):** 27,730 (growth rate: 0.3%); birth rate: 10.6/1000; infant mortality rate: 6.1/1000; density per sq mi: 1,174
**Capital and largest city (1992 est.):** San Marino, 2,397. **Monetary unit:** Euro. **Language:** Italian. **Ethnicity/race:** Sammarinese, Italian. **Religion:** Roman Catholic. **Literacy rate:** 96% (1976)
**Economic summary: GDP/PPP** (2000 est.): $860 million; per capita $32,000. **Real growth rate:** 8%. **Inflation:** 2.2% (2000). **Unemployment:** 3% (1999). **Arable land:** 17%. **Agriculture:** wheat, grapes, corn, olives; cattle, pigs, horses, beef, cheese, hides. **Labor force:** 18,500 (1999); services 60%, industry 38%, agriculture 2% (1998 est.). **Industries:** tourism, banking, textiles, electronics, ceramics, cement, wine. **Natural resources:** building stone. **Exports:** trade data are included with the statistics for Italy: building stone, lime, wood, chestnuts, wheat, wine, baked goods, hides, ceramics. **Imports:** trade data are included with the statistics for Italy: wide variety of consumer manufactures, food.

**Geography** One-tenth the size of New York City, San Marino is surrounded by Italy. It is situated in the Apennines, a little inland from the Adriatic Sea near Rimini.

**Government** Republic.

**History** According to tradition, San Marino was founded about A.D. 350 and had the good luck for centuries to stay out of the many wars and feuds on the Italian peninsula. It is the oldest republic in the world. San Marino has survived completely intact attacks by the unification of Italy, and two world wars. Those born in San Marino remain citizens and can vote no matter where they live. Throughout the 1990s San Marino has taken a more active role in international diplomacy, establishing strong diplomatic and economic ties to a host of other countries.

# São Tomé and Príncipe

### DEMOCRATIC REPUBLIC OF SÃO TOMÉ AND PRÍNCIPE
**President:** Fradique de Menezes (2001)
**Prime Minister:** Maria das Neves (2002)
**Area:** 386 sq mi (1,001 sq km)
**Population (2002 est.):** 170,372 (growth rate: 3.5%); birth rate: 42.3/1000; infant mortality rate: 47.5/1000;

density per sq mi: 441
**Capital and largest city (1990 est.):** São Tomé, 43,420.
**Monetary unit:** Dobra. **Language:** Portuguese.
**Ethnicity/race:** mestico, angolares (descendants of Angolan slaves), forros (descendants of freed slaves), servicais (contract laborers from Angola, Mozambique, and Cape Verde), tongas (children of servicais born on the islands), Europeans (primarily Portuguese).
**Religions:** Roman Catholic, Evangelical Protestant, Seventh-Day Adventist. **Literacy rate:** 57% (1981)
**Economic summary: GDP/PPP** (2000 est.): $178 million; per capita $1,100. **Real growth rate:** 3%. **Inflation:** 5%. **Unemployment:** n.a. **Arable land:** 2%. **Agriculture:** cocoa, coconuts, palm kernels, copra, cinnamon, pepper, coffee, bananas, papayas, beans; poultry; fish. **Labor force:** n.a.; population mainly engaged in subsistence agriculture and fishing; note: shortages of skilled workers. **Industries:** light construction, textiles, soap, beer; fish processing; timber. **Natural resources:** fish, hydropower. **Exports:** $3.2 million (f.o.b., 2000 est.): cocoa 90%, copra, coffee, palm oil. **Imports:** $40 million (f.o.b., 2000 est.): machinery and electrical equipment, food products, petroleum products. **Major trading partners:** Netherlands, Germany, Portugal, U.S., South Africa.

**Geography** The tiny volcanic islands of São Tomé and Príncipe lie in the Gulf of Guinea about 150 mi (240 km) off West Africa. São Tomé (about 330 sq mi; 859 sq km) is covered by a dense mountainous jungle, out of which have been carved large plantations. Príncipe (about 40 sq mi; 142 sq km) consists of jagged mountains. Other islands in the republic are Pedras Tinhosas and Rolas. About 95% of the population lives on São Tomé.

**Government** Republic.

**History** São Tomé and Príncipe, believed to have been originally uninhabited, were explored by Portuguese navigators in 1471 and settled by the end of the century. Intensive cultivation by slave labor made the islands a major producer of sugar during the 17th century but output declined until the introduction of coffee and cocoa in the 19th century brought new prosperity. The island of São Tomé was the world's largest producer of cocoa in 1908, and the crop is still the most important. Working conditions for laborers, however, were horrendous, and in 1909 British and German chocolate manufacturers boycotted São Tomé cocoa in protest. An exile liberation movement was formed in 1953 after Portuguese landowners quelled labor riots by killing several hundred African workers.

The Portuguese revolution of 1974 brought the end of the overseas empire, and the new Lisbon government transferred power to the liberation movement July IV, 1975. A former prime minister and dissident, Miguel Trovoada, was elected president in March 1991 after the withdrawal of the two other candidates.

In April 1995 Príncipe became autonomous. In Aug. a bloodless military coup was reversed through Angolan mediation. In Dec. an agreement was struck on forming a coalition government. President Trovoada won reelection in July 1996 against challenger and former president Manuel Pinto da Costa. Protests erupted in April 1997 when the government, in response to its inability to pay for imported oil, raised gasoline prices 140% in order to stem demand. The center-left government made economic improvement a major goal, including the expansion of agriculture and the exploration of potential offshore oil reserves. Businessman Fradique de Menezes won the presidential election in 2001.

# Saudi Arabia

**KINGDOM OF SAUDI ARABIA**

**National name:** Al-Mamlaka al-'Arabiya as-Sa'udiya
**Sovereign:** King Fahd bin 'Abdulaziz (1982)
**Area:** 756,981 sq mi (1,960,582 sq km)
**Population (2002 est.):** 23,513,330 (growth rate: 3.1%);
birth rate: 37.2/1000; infant mortality rate: 49.6/1000;
density per sq mi: 31
**Capital:** Riyadh. **Largest cities (1993):** Riyadh,
3,000,000; Jeddah, 2,500,000; Makkah (Mecca) (1994
est.), 550,000. **Monetary unit:** Riyal. **Languages:**
Arabic, English widely spoken. **Ethnicity/race:** Arab
90%, Afro-Asian 10%. **Religion:** Islam 100%. **Literacy
rate:** 62% (1990)
**Economic summary: GDP/PPP** (2000 est.): $232
billion; per capita $10,500. **Real growth rate:** 4%.
**Inflation:** 0.5% (2000). **Unemployment:** n.a. **Arable
land:** 2%. **Agriculture:** wheat, barley, tomatoes,
melons, dates, citrus; mutton, chickens, eggs, milk.
**Labor force:** 7 million; note: 35% of the population in
the 15–64 age group is non-national (July 1998 est.);
agriculture 12%, industry 25%, services 63% (1999
est.). **Industries:** crude oil production, petroleum
refining, basic petrochemicals, cement, construction,
fertilizer, plastics. **Natural resources:** petroleum,
natural gas, iron ore, gold, copper. **Exports:** $81.2
billion (f.o.b., 2000): petroleum and petroleum products
90%. **Imports:** $30.1 billion (f.o.b., 2000): machinery
and equipment, foodstuffs, chemicals, motor vehicles,
textiles. **Major trading partners:** Japan, U.S., France,
South Korea, Singapore, India, Germany, Italy, UK.

**Geography** Saudi Arabia occupies most of the Arabian Peninsula, with the Red Sea and the Gulf of
Aqaba to the west, and the Arabian Gulf to the east.
Neighboring countries are Jordan, Iraq, Kuwait, Qatar,
the United Arab Emirates, the Sultanate of Oman,
Yemen, and Bahrain, connected to the Saudi mainland
by a causeway. Saudi Arabia contains the world's largest continuous sand desert, the Rub Al-Khali, or
Empty Quarter. Its oil region lies primarily in the eastern province along the Arabian Gulf.

**Government** Saudi Arabia was an absolute monarchy until 1992, at which time the Sa'ud royal
family introduced the country's first constitution.
The legal system is based on the *sharia* (Islamic
law).

**History** Saudi Arabia is not only the homeland of
the Arab peoples—it is thought that the first Arabs
originated on the Arabian peninsula—but the
homeland of Islam, the world's second-largest
religion. Muhammad founded Islam there, and it
is the location of the two holy pilgrimage cities of
Mecca and Medina. The Islamic calendar begins
in 622, the year of the hegira, or Muhammad's
flight from Mecca. A succession of invaders
attempted to control the peninsula, but by 1517
the Ottoman Empire dominated, and in the middle
of the 18th century, it was divided into separate
principalities. In 1745 Muhammad ibn 'Abd
al-Wahhab began calling for the purification and
reform of Islam, and the Wahhabi movement
swept across Arabia. By 1811, Wahhabi leaders
had waged a *jihad*—a holy war—against other
forms of Islam on the peninsula, and succeeded in
uniting much of it. By 1818, however, the Wah-
habis had been driven out of power again by the
Ottomans and their Egyptian allies.
   The kingdom of Saudi Arabia is almost entirely the
creation of King Ibn Saud (1882–1953). A descendant
of Wahhabi leaders, he seized Riyadh in 1901 and set

himself up as leader of the Arab nationalist movement.
By 1906 he had established Wahhabi dominance in
Nejd and conquered Hejaz in 1924–25. Hejaz and
Nejd were merged to form the kingdom of Saudi Arabia in 1932, which was an absolute monarchy ruled by
sharia, Islamic law. A year later the region of Asir was
incorporated into the kingdom.
   Oil was discovered in 1936, and commercial production began during World War II. Its wealth allowed
the country to provide free health care and education
while not collecting any taxes from its people. Saudi
Arabia was neutral until nearly the end of the war, but
it was permitted to be a charter member of the United
Nations. The country joined the Arab League in 1945
and took part in the 1948–49 war against Israel. Saudi
Arabia still does not recognize the state of Israel. On
Ibn Saud's death in 1953, his eldest son, Saud, began
an 11-year reign marked by an increasing hostility
toward the radical Arabism of Egypt's Gamal Abdel
Nasser. In 1964, the ailing Saud was deposed and
replaced by the premier, Crown Prince Faisal, who
gave vocal support but no military help to Egypt in the
1967 Arab-Israeli war.
   Faisal's assassination by a deranged kinsman in
1975 shook the Middle East, but it failed to alter his
kingdom's course. His successor was his brother,
Prince Khalid. Khalid gave influential support to
Egypt during negotiations on Israeli withdrawal from
the Sinai Desert. King Khalid died of a heart attack in
1982, and was succeeded by his half-brother, Prince
Fahd bin 'Abdulaziz, who had exercised the real
power throughout Khalid's reign. King Fahd, a pro-
Western modernist, chose his 58-year-old half-brother,
Abdullah, as crown prince.
   Saudi Arabia and the smaller, oil-rich Arab states on
the Persian Gulf, fearful that they might become Ayatollah Ruhollah Khomeini's next targets if Iran conquered Iraq, made large financial contributions to the
Iraqi war effort during the 1980s. At the same time,
cheating by other members of the Organization of
Petroleum Exporting Countries (OPEC), competition
from nonmember oil producers, and conservation
efforts by consuming nations combined to drive down
the world price of oil. Saudi Arabia has one-third of
all known oil reserves, but falling demand and rising
production outside OPEC combined to reduce its oil
revenues from $120 billion in 1980 to less than $25
billion in 1985, threatening the country with domestic
unrest and undermining its influence in the Gulf area.
   At the start of 1996, King Fahd passed authority to
Crown Prince Abdullah, saying he needed rest.
Although not an abdication, it was unclear how long
the king would be absent. In 1998 the country's oil
income fell by 40% because of a worldwide decline in
prices, and it entered its first recession in 6 years.
   In 2000, Saudi Arabia, along with other OPEC
nations experiencing a recession, decided to reduce
production to raise oil prices. In 2001, OPEC cut oil
production three additional times.
   Saudi Arabia's relations with the U.S. were strained
after the Sept. 11, 2001, terrorist attacks—15 of the
suicide bombers involved were Saudis. Despite the
monarchy's close ties to the West, much of the
extremely influential religious establishment has supported anti-Americanism and Islamic militancy.
   In March 2002, Crown Prince Abdullah of Saudi
Arabia offered a Middle East peace plan at the annual
Arab summit: all Arab governments would offer "normal relations and the security of Israel in exchange for
a full Israeli withdrawal from all occupied Arab lands,
recognition of an independent Palestinian state with
noble Jerusalem as its capital, and the return of the

Palestinian refugees." An extraordinary offer because it promised the backing of the entire Arab world, the Saudi plan nevertheless seemed unrealistic in the concessions it expected from Israel. And without a cease-fire, much less an agreement to negotiate between the Israelis and Palestinians, the plan languished.

# Senegal

### REPUBLIC OF SENEGAL

**National name:** République du Sénegal
**President:** Abdoulaye Wade (2000)
**Prime Minister:** Mame Madior Boye (2001)
**Area:** 75,749 sq mi (196,190 sq km)
**Population (2002 est.):** 9,979,752 (growth rate: 2.9%); birth rate: 37.0/1000; infant mortality rate: 55.4/1000; density per sq mi: 132
**Capital and largest city (1994 est.):** Dakar, 1,729,823.
**Monetary unit:** CFA Franc. **Languages:** French (official); Wolof, Serer, other ethnic dialects. **Ethnicity/race:** Wolof 36%, Fulani 17%, Serer 17%, Toucouleur 9%, Diola 9%, Mandingo 9%, European and Lebanese 1%, other 2%. **Religions:** Islam 92%, indigenous 6%, Christian 2%. **Literacy rate:** 38% (1990)
**Economic summary: GDP/PPP** (2000 est.): $16 billion; per capita $1,600. **Real growth rate:** 5.7%. **Inflation:** 1.5%. **Unemployment:** n.a.; urban youth 40%. **Arable land:** 12%. **Agriculture:** peanuts, millet, corn, sorghum, rice, cotton, tomatoes, green vegetables; cattle, poultry, pigs; fish. **Labor force:** n.a.; agriculture 60%. **Industries:** agricultural and fish processing, phosphate mining, fertilizer production, petroleum refining, construction materials. **Natural resources:** fish, phosphates, iron ore. **Exports:** $959 million (f.o.b., 2000): fish, ground nuts (peanuts), petroleum products, phosphates, cotton. **Imports:** $1.3 billion (f.o.b., 2000): foods and beverages, consumer goods, capital goods, petroleum products. **Major trading partners:** France, India, Italy, Spain, Mali, Côte d'Ivoire, Nigeria, Thailand, Germany, U.S.

**Geography** The capital of Senegal, Dakar, is the westernmost point in Africa. The country, slightly smaller than South Dakota, surrounds Gambia on three sides and is bordered on the north by Mauritania, on the east by Mali, and on the south by Guinea and Guinea-Bissau.

Senegal is mainly a low-lying country, with a semi-desert area in the north and northeast and forests in the southwest. The largest rivers include the Senegal in the north and the Casamance in the south tropical climate region.

**Government** Multiparty democractic republic.

**History** The Toucouleur people, among the early inhabitants of Senegal, converted to Islam in the 11th century, although their religious beliefs retained strong elements of animism. The Portuguese had settlements on the banks of the Senegal River in the 15th century, and the first French settlement was made at Saint-Louis in 1659. Gorée Island became a major center for the Atlantic slave trade through the 1700s, and millions of Africans were shipped from there to the New World. The British took parts of Senegal at various times, but the French gained possession in 1840 and made it part of French West Africa in 1895. In 1946, together with other parts of French West Africa, Senegal became an overseas territory of France. On June 20, 1960, it became an independent republic federated with Mali, but the federation collapsed within four months.

Although Senegal is neither a large nor a strategically located country, it has nonetheless played a prominent role in African politics since its independence. As a black nation that is more than 90% Muslim, Senegal has been a diplomatic and cultural bridge between the Islamic and black African worlds. Senegal has also maintained closer economic, political, and cultural ties to France than probably any other former French African colony.

Senegal's first president, Léopold Sédar Senghor, towered over the country's political life until his voluntary retirement in 1981. He replaced multiparty democracy with an authoritarian regime. An acclaimed poet, Senghor sought to become a "black-skinned Frenchman," a quest he ultimately discovered to be impossible. An advocate of "African socialism," Senghor increased government involvement in the economy through a series of four-year plans.

In 1973 Senegal and six other nations created the West African Economic Community. When rising oil prices and fluctuations in the price of peanuts, a major export crop, ruined the economy in the 1970s, Senghor reversed course. He emphasized new industries such as tourism and fishing. Politically, the so-called passive revolution allowed limited opposition.

When the economy continued to stagnate, and with it Senghor's popularity, he resigned after 20 years at the helm in favor of his protégé, Abdou Diouf. Diouf, who led the country for the next 20 years, initiated further economic and political liberalization, including the sale of government companies and permitting the existence of political parties. In March 2000, opposition party challenger Abdoulaye Wade won 60% of the vote in multiparty elections. Diouf stepped aside in what was hailed as a rare smooth transition of power in Africa. In Jan. 2001, the Senegalese voted in a new constitution that legalized opposition parties and granted women equal property rights with men.

# Serbia and Montenegro

*SEE* YUGOSLAVIA.

# Seychelles

### REPUBLIC OF SEYCHELLES

**President:** France-Albert René (1977)
**Area:** 176 sq mi (455 sq km)
**Population (2002 est.):** 80,098 (growth rate: 1.1%); birth rate: 17.3/1000; infant mortality rate: 16.9/1000; density per sq mi: 456
**Capital and largest city (1993 est.):** Victoria, 25,000.
**Monetary unit:** Seychelles rupee. **Languages:** English and French (both official), and Seselwa (a creole). **Ethnicity/race:** Seychellois (mixture of Asians, Africans, Europeans). **Religions:** Roman Catholic 90%, Anglican 8%. **Literacy rate:** 58% (1971)
**Economic summary: GDP/PPP** (1999 est.): $610 million; per capita $7,700. **Real growth rate:** 1.5%. **Inflation:** 6% (1999 est.). **Unemployment:** n.a. **Arable land:** 2%. **Agriculture:** coconuts, cinnamon, vanilla, sweet potatoes, cassava (tapioca), bananas; broiler chickens; tuna fish. **Labor force:** 30,900 (1996); industry 19%, services 71%, agriculture 10% (1989). **Industries:** fishing; tourism; processing of coconuts and vanilla, coir (coconut fiber) rope, boat building, printing, furniture; beverages. **Natural resources:** fish, copra, cinnamon trees. **Exports:** $111 million (f.o.b., 1999): fish, cinnamon bark, copra, petroleum products (reexports). **Imports:** $440 million (c.i.f., 1999): machinery and equipment, foodstuffs, petroleum products, chemicals. **Major trading partners:** France, UK, Netherlands, Italy, China, Germany, Japan, South Africa, Singapore. **Member of Commonwealth of Nations**

**Geography** Seychelles consist of an archipelago of about 100 islands in the Indian Ocean northeast of Madagascar. The principal islands are Mahé (55 sq mi; 142 sq km), Praslin (15 sq mi; 38 sq km), and La Digue (4 sq mi; 10 sq km). The Aldabra, Farquhar, and Desroches groups are included in the territory of the republic.

**Government** Socialist multiparty republic.

**History** The Seychelles were uninhabited when the British East India Company became the first visitors to the archipelago in 1609. Thereafter, they became a favorite pirate haven. The French claimed the islands in 1756 and administered them as part of the colony of Mauritius. The British gained control of the islands through the Treaty of Paris (1814), and changed the islands' name from the French Séchelles to the Anglicized Seychelles.

The islands became self-governing in 1975 and independent on June 29, 1976. They have remained a member of the Commonwealth of Nations. Their first president, James Mancham, was overthrown in 1977 by the prime minister, France-Albert René. At first René created a socialist state with a one-party system, but later he reintroduced a multiparty system as well as various reforms.

To increase revenue the government in 1996 quietly initiated an Economic Citizenship Program that provides foreigners with the opportunity to obtain a Seychelles passport upon payment of $25,000. A new law in late 1995 granted immunity from criminal prosecution to anyone investing $10 million in the country.

In elections held in March 1998, President France-Albert René was reelected with 66.6% of the vote.

In Sept. 2001, President René was reelected for another five years, defeating Wavel Ramkalawan, an Anglican priest.

# Sierra Leone

### REPUBLIC OF SIERRA LEONE

**President:** Ahmad Tejan Kabbah (1998)
**Area:** 27,699 sq mi (71,740 sq km)
**Population (2002 est.):** 5,614,743 (growth rate: 2.6%); birth rate: 44.6/1000; infant mortality rate: 144.4/1000; density per sq mi: 203
**Capital and largest city (1994 est.):** Freetown, 1,300,000. **Monetary unit:** Leone. **Languages:** English (official), Mende, Temne, Krio. **Ethnicity/race:** 18 native African tribes 99% (Temne 30%, Mende 30%, other 39%), Creole, European, Lebanese, and Asian 1%. **Religions:** Islam 40%, Christian 35%, Indigenous 20%. **Literacy rate:** 21% (1990)
**Economic summary:** GDP/PPP (2000 est.): $2.7 billion; per capita $510. **Real growth rate:** 4.2%. **Inflation:** 15%. **Unemployment:** n.a. **Arable land:** 7%. **Agriculture:** rice, coffee, cocoa, palm kernels, palm oil, peanuts; poultry, cattle, sheep, pigs; fish. **Labor force:** 1.369 million (1981 est.); note: only about 65,000 wage earners (1985). **Industries:** mining (diamonds); small-scale manufacturing (beverages, textiles, cigarettes, footwear); petroleum refining. **Natural resources:** diamonds, titanium ore, bauxite, iron ore, gold, chromite. **Exports:** $65 million (f.o.b., 2000 est.): diamonds, rutile, cocoa, coffee, fish. **Imports:** $145 million (f.o.b., 2000 est.): foodstuffs, machinery and equipment, fuels and lubricants, chemicals. **Major trading partners:** Belgium, U.S., Italy, UK, Italy, Nigeria.
**Member of Commonwealth of Nations**

**Geography** Sierra Leone, on the Atlantic Ocean in West Africa, is half the size of Illinois. Guinea, in the north and east, and Liberia, in the south, are its neigh-bors. Mangrove swamps lie along the coast, with wooded hills and a plateau in the interior. The eastern region is mountainous.

**Government** Constitutional democracy.

**History** The Bulom people were thought to have been the earliest inhabitants of Sierra Leone, followed by the Mende and Temne peoples in the 15th century, and thereafter the Fulani. The Portuguese were the first Europeans to explore the land and gave Sierra Leone its name, which means "lion mountains." Freetown, on the coast, was ceded to English settlers in 1787 as a home for blacks discharged from the British armed forces and also for runaway slaves who had found asylum in London. In 1808 the coastal area became a British colony, and in 1896 a British protectorate was proclaimed over the hinterland.

Sierra Leone became an independent nation on April 27, 1961. A military coup overthrew the civilian government in 1967, which was in turn replaced by civilian rule a year later. The country declared itself a republic on April 19, 1971.

A coup attempt early in 1971 led to then prime minister Siaka Stevens calling in troops from neighboring Guinea's army, which remained for two years. Stevens turned the government into a one-party state under the aegis of the All People's Congress Party in April 1978. In 1992 rebel soldiers overthrew Stevens's successor, Joseph Momoh, calling for a return to a multiparty system. In 1996, another military coup ousted the country's military leader and president. Nevertheless, a multiparty presidential election proceeded in 1996, and People's Party candidate Ahmad Tejan Kabbah won with 59.4% of the vote, becoming Sierra Leone's first democratically elected president.

But a violent military coup ousted President Kabbah's civilian government in May 1997. The leader of the coup, Lieut. Col. Johnny Paul Koroma, assumed the title "Head of the Armed Forces Revolutionary Council" (AFRC). Koroma began a reign of terror, destroying the economy and murdering enemies. The Commonwealth of Nations demanded the reinstatement of Kabbah, and ECOMOG, the Nigerian-led peacekeeping force, intervened. On March 10, 1998, after ten months in exile, Kabbah resumed his rule over Sierra Leone. The ousted junta and other rebel forces continued to wage attacks, many of which included the torture, rape, and brutal maimings of thousands of civilians, including countless children—amputation by machete is the horrific signature of the rebels. In addition to political power, the rebels are after control of Sierra Leone's rich diamond fields.

In Jan. 1999, rebels and Liberian mercenaries stormed the capital, demanding the release of the imprisoned Revolutionary United Front (RUF) leader, Foday Sankoh. ECOMOG regained control of Freetown, but President Kabbah later released Sankoh so he could participate in peace negotiations. Pressured by Nigeria and the U.S., among other countries, Kabbah agreed to an untenable power-sharing agreement in July 1999, which made Sankoh vice president of the country—and in charge of the diamond mines. The accord dissolved in May 2000 after the RUF abducted about 500 UN peacekeepers and attacked Freetown. Sankoh was captured and remains in government custody, where he awaits trial for war crimes.

The conflict was officially declared over in Jan. 2002—an estimated 50,000 people were killed in the decade-long civil war. The UN has installed its largest peacekeeping force in the country (17,000 troops) and 45,000 soldiers have been disarmed. In May, President Kabbah was reelected with 70% of the vote.

# Singapore

**REPUBLIC OF SINGAPORE**

**President:** S. R. Nathan (1999)
**Prime Minister:** Goh Chok Tong (1990)
**Area:** 250 sq mi (648 sq km)
**Population (2002 est.):** 4,452,732 (growth rate: 0.9%);
birth rate: 12.8/1000; infant mortality rate: 3.6/1000;
density per sq mi: 17,797
**Capital (1996 est.):** Singapore, 3,044,000. **Monetary
unit:** Singapore dollar. **Languages:** Malay, Chinese
(Mandarin), Tamil, English (all official). **Ethnicity/race:**
Chinese 76.4%, Malay 14.9%, Indian 6.4%, other
2.3%. **Religions:** Islam, Christian, Buddhist, Hindu,
Taoist. **Literacy rate:** 90% (1990)
**Economic summary: GDP/PPP** (2000 est.): $109.8
billion; per capita $26,500. **Real growth rate:** 10.1%.
**Inflation:** 1.4% (2000). **Unemployment:** 3% (2000
est.). **Arable land:** 2%. **Agriculture:** rubber, copra,
fruit, orchids, vegetables; poultry, eggs, fish,
ornamental fish. **Labor force:** 2.1 million (2000);
financial, business, and other services 35%,
manufacturing 21%, construction 13%, transportation
and communication 9%. **Industries:** electronics,
chemicals, financial services, oil drilling equipment,
petroleum refining, rubber processing and rubber
products, processed food and beverages, ship repair,
entrepot trade, biotechnology. **Natural resources:**
fish, deepwater ports. **Exports:** $137 billion (f.o.b.,
2000): machinery and equipment (including
electronics), chemicals, mineral fuels. **Imports:** $127
billion (f.o.b., 2000): machinery and equipment,
mineral fuels, chemicals, foodstuffs. **Major trading
partners:** U.S., Malaysia, Hong Kong, Japan, Taiwan,
Thailand, UK, Netherlands, China, South Korea,
Germany, Saudi Arabia. **Member of Commonwealth
of Nations**

**Geography** The Republic of Singapore consists of
the main island of Singapore, off the southern tip of
the Malay Peninsula between the South China Sea and
the Indian Ocean, and 58 nearby islands.

**Government** Parliamentary republic.

**History** Inhabitants of the Malaysian peninsula and
the island of Singapore first migrated to the area
between 2500 and 1500 B.C. (*see* Malaysia). British
and Dutch interest in the region grew with the spice
trade, and the trading post of Singapore was founded
in 1819 by Sir Stamford Raffles. It was made a separate Crown colony of Britain in 1946, when the
former colony of the Straits Settlements was dissolved. The other two settlements on the peninsula—
Penang and Malacca—became part of the Union of
Malaya, and the small island of Labuan was transferred to North Borneo. The Cocos (or Keeling)
Islands and Christmas Island were turned over to
Australia in 1955 and in 1958, respectively.

Singapore attained full internal self-government in
1959, and Lee Kwan Yew, an economic visionary with
an authoritarian streak, took the helm as prime minister. On Sept. 16, 1963, Singapore joined Malaya,
Sabah (North Borneo), and Sarawak in the Federation
of Malaysia. It withdrew from the Federation on Aug.
9, 1965, and a month later proclaimed itself a republic.

Under Lee, Singapore developed into one of the
cleanest, safest, and most economically prosperous
cities in Asia. However, Singapore's strict rules of
civil obedience also drew criticism from those who
said the nation's prosperity was achieved at the
expense of individual freedoms. In 1990, Lee
stepped down as prime minister but remained "senior

minister" with considerable influence over his successor, Goh Chok Tong, who continued to preside
over Singapore through difficult economic times in
1998. The first direct presidential election took place
in Aug. 1993. Before then, Parliament chose the
president.

S. R. Nathan was declared president without an
election when he was certified as the only candidate
eligible to run in the elections originally scheduled for
Aug. 28, 1999. Singapore turned in its worst economic
performance in history in 2001, with its gross domestic product shrinking by 2%. The island nation seemed
poised to recover in 2002, however, with the Trade
and Industry Ministry predicting growth of between
2% and 4%.

# Slovakia

**REPUBLIC OF SLOVAKIA**

**President:** Rudolf Schuster (1999)
**Prime Minister:** Mikulás Dzurinda (1998)
**Area:** 18,859 sq mi (48,845 sq km)
**Population (2002 est.):** 5,422,366 (growth rate: 0.1%);
birth rate: 10.1/1000; infant mortality rate: 8.8/1000;
density per sq mi: 288
**Capital and largest city (1993 est.):** Bratislava,
446,600. **Other large city (1993 est.):** Kosice,
237,300. **Monetary unit:** Koruna. **Languages:** Slovak
(official), Hungarian. **Ethnicity/race:** Slovak 85.7%,
Hungarian 10.7%, Gypsy 1.5%, Czech 1%, Ruthenian
0.3%, Ukrainian 0.3%, German 0.1%, Polish 0.1%.
**Religions:** Roman Catholic 60.3%, atheist 9.7%,
Protestant 8.4%, Orthodox 4.1%, other 17.5%.
**Literacy rate:** 99%
**Economic summary: GDP/PPP** (2000 est.): $55.3
billion; per capita $10,200. **Real growth rate:** 2.2%.
**Inflation:** 12.2%. **Unemployment:** 17%. **Arable land:**
31%. **Agriculture:** grains, potatoes, sugar beets,
hops, fruit; pigs, cattle, poultry; forest products. **Labor
force:** 3 million (1999); industry 29.3%, agriculture
8.9%, construction 8%, transport and communication
8.2%, services 45.6% (1994). **Industries:** metal and
metal products; food and beverages; electricity, gas,
coke, oil, nuclear fuel; chemicals and manmade fibers;
machinery; paper and printing; earthenware and
ceramics; transport vehicles; textiles; electrical and
optical apparatus; rubber products. **Natural
resources:** brown coal and lignite; small amounts of
iron ore, copper and manganese ore; salt; arable land.
**Exports:** $12 billion (f.o.b., 2000 est.): machinery and
transport equipment 39.4%, intermediate
manufactured goods 27.5%, miscellaneous
manufactured goods 13% (1999). **Imports:** $12.8
billion (f.o.b., 2000 est.): machinery
and transport equipment 37.7%, intermediate
manufactured goods 18%, fuels 13%, chemicals 11%
(1999), miscellaneous manufactured goods 9.5% (1999).
**Major trading partners:** EU, Czech Republic, Russia
(1999).

**Geography** Slovakia is located in central Europe.
The land has rugged mountains, rich in mineral
resources, with vast forests and pastures. The Carpathian Mountains dominate the topography of Slovakia, with lowland areas in the southern region.
Slovakia is about twice the size of the state of Maryland.

**Government** Parliamentary democracy.

**History** Present-day Slovakia was settled by Slavic
Slovaks about the 6th century. They were politically
united in the Moravian empire in the 9th century. In
907, the Germans and the Magyars conquered the

Moravian state, and the Slovaks fell under Hungarian control from the 10th century up until 1918. When the Hapsburg-ruled empire collapsed in 1918 following World War I, the Slovaks joined the Czech lands of Bohemia, Moravia, and part of Silesia to form the new joint state of Czechoslovakia. In March 1939, Germany occupied Czechoslovakia, established a German "protectorate," and created a puppet state out of Slovakia with Monsignor Josef Tiso as premier. The country was liberated from the Germans by the Soviet army in the spring of 1945, and Slovakia was restored to its prewar status and rejoined to a new Czechoslovakian state.

After the Communist Party took power in Feb. 1948, Slovakia was again subjected to a centralized Czech-dominated government, and antagonism between the two republics developed. On Jan. 1969, the nation became the Slovak Socialist Republic of Czechoslovakia.

Nearly 42 years of Communist rule for Slovakia ended when Vaclav Havel became president of Czechoslovakia in 1989 and democratic political reform began. However, with the demise of Communist power, a strong Slovak nationalist movement resurfaced, and the rival relationship between the two states increased. By the end of 1991, discussions between Slovak and Czech political leaders turned to whether the Czech and Slovak republics should continue to coexist within the federal structure or be divided into two independent states.

After the general election in June 1992, it was decided that two fully independent republics would be created. The Republic of Slovakia came into existence on Jan. 1, 1993. The Parliament in February elected Michal Kovac as president.

Vladimir Meciar, who served three times as Slovakia's prime minister, exhibited increasingly authoritarian behavior, and was cited as the reason Slovakia was eliminated from consideration for both the EU and NATO. A referendum in May 1997 on whether the country should join NATO was boycotted by 90% of the electorate after it turned into a showdown between the prime minister and the president, who wanted a question about direct election of the president placed on the ballot. For more than a year, Slovakia was without a president after Michal Kovac finished his term. Finally, the constitution was changed to allow for direct vote, and Rudolf Schuster was elected in May 1999.

Populist prime minister Meciar was unseated in 1998 elections by the reformist government of Mikulás Dzurinda. Meciar has been blamed for Slovakia's very low influx of foreign capital because of his government's lack of transparency. In April 2000 Meciar was arrested and charged with paying illegal bonuses to his cabinet ministers while in office. A three-week standoff with police preceded the arrest, ending only when police commandos blew open the door on Meciar's house and seized him. He was also questioned about his alleged involvement in the 1995 kidnapping of the son of Slovakia's former president, Michal Kovac.

Dzurinda has improved Slovakia's reputation in the West. The country has again been invited to apply for EU membership, and hopes to become part of NATO as well. But Dzurinda's tough economic measures have made him unpopular within the country. In Sept. 2002 elections, the ruling coalition held onto power, despite Meciar coming out ahead in the vote.

# Slovenia

**REPUBLIC OF SLOVENIA**
**President:** Milan Kucan (1990)
**Prime Minister:** Janez Drnovsek (2000)
**Area:** 7,820 sq mi (20,253 sq km)
**Population (2002 est.):** 1,932,917 (growth rate: –0.1%); birth rate: 9.3/1000; infant mortality rate: 4.5/1000; density per sq mi: 247
**Capital and largest city (1996 est.):** Ljubljana, 330,000. **Other large city:** Maribor, 103,512. **Monetary unit:** Slovenian tolar. **Languages:** Slovenian; most can also speak Serbo-Croatian. **Ethnicity/race:** Slovene 91%, Serbo-Croatian 6%, other 3%. **Religions:** Roman Catholic 70.8% (including 2% Uniate), Lutheran 1%, Muslim 1%, other 27.2%. **Literacy rate:** 99%
**Economic summary:** GDP/PPP (2000 est.): $22.9 billion; per capita $12,000. **Real growth rate:** 4.5%. **Inflation:** 8.9%. **Unemployment:** 7.1% (1997 est.). **Arable land:** 12%. **Agriculture:** potatoes, hops, wheat, sugar beets, corn, grapes; cattle, sheep, poultry. **Labor force:** 857,400; agriculture n.a., industry n.a., services n.a. **Industries:** ferrous metallurgy and rolling mill products, aluminum reduction and rolled products, lead and zinc smelting, electronics (including military electronics), trucks, electric power equipment, wood products, textiles, chemicals, machine tools. **Natural resources:** lignite coal, lead, zinc, mercury, uranium, silver, hydropower. **Exports:** $8.9 billion (f.o.b., 2000): manufactured goods, machinery and transport equipment, chemicals, food. **Imports:** $9.9 billion (f.o.b., 2000): machinery and transport equipment, manufactured goods, chemicals, fuels and lubricants, food. **Major trading partners:** Germany, Italy, Croatia, Austria, France, Hungary, Russia.

**Geography** Slovenia occupies an area about the size of the state of Massachusetts. It is largely a mountainous republic and almost half of the land is forested, with hilly plains spread across the central and eastern regions. Mount Triglav, the highest peak, rises to 9,393 ft (2,864 m).

**Government** Parliamentary democractic republic.

**History** Slovenia was originally settled by Illyrian and Celtic peoples. It became part of the Roman empire in the first century B.C.

The Slovenes were a south Slavic group that settled in the region during the 6th century A.D. During the 7th century, the Slavs established the Slavic state of Samu, which owed its allegiance to the Avars, who dominated the Hungarian plain until Charlemagne defeated them in the late 8th century.

When the Hungarians were defeated by the Turks in 1526, Hungary accepted Austrian Hapsburg rule in order to escape Turkish domination; the Hapsburg monarchy was the first to include all of the Slovene regions. Thus, Slovenia and Croatia became part of the Austro-Hungarian kingdom when the dual-monarchy was established in 1867. Like Croatia and unlike the other Balkan states, it is primarily Roman Catholic.

Following the defeat and collapse of Austria-Hungary in World War I, Slovenia declared its independence. It formally joined with Montenegro, Serbia, and Croatia on Dec. 4, 1918, to form the new nation called the Kingdom of the Serbs, Croats, and Slovenes. The name was later changed to Yugoslavia in 1929.

During World War II, Germany occupied Yugoslavia, and Slovenia was divided among Germany, Italy, and Hungary. For the duration of the war many Slovenes fought a guerrilla war against the Nazis under the leadership of the Croatian-born Communist resistance leader, Marshal Tito. After the final defeat of the Axis powers in 1945, Slovenia was again made into a republic of the newly established Communist nation of Yugoslavia.

In the 1980s, Slovenia agitated for greater autonomy and occasionally threatened to secede. It introduced a multiparty system and in 1990 elected a non-Communist government. Slovenia declared its independence from Yugoslavia on June 25, 1991. The Serbian-dominated Yugoslavian army tried to keep Slovenia in line and some brief fighting took place, but the army then withdrew its forces. Unlike Croatia and Bosnia, Slovenia was able to sever itself from Yugoslavia with relatively little violence. With recognition of its independence granted by the European Community in 1992, the country began realigning its economy and society toward western Europe. Slovenia is considered one of the most promising candidates for EU admission and expects to join by 2003.

between them, but later Britain was given control of the entire territory. The Japanese invaded the islands in World War II, and they became the scene of some of the bloodiest battles in the Pacific theater, most famously the battle of Guadalcanal. The British gained control of the island again in 1945. In 1976 the islands became self-governing, and gained independence in 1978.

Since early 1999, the Isatabus, natives of Guadalcanal, have expelled more than 20,000 Malaitans from the island. The Malaitans had migrated from nearby Malaita, and many secured jobs in the capital, Honiara, stirring resentment among Isatabus that has grown steadily since independence. Ethnic tensions reached their height in June 2000, when the Malaita Eagle Force stole police weapons, forced Prime Minister Bartholomew Ulufa'alu to resign, and seized control of Honiara. The rival groups agreed to a cease-fire in June 2000, barely averting a civil war. Although a peace agreement has been signed and elections have taken place, the country continues to suffer from lawlessness.

## Solomon Islands

**Sovereign:** Queen Elizabeth II (1952).
**Governor-General:** Sir John Lapli (1999)
**Prime Minister:** Sir Allan Kemakeza (2001)
**Area:** 10,985 sq mi (28,450 sq km)
**Population (2002 est.):** 494,786 (growth rate: 2.9%); birth rate: 33.3/1000; infant mortality rate: 23.7/1000; density per sq mi: 45
**Capital and largest city (1990 est.):** Honiara (on Guadalcanal), 35,288. **Monetary unit:** Solomon Islands dollar. **Languages:** English, Solomon Pijin (an English pidgin), over 60 indigenous Melanesian languages. **Ethnicity/race:** Melanesian 93%, Polynesian 4%, Micronesian 1.5%, European 0.8%, Chinese 0.3%, other 0.4%. **Religions:** Anglican, Roman Catholic, South Seas Evangelical, Seventh-Day Adventist, United (Methodist) Church, other Protestant. **Literacy rate:** 30%
**Economic summary: GDP/PPP** (2000 est.): $900 million; per capita $2,000. **Real growth rate:** 1%. **Inflation:** 10% (1999 est.). **Unemployment:** n.a. **Arable land:** 1%. **Agriculture:** cocoa, beans, coconuts, palm kernels, rice, potatoes, vegetables, fruit; cattle, pigs; timber; fish. **Labor force:** 26,842; agriculture n.a., industry n.a., services n.a. **Industries:** fish (tuna), mining, timber. **Natural resources:** fish, forests, gold, bauxite, phosphates, lead, zinc, nickel. **Exports:** $165 million (f.o.b., 1999 est.): timber, fish, palm oil, cocoa, copra. **Imports:** $152 million (f.o.b., 1999 est.): plant and equipment, manufactured goods, food and live animals, fuels, chemicals. **Major trading partners:** Japan, other Asian countries, Australia, Singapore, New Zealand. **Member of British Commonwealth.**

**Geography** A scattered archipelago of mountainous islands and low-lying coral atolls, the Solomon Islands lie east of Papua New Guinea and northeast of Australia in the south Pacific. The islands include Guadalcanal, Malaita, Santa Isabel, San Cristóbal, Choiseul, New Georgia, the Santa Cruz group, and numerous smaller islands.

**Government** Parliamentary democracy.

**History** It is thought that people have lived in the Solomon Islands since at least 2000 B.C. Explored in 1568 by Alvaro de Mendaña of Spain, the Solomons were not visited again for about 200 years. In 1886, Great Britain and Germany divided the islands

## Somalia

**SOMALI DEMOCRATIC REPUBLIC**

**National name:** Al Jumhouriya As-Somalya al-Dimocradia
**Prime Minister:** Hassan Abshir Farah (2001)
**Area:** 246,199 sq mi (637,657 sq km)
**Population (2002 est.):** 7,753,310 (growth rate: 2.9%); birth rate: 46.8/1000; infant mortality rate: 122.2/1000; density per sq mi: 31
**Capital and largest city (1990 est.):** Mogadishu, 900,000. **Monetary unit:** Somali shilling. **Languages:** Somali (official), Arabic, English, Italian. **Ethnicity/race:** Somali 85%, Bantu, Arabs. **Religion:** Islam (Sunni). **Literacy rate:** 24% (1990)
**Economic summary: GDP/PPP** (2000 est.): $4.3 billion; per capita $600. **Real growth rate:** n.a. **Inflation:** over 100% (businesses print their own money). **Unemployment:** n.a. **Arable land:** 2%. **Agriculture:** cattle, sheep, goats; bananas, sorghum, corn, sugarcane, mangoes, sesame seeds, beans; fish. **Labor force:** 3.7 million (very few are skilled laborers) (1993 est.); agriculture (mostly pastoral nomadism) 71%, industry and services 29%. **Industries:** a few small industries, including sugar refining, textiles, petroleum refining (mostly shut down), wireless communication. **Natural resources:** uranium and largely unexploited reserves of iron ore, tin, gypsum, bauxite, copper, salt. **Exports:** $186 million (f.o.b., 1999 est.): livestock, bananas, hides, fish (1999). **Imports:** $314 million (f.o.b., 1999 est.): manufactures, petroleum products, foodstuffs, construction materials (1995). **Major trading partners:** Saudi Arabia, Yemen, UAE, Italy, Pakistan, Djibouti, Kenya, Brazil, India.

**Geography** Somalia, situated in the Horn of Africa, lies along the Gulf of Aden and the Indian Ocean. It is bounded by Djibouti in the northwest, Ethiopia in the west, and Kenya in the southwest. In area it is slightly smaller than Texas. Generally arid and barren, Somalia has two chief rivers, the Shebelle and the Juba.

**Government** Between Jan. 1991 and Aug. 2000, Somalia had no working government. A fragile parliamentary government was formed Aug. 22, 2000.

**History** From the 7th to the 10th century, Arab and Persian trading posts were established along the coast of present-day Somalia. Nomadic tribes occupied the interior, occasionally pushing into Ethiopian territory.

In the 16th century, Turkish rule extended to the northern coast, and the Sultans of Zanzibar gained control in the south.

After British occupation of Aden in 1839, the Somali coast became its source of food. The French established a coal mining station in 1862 at the site of Djibouti, and the Italians planted a settlement in Eritrea. Egypt, which for a time claimed Turkish rights in the area, was succeeded by Britain. By 1920, a British protectorate and an Italian protectorate occupied what is now Somalia. The British ruled the entire area after 1941, with Italy returning in 1950 to serve as United Nations trustee for its former territory.

By 1960, Britain and Italy granted independence to their respective sectors, enabling the two to join as the Republic of Somalia on July 1, 1960. Somalia broke diplomatic relations with Britain in 1963 when the British granted the Somali-populated Northern Frontier District of Kenya to the Republic of Kenya.

On Oct. 15, 1969, President Abdi Rashid Ali Shermarke was assassinated and the army seized power, dissolving the legislature and arresting all government leaders. Maj. Gen. Mohamed Siad Barre, as president of a renamed Somali Democratic Republic, leaned heavily toward the USSR. In 1977, Somalia openly backed rebels in the easternmost area of Ethiopia, the Ogaden Desert, which had been seized by Ethiopia at the turn of the century. Somalia acknowledged defeat in an eight-month war against the Ethiopians that year, having lost much of its 32,000-man army and most of its tanks and planes. President Siad Barre fled the country in late Jan. 1991. His departure left Somalia in the hands of a number of clan-based guerrilla groups, none of which trusted each other.

Africa's worst drought occurred in 1992, and coupled with the devastation of civil war, Somalia was plunged into a severe famine—an estimated one-third of the population was in danger of dying from starvation. U.S. troops were sent in to protect the delivery of food in Dec. 1992. In May the UN took control of the relief efforts from the U.S. The warlord Mohamed Farah Aidid ambushed UN troops and dragged American bodies through the streets, causing an about-face in America's willingness to involve itself in the fate of this anarchic country. Peace talks in Kenya appeared to be moving slowly but steadily toward an agreement on an interim government, at least in principle, when on March 23, 1994, they collapsed. The last of the U.S. troops left in late March, leaving 19,000 UN troops behind.

Since 1991 Somalia has been engulfed in anarchy. Years of peace negotiations between the various factions have been fruitless, and warlords rule over individual swathes of land. In 1991, a breakaway nation, the Somaliland Republic, proclaimed its independence. Since then several warlords have set up their own ministates—Colonel Jama Ali Jama is president of breakaway Puntland, and Mohamed "General Morgan" Said Hersi has ruled Jubaland since the fall of 1998. Although internationally unrecognized, these states have been peaceful and stable.

In Aug. 2000, a parliament convened in nearby Djibouti and elected Somalia's first government in nearly a decade. After its first year in office, the new government still controlled only 10% of the country. But it had made significant advances for a country starting over: a national police force and army are in place and half of the 20,000 militias roaming the country have been demobilized.

In Nov. 2001, the U.S. froze the assets of Somalia's largest financial company, al-Barakaat, because of its alleged association with al-Qaeda terrorists. The company is a money-wiring business that transfers millions of dollars annually from Somali immigrants abroad to their relatives in Somalia. The freeze has severely damaged the fragile Somalian economy.

# South Africa

### REPUBLIC OF SOUTH AFRICA

**National name:** Republic of South Africa
**President:** Thabo Mbeki (1999)
**Area:** 471,008 sq mi (1,219,912 sq km)
**Population (2002 est.):** 43,647,658 (growth rate: 0.2%); birth rate: 20.6/1000; infant mortality rate: 61.8/1000; density per sq mi: 93
**Administrative capital:** Pretoria; **Legislative capital:** Cape Town; **Judicial capital:** Bloemfontein. No decision has been made to relocate the seat of government. South Africa is demarcated into nine provinces, consisting of the Gauteng, Northern Province, Mpumalanga, North West, KwaZulu/Natal, Eastern Cape, Western Cape, Northern Cape, and Free State. Each province has its own capital. **Largest metropolitan areas (1995):** Johannesburg (2000 est.), 5,700,000 (metro. area); Cape Peninsula, 2,350,157; East Rand, 1,378,792 (part of Johannesburg metro. area); Durban/Pinetown, 1,137,378; Pretoria, 1,080,187. **Monetary unit:** Rand. **Languages:** Xhosa and Zulu (official), English, Afrikaans, Ndebele, Sesotho sa Leboa, Sesotho, Swati, Tsonga, Setswana, Tshivenda. **Ethnicity/race:** black 75.2%, white 13.6%, Colored 8.6%, Indian 2.6%. **Religions:** Christian; Hindu; Islam. **Literacy rate:** 60% (1980)
**Economic summary: GDP/PPP** (2000 est.): $369 billion; per capita $8,500. **Real growth rate:** 3%. **Inflation:** 5.3%. **Unemployment:** 30%. **Arable land:** 10%. **Agriculture:** corn, wheat, sugarcane, fruits, vegetables; beef, poultry, mutton, wool, dairy products. **Labor force:** 17 million economically active (2000); agriculture 30%, industry 25%, services 45% (1999 est.). **Industries:** mining (world's largest producer of platinum, gold, chromium), automobile assembly, metalworking, machinery, textile, iron and steel, chemicals, fertilizer, foodstuffs. **Natural resources:** gold, chromium, antimony, coal, iron ore, manganese, nickel, phosphates, tin, uranium, gem diamonds, platinum, copper, vanadium, salt, natural gas. **Exports:** $30.8 billion (f.o.b., 2000 est.): gold, diamonds, other metals and minerals, machinery and equipment. **Imports:** $27.6 billion (f.o.b., 2000 est.): machinery, foodstuffs and equipment, chemicals, petroleum products, scientific instruments. **Major trading partners:** UK, Italy, Japan, U.S., Germany.

**Geography** South Africa, on the continent's southern tip, is bordered by the Atlantic Ocean on the west and by the Indian Ocean on the south and east. Its neighbors are Namibia in the northwest, Zimbabwe and Botswana in the north, and Mozambique and Swaziland in the northeast. The kingdom of Lesotho forms an enclave within the southeast part of South Africa, which occupies an area nearly three times that of California.

The southernmost point of Africa is Cape Agulhas, located in the Western Cape Province about 100 mi (161 km) southeast of the Cape of Good Hope.

**Government** Republic.

**History** The San people were the first settlers. The Dutch East India Company landed the first European settlers on the Cape of Good Hope in 1652, launching a colony that by the end of the 18th century numbered only about 15,000. Known as Boers or Afrikaners, speaking a Dutch dialect known as Afrikaans, the settlers as early as 1795 tried to establish an independent republic.

After occupying the Cape Colony in that year, Britain took permanent possession in 1814 at the end of the Napoleonic Wars, bringing in 5,000 settlers. Anglicization of government and the freeing of slaves in 1833 drove about 12,000 Afrikaners to make the "great trek" north and east into African tribal territory, where they established the republics of the Transvaal and the Orange Free State.

The discovery of diamonds in 1867 and gold nine years later brought an influx of "outlanders" into the republics and spurred Cape Colony prime minister Cecil Rhodes to plot annexation. Rhodes's scheme of sparking an "outlander" rebellion, to which an armed party under Leander Starr Jameson would ride to the rescue, misfired in 1895, forcing Rhodes to resign. What British expansionists called the "inevitable" war with the Boers eventually broke out on Oct. 11, 1899. The defeat of the Boers in 1902 led in 1910 to the Union of South Africa, composed of four provinces, the two former republics, and the old Cape and Natal colonies. Louis Botha, a Boer, became the first prime minister. Organized political activity among Africans started with the establishment of the African National Congress in 1912.

Jan Christiaan Smuts brought the nation into World War II on the Allied side against Nationalist opposition, and South Africa became a charter member of the United Nations in 1945, but refused to sign the Universal Declaration of Human Rights. Apartheid—racial separation—dominated domestic politics as the Nationalists gained power and imposed greater restrictions on Bantus, Asians, and Coloreds (in South Africa the term meant any nonwhite person). African voters were removed from the voter rolls in 1936.

Afrikaner hostility to Britain triumphed in 1961 with the declaration on May 31 of the Republic of South Africa and the severing of ties with the Commonwealth. Nationalist prime minister H. F. Verwoerd's government in 1963 asserted the power to restrict the freedom of those who opposed rigid racial laws. Three years later, amid increasing racial tension and criticism from the outside world, Verwoerd was assassinated. His Nationalist successor, Balthazar J. Vorster, launched a campaign of conciliation toward conservative black African states, offering development loans and trade concessions.

Elections on May 7, 1987, improved the prime minister President P. W. Botha's Nationalist Party while enabling the far-right Conservative Party to replace the liberal Progressives as the official opposition. The results of the whites-only vote indicated a strong conservative reaction against Botha's policy of limited reform.

A stroke led Botha to step down as leader of his party in 1989 in favor of F. W. de Klerk. De Klerk accelerated the pace of reform. He removed the ban from the African National Congress, the principal anti-apartheid organization, and released Nelson Mandela, the ANC deputy president, after 27 years of imprisonment. Negotiations between the government and the ANC commenced.

On June 5, 1991, the Parliament scrapped the country's apartheid laws concerning property ownership.

On June 17 the Parliament did the same for the Population Registration Act of 1950, which classified all South Africans at birth by race. In Feb. 1993 the ANC approved a plan that would allow minority parties to participate in the government for five years after the end of white rule. Also in February, the first nonwhites entered the cabinet in an apparent bid to broaden the base of the ruling National Party.

The 1994 election, as expected, resulted in a massive victory for Mandela and his ANC. The new government included six ministers from the National Party and three from the Inkatha Freedom Party.

In 1997 the Truth and Reconciliation Commission, chaired by Desmond Tutu, began hearings regarding human rights violations between 1960 and 1993. The commission promised amnesty to those who confessed their crimes under the apartheid system. In 1998 F. W. de Klerk, P. W. Botha, and leaders of the ANC appeared before the commission, and the nation continued to grapple with its enlightened but often painful and divisive process of national recovery.

Nelson Mandela, whose term as president cemented his reputation as one of the world's most enlightened statesmen, retired in 1999. On June 2, 1999, Thabo Mbeki, the pragmatic deputy president of South Africa and leader of the African National Congress, was elected president in a landslide, having already assumed many of Mandela's governing responsibilities.

In 2000 and 2001, Mbeki wrestled with a slumping economy, a skyrocketing crime rate, and the country's rising AIDS epidemic. South Africa, which has the highest number of HIV-positive people in the world, has been hampered in fighting the epidemic by its president's highly controversial views. Mbeki has denied the link between HIV and AIDS, claimed that the West has exaggerated the epidemic to sell drugs, and charged that Western AIDS activists consider "Africans to be germ carriers and human beings of a lower order." The international community as well as most South African leaders, including Nelson Mandela and Desmond Tutu, have admonished Mbeki on his lack of leadership in combating AIDS. In April 2002, Mbeki's administration slightly reversed its policy, announcing plans to provide nationwide access to drugs that help prevent women from infecting their babies with HIV during childbirth.

# Spain

### KINGDOM OF SPAIN

**National name:** Reino de España

**Ruler:** King Juan Carlos I (1975)

**Prime Minister:** José María Aznar (1996)

**Area:** 194,881 sq mi (504,782 sq km)

**Population (2002 est.):** 40,077,100 (growth rate: 0.0%); birth rate: 9.3/1000; infant mortality rate: 4.8/1000; density per sq mi: 206

**Capital and largest city (2000 est.).:** Madrid, 5,050,000 (metro. area). **Other large cities:** Barcelona, 1,630,867; Valencia, 764,293; Seville, 714,148.

**Monetary units:** Euro (formerly peseta). **Languages:** Castilian Spanish 74% (official), Catalan 17%, Galician 7%, Basque 2%. **Ethnicity/race:** composite of Mediterranean and Nordic types. **Religion:** Roman Catholic 99%. **Literacy rate:** 95% (1991)

**Economic summary: GDP/PPP** (2000 est.): $720.8 billion; per capita $18,000. **Real growth rate:** 4%. **Inflation:** 3.4%. **Unemployment:** 14%. **Arable land:** 30%. **Agriculture:** grain, vegetables, olives, wine grapes, sugar beets, citrus; beef, pork, poultry, dairy products; fish. **Labor force:** 17 million (2000); services

64%, manufacturing, mining, and construction 28%, agriculture 8% (1997 est.). **Industries:** textiles and apparel (including footwear), food and beverages, metals and metal manufactures, chemicals, shipbuilding, automobiles, machine tools, tourism. **Natural resources:** coal, lignite, iron ore, uranium, mercury, pyrites, fluorspar, gypsum, zinc, lead, tungsten, copper, kaolin, potash, hydropower, arable land. **Exports:** $120.5 billion (f.o.b., 2000 est.): machinery, motor vehicles; foodstuffs, other consumer goods. **Imports:** $153.9 billion (f.o.b., 2000 est.): machinery and equipment, fuels, chemicals, semifinished goods; foodstuffs, consumer goods (1997). **Major trading partners:** EU, Latin America, U.S., OPEC, Japan.

1. Including the Balearic and Canary Islands.

**Geography** Spain occupies 85% of the Iberian Peninsula, which it shares with Portugal, in southwest Europe. Africa is less than 10 mi (16 km) south at the Strait of Gibraltar. A broad central plateau slopes to the south and east, crossed by a series of mountain ranges and river valleys. Principal rivers are the Ebro in the northeast, the Tajo in the central region, and the Guadalquivir in the south. Off Spain's east coast in the Mediterranean are the Balearic Islands (1,936 sq mi; 5,014 sq km), the largest of which is Majorca. Sixty mi (97 km) west of Africa are the Canary Islands (2,808 sq mi; 7,273 sq km).

**Government** Parliamentary monarchy.

**History** Spain, originally inhabited by Celts, Iberians, and Basques, became a part of the Roman Empire in 206 B.C., when it was conquered by Scipio Africanus. In A.D. 412, the barbarian Visigothic leader At, ulf crossed the Pyrenees and ruled Spain, first in the name of the Roman emperor and then independently. In 711, the Muslims under Tariq entered Spain from Africa and within a few years completed the subjugation of the country. In 732, the Franks, led by Charles Martel, defeated the Muslims near Poitiers, thus preventing the further expansion of Islam in southern Europe. Internal dissension of Spanish Islam invited a steady Christian conquest from the north.

Aragon and Castile were the most important Spanish states from the 12th to the 15th century, consolidated by the marriage of Ferdinand II and Isabella I in 1469. The last Muslim stronghold, Granada, was captured in 1492. Roman Catholicism was established as the official state religion and most Jews (1492) and Muslims (1502) were expelled. In the era of exploration, discovery, and colonization, Spain amassed tremendous wealth and a vast colonial empire through the conquest of Peru by Pizarro (1532–33) and of Mexico by Cortés (1519–21). The Spanish Hapsburg monarchy became for a time the most powerful in the world. In 1588, Philip II sent his invincible Armada to invade England, but its destruction cost Spain its supremacy on the seas and paved the way for England's colonization of America. Spain then sank rapidly to the status of a second-rate power under the rule of weak Hapsburg kings, and never again played a major role in European politics. The War of the Spanish Succession (1701–14) resulted in Spain's loss of Belgium, Luxembourg, Milan, Sardinia, and Naples. Its colonial empire in the Americas and the Philippines vanished in wars and revolutions during the 18th and 19th centuries.

In World War I, Spain maintained a position of neutrality. In 1923, Gen. Miguel Primo de Rivera became dictator. In 1930, King Alfonso XIII revoked the dic-

tatorship, but a strong antimonarchist and republican movement led to his leaving Spain in 1931. The new constitution declared Spain a workers' republic, broke up the large estates, separated church and state, and secularized the schools. The elections held in 1936 returned a strong Popular Front majority, with Manuel Azaña as president.

On July 18, 1936, a conservative army officer in Morocco, Francisco Franco Bahamonde, led a mutiny against the government. The civil war that followed lasted three years and cost the lives of nearly a million people. Franco was aided by Fascist Italy and Nazi Germany, while Soviet Russia helped the Loyalist side. Several hundred leftist Americans served in the Abraham Lincoln Brigade on the side of the republic. The war ended when Franco took Madrid on March 28, 1939. Franco became head of the state, national chief of the Falange Party (the governing party), and premier and caudillo (leader). In a referendum in 1947, the Spanish people approved a Franco-drafted succession law declaring Spain a monarchy again. Franco, however, continued as chief of state.

In 1969, Franco and the Cortes designated Prince Juan Carlos Alfonso Victor María de Borbón (who married Princess Sophia of Greece on May 14, 1962) to become king of Spain when the provisional government headed by Franco came to an end. Franco died of a heart attack on Nov. 20, 1975, after more than a year of ill health, and Juan Carlos was proclaimed king seven days later.

Under pressure from Catalonian and Basque nationalists, Premier Adolfo Suárez granted home rule to these regions in 1979. Basque separatists committed hundreds of terrorist bombings and kidnappings that continue to the present. With the overwhelming election of Prime Minister Felipe González Márquez and his Spanish Socialist Workers Party in the Oct. 20, 1982, parliamentary elections, the Franco past was finally buried.

Spain entered NATO in 1982. A treaty admitting Spain, along with Portugal, to the European Economic Community, now the European Union, took effect on Jan. 1, 1986. Later that year, Spain voted to remain in NATO but outside of its military command. General elections in March 1996 produced a victory for the conservative Popular Party, which, although lacking an absolute majority in the Cortes, received the backing of regional parties for a coalition government with José María Aznar as prime minister.

On Oct. 16, 1998, Spain issued a warrant for the extradition of former Chilean dictator Augusto Pinochet, charging him with the genocide, torture, and kidnapping of thousands of people, including Spanish nationals, during his 17-year rule. Eventually, Pinochet was returned to Chile where he was deemed unfit to stand trial.

In March 2000, Prime Minister Aznar of the center-right People's Party easily won reelection.

In July 2002, Morocco invaded a tiny, uninhabited island claimed by Spain off its Mediterranean coast. Spain promptly seized it back.

In Aug. 2002, Batasuna, the political wing of the Basque terrorist organization ETA, was banned. The wisdom of driving the party underground instead of permitting it a legitimate political outlet has been questioned.

# Sri Lanka

**DEMOCRATIC SOCIALIST REPUBLIC OF SRI LANKA**

**President:** Chandrika B. Kumaratunga (1994)
**Prime Minister:** Ranil Wickremesinghe (2001)
**Area:** 25,332 sq mi (65,610 sq km)
**Population (2002 est.):** 19,576,783 (growth rate: 1.0%); birth rate: 16.4/1000; infant mortality rate: 15.7/1000; density per sq mi: 773
**Capitals and largest city (1992 est.):** Colombo (official) 1,994,000; Sri Jayawardenepura Kotte (legislative and judicial), 107,000 (1988 est.). **Other large cities (1992 est.):** Gampaha, 1,543,000; Kurunegala, 1,445,000; Kandy, 1,257,000. **Monetary unit:** Sri Lanka rupee. **Languages:** Sinhala (official), Tamil, English. **Ethnicity/race:** Sinhalese 74%, Tamil 18%, Moor 7%, Burgher, Malay, and Vedda 1%. **Religions:** Buddhist 69%, Hindu 15%, Islam 8%, Christian 8%. **Literacy rate:** 88% (1990)
**Economic summary:** GDP/PPP (2000 est.): $62.7 billion; per capita $3,250. **Real growth rate:** 5.6%. **Inflation:** 8.5%. **Unemployment:** 8.8% (1999 est.). **Arable land:** 14%. **Agriculture:** rice, sugarcane, grains, pulses, oilseed, spices, tea, rubber, coconuts; milk, eggs, hides, beef. **Labor force:** 6.6 million (1998); services 45%, agriculture 38%, industry 17% (1998 est.). **Industries:** processing of rubber, tea, coconuts, and other agricultural commodities; clothing, cement, petroleum refining, textiles, tobacco. **Natural resources:** limestone, graphite, mineral sands, gems, phosphates, clay, hydropower. **Exports:** $5.2 billion (f.o.b., 2000): textiles and apparel, tea, diamonds, coconut products, petroleum products. **Imports:** $6.1 billion (f.o.b., 2000): machinery and equipment, textiles, petroleum, foodstuffs. **Major trading partners:** U.S., UK, Middle East, Germany, Japan, India, Hong Kong, Singapore, South Korea. **Member of Commonwealth of Nations**

**Geography** An island in the Indian Ocean off the southeast tip of India, Sri Lanka is about half the size of Alabama. Most of the land is flat and rolling; mountains in the south-central region rise to over 8,000 ft (2,438 m).

**Government** Republic.

**History** Indo-Aryan emigration from India in the 5th century B.C. came to form the largest ethnic group on Sri Lanka today, the Sinhalese. Tamils, the second-largest ethnic group on the island, were originally from the Tamil region of India, and emigrated between the 3rd century B.C. and A.D. 1200. Until colonial powers controlled Ceylon (the country's name until 1972), Sinhalese and Tamil rulers fought for dominance over the island. The Tamils, primarily Hindus, claimed the northern section of the island and the Sinhalese, who are predominantly Buddhist, controlled the south. In 1505 the Portuguese took possession of Ceylon until the Dutch India Company usurped control (1658–1796). The British took over in 1796, and Ceylon became an English Crown colony in 1802. The British developed coffee, tea, and rubber plantations. On Feb. 4, 1948, after pressure from Ceylonese nationalist leaders (which briefly unified the Tamil and Sinhalese), Ceylon became a self-governing dominion of the Commonwealth of Nations.

S. W. R. D. Bandaranaike became prime minister in 1956 and championed Sinhalese nationalism, making Sinhala the country's only official language and including state support of Buddhism, further marginalizing the Tamil minority. He was assassinated in 1959 by a Buddhist monk. His widow, Sirimavo Bandaranaike, became the world's first female prime min-

ister in 1960. The name *Ceylon* was changed to Sri Lanka on May 22, 1972, which was its original name and means "resplendent island."

The Tamil minority's mounting resentment toward the Sinhalese majority's monopoly on political and economic power, exacerbated by cultural and religious differences, erupted in bloody violence in 1983. By the end of 2001, the civil war, showing no signs of ceasing, had claimed 62,000 lives. Tamils make up about 18% of the population in Sri Lanka, whereas approximately three-quarters of Sri Lanka's 18 million people are Sinhalese. Tamil rebel groups, the strongest of which are the Liberation Tigers of Tamil Eelam, or Tamil Tigers, are fighting for a separate nation.

India had sent a peacekeeping force in July 1987 to help maintain an accord granting the Tamil minority limited autonomy. The agreement failed, and Indian troops withdrew at the end of 1989.

President Ranasinghe Premadasa was assassinated at a May Day political rally in 1993, when a Tamil rebel detonated explosives strapped to himself. Tamil extremists have frequently resorted to terrorist attacks against civilians and are renowned for suicide bombers that target government officials. The next president, Chandrika Kumaratunga, vowed to restore peace to the country. In Dec. 1999, she was herself wounded in a terrorist attack. By early 2000, 18 years of war had claimed the lives of more than 64,000, mostly civilians.

In Dec. 2001 elections, Ranil Wickremesinghe, longtime bitter rival of President Kumaratunga, was sworn in as prime minister. Wickremesinghe's victory precipitated a formal cease-fire with the Tamil rebels. Norway brokered the fragile peace agreement, which was signed in Feb. 2002 by Wickremesinghe and rebel leader Velupillai Prabhakaran. In March Wickremesinghe became the first prime minister in 20 years to visit Jaffna, the Tamil stronghold. In April, in his first press conference since 1990, Prabhakaran said he hoped the two parties could reach a political settlement to end the 18-year war. After an August meeting between a Tiger rebel leader and government officials in Oslo, Sri Lanka announced it would formally lift its ban on the group, and talks began in September.

# Sudan

**REPUBLIC OF THE SUDAN**

**National name:** Jamhuryat es-Sudan
**President:** Lt. Gen. Omar Hassan Ahmad al-Bashir (1989)
**Area:** 967,493 sq mi (2,505,810 sq km)
**Population (2002 est.):** 37,090,298 (growth rate: 2.7%); birth rate: 37.2/1000; infant mortality rate: 67.1/1000; density per sq mi: 38
**Capital (1993 est.):** Khartoum, 924,505. **Largest cities:** Omdurman, 1,267,077; Port Sudan, 305,000; **Monetary unit:** Dinar. **Languages:** Arabic (official), English, tribal dialects. **Ethnicity/race:** black 52%, Arab 39%, Beja 6%, foreigners 2%, other 1%. **Religions:** Islam (Sunni) 70%, indigenous 20%, Christian 5%. **Literacy rate:** 27% (1990)
**Economic summary:** GDP/PPP (2000 est.): $35.7 billion; per capita $1,000. **Real growth rate:** 7%. **Inflation:** 10%. **Unemployment:** 4% (1996 est.). **Arable land:** 5%. **Agriculture:** cotton, groundnuts (peanuts), sorghum, millet, wheat, gum arabic, sugarcane, cassara, mangos, papaya, bananas, sweet potatoes, sesame; sheep, livestock. **Labor force:** 11 million (1996 est.); agriculture 80%, industry and commerce 10%, government 6%, unemployed 4% (1996 est.). **Industries:** cotton ginning, textiles, cement; edible oils, sugar, soap distilling, shoes, petroleum refining, pharmaceuticals, armaments.

**Natural resources:** petroleum; small reserves of iron ore, copper, chromium ore, zinc, tungsten, mica, silver, gold, hydropower. **Exports:** $1.7 billion (f.o.b., 2000 est.): oil and petroleum products, cotton, sesame, livestock, groundnuts, gum arabic, sugar. **Imports:** $1.2 billion (f.o.b., 2000 est.): foodstuffs, manufactured goods, machinery and transport equipment, medicines and chemicals, textiles. **Major trading partners:** Saudi Arabia, Italy, Germany, France, Thailand, China, Libya, UK.

**Geography** The Sudan, in northeast Africa, is the largest country on the continent, measuring about one-fourth the size of the United States. Its neighbors are Chad and the Central African Republic on the west, Egypt and Libya on the north, Ethiopia and Eritrea on the east, and Kenya, Uganda, and Democratic Republic of the Congo on the south. The Red Sea washes about 500 mi of the eastern coast. It is traversed from north to south by the Nile.

**Government** Military government.

**History** What is now northern Sudan was in ancient times the kingdom of Nubia, which came under Egyptian rule after 2600 B.C. An Egyptian and Nubian civilization called Kush flourished until A.D. 350. Missionaries converted the region to Christianity in the 6th century, but an influx of Muslim Arabs, who had already conquered Egypt, eventually controlled the area and replaced Christianity with Islam. During the 1500s a people called the Funj conquered much of Sudan, and several other black African groups settled in the south, including the Dinka, Shilluk, Nuer, and Azande. Egyptians again conquered the Sudan in 1874, and after Britain occupied Egypt in 1882, it took over Sudan in 1898, ruling the country in conjunction with Egypt. It was known as the Anglo-Egyptian Sudan between 1898 and 1955.

The 20th century saw the growth of Sudanese nationalism, and in 1953 Egypt and Britain granted the Sudan self-government. Independence was proclaimed on Jan. 1, 1956. Since independence, the Sudan has been ruled by a series of unstable parliamentary governments and military regimes. Under Maj. Gen. Gaafar Mohamed Nimeiri, the Sudan instituted fundamentalist Islamic law in 1983. This exacerbated the rift between the Arab North, the seat of the government, and the black African animists and Christians in the South. Differences in language, religion, ethnicity, and political power erupted in an unending civil war between government forces, strongly influenced by the National Islamic Front (NIF), and the southern rebels, whose most influential faction is the Sudan People's Liberation Army (SPLA). Neither side has gained the upper hand, and more than an estimated 1 million people have died in battle or from famines and disease resulting from war. Human rights violations, religious persecution, and allegations that the Sudan has been a safe haven for terrorists have isolated the country from most of the international community. In 1995, the UN imposed sanctions against it.

On Aug. 20, 1998, the United States launched cruise missiles that destroyed a pharmaceutical manufacturing facility in Khartoum that allegedly manufactured chemical weapons. The U.S. contended that the Sudanese factory was financed by Islamic militant Osama Bin Laden.

Since 1999 international attention has been focused on evidence that slavery is widespread throughout Sudan. Arab raiders from the north of the country have enslaved thousands of southerners, who are black. The Dinka people have been the hardest hit. Some sources point out that the raids intensified in the 1980s along with the civil war between north and south. Since the early 1990s, several international human rights organizations have engaged in the controversial practice of buying back slaves from the traders. Some contend this may inadvertently encourage slavery since slave redemption has become profitable. The antislavery organizations counter that in the absence of a political solution, buying back slaves is the only hope for thousands of Sudanese.

Ever since Bashir's military coup in 1989, the de facto ruler of Sudan had been Hassan el-Turabi, a cleric and political leader who is a major figure in the pan-Arabic Islamic fundamentalist resurgence. In 1999, however, Bashir ousted Turabi and placed him under house arrest. Since then Bashir has made overtures to the West, and in Sept. 2001, the UN lifted its five-year-old sanctions. The U.S., however, still officially considers it a terrorist state.

After 19 years of brutal civil war, a cease-fire was declared between the Sudanese government and the Sudan People's Liberation Army (SPLA) in July 2002. In peace talks, the government has agreed to a power-sharing government for the next six years, to be followed by a referendum on self-determination for the south. Much skepticism remains whether the government will make good on its promises—it has violated agreements made in 1997 and 1998 and seems determined to hold on to Sudan's oil fields, 75% of which are located in the south. Fighting on both sides continued throughout the peace negotiations. More than 2 million people have died as a result of the civil war, mostly from starvation and disease.

# Suriname

### REPUBLIC OF SURINAME

**President:** Ronald Venetiaan (2000)
**Prime Minister:** Jules Ajodhia (2000)
**Area:** 63,039 sq mi (163,270 sq km)
**Population (2002 est.):** 436,494 (growth rate: 1.4%); birth rate: 20.0/1000; infant mortality rate: 23.5/1000; density per sq mi: 7
**Capital and largest city (1993 est.):** Paramaribo, 200,970. **Monetary unit:** Suriname guilder. **Languages:** Dutch (official), Surinamese (lingua franca), English widely spoken. **Ethnicity/race:** East Indians, also known locally as Hindustanis (their ancestors emigrated from northern India in the latter part of the 19th century) 37%, Creole (mixed European and African ancestry) 31%, Javanese 15.3%, "Bush Negroes," also known as Maroons (their ancestors were brought to the country in the 17th and 18th centuries as slaves) 10.3%, Amerindian 2.6%, Chinese 1.7%, Europeans 1%, other 1.1%. **Religions:** Protestant 25.2%, Roman Catholic 22.8%, Hindu 27.4%, Islam 19.6%, indigenous about 5%. **Literacy rate:** 95% (1990)
**Economic summary: GDP/PPP (1999 est.):** $1.48 billion; per capita $3,400. **Real growth rate:** –1%. **Inflation:** 78% (2000 est.). **Unemployment:** 20% (1997). **Arable land:** 0%. **Agriculture:** paddy rice, bananas, palm kernels, coconuts, plantains, peanuts; beef, chickens; forest products; shrimp. **Labor force:** 100,000; agriculture n.a., industry n.a., services n.a. **Industries:** bauxite and gold mining, alumina production, lumbering, food processing, fishing. **Natural resources:** timber, hydropower, fish, kaolin, shrimp, bauxite, gold, and small amounts of nickel, copper, platinum, iron ore. **Exports:** $443 million (f.o.b., 1999): alumina, crude oil, lumber, shrimp and fish, rice, bananas. **Imports:** $525 million (f.o.b., 1999): capital equipment, petroleum, foodstuffs, cotton, consumer goods. **Major trading partners:** U.S., Norway, Netherlands, France, Japan, UK, Trinidad and Tobago, Brazil.

**Geography** Suriname lies on the northeast coast of South America, with Guyana to the west, French Guiana to the east, and Brazil to the south. It is about one-tenth larger than Michigan. The principal rivers are the Corantijn on the Guyana border, the Marowijne in the east, and the Suriname, on which the capital city of Paramaribo is situated.

**Government** Constitutional democracy.

**History** Suriname's earliest inhabitants were the Surinen Indians, after whom the country is named. By the 16th century they had been supplanted by other South American Indians. Spain explored Suriname in 1593, but by 1602 the Dutch began to settle the land, followed by the English. The English transferred sovereignty to the Dutch in 1667 (the Treaty of Breda) in exchange for New Amsterdam (New York). Colonization was confined to a narrow coastal strip, and until the abolition of slavery in 1863, African slaves furnished the labor for the coffee and sugarcane plantations. Escaped African slaves fled into the interior, reconstituted their western African culture, and came to be called "Bush Negroes" by the Dutch. After 1870, East Indian laborers were imported from British India and Javanese from the Dutch East Indies.

Known as Dutch Guiana, the colony was integrated into the kingdom of the Netherlands in 1948. Two years later Dutch Guiana was granted home rule, except for foreign affairs and defense. After race rioting over unemployment and inflation, the Netherlands granted Suriname complete independence on Nov. 25, 1975. A coup d'état in 1980 brought military rule. During much of the 1980s Suriname was under the repressive control of Lieut. Col. Dési Bouterse. The Netherlands stopped all aid in 1982 when Suriname soldiers killed 15 journalists, politicians, lawyers, and union officials. Defense spending increased significantly, and the economy suffered. A guerrilla insurgency by the Jungle Commando (a Bush Negro guerrilla group) threatened to destabilize the country and was harshly suppressed by Bouterse. Free elections were held on May 25, 1991, depriving the military of much of its political power. In 1992 a peace treaty was signed between the government and several guerrilla groups. In March 1997, the president announced new economic measures, including eliminating import tariffs on most basic goods coupled with strict price controls. Later that year, the Netherlands said it would prosecute Bouterse for cocaine trafficking.

Public discontent over the 70% inflation rate prompted President Jules Wijdenbosch to hold elections in May 2000, one year ahead of schedule. The New Front for Democracy and Development, a coalition led by former president Ronald Venetiaan, won the election. Suriname has earned a reputation as a center for drug trafficking; in 1998, former dictator Bouterse was sentenced in absentia in the Netherlands for transporting cocaine.

# Swaziland

### KINGDOM OF SWAZILAND

**Ruler:** King Mswati III (1986)
**Prime Minister:** Barnabas Sibusiso Dlamini (1996)
**Area:** 6,704 sq mi (17,363 sq km)
**Population (2002 est.):** 1,123,605 (growth rate: 1.6%); birth rate: 39.6/1000; infant mortality rate: 109.4/1000; density per sq mi: 168
**Capital and largest city (1990 est.):** Mbabane 47,020.
**Monetary unit:** Lilangeni. **Languages:** English and Swazi (official). **Ethnicity/race:** African 97%, European 3%. **Religions:** Christian 60%, indigenous 40%.
**Literacy rate:** 70% (1986)

**Economic summary: GDP/PPP** (2000 est.): $4.4 billion; per capita $4,000. **Real growth rate:** 2.4%. **Inflation:** 6.4%. **Unemployment:** 22% (1995 est.). **Arable land:** 11%. **Agriculture:** sugarcane, cotton, corn, tobacco, rice, citrus, pineapples, sorghum, peanuts; cattle, goats, sheep. **Labor force:** n.a.; private sector 70%, public sector 30%. **Industries:** mining (coal and asbestos), wood pulp, sugar, soft drink concentrates. **Natural resources:** asbestos, coal, clay, cassiterite, hydropower, forests, small gold and diamond deposits, quarry stone, and talc. **Exports:** $881 million (f.o.b., 2000): soft drink concentrates, sugar, wood pulp, cotton yarn, refrigerators, citrus and canned fruit. **Imports:** $928 million (f.o.b., 2000): motor vehicles, machinery, transport equipment, foodstuffs, petroleum products, chemicals. **Major trading partners:** South Africa, EU, Mozambique, U.S., North Korea, Japan, Singapore. **Member of Commonwealth of Nations**

**Geography** Swaziland, which is about 85% the size of New Jersey, is surrounded by South Africa and Mozambique. The country consists of a high veld in the west and a series of plateaus descending from 6,000 ft (1,829 m) to a low veld of 1,500 ft (457 m).

**Government** Absolute monarchy.

**History** Bantu peoples migrated southwest to the area of Mozambique in the 16th century. A number of clans broke away from the main body in the 18th century and settled in Swaziland. In the 19th century these clans organized as a tribe, partly because they were in constant conflict with the Zulu. Their ruler, Mswazi, appealed to the British in the 1840s for help against the Zulu. The British and the Transvaal governments guaranteed the independence of Swaziland in 1881.

South Africa held Swaziland as a protectorate from 1894 to 1899, but after the Boer War, in 1902, Swaziland was transferred to British administration. The paramount chief was recognized as the native authority in 1941. In 1963, the territory was constituted a protectorate, and on Sept. 6, 1968, it became the independent nation of Swaziland.

Since 1986, King Mswati III has ruled as sub-Saharan Africa's last absolute monarch. Political parties are banned and the king appoints 10 of the 65 members of Parliament as well as the prime minister. King Mswati can veto any law passed by the legislature and frequently rules by decree.

With a modern infrastructure, Swaziland boasts one of the largest per capita manufacturing sectors in Africa. It is one of the few countries on the continent never to face an economic crisis severe enough to warrant imposition of a World Bank adjustment program. Many of the businesses in Swaziland moved there from South Africa in the 1980s in an effort to avoid international sanctions against apartheid.

In 1992, hundreds of thousands of Swazis faced starvation. Two years of drought as well as bad planning and agricultural practices were blamed for the crisis. The government has come under criticism for buying the king a $50 million-dollar luxury jet—a quarter of the national budget—while famine is looming.

# Sweden

### KINGDOM OF SWEDEN

**National name:** Konungariket Sverige
**Sovereign:** King Carl XVI Gustaf (1973)
**Prime Minister:** Göran Persson (1996)
**Area:** 173,731 sq mi (449,964 sq km)
**Population (2002 est.):** 8,876,744 (growth rate: –0.1%); birth rate: 9.8/1000; infant mortality rate: 3.4/1000; density per sq mi: 51

**Capital and largest city (1994):** Stockholm, 703,627. **Largest cities:** Göteborg, 444,553; Malmö, 242,706; Uppsala, 181,191. **Monetary unit:** Krona. **Language:** Swedish. **Ethnicity/race:** white 88%, Lapp (Sami), foreign-born or first-generation immigrants (Finns, Yugoslavs, Danes, Norwegians, Greeks, Turks) 12%. **Religions:** Evangelical Lutheran 94%, Roman Catholic 1.5%, Pentecostal 1%, other 3.5%. **Literacy rate:** 99% (1979)
**Economic summary: GDP/PPP** (2000 est.): $197 billion; per capita $22,200. **Real growth rate:** 4.3%. **Inflation:** 1.2%. **Unemployment:** 6%. **Arable land:** 7%. **Agriculture:** grains, sugar beets, potatoes; meat, milk. **Labor force:** 4.4 million; agriculture 2%, industry 24%, services 74% (2000 est.). **Industries:** iron and steel, precision equipment (bearings, radio and telephone parts, armaments), wood pulp and paper products, processed foods, motor vehicles. **Natural resources:** zinc, iron ore, lead, copper, silver, timber, uranium, hydropower. **Exports:** $95.5 billion (f.o.b., 2000): machinery 35%, motor vehicles, paper products, pulp and wood, iron and steel products, chemicals. **Imports:** $80 billion (f.o.b., 2000): machinery, petroleum and petroleum products, chemicals, motor vehicles, iron and steel; foodstuffs, clothing. **Major trading partners:** EU, U.S., Norway.

**Geography** Sweden, which occupies the eastern part of the Scandinavian peninsula, is the fourth-largest country in Europe, and is one-tenth larger than California. The country slopes eastward and southward from the Kjölen Mountains along the Norwegian border, where the peak elevation is Kebnekaise at 6,965 ft (2,123 m) in Lapland. In the north are mountains and many lakes. To the south and east are central lowlands and south of them are fertile areas of forest, valley, and plain. Along Sweden's rocky coast, chopped up by bays and inlets, are many islands, the largest of which are Gotland and Öland.

**Government** Constitutional monarchy.

**History** The earliest historical mention of Sweden is found in Tacitus's *Germania,* where reference is made to the powerful king and strong fleet of the Sviones. In the 11th century, Olaf Sköttkonung became the first Swedish king to be baptized as a Christian. Around 1400, an attempt was made to unite Sweden, Norway, and Denmark into one kingdom, but this led to bitter strife between the Danes and the Swedes. In 1520, the Danish king Christian II conquered Sweden and in the "Stockholm Bloodbath" put leading Swedish personages to death. Gustavus Vasa (1523–60) broke away from Denmark and fashioned the modern Swedish state. He also confiscated property from the Roman Catholic Church in Sweden to pay Sweden's war debts. The king justified his actions on the basis of Martin Luther's doctrines, which were being accepted nationwide with royal encouragement. The Lutheran Swedish church was eventually adopted as the state church.

Sweden played a leading role in the second phase (1630–35) of the Thirty Years' War (1618–48). By the Treaty of Westphalia (1648), Sweden obtained western Pomerania and some neighboring territory on the Baltic. In 1700, a coalition of Russia, Poland, and Denmark united against Sweden and by the Peace of Nystad (1721) forced it to relinquish Livonia, Ingria, Estonia, and parts of Finland. Sweden emerged from the Napoleonic Wars with the acquisition of Norway from Denmark and with a new royal dynasty stemming from Marshal Jean Bernadotte of France, who became King Charles XIV (1818–44). The artificial union between Sweden and Norway led to an uneasy

relationship, and the union was finally dissolved in 1905. Sweden maintained a position of neutrality in both world wars.

An elaborate structure of welfare legislation, imitated by many larger nations, began with the establishment of old-age pensions in 1911. Economic prosperity based on its neutralist policy enabled Sweden, together with Norway, to pioneer in public health, housing, and job security programs. Forty-four years of Socialist government were ended in 1976 with the election of a conservative coalition headed by Thorbjörn Fälldin. The Socialists were returned to power in the election of 1982, but Prime Minister Olof Palme, a Socialist, was assassinated by a gunman on Feb. 28, 1986, leaving Sweden stunned. Palme's Socialist domestic policies were carried out by his successor, Ingvar Carlsson. Elections in Sept. 1991 ousted the Social Democrats (Socialists) from power. The new coalition of four conservative parties pledged to reduce taxes and cut back on the welfare state but not alter Sweden's traditional neutrality. In Sept. 1994 the Social Democrats emerged again after three years as the opposition party.

In a 1994 referendum voters approved joining the European Union. Although supportive of a European monetary union, Sweden decided not to adopt the euro when it debuted in 1999.

The Social Democrat party, and its leader, Prime Minister Persson, easily won the Sept. 2002 elections. The center-left Social Democrats have run the government for 61 out of the last 70 years.

# Switzerland

### SWISS CONFEDERATION

**National name:** Schweiz/Suisse/Svizzera/Svizra
**President:** Kaspar Villiger (2002)
**Area:** 15,942 sq mi (41,290 sq km)
**Population (2002 est.):** 7,301,994 (growth rate: 0.1%); birth rate: 9.8/1000; infant mortality rate: 4.4/1000; density per sq mi: 458
**Capital (1994 est.):** Bern, 129,423. **Largest cities:** Zurich, 343,045; Basel, 176,220; Geneva, 171,744; Lausanne, 117,153. **Monetary unit:** Swiss franc. **Languages:** German, French, Italian (all official), Romansch. **Ethnicity/race:** German 65%, French 18%, Italian 10%, Romansch 1%, other 6%. **Religions:** Roman Catholic 49%, Protestant 40%, other 5%, no religion 8.3%. **Literacy rate:** 99% (1980)
**Economic summary: GDP/PPP** (2000 est.): $207 billion; per capita $28,600. **Real growth rate:** 3%. **Inflation:** 1.5%. **Unemployment:** 1.9%. **Arable land:** 10%. **Agriculture:** grains, fruits, vegetables; meat, eggs. **Labor force:** 3.9 million (964,000 foreign workers, mostly Italian) (1998 est.); services 69.1%, industry 26.3%, agriculture 4.6% (1998 est.). **Industries:** machinery, chemicals, watches, textiles, precision instruments. **Natural resources:** hydropower potential, timber, salt. **Exports:** $91.3 billion (f.o.b., 2000): machinery, chemicals, metals, watches, agricultural products. **Imports:** $91.6 billion (f.o.b., 2000): machinery, chemicals, vehicles, metals; agricultural products, textiles. **Major trading partners:** EU, U.S., Japan.

**Geography** Switzerland, in central Europe, is the land of the Alps. Its tallest peak is the Dufourspitze at 15,203 ft (4,634 m) on the Swiss side of the Italian border, one of 10 summits of the Monte Rosa massif. The tallest peak in all of the Alps, Mont Blanc (15,771 ft; 4,807 m), is actually in France. Most of Switzerland is composed of a mountainous plateau bordered by the great bulk of the Alps on the south and by the Jura Mountains on the northwest. The country's largest lakes—Geneva, Constance (Bodensee), and Maggiore—straddle the French, German-Austrian, and Italian borders, respectively. The Rhine, navigable from Basel to the North Sea, is the principal inland waterway.

**Government** Federal republic.

**History** Called Helvetia in ancient times, Switzerland in 1291 was a league of cantons in the Holy Roman Empire. Fashioned around the nucleus of three German forest districts of Schwyz, Uri, and Unterwalden, the Swiss Confederation slowly added new cantons. In 1648 the Treaty of Westphalia gave Switzerland its independence from the Holy Roman Empire.

French revolutionary troops occupied the country in 1798 and named it the Helvetic Republic, but Napoleon in 1803 restored its federal government. By 1815, the French- and Italian-speaking peoples of Switzerland had been granted political equality.

In 1815, the Congress of Vienna guaranteed the neutrality and recognized the independence of Switzerland. In the revolutionary period of 1847, the Catholic cantons seceded and organized a separate union called the *Sonderbund*, but they were defeated and rejoined the federation.

In 1848, the new Swiss constitution established a union modeled upon that of the U.S. The federal constitution of 1874 established a strong central government while giving large powers of control to each canton. National unity and political conservatism grew as the country prospered from its neutrality. Its banking system became the world's leading repository for international accounts.

Strict neutrality was its policy in both world wars. Geneva was the seat of the League of Nations (later the European headquarters of the United Nations) and of a number of international organizations.

Allegations in the 1990s concerning secret assets of Jewish Holocaust victims deposited in Swiss banks led to international criticism and the establishment of a fund to reimburse the victims and their families.

Surprisingly, women were not given the right to vote or to hold office until 1971. Switzerland's first woman president—as well as the first Jew to assume the position—was Ruth Dreifuss in 1999.

In Sept. 2000, the Swiss voted against a plan to cut the number of foreigners in the country to 18% of the population (in 2000 foreigners made up 19.3%). Since 1970, four similar anti-immigration plans have failed. With unemployment at 1.8%, the lowest in eight years, few Swiss feel threatened by the inroads rapid influx of foreign workers.

On Sept 10, 2002, the Swiss abandoned their long-held neutrality to become the 190th member of the UN.

# Syria

**SYRIAN ARAB REPUBLIC**
**National name:** Al-Jamhouriya al Arabiya As-Souriya
**President:** Bashar al-Assad (2000)
**Prime Minister:** Muhammad Mustafa Miro (2000)
**Area:** 71,498 sq mi (185,180 sq km)
**Population (2002 est.):** 17,155,814 (growth rate: 2.5%); birth rate: 30.1/1000; infant mortality rate: 32.7/1000; density per sq mi: 240
**Capital (1994 est.):** Damascus, 1,549,932. **Largest cities:** Aleppo, 1,591,400; Homs, 644,204; Latakia, 306,535; Hama, 229,000. **Monetary unit:** Syrian pound. **Languages:** Arabic (official), French and English widely understood. **Ethnicity/race:** Arab 90.3%, Kurds, Armenians, and other 9.7%. **Religions:** Islam 90%, Christian 10%. **Literacy rate:** 65% (1990) **Economic summary: GDP/PPP** (2000 est.): $50.9 billion; per capita $3,100. **Real growth rate:** 3.5%. **Inflation:** 1.5%. **Unemployment:** 20% (2000 est.). **Arable land:** 28%. **Agriculture:** wheat, barley, cotton, lentils, chickpeas, olives, sugar beets; beef, mutton, eggs, poultry, milk. **Labor force:** 4.7 million (1998 est.); agriculture 40%, industry 20%, services 40% (1996 est.). **Industries:** petroleum, textiles, food processing, beverages, tobacco, phosphate rock mining. **Natural resources:** petroleum, phosphates, chrome and manganese ores, asphalt, iron ore, rock salt, marble, gypsum, hydropower. **Exports:** $4.8 billion (f.o.b., 2000 est.): petroleum 65%, textiles 10%, manufactured goods 10%, fruits and vegetables 7%, raw cotton 5%, live sheep 2%, phosphates 1% (1998 est.). **Imports:** $3.5 billion (f.o.b., 2000 est.): machinery and equipment 23%, foodstuffs/animals 20%, metal and metal products 15%, textiles 10%, chemicals 10% (1998 est.). **Major trading partners:** Germany, Italy, France, Saudi Arabia, Turkey, China.

**Geography** Slightly larger than North Dakota, Syria lies at the eastern end of the Mediterranean Sea. It is bordered by Lebanon and Israel on the west, Turkey on the north, Iraq on the east, and Jordan on the south. Coastal Syria is a narrow plain, in back of which is a range of coastal mountains, and still farther inland a steppe area. In the east is the Syrian Desert, and in the south is the Jebel Druze Range. The highest point in Syria is Mount Hermon (9,232 ft; 2,814 m) on the Lebanese border.

**Government** Republic under a military regime since March 1963.

**History** Ancient Syria was conquered by Egypt about 1500 B.C., and after that by Hebrews, Assyrians, Chaldeans, Persians, and Alexander the Great of Macedonia. From 64 B.C. until the Arab conquest in A.D. 636, it was part of the Roman Empire except during brief periods. The Arabs made it a trade center for their extensive empire, but it suffered severely from the Mongol invasion in 1260 and fell to the Ottoman Turks in 1516. Syria remained a Turkish province until World War I.

A secret Anglo-French pact of 1916 put Syria in the French zone of influence. The League of Nations gave France a mandate over Syria after World War I, but the French were forced to put down several nationalist uprisings. In 1930, France recognized Syria as an independent republic but still subject to the mandate. After nationalist demonstrations in 1939, the French high commissioner suspended the Syrian constitution. In 1941, British and Free French forces invaded Syria to eliminate Vichy control. During the rest of World War II, Syria was an Allied base. Again in 1945, nationalist demonstrations broke into actual fighting, and British troops had to restore order. Syrian forces met a series of reverses while participating in the Arab invasion of Palestine in 1948. In 1958, Egypt and Syria formed the United Arab Republic, with Gamal Abdel Nasser of Egypt as president. However, Syria became independent again on Sept. 29, 1961, following a revolution.

In the Arab-Israeli War of 1967, Israel quickly vanquished the Syrian army. Before acceding to the UN cease-fire, the Israeli forces took control of the fortified Golan Heights. Syria joined Egypt in attacking

Israel in Oct. 1973 in the fourth Arab-Israeli war, but was pushed back from initial successes on the Golan Heights and ended up losing more land. However, in the settlement worked out by U.S. secretary of state Henry A. Kissinger in 1974, the Syrians recovered all the territory lost in 1973 and a token amount of land, including the deserted town of Quneitra, lost in 1967.

In the mid-1970s Syria sent some 20,000 troops to support Muslim Lebanese in their armed conflict with Christian militants supported by Israel during the civil war in Lebanon. Syrian troops frequently clashed with Israeli troops during Israel's 1982 invasion of Lebanon and remained thereafter as occupiers of large portions of Lebanon.

The first Arab country to condemn Iraq's invasion of Kuwait, Syria sent troops to help defend Saudi Arabia from possible Iraqi attack.

In 1990, President Assad ruled out any possibility of legalizing opposition political parties. In Dec. 1991 voters approved a fourth term for Assad, giving him 99.98% of the vote.

In the 1990s, the slowdown in the Israeli-Palestinian peace process was echoed in the lack of progress in Israeli-Syrian relations. Confronted with a steadily strengthening strategic partnership between Israel and Turkey, Syria took steps to construct a countervailing alliance by improving relations with Iraq, strengthening ties with Iran, and collaborating more closely with Saudi Arabia. In Dec. 1999, Israeli-Syrian talks resumed after a nearly four-year hiatus, with the aging Assad (who would die seven months later) attempting to shore up his legacy. From Syria's point of view, normalization of relations between the two countries largely depended on Israel's withdrawal from the Golan Heights, which was territory that Israel had captured from Syria during the Arab-Israeli War of 1967. By Jan. 2000, however, talks broke down when Syria demanded a detailed discussion about the return of the entire Golan Heights.

On June 10, 2000, President Hafez al-Assad died. He had ruled with an iron fist since taking power in a military coup in 1970. His son, Bashar al-Assad, an ophthalmologist by training, succeeded him. In his first two years in office, Assad freed hundreds of political prisoners locked up by his father. But approximately 1,000 remain in prison.

In the summer of 2001, Syria withdrew nearly all of its 25,000 troops from Beirut. Syrian soldiers, however, remain in the Lebanese countryside.

# Taiwan

**REPUBLIC OF CHINA**

**President:** Chen Shui-bian (2000)
**Prime Minister:** Yu Shyi-kun (2002)
**Area:** 13,892 sq mi (35,980 sq km)
**Population (2002 est.):** 22,548,009 (growth rate: 0.8%); birth rate: 14.2/1000; infant mortality rate: 6.8/1000; density per sq mi: 1,623
**Capital and largest city (2000 est.):** Taipei, 7,700,000 (metro. area). **Largest cities:** Kaohsiung, 1,423,163; Tai Chung, 848,320; Tainan, 705,565; Keelung, 367,668. **Monetary unit:** Taiwan dollar. **Language:** Chinese (Mandarin). **Ethnicity/race:** Taiwanese 84%, mainland Chinese 14%, aborigine 2%. **Religions:** Buddhist 4.86 million, Taoist 3.3 million, Protestant 422,000, Catholic 304,000. **Literacy rate:** 92% (1990)
**Economic summary: GDP/PPP** (2000 est.): $386 billion; per capita $17,400. **Real growth rate:** 6.3%. **Inflation:** 1.3%. **Unemployment:** 3%. **Arable land:** 24%. **Agriculture:** rice, corn, vegetables, fruit, tea; pigs, poultry, beef, milk; fish. **Labor force:** 9.8 million

(2000 est.); services 55%, industry 37%, agriculture 8% (1999 est.). **Industries:** electronics, petroleum refining, chemicals, textiles, iron and steel, machinery, cement, food processing. **Natural resources:** small deposits of coal, natural gas, limestone, marble, and asbestos. **Exports:** $148.38 billion (f.o.b., 2000): machinery and electrical equipment 51%, metals, textiles, plastics, chemicals. **Imports:** $140.01 billion (c.i.f., 2000): machinery and electrical equipment 51%, minerals, precision instruments. **Major trading partners:** U.S., Hong Kong, Europe, Association of Southeast Asian Nations, Japan.

**Geography** The Republic of China today consists of the island of Taiwan, an island 100 mi (161 km) off the Asian mainland in the Pacific; two off-shore islands, Kinmen (Quemoy) and Matsu; and the nearby islets of the Pescadores chain. It is slightly larger than the combined areas of Massachusetts and Connecticut. Taiwan is divided by a central mountain range that runs from north to south, rising sharply on the east coast and descending gradually to a broad western plain, where cultivation is concentrated.

**Government** Multiparty democracy.

**History** Taiwan was inhabited by aborigines of Malayan descent when Chinese from the areas now designated as Fukien and Kwangtung began settling it in the 7th century, becoming the majority. The Portuguese explored the area in 1590, naming it "the Beautiful" (Formosa). In 1624 the Dutch set up forts in the south, the Spanish in the north. The Dutch forced out the Spanish in 1641 and controlled the island until 1661, when Chinese general Koxinga took it over and established an independent kingdom. The Manchus seized the island in 1683 and held it until 1895, when it passed to Japan after the first Sino-Japanese War. Japan developed and exploited Formosa. It was the target of heavy American bombing during World War II, and at the close of the war the island was restored to China.

After the defeat of its armies on the mainland, the Nationalist government of Generalissimo Chiang Kai-shek retreated to Taiwan in Dec. 1949. Chiang dominated the island, even though only 15% of the population consisted of the 1949 immigrants, the Kuomintang. He maintained a 600,000-man army in the hope of eventually recovering the mainland. Beijing viewed the Taiwanese government with suspicion and anger, referring to Taiwan as a breakaway province of China.

The UN seat representing all of China was held by the Nationalists for over two decades before being lost in Oct. 1971, when the People's Republic of China was admitted and Taiwan was forced to abdicate its seat to Beijing.

Chiang died at 87 of a heart attack on April 5, 1975. His son, Chiang Ching-kuo, continued as premier and was a dominant figure in the Taipei regime. In April 1991, President Lee Teng-hui formally declared an end to emergency rule, which had existed since Chiang's forces originally occupied the island. In the first full election in many decades, the governing Kuomintang in Dec. 1991 won 71% of the vote, affirming the island's opposition to reunification with China. In Feb. 1993 the president, himself a native Taiwanese, nominated Lien Chan, another native, to be prime minister, marking a further generational shift away from the mainland exiles.

In the island's first free presidential election, voters defied mainland intimidation and gave 54% of the vote to incumbent president Lee Teng-hui. The second-place finisher, with 21%, advocated complete independence from China.

In 1998, Taiwan renewed its push for a separate UN seat—its sixth attempt in recent years. The move has been blocked each time by the Beijing government.

President Lee Teng-hui rankled mainland China by announcing in July 1999 that he was abandoning the longstanding "One China" policy that has kept the peace between the small island and its powerful neighbor, and would from now on deal with China on a "state-to-state basis." China, which has vowed to someday unite Taiwan with the mainland, has threatened to use force against Taiwan, and in late August conducted submarine warfare exercises and missile tests near the island in an effort to intimidate its tiny brazen neighbor, as it had once before in 1996.

In March 2000 elections—Taiwan's second free presidential elections—voters elected pro-independence candidate Chen Shui-bian of the Democratic Progressive Party, ending more than 50 years of Nationalist rule.

Taiwan joined the World Trade Organization in Jan. 2002, just one day after China gained entry. In August President Chen outraged China when he asserted that Taiwan and China are separate countries and that a referendum on independence for Taiwan is a "basic human right."

# Tajikistan

**REPUBLIC OF TAJIKISTAN**

**President:** Imomali Rakhmonov (1992)
**Prime Minister:** Akil Akilov (1999)
**Area:** 55,251 sq mi (143,100 sq km)
**Population (2002 est.):** 6,719,567 (growth rate: 2.5%); birth rate, 33.0/1000; infant mortality rate: 114.8/1000; density per sq mi: 122
**Capital and largest city (1994 est.):** Dushanbe, 524,000.
**Other large city:** Khodzhent (Leninabad), 164,500.
**Monetary unit:** Tajik ruble. **Language:** Tajik. **Ethnicity/ race:** Tajik 64.9%, Uzbek 25%, Russian 3.5% (declining because of emigration), other 6.6%. **Religion:** Sunni Muslim 80%. **Literacy rate:** 98% (1989)
**Economic summary: GDP/PPP** (2000 est.): $7.3 billion; per capita $1,140. **Real growth rate:** 5.1%. **Inflation:** 33%. **Unemployment:** 5.7%; includes only officially registered unemployed; also large numbers of underemployed workers and unregistered unemployed people (Dec. 1998). **Arable land:** 6%. **Agriculture:** cotton, grain, fruits, grapes, vegetables; cattle, sheep, goats. **Labor force:** 1.9 million (1996); agriculture and forestry 50%, industry 20%, services 30% (1997 est.). **Industries:** aluminum, zinc, lead, chemicals and fertilizers, cement, vegetable oil, metal-cutting machine tools, refrigerators and freezers. **Natural resources:** hydropower, some petroleum, uranium, mercury, brown coal, lead, zinc, antimony, tungsten, silver, gold. **Exports:** $761 million (f.o.b. 2000 est.): aluminum, electricity, cotton, fruits, vegetable oil, textiles. **Imports:** $782 million (f.o.b. 2000 est.): electricity, petroleum products, aluminum oxide, machinery and equipment, foodstuffs. **Major trading partners:** Liechtenstein, Uzbekistan, Russia.

**Geography** Ninety-three percent of Tajikistan's territory is mountainous, and the mountain glaciers are the source of its rivers. Tajikistan is an earthquake-prone area. The republic is bounded by China in the east, Afghanistan to the south, Uzbekistan and Kyrgyzstan to the west and north. The central Asian republic also includes the Gorno-Badakh Shan Autonomous region. Tajikistan is slightly larger than the state of Illinois.

**Government** Republic.

**History** The Tajiks, whose language is nearly identical with Persian, were part of the ancient Persian empire that was ruled by Darius I and later conquered by Alexander the Great (333 B.C.). In the 7th and 8th centuries, Arabs conquered the region and brought Islam. The Tajiks were successively ruled by Uzbeks and then Afghans until claimed by Russia in the 1860s. In 1924, Tajikistan was consolidated into a newly formed Tajik Autonomous Soviet Socialist Republic, which was administratively part of the Uzbek SSR until the Tajik ASSR gained full-fledged republic status in 1929.

Tajikistan declared its sovereignty in Aug. 1990. In 1991, the republic's Communist leadership supported the attempted coup against Soviet president Mikhail Gorbachev. Tajikistan joined with ten other former Soviet republics in the Commonwealth of Independent States on Dec. 21, 1991. A parliamentary republic was proclaimed and presidential rule abolished in Nov. 1992. After independence, Tajikistan experienced sporadic conflict as the Communist-dominated government struggled to combat an insurgency by Islamic and democratic opposition forces. Despite continued international efforts to end the civil war, periodic fighting continued. About 60,000 people lost their lives in Tajikistan's civil war. The conflict ended officially on June 27, 1997, with the signing in Moscow of peace accords between the government of President Imomali Rakhmonov and the United Tajik Opposition (UTO), a coalition of largely Islamic groups. Since then, however, peace has been tenuous, marred regularly by killing sprees by various opposition groups.

In 2000, Tajikistan allowed approximately 25,000 Russian troops into the country to help stem the violence by helping to patrol the long border with Taliban-run Afghanistan. The Tajiks had long supported Afghanistan's Northern Alliance fighters in their battle against the militantly Islamist Taliban, and the Taliban's fall in Dec. 2001 has returned a measure of security to this war-ravaged and impoverished country.

# Tanzania

**UNITED REPUBLIC OF TANZANIA**

**President:** Benjamin William Mkapa (1995)
**Prime Minister:** Frederick Tluway Sumaye (1995)
**Area:** 364,898 sq mi (945,087 sq km)[1]
**Population (2002 est.):** 37,187,939 (growth rate: 2.6%); birth rate: 39.1/1000; infant mortality rate: 77.8/1000; density per sq mi: 102
**Capitals and largest city (1988):** Dar es Salaam (administrative), 1,360,850; Dodoma (official) 45,807 (1988). Commercial: Dar es Salaam, capital.
**Languages:** Swahili and English (both official), local languages. **Ethnicity/race:** mainland: native African (95% Bantu, consisting of well over 100 tribes) 99%, Asian, European, and Arab 1%. Zanzibar: Arab, mixed Arab and native African, native African. **Religions:** Christian 40%, Muslim 33%. **Literacy rate:** 52% (1988)
**Economic summary: GDP/PPP** (2000 est.): $25.1 billion; per capita $710. **Real growth rate:** 5.2%. **Inflation:** 6%. **Unemployment:** n.a. **Arable land:** 3%. **Agriculture:** coffee, sisal, tea, cotton, pyrethrum (insecticide made from chrysanthemums), cashew nuts, tobacco, cloves (Zanzibar), corn, wheat, cassava (tapioca), bananas, fruits, vegetables; cattle, sheep, goats. **Labor force:** 13.495 million; agriculture 80%, industry and commerce 20% (2000 est.). **Industries:** primarily agricultural processing (sugar, beer,

cigarettes, sisal twine), diamond and gold mining, oil refining, shoes, cement, textiles, wood products, fertilizer, salt. **Natural resources:** hydropower, tin, phosphates, iron ore, coal, diamonds, gemstones, gold, natural gas, nickel. **Exports:** $937 million (f.o.b., 2000 est.): coffee, manufactured goods, cotton, cashew nuts, minerals, tobacco, sisal (1996). **Imports:** $1.57 billion (f.o.b., 2000 est.): consumer goods, machinery and transportation equipment, industrial raw materials, crude oil. **Major trading partners:** India, UK, Germany, Japan, Netherlands, Belgium, South Africa, Kenya, U.S. **Member of Commonwealth of Nations**

1. Including Zanzibar.

**Geography** Tanzania is in East Africa on the Indian Ocean. To the north are Uganda and Kenya; to the west, Burundi, Rwanda, and Congo; and to the south, Mozambique, Zambia, and Malawi. Its area is three times that of New Mexico. Tanzania contains three of Africa's best-known lakes—Victoria in the north, Tanganyika in the west, and Nyasa in the south. Mount Kilimanjaro in the north, 19,340 ft (5,895 m), is the highest point on the continent. The island of Zanzibar is separated from the mainland by a 22-mile channel.

**Government** Republic.

**History** Arab traders first began to colonize the area in 700. Portuguese explorers reached the coastal regions in 1500 and held some control until the 17th century, when the sultan of Oman took power. With what are now Burundi and Rwanda, Tanganyika became the colony of German East Africa in 1885. After World War I, it was administered by Britain under a League of Nations mandate and later as a UN trust territory.

Although not mentioned in old histories until the 12th century, Zanzibar was always believed to have had connections with southern Arabia. The Portuguese made it one of their tributaries in 1503 and later established a trading post, but they were driven from Oman by Arabs in 1698. Zanzibar was declared independent of Oman in 1861 and, in 1890, it became a British protectorate.

Tanganyika became independent on Dec. 9, 1961; Zanzibar on Dec. 10, 1963. On April 26, 1964, the two nations merged into the United Republic of Tanganyika and Zanzibar. The name was changed to Tanzania six months later.

An invasion by Ugandan troops in Nov. 1978 was followed by a counterattack in Jan. 1979, in which 5,000 Tanzanian troops were joined by 3,000 Ugandan exiles opposed to President Idi Amin. Within a month, full-scale war developed. Tanzanian president Julius Nyerere kept troops in Uganda in open support of former Ugandan president Milton Obote, despite protests from opposition groups, until the national elections in Dec. 1980.

In Nov. 1985, Nyerere stepped down as president. Ali Hassan Mwinyi, his vice president, succeeded him. Running unopposed, Mwinyi was elected president in October. Shortly thereafter plans were announced to study the benefits of instituting a multiparty democracy, and in Oct. 1995 the country's first multiparty elections since independence took place.

On Aug. 7, 1998, the U.S. embassy in Dar es Salaam was bombed by terrorists, killing 10. The same day an even more devastating explosion destroyed the U.S. embassy in neighboring Kenya.

Since taking office in 1995 President Benjamin William Mkapa has sought to increase economic productivity while dealing with serious pollution problems and deforestation. With more than one million people

infected with HIV, AIDS care and prevention have been major public health issues. On foreign policy, Tanzania has taken a leading diplomatic role in East Africa, hosting peace talks for the factions fighting in neighboring Burundi. The UN International Criminal Tribunal for Rwanda (ICTR) is located in the town of Arusha. In Oct. 2000, Mkapa was easily reelected.

# Thailand

### KINGDOM OF THAILAND

**Ruler:** King Bhumibol Adulyadej (1946)
**Prime Minister:** Thaksin Shinawatra (2001)
**Area:** 198,455 sq mi (514,000 sq km)
**Population (2002 est.):** 62,354,402 (growth rate: 0.9%); birth rate: 16.4/1000; infant mortality rate: 29.5/1000; density per sq mi: 314
**Capital and largest city (2000 est.):** Bangkok, 7,200,000 (metro. area). **Other large cities:** Nonthanburi, 261,335; Chiang Mai, 170,397.
**Monetary unit:** baht. **Languages:** Thai (Siamese), Chinese, English. **Ethnicity/race:** Thai 75%, Chinese 14%, other 11%. **Religions:** Buddhist 94.4%, Islam 4%, Hindu 1.1%, Christian 0.5%. **Literacy rate:** 93% (1990)
**Economic summary: GDP/PPP** (2000 est.): $413 billion; per capita $6,700. **Real growth rate:** 4.2%. **Inflation:** 2.1%. **Unemployment:** 3.7%. **Arable land:** 34%. **Agriculture:** rice, cassava (tapioca), rubber, corn, sugarcane, coconuts, soybeans. **Labor force:** 32.6 million (1997 est.); agriculture 54%, industry 15%, services 31% (1996 est.). **Industries:** tourism; textiles and garments, agricultural processing, beverages, tobacco, cement, light manufacturing, such as jewelry; electric appliances and components, computers and parts, integrated circuits, furniture, plastics; world's second-largest tungsten producer and third-largest tin producer. **Natural resources:** tin, rubber, natural gas, tungsten, tantalum, timber, lead, fish, gypsum, lignite, fluorite, arable land. **Exports:** $68.2 billion (f.o.b., 2000 est.): computers and parts, textiles, integrated circuits, rice. **Imports:** $61.8 billion (f.o.b., 2000 est.): capital goods, intermediate goods and raw materials, consumer goods, fuels. **Major trading partners:** U.S., Japan, Singapore, Hong Kong, Netherlands, Malaysia, UK, China, Taiwan.

**Geography** Thailand occupies the western half of the Indochinese peninsula and the northern two-thirds of the Malay Peninsula in southeast Asia. Its neighbors are Burma (Myanmar) on the north and west, Laos on the north and northeast, Cambodia on the east, and Malaysia on the south. Thailand is about the size of France.

**Government** Constitutional monarchy.

**History** The Thais first began settling their present homeland in the 6th century, and by the end of the 13th century ruled most of the western portion. During the next 400 years, they fought sporadically with the Cambodians to the east and Burmese to the west. Formerly called Siam, Thailand has never experienced foreign rule. The British gained a colonial foothold in the region in 1824, but by 1896 an Anglo-French accord guaranteed the independence of Thailand. A coup in 1932 demoted the monarchy to titular status and established representative government with universal suffrage.

At the outbreak of World War II, Japanese forces attacked Thailand. After five hours of token resistance Thailand yielded to Japan on Dec. 8, 1941, subsequently becoming a staging area for the Japanese campaign against Malaya. Following the demise of a pro-Japanese puppet government in July 1944, Thailand repudiated the declaration of war it had been forced to make in 1942 against Britain and the U.S.

By the late 1960s the nation's problems largely stemmed from conflicts brewing in neighboring Cambodia and Vietnam. Although Thailand had received $2 billion in U.S. economic and military aid since 1950, and had sent troops (paid by the U.S.) to Vietnam while permitting U.S. bomber bases on its territory, the collapse of South Vietnam and Cambodia in spring 1975 brought rapid changes in the country's diplomatic posture. At the Thai government's insistence, the U.S. agreed to withdraw all 23,000 U.S. military personnel remaining in Thailand by March 1976.

Three years of civilian government ended with a military coup on Oct. 6, 1976. Political parties, banned after the coup, gained limited freedom in 1980. The same year, the National Assembly elected Gen. Prem Tinsulananda as prime minister. Prem continued as prime minister following 1983 and 1986 elections.

Fleeing from Laos, Vietnam, and the murderous regime of Cambodia's Pol Pot, refugees flooded into Thailand in 1978 and 1979. Despite efforts by the United States and other Western countries to resettle them, a total of 130,000 Laotians and Vietnamese were living in camps along the Cambodian border in mid-1980.

On April 3, 1981, a military coup against the Prem government failed. Another coup attempt on Sept. 9, 1985, was crushed by loyal troops after 10 hours of fighting in Bangkok. In Feb. 1991, yet another coup yielded another junta, which declared a state of emergency and abolished the constitution. A scandal over a land-reform program caused the fall of the government in May 1995. A succession of governments followed.

Following several years of unprecedented economic growth, Thailand's economy, once one of the strongest in the region, collapsed under the weight of foreign debt in 1997. The Thai economy's downfall set off a chain reaction in the region, sparking the Asian currency crisis. The Thai government quickly accepted restructuring guidelines as a condition of the International Monetary Fund's $17 billion bailout. Thailand's economy, while far from completely recovered, continued to improve over the next several years. The Thai Rak Thai ("Thais Love Thais") party won elections in Jan. 2001 and formed a coalition government with the Chart Thai and New Aspiration Parties. Thaksin Shinawatra became prime minister. The hugely popular Thaksin, a billionaire telecommunications mogul, was indicted in Dec. 2000 on corruption charges but was acquitted in Aug. 2001. Thailand's Finance Ministry predicted growth of up to 5% for 2002.

# Togo

#### REPUBLIC OF TOGO

**National name:** République Togolaise
**President:** Gen. Gnassingbé Eyadema (1967)
**Prime Minister:** Koffi Sama (2002)
**Area:** 21,925 sq mi (56,785 sq km)
**Population (2002 est.):** 5,285,501 (growth rate: 2.5%); birth rate: 36.1/1000; infant mortality rate: 69.3/1000; density per sq mi: 241
**Capital and largest city (1983):** Lomé, 366,476.
  **Monetary unit:** CFA Franc. **Languages:** French (official), Ewé, Mina (south), Kabyé, Cotocoli (north), and many dialects. **Ethnicity/race:** native African (37 tribes; largest and most important are Ewe, Mina, and Kabre) 99%, European and Syrian-Lebanese less than 1%. **Religions:** Indigenous beliefs 70%, Christian

20%, Islam 10%. **Literacy rate:** 43% (1990)
**Economic summary: GDP/PPP** (2000 est.): $7.3 billion; per capita $1,500. **Real growth rate:** 3.4%. **Inflation:** 2.5%. **Unemployment:** n.a. **Arable land:** 38%. **Agriculture:** coffee, cocoa, cotton, yams, cassava (tapioca), corn, beans, rice, millet, sorghum; livestock; fish. **Labor force:** 1.74 million (1996); agriculture 65%, industry 5%, services 30% (1998 est.). **Industries:** phosphate mining, agricultural processing, cement; handicrafts, textiles, beverages. **Natural resources:** phosphates, limestone, marble, arable land. **Exports:** $336 million (f.o.b., 2000): cotton, phosphates, coffee, cocoa. **Imports:** $452 million (f.o.b., 2000): machinery and equipment, foodstuffs, petroleum products. **Major trading partners:** Nigeria, Brazil, Canada, Philippines, Ghana, China, France, Côte d'Ivoire.

**Geography** Togo, twice the size of Maryland, is on the south coast of West Africa bordering on Ghana to the west, Burkina Faso to the north, and Benin to the east. The Gulf of Guinea coastline, only 32 mi long (51 km), is low and sandy. The only port is at Lomé. The Togo hills traverse the central section.

**Government** Republic transitioning to multiparty democratic rule.

**History** The Voltaic peoples and the Kwa were the earliest known inhabitants. The Ewe followed in the 14th century, and the Ane in the 18th century. The Danish claimed the land in the 18th century, but by 1884 it was established as a German colony (Togoland). The area was split between the British and French under League of Nations mandates after World War I and subsequently administered as UN trusteeships. The British portion voted for incorporation with Ghana. The French portion became Togo, which declared its independence on April 27, 1960.

Togo's first democratically elected president, Sylvano Olympius, was overthrown in 1963. He was shot by Sgt. Etienne Eyadema while he attempted to scale the walls of the American Embassy to seek asylum. The government of Nicolas Grunitzky was overthrown in a bloodless coup on Jan. 13, 1967, led by Lt. Col. Etienne Eyadema (now called Gen. Gnassingbé Eyadema). A National Reconciliation Committee was set up to rule the country, but in April, Eyadema dissolved the committee and took over as president. He suspended the constitution, banned political parties, and created a cult of personality around his presidency—his official biography describes him as a "force of nature." Under pressure from the West, Eyadema legalized opposition parties in 1993, but the first multiparty presidential election in Aug. 1993 (which gave Eyadema more than 96% of the vote) was considered fraudulent, as was his 1998 reelection. In 2002, Eyadema was the longest-serving ruler in Africa. In June 2002, Eyadema replaced prime minister Agbeyome Messan Kodjo with Koffi Sama.

# Tonga

#### KINGDOM OF TONGA

**Sovereign:** King Taufa'ahau Tupou IV (1965)
**Prime Minister:** Prince Lavaka Ata Ulukalala (2000)
**Area:** 289 sq mi (748 sq km)
**Population (2002 est.):** 106,137 (growth rate: 1.8%); birth rate: 24.1/1000; infant mortality rate: 13.7/1000; density per sq mi: 368
**Capital and largest city (1990 est.):** Nuku'alofa, 34,000. **Monetary unit:** Pa'anga. **Languages:** Tongan (an Austronesian language), English. **Ethnicity/race:** Polynesian, European (about 300). **Religions:** Christian; Free Wesleyan Church claims over 30,000

adherents. **Literacy rate:** 98.5%
**Economic summary: GDP/PPP** (2000 est.): $225 million; per capita $2,200. **Real growth rate:** 5%. **Inflation:** 7%. **Unemployment:** 13.3% (FY96/97). **Arable land:** 24%. **Agriculture:** squash, coconuts, copra, bananas, vanilla beans, cocoa, coffee, ginger, black pepper; fish. **Labor force:** 34,000 (FY96/97); agriculture 65% (1997 est.). **Industries:** tourism, fishing. **Natural resources:** fish, fertile soil. **Exports:** $8 million (f.o.b., 1998): squash, fish, vanilla beans. **Imports:** $69 million (f.o.b., 1998): foodstuffs, machinery and transport equipment, fuels, chemicals. **Major trading partners:** Japan, U.S., New Zealand, Australia, UK. **Member of Commonwealth of Nations**

**Geography** Situated east of the Fiji Islands in the South Pacific, Tonga (also called the Friendly Islands) consists of some 150 islands, of which 36 are inhabited. Most of the islands contain active volcanic craters; others are coral atolls.

**Government** Hereditary constitutional monarchy.

**History** Polynesians have lived on Tonga for at least 3,000 years. The Dutch were the first to explore the islands, landing on Tafahi in 1616. British explorer James Cook landed on islands in 1773 and 1777, and dubbed them the Friendly Islands. The current royal dynasty of Tonga was founded in 1831 by Taufa'ahau Tupou, who took the name George I. He consolidated the kingdom by conquest and in 1875 granted a constitution. In 1900, his great-grandson, George II, signed a treaty of friendship with Britain, and the country became a British protected state. The treaty was revised in 1959. Tonga became independent on June 4, 1970.

The government is largely controlled by the king, his nominees, and a small group of hereditary nobles. In the 1990s a movement began aimed at curtailing the powers of the monarchy, and the Tongan Pro-Democracy Movement (TPDM) has continued to gain in popular support. In 1999, Tonga gained UN membership.

# Trinidad and Tobago

**REPUBLIC OF TRINIDAD AND TOBAGO**
**President:** Arthur N. R. Robinson (1997)
**Prime Minister:** Patrick Manning (2001)
**Area:** 1,980 sq mi (5,128 sq km)
**Population (2002 est.):** 1,163,724 (growth rate: 0.5%); birth rate: 13.7/1000; infant mortality rate: 24.2/1000; density per sq mi: 588
**Capital and largest city (1995):** Port-of-Spain, 52,451.
**Monetary unit:** Trinidad and Tobago dollar.
**Languages:** English (official), Hindi, French, Spanish.
**Ethnicity/race:** black 43%, East Indian (a local term—primarily immigrants from northern India) 40%, mixed 14%, white 1%, Chinese 1%, other 1%.
**Religions:** Roman Catholic 33%, Hindu 25%, Anglican 15%, other Christian 14%, Muslim 6%. **Literacy rate:** 95% (1980)
**Economic summary: GDP/PPP** (2000 est.): $11.2 billion; per capita $9,500. **Real growth rate:** 5%. **Inflation:** 3.2%. **Unemployment:** 12.8% (2000). **Arable land:** 15%. **Agriculture:** cocoa, sugarcane, rice, citrus, coffee, vegetables; poultry. **Labor force:** 558,700 (1998); construction and utilities 12.4%, manufacturing, mining, and quarrying 14%, agriculture 9.5%, services 64.1% (1997 est.). **Industries:** petroleum, chemicals, tourism, food processing, cement, beverage, cotton textiles. **Natural resources:** petroleum, natural gas, asphalt.

**Exports:** $3.2 billion (f.o.b., 2000): petroleum and petroleum products, chemicals, steel products, fertilizer, sugar, cocoa, coffee, citrus, flowers. **Imports:** $3 billion (f.o.b., 2000 est.): machinery, transportation equipment, manufactured goods, food, live animals. **Major trading partners:** U.S., Caricom countries, Latin America, EU. **Member of Commonwealth of Nations**

**Geography** Trinidad and Tobago lie in the Caribbean Sea off the northeast coast of Venezuela. Trinidad, the larger at 1,864 sq mi (4,828 sq km), is mainly flat and rolling, with mountains in the north that reach a height of 3,085 ft (940 m) at Mount Aripo. Tobago, at just 116 sq mi (300 sq km), is heavily forested with hardwood trees.

**Government** Parliamentary democracy.

**History** When Trinidad was explored by Columbus in 1498, it was inhabited by the Arawaks; Carib Indians inhabited Tobago. Trinidad remained in Spanish possession, despite raids by other European nations, until it was ceded to Britain in 1802. Tobago passed between Britain and France several times, but it was ultimately given to Britain in 1814. Slavery was abolished in 1834. Between 1845 and 1917, thousands of indentured workers were brought from India to work on sugarcane plantations. In 1889 Trinidad and Tobago were made a single colony.

Partial self-government was instituted in 1925, and from 1958 to 1962 the nation was part of the West Indies Federation. On Aug. 31, 1962, it became independent and on Aug. 1, 1976, Trinidad and Tobago became a republic, remaining within the Commonwealth. While the country is a stable democracy and enjoys the highest living standards in the Caribbean thanks to oil revenue, tension between East Indians and blacks has underlined much of political life. In 1970 rioting and an army mutiny against the East Indian population prompted a state of emergency, which lasted for two years.

Eric Williams, "Father of the Nation" and leader of the People's National Movement (PNM), which is largely supported by blacks, governed from 1956 until his death in 1981. In Dec. 1986 the multiracial National Alliance for Reconstruction (NAR), based in Tobago, won a parliamentary majority, promising to sell most state-owned companies, reorganize the civil service, and reduce dependence on oil.

In 1990, to protest the NAR government, some 100 radical black Muslims blew up the police station in an attempted coup, in which the prime minister and other officials were held hostage for six days. The NAR was defeated in 1991, and the PNM returned to power. In 1995, the East Indian–based party, the United National Congress (UNC), led by Basdeo Panday, formed a coalition government with the NAR. In 2000, Panday narrowly won another term.

In Dec. 2001 elections, both the governing UNC party and the People's National Movement (PNM) party gained 18 seats each. The two parties agreed to allow President Robinson to select the prime minister to end the impasse. But when Robinson selected Patrick Manning of the PNM because of his "moral and spiritual values," the opposition angrily called for new elections.

# Tunisia

**REPUBLIC OF TUNISIA**
**National name:** Al-Joumhouria Attunisia
**President:** Zine al-Abidine Ben Ali (1987)
**Prime Minister:** Mohamed Ghannouchi (1999)
**Area:** 63,170 sq mi (163,610 sq km)
**Population (2002 est.):** 9,815,644 (growth rate: 1.2%);
birth rate: 16.8/1000; infant mortality rate: 28.0/1000;
density per sq mi: 155
**Capital and largest city (1994):** Tunis, 887,800.
**Monetary unit:** Tunisian dinar. **Languages:** Arabic
(official), French. **Ethnicity/race:** Arab-Berber 98%,
European 1%, Jewish less than 1%. **Religions:** Islam
(Sunni) 98%, Christian 1%, Jewish, less than 1%.
**Literacy rate:** 65% (1990)
**Economic summary: GDP/PPP** (2000 est.): $62.8
billion; per capita $6,500. **Real growth rate:** 5%.
**Inflation:** 3%. **Unemployment:** 15.6%. **Arable land:**
19%. **Agriculture:** olives, olive oil, grain, dairy
products, tomatoes, citrus fruit, beef, sugar beets,
dates, almonds. **Labor force:** 2.65 million (2000 est.);
note: shortage of skilled labor; services 55%, industry
23%, agriculture 22% (1995 est.). **Industries:**
petroleum, mining (particularly phosphate and iron
ore), tourism, textiles, footwear, food, beverages.
**Natural resources:** petroleum, phosphates, iron ore,
lead, zinc, salt. **Exports:** $6.1 billion (f.o.b., 2000 est.):
textiles, mechanical goods, phosphates and
chemicals, agricultural products, hydrocarbons.
**Imports:** $8.4 billion (f.o.b., 2000 est.): machinery and
equipment, hydrocarbons, chemicals, food. **Major
trading partners:** Germany, France, Italy, Belgium,
Libya.

**Geography** Tunisia, at the northernmost bulge of
Africa, thrusts out toward Sicily to mark the division
between the eastern and western Mediterranean Sea.
Twice the size of South Carolina, it is bordered on the
west by Algeria and by Libya on the south. Coastal
plains on the east rise to a north-south escarpment that
slopes gently to the west. The Sahara Desert lies in the
southernmost part. Tunisia is more mountainous in the
north, where the Atlas range continues from Algeria.

**Government** Republic.

**History** Tunisia was settled by the Phoenicians in the
12th century B.C. By the sixth and fifth centuries B.C.,
the great city-state of Carthage (derived from the
Phoenician name for "new city") dominated much of
the western Mediterranean. The three Punic Wars
between Rome and Carthage (the second was the most
famous, pitting the Roman general Scipio Africanus
against Carthage's Hannibal) led to the complete
destruction of Carthage by 146 B.C.
Except for an interval of Vandal conquest in A.D.
439-533, Tunisia was part of the Roman Empire
until the Arab conquest of 648-69. It was then ruled
by various Arab and Berber dynasties, followed by the
Turks, who took it in 1570-74 and made it part of the
Ottoman Empire until the 19th century. In the late
16th century, it was a stronghold for the Barbary
pirates. French troops occupied the country in 1881,
and the bey, the local Tunisian ruler, signed a treaty
acknowledging it as a French protectorate.
Nationalist agitation forced France to recognize
Tunisian independence and sovereignty in 1956. The
Constituent Assembly deposed the bey on July 25,
1957, declared Tunisia a republic, and elected Habib
Bourguiba as president. Bourguiba maintained a pro-
Western foreign policy that earned him enemies. Tuni-
sia refused to break relations with the U.S. during the
Arab-Israeli War in June 1967. Concerned with

Islamic fundamentalist plots against the state, the government stepped up efforts to eradicate the movement,
including censorship and frequent detention of suspects.
In 1987, the aged Bourguiba was declared mentally
unfit to continue as president and was removed from
office. He was succeeded as president by General Zine
al-Abidine Ben Ali, whose tenure was marked by a
rise in Islamic fundamentalism and growing anti-
Western sentiments among the populace. Ben Ali was
reelected in Oct. 1999 with 99% of the vote in an
election criticized by many human rights observers. In
May 2000 Ben Ali's Constitutional Democratic
Assembly Party swept local elections with 92% of the
vote, in a contest many opposition leaders boycotted.
However, Tunisia's economy continued to improve in
the late 1990s, making the country one of the most
attractive in Africa for foreign investors.
On April 11, 2002, a suicide attack on an ancient
synagogue on the Tunisian island of Djerba killed 19
people, most of them German tourists. The al-Qaeda
terrorist network claimed responsibility.

# Turkey

**REPUBLIC OF TURKEY**
**National name:** Türkiye Cumhuriyeti
**President:** Ahmet Necdet Sezer (2000)
**Prime Minister:** Bulent Ecevit (1999)
**Area:** 301,382 sq mi (incl. 9,121 in Europe) (780,580 sq
km)
**Population (2002 est.):** 67,308,928 (growth rate: 1.2%);
birth rate: 17.9/1000; infant mortality rate: 45.8/1000;
density per sq mi: 223
**Capital (1996 est.):** Ankara, 2,890,025. **Largest cities:**
Istanbul (2000 est.), 10,250,000 (metro. area); Izmir,
1,920,807; Adana, 1,010,363; Bursa, 949,810;
Gaziantep, 683,557. **Monetary unit:** Turkish lira.
**Language:** Turkish. **Ethnicity/race:** Turkish 80%,
Kurdish 20%. **Religion:** Islam (mostly Sunni) 98%.
**Literacy rate:** 81% (1990)
**Economic summary: GDP/PPP** (2000 est.): $444
billion; per capita $6,800. **Real growth rate:** 6%.
**Inflation:** 39%. **Unemployment:** 5.6% (plus
underemployment of 5.6%) (2000 est.). **Arable land:**
32%. **Agriculture:** tobacco, cotton, grain, olives, sugar
beets, pulse, citrus; livestock. **Labor force:** 23 million
(2000 est.); note: about 1.2 million Turks work abroad
(1999); agriculture 38%, services 38%, industry 24%
(2000). **Industries:** textiles, food processing, autos,
mining (coal, chromite, copper, boron), steel,
petroleum, construction, lumber, paper. **Natural
resources:** antimony, coal, chromium, mercury,
copper, borate, sulfur, iron ore, arable land,
hydropower. **Exports:** $26.9 billion (f.o.b., 2000 est.):
apparel 25.9%, foodstuffs 18.1%, textiles 17.0%, metal
manufactures 8.6%, transport equipment 8.1% (1998).
**Imports:** $55.7 billion (c.i.f., 2000 est.): machinery
28.3%, chemicals 15.2%, semi-finished goods 14.5%,
fuels 11%, transport equipment 9.5% (1999). **Major
trading partners:** Germany, U.S., UK, Italy, France,
Russia.

**Geography** Turkey is at the northeast end of the
Mediterranean Sea in southeast Europe and southwest
Asia. To the north is the Black Sea and to the west is
the Aegean Sea. Its neighbors are Greece and Bulgaria
to the west, Russia and Ukraine to the north (through
the Black Sea), Georgia, Armenia, Azerbaijan, and
Iran to the east, and Syria and Iraq to the south. The
Dardanelles, the Sea of Marmara, and the Bosporus
divide the country. Turkey in Europe comprises an
area about equal to the state of Massachusetts. Turkey

in Asia is about the size of Texas. Its center is a tree-less plateau rimmed by mountains.

**Government** Republican parliamentary democracy.

**History** Anatolia (Turkey in Asia) was occupied in about 1900 B.C. by the Indo-European Hittites and, after the Hittite empire's collapse in 1200 B.C., by Phrygians and Lydians. The Persian Empire occupied the area in the 6th century B.C., giving way to the Roman Empire, then later the Byzantine Empire. The Ottoman Turks first appeared in the early 13th century, subjugating Turkish and Mongol bands pressing against the eastern borders of Byzantium and making the Christian Balkan states their vassals. They gradually spread through the Near East and Balkans, capturing Constantinople in 1453 and storming the gates of Vienna two centuries later. At its height, the Ottoman Empire stretched from the Persian Gulf to western Algeria. Lasting for 600 years, the Ottoman Empire was not only one of the most powerful empires in the history of the Mediterranean region, but it generated a great cultural outpouring of Islamic art, architecture, and literature.

After the reign of Sultan Süleyman I the Magnificent (1494–1566), the Ottoman Empire began to decline politically, administratively, and economically. By the 18th century, Russia was seeking to establish itself as the protector of Christians in Turkey's Balkan territories. Russian ambitions were checked by Britain and France in the Crimean War (1854–56), but the Russo-Turkish War (1877–78) gave Bulgaria virtual independence and Romania and Serbia liberation from their nominal allegiance to the sultan. Turkish weakness stimulated a revolt of young liberals known as the Young Turks in 1909. They forced Sultan Abdul Hamid to grant a constitution and install a liberal government. However, reforms were no barrier to further defeats in a war with Italy (1911–12) and the Balkan Wars (1912–13). Turkey sided with Germany in World War I, and, as a result, lost territory at the conclusion of the war.

Turkey's current boundaries were drawn in 1923 at the Conference of Lausanne, and Turkey became a republic with Kemal Atatürk as the first president. The Ottoman sultanate and caliphate were abolished, and modernization, reform, and industrialization began under Atatürk's direction. He secularized Turkish society, reducing Islam's dominant role and replacing Arabic with the Latin alphabet for writing the Turkish language. After Atatürk's death in 1938, parliamentary government and a multiparty system gradually took root in Turkey, despite periods of instability and brief intervals of military rule. Neutral during most of World War II, Turkey, on Feb. 23, 1945, declared war on Germany and Japan, but it took no active part in the conflict. Turkey became a full member of NATO in 1952, was a signatory in the Balkan Entente (1953), joined the Baghdad Pact (1955; later CENTO), joined the Organization for European Economic Cooperation (OEEC) and the Council of Europe, and became an associate member of the European Common Market in 1963.

Turkey invaded Cyprus by sea and air on July 20, 1974, following the failure of diplomatic efforts to resolve conflicts between Turkish and Greek Cypriots. Turkey unilaterally announced a cease-fire on Aug. 16, after having gained control of 40% of the island. Turkish Cypriots established their own state in the north on Feb. 13, 1975. In July 1975, after a 30-day warning, Turkey took control of all the U.S. installations except the joint defense base at Incirlik, which it reserved for "NATO tasks alone."

The establishment of military government in Sept. 1980 stopped the slide toward anarchy and brought some improvement in the economy. A Constituent Assembly, consisting of the six-member National Security Council and members appointed by them, drafted a new constitution that was approved by an overwhelming (91.5%) majority of the voters in a Nov. 6, 1982, referendum. Martial law was gradually lifted.

About 12 million Kurds, roughly 20% of Turkey's population, live in the southeast region of Turkey. Turkey, however, does not officially recognize Kurds as a minority group and is therefore exempted from protecting their rights. Oppression of Kurds and Kurdish culture led to the emergence in 1984 of the Kurdistan Workers' Party (PKK), a militant Kurdish terrorist campaign under the leadership of Abdullah Ocalan. Although the guerrilla movement sought independence at first, by the late 1980s the rebel Kurds were willing to accept an autonomous state or a federation with Turkey. In March 1995, Turkish troops moved into northern Iraq seeking to root out Kurdish rebels, who had used Iraq as a base. About 35,000 have died in clashes between the military and the PKK during the 1980s and '90s. On Feb. 16, 1999, Ocalan was captured, tried, and convicted of treason and separatism on June 2, 1999, and sentenced to death.

On Aug. 17, 1999, western Turkey was devastated by an earthquake (magnitude 7.4) that left more than 17,000 dead and 200,000 homeless. The government was decried for lax control of builders whose faulty construction increased the destruction and added to the death toll. Another huge earthquake struck in November.

In June 2002, Turkey became the major international peacekeeping force in war-ravaged Afghanistan, taking over the command from the UK.

In the summer of 2002, Prime Minister Bulent Ecevit, despite grave illness, refused to step down or pave the way for a successor. His intransigence led to the resignations of numerous key officials in his three-party coalition government. The prime minister finally relented, setting new elections for Nov. 3.

In Sept. 2002, construction on a $3 billion, 1,000-mile oil pipeline running from Baku, Azerbaijan, to the Mediterranean port city of Ceyhan was begun, and it is expected to bolster the economy.

# Turkmenistan

**TURKMENISTAN**

**President-for-Life:** Saparmurad A. Niyazov (1990)
**Area:** 188,455 sq mi (488,100 sq km)
**Population (2002 est.):** 4,688,963 (growth rate: 1.9%); birth rate: 28.3/1000; infant mortality rate: 73.2/1000; density per sq mi: 25
**Capital and largest city (1994 est.):** Ashgabat, 518,000. **Other large cities:** Chardzhou, 166,400; Tashauz, 117,000. **Monetary unit:** Manat.
**Languages:** Turkmen, 72%; Russian, 12%; Uzbek, 9%. **Ethnicity/race (1995):** Turkmen 77%, Uzbek 9.2%, Russian 6.7%, Kazak 2%, other 5.1%.
**Religions:** Muslim 89%, Eastern Orthodox 9%, unknown 2%. **Literacy rate:** 98% (1989)
**Economic summary:** GDP/PPP (2000 est.): $19.6 billion; per capita $4,300. **Real growth rate:** 16%. **Inflation:** 14%. **Unemployment:** n.a. **Arable land:** 3%. **Agriculture:** cotton, grain; livestock. **Labor force:** 2.34 million (1996); agriculture 44%, industry 19%, services 37% (1996). **Industries:** natural gas, oil, petroleum products, textiles, food processing. **Natural resources:** petroleum, natural gas, coal, sulfur, salt. **Exports:** $2.4 billion (f.o.b., 2000 est.): gas 33%, oil

30%, cotton fiber 18%, textiles 8% (1999). **Imports:** $1.65 billion (c.i.f., 2000 est.): machinery and equipment 60%, foodstuffs 15% (1999). **Major trading partners:** Ukraine, Iran, Turkey, Russia, Kazakhstan, Tajikstan, Azerbaijan, Germany, U.S., Uzbekistan.

**Geography** Turkmenistan (formerly Turkmenia) is bounded by the Caspian Sea in the west, Kazakhstan in the north, Uzbekistan in the east, and Iran and Afghanistan in the south. About nine-tenths of Turkmenistan is desert, chiefly the Kara-Kum. One of the world's largest sand deserts, it is approximately 138,966 sq mi (360,000 sq km). Many irrigation canals and reservoirs have been built, including the Kara-Kum Canal, which runs from the Amu Darya River westward to the Caspian Sea.

**Government** One-party republic.

**History** Turkmenistan was once part of the ancient Persian Empire. The Turkmen people were originally pastoral nomads and some of them continued this way of life up into the 20th century, living in transportable dome-shaped felt tents. The territory was ruled by the Seljuk Turks in the 11th century. The Mongols of Ghenghis Khan conquered the land in the 13th century and dominated the area for the next two centuries until they were deposed in the late 15th century by invading Uzbeks. Prior to the 19th century, Turkmenia was divided into two lands, one belonging to the khanate of Khiva and the other belonging to the khanate of Bukhara. In 1868, the khanate of Khiva was made part of the Russian empire and Turkmenia became known as the Transcaspia Region of Russian Turkistan. Turkmenistan was later founded out of the Turkistan Autonomous Soviet Socialist Republic, founded in 1922, and was made an independent Soviet Socialist Republic on May 13, 1925. It was the poorest of the Soviet republics.

Turkmenistan declared its sovereignty in Aug. 1990 and became a member of the Commonwealth of Independent States on Dec. 21, 1991, together with ten other former Soviet republics. It established a government more authoritarian than those functioning in the other newly independent central Asian republics. President Saparmurad A. Niyazov, also called the Turkmenbashy (Leader of All Turkmens), has attempted to create a cult of personality through extravagant self-promotion. Cities, aftershave, and a meteor now bear his name. In 2002, he renamed all the months of the calendar. Jan. is now called by his preferred name, Turkmenbashi; April is named after his mother. Protests against his authoritarian rule and practices notwithstanding, Niyazov was named president for life by his rubber stamp Parliament in 1999.

In the 1990s, Turkmenistan exported gas through a Russian pipeline, bringing in about $1 billion per year. But in 1993, Russia closed down Turkmenistan's only pipeline because it competed with Russia's own gas exportation. Turkmenistan was limited to exporting gas to its impoverished central Asian neighbors, who were unable to pay their bills. The nation then opened a pipeline route to Iran, generally agreed to be the most economical route for exporting Caspian oil, and thus ruffled the feathers of Iran's enemy, the U.S. So far, the new plan has not brought in money, and the country is living off loans from Western countries such as Germany who hope to partner with the oil-rich, money-poor country.

# Tuvalu

**Sovereign:** Queen Elizabeth II (1952)
**Governor-General:** Sir Tomasi Puapua (1998)
**Prime Minister:** Saufatu Sopoanga (2002)
**Area:** 10 sq mi (26 sq km)
**Population (2002 est.):** 11,146 (growth rate: 1.4%); birth rate: 21.4/1000; infant mortality rate: 22.0/1000; density per sq mi: 1,110
**Capital and largest city (1991):** Funafuti, 3,839.
**Monetary unit:** Australian dollar. **Languages:** Tuvaluan, English. **Ethnicity/race:** Polynesian 96%. **Religion:** Church of Tuvalu (Congregationalist) 97%. **Literacy rate:** less than 50%
**Economic summary: GDP/PPP** (1999 est.): $11.6 million; per capita $1,100. **Real growth rate:** 3%. **Inflation:** 7% (1999 est.). **Unemployment:** n.a. **Arable land:** 0%. **Agriculture:** coconuts; fish. **Labor force:** n.a.; people make a living mainly through exploitation of the sea, reefs, and atolls and from wages sent home by those working abroad (mostly workers in the phosphate industry and sailors). **Industries:** fishing, tourism, copra. **Natural resources:** fish. **Exports:** $165,000 (f.o.b., 1989): copra. **Imports:** $4.4 million (c.i.f., 1989): food, animals, mineral fuels, machinery, manufactured goods. **Major trading partners:** Fiji, Australia, New Zealand. **Member of Commonwealth of Nations**

**Geography** Tuvalu consists of nine small islands scattered over 500,000 sq mi of the western Pacific, just south of the equator. The islands include Niulakita, Nukulaelae, Funafuti, Nukufetau, Vaitupu, Nui, Niutao, Nanumaga (Nanumanga), and Nanumea.

**Government** Constitutional monarchy with a parliamentary democracy.

**History** Formerly the Ellice Islands, Tuvalu's first Polynesian settlers were probably Samoans or Tongans. The Ellice Islands became a British protectorate in 1892 and were annexed by Britain in 1915–16 as part of the Gilbert and Ellice Islands Colony. The Ellice Islands were separated from the Gilberts in 1975, given home rule, and renamed Tuvalu. Full independence was granted on Sept. 30, 1978, but it remained part of the Commonwealth. In 1979, the U.S. gave Tuvalu four islands that had been U.S. territory.

In 1997, the government adopted a strong stance on the need to control emissions of greenhouse gases in order to ensure the survival of low-lying island nations, which are threatened by rising sea levels—Tuvalu's highest point is just 16 ft above sea level. In 2000, Tuvalu became a member of the United Nations.

# Uganda

### REPUBLIC OF UGANDA

**President:** Yoweri Museveni (1986)
**Prime Minister:** Apolo Nsibambi (1999)
**Area:** 91,135 sq mi (236,040 sq km)
**Population (2002 est.):** 24,699,073 (growth rate: 3.0%); birth rate: 47.1/1000; infant mortality rate: 89.3/1000; density per sq mi: 271
**Capital and largest city (1991 est.):** Kampala, 773,463.
**Monetary unit:** Ugandan new shilling. **Languages:** English (official), Swahili, Luganda, Ateso, Luo. **Ethnicity/race:** Baganda 17%, Karamojong 12%, Basogo 8%, Iteso 8%, Langi 6%, Rwanda 6%, Bagisu 5%, Acholi 4%, Lugbara 4%, Bunyoro 3%, Batobo 3%, European, Asian, Arab 1%, other 23%. **Religions:** Christian 66%, Islam 16%. **Literacy rate:** 54% (1991)
**Economic summary: GDP/PPP** (2000 est.): $26.2

billion; per capita $1,100. **Real growth rate:** 6%.
**Inflation:** 6.5% (2000). **Unemployment:** n.a. **Arable land:** 25%. **Agriculture:** coffee, tea, cotton, tobacco, cassava (tapioca), potatoes, corn, millet, pulses; beef, goat meat, milk, poultry. **Labor force:** 8.361 million (1993 est.); agriculture 82%, industry 5%, services 13% (1999 est.). **Industries:** sugar, brewing, tobacco, cotton textiles, cement. **Natural resources:** copper, cobalt, hydropower, limestone, salt, arable land. **Exports:** $500.1 million (f.o.b., 1999): coffee, fish and fish products, tea; electrical products, iron and steel. **Imports:** $1.1 billion (f.o.b., 1999): vehicles, petroleum, medical supplies; cereals. **Major trading partners:** Spain, Germany, Belgium, Netherlands, Hungary, Kenya, U.S., France, UK, India. **Member of the Commonwealth of Nations**

**Geography** Uganda, twice the size of Pennsylvania, is in East Africa. It is bordered on the west by Congo, on the north by the Sudan, on the east by Kenya, and on the south by Tanzania and Rwanda. The country, which lies across the equator, is divided into three main areas—swampy lowlands, a fertile plateau with wooded hills, and a desert region. Lake Victoria forms part of the southern border.

**Government** Multiparty democractic republic.

**History** About 500 B.C. Bantu-speaking peoples migrated to the area now called Uganda. By the 14th century, three kingdoms dominated, Buganda (meaning "state of the Gandas"), Bunyoro, and Ankole. Uganda was first explored by Europeans as well as Arab traders in 1844. An Anglo-German agreement of 1890 declared it to be in the British sphere of influence in Africa, and the Imperial British East Africa Company was chartered to develop the area. The company did not prosper financially, and in 1894 a British protectorate was proclaimed. Few Europeans permanently settled in Uganda, but it attracted Indians, Pakistanis, and Goans, who became important players in Ugandan commerce.

Uganda became independent on Oct. 9, 1962. Sir Edward Mutesa, the king of Buganda (Mutesa II), was elected the first president, and Milton Obote the first prime minister of the newly independent country. With the help of a young army officer, Col. Idi Amin, Prime Minister Obote seized control of the government from President Mutesa four years later.

On Jan. 25, 1971, Colonel Amin deposed President Obote. Obote went into exile in Tanzania. Amin expelled Asian residents and launched a reign of terror against Ugandan opponents, torturing and killing tens of thousands. In 1976, he had himself proclaimed "President for Life." In 1977, Amnesty International estimated that 300,000 may have died under his rule, including church leaders and recalcitrant cabinet ministers.

After Amin held military exercises on the Tanzanian border, angering Tanzania's president, Julius Nyerere, a combined force of Tanzanian troops and Ugandan exiles loyal to former president Obote invaded Uganda and chased Amin into exile in Saudi Arabia. After a series of interim administrations, President Obote led his People's Congress Party to victory in 1980 elections that opponents charged were rigged. On July 27, 1985, army troops staged a coup and took over the government. Obote fled into exile. The military regime installed Gen. Tito Okello as chief of state.

The National Resistance Army (NRA), an anti-Obote group led by Yoweri Museveni, kept fighting after it had been excluded from the new regime. It seized Kampala on Jan. 29, 1986, and Museveni was declared president. Museveni has transformed the ruins of Idi Amin and Milton Obote's Uganda into an economic miracle, preaching a philosophy of self-sufficiency and anticorruption. Western countries have flocked to assist him in the country's transformation. Nevertheless, it remains one of Africa's poorest countries. A ban on political parties was lifted in 1996, and the incumbent Museveni won 72% of the vote, reflecting his popularity due to the country's economic recovery.

Uganda has waged an enormously successful campaign against AIDS, dramatically reducing the rate of new infections through an intensive public health and education campaign. Museveni won reelection in March 2001 with 70% of the vote, following a nasty and spirited campaign.

Close ties with Rwanda (many Rwandan Tutsi exiles helped Museveni come to power) led to the cooperation of Uganda and Rwanda in the ousting of Zaire's Mobutu Sese Seko in 1997, and a year later, in efforts to unseat his successor, Laurent Kabila, whom both countries originally supported but from whom they grew estranged. But in 1999, Uganda and Rwanda quarreled over strategy in the Congo, and began fighting each other. The two countries mended their differences in 2002. Uganda also signed a peace accord with the Congo in Sept. 2002.

Throughout 2002, Uganda continued its 15-year battle against the extremist rebel group, the Lord's Resistance Army (LRA), based in Sudan. Between 8,000 and 10,000 children have been abducted by the LRA and form the army of "prophet" Joseph Kony, whose aim is to take over Uganda and run it according to his vision of Christianity.

# Ukraine

### UKRAINE

**President:** Leonid D. Kuchma (1994)
**Prime Minister:** Anatoli Kinakh (2001)
**Area:** 233,089 sq mi (603,700 sq km)
**Population (2002 est.):** 48,396,470 (growth rate: –0.7%): birth rate: 9.6/1000; infant mortality rate: 21.1/1000; density per sq mi: 208
**Capital:** Kyiv (Kiev), 2,637,000. **Other large cities:** Kharkiv, 1,622,000; Donetske, 1,121,000; Odessa, 1,104,000; Lviv, 803,000. **Monetary unit:** Hryvna. **Language:** Ukrainian. **Ethnicity/race:** Ukrainian 73%, Russian 22%, Jewish 1%, other 4%. **Religions:** Orthodox 76%, Ukrainian Catholic (Uniate) 13.5%, Jewish 2.3%, Baptist, Mennonite, Protestant, and Muslim 8.2%. **Literacy rate:** 100% (1979)
**Economic summary: GDP/PPP** (2000 est.): $189.4 billion; per capita $3,850. **Real growth rate:** 6%. **Inflation:** 25.8%. **Unemployment:** 4.3% officially registered; large number of unregistered or underemployed workers (Dec. 1999). **Arable land:** 58%. **Agriculture:** grain, sugar beets, sunflower seeds, vegetables; beef, milk. **Labor force:** 22.8 million (year-end 1997); industry 32%, agriculture 24%, services 44% (1996). **Industries:** coal, electric power, ferrous and nonferrous metals, machinery and transport equipment, chemicals, food processing (especially sugar). **Natural resources:** iron ore, coal, manganese, natural gas, oil, salt, sulfur, graphite, titanium, magnesium, kaolin, nickel, mercury, timber, arable land. **Exports:** $14.6 billion (2000 est.): ferrous and nonferrous metals, fuel and petroleum products, machinery and transport equipment, food products. **Imports:** $15 billion (2000 est.): energy, machinery and parts, transportation equipment, chemicals. **Major trading partners:** Russia, Europe, U.S.

**Geography** Located in southeast Europe, the country consists largely of fertile black soil steppes. Mountainous areas include the Carpathians in the southwest and the Crimean chain in the south. There are forest lakes in the north. Ukraine is bordered by Belarus on the north, by Russia on the north, northeast, and east, by the Sea of Azov and the Black Sea on the south, by Moldova and Romania on the southwest, and by Hungary, Slovakia, and Poland on the west.

**Government** Constitutional republic.

**History** Ukraine was known as "Kievan Rus" (from which *Russia* is a derivative) up until the 16th century. In the 9th century, Kiev was the major political and cultural center in eastern Europe. Kievan Rus reached the height of its power in the 10th century and adopted Byzantine Christianity, the Church Slavonic written language, and the Cyrillic alphabet during that period. The Mongol conquest in 1240 ended Kievan power. From the 13th to the 16th century, Kiev was under the influence of Poland and western Europe. The negotiation of the Union of Brest-Litovsk in 1596 divided the Ukrainians into Orthodox and Ukrainian Catholic faithful. In 1654, Ukraine asked the czar of Moscovy for protection against Poland, and the Treaty of Pereyasav signed that year recognized the suzerainty of Moscow. The agreement was interpreted by Moscow as an invitation to take over Kiev, and the Ukrainian state was eventually absorbed into the Russian empire.

After the Russian Revolution, Ukraine declared its independence from Russia on Jan. 28, 1918, and several years of warfare ensued with several groups. The Red Army finally was victorious over Kiev, and in 1920 Ukraine became a Soviet republic. In 1922, Ukraine became one of the founders of the Union of Soviet Socialist Republics. In the 1930s, the Soviet government's enforcement of collectivization met with peasant resistance, which in turn prompted the confiscation of grain from Ukrainian farmers by Soviet authorities; the resulting famine took an estimated 5 million lives. Ukraine was one of the most devastated Soviet republics after World War II. (For details on World War II, *see* Headline History, World War II.) On April 26, 1986, the nation's nuclear power plant at Chernobyl was the site of the world's worst nuclear accident. On Oct. 29, 1991, the Ukrainian Parliament voted to shut down the reactor within two years' time and asked for international assistance in dismantling it.

When President Leonid Kravchuk was elected by the Ukrainian Parliament in 1990, he vowed to seek Ukrainian sovereignty. Ukraine declared its independence on Aug. 24, 1991. In Dec. 1991, Ukrainian, Russian, and Belorussian leaders cofounded a new Commonwealth of Independent States with the new capital to be situated in Minsk, Belarus. The new country's government was slow to reform the Soviet-era state-run economy, which was plagued by declining production, rising inflation, and widespread unemployment in the years following independence. The U.S. announced in Jan. 1994 that an agreement had been reached with Russia and Ukraine for the destruction of Ukraine's entire nuclear arsenal. In Oct. 1994, Ukraine began a program of economic liberalization and moved to reestablish central authority over Crimea. In 1995, Crimea's separatist leader was removed and the Crimean constitution revoked.

In June 1996, the last strategic nuclear warhead was removed to Russia. Also that month Parliament approved a new constitution that allowed for private ownership of land. An agreement was signed in May 1997 on the future of the Black Sea fleet, by which Ukrainian and Russian ships will share the port of Sevastopol for 20 years. Ukraine and Russia also signed a 10-year political treaty three days later, by which, among other provisions, Russia recognized the political and territorial integrity of Ukraine, including the Crimean Peninsula.

The Russian financial crisis in fall 1998 led to severe problems for the Ukrainian economy, which is dependent on Russia for 40% of its foreign trade. Ukraine remains saddled with its Soviet-era economy, and most of its major industries are still under state control. Corruption is rampant, and Western investors have shown only minimal interest. The election of the reform-minded Viktor Yushchenko as prime minister in Dec. 1999, however, was greeted with optimism by the West. He was also highly popular among ordinary Ukrainians. But in April 2001, he was dismissed in a no-confidence vote engineered by Communist hardliners and Ukrainian big business.

In the winter of 2001 violent demonstrations rocked Ukraine, with protesters demanding the resignation and impeachment of authoritarian president Leonid Kuchma. Critics accused Kuchma of involvement in the murder of a journalist critical of government corruption. Kuchma was recorded on tape urging that the journalist be disposed of. The president is also believed to have shipped military equipment to Iraq despite the international embargo. In April 2002 parliamentary elections, Kuchma's party failed to gain a clear majority. In Sept. 2002, tens of thousands of disillusioned Ukrainians demonstrated, calling for Kuchma to step down.

# United Arab Emirates

**President:** Sheikh Zayed bin Sultan al-Nahyan (1971)
**Prime Minister:** Sheikh Maktoum bin Rashid al-Maktoum (1990)
**Area:** 32,000 sq mi (82,880 sq km)
**Population (2002 est.):** 2,445,989 (growth rate: 1.4%); birth rate: 18.3/1000; infant mortality rate: 16.1/1000; density per sq mi: 76
**Capital and largest city (1989 est.):** Abu Dhabi, 363,432. **Monetary unit:** U.A.E. dirham. **Languages:** Arabic (official), English as a second language.
**Ethnicity/race:** Emiri 19%, other Arab and Iranian 23%, South Asian 50%, other expatriates (includes Westerners and East Asians) 8% (1982). **Religions:** Islam (Sunni 80%, Shi'ite 16%), others 4%. **Literacy rate:** 68% (1980)
**Economic summary:** GDP/PPP (2000 est.): $54 billion; per capita $22,800. **Real growth rate:** 4%. **Inflation:** 4.5%. **Unemployment:** n.a. **Arable land:** 0%. **Agriculture:** dates, vegetables, watermolons; poultry, eggs, dairy products; fish. **Labor force:** 1.4 million (1998 est.); note: 75% of the population in the 15-64 age group is non-national (July 1998 est.): services 60%, industry 32%, agriculture 5% (1993 est.). **Industries:** petroleum, fishing, petrochemicals, construction materials, some boat building, handicrafts, pearling. **Natural resources:** petroleum, natural gas. **Exports:** $46 billion (f.o.b., 2000 est.): crude oil 45%, natural gas, reexports, dried fish, dates. **Imports:** $34 billion (f.o.b., 2000 est.): machinery and transport equipment, chemicals, food. **Major trading partners:** Japan, India, Singapore, South Korea, Oman, Iran, U.S., UK, Italy, Germany.

**Geography** The United Arab Emirates, in the eastern part of the Arabian Peninsula, extends along part of the Gulf of Oman and the southern coast of the Persian Gulf. The nation is the size of Maine. Its neighbors are Saudi Arabia to the west and south, Qatar to the north, and Oman to the east. Most of the land is barren and sandy.

**Government** Federation formed in 1971 by seven emirates known as the Trucial States—Abu Dhabi (the largest), Dubai, Sharjah, Ajman, Fujairah, Ras al Khaimah, and Umm al-Qaiwain.

**History** Originally the area was inhabited by a seafaring people who were converted to Islam in the 7th century. Later, a dissident sect, the Carmathians, established a powerful sheikdom, and its army conquered Mecca. After the sheikdom disintegrated, its people became pirates. Threatening the Sultanate of Muscat and Oman early in the 19th century, the pirates provoked the intervention of the British, who in 1820 enforced a partial truce and in 1853 a permanent truce. Thus what had been called the Pirate Coast was renamed the Trucial Coast. The British provided the nine Trucial states with protection but did not formally administer them as a colony.

The British withdrew from the Persian Gulf in 1971, and the Trucial states became a federation called the United Arab Emirates (UAE). Two of the Trucial states, Bahrain and Oman, chose not to join the federation, reducing the number of states to seven.

The country signed a military defense agreement with the U.S. in 1994 and one with France in 1995. In 1997, UAE officials protested Iranian military activities in the Persian Gulf, especially in regard to the ownership of three Gulf islands, which had been the subject of disputes for many years.

In 2000, one of the biggest arms deals in history took place, with the United Arab Emirates buying 80 fighter jets and missiles from Lockheed Martin for nearly $8 billion.

After the Sept. 11 terrorist attacks on New York and Washington, DC, the UAE was identified as a major financial center used by al-Qaeda in transferring money to the hijackers. The nation immediately cooperated with the U.S., freezing accounts tied to suspected terrorists and strongly clamping down on money laundering.

# United Kingdom

**UNITED KINGDOM OF GREAT BRITAIN AND NORTHERN IRELAND**

**Sovereign:** Queen Elizabeth II (1952)
**Prime Minister:** Tony Blair (1997)
**Area:** 94,525 sq mi (244,820 sq km)
**Population (2002 est.):** 59,778,002 (growth rate: 0.1%); birth rate: 11.3/1000; infant mortality rate: 5.5/1000; density per sq mi: 632
**Capital and largest city (2000 est.):** London, 11,800,000 (metro. area). **Other large cities:** Birmingham, 1,009,100; Leeds, 721,800; Glasgow, 681,470; Liverpool, 479,000; Bradford, 477,500; Edinburgh, 441,620; Manchester, 434,600; Bristol, 396,600. **Monetary unit:** Pound sterling (£).
**Languages:** English, Welsh, Scots Gaelic. **Ethnicity/race:** English 81.5%; Scottish 9.6%; Irish 2.4%; Welsh 1.9%; Ulster 1.8%; West Indian, Indian, Pakistani, and other 2.8%. **Religions:** Church of England (established church), Church of Wales (disestablished), Church of Scotland (established church—Presbyterian), Church of Ireland (disestablished), Roman Catholic, Methodist, Congregational, Baptist, Jewish. **Literacy rate:** 99% (1978)
**Economic summary:** GDP/PPP (2000 est.): $1.36 trillion; per capita $22,800. **Real growth rate:** 3%. **Inflation:** 2.4%. **Unemployment:** 5.5%. **Arable land:** 25%. **Agriculture:** cereals, oilseed, potatoes, vegetables; cattle, sheep, poultry; fish. **Labor force:**

29.2 million (1999); agriculture 1%, industry 19%, services 80% (1996 est.). **Industries:** machine tools, electric power equipment, automation equipment, railroad equipment, shipbuilding, aircraft, motor vehicles and parts, electronics and communications equipment, metals, chemicals, coal, petroleum, paper and paper products, food processing, textiles, clothing, and other consumer goods. **Natural resources:** coal, petroleum, natural gas, tin, limestone, iron ore, salt, clay, chalk, gypsum, lead, silica, arable land. **Exports:** $282 billion (f.o.b., 2000): manufactured goods, fuels, chemicals; food, beverages, tobacco. **Imports:** $324 billion (f.o.b., 2000): manufactured goods, machinery, fuels; foodstuffs. **Major trading partners:** EU, U.S., Japan.

**Geography** The United Kingdom, consisting of England, Wales, Scotland, and Northern Ireland, is twice the size of New York State. England, in the southeast part of the British Isles, is separated from Scotland on the north by the granite Cheviot Hills; from them the Pennine chain of uplands extends south through the center of England, reaching its highest point in the Lake District in the northwest. To the west along the border of Wales—a land of steep hills and valleys—are the Cambrian Mountains, while the Cotswolds, a range of hills in Gloucestershire, extend into the surrounding shires.

Important rivers flowing into the North Sea are the Thames, Humber, Tees, and Tyne. In the west are the Severn and Wye, which empty into the Bristol Channel and are navigable, as are the Mersey and Ribble.

**Government** The United Kingdom is a constitutional monarchy and parliamentary democracy, with a queen and a Parliament that has two houses: the House of Lords, with 574 life peers, 92 hereditary peers, 26 bishops, and the House of Commons, which has 651 popularly elected members. Supreme legislative power is vested in Parliament, which sits for five years unless sooner dissolved. The House of Lords was stripped of most of its power in 1911, and now its main function is to revise legislation. In Nov. 1999 hundreds of hereditary peers were expelled in an effort to make the body more democratic. The executive power of the Crown is exercised by the cabinet, headed by the prime minister.

**Ruler** Queen Elizabeth II, born April 21, 1926, elder daughter of King George VI and Queen Elizabeth, succeeded to the throne on the death of her father on Feb. 6, 1952. On Nov. 20, 1947, she married Prince Philip, duke of Edinburgh, born June 10, 1921. Their children are Prince Charles[1] (heir apparent), born Nov. 14, 1948; Princess Anne, born Aug. 15, 1950; Prince Andrew, born Feb. 19, 1960; and Prince Edward, born March 10, 1964. Prince William Arthur Philip Louis, son of Prince Charles and the late princess of Wales and second in line to the throne, was born June 21, 1982. A second son, Prince Henry Charles Albert David, was born Sept. 15, 1984, and is third in line.

**History** Stonehenge and other examples of prehistoric culture are what remains of the earliest inhabitants of Britain. Celtic peoples followed. Roman invasions of the 1st century B.C. brought Britain into contact with continental Europe. When the Roman legions withdrew in the 5th century A.D., Britain fell easy prey to the invading hordes of Angles, Saxons,

---

1. The title Prince of Wales, which is not inherited, was conferred on Prince Charles by his mother on July 26, 1958. The investiture ceremony took place on July 1, 1969. The previous Prince of Wales was Prince Edward Albert, who held the title from 1911 to 1936 before he became Edward VIII.

## Rulers of England and Great Britain

| Name | Born | Ruled[1] | Name | Born | Ruled[1] |
|---|---|---|---|---|---|
| SAXONS[2] | | | Henry VI | 1421 | 1422–1461[5] |
| Egbert[3] | c. 775 | 802–839 | HOUSE OF YORK | | |
| Ethelwulf | ? | 839–858 | Edward IV | 1442 | 1461–1483[5] |
| Ethelbald | ? | 858–860 | Edward V | 1470 | 1483–1483 |
| Ethelbert | ? | 860–865 | Richard III | 1452 | 1483–1485 |
| Ethelred I | ? | 865–871 | HOUSE OF TUDOR | | |
| Alfred the Great | 849 | 871–899 | Henry VII | 1457 | 1485–1509 |
| Edward the Elder | c. 870 | 899–924 | Henry VIII | 1491 | 1509–1547 |
| Athelstan | 895 | 924–939 | Edward VI | 1537 | 1547–1553 |
| Edmund I the Deed-doer | 921 | 939–946 | Jane (Lady Jane Grey)[6] | 1537 | 1553–1553 |
| Edred | c. 925 | 946–955 | Mary I ("Bloody Mary") | 1516 | 1553–1558 |
| Edwy the Fair | c. 943 | 955–959 | Elizabeth I | 1533 | 1558–1603 |
| Edgar the Peaceful | 943 | 959–975 | HOUSE OF STUART | | |
| Edward the Martyr | c. 962 | 975–978 | James I[7] | 1566 | 1603–1625 |
| Ethelred II the Unready | 968 | 978–1016 | Charles I | 1600 | 1625–1649 |
| Edmund II Ironside | c. 993 | 1016 | COMMONWEALTH | | |
| DANES | | | Council of State | — | 1649–1653 |
| Canute | 995 | 1016–1035 | Oliver Cromwell[8] | 1599 | 1653–1658 |
| Harold I Harefoot | c.1016 | 1035–1040 | Richard Cromwell[8] | 1626 | 1658–1659[9] |
| Hardecanute | c.1018 | 1040–1042 | RESTORATION OF HOUSE OF STUART | | |
| SAXONS | | | Charles II | 1630 | 1660–1685 |
| Edward the Confessor | c.1004 | 1042–1066 | James II | 1633 | 1685–1688[10] |
| Harold II | c.1020 | 1066 | William III[11] | 1650 | 1689–1702 |
| HOUSE OF NORMANDY | | | Mary II[11] | 1662 | 1689–1694 |
| William I the Conqueror | 1027 | 1066–1087 | Anne | 1665 | 1702–1714 |
| William II Rufus | c.1056 | 1087–1100 | HOUSE OF HANOVER | | |
| Henry I Beauclerc | 1068 | 1100–1135 | George I | 1660 | 1714–1727 |
| Stephen of Boulogne | c.1100 | 1135–1154 | George II | 1683 | 1727–1760 |
| HOUSE OF PLANTAGENET | | | George III | 1738 | 1760–1820 |
| Henry II | 1133 | 1154–1189 | George IV | 1762 | 1820–1830 |
| Richard I Coeur de Lion | 1157 | 1189–1199 | William IV | 1765 | 1830–1837 |
| John Lackland | 1167 | 1199–1216 | Victoria | 1819 | 1837–1901 |
| Henry III | 1207 | 1216–1272 | HOUSE OF SAXE-COBURG[12] | | |
| Edward I Longshanks | 1239 | 1272–1307 | Edward VII | 1841 | 1901–1910 |
| Edward II | 1284 | 1307–1327 | HOUSE OF WINDSOR[12] | | |
| Edward III | 1312 | 1327–1377 | George V | 1865 | 1910–1936 |
| Richard II | 1367 | 1377–1399[4] | Edward VIII | 1894 | 1936[13] |
| HOUSE OF LANCASTER | | | George VI | 1895 | 1936–1952 |
| Henry IV Bolingbroke | 1367 | 1399–1413 | Elizabeth II | 1926 | 1952– |
| Henry V | 1387 | 1413–1422 | | | |

1. Year of end of rule is also that of death, unless otherwise indicated. 2. Dates for Saxon kings are still subject of controversy. 3. Became king of West Saxons in 802; considered (from 828) first king of all England. 4. Died 1400. 5. Henry VI reigned again briefly 1470–71. 6. Nominal queen for 9 days; not counted as queen by some authorities. She was beheaded in 1554. 7. Ruled in Scotland as James VI (1567–1625). 8. Lord Protector. 9. Died 1712. 10. Died 1701. 11. Joint rulers (1689–1694). 12. Name changed from Saxe-Coburg to Windsor in 1917. 13. Was known after his abdication as the duke of Windsor, died 1972.

and Jutes from Scandinavia and the Low Countries. The invasions had little effect on the Celtic peoples of Wales and Scotland. Seven large Anglo-Saxon kingdoms were established, and the original Britons were forced into Wales and Scotland. It was not until the 19th century that the country slowly became united under the kings of Wessex. Following the death of Edward the Confessor (1066), a dispute about the succession arose, and William, duke of Normandy, invaded England, defeating the Saxon king, Harold II, at the Battle of Hastings (1066). The Norman conquest introduced Norman French law and feudalism.

The reign of Henry II (1154–89), first of the Plantagenets, saw an increasing centralization of royal power at the expense of the nobles, but in 1215 King John (1199–1216) was forced to sign the Magna Carta, which awarded the people, especially the nobles, certain basic rights. Edward I (1272–1307) continued the conquest of Ireland, reduced Wales to subjection, and made some gains in Scotland. In 1314, however, English forces led by Edward II were ousted from Scotland after the Battle of Bannockburn. The late 13th and early 14th centuries saw the development of a separate House of Commons with tax-raising powers. Edward III's claim to the throne of France led to the Hundred Years' War (1338–1453) and the loss of almost all the large English territory in France. In England, the great poverty and discontent caused by the war were intensified by the Black Death, a plague that reduced the population by about one third. The Wars of the Roses (1455–85), a struggle for the throne between the House of York and the House of Lancaster, ended with the victory of Henry Tudor (Henry VII) at Bosworth Field (1485).

During the reign of Henry VIII (1509–47), the church in England asserted its independence from the Roman Catholic Church. Under Edward VI and Mary, the two extremes of religious fanaticism were reached, and it remained for Henry's daughter, Elizabeth I (1558–1603), to set up the Church of England on a moderate basis. In 1588, the Spanish Armada, a fleet sent out by Catholic King Philip II of Spain, was defeated by the English and destroyed during a storm. During Elizabeth's reign, England became a world

## British Prime Ministers Since 1770

| Name | Term | Name | Term |
|------|------|------|------|
| Lord North (Tory) | 1770–1782 | William E. Gladstone (Liberal) | 1886–1886 |
| Marquis of Rockingham (Whig) | 1782–1782 | Marquis of Salisbury (Conservative) | 1886–1892 |
| Earl of Shelburne (Whig) | 1782–1783 | William E. Gladstone (Liberal) | 1892–1894 |
| Duke of Portland (Coalition) | 1783–1783 | Earl of Rosebery (Liberal) | 1894–1895 |
| William Pitt, the Younger (Tory) | 1783–1801 | Marquis of Salisbury (Conservative) | 1895–1902 |
| Henry Addington (Tory) | 1801–1804 | Arthur James Balfour (Conservative) | 1902–1905 |
| William Pitt, the Younger (Tory) | 1804–1806 | Sir H. Campbell-Bannerman (Liberal) | 1905–1908 |
| Baron Grenville (Whig) | 1806–1807 | Herbert H. Asquith (Liberal) | 1908–1915 |
| Duke of Portland (Tory) | 1807–1809 | Herbert H. Asquith (Coalition) | 1915–1916 |
| Spencer Perceval (Tory) | 1809–1812 | David Lloyd George (Coalition) | 1916–1922 |
| Earl of Liverpool (Tory) | 1812–1827 | Andrew Bonar Law (Conservative) | 1922–1923 |
| George Canning (Tory) | 1827–1827 | Stanley Baldwin (Conservative) | 1923–1924 |
| Viscount Goderich (Tory) | 1827–1828 | James Ramsay MacDonald (Labour) | 1924–1924 |
| Duke of Wellington (Tory) | 1828–1830 | Stanley Baldwin (Conservative) | 1924–1929 |
| Earl Grey (Whig) | 1830–1834 | James Ramsay MacDonald (Labour) | 1929–1931 |
| Viscount Melbourne (Whig) | 1834–1834 | James Ramsay MacDonald (Coalition) | 1931–1935 |
| Sir Robert Peel (Tory) | 1834–1835 | Stanley Baldwin (Coalition) | 1935–1937 |
| Viscount Melbourne (Whig) | 1835–1841 | Neville Chamberlain (Coalition) | 1937–1940 |
| Sir Robert Peel (Tory) | 1841–1846 | Winston Churchill (Coalition) | 1940–1945 |
| Earl Russell (Whig) | 1846–1852 | Clement R. Attlee (Labour) | 1945–1951 |
| Earl of Derby (Tory) | 1852–1852 | Sir Winston Churchill (Conservative) | 1951–1955 |
| Earl of Aberdeen (Coalition) | 1852–1855 | Sir Anthony Eden (Conservative) | 1955–1957 |
| Viscount Palmerston (Liberal) | 1855–1858 | Harold Macmillan (Conservative) | 1957–1963 |
| Earl of Derby (Conservative) | 1858–1859 | Sir Alec Frederick Douglas-Home | 1963–1964 |
| Viscount Palmerston (Liberal) | 1859–1865 | (Conservative) | |
| Earl Russell (Liberal) | 1865–1866 | Harold Wilson (Labour) | 1964–1970 |
| Earl of Derby (Conservative) | 1866–1868 | Edward Heath (Conservative) | 1970–1974 |
| Benjamin Disraeli (Conservative) | 1868–1868 | Harold Wilson (Labour) | 1974–1976 |
| William E. Gladstone (Liberal) | 1868–1874 | James Callaghan (Labour) | 1976–1979 |
| Benjamin Disraeli (Conservative) | 1874–1880 | Margaret Thatcher (Conservative) | 1979–1990 |
| William E. Gladstone (Liberal) | 1880–1885 | John Major (Conservative) | 1990–1997 |
| Marquis of Salisbury (Conservative) | 1885–1886 | Tony Blair (Labour) | 1997– |

power. Elizabeth's heir was a Stuart—James VI of Scotland—who joined the two crowns as James I (1603–25). The Stuart kings incurred large debts and were forced either to depend on Parliament for taxes or to raise money by illegal means. In 1642, war broke out between Charles I and a large segment of the Parliament; Charles was defeated and executed in 1649, and the monarchy was then abolished. After the death in 1658 of Oliver Cromwell, the lord protector, the Puritan Commonwealth fell to pieces and Charles II was placed on the throne in 1660. The struggle between the king and Parliament continued, but Charles II knew when to compromise. His brother, James II (1685–88), possessed none of his ability and was ousted by the Revolution of 1688, which confirmed the primacy of Parliament. James's daughter, Mary, and her husband, William of Orange, then became the rulers.

Queen Anne's reign (1702–14) was marked by the duke of Marlborough's victories over France at Blenheim, Oudenarde, and Malplaquet in the War of the Spanish Succession. England and Scotland meanwhile were joined by the Act of Union (1707). Upon the death of Anne, the distant claims of the elector of Hanover were recognized, and he became king of Great Britain and Ireland as George I. The unwillingness of the Hanoverian kings to rule resulted in the formation by the royal ministers of a cabinet, headed by a prime minister, which directed all public business. Abroad, the constant wars with France expanded the British Empire all over the globe, particularly in North America and India. This imperial growth was checked by the revolt of the American colonies (1775–81). Struggles with France broke out

again in 1793 and during the Napoleonic Wars, which ended at Waterloo in 1815.

The Victorian era, named after Queen Victoria (1837–1901), saw the growth of a democratic system of government that had begun with the Reform Bill of 1832. The two important wars in Victoria's reign were the Crimean War against Russia (1853–56) and the Boer War (1899–1902), the latter enormously extending Britain's influence in Africa. Increasing uneasiness at home and abroad marked the reign of Edward VII (1901–10). Within four years after the accession of George V in 1910, Britain entered World War I when Germany invaded Belgium. The nation was led by coalition cabinets, headed first by Herbert Asquith and then, starting in 1916, by the Welsh statesman David Lloyd George. Postwar labor unrest culminated in the general strike of 1926.

King Edward VIII succeeded to the throne on Jan. 20, 1936, at his father's death, but abdicated on Dec. 11, 1936 (in order to marry an American divorcée, Wallis Warfield Simpson) in favor of his brother, who became George VI.

The efforts of Prime Minister Neville Chamberlain to stem the rising threat of Nazism in Germany failed with the German invasion of Poland on Sept. 1, 1939, which was followed by Britain's entry into World War II on Sept. 3. Allied reverses in the spring of 1940 led to Chamberlain's resignation and the formation of another coalition war cabinet by the Conservative leader, Winston Churchill, who led Britain through most of World War II. Churchill resigned shortly after V-E Day, May 7, 1945, but then formed a "caretaker" government that remained in office until after the parliamentary elections in July, which the Labour Party won overwhelmingly. The new government, formed by Clement R. Attlee, began a moderate socialist program.

In 1951, Churchill again became prime minister at the head of a Conservative government. George VI died on Feb. 6, 1952, and was succeeded by his daughter, Elizabeth II. Churchill stepped down in 1955 in favor of Sir Anthony Eden, who resigned on grounds of ill health in 1957 and was succeeded by Harold Macmillan and Sir Alec Douglas-Home. In 1964, Harold Wilson led the Labour Party to victory. A lagging economy brought the Conservatives back to power in 1970. Prime Minister Edward Heath won Britain's admission to the European Community. Margaret Thatcher became Britain's first woman prime minister as the Conservatives won 339 seats on May 3, 1979.

An Argentine invasion of the Falkland Islands on April 2, 1982, involved Britain in a war 8,000 mi from the home islands. Argentina had long claimed the Falklands, known as the *Malvinas* in Spanish, which had been occupied by the British since 1832. Britain won a decisive victory within six weeks when more than 11,000 Argentine troops on the Falklands surrendered on June 14, 1982.

Although there were continuing economic problems and foreign policy disputes, an upswing in the economy in 1986–87 led Thatcher to call elections in June, and she won a near-unprecedented third consecutive term. The unpopularity of Thatcher's poll tax together with an uncompromising position toward further European integration eroded support within her own party. When John Major won the Conservative Party leadership in November, Thatcher resigned, paving the way for Major to form a government.

Eighteen years of Conservative rule ended in May 1997 when Tony Blair and the Labour Party triumphed in the British elections. Blair has been compared to former U.S. president Bill Clinton for his youthful, telegenic personality and centrist views. He produced constitutional reform that partially decentralized the UK, leading to the formation of separate Parliaments in Wales and Scotland by 1999. Britain turned over its colony Hong Kong to China in July 1997.

Blair's controversial meeting in Oct. 1997 with Sinn Fein's president, Gerry Adams, was the first meeting in 76 years between a British prime minister and a Sinn Fein leader. It infuriated numerous factions but was a symbolic gesture in support of the nascent peace talks in Northern Ireland. In 1998 the Good Friday Agreement, strongly supported by Tony Blair, held out the promise of peace between Catholics and Protestants, but talks ran aground in 1999.

Along with the U.S., Britain launched air strikes against Iraq in Dec. 1998 after Saddam Hussein expelled UN arms inspectors. Low-grade bombing of Iraq continued into 2002. In the spring of 1999, Britain spearheaded the NATO operation in Kosovo, which resulted in Yugoslavian president Slobodan Milosevic's withdrawal from the territory. British peacekeeping forces remain in Kosovo.

In the fall of 1999, Britain and France argued heatedly about France's refusal to allow the importation of British beef. France remained leery of the possibility of infection from bovine spongiform encephalopathy (BSE), commonly known as mad cow disease, despite the fact that the EU had lifted the three-year ban on British beef in August.

In Feb. 2001, foot-and-mouth disease broke out among British livestock, prompting other nations to ban British meat import and forcing the slaughter of thousands of cattle, pigs, and sheep in an effort to stem

the highly contagious disease. The episode cost farmers and the tourist industry billions of dollars.

In June 2001, Blair won a second landslide victory, with the Labour Party capturing 413 seats in Parliament.

Britain became the U.S.'s staunchest ally after the Sept. 11 attacks on New York and Washington, DC. British troops joined the U.S. in the bombing campaign against Afghanistan in Oct. 2001, after the Taliban-led government refused to turn over the prime suspect in the terrorist attacks, Osama bin Laden. After the Taliban was toppled two months later, the UK led the peacekeeping forces stationed in Afghanistan, the International Security Assistance Force (ISAF), from Jan. to June 2002. The UK also sent additional troops to fight against remaining Taliban and al-Qaeda troops.

Blair again proved himself to be the U.S.'s strongest international supporter in Sept. 2002, when he became the first foreign leader to support President Bush's threat to wage war against Iraq. Blair maintained that military action was justified because Iraq is developing weapons of mass destruction that were a direct threat to its enemies.

## Northern Ireland

**Status:** Part of United Kingdom
**First Minister:** David Trimble (2001)
**Area:** 5,452 sq mi (14,121 sq km)
**Population (1998 est.):** 1,688,600
**Capital and largest city (1992):** Belfast, 287,500.
  **Monetary unit:** British pound sterling (£). **Language:** English. **Religions:** Presbyterian, Church of Ireland, Roman Catholic, Methodist.

**Geography** Northern Ireland is composed of 26 districts, derived from the boroughs of Belfast and Londonderry and the counties of Antrim, Armagh, Down, Fermanagh, Londonderry, and Tyrone. Together they are commonly called Ulster, though the territory does not include the entire ancient province of Ulster. It is slightly larger than Connecticut.

**Government** Northern Ireland is an integral part of the United Kingdom (it has 12 representatives in the British House of Commons), but under the terms of the Government of Ireland Act in 1920, it had a semiautonomous government. In 1972, however, after three years of sectarian violence between Protestants and Catholics that resulted in more than 400 dead and thousands injured, Britain suspended the Ulster Parliament. The Ulster counties were governed directly from London after an attempt to return certain powers to an elected assembly in Belfast.

As a result of the Good Friday Agreement of 1998, a new coalition government was formed on Dec. 2, 1999, with the British government formally transferring governing power to the Northern Irish Parliament. David Trimble, Protestant leader of the Ulster Unionist Party (UUP) and winner of the 1998 Nobel Peace Prize, became first minister.

**History** Ulster was part of Catholic Ireland until the reign of Elizabeth I (1558–1603) when, after suppressing three Irish rebellions, the Crown confiscated lands in Ireland and settled the Scots Presbyterians in Ulster. Another rebellion in 1641–51, brutally crushed by Oliver Cromwell, resulted in the settlement of Anglican Englishmen in Ulster. Subsequent political policy favoring Protestants and disadvantaging Catholics encouraged further Protestant settlement in Northern Ireland.

Northern Ireland did not separate from the South until William Gladstone presented, in 1886, his proposal for home rule in Ireland. The Protestants in the North feared domination by the Catholic majority. Industry, moreover, was concentrated in the North and dependent on the British market. When World War I began, civil war threatened between the regions. Northern Ireland, however, did not become a political entity until the six counties accepted the Home Rule Bill of 1920. This set up a semiautonomous Parliament in Belfast and a Crown-appointed governor advised by a cabinet of the prime minister and eight ministers, as well as a 12-member representation in the House of Commons in London.

When the Republic of Ireland gained sovereignty in 1922, relations improved between North and South, although the Irish Republican Army (IRA), outlawed in recent years, continued the struggle to end the partition of Ireland. In 1966–69, rioting and street fighting between Protestants and Catholics occurred in Londonderry, fomented by extremist nationalist Protestants, who feared the Catholics might attain a local majority, and by Catholics demonstrating for civil rights. These confrontations became known as "the Troubles."

The religious communities, Catholic and Protestant, became hostile armed camps. British troops were brought in to separate them, but themselves became a target of Catholics, particularly by the IRA, which by this time had turned into a full-fledged terrorist movement. The goal of the IRA was to eject the British and unify Northern Ireland with the Irish Republic to the south. The Protestants remained tenaciously loyal to the United Kingdom, and various Protestant terrorist organizations pursued the Unionist cause through violence. Various attempts at representational government and power-sharing foundered during the 1970s, and both sides were further polarized. Direct rule from London and the presence of British troops failed to stop the violence.

In Oct. 1977, the 1976 Nobel Peace Prize was awarded to Mairead Corrigan and Betty Williams, founders of the Community of Peace People, a nonsectarian organization dedicated to creating peace in Northern Ireland. Intermittent violence continued, however, and on Aug. 27, 1979, an IRA bomb killed Lord Mountbatten as he was sailing off southern Ireland, heightening tensions. Catholic protests over the death of IRA hunger striker Bobby Sands in 1981 fueled more violence. Riots, sniper fire, and terrorist attacks killed more than 3,200 people between 1969 and 1998. Among the attempts at reconciliation undertaken during the 1980s was the Anglo-Irish Agreement (1985), which, to the dismay of Unionists, marked the first time the Republic of Ireland had been given an official consultative role in the affairs of the province.

In 1997, Northern Ireland made a significant step in the direction of stemming sectarian strife. The first formal peace talks began on Oct. 6 with representatives of eight major Northern Irish political parties participating, a feat that in itself required three years of negotiations. Two smaller Protestant parties, including hard-liner Ian Paisley's Democratic Unionists, boycotted the talks. For the first time, Sinn Fein, the political wing of the IRA, won two seats in the British Parliament, which went to Sinn Fein president Gerry Adams and second-in-command, Martin McGuinness. Although the election strengthened the IRA's political legitimacy, it was the IRA's resumption of the 17-month cease-fire, which had collapsed in Feb. 1996, that gained them a place at the negotiating table.

A landmark settlement, the Good Friday Agreement of April 10, 1998, came after 19 months of intensive negotiations that involved eight of the ten major Irish political parties. The accord called for Protestants to share political power with the minority Catholics, and it gave the Republic of Ireland a voice in Northern Irish affairs. In turn, Catholics were to suspend the goal of a united Ireland—a territorial claim that was the raison d'être of the IRA and was written into the Irish Republic's constitution—unless the largely Protestant North voted in favor of such an arrangement, an unlikely occurrence.

The resounding commitment to the settlement was demonstrated in a dual referendum on May 22, 1998: the North approved the accord by a vote of 71% to 29%, and in the Irish Republic 94% favored it. In October, the Nobel Peace Prize was awarded to John Hume and David Trimble, leaders of the largest Catholic and Protestant political parties, an incentive for all sides to ensure that this time the peace would last.

In Dec. 1998 the rival Northern Ireland politicians agreed on the organization and contents of the new coalition government, but in June 1999 the peace process again hit an impasse when the IRA refused to disarm prior to the assembly of Northern Ireland's new provincial cabinet. Sinn Fein insisted the IRA would only begin giving up its illegal weapons after the formation of the new government; Unionists demanded disarmament first. As a result, the Ulster Unionists boycotted the assembly session that would have nominated the cabinet to run the new coalition government. The nascent Northern Irish government was stillborn in July 1999.

Subsequent talks on the agreement, which would have ended three decades of direct rule from London, seemed to go nowhere. Finally, at the end of November, David Trimble, leader of the Ulster Unionists, abandoned the seemingly sacrosanct "no guns, no government" position, and took a difficult leap of faith in agreeing to form a government prior to Sinn Fein's disarmament. If the IRA did not begin the destruction of their weapons by Jan. 31, 2000, however, the Ulster Unionists threatened they would withdraw from the Northern Irish Parliament, shutting down the new government. With this compromise in place, the new government was quickly formed, and on Dec. 2, 1999, the British government formally transferred governing power to the Northern Irish Parliament. David Trimble became first minister. Two leaders of Sinn Fein, Gerry Adams and Martin McGuinness, received seats in the 4-party, 12-member Parliament. But by the deadline, Sinn Fein had made little progress toward disarmament, and claimed it had not made any such commitment. As a result, the British government suspended Parliament on Feb. 12, 2000, and once again imposed direct rule. In July 2001, after issuing one last ultimatum to the IRA to begin destroying its weapons stores, Ulster Unionist leader David Trimble resigned his post as first minister.

Following Trimble's departure, the IRA offered another vague and open-ended disarmament plan, only to withdraw it. But on Oct. 23, days before Britain was to suspend the assembly, Sinn Fein leader Gerry Adams dramatically announced that the IRA had indeed begun disarming. Partially in response to the Sept. 11 attacks, which made the IRA's claim to weapons of terror seem even more senselessly brutal, Sinn Fein chose to embrace the promise of a political solution to the Northern Irish troubles. On Nov. 6, David Trimble was reelected as first minister.

On April 8, 2002, international weapons inspectors announced that the IRA had put more stockpiled munitions "beyond use," the euphemistic phrase used in the negotiations to mean disarmament. British and Irish leaders hoped that Protestant guerrilla groups would also begin to surrender their weapons. However, in mid-June British and Irish political leaders called emergency talks to stem the rising tide of violence in Belfast. On July 16, the IRA issued a public apology to the families of the 650 civilians killed by the IRA since the late 1960s.

## Scotland

**Status:** Part of United Kingdom
**First Minister:** Jack McConnell (2001)
**Area:** 30,414 sq mi (78,772 sq km)
**Population (1996 est.):** 5,128,000; density per sq mi: 168.6
**Capital (1995 est.):** Edinburgh, 441,620. **Largest city:** Glasgow, 681,470. **Monetary unit:** British pound sterling (£). **Languages:** English, Scots Gaelic.
**Religions:** Church of Scotland (established church—Presbyterian), Roman Catholic, Scottish Episcopal Church, Baptist, Methodist

**Geography** Scotland occupies the northern third of the island of Great Britain. It is bounded by England in the south and on the other three sides by water: by the Atlantic Ocean on the west and north and by the North Sea on the east. Scotland is divided into three physical regions—the Highlands; the Central Lowlands, containing two-thirds of the population; and the Southern Uplands. The western Highland coast is intersected throughout by long, narrow sea lochs, or fjords. Scotland also includes the Outer and Inner Hebrides and other islands off the west coast and the Orkney and Shetland Islands off the north coast. The famous Scottish Highlands include a series of lochs (or lakes), the largest of which is Loch Ness, famous for its mythical monster.

**Government** England and Scotland have shared a monarch since 1603 and a Parliament since 1707, but in May 1999, Scotland elected its own Parliament for the first time in three centuries. The new Scottish legislature was in part the result of British prime minister Tony Blair's campaign promise to permit devolution, the transfer of local powers from London to Edinburgh. In a Sept. 1997 referendum, 74% of Scotland voted in favor of their own Parliament, which controls most domestic affairs, including health, education, and transportation, and has powers to legislate and raise taxes. Queen Elizabeth opened the new Parliament on July 2, 1999.

**History** The first inhabitants of Scotland were the Picts, a Celtic tribe, before another tribe, the Romans invaded Scotland, naming it Caledonia. Roman influence over the land, however, was minimal. The Scots, a Celtic tribe from Ireland, migrated to the west coast of Scotland in about 500. Kenneth McAlpin, King of the Scots, ascended the throne of the Pictish kingdom in about 843, thereby uniting the various Scots and Pictish tribes under one kingdom called Alba. By the 11th century, the monarchy had extended its borders to include much of what is Scotland today.

English influence in the region expanded when Malcolm III, king of Scotland from 1057–93, married an English princess. England's appetite for Scottish land began to grow over the 12th and 13th centuries, and in 1296 King Edward I of England successfully invaded Scotland. The following year Robert the Bruce led a revolt for independence, was crowned king of Scotland (Robert I) in 1306, and after years of battle defeated the English in 1314 at the Battle of Bannockburn. In 1328 the English finally recognized Scottish independence.

In the 16th century John Knox introduced the Scottish reformation, and the Presbyterian church replaced Catholicism as the official religion. In 1567, Mary, Queen of Scots, a Catholic, was forced to abdicate the Scottish throne, and was later executed by Elizabeth I of England. Mary's son, James VI, was raised as a Protestant, and in 1603 he succeeded Elizabeth on the English throne as King James I of England. James thus became ruler of both Scotland and England, though the countries remained separate. In 1707, after a century of turmoil, Scotland and England passed the Act of Union, which united Scotland, England, and Wales under one rule as the Kingdom of Great Britain. The House of Hanover replaced the Stuart lineage on the throne in 1714, which caused a rebellion among Scots who still supported the Stuarts. The Jacobites, as the rebels were called, led two uprisings, in 1715 and again in 1745.

With the advent of the Industrial Revolution, Scotland, whose chief product had been textiles, began developing the industries of shipbuilding, coal mining, iron, and steel. In the late 20th century Scotland concentrated on electronics and high-tech industries. The North Sea has also become an important source of oil and gas.

In May 1999, Scotland elected its first separate Parliament in three centuries. Labour won the largest number of seats in Parliament, defeating the Scottish National Party (SNP), which supports Scotland's independence from Britain. A year later, however, the new Parliament had not lived up to its new promise—a BBC poll found that only 27% of the populace thought Parliament's performance had been good, and 31% considered it poor. At the same time, however, 62% said they wanted Parliament to have even greater powers.

## Wales

**Status:** Part of United Kingdom
**First Secretary:** Rhodri Morgan (2000)
**Area:** 8,019 sq mi (20,768 sq km)
**Population (1993 est.):** 2,906,500
**Capital and largest city (1996 est.):** Cardiff, 306,600.
**Monetary unit:** British pound sterling (£). **Languages:** English, Welsh. **Religions:** Calvinistic Methodist, Church of Wales (disestablished—Anglican), Roman Catholic

**Geography** Wales lies west of England and is separated from England by the Cambrian Mountains. It is bounded on the north and west by the Irish Sea and on the northeast and east by England. Wales is generally hilly; the Snowdon range in the northern part culminates in Mount Snowdon (3,560 ft, 1,005 m), Wales's highest peak.

**Government** Until 1999, Wales was ruled solely by the UK government and a secretary of state. In the referendum of Sept. 18, 1997, Welsh citizens voted to establish a National Assembly. Wales will remain part of the UK, and the secretary of state for Wales and members of Parliament from Welsh constituencies will continue to have seats in Parliament. Although Wales will control most of its local affairs, unlike Scotland, which in 1999 voted to have its own Parliament, the National Assembly will not be able to legislate and raise taxes. The Welsh assembly officially opened on July 1, 1999.

**History**  The prehistoric peoples of Wales left behind megaliths and other impressive monuments. They were followed by settlements of Celts in the region. The Romans occupied the region from the 1st to the 5th century A.D. Thereafter Angles, Saxons, and Jutes invaded the British island, but they left Wales virtually untouched. Beginning in the 8th century, the various Welsh tribes fought with their Anglo-Saxon neighbors to the east, but the Welsh were able to thwart attempted invasions. After William the Conqueror subdued England in 1066, however, his Norman armies marched into Wales in 1093 and occupied portions of it. By 1282, the English conquest of Wales was complete, and in 1284, the Statute of Rhuddlan formalized England's sovereignty over Wales. In 1301, King Edward I gave his son, who later became Edward II, the title Prince of Wales, a gesture meant to indicate the unity and relationship between the two lands. With the exception of Edward II, all subsequent British monarchs have given this title to their eldest son.

In 1400, the Welsh prince Owen Glendower led a revolt against the English, expelling them from much of Wales in just four years. By 1410, however, his rebellion was crushed. In 1485, Henry VII became king of England. A Welshman and the first in the Tudor line, Henry's reign, and that of subsequent Tudors, made English rule more palatable to the Welsh. His son, King Henry VIII, joined England and Wales under the Act of Union in 1536.

The Industrial Revolution of the 19th century transformed Wales and threatened the traditional livelihood of farmers and shepherds. In the 20th century, the economy of Wales was based primarily on coal production. After World War I, coal prices dropped; this, coupled with the Great Depression, fueled high unemployment rates and economic uncertainty.

In recent years, a resurgence of the Welsh language and culture has demonstrated a stronger national identity among the Welsh, and politically the country moved toward greater self-government (devolution). In 1999, with the strong support of Britain's prime minister, Tony Blair, Wales opened the Welsh National Assembly, the first real self-government Wales has had in more than six hundred years.

## Overseas Territories and Crown Dependencies of the United Kingdom

### Anguilla

**Status:** Overseas territory
**Governor:** Peter Johnstone (2000)
**Chief Minister:** Osbourne Fleming (2000)
**Area:** 35.14 sq mi (91 sq km)
**Population (2002 est.):** 12,446; (growth rate: 1.0%); birth rate: 14.9/1000; infant mortality rate: 23.7/1000; density per sq mi: 354
**Capital (1992):** The Valley, 1,400. **Monetary unit:** East Caribbean dollar. **Ethnicity/race:** black African. **Literacy:** 95% (1984)
**Economic summary:** GDP/PPP (1999 est.): $96 million; per capita $8,200. **Real growth rate:** 7%. **Inflation:** 2.5% (1998 est.). **Unemployment:** 7% (1992 est.). **Arable land:** 0%. **Agriculture:** small quantities of tobacco, vegetables; cattle raising. **Labor force:** 4,400 (1992); commerce 36%, services 29%, construction 18%, transportation and utilities 10%, manufacturing 3%, agriculture/fishing/forestry/mining 4%. **Industries:** tourism, boat building, offshore financial services. **Natural resources:** salt, fish, lobster. **Exports:** $4.5 million (1998): lobster, fish, livestock, salt. **Imports:** $57.6 million (1998). **Major trading partners:** n.a.

Anguilla was first colonized in 1650 by English settlers from St. Christopher (St. Kitts) and has since remained a British territory. It was originally part of the West Indies Associated States as a component of the St. Kitts-Nevis-Anguilla Federation. In 1967, Anguilla declared its independence from the federation but Britain did not recognize this action. In Feb. 1969, Anguilla voted to cut all ties with Britain and become an independent republic. In March, Britain landed troops on the island and, on March 30, a truce was signed. In July 1971, Anguilla became a dependency of Britain and two months later Britain ordered the withdrawal of all its troops. A new constitution for Anguilla, effective in Feb. 1976, provided for separate administration and a government of elected representatives. The Associated State of St. Kitts-Nevis-Anguilla ended in 1980, and in 1982 a new Anguillan constitution took effect.

### Bermuda

**Status:** Overseas territory
**Governor:** Sir John Vereker (2002)
**Premier:** Jennifer Smith (1998)
**Area:** 23 sq mi (59 sq km)
**Population (2002 est.):** 63,960; (growth rate: 0.4%); birth rate: 11.8/1000; infant mortality rate: 9.3/1000; density per sq mi: 2,817
**Capital (1994 est.):** Hamilton, 1,100. **Monetary unit:** Bermuda dollar. **Ethnicity/race:** black African 61%, white and other 39%. **Literacy rate:** 98% (1970)
**Economic summary:** GDP/PPP (2000 est.): $2.1 billion; per capita $33,000. **Real growth rate:** 1.5%. **Inflation:** 2.7%. **Unemployment:** negl. (1995). **Arable land:** 6%. **Agriculture:** bananas, vegetables, citrus, flowers; dairy products. **Labor force:** 35,296 (1997); clerical 23%, services 22%, laborers 17%, professional and technical 17%, administrative and managerial 12%, sales 7%, agriculture and fishing 2% (1996). **Industries:** tourism, finance, insurance, structural concrete products, paints, perfumes, pharmaceuticals, ship repairing. **Natural resources:** limestone, pleasant climate fostering tourism. **Exports:** $56 million (2000 est.): reexports of pharmaceuticals. **Imports:** $739 million (2000 est.): machinery and transport equipment, construction materials, chemicals, food and live animals. **Major trading partners:** UK, U.S., Mexico.

Bermuda is an archipelago of about 360 small islands, 580 mi (934 km) east of North Carolina. The largest is (Great) Bermuda, or Main Island. Explored by Juan de Bermúdez, a Spaniard, the islands were settled in 1612 by an offshoot of the Virginia Company. Bermuda became a Crown colony in 1684.

In 1968, Bermuda was granted a new constitution, its first prime minister, and autonomy, except for foreign relations, defense, and internal security. The predominantly white United Bermuda Party has retained power in four elections against the opposition—the black-led Progressive Labour Party—although Bermuda's population is 61% black. U.S. air and navy bases, which had been leased in 1941 for 99-year terms, closed in 1995, along with Canadian, British army, and Royal Navy bases. In a referendum held in Aug. 1995, nearly three-fourths of those voting opposed independence. The prime minister's unexpected resignation in March 1997 led the ruling United Bermuda Party to name Pamela Gordon the country's first female and youngest premier. She was succeeded in 1998 by Jennifer Smith.

## British Indian Ocean Territory

**Status:** Overseas territory
**Commissioner:** John White (1998)
**Administrative headquarters:** Victoria, Seychelles
**Area:** 85 sq mi (220 sq km)

This territory, consisting of the Chagos Archipelago and other small island groups, was formed in 1965 by agreement with Mauritius and the Seychelles. There is no permanent civilian population in the territory. One of its islands, Diego Garcia (17 sq mi), is a joint U.S.-UK refueling and support station that was used during the Persian Gulf War (1991).

## British Virgin Islands

VIRGIN ISLANDS
**Status:** Overseas territory
**Governor:** Tom Macan (2002)
**Chief Minister:** Ralph O'Neal (1995)
**Area:** 58 sq mi (150 sq km)
**Population (2002 est.):** 21,272; (growth rate: 1.1%); birth rate: 15.1/1000; infant mortality rate: 19.6/1000; density per sq mi: 367
**Capital (1991 census):** Road Town (on Tortola): 3,983.
**Monetary unit:** U.S. dollar. **Literacy rate:** 98% (1970)
**Economic summary: GDP/PPP** (2000 est.): $311 million; per capita $16,000. **Real growth rate:** 6%. **Inflation:** 2%. **Unemployment:** 3% (1995). **Arable land:** 20%. **Agriculture:** fruits, vegetables; livestock, poultry; fish. **Labor force:** 4,911 (1980). **Industries:** tourism, light industry, construction, rum, concrete block, offshore financial center. **Natural resources:** negl. **Exports:** $6.2 million (2000 est.): rum, fresh fish, fruits, animals; gravel, sand. **Imports:** $220 million (2000 est.): building materials, automobiles, foodstuffs, machinery. **Major trading partners:** U.S. Virgin Islands., Puerto Rico, U.S.

Some 36 islands (more than 20 are uninhabited) in the Caribbean Sea northeast of Puerto Rico and west of the Leeward Islands, the British Virgin Islands are economically interdependent with the U.S. Virgin Islands to the south. The principal islands are Tortola, Virgin Gorda, Anegada, and Jost Van Dyke. When Christopher Columbus explored the islands in 1493, he found the Carib people living there. By 1596 most of the Caribs had fled or been killed.

The British Virgin Islands were annexed in 1672. The English planters' slave-based sugar plantations declined after slavery was abolished in the first half of the 19th century. The islands received a separate administration in 1956 as a Crown colony. Tourism is the islands' mainstay.

## Cayman Islands

**Status:** Overseas territory
**Governor:** Peter Dinwiddy, (2000)
**Area:** 100 sq mi (259 sq km)
**Population (2002 est.):** 35,527 (growth rate: 0.8%); birth rate: 13.4/1000; infant mortality rate: 9.9/1000; density per sq mi: 355
**Capital (1992 est.):** George Town (on Grand Cayman), 15,000. **Monetary unit:** Cayman Islands dollar.
**Literacy rate:** 98% (1970)
**Economic summary: GDP/PPP** (1997 est.): $930 million; per capita $24,500. **Real growth rate:** 4.9% (1999 est.) **Inflation:** 3% (1998). **Unemployment:** 4.1% (1997). **Arable land:** 0%. **Agriculture:** vegetables, fruit; livestock, turtle farming. **Labor force:** 19,820 (1995); agriculture 1.4%, industry 12.6%, services 86% (1995). **Industries:** tourism, banking, insurance and finance, construction, construction materials, furniture. **Natural resources:** fish, climate and beaches that foster tourism. **Exports:** $1.5 million

(1998): turtle products, manufactured consumer goods. **Imports:** $507.6 million (1998): foodstuffs, manufactured goods. **Major trading partners:** U.S., Trinidad and Tobago, UK, Netherlands Antilles, Japan.

The Caymans consist of three islands—Grand Cayman (76 sq mi; 197 sq km), Cayman Brac (22 sq mi; 57 sq km), and Little Cayman (20 sq mi; 52 sq km)—situated about 180 mi (290 km) northwest of Jamaica. They were dependencies of Jamaica until 1959, when they became a unit territory within the Federation of the West Indies. In 1962, upon the dissolution of the federation, the Cayman Islands became a British dependency, and a new constitution approved in 1972 provided for a greater degree of autonomy. Tourism and finance are the Cayman Islands' major industries. For a time, the Cayman Islands were blacklisted by the Paris-based Financial Action Task Force (FATF) for its alleged loose policy concerning money laundering. It was removed from the list in 2001.

## Channel Islands: Jersey and Guernsey

**Status:** Crown dependencies
**Lieutenant Governor of Jersey:** Sir Michael Wilkes (1995)
**Lieutenant Governor of Guernsey:** Vice Adm. Sir John Coward (1994)
**Area:** 45 sq mi (116 sq km)
**Populations (2002 est.):** Jersey, 89,775; Guernsey, 64,587
**Capital of Jersey (1991):** St. Helier, 28,123
**Capital of Guernsey (1991):** St. Peter Port, 16,648.
**Monetary units:** Guernsey pound; Jersey pound

This group of islands, lying in the English Channel off the northwest coast of France, belonged to the Duchy of Normandy until it passed to the English Crown with the Norman conquest of 1066. It was the only British possession occupied by Germany during World War II. English and French are commonly spoken (though use of the latter is declining), and a Norman-French patois survives.

For administrative purposes, the islands are divided into the Bailiwick of Jersey (45 sq mi; 117 sq km), including the Ecrehous rocks and Les Minquiers, and the Bailiwick of Guernsey (30 sq mi; 78 sq km), including Alderney (3 sq mi; 7.8 sq km), Sark (2 sq mi; 5.2 sq km), Herm, Jethou, Brechou, and other smaller islands. The Channel Islands enjoy tax sovereignty, and their exports are protected by British tariff barriers. Financial services, tourism, market gardening, and dairy farming are important industries.

## Falkland Islands

**Status:** Overseas territory
**Governor:** Howard Pearce (?00?)
**Chief Executive:** A. M. Gurr
**Area:** 4,700 sq mi (12,173 sq km)
**Population (July 2001 est.):** 2,895
**Capital (1991):** Stanley (on East Falkland), 1,643.
**Monetary unit:** Falkland Island pound
**Economic summary: GDP/PPP** (FY95/96 est.): $52 million; per capita $19,000. **Real growth rate:** 1%. **Inflation:** 3.6% (1998). **Unemployment:** full employment; labor shortage. **Arable land:** 0%. **Agriculture:** fodder and vegetable crops; sheep, dairy products. **Labor force:** 1,100 (est.); agriculture 95% (mostly sheepherding and fishing). **Industries:** wool and fish processing; sale of stamps and coins. **Natural resources:** fish, wildlife. **Exports:** $7.6 million (1995): wool, hides, meat. **Imports:** $24.7 million (1995): fuel, food and drink, building materials, clothing. **Major trading partners:** UK, Japan, Chile, New Zealand.

COUNTRIES OF THE WORLD

This sparsely inhabited dependency consists of a group of islands in the South Atlantic, about 250 mi (402 km) east of the South American mainland. The largest islands are East Falkland and West Falkland. The English captain John Strong made the first recorded landing in the Falklands in 1690. The islands passed between the French, Spanish, and British until 1820, when the Argentine government proclaimed its sovereignty. In 1833 a British force expelled the few remaining Argentine officials from the island without firing a shot, and in 1841 a British civilian lieutenant-governor was appointed for the Falklands. Colonial status was granted to the Falklands in 1892. Argentina, calling the islands *Las Islas Malvinas*, regularly protested Britain's occupation of the islands. On April 2, 1982, Argentina's military government invaded the Falklands. The Falkland Islands war ended 10 weeks later with the surrender of the Argentine forces at Stanley to British troops, who had forcibly reoccupied the islands. Argentina still claims the islands. But an agreement between Argentina and the United Kingdom in 1995 sought to defuse licensing and sovereignty conflicts that would dampen foreign interest in exploiting the Falkland Islands' potential oil reserves.

## Gibraltar

**Status:** Overseas territory
**Governor:** David Durie (2000)
**Chief Minister:** Peter Caruana (1996)
**Area:** 2.51 sq mi (6.5 sq km)
**Population (2002 est.):** 27,714 (growth rate: 0.2%); birth rate: 11.2/1000; infant mortality rate: 5.4/1000; density per sq mi: 11,043. **Monetary unit:** Gibraltar pound. **Literacy rate:** 99%
**Economic summary: GDP/PPP** (1997 est.): $500 million; per capita $17,500. **Real growth rate:** n.a. **Inflation:** 1.5% (1998). **Unemployment:** 13.5% (1996). **Arable land:** 0%. **Agriculture:** none. **Labor force:** 14,800 (including non-Gibraltar laborers); services 60%, industry 40%, agriculture negl. **Industries:** tourism, banking and finance, ship-building and repairing; support to large UK naval and air bases; tobacco, mineral water, beer, canned fish. **Natural resources:** negl. **Exports:** $81.1 million (f.o.b., 1997): (principally reexports) petroleum 51%, manufactured goods 41%, other 8%. **Imports:** $492 million (c.i.f., 1997): fuels, manufactured goods, and foodstuffs. **Major trading partners:** UK, Morocco, Portugal, Netherlands, Spain, U.S., Germany, Japan.

Gibraltar, at the south end of the Iberian Peninsula, is a rocky promontory commanding the western entrance to the Mediterranean. Aside from its strategic importance, it is also a free port, naval base, and coaling station. It was captured by the Moorish leader Tarik, crossing from Africa into Spain in 711, and its name is derived from the Arabic, *Jabal-al-Tarik* (Mount of Tarik). In the 15th century, it passed to the Moorish ruler of Granada and later became Spanish. It was captured by an Anglo-Dutch force in 1704 during the War of the Spanish Succession and passed to Great Britain by the Treaty of Utrecht in 1713. Since then Spain has continually laid claims to it. Most of the inhabitants of Gibraltar are of Spanish, Italian, and Maltese descent, and in 1981 Gibraltarians were granted full British citizenship.

Spanish efforts to recover Gibraltar culminated in a referendum in 1967, in which the residents voted overwhelmingly to retain their link with Britain. In response, Spain sealed Gibraltar's land border between 1969 and 1985. In 2002, Britain and Spain discussed sharing the sovereignty of Gibraltar. In response, the government of Gibraltar scheduled a

Nov. 7, 2002, referendum to poll the population, in a move meant to demonstrate to both Britain and Spain that shared sovereignty was an idea highly unpopular with Gibraltarians.

## Isle of Man

**Status:** Crown dependency
**Lieutenant Governor:** Ian David Macfadyen (2000)
**Chief Minister:** Donald James Gelling (1996)
**Area:** 221 sq mi (572 sq km)
**Population (2002 est.):** 73,873 (growth rate: 0.0%); birth rate: 11.5/1000; infant mortality rate: 6.3/1000; density per sq mi: 334
**Capital (1991):** Douglas, 22,214. **Monetary unit:** Isle of Man pound

The Isle of Man is situated in the Irish Sea, equidistant from Scotland, Ireland, and England. Among its earliest inhabitants were Celts, and their language, Manx, which is closely related to Irish and Scottish Gaelic, remained the everyday speech of the people until the first half of the 19th century. Manx now has no native speakers. Norse (Viking) invasions began about 800, and the island was a dependency of Norway until 1266. During this period the Isle of Man came under a Scandinavian system of government that has remained practically unchanged ever since. The island came under the control of England in 1341. After allowing a succession of feudal lords to rule the island, the British Parliament purchased sovereignty over the island in 1765. The Isle of Man continues to be administered according to its own laws by a government composed of the lieutenant governor, a legislative council, and a House of Keys, one of the most ancient legislative assemblies in the world.

## Montserrat

**Status:** Overseas territory
**Governor:** Tony Longrigg (2001)
**Chief Minister:** John Osborne (2001)
**Area:** 39 sq mi (100 sq km)
**Population (2002 est.):** 8,437 (growth rate: 1.0%); birth rate: 17.5/1000; infant mortality rate: 8.0/1000; density per sq mi: 219
**Capital (1991 est.):** Plymouth, 2,500. **Monetary unit:** East Caribbean dollar
**Economic summary: GDP/PPP** (1999 est.): $31 million; per capita $5,000. **Real growth rate:** −1.5%. **Inflation:** 5% (1998). **Unemployment:** 20% (1996 est.). **Arable land:** 20%. **Agriculture:** cabbages, carrots, cucumbers, tomatoes, onions, peppers; livestock products. **Labor force:** 4,521 (1992); note—recently lowered by flight of people from volcanic activity; agriculture n.a., industry n.a., services n.a. **Industries:** tourism, rum, textiles, electronic appliances. **Natural resources:** negl. **Exports:** $1.5 million (1998): electronic components, plastic bags, apparel, hot peppers, live plants, cattle. **Imports:** $26 million (1998): machinery and transportation equipment, foodstuffs, manufactured goods, fuels, lubricants, and related materials. **Major trading partners:** U.S., Antigua and Barbuda, UK, Trinidad and Tobago, Japan, Canada.

The island of Montserrat is in the Lesser Antilles of the West Indies. Until 1956, it was a division of the Leeward Islands. In 1958 Montserrat joined the Federation of the West Indies, remaining a member until that organization's dissolution in 1962. Unlike most other British West Indies possessions, Montserrat, with its weak economy, has not vigorously sought independence. The Soufrière Hills volcano began erupting in 1995, and the situation continued to worsen through 1998, with the capital, Plymouth, destroyed and the southern and central parts of the British colony having been evacuated. Only about 4,000 people were left in the northern "safe zone" in 1998 after thousands had moved to nearby Antigua, Britain, or other parts of the Caribbean. The volcano continued to erupt throughout 2002.

## Pitcairn Island

**Status:** Overseas territory
**Governor:** Martin Williams (nonresident) (1998)
**Island Magistrate:** Jay Warren (1993)
**Area:** 18.15 sq mi (47 sq km)
**Population (July 2001 est.):** 47; density per sq mi: 3
**Capital:** Adamstown

Pitcairn Island, in the South Pacific about midway between Australia and South America, consists of the island of Pitcairn and the three uninhabited islands of Henderson, Duicie, and Oeno. Pitcairn was settled in 1790 by British mutineers from the ship *Bounty*, commanded by Capt. William Bligh. One of the most remote islands in the world, it was annexed as a British colony in 1838. Overpopulation forced removal of the settlement to Norfolk Island in 1856, but about 40 persons soon returned.

The descendants of First Mate Fletcher Christian, the 8 other mutineers, and the dozen or so Tahitians who accompanied them still inhabit the island. In addition to English, the residents of Pitcairn speak a dialect that is a mixture of Tahitian and 18th-century English.

## St. Helena

**Status:** Overseas territory
**Governor:** David Hollamby (1999)
**Area:** 158 sq mi (410 sq km)
**Population (2002 est.):** 7,317 (growth rate: 0.7%); birth rate: 13.3/1000; infant mortality rate: 21.5/1000; density per sq mi: 46
**Capital (1987):** Jamestown, 1,332. **Monetary unit:** Pound sterling. **Literacy rate:** 97% (1987)

St. Helena is a remote volcanic island in the South Atlantic about 1,100 mi (1,770 km) from the west coast of Africa. It is famous as Napoleon's place of exile (1815–21). The island was discovered in 1502 by João da Nova, a Spanish navigator in the service of Portugal. It was taken for England in 1659 by the East India Company and was brought under the direct government of the Crown in 1834. After the opening of the Suez Canal, in 1870, St. Helena's importance as a port of call diminished. About two-thirds of the colony's budget is provided by the United Kingdom in the form of a subsidy.

St. Helena has two dependencies: Ascension (34 sq mi; 88 sq km), an island about 700 mi (1,127 km) northwest of St. Helena; and Tristan da Cunha (40 sq mi; 104 sq km), a group of six islands about 1,500 mi (2,414 km) south-southwest of St. Helena.

## South Georgia and the South Sandwich Islands

**Status:** Overseas territory
**Commissioner:** Donald A. Lamont (1000)
**Area:** 1,506 sq mi (3,903 sq km)
**Population:** no indigenous inhabitants

The islands are located in the South Atlantic Ocean, east of the tip of South America, approximately 1,000 km east of the Falkland Islands, from which they are administered. In addition to South Georgia Island and the nine South Sandwich Islands, the island group includes Shag Rocks, Black Rock, Clerke Rocks, and Bird Island. A small military garrison on South Georgia withdrew in March 2001 and was replaced by a permanent group of scientists of the British Antarctic Survey.

## Turks and Caicos Islands

**Status:** Overseas territory
**Governor:** Mervyn Jones (2000)
**Chief Minister:** Derek H. Taylor (1995)
**Area:** 166 sq mi (430 sq km)
**Population (2002 est.):** 18,738 (growth rate: 2.0%); birth rate: 24.2/1000; infant mortality rate: 17.5/1000; density per sq mi: 113
**Capital (1990):** Cockburn Town, 3,720. **Monetary unit:** U.S. dollar. **Literacy rate:** 98% (1970)
**Economic summary: GDP/PPP** (1999 est.): $128 million; per capita $7,300. **Real growth rate:** 8.7%. **Inflation:** 4% (1995). **Unemployment:** 10% (1997 est.). **Arable land:** 2%. **Agriculture:** corn, beans, cassava (tapioca), citrus fruits; fish. **Labor force:** 4,848 (1990 est.); about 33% in government and 20% in agriculture and fishing; significant numbers in tourism, financial, and other services (1997 est.). **Industries:** tourism, offshore financial services. **Natural resources:** spiny lobster, conch. **Exports:** $4.7 million (1993): lobster, dried and fresh conch, conch shells. **Imports:** $46.6 million (1993): food and beverages, tobacco, clothing, manufactures, construction materials. **Major trading partners:** U.S., UK.

These two groups of islands are near the Bahamas in the Caribbean. The principal islands in the Turks group are Grand Turk and Salt Cay; the principal islands in the Caicos group are South Caicos, East Caicos, Middle (or Grand) Caicos, North Caicos, Providenciales, and West Caicos. The islands were not settled by Europeans until 1678, when British colonists from Bermuda established a salt-panning industry. The islands were at first placed under the Bahamian government, but in 1874 they became dependencies of the colony of Jamaica. Following Jamaica's independence, they became a British Crown colony. The salt production industry, the islands' economic mainstay, ceased in 1964 and gave way to tourism, offshore financial services, and fishing.

# United States

THE UNITED STATES OF AMERICA

**President:** George W. Bush (2001)
**Vice President:** Richard B. Cheney (2001)
**Area (2000):** 3,794,083 sq mi (9,826,675 sq km)
**Population (July 1, 2001 est.):** 284,796,887
**Population (2000 census):** 280,562,489 (change 1990–2000: 13.2%) (growth rate: 0.5%); birth rate: 14.1/1000; infant mortality rate: 6.7/1000; density per sq mi: 79.6
**Capital (2000 census):** Washington, DC, 572,059. **Largest cities (2000 census):** New York: city proper, 8,008,278; metro. area, 21,199,865; Los Angeles: city proper, 3,694,820; metro. area, 16,373,645; Chicago, city proper, 3,896,016; metro area, 9,157,540; Houston, 1,953,631; Philadelphia, 1,517,550; Phoenix, 1,321,045; San Diego, 1,223,400; Dallas, 1,188,580; San Antonio, 1,144,646; Detroit, 951,270. **Monetary unit:** dollar. **Languages:** English, sizable Spanish-speaking minority. **Ethnicity/race:** White: 211,460,626 (75.1%); Black: 34,658,190 (12.3%); American Indian and Alaska Native: 2,475,956 (0.9%); Asian: 10,242,998 (3.6%); Native Hawaiian and Other Pacific Islander: 398,835 (0.1%); Other race: 15,359,073 (5.5%); Hispanic origin:[1] 35,305,818 (12.5%). **Religions:** Protestant, 61%; Roman Catholic, 25%; Jewish, 2%; other, 5%; none, 7%. **Literacy rate:** 97% (1980)
**Economic summary: GDP/PPP** (2000 est.): $9.963 trillion; per capita $36,200. **Real growth rate:** 5%. **Inflation:** 3.4% (2000). **Unemployment:** 4% (2000). **Arable land:** 19%. **Agriculture:** wheat, other grains,

corn, fruits, vegetables, cotton; beef, pork, poultry, dairy products; forest products; fish. **Labor force:** 140.9 million (includes unemployed) (2000); managerial and professional 30.2%, technical, sales and administrative support 29.2%, services 13.5%, manufacturing, mining, transportation, and crafts 24.6%, farming, forestry, and fishing 2.5% (2000). **Industries:** leading industrial power in the world, highly diversified and technologically advanced; petroleum, steel, motor vehicles, aerospace, telecommunications, chemicals, electronics, food processing, consumer goods, lumber, mining. **Natural resources:** coal, copper, lead, molybdenum, phosphates, uranium, bauxite, gold, iron, mercury, nickel, potash, silver, tungsten, zinc, petroleum, natural gas, timber. **Exports:** $776 billion (f.o.b., 2000 est.): capital goods, automobiles, industrial supplies and raw materials, consumer goods, agricultural products. **Imports:** $1.223 trillion (f.o.b., 2000 est.): crude oil and refined petroleum products, machinery, automobiles, consumer goods, industrial raw materials, food and beverages. **Major trading partners:** Canada, Mexico, Japan, UK, Germany, France, Netherlands, China, Taiwan.

1. Persons of Hispanic origin can be of any race.

**Government** Federal republic.

The president is elected for a four-year term and may be reelected only once. The bicameral Congress consists of the 100-member Senate, elected to a six-year term with one-third of the seats becoming vacant every two years, and the 435-member House of Representatives, elected every two years. The minimum voting age is 18. (*See also* Profile of the United States, U.S. States, U.S. Cities, U.S. Statistics, and U.S. Government and History.)

# U.S. Territories and Outlying Areas

## Puerto Rico
### COMMONWEALTH OF PUERTO RICO

**Status:** Commonwealth
**Governor:** Sila María Calderón (2001)
**Capital and largest city (1990 pop.):** San Juan, 437,745. **Other large cities (1990 pop.):** Bayamón, 220,262; Ponce, 190,900; Carolina, 177,806
**Land area:** 3,515 sq mi (9,104 sq km)
**Population (est. 2002):** 3,957,988 (growth rate: 0.7%); birth rate: 15.0/1000; infant mortality rate: 9.3/1000; density per sq mi: 1,126. **Currency:** U.S. dollars.
**Languages:** Spanish and English (both official).
**Ethnicity/race:** Almost entirely Hispanic. **Religions:** Roman Catholic 85%, Protestant denominations and other 15%. **Literacy rate:** 89% (1980)
**Economic summary: GDP/PPP** (2000 est.): $39 billion; per capita $10,000. **Real growth rate:** 2.8%. **Inflation:** 5.7%. **Unemployment:** 9.5% (2000). **Arable land:** 4%. **Agriculture:** sugarcane, coffee, pineapples, plantains, bananas; livestock products, chickens. **Labor force:** 1.3 million (2000); agriculture 3%, industry 20%, services 77% (2000 est.). **Industries:** pharmaceuticals, electronics, apparel, food products; tourism. **Natural resources:** some copper and nickel; potential for onshore and offshore oil. **Exports:** $38.5 billion (f.o.b., 2000): pharmaceuticals, electronics, apparel, canned tuna, rum, beverage concentrates, medical equipment. **Imports:** $27 billion (c.i.f., 2000): chemicals, machinery and equipment, clothing, food, fish, petroleum products. **Major trading partner:** U.S.

The Commonwealth of Puerto Rico is located in the Caribbean Sea, about 1,000 mi east-southeast of Miami, Fla. A possession of the United States, it consists of the island of Puerto Rico plus the adjacent islets of Vieques, Culebra, and Mona. Puerto Rico has a mountainous, tropical ecosystem with very little flat land and few mineral resources.

Puerto Rico's governor is elected directly for a four-year term. A bicameral legislature consists of a 27-member Senate and a 51-member House of Representatives, all elected for four-year terms. From 1940 to 1968, Puerto Rican politics was dominated by a party advocating voluntary association with the U.S. Since then, the New Progressive Party, a party favoring U.S. statehood, has won five of the last eight gubernatorial elections. Puerto Ricans have twice voted to determine their political status. In 1967, the outcome was Commonwealth 60%; statehood 39%; independence 1%. In 1993, Commonwealth dropped to 48.6%; statehood rose to 46.3%; independence polled 4.4%; and 0.6% of the ballots were blank or spoiled.

Under the Commonwealth formula, residents of Puerto Rico lack voting representation in Congress and do not participate in presidential elections. As U.S. citizens, Puerto Ricans are subject to military service and most federal laws. Residents of the Commonwealth pay no federal income tax on locally generated earnings, but Puerto Rico government income-tax rates are set at a level that closely parallels federal-plus-state levies on the mainland.

When Christopher Columbus arrived there in 1493, the island was inhabited by the peaceful Arawak Indians, who were being challenged by the warlike Carib Indians. Puerto Rico remained economically undeveloped until 1830, when sugarcane, coffee, and tobacco plantations were gradually developed. After Puerto Ricans began to press for independence, Spain granted the island broad powers of self-government in 1897. But during the Spanish-American War of 1898 American troops invaded the island and Spain ceded it to the U.S. Since then, Puerto Rico has remained an unincorporated U.S. territory. Its people were granted American citizenship under the Jones Act in 1917; were permitted to elect their own governor, beginning in 1948; and now fully administer their internal affairs under a constitution approved by the U.S. Congress in 1952. In spite of broad popular support for the autonomy of the Commonwealth government and a rapidly modernizing industrial society, there were expressions of dissatisfaction. Puerto Rican extremists dramatized their desire for independence with an attempt to assassinate President Truman on Nov. 1, 1950, and on March 1, 1954, they wounded five congressmen in an attack on the U.S. Capitol.

A self-help program of economic development and social welfare (called "Operation Bootstrap") was forged in the 1940s by four-time governor Luis Muñoz Marín. In a little more than four decades, much of the island's crushing poverty was eliminated. This was done partly through the development of manufacturing and service industries, the latter related to an enormous growth in tourism. Also, many Puerto Ricans migrated to large cities on the mainland U.S.

Puerto Rico is a major hub of Caribbean commerce, finance, tourism, and communications. San Juan is one of the world's busiest cruise-ship ports, and Puerto Rico's standard of living continues to be among the highest in the hemisphere. Its future political status, however, remains unclear. On March 4, 1998, the U.S. House of Representatives passed a bill that called for binding elections in Puerto Rico to decide the island's permanent political status.

Since the 1940s, the U.S. Navy has used Vieques island as a bombing range. Protests against the exercises have grown in recent years, and in a July 2001 referendum residents of the island voted overwhelmingly to close the base immediately. President Bush has promised that the Navy will withdraw from Vieques by May 2003.

## Guam
### TERRITORY OF GUAM

**Status:** Territory
**Governor:** Carl T. C. Gutierrez (1995)
**Capital:** Agaña; population (1990) 1,139
**Land area:** 212 sq mi (549 sq km)
**Population (2002 est.):** 160,796 (growth rate: 2.0%); birth rate: 24.1/1000; infant mortality rate: 6.6/1000; density per sq mi: 759. **1996 est. net migration:** 3 migrants per 1,000 population. **Languages:** English and Chamorro; note: most residents are bilingual; Japanese also widely spoken. **Ethnicity/race:** Chamorro 47%, Filipino 25%, Caucasian 10%, Chinese, Japanese, Korean, and other, 18%. **Religions:** Roman Catholic 98%, other 2%. **Literacy rate:** 96% (1980). **Currency:** U.S. dollars
**Economic summary: GDP/PPP** (2000 est.): $3.2 billion; per capita $21,000. **Real growth rate:** n.a. **Inflation:** 0% (1999 est.). **Unemployment:** 15% (2000 est.). **Arable land:** 11%. **Agriculture:** fruits, copra, vegetables; eggs, pork, poultry, beef. **Labor force:** 60,000 (2000 est.); federal and territorial government 26%, private 74% (trade 24%, other services 40%, industry 10%) (2000 est.). **Industries:** U.S. military, tourism, construction, transshipment services, concrete products, printing and publishing, food processing, textiles. **Natural resources:** fishing (largely undeveloped), tourism (especially from Japan). **Exports:** $75.7 million (f.o.b., 1999): mostly transshipments of refined petroleum products; construction materials, fish, food and beverage products. **Imports:** $203 million (f.o.b., 1999 est.): petroleum and petroleum products, food, manufactured goods. **Major trading partners:** U.S., Japan.

Guam is the largest and southernmost island in the Marianas Archipelago. The island is divided into a northern coralline limestone plateau and a southern chain of volcanic hills. Today Guam is an unincorporated, organized territory of the United States. The people of Guam have been U.S. citizens since 1950. They have been represented in the U.S. Congress since 1973 by a nonvoting delegate, but do not participate in presidential elections. The executive branch includes a popularly elected governor, who serves a four-year term. The legislative branch is a 21-member unicameral legislature whose members are elected every two years.

Guam was probably visited by the Portuguese navigator Ferdinand Magellan (sailing for Spain) in 1521. The island was formally claimed by Spain in 1565, and its people were forced into submission and conversion to Roman Catholicism beginning in 1668. After the Spanish-American War of 1898, Spain ceded Guam to the United States. From 1899 to 1949, the U.S. Navy administered Guam, except during the Japanese occupation from 1941–44. Guam was liberated by American military forces in the summer of 1944. Guam's economy is based on tourism and U.S. military spending (U.S. naval and air force bases occupy one-third of the land on Guam).

## U.S. Virgin Islands
### VIRGIN ISLANDS OF THE UNITED STATES

**Status:** Territory
**Governor:** Charles Turnbull (1999)
**Capital:** Charlotte Amalie (on St. Thomas), population (1990): 12,331
**Land area:** 136 sq mi (352 sq km)
**Population (est. 2002):** 123,498 (growth rate: 1.0%); birth rate: 15.8/1000; infant mortality rate: 9.2/1000; density per sq mi: 909. **Languages:** English (official), but Spanish and French are also spoken. **Ethnicity/race:** West Indian 74% (45% born in the Virgin Islands and 29% born elsewhere in the West Indies), U.S. mainland 13%, Puerto Rican 5%, other 8%, black 80%, white 15%, other 5%, 14% of Hispanic origin. **Religions:** Baptist 42%, Roman Catholic 34%, Episcopalian 17%, other 7%. **Literacy rate:** 90%. **Currency:** U.S. dollars
**Economic summary: GDP/PPP** (2000 est.): $1.8 billion; per capita $15,000. **Real growth rate:** n.a. **Inflation:** n.a. **Unemployment:** 4.9% (March 1999). **Arable land:** 15%. **Agriculture:** fruit, vegetables, sorghum; Senepol cattle. **Labor force:** 47,443 (1990 est.); agriculture 1%, industry 20%, services 79% (1990 est.). **Industries:** tourism, petroleum refining, watch assembly, rum distilling, construction, pharmaceuticals, textiles, electronics. **Natural resources:** sun, sand, sea, surf. **Exports:** $n.a.: refined petroleum products. **Imports:** $n.a.: crude oil, foodstuffs, consumer goods, building materials. **Major trading partners:** U.S., Puerto Rico.

The Virgin Islands, consisting of nine main islands and some 75 islets, were explored by Columbus in 1493. They were originally inhabited by the Carib Indians. Since 1666, England has held six of the main islands; the remaining three (St. Croix, St. Thomas, and St. John), as well as about 50 of the islets, were eventually acquired by Denmark, which named them the Danish West Indies. In 1917, these islands were purchased by the U.S. from Denmark for $25 million.

Congress granted U.S. citizenship to Virgin Islanders in 1927. Universal suffrage was given in 1936 to all persons who could read and write English. The governor was elected by popular vote for the first time in 1970; previously he had been appointed by the U.S. president. A unicameral 15-person legislature serves the Virgin Islands, and congressional legislation gave the islands a nonvoting representative in Congress. Residents of the islands substantially enjoy the same rights as those enjoyed by mainlanders, but they may not vote in presidential elections.

Tourism is the primary economic activity, accounting for most of the GDP and 70% of employment. All goods made in the Virgin Islands qualify for duty-free entry into the United States.

## American Samoa
### TERRITORY OF AMERICAN SAMOA

**Status:** Territory
**Governor:** Tauese Pita Sunia (1997)
**Capital:** Pago Pago, population 1990: 3,519
**Land area:** 77 sq mi (199 sq km)
**Population (2002 est.):** 68,688 (growth rate: 2.0%); birth rate 24.0/1000; infant mortality rate: 10.1/1000; density per sq mi: 894. **Languages:** Samoan (closely related to Hawaiian and other Polynesian languages) and English; most people are bilingual. **Ethnicity/race:** Samoan (Polynesian) 89%, Tongan 4%, Caucasian 2%, other 6%. **Religions:** Christian Congregationalist 50%, Roman Catholic 20%, Protestant denominations and other 30%. **Literacy rate:** 97% (1980). **Currency:** U.S. dollars

**Economic summary: GDP/PPP** (2000 est.): $500 million; per capita $8,000. **Real growth rate:** n.a. **Inflation:** n.a. **Unemployment:** 16% (1993). **Arable land:** 5%. **Agriculture:** bananas, coconuts, vegetables, taro, breadfruit, yams, copra, pineapples, papayas; dairy products, livestock. **Labor force:** 14,000 (1996); government 33%, tuna canneries 34%, other 33% (1990). **Industries:** tuna canneries (largely dependent on foreign fishing vessels), handicrafts. **Natural resources:** pumice, pumicite. **Exports:** $500 million (1998): canned tuna 93%. **Imports:** $471 million (1996): materials for canneries 56%, food 8%, petroleum products 7%, machinery and parts 6%. **Major trading partners:** U.S., Japan, New Zealand, Australia, Fiji.

American Samoa, a group of five volcanic islands and two coral atolls located some 2,600 mi south of Hawaii in the South Pacific, is an unincorporated, unorganized territory of the U.S. It includes the eastern Samoan islands of Tutuila, Aunu'u, and Rose; three islands (Ta'u, Olosega, and Ofu) of the Manu'a group; and Swains Island. Around 1000 B.C. Proto-polynesians established themselves in the islands, and their descendants are one of the few remaining Polynesian societies. The Dutch navigator Jacob Roggeveen sighted the Manu'a Islands in 1722. American Samoa has been a territory of the United States since April 17, 1900, when the High Chiefs of Tutuila signed the first of two Deeds of Cession for the islands to the U.S. (Congress ratified the Deeds in 1929.) Swains Island, which is privately owned, came under U.S. administration in 1925.

Until World War II the United States operated a coaling station and naval base in Pago Pago. During the war, the islands were an important U.S. Marines staging area. In 1960 American Samoa ratified its territorial constitution and has since developed a modern, self-governing political system. American Samoans elect a governor, lieutenant governor, and legislature. The legislature (Fono) consists of two houses: the Senate, selected by village chiefs (matai) for four-year terms, and the House of Representatives, elected by the general population for two-year terms. The people of American Samoa are U.S. nationals, not U.S. citizens, but many have become naturalized American citizens. American Samoa does 80%–90% of its foreign trade with the U.S. Canned tuna is the primary export, earning $300 million annually. Transfers from the U.S. government add substantially to American Samoa's economic well-being.

## Northern Mariana Islands

### THE COMMONWEALTH OF THE NORTHERN MARIANA ISLANDS, OR CNMI

**Status:** Commonwealth
**Governor:** Juan N. Babautu (2002)
**Capital:** Chalan Kanoa (on Saipan)
**Total area:** 184 sq mi (477 sq km)
**Population (2002 est.):** 77,311 (growth rate: 1.8%); birth rate: 20.3/1000; infant mortality: 5.6/1000; density per sq mi: 420. **Languages:** English (official), Chamorro, Carolinian. **Ethnicity/race:** Chamorro, Carolinians, other Micronesians, Caucasian, Japanese, Chinese, Korean. **Religion:** Primarily Roman Catholic. **Literacy rate:** 97% (1980). **Currency:** U.S. dollars
**Economic summary: GDP/PPP** (2000 est.): $900 million; note: GDP numbers reflect U.S. spending; per capita $12,500. **Real growth rate:** n.a. **Inflation:** 1.2% (1997 est.). **Unemployment:** n.a. **Arable land:** 21%. **Agriculture:** coconuts, fruits, vegetables; cattle. **Labor force:** 6,006 total indigenous labor force; 2,699 unemployed; 28,717 foreign workers (1995).

**Industries:** tourism, construction, garments, handicrafts. **Natural resources:** arable land, fish. **Exports:** $n.a.: garments. **Imports:** $n.a.: food, construction equipment and materials, petroleum products. **Major trading partners:** U.S., Japan.

The Northern Mariana Islands, east of the Philippines and south of Japan, include the islands of Rota, Saipan, Tinian, Pagan, Guguan, Agrihan, and Aguijan. Although sighted by Ferdinand Magellan in 1521 as he sailed for Spain, the islands were not settled by Europeans until 1668, when missionaries converted the indigenous Chamorro people to Catholicism. They were ruled successively by Spain, Germany, and Japan before they became a UN Trusteeship (administered by the U.S.) after World War II. The Commonwealth of the Northern Mariana Islands (CNMI) became part of the United States in Nov. 1986. Spanish cultural traditions remain strong.

In recent years, Saipan's garment industry has been accused of exploiting thousands of Asian immigrants. Saipan's territorial status enables its employers to claim their clothing is "Made in the USA," while paying workers low wages and sidestepping import duties and tariffs.

## Midway Islands

**Status:** Territory
**Total area:** 2 sq mi (5 sq km)
**Population (1995 est.):** no indigenous inhabitants; 453 U.S. military personnel.

The Midway Islands consist of a circular atoll, 6 mi in diameter, that encloses two islands. Lying about 1,150 mi west-northwest of Hawaii, the islands were first explored by Captain N. C. Brooks on July 5, 1859, in the name of the U.S. The atoll was declared a U.S. possession in 1867, and in 1903 Theodore Roosevelt made it a naval reservation. The island was renamed "Midway" by the U.S. Navy in recognition of its geographic location on the route between California and Japan. Air traffic across the Pacific increased the island's importance in the mid-1930s; the San Francisco–Manila mail route included a regular stop on Midway. Its military importance was soon recognized, and the navy began building an air and submarine base there in 1940. The Battle of Midway, which took place from June 3–6, 1942, was considered a turning point in World War II. After the war, the strategic importance of the island declined; the Midway stop for commercial air traffic was eliminated in 1950, and the air base closed in 1992.

## Wake Island

**Status:** Territory
**Total area:** 2.51 sq mi (6.5 sq km)
**Comparative size:** about 11 times the size of the Mall in Washington, DC
**Population (1995 est.):** no indigenous inhabitants; 302 U.S. military personnel and civilian contractors.
**Economy:** The economic activity is limited to providing services to U.S. military personnel and contractors on the island. All food and manufactured goods must be imported.

Wake Island, about halfway between Midway and Guam, is an atoll consisting of the three islets of Wilkes, Peale, and Wake. They were discovered by the British in 1796 and annexed by the U.S. in 1899. In 1938, Pan American Airways established a seaplane base, and Wake Island was used as a commercial base for several years. On Dec. 8, 1941, it was attacked by the Japanese, who finally took possession on Dec. 23. It was surrendered by the Japanese on Sept. 4, 1945.

## Johnston Atoll

**Status:** Territory
**Land area:** 1.08 sq mi (2.8 sq km); density per sq mi: 1,111
**Population (July 1997 est.):** no indigenous inhabitants; 1,200 U.S. military and civilian personnel

Johnston is a coral atoll about 700 mi southwest of Hawaii. It consists of four small islands—Johnston Island, Sand Island, Hikina Island, and Akau Island—which lie on a 9-mile-long reef. The atoll was discovered by Capt. Charles James Johnston of HMS *Cornwallis* in 1807. In 1858 it was claimed by Hawaii, and later became a U.S. possession. Johnston Atoll is a Naval Defensive Sea Area and Airspace Reservation and is closed to the public. In the early 1990s, the U.S. government opened a facility for destroying chemical weapons on Johnston Atoll.

## Baker, Howland, and Jarvis Islands

**Status:** Territory

These Pacific islands were claimed by the United States under the Guano Act of 1856 on May 13, 1936. Guano, composed of phosphates, was used as fertilizer in the 19th century, and its collection was highly lucrative. Through the Guano Act the U.S. gained 79 tiny territories around the world; it still controls eight of them. Baker Island is a saucer-shaped atoll with an area of approximately one square mile about 1,650 mi from Hawaii. Howland Island, 36 mi to the northwest, is 1 mile long and half a mile wide. On their round-the-world flight in 1937, Amelia Earhart and Fred J. Noonan were headed for Howland when they disappeared. Jarvis Island is several hundred mi to the east.

## Kingman Reef

**Status:** Territory

Kingman Reef, located about 1,000 mi south of Hawaii, was discovered by Capt. E. Fanning in 1798, but named for Capt. W. E. Kingman, who rediscovered it in 1853. Triangular in shape, it is about 9.5 mi long. A U.S. possession since 1922, Kingman Reef is a Naval Defensive Sea Area and Airspace Reservation, and is closed to the public.

## Navassa Island

**Status:** Territory

Navassa Island is located in the Caribbean Sea, 99.4 mi (160 km) south of the U.S. naval base at Guantanamo, Cuba, between Cuba, Haiti, and Jamaica. The island has a total area of 2.01 sq mi (5.2 sq km). It was claimed for the U.S. under the Guano Act in 1857. The Navassa Phosphate Company mined the island until 1900, enlisting hundreds of freed American slaves to dig out several tons of guano. Working conditions were so brutal that the laborers finally revolted in 1889, killing their supervisors. The island is also claimed by Haiti.

## Palmyra Atoll

**Status:** Territory

Palmyra Atoll is an incorporated territory of the U.S. and privately owned. The atoll has a total area of 4.6 sq mi (11.9 sq km) and is located in the North Pacific Ocean, 994 mi (1,600 km) southwest of Honolulu. It was a U.S. military base during World War II but was not attacked.

# Uruguay

### ORIENTAL REPUBLIC OF URUGUAY

**National name:** República Oriental del Uruguay
**President:** Jorge Batlle (2000)
**Area:** 68,039 sq mi (176,220 sq km)
**Population (2002 est.):** 3,386,575 (growth rate: 0.8%); birth rate: 17.3/1000; infant mortality rate: 14.2/1000; density per sq mi: 50
**Capital and largest city (1998):** Montevideo, 1,330,440.
**Monetary unit:** Uruguay peso. **Language:** Spanish.
**Ethnicity/race:** white 88%, mestizo 8%, black 4%.
**Religions:** Roman Catholic 66%, Protestant 2%, Jewish 2%. **Literacy rate:** 96% (1990)
**Economic summary: GDP/PPP** (2000 est.): $31 billion; per capita $9,300. **Real growth rate:** –1.1%.
**Inflation:** 4.8%. **Unemployment:** 14%. **Arable land:** 7%. **Agriculture:** wheat, rice, barley, corn, sorghum; livestock; fish. **Labor force:** 1.5 million (1999 est.); agriculture n.a., industry n.a., services n.a. **Industries:** food processing, electrical machinery, transportation equipment, petroleum products, textiles, chemicals, beverages. **Natural resources:** arable land, hydropower, minor minerals, fisheries. **Exports:** $2.6 billion (f.o.b., 2000 est.): meat, rice, leather products, vehicles, dairy products, wool, electricity. **Imports:** $3.4 billion (f.o.b., 2000 est.): road vehicles, electrical machinery, metal manufactures, heavy industrial machinery, crude petroleum. **Major trading partners:** Mercosur partners, EU, U.S.

**Geography** Uruguay, on the east coast of South America south of Brazil and east of Argentina, is comparable in size to Oklahoma. The country consists of a low, rolling plain in the south and a low plateau in the north. It has a 120-mile (193 km) Atlantic shoreline, a 235-mile (378 km) frontage on the Rio de la Plata, and 270 mi (435 km) on the Uruguay River, its western boundary.

**Government** Constitutional republic.

**History** Prior to European settlement, Uruguay was inhabited by indigenous people, the Charrúas. Juan Díaz de Solis, a Spaniard, visited Uruguay in 1516, but the Portuguese were first to settle it when they founded the town of Colonia del Sacramento in 1680. After a long struggle, Spain wrested the country from Portugal in 1778, by which time almost all of the indigenous people had been exterminated. Uruguay revolted against Spain in 1811, only to be conquered in 1817 by the Portuguese from Brazil. Independence was reasserted with Argentine help in 1825, and the republic was set up in 1828.

A revolt in 1836 touched off nearly 50 years of factional strife, including an inconclusive civil war (1839–51) and a war with Paraguay (1865–70) accompanied by occasional armed intervention by Argentina and Brazil. Uruguay, made prosperous by meat and wool exports, founded a welfare state early in the 20th century under President José Batlle y Ordóñez, who ruled from 1903 to 1929. A decline began in the 1950s as successive governments struggled to maintain a large bureaucracy and costly social benefits. Economic stagnation and left-wing terrorist activity followed.

A military coup ousted the civilian government in 1973. The military dictatorship that followed used fear and terror to demoralize the population, taking thousands of political prisoners. After ruling for 12 years, the brutal military regime permitted election of a civilian government in Nov. 1984 and relinquished rule in March 1985; full political and civil rights were then restored.

Subsequent leaders contended with high inflation and a mammoth national debt. Presidential and legislative elections in Nov. 1994 resulted in a narrow victory for the center-right Colorado Party and its presidential candidate, Julio Sanguinetti Cairolo, who had been president in 1985–90. He pushed for constitutional and economic reforms aimed at reducing inflation and the size of the public sector, including tax increases and privatization. In Nov. 1999 Jorge Batlle, of the center-right Colorado Party, won the presidency. In Aug. 2000 a commission began investigating the disappearances of 160 people who vanished during the military regime.

In 2002, Uruguay entered its fourth year of recession. Economic troubles in neighboring Argentina caused a staggering 90% drop in tourists, devastating Uruguay's important tourism industry. Agricultural exports were hurt by the 2001 foot-and-mouth outbreak among cattle. Batlle also faced a sizable budget deficit, a growing public debt, and a weakening of the peso on international markets.

# Uzbekistan

### REPUBLIC OF UZBEKISTAN

**National name:** Uzbekistan Respublikasi
**President:** Islam A. Karimov (1990)
**Prime Minister:** Otkir Sultonov (1995)
**Area:** 172,741 sq mi (447,400 sq km)
**Population (2002 est.):** 25,563,441 (growth rate: 1.8%); birth rate: 26.1/1000; infant mortality rate: 71.7/1000; density per sq mi: 148
**Capital and largest city (1992 est.):** Tashkent, 2,106,000. **Other large cities:** Samarkand, 372,000; Andijon, 302,000. **Monetary unit:** Uzbekistani sum.
**Languages:** Uzbek 74.3%, Russian 14.2%, Tajik 4.4%, other 7.1%. **Ethnicity/race (1996 est.):** Uzbek 80%, Russian 5.5%, Tajik 5%, Kazak 3%, Karakalpak 2.5%, Tatar 1.5%, other 2.5%. **Religions:** Muslim (mostly Sunnis) 88%, Eastern Orthodox 9%, other 3%. **Literacy rate:** 99% (1996)
**Economic summary:** GDP/PPP (2000 est.): $$60 billion; per capita $2,400. **Real growth rate:** 2.1%. **Inflation:** 40%. **Unemployment:** 10% plus another 20% underemployed (1999 est.). **Arable land:** 9%. **Agriculture:** cotton, vegetables, fruits, grain; livestock. **Labor force:** 11.9 million (1998 est.); agriculture 44%, industry 20%, services 36% (1995). **Industries:** textiles, food processing, machine building, metallurgy, natural gas, chemicals. **Natural resources:** natural gas, petroleum, coal, gold, uranium, silver, copper, lead and zinc, tungsten, molybdenum. **Exports:** $2.9 billion (f.o.b., 2000 est.): cotton, gold, natural gas, mineral fertilizers, ferrous metals, textiles, food products, automobiles. **Imports:** $2.6 billion (f.o.b., 2000 est.): machinery and equipment, chemicals, metals; foodstuffs. **Major trading partners:** Russia, Switzerland, UK, Belgium, Kazakhstan, Tajikistan, South Korea, Germany, U.S., Turkey.

**Geography** Uzbekistan is situated in central Asia between the Amu Darya and Syr Darya Rivers, the Aral Sea, and the slopes of the Tien Shan Mountains. It is bounded by Kazakhstan in the north and northwest, Kyrgyzstan and Tajikistan in the east and southeast, Turkmenistan in the southwest, and Afghanistan in the south. The republic also includes the Karakalpakstan Autonomous Republic, with its capital, Nukus (1992 est. pop., 182,000). The country is about one-tenth larger in area than the state of California.

**Government** Republic; authoritarian presidential rule.

**History** The Uzbekistan land was once part of the ancient Persian empire and was later conquered by Alexander the Great in the 4th century B.C. During the 8th century, the nomadic Turkic tribes living there were converted to Islam by invading Arab forces who dominated the area. The Mongols under Ghengis Khan took over the region from the Seljuk Turks in the 13th century, and it later became part of Tamerlane the Great's empire and that of his successors until the 16th century. The Uzbeks invaded the territory in the early 16th century and merged with the other inhabitants in the area. Their empire broke up into separate Uzbek principalities, the khanates of Khiva, Bukhara, and Kokand. These city-states resisted Russian expansion into the area but were conquered by the Russian forces in the mid-19th century.

The territory was made into the Uzbek Republic in 1924 and became the independent Uzbekistan Soviet Socialist Republic in 1925. Under Soviet rule, Uzbekistan concentrated on growing cotton with the help of irrigation, mechanization, and chemical fertilizers and pesticides, causing serious environmental damage.

In June 1990, Uzbekistan became the first central Asian republic to declare that its own laws had sovereignty over those of the central Soviet government. Uzbekistan became fully independent and joined with ten other former Soviet republics on Dec. 21, 1991, in the Commonwealth of Independent States.

Vozrozhdeniye, an island in the Aral Sea, was a secret test site for biological weapons during the Soviet era. In 1988, the Soviets attempted to bury the evidence on the island, a frightening legacy that Uzbekistan inherited upon independence. U.S. scientists have confirmed that the island contains live anthrax and other deadly poisons.

In Feb. 1992, President Karimov, a former Communist Party boss, affirmed his commitment to democracy and human rights, but he effectively suppressed opposition parties in mid-1993. The criminal code was amended to impose stricter penalties for antigovernment activity. Opposition groups were largely excluded in future elections while the ruling party continued to post decisive victories.

In 1999, the country battled against militant Islamic groups bent on the overthrow of the secular government. In Feb. 1999, a series of bomb blasts killed 16 and injured hundreds in the capital, Tashkent. Militant Islamic gunmen remain stationed across the border in southern Kyrgyzstan, and Uzbek fighter planes have been unable to rout them. In 2000, Russia offered to help Uzbekistan "liquidate" the Islamic extremists, and Russia has also offered to send at least $30 million worth of weapons.

In 2001, Uzbekistan provided the United States with a base to fight against Taliban and al-Qaeda forces in neighboring Afghanistan. About 1,000 U.S. soldiers were stationed there in 2002.

# Vanuatu

### REPUBLIC OF VANUATU

**President:** John Bani (1999)
**Prime Minister:** Edward Natapei (2001)
**Area:** 4,710 sq mi (12,200 sq km)
**Population (2002 est.):** 196,178 (growth rate: 1.7%); birth rate: 24.8/1000; infant mortality rate: 59.6/1000; density per sq mi: 42
**Capital and largest city (1993 est.):** Port Vila, 26,100. **Monetary unit:** Vatu. **Languages:** Bislama (a Melanesian pidgin English), English, French (all 3 official). **Ethnicity/race:** indigenous Melanesian 94%, French 4%, Vietnamese, Chinese, other Pacific

Islanders. **Religions:** Presbyterian 36.7%, Roman Catholic 15%, Anglican 15%, other Christian 10%, indigenous beliefs 7.6%, other 15.7%. **Literacy rate:** 55% (1979)
**Economic summary: GDP/PPP** (1999 est.): $245 million; per capita $1,300. **Real growth rate:** –2.5%. **Inflation:** 2.5%. **Unemployment:** n.a. **Arable land:** 2%. **Agriculture:** copra, coconuts, cocoa, coffee, taro, yams, coconuts, fruits, vegetables; fish, beef. **Labor force:** n.a.; agriculture 65%, services 32%, industry 3% (1995 est.). **Industries:** food and fish freezing, wood processing, meat canning. **Natural resources:** manganese, hardwood forests, fish. **Exports:** $25.3 million (f.o.b., 1999): copra, kava, beef, cocoa, timber, coffee. **Imports:** $77.2 million (f.o.b., 1999): machinery and equipment, foodstuffs, fuels. **Major trading partners:** Japan, Germany, Spain, New Caledonia, Australia, Singapore, New Zealand, France, Fiji.

**Geography** Vanuatu is an archipelago of 83 islands lying between New Caledonia and Fiji in the South Pacific. Largest of the islands is Espiritu Santo (875 sq mi; 2,266 sq km); others are Efate, Malekula, Malo, Pentecost, and Tanna.

**Government** Republic.

**History** The first settlers were believed to have arrived approximately 3,500 years ago from New Guinea and the Solomon Islands by canoe. The islands were sighted by Pedro Fernandes de Queiros of Portugal in 1606 and were charted by the British navigator James Cook in 1774, who named the archipelago New Hebrides, after the northern Scottish islands. Competing British and French claims to the islands led to the formation of a condominium government, allowing for joint British-French rule in 1906. The islands' plantation economy, based on imported Vietnamese labor, was prosperous until the 1920s, when markets for its products declined. Diseases brought by missionaries, sandalwood traders, and others helped reduce the population from approximately 1 million in 1800 to 45,000 in 1935. The islands served as a major Allied base in World War II. After World War II, the indigenous Melanesians began lobbying for independence. In 1980 the country achieved independence and was renamed Vanuatu.

A brief rebellion by French settlers and plantation workers on Espiritu Santo took place in May 1980. Britain, France, and Papua New Guinea sent soldiers, who quelled the revolt, which the new government said was financed by the Phoenix Foundation, a right-wing U.S. group.

# Vatican City (Holy See)

**National name:** Stato della Città del Vaticano
**Ruler:** Pope John Paul II (1978)
**Area:** 0.17 sq mi (0.44 sq km)
**Population** (July 2001 est.): 890; population growth rate: 1.2%; density per sq mi: 5,239. **Monetary unit:** Euro.
**Languages:** Latin, Italian, and various other languages.
**Ethnicity/race:** Italians, Swiss. **Religion:** Roman Catholic.
**Labor force:** dignitaries, priests, nuns, guards, and 3,000 lay workers who live outside the Vatican.
**Budget (1997):** Revenues: $209.6 million; expenditures: $198.5 million, including capital expenditures.

**Geography** The Vatican City State is situated on the Vatican hill, on the right bank of the Tiber River, within the city of Rome.

**Government** The pope has full legal, executive, and judicial powers. Executive power over the area is in the hands of a commission of cardinals appointed by the pope. The College of Cardinals is the pope's chief advisory body, and upon his death the cardinals elect his successor for life.

**History** The Vatican City State, sovereign and independent, is the survivor of the papal states that in 1859 comprised an area of some 17,000 sq mi (44,030 sq km). During the struggle for Italian unification, from 1860 to 1870, most of this area became part of Italy. By an Italian law of May 13, 1871, the temporal power of the pope was abrogated, and the territory of the papacy was confined to the Vatican and Lateran palaces and the villa of Castel Gandolfo. The popes consistently refused to recognize this arrangement. The Lateran Treaty of Feb. 11, 1929, between the Vatican and the kingdom of Italy established the autonomy of the Holy See.

The first session of Ecumenical Council Vatican II was opened by John XXIII on Oct. 11, 1962, to plan and set policies for the modernization of the Roman Catholic Church. Pope Paul VI continued the council, presiding over the last three sessions. Vatican II, as it is called, revolutionized some of the church's practices. Power was decentralized, giving bishops a larger role, the liturgy was vernacularized, and laymen were given a larger part in church affairs.

On Aug. 26, 1978, Cardinal Albino Luciani was chosen by the College of Cardinals to succeed Paul VI, who had died of a heart attack on Aug. 6. The new pope took the name John Paul I. Only 34 days after his election, John Paul I died of a heart attack, ending the shortest reign in 373 years. On Oct. 16, Cardinal Karol Wojtyla, 58, was chosen pope and took the name John Paul II. Pope John Paul II became the first Polish pope and the first non-Italian pope since the 16th century. His rule has been characterized by conservatism regarding church doctrine. He has been the Vatican's greatest ambassador, traveling to more than 115 countries.

On May 13, 1981, a Turkish terrorist shot the pope in St. Peter's Square, the first assassination attempt against the pontiff in modern times. On June 3, 1985, the Vatican and Italy ratified a new church-state treaty, known as a concordat, replacing the Lateran Pact of 1929. The new accord affirmed the independence of Vatican City but ended a number of privileges the Catholic Church had in Italy, including its status as the state religion. The treaty ended Rome's status as a "sacred city."

In March 2000, the pope issued an apology for sins committed by Catholics over the past 2,000 years, including religious persecutions and discrimination against women. Several groups criticized the vagueness of the apology, wishing the pope had specified the church's particularly egregious sins.

The pope remained circumspect about the U.S. church's sexual abuse scandals in 2002, calling pedophilia an "appalling sin" and describing the crisis as "a dark shadow of suspicion . . . cast over all the other fine priests who perform their ministry with honesty and integrity and often with heroic self-sacrifice."

For a list of all the popes, *see* pp. 438–440.

# Venezuela

**REPUBLIC OF VENEZUELA**

**National name:** Republica de Venezuela
**President:** Hugo Chavez (2002)
**Area:** 352,143 sq mi (912,050 sq km)
**Population (2002 est.):** 24,287,670 (growth rate: 1.5%); birth rate: 20.2/1000; infant mortality rate: 24.6/1000; density per sq mile: 69
**Capital:** Caracas. **Largest cities (1990 est.):** Caracas, city, 1,824,892, metro area, 2,784,042; Maracaibo, 1,206,726; Valencia, 616,000; Barquisimeto, 723,587.
**Monetary unit:** bolivar. **Languages:** Spanish (official), various indigenous languages in the remote interior.
**Ethnicity/race:** mestizo 67%, white 21%, black 10%, Amerindian 2%. **Religions:** Roman Catholic 96%, Protestant 2%. **Literacy rate:** 91% (1990)
**Economic summary: GDP/PPP** (2000 est.): $146.2 billion; per capita $6,200. **Real growth rate:** 3.2%. **Inflation:** 13% (2000). **Unemployment:** 14% (2000 est.). **Arable land:** 4%. **Agriculture:** corn, sorghum, sugarcane, rice, bananas, vegetables, coffee; beef, pork, milk, eggs; fish. **Labor force:** 9.9 million (1999); services 64%, industry 23%, agriculture 13% (1997 est.). **Industries:** petroleum, iron ore mining, construction materials, food processing, textiles, steel, aluminum, motor vehicle assembly. **Natural resources:** petroleum, natural gas, iron ore, gold, bauxite, other minerals, hydropower, diamonds.
**Exports:** $32.8 billion (f.o.b., 2000): petroleum, bauxite and aluminum, steel, chemicals, agricultural products, basic manufactures. **Imports:** $14.7 billion (f.o.b., 2000): raw materials, machinery and equipment, transport equipment, construction materials. **Major trading partners:** U.S., Puerto Rico, Colombia, Brazil, Japan, Germany, Netherlands, Italy, France, Canada.

**Geography** Venezuela, a third larger than Texas, occupies most of the northern coast of South America on the Caribbean Sea. It is bordered by Colombia to the west, Guyana to the east, and Brazil to the south. Mountain systems break Venezuela into four distinct areas: (1) the Maracaibo lowlands; (2) the mountainous region in the north and northwest; (3) the Orinoco basin, with the llanos (vast grass-covered plains) on its northern border and great forest areas in the south and southeast; (4) the Guiana Highlands, south of the Orinoco, accounting for nearly half the national territory.

**Government** Federal republic.

**History** When Columbus explored Venezuela on his third voyage in 1498, the area was inhabited by Arawak, Carib, and Chibcha Indians. A subsequent Spanish explorer gave the country its name, meaning "Little Venice." Caracas was founded in 1567. Simón Bolívar, who led the liberation of much of the continent from Spain, was born in Caracas in 1783. With Bolívar taking part, Venezuela was one of the first South American colonies to revolt in 1810, winning independence in 1821. Federated at first with Colombia and Ecuador as the Republic of Greater Colombia, Venezuela became a republic in 1830. A period of unstable dictatorships followed. Antonio Guzman Blanco governed from 1870 to 1888, developing an infrastructure, expanding agriculture, and welcoming foreign investment.

Gen. Juan Vicente Gómez was dictator from 1908 to 1935, when Venezuela became a major oil exporter. A military junta ruled after his death. Leftist Dr. Rómulo Betancourt and the Democratic Action Party won a majority of seats in a constituent assembly to draft a new constitution in 1946. A well-known writer, Rómulo Gallegos, candidate of Betancourt's party, became Venezuela's first democratically elected president in 1947. Within eight months, Gallegos was overthrown by a military-backed coup led by Marcos Peréz Jiménez, who was ousted himself in 1958. Since 1959, Venezuela has been one of the most stable democracies in Latin America. Betancourt served from 1959–64, while Rafael Caldera Rodríguez, president from 1969 to 1974, legalized the Communist Party and established diplomatic relations with Moscow.

Venezuela benefited from the oil boom of the early 1970s. In 1974, President Carlos Andrés Pérez took office, and in 1976 Venezuela nationalized foreign-owned oil and steel companies, offering compensation. Luis Herrera Campíns took office in 1978. Declining world oil prices sent Venezuela's economy into a tail-spin, increasing the country's foreign debt. Pérez was reelected to a nonconsecutive term in 1988 and launched an unpopular austerity program. Military officers staged two unsuccessful coup attempts in 1992, while the following year Congress impeached Pérez on corruption charges. President Rafael Caldera Rodríguez was elected in Dec. 1993 to face the 1994 collapse of half of the country's banking sector, falling oil prices, foreign debt repayment, and inflation. In 1997, the government announced an expansion of gold and diamond mining to reduce reliance on oil.

Leftist president Hugo Chavez took office in 1999, pledging political and economic reforms to give the poor a greater share of the country's oil wealth. A constituent assembly was formed to rewrite the constitution in July 1999, followed by the creation of a constitutional assembly made up of Chavez's allies that replaced the democratically elected Congress. Chavez's assumption of greater power prompted charges that he is establishing a left-wing dictatorship.

Chavez was reelected to a six-year term in July 2000. Troops were called in to quell serious protests over the election in several cities. In 2000 Chavez visited other OPEC countries, becoming the first foreign head of state to visit Iraq since the 1991 Gulf War. He is close to President Fidel Castro of Cuba, which receives Venezuelan oil at reduced prices.

In Dec. 2001, business and labor organizations held a work stoppage to protest Chavez's increasingly authoritarian government. In April 2002, tensions reached a boiling point as workers reduced oil production to protest Chavez policies. Following a massive anti-Chavez demonstration during which 12 people were killed, a coalition of business and military leaders forced Chavez from power for two days, hoping to install an interim government leading to elections. However, international criticism of the coup, especially from Latin America, and an outpouring of support for Chavez from Venezuela's poor, returned Chavez to power. After the coup, Chavez remained highly popular among the poor, despite the desperate state of the economy. Other Venezuelans and a good part of the military were far less enchanted with his continued rule.

# Vietnam

**SOCIALIST REPUBLIC OF VIETNAM**

**National name:** Công Hòa Xa Hôi Chú Nghia Viêt Nam
**President:** Tran Duc Luong (1997)
**Prime Minister:** Phan Van Khai (1997)
**Area:** 127,243 sq mi (329,560 sq km)
**Population (2002 est.):** 81,098,416 (growth rate: 1.5%); birth rate: 20.9/1000; infant mortality rate: 29.3/1000; density per sq mi: 637

**Capital:** Hanoi. **Largest cities (1992 est.):** Ho Chi Minh City (Saigon), 3,015,743; Hanoi, 1,073,760. Other large cities (1989): Haiphong, 456,049; Da Nang, 370,670; Nha Trang, 213,687; Qui Nho'n, 160,091; Hué 211,085. **Monetary unit:** Dong. **Languages:** Vietnamese (official), French, English, Khmer, Chinese. **Ethnicity/race:** Vietnamese 85%–90%, Chinese 3%, Muong, Thai, Meo, Khmer, Man, Cham. **Religions:** Buddhist, Roman Catholic, Islam, Taoist, Confucian, Animist. **Literacy rate:** 94% (1995) **Economic summary: GDP/PPP** (2000 est.): $154.4 billion; per capita $1,950. **Real growth rate:** 5.5%. **Inflation:** –0.6%. **Unemployment:** 25% (1995 est.). **Arable land:** 17%. **Agriculture:** paddy rice, corn, potatoes, rubber, soybeans, coffee, tea, bananas, sugar; poultry, pigs; fish. **Labor force:** 38.2 million (1998 est.); agriculture 67%, industry and services 33% (1997 est.). **Industries:** food processing, garments, shoes, machine building, mining, cement, chemical fertilizer, glass, tires, oil, coal, steel, paper. **Natural resources:** phosphates, coal, manganese, bauxite, chromate, offshore oil and gas deposits, forests, hydropower. **Exports:** $14.3 billion (f.o.b., 2000 est.): crude oil, marine products, rice, coffee, rubber, tea, garments, shoes. **Imports:** $15.2 billion (f.o.b., 2000 est.): machinery and equipment, petroleum products, fertilizer, steel products, raw cotton, grain, cement, motorcycles. **Major trading partners:** China, Japan, Germany, Australia, U.S., France, Singapore, UK, Taiwan, South Korea, Thailand, Hong Kong, Malaysia, Indonesia, Sweden.

**Geography** Vietnam occupies the eastern and southern part of the Indochinese peninsula in Southeast Asia, with the South China Sea along its entire coast. China is to the north and Laos and Cambodia to the west. Long and narrow on a north-south axis, Vietnam is about twice the size of Arizona. The Mekong River delta lies in the south.

**Government** Communist state.

**History** The Vietnamese are descendants of nomadic Mongols from China and migrants from Indonesia. According to mythology, the first ruler of Vietnam was Hung Vuong, who founded the nation in 2879 B.C. China ruled the nation then known as Nam Viet as a vassal state from 111 B.C. until the 15th century, an era of nationalistic expansion, when Cambodians were pushed out of the southern area of what is now Vietnam.

A century later, the Portuguese were the first Europeans to enter the area. France established its influence early in the 19th century, and within 80 years conquered the three regions into which the country was then divided—Cochin-China in the south, Annam in the central region, and Tonkin in the north France first unified Vietnam in 1887, when a single governor-generalship was created, followed by the first physical links between north and south—a rail and road system. Even at the beginning of World War II, however, there were internal differences among the three regions. Japan took over military bases in Vietnam in 1940, and a pro-Vichy French administration remained until 1945. Veteran Communist leader Ho Chi Minh organized an independence movement known as the Vietminh to exploit the confusion surrounding France's weakened influence in the region. At the end of the war, Ho's followers seized Hanoi and declared a short-lived republic, which ended with the arrival of French forces in 1946.

Paris proposed a unified government within the French Union under the former Annamite emperor, Bao Dai. Cochin-China and Annam accepted the proposal, and Bao Dai was proclaimed emperor of all Vietnam in 1949. Ho and the Vietminh withheld support, and the revolution in China gave them the outside help needed for a war of resistance against French and Vietnamese troops armed largely by a United States worried about cold war Communist expansion.

A bitter defeat at Dien Bien Phu in northwest Vietnam on May 5, 1954, broke the French military campaign and resulted in the division of Vietnam. In the new South, Ngo Dinh Diem, premier under Bao Dai, deposed the monarch in 1955 and made himself president. Diem used strong U.S. backing to create an authoritarian regime that suppressed all opposition but could not eradicate the Northern-supplied Communist Viet Cong.

Skirmishing grew into a full-scale war, with escalating U.S. involvement. A military coup, U.S.-inspired in the view of many, ousted Diem on Nov. 1, 1963, and a kaleidoscope of military governments followed. The most savage fighting of the war occurred in early 1968 during the Vietnamese New Year, known as Tet. Although the so-called Tet Offensive ended in a military defeat for the North, its psychological impact changed the course of the war.

U.S. bombing and an invasion of Cambodia in the summer of 1970—an effort to destroy Viet Cong bases in the neighboring state—marked the end of major U.S. participation in the fighting. Most American ground troops were withdrawn from combat by mid-1971 when the U.S. conducted heavy bombing raids on the Ho Chi Minh Trail—a crucial North Vietnamese supply line. In 1972, secret peace negotiations led by Secretary of State Henry A. Kissinger took place, and a peace settlement was signed in Paris on Jan. 27, 1973.

By April 9, 1975, Hanoi's troops marched within 40 miles of Saigon, the South's capital. South Vietnam's president Thieu resigned on April 21 and fled. Gen. Duong Van Minh, the new president, surrendered Saigon on April 30, ending a war that claimed the lives of 1.3 million Vietnamese and 58,000 Americans. In 1977, border clashes between Vietnam and Cambodia intensified, as well as accusations by its former ally Beijing that Chinese residents of Vietnam were being subjected to persecution. Beijing cut off all aid and withdrew 800 technicians.

Hanoi was also preoccupied with a continuing war in Cambodia, where 60,000 Vietnamese troops had invaded and overthrown the country's Communist leader Pol Pot and his pro-Chinese regime. In early 1979, Vietnam was conducting a two-front war: defending its northern border against a Chinese invasion, and supporting its army in Cambodia, which was still fighting Pol Pot's Khmer Rouge guerrillas. Hanoi's Marxist policies combined with the destruction of the country's infrastructure during the decades of fighting devastated Vietnam's economy. However, it started to pick up in 1986 under *do Maui* (economic renovation), an effort at limited privatization. Vietnamese troops began limited withdrawals from Laos and Cambodia in 1988, and Vietnam supported the Cambodian peace agreement signed in Oct. 1991.

The U.S. lifted a Vietnamese trade embargo in Feb. 1994 that had been in place since U.S. involvement in the war. Full diplomatic relations were announced between the two countries in July 1995. In April 1997, a pact was signed with the U.S. concerning repayment of the $146 million wartime debt incurred by the South Vietnamese government, and the following year the nation began a drive to eliminate inefficient bureaucrats and streamline the approval process for direct foreign investment. Efforts of reform-minded officials toward political and economic change have been thwarted by Vietnam's ruling Communist Party. In April 2001, however, reform-minded Nong Duc Manh was appointed general secretary of the ruling Communist Party, succeeding Le Kha Phieu. Even with a reformer at the helm of the party, any change will come slowly and cautiously. Manh previously served as chairman of the National Assembly.

In Nov. 2001, Vietnam's National Assembly approved a trade agreement that opens U.S. markets to Vietnam's goods and services. Tariffs on Vietnam's products dropped to about 4% from rates as high as 40%. Vietnam in return opened its state markets to foreign competition and agreed to meet international standards on copyright and investment issues. The pact took effect in early December.

In July 2002, the National Assembly reappointed President Tran Duc Luong and Prime Minister Phan Van Khai.

(For a Vietnam War chronology, *see* Headline History.)

# Western Sahara (proposed state)

### WESTERN SAHARA
**Area:** 102,703 sq mi (266,000 sq km)
**Population (2002 est.):** 256,177; growth rate: n.a.%; birth rate: n.a./1000; infant mortality rate: n.a./1000; density per sq mi: 2
**Largest cities (1991):** El Aaiun (20,010). **Monetary unit:** Tala. **Languages:** Hassaniya Arabic, Moroccan Arabic. **Ethnicity/race:** Saharawi, Arab, Berber. **Religion:** Muslim
**Economic summary: GDP/PPP:** n.a. **Arable land:** 0%. **Agriculture:** fruits and vegetables (grown in the few oases); camels, sheep, goats (kept by nomads). **Labor force:** 12,000; animal husbandry and subsistence farming 50%. **Industries:** phosphate mining, handicrafts. **Natural resources:** phosphates, iron ore. **Exports:** $n.a.: phosphates 62%. **Imports:** $n.a.: fuel for fishing fleet, foodstuffs. **Major trading partners:** Morocco claims and administers Western Sahara, so trade partners are included in overall Moroccan accounts.

**Geography** Located in northern Africa on the Atlantic Ocean, Western Sahara is surrounded by Algeria to the east, Morocco to the north, and Mauritania to the south. About the size of Colorado, it is mostly low, flat desert with some small mountains in the south and northeast.

**Government** Legal status of the territory is disputed and sovereignty unresolved; a UN referendum on the issue is planned. The territory is contested by Morocco and the Polisario Front, which in Feb. 1976 formerly proclaimed a government-in-exile of the Saharawi Arab Democratic Republic, now officially recognized by about 55 countries.

**History** Little is known about Western Sahara until the 4th century B.C. when trade with Europe began. During the Middle Ages it was occupied first by Berbers and then by the Arabic-speaking Muslim Bedouins. In the 19th century the Spanish laid claim to the southern coastal region, called Rio de Oro, and later occupied the northern interior region, Saguia el Hamra, in 1934. The Spanish formally united the two regions, and it became known as Spanish Sahara in 1958. Both Morocco and Mauritania sought to control the territory, and when the Spanish departed in 1976 they divided the territory between them. In the meantime, the indigenous Saharawis began fighting for

independence. In 1976, the insurgents, called the Polisario Front, declared a government-in-exile (the Saharawi Arab Democratic Republic) from their base in Algeria. Mauritania reached a peace agreement with the Polisario in 1979, but Morocco then seized the land given up by Mauritania and now exerts administrative control over the entire region. The Polisario Front fought Morocco to a stalemate, and agreed in Sept. 1991 to a cease-fire, which was contingent on a referendum regarding independence. For the past decade, however, the UN has failed to hold the referendum; disputes over voter eligibility have been the major stumbling block, as well as Morocco's opposition to the referendum. In Aug. 2001, former secretary of state James A. Baker III, special UN envoy to the Western Sahara, proposed that instead of a referendum on independence, Western Sahara consider becoming an autonomous region of Morocco. The Western Sahara government rejected the new proposal, which it saw as a reversal of the UN's decade-old promise to hold a referendum on self-determination. In 2002, King Mohammed VI of Morocco reasserted that he "will not renounce an inch of" the Western Sahara.

# Yemen

### REPUBLIC OF YEMEN
**National name:** Al Jumhuriyahal Yamaniyah
**President:** Ali Abdullah Saleh (1990)
**Prime Minister:** Abdel Qadir Bajamal (2001)
**Area:** 203,849 sq mi (527,970 sq km)
**Population (2002 est.):** 18,701,257 (growth rate: 3.4%); birth rate: 43.3/1000; infant mortality rate: 66.8/1000; density per sq mi: 92
**Capital (1995):** Sanaá, 972,011. **Largest cities (1995):** Tiaz, 2,205,947; Hodiedah, 1,749,944; Aden, 562,162.
**Monetary unit:** Rial. **Language:** Arabic. **Ethnicity/race:** predominantly Arab; Afro-Arab concentrations in western coastal locations; South Asians in southern regions; small European communities in major metropolitan areas. **Religion:** Islam (Sunni and Shi'ite). **Literacy rate:** 39% (1990)
**Economic summary: GDP/PPP** (2000 est.): $14.4 billion; per capita $820. **Real growth rate:** 6%. **Inflation:** 10%. **Unemployment:** 30% (1995 est.). **Arable land:** 3%. **Agriculture:** grain, fruits, vegetables, pulses, qat (mildly narcotic shrub), coffee, cotton; dairy products, livestock (sheep, goats, cattle, camels), poultry; fish. **Labor force:** n.a.; most people are employed in agriculture and herding or as expatriate laborers; services, construction, industry, and commerce account for less than one-half of the labor force. **Industries:** crude oil production and petroleum refining; small-scale production of cotton textiles and leather goods; food processing; handicrafts; small aluminum products factory; cement. **Natural resources:** petroleum, fish, rock salt, marble, small deposits of coal, gold, lead, nickel, and copper, fertile soil in west. **Exports:** $4.2 billion (f.o.b. 2000 est.): crude oil, coffee, dried and salted fish. **Imports:** $2.7 billion (f.o.b. 2000 est.): food and live animals, machinery and equipment. **Major trading partners:** Thailand, China, South Korea, Japan, Saudi Arabia, UAE, U.S., France, Italy.

**Geography** Formerly divided into two nations, the People's Democratic Republic of Yemen and the Yemen Arab Republic, the Republic of Yemen occupies the southwest tip of the Arabian Peninsula on the Red Sea opposite Ethiopia, and extends along the southern part of the Arabian Peninsula on the Gulf of Aden and the Indian Ocean. Saudi Arabia is to the north and Oman is to the east. The country is about the size of France. A 700-mile (1,130-km) narrow coastal plain in the south gives way to a mountainous region and then a plateau area. Some of the interior highlands in the west attain a height of 12,000 ft (3,660 m).

**Government** Parliamentary republic.

**History** The history of Yemen dates back to the Minaean (1200–650 B.C.) and Sabaean (750–115 B.C.) kingdoms. Ancient Yemen (centered around the port of Aden) engaged in the lucrative myrrh and frankincense trade. It was invaded by the Romans (1st century A.D.) as well as the Ethiopians and Persians (6th century A.D.). In A.D. 628 it converted to Islam and in the 10th century came under the control of the Rassite dynasty of the Zaidi sect, which remained involved in North Yemeni politics until 1962. The Ottoman Turks nominally occupied the area from 1538 to the decline of their empire in 1918.

The northern portion of Yemen was ruled by imams until a pro-Egyptian military coup took place in 1962. The junta proclaimed the Yemen Arab Republic, and after a civil war in which Egypt's Nasser and the USSR supported the revolutionaries, and King Saud of Saudi Arabia and King Hussein of Jordan supported the royalists, the royalists were finally defeated in mid-1969.

The southern port of Aden, strategically located at the opening of the Red Sea, was colonized by Britain in 1839, and by 1937, with an expansion of its territory, it was known as the Aden Protectorate. In the 1960s the Nationalist Liberation Front (NLF) fought against British rule, which led to the establishment of the People's Republic of Southern Yemen on Nov. 30, 1967. In 1979, under strong Soviet influence, the country became the only Marxist state in the Arab world.

The Republic of Yemen was established on May 22, 1990, when pro-Western Yemen and the Marxist Yemen Arab Republic merged after 300 years of separation to form the new nation. The poverty and decline in Soviet economic support in the south was an important incentive for the merger. The new president, Ali Abdullah Saleh, was elected by the Parliaments of both countries.

Differences over power sharing and the pace of integration between the north and the south came to a head in 1994, resulting in a civil war. The north's superior forces quickly overwhelmed the south in May and early June despite the south's brief declaration of succession. The victorious north presented a reconciliation plan providing for a general amnesty and pledges to protect political democracy.

The president's party, the General People's Congress, won an enormous victory in the April 1997 parliamentary elections, the first since the civil war. In 1998–99, a militant Islamic group, the Aden-Abyan Islamic Army, kidnapped several groups of Western tourists, which led to the deaths of several during a poorly orchestrated rescue attempt. The group's leader, Zein Al-Abidine al-Mihdar, threatened to continue attacks on tourists and government officials. The goal of the militants is to overthrow the government and turn Yemen into an Islamic state.

On Oct. 12, 2000, 17 Americans died and 37 were wounded when suicide bombers attacked the U.S. Navy destroyer *Cole*, which was refueling in Aden, Yemen. The U.S. has had numerous clashes with Yemeni authorities during the investigation of the terrorist act. After the Sept. 11 terrorist attacks on the U.S., however, Yemen increased its cooperation with the U.S. and assisted in antiterrorism measures.

# Yugoslavia

**FEDERAL REPUBLIC OF YUGOSLAVIA**

**National name:** Savezna Republica Jugoslavija
**President:** Vojislav Kostunica (2000)
**Prime Minister:** Dragisa Pesic (2001)
**Area:** 39,517 sq mi (102,350 sq km)
**Population (2002 est.):** 10,656,929 (Montenegro: 677,177, Serbia: 9,979,752) (growth rate: Montenegro: 0.7%, Serbia: 0.2%); birth rate: Montenegro: 14.7/1000, Serbia: 12.7/1000; infant mortality rate: Montenegro: 10.5/1000, Serbia: 17.9/1000; density per sq mi: 92
**Capital and largest city (1994 est.):** Belgrade, 1,168,454. **Other large cities:** Novi Sad, 179,626; Nis, 175,391; Pristina, 155,499. **Monetary unit:** Yugoslav new dinar. **Languages:** Serbian 95%, Albanian 5%. What was once known as Serbo-Croatian is now known as Serbian, Croatian, or Bosnian, depending on the speaker's political and ethnic affiliation. It is written in Latin and Cyrillic.
**Ethnicity/race:** Serbs 63%, Albanians 14%, Montenegrins 6%, Hungarians 4%, other 13%.
**Religions:** Orthodox 65%, Muslim 19%, Roman Catholic 4%, Protestant 1%, other 11%. **Literacy rate:** 91%
**Economic summary:** GDP/PPP (2000 est.): $24.2 billion; per capita $2,300. **Real growth rate:** 15%. **Inflation:** 42% (1999 est.). **Unemployment:** 30% (2000 est.). **Arable land:** 40%. **Agriculture:** cereals, fruits, vegetables, tobacco, olives; cattle, sheep, goats. **Labor force:** 1.6 million (1999 est.); agriculture n.a., industry n.a., services n.a. **Industries:** machine building (aircraft, trucks, and automobiles; tanks and weapons; electrical equipment; agricultural machinery); metallurgy (steel, aluminum, copper, lead, zinc, chromium, antimony, bismuth, cadmium); mining (coal, bauxite, nonferrous ore, iron ore, limestone); consumer goods (textiles, footwear, foodstuffs, appliances); electronics; petroleum products, chemicals, and pharmaceuticals. **Natural resources:** oil, gas, coal, antimony, copper, lead, zinc, nickel, gold, pyrite, chrome, hydropower, arable land. **Exports:** $1.5 billion (1999): manufactured goods, food and live animals, raw materials. **Imports:** $3.3 billion (1999): machinery and transport equipment, fuels and lubricants, manufactured goods, chemicals, food and live animals, raw materials. **Major trading partners:** Bosnia and Herzegovina, Italy, the Former Yugoslav Republic of Macedonia, Germany, Russia.

**Geography** Serbia and Montenegro are about the size of the state of Kentucky and largely mountainous. The northeast section of Serbia is part of the rich, fertile Danubian Plain drained by the Danube, Tisa, Sava, and Morava River systems. Montenegro is a jumbled mass of mountains, containing also some grassy slopes and fertile river valleys.

**Government** The current federation is the third state to call itself by the name Yugoslavia, officially referring to itself as the Federal Republic of Yugoslavia. The United States, however, does not recognize it by that name because the U.S. does not consider the Serbian and Montenegrin federation the successor state of Yugoslavia. Serbia and Montenegro are a federal republic.

**History** Yugoslavia was formed on Dec. 4, 1918, from the patchwork of Balkan states and territories. World War I began there with the assassination of Archduke Franz Ferdinand of Austria at Sarajevo on June 28, 1914. The new kingdom of Serbs, Croats, and Slovenes included the former kingdoms of Serbia and

Montenegro; Bosnia-Herzegovina, previously administered jointly by Austria and Hungary; Croatia-Slavonia, a semiautonomous region of Hungary; and Dalmatia, formerly administered by Austria. King Peter I of Serbia became the first monarch; his son, Alexander I, succeeded him on Aug. 16, 1921. Croatian demands for a federal state forced Alexander to assume dictatorial powers in 1929 and to change the country's name to Yugoslavia. Serbian dominance continued despite his efforts, amid the resentment of other regions. A Macedonian associated with Croatian dissidents assassinated Alexander in Marseilles, France, on Oct. 9, 1934, and his cousin, Prince Paul, became regent for the king's son, Prince Peter.

Paul's pro-Axis policy brought Yugoslavia to sign the Axis Pact on March 25, 1941, and opponents overthrew the government two days later. On April 6 the Nazis occupied the country, and the young king and his government fled. Two guerrilla armies—the Chetniks under Draza Mihajlovic supporting the monarchy, and the Partisans under Tito (Josip Broz) leaning toward the USSR—fought the Nazis for the duration of the war. In 1943, Tito established an Executive National Committee of Liberation to function as a provisional government. Tito won the election held in the fall of 1945, as monarchists boycotted the vote. A new Assembly abolished the monarchy and proclaimed the Federal People's Republic of Yugoslavia, with Tito as prime minister. Tito ruthlessly eliminated the opposition and broke with the Soviet bloc in 1948. Yugoslavia followed a middle road, combining orthodox Communist control of politics and general overall economic policy with a varying degree of freedom in the arts, travel, and individual enterprise. Tito became president in 1953 and president-for-life under a revised constitution adopted in 1963.

After Tito's death on May 4, 1980, a rotating presidency designed to avoid internal dissension was put into effect immediately, and the feared clash of Yugoslavia's multiple nationalities and regions appeared to have been averted. In May 1991 Croatian voters supported a referendum calling for their republic to become an independent nation. A similar referendum passed in December in Slovenia. In June the respective Parliaments in both republics passed declarations of independence. Ethnic violence flared almost immediately. The largely Serbian-led Yugoslav military pounded breakaway Bosnia and Herzegovina, leading the UN Security Council in May 1992 to impose economic sanctions on the Belgrade government.

Despite rampant inflation reaching approximately 3,000% per month in Dec. 1993, the Serbian government of Slobodan Milosevic maintained its effective control over the rump Yugoslavia. Trade sanctions were lifted in Dec. 1995 following the signing of the Dayton Accords. In June 1996, the UN Security Council lifted its heavy weapons embargo. Large groups of demonstrators in 1996–97 engaged in several months of daily protests after Slobodan Milosevic refused to recognize opposition victories in local elections and in elections in Montenegro. Constitutionally barred from another term as president of Serbia, Milosevic became president of the Federal Republic of Yugoslavia (Serbia and Montenegro) in July 1997.

The situation in Serbia's provinces of Montenegro and Kosovo grew divisive in 1997 and 1998. In May 1998, Montenegro elected the reform-minded Milo Djukanovic as president. Not only was he an outspoken critic of Yugoslav president Milosevic but he has openly contemplated secession.

In Feb. 1998 the Yugoslav army and Serbian police began fighting against the separatist Kosovo Liberation Army, but their scorched-earth tactics were concentrated on ethnic Albanian civilians—Muslims who make up 90% of Kosovo's population. More than 900 Kosovars were killed in the fighting, and the hundreds of thousands forced to flee their homes were without adequate food and shelter. Although Serbs make up only 10% of Kosovo's population, the region figures strongly in Serbian nationalist mythology.

NATO was reluctant to intervene because Kosovo—unlike Bosnia in 1992—was legally a province of Yugoslavia. The proof of civilian massacres finally gave NATO the impetus to intervene for the first time ever in the dealings of a sovereign nation with its own people. In an Oct. 12, 1998, truce brokered by American diplomat Richard Holbrooke, and under the threat of a military air strike—for which there was little enthusiasm among several NATO countries—President Milosevic agreed to the withdrawal of military forces. Fighting continued, however, and neither side accepted Washington's proposal for the province—Kosovars demanded full independence while Serb leaders would agree only to limited autonomy.

After negotiations in Feb. and March 1999 went nowhere, on March 24, 1999, NATO began launching air strikes. Weeks of daily bombings destroyed significant Serbian military targets, yet Milosevic showed no signs of relenting. In fact, Serbian militia stepped up civilian massacres and deportations in Kosovo—by the end of the conflict, the UN high commissioner for refugees estimated that at least 850,000 people had fled Kosovo. The refugee crisis put a heavy burden on neighboring countries such as Albania and Macedonia. Many wondered whether the NATO strikes had actually exacerbated the violence. As effective as NATO airpower might be against Serbian targets, it was utterly helpless in preventing Serb soldiers and paramilitaries from wreaking havoc on Kosovo's civilians.

World opinion was divided over the effectiveness of conducting airstrikes without deploying ground troops, but NATO countries remained reluctant to do so, fearing that the inevitable casualties would dampen the public's support for troops on foreign soil. The initial reason NATO gave for involvement in Kosovo was to avoid a wider Balkan war, but once Serbia began accelerating its campaign of ethnic cleansing in Kosovo, NATO's reason for fighting changed to preventing a human rights calamity. Yet without a concomitant change in military strategy—sending in ground troops—many wondered whether there would be any Kosovars left to save. NATO's hesitation in committing to a land battle—and therefore putting its troops at greater risk—ultimately paid off. Serbia finally agreed to sign a UN-approved peace agreement with NATO on June 3, ending the 11-week war. As Serbian forces withdrew, a five-nation NATO peacekeeping force entered Kosovo and began monitoring the return of refugees. Russia complicated NATO's efforts by demanding a role as a peacekeeper yet refusing to answer to NATO. A new group of refugees, Kosovar's Serbs, began fleeing the province, fearing vengeance from ethnic Albanians. Milosevic, who was indicted as a war criminal by the UN tribunal for the deportation of ethnic Albanians from Kosovo, held fast to the presidency as opposition groups remained disorganized and focused on internecine politics.

In Feb. 2000 fighting broke out between Serbs and Albanians in Mitrovica, Kosovo. NATO peacekeepers struggled to contain the violence.

In Sept. 2000, federal elections in Yugoslavia formally ended the autocratic rule of Milosevic, who had entangled his country in almost continuous war, first

(1991–1995) and then in the Serbian province of Kosovo in 1998. Despite dragging Yugoslavia into economic collapse and relegating it to pariah status throughout much of the world, Milosevic had managed to hold fast to the presidency after the Kosovo debacle.

In the Sept. 24 elections, Vojislav Kostunica, a constitutional law professor and political outsider, won the presidency in spite of widespread reports of fraud and voter intimidation. When Milosevic refused to honor the results and demanded a runoff election, the country erupted in massive public demonstrations, ultimately forcing Milosevic to step down on Oct. 5. Milosevic's Socialist Party, with its monopoly on political clout, thereafter agreed to share power with the two opposition parties.

The U.S. and the European Union quickly lifted some economic sanctions against Yugoslavia, and the new government was recognized by Russia and China, both of whom had been strong allies of Milosevic's Socialist Party government. But Kostunica was quick to assert himself as a true-believing Serb nationalist with no plans for becoming the darling of the West. He faced a daunting task in revitalizing the nation's shattered economy and in rebuilding the infrastructure destroyed during the NATO bombing.

Milosevic was arrested on April 1, 2001, by Yugoslavian authorities and charged with corruption and abuse of power. The arrest of Milosevic prompted the U.S. to release $50 million in aid to Yugoslavia, which had been withheld pending cooperation on human rights abuses. In June Milosevic was turned over to the United Nations International Criminal Tribunal for the former Yugoslavia in The Hague, where he has been on trial throughout 2002, charged with crimes against humanity. The UN Security Council lifted the arms embargo on Yugoslavia in Sept. 2001, removing the last sanction by the international community against the country.

In March 2002, the nation agreed to form a new state, replacing Yugoslavia with a loose federation called Serbia and Montenegro. The agreement, ratified by the federal parliament in May, would allow Montenegro to hold a referendum on independence in three years' time. This new arrangement was made to placate Montenegro's restive stirrings for independence.

# Zaire

*SEE* CONGO, DEMOCRATIC REPUBLIC OF.

# Zambia

**REPUBLIC OF ZAMBIA**

**President:** Levy Mwanawasa (2002)
**Area:** 290,584 sq mi (752,614 sq km)
**Population (2002 est.):** 9,959,037 (growth rate: 1.9%); birth rate: 41.0/1000; infant mortality rate: 09.4/1000; density per sq mi: 34
**Capital:** Lusaka. **Largest cities (1997):** Lusaka, 1.6 million (1990 est.); Kitwe, 338,207; Ndola, 376,311; Chingola, 167,954. **Monetary unit:** Kwacha.
**Languages:** English (official) and local dialects.
**Ethnicity/race:** African 98.7%, European 1.1%, other 0.2%. **Religions:** Christian 50%–75%, Islam and Hindu 24$–49%, remainder indigenous beliefs.
**Literacy rate:** 73% (1990)
**Economic summary:** GDP/PPP (2000 est.): $8.5 billion, per capita $880. **Real growth rate:** 4%. **Inflation:** 27.3%. **Unemployment:** 50%. **Arable land:** 7%.
**Agriculture:** corn, sorghum, rice, peanuts, sunflower seed, vegetables, flowers, tobacco, cotton, sugarcane, cassava (tapioca); cattle, goats, pigs, poultry, milk, eggs, hides; coffee. **Labor force:** 3.4 million; agriculture 85%, industry 6%, services 9%. **Industries:** copper mining and processing, construction, foodstuffs, beverages, chemicals, textiles, fertilizer. **Natural resources:** copper, cobalt, zinc, lead, coal, emeralds, gold, silver, uranium, hydropower. **Exports:** $928 million (f.o.b., 2000 est.): copper, cobalt, electricity, tobacco. **Imports:** $1.05 billion (f.o.b., 2000 est.): machinery, transportation equipment, fuels, petroleum products, electricity, fertilizer; foodstuffs, clothing. **Major trading partners:** Japan, Saudi Arabia, India, Thailand, South Africa, U.S., Malaysia, UK, Zimbabwe.

**Geography** Zambia, a landlocked country in south-central Africa, is about one-tenth larger than Texas. It is surrounded by Angola, Zaire, Tanzania, Malawi, Mozambique, Zimbabwe, Botswana, and Namibia. The country is mostly a plateau that rises to 8,000 ft (2,434 m) in the east.

**Government** Republic.

**History** Early humans inhabited present-day Zambia between one and two million years ago. Today the country is made up almost entirely of Bantu-speaking peoples. Empire builder Cecil Rhodes obtained mining concessions in 1889 from King Lewanika of the Barotse and sent settlers to the area soon thereafter. The region was ruled by the British South Africa Company, which he established, until 1924, when the British government took over the administration.

From 1953 to 1964, Northern Rhodesia was federated with Southern Rhodesia and Nyasaland (now Malawi) in the Federation of Rhodesia and Nyasaland. On Oct. 24, 1964, Northern Rhodesia became the independent nation of Zambia.

Kenneth Kaunda, the first president, kept Zambia within the Commonwealth of Nations. The country's economy, dependent on copper exports, was threatened when Rhodesia declared its independence from British rule in 1965 and defied UN sanctions, which Zambia supported, an action that deprived Zambia of its trade route through Rhodesia. The U.S., Britain, and Canada organized an airlift in 1966 to ship gasoline into Zambia.

In 1972 Kaunda outlawed all opposition political parties. The world copper market collapsed in 1975. The Zambian economy was devastated—it had been the third-largest miner of copper in the world after the United States and Soviet Union.

With a soaring debt and inflation rate in 1991, riots took place in Lusaka, resulting in a number of killings. Mounting domestic pressure forced Kaunda to move Zambia toward multiparty democracy.

National elections on Oct. 31, 1991, brought a stunning defeat to long-serving President Kaunda and a repudiation of his persistent belief in a one-party state. The newly elected chief executive, Frederick Chiluba, called for sweeping economic reforms, including privatization and the establishment of a stock market. He was reelected in Nov. 1996. Chiluba declared martial law in 1997 and arrested Kaunda following a failed coup attempt. The 1999 slump in world copper prices depressed the economy since copper provides 80% of Zambia's export earnings.

In 2001 Chiluba contemplated changing the constitution to allow him to run for another presidential term. After protests he relented, and selected Levy Mwanawasa, a former vice president with whom he had fallen out, as his successor. Mwanawasa became president in Jan. 2002; opposition parties protested over alleged fraud. In June 2002, Mwanawasa, once seen as a pawn of Chiluba, accused the former president of stealing millions from the government while in office.

Although the country faced the threat of famine in 2002, the president refused to accept any international donations of food that had been genetically modified, which Mwanawasa considered "poison."

# Zimbabwe

**REPUBLIC OF ZIMBABWE**

**President:** Robert Mugabe (1987)
**Area:** 150,803 sq mi (390,580 sq km)
**Population (2002 est.):** 11,376,676 (growth rate: 0.1%); birth rate: 24.6/1000; infant mortality rate: 63.0/1000; density per sq mi: 75
**Capital and largest city (1992):** Harare, 1,184,169. **Other large cities:** Bulawayo, 621,000; Chitungwiza, 274,035. **Monetary unit:** Zimbabwean dollar.
**Languages:** English (official), Ndebele, Shona (85%).
**Ethnicity/race:** African 98% (Shona 71%, Ndebele 16%, other 11%), white 1%, mixed and Asian 1%.
**Religions:** Christian 25%, Animist 24%, Syncretic 50%. **Literacy rate:** 80% (1992)
**Economic summary:** GDP/PPP (2000 est.): $28.2 billion; per capita $2,500. **Real growth rate:** –6.1%. **Inflation:** 60%. **Unemployment:** 50%. **Arable land:** 7%. **Agriculture:** corn, cotton, tobacco, wheat, coffee, sugarcane, peanuts; cattle, sheep, goats, pigs. **Labor force:** 5.5 million (2000 est.); agriculture 66%, services 24%, industry 10% (1996 est.). **Industries:** mining (coal, gold, copper, nickel, tin, clay, numerous metallic and nonmetallic ores), steel, wood products, cement, chemicals, fertilizer, clothing and footwear, foodstuffs, beverages. **Natural resources:** coal, chromium ore, asbestos, gold, nickel, copper, iron ore, vanadium, lithium, tin, platinum group metals.
**Exports:** $1.8 billion (f.o.b., 2000 est.): tobacco 29%, gold 7%, ferroalloys 7%, cotton 5% (1999 est.).
**Imports:** $1.3 billion (f.o.b., 2000 est.): machinery and transport equipment 35%, other manufactures 18%, chemicals 17%, fuels 14% (1999 est.). **Major trading partners:** South Africa, UK, Malawi, Botswana, Japan, China, Germany, U.S.

**Geography** Zimbabwe, a landlocked country in south-central Africa, is slightly smaller than California. It is bordered by Botswana on the west, Zambia on the north, Mozambique on the east, and South Africa on the south.

**Government** Parliamentary democracy.

**History** The remains of early humans, dating back 500,000 years, have been discovered in present-day Zimbabwe. The land's earliest settlers, the Khoisan, date back to 200 B.C. After a period of Bantu domination, the Shona people ruled, followed by the Nguni and Zulu peoples. By the mid-19th century the descendants of the Nguni and Zulu, the Ndebele, had established a powerful warrior kingdom.

The first British explorers, colonists, and missionaries arrived in the 1850s, and the massive influx of foreigners led to the establishment of the territory Rhodesia, named after Cecil Rhodes of the British South Africa Company. In 1923, European settlers voted to become the self-governing British colony of Southern Rhodesia. After a brief federation with Northern Rhodesia and Nyasaland (now Malawi) in the post–World War II period, Southern Rhodesia (also known as Rhodesia) chose to remain a colony when its two partners voted for independence in 1963.

On Nov. 11, 1965, the conservative white-minority government of Rhodesia declared its independence from Britain. The country resisted the demands of black Africans, and Prime Minister Ian Smith withstood British pressure, economic sanctions, and guerrilla attacks to uphold white supremacy. On March 1, 1970, Rhodesia formally proclaimed itself a republic. Heightened guerrilla war and a withdrawal of South African military aid in 1976 marked the beginning of the collapse of Smith's 11 years of resistance.

Black nationalist movements were led by Bishop Abel Muzorewa of the African National Congress and Ndabaningi Sithole, who were moderates, and guerrilla leaders Robert Mugabe of the Zimbabwe African National Union (ZANU) and Joshua Nkomo of the Zimbabwe African People's Union (ZAPU), who advocated revolution.

On March 3, 1978, Smith, Muzorewa, Sithole, and Chief Jeremiah Chirau signed an agreement to transfer power to the black majority by Dec. 31, 1978. They constituted themselves an Executive Council, with chairmanship rotating but with Smith retaining the title of prime minister. Blacks were named to each cabinet ministry, serving as coministers with the whites already holding these posts. African nations and rebel leaders immediately denounced the action, but Western governments were more reserved, although none granted recognition to the new regime.

The white minority finally consented to hold multiracial elections in 1980, and Robert Mugabe won a landslide victory. The country achieved independence on April 17, 1980, under the name Zimbabwe. Mugabe eventually established a one-party socialist state, but by 1990 he had instituted multiparty elections and in 1991 deleted all references to Marxism-Leninism and scientific socialism from the constitution. Parliamentary elections in April 1995 gave Mugabe's party a stunning victory with 63 of the 65 contested seats, and in 1996 Mugabe won another six-year term as president.

One-third of Zimbabwe's arable land is owned by 4,000 white farmers. In Feb. 2000 President Mugabe's government lost a referendum on a constitutional amendment that would have allowed the seizure of this land without compensation. Despite the defeat, the government supported the land-taking. Veterans of Zimbabwe's war for independence in the 1970s began squatting on the land and attacking the whites in an effort to reclaim land taken under British colonization. Mugabe's support for the squatters and his repressive rule has led to foreign sanctions against Zimbabwe. Once heralded as a champion of the anticolonial movement, Mugabe is now viewed by much of the international community as an authoritarian responsible for egregious human rights abuses and for running the economy of his country into the ground.

On March 13, 2002, Mugabe was reelected president for another six years in a blatantly rigged election whose results were enforced by the president's militia. His opponent, Morgan Tsvangirai of the Movement for Democratic Change (MDC), was arrested and charged with treason.

In Aug. 2002, Mugabe ordered nearly 4,000 white commercial farmers to leave their land without compensation. Many of the farmers initially defied the order, but by October 90% of the farmers had been forced to leave.

# United Nations

## Preamble of the United Nations Charter

The Charter of the United Nations was adopted at the San Francisco Conference of 1945. The complete text is available on the UN website, www.un.org/aboutun/charter.

We the peoples of the United Nations determined to save succeeding generations from the scourge of war, which twice in our lifetime has brought untold sorrow to mankind, and

To reaffirm faith in fundamental human rights, in the dignity and worth of the human person, in the equal rights of men and women and of nations large and small, and

To establish conditions under which justice and respect for the obligations arising from treaties and other sources of international law can be maintained, and

To promote social progress and better standards of life in larger freedom, and for these ends

To practice tolerance and live together in peace with one another as good neighbors, and

To unite our strength to maintain international peace and security, and

To insure, by the acceptance of principles and the institution of methods, that armed force shall not be used, save in the common interest, and

To employ international machinery for the promotion of the economic and social advancement of all peoples, have resolved to combine our efforts to accomplish these aims.

Accordingly, our respective Governments, through representatives assembled in the city of San Francisco, who have exhibited their full powers found to be in good and due form, have agreed to the present Charter of the United Nations and do hereby establish an international organization to be known as the United Nations.

## Principal Organs of the United Nations

### Secretariat

This is the directorate on UN operations, apart from political decisions. The staff works under the secretary-general, whom it assists and advises.

**Secretaries-General**

Kofi Annan, Ghana, Jan. 1, 1997.

Boutros Boutros-Ghali, Egypt, Jan. 1, 1992–Dec. 31, 1996.

Javier Pérez de Cuéllar, Peru, Jan. 1, 1982–Dec. 31, 1991.

Kurt Waldheim, Austria, Jan. 1, 1972–Dec. 31, 1981.

U Thant, Burma (Myanmar), Nov. 3, 1961–Dec. 31, 1971.

Dag Hammarskjöld, Sweden, April 11, 1953–Sept. 17, 1961.

Trygve Lie, Norway, Feb. 1, 1946–April 10, 1953.

### General Assembly

The General Assembly is the world's forum for discussing matters affecting world peace and security, and for making recommendations concerning them. It has no power of its own to enforce decisions. It is composed of the 51 original member nations and those admitted since, a total of 189. On important questions including international peace and security, a two-thirds majority of those present and voting is required. Decisions on other questions are made by a simple majority. Emphasis is given on questions relating to international peace and security brought before it by any member, the Security Council, or nonmembers. It also maintains a broad program of international cooperation in economic, social, cultural, educational, and health fields, and for assisting in human rights and freedoms.

### International Court of Justice

The International Court of Justice is the UN's principal judicial organ. Based in The Hague, Netherlands, the Court pursues two primary objectives: (1) settling legal disputes submitted by states in accordance with international law, and (2) advising on legal questions brought by authorized international organs and agencies. The Court consists of 15 judges elected to nine-year terms by the United Nations General Assembly and the Security Council during independent sittings.

### Security Council

The Security Council is the primary instrument for establishing and maintaining international peace. Its main purpose is to prevent war by settling disputes between nations. Under the charter, the council is permitted to dispatch a UN force to stop aggression. All members must make endeavors to make available armed forces, assistance, and facilities to maintain international peace and security (*see* p. 900 for list of UN Peacekeeping Operations).

The Security Council has 15 members. There are five permanent members: the United States, the Russian Federation, Britain, France, and China; and 10 temporary members elected by the General Assembly for two-year terms, from five different regions of the world. Voting on procedural matters requires a nine-vote majority to carry. However, on questions of substance, the vote of each of the five permanent members is required. As of Jan. 2002, the ten elected nonpermanent members were Bulgaria, Cameroon, Colombia, Guinea, Ireland, Mauritius, Mexico, Norway, Singapore, and Syria.

## Economic and Social Council

This council is composed of 54 members elected by the General Assembly to three-year terms. It works under the authority of the General Assembly and seeks to promote progress in terms of higher standards of living, full employment, and economic and social viability; it also seeks solutions to international socioeconomic, health, and other problems through international and cultural cooperation. Finally, it advocates for the universal respect for and observance of human rights and fundamental freedoms for all.

## Trusteeship Council

The UN charter originally established the Trusteeship Council as a main organ of the UN and entrusted it with the administration of territories placed under the trusteeship system.

The Trusteeship Council suspended operations on Nov. 1, 1994, after the October independence of Palau, the last UN territory.

## UN Peacekeeping Missions

Since 1948 there have been 54 UN peacekeeping operations. 41 of these operations have been created by the United Nations Security Council in the last 12 years. Thus far, 123 nations have contributed personnel at various times; 89 are currently providing peacekeepers. As of May 31, 2002, the top contributors of military and civilian personnel to current missions were: Bangladesh (5,479), Pakistan (4,831), Nigeria (3,489), India (3,019), Ghana (2,489). In 2002, there were 15 peacekeeping operations underway.

## Current UN Peacekeeping Operations

| Region/Country | Duration | Region/Country | Duration |
|---|---|---|---|
| **AFRICA** | | **ASIA** | |
| Western Sahara | April 1991–present | India/Pakistan | Jan. 1949–present |
| Sierra Leone | Oct. 1999–present | East Timor | May 2002–present |
| Democratic Republic | Dec. 1999–present | **EUROPE** | |
| of the Congo | | Cyprus | March 1964–present |
| Ethiopia and Eritrea | July 2000–present | Georgia | Aug. 1993–present |
| **MIDDLE EAST** | | Bosnia & Herzegovina | Dec. 1995–present |
| Middle East | June 1948–present | Croatia | Feb. 1996–present |
| Golan Heights | June 1974–present | Kosovo | June 1999–present |
| Lebanon | March 1978–present | | |
| Iraq/Kuwait | April 1991–present | | |

## Completed UN Peacekeeping Operations

| Region/Country | Duration | Region/Country | Duration |
|---|---|---|---|
| **AFRICA** | | **AMERICAS** | |
| Congo | July 1960–June 1964 | Dominican Republic | May 1965–Oct. 1966 |
| Angola | Dec. 1988–May 1991 | Central America | Nov. 1989–Jan. 1992 |
| Namibia | April 1989–March 1990 | Observer Group | |
| Angola | May 1991–Feb. 1995 | El Salvador | July 1991–April 1995 |
| Somalia | April 1992–March 1993 | Haiti | Sept. 1993–June 1996 |
| Mozambique | Dec. 1992–Dec. 1994 | Haiti | July 1996–July 1997 |
| Somalia | March 1993–March 1995 | Guatemala | Jan.–May 1997 |
| Rwanda/Uganda | June 1993–Sept. 1994 | Haiti | Aug.–Nov. 1997 |
| Liberia | Sept. 1993–Sept. 1997 | Haiti | Dec. 1997–March 2000 |
| Rwanda | Oct. 1993–March 1996 | **ASIA** | |
| Chad/Libya | May–June 1994 | West New Guinea | Oct. 1962–April 1963 |
| Angola | Feb. 1995–June 1997 | India/Pakistan | Sept. 1965–March 1966 |
| Angola | June 1997–Feb. 1999 | Afghanistan/Pakistan | May 1988–March 1990 |
| Sierra Leone | July 1998–Oct. 1999 | Cambodia | Oct. 1991–March 1992 |
| Central African Republic | April 1998–Feb. 2000 | Cambodia | March 1992–Sept. 1993 |
| **MIDEAST** | | Tajikistan | Dec. 1994–May 2000 |
| Middle East—1st UN | Nov. 1956–June 1967 | East Timor | Oct. 1999–May 2002 |
| Emergency Force | | **EUROPE** | |
| Lebanon | June–Dec. 1958 | Former Yugoslavia | Feb. 1992–March 1995 |
| Yemen | July 1963–Sept. 1964 | Croatia | March 1995–Jan. 1996 |
| Middle East—2nd UN | Oct. 1973–July 1979 | Former Yugoslavia | March 1995–Feb. 1999 |
| Emergency Force | | Rep. of Macedonia | |
| Iran/Iraq | Aug. 1988–Feb. 1991 | Croatia | Jan. 1996–Jan. 1998 |
| | | Croatia | Jan. 1998–Oct. 1998 |

*Source:* United Nations Dept. of Public Information.

# Members of the United Nations (191 nations)

| Country | Joined UN[1] | Country | Joined UN[1] | Country | Joined UN[1] |
|---|---|---|---|---|---|
| Afghanistan | 1946 | Georgia | 1992 | Norway | 1945 |
| Albania | 1955 | Germany | 1973 | Oman | 1971 |
| Algeria | 1962 | Ghana | 1957 | Pakistan | 1947 |
| Andorra | 1993 | Greece | 1945 | Palau | 1994 |
| Angola | 1976 | Grenada | 1974 | Panama | 1945 |
| Antigua and Barbuda | 1981 | Guatemala | 1945 | Papua New Guinea | 1975 |
| Argentina | 1945 | Guinea | 1958 | Paraguay | 1945 |
| Armenia | 1992 | Guinea-Bissau | 1974 | Peru | 1945 |
| Australia | 1945 | Guyana | 1966 | Philippines | 1945 |
| Austria | 1955 | Haiti | 1945 | Poland | 1945 |
| Azerbaijan | 1992 | Honduras | 1945 | Portugal | 1955 |
| Bahamas | 1973 | Hungary | 1955 | Qatar | 1971 |
| Bahrain | 1971 | Iceland | 1946 | Romania | 1955 |
| Bangladesh | 1974 | India | 1945 | Russian Federation | 1945 |
| Barbados | 1966 | Indonesia | 1950 | Rwanda | 1962 |
| Belarus | 1945 | Iran | 1945 | St. Kitts and Nevis | 1983 |
| Belgium | 1945 | Iraq | 1945 | St. Lucia | 1979 |
| Belize | 1981 | Ireland | 1955 | St. Vincent and the | |
| Benin | 1960 | Israel | 1949 | Grenadines | 1980 |
| Bhutan | 1971 | Italy | 1955 | Samoa, Western | 1976 |
| Bolivia | 1945 | Jamaica | 1962 | San Marino | 1992 |
| Bosnia and Herzegovina | 1992 | Japan | 1956 | São Tomé and Príncipe | 1975 |
| Botswana | 1966 | Jordan | 1955 | Saudi Arabia | 1945 |
| Brazil | 1945 | Kazakhstan | 1992 | Senegal | 1960 |
| Brunei Darussalam | 1984 | Kenya | 1963 | Seychelles | 1976 |
| Bulgaria | 1955 | Kiribati | 1999 | Sierra Leone | 1961 |
| Burkina Faso | 1960 | North Korea | 1991 | Singapore | 1965 |
| Burma (Myanmar) | 1948 | South Korea | 1991 | Slovakia[4] | 1993 |
| Burundi | 1962 | Kuwait | 1963 | Slovenia | 1992 |
| Cambodia | 1955 | Kyrgyzstan | 1992 | Solomon Islands | 1978 |
| Cameroon | 1960 | Laos | 1955 | Somalia | 1960 |
| Canada | 1945 | Latvia | 1991 | South Africa | 1945 |
| Cape Verde | 1975 | Lebanon | 1945 | Spain | 1955 |
| Central African Republic | 1960 | Lesotho | 1966 | Sri Lanka | 1955 |
| Chad | 1960 | Liberia | 1945 | Sudan | 1956 |
| Chile | 1945 | Libya | 1955 | Suriname | 1975 |
| China[2] | 1945 | Liechtenstein | 1990 | Swaziland | 1968 |
| Colombia | 1945 | Lithuania | 1991 | Sweden | 1946 |
| Comoros | 1975 | Luxembourg | 1945 | Switzerland[6] | 2002 |
| Congo | 1960 | Macedonia[3] | 1993 | Syria | 1945 |
| Congo, Dem. Rep. | 1960 | Madagascar | 1960 | Tajikistan | 1992 |
| Costa Rica | 1945 | Malawi | 1064 | Tanzania | 1961 |
| Côte d'Ivoire | 1960 | Malaysia | 1957 | Thailand | 1946 |
| Croatia | 1992 | Maldives | 1965 | Togo | 1960 |
| Cuba | 1945 | Mali | 1960 | Tonga | 1999 |
| Cyprus | 1960 | Malta | 1964 | Trinidad and Tobago | 1962 |
| Czech Republic[4] | 1993 | Marshall Islands | 1991 | Tunisia | 1956 |
| Denmark | 1945 | Mauritania | 1961 | Turkey | 1945 |
| Djibouti | 1977 | Mauritius | 1968 | Turkmenistan | 1992 |
| Dominica | 1978 | Mexico | 1045 | Tuvalu | 2000 |
| Dominican Republic | 1945 | Micronesia | 1991 | Uganda | 1962 |
| East Timor[6] | 2002 | Moldova | 1992 | Ukraine | 1945 |
| Ecuador | 1945 | Monaco | 1993 | United Arab Emirates | 1971 |
| Egypt | 1945 | Mongolia | 1961 | United Kingdom | 1945 |
| El Salvador | 1945 | Morocco | 1956 | United States | 1945 |
| Equatorial Guinea | 1968 | Mozambique | 1975 | Uruguay | 1945 |
| Eritrea | 1993 | Namibia | 1990 | Uzbekistan | 1992 |
| Estonia | 1991 | Nauru | 1999 | Vanuatu | 1981 |
| Ethiopia | 1945 | Nepal | 1955 | Venezuela | 1945 |
| Fiji | 1970 | Netherlands | 1945 | Viet Nam | 1977 |
| Finland | 1955 | New Zealand | 1945 | Yemen, Republic of | 1947 |
| France | 1945 | Nicaragua | 1945 | Yugoslavia[5] | 2000 |
| Gabon | 1960 | Niger | 1960 | Zambia | 1964 |
| Gambia | 1965 | Nigeria | 1960 | Zimbabwe | 1980 |

1. The UN officially came into existence on Oct. 24, 1945. 2. On Oct. 25, 1971, the UN voted membership to the People's Republic of China, which replaced the Republic of China (Taiwan) in the world body. 3. The General Assembly on April 8, 1993, decided to admit the state provisionally being referred to as "The Former Yugoslav Republic of Macedonia" pending settlement of the difference that has arisen over its name. 4. Czechoslovakia was an original member of the United Nations from Oct. 24, 1945. As of Dec. 31, 1992, it ceased to exist and the Czech Republic and Slovakia as successor states were admitted Jan. 19, 1993. 5. The Socialist Federal Republic of Yugoslavia was a charter member; after its dissolution, the Federal Republic of Yugoslavia was admitted Nov. 1, 2000. 6. Newest members.

## U.S. Representatives to the United Nations

| Year | Ambassador | Year | Ambassador |
|---|---|---|---|
| 1946 | Edward R. Stettinius, Jr. | 1975–76 | Daniel P. Moynihan |
| 1946–47 | Herschel V. Johnson (acting) | 1976–77 | William W. Scranton |
| 1947–53 | Warren R. Austin | 1977–79 | Andrew Young |
| 1953–60 | Henry Cabot Lodge, Jr. | 1979–81 | Donald McHenry |
| 1960–61 | James J. Wadsworth | 1981–85 | Jeane J. Kirkpatrick |
| 1961–65 | Adlai E. Stevenson | 1985–89 | Vernon A. Walters |
| 1965–68 | Arthur J. Goldberg | 1989–92 | Thomas J. Pickering |
| 1968 | George W. Ball | 1992–93 | Edward J. Perkins |
| 1968–69 | James Russell Wiggins | 1993–96 | Madeleine K. Albright |
| 1969–71 | Charles W. Yost | 1997–98 | Bill Richardson |
| 1971–73 | George Bush | 1999–2001 | Richard Holbrooke |
| 1973–75 | John A. Scali | 2001– | John D. Negroponte |

## Selected International Organizations

### Arab League (AL)
*Members:* (21 plus the Palestine Liberation Organization) Algeria, Bahrain, Comoros, Djibouti, Egypt, Iraq, Jordan, Kuwait, Lebanon, Libya, Mauritania, Morocco, Oman, Qatar, Saudi Arabia, Somalia, Sudan, Syria, Tunisia, UAE, Yemen, Palestine Liberation Organization

### Association of Southeast Asian Nations (ASEAN)
*Members:* (10) Brunei, Burma, Cambodia, Indonesia, Laos, Malaysia, Philippines, Singapore, Thailand, Vietnam
*Observers:* (1) Papua New Guinea
*Consultative partners:* (2) China, Russia

### Group of 8 (G-8)
*Members:* (9) Canada, EU (as one member), France, Germany, Italy, Japan, Russia, UK, U.S.

### Commonwealth of Nations
*Members:* (53) Antigua and Barbuda, Australia, the Bahamas, Bangladesh, Barbados, Belize, Botswana, Brunei, Cameroon, Canada, Cyprus, Dominica, Fiji, the Gambia, Ghana, Grenada, Guyana, India, Jamaica, Kenya, Kiribati, Lesotho, Malawi, Malaysia, Maldives, Malta, Mauritius, Mozambique, Namibia, Nauru, New Zealand., Nigeria, Pakistan (suspended), Papua New Guinea, Saint Kitts and Nevis, Saint Lucia, Saint Vincent and the Grenadines, Samoa, Seychelles, Sierra Leone, Singapore, Solomon Islands, South Africa, Sri Lanka, Swaziland, Tanzania, Tonga, Trinidad and Tobago, Uganda, UK, Vanuatu, Zambia, Zimbabwe
*Special members:* (1) Tuvalu

### Commonwealth of Independent States (CIS)
*Members:* (12) Armenia, Azerbaijan, Belarus, Georgia, Kazakhstan, Kyrgyzstan, Moldova, Russia, Tajikistan, Turkmenistan, Ukraine, Uzbekistan

### European Union (EU)
*Members:* (15) Austria, Belgium, Denmark, Finland, France, Germany, Greece, Ireland, Italy, Luxembourg, Netherlands, Portugal, Spain, Sweden, UK
*Membership applicants:* (13) Bulgaria, Cyprus, Czech Republic, Estonia, Hungary, Latvia, Lithuania, Malta, Poland, Romania, Slovakia, Slovenia, Turkey

### North Atlantic Treaty Organization (NATO)
*Members:* (19) Belgium, Canada, Czech Republic, Denmark, France, Germany, Greece, Hungary, Iceland, Italy, Luxembourg, Netherlands, Norway, Poland, Portugal, Spain, Turkey, UK, U.S.

### African Union (AU)[1]
*Members:* (53) Algeria, Angola, Benin, Botswana, Burkina Faso, Burundi, Cameroon, Cape Verde, Central African Republic, Chad, Comoros, Congo, Democratic Republic of the Congo, Côte d'Ivoire, Djibouti, Egypt, Equatorial Guinea, Eritrea, Ethiopia, Gabon, The Gambia, Ghana, Guinea, Guinea-Bissau, Kenya, Lesotho, Liberia, Libya, Madagascar, Malawi, Mali, Mauritania, Mauritius, Mozambique, Namibia, Niger, Nigeria, Rwanda, São Tomé and Príncipe, Senegal, Seychelles, Sierra Leone, Somalia, South Africa, Sudan, Swaziland, Tanzania, Togo, Tunisia, Uganda, Western Sahara, Zambia, Zimbabwe

### Organization of Petroleum Exporting Countries (OPEC)
*Members:* (11) Algeria, Indonesia, Iran, Iraq, Kuwait, Libya, Nigeria, Qatar, Saudi Arabia, UAE, Venezuela

1. The Organization of African Unity (OAU), the African Union's predecessor, was formally disbanded on July 8, 2002. The AU was inaugurated July 9, 2002. The 53 member nations remain the same.

## Foreign Embassies in the United States

*Source:* U.S. Department of State

**Embassy of Afghanistan,** 200 L St., N.W., Suite 200, Washington, D.C. 20036. Phone: 202-416-1620.

**Embassy of the Republic of Albania,** 2100 S St., N.W., Washington, D.C. 20008. Phone: 202-223-4942.

**Embassy of the Democratic & Popular Republic of Algeria,** 2118 Kalorama Rd., N.W., Washington, D.C. 20008. Phone: 202-265-2800.

**Embassy of Andorra/Permanent Mission to the UN,** 2 United Nations Plaza, 25th flr. New York, N.Y. 10017. Phone: 212-750-8064.

**Embassy of the Republic of Angola,** 2100-2108 16th St., N.W., Washington, D.C. 20009. Phone: 202-785-1156.

**Embassy of Antigua & Barbuda,** 32 New Mexico Ave., N.W., Washington, D.C. 20016. Phone: 202-362-5122.

**Embassy of the Argentine Republic,** 1600 New Hampshire Ave., N.W., Washington, D.C. 20009. Phone: 202-238-6400.

**Embassy of the Republic of Armenia,** 2225 R Street, N.W., Washington, D.C. 20008. Phone: 202-319-1976.

**Embassy of Australia,** 1601 Massachusetts Ave., N.W., Washington, D.C. 20036. Phone: 202-797-3000.

**Embassy of Austria,** 3524 International Court, N.W., Washington, D.C. 20008-3027. Phone: 202-895-6700.

**Embassy of the Republic of Azerbaijan,** 2741 34th St., N.W., Washington, D.C. 20008. Phone: 202-337-3500.

**Embassy of the Commonwealth of the Bahamas,** 2220 Massachusetts Ave., N.W., Washington, D.C. 20008. Phone: 202-319-2660.

**Embassy of the Kingdom of Bahrain,** 3502 International Dr., N.W., Washington, D.C. 20008. Phone: 202-342-0741.

**Embassy of the People's Republic of Bangladesh,** 3510 International Drive, N.W., Washington, D.C. 20008. Phone: 202-244-0183.

**Embassy of Barbados,** 2144 Wyoming Ave., N.W., Washington, D.C. 20008. Phone: 202-939-9200 to 9202.

**Embassy of the Republic of Belarus,** 1619 New Hampshire Ave., N.W., Washington, D.C. 20009. Phone: 202-986-1604.

**Embassy of Belgium,** 3330 Garfield St., N.W., Washington, D.C. 20008. Phone: 202-333-6900.

**Embassy of Belize,** 2535 Massachusetts Ave., N.W., Washington, D.C. 20008. Phone: 202-332-9636.

**Embassy of the Republic of Benin,** 2124 Kalorama Road, N.W., Washington, D.C. 20008. Phone: 202-232-6656 to 6658.

**Embassy of Bolivia,** 3014 Massachusetts Ave., N.W., Washington, D.C. 20008. Phone: 202-483-4410.

**Embassy of Bosnia and Herzegovina,** 2109 E St. N.W., Washington, D.C. 20037. Phone: 202-337-1500.

**Embassy of Botswana,** 1531–1533 New Hampshire Ave., N.W., Washington, D.C. 20036. Phone: 202-244-4990.

**Brazilian Embassy,** 3006 Massachusetts Ave., N.W., Washington, D.C. 20008. Phone: 202-238-2700.

**Embassy of Brunei Darussalam,** 3520 International Court, N.W., Washington, D.C. 20008. Phone: 202-237-1838.

**Embassy of the Republic of Bulgaria,** 1621 22nd St., N.W., Washington, D.C. 20008. Phone: 202-387-0174.

**Embassy of Burkina Faso,** 2340 Massachusetts Ave., N.W., Washington, D.C. 20008. Phone: 202-332-5577.

**Embassy of the Union of Burma (Myanmar),** 2300 S St., N.W., Washington, D.C. 20008. Phone: 202-332-9044.

**Embassy of the Republic of Burundi,** 2233 Wisconsin Ave., N.W., Suite 212, Washington, D.C. 20007. Phone: 202-342-2574.

**Embassy of the Kingdom of Cambodia,** 1500 M St., N.W., Washington, D.C. 20011. Phone: 202-726-7742.

**Embassy of the Republic of Cameroon,** 2349 Massachusetts Ave., N.W., Washington, D.C. 20008. Phone: 202-265-8790.

**Embassy of Canada,** 501 Pennsylvania Ave., N.W., Washington, D.C. 20001. Phone: 202-682-1740.

**Embassy of the Republic of Cape Verde,** 3415 Massachusetts Ave., N.W., Washington, D.C. 20007. Phone: 202-965-6820.

**Embassy of Central African Republic,** 1618 22nd St. N.W., Washington, D.C. 20008. Phone: 202-483-7800.

**Embassy of the Republic of Chad,** 2002 R St., N.W., Washington, D.C. 20009. Phone: 202-462-4009.

**Embassy of Chile,** 1732 Massachusetts Ave., N.W., Washington, D.C. 20036. Phone: 202-785-1746.

**Embassy of the People's Republic of China,** 2300 Connecticut Ave., N.W., Washington, D.C. 20008. Phone: 202-328-2500 (to 2502).

**Embassy of Colombia,** 2118 Leroy Pl., N.W., Washington, D.C. 20008. Phone: 202-387-8338.

**Embassy of the Federal and Islamic Republic of Comoros,** c/o Permanent Mission of the Federal and Islamic Republic of Comoros to the United Nations, 420 E. 50th St., New York, N.Y. 10022. Phone: 212-972-8010.

**Embassy of the Democratic Republic of Congo,** 1800 New Hampshire Ave., N.W., Washington, D.C. 20009. Phone: 202-234-7690.

**Embassy of the Republic of Congo,** 4891 Colorado Ave., N.W., Washington, D.C. 20011. Phone: 202-726-0825.

**Embassy of Costa Rica,** 2114 S St., N.W., Washington, D.C. 20008. Phone: 202-234-2945.

**Embassy of the Republic of Côte d'Ivoire,** 2424 Massachusetts Ave., N.W., Washington, D.C. 20008. Phone: 202-797-0300.

**Embassy of the Republic of Croatia,** 2343 Massachusetts Ave., N.W., Washington, D.C. 20008-2853. Phone: 202-588-5899.

**Cuban Interests Section,** 2639 16th St., N.W., Washington, D.C. 20009. Phone: 202-797-0748.

**Embassy of the Republic of Cyprus,** 2211 R St. N.W., Washington, D.C. 20008. Phone: 202-462-5772.

**Embassy of the Czech Republic,** 3900 Spring of Freedom St., N.W., Washington, D.C. 20008. Phone: 202-274-9100.

**Royal Danish Embassy,** 3200 Whitehaven St., N.W., Washington, D.C. 20008. Phone: 202-234-4300.

**Embassy of the Republic of Djibouti,** 1156 15th St., N.W., Suite 515, Washington, D.C. 20005. Phone: 202-331-0270.

**Embassy of the Commonwealth of Dominica,** 3216 New Mexico Ave., N.W., Washington, D.C. 20016. Phone: 202-364-6781/2.

**Embassy of the Dominican Republic,** 1715 22nd St., N.W., Washington, D.C. 20008. Phone: 202-332-6280.

**Embassy of Ecuador,** 2535 15th St., N.W., Washington, D.C. 20009. Phone: 202-234-7200.

**Embassy of the Arab Republic of Egypt,** 3521 International Court, N.W., Washington, D.C. 20008. Phone: 202-895-5400.

**Embassy of El Salvador,** 2308 California St., N.W., Washington, D.C. 20008. Phone: 202-265-9671.

**Embassy of Equatorial Guinea,** 1712 I St., N.W., Suite 410, Washington, D.C. 20006. Phone: 202-296-4174.

**Embassy of the State of Eritrea,** 1708 New Hampshire Ave., N.W., Washington, D.C., 20009. Phone: 202-319-1991.

**Embassy of Estonia,** 1730 M St., N.W., Washington, D.C. 20036. Phone: 202-588-0101.

**Embassy of Ethiopia,** 3506 International Dr., N.W., Washington, D.C. 20008. Phone: 202-364-1200.

**European Union Delegation,** 2300 M St., N.W., Washington, D.C. 20037. Phone: 202-862-9500.

**Embassy of Fiji,** 2233 Wisconsin Ave., N.W., Suite 240, Washington, D.C. 20007. Phone: 202-337-8320.

**Embassy of Finland,** 3301 Massachusetts Ave., N.W., Washington, D.C. 20008. Phone: 202-298-5800.

**Embassy of France,** 4101 Reservoir Rd., N.W., Washington, D.C. 20007. Phone: 202-944-6000.

**Embassy of the Gabonese Republic,** 2034 20th St., N.W., Suite 200, Washington, D.C. 20009. Phone: 202-797-1000.

**Embassy of the Republic of the Gambia,** 1156 15th St., N.W., Suite 905, Washington, D.C. 20005-2076.

Phone: 202-785-1399.

**Embassy of the Republic of Georgia,** 1615 New Hampshire Ave., N.W., Suite 300, Washington, D.C. 20009. Phone: 202-387-2390.

**Embassy of Germany,** 4645 Reservoir Rd., N.W., Washington, D.C. 20007-1998. Phone: 202-298-4000.

**Embassy of Ghana,** 3512 International Dr., N.W., Washington, D.C. 20008. Phone: 202-686-4520 to 4026.

**Embassy of Greece,** 2221 Massachusetts Ave., N.W., Washington, D.C. 20008. Phone: 202-939-5800.

**Embassy of Grenada,** 1701 New Hampshire Ave., N.W., Washington, D.C. 20009. Phone: 202-265-2561.

**Embassy of Guatemala,** 2220 R St., N.W., Washington, D.C. 20008. Phone: 202-745-4952 to 4954.

**Embassy of the Republic of Guinea,** 2112 Leroy Pl., N.W., Washington, D.C. 20008. Phone: 202-483-9420.

**Embassy of the Republic of Guinea-Bissau,** 15929 Yunkon Lane, Rockville, Md. 20855. Phone: 301-947-3958.

**Embassy of Guyana,** 2490 Tracy Pl., N.W., Washington, D.C. 20008. Phone: 202-265-6900.

**Embassy of the Republic of Haiti,** 2311 Massachusetts Ave., N.W., Washington, D.C. 20008. Phone: 202-332-4090 to 4092.

**Apostolic Nunciature of the Holy See,** 3339 Massachusetts Ave., N.W., Washington, D.C. 20008. Phone: 202-333-7121.

**Embassy of Honduras,** 3007 Tilden St., N.W., Suite 4-M, Washington, D.C. 20008. Phone: 202-966-7702.

**Embassy of the Republic of Hungary,** 3910 Shoemaker St., N.W., Washington, D.C. 20008. Phone: 202-364-8218.

**Embassy of Iceland,** 1156 15th St., N.W., Suite 1200, Washington, D.C. 20005-1704. Phone: 202-265-6653 to 6655.

**Embassy of India,** 2107 Massachusetts Ave., N.W., Washington, D.C. 20008. Phone: 202-939-7000.

**Embassy of the Republic of Indonesia,** 2020 Massachusetts Ave., N.W., Washington, D.C. 20036. Phone: 202-775-5200.

**Iranian Interests Section,** 2209 Wisconsin Ave., N.W., Washington, D.C. 20007. Phone: 202-965-4990.

**Iraqi Interests Section,** 1801 P St., N.W., Washington, D.C. 20036. Phone: 202-483-7500.

**Embassy of Ireland,** 2234 Massachusetts Ave., N.W., Washington, D.C. 20008. Phone: 202-462-3939.

**Embassy of Israel,** 3514 International Dr., N.W., Washington, D.C. 20008. Phone: 202-364-5500.

**Embassy of Italy,** 3000 Whitehaven St., N.W., Washington, D.C. 20008. Phone: 202-612-4400.

**Embassy of Jamaica,** 1520 New Hampshire Ave., N.W., Washington, D.C. 20036. Phone: 202-452-0660.

**Embassy of Japan,** 2520 Massachusetts Ave., N.W., Washington, D.C. 20008. Phone: 202-238-6700.

**Embassy of the Hashemite Kingdom of Jordan,** 3504 International Dr., N.W., Washington, D.C. 20008. Phone: 202-966-2664.

**Embassy of the Republic of Kazakhstan,** (temporary) 1401 16th St., N.W., Washington, D.C. 20036. Phone: 202-232-5488.

**Embassy of the Republic of Kenya,** 2249 R St., N.W., Washington, D.C. 20008. Phone: 202-387-6101.

**Embassy of the Republic of Korea,** 2450 Massachusetts Ave., N.W., Washington, D.C. 20008. Phone: 202-939-5600.

**Embassy of the State of Kuwait,** 2904 Tilden St., N.W., Washington, D.C. 20008. Phone: 202-966-0702.

**Embassy of the Kyrgyz Republic,** 1732 Wisconsin Ave., Washington, D.C. 20007. Phone: 202-338-5141.

**Embassy of the Lao People's Democratic Republic,** 2222 S St., N.W., Washington, D.C. 20008. Phone: 202-332-6416.

**Embassy of Latvia,** 4325 17th St., N.W., Washington, D.C. 20011. Phone: 202-726-8213.

**Embassy of Lebanon,** 2560 28th St., N.W., Washington, D.C. 20008. Phone: 202-939-6300.

**Embassy of the Kingdom of Lesotho,** 2511 Massachusetts Ave., N.W., Washington, D.C. 20008. Phone: 202-797-5533 to 5536.

**Embassy of the Republic of Liberia,** 5201 16th St., N.W., Washington, D.C. 20011. Phone: 202-723-0437.

**Embassy of the Republic of Lithuania,** 2622 16th St., N.W., Washington, D.C. 20009. Phone: 202-234-5860.

**Embassy of Luxembourg,** 2200 Massachusetts Ave., N.W., Washington, D.C. 20008. Phone: 202-265-4171.

**Embassy of the Republic of Macedonia,** 3050 K St., N.W., Suite 210, Washington, D.C. 20007. Phone: 202-337-3063.

**Embassy of the Republic of Madagascar,** 2374 Massachusetts Ave., N.W., Washington, D.C. 20008. Phone: 202-265-5525, 5526.

**Embassy of Malawi,** Bristol House, 1400 20th Street, N.W., Washington, D.C. 20036. Phone: 202-223-4814.

**Embassy of Malaysia,** 2401 Massachusetts Ave., N.W., Washington, D.C. 20008. Phone: 202-328-2700.

**Embassy of the Republic of Mali,** 2130 R St., N.W., Washington, D.C. 20009. Phone: 202-332-2249.

**Embassy of Malta,** 2017 Connecticut Ave., N.W., Washington, D.C. 20008. Phone: 202-462-3611.

**Embassy of the Republic of the Marshall Islands,** 2433 Massachusetts Ave., N.W., Washington, D.C. 20008. Phone: 202-234-5414.

**Embassy of the Islamic Republic of Mauritania,** 2129 Leroy Pl., N.W., Washington, D.C. 20008. Phone: 202-232-5700, 5701.

**Embassy of the Republic of Mauritius,** 4301 Connecticut Ave., N.W., Suite 441, Washington, D.C. 20008. Phone: 202-244-1491.

**Embassy of Mexico,** 1911 Pennsylvania Ave., N.W., Washington, D.C. 20006. Phone: 202-728-1600.

**Embassy of the Federated States of Micronesia,** 1725 N St., N.W., Washington, D.C. 20036. Phone: 202-223-4383.

**Embassy of the Republic of Moldova,** 2101 S St., N.W., Washington, D.C. 20008. Phone: 202-667-1130, 1131, 1137.

**Embassy of Mongolia,** 2833 M St., N.W., Washington, D.C. 20007. Phone: 202-333-7117.

**Embassy of the Kingdom of Morocco,** 1601 21st St., N.W., Washington, D.C. 20009. Phone: 202-462-7979 to 7982, inclusive.

**Embassy of the Republic of Mozambique,** 1990 M St., N.W., Suite 570, Washington, D.C. 20036. Phone: 202-293-7146.

**Embassy of the Republic of Namibia,** 1605 New Hampshire Ave., N.W., Washington, D.C. 20009. Phone: 202-986-0540.

**Embassy of Nepal,** 2131 Leroy Pl., N.W., Washington, D.C. 20008. Phone: 202-667-4550.

**Embassy of the Netherlands,** 4200 Linnean Ave., N.W., Washington, D.C. 20008. Phone: 202-244-5300.

**Embassy of New Zealand,** 37 Observatory Circle, N.W., Washington, D.C. 20008. Phone: 202-328-4800.

**Embassy of Nicaragua,** 1627 New Hampshire Ave., N.W., Washington, D.C. 20009. Phone: 202-939-6570.

**Embassy of the Republic of Niger,** 2204 R St., N.W., Washington, D.C. 20008. Phone: 202-483-4224 to 4227, inclusive.

**Embassy of the Federal Republic of Nigeria,** 1333 16th St., N.W., Washington, D.C. 20036. Phone: 202-986-8400.

**Royal Embassy of Norway,** 2720 34th St., N.W., Washington, D.C. 20008. Phone: 202-333-6000.

**Embassy of the Sultanate of Oman,** 2535 Belmont Rd., N.W., Washington, D.C. 20008. Phone: 202-387-1980.

**Embassy of the Islamic Republic of Pakistan,** 2315 Massachusetts Ave., N.W., Washington, D.C. 20008. Phone: 202-939-6200.

**Embassy of the Republic of Palau,** 1150 18th St., N.W., #750, Washington, D.C. 20036. Phone: 202-452-6814.

**Embassy of the Republic of Panama,** 2862 McGill Terrace, N.W., Washington, D.C. 20008. Phone: 202-483-1407.

**Embassy of Papua New Guinea,** 1779 Massachusetts Ave., N.W., Suite 805, Washington, D.C. 20036. Phone: 202-745-3680.

**Embassy of Paraguay,** 2400 Massachusetts Ave., N.W., Washington, D.C. 20008. Phone: 202-483-6960.

**Embassy of Peru,** 1700 Massachusetts Ave., N.W., Washington, D.C. 20036. Phone: 202-833-9860 to 9869.

**Embassy of the Philippines,** 1600 Massachusetts Ave., N.W., Washington, D.C. 20036. Phone: 202-467-9300.

**Embassy of the Republic of Poland,** 2640 16th St., N.W., Washington, D.C. 20009. Phone: 202-234-3800 to 3802.

**Embassy of Portugal,** 2125 Kalorama Rd., N.W., Washington, D.C. 20008. Phone: 202-328-8610.

**Embassy of the State of Qatar,** 4200 Wisconsin Ave., N.W., Washington, D.C. 20016. Phone: 202-274-1600.

**Embassy of Romania,** 1607 23rd St., N.W., Washington, D.C. 20008. Phone: 202-332-2879.

**Embassy of the Russian Federation,** 2650 Wisconsin Ave., N.W., Washington, D.C. 20007. Phone: 202-298-5700.

**Embassy of the Republic of Rwanda,** 1714 New Hampshire Ave., N.W., Washington, D.C. 20009. Phone: 202-232-2882.

**Embassy of Saint Kitts and Nevis,** 3216 New Mexico Ave., N.W., Washington, D.C. 20016. Phone: 202-686-2636.

**Embassy of Saint Lucia,** 3216 New Mexico Ave., N.W., Washington, D.C. 20016. Phone: 202-364-6792 to 6795.

**Embassy of Saint Vincent and the Grenadines,** 3216 New Mexico Ave., N.W., Washington, D.C. 20016. Phone: 202-364-6730.

**Royal Embassy of Saudi Arabia,** 601 New Hampshire Ave., N.W., Washington, D.C. 20037. Phone: 202-337-4076/4134.

**Embassy of the Republic of Senegal,** 2112 Wyoming Ave., N.W., Washington, D.C. 20008. Phone: 202-234-0540, 0541.

**Embassy of the Republic of Seychelles,** 800 Second Ave., Suite 400C, New York, N.Y. 10017. Phone: 212-687-9766.

**Embassy of Sierra Leone,** 1701 19th St., N.W., Washington, D.C. 20009. Phone: 202-939-9261.

**Embassy of the Republic of Singapore,** 3501 International Pl., N.W., Washington, D.C. 20008. Phone: 202-537-3100.

**Embassy of the Slovak Republic,** 3523 International Court, N.W., Washington, D.C. 20008. Phone: 202-237-1054.

**Embassy of the Republic of Slovenia,** 1525 New Hampshire Ave., N.W., Washington, D.C. 20036. Phone: 202-667-5363.

**Embassy of the Republic of South Africa,** 3051 Massachusetts Ave., N.W., Washington, D.C. 20008. Phone: 202-232-4400.

**Embassy of Spain,** 2375 Pennsylvania Ave., N.W., Washington, D.C. 20037. Phone: 202-728-2330.

**Embassy of Sri Lanka,** 2148 Wyoming Ave., N.W., Washington, D.C. 20008. Phone: 202-483-4025 to 4028.

**Embassy of the Republic of the Sudan,** 2210 Massachusetts Ave., N.W., Washington, D.C. 20008. Phone: 202-338-8565.

**Embassy of the Republic of Suriname,** 4301 Connecticut Ave., N.W., Suite 460, Washington, D.C. 20008. Phone: 202-244-7488.

**Embassy of the Kingdom of Swaziland,** 3400 International Drive, N.W., Washington, D.C. 20008. Phone: 202-362-6683.

**Embassy of Sweden,** 1501 M St., N.W., Washington, D.C. 20005. Phone: 202-467-2600.

**Embassy of Switzerland,** 2900 Cathedral Ave., N.W., Washington, D.C. 20008. Phone: 202-745-7900.

**Embassy of the Syrian Arab Republic,** 2215 Wyoming Ave., N.W., Washington, D.C. 20008. Phone: 202-232-6313.

**The Republic of China on Taiwan,** 4201 Wisconsin Ave., N.W., Washington, D.C. 20016. Phone: 202-895-1800.

**Embassy of the United Republic of Tanzania,** 2139 R St., N.W., Washington, D.C. 20008. Phone: 202-884-1080.

**Royal Thai Embassy,** 1024 Wisconsin Ave., N.W., Washington, D.C. 20007. Phone: 202-944-3600.

**Embassy of the Republic of Togo,** 2208 Massachusetts Ave., N.W., Washington, D.C. 20008. Phone: 202-234-4212.

**Embassy of the Republic of Trinidad and Tobago,** 1708 Massachusetts Ave., N.W., Washington, D.C. 20036. Phone: 202-467-6490.

**Embassy of Tunisia,** 1515 Massachusetts Ave., N.W., Washington, D.C. 20005. Phone: 202-862-1850.

**Embassy of the Republic of Turkey,** 2525 Massachusetts Ave., N.W., Washington, D.C. 20008. Phone: 202-612-6700.

**Embassy of Turkmenistan,** 2207 Massachusetts Ave., N.W., Washington, D.C. 20008. Phone: 202-588-1500.

**Embassy of the Republic of Uganda,** 5911 16th St., N.W., Washington, D.C. 20011. Phone: 202-726-7100.

**Embassy of Ukraine,** 3350 M St., N.W., Washington, D.C. 20007. Phone: 202-333-0606.

**Embassy of the United Arab Emirates,** 3522 International Court, N.W., #300, Washington, D.C. 20008. Phone: 202-328-4536.

**United Kingdom of Great Britain & Northern Ireland—British Embassy,** 3100 Massachusetts Ave., N.W., Washington, D.C. 20008. Phone: 202-588-6500.

**Embassy of Uruguay,** 2715 M St., N.W., Washington, D.C. 20007. Phone: 202-331-1313.

**Embassy of the Republic of Uzbekistan,** 1746 Massachusetts Ave., N.W., Washington, D.C. 20036. Phone: 202-887-5300.

Embassy of the Republic of Venezuela, 1099 30th St., N.W., Washington D.C. 20007. Phone: 202-342-2214.

Embassy of the Socialist Republic of Vietnam, 1233 20th St., N.W., Suite 400, Washington, D.C. 20036. Phone: 202-861-0737.

Embassy of the Republic of Yemen, 2600 Virginia Ave., N.W., Suite 705, Washington, D.C. 20037. Phone: 202-965-4760.

Embassy of the Federal Republic of Yugoslavia, 2134 Kalorama Rd., N.W., Washington, D.C. 20008. Phone: 202-332-0333.

Embassy of the Republic of Zambia, 2419 Massachusetts Ave., N.W., Washington, D.C. 20008. Phone: 202-265-9717.

Embassy of the Republic of Zimbabwe, 1608 New Hampshire Ave., N.W., Washington, D.C. 20009. Phone: 202-332-7100.

## Diplomatic Personnel to and from the U.S.

| Country | U.S. Representative to[1] | Rank | Representative from[1] | Rank |
|---|---|---|---|---|
| Afghanistan | Robert P. Finn | Amb. | Haron Amin | Cd'A |
| Albania | Joseph Limprecht | Amb. | Fatos Tarifa | Amb. |
| Algeria | Janet A. Sanderson | Amb. | Idriss Jazairy | Amb. |
| Andorra | George Argyros | Amb. | Juli Minoves Triquell | Amb. |
| Angola | Christopher Dell | Amb. | Josefina Pitra Diakité | Amb. |
| Antigua and Barbuda[2] | Marcia Bernicat | Cd'A | Lionel Alexander Hurst | Amb. |
| Argentina | James D. Walsh | Amb. | Diego Ramiro Guelar | Amb. |
| Armenia | John M. Ordway | Amb. | Arman Kirakossian | Amb. |
| Australia | John Thomas Schieffer | Amb. | Michael J. Thawley | Amb. |
| Austria | Lyons Brown, Jr. | Amb. | Peter Moser | Amb. |
| Azerbaijan | Ross L. Wilson | Amb. | Hafiz Mir Jalal Pashayev | Amb. |
| Bahamas | Richard Blankenship | — | Joshua Sears | Amb. |
| Bahrain | Ronald Neumann | Amb. | Shaikh Khalifa Bin Ali Al-Khalifa | Amb. |
| Bangladesh | Mary Ann Peters | Amb. | Syed Hassan Almad | Amb. |
| Barbados[2] | Marcia Bernicat | Cd'A | Michael King | Amb. |
| Belarus | Michael G. Kozak | Amb. | Sergei A. Rachkov | Cd'A |
| Belgium | Stephen F. Brauer | Amb. | Alexis Reyn | Amb. |
| Belize | Russell Freeman | Amb. | Lisa Shoman | Amb. |
| Benin | Pamela Bridgewater | — | Lucien Tonoukouin | Amb. |
| Bolivia | V. Manuel Rocha | Amb. | Marlene Fernandez Del Granado | Amb. |
| Bosnia-Herzegovina | Clifford G. Bond | Amb. | Igor Davidovic | Amb. |
| Botswana | John E. Lange | Amb. | Kgosi Seepapitso IV | Amb. |
| Brazil | Donna Hrinak | Amb. | Rubens Antonio Barbosa | Amb. |
| Brunei | Sylvia Gaye Stanfield | Amb. | Pengiran Anak Dato Puteh | Amb. |
| Bulgaria | James W. Pardew | Amb. | Elena Poptodorova | Amb. |
| Burkina Faso | Jimmy J. Kolker | Amb. | Tertius Zongo | Amb. |
| Burma (Myanmar) | Priscilla A. Clapp | Cd'A | Linn Myaing | Amb. |
| Burundi | Mary C. Yates | Amb. | Thomas Ndikumana | Amb. |
| Cambodia | Kent M. Wiedemann | Amb. | Roland Eng | Amb. |
| Cameroon | George M. Staples | Amb. | Jerome Mendouga | Amb. |
| Canada | Paul Cellucci | Amb. | Michael Kergin | Amb. |
| Cape Verde | Michael D. Metelits | Amb. | Amilcar Spencer Lopes | Amb. |
| Central African Republic | Mattie Sharpless | Amb. | Emmanual Touaboy | Amb. |
| Chad | Christopher E. Goldthwait | Amb. | Ahmat Soubiane | Amb. |
| Chile | William R. Brownfield | Amb. | Andrés Bianchi | Amb. |
| China | Clark J. Randt, Jr. | Amb. | Yang Jiechi | Amb. |
| Colombia | Anne W. Patterson | Amb. | Luis Alberto Moreno | Amb. |
| Comoros | Bisa Williams | Cd'A | Ahmed Djabir | Amb. |
| Congo, Dem. Rep. of | Aubrey Hooks | Amb. | Faida Mitifu | Amb. |
| Congo, Rep. of | David H. Kaeuper | Amb. | Serge Mombouli | Amb. |
| Costa Rica | John J. Danilovich | Amb. | Jaime Daremblum | Amb. |
| Côte d'Ivoire | Arlene Render | Amb. | Moise Kaffi Koumove | Amb. |
| Croatia | Lawrence G. Rossin | Amb. | Ivan Grdesic | Amb. |
| Cuba | Vicki Huddleston | P.O. | — | — |
| Cyprus | Donald Bandler | Amb. | Erato Kozakou-Marcoullis | Amb. |
| Czech Republic | Craig R. Stapleton | Amb. | Martin Palous | Amb. |
| Denmark | Stuart Bernsein | Amb. | Ulrik Andreas Federspiel | Amb. |
| Djibouti | Donald Yamamoto | Amb. | Roble Olhaye | Amb. |
| Dominica[2] | Marcia Bernicat | Cd'A | Dr. Nicholas J. O. Liverpool | Amb. |
| Dominican Republic | Hans R. Hertell | Amb. | Roberto B. Saladin Selin | Amb. |
| East Timor | Shari Villarosa | Cd'A | — | — |
| Ecuador | Larry Palmer | Cd'A | Ivonne A-Baki | Amb. |
| Egypt | C. David Welch | Amb. | M. Nabil Fahmy | Amb. |
| El Salvador | Rose M. Likins | Amb. | Rene A. Rodriguez | Amb. |
| Equatorial Guinea | George M. Staples | Amb. | Micha Ondo Bile | Amb. |
| Eritrea | Donald McConnell | Amb. | Girma Asmerom | Amb. |
| Estonia | Joseph DeThomas | Amb. | Sven Juergenson | Amb. |

| Country | U.S. Representative to[1] | Rank | Representative from[1] | Rank |
|---|---|---|---|---|
| Ethiopia | Tibor P. Nagy | Amb. | Kassahun Ayele | — |
| EU Delegation | Rockwell Schnabel | Amb. | Günther Burghardt | Amb. |
| Fiji [3] | Robert McMullen | Cd'A | Napolioni Masirewa | Amb. |
| Finland | Bonnie McElveen-Hunter | Amb. | Jukka Valtasaari | Amb. |
| France | Howard A. Leach | Amb. | François Bujon de l'Estang | Amb. |
| Gabon | Kenneth P. Moorefield | Amb. | Paul Boundoukou-Latha | Amb. |
| Gambia, The | Jackson McDonald | Amb. | — | — |
| Georgia | Richard Miles | Amb. | Tedo Japaridze | Amb. |
| Germany | Daniel R. Coats | Amb. | Wolfgang Ischinger | Amb. |
| Ghana | Nancy Powell | Amb. | Alan Kyerematen | Amb. |
| Greece | Thomas J. Miller | Amb. | Alexander Philon | Amb. |
| Grenada[2] | Marcia Bernicat | Cd'A | Denis G. Antoine | Amb. |
| Guatemala | Prudence Bushnell | Amb. | Ariel Rivera | Amb. |
| Guinea | R. Barrie Walkley | Amb. | Mohamed Aly Thiam | Amb. |
| Guinea-Bissau | — | — | Mario Lopes Da Rosa | Amb. |
| Guyana | Ronald D. Godard | Amb. | Dr. Odeen Ishmael | Amb. |
| Haiti | Brian D. Curran | Amb. | Louis Harold Joseph | Cd'A |
| Holy See | Jim Nicholson | Amb. | Gabriel Montalvo | Pap. Nun. |
| Honduras | Frank Almaguer | Amb. | Dr. Hugo Noe Pino | Amb. |
| Hong Kong | Michael Klosson | C.G. | — | — |
| Hungary | Nancy Goodman Brinker | Amb. | Geza Jeszenszky | Amb. |
| Iceland | Barbara J. Griffiths | Amb. | Jon Baldvin Hannibalsson | Amb. |
| India | Robert D. Blackwill | Amb. | Lalit Mansingh | Amb. |
| Indonesia | Ralph L. Boyce | Amb. | Soemadi Djoko Moerdjono Bro-todiningrat | Amb. |
| Iran | — | — | Fariborz Jahansuzan[4] | — |
| Ireland | Richard Egan | Amb. | Sean O'Huiginn | Amb. |
| Israel | Daniel C. Kurtzer | Amb. | David Elekana Ivry | Amb. |
| Italy | Mel Sembler | Amb. | Ferdinando Salleo | Amb. |
| Jamaica | Sue McCourt Cobb | Amb. | Seymour Mullings | Amb. |
| Japan | Howard S. Baker | Amb. | Ryozo Kato | Amb. |
| Jordan | Edward Gnehm, Jr. | Amb. | Marwan Muasher | Amb. |
| Kazakhstan | Larry C. Napper | Amb. | Kanat Saudabayev | Amb. |
| Kenya | Johnnie Carson | Amb. | Yusuf A. Nzibo | Amb. |
| Kiribati, Republic of | Michael J. Senko | Amb. | — | — |
| Korea | Thomas C. Hubbard | Amb. | Sung-Chul Yang | Amb. |
| Kuwait | Richard H. Jones | Amb. | Muhammed Sabah Al Salim Al Sabah | Amb. |
| Kyrgyz Republic | John M. O'Keefe | Amb. | Baktybek Abdrisaev | Amb. |
| Laos | Douglas A. Hartwick | Amb. | Phanthong Phommahaxay | Amb. |
| Latvia | Brian E. Carlson | Amb. | Aivis Ronis | Amb. |
| Lebanon | Vincent Battle | Amb. | Farid Abboud | Amb. |
| Lesotho | Robert D. Loftis | Amb. | Dr. Lebohang K. Moleko | Amb. |
| Liberia | Bismarck Myrick | Amb. | William Bull | Amb. |
| Lithuania | John F. Tefft | Amb. | Vygaudas Usackas | Amb. |
| Luxembourg | Peter Terpeluk, Jr. | — | Arlette Conzemius | Amb. |
| Macedonia | Lawrence Butler | Amb. | Ljubica Z. Acevska | Amb. |
| Madagascar | Wanda L. Nesbitt | Amb. | Zina Andrianarivelo-Razafy | Amb. |
| Malawi | Roger A. Meece | Amb. | Paul T. S. Kandiero | Amb. |
| Malaysia | Marie T. Huhtala | Amb. | Dato' Sheikh Abdul Khalid Ghaz-zali | Amb. |
| Mali | Michael E. Ranneberger | Amb. | Cheick Oumar Diarrah | Amb. |
| Malta | Anthony Gioia | Amb. | George Saliba | Amb. |
| Marshall Islands | Michael J. Senko | Amb. | Banny de Brum | Amb. |
| Mauritania | John W. Limbert | Amb. | Mohamedou Ould Michel | Amb. |
| Mauritius | Bisa Williams | Cd'A | Chitmansing Jesseramsing | Amb. |
| Mexico | Jeffrey Davidow | Amb. | Juan José Bremer Martino | Amb. |
| Micronesia | Larry Miles Dinger | Amb | Jesse B. Marehalau | Amb. |
| Moldova | Pamela Hyde Smith | Amb. | Mihai Manoli | Amb. |
| Mongolia | John Dinger | Amb. | Jalbuu Choinhor | Amb. |
| Morocco | Margaret DeB. Tutwiler | Amb. | Abdullah Maaroufi | Amb. |
| Mozambique | Sharon Wilkinson | Amb. | Marcos Geraldo Namashulua | Amb. |
| Namibia | Kevin J. McGuire | Amb. | Leonard Nangolo Iipumbu | Amb. |
| Nepal | Michael Malinowski | Amb. | Tai Prataprana | Amb. |
| Netherlands | Clifford Sobel | Amb. | Boudewijn Johannes Van Eenennaam | Amb. |
| New Zealand | Charles J. Swindells | Amb. | John Wood | Amb. |
| Nicaragua | Oliver P. Garza | Amb. | Carlos Ulvert | Amb. |
| Niger | Barbro A. Owens-Kirkpatrick | Amb. | Joseph Diatta | Amb. |
| Nigeria | Howard Jeter | Amb. | Jibril Muhammad Aminu | Amb. |

| Country | U.S. Representative to[1] | Rank | Representative from[1] | Rank |
|---|---|---|---|---|
| Norway | John Doyle Ong | Amb. | Knut Vollbaek | Amb. |
| Oman | John Bruce Craig | Amb. | Abdulla Moh'd Aqeel Al Dhahab | Amb. |
| Pakistan | Marcy Powell | Cd'A. | Dr. Maleeha Lodhi | Amb. |
| Palau | Francis Ricciardone, Jr. | Amb. | Hersey Kyota | Amb. |
| Panama | Frederick A. Becker | Cd'A | Guillermo Alfredo Ford Boyd | Amb. |
| Papua New Guinea | Susan Jacobs | Amb. | Nagora Y. Bogan, KBE | Amb. |
| Paraguay | David N. Greenlee | Amb. | Leila Rachid | Amb. |
| Peru | John R. Hamilton | Amb. | Allan Wagner | Amb. |
| Philippines | Francis Ricciardone, Jr. | Amb. | Albert Del Rosario | Amb. |
| Poland | Christopher R. Hill | Amb. | Przemyslaw Grudzinski | Amb. |
| Portugal | John N. Palmer | Amb. | Joao Rocha Paris | Amb. |
| Qatar | Maureen Quinn | Amb. | Baderomar al-Dafa | Amb. |
| Romania | Michael Guest | Amb. | Sorin Ducaru | Amb. |
| Russia | Alexander Vershbow | Amb. | Yuriy Viktorovich Ushakov | Amb. |
| Rwanda | Margaret K. McMillion | Amb. | Dr. Richard Sezibera | Amb. |
| Saint Kitts and Nevis[2] | Marcia Bernicat | Cd'A | Osbert Liburd | Amb. |
| Saint Lucia[2] | Marcia Bernicat | Cd'A | Sonia Merlyn Johnny | Amb. |
| Saint Vincent and the Grenadines[2] | Marcia Bernicat | Cd'A | Ellsworth John | Amb. |
| Samoa, Western | Charles Swindells | Amb. | Tuiloma Slade | Amb. |
| São Tomé and Príncipe, Dem. Rep. of | James V. Ledesma | Amb. | Domingos Augusto Ferreira | Cd'A |
| Saudi Arabia | Robert Jordan | Amb. | H.R.H. Prince Bandar Bin Sultan | Amb. |
| Senegal | Harriet L. Elam-Thomas | Amb. | Mamadou Mansour Seck | Amb. |
| Serbia Montenegro | Richard Miles | Cd'A | — | — |
| Seychelles | Bisa Williams | Cd'A | Claude Morel | Amb. |
| Sierra Leone | Peter Chaveas | Amb. | John Ernest Leigh | Amb. |
| Singapore | Franklin Lavin | Amb. | Heng Chee Chan | Amb. |
| Slovakia | Ronald Weiser | Amb. | Martin Butora | Amb. |
| Slovenia | Johnny Young | Amb. | Davorin Kracun | Amb. |
| Solomon Islands | Arma Jane Karaer | Amb. | Jeremiah Manele | Cd'A |
| South Africa | Cameron R. Hume | Amb. | Sheila Sisulu | Amb. |
| Spain | George Argyros | Amb. | Javier Ruperez | Amb. |
| Sri Lanka | E. Ashley Wills | Amb. | Dr. Warnasena Rasaputram | Amb. |
| Sudan | Linda Clark | Amb. | Khidr Haroun | Cd'A |
| Suriname | Daniel A. Johnson | Amb. | Henry Illes | Amb. |
| Swaziland | James D. McGee | Amb. | Mary Madzandza Kanya | Amb. |
| Sweden | Charles Helmbold, Jr. | Amb. | Jan Eliasson | Amb. |
| Switzerland | Mercer Reynolds | Amb. | Christian Blickenstorfer | Amb. |
| Syria | Theodore Kattouf | Amb. | Dr. Rostom Al Zoubi | Cd'A |
| Tajikistan | Franklin Huddle | Amb. | Rashid Alimov | Amb. |
| Tanzania | Robert V. Royall | Amb. | Mustafa Salim Nyang'anyi | Amb. |
| Thailand | Darryl N. Johnson | Amb. | Sakthip Krairiksh | Amb. |
| Togo | Karl W. Hofmann | Amb. | Akoussou Lelou Bodjana | Amb. |
| Tonga | — | — | Sonatane T. T. Tupou | — |
| Trinidad and Tobago | Roy L. Austin | Amb. | Michael A. Arneaud | Amb. |
| Tunisia | Rust Deming | Amb. | Hatem Atallah | Amb. |
| Turkey | W. Robert Pearson | Amb. | O. Faruk Logoglu | Amb. |
| Turkmenistan | Laura E. Kennedy | Amb. | Meret Orazov | Amb. |
| Uganda | Martin G. Brennan | Amb. | Edith Grace Ssempala | Amb. |
| Ukraine | Carlos E. Pascual | Amb. | Kostyantyn Gryshchenko | Amb. |
| United Arab Emirates | Marcelle Wahba | Amb. | Asri Said Ahman Al-Dhariri | Amb. |
| United Kingdom | William Farish | Amb. | Sir Christopher Meyer | Amb. |
| Uruguay | Martin J. Silverstein | Amb. | Hugo Fernandez Faingold | Amb. |
| Uzbekistan | John Edward Herbst | Amb. | Shavkat S. Khamrakiilov | Amb. |
| Vanuatu | Arma Jane Karaer | Amb. | — | — |
| Venezuela | Charles S. Shapiro | Amb. | Luís Hererra Marcano | Cd'A |
| Vietnam | Raymond Burghardt | Amb. | Nguyen Tam Chien | Amb. |
| Yemen | Edmund J. Hull | Amb. | Abdulwahab Al-Hajjri | Amb. |
| Yugoslavia | William D. Mongtomery | Amb. | Ivan Zivkovic | Cd'A |
| Zambia | David B. Dunn | Amb. | Atan Shansonga | Amb. |
| Zimbabwe | Joseph G. Sullivan | Amb. | Simbi Yeke Mubako | Amb. |

1. As of June 2002. 2. The U.S. embassy in Barbados currently serves seven independent nations of the Eastern Caribbean (Barbados, Antigua and Barbuda, Dominica, Grenada, St. Kitts and Nevis, St. Lucia, and St. Vincent and the Grenadines) and provides consular services to American citizens in the nearby European dependent territories. 3. Ambassador to Fiji, Nauru; Tonga, and Tuvalu. 4. Head of Interests Section in U.S. NOTE: Amb.=Ambassador; Cd'A=Charge d'Affaires; C.G.=Consul General; Pap. Nun.=Papal Nuncio; P.O.=Principal Officer. *Source:* U.S. Department of State.

# The Olympic Games

| | | |
|---|---|---|
| 1896 Athens, Greece | 1948 St. Moritz, Switzerland (W) | 1980 Lake Placid, United States (W) |
| 1900 Paris, France | 1948 London, Great Britain (S) | 1980 Moscow, USSR (S) |
| 1904 St. Louis, United States | 1952 Oslo, Norway (W) | 1984 Sarajevo, Yugoslavia (W) |
| 1906 Athens, Greece | 1952 Helsinki, Finland (S) | 1984 Los Angeles, United States (S) |
| 1908 London, Great Britain | 1956 Cortina d'Ampezzo, Italy (W) | 1988 Calgary, Canada (W) |
| 1912 Stockholm, Sweden | 1956 Melbourne, Australia (S) | 1988 Seoul, South Korea (S) |
| 1920 Antwerp, Belgium | 1960 Squaw Valley, United States (W) | 1992 Albertville, France (W) |
| 1924 Chamonix, France (W) | 1960 Rome, Italy (S) | 1992 Barcelona, Spain (S) |
| 1924 Paris, France (S) | 1964 Innsbruck, Austria (W) | 1994 Lillehammer, Norway (W) |
| 1928 St. Moritz, Switzerland (W) | 1964 Tokyo, Japan (S) | 1996 Atlanta, United States (S) |
| 1928 Amsterdam, Netherlands (S) | 1968 Grenoble, France (W) | 1998 Nagano, Japan (W) |
| 1932 Lake Placid, United States (W) | 1968 Mexico City, Mexico (S) | 2000 Sydney, Australia (S) |
| 1932 Los Angeles, United States (S) | 1972 Sapporo, Japan (W) | 2002 Salt Lake City, United States (W) |
| 1936 Garmisch-Partenkirchen, | 1972 Munich, Germany (S) | 2004 Athens, Greece (S) |
|     Germany (W) | 1976 Innsbruck, Austria (W) | 2006 Turin, Italy (W) |
| 1936 Berlin, Germany (S) | 1976 Montreal, Canada (S) | 2008 Beijing, China (S) |

(W)—Site of Winter Games. (S)—Site of Summer Games

The first Olympic Games of which there is record were held in 776 B.C., and consisted of one event, a great foot race of about 200 yards held on a plain by the River Alpheus (now the Ruphia) just outside the little town of Olympia in Greece. It was from that date the Greeks began to keep their calendar by "Olympiads," the four-year spans between the celebrations of the famous games.

The modern Olympic Games, which started in Athens in 1896, are the result of the devotion of a French educator, Baron Pierre de Coubertin, to the idea that, since young people and athletics have gone together through the ages, education and athletics might go hand-in-hand toward a better international understanding.

The principal organization responsible for the staging of the Games is the International Olympic Committee (IOC). Other important roles are played by the National Olympic Committees in each participating country, international sports federations, and the organizing committee of the host city.

The Olympic motto is "Citius, Altius, Fortius,"— "Faster, Higher, Stronger." The Olympic symbol is five interlocking circles colored blue, yellow, black, green, and red, on a white background, representing the five continents. At least one of those colors appears in the national flag of every country.

Beginning in 1994, the IOC decided to change the format of having both the Summer and Winter Games in the same year. Summer and Winter Olympics now alternate every two years.

In Feb. 1998 the IOC announced that new sports added to the games must include women's events.

## Winter Games: Gold Medals

### FIGURE SKATING–MEN

| | |
|---|---|
| 1908 | Ulrich Salchow, Sweden |
| 1920 | Gillis Grafström, Sweden |
| 1924 | Gillis Grafström, Sweden |
| 1928 | Gillis Grafström, Sweden |
| 1932 | Karl Schäfer, Austria |
| 1936 | Karl Schäfer, Austria |
| 1948 | Dick Button, United States |
| 1952 | Dick Button, United States |
| 1956 | Hayes Alan Jenkins, United States |
| 1960 | David Jenkins, United States |
| 1964 | Manfred Schnelldorfer, Germany |
| 1968 | Wolfgang Schwarz, Austria |
| 1972 | Ondrej Nepela, Czechoslovakia |
| 1976 | John Curry, Great Britain |
| 1980 | Robin Cousins, Great Britain |
| 1984 | Scott Hamilton, United States |
| 1988 | Brian Boitano, United States |
| 1992 | Viktor Petrenko, Unified Team* |
| 1994 | Alexei Urmanov, Russia |
| 1998 | Ilia Kulik, Russia |
| 2002 | Alexei Yagudin, Russia |

*Former Soviet Union team.

### FIGURE SKATING–WOMEN

| | |
|---|---|
| 1908 | Madge Syers, Britain |
| 1920 | Magda Julin-Mauroy, Sweden |
| 1924 | Herma Planck-Szabó, Austria |
| 1928 | Sonja Henie, Norway |
| 1932 | Sonja Henie, Norway |
| 1936 | Sonja Henie, Norway |
| 1948 | Barbara Ann Scott, Canada |
| 1952 | Jeanette Altwegg, Great Britain |
| 1956 | Tenley Albright, United States |
| 1960 | Carol Heiss, United States |
| 1964 | Sjoukje Dijkstra, Netherlands |
| 1968 | Peggy Fleming, United States |
| 1972 | Beatrix Schuba, Austria |
| 1976 | Dorothy Hamill, United States |
| 1980 | Anett Pötzsch, East Germany |
| 1984 | Katarina Witt, East Germany |
| 1988 | Katarina Witt, East Germany |
| 1992 | Kristi Yamaguchi, United States |
| 1994 | Oksana Baiul, Ukraine |
| 1998 | Tara Lipinski, United States |
| 2002 | Sarah Hughes, United States |

## SPEED SKATING–MEN
### (U.S. winners only)

**500 Meters**

| | | |
|---|---|---|
| 1924 | Charles Jewtraw | 44.00 |
| 1932 | Jack Shea | 43.40 |
| 1952 | Ken Henry | 43.20 |
| 1964 | Terry McDermott | 40.10 |
| 1980 | Eric Heiden | 38.03 |
| 2002 | Casey FitzRandolph | 69.23[1] |

**1,000 Meters**

| | | |
|---|---|---|
| 1976 | Peter Mueller | 1:19.32 |
| 1980 | Eric Heiden | 1:15.18 |
| 1994 | Dan Jansen | 1:12.43[2] |

**1,500 Meters**

| | | |
|---|---|---|
| 1932 | Jack Shea | 2:57.50 |
| 1980 | Eric Heiden | 1:55.44 |
| 2002 | Derek Parra | 1:43.95[2] |

**5,000 Meters**

| | | |
|---|---|---|
| 1932 | Irving Jaffee | 9:40.80 |
| 1980 | Eric Heiden | 7:02.29 |

**10,000 Meters**

| | | |
|---|---|---|
| 1932 | Irving Jaffee | 19:13.60 |
| 1980 | Eric Heiden | 14:28.13 |

1. Combined time of two races. 2. World record.

## SPEED SKATING–WOMEN
### (U.S. winners only)

**500 Meters**

| | | |
|---|---|---|
| 1972 | Anne Henning | 43.33 |
| 1976 | Sheila Young | 42.76 |
| 1988 | Bonnie Blair | 39.10 |
| 1992 | Bonnie Blair | 40.33 |
| 1994 | Bonnie Blair | 39.25 |

**1,000 Meters**

| | | |
|---|---|---|
| 1992 | Bonnie Blair | 1:21.90 |
| 1994 | Bonnie Blair | 1:18.74 |
| 2002 | Chris Witty | 1:13.83[1] |

**1,500 Meters**

| | | |
|---|---|---|
| 1972 | Dianne Holum | 2:20.85 |

1. World record.

## SKIING, ALPINE–MEN

**Downhill**

| | | |
|---|---|---|
| 1948 | Henri Oreiller, France | 2:55.00 |
| 1952 | Zeno Colò, Italy | 2:30.80 |
| 1956 | Toni Sailer, Austria | 2:52.20 |
| 1960 | Jean Vuarnet, France | 2:06.00 |
| 1964 | Egon Zimmermann, Austria | 2:18.16 |
| 1968 | Jean-Claude Killy, France | 1:59.85 |
| 1972 | Bernhard Russi, Switzerland | 1:51.43 |
| 1976 | Franz Klammer, Austria | 1:45.73 |
| 1980 | Leonhard Stock, Austria | 1:45.50 |
| 1984 | Bill Johnson, United States | 1:45.59 |
| 1988 | Pirmin Zurbriggen, Switzerland | 1:59.63 |
| 1992 | Patrick Ortlieb, Austria | 1:50.37 |
| 1994 | Tommy Moe, United States | 1:45.75 |
| 1998 | Jean-Luc Cretier, France | 1:50.11 |
| 2002 | Fritz Strobl, Austria | 1:39.13 |

**Slalom**

| | | |
|---|---|---|
| 1948 | Edi Reinalter, Switzerland | 2:10.30 |
| 1952 | Othmar Schneider, Austria | 2:00.00 |
| 1956 | Toni Sailer, Austria | 3:14.70 |
| 1960 | Ernst Hinterseer, Austria | 2:08.90 |
| 1964 | Pepi Stiegler, Austria | 2:11.13 |
| 1968 | Jean-Claude Killy, France | 1:39.73 |
| 1972 | Francisco Ochoa, Spain | 1:49.27 |
| 1976 | Piero Gros, Italy | 2:03.29 |
| 1980 | Ingemar Stenmark, Sweden | 1:44.26 |
| 1984 | Phil Mahre, United States | 1:39.41 |
| 1988 | Alberto Tomba, Italy | 1:39.47 |
| 1992 | Finn Christian Jagge, Norway | 1:44.39 |
| 1994 | Thomas Stangassinger, Austria | 2:02.02 |

| | | |
|---|---|---|
| 1998 | Hans-Petter Buraas, Norway | 1:49.31 |
| 2002 | Jean-Pierre Vidal, France | 1:41.06 |

**Giant Slalom**

| | | |
|---|---|---|
| 1952 | Stein Eriksen, Norway | 2:25.00 |
| 1956 | Toni Sailer, Austria | 3:00.10 |
| 1960 | Roger Staub, Switzerland | 1:48.30 |
| 1964 | François Bonlieu, France | 1:46.71 |
| 1968 | Jean-Claude Killy, France | 3:29.28 |
| 1972 | Gustav Thöni, Italy | 3:09.62 |
| 1976 | Heini Hemmi, Switzerland | 3:26.97 |
| 1980 | Ingemar Stenmark, Sweden | 2:40.74 |
| 1984 | Max Julen, Switzerland | 2:41.18 |
| 1988 | Alberto Tomba, Italy | 2:06.37 |
| 1992 | Alberto Tomba, Italy | 2:06.98 |
| 1994 | Markus Wasmeier, Germany | 2:52.46 |
| 1998 | Hermann Maier, Austria | 2:38.51 |
| 2002 | Stephan Eberharter, Austria | 2:23.28 |

**Super Giant Slalom**

| | | |
|---|---|---|
| 1988 | Frank Piccard, France | 1:39.66 |
| 1992 | Kjetil Andre Aamodt, Norway | 1:13.04 |
| 1994 | Markus Wasmeier, Germany | 1:32.53 |
| 1998 | Hermann Maier, Austria | 1:34.84 |
| 2002 | Kjetil Andre Aamodt, Norway | 1:21.58 |

**Men's Combined (Downhill and Slalom)**

| | | Points |
|---|---|---|
| 1936 | Franz Pfnür, Germany | 99.25 |
| 1948 | Henri Oreiller, France | 3.27 |
| 1952–1984 | Not held | |
| 1988 | Hubert Strolz, Austria | 36.55 |
| 1992 | Josef Polig, Italy | 14.58 |

| | | Time |
|---|---|---|
| 1994 | Lasse Kjus, Norway | 3:17.53 |
| 1998 | Mario Reiter, Austria | 3:08.06 |
| 2002 | Kjetil Andre Aamodt, Norway | 3:17.56 |

## SKIING, ALPINE–WOMEN

**Downhill**

| | | |
|---|---|---|
| 1948 | Hedy Schlunegger, Switzerland | 2:28.30 |
| 1952 | Trude Jochum-Beiser, Austria | 1:47.10 |
| 1956 | Madeleine Berthod, Switzerland | 1:40.70 |
| 1960 | Heidi Biebl, Germany | 1:37.60 |
| 1964 | Christl Haas, Austria | 1:55.39 |
| 1968 | Olga Pall, Austria | 1:40.87 |
| 1972 | Marie-Theres Nadig, Switzerland | 1:36.68 |
| 1976 | Rosi Mittermaier, West Germany | 1:46.16 |
| 1980 | Annemarie Moser-Pröll, Austria | 1:37.52 |
| 1984 | Michela Figini, Switzerland | 1:13.36 |
| 1988 | Marina Kiehl, West Germany | 1:25.86 |
| 1992 | Kerrin Lee-Gartner, Canada | 1:52.55 |
| 1994 | Katja Seizinger, Germany | 1:35.93 |
| 1998 | Katja Seizinger, Germany | 1:28.89 |
| 2002 | Carole Montillet, France | 1:39.56 |

**Slalom**

| | | |
|---|---|---|
| 1948 | Gretchen Fraser, United States | 1:57.20 |
| 1952 | Andrea Mead Lawrence, United States | 2:10.60 |
| 1956 | Renée Colliard, Switzerland | 1:52.30 |
| 1960 | Anne Heggtveit, Canada | 1:49.60 |
| 1964 | Christine Goitschel, France | 1:29.86 |
| 1968 | Marielle Goitschel, France | 1:25.86 |
| 1972 | Barbara Cochran, United States | 1:31.24 |
| 1976 | Rosi Mittermaier, West Germany | 1:30.54 |
| 1980 | Hanni Wenzel, Liechtenstein | 1:25.09 |
| 1984 | Paoletta Magoni, Italy | 1:36.47 |
| 1988 | Vreni Schneider, Switzerland | 1:36.69 |
| 1992 | Petra Kronberger, Austria | 1:32.68 |
| 1994 | Vreni Schneider, Switzerland | 1:56.01 |
| 1998 | Hilde Gerg, Germany | 1:32.40 |
| 2002 | Janica Kostelic, Croatia | 1:46.10 |

**Giant Slalom**

| | | |
|---|---|---|
| 1952 | Andrea Mead Lawrence, United States | 2:06.80 |
| 1956 | Ossi Reichert, Germany | 1:56.50 |
| 1960 | Yvonne Rügg, Switzerland | 1:39.90 |
| 1964 | Marielle Goitschel, France | 1:52.24 |

1968  Nancy Greene, Canada ........................ 1:51.97
1972  Marie-Theres Nadig, Switzerland ......... 1:29.90
1976  Kathy Kreiner, Canada ....................... 1:29.13
1980  Hanni Wenzel, Liechtenstein ............... 2:41.66
1984  Debbie Armstrong, United States ......... 2:20.98
1988  Vreni Schneider, Switzerland .............. 2:06.49
1992  Pernilla Wiberg, Sweden ..................... 2:12.74
1994  Deborah Compagnoni, Italy ................. 2:30.97
1998  Deborah Compagnoni, Italy ................. 2:50.59
2002  Janica Kostelic, Croatia ...................... 2:30.01

**Super Giant Slalom**
1988  Sigrid Wolf, Austria ........................... 1:19.03
1992  Deborah Compagnoni, Italy ................. 1:21.22
1994  Diann Roffe-Steinrotter, United States ... 1:22.15
1998  Picabo Street, United States ............... 1:18.02
2002  Daniela Ceccarelli, Italy ..................... 1:13.59

**Combined (Downhill and Slalom)**    **Points**
1936  Christl Cranz, Germany ...................... 97.06
1948  Trude Beiser, Austria ......................... 6.58
1952-84 Not held
1988  Anita Wachter, Austria ....................... 29.25
1992  Petra Kronberger, Austria ................... 2.55
                                                          **Time**
1994  Pernilla Wiberg, Sweden ..................... 3:05.16
1998  Katja Seizinger, Germany ................... 2:40.74
2002  Janica Kostelic, Croatia ...................... 2:43.28

## ICE HOCKEY

**MEN**
| | | | |
|---|---|---|---|
| 1920 | Canada | 1976 | USSR |
| 1924 | Canada | 1980 | United States |
| 1928 | Canada | 1984 | USSR |
| 1932 | Canada | 1988 | USSR |
| 1936 | Great Britain | 1992 | Unified Team* |
| 1948 | Canada | 1994 | Sweden |
| 1952 | Canada | 1998 | Czech Republic |
| 1956 | USSR | 2002 | Canada |
| 1960 | United States | **WOMEN** | |
| 1964 | USSR | 1998 | United States |
| 1968 | USSR | 2002 | Canada |
| 1972 | USSR | | |

*Former Soviet Union team.

**2002 Men's Championship**
Canada 5, United States 2
**2002 Women's Championship**
Canada 3, United States 2

## FREESTYLE SKIING—MEN

**Moguls**
1992  Edgar Grospiron, France
1994  Jean-Luc Brassard, Canada
1998  Jonny Moseley, United States
2002  Janne Lahtela, Finland

**Aerials**
1994  Andreas Schoenbaechler, Switzerland
1998  Eric Bergoust, United States
2002  Ales Valenta, Czech Republic

## FREESTYLE SKIING—WOMEN

**Moguls**
1992  Donna Weinbrecht, United States
1994  Stine Lise Hattestad, Norway
1998  Tae Satoya, Japan
2002  Kari Traa, Norway

**Aerials**
1994  Lina Cherjazova, Uzbekistan
1998  Nikki Stone, United States
2002  Alisa Camplin, Australia

## DISTRIBUTION OF MEDALS
## 2002 WINTER OLYMPIC GAMES
(Salt Lake City, Utah)

| | Gold | Silver | Bronze | Total |
|---|---|---|---|---|
| Germany | 12 | 16 | 7 | 35 |
| United States | 10 | 13 | 11 | 34 |
| Norway | 11 | 7 | 6 | 24 |
| Canada | 6 | 3 | 8 | 17 |
| Austria | 2 | 4 | 10 | 16 |
| Russia | 6 | 6 | 4 | 16 |
| Italy | 4 | 4 | 4 | 12 |
| France | 4 | 5 | 2 | 11 |
| Switzerland | 3 | 2 | 6 | 11 |
| China | 2 | 2 | 4 | 8 |
| Netherlands | 3 | 5 | 0 | 8 |
| Finland | 4 | 2 | 1 | 7 |
| Sweden | 0 | 2 | 4 | 6 |
| Croatia | 3 | 1 | 0 | 4 |
| Korea | 2 | 2 | 0 | 4 |
| Bulgaria | 0 | 1 | 2 | 3 |
| Estonia | 1 | 1 | 1 | 3 |
| Great Britain | 1 | 0 | 2 | 3 |
| Australia | 2 | 0 | 0 | 2 |
| Czech Republic | 1 | 0 | 1 | 2 |
| Japan | 0 | 1 | 1 | 2 |
| Poland | 0 | 1 | 1 | 2 |
| Spain | 0 | 0 | 1 | 1 |
| Belarus | 0 | 0 | 1 | 1 |
| Slovenia | 0 | 0 | 1 | 1 |

## 2002 UNITED STATES MEDALISTS

**Alpine Skiing**
Men's Combined—SILVER—Bode Miller
Men's Giant Slalom—SILVER—Bode Miller

**Bobsleigh**
Four-Man—SILVER—Todd Hayes, Bill Schuffenhauer, Garrett Hines, Randy Jones
Four-Man—BRONZE—Mike Kohn, Doug Sharp, Brian Shimer, Dan Steele
Women—GOLD—Jill Bakken, Vonetta Flowers

**Figure Skating**
Women—GOLD—Sarah Hughes
Women—BRONZE—Michelle Kwan
Men—BRONZE—Timothy Goebel

**Freestyle Skiing**
Men's Aerials—SILVER—Joe Pack
Men's Moguls—SILVER—Travis Mayer
Women's Moguls—SILVER—Shannon Bahrke

**Hockey**
Men—SILVER—Tom Barrasso, Brian Rolston, Mike York, Tony Amonte, Chris Chelios, Chris Drury, Mike Dunham, Bill Guerin, Brett Hull, John LeClair, Brian Leetch, Mike Modano, Brian Rafalski, Jeremy Roenick, Gary Suter, Keith Tkachuk, Doug Weight, Scott Young, Tom Poti, Mike Richter, Phil Housley, Adam Deadmarsh, Aaron Miller
Women—Silver—Chris Bailey, Laurie Baker, Karyn Bye, Julie Chu, Natalie Darwitz, Sara DeCosta, Tricia Dunn, Cammi Granato, Courtney Kennedy, Andrea Kilbourne, Katie King, Shelley Looney, Sue Merz, Allison Mleczko, Tara Mounsey, Jenny Potter, Angela Ruggiero, Sara Tueting, Lyndsay Wall, Krissy Wendell

**Luge**
Men's Doubles—SILVER—Brian Martin, Mark Grimmette
Men's Doubles—BRONZE—Clay Ives

**Short Track Speed Skating**
Men's 1,000 m—SILVER—Apolo Anton Ohno
Men's 1,500 m—GOLD—Apolo Anton Ohno
Men's 500 m—BRONZE—Rusty Smith

**Skeleton**
Men—GOLD—Jim Shea
Women—GOLD—Tristan Gale
Women—SILVER—Lea Ann Parsley

**Snowboarding**
Men's Halfpipe—GOLD—Ross Powers
Men's Halfpipe—SILVER—Danny Kass

Men's Halfpipe—BRONZE—Jarret Thomas
Men's Parallel Giant Slalom—BRONZE—Chris Klug
Women's Halfpipe—GOLD—Kelly Clark

**Speed Skating**
Women's 1,000 m—GOLD—Chris Witty
Women's 1,000 m—BRONZE—Jennifer Rodriguez
Women's 1,500 m—BRONZE—Jennifer Rodriguez
Men's 1,000 m—BRONZE—Joey Cheek
Men's 1,500 m—GOLD—Derek Parra
Men's 500 m—GOLD—Casey FitzRandolph
Men's 500 m—BRONZE—Kip Carpenter
Men's 5,000 m—SILVER—Derek Parra

## Other 2002 Winter Olympic Games Champions

**Biathlon**
Men's 10 km Sprint—Ole Einar Bjoerndalen, Norway
Men's 12.5 km Pursuit—Ole Einar Bjoerndalen, Norway
Men's 20 km Individual—Ole Einar Bjoerndalen, Norway
Men's 4 × 7.5 km Relay—Norway
Women's 10 km Pursuit—Olga Pyleva, Russia
Women's 15 km Individual—Andrea Henkel, Germany
Women's 4 × 7.5 km Relay—Germany
Women's 7.5 km Sprint—Kati Wilhelm, Germany

**Bobsledding**
2-man—Germany
4-man—Germany
Women—United States

**Cross-Country Skiing**
Men's 10 km Free Pursuit—Johann Muehlegg, Spain
Men's 15 km Classical—Andrus Veerpalu, Estonia
Men's 30 km Free Mass Start—Johann Muehlegg, Spain
Men's 4 × 10 km Relay—Norway
Men's 50 km Classical—Mikhail Ivanov, Russia
Men's Sprint—Tor Arne Hetland, Norway
Women's 10 km Classical—Bente Skari, Norway
Women's 15 km Free Mass Start—Stefania Belmondo, Italy
Women's 30 km Classical—Gabriella Paruzzi, Italy
Women's 4 × 5 km Relay—Germany
Women's 5 km Free Pursuit—Olga Danilova, Russia
Women's Sprint—Julija Tchopalova, Russia

**Curling**
Men—Norway
Women—Germany

**Figure Skating**
Pairs—David Pelletier and Jamie Sale, Canada; Elena
  Berezhnaya and Anton Sikharulidze, Russia
Ice dancing—Marina Anissina and Gwendal Peizerat,
  France

**Skeleton**
Men—Jim Shea, United States
Women—Tristan Gale, United States

**Luge**
Men's Doubles—Germany
Men's Singles—Armin Zoeggeler, Italy
Women's Singles—Sylke Otto, Germany

**Nordic Combined**
Individual 15 km—Samppa Lajunen, Finland
Sprint 7.5 km—Samppa Lajunen, Finland
Team 4 × 5 km Relay—Finland

**Short Track Speed Skating**
Women's 1,000 km—Yang Yang (A), China
Women's 1,500 km—Gi-Hyun Ko, Korea
Women's 3,000 km Relay—Korea
Women's 500 m—Yang Yang (A), China
Men's 1,000 m—Steven Bradbury, Australia
Men'1 1,500 m—Apolo Anton Ohno, United States
Men's 500 m—Marc Gagnon, Canada
Men's 5,000 m Relay—Canada

**Ski Jumping**
Individual K120—Simon Ammann, Switzerland
Individual K90—Simon Ammann, Switzerland
Team K120-Germany

**Snowboarding**
Men's Halfpipe—Ross Powers, United States
Men' Parallel Giant Slalom—Philipp Schoch, Switzerland
Women's Halfpipe—Kelly Clark, United States
Women's Parallel Giant Slalom—Isabelle Blanc, France

**Speed Skating**
Women's 1,500 m—Anni Friesinger, Germany
Women's 3,000 m—Claudia Pechstein, Germany
Women's 500 m—Catriona LeMay Doan, Canada
Women's 5,000 m—Claudia Pechstein, Germany
Men's 1,000 m—Gerard van Velde, Netherlands
Men's 10,000 m—Jochem Uytdehaage, Netherlands
Men's 5,000 m—Jochem Uytdehaage, Netherlands

## Summer Games: Gold Medals

### TRACK AND FIELD—MEN

**100-Meter Dash**

| | | |
|---|---|---:|
| 1896 | Thomas Burke, United States | 12.00 |
| 1900 | Francis W. Jarvis, United States | 10.80 |
| 1904 | Archie Hahn, United States | 11.00 |
| 1906 | Archie Hahn, United States | 11.20 |
| 1908 | Reginald Walker, South Africa | 10.80 |
| 1912 | Ralph Craig, United States | 10.80 |
| 1920 | Charles Paddock, United States | 10.80 |
| 1924 | Harold Abrahams, Great Britain | 10.60 |
| 1928 | Percy Williams, Canada | 10.80 |
| 1932 | Eddie Tolan, United States | 10.30 |
| 1936 | Jesse Owens, United States | 10.30[1] |
| 1948 | Harrison Dillard, United States | 10.30 |
| 1952 | Lindy Remigino, United States | 10.40 |
| 1956 | Bobby Morrow, United States | 10.50 |
| 1960 | Armin Hary, Germany | 10.20 |
| 1964 | Robert Hayes, United States | 10.00 |
| 1968 | James Hines, United States | 09.90 |
| 1972 | Valery Borzow, USSR | 10.14 |
| 1976 | Hasely Crawford, Trinidad and Tobago | 10.06 |
| 1980 | Allan Wells, Britain | 10.25 |
| 1984 | Carl Lewis, United States | 09.99 |
| 1988 | Carl Lewis, United States | 09.92[2] |
| 1992 | Linford Christie, Great Britain | 09.96 |
| 1996 | Donovan Bailey, Canada | 09.84[3] |
| 2000 | Maurice Greene, United States | 09.87 |

1. Wind assisted. 2. Lewis was awarded the gold medal when Ben Johnson of Canada, the original winner in 09.79s, was stripped of the medal after testing positive for steroid use. 3. World record.

## 200-Meter Dash

| | | |
|---|---|---|
| 1900 | John Tewksbury, United States | 22.20 |
| 1904 | Archie Hahn, United States | 21.60 |
| 1908 | Robert Kerr, Canada | 22.60 |
| 1912 | Ralph Craig, United States | 21.70 |
| 1920 | Allan Woodring, United States | 22.00 |
| 1924 | Jackson Scholz, United States | 21.60 |
| 1928 | Percy Williams, Canada | 21.80 |
| 1932 | Eddie Tolan, United States | 21.20 |
| 1936 | Jesse Owens, United States | 20.70 |
| 1948 | Melvin E. Patton, United States | 21.10 |
| 1952 | Andrew Stanfield, United States | 20.70 |
| 1956 | Bobby Morrow, United States | 20.60 |
| 1960 | Livio Berruti, Italy | 20.50 |
| 1964 | Henry Carr, United States | 20.30 |
| 1968 | Tommie Smith, United States | 19.80 |
| 1972 | Vallery Borzov, USSR | 20.00 |
| 1976 | Don Quarrie, Jamaica | 20.23 |
| 1980 | Pietro Mennea, Italy | 20.19 |
| 1984 | Carl Lewis, United States | 19.80 |
| 1988 | Joe DeLoach, United States | 19.75 |
| 1992 | Mike Marsh, United States | 20.01 |
| 1996 | Michael Johnson, United States | 19.32[1] |
| 2000 | Konstantinos Kenteris, Greece | 20.09 |

1. World record.

## 400-Meter Dash

| | | |
|---|---|---|
| 1896 | Thomas Burke, United States | 54.20 |
| 1900 | Maxwell Long, United States | 49.40 |
| 1904 | Harry Hillman, United States | 49.20 |
| 1906 | Paul Pilgrim, United States | 53.20 |
| 1908 | Wyndham Halswelle, Great Britain (walkover) | 50.00 |
| 1912 | Charles Reidpath, United States | 48.20 |
| 1920 | Bevil Rudd, South Africa | 49.60 |
| 1924 | Eric Liddell, Great Britain | 47.60 |
| 1928 | Ray Barbuti, United States | 47.80 |
| 1932 | William Carr, United States | 46.20 |
| 1936 | Archie Williams, United States | 46.50 |
| 1948 | Arthur Wint, Jamaica, B.W.I. | 46.20 |
| 1952 | George Rhoden, Jamaica, B.W.I. | 45.90 |
| 1956 | Charles Jenkins, United States | 46.70 |
| 1960 | Otis Davis, United States | 44.00 |
| 1964 | Mike Larrabee, United States | 45.10 |
| 1968 | Lee Evans, United States | 43.80 |
| 1972 | Vincent Matthews, United States | 44.66 |
| 1976 | Alberto Juantorena, Cuba | 44.26 |
| 1980 | Viktor Markin, USSR | 44.60 |
| 1984 | Alonzo Babers, United States | 44.27 |
| 1988 | Steve Lewis, United States | 43.87 |
| 1992 | Quincy Watts, United States | 43.50 |
| 1996 | Michael Johnson, United States | 43.49 |
| 2000 | Michael Johnson, United States | 43.84 |

## 800-Meter Run

| | | |
|---|---|---|
| 1896 | Edwin Flack, Australia | 2:11.00 |
| 1900 | Alfred Tysoe, Great Britain | 2:01.40 |
| 1904 | James Lightbody, United States | 1:56.00 |
| 1906 | Paul Pilgrim, United States | 2:01.00 |
| 1908 | Mel Sheppard, United States | 1:52.80 |
| 1912 | Ted Meredith, United States | 1:51.90 |
| 1920 | Albert Hill, Great Britain | 1:53.40 |
| 1924 | Douglas Lowe, Great Britain | 1:52.40 |
| 1928 | Douglas Lowe, Great Britain | 1:51.80 |
| 1932 | Thomas Hampson, Great Britain | 1:49.80 |
| 1936 | John Woodruff, United States | 1:52.90 |
| 1948 | Malvin Whitfield, United States | 1:49.20 |
| 1952 | Malvin Whitfield, United States | 1:49.20 |
| 1956 | Tom Courtney, United States | 1:47.70 |
| 1960 | Peter Snell, New Zealand | 1:46.30 |
| 1964 | Peter Snell, New Zealand | 1:45.10 |
| 1968 | Ralph Doubell, Australia | 1:44.30 |
| 1972 | David Wottle, United States | 1:45.90 |
| 1976 | Alberto Juantorena, Cuba | 1:43.50 |
| 1980 | Steve Ovett, Britain | 1:45.40 |
| 1984 | Joaquin Cruz, Brazil | 1:43.00 |

| | | |
|---|---|---|
| 1988 | Paul Ereng, Kenya | 1:43.45 |
| 1992 | William Tanui, Kenya | 1:43.66 |
| 1996 | Vebjoern Rodal, Norway | 1:42.58 |
| 2000 | Nils Schumann, Germany | 1:45.08 |

## 1,500-Meter Run

| | | |
|---|---|---|
| 1896 | Edwin Flack, Australia | 4:33.20 |
| 1900 | Charles Bennett, Great Britain | 4:06.00 |
| 1904 | James Lightbody, United States | 4:05.40 |
| 1906 | James Lightbody, United States | 4:12.00 |
| 1908 | Mel Sheppard, United States | 4:03.40 |
| 1912 | Arnold Jackson, Great Britain | 3:56.80 |
| 1920 | Albert Hill, Great Britain | 4:01.80 |
| 1924 | Paavo Nurmi, Finland | 3:53.60 |
| 1928 | Harry Larva, Finland | 3:53.20 |
| 1932 | Luigi Becali, Italy | 3:51.20 |
| 1936 | Jack Lovelock, New Zealand | 3:47.80 |
| 1948 | Henri Eriksson, Sweden | 3:49.80 |
| 1952 | Joseph Barthel, Luxembourg | 3:45.20 |
| 1956 | Ron Delany, Ireland | 3:41.20 |
| 1960 | Herb Elliott, Australia | 3:35.60 |
| 1964 | Peter Snell, New Zealand | 3:38.10 |
| 1968 | Kipchoge Keino, Kenya | 3:34.90 |
| 1972 | Pekka Vasala, Finland | 3:36.30 |
| 1976 | John Walker, New Zealand | 3:39.17 |
| 1980 | Sebastian Coe, Britain | 3:38.40 |
| 1984 | Sebastian Coe, Britain | 3:32.53 |
| 1988 | Peter Rono, Kenya | 3:35.96 |
| 1992 | Fermin Cacho Ruiz, Spain | 3:40.12 |
| 1996 | Noureddine Morceli, Algeria | 3:35.78 |
| 2000 | Noah Ngeny, Kenya | 3:32.07 |

## 5,000-Meter Run

| | | |
|---|---|---|
| 1912 | Hannes Kolehmainen, Finland | 14:36.60 |
| 1920 | Joseph Guillemot, France | 14:55.60 |
| 1024 | Paavo Nurmi, Finland | 14:31.20 |
| 1928 | Willie Ritola, Finland | 14:38.00 |
| 1932 | Lauri Lehtinen, Finland | 14:30.00 |
| 1936 | Gunnar Hockert, Finland | 14:22.20 |
| 1948 | Gaston Reiff, Belgium | 14:17.60 |
| 1952 | Emil Zatopek, Czechoslovakia | 14:06.60 |
| 1956 | Vladimir Kuts, USSR | 13:30.60 |
| 1960 | Murray Halberg, New Zealand | 13:43.40 |
| 1964 | Bob Schul, United States | 13:48.80 |
| 1968 | Mohamed Gammoudi, Tunisia | 14:05.00 |
| 1972 | Lasse Viren, Finland | 13:26.40 |
| 1976 | Lasse Viren, Finland | 13:24.76 |
| 1980 | Miruts Yifter, Ethiopia | 13:21.00 |
| 1984 | Saud Aouita, Morocco | 13:05.59 |
| 1988 | John Ngugi, Kenya | 13:11.70 |
| 1992 | Dieter Baumann, Germany | 13:12.52 |
| 1996 | Venuste Niyongabo, Burundi | 13:07.96 |
| 2000 | Millon Wolde, Ethiopia | 13:35.49 |

## 10,000-Meter Run

| | | |
|---|---|---|
| 1912 | Hannes Kolehmainen, Finland | 31:20.80 |
| 1920 | Paavo Nurmi, Finland | 31:45.80 |
| 1924 | Willie Ritola, Finland | 30:23.20 |
| 1928 | Paavo Nurmi, Finland | 30:18.80 |
| 1932 | Janusz Kusocinski, Poland | 30:11.40 |
| 1936 | Ilmari Salminen, Finland | 00.15.40 |
| 1940 | Emil Zatopek, Czechoslovakia | 29:59.60 |
| 1952 | Emil Zatopek, Czechoslovakia | 29:17.00 |
| 1956 | Vladimir Kuts, USSR | 28:45.60 |
| 1960 | Peter Bolotnikov, USSR | 28:32.20 |
| 1964 | Billy Mills, United States | 28:24.40 |
| 1968 | Nartali Temu, Kenya | 29:27.40 |
| 1972 | Lasse Viren, Finland | 27:38.40 |
| 1976 | Lasse Viren, Finland | 27:40.38 |
| 1980 | Miruts Yifter, Ethiopia | 27:42.70 |
| 1984 | Alberto Cova, Italy | 27:47.50 |
| 1988 | Mly Brahim Boutaib, Morocco | 27:21.46 |
| 1992 | Khalid Skah, Morocco | 27:47.70 |
| 1996 | Haile Gebrselassie, Ethiopia | 27:07.34 |
| 2000 | Haile Gebrselassie, Ethiopia | 21:18.20 |

## Marathon

| | | |
|---|---|---|
| 1896 | Spiridon Loues, Greece | 2:58:50.00 |
| 1900 | Michel Teato, France | 2:59:45.00 |
| 1904 | Thomas Hicks, United States | 3:28:53.00 |
| 1906 | William J. Sherring, Canada | 2:51:23.65 |
| 1908 | John J. Hayes, United States | 2:55:18.40 |
| 1912 | Kenneth McArthur, South Africa | 2:36:54.80 |
| 1920 | Hannes Kolehmainen, Finland | 2:32:35.80 |
| 1924 | Albin Stenroos, Finland | 2:41:22.60 |
| 1928 | A.B. El Quafi, France | 2:32:57.00 |
| 1932 | Juan Zabala, Argentina | 2:31:36.00 |
| 1936 | Kitei Son, Japan | 2:29:19.20 |
| 1948 | Delfo Cabrera, Argentina | 2:34:51.60 |
| 1952 | Emil Zatopek, Czechoslovakia | 2:23:30.20 |
| 1956 | Alain Mimoun, France | 2:25:00.00 |
| 1960 | Abebe Bikila, Ethiopia | 2:15:16.20 |
| 1964 | Abebe Bikila, Ethiopia | 2:12:11.20 |
| 1968 | Mamo Wold, Ethiopia | 2:20:26.40 |
| 1972 | Frank Shorter, United States | 2:12:19.80 |
| 1976 | Walter Cierpinski, East Germany | 2:09:55.00 |
| 1980 | Walter Cierpinski, East Germany | 2:11:30.00 |
| 1984 | Carlos Lopes, Portugal | 2:09:21.00 |
| 1988 | Gelindo Bordin, Italy | 2:10:47.00 |
| 1992 | Hwang Young-Cho, South Korea | 2:13:23.00 |
| 1996 | Josia Thugwane, South Africa | 2:12:36.00 |
| 2000 | Gezahgne Abera, Ethiopia | 2:10:11.00 |

## 110-Meter Hurdles

| | | |
|---|---|---|
| 1896 | Thomas Curtis, United States | 17.60 |
| 1900 | Alvin Kraenzlein, United States | 15.40 |
| 1904 | Frederick Schule, United States | 16.00 |
| 1906 | R.G. Leavitt, United States | 16.20 |
| 1908 | Forrest Smithson, United States | 15.00 |
| 1912 | Frederick Kelly, United States | 15.10 |
| 1920 | Earl Thomson, Canada | 14.80 |
| 1924 | Daniel Kinsey, United States | 15.00 |
| 1928 | Sydney Atkinson, South Africa | 14.80 |
| 1932 | George Saling, United States | 14.60 |
| 1936 | Forrest Towns, United States | 14.20 |
| 1948 | William Porter, United States | 13.90 |
| 1952 | Harrison Dillard, United States | 13.70 |
| 1956 | Lee Calhoun, United States | 13.50 |
| 1960 | Lee Calhoun, United States | 13.80 |
| 1964 | Hayes Jones, United States | 13.60 |
| 1968 | Willie Davenport, United States | 13.30 |
| 1972 | Rodney Milburn, United States | 13.24 |
| 1976 | Guy Drut, France | 13.30 |
| 1980 | Thomas Munkett, East Germany | 13.20 |
| 1984 | Roger Kingdom, United States | 13.20 |
| 1988 | Roger Kingdom, United States | 12.98 |
| 1992 | Mark McCoy, Canada | 13.12 |
| 1996 | Allen Johnson, United States | 12.95 |
| 2000 | Anier Garcia, Cuba | 13.00 |

## 200-Meter Hurdles

| | | |
|---|---|---|
| 1900 | Alvin Kraenzlein, United States | 25.40 |
| 1904 | Harry Hillman, United States | 24.60 |

## 400-Meter Hurdles

| | | |
|---|---|---|
| 1900 | John Tewksbury, United States | 57.60 |
| 1904 | Harry Hillman, United States | 53.00 |
| 1908 | Charles Bacon, United States | 55.00 |
| 1920 | Frank Loomis, United States | 54.00 |
| 1924 | F. Morgan Taylor, United States | 52.60 |
| 1928 | Lord David Burghley, Great Britain | 53.40 |
| 1932 | Robert Tisdall, Ireland | 51.80[1] |
| 1936 | Glenn Hardin, United States | 52.40 |
| 1948 | Roy Cochran, United States | 51.10 |
| 1952 | Charles Moore, United States | 50.80 |
| 1956 | Glenn Davis, United States | 50.10 |
| 1960 | Glenn Davis, United States | 49.30 |
| 1964 | Rex Cawley, United States | 49.60 |
| 1968 | David Hemery, Great Britain | 48.10 |
| 1972 | John Akii-Bua, Uganda | 47.80 |
| 1976 | Edwin Moses, United States | 47.64 |
| 1980 | Volker Beck, East Germany | 48.70 |

| | | |
|---|---|---|
| 1984 | Edwin Moses, United States | 47.75 |
| 1988 | Andre Phillips, United States | 47.19 |
| 1992 | Kevin Young, United States | 46.78 |
| 1996 | Derrick Adkins, United States | 47.54 |
| 2000 | Angelo Taylor, United States | 47.50 |

1. Record not allowed.

## 2,500-Meter Steeplechase

| | | |
|---|---|---|
| 1900 | George Orton, United States | 7:34.00 |
| 1904 | James Lightbody, United States | 7:39.60 |

## 3,000-Meter Steeplechase

| | | |
|---|---|---|
| 1920 | Percy Hodge, Great Britain | 10:00.40 |
| 1924 | Willie Ritola, Finland | 09:33.60 |
| 1928 | Toivo Loukola, Finland | 09:21.80 |
| 1932 | Volmari Iso-Hollo, Finland | 10:33.40[1] |
| 1936 | Volmari Iso-Hollo, Finland | 09:03.80 |
| 1948 | Thure Sjoestrand, Sweden | 09:04.60 |
| 1952 | Horace Ashenfelter, United States | 08:45.40 |
| 1956 | Chris Brasher, Great Britain | 08:41.20 |
| 1960 | Zdzislaw Krzyskowiak, Poland | 08:34.20 |
| 1964 | Gaston Roelants, Belgium | 08:30.80 |
| 1968 | Amos Biwott, Kenya | 08:51.00 |
| 1972 | Kipchoge Keino, Kenya | 08:23.60 |
| 1976 | Anders Gardervd, Sweden | 08:08.02 |
| 1980 | Bronislaw Malinowski, Poland | 08:09.70 |
| 1984 | Julius Korir, Kenya | 08:11.80 |
| 1988 | Julius Karluki, Kenya | 08:05.51 |
| 1992 | Matthew Birir, Kenya | 08:08.84 |
| 1996 | Joseph Keter, Kenya | 08:07.12 |
| 2000 | Reuben Kosgei, Kenya | 08:21.43 |

1. About 3,450 meters-extra lap by error.

## 10,000-Meter Walk

| | | |
|---|---|---|
| 1912 | George Goulding, Canada | 46:28.40 |
| 1920 | Ugo Frigerio, Italy | 48:06.20 |
| 1924 | Ugo Frigerio, Italy | 47:49.00 |
| 1948 | John Mikaelsson, Sweden | 45:13.20 |
| 1952 | John Mikaelsson, Sweden | 45:02.80 |

## 20,000-Meter Walk

| | | |
|---|---|---|
| 1956 | Leonid Spirin, USSR | 1:31:27.40 |
| 1960 | Vladimir Golubnichy, USSR | 1:34:07.20 |
| 1964 | Ken Mathews, Great Britain | 1:29:34.00 |
| 1968 | Vladimir Golubnichy, USSR | 1:33:58.40 |
| 1972 | Peter Frenkel, East Germany | 1:26:42.40 |
| 1976 | Daniel Bautista, Mexico | 1:24:40.60 |
| 1980 | Maurizio Damiliano, Italy | 1:23:35.50 |
| 1984 | Ernesto Conto, Mexico | 1:23.13.00 |
| 1988 | Jozef Pribilinec, Czechoslovakia | 1:19:57.00 |
| 1992 | Daniel Plaza, Spain | 1:21:45.00 |
| 1996 | Jefferson Perez, Ecuador | 1:20:07.00 |
| 2000 | Robert Korzeniowski, Poland | 1:18.59.00 |

## 50,000-Meter Walk

| | | |
|---|---|---|
| 1932 | Thomas W. Green, Great Britain | 4:50:10.00 |
| 1936 | Harold Whitlock, Great Britain | 4:30:41.10 |
| 1948 | John Ljunggren, Sweden | 4:41:52.00 |
| 1952 | Giuseppe Dordoni, Italy | 4:28:07.80 |
| 1956 | Norman Read, New Zealand | 4:30:42.80 |
| 1960 | Donald Thompson, Great Britain | 4:25:30.00 |
| 1964 | Abdon Pamich, Italy | 4:11:12.40 |
| 1968 | Christoph Hohne, East Germany | 4:20:13.60 |
| 1972 | Bern Kannernberg, West Germany | 3:56:11.60 |
| 1980 | Hartwig Guader, East Germany | 3:49:24.00 |
| 1984 | Raul Gonzalez, Mexico | 3:37:26.00 |
| 1988 | Viacheslau Ivanenko, USSR | 3:48:29.00 |
| 1992 | Andrei Perlov, Unified Team[1] | 3:50:13.00 |
| 1996 | Robert Korzeniowski, Poland | 3:43:30.00 |
| 2000 | Robert Korzeniowski, Poland | 3:42.22.00 |

1. Former Soviet Union team.

## 400-Meter Relay (4x100)

| | | |
|---|---|---|
| 1912 | Great Britain | 42.40 |
| 1920 | United States | 42.20 |
| 1924 | United States | 41.00 |
| 1928 | United States | 41.00 |
| 1932 | United States | 40.00 |
| 1936 | United States | 39.80 |

| | | |
|---|---|---|
| 1948 | United States | 40.60 |
| 1952 | United States | 40.10 |
| 1956 | United States | 39.50 |
| 1960 | Germany | 39.50 |
| 1964 | United States | 39.00 |
| 1968 | United States | 38.20 |
| 1972 | United States | 38.19 |
| 1976 | United States | 38.33 |
| 1980 | USSR | 38.26 |
| 1984 | United States | 37.83 |
| 1988 | USSR | 38.19 |
| 1992 | United States | 37.40[1] |
| 1996 | Canada | 37.69 |
| 2000 | United States | 37.61 |

1. World record.

## 1,600-Meter Relay (4x400)

| | | |
|---|---|---|
| 1912 | United States | 3:16.60 |
| 1920 | Great Britain | 3:22.20 |
| 1924 | United States | 3:16.00 |
| 1928 | United States | 3:14.20 |
| 1932 | United States | 3:08.20 |
| 1936 | Great Britain | 3:09.00 |
| 1948 | United States | 3:10.40 |
| 1952 | Jamaica, B.W.I. | 3:03.90 |
| 1956 | United States | 3:04.80 |
| 1960 | United States | 3:02.20 |
| 1964 | United States | 3:00.70 |
| 1968 | United States | 2:56.10 |
| 1972 | Kenya | 2:59.80 |
| 1976 | United States | 2:58.65 |
| 1980 | USSR | 3:01.10 |
| 1984 | United States | 2:57.91 |
| 1988 | United States | 2:56.16 |
| 1992 | United States | 2:55.74[1] |
| 1996 | United States | 2:55.99 |
| 2000 | United States | 2:56.35 |

1. World record.

## Team Race

| | | Pts |
|---|---|---|
| 1900 | Great Britain (5,000 meters) | 26 |
| 1904 | United States (4 miles) | 27 |
| 1908 | Great Britain (3 miles) | 6 |
| 1912 | United States (3,000 meters) | 9 |
| 1920 | United States (3,000 meters) | 10 |
| 1924 | Finland (3,000 meters) | 9 |

## Standing High Jump

| | | |
|---|---|---|
| 1900 | Ray Ewry, United States | 5 ft 5 in |
| 1904 | Ray Ewry, United States | 4 ft 11 in |
| 1906 | Ray Ewry, United States | 5 ft 1⅝ in |
| 1908 | Ray Ewry, United States | 5 ft 2 in |
| 1912 | Platt Adams, United States | 5 ft 4⅛ in |

## Running High Jump

| | | |
|---|---|---|
| 1896 | Ellery Clark, United States | 5 ft 11¼ in |
| 1900 | Irving Baxter, United States | 6 ft 2¾ in |
| 1904 | Samuel Jones, United States | 5 ft 11 in |
| 1906 | Con Leahy, Ireland | 5 ft 9⅞ in |
| 1908 | Harry Porter, United States | 6 ft 3 in |
| 1912 | Alma Richards, United States | 6 ft 4 in |
| 1920 | Richmond Landon, United States | 6 ft 4¼ in |
| 1924 | Harold Osborn, United States | 6 ft 5¹⁵⁄₁₆ in |
| 1928 | Robert W. King, United States | 6 ft 4⅜ in |
| 1932 | Duncan McNaughton, Canada | 6 ft 5⅝ in |
| 1936 | Cornelius Johnson, United States | 6 ft 7¹⁵⁄₁₆ in |
| 1948 | John Winter, Australia | 6 ft 6 in |
| 1952 | Walter David, United States | 6 ft 8¹⁵⁄₁₆ in |
| 1956 | Charles Damas, United States | 6 ft 11¼ in |
| 1960 | Robert Shavlakadze, USSR | 7 ft 1 in |
| 1964 | Valeri Brumel, USSR | 7 ft 1¾ in |
| 1968 | Dick Fosbury, United States | 7 ft 4¼ in |
| 1972 | Yuri Tarmak, USSR | 7 ft 3¾ in |
| 1976 | Jacek Wszola, Poland | 7 ft 4½ in |
| 1980 | Gerd Wessig, East Germany | 7 ft 8¾ in |
| 1984 | Dietmar Mogenburg, West Germany | 7 ft 8½ in |
| 1988 | Guennadi Avdeenko, USSR | 7 ft ½ in |

| | | |
|---|---|---|
| 1992 | Javier Sotomayor, Cuba | 7 ft 8½ in |
| 1996 | Charles Austin, United States | 7 ft 10 in |
| 2000 | Sergey Kliugin, Russia | 7 ft 8½ in |

## Long Jump

| | | |
|---|---|---|
| 1896 | Ellery Clark, United States | 20 ft 9¾ in |
| 1900 | Alvin Kraenzlein, United States | 23 ft 6⅞ in |
| 1904 | Myer Prinstein, United States | 24 ft 1 in |
| 1906 | Myer Prinstein, United States | 23 ft 7½ in |
| 1908 | Frank Irons, United States | 24 ft 6½ in |
| 1912 | Albert Gutterson, United States | 24 ft 11¼ in |
| 1920 | William Petterssen, Sweden | 23 ft 5½ in |
| 1924 | DeHart Hubbard, United States | 24 ft 5⅛ in |
| 1928 | Edward B. Hamm, United States | 25 ft 4¾ in |
| 1932 | Edward Gordon, United States | 25 ft ¾ in |
| 1936 | Jesse Owens, United States | 26 ft 5⁵⁄₁₆ in |
| 1948 | Willie Steele, United States | 25 ft 8 in |
| 1952 | Jerome Biffle, United States | 24 ft 10 in |
| 1956 | Gregory Bell, United States | 25 ft 8¼ in |
| 1960 | Ralph Boston, United States | 26 ft 7¾ in |
| 1964 | Lynn Davies, Great Britain | 26 ft 5¾ in |
| 1968 | Bob Beamon, United States | 29 ft 2½ in |
| 1972 | Randy Williams, United States | 27 ft ½ in |
| 1976 | Arnie Robinson, United States | 24 ft 7¾ in |
| 1980 | Lutz Dombrowski, E. Germany | 28 ft ¼ in |
| 1984 | Carl Lewis, United States | 28 ft ¼ in |
| 1988 | Carl Lewis, United States | 28 ft 7¼ in |
| 1992 | Carl Lewis, United States | 28 ft 5½ in |
| 1996 | Carl Lewis, United States | 27 ft 10¾ in |
| 2000 | Ivan Pedroso, Cuba | 28 ft ¾ in |

## Triple Jump

| | | |
|---|---|---|
| 1896 | James B. Connolly, United States | 45 ft |
| 1900 | Myer Prinstein, United States | 47 ft 4¼ in |
| 1904 | Myer Prinstein, United States | 47 ft |
| 1906 | P.G. O'Connor, Ireland | 46 ft 2 in |
| 1908 | Timothy Ahearne, Great Britain | 48 ft 1¼ in |
| 1912 | Gustaf Lindblom, Sweden | 48 ft 5⅛ in |
| 1920 | Vilho Tuulos, Finland | 47 ft 6⅞ in |
| 1924 | Archie Winter, Australia | 50 ft 11⅛ in |
| 1928 | Mikio Oda, Japan | 49 ft 10¹³⁄₁₆ in |
| 1932 | Chuhei Nambu, Japan | 51 ft 7 in |
| 1936 | Naoto Tajima, Japan | 52 ft 5⅞ in |
| 1948 | Arne Ahman, Sweden | 50 ft 6¼ in |
| 1952 | Adhemar da Silva, Brazil | 53 ft 2½ in |
| 1956 | Adhemar da Silva, Brazil | 53 ft 7½ in |
| 1960 | Jozef Schmidt, Poland | 55 ft 1¾ in |
| 1964 | Jozef Schmidt, Poland | 55 ft 3¼ in |
| 1968 | Viktor Saneyev, USSR | 57 ft ¾ in |
| 1972 | Viktor Saneyev, USSR | 56 ft 11 in |
| 1976 | Viktor Saneyev, USSR | 56 ft 8¾ in |
| 1980 | Jaak Uudmae, USSR | 56 ft 11⅛ in |
| 1984 | Al Joyner, United States | 56 ft 7½ in |
| 1988 | Hristo Markov, Bulgaria | 57 ft 9¼ in |
| 1992 | Mike Conley, United States | 59 ft 7½ in |
| 1996 | Kenny Harrison, United States | 59 ft 4¼ in |
| 2000 | Jonathan Edwards, Great Britain | 58 ft 1¼ in |

## Pole Vault

| | | |
|---|---|---|
| 1896 | William Hoyt, United States | 10 ft 9¾ in |
| 1900 | Irving Baxter, United States | 10 ft 9⅞ in |
| 1904 | Charles Dvorak, United States | 11 ft 6 in |
| 1906 | Fernand Gouder, France | 11 ft 0 in |
| 1908 | Alfred Gilbert, United States, and Edward Cook, United States (tie) | 12 ft 2 in |
| 1912 | Harry Babcock, United States | 12 ft 11½ in |
| 1920 | Frank Foss, United States | 13 ft 5 ⁹⁄₁₆ in |
| 1924 | Lee Barnes, United States | 12 ft 11½ in |
| 1928 | Sabin W. Carr, United States | 13 ft 9⅜ in |
| 1932 | William Miller, United States | 14 ft 1⅞ in |
| 1936 | Earle Meadows, United States | 14 ft 3¼ in |
| 1948 | Guinn Smith, United States | 14 ft ¼ in |
| 1952 | Robert Richards, United States | 14 ft 11⅛ in |
| 1956 | Robert Richards, United States | 14 ft 11½ in |
| 1960 | Don Bragg, United States | 15 ft 5⅛ in |
| 1964 | Fred Hansen, United States | 16 ft 8¾ in |

| | | |
|---|---|---|
| 1968 | Bob Seagren, United States | 17 ft 8½ in |
| 1972 | Wolfgang Nordwig, East Germany | 18 ft ½ in |
| 1976 | Tadeusz Slusarski, Poland | 18 ft ½ in |
| 1980 | Wladyslaw Kozakiewics, Poland | 18 ft 11½ in |
| 1984 | Pierre Quinon, France | 18 ft 10¼ in |
| 1988 | Sergei Bubka, USSR | 19 ft 4¼ in |
| 1992 | Maxim Tarassov, Unified Team[1] | 19 ft 0¼ in |
| 1996 | Jean Galfione, France | 19 ft 5¼ in |
| 2000 | Nick Hysong, United States | 19 ft 4¼ in |

1. Former Soviet Union team.

### 16-lb Shot-Put

| | | |
|---|---|---|
| 1896 | Robert Garrett, United States | 36 ft 9¾ in |
| 1900 | Richard Sheldon, United States | 46 ft 3⅛ in |
| 1904 | Ralph Rose, United States | 48 ft 7 in |
| 1906 | Martin Sheridan, United States | 40 ft 4⅘ in |
| 1908 | Ralph Rose, United States | 46 ft 7½ in |
| 1912 | Pat McDonald, United States | 50 ft 4 in |
| 1920 | Ville Porhola, Finland | 48 ft 7⅛ in |
| 1924 | Clarence Houser, United States | 49 ft 2½ in |
| 1928 | John Kuck, United States | 52 ft 11¹¹⁄₁₆ in |
| 1932 | Leo Sexton, United States | 52 ft 6³⁄₁₆ in |
| 1936 | Hans Woellke, Germany | 53 ft 1¾ in |
| 1948 | Wilbur Thompson, United States | 56 ft 2 in |
| 1952 | Parry O'Brien, United States | 57 ft 1½ in |
| 1956 | Parry O'Brien, United States | 60 ft 11 in |
| 1960 | Bill Nieder, United States | 64 ft 6¾ in |
| 1964 | Dallas Long, United States | 66 ft 8¼ in |
| 1968 | Randy Matson, United States | 67 ft 4¾ in |
| 1972 | Wladyslaw Komar, Poland | 69 ft 6 in |
| 1976 | Udo Beyer, East Germany | 69 ft ¾ in |
| 1980 | Vladmir Klselyov, USSR | 70 ft ½ in |
| 1984 | Alessandro Andrei, Italy | 69 ft 9 in |
| 1988 | Uhf Timmerman, East Germany | 73 ft 8¾ in |
| 1992 | Michael Stulze, United States | 71 ft 2½ in |
| 1996 | Randy Barnes, United States | 70 ft 11¼ in |
| 2000 | Arsi Harju, Finland | 69 ft 10¼ in |

### Discus Throw

| | | |
|---|---|---|
| 1896 | Robert Garrett, United States | 95 ft 7½ in |
| 1900 | Rudolf Bauer, Hungary | 118 ft 2⅞ in |
| 1904 | Martin Sheridan, United States | 128 ft 10½ in |
| 1906 | Martin Sheridan, United States | 136 ft ⅓ in |
| 1908 | Martin Sheridan, United States | 134 ft 2 in |
| 1912 | Armas Taipale, Finland | 145 ft ⁹⁄₁₆ in |
| 1920 | Elmer Niklander, Finland | 146 ft 7 in |
| 1924 | Clarence Houser, United States | 151 ft 5¼ in |
| 1928 | Clarence Houser, United States | 155 ft 2⅘ in |
| 1932 | John Anderson, United States | 162 ft 4⅞ in |
| 1936 | Ken Carpenter, United States | 165 ft 7⅜ in |
| 1948 | Adolfo Consolini, Italy | 173 ft 2 in |
| 1952 | Simeon Iness, United States | 180 ft 6½ in |
| 1956 | Al Oerter, United States | 184 ft 10½ in |
| 1960 | Al Oerter, United States | 194 ft 2 in |
| 1964 | Al Oerter, United States | 200 ft 1½ in |
| 1968 | Al Oerter, United States | 212 ft 6 in |
| 1972 | Ludvik Danek, Czechoslovakia | 211 ft 3 in |
| 1976 | Mac Wilkins, United States | 221 ft 5 in |
| 1980 | Viktor Rashchupkin, USSR | 218 ft 8 in |
| 1984 | Rolf Dannenberg, West Germany | 218 ft 6 in |
| 1988 | Jurgen Schult, East Germany | 225 ft 9¼ in |
| 1992 | Romas Ubartas, Lithuania | 213 ft 7¾ in |
| 1996 | Lars Riedel, Germany | 227 ft 8 in |
| 2000 | Virgilijus Alekna, Lithuania | 227 ft 4in |

### Javelin Throw

| | | |
|---|---|---|
| 1906 | Eric Lemming, Sweden | 175 ft 6 in |
| 1908 | Eric Lemming, Sweden | 179 ft 10½ in |
| 1912 | Eric Lemming, Sweden | 198 ft 11¼ in |
| 1920 | Jonni Myyra, Finland | 215 ft 9¾ in |
| 1924 | Jonni Myyra, Finland | 206 ft 6¾ in |
| 1928 | Eric Lundquist, Sweden | 218 ft 6⅛ in |
| 1932 | Matti Jarvinen, Finland | 238 ft 7 in |
| 1936 | Gerhard Stoeck, Germany | 235 ft 8⁵⁄₁₆ in |
| 1948 | Kaj Rautavaara, Finland | 228 ft 10½ in |
| 1952 | Cy Young, United States | 242 ft¾ in |

| | | |
|---|---|---|
| 1956 | Egil Danielsen, Norway | 281 ft 2¼ in |
| 1960 | Viktor Tsibuelnko, USSR | 277 ft 8⅜ in |
| 1964 | Pauli Nevala, Finland | 271 ft 2¼ in |
| 1968 | Janis Lusis, USSR | 295 ft 7 in |
| 1972 | Klaus Wolfermann, West Germany | 296 ft 10 in |
| 1976 | Miklos Nemeth, Hungary | 310 ft 4 in |
| 1980 | Dainis Kula, USSR | 299 ft 2⅜ in |
| 1984 | Arto Haerkoenen, Finland | 284 ft 8 in |
| 1988 | Tapio Korjus, Finland | 276 ft 6 in |
| 1992 | Jan Zelezny, Czechoslovakia | 294 ft 2 in |
| 1996 | Jan Zelezny, Czech Republic | 289 ft 3 in |
| 2000 | Jan Zelezny, Czech Republic | 295 ft 9½ in |

### 16-lb Hammer Throw

| | | |
|---|---|---|
| 1900 | John Flanagan, United States | 167 ft 4 in |
| 1904 | John Flanagan, United States | 168 ft 1 in |
| 1908 | John Flanagan, United States | 170 ft 4¼ in |
| 1912 | Matt McGrath, United States | 179 ft 7⅛ in |
| 1920 | Pat Ryan, United States | 173 ft 5⅝ in |
| 1924 | Fred Tootell, United States | 174 ft 10¼ in |
| 1928 | Patrick O'Callaghan, Ireland | 168 ft 7½ in |
| 1932 | Patrick O'Callaghan, Ireland | 176 ft 11⅛ in |
| 1936 | Karl Hein, Germany | 185 ft 4 in |
| 1948 | Imre Nemeth, Hungary | 183 ft 11½ in |
| 1952 | Jozsef Csermak, Hungary | 197 ft 11⁹⁄₁₆ in |
| 1956 | Harold Connolly, United States | 207 ft 2¾ in |
| 1960 | Vasily Rudenkov, USSR | 220 ft 1⅝ in |
| 1964 | Romuald Klim, USSR | 228 ft 9½ in |
| 1968 | Gyula Zsivotzky, Hungary | 240 ft 8 in |
| 1972 | Anatoly Bondarchuk, USSR | 247 ft 8½ in |
| 1976 | Yuri Sedykh, USSR | 254 ft 4 in |
| 1980 | Yuri Sedykh, USSR (81.80m) | 268 ft 4½ in |
| 1984 | Juha Tiainen, Finland | 256 ft 2 in |
| 1988 | Sergei Litvinov, USSR | 278 ft 2½ in |
| 1992 | Andrey Abduvaliyev, Unified Team[1] | 270 ft 9½ in |
| 1996 | Balazs Kiss, Hungary | 266 ft 6 in |
| 2000 | Szymon Ziolkowski, Poland | 262 ft 6 in |

1. Former Soviet Union team.

### Decathlon

| | | |
|---|---|---|
| 1912 | Jim Thorpe, United States | — |
| | Hugo Wieslander, Sweden | — |
| 1920 | Helge Lovland, Norway | 6,804.35 pts. |
| 1924 | Harold Osborn, United States | 7,710.775 pts. |
| 1928 | Paavo Yrjola, Finland | 8,053.29 pts. |
| 1932 | James Bausch, United States | 8,462.23 pts. |
| 1936 | Glenn Morris, United States | 7,900 pts.[1] |
| 1948 | Robert B. Mathias, United States | 7,139 pts. |
| 1952 | Robert B. Mathias, United States | 7,887 pts. |
| 1956 | Milton Campbell, United States | 7,937 pts. |
| 1960 | Rafer Johnson, United States | 8,392 pts. |
| 1964 | Willi Holdorf, Germany | 7,887 pts.[1] |
| 1968 | Bill Toomey, United States | 8,193 pts. |
| 1972 | Nikolai Avilov, USSR | 8,454 pts. |
| 1976 | Bruce Jenner, United States | 8,618 pts. |
| 1980 | Daley Thompson, Great Britain | 8,495 pts. |
| 1984 | Daley Thompson, Great Britain | 8,797 pts. |
| 1988 | Christian Schenk, East Germany | 8,488 pts. |
| 1992 | Robert Zmelik, Czechoslovakia | 8,611 pts. |
| 1996 | Dan O'Brien, United States | 8,824 pts. |
| 2000 | Erki Nool, Estonia | 8,641 pts. |

1. Point system revised.

# TRACK AND FIELD–WOMEN

### 100-Meter Dash

| | | |
|---|---|---|
| 1928 | Elizabeth Robinson, United States | 12.20 |
| 1932 | Stella Walsh, Poland | 11.90 |
| 1936 | Helen Stephens, United States | 11.50 |
| 1948 | Fanny Blankers-Koen, Netherlands | 11.90 |
| 1952 | Marjorie Jackson, Australia | 11.50 |
| 1956 | Betty Cuthbert, Australia | 11.50 |
| 1960 | Wilma Rudolph, United States | 11.00 |
| 1964 | Wyomia Tyus, United States | 11.40 |
| 1968 | Wyomia Tyus, United States | 11.00 |
| 1972 | Renate Stecher, East Germany | 11.07 |

| | | |
|---|---|---|
| 1976 | Annegret Richter, West Germany | 11.08 |
| 1980 | Lyudmila Kondratyeva, USSR | 11.06 |
| 1984 | Evelyn Ashford, United States | 10.97 |
| 1988 | Florence Griffith-Joyner, United States | 10.54 |
| 1992 | Gail Devers, United States | 10.82 |
| 1996 | Gail Devers, United States | 10.94 |
| 2000 | Marion Jones, United States | 10.75 |

### 200-Meter Dash

| | | |
|---|---|---|
| 1948 | Fanny Blankers-Koen, Netherlands | 24.40 |
| 1952 | Marjorie Jackson, Australia | 23.70 |
| 1956 | Betty Cuthbert, Australia | 23.40 |
| 1960 | Wilma Rudolph, United States | 24.00 |
| 1964 | Edith McGuire, United States | 23.00 |
| 1968 | Irena Szewinska, Poland | 22.50 |
| 1972 | Renate Stecher, East Germany | 22.40 |
| 1976 | Baerbel Eckert, East Germany | 22.37 |
| 1980 | Barbara Wockel, East Germany | 22.03 |
| 1984 | Valerie Brisco-Hooks, United States | 21.81 |
| 1988 | Florence Griffith-Joyner, United States | 21.34 |
| 1992 | Gwen Torrence, United States | 21.81 |
| 1996 | Marie-Jose Perec, France | 22.12 |
| 2000 | Marion Jones, United States | 21.84 |

### 400-Meter Dash

| | | |
|---|---|---|
| 1964 | Betty Cuthbert, Australia | 52.00 |
| 1968 | Colette Besson, France | 52.00 |
| 1972 | Monika Zehrt, East Germany | 51.08 |
| 1976 | Irena Szewinska, Poland | 49.29 |
| 1980 | Marita Koch, East Germany | 48.88 |
| 1984 | Valerie Brisco-Hooks, United States | 48.83 |
| 1988 | Olga Bryzguina, USSR | 48.65 |
| 1992 | Marie Jose-Perec, France | 48.83 |
| 1996 | Marie Jose-Perec, France | 48.25 |
| 2000 | Cathy Freeman, Australia | 49.11 |

### 800-Meter Run

| | | |
|---|---|---|
| 1928 | Lina Radke, Germany | 2:16.80 |
| 1960 | Ljudmila Shevcova, USSR | 2:04.30 |
| 1964 | Ann Packer, Great Britain | 2:01.10 |
| 1968 | Madeline Manning, United States | 2:00.90 |
| 1972 | Hildegard Falck, West Germany | 1:58.60 |
| 1976 | Tatiana Kazankina, USSR | 1:54.94 |
| 1980 | Nadezhda Olizarenko, USSR | 1:53.50 |
| 1984 | Doina Melinte, Romania | 1:57.60 |
| 1988 | Sigrun Wodars, East Germany | 1:56.10 |
| 1992 | Ellen Van Langen, Netherlands | 1:55.54 |
| 1996 | Svetlana Masterkova, Russia | 1:57.73 |
| 2000 | Maria Mutola, Mozambique | 1:56.15 |

### 1,500-Meter Run

| | | |
|---|---|---|
| 1972 | Ludmila Bragina, USSR | 4:01.40 |
| 1976 | Tatiana Kazankina, USSR | 4:05.48 |
| 1980 | Tatiana Kazankina, USSR | 3:56.60 |
| 1984 | Gabriella Dorio, Italy | 4:03.25 |
| 1988 | Paula Ivan, Romania | 3:53.96 |
| 1992 | Hassiba Boulmerka, Algeria | 3:55.30 |
| 1996 | Svetlana Masterkova, Russia | 4:00.83 |
| 2000 | Nouria Merah-Benida, Algeria | 4:05.10 |

### 5,000-Meter Run

| | | |
|---|---|---|
| 1996 | Wang, Jun Xia, China | 14:59.88 |
| 2000 | Gabriela Szabo, Romania | 14:40.79 |

### 10,000-Meter Run

| | | |
|---|---|---|
| 1992 | Derartu Tulu, Ethiopia | 31:60.02 |
| 1996 | Fernanda Ribeiro, Portugal | 31:01.63 |
| 2000 | Derartu Tulu, Ethiopia | 30:17.49 |

### 80-Meter Hurdles

| | | |
|---|---|---|
| 1932 | Mildred Didrikson, United States | 11.70 |
| 1936 | Trebisonda Valla, Italy | 11.70 |
| 1948 | Fanny Blankers-Koen, Netherlands | 11.20 |
| 1952 | Shirley S. de la Hunty, Australia | 10.90 |
| 1956 | Shirley S. de la Hunty, Australia | 10.70 |
| 1960 | Irina Press, USSR | 10.80 |
| 1964 | Karin Balzer, Germany | 10.50[1] |
| 1968 | Maureen Caird, Australia | 10.30 |

1. Wind assisted.

### 100-Meter Hurdles

| | | |
|---|---|---|
| 1972 | Annelie Ehrhardt, East Germany | 12.59 |
| 1976 | Johanna Schaller, East Germany | 12.77 |
| 1980 | Vera Komisova, USSR | 12.56 |
| 1984 | Benita Fitzgerald-Brown, United States | 12.84 |
| 1988 | Jordanka Donkova, Bulgaria | 12.38 |
| 1992 | Paraskevi Patoulidou, Greece | 12.64 |
| 1996 | Ludmila Engquist, Sweden | 12.58 |
| 2000 | Olga Shishigina, Kazakhstan | 12.65 |

### 400-Meter Hurdles

| | | |
|---|---|---|
| 1984 | Nawai El Moutawakel, Morocco | 54.61 |
| 1988 | Debra Flintoff-King, Australia | 53.17 |
| 1992 | Sally Gunnell, Great Britain | 53.23 |
| 1996 | Deon Hemmings, Jamaica | 52.82 |
| 2000 | Irina Privalova, Russia | 53.02 |

### 400-Meter Relay

| | | |
|---|---|---|
| 1928 | Canada | 48.40 |
| 1932 | United States | 47.00 |
| 1936 | United States | 46.90 |
| 1948 | Netherlands | 47.50 |
| 1952 | United States | 45.90 |
| 1956 | Australia | 44.50 |
| 1960 | United States | 44.50 |
| 1964 | Poland | 43.60 |
| 1968 | United States | 42.80 |
| 1972 | West Germany | 42.81 |
| 1976 | East Germany | 42.50 |
| 1980 | East Germany | 41.60 |
| 1984 | United States | 41.65 |
| 1988 | United States | 41.98 |
| 1992 | United States | 42.11 |
| 1996 | United States | 41.95 |
| 2000 | Bahamas | 41.95 |

### 1,600-Meter Relay

| | | |
|---|---|---|
| 1972 | East Germany | 3:23.00 |
| 1976 | East Germany | 3:19.23 |
| 1980 | USSR | 3:20.20 |
| 1984 | United States | 3:18.29 |
| 1988 | USSR | 3:15.18 |
| 1992 | Unified Team[1] | 3:20.20 |
| 1996 | United States | 3:20.91 |
| 2000 | United States | 3:22.62 |

1. Former Soviet Union team.

### 10,000-Meter Walk

| | | |
|---|---|---|
| 1992 | ChenYue-Ling, China | 44:32 |
| 1996 | Yelena Nikolayeva, Russia | 41:49 |

### 20,000-Meter Walk

| | | |
|---|---|---|
| 2000 | Liping Wang, China | 1:29.05 |

### Marathon

| | | |
|---|---|---|
| 1984 | Joan Benoit, United States | 2:24:52 |
| 1988 | Rose Mota, Portugal | 2:25.40 |
| 1992 | Valentina Yegorova, Unified Team | 2:32.41 |
| 1996 | Fatuma Roba, Ethiopia | 2:26.05 |
| 2000 | Naoko Takahashi, Japan | 2:23.14 |

### Running High Jump

| | | |
|---|---|---|
| 1928 | Ethel Catherwood, Canada | 5 ft 3 in |
| 1932 | Jean Shiley, United States | 5 ft 5¼ in |
| 1936 | Ibolya Csak, Hungary | 5 ft 3 in |
| 1948 | Alice Coachman, United States | 5 ft 6⅛ in |
| 1952 | Ester Brand, South Africa | 5 ft 5¾ in |
| 1956 | Mildred McDaniel, United States | 5 ft 9¼ in |
| 1960 | Iolanda Balas, Romania | 6 ft ¾ in |
| 1964 | Iolanda Balas, Romania | 6 ft 2¾ in |
| 1968 | Miloslava Rezkova, Czechoslovakia | 5 ft 11¾ in |
| 1972 | Ulrike Meyfarth, West Germany | 6 ft 3⅝ in |
| 1976 | Rosemarie Ackerman, E. Germany | 6 ft 4 in |
| 1980 | Sara Simeoni, Italy | 6 ft 5½ in |
| 1984 | Ulrike Meyfarth, West Germany | 6 ft 7½ in |
| 1988 | Louise Ritter, United States | 6 ft 8 in |
| 1992 | Heike Henkel, Germany | 6 ft 7½ in |
| 1996 | Stefka Kostadinova, Bulgaria | 6 ft 8¾ in |
| 2000 | Yelena Yelesina, Russia | 6 ft 7 in |

### Long Jump

| | | |
|---|---|---|
| 1948 | Olga Gyarmati, Hungary | 18 ft 8¼ in |
| 1952 | Yvette Williams, New Zealand | 20 ft 5¾ in |
| 1956 | Elzbieta Krzesinska, Poland | 20 ft 9¾ in |
| 1960 | Vera Krepkina, USSR | 20 ft 10¾ in |
| 1964 | Mary Rand, Great Britain | 22 ft 2 in |
| 1968 | Viorica Ciscopoleanu, Romania | 22 ft 4½ in |
| 1972 | Heidemarie Rosendahl, West Germany | 22 ft 3 in |
| 1976 | Angela Voigt, East Germany | 22 ft ½ in |
| 1980 | Tatiana Kolpakova, USSR | 23 ft 2 in |
| 1984 | Anisoara Stanciu, Romania | 22 ft 10 in |
| 1988 | Jackie Joyner-Kersee, United States | 24 ft 3½ in |
| 1992 | Heike Drechsler, Germany | 23 ft 5¼ in |
| 1996 | Chioma Ajunwa, Nigeria | 23 ft 4½ in |
| 2000 | Heike Drechsler, Germany | 22 ft 11¼ in |

### Triple Jump

| | | |
|---|---|---|
| 1996 | Inessa Kravets, Ukraine | 50 ft 3½ in |
| 2000 | Tereza Marinova, Belarus | 49 ft 10 ½ in |

### Shot-Put

| | | |
|---|---|---|
| 1948 | Micheline Ostermeyer, France | 45 ft 1½ in |
| 1952 | Galina Zybina, USSR | 50 ft 1½ in |
| 1956 | Tamara Tishkyevich, USSR | 54 ft 5 in |
| 1960 | Tamara Press, USSR | 56 ft 9⅞ in |
| 1964 | Tamara Press, USSR | 59 ft 6 in |
| 1968 | Margitta Gummel, East Germany | 64 ft 4 in |
| 1972 | Nadezhda Chizhova, USSR | 69 ft |
| 1976 | Ivanka Christova, Bulgaria | 69 ft 5 in |
| 1980 | Ilona Sluplanek, East Germany | 73 ft 6 in |
| 1984 | Claudia Losch, West Germany | 67 ft 2¼ in |
| 1988 | Natalya Lisovskaya, USSR | 72 ft 11½ in |
| 1992 | Svetlana Kriveleva, Unified Team[1] | 69 ft 1¼ in |
| 1996 | Astrid Kumbernuss, Germany | 67 ft 5½ in |
| 2000 | Yanina Korolchik, Belarus | 67 ft 5½ in |

1. Former Soviet Union team.

### Discus Throw

| | | |
|---|---|---|
| 1928 | Helena Konopacka, Poland | 129 ft 11⅞ in |
| 1932 | Lillian Copeland, United States | 133 ft 2 in |
| 1936 | Gisela Mauermayer, Germany | 156 ft 3³⁄₁₆ in |
| 1948 | Micheline Ostermeyer, France | 137 ft 6½ in |
| 1956 | Olga Fikotova, Czechoslovakia | 176 ft 1½ in |
| 1960 | Nina Ponomareva, USSR | 180 ft 8¼ in |
| 1964 | Tamara Press, USSR | 187 ft 10¾ in |
| 1968 | Lia Manoliu, Romania | 191 ft 2½ in |
| 1972 | Faina Melnik, USSR | 218 ft 7 in |
| 1976 | Evelin Schlaak, East Germany | 226 ft 4 in |
| 1980 | Evelin Jahl, East Germany | 229 ft 6½ in |
| 1984 | Ria Stalman, Netherlands | 214 ft 5 in |
| 1988 | Martina Hellmann, East Germany | 237 ft 2¼ in |
| 1992 | Maritza Marten, Cuba | 229 ft 10¼ in |
| 1996 | Ilke Wyludda, Germany | 228 ft 6½ in |
| 2000 | Ellina Zvereva, Belarus | 224 ft 5 in |

### Javelin Throw

| | | |
|---|---|---|
| 1932 | Mildred Didrikson, United States | 143 ft 4 in |
| 1936 | Tilly Fleischer, Germany | 148 ft 2¾ in |
| 1948 | Herma Bauma, Austria | 149 ft 6 in |
| 1952 | Dana Zatopek, Czechoslovakia | 165 ft 7 in |
| 1956 | Inessa Janzeme, USSR | 176 ft 8 in |
| 1960 | Elvira Ozolina, USSR | 183 ft 8 in |
| 1964 | Mihaela Penes, Romania | 198 ft 7½ in |
| 1968 | Angela Nemeth, Hungary | 198 ft |
| 1972 | Ruth Fuchs, East Germany | 209 ft 7 in |
| 1976 | Ruth Fuchs, East Germany | 216 ft 4 in |
| 1980 | Maria Colon, Cuba | 224 ft 5 in |
| 1984 | Tessa Sanderson, Britain | 228 ft 2 in |
| 1988 | Petra Felke, East Germany | 245 ft |
| 1992 | Silke Renke, Germany | 224 ft 2½ in |
| 1996 | Heli Rantanen, Finland | 222 ft 11 in |
| 2000 | Trine Hattestad, Norway | 226 ft 1 in |

### Hammer Throw

| | | |
|---|---|---|
| 2000 | Kamila Skolimowska, Poland | 233 ft 5 ¾ in |

### Pole Vault

| | | |
|---|---|---|
| 2000 | Stacy Dragila, United States | 15 ft 1 in |

### Pentathlon

| | | |
|---|---|---|
| 1964 | Irina Press, USSR | 5,246 pts. |
| 1968 | Ingrid Becker, West Germany | 5,098 pts. |
| 1972 | Mary Peters, Britain | 4,801 pts. |
| 1976 | Siegrun Siegl, East Germany | 4,745 pts. |
| 1980 | Nadyeszhda Tkachenko, USSR | 5,083 pts. |
| 1984 | Daniele Masala, Italy | 5,469 pts. |
| 1988 | Jackie Joyner-Kersee, United States | 7,291 pts. |

### Heptathlon

| | | |
|---|---|---|
| 1992 | Jackie Joyner-Kersee, United States | 7,044 pts. |
| 1996 | Ghada Shouaa, Syria | 6,780 pts. |
| 2000 | Denise Lewis, Great Britain | 6,584 pts. |

## SWIMMING–MEN

### 50-Meter Freestyle

| | | |
|---|---|---|
| 1988 | Matt Biondi, United States | 22.14 |
| 1992 | Alexander Popov, Unified Team[1] | 21.91 |
| 1996 | Alexander Popov, Russia | 22.13 |
| 2000 | Anthony Ervin and Gary Hall, Jr., United States | 21.98 |

1. Former Soviet Union team.

### 100-Meter Freestyle

| | | |
|---|---|---|
| 1896 | Alfred Hajos, Hungary | 1:22.20 |
| 1904 | Zoltan de Halmay, Hungary | 1:02.80[1] |
| 1906 | Charles Daniels, United States | 1:13.00 |
| 1908 | Charles Daniels, United States | 1:05.60 |
| 1912 | Duke P. Kahanamoku, United States | 1:03.40 |
| 1920 | Duke P. Kahanamoku, United States | 1:01.40 |
| 1924 | John Weissmuller, United States | 0:59.00 |
| 1928 | John Weissmuller, United States | 0:58.60 |
| 1932 | Yasuji Miyazaki, Japan | 0:58.20 |
| 1936 | Ferenc Csik, Hungary | 0:57.60 |
| 1948 | Walter Ris, United States | 0:57.30 |
| 1952 | Clarke Scholes, United States | 0:57.40 |
| 1956 | Jon Henricks, Australia | 0:55.40 |
| 1960 | John Devitt, Australia | 0:55.20 |
| 1964 | Don Schollander, United States | 0:53.40 |
| 1968 | Michael Wenden, Australia | 0:52.20 |
| 1972 | Mark Spitz, United States | 0:51.22 |
| 1976 | Jim Montgomery, United States | 0:49.99 |
| 1980 | Jorg Woithe, East Germany | 0:50.40 |
| 1984 | Rowdy Gaines, United States | 0:49.80 |
| 1988 | Matt Biondi, United States | 0:48.63 |
| 1992 | Alexander Popov, Unified Team[2] | 0:49.02 |
| 1996 | Alexander Popov, Russia | 0:48.74 |
| 2000 | Pieter van den Hoogenband, Netherlands | 0:48.30 |

1. 100 yards. 2. Former Soviet Union team.

### 200-Meter Freestyle

| | | |
|---|---|---|
| 1900 | Frederick Lane, Australia | 2:25.20 |
| 1904 | Charles Daniels, United States | 2:44.20[1] |
| 1968 | Michael Wenden, Australia | 1:55.20 |
| 1972 | Mark Spitz, United States | 1:52.78 |
| 1976 | Bruce Furniss, United States | 1:50.29 |
| 1980 | Sergei Kopiliakov, USSR | 4:49.81 |
| 1984 | Michael Gross, West Germany | 1:47.44 |
| 1988 | Duncan Armstrong, Australia | 1:47.25 |
| 1992 | Evgueni Sadovyi, Unified Team[2] | 1:46.70 |
| 1996 | Danyon Loader, New Zealand | 1:47.63 |
| 2000 | Pieter van den Hoogenband, Netherlands | 1:45.35[3] |

1. 220 yards 2. Former Soviet Union team. 3. World record.

### 400-Meter Freestyle

| | | |
|---|---|---|
| 1896 | Paul Neumann, Austria | 8:12.60[1] |
| 1904 | Charles Daniels, United States | 6:16.20[2] |
| 1906 | Otto Sheff, Austria | 6:23.80 |
| 1908 | Henry Taylor, Great Britain | 5:36.80 |
| 1912 | George Hodgson, Canada | 5:24.40 |
| 1920 | Norman Ross, United States | 5:26.80 |
| 1926 | John Weissmuller, United States | 5:04.20 |
| 1928 | Albert Zorilla, Argentina | 5:01.60 |
| 1932 | Clarence Crabbe, United States | 4:48.40 |

| | | |
|---|---|---|
| 1936 | Jack Medica, United States | 4:44.50 |
| 1948 | William Smith, United States | 4:41.00 |
| 1952 | Jean Bolteux, France | 4:30.70 |
| 1956 | Murray Rose, Australia | 4:27.30 |
| 1960 | Murray Rose, Australia | 4:18.30 |
| 1964 | Don Schollander, United States | 4:12.20 |
| 1968 | Mike Burton, United States | 4:09.00 |
| 1972 | Bradford Cooper, Australia | 4:00.27[3] |
| 1976 | Brian Goodell, United States | 3:51.93 |
| 1980 | Vladimir Salnikov, USSR | 3:51.31 |
| 1984 | George DiCarlo, United States | 3:51.23 |
| 1988 | Uwe Dassier, East Germany | 3:46.95 |
| 1992 | Evgueni Sadovyi, Unified Team | 3:45.00[4] |
| 1996 | Danyon Loader, New Zealand | 3:47.97 |
| 2000 | Ian Thorpe, Australia | 3:40.59[4] |

1. 500 meters. 2. 440 yards. 3. Rich DeMont, United States, won but was disqualified following day for medical reasons. 4. World record.

## 1,500-Meter Freestyle

| | | |
|---|---|---|
| 1904 | Emil Rausch, Germany | 27:18.20[1] |
| 1906 | Henry Taylor, Great Britain | 28:28.00[2] |
| 1908 | Henry Taylor, Great Britain | 22:48.40 |
| 1912 | George Hodgson, Canada | 22:00.00 |
| 1920 | Norman Ross, United States | 22:23.20 |
| 1924 | Andrew Charlton, Australia | 20:06.60 |
| 1928 | Arne Borg, Sweden | 19:51.80 |
| 1932 | Kusuo Kitamura, Japan | 19:12.40 |
| 1936 | Noboru Terada, Japan | 19:13.70 |
| 1948 | James McLane, United States | 19:18.50 |
| 1952 | Ford Konno, United States | 18:30.00 |
| 1956 | Murray Rose, Australia | 17:58.90 |
| 1960 | Jon Konrads, Australia | 17:19.60 |
| 1964 | Robert Windle, Australia | 17:01.70 |
| 1968 | Michael Burton, United States | 16:38.90 |
| 1972 | Michael Burton, United States | 15:52.58 |
| 1976 | Brian Goodell, United States | 15:02.40 |
| 1980 | Vladimir Salnikov, USSR | 14:58.27 |
| 1984 | Michael O'Brien, United States | 15:05.20 |
| 1988 | Vladimir Salnikov, USSR | 15:00.40 |
| 1992 | Kieren Perkins, Australia | 14:43.48 |
| 1996 | Kieren Perkins, Australia | 14:56.40 |
| 2000 | Grant Hackett, Australia | 14:48.33 |

1. One mile. 2. 1,600 meters

## 100-Meter Backstroke

| | | |
|---|---|---|
| 1904 | Walter Brack, Germany | 1:16.80[1] |
| 1908 | Arno Bieberstein, Germany | 1:24.60 |
| 1912 | Harry Hebner, United States | 1:21.20 |
| 1920 | Warren Kealoha, United States | 1:15.20 |
| 1924 | Warren Kealoha, United States | 1:13.20 |
| 1928 | George Kojac, United States | 1:08.20 |
| 1932 | Masaji Kiyokawa, Japan | 1:08.60 |
| 1936 | Adolph Kiefer, United States | 1:05.90 |
| 1948 | Allen Stack, United States | 1:06.40 |
| 1952 | Yoshinobu Oyakawa, United States | 1:05.40 |
| 1956 | David Thiele, Australia | 1:02.20 |
| 1960 | David Thiele, Australia | 1:01.90 |
| 1968 | Roland Matthes, East Germany | 0:58.70 |
| 1972 | Roland Matthes, East Germany | 0:56.58 |
| 1976 | John Naber, United States | 0:55.49 |
| 1980 | Bengt Baron, Sweden | 0:56.53 |
| 1984 | Rick Carey, United States | 0:55.79 |
| 1988 | Daichi Suzuki, Japan | 0:55.05 |
| 1992 | Mark Tewksbury, Canada | 0:53.98 |
| 1996 | Jeff Rouse, United States | 0:54.10 |
| 2000 | Lenny Krayzelburg, United States | 0:53.72 |

1. 100 yards

## 200-Meter Backstroke

| | | |
|---|---|---|
| 1900 | Ernst Hoppenberg, Germany | 2:47.00 |
| 1964 | Jed Graef, United States | 2:10.30 |
| 1968 | Roland Matthes, East Germany | 2:09.60 |
| 1972 | Roland Matthes, East Germany | 2:02.82 |
| 1976 | John Naber, United States | 1:59.19 |
| 1980 | Sandor Wladar, Hungary | 2:01.93 |

| | | |
|---|---|---|
| 1984 | Rick Carey, United States | 2:00.23 |
| 1988 | Igor Polianski, USSR | 1:59.37 |
| 1992 | Martin Lopez Zubero, Spain | 1:58.47 |
| 1996 | Brad Bridgewater, United States | 1:58.54 |
| 2000 | Lenny Krayzelburg, United States | 1:56.76 |

## 100-Meter Breaststroke

| | | |
|---|---|---|
| 1968 | Donald McKenzie, United States | 1:07.70 |
| 1972 | Nobutaka Taguchi, Japan | 1:04.94 |
| 1976 | John Hencken, United States | 1:03.11 |
| 1980 | Duncan Goodhew, Britain | 1:03.34 |
| 1984 | Steve Lindquist, United States | 1:01.65 |
| 1988 | Adrian Moorhouse, Great Britain | 1:02.04 |
| 1992 | Nelson Diebel, United States | 1:01.50 |
| 1996 | Fred Deburghgraeve, Belgium | 1:00.60[1] |
| 2000 | Domenico Fioravanti, Italy | 1:00.46 |

1. World record.

## 200-Meter Breaststroke

| | | |
|---|---|---|
| 1908 | Frederick Holman, Great Britain | 3:09.20 |
| 1912 | Walter Bathe, Germany | 3:01.80 |
| 1920 | Haken Malmroth, Sweden | 3:04.40 |
| 1924 | Robert Skelton, United States | 2:56.60 |
| 1928 | Yoshiyuki Tsuruta, Japan | 2:48.80 |
| 1932 | Yoshiyuki Tsuruta, Japan | 2:45.40 |
| 1936 | Tetsuo Hamuro, Japan | 2:41.50 |
| 1948 | Joseph Verdeur, United States | 2:39.30 |
| 1952 | John Davies, Australia | 2:34.40 |
| 1956 | Masaura Furukawa, Japan | 2:34.70 |
| 1960 | Bill Muliken, United States | 2:37.40 |
| 1964 | Ian O'Brien, Australia | 2:07.80 |
| 1968 | Felipe Munoz, Mexico | 2:28.70 |
| 1972 | John Hencken, United States | 2:21.55 |
| 1976 | David Willkie, Britain | 2:15.11 |
| 1980 | Robertas Zulpa, USSR | 2:15.85 |
| 1984 | Victor Davis, Canada | 2:13.34 |
| 1988 | Jozef Szabo, Hungary | 2:13.52 |
| 1992 | Mike Barrowman, United States | 2:10.16 |
| 1996 | Norbert Rozsa, Hungary | 2:12.57 |
| 2000 | Domenico Fioravanti, Italy | 2:10.87 |

## 100-Meter Butterfly

| | | |
|---|---|---|
| 1968 | Douglas Russell, United States | 55.90 |
| 1972 | Mark Spitz, United States | 54.27 |
| 1976 | Matt Vogel, United States | 54.35 |
| 1980 | Par Arvidsson, Sweden | 54.92 |
| 1984 | Michael Gross, West Germany | 53.08 |
| 1988 | Anthony Nesty, Surinam | 53.00 |
| 1992 | Pablo Morales, United States | 53.32 |
| 1996 | Denis Pankratov, Russia | 52.27[1] |
| 2000 | Lars Froelander, Sweden | 52.00 |

1. World record.

## 200-Meter Butterfly

| | | |
|---|---|---|
| 1956 | Bill Yorzyk, United States | 2:19.30 |
| 1960 | Mike Troy, United States | 2:12.80 |
| 1964 | Kevin Berry, Australia | 2:06.60 |
| 1968 | Carl Robie, United States | 2:08.70 |
| 1972 | Mark Spitz, United States | 2:00.70 |
| 1976 | Mike Bruner, United States | 1:59.20 |
| 1980 | Sergei Fesenko, USSR | 1:59.76 |
| 1984 | Jon Sieben, Australia | 1:57.00 |
| 1988 | Michael Gross, East Germany | 1:56.94 |
| 1992 | Mel Stewart, United States | 1:56.26 |
| 1996 | Denis Pankratov, Russia | 1:56.51 |
| 2000 | Tom Malchow, United States | 1:55.35 |

## 200-Meter Individual Medley

| | | |
|---|---|---|
| 1968 | Charles Hickcox, United States | 2:12.00 |
| 1972 | Gunnar Larsson, Sweden | 2:07.17 |
| 1988 | Tamas Darnyi, Hungary | 2:00.17 |
| 1992 | Tamas Darnyi, Hungary | 2:00.76 |
| 1996 | Attila Czene, Hungary | 1:59.91 |
| 2000 | Massimiliano Rosolino, Italy | 1:58.98 |

## 400-Meter Individual Medley

| | | |
|---|---|---|
| 1964 | Dick Roth, United States | 4:45.40 |
| 1968 | Charles Hickox, United States | 4:48.40 |
| 1972 | Gunnar Larsson, Sweden | 4:31.98 |

| | | |
|---|---|---|
| 1976 | Rod Strachan, United States | 4:23.68 |
| 1980 | Aleksandr Sidorenko, USSR | 4:22.80 |
| 1984 | Alex Baumann, Canada | 4:17.41 |
| 1988 | Tamas Darnyi, Hungary | 4:14.75 |
| 1992 | Tamas Darnyi, Hungary | 4:14.23 |
| 1996 | Tom Dolan, United States | 4:14.90 |
| 2000 | Tom Dolan, United States | 4:11.76[1] |

1. World record.

**400-Meter Freestyle Relay**

| | | |
|---|---|---|
| 1964 | United States | 3:32.20 |
| 1968 | United States | 3:31.70 |
| 1972 | United States | 3:26.42 |
| 1988 | United States | 3:16.52 |
| 1992 | United States | 3:16.74 |
| 1996 | United States | 3:15.41 |
| 2000 | Australia | 3:13.67[1] |

1. World record.

**800-Meter Freestyle Relay**

| | | |
|---|---|---|
| 1908 | Great Britain | 10:55.60 |
| 1912 | Australia | 10:11.20 |
| 1920 | United States | 10:04.40 |
| 1924 | United States | 09:53.40 |
| 1928 | United States | 09:36.20 |
| 1932 | Japan | 08:58.40 |
| 1936 | Japan | 08:51.50 |
| 1948 | United States | 08:46.10 |
| 1952 | United States | 08:31.10 |
| 1956 | Australia | 08:23.60 |
| 1960 | United States | 08:10.20 |
| 1964 | United States | 07:52.10 |
| 1968 | United States | 07:52.30 |
| 1972 | United States | 07:35.78 |
| 1976 | United States | 07:23.22 |
| 1980 | USSR | 07:23.50 |
| 1984 | United States | 07:16.59 |
| 1988 | United States | 07:12.51 |
| 1992 | Unified Team[1] | 07:11.95 |
| 1996 | United States | 07:14.84 |
| 2000 | Australia | 07:07.05[2] |

1. Former Soviet Union team. 2. World record.

**400-Meter Medley Relay**

| | | |
|---|---|---|
| 1960 | United States | 4:05.40 |
| 1964 | United States | 3:58.40 |
| 1968 | United States | 3:54.90 |
| 1972 | United States | 3:48.16 |
| 1976 | United States | 3:42.22 |
| 1980 | Australia | 3:45.70 |
| 1984 | United States | 3:39.30 |
| 1988 | United States | 3:36.93 |
| 1992 | United States | 3:36.93 |
| 1996 | United States | 3:34.84 |
| 2000 | United States | 3:33.73[1] |

1. World record.

**Springboard Dive** — **Points**

| | | |
|---|---|---|
| 1908 | Albert Zuerner, Germany | 85.50 |
| 1912 | Paul Guenther, Germany | 79.23 |
| 1920 | Louis Kuehn, United States | 675.00 |
| 1924 | Albert White, United States | 696.40 |
| 1928 | Pete Desjardins, United States | 185.04 |
| 1932 | Michael Galitzen, United States | 161.38 |
| 1936 | Richard Degener, United States | 163.57 |
| 1948 | Bruce Harlan, United States | 163.64 |
| 1952 | David Browning, United States | 205.59 |
| 1956 | Robert Clotworthy, United States | 159.56 |
| 1960 | Gary Tobian, United States | 170.00 |
| 1964 | Ken Sitzberger, United States | 159.90 |
| 1968 | Bernard Wrightson, United States | 170.15 |
| 1972 | Vladimir Vasin, USSR | 594.09 |
| 1976 | Phil Boggs, United States | 619.05 |
| 1980 | Alexsandr Portnov, USSR | 905.02 |
| 1984 | Greg Louganis, United States | 754.41 |
| 1988 | Greg Louganis, United States | 730.80 |
| 1992 | Mark Lenzi, United States | 676.53 |

| | | |
|---|---|---|
| 1996 | Xiong Ni, China | 701.46 |
| 2000 | Xiong Ni, China | 708.72 |

**Platform Dive** — **Points**

| | | |
|---|---|---|
| 1904 | G.E. Sheldon, United States | 12.75 |
| 1906 | Gottlob Walz, Germany | 156.00 |
| 1908 | Hialmar Johansson, Sweden | 83.75 |
| 1912 | Erik Adlerz, Sweden | 73.94 |
| 1920 | Clarence Pinkston, United States | 100.67 |
| 1924 | Albert White, United States | 487.30 |
| 1928 | Pete Desjardins, United States | 98.74 |
| 1932 | Harold Smith, United States | 124.80 |
| 1936 | Marshall Wayne, United States | 113.58 |
| 1948 | Samuel Lee, United States | 130.05 |
| 1952 | Samuel Lee, United States | 156.28 |
| 1956 | Joaquin Capilla, Mexico | 152.44 |
| 1960 | Bob Webster, United States | 165.56 |
| 1964 | Bob Webster, United States | 148.58 |
| 1968 | Klaus Dibiasi, Italy | 164.18 |
| 1972 | Klaus Dibiasi, Italy | 504.12 |
| 1976 | Klaus Dibiasi, Italy | 600.51 |
| 1980 | Falk Hoffman, E. Germany | 835.65 |
| 1984 | Greg Louganis, United States | 710.91 |
| 1988 | Greg Louganis, United States | 638.61 |
| 1992 | Sun, Shu-Wei, China | 677.31 |
| 1996 | Dmitri Saoutine, Russia | 692.34 |
| 2000 | Tian Liang, China | 724.53 |

**Synchronized 3m Springboard Dive** — **Points**

| | | |
|---|---|---|
| 2000 | Xiao Hailiang and Xiong Ni, China | 365.58 |

**Synchronized 10m Platform Dive** — **Points**

| | | |
|---|---|---|
| 2000 | Igor Loukachine and Dmitri Saoutine, Russia | 365.04 |

# SWIMMING–WOMEN

**50-Meter Freestyle**

| | | |
|---|---|---|
| 1988 | Kristin Otto, East Germany | 25.49 |
| 1992 | Yang, Wen-Yi, China | 24.79 |
| 1996 | Amy Van Dyken, United States | 24.87 |
| 2000 | Inge de Bruijn, Netherlands | 24.32 |

**100-Meter Freestyle**

| | | |
|---|---|---|
| 1912 | Fanny Durack, Australia | 1:22.20 |
| 1920 | Ethelda Bleibtrey, United States | 1:13.60 |
| 1924 | Ethel Lackie, United States | 1:12.40 |
| 1928 | Albina Osipowich, United States | 1:11.00 |
| 1932 | Helene Madison, United States | 1:06.80 |
| 1936 | Hendrika Mastenbroek, Netherlands | 1:05.90 |
| 1948 | Greta Andersen, Denmark | 1:06.30 |
| 1952 | Katalin Szoke, Hungary | 1:06.80 |
| 1956 | Dawn Fraser, Australia | 1:02.00 |
| 1960 | Dawn Fraser, Australia | 1:01.20 |
| 1964 | Dawn Fraser, Australia | 0:59.50 |
| 1968 | Marge Jan Henne, United States | 1:00.00 |
| 1972 | Sandra Neilson, United States | 0:58.59 |
| 1976 | Kornelia Ender, East Germany | 0:55.65 |
| 1980 | Barbara Krause, East Germany | 0:54.79 |
| 1984 | Carrie Steinseifer, United States | 0:55.92 |
| 1988 | Kristin Otto, East Germany | 0:54.93 |
| 1992 | Zhuang Yong, China | 0:54.64 |
| 1996 | Le Jingyi, China | 0:54.50 |
| 2000 | Inge de Bruijn, Netherlands | 0:58.83 |

**200-Meter Freestyle**

| | | |
|---|---|---|
| 1968 | Debbie Meyer, United States | 2:10.50 |
| 1972 | Shane Gould, Australia | 2:03.56 |
| 1976 | Kornelia Ender, East Germany | 1:59.26 |
| 1980 | Barbara Krause, East Germany | 1:58.33 |
| 1984 | Mary Wayle, United States | 1:59.23 |
| 1988 | Heike Friedrich, East Germany | 1:57.65 |
| 1992 | Nicole Haislett, United States | 1:57.90 |
| 1996 | Claudia Poll, Costa Rica | 1:58.16 |
| 2000 | Susie O'Neill, Australia | 1:58.24 |

**400-Meter Freestyle**

| | | |
|---|---|---|
| 1920 | Ethelda Bleibtrey, United States | 4:34.00[1] |
| 1924 | Martha Norelius, United States | 6:02.20 |
| 1928 | Martha Norelius, United States | 5:42.80 |

| | | |
|---|---|---|
| 1932 | Helene Madison, United States | 5:28.50 |
| 1936 | Hendrika Mastenbroek, Netherlands | 5:26.40 |
| 1948 | Ann Curtis, United States | 5:17.80 |
| 1952 | Valerie Gyenge, Hungary | 5:12.10 |
| 1956 | Lorraine Crapp, Australia | 4:54.60 |
| 1960 | Chris von Saltza, United States | 4:50.60 |
| 1964 | Ginny Duenkel, United States | 4:43.30 |
| 1968 | Debbie Meyer, United States | 4:31.80 |
| 1972 | Shane Gould, Australia | 4:19.04 |
| 1976 | Petra Thumer, East Germany | 4:09.89 |
| 1980 | Ines Diers, East Germany | 4:08.76 |
| 1984 | Tiffany Cohen, United States | 4:07.10 |
| 1988 | Janet Evans, United States | 4:03.85 |
| 1992 | Dagmar Hase, Germany | 4:07.18 |
| 1996 | Michelle Smith, Ireland | 4:07.25 |
| 2000 | Brooke Bennett, United States | 4:05.80 |

1. 300 meters.

### 800-Meter Freestyle

| | | |
|---|---|---|
| 1968 | Debbie Meyer, United States | 9:24.00 |
| 1972 | Keena Rothhammer, United States | 8:53.68 |
| 1976 | Petra Thumer, East Germany | 8:37.14 |
| 1980 | Michelle Ford, Australia | 8:28.90 |
| 1984 | Tiffany Cohen, United States | 8:24.95 |
| 1988 | Janet Evans, United States | 8:20.20 |
| 1992 | Janet Evans, Unites States | 8:25.52 |
| 1996 | Brooke Bennett, Unites States | 8:27.89 |
| 2000 | Brooke Bennett, United States | 8:19.67 |

### 100-Meter Backstroke

| | | |
|---|---|---|
| 1924 | Sybil Bauer, United States | 1:23.20 |
| 1928 | Marie Braun, Netherlands | 1:22.00 |
| 1932 | Eleanor Holm, United States | 1:19.40 |
| 1936 | Dina Senff, Netherlands | 1:18.90 |
| 1948 | Karen Harup, Denmark | 1:14.40 |
| 1952 | Joan Harrison, South Africa | 1:14.30 |
| 1956 | Judy Grinham, Great Britain | 1:12.90 |
| 1960 | Lynn Burke, United States | 1:09.30 |
| 1964 | Cathy Ferguson, United States | 1:07.70 |
| 1968 | Kaye Hall, United States | 1:06.20 |
| 1972 | Melissa Belote, United States | 1:05.78 |
| 1976 | Ulrike Richter, East Germany | 1:01.83 |
| 1980 | Rica Reinisch, East Germany | 1:00.86 |
| 1984 | Theresa Andrews, United States | 1:02.55 |
| 1988 | Kristin Otto, East Germany | 1:00.89 |
| 1992 | Krisztina Egerszegi, Hungary | 1:00.68 |
| 1996 | Beth Botsford, United States | 1:01.19 |
| 2000 | Diana Mocanu, Romania | 1:00.21 |

### 200-Meter Backstroke

| | | |
|---|---|---|
| 1968 | Pokey Watson, United States | 2:24.80 |
| 1972 | Melissa Belote, United States | 2:19.19 |
| 1976 | Ulrike Richter, East Germany | 2:13.43 |
| 1980 | Rica Reinisch, East Germany | 2:11.77 |
| 1984 | Jolanda DeRover, Netherlands | 2:12.38 |
| 1988 | Krisztina Egerszegi, Hungary | 2:09.29 |
| 1992 | Krisztina Egerszegi, Hungary | 2:07.06 |
| 1996 | Krisztina Egerszegi, Hungary | 2:07.83 |
| 2000 | Diana Mocanu, Romania | 2:08.16 |

### 100-Meter Breaststroke

| | | |
|---|---|---|
| 1968 | Djurdjica Bjedov, Yugoslavia | 1:15.80 |
| 1972 | Catherine Carr, United States | 1:13.58 |
| 1976 | Hannelore Anke, East Germany | 1:11.16 |
| 1980 | Ute Geweniger, East Germany | 1:10.22 |
| 1984 | Petra Van Staveren, Netherlands | 1:09.88 |
| 1988 | Tainia Dangalakova, Bulgaria | 1:07.95 |
| 1992 | Elena Roudkovskaia, Unified Team | 1:08.00 |
| 1996 | Penny Heyns, South Africa | 1:07.73 |
| 2000 | Megan Quann, United States | 1:07.05 |

### 200-Meter Breaststroke

| | | |
|---|---|---|
| 1924 | Lucy Morton, Great Britain | 3:33.20 |
| 1928 | Hilde Schrader, Germany | 3:12.60 |
| 1932 | Clare Dennis, Australia | 3:06.30 |
| 1936 | Hideko Maehata, Japan | 3:03.60 |
| 1948 | Nel van Vliet, Netherlands | 2:57.20 |
| 1952 | Eva Szekely, Hungary | 2:51.70 |

| | | |
|---|---|---|
| 1956 | Ursala Happe, Germany | 2:53.10 |
| 1960 | Anita Lonsbrough, Great Britain | 2:49.50 |
| 1964 | Galina Prozumenschikova, USSR | 2:46.40 |
| 1968 | Sharon Wichman, United States | 2:44.40 |
| 1972 | Beverly Whitfield, Australia | 2:41.71 |
| 1976 | Marina Koshevaia, USSR | 2:33.35 |
| 1980 | Lina Kachushite, USSR | 2:29.54 |
| 1984 | Anne Ottenbrite, Canada | 2:30.38 |
| 1988 | Silke Hoerner, East Germany | 2:26.71 |
| 1992 | Kyoko Iwasaki, Japan | 2:26.65 |
| 1996 | Penny Heyns, South Africa | 2:25.41 |
| 2000 | Agnes Kovacs, Hungary | 2:24.35 |

### 100-Meter Butterfly

| | | |
|---|---|---|
| 1956 | Shelley Mann, United States | 1:11.00 |
| 1960 | Carolyn Schuler, United States | 1:09.50 |
| 1964 | Sharon Stouder, United States | 1:04.70 |
| 1968 | Lynn McClements, Australia | 1:05.50 |
| 1972 | Mayumi Aoki, Japan | 1:03.34 |
| 1976 | Kornelia Ender, East Germany | 1:00.13 |
| 1980 | Caren Metschuck, East Germany | 1:00.42 |
| 1984 | Mary Meagher, United States | 0:59.26 |
| 1988 | Kristin Otto, East Germany | 0:59.00 |
| 1992 | Qian Hong, China | 0:58.62 |
| 1996 | Amy Van Dyken, United States | 0:59.13 |
| 2000 | Inge de Bruijn, Netherlands | 0:56.61[1] |

1. World record.

### 200-Meter Butterfly

| | | |
|---|---|---|
| 1968 | Ada Kok, Netherlands | 2:24.70 |
| 1972 | Karen Moe, United States | 2:15.57 |
| 1976 | Andrea Pollack, East Germany | 2:11.41 |
| 1980 | Ines Geissler, East Germany | 2:10.44 |
| 1984 | Mary Meagher, United States | 2:06.90 |
| 1988 | Kathleen Nord, East Germany | 2:09.51 |
| 1992 | Summer Sanders, United States | 2:06.67 |
| 1996 | Susan O'Neill, Australia | 2:07.76 |
| 2000 | Misty Hyman, United States | 2:05.88 |

### 200-Meter Individual Medley

| | | |
|---|---|---|
| 1968 | Claudia Kolb, United States | 2:24.70 |
| 1972 | Shane Gould, Australia | 2:23.07 |
| 1984 | Tracy Caulkins, United States | 2:12.64 |
| 1988 | Daniela Hunger, East Germany | 2:12.59 |
| 1992 | Lin Lee, China | 2:11.55[1] |
| 1996 | Michelle Smith, Ireland | 2:13.93 |
| 2000 | Yana Klochkova, Ukraine | 2:10.68 |

1. World record.

### 400-Meter Individual Medley

| | | |
|---|---|---|
| 1964 | Donna de Varona, United States | 5:18.70 |
| 1968 | Claudia Kolk, United States | 5:08.50 |
| 1972 | Gail Neall, Australia | 5:02.97 |
| 1976 | Ulrike Tauber, East Germany | 4:42.77 |
| 1980 | Petra Schneider, East Germany | 4:36.29 |
| 1984 | Tracy Caulkins, United States | 4:39.21 |
| 1988 | Janet Evans, United States | 4:37.76 |
| 1992 | Krisztina Egerszegi, Hungary | 4:36.54 |
| 1996 | Michelle Smith, Ireland | 4:39.18 |
| 2000 | Yana Klochkova, Ukraine | 4:33.59[1] |

1. World record.

### 400-Meter Freestyle Relay

| | | |
|---|---|---|
| 1912 | Great Britain | 5:52.80 |
| 1920 | United States | 5:11.60 |
| 1924 | United States | 4:58.80 |
| 1928 | United States | 4:47.60 |
| 1932 | United States | 4:38.00 |
| 1936 | Netherlands | 4:36.00 |
| 1948 | United States | 4:29.20 |
| 1952 | Hungary | 4:24.40 |
| 1956 | Australia | 4:17.10 |
| 1960 | United States | 4:08.90 |
| 1964 | United States | 4:03.80 |
| 1968 | United States | 4:02.50 |
| 1972 | United States | 3:55.19 |

| | | |
|---|---|---|
| 1976 | United States | 3:44.82 |
| 1980 | East Germany | 3:42.71 |
| 1984 | United States | 3:44.43 |
| 1988 | East Germany | 3:40.63 |
| 1992 | United States | 3:39.46 |
| 1996 | United States | 3:39.29 |
| 2000 | United States | 3:36.61[1] |

1. World record.

**800-Meter Freestyle Relay**

| | | |
|---|---|---|
| 1996 | United States | 7:59.87 |
| 2000 | United States | 7:57.80 |

**400-Meter Medley Relay**

| | | |
|---|---|---|
| 1960 | United States | 4:41.10 |
| 1964 | United States | 4:33.90 |
| 1968 | United States | 4:28.30 |
| 1972 | United States | 4:20.75 |
| 1976 | East Germany | 4:07.95 |
| 1980 | East Germany | 4:06.67 |
| 1984 | United States | 4:08.34 |
| 1988 | East Germany | 4:03.74 |
| 1992 | United States | 4:02.54 |
| 1996 | United States | 4:02.88 |
| 2000 | United States | 3:58.30[1] |

1. World record.

**Springboard Dive** — **Points**

| | | |
|---|---|---|
| 1920 | Aileen Riggin, United States | 539.90 |
| 1924 | Elizabeth Becker, United States | 474.50 |
| 1928 | Helen Meany, United States | 78.62 |
| 1932 | Georgia Coleman, United States | 87.52 |
| 1936 | Marjorie Gestring, United States | 89.27 |
| 1948 | Victoria M. Draves, United States | 108.74 |
| 1952 | Patricia McCormick, United States | 147.30 |
| 1956 | Patricia McCormick, United States | 142.36 |
| 1960 | Ingrid Kramer, Germany | 155.81 |
| 1964 | Ingrid Kramer Engel, Germany | 145.00 |
| 1968 | Sue Gossick, United States | 150.77 |
| 1972 | Micki King, United States | 450.03 |
| 1976 | Jennifer Chandler, United States | 506.19 |
| 1980 | Irina Kalinina, USSR | 725.91 |
| 1984 | Sylvie Bernier, Canada | 530.70 |
| 1988 | Gao Min, China | 580.23 |
| 1992 | Gao Min, China | 572.40 |
| 1996 | Fu Ming-Xia, China | 547.68 |
| 2000 | Fu Ming-Xia, China | 609.42 |

**Platform Dive** — **Points**

| | | |
|---|---|---|
| 1912 | Greta Johansson, Sweden | 39.90 |
| 1920 | Stefani Fryland, Denmark | 34.60 |
| 1924 | Caroline Smith, United States | 166.00 |
| 1928 | Elizabeth B. Pinkston, United States | 31.60 |
| 1932 | Dorothy Poynton, United States | 40.26 |
| 1936 | Dorothy Poynton Hill, United States | 33.92 |
| 1948 | Victoria M. Draves, United States | 68.87 |
| 1952 | Patricia McCormick, United States | 79.37 |
| 1956 | Patricia McCormick, United States | 84.85 |
| 1960 | Ingrid Kramer, Germany | 91.28 |
| 1964 | Lesley Bush, United States | 99.80 |
| 1968 | Milena Duchkova, Czechoslovakia | 109.59 |
| 1972 | Ulrika Knape, Sweden | 390.00 |
| 1976 | Elena Vaytsekhovskaia, USSR | 406.59 |
| 1980 | Martina Jaschke, East Germany | 596.25 |
| 1984 | Zhou Ji-Hong, China | 435.51 |
| 1988 | Xu Yan-Mei, China | 445.20 |
| 1992 | Fu Ming-Xia, China | 461.43 |
| 1996 | Fu Ming-Xia, China | 521.58 |
| 2000 | Laura Wilkinson, United States | 543.75 |

**Synchronized 3m Springboard Dive** — **Points**

| | | |
|---|---|---|
| 2000 | Vera Ilina and Ioulia Pakhalina, Russia | 332.64 |

**Synchronized 10m Platform Dive** — **Points**

| | | |
|---|---|---|
| 2000 | Li Na and Sang Xue, China | 345.12 |

## BASKETBALL–MEN

| | | | | |
|---|---|---|---|---|
| 1904 | United States | | 1972 | USSR |
| 1936 | United States | | 1976 | United States |
| 1948 | United States | | 1980 | Yugoslavia |
| 1952 | United States | | 1984 | United States |
| 1956 | United States | | 1988 | USSR |
| 1960 | United States | | 1992 | United States |
| 1964 | United States | | 1996 | United States |
| 1968 | United States | | 2000 | United States |

## BASKETBALL–WOMEN

| | | | | |
|---|---|---|---|---|
| 1976 | USSR | | 1992 | Unified Team[1] |
| 1980 | USSR | | 1996 | United States |
| 1984 | United States | | 2000 | United States |
| 1988 | United States | | | |

1. Former Soviet Union team.

## BOXING

### (U.S. winners only)

NOTE: U.S. boycotted Olympics in 1980.

**Flyweight-112 pounds (51 kg)**

| | | | | |
|---|---|---|---|---|
| 1904 | George Finnegan | | 1952 | Nate Brooks |
| 1920 | Frank De Genaro | | 1976 | Leo Randolph |
| 1924 | Fidel La Barba | | 1984 | Steve McCrory |

**Bantamweight-119 (54 kg)**

| | | | | |
|---|---|---|---|---|
| 1904 | O.L. Kirk | | 1988 | Kennedy McKinney |

**Featherweight-126 pounds (57 kg)**

| | | | | |
|---|---|---|---|---|
| 1904 | O.L. Kirk | | 1984 | Meldrick Taylor |
| 1924 | Jackie Fields | | | |

**Lightweight-132 pounds (60 kg)**

| | | | | |
|---|---|---|---|---|
| 1904 | H.J. Spanger | | 1976 | Howard Davis |
| 1920 | Samuel Mosberg | | 1984 | Pernell Whitaker |
| 1968 | Ronnie Harris | | 1992 | Oscar De La Hoya |

**Light Welterweight-140 pounds (63.5 kg)**

| | | | | |
|---|---|---|---|---|
| 1952 | Charles Adkins | | 1976 | Ray Leonard |
| 1972 | Ray Seales | | 1984 | Jerry Page |

**Welterweight-148 pounds (67 kg)**

| | | | | |
|---|---|---|---|---|
| 1904 | Al Young | | 1984 | Mark Breland |
| 1932 | Edward Flynn | | | |

**Light Middleweight-157 pounds (71 kg)**

| | | | | |
|---|---|---|---|---|
| 1960 | Wilbert McClure | | 1996 | David Reid |
| 1984 | Frank Tate | | | |

**Middleweight-165 pounds (75 kg)**

| | | | | |
|---|---|---|---|---|
| 1904 | Charles Mayer | | 1960 | Eddie Cook |
| 1932 | Carmen Barth | | 1976 | Michael Spinks |
| 1952 | Floyd Patterson | | | |

**Light Heavyweight-179 pounds (81 kg)**

| | | | | |
|---|---|---|---|---|
| 1920 | Edward Eagan | | 1960 | Cassius Clay |
| 1952 | Norvel Lee | | 1976 | Leon Spinks |
| 1956 | James Boyd | | 1988 | Andrew Maynard |

**Heavyweight-201 pounds (91 kg)**

| | | | | |
|---|---|---|---|---|
| 1904 | Sam Berger | | 1968 | George Foreman |
| 1952 | Edward Sanders | | 1984 | Henry Tilman |
| 1956 | Pete Rademacher | | 1988 | Ray Mercer |
| 1964 | Joe Frazier | | | |

**Super Heavyweight (unlimited)**

| | | |
|---|---|---|
| 1984 | Tyrell Biggs | |

## DISTRIBUTION OF MEDALS—2000 SUMMER GAMES

| Country | Gold | Silver | Bronze | Total | Country | Gold | Silver | Bronze | Total |
|---|---|---|---|---|---|---|---|---|---|
| United States | 39 | 25 | 33 | 97 | Iran | 3 | 0 | 1 | 4 |
| Russia | 32 | 28 | 28 | 88 | Turkey | 3 | 0 | 1 | 4 |
| China | 28 | 16 | 15 | 59 | Finland | 2 | 1 | 1 | 4 |
| Australia | 16 | 25 | 17 | 58 | Uzbekistan | 1 | 1 | 2 | 4 |
| Germany | 14 | 17 | 26 | 57 | New Zealand | 1 | 0 | 3 | 4 |
| France | 13 | 14 | 11 | 38 | Argentina | 0 | 2 | 2 | 4 |
| Italy | 13 | 8 | 13 | 34 | Korea | 0 | 1 | 3 | 4 |
| Cuba | 11 | 11 | 7 | 29 | Austria | 2 | 1 | 0 | 3 |
| Great Britain | 11 | 10 | 7 | 28 | Azerbaijan | 2 | 0 | 1 | 3 |
| Korea | 8 | 9 | 11 | 28 | Latvia | 1 | 1 | 1 | 3 |
| Romania | 11 | 6 | 9 | 26 | Yugoslavia | 1 | 1 | 1 | 3 |
| Netherlands | 12 | 9 | 4 | 25 | Estonia | 1 | 0 | 2 | 3 |
| Ukraine | 3 | 10 | 10 | 23 | Thailand | 1 | 0 | 2 | 3 |
| Japan | 5 | 8 | 5 | 18 | Nigeria | 0 | 3 | 0 | 3 |
| Hungary | 8 | 6 | 3 | 17 | Slovenia | 2 | 0 | 0 | 2 |
| Belarus | 3 | 3 | 11 | 17 | Bahamas | 1 | 1 | 0 | 2 |
| Poland | 6 | 5 | 3 | 14 | Croatia | 1 | 0 | 1 | 2 |
| Canada | 3 | 3 | 8 | 14 | Saudi Arabia | 0 | 1 | 1 | 2 |
| Bulgaria | 5 | 6 | 2 | 13 | Moldova | 0 | 1 | 1 | 2 |
| Greece | 4 | 6 | 3 | 13 | Trinidad & Tobago | 0 | 1 | 1 | 2 |
| Sweden | 4 | 5 | 3 | 12 | Costa Rica | 0 | 0 | 2 | 2 |
| Brazil | 0 | 6 | 6 | 12 | Portugal | 0 | 0 | 2 | 2 |
| Spain | 3 | 3 | 5 | 11 | Cameroon | 1 | 0 | 0 | 1 |
| Norway | 4 | 3 | 3 | 10 | Colombia | 1 | 0 | 0 | 1 |
| Switzerland | 1 | 6 | 2 | 9 | Mozambique | 1 | 0 | 0 | 1 |
| Ethiopia | 4 | 1 | 3 | 8 | Ireland | 0 | 1 | 0 | 1 |
| Czech Republic | 2 | 3 | 3 | 8 | Uruguay | 0 | 1 | 0 | 1 |
| Kazakhstan | 3 | 4 | 0 | 7 | Vietnam | 0 | 1 | 0 | 1 |
| Kenya | 2 | 3 | 2 | 7 | Armenia | 0 | 0 | 1 | 1 |
| Jamaica | 0 | 4 | 3 | 7 | Barbados | 0 | 0 | 1 | 1 |
| Denmark | 2 | 3 | 1 | 6 | Chile | 0 | 0 | 1 | 1 |
| Indonesia | 1 | 3 | 2 | 6 | India | 0 | 0 | 1 | 1 |
| Mexico | 1 | 2 | 3 | 6 | Iceland | 0 | 0 | 1 | 1 |
| Georgia | 0 | 0 | 6 | 6 | Israel | 0 | 0 | 1 | 1 |
| Lithuania | 2 | 0 | 3 | 5 | Kyrgyzstan | 0 | 0 | 1 | 1 |
| Slovakia | 1 | 3 | 1 | 5 | Kuwait | 0 | 0 | 1 | 1 |
| Algeria | 1 | 1 | 3 | 5 | Macedonia | 0 | 0 | 1 | 1 |
| Belgium | 0 | 2 | 3 | 5 | Qatar | 0 | 0 | 1 | 1 |
| South Africa | 0 | 2 | 3 | 5 | Sri Lanka | 0 | 0 | 1 | 1 |
| Morocco | 0 | 1 | 4 | 5 | **Total** | **301** | **299** | **328** | **928** |
| Chinese Taipei | 0 | 1 | 4 | 5 | | | | | |

# Other 2000 Summer Olympic Games Champions

## Archery

Women's individual—Yun Mi-jin, South Korea

Women's team—South Korea

Men's individual—Simon Fairweather, Australia

Men's team—South Korea

## Badminton

Men's singles—Ji Xinpeng, China

Men's doubles—Indonesia (Tony Gunawan, Candra Wijaya)

Women's singles—Gong Zhichao, China

Women's doubles—China (Ge Fei, Gu Jun)

Mixed doubles—China (Jun Zhang, Ling Gao)

## Baseball

Men—United States

## Beach Volleyball

Women—Australia (Natalie Cook, Kerri Pottharst)

Men—United States (Dain Blanton, Eric Fonoimoana)

## Boxing

Light flyweight—Brahim Asloum, France

Flyweight—Wijan Ponlid, Thailand

Bantamweight—Guillermo Rigondeaux, Cuba

Featherweight—Bekzat Sattarkhanov, Kazakhstan

Lightweight—Mario Kindelan, Cuba

Light welterweight—Mahamadkadyz Abdullaev, Uzbekistan

Welterweight—Oleg Saitov, Russia

Light middleweight—Yermakhan Ibraimov, Kazakhstan

Middleweight—Jorge Gutierrez, Cuba

Light heavyweight—Alexander Lebziak, Russia

Heavyweight—Felix Savon, Cuba

Super heavyweight—Audley Harrison, Great Britain

## Cycling—Men

1 km time trial (track)—Jason Queally, Great Britain

Individual pursuit (track)—Robert Bartko, Germany

Team pursuit (track)—Germany

Individual points race (track)—Juan Llaneras, Spain

Individual sprint (track)—Marty Nothstein, United States

Olympic sprint (track)—France

Madison (track)—Australia

Keirin (track)—Florian Rousseau, France

Mountain bike—Miguel Martinez, France

Individual road race—Jan Ullrich, Germany

Individual time trial (road)—Viacheslav Ekimov, Russia

## Cycling—Women
500m time trial (track)—Felicia Ballanger, France
Individual pursuit (track)—Leontien Zijlaard, Netherlands
Sprint (track)—Felicia Ballanger, France
Points race (track)—Antonella Bellutti, Italy
Mountain bike—Paola Pezzo, Italy
Road race—Leontien Zijlaard, Netherlands
Individual time trial (road)—Leontien Zijlaard, Netherlands

## Equestrian
Individual three-day—David O'Connor, United States
Three-day team event—Australia
Individual dressage—Anky van Grunsven, Netherlands
Team dressage—Germany
Individual jumping—Jeroen Dubbeldam, Netherlands
Team jumping—Germany

## Fencing—Men
Individual epee—Pavel Kolobkov, Russia
Individual foil—Kim Young-ho, South Korea
Individual sabre—Mihai Claudiu Covaliu, Romania
Team epee—Italy
Team foil—France
Team sabre—Russia

## Fencing—Women
Individual epee—Timea Nagy, Hungary
Individual foil—Valentina Vezzali, Italy
Team epee—Russia
Team foil—Italy

## Field Hockey
Men—Netherlands
Women—Australia

## Gymnastics—Men
All-around—Alexei Nemov, Russia
Floor exercise—Igors Vihrovs, Latvia
Pommel horse—Marius Urzica, Romania
Rings—Szilveszter Csollany, Hungary
Horizontal bar—Alexei Nemov, Russia
Parallel bars—Li Xiaopeng, China
Vault—Gervasio Deferr, Spain
Team—China

## Gymnastics—Women
All-around—Simona Amanar, Romania
Uneven bars—Svetlana Khorkina, Russia
Balance beam—Liu Xuan, China
Floor exercise—Elena Zamolodtchikova, Russia
Vault—Elena Zamolodtchikova, Russia
Team—Romania

## Judo—Men
Extra-lightweight (60kg)—Tadahiro Nomura, Japan
Half-lightweight (66kg)—Huseyin Ozkan, Turkey
Lightweight (73kg)—Giuseppe Maddaloni, Italy
Half-middleweight (81kg)—Makoto Takimoto, Japan

Middleweight (90kg)—Mark Huizinga, Netherlands
Half-heavyweight (100kg)—Kosei Inoue, Japan
Heavyweight (100kg+)—David Douillet, France

## Judo—Women
Extra-lightweight (48kg)—Ryoko Tamura, Japan
Half-lightweight (52kg)—Legna Verdecia, Cuba
Lightweight (57kg)—Isabel Fernandez, Spain
Half-middleweight (63kg)—Severine Vandenhende, France
Middleweight (70kg)—Sibelis Veranes, Cuba
Half-heavyweight (78kg)—Tang Lin, China
Heavyweight (78kg+)—Yuan Hua, China

## Kayak-Canoe—Men
Canoe singles 500m—Gyorgy Kolonics, Hungary
Canoe pairs 500m—Hungary
Kayak singles 500m—Knut Holmann, Norway
Kayak pairs 500m—Hungary
Kayak singles 1,000m—Knut Holmann, Norway
Canoe singles 1,000m—Andreas Dittmer, Germany
Kayak pairs 1,000m—Italy
Canoe pairs 1,000m—Romania
Kayak fours 1,000m—Hungary
Canoe slalom singles—Tony Estanguet, France
Canoe slalom pairs—Slovakia
Kayak slalom singles—Thomas Schmidt, Germany

## Kayak—Women
500m singles—Josefa Idem Guerrini, Italy
500m pairs—Germany
500m fours—Germany
Single slalom—Stepanka Hilgertova, Czech Republic

## Modern Pentathlon
Men—Dmitri Svatkovsky, Russia
Women—Stephanie Cook, Great Britain

## Rhythmic Gymnastics
Individual—Yulia Barslukova, Russia
Team—Russia

## Rowing—Men
Single sculls—Rob Waddell, New Zealand
Lightweight double sculls—Poland
Heavyweight double sculls—Slovenia
Quadruple sculls—Italy
Coxless pair—France
Lightweight coxless four—France
Heavyweight coxless four—Great Britain
Eight—Great Britain

## Rowing—Women
Single sculls—Ekaterina Karsten, Belarus
Lightweight double sculls—Romania
Heavyweight double sculls—Germany
Quadruple sculls—Germany

Coxless pair—Romania
Eight—Romania

## Sailing
Open Tornado—Austria
Open 49er—Finland
Open Laser—Ben Ainslie, Great Britain
Open Star—United States
Open Soling—Denmark
Men's Mistral—Christoph Sieber, Austria
Men's 470 fleet—Australia
Men's Finn—Iain Percy, Great Britain
Women's Mistral—Alessandra Sensini, Italy
Women's 470 fleet—Australia
Women's Europe—Shirley Robertson, Great Britain

## Shooting—Men
Air pistol—Franck Dumoulin, France
Free pistol—Tanyu Kiriakov, Bulgaria
Rapid fire pistol—Serguei Alifirenko, Russia
Trap—Michael Diamond, Australia
Double trap—Richard Faulds, Great Britain
Air rifle—Cai Yalin, China
Running target—Yang Ling, China
Rifle prone—Jonas Edman, Sweden
Rifle 3-position—Rajmond Debevec, Slovenia
Skeet shooting—Mykola Milchev, Ukraine

## Shooting—Women
Air pistol—Tao Luna, China
Sport pistol—Maria Grozdeva, Bulgaria
Air rifle—Nancy Johnson, United States
Rifle three position—Renata Maier-Rozanska, Poland
Trap—Daina Gudzineviciute, Lithuania
Double trap—Pia Hansen, Sweden
Skeet—Zemfira Meftakhetdinova, Azerbaijan

## Soccer
Men—Cameroon
Women—Norway

## Softball
United States

## Synchronized Swimming
Duet—Russia
Team—Russia

## Table Tennis
Men's singles—Kong Linghui, China
Men's doubles—China
Women's singles—Wang Nan, China
Women's doubles—China

## Taekwondo
Men 58kg—Michail Mouroutsos, Greece
Men 68kg—Steven Lopez, United States
Men 80kg—Angel Matos Fuentes, Cuba
Men 80kg+—Kim Kyong-hun, South Korea
Women 49kg—Lauren Burns, Australia
Women 57kg—Jung Jae-eun, South Korea
Women 67kg—Lee Sun-Hee, South Korea
Women 67kg+—Chen Zhong, China

| | | |
|---|---|---|
| **Team Handball** | **Volleyball** | 69kg—Lin Weining, China |
| Men—Russia | Men—Yugoslavia | 75kg—Maria Urrutia, Colombia |
| Women—Denmark | Women—Cuba | 75kg+—Ding Meiyuan, China |

**Tennis**

Men's singles—Yevgeny Kafelnikov, Russia

Men's doubles—Canada

Women's singles—Venus Williams, United States

Women's doubles—United States

**Trampoline**

Men—Alexandre Moskalenko, Russia

Women—Irina Karavaeva, Russia

**Triathlon**

Men—Simon Whitfield, Canada

Women—Brigitte McMahon, Switzerland

**Water Polo**

Men—Hungary

Women—Australia

**Weightlifting—Men**

56kg—Halil Mutlu, Turkey

62kg—Nikolay Pechalov, Croatia

69kg—Galabin Boevski, Bulgaria

77kg—Zhan Xugang, China

85kg—Pyrros Dimas, Greece

94kg—Akakios Kakiasvilis, Greece

105kg—Hossein Tavakoli, Iran

105kg+—Hossein Rezazadeh, Iran

**Weightlifting—Women**

48kg—Tara Nott, United States

53kg—Yang Xia, China

58kg—Soraya Jimenez, Mexico

63kg—Xiaomin Chen, China

**Wrestling—Freestyle**

54kg—Namig Abdullayev, Azerbaijan

63kg—Mourad Oumakhanov, Russia

58kg—Alireza Dabir, Iran

69kg—Daniel Igali, Canada

76kg—Alexander Leipold, Germany

85kg—Adam Saitiev, Russia

97kg—Saghid Mourtasaliyev, Russia

130kg—David Moussoulbes, Russia

**Wrestling—Greco-Roman**

54kg—Sim Kwon Ho, South Korea

58kg—Armen Nazarian, Bulgaria

63kg—Varteres Samourgachev, Russia

69kg—Filiberto Azcuy, Cuba

76kg—Mourat Kardanov, Russia

85kg—Hamza Yerlikaya, Turkey

97kg—Mikael Ljungberg, Sweden

130kg—Rulon Gardner, United States

# Football

The pastime of kicking around a ball goes back beyond the limits of recorded history. Ancient savage tribes played football of a primitive kind. There was a ball-kicking game played by Athenians, Spartans, and Corinthians 2,500 years ago, which the Greeks called *Episkuros*. The Romans had a somewhat similar game called *Harpastum* and are supposed to have carried the game with them when they invaded the British Isles in the first century B.C.

Undoubtedly the game known in the United States as football traces directly to the English game of rugby, though the modifications have been many. Informal football was played on college lawns well over a century ago, and an annual freshman-sophomore series of "scrimmages" began at Yale in 1840. The first formal intercollegiate football game was the Princeton-Rutgers contest at New Brunswick, N.J., on Nov. 6, 1869, with Rutgers winning by 6 goals to 4.

In those days, games were played with 25, 20, 15, or 11 men on a side. In 1880, there was a conven-

tion at which Walter Camp of Yale persuaded the delegates to agree to 11 players on a side.

The first professional game was played in 1895 at Latrobe, Pa. The National Football League was founded in 1921. The All-American Conference went into action in 1946. At the end of the 1949 season the two circuits merged, retaining the name of the older league. In 1960, the American Football League began operations. In 1970, the leagues merged. The United States Football League played its first season in 1983, from March to July. It suspended spring operations after the 1985 season, and planned a 1986 move to fall, but suspended operations again.

In March 1991, another effort at spring football was launched. This time the ten-team World League of American Football had the backing of the National Football League. After two seasons it was suspended. The league returned in 1995, with six teams in Europe. In 1998, it was renamed the NFL Europe League.

## College Football

### NATIONAL COLLEGE FOOTBALL CHAMPIONS

The "National Collegiate Athletic Association Football Guide" recognizes as unofficial national

champion the team selected each year by press association polls of writers and coaches.

| | | | | |
|---|---|---|---|---|
| 1936 | Minnesota | 1952 | Mich. State | 1965 Alabama and | 1977 Notre Dame | 1991 Miami (Fla.) and |
| 1937 | Pittsburgh | 1953 | Maryland | Mich. State | 1978 Alabama and | Washington |
| 1938 | Texas Christian | 1954 | Ohio State and | 1966 Notre Dame | So. Calif. | 1992 Alabama |
| 1939 | Texas A & M | | UCLA | 1967 So. Calif. | 1979 Alabama | 1993 Florida State |
| 1940 | Minnesota | 1955 | Oklahoma | 1968 Ohio State | 1980 Georgia | 1994 Nebraska |
| 1941 | Minnesota | 1956 | Oklahoma | 1969 Texas | 1981 Clemson | 1995 Nebraska |
| 1942 | Ohio State | 1957 | Auburn and | 1970 Texas and | 1982 Penn State | 1996 Univ. of Florida |
| 1943 | Notre Dame | | Ohio State | Nebraska | 1983 Miami (Fla.) | 1997 Michigan and |
| 1944 | Army | 1958 | Louisiana State | 1971 Nebraska | 1984 Brigham Young | Nebraska |
| 1945 | Army | 1959 | Syracuse | 1972 So. Calif. | 1985 Oklahoma | 1998 Tennessee |
| 1946 | Notre Dame | 1960 | Minnesota | 1973 Notre Dame | 1986 Penn State | 1999 Florida State |
| 1947 | Notre Dame | 1961 | Alabama | and U. of Ala. | 1987 Miami (Fla.) | 2000 Oklahoma |
| 1948 | Michigan | 1962 | So. Calif. | 1974 Oklahoma and | 1988 Notre Dame | 2001 Miami (Fla.) |
| 1949 | Notre Dame | 1963 | Texas | So. Calif. | 1989 Miami (Fla.) | |
| 1950 | Oklahoma | 1964 | Alabama | 1975 Oklahoma | 1990 Colorado and | |
| 1951 | Tennessee | | | 1976 Pittsburgh | Georgia Tech | |

# RECORD OF ANNUAL MAJOR COLLEGE FOOTBALL BOWL GAMES

## Rose Bowl (At Pasadena, Calif.)

1902 Michigan 49, Stanford 0
1916 Washington State 14, Brown 0
1917 Oregon 14, Pennsylvania 0
1918 Mare Island Marines 19, Camp Lewis 7
1919 Great Lakes 17, Mare Island Marines 0
1920 Harvard 7, Oregon 6
1921 California 28, Ohio State 0
1922 Washington and Jefferson 0, California 0
1923 So. Calif. 14, Penn State 3
1924 Navy 14, Washington 14
1925 Notre Dame 27, Stanford 10
1926 Alabama 20, Washington 19
1927 Alabama 7, Stanford 7
1928 Stanford 7, Pittsburgh 6
1929 Georgia Tech 8, California 7
1930 So. Calif. 47, Pittsburgh 14
1931 Alabama 24, Wash. State 0
1932 So. Calif. 21, Tulane 12
1933 So. Calif. 35, Pittsburgh 0
1934 Columbia 7, Stanford 0
1935 Alabama 29, Stanford 13
1936 Stanford 7, So. Methodist 0
1937 Pittsburgh 21, Washington 0
1938 California 13, Alabama 0
1939 So. Calif. 7, Duke 3
1940 So. Calif. 14, Tennessee 0
1941 Stanford 21, Nebraska 13
1942 Oregon State 20, Duke 16[1]
1943 Georgia 9, UCLA 0
1944 So. Calif. 29, Washington 0
1945 So. Calif. 25, Tennessee 0
1946 Alabama 34, So. Calif. 14
1947 Illinois 45, UCLA 14
1948 Michigan 49, So. Calif. 0
1949 Northwestern 20, California 14
1950 Ohio State 17, California 14
1951 Michigan 14, California 6
1952 Illinois 40, Stanford 7
1953 So. Calif. 7, Wisconsin 0
1954 Michigan State 28, UCLA 20
1955 Ohio State 20, So. Calif. 7
1956 Michigan State 17, UCLA 14
1957 Iowa 35, Oregon State 19
1958 Ohio State 10, Oregon 7
1959 Iowa 38, California 12
1960 Washington 44, Wisconsin 8
1961 Washington 17, Minnesota 7
1962 Minnesota 21, UCLA 3
1963 So. Calif. 42, Wisconsin 37
1964 Illinois 17, Washington 7
1965 Michigan 34, Oregon State 7
1966 UCLA 14, Michigan State 12
1967 Purdue 14, So. Calif. 13
1968 So. Calif. 14, Indiana 3
1969 Ohio State 27, So. Calif. 16
1970 So. Calif. 10, Michigan 3
1971 Stanford 27, Ohio State 17
1972 Stanford 13, Michigan 12
1973 So. Calif. 42, Ohio State 17
1974 Ohio State 42, So. Calif. 21
1975 So. Calif. 18, Ohio State 17
1976 UCLA 23, Ohio State 10
1977 So. Calif. 14, Michigan 6
1978 Washington 27, Michigan 20
1979 So. Calif. 17, Michigan 10
1980 So. Calif. 17, Ohio State 16
1981 Michigan 23, Washington 6

1982 Washington 28, Iowa 0
1983 UCLA 24, Michigan 14
1984 UCLA 45, Illinois 9
1985 So. Calif. 20, Ohio St. 17
1986 UCLA 45, Iowa 28
1987 Arizona State 22, Michigan 15
1988 Michigan State 20, So. Calif. 17
1989 Michigan 22, So. Calif. 14
1990 So. Calif. 17, Michigan 10
1991 Washington 46, Iowa 34
1992 Washington 34, Michigan 14
1993 Michigan 38, Washington 31
1994 Wisconsin 21, UCLA 16
1995 Penn State 38, Oregon 20
1996 So. Calif. 41, Northwestern 32
1997 Ohio State 20, Arizona State 17
1998 Michigan 21, Washington State 16
1999 Wisconsin 38, UCLA 31
2000 Wisconsin 17, Stanford 9
2001 Washington 34, Purdue 24
2002 Miami 37, Nebraska 14
1. Played at Durham, N.C.

## Orange Bowl (At Miami)

1933 Miami (Fla.) 7, Manhattan 0
1934 Duquesne 33, Miami (Fla.) 7
1935 Bucknell 26, Miami (Fla.) 0
1936 Catholic 20, Mississippi 19
1937 Duquesne 13, Mississippi State 12
1938 Auburn 6, Michigan State 0
1939 Tennessee 17, Oklahoma 0
1940 Georgia Tech 21, Missouri 7
1941 Mississippi State 14, Georgetown 7
1942 Georgia 40, Texas Christian 26
1943 Alabama 37, Boston College 21
1944 Louisiana State 19, Texas A & M 14
1945 Tulsa 26, Georgia Tech 12
1946 Miami (Fla.) 13, Holy Cross 6
1947 Rice 8, Tennessee 0
1948 Georgia Tech 20, Kansas 14
1949 Texas 41, Georgia 28
1950 Santa Clara 21, Kentucky 13
1951 Clemson 15, Miami (Fla.) 14
1952 Georgia Tech 17, Baylor 14
1953 Alabama 61, Syracuse 6
1954 Oklahoma 7, Maryland 0
1955 Duke 34, Nebraska 7
1956 Oklahoma 20, Maryland 6
1957 Colorado 27, Clemson 21
1958 Oklahoma 48, Duke 21
1959 Oklahoma 21, Syracuse 6
1960 Georgia 14, Missouri 0
1961 Missouri 21, Navy 14
1962 Louisiana State 25, Colorado 7
1963 Alabama 17, Oklahoma 0
1964 Nebraska 13, Auburn 7
1965 Texas 21, Alabama 17
1966 Alabama 39, Nebraska 28
1967 Florida 27, Georgia Tech 12
1968 Oklahoma 26, Tennessee 24
1969 Penn State 15, Kansas 14
1970 Penn State 10, Missouri 3
1971 Nebraska 17, Louisiana State 12
1972 Nebraska 38, Alabama 6
1973 Nebraska 40, Notre Dame 6
1974 Penn State 16, Louisiana State 9

1975 Notre Dame 13, Alabama 11
1976 Oklahoma 14, Michigan 6
1977 Ohio State 27, Colorado 10
1978 Arkansas 31, Oklahoma 6
1979 Oklahoma 31, Nebraska 24
1980 Oklahoma 24, Florida State 7
1981 Oklahoma 18, Florida State 17
1982 Clemson 22, Nebraska 15
1983 Nebraska 21, Louisiana State 20
1984 Miami (Fla.) 31, Nebraska 30
1985 Washington 28, Oklahoma 17
1986 Oklahoma 25, Penn State 10
1987 Oklahoma 42, Arkansas 8
1988 Miami (Fla.) 20, Oklahoma 14
1989 Miami (Fla.) 23, Nebraska 3
1990 Notre Dame 21, Colorado 6
1991 Colorado 10, Notre Dame 9
1992 Miami (Fla.) 22, Nebraska 0
1993 Florida State 27, Nebraska 14
1994 Florida State 18, Nebraska 16
1995 Nebraska 24, Miami (Fla.) 17
1996 Florida State 31, Notre Dame 26
1997 Nebraska 41, Virginia Tech 21
1998 Nebraska 42, Tennessee 17
1999 Florida 31, Syracuse 10
2000 Michigan 35, Alabama 34
2001 Oklahoma 13, Florida State 2
2002 Florida 56, Maryland 23

## Sugar Bowl (At New Orleans)

1935 Tulane 20, Temple 14
1936 Texas Christian 3, Louisiana State 2
1937 Santa Clara 21, Louisiana State 14
1938 Santa Clara 6, Louisiana State 0
1939 Texas Christian 15, Carnegie Tech 7
1940 Texas A & M 14, Tulane 13
1941 Boston College 19, Tennessee 13
1942 Fordham 2, Missouri 0
1943 Tennessee 14, Tulsa 7
1944 Georgia Tech 20, Tulsa 18
1945 Duke 29, Alabama 26
1946 Oklahoma A & M 33, St. Mary's (Calif.) 13
1947 Georgia 20, North Carolina 10
1948 Texas 27, Alabama 7
1949 Oklahoma 14, North Carolina 6
1950 Oklahoma 35, Louisiana State 0
1951 Kentucky 13, Oklahoma 7
1952 Maryland 28, Tennessee 13
1953 Georgia Tech 24, Mississippi 7
1954 Georgia Tech 42, West Virginia 19
1955 Navy 21, Mississippi 0
1956 Georgia Tech 7, Pittsburgh 0
1957 Baylor 13, Tennessee 7
1958 Mississippi 39, Texas 7
1959 Louisiana State 7, Clemson 0
1960 Mississippi 21, Louisiana State 0
1961 Mississippi 14, Rice 6
1962 Alabama 10, Arkansas 3
1963 Mississippi 17, Arkansas 13
1964 Alabama 12, Mississippi 7
1965 Louisiana State 13, Syracuse 10
1966 Missouri 20, Florida 18

Banonis, Vince—Detroit, 1941
Barnes, Stanley—So. Calif., 1921
Barrett, Charles—Cornell, 1915
Baston, Bert—Minnesota, 1916
Battles, Cliff—W. Va. Wesleyan, 1931
Baugh, Sammy—Texas Christian, 1936
Baughan, Maxie—Georgia Tech, 1959
Bausch, James—Kansas, 1930
Beagle, Ron—Navy, 1955
Beasley, Terry—Auburn, 1971
Beban, Gary—UCLA, 1967
Bechtol, Hub—Texas Tech, 1946
Beck, Ray—Georgia Tech, 1951
Beckett, John—Oregon, 1913
Bednarik, Chuck—Pennsylvania 1948
Behm, Forrest—Nebraska, 1940
Bell, Bobby—Minnesota, 1962
Bellino, Joe—Navy, 1960
Below, Marty—Wisconsin, 1923
Benbrook, A.—Michigan, 1911
Bentrim, Jeff—North Dakota State, 1986
Bertelli, A.—Notre Dame, 1943
Berry, Charlie—Lafayette, 1924
Berwanger, John (Jay)—Chicago, 1935
Bettencourt, Larry—St. Mary's, 1927
Biletnikoff, Fred—Florida State, 1964
Blanchard, Felix (Doc)—Army, 1946
Blazine, Tony—Ill. Wesleyan, 1934
Bock, Ed—Iowa State, 1938
Bomar, Lynn—Vanderbilt, 1924
Bomeisler, Doug (Bo)—Yale, 1913
Booth, Albie—Yale, 1931
Bork, George—Northern Illinois, 1963
Borries, Fred—Navy, 1934
Bosely, Bruce—West Virginia, 1955
Bosseler, Don—Miami (Fla.), 1956
Bottari, Vic—California, 1939
Boynton, Ben—Williams, 1920
Bozis, Al—Georgetown, 1941
Bradshaw, Terry—Louisiana Tech, 1969
Brewer, Charles—Harvard, 1895
Bright, John—Drake, 1951
Brodie, John—Stanford, 1956
Brooke, George—Pennsylvania, 1895
Brosky, Al—Illinois, 1952
Brown, Bob—Nebraska, 1963
Brown, George—Navy/San Diego State, 1947
Brown, Gordon—Yale, 1900
Brown, Jim—Syracuse, 1956
Brown, John, Jr.—Navy, 1913
Brown, Johnny Mack—Alabama, 1925
Brown, Raymond (Tay)—So. Calif., 1932
Browner, Ross—Notre Dame, 1977
Bruner, Teel—Centre College (Ky.), 1985
Buchanan, Buck—Grambling State, 1962
Budde, Brad—So. Calif., 1979
Bunker, Paul—Army, 1902
Burford, Chris—Stanford, 1959
Burris, Kurt—Oklahoma, 1954
Burton, Ron—Northwestern, 1956
Butkus, Dick—Illinois, 1964
Butler, Kevin—Georgia, 1984
Butler, Robert—Wisconsin, 1912
Cafego, George—Tennessee, 1939
Cagle, Chris—SW La./Army, 1929
Cain, John—Alabama, 1932
Cameron, Eddie—Wash. & Lee, 1924
Campbell, David C.—Harvard, 1901
Campbell, Earl—Texas, 1977
Cannon, Billy—Louisiana State, 1959
Cannon, Jack—Notre Dame, 1929
Cappelletti, John—Penn State, 1973
Carideo, Frank—Notre Dame, 1930
Caroline, J.C.—Illinois, 1954
Carney, Charles—Illinois, 1921
Carpenter, Bill—Army, 1959
Carpenter, C. Hunter—VPI, 1905
Carroll, Charles—Washington, 1928
Carson, Harry—So. Carolina State, 1975
Carter, Anthony—Michigan, 1982

Casanova, Tommy—Louisiana State, 1971
Casey, Edward L.—Harvard, 1919
Cason, Rod—Angelo State, 1971
Cassady, Howard—Ohio State, 1955
Chamberlain, Guy—Nebraska, 1915
Chapman, Sam—Cal.-Berkeley, 1938
Chappuis, Bob—Michigan, 1947
Christman, Paul—Missouri, 1940
Cichy, Joe—North Dakota State, 1970
Clark, Earl (Dutch)—Colo. College, 1929
Cleary, Paul—So. Calif., 1947
Clevenger, Zora—Indiana, 1903
Cloud, Jack—William & Mary, 1948
Cochran, Gary—Princeton, 1895
Cody, Josh—Vanderbilt, 1920
Coleman, Don—Mich. State, 1951
Conerly, Chuck—Mississippi, 1947
Connor, George—Notre Dame, 1947
Cooper, Bill—Muskingum (Ohio), 1960
Corbin, W.—Yale, 1888
Corbus, William—Stanford, 1933
Cowan, Hector—Princeton, 1889
Coy, Edward H. (Tad)—Yale, 1909
Crawford, Brad—Franklin (Ind.), 1977
Crawford, Fred—Duke, 1933
Crow, John D.—Texas A & M, 1957
Crowley, James—Notre Dame, 1924
Csonka, Larry—Syracuse, 1967
Cutter, Slade—Navy, 1934
Czarobski, Ziggie—Notre Dame, 1947
Dale, Carroll—Virginia Tech, 1959
Dalrymple, Gerald—Tulane, 1931
Dalton, John—Navy, 1912
Daly, Charles—Harvard/Army, 1902
Daniell, Averell—Pittsburgh, 1936
Daniell, James—Ohio State, 1941
Davies, Tom—Pittsburgh, 1921
Davis, Ernest—Syracuse, 1961
Davis, Glenn—Army, 1946
Davis, Robert T.—Georgia Tech, 1947
Dawkins, Pete—Army, 1958
Delaney, Joe—Northwestern State, 1980
Deery, Tom—Widener, 1981
DeLong, Steve—Tennessee, 1964
Dement, Kenneth—SE Missouri, 1954
Den Herder, Vern—Central (Iowa), 1970
De Rogatis, Al—Duke, 1940
DesJardien, Paul—Chicago 1914
Devino, Aubrey—Iowa, 1921
DeWitt, John—Princeton, 1903
Dial, Buddy—Rice, 1958
Dicus, Chuck—Arkansas, 1970
Dierdorf, Dan—Michigan, 1970
Ditka, Mike—Pittsburgh, 1960
Dobbs, Glenn—Tulsa, 1942
Dodd, Bobby—Tennessee, 1930
Donan, Holland—Princeton, 1950
Donchess, Joseph—Pittsburgh, 1929
Dorsett, Tony—Pittsburgh, 1976
Dougherty, Nathan—Tennessee, 1909
Dove, Bob—Notre Dame, 1942
Drahos, Nick—Cornell, 1940
Driscoll, Paddy—Northwestern, 1917
Finny, Illinois/Mich. St. Col., 1927
Dryer, Fred—San Diego State, 1968
Dudek, Joe—Plymouth State, 1985
Dudon, Dick—Navy, 1945
Dudley, William (Bill)—Virginia, 1941
Duncan, Randy—Iowa, 1958
Easley, Ken—UCLA, 1980
Eckersall, Walter—Chicago, 1906
Edwards, Turk—Washington State, 1931
Edwards, William—Princeton, 1900
Eichenlaub, R.—Notre Dame, 1913
Eisenhauer, Steve—Navy, 1953
Elking, Larry—Baylor, 1964
Elliott, Chalmers—Purdue, 1944 & Mich., 1947
Elliott, Pete—Michigan, 1948
Elmendorf, Dave—Texas A & M, 1970
Elway, John—Stanford, 1982

Evans, Ray—Kansas, 1947
Exendine, Albert—Carlisle, 1908
Falaschi, Nello—Santa Clara, 1937
Fears, Tom—Santa Clara/UCLA, 1947
Feathers, Beattie—Tennessee, 1933
Fenimore, Robert—Oklahoma State, 1947
Fenton, G.E. (Doc)—Louisiana State, 1910
Ferguson, Bob—Ohio State, 1961
Ferraro, John—So. Calif., 1944
Fesler, Wesley—Ohio State, 1930
Fincher, Bill—Georgia Tech, 1920
Fischer, Bill—Notre Dame, 1948
Fish, Hamilton—Harvard, 1909
Fisher, Robert—Harvard, 1911
Flowers, Abe—Georgia Tech, 1920
Flowers, Charlie—Mississippi, 1959
Floyd, George—Eastern Kentucky, 1981
Fortmann, Daniel—Colgate, 1935
Fralic, Bill—Pittsburgh, 1984
Francis, Sam—Nebraska, 1936
Franck, George (Sonny)—Minnesota, 1940
Franco, Edmund (Ed)—Fordham, 1937
Frank, Clint—Yale, 1937
Franz, Rodney—California, 1949
Frederickson, Tucker—Auburn, 1964
Friedman, Benny—Michigan, 1926
Gabriel, Roman—North Carolina St., 1961
Gain, Bob—Kentucky, 1950
Galiffa, Arnold—Army, 1949
Galimore, Willie—Florida A & M, 1956
Gallarneau, Hugh—Stanford, 1941
Gamble, Kenny—Colgate, 1987
Garbisch, Edgar—Army, 1924
Garrett, Mike—So. Calif., 1965
Gelbert, Charles—Pennsylvania, 1896
Geyer, Forest—Oklahoma, 1915
Gibbs, Jake—Mississippi, 1960
Giel, Paul—Minnesota, 1953
Gifford, Frank—So. Calif., 1951
Gilbert, Chris—Texas, 1968
Gilbert, Walter—Auburn, 1936
Gilmer, Harry—Alabama, 1947
Gipp, George—Notre Dame, 1920
Gladchuk, Chet—Boston College, 1940
Glass, Bill—Baylor, 1956
Glover, Rich—Nebraska, 1972
Goldberg, Marshall—Pittsburgh, 1938
Goodreault, Gene—Boston College, 1940
Gordon, Walter—California, 1918
Governale, Paul—Columbia, 1942
Grabowski, Jim—Illinois, 1965
Graham, Otto—Northwestern, 1943
Gradishar, Randy—Ohio State, 1973
Grange, Harold (Red)—Illinois, 1925
Grayson, Roberty—Stanford, 1935
Green, Charles—Wittenberg, 1964
Green, Hugh—Pittsburgh, 1980
Green, Joe—North Texas State, 1968
Green, Tim—Syracuse, 1985
Gregg, Bob—Purdue, 1950
Griffin, Archie—Ohio State, 1975
Grinnell, William—Tufts, 1934
Gream, Jerry—Notre Dame, 1956
Guglielmi, Ralph—Notre Dame, 1954
Gulick, Merel—Hobart, 1929
Guyon, Joe—Georgia Tech, 1919
Hadl, John—Kansas, 1961
Hale, Edwin—Mississippi Col., 1921
Hall, Parker—Mississippi, 1938
Ham, Jack—Penn State, 1970
Hamilton, Robert (Bones)—Stanford, 1935
Hamilton, Tom—Navy, 1925
Hannah, John—Alabama, 1972
Hanson, Vic—Syracuse, 1926
Harder, Pat—Wisconsin, 1942
Hardwick, H. (Tack)—Harvard, 1914

Hare, T. Truxton—Pennsylvania, 1900
Harley, Chick—Ohio State, 1919
Harmon, Tom—Michigan, 1940
Harpster, Howard—Carnegie Tech, 1928
Hart, Edward J. Princeton, 1911
Hart, Leon—Notre Dame, 1949
Hartman, Bill—Georgia, 1937
Haslett, Jim—Indiana (Pa.), 1978
Hawkins, Frank—Nevada, 1980
Haynes, Michael—Arizona State, 1975
Hazel, Homer—Rutgers, 1924
Healey, Ed—Dartmouth, 1916
Heffelfiner, W. (Pudge)—Yale, 1891
Hein, Mel—Washington State, 1930
Heinrich, Don—Washington, 1952
Hendricks, Ted—Miami, 1968
Henry, Wilbur—Wash. & Jefferson, 1919
Herschberger, Clarence—Chicago, 1899
Herwig, Robert—California, 1937
Heston, Willie—Michigan, 1904
Hickman, Herman—Tennessee, 1931
Hickok, William—Yale, 1895
Hicks, John—Ohio State, 1973
Hill, Dan—Duke, 1938
Hillebrand, A.R. (Doc)—Princeton, 1900
Hinkey, Frank—Yale, 1894
Hinkle, Carl—Vanderbilt, 1937
Hinkle, Clark—Bucknell, 1932
Hirsch, Elroy—Wisconsin/Michigan, 1943
Hitchcock, James—Auburn, 1932
Hoage, Terry—Georgia, 1983
Hoffman, Frank—Notre Dame, 1931
Hogan, James J.—Yale, 1904
Holland, Jerome (Brud)—Cornell, 1938
Holleder, Don—Army, 1955
Hollenbeck, William—Pennsylvania, 1908
Holovak, Michael—Boston College, 1942
Holt, Pierce—Angelo State, 1980
Holub, E.J.—Texas Tech, 1960
Hornung, Paul—Notre Dame, 1956
Horrell, Edwin—California, 1924
Horvath, Les—Ohio State, 1944
Howe Arthur—Yale, 1911
Howell, Millard (Dixie)—Alabama, 1934
Hubbard, Cal—Centenary, 1926
Hubbard, John—Amherst, 1906
Hubert, Allison—Alabama, 1925
Huff, Robert Lee (Sam)—W. Va., 1955
Humble, Weldon G.—Rice, 1946
Hunley, Ricky—Arizona, 1983
Hunt, Joel—Texas A & M, 1927
Huntington, Ellery—Colgate, 1914
Hutson, Don—Alabama, 1934
Ingram, James—Navy, 1906
Iacavazzi, Cosmo—Princeton, 1964
Isbell, Cecil—Purdue, 1937
Jablonsky, Harvey—Wash. U./Army, 1933
Jackson, Bo—Auburn, 1985
Jackson, Keith—Oklahoma, 1987
Janowicz, Vic—Ohio State, 1951
Jefferson, John—Arizona State, 1977
Jenkins, Darold—Missouri, 1941
Jensen, Jack—Cal.-Berkeley, 1948
Joesting, Herbert—Minnesota, 1927
Johnson, Billy—Widener, 1973
Johnson, Gary—Grambling State, 1974
Johnson, James—Carlisle, 1903
Johnson, Robert—Tennessee, 1967
Johnson, Ron—Michigan, 1968
Jones, Brent—Santa Clara, 1985
Jones, Calvin—Iowa, 1955
Jones, Gormer—Ohio State, 1935
Jones, Stan—Maryland, 1953
Jordan, Lee Roy—Alabama, 1962
Juhan, Frank—Univ. of South, 1910
Justice, Charlie—North Carolina, 1949
Kaer, Mort—So. Calif., 1926
Karras, Alex—Iowa, 1957
Kavanaugh, Kenneth—Louisiana State, 1939
Kaw, Edgar—Cornell, 1922

Kazmaier, Richard—Princeton, 1951
Keck, James—Princeton, 1921
Kelley, Larry—Yale, 1936
Kelly, William—Montana, 1926
Kenna, Ed—Syracuse, 1966
Kern, George—Boston College, 1941
Ketcham, Henry—Yale, 1913
Keyes, Leroy—Purdue, 1968
Killinger, William—Penn State, 1922
Kilmer, Billy—UCLA, 1960
Kimbrough, John—Texas A & M, 1940
Kinard, Frank—Mississippi, 1937
Kinard, Terry—Clemson, 1982
Kiner, Steve—Tennessee, 1969
King, Philip—Princeton, 1893
Kinnick, Nile—Iowa, 1939
Kipke, Harry—Michigan, 1923
Kirkpatrick, John Reed—Yale, 1910
Kitzmiller, John—Oregon, 1929
Koch, Barton—Baylor, 1931
Kitner, Malcolm—Texas, 1942
Kramer, Ron—Michigan, 1956
Kroll, Alex—Rutgers, 1961
Krueger, Charlie—Texas A & M, 1957
Kwalick, Ted—Penn State, 1968
Lach, Steve—Duke, 1941
Lane, Myles—Dartmouth, 1927
Lanier, Sr., Willie—Morgan State, 1966
Lattner, Joseph J.—Notre Dame, 1953
Lauricella, Hank—Tennessee, 1952
Lautenschlaeger—Tulane, 1925
Layden, Elmer—Notre Dame, 1924
Layne, Bobby—Texas, 1947
Lea, Langdon—Princeton, 1895
LeBaron, Eddie—Univ. of Pacific, 1949
LeClair, Jim—North Dakota, 1971
Leech, James—Va. Mil. Inst., 1920
Lester, Darrell—Texas Christian, 1935
Lewis, D. D.—Mississippi State, 1968
Lilly, Bob—Texas Christian, 1960
Little, Floyd—Syracuse, 1966
Lio, Augie—Georgetown, 1940
Lockbaum, Gordie—Holy Cross, 1987
Locke, Gordon—Iowa, 1922
Lomax, Neil—Portland (Ore.) State, 1980
Long, Chuck—Iowa, 1985
Long, Mel—Toledo, 1971
Loria, Frank—Virginia Tech, 1967
Lott, Ronnie—So. Calif., 1980
Lourie, Don—Princeton, 1921
Lucas, Richard—Penn State, 1959
Luckman, Sid—Columbia, 1938
Lujack, John—Notre Dame, 1947
Lund, J.L. (Pug)—Minnesota, 1934
Lynch, Jim—Notre Dame, 1966
MacAfee, Ken—Notre Dame, 1977
Macomber, Bart—Illinois, 1915
MacLeod, Robert—Dartmouth, 1938
Maegle, Dick—Rice, 1954
Mahan, Edward W.—Harvard, 1915
Majors, John—Tennessee, 1956
Mallory, William—Yale, 1893
Mancha, Vaughn—Alabama, 1947
Mann, Gerald—So. Methodist, 1927
Manning, Archie—Mississippi, 1970
Manske, Edgar—Northwestern, 1933
Marinaro, Ed—Cornell, 1971
Marino, Dan—Pittsburgh, 1982
Markov, Vic—Washington, 1937
Marshall, Robert—Minnesota, 1907
Martin, Jim—Notre Dame, 1949
Matson, Ollie—San Fran. U., 1952
Matthews, Ray—Texas Christian, 1928
Maulbetsch, John—Michigan, 1914
Mauthe, J.L. (Pete)—Penn State, 1912
Maxwell, Robert—Chicago/Swarthmore, 1906
McAfee, George—Duke, 1939
McCallum, Napoleon—Navy, 1985
McCauley, Don—North Carolina, 1970
McClung, Thomas L.—Yale, 1891
McColl, William F.—Stanford, 1951
McCormick, James B.—Princeton, 1907

McDonald, Tom—Oklahoma, 1956
McDowall, Jack—No. Carolina State, 1927
McElhenny, Hugh—Washington, 1951
McEver, Gene—Tennessee, 1931
McEwan, John—Minn./Army, 1916
McFadden, J.B.—Clemson, 1939
McFadin, Bud—Texas, 1950
McGee, Mike—Duke, 1959
McGinley, Edward—Pennsylvania, 1924
McGovern, J.—Minnesota, 1910
McGraw, Thurman—Colorado State, 1949
McGriff, Tyrone—Florida A & M, 1979
McKeever, Mike—So. Calif., 1960
McKenzie, Reggie—Michigan, 1971
McLaren, George—Pittsburgh, 1918
McMahon, Jim—Brigham Young, 1981
McMillan, Dan—So. Calif./California, 1922
McMillin, A.N. (Bo)—Centre, 1921
McWhorter, Robert—Georgia, 1913
Mercer, Leroy—Pennsylvania, 1912
Meredith, Don—So. Methodist, 1959
Merritt, Frank—Army, 1943
Metzger, Bert—Notre Dame, 1930
Meyland, Wayne—Nebraska, 1967
Michaels, Lou—Kentucky, 1957
Michels, John—Tennessee, 1952
Mickal, Abe—Louisiana State, 1935
Miller, Creighton—Notre Dame, 1943
Miller, Don—Notre Dame, 1925
Miller, Edgar (Rip)—Notre Dame, 1924
Miller, Eugene—Penn State, 1913
Miller, Fred—Notre Dame, 1928
Millner, Wayne—Notre Dame, 1935
Milstead, Century—Wabash/Yale, 1923
Minds, John—Pennsylvania, 1897
Minisi, Anthony—Navy/Pennsylvania, 1947
Modzelewski, Dick—Maryland, 1952
Moffatt, Alex—Princeton, 1884
Molinski, Ed—Tennessee, 1940
Montgomery, Cliff—Columbia, 1933
Montgomery, Wilbert—Abilene Christian, 1976
Moomaw, Donn—UCLA, 1952
Morley, William—Columbia, 1903
Morris, George—Georgia Tech, 1952
Morris, Larry—Georgia Tech, 1954
Morton, Craig—California, 1964
Morton, William—Dartmouth, 1931
Moscrip, Monk—Stanford, 1935
Muller, Harold (Brick)—Calif., 1922
Musso, Johnny—Alabama, 1971
Nagurski, Bronko—Minnesota, 1929
Nevers, Ernie—Stanford, 1925
Newell, Marshall—Harvard, 1893
Newman, Harry—Michigan, 1932
Newsome, Ozzie—Alabama, 1977
Nielsen, Gifford—Brigham Young, 1976
Nobis, Tommy—Texas, 1965
Nomellini, Leo—Minnesota, 1949
Oberland, Andrew—Dartmouth, 1925
O'Brien, Davey—Texas Christian, 1938
O'Brien, Ken—Cal.-Davis, 1982
O'Dea, Pat—Wisconsin, 1899
Odell, Robert—Pennsylvania, 1943
O'Hearn, J.—Cornell, 1915
Olds, Robin—Army, 1942
Oliphant, Elmer—Purdue/Army, 1917
Olsen, Merlin—Utah State, 1961
Onkotz, Dennis—Penn State, 1969
Oosterbaan, Ben—Michigan, 1927
O'Rourke, Charles—Boston College, 1940
Orsi, John—Colgate, 1931
Osgood, W.D.—Cornell/Pennsylvania, 1895
Osmanski, William—Holy Cross, 1938
Outland, John—Kansas/Pennsylvania, 1899
Owen, George—Harvard, 1922
Owens, Jim—Oklahoma, 1949

Owens, Steve—Oklahoma, 1969
Page, Alan—Notre Dame, 1966
Palumbo, Joe—U. of Virginia, 1951
Pardee, Jack—Texas A & M, 1956
Parilli, Vito (Babe)—Kentucky, 1951
Parker, Clarence (Ace)—Duke, 1936
Parker, Jackie—Miss. State, 1953
Parker, James—Ohio State, 1956
Payton, Walter—Jackson State, 1974
Pazzetti, V.J.—Wesleyan/Lehigh, 1912
Peabody, Endicott—Harvard, 1941
Peck, Robert—Pittsburgh, 1916
Pellegrini, Bob—Maryland, 1955
Pennock, Stanley B.—Harvard, 1914
Pfann, George—Cornell, 1923
Phillips, H.D.—Univ. of South, 1904
Phillips, Loyd—Arkansas, 1966
Pingel, John—Michigan State, 1938
Pihos, Pete—Indiana, 1945
Pinckert, Ernie—So. Calif., 1931
Plunkett, Jim—Stanford, 1970
Poe, Arthur—Princeton, 1899
Pollard, Fritz—Brown, 1916
Poole, Barney—Miss./Army, 1947
Powell, Marvin—So. Calif., 1976
Pregulman, Merv—Michigan, 1943
Price, Eddie—Tulane, 1949
Pruitt, Greg—Oklahoma, 1972
Pugh, Larry—Westminster, Pa., 1964
Pund, Henry—Georgia Tech, 1928
Ramsey, Gerrard—Wm. & Mary, 1942
Reasons, Gary—Northwestern State (La.), 1983
Redell, Bill—Occidental, 1963
Redman, Rick—Washington, 1964
Reeds, Claude—Oklahoma, 1913
Reid, Mike—Penn State, 1970
Reid, Steve—Northwestern, 1936
Reid, William—Harvard, 1900
Reifsnyder, Bob—Navy, 1958
Renfro, Mel—Oregon, 1963
Rentner, Ernest—Northwestern, 1932
Ressler, Glenn—Penn State, 1964
Reynolds, Robert—Nebraska, 1952
Reynolds, Robert—Stanford, 1935
Rhino, Randy—Georgia Tech, 1974
Rhome, Jerry—Tulsa, 1964
Richter, Les—California, 1951
Richter, Pat—Wisconsin, 1962
Riley, John—Northwestern, 1931
Rimington, Dave—Nebraska, 1982
Rinehart, Charles—Lafayette, 1897
Ritchie, Richard—Texas A & M, 1977
Ritcher, Jim—No. Carolina St., 1979
Roberts, J.D.—Oklahoma, 1953
Robeson, Paul—Rutgers, 1918
Robinson, Dave—Penn State, 1962
Robinson, Jerry—UCLA, 1978
Rodgers, Ira—West Virginia, 1919
Rodgers, Johnny—Nebraska, 1972
Rogers, Edward L.—Minnesota, 1903
Rogers, George—South Carolina, 1980
Roland, Johnny—Missouri, 1965
Romig, Joe—Colorado, 1961
Rosenberg, Aaron—So. Calif., 1934
Rote, Kyle—So. Methodist, 1950
Routt, Joe—Texas A & M, 1937
Salmon, Louis—Notre Dame, 1904
Sarkisian, Alex—Northwestern, 1948
Sauer, George—Nebraska, 1933
Savitsky, George—Pennsylvania, 1947
Saxon, Jimmy—Texas, 1961
Sayers Gale—Kansas, 1964
Scarbath, Jack—Maryland, 1952
Scarlett, Hunter—Pennsylvania, 1909
Schloredt, Bob—Washington, 1960
Schmidt, Joe—Pittsburgh, 1952
Schoonover, Wear—Arkansas, 1929
Schreiner, Dave—Wisconsin, 1942
Schultz, Adolf (Germany)—Mich., 1908
Schwab, Frank—Lafayette, 1922
Schwartz, Marchmont—Notre Dame, 1931

Schwegler, Paul—Washington, 1931
Scott, Clyde—Arkansas, 1949
Scott, Freddie—Amherst, 1973
Scott, Richard—Navy, 1947
Scott, Tom—Virginia, 1953
Seibels, Henry—Sewanee, 1899
Sellers, Ron—Florida State, 1968
Selmon, Lee Roy—Oklahoma, 1975
Sewell, Harley—Texas, 1952
Shakespeare, Bill—Notre Dame, 1935
Shell, Donnie—So. Carolina St., 1973
Shelton, Murray—Cornell, 1915
Shevlin, Tom—Yale, 1905
Shively, Bernie—Illinois, 1926
Simons, Claude—Tulane, 1934
Sims, Billy—Oklahoma, 1979
Simpson, O.J.—So. Calif., 1968
Singletary, Mike—Baylor, 1980
Sington, Fred—Alabama, 1930
Sinkwich, Frank—Georgia, 1942
Sisemore, Jerry—Texas, 1972
Sitko, Emil—Notre Dame, 1949
Skladany, Joe—Pittsburgh, 1933
Slater, F.F. (Duke)—Iowa, 1921
Smith, Billy Ray—Arkansas, 1982
Smith, Bruce—Minnesota, 1941
Smith, Bubba—Michigan State, 1966
Smith, Ernie—So. Calif., 1932
Smith, Harry—So. Calif., 1939
Smith, Jim Ray—Baylor, 1954
Smith, John (Clipper)—Notre Dame, 1927
Smith, Riley—Alabama, 1935
Smith, Vernon—Georgia, 1931
Snow, Neil—Michigan, 1901
Spani, Gary—Kansas State, 1977
Sparlis, Al—UCLA, 1945
Spears, Clarence W.—Dartmouth, 1915
Spears, W.D.—Vanderbilt, 1927
Sprackling, William—Brown, 1911
Sprague, M. (Bud)—Texas/Army, 1928
Spurrier, Steve—Florida, 1966
Stafford, Harrison—Texas, 1932
Stagg, Amos Alonzo—Yale, 1889
Stanfill, Bill—Georgia, 1968
Starcevich, Max—Washington, 1936
Staubach, Roger—Navy, 1963
Steffen, Walter—Chicago, 1908
Steffy, Joe—Army, 1947
Stein, Herbert—Pittsburgh, 1921
Steuber, Robert—Missouri, 1943
Stevens, Mal—Yale, 1923
Stevenson, Vincent—Pennsylvania, 1905
Stillwagon, Jim—Ohio State, 1970
Stinchcomb, Gaylord—Ohio State, 1920
Strom, Brock—Air Force, 1959
Strong, Ken—New York Univ., 1928
Strupper, George—Georgia Tech, 1917
Stuhldreher, Harry—Notre Dame, 1924
Stydahar, Joe—West Virginia, 1935
Suffridge, Robert—Tennessee, 1940
Suhey, Steve—Penn State, 1947
Sullivan, Pat—Auburn, 1971
Sundstrom, Frank—Cornell, 1920
Swann, Lynn—So. Calif., 1973
Swanson, Clarence—Nebraska, 1921
Swiacki, Bill—Holy Cross/Colombia, 1947
Swink, Jim—Texas Christian, 1956
Talboom, Eddie—Wyoming, 1950
Taliafarro, George—Indiana, 1948
Tarkenton, Fran—Georgia, 1960
Tavener, John—Indiana, 1944
Taylor, Bruce—Boston Univ., 1969
Taylor, Charles—Stanford, 1942
Thomas, Aurelius—Ohio State, 1957
Thompson, Joe—Pittsburgh, 1907
Thomsen, Lynn—Austana, 1986
Thorne, Samuel B.—Yale, 1906
Thorpe, Jim—Carlisle, 1912
Ticknor, Ben—Harvard, 1930

Tigert, John—Vanderbilt, 1904
Tinsley, Gaynell—Louisiana State, 1936
Tipton, Eric—Duke, 1938
Tonnemaker, Clayton—Minnesota, 1949
Torrey, Robert—Pennsylvania, 1906
Trautman, Randy—Boise State, 1981
Travis, Ed Tarkio—Missouri, 1920
Trippi, Charles—Georgia, 1946
Tryon, J. Edward—Colgate, 1925
Tubbs, Jerry—Oklahoma, 1956
Utay, Joe—Texas A & M, 1907
Van Brocklin, Norm—Oregon, 1948
Van Pelt, Brad—Michigan State, 1972
Van Sickel, Dale—Florida, 1929
Van Surdam, Henderson—Wesleyan, 1905
Very, Dexter—Penn State, 1912
Vessels, Billy—Oklahoma, 1952
Vick, Ernie—Michigan, 1921
Wagner, Huber—Pittsburgh, 1913
Walker, Doak—So. Methodist, 1949
Walker, Herschel—Georgia, 1982
Wallace, Bill—Rice, 1935
Walsh, Adam—Notre Dame, 1924
Warburton, I. (Cotton)—So. Calif., 1934
Ward, Robert (Bob)—Maryland, 1951
Warner, William—Cornell, 1903
Washington, Ken—UCLA, 1939
Weatherall, Jim—Oklahoma, 1951
Webster, George—Mich. State, 1966
Wedemeyer, Herman J.—St. Mary's, 1947
Weekes, Harold—Columbia, 1902
Weiner, Art—North Carolina, 1949
Weir, Ed—Nebraska, 1925
Welch, Gus—Carlisle, 1914
Weller, John—Princeton, 1935
Wendell, Percy—Harvard, 1913
West, D. Belford—Colgate, 1919
Westfall, Bob—Michigan, 1941
Weyand, Alex—Army, 1915
Wharton, Charles—Pennsylvania, 1896
Wheeler, Arthur—Princeton, 1894
White, Byron (Whizzer)—Colorado, 1937
White, Charles—So. Calif., 1979
White, Danny—Arizona State, 1973
White, Ed—California-Berkeley, 1968
White, Randy—Maryland, 1974
White, Reggie—Tennessee, 1983
Whitmire, Don—Alabama/Navy, 1944
Wickhorst, Frank—Navy, 1926
Widseth, Ed—Minnesota, 1936
Wildung, Richard—Minnesota, 1942
Williams, Bob—Notre Dame, 1950
Williams, Doug—Grambling, 1977
Williams, James—Rice, 1949
Willis, William—Ohio State, 1945
Wilson, George—Washington, 1925
Wilson, George—Lafayette, 1928
Wilson, Harry—Penn State/Army, 1923
Wilson, Marc—Brigham Young, 1979
Winslow, Kellen—Missouri, 1978
Wistert, Albert A.—Michigan, 1942
Wistert, Al Michigan, 1949
Wistert, Frank (Whitey) Michigan, 1933
Wood, Barry—Harvard, 1931
Wojciechowicz, Alex—Fordham, 1936
Wyant, Andrew—Bucknell/Chicago, 1894
Wyatt, Bowden—Tennessee, 1938
Wyckoff, Clint—Cornell, 1896
Yarr, Tom—Notre Dame, 1931
Yary, Ron—So. Calif., 1968
Yoder, Lloyd—Carnegie Tech, 1926
Young, Claude (Buddy)—Illinois, 1946
Young, Harry—Wash. & Lee, 1916
Young, Steve—Brigham Young, 1983
Young, Walter—Oklahoma, 1938
Youngblood, Jack—Florida, 1970
Youngblood, Jim—Tennessee, 1972
Zarnas, Gus—Ohio State, 1937

## Coaches

| | | | | |
|---|---|---|---|---|
| Bill Alexander | Bobby Dodd | Howard Jones | Frank Murray | Buck Shaw |
| Dr. Ed Anderson | Terry Donahue | L. (Biff) Jones | William Murray | Edgar Sherman |
| Ike Armstrong | Michael Donohue | Thomas (Tad) Jones | Ed (Hooks) Mylin | Andrew L. Smith |
| Chris Ault | Vince Dooley | Ralph (Shug) Jordan | Earle (Greasy) Neale | Carl Snavely |
| Earl Banks | Gus Dorais | Bob Keade | Jess Neely | Jim Sochor |
| Harry Baujan | Bill Edwards | Andy Kerr | David Nelson | Amos A. Stagg |
| Matty Bell | Charles (Rip) Engle | Chuck Klausing | Robert Neyland | Gilbert Steinke |
| Hugo Bezdek | Forest Evashevski | Frank Kush | Billy Nicks | Jock Sutherland |
| Dana X. Bible | Don Faurot | Frank Leahy | Homer Norton | Barry Switzer |
| Bernie Bierman | Joseph Fusco | George E. Little | Frank (Buck) O'Neill | James Tatum |
| Bob Blackman | Jake Gaither | Lou Little | Tom Osborne | Grant Teaff |
| Earl (Red) Blaik | Sid Gillman | El (Slip) Madigan | Bennie Owen | Frank W. Thomas |
| Frank Broyles | Ernest Godfrey | Fred Martinelli | Ara Parseghian | Lee Tressell |
| Earle Bruce | Ray Graves | Dave Maurer | Doyt Perry | Thad Vann |
| Paul "Bear" Bryant | Andy Gustafson | Charley McClendon | James Phalea | John H. Vaught |
| Harold Burry | Jack Harding | Herbert McCracken | Tommy Prothro | Wallace Wade |
| Jim Butterfield | Edward K. Hall | Daniel McGugin | John Ralston | Lynn Waldorf |
| James "Wally" Butts | Richard Harlow | John McKay | E.N. Robinson | Glenn (Pop) Warner |
| Charles W. Caldwell | Jesse Harper | Allyn McKeen | Knute Rockne | Frank Waters |
| Walter Camp | Percy Haughton | DeOrmond (Tuss) | E.L. (Dick) Romney | E.E. (Tad) Wieman |
| Len Casanova | Woody Hayes | McLaughry | William W. Roper | John W. Wilce |
| Frank Cavanaugh | John W. Heisman | John Merritt | Darrell Royal | Bud Wilkinson |
| Jerry Claiborne | R.A. (Bob) Higgins | L.R. (Dutch) Meyer | Ad Rutschman | Henry L. Williams |
| Richard Colman | Paul Hoernemann | Bernie Moore | Henry (Red) Sanders | George W. Woodruff |
| Don Coryell | Orin E. Hollingbery | Scrappy Moore | George F. Sanford | Warren Woodson |
| Carmen Cozza | Frank Howard | Jack Mollenkopf | Bo Schembechler | Bowden Wyatt |
| Fritz Crisler | Marcelino (Chelo) | Ray Morrison | Ron Schipper | Bill Yeoman |
| Duffy Daugherty | Huerta | Darrell Mudra | Francis A. Schmidt | Fielding H. Yost |
| Bob Devaney | William Ingram | Arnett "Ace" Mumford | Floyd (Ben) | Jim Young |
| Dan Devine | Don James | George A. Munger | Schwartzwalder | Robert Zuppke |
| Gil Dobie | Morley Jennings | Clarence Munn | Clark Shaughnessy | |

# Professional Football

## SUPER BOWLS I-XXXVI

| Game | Date | Winner | Loser | Site | Attendance |
|---|---|---|---|---|---|
| XXXVI | Feb. 3, 2002 | New England (AFC) 20 | St. Louis (NFC) 17 | Superdome, New Orleans | 72,922 |
| XXXV | Jan. 28, 2001 | Baltimore (AFC) 34 | New York Giants (NFC) 7 | Raymond James Stadium, Tampa, Fla. | 71,921 |
| XXXIV | Jan. 30, 2000 | St. Louis (NFC) 23 | Tennessee (AFC) 16 | Georgia Dome, Atlanta, Ga. | 72,625 |
| XXXIII | Jan. 31, 1999 | Denver (AFC) 34 | Atlanta (NFC) 19 | Pro Player Stadium, Miami, Fla. | 74,803 |
| XXXII | Jan. 25, 1998 | Denver (AFC) 31 | Green Bay (NFC) 24 | Qualcomm Stadium, San Diego, Calif. | 68,912 |
| XXXI | Jan. 26, 1997 | Green Bay (NFC) 35 | New England (AFC) 21 | Superdome, New Orleans, La. | 72,301 |
| XXX | Jan. 28, 1996 | Dallas (NFC) 27 | Pittsburgh (AFC) 17 | Sun Devil Stadium, Tempe, Ariz. | 76,347 |
| XXIX | Jan. 29, 1995 | San Francisco (NFC) 49 | San Diego (AFC) 26 | Joe Robbie Stadium, Miami, Fla. | 74,107 |
| XXVIII | Jan. 30, 1994 | Dallas (NFC) 30 | Buffalo (AFC) 13 | Georgia Dome, Atlanta, Ga. | 72,817 |
| XXVII | Jan. 31, 1993 | Dallas (NFC) 52 | Buffalo (AFC) 17 | Rose Bowl, Pasadena, Calif. | 98,374 |
| XXVI | Jan. 26, 1992 | Washington (NFC) 37 | Buffalo (AFC) 24 | Metrodome, Minneapolis, Minn. | 63,130 |
| XXV | Jan. 27, 1991 | Giants (NFC) 20 | Buffalo (AFC) 19 | Tampa Stadium, Tampa, Fla. | 73,813 |
| XXIV | Jan. 28, 1990 | San Francisco (NFC) 55 | Denver (AFC) 10 | Superdome, New Orleans | 72,919 |
| XXIII | Jan. 22, 1989 | San Francisco (NFC) 20 | Cincinnati (AFC) 16 | Joe Robbie Stadium, Miami, Fla. | 75,179 |
| XXII | Jan. 31, 1988 | Washington (NFC) 42 | Denver (AFC) 10 | Jack Murphy Stadium, San Diego, Calif. | 73,302 |
| XXI | Jan. 25, 1987 | Giants (NFC) 39 | Denver (AFC) 20 | Rose Bowl, Pasadena, Calif. | 101,063 |
| XX | Jan. 26, 1986 | Chicago (NFC) 46 | New England (AFC) 10 | Superdome, New Orleans | 73,818 |
| XIX | Jan. 20, 1985 | San Francisco (NFC) 38 | Miami (AFC) 16 | Stanford Stadium, Palo Alto, Calif. | 84,059 |
| XVIII | Jan. 22, 1984 | Los Angeles Raiders (AFC) 38 | Washington (NFC) 9 | Tampa Stadium, Tampa, Fla | 72,920 |
| XVII | Jan. 30, 1983 | Washington (NFC) 27 | Miami (AFC) 17 | Rose Bowl, Pasadena, Calif. | 103,667 |
| XVI | Jan. 24, 1982 | San Francisco (NFC) 26 | Cincinnati (AFC) 21 | Silverdome, Pontiac, Mich. | 81,270 |
| XV | Jan. 25, 1981 | Oakland (AFC) 27 | Philadelphia (NFC) 10 | Superdome, New Orleans | 75,500 |
| XIV | Jan. 20, 1980 | Pittsburgh (AFC) 31 | Los Angeles (NFC) 19 | Rose Bowl, Pasadena | 103,985 |
| XIII | Jan. 21, 1979 | Pittsburgh (AFC) 35 | Dallas (NFC) 31 | Orange Bowl, Miami | 79,484 |
| XII | Jan. 15, 1978 | Dallas (NFC) 27 | Denver (AFC) 10 | Superdome, New Orleans | 75,583 |
| XI | Jan. 9, 1977 | Oakland (AFC) 32 | Minnesota (NFC) 14 | Rose Bowl, Pasadena | 103,424 |
| X | Jan. 18, 1976 | Pittsburgh (AFC) 21 | Dallas (NFC) 17 | Orange Bowl, Miami | 80,187 |
| IX | Jan. 12, 1975 | Pittsburgh (AFC) 16 | Minnesota (NFC) 6 | Tulane Stadium, New Orleans | 80,997 |
| VIII | Jan. 13, 1974 | Miami (AFC) 24 | Minnesota (NFC) 7 | Rice Stadium, Houston | 71,882 |
| VII | Jan. 14, 1973 | Miami (AFC) 14 | Washington (NFC) 7 | Memorial Coliseum, Los Angeles | 90,182 |
| VI | Jan. 16, 1972 | Dallas (NFC) 24 | Miami (AFC) 3 | Tulane Stadium, New Orleans | 81,591 |
| V | Jan. 17, 1971 | Baltimore (AFC) 16 | Dallas (NFC) 13 | Orange Bowl, Miami | 79,204 |
| IV | Jan. 11, 1970 | Kansas City (AFL) 23 | Minnesota (NFL) 7 | Tulane Stadium, New Orleans | 80,562 |
| III | Jan. 12, 1969 | New York (AFL) 16 | Baltimore (NFL) 7 | Orange Bowl, Miami | 75,389 |
| II | Jan. 14, 1968 | Green Bay (NFL) 33 | Oakland (AFL) 14 | Orange Bowl, Miami | 75,546 |
| I | Jan. 15, 1967 | Green Bay (NFL) 35 | Kansas City (AFL) 10 | Memorial Coliseum, Los Angeles | 61,946 |

NOTE: Super Bowls I to IV were played before the American Football League and National Football League merged into the NFL, which was divided into two conferences, the NFC and AFC.

# NATIONAL FOOTBALL LEAGUE FINAL STANDINGS 2001

## AMERICAN FOOTBALL CONFERENCE

### Eastern Division

| | W | L | T | Pct | PF | PA |
|---|---|---|---|---|---|---|
| New England Patriots[1] | 11 | 5 | 0 | .688 | 371 | 272 |
| Miami Dolphins[2] | 11 | 5 | 0 | .688 | 344 | 290 |
| New York Jets[2] | 10 | 6 | 0 | .625 | 308 | 295 |
| Indianapolis Colts | 6 | 10 | 0 | .375 | 413 | 486 |
| Buffalo Bills | 3 | 13 | 0 | .188 | 265 | 420 |

### Central Division

| | W | L | T | Pct | PF | PA |
|---|---|---|---|---|---|---|
| Pittsburgh Steelers[1] | 13 | 3 | 0 | .812 | 352 | 212 |
| Baltimore Ravens[2] | 10 | 6 | 0 | .625 | 303 | 265 |
| Cleveland Browns | 7 | 9 | 0 | .438 | 285 | 319 |
| Tennessee Titans | 7 | 9 | 0 | .438 | 336 | 388 |
| Jacksonville Jaguars | 6 | 10 | 0 | .375 | 294 | 286 |
| Cincinnati Bengals | 6 | 10 | 0 | .375 | 226 | 309 |

### Western Division

| | W | L | T | Pct | PF | PA |
|---|---|---|---|---|---|---|
| Oakland Raiders[1] | 10 | 6 | 0 | .625 | 399 | 327 |
| Seattle Seahawks | 9 | 7 | 0 | .562 | 301 | 324 |
| Denver Broncos | 8 | 8 | 0 | .500 | 340 | 339 |
| Kansas City Chiefs | 6 | 10 | 0 | .375 | 320 | 344 |
| San Diego Chargers | 5 | 11 | 0 | .312 | 332 | 321 |

1. Division champion. 2. Wild card qualifier for playoffs. **Wild card:** Oakland 38, N.Y. 24; Baltimore 20, Miami 3. **Division:** Pittsburgh 27, Baltimore 10; New England 16, Oakland 13 (OT). **Conference:** New England 24, Pittsburgh 17.

## NATIONAL FOOTBALL CONFERENCE

### Eastern Division

| | W | L | T | Pct | PF | PA |
|---|---|---|---|---|---|---|
| Philadelphia Eagles[1] | 11 | 5 | 0 | .688 | 343 | 208 |
| Washington Redskins | 8 | 8 | 0 | .500 | 256 | 303 |
| New York Giants | 7 | 9 | 0 | .438 | 294 | 321 |
| Arizona Cardinals | 7 | 9 | 0 | .438 | 295 | 343 |
| Dallas Cowboys | 5 | 11 | 0 | .312 | 246 | 338 |

### Central Division

| | W | L | T | Pct | PF | PA |
|---|---|---|---|---|---|---|
| Chicago Bears [1] | 13 | 3 | 0 | .812 | 338 | 203 |
| Green Bay Packers[2] | 12 | 4 | 0 | .750 | 390 | 266 |
| Tampa Bay Buccaneers[2] | 9 | 7 | 0 | .562 | 324 | 280 |
| Minnesota Vikings | 5 | 11 | 0 | .312 | 290 | 390 |
| Detroit Lions | 2 | 14 | 0 | .125 | 270 | 424 |

### Western Division

| | W | L | T | Pct | PF | PA |
|---|---|---|---|---|---|---|
| St. Louis Rams[1] | 14 | 2 | 0 | .875 | 503 | 273 |
| San Francisco 49ers[2] | 12 | 4 | 0 | .750 | 409 | 282 |
| New Orleans Saints | 7 | 9 | 0 | .438 | 333 | 409 |
| Atlanta Falcons | 7 | 9 | 0 | .438 | 291 | 377 |
| Carolina Panthers | 1 | 15 | 0 | .062 | 253 | 410 |

1. Division champion. 2. Wild card qualifier for playoffs. **Wild card:** Philadelphia 31, Tampa Bay 9; Green Bay 25, San Francisco 15. **Division:** Philadelphia 33, Chicago 19; St. Louis 45, Green Bay 17. **Conference:** St. Louis 29, Philadelphia 24.

## LEAGUE CHAMPIONSHIP—SUPER BOWL XXXVI

(Feb. 3, 2002, Superdome, New Orleans, La. Attendance: 72,922. Time: 3:24)

### Scoring

| | 1st Q | 2nd Q | 3rd Q | 4th Q | Final |
|---|---|---|---|---|---|
| St. Louis | 3 | 0 | 0 | 14 | 17 |
| New England | 0 | 14 | 3 | 3 | 20 |

**1st:** STL—Jeff Wilkins 50-yd field goal, 11:50. Key plays: Warner 8-yd pass to Holt to STL 28. Warner 11-yd pass to Bruce to STL 47. Warner 14-yd pass to M. Faulk to NE 39.

**2nd:** NE—TD: Law 47-yd interception return (Vinatieri kick), 6:11. NE—TD: Patten 8-yd pass from Brady (Vinatieri kick), 14:29. Key plays: Buckley 15-yd return of Proehl fumble to STL 40. Brady 16-yd pass to Brown to STL 24. Brady 8-yd pass to Wiggins to STL 16. K. Faulk 8-yd run to STL 8.

**3rd:** NE—Vinatieri 37-yd field goal, 13:42. Key plays: O. Smith 30-yd interception return to STL 33. Brady 11-yd pass to brown to STL 22. K. Faulk 7-yd run to STL 19.

**4th:** STL—TD: Warner 2-yd run (Wilkins kick), 5:29. Key plays: Warner 15-yd pass to Bruce to STL 38. Warner 14-yd pass to Hakim to NE 43. Warner 22-yd pass to M. Faulk to NE 9. Defensive holding on NE McGinest nullifies fumble return for TD by NE's Jones. STL—TD: Proehl 26-yd pass from Warner (Wilkins kick), 13:30. Key plays: Warner 30-yd punt to STL 45. Warner 18-yd pass to Hakim to NE 37. Warner 11-yd pass to Murphy to NE 26. —Vinatieri 48-yd field goal, 15:00. Key plays: Brady 5-yd pass to Hedmond to NE 22. Brady 8-yd pass to Redmond to NE 30. Brady 11-yd pass to Redmond to NE 41. Brady 23-yd pass to Brown to STL 36. Brady 6-yd pass to Wiggins to STL 30.

### Individual Statistics

**Passing:** STL—K. Warner 28–44 for 365 yds. NE—T. Brady 16–27 for 145 yds.

**Rushing:** STL—M. Faulk 17–76, K. Warner 3–6, A-Z Hakim 1–5, J. Hodgins 1–3. NE—A. Smith 18–92, D. Patten 1–22, K. Faulk 2–15, M Edwards 2–5, T. Brady 1–3, J. R. Redmond 1–(-4).

**Receiving:** STL—A-Z Hakim 5–90, R. Proehl 3–71, Isaac Bruce 5–56, M. Faulk 4–54, T. Holt 5–49, J. Robinson 2–18, Y. Murphy 1–11, E.. Conwell 2–8, J., Hodgins 1–8. NE—T. Brown 6–89, J. R. Redmond 3–24, J. Wiggins 2–14, D. Patten 1–8, M. Edwards 2–7, A. Smith 1–4, K. Faulk 1–(-1).

**Field goals:** STL—J. Wilkins 1–2. NE—A. Vinatieri 2–2.

**Punting:** STL—J. Baker 4. NE: K. Walker 8.

**Kick/Punt Returns:** STL—Y. Murphy 3–81, M. Faulk 1–1, Dre' Bly 0–0. NE—P. Pass 3–85, T. Brown 1–15.

**Interceptions:** NE—T. Law 1–47, O. Smith 1–30.

**MVP:** Tom Brady, New England quarterback.

### Statistics of the Game

| | Rams | Patriots |
|---|---|---|
| First downs | 26 | 15 |
| 3rd down efficiency | 5/13 | 2/11 |
| Total offense (net yards) | 427 | 267 |
| Plays | 66 | 52 |
| Average gain | 6.5 | 5.1 |
| Rushing yards (net) | 90 | 133 |
| Rushes | 22 | 25 |
| Average per rush | 4.1 | 5.3 |
| Passing yards (net) | 337 | 134 |
| Completions/attempts | 28/44 | 16/27 |
| Yards per pass | 8.3 | 5.4 |
| Times sacked | 3 | 2 |
| Yards lost to sacks | 28 | 11 |
| Had intercepted | 2 | 0 |
| Punts | 4 | 8 |
| Average punt | 38.8 | 42.4 |
| Penalties | 6 | 5 |
| Penalty yards | 39 | 31 |
| Fumbles | 2 | 0 |
| Fumbles lost | 1 | 0 |
| Time of possession | 33:30 | 26:30 |

## NATIONAL LEAGUE CHAMPIONS

| Year | Champion | (W-L-T) | Year | Champion | (W-L-T) | Year | Champion | (W-L-T) |
|------|----------|---------|------|----------|---------|------|----------|---------|
| 1921 | Chicago Bears (Staley's) | (10-1-1) | 1926 | Frankford Yellow Jackets | (14-1-1) | 1930 | Green Bay Packers | (10-3-1) |
| 1922 | Canton Bulldogs | (10-0-2) | 1927 | New York Giants | (11-1-1) | 1931 | Green Bay Packers | (12-2-0) |
| 1923 | Canton Bulldogs | (11-0-1) | 1928 | Providence | (8-1-2) | 1932 | Chicago Bears | (7-1-6) |
| 1924 | Cleveland Indians | (7-1-1) | | Steamrollers | | | | |
| 1925 | Chicago Cardinals | (11-2-1) | 1929 | Green Bay Packers | (12-0-1) | | | |

| Year | Eastern Conference winners (W-L-T) | Western Conference winners (W-L-T) | League champion playoff results |
|------|-------------------------------------|-------------------------------------|----------------------------------|
| 1933 | New York Giants (11-3-0) | Chicago Bears (10-2-1) | Chicago Bears 23, New York 21 |
| 1934 | New York Giants (8-5-0) | Chicago Bears (13-0-0) | New York 30, Chicago Bears 13 |
| 1935 | New York Giants (9-3-0) | Detroit Lions (7-3-2) | Detroit 26, New York 7 |
| 1936 | Boston Redskins (7-5-0) | Green Bay Packers (10-1-1) | Green Bay 21, Boston 6 |
| 1937 | Washington Redskins (8-3-0) | Chicago Bears (9-1-1) | Washington 28, Chicago Bears 21 |
| 1938 | New York Giants (8-2-1) | Green Bay Packers (8-3-0) | New York 23, Green Bay 17 |
| 1939 | New York Giants (9-1-1) | Green Bay Packers (9-2-0) | Green Bay 27, New York 0 |
| 1940 | Washington Redskins (9-2-0) | Chicago Bears (8-3-0) | Chicago Bears 73, Washington 0 |
| 1941 | New York Giants (8-3-0) | Chicago Bears (10-1-1)[2] | Chicago Bears 37, New York 9 |
| 1942 | Washington Redskins (10-1-1) | Chicago Bears (11-0-0) | Washington 14, Chicago Bears 6 |
| 1943 | Washington Redskins (6-3-1)[2] | Chicago Bears (8-1-1) | Chicago Bears 41, Washington 21 |
| 1944 | New York Giants (8-1-1) | Green Bay Packers (8-2-0) | Green Bay 14, New York 7 |
| 1945 | Washington Redskins (8-2-0) | Cleveland Rams (9-1-0) | Cleveland 15, Washington 14 |
| 1946 | New York Giants (7-3-1) | Chicago Bears (8-2-1) | Chicago Bears 24, New York 14 |
| 1947 | Philadelphia Eagles (8-4-0)[2] | Chicago Cardinals (9-3-0) | Chicago Cardinals 28, Philadelphia 21 |
| 1948 | Philadelphia Eagles (9-2-1) | Chicago Cardinals (11-1-0) | Philadelphia 7, Chicago Cardinals 0 |
| 1949 | Philadelphia Eagles (11-1-0) | Los Angeles Rams (8-2-2) | Philadelphia 14, Los Angeles 0 |
| 1950[1] | Cleveland Browns (10-2-0)[2, 3] | Los Angeles Rams (9-3-0)[2] | Cleveland 30, Los Angeles 28 |
| 1951[1] | Cleveland Browns (11-1-0) | Los Angeles Rams (8-4-0) | Los Angeles 24, Cleveland 17 |
| 1952[1] | Cleveland Browns (8-4-0) | Detroit Lions (9-3-0)[2] | Detroit 17, Cleveland 7 |
| 1953 | Cleveland Browns (11-1-0) | Detroit Lions (10-2-0) | Detroit 17, Cleveland 16 |
| 1954 | Cleveland Browns (9-3-0) | Detroit Lions (9-2-1) | Cleveland 56, Detroit 10 |
| 1955 | Cleveland Browns (9-2-1) | Los Angeles Rams (8-3-1) | Cleveland 38, Los Angeles 14 |
| 1956 | New York Giants (8-3-1) | Chicago Bears (9-2-1) | New York 47, Chicago Bears 7 |
| 1957 | Cleveland Browns (9-2-1) | Detroit Lions (8-4-0)[2] | Detroit 59, Cleveland 14 |
| 1958 | New York Giants (9-3-0)[2] | Baltimore Colts (9-3-0) | Baltimore 23, New York 17[4] |
| 1959 | New York Giants (10-2-0) | Baltimore Colts (9-3-0) | Baltimore 31, New York 16 |
| 1960 | Philadelphia Eagles (10-2-0) | Green Bay Packers (8-4-0) | Philadelphia 17, Green Bay 13 |
| 1961 | New York Giants (10-3-1) | Green Bay Packers (11-3-0) | Green Bay 37, New York 0 |
| 1962 | New York Giants (12-2-0) | Green Bay Packers (13-1-0) | Green Bay 16, New York 7 |
| 1963 | New York Giants (11-3-0) | Chicago Bears (11-1-2) | Chicago 14, New York 10 |
| 1964 | Cleveland Browns (10-3-1) | Baltimore Colts (12-2-0) | Cleveland 27, Baltimore 0 |
| 1965 | Cleveland Browns (11-3-0) | Green Bay Packers (11-3-1)[2] | Green Bay 23, Cleveland 12 |
| 1966 | Dallas Cowboys (10-3-1) | Green Bay Packers (12-2-0) | Green Bay 34, Dallas 27 |
| 1967 | Dallas Cowboys (9-5-0) | Green Bay Packers (9-4-1)[2] | Green Bay 21, Dallas 17 |
| 1968 | Cleveland Browns (10-4-0)[2] | Baltimore Colts (13-1-0)[2] | Baltimore 34, Cleveland 0 |
| 1969 | Cleveland Browns (10-3-1)[2] | Minnesota Vikings (12-2-0)[2] | Minnesota 27, Cleveland 7 |

1. League was divided into American and National Conferences, 1950-52 and again in 1970, when leagues merged. 2. Won divisional playoff. 3. Cleveland Browns and San Francisco 49ers joined league after All-America Football Conference (1946–1949) folded. 4. Won at 8:15 of sudden death overtime period.

## NATIONAL CONFERENCE CHAMPIONS

| Year | Eastern Division | Central Division | Western Division | Champion |
|------|------------------|------------------|-------------------|----------|
| 1970 | Dallas Cowboys (10-4-0) | Minnesota Vikings (12-2-0) | San Francisco 49ers (10-3-1) | Dallas |
| 1971 | Dallas Cowboys (11-3-0) | Minnesota Vikings (11-3-0) | San Francisco 49ers (9-5-0) | Dallas |
| 1972 | Washington Redskins (11-3-0) | Green Bay Packers (10-4-0) | San Francisco 49ers (8-5-1) | Washington |
| 1973 | Dallas Cowboys (10-4-0) | Minnesota Vikings (12-2-0) | Los Angeles Rams (12-2-0) | Minnesota |
| 1974 | St. Louis Cardinals (10-4-0) | Minnesota Vikings (10-4-0) | Los Angeles Rams (10-4-0) | Minnesota |
| 1975 | St. Louis Cardinals (11-3-0) | Minnesota Vikings (12-2-0) | Los Angeles Rams (12-2-0) | Dallas[1] |
| 1976 | Dallas Cowboys (11-3-0) | Minnesota Vikings (11-2-1) | Los Angeles Rams (10-3-1) | Minnesota |
| 1977 | Dallas Cowboys (12-2-0) | Minnesota Vikings (9-5-0) | Los Angeles Rams (10-4-0) | Dallas |
| 1978 | Dallas Cowboys (12-4-0) | Minnesota Vikings (8-7-1) | Los Angeles Rams (12-4-0) | Dallas |
| 1979 | Dallas Cowboys (11-5-0) | Tampa Bay Buccaneers (10-6-0) | Los Angeles Rams (9-7-0) | Los Angeles |
| 1980 | Philadelphia Eagles (12-4-0) | Minnesota Vikings (9-7-0) | Atlanta Falcons (12-4-0) | Philadelphia |
| 1981 | Dallas Cowboys (12-4-0) | Tampa Bay Buccaneers (9-7-0) | San Francisco 49ers (13-3-0) | San Francisco |
| 1982[2] | | | | |
| 1983 | Washington Redskins (14-2-0) | Detroit Lions (8-8-0) | San Francisco 49ers (10-6-0) | Washington |
| 1984 | Washington Redskins (11-5-0) | Chicago Bears (10-6-0) | San Francisco 49ers (15-1-0) | San Francisco |
| 1985 | Dallas Cowboys (10-6-0) | Chicago Bears (15-1-0) | Los Angeles Rams (11-5-0) | Chicago |
| 1986 | New York Giants (14-2-0) | Chicago Bears (14-2-0) | San Francisco 49ers (10-5-1) | New York |
| 1987 | Washington Redskins (11-4-0) | Chicago Bears (11-4-0) | San Francisco 49ers (13-2-0) | Washington |
| 1988 | Philadelphia Eagles (10-6-0) | Chicago Bears (12-4-0) | San Francisco 49ers (10-6-0) | San Francisco |

| Year | Eastern Division | Central Division | Western Division | Champion |
|---|---|---|---|---|
| 1989 | New York Giants (12-4-0) | Minnesota Vikings (10-6-0) | San Francisco 49ers (14-2-0) | San Francisco |
| 1990 | New York Giants (13-3-0) | Chicago Bears (11-5-0) | San Francisco 49ers (14-2-0) | New York |
| 1991 | Washington (14-2-0) | Detroit Lions (12-4-0) | New Orleans Saints (11-5-0) | Washington |
| 1992 | Dallas Cowboys (13-3-0) | Minnesota Vikings (11-5-0) | San Francisco 49ers (14-2-0) | Dallas |
| 1993 | Dallas Cowboys (12-4-0) | Detroit Lions (10-6-0) | San Francisco 49ers (10-6-0) | Dallas |
| 1994 | Dallas Cowboys (12-4-0) | Minnesota Vikings (10-6-0) | San Francisco 49ers (13-3-0) | San Francisco |
| 1995 | Dallas Cowboys (12-4-0) | Green Bay Packers (11-5-0) | San Francisco 49ers (11-5-0) | Dallas |
| 1996 | Dallas Cowboys (10-6-0) | Green Bay Packers (13-3-0) | Carolina Panthers (12-4-0) | Green Bay |
| 1997 | New York Giants (10-5-1) | Green Bay Packers (13-3-0) | San Francisco 49ers (13-3-0) | Green Bay |
| 1998 | Dallas Cowboys (10-6-0) | Minnesota Vikings (15-1-0) | Atlanta Falcons (14-2-0) | Atlanta |
| 1999 | Washington Redskins (10-6-0) | Tampa Bay Buccaneers (11-5-0) | St. Louis Rams (13-3-0) | St. Louis |
| 2000 | New York Giants (12-4-0) | Minnesota Vikings (11-5-0) | New Orleans Saints (10-6-0) | New York |
| 2001 | Philadelphia Eagles (11-5-0) | Chicago Bears (13-3-0) | St. Louis Rams (14-2-0) | St. Louis |

1. Wild card. 2. Schedule reduced to 9 games from usual 16, with no standings kept in Eastern, Central, and Western Divisions, because of 57-day player strike. Washington Redskins won conference title and also had best regular-season record (8-1-0).

## AMERICAN LEAGUE CHAMPIONS

| Year | Eastern Division (W-L-T) | Western Division (W-L-T) | League champion, playoff results |
|---|---|---|---|
| 1960 | Houston Oilers (10-4-0) | Los Angeles Chargers (10-4-0) | Houston 24, Los Angeles 16 |
| 1961 | Houston Oilers (10-3-1) | San Diego Chargers (12-2-0) | Houston 10, San Diego 3 |
| 1962 | Houston Oilers (11-3-0) | Dallas Texans (11-3-0) | Dallas 20, Houston 17[1] |
| 1963 | Boston Patriots (8-6-1)[2] | San Diego Chargers (11-3-0) | San Diego 51, Boston 10 |
| 1964 | Buffalo Bills (12-2-0) | San Diego Chargers (8-5-1) | Buffalo 20, San Diego 7 |
| 1965 | Buffalo Bills (10-3-1) | San Diego Chargers (9-2-3) | Buffalo 23, San Diego 0 |
| 1966 | Buffalo Bills (9-4-1) | Kansas City Chiefs (11-2-1) | Kansas City 31, Buffalo 7 |
| 1967 | Houston Oilers (9-4-1) | Oakland Raiders (13-1-0) | Oakland 40, Houston 7 |
| 1968 | New York Jets (11-3-0) | Oakland Raiders (12-2-0)[2] | New York 27, Oakland 23 |
| 1969 | New York Jets (10-4-0) | Oakland Raiders (12-1-1) | Kansas City 17, Oakland 7[3] |

1. Won at 2:45 of second sudden death overtime period. 2. Won divisional playoff. 3. Kansas City defeated New York, 13-6, and Oakland defeated Houston, 56-7, in interdivisional playoffs.

## AMERICAN CONFERENCE CHAMPIONS

| Year | Eastern Division | Central Division | Western Division | Champion |
|---|---|---|---|---|
| 1970 | Baltimore Colts (11-2-1) | Cincinnati Bengals (8-6-0) | Oakland Raiders (8-4-2) | Baltimore |
| 1971 | Miami Dolphins (10-3-1) | Cleveland Browns (9-5-0) | Kansas City Chiefs (10-3-1) | Miami |
| 1972 | Miami Dolphins (14-0-0) | Pittsburgh Steelers (11-3-0) | Oakland Raiders (10-3-1) | Miami |
| 1973 | Miami Dolphins (12-2-0) | Cincinnati Bengals (10-4-0) | Oakland Raiders (9-4-1) | Miami |
| 1974 | Miami Dolphins (11-3-0) | Pittsburgh Steelers (10-3-1) | Oakland Raiders (12-2-0) | Pittsburgh |
| 1975 | Baltimore Colts (10-4-0) | Pittsburgh Steelers (12-2-0) | Oakland Raiders (12-2-0) | Pittsburgh |
| 1976 | Baltimore Colts (11-3-0) | Pittsburgh Steelers (10-4-0) | Oakland Raiders (13-1-0) | Oakland |
| 1977 | Baltimore Colts (10-4-0) | Pittsburgh Steelers (9-5-0) | Denver Broncos (12-2-0) | Denver |
| 1978 | New England Patriots (11-5-0) | Pittsburgh Steelers (14-2-0) | Denver Broncos (10-6-0) | Pittsburgh |
| 1979 | Miami Dolphins (10-6-0) | Pittsburgh Steelers (12-4-0) | San Diego Chargers (12-4-0) | Pittsburgh |
| 1980 | Buffalo Bills (11-5-0) | Cleveland Browns (11-5-0) | San Diego Chargers (11-5-0) | Oakland[1] |
| 1981 | Miami Dolphins (11-4-1) | Cincinnati Bengals (12-4-0) | San Diego Chargers (10-6-0) | Cincinnati |
| 1982[2] | Miami Dolphins won the conference title, but the Los Angeles Raiders had best regular-season record (8-1-0). | | | |
| 1983 | Miami Dolphins (12-4-0) | Pittsburgh Steelers (10-6-0) | Los Angeles Raiders (12-4-0) | Los Angeles |
| 1984 | Miami Dolphins (14-2-0) | Pittsburgh Steelers (9-7-0) | Denver Broncos (13-3-0) | Miami |
| 1985 | Miami Dolphins (12-4-0) | Cleveland Browns (8-8) | Los Angeles Raiders (12-4-0) | New England[1] |
| 1986 | New England Patriots (11-5-0) | Cleveland Browns (12-4-0) | Denver Broncos (11-5-0) | Denver |
| 1987 | Indianapolis Colts (9-6-0) | Cleveland Browns (10-5-0) | Denver Broncos (10-4-1) | Denver |
| 1988 | Buffalo Bills (12-4-0) | Cincinnati Bengals (12-4-0) | Seattle Seahawks (9-7-0) | Cincinnati |
| 1989 | Buffalo Bills (9-7-0) | Cleveland Browns (9-6-1) | Denver Broncos (11-5-0) | Denver |
| 1990 | Buffalo Bills (13-3-0) | Cincinnati Bengals (9-7-0) | Los Angeles Raiders (12-4-0) | Buffalo |
| 1991 | Buffalo Bills (13-3-0) | Houston Oilers (11-5-0) | Denver Broncos (12-4-0) | Buffalo |
| 1992 | Miami Dolphins (11-5-0) | Pittsburgh Steelers (11-5-0) | San Diego Chargers (11-5-0) | Buffalo[1] |
| 1993 | Buffalo Bills (12-4-0) | Houston Oilers (12-4-0) | Kansas City Chiefs (11-5-0) | Buffalo |
| 1994 | Miami Dolphins (10-6-0) | Pittsburgh Steelers (12-4-0) | San Diego Chargers (11-5-0) | San Diego |
| 1995 | Buffalo Bills (10-6-0) | Pittsburgh Steelers (11-5-0) | Kansas City Chiefs (13-3-0) | Pittsburgh |
| 1996 | New England Patriots (11-5-0) | Pittsburgh Steelers (10-6-0) | Denver Broncos (13-3-0) | New England |
| 1997 | New England Patriots (10-6-0) | Pittsburgh Steelers (11-5-0) | Kansas City Chiefs (13-3-0) | Denver[1] |
| 1998 | New York Jets (12-4-0) | Jacksonville Jaguars (11-5-0) | Denver Broncos (14-2-0) | Denver |
| 1999 | Indianapolis Colts (13-3-0) | Jacksonville Jaguars (14-2-0) | Seattle Seahawks (9-7-0) | Tennessee[1] |
| 2000 | Miami Dolphins (11-5-0) | Tennessee Titans (13-3-0) | Oakland Raiders (12-4-0) | Baltimore[1] |
| 2001 | New England Patriots (11-5-0) | Pittsburgh Steelers (13-3-0) | Oakland Raiders (10-6-0) | New England |

1. Wild card. 2. Schedule reduced to 9 games from usual 16, with no standings kept in Eastern, Central, and Western Divisions, because of 57-day player strike.

## NFL INDIVIDUAL LIFETIME, SEASON, AND GAME RECORDS

(American Football League records were incorporated into NFL records after merger of the leagues.) Players listed in boldface were active during the 2001 season. The NFL does not recognize records from the All-American Football Conference (AAFC) which existed from 1946 to 1949. The 49ers, Browns, and Colts merged with the NFL in 1949.

### All-Time Leading Touchdown Scorers
### (Through 2001)

| | | Yrs | Rush | Rec | Ret | Total |
|---|---|---|---|---|---|---|
| 1. | **Jerry Rice** | 17 | 10 | 185 | 1 | 196 |
| 2. | **Emmitt Smith** | 12 | 148 | 11 | 0 | 159 |
| 3. | Marcus Allen | 16 | 123 | 21 | 1 | 145 |
| 4. | **Cris Carter** | 15 | 0 | 129 | 1 | 130 |
| 5. | Jim Brown | 9 | 106 | 20 | 0 | 126 |
| 6. | Walter Payton | 13 | 110 | 15 | 0 | 125 |
| 7. | John Riggins | 14 | 104 | 12 | 0 | 116 |
| 8. | Lenny Moore | 12 | 63 | 48 | 2 | 113 |
| 9. | **Marshall Faulk** | 8 | 79 | 31 | 0 | 110 |
| 10. | Barry Sanders | 10 | 99 | 10 | 0 | 109 |
| 11. | Don Hutson | 11 | 3 | 99 | 3 | 105 |
| 12. | Steve Largent | 14 | 1 | 100 | 0 | 101 |
| 13. | Franco Harris | 13 | 91 | 9 | 0 | 100 |
| | **Tim Brown** | 14 | 1 | 95 | 4 | 100 |
| 15. | Eric Dickerson | 11 | 90 | 6 | 0 | 96 |

### All-Time Leading Receivers
### (Through 2001)

| | | Yrs | No | Yards | Avg | TD |
|---|---|---|---|---|---|---|
| 1. | **Jerry Rice** | 17 | 1364 | 20,386 | 14.9 | 185 |
| 2. | **Cris Carter** | 15 | 1093 | 13,833 | 12.7 | 129 |
| 3. | Andre Reed | 16 | 951 | 13,198 | 13.9 | 87 |
| 4. | Art Monk | 16 | 940 | 12,721 | 13.5 | 68 |
| 5. | **Tim Brown** | 14 | 937 | 13,237 | 14.1 | 95 |
| 6. | Irving Fryar | 17 | 851 | 12,785 | 15.0 | 84 |
| 7. | Steve Largent | 14 | 819 | 13,089 | 16.0 | 100 |
| 8. | Henry Ellard | 16 | 814 | 13,777 | 16.9 | 65 |
| 9. | **Larry Centers** | 12 | 765 | 6,303 | 8.2 | 27 |
| 10. | James Lofton | 16 | 764 | 14,004 | 18.3 | 75 |
| 11. | Charlie Joiner | 18 | 750 | 12,146 | 16.2 | 65 |
| | Michael Irvin | 12 | 750 | 11,904 | 15.9 | 65 |
| 13. | Andre Rison | 12 | 743 | 10,205 | 13.7 | 84 |
| 14. | Gary Clark | 11 | 699 | 10,856 | 15.5 | 65 |
| 15. | **Shannon Sharpe** | 12 | 692 | 8,604 | 12.4 | 51 |

### All-Time Leading Passers
### (Minimum 1,500 attempts. Through 2001)

| | | Yrs | Att | Cmp | Cmp% | Yards | Avg Gain | TD | TD% | Int | Int% | Rating |
|---|---|---|---|---|---|---|---|---|---|---|---|---|
| 1. | Steve Young | 15 | 4,149 | 2,667 | 64.4 | 33,124 | 7.98 | 232 | 5.6 | 107 | 2.6 | 96.8 |
| 2. | Joe Montana | 15 | 5,391 | 3,409 | 63.2 | 40,551 | 7.52 | 273 | 5.1 | 139 | 2.6 | 92.3 |
| 3. | **Brett Favre** | 11 | 5,442 | 3,311 | 60.8 | 38,627 | 7.10 | 287 | 5.3 | 172 | 3.2 | 86.8 |
| 4. | Dan Marino | 17 | 8,358 | 4,967 | 59.4 | 61,361 | 7.34 | 420 | 5.0 | 252 | 3.0 | 86.4 |
| 5. | **Peyton Manning** | 4 | 2,226 | 1,357 | 61.0 | 16,418 | 7.38 | 111 | 5.0 | 81 | 3.6 | 85.1 |
| 6. | **Mark Brunell** | 8 | 3,145 | 1,897 | 60.3 | 22,521 | 7.16 | 125 | 4.0 | 79 | 2.5 | 85.0 |
| 7. | Jim Kelly | 11 | 4,779 | 2,874 | 60.1 | 35,467 | 7.42 | 237 | 5.0 | 175 | 3.7 | 84.4 |
| 8. | Roger Staubach | 11 | 2,958 | 1,685 | 57.0 | 22,700 | 7.67 | 153 | 5.2 | 109 | 3.7 | 83.4 |
| 9. | **Brad Johnson** | 10 | 2,380 | 1,466 | 61.6 | 16,379 | 6.88 | 92 | 3.9 | 68 | 2.9 | 83.069 |
| 10. | **Rich Gannon** | 14 | 3,295 | 1,949 | 59.2 | 22,256 | 6.75 | 145 | 4.4 | 88 | 2.7 | 83.060 |
| 11. | Neil Lomax | 8 | 3,153 | 1,817 | 57.6 | 22,771 | 7.22 | 136 | 4.3 | 90 | 2.9 | 82.7 |
| 12. | Sonny Jurgensen | 18 | 4,262 | 2,433 | 57.1 | 32,224 | 7.56 | 255 | 6.0 | 189 | 4.4 | 82.625 |
| 13. | Len Dawson | 19 | 3,741 | 2,136 | 57.1 | 28,711 | 7.67 | 239 | 6.4 | 183 | 4.9 | 82.555 |
| 14. | Ken Anderson | 16 | 4,475 | 2,654 | 59.3 | 32,838 | 7.34 | 197 | 4.4 | 160 | 3.6 | 81.858 |
| 15. | Bernie Kosar | 12 | 3,365 | 1,994 | 59.3 | 23,301 | 6.92 | 124 | 3.7 | 87 | 2.6 | 81.8 |

**Note:** If the NFL recognized records from the AAFC, **Otto Graham** would rank 4th (after Favre) with the following stats: 10 Yrs; 2,626 Att; 1,464 Comp; 55.8 Comp Pct; 23,584 Yards; 8.98 Avg Gain; 174 TD; 6.6 TD Pct; 135 Int; 5.1 Int Pct; and 86.6 Rating Pts.

### All-Time Leading Scorers
### (Through 2001)

| | | Yrs | TD | FG | PAT | Total |
|---|---|---|---|---|---|---|
| 1. | **Gary Anderson** | 20 | 0 | 476 | 705 | 2,133 |
| 2. | **Morten Andersen** | 20 | 0 | 464 | 644 | 2,036 |
| 3. | George Blanda | 26 | 9 | 335 | 943 | 2,002 |
| 4. | Norm Johnson | 18 | 0 | 366 | 638 | 1,736 |
| 5. | Nick Lowery | 18 | 0 | 383 | 562 | 1,711 |
| 6. | Jan Stenerud | 19 | 0 | 373 | 580 | 1,699 |
| 7. | Eddie Murray | 19 | 0 | 352 | 538 | 1,594 |
| 8. | Al Del Greco | 17 | 0 | 347 | 543 | 1,584 |
| 9. | Pat Leahy | 18 | 0 | 304 | 558 | 1,470 |
| 10. | Jim Turner | 16 | 1 | 304 | 521 | 1,439 |
| 11. | Matt Bahr | 17 | 0 | 300 | 522 | 1,422 |
| 12. | Mark Moseley | 16 | 0 | 300 | 482 | 1,382 |
| 13. | Jim Bakken | 17 | 0 | 282 | 534 | 1,380 |
| 14. | Fred Cox | 15 | 0 | 282 | 519 | 1,365 |
| 15. | Lou Groza | 17 | 1 | 234 | 641 | 1,349 |

### All-Time Leading Rushers
### (Through 2001)

| | | Yrs | Car | Yards | Avg | TD |
|---|---|---|---|---|---|---|
| 1. | Walter Payton | 13 | 3,838 | 16,726 | 4.4 | 110 |
| 2. | **Emmitt Smith** | 12 | 3,798 | 16,187 | 4.3 | 148 |
| 3. | Barry Sanders | 10 | 3,062 | 15,269 | 5.0 | 99 |
| 4. | Eric Dickerson | 11 | 2,996 | 13,259 | 4.4 | 90 |
| 5. | Tony Dorsett | 12 | 2,936 | 12,739 | 4.3 | 77 |
| 6. | Jim Brown | 9 | 2,359 | 12,312 | 5.2 | 106 |
| 7. | Marcus Allen | 16 | 3,022 | 12,243 | 4.1 | 123 |
| 8. | Franco Harris | 13 | 2,949 | 12,120 | 4.1 | 91 |
| 9. | Thurman Thomas | 13 | 2,877 | 12,074 | 4.2 | 65 |
| 10. | John Riggins | 14 | 2,916 | 11,352 | 3.9 | 104 |
| 11. | O.J. Simpson | 11 | 2,404 | 11,236 | 4.7 | 61 |
| 12. | **Jerome Bettis** | 9 | 2,686 | 10,876 | 4.0 | 53 |
| 13. | **Ricky Watters** | 10 | 2,622 | 10,643 | 4.1 | 78 |
| 14. | Ottis Anderson | 14 | 2,562 | 10,273 | 4.0 | 81 |
| 15. | **Marshall Faulk** | 8 | 2,155 | 9,442 | 4.4 | 79 |

## Scoring

Most points scored, lifetime—2,133, Gary Anderson, Pittsburgh, 1982–94; Philadelphia, 1995–96; San Francisco, 1997; Minnesota, 1998–2001.

Most points, season—176, Paul Hornung, Green Bay, 1960 (15 td, 41 pat, 15 fg).

Most points, game—40, Ernie Nevers, Chicago Cardinals, 1929 (6 td, 4 pat).

Most touchdowns, lifetime—196, Jerry Rice, San Francisco, 1985–2000; Oakland 2001.

Most touchdowns, season—26, Marshall Faulk, St. Louis, 2000.

Most points after touchdown, lifetime—943, George Blanda, Chicago Bears, 1949–58; Baltimore, 1950; Houston, 1960–66; Oakland, 1967–75.

Most field goals, lifetime—476, Gary Anderson, Pittsburgh, 1982–94; Philadelphia, 1995–96; San Francisco, 1997; Minnesota, 1998–2001.

Most field goals, season—39, Olindo Mare, Miami, 1999.

Most field goals, game—7, Jim Bakken, St. Louis, 1967; Rich Karlis, Minnesota, 1989; and Chris Boniol, Dallas, 1996.

Longest field goal—63 yards, Tom Dempsey, New Orleans, 1970; Jason Elam, Denver, 1998.

## Rushing

Most yards gained, lifetime—16,726, Walter Payton, Chicago Bears, 1975–87.

Most yards gained, season—2,105, Eric Dickerson, Los Angeles, 1984.

Most yards gained, game—278, Corey Dillon, Cincinnati, 2000.

Most touchdowns, lifetime—148, Emmitt Smith, Dallas, 1990–2001.

Most touchdowns, season—25, Emmitt Smith, Dallas, 1995.

Most touchdowns, game—6, Ernie Nevers, Chicago Cardinals, 1929.

Longest run from scrimmage—99 yards, Tony Dorsett, Dallas, 1983.

## Receiving

Most pass receptions, lifetime—1,364, Jerry Rice, San Francisco, 1985–2000; Oakland 2001.

Most pass receptions, season—123, Herman Moore, Detroit, 1995.

Most pass receptions, game—20, Terrell Owens, San Francisco, 2000.

Most yards gained, pass receptions, lifetime—20,386, Jerry Rice, San Francisco, 1985–2000; Oakland 2001.

Most yards gained, receptions, season—1,848, Jerry Rice, San Francisco, 1995.

Most yards gained, receptions, game—336, Flipper Anderson, Los Angeles Rams, 1989.

Most touchdown receptions, lifetime—185, Jerry Rice, San Francisco, 1985–2000; Oakland 2001.

Most touchdown pass receptions, season—22, Jerry Rice, San Francisco, 1987.

Most touchdown pass receptions, game—5, Bob Shaw, Chicago Cards, 1950; Kellen Winslow, San Diego, 1981; Jerry Rice, San Francisco, 1990.

## Interceptions

Most pass interceptions, lifetime—81, Paul Krause, Washington, 1964-67; Minnesota, 1968-79.

Most pass interceptions, season—14, Richard (Night Train) Lane, Detroit, 1952.

Most pass interceptions, game—4, by 18 players.

Longest pass interception return—104 yards, James Willis, Philadelphia, 1996.

## Kicking

Highest average punting, lifetime—45.1 yards, Sammy Baugh, Washington, 1937–52.

Longest punt return—103 yards, Robert Bailey, L.A. Rams, 1994.

Longest kick-off return—106 yards, Roy Green, St. Louis, 1979; Al Carmichael, Green Bay, 1956; Noland Smith, Kansas City, 1967.

## Passing

Most touchdown passes, lifetime—420, Dan Marino, Miami, 1983–99.

Most touchdown passes, season—48, Dan Marino, Miami, 1984.

Most touchdown passes, game—7, Sid Luckman, Chicago Bears, 1943; Adrian Burk, Philadelphia, 1954; George Blanda, Houston, 1961; Y. A. Tittle, N.Y. Giants, 1962; Joe Kapp, Minnesota, 1969.

Longest pass completion—99 yards, Frank Filchock (to Andy Farkas), Washington, 1939; George Izo (to Bob Mitchell), Washington, 1963; Karl Sweetan (to Pat Studstill), Detroit, 1966; Sonny Jurgensen (to Gerry Allen), Washington, 1968; Jim Plunkett (to Cliff Branch) L.A. Raiders, 1983; Ron Jaworski (to Mike Quick), Philadelphia, 1985; Stan Humphries (to Tony Martin), San Diego, 1994; Brett Favre (to Robert Brooks), Green Bay, 1995.

Most passes completed, lifetime—4,967, Dan Marino, Miami, 1983–99.

Most passes completed, season—404, Warren Moon, 1991.

Most passes completed, game—45, Drew Bledsoe, New England, 1994.

Most yards gained, lifetime—61,361, Dan Marino, Miami, 1983–99.

Most yards gained, season—5,084, Dan Marino, Miami, 1984.

Most yards gained, game—554, Norm Van Brocklin, Los Angeles, 1951.

## PRO FOOTBALL HALL OF FAME

(National Football Museum, Canton, Ohio)

Teams named are those with which player is best identified; figures in parentheses indicate number of playing seasons.

| | |
|---|---|
| Adderley, Herb, defensive back, Packers, Cowboys (10) | 1961-72 |
| Allen, George, coach, Rams, Redskins (12) | 1966-77 |
| Alworth, Lance, wide receiver, Chargers, Cowboys (12) | 1961–72 |
| Atkins, Doug, defensive end, Browns, Bears, Saints (17) | 1953–69 |
| Badgro, Morris, end, N.Y. Yankees, Giants, Brooklyn Dodgers (8) | 1927, 1930–36 |
| Barney, Lem, defensive back, Lions (11) | 1967–78 |
| Battles, Cliff, back, Redskins (6) | 1932–37 |
| Baugh, Sammy, quarterback, Redskins (16) | 1936–52 |
| Bednarik, Chuck, center-linebacker, Eagles (14) | 1949–62 |
| Bell, Bert, NFL founder, Eagles and Steelers, NFL Commissioner | 1946–59 |
| Bell, Bobby, linebacker, Chiefs (12) | 1963–74 |
| Berry, Raymond, end, Colts (13) | 1955–67 |
| Bidwell, Charles W., owner, Chicago Cardinals | 1933–47 |

| | |
|---|---|
| Biletnikoff, Fred, wide receiver, Raiders (14) | 1965–78 |
| Blanda, George, quarterback-kicker, Bears, Oilers, Raiders (27) | 1949–75 |
| Blount, Mel, cornerback, Pittsburgh Steelers (14) | 1970–83 |
| Bradshaw, Terry, quarterback, Pittsburgh Steelers (14) | 1970–83 |
| Brown, Jim, fullback, Browns (9) | 1957–65 |
| Brown, Paul E., coach, Browns (1946–62), Bengals (1968–75) | 1946–75 |
| Brown, Roosevelt, tackle, Giants (13) | 1953–65 |
| Brown, Willie, cornerback, Broncos, Raiders (16) | 1963–78 |
| Buchanan, Buck, tackle, Chiefs (13) | 1963–73 |
| Buoniconti, Nick, linebacker, Patriots, Dolphins (14) | 1962–74, 1976 |
| Butkus, Dick, linebacker, Bears (9) | 1965–73 |
| Campbell, Earl, running back, Oilers, Saints (8) | 1978–85 |
| Canadeo, Tony, back, Packers (11) | 1941–52 |
| Carr, Joe, NFL president (18) | 1921–39 |

| | | | |
|---|---|---|---|
| Shula, Don, coach, Colts, Dolphins (33) | 1963–95 | Tunnell, Emlen, defensive back, Giants, Packers (14) | 1948–61 |
| Simpson, O.J., back, Bills, 49ers (11) | 1969–79 | Turner, Clyde (Bulldog), center, Bears (13) | 1940–52 |
| Singletary, Mike, linebacker, Bears (12) | 1981–92 | Unitas, John, quarterback, Colts (18) | 1956–73 |
| Slater, Jackie, tackle, Rams (20) | 1976–95 | Upshaw, Gene, guard, Raiders (15) | 1967–81 |
| Smith, Jackie, tight end, Cardinals, Cowboys (16) | 1963–78 | Van Brocklin, Norm, quarterback, Rams, Eagles (12) | 1949–60 |
| Stallworth, John, wide receiver, Steelers (14) | 1974–87 | Van Buren, Steve, back, Eagles (8) | 1944–51 |
| Starr, Bart, quarterback, coach, Packers (16) | 1956–71 | Walker, Doak, running back, def. back, kicker, Lions (6) | 1950–55 |
| Staubach, Roger, quarterback, Cowboys (11) | 1969–79 | Walsh, Bill, coach, 49ers (10) | 1979–88 |
| Stautner, Ernie, defensive tackle, Steelres (14) | 1950–63 | Warfield, Paul, wide receiver, Browns, Dolphins (13) | 1964–74, 76–77 |
| Stenerud, Jan, placekicker, Chiefs, Packers, Vikings (19) | 1967–85 | Waterfield, Bob, quarterback, Rams (8) | 1945–52 |
| Stephenson, Dwight, center, Dolphins (8) | 1980–87 | Webster, Mike, center, Steelers, Chiefs (17) | 1974–90 |
| Strong, Ken, back, Giants, Yankees (14) | 1929–47 | Weinmeister, Arnie, tackle, N.Y. Yankees, Giants (6) | 1948–53 |
| Stydahar, Joe, tackle, Bears (9); coach, Rams, Cardinals (5) | 1936–54 | White, Randy, defensive tackle, Cowboys (14) | 1975–88 |
| Swann, Lynn, wide receiver, Steelers (9) | 1974–82 | Wilcox, Dave, linebacker, 49ers (11) | 1964–74 |
| Tarkenton, Fran, quarterback, Vikings, Giants (18) | 1961–78 | Willis, Bill, guard, Browns (8) | 1946–53 |
| Taylor, Charlie, wide receiver, Redskins (14) | 1964–77 | Wilson, Larry, defensive back, Cardinals (13) | 1960–72 |
| Taylor, Jim, fullback, Packers, Saints (10) | 1958–67 | Winslow, Kellen, tight end, Chargers (9) | 1979–87 |
| Taylor, Lawrence, linebacker, Giants (13) | 1981–93 | Wood, Willie, safety, Packers (12) | 1960–71 |
| Thorpe, Jim, back, 7 teams (12) | 1915–28 | Wojciechowicz, Alex, center, Lions, Eagles (13) | 1938–50 |
| Tittle, Y.A., quarterback, Colts, 49ers, Giants (17) | 1948–64 | Yary, Ron, tackle, Vikings, Rams (15) | 1968–82 |
| Trafton, George, center, Bears (13) | 1920–32 | Youngblood, Jack, defensive end, Rams (14) | 1971–84 |
| Trippi, Charley, back, Chicago Cardinals (9) | 1947–55 | | |

# Basketball

Basketball is one of the few sports whose exact origin is definitely known. In the winter of 1891–1892, Dr. James Naismith, an instructor in the YMCA. Training College (now Springfield College) at Springfield, Mass., deliberately invented the game of basketball in order to provide indoor exercise and competition for the students between the closing of the football season and the opening of the baseball season. He affixed peach baskets overhead on the walls at opposite ends of the gymnasium and organized teams to play his new game in which the purpose was to toss an association (soccer) ball into one basket and prevent the opponents from tossing the ball into the other basket. Because Dr. Naismith had eighteen available players when he invented the game, the first rule was: "There shall be nine players on each side." Later the number of players became optional, depending upon the size of the available court, but the five-player standard was adopted when the game spread over the country. U.S. soldiers brought basketball to Europe in World War I, and it soon became a worldwide sport.

## College Basketball

### NCAA CHAMPIONS

| | | | | | | | |
|---|---|---|---|---|---|---|---|
| 1938 | Temple | 1949 | Kentucky | 1962 | Cincinnati | 1979 | Michigan State |
| 1939 | Oregon | 1950 | C.C.N.Y. | 1963 | Loyola (Chi- | 1980 | Louisville |
| 1940 | Indiana & USC | 1951 | Kentucky | | cago) | 1981 | Indiana |
| 1941 | Wisconsin | 1952 | Kansas | 1964 | UCLA | 1982 | North Carolina |
| 1942 | Stanford | 1953 | Indiana | 1965 | UCLA | 1983 | North Carolina |
| 1943 | Wyoming | 1954 | La Salle | 1966 | Texas Western | | State |
| 1944 | Utah | 1955 | San Francisco | 1967–73 | UCLA | 1984 | Georgetown |
| 1945 | Oklahoma | 1956 | San Francisco | 1974 | North Carolina | 1985 | Villanova |
| | A & M | 1957 | North Carolina | | State | 1986 | Louisville |
| 1946 | Oklahoma | 1958 | Kentucky | 1975 | UCLA | 1987 | Indiana |
| | A & M | 1959 | California | 1976 | Indiana | 1988 | Kansas |
| 1947 | Holy Cross | 1960 | Ohio State | 1977 | Marquette | 1989 | Michigan |
| 1948 | Kentucky | 1961 | Cincinnati | 1978 | Kentucky | 1990 | UNLV |
| | | | | | | 1991 | Duke |
| | | | | | | 1992 | Duke |
| | | | | | | 1993 | North Carolina |
| | | | | | | 1994 | Arkansas |
| | | | | | | 1995 | UCLA |
| | | | | | | 1996 | Kentucky |
| | | | | | | 1997 | Arizona |
| | | | | | | 1998 | Kentucky |
| | | | | | | 1999 | Connecticut |
| | | | | | | 2000 | Michigan State |
| | | | | | | 2001 | Duke |
| | | | | | | 2002 | Maryland |

### NATIONAL INVITATION TOURNAMENT (NIT) CHAMPIONS

| | | | | | | | |
|---|---|---|---|---|---|---|---|
| 1938 | Temple | 1953 | Seton Hall | 1965 | St. John's | 1978 | Texas | 1992 | Virginia |
| 1939 | Long Island U. | 1954 | Holy Cross | | (N.Y.C.) | 1979 | Indiana | 1993 | Minnesota |
| 1940 | Colorado | 1955 | Duquesne | 1966 | Brigham Young | 1980 | Virginia | 1994 | Villanova |
| 1941 | Long Island U. | 1956 | Louisville | 1967 | So. Illinois | 1981 | Tulsa | 1995 | Virginia Tech |
| 1942 | West Virginia | 1957 | Bradley | 1968 | Dayton | 1982 | Bradley | 1996 | Nebraska |
| 1943–44 | St. John's | 1958 | Xavier (Cincin- | 1969 | Temple | 1983 | Fresno State | 1997 | Michigan |
| (N.Y.C.) | | | nati) | 1970 | Marquette | 1984 | Michigan | 1998 | Minnesota |
| 1945 | DePaul | 1959 | St. John's | 1971 | North Carolina | 1985 | UCLA | 1999 | California |
| 1946 | Kentucky | | (N.Y.C.) | 1972 | Maryland | 1986 | Ohio State | 2000 | Wake Forest |
| 1947 | Utah | 1960 | Bradley | 1973 | Virginia Tech | 1987 | So. Mississippi | 2001 | Tulsa |
| 1948 | St. Louis | 1961 | Providence | 1974 | Purdue | 1988 | Connecticut | 2002 | Memphis |
| 1949 | San Francisco | 1962 | Dayton | 1975 | Princeton | 1989 | St. John's | | |
| 1950 | C.C.N.Y. | 1963 | Providence | 1976 | Kentucky | | (N.Y.C.) | | |
| 1951 | Brigham Young | 1964 | Bradley | 1977 | St. Bonaven- | 1990 | Vanderbilt | | |
| 1952 | La Salle | | | | ture | 1991 | Stanford | | |

## MEN'S NCAA BASKETBALL CHAMPIONSHIPS, 2002

### Division I

**First Round—East**
Kentucky 83, Valparaiso 68
Marquette 69, Tulsa 71
No. Carolina State 69, Michigan State 58
Connecticut 78, Hampton 67
Wisconsin 80, St. John's 70
Maryland 85, Siena 70
Texas Tech 68, Southern Illinois 76
Georgia 85, Murray State 68

**First Round—Midwest**
Kansas 70, Holy Cross 59
Stanford 84, Western Kentucky 68
Wake Forest 83, Pepperdine 74
Oregon 81, Montana 62
Florida 82, Creighton 83 (2OT)
Illinois 93, San Diego St. 64
Mississippi State 70, McNeese State 58
Texas 70, Boston College 57

**First Round—South**
Oklahoma State 61, Kent State 69
Alabama 86, Florida Atlantic 78
Notre Dame 82, Charlotte 63
Duke 84, Winthrop 37
Southern Cal 89, UNC-Wilmington 93
Indiana 75, Utah 56
Pittsburgh 71, Central Conn. State 54
California 82, Pennsylvania 75

**First Round—West**
Missouri 93, Miami Florida 80
Ohio State 69, Davidson 64
Gonzaga 66, Wyoming 73
Arizona 86, Santa Barbara 81
Cincinnati 90, Boston 52
UCLA 80, Mississippi 58
Oklahoma 71, Ill.-Chicago 63
Xavier 70, Hawaii 58

**Second Round—East**
Kentucky 87, Tulsa 82
Connecticut 77, No. Carolina State 74
Maryland 87, Wisconsin 57
Southern Illinois 77, Georgia 75

**Second Round—Midwest**
Kansas 86, Stanford 63
Oregon 92, Wake Forest 87
Illinois 72, Creighton 60
Mississippi State 64, Texas 68

**Second Round—South**
Duke 84, Notre Dame 77
Alabama 58, Kent State 71
UNC-Wilmington 67, Indiana 76
Pittsburgh 63, California 50

**Second Round—West**
Missouri 83, Ohio State 67
Wyoming 60, Arizona 68
Cincinnati 101, UCLA 105 (2OT)
Xavier 65, Oklahoma 78

**Third Round—East**
Connecticut 71, Southern Illinois 59
Maryland 78, Kentucky 68

**Third Round—Midwest**
Oregon 72, Texas 70
Kansas 73, Illinois 69

**Third Round—South**
Indiana 74, Duke 73
Kent State 78, Pittsburgh 73 (OT)

**Third Round—West**
Oklahoma 88, Arizona 67
Missouri 82, UCLA 73

**Regional Finals**
East—Maryland 90, Connecticut 82
Midwest—Kansas 104, Oregon 86
South—Indiana 81, Kent State 69
West—Oklahoma 81, Missouri 75

**Final Four**
(March 30, 2002, Atlanta, Ga.)
Indiana 73, Oklahoma 64
Kansas 88, Maryland 97

**National Final**
(April 1, 2002, Atlanta, Ga.)
Indiana 52, Maryland 64

### Division II

**Semifinals**
Indiana (Pa.) 52, Metro State 82
Shaw 92, Kentucky Wesleyan 101

**Championship**
Metro State 80, Kentucky Wesleyan 72

## LEADING NCAA DIVISION I MEN, 2001–2002

### POINTS PER GAME

| | FGM | 3FG | FT | PTS | PPG |
|---|---|---|---|---|---|
| Jason Conley, VMI | 285 | 79 | 171 | 820 | 29.3 |
| Henry Domercant, Eastern III. | 262 | 104 | 189 | 817 | 26.4 |
| Mire Chatman, Tex.-Pan American | 265 | 65 | 165 | 760 | 26.2 |
| Ernest Bremer, St. Bonaventure | 231 | 88 | 188 | 738 | 24.6 |
| Melvin Ely, Fresno St. | 246 | 0 | 161 | 653 | 23.3 |

### FIELD-GOAL PERCENTAGE

| | G | FGM | FGA | FG% |
|---|---|---|---|---|
| Adam Mark, Belmont | 26 | 150 | 212 | 70.8% |
| Carlos Boozer, Duke | 35 | 230 | 346 | 66.5 |
| David Harrison, Colorado | 27 | 139 | 218 | 63.8 |
| Rolan Roberts, Southern Ill. | 36 | 209 | 346 | 60.4 |
| Jermaine Hall, Wagner | 29 | 240 | 400 | 60.0 |

### REBOUNDING

| | G | REB | RPG |
|---|---|---|---|
| Jeremy Bishop, Quinnipiac | 29 | 347 | 12.0 |
| Bruce Jenkins, N.C. A&T | 28 | 329 | 11.8 |
| Curtis Borchardt, Stanford | 29 | 332 | 11.4 |
| Drew Gooden, Kansas | 37 | 423 | 11.4 |
| Corey Jackson, Nevada | 29 | 323 | 11.1 |

### ASSISTS

| | G | AST | APG |
|---|---|---|---|
| T. J. Ford, Texas | 33 | 273 | 8.3 |
| Steve Blake, Maryland | 36 | 286 | 7.9 |
| Edward Scott, Clemson | 30 | 238 | 7.9 |
| Sean Kennedy, Marist | 28 | 222 | 7.9 |
| Chris Thomas, Notre Dame | 33 | 252 | 7.6 |

### FREE-THROW PERCENTAGE

| | G | FT | FTA | FT% |
|---|---|---|---|---|
| Cary Cochran, Nebraska | 28 | 71 | 77 | 92.2% |
| Gary Buchanan, Villanova | 32 | 112 | 123 | 91.1 |
| Cain Doliboa, Wright St. | 28 | 80 | 88 | 90.9 |
| Salim Stoudamire, Arizona | 34 | 103 | 114 | 90.4 |
| Jake Sullivan, Iowa St. | 28 | 117 | 130 | 90.0 |

### THREE-PT FIELD-GOAL PERCENTAGE

| | G | 3FG | 3FGA | 3FG% |
|---|---|---|---|---|
| Dante Swanson, Tulsa | 33 | 73 | 149 | 49.0% |
| Cain Doliboa, Wright St. | 28 | 104 | 217 | 47.9 |
| Jake Sullivan, Iowa St. | 28 | 60 | 127 | 47.2 |
| Jeff Boschee, Kansas | 37 | 110 | 237 | 46.4 |
| Ray Abellard, UCF | 29 | 80 | 173 | 46.2 |

## NCAA DIVISION I SINGLE-GAME SCORING MARKS

| | Year | Pts |
|---|---|---|
| Kevin Bradshaw, US Int'l vs. Loyola-CA | 1991 | 72 |
| Pete Maravich, LSU vs. Alabama | 1970 | 69 |
| Calvin Murphy, Niagara vs. Syracuse | 1969 | 68 |
| Jay Handlan, Wash. & Lee vs. Furman | 1951 | 66 |
| Pete Maravich, LSU vs. Tulane | 1969 | 66 |
| Anthony Roberts, Oral Rbts. vs. N.C. A.&T. | 1977 | 66 |

| | Year | Pts |
|---|---|---|
| Anthony Roberts, Oral Rbts. vs. Oregon | 1977 | 65 |
| Scott Haffner, Evansville vs. Dayton | 1989 | 65 |
| Pete Maravich, LSU vs. Kentucky | 1970 | 64 |
| Johnny Neumann, Ole Miss vs. LSU | 1971 | 63 |
| Hersey Hawkins, Bradley vs. Detroit | 1988 | 63 |

## NCAA DIVISION I INDIVIDUAL CAREER RECORDS

### SCORING—TOTAL POINTS

| | Yrs | Last | Gm | Pts |
|---|---|---|---|---|
| Pete Maravich, LSU | 3 | 1970 | 83 | 3,667 |
| Freeman Williams, Port. St. | 4 | 1978 | 106 | 3,249 |
| Lionel Simmons, La Salle | 4 | 1990 | 131 | 3,217 |
| Alphonso Ford, Miss. Val. St. | 4 | 1993 | 109 | 3,165 |
| Harry Kelly, Texas Southern | 4 | 1983 | 110 | 3,066 |
| Hersey Hawkins, Bradley | 4 | 1988 | 125 | 3,008 |
| Oscar Robertson, Cincinnati | 3 | 1960 | 88 | 2,973 |
| Danny Manning, Kansas | 4 | 1988 | 147 | 2,951 |
| Alfredrick Hughes, Loyola-Ill. | 4 | 1985 | 120 | 2,914 |
| Elvin Hayes, Houston | 3 | 1968 | 93 | 2,884 |

### SCORING—AVERAGE POINTS

| | Yrs | Last | Pts | Avg |
|---|---|---|---|---|
| Pete Maravich, LSU | 3 | 1970 | 3,667 | 44.2 |
| Austin Carr, Notre Dame | 3 | 1971 | 2,560 | 34.6 |
| Oscar Robertson, Cinn. | 3 | 1960 | 2,973 | 33.8 |
| Calvin Murphy, Niagara | 3 | 1970 | 2,548 | 33.1 |
| Dwight Lamar, SW La. | 2 | 1973 | 1,862 | 32.7 |
| Frank Selvy, Furman | 3 | 1954 | 2,538 | 32.5 |
| Rick Mount, Purdue | 3 | 1970 | 2,323 | 32.3 |
| Darrell Floyd, Furman | 3 | 1956 | 2,281 | 32.1 |
| Nick Werkman, Seton Hall | 3 | 1964 | 2,273 | 32.0 |
| Willie Humes, Idaho St. | 2 | 1971 | 1,510 | 31.5 |

### BLOCKED SHOTS—AVERAGE

| | Yrs | Last | No | Avg |
|---|---|---|---|---|
| Keith Closs, Cen. Conn. St. | 2 | 1996 | 317 | 5.87 |
| Adonal Foyle, Colgate | 3 | 1997 | 492 | 5.66 |
| David Robinson, Navy | 2 | 1987 | 351 | 5.24 |
| Shaquille O'Neal, LSU | 3 | 1992 | 412 | 4.58 |
| Troy Murphy, Notre Dame | 3 | 2001 | 425 | 4.52 |

**Note**: minimum 225 blocked shots.

### REBOUNDS—TOTAL, SINCE 1973

| | Yrs | Last | Gm | No |
|---|---|---|---|---|
| Tim Duncan, Wake Forest | 4 | 1997 | 128 | 1,570 |
| Derrick Coleman, Syracuse | 4 | 1990 | 143 | 1,537 |
| Malik Rose, Drexel | 4 | 1996 | 120 | 1,514 |
| Ralph Sampson, Virginia | 4 | 1983 | 132 | 1,511 |
| Pete Padgett, Nevada-Reno | 4 | 1976 | 104 | 1,464 |
| Lionel Simmons, La Salle | 4 | 1990 | 131 | 1,429 |
| Anthony Bonner, St. Louis | 4 | 1990 | 133 | 1,424 |
| Tyrone Hill, Xavier-Ohio | 4 | 1990 | 126 | 1,380 |
| Popeye Jones, Murray St. | 4 | 1992 | 123 | 1,374 |
| Michael Brooks, La Salle | 4 | 1980 | 114 | 1,372 |

### ASSISTS—TOTAL

| | Yrs | Last | Gm | No |
|---|---|---|---|---|
| Bobby Hurley, Duke | 4 | 1993 | 140 | 1,076 |
| Chris Corchiani, N.C. State | 4 | 1991 | 124 | 1,038 |
| Ed Cota, N. Carolina | 4 | 2000 | 138 | 1,030 |
| Keith Jennings, E. Tenn. St. | 4 | 1991 | 127 | 983 |
| Sherman Douglas, Syracuse | 4 | 1989 | 138 | 960 |
| Tony Miller, Marquette | 4 | 1995 | 123 | 956 |
| Greg Anthony, Portland/UNLV | 4 | 1991 | 138 | 950 |
| Doug Gottlieb, ND/Okla St. | 4 | 2000 | 124 | 947 |
| Gary Payton, Oregon St. | 4 | 1990 | 120 | 938 |
| Orlando Smart, San Fran. | 4 | 1994 | 116 | 902 |

### STEALS—AVERAGE

| | Yrs | Last | No | Avg |
|---|---|---|---|---|
| Mookie Blaylock, Oklahoma | 2 | 1989 | 281 | 3.80 |
| Ronn McMahon, Eastern Wash. | 3 | 1990 | 225 | 3.52 |
| Eric Murdock, Providence | 4 | 1991 | 376 | 3.21 |
| Van Usher, Tennessee Tech | 3 | 1992 | 270 | 3.18 |
| Pepe Sanchez, Temple | 4 | 2000 | 365 | 3.15 |

**Note**: minimum 225 steals.

## WOMEN'S NCAA CHAMPIONSHIPS, 2002

### Division I
**First Round—Mideast**
Creighton 58, Florida International 73
Chattanooga 67, Penn State 82
Clemson 68, Arkansas 78
Kent State 65, Kansas State 93
Iowa 69, Virginia 62
Connecticut 86, St. Francis, Pa. 37
Old Dominion 68, Georgia 54
Purdue 80, Austin Peay 49
**First Round—Midwest**
New Mexico 44, Notre Dame 58
Georgia State 68, Tennessee 98
UNLV 54, Minnesota 71
Harvard 58, North Carolina 85
BYU 00, Florida 52
Tulsa 67, Iowa State 72
Arizona State 73, Wisconsin 70
Oakland 38, Vanderbilt 63
**First Round—East**
Santa Barbara 57, Louisiana Tech 56
Wisconsin-Green Bay 55, Texas 60
Indiana 45, TCU 55
Norfolk State 48, Duke 95
Syracuse 69, Drake 87
Bucknell 56, Baylor 80
St. Peter's 63, Cincinnati 76
Liberty 61, South Carolina 69
**First Round—West**
Mississippi State 65, Boston College 59
Stephen F. Austin 63, Texas Tech 84

Southern 61, Colorado 88
Santa Clara 78, LSU 84
Villanova 67, Pepperdine 46
Hartford 52, Oklahoma 84
Tulane 73, Colorado State 69
Weber State 51, Stanford 76
**Second Round—Mideast**
Penn State 96, Florida International 76
Kansas State 64, Arkansas 68
Connecticut 86, Iowa 46
Old Dominion 74, Purdue 70
**Second Round—Midwest**
Tennessee 89, Notre Dame 50
Minnesota 69, North Carolina 72
Vanderbilt 61, Arizona State 35
BYU 76, Iowa State 69
**Second Round—East**
Duke 76, TCU 66
Drake 76, Baylor 72
Texas 76, Santa Barbara 00
South Caorlina 75, Cincinnati 56
**Second Round—West**
Texas Tech 77, Mississippi State 55
Colorado 69, LSU 58
Oklahoma 66, Villanova 53
Stanford 77, Tulane 55
**Third Round—Mideast**
Penn State 64, Connecticut 82
Old Dominion 88, Kansas State 62
**Third Round—Midwest**
Tennessee 68, Brigham Young 57
Vanderbilt 71, North Carolina 60

**Third Round—East**
Drake 65, South Carolina 79
Texas 46, Duke 62
**Third Round—West**
Colorado 62, Stanford 59
Oklahoma 72, Texas Tech 62
**Regional Finals**
Mideast—Connecticut 85, Old Dominion 64
Midwest—Tenneessee 68, Vanderbilt 63
East—Duke 77, South Carolina 68
West—Oklahoma 94, Colorado 60
**Final Four**
(March 29, 2002, San Antonio, Tex.)
Duke 71, Oklahoma 86
Tennessee 60, Connecticut 79
**National Championship**
(March 31, 2002, San Antonio, Tex.)
Oklahoma 70, Connecticut 82

### Division II
**Semifinals**
Cal Poly Pomona 74, Glenville State, W. Va. 62
South Dakota State 67, SE Oklahoma State 77
**Championship**
Cal Poly Pomona 73, SE Oklahoma State 62

## LEADING NCAA DIVISION I WOMEN, 2001–2002

**POINTS PER GAME**

| | FGM | 3FG | FT | PTS | PPG |
|---|---|---|---|---|---|
| Kelly Mazzante, Penn St. | 313 | 102 | 144 | 872 | 24.9 |
| LaToya Thomas, Mississippi St. | 286 | 1 | 190 | 763 | 24.6 |
| Janet Holt, Tennessee Tech | 255 | 21 | 183 | 714 | 23.8 |
| Susan Moran, St. Joseph's | 264 | 8 | 208 | 744 | 23.3 |
| Chandi Jones, Houston | 277 | 47 | 165 | 766 | 22.5 |

**FIELD-GOAL PERCENTAGE**

| | G | FGM | FGA | FG% |
|---|---|---|---|---|
| Angie Welle, Iowa St. | 33 | 244 | 369 | 66.1% |
| Chantelle Anderson, Vanderbilt | 37 | 295 | 456 | 64.7 |
| Teana McKiver, Tulane | 35 | 235 | 377 | 62.3 |
| Thea Herring, Troy St. | 28 | 171 | 275 | 62.2 |
| Jocelyn Penn, South Carolina | 32 | 218 | 351 | 62.1 |

**THREE-POINT FIELD-GOAL PERCENTAGE**

| | G | 3FG | 3FGA | 3FG% |
|---|---|---|---|---|
| Lindsay Herbert, Utah | 27 | 70 | 145 | 48.3% |
| Sara Boyer, Wis.-Green Bay | 31 | 64 | 134 | 47.8 |
| Kristin Rethman, Kansas St. | 34 | 69 | 145 | 47.6 |
| Jenia Dimitrova, New Mexico St. | 28 | 62 | 131 | 47.3 |
| Kerri Nakamoto, San Diego | 28 | 64 | 139 | 46.0 |

**FREE-THROW PERCENTAGE**

| | G | FT | FTA | FT% |
|---|---|---|---|---|
| Sue Bird, Connecticut | 39 | 98 | 104 | 94.2% |
| Kandi Brown, Morehead St. | 29 | 74 | 79 | 93.7 |
| Jennifer Mitchell, Loyola (Md.) | 29 | 90 | 98 | 91.8 |
| Carey Sauer, San Francisco | 30 | 90 | 98 | 91.8 |
| Sarah Judd, Oakland | 31 | 125 | 137 | 91.2 |

**REBOUNDS PER GAME**

| | G | REB | RPG |
|---|---|---|---|
| Mandi Carver, Idaho St. | 27 | 336 | 12.4 |
| Jermisha Dosty, St. Mary's (Cal.) | 29 | 344 | 11.9 |
| Rosalee Mason, Manhattan | 29 | 344 | 11.9 |
| Vanessa Hayden, Florida | 29 | 343 | 11.8 |
| Jennifer Butler, Massachusetts | 30 | 353 | 11.8 |

**ASSISTS PER GAME**

| | G | AST | APG |
|---|---|---|---|
| La'Terrica Dobin, Northwestern St. | 29 | 250 | 8.6 |
| Sara Nord, Louisville | 30 | 235 | 7.8 |
| Temeka Johnson, LSU | 24 | 179 | 7.5 |
| Michele Koclanes, Richmond | 30 | 221 | 7.4 |
| Becki Ashbaugh, Santa Clara | 31 | 227 | 7.3 |

## OTHER TOURNAMENTS, 2001–2002

**MEN**

NIT—Memphis 72, South Carolina 62
NAIA Div. I—Science and Arts 96, Oklahoma Baptist 79
NAIA Div. II—Evangel (Mo.) 84, Robert Morris (Ill.) 61

**WOMEN**

NIT—Oregon 54, Houston 52
NAIA Div. I—Oklahoma City 82, Southern Nazarene 73
NAIA Div. II—Hastings (Neb.) 73, Cornerstone (Mich.) 69

# Professional Basketball

## NATIONAL BASKETBALL ASSOCIATION CHAMPIONS

The National Basketball Association was originally the Basketball Association of America. It took its current name in 1949 when it merged with the National Basketball League.

| Year | Eastern Conference | Western Conference | Winner (Series) |
|---|---|---|---|
| 1947 | Philadelphia Warriors | Chicago Stags | Philadelphia Warriors (4–1) |
| 1948 | Philadelphia Warriors | Baltimore Bullets | Baltimore Bullets (4–2) |
| 1949 | Washington Capitols | Minneapolis Lakers | Minneapolis Lakers (4–2) |
| 1950 | Syracuse Nationals | Minneapolis Lakers | Minneapolis Lakers (4–2) |
| 1951 | New York Knickerbockers | Rochester Royals | Rochester Royals (4–3) |
| 1952 | New York Knickerbockers | Minneapolis Lakers | Minneapolis Lakers (4–3) |
| 1953 | New York Knickerbockers | Minneapolis Lakers | Minneapolis Lakers (4–1) |
| 1954 | Syracuse Nationals | Minneapolis Lakers | Minneapolis Lakers (4–3) |
| 1955 | Syracuse Nationals | Ft. Wayne Pistons | Syracuse Nationals (4–3) |
| 1956 | Philadelphia Warriors | Ft. Wayne Pistons | Philadelphia Warriors (4–1) |
| 1957 | Boston Celtics | St. Louis Hawks | Boston Celtics (4–3) |
| 1958 | Boston Celtics | St. Louis Hawks | St. Louis Hawks (4–2) |
| 1959 | Boston Celtics | Minneapolis Lakers | Boston Celtics (4–0) |
| 1960 | Boston Celtics | St. Louis Hawks | Boston Celtics (4–3) |
| 1961 | Boston Celtics | St. Louis Hawks | Boston Celtics (4–1) |
| 1962 | Boston Celtics | Los Angeles Lakers | Boston Celtics (4–3) |
| 1963 | Boston Celtics | Los Angeles Lakers | Boston Celtics (4–2) |
| 1964 | Boston Celtics | San Francisco Warriors | Boston Celtics (4–1) |
| 1965 | Boston Celtics | Los Angeles Lakers | Boston Celtics (4–1) |
| 1966 | Boston Celtics | Los Angeles Lakers | Boston Celtics (4–3) |
| 1967 | Philadelphia 76ers | SF Warriors | Philadelphia 76ers (4–2) |
| 1968 | Boston Celtics | Los Angeles Lakers | Boston Celtics (4–2) |
| 1969 | Boston Celtics | Los Angeles Lakers | Boston Celtics (4–3) |
| 1970 | New York Knickerbockers | Los Angeles Lakers | New York Knickerbockers (4–3) |
| 1971 | Baltimore Bullets | Milwaukee Bucks | Milwaukee Bucks (4–0) |
| 1972 | New York Knickerbockers | Los Angeles Lakers | Los Angeles Lakers (4–1) |
| 1973 | New York Knickerbockers | Los Angeles Lakers | New York Knickerbockers (4–1) |
| 1974 | Boston Celtics | Milwaukee Bucks | Boston Celtics (4–3) |

| Year | Eastern Conference | Western Conference | Winner (Series) |
|---|---|---|---|
| 1975 | Washington Bullets | Golden State Warriors | Golden State Warriors (4–0) |
| 1976 | Boston Celtics | Phoenix Suns | Boston Celtics (4–2) |
| 1977 | Philadelphia 76ers | Portland Trail Blazers | Portland Trail Blazers (4–2) |
| 1978 | Washington Bullets | Seattle SuperSonics | Washington Bullets (4–3) |
| 1979 | Washington Bullets | Seattle SuperSonics | Seattle SuperSonics (4–1) |
| 1980 | Philadelphia 76ers | Los Angeles Lakers | Los Angeles Lakers (4–2) |
| 1981 | Boston Celtics | Houston Rockets | Boston Celtics (4–2) |
| 1982 | Philadelphia 76ers | Los Angeles Lakers | Los Angeles Lakers (4–2) |
| 1983 | Philadelphia 76ers | Los Angeles Lakers | Philadelphia 76ers (4–0) |
| 1984 | Boston Celtics | Los Angeles Lakers | Boston Celtics (4–3) |
| 1985 | Boston Celtics | Los Angeles Lakers | Los Angeles Lakers (4–2) |
| 1986 | Boston Celtics | Houston Rockets | Boston Celtics (4–2) |
| 1987 | Boston Celtics | Los Angeles Lakers | Los Angeles Lakers (4–2) |
| 1988 | Detroit Pistons | Los Angeles Lakers | Los Angeles Lakers (4–3) |
| 1989 | Detroit Pistons | Los Angeles Lakers | Detroit Pistons (4–0) |
| 1990 | Detroit Pistons | Portland Trail Blazers | Detroit Pistons (4–1) |
| 1991 | Chicago Bulls | Los Angeles Lakers | Chicago Bulls (4–1) |
| 1992 | Chicago Bulls | Portland Trail Blazers | Chicago Bulls (4–2) |
| 1993 | Chicago Bulls | Phoenix Suns | Chicago Bulls (4–2) |
| 1994 | New York Knickerbockers | Houston Rockets | Houston Rockets (4–3) |
| 1995 | Orlando Magic | Houston Rockets | Houston Rockets (4–0) |
| 1996 | Chicago Bulls | Seattle SuperSonics | Chicago Bulls (4–2) |
| 1997 | Chicago Bulls | Utah Jazz | Chicago Bulls (4–2) |
| 1998 | Chicago Bulls | Utah Jazz | Chicago Bulls (4–2) |
| 1999 | New York Knickerbockers | San Antonio Spurs | San Antonio Spurs (4–1) |
| 2000 | Indiana Pacers | Los Angeles Lakers | Los Angeles Lakers (4–2) |
| 2001 | Philadelphia 76ers | Los Angeles Lakers | Los Angeles Lakers (4–1) |
| 2002 | New Jersey Nets | Los Angeles Lakers | Los Angeles Lakers (4–0) |

## INDIVIDUAL NBA SCORING CHAMPIONS

| Season | Player, Team | G | FG | FT | Pts | Avg |
|---|---|---|---|---|---|---|
| 1953–54 | Neil Johnston, Philadelphia Warriors | 72 | 591 | 577 | 1,759 | 24.4 |
| 1954–55 | Neil Johnston, Philadelphia Warriors | 72 | 521 | 589 | 1,631 | 22.7 |
| 1955–56 | Bob Pettit, St. Louis Hawks | 72 | 646 | 557 | 1,849 | 25.7 |
| 1956–57 | Paul Arizin, Philadelphia Warriors | 71 | 613 | 591 | 1,817 | 25.6 |
| 1957–58 | George Yardley, Detroit Pistons | 72 | 673 | 655 | 2,001 | 27.8 |
| 1958–59 | Bob Pettit, St. Louis Hawks | 72 | 719 | 667 | 2,105 | 29.2 |
| 1959–60 | Wilt Chamberlain, Philadelphia Warriors | 72 | 1,065 | 577 | 2,707 | 37.6 |
| 1960–61 | Wilt Chamberlain, Philadelphia Warriors | 79 | 1,251 | 531 | 3,033 | 38.4 |
| 1961–62 | Wilt Chamberlain, Philadelphia Warriors | 80 | 1,597 | 835 | 4,029 | 50.4 |
| 1962–63 | Wilt Chamberlain, San Francisco Warriors | 80 | 1,463 | 660 | 3,586 | 44.8 |
| 1963–64 | Wilt Chamberlain, San Francisco Warriors | 80 | 1,204 | 540 | 2,948 | 36.9 |
| 1964–65 | Wilt Chamberlain, San Francisco Warriors/Phila. 76ers | 73 | 1,063 | 408 | 2,534 | 34.7 |
| 1965–66 | Wilt Chamberlain, Philadelphia 76ers | 79 | 1,074 | 501 | 2,649 | 33.5 |
| 1966–67 | Rick Barry, San Francisco Warriors | 78 | 1,011 | 753 | 2,775 | 35.6 |
| 1967–68 | Dave Bing, Detroit Pistons | 79 | 835 | 472 | 2,142 | 27.1 |
| 1968–69 | Elvin Hayes, San Diego Rockets | 82 | 930 | 467 | 2,327 | 28.4 |
| 1969–70 | Jerry West, Los Angeles Lakers | 74 | 831 | 647 | 2,309 | 31.2 |
| 1970–71 | Lew Alcindor,[1] Milwaukee Bucks | 82 | 1,063 | 470 | 2,596 | 31.7 |
| 1971–72 | Kareem Abdul-Jabbar, Milwaukee Bucks | 81 | 1,159 | 504 | 2,822 | 34.8 |
| 1972–73 | Nate Archibald, Kansas City/Omaha Kings | 80 | 1,028 | 663 | 2,719 | 34.0 |
| 1973–74 | Bob McAdoo, Buffalo Braves | 74 | 901 | 459 | 2,261 | 30.8 |
| 1974–75 | Bob McAdoo, Buffalo Braves | 82 | 1,005 | 641 | 2,831 | 34.5 |
| 1975–76 | Bob McAdoo, Buffalo Braves | 78 | 934 | 559 | 2,427 | 31.1 |
| 1976–77 | Pete Maravich, New Orleans Jazz | 73 | 886 | 501 | 2,273 | 31.1 |
| 1977–78 | George Gervin, San Antonio Spurs | 82 | 864 | 504 | 2,232 | 27.2 |
| 1978–79 | George Gervin, San Antonio Spurs | 80 | 947 | 471 | 2,365 | 29.0 |
| 1979–80 | George Gervin, San Antonio Spurs | 78 | 1,024 | 505 | 2,585 | 33.1 |
| 1980–81 | Adrian Dantley, Utah Jazz | 80 | 909 | 632 | 2,452 | 30.7 |
| 1981–82 | George Gervin, San Antonio Spurs | 79 | 993 | 555 | 2,551 | 32.3 |
| 1982–83 | Alex English, Denver Nuggets | 82 | 959 | 406 | 2,326 | 28.4 |
| 1983–84 | Adrian Dantley, Utah Jazz | 79 | 802 | 813 | 2,418 | 30.6 |
| 1984–85 | Bernard King, New York Knicks | 55 | 691 | 426 | 1,809 | 32.9 |
| 1985–86 | Dominique Wilkins, Atlanta Hawks | 78 | 888 | 527 | 2,366 | 30.3 |
| 1986–87 | Michael Jordan, Chicago Bulls[2] | 82 | 1,098 | 833 | 3,041 | 37.1 |
| 1987–88 | Michael Jordan, Chicago Bulls[3] | 82 | 1,069 | 723 | 2,868 | 35.0 |
| 1988–89 | Michael Jordan, Chicago Bulls[4] | 81 | 966 | 674 | 2,633 | 32.5 |
| 1989–90 | Michael Jordan, Chicago Bulls[5] | 82 | 1,034 | 593 | 2,753 | 33.6 |
| 1990–91 | Michael Jordan, Chicago Bulls[6] | 82 | 990 | 571 | 2,580 | 31.5 |
| 1991–92 | Michael Jordan, Chicago Bulls[7] | 80 | 943 | 491 | 2,404 | 30.1 |

| Season | Player, Team | G | FG | FT | Pts | Avg |
|--------|--------------|---|----|----|-----|-----|
| 1992–93 | Michael Jordan, Chicago Bulls[8] | 78 | 992 | 476 | 2,541 | 32.6 |
| 1993–94 | David Robinson, San Antonio Spurs[9] | 80 | 840 | 693 | 2,383 | 29.8 |
| 1994–95 | Shaquille O'Neal, Orlando Magic[10] | 79 | 930 | 455 | 2,315 | 29.3 |
| 1995–96 | Michael Jordan, Chicago Bulls[11] | 82 | 916 | 548 | 2,491 | 30.4 |
| 1996–97 | Michael Jordan, Chicago Bulls[11] | 82 | 920 | 480 | 2,431 | 29.6 |
| 1997–98 | Michael Jordan, Chicago Bulls[12] | 82 | 881 | 565 | 2,357 | 28.7 |
| 1998–99 | Allen Iverson, Philadelphia 76ers[13] | 48 | 435 | 356 | 1,284 | 26.8 |
| 1999–2000 | Shaquille O'Neal, L.A. Lakers | 79 | 956 | 432 | 2,344 | 29.7 |
| 2000–01 | Allen Iverson, Philadelphia 76ers[14] | 71 | 762 | 585 | 2,207 | 31.1 |
| 2001–02 | Allen Iverson, Philadelphia 76ers[15] | 60 | 665 | 475 | 1,883 | 31.4 |

1. (Kareem Abdul-Jabbar). 2. Also had 12 3-point field goals. 3. Also had 7 3-point field goals. 4. Also had 27 3-point field goals. 5. Also had 92 3-point field goals. 6. Also had 29 3-point field goals. 7. Attempted 27 3-point field goals. 8. Also had 81 3-point field goals. 9. Also had 10 3-point field goals. 10. O'Neal scored no 3-point field goals in 1994–1995. 11. Also had 111 3-point field goals in both 1995–1996 and 1996–1997. 12. Also had 30 3-point field goals. 13. Also had 58 3-point field goals. 14. Also had 98 3-point field goals. 15. Also had 78 3-point field goals.

## NBA MOST VALUABLE PLAYERS

| | | |
|---|---|---|
| 1956 Bob Pettit, St. Louis | 1975 Bob McAdoo, Buffalo | 1991 Michael Jordan, Chicago |
| 1957 Bob Cousy, Boston | 1976–77 Kareem Abdul-Jabbar, L.A. Lakers | 1992 Michael Jordan, Chicago |
| 1958 Bill Russell, Boston | | 1993 Charles Barkley, Phoenix |
| 1959 Bob Pettit, St. Louis | 1978 Bill Walton, Portland | 1994 Hakeem Olajuwon, Houston |
| 1960 Wilt Chamberlain, Philadelphia | 1979 Moses Malone, Houston | 1995 David Robinson, San Antonio |
| 1961–63 Bill Russell, Boston | 1980 Kareem Abdul-Jabbar, L.A. Lakers | 1996 Michael Jordan, Chicago |
| 1964 Oscar Robertson, Cincinnati | | 1997 Karl Malone, Utah |
| 1965 Bill Russell, Boston | 1981 Julius Erving, Philadelphia | 1998 Michael Jordan, Chicago |
| 1966–68 Wilt Chamberlain, Philadelphia | 1982 Moses Malone, Houston | 1999 Karl Malone, Utah |
| | 1983 Moses Malone, Philadelphia | 2000 Shaquille O'Neal, L.A. Lakers |
| 1969 Wes Unseld, Baltimore | 1984 Larry Bird, Boston | 2001 Allen Iverson, Philadelphia |
| 1970 Willis Reed, New York | 1985 Larry Bird, Boston | 2002 Tim Duncan, San Antonio |
| 1971–72 Lew Alcindor (Kareem Abdul-Jabbar), Milwaukee | 1986 Larry Bird, Boston | |
| | 1987 Earvin Johnson, L.A. Lakers | |
| 1973 Dave Cowens, Boston | 1988 Michael Jordan, Chicago | |
| 1974 Kareem Abdul-Jabbar, Milwaukee | 1989 Earvin Johnson, L.A. Lakers | |
| | 1990 Earvin Johnson, L.A. Lakers | |

## NBA LIFETIME LEADERS

(Through 2002 season)

Players in bold face active in 2001–2002 season

### POINTS

| | Yrs | Gm | Pts | Avg |
|---|-----|-----|-----|-----|
| Kareem Abdul-Jabbar | 20 | 1,560 | 38,387 | 24.6 |
| **Karl Malone** | 17 | 1,353 | 34,707 | 25.7 |
| Wilt Chamberlain | 14 | 1,045 | 31,419 | 30.1 |
| **Michael Jordan** | 14 | 990 | 30,652 | 31.0 |
| Moses Malone | 19 | 1,329 | 27,409 | 20.6 |
| Elvin Hayes | 16 | 1,303 | 27,313 | 21.0 |
| **Hakeem Olajuwon** | 18 | 1,238 | 26,946 | 21.8 |
| Oscar Robertson | 14 | 1,040 | 26,710 | 25.7 |
| Dominique Wilkins | 15 | 1,074 | 26,668 | 24.8 |
| John Havlicek | 16 | 1,270 | 26,395 | 20.8 |

### FIELD GOALS

| | Yrs | FG | Att | Pct |
|---|-----|-----|-----|-----|
| Kareem Abdul-Jabbar | 20 | 15,837 | 28,307 | .559 |
| Wilt Chamberlain | 14 | 12,681 | 23,497 | .540 |
| **Karl Malone** | 17 | 12,737 | 24,521 | .519 |
| **Michael Jordan** | 14 | 11,513 | 23,010 | .500 |
| Elvin Hayes | 16 | 10,976 | 24,272 | .452 |
| Alex English | 15 | 10,659 | 21,036 | .507 |
| John Havlicek | 16 | 10,513 | 23,930 | .439 |
| **Hakeem Olajuwon** | 18 | 10,749 | 20,991 | .512 |
| Dominique Wilkins | 15 | 9,963 | 21,589 | .461 |
| Robert Parish | 21 | 9,614 | 17,914 | .537 |

### SCORING AVERAGE

**Minimum of 400 games or 10,000 points**

| | Yrs | Gm | Pts | Avg |
|---|-----|-----|-----|-----|
| **Michael Jordan** | 14 | 990 | 30,652 | 31.0 |
| Wilt Chamberlain | 14 | 1,045 | 31,419 | 30.1 |
| **Shaquille O'Neal** | 10 | 675 | 18,634 | 27.6 |
| Elgin Baylor | 14 | 846 | 23,149 | 27.4 |
| Jerry West | 14 | 932 | 25,192 | 27.0 |
| **Allen Iverson** | 6 | 405 | 10,908 | 26.9 |
| Bob Pettit | 11 | 792 | 20,880 | 26.4 |
| George Gervin | 10 | 791 | 20,708 | 26.2 |
| Oscar Robertson | 14 | 1,040 | 26,710 | 25.7 |
| **Karl Malone** | 17 | 1,353 | 34,707 | 25.7 |

### FREE THROWS

| | Yrs | FT | Att | Pct |
|---|-----|-----|-----|-----|
| **Karl Malone** | 17 | 9,145 | 12,342 | .741 |
| Moses Malone | 19 | 8,531 | 11,090 | .769 |
| Oscar Robertson | 14 | 7,694 | 9,185 | .838 |
| Jerry West | 14 | 7,160 | 8,801 | .814 |
| **Michael Jordan** | 14 | 7,061 | 8,448 | .836 |
| Dolph Schayes | 16 | 6,979 | 8,273 | .844 |
| Adrian Dantley | 15 | 6,832 | 8,351 | .818 |
| Kareem Abdul-Jabbar | 20 | 6,712 | 9,304 | .721 |
| Charles Barkley | 16 | 6,349 | 8,643 | .734 |
| Bob Pettit | 11 | 6,182 | 8,119 | .761 |

## MOST GAMES PLAYED

| | | | |
|---|---|---|---|
| Robert Parish | 1,611 | | |
| Kareem Abdul-Jabbar | 1,560 | | |
| John Stockton | 1,422 | | |
| Karl Malone | 1,353 | | |
| Moses Malone | 1,329 | | |

## PERSONAL FOULS

| | |
|---|---|
| Kareem Abdul-Jabbar | 4,657 |
| Robert Parish | 4,443 |
| Hakeem Olajuwon | 4,383 |
| Charles Oakley | 4,323 |
| Buck Williams | 4,267 |

## REBOUNDS

| | | | |
|---|---|---|---|
| Wilt Chamberlain | 23,924 | Robert Parish | 14,715 |
| Bill Russell | 21,620 | Nate Thurmond | 14,464 |
| Kareem Abdul-Jabbar | 17,440 | Walt Bellamy | 14,241 |
| Elvin Hayes | 16,279 | Karl Malone | 13,973 |
| Moses Malone | 16,212 | Wes Unseld | 13,769 |

## BLOCKED SHOTS

| | |
|---|---|
| Hakeem Olajuwon | 3,830 |
| Kareem Abdul-Jabbar | 3,189 |
| Mark Eaton | 3,064 |
| Patrick Ewing | 2,894 |
| David Robinson | 2,843 |

## STEALS

| | |
|---|---|
| John Stockton | 3,128 |
| Michael Jordan | 2,391 |
| Maurice Cheeks | 2,310 |
| Clyde Drexler | 2,207 |
| Scottie Pippen | 2,181 |

## ASSISTS

| | | | |
|---|---|---|---|
| John Stockton | 15,177 | Rod Strickland | 7,490 |
| Magic Johnson | 10,141 | Maurice Cheeks | 7,392 |
| Oscar Robertson | 9,887 | Lenny Wilkens | 7,211 |
| Mark Jackson | 9,840 | Bob Cousy | 6,955 |
| Isiah Thomas | 9,061 | Gary Payton | 6,927 |

## NBA INDIVIDUAL RECORDS, GAME

### (Through 2001–2002 season)

Most points, game—100, Wilt Chamberlain, Philadelphia vs. New York, 1962

Most free throws, game—28, Wilt Chamberlain, Philadelphia vs. New York, 1962; 28, Adrian Dantley, Utah vs. Houston, 1984

Most field goals, game—36, Wilt Chamberlain, Philadelphia vs. New York, 1962

Most assists, game—30, Scott Skiles, Orlando vs. Denver, 1990

Most rebounds, game—55, Wilt Chamberlain, Philadelphia vs. Boston, 1960

Most 3-pt. field goals, game—11, Dennis Scott, Orlando vs. Atlanta, 1996

Most blocked shots, game—17, Elmore Smith, Los Angeles vs. Portland, 1973

Most steals, game—11, Larry Kenon, San Antonio vs. Kansas City, 1976; 11, Kendall Gill, New Jersey vs. Miami, 1999

## NATIONAL BASKETBALL ASSOCIATION FINAL STANDINGS, 2001–2002

### EASTERN CONFERENCE

| Atlantic Division | W | L | Pct | GB |
|---|---|---|---|---|
| New Jersey Nets[1] | 52 | 30 | .634 | — |
| Boston Celtics[2] | 49 | 33 | .598 | 3 |
| Orlando Magic[2] | 44 | 38 | .537 | 8 |
| Philadelphia 76ers[2] | 43 | 39 | .524 | 9 |
| Washington Wizards | 37 | 45 | .451 | 15 |
| Miami Heat | 36 | 46 | .439 | 16 |
| New York Knicks | 30 | 52 | .366 | 22 |

| Central Division | W | L | Pct | GB |
|---|---|---|---|---|
| Detroit Pistons[1] | 50 | 32 | .610 | — |
| Charlotte Hornets[2] | 44 | 38 | .537 | 6 |
| Toronto Raptors[2] | 42 | 40 | .512 | 8 |
| Indiana Pacers[2] | 42 | 40 | .512 | 8 |
| Milwaukee Bucks | 41 | 41 | .500 | 9 |
| Atlanta Hawks | 33 | 49 | .402 | 17 |
| Cleveland Cavaliers | 29 | 53 | .354 | 21 |
| Chicago Bulls | 21 | 61 | .256 | 29 |

### WESTERN CONFERENCE

| Midwest Division | W | L | Pct | GB |
|---|---|---|---|---|
| San Antonio Spurs[1] | 58 | 24 | .707 | — |
| Dallas Mavericks[2] | 57 | 25 | .695 | 1 |
| Minnesota Timberwolves[2] | 50 | 32 | .610 | 8 |
| Utah Jazz[2] | 44 | 38 | .537 | 14 |
| Houston Rockets | 28 | 54 | .341 | 30 |
| Denver Nuggets | 27 | 55 | .329 | 31 |
| Memphis Grizzlies | 23 | 59 | .280 | 35 |

| Pacific Division | W | L | Pct | GB |
|---|---|---|---|---|
| Sacramento Kings[1] | 61 | 21 | .744 | — |
| L.A. Lakers[2] | 58 | 24 | .707 | 3 |
| Portland Trail Blazers[2] | 49 | 33 | .598 | 12 |
| Seattle SuperSonics[2] | 45 | 37 | .549 | 16 |
| L.A. Clippers | 39 | 43 | .476 | 22 |
| Phoenix Suns | 36 | 46 | .439 | 25 |
| Golden State Warriors | 21 | 61 | .256 | 40 |

1. Division champion. 2. Playoff qualifier.

## NBA PLAYOFFS, 2002

### EASTERN CONFERENCE

**First Round**
(Best of 5)
New Jersey Nets defeated Indiana Pacers, 3 games to 2
Detroit Pistons defeated Toronto Raptors, 3 games to 2
Boston Celtics defeated Philadelphia 76ers, 3 games to 2
Charlotte Hornets defeated Orlando Magic, 3 games to 1

**Conference Semifinals**
(Best of 7)
New Jersey Nets defeated Charlotte Hornets, 4 games to 1
Boston Celtics defeated Detroit Pistons, 4 games to 1

**Conference Finals**
(Best of 7)
New Jersey Nets defeated Boston Celtics, 4 games to 2

### WESTERN CONFERENCE

**First Round**
(Best of 5)
Sacramento Kings defeated Utah Jazz, 3 games to 1
San Antonio Spurs defeated Seattle SuperSonics, 3 games to 2
L.A. Lakers defeated Portland Trail Blazers, 3 games to 0
Dallas Mavericks defeated Minnesota Timberwolves, 3 games to 0

**Conference Semifinals**
(Best of 7)
Sacramento Kings defeated Dallas Mavericks, 4 games to 1
L.A. Lakers defeated San Antonio Spurs, 4 games to 1

**Conference Finals**
(Best of 7)
L.A. Lakers defeated Sacramento Kings, 4 games to 3

## NBA CHAMPIONSHIPS

Los Angeles Lakers defeated New Jersey Nets, 4 games to 0
Shaquille O'Neal, Los Angeles, named Finals MVP

June 5—Los Angeles 99, New Jersey 94
June 7—Los Angeles 106, New Jersey 83

June 9—Los Angeles 106, New Jersey 103
June 12—Los Angeles 113, New Jersey 107

## NBA INDIVIDUAL LEADERS, 2001–2002 SEASON

### POINTS PER GAME
Minimum of 49 games played

| | Gm | Pts | Avg |
|---|---|---|---|
| Allen Iverson, Philadelphia | 60 | 1,883 | 31.4 |
| Shaquille O'Neal, L.A. Lakeres | 67 | 1,822 | 27.2 |
| Paul Pierce, Boston | 82 | 2,144 | 26.1 |
| Tracy McGrady, Orlando | 76 | 1,948 | 25.6 |
| Tim Duncan, San Antonio | 82 | 2,089 | 25.5 |
| Kobe Bryant, L.A. Lakers | 80 | 2,019 | 25.2 |
| Vince Carter, Toronto | 60 | 1,484 | 24.7 |
| Dirk Nowitzki, Dallas | 76 | 1,779 | 23.4 |
| Karl Malone, Utah | 80 | 1,788 | 22.4 |
| Antoine Walker, Boston | 81 | 1,794 | 22.1 |

### ASSISTS PER GAME
Minimum of 49 games played

| | Gm | Avg | Ast |
|---|---|---|---|
| Andre Miller, Cleveland | 81 | 882 | 10.9 |
| Jason Kidd, New Jersey | 82 | 808 | 9.9 |
| Gary Payton, Seattle | 82 | 737 | 9.0 |
| Baron Davis, Charlotte | 82 | 698 | 8.5 |
| John Stockton, Utah | 82 | 674 | 8.2 |
| Stephon Marbury, New Jersy | 82 | 666 | 8.1 |
| Jamaal Tinsley, Indiana | 80 | 647 | 8.1 |
| Jason Williams, Memphis | 65 | 519 | 8.0 |
| Steve Nash, Dallas | 82 | 634 | 7.7 |
| Mark Jackson, New York | 82 | 605 | 7.4 |

### REBOUNDS PER GAME
Minimum of 49 games played

| | Gm | Reb | RPG |
|---|---|---|---|
| Ben Wallace, Detroit | 80 | 1,039 | 13.0 |
| Tim Duncan, San Antonio | 82 | 1,042 | 12.7 |
| Kevin Garnett, Minnesota | 81 | 981 | 12.1 |
| Danny Fortson, Golden State | 77 | 899 | 11.7 |
| Elton Brand, L.A. Clippers | 80 | 925 | 11.6 |
| Dikembe Mutombo, Philadelphia | 80 | 863 | 10.8 |
| Jermaine O'Neal, Indiana | 72 | 757 | 10.5 |
| Dirk Nowitzki, Dallas | 76 | 755 | 9.9 |
| Shawn Marion, Phoenix | 81 | 804 | 9.9 |
| P. J. Brown, Charlotte | 80 | 786 | 9.8 |

### FIELD GOAL PERCENTAGE
Minimum of 288 field goals made

| | FGM | FGA | Pct |
|---|---|---|---|
| Shaquille O'Neal, L.A. Lakers | 712 | 1,229 | .579 |
| Elton Brand, L.A. Clippers | 532 | 1,010 | .527 |
| Donyell Marshall, Utah | 343 | 661 | .519 |
| Pau Gasol, Memphis | 551 | 1,064 | .518 |
| John Stockton, Utah | 401 | 775 | .517 |
| Alonzo Mourning, Miami | 447 | 866 | .516 |
| Ruben Patterson, Portland | 319 | 619 | .515 |
| Corliss Williamson, Detroit | 411 | 806 | .510 |
| Tim Duncan, San Antonio | 764 | 1,504 | .508 |
| Brent Barry, Seattle | 401 | 790 | .508 |

### FREE-THROW PERCENTAGE
Minimum of 120 free throws made

| | FTM | FTA | Pct |
|---|---|---|---|
| Reggie Miller, Indiana | 296 | 325 | .911 |
| Richard Hamilton, Washington | 300 | 337 | .890 |
| Darrell Armstrong, Orlando | 182 | 205 | .888 |
| Damon Stoudamire, Portland | 174 | 196 | .888 |
| Steve Nash, Dallas | 260 | 293 | .887 |
| Chauncey Billups, Minnesota | 207 | 234 | .885 |
| Chris Whitney, Washington | 154 | 175 | .880 |
| Steve Smith, San Antonio | 159 | 181 | .878 |
| Predrag Stojakovic, Sacramento | 283 | 323 | .876 |
| Troy Hudson, Orlando | 176 | 201 | .876 |
| Jamal Mashburn, Charlotte | 211 | 241 | .876 |

### 3-POINT FIELD GOAL PERCENTAGE
Minimum of 55 3-point field goals made

| | 3FGM | 3FGA | Pct |
|---|---|---|---|
| Steve Smith, San Antonio | 116 | 246 | .472 |
| Jon Barry, Detroit | 121 | 258 | .469 |
| Eric Piatkowski, L.A. Clippers | 111 | 238 | .466 |
| Wally Szczerbiak, Minnesota | 87 | 191 | .455 |
| Steve Nash, Dallas | 156 | 343 | .455 |
| Hubert Davis, Washington | 57 | 126 | .452 |
| Tyronn Lue, Washington | 63 | 141 | .447 |
| Michael Redd, Milwaukee | 88 | 198 | .444 |
| Ray Allen, Milwaukee | 229 | 528 | .434 |

### BLOCKED SHOTS
Minimum of 49 games played or 96 block shots

| | Gm | Blk | BPG |
|---|---|---|---|
| Ben Wallace, Detroit | 80 | 278 | 3.47 |
| Raef LaFrentz, Denver | 78 | 213 | 2.73 |
| Alonzo Mourning, Miami | 75 | 186 | 2.48 |
| Tim Duncan, San Antonio | 82 | 203 | 2.48 |
| Dikembe Mutombo, Philadelphia | 80 | 190 | 2.38 |
| Jermaine O'Neal, Indiana | 72 | 166 | 2.31 |
| Erick Dampier, Golden State | 73 | 167 | 2.29 |
| Adonal Foyle, Golden State | 79 | 168 | 2.13 |
| Pau Gasol, Memphis | 82 | 169 | 2.06 |
| Shaquille O'Neal, L.A. Lakers | 67 | 137 | 2.04 |

### STEALS
Minimum of 49 games played or 120 steals

| | Gm | Stl | SPG |
|---|---|---|---|
| Allen Iverson, Philadelphia | 60 | 168 | 2.80 |
| Ron Artest, Chicao | 55 | 141 | 2.56 |
| Jason Kidd, New Jersey | 82 | 175 | 2.13 |
| Baron Davis, Charlotte | 82 | 172 | 2.10 |
| Doug Christie, Sacramento | 81 | 160 | 1.98 |
| Darrell Armstrong, Orlando | 82 | 157 | 1.91 |
| Karl Malone, Utah | 80 | 152 | 1.90 |
| Paul Pierce, Boston | 82 | 154 | 1.88 |
| Kenny Anderson, Boston | 76 | 141 | 1.86 |
| John Stockton, Utah | 82 | 152 | 1.85 |

# Women's Professional Basketball

## WOMEN'S NATIONAL BASKETBALL ASSOCIATION, 2002 SEASON

### Eastern Conference

| | W | L | Pct | GB | Home | Road |
|---|---|---|---|---|---|---|
| New York Liberty[1] | 18 | 14 | .563 | — | 10–6 | 8–8 |
| Charlotte Sting[1] | 18 | 14 | .563 | — | 11–5 | 7–9 |
| Washington Mystics[1] | 17 | 15 | .531 | 1 | 9–7 | 8–8 |
| Indiana Fever[1] | 16 | 16 | .500 | 2 | 10–6 | 6–10 |
| Orlando Miracle | 16 | 16 | .500 | 2 | 10–6 | 6–10 |
| Miami Sol | 15 | 17 | .469 | 3 | 9–7 | 6–10 |
| Cleveland Rockers | 10 | 22 | .313 | 8 | 4–12 | 6–10 |
| Detroit Shock | 9 | 23 | .281 | 9 | 7–9 | 2–14 |

### Western Conference

| | W | L | Pct | GB | Home | Road |
|---|---|---|---|---|---|---|
| Los Angeles Sparks[1] | 25 | 7 | .781 | — | 12–4 | 13–3 |
| Houston Comets[1] | 24 | 8 | .750 | 1 | 14–2 | 10–6 |
| Utah Starzz[1] | 20 | 12 | .625 | 5 | 12–4 | 8–8 |
| Seattle Storm[1] | 17 | 15 | .531 | 8 | 10–6 | 7–9 |
| Portland Fire | 16 | 16 | .500 | 9 | 9–7 | 7–9 |
| Sacramento Monarchs | 14 | 18 | .438 | 11 | 10–6 | 4–12 |
| Phoenix Mercury | 11 | 21 | .344 | 14 | 10–6 | 1–15 |
| Minnesota Lynx | 10 | 22 | .313 | 15 | 7–9 | 3–13 |

NOTE: GB refers to Games Behind leader. 1. Playoff qualifier.

### Conference Championship Series (Best of 3)

#### EASTERN CONFERENCE

| Date | Result |
|---|---|
| Aug. 22 | Washington 79, New York 74 |
| Aug. 24 | New York 96, Washington 79 |
| Aug. 25 | New York 64, Washington 57 |
| | New York wins series, 2–1 |

#### WESTERN CONFERENCE

| Date | Result |
|---|---|
| Aug. 22 | Los Angeles 75, Utah 67 |
| Aug. 24 | Los Angeles 103, Utah 77 |
| | Los Angeles wins series, 2–0 |

### League Championship Series (Best of 3)
### Los Angeles wins championship, 2 games to 0

| Date | Result |
|---|---|
| Aug. 29 | Los Angeles 71, New York 63 |
| Aug. 31 | Los Angeles 69, New York 66 |

## WNBA ANNUAL AWARDS, 2002 SEASON

**Most Valuable Player:** Sheryl Swoopes, Houston
**Rookie of the Year:** Tamika Catchings, Indiana
**Defensive Player of the Year:** Sheryl Swoopes, Houston
**Most Improved Player of the Year:** Coco Miller, Washington

**Coach of the Year:** Marianne Stanley, Washington
**Sportsmanship Award:** Jennifer Gillom, Phoenix
**Bud Light Scoring Average and Rebounds per Game:** Chamique Holdsclaw, Washingon

## 2002 WNBA LEAGUE LEADERS

### POINTS PER GAME

| | Gm | Pts | PPG |
|---|---|---|---|
| Chamique Holdsclaw, Washington | 20 | 397 | 19.9 |
| Tamika Catchings, Indiana | 32 | 594 | 18.6 |
| Sheryl Swoopes, Houston | 32 | 592 | 18.5 |
| Lauren Jackson, Seattle | 28 | 482 | 17.2 |
| Lisa Leslie, Los Angeles | 31 | 523 | 16.9 |

### STEALS PER GAME

| | Gm | Stl | SPG |
|---|---|---|---|
| Tamika Catchings, Indiana | 32 | 94 | 2.94 |
| Sheryl Swoopes, Houston | 32 | 88 | 2.75 |
| Ticha Penicheiro, Sacramento | 24 | 64 | 2.67 |
| Sheri Sam, Miami | 32 | 69 | 2.16 |
| Nykesha Sales, Orlando | 32 | 60 | 1.88 |

### REBOUNDS PER GAME

| | Gm | Reb | RPG |
|---|---|---|---|
| Chamique Holdsclaw, Washington | 20 | 232 | 11.6 |
| Lisa Leslie, Los Angeles | 31 | 322 | 10.4 |
| Margo Dydek, Utah | 30 | 262 | 8.7 |
| Tamika Catchings, Indiana | 32 | 276 | 8.6 |
| Natalie Williams, Utah | 31 | 273 | 8.7 |

### FIELD GOAL PERCENTAGE

| | FGM | FGA | FG% |
|---|---|---|---|
| Alisa Burras, Portland | 117 | 186 | .629 |
| Tamika Williams, Minnesota | 124 | 221 | .561 |
| Ann Wauters, Cleveland | 120 | 217 | .553 |
| Tammy Sutton-Brown, Charlotte | 129 | 243 | .531 |
| Tamicha Jackson, Sacramento | 97 | 178 | .520 |

### ASSISTS PER GAME

| | Gm | Ast | APG |
|---|---|---|---|
| Ticha Penicheiro, Sacramento | 24 | 192 | 8.0 |
| Sue Bird, Seattle | 32 | 191 | 6.0 |
| Teresa Weatherspoon, New York | 32 | 181 | 5.7 |
| Shannon Johnson, Orlando | 31 | 163 | 5.3 |
| Dawn Staley, Charlotte | 32 | 164 | 5.1 |

### 3-POINT FIELD GOAL PERCENTAGE

| | 3FGM | 3FGA | 3FG% |
|---|---|---|---|
| Kelly Miller, Charlotte | 24 | 51 | .471 |
| Jennifer Azzi, Utah | 41 | 92 | .446 |
| Coquese Washington, Indiana | 22 | 52 | .423 |
| Vickie Johnson, New York | 32 | 76 | .421 |
| DeLisha Milton, Los Angeles | 21 | 50 | .420 |

### BLOCKS PER GAME

| | Gm | Blk | BPG |
|---|---|---|---|
| Margo Dydek, Utah | 30 | 107 | 3.57 |
| Lisa Leslie, Los Angeles | 31 | 90 | 2.90 |
| Lauren Jackson, Seattle | 28 | 81 | 2.89 |
| Ruth Riley, Miami | 26 | 41 | 1.58 |
| Tangela Smith, Sacramento | 32 | 46 | 1.44 |

### FREE THROW PERCENTAGE

| | FTM | FTA | FT% |
|---|---|---|---|
| Sue Bird, Seattle | 102 | 112 | .911 |
| Ukari Figgs, Portland | 59 | 65 | .908 |
| Janeth Arcain, Houston | 98 | 111 | .883 |
| Katie Douglas, Orlando | 58 | 67 | .866 |
| Tamara Moore, Minnesota | 54 | 63 | .857 |

# Sports Personalities

A name in parentheses is the original name or form of name. Localities are places of birth. Dates of birth appear as month/day/year. **Boldface** years in parentheses are dates of **(birth–death)**.

Information has been gathered from many sources, including the individuals themselves. However, the almanac cannot guarantee the accuracy of every individual item.

**Aaron,** Hank (Henry) (baseball); Mobile, Ala., 2/5/34
**Abdul-Jabbar,** Kareem (Lewis Ferdinand Alcindor, Jr.) (basketball); New York City, 4/16/47
**Affleck,** Francis (auto racing) **(1951–1985)**
**Agassi,** Andre (tennis); Las Vegas, Nev., 4/29/70
**Aikman,** Troy (football); Henryetta, Okla., 11/21/66
**Ali,** Muhammad (Cassius Clay) (boxing); Louisville, Ky., 1/18/42
**Allen,** Dick (Richard Anthony) (baseball); Wampum, Pa., 3/8/42
**Allen,** George (football) **(1918–1990)**
**Allison,** Bobby (Robert Arthur) (auto racing); Hueytown, Ala., 12/3/37
**Allison,** Davey (auto racing); Hueytown, Ala. **(1961–1993)**
**Alston,** Walter (baseball); Venice, Ohio **(1911–1984)**
**Alworth,** Lance (football); Houston, 8/3/40
**Ameche,** Alan (football); Houston, Tex. **(1933–1988)**
**Anderson,** Sparky (George) (baseball); Bridgewater, S.D., 2/22/34
**Andretti,** Mario (auto racing); Montona, Trieste, Italy, 2/28/40
**Anthony,** Earl (bowling); Kent, Wash. **(1939–2001)**
**Appling,** Luke (baseball); High Point, N.C. **(1907–1990)**
**Arcaro,** Eddie (George Edward) (jockey); Cincinnati **(1916–1997)**
**Armstrong,** Lance (bicycling); Plano, Tex., Sept. 18, 1971
**Ashe,** Arthur (tennis); Richmond, Va. **(1943–1993)**
**Ashford,** Evelyn (track & field); Shreveport, La., 4/15/57
**Austin,** Tracy (tennis); Rolling Hills, Calif., 12/2/62
**Averill,** Earl (baseball); Everett, Wash. **(1915–1983)**
**Babashoff,** Shirley (swimming); Whittier, Calif., 1/31/57
**Baer,** Max (boxing); Omaha, Neb. **(1909–1959)**
**Bailey,** Donovan (track); Canada, 12/16/67
**Banks,** Ernie (baseball); Dallas, 1/31/31
**Bannister,** Roger (runner); Harrow, England, 3/24/29
**Barkley,** Charles (basketball); Leeds, Ala., 2/20/63
**Barry,** Rick (Richard) (basketball); Elizabeth, N.J., 3/28/44
**Bauer,** Hank (Henry) (baseball); East St. Louis, Ill., 7/31/22
**Baugh,** Sammy (football); Temple, Tex., 3/17/14
**Baylor,** Elgin (basketball); Washington, D.C., 9/16/34
**Beamon,** Bob (long jumper); New York City, 8/2/46
**Becker,** Boris (tennis); Leiman, W. Germany, 11/22/67
**Bee,** Clair (basketball); Cleveland, Ohio **(1896–1983)**
**Beliveau,** Jean (hockey); Three Rivers, Quebec, Canada, 8/31/31
**Belle,** Albert (baseball); Shreveport, La., 8/25/66
**Beman,** Deane (golf); Washington, D.C., 4/22/38
**Bench,** Johnny (Johnny Lee) (baseball); Oklahoma City, 12/7/47
**Berg,** Patty (Patricia Jane) (golf); Minneapolis, 2/13/18
**Berra,** Yogi (Lawrence) (baseball); St. Louis, 5/12/25
**Biletnikoff,** Frederick (football); Erie, Pa., 2/23/43
**Bing,** Dave (basketball); Washington, D.C., 11/24/43
**Bird,** Larry (basketball); French Lick, Ind., 12/7/56
**Blaik,** Earl H. (football); Detroit **(1897–1989)**
**Blanda,** George Frederick (football); Youngwood, Pa., 9/17/27
**Bledsoe,** Drew (football); Walla Walla, Wash., 2/14/72
**Blue,** Vida (baseball); Mansfield, La., 7/28/49
**Bodine,** Brett (auto racing); Chemung, N.Y., 1/11/59
**Bodine,** Geoff (auto racing); Chemung, N.Y., 4/18/49
**Boggs,** Wade (baseball); Omaha, Neb., 6/15/58
**Bonds,** Barry (baseball); Riverside, Calif., 7/24/64
**Borg,** Björn (tennis); Stockholm, Sweden, 6/6/56
**Boros,** Julius (golf); Fairfield, Conn. **(1920–1994)**
**Bossy,** Mike (hockey); Montreal, 1/22/57
**Boston,** Ralph (long jumper); Laurel, Miss., 5/9/39
**Bourque,** Ray (hockey); Montreal, Que., 12/28/60
**Bradley,** Bill (William Warren) (basketball); Crystal City, Mo., 7/28/43
**Bradley,** Pat (golf); Westford, Mass., 3/24/51
**Bradshaw,** Terry (football); Shreveport, La., 9/2/48
**Breedlove,** Craig (Norman) (speed driving); Los Angeles, 3/23/38
**Brett,** George (baseball); Glendale, W. Va., 5/15/53
**Brock,** Louis Clark (baseball); El Dorado, Ark., 6/18/39
**Brown,** Jim (football); St. Simon Island, Ga., 2/17/36
**Brumel,** Valeri (high jumper); Tolbuzino, Siberia, 4/14/42
**Bryant,** Paul "Bear" (football); Morro Bottom, Ark. **(1913–1983)**
**Bryant,** Rosalyn Evette (track); Chicago, 1/7/56
**Burton,** Michael (swimming); Des Moines, Iowa, 7/3/47
**Butkus,** Dick (Richard Marvin) (football); Chicago, 12/9/42
**Calipari,** John (basketball); Moon, Pa., 2/10/59
**Campanella,** Roy (baseball); Homestead, Pa. **(1921–1993)**
**Campbell,** Earl (football); Tyler, Tex., 3/29/55
**Canseco,** Jose (baseball); Havana, Cuba, 7/2/64
**Caponi,** Donna Maria (golf); Detroit, 1/29/45
**Cappelletti,** Gino (football); Keewatin, Minn., 3/26/34
**Capriati,** Jennifer (tennis); New York, N.Y., 3/29/76
**Carew,** Rod (Rodney Cline) (baseball); Gatun, Panama, 10/1/45

**Carlos,** John (sprinter); New York City, 6/5/45
**Carlton,** Steven Norman (baseball); Miami, Fla., 12/22/44
**Carner,** Joanne Gunderson, Mrs. Don (golf); Kirkland, Wash., 3/4/39
**Casals,** Rosemary (tennis); San Francisco, 9/16/48
**Casper,** Billy (golf); San Diego, Calif., 6/24/31
**Caulkins,** Tracy (swimming); Winona, Minn., 1/11/63
**Cauthen,** Steve (jockey); Covington, Ky., 5/1/60
**Chamberlain,** Wilt (Wilton) (basketball); Philadelphia **(1936–1999)**
**Chandler,** A.B. (Happy) (baseball); Louisville, Ky. **(1899–1991)**
**Chandler,** Spud (baseball); Commerce, Ga. **(1907–1990)**
**Chang,** Michael (tennis); Hoboken, N.J., 2/22/72
**Chapot,** Frank (equestrian); Camden, N.J., 2/24/34
**Chastain,** Brandi (soccer); San Jose, Calif., 7/21/68
**Chinaglia,** Giorgio (soccer); Carrara, Italy, 1/24/47
**Clarke,** Bobby (Robert Earle) (hockey); Flin Flon, Manitoba, Canada, 8/13/49
**Clemens,** Roger (baseball); Dayton, Ohio, 8/4/62
**Clemente,** Roberto Walker (baseball); Carolina, Puerto Rico **(1934–1972)**
**Cobb,** Ty (Tyrus Raymond) (baseball); Narrows, Ga. **(1886–1961)**
**Cochran,** Barbara Ann (skiing); Claremont, N.H., 1/14/51
**Cochran,** Marilyn (skiing); Burlington, Vt., 2/7/50
**Cochran,** Robert (skiing); Claremont, N.H., 12/11/51
**Coe,** Sebastian Newbold (track); London, England, 9/29/56
**Coffey,** Paul (hockey); Weston, Ont., 6/1/61
**Colavito,** Rocky (Rocco Domenico) (baseball); New York City, 8/10/33
**Coleman,** Derrick (basketball); Mobile, Ala., 6/21/67
**Comaneci,** Nadia (gymnast); Onesti, Romania, 11/12/61
**Conigliaro,** Tony (baseball); Revere, Mass. **(1945–1990)**
**Connors,** Jimmy (James Scott) (tennis); East St. Louis, Ill., 9/2/52
**Cooper,** Cynthia (basketball); Chicago, Ill., 4/14/63
**Cordero,** Angel (jockey); Santurce, Puerto Rico, 5/8/42
**Cosell,** Howard (broadcaster); Winston-Salem, N.C. **(1918–1995)**
**Courier,** Jim (tennis); Sanford, Fla., 8/17/70
**Cournoyer,** Yvan Serge (hockey); Drummondville, Quebec, Canada, 11/22/43
**Court,** Margaret Smith (tennis); Albury, New South Wales, Australia, 7/16/42
**Cousy,** Bob (basketball); New York City, 8/9/28
**Crabbe,** Buster (swimming); Scottsdale, Ariz. **(1908–1983)**
**Crenshaw,** Ben (golf); Austin, Tex., 1/11/52
**Cronin,** Joe (baseball executive); San Francisco **(1906–1984)**
**Cruyff,** Johan (soccer); Amsterdam, Netherlands, 4/25/47
**Csonka,** Larry (Lawrence Richard) (football); Stow, Ohio, 12/25/46
**Dancer,** Stanley (harness racing); New Egypt, N.J., 7/25/27
**Dark,** Alvin (baseball); Comanche, Okla., 1/7/22
**Davenport,** Willie (track); Troy, Ala. **(1943–2002)**
**Dawson,** Andre (baseball); Miami, Fla., 7/10/54
**Dawson,** Leonard Ray (football); Alliance, Ohio, 6/20/35
**Dean,** Dizzy (Jay Hanna) (baseball); Lucas, Ark. **(1911–1974)**
**DeBusschere,** Dave (basketball); Detroit, 10/16/40
**De La Hoya,** Oscar (boxing); East Los Angeles, Calif., 2/4/73
**Delvecchio,** Alex Peter (hockey); Fort William, Ontario, Canada, 12/4/31
**Demaret,** Jim (golf); Houston **(1910–1983)**
**Dempsey,** Jack (William H.) (boxing); Manassa, Colo. **(1895–1983)**
**DeVicenzo,** Roberto (golf); Buenos Aires, 4/14/23
**Dibbs,** Edward George (tennis); Brooklyn, New York, 2/23/51
**Dietz,** James W. (rowing); New York, N.Y., 1/12/49
**DiMaggio,** Joe (baseball); Martinez, Calif. **(1914–1999)**
**Dionne,** Marcel (hockey); Drummondville, Quebec, Canada, 8/3/51
**Dorsett,** Tony (football); Rochester, Pa., 4/7/54
**Dryden,** Kenneth (hockey); Hamilton, Ontario, Canada, 8/4/47
**Drysdale,** Don (baseball); Van Nuys, Calif. **(1936–1993)**
**Duran,** Roberto (boxing); Panama City, 6/16/51
**Durocher,** Leo (baseball); West Springfield, Mass. **(1906–1991)**
**Durr,** Francois (tennis); Algiers, Algeria, 12/25/42
**Earnhardt,** Dale (auto racing); Concord, N.C. **(1951–2001)**
**Eckersley,** Dennis (baseball); Oakland, Calif., 10/3/54
**Elder,** Lee (golf); Dallas, 7/14/34
**Elway,** John (football); Port Angeles, Wash., 6/28/60
**Emerson,** Roy (tennis); Kingsway, Australia, 11/3/36
**Ender,** Kornelia (swimming); Plauen, East Germany, 10/25/58
**Erving,** Julius ("Dr. J") (basketball); Roosevelt, N.Y., 2/22/50
**Esposito,** Phil (Philip Anthony) (hockey); Sault Ste. Marie, Ontario, Canada, 2/20/42
**Evans,** Lee (runner); Mandena, Calif., 2/25/47
**Evert,** Chris (Christine Marie) (tennis); Fort Lauderdale, Fla., 12/21/54
**Ewbank,** Weeb (football); Richmond, Ind. **(1907–1998)**

Ewing, Patrick (basketball); Kingston, Jamaica, 8/5/62
Favro, Brett (football); Gulfport, Miss., 10/10/69
Feller, Robert (Bob) (baseball); Van Meter, Iowa, 11/3/18
Feuerbach, Allan Dean (track); Preston, Iowa, 1/12/48
Finley, Charles O. (sportsman); Ensley, Ala. (1918–1996)
Fischer, Bobby (chess); Chicago, 3/9/43
Fitzsimmons, Bob (Robert Prometheus) (boxing); Cornwall, England (1862–1917)
Fleming, Peggy Gale (ice skating); San Jose, Calif., 7/27/48
Ford, Whitey (Edward) (baseball); New York City, 10/21/28
Foreman, George (boxing); Marshall, Tex., 1/10/49
Fosbury, Richard (high jumper); Portland, Ore., 3/6/47
Fox, Nellie (Jacob Nelson) (baseball); St. Thomas, Pa. (1927–1975)
Foxx, James Emory (baseball); Sudlersville, Md. (1907–1967)
Foyt, A. J. (auto racing); Houston, 1/16/35
Frazier, Joe (boxing); Beauford, S.C., 1/17/44
Frazier, Walt (basketball); Atlanta, 3/29/45
Freeman, Cathy (track & field); Mackay, Queensland, Australia, 2/16/73
Frick, Ford C. (baseball); Wawaka, Ind. (1894–1978)
Furniss, Bruce (swimming); Fresno, Calif., 5/27/57
Gable, Dan (wrestling); Waterloo, Iowa, 10/25/45
Gabriel, Roman (football); Wilmington, N.C., 8/5/40
Gallagher, Michael Donald (skiing); Yonkers, N.Y., 10/3/41
Garvey, Steve (baseball); Tampa, Fla., 12/22/48
Gehrig, Lou (Henry Louis) (baseball); New York City (1903–1941)
Gehringer, Charlie (baseball); Fowlerville, Mich. (1903–1993)
Geoffrion, "Boom Boom" (Bernie) (hockey); Montreal, 2/14/31
Gerulaitis, Vitas (tennis); Brooklyn, N.Y. (1954–1994)
Gervin, George (basketball); Long Beach, Calif., 4/27/52
Giacomin, Ed (hockey); Sudbury, Ontario, Canada, 6/6/39
Giamatti, A. Bartlett (baseball); South Hadley, Mass. (1938–1989)
Gibson, Bob (baseball); Omaha, Neb., 11/9/35
Gifford, Frank (football); Santa Monica, Calif., 8/16/30
Gilbert, Rod (Rodrique) (hockey); Montreal, 7/1/41
Gilmore, Artis (basketball); Chipley, Fla., 9/21/49
Glance, Harvey (track); Phenix City, Ala., 3/28/57
Gonzalez, Pancho (tennis); Los Angeles (1928–1995)
Goodell, Brian Stuart (swimming); Stockton, Calif., 4/2/59
Gooden, Dwight (baseball); Tampa, Fla., 11/16/64
Goodrich, Gail (basketball); Los Angeles, 4/23/43
Goolagong, Cawley, Evonne (tennis); Griffith, Australia, 7/31/51
Gordon, Jeff (auto racing); Vallejo, Calif., 8/4/71
Gossage, "Goose" (Rich) (baseball); Colorado Springs, Colo., 4/5/51
Graf, Steffi (tennis); Mannheim, W. Germany, 6/14/69
Graham, David (golf); Windson, Australia, 5/23/46
Graham, Otto Everett (football); Waukegan, Ill., 12/6/21
Grange, Red (Harold) (football); Forksville, Pa. (1904–1991)
Green, Hubert (golf); Birmingham, Ala., 12/28/46
Greene, Charles E. (sprinter); Pine Bluff, Ark., 3/21/45
Greene, "Mean" (Joe) (football); Temple, Tex., 9/24/46
Gretzky, Wayne (hockey); Brantford, Ont., 1/26/61
Griese, Bob (Robert Allen) (football); Evansville, Ind., 2/3/45
Griffey, Ken, Jr. (baseball); Donora, Pa., 11/21/69
Grove, Lefty (Robert Moses) (baseball); Lonaconing, Md. (1900–1975)
Groza, Lou (football); Martins Ferry Ohio (1924–2000)
Guidry, Ronald Ames (baseball); Lafayette, La., 8/28/50
Gwynn, Tony (baseball); Los Angeles, Calif., 5/9/60
Halas, George (football); Chicago (1895–1983)
Hall, Gary (swimming); Fayetteville, N.C., 8/7/51
Hamill, Dorothy (figure skating); Chicago, 7/26/56
Hamilton, Scott (figure skating); Bowling Green, Ohio, 8/28/58
Hamm, Mia (soccer); Selma, Ala., 3/17/72
Hammond, Kathy (runner); Sacramento, Calif., 11/2/51
Hardaway, Anfernee (basketball); Memphis, Tenn., 7/18/72
Harding, Tonya (figure skating); Portland, Ore., 11/12/70
Harris, Franco (football); Ft. Dix, N.J., 3/7/50
Hartack, William, Jr. (jockey); Colver, Pa., 12/9/32
Hasek, Dominik (hockey); Pardubice, Czechoslovakia, 1/29/65
Haughton, William (harness racing); Gloversville, N.Y. (1923–1986)
Havlicek, John (basketball); Martins Ferry, Ohio, 4/8/40
Hayes, Elvin (basketball); Rayville, La., 11/17/45
Hayes, Woody (football); Upper Arlington, Ohio (1913–1987)
Heiden, Eric (speed skating); Madison, Wis., 6/14/58
Hencken, John (swimming); Culver City, Calif., 5/29/54
Henderson, Rickey (baseball); Chicago, 12/25/58
Henie, Sonja (ice skater); Oslo (1912–1969)
Herman, Floyd Caves (Babe) (baseball); Buffalo, N.Y. (1903–1987)
Hernandez, Keith (baseball); San Francisco, 10/20/53
Hershiser, Orel (baseball); Buffalo, N.Y., 9/16/58
Hickcox, Charles (swimming); Phoenix, Ariz., 2/6/47
Hines, James (sprinter); Dumas, Ark., 9/10/46
Hingis, Martina (tennis); Kosice, Slovakia, 9/30/80
Hodges, Gil (baseball); Princeton, Ind. (1924–1972)
Hogan, Ben (golf); Dublin, Tex. (1912–1997)
Holmes, Larry (boxing); Cuthert, Ga., 11/3/49
Holyfield, Evander (boxing); Atlanta, Ga., 10/19/62
Hornsby, Rogers (baseball); Winters, Tex. (1896–1963)

Hornung, Paul (football); Louisville, Ky., 12/23/35
Houk, Ralph (baseball); Lawrence, Kan., 8/9/19
Howard, Elston (baseball); St. Louis (1929–1980)
Howe, Gordon (hockey); Floral, Sask., Canada, 3/31/28
Howell, Jim Lee (football); Lonoke, Ark. (1914–1995)
Howser, Dick (baseball); Miami, Fla. (1937–1987)
Hubbell, Carl (baseball); Carthage, Mo. (1903–1988)
Huff, Sam (Robert Lee) (football); Morgantown, W. Va., 10/4/34
Hull, Bobby (hockey); Point Anne, Ontario, Canada, 1/3/39
Hunter, "Catfish" (Jim) (baseball); Hertford, N.C. (1946–1999)
Hutson, Donald (football); Pine Bluff, Ark. (1913–1997)
Irwin, Hale (golf); Joplin, Mo., 6/3/45
Jacobs, Helen Hull (tennis); Globe, Ariz. (1908–1997)
Jackson, Phil (basketball coach); Deer Lodge, Mont., 9/17/45
Jackson, Reggie (baseball); Wyncote, Pa., 5/18/46
Jagr, Jaromir (hockey); Kladno, Czechoslovakia, 2/15/72
Jeffries, James J. (boxing); Carroll, Ohio (1875–1953)
Jenkins, Ferguson Arthur (baseball); Chatham, Ontario, Canada, 12/13/43
Jenner, (W.) Bruce (track); Mt. Kisco, N.Y., 10/28/49
Jezek, Linda (swimming); Palo Alto, Calif., 3/10/60
Johnson, "Magic" (Earvin) (basketball); E. Lansing, Mich., 8/14/59
Johnson, Anthony (rowing); Washington, D.C., 11/16/40
Johnson, Jack (John Arthur) (boxing); Galveston, Tex. (1876–1946)
Johnson, Jimmy (football); Port Arthur, Tex., 8/14/43
Johnson, Michael (track); Dallas, Tex., 9/13/67
Johnson, Rafer (decathlon); Hillsboro, Tex. 8/18/35
Johnson, Randy (baseball); Walnut Creek, Calif., 9/10/63
Johnson, Wilham Julius (Judy) (baseball); Wilmington, Del. (1899–1989)
Jones, Cobi (soccer); Detroit, Mich., 6/16/70
Jones, Deacon (David) (football); Eatonville, Fla., 12/9/38
Jones, Marion (track & field); Los Angeles, Calif., 10/12/75
Jordan, Michael (basketball); Brooklyn, N.Y., 2/17/63
Joyner, Florence Griffith (sprinter); Mojave Desert, Calif. (1959–1998)
Joyner-Kersee, Jackie (track); East St. Louis, Ill., 3/3/62
Juantoreno, Alberto (track); Santiago, Cuba, 12/3/51
Jurgensen, Sonny (football); Wilmington, N.C., 8/23/34
Justice, Dave (baseball); Cincinnati, Ohio, 4/14/66
Kaat, Jim (baseball); Zeeland, Mich., 11/7/38
Kaline, Al (Albert) (baseball); Baltimore, 12/19/34
Keino, Kipchoge (runner); Kapchemoiymo, Kenya, 1/17/40
Kelly, Leroy (football); Philadelphia, 5/20/42
Kelly, Red (Leonard Patrick) (hockey); Simcoe, Ontario, Canada, 7/9/27
Kerrigan, Nancy (figure skating); Woburn, Mass., 10/13/69
Killebrew, Harmon (baseball); Payette, Idaho, 6/29/36
Killy, Jean-Claude (skiing); Saint-Cloud, France, 8/30/43
Kilmer, Bill (William Orland) (football); Topeka, Kan., 9/5/39
King, Bille Jean (Bille Jean Moffitt) (tennis); Long Beach, Calif., 11/22/43
Kinsella, John (swimming); Oak Park, Ill., 8/26/52
Kluszewski, Ted (baseball); Argo, Ill. (1924–1988)
Kodes, Jan (tennis); Prague, 3/1/46
Kolb, Claudia (swimming); Hayward, Calif., 12/19/49
Korbut, Olga (gymnast); Grodno, Byelorussia, USSR, 5/16/55
Koufax, Sandy (Sanford) (baseball); Brooklyn, N.Y., 12/30/35
Kramer, Jack (tennis); Las Vegas, Nev., 8/1/21
Kramer, Jerry (football); Jordan, Mont., 1/23/36
Krayzelburg, Lenny (swimming); Odessa, Ukraine, 9/28/75
Kuenn, Harvey (baseball); West Allis, Wis. (1930–1988)
Kuhn, Bowie Kent (baseball); Takoma Park, Md., 10/28/26
Kwan, Michelle (figure skating); Torrance, Calif., 7/7/80
Lafleur, Guy Damien (hockey); Thurson, Quebec, Canada, 8/20/51
Laird, Ronald (walker); Louisville, Ky., 5/31/35
Lalas, Alexi (soccer); Birmingham, Mich., 6/1/70
Lamonica, Daryle (football); Fresno, Calif., 7/17/41
Landis, Kenesaw Mountain (1st baseball commissioner); Millville, Ohio (1866–1944)
Landry, Tom (football); Mission, Tex. (1924–2000)
Landy, John (runner); Australia, 4/4/30
Larrieu, Francie (track); Palo Alto, Calif., 11/28/52
La Russa, Tony (baseball); Tampa, Fla. 10/4/44
Lasorda, Tom (baseball); Norristown, Pa., 9/22/27
Laver, Rod (tennis); Rockhampton, Australia, 8/9/38
Layne, Bobby (football); Lubbock, Texas (1927–1986)
Leetch, Brian (hockey); Corpus Christi, Tex., 3/3/68
Lemieux, Mario (hockey); Montreal, Quebec, Canada, 10/5/65
Lendl, Ivan (tennis); Prague, 3/7/60
Leonard, Benny (Benjamin Leiner) (boxing); New York City (1896–1947)
Leonard, Sugar Ray (boxing); Wilmington, N.C., 5/17/56
Lewis, Carl (track); Willingboro, N.J., 7/1/61
Lindros, Eric (hockey); London, Ont., 2/28/73
Lipinski, Tara (figure skating); Philadelphia, Pa., 6/10/82
Liquori, Marty (runner); Montclair, N.J., 9/11/49
Little, Lou (football); Leominster, Mass. (1893–1979)
Littler, Gene (golf); La Jolla, Calif., 7/21/30

**Lobo,** Rebecca (basketball); Southwick, Mass., 10/6/73
**Lombardi,** Vince (football); Brooklyn, N.Y. **(1913–1970)**
**Longden,** Johnny (horse racing); Wakefield, England, 2/14/07
**Lopat,** Eddie (baseball); New York, N.Y. **(1918–1992)**
**Lopez,** Al (baseball); Tampa, Fla., 8/20/08
**Lopez,** Nancy (golf); Torrance, Calif., 1/6/57
**Louis,** Joe (Joe Louis Barrow) (boxing); Lafayette, Ala. **(1914–1981)**
**Lukas,** D. Wayne (horse racing); Antigo, Wis., 9/2/35
**Lynn,** Frederic Michael (baseball); Chicago, Ill., 2/3/52
**Lynn,** Janet (figure skating); Rockford, Ill., 4/6/53
**Mack,** Connie (Cornelius Alexander McGillicuddy) (baseball executive); East Brookfield, Mass. **(1862–1956)**
**Mackey,** John (football); New York City, 9/24/41
**Maddux,** Greg (baseball); San Angelo, Texas, 4/14/66
**Mahovlich,** Frank (Francis William) (hockey); Timmins, Ontario, Canada, 1/10/38
**Mahre,** Phil (skiing); White Pass, Wash., 5/10/57
**Malone,** Karl (basketball); Summerfield, La., 7/24/63
**Malone,** Moses (basketball); Petersburg, Va., 3/23/55
**Mandlikova,** Hana (tennis); Prague, Czechoslovakia, 2/62
**Mann,** Carol (golf); Buffalo, N.Y., 2/3/41
**Manning,** Madeline (runner); Cleveland, 1/11/48
**Mantle,** Mickey Charles (baseball); Spavinaw, Okla. **(1931–1995)**
**Maravich,** "Pistol Pete" (Peter) Aliquippa, Pa. **(1948–1988)**
**Marble,** Alice (tennis); Palm Springs, Calif. **(1913–1990)**
**Marciano,** Rocky (boxing); Brockton, Mass. **(1923–1969)**
**Marichal,** Juan (baseball); Laguna Verde, Montecristi, Dominican Republic, 10/20/37
**Marino,** Dan (football); Pittsburgh, Pa., 9/15/61
**Maris,** Roger (baseball); Hibbing, Minn. **(1934–1985)**
**Martin,** Billy (Alfred Manuel) (baseball); Berkeley, Calif. **(1928–1989)**
**Martin,** Christy (boxing); Mullers, W.Va., 6/12/68
**Martin,** Rick (Richard Lionel) (hockey); Verdun, Quebec, Canada, 7/26/51
**Mathews,** Ed (Edwin) (baseball); Texarkana, Tex. **(1931–2001)**
**Mattingly,** Don (baseball); Evansville, Ind., 4/20/61
**Matson,** Randy (shot putter); Kilgore, Tex., 3/5/45
**Mays,** Willie (baseball); Westfield, Ala., 5/6/31
**McAdoo,** Bob (basketball); Greensboro, N.C., 9/25/51
**McCarthy,** Joe (Joseph Vincent) (baseball); Philadelphia **(1887–1978)**
**McCovey,** Willie Lee (baseball); Mobile, Ala., 1/10/38
**McDonald,** Lanny (hockey); Hanna, Alberta, Canada, 2/16/53
**McDowell,** Jack (baseball); Van Nuys, Calif., 1/16/66
**McEnroe,** John Patrick, Jr. (tennis); Wiesbaden, Germany, 2/16/59
**McGraw,** John Joseph (baseball); Truxton, N.Y. **(1873–1934)**
**McGwire,** Mark (baseball); Pomona, Calif., 10/1/63
**McLain,** Dennis (baseball); Chicago, 3/24/44
**McMillan,** Kathy Laverne (track); Raeford, N.C., 11/7/57
**Merrill,** Janice (track); New London, Conn., 6/18/62
**Messier,** Mark (hockey); Edmonton, Alberta, Canada, 1/18/61
**Meyer,** Deborah (swimming); Haddonfield, N.J., 8/14/52
**Meyers,** Anne (basketball); San Diego, Calif., 3/26/55
**Middlecoff,** Cary (golf); Halls, Tenn. **(1921–1998)**
**Mikita,** Stan (hockey); Sokolce, Czechoslovakia, 5/20/40
**Milburn,** Rodney, Jr. (hurdler); Opelousas, La., 5/18/50
**Miller,** Cheryl (basketball); Riverside, Calif., 1/3/64
**Miller,** Johnny (golf); San Francisco, 4/29/47
**Miller,** Reggie (basketball); Riverside, Calif., 8/24/65
**Montana,** Joe (football); New Eagle, Pa., 6/11/56
**Montgomery,** Jim (swimming); Madison, Wis., 1/24/55
**Montgomery,** Tim (track); Gaffney, S.C., 1/25/75
**Moody,** Helen Wills (tennis); Centerville, Calif. **(1906–1998)**
**Moore,** Archie (boxing); Benoit, Miss. **(1916–1998)**
**Morgan,** Joe Leonard (baseball); Bonham, Tex., 9/19/43
**Morrall,** Earl (football); Muskegon, Mich., 5/17/34
**Morton,** Craig L. (football); Flint, Mich., 2/5/43
**Mosconi,** Willie (pocket billiards); Philadelphia **(1913–1993)**
**Moses,** Edwin Corley (track); Dayton, Ohio, 8/31/58
**Mungo,** Van Lingo (baseball); Pageland, S.C. **(1911–1985)**
**Munson,** Thurman (baseball); Akron, Ohio **(1947–1979)**
**Murphy,** Calvin (basketball); Norwalk, Conn., 5/9/48
**Murray,** Eddie (baseball); Los Angeles, Calif., 2/24/56
**Musial,** Stan (baseball); Donora, Pa., 11/21/20
**Myers,** Linda (archery); York, Pa., 6/19/47
**Naber,** John (swimming); Evanston, Ill., 1/20/56
**Namath,** Joe (Joseph William) (football); Beaver Falls, Pa., 5/31/43
**Nastase,** Ilie (tennis); Bucharest, 7/19/46
**Navratilova,** Martina (tennis); Prague, 10/18/56
**Nehemiah,** Renaldo (track); Newark, N.J., 3/24/59
**Nelson,** Cindy (skiing); Lutsen, Minn., 8/19/55
**Newcombe,** John (tennis); Sydney, Australia, 5/23/43
**Niekro,** Phil (baseball); Lansing, Ohio, 4/1/39
**Nicklaus,** Jack (golf); Columbus, Ohio, 1/21/40
**Norman,** Gregory (golf); Mount Isa, Australia, 2/10/55
**Oerter,** Al (discus thrower); New York City, 9/19/36
**Olajuwon,** Hakeem (basketball); Lagos, Nigeria, 1/21/63
**Oldfield,** Barney (racing driver); Fulton County, Ohio **(1878–1946)**

**Oliva,** Tony (Pedro) (baseball); Pinar Del Rio, Cuba, 7/20/40
**Olsen,** Merlin Jay (football); Logan, Utah, 9/15/40
**O'Malley,** Walter (baseball executive); New York City **(1903–1979)**
**O'Neal,** Shaquille (basketball); Newark, N.J., 3/6/72
**Orantes,** Manuel (tennis); Granada, Spain, 2/6/49
**Orr,** Bobby (hockey); Parry Sound, Ontario, Canada, 3/20/48
**Ovett,** Steve (track); Brighton, England, 10/9/55
**Owens,** Jesse (track); Decatur, Ala. **(1914–1980)**
**Paige,** Satchel (Leroy) (baseball); Mobile, Ala. **(1906–1982)**
**Palmer,** Arnold (golf); Latrobe, Pa., 9/10/29
**Palmer,** James Alvin (baseball); New York City, 10/15/45
**Parcells,** Bill (football coach); Englewood, N.J., 8/22/41
**Parent,** Bernard Marcel (hockey); Montreal, 4/3/45
**Park,** Brad (Douglas Bradford) (hockey); Toronto, Ontario, Canada, 7/6/48
**Parseghian,** Ara (football); Akron, Ohio, 5/21/23
**Pasarell,** Charles (tennis); San Juan, Puerto Rico, 2/12/44
**Patterson,** Floyd (boxing); Waco, N.C., 1/4/35
**Peete,** Calvin (golf); Detroit, Mich., 7/18/43
**Pelé** (Edson Arantes do Nascimento) (soccer); Tres Coracoes, Brazil, 10/23/40
**Perry,** Gaylord (baseball); Williamston, N.C., 9/15/38
**Perry,** Jim (baseball); Williamston, N.C., 10/30/36
**Pettit,** Bob (basketball); Baton Rouge, La., 12/12/32
**Petty,** Richard Lee (auto racing); Randleman, N.C., 7/2/37
**Pincay,** Laffit, Jr. (jockey); Panama City, Panama, 12/29/46
**Pippen,** Scottie (basketball); Trenton, N.J., 9/25/65
**Plager,** Barclay (ice hockey); Kirkland Lake, Ontario **(1941–1988)**
**Plante,** Jacques (hockey); Sahwinigan Falls, Quebec, Canada, 1/17/29
**Player,** Gary (golf); Johannesburg, South Africa, 11/1/35
**Plunkett,** Jim (football); San Jose, Calif., 12/5/47
**Potvin,** Denis Charles (hockey); Hull, Quebec, Canada, 10/29/53
**Powell,** Boog (John) (baseball); Lakeland, Fla., 8/17/41
**Powell,** Mike (track); Philadelphia, 11/10/63
**Prefontaine,** Steve Roland (runner); Coos Bay, Ore. **(1951–1975)**
**Prince,** Bob (baseball announcer); Pittsburgh **(1917–1985)**
**Proell,** Annemarie Moser (Alpine skier); Kleinarl, Austria, 3/27/53
**Rafter,** Patrick (tennis); Brisbane, Australia, 12/28/72
**Ralston,** Dennis (tennis); Bakersfield, Calif., 7/27/42
**Rankin,** Judy Torluemke (golf); St. Louis, Mo., 2/18/45
**Raschi,** Vic (baseball); West Springfield, Mass. **(1919–1988)**
**Ratelle,** Jean (Joseph Gilbert Yvon Jean) (hockey); St. Jean, Quebec, Canada, 10/29/53
**Rawls,** Betsy (Elizabeth Earle) (golf); Spartanburg, S.C., 5/4/28
**Reed,** Willis (basketball); Hico, La., 6/25/42
**Reese,** Pee Wee (Harold) (baseball); Ekron, Ky. **(1919–1999)**
**Resch,** Glenn "Chico" (hockey); Moose Jaw, Saskatchewan, Canada, 7/10/48
**Rice,** Jerry (football); Crawford, Miss., 10/13/62
**Richard,** Maurice (hockey); Montreal, 8/14/24
**Riessen,** Martin (tennis); Hinsdale, Ill., 12/4/41
**Rigney,** William (baseball); Alameda, Calif. **(1918–2001)**
**Rios,** Marcelo (tennis); Santiago, Chile, 12/26/75
**Ripken,** Cal, Jr. (baseball); Havre de Grace, Md., 8/24/60
**Rizzuto,** Phil (baseball); New York City, 9/25/18
**Robertson,** Oscar (basketball); Charlotte, Tenn., 11/24/38
**Robinson,** Arnie (track); San Diego, Calif., 4/7/48
**Robinson,** Brooks (baseball); Little Rock, Ark., 5/18/37
**Robinson,** David (basketball); Key West, Fla., 8/6/65
**Robinson,** Frank (baseball); Beaumont, Tex., 8/31/35
**Robinson,** Jackie (baseball); Cairo, Ga. **(1919–1972)**
**Robinson,** Larry Clark (hockey); Marvelville, Ontario, Canada, 6/2/51
**Robinson,** "Sugar" Ray (boxing); Detroit **(1920–1989)**
**Rockne,** Knute Kenneth (football); Voss, Norway **(1888–1931)**
**Rockwell,** Martha (skiing); Providence, R.I., 4/26/44
**Rodman,** Dennis (basketball); Trenton, N.J., 5/13/61
**Ronaldo** (soccer); Bento Ribeiro, Brazil, 9/22/76
**Rono,** Harry (track); Kiptaragon, Kenya, 2/12/52
**Rooney,** Art (football); Pittsburgh, Pa. **(1901–1988)**
**Rose,** Pete (Peter Edward) (baseball); Cincinnati, 4/14/41
**Rosenbloom,** Maxie (boxing); New York City **(1904–1976)**
**Rosewall,** Ken (tennis); Sydney, Australia, 11/2/34
**Rote,** Kyle (football); San Antonio, 10/27/28
**Roush,** Edd (baseball); Oakland City, Ind. **(1893–1988)**
**Rozelle,** Pete (Alvin Ray) (commissioner of National Football League); South Gate, Calif. **(1926–1996)**
**Rudolph,** Wilma Glodean (sprinter); St. Bethlehem, Tenn. **(1940–1994)**
**Russell,** Bill (basketball); Monroe, La., 2/12/34
**Ruth,** Babe (George Herman Ruth) (baseball); Baltimore **(1895–1948)**
**Rutherford,** Johnny (auto racing); Fort Worth, 3/12/38
**Ryan,** Nolan (Lynn Nolan, Jr.) (baseball); Refugio, Tex., 1/31/47
**Ryon,** Luann (archery); Long Beach, Calif., 1/13/53
**Ryun,** Jim (runner); Wichita, Kan., 4/29/47
**Salazar,** Alberto (track); Havana, 8/7/58
**Sampras,** Pete (tennis); Washington, D.C., 8/12/71
**Samuels,** Howard (horse racing soccer); New York City **(1920–1984)**
**Sanders,** Barry (football); Wichita, Kan., 7/16/68

**Sanders,** Deion (baseball/football); Ft. Myers, Fla., 8/9/67
**Santana,** Manuel (Manuel Santana Martinez) (tennis); Chamartin, Spain, 5/10/38
**Sayers,** Gale (football); Wichita, Kan., 5/30/43
**Schmidt,** Mike (baseball); Dayton, Ohio, 9/27/49
**Schoendienst,** Red (Albert) (baseball); Germantown, Ill., 2/2/23
**Schollander,** Donald (swimming); Charlotte, N.C., 4/30/46
**Scurry,** Briana (soccer); Minneapolis, Minn., 9/7/71
**Seagren,** Bob (Robert Lloyd) (pole vaulter); Pomona, Calif., 10/17/46
**Seau,** Junior (football); Oceanside, Calif., 1/19/69
**Seaver,** Tom (baseball); Fresno, Calif., 11/17/44
**Seidler,** Maren (track); Brooklyn, N.Y., 6/11/62
**Seles,** Monica (tennis); Novi Sad, Yugoslavia, 12/2/73
**Selke,** Frank (ice hockey); Canada **(1893–1985)**
**Sewell,** Joe (baseball); Titus, Ala. **(1898–1990)**
**Shepherd,** Lee (auto racing) **(1945–1985)**
**Shero,** Fred (hockey); Camden, N.J. **(1925–1990)**
**Shoemaker,** Willie (jockey); Fabens, Tex., 8/19/31
**Shore,** Eddie (ice hockey); Saskatchewan, Canada **(1902–1985)**
**Shorter,** Frank (runner); Munich, Germany, 10/31/47
**Shriver,** Pam (tennis); Baltimore, 7/4/62
**Shula,** Don (Donald Francis) (football); Grand River, Ohio, 1/4/30
**Silvester,** Jay (discus thrower); Tremonton, Utah, 2/27/37
**Simpson,** O.J. (Orenthal James) (football); San Francisco, 7/9/47
**Sims,** Billy (football); St. Louis, 9/18/55
**Smith,** Bubba (Charles Aaron) (football); Orange, Tex., 2/28/45
**Smith,** Emmitt (football); Pensacola, Fla., 5/15/69
**Smith,** Ozzie (baseball); Mobile, Ala., 12/26/54
**Smith,** Ronnie Ray (sprinter); Los Angeles, 3/28/49
**Smith,** Stanley Roger (tennis); Pasadena, Calif., 12/14/46
**Smith,** Tommie (sprinter); Clarksville, Tex., 6/5/44
**Smoke,** Marcia Jones (canoeing); Oklahoma City, 7/18/41
**Snead,** Sam (golf); Hot Springs, Va. **(1912–2002)**
**Sneva,** Tom (auto racing); Spokane, Wash., 6/1/48
**Snider,** Duke (Edwin) (baseball); Los Angeles, 9/19/26
**Solomon,** Harold (tennis); Washington, D.C., 9/17/52
**Sosa,** Sammy (Samuel) (baseball); San Pedro de Macoris, Dominican Republic, 11/12/68
**Spahn,** Warren (baseball); Buffalo, N.Y., 4/23/21
**Speaker,** Tristram (baseball); Hubbard City, Tex. **(1888–1958)**
**Spencer,** Brian (ice hockey); Fort St. James, British Columbia **(1949–1988)**
**Spinks,** Leon (boxing); St. Louis, 7/11/53
**Spitz,** Mark (swimming); Modesto, Calif., 2/10/50
**Stabler,** Kenneth (football); Foley, Ala., 12/25/45
**Stagg,** Amos Alonzo (football); West Orange, N.J. **(1862–1965)**
**Stargell,** Willie (Wilver Dornell) (baseball); Earlsboro, Okla. **(1941–2001)**
**Starr,** Bart (football); Montgomery, Ala., 1/9/34
**Staub,** "Rusty" (Daniel) (baseball); New Orleans, 4/4/44
**Staubach,** Roger (football); Cincinnati, 2/5/42
**Steinkraus,** William C. (equestrian); Cleveland, 10/12/25
**Stenerud,** Jan (football); Fetsund, Norway, 11/26/42
**Stengel,** Casey (Charles Dillon) (baseball); Kansas City, Mo. **(1891–1975)**
**Stenmark,** Ingemar (Alpine skier); Tarnaby, Sweden, 3/18/56
**Stevens,** Scott (hockey); Completon, New Brunswick, 5/4/66
**Stockton,** Richard LaClede (tennis); New York City, 2/18/51
**Stones,** Dwight Edwin (track); Los Angeles, 12/6/53
**Strawberry,** Darryl (baseball); Los Angeles, 3/12/62
**Street,** Picabo (skiing); Triumph, Idaho, 4/3/71
**Sullivan,** John Lawrence (boxing); Boston **(1858–1918)**
**Summitt,** Pat (basketball); Henrietta, Tenn., 6/14/52
**Sutton,** Don (Donald Howard) (baseball); Clio, Ala., 4/2/45
**Swann,** Lynn (football); Alcoa, Tenn., 3/7/52
**Swoopes,** Sheryl (basketball); Brownfield, Tex., 3/25/71
**Tanner,** Leonard Roscoe III (tennis); Chattanooga, Tenn., 10/15/51
**Tarkenton,** Fran (Francis) (football); Richmond, Va., 2/3/40
**Tebbetts,** Birdie (George R.) (baseball); Nashua, N.H. **(1914–1999)**
**Theismann,** Joe (football); New Brunswick, N.J., 9/9/49

**Thomas,** Frank (baseball); Columbus, Ga., 5/27/68
**Thomas,** Isiah (basketball); Chicago, Ill., 4/30/61
**Thomas,** Thurman (football); Houston, Texas, 5/16/66
**Thompson,** David (basketball); Shelby, N.C., 7/13/54
**Thorpe,** Ian (swimming); Sydney, New South Wales, Australia, 10/13/82
**Thorpe,** Jim (James Francis) (all-around athlete); nr. Prague, Okla. **(1888–1953)**
**Tilden,** William Tatem II (tennis); Philadelphia **(1893–1953)**
**Tittle,** Y. A. (Yelberton Abraham) (football); Marshall, Tex., 10/24/26
**Toomey,** William (decathlon); Philadelphia, 1/10/39
**Trevino,** Lee (golf); Dallas, 12/1/39
**Trottier,** Bryan (hockey); Val Marie, Sask., Canada, 7/17/56
**Tunney,** Gene (James J.) (boxing); New York City **(1898–1978)**
**Tyson,** Mike (boxing); Brooklyn, N.Y., 6/30/66
**Tyus,** Wyomia (runner); Griffin, Ga., 8/29/45
**Ueberroth,** Peter (baseball); Evanston, Ill., 9/2/37
**Unitas,** John (football); Pittsburgh **(1933–2002)**
**Unser,** Al (auto racing); Albuquerque, N. Mex., 5/29/39
**Unser,** Bobby (auto racing); Albuquerque, N. Mex., 2/20/34
**Valenzuela,** Fernando (baseball); Sonora, Mexico, 11/1/60
**Valvano,** Jim (basketball); New York, N.Y. **(1946–1993)**
**Van Brocklin,** Norm (football); Eagle Butte, S. Dak. **(1926–1983)**
**Vaughn,** Mo (baseball); Norwalk, Conn., 12/15/67
**Vilas,** Guillermo (tennis); Mar del Plata, Argentina, 8/17/52
**Viola,** Frank (baseball); Hempstead, N.Y., 4/19/60
**Viren,** Lasse (track); Myrskyla, Finland, 7/12/49
**Vitale,** Dick (basketball); E. Rutherford, N.J., 6/9/39
**Wade,** Virginia (tennis); Bournemouth, England, 7/10/45
**Wagner,** Honus (John Peter Honus) (baseball); Carnegie, Pa. **(1867–1955)**
**Waitz,** Grete (Andersen) (running); Oslo, Norway, 10/1/53
**Walcott,** Jersey Joe (Arnold Cream) (boxing); Merchantville, N.J. **(1914–1994)**
**Wallace,** Rusty (auto racing); St. Louis, Mo., 8/14/56
**Walsh,** Adam (football) **(1902–1985)**
**Walton,** Bill (basketball); La Mesa, Calif., 11/5/52
**Waterfield,** Bob (football); Burbank, Calif **(1921–1983)**
**Watson,** Martha Rae (track); Long Beach, Calif., 8/19/46
**Watson,** Tom (golf); Kansas City, Mo., 9/4/49
**Weaver,** Earl (baseball); St. Louis, 8/14/30
**Weiskopf,** Tom (golf); Massillon, Ohio, 11/9/42
**Weiss,** George (baseball executive); New Haven, Conn. **(1895–1972)**
**Weissmuller,** Johnny (swimmer and actor); Windber, Pa. **(1904–1984)**
**West,** Jerry (basketball); Cheylan, W. Va., 5/28/38
**White,** Reggie (football); Chattanooga, Tenn., 12/19/61
**White,** Willye B. (long jumper); Money, Miss., 1/1/36
**Whitworth,** Kathy (golf); Monahans, Tex., 9/27/39
**Wilkens,** Mac Maurice (track); Eugene, Ore., 11/15/50
**Wilkins,** Lennie (basketball) 11/25/37
**Wilkinson,** Bud (football); Minneapolis **(1916–1994)**
**Williams,** Dick (baseball); St. Louis, 5/7/29
**Williams,** Serena (tennis); Saginaw, Mich., 9/26/81
**Williams,** Ted (baseball); San Diego, Calif. **(1918–2002)**
**Williams,** Venus (tennis); Lynnwood, Calif., 6/17/80
**Wills,** Maury (baseball); Washington, D.C., 10/2/32
**Winfield,** Dave (baseball); St. Paul, Minn., 10/3/51
**Wohlhuter,** Richard C. (runner); Geneva, Ill., 12/23/45
**Wood,** "Smokey Joe" (Joseph) (baseball); Kansas City, Mo. **(1890–1985)**
**Woods,** Tiger (Eldrick) (golf); Long Beach, Calif., 12/30/75
**Wottle,** David James (runner); Canton, Ohio, 8/7/50
**Wright,** Mickey (Mary Kathryn) (golf); San Diego, Calif., 2/14/35
**Yarborough,** Cale (William Caleb) (auto racing); Timmonsville, S.C., 3/27/39
**Yastrzemski,** Carl (baseball); Southampton, N.Y., 8/22/39
**Young,** Cy (Denton True) (baseball); Gilmore, Ohio **(1867–1955)**
**Young,** Sheila (speed skater, bicycle racer); Detroit, 10/14/50
**Young,** Steve (football); Salt Lake City, Utah, 10/11/61
**Zaharias,** Babe Didrikson (golf); Port Arthur, Tex. **(1913–1956)**

# Hockey

Ice hockey, by birth and upbringing a Canadian game, is an offshoot of field hockey. Some historians say that the first ice hockey game was played in Montreal in Dec. 1879 between two teams composed almost exclusively of McGill University students, but others assert that earlier hockey games took place in Kingston, Ontario, or Halifax, Nova Scotia. In the Montreal game of 1879, there were fifteen players on a side, who used an assortment of crude sticks to keep the puck in motion. Early rules allowed nine men on a side, but the number was reduced to seven in 1886 and later to six.

The first governing body of the sport was the Amateur Hockey Association of Canada, organized in 1887. In the winter of 1894–1895, a group of college students from the United States visited Canada and saw hockey played. They became enthusiastic about the game and introduced it as a winter sport when they returned home. The first professional league was the International Hockey League, which operated in northern Michigan in 1904–1906.

Until 1910, professionals and amateurs were allowed to play together on "mixed teams," but this arrangement ended with the formation of the first "big league," the National Hockey Association, in eastern Canada in 1910. The Pacific Coast League was organized in 1911 for western Canadian hockey. The league included Seattle and later other American cities. The National Hockey League replaced the National Hockey Association in 1917. Boston, in 1924, was the first American city to join that circuit. The league expanded to include western cities in 1967. The Stanley Cup was competed for by "mixed teams" from 1894 to 1910, thereafter by professionals. It was awarded to the winner of the NHL playoffs from 1926–1967 and now to the league champion.

The World Hockey Association was organized in Oct. 1972 and was dissolved after the 1978–1979 season when the NHL absorbed four of the teams.

Rule changes have been implemented to steer the league from its violent reputation in order to better showcase the world's most talented stars.

Hockey, once considered a cold-weather sport, has taken major strides in increasing its fan base to the southern and western part of the United States as well. In the 1995–1996 season, Florida and Colorado battled in the Stanley Cup Finals, the San Jose Sharks sold out all 41 of their home games, and the second team in two years (Winnipeg) migrated from Canada to the Southwest region of the U.S. (Phoenix).

The league continued to expand when the Nashville Predators joined the league in the 1998–1999 season. The 1999–2000 season included the new Atlanta Thrashers and the 2000–2001 season introduced the Columbus Blue Jackets and the Minnesota Wild.

## STANLEY CUP WINNERS

### Emblematic of World Professional Championship; NHL Championship after 1967

| | | |
|---|---|---|
| 1893  Montreal A.A.A. | 1925  Victoria Cougars | 1962–64 Toronto Maple Leafs |
| 1894  Montreal A.A.A. | 1926  Montreal Maroons | 1965–66 Montreal Canadiens |
| 1895  Montreal Victorias | 1927  Ottawa Senators | 1967  Toronto Maple Leafs |
| 1896  (Feb.) Winnipeg Victorias | 1928  N.Y. Rangers | 1968–69 Montreal Canadiens |
| 1896  (Dec.) Montreal Victorias | 1929  Boston Bruins | 1970  Boston Bruins |
| 1897–99 Montreal Victorias | 1930–31 Montreal Canadiens | 1971  Montreal Canadiens |
| 1899–1900 Montreal Shamrocks | 1932  Toronto Maple Leafs | 1972  Boston Bruins |
| 1901  Winnipeg Victorias | 1933  N.Y. Rangers | 1973  Montreal Canadiens |
| 1902  Montreal A.A.A. | 1934  Chicago Blackhawks | 1974–75 Philadelphia Flyers |
| 1903–05 Ottawa Silver Seven | 1935  Montreal Maroons | 1976–79 Montreal Canadiens |
| 1906  Montreal Wanderers | 1936–37 Detroit Red Wings | 1980–83 N.Y. Islanders |
| 1907  (Jan.) Kenora Thistles | 1938  Chicago Red Hawks | 1984–85 Edmonton Oilers |
| 1907  (March) Montreal Wanderers | 1939  Boston Bruins | 1986  Montreal Canadiens |
| 1908  Montreal Wanderers | 1940  N.Y. Rangers | 1987–88 Edmonton Oilers |
| 1909  Ottawa Senators | 1941  Boston Bruins | 1989  Calgary Flames |
| 1910  Montreal Wanderers | 1942  Toronto Maple Leafs | 1990  Edmonton Oilers |
| 1911  Ottawa Senators | 1943  Detroit Red Wings | 1991–92 Pittsburgh Penguins |
| 1912–13 Quebec Bulldogs | 1944  Montreal Canadiens | 1993  Montreal Canadiens |
| 1914  Toronto Blueshirts | 1945  Toronto Maple Leafs | 1994  N.Y. Rangers |
| 1915  Vancouver Millionaries | 1946  Montreal Canadiens | 1995  N.J. Devils |
| 1916  Montreal Canadiens | 1947–49 Toronto Maple Leafs | 1996  Colorado Avalanche |
| 1917  Seattle Metropolitans | 1950  Detroit Red Wings | 1997–98 Detroit Red Wings |
| 1918  Toronto Arenas | 1951  Toronto Maple Leafs | 1999  Dallas Stars |
| 1919  No champion | 1952  Detroit Red Wings | 2000  N.J. Devils |
| 1920–21 Ottawa Senators | 1953  Montreal Canadiens | 2001  Colorado Avalanche |
| 1922  Toronto St. Patricks | 1954–55 Detroit Red Wings | 2002  Detroit Red Wings |
| 1923  Ottawa Senators | 1956–60 Montreal Canadiens | |
| 1924  Montreal Canadiens | 1961  Chicago Blackhawks | |

## NHL CHAMPIONS

| **Wales Trophy** | 1958–62 Montreal | 1971–72 Boston | 1982–84 N.Y. | 1993  Montreal |
|---|---|---|---|---|
| 1939–41 Boston | 1963  Toronto | 1973  Montreal | Islanders | 1994  N.Y. Rangers |
| 1942  New York | 1964  Montreal | 1974  Boston | 1985  Philadelphia | 1995  New Jersey |
| 1943  Detroit | 1965  Detroit | **Eastern Conference**[1] | 1986  Montreal | 1996  Florida |
| 1944–47 Montreal | 1966  Montreal | 1975  Buffalo | 1987  Philadelphia | 1997  Philadelphia |
| 1948  Toronto | 1967  Chicago | 1976–79 Montreal | 1988  Boston | 1998  Washington |
| 1948–55 Detroit | **Eastern Division** | 1980  Buffalo | 1989  Montreal | 1999  Buffalo |
| 1956  Montreal | 1968–69 Montreal | 1981  Montreal | 1990  Boston | 2000–01 New |
| 1957  Detroit | 1970  Chicago | | 1991–92 Pittsburgh | Jersey |
| | | | | 2002  Carolina |

1. Prior to 1994 was the Wales Conference.

## CAMPBELL BOWL

| **Western Division** | 1978–79 N.Y. Islanders | 1989  Calgary | 1995  Detroit |
|---|---|---|---|
| 1968–70 St. Louis | 1980  Philadelphia | 1990  Edmonton | 1996  Colorado |
| 1971–73 Chicago | 1981  N.Y. Islanders | 1991  Minnesota | 1997–98 Detroit |
| 1974  Philadelphia | 1982–85 Edmonton | 1992  Chicago | 1999–2000 Dallas |
| **Western Conference**[2] | 1986  Calgary | 1993  Los Angeles | 2001  Colorado |
| 1975–77 Philadelphia | 1987–88 Edmonton | 1994  Vancouver | 2002  Detroit |

2. Prior to 1994 was the Campbell Conference.

# NATIONAL HOCKEY LEAGUE YEARLY TROPHY WINNERS

## The Hart Trophy—Most Valuable Player

1924  Frank Nighbor, Ottawa
1925  Billy Burch, Hamilton
1926  Nels Stewart, Montreal Maroons
1927  Herb Gardiner, Montreal Canadiens
1928  Howie Morenz, Montreal Canadiens
1929  Roy Worters, N.Y. Americans
1930  Nels Stewart, Montreal Maroons
1931–32  Howie Morenz, Montreal Canadiens
1933  Eddie Shore, Boston
1934  Aurel Joliat, Montreal Canadiens
1935–36  Eddie Shore, Boston
1937  Babe Siebert, Montreal Canadiens
1938  Eddie Shore, Boston
1939  Toe Blake, Montreal Canadiens
1940  Ebbie Goodfellow, Detroit
1941  Bill Cowley, Boston
1942  Tommy Anderson, N.Y. Americans
1943  Bill Cowley, Boston
1944  Babe Pratt, Toronto
1945  Elmer Lach, Montreal Canadiens
1946  Max Bentley, Chicago
1947  Maurice Richard, Montreal Canadiens
1948  Buddy O'Connor, N.Y. Rangers
1949  Sid Abel, Detroit
1950  Chuck Rayner, N.Y. Rangers
1951  Milt Schmidt, Boston
1952–53  Gordie Howe, Detroit
1954  Al Rollins, Chicago
1955  Ted Kennedy, Toronto
1956  Jean Belveau, Montreal Canadiens
1957–58  Gordie Howe, Detroit
1959  Andy Bathgate, N.Y. Rangers
1960  Gordie Howe, Detroit
1961  Bernie Geoffrion, Montreal Canadiens
1962  Jacques Plante, Montreal Canadiens
1963  Gordon Howe, Detroit
1964  Jean Beliveau, Montreal Canadiens
1965–66  Bobby Hull, Chicago
1967–68  Stan Mikita, Chicago
1969  Phil Esposito, Boston
1970–72  Bobby Orr, Boston
1973  Bobby Clarke, Philadelphia
1974  Phil Esposito, Boston
1975–76  Bobby Clarke, Philadelphia
1977–78  Guy Lafleur, Montreal
1979  Bryan Trottier, N.Y. Islanders
1980–87  Wayne Gretzky, Edmonton
1988  Mario Lemieux, Pittsburgh
1989  Wayne Gretzky, Los Angeles
1990  Mark Messier, Edmonton
1991  Brett Hull, St. Louis
1992  Mark Messier, N.Y. Rangers
1993  Mario Lemieux, Pittsburgh
1994  Sergei Fedorov, Detroit
1995  Eric Lindros, Philadelphia
1996  Mario Lemieux, Pittsburgh
1997–98  Dominik Hasek, Buffalo
1999  Jaromir Jagr, Pittsburgh
2000  Chris Pronger, St. Louis
2001  Joe Sakic, Colorado
2002  Jose Theodore, Montreal

## Vezina Trophy—Leading Goalkeeper

1956–60  Jacques Plante, Montreal
1961  Johnny Bower, Toronto
1962  Jacques Plante, Montreal
1963  Glenn Hall, Chicago
1964  Charlie Hodge, Montreal
1965  Terry Sawchuk—Johnny Bower, Toronto
1966  Gump Worsley—Charlie Hodge, Montreal
1967  Glen Hall—Denis Dejordy, Chicago
1968  Gump Worsley—Rogie Vachon, Montreal
1969  Glenn Hall—Jacques Plante, St. Louis
1970  Tony Esposito, Chicago
1971  Ed Giacomin—Gilles Villemure, N.Y. Rangers
1972  Tony Esposito—Gary Smith, Chicago
1973  Ken Dryden, Montreal
1974  Bernie Parent, Philadelphia and Tony Esposito, Chicago
1975  Bernie Parent, Philadelphia
1976  Ken Dryden, Montreal
1977–79  Ken Dryden—Bunny Larocque, Montreal
1980  Bob Sauve—Don Edwards, Buffalo
1981  Richard Sevigny—Denis Herron—Bunny Larocque, Montreal
1982  Billy Smith, N.Y. Islanders
1983  Pete Peeters, Boston
1984  Tom Barrasso, Buffalo
1985  Pelle Lindbergh, Philadelphia
1986  John Vanbiesbrouck, N.Y. Rangers
1987  Ron Hextall, Philadelphia
1988  Grant Fuhr, Edmonton
1989–90  Patrick Roy, Montreal
1991  Ed Belfour, Chicago
1992  Patrick Roy, Montreal
1993  Ed Belfour, Chicago
1994  Dominik Hasek, Buffalo
1996  Jim Carey, Washington
1997–99  Dominik Hasek, Buffalo
2000  Olaf Kolzig, Washington
2001  Dominik Hasek, Buffalo
2002  Jose Theodore, Montreal

## James Norris Trophy—Defenseman

1954  Red Kelly, Detroit
1955–58  Doug Harvey, Montreal
1959  Tom Johnson, Montreal
1960–62  Doug Harvey, Montreal, N.Y. Rangers (62)
1963–65  Pierre Pilote, Chicago
1966  Jacques Laperriere, Montreal
1967  Harry Howell, N.Y. Rangers
1968–75  Bobby Orr, Boston
1976  Denis Potvin, N.Y. Islanders
1977  Larry Robinson, Montreal
1978–79  Denis Potvin, N.Y. Islanders
1980  Larry Robinson, Montreal
1981  Randy Carlyle, Pittsburgh
1982  Doug Wilson, Chicago
1983–84  Rod Langway, Washington
1985–86  Paul Coffey, Edmonton
1987–88  Ray Bourque, Boston
1989  Chris Chelios, Montreal
1990–91  Ray Bourque, Boston
1992  Brian Leetch, N.Y. Rangers
1993  Chris Chelios, Chicago
1994  Ray Bourque, Boston
1995  Paul Coffey, Detroit
1996  Chris Chelios, Chicago
1997  Brian Leetch, N.Y. Rangers
1998  Rob Blake, Los Angeles
1999  Al MacInnis, St. Louis
2000  Chris Pronger, St. Louis
2001–2002  Nicklas Lidstrom, Detroit

## Lady Byng Trophy—Sportsmanship

1960  Don McKenney, Boston
1961  Red Kelly, Toronto
1962–63  Dave Keon, Toronto
1964  Ken Wharram, Chicago
1965  Bobby Hull, Chicago
1966  Alex Delvecchio, Detroit
1967–68  Stan Mikita, Chicago
1969  Alex Delvecchio, Detroit
1970  Phil Goyette, St. Louis
1971  Johnny Bucyk, Boston
1972  Jean Ratelle, N.Y. Rangers
1973  Gilbert Perreault, Buffalo
1974  Johnny Bucyk, Boston
1975  Marcel Dionne, Detroit
1976  Jean Ratelle, N.Y. Rangers, Boston
1977  Marcel Dionne, Los Angeles
1978  Butch Goring, Los Angeles
1979  Bob MacMillan, Atlanta
1980  Wayne Gretzky, Edmonton
1981  Rick Kehoe, Pittsburgh
1982  Rick Middleton, Boston
1983–84  Mike Bossy, N.Y. Islanders
1985  Jarl Kurri, Edmonton
1986  Mike Bossy, N.Y. Islanders
1987  Joey Mullen, Calgary
1988  Mats Naslund, Montreal
1989  Joey Mullen, Calgary
1990  Brett Hull, St. Louis
1991–92  Wayne Gretzky, Los Angeles
1993  Pierre Turgeon, N.Y. Islanders
1994  Wayne Gretzky, Los Angeles
1995  Ron Francis, Pittsburgh
1996–97  Paul Kariya, Anaheim
1998  Ron Francis, Pittsburgh
1999  Wayne Gretzky, N.Y. Rangers
2000  Pavol Demitra, St. Louis
2001  Joe Sakic, Colorado
2002  Ron Francis, Carolina

## Calder Trophy—Rookie

1962  Bobby Rousseau, Montreal
1963  Kent Douglas, Toronto

| | | | | |
|---|---|---|---|---|
| 1964 | Jacques Laperriere, Montreal | 1988 | Joe Nieuwendyk, Calgary | |
| 1965 | Roger Crozier, Detroit | 1989 | Brian Leetch, N.Y. Rangers | |
| 1966 | Brit Selby, Toronto | 1990 | Sergei Makarov, Calgary | |
| 1967 | Bobby Orr, Boston | 1991 | Ed Belfour, Chicago | |
| 1968 | Derek Sanderson, Boston | 1992 | Pavel Bure, Vancouver | |
| 1969 | Danny Grant, Minnesota | 1993 | Teemu Selanne, Winnipeg | |
| 1970 | Tony Esposito, Chicago | 1994 | Martin Brodeur, N.J. Devils | |
| 1971 | Gilbert Perreault, Buffalo | 1995 | Peter Forsberg, Quebec | |
| 1972 | Ken Dryden, Montreal | 1996 | Daniel Alfredsson, Ottawa | |
| 1973 | Steve Vickers, N.Y. Rangers | 1997 | Bryan Berard, N.Y. Islanders | |
| 1974 | Denis Potvin, N.Y. Islanders | 1998 | Sergei Samsonov, Boston | |
| 1975 | Eric Vail, Atlanta | 1999 | Chris Drury, Colorado | |
| 1976 | Bryan Trottier, N.Y. Islanders | 2000 | Scott Gomez, New Jersey | |
| 1977 | Willi Plett, Atlanta | 2001 | Evgeni Nabokov, San Jose | |
| 1978 | Mike Bossy, N.Y. Islanders | 2002 | Dany Heatley, Atlanta | |

Hockey leaders columns:

| Year | Scoring leader | Year | Scoring leader | Year | Scoring leader |
|---|---|---|---|---|---|
| 1964 | Jacques Laperriere, Montreal | 1988 | Joe Nieuwendyk, Calgary | 1962 | Bobby Hull, Chicago |
| 1965 | Roger Crozier, Detroit | 1989 | Brian Leetch, N.Y. Rangers | 1963 | Gordie Howe, Detroit |
| 1966 | Brit Selby, Toronto | 1990 | Sergei Makarov, Calgary | 1964–65 | Stan Mikita, Chicago |
| 1967 | Bobby Orr, Boston | 1991 | Ed Belfour, Chicago | 1966 | Bobby Hull, Chicago |
| 1968 | Derek Sanderson, Boston | 1992 | Pavel Bure, Vancouver | 1967–68 | Stan Mikita, Chicago |
| 1969 | Danny Grant, Minnesota | 1993 | Teemu Selanne, Winnipeg | 1969 | Phil Esposito, Boston |
| 1970 | Tony Esposito, Chicago | 1994 | Martin Brodeur, N.J. Devils | 1970 | Bobby Orr, Boston |
| 1971 | Gilbert Perreault, Buffalo | 1995 | Peter Forsberg, Quebec | 1971–74 | Phil Esposito, Boston |
| 1972 | Ken Dryden, Montreal | 1996 | Daniel Alfredsson, Ottawa | 1975 | Bobby Orr, Boston |
| 1973 | Steve Vickers, N.Y. Rangers | 1997 | Bryan Berard, N.Y. Islanders | 1976–78 | Guy Lafleur, Montreal |
| 1974 | Denis Potvin, N.Y. Islanders | 1998 | Sergei Samsonov, Boston | 1979 | Bryan Trottier, N.Y. Islanders |
| 1975 | Eric Vail, Atlanta | 1999 | Chris Drury, Colorado | 1980 | Marcel Dionne, Los Angeles |
| 1976 | Bryan Trottier, N.Y. Islanders | 2000 | Scott Gomez, New Jersey | 1981–87 | Wayne Gretzky, Edmonton |
| 1977 | Willi Plett, Atlanta | 2001 | Evgeni Nabokov, San Jose | 1988–89 | Mario Lemieux, Pittsburgh |
| 1978 | Mike Bossy, N.Y. Islanders | 2002 | Dany Heatley, Atlanta | 1990–91 | Wayne Gretzky, Los Angeles |
| 1979 | Bobby Smith, Minnesota | | | 1992–93 | Mario Lemieux, Pittsburgh |
| 1980 | Ray Bourque, Boston | **Art Ross Trophy—Leading Scorer** | | 1994 | Wayne Gretzky, Los Angeles |
| 1981 | Peter Stastny, Quebec | | | 1995 | Jaromir Jagr, Pittsburgh |
| 1982 | Dale Hawerchuk, Winnipeg | 1955 | Bernie Geoffrion, Montreal | 1996–97 | Mario Lemieux, Pittsburgh |
| 1983 | Steve Larmer, Chicago | 1956 | Jean Beliveau, Montreal | 1998–2001 | Jaromir Jagr, Pittsburgh |
| 1984 | Tom Barrasso, Buffalo | 1957 | Gordie Howe, Detroit | 2002 | Jarome Iginla, Calgary |
| 1985 | Mario Lemieux, Pittsburgh | 1958–59 | Dickie Moore, Montreal | | |
| 1986 | Gary Suter, Calgary | 1960 | Bobby Hull, Chicago | | |
| 1987 | Luc Robitaille, Los Angeles | 1961 | Bernie Geoffrion, Montreal | | |

## STANLEY CUP PLAYOFFS—2002

### NOTE: Home teams are in capitals.

### EASTERN CONFERENCE

**Quarterfinals**

Montreal Canadiens defeated Boston Bruins,
  4 games to 2
Ottawa Senators defeated Philadelphia Flyers,
  4 games to 1
Carolina Hurricanes defeated New Jersey Devils,
  4 games to 2
Toronto Maple Leafs defeated New York Islanders,
  4 games to 3

**Semifinals**

Carolina Hurricanes defeated Montreal Canadiens,
  4 games to 2
Toronto Maple Leafs defeated Ottawa Senators,
  4 games to 3

**Finals**

Carolina Hurricanes defeated Toronto Maple Leafs,
  4 games to 2
May 16—Toronto 2, CAROLINA 1
May 19—CAROLINA 2, Toronto 1 (OT)
May 21—Carolina 2, TORONTO 1 (OT)
May 23—Carolina 3, TORONTO 0
May 25—Toronto 1, CAROLINA 0
May 28—Carolina 2, TORONTO 1 (OT)

### WESTERN CONFERENCE

**Quarterfinals**

Detroit Red Wings defeated Vancouver Canucks,
  4 games to 2
Colorado Avalanche defeated Los Angeles Kings,
  4 games to 3
San Jose Sharks defeated Phoenix Coyotes,
  4 games to 1
St. Louis Blues defeated Chicago Blackhawks,
  4 games to 1

**Semifinals**

Detroit Red Wings defeated St. Louis Blues,
  4 games to 1
Colorado Avalanche defeated San Jose Sharks,
  4 games to 3

**Finals**

Detroit Red Wings defeated Colorado Avalanche,
  4 games to 3
May 18—DETROIT 5, Colorado 3
May 20—Colorado 4, DETROIT 3 (OT)
May 22—Detroit 2, COLORADO 1 (OT)
May 25—COLORADO 3, Detroit 2
May 27—Colorado 2, DETROIT 1 (OT)
May 29—Detroit 2, COLORADO 0
May 31—DETROIT 7, Colorado 0

## STANLEY CUP CHAMPIONSHIP FINALS

### Detroit Red Wings defeated Carolina Hurricanes, 4 games to 1

June 4—Carolina 3, DETROIT 2 (OT)
June 6—DETROIT 3, Carolina 1
June 8—Detroit 3, CAROLINA 2 (3OT)

June 10—Detroit 3, Carolina 0
June 13—DETROIT 3, Carolina 1

Conn Smythe Trophy for most valuable player in the playoffs: Nicklas Lidstrom, Detroit

## OTHER NHL AWARDS—2002

Frank Selke Trophy (Top defensive forward)—Michael Peca, N.Y. Islanders
King Clancy Trophy (Humanitarian community involvement)—Ron Francis, Carolina

Jack Adams Award (Coach of the Year)—Bob Francis, Phoenix
Bill Masterson Trophy (Perseverance, sportsmanship, and dedication to hockey)—Saku Koivu, Montreal

## NATIONAL HOCKEY LEAGUE FINAL STANDINGS OF THE CLUBS: 2001–2002

### EASTERN CONFERENCE

**Northeast Division**

| | W | L | T | Pts | GF | GA |
|---|---|---|---|---|---|---|
| Boston Bruins[1] | 43 | 24 | 6 | 101 | 236 | 201 |
| Toronto Maple Leafs[2] | 43 | 25 | 10 | 100 | 249 | 207 |
| Ottawa Senators[2] | 39 | 27 | 9 | 94 | 243 | 208 |
| Montreal Canadiens[2] | 36 | 31 | 12 | 87 | 207 | 209 |
| Buffalo Sabres | 35 | 35 | 11 | 82 | 213 | 200 |

**Atlantic Division**

| | W | L | T | Pts | GF | GA |
|---|---|---|---|---|---|---|
| Philadelphia Flyers[1] | 42 | 27 | 10 | 97 | 234 | 192 |
| N.Y. Islanders[2] | 42 | 28 | 8 | 96 | 239 | 220 |
| New Jersey Devils[2] | 41 | 28 | 9 | 95 | 205 | 187 |
| N.Y. Rangers | 36 | 38 | 4 | 80 | 227 | 258 |
| Pittsburgh Penguins | 28 | 41 | 8 | 69 | 198 | 249 |

**Southeast Division**

| | W | L | T | Pts | GF | GA |
|---|---|---|---|---|---|---|
| Carolina Hurricanes[1] | 35 | 26 | 16 | 91 | 217 | 217 |
| Washington Capitals | 36 | 33 | 11 | 85 | 228 | 240 |
| Tampa Bay Lightning | 27 | 40 | 11 | 69 | 178 | 219 |
| Florida Panthers | 22 | 44 | 10 | 60 | 180 | 250 |
| Atlanta Thrashers | 19 | 47 | 11 | 54 | 187 | 288 |

1. Division champion. 2. Playoff qualifier.

### WESTERN CONFERENCE

**Central Division**

| | W | L | T | Pts | GF | GA |
|---|---|---|---|---|---|---|
| Detroit Red Wings[1] | 51 | 17 | 10 | 116 | 251 | 187 |
| St. Louis Blues[2] | 43 | 27 | 8 | 98 | 227 | 188 |
| Chicago Blackhawks[2] | 41 | 27 | 13 | 96 | 216 | 207 |
| Nashville Predators | 28 | 41 | 13 | 69 | 196 | 230 |
| Columbus Blue Jackets | 22 | 47 | 8 | 57 | 164 | 255 |

**Pacific Division**

| | W | L | T | Pts | GF | GA |
|---|---|---|---|---|---|---|
| San Jose Sharks[1] | 44 | 27 | 8 | 99 | 248 | 199 |
| Phoenix Coyotes[2] | 40 | 27 | 9 | 95 | 228 | 210 |
| Los Angeles Kings[2] | 40 | 27 | 11 | 95 | 214 | 190 |
| Dallas Stars | 36 | 28 | 13 | 90 | 215 | 213 |
| Anaheim Mighty Ducks | 29 | 42 | 8 | 69 | 175 | 198 |

**Northwest Division**

| | W | L | T | Pts | GF | GA |
|---|---|---|---|---|---|---|
| Colorado Avalanche[1] | 45 | 28 | 8 | 99 | 212 | 169 |
| Vancouver Canucks[2] | 42 | 30 | 7 | 94 | 254 | 211 |
| Edmonton Oilers | 38 | 28 | 12 | 92 | 205 | 182 |
| Calgary Flames | 32 | 35 | 12 | 79 | 201 | 220 |
| Minnesota Wild | 26 | 35 | 12 | 73 | 195 | 238 |

### NHL LEADING SCORERS: 2001–2002

| | Gm | G | A | Pts |
|---|---|---|---|---|
| Jarome Iginla, Calgary | 82 | 52 | 44 | 96 |
| Markus Naslund, Vancouver | 81 | 40 | 50 | 90 |
| Todd Bertuzzi, Vancouver | 72 | 36 | 49 | 85 |
| Mats Sundin, Toronto | 82 | 41 | 39 | 80 |
| Jaromir Jagr, Washington | 69 | 31 | 48 | 79 |
| Joe Sakic, Colorado | 82 | 26 | 53 | 79 |
| Pavol Demitra, St. Louis | 82 | 35 | 43 | 78 |
| Adam Oates, Washington-Philadelphia | 80 | 14 | 64 | 78 |
| Mike Modano, Dallas | 78 | 34 | 43 | 77 |
| Ron Francis, Carolina | 80 | 27 | 50 | 77 |

### NHL CAREER SCORING LEADERS

#### (Through 2001–2002 season)

| | | Yrs | Gm | G | A | Pts |
|---|---|---|---|---|---|---|
| 1 | Wayne Gretzky | 20 | 1,487 | 894 | 1,963 | 2,857 |
| 2 | Gordie Howe | 26 | 1,767 | 801 | 1,049 | 1,850 |
| 3 | **Mark Messier** | 23 | 1,602 | 658 | 1,146 | 1,804 |
| 4 | Marcel Dionne | 18 | 1,348 | 731 | 1,040 | 1,771 |
| 5 | **Ron Francis** | 21 | 1,569 | 514 | 1,187 | 1,701 |
| 6 | **Steve Yzerman** | 19 | 1,362 | 658 | 1,004 | 1,662 |
| 7 | **Mario Lemieux** | 14 | 812 | 654 | 947 | 1,601 |
| 8 | Phil Esposito | 18 | 1,282 | 717 | 873 | 1,590 |
| 9 | Ray Bourque | 22 | 1,612 | 410 | 1,169 | 1,579 |
| 10 | **Paul Coffey** | 21 | 1,409 | 396 | 1,135 | 1,531 |

Players active during 2001–2002 season in **bold** type.

### NHL LEADING GOALTENDERS: 2001–2002

#### (Minimum 26 games played)

| | Gm | Min | GAA | GA | Shots |
|---|---|---|---|---|---|
| Patrick Roy, Colorado | 63 | 3,773 | 1.94 | 122 | 1,629 |
| Roman Cechmanek, Philadelphia | 46 | 2,600 | 2.05 | 89 | 1,131 |
| Marty Turco, Dallas | 31 | 1,519 | 2.09 | 53 | 670 |
| José Théodore, Montreal | 67 | 3,864 | 2.11 | 136 | 1,972 |
| Jean-Sebastien Giguere, Anaheim | 53 | 3,127 | 2.13 | 111 | 1,384 |
| Martin Brodeur, New Jersey | 73 | 4,347 | 2.15 | 156 | 1,655 |
| Dominik Hasek, Detroit | 65 | 3,872 | 2.17 | 140 | 1,654 |
| Brent Johnson, St. Louis | 58 | 3,491 | 2.18 | 127 | 1,293 |
| Byron Dafoe, Boston | 64 | 3,827 | 2.21 | 141 | 1,520 |
| Martin Biron, Buffalo | 72 | 4,085 | 2.22 | 151 | 1,781 |

### NHL CAREER GOALTENDING WINS LEADERS

#### (Through 2001–2002 season)

| | | Yrs | Gm | W | L | T | Pct |
|---|---|---|---|---|---|---|---|
| 1 | Patrick Roy | 17 | 1,011 | 516 | 300 | 116 | .618 |
| 2 | Terry Sawchuk | 21 | 971 | 447 | 330 | 172 | .562 |
| 3 | Jacques Plante | 18 | 837 | 434 | 247 | 146 | .614 |
| 4 | Tony Esposito | 16 | 886 | 423 | 306 | 152 | .566 |
| 5 | Glenn Hall | 18 | 906 | 407 | 326 | 163 | .545 |
| 6 | Grant Fuhr | 19 | 868 | 403 | 295 | 114 | .567 |
| 7 | **Mike Vernon** | 19 | 781 | 385 | 273 | 92 | .575 |
| 8 | **J. Vanbiesbrouck** | 20 | 882 | 374 | 346 | 119 | .517 |
| 9 | Andy Moog | 18 | 713 | 372 | 209 | 88 | .622 |
| 10 | **Tom Barrasso** | 18 | 771 | 368 | 273 | 86 | .565 |

Players active during 2001–2002 season in **bold** type.

# Chess

## WORLD CHAMPIONS

| | | | |
|---|---|---|---|
| 1894– | Emanuel Lasker, Germany | 1969–71 | Boris Spassky, USSR |
| 1921 | | 1972–74 | Bobby Fischer, United States |
| 1921–27 | Jose R. Capablanca, Cuba | 1975 | Bobby Fischer, United States[2]; Anatoly |
| 1927–35 | Alexander A. Alekhine, USSR | | Karpov, USSR |
| 1935–37 | Dr. Max Euwe, Netherlands | 1976–85 | Anatoly Karpov, USSR[3] |
| 1937–46 | Alexander A. Alekhine, USSR[1] | 1985– | Garry Kasparov, Russia[4] |
| 1948–57 | Mikhail Botvinnik, USSR | 2000 | |
| 1957–58 | Vassily Smyslov, USSR | 1993–99 | Anatoly Karpov, Russia[5] |
| 1958–60 | Mikhail Botvinnik, USSR | 1999 | Alexander Khalifman, Russia[5] |
| 1960–61 | Mikhail Tal, USSR | 2000 | Viswanathan Anand, India[5] |
| 1961–63 | Mikhail Botvinnik, USSR | | Vladimir Kramnik, Russia[6] |
| 1963–68 | Tigran Petrosian, USSR | 2001–02 | Ruslan Ponomariov, Ukraine[5] |

1. Alekhine died while champion. 2. Relinquished title. 3. In 1978, Karpov defeated Viktor Korchnoi 6 games to 5. 4. Kasparov broke away from FIDE (International Chess Federation) and formed the PCA (Professional Chess Association) in 1993. He was PCA champion after 1993. 5. FIDE world champion. 6. PCA world champion.

## UNITED STATES CHAMPIONS

| | | | |
|---|---|---|---|
| 1909–36 | Frank J. Marshall, New York | 1986 | Yasser Seirawan, Seattle, Wash. |
| 1936–44 | Samuel Reshevsky, New York[1] | 1987 | Tie, Nick Defirmian, San Francisco |
| 1944–46 | Arnold S. Denker, New York | | Joel Benjamin, Brooklyn, N.Y. |
| 1946 | Samuel Reshevsky, Boston | 1988 | Michael Wilder, Princeton, N.J. |
| 1948 | Herman Steiner, Los Angeles | 1989 | Tie, Stuart Rachels, Birmingham, Ala. |
| 1951–52 | Larry Evans, New York | | Yasser Seirawan, Seattle, Wash. |
| 1954–57 | Arthur Bisguier, New York | | Roman Dzindzichashvili, New York, N.Y. |
| 1958–61 | Bobby Fischer, Brooklyn, N.Y. | 1990–91 | Lev Alburt, New York, N.Y. |
| 1962 | Larry Evans, New York | 1992 | Gata Kamsky, Brooklyn, N.Y. |
| 1963–67 | Bobby Fischer, New York | | Patrick Wolff, Somerville, Mass. |
| 1968 | Larry Evans, New York | 1993 | Tie, Alexander Shabalov, Pittsburgh, Pa. |
| 1969–71 | Samuel Reshevsky, Spring Valley, N.Y. | | Alex Yermolinski, Edison, N.J. |
| 1972 | Robert Byrne, Ossining, N.Y. | 1994 | Boris Gulko, Fairlawn, N.J. |
| 1973 | Lubomir Kavelek, Washington; | 1995 | Patrick Wolff, Somerville, Mass. |
| | John Grefe, San Francisco | 1996 | Alex Yurmolinsky, Cleveland, Ohio |
| 1974–77 | Walter Browne, Berkeley, Calif. | 1997 | Joel Benjamin, N.Y. (men) |
| 1978–79 | Lubomir Kavalek, New York | | Esther Epstein, Mass. (women) |
| 1980 | Tie, Walter Browne, Berkeley, Calif. | 1998 | Nick de Firmian, New York City (men) |
| | Larry Christiansen, Modesto, Calif. | | Irina Krush, Brooklyn, N.Y. (women) |
| | Larry Evans, Reno, Nev. | 1999 | Boris Gulko, Fairlawn, N.J. (men) |
| 1981–82[2] | Tie, Walter Browne, Berkeley, Calif. | | Anjelina Belakovskaia, Brooklyn, N.Y. (women) |
| | Yasser Seirawan, Seattle, Wash. | 2000 | Joel Benjamin, New York, N.Y. (men) |
| 1983 | Tie, Walter Browne, Berkeley, Calif. | | Camilla Baginskaite, Vilnius, Lithuania |
| | Larry Christiansen, Los Angeles, Calif., | | (women) |
| | Roman Dzindzichashvili, Corona, N.Y. | 2001 | Larry Christiansen, Riverside, Calif. (men) |
| 1984–85 | Lev Alburt, New York City | | Jennifer Shahade, Philadelphia, Pa. (women) |

1. In 1942, Isaac I. Kashdan of New York was co-champion for a while because of a tie with Reshevsky in that year's tournament. Reshevsky won the play-off. 2. Championship not contested in 1982.

# Bowling

The game of bowling in the United States is an indoor development of the more ancient outdoor game that survives as lawn bowling. The outdoor game is prehistoric in origin and probably goes back to primitive man and round stones that were rolled at some target. It is believed that a game something like nine-pins was popular among the Dutch, Swiss, and Germans as long ago as A.D. 1200. The game was played outdoors with an alley consisting of a single plank 12 to 18 inches wide, along which a ball was rolled toward three rows of three pins each placed at the far end of the alley. When the first indoor alleys were built and how the game was modified from time to time are matters of dispute.

It is supposed that the early settlers of New Amsterdam (New York City), being Dutch, brought their two bowling games with them. About a century ago the game of nine-pins was flourishing in the United States but was so corrupted by gambling on matches that it was barred by law in New York and Connecticut. Since the law specifically barred "nine-pins," it was eventually evaded by adding another pin and thus legally making it a new game.

Various organizations were formed to make rules for bowling and supervise competition in the United States, but none was successful until the American Bowling Congress, organized Sept. 9, 1895, became the ruling body.

## AMERICAN BOWLING CONGRESS CHAMPIONS

| Year | Singles | All-events | Year | Singles | All-events |
|---|---|---|---|---|---|
| 1959 | Ed Lubanski | Ed Lubanski | 1982 | Bruce Bohm | Rich Wonders |
| 1960 | Paul Kulbaga | Vince Lucci | 1983 | Rick Kendrick | Tony Cariello |
| 1961 | Lyle Spooner | Luke Karen | 1984 | Bob Antczak and Neal Young (tie) | Bob Goike |
| 1962 | Andy Renaldo | Billy Young | 1985 | Glen Harbison | Barry Asher |
| 1963 | Fred Delello | Bus Owalt | 1986 | Jess Mackey | Ed Marazka |
| 1964 | Jim Stefanich | Les Zikes, Jr. | 1987 | Terry Taylor | Ryan Schafer |
| 1965 | Ken Roeth | Tom Hathaway | 1988 | Steve Hutkowski | Rick Steelsmith |
| 1966 | Don Chapman | John Wilcox | 1989 | Paul Tetreault | George Hall |
| 1967 | Frank Perry | Gary Lewis | 1990 | Bob Hochrein | Mike Neumann |
| 1968 | Wayne Kowalski | Vince Mazzanti | 1991 | Ed Deines | Tom Howery |
| 1969 | Greg Campbell | Eddie Jackson | 1992 | Bob Youker and Gary Blatchford (tie) | Mike Tucker |
| 1970 | Jake Yoder | Mike Berlin | 1993 | Dan Bock | Jeff Nimke |
| 1971 | Al Cohn | Al Cohn | 1994 | John Weltzien | Thomas Holt |
| 1972 | Bill Pointer | Mac Lowry | 1995 | Matt Surina | Jeff Kwiatkowski |
| 1973 | Ed Thompson | Ron Woolet | 1996 | Donald Scudder, Jr. | Scott Kurtz |
| 1974 | Gene Krause | Bob Hart | 1997 | John Socha | Jeff Richgels |
| 1975 | Jim Setser | Bobby Meadows | 1998 | John Gaines | Chris Barnes |
| 1976 | Mike Putzer | Jim Lindquist | 1999 | Dan Winter | Thomas A. Jones |
| 1977 | Frank Gadaleto | Bud Debenham | 2000 | Garran Hein | Roy Daniels |
| 1978 | Rich Mersek | Chris Cobus | 2001 | Nicholas Hoagland | D. J. Archer |
| 1979 | Rick Peters | Bob Basacchi | 2002 | Mark Millsap | Stephen A. Hardy |
| 1980 | Mike Eaton | Steve Fehr | | | |
| 1981 | Rob Vital | Rod Toft | | | |

## PROFESSIONAL BOWLERS ASSOCIATION

### National Championship Tournament[1]

| | | | | | | | |
|---|---|---|---|---|---|---|---|
| 1960 | Don Carter | 1971 | Mike Lemongello | 1982 | Earl Anthony | 1993 | Ron Palombi |
| 1961 | Dave Soutar | 1972 | Johnny Guenther | 1983 | Earl Anthony | 1994 | David Traber |
| 1962 | Carmen Salvino | 1973 | Earl Anthony | 1984 | Bob Chamberlain | 1995 | Scott Alexander |
| 1963 | Billy Hardwick | 1974 | Earl Anthony | 1985 | Mike Aulby | 1996 | Butch Soper |
| 1964 | Bob Strampe | 1975 | Earl Anthony | 1986 | Tom Crites | 1997 | Rich Steelsmith |
| 1965 | Dave Davis | 1976 | Paul Colwell | 1987 | Randy Pedersen | 1998 | Pete Weber |
| 1966 | Wayne Zahn | 1977 | Tommy Hudson | 1988 | Brian Voss | 1999 | Tim Criss |
| 1967 | Dave Davis | 1978 | Warren Nelson | 1989 | Pete Weber | 2000 | Norm Duke |
| 1968 | Wayne Zahn | 1979 | Mike Aulby | 1990 | Jim Pencak | 2001 | Walter Ray Williams, Jr. |
| 1969 | Mike McGrath | 1980 | Johnny Petraglia | 1991 | Mike Miller | | |
| 1970 | Mike McGrath | 1981 | Earl Anthony | 1992 | Eric Forkel | 2002 | Doug Kent |

1. Changed to PBA World Championship in 2002.

## BOWLING PROPRIETORS' ASSOCIATION OF AMERICA—MEN

### United States Open[1]

| | | | | | | | |
|---|---|---|---|---|---|---|---|
| 1971 | Mike Lemongello | 1979 | Joe Berardi | 1987 | Del Ballard | 1995 | Dave Husted |
| 1972 | Don Johnson | 1980 | Steve Martin | 1988 | Pete Weber | 1996 | Dave Husted |
| 1973 | Mike McGrath | 1981 | Marshall Holman | 1989 | Mike Aulby | 1997 | Not held |
| 1974 | Larry Laub | 1982 | Dave Husted | 1990 | Ron Palumbi, Jr. | 1998 | Walter Ray Williams, Jr. |
| 1975 | Steve Neff | 1983 | Gary Dickinson | 1991 | Pete Weber | | |
| 1976 | Paul Moser | 1984 | Mark Roth | 1992 | Robert Lawrence | 1999 | Bob Learn, Jr. |
| 1977 | Johnny Petraglia | 1985 | Marshall Holman | 1993 | Del Ballard, Jr. | 2000 | Robert Smith |
| 1978 | Nelson Burton, Jr. | 1986 | Steve Cook | 1994 | Justin Hromek | 2001[2] | Mika Koivuniemi |

1. Replaced All-Star tournament and is rolled as part of PBA tour. 2. 2002–2003 tournament held Jan. 27–Feb. 2, 2003, after almanac went to press.

## WOMEN'S INTERNATIONAL BOWLING CONGRESS CHAMPIONS

| Year | Singles | All events | Year | Singles | All events |
|---|---|---|---|---|---|
| 1959 | Mae Bolt | Pat McBride | 1966 | Gloria Bouvia | Kate Helbig |
| 1960 | Marge McDaniels | Judy Roberts | 1967 | Gloria Paeth | Carol Miller |
| 1961 | Elaine Newton | Evelyn Teal | 1968 | Norma Parks | Susie Reichley |
| 1962 | Martha Hoffman | Flossie Argent | 1969 | Joan Bender | Helen Duval |
| 1963 | Dot Wilkinson | Helen Shablis | 1970 | Dorothy Fothergill | Dorothy Fothergill |
| 1964 | Jean Havlish | Jean Havlish | 1971 | Mary Scruggs | Lorrie Nichols |
| 1965 | Doris Rudell | Donna Zimmerman | 1972 | D. D. Jacobson | Mildred Martorella |

| Year | Singles | All events | Year | Singles | All events |
|---|---|---|---|---|---|
| 1973 | Bobby Buffaloe | Toni Calvery | 1989 | Lorraine Anderson | Nancy Fehn |
| 1974 | Shirley Garms | Judy C. Soutar | 1990 | Dana Miller-Mackie and Paula Carter (tie) | Carol Norman |
| 1975 | Barbara Leicht | Virginia Norton | | | |
| 1976 | Bev Shonk | Betty Morris | 1991 | Debbie Kuhn | Debbie Kuhn |
| 1977 | Akiko Yamaga | Akiko Yamaga | 1992 | Patty Ann | Mitsuko Tokimoto |
| 1978 | Mae Bolt | Annese Kelly | 1993 | Karen Collurs and Kari Murph (tie) | Bertha Blackshur and Sharon Davis (tie) |
| 1979 | Betty Morris | Betty Morris | | | |
| 1980 | Betty Morris | Cheryl Robinson | 1994 | Vicki Fifield | Wendy Macpherson-Papanos |
| 1981 | Virginia Norton | Virginia Norton | | | |
| 1982 | Gracie Freeman | Aleta Rzepecki | 1995 | Beth Owen | Beth Owen |
| 1983 | Aleta Rzepecki | Virginia Norton | 1996 | Cindy Berlanga | Lorrie Nichols |
| 1984 | Freida Gates | Shinobu Saitoh | 1997 | Jean Schmidt | Kendra Cameron |
| 1985 | Polly Schwarzel | Aleta Sill | 1998 | Nellie Glandon | Liz Johnson |
| 1986 | Dana Stewart | Robin Romeo and Maria Lewis (tie) | 1999 | Maggie Matheson | Marlene Walls |
| | | | 2000 | Cathy Krasner | Carolyn Dorin-Ballard |
| 1987 | Regi Junak | Leanne Barrette | 2001 | Lisa Wagner | Jonquay Armon |
| 1988 | Michelle Meyer-Welty | Lisa Wagner | 2002 | Theresa Smith | Cara Honeychurch |

## BOWLING PROPRIETORS' ASSOCIATION OF AMERICA—WOMEN

**United States Open**

| | | | | | | | |
|---|---|---|---|---|---|---|---|
| 1971 | Paula Carter | 1979 | Diana Silva | 1987 | Carol Nurman | 1995 | Tish Johnson |
| 1972 | Lorrie Nichols | 1980 | Pat Costello (Calif.) | 1988 | Lisa Wagner | 1996 | Liz Johnson |
| 1973 | Mildred Martorella | 1981 | Donna Adamek | 1989 | Robin Romeo | 1997 | Not held |
| 1974 | Pat Costello (Calif.) | 1982 | Shinobu Saitoh | 1990 | Dana Miller-Mackie | 1998 | Aleta Sill |
| 1975 | Paula Carter | 1983 | Dana Miller | 1991 | Anne Marie Duggan | 1999 | Kim Adler |
| 1976 | Patty Costello (Pa.) | 1984 | Karen Ellingsworth | 1992 | Tish Johnson | 2000 | Tennelle Grijalva |
| 1977 | Betty Morris | 1985 | Pat Mercatanti | 1993 | Dede Davidson | 2001 | Kim Terrell |
| 1978 | Donna Adamek | 1986 | Wendy Macpherson | 1994 | Aleta Sill | | |

## WIBC QUEENS TOURNAMENT CHAMPIONS

| | | | | | | | |
|---|---|---|---|---|---|---|---|
| 1961 | Janet Harman | 1972 | Dorothy Fothergill | 1983 | Aleta Rzepecki | 1994 | Anne Marie Duggan |
| 1962 | Dorothy Wilkinson | 1973 | Dorothy Fothergill | 1984 | Kazue Inahashi | 1995 | Sandy Postma |
| 1963 | Irene Monterosso | 1974 | Judy Soutar | 1985 | Aleta Sill | 1996 | Lisa Wagner |
| 1964 | D.D. Jacobson | 1975 | Cindy Powell | 1986 | Cora Fiebig | 1997 | Sandra-Jo Shiery-Odom |
| 1965 | Betty Kuczynski | 1976 | Pamela Buckner | 1987 | Cathy Almeida | | |
| 1966 | Judy Lee | 1977 | Dana Stewart | 1988 | Wendy Macpherson | 1998 | Lynda Norry |
| 1967 | Mildred Martorella | 1978 | Loa Boxberger | 1989 | Carol Gianotti | 1999 | Leanne Barrette |
| 1968 | Phyllis Massey | 1979 | Donna Adamek | 1990 | Patty Ann | 2000 | Wendy Macpherson |
| 1969 | Ann Feigel | 1980 | Donna Adamek | 1991 | Dede Davidson | 2001 | Carolyn Dorin-Ballard |
| 1970 | Mildred Martorella | 1981 | Katsuko Sugimoto | 1992 | Cindy Coburn-Carroll | 2002 | Kim Terrell |
| 1971 | Mildred Martorella | 1982 | Katsuko Sugimoto | 1993 | Jan Schmidt | | |

## PBA WORLD CHAMPIONSHIP—2002

### (March 3, 2002, Toledo, Ohio)

Winner—Doug Kent, Newark, N.Y., defeated Lonnie Waliczek, Wichita, Kans., 215–160 in title match.

3. Rick Steelsmith, Wichita, Kans. and T. Brian Voss, Atlanta, Ga.

## AMERICAN BOWLING CONGRESS TOURNAMENT—2002

### (Feb. 9–June 22, 2002, Billings, Mont.)

| | |
|---|---|
| Singles—Mark Millsap, Portage, Ind. | 823 |
| Doubles—Fred Mattson, Tacoma, Wash., and Chris Warren, Puyallup, Wash. | 1,534 |
| Team—Brunos Pizza #1, Lafayette, Ind. | 3,473 |
| All Events—Stephen A. Hardy, Manchester, N.H. | 2,279 |

## WOMEN'S INTERNATIONAL BOWLING CONGRESS TOURNAMENT—2002

### (April 13–June 10, 2002, Milwaukee, Wis.)

| | |
|---|---|
| Singles—Theresa Smith, Indianapolis, Ind. | 752 |
| Doubles—Jody Ellis, Pembroke Pines, Fla., and Kathy Tribbey, Newberg, Ore. | 1,434 |
| Team—High Roller, Cherry Hill N.J., Henderson, Nev. | 3,327 |
| All Events—Cara Honeychurch, Australia | 2,150 |

## WOMEN'S INTERNATIONAL BOWLING CONGRESS QUEENS TOURNAMENT—2002

### (May 6–10, 2002, Wauwatosa, Wis.)

Winner—Kim Terrell, Daly City, Calif., defeated Kim Adler, Cocoa, Fla., 227–214 in title match.
3. Kari Schwager, Montgomery, Ill.
4. Kirsten Penny, England
5. Cara Honeychurch, Australia

# Skiing

## HISTORY OF SKIING IN THE UNITED STATES

Skis were devised for utility, to aid those who had to travel over snow. The Norwegians, Swedes, Lapps, and other inhabitants of northern lands used skis for many centuries before skiing became a sport. Emigrants from these countries brought skis to the United States with them. The first skier of record in the United States was a mailman by the name of "Snowshoe" Thompson, born and raised in Telemarken, Norway, who came to the United States and, beginning in 1850, used skis through 20 successive winters in carrying mail from Northern California to Carson Valley, Idaho.

Ski clubs sprang up over 100 years ago where there were Norwegian and Swedish settlers in Wisconsin and Minnesota, and ski contests were held in that territory in 1886. On Feb. 21, 1904, at Ishpenning, Mich., a small group of skiers organized the National Ski Association. In 1961 it was renamed the United States Ski Association. In the 1990s it became the United States Ski and Snowboard Association and included freestyle and disabled skiing.

## ALPINE SKIING

### 2002 Chevy Truck U.S. Alpine Championships
(March 14–19, 2002, Squaw Valley, Calif.)

**Men**

Downhill—Cancelled.

Slalom—1. Bode Miller, Franconia, N.H.; 2. Erik Schlopy, Park City, Utah; 3. Paul Casey Puckett, Aspen, Colo.

Super G—1. Marco Sullivan, Squaw Valley, Calif.; 2. TJ Lanning, Park City, Utah; 3. Steve Nyman, Sundance, Utah

Giant Slalom—1. Thomas Vonn, Newburgh, N.Y.; 2. Tom Rothrock, Cashmere, Wash.; 3. Erk Schlopy, Park City, Utah

Combined—1. Bode Miller, Franconia, N.H.; 2. Erik Schlopy, Park City, Utah; 3. TJ Lanning, Park City, Utah

**Women**

Downhill—Cancelled

Slalom—1. Sarah Schleper, Vail, Colo.; 2. Caroline Lalive, Steamboat Springs, Colo.; 3. Julia Mancuso, Squaw Valley, Calif.

Giant Slalom—1. Jonna Mendes, Heavenly, Calif.; 2. Caroline Lalive, Steamboat Springs, Colo.; 3. Julia Mancuso, Squaw Valley, Calif.

Super G—1. Caroline Lalive, Steamboat Springs, Colo.; 2. Jonna Mendes, Heavenly, Calif.; 3. Julia Mancuso, Squaw Valley, Calif.

Combined —1. Caroline Lalive, Steamboat Springs, Colo.; 2. Julia Mancuso, Squaw Valley, Calif.; 3. Sarah Schleper, Vail, Colo.

### 2002 Alpine World Cup Champions

| Men | Pts | Women | Pts |
|---|---|---|---|
| Overall—Stephan Eberharter, Austria | 1,702 | Overall—Michaela Dorfmeister, Austria | 1,271 |
| Downhill—Stephan Eberharter, Austria | 810 | Downhill—Isolde Kostner, Italy | 568 |
| Slalom—Ivica Kostelic, Croatia | 611 | Slalom—Laure Pequegnot, France | 597 |
| Giant Slalom—Frederic Covili, France | 471 | Giant Slalom—Sonja Nef, Switzerland | 574 |
| Super G—Stephan Eberharter, Austria | 470 | Super G—Hilde Gerg, Germany | 355 |
| Combined—Kjetil Andre Aamodt, Norway | 200 | Combined—Renate Goetschl, Austria | 200 |

### 2002 Alpine Skiing Paralympics
(March 7–16, 2002, Salt Lake City, Utah)

Skiers are placed in categories appropriate to their disability. There are 3 blind classes, 11 standing classes, and 5 sitting classes. When several classes combine in competition, a factor system is used to calculate results.

**Gold Medals—Men**

Downhill—**Blind:** Bart Bunting, Australia. **Sitting:** Martin Braxenthaler, Germany; Harald Eder, Austria; Kevin Bramble, United States. **Standing:** Michael Milton, Australia; Gerd Schoenfelder, Germany; Hans Burk, Switzerland; Rolf Heinzmann, Switzerland

Slalom—**Blind:** Eric Villalon, Spain; Chris Williamson, Canada. **Sitting:** Martin Braxenthaler, Germany; Denis Barbet, France; Daniel Wesley, Canada. **Standing:** Michael Milton, Australia; Gerd Schoenfelder, Germany; Hubert Mandl, Austria; Wolfgang Moosbrugger, Austria

Giant Slalom—**Blind:** Eric Villalon, Spain; Yon Santacana, Spain. **Sitting:** Martin Braxenthaler, Germany; Harald Eder, Austria; Hans-Joerg Arnold, Switzerland. **Standing:** Michael Milton, Australia; Gerd Schoenfelder, Germany; Steven Bayley, New Zealand; Rolf Heinzmann, Switzerland

Super G—**Blind:** Bart Bunting, Australia. **Sitting:** Martin Braxenthaler, Germany; Fabrizio Zardini, Italy; Chris Devlin-Young, United States. **Standing:** Michael Milton, Australia; Gerd Schoenfelder, Germany; Hubert Mandl, Austria; Rolf Heinzmann, Switzerland

**Gold Medals—Women**

Downhill—**Blind:** Pascale Casanova, France. **Sitting:** Sarah Will, United States. **Standing:** Danja Haslacher, Austria; Rachael Battersby, New Zealand

Slalom—**Blind:** Gabriele Huemer, Austria. **Sitting:** Sarah Will, United States. **Standing:** Danja Haslacher, Austria; Lauren Woolstencroft, Canada; Rachael Battersby, New Zealand

Giant Slalom—**Blind:** Katerina Tepla, Czech Republic. **Sitting:** Sarah Will, United States; Allison Pearl, United States. **Standing:** Danja Haslacher, Austria; Mary Riddell, United States; Rachael Battersby, New Zealand

Super G—**Blind:** Katerina Tepla, Czech Republic; **Sitting:** Sarah Will, United States; **Standing:** Sarah Billmeier, United States; Lauren Woolstencroft, Canada

## NORDIC SKIING/SKI JUMPING/CROSS COUNTRY

### 2002 Chevy Truck U.S. Ski Jumping/Nordic Combined Championships
(March 27–28, 2002, Steamboat Springs, Colo.)

**Men**

Nordic Combined (K90m jumping–10k race)—1. Bill Demong, Vermontville, N.Y.; 2. Todd Lodwick, Steamboat Springs, Colo.; 3. Matt Dayton, Breckenridge, Colo.

Normal Hill (K90m)—1. Alan Alborn, Anchorage, Alaska; 2. Clint Jones, Steamboat Springs, Colo.; 3. Bill Demong, Vermontville, N.Y.

Large Hill (K114m)—1. Alan Alborn, Anchorage, Alaska; 2. Bill Demong, Vermontville, N.Y.; 3. Clint Jones, Steamboat Springs, Colo.

**Women**

Normal Hill (K90m)—1. Jessica Jerome, Park City, Utah; 2. Lindsay Van, Park City, Utah; 3. Liz Syotori, Saugerties, N.Y.

Large Hill (K114 m)—1. Jessica Jerome, Park City, Utah; 2. Lindsay Van, Park City, Utah; 3. Liz Syotori, Saugerties, N.Y.

### 2002 Cross Country World Cup

**Men**

Sprint—Trond Iversen, Norway

Overall—Per Elofsson, Sweden.

**Women**

Sprint—Bente Skari, Norway

Overall—Bente Skari, Norway

## FREESTYLE SKIING

### 2002 Freestyle Skiing World Cup Champions

**Men**

Aerials—Eric Bergoust, United States

Moguls—Jeremy Bloom, United States

Dual Moguls—Richard Gay, France

Overall—Eric Bergoust, United States

**Women**

Aerials—Alla Tsuper, Belarus

Moguls—Kari Traa, Norway

Dual Moguls—Christine Gerg, Germany

Overall—Kari Traa, Norway

### 2002 Chevy Truck U.S. Freestyle Championships

(March 22–24, 2002, Bogus Basin, Idaho)

**Men**

Aerials—Ryan St. Onge, Winter Park, Colo.

Moguls—Travis Ramos, South Lake Tahoe, Calif.

Dual Moguls—Toby Dawson, Vail, Colo.

**Women**

Aerials—Tracy Evans, Park City, Utah

Moguls—Shannon Bahrke, Tahoe City, Calif.

Dual Moguls—Shannon Bahrke, Tahoe City, Calif.

## SNOWBOARDING

### 2002 World Cup Snowboard Champions

**Men**

Big Air—Jukka Eratuli, Finland

Halfpipe—Jan Michaelis, Germany

Giant Slalom—Dejan Kosir, Slovenia

Parallel Slalom—Mathieu Bozzetto, France

Parallel Giant Slalom—Dejan Josir, Slovenia

Snowboard Cross—Jasey Jay Anderson, Canada

Overall—Jasey Jay Anderson, Canada

**Women**

Halfpipe—Nicola Pederzolli, Austria

Giant Slalom—Steffi von Siebenthal, Switzerland

Parallel Slalom—Karine Ruby, France

Parallel Giant Slalom—Isabelle Blanc, France

Snowboard Cross—Doris Krings, Austria

Overall—Karine Ruby, France

### 2002 X-Nix U.S. Snowboard Championships

(March 28–31, 2002, Northstar-at-Tahoe, Calif.)

**Men**

Slalom—Chris Klug, Aspen, Colo

Parallel Giant Slalom—Jasey Jay Anderson, Canada

Snowboard cross—Seth Wescott, Kingfield, Maine

Halfpipe—Wyatt Caldwell, Sun Valley, Idaho

**Women**

Slalom—Stacey Hookom, Edwards, Colo.

Parallel Giant Slalom—Stacey Hookom, Edwards, Colo.

Snowboard Cross—Lindsey Jacobellis, Stratton Mountain, Vt.

Halfpipe—Gretchen Bleiler, Snowmass Village, Colo.

## JAMES E. SULLIVAN MEMORIAL AWARD WINNERS

**(Amateur Athlete of the Year Chosen in Amateur Athletic Union Poll)**

| | | | | | | |
|---|---|---|---|---|---|---|
| 1930 | Robert Tyre Jones, Jr. | Golf | | 1943 | Gilbert L. Dodds | Track and field |
| 1931 | Bernard E. Berlinger | Track and field | | 1944 | Ann Curtis | Swimming |
| 1932 | James A. Bausch | Track and field | | 1945 | Felix (Doc) Blanchard | Football |
| 1933 | Glenn Cunningham | Track and field | | 1946 | Y. Arnold Tucker | Football |
| 1934 | William R. Bonthron | Track and field | | 1947 | John B. Kelly, Jr. | Rowing |
| 1935 | W. Lawson Little, Jr. | Golf | | 1948 | Robert B. Mathias | Track and field |
| 1936 | Glenn Morris | Track and field | | 1949 | Richard T. Button | Figure skating |
| 1937 | J. Donald Budge | Tennis | | 1950 | Fred Wilt | Track and field |
| 1938 | Donald R. Lash | Track and field | | 1951 | Robert E. Richards | Track and field |
| 1939 | Joseph W. Burk | Rowing | | 1952 | Horace Ashenfelter | Track and field |
| 1940 | J. Gregory Rice | Track and field | | 1953 | Sammy Lee | Diving |
| 1941 | Leslie MacMitchell | Track and field | | 1954 | Malvin Whitfield | Track and field |
| 1942 | Cornelius Warmerdam | Track and field | | 1955 | Harrison Dillard | Track and field |

| 1956 | Patricia McCormick | Diving |
|---|---|---|
| 1957 | Bobby Jo Morrow | Track and field |
| 1958 | Glenn Davis | Track and field |
| 1959 | Parry O'Brien | Track and field |
| 1960 | Rafer Johnson | Track and field |
| 1961 | Wilma Rudolph Ward | Track and field |
| 1962 | Jim Beatty | Track and field |
| 1963 | John Pennel | Track and field |
| 1964 | Don Schollander | Swimming |
| 1965 | Bill Bradley | Basketball |
| 1966 | Jim Ryun | Track and field |
| 1967 | Randy Matson | Track and field |
| 1968 | Debbie Meyer | Swimming |
| 1969 | Bill Toomey | Decathlon |
| 1970 | John Kinsella | Swimming |
| 1971 | Mark Spitz | Swimming |
| 1972 | Frank Shorter | Marathon |
| 1973 | Bill Walton | Basketball |
| 1974 | Rick Wohlhuter | Track and field |
| 1975 | Tim Shaw | Swimming |
| 1976 | Bruce Jenner | Track and field |
| 1977 | John Naber | Swimming |
| 1978 | Tracy Caulkins | Swimming |
| 1979 | Kurt Thomas | Gymnastics |
| 1980 | Eric Heiden | Speed skating |
| 1981 | Carl Lewis | Track and field |
| 1982 | Mary Decker Tabb | Track and field |
| 1983 | Edwin Moses | Track and field |
| 1984 | Greg Louganis | Diving |
| 1985 | Joan Benoit-Samuelson | Marathon |
| 1986 | Jackie Joyner-Kersee | Heptathlon |
| 1987 | Jim Abbott | Baseball |
| 1988 | Florence Griffith-Joyner | Track and field |
| 1989 | Janet Evans | Swimming |
| 1990 | John Smith | Wrestling |
| 1991 | Mike Powell | Track and field |
| 1992 | Bonnie Blair | Speed skating |
| 1993 | Charles Ward | Football/Basketball |
| 1994 | Dan Jansen | Speed skating |
| 1995 | Bruce Baumgartner | Wrestling |
| 1996 | Michael Johnson | Track and field |
| 1997 | Peyton Manning | Football |
| 1998 | Chamique Holdsclaw | Basketball |
| 1999 | Kelly and Coco Miller | Basketball |
| 2000 | Rulon Gardner | Wrestling |
| 2001 | Michelle Kwan | Figure skating |

# Speed Skating

## WORLD SPEED SKATING RECORDS (LONG TRACK)

| Distance | Time | Skater | Place | Date |
|---|---|---|---|---|
| **Men** | | | | |
| 500 m | 34.32 | Hiroyasu Shimizu, Japan | Salt Lake City | March 10, 2001 |
| 1,000 m | 1:07.18 | Gerard van Velde, Netherlands | Salt Lake City | Feb. 16, 2002 |
| 1,500 m | 1:43.95 | Derek Parra, United States | Salt Lake City | Feb. 19, 2002 |
| 3,000 m | 3:42.75 | Gianni Romme, Netherlands | Calgary, Canada | September 11, 2000 |
| 5,000 m | 6:14.66 | Jochem Uytdehaage, Netherlands | Salt Lake City | Feb. 9, 2002 |
| 10,000 m | 12:58.92 | Jochem Uytdehaage, Netherlands | Salt Lake City | Feb. 22, 2002 |
| **Women** | | | | |
| 500 m | 37.22 | Catriona LeMay Doan, Canada | Calgary, Canada | Dec. 9, 2001 |
| 1,000 m | 1:13.83 | Chris Witty, United States | Salt Lake City | Feb. 17, 2002 |
| 1,500 m | 1:54.02 | Anna "Anni" Friesinger, Germany | Salt Lake City | Feb. 20, 2002 |
| 3,000 m | 3:57.70 | Claudia Pechstein, Germany | Salt Lake City | Feb. 10, 2002 |
| 5,000 m | 6:46.91 | Claudia Pechstein, Germany | Salt Lake City | Feb. 23, 2002 |

## WORLD SPEED SKATING RECORDS (SHORT TRACK)

| Distance | Time | Skater | Place | Date |
|---|---|---|---|---|
| **Men** | | | | |
| 500 m | 41.514 | Jeffrey Scholten, Canada | Calgary, Canada | Oct. 13, 2001 |
| 1,000 m | 1:25.985 | Steve Robillard, Canada | Calgary, Canada | Oct. 14, 2001 |
| 1,500 m | 2:13.728 | Apolo Anton Ohno, United States | Salt Lake City | Dec. 15, 2001 |
| 3,000 m | 4:46.727 | Dong-Sung Kim, Korea | Szekesfehervar, Hungary | Nov. 8, 1998 |
| 5,000 m relay | 6:43.730 | Canada | Calgary, Canada | Oct. 14, 2001 |
| **Women** | | | | |
| 500 m | 43.671 | Evgenia Radanova, Bulgaria | Calgary, Canada | Oct. 19, 2001 |
| 1,000 m | 1:31.871 | Yang Yang (A), China | Calgary, Canada | Oct. 20, 2001 |
| 1,500 m | 2:21.844 | Moon-Yung Kim, Korea | Montreal, Canada | Jan. 17, 1999 |
| 3,000 m | 5:01.976 | Eun Kyung Choi, Korea | Calgary, Canada | Oct. 22, 2000 |
| 3,000 m relay | 4:13.541 | China | Calgary, Canada | Oct. 19, 2001 |

## WORLD SPEED SKATING CHAMPIONSHIPS—2002

### (March 14–17, 2002, Heerenveen, Netherlands)

| Men | Time | Women | Time |
|---|---|---|---|
| 500 m—Petter Andersen, Norway | 36.39 | 500 m—Jennifer Rodriguez, United States | 38.59 |
| 1,500 m—Dmitry Shepel, Russia | 1:48.44 | 1,500 m—Anni Friesinger, Germany | 1:56.43 |
| 5,000 m—Jochem Uytdehaage, Netherlands | 6:30.27 | 3,000 m—Anni Friesinger, Germany | 4:08.02 |
| 10,000 m—Jochem Uytdehaage, Netherlands | 13:27.25 | 5,000 m—Claudia Pechstein, Germany | 7:01.31 |

## WORLD SHORT TRACK CHAMPIONSHIPS—2002
### (April 5–7, 2002, Montreal, Canada)

| Men | Time | Women | Time |
|---|---|---|---|
| 500 m—Dong-Sung Kim, Korea | 41.930 | 500 m—Yang Yang (A), China | 44.460 |
| 1,000 m—Dong-Sung Kim, Korea | 1:31.361 | 1,000 m—Yang Yang (A), China | 1:34.732 |
| 1,500 m—Dong-Sung Kim, Korea | 2:21.736 | 1,500 m—Yang Yang (A), China | 2:31.630 |
| 3,000 m—Dong-Sung Kim, Korea | 5:19.041 | 3,000 m—Eun-Kyung Choi, Korea | 5:17.678 |
| Relay—Korea | 7:10.751 | Relay—Korea | 4:18.599 |

# Figure Skating

## WORLD CHAMPIONS

**Men**

| | |
|---|---|
| 1960 | Alain Giletti, France |
| 1961 | No competition |
| 1962 | Donald Jackson, Canada |
| 1963 | Don McPherson, Canada |
| 1964 | Manfred Schnelldorfer, West Germany |
| 1965 | Alain Calmat, France |
| 1966–68 | Emmerich Danzer, Austria |
| 1969–70 | Tim Wood, United States |
| 1971–73 | Ondrej Nepela, Czechoslovakia |
| 1974 | Jan Hoffman, East Germany |
| 1975 | Sergei Yolkov, USSR |
| 1976 | John Curry, Britain |
| 1977 | Vladimir Kovalev, USSR |
| 1978 | Charles Tickner, United States |
| 1979 | Vladimir Kovalev, USSR |
| 1980 | Jan Hoffman, East Germany |
| 1981–84 | Scott Hamilton, United States |
| 1985 | Alexandr Fadeev, USSR |
| 1986 | Brian Boitano, United States |
| 1987 | Brian Orser, Canada |
| 1988 | Brian Boitano, United States |
| 1989–91 | Kurt Browning, Canada |
| 1992 | Viktor Petrenko, Unified Team |
| 1993 | Kurt Browning, Canada |
| 1994–95 | Elvis Stojko, Canada |
| 1996 | Todd Eldredge, United States |
| 1997 | Elvis Stojko, Canada |
| 1998–2000 | Alexei Yagudin, Russia |
| 2001 | Evgeni Plushenko, Russia |
| 2002 | Alexei Yagudin, Russia |

**Women**

| | |
|---|---|
| 1956–60 | Carol Heiss, United States |
| 1961 | No competition |
| 1962–64 | Sjoukje Dijkstra, Netherlands |
| 1965 | Petra Burka, Canada |
| 1966–68 | Peggy Fleming, United States |
| 1969–70 | Gabriele Seyfert, East Germany |
| 1971–72 | Beatrix Schuba, Austria |
| 1973 | Karen Magnusson, Canada |
| 1974 | Christine Errath, East Germany |
| 1975 | Dianne de Leeuw, Netherlands |
| 1976 | Dorothy Hamill, United States |
| 1977 | Linda Fratianne, United States |
| 1978 | Anett Poetzsch, East Germany |
| 1979 | Linda Fratianne, United States |
| 1980 | Anett Poetzsch, East Germany |
| 1981 | Denise Beillmann, Switzerland |
| 1982 | Elaine Zayak, United States |
| 1983 | Rosalynn Sumners, United States |
| 1984–85 | Katarina Witt, East Germany |
| 1986 | Debi Thomas, United States |
| 1987–88 | Katarina Witt, East Germany |
| 1989 | Midori Ito, Japan |
| 1990 | Jill Trenary, United States |
| 1991–92 | Kristi Yamaguchi, United States |
| 1993 | Oksana Baiul, Ukraine |
| 1994 | Yuka Sato, Japan |
| 1995 | Chen Lu, China |
| 1996 | Michelle Kwan, United States |
| 1997 | Tara Lipinski, United States |
| 1998 | Michelle Kwan, United States |
| 1999 | Maria Butyrskaya, Russia |
| 2000–01 | Michelle Kwan, United States |
| 2002 | Irina Slutskaya, Russia |

## U.S. CHAMPIONS

**Men**

| | |
|---|---|
| 1946–52 | Richard Button |
| 1953–56 | Hayes Jenkins |
| 1957–60 | David Jenkins |
| 1961 | Bradley Lord |
| 1962 | Monty Hoyt |
| 1963 | Tommy Liz |
| 1964 | Scott Allen |
| 1965 | Gary Visconti |
| 1966 | Scott Allen |
| 1967 | Gary Visconti |
| 1968–70 | Tim Wood |
| 1971 | John M. Petkevich |
| 1972 | Ken Shelley |
| 1973–75 | Gordon McKellen |
| 1976 | Terry Kubicka |
| 1977–80 | Charles Tickner |
| 1981–84 | Scott Hamilton |
| 1985–88 | Brian Boitano |
| 1989 | Christopher Bowman |
| 1990–91 | Todd Eldredge |
| 1992 | Christopher Bowman |
| 1993–94 | Scott Davis |
| 1995 | Todd Eldredge |
| 1996 | Rudy Galindo |
| 1997–98 | Todd Eldredge |
| 1999–2000 | Michael Weiss |
| 2001 | Timothy Goebel |
| 2002 | Todd Eldredge |

**Women**

| | |
|---|---|
| 1943–48 | Gretchen Merrill |
| 1949–50 | Yvonne Sherman |
| 1951 | Sonya Klopfer |
| 1952–56 | Tenley Albright |
| 1957–60 | Carol Heiss |
| 1961 | Laurence Owen |
| 1962 | Barbara Roles Pursley |
| 1963 | Lorraine Hanlon |
| 1964–68 | Peggy Fleming |
| 1969–73 | Janet Lynn |
| 1974–76 | Dorothy Hamill |
| 1977–80 | Linda Fratianne |
| 1981 | Elaine Zayak |
| 1982–84 | Rosalynn Sumners |
| 1985 | Tiffany Chin |
| 1986 | Debi Thomas |
| 1987 | Jill Trenary |
| 1988 | Debi Thomas |
| 1989–90 | Jill Trenary |
| 1991 | Tonya Harding |
| 1992 | Kristi Yamaguchi |
| 1993 | Nancy Kerrigan |
| 1994 | Tonya Harding |
| 1995 | Nicole Bobek |
| 1996 | Michelle Kwan |
| 1997 | Tara Lipinski |
| 1998–2002 | Michelle Kwan |

## 2002 UNITED STATES CHAMPIONSHIPS
### (Jan. 16–13, 2002, Los Angeles, Calif.)

**Men's singles**
1. Todd Eldredge, Lake Angelus, Mich.
2. Timothy Goebel, Rolling Meadows, Ill.
3. Michael Weiss, Fairfax, Va.

**Women's singles**
1. Michelle Kwan, Lake Arrowhead, Calif.
2. Sasha Cohen, Laguna Niguel, Calif.
3. Sarah Hughes, Great Neck, N.Y.

**Pairs**
1. Kyoko Ina, Greenwich, Conn., and John Zimmerman, Birmingham, Ala.
2. Tiffany Scott, Hanson, Mass., and Philip Dulebohn, Germantown, Md.
3. Stephanie Kalesavich, Rochester Hills, Minn., and Aaron Parchem, Oak Park, Ill.

**Dance**
1. Naomi Lang, Allegan, Mich., and Peter Tchernyshev, St. Petersburg, Russia
2. Tanith Belbin, Bloomfield Hills, Mich., and Benjamin Agosto, Beverly Hills, Mich.
3. Melissa Gregory, Broadmoor SC, and Denis Petukhov, Skokie Valley SC

## 2002 WORLD CHAMPIONSHIPS
### (March 16–24, 2002, Nagano, Japan)

**Men's singles**
1. Alexei Yagudin, Russia
2. Timothy Goebel, United States
3. Takeshi Honda, Japan

**Women's singles**
1. Irina Slutskaya, Russia
2. Michelle Kwan, United States
3. Fumie Suguri, Japan

**Pairs**
1. Xue Shen and Hongbo Zhao, China
2. Tatiana Totmianina and Maxim Marinin, Russia
3. Kyoko Ina and John Zimmerman, United States

**Dance**
1. Irina Lobacheva and Ilia Averbukh, Russia
2. Shae-Lynn Bourne and Victor Kraatz, Canada
3. Galit Chait and Sergei Sakhnovski, Israel

# Swimming

## WORLD LONG COURSE RECORDS—MEN
### (Through Sept. 19, 2002)

| Distance | Record | Holder | Country | Date |
|---|---|---|---|---|
| **Freestyle** | | | | |
| 50 m | 0:21.64 | Alexander Popov | Russia | June 16, 2000 |
| 100 m | 0:47.84 | Pieter van den Hoogenband | Netherlands | Sept. 19, 2000 |
| 200 m | 1:44.06 | Ian Thorpe | Australia | July 25, 2001 |
| 400 m | 3:40.08 | Ian Thorpe | Australia | July 30, 2002 |
| 800 m | 7:39.16 | Ian Thorpe | Australia | July 24, 2001 |
| 1,500 m | 14:34.56 | Grant Hackett | Australia | July 29, 2001 |
| **Backstroke** | | | | |
| 50 m | 0:24.99 | Lenny Krayzelburg | United States | Aug. 28, 1999 |
| 100 m | 0:53.60 | Lenny Krayzelburg | United States | Aug. 24, 1999 |
| 200 m | 1:55.15 | Aaron Peirsol | United States | March 20, 2002 |
| **Breaststroke** | | | | |
| 50 m | 0:27.18 | Oleg Lisogur | Ukraine | Aug. 1, 2002 |
| 100 m | 0:59.94 | Roman Sloudnov | Russia | July 23, 2001 |
| 200 m | 2:10.16 | Mike Barrowman | United States | July 29, 1992 |
| **Butterfly** | | | | |
| 50 m | 0:23.44 | Geoff Huegill | Australia | July 27, 2001 |
| 100 m | 0:51.81 | Michael Klim | Australia | Dec. 12, 1999 |
| 200 m | 1:54.58 | Michael Phelps | United States | July 01, 2001 |
| **Individual medley** | | | | |
| 200 m | 1:58.16 | Jani Sievinen | Finland | Sept. 11, 1994 |
| 400 m | 4:11.09 | Michael Phelps | United States | Aug. 15, 2002 |
| **Medley relay** | | | | |
| 400 m | 3:33.48 | National Team | United States | Aug. 29, 2002 |
| **Freestyle relay** | | | | |
| 400 m | 3:13.67 | Olympic Team | Australia | Sept. 16, 2000 |
| 800 m | 7:04.66 | National Team | Australia | July 27, 2001 |

Approved by the International Swimming Federation (FINA). (FINA discontinued acceptance of records in yards in 1968.)
*Source:* FINA.

## WORLD LONG COURSE RECORDS—WOMEN
### (Through Sept. 19, 2002)

| Distance | Record | Holder | Country | Date |
|---|---|---|---|---|
| **Freestyle** | | | | |
| 50 m | 0:24.13 | Inge de Bruijn | Netherlands | Sept. 22, 2000 |
| 100 m | 0:53.77 | Inge de Bruijn | Netherlands | Sept. 20, 2000 |
| 200 m | 1:56.64 | Franziska van Almsick | Germany | Aug. 3, 2002 |
| 400 m | 4:03.85 | Janet Evans | United States | Sept. 22, 1988 |
| 800 m | 8:16.22 | Janet Evans | United States | Aug. 20, 1989 |
| 1,500 m | 15:52.10 | Janet Evans | United States | March 26, 1988 |
| **Backstroke** | | | | |
| 50 m | 0:28.25 | Sandra Voelker | Germany | June 17, 2000 |
| 100 m | 0:59.58[1] | Natalie Coughlin | United States | Aug. 13, 2002 |
| 200 m | 2:06.62 | Krisztina Egerszegi | Hungary | Aug. 25, 1991 |
| **Breaststroke** | | | | |
| 50 m | 0:30.57 | Zoe Baker | Great Britain | July 30, 2002 |
| 100 m | 1:06.52 | Penny Heyns | South Africa | Aug. 23, 1999 |
| 200 m | 2:22.99 | Hui Qi | China | April 13, 2001 |
| **Butterfly** | | | | |
| 50 m | 0:25.57 | Anna-Karin Kammerling | Sweden | July 30, 2000 |
| 100 m | 0:56.61 | Inge de Bruijn | Netherlands | Sept. 17, 2000 |
| 200 m | 2:05.78 | Otylia Jedrzejczak | Poland | Aug. 4, 2002 |
| **Individual medley** | | | | |
| 200 m | 2:09.72 | Yanyan Wu | China | Oct. 17, 1997 |
| 400 m | 4:33.59 | Yana Klochkova | Ukraine | Sept. 16, 2000 |
| **Medley relay** | | | | |
| 400 m | 3:58.30 | Olympic Team | United States | Sept. 23, 2000 |
| **Freestyle relay** | | | | |
| 400 m | 3:36.00 | National Team | Germany | July 29, 2002 |
| 800 m | 7:55.47 | National Team | East Germany | Aug. 18, 1987 |

Approved by the International Swimming Federation (FINA). (FINA discontinued acceptance of records in yards in 1968.)
*Source:* FINA.

## AMERICAN LONG COURSE SWIMMING RECORDS
### (Through Sept. 19, 2002)

| Distance | Record | Holder | Date | Distance | Record | Holder | Date |
|---|---|---|---|---|---|---|---|
| **MEN** | | | | **WOMEN** | | | |
| **Freestyle** | | | | **Freestyle** | | | |
| 50 m | 0:21.76 | Gary Hall, Jr. | Aug. 15, 2000 | 50 m | 0:24.63 | Dara Torres | Sept. 23, 2000 |
| 100 m | 0:48.33 | Anthony Ervin | July 27, 2001 | 100 m | 0:53.99 | Natalie Coughlin | Aug. 29, 2002 |
| 200 m | 1:46.73 | Josh Davis | Sept. 18, 2000 | 200 m | 1:57.90 | Nicole Haislett | July 27, 1992 |
| 400 m | 3:47.00 | Klete Keller | Sept. 16, 2000 | 400 m | 4:03.85 | Janet Evans | Sept. 22, 1988 |
| 800 m | 7:52.05 | Larsen Jensen | Aug. 25, 2002 | 800 m | 8:16.22 | Janet Evans | Aug. 20, 1989 |
| 1,500 m | 14:56.81 | Chris Thompson | Sept. 23, 2000 | 1,500 m | 15:52.10 | Janet Evans | March 26, 1988 |
| **Backstroke** | | | | **Backstroke** | | | |
| 50 m | 0:24.99 | Lenny Krayzelburg | Aug. 28, 1999 | 50 m | 0:28.49 | Natalie Coughlin | July 23, 2001 |
| 100 m | 0:53.60 | Lenny Krayzelburg | Aug. 24, 1999 | 100 m | 0:59.58 | Natalie Coughlin | Aug. 13, 2002 |
| 200 m | 1:55.15 | Aaron Peirsol | March 20, 2002 | 200 m | 2:08.53 | Natalie Coughlin | Aug. 16, 2002 |
| **Breaststroke** | | | | **Breaststroke** | | | |
| 50 m | 0:27.39 | Ed Moses | March 31, 2001 | 50 m | 0:31.34 | Megan Quann | Aug. 11, 2000 |
| 100 m | 1:00.29 | Ed Moses | March 28, 2001 | 100 m | 1:07.05 | Megan Quann | Sept. 18, 2000 |
| 200 m | 2:10.16 | Mike Barrowman | July 29, 1992 | 200 m | 2:24.56 | Kristy Kowal | Sept. 21, 2000 |
| **Butterfly** | | | | **Butterfly** | | | |
| 50 m | 0:23.85 | Ian Crocker | July 28, 2001 | 50 m | 0:26.50 | Dara Torres | Aug. 9, 2000 |
| 100 m | 0:51.88 | Michael Phelps | Aug. 16, 2002 | 100 m | 0:57.58 | Dara Torres | Aug. 9, 2000 |
| 200 m | 1:54.58 | Michael Phelps | July 24, 2001 | 200 m | 2:05.88 | Misty Hyman | Sept. 20, 2000 |
| **Individual medley** | | | | **Individual medley** | | | |
| 200 m | 1:58.68 | Michael Phelps | Aug. 12, 2002 | 200 m | 2:11.91 | Summer Sanders | July 30, 1992 |
| 400 m | 4:11.09 | Michael Phelps | Aug. 15, 2002 | 400 m | 4:37.58 | Summer Sanders | July 26, 1992 |
| **Medley relay** | | | | **Medley relay** | | | |
| 400 m | 3:33.73 | U.S. Olympic Team | Sept. 23, 2000 | 400 m | 3:58.30 | U.S. Olympic Team | Sept. 23, 2000 |
| **Freestyle relay** | | | | **Freestyle relay** | | | |
| 400 m | 3:13.86 | U.S. Olympic Team | Sept. 16, 2000 | 400 m | 3:36.61 | U.S. Olympic Team | Sept. 16, 2000 |
| 800 m | 7:11.81 | U.S. National Team | Aug. 8, 2002 | 800 m | 7:56.53 | U.S. National Team | July 25, 2001 |

*Source:* United States Swim Team, FINA.

## FINA DIVING WORLD CUP, 2002

### (Seville, Spain, June 25–29, 2002)

| Men | Points | Women | Points |
|---|---|---|---|
| 1-m springboard—Xiang Xu, China | 421.80 | 1-m springboard—Jing Jing Guo, China | 312.84 |
| 3-m springboard—Dmitry Sautin, Russia | 519.06 | 3-m springboard—Jing Jing Guo, China | 355.08 |
| 3-m springboard synchronized—Tianling Wang and Feng Wang, China | 363.24 | 3-m springboard synchronized—Vera Ilyina and Julia Pakhalina, Russia | 329.31 |
| 10-m platform—Liang Tian, China | 558.84 | 10-m platform—Lishi Lao, China | 377.88 |
| 10-m platform synchronized—Liang Tian and Yu Tong Luo, China | 353.31 | 10-m platform synchronized—Lishi Lao and Ting Li, China | 317.16 |
| Team trophy ranking: | | Team trophy ranking: | |
| 1. China | 265 | 1. China | 288 |
| 2. Russia | 118 | 2. Russia | 140 |
| 3. Great Britain | 115 | 3. United States | 132 |

## FINA SHORT COURSE WORLD CHAMPIONSHIPS, 2002

### (April 3–7, 2002, Moscow, Russia)

| Men | Time | Women | Time |
|---|---|---|---|
| 50-m freestyle—Jose Martin Meolans, Argentina | 0:21.36 | 50-m freestyle—Therese Alshammar, Sweden | 0:24.16 |
| 100-m freestyle—Ashley Callus, Australia | 0:46.99 | 100-m freestyle—Therese Alshammar, Sweden | 0:52.89 |
| 200-m freestyle—Klete Keller, United States | 1:44.36 | 200-m freestyle—Lindsay Benko, United States | 1:54.04 |
| 400-m freestyle—Grant Hackett, Australia | 3:38.29 | 400-m freestyle—Yana Klochkova, Ukraine | 4:01.26 |
| 1,500-m freestyle—Grant Hackett, Australia | 14:33.94 | 800-m freestyle—Hua Chen, China | 8:16.34 |
| 50-m backstroke—Matt Welsh, Australia | 0:23.66 | 50-m backstroke—Jennifer Carroll, Canada | 0:27.38 |
| 100-m backstroke—Matt Welsh, Australia | 0:51.26 | 100-m backstroke—Haley Cope, United States | 0:59.07 |
| 200-m backstroke—Aaron Peirsol, United States | 1:51.17 | 200-m backstroke—Lindsay Benko, United States | 2:04.97 |
| 50-m breaststroke—Oleg Lisogor, Ukraine | 0:26.42 | 50-m breaststroke—Emma Igelstrom, Sweden | 0:29.96 |
| 100-m breaststroke—Oleg Lisogor, Ukraine | 0:58.33 | 100-m breaststroke—Emma Igelstrom, Sweden | 1:05.38 |
| 200-m breaststroke—Jim Piper, United States | 2:07.16 | 200-m breaststroke—Hui Qi, China | 2:20.91 |
| 50-m butterfly—Geoff Huegill, Australia | 0:22.89 | 50-m butterfly—A. Kammerling, Sweden | 0:25.55 |
| 100-m butterfly—Geoff Huegill, Australia | 0:50.95 | 100-m butterfly—Martina Moravcova, Slovak Republic | 0:57.04 |
| 200-m butterfly—James Hickman, Great Britain | 1:53.14 | 200-m butterfly—Petria Thomas, Australia | 2:05.76 |
| 100-m individual medley—Peter Mankoc, Slovenia | 0:52.90 | 100-m individual medley—Martina Moravcova, Slovak Republic | 0:59.91 |
| 200-m individual medley—Jani Sievinen, Finland | 1:55.45 | 200-m individual medley—Yana Klochkova, Ukraine | 2:08.82 |
| 400-m individual medley—Thomas Wilkens, United States | 4:04.82 | 400-m individual medley—Yana Klochkova, Ukraine | 4:30.63 |
| 4×100-m medley relay—United States | 3:29.00 | 4×100-m medley relay—Sweden | 3:55.78 |
| 4×100-m free relay—United States | 3:10.64 | 4×100-m free relay—Sweden | 3:35.09 |
| 4×200-m free relay—Australia | 7:00.36 | 4×200-m free relay—China | 7:46.30 |

# Boxing

Whether it be called pugilism, prize fighting, or boxing, there is no tracing "the Sweet Science" to any definite source. Tales of rivals exchanging blows for fun, fame, or money go back to earliest recorded history and classical legend. There was a mixture of boxing and wrestling called the "pancratium" in the ancient Olympic Games; in such contests rivals belabored one another with hands fortified by heavy leather wrappings that were sometimes studded with metal. More than one Olympic competitor lost his life in this brutal exercise.

There was little law or order in pugilism until Jack Broughton, one of the early champions of England, drew up a set of rules for the game in 1743. Broughton, called "the father of English box-

ing" also is credited with inventing boxing muffs or gloves. However, these gloves—or "mufflers" as they were called—were used only in teaching "the manly art of self-defense" or in training bouts. All professional championship fights were contested with bare knuckles until 1892, when John L. Sullivan lost the heavyweight championship of the world to James J. Corbett in New Orleans in a bout in which both contestants wore regulation gloves.

The Broughton Rules were superseded by the London Prize Ring Rules of 1838. In 1884 the eighth marquis of Queensberry, with the help of John G. Chambers, put forward the Queensberry Rules, a code that called for gloved contests. Amateurs took to the Queensberry Rules more quickly than the professionals did.

# HISTORY OF WORLD HEAVYWEIGHT CHAMPIONSHIP FIGHTS

## (Bouts in which a new champion was crowned)

| Date | Where held | Winner, weight (age) | Loser, weight (age) | Rounds |
|------|-----------|---------------------|--------------------|--------|
| Sept. 7, 1892 | New Orleans, La. | James J. Corbett, 178 (26) | John L. Sullivan, 212 (33) | 21 |
| March 17, 1897 | Carson City, Nev. | Bob Fitzsimmons, 167 (34) | James J. Corbett, 183 (30) | KO 14 |
| June 9, 1899 | Coney Island, N.Y. | James J. Jeffries, 206 (24)[1] | Bob Fitzsimmons, 167 (37) | KO 11 |
| Feb. 23, 1906 | Los Angeles | Tommy Burns, 180 (24)[2] | Marvin Hart, 188 (29) | 20 |
| Dec. 26, 1908 | Sydney, Australia | Jack Johnson, 196 (30) | Tommy Burns, 176 (27) | KO 14 |
| April 5, 1915 | Havana, Cuba | Jess Willard, 230 (33) | Jack Johnson, 205½ (37) | KO 26 |
| July 4, 1919 | Toledo, Ohio | Jack Dempsey, 187 (24) | Jess Willard, 245 (37) | KO 3 |
| Sept. 23, 1926 | Philadelphia | Gene Tunney, 189 (28)[3] | Jack Dempsey, 190 (31) | 10 |
| June 12, 1930 | New York | Max Schmeling, 188 (24) | Jack Sharkey, 197 (27) | WF 4 |
| June 21, 1932 | Long Island City | Jack Sharkey, 205 (29) | Max Schmeling, 188 (26) | 15 |
| June 29, 1933 | Long Island City | Primo Carnera, 260½ (26) | Jack Sharkey, 201 (30) | KO 6 |
| June 14, 1934 | Long Island City | Max Baer, 209½ (25) | Primo Carnera, 263¼ (27) | KO 11 |
| June 13, 1935 | Long Island City | Jim Braddock, 193¾ (29) | Max Baer, 209½ (26) | 15 |
| June 22, 1937 | Chicago | Joe Louis, 197¼ (23) | Jim Braddock, 197 (31) | KO 8 |
| June 22, 1949 | Chicago | Ezzard Charles, 181¾ (27)[4] | Joe Walcott, 195½ (35) | 15 |
| Sept. 27, 1950 | New York | Ezzard Charles, 184½ (29)[5] | Joe Louis, 218 (36) | 15 |
| July 18, 1951 | Pittsburgh | Joe Walcott, 194 (37) | Ezzard Charles, 182 (30) | KO 7 |
| Sept. 23, 1952 | Philadelphia | Rocky Marciano, 184 (29)[6] | Joe Walcott, 196 (38) | KO13 |
| Nov. 30, 1956 | Chicago | Floyd Patterson, 182¼ (21) | Archie Moore, 187¾ (42) | KO 5 |
| June 26, 1959 | New York | Ingemar Johansson, 196 (26) | Floyd Patterson, 182 (24) | KO 3 |
| June 20, 1960 | New York | Floyd Patterson, 190 (25) | Ingemar Johansson, 194¾ (27) | KO 5 |
| Sept. 25, 1962 | Chicago | Sonny Liston, 214 (28) | Floyd Patterson, 189 (27) | KO 1 |
| Feb. 25, 1964 | Miami Beach, Fla. | Cassius Clay (Muhammad Ali), 210 (22)[7] | Sonny Liston, 218 (30) | KO 7 |
| March 4, 1968 | New York | Joe Frazier, 204½ (24)[8] | Buster Mathis, 243½ (23) | KO 11 |
| April 27, 1968 | Oakland, Calif. | Jimmy Ellis, 197 (28)[9] | Jerry Quarry, 195 (22) | 15 |
| Feb. 16, 1970 | New York | Joe Frazier, 205 (26)[10] | Jimmy Ellis, 201 (29) | KO 5 |
| Jan. 22, 1973 | Kingston, Jamaica | George Foreman, 217½ (24) | Joe Frazier, 214 (29) | KO 2 |
| Oct. 30, 1974 | Kinshasa, Zaire | Muhammad Ali, 216½ (32) | George Foreman, 220 (26) | KO 8 |
| Feb. 15, 1978 | Las Vegas, Nev. | Leon Spinks, 197 (25) | Muhammad Ali, 224½ (36) | 15 |
| June 9, 1978 | Las Vegas, Nev. | Larry Holmes, 212 (28)[11] | Ken Norton, 220 (32) | 15 |
| Sept. 15, 1978 | New Orleans | Muhammad Ali, 221 (36)[12] | Leon Spinks, 201 (25) | 15 |
| Oct. 20, 1979 | Pretoria, S. Africa | John Tate, 240 (24)[13] | Gerrie Coetzee, 222 (24) | 15 |
| March 31, 1980 | Knoxville, Tenn. | Mike Weaver, 207½ (27) | John Tate, 232 (25) | KO 15 |
| Dec. 10, 1982 | Las Vegas, Nev. | Michael Dokes, 216 (24) | Mike Weaver, 209½ (30) | KO 1 |
| Sept. 23, 1983 | Richfield, Ohio | Gerrie Coetzee, 215 (28) | Michael Dokes, 217 (25) | KO 10 |
| March 9, 1984 | Las Vegas, Nev. | Tim Witherspoon, 220½ (26)[14] | Greg Page, 239½ (25) | 12 |
| Aug. 31, 1984 | Las Vegas, Nev. | Pinklon Thomas, 216 (26) | Tim Witherspoon, 217 (26) | 12 |
| Nov. 9, 1984 | Las Vegas, Nev. | Larry Holmes, 221½ (35)[15] | James Smith, 227 (31) | KO 12 |
| Dec. 1, 1984 | Sun City, S. Africa | Greg Page, 236 (25)[16] | Gerry Coetzee, 217 (29) | KO 8 |
| April 29, 1985 | Buffalo, N.Y. | Tony Tubbs, 229 (26)[16] | Greg Page, 239½ (26) | 15 |
| Sept. 21,1985 | Las Vegas, Nev. | Michael Spinks, 200 (29) | Larry Holmes, 221 (35) | 15 |
| Jan. 17, 1986 | Atlanta, Ga. | Tim Witherspoon, 227 (28) | Tony Tubbs, 229 (27) | 15 |
| Nov. 23, 1986 | Las Vegas, Nev. | Mike Tyson, 217 (20)[17] | Trevor Berbick, 220 (29) | KO 2 |
| Dec. 12, 1986 | New York, N.Y. | James Smith, 230 (33)[16] | Tim Witherspoon, 218 (29) | KO 1 |
| March 7, 1987 | Las Vegas, Nev. | Mike Tyson, 217 (20)[16] | James Smith, 230 (33) | 12 |
| Feb. 10, 1990 | Tokyo | James "Buster" Douglas, 231½ (29)[18] | Mike Tyson, 220 (23) | KO 10 |
| Oct. 25, 1990 | Las Vegas, Nev. | Evander Holyfield, 208 (28) | James "Buster" Douglas, 246 (30) | KO 3 |
| Nov. 13, 1992 | Las Vegas, Nev. | Riddick Bowe,[19] 235 (25) | Evander Holyfield, 205 (30) | 12 |
| Nov. 6, 1993 | Las Vegas, Nev. | Evander Holyfield, 217 (30) | Riddick Bowe, 246 (26) | 12 |
| April 22, 1994 | Las Vegas, Nev. | Michael Moorer, 214 (26) | Evander Holyfield,[20] 214 (31) | 12 |
| Sept 24, 1994 | London | Oliver McCall,[21] 228 (29) | Lennox Lewis, 238 (28) | 2 |
| Nov. 5, 1994 | Las Vegas, Nev. | George Foreman,[22] 250 (45) | Michael Moorer, 222 (26) | 10 |
| April 8, 1995 | Las Vegas, Nev. | Bruce Seldon,[23] 232 (28) | Tony Tucker, 238 (36) | 7 |
| Dec.9, 1995 | Stuttgart, Ger. | Frans Botha,[24] 227 (28) | Axel Schulz, 222 (27) | 12 |
| March 16, 1996 | Las Vegas, Nev. | Mike Tyson,[25] 220 (29) | Frank Bruno, 247 (34) | 3 |
| June 22, 1996 | Dortmund, Ger. | Michael Moorer, 222 (28) | Axel Schulz, 222 (27) | 12 |
| Sept. 7, 1996 | Las Vegas, Nev. | Mike Tyson, 219 (30) | Bruce Seldon, 229 (29) | 1 |
| Nov. 9, 1996 | Las Vegas, Nev. | Evander Holyfield,[23] 215 (34) | Mike Tyson, 222 (30) | 11 |
| Feb. 7, 1997 | Las Vegas, Nev. | Lennox Lewis,[25] 251 (31) | Oliver McCall, 237 (30) | 5 |
| Nov. 8, 1997 | Las Vegas, Nev. | Evander Holyfield,[26] 214 (35) | Michael Moorer, 223 (30) | 8 |
| Nov. 13, 1999 | Las Vegas, Nev. | Lennox Lewis,[23, 27] 240 (33) | Evander Holyfield, 217 (36) | 12 |
| Aug. 12, 2000 | Las Vegas, Nev. | Evander Holyfield,[23] 221 (37) | John Ruiz, 224 (24) | 12 |
| March 3, 2001 | Las Vegas, Nev. | John Ruiz,[23] 227 (27) | Evander Holyfield, 217 (38) | 12 |
| Apr. 21, 2001 | Carnival City, South Africa | Hasim Rahman, [25, 26] 237 (28) | Lennox Lewis, 253 (35) | KO 5 |
| Nov. 17, 2001 | Las Vegas, Nev. | Lennox Lewis,[25, 26] 246 (36) | Hasim Rahman, 236 (29) | KO 4 |

1. Jeffries retired as champion in March 1905. He named Marvin Hart and Jack Root as leading contenders and agreed to referee their fight in Reno, Nev., on July 3, 1905, with the stipulation that he would term the winner the champion. Hart, 190 (28), knocked out Root, 171 (29), in the 12th round. 2. Burns claimed the title after defeating Hart. 3. Tunney retired as champion after defeating Tom Heeney on July 26, 1928. 4. After Louis announced his retirement as champion on March 1,

1949, Charles won recognition from the National Boxing Association as champion by defeating Walcott. 5. Charles gained undisputed recognition as champion by defeating Louis, who came out of retirement. 6. Retired as champion April 27, 1956. 7. The World Boxing Association (WBA) later withdrew its recognition of Clay as champion and declared the winner of a bout between Ernie Terrell and Eddie Machen would gain its version of the title. Terrell, 199 (25), won a 15-round decision from Machen, 192 (32), in Chicago on March 5, 1965. Clay, 212¼ (25) and Terrell, 212½ (27), met in Houston on Feb. 6, 1967, Clay winning a 15-round decision. 8. Winner recognized by N.Y., Mass., Maine, Ill., Tex. and Pa. to fill vacated title when Clay was stripped of championship for failing to accept U.S. Induction. 9. Bout was final of eight-man tournament to fill Clay's place and is recognized by World Boxing Association. 10. Bout settled controversy over title. 11. Holmes won World Boxing Council title after WBC had withdrawn recognition of Spinks, March 18, 1978, and awarded its title to Norton. WBC said Spinks had reneged on agreement to fight Norton. 12. Ali regained World Boxing Association championship. 13. Tate won WBA title after Ali retired and left it vacant. 14. Tim Witherspoon and Greg Page fought for the WBC heavyweight title vacated by Larry Holmes, who could not come to agreement on a deal to fight Page, the No. 1 contender. Holmes declared he would fight under the banner of the International Boxing Federation (IBF). Several dates were set and postponed for fights between Holmes and Gerry Coetzee, the WBA champ, the latest being Nov. 16, 1984. 15. First fight under banner of International Boxing Federation. 16. New WBA champion. 17. New WBC champion. 18. New undisputed champion. 19. The WBC stripped Bowe of its version of the title in December 1992 and named Lennox Lewis champion. 20. After the loss, Holyfield retired. 21. New WBC champion. Lennox Lewis had been named champion in 1992 and had won three title defenses before losing to McCall. 22. For combined WBA/IBF titles. Later WBA stripped Foreman of title for failing to fight no. 1 contender Tony Tucker. IBF also stripped Foreman on June 29, 1995. 23. New WBA champion. 24. Botha later tested positive for steroids and was stripped of the title. 25. New WBC champion. 26. New IBF champion. 27. Surrendered WBA title to fight Michael Grant in unsanctioned bout.

## OTHER WORLD BOXING TITLEHOLDERS
### (Through Aug. 13, 2002)

### Light Heavyweight

| | | |
|---|---|---|
| 1903 | Jack Root, George Gardner | |
| 1903–05 | Bob Fitzsimmons | |
| 1905–12 | Philadelphia Jack O'Brien[1] | |
| 1912–16 | Jack Dillon | |
| 1916–20 | Battling Levinsky | |
| 1920–22 | Georges Carpentier | |
| 1923 | Battling Siki | |
| 1923–25 | Mike McTigue | |
| 1925–26 | Paul Berlenbach | |
| 1926–27 | Jack Delaney[2] | |
| 1927 | Mike McTigue | |
| 1927–29 | Tommy Loughran | |
| 1930 | Jimmy Slattery | |
| 1930–34 | Maxie Rosenbloom | |
| 1934–35 | Bob Olin | |
| 1935–39 | John Henry Lewis | |
| 1939 | Melio Bettina | |
| 1939–41 | Billy Conn[2] | |
| 1941 | Anton Christoforidis (NBA) | |
| 1941–48 | Gus Lesnevich | |
| 1948–50 | Freddie Mills | |
| 1950–52 | Joey Maxim | |
| 1952–61 | Archie Moore[3] | |
| 1961–63 | Harold Johnson | |
| 1963–65 | Willie Pastrano | |
| 1965–66 | José Torres | |
| 1966–67 | Dick Tiger | |
| 1968 | Dick Tiger, Bob Foster | |
| 1969–70 | Bob Foster | |
| 1971 | Vicente Rondon (WBA), Bob Foster (WBC) | |
| 1972–73 | Bob Foster (WBA, WBC) | |
| 1974 | John Conteh (WBA), Bob Foster (WBC)[1, 4] | |
| 1975–76 | Victor Galindez (WBA), John Conteh (WBC) | |
| 1977 | Victor Galindez (WBA), John Conteh (WBC)[4], Miguel Cuello (WBC) | |
| 1978 | Victor Galindez (WBA), Mike Rossman (WBA), Miguel Cuello (WBC), Mate Parlov (WBC), Marvin Johnson (WBC) | |
| 1979 | Mike Rossman (WBA), Victor Galindez (WBA), Marvin Johnson (WBC), Matthew (Franklin) Saad Muhammad (WBC) | |

| | | |
|---|---|---|
| 1980 | Matthew Saad Muhammad (WBC), Marvin Johnson (WBA), Eddie (Gregory) Mustafa Muhammad (WBA) | |
| 1981 | Matthew Saad Muhammad (WBC), Eddie Mustafa Muhammad (WBA), Michael Spinks (WBA), Dwight Braxton (WBC) | |
| 1982 | Dwight Braxton (WBC), Michael Spinks (WBA) | |
| 1983 | Michael Spinks (undisputed) | |
| 1984 | Michael Spinks (undisputed) | |
| 1985 | Michael Spinks (undisputed)[5] | |
| 1986 | Marvin Johnson (WBA), Dennis Andries (WBC) | |
| 1987 | Thomas Hearns (WBC), Virgil Hill (WBA), Bobby Czyz (IBF) | |
| 1988 | Charles Williams (IBF), Virgil Hill (WBA), Donny LaLonde (WBC), Sugar Ray Leonard (WBC) | |
| 1989 | Dennis Andries (WBC), Virgil Hill (WBA), Charles Williams (IBF), Jeff Harding (WBC) | |
| 1990 | Virgil Hill (WBA), Charles Williams (IBF), Jeff Harding (WBC), Dennis Andries (WBC) | |
| 1991 | Virgil Hill (WBA), Thomas Hearns (WBA), Dennis Andries (WBC), Charles Williams (IBF) | |
| 1992 | Charles Williams (IBF), James Waring (IBF), Jeff Harding (WBC) | |
| 1993 | Virgil Hill (WBA), Jeff Harding (WBC), Henry Maske (IBF) | |
| 1994 | Virgil Hill (WBA), Mike McCallum (WBC), Henry Maske (IBF) | |

| | | |
|---|---|---|
| 1995 | Virgil Hill (WBA), Fabio Tiozzo (WBC), Henry Maske (IBF) | |
| 1996–97 | Virgil Hill (WBA), Fabio Tiozzo (WBC), Henry Maske (IBF) | |
| 1998 | Roy Jones (WBA, WBC), Reggie Johnson (IBF) | |
| 1999–2001 | Roy Jones (WBA, WBC, IBF) | |
| 2002 | Bruno Girard (WBA), Roy Jones (WBC, IBF) | |

### Middleweight

| | | |
|---|---|---|
| 1867–72 | Tom Chandler | |
| 1872–81 | George Rooke | |
| 1881–82 | Mike Donovan[1] | |
| 1884–91 | Jack (Nonpareil) Dempsey | |
| 1891–97 | Bob Fitzsimmons[2] | |
| 1908 | Stanley Ketchel, Billy Papke | |
| 1908–10 | Stanley Kotohol[3] | |
| 1913 | Frank Klaus | |
| 1913–14 | George Chip | |
| 1914–17 | Al McCoy | |
| 1917–20 | Mike O'Dowd | |
| 1920–23 | Johnny Wilson | |
| 1923–26 | Harry Greb | |
| 1926 | Tiger Flowers | |
| 1926–31 | Mickey Walker[2] | |
| 1931–41 | Gorilla Jones, Ben Jeby, Marcel Thil, Lou Brouillard, Vince Dundee, Teddy Yarosz, Babe Risko, Freddy Steele, Al Hostak, Solly Krelger, Fred Apostoli, Cerferino Garcia, Ken Overlin, Billy Soose, Tony Zale[4] | |
| 1941–47 | Tony Zale | |
| 1947–48 | Rocky Graziano | |
| 1948 | Tony Zale | |
| 1948–49 | Marcel Cerdan | |
| 1949–51 | Jake LaMotta | |
| 1951–52 | Ray Robinson[1] | |
| 1952 | Ray Robinson, Randy Turpin | |
| 1953–55 | Carl Olson | |
| 1955–57 | Ray Robinson[5] | |
| 1957 | Gene Fullmer, Ray Robinson | |
| 1957–58 | Carmen Basilio | |
| 1958–60 | Ray Robinson[6] | |
| 1959–62 | Gene Fullmer (NBA) | |
| 1960–61 | Paul Pender[7] | |
| 1961–62 | Terry Downes[1] | |
| 1962 | Paul Pender[1] | |
| 1962–63 | Dick Tiger | |

---

1. Retired. 2. Abandoned title. 3. NBA withdrew recognition in 1961, New York Commission in 1962; recognized thereafter only by California and Europe. 4. WBC withdrew recognition. 5. Spinks relinquished title in 1985 to fight for heavyweight title.

| | |
|---|---|
| 1963–65 | Joey Giardello |
| 1965–66 | Dick Tiger |
| 1966 | Emile Griffith |
| 1967 | Nino Benvenuti, Emile Griffith |
| 1968 | Emile Griffith, Nino Benvenuti |
| 1969 | Nino Benvenuti |
| 1970 | Nino Benvenuti, Carlos Monzon |
| 1971–73 | Carlos Monzon |
| 1974–75 | Carlos Monzon (WBA), Rodrigo Valdez (WBC) |
| 1976 | Carlos Monzon (WBA, WBC), Rodrigo Valdez (WBC) |
| 1977 | Carlos Monzon (WBA, WBC),[1] Rodrigo Valdez (WBA, WBC) |
| 1978 | Rodrigo Valdez, Hugo Corro |
| 1979 | Hugo Corro, Vito Antuofermo |
| 1980 | Vito Antuofermo, Alan Minter, Marvin Hagler |
| 1981 | Marvin Hagler |
| 1982–86 | Marvin Hagler (undisputed) |
| 1987 | Marvin Hagler (undisputed), Sugar Ray Leonard (undisputed) |
| 1988 | Sumbu Kalambay (WBA), Thomas Hearns (WBC), Iran Barkley (WBC), Frank Tate (IBF), Michael Nunn (IBF), James Kinchen (NABF) |
| 1989 | Michael Nunn (IBF), Mike McCallum (WBA), Iran Barkley (WBC), Roberto Duran (WBC) |
| 1990 | Michael McCallum (WBA), Michael Nunn (IBF), Iran Barkley (WBC) |
| 1991 | Michael Nunn (IBF), James Toney (IBF), Michael McCallum (WBA) |
| 1992 | James Toney (IBF), Julian Jackson (WBC), Reggie Johnson (WBA) |
| 1993 | Reggie Johnson (WBA), Gerald McClellan (WBA), Roy Jones (IBF) |
| 1994 | Julian Jackson (WBA), Gerald McClellan (WBA), Roy Jones (IBF) |
| 1995 | Jorge Castro (WBA), Julian Jackson (WBC), Bernard Hopkins (IBF) |
| 1996 | William Joppy (WBA), Keith Holmes (WBC), Bernard Hopkins (IBF) |
| 1997 | Shinji Takehara (WBA), Quincy Taylor (WBC), Bernard Hopkins (IBF) |
| 1998 | William Joppy (WBA), Hassine Cherifi (WBC), Bernard Hopkins (IBF) |
| 1999–2000 | William Joppy (WBA), Keith Holmes (WBC), Bernard Hopkins (IBF) |
| 2001 | Felix Trinidad (WBA), Bernard Hopkins (WBC, IBF) |
| 2002 | William Joppy (WBA), Bernard Hopkins (WBC, IBF) |

1. Retired. 2. Abandoned title. 3. Died. 4. National Boxing Association and New York Commission disagreed on champions. Those listed were accepted by one or the other until Zale gained world-wide recognition. 5. Ended retirement in 1954. 6. NBA withdrew recognition. 7. Recognized by New York, Massachusetts, and Europe.

## Welterweight

| | |
|---|---|
| 1892–94 | Mysterious Billy Smith |
| 1894–96 | Tommy Ryan |
| 1896 | Kid McCoy[1] |
| 1896– 1900 | Mysterious Billy Smith |
| 1900 | Rube Ferns |
| 1900–01 | Matty Matthews |
| 1901 | Ruby Ferns |
| 1901–04 | Joe Walcott |
| 1904 | Dixie Kid[1] |
| 1904–06 | Joe Walcott |
| 1906–07 | Honey Mellody |
| 1907 | Mike (Twin) Sullivan[1] |
| 1915–19 | Ted Lewis |
| 1919–22 | Jack Britton |
| 1922–26 | Mickey Walker |
| 1926–27 | Pete Latzo |
| 1927–29 | Joe Dundee |
| 1929–30 | Jackie Fields |
| 1930 | Young Jack Thompson |
| 1930–31 | Tommy Freeman |
| 1931 | Young Jack Thompson |
| 1931–32 | Lou Brouillard |
| 1932–33 | Jackie Fields |
| 1933 | Young Corbett 3rd |
| 1933–34 | Jimmy McLarnin, Barney Ross |
| 1934–35 | Jimmy McLarnin |
| 1935–38 | Barney Ross |
| 1938–40 | Henry Armstrong |
| 1940–41 | Fritzie Zivic |
| 1941–46 | Freddie Cochrane |
| 1946 | Marty Servo[2] |
| 1946–51 | Ray Robinson[1] |
| 1951 | Johnny Bratton (NBA) |
| 1951–54 | Kid Gavilan |
| 1954–55 | Johnny Saxton |
| 1955 | Tony DeMarco |
| 1955–56 | Carmen Basilio |
| 1956 | Johnny Saxton |
| 1956–57 | Carmen Basilio[1] |
| 1958 | Virgil Akins |
| 1959–60 | Don Jordan |
| 1960–61 | Benny (Kid) Paret |
| 1961 | Emile Griffith |
| 1961–62 | Benny (Kid) Paret |
| 1962–63 | Emile Griffith, Luis Rodriguez |
| 1963–66 | Emile Griffith[1] |
| 1966–69 | Curtis Cokes |
| 1969 | Curtis Cokes, José Napoles |
| 1970 | José Napoles, Billy Backus |
| 1971 | Billy Backus, José Napoles |
| 1972–74 | José Napoles |
| 1975 | José Napoles (WBA, WBC),[3] Angel Espada (WBA), John Stracey (WBC) |
| 1976 | Angel Espada (WBA), José Cuevas (WBA), John Stracey (WBC), Carlos Palomino |
| 1977–78 | José Cuevas (WBA), Carlos Palomino (WBC) |
| 1979 | José Cuevas (WBA), Carlos Palomino (WBC), Wilfredo Benitez (WBC) |
| 1980 | José Cuevas (WBA), Ray Leonard (WBC), Roberto Duran (WBC), Thomas Hearns (WBA) |
| 1981 | Ray Leonard (WBC), Thomas Hearns (WBA), Ray Leonard (WBC, WBA) |
| 1982 | Ray Leonard |
| 1983–85 | Donald Curry (WBA), Milton McCrory (WBC) |
| 1985–86 | Donald Curry (undisputed) |
| 1987 | Mark Breland (WBA), Marlon Starling (WBA), Lloyd Honeyghan (IBF) |
| 1988 | Marlon Starling (WBA), Tomas Molinares (WBA), Lloyd Honeyghan (WBC), Simon Brown (IBF) |
| 1989 | Mark Breland (WBA), Marlon Starling (WBC), Simon Brown (IBF) |
| 1990 | Mark Breland (WBA), Aaron Davis (WBA), Simon Brown (IBF), Marlon Starling (WBC), Maurice Blocker (WBC) |
| 1991 | Meldrick Taylor (WBA), Simon Brown (IBF, WBC) |
| 1992 | Meldrick Taylor (WBA), James "Buddy" McGirt (WBC), Maurice Blocker (IBF) |
| 1993 | Cristianto Espana (WBA), Pernell Whitaker (WBC), Felix Trinidad (IBF) |
| 1994 | Ike Quartey (WBA), Pernell Whitaker (WBC), Felix Trinidad (IBF) |
| 1995 | Ike Quartey (WBA), Pernell Whitaker (WBC), Felix Trinidad (IBF) |
| 1996–97 | Ike Quartey (WBA), Pernell Whitaker (WBC), Felix Trinidad (IBF) |
| 1998 | Ike Quartey (WBA), Oscar De La Hoya (WBC), Felix Trinidad (IBF) |
| 1999 | James Page (WBA), Oscar De La Hoya (WBC), Felix Trinidad (IBF, WBC) |
| 2000 | James Page (WBA), Shane Mosley (WBC), Vacant (IBF) |
| 2001 | Andrew Lewis (WBA), Shane Mosley (WBC), Vernon Forrest (IBF) |
| 2002 | Ricardo Mayorga (WBA), Vernon Forrest (WBC), Michele Piccirillo (IBF) |

1. Retired. 2. Abandoned title. 3. WBA withdrew recognition.

## Lightweight

| | |
|---|---|
| 1869–99 | Kid Lavigne |
| 1899– 1902 | Frank Erne |
| 1902–08 | Joe Gans |
| 1908–10 | Battling Nelson |
| 1910–12 | Ad Wolgast |
| 1912–14 | Willie Ritchie |
| 1914–17 | Freddy Welsh |
| 1917–25 | Benny Leonard[1] |
| 1925 | Jimmy Goodrich |
| 1925–26 | Rocky Kansas |
| 1926–30 | Sammy Mandell |
| 1930 | Al Singer |
| 1930–33 | Tony Canzoneri |
| 1933–35 | Barney Ross[2] |
| 1935–36 | Tony Canzoneri |
| 1936–38 | Lou Ambers |
| 1938–39 | Henry Armstrong |
| 1939–40 | Lou Ambers |

| 1940–41 | Lew Jenkins |
| 1941–42 | Sammy Angott[1] |
| 1943–47 | Beau Jack (N.Y.), |
| | Bob Montgomery (N.Y.), |
| | Sammy Angott (NBA), |
| | Juan Zurita (NBA), |
| | Ike Williams (NBA) |
| 1947–51 | Ike Williams |
| 1951–52 | James Carter |
| 1952 | Lauro Salas |
| 1952–54 | James Carter |
| 1954 | Paddy DeMarco |
| 1954–55 | James Carter |
| 1955–56 | Wallace Smith |
| 1956–62 | Joe Brown |
| 1962–65 | Carlos Ortiz |
| 1965 | Ismael Laguna |
| 1965–68 | Carlos Ortiz |
| 1968 | Teo Cruz |
| 1969 | Teo Cruz, |
| | Mando Ramos |
| 1970 | Mando Ramos, |
| | Ismael Laguna, |
| | Ken Buchanan |
| 1971 | Ken Buchanan (WBA), |
| | Mando Ramos (WBC), |
| | Pedro Carrasco (WBC) |
| 1972 | Ken Buchanan (WBA), |
| | Roberto Duran (WBA), |
| | Pedro Carrasco (WBC), |
| | Mando Ramos (WBC), |
| | Chango Carmona (WBC), |
| | Rodolfo Gonzalez (WBC) |
| 1973 | Roberto Duran (WBA), |
| | Rodolfo Gonzalez (WBC) |
| 1974 | Roberto Duran (WBA), |
| | Rodolfo Gonzalez (WBC), |
| | Guts Ishimatsu (WBC) |
| 1975 | Roberto Duran (WBA), |
| | Guts Ishimatsu (WBC) |
| 1976 | Roberto Duran (WBA), |
| | Guts Ishimatsu (WBC), |
| | Esteban De Jesus (WBC) |
| 1977 | Roberto Duran (WBA), |
| | Esteban De Jesus (WBC) |
| 1978 | Roberto Duran (WBA, |
| | WBC) |
| 1979 | Roberto Duran,[2] |
| | Jim Watt (WBC), |
| | Ernesto Espana (WBA) |
| 1980 | Ernesto Espana (WBA), |
| | Hilmer Kenty (WBA), |
| | Jim Watt (WBC) |
| 1981 | Hilmer Kenty (WBA), |
| | Sean O'Grady (WBA), |
| | James Watt (WBC), |
| | Alexis Arguello (WBC), |
| | Arturo Frias (WBA) |
| 1982 | Arturo Frias (WBA), |
| | Ray Mancini (WBA), |
| | Alexis Arguello (WBC) |
| 1983 | Edwin Rosario (WBC), |
| | Ray Mancini (WBA) |
| 1984 | Edwin Rosario (WBC), |
| | Livingstone Bramble |
| | (WBA) |
| 1985 | Jose Luis Ramirez (WBC), |
| | Hector Camacho (WBC), |
| | Livingstone Bramble |
| | (WBA) |
| 1986 | Hector Camacho (WBC), |
| | Livingstone Bramble |
| | (WBA), |
| | Jim Paul (IBF) |
| 1987 | Edwin Rosario (WBA), |
| | Jose Luis Ramirez (WBC), |
| | Greg Haugen (IBF) |
| 1988 | Jose Luis Ramirez (WBC), |
| | Julio Cesar Chavez |
| | (WBA), |
| | Greg Haugen (IBF), |
| | Julio Cesar Chavez (WBC |
| | & WBA title unified) |

| 1989 | Pernell Whitaker (IBF, |
| | WBC), |
| | Edwin Rosario (WBA) |
| 1990 | Pernell Whitaker (IBF, |
| | WBC), |
| | Juan Nazario (WBA) |
| 1991 | Pernell Whitaker (IBF, |
| | WBA, WBC) |
| 1992 | Pernell Whitaker (IBF, |
| | WBA, WBC),[3] |
| | Joey Gamache (WBA) |
| 1993 | Dingaan Thobela (WBA), |
| | Angel Gonzalez (WBC), |
| | Freddie Pendleton (IBF) |
| 1994 | Orzubek Nazarov (WBA), |
| | Angel Gonzalez (WBC), |
| | Rafael Ruelas (IBF) |
| 1995 | Orzubek Nazarov (WBA), |
| | Angel Gonzalez (WBC), |
| | Oscar De La Hoya (IBF) |
| 1996 | Gusshie Nazarov (WBA), |
| | Jean Baptiste Mendy |
| | (WBC), |
| | Phillip Holiday (IBF) |
| 1997 | Orzubek Nazarov (WBA), |
| | Jean Baptiste Mendy |
| | (WBC), |
| | Philip Holiday (IBF) |
| 1998 | Jean Baptiste Mendy |
| | (WBA), |
| | Cesar Bazan (WBC), |
| | Shane Mosley (IBF) |
| 1999 | Stefano Zoff (WBA), |
| | Stevie Johnston (WBC), |
| | Paul Spadafora (IBF) |
| 2000 | Takanori Hatakeyama |
| | (WBA), Jose Luis Castillo |
| | (WBC), Paul Spadafora |
| | (IBF) |
| 2001 | Julien Lorcy (WBA), |
| | Jose Luis Castillo (WBC), |
| | Paul Spadafora (IBF) |
| 2002 | Leonard Dorin (WBA), |
| | Floyd Mayweather (WBC), |
| | Paul Spadafora (IBF) |

1. Retired. 2. Abandoned title. 3. Moving up in weight class, so resigned titles.

## Featherweight

| 1889 | Dal Hawkins[1] |
| 1890 | Billy Murphy |
| 1892– | |
| 1900 | George Dixon |
| 1900–01 | Terry McGovern |
| 1901 | Young Corbett[1] |
| 1901–12 | Abe Attell |
| 1912–23 | Johnny Kilbane |
| 1923 | Eugene Criqui |
| 1923–25 | Johnny Dundee[1] |
| 1925–27 | Louis (Kid) Kaplan[1] |
| 1927–28 | Benny Bass |
| 1928 | Tony Canzoneri |
| 1928–29 | Andre Routis |
| 1929–32 | Battling Battalino[1] |
| 1932 | Tommy Paul (NBA), |
| | Kid Chocolate (N.Y.) |
| 1933–36 | Freddie Miller |
| 1936–37 | Petey Sarron |
| 1937–38 | Henry Armstrong[1] |
| 1938–40 | Joey Archibald |
| 1940–41 | Harry Jefra, |
| | Joey Archibald |
| 1941–42 | Chalky Wright |
| 1942–48 | Willie Pep |
| 1948–49 | Sandy Saddler[2] |
| 1949–50 | Willie Pep |
| 1950–57 | Sandy Saddler |
| 1957–59 | Kid Bassey |
| 1959–63 | Davey Moore |
| 1963–64 | Sugar Ramos |
| 1964–67 | Vicente Saldivar[2] |

| 1968 | Howard Winstone, |
| | José Legra,[3] |
| | Paul Rojas (WBA), |
| | Sho Saijo (WBA) |
| 1969 | Sho Saijo (WBA), |
| | Johnny Famechon[3] |
| 1970 | Sho Saijo (WBA), |
| | Johnny Famechon,[3] |
| | Vicente Salvidar,[3] |
| | Kuniaki Shibata[3] |
| 1971 | Sho Saijo (WBA), |
| | Antonio Gomez (WBA), |
| | Kuniaki Shibata (WBC) |
| 1972 | Antonio Gomez (WBA), |
| | Ernesto Marcel (WBA), |
| | Kuniaki Shibata (WBC), |
| | Clemente Sanchez |
| | (WBC), |
| | José Legra (WBC) |
| 1973 | Ernesto Marcel (WBA), |
| | José Legra (WBC), |
| | Eder Jofre (WBC) |
| 1974 | Ernesto Marcel (WBA),[2] |
| | Ruben Olivares (WBA), |
| | Alexis Arguello (WBA), |
| | Eder Jofre (WBC) |
| 1975 | Alexis Arguello (WBA), |
| | Bobby Chacon (WBC), |
| | Ruben Olivares (WBC), |
| | David Kotey (WBC) |
| 1976 | Alexis Arguello (WBA),[2] |
| | David Kotey (WBC), |
| | Danny Lopez (WBC) |
| 1977 | Rafael Ortega (WBA), |
| | Danny Lopez (WBC) |
| 1978 | Rafael Ortega (WBA), |
| | Cecilio Lastra (WBA), |
| | Eusebio Pedroza (WBA), |
| | Danny Lopez (WBC) |
| 1979 | Eusebio Pedroza (WBA), |
| | Danny Lopez (WBC) |
| 1980 | Eusebio Pedroza (WBA), |
| | Danny Lopez (WBC), |
| | Salvador Sanchez (WBC) |
| 1981 | Eusebio Pedroza (WBA), |
| | Salvador Sanchez (WBC) |
| 1982 | Eusebio Pedroza (WBA), |
| | Salvador Sanchez (WBC)[4] |
| 1983 | Juan Laporte (WBC), |
| | Eusebio Pedroza (WBA) |
| 1984 | Wilfred Gomez (WBC), |
| | Eusebio Pedroza (WBA) |
| 1985 | Eusebio Pedroza (WBA), |
| | Barry McGuigan (WBA), |
| | Azumah Nelson (WBC) |
| 1986 | Barry McGuigan (WBA), |
| | Stevie Cruz (WBA), |
| | Azumah Nelson (WBC) |
| 1987 | Azumah Nelson (WBC), |
| | Antonio Esparragoza |
| | (WBA) |
| 1988 | Calvin Grove (IBF), |
| | Jorge Paez (IBF), |
| | Antonio Esparragoza |
| | (WBA), |
| | Jeff Fenech (WBC) |
| 1989 | Jorge Paez (IBF), |
| | Antonio Esparragoza |
| | (WBA), |
| | Jeff Fenech (WBC) |
| 1990 | Marcos Villasana (WBC), |
| | Antonio Esparragoza |
| | (WBA), |
| | Jorge Paez (IBF) |
| 1991 | Yung-Kyun Park (WBA), |
| | Troy Dorsey (IBF), |
| | Marcos Villagana (WBC) |
| 1992 | Paul Hodkinson (WBC), |
| | Manuel Medina (IBF), |
| | Yung-Kyun Park (WBA) |

| | | | | | |
|---|---|---|---|---|---|
| 1993 | Yung-Kyun Park (WBA), Goyo Vargas (WBC), Tom Johnson (IBF) | 1937 | Sixto Escobar, Harry Jeffra | 1981 | Lupe Pintor (WBC), Jeff Chandler (WBA) |
| 1994 | Eloy Rojas (WBA), Kevin Kelley (WBC), Tom Johnson (IBF) | 1938 | Harry Jeffra, Sixto Escobar | 1982 | Lupe Pintor (WBC), Jeff Chandler (WBA) |
| 1995 | Eloy Rojas (WBA), Alejandro Gonzalez (WBC), Tom Johnson (IBF) | 1939–40 | Sixto Escobar[2] | 1983 | Jeff Chandler (WBA), Albert Dauila (WBC) |
| | | 1940–42 | Lou Salica | 1984 | Richie Sandqual (WBA), Albert Dauila (WBC) |
| 1996 | Wilfredo Vázquez (WBA), Luisto Espinoza (WBC), Tom Johnson (IBF) | 1942–46 | Manuel Ortiz | 1985 | Richard Sandoval (WBA), Daniel Zaragoza (WBC), Miguel Lora (WBC) |
| | | 1947 | Manuel Ortiz, Harold Dade | | |
| 1997 | Elroy Rojas (WBA), Luisito Espinoza (WBC), Tom Johnson (IBF) | 1948–50 | Manuel Ortiz | 1986 | Richard Sandoval (WBA), Bernardo Pinango (WBA), Jeff Fenech (IBF) |
| | | 1950–52 | Vic Toweel | | |
| 1998 | vacant (WBA), Luisito Espinoza (WBC), Manuel Medina (IBF) | 1952–54 | Jimmy Carruthers[2] | 1987 | Bernardo Pinango (WBA), Takuya Muguruma (WBA), Miguel Lora (WBC) |
| | | 1954–55 | Robert Cohen | | |
| 1999 | Freddie Norwood (WBA), Cesar Soto (WBC), Manuel Medina (IBF) | 1956 | Robert Cohen, Mario D'Agata, Raul Macias (NBA) | 1988 | Wilfredo Vásquez (WBA), Jibaro Perez (WBC), Moon Sung-gil (WBA), Orlando Canizales (IBF) |
| 2000 | Freddie Norwood (WBA), Guty Espadas (WBC), Paul Ingle (IBF) | 1957 | Mario D'Agata, Alphonse Halimi | 1989 | Jibaro Perez (WBC), Moon Sung-gil (WBA), Orlando Canizales (IBF), Kaokor Galaxy (WBA), Luis Espinosa (WBA) |
| | | 1958–59 | Alphonse Halimi | | |
| 2001 | Derrick Gainer (WBA), Erik Morales (WBC), Frankie Toledo (IBF) | 1959–60 | Jose Becerra[2] | | |
| | | 1960–61 | Alphonse Halimi[4] | | |
| | | 1961–62 | Johnny Caldwell[4] | 1990 | Orlando Canizales (IBF), Jibaro Perez (WBC), Luis Espinosa (WBA) |
| 2002 | Derrick Gainer (WBA), vacant (WBC), Johnny Tapia (IBF) | 1961–65 | Eder Jofre | | |
| | | 1965–68 | Masahika "Fighting" Harada | 1991 | Greg Richardson (WBC), Orlando Canizales (IBF), Luis Espinosa (WBA) |
| | | 1968 | Masahika "Fighting" Harada, Lionel Rose | | |
| | | 1969 | Lionel Rose, Ruben Olivares | 1992 | Joichiro Tatsuyoshi (WBC), Victor Manuel Rabanales (WBC), Eddie Cook (WBA), Orlando Gonzales (IBF) |
| | | 1970 | Ruben Olivares, Chucho Castillo | | |
| | | 1971 | Chucho Castillo, Ruben Olivares | 1993 | Jorge Julio (WBA), Byun-Jong-il (WBC), Orlando Canizales (IBF) |
| | | 1972 | Ruben Olivares, Rafael Herrera, Enrique Pinder | 1994 | John Michael Johnson (WBA), Yasuei Yakushiji (WBC), Orlando Canizales (IBF) |
| | | 1973 | Enrique Pinder (WBA), Romeo Anaya (WBA), Arnold Taylor (WBA), Rodolfo Martinez (WBC), Rafael Herrera | 1995 | Daorun Chuwatang (WBA), Yasuei Yakushiji (WBC), Mbulelo Botile (IBF) |
| | | 1974 | Arnold Taylor (WBA), Soo Hwan Hong (WBA), Rafael Herrera (WBC), Rodolfo Martinez (WBC) | 1996–97 | Nana Konadu (WBA), Wayne McCullough (WBC), Mbulelo Botile (IBF) |
| | | 1975 | Soo Hwan Hong (WBA), Alfonso Zamora (WBA), Rodolfo Martinez (WBC) | 1998 | Nana Konadu (WBA), Joichiro Tatsuyoshi (WBC), Tim Austin (IBF) |
| | | 1976 | Alfonso Zamora (WBA), Rodolfo Martinez (WBC), Carlos Zarate (WBC) | 1999– 2001 | Paulie Ayala (WBA), Veeraphol Sahaprom (WBC), Tim Austin (IBF) |
| | | 1977 | Alfonso Zamora (WBA), Jorge Lujan (WBA), Carlos Zarate (WBC) | 2002 | Johnny Bredahl (WBA), Veeraphol Sahaprom (WBC), Tim Austin (IBF) |
| | | 1978 | Jorge Lujan (WBA), Carlos Zarate (WBC) | | |

1. Abandoned title. 2. Retired. 3. Recognized in Europe, Mexico, and Orient. 4. Killed in auto accident.

**Bantamweight**

| | |
|---|---|
| 1890–92 | George Dixon[1] |
| 1894–99 | Jimmy Barry[2] |
| 1899– | |
| 1900 | Terry McGovern[1] |
| 1901 | Harry Harris[1] |
| 1902–03 | Harry Forbes |
| 1903–04 | Frankie Neil |
| 1904 | Joe Bowker[1] |
| 1905–07 | Jimmy Walsh[1] |
| 1910–14 | Johnny Coulon |
| 1914–17 | Kid Williams |
| 1917–20 | Pete Herman |
| 1920 | Joe Lynch |
| 1920–21 | Joe Lynch, Pete Herman, Johnny Buff |
| 1922 | Johnny Buff, Joe Lynch |
| 1923 | Joe Lynch |
| 1924 | Joe Lynch, Abe Goldstein, Eddie "Cannonball" Martin |
| 1925 | Eddie "Cannonball" Martin, Charlie (Phil) Rosenberg[3] |
| 1927–28 | Bud Taylor (NBA)[1] |
| 1929–34 | Al Brown |
| 1935 | Al Brown, Baltazar Sangchili |
| 1936 | Baltazar Sangchili, Tony Marino, Sixto Escobar |

(1979: Jorge Lujan (WBA), Carlos Zarate (WBC), Lupe Pintor (WBC); 1980: Jorge Lujan (WBA), Lupe Pintor (WBC), Julian Solis (WBA), Jeff Chandler (WBA))

1. Abandoned title. 2. Retired. 3. Deprived of title for failing to make weight. 4. Recognized in Europe.

# Horse Racing

Ancient drawings on stone and bone prove that horse racing is at least 3,000 years old, but thoroughbred racing is a modern development. Practically every thoroughbred in training today traces its registered ancestry back to one or more of three sires that arrived in England about 1728 from the Near East and became known, from the names of their owners, as the Byerly Turk, the Darley Arabian, and the Godolphin Arabian. The Jockey Club (English) was founded at Newmarket in 1750 or 1751 and became the custodian of the Stud Book as well as the court of last resort in deciding turf affairs.

Horse racing took place in this country before the Revolution, but the great lift to the breeding industry came with the importation in 1798, by Col. John Hoomes of Virginia, of Diomed, winner of the Epsom Derby of 1780. Diomed's lineal descendants included such famous 19th-century stars of the American turf as American Eclipse, Sir Archy, and Lexington. From 1800 to the time of the Civil War there were race courses and breeding establishments plentifully scattered through Virginia, North Carolina, South Carolina, Tennessee, Kentucky, and Louisiana.

The oldest stake event in North America is the Queen's Plate, a Canadian fixture that was first run in the Province of Quebec in 1836. The oldest stake event in the United States is the Travers, which was first run at Saratoga in 1864. The gambling that goes with horse racing and trickery by jockeys, trainers, owners, and track officials caused attacks on the sport by reformers and a demand among horse racing enthusiasts for an honest and effective control of some kind, but nothing of lasting value to racing came of this until the formation in 1894 of the Jockey Club (American).

## "TRIPLE CROWN" WINNERS IN THE UNITED STATES
### (Kentucky Derby, Preakness, and Belmont Stakes)

| Year | Horse | Owner | Year | Horse | Owner |
|---|---|---|---|---|---|
| 1919 | Sir Barton | J. K. L. Ross | 1946 | Assault | Robert J. Kleberg |
| 1930 | Gallant Fox | William Woodward | 1948 | Citation | Warren Wright |
| 1935 | Omaha | William Woodward | 1973 | Secretariat | Meadow Stable |
| 1937 | War Admiral | Samuel D. Riddle | 1977 | Seattle Slew | Karen Taylor |
| 1941 | Whirlaway | Warren Wright | 1978 | Affirmed | Louis Wolfson |
| 1943 | Count Fleet | Mrs. John Hertz | | | |

## KENTUCKY DERBY
### Churchill Downs; 3-year-olds; 1¼ mi.

| Year | Winner | Jockey | Year | Winner | Jockey | Year | Winner | Jockey |
|---|---|---|---|---|---|---|---|---|
| 1875 | Aristides | O. Lewis | 1920 | Paul Jones | T. Rice | 1964 | Northern | |
| 1876 | Vagrant | R. Swim | 1921 | Behave Yourself | C. Thompson | | Dancer | W. Hartack |
| 1877 | Baden Baden | W. Walker | 1922 | Morvich | A. Johnson | 1965 | Lucky Debonair | W. Shoemaker |
| 1878 | Day Star | J. Carter | 1923 | Zev | E. Sande | 1966 | Kauai King | D. Brumfield |
| 1879 | Lord Murphy | C. Shauer | 1924 | Black Gold | J. D. Mooney | 1967 | Proud Clarion | R. Ussery |
| 1880 | Fonso | G. Lewis | 1925 | Flying Ebony | E. Sande | 1968 | Forward Pass[1] | I. Valenzuela |
| 1881 | Hindoo | J. McLaughlin | 1926 | Bubbling Over | A. Johnson | 1969 | Majestic Prince | W. Hartack |
| 1882 | Apollo | B. Hurd | 1927 | Whiskery | L. McAtee | 1970 | Dust Com- | |
| 1883 | Leonatus | W. Donohue | 1928 | Reigh Count | C. Lang | | mander | M. Manganello |
| 1884 | Buchanan | I. Murphy | 1929 | Clyde Van | | 1971 | Canonero II | G. Avila |
| 1885 | Joe Cotton | B. Henderson | | Dusen | L. McAtee | 1972 | Riva Ridge | R. Turcotte |
| 1886 | Ben Ali | P. Duffy | 1930 | Gallant Fox | E. Sande | 1973 | Secretariat | R. Turcotte |
| 1887 | Montrose | I. Lewis | 1931 | Twenty Grand | C. Kurtsinger | 1974 | Cannonade | A. Cordero, Jr. |
| 1888 | Macbeth II | G. Covington | 1932 | Burgoo King | E. James | 1975 | Foolish Plea- | |
| 1889 | Spokane | T. Kiley | 1933 | Brokers Tip | D. Meade | | sure | J. Vasquez |
| 1890 | Riley | I. Murphy | 1934 | Cavalcade | M. Garner | 1976 | Bold Forbes | A. Cordero, Jr. |
| 1891 | Kingman | I. Murphy | 1935 | Omaha | W. Saunders | 1977 | Seattle Slew | J. Cruguet |
| 1892 | Azra | L. Clayton | 1936 | Bold Venture | I. Hanford | 1978 | Affirmed | S. Cauthen |
| 1893 | Lookout | E. Kunze | 1937 | War Admiral | C. Kurtsinger | 1979 | Spectacular Bid | R. Franklin |
| 1894 | Chant | F. Goodale | 1938 | Lawrin | E. Arcaro | 1980 | Genuine Risk | J. Vasquez |
| 1895 | Halma | S. Perkins | 1939 | Johnstown | J. Stout | 1981 | Pleasant Colony | J. Velasquez |
| 1896 | Ben Brush | W. Simms | 1940 | Gallahadion | C. Bierman | 1982 | Gato del Sol | E. Delahoussaye |
| 1897 | Typhoon II | B. Garner | 1941 | Whirlaway | E. Arcaro | 1983 | Sunny's Halo | E. Delahoussaye |
| 1898 | Plaudit | W. Simms | 1942 | Shut Out | W. D. Wright | 1984 | Swale | L. Pincay, Jr. |
| 1899 | Manuel | F. Taral | 1943 | Count Fleet | J. Longden | 1985 | Spend a Buck | A. Cordero, Jr. |
| 1900 | Lieut. Gibson | J. Boland | 1944 | Pensive | C. McCreary | 1986 | Ferdinand | W. Shoemaker |
| 1901 | His Eminence | J. Winkfield | 1945 | Hoop Jr. | E. Arcaro | 1987 | Alysheba | C. McCarron |
| 1902 | Alan-a-Dale | J. Winkfield | 1946 | Assault | W. Mehrtens | 1988 | Winning Colors | G. Stevens |
| 1903 | Judge Himes | H. Booker | 1947 | Jet Pilot | F. Guerin | 1989 | Sunday Silence | P. Valenzuela |
| 1904 | Elwood | F. Prio | 1948 | Citation | E. Arcaro | 1990 | Unbridled | C. Perret |
| 1905 | Agile | J. Martin | 1949 | Ponder | S. Brooks | 1991 | Strike the Gold | C. Antley |
| 1906 | Sir Huon | R. Troxler | 1950 | Middleground | W. Boland | 1992 | Lil E. Tee | P. Day |
| 1907 | Pink Star | A. Minder | 1951 | Count Turf | O. McCreary | 1993 | Sea Hero | J. Bailey |
| 1908 | Stone Street | A. Pickens | 1952 | Hill Gail | E. Arcaro | 1994 | Go For Gin | C. McCarron |
| 1909 | Wintergreen | V. Powers | 1953 | Dark Star | H. Moreno | 1995 | Thunder Gulch | G. Stevens |
| 1910 | Donau | F. Herbert | 1954 | Determine | R. York | 1996 | Grindstone | J. Bailey |
| 1911 | Meridian | G. Archibald | 1955 | Swaps | W. Shoemaker | 1997 | Silver Charm | G. Stevens |
| 1912 | Worth | C. H. Shilling | 1956 | Needles | D. Erb | 1998 | Real Quiet | K. Desormeaux |
| 1913 | Donerail | R. Goose | 1957 | Iron Liege | W. Hartack | 1999 | Charismatic | C. Antley |
| 1914 | Old Rosebud | J. McCabe | 1958 | Tim Tam | I. Valenzuela | 2000 | Fusaichi | |
| 1915 | Regret | J. Notter | 1959 | Tomy Lee | W. Shoemaker | | Pegasus | K. Desormeaux |
| 1916 | George Smith | J. Loftus | 1960 | Venetian Way | W. Hartack | 2001 | Monarchos | J. Chavez |
| 1917 | Omar Khayyam | C. Borel | 1961 | Carry Back | J. Sellers | 2002 | War Emblem | V. Espinoza |
| 1918 | Exterminator | W. Knapp | 1962 | Decidedly | W. Hartack | | | |
| 1919 | Sir Barton | J. Loftus | 1963 | Chateaugay | B. Baeza | | | |

1. Dancer's Image finished first but was disqualified after traces of drug were found in his system.

# PREAKNESS STAKES
**Pimlico; 3-year-olds; 1³⁄₁₆ mi.**

| Year | Winner | Jockey | Year | Winner | Jockey | Year | Winner | Jockey |
|------|--------|--------|------|--------|--------|------|--------|--------|
| 1873 | Survivor | G. Barbee | 1918 | Jack Hare Jr. | C. Peak | 1962 | Greek Money | J. Rotz |
| 1874 | Culpepper | W. Donohue | 1919 | Sir Barton | J. Loftus | 1963 | Candy Spots | W. Shoemaker |
| 1875 | Tom Ochiltree | L. Hughes | 1920 | Man o' War | C. Kummer | 1964 | Northern Dancer | W. Hartack |
| 1876 | Shirley | G. Barbee | 1921 | Broomspun | F. Coltiletti | 1965 | Tom Rolfe | R. Turcotte |
| 1877 | Cloverbrook | C. Holloway | 1922 | Pillory | L. Morris | 1966 | Kauai King | D. Brumfield |
| 1878 | Duke of Magenta | C. Holloway | 1923 | Vigil | B. Marinelli | 1967 | Damascus | W. Shoemaker |
| 1879 | Harold | L. Hughes | 1924 | Nellie Morse | J. Merimee | 1968 | Forward Pass | I. Valenzuela |
| 1880 | Grenada | L. Hughes | 1925 | Coventry | C. Kummer | 1969 | Majestic Prince | W. Hartack |
| 1881 | Saunterer | T. Costello | 1926 | Display | J. Maiben | 1970 | Personality | E. Belmonte |
| 1882 | Vanguard | T. Costello | 1927 | Bostonian | W. Abel | 1971 | Canonero II | G. Avila |
| 1883 | Jacobus | G. Barbee | 1928 | Victorian | S. Workman | 1972 | Bee Bee Bee | E. Nelson |
| 1884 | Knight of Ellerslie | S. Fisher | 1929 | Dr. Freeland | L. Schaefer | 1973 | Secretariat | R. Turcotte |
| 1885 | Tecumseh | J. McLaughlin | 1930 | Gallant Fox | E. Sande | 1974 | Little Current | M. Rivera |
| 1886 | The Bard | S. Fisher | 1931 | Mate | G. Ellis | 1975 | Master Derby | D. McHargue |
| 1887 | Dunboyne | W. Donohue | 1932 | Burgoo King | E. James | 1976 | Elocutionist | J. Lively |
| 1888 | Refund | F. Littlefield | 1933 | Head Play | C. Kurtsinger | 1977 | Seattle Slew | J. Cruguet |
| 1889 | Buddhist | W. Anderson | 1934 | High Quest | R. Jones | 1978 | Affirmed | S. Cauthen |
| 1890 | Montague | W. Martin | 1935 | Omaha | W. Saunders | 1979 | Spectacular Bid | R. Franklin |
| 1891-93 | Not held | | 1936 | Bold Venture | G. Woolf | 1980 | Codex | A. Cordero |
| 1894 | Assignee | F. Taral | 1937 | War Admiral | C. Kurtsinger | 1981 | Pleasant Colony | J. Velasquez |
| 1895 | Belmar | F. Taral | 1938 | Dauber | M. Peters | 1982 | Aloma's Ruler | J. Kaenel |
| 1896 | Margrave | H. Griffin | 1939 | Challedon | G. Seabo | 1983 | Deputed | |
| 1897 | Paul Kauvar | T. Thorpe | 1940 | Bimelech | F.A. Smith | | Testamony | D. Miller |
| 1898 | Sly Fox | W. Simms | 1941 | Whirlaway | E. Arcaro | 1984 | Gate Dancer | A. Cordero |
| 1899 | Half Time | R. Clawson | 1942 | Alsab | B. James | 1985 | Tank's Prospect | P. Day |
| 1900 | Hindus | H. Spencer | 1943 | Count Fleet | J. Longden | 1986 | Snow Chief | A. Solis |
| 1901 | The Parader | F. Landry | 1944 | Pensive | C. McCreary | 1987 | Alysheba | C. McCarron |
| 1902 | Old England | L. Jackson | 1945 | Polynesian | W.D. Wright | 1988 | Risen Star | E. Delahoussaye |
| 1903 | Flocarline | W. Gannon | 1946 | Assault | W. Mehrtens | 1989 | Sunday Silence | P. Valenzuela |
| 1904 | Bryn Mawr | E. Hildebrand | 1947 | Faultless | D. Dodson | 1990 | Summer Squall | P. Day |
| 1905 | Cairngorm | W. Davis | 1948 | Citation | E. Arcaro | 1991 | Hansel | J. Bailey |
| 1906 | Whimsical | W. Miller | 1949 | Capot | T. Atkinson | 1992 | Pine Bluff | C. McCarron |
| 1907 | Don Enrique | G. Mountain | 1950 | Hill Prince | E. Arcaro | 1993 | Prairie Bayou | M. Smith |
| 1908 | Royal Tourist | E. Dugan | 1951 | Bold | E. Arcaro | 1994 | Tabasco Cat | P. Day |
| 1909 | Effendi | W. Doyle | 1952 | Blue Man | C. McCreary | 1995 | Timber Country | P. Day |
| 1910 | Layminster | R. Estep | 1953 | Native Dancer | E. Guerin | 1996 | Louis Quatorze | P. Day |
| 1911 | Watervale | E. Dugan | 1954 | Hasty Road | J. Adams | 1997 | Silver Charm | G. Stevens |
| 1912 | Colonel Holloway | C. Turner | 1955 | Nashua | E. Arcaro | 1998 | Real Quiet | K. Desormeaux |
| 1913 | Buskin | J. Butwell | 1956 | Fabius | W. Hartack | 1999 | Charismatic | C. Antley |
| 1914 | Holiday | A. Schuttinger | 1957 | Bold Ruler | E. Arcaro | 2000 | Red Bullet | J. Bailey |
| 1915 | Rhine Maiden | D. Hoffman | 1958 | Tim Tam | I. Valenzuela | 2001 | Point Given | G. Stevens |
| 1916 | Damrosch | L. McAtee | 1959 | Royal Orbit | W. Harmatz | 2002 | War Emblem | V. Espinoza |
| 1917 | Kalitan | E. Haynes | 1960 | Bally Ache | R. Ussery | | | |
| 1918 | War Cloud | J. Loftus | 1961 | Carry Back | J. Sellers | | | |

# BELMONT STAKES
**Belmont Park; 3-year-olds; 1½ mi.**

Run at Jerome Park 1867 to 1890; at Morris Park 1890–94; at Belmont Park 1905–62; at Aqueduct 1963–67. Distance 1⅝ mi prior to 1874; reduced to 1½ mi, 1874; reduced to 1¼ mi, 1890; reduced to 1⅛ mi, 1893; increased to 1¼ mi, 1895; increased to 1⅜ mi, 1896; reduced to 1¼ mi in 1904; increased to 1½ mi, 1926.

| Year | Winner | Jockey | Year | Winner | Jockey | Year | Winner | Jockey |
|------|--------|--------|------|--------|--------|------|--------|--------|
| 1867 | Ruthless | J. Gilpatrick | 1878 | Duke of Magenta | L. Hughes | 1889 | Eric | W. Hayward |
| 1868 | General Duke | B. Swim | 1879 | Spendthrift | G. Evans | 1890 | Burlington | P. Barnes |
| 1869 | Fenian | C. Miller | 1880 | Grenada | L. Hughes | 1891 | Foxford | E. Garrison |
| 1870 | Kingfisher | W. Dick | 1881 | Saunterer | T. Costello | 1892 | Patron | W. Hayward |
| 1871 | Harry Bassett | W. Miller | 1882 | Forester | J. McLaughlin | 1893 | Commanche | W. Simms |
| 1872 | Joe Daniels | J. Roe | 1883 | George Kinney | J. McLaughlin | 1894 | Henry of Navarre | W. Simms |
| 1873 | Springbok | J. Roe | 1884 | Panique | J. McLaughlin | | (11/2) | |
| 1874 | Saxon | G. Barbee | 1885 | Tyrant | P. Duffy | 1895 | Belmar | F. Taral |
| 1875 | Calvin | B. Swim | 1886 | Inspector B | J. McLaughlin | 1896 | Hastings | H. Griffin |
| 1876 | Algerine | B. Donohue | 1887 | Hanover | J. McLaughlin | 1897 | Scottish Chieftain | J. Scherrer |
| 1877 | Cloverbrook | C. Holloway | 1888 | Sir Dixon | J. McLaughlin | 1898 | Bowling Brook | F. Littlefield |

| Year | Winner | Jockey | Year | Winner | Jockey | Year | Winner | Jockey |
|---|---|---|---|---|---|---|---|---|
| 1899 | Jean Beraud | R. Clawson | 1936 | Granville | J. Stout | 1971 | Pass Catcher | R. Blum |
| 1900 | Ildrim | N. Turner | 1937 | War Admiral | C. Kurtsinger | 1972 | Riva Ridge | R. Turcotte |
| 1901 | Commando | H. Spencer | 1938 | Pasteurized | J. Stout | 1973 | Secretariat | R. Turcotte |
| 1902 | Masterman | J. Bullman | 1939 | Johnstown | J. Stout | 1974 | Little Current | M. Rivera |
| 1903 | Africander | J. Bullman | 1940 | Bimelech | F.A. Smith | 1975 | Avatar | W. Shoemaker |
| 1904 | Delhi | G. Odom | 1941 | Whirlaway | E. Arcaro | 1976 | Bold Forbes | A. Cordero, Jr. |
| 1905 | Tanya | E. Hildebrand | 1942 | Shut Out | E. Arcaro | 1977 | Seattle Slew | J. Cruguet |
| 1906 | Burgomaster | L. Lyne | 1943 | Count Fleet | J. Longden | 1978 | Affirmed | S. Cauthen |
| 1907 | Peter Pan | G. Mountain | 1944 | Bounding Home | G.L. Smith | 1979 | Coastal | R. Hernandez |
| 1908 | Colin | J. Notter | 1945 | Pavot | E. Arcaro | 1980 | Temperence Hill | E. Maple |
| 1909 | Joe Madden | E. Dugan | 1946 | Assault | W. Mehrtens | 1981 | Summing | G. Martens |
| 1910 | Sweep | J. Butwell | 1947 | Phalanx | R. Donoso | 1982 | Conquistador | |
| 1911-12 | Not held | | 1948 | Citation | E. Arcaro | | Cielo | L. Pincay, Jr. |
| 1913 | Prince Eugene | R. Troxler | 1949 | Capot | T. Atkinson | 1983 | Caveat | L. Pincay, Jr. |
| 1914 | Luke McLuke | M. Buxton | 1950 | Middleground | W. Boland | 1984 | Swale | L. Pincay, Jr. |
| 1915 | The Finn | G. Byrne | 1951 | Counterpoint | D. Gorman | 1985 | Creme Fraiche | E. Maple |
| 1916 | Friar Rock | E. Haynes | 1952 | One Count | E. Arcaro | 1986 | Danzig | |
| 1917 | Hourless | J. Butwell | 1953 | Native Dancer | E. Guerin | | Connection | C. McCarron |
| 1918 | Johren | F. Robinson | 1954 | High Gun | E. Guerin | 1987 | Bet Twice | C. Perret |
| 1919 | Sir Barton | J. Loftus | 1955 | Nashua | E. Arcaro | 1988 | Risen Star | E. Delahoussaye |
| 1920 | Man o' War | C. Kummer | 1956 | Needles | D. Erb | 1989 | Easy Goer | P. Day |
| 1921 | Grey Lag | E. Sande | 1957 | Gallant Man | W. Shoemaker | 1990 | Go And Go | M. Kinane |
| 1922 | Pillory | C.H. Miller | 1958 | Cavan | P. Anderson | 1991 | Hansel | J. Bailey |
| 1923 | Zev | E. Sande | 1959 | Sword Dancer | W. Shoemaker | 1992 | A.P. Indy | E. Delahoussaye |
| 1924 | Mad Play | E. Sande | 1960 | Celtic Ash | W. Hartack | 1993 | Colonial Affair | J. Krone |
| 1925 | American Flag | A. Johnson | 1961 | Sherluck | B. Baeza | 1994 | Tabasco Cat | P. Day |
| 1926 | Crusader | A. Johnson | 1962 | Jaipur | W. Shoemaker | 1995 | Thunder Gulch | G. Stevens |
| 1927 | Chance Shot | E. Sande | 1963 | Chateaugay | B. Baeza | 1996 | Editor's Note | R. Douglas |
| 1928 | Vito | C. Kummer | 1964 | Quadrangle | M. Ycaza | 1997 | Touch Gold | C. McCarron |
| 1929 | Blue Larkspur | M. Garner | 1965 | Hail to All | J. Sellers | 1998 | Victory Gallop | G. Stevens |
| 1930 | Gallant Fox | E. Sande | 1966 | Amberoid | W. Boland | 1999 | Lemon Drop Kid | J. Santos |
| 1931 | Twenty Grand | C. Kurtsinger | 1967 | Damascus | W. Shoemaker | 2000 | Commendable | P. Day |
| 1932 | Faireno | T. Malley | 1968 | Stage Door | | 2001 | Point Given | G. Stevens |
| 1933 | Hurryoff | M. Garner | | Johnny | H. Gustines | 2002 | Sarava | E. Prado |
| 1934 | Peace Chance | W. D. Wright | 1969 | Arts and Letters | B. Baeza | | | |
| 1935 | Omaha | W. Saunders | 1970 | High Echelon | J. Rotz | | | |

## TRIPLE CROWN RACES—2002

**Kentucky Derby** (Churchill Downs, Louisville, Ky., May 4, 2002). Purse: $1,000,000. Distance: 1¼ mi. Order of finish: 1. War Emblem (Espinoza), mutuel returns: $43.00, $22.80, $13.60. 2. Proud Citizen (Smith), $24.60, $13.40. 3. Perfect Drift (Delahoussaye), $6.40. 4. Medaglia d'Oro (Pincay, Jr.). 5. Request for Parole (Albarado). 6. Came Home (McCarron). 7. Harlan's Holiday (Prado). 8. Johannesburg (Stevens). 9. Essence of Dubai (Flores). 10. Saarland (Velazquez). 112. Blue Burner (Day). 12. Castle Gandolfo (Bailey). 13. Easy Grades (Chavez). 14. Private Emblem (Meche). 15. Lusty Latin (Corbett). 16. It'sallinthechase (Martin, Jr.). 17. Ocean Sound (Solis). 18. Wild Horses (Douglas). Winner's purse: $875,000.

**Preakness Stakes** (Pimlico, Baltimore, Md., May 18, 2002). Purse: $1,000,000. Distance: 1³⁄₁₆ mi. Order of finish: 1. War Emblem (Espinoza), mutuel returns: $7.60, $6.00, $4.40. 2. Magic Weisner (Migliore), $30.00, $14.00. 3. Proud Citizen, $5.00. 4. Harlan's Holiday (Prado). 5. Easyfromthegitgo (Meche). 6. U S S Tinosa (Desormeaux). 7. Crimson Hero (McCarron). 8. Medaglia d'Oro (Bailey). 9. Straight Gin (Albarado). 10. Menacing Dennis (Pino). 11. Table Limit (Stevens). 12. Booklet (Day). 13. Equality (Dominguez). Winner's purse: $650,000. Margin of victory: ¾ length. Time of race: 1:56.36.

**Belmont Stakes** (Belmont Park, Elmont, N.Y., June 8, 2002). Gross purse: $1,000,000. Distance: 1½ mi. Order of finish: 1. Sarava (Prado), mutuel returns: $120.00, $50.00, $22.40. 2. Medaglia d'Oro (Desormeaux), $16.00, $10.60. 3. Sunday Break (Stevens), $7.10. 4. Magic Weisner (Migliore). 5. Proud Citizen (Smith). 6. Essence of Dubai (Bailey). 7. Like a Hero (Day). 8. War Emblem (Espinoza). 9. Wiseman's Ferry (Chavez). 10. Perfect Drift (Delahoussaye). 11. Artax Too (Santos). Winner's purse: $600,000. Margin of victory: ½ length. Time of race: 2:29⅗.

## ECLIPSE AWARDS—2002

### (Presented on Feb. 18, 2002)

| | |
|---|---|
| Horse of the Year | Point Given |
| 2-year-old colt | Johannesburg |
| 2-year-old filly | Tempera |
| 3-year-old colt | Point Given |
| 3-year-old filly | Xtra Heat |
| Older male | Tiznow |
| Older female | Gourmet Girl |
| Male turf | Fantastic Light |
| Female turf | Banks Hill |
| Steeplechase | Pompeyo |
| Owner | Richard Englander |
| Breeder | Juddmonte Farms |
| Jockey | Jerry Bailey |
| Apprentice jockey | Jeremy Rose |
| Trainer | Bobby Frankel |

(Based on vote by the Thoroughbred Racing Associations, the *Daily Racing Form*, and the National Turf Writers Association.)

# Track and Field

## WORLD OUTDOOR RECORDS—MEN

### (Through Sept. 19, 2002)

Recognized by the International Athletic Federation. The IAAF decided late in 1976 not to recognize records in yards except for the one-mile run.

The IAAF also requires automatic timing for all records for races of 400 meters or less.

| Event | Record | Holder | Home country | Where made | Date |
|---|---|---|---|---|---|
| **Running** | | | | | |
| 100 m | 0:09.78 | Tim Montgomery | United States | Paris, France | Sept. 14, 2002 |
| 200 m | 0:19.32 | Michael Johnson | United States | Atlanta, Ga. | Aug. 1, 1996 |
| 400 m | 0:43.18 | Michael Johnson | United States | Seville, Spain | Aug. 26, 1999 |
| 800 m | 1:41.11 | Wilson Kipketer | Denmark | Köln, Germany | Aug. 24, 1997 |
| 1,000 m | 2:11.96 | Noah Ngeny | Kenya | Rieti, Italy | Sept. 5, 1999 |
| 1,500 m | 3:26.00 | Hicham El Guerrouj | Morocco | Rome, Italy | July 14, 1998 |
| 1 mile | 3:43.13 | Hicham El Guerrouj | Morocco | Rome, Italy | July 7, 1999 |
| 2,000 m | 4:44.79 | Hicham El Guerrouj | Morocco | Berlin, Germany | Sept. 7, 1999 |
| 3,000 m | 7:20.67 | Daniel Komen | Kenya | Rieti, Italy | Sept. 1, 1996 |
| 3,000 m steeplechase | 7:53.17 | Brahim Boulami | Morocco | Zürich, Switzerland | Aug. 16, 2002 |
| 5,000 m | 12:39.36 | Haile Gebrselassie | Ethiopia | Helsinki, Finland | June 13, 1998 |
| 10,000 m | 26:22.75 | Haile Gebrselassie | Ethiopia | Hengelo, Netherlands | June 1, 1998 |
| 20,000 m | 56:55.60 | Arturo Barrios | Mexico | La Fleche, France | March 30, 1991 |
| 25,000 m | 1:13:55.80 | Toshihiko Seko | Japan | Christchurch, N.Z. | March 22, 1981 |
| 30,000 m | 1:29:18.80 | Toshihiko Seko | Japan | Christchurch, N.Z. | March 22, 1981 |
| 1 hour | 21,101 m | Arturo Barrios | Mexico | La Fleche, France | March 30, 1991 |
| Marathon[1] | 2:05.38 | Khalid Khannouchi | United States | London, England | April 14, 2002 |
| **Walking** | | | | | |
| 20,000 m | 1:17:25.60 | Bernardo Segura | Mexico | Bergen, Norway | May 7, 1994 |
| 30,000 m | 2:01:44.10 | Maurizio Damilano | Italy | Cuneo, Italy | Oct. 3, 1992 |
| 50,000 m | 3:40:57.90 | Thierry Toutain | France | Héricourt, France | Sept. 29, 1996 |
| 2 hours | 29,572 m | Maurizio Damilano | Italy | Cuneo, Italy | Oct. 3, 1992 |
| **Hurdles** | | | | | |
| 110 m | 0:12.91 | Colin Jackson | Great Britain | Stuttgart, Germany | Aug. 20, 1993 |
| 400 m | 0:46.78 | Kevin Young | United States | Barcelona, Spain | Aug. 6, 1992 |
| **Relay races** | | | | | |
| 400 m (4 × 100) | 0:37.40 | National Team | United States | Barcelona, Spain | Aug. 8, 1992 |
| | 0:37.40 | National Team | United States | Stuttgart, Germany | Aug. 21, 1993 |
| 800 m (4 × 200) | 1:18.68 | Santa Monica T.C. | United States | Walnut, Calif. | April 17, 1994 |
| 1,600 m (4 × 400) | 2:54.20 | National Team | United States | New York, N.Y. | July 22, 1998 |
| 3,200 m (4 × 800) | 7:03.89 | National Team | Britain | London, England | Aug. 30, 1982 |
| 6,000 m | 14:38.80 | National Team | West Germany | Köln, Germany | Aug. 17, 1977 |
| **Field events** | | | | | |
| High jump | 2.45 m | Javier Sotomayor | Cuba | Salamanca, Spain | July 27, 1993 |
| Long jump | 8.95 m | Mike Powell | United States | Tokyo, Japan | Aug. 30, 1991 |
| Triple jump | 18.29 m | Jonathan Edwards | Great Britain | Goteborg, Sweden | Aug. 7, 1995 |
| Pole vault | 6.14 m | Sergey Bubka | Ukraine | Sestriere, Italy | July 31, 1994 |
| Shot-put | 23.12 m | Randy Barnes | United States | Los Angeles, Calif. | May 20, 1990 |
| Discus throw | 74.08 m | Jürgen Schult | East Germany | Neubrandenburg, E. Germany | June 6, 1986 |
| Hammer throw | 86.74 m | Yuriy Sedykh | USSR | Stuttgart, Germany | Aug. 30, 1986 |
| Javelin throw | 98.48 m | Jan Zelezny | Czech Republic | Jena, Germany | May 25, 1996 |
| Decathlon | 9,026 pts. | Roman Sebrle | Czech Republic | Götzis, Austria | May 27, 2001 |

1. Not recognized by IAAF as world record, but considered to be "world-best performance."

## WORLD OUTDOOR RECORDS—WOMEN

### (Through Oct. 13, 2002)

| Event | Record | Holder | Home country | Where made | Date |
|---|---|---|---|---|---|
| **Running** | | | | | |
| 100 m | 0:10.49 | Florence Griffith-Joyner | United States | Indianapolis, Ind. | July 16, 1988 |
| 200 m | 0:21.34 | Florence Griffith-Joyner | United States | Seoul, South Korea | Sept. 29, 1988 |
| 400 m | 0:47.60 | Martina Koch | East Germany | Canberra, Australia | Oct. 6, 1985 |
| 800 m | 1:53.28 | Jarmila Kratochvilova | Czechoslovakia | Munich, W. Germany | July 26, 1983 |
| 1000 m | 2:28.98 | Svetlana Masterkova | Russia | Brussels, Belgium | Aug. 23, 1996 |
| 1,500 m | 3:50.46 | Qu Yunxia | China | Beijing, China | Sept. 11, 1993 |
| 1 mile | 4:12.56 | Svetlana Masterkova | Russia | Zurich, Switzerland | Aug. 14, 1996 |

| Event | Record | Holder | Home country | Where made | Date |
|---|---|---|---|---|---|
| 2,000 m | 5:25.36 | Sonia O'Sullivan | Ireland | Edinburgh, Scotland | July 8, 1994 |
| 3,000 m | 8:06.11 | Wang Junxia | China | Beijing, China | Sept. 13, 1993 |
| 5,000 m | 14:28.09 | Jiang Bo | China | Shanghai, China | Oct. 23, 1997 |
| 10,000 m | 29:31.78 | Wang Junxia | China | Beijing, China | Sept. 8, 1993 |
| 20,000 m | 1:05:26.60 | Tegla Loroupe | Kenya | Borgholzhausen, Germany | Sept. 3, 2000 |
| 25,000 m | 1:29:29.20 | Karolina Szabo | Hungary | Budapest, Hungary | April 22, 1988 |
| 30,000 m | 1:47:05.60 | Karolina Szabo | Hungary | Budapest, Hungary | April 22, 1988 |
| 1 hour | 18.340 | Tegla Loroupe | Kenya | Borgholzhausen, Germany | July 8, 1999 |
| 3,000 m steeplechase | 9:16.51 | Alesya Turova | Belarus | Gdansk, Poland | July 27, 2002 |
| Marathon[1] | 2:17:18 | Paula Radcliffe | Great Britain | Chicago, Ill. | Oct. 13, 2002 |
| **Walking** | | | | | |
| 5,000 m | 20:13.26 | Kerry Saxby-Junna | Australia | Hobart, Australia | Feb. 25, 1996 |
| 10,000 m | 41:56.23 | Nadezhda Ryashkina | Russia | Seattle, Wash. | July 24, 1990 |
| 20,000 m | 1:26:52.30 | Olimpiada Ivanova | Russia | Brisbane, Australia | Sept. 6, 2001 |
| **Hurdles** | | | | | |
| 100 m | 0:12.21 | Yordanka Donkova | Bulgaria | Stara Zagora, Bulgaria | Aug. 20, 1988 |
| 400 m | 0:52.61 | Kim Batten | United States | Goteborg, Sweden | Aug. 11, 1995 |
| **Relay races** | | | | | |
| 400 m (4 × 100) | 0:41.37 | East Germany | E. Germany | Canberra, Australia | Oct. 6, 1985 |
| 800 m (4 × 200) | 1:27.46 | United States "Blue" | United States | Philadelphia, Pa. | April 29, 2000 |
| 1,600 m (4 × 400) | 3:15.17 | USSR | USSR | Seoul, South Korea | Oct. 1, 1988 |
| 3,200 m (4 × 800) | 7:50.17 | USSR | USSR | Moscow, USSR | Aug. 5, 1984 |
| **Field events** | | | | | |
| High jump | 2.09 m | Stefka Kostadinova | Bulgaria | Rome, Italy | Aug. 30, 1987 |
| Pole vault | 4.81 m | Stacy Dragila | United States | Palo Alto, Calif. | June 9, 2001 |
| Long jump | 7.52 m | Galina Chistyakova | USSR | Leningrad, Russia | June 11, 1988 |
| Triple jump | 15.50 m | Inessa Kravets | Ukraine | Goteborg, Sweden | Aug. 10, 1995 |
| Shot-put | 22.63 m | Natalya Lisovskaya | USSR | Moscow, Russia | June 7, 1987 |
| Discus throw | 76.80 m | Gabriele Reinsch | East Germany | Neubrandenburg, E. Ger. | July 9, 1988 |
| Hammer throw | 76.07 m | Mihaela Melinte | Romania | Rüdlingen, Switzerland | Aug. 29, 1999 |
| Javelin throw | 71.54 m | Osleidys Menéndez | Cuba | Réthymno, Greece | July 1, 2001 |
| Heptathlon | 7,291 pts | Jackie Joyner-Kersee | United States | Seoul, South Korea | Sept. 24, 1988 |

1. Not recognized by IAAF as world record, but considered to be "world-best performance."

## AMERICAN OUTDOOR RECORDS—MEN

### (Through Sept. 19, 2002)

| Event | Record | Holder | Where Made | Date |
|---|---|---|---|---|
| **Running** | | | | |
| 100 m | 0:09.78 | Tim Montgomery | Paris, France | Sept. 14 ,2002 |
| 200 m | 0:19.32 | Michael Johnson | Atlanta, Ga. | Aug. 1, 1996 |
| 400 m | 0:43.18 | Michael Johnson | Seville, Spain | Aug. 26, 1999 |
| 800 m | 1:42.60 | Johnny Gray | Koblenz, W. Germany | Aug. 29, 1985 |
| 1,000 m | 2:13.90 | Richard Wohlhuter | Oslo, Norway | July 30, 1974 |
| 1,500 m | 3:29.77 | Sydney Maree | Cologne, W. Germany | Aug. 25, 1985 |
| 1 mile | 3:47.69 | Steve Scott | Oslo, Norway | July 7, 1982 |
| 2,000 m | 4:52.44 | Jim Spivey | Lausanne, Switzerland | Sept. 15, 1987 |
| 3,000 m | 7:35.84 | Bob Kennedy | Monaco | Aug. 8, 1996 |
| 5,000 m | 12:58.21 | Bob Kennedy | Zurich, Switzerland | Aug. 14, 1996 |
| 10,000 m | 27:13.98 | Meb Keflezighi | Stanford, Calif. | May 4, 2001 |
| 3,000-m steeplechase | 8:09.17 | Henry Marsh | Koblenz, W. Ger. | Aug. 29, 1985 |
| Marathon | 2:05:38 | Khalid Khannouchi | London, England | April 14, 2002 |
| **Hurdles** | | | | |
| 110 m | 0:12.92 | Roger Kingdom | Berlin, Germany | Aug. 16, 1989 |
| | | Allen Johnson | Atlanta, Ga. | June 23, 1996 |
| 400 m | 0:46.78 | Kevin Young | Barcelona | Aug. 6, 1992 |
| **Relay races** | | | | |
| 400 m (4 × 100) | 0:37.40 | Olympic Team | Barcelona, Spain | Aug. 8, 1992 |
| | | USA National Team | Stuttgart, Germany | Aug. 21, 1993 |
| 800 m (4 × 200) | 1:18.68 | Santa Monica T.C. | Walnut, Calif. | April 17, 1994 |
| 1,600 m (4 × 400) | 2:54.20 | USA National Team | New York, N.Y. | July 22, 1998 |
| 3,200 m (4 × 800) | 7:06.50 | Santa Monica T.C. | Walnut, Calif. | Apr. 26, 1986 |
| 6,000 m (4 × 1,500) | 14:46.30 | National Team | Bourges, France | June 24, 1979 |

| Event | Record | Holder | Where Made | Date |
|---|---|---|---|---|
| **Field events** | | | | |
| High jump | 7 ft. 10½ in. | Charles Austin | Zurich, Switzerland | Aug. 7, 1991 |
| Long jump | 29 ft. 4½ in. | Mike Powell | Tokyo, Japan | Aug. 30, 1991 |
| Triple jump | 59 ft. 4 in. | Kenny Harrison | Atlanta, Ga. | July 27, 1996 |
| Pole vault | 19 ft. 9 ¼in. | Jeff Hartwig | Jonesboro, Ark. | June 14, 2000 |
| Shot-put | 75 ft. 10¼ in. | Randy Barnes | Los Angeles | May 20, 1990 |
| Discus throw | 237 ft. 4 in. | Ben Plucknett | Stockholm, Swe. | July 7, 1981 |
| Javelin throw | 285 ft. 10 in. | Tom Pukstys | Jena, Germany | May 25, 1997 |
| Hammer throw | 270 ft. 9 in. | Lance Deal | Milan, Italy | July 9, 1996 |
| Decathlon | 8,891 pts | Dan O'Brien | Talence, France | Sept. 4–5, 1992 |

## AMERICAN OUTDOOR RECORDS—WOMEN

### (Through Sept. 19, 2002)

| Event | Record | Holder | Where Made | Date |
|---|---|---|---|---|
| **Running** | | | | |
| 100 m | 0:10.49 | Florence Griffith Joyner | Indianapolis, Ind. | July 16, 1988 |
| 200 m | 21.34 | Florence Griffith Joyner | Seoul, South Korea | Sept. 29, 1988 |
| 400 m | 0:48.83 | Valerie Brisco | Los Angeles, Calif. | Aug. 6, 1984 |
| 800 m | 1:56.40 | Jearl Miles-Clark | Zurich, Switzerland | Aug. 11, 1999 |
| 1,000 m | 2:31.80 | Regina Jacobs | Brunswick, Maine | July 3, 1999 |
| 1,500 m | 3:57.12 | Mary Slaney | Stockholm, Sweden. | July 26, 1983 |
| 2,000 m | 5:32.70 | Mary Slaney | Eugene, Ore. | Aug. 3, 1984 |
| 1 mile | 4:16.71 | Mary Decker Slaney | Zurich, Switzerland | Aug. 21, 1985 |
| 3,000 m | 8:29.69 | Mary Decker Slaney | Cologne, Germany | Aug. 25, 1985 |
| 5,000 m | 14:45.38 | Regina Jacobs | Sacramento, Calif. | July 21, 2000 |
| 10,000 m | 30:50.32 | Deena Drossin | Palo Alto, Calif. | May 3, 2002 |
| 3,000 m steeplechase | 9:41.94 | Elizabeth Jackson | Brisbane, Australia | Sept. 4, 2001 |
| Marathon | 2:21:21 | Joan Samuelson | Chicago, Ill. | Oct. 20, 1985 |
| **Hurdles** | | | | |
| 100 m | 0:12.33 | Gail Devers | Sacramento, Calif. | July 23, 2000 |
| 400 m | 0:52.61 | Kim Batten | Goteborg, Sweden | Aug. 11, 1995 |
| **Relay races** | | | | |
| 400 m (4 × 100) | 41.47 | U.S.A. National Team | Athens, Greece | Aug. 9, 1997 |
| 800 m (4 × 200) | 1:27.46 | United States Blue Team | Philadelphia, Pa. | April 29, 2000 |
| 1,600 m (4 × 400) | 3:15.51 | U.S. Olympic Team | Seoul, South Korea | Oct. 1, 1988 |
| **Field events** | | | | |
| Pole vault | 15 ft 2 ¼ in. | Stacy Dragila | Sacramento, Calif. | July 23, 2000 |
| High jump | 6 ft 8 in. | Louise Ritter | Austin, Tex. | July 9, 1988 |
| Long jump | 24 ft 7 in. | Jackie Joyner-Kersee | New York, N.Y. | May 22, 1994 |
| Triple jump | 47 ft 3½ in. | Sheila Hudson | Stockholm, Sweden | July 8, 1996 |
| Shot-put | 66 ft 2½ in. | Ramon Pagel | San Diego, Calif. | June 25, 1988 |
| Discus throw | 227 ft 10 in. | Suzy Powell | La Jolla, Calif. | April 27, 2002 |
| Hammer throw | 235 ft 0 in. | Anna Norgren-Mahon | West Point, N.Y. | June 8, 2002 |
| Javelin throw (old) | 227 ft 5 in. | Kate Schmidt | Fürth, W. Ger. | Sept. 10, 1977 |
| Javelin throw (new) | 197 ft 0 in. | Serene Ross | Palo Alto, Calif. | June 21, 2002 |
| Heptathlon | 7,291 pts | Jackie Joyner-Kersee | Seoul, South Korea | Sept. 23–24, 1988 |

## HISTORY OF THE RECORD FOR THE MILE RUN

(Under 4 minutes) *Source:* USA Track & Field.

| Time | Athlete | Country | Year | Location |
|---|---|---|---|---|
| 3:59.4 | Roger Bannister | England | 1954 | Oxford, England |
| 3:58.0 | John Landy | Australia | 1954 | Turku, Finland |
| 3:57.2 | Derek Ibbotson | England | 1957 | London |
| 3:54.5 | Herb Elliott | Australia | 1958 | Dublin |
| 3:54.4 | Peter Snell | New Zealand | 1962 | Wanganui, N.Z. |
| 3:54.1 | Peter Snell | New Zealand | 1964 | Auckland, N.Z. |
| 3:53.6 | Michel Jazy | France | 1965 | Rennes, France |
| 3:51.3 | Jim Ryun | United States | 1966 | Berkeley, Calif. |
| 3:51.1 | Jim Ryun | United States | 1967 | Bakersfield, Calif. |
| 3:51.0 | Filbert Bayi | Tanzania | 1975 | Kingston, Jamaica |
| 3:49.4 | John Walker | New Zealand | 1975 | Goteborg, Sweden |
| 3:49.0 | Sebastian Coe | England | 1979 | Oslo |
| 3:48.8 | Steve Ovett | England | 1980 | Oslo |
| 3:48.53 | Sebastian Coe | England | 1981 | Zurich, Switzerland |
| 3:48.40 | Steve Ovett | England | 1981 | Koblenz, W. Ger. |
| 3:47.33 | Sebastian Coe | England | 1981 | Brussels |
| 3:46.31 | Steve Cram | England | 1985 | Oslo |
| 3:44.39 | Noureddine Morceli | Algeria | 1993 | Rieti, Italy |
| 3:43.13 | Hicham El Guerrouj | Morocco | 1999 | Rome, Italy |

## TOP TEN WORLD'S FASTEST INDOOR MILES

*Source:* USA Track & Field.

| Time | Athlete | Country | Date | Location |
|------|---------|---------|------|----------|
| 3:48.45 | Hicham El Guerrouj | Morocco | Feb. 12, 1997 | Gent, Netherlands |
| 3:49.78 | Eamonn Coghlan | Ireland | Feb. 27, 1983 | East Rutherford, N.J. |
| 3:50.6 | Eamonn Coghlan | Ireland | Feb. 20, 1981 | San Diego |
| 3:50.7 | Noureddine Morceli | Algeria | Feb. 20, 1993 | Birmingham, England |
| 3:50.94 | Marcus O'Sullivan | Ireland | Feb. 13, 1988 | East Rutherford, N.J. |
| 3:51.2 | Ray Flynn[1] | Ireland | Feb. 27, 1983 | East Rutherford, N.J. |
| 3:51.66 | Marcus O'Sullivan | Ireland | Feb. 10, 1989 | East Rutherford, N.J. |
| 3:51.8 | Steve Scott[1] | United States | Feb. 20, 1981 | San Diego |
| 3:52.28 | Steve Scott[2] | United States | Feb. 27, 1983 | East Rutherford, N.J. |
| 3:52.30 | Frank O'Mara | Ireland | Feb. 1986 | New York |

1. Finished second. 2. Finished third.

## 2002 USA OUTDOOR CHAMPIONSHIPS

### (June 21–23, 2002, Palo Alto, Calif.)

**Men's Events**

| Event, athlete, team | Results |
|----------------------|---------|
| 100 m dash—Maurice Greene, adidas | 9.88 |
| 200 m dash—Ramon Clay, adidas | 20.27 |
| 400 m dash—Alvin Harrison, Nike | 44.62 |
| 800 m run—David Krummenacker, adidas | 1:47.24 |
| 1,500 m run—Seneca Lassiter, Nike | 3:40.90 |
| 5,000 m run—Alan Culpepper, adidas | 13:27.52 |
| 10,000 m run—Mebrahtom Keflezighi, Nike | 27:41.68 |
| 3,000 m steeplechase—Anthoney Famiglietti, adidas | 8:19.07 |
| 110 m hurdles—Allen Johnson, Nike | 13.08 |
| 400 m hurdles—James Carter, Nike | 48.12 |
| 20,000 m race walk—Tim Seaman, New York AC | 1:26:40.36 |
| Hammer throw—Lance Deal, New York AC | 74.49 m |
| Javelin throw—Breaux Greer, adidas | 81.78 m |
| Long jump—Savante Stringfellow, Nike | 8.52 m |
| Discus throw—Adam Setliff, Nike | 63.74 m |
| Pole vault—Jeff Hartwig, Nike | 5.84 m |
| Triple jump—Walter Davis, LSU | 17.59 m |
| Shot put—Adam Nelson, Nike | 22.22 m |
| High jump—Nathan Leeper, Nike | 2.32 m |

**Women's Events**

| Event, athlete, team | Results |
|----------------------|---------|
| 100 m dash—Marion Jones, Nike | 11.01 |
| 200 m dash—Marion Jones, Nike | 22.35 |
| 400 m dash—Jearl Miles Clark, New Balance | 50.91 |
| 800 m run—Nicole Teter, Nike Farm Team | 1:58.83 |
| 1,500 m run—Regina Jacobs, Nike | 4:09.57 |
| 5,000 m run—Marla Runyan, Nike | 15:07.19 |
| 10,000 m run—Jen Rhines, adidas | 31:57.38 |
| 3,000 m steeplechase—Elizabeth Jackson, Nike | 9:47.35 |
| 100 m hurdles—Gail Devers, Nike | 12.51 |
| 400 m hurdles—Sandra Glover, Nike | 55.22 |
| 20,000 m race walk—Joanne Dow, adidas | 1:34:46.52 |
| Hammer throw—Anna Mahon, unattached | 70.27 m |
| Javelin throw—Serene Ross, unattached | 60.06 m |
| Long jump—Brianna Glenn, Tucson Elite | 6.46 m |
| Discus throw—Kris Kuehl, Nike | 64.44 m |
| Pole vault—Stacy Dragila, Nike | 4.65 m |
| Triple jump—Brandi Prieto, unattached | 13.03 m |
| Shot put—Teri Steer, Nike | 19.20 m |
| High jump—Tisha Waller, Nike | 1.96 m |

# Tennis

Lawn tennis is a comparatively modern modification of the ancient game of court tennis. Maj. Walter Clopton Wingfield thought that something like court tennis might be played outdoors on lawns, and in Dec. 1873, at Nantclwyd, Wales, he introduced his new game under the name of *Sphairistike* at a lawn party. The game was a success and spread rapidly but the name was a total failure and almost immediately disappeared when all the players and spectators began to refer to the new game as *lawn tennis.* In the early part of 1874, a young lady named Mary Ewing Outerbridge returned from Bermuda to New York, bringing with her the implements and necessary equipment of the new game, which she had obtained from a British Army supply store in Bermuda. Miss Outerbridge and friends played the first game of lawn tennis in the United States on the grounds of the Staten Island Cricket and Baseball Club in the spring of 1874.

For a few years, the new game went along in haphazard fashion until about 1880, when standard measurements for the court and standard equipment

within definite limits became the rule. In 1881, the U.S. Lawn Tennis Association (whose name was changed in 1975 to the U.S. Tennis Association) was formed and conducted the first national championship at Newport, R.I. The international matches for the Davis Cup began with a series between the British and U.S. players on the courts of the Longwood Cricket Club, Chestnut Hill, Mass., in 1900, with the home players winning.

Professional tennis, which got its start in 1926 when the French star Suzanne Lenglen was paid $50,000 for a tour, received full recognition in 1968. Staid old Wimbledon, the London home of what are considered the world championships, let the pros compete. This decision ended a long controversy over open tennis and changed the format of the competition. The U.S. championships were also opened to the pros and the site of the event, long held at Forest Hills, N.Y., was shifted to the National Tennis Center in Flushing Meadows, N.Y., in 1978. Pro tours for men and women became worldwide in play that continued throughout the year.

## DAVIS CUP CHAMPIONSHIPS

### No matches in 1901, 1910, 1915–1918, and 1940–1945

| | | |
|---|---|---|
| 1900 United States 3, British Isles 0 | 1937 United States 4, Great Britain 1 | 1973 Australia 5, United States 0 |
| 1902 United States 3, British Isles 2 | 1938 United States 3, Australia 2 | 1974 South Africa (Default by India) |
| 1903 British Isles 4, United States 1 | 1939 Australia 3, United States 2 | 1975 Sweden 3, Czechoslovakia 2 |
| 1904 British Isles 5, Belgium 0 | 1946 United States 5, Australia 0 | 1976 Italy 4, Chile 1 |
| 1905 British Isles 5, United States 0 | 1947 United States 4, Australia 1 | 1977 Australia 3, Italy 1 |
| 1906 British Isles 5, United States 0 | 1948 United States 5, Australia 0 | 1978 United States 4, Britain 1 |
| 1907 Australasia 3, British Isles 2 | 1949 United States 4, Australia 1 | 1979 United States 5, Italy 0 |
| 1908 Australasia 3, United States 2 | 1950 Australia 4, United States 1 | 1980 Czechoslovakia 3, Italy 2 |
| 1909 Australasia 5, United States 0 | 1951 Australia 3, United States 2 | 1981 United States 3, Argentina 1 |
| 1911 Australasia 5, United States 0 | 1952 Australia 4, United States 1 | 1982 United States 3, France 0 |
| 1912 British Isles 3, Australasia 2 | 1953 Australia 3, United States 2 | 1983 Australia 3, Sweden 2 |
| 1913 United States 3, British Isles 2 | 1954 United States 3, Australia 2 | 1984 Sweden 4, United States 1 |
| 1914 Australasia 3, United States 2 | 1955 Australia 5, United States 0 | 1985 Sweden 3, West Germany 2 |
| 1919 Australasia 4, British Isles 1 | 1956 Australia 5, United States 0 | 1986 Australia 3, Sweden 2 |
| 1920 United States 5, Australasia 0 | 1957 Australia 3, United States 2 | 1987 Sweden 5, India 0 |
| 1921 United States 5, Japan 0 | 1958 United States 3, Australia 2 | 1988 West Germany 4, Sweden 1 |
| 1922 United States 4, Australasia 1 | 1959 Australia 3, United States 2 | 1989 West Germany 3, Sweden 2 |
| 1923 United States 4, Australasia 1 | 1960 Australia 4, Italy 1 | 1990 United States 3, Australia 2 |
| 1924 United States 5, Australasia 0 | 1961 Australia 5, Italy 0 | 1991 France 3, United States 1 |
| 1925 United States 5, France 0 | 1962 Australia 5, Mexico 0 | 1992 United States 3, Switzerland 1 |
| 1926 United States 4, France 1 | 1963 United States 3, Australia 2 | 1993 Germany 4, Australia 1 |
| 1927 France 3, United States 2 | 1964 Australia 3, United States 2 | 1994 Sweden 4, Russia 1 |
| 1928 France 4, United States 1 | 1965 Australia 4, Spain 1 | 1995 United States 3, Russia 1 |
| 1929 France 3, United States 2 | 1966 Australia 4, India 1 | 1996 France 3, Sweden 2 |
| 1930 France 4, United States 1 | 1967 Australia 4, Spain 1 | 1997 Sweden 5, United States 0 |
| 1931 France 3, Great Britain 2 | 1968 United States 4, Australia 1 | 1998 Sweden 4, Italy 1 |
| 1932 France 3, United States 2 | 1969 United States 5, Romania 0 | 1999 Australia 3, France 2 |
| 1933 Great Britain 3, France 2 | 1970 United States 5, West Germany 0 | 2000 Spain 3, Australia 1 |
| 1934 Great Britain 4, United States 1 | 1971 United States 3, Romania 2 | 2001 France 3, Australia 2 |
| 1935 Great Britain 5, United States 0 | 1972 United States 3, Romania 2 | |
| 1936 Great Britain 3, Australia 2 | | |

## FEDERATION CUP CHAMPIONSHIPS

### World team competition for women conducted by International Lawn Tennis Federation

| | | |
|---|---|---|
| 1963 United States 2, Australia 1 | 1978 United States 2, Australia 1 | 1989 United States 3, Spain 0 |
| 1964 Australia 2, United States 1 | 1979 United States 3, Australia 0 | 1990 United States 2, Soviet Union 1 |
| 1965 Australia 2, United States 1 | 1980 United States 3, Australia 0 | 1991 Spain 2, United States 1 |
| 1966 United States 3, West Germany 0 | 1981 United States 3, Britain 0 | 1992 Germany 2, Spain 1 |
| 1967 United States 2, Britain 0 | 1982 United States 3, West Germany 0 | 1993 Spain 3, Australia 0 |
| 1968 Australia 3, Netherlands 0 | 1983 Czechoslovakia 2, West Germany 1 | 1994 Spain 3, United States 0 |
| 1969 United States 2, Australia 1 | 1984 Czechoslovakia 2, Australia 1 | 1995 Spain 3, United States 2 |
| 1970 Australia 3, West Germany 0 | 1985 Czechoslovakia 2, United States 1 | 1996 United States 5, Spain 2 |
| 1971 Australia 3, Britain 0 | 1986 United States 3, Czechoslovakia 0 | 1997 France 4, Netherlands 1 |
| 1972 South Africa 2, Britain 1 | 1987 West Germany 2, United States 1 | 1998 Spain 3, Switzerland 2 |
| 1973 Australia 3, South Africa 0 | 1988 Czechoslovakia 2, Soviet Union 1 | 1999 United States 4, Russia 1 |
| 1974 Australia 2, United States 1 | | 2000 United States 5, Spain 0 |
| 1975 Czechoslovakia 3, Australia 0 | | 2001 Belgium 2, Russia 1 |
| 1976 United States 2, Australia 1 | | |
| 1977 United States 2, Australia 1 | | |

## U.S. NATIONAL AND OPEN CHAMPIONS

### SINGLES—MEN

| NATIONAL | | | | | |
|---|---|---|---|---|---|
| 1881–87 Richard D. Sears | 1907–11 William A. Larned | 1933–34 Fred J. Perry | 1951–52 Frank Sedgman |
| 1888–89 Henry Slocum, Jr. | 1912–13 Maurice McLoughlin[1] | 1935 Wilmer L. Allison | 1953 Tony Trabert |
| 1890–92 Oliver S. Campbell | 1914 R. N. Williams II | 1936 Fred J. Perry | 1954 Vic Seixas |
| 1893–94 Robert D. Wrenn | 1915 William Johnston | 1937–38 Don Budge | 1955 Tony Trabert |
| 1895 Fred H. Hovey | 1916 R. N. Williams II | 1939 Robert L. Riggs | 1956 Ken Rosewall |
| 1896–97 Robert D. Wrenn | 1917–18 R. Lindley Murray[2] | 1940 Donald McNeill | 1957 Mal Anderson |
| 1898– 1900 Malcolm Whitman | 1919 William Johnston | 1941 Robert L. Riggs | 1958 Ashley Cooper |
| 1901–02 William A. Larned | 1920–25 Bill Tilden | 1942 Fred Schroeder | 1959–60 Neale Fraser |
| 1903 Hugh L. Doherty | 1926–27 Jean Rene Lacoste | 1943 Joseph Hunt | 1961 Roy Emerson |
| 1904 Holcombe Ward | 1928 Henri Cochet | 1944–45 Frank Parker | 1962 Rod Laver |
| 1905 Beals C. Wright | 1929 Bill Tilden | 1946–47 Jack Kramer | 1963 Rafael Osuna |
| 1906 William J. Clothier | 1930 John H. Doeg | 1948–49 Richard Gonzales | 1964 Roy Emerson |
| | 1931–32 Ellsworth Vines | 1950 Arthur Larsen | 1965 Manuel Santana |

| | | | | | | | |
|---|---|---|---|---|---|---|---|
| 1966 | Fred Stolle | 1972 | Ilie Nastase | 1983 | Jimmy Connors | 1995 | Pete Sampras |
| 1967 | John Newcombe | 1973 | John Newcombe | 1984 | John McEnroe | 1996 | Pete Sampras |
| 1968 | Arthur Ashe | 1974 | Jimmy Connors | 1985–87 | Ivan Lendl | 1997–98 | Patrick Rafter |
| 1969 | Rod Laver | 1975 | Manuel Orantes | 1988 | Mats Wilander | 1999 | Andre Agassi |
| | | 1976 | Jimmy Connors | 1989 | Boris Becker | 2000 | Marat Safin |
| **OPEN** | | 1977 | Guillermo Vilas | 1990 | Pete Sampras | 2001 | Lleyton Hewitt |
| 1968 | Arthur Ashe | 1978 | Jimmy Connors | 1991 | Stefan Edberg | 2002 | Pete Sampras |
| 1969 | Rod Laver | 1979 | John McEnroe | 1992 | Stefan Edberg | | |
| 1970 | Ken Rosewall | 1980–81 | John McEnroe | 1993 | Pete Sampras | | |
| 1971 | Stan Smith | 1982 | Jimmy Connors | 1994 | Andre Agassi | | |

1. Challenge Round abandoned in 1912. 2. Patriotic Tournament in 1917.

## SINGLES—WOMEN

**NATIONAL**

| | | | | | | | |
|---|---|---|---|---|---|---|---|
| 1887 | Ellen F. Hansel | 1912–14 | Mary K. Browne | 1948–50 | Margaret Osborne duPont | 1975–78 | Chris Evert |
| 1888–89 | Bertha Townsend | 1915–18 | Molla Bjurstedt | 1951–53 | Maureen Connolly | 1979 | Tracy Austin |
| 1890 | Ellen C. Roosevelt | 1919 | Hazel Hotchkiss Wightman | 1954–55 | Doris Hart | 1980 | Chris Evert-Lloyd |
| 1891–92 | Mabel E. Cahill | 1920–22 | Molla Bjurstedt Mallory | 1956 | Shirley Fry | 1981 | Tracy Austin |
| 1893 | Aline M. Terry | | | 1957–58 | Althea Gibson | 1982 | Chris Evert-Lloyd |
| 1894 | Helen R. Helwig | 1923–25 | Helen N. Wills | 1959 | Maria Bueno | 1983–84 | Martina Navratilova |
| 1895 | Juliette P. Atkinson | 1926 | Molla B. Mallory | 1960–61 | Darlene Hard | 1985 | Hana Mandlikova |
| 1896 | Elisabeth H. Moore | 1927–29 | Helen N. Wills | 1962 | Margaret Smith | 1986–87 | Martina Navratilova |
| 1897–98 | Juliette P. Atkinson | 1930 | Betty Nuthall | 1963–64 | Maria Bueno | 1988 | Steffi Graf |
| 1899 | Marion Jones | 1931 | Helen Wills Moody | 1965 | Margaret Smith | 1989 | Steffi Graf |
| 1900 | Myrtle McAteer | 1932–35 | Helen Jacobs | 1966 | Maria Bueno | 1990 | Grabriela Sabatini |
| 1901 | Elisabeth H. Moore | 1936 | Alice Marble | 1967 | Billie Jean King | 1991 | Monica Seles |
| 1902 | Marion Jones | 1937 | Anita Lizana | 1968–69 | Margaret Smith Court[1] | 1992 | Monica Seles |
| 1903 | Elisabeth H. Moore | 1938–40 | Alice Marble | | | 1993 | Steffi Graf |
| 1904 | May Sutton | 1941 | Sarah Palfrey Cooke | **OPEN** | | 1994 | Arantxa Sanchez Vicario |
| 1905 | Elisabeth H. Moore | 1942–44 | Pauline Betz | 1968 | Virginia Wade | 1995 | Steffi Graf |
| 1906 | Helen Homans | 1945 | Sarah Cooke | 1969–70 | Margaret Court | 1996 | Steffi Graf |
| 1907 | Evelyn Sears | 1946 | Pauline Betz | 1971–72 | Billie Jean King | 1997 | Martina Hingis |
| 1908 | Maud Bargar-Wallach | 1947 | Louise Brough | 1973 | Margaret Court | 1998 | Lindsay Davenport |
| 1909–11 | Hazel V. Hotchkiss | | | 1974 | Billie Jean King | 1999 | Serena Williams |
| | | | | | | 2000–01 | Venus Williams |
| | | | | | | 2002 | Serena Williams |

1. With the inaugural of the Open Tournament in 1968, the United States Lawn Tennis Association held a championship at Longwood, Chestnut Hill, Mass., which barred contract professionals in 1968 and 1969.

## DOUBLES—MEN

**NATIONAL**

| | | | | | | |
|---|---|---|---|---|---|---|
| 1920 | Bill Johnston-C. J. Griffin | 1950 | John Bromwich-Frank Sedgman | 1972 | Cliff Drysdale-Roger Taylor |
| 1921–22 | Bill Tilden-Vincent Richards | 1951 | Frank Sedgman-Ken McGregor | 1973 | John Newcombe-Owen Davidson |
| 1923 | Bill Tilden-B. I. C. Norton | 1952 | Vic Seixas-Mervyn Rose | 1974 | Bob Lutz-Stan Smith |
| 1924 | H. O. Kinsey-R. G. Kinsey | 1953 | Mervyn Rose-Rex Hartwig | 1975 | Jimmy Connors-Ilie Nastase |
| 1925–26 | Vincent Richards-R. N. Williams II | 1954 | Vic Seixas-Tony Trabert | 1976 | Marty Riessen-Tom Okker |
| 1927 | Bill Tilden-Frank Hunter | 1955 | Kosei Kamo-Atsushi Miyagi | 1977 | Frew McMillan-Bob Hewitt |
| 1928 | G. M. Lott, Jr.-V. Hennessy | 1956 | Lewis Hoad-Ken Rosewall | 1978 | Bob Lutz-Stan Smith |
| 1929–30 | G. M. Lott, Jr.-J. H. Doeg | 1957 | Ashley Cooper-Neale Fraser | 1979 | John McEnroe-Peter Fleming |
| 1931 | W. L. Allison-John Van Ryn | 1958 | Ham Richardson-Alex Olmedo | 1980 | Stan Smith-Bob Lutz |
| 1932 | E. H. Vines, Jr.-Keith Gledh | 1959–60 | Neale Fraser-Roy Emerson | 1981 | John McEnroe-Peter Fleming |
| 1933–34 | G. M. Lott, Jr.-L. R. Stoefen | 1961 | Chuck McKinley-Dennis Ralston | 1982 | Kevin Curren-Steve Denton |
| 1935 | W. L. Allison-John Van Ryn | | | 1983 | John McEnroe-Peter Fleming |
| 1936 | Don Budge-Gene Mako | 1962 | Rafael Osuna-Antonio Palafox | 1984 | John Fitzgerald-Tomas Smid |
| 1937 | G. von Cramm-H. Henkel | 1963–64 | Chuck McKinley-Dennis Ralston | 1985 | Ken Flach-Robert Seguso |
| 1938 | Don Budge-Gene Mako | 1965–66 | Fred Stolle-Roy Emerson | 1986 | Andres Gomez-Slobodan Zivojinovic |
| 1939 | A. K. Quist-J. E. Bromwich | 1967 | John Newcombe-Tony Roche | 1987 | Stefan Edberg-Anders Jarryd |
| 1940–41 | Jack Kramer-F. R. Schroeder | 1968 | Stan Smith-Bob Lutz[1] | 1988 | Sergio Casal-Emilio Sanchez |
| 1942 | Gardnar Mulloy-Bill Talbert | 1969 | Richard Crealy-Allan Stone[1] | 1989 | John McEnroe-Mark Woodforde |
| 1943 | Jack Kramer-Frank Parker | | | 1990 | Pieter Aldrich-Danie Visser |
| 1944 | Don McNeill-Bob Falkenburg | **OPEN** | | 1991 | John Fitzgerald-Anders Jarryd |
| 1945 | Gardnar Mulloy-Bill Talbert | 1968 | Stan Smith-Bob Lutz | | |
| 1946 | Gardnar Mulloy-Bill Talbert | 1969 | Fred Stolle-Ken Rosewall | 1992 | Jim Grabb-Richey Reneberg |
| 1947 | Jack Kramer-Fred Schroeder | 1970 | Nikki Pilic-Fred Barthes | 1993 | Ken Flach-Rick Leach |
| 1948 | Gardnar Mulloy-Bill Talbert | 1971 | John Newcombe-Roger Taylor | | |
| 1949 | John Bromwich-William Sidwell | | | | |

| 1994 | Jacco Hingh–Paul Haarhuis | 1998 | Sandon Stolle–Cyril Zuk | 2002 | Mahesh Bhupathi–Max |
| 1995–96 | Todd Woodbridge–Mark Woodforde | 1999 | Sebastien Lareau–Alex O'Brien | | Mirnyi |
| 1997 | Yevgeny Kafelnikov–Daniel Vacek | 2000 | Lleyton Hewitt–Max Mirnyi | | |
| | | 2001 | Wayne Black–Kevin Ullyett | | |

1. With the inaugural of the Open Tournament in 1968, the United States Lawn Tennis Association held a national championship at Longwood, Chestnut Hill, Mass., which barred contract professionals in 1968 and 1969.

## DOUBLES—WOMEN

**NATIONAL**

| 1924 | G. W. Wightman–Helen Wills |
| 1925 | Mary K. Browne–Helen Wills |
| 1926 | Elizabeth Ryan–Eleanor Goss |
| 1927 | L. A. Godfree–Ermyntrude Harvey |
| 1928 | Hazel Hotchkiss Wightman–Helen Wills |
| 1929 | Phoebe Watson–L. R. C. Michell |
| 1930 | Betty Nuthall–Sarah Palfrey |
| 1931 | Betty Nuthall–E. B. Wittingstall |
| 1932 | Helen Jacobs–Sarah Palfrey |
| 1933 | Betty Nuthall–Freda James |
| 1934 | Helen Jacobs–Sarah Palfrey |
| 1935 | Helen Jacobs–Sarah Palfrey Fabyan |
| 1936 | Marjorie G. Van Ryn–Carolin Babcock |
| 1937–40 | Sarah Palfrey Fabyan–Alice Marble |
| 1941 | Sarah Palfrey Cooke–Margaret Osborne |
| 1942–47 | A. Louise Brough–Margaret Osborne |
| 1948–50 | A. Louise Brough–Margaret O. duPont |
| 1951–54 | Doris Hart–Shirley Fry |
| 1955–57 | A. Louise Brough–Margaret O. duPont |
| 1958–59 | Darlene Hard–Jeanne Arth |
| 1960 | Darlene Hard–Maria Bueno |
| 1961 | Darlene Hard–Lesley Turner |
| 1962 | Darlene Hard–Maria Bueno |

| 1963 | Margaret Smith–Robyn Ebbern |
| 1964 | Karen Hantze Susman–Billie Jean Moffitt |
| 1965 | Nancy Richey–Carole Caldwell Graebner |
| 1966 | Nancy Richey–Maria Bueno |
| 1967 | Billie Jean King–Rosemary Casals |
| 1968 | Margaret Court–Maria Bueno[1] |
| 1969 | Margaret Court–Virginia Wade[1] |

**OPEN**

| 1968 | Maria Bueno–Margaret Court |
| 1969 | Darlene Hard–Francoise Durr |
| 1970 | Margaret Court–Judy Dalton |
| 1971 | Rosemary Casals–Judy Dalton |
| 1972 | Francoise Durr–Betty Stove |
| 1973 | Margaret Court–Virginia Wade |
| 1974 | Billie Jean King–Rosemary Casals |
| 1975 | Margaret Court–Virginia Wade |
| 1976 | Linky Boshoff–Ilana Kloss |
| 1977 | Martina Navratilova–Betty Stove |
| 1978 | Billie Jean King–Martina Navratilova |
| 1979 | Betty Stove–Wendy Turnbull |
| 1980 | Billie Jean King–Martina Navratilova |
| 1981 | Kathy Jordan–Anne Smith |

| 1982 | Rosemary Casals–Wendy Turnbull |
| 1983–84 | Martina Navratilova–Pam Shriver |
| 1985 | Claudia Khode-Kilsch–Helena Sukova |
| 1986–87 | Martina Navratilova–Pam Shriver |
| 1988 | Gigi Fernandez–Robin White |
| 1989 | Hana Mandlikova–Martina Navratilova |
| 1990 | Gigi Fernandez–Martina Navratilova |
| 1991 | Pam Shriver–Natalia Zvereva |
| 1992 | Gigi Fernandez–Natalia Zvereva |
| 1993 | Arantxa Sanchez Vicario–Helena Sukova |
| 1994 | Jana Novotna–Arantxa Sanchez Vicario |
| 1995 | Gigi Fernandez–Natasha Zvereva |
| 1996 | Gigi Fernandez–Natasha Zvereva |
| 1997 | Lindsay Davenport–Jana Novotna |
| 1998 | Martina Hingis–Jana Novotna |
| 1999 | Serena Williams–Venus Williams |
| 2000 | Julie-Halard Decugis–Ai Sugiyama |
| 2001 | Lisa Raymond–Renae Stubbs |
| 2002 | Virginia Ruano Pascual–Paola Suarez |

1. With the inaugural of the Open Tournament in 1968, the United States Lawn Tennis Association held a national championship at Longwood, Chestnut Hill, Mass., which barred contract professionals in 1968 and 1969.

### U.S. OPEN, 2002
### (Flushing Meadow, N.Y., Aug. 26–Sept. 8, 2002)

Men's singles—Pete Sampras defeated Andre Agassi, 6–3, 6–4, 5–7, 6–4.

Women's singles—Serena Williams defeated Venus Williams, 6–4, 6–3.

Men's doubles—Mahesh Bhupathi and Max Mirnyi defeated Jiri Novak and Radek Stepanek, 6–3, 3–6, 6–4.

Women's doubles—Virginia Ruano Pascual and Paola Suarez defeated Elena Dementieva and Janette Husarova, 6–2, 6–1.

Mixed doubles—Lisa Raymond and Mike Bryan defeated Katarina Srebotnik and Bob Bryan, 7–6 (11–9), 7–6 (7–1).

### BRITISH (WIMBLEDON) CHAMPIONS
#### (Amateur from inception in 1877 through 1967)
### SINGLES—MEN

| 1908–09 | Arthur Gore | 1925 | Rene Lacoste | 1933 | J. H. Crawford | 1950 | Budge Patty |
| 1910–13 | A. F. Wilding | 1926 | Jean Borotra | 1934–36 | Fred Perry | 1951 | Richard Savitt |
| 1914 | N. E. Brookes | 1927 | Henri Cochet | 1937–38 | Don Budge | 1952 | Frank Sedgman |
| 1919 | G. L. Patterson | 1928 | Rene Lacoste | 1939 | Robert L. Riggs | 1953 | Vic Siexas |
| 1920–21 | Bill Tilden | 1929 | Jean Cochet | 1946 | Yvon Petra | 1954 | Jaroslav Drobny |
| 1922 | G. L. Patterson | 1930 | Bill Tilden | 1947 | Jack Kramer | 1955 | Tony Trabert |
| 1923 | William Johnston | 1931 | S. B. Wood | 1948 | R. Falkenburg | 1956–57 | Lewis Hoad |
| 1924 | Jean Borotra | 1932 | Ellsworth Vines | 1949 | Fred Schroeder | 1958 | Ashley Cooper |

| | | | | | | | | |
|------|------------------|---------|----------------|---------|-----------------|------|-------------------|
| 1959 | Alex Olmedo | 1970–71 | John Newcombe | 1983–84 | John McEnroe | 1993–95 | Pete Sampras |
| 1960 | Neale Fraser | 1972 | Stan Smith | 1985–86 | Boris Becker | 1996 | Richard Krajicek |
| 1961–62 | Rod Laver | 1973 | Jan Kodes | 1987 | Pat Cash | 1997– | |
| 1963 | Chuck McKinley | 1974 | Jimmy Connors | 1988 | Stefan Edberg | 2000 | Pete Sampras |
| 1964–65 | Roy Emerson | 1975 | Arthur Ashe | 1989 | Boris Becker | 2001 | Goran Ivanisevic |
| 1966 | Manuel Santana | 1976–80 | Bjorn Borg | 1990 | Stefan Edberg | 2002 | Lleyton Hewitt |
| 1967 | John Newcombe | 1981 | John McEnroe | 1991 | Michael Stich | | |
| 1968–69 | Rod Laver | 1982 | Jimmy Connors | 1992 | Andre Agassi | | |

## SINGLES—WOMEN

| | | | | | | | |
|------|-------------------|---------|------------------|---------|------------------|------|--------------------|
| 1919–23 | Suzanne Lenglen | 1939 | Alice Marble | 1964 | Maria Bueno | 1980 | Evonne Goolagong |
| 1924 | Kathleen McKane | 1946 | Pauline M. Betz | 1965 | Margaret Smith | | Cawley |
| 1925 | Suzanne Lenglen | 1947 | Margaret Osborne | 1966–68 | Billie Jean King | 1981 | Chris Evert-Lloyd |
| 1926 | Kathleen Godfree | 1948–50 | A. Louise Brough | 1969 | Ann Jones | 1982–87 | Martina Navratilova |
| 1927–29 | Helen Wills | 1951 | Doris Hart | 1970 | Margaret Court | 1988–89 | Steffi Graf |
| 1930 | Helen Wills Moody | 1952–54 | Maureen Connolly | 1971 | Evonne Goolagong | 1990 | Martina Navratilova |
| 1931 | Cilly Aussem | 1955 | A. Louise Brough | 1972–73 | Billie Jean King | 1991–93 | Steffi Graf |
| 1932–33 | Helen Wills Moody | 1956 | Shirley Fry | 1974 | Chris Evert | 1994 | Conchita Martinez |
| 1934 | D. E. Round | 1957–58 | Althea Gibson | 1975 | Billie Jean King | 1995–96 | Steffi Graf |
| 1935 | Helen Wills Moody | 1959–60 | Maria Bueno | 1976 | Chris Evert | 1997 | Martina Hingis |
| 1936 | Helen Jacobs | 1961 | Angela Mortimer | 1977 | Virginia Wade | 1998 | Jana Novotna |
| 1937 | D. E. Round | 1962 | Karen Susman | 1978–79 | Martina Navratilova | 1999 | Lindsay Davenport |
| 1938 | Helen Wills Moody | 1963 | Margaret Smith | | | 2000–01 | Venus Williams |
| | | | | | | 2002 | Serena Williams |

## DOUBLES—MEN

| | | | | | | |
|------|-----------------------------|---------|---------------------------|------|-----------------------------|
| 1953 | K. Rosewall–L. Hoad | 1972 | Bob Hewitt–Frew McMillan | 1986 | Joakim Nystrom–Mats |
| 1954 | R. Hartwig–M. Rose | 1973 | Jimmy Connors–Ilie Nastase | | Wilander |
| 1955 | R. Hartwig–L. Hoad | 1974 | John Newcombe–Tony | 1987 | Ken Flach–Robert Seguso |
| 1956 | L. Hoad–K. Rosewall | | Roche | 1988 | Ken Flach–Robert Seguso |
| 1957 | Gardnar Mulloy–Budge Patty | 1975 | Vitas Gerulaitis–Sandy | 1989 | John Fitzgerald–Anders |
| 1958 | Sven Davidson–Ulf Schmidt | | Mayer | | Jarryd |
| 1959 | Roy Emerson–Neale Fraser | 1976 | Brian Gottfried–Raul | 1990 | Rick Leach–Jim Pugh |
| 1960 | Dennis Ralston–Rafael | | Ramirez | 1991 | Anders Jarryd–John |
| | Osuna | 1977 | Ross Case–Geoff Masters | | Fitzgerald |
| 1961 | Roy Emerson–Neale Fraser | 1978 | Fred McMillan–Bob Hewitt | 1992 | John McEnroe–Michael |
| 1962 | Fred Stolle–Bob Hewitt | 1979 | Peter Fleming–John | | Stich |
| 1963 | Rafael Osuna–Antonio | | McEnroe | 1993–97 | Todd Woodbridge–Mark |
| | Palafox | 1980 | Peter McNamara–Paul | | Woodforde |
| 1964 | Fred Stolle–Bob Hewitt | | McNamee | 1998 | Jacco Eltingh–Paul Haarhuis |
| 1965 | John Newcombe–Tony | 1981 | John McEnroe–Peter | 1999 | Mahesh Bhupathi–Leander |
| | Roche | | Fleming | | Paes |
| 1966 | John Newcombe–Ken | 1982 | Paul McNamee–Peter | 2000 | Todd Woodbridge–Mark |
| | Fletcher | | McNamara | | Woodforde |
| 1967 | Bob Hewitt–Frew McMillan | 1983–84 | John McEnroe–Peter | 2001 | Donald Johnson–Jared |
| 1968–70 | John Newcombe–Tony | | Fleming | | Palmer |
| | Roche | 1985 | Heinz Gunthardt–Balazs | 2002 | Todd Woodbridge–Jonas |
| 1971 | Rod Laver–Roy Emerson | | Taroczy | | Bjorkman |

## DOUBLES—WOMEN

| | | | | | | |
|------|-----------------------------|---------|----------------------------|------|----------------------------|
| 1956 | Althea Gibson–Angela | 1972 | Billie Jean King–Betty Stove | 1986 | Pam Shriver–Martina |
| | Buxton | 1973 | Billie Jean King–Rosemary | | Navratilova |
| 1957 | Althea Gibson–Darlene Hard | | Casals | 1987 | Claudia Khode-Kilsch– |
| 1958 | Althea Gibson–Maria Bueno | 1974 | Evonne Goolagong–Peggy | | Helena Sukova |
| 1959 | Darlene Hard–Jeanne Arth | | Michel | 1988 | Steffi Graf–Gabriela Sabatini |
| 1960 | Darlene Hard–Maria Bueno | 1975 | Ann Kiyomura–Kazuko | 1989 | Jana Novotna–Helena |
| 1961 | Karen Hantze–Billie Jean | | Sawamatsu | | Sukova |
| | Moffitt | 1976 | Chris Evert–Martina | 1990 | Jana Novotna–Helena |
| 1962 | Karen Hantze Susman–Billie | | Navratilova | | Sukova |
| | Jean Moffitt | 1977 | Helen Cawley–JoAnne | 1991 | Pam Shriver–Natalia Zvereva |
| 1963 | Darlene Hard–Maria Bueno | | Russell | 1992 | Gigi Fernandez–Natalia |
| 1964 | Margaret Smith–Les | 1978 | Wendy Turnbull–Kerry Reid | | Zvereva |
| | Turnerley | 1979 | Billie Jean King–Martina | 1993 | Gigi Fernandez–Natalia |
| 1965 | Billie Jean Moffitt–Maria | | Navratilova | | Zvereva |
| | Bueno | 1980 | Kathy Jordan–Anne Smith | 1994 | Gigi Fernandez–Natalia |
| 1966 | Nancy Richey–Maria Bueno | 1981 | Martina Navratilova–Pam | | Zvereva |
| 1967–68 | Billie Jean King–Rosemary | | Shriver | 1995 | Jana Novotna–Arantxa |
| | Casals | 1982–84 | Pam Shriver–Martina | | Sanchez Vicario |
| 1969 | Margaret Court–Judy Tegart | | Navratilova | 1996 | Martina Hingis–Helena |
| 1970–71 | Billie Jean King–Rosemary | 1985 | Kathy Jordan–Elizabeth | | Sukova |
| | Casals | | Smylie | 1997 | Gigi Fernandez–Natasha |
| | | | | | Zvereva |

| 1998 | Martina Hingis–Jana Novotna | 2000 | Venus Williams–Serena Williams | 2002 | Serena Williams–Venus Williams |
|------|------|------|------|------|------|
| 1999 | Lindsay Davenport–Corina Morariu | 2001 | Lisa Raymond–Rennae Stubbs | | |

## WIMBLEDON CHAMPIONS, 2002
(Wimbledon, England, June 23–July 6, 2002)

Men's singles—Lleyton Hewitt defeated David Nalbandian, 6–1, 6–3, 6–2.

Women's singles—Serena Williams defeated Venus Williams, 7–6, 6–3.

Men's doubles—Todd Woodbridge and Jonas Bjorkman defeated Mark Knowles and Daniel Nestor, 6–1, 6–2, 6–7 (7–9), 7–5.

Women's doubles—Serena Williams and Venus Williams defeated Virgina Ruano Pascual and Paola Suarez, 6–2, 7–5.

Mixed doubles—Elena Likhovtseva and Mahesh Bhupathi defeated Daniela Hantuchova and Kevin Ullyett, 6–2, 1–6, 6–1.

## OTHER 2002 GRAND SLAM CHAMPIONS

### French Open
**(Paris, May 27–June 9, 2002)**

Men's singles—Albert Costa defeated Juan Carlos Ferrero, 6–1, 6–0, 4–6, 6–3.

Women's singles—Serena Williams defeated Venus Williams, 7–5, 6–3.

Men's doubles—Paul Haarhuir and Yevgeny Kafelnikov defeated Mark Knowles and Daniel Nestor, 7–5, 6–4.

Women's doubles—Virginia Ruano Pascual and Paola Suarez defeated Lisa Raymond and Rennae Stubbs, 6–4, 6–2.

Mixed doubles—Cara Black and Wayne Black defeated Elena Bovina and Mark Knowles, 6–3, 6–3.

### Australian Open
**(Melbourne, Australia, Jan. 14–27, 2002)**

Men's singles—Thomas Johansson defeated Marat Safin, 3–6, 6–4, 6–4, 7–6 (7–4).

Women's singles—Jennifer Capriati defeated Martina Hingis, 4–6, 7–6 (9–7), 6–2.

Men's doubles—Mark Knowles and Daniel Nestor defeated Michael Llodra and Fabrice Santor, 7–6 (7–4), 6–3.

Women's doubles—Martina Hingis and Anna Kournikova defeated Daniela Hantuchova and Arantxa Sanchez-Vicario, 6–2, 6–7 (4–7), 6–1.

Mixed doubles—Kevin Ullyett and Daniela Hantuchova defeated Gaston Etlis and Paola Suarez, 6–3, 6–2.

## OTHER WTA TOURNAMENTS, 2002

| Tournament | Singles champion |
|------|------|
| adidas International, Sydney, Australia | Martina Hingis |
| Toray Pan Pacific Open, Tokyo, Japan | Martina Hingis |
| Open Gaz de France, Paris, France | Venus Williams |
| Proximus Diamond Games, Antwerp, Belgium | Venus Williams |
| Dubai Duty Free, UAE | Amelie Mauresmo |
| State Farm Women's Tennis Classic, Scottsdale, Ariz. | Serena William |
| Abierto Mexicano Pegaso, Acapulco, Mexico | Katarina Srebotnik |
| Pacific Life Open, Indian Wells, Calif. | Daniela Hantuchova |
| NASDAQ-100 Open, Miami, Fla. | Serena Williams |
| Family Circle Cup, Charleston, S.C. | Iva Majoli |
| Betty Barclay Cup, Hamburg, Germany | Kim Clijsters |
| EUROCARD Ladies German Open, Berlin, Germany | Justine Henin |
| Tennis Masters Series, Rome, Italy | Serena Williams |
| Open de España, Madrid, Spain | Monica Seles |
| Britannic Asset Management Int'l Championships, Eastbourne, England | Chanda Rubin |
| Bank of the West Classic, Stanford, Calif. | Venus Williams |
| Acura Classic, San Diego, Calif. | Venus Williams |
| Rogers AT&T Cup, Montreal, Canada | Amelie Mauresmo |
| Pilot Pen Tennis, New Haven Conn. | Venus Williams |

*Source:* www.wtatour.com.

## WOMEN'S TOP 5 MONEY WINNERS, 2002

| | | |
|---|---|---|
| 1. | Serena Williams | $3,073,076 |
| 2. | Venus Williams | 2,043,761 |
| 3. | Jennifer Capriati | 1,400,679 |
| 4. | Martina Hingis | 1,046,024 |
| 5. | Daniela Hantuchova | 1,013,279 |

As of Sept. 10, 2002. *Source:* www.wtatour.com.

## OTHER ATP TOURNAMENTS, 2002

| Tournament | Singles champion |
|------|------|
| Marseille, France | Thomas Enqvist |
| Memphis, Tenn. | Andy Roddick |
| Rotterdam, Netherlands | Nicolas Escude |
| Dubai, UAE | Fabrice Santoro |
| Acapulco, Mexico | Carlos Moya |
| Indian Wells, Calif. | Lleyton Hewitt |
| Miami, Fla. | Andre Agassi |
| Monte Carlo, Monaco | Juan Carlos Ferrero |
| Barcelona, Spain | Gaston Gaudio |
| Rome, Italy | Andre Agassi |
| Hamburg, Germany | Roger Federer |
| London/Queen's Club, England | Lleyton Hewitt |
| Halle, Germany | Yevgeny Kafelnikov |
| Gstaad, Switzerland | Alex Corretja |
| Kitzbuhel, Austria | Alex Corretja |
| Toronto, Canada | Guillermo Canas |
| Cincinnati, Ohio | Carlos Moya |
| Washington, DC | James Blake |
| Indianapolis, Ind. | Greg Rusedski |

*Source:* www.atptour.com.

## MEN'S TOP 5 MONEY WINNERS, 2002

| | | |
|---|---|---|
| 1. | Lleyton Hewitt | $2,113,989 |
| 2. | Andre Agassi | 1,639,486 |
| 3. | Pete Sampras | 1,222,999 |
| 4. | Albert Costa | 1,162,839 |
| 5. | Juan Carlos Ferrero | 1,125,498 |

As of Sept. 10, 2002. *Source:* www.atptour.com.

# Harness Racing

Oliver Wendell Holmes, the famous Autocrat of the Breakfast Table, wrote that the running horse was a gambling toy but the trotting horse was useful and, furthermore, "horse-racing is not a republican institution; horse-trotting is." Oliver Wendell Holmes was a born-and-bred New Englander, and New England was the nursery of the harness racing sport in America. Pacers and trotters were matters of local pride and prejudice in colonial New England, and, shortly after the Revolution, the Messenger and Justin Morgan strains produced many winners in harness racing "matches" along the turnpikes of New York, Connecticut, Rhode Island, Massachusetts, Vermont, and New Hampshire.

There was English thoroughbred blood in Messenger and Justin Morgan, and, many years later, it was blended in Rysdyk's Hambletonian, foaled in 1849. Hambletonian was not particularly fast under harness but his descendants have had almost a monopoly of prizes, titles, and records in the harness racing game. Hambletonian was purchased as a foal with its dam for a total of $124 by William Rysdyk of Goshen, N.Y., and made a modest fortune for the purchaser.

Trotters and pacers often were raced under saddle in the old days, and, in fact, the custom still survives in some places in Europe. Dexter, the great trotter that lowered the mile record from 2:19¾ to 2:17 ¼ in 1867, was said to handle just as well under saddle as when pulling a sulky. But as sulkies were lightened in weight and improved in design, trotting under saddle became less common and finally faded out in this country.

## HISTORY OF TRADITIONAL HARNESS RACING STAKES

## THE HAMBLETONIAN

| Year | Winner | Driver | Best time | Total purse |
|------|--------|--------|-----------|-------------|
| 1967 | Speedy Streak | Del Cameron | 2:00 | $122,650 |
| 1968 | Nevele Pride | Stanley Dancer | 1:59.2 | 116,190 |
| 1969 | Lindy's Pride | Howard Beissinger | 1:57 .3 | 124,910 |
| 1970 | Timothy T. | John Simpson, Jr. | 1:58.2[1] | 143,630 |
| 1971 | Speedy Crown | Howard Beissinger | 1:57.2 | 129,770 |
| 1972 | Super Bowl | Stanley Dancer | 1:56.2 | 119,090 |
| 1973 | Flirth | Ralph Baldwin | 1:57.1 | 144,710 |
| 1974 | Christopher T | Billy Haughton | 1:58.3 | 160,150 |
| 1975 | Bonefish | Stanley Dancer | 1:59[2] | 232,192 |
| 1976 | Steve Lobell | Billy Haughton | 1:56.2 | 263,524 |
| 1977 | Green Speed | Billy Haughton | 1:55.3 | 284,131 |
| 1978 | Speedy Somolli | Howard Beissinger | 1:55[3] | 241,280 |
| 1979 | Legend Hanover | George Sholty | 1:56.1 | 300,000 |
| 1980 | Burgomeister | Billy Haughton | 1:56.3 | 293,570 |
| 1981 | Shiaway St. Pat | Ray Remmen | 2:01.1[4] | 838,000 |
| 1982 | Speed Bowl | Tommy Haughton | 1:56.4 | 875,750 |
| 1983 | Duenna | Stanley Dancer | 1:57.2 | 1,000,000 |
| 1984 | Historic Freight | Ben Webster | 1:56.2[5] | 1,219,000 |
| 1985 | Prakas | Bill O'Donnell | 1:54.3 | 1,272,000 |
| 1986 | Nuclear Kosmos | Ulf Thoresen | 1:55.2[6] | 1,172,082 |
| 1987 | Mack Lobell | John Campbell | 1:53.3 | 1,046,300 |
| 1988 | Armbro Goal | John Campbell | 1:54.3 | 1,156,800 |
| 1989 | Park Avenue Joe and Probe* | Ron Wayples Bill Fahy | 1:54.3 | 1,131,000 |
| 1990 | Harmonious | John Campbell | 1:54.1 | 1,346,000 |
| 1991 | Giant Victory | Jack Moiseyev | 1:54.4 | 1,238,000 |
| 1992 | Alf Palema | Mickey McNichol | 1:56.2[7] | 1,200,000 |
| 1993 | American Winner | Ron Pierce | 1:53.1 | 1,200,000 |
| 1994 | Victory Dream | Mike Lachance | 1:53.4 | 1,200,000 |
| 1995 | Tagliabue | John Campbell | 1:54.4 | 1,200,000 |
| 1996 | Continentalvictory | Mike Lachance | 1:52.1 | 1,200,000 |
| 1997 | Malabar Man | Malvern Burroughs | 1:53.4 | 1,000,000 |
| 1998 | Muscles Yankee | John Campbell | 1:52.2 | 1,000,000 |
| 1999 | Self Possessed | Mike Lachance | 1:51.3 | 1,000,000 |
| 2000 | Yankee Paco | Travor Ritchie | 1:53.2 | 1,000,000 |
| 2001 | Scarlet Knight | Stefan Melander | 1:53.4 | 1,000,000 |
| 2002 | Chip Chip Hooray | Eric Ledford | 1:53.3 | 1,000,000 |

Three-year-old trotters. One mile. Guy McKinney won first race at Syracuse in 1926; held at Goshen, N.Y., 1930–1942, 1944–1956; at Yonkers, N.Y., 1943; at Du Quoin, Ill., 1957–1980. Since 1981, the race has been held at The Meadowlands in East Rutherford, N.J. *Cowinners. Fastest heat won by: 1. By Formal Notice. 2. By Yankee Bambino. 3. By Speedy Somolli and Florida Pro. 4. By Super Juan. 5. Delvin G. Hanover. 6. Royal Prestige. 7. Baltic Sonata.

# LITTLE BROWN JUG

| Year | Winner | Driver | Best time | Total purse |
|------|--------|--------|-----------|-------------|
| 1967 | Best of All | Jim Hackett | 1:59[1] | $84,778 |
| 1968 | Rum Customer | Billy Haughton | 1:59.3 | 104,226 |
| 1969 | Laverne Hanover | Billy Haughton | 2:00.2 | 109,731 |
| 1970 | Most Happy Fella | Stanley Dancer | 1:57.1 | 100,110 |
| 1971 | Nansemond | Herve Filion | 1:57.2 | 102,994 |
| 1972 | Strike Out | Keith Waples | 1:56.3 | 104,916 |
| 1973 | Melvin's Woe | Joe O'Brien | 1:57.3 | 120,000 |
| 1974 | Ambro Omaha | Billy Haughton | 1:57 | 132,630 |
| 1975 | Seatrain | Ben Webster | 1:57[2] | 147,813 |
| 1976 | Keystone Ore | Stanley Dancer | 1:56.4[3] | 153,799 |
| 1977 | Governor Skipper | John Chapman | 1:56.1 | 150,000 |
| 1978 | Happy Escort | William Popfinger | 1:55.2[4] | 186,760 |
| 1979 | Hot Hitter | Herve Filion | 1:55.3 | 226,455 |
| 1980 | Niatross | Clint Galbraith | 1:54.4 | 207,361 |
| 1981 | Fan Hanover | Glen Garnsey | 1:56[5] | 243,799 |
| 1982 | Merger | John Campbell | 1:56.3 | 328,900 |
| 1983 | Ralph Hanover | Ron Waples | 1:55.3 | 358,800 |
| 1984 | Colt 46 | Norman Boring | 1:53.3 | 366,717 |
| 1985 | Nihilator | Bill O'Donnell | 1:52.1 | 350,730 |
| 1986 | Barberry Spur | Bill O'Donnell | 1:52.4 | 407,684 |
| 1987 | Jaguar Spur | Richard Stillings | 1:55.3 | 412,330 |
| 1988 | B.J. Scoot | Mike Lachance | 1:52.3 | 486,050 |
| 1989 | Goalie Jeff | Mike Lachance | 1:54.1 | 500,200 |
| 1990 | Beach Towel | Ray Remmen | 1:53.3 | 253,049 |
| 1991 | Precious Bunny | Jack Moiseyev | 1:54.1 | 575,150 |
| 1992 | Fake Left | Ron Waples | 1:54.2 | 556,210 |
| 1993 | Life Sign | John Campbell | 1:52 | 465,500 |
| 1994 | Magical Mike | Mike Lachance | 1:52.3 | 512,830 |
| 1995 | Nick's Fantasy | John Campbell | 1:51.2 | 543,670 |
| 1996 | Armbro Operative | Jack Moiyesev | 1:52.3 | 542,220 |
| 1997 | Western Dreamer | Mike Lachance | 1:51.1 | 605,210 |
| 1998 | Shady Character | Ron Pierce | 1:52.3 | 566,630 |
| 1999 | Blissfull Hall | Ron Pierce | 1:55.3 | 543,980 |
| 2000 | Astreos | Chris Christoforou | 1:55.3 | 547,972 |
| 2001 | Bettor's Delight | Mike Lachance | 1:51.4 | 646,050 |
| 2002 | Million Dollar Cam | Luc Ouellette | 1:50.2 | 618,625 |

Three-year-old pacers. One Mile. Raced at Delaware County Fair Grounds, Delaware, Ohio. 1. By Nardin's Byrd. 2. By Albert's Star. 3. By Armbro Ranger. 4. By Falcon Almahurst. 5. By Seahawk Hanover.

# HARNESS HORSE OF THE YEAR

| | | | | | |
|------|--------|------|--------|------|--------|
| 1959 | Bye Bye Byrd, Pacer | 1976 | Keystone Ore, Pacer | 1990 | Beach Towell |
| 1960–61 | Adios Butler, Pacer | 1977 | Green Speed, Trotter | 1991 | Precious Bunny |
| 1962 | Su Mac Lad, Trotter | 1978 | Abercrombie, Pacer | 1992 | Artsplace |
| 1963 | Speedy Scot, Trotter | 1979–80 | Niatross, Pacer | 1993 | Staying Together |
| 1964–66 | Bret Hanover, Pacer | 1981 | Fan Hanover, Pacer | 1994 | Cam's Card Shark |
| 1967–69 | Nevele Pride, Trotter | 1982–83 | Cam Fella, Pacer | 1995 | CR Kay Suzie |
| 1970 | Fresh Yankee, Trotter | 1984 | Fancy Crown, Trotter | 1996 | Continentalvictory |
| 1971–72 | Albatross, Pacer | 1985 | Nihilator, Trotter | 1997 | Malabar Man |
| 1973 | Sir Dalrae, Pacer | 1986 | Forrest Skipper | 1998–99 | Moni Maker |
| 1974 | Delmonica Hanover, Trotter | 1987–88 | Mack Lobell | 2000 | Gallo Blue Chip |
| 1975 | Savoir, Trotter | 1989 | Matt's Scooter | 2001 | Bunny Lake |

Chosen in poll conducted by U.S. Trotting Association in conjunction with the U.S. Harness Writers Association.

# Golf

It may be that golf originated in Holland—historians believe it did—but certainly Scotland fostered the game and is famous for it. In fact, in 1457 the Scottish Parliament, disturbed because football and golf had lured young Scots from the more soldierly exercise of archery, passed an ordinance that "futeball and golf be utterly cryit doun and nocht usit." James I and Charles I of the royal line of Stuarts were golf enthusiasts, whereby the game came to be known as "the royal and ancient game of golf."

The golf balls used in the early games were leather-covered and stuffed with feathers. Clubs of all kinds were fashioned by hand to suit individual players. The great step in spreading the game came with the change from the feather ball to the gutta-percha ball about 1850. In 1860, formal competition began with the establishment of an annual tournament for the British Open championship. There are records of "golf clubs" in the United States as far

back as colonial days but no proof of actual play before John Reid and some friends laid out six holes on the Reid lawn in Yonkers, N.Y., in 1888 and played there with golf balls and clubs brought over from Scotland by Robert Lockhart. This group then formed the St. Andrews Golf Club of Yonkers, and golf was established in this country.

However, it remained a rather sedate and almost aristocratic pastime until a 20-year-old ex-caddy, Francis Ouimet of Boston, defeated two great British professionals, Harry Vardon and Ted Ray, in the United States Open championship at Brookline, Mass., in 1913. This feat put the game and Francis Ouimet on the front pages of the newspapers and stirred a wave of enthusiasm for the sport. The greatest feat so far in golf history is that of Robert Tyre Jones, Jr., of Atlanta, who won the British Open, the British Amateur, the U.S. Open, and the U.S. Amateur titles in one year, 1930.

## THE MASTERS TOURNAMENT WINNERS

### Augusta National Golf Club, Augusta, Ga.

| Year | Winner | Score | Year | Winner | Score | Year | Winner | Score |
|------|--------|-------|------|--------|-------|------|--------|-------|
| 1934 | Horton Smith | 284 | 1959 | Art Wall, Jr. | 284 | 1982 | Craig Stadler[1] | 284 |
| 1935 | Gene Sarazen[1] | 282 | 1960 | Arnold Palmer | 282 | 1983 | Severiano Ballesteros | 280 |
| 1936 | Horton Smith | 285 | 1961 | Gary Player | 280 | 1984 | Ben Crenshaw | 277 |
| 1937 | Byron Nelson | 283 | 1962 | Arnold Palmer[1] | 280 | 1985 | Bernhard Langer | 282 |
| 1938 | Henry Picard | 285 | 1963 | Jack Nicklaus | 286 | 1986 | Jack Nicklaus | 279 |
| 1939 | Ralph Guldahl | 279 | 1964 | Arnold Palmer | 276 | 1987 | Larry Mize[1] | 285 |
| 1940 | Jimmy Demaret | 280 | 1965 | Jack Nicklaus | 271 | 1988 | Sandy Lyle | 281 |
| 1941 | Craig Wood | 280 | 1966 | Jack Nicklaus[1] | 288 | 1989 | Nick Faldo[1] | 283 |
| 1942 | Byron Nelson[1] | 280 | 1967 | Gay Brewer, Jr. | 280 | 1990 | Nick Faldo | 278 |
| 1943–45 No Tournaments | | | 1968 | Bob Goalby | 277 | 1991 | Ian Woosnam | 277 |
| 1946 | Herman Keiser | 282 | 1969 | George Archer | 281 | 1992 | Fred Couples | 275 |
| 1947 | Jimmy Demaret | 281 | 1970 | Billy Casper[1] | 279 | 1993 | Bernard Langer | 277 |
| 1948 | Claude Harmon | 279 | 1971 | Charles Coody | 279 | 1994 | Jose Maria Olazabal | 279 |
| 1949 | Sam Snead | 282 | 1972 | Jack Nicklaus | 286 | 1995 | Ben Crenshaw | 274 |
| 1950 | Jimmy Demaret | 283 | 1973 | Tommy Aaron | 283 | 1996 | Nick Faldo | 276 |
| 1951 | Ben Hogan | 280 | 1974 | Gary Player | 278 | 1997 | Tiger Woods | 270 |
| 1952 | Sam Snead | 286 | 1975 | Jack Nicklaus | 276 | 1998 | Mark O'Meara | 279 |
| 1953 | Ben Hogan | 274 | 1976 | Ray Floyd | 271 | 1999 | Jose Maria Olazabal | 280 |
| 1954 | Sam Snead[1] | 289 | 1977 | Tom Watson | 276 | 2000 | Vijay Singh | 278 |
| 1955 | Cary Middlecoff | 279 | 1978 | Gary Player | 277 | 2001 | Tiger Woods | 272 |
| 1956 | Jack Burke | 289 | 1979 | Fuzzy Zoeller[1] | 280 | 2002 | Tiger Woods | 276 |
| 1957 | Doug Ford | 283 | 1980 | Severiano Ballesteros | 275 | | | |
| 1958 | Arnold Palmer | 284 | 1981 | Tom Watson | 280 | | | |

1. Winner in playoff.

## U.S. OPEN CHAMPIONS

| Year | Winner | Score | Where played | Year | Winner | Score | Where played |
|------|--------|-------|--------------|------|--------|-------|--------------|
| 1895 | Horace Rawlins | 173 | Newport | 1910 | Alex Smith[1] | 298 | Philadelphia |
| 1896 | James Foulis | 152 | Shinnecock Hills | 1911 | John McDermott[1] | 307 | Chicago |
| 1897 | Joe Lloyd | 162 | Chicago | 1912 | John McDermott | 294 | Buffalo |
| 1898[3] | Fred Herd | 328 | Myopia | 1913 | Francis Ouimet[1, 2] | 304 | Brookline |
| 1899 | Willie Smith | 315 | Baltimore | 1914 | Walter Hagen | 290 | Midlothian |
| 1900 | Harry Vardon | 313 | Chicago | 1915 | Jerome D. Travers[2] | 297 | Baltusrol |
| 1901 | Willie Anderson[1] | 331 | Myopia | 1916 | Charles Evans, Jr.[2] | 286 | Minikahda |
| 1902 | Laurie Auchterlonie | 307 | Garden City | 1917–18 | No tournaments[4] | | |
| 1903 | Willie Anderson[1] | 307 | Baltusrol | 1919 | Walter Hagen[2] | 301 | Brae Burn |
| 1904 | Willie Anderson | 303 | Glen View | 1920 | Edward Ray | 295 | Inverness |
| 1905 | Willie Anderson | 314 | Myopia | 1921 | Jim Barnes | 289 | Columbia |
| 1906 | Alex Smith | 295 | Onwentsia | 1922 | Gene Sarazen | 288 | Skokie |
| 1907 | Alex Ross | 302 | Philadelphia | 1923 | R. T. Jones, Jr.[1, 2] | 296 | Inwood |
| 1908 | Fred McLeod[1] | 322 | Myopia | 1924 | Cyril Walker | 297 | Oakland Hills |
| 1909 | George Sargent | 290 | Englewood | 1925 | Willie Macfarlane[1] | 291 | Worcester |

| Year | Winner | Score | Where played | Year | Winner | Score | Where played |
|---|---|---|---|---|---|---|---|
| 1926 | R. T. Jones, Jr.[2] | 293 | Scioto | 1967 | Jack Nicklaus | 275 | Baltusrol |
| 1927 | Tommy Armour[1] | 301 | Oakmont | 1968 | Lee Trevino | 275 | Oak Hill |
| 1928 | Johnny Farrell[1] | 294 | Olympia Fields | 1969 | Orville Moody | 281 | Champions G.C. |
| 1929 | R. T. Jones, Jr.[1,2] | 294 | Winged Foot | 1970 | Tony Jacklin | 281 | Hazeltine |
| 1930 | R. T. Jones, Jr.[2] | 287 | Interlachen | 1971 | Lee Trevino[1] | 280 | Merion |
| 1931 | Billy Burke[1] | 292 | Inverness | 1972 | Jack Nicklaus | 290 | Pebble Beach |
| 1932 | Gene Sarazen | 286 | Fresh Meadow | 1973 | Johnny Miller | 279 | Oakmont |
| 1933 | John Goodman[2] | 287 | North Shore | 1974 | Hale Irwin | 287 | Winged Foot |
| 1934 | Olin Dutra | 293 | Merion | 1975 | Lou Graham[1] | 287 | Medinah |
| 1935 | Sam Parks, Jr. | 299 | Oakmont | 1976 | Jerry Pate | 277 | Atlanta A.C. |
| 1936 | Tony Manero | 282 | Baltusrol | 1977 | Hubert Green | 278 | Southern Hills |
| 1937 | Ralph Guldahl | 281 | Oakland Hills | 1978 | Andy North | 285 | Cherry Hills |
| 1938 | Ralph Guldahl | 284 | Cherry Hills | 1979 | Hale Irwin | 284 | Inverness |
| 1939 | Byron Nelson[1] | 284 | Philadelphia | 1980 | Jack Nicklaus | 272 | Baltusrol |
| 1940 | Lawson Little[1] | 287 | Canterbury | 1981 | David Graham | 273 | Merion |
| 1941 | Craig Wood | 284 | Colonial | 1982 | Tom Watson | 282 | Pebble Beach |
| 1942–45 | No tournaments[5] | | | 1983 | Larry Nelson | 280 | Oakmont |
| 1946 | Lloyd Mangrum[1] | 284 | Canterbury | 1984 | Fuzzy Zoeller[1] | 276 | Winged Foot |
| 1947 | Lew Worsham[1] | 282 | St. Louis | 1985 | Andy North | 279 | Oakland Hills |
| 1948 | Ben Hogan | 276 | Riviera | 1986 | Ray Floyd | 279 | Shinnecock Hills |
| 1949 | Cary Middlecoff | 286 | Medinah | 1987 | Scott Simpson | 277 | Olympic Golf Club |
| 1950 | Ben Hogan[1] | 287 | Merion | 1988 | Curtis Strange[1] | 278 | The Country Club |
| 1951 | Ben Hogan | 287 | Oakland Hills | 1989 | Curtis Strange | 278 | Oak Hill Country Club |
| 1952 | Julius Boros | 281 | Northwood | | | | |
| 1953 | Ben Hogan | 283 | Oakmont | 1990 | Hale Irwin[1] | 280 | Medinah C.C. |
| 1954 | Ed Furgol | 284 | Baltusrol | 1991 | Payne Stewart[1] | 282 | Hazeltine |
| 1955 | Jack Fleck[1] | 287 | Olympic | 1992 | Tom Kite | 285 | Pebble Beach |
| 1956 | Cary Middlecoff | 281 | Oak Hill | 1993 | Lee Janzen | 272 | Baltusrol |
| 1957 | Dick Mayer[1] | 298 | Inverness | 1994 | Ernie Els | 279 | Oakmont |
| 1958 | Tommy Bolt | 283 | Southern Hills | 1995 | Corey Pavin | 280 | Shinnecock Hills |
| 1959 | Bill Casper, Jr. | 282 | Winged Foot | 1996 | Steve Jones | 278 | Oakland Hills |
| 1960 | Arnold Palmer | 280 | Cherry Hills | 1997 | Ernie Els | 276 | Congressional C.C. |
| 1961 | Gene Littler | 281 | Oakland Hills | 1998 | Lee Janzen | 280 | Olympic Country Club |
| 1962 | Jack Nicklaus[1] | 283 | Oakmont | | | | |
| 1963 | Julius Boros[1] | 293 | Country Club | 1999 | Payne Stewart | 279 | Pinehurst |
| 1964 | Ken Venturi | 278 | Congressional | 2000 | Tiger Woods | 272 | Pebble Beach |
| 1965 | Gary Player[1] | 282 | Bellerive | 2001 | Retief Goosen | 276 | Southern Hills |
| 1966 | Bill Casper[1] | 278 | Olympic | 2002 | Tiger Woods | 277 | Bethpage Black |

1. Winner in playoff. 2. Amateur. 3. In 1898, competition was extended to 72 holes. 4. In 1917, Jock Hutchison, with a 292, won an Open Patriotic Tournament for the benefit of the American Red Cross at Whitemarsh Valley Country Club. 5. In 1942, Ben Hogan, with a 271 won a Hale American National Open Tournament for the benefit of the Navy Relief Society and USO at Ridgemoor Country Club.

## U.S. AMATEUR CHAMPIONS

|  |  |  |  |  |  |  |  |
|---|---|---|---|---|---|---|---|
| 1895 | Charles B. Macdonald | 1924–25 | R. T. Jones, Jr. | 1954 | Arnold Palmer | 1978 | John Cook |
| | | 1926 | George Von Elm | 1955–56 | Harvie Ward | 1979 | Mark O'Meara |
| 1896–97 | H. J. Whigham | 1927–28 | R. T. Jones, Jr. | 1957 | Hillman Robbins | 1980 | Hal Sutton |
| 1898 | Findlay S. Douglas | 1929 | H. R. Johnston | 1958 | Charles Coe | 1981 | Nathaniel Crosby |
| 1899 | H. M. Harriman | 1930 | R. T. Jones, Jr. | 1959 | Jack Nicklaus | 1982 | Jay Sigel |
| 1900–01 | Walter J. Travis | 1931 | Francis Ouimet | 1960 | Deane Beman | 1983 | Jay Sigel |
| 1902 | Louis N. James | 1932 | Ross Somerville | 1961 | Jack Nicklaus | 1984 | Scott Verplank |
| 1903 | Walter J. Travis | 1933 | G. T. Dunlap, Jr. | 1962 | Labron Harris, Jr. | 1985 | Sam Randolph |
| 1904–05 | H. Chandler Egan | 1934–35 | Lawson Little | 1963 | Deane Beman | 1986 | Buddy Alexander |
| 1906 | Eben M. Byers | 1936 | John W. Fischer | 1964 | Bill Campbell | 1987 | Bill Mayfair |
| 1907–08 | Jerome D. Travers | 1937 | John Goodman | 1965[2] | Robert Murphy, Jr. | 1988 | Eric Meeks |
| 1909 | Robert A. Gardner | 1938 | Willie Turnesa | 1966 | Gary Cowan[1] | 1989 | Chris Patton |
| 1910 | W. C. Fownes, Jr. | 1939 | Marvin H. Ward | 1967 | Bob Dickson | 1990 | Phil Mickelson |
| 1911 | Harold H. Hilton | 1940 | R. D. Chapman | 1968 | Bruce Fleisher | 1991 | Mitch Voges |
| 1912–13 | Jerome D. Travers | 1941 | Marvin H. Ward | 1969 | Steven Melnyk | 1992 | Justin Leonard |
| 1914 | Francis Ouimet | 1946 | Ted Bishop | 1970 | Lanny Wadkins | 1993 | John Harris |
| 1915 | Robert A. Gardner | 1947 | Robert Riegel | 1971 | Gary Cowan | 1994–96 | Tiger Woods |
| 1916 | Charles Evans, Jr. | 1948 | Willie Turnesa | 1972 | Vinny Giles 3d | 1997 | Matthew Kuchar |
| 1919 | S. D. Herron | 1949 | Charles Coe | 1973[3] | Craig Stadler | 1998 | Hank Kuehne |
| 1920 | Charles Evans, Jr. | 1950 | Sam Urzetta | 1974 | Jerry Pate | 1999 | David Gossett |
| 1921 | Jesse P. Guilford | 1951 | Billy Maxwell | 1975 | Fred Ridley | 2000 | Jeff Quinney |
| 1922 | Jess W. Sweetser | 1952 | Jack Westland | 1976 | Bill Sander | 2001 | Bubba Dickerson |
| 1923 | Max R. Marston | 1953 | Gene Littler | 1977 | John Fought | 2002 | Ricky Barnes |

1. Winner in playoff. 2. Tourney switched to medal play through 1972. 3. Return to match play.

## U.S. PGA CHAMPIONS

| | | | | | | | |
|---|---|---|---|---|---|---|---|
| 1916 | Jim Barnes | 1945 | Byron Nelson | 1965 | Dave Marr | 1985 | Hubert Green |
| 1919 | Jim Barnes | 1946 | Ben Hogan | 1966 | Al Geiberger | 1986 | Bob Tway |
| 1920 | Jock Hutchison | 1947 | Jim Ferrier | 1967 | Don January[1] | 1987 | Larry Nelson |
| 1921 | Walter Hagen | 1948 | Ben Hogan | 1968 | Julius Boros | 1988 | Jeff Sluman |
| 1922–23 | Gene Sarazen | 1949 | Sam Snead | 1969 | Ray Floyd | 1989 | Payne Stewart |
| 1924–27 | Walter Hagen | 1950 | Chandler Harper | 1970 | Dave Stockton | 1990 | Wayne Grady |
| 1928–29 | Leo Diegel | 1951 | Sam Snead | 1971 | Jack Nicklaus | 1991 | John Daly |
| 1930 | Tommy Armour | 1952 | Jim Turnesa | 1972 | Gary Player | 1992 | Nick Price |
| 1931 | Tom Creavy | 1953 | Walter Burkemo | 1973 | Jack Nicklaus | 1993 | Paul Azinger[1] |
| 1932 | Olin Dutra | 1954 | Chick Harbert | 1974 | Lee Trevino | 1994 | Nick Price |
| 1933 | Gene Sarazen | 1955 | Doug Ford | 1975 | Jack Nicklaus | 1995 | Steve Elkington |
| 1934 | Paul Runyan | 1956 | Jack Burke, Jr. | 1976 | Dave Stockton | 1996 | Mark Brooks[1] |
| 1935 | Johnny Revolta | 1957 | Lionel Hebert | 1977 | Lanny Wadkins[1] | 1997 | Davis Love III |
| 1936–37 | Denny Shute | 1958[2] | Dow Finsterwald | 1978 | John Mahaffey | 1998 | Vijay Singh |
| 1938 | Paul Runyan | 1959 | Bob Rosburg | 1979 | David Graham[1] | 1999– | |
| 1939 | Henry Picard | 1960 | Jay Hebert | 1980 | Jack Nicklaus | 2000 | Tiger Woods |
| 1940 | Byron Nelson | 1961 | Jerry Barber[1] | 1981 | Larry Nelson | 2001 | David Toms |
| 1941 | Victor Ghezzi | 1962 | Gary Player | 1982 | Ray Floyd | 2002 | Rich Beem |
| 1942 | Sam Snead | 1963 | Jack Nicklaus | 1983 | Hal Sutton | | |
| 1944 | Bob Hamilton | 1964 | Bobby Nichols | 1984 | Lee Trevino | | |

1. Winner in playoff. 2. Switched to medal play.

## U.S. WOMEN'S AMATEUR CHAMPIONS

| | | | | | | | |
|---|---|---|---|---|---|---|---|
| 1916 | Alexa Stirling | 1946 | Mildred Zaharias | 1965 | Jean Ashley | 1984 | Deb Richard |
| 1919–20 | Alexa Stirling | 1947 | Louise Suggs | 1966 | JoAnne Gunderson | 1985 | Michiko Hattori |
| 1921 | Marion Hollins | 1948 | Grace Lenczyk | 1967 | Lou Dill | 1986 | Kay Cockerill |
| 1922 | Glenna Collett | 1949 | Mrs. D. G. Porter | 1968 | JoAnne G. Carner | 1987 | Kay Cockerill |
| 1923 | Edith Cummings | 1950 | Beverly Hanson | 1969 | Catherine LaCoste | 1988 | Pearl Sinn |
| 1924 | Dorothy Campbell Hurd | 1951 | Dorothy Kirby | 1970 | Martha Wilkinson | 1989 | Vicki Goetze |
| | | 1952 | Jacqueline Pung | 1971 | Laura Baugh | 1990 | Pat Hurst |
| 1925 | Glenna Collett | 1953 | Mary Lena Faulk | 1972 | Mary Ann Budke | 1991 | Amy Fruhwirth |
| 1926 | Helen Stetson | 1954 | Barbara Romack | 1973 | Carol Semple | 1992 | Vicki Goetze |
| 1927 | Mrs. M. B. Horn | 1955 | Patricia Lesser | 1974 | Cynthia Hill | 1993 | Jill McGill |
| 1928–30 | Glenna Collett | 1956 | Marlene Stewart | 1975 | Beth Daniel | 1994 | Wendy Ward |
| 1931 | Helen Hicks | 1957 | JoAnne Gunderson | 1976 | Donna Horton | 1995 | Kelli Kuehne |
| 1932–34 | Virginia Van Wie | 1958 | Anne Quast | 1977 | Beth Daniel | 1996 | Kelli Kuehne |
| 1935 | Glenna Collett Vare | 1959 | Barbara McIntire | 1978 | Cathy Sherk | 1997 | Silvia Cavalleri |
| 1936 | Pamela Barton | 1960 | JoAnne Gunderson | 1979 | Carolyn Hill | 1998 | Grace Park |
| 1937 | Mrs. J. A. Page, Jr. | 1961 | Anne Quast Decker | 1980 | Juli Inkster | 1999 | Dorothy Delasin |
| 1938 | Patty Berg | 1962 | JoAnne Gunderson | 1981 | Juli Inkster | 2000 | Marcy Newton |
| 1939–40 | Betty Jameson | 1963 | Anne Quast Welts | 1982 | Juli Inkster | 2001 | Meredith Duncan |
| 1941 | Mrs. Frank Newell | 1964 | Barbara McIntire | 1983 | Joanne Pacillo | 2002 | Becky Lucidi |

## U.S. WOMEN'S OPEN CHAMPIONS

| Year | Winner | Score | Year | Winner | Score | Year | Winner | Score |
|---|---|---|---|---|---|---|---|---|
| 1946 | Patty Berg (match play) | — | 1965 | Carol Mann | 290 | 1985 | Kathy Baker | 280 |
| | | | 1966 | Sandra Spuzich | 297 | 1986 | Jane Geddes[1] | 287 |
| 1947 | Betty Jameson | 295 | 1967 | Catherine LaCoste[2] | 294 | 1987 | Laura Davies[1] | 285 |
| 1948 | Mildred D. Zaharias | 300 | 1968 | Susie Berning | 289 | 1988 | Liselotte Neumann | 277 |
| 1949 | Louise Suggs | 291 | 1969 | Donna Caponi | 294 | 1989 | Betsy King | 278 |
| 1950 | Mildred D. Zaharias | 291 | 1970 | Donna Caponi | 287 | 1990 | Betsy King | 284 |
| 1951 | Betsy Rawls | 293 | 1971 | JoAnne Carner | 288 | 1991 | Meg Mallon | 283 |
| 1952 | Louise Suggs | 284 | 1972 | Susie Berning | 299 | 1992 | Patty Sheehan | 280 |
| 1953 | Betsy Rawls[1] | 302 | 1973 | Susie Berning | 290 | 1993 | Lauri Merten | 280 |
| 1954 | Mildred D. Zaharias | 291 | 1974 | Sandra Haynie | 295 | 1994 | Patty Sheehan | 277 |
| 1955 | Fay Crocker | 299 | 1975 | Sandra Palmer | 295 | 1995 | Annika Sorenstam | 278 |
| 1956 | Katherine Cornelius[1] | 302 | 1976 | JoAnne Carner[1] | 292 | 1996 | Annika Sorenstam | 272 |
| 1957 | Betsy Rawls | 299 | 1977 | Hollis Stacy | 292 | 1997 | Alison Nicholas | 274 |
| 1958 | Mickey Wright | 290 | 1978 | Hollis Stacy | 289 | 1998 | Se Ri Pak | 290 |
| 1959 | Mickey Wright | 287 | 1979 | Jerilyn Britz | 284 | 1999 | Juli Inkster | 272 |
| 1960 | Betsy Rawls | 291 | 1980 | Amy Alcott | 280 | 2000 | Karrie Webb | 282 |
| 1961 | Mickey Wright | 293 | 1981 | Pat Bradley | 279 | 2001 | Karrie Webb | 273 |
| 1962 | Murle Lindstrom | 301 | 1982 | Janet Alex | 283 | 2002 | Juli Inkster | 276 |
| 1963 | Mary Mills | 289 | 1983 | Jan Stephenson | 290 | | | |
| 1964 | Mickey Wright[1] | 290 | 1984 | Hollis Stacy | 290 | | | |

1. Winner in playoff. 2. Amateur.

# BRITISH OPEN CHAMPIONS

## (First tournament, held in 1860, was won by Willie Park, Sr.)

| Year | Winner | Score | Year | Winner | Score | Year | Winner | Score |
|---|---|---|---|---|---|---|---|---|
| 1920 | George Duncan | 303 | 1952 | Bobby Locke | 287 | 1978 | Jack Nicklaus | 281 |
| 1921 | Jock Hutchison | 296 | 1953 | Ben Hogan | 282 | 1979 | Severiano Ballesteros | 283 |
| 1922 | Walter Hagen | 300 | 1954 | Peter Thomson | 283 | 1980 | Tom Watson | 271 |
| 1923 | A. G. Havers | 295 | 1955 | Peter Thomson | 281 | 1981 | Bill Rogers | 276 |
| 1924 | Walter Hagen | 301 | 1956 | Peter Thomson | 286 | 1982 | Tom Watson | 284 |
| 1925 | Jim Barnes | 300 | 1957 | Bobby Locke | 279 | 1983 | Tom Watson | 275 |
| 1926 | R. T. Jones, Jr. | 291 | 1958 | Peter Thomson | 278 | 1984 | Severiano Ballesteros | 276 |
| 1927 | R. T. Jones, Jr. | 285 | 1959 | Gary Player | 284 | 1985 | Sandy Lyle | 282 |
| 1928 | Walter Hagen | 292 | 1960 | Kel Nagle | 278 | 1986 | Greg Norman | 280 |
| 1929 | Walter Hagen | 292 | 1961 | Arnold Palmer | 284 | 1987 | Nick Faldo | 279 |
| 1930 | R. T. Jones, Jr. | 291 | 1962 | Arnold Palmer | 276 | 1988 | Seve Ballesteros | 273 |
| 1931 | Tommy Armour | 296 | 1963 | Bob Charles | 277 | 1989 | Mark Calcavecchia | 275 |
| 1932 | Gene Sarazen | 283 | 1964 | Tony Lema | 279 | 1990 | Nick Faldo | 270 |
| 1933 | Denny Shute | 292 | 1965 | Peter Thomson | 285 | 1991 | Ian Baker-Finch | 272 |
| 1934 | Henry Cotton | 283 | 1966 | Jack Nicklaus | 282 | 1992 | Nick Faldo | 272 |
| 1935 | A. Perry | 283 | 1967 | Roberto de Vicenzo | 278 | 1993 | Greg Norman | 267 |
| 1936 | A. H. Padgham | 287 | 1968 | Gary Player | 289 | 1994 | Nick Price | 268 |
| 1937 | Henry Cotton | 290 | 1969 | Tony Jacklin | 280 | 1995 | John Daly | 282 |
| 1938 | R. A. Whitcombe | 295 | 1970 | Jack Nicklaus | 283 | 1996 | Tom Lehman | 271 |
| 1939 | R. Burton | 290 | 1971 | Lee Trevino | 278 | 1997 | Justin Leonard | 272 |
| 1940 | Sam Snead | 290 | 1972 | Lee Trevino | 278 | 1998 | Mark O'Meara | 280 |
| 1947 | Fred Daly | 294 | 1973 | Tom Weiskopf | 276 | 1999 | Paul Lawrie | 290 |
| 1948 | Henry Cotton | 283 | 1974 | Gary Player | 282 | 2000 | Tiger Woods | 269 |
| 1949 | Bobby Locke | 283 | 1975 | Tom Watson | 279 | 2001 | David Duval | 274 |
| 1950 | Bobby Locke | 279 | 1976 | Johnny Miller | 279 | 2002 | Ernie Els | 278 |
| 1951 | Max Faulkner | 285 | 1977 | Tom Watson | 268 | | | |

## OTHER 2002 PGA TOUR WINNERS

### (Through Sept. 29, 2002)

| Tournament—winner | First place prize money |
|---|---|
| Mercedes Championship—Sergio Garcia | $ 720,000 |
| Sony Open in Hawaii—Jerry Kelly | 720,000 |
| Bob Hope Chrysler Classic—Phil Mickelson | 720,000 |
| Phoenix Open—Chris DiMarco | 720,000 |
| AT&T Pebble Beach National Pro-Am—Matt Gogel | 720,000 |
| Genuity Championship—Ernie Els | 846,000 |
| Honda Classic—Matt Kuchar | 630,000 |
| THE PLAYERS Championship—Craig Perks | 1,080,000 |
| BellSouth Classic—Retief Goosen | 684,000 |
| Verizon Byron Nelson Classic—Shigeki Maruyama | 864,000 |
| Bay Hill Invitational—Tiger Woods | 720,000 |
| Shell Houston Open—Vijay Singh | 720,000 |
| Compaq Classic of New Orleans—K. J. Choi | 810,000 |
| MasterCard Colonial—Nick Price | 774,000 |
| Memorial Tournament—Jim Furyk | 810,000 |
| Buick Classic—Chris Smith | 630,000 |
| Canon Greater Hartford Open—Phil Mickelson | 720,000 |
| The INTERNATIONAL Presented by Qwest—Rich Beem | 810,000 |
| Buick Open—Tiger Woods | 594,000 |
| Bell Canadian Open—John Rollins | 720,000 |
| Air Canada Championship—Gene Sauers | 630,000 |
| American Express Championship—Tiger Woods | 1,000,000 |

Ryder Cup—Europe 15½ pts, America 12½ pts
*Source:* www.golfweb.com.

## OTHER 2002 LPGA TOUR WINNERS

### (Through Sept. 29, 2002)

| Tournament—winner | First place prize money |
|---|---|
| Takefuji Classic—Annika Sörenstam | $135,000 |
| Ping Banner Health—Rachel Teske | 150,000 |
| Welch's-Circle K Championship—Laura Diaz | 120,000 |
| Kraft Nabisco Championship—Annika Sörenstam | 225,000 |
| The Office Depot—Se Ri Pak | 150,000 |
| Chick-fil-A Charity Championship—Juli Inkster | 180,000 |
| Asahi Ryokuken International—Janice Moodie | 180,000 |
| LPGA Corning Classic—Laura Diaz | 150,000 |
| Kellogg-Keebler Classic—Annika Sörenstam | 180,000 |
| McDonald's LPGA Championship—Se Ri Pak | 225,000 |
| Evian Masters—Annika Sörenstam | 315,000 |
| Wegman's Rochester LPGA—Karrie Webb | 180,000 |
| Shoprite LPGA Classic—Annika Sörenstam | 180,000 |
| Jamie Farr Kroger Classic—Rachel Teske | 150,000 |
| Sybase Big Apple Classic—Gloria Park | 142,500 |
| Wendy's Championship for Children—Mi Hyun Kim | 150,000 |
| Weetabix Women's British Open—Karrie Webb | 225,000 |
| Giant Eagle LPGA Classic—Mi Hyun Kim | 150,000 |
| Bank of Montreal Canadian Women's Open—Meg Mallon | 180,000 |
| First Union Betsy King Classic—Se Ri Pak | 180,000 |
| State Farm Classic—Patricia Meunier-Lebouc | 165,000 |
| Williams Championship—Annika Sörenstam | 150,000 |
| Safeway Classic—Annika Sörenstam | 150,000 |

Solheim Cup—America 15½ pts, Europe 12½ pts
*Source:* Ladies Professional Golf Association.
Web: www.lpga.com.

# Auto Racing

## INDIANAPOLIS 500

| Year | Winner | Car | Time | mph | Second place |
|------|--------|-----|------|-----|--------------|
| 1911 | Ray Harroun | Marmon | 6:42:08.000 | 74.590 | Ralph Mulford |
| 1912 | Joe Dawson | National | 6:21:06.000 | 78.720 | Teddy Tetzloff |
| 1913 | Jules Goux | Peugeot | 6:35:05.000 | 75.930 | Spencer Wishart |
| 1914 | René Thomas | Delage | 6:03:45.000 | 82.470 | Arthur Duray |
| 1915 | Ralph DePalma | Mercedes | 5:33:55.510 | 89.840 | Dario Resta |
| 1916[1] | Dario Resta | Peugeot | 3:34:17.000 | 84.000 | Wilbur D'Alene |
| 1919 | Howard Wilcox | Peugeot | 5:40:42.870 | 88.050 | Eddie Hearne |
| 1920 | Gaston Chevrolet | Monroe | 5:38:32.000 | 88.620 | René Thomas |
| 1921 | Tommy Milton | Frontenac | 5:34:44.650 | 89.620 | Roscoe Sarles |
| 1922 | Jimmy Murphy | Murphy Special | 5:17:30.790 | 94.480 | Harry Hartz |
| 1923 | Tommy Milton | H. C. S. Special | 5:29.50.170 | 90.950 | Harry Hartz |
| 1924 | L. L. Corum-Joe Boyer | Dusenberg Special | 5:05:23.510 | 98.230 | Earl Cooper |
| 1925 | Peter DePaolo | Dusenberg Special | 4:56:39.450 | 101.130 | Dave Lewis |
| 1926[2] | Frank Lockhart | Miller Special | 4:10:14.950 | 95.904 | Harry Hartz |
| 1927 | George Souders | Dusenberg Special | 5:07:33.080 | 97.540 | Earl DeVore |
| 1928 | Louis Meyer | Miller Special | 5:01:33.750 | 99.480 | Lou Moore |
| 1929 | Ray Keech | Simplex Special | 5:07:25.420 | 97.580 | Louis Meyer |
| 1930 | Billy Arnold | Miller-Hartz Special | 4:58:39.720 | 100.448 | Shorty Cantlon |
| 1931 | Louis Schneider | Bowes Special | 5:10:27.930 | 96.629 | Fred Frame |
| 1932 | Fred Frame | Miller-Hartz Special | 4:48:03.790 | 104.144 | Howard Wilcox |
| 1933 | Louis Meyer | Tydol Special | 4:48:00.750 | 104.162 | Wilbur Shaw |
| 1934 | Bill Cummings | Boyle Products Special | 4:46:05.200 | 104.863 | Mauri Rose |
| 1935 | Kelly Petillo | Gilmore Special | 4:42:22.710 | 106.240 | Wilbur Shaw |
| 1936 | Louis Meyer | Ring Free Special | 4:35:03.390 | 109.069 | Ted Horn |
| 1937 | Wilbur Shaw | Shaw-Gilmore Special | 4:24:07.800 | 113.580 | Ralph Hepburn |
| 1938 | Floyd Roberts | Burd Piston Ring Special | 4:15:58.400 | 117.200 | Wilbur Shaw |
| 1939 | Wilbur Shaw | Boyle Special | 4:20:47.390 | 115.035 | Jimmy Snyder |
| 1940 | Wilbur Shaw | Boyle Special | 4:22:31.170 | 114.277 | Rex Mays |
| 1941 | Floyd Davis-Mauri Rose | Noc-Out Hose Clamp Special | 4:20:36.240 | 115.117 | Rex Mays |
| 1946 | George Robson | Thorne Engineering Special | 4:21:26.710 | 114.820 | Jimmy Jackson |
| 1947 | Mauri Rose | Blue Crown Special | 4:17:52.170 | 116.338 | Bill Holland |
| 1948 | Mauri Rose | Blue Crown Special | 4:10:23.330 | 119.814 | Bill Holland |
| 1949 | Bill Holland | Blue Crown Special | 4:07:15.970 | 121.327 | Johnny Parsons |
| 1950[3] | Johnnie Parsons | Wynn's Friction Proof Special | 2:46:55.970 | 124.002 | Bill Holland |
| 1951 | Lee Wallard | Belanger Special | 3:57:38.050 | 126.244 | Mike Nazaruk |
| 1952 | Troy Ruttman | Agajanian Special | 3:52:41.880 | 128.922 | Jim Rathmann |
| 1953 | Bill Vukovich | Fuel Injection Special | 3:53:01.690 | 128.740 | Art Cross |
| 1954 | Bill Vukovich | Fuel Injection Special | 3:49:17.270 | 130.840 | Jim Bryan |
| 1955 | Bob Sweikert | John Zink Special | 3:53:59.13 | 128.209 | Tony Bettenhausen |
| 1956 | Pat Flaherty | John Zink Special | 3:53:28.840 | 128.490 | Sam Hanks |
| 1957 | Sam Hanks | Belond Exhaust Special | 3:41:14.250 | 135.601 | Jim Rathmann |
| 1958 | Jimmy Bryan | Belond A-P Special | 3:44:13.800 | 133.791 | George Amick |
| 1959 | Rodger Ward | Leader Card 500 Roadster | 3:40:49.200 | 135.857 | Jim Rathmann |
| 1960 | Jim Rathmann | Ken-Paul Special | 3:36:11.360 | 138.767 | Rodger Ward |
| 1961 | A. J. Foyt | Bowes Special | 3:35:37.490 | 139.130 | Eddie Sachs |
| 1962 | Rodger Ward | Leader Card Special | 3:33:50.330 | 140.293 | Len Sutton |
| 1963 | Parnelli Jones | Agajanian Special | 3:29:35.400 | 143.137 | Jim Clark |
| 1964 | A. J. Foyt | Sheraton-Thompson Spl. | 3:23:35.830 | 147.350 | Rodger Ward |
| 1965 | Jim Clark | Lotus-Ford | 3:19:05.340 | 150.686 | Parnelli Jones |
| 1966 | Graham Hill | Red Ball Lola-Ford | 3:27:52.530 | 144.317 | Jim Clark |
| 1967[4] | A. J. Foyt | Sheraton-Thompson Coyote-Ford | 3:18:24.220 | 151.207 | Al Unser |
| 1968 | Bobby Unser | Hislone Eagle-I Offenhauser | 3:16:13.760 | 152.882 | Dan Gurney |
| 1969 | Mario Andretti | STP Hawk-Ford | 3:11:14.710 | 156.867 | Dan Gurney |
| 1970 | Al Unser | Johnny Lightning P. J. Colt-Ford | 3:12:37.040 | 155.749 | Mark Donohue |
| 1971 | Al Unser | Johnny Lightning P. J. Colt-Ford | 3:10:11.560 | 157.735 | Peter Revson |
| 1972 | Mark Donohue | Sunoco McLaren-Offenhauser | 3:04:05.540 | 162.962 | Al Unser |
| 1973[5] | Gordon Johncock | STP Eagle-Offenhauser | 2:05:26.590 | 159.036 | Bill Vukovich, Jr. |
| 1974 | Johnny Rutherford | McLaren-Offenhauser | 3:09:10.060 | 158.589 | Bobby Unser |
| 1975[6] | Bobby Unser | Jorgensen Eagle-Offenhauser | 2:54:55.080 | 149.213 | Johnny Rutherford |
| 1976[7] | Johnny Rutherford | Hy-gain McLaren-Offenhauser | 1:42:52.480 | 148.725 | A. J. Foyt |
| 1977 | A. J. Foyt | Gilmore Coyote-Foyt | 3:05:57.160 | 161.331 | Tom Sneva |
| 1978 | Al Unser | 1st Nat'l City Lola-Cosworth | 3:05:54.990 | 161.363 | Tom Sneva |
| 1979 | Rick Mears | Gould Penske-Cosworth | 3:08:27.970 | 158.899 | A. J. Foyt |
| 1980 | Johnny Rutherford | Pennzoil Chaparral-Cosworth | 3:29:59.560 | 142.862 | Tom Sneva |
| 1981[8] | Bobby Unser | Norton Penske-Cosworth | 3:35:41.780 | 139.029 | Mario Andretti |
| 1982 | Gordon Johncock | STP Wildcat-Cosworth | 3:05:09.140 | 162.029 | Rick Mears |
| 1983 | Tom Sneva | Texaco Star March-Cosworth | 3:05:03.060 | 162.117 | Al Unser |
| 1984 | Rick Mears | Pennzoil March-Cosworth | 3:03:21.000 | 162.962 | Roberto Guerrero |
| 1985 | Danny Sullivan | Miller March-Cosworth | 3:16:06.069 | 152.982 | Mario Andretti |

| Year | Winner | Car | Time | mph | Second place |
|---|---|---|---|---|---|
| 1986 | Bobby Rahal | Budweiser March-Cosworth | 2:55:43.480 | 170.722 | Kevin Cogan |
| 1987 | Al Unser, Sr. | Cummins March-Cosworth | 3:04:59.147 | 162.175 | Roberto Guerrero |
| 1988 | Rick Mears | Pennzoil Penske P.C.17-Chevrolet | 3:27:10.204 | 144.809 | Emerson Fittipaldi |
| 1989 | Emerson Fittipaldi | Marlboro Penske-Cosworth | 2:59:01.040 | 167.581 | Al Unser, Jr. |
| 1990 | Arie Luyendyk | Domino's Pizza Lola-Cosworth | 2:41:18.248 | 185.987 | Bobby Rahal |
| 1991 | Rick Mears | Marlboro Penske-Cosworth | 2:50:01.018 | 176.460 | Michael Andretti |
| 1992 | Al Unser, Jr. | Valvoline-Chevrolet | 3:43.05.148 | 134.477 | Scott Goodyear |
| 1993 | Emerson Fittipaldi | Penske-Chevrolet | 3:10:49.860 | 157.207 | Arie Luyendyk |
| 1994 | Al Unser, Jr. | Penske-Mercedes | 3:06:29.006 | 160.872 | Jacques Villeneuve |
| 1995 | Jacques Villeneuve | Reynard-Ford | 3:15:17.561 | 156.616 | Christian Fittipaldi |
| 1996 | Buddy Lazier | Reynard-Ford | 3:22:45.753 | 147.956 | Davy Jones |
| 1997 | Arie Luyendyk | G Force-Aurora | 3:25:43.388 | 145.827 | Scott Goodyear |
| 1998 | Eddie Cheever | Dallara-Aurora | 3:26:40.524 | 145.155 | Buddy Lazier |
| 1999 | Kenny Brack | Dallara-Aurora-Goodyear | 3:15:51.182 | 153.176 | Jeff Ward |
| 2000 | Juan Montoya | GForce-Aurora-Firestone | 2:58:59.431 | 167.607 | Buddy Lazier |
| 2001 | Helio Castroneves | Dallara-Aurora-Firestone | 3:31:54.180 | 153.601 | Gil de Ferran |
| 2002 | Helio Castroneves | Dallara-Chevrolet-Firestone | 3:00:10.000 | 166.499 | Paul Tracy |

1. 300 miles. 2. Race ended at 400 miles because of rain. 3. Race ended at 345 miles because of rain. 4. Race, postponed after 18 laps because of rain on May 30, was finished on May 31. 5. Race postponed May 28 and 29 was cut to 332.5 miles because of rain, May 30. 6. Race ended at 435 miles because of rain. 7. Race ended at 255 miles because of rain. 8. Andretti was awarded the victory the day after the race after Bobby Unser, whose car finished first, was penalized one lap and dropped from first place to second for passing other cars illegally under a yellow caution flag. Unser appealed the decision to the U.S. Auto Club and was upheld. A panel ruled the penalty was too severe and instead fined Unser $40,000, but restored the victory to him.

## 2002 NASCAR WINSTON CUP RACES

| Date | Race | Raceway | Winner |
|---|---|---|---|
| Feb. 17 | Daytona 500 | Daytona International Speedway | Ward Burton |
| Feb. 24 | Subway 400 | North Carolina Speedway | Matt Kenseth |
| March 3 | UAW-DaimlerChrysler 400 | Las Vegas Motor Speedway | Sterling Marlin |
| March 10 | MBNA America 500 | Atlanta Motor Speedway | Tony Stewart |
| March 17 | Carolina Dodge Dealers 400 | Darlington Raceway | Sterling Marlin |
| March 24 | Food City 500 | Bristol Motor Speedway | Kurt Busch |
| April 8 | Samsung/RadioShack 500 | Texas Motor Speedway | Matt Kenseth |
| April 14 | Virginia 500 | Martinsville Speedway | Bobby Labonte |
| April 21 | Aaron's 499 | Talladega Superspeedway | Dale Earnhardt, Jr. |
| April 28 | NAPA Auto Parts 500 | California Speedway | Jimmie Johnson |
| May 5 | Pontiac Excitement 400 | Richmond International Raceway | Tony Stewart |
| May 26 | Coca-Cola Racing Family 600 | Lowe's Motor Speedway | Mark Martin |
| June 2 | MBNA Platinum 400 | Dover Downs International Speedway | Jimmie Johnson |
| June 9 | Pocono 500 | Pocono Raceway | Dale Jarrett |
| June 16 | Sirius Satellite Radio 400 | Michigan International Speedway | Matt Kenseth |
| June 23 | Dodge/Save Mart 350 | Infineon Raceway | Ricky Rudd |
| July 6 | Pepsi 400 | Daytona International Speedway | MichaelWaltrip |
| July 14 | Tropicana 400 | Chicagoland Speedway | Kevin Harvick |
| July 21 | New England 300 | New Hampshire International Speedway | Ward Burton |
| July 28 | Pennsylvania 500 | Pocono Raceway | Bill Elliott |
| Aug. 4 | Brickyard 400 | Indianapolis Motor Speedway | Bill Elliott |
| Aug. 11 | Sirius Satellite Radio at The Glen | Watkins Glen International | Tony Stewart |
| Aug. 18 | Pepsi 400 presented by Farmer Jack | Michigan International Speedway | Dale Jarrett |
| Aug. 24 | Sharpie 500 | Bristol Motor Speedway | Jeff Gordon |
| Sept. 1 | Mountain Dew Southern 500 | Darlington Raceway | Jeff Gordon |
| Sept. 7 | Chevy Monte Carlo 400 | Richmond International Raceway | Matt Kenseth |
| Sept. 15 | New Hampshire 300 | New Hampshire International Speedway | Ryan Newman |
| Sept. 22 | MBNA All–American Heroes 400 | Dover International Speedway | Jimmie Johnson |
| Sept. 29 | Protection One 400 | Kansas Speedway | Jeff Gordon |
| Oct. 6 | EA SPORTS 500 | Talladega Superspeedway | Dale Earnhardt, Jr. |

## NATIONAL ASSOCIATION FOR STOCK CAR AUTO RACING
## WINSTON CUP CHAMPIONS

| Year | Champion | Year | Champion | Year | Champion | Year | Champion |
|---|---|---|---|---|---|---|---|
| 1949 | Red Byron | 1964 | Richard Petty | 1981 | Darrell Waltrip | 1993 | Dale Earnhardt |
| 1950 | Bill Rexford | 1965 | Ned Jarrett | 1982 | Darrell Waltrip | 1994 | Dale Earnhardt |
| 1951 | Herb Thomas | 1966 | David Pearson | 1983 | Bobby Allison | 1995 | Jeff Gordon |
| 1952 | Tim Flock | 1967 | Richard Petty | 1984 | Terry Labonte | 1996 | Terry Labonte |
| 1953 | Herb Thomas | 1968–69 | David Pearson | 1985 | Darrell Waltrip | 1997–98 | Jeff Gordon |
| 1954 | Lee Petty | 1970 | Bobby Isaac | 1986 | Dale Earnhardt | 1999 | Dale Jarrett |
| 1955 | Tim Flock | 1971–72 | Richard Petty | 1987 | Dale Earnhardt | 2000 | Bobby Labonte |
| 1956–57 | Buck Baker | 1973 | Benny Parsons | 1988 | Bill Elliott | 2001 | Jeff Gordon |
| 1958–59 | Lee Petty | 1974–75 | Richard Petty | 1989 | Rusty Wallace | 2002[1] | Tony Stewart |
| 1960 | Rex White | 1976–78 | Cale Yarborough | 1990 | Dale Earnhardt | | |
| 1961 | Ned Jarrett | 1979 | Richard Petty | 1991 | Dale Earnhardt | | |
| 1962–63 | Joe Weatherly | 1980 | Dale Earnhardt | 1992 | Alan Kulwicki | | |

1. As of Oct. 6, 2002.

## 2002 NASCAR LEADING POINT WINNERS
### (as of Oct. 6, 2002)

| Driver | Pts | Winnings | Driver | Pts | Winnings |
|--------|-----|----------|--------|-----|----------|
| 1. Tony Stewart | 3,958 | $4,042,800 | 11. Kurt Busch | 3,634 | $2,834,720 |
| 2. Mark Martin | 3,886 | 4,586,960 | 12. Dale Jarrett | 3,594 | 3,382,270 |
| 3. Jimmie Johnson | 3,876 | 2,506,930 | 13. Dale Earnhardt, Jr. | 3,481 | 3,104,080 |
| 4. Ryan Newman | 3,821 | 3,897,400 | 14. Jeff Burton | 3,417 | 3,174,570 |
| 5. Rusty Wallace | 3,786 | 3,454,590 | 15. Michael Waltrip | 3,362 | 2,484,750 |
| 6. Matt Kenseth | 3,757 | 3,317,400 | 16. Ricky Craven | 3,292 | 2,160,040 |
| 7. Jeff Gordon | 3,757 | 4,228,340 | 17. Jeff Green | 3,224 | 1,866,240 |
| 8. Bill Elliott | 3,729 | 3,316,110 | 18. Bobby Labonte | 3,111 | 3,243,950 |
| 9. Ricky Rudd | 3,712 | 3,444,790 | 19. Robby Gordon | 3,089 | 2,617,830 |
| 10. Sterling Marlin | 3,703 | 3,711,150 | 20. Dave Blaney | 3,025 | 2,257,820 |

## INDYCAR CHAMPIONS

| | | | | | | | |
|---|---|---|---|---|---|---|---|
| 1910 | Ray Harroun | 1933 | Louis Meyer | 1962 | Rodger Ward | 1986–87 | Bobby Rahal |
| 1911 | Ralph Mulford | 1934 | Bill Cummings | 1963–64 | A. J. Foyt | 1988 | Danny Sullivan |
| 1912 | Ralph DePalma | 1935 | Kelly Petillo | 1965–66 | Mario Andretti | 1989 | Emerson Fitti- |
| 1913 | Earl Cooper | 1936 | Mauri Rose | 1967 | A. J. Foyt | | paldi |
| 1914 | Ralph DePalma | 1937 | Wilbur Shaw | 1968 | Bobby Unser | 1990 | Al Unser, Jr. |
| 1915 | Earl Cooper | 1938 | Floyd Roberts | 1969 | Mario Andretti | 1991 | Michael Andretti |
| 1916 | Dario Resta | 1939 | Wilbur Shaw | 1970 | Al Unser | 1992 | Bobby Rahal |
| 1917 | Earl Cooper | 1940–41 | Rex Mays | 1971–72 | Joe Leonard | 1993 | Nigel Mansell |
| 1918 | Ralph Mulford | 1946–48 | Ted Horn | 1973 | Roger McCluskey | 1994 | Al Unser, Jr. |
| 1919 | Howard Wilcox | 1949 | Johnnie Parsons | 1974 | Bobby Unser | 1995 | Jacques Ville- |
| 1920 | Gaston Chevrolet | 1950 | Henry Banks | 1975 | A. J. Foyt | | neuve |
| 1921 | Tommy Milton | 1951 | Tony Betten- | 1976 | Gordon Johncock | 1996 | Jimmy Vasser |
| 1922 | James Murphy | | hausen | 1977–78 | Tom Sneva | 1997–98 | Alessandro |
| 1923 | Eddie Hearne | 1952 | Chuck Stevenson | 1979 | Rick Mears | | Zanardi |
| 1924 | James Murphy | 1953 | Sam Hanks | | (CART), A.J. Foyt | 1999 | Juan Montoya |
| 1925 | Peter DePaolo | 1954 | Jimmy Bryan | | (USAC)[1] | 2000 | Gil de Ferran |
| 1926 | Harry Hartz | 1955 | Bob Sweikert | 1980 | Johnny Ruther- | 2001 | Kenny Brack |
| 1927 | Peter DePaolo | 1956–57 | Jimmy Bryan | | ford | 2002 | Cristiano da |
| 1928–29 | Louis Meyer | 1958 | Tony Betten- | 1981–82 | Rick Mears | | Matta |
| 1930 | Billy Arnold | | hausen | 1983 | Al Unser | | |
| 1931 | Louis Schneider | 1959 | Rodger Ward | 1984 | Mario Andretti | | |
| 1932 | Bob Carey | 1960–61 | A. J. Foyt | 1985 | Al Unser | | |

1. Two separate series were held in 1979. NOTE: There have been three sanctioning bodies for the series: the Automobile Association of America (1909–1955), the U.S. Auto Club (1956–1979), and the Championship Auto Racing Team (CART), 1979–present.

## 2002 INDY RACING LEAGUE POINT WINNERS

| Driver | Pts | Driver | Pts | Driver | Pts |
|--------|-----|--------|-----|--------|-----|
| 1. Sam Hornish, Jr. | 531 | 9. Airton Dare | 304 | 17. Robbie Buhl | 177 |
| 2. Helio Castroneves | 511 | 10. Eddie Cheever, Jr. | 280 | 18. Sarah Fisher | 161 |
| 3. Gil de Ferran | 443 | 11. Jeff Ward | 268 | 19. Raul Boesel | 158 |
| 4. Felipe Giaffone | 432 | 12. Laurent Redon | 229 | 20. Eliseo Salazar | 157 |
| 5. Alex Barron | 366 | 13. Billy Boat | 225 | 21. Hobby McGehee | 142 |
| 6. Scott Sharp | 332 | 14. Tomas Scheckter | 210 | 22. Buddy Rice | 140 |
| 7. Al Unser, Jr. | 311 | 15. Richie Hearn | 204 | 23. Greg Ray | 128 |
| 8. Buddy Lazier | 305 | 16. George Mack | 184 | 24. Tony Renna | 121 |

## WORLD GRAND PRIX DRIVER CHAMPIONS

| | | | |
|---|---|---|---|
| 1950 | Giuseppe Farina, Italy, Alfa Romeo | 1964 | John Surtees, England, Ferrari |
| 1951 | Juan Fangio, Argentina, Alfa Romeo | 1965 | Jim Clark, Scotland, Lotus-Ford |
| 1952 | Alberto Ascari, Italy, Ferrari | 1966 | Jack Brabham, Australia, Brabham-Repco |
| 1953 | Alberto Ascari, Italy, Ferrari | 1967 | Denis Hulme, New Zealand, Brabham-Repco |
| 1954 | Juan Fangio, Argentina, Maserati, Mercedes-Benz | 1968 | Graham Hill, England, Lotus-Ford |
| 1955 | Juan Fangio, Argentina, Mercedes-Benz | 1969 | Jackie Stewart, Scotland, Matra-Ford |
| 1956 | Juan Fangio, Argentina, Lancia-Ferrari | 1970 | Jochen Rindt, Austria, Lotus-Ford |
| 1957 | Juan Fangio, Argentina, Maserati | 1971 | Jackie Stewart, Scotland, Tyrrell-Ford |
| 1958 | Mike Hawthorn, England, Ferrari | 1972 | Emerson Fittipaldi, Brazil, Lotus-Ford |
| 1959 | Jack Brabham, Australia, Cooper | 1973 | Jackie Stewart, Scotland, Tyrrell-Ford |
| 1960 | Jack Brabham, Australia, Cooper | 1974 | Emerson Fittipaldi, Brazil, McLaren-Ford |
| 1961 | Phil Hill, United States, Ferrari | 1975 | Niki Lauda, Austria, Ferrari |
| 1962 | Graham Hill, England, BRM | 1976 | James Hunt, Britain, McLaren-Ford |
| 1963 | Jim Clark, Scotland, Lotus-Ford | 1977 | Niki Lauda, Austria, Ferrari |

| | |
|---|---|
| 1978 Mario Andretti, United States, Lotus | 1991 Aryton Senna, Brazil, McLaren-Honda |
| 1979 Jody Scheckter, South Africa, Ferrari | 1992 Nigel Mansell, Britain, Williams-Renault |
| 1980 Alan Jones, Australia, Williams-Ford | 1993 Alain Prost, France, Williams-Renault |
| 1981 Nelson Piquet, Brazil, Brabham-Ford | 1994 Michael Schumacher, Germany, Benetton |
| 1982 Keke Rosberg, Finland, Williams-Ford | 1995 Michael Schumacher, Germany, Benetton Renault |
| 1983 Nelson Piquet, Brazil. Brabham-BMW | 1996 Damon Hill, Britain, Williams |
| 1984 Niki Lauda, Austria, McLaren-Porsche | 1997 Jacques Villeneuve, Canada, Williams-Renault |
| 1985 Alain Prost, France, McLaren-Porsche | 1998 Mika Hakkinen, Finland, McLaren-Mercedes |
| 1986 Alain Prost, France, McLaren-Porsche | 1999 Mika Hakkinen, Finland, McLaren-Mercedes |
| 1987 Nelson Piquet, Brazil, Williams-Honda | 2000 Michael Schumacher, Germany, Ferrari |
| 1988 Aryton Senna, Brazil, McLaren-Honda | 2001 Michael Schumacher, Germany, Ferrari |
| 1989 Alain Prost, France, McLaren-Honda | 2002 Michael Schumacher, Germany, Ferrari |
| 1990 Ayrton Senna, Brazil, McLaren-Honda | |

# Yachting

## AMERICA'S CUP RECORD

First race in 1851 around Isle of Wight, Cowes, England. First defense and all others through 1920 held 30 miles off New York Bay. Races since 1930 held 30 miles off Newport, R.I. Conducted as one race only in 1851 and 1870; best four-of-seven basis, 1871; best two-of-three, 1876–1887; best three-of-five, 1893–1901; best four-of-seven, since 1930. Figures in parentheses indicate number of races won. The next America's Cup is scheduled to begin Feb. 15, 2003.

| Year Winner and owner | Loser and owner |
|---|---|
| 1851 AMERICA (1), John C. Stevens, U.S. | AURORA, T. Le Marchant, England[1] |
| 1870 MAGIC (1), Franklin Osgood, U.S. | CAMBRIA, James Ashbury, England[2] |
| 1871 COLUMBIA (2), Franklin Osgood, U.S.[3] SAPPHO (2), William P. Douglas, U.S. | LIVONIA (1), James Ashbury, England |
| 1876 MADELEINE (2), John S. Dickerson, U.S. | COUNTESS OF DUFFERIN, Chas. Gifford, Canada |
| 1881 MISCHIEF (2), J. R. Busk, U.S. | ATALANTA, Alexander Cuthbert, Canada |
| 1885 PURITAN (2), J. M. Forbes-Gen. Charles Paine, U.S. | GENESTA, Sir Richard Sutton, England |
| 1886 MAYFLOWER (2), Gen. Charles Paine, U.S. | GALATEA, Lt. William Henn, England |
| 1887 VOLUNTEER (2), Gen. Charles Paine, U.S. | THISTLE, James Bell et al., Scotland |
| 1893 VIGILANT (3), C. Oliver Iselin et al., U.S. | VALKYRIE II, Lord Dunraven, England |
| 1895 DEFENDER (3), C. O. Iselin–W. K. Vanderbilt–E. D. Morgan, U.S. | VALKYRIE III, Lord Dunraven–Lord Lonsdale–Lord Wolverton, England |
| 1899 COLUMBIA (3), J. P. Morgan–C. O. Iselin, U.S. | SHAMROCK I, Sir Thomas Lipton, Ireland |
| 1901 COLUMBIA (3), Edwin D. Morgan, U.S. | SHAMROCK II, Sir Thomas Lipton, Ireland |
| 1903 RELIANCE (3), Cornelius Vanderbilt et al., U.S. | SHAMROCK III, Sir Thomas Lipton, Ireland |
| 1920 RESOLUTE (3), Henry Walters et al., U.S. | SHAMROCK IV (2), Sir Thomas Lipton, Ireland |
| 1930 ENTERPRISE (4), Harold S. Vanderbilt et al., U.S. | SHAMROCK V, Sir Thomas Lipton, Ireland |
| 1934 RAINBOW (4), Harold S. Vanderbilt, U.S. | ENDEAVOUR (2), T. O. M. Sopwith, England |
| 1937 RANGER (4), Harold S. Vanderbilt, U.S. | ENDEAVOUR II, T. O. M. Sopwith, England |
| 1958 COLUMBIA (4), Henry Sears et al., U.S. | SCEPTRE, Hugh Goodson et al., England |
| 1962 WEATHERLY (4), Henry D. Mercer et al., U.S. | GRETEL (1), Sir Frank Packer et al., Australia |
| 1964 CONSTELLATION (4), New York Y.C. Syndicate, U.S. | SOVEREIGN (0), J. Anthony Bowden, England |
| 1967 INTREPID (4), New York Y.C. Syndicate, U.S. | DAME PATTIE (0), Sydney (Aust.) Syndicate |
| 1970 INTREPID (4), New York Y.C. Syndicate, U.S. | GRETEL II (1), Sydney (Aust.) Syndicate |
| 1974 COURAGEOUS (4), New York, N.Y. Syndicate, U.S. | SOUTHERN CROSS (0), Sydney (Aust.) Syndicate |
| 1977 COURAGEOUS (4), New York, N.Y. Syndicate, U.S. | AUSTRALIA (0), Sun City (Aust.) Syndicate |
| 1980 FREEDOM (4), New York, N.Y. Syndicate, U.S. | AUSTRALIA (1), Alan Bond et al, Australia |
| 1983 AUSTRALIA II (4), Alan Bond et al., Australia | LIBERTY, (3) New York, N.Y. Syndicate, U.S. |
| 1987 STARS & STRIPES (4), Dennis Conner et al., United States | KOOKABURRA III (0), Iain Murray et al., Australia |
| 1988[4] STARS & STRIPES, Dennis Conner, et al., United States | NEW ZEALAND, Michael Fay, et al., New Zealand |
| 1992 AMERICA 3, Bill Koch, et al., United States | IL MORO DI VENEZIA, Paul Cayard, et al., Italy |
| 1995 BLACK MAGIC, Peter Blake, et al., New Zealand | YOUNG AMERICA, Dennis Conner, et al., United States |
| 2000 NEW ZEALAND, Peter Blake, et al., New Zealand | LUNA ROSSA, Patrizio Bertelli, et al., Italy |

1. Fourteen British yachts started against America; Aurora finished second. 2. Cambria sailed against 23 U.S. yachts and finished tenth. 3. Columbia was disabled in the third race, after winning the first two; Sappho substituted and won the fourth and fifth. 4. Shortly after Dennis Conner and his 60-foot, twin-hulled catamaran easily defeated the challenge of the New Zealand, a 133-foot, single-hulled yacht in the waters off San Diego in early September 1988, a New York State Supreme Court judge ruled that the Americans did not live up to the America's Cup Deed of Gift, which means competing boats must be similar. The judge ruled that the Americans had an unfair advantage over the monohulled ship, and awarded the Cup to New Zealand. However, an Appeal awarded the Cup to the United States.

# Bicycling

## TOUR DE FRANCE–2002
### (July 6–28, 2002)

| | Team | Behind | | | Team | Behind |
|---|---|---|---|---|---|---|
| 1. Lance Armstrong, United States | U.S. Postal | (1) | | 6. Jose Azevedo, Portugal | Once | 15:44 |
| | | | | 7. Francisco Mancebo, Spain | ibanesto.com | 16:05 |
| 2. Joseba Beloki, Spain | Once | 07:17 | | 8. Levi Leipheimer, United States | Rabobank | 17:11 |
| 3. Raimondas Rumsas, Lithuania | Lampre | 08:17 | | 9. Roberto Heras Hernandez, Spain | U.S. Postal | 17:12 |
| 4. Santiago Botero, Colombia | Kelme | 13:10 | | | | |
| 5. Igor Gonzalez de Galdeano, Spain | Once | 13:54 | | 10. Carlos Sastre, Spain | CSC-Tiscali | 19:05 |

1. Completed course in 82 hours, 5 minutes, 12 seconds.

# Marathons

## BOSTON MARATHON
### (April 15, 2002)

| Men | Time | Women | Time |
|---|---|---|---|
| Rodgers Rop, Kenya | 2:09:02 | Margaret Okayo, Kenya | 2:20:43 |
| Wheelchair—Ernst Van Dyk, South Africa | 1:23:19 | Wheelchair—Edith Hunkeler, Switzerland | 1:45:57 |

### OTHER 2002 MARATHONS

**Chicago (Oct. 13, 2002)**

| Men | Time |
|---|---|
| Khalid Khannouchi, Ossining, N.Y. | 2:05:56 |
| Wheelchair—Adam Bleakney, Savoy, Ill. | 1:40:14 |
| Women | |
| Paula Radcliffe, Great Britain | 2:17:18* |
| Wheelchair—Tricia Downing, Denver, Colo. | 2:39:54 |

*World record.

**London (April 14, 2002)**

| Men | Time |
|---|---|
| Khalid Khannouchi, United States | 2:05:38 |
| Wheelchair—D. Weir, Great Britain | 1:39:44 |
| Women | |
| Paula Radcliffe, Great Britain | 2:18:56 |
| Wheelchair—T. Grey-Thompson, Great Britain | 2:22:51 |

**Paris (April 7, 2002)**

| Men | Time |
|---|---|
| Benoit Zwierzchlewski, France | 2:08:18 |
| Women | |
| Marleen Renders, Belgium | 2:23:05 |

**Los Angeles (March 3, 2002)**

| Men | Time |
|---|---|
| Stephen Ndungu, Kenya | 2:10:27 |
| Wheelchair—Ernst Van Dyk, South Africa | 1:28:44 |
| Women | |
| Lyubov Denisova, Russia | 2:28:49 |
| Wheelchair—Ariadne Hernandez, Mexico | 1:55:01 |

# Little League

## LITTLE LEAGUE WORLD SERIES CHAMPIONS

| Year | Champion | Runner-up | Score | Year | Champion | Runner-up | Score |
|---|---|---|---|---|---|---|---|
| 1947 | Williamsport, Pa. | Lock Haven, Pa. | 16–7 | 1965 | Windsor Locks, Conn. | Stoney Creek, Can. | 3–1 |
| 1948 | Lock Haven, Pa. | St. Petersburg, Fla. | 6–5 | 1966 | Houston, Tex. | W. New York, N.J. | 8–2 |
| 1949 | Hammontown, N.J. | Pensacola, Fla. | 5–0 | 1967 | West Tokyo, Japan | Chicago, Ill. | 4–1 |
| 1950 | Houston, Tex. | Bridgeport, Conn. | 2–1 | 1968 | Osaka, Japan | Richmond, Va. | 1–0 |
| 1951 | Stamford, Conn. | Austin, Tex. | 3–0 | 1969 | Taipei, Taiwan | Santa Clara, Calif. | 5–0 |
| 1952 | Norwalk, Conn. | Monongahela, Pa. | 4–3 | 1970 | Wayne, N.J. | Campbell, Calif. | 2–0 |
| 1953 | Birmingham, Ala. | Schenectady, N.Y. | 1–0 | 1971 | Tainan, Taiwan | Gary, Ind. | 12–3 |
| 1954 | Schenectady, N.Y. | Colton, Calif. | 7–5 | 1972 | Taipei, Taiwan | Hammond, Ind. | 6–0 |
| 1955 | Morrisville, Pa. | Merchantville, N.J. | 4–3 | 1973 | Tainan City, Taiwan | Tucson, Ariz. | 12–0 |
| 1956 | Roswell, N.M. | Merchantville, N.J. | 3–1 | 1974 | Kao Hsiung, Taiwan | El Cajon, Calif. | 7–2 |
| 1957 | Monterrey, Mex. | LaMesa, Calif. | 4–0 | 1975 | Lakewood, N.J. | Tampa, Fla. | 4–3 |
| 1958 | Monterrey, Mex. | Kankakee, Ill. | 10–1 | 1976 | Tokyo, Japan | Campbell, Calif. | 10–3 |
| 1959 | Hamtramck, Mich. | Auburn, Calif. | 12–0 | 1977 | Kao Hsiung, Taiwan | El Cajon, Calif. | 7–2 |
| 1960 | Levittown, Pa. | Ft. Worth, Tex. | 5–0 | 1978 | Pin-Tung, Taiwan | Danville, Calif. | 11–1 |
| 1961 | El Cajon, Calif. | El Campo, Tex. | 4–2 | 1979 | Hsien, Taiwan | Campbell, Calif. | 2–1 |
| 1962 | San Jose, Calif. | Kankakee, Ill. | 3–0 | 1980 | Hua Lian, Taiwan | Tampa, Fla. | 4–3 |
| 1963 | Granada Hills, Calif. | Stratford, Conn. | 2–1 | 1981 | Tai-Chung, Taiwan | Tampa, Fla. | 4–2 |
| 1964 | Staten Island, N.Y. | Monterrey, Mex. | 4–0 | 1982 | Kirkland, Wash. | Hsien, Taiwan | 6–0 |

| Year | Champion | Runner-up | Score | Year | Champion | Runner-up | Score |
|------|----------|-----------|-------|------|----------|-----------|-------|
| 1983 | Marietta, Ga. | Barahona, Dom. Rep. | 3–1 | 1994 | Maracaibo, Venezuela | Northridge, Calif. | 4–3 |
| 1984 | Seoul, S. Korea | Altamonte Springs, Fla. | 6–2 | 1995 | Tainan, Taiwan | Spring, Texas | 17–3 |
| | | | | 1996 | Kao-Hsuing City, Taipei | Cranston, R.I. | 13–3 |
| 1985 | Seoul, S. Korea | Mexicali, Mex. | 7–1 | | | | |
| 1986 | Tianan Park, Taiwan | Tucson, Ariz. | 12–0 | 1997 | Guadalupe, Mexico | South Mission Viejo, Calif. | 5–4 |
| 1987 | Hua Lian, Taiwan | Irvine, Calif. | 21–1 | | | | |
| 1988 | Tai-Chung, Taiwan | Pearl City, Haw. | 10–0 | 1998 | Toms River, N.J. | Kashima, Japan | 12–9 |
| 1989 | Trumbull, Conn. | Kaohsiung, Taiwan | 5–2 | 1999 | Hirakata, Osaka, Japan | Phenix City, Ala. | 5–0 |
| 1990 | Taipei, Taiwan | Shippensburg, Pa. | 9–0 | | | | |
| 1991 | Tai-Chung, Taiwan | San Ramon Valley, Calif. | 11–0 | 2000 | Maracaibo, Venezuela | Bellaire, Tex. | 3–2 |
| | | | | 2001 | Tokyo Kitasuna, Tokyo, Japan | Apopka, Fla. | 2–1 |
| 1992* | Long Beach, Calif. | Zamboanga, Phil. | 6–0 | | | | |
| 1993 | Long Beach, Calif. | David Chiriqui, Pan. | 3–2 | 2002 | Louisville, Ky. | Sendai, Japan | 1–0 |

* Long Beach declared a 6–0 winner after the international tournament committee determined that Zamboanga City had used players that were not within its city limits.

# Baseball

The popular tradition that baseball was invented by Abner Doubleday at Cooperstown, N.Y., in 1839 has been enshrined in the Hall of Fame and National Museum of Baseball erected in that town, but research has proved that a game called "Base Ball" was played in this country and England before 1839. The first team baseball as we know it was played at the Elysian Fields, Hoboken, N.J., on June 19, 1846, between the Knickerbockers and the New York Nine. The next fifty years saw a gradual growth of baseball and an improvement of equipment and playing skill.

Historians have it that the first pitcher to throw a curve was William A. (Candy) Cummings in 1867. The Cincinnati Red Stockings were the first all-professional team, and in 1869 they played 64

games without a loss. The standard ball of the same size and weight, still the rule, was adopted in 1872. The first catcher's mask was worn in 1875. The National League was organized in 1876. The first chest protector was worn in 1885. The three-strike rule was put on the books in 1887, and the four-ball ticket to first base was instituted in 1889. The pitching distance was lengthened to 60 feet 6 inches in 1893, and the rules have been modified only slightly since that time.

The American League, under the vigorous leadership of B. B. Johnson, became a major league in 1901. Judge Kenesaw Mountain Landis, by action of the two major leagues, became Commissioner of Baseball in 1921.

## MAJOR LEAGUE ALL-STAR GAME

| Year | Date | Winning league and manager | Runs | Losing league and manager | Runs | Winning pitcher | Losing pitcher | Site | Paid attendance |
|------|------|----------------------------|------|----------------------------|------|-----------------|----------------|------|-----------------|
| 1933 | July 6 | A.L. (Mack) | 4 | N.L. (McGraw) | 2 | Gomez | Hallahan | Chicago A.L. | 47,595 |
| 1934 | July 10 | A.L. (Cronin) | 9 | N.L. (Terry) | 7 | Harder | Mungo | New York N.L. | 48,363 |
| 1935 | July 8 | A.L. (Cochrane) | 4 | N.L. (Frisch) | 1 | Gomez | Walker | Cleveland A.L. | 69,831 |
| 1936 | July 7 | N.L. (Grimm) | 4 | A.L. (McCarthy) | 3 | J. Dean | Grove | Boston N.L. | 25,556 |
| 1937 | July 7 | A.L. (McCarthy) | 8 | N.L. (Terry) | 3 | Gomez | J. Dean | Washington A.L. | 31,391 |
| 1938 | July 6 | N.L. (Terry) | 4 | A.L. (McCarthy) | 1 | Vander Meer | Gomez | Cincinnati N.L. | 27,067 |
| 1939 | July 11 | A.L. (McCarthy) | 3 | N.L. (Hartnett) | 1 | Bridges | Lee | New York A.L. | 62,892 |
| 1940 | July 9 | N.L. (McKechnie) | 4 | A.L. (Cronin) | 0 | Derringer | Ruffing | St. Louis N.L. | 32,373 |
| 1941 | July 8 | A.L. (Baker) | 7 | N.L. (McKechnie) | 5 | E. Smith | Passeau | Detroit A.L. | 54,674 |
| 1942 | July 6 | A.L. (McCarthy) | 3 | N.L. (Durocher) | 1 | Chandler | Cooper | New York N.L. | 34,178 |
| 1943 | July 13 | A.L. (McCarthy) | 5 | N.L. (Southworth) | 3 | Leonard | Cooper | Philadelphia A.L. | 31,938 |
| 1944 | July 11 | N.L. (Southworth) | 7 | A.L. (McCarthy) | 1 | Raffensberger | Hughson | Pittsburgh N.L. | 29,589 |
| 1946 | July 9 | A.L. (O'Neill) | 12 | N.L. (Grimm) | 0 | Feller | Passeau | Boston A.L. | 34,906 |
| 1947 | July 8 | A.L. (Cronin) | 2 | N.L. (Dyer) | 1 | Shea | Sain | Chicago N.L. | 41,123 |
| 1948 | July 13 | A.L. (Harris) | 5 | N.L. (Durocher) | 2 | Raschi | Schmitz | St. Louis A.L. | 34,009 |
| 1949 | July 12 | A.L. (Boudreau) | 11 | N.L. (Southworth) | 7 | Trucks | Newcombe | Brooklyn N.L. | 32,577 |
| 1950 | July 11 | N.L. (Shotton) | 4 | A.L. (Stengel) | 3[1] | Blackwell | Gray | Chicago A.L. | 46,127 |
| 1951 | July 10 | N.L. (Sawyer) | 8 | A.L. (Stengel) | 3 | Maglie | Lopat | Detroit A.L. | 52,075 |
| 1952 | July 8 | N.L. (Durocher) | 3 | A.L. (Stengel) | 2[2] | Rush | Lemon | Philadelphia N.L. | 32,785 |
| 1953 | July 14 | N.L. (Dressen) | 5 | A.L. (Stengel) | 1 | Spahn | Reynolds | Cincinnati N.L. | 30,846 |
| 1954 | July 13 | A.L. (Stengel) | 11 | N.L. (Alston) | 9 | Stone | Conley | Cleveland A.L. | 68,751 |
| 1955 | July 12 | N.L. (Durocher) | 6 | A.L. (Lopez) | 5[3] | Conley | Sullivan | Milwaukee N.L. | 45,643 |
| 1956 | July 10 | N.L. (Alston) | 7 | A.L. (Stengel) | 3 | Friend | Pierce | Washington A.L. | 28,843 |
| 1957 | July 9 | A.L. (Stengel) | 6 | N.L. (Alston) | 5 | Bunning | Simmons | St. Louis N.L. | 30,693 |
| 1958 | July 8 | A.L. (Stengel) | 4 | N.L. (Haney) | 3 | Wynn | Friend | Baltimore A.L. | 48,829 |
| 1959[4] | July 7 | N.L. (Haney) | 5 | A.L. (Stengel) | 4 | Antonelli | Ford | Pittsburgh N.L. | 35,277 |
| | Aug. 3 | A.L. (Stengel) | 5 | N.L. (Haney) | 3 | Walker | Drysdale | Los Angeles N.L. | 55,105 |
| 1960[4] | July 11 | N.L. (Alston) | 5 | A.L. (Lopez) | 3 | Friend | Monbouquette | Kansas City A.L. | 30,619 |
| | July 13 | N.L. (Alston) | 6 | A.L. (Lopez) | 0 | Law | Ford | New York A.L. | 38,362 |
| 1961[4] | July 11 | N.L. (Murtaugh) | 5 | A.L. (Richards) | 4[5] | Miller | Wilhelm | San Francisco N.L. | 44,115 |
| | July 31 | N.L. (Murtaugh) | 1 | A.L. (Richards) | 1[6] | — | — | Boston A.L. | 31,851 |

| Year | Date | Winning league and manager | Runs | Losing league and manager | Runs | Winning pitcher | Losing pitcher | Site | Paid attendance |
|------|------|------|------|------|------|------|------|------|------|
| 1962[4] | July 10 | N.L. (Hutchinson) | 3 | A.L. (Houk) | 1 | Marichal | Pascual | Washington A.L. | 45,480 |
| | July 30 | A.L. (Houk) | 9 | N.L. (Hutchinson) | 4 | Herbert | Mahaffey | Chicago N.L. | 38,359 |
| 1963 | July 9 | N.L. (Dark) | 5 | A.L. (Houk) | 3 | Jackson | Bunning | Cleveland A.L. | 44,160 |
| 1964 | July 7 | N.L. (Alston) | 7 | A.L. (Lopez) | 4 | Marichal | Radatz | New York N.L. | 50,850 |
| 1965 | July 13 | N.L. (March) | 6 | A.L. (Lopez) | 5 | Koufax | McDowell | Minnesota A.L. | 46,706 |
| 1966 | July 12 | N.L. (Alston) | 2 | A.L. (Mele) | 1[5] | Perry | Rickert | St. Louis N.L. | 49,926 |
| 1967 | July 11 | N.L. (Alston) | 2 | A.L. (Bauer) | 1[7] | Drysdale | Hunter | Anaheim A.L. | 46,309 |
| 1968 | July 9 | N.L. (Schoendienst) | 1 | A.L. (Williams) | 0 | Drysdale | Tiant | Houston N.L. | 48,321 |
| 1969 | July 23 | N.L. (Schoendienst) | 9 | A.L. (M. Smith) | 3 | Carlton | Stottlemyre | Washington A.L. | 45,259 |
| 1970 | July 14 | N.L. (Hodges) | 5 | A.L. (Weaver) | 4 | Osteen | Wright | Cincinnati N.L. | 51,838 |
| 1971 | July 13 | A.L. (Weaver) | 6 | N.L. (Anderson) | 4 | Blue | Ellis | Detroit A.L. | 53,559 |
| 1972 | July 25 | N.L. (Murtaugh) | 4 | A.L. (Weaver) | 3[5] | McGraw | McNally | Atlanta N.L. | 53,107 |
| 1973 | July 24 | N.L. (Anderson) | 7 | A.L. (Williams) | 1 | Wise | Blyleven | Kansas City A.L. | 40,849 |
| 1974 | July 23 | N.L. (Berra) | 7 | A.L. (Williams) | 2 | Brett | Tiant | Pittsburgh N.L. | 50,706 |
| 1975 | July 15 | N.L. (Alston) | 6 | A.L. (Dark) | 3 | Matlack | Hunter | Milwaukee A.L. | 51,540 |
| 1976 | July 13 | N.L. (Anderson) | 7 | A.L. (D. Johnson) | 1 | R. Jones | Fidrych | Philadelphia N.L. | 63,974 |
| 1977 | July 19 | N.L. (Anderson) | 7 | A.L. (Martin) | 5 | Sutton | Palmer | New York A.L. | 56,683 |
| 1978 | July 11 | N.L. (Lasorda) | 7 | A.L. (Martin) | 3 | Sutter | Gossage | San Diego N.L. | 51,549 |
| 1979 | July 17 | N.L. (Lasorda) | 7 | A.L. (Lemon) | 6 | Sutter | Kern | Seattle A.L. | 58,905 |
| 1980 | July 8 | N.L. (Tanner) | 4 | A.L. (Weaver) | 2 | Reuss | John | Los Angeles N.L. | 56,088 |
| 1981[8] | Aug. 9 | N.L. (Green) | 5 | A.L. (Frey) | 4 | Blue | Fingers | Cleveland A.L. | 72,086 |
| 1982 | July 13 | N.L. (Lasorda) | 4 | A.L. (Martin) | 1 | Rogers | Eckersley | Montreal N.L. | 59,057 |
| 1983 | July 6 | A.L. (Kuenn) | 13 | N.L. (Herzog) | 3 | Steib | Soto | Chicago A.L. | 43,801 |
| 1984 | July 11 | A.L. (Owens) | 3 | N.L. (Altobelli) | 1 | Leg | Steib | San Francisco N.L. | 57,756 |
| 1985 | July 16 | N.L. (Williams) | 6 | A.L. (Anderson) | 1 | Hoyt | Morris | Minneapolis A.L. | 54,960 |
| 1986 | July 15 | A.L. (Howser) | 3 | N.L. (Herzog) | 2 | Clemens | Gooden | Houston N.L. | 45,774 |
| 1987 | July 14 | N.L. (Johnson) | 2 | A.L. (McNamara) | 0[9] | Smith | Howell | Oakland A.L. | 49,671 |
| 1988 | July 12 | A.L. (Kelly) | 2 | N.L. (Herzog) | 1 | Viola | Gooden | Cincinnati, N.L | 55,837 |
| 1989 | July 11 | A.L. (LaRussa) | 5 | N.L. (Lasorda) | 3 | Ryan | Smoltz | California A.L. | 64,036 |
| 1990 | July 10 | A.L. (LaRussa) | 2 | N.L. (Craig) | 0 | Saberhagen | Brantley | Chicago N.L. | 39,071 |
| 1991 | July 9 | A.L. (LaRussa) | 4 | N.L. (Piniella) | 2 | Key | Martinez | Toronto A.L. | 52,383 |
| 1992 | July 14 | A.L. (Kelly) | 13 | N.L. (Cox) | 6 | Brown | Glavine | San Diego N.L. | 59,372 |
| 1993 | July 13 | A.L. (Gaston) | 9 | N.L. (Cox) | 3 | McDowell | Burkett | Baltimore A.L. | 48,147 |
| 1994 | July 12 | N.L. (Fregosi) | 8 | A.L. (Gaston) | 7[5] | Jones | Bere | Pittsburgh N.L. | 59,568 |
| 1995 | July 11 | N.L. (Alou) | 3 | A.L. (Showalter) | 2 | Slocumb | Rogers | Texas A.L. | 50,920 |
| 1996 | July 9 | N.L. (Cox) | 6 | A.L. (Hargrove) | 0 | Smoltz | Nagy | Philadelphia N.L. | 62,670 |
| 1997 | July 8 | A.L. (Torre) | 3 | N.L. (Cox) | 1 | Johnson | Maddux | Cleveland A.L. | 44,916 |
| 1998 | July 7 | A.L. (Hargrove) | 13 | N.L. (Leyland) | 3 | Colon | Urbina | Denver N.L. | 51,267 |
| 1999 | July 13 | A.L. (Torre) | 4 | N.L. (Bochy) | 1 | P. Martinez | Schilling | Boston A.L. | 34,187 |
| 2000 | July 11 | A.L. (Torre) | 6 | N.L. (Cox) | 3 | Baldwin | Leiter | Atlanta N.L. | 51,323 |
| 2001 | July 10 | A.L. (Torre) | 4 | N.L. (Valentine) | 1 | Garcia | Park | Seattle A.L. | 47,364 |
| 2002 | July 9 | 7–7 tie after 11 innings. Bob Brenley, N.L. manager, Joe Torre, A.L. manager | | | | | | Milwaukee N.L. | 41,871 |

1. Fourteen innings. 2. Five innings, rain. 3. Twelve innings. 4. Two games. 5. Ten innings. 6. Called because of rain after nine innings. 7. Fifteen innings. 8. Game was originally scheduled for July 14, but was put off because of players' strike. 9. Thirteen innings. NOTE: No game in 1945.

## NATIONAL BASEBALL HALL OF FAME

### Cooperstown, N.Y.

### Fielders

| Member | Active years | Member | Active years | Member | Active years |
|------|------|------|------|------|------|
| Aaron, Henry (Hank) | 1954–1976 | Campanella, Roy | 1948–1957 | Delahanty, Edward | 1888–1903 |
| Anson, Adrian (Cap) | 1876–1897 | Carew, Rod | 1967–1985 | Dickey, William | 1928–1946 |
| Aparicio, Luis | 1956–1973 | Carey, Max | 1910–1929 | Dihigo, Martin[1] | 1923–1945 |
| Appling, Lucius (Luke) | 1930–1950 | Cepeda, Orlando | 1958–1974 | DiMaggio, Joseph | 1936–1951 |
| Ashburn, Richie | 1948–1962 | Chance, Frank | 1898–1914 | Doby, Larry | 1947–1959 |
| Averill, H. Earl | 1929–1941 | Charleston, Oscar[1] | 1915–1954 | Doerr, Bobby | 1937–1951 |
| Baker, J. Frank (Home Run) | 1908–1922 | Clarke, Fred | 1894–1915 | Duffy, Hugh | 1888–1906 |
| | | Clemente, Roberto | 1955–1972 | Ewing, William | 1880–1897 |
| Bancroft, David | 1915–1930 | Cobb, Tyrus | 1905–1928 | Evers, John | 1902–1919 |
| Banks, Ernest | 1953–1971 | Cochrane, Gordon (Mickey) | 1925–1937 | Ferrell, Rick | 1929–1947 |
| Beckley, Jacob | 1888–1907 | | | Fisk, Carlton | 1969–1991 |
| Bell, James (Cool Papa)[1] | 1920–1947 | Collins, Edward | 1906–1930 | Flick, Elmer | 1898–1910 |
| Bench, John | 1967–1983 | Collins, James | 1895–1908 | Fox, Nellie | 1947–1965 |
| Berra, Lawrence (Yogi) | 1946–1965 | Comiskey, Charles | 1882–1894 | Foxx, James | 1925–1945 |
| Bottomley, James | 1922–1937 | Combs, Earle | 1924–1935 | Frisch, Frank | 1919–1937 |
| Boudreau, Louis | 1938–1952 | Connor, Roger | 1880–1897 | Gehrig, H. Louis (Lou) | 1923–1939 |
| Bresnahan, Roger | 1897–1915 | Crawford, Samuel | 1899–1917 | Gehringer, Charles | 1924–1942 |
| Brett, George | 1973–1993 | Cronin, Joseph | 1926–1945 | Gibson, Josh[1] | 1929–1946 |
| Brock, Lou | 1961–1980 | Cuyler, Hazen (Kiki) | 1921–1938 | Goslin, Leon (Goose) | 1921–1938 |
| Brouthers, Dennis | 1879–1896 | Dandridge, Ray[1] | 1933–1953 | Greenberg, Henry (Hank) | 1933–1947 |
| Burkett, Jesse | 1890–1905 | Davis, George | 1890–1909 | Hafey, Charles (Chick) | 1924–1937 |

| Member | Active years | Member | Active years | Member | Active years |
|---|---|---|---|---|---|
| Hamilton, William | 1888–1901 | Matthews, Edwin | 1952–1968 | Simmons, Al | 1924–1944 |
| Hartnett, Charles (Gabby) | 1922–1941 | Mays, Willie | 1951–1973 | Sisler, George | 1915–1930 |
| Heilmann, Harry | 1914–1932 | Mazeroski, William Stan- | 1956–1972 | Slaughter, Enos | 1938–1959 |
| Herman, William | 1931–1947 | ley (Maz) | | Smith, Ozzie | 1978–1996 |
| Hooper, Harry | 1909–1925 | McCarthy, Thomas | 1884–1896 | Snider, Edwin D. (Duke) | 1947–1964 |
| Hornsby, Rogers | 1915–1937 | McCovey, Willie | 1959–1980 | Speaker, Tristram | 1907–1928 |
| Irvin, Monford (Monte)[1] | 1939–1956 | McGraw, John J. | 1891–1906 | Stargell, Willie | 1962–1982 |
| Jackson, Reggie | 1967–1987 | McPhee, John Alexander | 1882–1899 | Stearnes, Norman (Tur- | 1921–1942 |
| Jackson, Travis | 1922–1936 | (Bid) | | key) | |
| Jennings, Hugh | 1891–1918 | Medwick, Joseph (Ducky) | 1932–1948 | Terry, William | 1923–1936 |
| Johnson, William (Judy)[1] | 1921–1937 | Mize, John (The Big Cat) | 1936–1953 | Thompson, Samuel | 1885–1906 |
| Kaline, Albert W. | 1953–1974 | Morgan, Joe | 1963–1984 | Tinker, Joseph | 1902–1916 |
| Keeler, William (Wee | 1892–1910 | Musial, Stanley | 1941–1963 | Traynor, Harold (Pie) | 1920–1937 |
| Willie) | | O'Rourke, James | 1876–1894 | Vaughan, Arky | 1932–1948 |
| Kell, George | 1943–1957 | Ott, Melvin | 1926–1947 | Wagner, John (Honus) | 1897–1917 |
| Kelley, Joseph | 1891–1908 | Perez, Tony | 1964–1983 | Wallace, Roderick (Bobby) | 1894–1918 |
| Kelly, George | 1915–1932 | Puckett, Kirby | 1984–1995 | Waner, Lloyd | 1927–1945 |
| Kelly, Michael (King) | 1878–1893 | Reese, Harold (Pee Wee) | 1940–1958 | Waner, Paul | 1926–1945 |
| Killebrew, Harmon | 1954–1975 | Rice, Edgar (Sam) | 1915–1934 | Ward, John (Monte) | 1878–1894 |
| Kiner, Ralph | 1946–1955 | Rizzuto, Phil | 1941–1956 | Wells, Willie | 1924–1949 |
| Klein, Charles H. (Chuck) | 1928–1944 | Robinson, Brooks | 1955–1977 | Wheat, Zachariah | 1909–1927 |
| Lajoie, Napoleon | 1896–1916 | Robinson, Frank | 1956–1976 | Williams, Billy | 1959–1976 |
| Lazzeri, Tony | 1926–1939 | Robinson, Jack | 1947–1956 | Williams, Theodore | 1939–1960 |
| Leonard, Walter (Buck)[1] | 1933–1955 | Robinson, Wilbert | 1886–1902 | Wilson, Lewis R. (Hack) | 1923–1934 |
| Lindstrom, Frederick | 1924–1936 | Roush, Edd | 1913–1931 | Winfield, David Mark | 1973–1995 |
| Lloyd, John Henry (Pop)[1] | 1905–1931 | Ruth, Babe | 1914–1935 | Yastrzemski, Carl | 1961–1983 |
| Lombardi, Ernie | 1932–1947 | Schalk, Raymond | 1912–1929 | Youngs, Ross (Pep) | 1917–1926 |
| Mantle, Mickey | 1951–1968 | Schoendienst, Red | 1945–1963 | Yount, Robin | 1974–1993 |
| Manush, Henry (Heinie) | 1923–1939 | Schmidt, Mike | 1973–1989 | | |
| Maranville, Walter (Rabbit) | 1912–1935 | Sewell, Joseph | 1920–1933 | | |

1. Negro League player selected by special committee.

## Pitchers

| | | | | | |
|---|---|---|---|---|---|
| Alexander, Grover | 1911–1930 | Haines, Jesse | 1918–1937 | Radbourn, Charles (Hoss) | 1880–1891 |
| Bender, Charles (Chief) | 1903–1925 | Hoyt, Waite | 1918–1938 | Rixey, Eppa | 1912–1933 |
| Brown, Mordecai (3-Finger) | 1903–1916 | Hubbell, Carl | 1928–1943 | Roberts, Robert (Robin) | 1948–1966 |
| Bunning, Jim | 1955–1971 | Hunter, Jim (Catfish) | 1965–1979 | Rogan, Wilber | 1920–1938 |
| Carlton, Steve | 1965–1988 | Jenkins, Ferguson | 1965–1983 | Ruffing, Charles (Red) | 1924–1947 |
| Chesbro, John | 1899–1909 | Johnson, Walter | 1907–1927 | Rusie, Amos | 1889–1901 |
| Clarkson, John | 1882–1894 | Joss, Adrian | 1902–1910 | Ryan, Nolan, Jr. | 1966–1973 |
| Coveleski, Stanley | 1912–1928 | Keefe, Timothy | 1880–1893 | Seaver, Tom | 1967–1986 |
| Day, Leon | 1935–1955 | Koufax, Sanford (Sandy) | 1955–1966 | Smith, Hilton Lee | 1932–1948 |
| Dean, Jerome (Dizzy) | 1930–1947 | Lemon, Robert | 1946–1958 | Spahn, Warren | 1942–1965 |
| Drysdale, Don | 1956–1969 | Lyons, Theodore | 1923–1946 | Sutton, Don | 1966–1988 |
| Faber, Urban (Red) | 1914–1933 | Marichal, Juan | 1960–1975 | Vance, Arthur (Dazzy) | 1915–1935 |
| Feller, Robert | 1936–1956 | Marquard, Richard (Rube) | 1908–1924 | Waddell, Rube | 1897–1910 |
| Fingers, Rollie | 1968–1985 | Mathewson, Christopher | 1900–1916 | Walsh, Edward | 1904–1917 |
| Ford, Edward (Whitey) | 1950–1967 | McGinnity, Joseph | 1899–1908 | Welch, Michael (Mickey) | 1880–1892 |
| Foster, Andrew (Rube) | 1897–1926 | Newhouser, Hal | 1939–1955 | Wilhelm, Hoyt | 1952–1972 |
| Foster, Bill | 1923–1937 | Nichols, Charles (Kid) | 1890–1906 | Williams, Joseph | 1910–1932 |
| Galvin, James (Pud) | 1876–1892 | Niekro, Phil | 1959–1987 | Willis, Vic | 1898–1910 |
| Gibson, Bob | 1959–1975 | Paige, Leroy (Satchel)[1] | 1926–1965 | Wynn, Early | 1939–1963 |
| Gomez, Vernon (Lefty) | 1930–1943 | Palmer, Jim | 1965–1984 | Young, Denton (Cy) | 1890–1911 |
| Griffith, Clark | 1891–1914 | Pennock, Herbert | 1912–1934 | | |
| Grimes, Burleigh | 1916–1934 | Perry, Gaylord | 1962–1983 | | |
| Grove, Robert (Lefty) | 1925–1941 | Plank, Edward | 1901–1917 | | |

1. Negro League player selected by special committee.

## Officials and Others

| | | | | |
|---|---|---|---|---|
| Alston, Walter[1] | Comiskey, Charles[1] | Hanlon, Ned[3] | Lasorda, Tommy[1] | Selee, Frank G.[1] |
| Anderson, Sparky[1] | Conlan, John[3] | Harridge, William[3] | Lopez, Alfonso R.[7] | Spalding, Albert G.[2] |
| Barlick, Al[2] | Connolly, Thomas[2] | Harris, Stanley R.[7] | Mack, Connie[1, 3] | Stengel, Charles D.[7] |
| Barrow, Edward[1, 3] | Cummings, William A.[6] | Hubbard, R. Calvin[2] | MacPhail, Lee, Jr.[3] | Veeck, Bill[3] |
| Bulkeley, Morgan G.[3] | Durocher, Leo[1] | Huggins, Miller J.[1] | MacPhail, Leland S.[3] | Weaver, Earl[1] |
| Cartwright, Alexander[3] | Evans, William G.[2, 3] | Hulbert, William[3] | McCarthy, Joseph V.[1] | Weiss, George M.[3] |
| Chadwick, Henry[4] | Foster, Rube[3] | Johnson, B. Bancroft[3] | McGowan, Bill[2] | Wright, George[6] |
| Chandler, A. B.[5] | Frick, Ford C.[3, 5] | Klem, William[2] | McKechnie, William B.[1] | Wright, Harry[1, 6] |
| Chylak, Nestor, Jr.[2] | Giles, Warren C.[3] | Landis, Kenesaw M.[5] | Rickey, W. Branch[1, 3] | Yawkey, Thomas[3] |

1. Manager. 2. Umpire. 3. Executive. 4. Writer-statistician. 5. Commissioner. 6. Early player. 7. Player-manager.

## BASEBALL'S PERFECTLY PITCHED GAMES[1]
### (no opposing runner reached base)

| | |
|---|---|
| Lee Richmond—Worcester vs. Cleveland (N.L.) June 12, 1880 | (1–0) |
| John M. Ward—Providence vs. Buffalo (N.L.) June 17, 1880 | (5–0) |
| Cy Young—Boston vs. Philadelphia (A.L.) May 5, 1904 | (3–0) |
| Addie Joss—Cleveland vs. Chicago (A.L.) Oct. 2, 1908 | (1–0) |
| Ernest Shore[2]—Boston vs. Washington (A.L.) June 23, 1917 | (4–0) |
| Charles Robertson—Chicago vs. Detroit (A.L.) April 30, 1922 | (2–0) |
| Don Larsen[3]—New York (A.L.) vs. Brooklyn (N.L.) Oct. 8, 1956 | (2–0) |
| Jim Bunning—Philadelphia vs. New York (N.L.) June 21, 1964 | (6–0) |
| Sandy Koufax—Los Angeles vs. Chicago (N.L.) Sept. 9, 1965 | (1–0) |
| Jim Hunter—Oakland vs. Minnesota (A.L.) May 8, 1968 | (4–0) |
| Len Barker—Cleveland vs. Toronto (A.L.) May 15, 1981 | (3–0) |
| Mike Witt—California vs. Texas (A.L.) Sept. 30, 1984 | (1–0) |
| Tom Browning—Cincinnati vs. Los Angeles (N.L.) Sept. 16, 1988 | (1–0) |
| Dennis Martinez—Montreal vs. Los Angeles (N.L.) July 28, 1991 | (2–0) |
| Kenny Rogers—Texas vs. California (A.L.) July 28, 1994 | (4–0) |
| David Wells—New York vs. Minnesota (A.L.) May 17, 1998 | (4–0) |
| David Cone[4]—New York (A.L.) vs. Montreal (N.L.) July 18, 1999 | (6–0) |

1. Harvey Haddix, of Pittsburgh, pitched 12 perfect innings against Milwaukee (N.L.), May 26, 1959, but lost game in 13th on error and hit. Montreal's Pedro Martinez pitched nine perfect innings against the San Diego Padres on June 3, 1995 before surrendering a leadoff double to Bip Roberts in the 10th. Mel Rojas finished the game, and Montreal won, 1–0. 2. Shore, relief pitcher for Babe Ruth who walked first batter before being ejected by umpire, retired 26 batters who faced him and base-runner was out stealing. 3. World Series. 4. Interleague game.

## LIFETIME BATTING, PITCHING, AND BASE-RUNNING RECORDS
### (Records through 2002. Boldface indicates player active in 2002 season.)

**Hits (3,000+)**

| | |
|---|---|
| Pete Rose | 4,256 |
| Ty Cobb | 4,189 |
| Hank Aaron | 3,771 |
| Stan Musial | 3,630 |
| Tris Speaker | 3,514 |
| Carl Yastrzemski | 3,419 |
| Cap Anson | 3,418 |
| Honus Wagner | 3,415 |
| Paul Molitor | 3,319 |
| Eddie Collins | 3,315 |
| Willie Mays | 3,283 |
| Eddie Murray | 3,255 |
| Nap Lajoie | 3,242 |
| Cal Ripken, Jr. | 3,184 |
| George Brett | 3,154 |
| Paul Waner | 3,152 |
| Robin Yount | 3,142 |
| Tony Gwynn | 3,141 |
| Dave Winfield | 3,110 |
| Rod Carew | 3,053 |
| **Rickey Henderson** | **3,040** |
| Lou Brock | 3,023 |
| Wade Boggs | 3,010 |
| Al Kaline | 3,007 |
| Roberto Clemente | 3,000 |

**Earned Run Average (Minimum 1,500 innings pitched)**

| | |
|---|---|
| Ed Walsh | 1.82 |
| Addie Joss | 1.89 |
| Al Spalding | 2.04 |
| Mordecai Brown | 2.06 |
| John Ward | 2.10 |
| Christy Mathewson | 2.13 |
| Tommy Bond | 2.14 |
| Rube Waddell | 2.16 |
| Walter Johnson | 2.17 |
| Ed Reulbach | 2.28 |
| Will White | 2.28 |
| Ed Plank | 2.35 |
| Larry Corcoran | 2.36 |
| Ed Cicotte | 2.38 |
| Candy Cummings | 2.39 |
| Doc White | 2.39 |
| Nap Rucker | 2.42 |
| George Bradley | 2.43 |
| Jim McCormick | 2.43 |

**Runs Scored**

| | |
|---|---|
| **Rickey Henderson** | **2,288** |
| Ty Cobb | 2,246 |
| Hank Aaron | 2,174 |
| Babe Ruth | 2,174 |
| Pete Rose | 2,165 |
| Willie Mays | 2,062 |
| Cap Anson | 1,996 |
| Stan Musial | 1,949 |
| Lou Gehrig | 1,888 |
| Tris Speaker | 1,882 |
| Mel Ott | 1,859 |
| **Barry Bonds** | **1,830** |
| Frank Robinson | 1,829 |
| Eddie Collins | 1,821 |
| Carl Yastrzemski | 1,816 |
| Ted Williams | 1,798 |
| Paul Molitor | 1,782 |
| Charlie Gehringer | 1,774 |
| Jimmie Foxx | 1,751 |
| Honus Wagner | 1,736 |
| Jim O'Rourke | 1,729 |
| Jesse Burkett | 1,720 |
| Willie Keeler | 1,710 |
| Billy Hamilton | 1,691 |
| Bid McPhee | 1,678 |
| Mickey Mantle | 1,677 |
| Dave Winfield | 1,669 |
| Joe Morgan | 1,650 |

**Strikeouts, Pitching**

| | |
|---|---|
| Nolan Ryan | 5,714 |
| Steve Carlton | 4,136 |
| **Roger Clemens** | **3,909** |
| **Randy Johnson** | **3,746** |
| Bert Blyleven | 3,701 |
| Tom Seaver | 3,640 |
| Don Sutton | 3,574 |

| | |
|---|---|
| Gaylord Perry | 3,534 |
| Walter Johnson | 3,508 |
| Phil Niekro | 3,342 |
| Ferguson Jenkins | 3,192 |
| Bob Gibson | 3,117 |
| Jim Bunning | 2,855 |
| Mickey Lolich | 2,832 |
| Cy Young | 2,803 |
| Frank Tanana | 2,773 |
| David Cone | 2,655 |
| **Greg Maddux** | **2,641** |
| **Chuck Finley** | **2,610** |
| Warren Spahn | 2,583 |
| Bob Feller | 2,581 |
| Tim Keefe | 2,564 |
| Jerry Koosman | 2,556 |

**Home Runs (375+)**

| | |
|---|---|
| Hank Aaron | 755 |
| Babe Ruth | 714 |
| Willie Mays | 660 |
| **Barry Bonds** | **613** |
| Frank Robinson | 586 |
| Mark McGwire | 583 |
| Harmon Killebrew | 573 |
| Reggie Jackson | 563 |
| Mike Schmidt | 548 |
| Mickey Mantle | 536 |
| Jimmie Foxx | 534 |
| Willie McCovey | 521 |
| Ted Williams | 521 |
| Ernie Banks | 512 |
| Eddie Mathews | 512 |
| Mel Ott | 511 |
| Eddie Murray | 504 |
| **Sammy Sosa** | **499** |
| Lou Gehrig | 493 |
| **Rafael Palmeiro** | **490** |
| **Fred McGriff** | **478** |
| Stan Musial | 475 |
| Willie Stargell | 475 |
| **Ken Griffey, Jr.** | **468** |
| Dave Winfield | 465 |
| Jose Canseco | 462 |

| | |
|---|---|
| Carl Yastrzemski | 452 |
| Dave Kingman | 442 |
| Andre Dawson | 438 |
| Cal Ripken, Jr. | 431 |
| Billy Williams | 426 |
| Darrell Evans | 414 |
| Duke Snider | 407 |
| **Juan Gonzalez** | **405** |
| Al Kaline | 399 |
| Dale Murphy | 398 |
| Joe Carter | 396 |
| **Andres Galarraga** | **396** |
| Graig Nettles | 390 |
| Johnny Bench | 389 |
| Dwight Evans | 385 |
| Harold Baines | 384 |
| Frank Howard | 382 |
| Jim Rice | 382 |
| **Albert Belle** | **381** |
| **Jeff Bagwell** | **380** |
| Orlando Cepeda | 379 |
| Tony Perez | 379 |
| Norm Cash | 377 |
| Carlton Fisk | 376 |

**Shutouts**

| | |
|---|---|
| Walter Johnson | 110 |
| Grover Alexander | 90 |
| Christy Mathewson | 79 |
| Cy Young | 76 |
| Ed Plank | 69 |
| Warren Spahn | 63 |
| Nolan Ryan | 61 |
| Tom Seaver | 61 |
| Bert Blyleven | 60 |
| Don Sutton | 58 |
| Pud Galvin | 57 |
| Ed Walsh | 57 |
| Bob Gibson | 56 |
| Mordecai Brown | 55 |
| Steve Carlton | 55 |
| Jim Palmer | 53 |
| Gaylord Perry | 53 |
| Juan Marichal | 52 |

## Strikeouts, Batting

| | | | | | | | |
|---|---|---|---|---|---|---|---|
| Reggie Jackson | 2,597 | Mickey Mantle | 1,710 | Lance Parrish | 1,527 | Darrell Evans | 1,605 |
| **Andres Galarraga** | **2,007** | Harmon Killebrew | 1,699 | Willie Mays | 1,526 | Stan Musial | 1,599 |
| Jose Canseco | 1,942 | Chili Davis | 1,698 | | | Pete Rose | 1,566 |
| Willie Stargell | 1,936 | Dwight Evans | 1,697 | **Walks** | | Harmon Killebrew | 1,559 |
| Mike Schmidt | 1,883 | Dave Winfield | 1,686 | **Rickey Henderson** | **2,179** | Lou Gehrig | 1,508 |
| Tony Perez | 1,867 | **Rickey Henderson** | **1,678** | Babe Ruth | 2,062 | Mike Schmidt | 1,507 |
| **Sammy Sosa** | **1,834** | Gary Gaetti | 1,602 | Ted Williams | 2,019 | Eddie Collins | 1,499 |
| Dave Kingman | 1,816 | Mark McGwire | 1,596 | **Barry Bonds** | **1,922** | Willie Mays | 1,464 |
| **Fred McGriff** | **1,797** | Lee May | 1,570 | Joe Morgan | 1,865 | Jimmie Foxx | 1,452 |
| Bobby Bonds | 1,757 | Dick Allen | 1,556 | Carl Yastrzemski | 1,845 | Eddie Mathews | 1,444 |
| Dale Murphy | 1,748 | Willie McCovey | 1,550 | Mickey Mantle | 1,733 | Frank Robinson | 1,420 |
| Lou Brock | 1,730 | Dave Parker | 1,537 | Mel Ott | 1,708 | Wade Boggs | 1,412 |
| | | Frank Robinson | 1,532 | Eddie Yost | 1,614 | Hank Aaron | 1,402 |

# RECORD OF WORLD SERIES GAMES
## (through 2001)

Figures in parentheses for winning pitchers (WP) and losing pitchers (LP) indicate the game number in the series.

**1903**—Boston A.L. 5 (Jimmy Collins); Pittsburgh N.L. 3 (Fred Clarke). WP—Boston: Dinneen (2, 6, 8), Young (5, 7); Pittsburgh: Phillippe (1, 3, 4). LP—Boston: Young (1), Hughes (3), Dinneen (4); Pittsburgh: Leever (2, 6), Kennedy (5), Phillippe (7, 8).

**1904**—No series.

**1905**—New York N.L. 4 (John J. McGraw); Philadelphia A.L. 1 (Connie Mack). WP—New York: Mathewson (1, 3, 5); McGinnity (4); Phila.: Bender (2). LP—New York: McGinnity (2); Phila.: Plank (1, 4), Coakley (3), Bender (5).

**1906**—Chicago A.L. 4 (Fielder Jones); Chicago N.L. 2 (Frank Chance). WP—Chicago: A.L.: Altrock (1), Walsh (3, 5), White (6); Chicago: N.L.: Reulbach (2), Brown (4). LP—Chicago A.L.: White (2), Altrock. (4); Chicago: N.L.: Brown (1, 6), Pfeister (3, 5).

**1907**—Chicago N.L. 4 (Frank Chance); Detroit A.L. 0 (Hugh Jennings). First game tied 3–3, 12 innings. WP—Pfeister (2), Reulbach (3), Overall (4), Brown (5). LP—Mullin (2, 5), Siever (3), Donovan (4).

**1908**—Chicago N.L. 4 (Frank Chance); Detroit A.L. 1 (Hugh Jennings). WP—Chicago: Brown (1, 4), Overall (2, 5); Det.: Mullin (3). LP—Chicago: Pfeister (3); Det.: Summers (1, 4), Donovan (2, 5).

**1909**—Pittsburgh N.L. 4 (Fred Clarke); Detroit A.L. 3 (Hugh Jennings). WP—Pittsburgh: Adams (1, 5, 7), Maddox (3); Det.: Donovan (2), Mullin (4, 6). LP—Pittsburgh: Camnitz (2), Leifield (4), Willis (6); Det.: Mullin (1), Summers (3, 5), Donovan (7).

**1910**—Philadelphia A.L. 4 (Connie Mack); Chicago N.L. 1 (Frank Chance). WP—Phila.: Bender (1), Coombs (2, 3, 5); Chicago: Brown (4). LP—Phila.: Bender (4); Chicago: Overall (1), Brown (2), McIntyre (3).

**1911**—Philadelphia A.L. 4 (Connie Mack); New York N.L. 2 (John J. McGraw). WP—Phila.: Plank (2), Coombs (3), Bender (4, 6); New York: Mathewson (1), Crandall (5). LP—Phila.: Bender (1), Plank (5); New York: Marquard (2), Mathewson (3, 4), Ames (6).

**1912**—Boston A.L. 4 (J. Garland Stahl); New York N.L. 3 (John J. McGraw). Second game tied, 6–6, 11 innings. WP—Boston: Wood (1, 4, 8), Bedient (5); New York: Marquard (3, 6), Tesreau (7). LP—Boston: O'Brien (3, 6), Wood (7); New York: Tesreau (1, 4), Mathewson (5, 8).

**1913**—Philadelphia A.L. 4 (Connie Mack); New York N.L. 1 (John J. McGraw). WP—Phila.: Bender (1, 4), Bush (3), Plank (5); New York: Mathewson (2); LP—Phila.: Plank (2); New York: Marquard (1), Tesreau (3), Demaree (4), Mathewson (5).

**1914**—Boston N.L. 4 (George Stallings); Philadelphia A.L. 0 (Connie Mack). WP—Rudolph (1, 4), James (2, 3). LP—Bender (1), Plank (2), Bush (3), Shawkey (4).

**1915**—Boston A.L. 4 (Bill Carrigan); Philadelphia N.L. 1 (Pat Moran). WP—Boston: Foster (2, 5), Leonard (3), Shore (4); Phila.: Alexander (1). LP—Boston: Shore (1); Phila.:

Mayer (2), Alexander (3), Chalmers (4), Rixey (5).

**1916**—Boston A.L. 4 (Bill Carrigan); Brooklyn N.L. 1 (Wilbert Robinson). WP—Boston: Shore (1, 5), Ruth (2), Leonard (4); Brooklyn: Coombs (3). LP—Boston: Mays (3); Brooklyn: Marquard (1, 4), Smith (2), Pfeffer (5).

**1917**—Chicago A.L. 4 (Clarence Rowland); New York N.L. 2 (John J. McGraw). WP—Chicago: Cicotte (1), Faber (2, 5, 6); New York: Benton (3), Schupp (4), LP—Chicago: Cicotte (3), Faber (4); New York: Sallee (1, 5), Anderson (2), Benton (6).

**1918**—Boston A.L. 4 (Ed Barrow); Chicago N.L. 2 (Fred Mitchell). WP—Boston: Ruth (1, 4), Mays (3, 6); Chicago: Tyler (2), Vaughn (5). LP—Boston: Bush (2), Jones (5); Chicago: Vaughn (1, 3), Douglas (4), Tyler (6).

**1919**—Cincinnati N.L. 5 (Pat Moran); Chicago A.L. 3 (William Gleason). WP—Cincinnati: Ruether (1), Sallee (2), Ring (4), Eller (5, 8); Chicago: Kerr (3, 6), Cicotte (7). LP—Cincinnati: Fisher (3), Ring (6), Sallee (7); Chicago: Cicotte (1, 4), Williams (2, 5, 8).

**1920**—Cleveland A.L. 5 (Tris Speaker); Brooklyn N.L. 2 (Wilbert Robinson). WP—Cleve.: Coveleski (1, 4, 7), Bagby (5), Mails (6); Brooklyn: Grimes (2), Smith (3). LP—Cleve.: Bagby (2), Caldwell (4). Brooklyn: Marquard (1), Cadore (4), Grimes (5, 7), Smith (6).

**1921**—New York N.L. 5 (John J. McGraw); New York A.L. 3 (Miller Huggins). WP—New York N.L.: Barnes (3, 6), Douglas (4, 7), Nehf (8); New York A.L.: Mays (1), Hoyt (2, 5). LP—New York N.L.: Nehf (2, 5), Douglas (1). New York A.L.: Quinn (3), Mays (4, 7), Shawkey (6), Hoyt (8).

**1922**—New York N.L. 4 (John J. McGraw); New York A.L. 0 (Miller Huggins). Second game tied 3–3, 10 innings. WP—Ryan (1), Scott (3), McQuillan (4), Nehf (5); LP—Bush (1, 5), Hoyt (3), Mays (4).

**1923**—New York A.L. 4 (Miller Huggins); New York N.L. 2 (John J. McGraw). WP—New York A.L.: Pennock (2, 6), Shawkey (4), Bush (5); New York N.L.: Ryan (1), Nehf (3). LP—New York A.L.: Bush (1), Jones (3); New York N.L.: McQuillan (2), Scott (4), Bentley (5), Nehf (6).

**1924**—Washington A.L. 4 (Bucky Harris); New York N.L. 3 (John J. McGraw). WP—Washington: Zachary (2, 6), Mogridge (4), Johnson (7); New York: Nehf (1), McQuillan (3), Bentley (5). LP—Washington: Johnson (1, 5), Marberry (3); New York: Bentley (2, 7), Barnes (4), Nehf (6).

**1925**—Pittsburgh N.L. 4 (Bill McKechnie); Washington A.L. 3 (Bucky Harris). WP—Pittsburgh: Aldridge (2, 5), Kremer (6, 7); Washington: Johnson (1, 4), Ferguson (3). LP—Pittsburgh: Meadows (1), Kremer (3), Yde (4); Washington: Coveleski (2, 5), Ferguson (6), Johnson (7).

**1926**—St. Louis N.L. 4 (Rogers Hornsby); New York A.L. 3 (Miller Huggins). WP—St. Louis: Alexander (2, 6), Haines (3, 7); New York: Pennock (1, 5), Hoyt (4). LP—St. Louis: Sherdel (1, 5), Reinhart (4); New York: Shocker (2),

Ruether (3), Shawkey (6), Hoyt (7).

**1927**—New York A.L. 4 (Miller Huggins); Pittsburgh N.L. 0 (Donie Bush). WP—Hoyt (1), Pipgras (2), Pennock (3), Moore (4). LP—Kremer (1), Aldridge (2), Meadows (3), Miljus (4).

**1928**—New York A.L. 4 (Miller Huggins); St. Louis N.L. 0 (Bill McKechnie). WP—Hoyt (1, 4), Pipgras (2), Zachary (3). LP—Sherdel (1, 4), Alexander (2), Haines (3).

**1929**—Philadelphia A.L. 4 (Connie Mack); Chicago N.L. 1 (Joe McCarthy). WP—Phila.: Ehmke (1), Earnshaw (2), Rommel (4), Walberg (5); Chicago: Bush (3). LP—Phila.: Earnshaw (3) Chicago: Root (1), Malone (2, 5), Blake (4).

**1930**—Philadelphia A.L. 4 (Connie Mack); St. Louis N.L. 2 (Gabby Street). WP—Phila.: Grove (1, 5), Earnshaw (2, 6); St. Louis: Hallahan (3), Haines (4). LP—Phila.: Walberg (3), Grove (4); St. Louis: Grimes (1, 5), Rhem (2), Hallahan (6).

**1931**—St. Louis N.L. 4 (Gabby Street); Philadelphia A.L. 3 (Connie Mack). WP—St. Louis: Hallahan (2, 5), Grimes (3, 7); Phila.: Grove (1, 6), Earnshaw (4). LP—St. Louis: Derringer (1, 6), Johnson (4); Phila.: Earnshaw (2, 7), Grove (3), Hoyt (5).

**1932**—New York A.L. (Joe McCarthy); Chicago N.L. 0 (Charles Grimm). WP—Ruffing (1), Gomez (2), Pipgras (3), Moore (4). LP—Bush (1), Warneke (2), Root (3), May (4).

**1933**—New York N.L. 4 (Bill Terry); Washington A.L. 1 (Joe Cronin.). WP—New York: Hubbell (1, 4), Schumacher (2), Luque (5); Washington: Whitehill (3). LP—New York: Fitzsimmons (3); Washington: Stewart (1), Crowder (2), Weaver (4), Russell (5).

**1934**—St. Louis N.L. 4 (Frank Frisch); Detroit A.L. 3 (Mickey Cochrane). WP—St. Louis: J. Dean (1, 7), P. Dean (3, 6); Det.: Rowe (2), Auker (4), Bridges (5). LP—St. Louis: W. Walker (2, 4), J. Dean (5); Det.: Crowder (1), Bridges (3), Rowe (6), Auker (7).

**1935**—Detroit A.L. 4 (Mickey Cochrane); Chicago N.L. 2 (Charles Grimm). WP—Det.: Bridges (2, 6), Rowe (3), Crowder (4); Chicago: Warneke (1, 5); LP—Det.: Rowe (1, 5), Chicago: Root (1), French (3, 6), Carleton (4).

**1936**—New York A.L. 4 (Joe McCarthy); New York N.L. 2 (Bill Terry). WP—New York A.L.: Gomez (2, 6), Hadley (3), Pearson (4); New York N.L.: Hubbell (1), Schumacher (5); LP—New York A.L.: Ruffing (1), Malone (5); New York N.L.: Schumacher (2), Fitzsimmons (3, 6), Hubbell (4).

**1937**—New York A.L. 4 (Joe McCarthy); New York N.L. 1 (Bill Terry). WP—New York A.L.: Gomez (1, 5), Ruffing (2), Pearson (3); New York N.L.: Hubbell (4). LP—New York A.L.: Hadley (4); New York N.L.: Hubbell (1), Melton (2, 5), Schumacher (3).

**1938**—New York A.L. 4 (Joe McCarthy); Chicago N.L. 0 (Gabby Hartnett). WP—Ruffing (1, 4), Gomez (2), Pearson (3) LP—Lee (1, 4), Dean (2), Bryant (3).

**1939**—New York A.L. 4 (Joe McCarthy); Cincinnati N.L. 0 (Bill McKechnie). WP—Ruffing (1), Pearson (2), Hadley (3), Murphy (4). LP—Derringer (1), Walters (2, 4), Thompson (3).

**1940**—Cincinnati N.L. 4 (Bill McKechnie); Detroit A.L. 3 (Del Baker). WP—Cincinnati: Walters (2, 6), Derringer (4, 7); Det.: Newsom (1, 5), Bridges (3). LP—Cincinnati: Derringer (1), Turner (3), Thompson (5); Det.: Rowe (2, 6), Trout (4), Newsom (7).

**1941**—New York A.L. 4 (Joe McCarthy); Brooklyn N.L. 1 (Leo Durocher). WP—New York: Ruffing (1), Russo (3), Murphy (4), Bonham (5); Bklyn: Wyatt (2). LP—New York: Chandler (2); Bklyn: Davis (1), Casey (3, 4), Wyatt (5).

**1942**—St. Louis N.L. 4 (Billy Southworth); New York A.L. 1 (Joe McCarthy). WP—St. Louis: Beazley (2, 5), White (3), Lanier (4); New York: Ruffing (1). LP—St. Louis: Cooper (1); New York: Bonham (2), Chandler (3), Donald (4), Ruffing (5).

**1943**—New York A.L. 4 (Joe McCarthy); St. Louis N.L. 1

(Billy Southworth). WP—New York: Chandler (1, 5), Borowy (3), Russo (4); St. Louis: Cooper (2). LP—New York: Bonham (2); St. Louis: Lanier (1), Brazle (3), Brecheen (4), Cooper (5).

**1944**—St. Louis N.L. 4 (Billy Southworth); St. Louis A.L. 2 (Luke Sewell). WP—St. Louis N.L.: Donnelly (2), Brecheen (4), Cooper (5), Lanier (6); St. Louis A.L.: Galehouse (1), Kramer (3). LP—St. Louis N.L.: Cooper (1), Wilks (3); St. Louis A.L.: Muncrief (2), Jakucki (4), Galehouse (5), Potter (6).

**1945**—Detroit A.L. 4 (Steve O'Neill); Chicago N.L. 3 (Charles Grimm). WP—Det.: Trucks (2), Trout (4), Newhouser (5, 7); Chicago: Borowy (1, 6), Passeau (3). LP—Det.: Newhouser (1), Overmire (3), Trout (6); Chicago: Wyse (2), Prim (4), Borowy (5, 7).

**1946**—St. Louis N.L. 4 (Eddie Dyer); Boston A.L. 3 (Joe Cronin). WP—St. Louis: Brecheen (2, 6, 7), Munger (4); Boston: Johnson (1), Ferriss (3), Dobson (5). LP—St. Louis: Pollet (1), Dickson (3), Brazle (5); Boston: Harris (2, 6), Hughson (4), Klinger (7).

**1947**—New York A.L. 4 (Bucky Harris); Brooklyn N.L. 3 (Burt Shotton). WP—New York: Shea (1, 5), Reynolds (2), Page (7); Brooklyn: Casey (3, 4), Branca (6). LP—New York: Newsom (3), Bevens (4), Page (6); Brooklyn: Branca (1), Lombardi (2), Barney (5), Gregg (7).

**1948**—Cleveland A.L. 4 (Lou Boudreau); Boston N.L. 2 (Billy Southworth). WP—Cleve.: Lemon (2, 6), Bearden (3), Gromek (4); Boston: Sain (1), Spahn (5). LP—Cleve.: Feller (1, 5); Boston: Spahn (2), Bickford (3), Sain (4), Voiselle (6).

**1949**—New York A.L. 4 (Casey Stengel); Brooklyn N.L. 1 (Burt Shotton). WP—New York: Reynolds (1), Page (3), Lopat (4), Raschi (5); Brooklyn: Roe (2). LP—New York: Raschi (2); Brooklyn: Newcombe (1, 4), Branca (3), Barney (5).

**1950**—New York A.L. 4 (Casey Stengel); Philadelphia N.L. 0 (Eddie Sawyer). WP—Raschi (1), Reynolds (2), Ferrick (3), Ford (4). LP—Konstanty (1), Roberts (2), Meyer (3), Miller (4).

**1951**—New York A.L. 4 (Casey Stengel); New York N.L. 2 (Leo Durocher). WP—New York A.L.: Lopat (2, 5), Reynolds (4), Raschi (6); New York N.L.: Koslo (1), Hearn (3). LP—New York A.L.: Reynolds (1), Raschi (3); New York N.L.: Jansen (2, 5), Maglie (4), Koslo (6).

**1952**—New York A.L. 4 (Casey Stengel); Brooklyn N.L. 3 (Chuck Dressen). WP—New York: Raschi (2, 6), Reynolds (4, 7); Brooklyn: Black (1), Roe (3), Erskine (5). LP—New York: Reynolds (1), Lopat (3), Sain (5); Brooklyn: Erskine (2), Black (4, 7), Loes (6).

**1953**—New York A.L. 4 (Casey Stengel); Brooklyn N.L. 2 (Chuck Dressen). WP—New York: Sain (1), Lopat (2), McDonald (5), Reynolds (6); Brooklyn: Erskine (3), Loes (4). LP—New York: Raschi (3), Ford (4); Brooklyn: Labine (1, 6), Roe (2), Podres (5).

**1954**—New York N.L. 4 (Leo Durocher); Cleveland A.L. 0 (Al Lopez). WP—Grissom (1), Antonelli (2), Gomez (3), Liddle (4). LP—Lemon (2, 4), Wynn (3), Garcia (0)

**1955**—Brooklyn N.L. 4 (Walter Alston); New York A.L. 3 (Casey Stengel). WP—Brooklyn: Podres (3, 7), Labine (4), Craig (5); New York: Ford (1, 6), Byrne (2). LP—Brooklyn: Newcombe (1), Loes (2), Spooner (6); New York: Turley (3), Larsen (4), Grim (5), Byrne (7).

**1956**—New York A.L. 4 (Casey Stengel); Brooklyn N.L. 3 (Walter Alston). WP—New York: Ford (3), Sturdivant (4), Larsen (5), Kucks (7); Brooklyn: Maglie (1), Bessent (2), Labine (6). LP—New York: Ford (1), Morgan (2), Turley (6); Brooklyn: Craig (3), Erskine (4), Maglie (5), Newcombe (7).

**1957**—Milwaukee N.L. 4 (Fred Haney); New York A.L. 3 (Casey Stengel). WP—Milwaukee: Burdette (2, 5, 7), Spahn (4); New York: Ford (1), Larsen (3), Turley (6). LP—Milwaukee: Spahn (1), Buhl (3), Johnson (6); New York: Shantz (2), Grim (4), Ford (5), Larsen (7).

**1958**—New York A.L. 4 (Casey Stengel); Milwaukee N.L. 3 (Fred Haney). WP—New York: Larsen (3), Turley (5, 7), Duren (6); Milwaukee: Spahn (1, 4), Burdette (2). LP—New York: Duren (1), Turley (2), Ford (4); Milwaukee: Rush (3), Burdette (5, 7), Spahn (6).

**1959**—Los Angeles N.L. 4 (Walter Alston); Chicago A.L. 2 (Al Lopez). WP—Los Angeles: Podres (2), Drysdale (3), Sherry (4, 6); Chicago: Wynn (1), Shaw (5). LP—Los Angeles: Craig (1), Koufax (5); Chicago: Shaw (2), Donovan (3), Staley (4), Wynn (6).

**1960**—Pittsburgh N.L. 4 (Danny Murtaugh); New York A.L. 3 (Casey Stengel). WP—Pittsburgh: Law (1, 4), Haddix (5, 7); New York: Turley (2), Ford (3, 6). LP—Pittsburgh: Friend (2, 6), Mizell (3); New York: Ditmar (1, 5), Terry (4, 7).

**1961**—New York A.L. 4 (Ralph Houk); Cincinnati N.L. 1 (Fred Hutchinson). WP—New York: Ford (1, 4), Arroyo (3), Daley (5); Cincinnati: Jay (2). LP—New York: Terry (2); Cincinnati: O'Toole (1, 4), Purkey (5), Jay (5).

**1962**—New York A.L. 4 (Ralph Houk); San Francisco N.L. 3 (Al Dark). WP—New York: Ford (1), Stafford (3), Terry (5, 7); San Francisco Sanford (2), Larsen (4), Pierce (6). LP—New York: Terry (2), Coates (4), Ford (6); San Francisco: O'Dell (1), Pierce (3), Sanford (5, 7).

**1963**—Los Angeles N.L. 4 (Walter Alston); New York A.L. 0 (Ralph Houk). WP—Koufax (1, 4), Podres (2), Drysdale (3). LP—Ford (1, 4), Downing (2), Bouton (3).

**1964**—St. Louis N.L. 4 (Johnny Keane); New York A.L. 3 (Yogi Berra). WP—St. Louis: Sadecki (1), Craig (4), Gibson (5, 7); New York: Stottlemyre (2), Bouton (3, 6). LP—St. Louis: Gibson (2), Schultz (3), Simmons (4); New York: Ford (1), Downing (4), Mikkelsen (5), Stottlemyre (7).

**1965**—Los Angeles N.L. 4 (Walter Alston); Minnesota A.L. 3 (Sam Mele). WP—Los Angeles: Osteen (3), Drysdale (4), Koufax (5, 7); Minnesota: Grant (1, 6), Kaat (2). LP—Los Angeles: Drysdale (1), Koufax (2), Osteen (6); Minnesota: Pascual (3), Grant (4), Kaat (5, 7).

**1966**—Baltimore A.L. 4 (Hank Bauer); Los Angeles N.L. 0 (Walter Alston). WP—Drabowsky (1), Palmer (2), Bunker (3), McNally (4). LP—Drysdale (1, 4), Koufax (2), Osteen (3).

**1967**—St. Louis N.L. 4 (Red Schoendienst); Boston A.L. 3 (Dick Williams). WP—St. Louis: Gibson (1, 4, 7), Briles (3); Boston: Lonborg (2, 5); Wyatt (6). LP—St. Louis: Hughes (2), Carlton (5), Lamabe (6); Boston: Santiago (1, 4), Bell (3), Lonborg (7).

**1968**—Detroit A.L. 4 (Mayo Smith); St. Louis N.L. 3 (Red Schoendienst). WP—Det.: Lolich (2, 5, 7), McLain (6); St. Louis: Gibson (1, 4), Washburn (3), LP—Det.: McLain (1, 4), Wilson (3); St. Louis: Briles (2), Hoerner (5), Washburn (6), Gibson (7).

**1969**—New York N.L. 4 (Gil Hodges); Baltimore A.L. 1 (Earl Weaver). WP—New York: Koosman (2, 5), Gentry (3), Seaver (4); Baltimore: Cuellar (1). LP—New York: Seaver (1); Baltimore: McNally (2), Palmer (3), Hall (4), Watt (5).

**1970**—Baltimore A.L. 4 (Earl Weaver); Cincinnati N.L. 1 (Sparky Anderson) 1. WP—Baltimore: Palmer (1), Phoebus (2), McNally (3), Cuellar (5); Cincinnati: Carroll (4). LP—Cincinnati: Nolan (1), Wilcox (2), Cloninger (3), Merritt (5); Baltimore: Watt (4).

**1971**—Pittsburgh N.L. 4 (Danny Murtaugh); Baltimore A.L. 3 (Earl Weaver). WP—Pittsburgh: Blass (3, 7), Kison (4), Briles (5); Baltimore: McNally (1, 6), Palmer (2). LP—Pittsburgh: Ellis (1), R. Johnson (2), Miller (6); Baltimore: Cuellar (3, 7), Watt (4) McNally (5).

**1972**—Oakland A.L. 4 (Dick Williams); Cincinnati N.L. (Sparky Anderson) 3. WP—Oakland: Holtzman (1), Hunter (2, 7), Fingers (4); Cincinnati: Billingham (3), Grimsley (5). LP—Oakland: Odom (3), Fingers (5), Blue (6); Cincinnati: Nolan (1), Grimsley (2), Carroll (4), Borbon (7).

**1973**—Oakland A.L. 4 (Dick Williams): New York N.L. 3 (Yogi Berra). WP—Oakland: Holtzman (1, 7), Lindblad (3), Hunter (6). New York: McGraw (2), Matlack (4), Koosman (5). LP—Oakland: Fingers (2), Holtzman (4), Blue (5). New York: Matlack (1, 7) Parker (3), Seaver (6).

**1974**—Oakland A.L. 4 (Al Dark); Los Angeles N.L. 1 (Walter Alston). WP—Oakland: Fingers (1), Hunter (3), Holtzman (4), Odom (5). Los Angeles: Sutton (2). LP—Oakland: Blue (2), Los Angeles: Messersmith (1, 4), Downing (3), Marshall (5).

**1975**—Cincinnati N.L. 4 (Sparky Anderson); Boston A.L. 3 (Darrell Johnson). WP—Cincinnati: Eastwick (2, 3), Gullett (5), Carroll (7); Boston: Tiant (1, 4), Wise (6). LP—Cincinnati: Gullett (1), Norman (4), Darcy (6); Boston: Drago (2), Willoughby (3), Cleveland (5), Burton (7).

**1976**—Cincinnati N.L. 4 (Sparky Anderson); New York A.L. 0 (Billy Martin). WP—Gullett (1), Billingham (2), Zachry (3), Nolan (4). LP—Alexander (1), Hunter (2), Ellis (3), Figueroa (4).

**1977**—New York A.L. 4 (Billy Martin); Los Angeles N.L. 2 (Tom Lasorda). WP—New York: Lyle (1), Torrez (3, 6), Guidry (4); Los Angeles: Hooton (2), Sutton (5). LP—New York: Hunter (2), Gullett (5); Los Angeles: Rhoden (1), John (3), Rau (4), Hooton (6).

**1978**—New York A.L. 4 (Bob Lemon), Los Angeles N.L. 2 (Tom Lasorda). WP—New York: Guidry (3), Gossage (4); Beattie (5), Hunter (6); Los Angeles: John (1), Hooton (2). LP—New York: Figueroa (1), Hunter (2); Los Angeles: Sutton (3, 6), Welch (4), Hooton (5).

**1979**—Pittsburgh N.L. 4 (Chuck Tanner), Baltimore A.L. 3 (Earl Weaver); WP—Pittsburgh: D. Robinson (2), Blyleven (5), Candelaria (6), Jackson (7); Baltimore: Flanagan (1), McGregor (3), Stoddard (4). LP—Pittsburgh: Kison (1), Candelaria (3), Tekulve (4); Baltimore: Stanhouse (2), Flanagan (5), Palmer (6), McGregor (7).

**1980**—Philadelphia N.L. 4 (Dallas Green), Kansas City A.L. 2 (Jim Frey); WP—Philadelphia: Walk (1), Carlton (2), McGraw (5), Carlton (6); Kansas City: Quisenberry (3), Leonard (4). LP—Philadelphia: McGraw (3), Christenson (4); Kansas City: Leonard (1), Quisenberry (2), Quisenberry (5), Gale (6).

**1981**—Los Angeles N.L. 4 (Tom Lasorda), New York A.L. 2 (Bob Lemon); WP—Los Angeles: Valenzuela (3), Howe (4), Reuss (5), Hooton (6); New York: Guidry (1), John (2). LP—Los Angeles: Reuss (1), Hooton (2); New York: Frazier (3), Frazier (4), Guidry (5), Frazier (6).

**1982**—St. Louis N.L. 4 (Whitey Herzog), Milwaukee A.L. 3 (Harvey Kuenn); WP—St. Louis: Sutter (2), Andujar (3), Stuper (6), Andujar (7). Milwaukee: Caldwell (1), Slaton (4), Caldwell (5). LP—St. Louis: Forsch (1), Bair (4), Forsch (5). Milwaukee: McClure (2), Vuckovich (3), Sutton (6), McClure (7).

**1983**—Baltimore A.L. 4 (Joe Altobelli), Philadelphia N.L. 1 (Paul Owens); WP—Baltimore: Boddicker (2), Palmer (3), Davis (4), McGregor (5). Philadelphia: Denny (1).

**1984**—Detroit A.L. 4 (Sparky Anderson), San Diego N.L. 1 (Dick Williams); WP—Det.: Morris (1,4), Wilcox (3), Lopez (5), San Diego: Hawkins (2). LP—Det.: Petry (2), San Diego: Thurmond (1), Lollar (3), Show (4), Hawkins (5).

**1985**—Kansas City A.L. 4 (Dick Howser), St. Louis N.L. 3 (Whitey Herzog); WP—KC: Saberhagen (3,7) Quisenberry (6), Jackson (5). St. Louis: Tudor (1,4) Dayley (2). LP—KC: Jackson (1), Leibrandt (2), Black (4); St. Louis: Andujar (3), Forsch (5), Worrell (6), Tudor (7).

**1986**—New York N.L. 4 (Dave Johnson); Boston A.L. (John McNamara) 3 WP—New York—Ojeda (3), Darling (4), Aguilera (6), McDowell (7), Bos: Hurst (1, 5), Crawford (2). LP—New York Darling (1), Gooden (2, 5).

**1987**—Minnesota A.L. 4 (Tom Kelly); St. Louis N.L. (Whitey Herzog) 3. WP—Minnesota Viola (1, 7), Blyleven (2), Schatzeder (6), St. Louis: Tudor (3), Forsch (4), Cox (5). LP—Minnesota Berenguer (3), Viola (4), Blyleven (5); St. Louis: Magrane (1), Cox (2, 7), Tudor (6).

**1988**—Los Angeles N.L. 4 (Tommy Lasorda); Oakland A.L.

(Tony LaRussa) 1. WP—Los Angeles: Hershiser (2, 5), Pena (1), Belcher (4); Oakland: Honeycutt (3). LP—Los Angeles: Howell (3); Oakland: Davis (2, 5), Eckersley (1), Stewart (4).

**1989**—Oakland A.L. 4 (Tony LaRussa); San Francisco N.L. 0 (Roger Craig). WP—Oakland: Dave Stewart (1, 3), Mike Moore (2, 4). LP—San Francisco: Scott Garrelts (1, 3), Don Robinson (4), Rick Reuschel (2).

**1990**—Cincinnati N.L. 4 (Lou Piniella); Oakland A.L. 0 (Tony LaRussa). WP—Cincinnati: Jose Rijo (1, 4), Rob Dibble (2), Tom Browning (3). LP—Oakland: Dave Stewart (1, 4), Dennis Eckersley (2), Mike Moore (3).

**1991**—Minnesota A.L. 4 (Tom Kelly); Atlanta N.L. 3 (Bobby Cox). WP—Minnesota: Morris (1,7), Tapani (2), Aguilera (6). Atlanta: Clancy (3), Stanton (4), Glavine (5). LP—Minnesota: Aguilera (3), Gurhtie (4), Tapani (5). Atlanta: Leibrandt (1, 6), Glavine (5), Pena (7).

**1992**—Toronto A.L. 4 (Cito Gaston); Atlanta N.L. 2 (Bobby Cox). WP—Toronto: Ward (2, 3), Key (4, 6). Atlanta: Glavine (1), Smoltz (5). LP—Toronto: Morris (1, 5). Atlanta: Leibrandt (6), Reardon (2), Avery (3), Glavine (4).

**1993**—Toronto A.L. 4 (Cito Gaston); Philadelphia N.L. 2 (Jim Fregosi). WP—Toronto: Leiter (1), Hentgen (3), Castillo (4), Ward (6). Philadelphia: Mullholland (2), Schilling (5). LP—Toronto: Stewart (2), Guzman (5). Philadelphia: Schilling (1), Jackson (3), Williams (4, 6).

**1994**—World Series cancelled due to players' strike.

**1995**—Atlanta N.L. 4 (Bobby Cox); Cleveland A.L. 2 (Mike Hargrove). WP—Atlanta: Maddux (1), Glavine (2,6), Avery (4). Cleveland: Mesa (3), Hershiser (5).

LP—Atlanta: Pena (3), Maddux (5). Cleveland: Hershiser (1), Martinez (2), Hill (4), Poole (6).

**1996**—New York A.L. 4 (Joe Torre); Atlanta N.L. 2 (Bobby Cox). WP—New York: Cone (3), Lloyd (4), Pettitte (5), Key (6). Atlanta: Smoltz (1), Maddux (2). LP—New York: Pettitte (1), Key (2). Atlanta: Glavine (3), Avery (4), Smoltz (5), Maddux (6).

**1997**—Florida N.L. 4 (Jim Leyland); Cleveland A.L. 3 (Mike Hargrove). WP—Florida: Hernandez (1, 5), Cook (3), Powell (7). Cleveland: Ogea (2, 6), Wright (4). LP—Florida: Brown (2, 6), Saunders (4). Cleveland: Hershiser (1, 5), Plunk (3), Nagy (7).

**1998**—New York A.L. 4 (Joe Torre); San Diego N.L. 0 (Bruce Bochy). WP—New York: Wells (1), Hernandez (2), Mendoza (3), Pettitte (4). LP—San Diego: Wall (1), Ashby (2), Hoffman (3), Brown (4).

**1999**—New York A.L. 4 (Joe Torre); Atlanta N.L. 0 (Bobby Cox). WP—New York: Hernandez (1), Cone (2), Rivera (3), Clemens (4). LP—Atlanta: Maddux (1), Millwood (2), Remlinger (3), Smoltz (4).

**2000**—New York Yankees A.L. 4 (Joe Torre); New York Mets N.L. 1 (Bobby Valentine). WP—Yankees: Stanton (1, 5), Clemens (2), Nelson (4). Mets: Franco (3). LP—Wendell (1), Hampton (2), Jones (4), Leiter (5). Yankees: Hernandez (3).

**2001**—Arizona Diamondbacks N.L. 4 (Bob Brenly); New York Yankees A.L. 3 (Joe Torre). WP—Arizona: Schilling (1), Johnson (2, 6, 7). New York: Clemens (3), Rivera (4), Hitchcock (5). LP—New York: Mussina (1), Pettitte (2, 6), Rivera (7). Arizona: Anderson (3), Kim (4), Lopez (5).

## WORLD SERIES CLUB STANDINGS

### (through 2001)

| | Series | Won | Lost | Pct. | | Series | Won | Lost | Pct. |
|---|---|---|---|---|---|---|---|---|---|
| Toronto (A) | 2 | 2 | 0 | 1.000 | Kansas City (A) | 2 | 1 | 1 | .500 |
| Florida (N) | 1 | 1 | 0 | 1.000 | Detroit (A) | 9 | 4 | 5 | .444 |
| Arizona (N) | 1 | 1 | 0 | 1.000 | Cleveland (A) | 5 | 2 | 3 | .400 |
| Pittsburgh (N) | 7 | 5 | 2 | .714 | New York (N-Giants) | 14 | 5 | 9 | .357 |
| New York (A) | 38 | 26 | 12 | .684 | Washington (A) | 3 | 1 | 2 | .333 |
| Oakland (A) | 6 | 4 | 2 | .667 | Atlanta (N) | 5 | 1 | 4 | .200 |
| Minnesota (A) | 3 | 2 | 1 | .667 | Philadelphia (N) | 5 | 1 | 4 | .200 |
| Philadelphia (A) | 8 | 5 | 3 | .625 | Chicago (N) | 10 | 2 | 8 | .200 |
| St. Louis (N) | 15 | 9 | 6 | .600 | Brooklyn (N) | 9 | 1 | 8 | .111 |
| Boston (A) | 9 | 5 | 4 | .556 | St. Louis (A) | 1 | 0 | 1 | .000 |
| Los Angeles (N) | 9 | 5 | 4 | .556 | San Francisco (N) | 2 | 0 | 2 | .000 |
| Cincinnati (N) | 9 | 5 | 4 | .556 | Milwaukee (A) | 1 | 0 | 1 | .000 |
| New York (N-Mets) | 4 | 2 | 2 | .500 | San Diego (N) | 2 | 0 | 2 | .000 |
| Milwaukee (N) | 2 | 1 | 1 | .500 | | | | | |
| Boston (N) | 2 | 1 | 1 | .500 | **Recapitulation** | | | | **Won** |
| Chicago (A) | 4 | 2 | 2 | .500 | American League | | | | 56 |
| Baltimore (A) | 6 | 3 | 3 | .500 | National League | | | | 39 |

## LIFETIME WORLD SERIES RECORDS

(through 2001)

Most hits—71, Yogi Berra, New York A.L., 1947, 1949–53, 1955–56, 1960–64.

Most runs—42, Mickey Mantle, New York A.L., 1951–53, 1955–58, 1960–64.

Most runs batted in—40, Mickey Mantle, New York A.L., 1951–53, 1955–58, 1960–64.

Most home runs—18, Mickey Mantle, New York A.L., 1951–53, 1955–58, 1960–64.

Most bases on balls—43, Mickey Mantle, New York A.L., 1951–53, 1955–58, 1960–64.

Most strikeouts—54, Mickey Mantle, New York A.L., 1951–53, 1955–58, 1960–64.

Most stolen bases—14, Eddie Collins, Philadelphia A.L. 1910–11, 13–14; Chicago A.L., 1917, 1919. Lou Brock, St. Louis N.L., 1964, 67–68.

Most victories, pitcher—10, Whitey Ford, New York A.L., 1950, 1953, 1955–58 1960–64

Most times member of winning team—10, Yogi Berra, New York A.L., 1947, 1949–53, 1956, 1958, 1961–62.

Most victories, no defeats—6, Vernon Gomez, New York A.L., 1932, 1936(2), 1937(2), 1938.

Most shutouts—4, Christy Mathewson, New York N.L., 1905 (3), 1913.

Most innings pitched—146, Whitey Ford, New York A.L., 1950, 1953, 1955–58, 1960–1964

Most consecutive scoreless innings—33⅔, Whitey Ford, New York A.L., 1960 (18), 1961 (14), 1962 (1⅔).

Most strikeouts by pitcher—94, Whitey Ford, New York A.L., 1950, 1953, 1955–58, 1960–64.

## WORLD SERIES SINGLE GAME AND SINGLE SERIES RECORDS
### (through 2001)

Most hits game—5, Paul Molitor, Milwaukee A.L., first game vs. St. Louis N.L., 1982.

Most 4-hit games, series—2, Robin Yount, Milwaukee A.L., first and fifth games vs. St. Louis N.L., 1982.

Most hits inning—2, held by 17 players.

Most hits series—13 (7 games) Bobby Richardson, New York A.L., 1964; Lou Brock, St. Louis N.L., 1968; Marty Barrett, Boston A.L., 1986.

Most home runs, series—5 (6 games) Reggie Jackson, New York A.L., 1977; 4 (7 games) Babe Ruth, New York A.L., 1926; Duke Snider, Brooklyn N.L., 1952, 1955; Hank Bauer, New York A.L., 1958; Gene Tenace, Oakland A.L., 1972; 4 (4 games) Lou Gehrig, New York A.L., 1928; 4 (6 games) Willie Aikens, Kansas City A.L., 1980.

Most home runs, game—3, Babe Ruth, New York A.L., 1926 and 1928; Reggie Jackson, New York A.L., 1977.

Most strikeouts, series—12 (6 games) Willie Wilson, Kansas City A.L., 1980; 11 (7 games) Ed Mathews, Milwaukee N.L., 1958; Wayne Garrett, New York N.L., 1973; 9 (5 games) Carmelo Martinez, San Diego N.L., 1984; 7 (4 games) Bob Muesel, New York A.L., 1927; Ken Caminiti, San Diego N.L., 1998.

Most stolen bases, game—3, Honus Wagner, Pittsburgh N.L., 1909; Willie Davis, Los Angeles N.L., 1965; Lou Brock, St. Louis N.L., 1967 and 1968.

Most strikeouts by pitcher, game—17, Bob Gibson, St. Louis N.L. 1968.

Most strikeouts by pitcher in succession—6, Horace Eller, Cincinnati N.L., 1919; Moe Drabowsky, Baltimore A.L., 1966.

Most strikeouts by pitcher, series—35 (7 games) Bob Gibson, St. Louis N.L., 1968; 23 (4 games) Sandy Koufax, Los Angeles, 1963; 20 (6 games) Chief Bender, Philadelphia A.L., 1911; 18 (5 games) Christy Mathewson, New York N.L., 1905.

Most bases on balls, series—11 (7 games) Babe Ruth, New York A.L., 1926; Gene Tenace, Oakland A.L., 1973; 9 (6 games) Willie Randolph, New York A.L., 1981; 7 (5 games) James Sheckard, Chicago N.L., 1910; Mickey Cochrane, Philadelphia A.L., 1929; Joe Gordon, New York A.L., 1941; 7 (4 games) Hank Thompson, New York N.L., 1954.

Most consecutive scoreless innings one series—27, Christy Mathewson, New York N.L., 1905.

## AMERICAN LEAGUE HOME RUN CHAMPIONS

| Year | Player, team | No. | Year | Player, team | No. | Year | Player, team | No. |
|---|---|---|---|---|---|---|---|---|
| 1901 | Nap Lajoie, Philadelphia | 13 | 1937 | Joe DiMaggio, New York | 46 | 1970 | Frank Howard, Washington | 44 |
| 1902 | Ralph Seybold, Philadelphia | 16 | 1938 | Hank Greenberg, Detroit | 58 | 1971 | Bill Melton, Chicago | 33 |
| 1903 | Buck Freeman, Boston | 13 | 1939 | Jimmie Foxx, Boston | 35 | 1972 | Dick Allen, Chicago | 37 |
| 1904 | Harry Davis, Philadelphia | 10 | 1940 | Hank Greenberg, Detroit | 41 | 1973 | Reggie Jackson, Oakland | 32 |
| 1905 | Harry Davis, Philadelphia | 8 | 1941 | Ted Williams, Boston | 37 | 1974 | Dick Allen, Chicago | 32 |
| 1906 | Harry Davis, Philadelphia | 12 | 1942 | Ted Williams, Boston | 36 | 1975 | Reggie Jackson, Oakland; | 36 |
| 1907 | Harry Davis, Philadelphia | 8 | 1943 | Rudy York, Detroit | 34 | | George Scott, Milwaukee | |
| 1908 | Sam Crawford, Detroit | 7 | 1944 | Nick Etten, New York | 22 | 1976 | Graig Nettles, New York | 32 |
| 1909 | Ty Cobb, Detroit | 9 | 1945 | Vern Stephens, St. Louis | 24 | 1977 | Jim Rice, Boston | 39 |
| 1910 | J. Garland Stahl, Boston | 10 | 1946 | Hank Greenberg, Detroit | 44 | 1978 | Jim Rice, Boston | 46 |
| 1911 | Franklin Baker, Philadelphia | 9 | 1947 | Ted Williams, Boston | 32 | 1979 | Gorman Thomas, Milwaukee | 45 |
| 1912 | Franklin Baker, Philadelphia | 10 | 1948 | Joe DiMaggio, New York | 39 | 1980 | Reggie Jackson, New York; | 41 |
| 1913 | Franklin Baker, Philadelphia | 12 | 1949 | Ted Williams, Boston | 43 | | Ben Oglivie, Milwaukee | |
| 1914 | Franklin Baker, Philadelphia; | 8 | 1950 | Al Rosen, Cleveland | 37 | 1981[1] | Tony Armas, Oakland; | 22 |
| | Sam Crawford, Detroit | | 1951 | Gus Zernial, | 33 | | Dwight Evans, Boston; | |
| 1915 | Robert Roth, | 7 | | Chicago-Philadelphia | | | Bobby Grich, California; | |
| | Chicago-Cleveland | | 1952 | Larry Doby, Cleveland | 32 | | Eddie Murray, Baltimore (tie) | |
| 1916 | Wally Pipp, New York | 12 | 1953 | Al Rosen, Cleveland | 43 | 1982 | Gorman Thomas, | 39 |
| 1917 | Wally Pipp, New York | 9 | 1954 | Larry Doby, Cleveland | 32 | | Milwaukee; Reggie Jackson, | |
| 1918 | Babe Ruth, Boston; | 11 | 1955 | Mickey Mantle, New York | 37 | | California | |
| | Clarence Walker, | | 1956 | Mickey Mantle, New York | 52 | 1983 | Jim Rice, Boston | 39 |
| | Philadelphia | | 1957 | Roy Sievers, Washington | 42 | 1984 | Tony Armas, Boston | 43 |
| 1919 | Babe Ruth, Boston | 29 | 1958 | Mickey Mantle, New York | 42 | 1985 | Darrell Evans, Detroit | 40 |
| 1920 | Babe Ruth, New York | 54 | 1959 | Rocky Colavito, Cleveland; | 42 | 1986 | Jesse Barfield, Toronto | 40 |
| 1921 | Babe Ruth, New York | 59 | | Harmon Killebrew, | | 1987 | Mark McGwire, Oakland | 49 |
| 1922 | Ken Williams, St. Louis | 39 | | Washington | | 1988 | Jose Canseco, Oakland | 42 |
| 1923 | Babe Ruth, New York | 41 | 1960 | Mickey Mantle, New York | 40 | 1989 | Fred McGriff, Toronto | 36 |
| 1924 | Babe Ruth, New York | 46 | 1961 | Roger Maris, New York | 61 | 1990 | Cecil Fielder, Detroit | 51 |
| 1925 | Bob Meusel, New York | 33 | 1962 | Harmon Killebrew, | 48 | 1991 | Jose Canseco, Oakland; | 44 |
| 1926 | Babe Ruth, New York | 47 | | Minnesota | | | Cecil Fielder, Detroit (tie) | |
| 1927 | Babe Ruth, New York | 60 | 1963 | Harmon Killebrew, | 45 | 1992 | Juan Gonzalez, Texas | 43 |
| 1928 | Babe Ruth, New York | 54 | | Minnesota | | 1993 | Juan Gonzalez, Texas | 46 |
| 1929 | Babe Ruth, New York | 46 | 1964 | Harmon Killebrew, | 49 | 1994[2] | Ken Griffey, Jr., Seattle | 40 |
| 1930 | Babe Ruth, New York | 49 | | Minnesota | | 1995 | Albert Belle, Cleveland | 50 |
| 1931 | Lou Gehrig, New York; Babe | 46 | 1965 | Tony Conigliaro, Boston | 32 | 1996 | Mark McGwire, Oakland | 52 |
| | Ruth, New York | | 1966 | Frank Robinson, Baltimore | 49 | 1997 | Ken Griffey, Jr., Seattle | 56 |
| 1932 | Jimmie Foxx, Philadelphia | 58 | 1967 | Carl Yastrzemski, Boston; | 44 | 1998 | Ken Griffey, Jr., Seattle | 56 |
| 1933 | Jimmie Foxx, Philadelphia | 48 | | Harmon Killebrew, | | 1999 | Ken Griffey, Jr., Seattle | 48 |
| 1934 | Lou Gehrig, New York | 49 | | Minnesota | | 2000 | Tony Glaus, Anaheim | 47 |
| 1935 | Jimmie Foxx, Philadelphia; | 36 | 1968 | Frank Howard, Washington | 44 | 2001 | Alex Rodriguez, Texas | 52 |
| | Hank Greenberg, Detroit | | 1969 | Harmon Killebrew, | 49 | 2002 | Alex Rodriguez, Texas | 57 |
| 1936 | Lou Gehrig, New York | 49 | | Minnesota | | | | |

1. Split season because of players' strike. 2. Season ended on Aug. 12 because of players' strike.

## AMERICAN LEAGUE BATTING CHAMPIONS

| Year | Player, team | Avg. | Year | Player, team | Avg. | Year | Player, team | Avg. |
|---|---|---|---|---|---|---|---|---|
| 1901 | Nap Lajoie, Philadelphia | .422 | 1935 | Buddy Myer, Washington | .349 | 1969 | Rod Carew, Minnesota | .332 |
| 1902 | Ed Delahanty, Washington | .376 | 1936 | Luke Appling, Chicago | .388 | 1970 | Alex Johnson, California | .329 |
| 1903 | Nap Lajoie, Cleveland | .355 | 1937 | Charley Gehringer, Detroit | .371 | 1971 | Tony Oliva, Minnesota | .337 |
| 1904 | Nap Lajoie, Cleveland | .381 | 1938 | Jimmie Foxx, Boston | .349 | 1972 | Rod Carew, Minnesota | .318 |
| 1905 | Elmer Flick, Cleveland | .306 | 1939 | Joe DiMaggio, New York | .381 | 1973 | Rod Carew, Minnesota | .350 |
| 1906 | George Stone, St. Louis | .358 | 1940 | Joe DiMaggio, New York | .352 | 1974 | Rod Carew, Minnesota | .364 |
| 1907 | Ty Cobb, Detroit | .350 | 1941 | Ted Williams, Boston | .406 | 1975 | Rod Carew, Minnesota | .359 |
| 1908 | Ty Cobb, Detroit | .324 | 1942 | Ted Williams, Boston | .356 | 1976 | George Brett, Kansas City | .333 |
| 1909 | Ty Cobb, Detroit | .377 | 1943 | Luke Appling, Chicago | .328 | 1977 | Rod Carew, Minnesota | .388 |
| 1910 | Ty Cobb, Detroit | .385 | 1944 | Lou Boudreau, Cleveland | .327 | 1978 | Rod Carew, Minnesota | .333 |
| 1911 | Ty Cobb, Detroit | .420 | 1945 | George Sternweiss, New | .309 | 1979 | Fred Lynn, Boston | .333 |
| 1912 | Ty Cobb, Detroit | .410 | | York | | 1980 | George Brett, Kansas City | .390 |
| 1913 | Ty Cobb, Detroit | .390 | 1946 | Mickey Vernon, Washington | .353 | 1981[1] | Carney Lansford, Boston | .336 |
| 1914 | Ty Cobb, Detroit | .368 | 1947 | Ted Williams, Boston | .343 | 1982 | Willie Wilson, Kansas City | .332 |
| 1915 | Ty Cobb, Detroit | .369 | 1948 | Ted Williams, Boston | .369 | 1983 | Wade Boggs, Boston | .361 |
| 1916 | Tris Speaker, Cleveland | .386 | 1949 | George Kell, Detroit | .343 | 1984 | Don Mattingly, New York | .343 |
| 1917 | Ty Cobb, Detroit | .383 | 1950 | Billy Goodman, Boston | .354 | 1985 | Wade Boggs, Boston | .368 |
| 1918 | Ty Cobb, Detroit | .382 | 1951 | Ferris Fain, Philadelphia | .344 | 1986 | Wade Boggs, Boston | .357 |
| 1919 | Ty Cobb, Detroit | .384 | 1952 | Ferris Fain, Philadelphia | .327 | 1987 | Wade Boggs, Boston | .363 |
| 1920 | George Sisler, St. Louis | .407 | 1953 | Mickey Vernon, Washington | .337 | 1988 | Wade Boggs, Boston | .366 |
| 1921 | Harry Heilmann, Detroit | .394 | 1954 | Bobby Avila, Cleveland | .341 | 1989 | Kirby Puckett, Minnesota | .339 |
| 1922 | George Sisler, St. Louis | .420 | 1955 | Al Kaline, Detroit | .340 | 1990 | George Brett, Kansas City | .328 |
| 1923 | Harry Heilmann, Detroit | .403 | 1956 | Mickey Mantle, New York | .353 | 1991 | Julio Franco, Texas | .341 |
| 1924 | Babe Ruth, New York | .378 | 1957 | Ted Williams, Boston | .388 | 1992 | Edgar Martinez, Seattle | .343 |
| 1925 | Harry Heilmann, Detroit | .393 | 1958 | Ted Williams, Boston | .328 | 1993 | John Olerud, Toronto | .363 |
| 1926 | Heinie Manush, Detroit | .378 | 1959 | Harvey Kuenn, Detroit | .353 | 1994[2] | Paul O'Neill, New York | .359 |
| 1927 | Harry Heilmann, Detroit | .398 | 1960 | Pete Runnels, Boston | .320 | 1995 | Edgar Martinez, Seattle | .356 |
| 1928 | Goose Goslin, Washington | .379 | 1961 | Norman Cash, Detroit | .361 | 1996 | Alex Rodriguez, Seattle | .358 |
| 1929 | Lew Fonseca, Cleveland | .369 | 1962 | Pete Runnels, Boston | .326 | 1997 | Frank Thomas, Chicago | .347 |
| 1930 | Al Simmons, Philadelphia | .381 | 1963 | Carl Yastrzemski, Boston | .321 | 1998 | Bernie Williams, New York | .339 |
| 1931 | Al Simmons, Philadelphia | .390 | 1964 | Tony Oliva, Minnesota | .323 | 1999 | Nomar Garciaparra, Boston | .357 |
| 1932 | Dale Alexander, | .367 | 1965 | Tony Oliva, Minnesota | .321 | 2000 | Nomar Garciaparra, Boston | .372 |
| | Detroit-Boston | | 1966 | Frank Robinson, Baltimore | .316 | 2001 | Ichiro Suzuki, Seattle | .350 |
| 1933 | Jimmie Foxx, Philadelphia | .356 | 1967 | Carl Yastrzemski, Boston | .326 | 2002 | Manny Ramirez, Boston | .349 |
| 1934 | Lou Gehrig, New York | .363 | 1968 | Carl Yastrzemski, Boston | .301 | | | |

1. Split season because of players' strike. 2. Season ended on Aug. 12 because of players' strike.

## NATIONAL LEAGUE HOME RUN CHAMPIONS

| Year | Player, team | No. | Year | Player, team | No. | Year | Player, team | No. |
|---|---|---|---|---|---|---|---|---|
| 1876 | George Hall, Philadelphia Athletics | 5 | 1896 | Ed Delahanty, Philadelphia; Sam Thompson, Philadelphia | 13 | 1920 | Cy Williams, Philadelphia | 15 |
| 1877 | George Shaffer, Louisville | 3 | | | | 1921 | George Kelly, New York | 23 |
| 1878 | Paul Hines, Providence | 4 | 1897 | Nap Lajoie, Philadelphia | 10 | 1922 | Rogers Hornsby, St. Louis | 42 |
| 1879 | Charles Jones, Boston | 9 | 1898 | James Colins, Boston | 14 | 1923 | Cy Williams, Philadelphia | 41 |
| 1880 | James O'Rourke, Boston; Harry Stovey, Worcester | 6 | 1899 | John Freeman, Washington | 25 | 1924 | Jacques Fournier, Brooklyn | 27 |
| | | | 1900 | Herman Long, Boston | 12 | 1925 | Rogers Hornsby, St. Louis | 39 |
| 1881 | Dan Brouthers, Buffalo | 8 | 1901 | Sam Crawford, Cincinnati | 16 | 1926 | Hack Wilson, Chicago | 21 |
| 1882 | George Wood, Detroit | 7 | 1902 | Tom Leach, Pittsburgh | 6 | 1927 | Hack Wilson, Chicago; Cy Williams, Philadelphia | 30 |
| 1883 | William Ewing, New York | 10 | 1903 | James Sheckard, Brooklyn | 9 | | | |
| 1884 | Ed Williamson, Chicago | 27 | 1904 | Harry Lumley, Brooklyn | 9 | 1928 | Hack Wilson, Chicago; Jim Bottomley, St. Louis | 31 |
| 1885 | Abner Dalrymple, Chicago | 11 | 1905 | Fred Odwell, Cincinnati | 9 | | | |
| 1886 | Arthur Richardson, Detroit | 11 | 1906 | Tim Jordan, Brooklyn | 12 | 1929 | Chuck Klein, Philadelphia | 43 |
| 1887 | Roger Connor, New York; Wm. O'Brien, Washington | 17 | 1907 | David Brain, Boston | 10 | 1930 | Hack Wilson, Chicago | 56 |
| | | | 1908 | Tim Jordan, Brooklyn | 12 | 1931 | Chuck Klein, Philadelphia | 31 |
| 1888 | Roger Connor, New York | 14 | 1909 | John Murray, New York | 7 | 1932 | Chuck Klein, Philadelphia; Mel Ott, New York | 38 |
| 1889 | Sam Thompson, Philadelphia | 20 | 1910 | Fred Beck, Boston; Frank Schulte, Chicago | 10 | | | |
| | | | | | | 1933 | Chuck Klein, Philadelphia | 28 |
| 1890 | Tom Burns, Brooklyn; Mike Tiernan, New York | 13 | 1911 | Frank Schulte, Chicago | 21 | 1934 | Mel Ott, New York; Rip Collins, St. Louis | 35 |
| | | | 1912 | Henry Zimmerman, Chicago | 14 | | | |
| 1891 | Harry Stovey, Boston; Mike Tiernan, New York | 16 | 1913 | Cliff Cravath, Philadelphia | 19 | 1935 | Wally Berger, Boston | 34 |
| | | | 1914 | Cliff Cravath, Philadelphia | 19 | 1936 | Mel Ott, New York | 33 |
| 1892 | Jim Holliday, Cincinnati | 13 | 1915 | Cliff Cravath, Philadelphia | 24 | 1937 | Mel Ott, New York; Joe Medwick, St. Louis | 31 |
| 1893 | Ed Delahanty, Philadelphia | 19 | 1916 | Davis Robertson, New York; Fred Williams, Chicago | 12 | | | |
| 1894 | Hugh Duffy, Boston; Robert Lowe, Boston | 18 | | | | 1938 | Mel Ott, New York | 36 |
| | | | 1917 | Davis Robertson, New York; Cliff Cravath, Philadelphia | 12 | 1939 | John Mize, St. Louis | 28 |
| 1895 | Bill Joyce, Washington | 17 | | | | 1940 | John Mize, St. Louis | 43 |
| | | | 1918 | Cliff Cravath, Philadelphia | 8 | 1941 | Dolph Camilli, Brooklyn | 34 |
| | | | 1919 | Cliff Cravath, Philadelphia | 12 | 1942 | Mel Ott, New York | 30 |
| | | | | | | 1943 | Bill Nicholson, Chicago | 29 |

| Year | Player, team | No. | Year | Player, team | No. | Year | Player, team | No. |
|---|---|---|---|---|---|---|---|---|
| 1944 | Bill Nicholson, Chicago | 33 | 1963 | Hank Aaron, Milwaukee; Willie McCovey, San Francisco | 44 | 1982 | Dave Kingman, New York | 37 |
| 1945 | Tommy Holmes, Boston | 28 | | | | 1983 | Mike Schmidt, Philadelphia | 40 |
| 1946 | Ralph Kiner, Pittsburgh | 23 | | | | 1984 | Mike Schmidt, Philadelphia; Dale Murphy, Atlanta | 36 |
| 1947 | Ralph Kiner, Pittsburgh; John Mize, New York | 51 | 1964 | Willie Mays, San Francisco | 47 | | | |
| | | | 1965 | Willie Mays, San Francisco | 52 | 1985 | Dale Murphy, Atlanta | 37 |
| 1948 | Ralph Kiner, Pittsburgh; John Mize, New York | 40 | 1966 | Hank Aaron, Atlanta | 44 | 1986 | Mike Schmidt, Philadelphia | 37 |
| | | | 1967 | Hank Aaron, Atlanta | 39 | 1987 | Andre Dawson, Chicago | 49 |
| 1949 | Ralph Kiner, Pittsburgh | 54 | 1968 | Willie McCovey, San Francisco | 36 | 1988 | Darryl Strawberry, New York | 39 |
| 1950 | Ralph Kiner, Pittsburgh | 47 | | | | 1989 | Kevin Mitchell, San Francisco | 47 |
| 1951 | Ralph Kiner, Pittsburgh | 42 | 1969 | Willie McCovey, San Francisco | 45 | | | |
| 1952 | Ralph Kiner, Pittsburgh; Hank Sauer, Chicago | 37 | | | | 1990 | Ryne Sandberg, Chicago | 40 |
| | | | 1970 | Johnny Bench, Cincinnati | 45 | 1991 | Howard Johnson, New York | 38 |
| 1953 | Ed Mathews, Milwaukee | 47 | 1971 | Willie Stargell, Pittsburgh | 48 | 1992 | Fred McGriff, San Diego | 35 |
| 1954 | Ted Kluszewski, Cincinnati | 49 | 1972 | Johnny Bench, Cincinnati | 40 | 1993 | Barry Bonds, San Francisco | 46 |
| 1955 | Willie Mays, New York | 51 | 1973 | Willie Stargell, Pittsburgh | 44 | 1994² | Matt Williams, San Francisco | 43 |
| 1956 | Duke Snider, Brooklyn | 43 | 1974 | Mike Schmidt, Philadelphia | 36 | 1995 | Dante Bichette, Colorado | 40 |
| 1957 | Hank Aaron, Milwaukee | 44 | 1975 | Mike Schmidt, Philadelphia | 38 | 1996 | Andres Galarraga, Colorado | 40 |
| 1958 | Ernie Banks, Chicago | 47 | 1976 | Mike Schmidt, Philadelphia | 38 | 1997 | Larry Walker, Colorado | 49 |
| 1959 | Ed Mathews, Milwaukee | 46 | 1977 | George Foster, Cincinnati | 52 | 1998 | Mark McGwire, St. Louis | 70 |
| 1960 | Ernie Banks, Chicago | 41 | 1978 | George Foster, Cincinnati | 40 | 1999 | Mark McGwire, St. Louis | 65 |
| 1961 | Orlando Cepeda, San Francisco | 46 | 1979 | Dave Kingman, Chicago | 48 | 2000 | Sammy Sosa, Chicago | 50 |
| | | | 1980 | Mike Schmidt, Philadelphia | 48 | 2001 | Barry Bonds, San Francisco | 73 |
| 1962 | Willie Mays, San Francisco | 49 | 1981¹ | Mike Schmidt, Philadelphia | 31 | 2002 | Sammy Sosa, Chicago | 49 |

1. Split season because of players' strike. 2. Season ended on Aug. 12 because of players' strike.

## NATIONAL LEAGUE BATTING CHAMPIONS

| Year | Player, team | Avg. | Year | Player, team | Avg. | Year | Player, team | Avg. |
|---|---|---|---|---|---|---|---|---|
| 1876 | Roscoe Barnes, Chicago | .404 | 1914 | Jake Daubert, Brooklyn | .329 | 1954 | Willie Mays, New York | .345 |
| 1877 | Jim White, Boston | .385 | 1915 | Larry Doyle, New York | .320 | 1955 | Richie Ashburn, Philadelphia | .338 |
| 1878 | Abner Dalrymple, Milwaukee | .356 | 1916 | Hal Chase, Cincinnati | .339 | 1956 | Hank Aaron, Milwaukee | .328 |
| 1879 | Cap Anson, Chicago | .407 | 1917 | Edd Roush, Cincinnati | .341 | 1957 | Stan Musial, St. Louis | .351 |
| 1880 | George Gore, Chicago | .365 | 1918 | Zack Wheat, Brooklyn | .335 | 1958 | Richie Ashburn, Philadelphia | .350 |
| 1881 | Cap Anson, Chicago | .399 | 1919 | Edd Roush, Cincinnati | .321 | 1959 | Hank Aaron, Milwaukee | .355 |
| 1882 | Dan Brouthers, Buffalo | .367 | 1920 | Rogers Hornsby, St. Louis | .370 | 1960 | Dick Groat, Pittsburgh | .325 |
| 1883 | Dan Brouthers, Buffalo | .371 | 1921 | Rogers Hornsby, St. Louis | .397 | 1961 | Roberto Clemente, Pittsburgh | .351 |
| 1884 | James O'Rourke, Buffalo | .350 | 1922 | Rogers Hornsby, St. Louis | .401 | | | |
| 1885 | Roger Connor, New York | .371 | 1923 | Rogers Hornsby, St. Louis | .384 | 1962 | Tommy Davis, Los Angeles | .346 |
| 1886 | King Kelly, Chicago | .388 | 1924 | Rogers Hornsby, St. Louis | .424 | 1963 | Tommy Davis, Los Angeles | .326 |
| 1887 | Cap Anson, Chicago | .421 | 1925 | Rogers Hornsby, St. Louis | .403 | 1964 | Roberto Clemente, Pittsburgh | .339 |
| 1888 | Cap Anson, Chicago | .343 | 1926 | Gene Hargrave, Cincinnati | .353 | | | |
| 1889 | Dan Brouthers, Boston | .373 | 1927 | Paul Waner, Pittsburgh | .380 | 1965 | Roberto Clemente, Pittsburgh | .329 |
| 1890 | John Glasscock, New York | .336 | 1928 | Rogers Hornsby, Boston | .387 | | | |
| 1891 | William Hamilton, Philadelphia | .338 | 1929 | Lefty O'Doul, Philadelphia | .398 | 1966 | Matty Alou, Pittsburgh | .342 |
| | | | 1930 | Bill Terry, New York | .401 | 1967 | Roberto Clemente, Pittsburgh | .357 |
| 1892 | Dan Brouthers, Brooklyn; Clarence Childs, Cleveland | .335 | 1931 | Chick Hafey, St. Louis | .349 | | | |
| | | | 1932 | Lefty O'Doul, Brooklyn | .368 | 1968 | Pete Rose, Cincinnati | .335 |
| 1893 | Hugh Duffy, Boston | .378 | 1933 | Chuck Klein, Philadelphia | .368 | 1969 | Pete Rose, Cincinnati | .348 |
| 1894 | Hugh Duffy, Boston | .438 | 1934 | Paul Waner, Pittsburgh | .362 | 1970 | Rico Carty, Atlanta | .366 |
| 1895 | Jesse Burkett, Cleveland | .423 | 1935 | Arky Vaughan, Pittsburgh | .385 | 1971 | Joe Torre, St. Louis | .363 |
| 1896 | Jesse Burkett, Cleveland | .410 | 1936 | Paul Waner, Pittsburgh | .373 | 1972 | Billy Williams, Chicago | .333 |
| 1897 | Willie Keeler, Baltimore | .432 | 1937 | Joe Medwick, St. Louis | .374 | 1973 | Pete Rose, Cincinnati | .338 |
| 1898 | Willie Keeler, Baltimore | .379 | 1938 | Ernie Lombardi, Cincinnati | .342 | 1974 | Ralph Garr, Atlanta | .353 |
| 1899 | Ed Delahanty, Philadelphia | .408 | 1939 | John Mize, St. Louis | .349 | 1975 | Bill Madlock, Chicago | .354 |
| 1900 | Honus Wagner, Pittsburgh | .381 | 1940 | Debs Garms, Pittsburgh | .355 | 1976 | Bill Madlock, Chicago | .339 |
| 1901 | Jesse Burkett, St. Louis | .382 | 1941 | Pete Reiser, Brooklyn | .343 | 1977 | Dave Parker, Pittsburgh | .338 |
| 1902 | Clarence Beaumont, Pittsburgh | .357 | 1942 | Ernie Lombardi, Boston | .330 | 1978 | Dave Parker, Pittsburgh | .334 |
| | | | 1943 | Stan Musial, St. Louis | .357 | 1979 | Keith Hernandez, St. Louis | .344 |
| 1903 | Honus Wagner, Pittsburgh | .355 | 1944 | Dixie Walker, Brooklyn | .357 | 1980 | Bill Buckner, Chicago | .324 |
| 1904 | Honus Wagner, Pittsburgh | .349 | 1945 | Phil Cavarretta, Chicago | .355 | 1981¹ | Bill Madlock, Pittsburgh | .341 |
| 1905 | Cy Seymour, Cincinnati | .377 | 1946 | Stan Musial, St. Louis | .365 | 1982 | Al Oliver, Montreal | .331 |
| 1906 | Honus Wagner, Pittsburgh | .339 | 1947 | Harry Walker, St. Louis-Philadelphia | .363 | 1983 | Bill Madlock, Pittsburgh | .323 |
| 1907 | Honus Wagner, Pittsburgh | .350 | | | | 1984 | Tony Gwynn, San Diego | .351 |
| 1908 | Honus Wagner, Pittsburgh | .354 | 1948 | Stan Musial, St. Louis | .376 | 1985 | Willie McGee, St. Louis | .353 |
| 1909 | Honus Wagner, Pittsburgh | .339 | 1949 | Jackie Robinson, Brooklyn | .342 | 1986 | Tim Raines, Montreal | .334 |
| 1910 | Sherwood Magee, Philadelphia | .331 | 1950 | Stan Musial, St. Louis | .346 | 1987 | Tony Gwynn, San Diego | .370 |
| | | | 1951 | Stan Musial, St. Louis | .355 | 1988 | Tony Gwynn, San Diego | .313 |
| 1911 | Honus Wagner, Pittsburgh | .334 | 1952 | Stan Musial, St. Louis | .336 | 1989 | Tony Gwynn, San Diego | .336 |
| 1912 | Henry Zimmerman, Chicago | .372 | 1953 | Carl Furillo, Brooklyn | .344 | 1990 | Willie McGee, St. Louis | .335 |
| 1913 | Jake Daubert, Brooklyn | .350 | | | | 1991 | Terry Pendleton, Atlanta | .319 |

| Year | Player, team | Avg. | Year | Player, team | Avg. | Year | Player, team | Avg. |
|------|--------------|------|------|--------------|------|------|--------------|------|
| 1992 | Gary Sheffield, San Diego | .330 | 1996 | Tony Gwynn, San Diego | .353 | 2000 | Todd Helton, Colorado | .372 |
| 1993 | Andres Galarraga, Colorado | .370 | 1997 | Tony Gwynn, San Diego | .372 | 2001 | Larry Walker, Colorado | .350 |
| 1994[2] | Tony Gwynn, San Diego | .394 | 1998 | Larry Walker, Colorado | .363 | 2002 | Barry Bonds, San Francisco | .370 |
| 1995 | Tony Gwynn, San Diego | .368 | 1999 | Larry Walker, Colorado | .379 | | | |

1. Split season because of players' strike. 2. Season ended on Aug. 12 because of players' strike.

## MOST VALUABLE PLAYERS
### (Baseball Writers' Association selections)

**American League**

| | | |
|---|---|---|
| 1931 | Lefty Grove, Philadelphia | |
| 1932–33 | Jimmie Foxx, Philadelphia | |
| 1934 | Mickey Cochrane, Detroit | |
| 1935 | Hank Greenberg, Detroit | |
| 1936 | Lou Gehrig, New York | |
| 1937 | Charlie Gehringer, Detroit | |
| 1938 | Jimmie Foxx, Boston | |
| 1939 | Joe DiMaggio, New York | |
| 1940 | Hank Greenberg, Detroit | |
| 1941 | Joe DiMaggio, New York | |
| 1942 | Joe Gordon, New York | |
| 1943 | Spurgeon Chandler, New York | |
| 1944–45 | Hal Newhouser, Detroit | |
| 1946 | Ted Williams, Boston | |
| 1947 | Joe DiMaggio, New York | |
| 1948 | Lou Boudreau, Cleveland | |
| 1949 | Ted Williams, Boston | |
| 1950 | Phil Rizzuto, New York | |
| 1951 | Yogi Berra, New York | |
| 1952 | Bobby Shantz, Philadelphia | |
| 1953 | Al Rosen, Cleveland | |
| 1954–55 | Yogi Berra, New York | |
| 1956–57 | Mickey Mantle, New York | |
| 1958 | Jackie Jensen, Boston | |
| 1959 | Nellie Fox, Chicago | |
| 1960–61 | Roger Maris, New York | |
| 1962 | Mickey Mantle, New York | |
| 1963 | Elston Howard, New York | |
| 1964 | Brooks Robinson, Baltimore | |
| 1965 | Zoilo Versalles, Minnesota | |
| 1966 | Frank Robinson, Baltimore | |
| 1967 | Carl Yastrzemski, Boston | |
| 1968 | Dennis McLain, Detroit | |
| 1969 | Harmon Killebrew, Minnesota | |
| 1970 | John (Boog) Powell, Baltimore | |
| 1971 | Vida Blue, Oakland | |
| 1972 | Dick Allen, Chicago | |
| 1973 | Reggie Jackson, Oakland | |
| 1974 | Jeff Burroughs, Texas | |
| 1975 | Fred Lynn, Boston | |
| 1976 | Thurman Munson, New York | |
| 1977 | Rod Carew, Minnesota | |
| 1978 | Jim Rice, Boston | |
| 1979 | Don Baylor, California | |
| 1980 | George Brett, Kansas City | |
| 1981 | Rollie Fingers, Milwaukee | |

| | | |
|---|---|---|
| 1982 | Robin Yount, Milwaukee | |
| 1983 | Cal Ripken, Jr., Baltimore | |
| 1984 | Willie Hernandez, Detroit | |
| 1985 | Don Mattingly, New York | |
| 1986 | Roger Clemens, Boston | |
| 1987 | George Bell, Toronto | |
| 1988 | Jose Canseco, Oakland | |
| 1989 | Robin Yount, Milwaukee | |
| 1990 | Rickey Henderson, Oakland | |
| 1991 | Cal Ripken, Jr., Baltimore | |
| 1992 | Dennis Eckersley, Oakland | |
| 1993 | Frank Thomas, Chicago | |
| 1994 | Frank Thomas, Chicago | |
| 1995 | Mo Vaughn, Boston | |
| 1996 | Juan Gonzalez, Texas | |
| 1997 | Ken Griffey, Jr., Seattle | |
| 1998 | Juan Gonzalez, Texas | |
| 1999 | Ivan Rodriguez, Texas | |
| 2000 | Jason Giambi, Oakland | |
| 2001 | Ichiro Suzuki, Seattle | |

**National League**

| | | |
|---|---|---|
| 1931 | Frank Frisch, St. Louis | |
| 1932 | Chuck Klein, Philadelphia | |
| 1933 | Carl Hubbell, New York | |
| 1934 | Dizzy Dean, St. Louis | |
| 1935 | Gabby Hartnett, Chicago | |
| 1936 | Carl Hubbell, New York | |
| 1937 | Joe Medwick, St. Louis | |
| 1938 | Ernie Lombardi, Cincinnati | |
| 1939 | Bucky Walters, Cincinnati | |
| 1940 | Frank McCormick, Cincinnati | |
| 1941 | Dolph Camilli, Brooklyn | |
| 1942 | Mort Cooper, St. Louis | |
| 1943 | Stan Musial, St. Louis | |
| 1944 | Marty Marion, St. Louis | |
| 1945 | Phil Cavarretta, Chicago | |
| 1946 | Stan Musial, St. Louis | |
| 1947 | Bob Elliott, Boston | |
| 1948 | Stan Musial, St. Louis | |
| 1949 | Jackie Robinson, Brooklyn | |
| 1950 | Jim Konstanty, Philadelphia | |
| 1951 | Roy Campanella, Brooklyn | |
| 1952 | Hank Sauer, Chicago | |
| 1953 | Roy Campanella, Brooklyn | |
| 1954 | Willie Mays, New York | |
| 1955 | Roy Campanella, Brooklyn | |

| | | |
|---|---|---|
| 1956 | Don Newcombe, Brooklyn | |
| 1957 | Hank Aaron, Milwaukee | |
| 1958–59 | Ernie Banks, Chicago | |
| 1960 | Dick Groat, Pittsburgh | |
| 1961 | Frank Robinson, Cincinnati | |
| 1962 | Maury Wills, Los Angeles | |
| 1963 | Sandy Koufax, Los Angeles | |
| 1964 | Ken Boyer, St. Louis | |
| 1965 | Willie Mays, San Francisco | |
| 1966 | Roberto Clemente, Pittsburgh | |
| 1967 | Orlando Cepeda, St. Louis | |
| 1968 | Bob Gibson, St. Louis | |
| 1969 | Willie McCovey, San Francisco | |
| 1970 | Johnny Bench, Cincinnati | |
| 1971 | Joe Torre, St. Louis | |
| 1972 | Johnny Bench, Cincinnati | |
| 1973 | Pete Rose, Cincinnati | |
| 1974 | Steve Garvey, Los Angeles | |
| 1975–76 | Joe Morgan, Cincinnati | |
| 1977 | George Foster, Cincinnati | |
| 1978 | Dave Parker, Pittsburgh | |
| 1979 | Willie Stargell, Pittsburgh | |
| 1979 | Keith Hernandez, St. Louis | |
| 1980 | Mike Schmidt, Philadelphia | |
| 1981 | Mike Schmidt, Philadelphia | |
| 1982 | Dale Murphy, Atlanta | |
| 1983 | Dale Murphy, Atlanta | |
| 1984 | Ryne Sandberg, Chicago | |
| 1985 | Willie McGee, St. Louis | |
| 1986 | Mike Schmidt, Philadelphia | |
| 1987 | Andre Dawson, Chicago | |
| 1988 | Kirk Gibson, Los Angeles | |
| 1989 | Kevin Mitchell, San Francisco | |
| 1990 | Barry Bonds, Pittsburgh | |
| 1991 | Terry Pendleton, Atlanta | |
| 1992 | Barry Bonds, Pittsburgh | |
| 1993 | Barry Bonds, San Francisco | |
| 1994 | Jeff Bagwell, Houston | |
| 1995 | Barry Larkin, Cincinnati | |
| 1996 | Ken Caminiti, San Diego | |
| 1997 | Larry Walker, Colorado | |
| 1998 | Sammy Sosa, Chicago | |
| 1999 | Chipper Jones, Atlanta | |
| 2000 | Jeff Kent, San Francisco | |
| 2001 | Barry Bonds, San Francisco | |

## CY YOUNG AWARD

| | | |
|---|---|---|
| 1956 | Don Newcombe, Brooklyn N.L. | |
| 1957 | Warren Spahn, Milwaukee N.L. | |
| 1958 | Bob Turley, New York A.L. | |
| 1959 | Early Wynn, Chicago A.L. | |
| 1960 | Vernon Law, Pittsburgh N.L | |
| 1961 | Whitey Ford, New York A.L. | |
| 1962 | Don Drysdale, Los Angeles N.L. | |
| 1963 | Sandy Koufax, Los Angeles N.L. | |
| 1964 | Dean Chance, Los Angeles A.L. | |

| | | |
|---|---|---|
| 1965 | Sandy Koufax, Los Angeles N.L. | |
| 1966 | Sandy Koufax, Los Angeles N.L. | |
| 1967 | Jim Lonborg, Boston A.L.; Mike McCormick, San Francisco N.L. | |
| 1968 | Dennis McLain, Detroit A.L.; Bob Gibson, St. Louis N.L. | |

| | | |
|---|---|---|
| 1969 | Mike Cuellar, Baltimore A.L. and Dennis McLain, Detroit A.L. (tied); Tom Seaver, New York N.L. | |
| 1970 | Jim Perry, Minnesota A.L; Bob Gibson, St. Louis N.L. | |
| 1971 | Vida Blue, Oakland A.L.; Ferguson Jenkins, Chicago N.L. | |
| 1972 | Gaylord Perry, Cleveland A.L.; Steve Carlton, Philadelphia N.L. | |

| | | |
|---|---|---|
| 1973 Jim Palmer, Baltimore A.L.; Tom Seaver, New York N.L. | 1983 LaMarr Hoyt, Chicago A.L.; John Denny, Philadelphia N.L. | 1992 Dennis Eckersley, Oakland A.L.; Greg Maddux, Atlanta N.L. |
| 1974 Catfish Hunter, Oakland A.L.; Mike Marshall, Los Angeles N.L. | 1984 Willie Hernandez, Detroit A.L.; Rick Sutcliffe, Chicago N.L. | 1993 Jack McDowell, Chicago A.L.; Greg Maddux, Atlanta N.L. |
| 1975 Jim Palmer, Baltimore A.L.; Tom Seaver, New York N.L. | 1985 Bret Saberhagen, Kansas City A.L.; Dwight Gooden, New York N.L. | 1994 David Cone, Kansas A.L.; Greg Maddux, Atlanta N.L. |
| 1976 Jim Palmer, Baltimore A.L.; Randy Jones, San Diego N.L. | 1986 Roger Clemens, Boston A.L.; Mike Scott, Houston N.L. | 1995 Randy Johnson, Seattle A.L.; Greg Maddux, Atlanta N.L. |
| 1977 Sparky Lyle, New York A.L.; Steve Carlton, Philadelphia N.L. | 1987 Roger Clemens, Boston A.L.; Steve Bedrosian, Philadelphia N.L. | 1996 Pat Hentgen, Toronto A.L.; John Smoltz, Atlanta N.L. |
| 1978 Ron Guidry, New York A.L.; Gaylord Perry, San Diego N.L. | 1988 Frank Viola, Minnesota A.L.; Orel Hershiser, Los Angeles, N.L. | 1997 Roger Clemens, Toronto A.L.; Pedro Martinez, Montreal N.L. |
| 1979 Mike Flanagan, Baltimore A.L.; Bruce Sutter, Chicago N.L. | 1989 Bret Saberhagen, Kansas A.L.; Mark Davis, San Diego N.L. | 1998 Roger Clemens, Toronto A.L.; Tom Glavine, Atlanta N.L. |
| 1980 Steve Stone, Baltimore A.L.; Steve Carlton, Philadelphia N.L. | 1990 Bob Welch, Oakland A.L.; Doug Drabek, Pittsburgh N.L. | 1999– Pedro Martinez, Boston A.L.; 2000 Randy Johnson, Arizona N.L. |
| 1981 Rollie Fingers, Milwaukee A.L.; Fernando Valenzuela, Los Angeles N.L. | 1991 Roger Clemens, Boston A.L.; Tom Glavine, Atlanta N.L. | 2001 Roger Clemens, New York A.L.; Randy Johnson, Arizona N.L. |
| 1982 Pete Vuckovich, Milwaukee A.L.; Steve Carlton, Philadelphia N.L. | | |

# MAJOR LEAGUE LIFETIME RECORDS

## (through 2002)

### Wins
### (Boldface indicates player active in 2002)

### Leading Batters, by Batting Average

| | | W | L | ERA | G | | | G | AB | H | Avg. |
|---|---|---|---|---|---|---|---|---|---|---|---|
| 1 | Cy Young | 511 | 316 | 2.63 | 906 | 1 | Ty Cobb | 3,035 | 11,434 | 4,189 | .366 |
| 2 | Walter Johnson | 417 | 279 | 2.17 | 802 | 2 | Rogers Hornsby | 2,259 | 8,173 | 2,930 | .358 |
| 3 | Grover Alexander | 373 | 208 | 2.56 | 696 | 3 | Ed Delahanty | 1,835 | 7,505 | 2,596 | .346 |
| 4 | Christy Mathewson | 373 | 188 | 2.13 | 635 | 4 | Tris Speaker | 2,789 | 10,195 | 3,514 | .345 |
| 5 | Pud Galvin | 365 | 310 | 2.85 | 705 | 5 | Billy Hamilton | 1,591 | 6,269 | 2,159 | .344 |
| 6 | Warren Spahn | 363 | 245 | 3.09 | 750 | 5 | Ted Williams | 2,292 | 7,706 | 2,654 | .344 |
| 7 | Kid Nichols | 361 | 208 | 2.95 | 620 | 7 | Dan Brouthers | 1,673 | 6,711 | 2,296 | .342 |
| 8 | Tim Keefe | 342 | 225 | 2.62 | 600 | 7 | Harry Heilmann | 2,147 | 7,787 | 2,660 | .342 |
| 9 | Steve Carlton | 329 | 244 | 3.22 | 741 | 7 | Babe Ruth | 2,503 | 8,399 | 2,873 | .342 |
| 10 | John Clarkson | 328 | 178 | 2.81 | 531 | 10 | Willie Keeler | 2,123 | 8,591 | 2,932 | .341 |
| 11 | Eddie Plank | 326 | 194 | 2.35 | 623 | 10 | Bill Terry | 1,721 | 6,428 | 2,193 | .341 |
| 12 | Nolan Ryan | 324 | 292 | 3.19 | 807 | 12 | Lou Gehrig | 2,164 | 8,001 | 2,721 | .340 |
| 13 | Don Sutton | 324 | 256 | 3.26 | 774 | 12 | George Sisler | 2,055 | 8,267 | 2,812 | .340 |
| 14 | Phil Niekro | 318 | 274 | 3.35 | 864 | 14 | Jesse Burkett | 2,066 | 8,421 | 2,850 | .338 |
| 15 | Gaylord Perry | 314 | 265 | 3.11 | 777 | 14 | Tony Gwynn | 2,440 | 9,288 | 3,141 | .338 |
| 16 | Tom Seaver | 311 | 205 | 2.86 | 656 | 14 | Nap Lajoie | 2,480 | 9,589 | 3,242 | .338 |
| 17 | Charley Radbourn | 309 | 195 | 2.67 | 528 | 14 | Al Simmons | 2,215 | 8,759 | 2,927 | .334 |
| 18 | Mickey Welch | 307 | 210 | 2.71 | 565 | 18 | Cap Anson | 2,523 | 10,278 | 3,418 | .333 |
| 19 | Lefty Grove | 300 | 141 | 3.06 | 616 | 18 | Eddie Collins | 2,826 | 9,949 | 3,315 | .333 |
| 20 | Early Wynn | 300 | 244 | 3.54 | 691 | 18 | Paul Waner | 2,549 | 9,459 | 3,152 | .333 |
| 21 | Bobby Mathews | 297 | 248 | 2.85 | 578 | 21 | Stan Musial | 3,026 | 10,972 | 3,630 | .331 |
| 22 | **Roger Clemens** | **293** | **151** | **3.15** | **574** | 21 | Sam Thompson | 1,407 | 5,984 | 1,979 | .331 |
| 23 | Tommy John | 288 | 231 | 3.34 | 760 | 23 | Heinie Manush | 2,008 | 7,654 | 2,524 | .330 |
| 24 | Bert Blyleven | 287 | 250 | 3.31 | 692 | 24 | Wade Boggs | 2,440 | 9,180 | 3,010 | .328 |
| 25 | Robin Roberts | 286 | 245 | 3.41 | 676 | 24 | Rod Carew | 2,469 | 9,315 | 3,053 | .328 |

### Pitchers Active in 2002

### Players Active in 2002 (3,000 at-bats minimum)

| | | W | L | ERA | G | | | G | AB | H | Avg. |
|---|---|---|---|---|---|---|---|---|---|---|---|
| 1 | Roger Clemens | 293 | 151 | 3.15 | 574 | 1 | Nomar Garciaparra | 772 | 3,154 | 1,033 | .328 |
| 2 | Greg Maddux | 273 | 152 | 2.83 | 539 | 2 | Vladimir Guerrero | 892 | 3,369 | 1,085 | .322 |
| 3 | Tom Glavine | 242 | 143 | 3.37 | 505 | 3 | Mike Piazza | 1,393 | 5,116 | 1,641 | .321 |
| 4 | Randy Johnson | 224 | 106 | 3.06 | 436 | 4 | Derek Jeter | 1,093 | 4,388 | 1,390 | .317 |
| 5 | Chuck Finley | 200 | 173 | 3.85 | 524 | 4 | Edgar Martinez | 1,769 | 6,230 | 1,973 | .317 |
| 6 | David Wells | 185 | 121 | 4.05 | 526 | 4 | Larry Walker | 1,663 | 5,880 | 1,863 | .317 |
| 7 | Kevin Brown | 183 | 122 | 3.22 | 419 | 7 | Manny Ramirez | 1,229 | 4,435 | 1,400 | .316 |
| 8 | Mike Mussina | 182 | 102 | 3.54 | 355 | 8 | Frank Thomas | 1,698 | 6,065 | 1,902 | .314 |
| 9 | Bret Saberhagen | 167 | 117 | 3.34 | 399 | 9 | Jason Giambi | 1,108 | 3,958 | 1,224 | .309 |
| 10 | Jamie Moyer | 164 | 125 | 4.14 | 439 | 9 | Chipper Jones | 1,252 | 4,589 | 1,419 | .309 |

## MAJOR LEAGUE ALL-TIME PITCHING RECORDS

### (through 2002)

Most Games Won—511, Cy Young, Cleveland N.L., 1890–98, St. Louis N.L., 1899–1900, Boston A.L., 1901–08, Cleveland A.L., 1909–11, Boston N.L., 1911.

Most Games Won, Season—54, Al Spalding, Boston N.A., 1875. (Since 1900—41, Jack Chesbro, New York A.L., 1904.)

Most Consecutive Games Won—24, Carl Hubbell, New York N.L., 1936 (16) and 1937 (8).

Most Consecutive Games Won, Season—19, Tim Keefe, New York N.L., 1888; Rube Marquard, New York N.L., 1912.

Most Years Won 20 or More Games—16, Cy Young, Cleveland N.L., 1891–98, St. Louis N.L., 1899–1900, Boston A.L., 1901–04, 1907–08.

Most Shutouts—110, Walter Johnson, Washington A.L., 1907–27.

Most Shutouts, Season—16, Grover Alexander, Philadelphia N.L., 1916.

Most Consecutive Shutouts—6, Don Drysdale, Los Angeles N.L., 1968.

Most Consecutive Scoreless Innings—59, Orel Hershiser, Los Angeles Dodgers, 1988.

Most Strikeouts—5,714, Nolan Ryan, New York N.L., California A.L., Houston N.L., 1968–1988 Texas, 1989–93.

Most Strikeouts, Season—513, Matthew Kilroy, Baltimore A.A., 1886. (Since 1900—383, Nolan Ryan, California A.L., 1973.)

Most Strikeouts, Game—21, Tom Cheney, Washington A.L., 1962, 16 innings. Nine innings: 20, Roger Clemens, Boston A.L., 1986; Kerry Wood, Chicago N.L., 1998.

Most Consecutive Strikeouts—10, Tom Seaver, New York N.L. vs. San Diego, April 22, 1970.

Most Games, Season—106, Mike Marshall, Los Angeles N.L., 1974.

Most Complete Games, Season—75, William White, Cincinnati N.L., 1879. (Since 1900—48, Jack Chesbro, New York A.L., 1904.)

## MAJOR LEAGUE INDIVIDUAL ALL-TIME HITTING RECORDS

### (through 2002)

Highest Batting Average, Season—.440, Hugh Duffy, Boston N.L., 1894;.435, Tip O'Neill, St. Louis, A.A., 1887. (Since 1900—.426, Nap Lajoie, Phil. A.L., 1901); 424, Rogers Hornsby, St. Louis N.L., 1924.

Most Times at Bat—14,053, Pete Rose, Cincinnati N.L., 1963–78; Philadelphia N.L., 1979–83; Montreal N.L., 1984; Cincinnati N.L., 1984–86.

Most Years Batted .300 or Better—23, Ty Cobb, Detroit A.L., 1906–26, Philadelphia A.L., 1927–28.

Most Hits—4,256, Pete Rose, Cincinnati 1963–79, Philadelphia 1980–83, Montreal 1984, Cincinnati 1984–86.

Most Hits, Season—257, George Sisler, St. Louis A.L., 1920.

Most Hits in Succession—12, Mike Higgins, Boston A.L., in four games, 1938; Walt Dropo, Detroit A.L., in three games, 1952.

Most Consecutive Games Batted Safely—56, Joe DiMaggio, New York A.L., 1941.

Most Runs—2,288, Rickey Henderson, Oakland A.L., 1979–84, 1989–93, 1994–95, 1998; New York A.L., 1985–89; Toronto A.L., 1993; San Diego N.L., 1996, 1997, 2001; Anaheim A.L., 1997; New York N.L., 1999–2000; Seattle A.L., 2000; Boston A.L., 2002.

Most Runs, Season—196, William Hamilton, Philadelphia N.L., 1894. (Since 1900—177, Babe Ruth, New York A.L., 1921.)

Most Runs Batted In—2,297, Hank Aaron, Milwaukee N.L., 1954–1965; Atlanta N.L., 1966–74; Milwaukee A.L., 1975–76.

Most Runs Batted in, Season—191, Hack Wilson, Chicago N.L., 1930.

Most Home Runs—755, Hank Aaron, Milwaukee N.L., 1954–1965; Atlanta N.L., 1966–74; Milwaukee A.L., 1975–76.

Most Home Runs, Season—162-game season: 73, Barry Bonds, San Francisco N.L., 2001; 70, Mark McGwire, St. Louis N.L., 1998; 66, Sammy Sosa, Chicago N.L., 1998; 65, Mark McGwire, St. Louis N.L., 1999; 64, Sammy Sosa, Chicago N.L., 2001; 63, Sammy Sosa, Chicago N.L., 1999; 61, Roger Maris, New York A.L., 1961. 154-game season: 60, Babe Ruth, New York A.L., 1927.

Most Home Runs with Bases Filled—23, Lou Gehrig, New York A.L., 1927–39.

Most 2-Base Hits—792, Tris Speaker, Boston A.L., 1907–15, Cleveland A.L., 1916–26, Washington A.L., 1927, Philadelphia A.L., 1928.

Most 2-Base Hits, Season—67, Earl Webb, Boston A.L., 1931.

Most 3-Base Hits—309, Sam Crawford, Cincinnati N.L., 1899–1902, Detroit A.L., 1903–17.

Most 3-Base Hits, Season—36, Owen Wilson, Pittsburgh N.L., 1912.

Most Games Played—3,562, Pete Rose, Cincinnati N.L., Philadelphia N.L., Montreal N.L., 1964–86.

Most Consecutive Games Played—2,632, Cal Ripken, Jr., Baltimore Orioles A.L., 1981–1998.

Most Bases on Balls—2,179, Rickey Henderson, Oakland A.L., 1979–84, 1989–93, 1994–95, 1998; New York A.L., 1985–89; Toronto A.L., 1993; San Diego N.L., 1996, 1997, 2001; Anaheim A.L., 1997; New York N.L., 1999–2000; Seattle A.L., 2000; Boston A.L., 2002.

Most Bases on Balls, Season—198, Barry Bonds, San Francisco N.L., 2002.

Most Strikeouts, Season—189, Bobby Bonds, San Francisco N.L., 1970.

Most Stolen Bases, Lifetime—1,403, Rickey Henderson, Oakland A.L., 1979–84, 1989–93, 1994–95, 1998; New York A.L., 1985–89; Toronto A.L., 1993; San Diego N.L., 1996, 1997, 2001; Anaheim A.L., 1997; New York N.L., 1999–2000; Seattle A.L., 2000; Boston A.L., 2002.

Most Stolen Bases, Season—138, Hugh Nicol, Cincinnati A.A., 1887. Since 1900: 130, Rickey Henderson, Oakland A.L., 1982; 118, Lou Brock, St. Louis N.L., 1974.

Most Stolen Bases, Game—7, George Gore, Chicago N.L. 1881; William Hamilton, Philadelphia N.L. 1894. (Since 1900—6, Eddie Collins, Philadelphia A.L., 1912.) and Otis Nixon, Atlanta N.L., 1991.

Most Time Stealing Home, Lifetime—50, Ty Cobb, Detroit-Phil. A.L., 1905–28.

# ROOKIE OF THE YEAR
## (Baseball Writers' Association selections)

### American League

| | | | | | |
|---|---|---|---|---|---|
| 1949 | Roy Sievers, St. Louis | 1967 | Rod Carew, Minnesota | 1984 | Alvin Davis, Seattle |
| 1950 | Walt Dropo, Boston | 1968 | Stan Bahnsen, New York | 1985 | Ozzie Guillen, Chicago |
| 1951 | Gil McDougald, New York | 1969 | Lou Piniella, Kansas City | 1986 | Jose Canseco, Oakland |
| 1952 | Harry Byrd, Philadelphia | 1970 | Thurman Munson, New York | 1987 | Mark McGwire, Oakland |
| 1953 | Harvey Kuenn, Detroit | 1971 | Chris Chambliss, Cleveland | 1988 | Walter Weiss, Oakland |
| 1954 | Bob Grim, New York | 1972 | Carlton Fisk, Boston | 1989 | Gregg Olson, Baltimore |
| 1955 | Herb Score, Cleveland | 1973 | Alonzo Bumbry, Baltimore | 1990 | Sandy Alomar Jr., Cleveland |
| 1956 | Luis Aparicio, Chicago | 1974 | Mike Hargrove, Texas | 1991 | Chuck Knoblauch, Minnesota |
| 1957 | Tony Kubek, New York | 1975 | Fred Lynn, Boston | 1992 | Pat Listach, Milwaukee |
| 1958 | Albie Pearson, Washington | 1976 | Mark Fidrych, Detroit | 1993 | Tim Salmon, California |
| 1959 | Bob Allison, Washington | 1977 | Eddie Murray, Baltimore | 1994 | Bob Hamelin, Kansas City |
| 1960 | Ron Hansen, Baltimore | 1978 | Lou Whitaker, Detroit | 1995 | Marty Cordova, Minnesota |
| 1961 | Don Schwall, Boston | 1979 | Alfredo Griffin, Toronto | 1996 | Derek Jeter, New York |
| 1962 | Tom Tresh, New York | 1979 | John Castino, Minnesota | 1997 | Nomar Garciaparra, Boston |
| 1963 | Gary Peters, Chicago | 1980 | Joe Charboneau, Cleveland | 1998 | Ben Grieve, Oakland |
| 1964 | Tony Oliva, Minnesota | 1981 | Dave Righetti, New York | 1999 | Carlos Beltran, Kansas City |
| 1965 | Curt Blefary, Baltimore | 1982 | Cal Ripken, Jr., Baltimore | 2000 | Kazuhiro Sasaki, Seattle |
| 1966 | Tommy Agee, Chicago | 1983 | Ron Kittle, Chicago | 2001 | Ichiro Suzuki, Seattle |

### National League

| | | | | | |
|---|---|---|---|---|---|
| 1949 | Don Newcombe, Brooklyn | 1967 | Tom Seaver, New York | 1984 | Dwight Gooden, New York |
| 1950 | Sam Jethroe, Boston | 1968 | Johnny Bench, Cincinnati | 1985 | Vince Coleman, St. Louis |
| 1951 | Willie Mays, New York | 1969 | Ted Sizemore, Los Angeles | 1986 | Todd Worrell, St. Louis |
| 1952 | Joe Black, Brooklyn | 1970 | Carl Morton, Montreal | 1987 | Benito Santiago, San Diego |
| 1953 | Jim Gilliam, Brooklyn | 1971 | Earl Williams, Atlanta | 1988 | Chris Sabo, Cincinnati |
| 1954 | Wally Moon, St. Louis | 1972 | Jon Matlack, New York | 1989 | Jerome Walton, Chicago |
| 1955 | Bill Virdon, St. Louis | 1973 | Gary Matthews, San Francisco | 1990 | Dave Justice, Atlanta |
| 1956 | Frank Robinson, Cincinnati | 1974 | Bake McBride, St. Louis | 1991 | Jeff Baguell, Houston |
| 1957 | Jack Sanford, Philadelphia | 1975 | John Montefusco, San Francisco | 1992 | Eric Karros, Los Angeles |
| 1958 | Orlando Cepeda, San Francisco | 1976 | Pat Zachry, Cincinnati | 1993 | Mike Piazza, Los Angeles |
| 1959 | Willie McCovey, San Francisco | 1976 | Bruce Metzger, San Diego | 1994 | Raul Mondesi, Los Angeles |
| 1960 | Frank Howard, Los Angeles | 1977 | Andre Dawson, Montreal | 1995 | Hideo Nomo, Los Angeles |
| 1961 | Billy Williams, Chicago | 1978 | Bob Horner, Atlanta | 1996 | Todd Hollandsworth, Los Angeles |
| 1962 | Ken Hubbs, Chicago | 1979 | Rick Sutcliffe, Los Angeles | 1997 | Scott Rolen, Philadelphia |
| 1963 | Pete Rose, Cincinnati | 1980 | Steve Howe, Los Angeles | 1998 | Kerry Wood, Chicago |
| 1964 | Richie Allen, Philadelphia | 1981 | Fernando Valenzuela, Los Angeles | 1999 | Scott Williamson, Cincinnati |
| 1965 | Jim Lefebvre, Los Angeles | 1982 | Steve Sax, Los Angeles | 2000 | Rafael Furcal, Atlanta |
| 1966 | Tommy Helms, Cincinnati | 1983 | Darryl Strawberry, New York | 2001 | Albert Pujols, St. Louis |

# MOST HOME RUNS IN ONE SEASON
## (45 or More)

| HR | Player/Team | Year | HR | Player/Team | Year |
|---|---|---|---|---|---|
| 73 | Barry Bonds, San Francisco (N.L.) | 2001 | 51 | Ralph Kiner, Pittsburgh (N.L.) | 1947 |
| 70 | Mark McGwire, St. Louis (N.L.) | 1998 | 51 | John Mize, New York (N.L.) | 1947 |
| 66 | Sammy Sosa, Chicago (N.L.) | 1998 | 51 | Willie Mays, New York (N.L.) | 1955 |
| 65 | Mark McGwire, St. Louis (N.L.) | 1999 | 51 | Cecil Fielder (A.L.) | 1990 |
| 64 | Sammy Sosa, Chicago (N.L.) | 2001 | 50 | Jimmie Foxx, Boston (A.L.) | 1938 |
| 63 | Sammy Sosa, Chicago (N.L.) | 1999 | 50 | Albert Belle, Cleveland (A.L.) | 1995 |
| 61 | Roger Maris, New York (A.L.) | 1961 | 50 | Brady Anderson, Baltimore (A.L.) | 1996 |
| 60 | Babe Ruth, New York (A.L.) | 1927 | 50 | Sammy Sosa, Chicago (N.L.) | 2000 |
| 59 | Babe Ruth, New York (A.L.) | 1921 | 50 | Greg Vaughn, San Diego (N.L.) | 1998 |
| 58 | Jimmie Foxx, Philadelphia (A.L.) | 1932 | 49 | Babe Ruth, New York (A.L.) | 1930 |
| 58 | Hank Greenberg, Detroit (A.L.) | 1938 | 49 | Lou Gehrig, New York (A.L.) | 1934 |
| 58 | Mark McGwire, Oakland (A.L.), St. Louis (N.L.) | 1997 | 49 | Lou Gehrig, New York (A.L.) | 1936 |
| 57 | Luis Gonzalez, Arizona (N.L.) | 2001 | 49 | Ted Kluszewski, Cincinnati (N.L.) | 1954 |
| 57 | Alex Rodriguez, Texas (A.L.) | 2002 | 49 | Willie Mays, San Francisco (N.L.) | 1962 |
| 56 | Hack Wilson, Chicago (N.L.) | 1930 | 49 | Harmon Killebrew, Minnesota (A.L.) | 1964 |
| 56 | Ken Griffey, Jr., Seattle (A.L.) | 1997 | 49 | Frank Robinson, Baltimore (A.L.) | 1966 |
| 56 | Ken Griffey, Jr., Seattle (A.L.) | 1998 | 49 | Harmon Killebrew, Minnesota (A.L.) | 1969 |
| 54 | Babe Ruth, New York (A.L.) | 1920 | 49 | Mark McGwire, Oakland (A.L.) | 1987 |
| 54 | Babe Ruth, New York (A.L.) | 1928 | 49 | Andre Dawson, Chicago (N.L.) | 1987 |
| 54 | Ralph Kiner, Pittsburgh (N.L.) | 1949 | 49 | Ken Griffey, Jr., Seattle (A.L.) | 1996 |
| 54 | Mickey Mantle, New York (A.L.) | 1961 | 49 | Larry Walker, Colorado (N.L.) | 1997 |
| 52 | Mickey Mantle, New York (A.L.) | 1956 | 49 | Albert Belle, Chicago (A.L.) | 1998 |
| 52 | Willie Mays, San Francisco (N.L.) | 1965 | 49 | Barry Bonds, San Francisco (N.L.) | 2000 |
| 52 | George Foster, Cincinnati (N.L.) | 1977 | 49 | Shawn Green, Los Angeles (N.L.) | 2001 |
| 52 | Mark McGwire, Oakland (A.L.) | 1996 | 49 | Todd Helton, Colorado (N.L.) | 2001 |
| 52 | Alex Rodriguez, Texas (A.L.) | 2001 | 49 | Jim Thome, Cleveland (A.L.) | 2001 |
| 52 | Jim Thome, Cleveland (A.L.) | 2002 | 49 | Sammy Sosa, Chicago (N.L.) | 2002 |

| HR | Player/Team | Year | HR | Player/Team | Year |
|----|-------------|------|----|-------------|------|
| 48 | Jimmie Foxx, Philadelphia (A.L.) | 1933 | 46 | Babe Ruth, New York, (A.L.) | 1929 |
| 48 | Harmon Killebrew, Minnesota (A.L.) | 1962 | 46 | Babe Ruth, New York (A.L.) | 1931 |
| 48 | Frank Howard, Washington (A.L.) | 1969 | 46 | Lou Gehrig, New York (A.L.) | 1931 |
| 48 | Willie Stargell, Pittsburgh (N.L.) | 1971 | 46 | Joe DiMaggio, New York (A.L.) | 1937 |
| 48 | Dave Kingman, Chicago (N.L.) | 1979 | 46 | Ed Mathews, Milwaukee (N.L.) | 1959 |
| 48 | Mike Schmidt, Philadelphia (N.L.) | 1980 | 46 | Orlando Cepeda, San Francisco (N.L.) | 1961 |
| 48 | Albert Belle, Cleveland (A.L.) | 1996 | 46 | Jim Rice, Boston (A.L.) | 1978 |
| 48 | Ken Griffey, Jr., Seattle (A.L.) | 1999 | 46 | Juan Gonzalez, Texas (A.L.) | 1993 |
| 47 | Babe Ruth, New York (A.L.) | 1926 | 46 | Barry Bonds, San Francisco (N.L.) | 1993 |
| 47 | Ralph Kiner, Pittsburgh (N.L.) | 1950 | 46 | Jose Canseco, Toronto (A.L.) | 1998 |
| 47 | Ed Mathews, Milwaukee (N.L.) | 1953 | 46 | Vinnie Castilla, Colorado (N.L.) | 1998 |
| 47 | Ernie Banks, Chicago (N.L.) | 1958 | 46 | Barry Bonds, San Francisco (N.L.) | 2002 |
| 47 | Willie Mays, San Francisco (N.L.) | 1964 | 45 | Ernie Banks, Chicago (N.L.) | 1959 |
| 47 | Hank Aaron, Atlanta (N.L.) | 1971 | 45 | Harmon Killebrew, Minnesota (A.L.) | 1963 |
| 47 | Reggie Jackson, Oakland (A.L.) | 1969 | 45 | Willie McCovey, San Francisco (N.L.) | 1969 |
| 47 | George Bell, Toronto (A.L.) | 1987 | 45 | Johnny Bench, Cincinnati (N.L.) | 1970 |
| 47 | Kevin Mitchell, San Francisco (N.L.) | 1989 | 45 | Gorman Thomas, Milwaukee (A.L.) | 1979 |
| 47 | Andres Galarraga, Colorado (N.L.) | 1996 | 45 | Hank Aaron, Milwaukee (N.L.) | 1962 |
| 47 | Juan Gonzalez, Texas (A.L.) | 1996 | 45 | Ken Griffey, Jr., Seattle (A.L.) | 1993 |
| 47 | Rafael Palmeiro, Texas (A.L.) | 1999 | 45 | Juan Gonzalez, Texas (A.L.) | 1998 |
| 47 | Jeff Bagwell, Houston (N.L.) | 2000 | 45 | Manny Ramirez, Cleveland (A.L.) | 1998 |
| 47 | Troy Glaus, Anaheim (A.L.) | 2000 | 45 | Chipper Jones, Atlanta (N.L.) | 1999 |
| 47 | Rafael Palmeiro, Texas (A.L.) | 2001 | 45 | Greg Vaughn, Cincinnati (N.L.) | 1999 |
| 46 | Babe Ruth, New York (A.L.) | 1924 | | | |

## MAJOR LEAGUE BASEBALL—2002

## AMERICAN LEAGUE FINAL STANDINGS

### EASTERN DIVISION

| Team | W | L | Pct | GB |
|------|---|---|-----|-----|
| New York Yankees | 103 | 58 | .640 | — |
| Boston Red Sox | 93 | 69 | .574 | 10.5 |
| Toronto Blue Jays | 78 | 84 | .481 | 25.5 |
| Baltimore Orioles | 67 | 95 | .414 | 36.5 |
| Tampa Bay Devil Rays | 55 | 106 | .342 | 48.0 |

### CENTRAL DIVISION

| Team | W | L | Pct | GB |
|------|---|---|-----|-----|
| Minnesota Twins | 94 | 67 | .584 | — |
| Chicago White Sox | 81 | 81 | .500 | 13.5 |
| Cleveland Indians | 74 | 88 | .457 | 20.5 |
| Kansas City Royals | 62 | 100 | .383 | 32.5 |
| Detroit Tigers | 55 | 106 | .342 | 39.0 |

### WESTERN DIVISION

| Team | W | L | Pct | GB |
|------|---|---|-----|-----|
| Oakland Athletics | 103 | 59 | .636 | — |
| Anaheim Angels | 99 | 63 | .611 | 4.0 |
| Seattle Mariners | 93 | 69 | .574 | 10.0 |
| Texas Rangers | 72 | 90 | .444 | 31.0 |

## AMERICAN LEAGUE LEADERS, 2002

| | |
|---|---|
| Batting—Manny Ramirez, Boston | .349 |
| Home runs—Alex Rodriguez, Texas | 57 |
| Runs batted in—Alex Rodriguez, Texas | 142 |
| Runs—Alfonso Soriano, New York | 128 |
| Hits—Alfonso Soriano, New York | 209 |
| Stolen bases—Alfonso Soriano, New York | 41 |
| Doubles—Garret Anderson, Anaheim | 56 |
| Triples—Johnny Damon, Boston | 11 |
| Slugging percentage—Jim Thome, Cleveland | .677 |

### A.L. Pitching

| | |
|---|---|
| Wins—Barry Zito, Oakland | 23 |
| Earned run average—Pedro Martinez, Boston | 2.26 |
| Strikeouts—Pedro Martinez, Boston | 239 |
| Innings pitched—Roy Halladay, Toronto | 239 |
| Complete games—Paul Byrd, Kansas City | 7 |
| Shutouts—Jeff Weaver, New York | 3 |
| Saves—Eddie Guardado, Minnesota | 45 |

## NATIONAL LEAGUE FINAL STANDINGS

### EASTERN DIVISION

| Team | W | L | Pct | GB |
|------|---|---|-----|-----|
| Atlanta Braves | 101 | 59 | .631 | — |
| Montreal Expos | 83 | 79 | .512 | 19.0 |
| Philadelphia Phillies | 80 | 81 | .497 | 21.5 |
| Florida Marlins | 79 | 83 | .488 | 23.0 |
| New York Mets | 75 | 86 | .466 | 26.5 |

### CENTRAL DIVISION

| Team | W | L | Pct | GB |
|------|---|---|-----|-----|
| St. Louis Cardinals | 97 | 65 | .599 | — |
| Houston Astros | 84 | 78 | .519 | 13.0 |
| Cincinnati Reds | 78 | 84 | .481 | 19.0 |
| Pittsburgh Pirates | 72 | 89 | .447 | 24.5 |
| Chicago Cubs | 67 | 95 | .414 | 30.0 |
| Milwaukee Brewers | 56 | 106 | .346 | 41.0 |

### WESTERN DIVISION

| Team | W | L | Pct | GB |
|------|---|---|-----|-----|
| Arizona Diamondbacks | 98 | 64 | .605 | — |
| San Francisco Giants | 95 | 66 | .590 | 2.5 |
| Los Angeles Dodgers | 92 | 70 | .568 | 6.0 |
| Colorado Rockies | 73 | 89 | .451 | 25.0 |
| San Diego Padres | 66 | 96 | .407 | 32.0 |

## NATIONAL LEAGUE LEADERS, 2002

| | |
|---|---|
| Batting—Barry Bonds, San Francisco | .370 |
| Home runs—Sammy Sosa, Chicago | 49 |
| Runs batted in—Lance Berkman, Houston | 128 |
| Runs—Sammy Sosa, Chicago | 122 |
| Hits—Vladimir Guerrero, Montreal | 206 |
| Stolen bases—Luis Castillo, Florida | 48 |
| Doubles—Bobby Abreu, Philadelphia | 50 |
| Triples—Jimmy Rollins, Philadelphia | 10 |
| Slugging percentage—Barry Bonds, San Francisco | .799 |

### N.L. Pitching

| | |
|---|---|
| Wins—Randy Johnson, Arizona | 24 |
| Earned run average—Randy Johnson, Arizona | 2.32 |
| Strikeouts—Randy Johnson, Arizona | 334 |
| Innings pitched—Randy Johnson, Arizona | 260 |
| Complete games—Randy Johnson, Arizona | 8 |
| Shutouts—A. J. Burnett, Florida | 5 |
| Saves—John Smoltz, Atlanta | 55 |

### American League Division Series

Minnesota Twins defeated Oakland Athletics,
3 games to 2
Oct. 1—Minnesota 7, Oakland 5
Oct. 2—Oakland 9, Minnesota 1
Oct. 4—Oakland 6, Minnesota 3
Oct. 5—Minnesota 11, Oakland 2
Oct. 6—Minnesota 5, Oakland 4

Anaheim Angels defeated New York Yankees,
3 games to 1
Oct. 1—New York 8, Anaheim 5
Oct. 2—Anaheim 8, New York 6
Oct. 4—Anaheim 9, New York 6
Oct. 5—Anaheim 9, New York 5

### National League Division Series

San Francisco Giants defeated Atlanta Braves,
3 games to 2
Oct. 2—San Francisco 8, Atlanta 5
Oct. 3—Atlanta 7, San Francisco 3
Oct. 5—Atlanta 10, San Francisco 2
Oct. 6—San Francisco 8, Atlanta 3
Oct. 7—San Francisco 3, Atlanta 1

St. Louis Cardinals defeated Arizona Diamondbacks,
3 games to 0
Oct. 1—St. Louis 12, Arizona 2
Oct. 3—St. Louis 2, Arizona 1
Oct. 5—St. Louis 6, Arizona 3

## AMERICAN LEAGUE AVERAGES, 2002

### Team Pitching

| | W | L | ERA | SHO | H | R | SO |
|---|---|---|---|---|---|---|---|
| Oakland | 103 | 59 | 3.68 | 19 | 1,391 | 654 | 1,021 |
| Anaheim | 99 | 63 | 3.69 | 14 | 1,345 | 644 | 999 |
| Boston | 93 | 69 | 3.75 | 17 | 1,339 | 665 | 1,157 |
| New York | 103 | 58 | 3.87 | 11 | 1,441 | 697 | 1,135 |
| Seattle | 93 | 69 | 4.07 | 12 | 1,422 | 699 | 1,063 |
| Minnesota | 94 | 67 | 4.12 | 9 | 1,454 | 712 | 1,026 |
| Baltimore | 67 | 95 | 4.46 | 3 | 1,491 | 773 | 967 |
| Chicago | 81 | 81 | 4.55 | 7 | 1,422 | 798 | 945 |
| Toronto | 78 | 84 | 4.80 | 6 | 1,504 | 828 | 991 |
| Cleveland | 74 | 88 | 4.91 | 4 | 1,508 | 837 | 1,058 |
| Detroit | 55 | 106 | 4.92 | 7 | 1,593 | 864 | 794 |
| Texas | 72 | 90 | 5.15 | 4 | 1,528 | 882 | 1,030 |
| Kansas City | 62 | 100 | 5.21 | 6 | 1,587 | 891 | 909 |
| Tampa Bay | 55 | 106 | 5.29 | 3 | 1,567 | 918 | 925 |

### Team Batting

| | Avg. | AB | R | H | HR | RBI |
|---|---|---|---|---|---|---|
| Anaheim | .282 | 5,678 | 851 | 1,603 | 152 | 811 |
| Boston | .277 | 5,640 | 859 | 1,560 | 177 | 810 |
| New York | .275 | 5,601 | 897 | 1,540 | 223 | 857 |
| Seattle | .275 | 5,569 | 814 | 1,531 | 152 | 771 |
| Minnesota | .272 | 5,582 | 768 | 1,518 | 167 | 731 |
| Chicago | .270 | 5,847 | 927 | 1,578 | 226 | 867 |
| Texas | .269 | 5,618 | 843 | 1,510 | 230 | 806 |
| Oakland | .261 | 5,558 | 800 | 1,450 | 205 | 772 |
| Toronto | .261 | 5,581 | 813 | 1,457 | 187 | 771 |
| Kansas City | .256 | 5,535 | 737 | 1,415 | 140 | 695 |
| Tampa Bay | .253 | 5,605 | 673 | 1,419 | 133 | 641 |
| Cleveland | .249 | 5,423 | 739 | 1,349 | 192 | 706 |
| Detroit | .248 | 5,406 | 575 | 1,340 | 124 | 546 |
| Baltimore | .246 | 5,491 | 667 | 1,353 | 165 | 636 |

### Individual Pitching
(based on 10 decisions)

| | W | L | ERA | IP | H | BB | SO |
|---|---|---|---|---|---|---|---|
| B. Zito, Oakland | 23 | 5 | 2.75 | 229.1 | 182 | 78 | 182 |
| D. Lowe, Boston | 21 | 8 | 2.58 | 219.2 | 166 | 48 | 127 |
| P. Martinez, Boston | 20 | 4 | 2.26 | 199.1 | 144 | 40 | 239 |
| M. Buehrle, Chicago | 19 | 12 | 3.58 | 239.0 | 236 | 61 | 134 |
| R. Halladay, Toronto | 19 | 7 | 2.93 | 239.1 | 223 | 62 | 168 |
| M. Mulder, Oakland | 19 | 7 | 3.47 | 207.1 | 182 | 55 | 159 |
| D. Wells, New York | 19 | 7 | 3.75 | 206.1 | 210 | 45 | 137 |
| M. Mussina, New York | 18 | 10 | 4.05 | 215.2 | 208 | 48 | 182 |
| J. Washburn, Anaheim | 18 | 6 | 3.15 | 206.0 | 183 | 59 | 139 |
| P. Byrd, Kansas City | 17 | 11 | 3.90 | 228.1 | 224 | 38 | 129 |
| F. Garcia, Seattle | 16 | 10 | 4.39 | 223.2 | 227 | 63 | 181 |
| T. Hudson, Oakland | 15 | 9 | 2.98 | 238.1 | 237 | 62 | 152 |
| R. Lopez, Baltimore | 15 | 9 | 3.57 | 196.2 | 172 | 62 | 136 |
| R. Ortiz, Anaheim | 15 | 9 | 3.77 | 217.1 | 188 | 68 | 162 |
| R. Reed, Minnesota | 15 | 7 | 3.78 | 188.0 | 192 | 26 | 121 |
| K. Appier, Anaheim | 14 | 12 | 3.92 | 188.1 | 191 | 64 | 132 |
| J. Pineiro, Seattle | 14 | 7 | 3.24 | 194.1 | 189 | 54 | 136 |
| D. Wright, Chicago | 14 | 12 | 5.18 | 196.1 | 200 | 71 | 136 |

### Individual Batting
(based on 300 plate appearances)

| | Avg. | AB | R | H | HR | RBI |
|---|---|---|---|---|---|---|
| M. Ramirez, Boston | .349 | 436 | 84 | 152 | 33 | 107 |
| M. Sweeney, Kansas City | .340 | 471 | 81 | 160 | 24 | 86 |
| B. Williams, New York | .333 | 612 | 102 | 204 | 19 | 102 |
| I. Suzuki, Seattle | .321 | 647 | 111 | 208 | 8 | 51 |
| M. Ordonez, Chicago | .320 | 590 | 116 | 189 | 38 | 135 |
| J. Giambi, New York | .314 | 560 | 120 | 176 | 41 | 122 |
| A. Kennedy, Anaheim | .312 | 474 | 65 | 148 | 7 | 52 |
| N. Garciaparra, Boston | .310 | 635 | 101 | 197 | 24 | 120 |
| M. Tejada, Oakland | .308 | 662 | 108 | 204 | 34 | 131 |
| G. Anderson, Anaheim | .306 | 638 | 93 | 195 | 29 | 123 |
| P. Konerko, Chicago | .304 | 570 | 81 | 173 | 27 | 104 |
| J. Thome, Cleveland | .304 | 480 | 101 | 146 | 52 | 118 |
| S. Stewart, Toronto | .303 | 577 | 103 | 175 | 10 | 45 |
| E. Burks, Cleveland | .301 | 518 | 92 | 156 | 32 | 91 |
| R. Simon, Detroit | .301 | 482 | 51 | 145 | 19 | 82 |
| J. Jones, Minnesota | .300 | 577 | 96 | 173 | 27 | 85 |
| J. Olerud, Seattle | .300 | 553 | 85 | 166 | 22 | 102 |
| A. Rodriguez, Texas | .300 | 624 | 125 | 187 | 57 | 142 |
| A. Soriano, New York | .300 | 696 | 128 | 209 | 39 | 102 |
| R. Winn, Tampa Bay | .298 | 607 | 87 | 181 | 14 | 75 |

## NATIONAL LEAGUE AVERAGES, 2002

### Team Pitching

| | W | L | ERA | SHO | H | R | SO |
|---|---|---|---|---|---|---|---|
| Atlanta | 101 | 59 | 3.13 | 15 | 1,302 | 565 | 1,058 |
| San Francisco | 95 | 66 | 3.54 | 13 | 1,349 | 616 | 992 |
| Los Angeles | 92 | 70 | 3.69 | 15 | 1,311 | 643 | 1,132 |
| St. Louis | 97 | 65 | 3.70 | 9 | 1,355 | 648 | 1,009 |
| New York | 75 | 86 | 3.89 | 10 | 1,408 | 703 | 1,107 |
| Arizona | 98 | 64 | 3.92 | 10 | 1,361 | 674 | 1,303 |
| Montreal | 83 | 79 | 3.97 | 3 | 1,475 | 718 | 1,088 |
| Houston | 84 | 78 | 4.00 | 11 | 1,423 | 695 | 1,219 |
| Philadelphia | 80 | 81 | 4.17 | 9 | 1,381 | 724 | 1,075 |
| Pittsburgh | 72 | 89 | 4.23 | 7 | 1,447 | 730 | 920 |
| Cincinnati | 78 | 84 | 4.27 | 8 | 1,502 | 774 | 980 |
| Chicago | 67 | 95 | 4.29 | 9 | 1,373 | 759 | 1,333 |
| Florida | 79 | 83 | 4.36 | 12 | 1,449 | 763 | 1,104 |
| San Diego | 66 | 96 | 4.62 | 10 | 1,522 | 815 | 1,108 |
| Milwaukee | 56 | 106 | 4.72 | 4 | 1,468 | 821 | 1,026 |
| Colorado | 73 | 89 | 5.20 | 8 | 1,554 | 898 | 920 |

## Individual Pitching (based on 10 decisions)

| | W | L | ERA | IP | H | BB | SO | | W | L | ERA | IP | H | BB | SO |
|---|---|---|---|---|---|---|---|---|---|---|---|---|---|---|---|
| R. Johnson, Arizona | 24 | 5 | 2.32 | 260.0 | 197 | 71 | 334 | W. Miller, Houston | 15 | 4 | 3.28 | 164.2 | 151 | 62 | 144 |
| C. Schilling, Arizona | 23 | 7 | 3.23 | 259.1 | 218 | 33 | 316 | O. Perez, Los Angeles | 15 | 10 | 3.00 | 222.1 | 182 | 38 | 155 |
| R. Oswalt, Houston | 19 | 9 | 3.01 | 233.0 | 215 | 62 | 208 | K. Ishii, Los Angeles | 14 | 10 | 4.27 | 154.0 | 137 | 106 | 143 |
| T. Glavine, Atlanta | 18 | 11 | 2.96 | 224.2 | 210 | 78 | 127 | R. Ortiz, San Francisco | 14 | 10 | 3.61 | 214.1 | 191 | 94 | 137 |
| K. Millwood, Atlanta | 18 | 8 | 3.24 | 217.0 | 186 | 65 | 178 | V. Padilla, Philadelphia | 14 | 11 | 3.28 | 206.0 | 198 | 53 | 128 |
| M. Morris, St. Louis | 17 | 9 | 3.42 | 210.1 | 210 | 64 | 171 | K. Rueter, San Francisco | 14 | 8 | 3.23 | 203.2 | 204 | 54 | 76 |
| J. Jennings, Colorado | 16 | 8 | 4.52 | 185.1 | 201 | 70 | 127 | R. Jensen, San Francisco | 13 | 8 | 4.51 | 171.2 | 183 | 66 | 105 |
| G. Maddux, Atlanta | 16 | 6 | 2.62 | 199.1 | 194 | 45 | 118 | A. Leiter, New York | 13 | 13 | 3.48 | 204.1 | 194 | 69 | 172 |
| H. Nomo, Los Angeles | 16 | 6 | 3.39 | 220.1 | 189 | 101 | 193 | T. Ohka, Montreal | 13 | 8 | 3.18 | 192.2 | 194 | 45 | 118 |
| J. Haynes, Cincinnati | 15 | 10 | 4.12 | 196.2 | 210 | 81 | 126 | J. Schmidt, San Francisco | 13 | 8 | 3.45 | 185.1 | 148 | 73 | 196 |

## Team Batting

| | Avg. | AB | R | H | HR | RBI | | Avg. | AB | R | H | HR | RBI |
|---|---|---|---|---|---|---|---|---|---|---|---|---|---|
| Colorado | .274 | 5,512 | 778 | 1,508 | 152 | 726 | Atlanta | .260 | 5,495 | 708 | 1,428 | 164 | 669 |
| St. Louis | .268 | 5,505 | 787 | 1,475 | 175 | 758 | Philadelphia | .259 | 5,523 | 710 | 1,428 | 165 | 676 |
| Arizona | .267 | 5,508 | 819 | 1,471 | 165 | 783 | New York | .256 | 5,496 | 690 | 1,409 | 160 | 650 |
| San Francisco | .267 | 5,497 | 783 | 1,465 | 198 | 751 | Cincinnati | .253 | 5,470 | 709 | 1,386 | 169 | 678 |
| Los Angeles | .264 | 5,554 | 713 | 1,464 | 155 | 693 | Milwaukee | .253 | 5,415 | 627 | 1,369 | 139 | 597 |
| Houston | .262 | 5,503 | 749 | 1,441 | 167 | 719 | San Diego | .253 | 5,515 | 662 | 1,393 | 136 | 627 |
| Florida | .261 | 5,496 | 699 | 1,433 | 146 | 653 | Chicago | .246 | 5,496 | 706 | 1,351 | 200 | 676 |
| Montreal | .261 | 5,553 | 744 | 1,447 | 162 | 699 | Pittsburgh | .244 | 5,330 | 641 | 1,300 | 142 | 610 |

## Individual Batting (based on 300 plate appearances)

| | Avg. | AB | R | H | HR | RBI | | Avg. | AB | R | H | HR | RBI |
|---|---|---|---|---|---|---|---|---|---|---|---|---|---|
| B. Bonds, San Francisco | .370 | 403 | 117 | 149 | 46 | 110 | E. Alfonzo, New York | .308 | 490 | 78 | 151 | 16 | 56 |
| L. Walker, Colorado | .338 | 477 | 95 | 161 | 26 | 104 | G. Sheffield, Atlanta | .307 | 492 | 82 | 151 | 25 | 84 |
| V. Guerrero, Montreal | .336 | 614 | 106 | 206 | 39 | 111 | L. Castillo, Florida | .305 | 606 | 86 | 185 | 2 | 39 |
| T. Helton, Colorado | .329 | 553 | 107 | 182 | 30 | 109 | E. Renteria, St. Louis | .305 | 544 | 77 | 166 | 11 | 83 |
| C. Jones, Atlanta | .327 | 548 | 90 | 179 | 26 | 100 | J. Spivey, Arizona | .301 | 538 | 103 | 162 | 16 | 78 |
| J. Vidro, Montreal | .315 | 604 | 103 | 190 | 19 | 96 | R. Klesko, San Diego | .300 | 540 | 90 | 162 | 29 | 95 |
| A. Pujols, St. Louis | .314 | 590 | 118 | 185 | 34 | 127 | T. Walker, Cincinnati | .299 | 612 | 79 | 183 | 11 | 64 |
| J. Kent, San Francisco | .313 | 623 | 102 | 195 | 37 | 108 | B. Giles, Pittsburgh | .298 | 497 | 95 | 148 | 38 | 103 |
| J. Edmonds, St. Louis | .311 | 476 | 96 | 148 | 28 | 83 | L. Berkman, Houston | .292 | 578 | 106 | 169 | 42 | 128 |
| B. Abreu, Philadelphia | .308 | 572 | 102 | 176 | 20 | 85 | M. Kotsay, San Diego | .292 | 578 | 82 | 169 | 17 | 61 |

# AMERICAN LEAGUE CHAMPIONSHIP SERIES—2002

Anaheim Angels win series, 4 games to 1

### 1st Game, at Minnesota, Oct. 8, 2002

| | | | | R | H | E |
|---|---|---|---|---|---|---|
| Anaheim | 001 | 000 | 000 | — 1 | 4 | 0 |
| Minnesota | 010 | 010 | 00x | — 2 | 5 | 1 |

Pitchers—Anaheim: Appier, Donnelly, Schoeneweis, Weber. Minnesota: Mays, Guardado. Winner: Mays. Loser: Appier. Save: Guardado. Attendance: 55,562.

### 2nd Game, at Minnesota, Oct. 9, 2002

| | | | | R | H | E |
|---|---|---|---|---|---|---|
| Anaheim | 130 | 002 | 000 | — 6 | 10 | 0 |
| Minnesota | 000 | 003 | 000 | — 3 | 11 | 1 |

Pitchers—Anaheim: Ortiz, Donnelly, Rodriguez, Percival. Minnesota: Reed, Santana, Romero, Hawkins, Jackson. Winner: Ortiz. Loser: Reed. Save: Percival. Attendance: 55,990.

### 3rd Game, at Anaheim, Oct. 11, 2002

| | | | | R | H | E |
|---|---|---|---|---|---|---|
| Minnesota | 000 | 000 | 100 | — 1 | 6 | 0 |
| Anaheim | 010 | 000 | 01x | — 2 | 7 | 2 |

Pitchers—Minnesota: Milton, Hawkins, Santana, Jackson. Romero. Anaheim: Washburn, Rodriguez, Percival. Winner: Rodriguez. Loser: Romero. Save: Percival. Attendance: 44,234.

### 4th Game, at Anaheim, Oct. 12, 2002

| | | | | R | H | E |
|---|---|---|---|---|---|---|
| Minnesota | 000 | 000 | 001 | — 1 | 6 | 2 |
| Anaheim | 000 | 000 | 25x | — 7 | 10 | 0 |

Pitchers—Minnesota: Radke, Santana, Hawkins, Romero, Jackson, Wells. Anaheim: Lackey, Rodriguez, Weber. Winner: Lackey. Loser: Radke. Attendance: 44,830.

### 5th Game, at Anaheim, Oct. 13, 2002

| | | | | R | H | E |
|---|---|---|---|---|---|---|
| Minnesota | 110 | 000 | 300 | — 5 | 9 | 0 |
| Anaheim | 001 | 020 | 10x | — 13 | 18 | 0 |

Pitchers—Minnesota: Mays, Santana, Hawkins, Romero, Wells, Lohse. Anaheim: Appier, Donnelly, Rodriguez, Weber, Percival. Winner: Rodriguez. Loser: Santana. Attendance: 44,835.

Series MVP—Adam Kennedy

## NATIONAL LEAGUE CHAMPIONSHIP SERIES—2002
San Francisco Giants win series, 4 games to 1

**1st Game, at St. Louis, Oct. 9, 2002**

|  |  |  |  |  |  | R | H | E |
|---|---|---|---|---|---|---|---|---|
| San Francisco | 1 4 1 | 0 1 2 | 0 0 0 | — | 9 | 11 | 0 |
| St. Louis | 0 1 0 | 0 2 2 | 0 1 0 | — | 6 | 11 | 0 |

Pitchers—San Francisco: Rueter, Rodriguez, Worrell, Nen. St. Louis: Morris, Crudale, Veres, Kline. Winner: Rueter. Loser: Morris. Save: Nen. Attendance: 52,175.

**2nd Game, at St. Louis, Oct. 10, 2002**

|  |  |  |  |  |  | R | H | E |
|---|---|---|---|---|---|---|---|---|
| San Francisco | 1 0 0 | 0 2 0 | 0 0 1 | — | 4 | 7 | 0 |
| St. Louis | 0 0 0 | 0 0 0 | 0 1 0 | — | 1 | 6 | 0 |

Pitchers—San Francisco: Schmidt, Eyre, Nen. St. Louis: Williams, White, Fassero, Isringhausen. Winner: Schmidt. Loser: Williams. Save: Nen. Attendance: 52,195.

**3rd Game, at San Francisco, Oct. 12, 2002**

|  |  |  |  |  |  | R | H | E |
|---|---|---|---|---|---|---|---|---|
| St. Louis | 0 0 2 | 1 1 1 | 0 0 0 | — | 5 | 6 | 1 |
| San Francisco | 0 1 0 | 0 3 0 | 0 0 0 | — | 4 | 10 | 0 |

Pitchers—St. Louis: Finley, Veres, Kline, White, Isringhausen. San Francisco: Ortiz, Fultz, Witasick, Rodriguez, Eyre, Worrell. Winner: Finley. Loser: Witasick. Save: Isringhausen. Attendance: 42,177.

**4th Game, at San Francisco, Oct. 13, 2002**

|  |  |  |  |  |  | R | H | E |
|---|---|---|---|---|---|---|---|---|
| St. Louis | 2 0 0 | 0 0 0 | 0 0 1 | — | 3 | 12 | 9 |
| San Francisco | 0 0 0 | 0 0 2 | 0 2 x | — | 4 | 4 | 1 |

Pitchers—St. Louis: Benes, White, Kline. San Francisco: Hernandez, Rodriguez, Eyre, Worrell, Nen. Winner: Worrell. Loser: White. Save: Nen. Attendance: 42,676.

**5th Game, at San Francisco, Oct. 14, 2002**

|  |  |  |  |  |  | R | H | E |
|---|---|---|---|---|---|---|---|---|
| St. Louis | 0 0 0 | 0 0 0 | 1 0 0 | — | 1 | 9 | 0 |
| San Francisco | 0 0 0 | 0 0 0 | 0 1 1 | — | 2 | 7 | 0 |

Pitchers—St. Louis: Morris, Kline. San Francisco: Rueter, Rodriguez, Eyre, Worrell. Winner: Worrell. Loser: Morris. Attendance: 42,673.

Series MVP—Benito Santiago

## AMERICAN LEAGUE PENNANT WINNERS

| Year | Club | Manager | Won | Lost | Pct | Year | Club | Manager | Won | Lost | Pct |
|---|---|---|---|---|---|---|---|---|---|---|---|
| 1901 | Chicago | Clark C. Griffith | 83 | 53 | .610 | 1941 | New York[1] | Joseph V. McCarthy | 101 | 53 | .656 |
| 1902 | Philadelphia | Connie Mack | 83 | 53 | .610 | 1942 | New York | Joseph V. McCarthy | 103 | 51 | .669 |
| 1903 | Boston | Jimmy Collins | 91 | 47 | .659 | 1943 | New York[1] | Joseph V. McCarthy | 98 | 56 | .636 |
| 1904 | Boston[2] | Jimmy Collins | 95 | 59 | .617 | 1944 | St. Louis | Luke Sewell | 89 | 65 | .578 |
| 1905 | Philadelphia | Connie Mack | 92 | 56 | .622 | 1945 | Detroit[1] | Steve O'Neill | 88 | 65 | .575 |
| 1906 | Chicago[1] | Fielder A. Jones | 93 | 58 | .616 | 1946 | Boston | Joseph E. Cronin | 104 | 50 | .675 |
| 1907 | Detroit | Hugh A. Jennings | 92 | 58 | .613 | 1947 | New York[1] | Stanley R. Harris | 97 | 57 | .630 |
| 1908 | Detroit | Hugh A. Jennings | 90 | 63 | .588 | 1948 | Cleveland[1] | Lou Boudreau | 97 | 58 | .626 |
| 1909 | Detroit | Hugh A. Jennings | 98 | 54 | .645 | 1949 | New York[1] | Casey Stengel | 97 | 57 | .630 |
| 1910 | Philadelphia[1] | Connie Mack | 102 | 48 | .680 | 1950 | New York[1] | Casey Stengel | 98 | 56 | .636 |
| 1911 | Philadelphia[1] | Connie Mack | 101 | 50 | .669 | 1951 | New York[1] | Casey Stengel | 98 | 56 | .636 |
| 1912 | Boston[1] | J. Garland Stahl | 105 | 47 | .691 | 1952 | New York[1] | Casey Stengel | 95 | 59 | .617 |
| 1913 | Philadelphia[1] | Connie Mack | 96 | 57 | .627 | 1953 | New York[1] | Casey Stengel | 99 | 52 | .656 |
| 1914 | Philadelphia | Connie Mack | 99 | 53 | .651 | 1954 | Cleveland | Al Lopez | 111 | 43 | .721 |
| 1915 | Boston[1] | William F. Carrigan | 101 | 50 | .669 | 1955 | New York | Casey Stengel | 96 | 58 | .623 |
| 1916 | Boston[1] | William F. Carrigan | 91 | 63 | .591 | 1956 | New York[1] | Casey Stengel | 97 | 57 | .630 |
| 1917 | Chicago[1] | Clarence H. Rowland | 100 | 54 | .649 | 1957 | New York | Casey Stengel | 98 | 56 | .636 |
| 1918 | Boston[1] | Ed Barrow | 75 | 51 | .595 | 1958 | New York[1] | Casey Stengel | 92 | 62 | .597 |
| 1919 | Chicago | William Gleason | 88 | 52 | .629 | 1959 | Chicago | Al Lopez | 94 | 60 | .610 |
| 1920 | Cleveland[1] | Tris Speaker | 98 | 56 | .636 | 1960 | New York | Casey Stengel | 97 | 57 | .630 |
| 1921 | New York | Miller J. Huggins | 98 | 55 | .641 | 1961 | New York[1] | Ralph Houk | 109 | 53 | .673 |
| 1922 | New York | Miller J. Huggins | 94 | 60 | .610 | 1962 | New York[1] | Ralph Houk | 96 | 66 | .593 |
| 1923 | New York[1] | Miller J. Huggins | 98 | 54 | .645 | 1963 | New York | Ralph Houk | 104 | 57 | .646 |
| 1924 | Washington[1] | Stanley R. Harris | 92 | 62 | .597 | 1964 | New York | Yogi Berra | 99 | 63 | .611 |
| 1925 | Washington | Stanley R. Harris | 96 | 55 | .636 | 1965 | Minnesota | Sam Mele | 102 | 60 | .630 |
| 1926 | New York | Miller J. Huggins | 91 | 63 | .591 | 1966 | Baltimore[1] | Hank Bauer | 97 | 53 | .606 |
| 1927 | New York[1] | Miller J. Huggins | 110 | 44 | .714 | 1967 | Boston | Dick Williams | 92 | 70 | .568 |
| 1928 | New York[1] | Miller J. Huggins | 101 | 53 | .656 | 1968 | Detroit[1] | Mayo Smith | 103 | 59 | .636 |
| 1929 | Philadelphia[1] | Connie Mack | 104 | 46 | .693 | 1969 | Baltimore[3] | Earl Weaver | 109 | 53 | .673 |
| 1930 | Philadelphia[1] | Connie Mack | 102 | 52 | .662 | 1970 | Baltimore[1, 3] | Earl Weaver | 108 | 54 | .667 |
| 1931 | Philadelphia | Connie Mack | 107 | 45 | .704 | 1971 | Baltimore[4] | Earl Weaver | 101 | 57 | .639 |
| 1932 | New York[1] | Joseph V. McCarthy | 107 | 47 | .695 | 1972 | Oakland[1, 5] | Dick Williams | 93 | 62 | .600 |
| 1933 | Washington | Joseph E. Cronin | 99 | 53 | .651 | 1973 | Oakland[1, 6] | Dick Williams | 94 | 68 | .580 |
| 1934 | Detroit | Gordon Cochrane | 101 | 53 | .656 | 1974 | Oakland[1, 6] | Alvin Dark | 90 | 72 | .556 |
| 1935 | Detroit[1] | Gordon Cochrane | 93 | 58 | .616 | 1975 | Boston[4] | Darrell Johnson | 95 | 65 | .594 |
| 1936 | New York[1] | Joseph V. McCarthy | 102 | 51 | .667 | 1976 | New York[7] | Billy Martin | 97 | 62 | .610 |
| 1937 | New York[1] | Joseph V. McCarthy | 102 | 52 | .662 | 1977 | New York[1, 7] | Billy Martin | 100 | 62 | .617 |
| 1938 | New York[1] | Joseph V. McCarthy | 99 | 53 | .651 | 1978 | New York[1, 7] | Billy Martin and Bob Lemon | 100 | 63 | .613 |
| 1939 | New York[1] | Joseph V. McCarthy | 106 | 45 | .702 |  |  |  |  |  |  |
| 1940 | Detroit | Delmar D. Baker | 90 | 64 | .584 | 1979 | Baltimore[8] | Earl Weaver | 102 | 57 | .642 |

| Year | Club | Manager | Won | Lost | Pct |
|---|---|---|---|---|---|
| 1980 | Kansas City[9] | Jim Frey | 97 | 65 | .599 |
| 1981* | New York[10] | Gene Michael-Bob Lemon | 59 | 48 | .551 |
| 1982 | Milwaukee[11] | Harvey Kuenn | 95 | 67 | .586 |
| 1983 | Baltimore[1,12] | Joe Altobelli | 98 | 64 | .605 |
| 1984 | Detroit[1,13] | Sparky Anderson | 104 | 58 | .642 |
| 1985 | Kansas City[1,14] | Dick Howser | 91 | 71 | .562 |
| 1986 | Boston[11] | John McNamara | 95 | 66 | .590 |
| 1987 | Minnesota[15] | Tom Kelly | 85 | 77 | .525 |
| 1988 | Oakland[16] | Tony LaRussa | 104 | 58 | .642 |
| 1989 | Oakland[1,17] | Tony LaRussa | 99 | 63 | .611 |
| 1990 | Oakland[18] | Tony LaRussa | 103 | 59 | .636 |

| Year | Club | Manager | Won | Lost | Pct |
|---|---|---|---|---|---|
| 1991 | Minnesota[1,19] | Tom Kelly | 95 | 67 | .586 |
| 1992 | Toronto[1,10] | Cito Gaston | 96 | 66 | .593 |
| 1993 | Toronto[1,12] | Cito Gaston | 95 | 67 | .586 |
| 1994 | Strike ended season Aug. 11. No playoffs, no pennant winner. | | | | |
| 1995 | Cleveland[20] | Mike Hargrove | 100 | 44 | .694 |
| 1996 | New York[1,21] | Joe Torre | 92 | 70 | .568 |
| 1997 | Cleveland[6] | Mike Hargrove | 86 | 75 | .534 |
| 1998 | New York[1,22] | Joe Torre | 114 | 48 | .704 |
| 1999 | New York[1,23] | Joe Torre | 98 | 64 | .605 |
| 2000 | New York[1,24] | Joe Torre | 87 | 74 | .540 |
| 2001 | New York[20] | Joe Torre | 95 | 65 | .594 |
| 2002 | Anaheim[25] | Mike Scioscia | 99 | 63 | .611 |

*Split season because of players' strike. 1. World Series winner. 2. No World Series. 3. Defeated Minnesota, Western Division winner, in playoff. 4. Defeated Oakland, Western Division Leader, in playoff. 5. Defeated Detroit, Eastern Division winner, in playoff. 6. Defeated Baltimore, Eastern Division winner, in playoff. 7. Defeated Kansas City, Western Division winner, in playoff. 8. Defeated California, Western Division winner, in playoff. 9. Defeated New York, Eastern Division winner, in playoff. 10. Defeated Oakland, Western Division winner, in playoff. 11. Defeated California, Western Division winner, in playoff. 12. Defeated Chicago, Western Division winner, in playoff. 13. Defeated Kansas City, Western Division winner, in playoff. 14. Defeated Toronto, Eastern Division winner, in playoff. 15. Defeated Detroit, Eastern winner, in playoff. 16. Defeated Boston, Eastern division winner, in playoffs. 17. Defeated Toronto, Eastern Division winner, in playoffs. 18. Defeated Boston, Eastern Division winner, in playoffs. 19. Defeated Toronto, Eastern Division winner, in playoffs. 20. Defeated Seattle Mariners, Western Division winner, in playoffs. 21. Defeated Baltimore Orioles, Eastern Division wild-card team, in playoffs. 22. Defeated Cleveland Indians, Central Division winner, in playoffs. 23. Defeated Boston Red Sox, Eastern Division wild-card team, in playoffs. 24. Defeated Seattle Mariners, Western Division wild-card team, in playoffs. 25. Defeated Minnesota Twins, Central Division winner, in playoffs.

## NATIONAL LEAGUE PENNANT WINNERS

| Year | Club | Manager | Won | Lost | Pct |
|---|---|---|---|---|---|
| 1876 | Chicago | Albert G. Spalding | 52 | 14 | .788 |
| 1877 | Boston | Harry Wright | 31 | 17 | .646 |
| 1878 | Boston | Harry Wright | 41 | 19 | .683 |
| 1879 | Providence | George Wright | 55 | 23 | .705 |
| 1880 | Chicago | Adrian C. Anson | 67 | 17 | .798 |
| 1881 | Chicago | Adrian C. Anson | 56 | 28 | .667 |
| 1882 | Chicago | Adrian C. Anson | 55 | 29 | .655 |
| 1883 | Boston | John F. Morrill | 63 | 35 | .643 |
| 1884 | Providence | Frank C. Bancroft | 84 | 28 | .750 |
| 1885 | Chicago | Adrian C. Anson | 87 | 25 | .777 |
| 1886 | Chicago | Adrian C. Anson | 90 | 34 | .726 |
| 1887 | Detroit | W. H. Watkins | 79 | 45 | .637 |
| 1888 | New York | James J. Mutrie | 84 | 47 | .641 |
| 1889 | New York | James J. Mutrie | 83 | 43 | .659 |
| 1890 | Brooklyn | Wm. H. McGunnigle | 86 | 43 | .667 |
| 1891 | Boston | Frank G. Selee | 87 | 51 | .630 |
| 1892 | Boston | Frank G. Selee | 102 | 48 | .680 |
| 1893 | Boston | Frank G. Selee | 86 | 44 | .662 |
| 1894 | Baltimore | Edward H. Hanlon | 89 | 39 | .695 |
| 1895 | Baltimore | Edward H. Hanlon | 87 | 43 | .669 |
| 1896 | Baltimore | Edward H. Hanlon | 90 | 39 | .698 |
| 1897 | Boston | Frank G. Selee | 93 | 39 | .705 |
| 1898 | Boston | Frank G. Selee | 102 | 47 | .685 |
| 1899 | Brooklyn | Edward H. Hanlon | 101 | 47 | .682 |
| 1900 | Brooklyn | Edward H. Hanlon | 82 | 54 | .603 |
| 1901 | Pittsburgh | Fred C. Clarke | 90 | 49 | .647 |
| 1902 | Pittsburgh | Fred C. Clarke | 103 | 36 | .741 |
| 1903 | Pittsburgh | Fred C. Clarke | 91 | 49 | .650 |
| 1904 | New York[1] | John J. McGraw | 106 | 47 | .693 |
| 1905 | New York[2] | John J. McGraw | 105 | 48 | .686 |
| 1906 | Chicago | Frank L. Chance | 116 | 36 | .763 |
| 1907 | Chicago[2] | Frank L. Chance | 107 | 45 | .704 |
| 1908 | Chicago[2] | Frank L. Chance | 99 | 55 | .643 |
| 1909 | Pittsburgh[2] | Fred C. Clarke | 110 | 42 | .724 |
| 1910 | Chicago | Frank L. Chance | 104 | 50 | .675 |
| 1911 | New York | John J. McGraw | 99 | 54 | .647 |
| 1912 | New York | John J. McGraw | 103 | 48 | .682 |
| 1913 | New York | John J. McGraw | 101 | 51 | .664 |
| 1914 | Boston[2] | George T. Stallings | 94 | 59 | .614 |
| 1915 | Philadelphia | Patrick J. Moran | 90 | 62 | .592 |

| Year | Club | Manager | Won | Lost | Pct |
|---|---|---|---|---|---|
| 1916 | Brooklyn | Wilbert Robinson | 94 | 60 | .610 |
| 1917 | New York | John J. McGraw | 98 | 56 | .636 |
| 1918 | Chicago | Fred L. Mitchell | 84 | 45 | .651 |
| 1919 | Cincinnati[2] | Patrick J. Moran | 96 | 44 | .686 |
| 1920 | Brooklyn | Wilbert Robinson | 93 | 61 | .604 |
| 1921 | New York[2] | John J. McGraw | 94 | 59 | .614 |
| 1922 | New York[2] | John J. McGraw | 93 | 61 | .604 |
| 1923 | New York | John J. McGraw | 95 | 58 | .621 |
| 1924 | New York | John J. McGraw | 93 | 60 | .608 |
| 1925 | Pittsburgh[2] | Wm. B. McKechnie | 95 | 58 | .621 |
| 1926 | St. Louis[2] | Rogers Hornsby | 89 | 65 | .578 |
| 1927 | Pittsburgh | Donie Bush | 94 | 60 | .610 |
| 1928 | St. Louis | Wm. B. McKechnie | 95 | 59 | .617 |
| 1929 | Chicago | Joseph V. McCarthy | 98 | 54 | .645 |
| 1930 | St. Louis | Gabby Street | 92 | 62 | .597 |
| 1931 | St. Louis[2] | Gabby Street | 101 | 53 | .656 |
| 1932 | Chicago | Charles J. Grimm | 90 | 64 | .584 |
| 1933 | New York[2] | William H. Terry | 91 | 61 | .599 |
| 1934 | St. Louis[2] | Frank F. Frisch | 95 | 58 | .621 |
| 1935 | Chicago | Charles J. Grimm | 100 | 54 | .649 |
| 1936 | New York | William H. Terry | 92 | 62 | .597 |
| 1937 | New York | William H. Terry | 95 | 57 | .625 |
| 1938 | Chicago | Gabby Hartnett | 89 | 63 | .586 |
| 1939 | Cincinnati | Wm. B. McKechnie | 97 | 57 | .630 |
| 1940 | Cincinnati[2] | Wm. B. McKechnie | 100 | 53 | .654 |
| 1941 | Brooklyn | Leo E. Durocher | 100 | 54 | .649 |
| 1942 | St. Louis[2] | Wm. H. Southworth | 106 | 48 | .688 |
| 1943 | St. Louis | Wm. H. Southworth | 105 | 49 | .682 |
| 1944 | St. Louis[2] | Wm. H. Southworth | 105 | 49 | .682 |
| 1945 | Chicago | Charles J. Grimm | 98 | 56 | .636 |
| 1946 | St. Louis[2] | Edwin H. Dyer | 98 | 58 | .628 |
| 1947 | Brooklyn | Burton E. Shotton | 94 | 60 | .610 |
| 1948 | Boston | Wm. H. Southworth | 91 | 62 | .595 |
| 1949 | Brooklyn | Burton E. Shotton | 97 | 57 | .630 |
| 1950 | Philadelphia | Edwin M. Sawyer | 91 | 63 | .591 |
| 1951 | New York | Leo E. Durocher | 98 | 59 | .624 |
| 1952 | Brooklyn | Charles W. Dressen | 96 | 57 | .630 |
| 1953 | Brooklyn | Charles W. Dressen | 105 | 49 | .682 |
| 1954 | New York[2] | Leo E. Durocher | 97 | 57 | .630 |
| 1955 | Brooklyn[2] | Walter Alston | 98 | 55 | .641 |

| Year | Club | Manager | Won | Lost | Pct |
|------|------|---------|-----|------|-----|
| 1956 | Brooklyn | Walter Alston | 93 | 61 | .604 |
| 1957 | Milwaukee[2] | Fred Haney | 95 | 59 | .617 |
| 1958 | Milwaukee | Fred Haney | 92 | 62 | .597 |
| 1959 | Los Angeles[2] | Walter Alston | 88 | 68 | .564 |
| 1960 | Pittsburgh[2] | Danny Murtaugh | 95 | 59 | .617 |
| 1961 | Cincinnati | Fred Hutchinson | 93 | 61 | .604 |
| 1962 | San Francisco | Alvin Dark | 103 | 62 | .624 |
| 1963 | Los Angeles[2] | Walter Alston | 99 | 63 | .611 |
| 1964 | St. Louis[2] | Johnny Keane | 93 | 69 | .574 |
| 1965 | Los Angeles[2] | Walter Alston | 97 | 65 | .599 |
| 1966 | Los Angeles | Walter Alston | 95 | 67 | .586 |
| 1967 | St. Louis[2] | Red Schoendienst | 101 | 60 | .627 |
| 1968 | St. Louis | Red Schoendienst | 97 | 65 | .599 |
| 1969 | New York[2, 3] | Gil Hodges | 100 | 62 | .617 |
| 1970 | Cincinnati[4] | Sparky Anderson | 102 | 60 | .630 |
| 1971 | Pittsburgh[2, 5] | Danny Murtaugh | 97 | 65 | .599 |
| 1972 | Cincinnati[4] | Sparky Anderson | 95 | 59 | .617 |
| 1973 | New York[6] | Yogi Berra | 82 | 79 | .509 |
| 1974 | Los Angeles[4] | Walter Alston | 102 | 60 | .630 |
| 1975 | Cincinnati[2, 4] | Sparky Anderson | 108 | 54 | .667 |
| 1976 | Cincinnati[7, 2] | Sparky Anderson | 102 | 60 | .630 |
| 1977 | Los Angeles[7] | Tom Lasorda | 98 | 64 | .605 |
| 1978 | Los Angeles[7] | Tom Lasorda | 95 | 67 | .586 |
| 1979 | Pittsburgh[2, 6] | Chuck Tanner | 98 | 64 | .605 |

| Year | Club | Manager | Won | Lost | Pct |
|------|------|---------|-----|------|-----|
| 1980 | Philadelphia[2, 8] | Dallas Green | 91 | 71 | .562 |
| 1981* | Los Angeles[2 9] | Tom Lasorda | 63 | 47 | .573 |
| 1982 | St. Louis[2, 3] | Whitey Herzog | 92 | 70 | .568 |
| 1983 | Philadelphia[11] | Paul Owens | 90 | 72 | .556 |
| 1984 | San Diego[12] | Dick Williams | 92 | 70 | .568 |
| 1985 | St. Louis[11] | Whitey Herzog | 101 | 61 | .623 |
| 1986 | New York[2, 8] | Dave Johnson | 108 | 54 | .667 |
| 1987 | St. Louis[5] | Whitey Herzog | 95 | 67 | .586 |
| 1988 | Los Angeles[2, 10] | Tom Lasorda | 94 | 67 | .584 |
| 1989 | San Francisco[12] | Roger Craig | 92 | 70 | .568 |
| 1990 | Cincinnati[2, 4] | Lou Piniella | 91 | 71 | .562 |
| 1991 | Atlanta[4] | Bobby Cox | 94 | 68 | .580 |
| 1992 | Atlanta[4] | Bobby Cox | 98 | 64 | .605 |
| 1993 | Philadelphia[3] | Jim Fregosi | 97 | 65 | .599 |
| 1994 | Strike ended season Aug. 11. No playoffs, no pennant winner. |  |  |  |  |
| 1995 | Atlanta[2, 13] | Bobby Cox | 90 | 54 | .625 |
| 1996 | Atlanta[14] | Bobby Cox | 96 | 66 | .593 |
| 1997 | Florida[2, 15] | Jim Leyland | 92 | 70 | .568 |
| 1998 | San Diego[16] | Bruce Bochy | 98 | 64 | .605 |
| 1999 | Atlanta[17] | Bobby Cox | 103 | 59 | .636 |
| 2000 | New York[18] | Bobby Valentine | 94 | 68 | .580 |
| 2001 | Arizona[16] | Bob Brenly | 92 | 70 | .568 |
| 2002 | San Francisco[14] | Dusty Baker | 95 | 66 | .590 |

*Split season because of players' strike. 1. No World Series. 2. World Series winner. 3. Defeated Atlanta, Western Division winner, in playoff. 4. Defeated Pittsburgh, Eastern Division winner, in playoff. 5. Defeated San Francisco, Western Division winner, in playoff. 6. Defeated Cincinnati, Western Division winner, in playoff. 7. Defeated Philadelphia, Eastern Division winner, in playoff. 8. Defeated Houston, Western Division winner, in playoff. 9. Defeated Montreal, Eastern Division winner, in playoff. 10. Defeated New York, Eastern Division winner, in playoff. 11. Defeated Los Angeles, Western Division winner, in playoff. 12. Defeated Chicago, Eastern Division champion, in playoff. 13. Defeated Cincinnati, Central Division winner, in playoff. 14. Defeated St. Louis, Central Division winner, in playoff. 15. Eastern Division wildcard Florida defeated Atlanta, Eastern Division winner, in playoff. 16. Defeated Atlanta, Eastern Division winner, in playoff. 17. Defeated New York, Eastern Division wild card team, in playoff. 18. Eastern Division wild card New York defeated Central Division winner St. Louis in playoff.

## WORLD SERIES—2002

**Anaheim Angels win series, 4 games to 3**
**Series MVP—Troy Glaus**

### 1st Game—Anaheim, Oct. 19
### San Francisco 4, Anaheim 3

| San Francisco (N.L.) | AB | R | H | RBI | Anaheim (A.L.) | AB | R | H | RBI |
|------|----|----|----|-----|------|----|----|----|-----|
| Lofton cf | 3 | 0 | 0 | 0 | Eckstein, ss | 5 | 0 | 1 | 0 |
| Aurilia ss | 4 | 0 | 0 | 0 | Erstad cf | 5 | 0 | 1 | 0 |
| Kent 2b | 4 | 0 | 0 | 0 | Salmon rf | 4 | 0 | 0 | 0 |
| Bonds lf | 3 | 1 | 1 | 1 | Anderson lf | 4 | 0 | 1 | 0 |
| Santiago c | 4 | 0 | 1 | 0 | Glaus 3b | 4 | 2 | 2 | 2 |
| Sanders rf | 3 | 2 | 1 | 0 | Fullmer dh | 3 | 1 | 1 | 0 |
| Snow 1b | 3 | 1 | 1 | 2 | Spiezio 1b | 3 | 0 | 1 | 0 |
| Bell 3b | 4 | 0 | 0 | 0 | Figgins pr | 0 | 0 | 0 | 0 |
| Shinjo dh | 3 | 0 | 1 | 0 | Wooten 1b | 0 | 0 | 0 | 0 |
| Goodwin ph-dh | 1 | 0 | 0 | 0 | B. Molina c | 3 | 0 | 0 | 0 |
|  |  |  |  |  | Palmeiro ph | 1 | 0 | 0 | 0 |
|  |  |  |  |  | J. Molina c | 0 | 0 | 0 | 0 |
|  |  |  |  |  | Kennedy 2b | 4 | 0 | 2 | 1 |
| Totals | 32 | 4 | 6 | 4 | Totals | 36 | 3 | 9 | 3 |

|  |  | R | H | E |
|------|------|---|---|---|
| San Francisco | 0 2 0   0 0 2   0 0 0 — | 4 | 6 | 0 |
| Anaheim | 0 1 0   0 0 2   0 0 0 — | 3 | 9 | 0 |

2B—Anaheim: Kennedy, Spiezio. HR—San Francisco: Bonds (off Washburn), Sanders (off Washburn), Snow (off Washburn); Anaheim: Glaus 2 (both off Schmidt). RBI—San Francisco: Bonds, Sanders, Snow 2; Anaheim: Glaus 2, Kennedy. S—San Francisco: Lofton. SB—Anaheim: Fullmer. LOB—San Francisco: 5, Anaheim: 8.

|  | IP | H | R | ER | BB | SO | HR | ERA |
|------|----|----|----|----|----|----|----|-----|
| **San Francisco** |  |  |  |  |  |  |  |  |
| Schmidt (W, 1–0) | 5.2 | 9 | 3 | 3 | 1 | 6 | 2 | 4.76 |
| Rodriguez | 1.1 | 0 | 0 | 0 | 0 | 1 | 0 | 0.00 |
| Worrell | 1.0 | 0 | 0 | 0 | 1 | 1 | 0 | 0.00 |
| Nen (S, 1) | 1.0 | 0 | 0 | 0 | 0 | 1 | 0 | 0.00 |
| **Anaheim** |  |  |  |  |  |  |  |  |
| Washburn (L, 0–1) | 5.2 | 6 | 4 | 4 | 2 | 5 | 3 | 6.35 |

|  | IP | H | R | ER | BB | SO | HR | ERA |
|------|----|----|----|----|----|----|----|-----|
| Donnelly | 1.2 | 0 | 0 | 0 | 0 | 0 | 0 | 0.00 |
| Schoeneweis | 0.0 | 0 | 0 | 0 | 1 | 0 | 0 | 0.00 |
| Weber | 1.2 | 0 | 0 | 0 | 0 | 2 | 0 | 0.00 |

Umpires—HP: Jerry Crawford, 1B: Angel Hernandez, 2B: Tim Tschida, 3B: Mike Winters, LF: Mike Reilly, RF: Tim McClelland. T—3:44. Att.—44,603.

### 2nd Game—Anaheim, Oct. 20
### Anaheim 11, San Francisco 10

| San Francisco (N.L.) | AB | R | H | RBI | Anaheim (A.L.) | AB | R | H | RBI |
|------|----|----|----|-----|------|----|----|----|-----|
| Lofton cf | 5 | 0 | 1 | 0 | Eckstein ss | 5 | 3 | 3 | 0 |
| Aurilia ss | 5 | 1 | 1 | 0 | Erstad cf | 5 | 2 | 2 | 1 |
| Kent 2b | 5 | 1 | 1 | 1 | Salmon rf | 4 | 3 | 4 | 4 |
| Bonds lf | 2 | 3 | 1 | 1 | Ochoa rf | 0 | 0 | 0 | 0 |
| Santiago c | 5 | 1 | 1 | 0 | Anderson lf | 5 | 1 | 2 | 2 |
| Snow 1b | 4 | 2 | 2 | 2 | Glaus 3b | 4 | 1 | 2 | 0 |
| Sanders rf | 4 | 1 | 2 | 3 | Fullmer dh | 3 | 1 | 2 | 1 |
| Bell 3b | 4 | 1 | 2 | 2 | Spiezio 1b | 3 | 0 | 1 | 2 |
| Dunston dh | 4 | 0 | 1 | 1 | B. Molina c | 4 | 0 | 0 | 0 |
|  |  |  |  |  | Kennedy 2b | 4 | 0 | 0 | 0 |
| Totals | 38 | 10 | 12 | 10 | Totals | 37 | 11 | 16 | 10 |

|  |  | R | H | E |
|------|------|---|---|---|
| San Francisco | 0 4 1   0 4 0   0 0 1 — | 10 | 12 | 1 |
| Anaheim | 5 2 0   0 1 1   0 2 x — | 11 | 16 | 1 |

2B—San Francisco: Aurilia; Anaheim: Erstad 2, Glaus. HR—San Francisco: Sanders (off Appier), Bell (off Appier), Kent (off Appier), Bonds (off Percival); Anaheim: Salmon 2 (off Ortiz and Rodriguez). RBI—San Francisco: Sanders 3, Bell 2, Kent, Snow 2, Dunston, Bonds; Anaheim: Erstad, Anderson 2, Fullmer, Spiezio 2, Salmon 4. SF—Anaheim: Spiezio. GIDP—Anaheim: B. Molina. E—San Francisco: Lofton; Anaheim: Anderson. PB—San Francisco: Santiago. DP—San Francisco: (Bell-Kent-Snow); Anaheim: (Eckstein-Spiezio). LOB—San Francisco: 4, Anaheim: 5.

**San Francisco**

| | IP | H | R | ER | BB | SO | HR | ERA |
|---|---|---|---|---|---|---|---|---|
| Ortiz | 1.2 | 9 | 7 | 7 | 0 | 0 | 1 | 37.80 |
| Zerbe | 4.0 | 4 | 2 | 1 | 0 | 0 | 0 | 2.25 |
| Witasick | 0.0 | 0 | 0 | 0 | 1 | 0 | 0 | 0.00 |
| Fultz | 0.1 | 1 | 0 | 0 | 0 | 0 | 0 | 0.00 |
| Rodriguez (L, 0–1) | 1.2 | 2 | 2 | 2 | 1 | 0 | 1 | 6.00 |
| Worrell | 0.1 | 0 | 0 | 0 | 0 | 0 | 0 | 0.00 |

**Anaheim**

| | IP | H | R | ER | BB | SO | HR | ERA |
|---|---|---|---|---|---|---|---|---|
| Appier | 2.0 | 5 | 5 | 5 | 2 | 2 | 3 | 22.50 |
| Lackey | 2.1 | 2 | 2 | 2 | 1 | 1 | 0 | 7.71 |
| Weber | 0.2 | 4 | 2 | 2 | 0 | 1 | 0 | 7.71 |
| Rodriguez (W, 1–0) | 3.0 | 0 | 0 | 0 | 0 | 4 | 0 | 0.00 |
| Percival (S, 1) | 1.0 | 1 | 1 | 1 | 0 | 0 | 1 | 9.00 |

IBB—Bonds (by Lackey). Umpires—HP: Hernandez, 1B: Tschida, 2B: Winters, 3B: Reilly, LF: McClelland. RF: Crawford. T—3:57. Att.—44,584.

### 3rd Game—San Francisco, Oct. 22
### Anaheim 10, San Francisco 4

| Anaheim (A.L.) | AB | R | H | RBI | San Francisco (N.L.) | AB | R | H | RBI |
|---|---|---|---|---|---|---|---|---|---|
| Eckstein ss | 5 | 1 | 2 | 1 | Lofton cf | 4 | 1 | 0 | 0 |
| Erstad cf | 6 | 2 | 3 | 0 | Aurilia ss | 5 | 1 | 2 | 1 |
| Salmon rf | 4 | 2 | 1 | 1 | Kent 2b | 4 | 1 | 2 | 0 |
| Schoeneweis p | 0 | 0 | 0 | 0 | Bonds lf | 2 | 1 | 1 | 2 |
| Anderson lf | 6 | 0 | 1 | 1 | Santiago c | 4 | 0 | 0 | 1 |
| Glaus 3b | 5 | 2 | 2 | 1 | Snow 1b | 4 | 0 | 1 | 0 |
| Spiezio 1b | 5 | 1 | 2 | 3 | Sanders rf | 4 | 0 | 0 | 0 |
| Kennedy 2b | 5 | 1 | 2 | 1 | Bell 3b | 1 | 0 | 0 | 0 |
| B. Molina c | 2 | 1 | 2 | 1 | Hernandez p | 0 | 0 | 0 | 0 |
| Ortiz p | 3 | 0 | 0 | 0 | Witasick p | 0 | 0 | 0 | 0 |
| Wooten ph | 1 | 0 | 0 | 0 | Feliz ph | 1 | 0 | 0 | 0 |
| Donnelly p | 0 | 0 | 0 | 0 | Fultz p | 0 | 0 | 0 | 0 |
| Gil ph | 1 | 0 | 1 | 0 | Dunston ph | 1 | 0 | 0 | 0 |
| Ochoa rf | 0 | 0 | 0 | 0 | Rodriguez p | 0 | 0 | 0 | 0 |
| | | | | | Eyre p | 0 | 0 | 0 | 0 |
| | | | | | Martinez ph | 1 | 0 | 0 | 0 |
| **Totals** | 43 | 10 | 16 | 9 | **Totals** | 31 | 4 | 6 | 4 |

|  | | | | | | | | | | R | H | E |
|---|---|---|---|---|---|---|---|---|---|---|---|---|
| Anaheim | 004 | 401 | 010 | — | 10 | 16 | 0 |
| San Francisco | 100 | 030 | 000 | — | 4 | 6 | 2 |

2B—Anaheim: Kennedy, Erstad, Salmon. 3B—Anaheim: Spiezio. HR—San Francisco: Aurilia (off Ortiz), Bonds (off Ortiz). RBI—Anaheim: Salmon, Glaus, Spiezio 3, Anderson, Kennedy, B. Molina, Eckstein; San Francisco: Santiago, Aurilia, Bonds 2. S—San Francisco: Hernandez. GIDP—Anaheim: Spiezio; San Francisco: Bell. SB—Anaheim: Erstad, Salmon; San Francisco: Lofton. DP—Anaheim: (Eckstein-Kennedy-Spiezio); San Francisco: (Aurilia-Kent-Snow).

**Anaheim**

| | IP | H | R | ER | BB | SO | HR | ERA |
|---|---|---|---|---|---|---|---|---|
| Ortiz (W, 1–0) | 5.0 | 5 | 4 | 4 | 4 | 3 | 2 | 7.20 |
| Donnelly | 2.0 | 0 | 0 | 0 | 2 | 0 | 0 | 0.00 |
| Schoeneweiss | 2.0 | 1 | 0 | 0 | 0 | 2 | 0 | 0.00 |

**San Francisco**

| | IP | H | R | ER | BB | SO | HR | ERA |
|---|---|---|---|---|---|---|---|---|
| Hernandez (L, 0–1) | 3.2 | 5 | 6 | 5 | 5 | 3 | 0 | 12.27 |
| Witasick | 0.1 | 3 | 2 | 2 | 1 | 1 | 1 | 54.00 |
| Fultz | 2.0 | 3 | 1 | 1 | 1 | 0 | 0 | 3.86 |
| Rodriguez | 1.0 | 0 | 0 | 0 | 0 | 0 | 0 | 4.50 |
| Eyre | 2.0 | 4 | 1 | 0 | 1 | 1 | 0 | 0.00 |

IBB—Bonds (by Ortiz), B. Molina 2 (by Hernandez), Salmon (by Eyre). HBP—Kennedy (by Fultz). Umpires—HP: Tschida, 1B: Winters, 2B: Reilly, 3B: McClelland, LF: Crawford, RF: Hernandez. T—3:37. Att.—42,707.

### 4th Game—San Francisco, Oct. 23
### San Francisco 4, Anaheim 3

| Anaheim (A.L.) | AB | R | H | RBI | San Francisco (N.L.) | AB | R | H | RBI |
|---|---|---|---|---|---|---|---|---|---|
| Eckstein ss | 5 | 0 | 0 | 1 | Lofton cf | 4 | 1 | 3 | 0 |
| Erstad cf | 4 | 0 | 0 | 0 | Aurilia ss | 4 | 1 | 3 | 1 |
| Salmon rf | 4 | 0 | 1 | 0 | Kent 2b | 3 | 0 | 0 | 1 |
| Anderson lf | 4 | 1 | 2 | 0 | Bonds lf | 2 | 1 | 1 | 0 |
| Glaus 3b | 4 | 1 | 1 | 2 | Santiago c | 4 | 0 | 1 | 1 |
| Spiezio 1b | 4 | 0 | 1 | 0 | Snow 1b | 4 | 1 | 1 | 0 |
| Gil 2b | 3 | 1 | 2 | 0 | Sanders rf | 4 | 0 | 1 | 0 |

| Anaheim (A.L.) | AB | R | H | RBI | San Francisco (N.L.) | AB | R | H | RBI |
|---|---|---|---|---|---|---|---|---|---|
| Kennedy ph | 1 | 0 | 1 | 0 | Bell 3b | 4 | 0 | 2 | 1 |
| B. Molina c | 3 | 0 | 1 | 0 | Rueter p | 2 | 1 | 1 | 0 |
| Fullmer ph | 1 | 0 | 0 | 0 | Goodwin ph | 0 | 0 | 0 | 0 |
| Lackey p | 2 | 0 | 1 | 0 | Rodriguez p | 0 | 0 | 0 | 0 |
| Weber p | 0 | 0 | 0 | 0 | Worrell p | 0 | 0 | 0 | 0 |
| Palmeiro ph | 1 | 0 | 0 | 0 | Martinez ph | 1 | 0 | 0 | 0 |
| Rodriguez p | 0 | 0 | 0 | 0 | Nen p | 0 | 0 | 0 | 0 |
| **Totals** | 34 | 3 | 10 | 3 | **Totals** | 31 | 4 | 12 | 4 |

|  | | | | | | | | | | R | H | E |
|---|---|---|---|---|---|---|---|---|---|---|---|---|
| Anaheim | 012 | 000 | 000 | — | 3 | 10 | 1 |
| San Francisco | 000 | 030 | 01x | — | 4 | 12 | 1 |

2B—San Francisco: Aurilia. HR—Anaheim: Glaus (off Reuter). RBI—Anaheim: Eckstein, Glaus 2; San Francisco: Aurilia, Kent, Santiago, Bell. SF—Anaheim: Eckstein; San Francisco: Kent. GIDP—Anaheim: Glaus, B. Molina, Fullmer; San Francisco: Santiago 2. SB—San Francisco: Goodwin. CS—San Francisco: Bell. E—Anaheim: Salmon; San Francisco: Bell. DP—Anaheim: 3 (Eckstein-Gil-Spiezio), (B. Molina-Gil), (Eckstein-Spiezio); San Francisco: 3 (Aurilia-Kent-Snow), (Snow-Aurilia-Reuter), (Aurilia-Snow) LOB—Anaheim: 5; San Francisco: 8..

**Anaheim**

| | IP | H | R | ER | BB | SO | HR | ERA |
|---|---|---|---|---|---|---|---|---|
| Lackey | 5.0 | 9 | 3 | 3 | 3 | 2 | 0 | 6.14 |
| Weber | 1.0 | 1 | 0 | 0 | 1 | 0 | 0 | 5.40 |
| Rodriguez (L, 1–1) | 2.0 | 2 | 1 | 0 | 0 | 2 | 0 | 0.00 |

**San Francisco**

| | IP | H | R | ER | BB | SO | HR | ERA |
|---|---|---|---|---|---|---|---|---|
| Rueter | 6.0 | 9 | 3 | 3 | 2 | 1 | 1 | 4.50 |
| Rodriguez | 1.0 | 0 | 0 | 0 | 0 | 1 | 0 | 3.60 |
| Worrell (W, 1–0) | 1.0 | 1 | 0 | 0 | 0 | 0 | 0 | 0.00 |
| Nen (S, 2) | 1.0 | 0 | 0 | 0 | 0 | 1 | 0 | 0.00 |

IBB—Bonds (3 times by Lackey). Umpires—HP: Winters, 1B: Reilly, 2B: McClelland, 3B: Crawford, LF: Hernandez, RF: Tschida. T—3:02. Att.—42,703.

### 5th Game—San Francisco, Oct. 24
### San Francisco 16, Anaheim 4

| Anaheim (A.L.) | AB | R | H | RBI | San Francisco (N.L.) | AB | R | H | RBI |
|---|---|---|---|---|---|---|---|---|---|
| Eckstein ss | 4 | 1 | 2 | 1 | Lofton cf | 6 | 3 | 3 | 2 |
| Erstad cf | 4 | 0 | 1 | 1 | Eyre p | 0 | 0 | 0 | 0 |
| Salmon rf | 4 | 1 | 1 | 0 | Aurilia ss | 6 | 2 | 2 | 3 |
| Ochoa rf | 1 | 0 | 0 | 0 | Kent 2b | 5 | 4 | 3 | 4 |
| Anderson lf | 5 | 0 | 1 | 0 | Bonds lf | 4 | 2 | 3 | 1 |
| Glaus 3b | 4 | 0 | 1 | 1 | Santiago 3b | 3 | 0 | 1 | 3 |
| Spiezio 1b | 2 | 0 | 0 | 0 | Sanders rf | 1 | 0 | 0 | 1 |
| Shields p | 0 | 0 | 0 | 0 | Rodriguez p | 0 | 0 | 0 | 0 |
| Kennedy 2b | 4 | 0 | 0 | 0 | Dunston ph | 1 | 0 | 0 | 0 |
| B. Molina c | 4 | 1 | 1 | 0 | Worrell p | 0 | 0 | 0 | 0 |
| J. Molina c | 0 | 0 | 0 | 0 | Feliz ph | 1 | 0 | 0 | 0 |
| Washburn p | 1 | 0 | 0 | 0 | Goodwin rf | 0 | 0 | 0 | 0 |
| Palmeiro ph | 1 | 1 | 1 | 0 | Snow 1b | 4 | 2 | 2 | 0 |
| Donnelly p | 0 | 0 | 0 | 0 | Bell 3b | 3 | 2 | 2 | 1 |
| Gil ph | 1 | 0 | 1 | 0 | Schmidt p | 1 | 0 | 0 | 0 |
| Weber p | 0 | 0 | 0 | 0 | Zerbe | 0 | 0 | 0 | 0 |
| Wooten 1b | 0 | 0 | 0 | 0 | Shinjo rf-cf | 2 | 1 | 0 | 0 |
| **Totals** | 36 | 4 | 10 | 3 | **Totals** | 37 | 16 | 16 | 15 |

|  | | | | | | | | | | R | H | E |
|---|---|---|---|---|---|---|---|---|---|---|---|---|
| Anaheim | 000 | 031 | 000 | — | 4 | 10 | 2 |
| San Francisco | 030 | 003 | 44x | — | 16 | 16 | 0 |

2B—Anaheim: Palmeiro, Glaus, Gil; San Francisco: Bonds 2, Kent. 3B—San Francisco: Lofton. HR—San Francisco: Kent 2 (off Weber and Shields), Aurilia (off Shields). RBI—Anaheim: Erstad, Glaus, Eckstein; San Francisco: Bonds, Santiago 3, Bell, Sanders, Kent 4, Lofton 2, Aurilia 3. S—San Francisco: Schmidt, Shinjo. SF—Anaheim: Erstad; San Francisco: Santiago, Sanders. SB—Anaheim: Eckstein. E—Anaheim: Erstad, Glaus. LOB—Anaheim: 9; San Francisco: 8.

**Anaheim**

| | IP | H | R | ER | BB | SO | HR | ERA |
|---|---|---|---|---|---|---|---|---|
| Washburn (L, 0–2) | 4.0 | 6 | 6 | 6 | 5 | 1 | 0 | 9.31 |
| Donnelly | 1.0 | 0 | 0 | 0 | 0 | 2 | 0 | 0.00 |
| Weber | 1.1 | 5 | 5 | 5 | 1 | 2 | 1 | 13.50 |
| Shields | 1.2 | 5 | 5 | 1 | 0 | 1 | 2 | 5.40 |

| | IP | H | R | ER | BB | SO | HR | ERA |
|---|---|---|---|---|---|---|---|---|
| **San Francisco** | | | | | | | | |
| Schmidt | 4.2 | 7 | 3 | 3 | 3 | 8 | 0 | 5.23 |
| Zerbe (W, 1–0) | 1.0 | 2 | 1 | 1 | 0 | 0 | 0 | 3.60 |
| Rodriguez | 0.1 | 0 | 0 | 0 | 0 | 0 | 0 | 3.38 |
| Worrell | 2.0 | 1 | 0 | 0 | 0 | 2 | 0 | 0.00 |
| Eyre | 1.0 | 0 | 0 | 0 | 0 | 1 | 0 | 0.00 |

WP—Schmidt. IBB—Sanders (by Washburn), Bonds (by Washburn), Santiago (by Weber). HBP—Bell (by Weber). Umpires—HP: Reilly, 1B: McClelland, 2B: Crawford, 3B: Hernandez, LF: Tschida, RF: Winters. T—3:53. Att.—42,713.

### 6th Game—Anaheim, Oct. 26
### Anaheim 6, San Francisco 5

| San Francisco (N.L.) | AB | R | H | RBI | Anaheim (A.L.) | AB | R | H | RBI |
|---|---|---|---|---|---|---|---|---|---|
| Lofton cf | 5 | 2 | 2 | 0 | Eckstein, ss | 4 | 0 | 0 | 0 |
| Aurilia ss | 4 | 0 | 0 | 0 | Erstad cf | 3 | 1 | 1 | 1 |
| Kent 2b | 4 | 0 | 2 | 1 | Salmon rf | 4 | 0 | 2 | 0 |
| Bonds lf | 2 | 1 | 1 | 1 | Figgins pr | 0 | 1 | 0 | 0 |
| Santiago c | 3 | 0 | 0 | 0 | Ochoa rf | 0 | 0 | 0 | 0 |
| Snow 1b | 4 | 0 | 1 | 0 | Anderson lf | 4 | 1 | 1 | 0 |
| Sanders rf | 4 | 0 | 0 | 0 | Glaus 3b | 3 | 1 | 2 | 2 |
| Bell 3b | 4 | 1 | 1 | 0 | Fullmer dh | 4 | 1 | 1 | 0 |
| Dunston dh | 3 | 1 | 1 | 2 | Spiezio 1b | 3 | 1 | 1 | 3 |
| Goodwin ph-dh | 1 | 0 | 0 | 0 | B. Molina c | 2 | 0 | 0 | 0 |
| | | | | | Palmeiro ph | 1 | 0 | 0 | 0 |
| | | | | | J. Molina c | 0 | 0 | 0 | 0 |
| | | | | | Kennedy 2b | 4 | 0 | 2 | 0 |
| **Totals** | 34 | 5 | 8 | 4 | **Totals** | 32 | 6 | 10 | 6 |

| | | | | | | | R | H | E |
|---|---|---|---|---|---|---|---|---|---|
| San Francisco | 000 | 031 | 100 | — | | | 5 | 8 | 1 |
| Anaheim | 000 | 000 | 33x | — | | | 6 | 10 | 1 |

2B—San Francisco: Lofton; Anaheim: Glaus. HR—San Francisco: Dunston (off Appier), Bonds (off Rodriguez); Anaheim: Spiezio (off Rodriguez), Erstad (off Worrell). RBI—San Francisco: Dunston 2, Bonds, Kent; Anaheim: Spiezio 3, Erstad, Glaus 2. S—Anaheim: J. Molina. GIDP—San Francisco: Santiago; Anaheim: Anderson. E—San Francisco: Bonds; Anaheim: B. Molina. DP—San Francisco: (Kent-Aurilia-Snow); Anaheim: (Glaus-Kennedy-Spiezio). LOB—San Francisco: 6; Anaheim: 6.

| | IP | H | R | ER | BB | SO | HR | ERA |
|---|---|---|---|---|---|---|---|---|
| **San Francisco** | | | | | | | | |
| Ortiz | 6.1 | 4 | 2 | 2 | 2 | 2 | 0 | 10.13 |
| Rodriguez | 0.1 | 1 | 1 | 1 | 0 | 1 | 1 | 4.76 |
| Eyre | 0.0 | 1 | 0 | 0 | 0 | 0 | 0 | 0.00 |
| Worrell (L, 1–1) | 0.1 | 3 | 3 | 2 | 0 | 0 | 1 | 3.86 |
| Nan | 1.0 | 1 | 0 | 0 | 1 | 2 | 0 | 0.00 |

| | IP | H | R | ER | BB | SO | HR | ERA |
|---|---|---|---|---|---|---|---|---|
| **Anaheim** | | | | | | | | |
| Appier | 4.1 | 4 | 3 | 3 | 3 | 2 | 1 | 11.37 |
| Rodriguez | 2.2 | 4 | 2 | 2 | 0 | 4 | 1 | 2.35 |
| Donnelly (W, 1–0) | 1.0 | 0 | 0 | 0 | 1 | 2 | 0 | 0.00 |
| Percival (S, 2) | 1.0 | 0 | 0 | 0 | 0 | 2 | 0 | 4.50 |

WP—Rodriguez. IBB—Spiezio (by Nen), Bonds (by Appier). Umpires—HP: McClelland, 1B: Crawford, 2B: Hernandez, 3B: Tschida, LF: Winters, RF: Reilly. T—3:48. Att.—44,506.

### 7th Game—Anaheim, Oct. 27
### Anaheim 4, San Francisco 1

| San Francisco (N.L.) | AB | R | H | RBI | Anaheim (A.L.) | AB | R | H | RBI |
|---|---|---|---|---|---|---|---|---|---|
| Lofton cf | 4 | 0 | 0 | 0 | Eckstein ss | 3 | 1 | 1 | 0 |
| Aurilia ss | 4 | 0 | 0 | 0 | Erstad cf | 3 | 1 | 1 | 0 |
| Kent 2b | 4 | 0 | 0 | 0 | Salmon rf | 2 | 1 | 0 | 0 |
| Bonds lf | 3 | 0 | 1 | 0 | Ochoa rf | 0 | 0 | 0 | 0 |
| Santiago c | 3 | 1 | 2 | 0 | Anderson lf | 4 | 0 | 1 | 3 |
| Snow 1b | 4 | 0 | 3 | 0 | Glaus 3b | 2 | 0 | 0 | 0 |
| Sanders rf | 1 | 0 | 0 | 1 | Fullmer dh | 4 | 0 | 0 | 0 |
| Goodwin ph-rf | 2 | 0 | 0 | 0 | Spiezio 1b | 3 | 1 | 0 | 0 |
| Bell 3b | 3 | 0 | 0 | 0 | B. Molina c | 3 | 0 | 2 | 1 |
| Feliz dh | 3 | 0 | 0 | 0 | Kennedy 2b | 3 | 0 | 0 | 0 |
| Shinjo ph-dh | 1 | 0 | 0 | 0 | | | | | |
| **Totals** | 32 | 1 | 6 | 1 | **Totals** | 27 | 4 | 5 | 4 |

| | | | | | | | R | H | E |
|---|---|---|---|---|---|---|---|---|---|
| San Francisco | 010 | 000 | 000 | — | | | 1 | 6 | 0 |
| Anaheim | 013 | 000 | 00x | — | | | 4 | 5 | 0 |

2B—San Francisco: Snow; Anaheim: B. Molina 2, Anderson. RBI—San Francisco: Sanders; Anaheim: B. Molina, Anderson 3. SF—San Francisco: Sanders. S—Anaheim: Erstad. DP—San Francisco: (Lofton-Kent). LOB—San Francisco: 9; Anaheim: 6.

| | IP | H | R | ER | BB | SO | HR | ERA |
|---|---|---|---|---|---|---|---|---|
| **San Francisco** | | | | | | | | |
| Hernandez (L, 0–2) | 2.0 | 4 | 4 | 4 | 4 | 1 | 0 | 14.29 |
| Zerbe | 1.0 | 0 | 0 | 0 | 0 | 0 | 0 | 3.00 |
| Rueter | 4.0 | 1 | 0 | 0 | 1 | 3 | 0 | 2.70 |
| Worrell | 1.0 | 0 | 0 | 0 | 0 | 1 | 0 | 3.18 |
| **Anaheim** | | | | | | | | |
| Lackey (W, 1–0) | 5.0 | 4 | 1 | 1 | 1 | 4 | 0 | 4.38 |
| Donnelly | 2.0 | 1 | 0 | 0 | 1 | 2 | 0 | 0.00 |
| Rodriguez | 1.0 | 0 | 0 | 0 | 1 | 3 | 0 | 2.08 |
| Percival (S, 3) | 1.0 | 1 | 0 | 0 | 1 | 1 | 0 | 3.00 |

IBB—Glaus (by Hernandez). HBP—Salmon (by Hernandez). Umpires—HP: Crawford, 1B: Hernandez, 2B: Tschida, 3B: Winters, LF: Reilly, RF: McClelland. T—3:16. Att.—44,598.

## ROBERTO CLEMENTE AWARD

The Roberto Clemente Award is presented annually to the Major League Baseball player who combines outstanding baseball skills with work in the community. In 2002, Jim Thome of the Cleveland Indians received the award.

# Extreme Sports

## 2002 SUMMER EXTREME GAMES
### (Philadelphia, Pa., Aug. 15–19, 2002)

**Motocross:** Mike Metzger (big air), Tommy Clowers (step up), Mike Metzger (freestyle)

**Skateboarding:** Rodil de Araujo, Jr. (park), Pierre-Luc Gagnon (vert best trick), Tony Hawk/Andy Macdonald (vert doubles), Pierre-Luc Gagnon (vert), Rodil de Araujo, Jr. (street), Rodil de Araujo, Jr. (street best trick)

**BMX:** Ryan Nyquist (park), Martti Kuoppa (flatland), Dave Mirra (vert), Allan Cooke (dirt), Robbie Miranda (downhill)

**Wakeboarding:** Danny Harf (men), Emily Copeland (women)

**Agressive Inline:** Takeshi Yasutoko (men's vert), Jaren Grob (men's park), Martina Svobodova (women's park)

**Speed climbing:** Maxim Stenkovoy (men), Tori Allen (women)

# Soccer

The early history of the sport is uncertain. A form of the game in which a leather ball was dribbled was played in China as early as the 4th century B.C. The Romans played a variation of soccer which eventually spread throughout Europe. British schools and universities played soccer (known as football) during the 1800s, however, each school used different sets of rules and the number of players varied. This difficulty was corrected on Oct. 26, 1863, when the Football Association (FA) was formed in London for the purpose of unifying the rules of the game.

The Federation of International Football Associations (FIFA) was created in 1913 as a world governing body to coordinate all of the national associations in the world. The FIFA held the first World Cup Championship tournament in 1930 in Montevideo, Uruguay. Today, soccer is the world's most popular sport. The first FIFA Women's World Cup was held in 1991 with the United States winning the title.

## WORLD CUP
### (W) indicates Women's World Cup

| | | | |
|---|---|---|---|
| 1930 Uruguay | 1954 West Germany | 1978 Argentina | 1995 Norway (W) |
| 1934 Italy | 1958 Brazil | 1982 Italy | 1998 France |
| 1938 Italy | 1962 Brazil | 1986 Argentina | 1999 United States (W) |
| 1942 No competition | 1966 England | 1990 West Germany | 2002 Brazil |
| 1946 No competition | 1970 Brazil | 1991 United States (W) | |
| 1950 Uruguay | 1974 West Germany | 1994 Brazil | |

## WORLD CUP—2002

**QUARTERFINALS**
Brazil 2, England 1
Germany 1, United States 0
South Korea 0, Spain 0 (South Korea won 5–3 in shootout)
Turkey 1, Senegal 0

**SEMIFINALS**
Germany 1, South Korea 0
Brazil 1, Turkey 0

**THIRD PLACE**
Turkey 3, South Korea 2

**CHAMPIONSHIP**
Brazil 2, Germany 0
 **Goals scored:** Ronaldo 2 (67th min and 79th min)

### Championship game statistics

| Statistics | Brazil | Germany |
|---|---|---|
| Shots | 9 | 12 |
| Shots on goal | 7 | 4 |
| Fouls | 19 | 21 |
| Corner kicks | 3 | 13 |
| Free kicks | 1 | 2 |
| Penalty kicks | 0 | 0 |
| Offsides | 0 | 1 |
| Own goals | 0 | 0 |
| Cautions | 1 | 1 |
| Expulsions | 0 | 0 |
| Ball possession percentage | 44% | 56% |
| Actual playing time | 22 | 28 |

## WORLD CUP
### All-Time Top 10

| Country | App | Gm | Record (W–L–T) | Pts | GF | GA | Country | App | Gm | Record (W–L–T) | Pts | GF | GA |
|---|---|---|---|---|---|---|---|---|---|---|---|---|---|
| 1. Brazil | 17 | 87 | 60–13–14 | 141 | 191 | 82 | 7. France | 11 | 44 | 21–16–7 | 49 | 86 | 61 |
| 2. Germany | 15 | 85 | 50–17–18 | 123 | 176 | 106 | 8. Sweden | 10 | 42 | 15–16–10 | 42 | 71 | 65 |
| 3. Italy | 15 | 70 | 39–14–17 | 96 | 110 | 67 | 9. Russia | 9 | 37 | 17–14–6 | 41 | 64 | 44 |
| 4. Argentina | 13 | 60 | 30–19–11 | 72 | 102 | 71 | 10. Yugoslavia | 9 | 37 | 16–13–8 | 40 | 60 | 46 |
| 5. England | 11 | 50 | 26–13–15 | 61 | 68 | 45 | Uruguay | 10 | 40 | 15–15–10 | 40 | 65 | 57 |
| 6. Spain | 11 | 45 | 20–15–10 | 54 | 71 | 53 | | | | | | | |

## WOMEN'S WORLD CUP—1999

**SEMIFINALS**
United States 2, Brazil 0
China 5, Norway 0

**THIRD PLACE**
Brazil 0, Norway 0 (Brazil won 5–4 on penalty kicks)

**CHAMPIONSHIP**
United States 0, China 0 (The United States won 5–4 on penalty kicks)

## MAJOR LEAGUE SOCCER 2002 FINAL STANDINGS
The GF and GA columns refer to Goals For and Goals Against in regulation play.

### EASTERN CONFERENCE

| Team | W | L | T | Pts | GF | GA |
|---|---|---|---|---|---|---|
| New England Revolution[1] | 12 | 14 | 2 | 38 | 49 | 49 |
| Columbus Crew[2] | 11 | 12 | 5 | 38 | 44 | 43 |
| Chicago Fire[2] | 11 | 13 | 4 | 37 | 43 | 38 |
| MetroStars | 11 | 15 | 2 | 35 | 41 | 47 |
| DC United | 9 | 14 | 5 | 32 | 31 | 40 |

### WESTERN CONFERENCE

| Team | W | L | T | Pts | GF | GA |
|---|---|---|---|---|---|---|
| Los Angeles Galaxy[1] | 16 | 9 | 3 | 51 | 44 | 33 |
| San Jose Earthquakes[2] | 14 | 11 | 3 | 45 | 45 | 35 |
| Dallas Burn[2] | 12 | 9 | 7 | 43 | 44 | 43 |
| Colorado Rapids[2] | 13 | 11 | 4 | 43 | 43 | 48 |
| Kansas City Wizards[2] | 9 | 10 | 9 | 36 | 37 | 45 |

1. Conference champions. 2. Playoff qualifiers.

## MLS PLAYOFFS

3 points are awarded for a win, and 1 point for a tie. The winner of the series is the first to reach or exceed 5 points.

**Quarterfinals**
New England defeated Chicago, 6 points to 3
Colorado defeated Dallas, 6 points to 3
Los Angeles defeated Kansas City, 6 points to 3
Columbus defeated San Jose, 6 points to 0

**Semifinals**
New England defeated Columbus, 5 points to 2
Los Angeles defeated Colorado, 6 points to 0

## MLS CUP

**Oct. 20 at Foxboro, Mass.**
**Los Angeles Galaxy 1, New England Revolution 0**

| | 1st | 2nd | OT | Total |
|---|---|---|---|---|
| Los Angeles Galaxy | 0 | 0 | 1 | 1 |
| New England Revolution | 0 | 0 | 0 | 0 |

**Scoring:** Los Angeles: Carlos Ruiz, 113th min. **MVP:** Carlos Ruiz.

## 2002 REGULAR SEASON

### LEADING SCORERS

| | Gm | G | A | Pts |
|---|---|---|---|---|
| Taylor Twellman, New England | 28 | 23 | 6 | 52 |
| Carlos Ruiz, Los Angeles | 26 | 24 | 1 | 49 |
| Jeff Cunningham, Columbus | 27 | 16 | 5 | 37 |
| Ante Razov, Chicago | 25 | 14 | 8 | 36 |
| Ariel Graziani, San Jose | 28 | 14 | 5 | 33 |

### GOAL SCORING LEADERS

| | Gm | No |
|---|---|---|
| Carlos Ruiz, Los Angeles | 26 | 24 |
| Taylor Twellman, New England | 28 | 23 |
| Jeff Cunningham, Columbus | 27 | 16 |
| Ante Razov, Chicago | 25 | 14 |
| Ariel Graziani, San Jose | 28 | 14 |

### LEADING GOALKEEPERS

| | Gm | Shts | Svs | GA | GAA |
|---|---|---|---|---|---|
| Kevin Hartman, Los Angeles | 18 | 108 | 83 | 20 | 1.09 |
| Jon Busch, Columbus | 14 | 80 | 63 | 15 | 1.09 |
| Joe Cannon, San Jose | 26 | 136 | 100 | 29 | 1.10 |
| Zach Thornton, Chicago | 27 | 164 | 124 | 34 | 1.23 |
| Adin Brown, New England | 16 | 102 | 72 | 20 | 1.23 |

### ASSIST LEADERS

| | Gm | No |
|---|---|---|
| Steve Ralston, New England | 27 | 19 |
| Carlos Valderrama, Colorado | 27 | 16 |
| Andy Williams, MetroStars | 24 | 15 |
| Cobi Jones, Los Angeles | 19 | 13 |

1. Played for more than one team, most recent team listed.

## WOMEN'S UNITED SOCCER ASSOCIATION 2002 FINAL STANDINGS

The GF and GA columns refer to Goals For and Goals Against in regulation play. 3 points are awarded for a win, and 1 point for a tie.

| Team | W | L | T | Pts | GF | GF | Home | Road |
|---|---|---|---|---|---|---|---|---|
| Carolina Courage | 12 | 5 | 4 | 40 | 40 | 30 | 6–3–1 | 6–2–3 |
| Philadelphia Charge | 11 | 4 | 6 | 39 | 36 | 22 | 7–1–3 | 4–3–3 |
| Washington Freedom | 11 | 5 | 5 | 38 | 40 | 29 | 6–2–3 | 5–3–2 |
| Atlanta Beat | 11 | 9 | 1 | 34 | 34 | 29 | 6–3–1 | 5–6–0 |
| San Jose CyberRays | 8 | 8 | 5 | 29 | 34 | 30 | 7–3–1 | 1–5–4 |
| Boston Breakers | 6 | 8 | 7 | 25 | 36 | 35 | 5–0–5 | 1–8–2 |
| San Diego Spirit | 5 | 11 | 5 | 20 | 28 | 42 | 3–4–3 | 2–7–2 |
| New York Power | 3 | 17 | 1 | 10 | 31 | 62 | 1–10–0 | 2–7–1 |

## WUSA PLAYOFFS

Aug. 17—Carolina 2, Atlanta 1
Aug. 17—Washington 1, Philadelphia 0

**Championship**
Aug. 24, Atlanta, Ga.—Carolina 3, Washington 2

## 2002 REGULAR SEASON

### POINTS LEADERS

| | Gm | G | A | Pts |
|---|---|---|---|---|
| Katia, San Jose | 21 | 15 | 5 | 35 |
| Danielle Fotopoulos, Carolina | 21 | 11 | 10 | 32 |
| Birgit Prinz, Carolina | 15 | 12 | 8 | 32 |
| Maren Meinert, Boston | 21 | 7 | 16 | 30 |
| Abby Wambach, Washington | 19 | 10 | 9 | 29 |
| Marinette Pichon, Philadelphia | 18 | 14 | 1 | 29 |
| Kristine Lilly, Boston | 19 | 8 | 13 | 29 |

### ASSISTS LEADERS

| | Gm | Assists |
|---|---|---|
| Maren Meinert, Boston | 21 | 16 |
| Hege Riise, Carolina | 19 | 13 |
| Kristine Lilly, Boston | 19 | 13 |
| Danielle Fotopoulos, Carolina | 21 | 10 |
| Abby Wambach, Washington | 19 | 9 |
| Bettina Wiegmann, Boston | 20 | 9 |
| Sissi, San Jose | 21 | 9 |

### GOALS LEADERS

| | Gm | Goals |
|---|---|---|
| Katia, San Jose | 21 | 15 |
| Marinette Pichon, Philadelphia | 18 | 14 |
| Birgit Prinz, Carolina | 15 | 12 |
| Danielle Fotopoulos, Carolina | 21 | 11 |
| Charmaine Hooper, Atlanta | 19 | 11 |
| Dagny Mellgren, Boston | 20 | 11 |

### SHOTS LEADERS

| | Gm | Shots |
|---|---|---|
| Katia, San Jose | 21 | 96 |
| Danielle Fotopoulos, Carolina | 21 | 90 |
| Marinette Pichon, Philadelphia | 18 | 68 |
| Tiffeny Milbrett, New York | 19 | 62 |
| Kristine Lilly, Boston | 19 | 62 |

# History of the Income Tax in the United States

Source: Ernst & Young LLP

The nation had few taxes in its early history. From 1791 to 1802, the United States government was supported by internal taxes on distilled spirits, carriages, refined sugar, tobacco and snuff, property sold at auction, corporate bonds, and slaves. The high cost of the War of 1812 brought about the nation's first sales taxes on gold, silverware, jewelry, and watches. In 1817, however, Congress did away with all internal taxes, relying on tariffs on imported goods to provide sufficient funds for running the government.

In 1862, in order to support the Civil War effort, Congress enacted the nation's first income tax law. It was a forerunner of our modern income tax in that it was based on the principles of graduated, or progressive, taxation and of withholding income at the source. During the Civil War, a person earning from $600 to $10,000 per year paid tax at the rate of 3%. Those with incomes of more than $10,000 paid taxes at a higher rate. Additional sales and excise taxes were added, and an "inheritance" tax also made its debut. In 1866, internal revenue collections reached their highest point in the nation's 90-year history—more than $310 million, an amount not reached again until 1911.

The Act of 1862 established the office of Commissioner of Internal Revenue. The Commissioner was given the power to assess, levy, and collect taxes, and the right to enforce the tax laws through seizure of property and income and through prosecution. His powers and authority remain very much the same today.

In 1868, Congress again focused its taxation efforts on tobacco and distilled spirits and eliminated the income tax in 1872. It had a short-lived revival in 1894 and 1895. In the latter year, the U.S. Supreme Court decided that the income tax was unconstitutional because it was not apportioned among the states in conformity with the Constitution.

In 1913, the 16th Amendment to the Constitution made the income tax a permanent fixture in the U.S. tax system. The amendment gave Congress legal authority to tax income and resulted in a revenue law that taxed incomes of both individuals and corporations. In fiscal year 1918, annual internal revenue collections for the first time passed the billion-dollar mark, rising to $5.4 billion by 1920. With the advent of World War II, employment increased, as did tax collections—to $7.3 billion. The withholding tax on wages was introduced in 1943 and was instrumental in increasing the number of taxpayers to 60 million and tax collections to $43 billion by 1945.

In 1981, Congress enacted the largest tax cut in U.S. history, approximately $750 billion over six years. The tax reduction, however, was partially offset by two tax acts, in 1982 and 1984, that attempted to raise approximately $265 billion.

On Oct. 22, 1986, President Reagan signed into law the Tax Reform Act of 1986, one of the most far-reaching reforms of the United States tax system since the adoption of the income tax. In an attempt to remain revenue neutral, the act called for a $120 billion increase in business taxation and a corresponding decrease in individual taxation over a five-year period.

Following what seemed to be a yearly tradition of new tax acts that began in 1986, the Revenue Reconciliation Act of 1990 was signed into law on Nov. 5, 1990. As with the '87, '88, and '89 acts, the 1990 act, while providing a number of substantive provisions, was small in comparison with the 1986 act. The emphasis of the 1990 act was increased taxes on the wealthy.

On Aug. 10, 1993, President Clinton signed the Revenue Reconciliation Act of 1993 into law. The act's purpose was to reduce by approximately $496 billion the federal deficit that would otherwise accumulate in fiscal years 1994 through 1998.

On Aug. 5, 1997, President Clinton signed the Taxpayer Relief Act of 1997. The act included $152 billion in tax cuts, a cut in capital-gains tax for individuals, a $500 per child tax credit, estate tax relief, tax incentives for education, and a host of revenue-raising and tax-simplification provisions.

On June 7, 2001, President George W. Bush signed the Economic Growth and Tax Relief Reconciliation Act of 2001. The act included a variety of tax cuts and offered benefits to a broad range of taxpayers through relief provisions that included: married couples; families with children, who would receive tax cuts to help pay for education, childcare, and other expenses; single mothers; and seniors. The act also included tax cuts that completely eliminated the entire income tax liability for some families.

## Internal Revenue Service

The Internal Revenue Service (IRS), a bureau of the U.S. Treasury Department, is the federal agency charged with the administration of the tax laws passed by Congress. The IRS functions through a national office in Washington, 4 regional offices, 63 district offices, and 10 service centers.

Operations involving most taxpayers are carried out in the district offices and service centers. District offices are organized into Resources Management, Examination, Collection, Taxpayer Service, Employee Plans and Exempt Organizations, and Criminal Investigation. All tax returns are filed with the service centers, where the IRS computer operations are located.

IRS service centers are processing an ever increasing number of returns and documents. Prior to 1987, all tax return processing was performed by hand. This process was time consuming and costly. In an attempt to improve the speed and efficiency of the manual processing procedure, the IRS began testing an electronic return filing system beginning with the filing of 1985 returns.

## Internal Revenue Service

| | 2001 | 1996 | 1995 | 1994 | 1993 | 1970 |
|---|---|---|---|---|---|---|
| U.S. population (in thousands) | 288,058 | 266,109 | 263,730 | 261,698 | 259,015 | 204,878 |
| Number of IRS employees | 100,577 | 102,082 | 112,023 | 110,665 | 113,352 | 68,683 |
| Cost to govt. of collecting $100 in taxes | $0.41 | $0.49 | $0.55 | $0.58 | $0.60 | $0.45 |
| Tax per capita | $7,448.90 | $5,586.00 | $5,216.44 | $4,878.00 | $4,543.33 | $955.31 |
| Collections by principal sources (in thousands of dollars) | | | | | | |
| Total IRS collections | $2,128,831,182 | $1,486,546,674 | $1,375,731,835 | $1,276,466,776 | $1,176,685,625 | $195,722,096 |
| Income and profits taxes | | | | | | |
| Individual | $1,178,209,880 | $745,313,276 | $675,779,337 | $619,819,153 | $585,774,159 | $103,651,585 |
| Corporation | $186,731,643 | $189,054,791 | $174,422,173 | $154,204,684 | $131,547,509 | $35,036,983 |
| Employment taxes | $682,222,895 | $492,365,178 | $465,405,305 | $443,831,352 | $411,510,516 | $37,449,188 |
| Estate and gift taxes | $29,247,916 | $17,591,817 | $15,144,394 | $15,606,793 | $12,890,965 | $3,680,076 |
| Alcohol taxes | (1) | (1) | (1) | (1) | (1) | $4,746,382 |
| Tobacco taxes | (1) | (1) | (1) | (1) | (1) | $2,094,212 |
| Excise taxes[2] | $52,418,848 | $42,221,611 | $44,980,627 | $43,004,794 | $34,962,476 | $2,380,609 |

NOTE: For fiscal year ending Sept. 30th. 1. Alcohol and tobacco tax collections are now collected and reported by the Bureau of Alcohol, Tobacco, and Firearms. 2. Includes principal and interest paid on refunds. Represents overpayment refunds resulting from examination activity, and other refunds (except earned income credit refunds) required by law, including $35.51 billion in advance individual income tax refunds. *Source:* 2001 IRS Data Book.

The two most significant results of the test were that refunds for the electronically filed returns were issued more quickly and the tax processing error rate was significantly lower when compared to paper returns. Electronic filing of individual income tax returns with refunds became an operational program in selected areas for the 1987 processing year.

## Auditing Tax Returns

Most taxpayers' contacts with the IRS arise through the auditing of their tax returns. The Service has been empowered by Congress to inquire about all persons who may be liable for any tax and to obtain for review the books and/or records pertinent to those taxpayers' returns.

In 2002 the IRS announced a new auditing policy that will concentrate less on wage earners—particularly those earning less than $100,000, and instead focus more closely on the very wealthy and business owners, as well as on complex business partnerships, tax shelters, and offshore accounts. The revised strategy will take about two years to fully implement. A computer program will help to determine which returns have the potential for hidden or unreported income and thus merit an audit.

## The Appeals Process

Taxpayers who, after audit of their tax returns, disagree with a proposed change in their tax liabilities are entitled to an independent review of their cases. Taxpayers are able to seek an immediate, informal appeal with the Appeals Office. If, however, the dispute arises from a field audit and the amount in question exceeds $10,000, a taxpayer must submit a written protest. Alternatively, the taxpayer can wait for the examiner's report and then request consideration by the Appeals Office and file a protest if necessary. Taxpayers may represent themselves or be represented by an attorney, accountant, or any other adviser authorized to practice before the IRS. Taxpayers can forgo their right to the above process and await receipt of a deficiency notice. At this juncture, taxpayers can either (1) not pay the deficiency and petition the Tax Court by a required deadline or (2) pay the deficiency and file a claim for refund with the District Director's office. If the claim is not allowed, a suit for refund may be brought either in the District Court or the Claims Court.

## Percentages of Income Earned and Federal Individual Income Taxes Paid

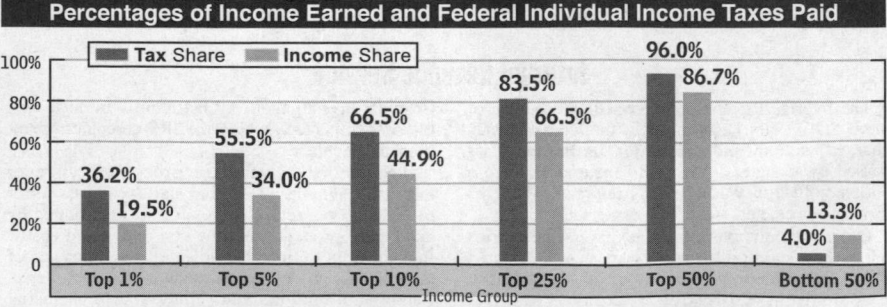

NOTE: Figures for 1999. *Source:* Tax Foundation, Special Report, No. 109, Feb. 2002. Web: http://taxfoundation.org.

# Federal Individual Income Tax

## Tax Brackets—2002 Taxable Income

| Joint return | Single taxpayer | Rate |
|---|---|---|
| $0–$12,000 | $0–$6,000 | 10.0% |
| 12,000–46,700 | 6,000–27,950 | 15.0 |
| 46,700–112,850 | 27,950–67,700 | 27.0 |
| 112,850–171,950 | 67,700–141,250 | 30.0 |
| 171,950–307,050 | 141,250–307,050 | 35.0 |
| 307,050 and up | 307,050 and up | 38.6 |

Source: Tax Foundation.

The federal individual income tax is levied on the worldwide income of U.S. citizens and resident aliens and on certain types of U.S. source income of nonresidents. For a nonitemizer, "tax table income" is adjusted gross income less $2,800 for each personal exemption and the standard deduction. If a taxpayer itemizes, tax table income is adjusted gross income minus total itemized deductions and personal exemptions. In addition, individuals may also be subject to the alternative minimum tax.

## Who Must File a Return[1]

| If your filing status is: | Age at end of 2001 | Gross income at least |
|---|---|---|
| Single | Under 65 | $7,450 |
| | 65 or older | 8,550 |
| Married filing jointly | Under 65 (both spouses) | 13,400 |
| | 65 or older (one spouse) | 14,300 |
| | 65 or older (both spouses) | 15,200 |
| Married filing separately | Any age | 2,900 |
| Head of household | Under 65 | 9,550 |
| | 65 or older | 10,650 |
| Qualifying widower | Under 65 | 10,500 |
| | 65 or older | 11,400 |

1. In 2001.

## Adjusted Gross Income

Gross income consists of wages and salaries, unemployment compensation, tips and gratuities, interest, dividends, annuities, rents and royalties, up to 85% of Social Security benefits if the recipient's income exceeds a base amount, and certain other types of income. Among the items excluded from gross income, and thus not subject to tax, are public assistance benefits and interest on exempt securities (mostly state and local bonds).

Adjusted gross income is determined by subtracting from gross income: alimony paid, penalties on early withdrawal of savings, payments to an IRA (reduced proportionally based upon adjusted gross income levels if taxpayer is an active participant in an employer maintained retirement plan), payments to a Keogh retirement plan, and self-employed health insurance payments and moving expenses.

## Itemized Deductions

Taxpayers may itemize deductions or take the standard deduction. The standard deduction amounts for 2001 were as follows: $4,550 for single persons, $6,650 for heads of household, $7,600 for married filing jointly or qualifying widower, and $3,800 for married filing separately. Taxpayers 65 and older or blind are entitled to an additional standard deduction of up to $6,750 for single persons, up to $11,200 for married persons filing jointly or qualifying widowers, up to $7,400 for married persons filing separately, and up to $8,850 for heads of households.

In itemizing deductions, the following are major items that may be deducted in 2001: state and local income and property taxes, charitable contributions, employee moving expenses, medical expenses (exceeding 7.5% of adjusted gross income), casualty losses (only the amount over the $100 floor which exceeds 10% of adjusted gross income), mortgage interest, and miscellaneous deductions (deductible only to the extent by which cumulatively they exceed 2% of adjusted gross income).

## Personal Exemptions

Personal exemptions are available to the taxpayer for himself, his spouse, and his dependents. The 2001 amount was $2,900 for each individual. No exemption is allowed to a taxpayer who can be claimed as a dependent on another taxpayer's return.

## Credits

Taxpayers can reduce their income tax liability by claiming the benefit of certain tax credits. Each dollar of tax credit offsets a dollar of tax liability. The following are a few of the available tax credits.

Certain low income households may claim an Earned Income Credit. The maximum Earned Income Credit for 2001 was $364 for taxpayers with no qualifying children, $2,428 for taxpayers with one qualifying child, $4,008 for taxpayers with two or more qualifying children. The maximum credit is reduced if earned income or adjusted gross income exceeds $13,100 for taxpayers with one or more children, or exceeds $5,950 for taxpayers with no children. For families with no qualifying children, the credit is zero if earned income or adjusted gross income exceeds $10,710; for families with one qualifying child, the credit is zero if earned income or adjusted gross income exceeds $28,281; and for taxpayers with two or more qualifying children, the credit is zero if earned income or adjusted gross income exceeds $32,121. The earned income credit is a refundable credit.

A credit for Child and Dependent Care Expenses is available for amounts paid to care for a qualifying child or other dependent so that the taxpayer can work or look for work. The credit is up to 30% (depending on adjusted gross income) of up to $2,400 of employment-related expenses for one qualifying child or dependent and up to $4,800 of employment-related expenses for two qualifying individuals.

## Number of Individual Income Tax Returns Filed Electronically

| Year | Number of returns (in thousands) | Percentage increase |
|---|---|---|
| 1995 | 11,807 | n.a. |
| 1996 | 14,968 | 26.8% |
| 1997 | 19,136 | 27.8 |
| 1998 | 24,580 | 28.4 |
| 1999 | 29,349 | 19.4 |
| 2000 | 35,394 | 20.6 |
| 2001 | 40,245 | 13.7 |

Source: 2001 IRS Data Book.

## State Taxes on Individuals

### (as of Dec. 31, 2001)

| State | Sales/use tax (percent)[1] | Income tax (percent)[2] | State | Sales/use tax (percent)[1] | Income tax (percent)[2] |
|---|---|---|---|---|---|
| Alabama | 4 | 2.0 – 5.0 | Nebraska | 5 | 2.51 – 6.68 |
| Alaska | none | none | Nevada | 6.5 | none |
| Arizona | 5 | 2.87 – 5.04 | New Hampshire | none | [5] |
| Arkansas | 5.125 | 1.0 – 7.0[3] | New Jersey | 6 | 1.4 – 6.37 |
| California | 6 | 1.0 – 9.3[3] | New Mexico | 5 | 1.7 – 8.2 |
| Colorado | 2.9 | 4.63 | New York | 4 | 4.0 – 6.85 |
| Connecticut | 6 | 3.0 – 4.5 | North Carolina | 4 | 6.0 – 8.75 |
| Delaware | none | 2.2 – 5.95 | North Dakota | 5 | 2.1 – 5.54 |
| Florida | 6 | none | Ohio | 5 | 0.743 – 7.5 |
| Georgia | 4 | 1.0 – 6.0 | Oklahoma | 4.5 | 0.5 – 6.75 |
| Hawaii | 4 | 1.5 – 8.5 | Oregon | none | 5.0 – 9.0 |
| Idaho | 5 | 1.6 – 7.8 | Pennsylvania | 6 | 2.8 |
| Illinois | 6.25 | 3.0 | Rhode Island | 7 | 26.0[6] |
| Indiana | 5 | 3.4 | South Carolina | 5 | 2.5 – 7.0 |
| Iowa | 5 | 0.36 – 8.98 | South Dakota | 4 | none |
| Kansas | 4.9 | 3.5 – 6.45 | Tennessee | 6 | [5] |
| Kentucky | 6 | 2.0 – 6.0 | Texas | 6.25 | none |
| Louisiana | 4 | 2.0 – 6.0 | Utah | 4.75 | 2.3 – 7.0 |
| Maine | 5 | 2.0 – 8.5 | Vermont | 5 | 24.0[6] |
| Maryland | 5 | 2.0 – 4.85 | Virginia | 3.5 | 2.0 – 5.75 |
| Massachusetts | 5 | 5.6 or 12.0[4] | Washington | 6.5 | none |
| Michigan | 6 | 4.2 | West Virginia | 6 | 3.0 – 6.5 |
| Minnesota | 6.5 | 5.35 – 7.85 | Wisconsin | 5 | 4.6 – 6.75 |
| Mississippi | 7 | 3.0 – 5.0 | Wyoming | 4 | none |
| Missouri | 4.225 | 1.5 – 6.0 | District of Columbia | 5.75 | 5.0 – 9.3 |
| Montana | none | 2.0 – 11.0 | | | |

1. Local and county taxes, if any, are additional. 2. Tax rate for individuals; unless otherwise noted, range denotes progressive structure; higher income pays higher rate. 3. Indexed for inflation. 4. 12% rate applies to short-term capital gains, long- and short-term capital gains on collectibles and pre-1996 installment sales classified as capital gain income. 5. State income tax is limited to dividends and interest. 6. Percentage of federal tax liability. *Source:* The Federation of Tax Administrators.

The elderly and those under 65 who are retired under total disability may be entitled to a credit of up to $750 (if single) or $1,125 (if married and filing jointly). No credit is available if the taxpayer is single and has adjusted gross income of $17,500 or more. Similarly, the credit is unavailable to a married couple filing jointly if their adjusted gross income exceeds $25,000.

Effective for tax years beginning after Dec. 1, 1997, taxpayers who have qualifying children for whom the taxpayer may claim a dependency exemption and who are less than 17 years old as of the close of the tax year are entitled to the child tax credit. The amount of the credit for 2000 was $500. The child credit begins to phase out when AGI reaches $110,000 for joint filers and $75,000 for singles. Taxpayers who have three or more qualifying children may also be entitled to an additional credit.

# Federal Estate and Gift Taxes

A Federal Estate Tax Return must generally be filed for the estate of every U.S. citizen or resident whose gross estate, taxable gifts, and specific exemptions exceed $1,000,000 for decedents dying in 2002, and according to the following table if dying in succeeding years:

| Decedent dying in | Exclusion amount |
|---|---|
| 2003 | $1,000,000 |
| 2004 and 2005 | 1,500,000 |
| 2006, 2007, and 2008 | 2,000,000 |
| 2009 | 3,500,000 |

A unified credit of $202,050 is available to offset both estate and gift taxes. Any part of the credit used to offset gift taxes is not available to offset estate taxes. As a result, although they are still taxable as gifts, lifetime taxable transfers no longer cushion the impact of progressive estate tax rates. Lifetime transfers and transfers made at death are combined for estate tax rate purposes.

Gift taxes are computed by applying the uniform rate schedule to lifetime taxable transfers (after deducting the unified credit) and subtracting the taxes payable for prior taxable periods. In general, estate taxes are computed by applying the uniform rate schedule to cumulative transfers and subtracting the gift taxes paid. An appropriate adjustment is made for taxes on lifetime transfers—such as certain gifts within three years of death—in a decedent's estate.

Among the deductions allowed in computing the amount of the estate subject to tax are funeral expenses, administrative costs, claims and bequests to religious, charitable, and fraternal organizations or government welfare agencies, and state inheritance taxes.

For 2002, an annual gift tax exclusion is provided that permits tax-free gifts to each donee of $11,000 for each year. A husband and wife who agree to treat gifts to third persons as joint gifts can exclude up to $22,000 a year to each donee. An unlimited exclusion for medical expenses and school tuition both paid directly to the institution for the benefit of any donee is also available in addition to the annual gift tax exclusion.

# Federal Corporation Taxes

Corporations are taxed under a graduated tax rate structure. If a corporation has taxable income in excess of $100,000, the amount of tax shall be increased by the lesser of 5% of such excess or $11,750. When a corporation has taxable income in excess of $15,000,000, the amount of tax shall be increased by an additional amount equal to the lesser of 3% of such excess or $100,000.

If the corporation qualifies, it may elect to be an S corporation. If it makes this election, the corporation will not (with certain exceptions) pay corporate tax on its income. Its income is instead passed through and taxed to its shareholders. There are sev-

eral requirements a corporation must meet to qualify as an S corporation, including having 75 or fewer shareholders and having only one class of stock.

## Corporate Tax Rates

| Taxable income | Tax rate |
|---|---|
| $0–$50,000 | 15% |
| $50,001–$75,000 | 25% |
| $75,001–$10,000,000 | 34% |
| $10,000,001 and up | 35% |

# State Corporation Income and Franchise Taxes

All states except Texas, Nevada, South Dakota, Washington, and Wyoming impose a tax on corporation net income. The majority of states impose the tax at flat rates ranging from 2.3% to approximately 10.75%. Several states have adopted a graduated basis of rates for corporations.

Nearly all states follow the federal law in defining net income. However, many states provide for varying exclusions and adjustments.

A state is empowered to tax all of the net income of its domestic corporations. With regard to non-

resident corporations, however, it may only tax the net income on business carried on within its boundaries. Corporations are, therefore, required to apportion their incomes among the states where they do business, and pay a tax to each of these states. Nearly all states provide an apportionment to their domestic corporations, too, in order that they not be unduly burdened. Several states tax unincorporated businesses separately.

## Federal Expenditures for Every Dollar of Taxes Sent to Washington

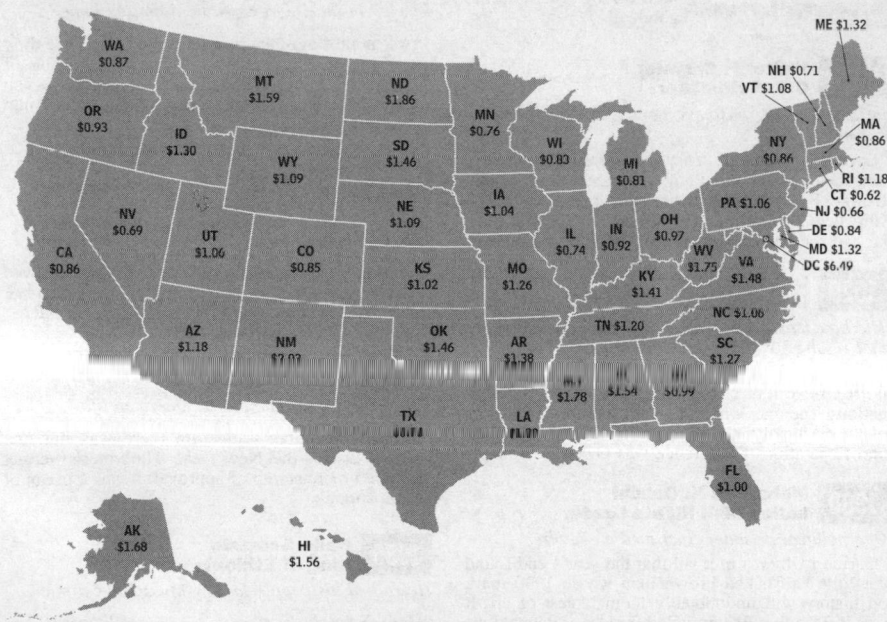

NOTE: For fiscal year 2000. *Source:* Tax Foundation. Web: http://taxfoundation.org/pr-fedtaxspendingratio.html.

# Seventy-Five Years of Great People

When the editors of TIME named Rudolph Giuliani the Person of the Year 2001 for his leadership after the tragic events of Sept. 11, the mayor of New York City became the 75th recipient of this annual designation. It was in 1927 that TIME's editors named pioneering aviator Charles Lindbergh as the magazine's first Man of the Year.

The Person of the Year program reflects TIME's emphasis on the power of individuals to shape history. The designation is not necessarily an honor, for it is bestowed on the person "who has done the most to influence the events of the year—for better or for worse, for good or for ill." Indeed, such villains of history as Adolf Hitler, Joseph Stalin, and Ayatollah Khomeini have been named Man of the Year, alongside such heroes as Mohandas Gandhi, Martin Luther King Jr., and Winston Churchill. At the end of the millennium, TIME's editors named Albert Einstein the Person of the Century; the two runners-up were Franklin D. Roosevelt and Mohandas Gandhi.

### 1927 Charles Lindbergh
#### U.S. Aviator

*His solo Atlantic crossing thrilled the world.*

"Height: 6 ft. 2 in. Age: 25. Characteristics: modesty, taciturnity, diffidence (women make him blush), singleness of purpose, courage, occasional curtness. To date he has flown to France, Belgium, England, Mexico, and Canada in the interests (his) of aviation progress and the interests (governmental) of international goodwill."

### 1928 Walter P. Chrysler
#### U.S. Automaker

*In an age of big business, he was the dominant businessman.*

"Last July, Walter P. Chrysler offered the public a new auto called the Plymouth. Later that month, Dodge Bros. turned over their business to the Chrysler Corp. From a motor man with one product, he had become one of the chief U.S. industrialists."

### 1929 Owen D. Young
#### U.S. Diplomat

*The broadcasting executive chaired the conference that resolved World War I reparations.*

"One man could and did perform the year's largest politico-economic job for the world's leading nations. The man who spent four months as foreman of the financial wrecking crew which was the Second Reparations Conference was Owen D. Young."

### 1930 Mohandas K. Gandhi
#### Indian Civil Rights Leader

*One political prisoner frustrated an empire.*

"Curiously, it was in a jail that the year's end found the little half-naked brown man whose 1930 mark on history will undoubtedly loom largest of all. It was in May that Britain jailed Gandhi at Poona. Last week he was still there, and some 30,000 members of his Independence movement were caged elsewhere. The British Empire was still wondering fearfully what to do about them."

### 1931 Pierre Laval
#### Premier of France

*He brought new direction to his nation.*

"He took a strong line against the customs union proposed by Germany and Austria, re-examined French policy in Indochina and showed his tough mettle by holding off Herbert Hoover's One-Year Moratorium on war reparations single-handed."

### 1932 Franklin D. Roosevelt
#### U.S. President

*Elected in the Depression, he promised hope.*

"Two months ago, the people of the U.S. chose their own Man of the Year. To millions and millions of 'Forgotten Men' he was a big-jawed, happy Messiah whose 'New Deal' would somehow put money into everybody's pocket."

### 1933 Hugh S. Johnson
#### U.S. Official

*His National Recovery Administration remade the U.S. economy.*

"Johnson's scowl, his broad mouth and furrowed brow, his pithy epithets, made acres of newspictures, miles of new copy every 24 hours. He *was* NRA."

### 1934 Franklin D. Roosevelt
#### U.S. President

*FDR's New Deal dominated American life.*

"In last November's election there was but one national issue—the New Deal. The voter's verdict was not a mere stamp of approval. It was a paean of acclamation."

### 1935 Haile Selassie
#### King of Ethiopia

*He rallied his people to defy Mussolini's armies.*

"Haile Selassie has created a general, warm, and blind sympathy for uncivilized Ethiopia throughout civilized Christendom."

### 1936 Mrs. Wallis Warfield Simpson
Socialite

*Britain's king abdicated his throne to marry her.*

"Mrs. Simpson was first in the news, first in the heart of Edward VIII, first in that historic British crisis—moral, emotional, political, religious—which aroused all civilization."

### 1937 Gen. and Mme. Chiang Kai-shek
Chinese Leaders

*The husband-and-wife team united China.*

"Every headline reader knows that in 1937 the Japanese War Machine was halted at Shanghai for 13 long weeks, its timetable shattered by the first Chinese War Machine worthy of the name which the modern world had ever seen."

### 1938 Adolf Hitler
German Führer

*He won Czechoslovakia in exchange for "peace for our time."*

"What Adolf Hitler and Co. did to the Germans left civilized men and women aghast. Civil rights and liberties have disappeared. Germany's 700,000 Jews have been tortured physically, robbed of homes and properties, denied a chance to earn a living, chased off the streets."

### 1939 Joseph Stalin
Leader of the U.S.S.R.

*His cynical pact with Hitler sparked World War II.*

"The Man of 1939 gained large slices of territory, but he also paid a big price. By becoming a partner of Adolf Hitler in aggression, Joseph Stalin matched himself with Hitler as the world's most hated man."

### 1940 Winston Churchill
Prime Minister of Britain

*He rallied besieged Britain against Germany.*

"He gave his countrymen exactly what he promised them—blood, toil, tears, sweat—and one thing more: untold courage. It was the last that counted."

### 1941 Franklin D. Roosevelt
U.S. President

*Pearl Harbor made FDR a wartime leader.*

"The intensity of his feeling for what America can be and therefore will be awakened the country to master its creeping paralysis in the Depression. On a far greater scale, for a far greater cause, those same qualities were called into play when the Japanese descended on Pearl Harbor."

### 1942 Joseph Stalin
Leader of the U.S.S.R.

*Betrayed by Hitler, he staved off German armies.*

"Only Joseph Stalin fully knew how close Russia stood to defeat in 1942, and only Joseph Stalin fully knew how he brought Russia through. Adolf Hitler found his past accomplishments turning into dust."

### 1943 George C. Marshall
U.S. General

*He built the greatest army in U.S. history.*

"In the year 1943 the Allies started to break the Axis. The cause was plain: the U.S. had actualized her strength. The man who, more than any other, could be said to have armed the Republic was George Catlett Marshall, Chief of Staff."

### 1944 Dwight D. Eisenhower
U.S. General

*He oversaw the Allied invasion of Normandy.*

"The invasion was the greatest gamble, the most complex operation in the history of war. The design of it was the product of hundreds of brains. The responsibility of it fell on the shoulders of one man—Dwight David Eisenhower."

### 1945 Harry Truman
U.S. President

*He decided to drop the atom bomb.*

"It was no scientist who, by historic accident, became more than any other man responsible for the bomb, its use in 1945 and in the future. It was an ordinary, incurious man without any pretensions to scientific knowledge, without many pretensions of any kind."

### 1946 James Byrnes
U.S. Diplomat

*He served on the front lines of the cold war.*

"Russia's Foreign Minister Molotov rode the postwar flood, whipping it with a hard wind of propaganda. Before the year was out, however, the Russian flood was contained. The dam's chief builder was James F. Byrnes, U.S. Secretary of State."

### 1947 George C. Marshall
U.S. Diplomat

*America's secretary of state helped save Europe.*

"On June 5, standing under the elms in Harvard Yard, George Marshall announced the beginning of the Marshall Plan. Then and there the U.S. at last set out to seize the initiative from Russia in the cold war."

### 1948 Harry Truman
U.S. President

*He won the greatest upset in U.S. history.*

"To millions of voters he seemed a simple, sincere man fighting against overwhelming odds. He was no orator. But his audiences knew just how he felt. 'Pour it on, Harry,' they cried. 'Give 'em hell!'"

## 1949 Winston Churchill
### British Statesman
### Man of the Half-Century

*He saved the West—and left his stamp on history.*

"That a free world survived in 1950, with a hope of more progress and less calamity, was due in large measure to his exertions."

## 1950 The U.S. Fighting Man
### Soldier

*He was TIME's first group Man of the Year.*

"1950's man was an American in the bitterly unwelcome role of the fighting man. It was not a role the Americans had sought. The U.S. fighting man was not civilization's crusader, but destiny's draftee."

## 1951 Mohammed Mossadegh
### Premier of Iran

*He nationalized Iran's oil industry.*

"There were millions inside and outside of Iran whom Mossadegh spoke for. They would rather see their own nations fall apart than continue their present relations with the West."

## 1952 Queen Elizabeth II
### British Monarch

*The Queen was crowned at age 26.*

"The British, as weary and discouraged as the rest of the world in 1952, saw in their new young Queen a reminder of a great past when they had carved out empires under Elizabeth I and Victoria, and dared to hope that she might be an omen of a great future."

## 1953 Konrad Adenauer
### Chancellor of West Germany

*He made West Germans face the past—and future.*

"In 1953, only eight years after the shame, horror, and impotence of defeat in mankind's bloodiest war, Germany came back. It was a world power once more."

## 1954 John Foster Dulles
### U.S. Diplomat

*The U.S. secretary of state challenged the Soviet Union.*

"Dulles pressed the Soviets with greater skill and force than any diplomat had ever shown in dealing with them. He spent 1954 in a ceaseless round of travel, reinforcing the free world's outposts."

## 1955 Harlowe Curtice
### U.S. Automaker

*In the prosperous 1950s, American pride was made in Detroit.*

"The U.S. rolled through 1955 in two-toned splendor to an all-time crest of prosperity, much of it directly attributable to the manufacture and sale of that quintessential American product, the automobile."

## 1956 The Hungarian Freedom Fighter
### Rebel

*Hungarian rebels were overwhelmed by the Russian military.*

"The Freedom Fighter's greatest triumph was moral: he demonstrated the needful truth that humanity is not necessarily forever bound and gagged by modern terrorist political techniques."

## 1957 Nikita Khrushchev
### Leader of the U.S.S.R.

*Russia's Sputnik was a huge propaganda victory.*

"Unquestionably, in the deadly give and take of the cold war, the high score for the year belongs to Russia. And unquestionably, the Man of the Year was Russia's stubby and bald, garrulous and brilliant ruler, Nikita Khrushchev."

## 1958 Charles de Gaulle
### Premier of France

*A World War II icon healed a fractured nation.*

"De Gaulle, with the support of his countrymen, has given France a new constitution, and has laid the groundwork for a fruitful new relationship between France and her one-time African colonies."

## 1959 Dwight D. Eisenhower
### U.S. President

*He traveled the world to visit America's allies.*

"In 1959, after years of hostile communist propaganda, spectacular Russian successes in space, threats of missiles and atomic war, the throngs of Europe, Asia, and Africa cast a durable vote for freedom and liberty."

## 1960 U.S. Scientists
### Seekers of Knowledge

*Science drove history in the 20th century.*

"Scientists in the U.S. and their colleagues in other free lands are the true 20th century adventurers, the real intellectuals of the day. At a time when science is at the apogee of its power for good or evil, they are the Men of the Year 1960."

## 1961 John F. Kennedy
### U.S. President

*He suffered setbacks, but also grew into his role.*

"The communist wall in Berlin caught the U.S. by surprise. Then he ordered an armored U.S. troop convoy to travel the Autobahn from West Germany through East German territory to West Berlin. For the first time Kennedy had backed up his urgent words with urgent action."

### 1962 Pope John XXIII
### Roman Catholic Pontiff

*The beloved Pope called his Church into Council, forcing change in a long-stagnant institution.*

"John set out to adapt his church's whole life and stance to the revolutionary changes in science, economics, morals, and politics that have swept the modern world: to make it, in short, more Catholic and less Roman."

### 1963 Martin Luther King, Jr.
### U.S. Civil Rights Leader

*His moral force moved millions.*

"The U.S. Negro made 1963 the year of his outcry for equality, of massive demonstrations, of sit-ins and speeches and street fighting, of soul-searching in the suburbs and psalm singing in jail cells. Martin Luther King, Jr., became to millions the symbol of that revolution."

### 1964 Lyndon B. Johnson
### U.S. President

*His Great Society electrified America.*

"He confounded the skeptics by surpassing almost all of his predecessors in first-year accomplishments. His remarkable legislative record was crowned by the historic Civil Rights Act. On Nov. 3, he won the greatest electoral victory since 1936."

### 1965 William Westmoreland
### U.S. General

*He oversaw U.S. troops in a faraway land.*

"He was the sinewy personification of the American fighting man in 1965, who served as the instrument of U.S. policy, quietly enduring the terror and discomfort of a conflict that was not yet a war, on a battlefield that was all no man's land."

### 1966 Twenty-Five and Under
### U.S. Youth

*America's restless young people demanded change.*

"No adult can or will tell the young what earlier generations were told: this is God, that is Good, this is Art that is Not Done. He has signaled his determination to live according to his own lights and rights."

### 1967 Lyndon B. Johnson
### U.S. President

*The war in Vietnam put him under siege.*

"The nation's discontent was focused upon its President. Week by week, his popularity plummeted. Rarely had the voices of dissent been raised so loud, or carried so far, or trained on so many issues."

### 1968 William Anders, Frank Borman, James Lovell
### U.S. Astronauts

*They were first to orbit the moon.*

"In the course of that first soaring escape from the planet that was no longer the world, it was the courage, grace, and cool proficiency of Borman, Lovell, and Anders that transfixed their fellow men."

### 1969 The Middle Americans
### U.S. Adults

*America's "silent majority" raised their voices.*

"No one celebrated them. Pornography, dissent, and drugs seemed to wash over them in waves, bearing some of their children away. But in 1969 they sought to reclaim their culture."

### 1970 Willy Brandt
### Chancellor of West Germany

*He engaged East Germany's communist regime.*

"Brandt has projected the most exciting and hopeful vision for Europe since the Iron Curtain crashed down. It is a daring vision, rekindling the dreams of unity that have inspired Europeans from Charlemagne to Napoleon."

### 1971 Richard Nixon
### U.S. President

*He announced he would visit China in 1972.*

"He embarked upon a dazzling round of summitry that will culminate in odysseys to Beijing and Moscow. He doggedly pursued his own slow timetable in withdrawing the nation's combat troops from their longest and most humiliating war."

### 1972 Richard Nixon & Henry Kissinger
### U.S. President and Diplomat

*Their mission to China made history.*

"It was a year of visitations and bold ventures with Russia and China, of a uniquely personal triumph at the polls for the President, of hopes raised and largely dashed for peace in Vietnam."

### 1973 John J. Sirica
### U.S. Jurist

*He proved that no American is above the law.*

"One judge, insisting that not all the panoply of the presidency entitled Nixon to withhold material evidence from the Watergate prosecutors, brought the White House tapes and documents out of hiding."

### 1974 King Faisal
### Monarch of Saudi Arabia

*Raising oil prices, he unleashed turmoil.*

"He was a principal factor in raising oil prices, and now holds more power than any other leader to lower them or raise them anew. He is also a spiritual leader of the world's 600 million Muslims."

### 1975 U.S. Women
### Civil Rights Pioneers

*American women won new freedom—and power.*

"Across the broad range of American life, women's lives are profoundly changing. In 1975 the women's drive matured beyond ideology to a new status of general—and often unconscious—acceptance."

## 1976 Jimmy Carter
### U.S. President-Elect

*A Washington outsider won the presidency.*

"When he was walking the icy streets of New Hampshire last January, as many as 40% of the voters did not even know who he was. Now, because of his impressive rise to power, James Earl Carter, Jr., is Man of the Year."

## 1977 Anwar Sadat
### President of Egypt

*He visited longtime foe Israel in quest of peace.*

"For his willingness to seize upon a fresh approach, for his display of personal and political courage, for his unshakable resolve to restore a momentum for peace in the Middle East, he is Man of the Year."

## 1978 Deng Xiaoping
### Vice Premier of China

*A 74-year-old visionary stabilized restless China.*

"Deng Xiaoping, only third in China's communist party heirarchy, is the principal architect of what has become known as the Four Modernizations—an attempt simultaneously to improve agriculture, industry, science and technology, and defense."

## 1979 Ayatollah Khomeini
### Imam of Iran

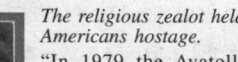

*The religious zealot held Americans hostage.*

"In 1979 the Ayatollah Ruhollah Khomeini gave the 20th century world a frightening lesson in the shattering power of irrationality, of the ease with which terrorism can be adopted as government policy. Khomeini joins a handful of other figures whose deeds are debatable—or worse—but who nonetheless branded a year as their own."

## 1980 Ronald Reagan
### U.S. President-Elect

*He sold voters on his optimistic vision of America.*

"Reagan is TIME's Man of the Year. He is also the idea of the year, his triumph being philosophical as well as personal. He has revived the Republican Party, and has garnered high initial hopes, both because of his personal style and because the U.S. is famished for cheer."

## 1981 Lech Walesa
### Polish Labor Union Leader

*He shook the Soviet hold on Eastern Europe.*

"As 1981 came to a close, the courageous little electrician from Gdansk stood out not only as the heart and soul of Poland's battle with a corrupt communist regime, but as an international symbol of the struggle for freedom and dignity."

## 1982 The Personal Computer
### Machine of the Year

*For the first time, the Person of the Year was not a person at all.*

"In 1982 a cascade of computers beeped and blipped their way into the American office, the American school, the American home. The 'information revolution' has arrived."

## 1983 Yuri Andropov & Ronald Reagan,
### Leader of the U.S.S.R. and U.S. President

*Deadlocked adversaries traded threats.*

"The deterioration of U.S.-Soviet relations to a frozen impasse overshadowed other events in 1983."

## 1984 Peter Ueberroth
### U.S. Olympics Organizer

*He reinvented the Olympics on a grand scale.*

"Despite the Soviet boycott, the Games became one of the greatest athletic spectacles in history. Ueberroth took over the stage of the global village, and he spectacularly presented the U.S. upon it."

## 1985 Deng Xiaoping
### Premier of China

*He transformed his nation for a second time.*

"Having essentially completed a transformation in the countryside, where 80% of China's masses live, Deng launched what may be the harder job of bringing change to China's cities."

## 1986 Corazon Aquino
### Philippine President

*Her "People Power" revolution ousted a hated dictator.*

"Cory Aquino, 53, stood in effect on a platform of faith, hope, and charity. Yet as all the global village looked on, President Ferdinand Marcos and his wife Imelda stumbled and fell in their ruthless campaign to extend their stolen empire."

## 1987 Mikhail Gorbachev
### Leader of the U.S.S.R.

*He unleashed change in a long-static Kremlin.*

"Gorbachev has reinvented the idea of a Soviet leader. Virtually everything about his country and its place in world affairs seems less ponderous, less opaque than it did before."

## 1988 Endangered Earth
### Planet of the Year

*Mankind's imperiled home was the year's central figure.*

"This year no single individual dominated headlines more than the clump of rock and soil and water and air that is our common home."

**1989** Mikhail Gorbachev
Leader of the U.S.S.R.
Man of the Decade

*He presided over a peaceful revolution.*

"The 1980s came to an end in what seemed like a magic act, performed on a world-historical stage. Trapdoors flew open, and whole regimes vanished. The wall that divided Berlin crumbled into souvenirs. The cold war was peacefully deconstructing before the world's eyes."

**1990** The Two George Bushes
U.S. President

*A bold leader abroad was out of touch at home.*

"He seemed almost to be two Presidents last year, turning to the world two faces. One was a foreign policy profile that was a study in resoluteness and mastery, the other a domestic visage just as strongly marked by wavering and confusion."

**1991** Ted Turner
Television News Pioneer

*His Cable News Network broadcast the bombing of Iraq—live.*

"In 1991, the very definition of news was rewritten—from something that *has happened* to something that *is happening* at the very moment you are hearing of it."

**1992** Bill Clinton
U.S. President-Elect

*A young governor promised to change America.*

"Clinton looked at very bad odds and gambled. He ran against an incumbent President whose re-election seemed, at the time, a mere technicality."

**1993** The Peacemakers:
Nelson Mandela, F.W. de Klerk,
Yitzhak Rabin, Yasir Arafat

*Four men defied history and groped toward peace.*

"The conflicts in the Middle East and South Africa were not ideological; they worked at a harder level, closer to bone and gene and skin. The struggles became prisons. The Men of the Year of 1993 did nothing more and nothing less than find a way to break out."

**1994** Pope John Paul II
Roman Catholic Pontiff

*He presided over an empire of the spirit.*

"His appearances generate an electricity unmatched by anyone else on earth. When he talks, it is not only to his flock of nearly a billion; he expects the world to listen. And the flock and the world listen, not always liking what they hear."

**1995** Newt Gingrich
Speaker of the House

*A onetime rebel shook up Congress—and America.*

"All year—ruthlessly, brilliantly, obnoxiously—he worked at hammering together inevitabilities: a balanced federal budget, for one."

**1996** Dr. David Ho
Medical Researcher

*A little-known scientist fought the scourge of AIDS.*

"Dr. David Ho is not a household name. But some people make headlines while others make history."

**1997** Andrew Grove
Physicist and Entrepreneur

*He left his fingerprints on a digital age.*

"The microchip has become the dynamo of a new economy marked by low unemployment, negligible inflation, and a rationally exuberant stock market."

**1998** Bill Clinton & Kenneth Starr
U.S. President and Independent
Counsel

*They battled over a scandal in the White House.*

"One man's loss of control inspired the other's, and we are no better for anything either of them did."

**1999** Jeff Bezos
Online Entrepreneur

*He built the Internet's biggest retail store.*

"Amazon is alive with uncounted species of insight, innovation, and intellect. Jeff Bezos has done more than construct an online mall. He's helped build the foundation of our future."

**1900–1999** Albert Einstein
Person of the Century

*His insights shaped our age.*

"The name that will prove the most enduring from our era will be that of Albert Einstein: genius, political refugee, humanitarian, locksmith of the mysteries of man and the universe."

**2000** George W. Bush
U.S. President-Elect

*He won one of the closest elections in U.S. history.*

"Lampooned as a feckless frat boy, he ran a disciplined race; he made his inexperience a virtue, his vagueness a shield, his sins a sign of sincerity."

**2001** Rudolph Giuliani
Mayor of New York City

*When the Twin Towers toppled, he was a pillar of strength*

"For having more faith in us than we had in ourselves, for being brave when required and rude where appropriate and tender without being trite, for not sleeping, not quitting, and not shrinking from the pain all around him, he is Person of the Year."

# People in the News, 2002

**Abdullah bin Abdul Aziz Saud,** crown prince of Saudi Arabia, put forward a Middle East peace initiative in February in which he proposed that Arab countries would agree to fully normalize relations with Israel if it withdrew from the West Bank, Gaza Strip, and other lands it occupied in the 1967 war. The framework, albeit vague, signaled an unprecedented willingness of the Saudi government to help solve the conflict between Palestinians and Israelis.

**Abu Nidal,** Palestinian terrorist, was found dead in Baghdad in August. Many questioned the determination that his death was a suicide when it was revealed that there were four bullet wounds in his head. Abu Nidal, an archenemy of Yasir Arafat, led the Fatah Revolutionary Council, a radical group that targeted Jews, Israel, the U.S., and England, as well as Arabs who were at all conciliatory toward Israel. He has been blamed for killing or injuring about 900 people worldwide.

**Terry Lynn Barton,** forest-service worker accused of starting the biggest wildfire in Colorado history, was arrested in July and charged with willfully and maliciously destroying U.S. property and causing personal injury. She could face up to 75 years in jail if found guilty of all charges. Barton initially told authorities she had discovered the fire and reported it. She later altered her story, saying she accidentally set it while burning a letter from her estranged husband. The fire consumed 135,000 acres.

**Lance Bass,** singer in the boy band 'N Sync, aspired to be the first celebrity in space when he began his training at the Johnson Space Center in August. He had planned to join three astronauts on a mission to the International Space Station, but his dreams were dashed when his sponsors failed to pony up the $20 million in fees for the trip.

**Ramzi bin al-Shibh,** alleged al-Qaeda member, was captured in September during a raid in Pakistan. U.S. officials said the 30-year-old from Yemen had planned to serve as the 20th hijacker in the Sept. 11 terrorist attacks but was denied a U.S. visa on four occasions. He was taken to a military base, where U.S. authorities began interrogating him, hoping to extract details about al-Qaeda and its operations.

**Robert Blake,** actor, was arrested in April and charged with murdering his wife, Bonnie Lee Bakley, who was shot in the head in a car parked outside a California restaurant in May 2001. Blake said he went back to the restaurant to retrieve a gun that had fallen out of his pocket and returned to the car to find his wife gravely injured. He was also charged with two counts of solicitation of murder and one count of conspiring with his bodyguard, Earle Caldwell. Blake and Bakley, by all accounts an unhappy couple, married after the June 2000 birth of their daughter.

**Hans Blix,** Swedish diplomat, headed the United Nations weapons inspection team that was preparing in October to return to Iraq to search the country for chemical, biological, and ballistic weapons. Blix negotiated the logistics of the mission as U.S. officials faced off with other members of the Security Council over the wording of a UN resolution.

**Martin Burnham,** missionary from Kansas, was killed in June during a fire fight in the Philippines between members of Muslim rebel group Abu Sayyaf and government troops. Filipino nurse Deborah Yap also died in the battle. Burnham's wife, Gracia, was wounded in the battle and later returned to the U.S. They had been held hostage since May 2001.

**Jimmy Carter,** former president, won the Nobel Peace Prize in October. He was cited for "his untiring effort to find peaceful solutions to international conflicts, to advance democracy and human rights, and to promote economic and social development." Another recent accomplishment was Carter's visit to Cuba in May—he became the first former or sitting U.S. president to travel there since Fidel Castro assumed power in 1959. He urged Castro to expand civil liberties and allow reform through elections. He also called on the U.S. government to lift sanctions against Cuba.

**Hugo Chávez,** firebrand president of Venezuela, was forced to resign in April after 12 people died in massive protests against his increasingly authoritarian government. However, international criticism of the coup, especially from Latin America, and an outpouring of support from Venezuela's poor, returned Chávez to power after only two days. After the coup, Chávez remained highly popular among the poor, despite the desperate state of the economy. Other Venezuelans and a good part of the military were far less enchanted with his continued rule.

**Bobby Frank Cherry,** former member of the Ku Klux Klan, was sentenced to life in prison in May after being convicted of first-degree murder in the 1963 bombing of the 16th Street Baptist Church that killed four black girls in Birmingham, Ala. The bombing is considered the most heinous crime of the civil rights era. An accomplice, Thomas Blanton, Jr., was found guilty of the same charges in 2001.

**Vincent "Buddy" Cianci,** flamboyant politician, resigned as mayor of Providence, R.I., in September after being sentenced to 64 months in prison. He was convicted of racketeering by a federal jury in June. Prosecutors alleged that Cianci ran a criminal organization from his city hall office and code-named their investigation "Operation Plunder Dome." Cianci is largely revered in Providence, credited with revitalizing the city's economy and image.

**Kelly Clarkson,** singer, was named America's newest idol in September on FOX's talent-search show, *American Idol.* In each episode, a parade of young crooners performed in front of a live audience, and viewers whittled the group down to two finalists, Clarkson and Justin Guarini. With the title, the 20-year-old Clarkson won a CD deal, a short spurt of media saturation, and fame, however fleeting.

**Herta Däubler-Gmelin,** German justice minister, outraged the Bush administration in September when she said that President Bush was focusing on a military strike against Iraq to shift attention away from domestic woes, just as Hitler did. The Bush administration said the comparison had "poisoned" relations between the two countries. Däubler-Gmelin, who said she had been misquoted, resigned her post.

**David Duncan,** former Arthur Andersen partner in charge of auditing Enron, pleaded guilty in April to obstruction of justice. He admitted to ordering the shredding of thousands of Enron-related documents in an effort to hide them from Securities and Exchange Commission investigators.

**Pim Fortuyn,** maverick right-wing Dutch politician, was assassinated in Hilversum, nine days before the May 15 general election. Fortuyn, who was openly gay and rabidly anti-immigration, headed the Lijst Pim Fortuyn party. His murder shocked the nation and rocked the normally bland political scene.

**Steve Fossett,** investment banker and adventurer, became the first person to circumnavigate the globe alone in an unmotorized balloon. The journey, which he completed in July, lasted 14 days, 19 hours. It was his sixth attempt.

**John Geoghan,** defrocked priest, was sentenced to nine to ten years in prison by a Massachusetts court following his conviction in January of indecent assault and battery for fondling a young boy in 1991. He is accused of sexually molesting about 130 children during his 30-year tenure as a priest. After Geoghan's case was made public, scores of other victims came forward throughout the country, and the Catholic church faced resounding criticism for its handling of the crisis.

**José Gusmão,** charismatic former rebel leader, won East Timor's first presidential election, held in April. An independent, he was the candidate of nine of East Timor's 16 political parties, an indication of his broad appeal. Gusmão took office on May 20, 2002, after the UN relinquished power. He became an active revolutionary in 1975, and directed an effective guerrilla war for independence. Gusmão was arrested in 1992 and imprisoned until 1999, winning release days after the East Timorese voted for independence from Indonesia.

**Steven Hatfill,** germ-weapons expert, was named a "person of interest" by justice department officials investigating the string of mail-based anthrax attacks that killed five people in 2001. FBI agents searched his Maryland home in June and again in August, reportedly finding no evidence to consider him a suspect. Hatfill accused the government of tipping off the media to the investigation and said repeated inquiries to former employers had destroyed his reputation. In September he was fired from his job as a researcher at Louisiana State University.

**Lucas Helder,** 21, college student, admitted to planting 18 pipe bombs in mailboxes in five states. Six people were injured in the attacks. It's not clear what motivated the Wisconsin college student to go on the spree, which took him to Illinois, Iowa, Nebraska, Colorado, and Texas before he was arrested near Reno, Nev., in May.

**Karen Hughes,** President Bush's director of communications, chief spokeswoman, and confidante, announced her resignation in April, saying her son and husband missed their home and friends in Texas. Hughes said she would continue to advise Bush from Austin. She has worked for Bush since 1994, when he was elected governor of Texas.

**Sarah Hughes,** 16, became the darling of the 2002 Winter Olympics when she won the overall women's skating competition in February. She beat out favorite Michelle Kwan and Russia's Irina Slutskaya. She also became the first woman to land two triple-triple jump combinations in one program. Hughes, who was in fourth place after the short program, staged a dramatic come-from-behind victory.

**Saddam Hussein,** president of Iraq, in September agreed to allow UN weapons inspectors to return to his country unconditionally after months of warnings of a preemptive military strike by the U.S. However, the defiant Hussein then reversed himself and refused to grant inspectors unfettered access to some sites, including his array of presidential palaces. As the UN Security Council wrangled over the wording of a resolution that calls for the disarmament of Iraq, Hussein continued to taunt the U.S. with his trademark bluster. "In targeting Iraq, America is acting for the Zionists who are killing the heroic people of Palestine, destroying their properties, murdering their children, and working to impose their domination on the whole world," he said in a letter to the United Nations. In October, days after he was reelected with 100% support in an election with no other candidates, Hussein granted amnesty to tens of thousands of prisoners.

**Hamid Karzai,** Afghan politician, was elected interim president in a landslide during June's *loya jirga,* or grand council, of 1,500 delegates. He'll serve until general elections in 2004. He promptly assembled a cabinet, selecting representatives from Afghanistan's many ethnic groups. Karzai's enormous popularity in the West led to the infusion of both financial assistance and troops to the war-ravaged country. However, his grasp on power within the country remains somewhat tenuous, with warlords maintaining tight regional control. He narrowly averted an assassination attempt in September.

**Alex and Derek King,** Florida teens, were convicted in September of second-degree murder in the killing of their father, Terry, who was blugeoned to death by a baseball bat in Nov. 2000. Another man, Ricky Chavis, 40, a former friend of the family, stood trial for the same murder but was acquitted. Chavis was also charged with molesting Alex and being an accessory in the murder. The judge, who heard both trials, threw out the boys' convictions in October, claiming that the prosecution's unusual tactic denied them due process and a fair trial. The judge ordered the two sides to try to work out the case in mediation.

**Marjorie Knoller,** California attorney, was convicted in March of second-degree murder in the death of Diane Whipple, 33, who was mauled to death in 2001 by a 120-pound Presa Canario dog. The conviction, however, was overturned in June when a San Francisco judge said the evidence did not justify the verdict. Knoller and her husband, Robert Noel, were caring for two Presa Canarios for Paul John Schneider, a 38-year-old inmate and white supremacist they had recently adopted. Knoller and Noel were also found guilty of involuntary manslaughter. The manslaughter verdicts were not overturned, and the pair were sentenced to four years in prison.

**Michael Kopper,** former Enron executive, admitted in August to paying kickbacks to the company's CFO, Andrew Fastow, from money he earned in running off-the-book partnerships that hid debt and led to the company's collapse. Kopper also pleaded guilty to wire fraud and money laundering and was ordered to pay the government $12 million—money that he earned in defrauding the company. Kopper's testimony was considered crucial in linking top Enron officials to the company's demise.

**L. Dennis Kozlowski,** former chief executive of Tyco International, was indicted in June on charges that he avoided more than $1 million in sales taxes on six pieces of art he purchased in 2001 for $13.1 million. He was indicted later in the month on charges of tampering with evidence in the first indictment. The charges allege that Kozlowski bought the art, including works by Monet and Renoir, for his Manhattan apartment but claimed the pieces were being sent to Tyco's New Hampshire headquarters in order to elude New York sales tax. Kozlowski was indicted a third time in September and charged with bilking the company out of $600 million in a stock-fraud scheme and using the money for personal purposes.

**Cardinal Bernard Law,** embattled archbishop of Boston, repeatedly refused to step down despite pressure from scores of Catholics, priests, and politicians amid a growing scandal involving sexual abuse by priests. The controversy began in January, when defrocked Massachusetts cleric John Geoghan was sentenced to nine to ten years in prison for sexual assault, and escalated in April with the release of hundreds of pages of documents that revealed that the archdiocese had reassigned Rev. Paul Shanley from parish to parish despite his history of sexual abuse. The scandal reached a fever pitch in late April, when the pope summoned U.S. cardinals to the Vatican for a historic meeting on the issue. In a deposition in May, Law said he had delegated most decision-making in the Geoghan case and claimed he had forgotten many of the details of the scandal.

**Amin Lawal,** Nigerian mother, was sentenced to death by stoning in March after an Islamic court convicted her of adultery. An Islamic appeals court upheld the decision in August. Lawal, 30, was arrested after giving birth more than nine months after divorcing her husband. The man she said was the father denied the charge and was acquitted of adultery. Lawal is the second Nigerian woman to be sentenced to death for adultery. The other woman, Safiya Hussaini, was acquitted on appeal.

**Kenneth Lay,** executive, resigned as chief executive and chairman of Enron, the beleaguered energy trading company that filed for bankruptcy in Dec. 2001. It was the largest such claim in U.S. history, resulting in the loss of about 5,000 jobs and leaving thousands of people financially ruined. Enron's downfall uncovered a flurry of scandals, including questionable accounting practices by Enron to hide losses and massive document-shredding by both Enron and its auditor, Arthur Andersen.

**Jean-Marie Le Pen,** far-right French politician, shocked the world in April with his second-place finish in the first round of France's presidential election. He took 17% of the vote, eliminating Lionel Jospin, the Socialist prime minister, who tallied 16%. Jospin, stunned by the result, announced that he was retiring from politics and threw his support behind incumbent President Jacques Chirac, who led the group of 16 candidates with 20% of the vote. Chirac won the final round in a landslide. Le Pen's party, the right-wing, anti-immigrant National Front party, failed to win any seats in parliament.

**David Letterman,** late-night talk-show host, flirted with taking his *Late Show* from CBS to ABC. In attempting to lure Letterman to its network, ABC, which is owned by the Walt Disney Company, considered displacing Ted Koppel's highly respected news show, *Nightline.* The move outraged the staff of ABC News, who claimed the network was placing profit over programming. Letterman announced in March that he would remain with CBS, where he makes an estimated $30 million a year hosting the show.

**John Walker Lindh,** 20, American Taliban soldier, reached a deal with U.S. prosecutors in July in which he avoided a life sentence by pleading guilty to serving in the Taliban's army. In exchange, the government dropped the charge that he conspired to kill U.S. citizens. Lindh was taken into custody in Nov. 2001, after a Taliban uprising at a prison compound in Mazar-e-Sharif. The U.S.'s first casualty, CIA officer Johnny Mike Spann, was killed during the revolt. Born in California's Marin County, Lindh traveled to Yemen and Pakistan to study Islam and Arabic, joined the Taliban, and trained at al-Qaeda terrorist camps in Afghanistan.

**Ray Marsh,** crematory operator, was arrested in February after investigators discovered several hundred rotting corpses on the grounds of the Tri-State Crematory in Noble, Ga. The crematory's furnace was not functioning for possibly up to ten years, yet the owners continued to accept bodies for cremation, sending families powdered cement and other substances instead of human remains. Marsh was charged with 16 felony counts of theft by fraud.

**Emma McLaughlin and Nicola Kraus,** writers, became instant celebrities with the March publication of their best-selling *The Nanny Diaries,* a novel about a babysitter who tends to Grayer, the four-year-old son of an outrageously wealthy and self-absorbed couple. McLaughlin and Kraus, who both had worked as nannies on Manhattan's Upper East Side, insisted that the book is a work of fiction.

**Slobodan Milosevic,** former president of Yugoslavia, began his trial at The Hague in February on charges of war crimes and crimes against humanity in Bosnia, Croatia, and Kosovo, as well as for committing genocide in Bosnia. He is the first head of state to face an international war-crimes court. Milosevic was diagnosed with severe heart disease and high blood pressure in July. The diagnosis will likely prolong the trial, which had been predicted to last for two years.

**Zacarias Moussaoui,** suspected terrorist and al-Qaeda member, pleaded guilty in federal court in July to six counts of conspiracy, but withdrew his plea after Judge Leonie Brinkema explained to him that he could not enter such a plea and deny playing a role in the Sept. 11 attacks. Officials believe that Moussaoui, the first person to be indicted on charges relating directly to the Sept. 11 attacks, had planned to participate in the hijackings. His attempts were thwarted by an Aug. 2001 arrest in Minnesota on immigration charges.

**Robert Mueller,** director of the FBI, acknowledged in May that the Sept. 11 terrorist attacks might have been forestalled had bureau headquarters followed through on tips from several field offices. He also outlined a reorganization plan that will have the bureau focus on counterterrorism rather than domestic crimes. His acknowledgement followed the publication of agent Coleen Rowley's "bombshell memo" that criticized the bureau's handling of information generated by field offices.

**Robert Mugabe,** president of Zimbabwe, in August ordered nearly 3,000 white commercial farmers to leave their land without compensation. Many of the farmers defied the order, and Mugabe threatened the farmers with arrest if they failed to comply. The land redistribution policy was denounced by the international community for contributing to food and economic crises.

**Pervez Musharraf,** president of Pakistan, proved to be an invaluable ally of the United States in its war on terrorism. But he faced bitter criticism at home, where a percentage of the population considers his pro-American stance collaborationist and a betrayal of Islam. Attacks by Islamic militants on Western and Christian sites increased after Musharraf began cozying up with the U.S. In April voters overwhelmingly approved a referendum to extend Musharraf's presidency for another five years. The vote, however, outraged opposing political parties and human rights groups that said the process was rigged. In August he made sweeping changes to the constitution that allow him to dissolve parliament and appoint supreme court justices and military leaders. In June Musharraf halted the infiltration of Muslim militants and weapons into India-controlled Kashmir—an attempt to thwart a nuclear confrontation with India.

**Rosie O'Donnell,** beleaguered celebrity, ended her acrimonious relationship in September with Gruner & Jahr USA, the company that copublished *Rosie.* "I cannot have my name on a magazine if I cannot be assured that it will represent my vision and ideas," she said. Gruner & Jahr countered that O'Donnell used the magazine to promote her own agenda and filed a breach of contract lawsuit against her in October. The company is seeking damages in excess of $100 million. The magazine, formerly *McCall's,* debuted in early 2001 and will shut down after the publication of the December issue. O'Donnell stepped down as host of her Emmy Award–winning eponymous talk show at the end of the 2002 season.

**Ozzy Osbourne,** aging rocker, opened his home and exposed his family to the world with the March debut of *The Osbournes,* MTV's latest reality show. The offbeat and often bizarre show became an instant hit, delivering about six million viewers a week to MTV, its largest audience in history. *The Osbournes* won an Emmy Award in September for best reality series.

**Daniel Pearl,** 38, *Wall Street Journal* foreign correspondent, was kidnapped and murdered in January in Karachi, Pakistan, where he was researching a story about alleged "shoe bomber" Richard Reid. British-born Islamic militant Ahmed Omar Sheikh, a leader of the National Movement for the Restoration of Pakistani Sovereignty, was sentenced to death in July after being convicted of kidnapping and murdering Pearl. Three others were given life sentences for their role in the slaying. DNA tests confirmed that a body found in May was indeed Pearl's.

**Pennsylvania Coal Miners** emerged in good health and spirits after enduring 77 grueling hours in a dark, flooded mine shaft 240 feet below ground in Quecreek. The nine workers—Randy Fogle, Dennis Hall, John Phillippi, Tom Foy, John Unger, Robert Pugh, Harry Mayhugh, Ron Hileman, and Mark Popernack—huddled together as millions of gallons of cold water from an adjacent mine rushed into their site, submerging them up to their necks.

**Charles Pickering, Sr.,** trial judge, was denied a promotion to a seat on the U.S. Court of Appeals for the Fifth Circuit by the Senate Judiciary Committee in March. Democrats, who hold a majority on the committee, banded together to thwart President Bush's first judicial nomination. They cited Pickering's decisions on racial issues in his 11 years as a judge in Hattiesburg, Miss., and also sought to discourage Bush from stacking courts with conservatives.

**Colin Powell,** secretary of state, emerged as the voice of moderation and multilateralism among the hawks and unilateralists in the Bush administration. As the country braced for a preemptive military strike against Iraq, Powell urged the UN Security Council to approve a resolution calling for unconditional access for weapons inspectors and the right to use force if Saddam Hussein failed to comply.

**Maria Teresa and Maria de Jesus Quiej-Alvarez,** One-year-old twins joined at the head, survived a 22-hour separation surgery in August. UCLA Medical Center doctors guardedly said they expected the Guatemalan girls to make a full recovery. More than 50 doctors and nurses participated in the marathon procedure.

**Richard Reid,** accused terrorist, said in October that he would plead guilty to eight terrorism-related charges, including attempted use of a weapon of mass destruction, attempted murder, and attempted destruction of an aircraft. He was arrested in Dec. 2001 after he tried to light a fuse extending from his shoe on an American Airlines Paris-to-Miami flight. Investigators found plastic explosives in both shoes. Reid is a British citizen who had converted to Islam and reportedly has links to al-Qaeda.

**Janet Reno,** former U.S. attorney general, lost her bid to become the governor of Florida when Bill McBride beat her in September's Democratic primary election, 44.5% to 43.9%. The vote was tainted by malfunctioning voting machines, voter disenfranchisement, and botched results, an embarrassing reminder of the 2000 presidential election debacle.

**Rebekah Revels,** beauty queen, was denied a chance to participate in September's Miss America Pageant. Revels had won the Miss North Carolina title in June but resigned after a former boyfriend notified pageant officials that he had a topless photo of her, evidence of "dishonest, immoral, and indecent behavior," which is prohibited by pageant rules. Misty Clymer, the runner-up in the state contest, thus inherited the crown. Revels changed her mind, however, and sued to regain the title. (Each state's pageant winner receives an invitation to participate in the national event.) In September a federal judge ruled that Miss America officials were not obligated to reinstate Revels as a contestant.

**John Rigas,** founder of Adelphia Communications Corp., was indicted in September on charges of bank, wire, and securities fraud. His sons, Timothy and Michael, and two other executives were also

charged. Prosecutors allege the executives hid $2.3 billion in liabilities from Adelphia investors and that the Rigases used company funds as their "personal piggy bank." The company filed for bankruptcy protection in June, after it had acknowledged that the Rigases had been given $3.1 billion in off-the-balance-sheet loans. John Rigas stepped down as CEO of the company in May.

**Coleen Rowley,** chief counsel of the FBI's Minneapolis field office, who, in a 13-page memo, outlined how FBI headquarters thwarted agents' attempts to investigate Zacarias Moussaoui, the alleged 20th hijacker. The "bombshell memo" led bureau chief Robert Mueller to reorganize the agency. She testified before the Senate Judiciary Committee in June about the FBI bureaucracy that frustrates agents' attempts at innovative investigation and mires them in paperwork.

**Yves Saint Laurent,** premier French fashion designer, announced his retirement in January, ending a 40-plus-year career as a trendsetting couturier. Saint Laurent introduced the chic beatnik look of the 1960s and popularized thigh-high boots, skin-tight trousers, and the sophisticated tweed suit.

**Jamie Salé and David Pelletier,** Canadian figure skaters, were belatedly awarded gold medals in the February Olympics after an investigation revealed the judging had been tainted. The pair delivered a flawless performance in the pairs long program but lost out to Russian skaters Yelena Berezhnaya and Anton Sikharulidze, who won the gold despite a number of errors in their presentation. After French judge Marie Reine Le Gougne admitted that she had been pressured to vote for the Russians as part of a vote-swapping arrangement, Salé and Pelletier traded in their silver medals for gold, thus sharing the top honor with Berezhnaya and Sikharulidze.

**Jonas Savimbi,** Angolan rebel leader, was killed by government soldiers in February. Savimbi won enormous loyalty in his fight for independence from Portugal, which was achieved in 1975. Hungry for power, however, he immersed the country in a brutal, protracted war against the ruling Popular Movement for the Liberation of Angola (MPLA). He dispensed with opponents as well as his own officers who challenged him, and hundreds of thousands of Angolan peasants died in the war, which was largely viewed as pointless. During the cold war, the United States and South Africa used Savimbi and his party, the CIA-funded National Union for the Total Independence of Angola (UNITA), as pawns to oust the Marxist MPLA. Six weeks after Savimbi's death, rebel leaders signed a cease-fire deal with the government, signalling the end of almost 30 years of civil war.

**Gerhard Schröder,** German politician, was reelected chancellor by a razor-thin margin in September, defeating conservative businessman Edmund Stoiber. Schröder, who early on trailed Stoiber in the polls, was buoyed in the weeks leading up to the election by his deft handling of Germany's catastrophic floods and his staunch opposition to any preemptive attack on Iraq by the United States. Schröder's Social Democrats and the Greens, headed by Foreign Minister Joschka Fischer, hung on to a majority of parliament, but only by nine seats.

**Charles Schwarz,** former New York police officer, in February had his convictions of obstructing justice and civil rights violations in the Abner Louima torture case overturned. He was granted a new trial for the charge of violating Louima's civil rights—he allegedly held down Louima while another officer sodomized him with a broken broomstick. In July, a federal jury deadlocked on the civil rights charges but convicted Schwarz of perjury. Rather than face another trial on the civil rights charges, Schwarz in September agreed to a five-year sentence for the perjury charge and prosecutors dropped the other charges. In addition, Schwarz, his lawyers, and family are barred from ever speaking publicly about the case.

**Paul Shanley,** Catholic priest, was arrested in May in San Diego and charged with three counts of child rape. He was extradited to Massachusetts, where he had served as a priest for 30 years. He was indicted in June in Massachusetts on charges of raping four children between 1979 and 1989. Documents released in April by the Boston archdiocese revealed that Shanley was a member of the North American Man-Boy Love Association and that archdiocese officials repeatedly transferred him from parish to parish, despite knowing that he was a child molester.

**Michael Skakel,** nephew of Ethel Kennedy, was found guilty in June by a Connecticut jury of the 1975 murder of Martha Moxley. Skakel was 15 when Moxley, also 15, was found bludgeoned to death outside her Greenwich, Conn., home. Skakel was sentenced to 20 years to life in prison in August.

**Lynne Stewart,** New York defense attorney, was indicted in April for allegedly helping client Omar Abdel Rahman, the Egyptian sheik convicted of planning the 1993 bombing of the World Trade Center, to pass messages to members of the Islamic Group, an Egypt-based fundamentalist terrorist organization.

**Martha Stewart,** queen of domesticity, found herself under the microscope over the summer and into the fall while being scrutinized by the Justice Department, the Securities and Exchange Commission, and a Congressional committee. The three were investigating whether she had inside information that prompted her to sell about 4,000 shares of ImClone stock. She made the trade the day before the FDA announced it had declined to review ImClone's new cancer drug—news that sent shares tumbling.

**Daw Aung San Suu Kyi,** Burmese opposition leader, was freed in May after 19 months of house arrest. In her first public speech, she promised to "make sure democracy comes to Burma." The military leader of Myanmar (formerly called Burma) said Suu Kyi would be allowed to travel freely within the country and face no restrictions on her political activities. While under house arrest in 1991, Suu Kyi won the Nobel Peace Prize for her pro-democracy efforts.

**Robert Torricelli,** U.S. senator from New Jersey, abandoned his reelection campaign in September, fearing a recent fund-raising scandal would cost him the race and Democrats control of the Senate. He was "severely admonished" by the Senate Ethics Committee in July for lapses in judgement in accepting lavish gifts from David Chang, a campaign contributor, who himself pleaded guilty in 2000 to making illegal donations to Torricelli's campaign fund.

**James Traficant,** maverick Congressman from Ohio, was sentenced to eight years in prison in July after being found guilty of bribery, racketeering, tax evasion, and obstruction of justice. In all, he was convicted on 10 federal charges. In July the U.S. House of Representatives voted, 420–1, to expel him.

**Alvaro Uribe,** lawyer, was elected president of Colombia in May. He promised to clamp down on drug traffickers and the left-wing rebel group Revolutionary Armed Forces of Colombia (FARC), which has frequently kidnapped and murdered politicians. Grenade attacks on the presidential palace and a nearby neighborhood killed at least 14 people during Uribe's inauguration in August. Officials suspected FARC guerrillas were responsible.

**Samuel Waksal,** founder of ImClone, a biotech company, pleaded guilty to six charges, including securities fraud, conspiracy, and perjury in October. The counts stem from two federal indictments that accused Waksal of tipping off family members and friends that the FDA had declined to review ImClone's new cancer drug, thus encouraging them to sell company shares before the news broke;

forged documents to secure a $44 million loan; and ordered ImClone employees to shred documents relating to a SEC investigation. He had earlier pleaded not guilty to the charges, along with seven others, for which he did not change the plea. The scandal also shed negative light on Martha Stewart, who sold nearly 4,000 shares of ImClone the day before the FDA decision was publicized.

**Sherron Watkins,** Enron vice president and whistleblower, testified before the House Energy and Commerce Committee in February about the Aug. 2001 memo she wrote to chairman Kenneth Lay, voicing concern about the company's off-the-book partnerships and questionable accounting practices. Watkins was widely hailed as a hero for exposing the level of corporate malfeasance that contributed to the collapse of the energy giant.

**John Welch, Jr.,** retired CEO, announced in September that he would pay former employer General Electric about $2.5 million a year for corporate perks, such as use of the company's jet and a luxurious Manhattan apartment, that were included in the retirement package he negotiated in 1996. The SEC is investigating the contract, which came to light in divorce papers filed by his wife, Jane Welch. GE had also been bankrolling court-side seats at several sports events, laundry services, and country club memberships. Welch retired from GE in 2001.

**David Westerfield,** California engineer, was convicted in August of kidnapping and murdering his neighbor, 7-year-old Danielle van Dam. The child was abducted from her bedroom in February while her father was sleeping and her mother was out. In September the jury recommended that Westerfield receive the death penalty.

**Kenneth Williams,** FBI agent, testified at a May Congressional hearing about a memo he wrote in July 2001, in which he had speculated that a large number of al-Qaeda members enrolled in U.S. flight schools could use their training to launch a terrorist attack on the country. FBI Director Robert Mueller didn't see the "Phoenix memo" until after the Sept. 11 attacks, and President Bush wasn't briefed on the memo until early May, prompting members of Congress to question whether the attacks could have been prevented.

**Serena and Venus Williams,** power-house professional tennis players, continued to dominate the courts throughout 2002 and propelled women's professional tennis to prime-time status. Serena won three consecutive Grand Slam tournaments: the French Open in June, Wimbledon in July—for the third straight time, and the U.S. Open in September, earning herself a No. 1 ranking. It hasn't been a bad year for Venus, either. She's ranked No. 2, and made it to the finals in three of the year's four Grand Slam events. She placed No. 2, behind little sister Serena, in the U.S. and French Opens.

**Oprah Winfrey,** media queen, sent shockwaves through the publishing industry with her April announcement that she would no longer regularly recommend books on her *Oprah Winfrey Show*. Nearly 50 titles have been featured since Oprah's Book Club debuted in 1996, and every one of them has rocketed up the bestseller lists. Many of the titles have featured women overcoming obstacles and dysfunction. "It has become harder and harder to find books on a monthly basis that I feel absolutely compelled to share," she said.

**Abu Zubaydah,** al-Qaeda chief of operations and top recruiter, was captured by Pakistani police forces during a bold raid in Faisalabad in March. Under intense interrogation by U.S. intelligence officials, the Saudi-born Palestinian revealed details of al-Qaeda plots against U.S. landmarks. Zubaydah was the third-highest-ranking al-Qaeda member.

# 2002 Deaths

(through October 24, 2002)

**Stephen Ambrose,** 66: military historian and writer who prolifically produced best-selling, authoritative war chronicles and biographies. His books, which focused mostly on World War II, include *D-Day, June 6, 1944: The Climactic Battle of World War II* and *Citizen Solders.* HBO's highly acclaimed miniseries *Band of Brothers,* which won an Emmy Award in September, was based on his 1992 book. In early 2002 Ambrose faced criticism for using passages in his works that closely resembled those that had appeared in other sources. Oct. 13, 2002

**Walter Annenberg,** 94: publisher, philanthropist, and art collector who presided over media empire Triangle Publications from 1942, when he inherited it from his father, until 1988, when he sold the business to Rupert Murdoch for $3.2 billion. Triangle published the *Philadelphia Inquirer* and *TV Guide* and owned several radio and TV stations. A loyal Republican, he served as ambassador to Britain under President Nixon. His art collection, valued at more than $1 billion, included works by Monet, Renoir, van Gogh, Manet, Picasso, and Rodin. Oct. 1, 2002

**Kenneth Armitage,** 85: British sculptor known for his offbeat, semi-abstract bronze figures. Jan. 22, 2002

**Joaquín Balaguer,** 95: lawyer who served as president of the Dominican Republic for 22 years—six terms—between 1960 and 1996. July 14, 2002

**David W. Barry,** 58: scientist who codiscovered AZT, the antiviral drug that is considered the first effective treatment for AIDS. Jan. 28, 2002

**Mildred Benson,** 96: author, under the name Carolyn Keene, of 23 of the first 30 Nancy Drew mystery novels. She wrote the books, churning out as many as 13 a year, as a side job while working as a newspaper reporter. May 28, 2002

**Milton Berle,** 93: Emmy Award-winning actor who began his career as a vaudeville performer before moving on to radio. He made his mark in television, however, starring in *Texaco Star Theater.* Berle's broad appeal helped spark the popularity of television and earned him the nickname "Mr. Television." His film credits include *It's a Mad Mad Mad Mad World, Always Leave Them Laughing,* and *Broadway Danny Rose.* March 27, 2002

**Theresa Bernstein,** 111?: painter of the Ash Can school and one of the first women to paint in the Realist style. She was known for her urban landscapes. Feb. 12, 2002

**Abdullah bin Laden,** 75: patriarch of the wealthy Saudi family and uncle of suspected terrorist Osama bin Laden. The family broke all ties with Osama in 1994, and Abdullah condemned the Sept. 11 attacks on the U.S. He headed the Saudi Binladin Group, a company that included construction, mining, and telecommunications interests. March 21, 2002

**Prince Ahmed bin Salman,** 43: businessman and nephew of Saudi Arabia's King Fahd. A publishing magnate, bin Salman also owned War Emblem, the horse that won 2002's Kentucky Derby and Preakness Stakes. He died of a heart attack. His cousin, Prince Sultan bin Faisal, died in a car accident on the way to bin Salman's funeral. July 22, 2002

**Otis Blackwell,** 70: songwriter who penned hits that were made famous by Elvis ("Don't Be Cruel"), Jerry Lee Lewis ("Great Balls of Fire"), and James Taylor ("Handy Man"). May 6, 2002

**James Blackwood,** 82: gospel musician who was a founding member of the Blackwood Brothers Quartet. He recorded 200 albums and won nine Grammy Awards. Feb. 3, 2002

**Bill Blass,** 79: fashion designer known for his classic yet elegant designs favored by Nancy Reagan, Brooke Astor, and Jessye Norman. He was also an adept marketer, putting his name on products ranging from chocolates to perfume to Lincoln Continentals. June 12, 2002

**Nils Bohlin,** 82: engineer who invented the three-point seat belt in the late 1950s as Volvo's chief safety engineer. He was inducted into the National Inventors Hall of Fame on the day he died. Sept. 21, 2002

**Joe Bonanno,** 97: Sicilian-born Mafia don of one of New York's original five crime families. May 11, 2002

**Linda Boreman,** 53: former porn star who, under the name Linda Lovelace, starred in 1972's classic adult film *Deep Throat,* which has earned about $600 million. April 22, 2002

**Robert Borkenstein,** 89: scientist who invented the Breathalyzer, which provided prosecutors with concrete evidence of intoxication. Aug. 10, 2002

**Claude Brown,** 64: writer who vividly chronicled his experiences growing up poor in Harlem alongside drug dealers, murderers, and prostitutes in his 1965 bestseller *Manchild in the Promised Land.* The book reached a wide audience and exposed the masses to inner-city black culture. Feb. 2, 2002

**J. Carter Brown,** 67: director of Washington, DC's National Gallery of Art who helped to transform the museum into a venue for blockbuster exhibits, such as King Tut and Andrew Wyeth's "Helga" nudes. June 17, 2002

**Norman O. Brown,** 89: philosopher and critic who analyzed history, drawing on theories by such disparate figures as Freud and Marx, to produce scholarly and often mystical works that appealed to members of the 1960s counterculture. His books include *Closing Time* and *Life Against Death.* Oct. 2, 2002

**Charles Burton,** 59: British explorer who was a member of the first pole-to-pole expedition. The group completed the 52,000-mile trip in two-and-a-half years. July 15, 2002

**Howard Cannon,** 90: World War II pilot and Democratic politician who served four terms as a U.S. senator from Nevada. He lost his 1982 bid for reelection after Teamster officials were convicted of offering him a bribe. Cannon was never indicted in the scandal. March 8, 2002

**Camilo José Cela,** 85: Spanish writer who won the 1989 Nobel Prize in Literature and Spain's highest literary honor, the Cervantes Prize, in 1995. He's best known for his first book, *The Family of Pascual Duarte,* an example of his raw, intense, and experimental style. Jan. 17, 2002

**Rosemary Clooney,** 74: deep-voiced singer and actress who was one of the country's premier jazz and pop singers of the 1950s and '60s. Her hits include "Come on-a My House" and "Mambo Italiano." Her films include *White Christmas* and *Here Come the Girls.* Clooney won a lifetime achievement Grammy Award in 2002. June 29, 2002

**Elizabeth Coblentz,** 66: syndicated columnist who handwrote her homespun prose from her Missouri home deep in Amish country. Her column, which appeared in 105 newspapers and primarily covered food and recipes, provided a peek into the traditional and austere Amish lifestyle. Sept. 17, 2002

**Ray Conniff,** 85: Grammy Award–winning composer, bandleader, and trombonist whose recordings defined the lounge-singing style of the 1950s and 1960s. He produced 25 Top 40 albums. His recordings include "Somewhere My Love" and "'S' Wonderful." Oct. 12, 2002

**George Cooper,** 85: naval officer who was a member of the Golden 13, the first group of black U.S. Navy officers to earn their commissions. May 20, 2002

**Jeff Corey,** 88: versatile character actor who, after being blacklisted in the 1950s for refusing to cooperate with the House Committee on Un-American Activities, emerged as one of Hollywood's most desired acting coaches. August 16, 2002

**Norman Davidson,** 85: scientist whose work in molecular biology paved the way for the mapping of the human genome. He won the National Medal of Science in 1996. Feb. 14, 2002

**Benjamin Davis, Jr.,** 89: the first black U.S. Air Force general, who, during World War II, led the Tuskegee Airmen, the pioneering group of all-black fighter pilots. The success of the Airmen led to the integration of the military. Davis graduated from West Point in 1936, the first black cadet to do so in the 20th century. His father was the U.S. Army's first black general. July 4, 2002

**Jan de Hartog,** 88: Dutch writer whose play *The Fourposter* won the 1952 Tony Award for Best Play. He frequently wrote about fleeing from the Nazis during World War II and about his exploits at sea as a young man. Sept. 22, 2002

**Ted Demme,** 38: director who helmed the films *Beautiful Girls* and *Blow.* He died while playing in a celebrity basketball game. He was the nephew of director Jonathan Demme. Jan. 13, 2002

**Niki de Saint Phalle,** 71: French-born artist and feminist known for her *nanas* sculptures, papier-mâché figures of enormous, voluptuous women. One of the Nouveaux Réalistes of the early 1960s, de Saint Phalle also earned fame for her "shooting paintings," works created by firing a gun at her sculptures, which contained bags of paint. May 21, 2002

**Indra Devi (Eugenie Peterson),** 102: renowned yoga instructor who taught all over the world. Her students included Gloria Swanson, Greta Garbo, and Madame Chiang Kai-shek. Devi was the first female student of Sri Tirumalai Krishnamacharya. April 25, 2002

**Burton Edelson,** 75: satellite expert and NASA official who directed the Hubble Space Telescope project. He created George Washington University's Institute for Applied Space Research after he retired from NASA in 1987. Jan. 6, 2002

**Elizabeth (Elizabeth Angela Marguerite Bowes-Lyon),** 101: Queen Mother who was perhaps the most popular member of England's royal family. She became queen of England in 1936, when her husband, George VI, ascended to the throne following the abdication of his brother, Edward VIII. March 30, 2002

**John Entwistle,** 57: bassist for the Who whose disciplined demeanor onstage balanced the theatrical, often outrageous styles of bandmates Roger Daltrey, Keith Moon, and Pete Townshend. Entwistle, widely considered one of the most influential bassists of all time, died of a heart attack. June 27, 2002

**Juan García Esquivel,** 83: composer and arranger whose experimental recordings of the 1950s and '60s regained popularity during the revival of lounge music in the 1990s. His albums include *Other Worlds, Other Sounds* and *Exploring New Sounds in Stereo.* Jan. 3, 2002

**Eileen Farrell,** 82: earthy dramatic soprano who lent her rich voice to such productions as the Metropolitan Opera's *Alceste* and Carnegie Hall's *Wozzeck.* March 23, 2002

**María Félix,** 87: Mexican actress whose beauty and flamboyant personality propelled her to international fame and icon status. Her credits include *Woman Without a Soul* and *La Generala.* April 8, 2002

**Sir Raymond Firth,** 100: British social anthropologist who was an expert on Polynesian culture, focusing on its social organization and economic systems. Feb. 22, 2002

**John Frankenheimer,** 72: acclaimed director known for his social dramas and thrillers, such as *The Birdman of Alcatraz* and *The Manchurian Candidate.* He won Emmy Awards for the cable television films *The Burning Season* and *George Wallace.* July 6, 2002

**Uzi Gal,** 79: Israeli arms expert who, in the 1950s, invented the Uzi, a 9-millimeter submachine gun. He moved to the United States in the 1970s after retiring from an Israeli weapons-manufacturing company. Sept. 7, 2002

**John W. Gardner,** 89: American public official who, as secretary of Health, Education, and Welfare under President Johnson, created Medicare. He also established Common Cause, the nonpartisan grassroots organization. Feb. 16, 2002

**Emily Genauer,** 91: Pulitzer Prize–winning art critic who promoted the works of such 20th-century artists as Marc Chagall and Diego Rivera. Aug. 23, 2002

**Cliff Gorman,** 65: explosive film, stage, and television actor who won a 1972 Tony Award for his portrayal of Lenny Bruce in the play *Lenny.* Sept. 5, 2002

**John Gotti,** 61: cocky mobster who headed the Gambino crime family from 1985 to 1992, when he was sentenced to life in prison on charges of racketeering and conspiring to commit murder. His swagger and ability to avoid prosecution earned him the nickname "Teflon Don." June 10, 2002

**Stephen Jay Gould,** 60: revered paleontologist and science writer whose theories, including punctuated equilibrium (developed with Niles Eldredge), which asserted that evolutionary change in the fossil record occurred suddenly rather than gradually, provoked heated debate and earned him a mainstream following not typical for evolutionary biologists. A Harvard professor since 1967, Gould wrote hundreds of essays and several books, including *Mismeasure of Man* and *Wonderful Life.* May 20, 2002

**Charles Guggenheim,** 78: Academy Award–winning documentary filmmaker and producer of political campaign commercials. His film credits include *The Johnstown Flood* and *Robert Kennedy Remembered.* He made commercials for Adlai Stevenson, Walter Mondale, and Ernest Hollings before he quit the profession in the mid-1980s, calling it "sick." Oct. 9, 2002

**Carrie Hamilton,** 38: actress and musician whose substance abuse as a teen led her parents, Carol Burnett and Joe Hamilton, to crusade against drugs. Hamilton appeared on the television shows *Fame* and *The X-Files.* Jan. 20, 2002

**Lionel Hampton,** 94: dynamic jazz vibraphonist whose rollicking delivery and backbeat influenced generations of jazz musicians and helped to usher in rock and roll. He also played piano and drums and frequently collaborated with Benny Goodman and Louis Armstrong. He's known for the 1942 classic "Flying Home." Aug. 31, 2002

**Ruth Handler,** 85: cofounder of Mattel and creator of the Barbie doll. The buxom doll debuted in 1959 and became an instant hit, offering girls a mature alternative to baby dolls. More than 1 billion Barbies have been sold in 150 countries. April 27, 2002

**John Harper,** 78: rector of Washington, DC's St. John's Episcopal Church who preached to eight presidents, from Kennedy to Clinton, in his 30-year career with the church. Sept. 13, 2002

**Richard Harris,** 72: versatile Irish actor who received Oscar nominations for his roles in *This Sporting Life* and *The Field.* Known for his disdain of film stars, Harris was nevertheless a prolific screen presence. His other films include *Camelot* and *Harry Potter and the Sorcerer's Stone.* Oct. 25, 2002

**Signe Hasso,** 91: Swedish-born stage and screen actress who played the obsessive wife of an actor in *A Double Life.* June 7, 2002

**Ed Headrick,** 78: toy designer who modified the Pluto Platter, a clunky flying disc, and created the modern, aerodynamic Frisbee. Aug. 12, 2002

**Thor Heyerdahl,** 87: Norwegian explorer and anthropologist who, in 1947, traveled 4,300 miles from Peru to the Tuamotu Archipelago near Tahiti in a primitive raft he called the *Kon-Tiki* to support his theory that the first Polynesian settlers were from South America. His memoir, *Kon-Tiki,* became an international bestseller, and the documentary on the epic voyage won an Oscar. April 18, 2002

**Harlan Howard,** 74: country-music composer who wrote more than 100 Top 10 hits, including "Busted" and "I Fall to Pieces." March 3, 2002

**Roy Huggins,** 87: television writer and producer responsible for such hits as *Maverick, The Fugitive,* and *The Rockford Files.* He also wrote the novel *The Doubletake.* April 3, 2002

**Kim Hunter,** 79: actress famous for her Oscar-winning role as Stella in the film and stage versions of Tennessee Williams's *A Streetcar Named Desire,* opposite Marlon Brando. She also played Dr. Zira in *Planet of the Apes.* Hunter was blacklisted in the early 1950s, but reemerged in 1956, starring opposite Bette Davis in *Storm Center.* Sept. 11, 2002

**Waylon Jennings,** 64: country musician who, with Willie Nelson, epitomized the genre's outlaw movement of the 1960s and early '70s. He recorded 60 albums and boasted 16 No. 1 hits, including "Mamas Don't Let Your Babies Grow Up to Be Cowboys" and "I'm a Ramblin' Man." Feb. 13, 2002

**Chuck Jones,** 89: animator of such classic cartoon characters as Bugs Bunny, Daffy Duck, and Elmer Fudd. Jones spent 30 of his 70 years in animation with Warner Bros., bringing to life the Looney Tunes and Merry Melodies series. He directed more than 300 films, and three of them, *For Scent-Imental Reasons, So Much for So Little,* and *The Dot and the Line,* won Oscars. Feb. 22, 2002

**Katy Jurado,** 78: Mexican actress best known in the U.S. for her roles as Gary Cooper's former mistress in *High Noon* and Spencer Tracy's wife in *Broken Lance.* July 5, 2002

**Martin Kamen,** 89: biochemist who discovered carbon-14, which is used to date archeological and anthropological artifacts and led to the understanding of carbon dioxide processes in plants and animals. He was fired from his job at the University of California at Berkeley in 1944 after being accused of leaking information about the atomic bomb to the Soviets. He eventually cleared his name and won the 1996 Enrico Fermi Award. Aug. 31, 2002

**Yousuf Karsh,** 93: photographer best known for his formal portraits of celebrities, World War II leaders, and artists. His subjects include Winston Churchill, Dwight Eisenhower, Ernest Hemingway, and Georgia O'Keeffe. July 14, 2002

**Thomas J. Kelly,** 72: engineer whose team of engineers at the Grumman Aircraft Corp. designed NASA's lunar module that landed Neil Armstrong and Edwin "Buzz" Aldrin on the moon on July 20, 1969. March 24, 2002

**Ward Kimball,** 88: animator who was one of Walt Disney's "nine old men," a group of elite artists. He cre-

ated Jiminy Cricket and was animation director on *Fantasia, Dumbo,* and *Cinderella.* His team won Oscars for the shorts *Toot, Whistle, Plunk, and Boom* and *It's Tough to Be a Bird.* July 8, 2002

**Caroline Knapp,** 42: writer and columnist whose candid best-selling memoir *Drinking: A Love Story* recounted her 20-year battle with alcoholism. She died of lung cancer. June 4, 2002

**Hildegard Knef,** 76: German actress and smoky-voiced singer who earned fame in the U.S. for her performance as a Soviet commissar in Cole Porter's *Silk Stockings.* She starred opposite Gregory Peck in *The Snows of Kilimanjaro.* February 1, 2002

**Kenneth Koch,** 77: poet, novelist, and playwright who, with John Ashbery and Frank O'Hara, created the New York school of poets in the 1950s. He wrote more than 20 volumes of poetry, and his work—witty, lyrical, and often erotic—covered topics as diverse as furniture, lipstick, and fudge. July 6, 2002

**Spyros Kyprianou,** 69: politician who served as president of Cyprus (1977–1988). March 12, 2002

**Ann Landers (Esther "Eppie" Lederer),** 83: syndicated columnist whose witty and frank advice reached about 90 million readers, the most in the world. Landers, who dispensed advice on such topics as AIDS, teen dating, and homosexuality, competed with her twin sister, Pauline, known as Dear Abby. June 22, 2002

**Peggy Lee (Norma Deloris Egstrom),** 81: jazz-pop singer, songwriter, and actress whose smooth, smoldering voice defined the genre. She performed with Benny Goodman's orchestra before setting out on a successful solo career. She earned an Oscar nomination for her role as an alcoholic singer in *Pete Kelly's Blues.* Jan. 21, 2002

**Flora Lewis,** 79: journalist and writer who covered momentous world events as a foreign correspondent for the *New York Times, Washington Post,* and other publications. June 2, 2002

**R.W.B. Lewis,** 84: biographer, literary critic, and scholar who won a Pulitzer Prize and a National Book Critics Circle Award for *Edith Wharton: A Biography.* June 13, 2002

**Astrid Lindgren,** 94: Swedish author who wrote the classic children's book *Pippi Longstocking.* Pippi, a headstrong, rude orphan who answered only to herself, caused quite a stir when she first debuted in Sweden in 1945 and the U.S. in 1950. Jan. 28, 2002

**Alan Lomax,** 87: folk-music collector, writer, and disc jockey, who, in addition to discovering Woodie Guthrie, Jelly Roll Morton, and Muddy Waters, preserved the folk tradition and inspired the folk revival in the U.S. and in Europe. July 19, 2002

**Lisa "Left Eye" Lopes,** 30: mercurial rapper and songwriter who was a member of the hip-hop band TLC. In 1994 Lopes was arrested for burning down the house of her boyfriend, Andre Rison, who played for the NFL's Atlanta Falcons. Lopes died in a car crash in Honduras. April 28, 2002

**Walter Lord,** 84: historian who penned the best-selling *A Night to Remember,* the definitive chronicle of the sinking of the *Titanic* and the basis for the 1997 film *Titanic.* Lord also wrote *Day of Infamy,* an account of the attack at Pearl Harbor. May 19, 2002

**Princess Margaret,** 71: free-spirited younger sister of Queen Elizabeth II of England who sparked a royal scandal in the 1950s when she nearly married a divorced man. Feb. 9, 2002

**Kathleen McGrath,** 50: U.S. Navy captain who became the first woman to command a warship. She led the USS *Jarrett* in a 6-month-long mission to the Persian Gulf to track down ships smuggling Iraqi oil. She died of lung cancer. Sept. 26, 2002

**Arthur Melin,** 77: entrepreneur who cofounded Wham-O, the toy company responsible for the Hula Hoop, the Frisbee, and the SuperBall. July 8, 2002

**César Milstein,** 74: Argentine-born immunologist who, with Niels K. Jerne and Georges J. F. Köhler, won the 1984 Nobel Prize in Medicine for their work in the "development and control of the immune system and the discovery of the principle for production of monoclonal antibodies." March 24, 2002

**Joshua Miner,** 81: educator who introduced Outward Bound to the United States in 1961. There were 80 students in the first course, and 600,000 have participated since. Jan. 29, 2002

**Patsy Mink,** 74: Democratic congresswoman who was the first Asian-American woman to serve in the House (1965–1977; 1990–2002). She was appointed assistant secretary for Oceans and Environmental Affairs in 1977 and reentered national politics in 1990. Sept. 28, 2002

**Dudley Moore,** 66: British actor known for his broad physical comedy and his hilarious high-brow performances with Peter Cook in the revue *Beyond the Fringe.* His films include *10* (1979), *Arthur* (1981), and *Micki and Maude* (1984). March 27, 2002

**Richard Mudd,** 101: physician who was consumed with clearing the name of his grandfather, Dr. Samuel Mudd, who was convicted by a military court of conspiring in the assassination of President Lincoln. Samuel Mudd set John Wilkes Booth's broken leg after the murder. May 21, 2002

**Lore Noto,** 79: producer who turned *The Fantasticks,* originally a one-act college production, into the world's longest-running musical. July 8, 2002

**Robert Nozick,** 63: political philosopher and Harvard professor who argued in his National Book Award–winning examination of the welfare system, *Anarchy, State, and Utopia,* that capitalist governments should have only a limited role in the lives and rights of citizens. Jan. 23, 2002

**LaWanda Page,** 81: actress who played wisecracking Aunt Esther on *Sanford and Son.* Sept. 14, 2002

**Bruce Paltrow,** 58: television and film director and producer who created and directed the acclaimed TV series *The White Shadow* and produced and directed *St. Elsewhere.* He also directed the film *Duets,* starring his daughter, Gwyneth Paltrow. His wife is the actress Blythe Danner. Oct. 3, 2002

**Dolores Olmedo Patiño,** 88. Mexican art patron who controlled the world's largest collection of works by Diego Rivera and Frida Kahlo. July 26, 2002

**Max Perutz,** 87: molecular biologist who shared the 1962 Nobel Prize in Chemistry with John Kendrew for "their studies of the structures of globular proteins." Feb. 6, 2002

**Julia Phillips,** 57: Oscar-winning producer who lambasted the Hollywood establishment in her 1991 incendiary book, *You'll Never Eat Lunch in This Town Again.* She won a Best Picture Oscar for *The Sting,* which she coproduced. She was the first woman to win the award. Her other producing credits include *Taxi Driver* and *Close Encounters of the Third Kind.* Jan. 1, 2002

**William Phillips,** 94: cofounder and editor of the *Partisan Review,* a political and literary forum for emerging journalists and writers. Sept. 13, 2002

**George Porter,** 81: British scientist who shared the 1967 Nobel Prize in Chemistry with Manfred Eigen and Ronald George Wreyford Norrish for their studies of "extremely fast chemical reactions, effected by disturbing the equilibrium by means of very short pulses of energy." Aug. 31, 2002

**Chaim Potok,** 73: novelist and rabbi whose bestselling book *The Chosen,* about a young man struggling with his obligation to follow in his father's footsteps and become a rabbi, offered the secular world a look at Hasidic Judaism. July 23, 2002

**Aleksandr Prokhorov,** 85: Russian physicist who won a 1964 Nobel Prize in Physics for his work in the field of quantum electronics. Jan. 8, 2002

**Dee Dee Ramone (Douglas Colvin),** 50: punk rocker who played bass and wrote songs for the Ramones. June 5, 2002

**David Riesman,** 92: sociologist whose 1950 book, *The Lonely Crowd: A Study of the Changing American Character,* became an unexpected and perennial bestseller. May 10, 2002

**Larry Rivers,** 78: experimental painter and sculptor who helped to define pop art. His works often parodied pieces by the old masters. His influential paintings include *Washington Crossing the Delaware* and *Dutch Masters and Cigars.* Aug. 14, 2002

**Matt Robinson,** 65: television writer and actor who wrote scripts for *The Cosby Show, Sanford and Son,* and *Eight Is Enough.* He was the first actor to play Gordon on *Sesame Street.* August 5, 2002

**Reginald Rose,** 81: Emmy Award–winning television writer who penned and coproduced *Twelve Angry Men.* He also wrote the screenplay for the film adaptation. April 19, 2002

**William Rosenberg,** 86: entrepreneur who expanded his Massachusetts coffee shop into Dunkin' Donuts, one of the biggest coffee chains in the world. The 5,000-location franchise, which debuted in 1948 as Open Kettle, operates across the United States and in 37 countries worldwide. Sept. 20, 2002

**Ted Ross,** 68: film, stage, and television actor who won a Tony Award for his 1975 role as the Cowardly Lion in *The Wiz.* Sept. 3, 2002

**Harold Russell,** 88: veteran and actor who won two Oscars—one for acting and a special award—for his performance as a disabled World War II soldier in the film *The Best Years of Our Lives.* Russell, a U.S. Army instructor, lost both hands during a training exercise. Jan. 29, 2002

**William Scholl,** 81: footwear designer who in the 1970s introduced Dr. Scholl's, the popular wooden sandals. March 15, 2002

**Earl Shaffer,** 83: outdoorsman who in 1948 became the first person to walk the entire Appalachian Trail in one trip. He made the 2,058-mile trek in 124 days, without a tent or stove. May 5, 2002

**George Sidney,** 85: director of such movie musicals as *Ziegfeld Follies, Annie Get Your Gun,* and *Kiss Me Kate.* He also directed *Anchors Aweigh,* the first film to combine live action and animation, and cofounded the animation house Hanna-Barbera. May 5, 2002

**Mia Slavenska,** 86: Croatian-born classically trained prima ballerina who performed with the Ballet Russe de Monte Carlo. Known for both her flawless technique and beauty, Slavenska won fame for her roles in *Giselle* and *Coppélia.* Oct. 5, 2002

**Howard K. Smith,** 87: opinionated broadcast journalist who covered WWII, the Nuremberg trials, the cold war, and the civil rights protests of the 1960s. In 1960 he moderated the first televised presidential debate, between Kennedy and Nixon. Feb. 15, 2002

**Sam Snead,** 89: professional golfer, whose effortless swing, unmatched success, and down-home sense of humor made him one of the most loved and admired athletes of the 20th century. He won three Masters, three PGA Championships, and one British Open. May 23, 2002

**Holly Solomon,** 68: influential art dealer who championed pop art and the early works of Robert Kushner, Robert Mapplethorpe, and Laurie Anderson. She was the subject of portraits by Andy Warhol, Robert Rauschenberg, and Roy Lichtenstein. June 6, 2002

**Layne Staley,** 34: lead singer of the grunge band Alice in Chains. The group was one of the first grunge bands to emerge from Seattle and has inspired scores of copycat bands. April 2002

**J. William Stanton,** 78: Republican congressman from Ohio who served in the House from 1964 until his retirement in 1983. April 11, 2002

**Rod Steiger,** 77: versatile, compelling character actor who won a Best Actor Oscar for his role as a Southern sheriff in 1968's *In the Heat of the Night.* An actor who totally immersed himself in the roles he played, Steiger also earned Oscar nominations for *On the Waterfront* and *The Pawnbroker.* July 9, 2002

**Joseph Steiner,** 95: cofounder of the Kenner toy company, which manufactured the Bubble Rocket and the Easy-Bake Oven. May 11, 2002

**Herman Talmadge,** 88: Democratic politician who served as governor of Georgia and four terms as a U.S. senator. March 21, 2002

**William Taylor,** 93: newspaper executive who was publisher of the *Boston Globe* from 1955 to 1978. Feb. 19, 2002

**John Thaw,** 60: British actor who played the title character in the *Inspector Morse* television series, based on the novels by Colin Dexter. Feb. 21, 2002

**Dave Thomas,** 69: founder of the Wendy's fast-food chain who built his business into the third-largest burger outlet in the country. Jan. 8, 2002

**Benjamin Thompson,** 84: architect who transformed Boston's dilapidated waterfront into the Faneuil Hall Marketplace, a popular tourist attraction. He duplicated the concept with equal success in Manhattan, Baltimore, and Washington. Aug. 17, 2002

**Floyd Thompson,** 69: Army Special Forces major who was the country's longest-serving prisoner of war, having endured nine years of isolation and starvation in South Vietnam. July 16, 2002

**J. Lee Thompson,** 88: British director who earned fame on these shores for *Guns of Navarone,* which was nominated for seven Oscars. His other credits include *Cape Fear.* Aug. 30, 2002

**Lawrence Tierney,** 82: actor who appeared in more than 70 films, often as a tough guy. He played the title role in 1945's *Dillinger.* He reemerged after several years away from the big screen in 1992's *Reservoir Dogs.* Feb. 26, 2002

**James Tobin,** 84: Nobel Prize–winning economist and Yale professor who was an influential adviser to President Kennedy, serving on his Council of Economic Advisers. Tobin won the 1981 Nobel for his Portfolio Selection Theory, which suggested that investors considered the risk factor when investing and varied the amount of risk. He once translated the theory in layman's terms: "Don't put your eggs in one basket." March 11, 2002

**Johnny Unitas,** 69: record-setting quarterback of the Baltimore Colts, whose black high-top cleats and dark crew cut remain indelible symbols of the franchise's success in the late 1950s and 1960s. He led the Colts to NFL titles in 1958 and 1959, and the 1959 overtime victory over the Giants is widely considered the greatest NFL game ever. Sept. 11, 2002

**Robert Urich,** 55: Emmy Award–winning actor who starred in the television series *Vega$* and *Spenser: For Hire.* His film credits include *Bob & Carol & Ted & Alice* and *Turk 182!* He died of synovial cell sarcoma, a rare form of cancer. April 16, 2002

**Cyrus Vance,** 84: public official and lawyer who served under presidents Kennedy and Johnson as secretary of the army (1961–62), deputy secretary of defense (1964–67), and U.S. negotiator to the Paris Peace Conference on the Vietnam War (1968–69). He resigned his post as President Carter's secretary of state in protest of the president's 1980 attempt to rescue the American hostages in Iran. Jan. 12, 2002

**Vernon Walters,** 85: public official and general who served under President Nixon as the deputy director of the CIA and under Reagan as ambassador to the UN. In all, Walters worked for seven presidents. He spoke eight languages, often using his linguistic gift on diplomatic missions. Feb. 10, 2002

**Lew Wasserman,** 89: legendary Hollywood mogul who served as chairman and CEO of MCA for four decades after World War II and permanently changed the landscape of the entertainment industry. As an agent, his client list included Marilyn Monroe, Jimmy Stewart, Clark Gable, and Betty Grable. In the 1940s, he convinced executives to abandon the stringent long-term contracts that held actors hostage to studios. June 3, 2002

**John Weitz,** 79: German-born fashion designer who also had a successful career as a writer and historian. Weitz was one of the first designers to license his name for products such as socks, ties, and cologne. He worked for the Office of Strategic Services before embarking on a career in fashion. His books include *Hitler's Diplomat: The Life and Times of Joachim von Ribbentrop.* His sons are the film directors Paul and Christopher Weitz. Oct. 3, 2002

**Paul Wellstone,** 58: popular Democrat from Minnesota who championed liberal causes during his two terms as a senator. Despite his left-leaning philosophy, Wellstone was widely liked and respected by Democrats and Republicans alike. He died in a plane crash. Oct. 25, 2002

**Byron White,** 84: college and professional football star who went on to become associate justice of the U.S. Supreme Court (1962–93). White, considered a "swing" justice who typically voted with liberals on civil-rights cases and with conservatives on personal liberty and criminal justice issues, was the last surviving member of the Warren Court. He was an All America halfback at the University of Colorado and signed with the Pittsburgh Pirates (now the Steelers) in 1938 for the then largest contract in pro history ($15,800). He went to Oxford on a Rhodes scholarship in 1939 and returned to the gridiron in 1940. White earned his law degree from Yale in 1946 and served as Robert Kennedy's deputy attorney general. April 15, 2002

**Nancy White,** 85: refined editor of *Harper's Bazaar* from 1958 to 1971 whose spreads by such photographers as Richard Avedon and Hiro helped to define the style of the era. May 25, 2002

**Timothy White,** 50: editor in chief of *Billboard* magazine. He wrote *Catch a Fire: The Life of Bob Marley.* He died of a heart attack. June 27, 2002

**Robert Whitehead,** 86: distinguished theatrical producer who staged many of the most important plays of the 20th century, including works by such luminaries as Arthur Miller, Tennessee Williams, Eugene O'Neill, and Thornton Wilder. June 15, 2002

**Billy Wilder (Samuel Wilder),** 95: Austrian-born director and producer known for his scathing satires of American mores. Wilder, who won six Academy Awards, was a versatile director who shifted seamlessly from drama to comedy to film noir. His Oscar-winning films include *The Lost Weekend, Sunset Boulevard,* and *The Apartment.* March 28, 2002

**Ted Williams,** 83: Boston Red Sox legend, whose passion for hitting was unrivaled, as were his results. His career .344 batting average is sixth-highest since 1900, he won the American League batting title six times, and his 521 career home runs place him 12th on the all-time list. Williams missed all or part of five seasons due to military service as a pilot in WWII and the Korean War. July 5, 2002

**Thomas Winship,** 81: crusading editor of the *Boston Globe* (1965–1984) who guided the paper to national recognition and 12 Pulitzer Prizes. March 14, 2002

**David Wisniewski,** 49: artist and author known for the layered, cut-paper technique he used to illustrate books, including *Golem,* which won the 1997 Caldecott Medal. Sept. 11, 2002

**Irene Worth,** 85: versatile British film and stage actress who won Tony Awards for her roles in Tennessee Williams' *Sweet Bird of Youth* and Neil Simon's *Lost in Yonkers.* March 10, 2002

*See first page of book for additional tabs.*